# DICTIONARY OF
# GARDENING

THE ROYAL HORTICULTURAL SOCIETY

# DICTIONARY OF GARDENING

## A PRACTICAL AND SCIENTIFIC ENCYCLOPAEDIA OF HORTICULTURE

*Edited by*

FRED J. CHITTENDEN, O.B.E., F.L.S., V.M.H.

*Assisted by Specialists*

*SECOND EDITION*
*by*
PATRICK M. SYNGE, M.A. (Cantab.), F.L.S.

**VOLUME II: CO—JA**

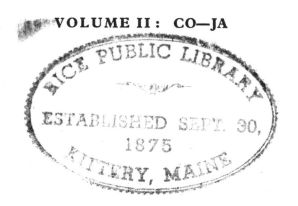
OXFORD
AT THE CLARENDON PRESS

*Oxford University Press, Walton Street, Oxford* OX2 6DP

OXFORD LONDON GLASGOW
NEW YORK TORONTO MELBOURNE WELLINGTON
IBADAN NAIROBI DAR ES SALAAM LUSAKA CAPE TOWN
KUALA LUMPUR SINGAPORE JAKARTA HONG KONG TOKYO
DELHI BOMBAY CALCUTTA MADRAS KARACHI

ISBN 0 19 869106 8

*First published 1951*
*Second edition 1956*
*Reprinted from corrected sheets of the*
*second edition 1965*
*Reprinted (with corrections) 1974, 1977*

*Printed in Great Britain*
*at the University Press, Oxford*
*by Vivian Ridler*
*Printer to the University*

# ABBREVIATIONS USED FOR TITLES OF WORKS CONTAINING ILLUSTRATIONS
## CITED IN THIS DICTIONARY

*(Works are octavo unless otherwise mentioned)*

A.B.G.C.    CALCUTTA, ROYAL BOTANIC GARDENS. Annals. Calcutta. 1887–1936. Vols. 1–14, pt. i. Folio.

A.B.R.    ANDREWS, HENRY C. The Botanist's Repository. London. 1797–1812. 10 vols. 4to. (For dates of publication, see *J. Bot.* (*London*), 54. 236; 1916.)

ADD.    Addisonia: coloured Illustrations and popular Descriptions of Plants. New York. 1916– . Vol. 1– . Ref. to plate nos.

A.G.    ANDREWS, HENRY C. Geraniums. London. 1805–24. 2 vols. 4to. Ref. to plate nos.

A.G.S.B.    ALPINE GARDEN SOCIETY. Bulletin. Capel, Surrey, &c., 1930– . Vol. I– .

A.H.    ANDREWS, HENRY C. The Heathery; or a Monograph of the Genus Erica. London. 1804–12. 6 vols. Ref. to plate nos.

A.P.J.    TAKEDA, HISAYOSHI. Alpine Plants of Japan. Tokyo. 1938. Ref. to plate nos.

ANN. MUS. LUGDUNO-BAT.    MIQUEL, FREDERIK ANTON WILHELM. Annales Musei botanici Lugduno-Batavorum. Amsterdam, &c. 1863–9. 4 vols. Folio. (For dates of publication see *J. Arnold Arb.* 6. 212; 1925.)

B.B.    BRITTON, NATHANIEL LORD, and BROWN, ADDISON. An Illustrated Flora of the Northern United States, Canada, and the British Possessions from Newfoundland to Virginia. New York. Ed. 2. 1913. 3 vols. Ref. to vol. and page.

B.C.F.    SCHNEIDER, GEORGE. The Book of choice Ferns. London. 1892–4. 3 vols.

B.H.    La Belgique Horticole. Liége. 1851–85. 35 vols. Ref. to date and plate nos.

B.J.O.    BOLUS, HARRY. Icones Orchidearum Austro-Africanarum extra-tropicarum. London. 1893–1913. 3 vols. Ref. to plate nos.

B.M.    Curtis's Botanical Magazine. London. 1787–1947. 164 vols. Ref. to plate nos.

B.M. n.s.    Idem 1948– . Vol. 165– . Ref. to plate nos.

B.O.    BATEMAN, JAMES. A Monograph of Odontoglossum. 1864–74. Folio. Ref. to plate nos.

B.O.M.G.    BATEMAN, JAMES. The Orchidaceae of Mexico and Guatemala. London. 1843. Folio.

B.R.    The Botanical Register by SYDENHAM EDWARDS. London. 1815–28. 14 vols. 8vo. *Cont.* as Botanical Register or Ornamental Flower Garden. Ed. by JOHN LINDLEY. 1829–47. 19 vols. Ref. to plate nos. for vols. 1–23 (1815–37), to vol. and plate nos. for vols. 24–47 (1838–49).

B.R.C.    BRITTON, NATHANIEL LORD, and ROSE, JOSEPH NELSON. The Cactaceae: Descriptions and Illustrations of Plants of the Cactus Family. Washington, D.C. 1919–23. 4 vols. 4to. Ref. to vol. and plate or fig. nos.

B.T.S.    BEAN, WILLIAM JACKSON. Trees and Shrubs hardy in the British Isles. 1914. 2 vols. Vol. 3. 1933. Ref. to vol. and page.

BAIRD, VIOL.    BAIRD, VIOLA BRAINERD. Wild Violets of North America. Berkeley and Los Angeles. 1942.

BULL. ALP. GARD. SOC.    *See* A.G.S.B. *above.*

C.B.    CLINTON-BAKER, HENRY WILLIAM. Illustrations of Conifers. Hertford. 1909–13. 3 vols. 4to. Ref. to vol. and plate nos.

C.B.J.    CLINTON-BAKER, HENRY WILLIAM, and JACKSON, ALBERT BRUCE. Illustrations of new Conifers. Hertford. 1935. 4to. Ref. to plate nos.

C.F.K.    COVENTRY, B.O. Wild Flowers of Kashmir. Calcutta, Simla, London. 1925–30. 3 vols.

C.H.P.    *See* H.I.H. *below.*

C.I.N.Z.    CHEESEMAN, THOMAS FREDERICK. Illustrations of the New Zealand Flora. Wellington, N.Z. 1914. 2 vols. 4to. Ref. to plate nos.

D.C.PL.G.    CANDOLLE, AUGUSTIN PYRAMUS DE. Plantarum succulentarum Historia; ou Histoire naturelle des Plantes grasses. Paris. 1798–1829. 2 vols. Folio. Ref. to plate nos. (For dates of publication, see *Cactus J.* 7. 37; 1938.)

D.J.C.    DALLIMORE, WILLIAM, and JACKSON, ALBERT BRUCE. A Handbook of Coniferae including Ginkgoaceae. London. 1923. Ref. to pages.

E.B.    SYME, JOHN THOMAS BOSWELL. English Botany. London. 1863–86. 12 vols. 8vo. Supplementary vol. (13) by NICHOLAS EDWARD BROWN. 1891–2. Ref. to plate nos.

E.H.    ELWES, HENRY JOHN, and HENRY, AUGUSTINE. The Trees of Great Britain and Ireland. Edinburgh. 1906–13. 7 vols. 4to. Ref. to plate nos.

E.L.    ELWES, HENRY JOHN. A Monograph of the Genus Lilium. London. 1877–80. Folio. Ref. to plate nos. (For dates of publication, see WOODCOCK, H. B. D., and STEARN, W. T., Lilies, 396; 1950.)

| | |
|---|---|
| E.L.S. | GROVE, ARTHUR STANLEY, and COTTON, ARTHUR DISBROWE. A Supplement to Elwes' Monograph of the Genus Lilium. London. 1934–40. Folio. Ref. to plate nos. |
| E.R.G. | FARRER, REGINALD. The English Rock-garden. London. 1919. 2 vols. Ref. to pages. |
| F.A.O. | FITZGERALD, ROBERT DAVID. Australian Orchids. Sydney. 1875–94. 2 vols. Folio. Ref. to vol. and part. |
| F. & S. | Flora and Sylva; a monthly Review for Lovers of Garden, Woodland, Tree or Flower. Ed. by WILLIAM ROBINSON. London. 1903–5. 3 vols. 4to. Ref. to vol. and plate nos. |
| F.B.A. | HOOKER, Sir WILLIAM JACKSON. Flora Boreali-Americana: or the Botany of the northern Parts of British America. London. 1829–40. 2 vols. 4to. Ref. to plate nos. (For dates of publication, see J. Bot. (London), 47. 106; 1909.) |
| F.B.I. | BEDDOME, RICHARD HENRY. The Ferns of British India. Madras. 1865–70. 3 vols. 4to. |
| F.C. | KNOWLES, GEORGE BEAUCHAMP, and WESTCOTT, FREDERIC. The Floral Cabinet and Magazine of exotic Beauty. London. 1837–40. 3 vols. 4to. |
| F.d.S. | Flore des Serres et des Jardins de l'Europe. Ghent. 1845–83. 23 vols. Ref. to plate nos. |
| F.G. | SIBTHORP, JOHN, and SMITH, Sir JAMES EDWARD. Flora Graeca: sive Plantarum rariorum Historia. London. 1806–40. 10 vols. Folio. Ref. to plate nos. |
| FL.ATL. | DESFONTAINES, RENÉ LOUICHE. Flora Atlantica. Paris. 1798–9. 2 vols. 4to. Ref. to plate nos. (For dates of publication, see J. Soc. Bibl. Nat. Hist. I. 147; 1938.) |
| F.M. | The Floral Magazine. London, 1st series 1861–71. 10 vols. 8vo. 2nd series 1872–81. 10 vols. 4to. |
| F.P.R. | BICKNELL, CLARENCE. Flowering Plants and Ferns of the Riviera and neighbouring Mountains. London. 1885. 4to. Ref. to plate nos. |
| F.P.S.A. | The Flowering Plants of South Africa. London &c. 1921–44. Vols. 1–24. Cont. as The Flowering Plants of Africa. Vol. 25– . 1945– . Ref. to plate nos. |
| F.S.A. | MARLOTH, RUDOLF. The Flora of South Africa: with synoptical Tables of the Genera of the Higher Plants. Cape Town and London. 1913–32. Vols. 1–4. 4to. Ref. to plate nos. |
| F.S.I. | BEDDOME, RICHARD HENRY. The Ferns of Southern India; being Descriptions and Plates of the Ferns of the Madras Presidency. Madras. 1863–4. Ref. to plate nos. |
| G. & F. | Garden and Forest: A Journal of Horticulture, Landscape, Art, and Forestry. New York. 1888–97. 10 vols. 4to. Ref. to vol. and plate nos. |
| G.C. | The Gardeners' Chronicle. London. 1841–3. 3 vols. 4to. The Gardeners' Chronicle and Agricultural Gazette. 1844–73. 30 vols. The Gardeners' Chronicle, new series 1874–86. 26 vols.; 3rd series 1887– . Vol. 1– . Ref. to vol., date, and page. |
| GEN. | WILKIE, DAVID. Gentians. London. 1936. |
| GENTES HERB. | BAILEY, LIBERTY HYDE. Gentes Herbarum. Ithaca, N.Y. 1920– . Vol. 1– . |
| G.F. | Gartenflora. Erlangen. 1852–85. 34 vols. Cont. as Gartenflora, Zeitschrift, &c. 1886–1938. Berlin. Vols. 35–87. Ref. to plate nos., or to vol. and page. |
| G.I. | Gardening Illustrated. London. |
| GN. | The Garden: an illustrated weekly Journal of Gardening in all its Branches. London. 1871–1927. 91 vols. 4to. Ref. to vol., date, and page. |
| GTF. | Gartenflora. See G.F. above. |
| H.B.F. | HOOKER, Sir WILLIAM JACKSON. The British Ferns. London. 1861. 8vo. Ref. to fig. nos. |
| H.C.I.S. | HU, HSEN-HSU, and CHUN, WOON YOUNG. Icones Plantarum Sinicarum. Shanghai. 1927–9. Folio. 2 parts. Ref. to plate nos. |
| H.E.F. | HOOKER, Sir WILLIAM JACKSON. Exotic Flora. Edinburgh. 1822–7. 3 vols. Ref. to plate nos. |
| HENSHAW MT.W.FL. | HENSHAW, JULIA WILLMOTTE. Wild Flowers of the North American Mountains. London and New York. 1916. |
| H.F.A. | HOOKER, Sir JOSEPH DALTON. Flora Antarctica. London. 1844–60. 2 vols. 4to. (For dates of publication, see J. Bot. (London), 51. 356; 1913.) |
| H.F.T. | HOOKER, Sir JOSEPH DALTON. Flora Tasmaniae. London. 1855–60. 2 vols. 4to. (For dates of publication, see J. Bot. (London), 51. 358: 1913.) |
| H.G.F. | HOOKER, Sir WILLIAM JACKSON. Genera Filicum; or Illustrations of Ferns. London. 1842. Ref. to fig. nos. |
| H.I.H. | HOOKER, Sir JOSEPH DALTON. Illustrations of Himalayan Plants. London. 1855. Folio. Ref. to plate nos. (For date of publication, see Calcutta, R. Bot. Gard., Anniv. Vol., 115; 1942.) |
| H.I.P. | HOOKER, Sir WILLIAM JACKSON. Icones Plantarum. London. 1837–53. 10 vols. 8vo. Cont. as Hooker's Icones Plantarum under various editors. Ref. to plate nos. |
| H.S. } H.S.F. } | HOOKER, Sir WILLIAM JACKSON. Species Filicum. London. 1846–64. 5 vols. Folio. |
| H.S.C.F. | HOOKER, Sir WILLIAM JACKSON. A Second Century of Ferns. London. 1860. |
| H.T. | HALL, Sir ALFRED DANIEL. The Genus Tulipa. London. 1940. Ref. to plate nos. |
| HOOK.I. | See H.I.P. above. |
| HOUSE, W. F. | HOUSE, HOMER DOLIVER. Wild Flowers of New York. New York. 1918. 4to. |

J.H.S.    HORTICULTURAL SOCIETY OF LONDON. Journal. London. 1846–55. 9 vols. Ref. to vol. and page.

J.L.    JORDAN, ALEXIS, and FOURREAU, JULES. Icones ad Floram Europæ novo fundamento instaurandam spectantes. Paris. 1866–1903. 3 vols. Folio. Ref. to plate nos.

J.L.S.    LINNEAN SOCIETY OF LONDON. Journal: Botany. London. 1865– . Vol. 8– . 8vo. Ref. to vol. and plate nos.

J.R.H.S.    ROYAL HORTICULTURAL SOCIETY. Journal. London. 1866. Vol. 1– . Ref. to vol. and page.

K.B.    KEW, ROYAL BOTANIC GARDENS. Bulletin of Miscellaneous Information. London. 1887. Ref. to date and page.

L.    LINDEN, JULES, and LINDEN, LUCIEN. Lindenia: Iconographie des Orchidées. Ghent. 1885–1901. 17 vols. Folio. Ref. to plate nos.

L.B.C.    LODDIGES, CONRAD. The Botanical Cabinet: coloured Delineations of Plants from all Countries. London. 1818–33. 20 vols. 4to. Ref. to plate nos.

L.F.    LOWE, EDWARD JOSEPH. Ferns British and exotic. London. 1856–60. 8 vols. 8vo. Ref. to vol. and plate nos.

L.Y.B.    ROYAL HORTICULTURAL SOCIETY. Lily Year Book. London. 1932– . Ref. to year and fig. nos.

LAING AND BLACKWELL    LAING, ROBERT MALCOLM, and BLACKWELL, E. W. Plants of New Zealand. Christchurch, N.Z. 1906. Ref. to pages.

M.A.S.    SALM-REIFFERSCHEID-DYCK, JOSEPH, Prince. Monographia Generum Aloes et Mesembryanthemi. Bonn. 1836–63. 2 vols. 4to. Ref. to vol. and plate nos. (For the modern names of the plants figured, see *Cactus J.* 1. 34–44, 66–85; 1938–9.)

M.C.    MAW, GEORGE. A Monograph of the Genus Crocus. London. 1886. 4to. Ref. to plate nos.

M.F.M.    MOGGRIDGE, JOHN TRAHERNE. Contributions to the Flora of Mentone. London. 1865–71. (3rd ed. 1874.) Ref. to plate nos.

MOGGRIDGE, FL. MENTONE    *See* M.F.M. *above.*

N.    BURBIDGE, FREDERICK WILLIAM, and BAKER, JOHN GILBERT. The Narcissus, its History and Culture. London. 1875. Ref. to plate nos.

N.E.BR.    BROWN, NATHANIEL EDWARD, FISCHER, A., and KARSTEN, M. C. Mesembryanthema. Ashford. 1931. 8vo. Ref. to pages.

N.F.S.    The New Flora and Silva. London. 1928–40. 12 vols. 8vo. Ref. to vol. and fig. nos.

N.R.B.G.E.    EDINBURGH, ROYAL BOTANIC GARDEN. Notes. Glasgow and Edinburgh. 1900– . Vol. 1– . Ref. to vol. and page.

O.R.    The Orchid Review: and illustrated monthly Journal devoted to Orchidology. London. 1893– . Vol. 1– . 8vo. Ref. to date and page.

P.F.G.    LINDLEY, JOHN, and PAXTON, Sir JOSEPH. Paxton's Flower Garden. London. 1850–3. 3 vols. 4to. Ref. to vol. and plate nos.

P.F.S.    POST, GEORGE EDWARD. Flora of Syria, Palestine and Sinai. Beirut. 1896. Ref. to pages.

P.L.    SALISBURY, RICHARD ANTHONY. Paradisus Londinensis. London. 1805–8. 2 vols. 4to. Ref. to plate nos.

P.M.B.    Paxton's Magazine of Botany. London. 1834–49. 16 vols. 4to. Ref. to vol. and plate nos.

PARSONS, WILD FLOWERS OF CALIFORNIA.    PARSONS, MARY ELIZABETH. The Wild Flowers of California, their Names, Haunts, and Habits. San Francisco. 1897.

PESCATOREA    LINDEN, JEAN JULES. Pescatorea: Iconographie des Orchidées. Brussels. 1860. Folio. Ref. to plate nos.

R.    SANDER, FREDERICK. Reichenbachia. St. Albans. 1888–94. 4 vols. Folio. Ref. to plate nos.

REF.B.    SAUNDERS, WILLIAM WILSON. Refugium Botanicum. London. 1869–73. 5 vols. Ref. to vol. and plate nos.

R.H.    La Revue Horticole. Paris. 1842– . 12mo. and 8vo. Ref. to date and plate nos.

R.H.B.    Revue de l'Horticulture belge et étrangère. 1875–1914. 40 vols. Ghent. Ref. to date and plate nos.

R.I.F.G.    REICHENBACH, HEINRICH GOTTLIEB, and others. Icones Florae Germanicae et Helveticae. Leipzig. 1834–1912. 25 vols. 4to. Ref. to vol. and plate nos.

R.L.    REDOUTÉ, PIERRE JOSEPH. Les Liliacées. Paris. 1807–16. 8 vols. Folio. Ref. to plate nos. (For dates of publication, see *J. Bot.* (*London*), 43. 26; 1905.)

R.M.F.    CLEMENTS, FREDERIC EDWARD, and CLEMENTS, EDITH SCHWARTZ. Rocky Mountain Flowers. New York. 1914. Ref. to fig. nos.

R.S.H.    HOOKER, Sir JOSEPH DALTON. The Rhododendrons of Sikkim-Himalaya. London. 1849–51. Folio. Ref. to plate nos.

R.X.O.    REICHENBACH, HENRICH GUSTAV. Xenia orchidacea. Leipzig. 1854–1900. 3 vols. 8vo. Ref. to plate nos.

RHODORA    NEW ENGLAND BOTANICAL CLUB. Rhodora. Boston. 1899– . Vol. 1– .

ROYLE ILL. B.H.    ROYLE, JOHN FORBES. Illustrations of the Botany of the Himalayan Mountains, and of the Flora of Cashmere. London. 1833–40. 2 vols. 4to. Ref. to plate nos. (For dates of publication, see *J. Arnold. Arb.* 24. 484; 1943.)

S.AFR.GARD.    South African Gardening. Cape Town. 1915– . Vols. 1– . 4to. Ref. to vol., date, and page.

S.B.F.G.    SWEET, ROBERT. The British Flower Garden. London. 1st series 1823–9. 3 vols. Ref. to plate nos.

| | |
|---|---|
| S.B.F.G.2 | SWEET, ROBERT. The British Flower Garden. London. 2nd series 1831–8. 4 vols. Ref. to plate nos. |
| S.C. | SWEET, ROBERT. Cistineae. London. 1825–30. Ref. to plate nos. |
| S.D. | *See* M.A.S. *above.* |
| S.E.B. | SMITH, Sir JAMES EDWARD. Exotic Botany. 1804–5. 2 vols. 4to. Ref. to plate nos. |
| S.G. | SWEET, ROBERT. Geraniaceae. London. 1820–30. 5 vols. Ref. to plate nos. |
| S.MAN. | SARGENT, CHARLES SPRAGUE. Manual of the Trees of North America (exclusive of Mexico). Boston. 1905. |
| S.P. | STERN, FREDERICK CLAUDE. A Study of the Genus Paeonia. London. 1946. 4to. Ref. to plate nos. |
| S.S. | SARGENT, CHARLES SPRAGUE. The Silva of North America. Boston. 1891–1902. 14 vols. 4to. Ref. to plate nos. |
| S.T.S. | SARGENT, CHARLES SPRAGUE. Trees and Shrubs; Illustrations of new or little known ligneous Plants. 1902–13. Boston and New York. 2 vols. 4to. |
| S.Z.F.J. | SIEBOLD, PHILIPP FRANZ VON, and ZUCCARINI, JOSEPH GERHARD. Flora Japonica. 1835–70. Leyden. 2 vols. Folio. Ref. to plate nos. (For dates of publication, see *Bot. Mag. Tokyo,* **40.** 362; 1926.) |
| SIBTH, SM., FL. GRAECA | *See* F.G. *above.* |
| STOKER, GARDENER'S PROGRESS. | |
| | STOKER, FRED. A Gardener's Progress. London. 1938. 8vo. Ref. to fig. nos. |
| T.A.P.E. | THOMPSON, HAROLD STUART. Alpine Plants of Europe: together with cultural Hints. London. 1911. Ref. to pages. |
| T.H.S. | HORTICULTURAL SOCIETY OF LONDON. Transactions. 1805–48. 10 vols. 4to. Ref. to vol. and plate nos. |
| T.L.S. | LINNEAN SOCIETY OF LONDON. Transactions. London. 1791–1876. 30 vols. 4to. 2nd series, Botany. 1875– . Vol. 1– . Ref. to vol. and plate nos. |

| | |
|---|---|
| T.S.A.P. | THOMPSON, HAROLD STUART. Sub-alpine Plants or Flowers of the Swiss Woods and Meadows. London. 1912. 8vo. Ref. to pages. |
| USEFUL PL. JAP. | AGRICULTURAL SOCIETY OF JAPAN. Useful Plants of Japan described and illustrated. Tokyo. 1895. 3 vols. of plates. 1 vol. of text. |
| W.A.P. | WOOSTER, DAVID. Alpine Plants. London. 1st series 1872. 2nd series 1874. 2 vols. 4to. Ref. to plate nos. |
| W.I.C.P. | WEBB, PHILIP BARKER, and BERTHELOT, SABIN. Histoire naturelle des Iles Canaries: Tome 3, Partie 2, Phytographia Canariensis. Paris. 1836–50. 3 vols. 4to. Ref. to plate nos. (For dates of publication, see *J. Soc. Bibl. Nat. Hist.* **1.** 49; 1937.) |
| W.I.I.B. | WRIGHT, ROBERT. Illustrations of Indian Botany. Madras. 1840–50. 2 vols. 4to. Ref. to plate nos. |
| W.O.A. | WARNER, ROBERT, &c. The Orchid Album. Coloured Figures and Descriptions of new, rare, and beautiful orchidaceous Plants. London. 1882–97. 11 vols. 4to. Ref. to plate nos. |
| W.P.A.R. | WALLICH, NATHANIEL. Plantae Asiaticae rariores. London. 1829–32. 3 vols. Folio. Ref. to plate nos. |
| W.R. | WILLMOTT, ELLEN ANN. The Genus Rosa. London. 1910–14. 2 vols. 4to. Ref. to plate nos. (For dates of publication, see *J. Arnold Arb.* **3.** 230; 1922.) |
| W.S. | WOODCOCK, HUBERT DRYSDALE, and STEARN, WILLIAM THOMAS. Lilies of the World, their Cultivation and Classification. London. 1950. Ref. to pages. |
| W.S.O. | WARNER, ROBERT. Select Orchidaceous Plants. London. 1862–5. 2nd series 1865–75. 3rd series 1878–91. Folio. Ref. to plate nos. |
| WIGHT ICON. | WIGHT, ROBERT. Icones Plantarum Indiae orientalis. Madras. 1838–40. 6 vols. 4to. Ref. to plate nos. (For dates of publication, see *J. Arnold Arb.* **22.** 222; 1941.) |

*See also Vol. I, p. xiv, for additions.*

# ABBREVIATIONS USED IN TEXT

**A** indicates entries to be found in the Additions, Part II of Supplement
**A→** indicates new headings to be found in the Additions, Part II of Supplement

| | | | | | |
|---|---|---|---|---|---|
| cal. | calyx | in. | inch (2·5 cm.) | rhiz. | rhizome |
| cau. | caudex (rootstock of ferns) | infl. | inflorescence | S. | South(ern) |
| Cent. | Central | infruct. | infructescence | SE. | South east(ern) |
| cor. | corolla | Is. | Isle(s), Island(s) | SW. | South west(ern) |
| Dist. | Distribution | l. | leaf (leaves) | seg. | segment(s) |
| E. | East(ern) | lflets. | leaflets | sep. | sepal(s) |
| FAM. | Botanical Family (formerly called Natural Order) | lvs. | leaves | sti. | stipe (leaf-stalk of ferns) |
| fl. | flower(s) | Mts. | Mountains | SYN. | Synonym |
| -fld. | -flowered | N. | North(ern) | W. | West(ern) |
| fr. | fruit | NE. | North east(ern) | * | of special merit |
| ft. | foot (approximately 30 cm.) | NW. | North west(ern) | × | hybrid |
| h. | high | per. | perianth | + | graft chimaera (graft hybrid) |
| | | pet. | petal(s) | | |

The scale of illustrations is indicated by the line e.g. ——— which is included
in each drawing and represents one inch.
The year given in many descriptions represents the date of first introduction
of the plant to Great Britain as far as is known.

**COCHEMI'EA** (after an Indian tribe which once inhabited Lower California). FAM. *Cactaceae*. Plants cylindrical, often much elongated; tubercles spirally arranged, not milky or grooved. Flowers borne in the axils of the tubercles, as in Mammillaria, but differing from that genus by being narrowly tubular, curved, and 2-lipped. Fruit round, red. **A**

**C. Hal'ei.** Plants elongated, growing in clusters; tubercles short, axils woolly; radial spines 10 to 20; centrals 3 or 4. *fl.* scarlet, up to 2 in. long. Islands of S. Lower California. (B.R.C. 4, f. 22.) SYN. *Mammillaria Halei.*

**C. Pond'ii.** Stems cylindrical, simple or branched; axils bristly; radial spines 15 to 25, white; centrals 8 to 11, much longer and stouter. *fl.* scarlet, slender, up to 2 in. long. Islands off the W. coast of N. Lower California. SYN. *Mammillaria Pondii.*

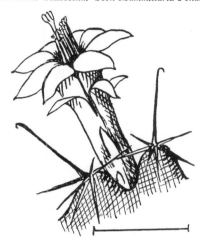

*Cochemiea Poselgeri*

**C. Posel'geri.** Stems numerous from a central root, spreading or prostrate, up to 6 ft. long; areoles and young axils woolly; tubercles somewhat flattened; radial spines 7 to 9, yellowish; central 1, hooked. *fl.* scarlet, shorter. Lower California. (B.R.C. 4, t. 2.) SYN. *Mammillaria Poselgeri.*

**C. setispi'na.** Stems erect, cylindrical; axils woolly; radial spines 10 to 12, white with black tips, slender; centrals 1 to 4, stouter, 1 hooked. *fl.* large, scarlet. S. Lower California. SYN. *Mammillaria setispina.*

V. H.

**cochinchinen'sis -is -e,** of Cochin-China.

**COCHINEAL.** Dye obtained from a scale insect which lives on Opuntia, Nopalea, &c., used also as a colouring agent in cooking.

**COCHINEAL FIG.** *See* **Nopalea cochenillifera.**

**COCHLEA'RIA** (*cochlear*, spoon; the leaves of many species are shaped like the bowl of a spoon). FAM. *Cruciferae*. Annual or perennial herbs with about 15 species in Europe and N. America, usually smooth and fleshy. Leaves very variable; radical leaves usually stalked; stem leaves often arrow-shaped and auricled. Flowers small, white, yellowish, or purplish, in racemes. Fruit an inflated silicula with very convex valves; seeds many. Few species are sufficiently beautiful to justify their cultivation but those that are cultivated grow freely in ordinary rich, damp, but well-drained soil, from seed sown in the open. All are hardy. *C. officinalis* is the Scurvy Grass so well known to sailors of old and valued for its anti-scorbutic properties; the green parts are acrid with a tarry flavour. *C. Armoracia*, Horse-radish, has recently been moved into other genera by different botanists, into Radicula, Roripa, and Nasturtium, and while this difference of opinion exists it seems best to retain it in this genus where it has for so long been well known. Some species may be grown on the rockgarden for they make neat rosettes of glossy leaves, *C. danica* and *C. officinalis* being typical and as good as any.

**C. Armorac'ia.** Horse-radish. Perennial. Root large, fleshy, its fangs going deeply into the soil. Stem about 2 ft. h. *l.* at base large, oblong, with rounded teeth; stem-l. lanceolate, more or less deeply toothed or cut. *fl.* white; cal. spreading. May. E. temperate Europe, naturalized in Britain. (E.B. 129.) *See* **Horse-radish.**

**C. dan'ica.** Annual, tufted, 6 to 8 in. h. *l.* radical, rounded kidney-shaped, rarely 1 in. long. *fl.* small, white, numerous. May, June. N. temperate and Arctic regions. (L.B.C. 1482.)

**C. officina'lis.** Common Scurvy Grass. Biennial, 2 to 12 in. h. Radical *l.* stalked, heart-shaped; stem-l. ovate, toothed, angled. *fl.* white. Spring. Northern parts of N. hemisphere. (E.B. 130.)

**C. saxat'ilis.** A synonym of *Kernera saxatilis.*

**cochlea'ris -is -e,** spoon-shaped.

**cochlea'tus -a -um,** twisted so as to resemble the shell of a snail.

**COCHLIO'DA** (*kochlion*, a little snail; in reference to the curiously shaped callus). FAM. *Orchidaceae*. A genus embracing about 10 species of evergreen, epiphytic Orchids, natives of the Andes. Flowers often red, disposed in loose racemes, pedicellate; sepals equal, spreading, free, or the lateral ones more or less connate; petals nearly similar; claw of the lip erect, the lamina spreading, the lateral lobes round and often reflexed, the middle one narrow, entire or emarginate, not exceeding the sepals; column erect, often slightly incurved; stigmatic surfaces 2, rather obscure; scapes from base of pseudobulbs. Leaves oblong or narrow, leathery, contracted into the petioles. Pseudobulbs 1- or 2-leaved. Cultural treatment, compost, &c. exactly as for *Odontoglossuma crispum*. The pseudobulbs and foliage are of slightly harder texture than that of true Odontoglossums with which genus Cochlioda readily intercrosses, the hybrids (Odontiodas) being valuable for their brilliant hues, obtained chiefly by the use of *C. densiflora*, better known as *C. Noezliana*.

**C. brasilien'sis.** A synonym of *Binotia brasiliensis.*

**C. densiflo'ra.*** *fl.* orange-scarlet, about 1 in. across; disk of lip yellow; lateral sep. narrower and longer than dorsal one and pet.; lip 3-lobed, mid-lobe bluntly-obcordate; column triquetrous, dark; peduncles nodding or pendulous, racemose, many-fld. *l.* linear-oblong, acute, 4 to 6 in. long. *Pseudobulbs* 1½ to 2 in. long, 1 or 2-lvd. S. America. 1891. (L. 266; W.O.A. 509; B.M. 7474.) SYN. *C. Noezliana, Odontoglossum Noezlianum.* var. **auranti'aca** has yellower *fl.* than type.

*Cochlioda sanguinea* (p. 514)

A*

**C. Flor'yi.** Possibly a natural hybrid between *C. densiflora* and *C. rosea. fl.* cinnabar-red, 1½ in. across; sep. lanceolate; pet. shorter, broader, elliptic-oblong; lip 3-lobed with a yellow crest. Peru. 1911.

**C. minia'ta.** Probably a natural hybrid between *C. densiflora* and *C. vulcanica.* (L. 562.)

**C. Noezlia'na.** A synonym of *C. densiflora.*

**C. ro'sea.** *fl.* rosy-carmine, except the white tip of the column, about 1 in. across; sep. and pet. oblong-elliptic; lip cuneate at base, the small lateral lobes enclosing the disk, which bears a 4-lobed callus, mid-lobe longer, linear, dilated at end; racemes drooping, 12- to 20-fld. Winter. *l.* ligulate-oblong. *Pseudobulbs* green, ovate, 2-edged. Peru. 1851. (B.M. 6084.) SYN. *Mesospinidium roseum, Odontoglossum roseum.*

**C. sanguin'ea.** *fl.* numerous, bright rose, waxy in appearance; lower sep. partially connate; racemes slender, drooping, slightly branched. Summer, autumn. *l.* 2, cuneate-ligulate. *Pseudobulbs* oval, compressed, sometimes banded with mottled brown. Peru and Ecuador. 1867. (B.M. 5627 as *Mesospinidium sanguineum.*)

**C. stric'ta.** *fl.* rose, numerous, erect, smaller than in *C. rosea* which they otherwise resemble; peduncle slender, erect. *l.* narrow, acute. *Pseudobulbs* ovate, compressed, bronzy-green. Colombia. 1897.

**C. vulcan'ica.*** *fl.* 1½ to 2 in. across; sep. and pet. dark rose; lip bright rose in front, paler on disk where there is a 4-keeled callus, side lobes roundish, mid-lobe emarginate; racemes erect, 12- to 20-fld.; peduncle slender, erect. *l.* oblong, keeled, 3 to 5 in. long. *Pseudobulbs* ovoid, compressed, more or less 2-edged. E. Peru. 1872. (B.M. 6001 as *Mesospinidium vulcanicum.*) var. **grandiflo'ra** has deep rose *fl.* in racemose spikes, larger than in type. 1893.
E. C.

*cochlio'des,* resembling Cochlioda.

**COCHLIOSTE'MA** (*kochlion,* spiral, *stema,* stamen; the stamens being spirally curved). FAM. *Commelinaceae.* A genus of 2 species (sometimes combined in one) of very handsome perennial, stemless, epiphytic herbs, natives of Ecuador, with the habit of a Billbergia. Leaves large, oblong-lanceolate, sheathing at base. Flowers large, in crowded terminal cymes forming large panicles in the leaf-axils. The individual flowers last but a short time and open successively over a long period. Sepals 3, concave; petals 3, nearly equal, wider than sepals, with long marginal hairs; staminodes 3, 2 erect, linear, 1 short, feathery; staminal column hooded, its incurved margins enclosing 3 spirally twisted anthers. The Cochliostemas are stove plants growing well in a compost of peat and loam in equal parts with a small quantity of sand and well-decayed sheep or cow manure. They need plenty of water, both overhead and by syringing, and perfect drainage, and though less water is needed in winter they must not be allowed to become dry. Propagation is by division of the plants in spring or by seed, sown as soon as ripe. To make certain of seed artificial pollination is necessary.

**C. Jacobia'num.*** *l.* oblong-lanceolate, 1 to 3 ft. long, 6 to 8 in. wide, rich dark green with a narrow purple margin. *fl.* blue, delicately sweet-scented, numerous, stalked, in crowded cymes. September. Ecuador. 1867. (B.M. 5705.)

**C. odoratis'simum.** Habit of *C. Jacobianum. l.* pale green above, margined red, red with deep red-violet lines beneath. *fl.* yellowish-green at base, reddish above; pet. deep blue with large white claw. More strongly scented than *C. Jacobianum.* Ecuador. (G.F. 590.)

**COCHLOSPERMA'CEAE.** Dicotyledons. A family of about 18 tropical trees in a single genus, Cochlospermum. Some species have a short, stout underground stem. Leaves usually palmately lobed, or digitate, alternate, stipulate. Flowers perfect, usually regular, in panicles; sepals and petals 4 or 5; stamens many; carpels 3 to 5, joined, with many ovules on parietal or central placentae. Fruit a capsule. Related to Bixaceae with which it was at one time united.

**COCHLOSPERM'UM** (*cochlo,* to twist, *sperma,* seed; in reference to the form of the seed). FAM. *Cochlospermaceae.* The only genus in its family, containing 18 magnificent trees, usually evergreen but in many species dropping their leaves in the dry season. For characters **see** Family. Flowers yellow, large. The plants grow

well in a compost of loam and peat and require stove treatment. Cuttings of ripe shoots made in April will root in sand under a bell-glass, but do not make such good trees as seedlings. **A**

**C. Gossyp'ium.** Tree up to 50 ft. *l.* 3- to 5-lobed, lobes acute, entire, hairy beneath. *fl.* yellow, large. India. 1822. SYN. *Bombax Gossypium.*

*Cockburnia'nus -a -um,* in honour of H. Cockburn, 1859–1932?, British consul in China, or Rev. G. Cockburn, of the Scottish church in China.

**COCKCHAFERS.** *See* **Chafers.**

**COCKLE BUR.** *See* **Xanthium.** **A**

**COCKROACHES.** The 5 kinds that are of economic importance in this country are the Common or Oriental (*Blatta orientalis*), the German (*Blatella germanica*), the American (*Periplaneta americana*) the Australian (*P. australasiae*), and *Leucophaea surinamensis.* The Common and German species are commonly found in dwelling-houses and are generally referred to as 'Black-beetles', while the other three occur in glasshouses and warehouses. They are omnivorous in their habits, being partial to a varied diet and, when short of food, may resort to cannibalism. The household species do more harm by tainting and spoiling food than from the actual amount of food consumed. They are nocturnal, swift runners, have very flat bodies that allows them to gain entrance into buildings through small cracks and crevices in brick- and wood-work, possess a large and broad upper segment of the thorax which almost entirely conceals the head, and very long antennae. Their eggs are laid in conspicuous, horny, purse-like sacs containing a varying number of eggs. The young nymphs resemble their parents but are wingless, the wing-buds lengthening as the insects develop—an exception being the female of the Common Cockroach which is practically wingless. The American and Australian species abound in glasshouses and forcing-pits where they eat seeds, seedlings, and leaves, and nibble the aerial roots of Orchids.

The presence of plant refuse beneath the staging of glasshouses encourages these pests, and all rubbish should be cleared from the houses. Trapping is a useful measure for reducing their numbers, and effective traps are made by sinking jam-jars in the borders and floor baited with stale beer and treacle or peeled Banana. The use of poisonous baits (Paris Green and bran or D.D.T. dust) or non-poisonous dressings (powdered borax and fresh pyrethrum powder) is desirable in heavy infestations (*see* F. Laing, Economic Series No. 12, British Museum (Natural History), Bulletin 'Cockroaches').

G. F. W.

**COCKSCOMB.** *See* **Celosia.** **A**

**COCKSFOOT GRASS.** *See* **Dactylis glomerata.**

**COCKSPUR FLOWER.** *See* **Plectranthus.**

**COCKSPUR THORN.** *See* **Crataegus Crus-galli.**

**COCKTAIL BEETLE.** *See* **Devil's Coach Horse.**

**COCO DE MER.** *See* **Lodoicea.**

**COCOA.** *See* **Theobroma Cacao.**

**COCOA PLUM.** *See* **Chrysobalanus Icaco.** **A**

**COCOA ROOTS.** Roots of *Caladium bicolor* and other species of Caladium.

*cocoi'des,* Cocos-like.

*cocoi'nus -a -um,* like coco-nut in some way, e.g. in odour.

**COCO-NUT.** The fruit of *Cocos nucifera.*

**COCO-NUT, DOUBLE.** *See* **Lodoicea.**

**COCO-NUT FIBRE.** The fibre between the outer skin and the shell of the coco-nut was at one time extensively used in horticulture and was most useful, but since the dried flesh of the nut (copra) is the form in which it is now commonly imported, instead of as the whole nut, little is available. It is free from acid, salts of any kind and tannin, or any other substance injurious to young plants and proved very suitable as a medium for the raising of cuttings of tender bedding plants which rooted readily in it. The fresher it is the longer it will last and therefore the better for all purposes. Being very light and easily handled it formed one of the best materials for plunging small pots in, either in the house or frame in winter and spring or outside at any time. It could be used for potting young bedding plants but not for permanent potting since it held water too tenaciously and decayed too quickly. It was frequently used for surfacing flower-beds in summer, and for protecting roots of tender plants in winter, and its cheapness was greatly in its favour, especially as it was also useful as an addition to stiff soils to lighten them, and to dry soils to enable them to hold more moisture. There is nothing that can quite take its place, a good peat being the nearest.

**CO'COS** (*coco*, Portuguese name for monkey, from the likeness of the end of the nut to a monkey's head). Fam. *Palmaceae*. Like many other genera of Palms Cocos has undergone many changes and the genus as understood by many botanists now contains but one species, *C. nucifera*, the Coco-nut. Other species once included in it have been distributed over the genera Arecastrum, Arikuryroba, Butia, Rhyticocos, and Syagrus and should be sought under these headings. For characters of *C. nucifera* see below. The Coco-nut Palm has, in its native home and in the many parts of the tropics in which it has become naturalized, been put to almost innumerable uses, its leaves for thatch, the outer part of its trunk as timber for various purposes (porcupine wood) and its fruit for divers purposes. The fruit is readily transported by ocean currents and, probably mainly by this means, the tree has spread far from its place of origin which is supposed to be Trop. America. Among the purposes it serves are the making of toddy and its derivatives from the sap which exudes from the end of the unopened spathe when its tip is sliced off (as it is day after day by the collectors). This is used fresh as a beverage, or as a source of alcohol, or sugar, or vinegar. The fibrous coat outside the shell of the nut provides Coir, used in the manufacture of cordage, for coco-nut matting, and for brooms. The third important product and the most important is Copra, made by drying the flesh of the nut either in the sun or by artificial heat, a source of fat and oil used in making soap, candles, and substitutes for butter. Desiccated coco-nut is exported from Ceylon, and a certain number, much smaller however than formerly, of the ripe nuts are also imported into this country. The coco-nut produces 1 seedling from the largest of the 3 soft disks at the end of the nut (2 of the 3 ovules contained in the flower aborting). It does not as a rule grow satisfactorily in this country, being more exacting in its requirements than many other Palms. It needs stove conditions, a compost of 2 parts rich loam, 1 of peat, and 1 of sand, much water during the growing season, and a gradually reduced supply as winter approaches. It is reproduced by the nuts.

**C. austra'lis.** A synonym of *Butia capitata.*

**C. capita'ta.** A synonym of *Butia capitata.*

**C. Da'til.** A synonym of *Arecastrum Romanzoffianum australe.*

**C. eriospa'tha.** A synonym of *Butia Yatay.*

**C. flexuo'sa.** A synonym of *Arecastrum Romanzoffianum australe.*

**C. leiospa'tha.** A synonym of *Butia leiospatha.*

**C. nucif'era.** Coco-nut Palm. Tree of 40 to 100 ft., slender, thickened at base. *l.* pinnate, 6 to 20 ft. long; lflets. linear-lanceolate, 2 to 3 ft. long, more or less pendent, leathery, bright glossy-green; stalk stout, 3 to 5 ft. long. Introduced from E. Indies. 1690. Native of Cocos and Keeling Is. and probably Trop. America. var. **au'rea,** sheaths, stalks, and midribs of *l.* orange-yellow.

**C. odora'ta.*** A synonym of *Butia capitata odorata.*

**C. petrae'a.** A synonym of *Syagrus petraea.*

**C. plumo'sa.** A synonym of *Arecastrum Romanzoffianum.*

**C. Procopia'na.** A synonym of *Syagrus macrocarpa.*

**C. Romanzoffia'na.** A synonym of *Arecastrum Romanzoffianum.*

**C. schizophyl'la.** A synonym of *Arikuryroba schizophylla.*

**C. Weddelia'na.** A synonym of *Syagrus Weddeliana.*

**C. Ya'tay.** A synonym of *B tia Yatay.*

**CODIAE'UM** (from the native name, *kodiho*, in Ternatea). Fam. *Euphorbiaceae.* A genus of perhaps 6 species of evergreen shrubs natives of Malaya and the Pacific Is. Leaves alternate, leathery, rather thick, glabrous, with slightly milky juice. Flowers monoecious, in slender axillary racemes; staminate flowers with 3 to 6 reflexed sepals (mostly 5); 5 petals, scale-like, shorter than sepals; 20 to 30 stamens; pistillate flowers without petals, sepals 5; ovary 3-celled, with 1 ovule in each cell. Only 1 species is in general cultivation, *C. variegatum,* and of that only the variety *pictum* of which there are a great number of forms, many of which have received names of Latin form as though they were species. Among plants with ornamental foliage few are as useful or striking as the forms of this plant. They are usually called Crotons (but differ in several ways from the true Crotons, particularly in having glabrous leaves, milky sap, and erect stamens). In addition to the remarkable range of bright colours found in these plants the leaves often assume singular forms, and except Dracaenas no group of plants of a similar type is more easily grown than Codiaeums; and, furthermore, they are available the year round. When wanted for table decorations the plants should be grown with a single stem. To obtain this the best way is to take off the tops of strong leading shoots and use them as cuttings. They may be struck by placing singly in small pots, covering with bell-glasses, in strong, moist heat, when they soon form roots losing none of the leaves that were on the shoots when they were inserted. When rooted they should be given a little air, gradually giving more until they can bear full exposure. The most useful size for table decoration is from 12 to 18 in. high. When used for this purpose the plants frequently lose their lowest leaves and when they reach this height it is best to make cuttings of their tops and start again. Besides this use for table decoration and for use in rooms generally Codiaeums are equally useful for conservatories and other cool houses during summer and autumn. For this purpose they must be gradually hardened before they are taken out of the stove heat as they are very susceptible to cold, and sudden changes cause their leaves to fall. The soil best suited for them is fibrous loam with a good sprinkling of sand to keep it open and porous. In this, given due attention to water-supply and temperature, they will grow very freely. The temperature most suitable in winter ranges from 60 to 70° F. according to the state of the weather. In order to bring out to the fullest extent their brilliant colourings it is necessary to give the plants plenty of light; they should be placed on pans or inverted pots to raise them above neighbouring plants which might shade them. Plants which it is desired should grow into large specimens should be encouraged to make plenty of side shoots by pinching the end of the leading shoots if they do not start freely without, but they usually grow naturally into bushy plants. They need a moist atmosphere and must be well attended to in regard to watering and syringing otherwise Red-spider-mites will become troublesome. This is one of the worst enemies of the Codiaeums and Thrips is another, and no pains should be spared to keep them in check. (See special headings.) For the different forms see Appendix.

**C. variega'tum pic'tum.** Croton. *l.* ovate to linear, marked with various colours, entire or lobed. (B.M. 3051; L.B.C. 870.) The l. may be plane or recurved, entire or lobed, the margins may also be crisped, or the l. spirally twisted, the blade may have a hair-like apical projection or this projection may terminate in a l.-like appendage and each of these forms has appeared in a great variety of colourings.

**CODLIN.** A smooth green or golden apple without stripes and with at most a faint flush of reddish colour on one side, usually early, usually sour, sometimes sweet, always juicy, with more or less acidity, excellent cookers and usually very fertile. The term is applied generally and also with a prefix, as Manx Codlin, English Codlin, to particular varieties of apple. Sometimes spelt Codling.

**CODLING MOTH,** *Cydia pomonella,* one of the most widespread Apple pests, occurs in almost every country where apples are grown. Its caterpillar was long known as the 'Apple Worm'. The chief food plant is the Apple, but it attacks Pear, Quince, Walnut, and some wild species of Pyrus. The moths, which have brownish-grey wings with a copper-coloured patch towards the ends of the fore-wings, are not well known for they fly at dusk and rest during the day on tree trunks, branches, and leaves where they are difficult to detect. The female lays her oval flat eggs singly on the developing fruitlets, leaves, spurs, and shoots. The young caterpillar enters the fruit either through the 'eye' or the side, and burrows down and round the core devouring the flesh and the pips. The larvae are fully fed in 3 to 4 weeks, and are then about $\frac{1}{2}$ to $\frac{3}{4}$ in. long, pinkish-white with a brown head. They burrow their way out of the fruits, which may still be attached to the tree or have fallen to the ground, and seek shelter in which to overwinter. Positions chosen for hibernation are cracks and crevices in the bark, beneath old grease-bands and in dry rubbish on the ground nearby, and there they spin whitish or brown cocoons in which they remain until the following spring when they pupate. There may occur a partial second brood of caterpillars in August and September, but the extended period of egg-laying—mid-June to early August—has resulted in mistaken statements to the effect that this pest is invariably 3-brooded in this country. Much confusion still exists between attacks by this pest and the Apple Sawfly (q.v.), but the following may enable one to distinguish between these pests. Damage by Codling moth occurs later in the season than Sawfly; unlike fruits injured by the Sawfly, those attacked by the moth larvae have no unpleasant odour; Codling caterpillars emit no black frass from their tunnels, and do not give rise to ribbon-like scars on the fruits; Codling caterpillars feed chiefly in the region of the core, those of the Sawfly eat out large irregular cavities in the flesh; and the number of legs differs—the Codling larva possesses 8 pairs (3 pairs of true or thoracic legs and 5 pairs of prolegs or 'sucker feet') while the Sawfly larva possesses 10 pairs (3 pairs and 7 pairs respectively).

Control measures include the collection and destruction of all fallen and maggoty fruit; clearance of all rubbish and dead leaves round and near the fruit trees; scraping loose bark from the trunks of old and neglected trees; spraying of moss- and lichen-covered trunks and branches with caustic alkali or tar-distillate wash; placing of trap-bands (corrugated paper or sacking) round the trunks in July and their removal and destruction in October; and spraying with arsenate of lead, which should be directed into the 'eye' or calyx-cup of the developing fruits, within 14 days of petal-fall. The later (July) brood may be controlled by spraying with a D.D.T. emulsion. **A** G. F. W.

**CODLINS AND CREAM.** *See* **Epilobium hirsutum.**

**CODONAN'THE** (*kodon,* bell, *anthos,* flower; from the shape of the corolla). FAM. *Gesneriaceae.* A genus of about 12 species of herbs or sub-shrubs, which creep or climb over rocks and trees in Trop. America. Leaves opposite, often rather small and fleshy. Flowers solitary in the leaf-axils, short-stalked, whitish; calyx of 5 linear, free sepals; corolla tube curved or bent downwards, rather broad at the throat, lobes 5, spreading, oblique. Fruit a berry. For cultivation of the two mentioned, which make good basket plants, *see* **Gesneria.**

**C. Devosia'na.** Nearly allied to *C. gracilis.* Branches many, pendent, slender, brown, rooting. *l.* rounded-oval, recurved at tip, fleshy, usually entire. *fl.* whitish-rose, 2-lipped, lower lip auricled at base; cor. tube velvety within, spotted golden-red in mouth; peduncles solitary or opposite. Organ Mts., Brazil. 1855. (I.H. 2 (1855), 56.)

**C. grac'ilis.** Stem branched, terete, purplish-brown, rooting below nodes. *l.* ovate, thick, fleshy, dark green above, pale and often blotched red beneath. *fl.* creamy-white, spotted orange on lower side of tube within; peduncles 1 or 2 in axils, short, red. June. Organ Mts., Brazil. 1850. (B.M. 4531 as *Hypocyrta gracilis.*)

*codono'des,* bell-bearing.

**CODONOP'SIS** (*kodon,* bell, *opsis,* resembling; from the shape of the corolla). FAM. *Campanulaceae.* A genus of about 20 species of herbs, often with twining stems, natives of Asia from the Himalaya to Japan, annual or perennial. Branches usually opposite. Leaves alternate or nearly opposite, ovate; stalks short. Flowers whitish, yellowish, or bluish, bell-shaped, often malodorous; stamens free of corolla; ovary inferior or half superior; stigma lobes 3, broad. Fruit opening regularly at top. The species are easily raised from seed, are generally hardy, and are best planted on a high bank so that the interior of the hanging flowers can be seen, for there the chief beauty of the flower lies, the outer colouring, except in the very beautiful and uncommon *C. convolvulacea* which is blue without and within, being usually somewhat indeterminate. Good, light soil, suits them best. **A**

**C. clematid'ea.** Perennial, 3 or 4 ft. h. *l.* ovate, slender-pointed, almost glabrous. *fl.* white, tinged blue. Mts. of Asia. (G.F. 167.)

*Codonopsis convolvulacea Forrestii* (p. 517)

**C. convolvula′cea.*** Perennial twiner. Stem slender, glabrous, slightly branched. *l.* usually smooth, alternate, ovate-lanceolate or ovate, ½ to 2 in. long, more or less acute, entire or nearly so; stalk slender, ⅛ to ½ in. long. *fl.* blue, bell-shaped, 1¼ to 2 in. across; lobes ¾ to 1½ in. long, oblanceolate, acute; cal. superior, tube about ⅓ in. long, lobes 5, triangular, acute. Himalaya, W. China. 1906. (B.M. 8178.) var. **Forrest′ii,** differs by its more robust habit and larger *l.* and *fl.*, *l.* firm, ovate. Yunnan, Szechwan. 1923. (B.M. 9581.) SYN. *C. Forrestii, C. tibetica.*

**C. Forrest′ii.** A variety of *C. convolvulacea.*

**C. lanceola′ta.** Perennial twiner, 2 to 3 ft. h. Stems purplish, roots tuberous. *l.* oblong-lanceolate, 1 to 2 in. long, sometimes with rounded teeth. *fl.* pale lilac without, violet within; segs. ovate-deltoid. China. 1851. (F.d.S. 927 as *Campanumoea lanceolata.*)

**C. Meleag′ris.** Perennial herb with a large, fleshy rootstock. Stems erect, somewhat flexuous in upper part, 6 to 14 in. h., with 1 or 2 *l. l.* crowded at base, often in rosettes, elliptic-oblong, sessile or nearly so, margins wavy, lower surface glaucous, softly hairy. *fl.* 1 or 2, nodding, bell-shaped, 1 to 1½ in. long, bluish to cream, netted chocolate-brown without, dull purple-violet from a narrow green base, sometimes spotted yellow within; lobes ovate, sub-acute, ⅔ in. long. August. Yunnan, China. 1916. (B.M. 9237.)

**C. mol′lis.** Tufted with many leafy ascending stems. *l.* small, ovate, greyish-green, softly hairy. *fl.* pale blue, nodding, without the unpleasant odour of most species; cor. tubular, expanding from middle, lobes short, triangular; peduncle slender, long, leafless, 1- to 4-fld. Tibet. 1924. (J.R.H.S. 70, f. 91; B.M. 9677.) A difficult plant, for the rock-garden.

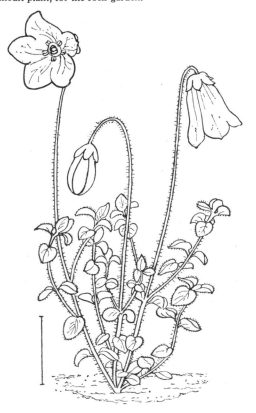

*Codonopsis ovata*

**C. ova′ta.** Perennial, 6 to 12 in. h., lower part of stem spreading, upper erect. *l.* ovate, up to ¾ in. long, hairy on both sides; stalks up to ¼ in. long. *fl.* pale blue, broadly bell-shaped, 1 to 1½ in. long; peduncles 3 to 6 in. long. Himalaya. 1856. (B.M. 9208.)

**C. rotundifo′lia.** Annual twiner, tall. *l.* ovate, rather blunt, stalked. *fl.* yellowish-green veined dark purple, larger, bell-shaped, widening inwards. Himalaya. (B.M. 4942.) var. **grandiflo′ra,** cor. more variegated than in type, resembling that of Deadly Nightshade. (B.M. 5018.)

**C. Tang′shen.** Perennial twiner, up to 10 ft. h. Stems slender, smooth or almost so; roots long, fleshy. *l.* ovate to ovate-lanceolate, 1½ to 2½ in. long, usually minutely downy, blunt, remotely crenate. *fl.* greenish, with purple stripes and spots within, bell-shaped, about 1½ in. long, lobes ¼ in. long. W. China. 1902. (B.M. 8090.) Root yields a tonic drug used in China.

**C. tibet′ica.** A synonym of *C. convolvulacea.*

**COELESTI′NA ageratoi′des.** A synonym of *Ageratum corymbosum.*                    **A**

*coelesti′nus -a -um,* blue.

*coeles′tis -is -e,* sky-blue.

*Coeli-ro′sa,* Rose of heaven.

*Codonopsis Tangshen*

**COE′LIA** (*koilos,* hollow; the 8 pollen masses were wrongly thought to be concave within). FAM. *Orchidaceae.* A genus of 6 or 7 species of epiphytic orchids in Cent. America, the W. Indies, and Mexico. The pseudobulbs are comparatively small, globose, bearing 3 or 4 narrow, ribbed leaves, narrowed below into sheathing foot-stalks. The flowers are produced from their bases in short, usually densely flowered, bracteate spikes. With the exception of *C. bella,* the flowers are small. The column is produced into a short foot to which the 2 lateral sepals are adnate at their bases; capsule 3-winged. The species succeed well in the cool house, but *C. bella* should have a winter temperature of 55° F. *C. macrostachya* requires a rather longer rest than the other species with softer bulbs. Compost as for Lycaste with greater proportions of Osmunda fibre and Sphagnum.

**C. Baueria′na.** *fl.* small, greenish-white, fragrant; racemes densely-fld.; bracts long. June. *l.* ensiform, 12 to 15 in. long. *Pseudobulbs* ovate. 1 ft. h. W. Indies, &c. 1790. (B.R. 28, 36.)

**C. bel′la.*** *fl.* 3 or 4, erect, 2 in. long; perianth yellowish-white, with rose-purple tips to seg., and having an orange mid-lobe to lip, tubular below, funnel-shaped above; scape 2 to 4 in. long, clothed with brown sheaths. Autumn to December. *l.* 3 or 4, 6 to 10 in. long, elongate-ensiform, acuminate. *Pseudobulbs* 1½ to 2 in. long, globose or ovoid. Ile St. Catherine. 1882. (B.M. 6628; W.O.A. ii. 51.) SYN. *Bifrenaria bella, Bothriochilus bellus.*

**C. densiflo′ra.** *fl.* pure white; anther-case yellow. Allied to *C. Baueriana* but differing in colour and in the shorter more densely-fld. infl. Guatemala. 1906.

**C. guatemalen′sis.** Spikes erect, bracteate, 4 in. h. *fl.* 4 or more, small, fleshy, soft rose; sep. forming a tube ½ in. long, concealing the pet. and lip, slightly reflexed at tips; pet. and lip whitish. The bases of the lip and lateral sep. form a blunt, tapered, straight spur, as long as the sepaline tube. Fl. in axil of a greenish boat-shaped, acuminate bract. *Pseudobulbs* globose-conical, 2 in. h. *l.* narrow, 12 in. long. Summer. Guatemala. 1939.

**C. macrostach′ya.*** *fl.* red; racemes many-fld.; bracts red-brown, linear-lanceolate, acute, squarrose; lip lanceolate, 2-saccate at base. April. *l.* ensiform, plicate. *Pseudobulbs* large, almost globose. 1½ ft. h. Guatemala. 1840. (B.M. 4712.)

**C. trip′tera.** A synonym of *C. Baueriana.*

E. C.

**COELIOP′SIS** (*Coelia*-like). FAM. *Orchidaceae.* The only species known is *C. hyacinthosma,* an epiphyte. Compost and cultivation should be as for Stanhopeas. The winter rest must not be drastic, and pots and pans may be used in place of baskets.

**C. hyacinthos'ma.*** *fl.* fragrant, fleshy, 12 to 20, closely set on short, lateral peduncles, produced from the base of the bulbs, about 1 in. across, broadly campanulate; sep. broadly lanceolate; pet. narrow; lip deeply saccate at the base, broadly rounded with the front lobe extended into a narrow reflexed tongue, white with the exception of deep ochre in the throat, a circular thin zone of purplish-red in front of it and a small anterior blotch of the same colour. Column stout, white, deep purplish-black on the basal half in front passing into the sac; slightly variable. Pollen masses 2. Spring. *Pseudobulbs* ovoid, 2 to 3 in. h., triphyllous. *l.* 15 to 18 in. long, lanceolate, plicate, contracted below into a channelled foot-stalk. Panama, Costa Rica. 1872.

E. C.

**COELOGLOS'SUM.** Included in **Habenaria.**

**COELOG'YNE** (*koilos*, hollow, and *gyne*, female; referring to the form of the stigma). FAM. *Orchidaceae.* A genus of 120 or more epiphytic species distributed from Ceylon, through the East. The species vary greatly, but in general they are pseudobulbous with bulbs from 1 to 6 in. high, usually diphyllous. The flowers solitary or racemose, erect or pendent, are in many species produced from the middle of the young growth, in others they do not fully develop until the pseudobulbs are complete. The sepals, larger than the petals, are free, but not always spreading; the petals in some species are so narrow as to be nearly filiform. The lip usually large and cucullate may be entire or 3-lobed, slightly saccate at the base with 2 or more longitudinal raised lines or keels; the side lobes are often comparatively large and erect. The column is curved and winged, often toothed on a membraneous margin, nearly parallel with the lip. Pollen masses 4.

The great variation in the genus and its wide distribution governs the temperatures required. The Bornean, New Guinea, and Far Eastern species require a warm house with a winter night temperature of at least 60° F. The Indian and many of the Burmese species can be grown in the cool house during summer but should not fall below 50° F. in the winter, though the greater number then require but infrequent waterings. The species with pendent spikes should be placed in baskets or pans which can be suspended. The smaller growing species, particularly those with clustered pseudobulbs, can be placed in pans or pots; a few with straggling habit should be accommodated on rafts. All need a compost of 3 parts of shredded Osmunda fibre to 1 part of Sphagnum moss. When the foliage is young and enfolded the syringe should not be used; with all, water may be freely given when growths and roots are active.

Botanically, Pleiones are very nearly related to Coelogyne, but they differ widely in habit and in the cultivation required and are therefore kept separate here.

**C. albolu'tea.** *fl.* fragrant; white with deep yellow markings on the lip. Allied to and resembling *C. Huettneriana.* India. 1896.

**C. annamen'sis.** Differs from *C. fuscescens* in that the sep. and pet. are pale buff and the buff lip is marked with deep orange-brown. Summer. Annam. 1894.

**C. Arthuria'na.** A synonym of *Pleione Arthuriana.*

**C. aspera'ta.*** *fl.* about 3 in. across; sep. and pet. pale cream, nearly equal; lip ground-colour the same, marked with chocolate and yellow streaks and veins, which radiate from an orange central ridge; raceme pendulous, 12 to 18 in. long, several-fld. Summer. 2 ft. h. Borneo. (L. 582; W.O.A. 311.)

**C. assam'ica.** *fl.* 6 to 10, ochre, 1½ in. across; pet. linear; lip 3-lobed, side lobes margined brown, mid-lobe spreading, darker on margins. Autumn. Assam. 1857. (X.O. 2, 134.) Very near *C. fuscescens.*

**C. barba'ta.*** *fl.* snow-white, large; lip 3-fid, with projecting triangular acute mid-lobe, 3 rows of narrow lamellae on the disk, and a border of cilia; the lamellae, cilia, and the top are sepia-brown, verging to black, which forms an exceedingly neat contrast to the white of the other parts of the fl.; spikes erect. Winter and spring. *l.* 9 to 15 in. long. Assam. 1837. (W.O.A. 143.) Cool or intermediate house.

**C. Bec'carii.** *fl.* 1 to 5, large, yellowish-white; sep. 1½ in. long; pet. much narrower; lip 3-lobed as long as the sep., with 5 to 7 reddish keels. New Guinea. var. **brachyp'tera,** *see* **C.brachyptera.**

**C. borneen'sis.** *fl.* about 1 in. long; sep. and narrow pet. whitish; lip marked with reddish-brown; raceme about 5 in. long. *l.* obovate. *Pseudobulbs* ovoid, 2-leaved. Borneo. 1893.

*Coelogyne brachyptera*

**C. brachyp'tera.** *fl.* 3 to 6; sep. green, 1½ in. long, narrowly lanceolate; pet. shorter, almost linear; lip resembling that of *C. pandurata,* green sprinkled with sepia-black, but smaller and lighter in colour, the front lobe whitish; column green, winged. *Pseudobulbs* 4-sided, 4 to 6 in. h., diphyllous. *l.* 6 in. long by 1½ in. broad. *Raceme* apical, erect or curved. Burma. 1881. (B.M. 8582.) SYN. *C. Beccarii brachyptera, C. Parishii brachyptera.*

**C. brun'nea.** A variety of *C. fuscescens.*

**C. burman'ica.** A synonym of *Pleione burmanica.*

**C. can'dida.** A synonym of *Pleione maculata.*

**C. carina'ta.** *fl.* sep. and pet. whitish-green, 1 in. long; lip spotted with brown, 3-lobed; scape 4 to 8 in. long, 6-fld. *l.* oblong-lanceolate, 5 in. long. *Pseudobulbs* 4-angled, 2 in. long, 2-leaved. New Guinea. 1895.

**C. chlorop'tera.** *fl.* 4 to 8, about 1 in. across; sep. and pet. bright greenish-yellow; the 3-lobed lip marked and keeled red-brown. *Pseudobulbs* obscurely 4-sided, 1 to 1½ in. h., diphyllous. *l.* 4 to 6 in. long, 1 in. broad. Philippines. 1883. (X.O. 3, 235.)

**C. cilia'ta.** *fl.* yellow and white, with brown markings. Autumn. Compact growing, with light green leaves, and *pseudobulbs* about 4 in. h. Philippines.

**C. cinnamo'mea.** *fl.* 3 to 4, yellowish-white, 1½ in. across; lip 3-lobed, side lobes brown with lighter stripes, margined yellow, mid-lobe viol-shape, bluntly pointed, reflexed at tip, brown and yellow. *rhiz.* creeping. *Pseudobulbs* about 3 in. h. *l.* 12 to 15 in. long, including foot-stalk, 1 to 1½ in. broad. Java. 1909.

**C. Clark'ei.** *fl.* sep. and pet. light brown; lip yellowish-brown, margined with brown. Allied to *C. prolifera.* Habitat ? 1893.

**C. con'color.** A synonym of *Pleione concolor.*

**C. corona'ria.** A synonym of *Eria coronaria.*

**C. corruga'ta.*** *fl.* 1½ in. wide, sep. and pet. pure white; lip white, with a yellow disk in front, and veined with orange; racemes erect, shorter than l. Autumn. *l.* twin, about 6 in. long, leathery. *Pseudobulbs* much corrugated, yellowish. India. 1866. Cool house, needing a decided rest. (B.M. 5601.)

**C. corymbo'sa.*** *fl.* 3 to 7, about 3 in. across; sep. and pet. white; lip white, pointed, with 2 ocellate yellow brown-edged blotches. June. *Pseudobulbs* 2 in. h., obscurely 4-sided. *l.* 4 to 6 in. Himalaya. 1876. (B.M. 6955; A.B.G.C. 8, 185.)

**C. crista'ta.*** *fl.* fragrant in some forms, 3 to 4 in. wide; sep. and pet. snow-white; lip white, with a large blotch of rich yellow in the middle, veins ornamented with a golden crest-like fringe; raceme somewhat drooping, 5- to 8-fld. December to March. *l.* twin, narrow, leathery, dark green. *Pseudobulbs* roundish oblong, smooth, shining, apple-green, 2 to 3 in. h. Nepal. 1837. (B.M. 8477; W.O.A. 501.) A very popular, showy, easily grown species. Though capable of resisting low temperatures better results are obtained when the plants are grown in the cool house during summer and in winter and spring kept at 50 to 55° F. Abundance of water is needed from early April to October but through the winter infrequently. Of rather straggling habit, it can be grown in shallow pans or on tree-fern sections. var. **al'ba,** *fl.* pure white throughout, *pseudobulbs* set at greater intervals on the rhizome. (L. 173; W.O.A. 54.); **Chats-worth,** *fl.* larger than in type, usually 8 on a spike; **citri'na,** a synonym of var. *Lemoniana;* **hololeu'ca,** a synonym of var. *alba;* **Lemonia'na,** middle of lip stained delicate lemon. Nepal; **ma'jor,** larger than type, with stouter sep. and pet. India; **max'ima,** sep. and pet. very broad, side lobes of lip shallow, 1886; **Woodland's var.,** *fl.* white, faintly tinged lemon-yellow in the throat.

**C. Cum'ingii.*** *fl.* 5 or 6; sep. and pet. white; lip white, with yellow down the middle. Summer. 2 ft. h. Singapore. 1840. (B.M. 4645; B.R. 27, 29.) A pretty species, retaining its beauty for a considerable period.

**C. cu'prea.** *fl.* somewhat resembling those of *C. speciosa,* but smaller, drooping; stalks bearing 5 to 8 bracts. *l.* oblong. *Pseudobulbs* 2 or 3 in. long. Sumatra. (X.O. 3, 263.) 1892.

**C. Daya'na.*** *fl.* light ochreous; sep. and pet. narrow, acute; lip broad, 3-lobed, the side lobes striped dark brown, wavy, the mid-lobe somewhat quadrate, point reflexed, crenulate, with a dark brown crescent, 2 keels run from base of lip to base of mid-lobe where they divide into 6; infl. 2 to 3 ft. long, many-fld. May, June. *l.* stalked, oblong, 18 to 24 in. long, acuminate, stiffly plicate. *Pseudobulbs* long, narrow, fusiform, 5 to 9 in. h. Borneo. 1884. (L. 687; W.O.A. 247.)

**C. ela'ta.*** *fl.* 5 to 12 opening in succession, medium-sized; sep. and pet. white, narrowish; lip white, with a forked, yellow band in centre, and 2 orange-striped crests on disk; racemes erect springing with the l. from the apex of the pseudobulbs. Spring. *l.* 12 to 18 in. long, 2 to 3 in. wide. *Pseudobulbs* 3 to 6 in. h., stout, oblong, angled. Tongoo, Darjeeling (8,000 to 9,000 ft.). 1837. (B.M. 5001; A.B.G.C. 8, 188.)

**C. el'egans.** A synonym of *C. Huettneriana.*

**C. fimbria'ta.** *fl.* sep. yellowish-green or brownish, ovate-lanceo-late, ¾ in. long; pet. filiform; lip yellow, streaked with reddish-brown, mid-lobe fringed; scape 1 to 2 in. long, 1- or 2-fld. Summer. *l.* sessile, 2 to 5 in. long, lanceolate. *Pseudobulbs* ovoid-oblong, ¾ to 1½ in. long. Khasia, China. (B.R. 868.)

**C. flac'cida.** *fl.* 1½ in. wide with a somewhat heavy odour; sep. and pet. whitish; lip white, stained with pale yellow in front, and streaked with crimson towards its base; racemes pendulous, 7- to 12-fld. Winter and spring. *l.* twin, dark green, leathery. *Pseudo-bulbs* oblong. Nepal. (B.M. 3318; B.R. 27, 31; A.B.G.C. 8, 183.) Requires a decided rest.

**C. flav'ida.** *fl.* 8 to 10, yellow, ½ in. across; spikes erect, bracteate; scape slender. Spring. *l.* 3 to 6 in. long, petiolate, narrow-lanceolate, acuminate. *Pseudobulbs* 1 to 2 in. long, distant, on a slender, scaly rhizome. Sikkim. 1838. (A.B.G.C. 8, 191.)

**C. flexuo'sa.** *fl.* ¾ in. across, white, with a slight yellow stain across middle of lip, extended as a narrow line on either side of disk to near base, where the lip is very sharply constricted, forming a narrow, transverse channel underneath. Java. 1892.

**C. Foersterman'nii.*** *fl.* white, with some yellowish-brown on disk of lip; sep. and pet. ligulate, acute; lip 3-fid, lateral lobes rounded, mid-lobe rounded, apiculate; peduncles sometimes 40-fld. *l.* cartilaginous, ribbed, 1½ ft. long, 3 in. or more wide, on very short petioles. Sunda Is. 1887.

**C. fuligino'sa.** *fl.* 1 to 3, expanding one at a time, 2 in. across; sep. and narrower pet. brownish-white, tinged rosy; lip similarly coloured, mid-lobe nearly covered and margined with sooty-black hairs; racemes shorter than l. Summer. *l.* broadly lanceolate, 5 to 7 in. long. *Pseudobulbs* 2 to 3 in. long. N. India. 1838. (B.M. 4440.) Habit straggling, suitable for a raft.

**C. fusces'cens.** *fl.* large; sep. and pet. pale yellowish, suffused with brown-red; tipped with white; lip edged with white and streaked with orange-yellow, and having on each side of base 2 spots of cinnamon-brown; raceme slightly pendulous, 6- to 12-fld. Winter. *l.* about 9 in. long, broad, dark green. *Pseudobulbs* about 4 or 5 in. h. Moulmein. (A.B.G.C. 8, 181; B.M. 5494.) var. **brun'nea,** *fl.* brown.

**C. Gardneria'na.*** *fl.* 10 to 15, large, pure white, except at base of lip, where they are stained with lemon; segs. narrow; raceme long, nodding; bracts large, white or brown, fleshy. Winter. *l.* twin, lanceolate, thin, bright green, 1 to 1½ ft. long, 3 in. wide. *Pseudo-bulbs* 4 to 6 in. long, narrow, tapering from the base upwards. Khasia. 1837. (W.O.A. 153.) Intermediate house in winter, cool in summer. SYN. *Neogyne Gardneriana.*

**C. glandulo'sa.** *fl.* pure white, 1½ in. across, in a nodding raceme; front lobe of lip ovate, marked on disk with yellow lines. *l.* oblong-lanceolate. *Pseudobulbs* ovate, sulcate. Nilghiri Hills. 1882.

**C. Gow'eri.*** *fl.* sep. and pet. snow-white; lip white, with 3 parallel raised lines and a lemon blotch on disk; raceme pendulous,

many-fld. Winter and spring. *l.* lanceolate, about 6 in. long, bright green. *Pseudobulbs* ovate, shining green. Assam. 1869. A lovely small species, suitable for cultivation on a block of wood; requiring cool treatment.

**C. graminifo'lia.** *fl.* nearly 2 in. across; sep. white, narrowly oblong-lanceolate, acute; pet. similar, but rather narrower; lip 3-lobed, lateral lobes white, streaked brown, oblong, mid-lobe orange-yellow, with 3 whitish ridges; raceme 2- to 4-fld.; scape 1 to 2 in. l., 2, grass-like, 1 to 1½ ft. long. *Pseudo-bulbs* 1 to 1½ in. long. Moulmein. 1888. (B.M. 7006.)

**C. Hookeria'na.** A synonym of *Pleione Hookeriana.*

**C. Huettneria'na.** *fl.* white, 8 to 10 in an arched raceme; lip toothed, with a rounded-ovate mid-lobe; bracts 1 in. long, cymbi-form; scape 7 in. long. Summer. *l.* petiolate, oblong-lanceolate. *Pseudobulbs* fusiform, much wrinkled. Tenasserim. (W.O.A. 459 as *C. lactea.*) SYN. *C. elegans.*

**C. hu'milis.** A synonym of *Pleione humilis.*

**C. integer'rima.** *fl.* 8 to 12, 1½ in. across, light green; lip with 4 brown bands. Summer. *Pseudobulbs* 1 to 2 in. h., smooth, some-what cylindrical. *l.* 3 to 5 in. long, 1 in. broad. *Racemes* arching. Philippines. 1890. (B.M. 8856.)

**C. lac'tea.** A synonym of *C. Huettneriana.*

**C. lagena'ria.** A synonym of *Pleione lagenaria.*

**C. lamella'ta.** *fl.* whitish-green; sep. and pet. oblong-lanceolate, keeled, 1½ in. long; lip 3-lobed, corrugated; scape erect, 3- to 5-fld. New Hebrides. 1895.

*Coelogyne Lawrenceana*

**C. Lawrencea'na.*** *fl.* large, showy; sep. 2½ in. long, ⅞ in. broad, tawny-yellow; pet. linear; lip 2 in. long, front lobe 1 in. broad or more, broadly ovate, white with crimped edges and central thickened tongue, slightly reflexed; side lobes erect, white, mar-gined and spotted brown; at base of winged, hooded, creamy-white green tinged column is a clear yellow blotch, bearing 5 raised fim-briated keels, with red-brown papillae more numerous and pro-nounced on an orange-yellow and sepia-brown ground. June. *Pseudobulbs* ovoid, 2 to 4 in. h., diphyllous. *l.* 7 to 12 in. long, 1 to 1½ in. broad; peduncle from apex of bulbs, 6 to 9 in. long, 1- to 2-fld. Annam. 1904. (B.M. 8164.) Winter temperature about 55° F. var. **super'ba,** *fl.* larger, finer.

**C. lentigino'sa.** *fl.* 1½ in. across; sep. and pet. straw-coloured or clear yellow; side lobes of lip margined brown, the larger mid-lobe white with orange blotches; broadly clawed; raceme 5- to 8-fld. (in-cluding scape) 4 to 5 in. long, sheathed up to fl. Summer. *l.* linear-oblong, 6 to 8 in. long. *Pseudobulbs* 3 to 4 in. long, obtusely 4-angled. Tenasserim. 1847. (B.M. 5958; W.O.A. 442.)

**C. Low'ii.** A synonym of *C. asperata*.

**C. macrobul'bon.** A synonym of *C. Rochussenii*.

**C. macula'ta.** A synonym of *Pleione maculata*.

**C. Massangea'na.\*** *fl.* sep. and pet. light ochre; lip 3-fid, marked with maroon-brown, and ochre-coloured veins; raceme pendulous, many, but loosely, fld. *Pseudobulbs* pyriform, bearing 2 Stanhopea-like l. Assam. 1879. (B.M. 6979; L. 548.) Intermediate to cool house.

**C. Mayeria'na.** *fl.* 3 to 7, 2½ in. across, with green sep. and pet., and a green and black lip, resembling those of *C. pandurata*, but smaller. *rhiz.* freely branching with pseudobulbs at intervals. Trop. Asia. 1894. Succeeds well on a tree-fern section.

**C. me'dia.\*** *fl.* on spikes 10 in. h.; sep. and pet. creamy-white; lip yellow and brown. *Pseudobulb* short, round. *l.* 7 in. long. Khasia. 1837. Pretty, small-growing, winter-flowering.

**C. Micholiczia'na.\*** *fl.* 2 to 4, opening successively, pure white except the thick, fleshy, raised, dark chocolate-brown disk. Summer. Resembling *C. speciosa* in habit but scapes taller. New Guinea. 1895. (X.O. 3. 256.)

**C. minia'ta.** *fl.* 3 to 7, small, cinnabar-red, on short erect spikes. *rhiz.* ascending. *Pseudobulbs* spaced, slender, obscurely ovate, red-shaded. *l.* 4 to 5 in. long, 1 in. broad. Java.

**C. Moorea'na.\*** *fl.* 4 to 12, on erect spikes, superficially resembling those of *C. cristata*; lip with golden hairs on disk, mid-lobe broadly ovate. *Pseudobulbs* ovate-globose, clustered, diphyllous. *l.* 12 to 16 in. long, rather fleshy. Annam. 1904. (B.M. 8297.) var. **magnif'ica,** has *fl.* 4 in. across; **Wes'tonbirt** has *fl.* larger than type.

**C. Mos'siae.\*** *fl.* pure white, 1½ in. across, with a yellow, crescent-shaped mark on lip; raceme 6 in. long, about 6-fld. Summer. *l.* 6 in. long. *Pseudobulbs* 1½ in. long, ovate, 2-leaved. Nilghiri Hills. 1894. (G.C. 15 (1894), 401.) Markings much as in *C. ocellata*.

**C. nervo'sa.** *fl.* 2 to 4, sep. and pet. white, acute, former 1 to 1¼ in. long; lip white and yellowish-brown; bracts very large; scape erect, sheathed up to the few fl. Summer. *l.* oblong-lanceolate, 4 to 6 in. long. *Pseudobulbs* 2 to 3 in. long, ovoid. Nilghiri Hills.

**C. ocella'ta.\*** *fl.* 5 to 7, sep. and pet. pure white; lip white, streaked and spotted with yellow and brown at base; side lobes with 2 bright yellow spots on each; column bordered with bright orange; racemes upright. March, April. *l.* long, narrow, bright green, longer than racemes. *Pseudobulbs* ovate. India. 1822. (B.M. 3767.) Pretty species for cool house. var. **max'ima** has a raceme of about 8 star-like fl., segs. lanceolate, lip saddle-shaped, with terminal lobe marked with yellow. 1879. (L. 243.)

**C. ochra'cea.\*** *fl.* 7 to 9, 1½ in. across, white, very fragrant, in erect racemes; lip with two bright ochreous-yellow, orange bordered, horseshoe-shaped blotches on disk. Spring. *l.* 2 or 3, lanceolate. *Pseudobulbs* 2 to 4 in. h., 4-sided. NE. India. 1844. (B.M. 4661; B.R. 32, 69; A.B.G.C. 8, 182.)

**C. odoratis'sima.\*** *fl.* 2 to 5, fragrant, pure white, except the centre of the lip, which is stained yellow; raceme slender. Summer. *l.* twin, pale green, lanceolate, about 4 in. long. *Pseudobulbs* thickly clustered about 1 in. h. India. 1864. (B.M. 5462.) This species grows freely in a cool house.

**C. ova'lis.** *fl.* 2 to 4. Very similar to *C. fimbriata* but stronger and with slightly larger fl. Himalaya. 1837. (A.B.G.C. 8, 187.) A

**C. pachybul'bon.** *fl.* about 9, 1½ in. across; sep. and narrower pet. straw-yellow; lip 3-lobed, side lobes erect, fuscous-brown and white, mid-lobe oblong, reflexed, light brown to yellow. *infl.* arching, 9 in. long. *Pseudobulbs* stout, brownish. *l.* 12 to 18 in. long. Malaya.

**C. pandura'ta.\*** *fl.* 5 to 15, up to 4 in. across, very fragrant; sep. and pet. of a very lively green; lip of same colour, with several deep velvety black, parallel, raised ridges upon its surface, oblong, but curiously bent down at sides, thus assuming somewhat the form of a violin; raceme 15 to 30 in. long, arching, longer than the l. June, July. *l.* bright shining green, 1 to 1½ ft. long. *Pseudobulbs* large, broadly ovate, compressed at edges, set at intervals. Borneo. 1853. (B.M. 5084; W.O.A. 63; L. 86.) Requires a basket or raft.

**C. Par'ishii.** *fl.* 3 to 5, about 3 in. across, resembling those of *C. pandurata* in form and colour; keels on lip fringed. Spring. Spike from apex of the *pseudobulbs*, which are diphyllous, 3 to 6 in. h. 4-sided. Moulmein. 1862. (B.M. 5323.) var. **brachyp'tera,** see **C. brachyptera.**

**C. peltas'tes.** *fl.* 4 to 6, 2½ to 3 in. across, resembling those of *C. pandurata*, except in the lip, which is creamy-white with yellowish-brown markings. Summer. *Pseudobulbs* crescent-shaped, compressed. Borneo. 1880. (L. 258.)

**C. peraken'sis.** *fl.* many, about 1 in. across; sep. buff-yellow; keeled; pet. greenish; lip light yellow with deeper yellow disk; scape erect. *l.* 7 in. long, oblong-lanceolate. Malaya. Before 1929. (B.M. 8203.)

**C. plantagin'ea.** A synonym of *C. Rochussenii*.

**C. pogonoi'des.** A synonym of *Pleione pogonoides*.

**C. prae'cox.** A synonym of *Pleione praecox*.

**C. prolif'era.** *fl.* greenish-yellow, small; scape long, slender, many-fld. *l.* 3 to 7 in. long, petiolate, lanceolate. *Pseudobulbs* 1½ to 2½ in. long, distant, ovoid or oblong, compressed. Trop. Himalaya. 1837. (A.B.G.C. 8, 196.)

**C. psittaci'na.\*** *fl.* 4 to 6, large; sep. 1½ in. long, like the filiform pet. greenish-yellow; lip large, orange-red at base with 3 ragged dark brown keels; mid-lobe broad, spreading, white, toothed; side lobes shaded and marked with brown. Summer. *Pseudobulbs* 3 to 5 in. h., somewhat conical. *l.* 12 to 15 in. long; scape taller. Amboina. (X.O. 2, 153.)

*Coelogyne pandurata*

**C. pulchel'la.\*** *fl.* about 1 in. across, pure white, except a brown-black blotch on disk of lip and a smaller at base; scapes terminal, slender, bearing several fl. close together. Spring. *l.* rather thick, oblong-lanceolate. *Pseudobulbs* ovoid-oblong, 2-leaved. Habitat? 1898. (B.M. n.s. 28.)

**C. purpuras'cens.** *fl.* nearly white, small; scape 3 to 4 in. long, 1-to 3-fld. *l.* 1 to 4 in. long, ⅛ to ½ in. broad, leathery, often purplish. *Pseudobulbs* very slender. *l.* 1. Ceylon. (H.I.P. 2110.)

**C. Reichenbachia'na.** A synonym of *Pleione Reichenbachiana*.

**C. Rhodea'na.** A synonym of *C. Rossiana*.

**C. rig'ida.** *fl.* yellow, with 3 red ridges on disk of lip; sep. ½ in. long; scape (with the drooping raceme) 6 to 8 in. long, rigid. *l.* petiolate, elliptic-lanceolate, 4 to 6 in. long. *Pseudobulbs* 3 to 5 in. long, narrow-oblong. Tenasserim.

**C. Rochus'senii.\*** *fl.* 1½ to 1¾ in. across; sep. lanceolate, the upper slightly broader; pet. narrower, all inclined forward and yellowish-green; lip 3-lobed, mid-lobe white, cordate, with toothed margins, side lobes white, lined with red-brown on their inner surfaces, crest with 3 or 4 white tomentose keels; column winged, toothed on upper margin. *Pseudobulbs* 8 in. h., cylindrical, tapered, diphyllous. *l.* 12 in. long by 5 in. broad, elliptical-oblong, narrowed to a short, channelled base. *Raceme* pendulous, 18 to 24 in. long, of 40 fl. or more. Java. (X.O. 1, 85.)

**C. Rossia'na.** *fl.* sep. and pet. creamy-white, ligulate, acute; lip mostly ochre, disk, broad claw, and top of mid-lobe white; column white with a brown mid-line in front; bracts linear, acuminate. Summer. *l.* 2, oblong-petiolate, cuneate-oblong-lanceolate, acute, over 1 ft. long and 1½ in. broad. *Pseudobulbs* 2 to 3 in. long, nearly pear-shaped. Burma. 1884. (B.M. 7176.)

**C. Rumph'ii.** *fl.* 1 or 2, spike 6 in. long; sep. and pet. greenish, sep. lanceolate, pet. linear; lip pandurate, side lobes spotted red, mid-lobe pure white. *l.* 1 ft. long, obovate. *Pseudobulbs* oblong. Amboina. 1896.

**C. San'derae.*** *fl.* 4 to 10, white, 2 in. across, with a yellow blotch on lip and a fringe of long, brown hairs on the 3 parallel keels; scapes erect. Summer. *l.* ovate-lanceolate. *Pseudobulbs* ovate, tapering, 3 to 4 in. long. Upper Burma. 1893. (R. 2, 56.)

**C. Sanderia'na.*** *fl.* 7 to 10, 3 in. across, snow-white, large and showy; sep. keeled, acute; pet. lanceolate, acute, dilated above; side lobes of lip marked with 3 brown stripes, mid-lobe yellow with a few white marks and yellow crests. Spring. *l.* petiolate, cuneate-oblong, acute, 10 to 15 in. long. *Pseudobulbs* ovoid, 2 to 4 in. long, diphyllous. Sunda Is. 1887.

**C. Schilleria'na.** A synonym of *Pleione Schilleriana.*

**C. siamen'sis.** *fl.* sep. and pet. pale green; lip yellow, marked with brown. Allied to *C. lentiginosa.* Siam. 1914.

**C. spar'sa.** *fl.* white; lip 3-lobed, having a brown spot in front of the keels, smaller ones on side lobes, and a yellow one at base; peduncle 1- to 7-fld. *l.* cuneate-oblong, acute, glaucous, 3 to 4 in. long, 1 in. broad. *Pseudobulbs* glaucous, fusiform. Philippines. 1883. Charming dwarf plant; fl. fragrant.

**C. specio'sa.*** *fl.* 1 to 3, over 3 in. across; peduncle slender; sep. and pet. brownish or olive-green, the latter much narrower than sep.; lip oblong, very beautiful both in the colour and marking, and in the exquisite fringe of the crests and margin, ground-colour yellow, variously veined with dark red, base dark brown, apex pure white. *l.* solitary, 9 in. long, 2 in. wide, oblong-lanceolate, thin, dark green. *Pseudobulbs* somewhat oblong, 1 to 3 in. long. Java, Sumatra. 1845. Almost a perpetual blossomer. (B.M. 4889; W.O.A. 494; B.R. 33, 23.) var. **al'ba,** sep. and pet. greenish, lip soft, flesh-colour. (B.M. 9539.) Java; **ma'jor,** *fl.* larger and deeper colour than the type. Java; **salmonic'olor,** *fl.* solitary, salmon, lip tessellated with brown, *l.* undulate, *pseudobulbs* tetragonal, pear-shaped. 1883.

**C. stella'ris.** *fl.* sep. and pet. green; lip white, marked with brown lines on side lobes. *Pseudobulbs* tetragonal. Borneo. 1886.

**C. suaveo'lens.** *fl.* 9 to 12, glistening white, fragrant, ½ in. wide; sep. lanceolate, keeled; pet. narrower; lip 3-lobed, side lobes erect, mid-lobe reflexed, oblong, tapered, with 5 obscure, crenulated laminae. *Pseudobulbs* 2½ in. h., conical, set at intervals on the rhizome, diphyllous. *l.* 8 to 10 in. long, 2 in. broad, lanceolate, conduplicate at base. Spike 6 in. h. from young growth. Shan States. (A.B.G.C. 5, 40.)

**C. sulphu'rea.** *fl.* 9 to 15, ¾ in. wide, yellowish-green; lip white with a yellow middle band and cleft mid-lobe; pet. linear reflexed; column with a yellow blotch at base. *Pseudobulbs* 1 to 2 in. h., conical. *l.* 6 to 10 in. long. Java. 1871.

**C. Swania'na.** *fl.* 12 to 20, 2 in. across; sep. white, 1 in. long; pet. white, narrower; lip pale brown, darker round margins and tips of lobes; column yellow; raceme 1 ft. long, pendent. May and June. *l.* 2, 6 to 8 in. long, elliptic-lanceolate; petioles 2 to 3 in. long. *Pseudobulbs* 3½ to 4 in. long, obtusely 4- to 6-angled. Philippines. 1892. (B.M. 7602; R. 2, 92.)

**C. ten'uis.** *fl.* light buff, small. Borneo. 1893. Allied to *C. borneensis,* but with slender scapes, and 1-lvd. pseudobulbs.

**C. testa'cea.** *fl.* 1½ in. across; sep. and pet. pale brown; side lobes of lip dark brown, margined white, narrow, mid-lobe broad; column white; raceme many-fld., pendulous. *l.* 2, 9 to 15 in. long, lanceolate, petiolate. *Pseudobulbs* 3 to 5 in. long, narrow-ovoid. Singapore. 1842. (B.M. 4785.)

**C. Thunia'na.** A synonym of *C. uniflora.*

**C. tomento'sa.*** *fl.* 15 to 30, 2 to 2½ in. across; sep. and pet. light orange-red; lip white, streaked red within, obovate, mid-lobe 3 keeled; racemes pendulous, rachis and pedicels reddish tomentose. Summer. *l.* 9 to 12 in. long, variable. *Pseudobulbs* elongate-ovoid, 2 to 3 in. long. Borneo. 1873.

**C. triplicat'ula.** *fl.* sep. 1½ in. long, over ½ in. wide at base, lanceolate, honey-yellow with a few brown lines; pet. filiform; lip 1½ in. long, side lobes erect, veined yellowish, flushed sepia-brown, front lobe rounded with reflexed, softly fringed margins, base with 3 yellow waved keels, the 2 outer extending on the blade, becoming black-brown and meeting; column winged, hooded, with a red-brown basal blotch. *Pseudobulbs* cylindrical, 4 in. h., diphyllous. *l.* 3 to 6 in. long. Burma. 1846. (X.O. 2, 166.) Habit of *C. fuliginosa* with which it has been confused, but always ascending.

**C. uniflo'ra.** *fl.* white or flesh-coloured; sep. 1 in. long; lip with 3 to 7 orange spots; scape ½ to 1 in. long, 1- or 2-fld. Summer. *l.* 3 to 6 in. long, erect, narrow-lanceolate. *Pseudobulbs* up to 1 in. long, ovoid, crowded. India. (A.B.G.C. 8, 192.) Syn. *C. Thuniana, Panisia uniflora.*

**C. val'ida.** *fl.* 4 or more, on a slender peduncle, 3 to 5 in. long, cream-white, except lip; sep. oblong, 1¼ to 1½ in. long, ½ in. wide at base, tapering to a blunt apex; pet. as long, very narrow; all segs. directed forwards; lip white, as long as sep., side lobes erect, upper margins parallel with column, front margins projecting, fringed, mid-lobe ½ in. long, deflexed, fringed and crimped on margin, base ochre, almost red, hairy, furnished with 2 curved, red-haired keels enclosing a yellow area. *Pseudobulbs* at intervals on rhizome, 3 to 4 in. h., oval, compressed, ribbed. *l.* 2, stalks 2 to 3 in. long, blade lanceolate, 9 to 15 in. long, 1½ to 2 in. wide. Summer. Assam. 1918. Intermediate house. *fl.* somewhat resemble those of *C. Sanderae,* but are larger.

**C. Veitch'ii.** *fl.* pure white, about 1 in. across; racemes drooping, 2 ft. long, many-fld. Summer. *l.* lanceolate, 6 in. long. *Pseudobulbs* fusiform, 3 to 4 in. long. New Guinea. 1895. (B.M. 7764.)

**C. venus'ta.*** *fl.* numerous, 1 to 1½ in. across; sep. and much narrower pet. buff-yellow; lip whitish with the side lobes and centre of the mid-lobe light yellow; base with 6 brown-tipped keels. Spring. *Pseudobulbs* at short intervals on the rhizome, 2 to 3 in. h., diphyllous. *l.* 5 to 8 in. long. *infl.* pendulous 10 or more in. long. Yunnan. 1904. (B.M. 8262.)

**C. vires'cens.** Closely allied to *C. Parishii.* *fl.* 3 to 7, with green sep. and pet; lip marked with deep sepia-brown. Summer. Annam. 1904.

**C. visco'sa.** *fl.* sep. and pet. white; lip white, side lobes broadly streaked with rich brown. Summer. *l.* dark green, tapering towards base. *Pseudobulbs* fusiform. India. 1870. Rare, near *C. flaccida.*

**C. Wallichia'na.** A synonym of *Pleione Wallichiana.*

**C. Zurowet'zii.** *fl.* about 3 in. across; sep. 1½ in. long, ½ in. broad, the lower somewhat falcate, with the narrower pet. bright yellow-green; lip 3-lobed, side lobes whitish, veined chestnut, erect, slightly incurved; mid-lobe shortly clawed, abruptly spreading, whitish suffused chestnut, palest at base, with warts white at first, then chestnut, except at apex, between lateral lobes are 2 white green-tipped keels. *rhiz.* ascending. *Pseudobulbs* overlapping, 3 in. long by 1½ in. broad. *l.* 10 in. long by 2 or more broad. Borneo. 1933. (O.R. 1934, 45.) Allied to *C. peltastes.*

E. C.

***coerules'cens,*** bluish.

***coeru'leus -a -um,*** blue.

**COF'FEA** (from the Arabic name of the beverage made from the dried seeds). Fam. *Rubiaceae.* A genus of perhaps 40 species of shrubs or small trees, natives of Trop. Asia and Africa. Leaves evergreen, opposite with interpetiolar stipules. Flower white or cream, fragrant, clustered in leaf-axils; calyx 5- or 4-parted; corolla salver-shaped, tube straight, throat often hairy, lobes oblong. Fruit a berry, globose or oblong, usually with 2 horny seeds. The seeds form the coffee 'beans' of commerce. Some species are grown for ornament but their main interest is as economic plants. They need stove or warm house conditions, plenty of water, ample pot room and a compost of turfy loam and sand. Best raised from ripe cuttings in sand under a bell-glass in moist heat, the plants thus raised flowering and fruiting better than seedlings.

**C. arab'ica.** Arabian Coffee. 5 to 15 ft. h. *l.* oblong, 3 to 6 in. long, rather thin, with a long slender point, dark glossy green above, paler beneath. *fl.* in clusters of 4 or 5, cor. 5-, rarely 4-parted. September. *fr.* deep crimson. Abyssinia, Angola. 1696. (B.M. 1303.) var. **variega'ta,** *l.* variegated.

**C. bengalen'sis.** Small shrub. *l.* ovate, slender-pointed, entire, spreading, almost sessile. *fl.* solitary or in pairs or threes, larger than in *C. arabica,* segs. scarcely twice as long as wide. India, Malaya. (B.M. 4917.) Little grown for its seeds now.

**C. Dewev'rei.** Tree up to 45 ft. h. *l.* ovate-oblong, 10 to 12 in. long, 4 to 6 in. wide. Cor. 5-parted, tube ⅜ in. long; stamens exserted. *fr.* red. Congo.

**C. laurin'a.** A synonym of *Craterispermum laurinum.*

**C. libe'rica.** Liberian Coffee. More robust than *C. arabica* with longer, wider *l.* with a shorter point. *fl.* in a dense cluster of 15 or more; cor. segs. usually 7. Liberia. 1875. With *C. arabica* the chief source of Coffee. It thrives in hot climates where *C. arabica* will not grow well.

**C. Maragogi'pa.** A S. American seedling of *C. arabica.*

**C. robus'ta.** Vigorous. *l.* large, ovate, apiculate. Congo. (G.C. 28 (1900), 311.)

**C. stenophyl'la.** About 10 ft. h. *l.* 4 to 6 in. long, relatively narrower than in *C. arabica* and with a longer, more tapering point, nearly sessile. *fl.* about ¾ in. long, solitary or in pairs or threes; pedicels short; cor. segs. usually 9. W. Africa. 1896. (B.M. 7475.)

**C. Zanguebar'iae.** About 6 ft. h., glabrous, branches ash-coloured. *l.* ovate or obovate, obtuse or shortly pointed, 2 to 4 in. long, veins in 6 pairs. *fl.* in dense clusters; cor. segs. 6 or 7. *Berry* red, becoming black. Trop. Africa.

***coffea'tus -a -um,*** coffee-coloured.

**COFFEE.** *See* **Coffea.**

**COFFEE-TREE.** *See* **Gymnocladus, Polyscias Guilfoylei.**

*Coggy'gria,* ancient Greek name.

*cogna'tus -a -um,* closely related.

*Cogniauxia'nus -a -um,* in honour of A. Cogniaux, 1841–1916, director of the botanical museum, Brussels.

**coherent,** members of one organ, e.g. petals, joined together (cf. adherent).

**cohesion,** union of like organs.

**COHUNE PALM.** *See* **Orbignya Cohune.**

*Coignet'iae,* in honour of Mme Coignet, *c.* 1883.

**COIR.** The outer fibrous pericarp of the coconut, used for rope-making, &c.

**CO'IX** (old Greek name for a reed-leaved plant). A genus of 3 E. Indian species of tall, broad-leaved grasses with a globular or oval leaf-sheath about ½ in. long at the end of each peduncle, which becomes hard and pearl-grey, from the apex of which project the staminate spikelets and the stigmas of the pistillate flower contained within the 'bead' as the very hard receptacle is called. *C. Lacryma-Jobi* is cultivated as a curiosity in the open sunny border, seed being sown under glass in heat in February or March or in the open in May.

**C. Lac'ryma-Jo'bi.** Job's Tears. Annual with smooth branching stems about 3 ft. h. *l.* ½ in. or more wide, sheath smooth, ligule very short, split. *fr.,* the 'tears', about ½ in. long. Autumn. Tropics. (B.M. 2479 as *C. Lachryma.*) var. **au'rea zebri'na** has yellow-striped l.-blades. (SYN. var. *variegata.*) The fr. are frequently used as beads, and are used as food in India, and medicinally in China.

*-cola,* suffix implying loving, as *rupicola,* rock-loving. **A**

**CO'LA** (from the native name). FAM. *Sterculiaceae.* A genus of about 40 species of evergreen trees, natives of Trop. Africa. Leaves entire or lobed. Flowers unisexual or polygamous, clustered in leaf-axils or in terminal cymes; calyx 5-cleft; petals absent. Fruit of 4 or 5 leathery or woody carpels. Grown largely in Africa and in the W. Indies for its nuts which are said to sustain the natives in feats of endurance, and are used in medicine and for other purposes. *C. acuminata* is the source of the Cola or Goora Nut. It will grow best in rich, light loam, and is increased by seeds.

**C. acumina'ta.** Tree to 40 ft. with spreading head. *l.* leathery, oblong-ovate, 4 to 6 in. long, variable. *fl.* yellow, ½ in. across, in panicles of about 15. January. *fr.* 5 to 6 in. long. Seed resembling the horse-chestnut, bitter. Trop. Africa. 1868. (B.M. 5699.)

**CO'LAX** (*Colax,* a parasite). FAM. *Orchidaceae.* A small epiphytic genus chiefly Brazilian, at times placed under Maxillaria, Lycaste, or Zygopetalum. Very closely related to Zygopetalum but the pollinia are slightly different. Several hybrids have been recorded between Colax and Zygopetalum under the name Zygocolax. Under cultivation the temperatures should be as for *Odontoglossum crispum.* Compost should be that advised for Odontoglossums, but about one-third of loam fibre should be added.

**C. jugo'sus.*** *fl.* 2 to 4, 2 to 3 in. across; sep. ovate-oblong, white; pet. nearly equal, white densely spotted with violet-purple; lip shortly clawed, 1 in. long, barely ¾ in. in breadth, 3-lobed, side lobes rounded, striated with violet-purple, front lobe rounded with numerous keels on the disk, striated and marked with violet-purple. *Pseudobulbs* 2 to 3 in. h., diphyllous. *l.* 6 to 10 in. long, 1 to 2 in. broad. *Peduncles* 4 to 8 in. h. Brazil. 1840. (B.M. 5661.) So far the most popular species of the genus. var. **puncta'tus,** *fl.* greenish-yellow, spotted reddish-black; **rufi'nus,** *fl.* yellowish-green, spotted black-purple; **vi'ridis,** a synonym of *C. viridis.*

**C. placan'therus.** *fl.* usually solitary; sep. over 1 in. long, ½ in. broad; pet. smaller, yellowish-green thickly spotted brown-purple; lip with a longer claw than that of *C. jugosus,* side lobes pale green, streaked with brown, mid-lobe with a whitish purple-flushed central area, greenish near tip, disk smooth. *Pseudobulbs* 2- or 3-phyllous, rather smaller than in *C. jugosus.* Brazil. 1843. (L. 76; B.M. 3173 as *Maxillaria placanthera.*)

**C. Puy'dtii.** Differs from *C. viridis* of which it is often considered a variety by the hair at the base of the column. Spring. Brazil. (I.H. 369.)

**C. trip'terus.** *fl.* 2; sep. and pet. light green; pet. densely speckled with dark brown; lip yellowish-white with lines of minute purple dots on the fleshy disk. Differs from *C. placantherus* by its 3-winged ovary and the broad fleshy callus on the lip. Brazil. 1905.

**C. vi'ridis.** *fl.* 1 to 2, sub-globose; sep. green; pet. green spotted with brown-purple; lip lilac, light or dark. *Pseudobulbs* ovoid. *l.* narrowly lanceolate, 5 to 7 in. long. Variable. Brazil. 1843. (B.R. 1510 as *Maxillaria viridis.*) SYN. *C. jugosus viridis.*

E. C.

*colchiciflo'rus -a -um,* with Colchicum-like flowers.

**COLCHICINE.** An alkaloid ($C_{22}H_{25}O_6N$) obtained from corms and seeds of *Colchicum autumnale.* It occurs in yellow flakes, crystals, or a whitish-yellow amorphous powder, soluble in water, alcohol, and chloroform. It is very poisonous and should be kept in the dark. It has found a use in horticulture, for if seeds are soaked for a time in a weak solution (0·2 to 0·4 per cent. for 4 to 10 days) before sowing the resulting plants are dwarfed and malformed owing to changes in the number of chromosomes in the cells or in some of them. In many cases the number of chromosomes in the pollen grains and the egg cells is doubled and the seedlings in the succeeding generation differ from the original plants, often being considerably larger. The exact strength of the solution and time of soaking must be ascertained for each species.

**COL'CHICUM** (from Colchis in Asia Minor). FAM. *Liliaceae.* A genus of between 50 and 60 species closely related to Bulbocodium and Merendera and bearing a great resemblance to Crocus from which the species are easily distinguished by their 6 instead of 3 stamens, and their superior ovary (underground at flowering time). In Colchicum and Bulbocodium the perianth segments are united to form a long tube, in Merendera they are free to the base. In Bulbocodium the 3 styles are joined but in Colchicum and Merendera they are quite separate. The species are widely distributed from Britain to Turkestan and Persia and occur most abundantly in the E. Mediterranean region.

The corms which are covered with a brown tunic drawn out into a longer or shorter neck should be planted in July or early August in a rich well-drained loam which does not dry out rapidly in summer. The flowers of many species precede the leaves and it is important that the latter should remain green as long as possible, until they die down naturally in June or July when the seed ripens. The very large foliage of some species, e.g. *C. speciosum,* makes them undesirable on the rock-garden, but others can well be used there. A sunny place is best for them but some, e.g. *C. autumnale,* will put up with partial shade and this species also succeeds in thin grass. The corms should be planted 3 or 4 inches deep and should be allowed to remain undisturbed unless it is desired to increase them quickly when they should be lifted every other year in July, divided, and immediately replanted. The other means of increase is by seed which should be sown either outdoors in a sheltered place on a good seed bed, covering the seed lightly with fine soil, or in pans in a cold frame. The seedlings should be watered in dry weather up to the end of July. They may be transplanted into nursery beds when 2 years old and there remain till they flower at the age of 3 to 5 years. They should be protected from slugs which are fond of some species and do much damage by the early destruction of the leaves.

The similarity of the flowers and the habit of several species of producing them in autumn has gained the name of Autumn Crocuses for several, and our own native *C. autumnale* has, because of its habitat and that same similarity, been called Meadow Saffron.

Much confusion exists regarding the names of the species comprising this genus partly because many have been originally described and named from dried specimens and partly because the distinguishing characters often need looking for. The following account has been drawn up largely from the *Monographie die Gattung Colchicum* by Stefanoff (1926) from which also the key given here has been adapted. Other good accounts of the genus are to be found in *A Handbook of Crocus and Colchicum* by E. A. Bowles (1952) and by G. B. Mallet in *Flora and Sylva*, i, p. 108 (1903).

Some very beautiful hybrids have recently been distributed from Holland, including the double lilac mauve Waterlily, raised by crossing *C. speciosum album* and *C. autumnale album plenum*; and the following derived from *C. speciosum giganteum* × *C. Sibthorpii*: Autumn Queen (tessellated on violet mauve), Giant (deep lilac mauve with white base), Lilac Wonder (violet mauve), Premier (tessellated on pinkish mauve), Princess Astrid (light violet), Violet Queen (deep purplish with white base). These are all large-flowered varieties blooming in autumn and good for pot cultivation as well as the outdoor garden. **A**

Colchicum foliage sometimes shows the black streaks due to the smut fungus *Urocystis colchici* which also attacks species of Muscari. Such plants cannot recover and should be destroyed by fire to prevent the spread of the fungus. The Grey Bulb Rot of Tulips (q.v.) also attacks them at times.

(D. E. G.)

KEY

| | |
|---|---|
| 1. *Anthers basifixed* | 2 |
| 1. *Anthers versatile* | 3 |
| 2. *Fl. yellow* | C. luteum |
| 2. *Fl. white* | C. Regelii |
| 3. *Fl. and lvs. together* | 4 |
| 3. *Fl. before lvs.* | 13 |
| 4. *Lvs. 2 from a sheath* | 5 |
| 4. *Lvs. 3 to 12* | 6 |
| 5. *Fl. vernal* | C. hungaricum |
| 5. *Fl. autumnal* | C. Cupani |
| 6. *Corm with more or less neck* | 7 |
| 6. *Corm with very short neck* | 8 |
| 7. *Fl. autumnal* | C. Steveni |
| 7. *Fl. vernal* | C. crocifolium |
| 8. *Segs. fimbriate-cristate at base* | C. Ritchii |
| 8. *Segs. not fimbriate-cristate* | 9 |
| 9. *Anthers yellow* | C. libanoticum |
| 9. *Anthers brownish* | 10 |
| 10. *Lvs. 3 to 7, fl. small white, rarely pale rose, many from a spathe* | C. fasciculare |
| 10. *Lvs.* 3 (4 *or* 5), *fl. lilac-rose,* 1 *to* 10 *from a spathe* | 11 |
| 11. *Lvs. lanceolate,* $\frac{1}{4}$ *to* $\frac{3}{8}$ *in. wide* | C. hydrophilum |
| 11. *Lvs. narrower,* $\frac{1}{10}$ *to* $\frac{3}{10}$ *in. wide* | 12 |
| 12. *L.-margin often scabrid-ciliate* | C. Biebersteinii |
| 12. *L. glabrous* | C. Catacuzenium |
| 13. *Stigmas at tip of styles* | 14 |
| 13. *Stigmas on one side of styles* | 18 |
| 14. *Corm small on end of underground shoot* | C. procurrens |
| 14. *Corm oblong, ovate, or round, not on shoot* | 15 |
| 15. *Fl. white or pale rose,* 3 *to* 12 *from spathe* | C. troodi |
| 15. *Fl. rose,* 1 *to* 4 *from spathe* | 16 |
| 16. *Fl. deep rose, faintly tessellated* | C. Sieheanum |
| 16. *Fl. pale rose, not tessellated* | 17 |
| 17. *Lvs.* 3 *to* 5, *fl. autumnal,* 1 *to* 4 *from spathe* | C. arenarium |
| 17. *Lvs.* 3, *fl. summer,* 1 (*rarely* 2 *or* 3) | C. alpinum |
| 18. *Stigmas on one side of styles, short* | 19 |
| 18. *Stigmas on one side of styles, distinct* | 23 |
| 19. *Fl. small, segs.* $\frac{3}{8}$ *to* 1 *in. long,* 5- *to* 11-*nerved* | 20 |
| 19. *Fl. medium, segs.* 1 *to* 2 *in. long,* 9- *to* 17-*nerved* | 21 |
| 20. *Lvs.* 3 *to* 5, *broad-lanceolate, anthers yellow* | C. umbrosum |
| 20. *Lvs.* 3 *to* 5, *linear-lanceolate, anthers black* | C. callicymbium |
| 20. *Lvs.* 2 *to* 3, *linear-lanceolate, anthers yellow* | C. corsicum |
| 21. *Lvs.* 5 *to* 12, *broad-linear* | C. Decaisnei |
| 21. *Lvs.* 3 *to* 5, *lingulate or broad-lanceolate* | 22 |
| 22. *Lvs. acute. Fl. rose* | C. laetum |
| 22. *Lvs. obtuse. Fl. pale rose or white* | C. Kotschyi |
| 23. *Fl. tessellated (if faintly then anthers brown)* | 24 |
| 23. *Fls. not tessellated (if faintly then anthers yellow)* | 29 |
| 24. *Lvs. linear* | 25 |
| 24. *Lvs. linear-lanceolate, lanceolate, or oblong* | 26 |
| 25. *Fl. segs.* 2 *to* 2$\frac{1}{2}$ *in., anthers brown* | C. Bivonae |
| 25. *Fl. segs.* 1$\frac{3}{8}$ *to* 1$\frac{4}{5}$ *in., anthers yellow* | C. neapolitanum var. |
| 26. *Fl. segs.* $\frac{4}{5}$ *to* 1$\frac{3}{8}$ *in., faintly tessellated* | C. lingulatum |
| 26. *Fl. segs.* 1$\frac{3}{8}$ *to* 2$\frac{3}{8}$ in. | 27 |
| 27. *Lvs.* 3 *to* 4, *glaucous green, undulate, prostrate. Fl. Oct.* | C. variegatum |
| 27. *Lvs.* 3 *to* 4, *slightly undulate, nearly upright. Fl. Aug.* | C. agrippinum |
| 27. *Lvs.* 3 *to* 5, *neither glaucous nor undulate* | 28 |
| 28. *Fl. segs. wide-elliptic,* 2 *to* 3$\frac{1}{4}$ *in. long* | C. latifolium |
| 28. *Fl. segs. oblong-lanceolate,* 1$\frac{3}{8}$ *to* 2 *in. long* | C. Tenorii |
| 29. *Lvs. large, wide-oblong or ovate-oblong,* 1 *to* 2$\frac{1}{2}$ *in. wide. Fl.* 1 *to* 4, segs. 2 *to* 3$\frac{1}{2}$ *in. long* | C. speciosum |
| 29. *Lvs. very large, plicate* 3 *to* 4 *in. wide. Fl.* 12 *to* 20, *segs. to* 2$\frac{1}{2}$ *in. long* | C. byzantinum |
| 29. *Lvs. large, plicate. Fl.* 20, *segs.* 2 *in. long, keeled* | C. cilicicum |
| 29. *Lvs. linear or lanceolate. Fl. segs. to* 2$\frac{1}{4}$ *in. long* | 30 |
| 30. *Fl. deep rose, per. tube about* 1 *in. above ground* | C. atropurpureum |
| 30. *Fl. pale rose, tube longer* | 31 |
| 31. *Lvs. linear-lanceolate* | 32 |
| 31. *Lvs. lanceolate or lingulate* | 33 |
| 32. *Lvs.* 3 *to* 9, $\frac{1}{3}$ *to* $\frac{2}{3}$ *in. wide. Fl.* 1 *or* 2, *segs.* $\frac{1}{3}$ *to* $\frac{1}{2}$ *in. wide* | C. neapolitanum |
| 32. *Lvs.* 3 *or* 4. *Fl.* 2 *to* 4, *segs.* $\frac{1}{8}$ *to* $\frac{1}{4}$ *in. wide* | C. neapolitanum var. |
| 33. *Lvs. lanceolate,* $\frac{3}{5}$ *to* 2 *in. wide* | C. autumnale |
| 33. *Lvs. oblong-lanceolate or lingulate* | C. lingulatum |

**C. agrippi'num.** *fl.* 2 or 3 to a spathe; per. tube whitish, about twice as long as segs. which are lilac-purple without orange spot (cf. *variegatum*), chequered with white, 1$\frac{3}{4}$ to 2$\frac{3}{4}$ in. long. Autumn. *l.* 3 or 4, vernal, nearly erect, slightly undulate, linear-lanceolate, 4 to 6 in. long. *Corm* ovoid, about 1 in. thick. Origin? (B.M. 1028 as *C. variegatum.*) Syn. *C. tessellatum.*

**C. alpi'num.** *fl.* 1 (rarely 2 or 3) to a spathe; per. tube 2 to 4 times as long as segs.; segs. elliptic, $\frac{3}{4}$ to 1$\frac{1}{4}$ in. long, $\frac{1}{4}$ in. wide, rose. Summer. *l.* 2 or 3, linear-lanceolate or lingulate, appearing after fl. *Corm* globose, $\frac{3}{4}$ in. long. 1820. SE. France, Italy, Sicily, Sardinia, Corsica. (R.I.F.G. 425, 946–8.) Syn. *C. alpinum parvulum.*

**C. arena'rium.** *fl.* 1 to 4 to a spathe, pale rose; per. tube 2 to 3 times segs.; segs. 1 to 1$\frac{1}{2}$ in. long, $\frac{1}{8}$ to $\frac{2}{5}$ in. wide, oblong; anthers yellow. September, October. *l.* 3 to 5, vernal, linear-lanceolate or lingulate. *Corm* 1 in. long with neck. Hungary. (R.I.F.G. 425, 944–5.) var. **umbro'sum.** A synonym of *C. umbrosum.*

**C. atropurpu'reum.** Similar to *C. autumnale* but *fl.* pale at first becoming red-magenta; per. tube only 1 in. and shorter than segs. Autumn. *l.* smaller and darker. 1771. (B.M. 8876.) Syn. *C. autumnale atropurpureum.*

**C. autumna'le.** Meadow Saffron. *fl.* 1 to 6 to a spathe, pale rose or white, sometimes obscurely tessellated; per. tube 3 or 4 times as long as segs.; segs. oblong-elliptic, 1$\frac{1}{4}$ to 2$\frac{1}{4}$ in. long; anthers yellow. Autumn. *l.* 3 to 8, vernal, lanceolate, 6 to 10 in. long, about 1 in. wide. *Corm* with neck 1$\frac{1}{2}$ in. long, ovate. Europe (Britain). (E.B. 1444, 1445.) A very variable plant; among the varieties **al'bum** (white), **album ple'num** (double white), **flore ple'no** (double lilac), are well worth growing. A striped variety (**stria'tum**) is sometimes seen. var. **atropurpu'reum.** A synonym of *C. atropurpureum.*

**C. Balan'sae** of gardens is perhaps *C. autumnale minus.*

**C. Bertolo'nii.** A synonym of *C. Cupani.*

**C. Bieberstein'ii.** *fl.* 2 to 4 to a spathe, rosy-lilac, per. tube twice as long as segs., segs. elliptic-oblong, $\frac{3}{5}$ to $\frac{4}{5}$ in. long. March. *l.* 3, with fls., linear, $\frac{1}{4}$ in. wide, more or less ciliate. *Corm* ovate $\frac{3}{5}$ to $\frac{4}{5}$ in. long with a short neck. S. Russia, Bulgaria, Asia Minor. Syn. *C. montanum.*

**C. Bivon'ae.** *fl.* rose-purple, beautifully chequered; per. tube 3 or 4 times as long as segs.; segs. elliptic, acute or obtuse, 2 to 3 in. long; anthers brown. September, October. *l.* 5 to 9, vernal, linear-lanceolate, 8 to 10 in. long, $\frac{1}{3}$ to $\frac{2}{3}$ in. wide. *Corm* ovate, 1 to 1$\frac{1}{2}$ in. long, 1 in. wide. Sicily, Sardinia.

**C. Bornmül'leri.** A synonym of *C. speciosum.*

**C. brachyphyl'lum.** A synonym of *C. fasciculare brachyphyllum.*

**C. bulbocodoi'des.** A synonym of *C. Biebersteinii, Merendera montana.*

**C. byzanti'num.** *fl.* up to 20 in a spathe, lilac-rose, very similar to those of *C. autumnale*, but larger, and more numerous. Autumn. *l.* vernal, 5 or 6, oblong, 12 to 16 in. long, 3 to 4 in. wide, dark green, often plicate. *Corm* very large, 2 in. or more long and wide. Transylvania and Constantinople. 1629. (B.M. 1122.) Syn. *C. autumnale major, C. veratrifolium.* var. **cilic'icum,** a synonym of *C. cilicicum.*

**C. callicym'bium.** *fl.* 2 to 4 to a spathe, pale violet-lilac with darker throat; per. tube twice as long as segs.; segs. oblanceolate, 1$\frac{1}{5}$ to 1$\frac{2}{5}$ in. long, $\frac{1}{3}$ to $\frac{1}{2}$ in. wide; anthers black. September. *l.* 3 to 5, with flowers, sub-erect, narrow. Greece, Bulgaria. 1902.

**C. can'didum.** A synonym of *C. Decaisnei.*

**C. Catacuze'nium.** *fl.* 1 to 6 to a spathe, lilac-rose or paler; per. tube 4 or 5 times as long as segs.; segs. narrow-elliptic, $\frac{4}{5}$ in. long, $\frac{1}{10}$ to $\frac{1}{4}$ in. wide; anthers brown. March, April. *l.* 3 or 4, vernal, wide linear, more or less undulate, 4 in. long, $\frac{1}{8}$ to $\frac{3}{8}$ in. wide. *Corm* small, $\frac{4}{5}$ in. long. Greece. 1938. (B.M. 9652.)

**C. caucas'icum.** A synonym of *Merendera trigyna.*

**C. cilic'icum.** *fl.* up to 25 to a sheath, rosy-lilac with yellowish-white keel; per. tube white, 6 to 10 in. long; segs. oblanceolate to obovate, 2 in. long; anthers golden-yellow. October. *l.* 5, vernal, broad-elliptic, 6 in. long, plicate, dark green. *Corm* ovoid, up to 2 in. h. Taurus Mts. 1896. (B.M. 9135.) Syn. *C. byzantinum cilicicum.*

**C. cor'sicum.** *fl.* 1 to a spathe, lilac-rose; segs. linear-elliptic, ¾ to 1 in. long; anthers yellow. September. *l.* 3 or 4, vernal, sub-erect, linear-lanceolate. *Corm* globose, ⅝ to ⅞ in. wide. Corsica.

**C. croat'icum.** A synonym of *C. hungaricum.*

**C. crociflo'rum.** A synonym of *C. Regelii.*

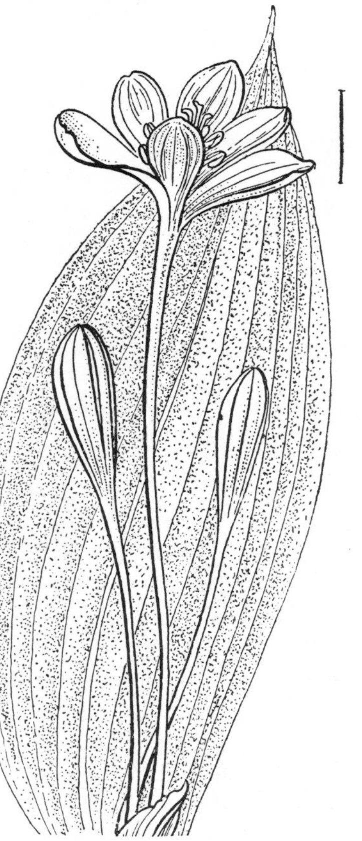

*Colchicum byzantinum* (p. 523)

**C. crocifo'lium.** *fl.* numerous, pale rose or white striped outside; per. tube much longer than segs.; segs. narrow, apex acute, ½ in. long; anthers yellow. February, March. *l.* 4 to 8, linear, 2 to 3½ in. long at flowering time. *Corm* oblong, with neck, ⅝ to 1 in. long. Iraq, S. Persia. 1904.

**C. Cupa'ni.** *fl.* 1 to 5 to a sheath, rarely up to 12, rose; per. tube 2 to 5 times as long as segs.; segs. linear-elliptic, ½ to 1 in. long; anthers brown. September. *l.* 2, with fl., linear or linear-lanceolate. *Corm* ovate, with short neck, ⅜ to ⅞ in. long. E. Mediterranean, Sicily, Sardinia, Algeria, Tunis. (R.I.F.G. 424, 942–3.) SYN. *C. Bertolonii.*

**C. Decais'nei.** *fl.* 3 to 6 (rarely to 12) to a sheath, white or pale rose; per. tube 3 to 5 times as long as segs.; segs. oblong-elliptic, obtuse, 1⅛ to 1½ in. long; anthers yellow. October. *l.* 5 to 12, vernal, wide linear, somewhat undulate, obtuse. *Corm* ovate, with neck, 1 to 1¼ in. long. Syria and Palestine. 1892. SYN. *C. laetum, C. candidum* of some lists.

**C. fascicula're.** *fl.* numerous, white or pale rose; per. tube 2 or 3 times as long as segs.; segs. linear-elliptic, ⅜ to 1⅛ in. long; anthers brown. January, February. *l.* 3 to 7, about 8 in. long, linear-lanceolate. *Corm* ovate-oblong, with short neck, ⅞ to 1⅛ in. long. 1896. Syria, Palestine. var. **brachyphyl'lum** has wider *l.* and a globose *corm.* Moist places near Aleppo and Lebanon.

**C. gigan'teum.** A synonym of *C. speciosum.*

**C. guadarramen'se.** Spanish form of *C. neapolitanum.*

**C. Haussknecht'ii.** A synonym of *C. Kotschyi.*

**C. hunga'ricum.** *fl.* 1 (rarely 2 to 8), pale rose or white; per. tube 2 or 3 times as long as the segs.; segs. oblong-elliptic, 1 in. long; anthers brownish. January, February. *l.* 2 (or 3), with the fl., linear or linear-lanceolate, acute. *Corm* oblong, with short neck, about 1 in. long. Hungary to Dalmatia. 1921. (R.I.F.G. 424, 940–1 as *C. Bertolonii*; B.M. n.s. 373.)

**C. hydroph'ilum.** *fl.* 3 to 8 to a spathe, pink; per. tube 3 to 4 times as long as the oblong-elliptic segs.; segs. ⅞ to 1⅛ in. long. May. *l.* 3 (2 to 4), with fl., lanceolate. *Corm* ovate with short neck, 1 in. long. Cappadocia. 1898. (B.M. 8040.)

**C. Kots'chyi.** *fl.* 3 to 12 to a spathe, pale rose or white; per. tube 3 to 5 times as long as the linear elliptic segs.; segs. 1 to 2 in. long; anthers yellow or brown. September. *l.* 3 or 4 (up to 10), vernal, broad lanceolate, 6 to 8 in. long. *Corm* ovate, with neck, 1¼ to 1¾ in. long. Persia and Armenia.

**C. lae'tum.** *fl.* 1 to 3 (rarely many) to a spathe, pale or deep rose; per. tube 3 times as long as the segs.; segs. oblong-elliptic, 1⅛ to 2 in. long, obtuse; anthers yellow. September. *l.* 3 to 5, vernal, lingulate, acute. *Corm* ovate-oblong with neck, 1½ in. long. Caucasus. 1897.

**C. latifo'lium.** *fl.* 1 to 7 to a spathe, lilac-purple, tessellated; per. tube 1½ to 3 times as long as the widely elliptic segs.; segs. 2 to 3½ in. long; anthers yellow or brown. September. *l.* 3 to 5, vernal, ovate-oblong, obtuse, 6 to 10 in. long. *Corm* 1½ in. long and wide, with short neck. Greece, Crete. (B.M. 7181, F.G. 1, 108 as *C. Sibthorpii.*)

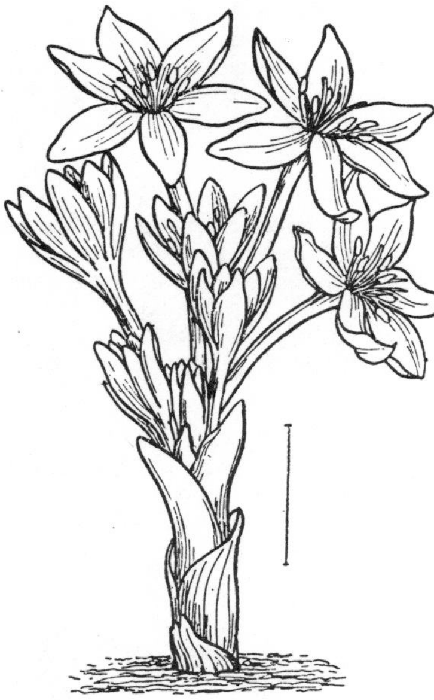

*Colchicum libanoticum*

**C. libanot'icum.** *fl.* 1 to 10 to a spathe, pale rose or white, starry; per. tube 2 to 4 times as long as segs.; segs. ¾ in. long, oblong, obtuse; anthers yellow or brown. February. *l.* 3 to 5, broad lanceolate, acute. *Corm* oblong, ⅞ in. long with short neck. Lebanon. 1904. (B.M. 8015.)

**C. lingula'tum.** *fl.* 1 to 4 (rarely to 10) to a spathe, rose, more or less distinctly chequered; per. tube 2 or 3 times as long as the oblong-elliptic segs.; segs. ⅞ to 1½ in. long; anthers yellow or brown. September, October. *l.* 4 to 6, vernal, lingulate, up to 6 in. long, obtuse. *Corm* ovate-oblong with neck, up to 2 in. long. Greece.

**C. lu'teum.** *fl.* 1 to 4 to a spathe, yellow, often tinged lilac outside at base of lanceolate segs.; per. tube tinged yellow or lilac, 2 to 4 times as long as segs.; segs. up to 1 in. long; anthers yellow. February, March. *l.* 2 to 5, short at flowering time, but eventually linear-lanceolate, up to 12 in. long. *Corm* ovate-oblong, with longish neck, ⅝ to 1¼ in. long. N. India, Afghanistan, Turkestan. (B.M. 6153.)

**C. monta'num.** This name has been applied to so many different species as well as to *Merendera Bulbocodium* that it is better discarded. var. **croat'icum,** a synonym of *C. hungaricum.*

**C. neapolita'num.** *fl.* 2 to 4 to a spathe, rose to deep rose, sometimes tessellated (var. *variopictum*), per. tube 3 times as long as segs.; segs. oblong, apex obtuse, 1⅛ to 1⅝ in. long; anthers yellow. August. *l.* 3 to 9, after fl., linear-lanceolate, obtuse, 8 to 10 in. long. *Corm* ovate 1½ in. long, with neck. Italy. A Spanish form has been called *C. longifolium.*

**C. Parkinson'ii.** A synonym of *C. variegatum.*

**C. par'vulum.** A synonym of *C. alpinum.*

**C. procur'rens.** *fl.* 1, deep rose; per. tube 3 times as long as segs.; segs. oblong-elliptic, obtuse, 1¼ to 1¾ in. long; anthers yellow. October. *l.* 3, vernal, linear, obtuse. *Corm* small, at end of underground shoot. Asia Minor. *C. procurrens* of gardens is *Merendera sobolifera.*

**C. Regel'ii.** *fl.* 1 to 4 to a spathe, white striped on back with purple; per. tube 3 times as long as segs.; segs. lanceolate, obtuse or acute, ⅝ to 1¼ in. long; anthers yellow, basifixed. February. *l.* 1 to 7, at flowering time short, later linear-lanceolate, obtuse or acute. *Corm* ovate-oblong, ⅞ to over 1 in. long with neck. Turkestan. 1905. (B.M. 8055 as *C. crociflorum.*)

**C. Ritch'ii.** *fl.* 1 to 7 to a spathe, pale rose or white; per. tube 3 to 5 times as long as segs.; segs. oblong, obtuse or acute, $\frac{3}{8}$ to 1 in. long, often fimbriate-cristate at base; anthers yellow or brown. January. *l.* 2 to 4, with l. linear, finally 4 to 8 in. long, sometimes undulate. *Corm* with short neck, up to 1 in. long. Palestine, Egypt, Tripoli.

**C. robus'tum.** A synonym of *Merendera robusta.*

**C. Sibthorp'ii.** A synonym of *C. latifolium.*

**C. Siehea'num.** *fl.* 1 to 3 to a spathe, deep rose, faintly tessellated; per. tube double length of segs.; segs. oblong-elliptic, 1 to $1\frac{1}{2}$ in. long, obtuse or acute; anthers yellow. September. *l.* vernal. *Corm* ovate with neck, about $\frac{3}{8}$ in. long. Cilicia.

**C. specio'sum.** *fl.* 3 or 4 to a spathe, rose, purple, or white; per. tube 3 to 5 times as long as the large broadly elliptic segs.; segs. $1\frac{1}{2}$ to $2\frac{1}{2}$ in. long, $\frac{3}{4}$ to $1\frac{1}{4}$ in. wide; anthers yellow or brown. August, September. *l.* 4 to 6, vernal, large, wide oblong, 12 to 16 in. long, sometimes larger, $1\frac{1}{2}$ to 3 in. wide. *Corm* very large, 2 in. long with neck. Persia, Caucasus, Asia Minor, Syria, Lebanon. 1850? (B.M. 6078.) SYN. *C. veratrifolium.* Many varieties occur. var. **ru'brum** (deep red) and **al'bum** (perhaps the best hardy white-fld. bulbous plant) were raised by Messrs. Backhouse of York. **C. giganteum** (F. & S. 1, 108) and **C. Bornmülleri** of lists are apparently forms of this species with green tubes. **C. speciosum max'imum** shows no white in the throat.

**C. Ste'veni.** *fl.* 2 to 10, fascicled, rose; per. tube 3 or 4 times as long as segs.; segs. oblong or linear-elliptic, $\frac{3}{8}$ to $1\frac{1}{4}$ in. long; anther yellow. January. *l.* 5 to 12, with the fl., narrow-linear, acute. *Corm* ovate or oblong, $\frac{3}{8}$ in. long, with neck. Coasts of Syria and Cilicia. 1904. (B.M. 8025.)

**C. Tenor'ii.** *fl.* 3 or 4 to a spathe, deep rose, more or less tessellated; per. tube pale, 2 or 3 times as long as segs.; segs. oblong-lanceolate, obtuse, 2 in. long; anthers brown. September. *l.* 5, vernal, erect, widely elliptic. *Corm* globose, over 1 in. long and wide. Italy.

**C. tessella'tum.** A synonym of *C. agrippinum, C. variegatum.*

**C. troo'di.** *fl.* 3 to 12 to a spathe, white; per. tube 2 or 3 times as long as segs.; segs. oblong-elliptic 1 to $1\frac{3}{8}$ in. long, obtuse; anthers yellow. October. *l.* 3 to 6, vernal, broad linear, 10 in. long, obtuse. *Corm* ovate, 1 in. long with neck. Cyprus. (B.M. 6901.)

**C. umbro'sum.** *fl.* 1 to 3 (rarely up to 5), rose; per. tube 2 to 4 times as long as segs.; segs. narrow-elliptic, about $1\frac{1}{4}$ in. long, obtuse; anthers yellow. August, September. *l.* 3 to 5, vernal, wide-lanceolate, up to 6 in. long, obtuse. *Corm* $\frac{1}{2}$ to $\frac{3}{4}$ in. long with neck. Caucasus, Kurdistan. (B.R. 541 as *C. arenarium umbrosum.*)

**C. variega'tum.** *fl.* 1 to 3 to a spathe, lilac-purple, beautifully chequered; per. tube white, about double length of segs.; segs. $1\frac{3}{4}$ to nearly 3 in. long, lanceolate-elliptic, acute; anthers brown. September, October, or later. *l.* 3 to 4, lanceolate, 4 to 6 in. long, undulate. *Corm* ovate, 1 in. long and wide, with neck. Asia Minor, Greece. (B.M. 6090 as *C. Parkinsonii.*) *See note under* **C. agrippinum.**

**C. veratrifo'lium.** A synonym of *C. speciosum, C. byzantinum.*

**C. vern'um.** A synonym of *Bulbocodium vernum.*

***col'chicus -a -um,*** of Colchis on the Black Sea.

**CO'LEA** (in honour of Gen. Sir G. Lowry Cole, 1772–1842, a Governor of Mauritius). FAM. *Bignoniaceae.* A genus of about 15 species of evergreen shrubs, natives of Mauritius, Madagascar, &c. Leaves opposite or whorled, unequally pinnate with 2 to many pairs of leaflets. Flowers in cymes or clusters; calyx somewhat bell-shaped, 5-toothed; corolla funnel-shaped, lobes 5, spreading. The Coleas need a moist, warm atmosphere, a compost of fibrous peat and loam with a little sand and charcoal, and may be propagated by cuttings of ripe wood in sand under a glass with moist bottom heat.

**C. Co'lei.** *l.* oblong, warted; lflets. in whorls of 3, elliptic-lanceolate, slender-pointed, almost sessile. *fl.* dark rose; cor. glabrous; pedicels short, clustered. Mauritius. SYN. *C. mauritiana.*

**C. floribun'da.** About 10 ft. h. *l.* whorled; lflets. in 8 pairs, oblong-lanceolate, acute. *fl.* yellowish-white, clustered on old wood, nearly sessile. Mauritius. 1839. (B.R. 27, 19.)

**C. mauritia'na.** A synonym of *C. Colei.*

**C. undula'ta.** Stem unbranched. *l.* whorled, 2 to 4 ft. long. *fl.* yellow and lilac in racemes on old wood. Summer. Madagascar. 1870. (G.F. 669 as *C. Commersonii.*)

F. G. P.

***colea'tus -a -um,*** sheath-like.

**COLEBROOK'EA** (in honour of Henry Thomas Colebrook, F.R.S., F.L.S., 1765–1837, Sanskrit scholar and naturalist). FAM. *Labiatae.* A genus of 1 species, an evergreen shrub, native of India, densely covered with reddish or whitish woolly hairs. Leaves oblong-elliptic, with roundish teeth. Flowers white, small with tubular corollas, contracted in middle. Cymes distinct, capitate, dense, sessile in stalked spikelets 1 to 3 in. long. *C. oppositifolia* needs greenhouse protection and a compost of 1 part peat, 2 loam with a little sand. Cuttings of half-ripe shoots taken in April or May will root in sand under a bell-glass.

**C. oppositifo'lia.** Shrub of 3 to 4 ft. *l.* opposite or in whorls of three, very woolly. India. 1820. (S.E.B. 115.) SYN. *C. ternifolia.*

**COLENSO'A** (in honour of the Rev. William Colenso, F.R.S., 1811–99, a great student of New Zealand flora, &c.). FAM. *Campanulaceae.* A genus of a single species of perennial herbaceous plant, woody at base, native of New Zealand. It is half-hardy, needs a rich, moist, sandy loam and shade. Propagated by rooted pieces, cuttings, or seed.

**C. physalo'des.** Rather straggly, 2 to 3 ft. h. *l.* elliptic-ovate, 4 to 6 in. long, doubly toothed, thin, stalked. *fl.* pale blue, $1\frac{1}{2}$ to 2 in. long, 2-lipped, upper lip with 2 linear lobes; stamens free of cor., filaments only slightly connate; racemes short, terminal, few-fld. Summer. *fr.* a violet berry, globose, crowned with the green, linear cal. teeth. 1886. (B.M. 6864.)

**COLEONE'MA** (*koleos*, a sheath, *nema*, a filament; referring to the filaments of the sterile stamens which are enfolded in the channels of the petals). FAM. *Rutaceae.* A genus of 4 or 5 species of evergreen shrubs, natives of S. Africa. Leaves alternate, linear or filiform, glandular-dotted. Flowers axillary, solitary; calyx 5-parted; petals 5, channelled below; stamens 10, 5 of them fertile, the other 5 sterile and hidden in the channelled petals; capsule 5-carpelled. Related to Diosma which has no sterile stamens. Cool greenhouse plants needing the same treatment as Barosma.

**C. al'bum.** Shrub 2 to 3 ft., much branched. *l.* very crowded, linear, $\frac{1}{4}$ to $\frac{1}{2}$ in. long, $\frac{1}{24}$ to $\frac{1}{16}$ in. wide, pointed, very minutely toothed with 2 or more rows of glandular dots beneath. *fl.* white, solitary in uppermost l.-axils, $\frac{1}{8}$ in. wide; pet. spoon-shaped. April. S. Africa. Fragrant shrub; grown in the open air at Tresco Abbey.

**C. juniperifo'lium.** Shrub $1\frac{1}{2}$ to 4 ft., branches many, erect, very slender, glabrous. *l.* $\frac{1}{6}$ to $\frac{3}{8}$ in. long, $\frac{1}{24}$ in. wide, erect, filiform, concave, and shining green above, convex below; with glandular dots in a row. *fl.* white, small, solitary in the axils of numerous uppermost l. S. Africa. Very distinct by its threadlike shoots and l.

**C. pul'chrum.*** Erect shrub, 4 to 6 ft., shoots very long and very slender. *l.* $\frac{1}{2}$ to $1\frac{1}{2}$ in. long, $\frac{1}{16}$ to $\frac{1}{24}$ in. wide, filiform, long-pointed, rounded, and with 2 lines of glandular dots beneath. *fl.* rose, $\frac{5}{8}$ to $\frac{3}{4}$ in. wide, solitary in the 6 to 12 uppermost l.-axils; pet. recurved, the colour deepening towards the base. April, May. S. Africa. (B.M. 3340.)

W. J. B.

**COLEOPH'ORA.** A genus of small moths. *See* **Case-bearer Moths.**

**COLEOP'TERA.** The largest family of Insects, including beetles and weevils.

**COLEORHIZA.** Sheath around base of root in many monocotyledons.

**COLEOSPO'RIUM.** A genus of Rust Fungi with alternate host plants, the aecidial stage being on 2-leaved Pines. Some species damage garden plants, e.g. those attacking Campanula and Cineraria (q.v.).

D. E. G.

**A→**

**CO'LEUS** (*koleos*, sheath; the filaments form a tube at their base, sheathing the style). FAM. *Labiatae.* A genus of about 150 species, natives of the tropics of the Old World, differing from Plectranthus only by the monadelphous stamens. Most species are perennial, a few annual, and a few sub-shrubby. Flowers rather small, usually bluish, in whorls, sometimes dense, sometimes loose, in spike-like terminal racemes.

The genus is generally represented in gardens by the many varieties of *C. Blumei*, characterized by their varied and brilliantly coloured leaves. At one time innumerable named varieties were in cultivation but there are now but few. Several other species, e.g. *C. Frederici*, *C. Penzigii*, *C. shirensis*, and *C. thyrsoideus*, are worth cultivating for their blue or purplish-blue flowers, the first and last being particularly good. The named varieties of *C. Blumei* are propagated by cuttings at almost any time of year. They are best inserted singly in thumb pots, kept moist, and shaded from the sun, when in a temperature of 55 to 60° F. they root rapidly. When rooted the young plants should be moved into 4-in. pots using a compost of 3 parts good loam and 1 of leaf-soil and sand; they should be stood in a sunny position well up to the glass. The tips should be pinched to induce a bushy habit, and they should be potted on as they require it. For the stages and for general decorative purposes good useful plants can be grown in 5- or 6-in. pots, but if large specimens are desired they should be potted on into 8-, 10-, or even 12-in. pots. They may be trained in bush or pyramid form; if the pyramid form be chosen, the leading shoot should be tied to a stake and not stopped, otherwise all shoots should be pinched occasionally to encourage branching. Before the plants are removed to the conservatory or greenhouse they should be given more air and less heat for a week or 10 days.

Young stock should be raised in September discarding the old plants as they get shabby and the young stock should be wintered in a minimum temperature of 55° F.

The variety *Verschaffeltii* of *C. Blumei* with purplish-red leaves is largely grown for summer-bedding and is very effective when used with grey foliage.

J. C.

**C. Autra'nii.** Perennial. Stem 3 ft. h., hairy at nodes. *l.* roundish ovate, sparsely and minutely toothed, bristly hairy above and more on veins beneath, 3 to 5 in. long, 2 to $2\frac{1}{2}$ in. wide. *infl.* a raceme-like spike, 6 to 8 in. long, $1\frac{1}{2}$ in. wide, lower cluster distant. *fl.* deep violet, nearly $\frac{3}{4}$ in. long, tube geniculate. Winter. Abyssinia. (B.M. 9605.)

**C. barba'tus.** Strongly scented in all parts. Perennial of about 2 ft. *l.* oval, narrowed to base, scalloped, downy, wrinkled. *fl.* brownish, lower lip nearly ovate, compressed, hairy. November. Abyssinia. (B.M. 2318 as *Plectranthus comosus*.)

**C. Blu'mei.** Perennial of 12 to 18 in. *l.* rhomboid-ovate, rather thin, deeply and coarsely toothed, with an entire slender point, yellowish-green, dull red, or purplish. *fl.* white and purple. Java. (B.M. 4754.) var. **Verschaffel'tii,** *l.* purplish-red. There are innumerable forms of this plant with variously coloured foliage derived from a Javanese garden plant which may be of hybrid origin.

**C. Frederi'ci.*** Annual or biennial herb to 4 ft. Stems 4-angled, roughly hairy. *l.* in unequal pairs, broadly ovate, blade decurrent on stalk especially on lower l., teeth rounded, bristly hairy. *fl.* deep blue in open panicles 4 or 5 in. long, fragrant, more or less papilionaceous, the vertical tube recurved into the 2-lobed upper lip, lower lip keel-like, about $\frac{1}{2}$ in. long, intensely blue. December. Angola. 1931. (B.M. 9421.)

**C. Mahon'ii.** A synonym of *Plectranthus Mahonii*.

**C. Pen'zigii.** Perennial, softly white, hairy. *l.* ovate, 2 to 3 in. long, abruptly narrowed to a winged stalk, teeth rounded. *fl.* bright violet, lower lip $\frac{1}{4}$ in. long, upper smaller, reflexed; raceme 6 to 8 in. long, loose. Autumn. Abyssinia.

**C. shiren'sis.** Perennial, densely hairy, 3 ft. h. Stems finally brown. *l.* scented, broad ovate, slender-pointed, 2 to 3 in. long, rather thin, teeth rounded, hairy especially beneath. *fl.* blue, in large, erect panicles. Winter. Cent. Africa. (B.M. 8024.)

**C. thyrsoi'deus.*** Perennial, hairy, about 3 ft. h. *Lower l.* ovate-cordate, up to 7 in. long, coarsely lobulate with rounded teeth, stalks about 2 in. long. *fl.* bright blue, about $\frac{1}{2}$ in. long, in a panicle about 3 in. wide, with sub-erect branches. Winter. Cent. Africa. 1897. (B.M. 7672.)

**COLEWORT.** Varieties of white cabbage before the hearts become solid, and cut for use at this stage. Often called Collard. Often grown from seed sown in July, thinned out but not transplanted.

**COLIC ROOT.** *See* **Aletris farinosa.**

**COLLA'BIUM** (*collum*, neck, *labium*, lip; the basal part of the lip encircles the column). FAM. *Orchidaceae.* A genus of 4 species of terrestrial Orchids, natives of India, Java, and Borneo. Flowers in a long raceme on a tall scape; lateral sepals adnate to the trumpet-shaped foot of the long, incurved column, to which the short lip is also jointed; pollinia 2. Leaf plicate. The compost should be as for Bletias with the addition of more leaf mould and Sphagnum moss. Careful watering is required in the winter months. A decided rest is not advisable. Stove plants.

**C. sim'plex.** *fl.* sep. and pet. greenish-yellow, with purple and brown blotches; lip white; column white, purple at base; peduncle tumid at base, racemose at apex. *l.* oblong, acute, wavy, green, with darker blotches. Borneo. 1881.

E. C.

**COLLAN'IA.** Included in **Bomarea.**

**COLLAR.** Junction between stem and root.

**COLLARD.** *See* **Colewort.**

**COLLAR-ROT.** Rotting at soil-level, often due to an attack by fungi or bacteria of which it is a symptom, this attack sometimes follows damage by insects or injury through water standing about the collar.

**COLLEM'BOLA.** An order of wingless Insects. *See* **Springtails.**

**COLLENCHYMA.** Consists of parenchymatous tissue with cellulose walls thickened at the angles of the cells. It occurs just below the surface of midribs, leaf-stalks, and young stems, especially (but not exclusively) in Dicotyledons and helps to give them firmness. Cf. **Sclerenchyma.**

**COLLET'IA** (in honour of Philibert Collet, a French botanist, 1643–1718). FAM. *Rhamnaceae.* A genus of some 20 species of S. American, deciduous, spiny shrubs. The spines are really modified branches borne in pairs. Leaves opposite, small, soon falling except on young seedlings. Flowers solitary or few in clusters at the base of the spines, tubular, whitish; petals small or absent. Fruit capsular, 3-parted. The 3 following species are hardy in sheltered places, but to flower freely they must have full sunshine. Propagated by cuttings of half-ripened wood.

**C. arma'ta.*** Shrub up to 8 or 10 ft., younger parts consisting mostly of slender, terete, rigid spines $\frac{1}{2}$ to $1\frac{1}{2}$ in. long, sharply pointed and more or less downy. *l.* often absent, $\frac{1}{8}$ to $\frac{1}{2}$ in. long. *fl.* waxy-white, tubular, $\frac{1}{8}$ in. long, fragrant, solitary or in twos or threes. *fr.* of 3 rounded capsules, $\frac{1}{8}$ in. wide, 1-seeded. Late autumn. Chile. 1882. (G.C. 60 (1916), 223.) Attractive late-fl. shrub. var. **ro'sea,** *fl.* pink-tinted.

**C. bictonen'sis.** A synonym of *C. cruciata*.

**C. crucia'ta.** Shrub up to 10 ft., of rigid habit. Branches armed with flat, triangular spines, each pair set at right angles to its neighbour, sharply pointed, $\frac{1}{2}$ to $1\frac{1}{2}$ in. long. *l.* ovate, toothed, $\frac{1}{4}$ in. long, usually absent. *fl.* yellowish-white, tubular, $\frac{1}{4}$ in. long, solitary to 4 or 6 in a cluster. On rare occasions this shrub will produce a shoot with bodkin-shaped spines. (*See* G.C. 60 (1906), 109.) Uruguay, S. Brazil. 1824. (B.M. 5033 as *C. bictonensis*.)

**C. hor'rida.** A synonym of *C. infausta*.

**C. infaus'ta.** Shrub up to 10 ft., younger parts consisting mostly of bodkin-shaped spines as in *C. armata*, but glabrous. *l.* (when present) $\frac{1}{8}$ to $\frac{1}{3}$ in. long. *fl.* dull white suffused with red, $\frac{1}{4}$ in. long, lobes recurved; anthers only half exposed. March to June. Chile. 1833. (B.M. 3644 as *C. horrida*.)

**C. spino'sa.** This name is often met with in horticultural literature, but the true thing is not in cult.

W. J. B.

**COLLETOT'RICHUM.** A genus of Fungi, some species of which cause diseases in plants. *See* **Bean Anthracnose.**

***Collet'tii,*** in honour of Col. Sir Henry Collett, K.C.B., 1836–1901, who collected in the Shan States.

**COLLIER.** The Bean Aphis. *See* **Aphis.** **A**

**A→**

**COLLINS'IA** (in honour of Zaccheus Collins, 1764–1831, Vice-President, Philadelphia Academy of Natural Sciences). FAM. *Scropulariaceae.* A genus of about

25 species of annuals, natives of Western N. America and Mexico, related to Penstemon but with the fifth stamen reduced to a gland. Leaves entire, opposite or whorled. Flowers axillary; calyx bell-shaped; corolla deeply 2-lipped, saccate at base, bright coloured. The following are hardy annuals succeeding in any good garden soil. In well-drained situations they may be sown in autumn, or in late March or April, the autumn-sown plants flowering earlier, the seedlings being thinned to about 4 in. apart.

*Collinsia bicolor*

**C. bi'color.\*** Stems more or less erect but rather weak, 1 to 2 ft. h. *l.* ovate-lanceolate, somewhat cordate at base, more or less toothed, sometimes downy, sessile. *fl.* upper lip and tube of cor. white, lower rose-purple, in whorls forming a raceme. August. California. 1833. (B.M. 3488; B.R. 1734.) Variable in colour. var. **al'ba**, *fl.* white with lower lip greenish; **candidis'sima**, *fl.* white; **multicol'or,** *fl.* variegated white, lilac, and rose, the form of this called **marmora'ta** being striped and spotted carmine. **A**

**C. grandiflo'ra.** Stems 6 to 12 in. h. *Lower l.* spatulate, *upper* oblong-linear, all rather thick. *fl.* pale purple, upper lip blue, in whorls of 3 to 9. May, June. California. 1826. (B.R. 1107.) var. **carmin'ea,** *fl.* carmine.

**C. tincto'ria.** Stems about 12 in. h. May. California. 1848. var. **purpu'rea,** *fl.* purple.

**C. ver'na.** 3 to 12 in. h. *l.* ovate or oblong to ovate-lanceolate, with distant teeth. *fl.* white with lower lip blue, on solitary pedicels longer than fl. May. Eastern U.S. America. 1871. (B.M. 4927.)

**COLLINSO'NIA** (in honour of Peter Collinson, English botanist, correspondent of Linnaeus and John Bartram, introducer of many plants). FAM. *Labiatae*. A genus of 3 species of rather coarse perennial herbs, natives of Eastern N. America. Roots thick. Leaves large, strongly though agreeably scented, ovate, toothed, usually with long stalks. Flowers yellow or whitish in long panicles or terminal racemes. Easily grown in common garden soil, preferring sandy peat, in a moist situation; of little beauty. Propagated by root divisions in spring.

**C. canaden'sis.** Branched, glabrous or nearly so, 1 to 2 ft. h. *l.* broadly ovate, slender-pointed, base rounded or somewhat heart-shaped. *fl.* yellow, 4 times as long as cal., in long, loose, many-fld. panicles. August. Eastern N. America. 1734. (B.B. ed. 2, 3, 153.)

*colli'nus -a -um,* growing on a hill.

**COLLOM'IA** (*kolla*, mucilage; from the mucilaginous character of the seed-coat of many species when wet). FAM. *Polemoniaceae*. A genus of 9 species of American annual herbs, related to Gilia but with membranous plicae between the calyx teeth. Flowers in dense heads with broad, ovate, entire bracts beneath them; corolla salver-shaped. Leaves alternate, nearly always entire. Collomias are easily grown in ordinary garden soil, treated like other hardy annuals.

KEY
1. *Lvs. usually undivided*    2
1. *Lvs. usually pinnately cut*    C. heterophylla
2. *Cor. 4 times as long as cal.*    C. grandiflora
2. *Cor. twice as long as cal.*    3
3. *Stem glabrous*    C. linearis
3. *Stem hairy at base*    C. biflora

*Collomia biflora*

**C. biflo'ra.** Stem erect, branched, 1 to 1½ ft. *l.* lanceolate or linear-lanceolate, 1½ to 2 in. long, ⅓ in. wide, entire or few-toothed. *fl.* scarlet or rarely yellow. Summer. Chile. 1831. (B.M. 3468 as *C. Cavanillesii;* B.R. 1622 as *C. coccinea.*)

**C. Cavanille'sii.** A synonym of *C. biflora.*

**C. coccin'ea.** A synonym of *C. biflora.*

**C. grandiflo'ra.** Stem erect, usually branched, 1½ to 2 ft., leafy, hairy above. *l.* linear-lanceolate, 2 in. long, ¼ to ⅓ in. wide. *fl.* in half-round, dense-fld., clammy heads, at first yellow then red. Summer. Western N. America. 1826. (B.R. 1174; B.M. 2894.)

**C. heterophyl'la.** Stem 8 or 9 in., branched from base, glandular above. *l.* hairy, lower 2-pinnately cut or lobed, upper with a few coarse teeth. *fl.* 6 to 10 in a terminal head, rose. July. Western N. America. 1828. (B.M. 2895; B.R. 1347.)

**C. linea'ris.** Erect, hairy, 9 to 12 in. *l.* narrow-lanceolate, hairy, entire. *fl.* in a many-fld. terminal head, yellowish-brown. (B.M. 2893; B.R. 1166.)

**COLMANA'RA** (in honour of Sir Jeremiah Colman, V.M.H., d. 1942, noted amateur grower of orchids, of Merstham, Surrey). FAM. *Orchidaceae*. Hybrids involving species of Miltonia, Oncidium, and Odontoglossum.

*colobo'des,* curtailed.

**COLOCA'SIA** (from Arabia *kolkas* or *kulkas*). FAM. *Araceae*. A genus of about 7 species of tuberous herbs or herbs with thick erect stems, natives of Trop. Asia. Leaves and scapes usually radical, leaves very large, cordate, or peltate, undivided. Flowers unisexual, naked, females at base of spadix, separated from males by some short ovoid neutral flowers, spathe ovoid or oblong, deciduous. For treatment, *see* **Caladium.**

**C. affin'is.** Tuber rounded, small. *l.* peltate, roundish-ovate, or ovate, 4 to 6 in. long, thinly membranous, green above, glaucous beneath; l.-stalk slender, 8 to 14 in. long. *Peduncle* solitary or many, 2 to 3 in. long. *Spathe* tube pale, blade linear-lanceolate with a long slender tip, 2 to 3 in. long. India. var. **Jennings'ii,** *l.-stalk* purplish with transverse lines of purple spots, *l.* cordate, spotted deep green or blackish-violet. Trop. Himalaya.

**C. antiquor'um.** Taro. Tuberous at base. *l.* peltate-ovate, cordate at base, about 20 in. long, thinly leathery; stalk about 3½ ft. long. *Peduncles* much shorter than l.-stalks. *Spathe* pale yellow, 6 to 14 in. long, tube green, oblong. E. Indies. 1551. Cultivated in S. Europe and throughout the tropics. A variable species. var. **esculen'ta,** *fl.* whitish, spadix shorter than the ovate-lanceolate spathe. Sandwich Is. 1739. Syn. *Caladium esculentum*; **Fontanes'ii,** *rhiz.* short, fleshy, l.-stalks reddish-purple or violet, blade large, oblong, dark green, margin and nerves violet. Ceylon. (B.M. 7732.); **illust'ris,** *l.-stalks* violet, blade large, oblong-ovate, with many dark green spots. Syn. *Alocasia illustris*; **nymphaeifo'lia,** tubers long, spadix longer than the white spathe, sagittate at the end. India. 1800.

**C. Devansaya'na.** A synonym of *Alocasia Devansayana*.

**C. × Marchal'lii** (*C. affinis* × *C. antiquorum*?). *l.* widely ovate or roundish-ovate, peltate, 5 to 7 in. long, margin somewhat undulate, green above, somewhat glaucous beneath, spots confluent, stalks pale green, 8 to 12 in. long. *Peduncle* 3 to 6 in. long, slender. *Spathe* linear-oblong, 1½ to 3 in. long. (G.I. 1878, 86 as *Alocasia hybrida*.)

**C. odora'ta.** A synonym of *Alocasia indica*.

## COLOCYNTH. *See* **Citrullus Colocynthis.**

*colocyn'this,* from Colocynth, the classical name of the plant.

*colo'nus -a -um,* mound.

## COLORADO BEETLE, *Leptinotarsa decemlineata,* is a dangerous foreign pest of Potatoes, the presence of which must be reported in writing *immediately* to the Ministry of Agriculture. The grubs are reddish-yellow, humpbacked, and feed for about 3 weeks on the leaves of Potato, eventually descending to the soil for pupation. The beetles, which are about twice the size of the common 7-spotted Ladybird, are yellowish with 10 black lines on the wing-cases and some black spots on the thorax. They appear in late July and August and, if weather conditions are favourable, eggs are laid on the leaves and a further generation of beetles occurs before the haulm dies down in autumn. This pest which may ruin a crop entirely has become established in several European countries within recent years.

Prompt and thorough steps under the direction of the Ministry of Agriculture must be taken as soon as the presence of the pest is seen.

G. F. W.

## COLORADO DOUGLAS FIR. *See* **Pseudotsuga glauca.**

*colo'rans, colora'tus -a -um,* coloured.

*colos'seus -a -um,* very large.

*colpo'des,* lap or hollow.

## COLQUHOUN'IA (in honour of Sir Robert Colquhoun, a patron of the Calcutta Botanic Garden in the early part of the 19th Century). Fam. *Labiatae.* A genus of 3 closely related species of evergreen, soft-wooded shrubs. Leaves opposite, stamens 4. *C. coccinea* is a free-growing shrub which is too tender for the open ground except in the south-west, but can be grown against a warm wall if covered in very cold weather. Easily propagated by cuttings.

**C. coccin'ea.** Evergreen shrub of loose habit up to 10 ft., shoots semi-woody, downy, 4-angled. *l.* ovate to lanceolate or cordate, 3 to 8 in. long, 1 to 4 in. wide, toothed, grey-white with down beneath. *fl.* 3 to 5 in axillary, short-stalked clusters, scarlet and yellow; cor. 1 in. long, tubular, 2-lipped; lower lip 3-lobed, upper lip erect, notched; cal. funnel-shaped, ⅓ in. long, 5-toothed, grey-downy. August to October. Himalaya. (B.M. 4514; B.M. n.s. 115.) var. **vesti'ta,** *l.* more woolly than in type; grows in drier localities.

**C. vesti'ta.** A variety of *C. coccinea*.

W. J. B.

## COLT'S FOOT. *See* **Tussilago Farfara.**

*colubri'nus -a -um,* snake-like.

*columba'rius -a -um,* dove-like.

*columbia'nus -a -um,* of British Columbia.

## COLUMBINE. *See* **Aquilegia.**

## COLUMBINE, FEATHERED or TUFTED. *See* **Thalictrum aquilegifolium.**

## COLUMEL'LA (after Columella, Roman writer on agriculture, 1st cent. B.C.). Fam. *Vitaceae.* A genus of about 16 species of climbing plants, usually shrubby, related to Vitis with which it is often combined, differing by the 4- (not 5-)merous flower; distinct from Cissus by the axillary (not leaf-opposed) tendrils and digitate or pedate leaves, and from Tetrastigma by the filiform style with a small stigma and larger, stalked leaflets from 2½ to 6 in. long. For cultivation, *see* **Cissus.**

**C. japon'ica.** Herbaceous tendril climber of rapid growth. Stem striate. *l.* usually glabrous, pedate; lflets. 5, roundish-oval, broad, terminal large, oval-elliptic, slender-pointed. *fl.* greenish, in forked cymes. *fr.* 2- to 4-seeded, as large as a small pea. Japan, Java, Australia. 1875. Half-hardy. Syn. *Cissus japonica, Vitis japonica.* var. **marmora'ta,** *l.* with broad, yellow blotches. **A**

**C. oligocar'pa.** Similar to *C. japonica* but with slender-pointed, more sharply and closely toothed lflets., finely downy when young. China. Syn. *Vitis oligocarpa.* **A**

## COLUMEL'LIA (derivation as Columella). Fam. *Columelliaceae.* A genus of 2 evergreen shrubs or small trees in the Andes of Peru and Ecuador. For characters see family. *C. oblonga* will grow in a mixture of loam, peat, leaf-soil, and sand and needs the protection of a greenhouse. Propagation is by half-ripe cuttings in the above compost in gentle heat under a bell-glass. **A**

**C. oblong'a.** Small tree to 20 ft. Shoots silky-downy, flattish cut podes. *l.* oblong, 1 to 2 in. long, toothed at top, narrowed at base, shining green above, silky glaucous below. *fl.* yellow, in terminal leafy corymbs, peduncles short; cor. rotate, 5-lobed, lobes equal. 1875. (B.M. 6183.)

## COLUMELLIA'CEAE. Dicotyledons. A family of 1 genus, Columellia, containing 2 species. Shrubs or small trees with evergreen, opposite, toothed leaves without stipules. Flowers perfect, nearly regular, in cymes; calyx and corolla 5- to 8-parted; stamens 2, short and thick with a broad irregular connective and 1 twisted pollen-sac. Ovary imperfectly 2-celled, superior. Fruit a many-seeded capsule enclosed in the calyx.

## COLUMN. The stamens and styles combined into a solid structure in the centre of the flower as seen in orchids.

*Colum'nae,* in honour of Fabio Colonna, 1567–1640, of Naples.

*columna'ris -is -e,* columnar, formed like a column.

## COLUM'NEA (in honour of Fabius Columna (Fabio Colonna), 1567–1640, author of *Phytobasanos*, the earliest botanical book with copper plates, published at Naples, 1592, &c.). Fam. *Gesneriaceae.* A genus of about 100 species of evergreen herbs, or sub-shrubs, natives of Trop. America, often creeping or climbing. Leaves opposite, often unequal, thickish, hairy or downy, somewhat toothed. Flowers axillary, solitary, or clustered; corolla tubular, nearly straight, swollen behind at base, upper lip erect, arching, lower 3-lobed, spreading. For cultivation, *see* **Aeschynanthus.** *C. crassifolia, C. glabra, C. magnifica,* and similar plants from the mountains of Costa Rica, should be grown cool in a compost of leaf-mould and coarse sand in equal parts, with pea-size crocks over good drainage topped by moss. **A**

**C. auranti'aca.** Creeping. *fl.* orange-yellow, long-stalked. June. Colombia. 1851. (F.d.S. 552.) A good basket plant, or for growing on a block of rotten wood.

**C. aureoni'tens.** Large species. *l.* broad-lanceolate, densely covered with silky golden hairs. *fl.* orange-red. September. Colombia. 1843. (B.M. 4294.)

**C. × Banks'ii** (*C. Oerstediana* × *C. Schiedeana*). As showy as *C. Oerstediana* with *fl.* of same colour, 3 in. long, 1½ in. across. *l.* smaller than those of *C. Schiedeana.* Of garden origin. 1918. (G.C. 63 (1918), 64.)

**C. crassifo'lia.** Erect shrub, about 1 ft. h., rooting at nodes. *l.* narrow, lanceolate, 4 to 5 in. long. *fl.* erect; cal. 1 in. long, cut to base; cor. 4 in. long, bright scarlet, yellow in mouth, covered with red hairs; peduncles 1-fld., short. Mexico? (B.M. 4330.)

**C. erythrophae'a.** Shrub, 2 ft. h. *l.* lanceolate, long-pointed, oblique at base, deep green. *fl.* solitary, bright red, large; cal. large, spreading, blotched red inside. November. Mexico. 1858. (R.H. 1867, 170.)

**C. glab'ra.*** Erect shrub, rooting at nodes. *l.* ovate-lanceolate, fleshy, glabrous, glossy. *fl.* very large, scarlet, stamens white; solitary in l.-axils. April. Costa Rica. (B.M. 8453.) May be grown in a hanging basket.

**C. glorio'sa.*** Epiphyte, growths pendulous, about 2 ft. long, fleshy. *l.* ovate, hairy. *fl.* large, tubular, fiery-red, yellow in throat. Winter. Costa Rica. 1915. (B.M. 8378.) var. **purpu'rea,** *l.* purplish when young, later bronze.

**C. hirsu'ta.** Climbing shrub. *l.* ovate, slender-pointed, toothed, hairy above. *fl.* usually twin; cor. purplish or pale red, about 1 in. long, hairy; sep. toothed. August to November. Jamaica. 1870. (B.M. 3081.)

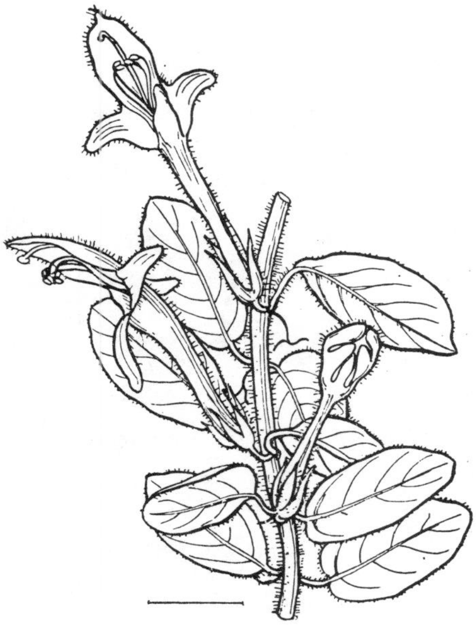

*Columnea hirta*

**C. hir'ta.** Epiphyte, rooting at nodes. Stem densely covered with reddish-brown hairs. *l.* elliptic to ovate-oblong or obovate-oblong, 1 to 2 in. long, up to nearly 1 in. wide, hairy on both sides; stalks up to ½ in. long. *fl.* solitary in l.-axils, shortly stalked; cor. about 3¼ in. long, vermilion, orange at base of lobes, hairy, hairs long, spreading; tube slender, gibbous behind at base; cal. toothed. Cent. America. (B.M. 9542.)

**C. Kalbreyeria'na.** Half-climbing shrub, stem fleshy. *l.* lanceolate, unequal, dull green above with pale yellow spots, deep claret beneath. *fl.* yellow, marked with red within; cal. yellow, 1½ to 2 in. long. February. Antioqua. 1882. (B.M. 6633.)

**C. magnif'ica.*** Habit and appearance of *C. glabra* but *l.* downy. Costa Rica. (B.M. 8225.)

**C. microphyl'la.*** Habit of *C. gloriosa. l.* small, orbicular-cordate, about ¼ in. long, covered with purplish hairs. *fl.* bright orange-scarlet. Costa Rica. 1925. (B.M. 9203.)

**C. Oerstedia'na.*** Habit of *C. gloriosa. l.* small, glossy, nearly glabrous, ovate-oblong, about ½ in. long, somewhat Box-like. *fl.* russet-orange, 2¾ in. long; cor. somewhat hairy without. February. Costa Rica. 1912. (B.M. 8344.)

**C. ova'ta.** *l.* small, oval, toothed. *fl.* large, crimson, solitary. Chile.

**C. pic'ta.** *fl.* mixed with large membranous coloured bracts. Colombia.

**C. rotundifo'lia.*** Pendulous, slender. *l.* small, broadly oval, entire, hairy. *fl.* large, long, crimson; sometimes twin. Winter. Trinidad. 1805

**C. ru'tilans.** Climbing shrub. *l.* ovate-lanceolate, toothed, rather rough to the touch, hairy, reddish beneath. *fl.* reddish-yellow, hairy; sep. jagged. August, September. Jamaica. 1823.

**C. scan'dens.** Climbing shrub. Stem 4-angled. *l.* ovate, acute, toothed, rather hairy; stalked. *fl.* scarlet, hairy; sep. toothed. August. Guiana. 1759. (B.M. 1614.)

**C. Schiedea'na.** Climbing herb with stems swollen at nodes, purple-hairy. *l.* oblong-lanceolate, entire, about 5 in. long, silky-hairy. *fl.* 2 in. long, glandular-hairy, variegated yellow and brown; sep. entire, spotted, hairy. June. Mexico. 1840. (B.M. 4045.)

**C. Tu'lae.** Climbing, with many aerial roots. *fl.* bright yellow (var. **fla'va**), hairy; cal. lobes ovate-acute, entire, hairy. *fr.* round, snow-white. W. Indies.

**C. × vedrairien'sis** (*C. magnifica* × *C. Schiedeana*). More vigorous than *C. magnifica* and with brighter *fl.* than *C. Schiedeana.* France. 1918. (R.H. 90, p. 168.)

**COLUR'IA** (*kolouros*, carved swan; from the position of the dying styles). FAM. *Rosaceae.* A genus of about 4 species of perennial mat-forming herbs, closely related to Waldsteinia and needing similar cultural treatment, differing by the persistent stamens curving together over the young fruits and by the numerous carpels. Natives of E. Asia.

**C. Laxman'nii.** Habit of Waldsteinia. *Basal l.* in a rosette, palmately cut into broad obovate-obtuse, coarsely double-toothed lobes, veins beneath and l.-stalks with long, outstanding hairs. *fl.* 1 to 3, erect or ascending, stems about 8 in. h., large, yellow; cal. funnel-shaped; pet. many times longer than sep. Altai, Siberia. SYN. *C. geoides, C. potentilloides.*

***colurn'us -a -um,*** hazel-nut.

**COLU'TEA** (Greek *Koloutea*). FAM. *Leguminosae.* Bladder Senna. A genus of 10 or more species of deciduous shrubs, natives of S. Europe eastward to the Himalaya. Leaves unequally pinnate, alternate. Leaflets 5 to 19, entire. Flowers yellow or brownish-red, papilionaceous, borne in long-stalked, few-flowered racemes. Pod inflated, bladder-like.

Easily cultivated shrubs enjoying full sunshine. *C. arborescens* and *C. media* are excellent for furnishing dry banks. All flower on the growths of the current season, continuing to do so for weeks or even months. They can be pruned back nearly to the older wood in February. Most of them ripen seeds; they can be propagated also from half-ripened short shoots in July.

KEY

| | |
|---|---|
| 1. *Pod closed at apex* | 2 |
| 1. *Pod open at apex* | 7 |
| 2. *Fl. mainly yellow* | 3 |
| 2. *Fl. more or less reddish or coppery* | C. × media |
| 3. *Wings of fl. not longer than keel* | 4 |
| 3. *Wings of fl. longer than keel* | 5 |
| 4. *Fl. ¾ in. long. Shrub to 12 ft. Lflets. ½ to 1¼ in. long* | C. arborescens |
| 4. *Fl. ½ in. long. Shrub of 3 to 4 ft. Lflets. smaller* | C. brevialata |
| 5. *Lflets. ½ to ¾ in. long* | 6 |
| 5. *Lflets. 9 to 15, ¼ to ⅜ in. long* | C. istria |
| 6. *Lflets. 9 to 13, slightly hairy beneath* | C. cilicica |
| 6. *Lflets. 7 to 11, more hairy. Cal. densely brown-hairy* | C. melanocalyx |
| 7. *Racemes drooping* | C. nepalensis |
| 7. *Racemes not drooping* | 8 |
| 8. *Shoots downy. Lflets. 7 or 9, pale glaucous. Fl. brownish or coppery* | C. orientalis |
| 8. *Shoots glabrous. Lflets. 5 to 11. Fl. yellow* | C. persica |

**C. arbores'cens.** Rounded, bushy shrub up to 12 ft., shoots downy. *l.* 3 to 6 in. long; lflets. 9 to 13, oval or obovate, notched at the apex, ½ to 1 in. long, downy beneath at first. *fl.* bright yellow, ¾ in. long, 3 to 7 in axillary, long-stalked racemes produced successively from June to September. *Pod* inflated, bladder-like, 3 in. long. S. Europe and Mediterranean region. 16th century. (B.M. 81.) var. **bulla'ta,** of dwarf dense habit; *lflets.* ¼ to ⅝ in. long; raceme 1 to 1½ in. long.

**C. breviala'ta.** Closely akin to *C. arborescens* but only 3 to 4 ft. h. *lflets.* usually 11, much smaller. *fl.* in racemes of 2 to 6, each only ½ in. long; wing pet. three-fourths the length of the keel and two-thirds that of the standard pet. *Pods* more attenuated. S. France.

**C. casp'ica.** A synonym of *Sphaerophysa salsula.*

**C. cilic'ica.** Similar to *C. arborescens* in growth and in the *l.* with its 9 to 13 lflets. *fl.* yellow, 3 to 5 together towards the end of a raceme, distinguished from *C. arborescens* by larger wing pet. which are longer than the keel. June onwards. Asia Minor. SYN. *C. longialata.* (G.C. 16 (1894), 155 as *C. melanocalyx.*)

**C. cruen'ta.** A synonym of *C. orientalis*.

**C. halep'ica.** A synonym of *C. istria*.

**C. is'tria.** Shrub 3 to 5 ft. *lflets*. 9 to 15, ¼ to ⅜ in. long, obovate, broadly oval, appressed hairy. *fl*. 2 to 5 together, coppery-yellow, ¾ in. long; standard pet. ⅝ in. wide; wing pet. as long as keel. May onwards. *Pod* 2 in. long. Asia Minor. 1752. SYN. *C. halepica*. Rather tender.

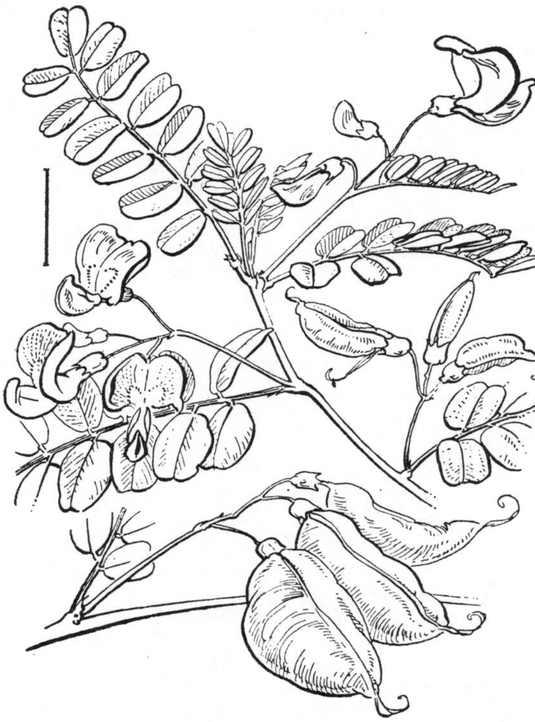

*Colutea arborescens* (p. 529)

**C. longiala'ta.** A synonym of *C. cilicica*.

**C. × me'dia** (*C. arborescens* × *C. orientalis*). Very similar to *C. arborescens* in general appearance. *lflets*. 9 to 13, obovate, ½ to 1 in. long, bluish-green, downy beneath at first. *fl*. brownish-red or orange-red; cal. resembling that of *C. orientalis* in being longer than that of *C. arborescens* and with linear-lanceolate teeth. *Pod* 3 in. long. Grown in the Berlin B.G. in 1790.

**C. melanoca'lyx.** Very closely akin to *C. arborescens*, from which it differs in the cal. which is longer (⅓ in.), more tubular, has broader triangular teeth, and is clothed with dark brown velvety down. *fl*. yellow, wing pet. as long as keel. Asia Minor.

**C. nepalen'sis.** Much like *C. arborescens* but less hardy and with drooping racemes. *lflets*. 9 to 13, ¼ to ½ in. long. *fl*. about ½ in. long. Nepal. (B.M. 2622; B.R. 1727.)

**C. orienta'lis.** Shrub of rounded compact growth, up to 6 ft., shoots downy. *l*. 3 to 4 in. long with usually 7 or 9 lflets. which are broadly ovate or roundish, ¼ to ⅝ in. long, very glaucous. *fl*. 2 to 5 in a raceme, brownish-red or coppery, ⅝ in. long; standard pet. ½ in. across, with a yellow spot; wing pet. shorter than keel. *Pod* 1½ in. long, open at end. Orient. 1710. SYN. *C. cruenta*. Distinct by its glaucous-white l.

**C. per'sica.** Shrub 6 to 8 ft., shoots glabrous. *l*. 1½ to 3 in. long; *lflets*. 5 to 11, obovate or obcordate, rounded or notched at the apex, ¼ to ½ in. long. *fl*. pure yellow, ¾ in. long, in racemes of 3 or 4; wing pet. longer than keel. *Pod* glabrous, 1½ to 2 in. long, open at apex. Persia and Kurdistan. var. **Buh'sei,** *pods* downy, *fl*. larger.

W. J. B.

**COLUTEOCARP'US** (*Colutea* and *carpon*, fruit; from the form of the capsule). FAM. *Cruciferae*. A genus of a single species with the characters described below, native of the eastern Mediterranean, related to Alyssum and Vesicaria. A rock-garden plant easily grown in light soil on a sunny bank or wall. Seed is abundantly produced.

**C. reticula'tus.** Dwarf tufted perennial with a woody base, glabrous. *l*. in rosettes, stiff, with a few sharp teeth. *fl*. golden yellow, numerous, in flattish heads, about 6 to 8 in. h. *fr*. large, round, bladder-like. Europe, Asia Minor.

***Colvil'ei,*** in honour of Sir James Colvile, F.R.S., Indian Judge, d. 1890.

**COLVIL'LEA** (in honour of Sir Charles Colville, Governor of Mauritius). FAM. *Leguminosae*. A genus of a single species of tree similar in aspect to *Poinciana regia* to which it is nearly related and which it rivals in brilliance, distinguished by its round, full, not flat, legume. It needs stove conditions and cultivation like that of a Caesalpinia.

**C. racemo'sa.** Tree of 40 to 50 ft. with long spreading branches. *l*. alternate, remote, oblong-ovate, about 3 ft. long, 2-pinnate; pinnae in 20 to 30 pairs, opposite, 4 in. long, with 20 to 28 pairs of linear lflets. ½ in. long. *fl*. bright scarlet, wings long, narrow, erect, standard the smallest pet., keel small, almost covered by the wings, stamens 10, free, exserted, yellow; raceme about 18 in. long, drooping with up to 200 crowded fls., those at the stem end of the raceme or its branches opening first. Madagascar. (B.M. 3325–6.)

***Colvil'lei,*** in honour of Mr. Colville, nurseryman of Chelsea, predecessor of Messrs. James Veitch. **A**

**COLY'SIS.** Included in **Polypodium.**

**COLZA-OIL.** Oil expressed from seed of Rape, *Brassica Napus*.

***co'mans,*** hairy.

**COMANTHOSPHA'CE** (*coma*, a tuft of hairs, *anthos*, flower, and *sphakos*, sage; in allusion to the character of the flower and its botanical relationship). FAM. *Labiatae*. A genus of 4 species of Japanese undershrubs or herbaceous perennials.

**C. japon'ica.** Small undershrub with 4-angled, downy stems. *l*. opposite, 3 to 5 in. long, ovate-lanceolate, slender-pointed, coarsely toothed, pale beneath. *fl*. in a slender, terminal, erect, downy spike up to 6 in. long; cor. yellow, tubular, ⅓ in. long with a ring of down inside, 5-lobed, 1 lobe much the largest; stamens 4, exserted ⅛ in. October. Japan. 1893. (B.M. 7463.)

**C. sublanceola'ta.** Herbaceous perennial, 3 or 4 ft., stems angled, glabrous. *l*. lanceolate, 3 to 6 in. long, ½ to 1¾ in. wide, base cuneate, apex slender-pointed; green on both surfaces, glabrous. *fl*. pale yellow, crowded on terminal spikes 2 to 3½ in. long; cor. tubular, ¼ in. long, stamens yellow, exserted ⅛ in. October. Japan.

W. J. B.

**COMAREL'LA.** Included in **Potentilla.**

**COMAROP'SIS.** Included in **Waldsteinia.**

**COMAROSTAPH'YLIS** (*Komaros*, the Arbutus, and *staphyle*, a grape; referring to the fruit clusters). FAM. *Ericaceae*. A genus of about 12 species of evergreen shrubs natives of California, Mexico, Guatemala. Leaves leathery, alternate. They are intermediate between Arbutus and Arctostaphylos. Bentham and Hooker sunk the genus under Arctostaphylos, but later authors have restored it because of the very different fruit which more resembles that of Arbutus. Cool greenhouse plants except in the south-west, thriving in a peaty or lime-free soil.

**C. arbutoi'des.*** Shrub 5 or 6 ft., shoots downy. *l*. entire, 2 to 3 in. long, ½ to ¾ in. wide, linear-oblong, pointed, rusty-downy beneath; stalk ⅛ to ⅓ in. long. *fl*. in terminal, pyramidal, downy panicles up to 6 in. long; cor. white, globose-ovoid (resembling Arbutus), ⅓ in. long, with 5 small, toothed reflexed lobes. May. Guatemala. 1840. (B.R. 29, 30.)

**C. diversifo'lia.** Shrub 6 to 15 ft., the parts minutely downy when young. *l*. of sterile shoots 1 to 2 in. long, oblong to oval, spiny-toothed, those of the flowering shoots smaller, spathulate-lanceolate, sometimes entire. *fl*. white, in solitary or clustered racemes; cal. with 5 lanceolate lobes; cor. ovate, ¼ in. long. *fr*. a berry-like drupe, ⅛ in. wide, red, granular, pulpy. May, June. S. California. Cultivated in Scilly Isles.

W. J. B.

**COMAR'UM** (*Komaros*, the Arbutus, in allusion to the similarity of the fruits). FAM. *Rosaceae*. Closely related to Potentilla with which it is often combined, distinguished by the spongy mature receptacle and the dull-purple flowers. A hardy herbaceous perennial growing by the water-side or in marshy places, easily propagated by division. The very astringent rootstock yields a yellow dye.

**C. palust're.** Marsh Cinquefoil. *l.* pinnate; lflets. broad, sharply toothed, green above, greyish beneath. *fl.* dark purplish-brown; pet. lanceolate, slender-pointed, much shorter than cal.; stalked, axillary and terminal. 12 to 18 in. h. June. N. Hemisphere, including Britain. (E.B. 437.) SYN. *Potentilla Comarum.*

F. P.

*coma'tus -a -um,* hairy.

## COMB FERN. *See* Schizaea.

*Comb'eri,* in honour of H. F. Comber who collected in the Andes (1925–7) and Tasmania (1930).

**COMBINED WASHES.** Sprays for a double purpose, such as insecticidal and fungicidal, combined into a single spray for application at the same time. *See* **Sprays, Spraying.** **A**

**COMBRETA'CEAE.** Dicotyledons. A family of about 450 tropical and sub-tropical trees and shrubs, often climbing, falling into 16 genera. Leaves opposite, simple, without stipules. Flowers in racemes, sometimes unisexual, regular; sepals and petals usually 4 or 5 (rarely 6 to 8), petals sometimes absent; stamens 4 or 5 or twice as many; ovary inferior, 1-celled; ovules 2 to 6. Fruit dry, 1-seeded, often with winged angles. The genera treated here are Calycopteris, Combretum, Conocarpus, Quisqualis, Terminalia. **A**

**COMBRE'TUM** (Pliny's name for a climbing plant, not now recognizable). FAM. *Combretaceae.* A genus of about 250 species of evergreen climbing or erect shrubs, rarely herbs, natives of the tropics excluding Australia and Polynesia, but including S. Africa. The species with convolute cotyledons are sometimes separated into a genus Poivrea, but are here included as their characters are generally similar. Leaves opposite or 3 or 4 in a whorl, rarely alternate, entire. Flowers almost sessile, bracteate, in a terminal panicle; petals 4 or 5; stamens 8 or 10. Best planted out in the border of the stove and trained up an upright pillar and up the rafters or on chains hung up in festoons along the house. The compost should be 3 parts of peat, 1 of loam, and 1 of leaf-mould. They require plenty of water in summer and thorough and frequent syringing in the early part of the season before flowering. After flowering they need considerable pruning and thinning, and at the same time the parts remaining must be thoroughly cleansed. Save for tying in, little attention is then needed during the winter. Propagation is by cuttings of stiffish side shoots with a heel, in sand, under a glass, in heat. **A**

**C. apicula'tum.** *l.* elliptic or oblong, glabrous, veins netted. *fl.* yellow, small; spikes as long as l.; pet. ciliate; stamens exserted as long as style; cal. bell-shaped. Summer. *fr.* cordate-ovate, golden yellow, wings a little larger at base, rather wavy. S. Africa.

**C. argen'teum.** *l.* broadly ovate to elliptic-oblong, 2 to 6 in. long, more or less scaly beneath. *fl.* blood-red, greenish-yellow, fragrant; spikes thick, dense, sometimes solitary. Guatemala. SYN. *C. erianthum.*

**C. bracteo'sum.** Hiccup-nut. *l.* ovate or ovate-oblong, acute at both ends. *fl.* reddish; spikes about 1 in. long on lateral branches; bracts green, leafy; pet. 5; stamens 10. *fr.* wingless. Summer. S. Africa. SYN. *Poivrea bracteosa.*

**C. coccin'eum.** *l.* oblong-lanceolate, acute, dark shining green. *fl.* scarlet, in loose secund panicles; stamens long exserted. June to December. Madagascar. (B.M. 2102, B.R. 429, L.B.C. 563 as *Poivrea coccinea.*) SYN. *C. purpureum.*

**C. como'sum.** About 20 ft. h. *l.* opposite, oblong, acute, rather heart-shaped; stalks short. *fl.* intense scarlet, on long spikes; bracts lanceolate. May to August. Sierra Leone 1822. (B.R. 1165.) SYN. *Poivrea intermedia.*

**C. decan'drum.** *l.* elliptic-oblong, slender-pointed, veins in 6 to 8 pairs, silky-hairy when young. *fl.* greenish-white, densely hairy; spikes about 1 in. long; bracts creamy-white, 1 to 2 in. long; cal. tube hairy. *fr.* 1 in. long, oblong with 5 papery wings. Summer. India, Burma.

**C. erythrophyl'lum.** Branches unarmed, glabrous finally, downy when young. *l.* alternate or opposite, ovate. *fl.* yellow; spikes cylindrical, shorter than l. S. Africa.

**C. flagrocar'pum.** Large climbing shrub. *l.* opposite, elliptic or ovate-lanceolate, 4 to 6 in. long, hairy and glandular beneath; stalk short. *fl.* in rusty hairy racemes, axillary and crowded towards ends of branches; cal. funnel-shaped above ovary, downy without; pet. obovate, much longer than cal. Bengal, Burma.

**C. grandiflo'rum.** Hairy. *l.* oblong. *fl.* scarlet, large; spikes short; pet. obovate, obtuse. May to July. Sierra Leone. 1824. (B.M. 2944.) SYN. *C. Afzelii.*

*Combretum comosum*

**C. latifo'lium.** *l.* large, oblong, slender-pointed, leathery. *fl.* red, small; spikes short, crowded; cal. downy, turbinate-bell-shaped; pet. obovate, obtuse; stamens shortly exserted. India. SYN. *C. macrophyllum.*

**C. racemo'sum.** *l.* ovate-oblong, acute, shining. *fl.* white, pedicels short; pet. lanceolate, obtuse; spikes long, tufted at tip. February to July. W. Africa. 1826.

F. G. P.

**COMESPERM'A** (*kome*, hair, and *sperma*, seed; in allusion to the terminal hair-tufts on the seeds). FAM. *Polygalaceae.* A genus of about 25 species of herbs, undershrubs, or shrubs, erect or twining, natives of Australia and Tasmania. Leaves alternate; petals 3; stamens 8 united to above the middle. *C. volubile* needs a compost of sandy loam and peat with thorough drainage. It can be propagated by cuttings of young shoots, under a bell-glass.

**C. volu'bile.*** Glabrous, twining, semi-woody climber, usually over shrubs 4 to 6 ft. h. Stems very slender, often tangled and intertwined. *l.* few, linear-lanceolate, up to 1 or 2 in. long. *fl.* densely set in abundant, axillary or terminal, spike-like racemes, 1 to 3 in. long; cor. ⅛ to ¼ in. long, usually of a lovely blue, but also purplish-blue or sometimes white with a purple keel. April. Australia, Tasmania. 1834. (P.M.B. 5, 145 as *C. gracile.*) Greenhouse.

W. J. B.

**COMFREY.** *See* Symphytum officinale.

*cominta'nus -a -um,* from the Spanish name of Batangas or Luzon.

**COMMELI'NA** (in honour of Kaspar, 1667–1731, and Johann, 1629–98, Commelin, Dutch botanists). FAM. *Commelinaceae.* A genus of about 100 species, allied to Tradescantia, but with 3 perfect stamens only. Herbaceous, upright, spreading, or procumbent perennials, more or less succulent, often rooting at nodes. Leaves alternate, ovate, lanceolate or linear, sessile or nearly so, stem-clasping. Flowers opening for a day, blue, yellowish, or rarely white, rather small, usually in 2-branched cymes, emerging one at a time from a terminal spathe, those of the upper branch of the cyme small, deciduous, of lower fertile; sepals 3, membranous, 2 inner often connate; petals longer, 1 larger, often clawed; stamens 3, perfect, 2 or 3 imperfect, filaments not hairy. The stove and greenhouse evergreen species are best grown in light, rich soil and are propagated by cuttings which will root in sand in gentle heat. The tuberous-rooted species, if grown in the open, should be taken up before autumn and stored like Dahlias, but should not become dry; but they will sometimes come through the winter safely outdoors in sheltered, well-drained places. The stored tubers should be started in gentle heat and planted out in the open towards the end of May; so treated they are stronger than seedlings. **A**

**C. africa'na.** Slender, terete, 1 to 3 ft. long, trailing and somewhat bushy. *l.* lanceolate. *fl.* tawny-yellow. May to October. S. Africa. 1759. (B.M. 1431; F.P.S.A. 321.) SYN. *C. lutea*. Greenhouse.

**C. angustifo'lia.** *See* **C. virginica.**

**C. benghalen'sis.** Trailer, evergreen. *l.* oval, green, contracted at base into a sheath, often ciliate, with reddish hairy and wavy margin. *fl.* blue, small; spathe green, hairy. Trop. and S. Africa. (F.P.S.A. 42; G.F. 1868, 592.) Stove.

*Commelina coelestis*

**C. coeles'tis.\*** About 1½ ft. h. *l.* oblong-lanceolate, sheath ciliate. *fl.* blue; peduncles hairy, spathe cordate acuminate, folded together. June. Mexico. (S.B.F.G. 3.) Half-hardy perennial. var. **al'ba,** *fl.* white; **variega'ta,** *fl.* blue and white.

**C. defic'iens variega'ta.** Low-growing, spreading perennial with round stems. *l.* ovate-lanceolate, freely striped with longitudinal white bands. *fl.* blue, small, terminal. Brazil. Stove. (B.M. 2644 shows type of species.)

**C. ellip'tica.** Stem ascending, rooting, red especially above nodes, hairy, 1½ to 2 ft. h., branched. *l.* lanceolate, slender-pointed, flat, glabrous, 7-nerved, channelled and bright green above, whitish beneath. *fl.* white; cal. glabrous; peduncles 2 in. long, straight, with line of reflexed hairs on inner side. July. Lima. (B.M. 3047 as *C. gracilis*.) SYN. *C. formosa*. Stove.

**C. erec'ta.** Robust, 2 to 4 ft. h. *l.* large, 3 to 7 in. long, 1 to 2 in. wide, oblong-lanceolate, rough backwards above, sheath ciliate with white hairs. *fl.* 2, posterior pet. blue, anterior much smaller, white; spathes crowded, hooded, top-shaped in fr. Summer. SE. United States. *C. hirtella* is a form of this. Hardy.

**C. formo'sa.** A synonym of *C. elliptica*.

**C. hirtel'la.** *See* **C. erecta.**

**C. lu'tea.** A synonym of *C. africana*.

**C. nudiflo'ra.** Compact, creeping perennial, rooting at nodes. *l.* lanceolate or ovate-lanceolate, more or less acute; sheath often ciliate. *fl.* showy, cobalt-blue, few in each cluster. Argentine. 1897. SYN. *C. Sellowii*. Greenhouse.

**C. pal'lida.** Hairy, erect, branched perennial. *l.* oblong, acute, narrowed to base, sheath tinged violet, ciliate. *fl.* blue, spathes oblong, slender pointed, folded in two, hairy. Mexico. SYN. *C. rubens*. Greenhouse.

**C. prostra'ta.** A synonym of *C. benghalensis*.

**C. ru'bens.** A synonym of *C. pallida*.

**C. Sellow'ii.** A synonym of *C. nudiflora*.

**C. tubero'sa.\*** Roots tuberous. *l.* oblong-lanceolate, acute, sheaths hairy, ciliate. *fl.* sky-blue, spathes ovate-cordate, long pointed, ciliate. June, July. Mexico. 1732. (B.M. 1695.) Half-hardy.

**C. virgin'ica.** Slender, erect or reclining and rooting at basal nodes. *l.* oblong or linear-lanceolate. *fl.* blue; spathes solitary or scattered, roundish heart-shaped when expanded, pointed, somewhat hood-like in fruit. Summer. S. United States. Hardy. *C. angustifolia* is a narrow-leaved form of this.

F. G. P.

**COMMELINA'CEAE.** Monocotyledons. A family of about 300 herbaceous plants in 25 genera, natives for the most part of the warmer parts of the world but a few in temperate regions. Stems jointed. Leaves alternate, flat and sheathing. Flowers usually in a cyme, perfect, usually regular and blue; sepals and petals 3; stamens 6; ovary superior, 3-celled, with a few ovules in each cell. Fruit a capsule. In many instances some of the stamens are absent or transformed into staminodes. The genera dealt with here are Cochliostema, Commelina, Cuthbertia, Cyanotis, Dichorisandra, Forrestia, Palisota, Rhoeo, Spironema, Tinantia, Tradescantia, Weldenia, Zebrina. **A**

**Commerson'ii,** in honour of Ph. Commerson, 1727–73, doctor-naturalist.

**A→**

**commix'tus -a -um,** mixed up.

**commu'nis -is -e,** common, growing in company.

**commuta'tus -a -um,** changed or altered.

**COMOCLA'DIA** (*kome*, hair, *klados*, branch; the leaves crowded near the top of the branch form a sort of head). FAM. *Anacardiaceae*. A genus of evergreen trees with clammy sap, natives of the hotter parts of America. Leaves unequally pinnate with opposite leaflets. Flowers purple, small, on short pedicels in loose panicles; petals 3 or 4, overlapping. Fruit a drupe. These stove trees need a compost of peat and loam or any rich light soil. Cuttings of ripe shoots will root in sand under glass in heat.

**C. denta'ta.** Maiden Plum. Tree to 30 ft. *lflets.* shortly stalked, oblong, with erose teeth, smooth above, downy beneath. W. Indies. 1790.

**C. ilicifo'lia.** Tree to 20 ft. *lflets.* 9 to 12, ovate or roundish, smooth, with 1 to 3 spines each side, sessile. *fr.* oblong. W. Indies. 1778.

**C. integrifo'lia.** Tree of 10 to 30 ft. *l.* about 2 ft. long; lflets. 8 to 12, lanceolate, entire, smooth, stalked. *fr.* oblong, dark purple. Trop. America. 1778.

F. G. P.

**comoren'sis -is -e,** of the Comoro Is., E. Africa.

**como'sus -a -um,** growing in tufts, or bearing a tuft (often of l.).

**compac'tus -a -um,** close-growing.

**COMPARET'TIA** (named after Andreas Comparetti, professor at Padua, and writer on vegetable physiology; 1746–1801). FAM. *Orchidaceae*. A genus of 6 elegant epiphytic Orchids, natives of the Andes of S. America, with handsome, generally drooping, racemes of small but brightly coloured flowers, which retain their beauty for a considerable period. Sepals erecto-patent, the dorsal one free, the lateral ones connate, produced at base into a long, slender spur which is free of the petals; lip continuous with the base of the column, produced at base into 2 long, linear spurs, which are concealed within the bases of the sepaline spur; the lateral lobes rather broad, erect, the middle one spreading, very broad. All are dwarf with small pseudobulbs, bearing usually a single leathery leaf. All flower in summer. They succeed well in small pans suspended from the roof of a moderately warm house, where they will not be fully exposed to the sun. Comparettias require a liberal supply of moisture during the growing season, and at no time should they be allowed to become dry. The compost should consist of Sphagnum moss mixed with equal quantities of finely pulled Osmunda fibre. Winter temperature 55 to 60° F.

*Comparettia coccinea*

**C. coccin'ea.*** *fl.* sep. and pet. brilliant scarlet; lip scarlet, tinged white at base; racemes 3- to 7-fld. *l.* bright green on upper surface, purple beneath. *Pseudobulbs* about 1 in. long. Brazil. 1838. (B.R. 24, 68.)

**C. falca'ta.*** *fl.* rich rosy-purple; lip thickly veined with a deeper shade. Colombia. 1836. Not very dissimilar from *C. coccinea,* but with broader *l.* and somewhat differently shaped fl. (B.M. 4980; W.O.A. 359; L. 163.) SYN. *C. rosea.*

**C. macroplec'tron.*** *fl.* pale rose, speckled with red, distichous, nearly 2 in. long from the tip of dorsal sep. or end of lip, spur 2 in. or more long; racemes pendulous. *l.* 2 or 3, 4 to 5 in. long by ½ to 1¼ in. broad, leathery, green above; pale, and faintly streaked with rusty-yellow beneath. Colombia. (B.M. 6679; L. 664; W.O.A. 65.)

**C. ro'sea.** A synonym of *C. falcata.*

**C. specio'sa.*** *fl.* large and numerous; sep. and pet. light orange with a cinnabar glow; lip cinnabar, orange at base, front lobe subquadrate and emarginate, about 1¼ in. wide, with a very short claw and a small keel between the basal auricles; spur minutely pilose, over 1½ in. long; racemes loose. Ecuador. 1877. (W.O.A. 233; L. 673.)

E. C.

**COMPASS PLANT.** *See* **Silphium laciniatum.** *Lactuca Scariola* growing in dry places behaves in the same way.

***complana'tus -a -um,*** flattened vertically to a level surface above and below.

**COMPLETE.** Flower furnished with calyx, corolla, stamens, and pistils.

**COMPLICATE, COMPLICATED.** Folded up upon itself.

**COMPOS'ITAE.** Dicotyledons. The largest family of flowering plants including over 13,000 species in over 800 genera, mostly herbs, sometimes shrubs and rarely trees, world-wide in distribution. Leaves alternate, rarely opposite, without stipules. Flowers usually in heads or very short crowded spikes, the heads surrounded by an involucre of bracts. The flowers are sometimes neuter, sometimes unisexual, sometimes perfect, and the distribution of the different forms in the heads varies greatly. The calyx is rarely distinct, sometimes absent, sometimes a 5-toothed rim at the top of the inferior ovary, usually a number of hairs or bristles which enlarge after fertilization to aid distribution of the single-seeded fruit. The corolla is of 5 connate petals, sometimes 2-lipped, sometimes strap-shaped, often regular. Stamens 5, growing on the tube of the corolla, the anthers joined into a tube (syngenesious) surrounding the style. Ovary inferior, style 1, stigmas 2, ovule 1. A few genera are of economic importance and many are very decorative. The genera dealt with here are Achillea, Actinella, Actinomeris, Adenostyles, Ageratum, Agroseris, Ainsliaea, Amellus, Ammobium, Amphoricarpus, Anacyclus, Anaphalis, Andryala, Antennaria, Anthemis, Aphanostephus, Arctotis, Argyroxiphium, Arnica, Artemisia, Aster, Athanasia, Athrixia, Baccharis, Baeria, Balsamorrhiza, Barnardesia, Bedfordia, Bellis, Bellium, Berardia, Berkheya, Berlandiera, Bidens, Bigelovia, Boltonia, Brachycome, Brachyglottis, Brickellia, Buphthalmum, Cacalia, Calendula, Callistephus, Calocephalus, Calotis, Carduncellus, Carduus, Carlina, Carthamus, Cassinia, Catananche, Celmisia, Cenia, Centaurea, Chaenactis, Chaetanthera, Chaptalia, Charieis, Chevreulia, Chiliotrichum, Chrysanthemum, Chrysocoma, Chrysogonum, Chrysopsis, Cichorium, Cineraria, Cirsium, Cladanthus, Cneorum, Coreopsis, Cosmos, Cotula, Cousinia, Craspedia, Cremanthodium, Crepis, Cryptostemma, Cynara, Dahlia, Dendroseris, Dimorphotheca, Diotis, Doronicum, Dysodia, Echinops, Emilia, Encelia, Engelmannia, Erigeron, Eriocephalus, Eriophyllum, Erlangea, Eruca, Espeletia, Ethulia, Eunomia, Eupatorium, Euryops, Felicia, Flaveria, Franseria, Gaillardia, Galactites, Gamolepis, Garuleum, Gazania, Gerbera, Gnaphalium, Grindelia, Guizotia, Gundelia, Gymnolomia, Gynura, Haplocarpha, Haplopappus, Helenium, Helianthus, Helichrysum, Heliopsis, Helipterum, Heteropappus, Heterospermum, Heterotheca, Hidalgoa, Hieracium, Hippia, Hippocrepis, Homogyne, Hulsea, Humea, Hyoseris, Hypochaeris, Hysterionica, Inula, Iostephane, Iva, Ixodia, Jurinea, Kleinia, Kuhnea, Lactuca, Lagascea, Lagenophora, Lasiospermum, Lasthenia, Layia, Leontopodium, Leuceria, Leucogenes, Leuzea, Leyssera, Liabum, Liatris, Lidbeckia, Ligularia, Lindheimera, Lonas, Madia, Mairia, Marshallia, Matricaria, Melanthera, Microglossa, Mikania, Monolopia, Montanoa, Moscharia, Mutisia, Myriactis, Myriocephalus, Odontospermum, Oedera, Oldenburgia, Olearia, Onopordon, Onoseris, Osteospermum, Othonna, Othonnopsis, Oxylobus, Palafoxia, Pallenis, Pectis, Pentachaeta, Perezia, Pericome, Pertya, Petalacte, Petasites, Petrobium, Phaenocoma, Picridium, Platycarpha, Podachaenium, Podolepis, Polymnia, Polypteris, Prenanthes, Proustia, Psilotrophe, Raillardia, Rudbeckia, Santolina, Sanvitalia, Sausurea, Sclerocarpus, Scolymus, Scorzonera, Senecio, Sericocarpus, Serratula, Siegesbeckia, Silphium, Silybum, Solidago, Sonchus, Stephanocoma, Stevia, Stifftia, Tagetes, Tanacetum, Taraxacum, Tarchonanthus, Thelesperma, Tithonia, Tolpis, Townsendia, Tragopogon, Tridax, Trilisa, Triptilion, Trixis, Tussilago, Urospermum, Ursinia, Venidium, Verbesina, Vernonia,

Viguieria, Villanova, Vittadinia, Waitzia, Wedelia, Werneria, Wulffia, Wyethia, Xanthisma, Xanthocephalum, Xeranthemum, Zacintha, Zexmenia, Zinnia.

**COMPOSTS.** A compost is a mixture of various ingredients in which to pot plants or with which to top-dress plants in pots or growing in the open ground. The mixture may or may not consist of or include manures. Potting-composts in the past varied considerably according to the plants dealt with and sometimes included a great variety of materials, though this was unusual. The chief constituents were loam, leaf-mould, peat, and sand with small quantities of charcoal, burnt earth, and various manures, and these things must form the basis of all potting composts, but it must be realized that each of the chief constituents is an exceedingly variable material. Experience of the nature of the materials available enabled intelligent growers to meet the requirements of the plants they grew so that the results obtained were usually beyond praise, but skill in using them, care in watering and in ventilation, doing the work required at the proper time all combined to produce the results, and no good results can follow without this combination. Composts which have been found suitable for most of the plants described in the Dictionary are given under their appropriate headings, but recent experiments, especially those carried out at the John Innes Horticultural Institution by Mr. J. C. Lawrence have shown that some simplification or standardization of potting composts is possible.

Large users of potting composts concerned with growing a few types of plants on a large scale have long endeavoured to secure uniform composts for their own requirements, but the composts arrived at after considerable experiment at the John Innes Horticultural Institution have been widely adopted for ordinary plants and purposes. Three ingredients form the bulk of the 'John Innes Composts': (1) moderately heavy loam prepared by stacking turves from pasture, grass side downwards, for from 6 to 12 months and riddled through a $\frac{3}{8}$-in. sieve before use; (2) coarse clean sand containing particles up to $\frac{1}{8}$ in. diameter; and (3) dust-free moss or sedge-peat, only partly decomposed and moderately coarse in texture. The last, which is usually free from bacteria and any harmful organisms, takes the place of leaf-mould, which, where care had not been taken was often a source of trouble in preparing composts. Before mixing these main ingredients the loam is steam-sterilized, i.e. harmful organisms are destroyed by heating to a temperature somewhat short of that of boiling water by driving steam through the dry soil so as to heat it quickly and thoroughly. Chemical changes are brought about in soil during the heating process which are apt to make it injurious to plants for a time but these are counteracted by the addition of superphosphate.

The composts are made up as follows: I. For seed-sowing, 2 parts by bulk of sifted sterilized loam, 1 part peat, and 1 part sand and to each cubic yard of the mixture 2 lb. superphosphate, 1 lb. powdered chalk. II. For general potting purposes, 7 parts by bulk of sifted sterilized loam, 3 parts peat, 2 parts sand and to each cubic yard of this mixture a mixture of fertilizers consisting of 2 lb. of finely ground hoof and horn, 2 lb. superphosphate, and 1 lb. powdered chalk.

Young seedlings need a compost intermediate between the seed-sowing compost and the general potting compost.

A full account of the making and use of these composts is given in the *John Innes Leaflets*, *1* and *2*, published by the John Innes Horticultural Institution.

Although these and other composts are designated 'standardized', it must be remembered that loam, sand, and peat are all variable substances, loam especially so, and therefore experience with the types available in different districts must be acquired before entire reliance can be placed upon the exact quantities of each to use. It must be further remembered that the plants cultivated in gardens differ greatly between themselves in their relation to the environment to which they are adapted. It is not to be expected that a compost suitable for the majority of plants grown for ordinary purposes will suit all the varied types from Orchids, Cacti, and Aquatics also, to say nothing of the sensitiveness shown by many S. American, Australian, and New Zealand plants as well as Ericaceae to the alkalinity of soils. Cultivators must still, therefore, use their discretion in compounding mixtures for growing various plants, but the composts mentioned have proved satisfactory for a great number of widely grown plants and have shown that various complex mixtures recommended in old books are unnecessary.

**COMPOST-HEAP.** The conversion of vegetable refuse into manure has become essential now that farmyard and stable manure is so much less abundant, for the maintenance of a high humus content in our soils is a necessity for high fertility for most of the plants we grow.

A

**COMPOST-YARD.** An enclosure in a garden, preferably near the potting-sheds, where different soils, manures, &c., are stored until required. Part of the area should be under cover, as an open shed, where composts can be made in wet weather and kept dry for use. This shed should have a concrete floor. Each material in the yard should have its proper place and the whole area should be kept tidy.

**compound,** formed of several comparable parts united in one common whole, as a leaf formed of several leaflets, or a fruit formed of several ripened ovaries, as a blackberry or a strawberry.

*compres'sus -a -um,* pressed together and flattened.

**COMPTON'IA** (after Henry Compton, Bishop of London, 1632–1713). FAM. *Myricaceae.* Sweet Fern. One species, closely akin to Myrica, with which it was united by Linnaeus. It is distinguished chiefly by its pinnately lobed leaves and by having stipules.

**C. asplenifo'lia.*** Deciduous shrub 2 to 4 ft., shoots hairy. *l.* 2 to $4\frac{1}{2}$ in. long, $\frac{1}{4}$ to $\frac{5}{8}$ in. wide, cleft almost to the midrib into oblique, rounded lobes, downy, fragrant. *Male catkins* $\frac{3}{4}$ in. long; *female infl.* globular, $\frac{1}{2}$ to 1 in. wide. March, April. *fr.* ovoid, $\frac{1}{8}$ in. long. Eastern N. America. 1714. SYN. *C. peregrina, Myrica asplenifolia.* Valued for its charming foliage and pleasant fragrance. Very hardy. Should be grown in peat or light loam free from lime; propagated by layering.

W. J. B.

*Comptonia'nus -a -um,* in honour of the family of the Marquis of Northampton, Compton, of Castle Ashby, Northampton, *c.* 1810.

*comp'tus -a -um,* ornamented, having a head-dress.

**CONAN'DRON** (*konos,* cone, *andron,* anther; the appendages of the anthers are united in a cone around the style). FAM. *Gesneriaceae.* A genus of a single species of Japanese herbaceous perennial related to Streptocarpus but having a straight instead of twisted fruit. Not quite hardy but excellent for shady crevices in the cool rock-garden under glass or for the alpine house in pots or pans of well-drained rich leafy soil; propagated by division or by the very small seed sown under glass and treated like Rhododendron seed.

**C. ramondioi'des.** Tuberous rooted. *l.* few, radical, sometimes solitary, ovate-oblong, acute, coarsely toothed, rugose. *Scapes* 6- to 12-fld., in drooping cymes, about 5 in. h.; *cal.* about $\frac{1}{2}$ in. long, downy; *cor.* lilac or white, rotate, about 1 in. across; eye golden. Summer. Japan. 1879. (B.M. 6484.) var. **leucan'themum,** *fl.* white.

**CONAN'THERA** (*konos,* cone, *anthera,* anther; the 6 anthers form a cone in the early stages of the flower). FAM. *Liliaceae.* A genus of 3 or 4 species of small

**C. Cneo'rum.*** Sub-shrub, 1 to 3 ft. h. Stem branched. *l.* lanceolate, covered with silvery-silky hairs. *fl.* pale pink, hairy without, in heads on short peduncles. May. S. Europe. 1640. (B.M. 459.) Beautiful. Needing hot sunny place with well-drained soil. Half-hardy. Pot plant in greenhouse.

**C. farino'sus.** Tender twining annual. Stem silky. *l.* distant, more or less sagittate, slender-pointed, 1½ to 3 in. long, toothed; stalk slender, ½ in. long. *fl.* pale rose, about ½ in. long, in axillary 3- to 7-fld. panicles. Summer. Trop. Africa. Half-hardy. Needs restricted root-room. (B.R. 1323.)

**C. inca'nus.** Stems procumbent or trailing, 1 to 3 ft. long, densely, finely hairy. *l.* lanceolate, usually with 2 to 4 spreading lobes at base, blunt or mucronulate; stalk short. *fl.* white to rose; sep. oblong, ¼ in. long; peduncles 1- or 2-fld. April to August. N. and S. America. (B.B. ed. 2, 3, 47.)

**C. linea'tus.*** Deciduous perennial about 6 in. h. *l.* lanceolate, acute, silky-hairy, lined; stalked. *fl.* pale reddish-purple, hairy without; sep. rather leafy, silky; peduncles shorter than l., 1- or 2-fld. June. S. Europe. 1770.

**C. ma'jor** of gardens. A synonym of *Ipomoea purpurea.*

**C. mauritan'icus.** Prostrate, twining perennial covered with soft white hairs. *l.* nearly ovate, alternate, distichous; stalk very short. *fl.* blue with white throat, about 1 in. across; cal. hairy with 5 linear sep., 2 rather smaller than others; anthers yellow; peduncles 1-, 2-, or 3-fld. Summer. N. Africa. (B.M. 5243; F.d.S. 2183.) Hardy in favoured places or basket plant for greenhouse.

**C. nit'idus.** Cushion-forming, 3 in. h. *l.* small, ovate, blunt, silvery-silky. *fl.* rosy-white, large; peduncles very short, 1- to 4-fld. Summer. Sierra Nevada, Spain. Rock-garden; not free in fl. Sun.

**C. Scammo'nia.** Deciduous perennial. Stem trailing, angled, glabrous. *l.* heart-arrow-shaped. *fl.* cream or very pale red, large, bell-shaped; sep. ovate, blunt, tip reflexed; peduncles usually 3-fld., exceeding l. July. E. Mediterranean. 1726. (F.G. 192.) Hardy. Root yields a purgative gum-resin.

**C. sic'ulus.** Annual. Stems many from a slender root-stock, procumbent or twining, 6 to 24 in. long, hairy. *l.* somewhat heart-shaped, acute, downy, stalked. *fl.* blue; cor. twice as long as cal.; peduncles hairy, 1-fld., as long as or longer than l.-stalk with 2 linear bracts at apex. April onwards. Mediterranean region. (B.R. 445.)

**C. spithamae'us.** Erect perennial, about 6 in. h. *l.* grey, oval, upper sessile, obtuse, 1 to 2 in. long, ½ to 1¼ in. wide. *fl.* white, nearly 2 in. long, solitary; cal. with a large oval, acutish bract at base. May to August. N. America. Syn. *Calystegia spithamaea.*

**C. tenuis'simus.** Perennial, shining or silvery hairy. Stems diffuse, twining at tip. *Lower l.* oblong-heart-shaped, bluntly crenate or lobed; *upper* palmately partite, lobes linear, otherwise entire; terminal longest. *fl.* solitary, axillary, rose; cor. hairy in angles. April to July. Greece. (F.G. 195.)

**C. tric'olor.** Dwarf Convolvulus. Annual, about 1 ft. h., branches declinate, with small, soft, white hairs. *l.* ovate-lanceolate or spatulate, hairy, ciliate. *fl.* blue with yellowish-white throat and white tube; sep. ovate-lanceolate, acute; peduncles 1-fld., exceeding l. July to September. Sicily, Spain, Portugal. 1629. (B.M. 27.) Variable in fl. colour. Hardy.

**C. undula'tus.** Annual, hairy. Root slender. Stem ascending, 2 to 6 in. long, leafy. *l.* obovate-oblong to oblong-lanceolate, narrowed at base, blunt. *fl.* solitary, axillary, blue, white at base, hairy without, ⅓ to ⅔ in. long. May, June. Mediterranean region. (R.I.F.G. 1342.)

**CONVOLVULUS HAWK MOTH.** *See* **Hawk Moths.**

***Conwen'tzii,*** in honour of H. W. Conwentz, 1855–1922, paleobotanist in Berlin.

***conyzoi'des,*** Conyza-like.

**COOK'IA.** Included in **Clausena.**

***Cook'ii,*** in honour of James Cook, 1728–79, the explorer.

**COOPERAN'THES.** Fam. *Amaryllidaceae.* Hybrids between species of Cooperia and Zephyranthes, raised first by Mr. Percy Lancaster of the Alipur Botanical Gardens, Calcutta, about 1900, and subsequently by his son, Mr. S. Percy Lancaster, by whom the best-known forms have been introduced. They are intermediate between the parents, tending sometimes to one, sometimes to the other genus in the form of foliage and flower and usually with modified colouring. Cultivation is as in Zephyranthes, and flowering is usually much more free than in Cooperias.

**C. × 'Alipore Beauty'** (*Cooperia Oberwettii* ♀ × *Zephyranthes robusta* ♂) is probably the best known. *l.* as in *Z. robusta*, ¼ in. wide, slightly glaucous. *fl.* upright, as long as in *Z. robusta*, soft lilac-rose on white, deeper pink without; segs. long; tube 3 in. long; scape 12 in. long, brownish-green at base.

***Coop'eri, Cooperia'nus -a -um,*** in honour of: 1. Mr. Cooper of Alpha House, Old Kent Road, collector and grower of orchids about 1865. 2. Edward Cooper, 1871– , author of many notes on orchids, including those in this Dictionary. 3. Joseph Cooper, gardener at Wentworth, Yorks. 4. Thomas Cooper, 1815–1913, collector in S. Africa for Mr. W. W. Saunders of Reigate.

**COOPER'IA** (in honour of Joseph Cooper, successful cultivator, one-time gardener to Earl Fitzwilliam, Wentworth, Yorks.). Fam. *Amaryllidaceae.* A genus of perhaps 6 species of N. American bulbous plants differing from Zephyranthes by the long perianth-tube, and erect, not versatile, anthers. Flowers solitary, primrose-scented, opening only at night. Treatment as for Zephyranthes, hardy only in very sheltered places.

**C. Drummond'ii.** *l.* twisted, linear, 10 to 15 in. long, glaucous. *fl.* erect, white, tube becoming red; tube 4 to 5 in. long; limb 1½ to 2 in. across, segs. ovate; scape 6 to 9 in. long. August. Texas. (B.R. 1835.)

**C. Oberwet'tii.** Similar to *C. Drummondii* but *l.* scarcely glaucous.

**C. peduncula'ta.** *l.* linear-oblong, obtuse, somewhat glaucous. *fl.* white, tube shorter and scape longer than in *C. Drummondii.* August. (B.M. 3727.)

**COPAIBA BALSAM.** *See* **Copaifera officinalis,** &c., **Copal.**

**COPAIF'ERA** (*Copaiba*, the Brazilian name for the balsam of Capevi, *fero*, to bear). Fam. *Leguminosae.* A genus of about 16 species of evergreen trees, natives of Trop. Africa and America, with pinnate, somewhat leathery leaves. Flowers in panicles, white, the 2 anterior petals not glandular, ovules only 1 or 2. They need stove treatment and grow well in sandy loam. Cuttings of firm shoots will root in sand in March in heat, under glass. *C. Gorskiana* and other species yield Copal. Of no horticultural importance, but interesting as economic plants.

**C. Gorskia'na.** Inhambane Copal. Tree. *l.* widely falcato-ovate, 3- or 4-nerved, leathery. *fl.* subsessile; bracts caducous. *Pod* 1½ in. long, 1 in. wide. E. Trop. Africa.

**C. Lansdorf'fii.** Balsam of Copaiba. Shrub or tree up to 60 ft., much branched. *lflets.* in 3 to 5 pairs, 1¼ in. long, broadly oval, glabrous. *fl.* white, in short spicate panicles. Brazil.

**C. officina'lis.** Balsam of Copaiba. Evergreen tree of about 20 ft. *lflets.* in 2 to 5 pairs, ovate, incurved, unequal-sided, bluntly pointed, with numerous pellucid dots. W. Indies, Trop. America. 1774.

**COPAI-YÉ WOOD.** *See* **Vochysia guianensis.**

**COPAL.** Resin used in varnish-making, &c., obtained from several species of Copaifera, *Hymenaea Courbaril,* and Trachylobium species, all members of the Leguminosae. The copal of Hymenaea and Trachylobium is often dug up in lumps from the soil near where the trees are growing or have been.

***copalli'nus -a -um,*** from Mexican *kopallis.*

***Copeland'ii,*** in honour of Edwin Bingham Copeland, 1873– , botanist, University of California, student of Philippine flora.

**COPERNIC'IA** (in honour of the Polish astronomer N. Kopernik, 1473–1543). Fam. *Palmaceae.* A genus of about 30 species of erect, almost unarmed Palms with fan-shaped leaves in a terminal crown, the stem covered with bases of old leaves, natives of Trop. America. Young leaves usually undivided, old palmately cut. Spadix axillary, much branched; flowers clustered or solitary; calyx tubular, 3-toothed. Fruit globose or ovoid, 1-seeded. For treatment, *see* **Corypha.**

**C. cerif'era.** Carnauba; Wax Palm of S. America. 25 to 35 ft. h. Stem slightly swollen at base. *l.* nearly round, 3 to 4 ft. across, palmately cut when old, stalk channelled above, margin often spiny. *Spadix* erect, branched. Trop. S. America. *l.* covered with wax which is obtained by shaking them and is an important article of commerce. The wood is among the hardest known and the upper part of the stem yields a kind of sago.

**COPIAPO'A** (from Copiapo, one of the provinces of Chile). FAM. *Cactaceae.* Plants usually solitary, round or elongated, ribbed, with dense soft wool at top. Flowers nearly hidden in the wool, yellow. Fruit small, smooth, crowned with green, persistent, sepal-like scales. All the species are found in Chile. **A**

**C. cineras'cens.** Plants globose, about 3 in. wide; ribs about 20, compressed; radial spines 8, centrals 1 or 2, stouter, up to 1 in. long, all yellowish. *fl.* yellow. Chile. SYN. *Echinocactus cinerascens.*

V. H.

**COPING.** Bricks, stone, or tiles used at the top of a wall for protection or ornamentation. For a dry stone wall the coping may well consist of random lengths of York stone flagging cut to an even width so as to project about 2 in. beyond the face of the wall.

J. E. G. W.

***copio'sus -a -um,*** abundant.

**COPPICE.** A small wood of trees cut over at intervals for furnishing pea-sticks, stakes, &c. Hazel and sweet chestnut are especially useful for these purposes. The period of cutting is usually 5, 7, or 14 years according to the purposes to be served.

**COPRI'NUS.** A genus of capped fungi (Agaricaceae) in which the gills break down into an inky fluid. One species with a dark-brown cap (*C. atramentarius*) has been used for ink, being in its later condition as black as Indian ink. The species are found commonly in groups in woods, pastures, roadsides, &c. *C. comatus*, the Shaggy Cap Mushroom, has shaggy scales on its domed cap and is good for eating if gathered while the gills are still pink. The cap should be peeled downwards and the stem rejected. *C. niveus* with a snow-white cap sometimes appears on mushroom beds so abundantly as to interfere with the growth of the mushroom crop.

D. E. G.

**COPROS'MA** (*kopros*, dung, *osme*, a smell; in allusion to the often foetid odour of the plants when bruised). FAM. *Rubiaceae.* A genus of about 60 species of small trees or shrubs whose headquarters are in New Zealand, but which are also natives of Australia, Tasmania, and numerous islands of the far Pacific. All the New Zealand species are evergreen and no others are in cultivation. Leaves opposite, varying from part of an inch to 9 in. in length. Flowers unisexual, the sexes on separate plants, small, inconspicuous, and of no beauty. Many of the species, however, are very handsome in fruit, this being a fleshy, oblong or globose drupe usually ¼ to ⅓ in. long, and varying in colour from pale blue to yellow, orange, red, and purple.

Very few species can be termed truly hardy. *C. acerosa*, perhaps, is the hardiest and *C. Petriei* succeeds in moderate climates, but the majority are seen at their best in the counties of the south and south-west. Many species seem to find themselves particularly at home in the moist conditions of Ireland. The variegated forms of *C. Baueri* are occasionally grown in greenhouses for the sake of their leaf colouring, but the unisexuality of the plants makes them generally inconvenient for indoor cultivation. Propagation is by cuttings.

KEY

| | | |
|---|---|---|
| 1. | *Prostrate or low shrubs* | 2 |
| 1. | *Shrubs or small trees of over 5 ft.* | 3 |
| 2. | *Lvs. up to ½ in. long. Fr. dark or bluish-purple* | 10 |
| 2. | *Lvs. up to ¾ in. long. Fr. blue* | C. acerosa |
| 3. | *Lvs. rarely 1 in. long* | 4 |
| 3. | *Lvs. mostly over 1 in. long* | 6 |
| 4. | *Lvs. linear* | C. propinqua |
| 4. | *Lvs. ovate, round, or obovate* | 5 |
| 5. | *Lvs. smooth. Fr. yellow* | C. rigida |
| 5. | *Lvs. downy both sides. Fr. red* | C. rotundifolia |
| 5. | *Lvs. orbicular, ⅓ in. long. Fr. white* | C. parviflora |
| 6. | *Lvs. 4 to 9 in. long, dull green* | C. grandifolia |
| 6. | *Lvs. rarely over 4 or 5 in. long* | 7 |
| 7. | *Lvs. linear. Fr. pale* | C. Cunninghamii |
| 7. | *Lvs. broader. Fr. yellow to orange* | 8 |
| 8. | *Lvs. obovate, shining* | C. lucida |
| 8. | *Lvs. ovate or oblong* | 9 |
| 9. | *Lvs. bright glossy green or variegated, obtuse* | C. Baueri |
| 9. | *Lvs. dark glossy green, usually pointed* | C. robusta |
| 10. | *Lvs. oblong to obovate. Fr. purple* | C. Petriei |
| 10. | *Lvs. oval to ovate-lanceolate. Fr. blue* | C. Moorei |

**C. acero'sa.** Low evergreen shrub, usually prostrate, occasionally up to 5 ft., often forming a mass of interlacing, wiry, minutely downy shoots. *l.* ¼ to ¾ in. long, $\frac{1}{20}$ in. wide, in opposite pairs or clusters, linear. *fl.* unisexual, males 1 to 4 in a cluster; females solitary. *fr.* a globose drupe, ¼ in. wide, pale translucent blue. New Zealand. var. **arena'ria,** shoots yellow-green, more slender; **brun'nea,** shoots brown, shorter, more widely separated. Considered the most ornamental.

**C. austra'lis.** A synonym of *C. Cunninghamii.*

**C. Bau'eri.** Shrub or small tree, 15 to 25 ft. *l.* 1 to 3 in. long, bright glossy green, stout, broadly ovate or oblong, blunt-ended. *Male fl.* in dense axillary clusters; *females* 3 to 6 together; cor. ¼ in. long, tubular, with short lobes. *fr.* ovoid ¼ to ⅓ in. long, orange-yellow. New Zealand. 1876. var. **pictura'ta,** *l.* marked with blotches of pale yellow and creamy-white which assume a variety of grotesque forms spreading out from the midrib; **variega'ta,** compact shrub, *l.* bright green in the centre with a broad margin of creamy-yellow, changing to white. 1866.

**C. Cunningham'ii.** Shrub 6 to 15 ft., shoots glabrous. *l.* ½ to 2 in. long, ⅛ to ¼ in. wide, linear to linear-cuneate, pointed to bluntish. *fl.* in stalkless clusters of 2 to 12 on short, stunted branches, inconspicuous. *fr.* ¼ in. long, pale, translucent. New Zealand. SYN. *C. australis.*

**C. grandifo'lia.** Shrub 8 to 15 ft. *l.* 4 to 9 in. long, 1½ to 3½ in. wide, oval-oblong to obovate-oblong, cuneate, pointed, dull green; stalk ¾ to 1½ in. long. *fl.* in axillary clusters on branched stalks 1 to 3 in. long. *fr.* ⅓ in. long, oblong, reddish-orange. New Zealand. Very distinct by its large l.

**C. lu'cida.*** Glabrous shrub, 4 to 15 ft. *l.* 2 to 5 in. long, ¾ to 2½ in. wide, elliptical-obovate to lanceolate-obovate, cuneate, pointed or bluntish, leathery, shining; stalk up to ¾ in. long. *fl.* on branching axillary stalks up to 2 in. long. *fr.* ⅓ to ½ in. long, oblong or obovoid, reddish-orange. New Zealand. Near *C. grandifolia* but the l. are shining and leathery, not so large. Very showy in fr.

**C. Moor'ei.** Dwarf glabrous creeping perennial, 3 to 4 in. h. *l.* oval to ovate-lanceolate, thick, shining, concave, acute, narrowed below to a short stalk about ¼ in. long. *fl.* solitary on short erect branches; cor. about $\frac{1}{12}$ in. long. May. *fr.* broad oblong, ¼ to ⅓ in. long, blue. Tasmania.

**C. parviflo'ra.** Spreading leafy shrub. *l.* opposite, orbicular, about ⅓ in. long, distinctly variegated towards midrib. *fl.* inconspicuous, in clusters of 2 to 4. *Berry* small, round, transparent, white, persisting till New Year. New Zealand. Hardy.

**C. Pet'riei.** Dwarf prostrate shrub forming matted patches 3 in. h. *l.* ⅛ to ¼ in. long, narrowly oblong or narrowly obovate, more or less hairy. *fl.* solitary, ⅕ to ⅓ in. long; cor. tubular, deeply 4-lobed. *fr.* ⅕ to ⅓ in. wide, globose, dark purple or bluish-purple. New Zealand. Suitable for the rock-garden.

**C. propin'qua.** Shrub or small tree up to 20 ft., shoots downy at first. *l.* ¼ to ½ in. long, $\frac{1}{12}$ to ⅛ in. wide, opposite or in opposite clusters on short twigs, linear to linear-obovate, narrowed to the base. *fl.* inconspicuous. *fr.* sky-blue to blackish-blue, ⅓ in. long, globose or broadly oblong. New Zealand. Akin to the prostrate *C. acerosa.* (B.M. 9286.)

**C. rig'ida.** Erect, sparsely leaved shrub, 5 to 15 ft., shoots glabrous except when quite young, slender, branching widely, often at right angles, sometimes much interlaced. *l.* ¼ to ¾ in. long, obovate, rounded at the apex, glabrous. *fl.* solitary or 2 to 4 in stalkless clusters. *fr.* ¼ to ⅓ in. long, oblong or obovoid, yellow. New Zealand.

**C. robus'ta.** Shrub 5 to 15 ft., glabrous. *l.* 1½ to 4 in. long, ¾ to 2 in. wide, oval-oblong to oval-lanceolate, cuneate, usually pointed, leathery, dark glossy green. *fl.* in simple or branched, shortly stalked clusters. *fr.* oblong or ovoid, ¼ to ⅓ in. long, yellowish or reddish-orange. New Zealand.

**C. rotundifo'lia.** Shrub 4 to 12 ft., shoots very slender, downy. *l.* sparse, ¼ to 1 in. long, often as much wide, but also ovate-oblong to broadly oblong, more or less downy on both sides. *fl.* very small, in stalkless clusters. *fr.* globose or broader than long, ⅛ in. wide, red. New Zealand. Distinct by its sparse, roundish, thin, membranous l. and small fr.

W. J. B.

***cop'ticus -a -um,*** Egyptian.

**COP'TIS** (*kopto*, to cut; in allusion to the much-cut leaves). FAM. *Ranunculaceae*. A genus of about 8 species of small, evergreen bog plants distributed over north temperate and arctic regions. Leaves radical, much-divided. Flowers whitish, on leafless 1- to 3-flowered scapes; sepals 5 or 6, regular, petaloid, deciduous; petals 5 or 6, small, hooded or linear; carpels many. Hardy plants for moist peat, or very sandy moist soil, increased by division or seeds in early spring.

**C. asplenifo'lia.** About 1 ft. h. *l.* 2-ternate; lflets. somewhat pinnatifid, sharply toothed. *fl.* white; pet. 5, long and narrow, dilated and hooded in middle, very slender upwards; scape 2-fld., at first shorter than l. NW. America, Japan.

**C. occidenta'lis.** 6 to 12 in. h. *l.* 3-foliolate; lflets. stalked, broadly ovate. *fl.* white; pet. about 6, not hooded; scape short, 3-fld. Rocky Mts.

**C. orienta'lis.** 3 to 9 in. h. *l.* ternate, the divisions pinnate at base, pinnatifid above; lobes deeply cut. *fl.* white; scape about 3-fld. Japan. 1873.

**C. trifo'lia.*** 3 to 5 in. h. *l.* 3-foliolate from a bright yellow, fibrous root; lflets. obovate, blunt-toothed, scarcely 3-lobed. N. Hemisphere. 1782. (L.B.C. 173.)

*coquimben'sis -is -e,* of Coquimbo, Chile.

**COQUITO PALM.** *See* **Jubaea spectabilis.**

*coracen'sis -is -e,* Korean.

*coraci'nus -a -um,* raven black.

**CORAL BELLS.** *See* **Heuchera sanguinea.**

**CORAL BERRY.** *See* **Symphoricarpos orbiculatus.**

**CORAL-BUSH.** *See* **Templetonia retusa.**

**CORAL SPOT.** The Coral Spot fungus, *Nectria cinnabarina*, is very common and can be seen growing as a saprophyte on dead twigs and branches of many kinds of trees and shrubs. From such dead material this fungus may enter living branches through wounds and cause serious injury. One way in which it attacks living trees is first to become established on a dead snag-end of wood, or on a dead shoot, from which it grows into the adjacent living tissue. In this way large branches may be killed. The fungus is easily recognized when it produces its numerous pinkish or red cushion-like masses of spores, but these only appear on dead tissue and will not be seen on the branch until it is dead. Vast numbers of spores are released from these red cushions, to infect, where possible, other trees. Ornamental and forest trees, apple, pear, plum, walnut, fig, currant, and gooseberry trees may be attacked. It is advisable to remove all dead and dying branches from valuable trees, especially those showing the red pustules, and burn them. The cuts made should be painted over with white lead paint or tar.

In fruit plantations Coral Spot is most destructive to currants, especially old Red Currant bushes. On these, large branches when heavy with fruit may suddenly wilt. The usual reason is that the Coral Spot fungus has entered some part of the branch through a dead snag or side shoot which may or may not show the red fructifications. The affected branch must be cut off well below the last-affected leaves. Where a complete bush collapses the fungus has probably got into the stem or collar and the whole bush must be grubbed up and burnt. Where large wounds are made by cutting off branches the cut surface should be protected with a coat of paint. Infected material should not be allowed to lie about, pea-sticks, &c., should be kept dry, and old posts, &c., receive a dressing of creosote. Weakened bushes suffer most and good cultivation of Red Currant plantations should not be neglected.

D. E. G.

**CORAL TREE.** *See* **Erythrina.**

*coralli'nus -a -um,* coral-red.

**CORALLOBOT'RYS** (*korallion*, coral, *botrys*, a cluster; in allusion to the colour and character of the inflorescence). FAM. *Ericaceae*. Monotypic genus. Differs from Vaccinium by producing its flowers in stalked, corymbose clusters. Cool greenhouse shrub, requiring a peaty or lime-free soil.

**C. acumina'ta.*** Epiphytic shrub, 2 to 4 ft. *l.* short-stalked, 4 to 6 (sometimes over 10) in. long, lanceolate, slender-pointed, cuneate, sparsely toothed, leathery, often purplish beneath. *fl.* rich coral-red, in drooping, short-stalked clusters of up to a dozen, each on a pedicel 1 in. long coloured as richly as the cor., which is globose, ⅜ in. wide. Khasia Mts., Bhotan. (B.M. 5010 as *Epigynium acuminatum*.)

W. J. B.

**CORALLODIS'CUS** (*korallion*, coral, *discus*; from the colour of the disk). FAM. *Gesneriaceae*. A genus of 2 or 3 species closely related to Didissandra and Haberlea, natives of W. China and Tibet. Differing from Haberlea by the calyx segments divided to the base, stamens affixed at middle of corolla-tube, capsule almost twice as long as calyx, and pericarp more membranous. From Petrocosmea clearly marked by having 4 or 5 stamens instead of 2. Treatment as for Haberlea. Alpine-house. As at first constituted the genus contained plants with solitary flowers but plants with many-flowered scapes have recently been added from Didissandra. **A**

**C. Kingia'nus.** Perennial with a thick rhiz. ¾ in. in diameter, covered by bases of old l.-stalks. *l.* in a dense rosette, flat, broadly lanceolate or ovate-lanceolate, acute, narrowed to base, 2 to 4½ in. long, leathery, glabrous above, cinnamon-hairy beneath. *fl.* blue or blue and white; cor.-tube ½ in. long, upper lobe of limb about ¼ in. wide, front lobe ½ in. long. Peduncles many, up to 2½ in. long, densely cinnamon-hairy, many-fld. May, June. Chungkien, &c. 1919. SYN. *Didissandra grandis*. (J.R.H.S. 73, 292; B.M. n.s. 6.)

**C. lanugino'sus.** Root-stock without stolons. *l.* radical or nearly so, ovate-oblong, up to 3 in. long, 1½ in. wide, entire or nearly so, hairy, reddish-hairy when young. *fl.* pale blue or purple, ¾ in. across, in branching cymes, woolly when young; cor. hairy without, cal. glabrous; scape 2 to 6 in. long. N. India. SYN. *Didissandra lanuginosa*, *Didymocarpus lanuginosus*.

*corallorrhi'zus -a -um,* with coral roots.

**CORBULAR'IA.** *See* **Narcissus.**

*Corbular'ia,* a little basket.

**COR'CHORUS** (derivation doubtful). FAM. *Tiliaceae*. A genus of about 30 species of little-branched, usually annual plants about 12 ft. h. Flowers small, yellow, with 4 glandless petals. Fruit a slender or globose capsule. Of no horticultural value but of economic importance since *C. capsularis* and *C. olitorius* are the chief source of jute, the fibre being obtained from the mature stems by retting. The young shoots of both species are used in some warm countries as pot herbs.

**C. capsula'ris.** Pod semi-globose. Warm parts of Asia.

**C. olito'rius.** Pod slender, long. Warm parts of Asia. (B.M. 2810.)

**COR'CHORUS japon'ica.** A synonym of *Kerria japonica*.

*corcovaden'sis -is -e,* of Corcovado, Chile.

*corcyren'sis -is -e,* of Corcyra, an island in the Aegean Sea.

*corda'tus -a -um, cordi-,* in compound words, cordate, heart-shaped.

*Corderoy'i,* in honour of Mr. Justus Corderoy of Blewbury, Didcot, a collector of succulent plants.

**CORD'IA** (in honour of Enricius Cordus, whose true name was Henricus Urbanus, 1486–1535, and Valerius, his son, 1515–44). FAM. *Boraginaceae*. A genus of about 250 species of evergreen and deciduous trees and shrubs, natives of tropical or warm temperate regions of Asia, Africa, Cent. and S. America. Leaves alternate, stalked, entire or toothed. Flowers sessile, usually in terminal sometimes axillary, clusters; corolla tubular to bell-shaped, with a lobed, usually spreading limb; stamens 5 to 10. Fruit a drupe. They require stove or greenhouse temperatures and like a compost of loam, peat, and sand. Propagated by cuttings. The species marked * are of great beauty.

**C. Collococ'ca.** Deciduous tree up to 30 ft. or a shrub with a spreading head of branches, wider than high. *l.* 2 to 6 in. long, oblong-obovate to oval, margin entire but wavy, tapering at base, glabrous and lustrous above, downy beneath. *fl.* in corymbose clusters; cor. white, lobes ¼ in. long. *fr.* purple, ⅓ in. wide. Jamaica. Stove.

**C. decan'dra.*** Shrub 3 ft., shoots and l. rough with short, stiff hairs. *l.* stalkless, linear-lanceolate, 1 to 2 in. long, ¼ to ½ in. wide, margins recurved. *fl.* in terminal corymbose clusters of 7 to 10, fragrant; stalks downy; cor. pure white, funnel-shaped, with a 10-lobed, spreading limb 1 to 1½ in. across; stamens 10. May. Chile. 1875. (B.M. 6279.)

**C. Gerascan'thus.** Spanish Elm. Tree, 30 ft., stellately downy. *l.* 3 to 6 in. long, oblong-lanceolate to elliptic-oblong, pointed, entire. *fl.* crowded in clusters forming spreading panicles; cor. white, salver-shaped, tube slender, limb 5-lobed, ½ in. wide, spreading. W. Indies, Mexico. 1789. Greenhouse.

**C. glab'ra.*** Shrub with shoots and infl. covered with stiff, minute down. *l.* lanceolate to oblong-obovate, 3 to 8 in. long, pointed, coarsely toothed to entire. *fl.* in terminal clusters; cor. pure white, 1½ in. long, broadly funnel-shaped at the base, limb 2 to 2½ in. across, 5-lobed; lobes spreading, margins frilled; stamens 5. Autumn. Brazil. 1868. (B.M. 5774.) Stove.

**C. Greg'gii.*** Compact, much-branched shrub, 5 to 8 ft. *l.* ½ to ¾ in. long, ovate, downy, sharply toothed. *fl.* in terminal panicles of 4 to 6, pure white, fragrant; cor. funnel-shaped at base with a 5-lobed limb 1 to 1¼ in. across; lobes rounded. N. Mexico. 1889. (G. & F. ii. 233; var. *Palmeri.*) Greenhouse.

**C. ipomoeaeflo'ra.*** Tall shrub or small tree up to 14 ft., shoots appressed-hairy. *l.* 12 to 16 in. long, 3 to 5 in. wide, obovate-lanceolate, tapering at base to a stalk 2 to 3 in. long, coarsely and unevenly toothed, downy on veins beneath. *Panicles* large, terminal, many-fld., stalks downy; cor. narrowly bell-shaped at the base, limb 1½ to 2 in. across, 5-lobed, creamy-white. Summer. Brazil? (B.M. 5027.) Stove.

**C. Myx'a.** Tree up to 40 ft. or a large shrub; shoots glabrous. *l.* ovate to ovate-orbicular, 2 to 4 in. long, shallowly toothed or slightly lobed, scabrous above, downy beneath. *fl.* in loose terminal panicles up to 8 in. across; cor. white, ⅜ in. wide, lobes narrow, reflexed; tube hairy within. India, Ceylon. 1640. Stove.

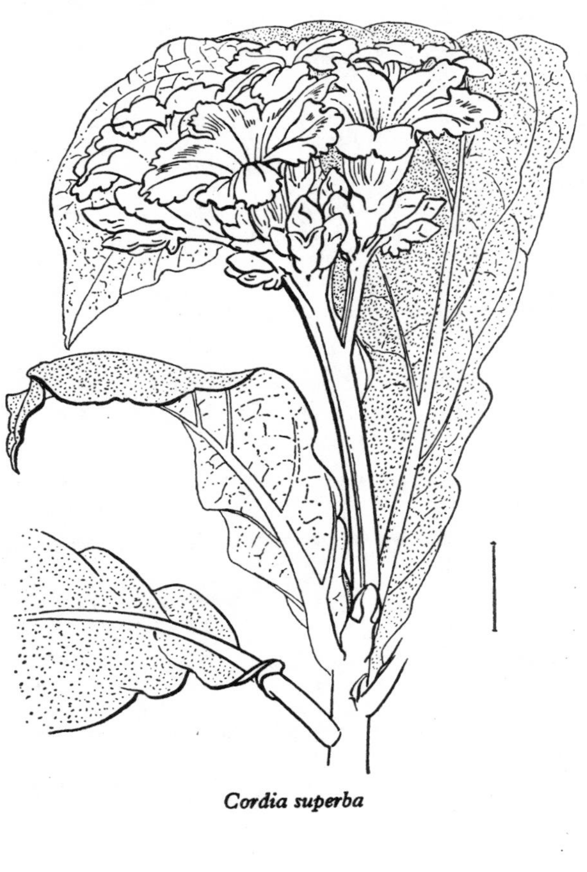

*Cordia superba*

**C. niv'ea.** Shrub 3 ft., stems, lf.-stalks, and fl.-stalks downy. *l.* 1½ to 2½ in. long, 1 to 1½ in. wide, ovate to ovate-oblong, upper part toothed; undersurface white with down. *fl.* in a terminal head or short spike; cor. white, funnel-shaped, 1½ in. long, limb 10-lobed, 1½ in. across. Brazil. Stove.

**C. Sebeste'na.** Shrub 10 to 12 ft. *l.* ovate, pointed, 5 to 8 in. long, 2 to 3½ in. wide, rounded to tapered at the base, slightly toothed to entire. *fl.* in a terminal corymb; cor. orange to dull scarlet, base tubular, expanding into a 5- to 8-lobed limb 1¾ in. across. July. W. Indies. 1728. (A.B.R. 157.) Stove.

**C. super'ba.*** Shrub with stout, glabrous, terete young shoots. *l.* clustered near the end, 6 to 8 in. long, 2 to 3 in. wide, oval to oblong-ovate, entire, slender-pointed, base cuneate, strongly veined beneath. *fl.* white, numerous in terminal long-stalked clusters; cor. 2 in. wide, bell-shaped at the base with a 5-lobed limb 2 in. wide. September. Brazil. (B.M. 4888.) Stove.

**C. ulmifo'lia.** Shrub 6 to 15 ft., shoots downy or velvety. *l.* 2 to 4 in. long, ovate to ovate-lanceolate, slender-pointed, sharply toothed; scabrous above, softly downy beneath. *fl.* axillary, in compact clusters or racemes; cor. white, ¼ in. long. W. Indies. Stove.

W. J. B.

**CORDON.** A form of tree trained to a single stem by cutting back all lateral branches to form fruiting spurs. A double cordon has 2 such stems. The stems may be erect, but are usually trained obliquely or sometimes horizontally. Only spur-bearing kinds and varieties lend themselves to this mode of training which permits a large number of trees to be grown in a small space, makes attention to spraying, thinning, and picking easier, and often produces finer fruits. Apples, pears, red currants, and gooseberries are most frequently so trained.

**CORDYLI'NE** (*kordyle*, a club; in allusion to the large fleshy roots of some of the species). FAM. *Liliaceae.* Several of the following species have been commonly known as Dracaena. A genus of about a dozen species of evergreen trees or shrubs, one of which is S. American, the rest wild in the vast area stretching from New Zealand and Australia, through Polynesia and Malaya, to India. Some have a single, simple or branched stem; others have the stems clustered. Leaves crowded at the top of the stem or sometimes more scattered, usually comparatively long and narrow. Flowers white or slightly coloured, borne in branched panicles. Perianth 6-parted, the segments narrow, stamens 6; stigma 3-lobed. Fruit a succulent, globose, 3-seeded berry.

They are easily cultivated in a good sandy loam with peat or leaf-soil added. The stove and greenhouse species and varieties are usually grown in pots and the coloured-leaved and variegated sorts make admirable decorative plants; they are propagated by cutting up the stems into pieces 1 to 2 in. long and placing them in light soil in a close propagating frame. The nearly hardy ones, *C. australis* and *C. indivisa*, can only be seen at their best when planted out. These are propagated by seed. *C. terminalis*, *C. australis*, and *C. indivisa* yield a tough fibre. *See also* **Dracaena** with which Cordyline is often confused.

**C. austra'lis.*** Tree up to 40 ft. with either a single, erect, cylindrical stem or one branching quite low down, each branch crowned with a dense cluster of *l.*, arching, 1 to 3 ft. long, 1 to 2½ in. wide, pointed, hard. *Panicle* 2 to 4 ft. long, half as wide, much-divided, the final divisions bearing creamy-white, fragrant fl. ¼ to ⅓ in. across; anthers yellow. *fr.* a white or bluish berry, globose, ¼ in. wide, seeds black. New Zealand. 1823. (B.M. 5636 (*not* 2835).) Hardy only in the milder counties. Admirable in Cornish gardens. var. **atropurpu'rea,** base of *l.* and midrib beneath purple; **aureostria'ta,** *l.* marked with a number of yellow longitudinal lines; **linea'ta,** *l.* wider than in type, sheathing base purple; **Veitch'ii,** base of *l.* and midrib beneath bright crimson.

**C. Banks'ii.** Shrub. Stems slender, occasionally branched, often clustered in clumps, 4 to 10 ft. *l.* 3 to 6 ft. long, 1½ to 3½ in. wide, linear-lanceolate, tapered at the base to a deeply channelled stalk 1 to 2 ft. long, 8 to 16 of the veins being green, red, or yellowish. *Panicles* 3 to 4 ft. long, mixed up with the l., made up sparsely of slender racemes of small pure white fl. New Zealand. 1860. (G.C. 41 (1907), 120.) Greenhouse. var. **erythrorach'is,** midrib red.

**C. Bau'eri.** Tree, 4 to 10 ft. Stem single, erect, crowned with a dense cluster of *l.* 1½ to 2 ft. long, sword-shaped, narrowed at the base, midrib broad, veins uniform. *fl.* white, ⅜ in. wide, sessile, fragrant, borne on a large panicle showing above the l. Norfolk Is. About 1820. (B.M. 2835 as *Dracaena australis.*) Differs from the true *C. australis* by the shorter, broader, uniformly veined l.

**C. Haagea'na.** Shrub up to 2 ft. or a little more. *l.* densely set, 4 to 8 in. long, 1½ to 2½ in. wide, abruptly narrowed at base to a stalk 3 or 4 in. long and deeply channelled. *Panicles* sparsely branched, 6 to 12 in. h. *fl.* ½ in. long, lilac-tinted white, resembling those of *C. terminalis.* Queensland. Greenhouse.

**C. indivi'sa.*** Tree up to 25 ft., usually with a single cylindrical stem. *l.* sessile, 3 to 6 ft. long, 4 to 6 in. wide, tapering to a long fine point; texture hard, veins prominent, midrib red or yellow; lower surface glaucous, the whole forming an imposing head up to 12 ft. across. *Panicle* pendulous, 2 to 4 ft. long, built up of numerous cylindrical racemes 4 to 6 in. long. *fl.* closely packed, ¼ in. wide, whitish, purple outside. *fr.* globose, ⅓ in. wide, purplish. New Zealand. (B.M. 9096.) Hardy only in the mildest counties.

**C. Pu'milio.** Shrub usually stemless, but sometimes with a slender stem of 1 to 3 ft. *l.* in a dense cluster of 40 or more, 1½ to 2½ ft. long, ¼ to ⅜ in. wide, narrowly linear, pointed, leathery; midrib prominent. *Panicle* 1 to 3 ft. long, terminal, slender, lax; *fl.* white or bluish-white, ⅛ in. long, thinly disposed, shortly stalked. New Zealand (north island). Greenhouse.

**C. ru'bra.** Slender, tree-like, 10 to 15 ft. *l.* closely set, oblanceolate, 12 to 15 in. long, 1½ to 1¾ in. wide above middle, thick, dull green, midrib conspicuous on both sides; stalk broad, deeply grooved, 4 to 6 in. long. *fl.* in a nodding panicle, lilac, about ¼ in. long. Habitat? *Dracaena* **Bruant'ii** belongs here. Of garden origin.

**C. stric'ta.** Shrub 3 to 8 ft. Stems erect, slender. *l.* closely set, 1 to 2 ft. long, ½ to 1 in. wide, linear-lanceolate. *Panicle* pyramidal, axillary, 1 to 2 ft. long, made up of spikes of lilac-coloured or blue *fl.* nearly or quite sessile, ⅜ in. long. Queensland and New S. Wales. (B.M. 2575.) Greenhouse. var. **dis'color,** *l.* dark-bronzy-purple; **gran'dis,** larger than type, *l.* highly coloured.

**C. termina'lis.*** Shrub 5 to 12 ft. Stems erect, slender, clustered. *l.* in terminal heads, 1 to 2 ft. long, 2 to 4 in. wide, normally green but developed by cultivation into numerous shades of reddish-purple, &c., stalk deeply grooved. *fl.* white or reddish, ½ in. long, borne on broad panicles 1 to 2 ft. long. *Berry* red, globose, ⅓ in. wide. Trop. Asia. (B.R. 1749 as *Dracaena terminalis.*) Once valued by the Maoris for the edible roots. Much cultivated in tropical countries for ornament. Stove.

A very large number of varieties have been raised or imported and listed as Dracaenas as a rule. Among them **ama'bilis,** *l.* broad, shining green, becoming spotted and tinged with rose and white; **Baptist'ii,** *l.* broad, recurved, deep green with pink and yellow stripes; **Guilfoyl'ei,** *l.* tapered to both ends, recurved, striped with red, pink, or white, white in lower half and margin of stalk; **May'i,** *l.* green, margined red, wholly red when young; **norwoodien'sis,** *l.* striped yellow and green with crimson margins and stalks.

W. J. B.

**CORE'MA** (*korema*, a broom, from the habit of the plant). FAM. *Empetraceae.* A genus of 2 species of low-growing, heath-like plants of rigid habit, closely related to Empetrum. Flowers dioecious; perianth segments 5 or 6, somewhat petaloid, overlapping; stamens 3, rarely 4; ovary sub-globose, 3-, rarely 2- or 4-celled. Fruit a nearly globose drupe. Treatment as for Empetrum.

**C. al'bum.** Heath-like, much-branched shrub about 1 ft. h. *l.* narrow with revolute margins, small, obtuse, gland-dotted. *fl.* white, small, in terminal groups. Spring. *fr.* white, 3-sided, globose. SW. Europe, Azores. 1774. Rock- or heath-garden.

**C. Conrad'ii.** 6 to 9 in. h. *l.* narrow-linear, scattered or nearly whorled. *fl.* with purple filaments, purple-brown anthers. April. N. America, including Newfoundland.

**COREOP'SIS** (*koris*, a bug, *opsis*, like; alluding to the appearance of the seed). FAM. *Compositae.* Tick-Seed. A genus of about 70 annual or perennial herbs. Leaves opposite, entire, or pinnately cut. Flower-heads rayed, pedunculate; involucral scales in 2 series, the outer narrower or shorter, the inner joined at base, broad-triangular-ovate or oblong, erect; ray-florets neutral or female. Achenes often winged, flat on one side, convex on other, pappus of 2 weak scales or bristles or none. Distinct from Bidens by the absence of teeth on the leaf-margins and the weak pappus scales. Mostly American but a few African. The annual species are easily raised from seed sown in late April outdoors or in March in gentle heat and planted out in ordinary soil. The perennial species need only ordinary soil, and can be raised from seed, by division in autumn or spring, or by cuttings of young growths in a frame. *C. gigantea* needs cool greenhouse treatment but is not of pleasing habit. The species with yellow flowers from Western N. America have often been known as Leptosyne and the annual species as Calliopsis.

A

**C. abyssin'ica.** Erect, corymbosely branched annual, about 2 ft. h. *l.* pinnatisect; lflets. lanceolate or linear-lanceolate, deeply toothed or cut, usually in 3 pairs, and a large terminal one. *fl.-heads* about 1 in. across, bright yellow; ray-fl. about ⅓ in. wide; inner involucral scales coloured, roughly hairy. Abyssinia. 1895.

**C. angustifo'lia.** Erect perennial, sparsely branched at top, 1 to 3 ft. h., glabrous. *l.* thickish, entire, basal oblanceolate, long-stalked, lower cauline, elliptical, upper narrow-spatulate or linear, sessile. *fl.-heads* 1 to 1½ in. across; ray-fl. yellow; disk dark purple. S. United States.

**C. Atkinsonia'na.** Annual or perennial 2 to 4 ft. h. *l.* all once or twice pinnately cut; lobes linear. *fl.-heads* as in *C. tinctoria.* Autumn. *fr.* with a narrow wing and very weak pappus. N. America. (B R. 1376.)

**C. auricula'ta.** Perennial, 1 to 1½ ft. h., stoloniferous, hairy. *l.* entire or sometimes 3-lobed. *fl.-heads* large; rays yellow with a band of purplish-brown round disk; peduncles long, slender. Summer. S. United States. 1699.

**C. bi'color.** A synonym of *C. tinctoria.*

**C. calliopsid'ea.** Stout, leafy annual of 1 to 2 ft. *l.-lobes* narrow-linear, sometimes cut. *fl.-heads* 3 in. across, bright yellow; rays broader and fewer than in *C. maritima*; peduncles long. Autumn. California. (R.H. 1873, 330 as *Leptosyne maritima.*) SYN. *Leptosyne calliopsidea.*

**C. cardaminifo'lia.** Glabrous annual branching from base, 6 to 24 in. h. *l.* pinnatifid, lobes of numerous lower l. usually oval, of upper l. narrower. *fl.-heads* as in *C. tinctoria*, often entirely dark, but smaller. Summer. *fr.* winged, pappus minute or absent. S. United States.

**C. corona'ta.** Slightly downy annual, often diffusely branched, 6 to 24 in. h. *l.* rather thick, lower pinnatifid or entire, upper spatulate, few, often entire. *fl.-heads* 1½ to 2 in. across; orange with a few brownish-purple lines near base of rays. Summer, autumn. *fr.* orbicular, winged, often toothed. Texas. 1835. (B.M. 3460.)

**C. delphinifo'lia.** Perennial, stouter than *C. verticillata. l.* segs. few and wider, mid-lobe of mid-seg. 1- or 3-partite, side-lobes simple or 2-partite; lobes linear, ⅛ in. wide. *fl.-head* with yellow rays and brown disk. E. United States. (B.M. 156.)

**C. diversifo'lia.** A synonym of *C. Drummondii.*

**C. Douglas'ii.** Annual, 9 to 12 in. h. *l.* 1 to 3 times cut into filiform segs., upper alternate. *fl.-heads* about 1 in. across, bright yellow; peduncles long. *Achenes* bristly. California. SYN. *Leptosyne Douglasii.*

**C. Drummond'ii.** Rather spreading, somewhat hairy annual about 1 ft. h. *l.* pinnatifid segs. short, few, elliptic in lower l., linear in upper. *fl.-heads* 1½ to 2 in. across, yellow with rich crimson circle round disk. Summer. *Achenes* oval, wingless. (B.M. 3474; S.B.F.G.s. 2, 315.) SYN. *C. diversifolia.*

**C. el'egans.** A synonym of *C. tinctoria.*

**C. gigan'tea.** Glabrous perennial, 2 to 8 ft. h. with a thick stem 1 to 5 in. through, somewhat woody at base and leafy only at top. *l.* pinnatifid; segs. narrow. *fl.-heads* yellow, about 1½ in. across, on short corymbose peduncles. California. 1895. SYN. *Leptosyne gigantea.* Greenhouse. An interesting variant but not elegant.

**C. grandiflo'ra.** Glabrous perennial, 1 to 2 ft. h., leafy throughout. *l.* connate and fringed with hair at base; lower few, spatulate or lanceolate, entire, upper with linear, entire segs. *fl.-heads* 1 to 2½ in. across, bright yellow; peduncles usually 1-fld. Summer. *fr.* orbicular, papillose, broadly winged. S. United States. 1826. (B.M. 3586; S.B.F.G. 175.) SYN. *C. longipes.* A double form (**fl. pl.**) is offered.

**C. lanceola'ta.** Perennial, 1 to 2 ft. h., sometimes hairy (var. **villo'sa**). Stems sometimes branched at base. *l.* few, large, oblong-spatulate, lower usually pinnatifid, upper entire. *fl.-heads* 1½ to 2½ in. across, bright yellow; peduncles long, usually 1-fld. Summer. *Achenes* as in *C. grandiflora.* E. United States. 1724. (B.M. 2451; S.B.F.G. 10.) A variable species.

**C. long'ipes.** A synonym of *C. grandiflora.*

**C. marit'ima.** Glabrous perennial. Rootstock thick. Stem about 1 ft. h. *l.* twice pinnate, lobes narrow-linear, about ⅛ in. wide. *fl.-heads* about 3½ in. across, bright yellow; rays 16 to 20, oblong; disk about 1 in. across. Autumn. *Achenes* not hairy. (B.M. 6241.) SYN. *Leptosyne maritima.*

**C. marmora'ta.** A synonym of *C. tinctoria.*

**C. nuda'ta.** Rush-like perennial, 2 to 4 ft. h. *l.* mostly basal, awl-shaped. *fl.-heads* about 2½ in. across, pale bluish, violet, or rose. August. *Achenes* with toothed wing. Florida, in swamps. 1879. (B.M. 6419.) Not hardy.

**C. palma'ta.** Tall, stout perennial, 2 to 3 ft. h., branched near top. *l.* 3-cleft to below middle, about 2½ in. long, lobes often again branched. *fl.-heads* 1½ to 2½ in. across, orange-yellow; involucral bracts all united at base. July to October. *Achenes* oblong, narrowly winged. Cent. United States.

**C. pubes'cens.** Tall, usually downy perennial, up to 4 ft. h., leafy throughout. *l.* thickish, oval to lanceolate, acute, entire or with small lobes, basal l. few. *fl.-heads* 1½ to 2½ in. across, yellow. Summer. *Achenes* as in *C. grandiflora.* S. United States. SYN. *C. auriculata* (not Linn.).

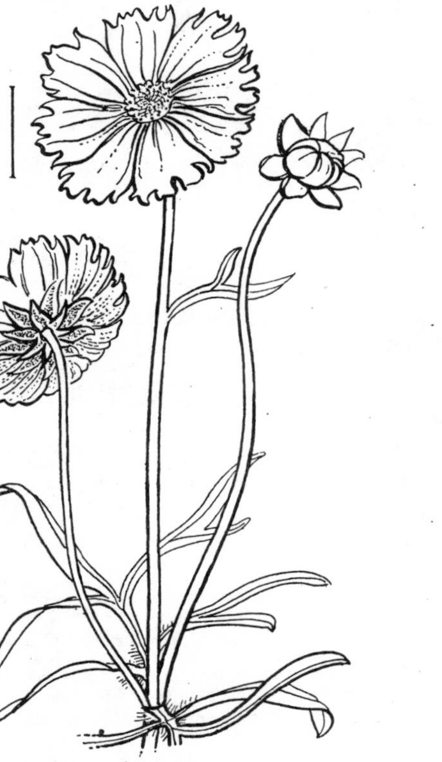

*Coreopsis grandiflora* (p. 543)

**C. ro'sea.** Perennial with slender, creeping rootstocks. Stem glabrous, 1 to 2 ft. h. *l.* narrow-linear, entire or lower sometimes with a few linear lobes. *fl.-heads* about 1 in. across; rays rose-red, lobed at apex; disk yellow. Summer. *Achenes* narrow-oblong, not winged. E. United States.

**C. senifo'lia.** Perennial up to 3 ft. h., stem stouter than in *C. verticillata. l.* 3-nate, about 3 in. long; segs. oblong or ovate-lanceolate, entire, sessile. *fl.-heads* with yellow rays; disk dull yellow. E. United States. (B.M. 3484.)

**C. Stillman'ii.** Stouter annual, more leafy below than *C. Douglasii. l.-lobes* linear, about 1/12 in. wide. *fl.-heads* bright yellow, 1½ in. across; ring of disk fl. not bearded as in *C. Douglasii. Achenes* not hairy. California. 1873. SYN. *Leptosyne Stillmanii.* var. **Golden Rosette** is a double form.

**C. tenuifo'lia.** A synonym of *C. verticillata.*

**C. tinctor'ia.** Erect, glabrous, branching annual, 1 to 3 ft. h. *l.* few or wanting at base, more numerous above, pinnatifid; segs. narrowly elliptical or cut into narrow-linear lobes. *fl.-heads* ¾ to 1½ in. across, rarely 2 in.; rays yellow with dark-purple base, jagged at tip. Summer. *Achenes* oblong, wingless. (B.M. 2512; B.R. 816.) SYN. *C. elegans.* Variable in colour. var. **atropurpu'rea,** ray-fl. almost entirely dark (B.M. 3511); **na'na,** dwarf, about 6 to 9 in. h.

**C. trip'teris.** Stout perennial 3 to 8 ft. h., glabrous, branched in upper part. *l.* 3- (or 5- to 7-)foliolate, the divisions lanceolate. *fl.-heads* about 1½ in. across; ray-fl. pale yellow; disk yellow or dark purple. Autumn. *Achenes* oblong with narrow wing. Cent. United States. (B.M. 3583 as *Chrysostemma tripteris.*)

**C. verticilla'ta.** Somewhat branched perennial, 1 to 2 ft. h. with furrowed stem. *l.* much divided into linear segs. about 1/16 in. wide. *fl.-heads* rich golden yellow, 1½ in. across or more, numerous, erect. Summer. *Achenes* oblong-obovate, narrowly winged. E. United States. 1780. (B.M. 156.) SYN. *C. tenuifolia.*

**CORETHROSTY'LIS.** *See* **Lasiopetalum bracteatum.**

***coria'ceus -a -um,*** thick and tough; leathery.

**CORIANDER** (*Coriandrum sativum*). An annual sometimes grown for its seeds which, when ripe, have a pleasant aroma. They have been used for flavouring alcoholic liquors such as gin, in confectionery, and abroad in bread, as an ingredient of curry powder, and of mixed spice. It should be sown, preferably on a warm, dry soil, in shallow drills in April, the drills being about 12 in. apart, thinned if necessary, and kept clear of weeds. The seeds (fruits) ripen about August, and the plants are then cut, dried in the shade, and threshed in dry weather. While unripe the seed has an unpleasant odour which disappears as they become dry. The drying may be completed, after threshing, on trays in the sun or by slight, artificial heat. The seed may be sown in autumn or under glass in heat in March for planting in May.

**CORIAN'DRUM** (*coris,* a bug; in allusion to the odour of the leaves). FAM. *Umbelliferae.* Annual. Leaves much-divided into linear segments. Flowers white or pale mauve; umbels without an involucre. Fruits globose, deeply furrowed. For cultivation, *see* **Coriander.**

**C. sati'vum.** Annual, about 18 in. h. Stem terete. *l.* shining bright green, glabrous, foetid. *fl.* in 5- to 10-rayed, short-stalked umbels without an involucre, involucels 3-lvd. S. Europe (naturalized in Britain). (E.B. 632.)

**CORIAR'IA** (*corium,* a hide or leather; in allusion to the use of some species for tanning). FAM. *Coriariaceae.* A genus constituting in itself a family of 6 or 7 species of trees, shrubs, sub-shrubs, and herbaceous plants, natives of S. Europe, N. Africa, India, China, Japan, New Zealand, and Temperate S. America. Stems angular, nearly always glabrous. Leaves opposite or ternate. Flowers perfect or unisexual, small, borne in axillary or terminal racemes. True fruits dry and 1-seeded but always enclosed by the 5 persistent, enlarged, fleshy petals. None of the species is genuinely hardy although most of them survive mild winters, especially if given artificial protection. They are usually hardy in Sussex and Hants. Easily grown and propagated by seeds or cuttings.

*C. myrtifolia* is very poisonous as are also the seeds of *C. thymifolia* and other species. The 'fruit'-juice of several species is apparently innocuous and the 'fruits' of *C. terminalis* have been eaten with impunity. But the genus as a whole should be treated with caution as food.

KEY

| | |
|---|---|
| 1. *Lvs. 1 in. or more long* | 2 |
| 1. *Densely leafy. Lvs.* ⅛ to ¾ *in. long* | C. thymifolia |
| 2. *Racemes mostly axillary* | 3 |
| 2. *Racemes terminal, large* | C. terminalis |
| 3. *Lvs. 3-nerved. Racemes up to 1½ in. long* | 4 |
| 3. *Lvs. 3- t. 5-nerved. Racemes 4 to 12 in. long* | C. ruscifolia |
| 3. *Lvs. 3- to 7-nerved. Racemes 2 to 6 in. long* | C. nepalensis |
| 4. *Shrub 4 ft. or more h. Lvs. ovate to oval* | 5 |
| 4. *Sub-shrub of 2 ft. Lvs. ovate-lanceolate* | C. japonica |
| 5. *Tall, coarse shrub. Lvs. 2 to 3½ in. long. Shoots warted* | C. sinica |
| 5. *Bushy shrubs. Lvs. 1 to 2½ in. long* | C. myrtifolia |

**C. japon'ica.*** Sub-shrub, 2 ft. or more. *l.* variable, 1 to 3½ in. long, ½ to 1¼ in. wide, ovate-lanceolate, slender-pointed, 3-veined. *Racemes* unisexual, 2 or 3 together at the joints of the year-old shoots, 1½ to 2½ in. long, the males the shorter; pet. at first green then, in females, after becoming thick and fleshy, bright red, finally purplish-black. Japan. 1893. (B.M. 7509.)

**C. myrtifo'lia.** Bushy shrub 4 to 6 ft., shoots 4-angled. *l.* in pairs or threes, 1 to 2½ in. long, ovate, pointed, 3-veined. *fl.* small, greenish, in racemes about 1 in. long, either axillary on the previous season's shoots, or terminal on young shoots; pet. becoming thick, fleshy, juicy, and, with the fr. they enclose, ⅕ in. wide, black. S. Europe, N. Africa. 1629.

**C. nepalen'sis.** Shrub with arching branches. *l.* ovate or elliptic, 1 to 2 in. long, 3- to 7-nerved, slender-pointed, minutely toothed. *fl.* in axillary racemes 2 to 6 in. long, small; stamens 10, carpels 5. *fr.* black; ¼ to ⅓ in. across. N. India. (W.P.A.R. 3, 289.) Warm house.

**C. ruscifo'lia.** Shrub or small tree, sometimes 20 ft., with a trunk 10 in. diam., shoots 4-angled. *l.* 1½ to 3 in. long, ¾ to 1½ in. wide, 3- or 5-nerved, ovate, pointed, base rounded or cordate. *Racemes* axillary on leafy shoots, 4 to 12 in. long, very slender. *fl.* small, pet. becoming enlarged, black, and juicy. New Zealand, Temperate S. America. 1823. (B.M. 2470 as *C. sarmentosa.*)

**C. sin'ica.** Deciduous shrub of coarse growth, up to 18 or 20 ft., shoots squarish, warted. *l.* oval, roundish-oval, or ovate, 3-veined, 1½ to 3½ in. long, pointed, base rounded. *fl.* in axillary racemes, 1 to 2 in. long; anthers of male plant red. *fr.* (including the fleshy, persistent pet.) black. Of little garden value. China. 1907.

**C. termina'lis.*** Sub-shrub, 2 to 4 ft., spreading by underground rhizomes. Twigs 4-angled, glandular-ciliate. *l.* ovate, 1½ to 3 in. long, shortly pointed, with 3 prominent veins and 2 or 4 minor ones. *Racemes* terminal, 4 to 6 in. long; pet. at first small, but after enlarging, becoming fleshy, and enclosing the fr. become ½ in. wide (collectively) and black. Sikkim, Tibet, China. var. **xanthocar'pa,*** *fr.* a beautiful translucent yellow. 1897. (B.M. 8525.)

*Coriaria japonica* (p. 544)

**C. thymifo'lia.*** Semi-shrubby or herbaceous plant up to 4 ft. Rootstock woody. Stems 4-angled, slightly downy. *l.* ovate, usually ¼ to ¾ in. long, densely set 6 to 10 to the in. *Racemes* very slender, up to 4 in. long, downy. *fl.* often unisexual, dark brown, pet. becoming fleshy, black, and (with the fr. enclosed) ⅛ in. wide. New Zealand and Temperate S. America. Foliage very elegant.

W. J. B.

**CORIARIA'CEAE.** Dicotyledons. A family of 1 genus, Coriaria, with a few species of shrubs or sub-shrubs widely distributed in temperate regions. Leaves opposite or whorled except sometimes at ends of shoots. Flowers inconspicuous in racemes, sometimes unisexual, with sepals and petals 5, stamens 10, carpels 5 to 8, superior, all free. The petals become fleshy after the flowers are fertilized, enclosing the carpels. Seeds 1 in each cell.

*coridifo'lius -a -um,* with Coris-like leaves.

**COR'IS** (name used by Dioscorides). FAM. *Primulaceae.* A genus of 2 sub-shrubby species, in the Mediterranean region, having the habit of a Thyme, with alternate linear leaves, on erect branching stems and smaller rosy flowers closely grouped in terminal racemes, the flowers, unlike those of most of the family, zygomorphic, the calyx lobes spiny and marked with large black spots. Perennial in their native homes, they are apt to be biennial in cultivation. They need a light, well-drained soil of sand and peat, in a sunny place, and are propagated by seed sown in a cold frame.

**C. hispan'ica.** Like *C. monspeliensis* but with the raceme elongated, the cal. teeth scarcely as long as the lobes and the fl. more regular and paler. S. Spain.

**C. monspelien'sis.** Densely leafy sub-shrub of 6 in., with ascending branches. *l.* leathery, linear, glabrous, finally reflexed. *fl.* in short racemes; cal. lobes deep, spines longer than lobes; cor. rose or lilac, 2-lobed. Mediterranean region. 1640. (B.M. 2131; B.R. 536.)

**CORK.** The outer layer of the bark of woody dicotyledonous and coniferous plants, consisting of layers of usually rectangular thin-walled cells, produced by the division of the cells of the cork cambium, the walls of which have become suberized and impervious to water. It forms a waterproof, elastic, flexible covering to the stem and roots as they become older and is occasionally very thick, as in the cork-tree (*see also under* **Bark**).

**CORK CAMBIUM.** *See* **Bark, Cork.**

**CORK-TREE.** *See* **Quercus Suber.**    A

**CORK-WOOD.** *See* **Ochroma Lagopus.**

**CORKY-SCAB.** A disease of Potatoes, now known as Powdery-Scab. *See* **Potato diseases.**

**CORM.** The solid, swollen part of a stem at or near ground level in which is stored reserve materials. It is sometimes annual, forming branches on the old one as in Crocus and Gladiolus, or at the side as in Eranthis and Colchicum; sometimes perennial as in Bowiea. It is often covered by a membranous coat as in Crocus when, until cut open, it strongly resembles a bulb. The corm produces a bud at the apex and gives rise to roots. Compare bulb and tuber, with which the corm is often confused.

**CORN BLUE-BOTTLE.** *See* **Centaurea Cyanus.**

**CORN FLAG.** *See* **Gladiolus.**

**CORN, INDIAN.** *See* **Zea Mays.**

**CORN MARIGOLD.** *See* **Chrysanthemum segetum.**

**CORN SALAD,** Lamb's Lettuce, Mâche (*Valerianella Locusta*). Annual salad plant, used more on the Continent than here; it is, however, a valuable addition to a salad and may, by sowing in February, April, August, and September, be had the year round from the open. The whole plant can be used in summer when growth is rapid, otherwise the leaves are picked off and used. The ground should be deeply dug and fairly rich as for all green salad plants. The seed should be sown in drills about 9 in. apart, and the seedlings thinned to 6 in. apart in the rows. The ground should be kept clear of weeds, and in winter, in hard weather, it is well to protect the plants by throwing some dry litter over the beds. The common corn salad with oblong-ovate leaves, the Round-leaved variety which is stronger and has larger leaves, and the Italian are the commonly grown varieties.

A→

**CORN VIOLET.** *See* **Specularia hybrida.**

**CORNA'CEAE.** Dicotyledons. A family of about 120 species, mostly shrubs, in 16 genera, chiefly in the north temperate zone. Leaves usually opposite, usually simple and entire, without stipules. Flowers small, usually in corymbs, umbels, or even heads with involucres; usually perfect but sometimes unisexual, regular; sepals, petals, and stamens 4, 5, or many; ovary inferior, usually 2-celled, with 1 ovule in each cell. Fruit a berry or drupe. Many species are ornamental. The genera dealt with are Aucuba, Cornus, Corokia, Curtisia, Davidia, Griselinia, Helwingia.

**CORNEL.** *See* **Cornus.**

**CORNELIAN CHERRY.** *See* **Cornus Mas.**

*corn'eus -a -um,* horny.

**CORNFLOWER** (*Centaurea Cyanus*). This annual is grown to some extent for cutting for market. Its cultivation is simple but it is important to give the plants plenty of room to develop and to keep the flowers cut as they open. Autumn-sown plants flower considerably earlier than those from seed sown in spring. Ordinary garden soil in good heart and well drained suits it and the blue forms are most appreciated. For the flower border, where cutting flowers is not an object, some twiggy shoots about 18 in. to 2 ft. long placed among the plants support them in wind. Powdery Mildew (*Erysiphe cichoracearum*) can be severe on cornflowers especially where the roots are dry and in severe cases spraying with Bordeaux mixture may be needed, but some method of supplying sufficient water to the roots (e.g. mulching) should also be considered. Rust disease, *Puccinia cyani*, may appear and affected plants which show brown pustules of spores are best destroyed as soon as seen.

(D. E. G.)

***corni-***, in compound words, signifying horn, as *cornigerus*, horn-bearing.

***cornicula'tus -a -um,*** having an appendage like a spur, or horn.

***cornifo'lius -a -um,*** with Cornus-like leaves.

**CORNISH MONEYWORT.** *See* **Sibthorpia europaea.**

***cor'nu-cer'vi,*** deer's horn.

***cornubien'sis -is -e,*** of Cornwall.

***cornuco'piae,*** full horn.

**COR'NUS** (Latin name for *C. Mas*). Cornel. FAM. *Cornaceae*. Deciduous or rarely evergreen trees, shrubs, or low herbs. Leaves opposite, rarely alternate, strongly parallel-veined, very often furnished with centrally attached, appressed hairs. Flowers with the parts in fours; in one group they come in terminal cymes or panicles without bracts, in a second group they are in small crowded umbels usually subtended by 4 bracts. Fruit a drupe. About 40 species are scattered over temperate parts of the Northern Hemisphere.

The cornels are mostly very hardy and grow in any soil of good or moderate quality. Some, like *C. alba* and *C. stolonifera*, are of too rampant growth for borders of mixed shrubs. Most of the shrubby species are easily propagated by cuttings or by layers. Seed is usually available for the tree species.

Owing to the variety seen in the inflorescences of different species here included in the genus some botanists have proposed to form other genera, restricting Cornus itself to the species in which the inflorescence is a corymbose cyme without bracts. The others it has been suggested should be divided into those with sessile flowers with petaloid bracts—where the fruits are free from one another forming the genus Cynoxylon, including *Cornus florida* and *C. Nuttallii* and some Mexican species not in cultivation here, and those with fruits connate into a fleshy syncarp in Dendrobenthamia including *C. capitata* and *C. Kousa*, while those with stalked flowers within petaloid bracts before flowering, when dioecious are included in Afrocania (not in cultivation), when hermaphrodite, if herbs, in Chamaepericlymenum (with *C. canadensis* and *C. suecica*), if trees, in Macrocarpium (with *C. Mas* and *C. sessilis*).

KEY

1. *Rootstock creeping, stems annual* 2
1. *Shrub or tree* 3
2. *Lvs. in pairs* C. suecica
2. *Lvs. clustered at top of stem* C. canadensis
3. *Lvs. evergreen* 4
3. *Lvs. deciduous* 5
4. *Lvs. grey-green. Fl. in panicles 3 in. h.* C. oblonga
4. *Lvs. shining green above. Fl. in crowded clusters. Fr. strawberry-like* C. capitata
5. *Lvs. alternate* 6
5. *Lvs. opposite* 7
6. *Veins in 5 or 6 pairs. Fl. small, clusters 2½ in. across* C. alternifolia
6. *Veins in 6 to 9 pairs. Fl. ½ in. wide, clusters up to 7 in. across* C. controversa
7. *Fl. in a dense umbel with an involucre beneath* 8
7. *Fl. in a loose cluster, cymose or paniculate, without an involucre* 13
8. *Fl. yellow, bracts yellow, not larger than fl., soon falling* 9
8. *Fl. greenish-yellow, bracts large, white or pink* 11
9. *Lvs. with tufts of hair in vein-axils beneath* 10
9. *Lvs. without tufts of hair in vein-axils* C. Mas
10. *Fr. scarlet* C. officinalis
10. *Fr. dark purple* C. sessilis
11. *Fr. in a dense cluster but separate* 12
11. *Fr. in fleshy globular heads, joined; bracts 4, 1 to 1½ in. long, slender-pointed* C. Kousa
12. *Bracts 4 to 8, usually 6, 1½ to 3 in. long, often slender-pointed* C. Nuttallii
12. *Bracts 4, 1½ to 2 in. long, obovate* C. florida
13. *Lvs. with appressed hairs beneath* 14
13. *Lvs. with spreading hairs beneath at least on veins* 21
14. *Lvs. whitish beneath* 15
14. *Lvs. green or slightly paler beneath* 19
15. *Shoots red, yellow, or green in winter* 16
15. *Shoots grey* C. candidissima
16. *Lvs. 2 to 5 in. long* 17
16. *Lvs. 4 to 7 in. long. Fl. in panicles* C. macrophylla
17. *Shoots smooth* 18
17. *Shoots downy* C. Hemsleyi
18. *Lvs. short-pointed* C. alba
18. *Lvs. long-pointed* C. stolonifera
19. *Of bushy habit* 20
19. *Tree; shoots soon glabrous, greenish- to reddish-brown* C. Walteri
20. *L.-veins in 2 or 3 pairs. Shoots 4-angled* C. paucinervis
20. *L.-veins in 3 to 5 pairs. Shoots glabrous, red-brown* C. glabrata
21. *Lvs. downy or woolly beneath, not scabrid* 22
21. *Lvs. more or less scabrid above* 28
22. *Lvs. green beneath* 23
22. *Lvs. whitish beneath* 24
23. *Lvs. slightly downy on both sides. Veins 3 to 5 pairs* C. sanguinea
23. *Lvs. rusty-downy on veins beneath. Veins 4 to 7 pairs* C. Amomum
24. *Branches purple or red-brown* 25
24. *Branches greenish, spotted purple* C. rugosa
25. *Shoots downy, at least at first* 26
25. *Shoots glabrous* C. pubescens
26. *Fr. blue or black* 27
26. *Fr. white* C. Baileyi
27. *L.-veins in 4 to 7 pairs. Fr. blue* C. obliqua
27. *L.-veins in 7 to 9 pairs. Fr. black* C. Monbeigii
28. *Lvs. rough with stiff hairs above. L.-veins in 5 pairs. Fr. white* C. asperifolia
28. *Lvs. slightly scabrid above. L.-veins in 5 to 7 pairs. Fr. blue-black* C. Bretschneideri

**C. al'ba.** Deciduous, wide-spreading shrub up to 10 ft., shoots glabrous, becoming red in winter. *l.* ovate to oval, short-pointed, 2 to 4½ in. long, glaucous beneath, minutely hairy on both sides, veins in 5 or 6 pairs. *fl.* small, yellowish-white, in clusters 1½ to 2 in. across. May, June. *fr.* white or tinged with blue, ¼ in. wide. Siberia. 1741. Too rampant for close association with other shrubs. SYN. *C. tatarica*. var. **atrosanguin'ea,*** habit dwarfer, stems brilliant crimson; **Gouchalt'ii,** *l.* margined yellow; **Kessel-ring'ii,** stems very dark purple; **sibi'rica,** not so vigorous, stems rich coral-red; there is a silver variegated form, SYN. *C. sibirica*; **Spaeth'ii,** best golden variegated variety.

**C. alternifo'lia.** Deciduous, flat-topped small tree up to 20 ft., or a shrub, branches horizontal. *l.* alternate, 2 to 5 in. long, often clustered at the end of the shoot, ovate or oval, slender-pointed, cuneate, glaucous and hairy beneath. *fl.* yellowish-white, small, of little beauty, in clusters 2½ in. across. June. *fr.* globose, ¼ in. wide, blue-black. N. America. 1760.

**C. Amo'mum.** Deciduous shrub up to 10 ft., shoots downy, purple. *l.* ovate to oval, 2 to 4 in. long, shortly pointed, reddish-downy on the veins beneath; veins in 4 to 7 pairs. *fl.* yellowish-white in flat clusters, 1½ to 2½ in. across. July. *fr.* pale blue, ¼ in. wide. N. America. 1683. SYN. *C. coerulea*.

**C. asperifo'lia.** Deciduous, erect shrub, 10 to 15 ft., sometimes a tree thrice as high, shoots reddish-brown. *l.* ovate, 2 to 4 in. long, rough with stiff hairs above, softly downy beneath; veins in about 5 pairs. *fl.* yellowish-white, in rounded clusters 1½ to 2½ in. wide. June. *fr.* white, ¼ in. wide. N. America. 1836.

**C. Bail'eyi.*** Deciduous shrub of erect habit, up to 10 ft., shoots downy, reddish-brown in winter. *l.* ovate-lanceolate, 2 to 5 in. long, glaucous and woolly beneath. *fl.* small, in downy clusters 1½ to 2 in. across. June. *fr.* white, orange-shaped, ⅓ in. wide. Near *C. stolonifera*, but differs by its woolly character and it is not stoloniferous. N. America. 1892.

**C. brachypo'da.** A synonym of *C. controversa*.

**C. Bretschneid'eri.** Deciduous shrub up to 15 ft., shoots downy when young, yellowish or reddish in winter. *l.* ovate, 2 to 4 in. long, slender-pointed, dull green above, grey-green beneath, more or less scabrid, especially beneath, veins in 5 to 7 pairs. *fl.* creamy-white, in clusters 2½ to 4 in. across. June. *fr.* blue-black, ¼ in. wide. N. China. 1887.

**C. canaden′sis.\*** Plant with a creeping horizontal rootstock, sending up annually erect stems 5 to 10 in. h. *l.* crowded at top about 6 together, oval, ovate, or obovate, with sometimes 1 or 2 pairs below, ¾ to 1¼ in. long; veins 5 or 7, longitudinal. *fl.* greenish-purple or violet, very small, clustered in a solitary terminal umbel, subtended by 4 ovate white bracts, ½ to ⅝ in. long. June. *fr.* bright red, ¼ in. wide, globose. N. America. 1774. (B.M. 880.) Syn. *Chamaepericlymenum canadense.* Distinct from *C. suecica* by the clustered l. Likes a damp soil.　**A**

**C. candidis′sima.** Shrub 8 to 15 ft. *l.* oval to ovate-lanceolate, cuneate, slender-pointed, 2 to 4 in. long, minutely appressed-downy, glaucous beneath; veins in 3 or 4 pairs. *fl.* small, white, profuse in cymose panicles 1½ to 2½ in. across terminating every shoot. July. *fr.* white, ¼ in. wide, depressed globose. N. America. 1758. Syn. *C. paniculata, C. racemosa.*

**C. capita′ta.\*** Evergreen tree 30 to 50 ft., usually more in diameter. *l.* oval-lanceolate, 2 to 5 in. long, dull grey-green, densely covered with minute appressed hairs. *fl.* inconspicuous, crowded densely in clusters ½ in. across; bracts 4 to 6, sulphur-yellow, obovate, 1½ to 2 in. long. June, July. *fr.* fleshy, strawberry-like, crimson, 1 to 1½ in. wide; ripe in October. Himalaya. 1825. (B.M. 4641 as *Benthamia fragifera*.) Syn. *Dendrobenthamia capitata.* Suitable only for the south and south-west.

**C. circina′ta.** A synonym of *C. rugosa.*

**C. coeru′lea.** A synonym of *C. Amomum.*

**C. controver′sa.\*** Deciduous tree 30 to 50 ft., branches in horizontal tiers. *l.* alternate, ovate or oval, shortly pointed, glaucous beneath, 3 to 6 in. long; veins in 6 to 9 pairs. *fl.* white, ½ in. wide, numerous in flattish clusters up to 7 in. across. June, July. *fr.* blue-black, globose, ¼ in. wide. Japan, China. 1880. (B.M. 8464.) Distinct from all other species except *C. alternifolia* by its alternate l. var. **variega′ta,** *l.* narrow, silver-variegated.

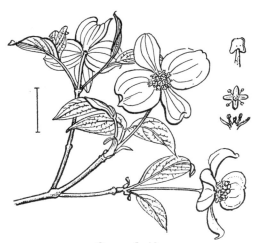

*Cornus florida*

**C. flo′rida.\*** Flowering Dogwood. Deciduous shrub or small tree, 10 to 20 ft. *l.* broadly oval or ovate, 3 to 6 in. long, half as wide, rather glaucous and downy beneath, turning orange and scarlet in autumn. *fl.* insignificant, greenish, crowded in a cluster ⅜ in. wide; bracts 4, obovate, 1½ to 2 in. long, white. May. (B.M. 526.) Syn. *Cynoxylon floridum.* var. **pen′dula,** branches stiffly pendulous; **ru′bra,\*** bracts rosy-red, very attractive. (B.M. 8315.) Beautiful and naturally very hardy trees but subject to injury by late frost and rarely a success except in the warmer counties.

**C. glabra′ta.** Deciduous bushy shrub up to 12 ft., shoots glabrous, red-brown. *l.* lanceolate or narrowly oval, 1¼ to 3 in. long, tapered to both ends, bright green, sparsely and minutely hairy; veins in 3 to 5 pairs. *fl.* dull white, in small clusters 1¼ in. or less wide. July. *fr.* white or bluish-white, ¼ in. wide. Western N. America. 1894.

**C. Hems′leyi.** Shrub or small tree, 12 to 25 ft., shoots downy, becoming red. *l.* roundish-ovate, 2 to 3 in. long, shortly pointed, grey-white and appressed-downy beneath; veins brownish downy, in 6 to 8 pairs. *fl.* small, white, in clusters 2 to 3 in. wide; anthers blue. July. *fr.* globose, ¼ in. wide, blue-black. China. 1908. Distinct by its brown downy veins.

**C. Kous′a.** Deciduous tree up to 20 ft., shoots glabrous. *l.* ovate, cuneate, pointed, 1½ to 3 in. long. *fl.* small and inconspicuous, crowded in a button-like mass, ½ in. wide; bracts 4, lanceolate, slender-pointed, spreading, 1 to 1½ in. long, creamy-white. June. Japan, Korea. 1875. Syn. *Dendrobenthamia japonica.* var. **chinen′sis,\*** tree up to 30 ft., bracts up to 2½ in. long, white then creamy-white. Superior to the Japanese type. China. 1907. (B.M. 8833.) Both are quite hardy.

**C. macrophyl′la.\*** Deciduous tree 30 to 50 ft. *l.* 4 to 7 in. long, ovate to roundish-oblong, long and slenderly pointed, dark lustrous green above, glaucous and with appressed hairs beneath; veins in 6 to 8 pairs. *fl.* yellowish-white, ½ in. wide in rounded panicles 4 to 6 in. across. July, August. *fr.* globose, ⅛ in. wide, blue. Himalaya, China, Japan. 1827. Attractive late-flowering small tree. (B.M. 8261.)

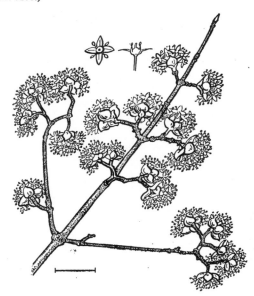

*Cornus Mas*

**C. Mas.\*** Cornelian Cherry. Deciduous shrub or small tree up to 25 ft., of spreading habit. *l.* ovate, 1½ to 2½ in. long, dull green, appressed-hairy on both sides; veins in 3 to 5 pairs. *fl.* yellow, ⅛ in. wide, in umbels ¾ in. across, enclosed at first in 4 downy, yellowish bracts. February, March. *fr.* bright red, oval, ⅝ in. long, edible. Europe. Long cultivated. Valued for its showy, early, yellow fl. (B.M. 2675.) Syn. *Macrocarpium Mas.* var. **au′rea,** *l.* yellowish; **aurea elegantis′sima,** *l.* wholly or partly yellow, tinged pink; **na′na,** habit dwarf, rounded; **variega′ta,** *l.* silver-variegated; **xanthocar′pa,** *fr.* yellow.

**C. Monbeig′ii.** Shrub 12 ft. and upwards. *l.* oval to roundish-ovate, 2½ to 4 in. long, dull green and very downy above, grey-white and more softly downy beneath, veins reddish in 7 to 9 pairs. *fl.* white, ⅓ in. wide, in clusters 3 to 4 in. across; stalk, cal., and pet. very downy. June. *fr.* black, ¼ in. wide, globose. China. 1917.

**C. Nuttal′lii.\*** Tree usually 15 to 25 ft. in cult., but 50 to 80 ft. in nature. *l.* oval or obovate, 3 to 5 in. long, appressed-downy; veins in 5 or 6 pairs. *fl.* very small, crowded in a mass ¾ in. across; bracts 4 to 8, usually 6, spreading, 1½ to 3 in. long, 1 to 2 in. wide, creamy-white, afterwards flushed pink. May. Western N. America. 1835. (B.M. 8311.) Syn. *Cynoxylon Nuttallii.* Noblest of the Cornels.

**C. obli′qua.** Very similar to *C. Amomum* but *l.* greyish beneath. N. America. 1888. Syn. *C. Purpusii.*

**C. oblon′ga.** Evergreen shrub or small tree up to 20 ft., shoots angular, very downy. *l.* 2 to 6 in. long, narrowly oval, dark lustrous green above, dull and grey-downy beneath; veins in 5 or 6 pairs. *fl.* white or purple-tinged, ¼ in. wide, fragrant, in panicles 3 in. h.; cal. and stalks downy. October to December. Himalaya, China. 1818. Happiest in the south and south-west.

**C. officina′lis.\*** Very closely akin to *C. Mas,* with quite similar yellow fl. in early spring, but generally more tree-like. *fr.* similar. Easily distinguished in summer by the l. having conspicuous patches of reddish down in or near the vein-axils beneath. Japan. 1877.

**C. panicula′ta.** A synonym of *C. candidissima.*

**C. pauciner′vis.\*** Deciduous shrub 6 to 10 ft., shoots 4-angled. *l.* narrowly oval, tapering equally to both ends, 1½ to 4 in. long, covered on both sides with minute appressed hairs; veins in 2 or 3 pairs. *fl.* creamy-white, ½ in. wide, in rounded clusters 3 in. across. July, August. *fr.* ¼ in. wide, globose, black. China. 1907. Distinct by the few l.-veins. (B.M. 9197.)

**C. pubes′cens.** Deciduous shrub, 6 to 18 ft., sometimes tree-like, shoots glabrous, purple. *l.* 1½ to 4 in. long, half as wide, dark green and slightly hairy above, woolly and glaucous beneath. *fl.* yellowish, crowded in compact, rounded clusters 2 in. wide. May, June. *fr.* white. California. 1874. Pretty in fl.

**C. Purpus′ii.** A synonym of *C. obliqua.*

**C. racemo′sa.** A synonym of *C. candidissima.*

**C. rugo'sa.*** Deciduous shrub up to 10 ft., sometimes of tree-like shape, shoots becoming purplish. *l.* roundish inclined to ovate, $2\frac{1}{2}$ to 5 in. long, densely grey-woolly beneath; veins in 6 to 8 pairs. *fl.* in clusters 2 to 3 in. wide, white. June. *fr.* pale blue, $\frac{1}{4}$ in. wide. N. America. 1784. Distinct by its roundish, woolly l., also pretty in fl. SYN. *C. circinata.*

**C. sanguin'ea.** Dogwood. Deciduous erect shrub, shoots minutely downy, dark red in winter. *l.* ovate to roundish-oval, $1\frac{1}{2}$ to $3\frac{1}{2}$ in. long, slender-pointed, thinly hairy on both sides, red in autumn; veins in 3 to 5 pairs. *fl.* dull white, heavily scented, in clusters 2 in. wide. June. *fr.* globose, $\frac{1}{4}$ in. wide, black, bitter. Europe (Britain). (E.B. 635.)

**C. ses'silis.** Deciduous, 10 to 15 ft., shoots and l. beneath thinly silky. *l.* 2 to $3\frac{1}{2}$ in. long, ovate to oval, with appressed hairs and tufts of down in the vein-axils beneath. *fl.* $\frac{1}{4}$ in. wide, yellow, in umbels of 20 to 30 opening on naked twigs in spring at first enclosed by 4 bracts. *fr.* oval, $\frac{1}{2}$ in. long, dark purple. Californian representative of *C. Mas* and *C. officinalis*. SYN. *Macrocarpium sessile.*

**C. sibir'ica.** A variety of *C. alba.*

**C. stolonif'era.** Rampant, suckering, deciduous shrub up to 8 ft., shoots dark purplish-red, glabrous. *l.* ovate, oval, or oval-lanceolate, long-pointed, 2 to 5 in. long, glaucous beneath; veins in about 5 pairs. *fl.* dull white, in clusters 1 to 2 in. wide. May, June. *fr.* white, globose, $\frac{1}{4}$ in. wide. N. America. 1656. var. **flaviram'ea,** shoots yellow.

**C. suec'ica.** Plant with creeping rootstocks sending up annually erect herbaceous stems 3 to 10 in. h., bearing several pairs of *l.* $\frac{1}{2}$ to $1\frac{1}{2}$ in. long, stalkless, ovate, pointed, 5- or 7-veined. *fl.* very small, in a terminal, solitary umbel surrounded by 4 ovate, spreading white bracts each $\frac{1}{4}$ to $\frac{1}{2}$ in. long. June, July. *fr.* globose-ovoid, red, clustered. Europe (Britain), N. America. (E.B. 634.) SYN. *Chamaepericlymenum suecicum.* Inhabits damp sites. *C. canadensis* differs by clustered whorled l.

**C. tata'rica.** A synonym of *C. alba.*

**C. Walt'eri.** Tree 35 to 40 ft. *l.* oval, 2 to 5 in. long, cuneate, slender-pointed, appressed-hairy on both surfaces, especially beneath; veins in 3 or 4 pairs. *fl.* white, $\frac{3}{8}$ in. wide, in clusters 3 in. across. June. *fr.* globose, $\frac{1}{4}$ in. wide, black. China. 1907. Interesting as a genuine tree.

W. J. B.

**CORNU'TIA** (in honour of Jacques Cornutus, 1606–51, a French physician, traveller in Canada and author of *Historia Plantarum Canadensium*). FAM. *Verbenaceae.* A genus of about 6 species of evergreen shrubs, natives of Trop. America, minutely downy or softly hairy, with usually 4-angled branches. Leaves opposite. Flowers in rather loose terminal panicles; corolla tube cylindrical, at most slightly curved, sometimes enlarged in upper part, lobes ovate; 2 perfect stamens on front of tube, sub-exserted, staminodes dorsal without anthers. Fruit a small, globose drupe.

A mixture of loam and peat suits *C. pyramidata* which can be propagated by cuttings which strike readily in sand under glass in bottom heat during February and March. It needs a warm greenhouse.

**C. pyramida'ta.** Shrub about 4 ft. Stems square, the angles winged. *l.* 3 to 4 in. long, broadly ovate, toothed, abruptly slender-pointed, softly downy above, more woolly beneath. *fl.* in axillary close clusters; cor. blue, slightly 2-lipped, base tubular, limb 4-lobed, $\frac{3}{8}$ in. across, with a yellow eye; cal. very small, downy, and indistinctly toothed; stamens 4, 2 of them barren. July. 1733. (B.M. 2611 as *C. punctata.*)

W. J. B.

***cornu'tus -a -um,*** horn-shaped, or having a horn-like process.

**COROK'IA** (*Korokia,* the Maori name). FAM. *Cornaceae.* A genus of 4 or 5 species of evergreen shrubs natives of New Zealand and the Chatham Islands; bark often black. Leaves alternate or clustered, entire. Flowers about $\frac{1}{2}$ in. wide, yellow, in axillary or terminal clusters, racemes, or panicles; petals 5, linear, spreading star-like; calyx turbinate, 5-lobed; stamens 5. Fruit a drupe, crowned by the persisting calyx. All the species are more or less tender, but *C. Cotoneaster* is excellent on a sunny wall although occasionally much injured even there in very severe winters. *C. virgata* will survive ordinary winters. All are perfectly at home in the south-west. Any fertile, well-drained soil suits them. Propagated by seeds or late summer cuttings.

KEY

| | |
|---|---|
| 1. *Lvs. 2 in. or more long* | 2 |
| 1. *Lvs. rarely up to 2 in. long* | 3 |
| 2. *Fl. in terminal panicles* | C. buddleioides |
| 2. *Fl. in axillary racemes* | C. macrocarpa |
| 3. *Shoots very tortuous and interlacing* | C. Cotoneaster |
| 3. *Shoots neither tortuous nor interlacing* | 4 |
| 4. *Fr. orange-yellow* | C. Cheesemanii |
| 4. *Fr. red* | C. virgata |

**C. buddleioi'des.** Shrub up to 10 ft., shoots grey-felted. *l.* linear-lanceolate, $1\frac{1}{2}$ to 5 in. long, $\frac{3}{16}$ to $\frac{5}{8}$ in. wide, tapered to a slender point, glossy green above, silvery-white-felted beneath. *fl.* $\frac{1}{2}$ in. wide, star-shaped, bright yellow, in terminal panicles 1 to 2 in. long; pet. linear, pointed, downy outside. May. *fr.* globose, blackish-red, $\frac{1}{4}$ in. wide. New Zealand. (B.M. 9019.) Hardy only in the south and south-west.

**C. Cheese'manii.** Shrub 5 to 12 ft., shoots neither tortuous nor interlacing, silvery-white-felted like the l. and infl. *l.* $\frac{3}{4}$ to 2 in. long, obovate to elliptic-oblong or oblanceolate; stalks flattened. *fl.* yellow, resembling those of *C. Cotoneaster* but with narrower pet.; in clusters of 2 to 4, axillary or terminal. May. *fr.* obovoid-oblong or oblong, $\frac{3}{8}$ in. long, $\frac{1}{4}$ in. wide, red. New Zealand. May be a natural hybrid between *C. Cotoneaster* and *C. buddleioides.*

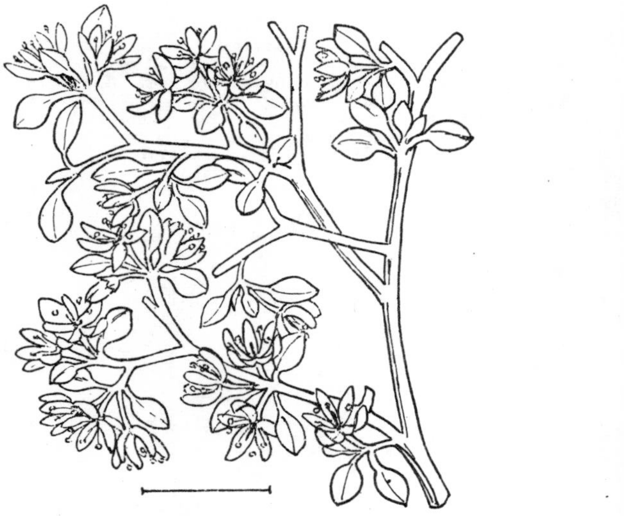

*Corokia Cotoneaster*

**C. Cotoneas'ter.** Evergreen, thinly leafy, rounded shrub, up to 8 ft., branches very tortuous and much interlaced, downy when young. *l.* $\frac{1}{2}$ to $\frac{3}{4}$ in. long, roundish, ovate, or obovate, dark green above, white-felted beneath; stalk flattened. *fl.* star-shaped, $\frac{1}{2}$ in. wide, bright yellow, borne 1 to 4 towards the end of short twigs; pet. linear, silky at the back. May. *fr.* red, roundish, $\frac{1}{4}$ in. long. New Zealand. 1875. (B.M. 8425.) The hardiest species but suffers in severe winters.

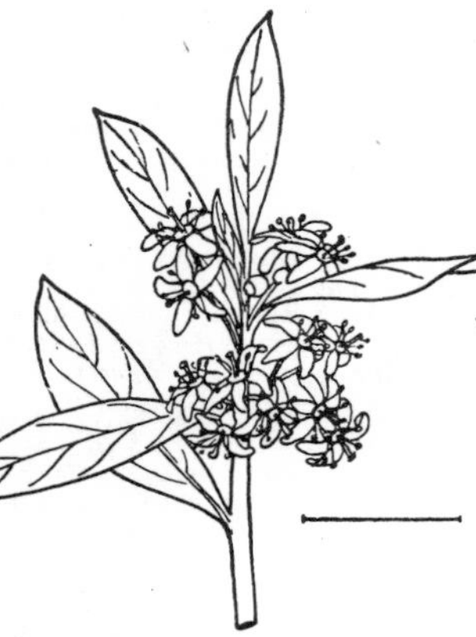

*Corokia macrocarpa*

**C. macrocar'pa.** Shrub up to 20 ft., shoots, fl.-stalks, and under-surface of l. covered with silvery-white felt. *l.* narrowly oval to oblong-lanceolate, 2 to 4 in. long, $\frac{1}{2}$ to 1 in. wide, tapered towards both ends. *fl.* starry, yellow, ⅓ to ½ in. wide, in axillary racemes of 3 to 8. June. *fr.* ⅝ in. long, broadly oblong, orange. Chatham Is. (B.M. 9168.) Hardy only in the south and south-west.

**C. virga'ta.** Shrub 10 ft. or more, shoots white with down when young, neither tortuous nor interlacing. *l.* oblanceolate, base more tapered than the apex, ½ to 1¾ in. long, ¼ to ⅜ in. wide, shining green above, white with appressed down beneath. *fl.* yellow, ½ in. wide, usually in threes near tips of shoots. May. *fr.* orange-yellow, ovoid, ¼ in. long. New Zealand. (B.M. 8466.) Suffers in hard winters.

W. J. B.

**COROLLA.** The inner whorl of leaves (petals) of the floral envelope, usually of a different colour from the calyx, the petals being free from one another (when the corolla is said to be polypetalous), or joined (gamopetalous).

***corolli'nus -a -um,*** with a conspicuous corolla.

***coromandelie'nus -a -um,*** of the E. coast of India.

**CORONA.** An appendage coming between the petals and the stamens, as the crown or cup of the Narcissus, or the rays of the Passion-flower, or the curious, usually nectar-producing appendages on the backs of the anthers in Asclepiadaceae.

***cor'onans,*** having a crown, or crown-like.

**CORONA'RIA.** Included in **Lychnis.**

***corona'rius -a -um,*** forming a crown, or crown-like.

***corona'tus -a -um,*** crowned.

**CORONIL'LA** (*corona*, a crown, in reference to the long-stalked umbels). FAM. *Leguminosae.* Shrubs or herbs, hardy, half-hardy, or greenhouse, evergreen or deciduous. Leaves alternate, unequally pinnate. Flowers in axillary or terminal umbels; the long claws of the petals furnish a distinctive character. Seed-pods slender, constricted between the seeds. About 20 species inhabiting Cent. and S. Europe, the Orient, N. Africa. The shrubby species like a sunny position and open, well-drained soil, and are propagated by late summer cuttings or by layers.

**C. cappado'cica.*** Prostrate herbaceous perennial. *lflets.* 9 to 11, obcordate, ciliate; stipules roundish, toothed. *fl.* large, yellow, in 7- or 8-fld. umbels. July. Asia Minor. 1822. (L.B.C. 789 as *C. iberica.*) Rock-garden. Hardy.

**C. corona'ta.** A synonym of *C. montana.*

**C. el'egans.** A synonym of *C. varia.*

**C. emeroi'des.** Shrub 4 to 5 ft., shoots angled. *lflets.* usually 7, obovate, ¼ to ¾ in. long. *fl.* ½ to ¾ in. long, yellow, in an umbel of 4 to 8 terminating a stalk 2 to 3 in. long. May onwards. *Pod* slender, 2 to 3 in. long. SE. Europe. Distinguished from *C. Emerus* by the more numerous fl. in the umbel.

**C. E'merus.** Scorpion Senna. Deciduous shrub, 5 to 7 ft., shoots angled, soon glabrous. *l.* 1 to 1½ in. long; lflets. 7 or 9, obovate, ⅓ to ¾ in. long. *fl.* yellow, ¾ in. long, 2 or 3 on a slender, axillary stalk 1 to 2 in. long. May to October. *Pod* 2 in. long, slender. Cent. and S. Europe. (B.M. 445.)

**C. glau'ca.*** Evergreen glabrous bush, 5 to 9 ft. *l.* 1 to 1½ in. long, very glaucous; lflets. 5 or 7, ¼ to ⅝ in. long, obovate, apex often notched. *fl.* rich yellow, ½ in. long, up to 10 clustered at the end of a stalk up to 2 in. long, fragrant by day only. April to June. *Pod* 1½ in. long. S. Europe. 1722. (B.M. 13.) Hardy in Sussex and westwards. Excellent cool greenhouse plant in colder localities. var. **pyg'maea,** 1½ to 2 ft. h., compact and rounded. There is a variegated form.

**C. ibe'rica.** A synonym of *C. cappadocica.*

**C. jun'cea.** Shrub 2 to 3 ft., sparsely leafy. Stems round, zigzag, forked, Ephedra-like. *l.* ¾ to ½ in. long; lflets. 5 or 7, narrowly oblong, ¼ to ½ in. long. *fl.* yellow, ⅓ in. long, from 6 to 12 in a globose umbel borne on an axillary and terminal stalk 3 or 4 in. long. *Pod* very slender, 1 in. long. S. Europe. 1656. (B.R. 822.) Needs the protection of a warm wall.

**C. min'ima.** Sub-shrub. Stem procumbent. *lflets.* 7 to 13, roundish-ovate, obtuse or retuse, lower remote from stem; stipules small, 2-toothed at tip. *fl.* yellow, fragrant, in 7- or 8-fld. umbels. June, July. SW. Europe. 1658. (B.M. 2179.) Half-hardy. Rock-garden.

**C. monta'na.** Erect or ascending sub-shrub, 1 to 2 ft. h. *lflets.* 7 to 13, obovate, mucronate, glaucous, lower near stem; stipules as in *C. minima. fl.* yellow, in many-fld. umbels. July, August. S. Europe, Caucasus. 1776. (B.M. 907 as *C. coronata.*) Greenhouse or rock-garden in sunny place.

**C. scorpioi'des.** Annual. *l.* 3-foliolate; lower lflet. small, roundish, close to stem, terminal largest, oval. *fl.* yellow, in a head. *Pod* somewhat curved. S. Europe. SYN. *Ornithopus scorpioides.* Hardy.

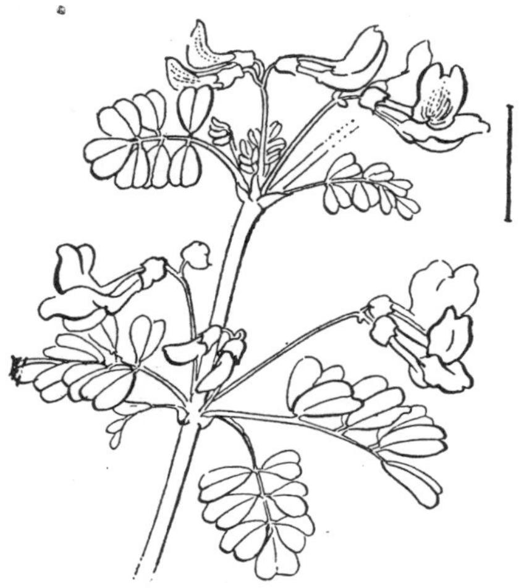

*Coronilla Emerus*

**C. valenti'na.*** Evergreen glabrous bush, 4 ft. or more. *l.* 1¼ to 2 in. long; stipules large; lflets. 7 to 11, obovate, ¼ to ¾ in. long, bright green, glaucous beneath. *fl.* rich yellow, ½ in. long, 10 to 14 in a cluster ending a stalk 3 in. long, fragrant. May to July. *Pod* slender, curved 1 to 1½ in. long. S. Europe. 1596. (B.M. 185.) SYN. *C. stipularis.* Differs from *C. glauca* by the more numerous lflets. and fl.; stipules much larger. Rather more tender.

**C. va'ria.** Diffuse herb with flexuous stems. *lflets.* 9 to 13, oblong, elliptic, mucronate, lower near stem. *fl.* pink and white, finally drooping, in 16- to 20-fld. umbels. June to November. Europe. 1640. (B.M. 258.) Hardy. Rock-garden.

**C. vimina'lis.** Trailing shrub. *lflets.* 13 to 21, obovate, notched. *fl.* pale red or white with red stripe on standard, in 6- to 10-fld. umbels. Summer. Algeria.

***coronilloi'des,*** Coronilla-like.

***coronopifo'lius -a -um,*** Coronopus-leaved.

**CORO'ZO** (native name of *C. oleifera*). FAM. *Palmaceae.* A genus of S. American palms related to Elaeis and at one time included in it. As with *E. guineensis* the fruits yield a valuable oil. Cultivation as for Elaeis.

**C. oleif'era.** Much resembling *Elaeis guineensis* in *l.* but smaller and somewhat decumbent, the stem rooting from the lower side where in contact with ground. Trop. America. 1821. SYN. *Elaeis melanococca.*

**COR'REA** (in honour of Jose Francesco Correa da Serra, Portuguese botanist, 1750–1823). FAM. *Rutaceae.* A genus of 5 or 6 species of evergreen shrubs, natives of Australia and Tasmania. Leaves opposite, stellately downy. Flowers 1 to 3, axillary or terminal; calyx cup-shaped, 4- to 8-toothed or 4-lobed; corolla made tubular by the union of 4 petals, with 4 short lobes at the top; stamens 8. Correas are easily cultivated. They like a peaty soil and in most localities require cool greenhouse conditions; they may be grown against walls in the south and south-west maritime counties and are grown fully in the open in S. Cornwall. They strike root readily from cuttings but it is the common practice to graft the better sorts on *C. alba.* A good many varieties have been raised under cultivation, most of them from *C. speciosa,* also hybrids with that species as one parent. Besides those mentioned below, the following are or have been grown: *bicolor, delicata, longifolia, magnifica, rosea-superba.* All have a long flowering season.

**C. al'ba.** Botany Bay Tea Tree. Evergreen shrub of stiff growth, 2 to 4 ft., shoots and underside of l. soft with dense down. *l.* ½ to 1½ in. long, ovate, roundish or obovate, cuneate, apex rounded. *fl.* ¾ to 1 in. across, white or pink, solitary or 2 or 3 at end of shoots. April to June. Australia, Tasmania. 1793. (B.R. 515.)

**C. Backhousia'na.** A variety of *C. speciosa.*

**C. cardina'lis.** A synonym of *C. speciosa.*

**C. ferrugin'ea.** A synonym of *C. Lawrenciana.*

**C. × Harris'ii.**\* A hybrid of shapely growth in which the characters inherited from *C. speciosa* predominate, including the bright scarlet fl. (P.M.B. vii. 79.)

**C. Lawrencia'na.** Slender shrub, sometimes a small tree, shoots scurfy, downy. *l.* oval-oblong to linear-oblong, cuneate, blunt-ended, ½ to 2 in. long, ¼ to ⅝ in. wide, downy beneath. *fl.* solitary or in twos or threes, terminating short lateral twigs; cor. tube ¾-in. long, greenish-yellow, lobes ovate; anthers well protruded. May onwards. Victoria, Tasmania. 1836. Syn. *C. ferruginea.*

**C. pulchel'la.** A variety of *C. speciosa.*

*Correa speciosa*

**C. specio sa.**\* Shrub up to 6 or 8 ft., usually much less, shoots and underside of l. stellately downy, sometimes almost flannelly. *l.* ovate to cordate, ½ to 1½ in. long, apex blunt, stalk very short. *fl.* terminal, solitary to 3; cor. red, the tube 1 in. long, ¼ in. wide; anthers yellow, protruded. April, May. Australia, Tasmania. 1804. (B.M. 1746; B.M. 4912 as *C. cardinalis.*) Variable. var. **Backhousia'na,** *l.* ovate, oblong, scarcely or not cordate. Syn. *C. Backhousiana;* **pulchel'la,**\* *fl.* rosy-red. 1824. (B.M. 4029 as *C. pulchella.*); **viridiflo'ra,**\* *fl.* green. (B.R. 3 as *C. virens.*)

**C. vi'rens.** See **C. speciosa.**

A→              W. J. B.

*correoi'des,* Correa-like.

**CORRIGIO'LA** (*corrigia,* a shoe-lace; from the slender prostrate stems). Fam. *Caryophyllaceae.* A genus of 5 species of prostrate, glabrous, annual or perennial herbs natives of Europe, Africa, and temperate America. Leaves alternate, linear or oblong. Flowers minute; sepals 5, connate at base, obtuse, margins membranous; petals 5, small, white; stamens 5. Fruit 3-angled, 1-seeded. Rock-garden plants in moist sandy soil.

**C. littora'lis.** Annual with many slender prostrate stems from root, 4 to 8 in. long. *l.* linear-lanceolate, about ⅓ in. long; stipules half-sagittate. *fl.* in crowded terminal cymes. Denmark southwards, including Britain. (E.B. 1170.)

**C. telephiifo'lia.** Perennial with a woody stem. Whole plant more robust than *C. littoralis.* *l.* grey-green, obovate-oblong, thick, more or less fleshy. *fl.* about twice as large as in *C. littoralis.* June to September. Mediterranean region.

**CORROSIVE SUBLIMATE** or Mercuric chloride ($HgCl_2$) is a violently poisonous crystalline white powder which is sometimes used as a 1 per cent. solution in water for treating seeds to destroy fungus spores, the seeds being steeped in the solution for ½ hour. It must not be confused with Mercurous chloride ($Hg_2Cl_2$), calomel (q.v.), which has several uses both as an insecticide and a fungicide.

*corruga'tus -a -um,* corrugate; wrinkled; irregularly crumpled.

**CORRYOCAC'TUS** (after T. A. Corry, Railway Engineer to the Peruvian Corporation). Fam. *Cactaceae.* Stems columnar, usually short, branching from the base, strongly ribbed, very spiny. Flowers large with a short tube and broad open throat, yellow or orange; tube and ovary spiny. Fruit naked, juicy.    **A**

**C. brachypet'alus.** Stems 6 to 10 ft. h., branching from the base; areoles woolly, spines almost black. *fl.* deep orange, broadly funnel-shaped. S. Peru. (B.R.C. 2, f. 100, 102–3.) Syn. *Cereus brachypetalus.*

**C. brevisty'lus.** Habit as above. *fl.* yellow, fragrant. S. Peru and N. Chile. (B.R.C. 2, f. 99, 101.) Syn. *Cereus brevistylus.*

**C. melanot'richus.** Habit similar but stems more slender; areoles with dark grey wool, long dark hairs, and yellowish spines. *fl.* pink. Bolivia. Syn. *Cereus melanotrichus.*

              V. H.

**CORSICAN PINE.** See **Pinus nigra calabrica.**

*cor'sicus -a -um,* of Corsica, the Mediterranean island.

*Cors'ii,* in honour of the Marquis Bardo Corsi Salvati, of Sesto, Florence, who had (*c.* 1920) the most complete collection of stove plants in Italy.

**CORTADER'IA** (*Cortadera,* the Argentine name for Pampas-grass). Fam. *Gramineae.* A genus of 6 species of large perennial grasses natives of tropical and temperate S. America. Leaves long, stiff, narrow. Inflorescence large, plume-like; spikelets 2- to 7-flowered. Dioecious grasses with silky-hairy female spikelets, glabrous male, the flowering-glumes with a long slender awn. The silky plumes of the female plants are much more beautiful than those of the male, furthermore considerable variation occurs in seedlings in habit, period of flowering, stature, and size of panicle. Propagation is therefore better done by division than by seed so that uniformity may be secured. Division and replanting are best carried out in April and the sites should be thoroughly prepared. The plants will grow in most soils but a deep, well-drained loam or a good deep, sandy soil suits them best, and for the finest results a sheltered position should be given. Nevertheless they make fine plants for isolated positions on lawns but in selecting sites regard should be paid to the danger of damage to passers-by from contact with the very sharply scabrid edges of the leaves. The plumes are useful for indoor decoration and for this purpose they should be cut as soon as the panicles have emerged, and in some districts it is found better to do this before emergence is complete. They are best dried at first in the sun if possible for 2 or 3 days and then laid on clean shelves in an airy shed until the stems are quite dry. If left too long the spikelets are apt to be shed and the beauty lost. In early spring the clumps should be trimmed over or even burnt to get rid of the dead matter which accumulates.

**C. argen'tea.** Pampas Grass. Densely tufted perennial. *l.* 3 to 9 ft. long, narrow, glaucous, edges very scabrid, more or less arching. Stems including panicle 6 to 10 ft. (taller in warm countries). *Panicle* 18 in. to 3 ft. long; male panicle rather narrow, oblong, female broader, pyramidal, hairy, usually silvery-white, but sometimes with a rose tint. Autumn. Temperate S. America. 1848. Syn. *C. Selloana, Gynerium argenteum.* var. **al'bo-linea'ta,** *l.* white-lined; **aur'eo-linea'ta,** *l.* yellow-lined; **carmin'ea Rendat'leri,** has purplish plumes; **car'nea,** plumes pinkish, near var. *rosea;* **compac'ta,** dwarf, near var. *pumila;* **monstro'sa,** a form with very large plumes; **pu'mila,** dwarf compact about 4 ft. h.; **ro'sea,** plumes tinged rose.

**C. conspic'ua.** See **Arundo conspicua.**

**C. juba'ta.** A synonym of *C. Quila.*

**C. Quil'a.** Characters generally similar to those of *C. argentea* but plume laxer, its branches more spreading, its lavender-*spikelets* smaller, 3- to 5-fld., narrower, its *l.* rather deeper green, and *fl.* earlier. Ecuador. More tender than *C. argentea.*

**C. Selloa'na.** A synonym of *C. argentea.*

**CORTEX.** Bark; more correctly the ring of tissue lying between the epidermis and the fibro-vascular bundles of the stem, generally green.

***cortica'lis -is -e,*** having a distinct bark.

***corticico'la,*** growing on bark.

**CORTI'CIUM.** A genus of Basidiomycetous Fungi containing some parasitic species, e.g. *C. Solani* (*Rhizoctonia Solani*) which attacks many kinds of cultivated plants, especially seedlings.

***cortico'sus -a -um,*** having a thick bark.

**CORTU'SA** (in honour of Jacobi Antonii Cortusi, 1513–93, director of the Botanic Garden at Padua). FAM. *Primulaceae.* A genus of 2 species, allied to Primula but with the stamens attached at the base of the corolla tube and the connective acute. Perennial, often hairy, herbs with long-stalked, roundish heart-shaped, lobed leaves; scapes much longer than the leaves, and rose or yellow flowers on long unequal pedicels. They are woodland plants and grow well in cool woodland and form good clumps which can be divided. Seed, if sown as soon as ripe, germinates freely in a cold frame.

**C. Matthio'li.** *l.* radical, more or less heart-shaped, 7- to 9-lobed, with rounded teeth; petiole much longer than blade. *Scape* 5- to 12-fld., about twice as long as l. *fl.* purple, drooping; bracts rarely toothed; cor. funnel-shaped to bell-shaped, tube short. July. Widely distributed on mts. of Europe and Asia. 1596. (B.M. 987.) Variable in form and hairiness. var. **pu'bens,** *l.* deeply cut, lobes wide, teeth large. Transsylvania. 1878; **villoso-hirsu'ta,** *l.* deeply lobed, lobes regularly toothed, more or less softly hairy. Distribution as type, except Japan and N. China.

**C. Semenov'ii.** Habit of *C. Matthioli* but *l.* hairy above and on veins. *fl.* yellow, bracts pinnatifid; style long exserted. Turkestan.

***coryan'drus -a -um,*** with helmet-like stamens.

**CORYAN'THES** (*korys*, helmet, and *anthos*, flower; referring to the shape of the lip). Helmet-flower. FAM. *Orchidaceae.* Very extraordinary and ornamental stove epiphytic Orchids. One of the most remarkable species is *C. macrantha*, and some idea of it may be gleaned from the following, which appeared in the *Botanical Register*, *t.* 1841: 'The plant has the habit of a Stanhopea, and pushes forth from the base of its pseudobulbs a pendulous scape, on which two or three flowers are developed; each flower is placed at the end of a long, stiff, cylindrical, furrowed ovary, and, when expanded, measures something more than 6 in. from the tip of one sepal to that of the opposite one. The sepals and petals are nearly of the same colour, being of an ochrey-yellow, spotted irregularly with dull purple. The lip is as fleshy and solid in texture as the sepals and petals are delicate; it is seated on a dark purple stalk, nearly 1 in. long. This stalk terminates in a hemispherical greenish-purple cup or cap, and the latter, contracting at its front edge, extends forward into a sort of second stalk of a very vivid blood-colour, the sides of which are thinner than the centre, turned back, and marked with four or five very deep, solid, sharp-edged plaits. These edges again expand and form a second cup, less lobed than the first, thinning away very much to the edges, of a broad conical figure, with a diameter of at least 2 in. at the orifice; this second cup is of an ochrey-yellow, streaked and spotted with pale crimson, and seems intended to catch a watery secretion, which drips into it from two succulent horns, taking their origin in the base of the column, and hanging over the centre of the cup.' The apex of the column is concealed in the further end of the second cup, really the blade or epichil of the lip, the first cup or cap representing the hypochil, the arm between it and the epichil, the mesochil. The shape of this epichil is such that while in some species capable of holding over a fluid ounce of the liquid secreted by the 2 glands, a passage is left through which an insect, usually a bee, falling into the cup (or bucket), must find egress often only by using considerable force. In so doing the pollen adheres to it and is left on the stigma of the same or a second flower visited, the clogged wings of the insect no doubt rendering it more susceptible to another fall. Should fertilization be effected shortly after the flowers open, the distillation of liquid ceases, the flowers endure for but a few days, the flimsy textured sepals and petals being particularly fugitive. The genus contains 12 to 15 species and is distributed through Trop. America. The species resemble Stanhopea in habit but the pseudobulbs are usually more decidedly conical, taller, more clearly furrowed, and paler, while the foliage 9 to 15 in. in length is less leathery. Many species produce masses of aerial roots which almost conceal the bulbs. For the species with pendent spikes, usually 2- or 3-flowered, baskets must take the place of pots. Some species, e.g. *C. elegantium* and *C. Wolfii*, have erect peduncles. Compost should consist of 2½ parts of Osmunda fibre, 1½ parts of Sphagnum moss, and some finely broken potsherds. When growing the plants revel in a moist warm atmosphere, tropical in temperature. After the pseudobulbs are matured water must be given infrequently, but the compost should never be allowed to become really dry. Even in winter atmospheric moisture is required, hence the winter night temperature should never be lower than 65°. Owing to the often strong reflexing of the sepals and petals and their often contorted wing-like appearance the exact sizes of the flowers cannot be given.

**C. Alberti'nae.** A variety of *C. maculata.*

**C. Balfouria'na.** *fl.* clear apricot-yellow with reddish spots on inner surface of mesochil; lateral sep. narrow, hood comparatively large, rounded, bucket somewhat oblong. Plant and fl. smaller than in *C. macrantha.* Habitat? 1911.

**C. biflo'ra.** *fl.* sep. and pet. yellowish; lateral sep. 2 to 2½ in. long; pet. shorter, narrower; lip with a rose-white hypochil and the epichil dark yellow, with purple spots within. Plant and fl. smaller than in most species. *l.*, including petiole, about 10 in. long, 1 in. broad. Brazil.

**C. Bungeroth'ii.*** *fl.* very large; sep. pale green, dotted with red, dorsal one 2½ in. long, lateral 6 in. long, with the lip orange, spotted with reddish-brown inside; pet. about 3 in. long, narrow, whiter than sep.; lip with the bucket-shaped part, yellow, shading to yellowish-brown and marked inside with large, reddish-brown spots. May. Venezuela. 1890. (L. 244.) A fine species.

**C. elegan'tium.** Allied to *C. Wolfii*; as in that species the fl. are on stout, erect spikes, the ovary being curved so that the bucket is inferior; hood solid and rather flat, hypochil stalk short; sep. and pet. yellow; lip purplish. Brazil. 1868.

**C. Field'ingii.*** *fl.* yellowish-brown with irregular spots and stains of cinnamon; lateral sep. 4 in. or more long, over 2 in. broad; dorsal sep. half as long; pet. slightly longer than the dorsal sep., very narrow. Brazil. 1847. (G.C. 22 (1897), 31 to 39.) Apparently not now in cultivation.

**C. leucocor'ys.*** *fl.* dorsal sep. greenish-yellow, tinted and striped purplish-brown, 1¾ in. across, lateral 2 in. wide, over 4 in. long, similarly coloured, curiously rolled over; pet. white, obscurely purple-striped, 2¾ in. long, ⅛ in. broad, falcate; pouch of lip whitish, marbled rosy-purple, hood ivory-white. June. Peru. 1891. (L. 293.)

**C. macranth'a.*** *fl.* large, ochre-yellow, spotted purple; lip purplish-yellow with purple flush. May, June, July. Caracas. (B.R. 1841; B.M. 7692.)

**C. macrocor'ys.*** *fl.* large, pale yellowish-white, spotted and dotted purple, and having a very elongated, thimble-shaped hood at the base of the lip, streaked and spotted with purple; lateral sep. concave, inclined towards lip. Peru. 1892. (L. 342.) A very distinct species.

**C. macula'ta.*** *fl.* variable, usually pale ochraceous-yellow, spotted with purple, lasting but 3 days in beauty; lateral sep. 4 in. long, 1½ in. wide. Summer. Demerara. 1829. (B.M. 3102.) var. **Alberti'nae,** *fl.* large, sep. pale greenish-yellow, densely purple-dotted, lip with a white, rose-spotted hypochil, epichil deep purple. Brazil. 1848; **Par'keri,** *fl.* much more purple. Brazil. 1840. (B.M. 3747.); **puncta'ta,** sep. and pet. yellowish, red-spotted, hypochil flushed with orange-red, often purple-spotted, epichil pale yellow, dotted and spotted red. (B.R. 1793; W.O.A. 98.); **splen'dens,** *fl.* large, sep. yellowish, flushed and dotted red, pet. whitish with red flushes and spots, hypochil whitish-rose, softly lined with purple, epichil yellowish rose-flushed, purple-spotted. Brazil. 1877. SYN. *C. splendens*; **vitri'na,** *fl.* light greenish-yellow, lip whitish touched with green.

**C. Mastersia'na.** *fl.* yellowish, stained with red, hypochil of lip deep glowing red, in a spike 1½ to 2 ft. long, lateral sep. 3½ to 4 in. long; lip consisting of a thick bell-shaped hypochil, a thick fleshy mesochil, and a large bell-shaped epichil; peduncles erect. *Pseudobulbs* 2-ld. Colombia. 1891. (G.C. 29 (1901), 19.)

**C. Par'keri.** A form of *C. maculata.*

**C. puncta'ta.** A form of *C. maculata.*

**C. specio'sa.*** *fl.* pale yellow; lateral sep. 2½ to 3 in. long; pet. shorter, narrower, lip orange flushed with red-brown, hairy; peduncle 12 to 20 in. long. Brazil. 1826. (B.M. 2755.) var. **al'ba,** *fl.* whitish; **exim'ia,** *fl.* smaller, sep. purple-spotted, hypochil yellowish passing to purple, mesochil orange-red lined purple, epichil purple-spotted on a whitish ground. Brazil. 1847. SYN. *C. eximia;* **vitelli'na,** *fl.* larger, inner surface of bucket spotted with purple like pet.

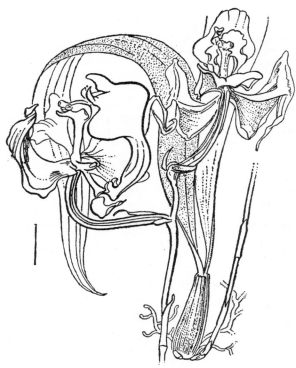

*Coryanthes speciosa*

**C. Wol'fii.** *fl.* yellow, mottled and stained with brownish-red, large, 3 to 6 in an erect spike, about 1½ ft. h. February and March. Colombia. 1891.

E. C.

**CORYD'ALIS** (*korydalis,* lark; the spur of the flower somewhat resembling the spur of a lark). FAM. *Papaveraceae.* A genus of about 20 species of annual or perennial, glabrous, usually glaucous herbs, natives of temperate regions of the N. Hemisphere. Roots fusiform, tuberous or fibrous. Leaves much-divided, alternate, or nearly opposite at tips of stems. Flowers in racemes terminal or opposite the leaves with a bract beneath each flower; petals 4, the outer 2 larger and 1 or both gibbous or spurred, often joined in 2 usually very unequal pairs. Easily increased by division, the bulbous species by offsets, the annuals by seed sown where the plants are to remain. A moist, well-drained, rather light soil suits them best, and most species thrive in semi-shade. Rock-garden plants, except the tallest, which are suitable for woodland.  **A**

**C. Al'lenii.** Perennial, about 10 in. h. *l.* much-divided; segs. slender, nearly 10 in. long over all. *fl.* rose, showy, in a dense terminal raceme about as long as *l.* NW. North America.

**C. angustifo'lia.** Perennial. *l.* 2-ternate, much cut. *fl.* flesh-coloured or white, about 1 in. long. April, May. Caucasus, Persia. (G.C. 35 (1904), 307.)

**C. au'rea.** Diffuse, branched annual or biennial about 6 in. h. *l.* glaucous, 2-pinnate, the pinnae pinnatifid; lobes oblong-linear. *fl.* golden-yellow, ½ in. long; spur blunt, shorter than pedicel; raceme short. N. America. The western form is more erect and tufted and with larger *fl.* (var. **occidenta'lis**).

**C. bractea'ta.** Perennial, about 9 in. h., unbranched. *l.* 2, 2-ternate; segs. cleft into linear lobes. *fl.* sulphur, 1 in. long, horizontal; spur longer than pedicel. May, June. Siberia. 1823. (B.M. 3242.)

**C. bulbo'sa.** A synonym of *C. solida.*

**C. ca'va.*** Perennial, about 6 in. h. Tuberous root hollow. Stem simple, without scales. *l.* 2, 2-ternate; segs. wedge-shaped, cleft. *fl.* purple, horizontal. February to May. Europe. 1596. (R.H. 1899, p. 555.) var. **albiflo'ra,** *fl.* white. Cf. *C. solida.*

**C. chaerophyl'la.** Perennial from a fusiform root, erect, 2 to 4 ft. h., branched, leafy. *l.* deltoid, much divided, 6 to 10 in. long, lower long-stalked. *fl.* golden yellow, ¾ in. long, in terminal panicles; spur slender. Sikkim to Kumaon.

**C. cheilanthifo'lia.*** Perennial. *l.* radical, about 8 in. long, nearly erect, fern-like. *fl.* yellow, about ½ in. long, in a many-fld. raceme usually taller than *l.* May. China. (Gn. 84 (1920), 234.)

**C. clavicula'ta.** Annual, climbing by branched tendrils, up to 4 ft. h. *l.* 2-pinnate; segs. oval, entire. *fl.* small, straw-coloured; spur short, blunt. June. Europe, including Britain. (E.B. 70.)

**C. densiflo'ra.** A synonym of *C. solida.*

**C. flav'ula.** Annual or biennial. Stem somewhat branched. 2-pinnatisect; lobes oblong, linear, glaucous. *fl.* yellowish. N. America.

**C. glau'ca.*** Annual of 12 to 18 in., erect. *l.* 2-pinnate, glaucous; segs. stalked, wedge-shaped, 3-fid. *fl.* red and yellow; spur blunt, much shorter than cor. July. Canada. 1683. (B.M. 179.)

**C. lu'tea.*** Perennial up to 1 ft. h. Stem branched, spreading. *l.* 2-ternate; segs. obovate, wedge-shaped, 3-fid at tip. *fl.* yellow. May. Europe, including Britain. (E.B. 69.) Walls, &c.

**C. nob'ilis.*** Perennial, about 9 in. h. Stem simple, erect, not scaly. *l.* 2-pinnate; segs. wedge-shaped, cut at tip. *fl.* pale yellow tipped green; spur long with blunt incurved tip. Siberia. 1783. (G.C. 35 (1904), 308.)

**C. ochroleu'ca.** About 12 in. h. *l.* much cut; stalk winged. *fl.* yellowish-white. June to September. Italy.

**C. ophiocar'pa.** Annual, 2 ft. or more h. Stem leafy. *l.* pinnatisect, 4 to 8 in. long, glaucous beneath. *fl.* yellow, in many-fld. loose racemes; sep. fimbriate. June. Himalaya.

**C. rupes'tris.** Near *C. ochroleuca* but *rhiz.* thick. *l.* oblong, rather fleshy, 2-pinnatisect; lobes very small; stalk up to 3 in. long. *fl.* in a short raceme, yellow; spur ½ in. long, swollen. Persia.

**C. rutifo'lia.** Perennial. Root tuberous. Stem not scaly below. *l.* 2-ternate; segs. large, ovate, entire or 3-cut. *fl.* deep rose; spur upturned. April, May. Asia Minor, Europe. (F.G. 667.)

*Corydalis thalictrifolia* (p. 553)

**C. Scou'leri.** Perennial with a tortuous root. Scaly at neck. Stem simple. *l.* few, lower stem-l. larger, upper small. *fl.* rose, 1 to 1½ in. long, in a loose raceme shorter than *l.* NW. America.

**C. sibir'ica.** Perennial up to 3 ft. h. Stem nearly erect, branched. *l.* 2-pinnate, greyish; segs. cut into oblong lobes. *fl.* yellow, usually recurved. June. Siberia. 1810.

**C. sol'ida.\*** Perennial with solid tuberous root, hollow in *C. cava.* Stem unbranched, scaly below, erect. *l.* 3 or 4, 2-ternate; segs. wedge-shaped or oblong, cut at tip. *fl.* purple, large. April, May. Europe, including Britain. (E.B. 68.) SYN. *C. bulbosa.*

**C. thalictrifo'lia.\*** *l.* large, from a long, woody rhizome, spreading, rigid, finely cut; stalk long. *fl.* yellow, in large spreading racemes which are opposite the l.; sep. ovate. China. (B.M. 7830.)

**C. tomentel'la.\*** Perennial. *l.* 2-pinnatisect; lobes oval, hairy, glaucous. *fl.* bright yellow, tinged green at tip, in erect racemes 6 to 8 in. long. May, June. Yunnan, China. 1894. (R.H. 1904, 189.)

**C. tomento'sa.\*** Perennial, about 6 in. h. *l.* radical, finely cut, 4 to 7 in. long, covered with pinkish-white hairs. *fl.* pale canary-yellow, about ¾ in. long, in erect racemes, 5 to 7 in. long; spur blunt, about ¼ in. long. China.

**C. verticilla'ris.\*** Stem from a tuber, simple, erect, 2 to 6 in. h. *Stem-l.* 2, opposite, deeply divided into 3 primary divisions, up to 4 in. long, primary divisions 3 or 4 times pinnate; ultimate segs. usually linear to narrow-elliptic, terminal lobe largest. *fl.* 2 to 12 in a simple terminal raceme, pale pink tipped maroon; cor. including the curved spur over 1 in. long. February, March. Persia, Iraq. 1932. (B.M. 9486.)

**C. vesica'ria.** Stem branching, climbing by petiolar tendrils. *fl.* yellow, one-spurred. *fr.* globose, inflated, netted. S. Africa.

**C. Wil'sonii.\*** Perennial, glabrous, usually glaucous. *l.* radical, much cut, about 5 in. long. *fl.* deep canary-yellow, about 1 in. long, in an erect, usually leafless raceme about 7 in. long; spur blunt, about ¼ in. long. China. (G.C. 65 (1919), 135; B.M. 7939.)

*coryli'nus -a -um,* Hazel-like.

# CORYLOP'SIS (*korylus,* the hazel, and *opsis,* like; alluding to the resemblance to Corylus). FAM. *Hamamelidaceae.* A genus of about 20 species of deciduous shrubs or small trees, usually of spreading habit; natives of NE. Asia. Leaves alternate, of uniform character, strongly parallel-veined, usually more or less cordate, bristle-toothed. Flowers fragrant and of some shade of soft yellow, produced in spring on the leafless shoots in drooping spikes 1 to 3 in. long, with large bracts at the base. Petals and stamens 5. Fruits woody, with 2 spreading, recurved beaks; seeds black.

Easily cultivated in a light loamy soil and propagated by cuttings. At their best they are charming in their soft fragrant beauty but are apt to be injured by spring frosts.

**C. glabres'cens.** Shrub or small tree up to 15 or 18 ft., shoots slender, glabrous. *l.* roundish cordate-ovate, abruptly short-pointed, 2 to 4 in. long, 1 to 3 in. wide, bristle-toothed; rather glaucous and nearly glabrous beneath. *fl.* pale yellow, fragrant, on pendent spikes 1 to 1½ in. long; pet. ⅜ in. wide; bracts appressed-silky inside. April. Japan. 1916. (Gn. 88 (1924), 419 as *C. Gotoana.*) The hardiest species.

**C. Gotoa'na.** A synonym of *C. glabrescens.*

**C. Griffith'ii.** Shrub or small tree, shoots closely, densely downy. *l.* cordate-ovate, 3 to 5 in. long, 1½ to 4 in. wide, pointed, toothed, downy beneath. *fl.* closely set on pendent spikes 1½ to 2 in. long, pale primrose-yellow; pet. spreading; basal bracts oblong, ½ to 1 in. long, silky inside. February, March. Himalaya. 1879. (B.M. 6779, as *C. himalayana.*) Half-hardy.

**C. himalaya'na.** A synonym of *C. Griffithii.*

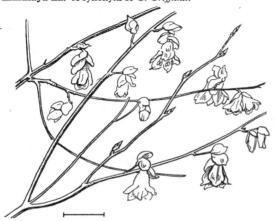

*Corylopsis pauciflora*

**C. pauciflo'ra.** Shrub 4 to 6 ft., shoots slender, glabrous. *l.* 1½ to 3 in. long, broadly ovate, cordate; bristle-toothed, pointed, rather

glaucous beneath. *fl.* 2 or 3 in short spikes, ⅝ in. wide; pet. roundish-obovate, spreading. March, April. Japan. 1874. (B.M. 7736.) Distinct by its few widely expanded fl. Rather tender.

**C. platypet'ala.** Shrub 6 to 9 ft., shoots glandular. *l.* 2 to 4 in. long, ovate (often broadly) to oval and roundish, cordate, abruptly pointed, bristle-toothed, soon nearly glabrous. *fl.* pale primrose-yellow, fragrant, in spikes 2 to 3 in. long; pet. roundish or kidney-shaped, ¼ in. long. April. Cent. China. 1908. (G.C. 95 (1934), 276.) var. **laev'is,** shoots not glandular.

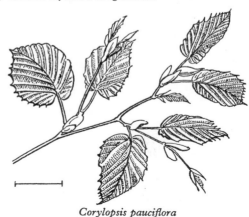

*Corylopsis pauciflora*

**C. sinen'sis.** Shrub or small tree, up to 15 ft., young shoots downy. *l.* obovate to obovate-oblong, 2 to 4 in. long, cordate, rather glaucous and downy beneath. *fl.* lemon-yellow, fragrant, 12 to 18 in spikes 1 to 2 in. long; pet. ⅓ in. long, roundish-ovate; anthers yellow; floral bracts large, downy. April. Cent. and W. China. 1901. (G.C. 39 (1906), 18.)

**C. spica'ta.\*** Shrub up to 6 ft., shoots silky-downy when young. *l.* 2 to 4 in. long, often nearly as wide, roundish-cordate, shortly bristle-toothed, glaucous and downy beneath; stalk and veins woolly. *fl.* yellow, 6 to 12 in drooping spikes 1 to 1½ in. long, fragrant, mainstalk downy; pet. ½ in. long, obovate, bracts greenish-yellow. Spring. Japan. 1863. (B.M. 5458.)

**C. Veitchia'na.** Shrub 5 or 6 ft., shoots reddish, glabrous. *l.* 3 to 4 in. long, 1½ to 2 in. wide, ovate to oval, pointed, slightly cordate, slender-toothed, reddish-purple, and sparingly downy beneath at first. *fl.* fragrant, crowded in spikes 1 to 1½ in. long; cal. greenish-yellow, hairy, ciliate; pet. primrose-yellow, spoon-shaped; anthers red-brown. April. Cent. China. 1900. (B.M. 8349.)

**C. Willmott'iae.** Shrub 6 to 12 ft., shoots slender, glabrous; winter buds pale shining green. *l.* ovate, roundish, or obovate, 1½ to 3½ in. long, short-pointed, pale or glaucous and at first hairy beneath. *fl.* fragrant, soft yellow, about 20 in spikes 2 to 3 in. long; pet. spoon-shaped, ⅜ in. wide; anthers yellow. April. W. China. 1909. (B.M. 8708, n.s. 438.)

**C. Wil'sonii.** Shrub or small tree, shoots stellately downy. *l.* cordate-obovate to ovate, 3 to 5 in. long, 1½ to 3 in. wide, abruptly slender-pointed, bristle-toothed, glaucous and ultimately glabrous beneath. *fl.* primrose-yellow, in spikes 2 to 3 in. long, bracts densely silky on both sides; pet. ¼ in. long. Spring. Cent. China. 1900.

**C. yunnanen'sis.** Shrub or small tree up to 20 ft., young shoots purplish, glabrous. *l.* 1½ to 3 in. long, roundish-cordate to ovate or obovate, short-pointed, minutely toothed, rather glaucous and more or less downy beneath. *fl.* pale to orange-yellow, densely set in spikes 1 to 1½ in. long; pet. roundish, ¼ in. long. April. W. China.

W. J. B.

# COR'YLUS (ancient Latin name). Hazel. FAM. *Betulaceae.* A genus of about 15 species scattered over the temperate parts of the N. Hemisphere. Deciduous trees and shrubs; leaves alternate, toothed, nearly always obovate or broadly ovate, shortly stalked. Flowers unisexual, without sepals or petals; the males in tail-like catkins mostly 2 to 3 in. long; stamens 4 to 8; females reduced to 2 very short red stigmas. Fruit a nut with a woody shell and more or less (sometimes wholly) enclosed by a conspicuous, often deeply lobed involucre (husk).

The tree species are handsome and even striking, but the shrubby ones are chiefly attractive in early spring, being profusely laden then with the yellow male catkins.

All the hazels are very hardy even in bleak places and grow well in loamy soil, even chalky. Seeds are desirable for the tree species, but the shrubby ones are best increased by layers, especially the varieties of garden origin.

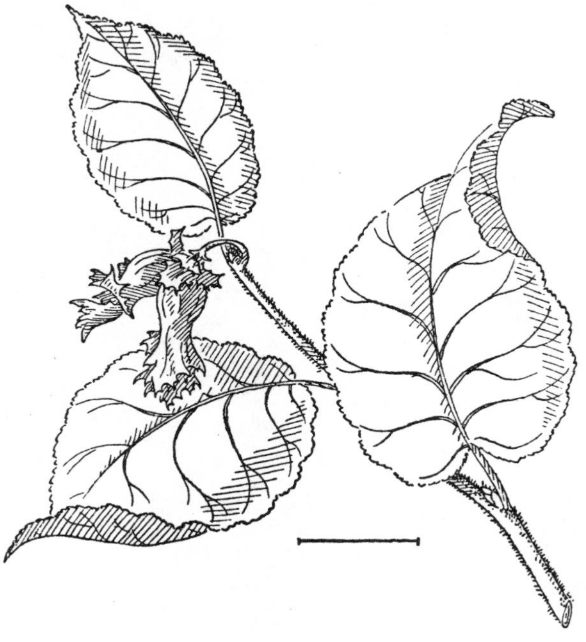

*Corylus americana*

**C. america'na.** American Hazel. Shrub 8 to 10 ft., shoots and l.-stalks glandular-hairy. *l.* 2½ to 5 in. long, broad-ovate, oval, or roundish, shortly pointed, downy beneath. *Nuts* in clusters of 2 to 6, ⅝ in. long; husk twice as long, downy, deeply lobed. Eastern N. America. 1798. Of little value in Britain.

**C. Avella'na.** Hazel or Cobnut. Shrub 12 to 20 ft. forming a dense thicket of erect stems copiously branched towards the top; shoots glandular-downy. *l.* roundish to broadly obovate, 2 to 4 in. long, toothed and often slightly lobed towards apex, downy, especially beneath. *Male catkins* up to 2½ in. long. *Nuts* in clusters of 2 to 4 or solitary, ¾ in. long; husk shorter. Europe (Britain), W. Asia. Much cultivated for its nuts and pliant shoots. *See* **Nuts.** (E.B. 1292.) var. **au'rea,** *l.* and shoots yellow; **contor'ta,** shoots curiously curled and twisted; found in a hedgerow near Frocester, Glos., in 1863; **lacinia'ta,** *l.* smaller, deeply lobed and sharply toothed; **pen'dula,** branches weeping; must have a leader trained up or be grafted on standards of *C. Colurna*; **purpu'rea,** *l.* purple, not so dark and effective as the corresponding var. of *C. maxima.*

**C. califor'nica.** A synonym of *C. rostrata californica.*

**C. chinen'sis.*** Chinese Hazel. Tree up to 120 ft., shoots, stalks, and midrib of l. glandular-hairy. *l.* 4 to 7 in. long, ovate to oval, oblique and cordate at base, evenly toothed, stalk ½ to 1 in. long. *Nuts* ⅝ in. wide, in clusters of 3 to 6; husk 1½ in. long, constricted above the nut into a short beak, toothed at end. China. 1900. The noblest of the hazels.

**C. Colur'na.*** Turkish Hazel. Tree 70 to 80 ft., bark scaling, grey, shoots glandular-downy. *l.* 3 to 6 in. long, broadly cordate-ovate, oval, or obovate, pointed, coarsely and doubly toothed, even slightly lobed, downy on midrib and veins. *Male catkins* 2 to 3 in. long. *Nuts* ½ to ⅝ in. wide, clustered 3 to 6 together; husks 1½ in. wide, fringed with numerous linear lobes ½ to 1 in. long, downy and glandular-bristly. SE. Europe, W. Asia. 1582. (B.M. 9469.)

**C. × colurnoi'des.** A hybrid between *C. Avellana* and *C. Colurna.*

**C. cornu'ta.** A synonym of *C. rostrata.*

**C. heterophyl'la.** Japanese Hazel. Shrub or small tree up to 20 ft., shoots and l.-stalks glandular-hairy. *l.* 2 to 4 in. long, roundish-obovate or ovate, cordate at base, short-pointed, unevenly toothed. *Nuts* in ones, twos, or threes; husk bell-shaped, ¾ to 1 in. long, conspicuously triangular-toothed. Japan, China. Akin to *C. Avellana,* but of little note in Britain.

**C. Jacquemon'tii.** Tree 40 to 50 ft. *l.* 6 to 8 in. long, up to 5 in. wide, obovate, shallowly lobed and sharply toothed. *Nuts* enclosed by a downy husk which is nearly or quite without glands, 2 in. long, with numerous curved subulate lobes. Himalaya. 1898. Closely akin to *C. Colurna* which has a conspicuously glandular husk.

**C. mandshu'rica.** Shrub 10 to 15 ft., shoots downy. *l.* 3 to 6 in. long, roundish-ovate to cordate-obovate, pointed, doubly toothed or shallowly lobed, downy on veins beneath; stalk ½ to 1 in. long. *Nuts* in clusters of 2 to 6, ⅓ in. long, ½ in. wide; husk bristly hairy, contracted above the nut into a slender beak up to 2 in. long. Manchuria, N. China. 1882. (B.M. 8623.) Near *C. rostrata* but l.-stalk twice as long.

**C. max'ima.** Filbert. Shrub 10 to 20 ft., shoots and l.-stalks glandular-hairy. *l.* broadly cordate-obovate or roundish, with a short slender point, 3 to 5½ in. long, nearly as wide, toothed and shallowly lobed. *Nuts* in ones, twos, or threes, completely enclosed by the tubular, much-lobed husk twice its length (in this respect differing from *C. Avellana.*) S. Europe (not Britain). W. Asia. Syn. *C. tubulosa. See* **Nuts.** var. **atropurpu'rea,*** *l.* dark purple, one of the hardiest, most easily grown shrubs of its colour.

**C. rostra'ta.** Beaked Hazel. Shrub 4 to 10 ft., shoots slightly hairy. *l.* up to 4 in. long, oval, ovate, or obovate, cordate at base, closely toothed, sometimes shallowly lobed, downy on midrib and veins. *Nuts* solitary or in pairs, ½ in. long; husk downy and bristly, ending in a slender cylindrical beak 1½ in. long. E. and Cent. United States. 1745. (G. & F. 8, 345.) Syn. *C. cornuta.* var. **califor'nica** has the l. more downy beneath and the husk shorter. Western N. America. 1910. Syn. *C. californica.*

**C. Sieboldia'na.** Shrub 10 to 15 ft., shoots hairy. *l.* 2 to 4 in. long, oval to obovate, doubly toothed and slightly lobed, downy on veins beneath. *Nuts* in ones, twos, or threes, conical, husk 1 to 1½ in. long, narrowed above nut, densely bristly. Japan. Akin to *C. mandshurica* but with a considerably shorter husk. var. **mandshu'rica.** A synonym of *C. mandshurica.*

**C. tibet'ica.** Tibetan Hazel. Tree 20 to 30 ft., shoots glabrous. *l.* broadly ovate or obovate, slenderly pointed, 2 to 5 in. long, sharply toothed, silky-hairy on veins beneath; stalk ½ to 1 in. long. *Nuts* in clusters of 3 to 6, husks covered with branching spines and making a prickly ball 1¾ in. wide. This chestnut-like burr distinguishes this from all the other hazels here mentioned. China. 1901. (R.H. 1910, 204.)

**C. tubulo'sa.** A synonym of *C. maxima.*

**C. × Vilmorin'ii.** A hybrid between *C. Avellana* and *C. chinensis.*

W. J. B.

**CORYMB.** An inflorescence of stalked flowers springing from different levels but making a flat head.

***corymbo'sus -a -um,*** with flowers in corymbs.

**CORYNEPH'ORUS** (*koryne,* club, *phoreo,* to bear; from the club-tipped awn). Fam. *Gramineae.* A genus of 2 species of annual grasses, with the habit of Aira, natives of W. Europe and the Mediterranean region. Leaves filiform. Inflorescence a panicle with capillary branches and small 2-flowered spikelets: Flowers hermaphrodite, the awn jointed in middle, clavate at tip. Any ordinary garden soil suits these graceful grasses.

**C. canes'cens.** Tufted annual, 3 to 12 in. h. *l.* setaceous, glaucous, clustered at base, margins convolute. Branches of infl. spreading. *Spikelets* few, glumes ⅛ in. long, nearly equal, awn jointed, filiform. May, June. Europe, including Britain. (E.B. 1729.) Syn. *Weingaertneria canescens.*

***coryno-,*** in compound words, signifying clubbed.

**CORYNOCARPA'CEAE.** Dicotyledons. A family of 1 species, *Corynocarpus laevigatus,* in New Zealand. A shrub or tree related to the hollies, with large, thickish, leathery, glossy, oblong-obovate leaves. Flowers in terminal panicles, small, perfect, regular, carpels 2, only 1 fruitful containing 1 ovule. Fruit a showy drupe.

**CORYNOCAR'PUS** (*koryne,* club, *corpos,* fruit; from the shape of the fruit). Fam. *Corynocarpaceae.* A monotypic genus, for the characters of which see its family. *C. laevigata* is hardy in Cornwall and Scilly, but in colder districts it needs a cool greenhouse. Ordinary good garden soil suits it.

**C. laeviga'ta.** Evergreen tree, 30 to 40 ft., glabrous. *l.* 3 to 8 in. long, ovate-oblong to ovate, entire, stout, and leathery; stalk short. *fl.* white, ⅛ in. wide, in stiff, erect, branched panicles 4 to 8 in. long. *fr.* an obovoid, fleshy drupe 1 to 1½ in. long, orange, edible; seeds poisonous unless steamed or steeped in salt water. N.Z. 1823. (B.M 4379.) var. **variega'ta,** *l.* bordered with golden yellow.

W. J. B.

**CORYNOPHAL'LUS.** Included in **Amorphophallus.**

**CORYNOSTY'LIS** (*koryne,* club, *stylos,* style; from the club-shaped style). Fam. *Violaceae.* A genus of 4 or 5 species of climbing shrubs, natives of Trop. America, with alternate leaves, and large white flowers. Petals 5, the lower one large, with a long, hollow pouch behind, which is compressed at sides, constricted in middle, twisted, and many-nerved. *C. Hybanthus* needs stove conditions and compost suitable for Stephanotis. It may be increased by cuttings of young wood in sand under glass with bottom heat, or by seeds.

**C. Aublet'ii.** A synonym of *C. Hybanthus*.

**C. Hyban'thus.** Stem striped, spotted white. *l.* oblong-ovate, slender-pointed. *fl.* large, white, horn about 2 in. long, in clustered racemes on slender thread-like pedicels. Trop. S. America. 1823. (B.M. 5960.)

**COR'YPHA** (*koryphe*, summit; from the terminal crown of leaves). FAM. *Palmaceae*. A genus of about 6 species of fan-leaved Palms with unarmed, ridged stems, generally very straight, and a terminal crown of large leaves, natives of Trop. Asia and the Malayan Archipelago. Flowers small, tubular, hermaphrodite; calyx cup-like, 3-toothed or -lobed; petals 3; stamens 6. Spadix solitary, erect, forming a very large panicle. Spathes many, tubular, sheathing. After flowering the tree dies. The Coryphas need stove conditions, and a compost of 2 parts loam, 1 peat, and 1 sand. They grow slowly and need thorough drainage and much water. Raised from seed. *See also* **Chamaerops, Livistona,** and **Sabal.**

**C. austra'lis.** A synonym of *Livistona australis*.

**C. ela'ta.** A synonym of *C. Utan*.

**C. Talier'a.** Trunk of about 30 ft. *l.* 6 ft. long, 15 ft. wide, 90- to 100-cleft; lobes deeper and broader than in *C. umbraculifera*, the middle ones 3 to 3½ ft. long, bases overlapping; stalks 5 to 10 ft. long, not spirally arranged. *fl.* in close clusters; spadix 20 ft. or more h. Bengal. 1823.

**C. umbraculif'era.** Talipot Palm. Trunk of up to 100 ft. *l.* very large, fan-shaped, plaited, forming a complete circle about 12 ft. wide; stalks about 6 ft. long, edges armed with small brown spiney teeth. S. India, Ceylon. *l.* used in making fans, umbrellas, thatching, writing material, &c.

**C. U'tan.** Trunk of about 60 to 70 ft., 2 ft. thick. *l.* 8 to 10 ft. across, 80- to 100-cleft to middle; lobes ensiform, obtuse or 2-fid; stalks 6 to 12 ft. long; spirally arranged. *fl.* in scattered clusters on the spreading branches of the spadix which is about 15 ft. h. India. 1825.

*coryphae'us -a -um,* leading.

**CORYPHAN'THA** (*koryphe*, summit, *anthos*, a flower; referring to the position of the flowers). FAM. *Cactaceae*. Round or cylindrical plants, solitary or growing in clusters; tubercles grooved on the upper surface for its full length. The flowers develop from the base of the groove on young areoles and are generally large and showy. The fruit is ovoid or oblong, greenish or yellowish, ripening slowly. This genus has given its name to the sub-tribe which includes the Mammillarias (*see under* **Cactus** (terrestrial) for cultivation).

**C. aggrega'ta.** Plants solitary or in clusters; radial spines numerous, white, pressed against the plant; several centrals which stand erect. *fl.* very large, purple. New Mexico, Arizona, and Sonora. (B.R.C. 4, t. 4, f. 47.) SYN. *Mammillaria aggregata*.

**C. arizon'ica.** Plants forming large clumps; tubercles 1 in. long, deeply grooved; radial spines 15 to 20, whitish; centrals 3 to 6, deep brown. *fl.* large, pink. Arizona. (B.R.C. 4, t. 5.) SYN. *Mammillaria arizonica*.

**C. bumam'ma.** Plants large, tubercles few but very large, axils very woolly when young; spines 5 to 8, brownish, all radial. *fl.* large, yellow. Mexico. (B.R.C. 4, t. 5, f. 29.) SYN. *Mammillaria bumamma*.

**C. chloran'tha.** Plants cylindric; tubercles closely set and entirely hidden by the densely matted spines. *fl.* small, yellow. Utah. (B.R.C. 4, t. 5.) SYN. *Mammillaria chlorantha*.

**C. cla'va.** Plant club-shaped; axils woolly; a red gland at the base of the groove; radial spines about 7, one central longer and stouter. *fl.* very large, pale yellow. Mexico. (B.M. 4358.) SYN. *Mammillaria clava*.

**C. compac'ta.** Plants solitary, round, depressed; tubercles crowded; radial spines 14 to 16, pressed against the plant and interlaced; centrals usually wanting. *fl.* small, yellow. Mexico. (B.R.C. 4, f. 33.) SYN. *Mammillaria compacta*.

**C. cornif'era.** Plants round, solitary; tubercles short and broad; radial spines 16 or 17, grey; 1 central stout, erect, and dark. *fl.* yellow, tinged with red. Mexico. (B.R.C. 4, t. 2.) SYN. *Mammillaria cornifera, M. scolymoides*.

**C. Desert'ii.** Plants usually cylindric, large; densely covered with whitish spines; centrals black to red towards the tip. *fl.* pale pink. California and Nevada. (B.R.C. 4, f. 44–6.) SYN. *Mammillaria Desertii, M. Alversonii*.

**C. durangen'sis.** Plants cylindric, solitary or in clusters; tubercles wide and flattened, axils very woolly; radial spines 6 to 8, short; central solitary, erect. *fl.* small, cream. Mexico. (B.R.C. 4, t. 5; f. 40–1.)

**C. Echi'nus.** Plants solitary, round; almost hidden by the spines which are closely pressed against the plant, whitish. *fl.* yellow. Texas. (B.R.C. 4, f. 31 b.) SYN. *Mammillaria Echinus*.

**C. elephan'tidens.** Plants hemispherical, solitary; tubercles very large, densely woolly in the axils; spines 8, all radial, short. *fl.* large, pink. Mexico. (Gn. 1 (1872), 396.) SYN. *Mammillaria elephantidens*.

**C. erec'ta.** Plants cylindric, growing in clusters, prostrate at the base but growing erect at the end; axils woolly when young; radial spines 8 to 14, awl-shaped; centrals 2. *fl.* large, yellow. Mexico. (B.R.C. 4, f. 30–1.) SYN. *Mammillaria erecta*.

**C. exsu'dans.** Plants short cylindric; yellow glands in the axils; radial spines 6 or 7, slender, yellow; 1 central yellow with a brown tip, occasionally hooked. *fl.* yellow. Mexico. SYN. *Mammillaria exsudans*.

**C. macrom'eris.** Plants large, growing in clusters; tubercles soft, loosely arranged; spines 10 to 17, the radials white, the centrals black, up to 2 in. long. *fl.* large, purple. Mexico and Texas. SYN. *Mammillaria macromeris*.

**C. Muehlenpford'tii.** Plants round, solitary, tubercles large with dark glands in the grooves; radial spines 6 to 16; centrals 1 to 4, variable in colour. *fl.* yellow. Mexico. (B.R.C. 4, f. 28.) SYN. *Echinocactus Muehlenpfordtii, Mammillaria Scheeri*.

**C. Nick'elsae.** Plants round, in large clusters, glaucous; tubercles almost hidden by the overlapping spines, all radial, 14 to 16, slender, yellow with dark tips. *fl.* bright yellow with a red centre. Mexico. (B.R.C. 4, t. 3.) SYN. *Mammillaria Nickelsae*.

**C. octacan'tha.** Plants cylindric, solitary; tubercles long, axils woolly, 1 or 2 red glands in the grooves; radial spines 8, centrals 1 or 2, stouter. *fl.* straw-coloured. Mexico. (B.M. 3634 as *M. Lehmannii*.) SYN. *Mammillaria octacantha*.

**C. Ot'tonis.** Plants round or elongated, glaucous; radial spines 8 to 12, centrals 3 or 4, longer and stouter. *fl.* white. Mexico. SYN. *Mammillaria Ottonis*.

**C. pal'lida.** Plants globular, solitary or in clusters; tubercles short and close set; radial spines 20 or more, white, short; centrals usually 3, 2 erect, the other curving downwards. *fl.* very large, pale yellow. Mexico. (B.R.C. 4, f. 38.)

**C. Palm'eri.** Plant globular, tubercles close set; radial spines 11 to 14, rather stout, yellowish; central 1 stout and hooked. *fl.* pale yellow. Mexico.

**C. pectina'ta.** Plants round, solitary; spines 16 to 24, all radials, recurved and pressed against the plant, interlacing, yellowish with dark tips. *fl.* yellow. Texas and Mexico. (B.R.C. 4, f. 31 a.) SYN. *Mammillaria pectinata*.

*Coryphantha Poselgeriana*

**C. Poselgeria'na.** Plants large, round, solitary; tubercles close set, strongly angled at base; lower radials spreading, reddish to black, upper radials weaker, erect, yellow with black tips; 1 central. *fl.* large, pinkish. Mexico. SYN. *Echinocactus Poselgerianus*.

**C. pycnacan'tha.** Plants round or cylindric, solitary; tubercles broad, glaucous; radial spines 10 to 12, slender; centrals 4, stouter. *fl.* yellowish. Mexico. (B.M. 3972.) Syn. *Mammillaria pycnacantha.*

**C. ra'dians.** Plants round, depressed, solitary; axils naked; spines all radial, 16 to 18, white or yellowish. *fl.* lemon-yellow. Mexico. (B.R.C. 4, f. 34.) Syn. *Mammillaria radians.*

**C. recurva'ta.** Plants round, depressed, forming large clusters; tubercles low; radial spines about 20, yellow to grey, with dark tips, recurved, pressed against the plant and interlacing; centrals 1 or 2. *fl.* lemon-yellow. Arizona and Mexico. (B.R.C. 4, f. 26–7.) Syn. *Mammillaria recurvata.*

**C. retu'sa.** Plants round, depressed, top very woolly; tubercles large; spines all radial, 6 to 12, curved backwards, yellowish. *fl.* yellow. Mexico. (B.R.C. 4, f. 36.) Syn. *Mammillaria retusa.*

**C. robustispi'na.** Plants round, solitary or in clusters, almost hidden by the spines; tubercles large, close; radial spines 12 to 15, 3 lowest very stout, upper weaker; central spine solitary, stout, erect, and curved, or even hooked, 1¼ in. long. *fl.* salmon. Arizona, New Mexico, and Mexico. Syn. *Mammillaria robustispina.*

**C. Run'yonii.** Plants forming large clumps with a thick tap-root; tubercles short and wide, loosely arranged; radial spines 6 or more, yellowish, variable in length; centrals 1-, 2-, 3-angled, up to 2 in. long. *fl.* large, purple. Texas. (B.R.C. 4, t. 1.)

**C. Salm-Dyckia'na.** Plants round, solitary or in clusters; tubercles short and close set; radial 15, whitish, centrals 1 to 4, reddish-black, the lowest curved downwards, up to 1 in. long. *fl.* yellow. Mexico. (B.R.C. 4, f. 37.) Syn. *Mammillaria Salm-Dyckiana.*

**C. sulcolana'ta.** Plants round, depressed, small; axils very woolly when young; spines all radial, 9 or 10, unequal in length, brownish. *fl.* large, yellow. Mexico. (B.R.C. 4, f. 35.) Syn. *Mammillaria sulcolanata, M. cornimamma.*

**C. vivip'ara.** Plants generally forming large clusters, with prominent tubercles; areoles woolly; radial spines 16, slender, white; centrals 4 to 6, much stouter, brown. *fl.* pinkish. Kansas, Texas, Colorado. (B.M. 7718.) Syn. *Mammillaria vivipara, M. radiosa.*

V. H.

**CORYSAN'THES** (*korys*, helmet, *anthos*, flower; flowers helmet-shaped). Fam. *Orchidaceae.* A genus of small, but very pretty, greenhouse terrestrial Orchids, allied to *Pterostylis*, and needing a compost of light sandy loam. There are about 60 species, distributed throughout Australia, New Zealand, New Guinea, Himalaya, Philippines, Malaya. All are small-growing plants with 1, sometimes 2, somewhat rounded, fleshy, usually flat leaves, seldom exceeding 2 in. in width, usually lying on the ground. The flowers are solitary, sessile or shortly pedicellate based by a small subtending bract. The dorsal sepal forms a helmet, shielding the small column, the labellum is at first tubular then expands into a blade, often reflexed with toothed or fringed margins. In the Australian species the petals and lateral sepals are very small.

**C. bicalcara'ta.** *fl.* helmet boat-shaped, dusky purple, sometimes white, completely concealing the labellum from above, the tube of which has two spurs at its base; ovary ¾ in. long. *l.* over 1 in. wide. Australia. (F.A.O. 1, pt. 2.)

**C. dilata'ta.** *fl.* helmet broad, fan-shaped, reddish purple, tube of lip longer than the blade which has dilated coarsely toothed margins; ovary ½ in. long, 1 in. wide. Australia.

**C. limba'ta.** *fl.* purple, white. Autumn. *l.* ovate, cordate, bright green, with reticulated white veins. 2 to 3 in. h. Java. 1863. (B.M. 5357.)

**C. pic'ta.**\* *fl.* with a very curious aspect, nearly sessile, 2-labiate; upper and hinder portion arched-ascending, stained with deep purple and yellow; lower lip divided into 4 long subulate segs., and a similar body, described as a bract, seated at base of the short ovary. *l.* solitary, cordate, ovate, reticulated. 3 or 4 in. h. Java. 1867.

**C. pruino'sa.** *fl.* helmet greyish-green, blade of lip fringed with dusky hairs; pet. and lateral sep. filiform, often projecting through the lip fringes; ovary ¾ in. long, under ½ in. across. *l.* 1 in. or over wide. Australia. (F.A.O. 1, pt. 1.)

E. C.

**CORYTHOLO'MA.** Included in **Gesneria.**

**COSCIN'IUM** (*koskinon*, a little sieve; in allusion to the pierced seed). Fam. *Menispermaceae.* A single species of climbing shrub native of Ceylon. It needs plenty of room in the stove to grow in or it will not flower well. A compost of light loam and peat suits it, and cuttings of young growths made in summer will root under a hand-glass.

**C. fenestra'tum.** False Calumba. *l.* alternate, cordate, entire, 5- to 7-nerved, smooth and shining above, very hoary beneath. *fl.* greenish; peduncles umbellate, several from the same bud. November. (B.M. 4658.) Syn. *Pereira medica.*

**COSMAN'THUS.** *See under* **Phacelia grandiflora.**

**COS'MEA.** A synonym of Cosmos.

**COSME'LIA** (*kosmeo*, to adorn; in allusion to its floral beauty). Fam. *Epacridaceae.* Monotypic genus, nearly akin to Epacris and similar in habit, differing chiefly by the leafy nature of the bracts, and by the anthers partially adnate to the corolla tube. Cultivation as for **Epacris.**

**C. ru'bra.** Evergreen glabrous shrub, 3 to 6 ft. *l.* ¼ to ⅜ in. long, ovate, sharply pointed, stiff and shining, the concave sheathing bases completely hiding the stem. *fl.* solitary, terminal, nodding; cor. ¾ in. long, red, tubular-flask-shaped and narrowing towards the 5-toothed limb, close beneath which the anthers are attached. May. W. Australia. 1826. (B.R. 1822.)

W. J. B.

**COSMIBUE'NA** (in honour of Cosimi Buena, Spanish physician, who wrote a Natural History of Peru). Fam. *Rubiaceae.* A genus of 6 species of trees, natives of Trop. America, related to Hillia but having a persistent calyx. Leaves somewhat succulent, stalked. Flowers with 5- or 6-toothed tubular or bell-shaped calyx, and 5- or 6-lobed salver- or funnel-shaped corolla with spreading lobes, tube long. They need stove conditions and a compost of loam, leaf-mould, and sand. Propagated by cuttings of ripe wood in sand, under a glass with bottom heat, or by seeds.

**C. obusifo'lia latifo'lia.** About 20 ft. h. *l.* opposite, 3 to 6 in. long, elliptic to obovate; stalked. *fl.* white, very fragrant, in terminal cymes; tube 3 in. long, about ⅛ in. wide at throat; peduncle stout, about ½ in. long. Colombia. 1876. (B.M. 6239.)

**COS'MOS** (*kosmos*, beautiful). Fam. *Compositae.* A genus of about 12 species of annual or perennial herbs, mostly natives of Trop. America. Leaves pinnate. Flower-heads solitary; receptacle with linear, acute, coloured bracteoles, equal to or longer than florets. Easily raised from seed sown in gentle heat in early

*Cosmos diversifolius* (p. 557)

spring. The seedlings should be pricked out into boxes, hardened off, and planted out in May. Perennials may be propagated like Dahlias, but need winter protection.

**C. atrosanguin'eus.** Perennial, tuberous, about 3 ft. h. *l.* pinnate, lower 8 to 9 in. long, lflets. 5 to 7, lower 2 to 2½ in. long, linear. *fl.-heads* dark blood-purple, large; ray-fl. elliptic, 3-toothed at tip; peduncles 18 in. long. September. Mexico. 1835. (B.M. 5227 as *C. diversifolius atrosanguineus.*)

**C. bipinna'tus.*** Annual, about 3 ft. h. *l.* pinnately cut; segs. narrow. *fl.-heads* rose or purple with yellow disk; peduncles axillary and terminal, leafy, rather short. Late summer. Mexico. 1799. var. **albiflo'rus,** *fl.-head* white. An earlier flowering race (**praecox**) has been developed and double-fld. forms with white and with coloured fl.-heads are offered.

**C. dahlioi'des.** A synonym of *C. diversifolius.*

**C. diversifo'lius.** Perennial herb, glabrous or nearly so, about 20 in. h. Roots tuberous, ½ to 1½ in. long. Stem branched. *l.* variable, opposite, lower lanceolate or oblanceolate, 2½ in. long, upper 3-partite or pinnatifid with 1 to 5 pairs of lflets. or segs., linear-lanceolate to oblanceolate. *fl.-heads* terminal, up to 2½ in. across; rays 7 to 9, white to rose, obovate-oblong, sometimes irregularly toothed; disk-florets fertile, yellow; anthers brown; involucral bracts in 2 series, each equal in number to ray-florets, with dark parallel lines; peduncles 18 in. long. Mexico. 1835. (B.M. 9180.) Syn. *Bidens dahlioides.*

**C. sulphu'reus.** Annual, about 2 ft. h. *l.* 2-pinnatipartite, lobes lanceolate, mucronate, rather rough on margin; stalks ciliate. *fl.-heads* sulphur; outer involucral bracts appressed, shorter and narrower than inner. Mexico. 1799. Syn. *Coreopsis parviflora.*

**COSSIG'NIA.** *See* **Cossinia.**

**COSSIN'IA** (in honour of Jos. Fr. Charpentier de Cossigny, 1730–89, French naturalist, once resident at Pondicherry, who presented Commerson with a herbarium of Coromandel plants). Fam. *Sapindaceae.* A genus of 3 species of shrubs or small trees with unequally pinnate leaves. *C. pinnata* is a stove plant grown for its ornamental foliage. It needs a compost of 2 parts loam and 1 each of peat and sand, thorough drainage and abundant water. It may be increased by cuttings of ripe wood but does not root readily.

**C. pinna'ta.** Tree of 10 to 20 ft. *lflets.* 3 to 5, oblong, entire, rough above, dark green, with bright orange-yellow veins beneath. *fl.* white in panicles. Mauritius. 1811. Syn. *C. borbonica.*

**COSSO'NIA africa'na.** A synonym of *Raffenaldia primuloides.*

**COS'SUS.** *See* **Goat Moth.**

**COSTA,** the midrib of a leaf.

***Cos'tae,*** in honour of Antonio Ciprianus Costa y Cuxart, 1817–86, Professor of Botany, Barcelona, student of the flora of Cataluna.

***costa'lis -is -e,*** with prominent ribs.

**COSTMARY** (*Chrysanthemum Balsamita*), also known as Alecost. The leaves were formerly put into ale and are sometimes used in salads, but their peculiar odour is not greatly in favour in this country. The plant is a hardy perennial and is best planted in early spring, dividing the old plant and planting 2 ft. apart in any good ordinary soil where it may remain safely for several years, if the situation is a warm one and the soil well drained. It is a native of the eastern Mediterranean region and is naturalized in S. Europe.

**COS'TUS** (ancient name, used by Pliny, probably from Arabic *Koost*). Fam. *Zingiberaceae.* A genus of about 100 tropical species of perennial herbs, nearly all with leafy stems and with the leaves spirally arranged, not in 2 ranks as in most other genera of the family. From Tapeinochilus, the only other genus in cultivation with leaves similarly arranged, Costus differs by its large bell-shaped labellum, petaloid filament much longer than the anther, and lack of lateral staminodes. The showy yellow, red, orange, or white flowers are in a dense terminal spike, usually with wide bracts. The roots are thickened and the leaves somewhat fleshy. Stove house conditions are necessary for their cultivation and a rich sandy soil with a little peat suits them best. They thrive in partial shade and may be propagated by division of the roots, or more quickly by cutting the stems into lengths of 1 or 2 in. and planting in fine peat or chopped Sphagnum and sand, lightly covering them.

KEY

| | | |
|---|---|---|
| 1. | *Lvs. scattered on stem* | 2 |
| 1. | *Lvs. clustered at top of stem or solitary* | 10 |
| 2. | *Bracts with a short point or recurved at tip* | C. Friedrichsenii |
| 2. | *Bracts without a short pointed piece* | 3 |
| 3. | *Bracts obtuse* | 4 |
| 3. | *Bracts acute* | 5 |
| 4. | *Lvs. silvery with silky hairs beneath* | C. Lucanusianus |
| 4. | *Lvs. not silky or silvery beneath* | C. afer |
| 5. | *Bracts not sharp-pointed* | 6 |
| 5. | *Bracts with a hard sharp tip or thickened below tip* | 8 |
| 6. | *Lvs. purple beneath* | C. discolor |
| 6. | *Lvs. not purple beneath* | 7 |
| 7. | *Lvs. lanceolate, not banded* | C. pictus |
| 7. | *Lvs. elliptic with darker bands* | C. Malortieanus |
| 8. | *Bracts hardened at tip* | C. speciosus |
| 8. | *Bracts hardened below tip* | 9 |
| 9. | *Spikes tapering* | C. spiralis |
| 9. | *Spikes cylindrical* | C. cylindricus |
| 10. | *Lvs. clustered at top of stem* | C. igneus |
| 10. | *Lvs. solitary* | C. Englerianus |

**C. a'fer.** Slender, up to 6 or 9 ft. h. *l.* lanceolate, slender-pointed, 4 to 6 in. long. *fl.* in a dense spike; cor. and lip white, lip deep yellow at base, cor. tube ¾ in. long, lobes 1 in. long. May. W. Africa. 1821. (B.R. 683; B.M. 4979.)

**C. cylin'dricus.** Variable in size, from 4 to 12 ft. h. *l.* oblanceolate, acute, 8 in. long, sometimes fringed with yellowish hairs. *fl.* at first in a globose head, later rather looser, bracts red; fl. yellow; lip up to about 2 in. long. W. Indies, Cent. and S. America.

**C. dis'color.** Stem glabrous, about 4 ft. h. *l.* oblong to elliptic, 4 to 8 in. long and about as wide, green above, purple beneath; ligule fringed with red hairs. *fl.* in an oval spike, bracts red and green; cor. white, lip white and yellow, often 2 in. long. June. Brazil. 1823. Distinct by the colour of its l.

**C. Engleria'nus.** *rhiz.* fleshy, stems 1-leaved. *l.* widely elliptic, about 6 in. long, rather fleshy, dark green. *fl.* few in a sessile spike; cor. white; lip about 1½ in. long, white with a yellow throat. Trop. W. Africa. 1892. Syn. *C. unifolius.* Unique by its single l.

**C. Friedrichsen'ii.** Stout, 5 to 6 ft. h. *l.* oblanceolate, about 14 in. long, softly hairy, flaccid. *fl.* in a conical spike about 4 in. long; cor. greenish-yellow, 3 to 4 in. long; lip 4 in. long, 5-lobed, deep yellow, passing to sulphur in throat with some red lines. Cent. America?

**C. ig'neus.*** Stout, about 15 in. h. *l.* oblong or oblong-lanceolate, 3 to 6 in. long, deep green above, reddish beneath. *fl.* few; cor. deep yellow to orange, tube 2 in. long; lip sub-orbicular, over 2 in. across, orange-scarlet. Brazil. 1884. (B.M. 6821.)

**C. Lucanusia'nus.** Stout, up to 6 ft. h. *l.* lanceolate, 8 to 10 in. long, silvery-hairy beneath, margin hairy. *Spike* variable; cor. white, tube ½ in. long, lobes 1 to 1¼ in.; lip about 2 in. wide, white with a broad red margin, yellow at base. Trop. W. Africa. 1892.

**C. Malortiea'nus.** Stout, nearly 5 ft. h. *l.* widely elliptic or obovate, acute, about 14 in. long, green with deeper zones above, glaucous beneath. *fl.* in a dense spike; cor. yellow, tube ¾ in. long, lobes nearly 2 in. long; lip golden yellow with brownish or reddish bands. Costa Rica. 1860. (B.M. 5894.)

**C. musa'icus.** *l.* 1-sided, lanceolate, 3 to 4 in. long, dark green in middle, chequered, silvery-grey elsewhere. Congo. 1887. A garden name and possibly identical with *C. zebrinus.*

**C. pic'tus.** Stem erect, about 18 in. h. *l.* oblong-lanceolate or oblanceolate, slender-pointed, about 8 in. long. *fl.* few in an ovate spike; cor. yellow, lip variegated with purple and golden yellow, 3-lobed. July. Mexico. 1832. (B.R. 1594.)

**C. Piso'nis.** A synonym of *C. spiralis.*

**C. specio'sus.** Woody at base, 6 to 9 ft. h., sometimes branched above. *l.* oblong or oblanceolate, slender-pointed, 6 to 8 in. long. *fl.* in an ovate spike about 5 in. long, bracts red; cor. tube short, lobes 2 in. long, white or red; lip white with an orange-red centre, nearly 4 in. long. India and E. Indies. 1799. A variable plant.

**C. spira'lis.** Moderately stout, about 4 ft. h. *l.* obovate-oblong, about 8 in. long, shining. *fl.* in a short spike; cor. red; lip about 1½ in. long. November. W. Indies, Ecuador. (B.R. 899 as *C. Pisonis.*)

**C. unifo'lius.** A synonym of *C. Englerianus.*

***cosyren'sis -is -e,*** of Cossyra, an island between Sicily and Africa, now Pantalaria.

**COTI'NUS.** Included in **Rhus.**

**COTONEAS'TER** (*kotoneon*, quince, *aster*, similar). FAM. *Rosaceae*. A genus of deciduous and evergreen shrubs, including a few trees, found wild in Europe, N. Africa, and N. Asia (not in Japan). The greatest aggregation of species is in W. and Cent. China and the Himalaya. Leaves alternate, entire, firm in texture, often woolly beneath. Flowers white or pinkish, nearly always $\frac{1}{4}$ to $\frac{3}{8}$ in. wide, sometimes solitary or in pairs, more often in clusters of 3 to 20, expanding mostly in May and June; sepals and petals 5; stamens 20. Fruit a red or black pome of globose, oval or obovoid shape, nearly always about $\frac{1}{4}$ in. wide, containing 2 to 5 seeds (pyrenes).

Cotoneasters are mostly hardy and easily grown. They make of course a finer display in good soils but no group of shrubs gives better results in poor ones. They thrive in a limy soil but are happy enough in peaty ones. The large red-fruited evergreen kinds such as Cornubia and Watereri, are admirable for quickly forming evergreen shelter-belts or screens up to 15 or 20 ft. high. They are also very effective as isolated specimens on spacious lawns. Propagation is effected by seeds or by late summer cuttings. Grafted stock, whether on hawthorn, quince, or other Cotoneasters, should be avoided. **A**

KEY

| | |
|---|---|
| 1. *Pet. upright, small, obovate, white or usually pinkish* | 2 |
| 1. *Pet. spreading, nearly round, white* | 24 |
| 2. *Fr. red or reddish-brown* | 3 |
| 2. *Fr. black or blackish-purple* | 18 |
| 3. *Fr. reddish-brown; deciduous shrub; lvs. 1 to 2 in. long, ovate to oval* | C. ignava |
| 3. *Fr. red* | 4 |
| 4. *Lvs. glabrous or nearly so, green beneath; fl. 1 to 4* | 5 |
| 4. *Lvs. hairy beneath, hairs on branches appressed; fl. 2 to many* | 11 |
| 5. *Deciduous or partly so* | 6 |
| 5. *Evergreen* | 16 |
| 6. *Prostrate shrub* | 7 |
| 6. *Upright or nearly so* | 8 |
| 7. *Lvs. broadly ovate to obovate, dull green; irregularly branched* | C. adpressa |
| 7. *Lvs. roundish oval, dark glossy green; regularly branched* | C. horizontalis |
| 8. *Lvs. usually less than $\frac{1}{2}$ in. long* | 9 |
| 8. *Lvs. up to $1\frac{1}{4}$ in. long* | 10 |
| 9. *Lvs. ovate to roundish, mucronate, somewhat hairy* | C. rotundifolia |
| 9. *Lvs. roundish to obovate, apiculate, nearly glabrous in age* | C. apiculata |
| 10. *Erect shrub; lvs. downy beneath* | C. Simonsii |
| 10. *Branches spreading; lvs. almost glabrous* | C. divaricata |
| 11. *Lvs. more or less plane, often hairy above* | 12 |
| 11. *Lvs. bullate above, downy beneath* | C. bullata |
| 12. *Lvs. up to $1\frac{1}{2}$ in. long* | 13 |
| 12. *Lvs. up to $2\frac{1}{4}$ in. long* | 15 |
| 13. *Shoots finally glabrous; cal. smooth or nearly so* | C. integerrima |
| 13. *Shoots very woolly; cal. woolly* | 14 |
| 14. *Lvs. obtuse; fl. 4 to 10 in cluster* | C. Zabelii |
| 14. *Lvs. acute; fl. 3 to 7 in cluster* | C. Dielsiana |
| 15. *Lvs. obtuse, whitish-hairy beneath; fl. 3 to 7 in cluster* | C. tomentosa |
| 15. *Lvs. acute, greyish-hairy beneath; fl. 2 to 5 in cluster* | C. acuminata |
| 16. *Bushy, shoots slender, rigid, woolly; lvs. $\frac{1}{3}$ to 1 in. long; fl. 3 to 5 in cluster* | C. amoena |
| 16. *Taller, spreading; lvs. $\frac{3}{4}$ to 2 in. long* | 17 |
| 17. *Lvs. up to $1\frac{1}{4}$ in. long, greyish or yellowish beneath; fl. 5 to 15 in cluster; fr. ovoid* | C. Franchetii |
| 17. *Lvs. up to 2 in. long, white-hairy beneath; fl. 10 to 15 in cluster; fr. obovoid* | C. Wardii |
| 18. *Fr. purplish-black; very leafy, lvs. usually obtuse, dark glossy green* | C. nitens |
| 18. *Fr. black* | 19 |
| 19. *Lvs. bullate above; fr. 10 to 30 in cluster* | C. moupinensis |
| 19. *Lvs. not bullate* | 20 |
| 20. *Lvs. more or less acute* | 21 |
| 20. *Lvs. often obtuse, whitish-hairy beneath; cal. glabrous* | C. melanocarpa |
| 21. *Lvs. more or less hairy above at first, dull green* | 22 |
| 21. *Lvs. glabrous and shining above; cal. glabrous or nearly so* | C. lucida |
| 22. *Lvs. $1\frac{1}{2}$ to 4 in. long; cal. densely hairy* | C. foveolata |
| 22. *Lvs. up to $2\frac{1}{4}$ in. long* | 23 |
| 23. *Cal. hairy; fr. with 2 stones* | C. acutifolia |

| | |
|---|---|
| 23. *Cal. glabrous or nearly so; fr. with 3 or 4 stones* | C. ambigua |
| 24. *Fr. black or brownish; deciduous shrubs* | 25 |
| 24. *Fr. red or orange* | 28 |
| 25. *Lvs. lanceolate, glaucous beneath, $1\frac{1}{2}$ to 4 in. long; branches soon glabrous* | C. Cooperi |
| 25. *Lvs. more or less oval* | 26 |
| 26. *Lvs. 2 to 5 in. long* | 27 |
| 26. *Lvs. 1 to 2 in. long, grey beneath, roundish-oval* | C. Lindleyi |
| 27. *Lvs. 3 to 5 in. long; young shoots woolly* | C. affinis |
| 27. *Lvs. 2 to 3 in. long; shoots nearly glabrous* | C. bacillaris |
| 28. *Deciduous shrub or tree* | 29 |
| 28. *Evergreen or partly so* | 35 |
| 29. *Lvs. 3 to 5 in. long, woolly beneath; fl.-clusters 2 to 3 in. across* | C. frigida |
| 29. *Lvs. less than 3 in. long* | 30 |
| 30. *Lvs. up to $2\frac{1}{2}$ in. long* | 31 |
| 30. *Lvs. rarely up to 2 in. long* | 32 |
| 31. *Lvs. finally glabrous, $\frac{3}{4}$ to $2\frac{1}{2}$ in. long, thin; fl. 3 to 12 in cluster* | C. multiflora |
| 31. *Lvs. pale shining green; shoots slender, downy; fl. 4 to 9 in cluster* | C. nitidifolia |
| 32. *Lvs. roundish to oval* | 33 |
| 32. *Lvs. ovate to oval; fl. 6 to 12 in cluster* | C. hupehensis |
| 33. *Lvs. woolly beneath, 1 to 2 in. long; fl. 3 to 7 in cluster* | C. tomentosa |
| 33. *Lvs. grey-hairy or glaucous beneath* | 34 |
| 34. *Lvs. glaucous beneath; fl. 7 to 20 in cluster* | C. hebephylla |
| 34. *Lvs. grey- or white-hairy beneath; fl. 3 to 12 in cluster* | C. racemiflora |
| 35. *Prostrate or dwarf shrubs* | 36 |
| 35. *Erect shrubs* | 41 |
| 36. *Lvs. not papillose beneath* | 37 |
| 36. *Lvs. papillose beneath* | 38 |
| 37. *Lvs. green, up to $1\frac{1}{2}$ in. long, soon glabrous; shoots prostrate, often rooting* | C. Dammeri |
| 37. *Lvs. elliptic to obovate, $\frac{1}{4}$ to $\frac{1}{2}$ in. long, dull green, tawny downy beneath* | C. buxifolia |
| 38. *Growth spreading* | 39 |
| 38. *Growth congested* | 40 |
| 39. *Lvs. ovate to obovate, downy beneath; fr. $\frac{1}{4}$ in. long* | C. microphylla |
| 39. *Forming a dense mat or more or less erect; fr. $\frac{3}{8}$ in. long* | C. conspicua |
| 40. *Lvs. obovate, margins revolute; fr. $\frac{1}{3}$ in. wide* | C. thymifolia |
| 40. *Lvs. oval to obovate, margins flat; fr. $\frac{1}{4}$ in. wide* | C. congesta |
| 41. *Mature lvs. glaucous beneath* | 42 |
| 41. *Mature lvs. more or less felted beneath* | 45 |
| 42. *Fl.-clusters up to $1\frac{1}{2}$ in. across* | 43 |
| 42. *Fl.-clusters 2 or 3 in. across* | 44 |
| 43. *Lvs. lanceolate, 2 to $4\frac{1}{2}$ in. long; shrub of 10 to 15 ft.* | C. glabrata |
| 43. *Lvs. oval, strongly veined, 1 to 3 in. long; shrub of about 6 ft.* | C. glaucophylla |
| 44. *Lvs. obovate to broadly oval, $1\frac{1}{2}$ to $2\frac{1}{2}$ in. long; fr. $\frac{3}{16}$ in. wide* | C. lactea |
| 44. *Lvs. oval, 1 to 3 in. long; fr. $\frac{1}{4}$ in. wide* | C. serotina |
| 45. *Lvs. elliptic-lanceolate, 4 to 6 in. long, more or less hairy beneath; fl.-clusters large; fr. bright red, abundant* | C. Cornubia; C. St. Monica; C. Watereri |
| 45. *Lvs. more or less felted beneath* | 46 |
| 46. *Felt under l. greyish or white* | 47 |
| 46. *Felt yellowish-brown; lvs. 1 to $2\frac{1}{2}$ in. long; fl.-clusters $1\frac{1}{2}$ in. wide* | C. Harroviana |
| 47. *Lvs. up to $1\frac{1}{4}$ in. long* | 48 |
| 47. *Lvs. up to $3\frac{1}{2}$ in. or more long* | 49 |
| 48. *Lvs. dull green, ovate to elliptic; fl. in clusters of 6 to 20* | C. pannosa |
| 48. *Lvs. dark glossy green, oval or obovate; fl. 1 to 3* | C. prostrata |
| 49. *Lvs. wrinkled or rugose above* | 50 |
| 49. *Lvs. not markedly rugose* | 51 |
| 50. *Lvs. lanceolate; fr. nearly round with 2 or 3 stones, bright red* | C. salicifolia |
| 50. *Lvs. oval lanceolate; fr. pear-shaped with 3 or 4 stones, orange-red* | C. rhytidophylla |
| 51. *Lvs. up to $4\frac{1}{2}$ in. long, narrow oval to obovate; fr. ovoid, dark crimson* | C. Henryana |
| 51. *Lvs. up to $2\frac{1}{2}$ in. long, narrow oval, dull green; fr. top-shaped, bright red* | C. turbinata |

**C. acumina′ta.** Deciduous shrub 10 to 20 ft., shoots densely woolly. *l.* ovate-lanceolate, 1 to $2\frac{1}{4}$ in. long, slender-pointed, dark dull green, sometimes colours well in autumn. *fl.* pink, 2 to 5 in a cluster, $\frac{3}{8}$ in. wide. *fr.* red, $\frac{1}{2}$ in. long, ovoid. Himalaya. 1820. (L.B.C. 919 as *Mespilus acuminata*.)

**C. acutifo′lia.** Deciduous shrub up to 10 ft., closely akin to *C. lucida* but differs by its *l.* being dull green, more or less pubescent above, and by its woolly cal. May, June. *fr.* black, oval, $\frac{1}{3}$ in. long. China. 1883. SYN. *C. pekinensis*.

**C. adpres'sa.** Prostrate, close-growing, rigidly branched, deciduous shrub, spreading widely, but only 1 to $1\frac{1}{2}$ ft. h. *l.* broadly ovate or obovate, $\frac{1}{4}$ to $\frac{5}{8}$ in. long, dull green. *fl.* solitary or in pairs, white, tipped with rose. June. *fr.* $\frac{1}{4}$ in. long, globose, bright red. China. 1895. Of no beauty in fl. and only second-rate in fr., but admirable for growing over declivities or as a curtain over rocks.

**C. affin'is.** Deciduous shrub between *C. bacillaris* and *C. frigida*, having the purplish-brown or nearly black *fr.* of the former and the woolly young l., wood, and fl.-stems of the latter. June. Himalaya. 1822. (L.B.C. 1522.)

**C. ambig'ua.** Deciduous shrub, 6 to 10 ft., shoots hairy. *l.* mostly ovate, finely pointed, 1 to $2\frac{1}{2}$ in. long, densely woolly beneath. *fl.* 5 to 10 in a cluster, white, tinged red. June. *fr.* globose to obovoid, black, $\frac{1}{3}$ to $\frac{1}{2}$ in. long. China. 1903. (B.M. 9106.)

**C. amoe'na.** Evergreen bushy shrub, 3 to 5 ft., shoots slender, rigid, woolly. *l.* oval to ovate, $\frac{1}{3}$ to 1 in. long, lustrous green, grey-woolly beneath. *fl.* white, $\frac{1}{3}$ in. wide in 6- to 10-fld. clusters; cal. woolly. June. *fr.* red, obovoid, $\frac{1}{4}$ in. long. China. 1904. (G.C. 51 (1912), 2.)

**C. apicula'ta.** Deciduous shrub up to 6 ft. *l.* orbicular to obovate, contracted at the apex to a short point, $\frac{1}{4}$ to $\frac{1}{2}$ in. long, shining green. *fl.* solitary, white or pinkish. June. *fr.* red, $\frac{1}{4}$ in. wide, globose. China. 1901.

**C. applana'ta.** A synonym of *C. Dielsiana.*

**C. bacilla'ris.** Deciduous shrub of spreading graceful habit, 15 ft. or more h. and usually more in width. *l.* ovate, oval, or obovate, pointed, 2 to 3 in. long. *fl.* in clusters 1 to 2 in. across. June. *fr.* globose, $\frac{1}{4}$ in. long, purplish-brown or nearly black. Vigorous, easily grown and one of the prettiest in fl. Himalaya. (G.C. 56 (1914), 412.) SYN. *C. affinis bacillaris.*

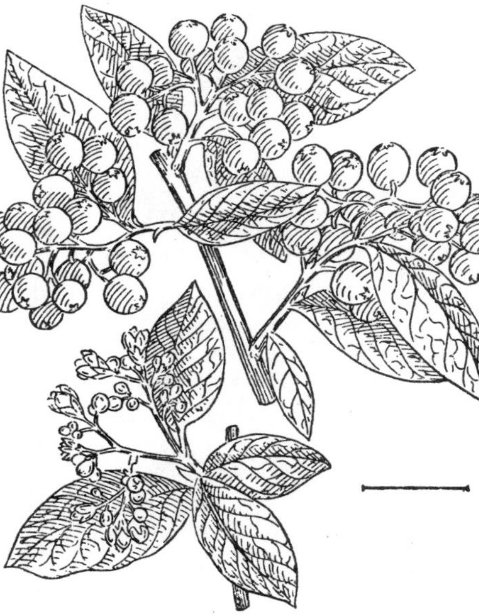

*Cotoneaster bullata*

**C. bulla'ta.*** Deciduous shrub up to 12 ft., young bark blackish-brown. *l.* ovate or oblong, 2 to $3\frac{1}{2}$ in. long, dark green and bullate above, downy beneath. *fl.* rosy-white, in clusters 1 to 2 in. wide of 10 to 30. June. *fr.* brilliant red, obovoid to globose, $\frac{1}{3}$ in. wide. China. 1898. The pet. soon fall but in fr. this is one of the handsomest species. (B.M. 8284 as *C. moupinensis floribunda.*) var. **macrophyl'la** has *l.* up to 5 in. long.

**C. buxifo'lia.** Evergreen rambling shrub, 1 to 2 ft., shoots densely downy. *l.* oval to obovate, $\frac{1}{4}$ to $\frac{1}{2}$ in. long, half as wide, dull green, densely tawny-downy beneath. *fl.* 2 to 7 in a cluster, white; anthers pink. *fr.* red, obovoid, $\frac{1}{4}$ in. long. Nilgiri Hills. (Ref. B. 52.) Much confused with *C. prostrata.* var. **villae'a,** procumbent, *l.* smaller. China. 1915.

**C. conges'ta.** Closely akin to, perhaps a var. of *C. microphylla*, but with a remarkably dwarf, congested habit, neither prostrate nor spreading. *l.* oval to obovate, $\frac{1}{3}$ in. long. *fl.* $\frac{1}{4}$ in. wide, pinkish. June. *fr.* globose, red, $\frac{1}{4}$ in. wide. Himalaya. 1868. (Ref. B. 51.) Differs from *C. thymifolia* by its flatter l. and larger, rounder fr. SYN. *C. microphylla glacialis, C. pyrenaica.*

**C. conspic'ua.*** Evergreen shrub akin to and similar in l. to *C. microphylla*, either erect and up to 6 ft. or quite prostrate and spreading. *fl.* solitary, white, $\frac{1}{2}$ in. wide, anthers red-purple. June. *fr.* obovoid to sub-globose, $\frac{3}{8}$ in. long. In fl. one of the prettiest species and the brilliant red fr. persist most of the winter. The prostrate var. **deco'ra** makes a dense mat and is especially attractive. SE. Tibet. 1934. (B.M. 9554.)

**C. Coop'eri.** Deciduous robust shrub, 10 to over 20 ft., soon quite glabrous. *l.* lanceolate, slender-pointed, $1\frac{1}{2}$ to 4 in. long, $\frac{1}{3}$ to $1\frac{1}{4}$ in. wide, glaucous beneath. *fl.* white, $\frac{1}{4}$ in. across, numerous, in clusters $1\frac{1}{2}$ in. wide. June. *fr.* obovoid, $\frac{1}{3}$ in. long, blue-black. Bhutan. 1915. var. **microcar'pa,** identical in shoot, *fl.* and *l.*, this differs by its smaller, globose, red *fr.* (B.M. 9478.)

**C. × Cornu'bia.*** Evergreen, widely-spreading shrub up to 20 or 25 ft., very vigorous and leafy. *C. frigida* is no doubt one of its parents and it is probably the finest of the hybrid group derived from that species which includes **St. Monica** and **Watereri.** The unusually large, brilliant red *fr.* come in heavy pendulous masses.

**C. Dam'meri.** Closely prostrate, self-rooting, evergreen shrub. *l.* obovate to roundish oval, $\frac{1}{2}$ to $1\frac{1}{4}$ in. long, dark glossy green, soon entirely glabrous. *fl.* usually solitary, white, $\frac{1}{3}$ to $\frac{1}{2}$ in. wide; anthers purple. June. *fr.* coral-red, $\frac{1}{4}$ in. across, globose to obovoid. China. 1900. Useful for overhanging rocks and steep banks.

**C. Davidia'na.** A synonym of *C. horizontalis.*

**C. Dielsia'na.*** Graceful, deciduous shrub, 6 to 8 ft., shoots slender, arching or pendulous, densely woolly. *l.* roundish oval, ovate or obovate, $\frac{1}{3}$ to 1 in. long, felted beneath, finely coloured in autumn. *fl.* pinkish, 3 to 7 in a cluster. June. *fr.* scarlet, globose to obovoid. China. 1900. SYN. *C. applanata.* var. **el'egans,** semi-evergreen, smaller and less woolly shrub. *fr.* coral-red.

**C. dis'ticha.** A synonym of *C. rotundifolia.*

**C. divarica'ta.*** Deciduous shrub, 6 ft. or more, of spreading habit. *l.* roundish oval, ovate, or obovate, $\frac{1}{3}$ to 1 in. long, glossy dark green, almost glabrous. *fl.* mostly in threes, pink. June. *fr.* ovoid, $\frac{1}{3}$ in. long, bright red. China. 1904. One of the best red-fruited species whose foliage sometimes turns good scarlet.

**C. foveola'ta.** Deciduous shrub, 10 to 12 fl., closely akin to *C. moupinensis* and with similar black, sub-globose *fr.* The *fl.*, however, are only 3 to 12 in a cluster (10 to 30 in *C. moupinensis*). June. China. 1907. Its chief garden value is in its autumn colour.

**C. Franchet'ii.** Evergreen shrub 8 to 10 ft., spreading and graceful, shoots very downy. *l.* oval to ovate, $\frac{3}{4}$ to $1\frac{1}{4}$ in. long, downy, especially beneath, ultimately bright green above. *fl.* in clusters of 5 to 15; pet. pink outside; cal. felted. May. *fr.* ovoid, $\frac{1}{4}$ to $\frac{1}{3}$ in. long, orange-scarlet. China. 1895. (B.M. 8571.) With little beauty of fl. but handsome in fr.

**C. frig'ida.*** Large deciduous spreading shrub, or a tree up to 30 ft. *l.* narrowly oval to obovate, 3 to 5 in. long, dull green, woolly beneath at first. *fl.* white, $\frac{1}{3}$ in. wide, numerous in clusters, 2 to 3 in. across. June. *fr.* abundant, bright red, $\frac{1}{4}$ in. wide. Himalaya. 1824. (B.R. 1229.) Very handsome when in fruit. var. **fruc'tu-lu'teo** has yellow *fr.*; **pen'dula** has pendulous branches; **Vica'ri*** has larger *fr.*

**C. glabra'ta.** Evergreen shrub 10 to 15 ft. *l.* leathery, lanceolate or oblanceolate, 2 to $4\frac{1}{2}$ in. long, bright green and glabrous above, glaucous beneath. *fl.* numerous in clusters, 1 to $1\frac{1}{2}$ in. across. June. *fr.* globose, orange-scarlet, $\frac{3}{16}$ in. wide. China. 1908. Similar in l. and akin to *C. salicifolia* which is much more downy.

**C. glaucophyl'la.** Evergreen shrub 6 ft. or more, much confused in gardens with *C. serotina*, from which it differs by its stiffer more strongly veined *l.* which are very glaucous beneath and tawny-woolly when quite young. *fl.* numerous, in clusters 1 in. wide. June. *fr.* obovoid, orange, $\frac{1}{4}$ in. long. China.

**C. Harrovia'na.** Evergreen shrub of loose, spreading habit, 6 ft. or more h. *l.* oval to obovate, 1 to $2\frac{1}{2}$ in. long, dark glossy green above, with yellowish-brown pubescence beneath. *fl.* numerous and closely clustered in corymbs $1\frac{1}{2}$ in. wide; pet. round, white; cal. woolly; anthers red-purple. June. *fr.* ovoid, red, $\frac{1}{4}$ in. long. China. 1899. One of the prettiest as regards blossom.

**C. hebephyl'la.*** Deciduous, spreading, sometimes tree-shaped shrub, 9 to 12 ft. *l.* oval to orbicular, $\frac{3}{4}$ to $1\frac{3}{4}$ in. long, glabrous above, glaucous beneath. *fl.* white, nearly $\frac{1}{2}$ in. wide, in clusters of 7 to 20; anthers violet. May. *fr.* oval, $\frac{1}{3}$ in. long, dark red. China. 1910. Handsome both in fl. and fr. var. **inca'na** is grey-downy beneath the l.; **monopyre'na** has only one stone to each fr. (B.M. 9389.)

**C. Henrya'na.*** Evergreen shrub up to 10 or 12 ft., branches pendulous, shoots downy. *l.* 2 to $4\frac{1}{2}$ in. long, narrowly oval or obovate, greyish, woolly beneath. *fl.* white, in clusters 2 to $2\frac{1}{2}$ in. across; stamens 20, anthers purple. June. *fr.* ovoid, $\frac{1}{4}$ in. long, rich crimson. China. 1901. (R.H. 1919, 264.) Handsome shrub with the largest l. of the evergreen species.

**C. horizonta'lis.*** Deciduous flat-growing shrub keeping within a few in. of the ground when young and increasing very slowly in height afterwards. *l.* roundish-oval, $\frac{1}{4}$ to $\frac{1}{2}$ in. long, dark glossy green. *fl.* single or in pairs, pinkish. May. *fr.* globose, bright red, $\frac{1}{5}$ in. long. Very distinct by its herring-bone-like branching. Can be used as a wall shrub without nailing, even on a N. wall. China. 1879. (R.H. 1889, 348.) SYN. *C. Davidiana.* var. **perpusil'la,** *l.* only $\frac{1}{4}$ in. long; **variega'ta,** *l.* prettily edged with white.

**C. humifu'sa.** A synonym of *C. Dammeri.*

**C. hupehen'sis.*** Deciduous shrub, 6 or 7 ft., with graceful arching branches. *l.* ovate to oval, 1 to $1\frac{1}{2}$ in. long, dark green, grey and thinly downy beneath. *fl.* white, $\frac{1}{2}$ in. wide, in 6- to 12-fld. clusters. May, June. *fr.* bright red, globose, $\frac{1}{3}$ to $\frac{1}{2}$ in. wide. China. 1907. Handsome species with large fl. and fr.

**C. igna'va.** Deciduous shrub, 5 or 6 ft. *l.* ovate to oval, 1 to 2 in. long, rounded at the base. *fl.* white, in clusters of 8 to 15; cal. and fl.-stalks downy. *fr.* red-brown, oval or obovoid. E. Turkestan. 1907. Acquires scarlet and orange tints in autumn.

**C. integer'rima.** Deciduous shrub 4 to 7 ft., interesting as the only species native of Britain. It has only been found on Gt. Orme's Head in Wales. *l.* ¾ to 1½ in. long. *fl.* 2 to 4 together. May. *fr.* globose, red, ¼ in. wide. Europe, N. Asia. (E.B. 477.) SYN. *C. vulgaris.* Of little garden value.

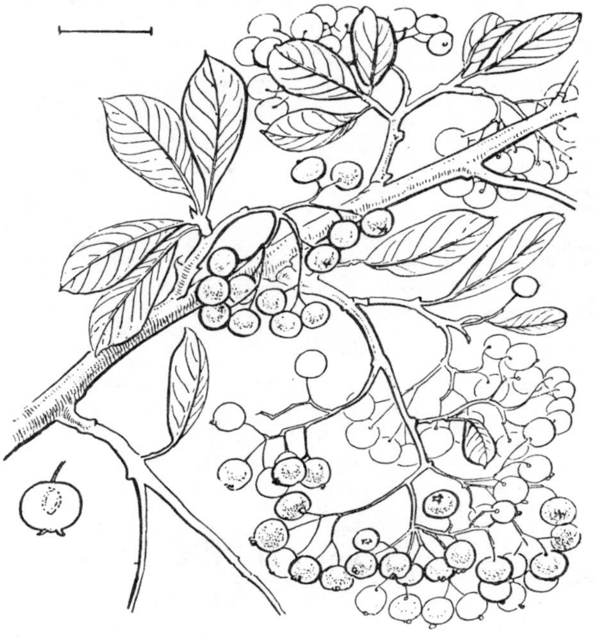

*Cotoneaster lactea*

**C. lac'tea.*** Evergreen shrub up to 12 ft., and more in width, shoots densely downy. *l.* obovate to broadly oval, 1½ to 2½ in. long, stout textured, veins 6 to 10 pairs. *fl.* in rounded corymbs, 2 to 3 in. wide, milky white; anthers pink. June, July. *fr.* obovoid, 3/16 in. long, red, late ripening. China. 1913. (B.M. 9454.)

**C. laxiflo'ra.** A synonym of *C. melanocarpa laxiflora.*

**C. Lind'leyi.** Deciduous shrub, 10 to 12 ft. *l.* roundish-oval to ovate, mucronate, 1 to 2 in. long, grey-felted beneath. *fl.* white, in clusters of 5 to 12. June. *fr.* purple-black, globose, ¼ in. wide. Himalaya. 1824. SYN. *C. nummularia.*

**C. lu'cida.** Deciduous shrub, 6 to 9 ft., shoots downy. *l.* ¾ to 2 in. long, ovate to oval, shining green and glabrous above. *fl.* rosy-white, in clusters of 3 to 10. May, June. *fr.* black, globose, ⅜ in. wide. Altai Mts. 1840. One of the best species with black fr.

**C. melanocar'pa.** Deciduous shrub up to 6 ft., of spreading habit. *l.* broadly ovate to ovate oblong, 1 to 2 in. long, grey-downy beneath. *fl.* pinkish-white in clusters of 3 to 8; cal. glabrous. May, June. *fr.* ¼ in. wide, black. Widely spread from Europe to Cent. and NE. Asia. 1826. (L.B.C. 1531.) SYN. *C. nigra.* var. **commix'ta,** *l.* ovate, *infl.* 8- to 15-fld. (B.M. 3519 as *C. laxiflora.*); **laxiflo'ra,*** *l.* larger, *fl.* in pendulous clusters of 20 to 40. (B.R. 1305 as *C. laxiflora.*) Attractive by its unusually large infl.

**C. microphyl'la.*** Evergreen low shrub, spreading to a width of 10 ft. or more, shoots woolly. *l.* ovate to obovate, ¼ to ⅜ in. long, deep shining green, grey and downy beneath. *fl.* white, ⅓ in. wide, usually solitary but occasionally 2 or 3. May, June. *fr.* globose, scarlet-red, ¼ in. wide. Very attractive and useful for covering slopes or for hanging as a curtain over supporting walls. Himalaya. 1824. (B.R. 1114; L.B.C. 1374.) var. **cochlea'ta,*** dwarf, creeping; **glacia'lis,** a synonym of *C. congesta.*

**C. moupinen'sis.** Very similar to *C. bullata* in habit. *l.* and pinkish *fl.* in June, but easily distinguished by its black, sub-globose to ovoid *fr.*, ¼ to ⅓ in. long. China. 1907.

**C. multiflo'ra.** Graceful small tree up to 10 or 12 ft. with arching or pendulous branches, or a large shrub. *l.* ovate to roundish, obtuse, ¾ to 2½ in. long, ½ to 1½ in. wide, thin in texture. *fl.* 3 to 12 in a cluster. May. *fr.* red, globose or obovoid. NW. China. 1837. Very attractive in habit. (B.T.S. i. 413.) SYN. *C. reflexa.* var. **calocar'pa** , and *fr.* larger. W. China. 1900; **granaten'sis,** *l.* more downy; cal. hairy. Spain.

**C. nig'ra.** A synonym of *C. melanocarpa.*

**C. ni'tens.** Deciduous, very leafy shrub, up to 6 ft., of dense habit, shoots tawny with down at first. *l.* roundish-oval, ½ to ⅞ in. long, dark glossy green. *fl.* pink, usually in threes. June. *fr.* ovoid-globose, ¼ to ⅓ in. long, purplish-black. China. 1910. Foliage sometimes scarlet in autumn.

**C. nitidifo'lia.** Deciduous shrub 5 to 8 ft., graceful, spreading, shoots slender, grey-downy. *l.* ovate-lanceolate, slender-pointed, 1½ to 2½ in. long, pale shining green, glabrous above. *fl.* white, ¼ in. wide, 4 to 9 in a cluster. June. *fr.* sub-globose to obovoid, crimson, ¼ in. long. China. 1924. Distinct by the pale glittering green of the l.; good autumn tints.

**C. nummular'ia.** A synonym of *C. Lindleyi* and *C. racemiflora nummularia.*

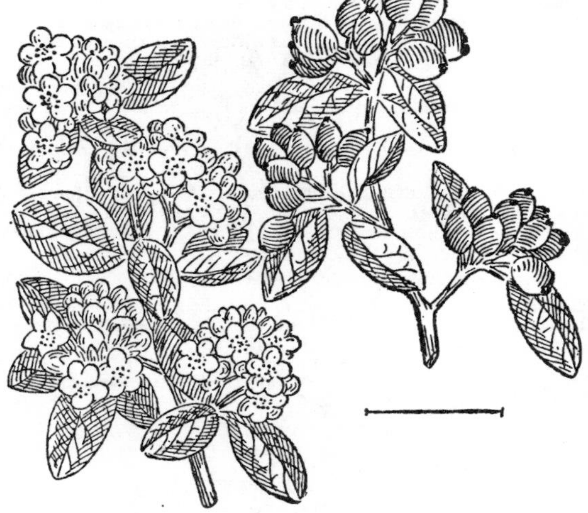

*Cotoneaster pannosa*

**C. panno'sa.** Evergreen or partly evergreen graceful shrub up to 8 or 10 ft., shoots woolly. *l.* ovate to elliptic, ½ to 1¼ in. long, dull green, white-felted beneath, stalk up to ¼ in. long. *fl.* white, ⅓ in. wide, about 20 in rounded clusters; cal. woolly. June. *fr.* oval to roundish, ¼ in. long, dull red, downy. China. 1888. (B.M. 8594.) Near *C. Franchetii,* but with the l.-stalk twice as long, whiter fl., and duller fr.

**C. pekinen'sis.** A synonym of *C. acutifolia.*

**C. prostra'ta.** Extremely vigorous evergreen shrub up to 10 or 12 ft. with long, spreading, sparsely-branched stems. *l.* ½ to 1 in. long, oval to obovate, dark glossy green, slightly woolly beneath. *fl.* white, ⅓ in. wide, solitary or in small clusters. June. *fr.* globose, red, ¼ in. wide. Himalaya. 1824. (B.R. 1187 as *C. microphylla Uva-ursi.*) var. **lana'ta,** *l.* more downy beneath, *fl.* in clusters of 3 to 8. SYN. *C. Wheeleri.*

**C. pyrena'ica.** A synonym of *C. congesta.*

**C. racemiflo'ra.** Deciduous shrub up to 8 ft. *l.* roundish to oval or obovate, ½ to 1½ in. long, grey or white with down beneath. *fl.* ⅓ in. wide, in 3- to 12-fld. clusters. May, June. *fr.* roundish, ⅓ in. wide, red. S. Europe and N. Africa to the Himalaya and Turkestan. 1829. A very variable species. var. **microcar'pa,** *fr.* smaller, ellipsoidal, ⅓ in. long. W. China. 1910; **nummular'ia,** has obtuse, more broadly rounded *l.*; **songa'rica,** *l.* oval, less downy, habit semipendulous, *fr.* persisting through the winter. W. China. 1910.

**C. reflex'a.** A synonym of *C. multiflora.*

**C. rhytidophyl'la.** Evergreen shrub up to 6 ft., graceful and spreading. *l.* oval-lanceolate, slender-pointed, 1½ to 3½ in. long, one-third as wide, dark shining green and glossy above, grey-woolly beneath. *fl.* white, in clusters of 10 to 12. June. *fr.* pear-shaped, orange-red, ¼ in. long. China. 1908.

**C. rotundifo'lia.*** Deciduous or semi-evergreen, stiff, spreading shrub 5 to 8 ft. *l.* ovate to roundish, mucronate, ⅓ to ½ in. long, dark lustrous green. *fl.* white, suffused with pink, ⅜ in. wide, single or in pairs. June. *fr.* ½ in. long, roundish-obovoid, scarlet. Himalaya. 1825. (B.M. 8010.) SYN. *C. disticha.* Retains its abundant handsome fr. till spring.

**C. × St. Mon'ica.*** Evergreen, red-fruited hybrid shrub up to 15 ft. or more, raised accidentally at St. Monica's Home, Bristol. *C. frigida* is evidently one of its parents and the one from which it inherits its vigour; its evergreen character is probably derived from *C. salicifolia* or one of its allies. *l.* elliptic-lanceolate, 4 to 6 in. long. *fr.* borne in pendulous masses.

**C. salicifo'lia.*** Graceful evergreen shrub up to 16 ft., shoots very slender, downy. *l.* lanceolate, slender-pointed, 1½ to 3 in. long, glossy green, white-felted beneath. *fl.* 3/16 in. wide, in corymbs 1½ in. across; anthers red. June. *fr.* bright red, globose, ¼ in. wide. China. 1908. A variable species especially in l. and stature. (B.M. 8999.) var. **prostra'ta,** dwarf, prostrate, with small narrow *l.*, useful for banks; **rugo'sa,** *l.* up to 3½ in. long and 1½ in. wide, more rugose, *fl.* and *fr.* larger. (B.M. 8694; G.C. 56 (1914), 412.)

**C. serot'ina.*** Evergreen shrub up to 10 ft., shoots downy. *l.* oval, 1 to 3 in. long, dark green, glabrous above and becoming so beneath. *fl.* on corymbs 2 to 3 in. wide, white, anthers red-brown. July, August. *fr.* bright red, obovoid, ¼ in. wide. China. (B.M. 8854 and 9171 as *C. glaucophylla serotina.*) Besides its late fl., its fr. persist until April.

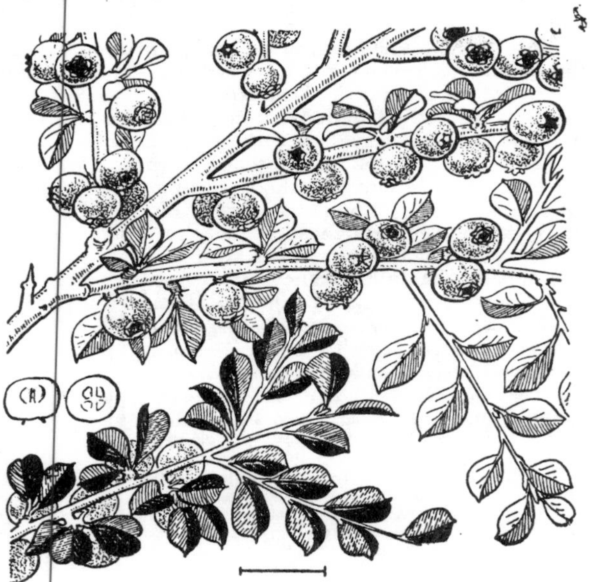

*Cotoneaster rotundifolia* (p. 560)

**C. Si'monsii.** Deciduous or semi-evergreen shrub up to 9 ft., shoots erect, brown-woolly. *l.* ¾ to 1¼ in. long, oval, roundish or obovate, dark glossy green, downy beneath. *fl.* 2 to 4 together, ⅓ in. wide, white. June. *fr.* scarlet, ⅓ in. long, obovoid. Khasia Mts. 1865. (Add. 91.) Useful for forming an unclipped screen or shelter belt.

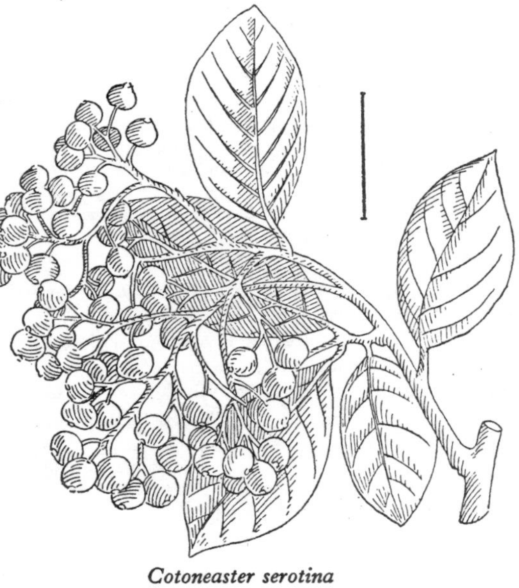

*Cotoneaster serotina*

**C. thymifo'lia.** Closely akin to, probably a var. of *C. microphylla*, but very distinct by its close, congested growth and dwarfed shape. *l.* ⅛ to ⅜ in. long, narrowly obovate, margins revolute. *fl.* pinkish, solitary or in pairs. May, June. *fr.* ⅕ in. wide, bright red. Himalaya. 1852. (Ref. B. 50.) Adapted for the rock-garden.

**C. tomento'sa.** Deciduous shrub 6 to 8 ft. *l.* 1 to 2 in. long, roundish to oval, very woolly beneath. *fl.* in short, nodding clusters of 3 to 7, white; cal. very woolly. May. *fr.* red, ⅓ in. wide, subglobose. Interesting as one of the few European species and perhaps the woolliest in the genus. 1759.

**C. turbina'ta.** Small pyramidal evergreen tree 10 ft. and upwards, or a large shrub. *l.* narrowly oval, tapering towards both ends, ¾ to 2½ in. long, about half as wide, dull green, grey-felted beneath. *fl.* ¼ in. wide, with rosy anthers, in hemispherical clusters 2 in. across. July, August. *fr.* top-shaped, red, ¼ in. long. China. 1910. (B.M. 8546.) Prettier in fl. than in fr. One of the latest to fl.

**C. Ward'ii.*** Evergreen shrub, 6 to 10 ft., shoots downy, afterwards shining brown. *l.* ovate, 1 to 2 in. long, half as wide, dark shining green above, white-felted beneath. *fl.* white or pinkish in clusters of 10 to 15. June. *fr.* bright orange-red, obovoid, ⅜ in. wide. SE. Tibet. 1913. The older l. often fade into bright orange shades in autumn.

**C. × Wa'tereri*** (*C. frigida* × *C. Henryana*). Evergreen hybrid shrub or small tree, very vigorous, 20 ft. h. and more in width. *l.* and *fr.* larger than in *C. frigida*, the latter scarlet. Should have an isolated position to show its magnificent crop of fr. borne on wide-spreading branches.

**C. Whee'leri.** A synonym of *C. prostrata.*

**C. Zabel'ii.** Deciduous shrub of arching, spreading growth up to 6 or 9 ft., shoots densely downy. *l.* ½ to 1½ in. long, oval or ovate to roundish, dull green above, yellowish- or grey-felted beneath. *fl.* small, rosy, in clusters of 4 to 10. May. *fr.* red, downy, obovoid, ⅓ in. long. China. 1907. var. **minia'ta,** *fr.* smaller, pale orange-scarlet, *l.* die off yellow.

W. J. B.

***Cottingham'ii,*** in honour of Capt. Cottingham, *c.* 1836.

**COTTON.** *See* **Gossypium.**

**COTTON GRASS.** *See* **Eriophorum.**

**COTTON GUM.** *See* **Nyssa aquatica.**

**COTTON SEDGE.** *See* **Eriophorum.**

**COTTON THISTLE.** *See* **Onopordum.**

**COTTON TREE.** *See* **Bombax malabaricum. A**

**COTTON TREE, SILK.** *See* **Ceiba Casearia.**

**COTTON-WOOD TREE.** *See* **Populus.**

**COTTON'IA** (in honour of Major-Gen. Cotton, Madras Engineers, collector and cultivator of Orchids, who found *C. macrostachya* at Malabar). FAM. *Orchidaceae.* A genus of 1 species differing from Vanda by its slender column and the shape of the lip which resembles that of *Ophrys aranifera.* For cultivation, *see* **Vanda.**

**C. Champio'nii.** A synonym of *Diploprora Championii.*

**C. macrostach'ya.** Stem 4 to 8 in. long, leafy. *l.* lorate, 5 to 6 in. long, ½ to ⅝ in. wide, recurved, obtusely 2-fid. *fl.* ¾ in. across; sep. sub-spatulate; pet. dirty orange with red streaks; lip dark purple and yellow with 2 finely hairy stripes; scape 1 to 1½ ft. h., erect; branches few, tipped by short racemes. May. India. 1840. (B.M. 7099.) SYN. *C. peduncularis, Vanda peduncularis.*

E. C.

**COT'ULA** (*kotule*, a small cup; the bases of the clasping leaves form a cup). FAM. *Compositae.* A genus of about 60 species, mostly natives of the S. Hemisphere. Leaves alternate, more or less pinnately cut. Flower-heads stalked, discoid, many-flowered, bell-shaped or hemispherical; outer florets without petals or nearly so, inner 4-toothed, sometimes male; receptacle naked. Pappus absent, achenes glabrous or compressed. The Cotulas, at one time placed under Leptinella, are hardy perennial carpeting plants for the rock-garden, especially for the waterside or as a carpet for bulbs. They are apt to spread unduly unless kept in check, and grow well in ordinary soil. Propagated by rooted pieces or by seed and generally easily established.

**C. acaenoi'des.** A synonym of *C. reptans.*

**C. barba'ta.** A synonym of *Cenia barbata.*

**C. coronopifo'lia.** Brass Buttons. Glabrous succulent perennia, with creeping, rooting stems ascending at tips, branched, 2 to 10 in. h. *l.* linear-lanceolate or oblong-lanceolate, ½ to 2 in. long, coarsely toothed, or lobed, sometimes entire, base clasping. *fl.-heads* bright yellow, up to ½ in. across; peduncles slender, longer than l.; female fl. in a single series without cor. *Achenes* of ray-fl. oblong, broadly winged, of disk-fl. smaller with much narrower wing. S. Temperate Zone.

**C. dioi'ca.** Stem creeping, rather stout, mat-forming; 2 to 3 in. h. *l.* linear or spatulate, deeply pinnately cut, obtuse, 1 to 2 in. long, dark green. *fl.-heads* pale yellowish, small, on slender scapes about as long as l. New Zealand .SYN. *Leptinella dioica*

**C. lana'ta.** Prostrate, woolly. *l.* oblong, obtuse, pinnatifid; segs. acute, upper pinnatifid-toothed. *fl.-heads* ¼ in. across; involucral bracts in 3 or 4 series, glabrous, glandular, roundish-elliptic; peduncles shorter than l. Lord Auckland Is. SYN. *Leptinella lanata*.

**C. mecel'leri.** A synonym of *C. potentillina*.

**C. plumo'sa.** About 6 in. h., erect. *l.* graceful, feathery, hairy, linear-oblong, 3-pinnatifid; ultimate segs. awl-shaped. *fl.-heads* about ¼ in. across, involucral bracts in one series; peduncles as long as l.-stalks. Lord Auckland's Is. SYN. *Leptinella plumosa*.

**C. potentilli'na.** Stem creeping, tips ascending. *l.* linear-obovate, 2 to 5 in. long, deeply pinnatifid, gland-dotted. *fl.-heads* about ⅓ in. across; peduncles shorter than l. New Zealand.

**C. pyrethrifo'lia.** Aromatic. Stout, often glabrous perennial with creeping rhizome and prostrate or finally ascending stems. *l.* ½ to 1½ in. long, pinnatifid; segs. 5 to 8 alternate, narrow linear to linear-oblong, obtuse, $\frac{1}{10}$ to ¼ in. long, fleshy. *fl.-heads* unisexual, up to ¾ in. across; female fl. 4-toothed, male 4-lobed. New Zealand.

**C. rep'tans.** Slender, creeping, glabrous perennial, with sometimes a few soft hairs, especially on peduncles. *l.* pinnate; segs. ovate, toothed or pinnately divided into short linear lobes. *fl.-heads* about ⅙ in. across; involucral bracts nearly orbicular; female fl. in several rows; cor. very short and broad, inflated, narrowed at mouth, 2- or 3-toothed; receptacle conical; peduncle longer than l. New S. Wales to Tasmania. var. **ma'jor,** rather coarser and parts larger. Victoria, Tasmania.

**C. scario'sa.** A synonym of **C. rep'tans.**

**C. squal'ida.*** Mat-forming with long creeping, slender, branched stems, silky or hairy. *l.* linear-obovate, 1 to 2 in. long, deeply pinnatifid; segs. recurved, deeply cut, usually along upper margin only. *fl.-heads* unisexual; male heads about ⅙ in., female ⅓ in. across; involucral bracts purplish, incurved over fl. in female heads, hiding them. New Zealand.

**COTYLEDON.** The first-formed leaves of the plant, forming part of the embryo in the seed.

**COTYLE'DON** (*kotyle*, a cavity; in reference to the cup-like leaves of *Cotyledon Umbilicus*, now *Umbilicus pendulinus*). FAM. *Crassulaceae*. Cotyledon, as now understood, includes some 30 species occurring in S. Africa (1 in Eritrea and Arabia), but formerly the genus also included a large number of species which are now separated into a number of different genera, viz. Adromischus, Chiastophyllum, Echeveria, Orostachys, Pachyphytum, Pistorinia, Rosularia, and Umbilicus. The true Cotyledons fall into two classes, those with shrubby growth whose leaves are opposite and persistent and others with much thickened, often fleshy stems and alternate leaves which are renewed annually; the leaves are always succulent, sometimes flattened, sometimes cylindrical, but the flowers of all are very similar in structure; the inflorescence is terminal, a false umbel; the flowers are pendent, 5-partite, the petals green, yellow, or red, united into a tube, the tips free and reflexed, the 10 stamens inserted at the base.

The genera allied to, but no longer included in Cotyledon may be roughly distinguished as follows:

ADROMISCHUS, habit similar but inflorescence a long slender spike with almost sessile, erect, narrowly tubular flowers, generally inconspicuous; 20 sp., S. Africa.

CHIASTOPHYLLUM, chiefly distinguished from Cotyledon by the unusual form of the styles; 1 sp., Caucasus.

ECHEVERIA, leaves in rosettes, inflorescence lateral, not terminal, corolla tube swollen at the base, pinched in near the mouth, usually brightly coloured; 150 sp., all American.

OROSTACHYS, leaves in rosettes, inflorescence very many flowered, terminal; more closely allied to Sedum; 10 sp., N. Asia.

PACHYPHYTUM, similar to Echeveria but the leaves in open rosettes and much thicker, often cylindrical; 8 sp., Mexico.

PISTORINIA, leaves cylindrical, inflorescence terminal; annuals; 2 sp., Spain and N. Africa.

ROSULARIA, leaves in rosettes, flowers bell-shaped, inconspicuous; more closely allied to Sedum; 20 sp., Asia Minor eastwards.

UMBILICUS, leaves alternate, usually stalked, often peltate with a central depression, flowers in a terminal, simple or branched raceme, flowers bell-shaped, inconspicuous; 16 sp., Europe and Asia.

Cotyledons need a sunny position in a cool house with a minimum temperature of 40 to 45° F.; the soil should be very well drained and water given in moderation; the deciduous species need no water in the summer when they are resting and leafless. The coloration of the leaves is intensified under dry conditions and in poor soil, but the lower leaves are then apt to fall; it is usually possible to cut off the leafy top and re-root it; the leafless base may throw out side shoots and should be retained for a time. Propagation is by seed, cuttings, or leaf cuttings; as Cotyledons hybridize easily seedlings may not be true. Normally these plants are free from pests but occasionally the inflorescence is attacked by Aphides; spraying with derris or nicotine will destroy this pest.

**C. adun'ca.** A synonym of *Pachyphytum Hookeri*.

**C. agavoi'des.** A synonym of *Echeveria agavoides*.

**C. Ai'zoon.** A synonym of *Rosularia Aizoon*.

**C. atropurpu'rea.** A synonym of *Echeveria atropurpurea*.

**C. Bar'beyi.** Shrubby, tall. *l.* obovate, 4 in. long, 2 to 3 in. wide, green. *fl.* 1 in. long, green and red, with glandular hairs. Eritrea and S. Arabia. 1892.

**C. cacalioi'des.** Stems stout, fleshy, bare below except for the persistent l. bases. *l.* alternate, in a rosette at top of stem, appearing only during the growing season (autumn to spring), 2½ in. long, slender, almost cylindrical, grey-green. *fl.* yellowish-red. Cape Province. Should be rested in summer.

**C. caespito'sa.** A synonym of *Echeveria caespitosa*.

**C. califor'nica.** A synonym of *Echeveria Cotyledon*.

**C. carnic'olor.** A synonym of *Echeveria carnicolor*.

**C. chrysan'tha.** A synonym of *Rosularia pallida*.

**C. clavifo'lia.** A synonym of *Adromischus clavifolius*.

**C. coccin'ea.** A synonym of *Echeveria coccinea*.

**C. Coo'peri.** A synonym of *Adromischus Cooperi*.

**C. Corderoy'i.** A synonym of *Echeveria Corderoyi*.

**C. crista'ta.** A synonym of *Adromischus cristatus*.

**C. ed'ulis.** A synonym of *Echeveria edulis*.

**C. el'egans.** A synonym of *Echeveria elegans*.

**C. farino'sa.** A synonym of *Echeveria farinosa*.

**C. fascicula'ris.** A synonym of *Cotyledon paniculata*.

**C. Flanagan'ii.** Stems stout, woody, branched. *l.* few, opposite, almost cylindrical, slender, 3 to 4 in. long, grey-green. *fl.* 1¼ in. long, red. Cape Province.

**C. gibbiflo'ra.** A synonym of *Echeveria gibbiflora*.

**C. glab'ra.** A synonym of *Rosularia glabra*.

**C. glau'ca.** A synonym of *Echeveria glauca*.

**C. globulariaefo'lia.** A synonym of *Rosularia globulariaefolia*.

**C. grandiflo'ra.** A synonym of *Echeveria grandiflora*.

**C. hemisphae'rica.** A synonym of *Adromischus hemisphaericus*.

**C. hispan'ica.** A synonym of *Pistorinia hispanica*.

**C. libanot'ica.** A synonym of *Rosularia Sempervivum*.

**C. linguaefo'lia.** A synonym of *Echeveria linguaefolia*.

**C. lusita'nica.** A synonym of *Umbilicus erectus*.

**C. macran'tha.** Shrubby type. *l.* opposite, rounded above, narrower at base, grass-green with a red edge. *fl.* ¾ in. long, red. Winter. Cape Province. (R.H. 1903, 452.)

**C. macula'ta.** A synonym of *Adromischus maculatus*.

**C. mamilla'ris.** A synonym of *Adromischus mamillaris*.

**C. nodulo'sa.** A synonym of *Echeveria nodulosa*.

**C. nu'da.** A synonym of *Echeveria nuda*.

**C. oppositifo'lia.** A synonym of *Chiastophyllum oppositifolium*.

**C. orbicula'ta.** Shrubby type. *l.* roundish above, narrowed to base, whitish-grey with a red edge. *fl.* ½ in. long, yellowish-red. Summer. Cape Province. (B.M. 321.) A variable species. var. **oophyl'la** has very small egg-shaped l.

**C. Pachyphy'tum.** A synonym of *Pachyphytum bracteosum*.

**C. panicula'ta.** Stem stout, fleshy, up to 5 ft. h. *l.* alternate, crowded into a rosette at the top of stem, wide and flat, 2 to 3 in. long, 1 to 2 in. wide, grey-green, deciduous. *fl.* 1 in. long, red with green border. Summer, during resting period. Cape Province. (B.M. 5602 as *C. fascicularis*.)

**C. Peacock'ii.** A synonym of *Echeveria Peacockii.*

**C. Pestaloz'zae.** A synonym of *Rosularia Sempervivum.*

**C. platyphyl'la.** A synonym of *Rosularia platyphylla.*

**C. pubes'cens.** A synonym of *Echeveria pubescens.*

**C. pulverulen'ta.** A synonym of *Echeveria pulverulenta.*

**C. pu'mila.** A synonym of *Echeveria pumila.*

**C. Purpus'ii.** A synonym of *Echeveria Purpusii.*

**C. reticula'ta.** Stem short and very broad, fleshy, covered with persistent remains of old infl. like thorns. *l.* alternate, 4 to 6, crowded at top of stem, deciduous, almost cylindrical, short, grey-green. *fl.* erect, ½ in. long, greenish-yellow striped with dull red. Summer. S. Africa. (G.C. 21 (1897), 282.) Rest during summer.

**C. ro'sea.** A synonym of *Echeveria rosea.*

**C. secun'da.** A synonym of *Echeveria secunda.*

**C. sedoi'des.** A synonym of *Sedum Candollei.*

**C. Sempervi'vum.** A synonym of *Rosularia Sempervivum.*

**C. serra'ta.** A synonym of *Rosularia serrata.*

**C. simplicifo'lia,** a garden name for *Chiastophyllum oppositifolium.*

**C. spino'sa.** A synonym of *Orostachys spinosus.*

**C. teretifo'lia.** Stem 4 to 6 in. h. *l.* opposite, 4 in. long, almost cylindrical, flattened at tip and pointed, covered with soft hairs, pale green. *fl.* yellow. Summer. Cape Province. (B.M. 6235.)

**C. tuberculo'sa.** Stem thick, fleshy, covered with old l. bases. *l.* almost cylindrical, scattered, deciduous. *fl.* 2 in. long, orange-red, hairy. Cape Province. (B.M. 2044 as *Cotyledon curviflora.*)

**C. turkestan'ica.** A synonym of *Rosularia turkestanica.*

**C. Umbil'icus.** A synonym of *Umbilicus pendulinus.*

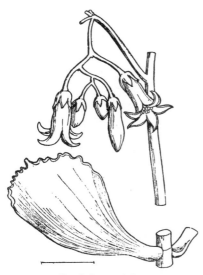

*Cotyledon undulata*

**C. undula'ta.\*** Shrubby type. *l.* narrowed at base, wider at top with a beautiful wavy edge, thickly covered with white meal. *fl.* ½ in. long, cream with a red stripe. Summer. Cape Province. (B.M. 7931.) The beauty of this plant depends on the perfect condition of the l.; watering overhead should be avoided or the meal will be washed off and the appearance spoiled.

**C. veluti'na.** Shrubby type. *l.* opposite, roundish, softly hairy at least when young. *fl.* yellow and red. Cape Province. (B.M. 5684.)

**C. Wallich'ii.** Stem stout, fleshy, branched, covered with old l. bases. *l.* alternate, crowded at top of branches, cylindrical, 2 to 4 in. long, grey-green, deciduous. *fl.* ½ in. long, greenish-yellow. Cape Province.

V. H.

**COUCH GRASS,** Quick, Twitch (*Agropyrum repens*). A noxious weed, very troublesome unless thorough means are taken to eradicate it. The long underground sharp-pointed stolons must be got rid of by forking out, taking care that no pieces are left behind since many nodes develop on them, every one of which is capable of forming a fresh plant. The stolons are not usually very deep-seated in heavy soil but often penetrate rather deeply in light soils where, however, they may be drawn out by means of suitable tools, such as the Simar cultivator, on areas large enough to warrant their use. The pieces should be turned to useful manure on the compost heap, not burned as was at one time the common and wasteful practice.

A

*Coulombie'ri,* in honour of M. Coulombier, nurseryman of Vitry-sur-Seine, *c.* 1887.

*Coult'eri,* in honour of Dr. T. Coulter of Dublin, 1793–1843, who collected in Mexico and California.

*coum,* possibly from a Hebrew name.

**COUMARIN.** An aromatic substance to which the scent of new-mown hay is due, abundant in, for example, sweet Vernal Grass, *Anthoxanthum odoratum.*

**COUNTRYMAN'S TREACLE.** *See* **Ruta graveolens.**

**COURAN'TIA.** An old name for **Echeveria Rosea.**

*Courba'ril,* W. Indian name.

**COUROUP'ITA** (native name). FAM. *Lecythidaceae.* A genus of about 9 species of Trop. American trees. Leaves alternate, oblong, entire or with rounded teeth. Flowers in racemes from the trunk or larger branches as a rule, showy; calyx tube top-shaped, limb 6-lobed; petals 6, unequal, spreading or recurved, borne on a disk; stamens many, in 2 sets—one in a ring in the middle of the flower around the ovary, the other from one side, longer. Fruit large, globular or nearly so, indehiscent, with many seeds embedded in pulp. *C. guianensis* needs stove conditions. It is interesting for the large fruit, the pulp of which is eaten by negroes and is used in making beverage while the shell is used for utensils.

**C. guianen'sis.** Cannon-ball Tree. Tall soft-wooded tree. *l.* oblong-obovate, elliptic or broadly-lanceolate, acute, entire or nearly so. *fl.* with concave pet. about 2 in. long, yellow, tinged red without, crimson-lilac within, very showy, in racemes 2 to 3 ft. long. *fr.* globular or nearly so, 6 to 8 in. across, reddish, hard without, pulpy within and with an unpleasant odour when ripe. Guiana. (B.M. 3158–9.)

**COURSONNE.** A small fruiting-lateral in pears or apples.

*Courtois'ii,* in honour of Richard J. Courtois, 1806–35, Professor of Botany, Lutlich, writer on horticulture.

**COUSIN'IA** (in honour of M. Cousin, a French botanist). FAM. *Compositae.* A genus of about 100 species of biennial and perennial, rarely annual, herbs. Easily grown and increased by division in spring or by seed sown in spring. Except *C. wolgensis* all are Asiatic, the exception a native of S. Russia.

**C. hys'trix.** Biennial about 2 ft. h. Stem branching at top. *l.* pinnatifid or pinnate, with spiny teeth, cobwebby on both surfaces. *fl.-heads* purplish, solitary, somewhat globose, woolly. June. E Mediterranean. 1838.

**COUSSAPO'A** (from *Coussapoui,* Caribbean name of 2 of the species). FAM. *Moraceae.* A genus of about 20 species of trees and shrubs with milky juice, sometimes climbing or epiphytic, natives of Trop. S. America. Leaves alternate, entire, leathery, pinnate- or 3-nerved. Flowers dioecious, in a globose head, solitary or in pairs in the leaf-axils; male heads few flowered, female heads large or small and clustered. For cultivation, *see* **Ficus.**

**C. dealba'ta.\*** *l.* elliptic, about 1 ft. long, 6 in. wide, deep green above, snowy white on account of a thick coat of silky hairs beneath especially on the young unfolding l. Peru. 1867. (I.H. 1870, 4.) SYN. *Ficus dealbata.* Very distinct and beautiful greenhouse shrub.

**COUTAR'EA** (native name in Guiana). FAM. *Rubiaceae.* A genus of about 5 species of evergreen trees or shrubs, natives of Trop. America. Leaves opposite, membranous, ovate, slender-pointed; stipules short, acute; stalks short. Flowers showy, scented, terminal, solitary or in cymes of 3; 5- or 6-merous. Needing stove conditions with a compost of loam, sand, and peat, and readily rooted from cuttings in the same soil under a hand-glass in heat.

**C. Scherffia'na.** Tall shrub with forked branches. *l.* ovate, narrowed to base, flat, shining; stipules broadly triangular. *fl.* white, solitary, in leafy cymes; cor. 2 in. long, tubular-bell-shaped, ribbed, lobes spreading. Colombia. 1876. (I.H. 1878, t. 321.)

**C. specio'sa.** Tree of about 25 ft. *l.* ovate, glabrous; stipules broad, short, acute; stalks very short. *fl.* purple, large, broad, funnel-shaped; cymes 3-fld. Guiana. 1803. SYN. *C. hexandra.*

**COUTOUB'EA** (native Caribbean name of 1 species). FAM. *Gentianaceae.* A genus of about 5 species of erect herbs natives of Trop. America. Leaves opposite, rarely whorled, thinnish, 1-nerved, sessile or stem-clasping on 4-angled, usually branched, branches usually opposite, thickened at nodes. Flowers white or purplish in terminal and lateral spikes or racemes, dense or loose, bracteate; corolla salver-shaped with an equal cylindrical tube, 4-lobed, naked in throat. Easily grown in the same way as other tender annuals.

**C. ramo'sa.** Stems spreading, 1 to 2 ft. h. *l.* oblong-lanceolate, narrowed to both ends. *fl.* white, remote, lower part leafy. Guiana. 1824.

**C. spica'ta.** 2 to 3 ft. h. *l.* lanceolate, narrowed to both ends. *fl.* rather close together, white, reddish in throat, spikes loose. July. Guiana. 1823.

**COUVE TRONCHUDA** (*Brassica oleracea costata*). Portuguese Cabbage. Grown for the midribs of its leaves which are cooked like Seakale and have an agreeable and distinct flavour. Seed should be sown in early February in gentle heat and a second sowing in mid-March in a frame or on a warm border outside with the usual precautions against insect pests and birds. The seedlings raised from the February sowing should be pricked out in rich soil, and in due course, hardened off and planted out in deeply dug rich soil 3½ ft. apart each way. Those of the March sowing should be transplanted the same distance apart as soon as large enough. Every effort should be made to induce strong growth by the use of liquid manure occasionally, or by a dressing of nitrate of soda or similar quick-acting nitrogenous manure.

**COW BELL.** *See* **Silene vulgaris** in Supplement.

**COW BERRY.** *See* **Vaccinium Vitis-Idaea.**

**COW ITCH.** *See* **Mucuna.**

**COW PARSLEY, COW PARSNIP.** *See* **Heracleum.**

**COW PEA.** *See* **Vigna sinensis.**

**COW TREE.** *See* **Brosimum Galactodendron.**

**COW WHEAT.** *See* **Melampyrum.**

**COWAGE.** *See* **Mucuna.**

**COW'ANIA** (in honour of James Cowan, a London merchant who introduced many plants from Mexico and Peru). FAM. *Rosaceae.* A genus of 4 or 5 species of evergreen shrubs inhabiting Mexico and SW. United States. Leaves alternate, often in clusters, lobed. Flowers rose-like, solitary, terminal on short side branchlets; sepals and petals 5; stamens numerous. Fruit with 1 to 12 pistils, each with a long persistent feathery style. They are sun-loving shrubs, on the tender side, and may be planted at the foot of a sunny wall in well-drained loam mixed with lime-rubble or mortar.

**C. mexica'na,** has been regarded both as a variety of, and a synonym for *C. Stansburiana* and no doubt most of the plants so called in gardens are *C. Stansburiana.*

**C. plica'ta.\*** Stiff shrub up to 6 or 7 ft., shoots reddish, woolly and glandular. *l.* ¼ to ⅜ in. long, obovate, pinnately 5- to 9-lobed, densely white-downy beneath, covered with stalked glands. *fl.*

rose-like, 1½ in. wide, solitary, terminal, rich rose-colour. June. Styles of the *fr.* (achene) silky-hairy, 1¼ in. long. New Mexico. SW. United States, usually on limestone. 1830. (B.M. 8889.)

*Cowania plicata*

**C. Stansburia'na.** Aromatic, evergreen shrub, 6 to 8 ft. of very stiff habit; shoots glandular. *l.* 3- or 5-lobed, ¼ to ½ in. long, lobes linear, margins revolute, glandular above, white-downy beneath. *fl.* solitary, terminal, white or pale yellow, ¾ in wide; cal. funnel-shaped with 5 downy lobes. July. *fr.* (achene) terminated by the persistent silky, feathery style 1 to 2 in. long. SW. United States.

W. J. B.

**COWDIE PINE.** *See* **Agathis australis.**

**COW-DUNG.** Highly valued for potting purposes, decaying somewhat slowly and therefore never raising the soil temperature rapidly or unduly. The dung should be collected and stored in a shed, frequently turned and allowed to become nearly dry before being used. For manure-water, fresh cow-dung may be used if plenty of clear water is added.

**COWHAGE.** *See* **Mucuna.**

**COWHAGE CHERRY.** *See* **Malpighia urens.**

**COWHORN ORCHID.** *See* **Myrmecophila tibicinis.**

**COWITCH CHERRY.** *See* **Malpighia urens.**

**COWL.** A tub for water.

**COW'S LUNGWORT.** An old name for **Verbascum Thapsus.**

**COWSLIP** (*Primula veris*). Grown in the same way as the Primrose and Polyanthus and producing large, sweet-scented trusses under cultivation.

**COW'S-TAIL PINE.** *See* **Cephalotaxus drupacea.**

**CRAB APPLE.** *See* **Malus pumila.**

**CRAB SPIDER.** *See* **Spiders.**

*Crab'ro,* hornet.

**CRAB'S EYE VINE.** *See* **Abrus precatorius.**

**CRAB-WOOD.** *See* **Schaeffera frutescens.**

**CRACK WILLOW.** *See* **Salix fragilis.**

**CRACKING** or **SPLITTING.** The causes of cracking in stems and fruits are many. Frost is probably the most serious and in severe weather splitting may occur in the bark of many fruit-trees, e.g. Apples, Rhododendrons, and in many woodland trees. In some heathers, splitting of the stems under such conditions, quickly kills the plants. In fruits the cracking of Apples is usually induced by early injury to the skin through attack by the Scab fungus (*see* **Apple Scab**) but some Apples not diseased may crack where the tree is weak and suffers great drought followed by heavy rain. Tomatoes which have been very dry at the roots and then heavily watered will quickly show fruit-splitting. In vegetables, Carrots and Potatoes are often badly cracked or split owing to similar very dry conditions checking growth, with the result that, following rain, the resumption of growth tends to cause cracking. *See* **Carrot diseases** and **Potato Hollow Heart.**

D. E. G.

**CRAM'BE** (Greek name for *Brassica oleracea*). FAM. *Cruciferae*. A genus of about 20 species of large annual or perennial herbs in Cent. and S. Europe, Asia Minor, Cent. Asia, and Trop. Africa. Stems often tall and branched, lower leaves very large, upper small or absent, flowers small, white or sulphur, very numerous, scented. Fruit 1-seeded, globose or ovoid. *C. maritima* is the Seakale (q.v.). The perennial species mentioned below are handsome hardy foliage plants, especially *C. cordifolia*, easily grown in good loam (not acid) and increased by division of the roots in spring or by seed. The perennial species flower in the third year from seed and thereafter annually.

KEY
1. Lower l. roundish or cordate     2
1. Lower l. deeply divided     3
2. Glabrous; l. elliptic or nearly round; corymbs
    close     C. maritima
2. Somewhat hairy; l. cordate; corymbs
    spreading     C. cordifolia
3. Racemes corymbose at fl.-time; l. irregularly
    deeply cut     C. tataria
3. Racemes loose at fl.-time. Lower l. pinnatisect     C. orientalis

**C. cordifo'lia.** Very large perennial herb. Stems 3 to 6 ft. h., branching. *l.* fleshy, cordate, 1 to 3 ft. long, unequally lobed or toothed, stalked; upper *l.* ovate, acute, more or less deeply toothed, almost smooth. *fl.* on a loose raceme in much-branched panicles. June. Caucasus. var. **Kotschya'na** has larger *fl.* on longer pedicels. Persia, Afghanistan, &c.

**C. jun'cea.** A variety of *C. orientalis*.

**C. Kotschya'na.** A variety of *C. cordifolia*.

**C. marit'ima.** Glabrous, glaucous, perennial with a thick root. Stem 1 to 2 ft. h., thick, branched. *l.* fleshy-elliptic or nearly round, wavy-lobed, stalked, 5 to 12 in. long. *fl.* in a close corymb. Europe, including Britain. (E.B. 80.) *See* **Seakale.**

**C. orienta'lis.** Perennial with a brown carrot-like root. Stem 2½ to 5 ft. h., branched from base, erect. *l.* at base large, pinnatipartite, end lobe obovate, teeth irregular, large, with appressed down above, softly hairy, becoming rough on veins beneath, stalks bristly; upper *l.* much smaller. *fl.* in a loose raceme. E. Mediterranean eastwards to Persia. var. **jun'cea,** more slender, 1 to 2½ ft. h., branches thin, *l.* smooth above. 1820.

**C. tata'ria.** Perennial with long blackish-brown carrot-like root. Stem erect 1 to 3 ft. h., branched from base. *l.* at base large, irregularly deeply divided and toothed, fleshy, grey-green; stalk bristly; veins reddish; upper *l.* much smaller. *fl.* in a corymbose panicle, close at first. E. Europe, Asia Minor. 1789.

**C. tatar'ica.** A synonym of *C. tataria*.

**CRANBERRIES.** There are several varieties of Cranberries (*Vaccinium*) known in America where Cranberry growing is practised, as well as that known as the American Cranberry (*V. macrocarpum*). The fruit is rather sour, but when cooked in tarts, &c., with sufficient sugar to sweeten, it is usually appreciated. When once established, little or no further attention is required, except preventing other trees or bushes from smothering the tough, wiry growths. The fruit, which is ripe in September, varies in colour from red to purple, and in form from round to oval. Propagation is usually effected by division in the early spring.

The cultivation of the Cranberry has not been seriously attempted in England, though those best capable of judging contend that it could be grown to profit in damp acid soils. In America the growing of the berries for market is chiefly done in Massachusetts and New Jersey. The land for growing Cranberries there is flooded from autumn to May with from 18 in. to 2 ft. of water. On the first of the latter month the water is drained away, and the plants soon flower.

**CRANBERRY.** *See* **Vaccinium Oxycoccus.**

**CRANE-FLIES** or **DADDY LONGLEGS.** These familiar insects are the parents of the ubiquitous Leather-jackets, which are especially troublesome on lawns and in freshly converted wasteland and pasture, and resemble Wire-worms in their wide range of food plants. They are particularly prevalent in the moister parts of the country and in soils which are inadequately drained, for Leather-jackets, especially when young, readily succumb to dry conditions. They attack a wide variety of crops, including cereals, grasses, vegetables, soft fruits, herbaceous and other plants, and feed chiefly on the roots and underground portions. Feeding occurs at night both above and below soil level, and they sever the base of the stems in a manner resembling that of Surface Caterpillars. The first sign of attack is the wilting of the plants and the presence of bare patches on lawns, greens, courts, and in cornfields. Leather-jackets are frequently introduced into potting composts and glass-house borders in loam owing to their 'earthy' colour which renders them difficult to detect. Not all species of Crane-flies are destructive in their larval stage to plants for some feed only on dead and decaying organic matter, rotting tree stumps, and in thatch. The species which occur most frequently in gardens are the Common Crane-fly, *Tipula oleracea*, the Marsh Crane-fly, *T. paludosa*, and the Common Spotted Crane-fly, *Pachyrrhina maculata*. The body colour of the first named is greyish, that of the second is reddish, while the last named has a yellow and black striped abdomen. The legless larvae of these species resemble one another and, when fully fed, are 1 to 1½ in. long, brownish, greyish, or nearly black, with a tough leathery skin. The adult flies appear throughout the summer, but are particularly abundant in late August and September. The small, black, oval, seed-like eggs are laid in the soil, one female being capable of laying as many as 300 eggs. The eggs hatch in about a fortnight, and the young Leather-jackets begin to feed on the roots of plants and continue to do so during the autumn, winter, and spring. Many succumb if the weather is warm and dry, but flourish in moist, cool weather. They become fully fed in early summer and pupate in the soil. In due course the pupae push themselves partly above ground to permit the emergence of the adult flies. Many birds, e.g. Lapwings, Rooks, and Starlings, feed on Leather-jackets, but the greatest mortality occurs when the young larvae are subjected to drought conditions in late summer. During a drought at this season the Crane-flies tend to lay their eggs on irrigated turf, e.g. cricket pitches and tennis-courts, in preference to parched pasture.

Cultural methods of control apply to these pests as to the Wire-worm, which they resemble in their choice of habitat. Newly broken grass- and waste-land should be broken up in spring and early summer and kept free from weeds before planting in autumn with such crops as Strawberry. The soil should be adequately drained, for a moist, sour, badly drained soil attracts the flies and provides conditions favourable to egg-laying. Frequent disturbance of the soil by regular hoeing will not only destroy wild food plants but injure many Leather-jackets through the mechanical action of the hoe-blade. Infested ground between crops may be treated with D.D.T. emulsion or dressed with 2 oz. of flake naphthalene to the square yard, and the preparation lightly forked or watered in. Good results will follow an application of a poison bait consisting of Paris green and bran (see **Surface Caterpillars**). Infested lawns should be thoroughly rolled, more especially in the autumn and preferably towards evening when the larvae are near the surface— this operation resulting both in the crushing of their bodies and in the consolidation of the soil which has been disturbed by their movements. Large numbers of larvae may be collected beneath tarpaulins and rubber-mats placed on the turf after a copious watering has been given.

G. F. W.

**CRANE'S-BILL.** *See* **Geranium**.

**CRANIOLAR'IA** an'nua. *See* **Martynia louisiana**. **C. frutico'sa.** *See* **Pentarhaphia Craniolaria**.

*Crantz'ii*, in honour of H. J. N. von Crantz, 1722–99, botanical writer.

**CRAPE FERN.** *See* **Todea**.

**CRAPE MYRTLE.** *See* **Lagerstroemia indica**.

**CRASPE'DIA** (*kraspedon*, a fringe; in allusion to the feathery pappus). FAM. *Compositae*. A genus of 4 or 5 species of perennial herbs. Leaves radical or alternate, entire. They are half-hardy or cold greenhouse plants. The following species may be treated as a half-hardy annual.

**C. uniflo'ra.** Perennial herb, more or less covered with woolly hairs. Radical *l.* obovate-oblong to lanceolate, long-stalked, 2 to 5 in. long, up to ½ in. wide; stem *l.* smaller, stem-clasping. *fl.-heads* closely packed in a globose, solitary, compound cluster, ½ to 1¼ in. wide, at top of an erect stalk 6 to 18 in. long, clear yellow. June. Australia, Tasmania, New Zealand. 1861. (B.M. 5271 as *C. Richea*; B.R. 1908 as *C. glauca*.) SYN. *C. pilosa*. var. **macroceph'ala**, tall, nearly glabrous, *fl.*-clusters larger. (B.M. 3415 as *C. macrocephala*.) Very variable species.

*crassi-*, in compound words, signifying thick.

**CRAS'SULA** (*crassus*, thick; referring to the thickened leaves). FAM. *Crassulaceae*. A large genus of some 300 species of succulent shrubs and herbs, mostly occurring in S. Africa, a few in Trop. E. Africa, Arabia, and Madagascar. The leaves are always opposite, sometimes crowded into basal rosettes, very varied in form and texture; the flowers usually have the parts in fives (but may be 3 to 9) and the number of stamens equals that of the petals which are free or shortly united at the base, spreading, small, white, yellow, or red. Only 1 species (*C. sarcocaulis*) is hardy in this country and hybrids are very uncommon. They need the same growing conditions as Cotyledon (q.v.) and may be propagated by seed, division, or leaf cuttings.

**C. abyssin'ica.** A synonym of *C. alba*. **A**

**C. acutifo'lia.** Stem woody, prostrate. *l.* small, cylindrical, green. *fl.* small. *infl.* terminal. S. Africa.

**C. al'ba.** Stem woody. *l.* flat, larger towards the base, ciliate. *fl.* white, small, in large corymbs. Eritrea and Abyssinia, south to the Transvaal. SYN. *C. abyssinica*.

**C. albiflo'ra.** Stem erect. *l.* ovate, papillose. *fl.* white. Cape Province. (B.M. 2391.)

**C. arbores'cens.** Shrubby, stem stout, 2 to 3 ft. h. *l.* rounded, narrowed at base, fleshy, grey-green with a red margin and fine dots all over the surface. *fl.* white, later turning red, in terminal panicles, rarely produced in cultivation. Cape Province. (B.M. 384.) SYN. *C. Cotyledon*. **A**

**C. argen'tea.** Shrubby, up to 10 ft. h. in nature. *l.* ovate, shining green. *fl.* pink, in terminal panicles. Cape Province. (D.C.Pl.Gr. 79.) SYN. *C. portulacea*.

**C. ar'ta.** Similar to *C. deceptrix* but smaller; the closely packed *l.* pale green with raised grey lines. Namaqualand.

**C. barba'ta.** Rosette stemless, 1½ in. across. *l.* wide, curved inwards, green with long white hairs along edge. *fl.* white, in small, close heads. S. Africa. The flowering rosette dies but others are usually formed around it.

**C. Bark'lyi.** Stems short, branching. *l.* concave, each pair at right angles, closely overlapping, forming a column ⅓ to ¾ in. wide, green. *fl.* white, scented, in a dense, sessile head. Cape Province. (B.M. 8421.)

**C. Bolus'ii.** A synonym of *C. Cooperi*.

**C. cephaloph'ora.** Stems short, branching. *l.* crowded, convex on both sides, 1 to 3 in. long, greenish-white. *fl.* white, in close panicles. Cape Province.

**C. coccin'ea.** A synonym of *Rochea coccinea*.

**C. columna'ris.** Stem very short. *l.* in 4 vertical rows, upper side concave, the edge turning in so that a close column is formed, ¾ to 1 in. wide, green with short white cilia along the edge. *fl.* white, scented, in a tight hemispherical, sessile head. Namaqualand. The plant dies after flowering and does not always make offsets.

**C. conges'ta.** Stem short. *l.* in 4 rows, incurved but not lying over one another. *fl.* white in a tight hemispherical head. Cape Province.

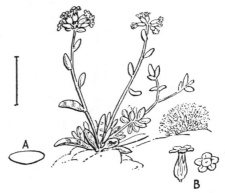

*Crassula Cooperi*

A, leaf section.  B, flower enlarged.

**C. Coo'peri.** Stems thin, branching freely, forming mats. *l.* crowded, about ½ in. long, pale green with dark depressed dots above, red beneath, ciliate. *fl.* pale pink, in few-fld. panicles. Cape Province, Transvaal. (B.M. 6194.) SYN. *C. Bolusii*.

**C. coralli'na.** Small plants with weak, prostrate stems and small, thick, elliptical *l.*, pale green, upper surface dusted with white wax like hoar frost. *fl.* yellow, from the axils of upper *l.* S. Africa. SYN. *C. dasyphylla*.

**C. corda'ta.** Stems slender, fleshy. *l.* heart-shaped, stalked, ¾ in. long, entire, covered with thick white meal, reddish at edge. *fl.* white. Cape Province. (D.C.Pl.Gr. 121.)

**C. corymbulo'sa.** Stems very short. *l.* crowded, narrow, green; the rosette elongates at flowering time and dies after, but fresh growths appear at the base. *fl.* white, in a long, open thyrse. Cape Province.

**C. Cotyle'don.** A synonym of *C. arborescens*.

**C. dasyphyl'la.** A synonym of *C. corallina*.

**C. decep'trix.** Stem very short, branching and forming clumps. *l.* crowded, very thick, ¾ in. long, flat above, almost hemispherical beneath, whitish-grey, covered with a raised network of lines. *fl.* white, in a slender-stemmed head. Namaqualand.

**C. deltoi'dea.** Stem short, branching. *l.* united at base, very thick, tapering, upper side channelled, lower bluntly keeled, grey-green and mealy. *fl.* small, dirty white, in a terminal infl. Namaqualand, S. Africa. SYN. *C. rhomboidea*.

**C. dichot'oma.** A synonym of *Vauanthes dichotoma*.

**C. falca'ta.** Stem erect, leafy to base, up to 2 ft. h. *l.* 3 to 4 in. long, sickle-shaped, oblique, grey. *fl.* scarlet, in close flat, showy, terminal corymbs. Cape Province. (B.M. 2035.) SYN. *Rochea falcata*. Useful as a decorative plant.

**C. Gill'ii.** Rosettes almost stemless, forming clumps. *l.* ovate, pointed, lying closely one above another, edge ciliate, glaucous green. *fl.* white, in a round head on a long, slender stalk. Natal.

**C. hemisphae'rica.** Rosettes stemless. *l.* rounded, thick, closely overlapping and turned downwards, ciliate, green, purple below. *fl.* small, white, in an open thyrsus. S. Africa.

**C. impres'sa.** A synonym of *C. Schmidtii*.

**C. in'dica.** A synonym of *Sedum indicum*.

**C. jasmin'ea.** A synonym of *Rochea jasminea*.

**C. Justi-Corderoy'i.** Stems short, erect, branching from base. *l.* narrow, tapering, flat above, lower beneath, dark green with dull red blotches, edge and surface papillose. *fl.* pink, in small corymbs. This plant is well known in cultivation but its origin is obscure; it may have been sent to Mr. Justus Corderoy of Blewbury, who collected succulent plants; the suggestion that it is a hybrid raised by him is unlikely.

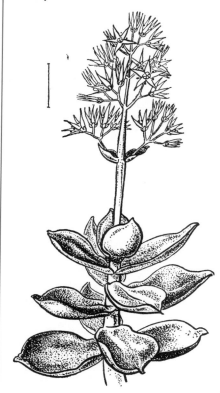

*Crassula lactea*

**C. lac'tea.*** Shrubby plant with thick stems, woody at the base. *l.* ovate, 1 to 1¼ in. long, smooth, dark green, usually with white dots. *fl.* white, starry, in loose terminal racemes. Natal, Transvaal. (B.M. 1171; D.C.Pl.Gr. 37.) Useful as a decorative plant.

**C. lycopodioi'des.** Stems up to 12 in. h., branching, entirely hidden by the 4 rows of tiny, scale-like, green *l.* so that it looks like a club moss. *fl.* minute, in l.-axils. SW. Africa.

**C. mesembrianthemop'sis.** Rosettes stemless, forming clumps. *l.* thick, triangular in section, the reddish-grey tops truncate, fitting into each other, the outermost the longest so that the tops are level. *fl.* white, in a close sessile head. Namaqualand.

**C. mesembrianthoi'des.** Stems low, woody at the base, leafy at the tips. *l.* crowded, very thick, triangular, blunt-edged, green. *fl.* small, in a few-fld. raceme. Namaqualand.

**C. multica'va.** Shrubby, stems lax, branched, up to 12 in. h. *l.* ovate, rounded, stalked, crenulate, green with a reddish tinge, surface pitted. *fl.* pink; adventitious buds often formed in the infl. S. Africa. SYN. *C. quadrifida.*

**C. nemoro'sa.** Stem slender, creeping. *l.* very small, stalked, heart-shaped, green with a red edge. *fl.* small, pink. Cape Province.

**C. obvalla'ta.** Stem woody at base. *l.* crowded, narrow, very thick, blunt, dark green with a reddish tinge. *fl.* small, white, in a round head on a slender stalk. Cape Colony. (D.C.Pl.Gr. 61.)

**C. orbicula'ris.** Similar to *C. rosularis* but smaller.

**C. perfolia'ta.** Stem short. *l.* narrow, tapering, the pairs at right angles becoming smaller up the stem, grey. *fl.* white or red, in a close, terminal corymb. Cape Province.

**C. perfora'ta.** Stem erect, branching from the base, up to 10 in. h. *l.* united in pairs through which the stem appears to be threaded, ovate, pointed, edge cartilaginous-ciliate, green, surface dotted with red. *fl.* small, yellowish, in an interrupted thyrse. Cape Province.

**C. perfos'sa.** Stem decumbent, branching from base, up to 12 in. h. *l.* united in pairs through which the stem appears to be threaded, ovate, pointed, flat above, convex below, entire, glaucous, reddish, dotted. *fl.* small, yellowish, in a loose, open thyrse. S. Africa. (D.C.Pl.Gr. 25.) **A**

**C. portula'cea.** A synonym of *C. argentea.*

**C. pseudolycopodioi'des.** Similar to *C. lycopodioides* but shorter, stouter, greyer-green.

**C. pyramid'alis.** Stem 1 to 3 in. h. *l.* in 4 rows, flat, broadly triangular, green, closely packed like a pile of tiles. *fl.* white, in a terminal, sessile head. Cape Province. (B.M. 7665.)

**C. quadrif'ida.** A synonym of *C. multicava.*

**C. rhomboi'dea.** A synonym of *C. deltoidea.*

**C. rosula'ris.** Rosette stemless. *l.* ovate or tapering, 2¼ to 3 in. long, blunt, not very fleshy, bright green. *fl.* white. Cape Province.

**C. rupes'tris.** Stem decumbent, woody at base, branched. *l.* united in pairs, triangular, concave, flat towards tip above, keeled beneath, very thick, glaucous, edge reddish. *fl.* small, white or pink, in a close terminal corymb. Cape Province.

**C. sarcocau'lis.*** Shrubby little plant, with erect stems, woody below. *l.* small, pointed, green. *fl.* pink in small, few-fld. cymes. S. Africa. The only Crassula that can be grown out of doors without protection in this country. Rock-garden.

**C. Schmidt'ii.** Stem low, branched at the base. *l.* in rosettes, 1½ in. long, slender, tapering, fleshy, green with dark dots, reddish beneath, white ciliate. *fl.* deep carmine. Cape Province. SYN. *C. impressa.*

**C. spatula'ta.** Stems long, prostrate or straggling, with long internodes. *l.* small, stalked, heart-shaped, finely serrate, bright green marked with red. *fl.* pink, in few-fld. cymes, freely produced. S. Africa.

**C. te'res.** Similar to *C. Barklyi* but with a translucent edge to *l.*

**C. tetrag'ona.** Shrubby, up to 2 ft. h. Stems erect, branching, breaking off easily, the broken shoots rooting readily. *l.* narrow, round or squarish in cross-section, tapering, 1 in. long, curving upwards, green. *fl.* small, white in few-fld. cymes. Cape Province. (D.C.Pl.Gr. 19.)

**C. trachysan'tha.** Stem erect, woody below. *l.* short, pointed, flat above, very convex below, covered with white papillae tipped with bristles. *fl.* whitish-yellow. Cape Province.

**C. ver'sicolor.** A synonym of *Rochea versicolor.*

V. H.

**CRASSULA'CEAE.** Dicotyledons. A family of about 600 species of succulent herbs or sub-shrubs in about 15 genera, distributed over the world but especially in S. Africa. Most species grow in dry places and show characteristic fleshy leaves and stem, often tufted growth, closely packed leaves with waxy surface, sunk stomata, and so on. The number of sepals, &c., may be anything from 3 to 30 and the parts, except sometimes the petals and carpels, are free; ovary superior. Fruit usually a group of follicles with many very small seeds. Many species are ornamental and several useful for the rock garden. The genera dealt with are Adromischus, Aeonium, Aichryson, Bryophyllum, Chiastophyllum, Cotyledon, Crassula, Echeveria, Greenovia, Kalanchoe, Monanthes, Orostachys, Pachyphytum, × Pachyveria, Pistorinia, Rochea, Rosularia, Sedum, Sempervivella, Sempervivum, Umbilicus, Vauanthes. **A**

**CRATAEGO-MESPILUS.** FAM. *Rosaceae.* A group of 3 deciduous trees—hybrids between hawthorn (*Crataegus Oxyacantha*) and medlar (*Mespilus germanica*). One is of natural origin, the others are graft hybrids.

**C. + Asniere'sii.*** Small, graceful tree with slender drooping branches, shoots woolly, occasionally spiny. *l.* ovate to broadly ovate, 1½ to 3 in. long, some entire, some deeply lobed, softly downy beneath. *fl.* white, 1 in. wide, in clusters of 3 to 12. *fr.* sub-globose, brown, about the size of common haws. (K.B. 1911, 269.) Originated in the garden of Mr. Dardar at Bronvaux, near Metz, about 1895, on a medlar tree grafted on hawthorn near the point of union between stock and scion. May, June. In fl. and fr. it resembles the hawthorn.

**C. + Dar'dari.** Small tree, shoots downy, more or less spiny. *l.* oblong to ovate, 1½ to 4 in. long, entire or minutely toothed, downy. *fl.* white, 1½ in. wide. *fr.* like a medlar but smaller and borne several together. (K.B. 1911, 268.) A graft hybrid which originated on the same tree and at the same time as *C. Asnieresii.* A single tree will occasionally bear shoots of true medlar and of *C.+Asnieresii.*

**C. × grandiflo'ra.*** Tree up to 30 ft., round-headed, free-flowering, shoots downy. *l.* oval to obovate, 2 to 3½ in. long, often lobed towards apex, downy beneath. *fl.* usually in twos or threes, 1 in. wide, pure white. May, June. *fr.* ¾ in. wide, globose-ovoid, yellow-brown, tasting like common haws. France (wild). 1800. (B.M. 3442 as *Mespilus lobata.*) SYN. *Mespilus grandiflora, M. Smithii, Pyrus lobata.*

W. J. B.

***crataegoi'des,*** Crataegus-like.

**CRATAE'GUS** (*kratos*, strength; in reference to the strength and hardness of the wood). Hawthorn. FAM. *Rosaceae*. Small deciduous trees or sometimes shrubs, almost always more or less spiny, sometimes fiercely so. Leaves alternate, simple, lobed or pinnatifid, and toothed, usually much larger and more deeply cut on the barren shoots than on the flowering ones. Flowers white, sometimes fading off into pink, but only genuinely pink or scarlet in the garden varieties of *C. monogyna* and *C. Oxyacantha*; they are produced in corymbs at the end of short, leafy shoots, rarely solitary; stamens 5 to 20; anthers pink, yellow, or white, styles 1 to 5. Fruit a pome, usually globose, oval, or pear-shaped, and red, yellow, or black, rarely blue. Each fruit (haw) contains 1 to 5 seeds ('stones'). The flowering time is May and June.

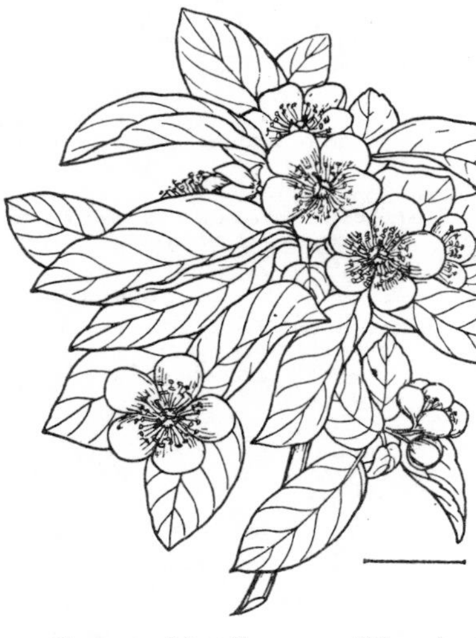

*Crataego-Mespilus × grandiflora* (p. 567)

The more distinctive characters relied on to differentiate the species are: the size, shape, and pubescence of the leaves; the size of the corymbs and the number of flowers they carry; the number of the stamens and the colour of their anthers; the shape, size and colour of the fruit and the number of seeds (stones) each contains, and the season at which they fall.

The genus is most strongly entrenched in E. and Central N. America, where over 950 species (many of doubtful standing) have been described. A well-marked group is established in Europe, Asia Minor, and N. Africa, but there is a curious dearth of them in Japan, China, Himalaya, and Western N. America. None come from south of the equator.

All the species mentioned in the following notes are quite hardy and should be grown in a sunny spot, preferably in a sound, open loamy soil, and it is immaterial whether it is limy or not. Many species of American origin, for the sake of gaining time, have been grafted on our common hawthorn (*C. monogyna*) which may explain why some of them appear to be comparatively short-lived in cultivation. Nearly all the species produce abundant seed which does not, however, germinate until the second spring after they ripen. Seeds have been known to lay dormant until the fourth spring and then germinate freely, but they must not be stored in dry places. The usual practice where large quantities of common hawthorn are required for hedge-making is to mix the haws when thoroughly ripe with sandy soil and leave them covered in a heap until the second spring. Where only small quantities are needed, the seeds can be sown in the ordinary way in autumn, placing the seed-pots or pans in a shady place (all the better if plunged in sand or ashes) to save labour in watering. Here the seeds may lie until the second spring when they can be brought out to germinate in a cold frame or given some other protection. **A**

Thorns may show a Powdery Mildew (*Podosphaera oxyacanthae*) very similar to that on Apples but of very little importance. The Honey Fungus (q.v.) may attack the roots. There is also a Leaf Blotch, *Sclerotinia crataegi*, which browns and rots the leaves and may in wet seasons be epidemic but does not seem to do permanent injury. The most important Hawthorn disease is Rust, caused by the fungus *Gymnosporangium clavariaeforme*. The teleutospore stage is perennial on the common Juniper and the aecidial on the Hawthorn where the cluster cups appear on the leaves, shoots, and fruits often causing distortion of the shoots. Another species, *G. confusum*, alternates in similar fashion between Hawthorn and *Juniperus Sabina*. Ornamental thorns are as likely to be attacked as the wild Hawthorn.

(D. E. G.)

**C. apiifo'lia.*** Parsley-leaved Thorn. Shrub or small tree, 10 to 20 ft., shoots downy, spines 1 in. long. *l.* triangular to reniform, coarsely toothed to pinnately lobed, 1 to 1¾ in. long, soon glabrous. *fl.* ¾ in. wide, in downy-stalked clusters of up to 12; stamens 20; anthers pink. May. *fr.* scarlet, oval, ⅓ in. long. S. United States. 1812. (S.S. 188.) One of the most attractive of Thorns for its deeply cut foliage.

**C. ap'rica.** Tree up to 20 ft. or a shrub, spines 1 to 1½ in. long. *l.* broadly obovate to oval, toothed in the terminal half, ¾ to 2 in. long, soon glabrous. *fl.* ¾ in. wide, in clusters of 3 to 6; stamens 10; anthers yellow. May. *fr.* globose, ½ in. wide, orange-red. N. America. 1900. (S.S. 698.) Distinct, free-flowering, and attractive small tree; autumn colour, deep purple.

**C. arkansa'na.** Tree up to 20 ft., often unarmed or with only a few spines ⅓ to ½ in. long. *l.* oblong-ovate to oval, 2 to 3 in. long, finally dull green and glabrous above. *fl.* 1 in. wide, in downy-stalked corymbs; stamens 20; anthers yellow. May. *fr.* ¾ to 1 in. long, shining crimson, sub-globose. Arkansas. 1902. (S.S. 660.) Autumn colour, clear yellow; fr. abundant and long persisting.

**C. arnoldia'na.*** Tree 15 to 20 ft. with zigzag branches, thorns abundant, 2 to 3 in. long. *l.* broadly ovate to oval, doubly toothed and shallowly lobed, downy especially beneath. *fl.* ¾ in. wide, in many-fld. clusters; stalks downy; stamens 10. May. *fr.* ½ in. wide, sub-globose, bright red, soon falling. Massachusetts. 1901. (S.S. 668.) One of the best of the newer species. (*C. mollis* group.)

**C. Aro'nia.** A synonym of *C. Azarolus*.

**C. Azaro'lus.** Azarole. Tree, 20 to 30 ft., shoots very downy, spines few or absent. *l.* 1½ to 3 in. long, nearly as wide, deeply 3- to 5-lobed, bright green, downy beneath; stalk ½ to 1 in. long. *fl.* ½ in. wide, in dense clusters 2 to 3 in. across; stamens 20; anthers purple. June. *fr.* ¾ to 1 in. wide, globose, orange to yellow, apple-flavoured. Orient. 1640. Cultivated in S. Europe for its edible fr. which vary from white to red. (R.H. 1856, 441; B.R. 1897 as *C. Aronia*.) var. **sina'ica,** *l.* glabrous, *fr.* smaller. Palestine.

**C. brachyacan'tha.** Pomette Bleue. Tree up to 40 or 50 ft., spines ⅓ to ½ in. long. *l.* oval to obovate, cuneate to truncate, rather finely toothed, 1 to 2 in. long. *fl.* ⅓ in. wide, pet. white, changing to orange before falling. June. *fr.* ⅓ to ½ in. wide, bright blue. SE. and Cent. United States. 1900. (S.S. 177.) Remarkable for its blue haws.

**C. Can'byi.** Bushy tree, 12 to 20 ft., thorns stout, ¾ to 1½ in. long. *l.* oblong, ovate to obovate, 2 to 2½ in. long, tapered and entire at base, toothed towards apex; stalk glandular, ½ to ¾ in. long. *fl.* ⅝ in. wide, long-stalked; cal. glandular, toothed; stamens 10 to 12; anthers rosy. May. *fr.* dark lustrous crimson, ½ to ⅝ in. long, sub-globose. N. America. 1901. (S.S. 638.)

**C. × Carrie'rei.*** Tree 15 to 20 ft., thorns few, 1 to 2 in. long, shoots downy. *l.* obovate or oval, 2 to 4½ in. long, coarsely toothed, glossy dark green, downy beneath; stalk ¼ to ¾ in. long. *fl.* 1 in. wide, in clusters 3 in. across; stamens 15 to 20; anthers red or yellow. June. *fr.* orange-red, ¾ in. wide, globose-pyriform, long persisting. Hybrid from *C. stipulacea* raised in the Jardin des Plantes, Paris, about 1870. (R.H. 1883, 108.) *C. × Lavallei*, is now considered to be the same.

**C. champlainen'sis.** Tree 15 to 20 ft., spines 1½ to 2 in. long. *l.* ovate, 2 to 3 in. long, toothed and shallowly 5- or 7-lobed, rounded or cordate at base, blue-green above, downy on veins beneath. *fl.* ¾ in. wide in few-fld. clusters; stalks very downy; stamens 10; anthers yellow. June. *fr.* obovoid, scarlet, ½ in. long. N. America. 1901. (S.S. 669.) Akin to *C. submollis* which has the l. tapered at base.

**C. chlorosar'ca.** Small tree, mostly unarmed, pyramidal, shoots brown-purple, buds blackish. *l.* 2 to 4 in. long, triangular to broadly ovate, shallowly 7- or 9-lobed and toothed, very dark glossy green above, downy beneath; stalk $\frac{1}{3}$ to $\frac{3}{4}$ in. long. *fl.* $\frac{1}{2}$ in. wide, in clusters 2 in. across; cal. minutely toothed; stamens 20; styles 5. May. *fr.* black, orange-shaped, $\frac{1}{2}$ in. wide. Manchuria.

**C. coccin'ea.** A synonym of *C. intricata* or *C. rotundifolia*.

**C. coccinoi'des.** Tree up to 20 ft., spines 1 to 2 in. long. *l.* broadly ovate, 2 to 3 in. long, rounded or truncate at base, toothed and shallowly lobed, soon glabrous. *fl.* $\frac{3}{4}$ in. wide, 5 to 7 in a cluster; stamens 20; anthers rose. May. *fr.* globose, $\frac{7}{8}$ in. wide, dark shining red, dotted. N. America. 1883. (S.S. 674.)

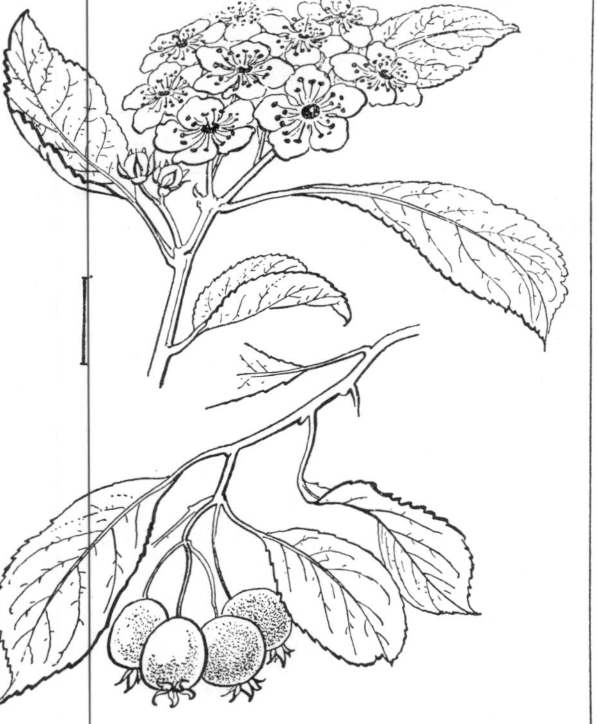

*Crataegus* × *Carrierei* (p. 568)

**C. corda'ta.** A synonym of *C. phaenopyrum*.

**C. crus-galli.*** Cockspur Thorn. Wide-spreading, often flat-topped tree up to 30 ft. (usually considerably less), glabrous in all its parts, spines $1\frac{1}{2}$ to 3 in. long. *l.* narrowly obovate, toothed towards apex only, 1 to $3\frac{1}{2}$ in. long, bright green; stalk $\frac{1}{4}$ to $\frac{1}{2}$ in. long. *fl.* $\frac{5}{8}$ in. wide, in clusters 2 to 3 in. across; stamens 10; anthers red. June. *fr.* sub-globose, $\frac{1}{2}$ in. wide, red, persisting till March. N. America. 1691. (S.S. 178; G.C. 28 (1900), 244.) vars. **linea'ris, pyracanthifo'lia** (S.S. 637), and **salicifo'lia** are all narrower-leaved forms, the last the narrowest. Distinct in habit and lasting long in fr.

**C. cupulif'era.** Small tree or shrub with numerous stems, occasionally 15 to 20 ft., shoots glabrous. *l.* obovate to rhombic, 2 to 3 in. long, doubly toothed, many-lobed. *fl.* cup-shaped, $\frac{5}{8}$ in. wide, in downy-stalked clusters. May. *fr.* scarlet, shining, $\frac{1}{2}$ in. wide, in pendulous clusters. N. America. 1913. Foliage rich crimson in autumn.

**C. × Dippelia'na.*** Small tree of hybrid origin with *C. tanacetifolia* as one parent. *l.* $1\frac{1}{2}$ to 3 in. long, 7- to 11-lobed, hairy above at first, permanently so beneath; stalk up to $\frac{5}{8}$ in. long. *fl.* $\frac{3}{4}$ to 1 in. across; cal. and fl.-stalk hairy; stamens about 20; anthers red. June. *fr.* globose, $\frac{5}{8}$ in. across, dull red. Appeared in Lee's nursery at Hammersmith about 1830. Very free-flowering and attractive. SYN. *C.* × *Leeana*.

**C. Douglas'ii.** Tree 30 to 40 ft., unarmed or nearly so, shoots slender, reddish-brown, glabrous. *l.* obovate to ovate, cuneate, slightly lobed or toothed, $1\frac{1}{2}$ to $3\frac{1}{2}$ in. long, dark glossy green and downy along the midrib above; stalk $\frac{1}{2}$ to $\frac{3}{4}$ in. long. *fl.* $\frac{1}{2}$ in. wide, in clusters 2 in. across. May. *fr.* black, $\frac{1}{3}$ in. wide. NW. America. 1828. (B.R. 1810; S.S. 175.) One of the tallest of Thorns, but one of the least attractive either in fl. or fr.

**C. Dun'barii.** Roundish shrub, 10 to 13 ft., spines red-brown, $1\frac{1}{2}$ to 2 in. long, reflexed. *l.* ovate to roundish, about 2 in. long, acutely lobed and toothed. *fl.* $\frac{1}{2}$ in. wide, hairy-stalked, in clusters of 10 to 14; stamens 10; anthers rose. May. *fr.* crimson, shining, dotted, sub-globose, $\frac{1}{2}$ in. wide. N. America. 1903.

**C. durobriven'sis.** Shrub 10 to 18 ft., soon glabrous; spines $1\frac{1}{2}$ to 2 in. long. *l.* broadly ovate, rounded, or cuneate at base, $1\frac{1}{2}$ to 3 in. long; stalk $\frac{1}{2}$ to $1\frac{1}{4}$ in. long. *fl.* $\frac{3}{4}$ to 1 in. wide; stamens 20; anthers pink; styles 5. May. *fr.* globose, $\frac{5}{8}$ in. wide, dark shining crimson. N. America. 1901. (S.T.S. 1, 2.) Attractive in fl.; the fr. persist until midwinter.

**C. Ellwangeria'na.** Tree up to 20 ft., spines $1\frac{1}{2}$ to 2 in. long. *l.* oval to ovate, $2\frac{1}{2}$ to $3\frac{1}{2}$ in. long, doubly toothed and shallowly lobed, at first downy. *fl.* 1 in. wide, in clusters of 9 to 12; stamens 10; anthers rose. May. *fr.* oval, 1 in. long, bright red. N. America. 1901. (S.S. 671; G.C. 47 (1910), 130; B.M. n.s. 105) Differs from *C. submollis* by the rosy anthers.

**C. glandulo'sa.** A synonym of *C. rotundifolia*.

**C. × grignonen'sis.*** Tree up to 20 ft., not, or but little spiny, shoots glabrous. *l.* 3 in. long, obovate, glossy green above, downy beneath, deeply lobed on maiden shoots. *fl.* $\frac{1}{2}$ to $\frac{3}{4}$ in. wide, numerous. May. *fr.* obovoid to globose, $\frac{5}{8}$ in. wide, bright red. Hybrid first noticed in 1873 at Grignon in France; probably derived from *C. crus-galli* and *C. stipulacea*. l. and fr. long persisting.

**C. heterophyl'la.*** Tree up to 20 ft., spines none or few. *l.* $1\frac{1}{2}$ to 3 in. long, deeply lobed like Hawthorn on barren shoots; much smaller and varying from entire to lobed on flowering ones, dark green. *fl.* $\frac{3}{4}$ in. wide, in clusters 2 to 3 in. across. May, June. *fr.* bright red, slenderly oval, $\frac{1}{2}$ to $\frac{5}{8}$ in. long. Orient. 1816. (B.R. 1161, 1847.) Handsome Thorn akin to *C. Oxyacantha*, distinct by the slender haws.

**C. Holmesia'na.** Tree up to 30 ft., spines few, $1\frac{1}{2}$ to 2 in. long. *l.* oval or ovate, doubly toothed and shallowly lobed, 2 to 4 in. long. *fl.* cup-shaped, $\frac{1}{2}$ to $\frac{3}{4}$ in. wide, 10 or more in a cluster; stamens mostly 5, sometimes more; anthers red-purple. May. *fr.* ovoid, crimson, shining, $\frac{1}{2}$ to $\frac{3}{4}$ in. long, falls early. N. America. 1903. (S.S. 676.)

**C. intrica'ta.** Shrub up to 10 ft. *l.* almost or quite glabrous, 1 to 3 in. long, ovate to broadly ovate, with 3 or 4 pairs of lobes. *fl.* $\frac{1}{2}$ in. wide, in clusters of 5 to 7; stamens 10; anthers yellow. May. *fr.* sub-globose, dark brownish-red. N. America. (B.B. ed. 2, 2, 307.) Associated with *C. rotundifolia* by Linnaeus under *C. coccinea*.

**C. Jack'ii.** Shrub 6 to 10 ft., round-topped, spines slender, 2 in. long. *l.* roundish-ovate to obovate, cuneate, 1 to 2 in. long, irregularly toothed, soon glabrous. *fl.* $\frac{3}{4}$ in. wide in clusters of 10 to 20; stamens usually 5, but sometimes up to 10; anthers pale yellow. May. *fr.* globose, dark dull-red, $\frac{1}{2}$ in. wide. Canada. 1903. (B.B. ed. 2, 2, 306.)

**C. Korolkow'i.** A synonym of *C. pinnatifida major*.

**C. × Laval'lei.** A synonym of *C.* × *Carrierei*.

**C. × Leea'na.** A synonym of *C.* × *Dippeliana*.

**C. macracan'tha.** Tree up to 15 ft., spines slender, numerous, 3 to 5 in. long. *l.* roundish-oval to obovate, 2 to $3\frac{1}{2}$ in. long, tapered at the base, sharply toothed and more or less lobed, dark green, slightly downy beneath. *fl.* $\frac{3}{4}$ in. wide, in clusters 2 to 3 in. across; stamens 10; anthers yellow. May, June. *fr.* globose, $\frac{1}{3}$ to $\frac{1}{2}$ in. wide, bright crimson. N. America. 1819. (S.S. 689; B.R. 1912 as *C. glandulosa macracantha*.) The most formidably armed of all Thorns.

**C. × me'dia.** Natural hybrid between the 2 British Thorns, *C. monogyna* and *C. Oxyacantha*.

**C. melanocar'pa.** A synonym of *C. pentagyna*.

**C. mexica'na.** A synonym of *C. stipulacea*.

**C. missourien'sis.** Shrub, sometimes a small tree, young shoots grey-downy, spines slender, $1\frac{1}{2}$ to 2 in. long. *l.* 1 to 3 in. long, obovate, ovate, or orbicular, coarsely and sharply toothed, downy and glossy above, more downy beneath; stalks only $\frac{1}{5}$ in. long. *fl.* $\frac{3}{4}$ in. wide, in clusters of 3 to 8; stalks white-downy; stamens 20; anthers pink. May. *fr.* $\frac{1}{3}$ in. wide, bright red, sub-globose to pyriform. S. United States. 1905.

**C. mol'lis.** Tree up to 30 ft., spines short and stout. *l.* ovate, $2\frac{1}{2}$ to 4 in. long, lobed and doubly toothed, very downy at first. *fl.* 1 in. wide; stamens 20; anthers pale yellow. June. *fr.* sub-globose, $\frac{3}{4}$ to 1 in. wide, red, downy. N. America. (S.S. 659.) Confused in gardens with the much commoner *C. submollis* which has only 10 stamens in each fl.

**C. monogy'na.** Hawthorn. Hedge-row Thorn. Tree up to 35 ft., usually much smaller, very thorny. *l.* deeply 3- to 7-lobed, the lobes narrow and deep, bright dark-green, glabrous. *fl.* $\frac{5}{8}$ in. wide, in clusters of 6 to 12, with 1 style only. *fr.* roundish-ovoid, $\frac{1}{3}$ in. long, containing 1 stone. Europe (Britain). June. (E.B. 480.) (*See also* **C. Oxyacantha.**) var. **au'rea,** *fr.* yellow; **filicifo'lia,** *l.* deeply cut; **flexuo'sa** (*tortuosa*), branches twisted and curled; **granaten'sis,** branches pendulous, thorns absent or few; **hor'rida,** thorns very abundant; **iner'mis,** dwarf and unarmed; **lacinia'ta,** *l.* very deeply lobed, lobes wide apart and doubly toothed; **lutescens,** *l.* yellow; **pen'dula,** branches gracefully pendulous; **prae'cox** (Glastonbury Thorn), *fl.* in winter and comes very early into l.; **semperflo'rens,** *fl.* at intervals up to August, *l.* very small, forms miniature trees and specimens 50 years old may be only 4 to 6 ft. h.; **Sesteria'na,** *fl.* red, double; **stric'ta** (*fastigiata*), branches erect; **variega'ta,** *l.* blotched with white.

**C. nig'ra.** Hungarian Thorn. Tree up to 30 ft., of rounded shape; thorns few, ½ in. long, shoots grey-felted. *l.* triangular to ovate, 1½ to 4 in. long, often nearly as wide, 7- to 11-lobed, dull green, very downy. *fl.* white, turning pinkish, ⅝ in. wide, in small clusters; stamens 20; anthers yellow. May. *fr.* globose, ½ in. wide, black, shining. Hungary. 1819. (L.B.C. 1021.) One of the most pubescent of Thorns.

**C. nit'ida.** Tree up to 30 ft., habit spreading, almost wholly glabrous, spines few, 1 to 1½ in. long. *l.* lanceolate to oblong-ovate, cuneate, toothed and lobed, dark shining green, 2 to 3 in. long. *fl.* ¾ in. wide, in clusters of 10 or more; stamens 15 to 20; anthers yellow. May. *fr.* roundish-oval, dull brick-red with a glaucous bloom, ½ to ⅝ in. long, persisting through the winter. United States. 1883. (S.S. 703.) Foliage turns scarlet in autumn. (*C. Mollis* group.)

**C. odoratis'sima.** A synonym of *C. orientalis*.

**C. Oliveria'na.** Tree 10 to 15 ft., shoots grey with down, spines few, short. *l.* 1 to 2 in. long, 3- or 5-lobed, the basal lobes deep, both surfaces downy but especially beneath. *fl.* ⅝ in. wide, in clusters 2 in. across; cal. and stalks very downy. June. *fr.* ½ in. long, ovoid, black-purple. SE. Europe, W. Asia. 1810. (B.R. 1933 as *C. Oxyacantha Oliveriana.*)

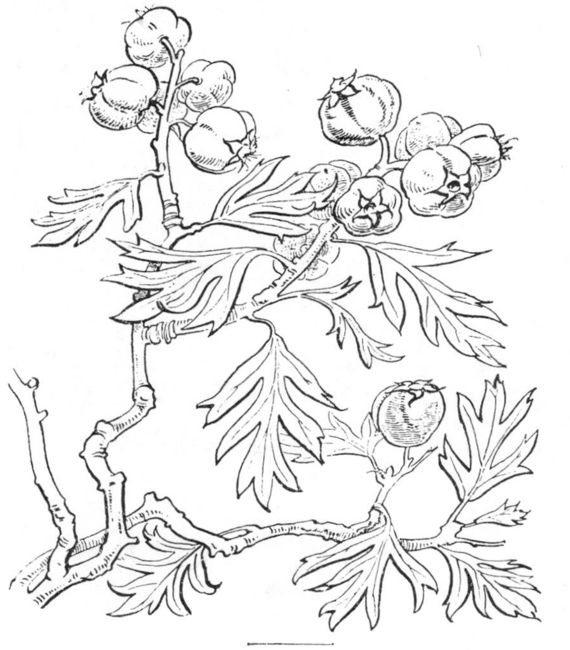

*Crataegus orientalis*

**C. orienta'lis.*** Tree 15 to 20 ft., almost unarmed, shoots downy. *l.* triangular to rhomboid, 1 to 2 in. long, nearly as wide, deeply and narrowly cut into 5 to 9 oblong lobes that are toothed at the end, downy above and beneath; stalk ¼ to ¾ in. long. *fl.* ¾ in. wide in clusters of 12 or more; cal. and stalks woolly; stamens 20. June. *fr.* coral-red or orange-red, ¾ in. wide, globose. Orient. 1810. (B.M. 2314 as *Mespilus odoratissima*; B.R. 1885 as *C. odoratissima.*) var. **sanguin'ea,** *l.* less downy, with broader lobes, *fr.* dull or purplish-red. (B.R. 1852 as *C. orientalis.*) Not so good as the type.

**C. Oxyacan'tha.** Hawthorn. Tree 15 to 20 ft., thorns about 1 in. long. *l.* mostly obovate, 3- or 5-lobed, ½ to 2¼ in. long, glabrous. On strong virgin shoots the lobing is much deeper. *fl.* ⅝ in. wide, in clusters of 6 to 12; stamens 20; anthers red; styles 2 (rarely 3). June. *fr.* roundish-ovoid, ⅜ to ⅝ in. long, red, containing 2 stones. Europe (Britain). It differs from the other, more common native Hawthorn, *C. monogyna* (which has only 1 stone to each haw) by being a smaller, less thorny tree with smaller, less deeply lobed l. (B.R. 1128 and E.B. 479 as *C. oxyacanthoides.*) var. **al'ba ple'na,*** *fl.* double, white changing to pink; **can'dida plena,** *fl.* double, remaining pure white; **coccin'ea** (SYN. *punicea*), *fl.* scarlet (L.B.C. 1363); **coccinea plena*** (Paul's Double Scarlet), *fl.* double, scarlet; **fructu-lu'teo** (*xanthocarpa*), *fr.* yellow; **Gireou'dii,** *l.* blotched white and pink; **Mas'kei,** *fl.* double, pale rose; **ro'sea,** *fl.* single, pink; **salisburifo'lia,** dwarf shrub with distorted branches and double red fl.

**C. oxyacanthoi'des.** A synonym of *C. Oxyacantha*.

**C. pentagy'na.** Tree up to 20 ft., shoots downy, thorns few and small. *l.* broadly ovate to rhomboid or obovate, 1 to 3 in. long, deeply lobed, at first downy, especially beneath. *fl.* ⅝ in. wide, in clusters 2 to 3 in. across; cal. and stalks downy; stamens 20; anthers red; styles 4 or 5. June. *fr.* black-purple, pyriform to oval, ½ in. long. SE. Europe, Caucasus. (R.H. 1901, 310.) SYN. *C. melanocarpa*.

**C. persis'tens.*** Tree 12 to 15 ft., wide-spreading, spines up to 2 in. long, shoots, l., and cal. glabrous. *l.* narrowly oval to obovate, cuneate, 2 to 3 in. long, terminal part toothed, dark shining green, persisting fresh till November. *fl.* ¾ in. wide, in clusters of 10 to 20; stamens 20; anthers whitish. *fr.* oval to pyriform, ¾ in. long, dull crimson, persisting through the winter. (S.T.S. 2, 190.) Origin unknown, but N. American; perhaps a hybrid of *C. crus-galli*.

**C. phaenopy'rum.*** Washington Thorn. Round-headed tree up to 30 ft., entirely glabrous, shoots slender, spines up to 3 in. long, slender. *l.* triangular, 3- or 5-lobed, sharply toothed, 1 to 3 in. long, nearly as wide, shining green. *fl.* ½ in. wide in clusters 2 to 3 in. across; stamens 20; anthers pink. July. *fr.* orange-shaped, ¼ in. wide, scarlet, long persisting. N. America. 1738. (B.T.S. i. 424; B.R. 1151 and S.S. 186 as *C. cordata.*) Autumn tints scarlet and orange.

**C. pinnatif'ida.** Tree 15 to 20 ft., shoots glabrous, thorns absent or quite small. *l.* 2 to 4 in. long and wide, broadly ovate, triangular or rhomboid, with 2 very deep lobes near the base, dark shining green, downy on midrib and veins; stalk 1 to 2¼ in. long. *fl.* ¾ in. wide, on downy clusters 3 in. across; stamens 20; anthers pink. May. *fr.* red, dotted, sub-globose or pyriform, ⅝ in. wide. NE. Asia. 1860. (R.H. 1901, 308.) var. **ma'jor,*** *l.* up to 6 in. long, with broader, shorter lobes, *fr.* 1 in. wide. One of the handsomest of all Thorns in fr. N. China. (R.H. 1901, 308 as *C. Korolkowi.*)

**C. pruino'sa.** Tree up to 20 ft., or a large shrub, spines 1 to 1½ in. long. *l.* broadly ovate, widely cuneate at the base, doubly toothed and triangularly lobed, 1 to 2½ in. long, glabrous. *fl.* ¾ to 1 in. wide; stamens 20; anthers pink. May. *fr.* globose, ⅝ in. wide, plum-coloured when young, finally dark purplish-red. N. America. 1820. (S.S. 648.)

**C. prunifo'lia.*** Rounded tree up to 20 ft., often leafy to ground-level, shoots glabrous, spines 1½ to 3 in. long. *l.* brilliant dark green, 1½ to 3½ in. long, roundish-ovate, oval, or obovate, slightly downy beneath. *fl.* ¾ in. wide, in rounded clusters 2½ to 3 in. across; stalks downy; anthers pink. June. *fr.* globose, ⅝ in. wide, rich crimson, containing 2 stones, falls in October. Origin unknown but may be a hybrid between *C. macracantha* and *C. crus-galli*. One of the most admirable of Thorns in its lush foliage, profuse blossom, finely coloured haws, and rich autumn colour. (B.R. 1868; G.C. 78 (1925), 146 as var. *splendens.*) var. **ovalifo'lia,** *l.* narrower, more downy. (B.R. 1860 as *C. crus-galli ovalifolia.*)

**C. pubes'cens stipula'cea.** A synonym of *C. stipulacea*.

**C. puncta'ta.*** Tree up to 35 ft., usually much smaller, spines few or absent, shoots downy at first. *l.* broadly ovate, 2 to 3½ in. long, lobed above middle; veins parallel in 5 to 10 pairs, sunken. *fl.* ¾ in. wide, in clusters 4 in. across; stamens 20. June. *fr.* deep red, dotted, ¾ to 1 in. wide, globose or obovoid. N. America. 1746. (S.S. 184.) One of the best species in regard to blossom. var. **au'rea** (*xanthocarpa*), *fr.* yellow; **ru'bra,** *fr.* cherry-red, finally almost black; **stria'ta,** *fr.* red with streaks of yellow. All the forms are distinct by the dotted fr. and deeply parallel-veined l.

**C. pyrifo'lia.** A synonym of *C. tomentosa*.

**C. rotundifo'lia.** Tree up to 20 ft., or a shrub with slender thorns 1 to 1½ in. long. *l.* roundish-ovate to obovate, 1½ to 2 in. long, coarsely double-toothed. *fl.* ½ to ¾ in. wide, in clusters 2 to 3 in. across; stalks downy; stamens 10; anthers pale yellow. May. *fr.* sub-globose, ½ in. wide, red. N. America. 1750. (B.R. 1957 as *C. coccinea* and L.B.C. 1012, G.C. 14 (1880), 557 as *C. glandulosa.*)

**C. salig'na.** Tree up to 20 ft., shoots glabrous, red, spines ¾ to 1½ in. long. *l.* rhombic and lanceolate to oval and obovate, cuneate, 1 to 2 in. long, toothed or lobed. *fl.* ⅝ in. wide, in clusters of 7 to 15; stamens 20; anthers yellow. June. *fr.* globose, ¼ in. wide, red, finally lustrous blue-black. Colorado. 1902. (S.S. 636.)

**C. sanguin'ea.** Tree up to 20 ft., mostly unarmed, shoots shining brown-purple, soon glabrous. *l.* diamond-shaped to ovate, 2 to 3½ in. long, shallowly 3-, 5-, or 7-lobed and toothed, slightly pubescent; stalk ¼ to ½ in. long. *fl.* ⅝ in. wide in dense clusters; stamens 20; anthers purple. May. *fr.* bright red, globose, ⅜ in. wide. Siberia. 1822.

**C. sina'ica.** A synonym of *C. Azarolus sinaica*.

**C. splen'dens.** A synonym of *C. prunifolia*.

**C. stipula'cea.** Tree 15 to 30 ft., usually unarmed, shoots downy. *l.* obovate to oval, cuneate, coarsely toothed, 2 to 4 in. long, downy beneath. *fl.* ¾ in. wide, in clusters of 10 to 15, 2 to 3 in. wide; stamens 15 to 20; anthers pink; stalks downy. June. *fr.* globose, yellow, dotted, 1 in. across, long persisting. Mexico. 1824. (B.M. 8589 as *C. pubescens stipulacea*; B.R. 1910 and S.B.F.G. 2, 300 as *C. mexicana.*) One of the parents of *C.* × *Carrierei*.

**C. submol'lis.** Tree up to 20 ft. armed with slender spines 2 to 3 in. long. *l.* softly downy beneath, ovate, 2 to 3½ in. long, doubly toothed and with 3 or 4 pairs of shallow lobes. *fl.* 1 in. across, in clusters 3 in. across on very downy stalks; stamens 10; anthers yellow. June. *fr.* broadly pyriform, ¾ in. long, bright orange-red, falling early. N. America. Long grown as *C. mollis*, which has 20 stamens.

**C. succulen'ta.** Tree 12 to 18 ft., shoots glabrous, spines 1½ to 2 in. long. *l.* roundish-obovate, cuneate, 2 to 3 in. long, toothed, lobed towards the apex, soon glabrous. *fl.* ¾ in. wide, in clusters 3 in. across; stalks downy; stamens 13 to 20; anthers pink. May. *fr.* globose, bright red, ¾ in. across. N. America. 1830. Akin to *C. tomentosa*. (Add. 123; S.S. 181 as *C. coccinea macracantha.*)

**C. tanacetifo'lia.*** Tansy-leaved Thorn. Tree up to 35 ft., shoots mostly unarmed, thickly grey-woolly. *l.* 1 to 2 in. long, obovate or rhomboid, but with 5 or 7 parallel, deep, narrow-oblong lobes, very downy. *fl.* 1 in. wide, in clusters of 6 to 8; cal. felted; stamens 20; anthers red; styles 5. June. *fr.* globose, yellow or reddish, $\frac{3}{4}$ to 1 in. wide, apple-scented, with one or more moss-like bracts beneath. Asia Minor. 1789. (B.R. 1884.) An attractive Thorn well marked by the very laciniate bracts beneath the haws.

**C. tomento'sa.*** Tree 15 to 20 ft., spines few or absent, 1 to 2 in. long, shoots downy. *l.* ovate to obovate, 2 to 5 in. long, coarsely toothed or slightly lobed, downy (especially beneath); stalk $\frac{1}{2}$ to $\frac{3}{4}$ in. long. *fl.* $\frac{5}{8}$ in. wide, in loose clusters 3 to 5 in. across; cal. and stalks woolly; stamens 15 to 20; anthers pink. June. *fr.* erect, pyriform, $\frac{1}{2}$ in. long, dull orange-yellow. N. America. 1765. (S.S. 183; B.R. 1877 as *C. pyrifolia.*) One of the best Thorns as regards blossom. Autumn colour good.

**C. uniflo'ra.** Shrub 5 to 8 ft., thorns slender, 1 to $1\frac{1}{4}$ in. long, shoots downy. *l.* obovate, always tapered at base, rounded and toothed at apex, 1 to 2 in. long. *fl.* creamy-white, $\frac{1}{2}$ to $\frac{3}{4}$ in. wide, solitary or in twos or threes; cal. and stalks shaggy; stamens 20; anthers whitish. May, June. *fr.* globose to pyriform, $\frac{1}{2}$ in. long, yellow. N. America. 1713. (S.S. 191.) Very distinct by its small size and often solitary fl.

**C. Wattia'na.** Tree 15 to 20 ft., unarmed or nearly so, young shoots brownish-purple, shining, glabrous. *l.* $1\frac{1}{2}$ to $3\frac{1}{2}$ in. long, ovate to triangular, deeply 3- to 5-lobed, the lobes sharply toothed, almost or quite glabrous. *fl.* $\frac{1}{2}$ in. wide, in clusters 2 to 3 in. across; stamens 15 to 20; anthers yellow; styles 5. May. *fr.* translucent yellow, globose, $\frac{1}{2}$ to $\frac{5}{8}$ in. across. Baluchistan. (B.M. 8818.)

**C. Wil'sonii.** Tree 20 to 25 ft., or a shrub, spines stout, $\frac{1}{2}$ to 1 in. long. *l.* ovate, shallowly lobed and finely toothed, cuneate to rounded at base, 2 to 4 in. long, dark shining green above, downy on veins beneath. *fl.* creamy-white, $\frac{1}{2}$ in. wide, crowded in clusters 2 in. across; stalks shaggy; stamens 20. June. *fr.* oval, $\frac{2}{5}$ in. long, shining red. China. 1907. Interesting in its close relationship to the American *C. tomentosa.*

W. J. B.

**CRATAEV'A** (after Cratevas, a Greek writer on medicinal plants 1st, century B.C.). FAM. *Capparidaceae.* A genus of about 10 species of evergreen or deciduous tropical trees and shrubs. Leaves 3-foliolate. Flowers in terminal cymes or racemes, large, garlic scented; sepals and petals 4; stamens 8 to 20; receptacle long with several carpels. Fruit an ovoid-globose berry. Stove conditions are necessary and a compost of loam, peat, and rotten manure. Cuttings root easily in sand in heat under a glass.

**C. gynan'dra.** Garlic Pear. Tree without spines. *lflets.* thin, entire. *fl.* with a stalk between cal. and stamens as in Cleome, pet. lanceolate. Jamaica. The bark raises blisters.

**C. religio'sa.** Deciduous tree without spines. *lflets.* 2 or 3 times as long as wide; l. long-stalked. *fl.* yellow, 2 or 3 in. across, showy, sometimes tinged purple; pet. long-clawed. Malabar, Society Is. Greenhouse. Regarded by natives as sacred; bark and l. used in stomach troubles.

***craten'sis -is -e,*** of Crato, Ceara, Brazil.

**crateriform,** goblet-shaped.

**CRATERISPERM'UM** (*krateros,* strong; *sperma,* seed). FAM. *Rubiaceae.* A genus of about 6 species.

**C. lauri'na.** Glabrous shrub. *l.* obovate-oval 2 to 9 in. long, $\frac{3}{4}$ to 3 in. wide, cuspidate, thinly leathery, base wedge-shaped. *fl.* white, funnel-shaped, about $\frac{1}{4}$ in. long, in dense clusters above the l.-axils, $\frac{1}{2}$ to 1 in. across; peduncles stout, $\frac{1}{2}$ to $\frac{3}{4}$ in. long. Sierra Leone, Senegambia.

**CRATEROSTIG'MA** (*krateros,* strong, stout; *stigma,* the stigma is conspicuous). FAM. *Scrophulariaceae.* A genus of 2 or 3 species of dwarf, almost stemless perennial herbs, natives of S. and Trop. E. Africa, closely related to Torenia. Leaves radical, Plantain-like, many-nerved, entire. Flowers in spikes, racemes, or rarely solitary; calyx tubular, 5-ribbed, 5-toothed; corolla tube enlarged above, dorsal lip concave, entire or emarginate, anterior one spreading, 3-lobed, lobes broad; style somewhat funnel-shaped at tip. Treatment as for Torenia.

**C. plantagin'eum.** *rhiz.* thick. *l.* in a basal rosette, ovate, $\frac{3}{4}$ to 3 in. long, nearly as wide, blunt, ciliate, densely hairy beneath, glabrous or almost so above. *fl.* yellow and white or yellow, white and purple or blue, $\frac{1}{2}$ in. long, upper lip $\frac{1}{4}$ in., lower $\frac{1}{3}$ in. long, wider than long. *infl.* racemose or corymbose; scape $\frac{3}{4}$ to $1\frac{3}{4}$ in. long, 4-angled. E. Trop. Africa, Arabia. Habit somewhat variable.

**C. pu'milum.** *l.* sessile, ovate in a radical rosette. *fl.* numerous, solitary on slender scapes, pale lilac, blotched purple and veined white on disk. Summer. Abyssinia. 1871 (F.M. 534.) SYN. *Torenia auriculaefolium.*

**CRATOXY'LON** (*krateros,* strong; *xylon,* wood). FAM. *Hypericaceae.* A genus of 12 species of trees and shrubs, natives of Trop. Asia. Leaves entire, rather thin, punctate. Flowers yellow, white or rose, on 1- to 5-flowered peduncles, or in terminal panicles; stamens in 3 bundles alternating with hypogynous glands; ovary 3-celled; cells with 4 to many ovules; seeds winged. Stove plants.

**C. polyan'thum.** Middle-sized tree, glabrous, thorny. *l.* deciduous, elliptic-lanceolate, 2 to 3 in. long, glaucous beneath. *fl.* pink or bright red, in 3-fld. axillary cymes or solitary; hypogynous glands nearly half length of pet. India.

**CRAWFURD'IA.** Included in **Gentiana.**

***Crawshaya'nus -a -um,*** in honour of de Barri Crawshay, noted amateur of orchids.

**CRAZY PAVING.** *See* **Paving.**

**CREAM FRUIT.** *See* **Strophanthus gratus.**

***cre'ber -ra -rum,*** thickly clustered.

***crebriflo'rus -a -um,*** with thickly clustered flowers.

**CREEPER** or Trailer differs from a Climber by running on the ground or drooping over rocks, often rooting at intervals. Such plants are often suitable for growing in hanging baskets and on banks, e.g. Ivy or Vinca (Periwinkle).

**CREEPER, VIRGINIAN.** *See* **Parthenocissus.**

**CREEPING JENNY.** *See* **Lysimachia nummularia.**

**CREEPING (climbing) LILY.** *See* **Gloriosa.**

**CREEPING SAILOR.** *See* **Saxifraga stolonifera.**

**CREEPING SNOWBERRY.** *See* **Chiogenes.**

**CREMANTHOD'IUM** (*kremannumi,* to swing from; the flower-heads are drooping). FAM. *Compositae.* A genus of about 6 species of rather large perennial herbs, natives of N. India, Tibet, and W. China. Leaves radical. Scape 1-headed. Flower-heads nodding, large; rays yellow or pinkish in 1 series; disk-florets hermaphrodite. Fairly hardy in ordinary garden soil. **A**

**C. Delavay'i.** About 18 in. h. Stems white, cobwebby in upper part. *l.* ovate-deltoid, $1\frac{1}{2}$ to 4 in. long, acute, cobwebby at first, finally glabrous and dark green above, lower long stalked. *fl.-heads* drooping, 1 to 3; ray-florets 10 to 14, in one series, bright yellow with dark veins, narrow lanceolate, $1\frac{1}{2}$ to 2 in. long, with 3 narrow teeth at apex. Autumn. Yunnan, Tibet. 1930? (B.M. 9398.)

**C. nob'ile.** About 12 in. h. Stem shortly red-hairy. *l.* entire, basal widely obovate, obtuse, glabrous. *fl.-heads* solitary, large, nodding; rays 3 times as long as involucre, yellow, linear-lanceolate, not narrowed to apex; pappus white, sub-plumose; involucral bracts widely margined, red-hairy. SW. China. Rather tender. Fragrant of Arnica.

**C. reniform'e.** About 15 in. h. from a thick, short rootstock. *l.* roundish heart-shaped or kidney-shaped, 3 to 8 in. long, with rounded teeth, glabrous. *fl.-heads* as large as in *Arnica montana*; rays 15 to 20, yellowish, $\frac{3}{4}$ to 1 in. long, entire; disk fl. numerous. Himalaya, W. Tibet.

***cremastogy'ne,*** having a pendent ovary.

**A→**

***crenati-,*** in compound words.

**crenature,** a tooth of a crenate margin.

***crena'tus -a -um,*** crenate; having rounded or convex flattish teeth.

**CREOSOTE.** Creosote is an oily, colourless liquid obtained by the distillation of wood-tar. It is insoluble in water but readily soluble in alcohol and alkalis, strongly caustic and poisonous, its action being similar to that of carbolic acid: indeed it is chemically a mixture of compounds closely related to carbolic acid. Its chief value in horticulture lies in its preservative properties, for it preserves wood properly treated with it from both insects and fungi. Its fumes are, however, liable to injure and even kill foliage, and its solutions are detrimental to all plant-life; it is therefore unsuitable for use in treating wood intended for frames or stakes or anything else with which plants may come into close proximity, and it is to be remembered that the fumes are given off slowly, so that wood so treated may be capable of causing damage for a considerable time.

**CREOSOTE PLANT.** *See* **Larrea tridentata.**

*crepida'tus -a -um,* sandal-shaped.

**CRE'PIS** (*krepis*, slipper). Fam. *Compositae.* A genus of about 170 species of annual, biennial, or perennial herbs, with milky sap, related to Hieracium, distributed over the N. Hemisphere. Flowers all ligulate; achenes cylindrical, striped, beak of varying length or absent; pappus hairs usually white, slender, simple, silky, in many series. Few of the species are worthy of a place in the garden: indeed most are weedy and some native species are persistent weeds of pastures and lawns. The following are quite hardy and need nothing special in the way of soil treatment. They may be readily increased by seed sown where the plants are to grow, and the perennials by division.

**C. au'rea.** Hardy perennial, 4 to 12 in. h. *l.* radical, spatulate, oblong, often runcinate, toothed, light green, shining. *fl.-heads* orange, usually solitary; involucre and stem covered with long, black hairs mixed with a few small white woolly ones. Autumn. European Alps. Rock-garden or border.

**C. blattaroi'des.** Hardy perennial. *l.* oblong, toothed; radical l. narrowed to base; stem-l. clasping, arrow-shaped at base. *fl.-heads* 1 to 6, almost corymbose, yellow; involucre hairy, outer bracts spreading. July, August. Jura. Rock-garden.

**C. pyg'maea.** Hardy perennial. Stems procumbent, branching from base. *l.* ovate, somewhat heart-shaped at base, toothed, stalked. *fl.-heads* yellow, few. July, August. European Alps. Rock-garden.

**C. ru'bra.** Annual, 6 to 12 in. h. *fl.-heads* red, usually solitary; involucre hispid, outer bracts scarious. Autumn. S. Europe. (S.B.F.G. 801 as *Barkhausia rubra.*) Border.

**C. terglouen'sis.** Hardy perennial, 8 to 16 in. h. from a short, truncate *rhiz. l.* all stalked, lower glabrous with rounded lobes, upper ciliate with acute lobes or linear. *fl.-heads* solitary, about 2 in. across, rays yellow, pappus white; peduncles thickened upwards. Alps and Carpathians.

*crep'itans,* rustling.

**CRESCENT'IA** (in honour of Pietro Crescenzi, 1230–1321, Italian, author of *Opus ruralium commodorum*). Fam. *Bignoniaceae.* A genus of about 5 species of large, spreading, evergreen trees. Leaves alternate, solitary or clustered, simple, entire. Flowers solitary, from the old wood of trunk or branches; large, somewhat bell-shaped; tube short, lobes toothed or curled. Fruit large, gourd-shaped, epicarp woody. After removal of the pulp of the fruit of *C. Cujete* the fruit forms a useful calabash. They need stove conditions and a compost of loam, peat, and sand. Unfortunately they do not flower until they have attained a large size and can therefore be grown with effect only in the largest of stoves. Cuttings of ripe wood can be rooted in sand under glass.

**C. Cujet'e.** Calabash Tree. Wide-spreading tree 20 to 40 ft. h., with clusters of l. at intervals along the scarcely divided branches. *l.* broadly lanceolate, 4 to 6 in. long tapered to base, dark glossy green. *fl.* solitary; cal. 2-partite; cor. narrow below middle, swollen above; stamens 4 or 5. *fr.* sometimes 18 to 20 in. through. Trop. America. (B.M. 3430.)

**CRESS, AMERICAN.** *See* **Land Cress.**

**CRESS, GARDEN** (*Lepidium sativum*). This useful salading is usually grown and eaten in the cotyledon stage with Mustard (q.v.). The seed should be sown in boxes about 1 ft. square and 3 in. deep, taking care that

there is a hole at the bottom of the box for drainage. The bottom of the box may be covered with roughage and the box should then be filled with friable soil to within ½ in. of the top. The seed should be sown thickly and evenly on the surface and gently pressed with a smooth flat board, but not covered with soil. A soil covering renders it difficult to cut the seedlings without grit. After watering gently the boxes should be covered with panes of glass and placed in a house or frame (with moderate warmth in winter) until germination has taken place. The seedlings will be ready for cutting in from 10 to 14 days. A succession may be kept up by frequent sowings and in summer the seed may be sown out of doors in a cool place. Mustard is treated in the same way but is sown 4 days later since it germinates more quickly.

Neither the plain or common Cress nor Mustard will remain long in perfection, but the curled Cress may, when more fully grown, be used for garnishing. It is treated like the common Cress. Golden or Australian Cress is sometimes grown but has little to recommend it. It is a dwarf, yellowish variety, needing a longer time to grow than either of the other two.

**CRESS, INDIAN.** *See* **Tropaeolum majus.**

**CRESS, LAND.** *See* **Land Cress.**

**CRESS, WATER.** *See* **Water Cress.**

**CREST.** A raised regular or irregular appendage on the surface of or terminating an organ.

*creta'ceus -a -um,* chalky.

*cret'icus -a -um,* of the island of Crete.

*Crew'ei,* in honour of the Rev. Harpur Crewe (1830–83), amateur of gardens, Rector of Drayton Beauchamp.

*cribro'sus -a -um,* pierced with holes, like a sieve.

**CRICKETS.** The 3 species of True Crickets found in this country are the Field, *Gryllus campestris,* the Wood, *Nemobius sylvestris,* and House, *Gryllus domesticus.* The last mentioned has been established in England for many centuries and, while found living normally in dwelling- and glass-houses, it will migrate into the open during hot summers and become a nuisance in and around rubbish dumps where breeding may occur and neighbouring houses be invaded by swarms of the pest. This Cricket is practically omnivorous, and in glass-houses damage is done to seedlings, foliage, stems, and the aerial roots of Orchids. It is active after dark and hides away during the day in warm corners and near hot-water pipes which are followed to reach other houses. The note emitted by this species is strident, and is caused by the scraping together of the margins of fore-wings. The insects are fully winged when adult, and the female is recognized by the presence of an elongated, bristle-like ovipositor.

This pest is encouraged in glass-houses by the presence of plant refuse beneath the staging. The methods of controlling it are by traps and poison baits—the former being a useful measure for reducing their numbers, the latter for complete eradication. An effective bait consists of ½ lb. of Paris green (an arsenical preparation) thoroughly mixed with 14 lb. of bran, and made attractive by the addition of mashed banana, fruit juice, or meat meal, the bait being evenly and thinly distributed towards evening on the paths, beneath the staging, and along the hot-water pipes.

G. F. W.

**CRICKET PITCH.** A cricket pitch is usually set out on a specially prepared and levelled turf area in the centre of the cricket field known as the playing table which should be from 80 to 150 ft. square, the distance between the wickets being 22 yards. The best type of wicket is obtained from turf growing on somewhat stiff loam over a clay or hard subsoil, provided that the drainage is good, and there is plenty of topsoil. Where the soil is naturally clayey and wet, excavate to a depth of 18 in. Replace the subsoil with rubble for drainage, and replace the topsoil. In the case of light soil excavate 9 in. and replace existing soil with good loam from yellow clay. After thorough consolidation and levelling, good quality turf which has been growing on stiff soil should be laid and well beaten. See **Lawn.**

J. E. G. W.

**CRIMSON CLOVER.** See **Trifolium incarnatum.**

**CRIMSON FLAG.** See **Schizostylis coccinea.**

*crini'tus -a -um* (*crini-,* in compound words), crinite, furnished with a tuft of long, weak hairs.

**CRINKLE.** A descriptive term for virus diseases causing puckering of the foliage of various plants, e.g. Potato Crinkle, Strawberry Crinkle.

D. E. G.

**CRINODEN'DRON.** See **Tricuspidaria.** A

**CRINODON'NA.** FAM. *Amaryllidaceae.* Hybrids produced by crossing species of Crinum and Amaryllis.

**C. × Cors'ii*** (*Amaryllis Belladonna × Crinum Moorei*). *fl.* rose, passing to white on the back, 3 to 4 in. across, funnel-shaped, slightly curved, with short tube; stamens declinate, fragrant, 8 to 12 in an umbel. September. *Bulb* 3 or 4 in. thick with long neck. *l.* evergreen, strap-shaped, recurved 24 by 1½ to 3 in., laterally grooved, 1½ to 3 ft. h. Raised by Dr. Ragioneri at Florence, and by Mr. F. Howard at Los Angeles (as *Amacrinum × Howardii*). 1921. (B.M. 9162.)

**CRI'NUM** (*krinon,* Greek name for Lily). FAM. *Amaryllidaceae.* A genus of possibly over 100 species of often very handsome bulbous plants, natives of the warmer parts of the world especially near the coasts, occasionally on stream sides or in marshes, much more rarely far inland. Their distribution has probably been facilitated by the large bulbiform seeds which might well be carried far by ocean currents. Leaves usually broad, sometimes distichous and then inner narrower, rarely in a rosette, usually lasting only through one growing season. Flowers regular or zygomorphic, tube narrow, segments 6, white or reddish, large, usually funnel-shaped, sessile or shortly stalked; stamens affixed to throat; ovules many in a cell; pedicels not lengthening in fruit. Most species need stove or greenhouse conditions, and as they usually have large bulbs and numerous fleshy roots, large pots or tubs are needed for plants of flowering size. Turfy loam, fibrous peat, and charcoal, all broken and used as lumpy as possible, make a good lasting compost in which the plants will grow and flower well for some years if given plenty of water and an annual top-dressing of good soil when growth begins in spring. Spring is the best season for re-potting such as need it. After potting or top-dressing the plants should be started in stove temperature or somewhat cooler for the less tropical species. They should be frequently syringed and liquid manure may be given to established plants occasionally. The flowering season varies considerably but is usually towards autumn, but some species flower more than once in a season. Sunshine rarely damages them, but some shade is advisable while the leaves are young. After flowering water should be partially withheld for the winter or rest period and the plants then fully exposed to the sun.

The hardy species need a rich soil in a sheltered south border with plenty of drainage. The bulbs should be of a good size before planting out and deep planting at the end of May is advisable, for then there is time for complete establishment before winter. A border at the foot of a warm house wall is a good site for them. They must be kept clean and watered when necessary. With the

onset of frost the necks of the bulbs should be protected by litter or some other means except in very favoured localities. Where safety outdoors cannot be ensured the bulbs should be lifted and stored in a cool house or shed for the winter, and replanted in the following May. The scape will need a stake in exposed places since the flowers are so heavy that without it they will be liable to damage by rough winds. C. *Moorei,* C. *bulbispermum,* and their varieties and hybrids (see **C. × Powellii**) are among the best for outdoor treatment; of the seedlings of this group those known as C. *Krelagei* and C. *haarlemense* are particularly pleasing; C. *asiaticum* and C. *Macowani,* while somewhat less hardy, will succeed in warm borders outside in some districts. Propagation is by seed or offsets. The seeds are often large and should be sown singly as soon as ripe in 3- or 4-in. pots to accommodate the large roots. Sandy loam and leafsoil suits the seeds best, and a temperature of 70 to 80° F. for all but the hardy species. The pots should be kept rather dry until germination occurs when more water will be needed. The young plants may be grown on with little rest as most species are evergreen or nearly so. Flowering size is, by this means, soon attained when once the seedlings are well started. Some species make offsets freely, others are rather shy, but where they can be obtained offsets reach flowering size more quickly than seedlings. They should be taken off when rather small, taking care to preserve the roots as far as possible. They should be potted separately and grown on in the same way as seedlings. The best position for the different species is indicated in the descriptions.

The characters of the species are not always clearly defined, and this is one of the genera that needs to be carefully studied afresh with the aid of living material. It may well be that such study will in some instances lead to a new conception of the status of some of the existing species and possibly to a new basis of classifying them. At present we follow the classification into three sections defined over 60 years ago by Mr. J. G. Baker in the *Gardeners' Chronicle,* vol. 15 (1881), p. 763. The sections are characterized as follows, and in the descriptions below the number immediately following the name of the species indicates the section into which it is placed.

SECTION 1. Flowers more or less erect. Perianth segments linear, not over ⅓ in. wide, spreading or reflexed. Filaments sub-erect, diverging equally on all sides from the ascending style.

SECTION 2. Flowers with perianth tube straight or slightly curved; segments lanceolate, at last spreading or ascending; filaments as in Section 1.

SECTION 3. Flowers with perianth tube more or less curved from the first; limb horizontal or sub-erect; segments oblong, permanently connivent or overlapping in lower half; filaments declined, close together, and nearly parallel with one another and with the style.

Hybrids between Crinum and Amaryllis and between Crinum and Hymenocallis have been recorded.

**C. abyssin'icum** (3). Bulb ovoid, 3 in. thick. *l.* about 6, linear, sub-erect, 1 ft. long, ½ to 1 in. wide, gradually narrowed, bluish-green. *fl.* white, fragrant; tube slender, curved, 1½ to 2 in. long; limb horizontal or sub-erect, 2 to 3 in. long; segs. ½ to ¾ in. wide; peduncle 4- to 6-fld., 1 to 2 ft. long. Abyssinia. 1892. (G.F. 1892, p. 412, f. 89.) Greenhouse.

**C. acau'le** (2?). *l.* linear, 18 in. long, ½ in. wide, firm, glossy. *fl.* white, keel red; tube cylindrical, erect, 2 in. long; segs. lanceolate, erect, recurved at end, 4 in. long, ½ to ¾ in. wide; peduncle 1-fld. Zululand.

**C. ama'bile** (1). Bulb small, neck about 1 ft. long. *l.* 25 to 30, lorate, 3 to 4 ft. long, 3 to 4 in. wide, gradually tapering to point. *fl.* very fragrant; tube bright red, cylindrical, 3 to 4 in. long; segs. white with a crimson central band, tinged purplish-red without, 3 to 4 in. long; stamens 1 in. shorter than segs.; scape 2 to 3 ft. long, 2-edged; umbel 20- to 30-fld. Summer. Sumatra. 1810. (B.M. 1605.) Stove.

**C. america'num** (2). Bulb ovoid, neck short, 3 to 4 in. thick. *l.* 6 to 10, lorate, arching, 2 to 3 ft. long, 1½ to 2 in. wide, toothed. *fl.* creamy-white, very fragrant; tube greenish, 4 to 5 in. long; segs. lanceolate, 3 to 4 in. long; scape 1½ to 2½ ft. long; umbel 3 to 6, pedicels very short. Summer. S. United States. 1752. (B.M. 1034.) Stove.

**C. amoe'num** (2). Bulb globose, 2 to 3 in. thick. *l.* linear, sub-erect, 1½ to 2 ft. long, 1 to 2 in. wide. *fl.* tube greenish, 3 to 5 in. long; segs. lanceolate, spreading, 2 to 3 in. long, pure white; scape 1 to 2 ft. long; umbel 6- to 12-fld. Summer. India. 1807. Stove. var. **Mears'ii**, very dwarf, *l.* narrow, about 1 ft. long, channelled-pointed, glaucous, *fl.* white, scape about 6 in. long, umbel 6-fld., plant floriferous. Burma. 1907.

**C. angustifo'lium** (2). Bulb nearly globose, neck very short. *l.* linear, 1½ to 2 ft. long, 1 to 1½ in. wide. *fl.* tube 3 to 4 in. long; segs. lanceolate, 2½ in. long, ½ in. wide; scape about 1 ft. long; umbels 5- to 6-fld. Summer. N. Australia. 1824. (B.M. 2355 as *C. arenarium.*) Greenhouse. var. **blan'dum**, *l.* broader, *fl.* with wider segs., filaments whitish (B.M. 2531 as *C. blandum*); **confer'tum**, *fl.* sessile, segs. 4 in. long, longer than tube. (B.M. 2522 as *C. confertum.*)

**C. aquat'icum.** A synonym of *C. campanulatum.*

**C. arenar'ium.** A synonym of *C. angustifolium.*

**C. asiat'icum** (1).* Asiatic Poison Bulb. Bulb 4 to 5 in. thick, neck 6 to 9 in. long or more. *l.* in a rosette, 20 to 30, 3 to 4 ft. long, 3 to 4 in. wide. *fl.* white; tube slender, cylindrical, 3 to 4 in. long, tinged green; segs. linear, 2½ to 3 in. long; scape 1½ to 2 ft. long, 2-edged; umbels about 20-fld. Almost continuously in flower. Trop. Asia. 1732. (B.M. 1073.) Greenhouse. The largest culti-vated species. A variable species to which many names have been given. var. **anom'alum** has a broad, membranous, striated, plaited wing to the *l.* (B.M. 2908 as *C. plicatum.*); **declina'tum,** bud declining, not erect, *fl.* tinged red. (B.M. 2231 as *C. declinatum.*); **pro'cerum,** larger than type, *l.* up to 5 ft. h., 6 in. wide, *fl.* tube and segs. about 5 in. long, segs. tinged red. (B.M. 2684.); **sin'icum,** bulb larger than type, 18 in. long, *l.* 5 in. wide, margin wavy, *fl.* longer than in type. China.

**C. augus'tum** (1). Bulb ovoid, about 1 ft. h., 6 in. thick. *l.* 20 to 30, lorate, 2 to 3 ft. long, 3 to 4 in. wide. *fl.* tinged red, 3 to 4 in. long; scape lateral, 2 to 3 ft. long, flattish; umbels 12- to 20-fld. Mauritius. 1818. (B.M. 2397.) Stove.

**C. Baines'ii.** A synonym of *Ammocharis heterostyla.*

**C. Balfour'ii** (2). Bulb 3 in. thick, neck short. *l.* 10 to 12, lorate, spreading, about 1 ft. long. *fl.* white with greenish tinge on tube, very fragrant; tube 2 in. long; segs. oblanceolate, 2 in. long, ½ in. wide; scape lateral, 18 in. long, flattish; umbel 10- to 12-fld. October. Socotra. 1880. (B.M. 6570.) Stove.

**C. blan'dum.** A variety of *C. angustifolium.*

**C. brachyne'ma** (3). Bulb ovoid, 2½ to 3 in. wide. *l.* lorate, developed after fl.,.1½ to 2 ft. long, 3 to 3½ in. wide. *fl.* white, tube green; tube 1½ to 1¾ in. long; segs. 2 in. long, oblanceolate, obtuse; scape 1 ft. long, nearly cylindrical; umbel 15- to 20-fld. India. 1840. (B.M. 5937.) Stove.

**C. bractea'tum** (1). Bulb ovoid, neck short. *l.* 6 to 8, 1 to 1½ ft. long, 3 to 4 in. wide. *fl.* white, tube tinged green, slightly scented; tube 2½ to 3 in. long; segs. linear, as long as tube; scape 1 ft. long, flattened; umbel 10- to 20-fld. July. Seychelles, Mauritius. 1810. (B.R. 179.) Stove.

**C. Braun'ii** (1). Bulbs 4 to 5 in. thick, scales dirty red, thick. *l.* about 1?., linear, 2½ to 3½ ft. long, 2 to 2½ in. wide, finely toothed, white-edged, channelled. *fl.* erect, scentless, white, tinged pink on margins, tube greenish below; tube narrow, 6 in. long; segs. linear, 4 in. long, 3½ in. wide. Madagascar. 1894.

**C. bulbisperm'um** (3).* Bulb ovoid, 3 to 4 in. thick. *l.* about 12, outer spreading, lorate, slender-pointed, 2 to 3 ft. long, 2 to 3 in. wide, glaucous, inner narrower. *fl.* white, flushed red at back; tube 3 to 4 in. long; segs. about as long, oblong, acute; scape about 1 ft. long; umbel 6- to 12-fld. S. Africa. 1752. (B.M. 661 as *Amaryllis longifolia.*) SYN. *C. capense, C. longifolium.* Hardy perennial. Variable and the parent of some fine hybrids. var. **al'bum,** *fl.* white.

**C. caf'frum.** A synonym of *C. campanulatum.*

**C. campanula'tum** (3). Bulb ovoid, small. *l.* linear, 3 to 4 ft. long, ½ to 1 in. wide, deeply channelled. *fl.* bright red-purple; tube 1½ to 2 in. long; limb bell-shaped, 1½ to 2 in. long; segs. oblong, obtuse; peduncles slender, 1 ft. long; umbel 5- or 6-fld. S. Africa. (B.M. 2532.) Stove. SYN. *C. aquaticum, C. caffrum.*

**C. capen'se.** A synonym of *C. bulbispermum.*

**C. Careya'num** (3). Bulb globose, 3 to 4 in. thick, neck short. *l.* 8 to 10, lorate, 1 to 2 ft. long, 2 to 3 in. wide. *fl.* white, tinged red towards middle of segs.; tube 3 to 4 in. long; limb about as long, horizontal; segs. oblong-lanceolate; scape 1 ft. long, somewhat flattened; umbel 4- to 6-fld. Seychelles, Mauritius. 1821. (B.M. 2466.) Greenhouse.

**C. Colen'soi.** A synonym of *C. Moorei.*

**C. crassifo'lium.** A synonym of *C. variabile.*

**C. cras'sipes** (3). Bulb very large, conical, up to 3 ft. long, 10 in. thick, without neck. *l.* strap-shaped, nearly erect, 3 to 4 ft. long, 4 in. wide, bright green. *fl.* white, with pink keel to segs., tube green; tube curved, 3 in. long; segs. oblanceolate, sub-erect, 2½ in. long, ½ in. wide; scape about 9 in. long, flattish; umbel 15- to 20-fld., pedicels 1 to 1½ in. long. July onwards. Trop. or sub-trop. Africa. 1887. Stove or warm house.

**C. cris'pum** (?). Bulb 2 to 2½ in. thick, neck 2 to 6 in. long. *l.* about 20, linear, up to 10 in. long, 2 in. wide, glabrous, margins waved. *fl.* white, pinkish without; tube 3½ in. long, cylindrical; segs. 2 in. long, somewhat tapered; scape 2 to 3½ in. long, flattish; umbel 5- to 6-fld. Transvaal. 1932.

**C. cruen'tum** (1). Bulb large. *l.* strap-shaped, 3 to 4 ft. long, 2 to 4 in. wide. *fl.* bright red; tube 7 to 8 in. long; segs. linear, 3 in. long; scape 2 ft. long, 2-edged, ½ in. thick near base; umbel 5- to 7-fld., pedicels very short. Mexico. 1810. (B.R. 171.) Stove. var. **Loddiges'ii,** segs. tipped dark purple, pedicels as long as ovary.

**C. declina'tum.** A variety of *C. asiaticum.*

**C. defix'um** (1). Bulb 2 to 3 in. thick. *l.* 6 to 8, linear, 2 to 3 ft. long, 1 in. wide. *fl.* white; tube greenish or tinged red, 2½ to 3 in. long; segs. linear; scape 1 to 1½ ft. long; umbel 6- to 16-fld. October. India. 1810. (B.M. 2208.) *C. ensifolium* (B.M. 2301) is very close to this and may be a variety. Stove.

**C. dis'tichum** (3). Bulb small, globose. *l.* about 10, 2-ranked, linear, 1 ft. long, tapering, channelled above, firm. *fl.* usually solitary, sessile, white, keeled, bright red; tube curved, 5 to 6 in. long; limb horizontal, about 4 in. long; segs. oblong, acute, connivent, 1 in. wide; stamens and style nearly reaching tips of segs. June. Sierra Leone. (B.M. 1253 as *Amaryllis ornata.*) Stove.

**C. Douglas'ii** (1). Related to *C. asiaticum,* differing by its columnar stem. *l.* several, 2½ ft. long, 4 to 5 in. wide, narrowed above middle to a blunt point. *fl.* white; tube about 5 in. long; segs. 3½ to 4 in. long, ½ in. wide, margins wavy; scape about 2½ ft. long, flattish, mottled dark green; umbels 20-fld., pedicels thick, as long as ovary. Thursday Is.

**C. erubes'cens** (2). Bulb ovoid, neck short. *l.* numerous, 2 to 3 ft. long, 2 to 2½ in. wide, strap-shaped. *fl.* white, tinted claret-purple outside; tube 5 in. long; segs. 2½ in. long, linear-lanceolate; scape 1½ to 2 ft. long; umbel 4- to 8-fld. Summer. Trop. America. 1780. (B.M. 1232.) Stove. A variable species.

**C. erythrophyl'lum** (2?). Bulb small, about 2½ in. thick. *l.* about 12 in. long, curling, sprawling, narrowed to a point, wine-coloured. *fl.* white; segs. 3 to 4 in. long, linear-lanceolate; scape slender, about 10 in. long; umbel 3- or 4-fld. Burma.

**C. falca'tum.** A synonym of *Cybistetes longifolia.*

**C. flac'cidum** (3). Bulb ovoid, 3 to 4 in. thick, neck very short. *l.* linear, 1½ to 2 ft. long, 1 to 1½ in. wide. *fl.* white; tube curved, 3 to 4 in. long; segs. oblong-lanceolate, 3 to 4 in. long, ¾ in. wide, acute; stamens much shorter than segs.; scape 1½ to 2 ft. long, flattish; umbel 6- to 8-fld. July. New S. Wales, S. Australia. 1819. (B.M. 2133; B.R. 426 as *Amaryllis australasica.*)

**C. Forbesia'num** (3). Bulb ovoid, 6 to 8 in. thick. *l.* 10 to 12 in rosette, strap-shaped, 3 to 4 ft. long, 3 to 4 in. wide, margin fimbriate. *fl.* white, tinged reddish outside, slightly scented; tube 3 in. long, limb funnel-shaped, 4 to 4½ in. long; segs. oblanceolate-oblong; scape scarcely 1 ft. long, stout; umbel 30- to 40-fld. October. Delagoa Bay. 1824. (B.M. 6545.) Stove.

**C. Forget'ii** (2). *l.* oblong-lanceolate, 14 in. long, nearly 3 in. wide, minutely toothed. *fl.* tube green, 8 in. long; segs. white, oblong, about 3 in. long, ½ in. wide, revolute; scape lateral, about 12 in. long, nearly round; umbel 5-fld. Peru.

**C. gigan'teum** (3). Bulb 5 to 6 in. thick. *l.* strap-shaped, 2 to 3 ft. long, 3 to 4 in. wide. *fl.* white, strongly vanilla-scented; tube 4 to 6 in. long; limb bell-shaped; 3 to 4 in. long; segs. oblong-obtuse, much overlapping; scape 2 to 3 ft. long, flattish; umbel 6-fld. Summer. W. Trop. Africa. 1792. (B.M. 923 as *Amaryllis ornata.*) Stove.

**C. × grandiflo'rum** (*C. bulbispermum × C. Careyanum*).

**C. × haarlemen'se.** A form of *C. × Powellii.* Hardy or nearly so.

**C. heterosty'lum.** A synonym of *Ammocharis heterostyla.*

**C. Hildebrandt'ii** (2). Bulb 2 to 3 in. thick, neck 6 in. long. *l.* 8 or 10, with fl., lanceolate, 1½ to 2 ft. long, firm. *fl.* white, erect; tube 6 to 7 in. long; segs. horizontally spreading, 2 to 3 in. long, less than ½ in. wide; scape 1 ft. long, 2-edged; umbel 6- to 10-fld. September. Comoro Is. (B.M. 6709; I.H. 1886, 115.)

**C. hu'mile** (2). Bulb small, globose, greenish, with a very short neck. *l.* linear, 1 ft. long, spreading, somewhat acute, thicker than *C. amoenum,* pitted on face. *fl.* drooping in bud, white; tube greenish, 3 in. long; segs. linear-lanceolate, spreading, 2 in. long, ⅓ in. wide; filaments bright red, longer than segs.; scape 1 ft. long, slender; umbels 6- to 9-fld., pedicels short. October. Trop. Asia. 1826. (B.M. 2636.)

**C. interme'dium** (2). Bulbs 2 to 3 in. thick, without aerial neck. *l.* obviously nerved, more or less blunt. *fl.* white; segs. tipped yellow; scape flattish, glaucous, tinged red at base. Wai Weir Is.

**C. jemen'se.** A synonym of *C. yemense.*

**C. Johnston'ii** (3). Bulbs globose, 3 to 4 in. thick, neck absent. *l.* about 20, 3 to 5 ft. long, outer ensiform, inner linear, about 2 in. wide, bright green. *fl.* white, tube greenish, segs. pinkish; tube slightly curved, 4 in. long; segs. rather shorter than tube, acute, ovate to oblong; stamens declinate; scape 2 ft. long; umbels many-fld., pedicels 1 in. long. British Cent. Africa. 1900. (B.M. 7812.)

**C. Kirk'ii** (3). Bulb globose, 6 to 8 in. thick. *l.* strap-shaped, 3½ to 4 ft. long, 4 to 4½ in. wide, margin crisped, white, ciliate. *fl.* white, striped red on back of segs., tube greenish; tube 4 in. long; limb horizontal, 5 in. long; segs. over 1 in. wide, slender-pointed; scape, more than one, 1 to 1½ ft. long, 2-edged; umbel 12- to 15-fld. September. Zanzibar. 1879. (B.M. 6512.) Stove.

**C. × Krelag'ei.** *See* **C. × Powellii.** Hardy or nearly so.

**C. Kunthian'um.** Bulb ovoid, 3 in. thick, neck short. *l.* about 20, strap-shaped, spreading, 12 to 20 in. long, 2 to 3 in. wide, bright green, margin wavy. *fl.* white, fragrant; tube 7 to 8 in. long; segs. lanceolate, 2½ in. long; scape 1 ft. long; umbels 4- to 5-fld. Colombia. 1890.

**C. Last'ii.** A synonym of *Ammocharis heterostyla*.

**C. latifo'lium** (3). Bulb sub-globose, 6 to 8 in. thick, neck short. *l.* numerous, strap-shaped, 2 to 3 ft. long, 3 to 4 in. wide. *fl.* white, faintly tinged red in middle of segs. both within and without, tube greenish; tube 3 to 4 in. long; segs. oblong-lanceolate, reflexed at tip; scape 1 to 2 ft. long; umbels 10- to 20-fld. Summer. India. 1806. (B.R. 1297; B.R. 579 as *C. insigne*; B.M. 2292 as *C. moluccanum*; B.M. 2217 as *C. speciosum*.) *C. yemense* with pure white fl. in large umbels, l. broad, shining green, Arabia, 1892, is very near *C. latifolium*, possibly only a variety of this variable species.

**C. leucophyl'lum** (1). Bulb nearly 6 in. thick. *l.* 12 to 14, forming a distichous column about 1 ft. long, 1½ to 2 ft. long, 5 to 6 in. wide, whitish-green, toothed. *fl.* pinkish, fragrant; tube cylindrical, 3 in. long; segs. linear, spreading, rather shorter than tube; scape from below l., 1 ft. long; umbel 40- to 50-fld., dense. August. Damaraland. 1880. (B.M. 6783.) Greenhouse.

**C. linear'e** (3). Bulb small, ovoid. *l.* linear, 1½ to 2 ft. long, ½ in. wide, glaucous-green, channelled above. *fl.* tube slender, curved, 1½ to 2½ in. long; segs. tinged red without, oblanceolate, 2 to 3 in. long, ⅓ to ½ in. wide, acute; scape slender, roundish, 1 ft. long; umbel 5- or 6-fld. September. S. Africa. (B.M. 623 and 915 as *Amaryllis revoluta*.) Greenhouse.

**C. Loddiges'ii.** A variety of *C. cruentum*.

**C. longiflo'rum** (3). Bulb ovoid, 4 to 5 in. thick. *l.* 6 to 8, linear, 1½ to 2 ft. long, 1½ to 2 in. wide. *fl.* white, tube greenish; tube 3 to 4 in. long; segs. lanceolate, ascending, nearly as long as tube; scape lateral, about 1½ ft. long; umbel 6- to 12-fld. India. (B.R. 1297.)

**C. longifo'lium.** A synonym of *C. bulbispermum*.

**C. Macken'ii.** A synonym of *C. Moorei*.

**C. Macow'anii** (3). Bulb 9 to 10 in. thick. *l.* 12 to 15, in a rosette, spreading, strap-shaped, 2 to 3 ft. long, 3 to 4 in. wide. *fl.* white, tinged purple, greenish on tube; tube 3 to 4 in. long; segs. oblong, acute, as long as tube, 1 to 1¾ in. wide; scape (sometimes more than one), 2 to 3 ft. long; umbel 10- to 15-fld. November. Natal. 1874. Greenhouse or nearly hardy.

**C. Makoyan'um.** A synonym of *C. Moorei*.

**C. mauritia'num** (1). 3 to 4 ft. h. *l.* numerous, glabrous, channelled. *fl.* small, white, segs. tipped pink, narrow linear; filaments pink; umbel 4-fld. about 9 in. across. April. Mauritius. 1817. (L.B.C. 650.)

**C. Mears'ii.** A variety of *C. amoenum*.

**C. Moor'ei** (3). Bulb ovoid, 6 in. thick. *l.* 12 to 15, spreading, strap-shaped, 2 to 3 ft. long, 3 to 4 in. wide. *fl.* white, with faint red flush, tube greenish; tube 3 to 4 in. long; limb funnel-shaped, as long as tube; segs. oblong-acute; scape 1½ to 2 ft. long; umbel 6- to 10-fld. Spring or autumn. Natal. 1874. (B.M. 6113, 6381 as *C. Macowanii*.) SYN. *C. Mackenii*, *C. Makoyanum*, *C. ornatum*. Greenhouse, or nearly hardy. var. **Schmidt'ii,** *fl.* pure white; **variega'tum,** *l.* striped yellow. 1895.

**C. orna'tum.** A synonym of *C. Moorei*.

**C. par'vum** (3). Bulb ovoid, small. *l.* 5 to 7, linear, 6 to 9 in. long, ½ in. wide, glabrous. *fl.* white, striped red; tube erect, 3 in. long; segs. narrow, 3 in. long, ½ in. wide; scape slender, 1-fld., about as long as l. Trop. Africa. 1896. *C. parvum* of gardens is *Ammocharis heterostyla*.

**C. peduncula'tum** (1). Bulb about 4 in. thick. *l.* 20, strap-shaped, 3 to 4 ft. long, 4 to 5 in. wide. *fl.* white, tube greenish; tube 2½ to 3 in. long; segs. linear, spreading horizontally; scape 2 to 3 ft. long, 2-edged; umbel 20- to 30-fld. E. Australia. 1790. (B.R. 52.) Greenhouse.

**C. plica'tum.** A variety of *C. asiaticum*.

**C. podophyl'lum** (3). Bulb nearly globose, up to 2 in. thick, without a neck. *l.* 5 or 6, lanceolate, 1 ft. long, 1½ to 2 in. wide. *fl.* white, tube greenish; tube 5 to 6 in. long; limb sub-erect, 3 in. long; segs. oblong-spatulate, acute, under 1 in. wide; scape, 8 to 9 in. long, flattish, 2-fld. November. Old Calabar. 1879. (B.M. 6483.) Stove.

**C. × Powellii*** (*C. bulbispermum* × *C. Moorei*). Bulb globose, neck short. *l.* about 20, spreading, ensiform, 3 to 4 ft. long, 3 to 4 in. wide near base, slender-pointed, bright green. *fl.* reddish, tube greenish; tube 3 in. long, curved; segs. oblanceolate, 4 in. long, 1 in. wide, acute; stamens much shorter than segs.; scape 2 ft. long, flattish, glaucous; umbel about 8-fld. Of garden origin. Hardy in S. England. A variable hybrid. (Gn. 37 (1890) 80, 81.) SYN. *C. × Lesemannii*. var. **al'bum,** *fl.* white, 8 to 15 in umbel. 1893; **Krelag'ei,** *fl.* very large, pink, segs. broad, overlapping, of good substance, umbels 10- to 12-fld. 1930.

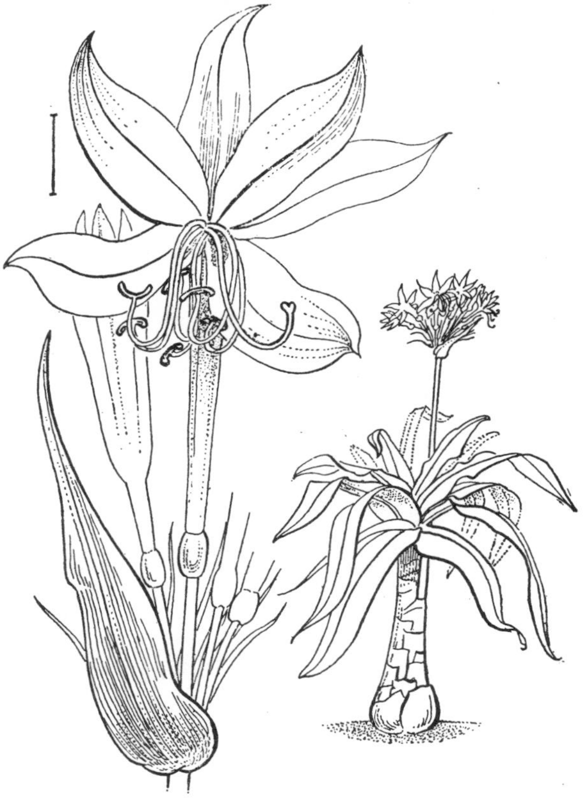

*Crinum Macowanii*

**C. × Prainia'num** (*C. Moorei* × *C. yemense*). *fl.* up to 12, rose.

**C. praten'se** (2). Bulb ovoid, 4 to 5 in. thick, neck short. *l.* 6 to 8, linear, nearly erect, 1½ to 2 ft. long, 1½ to 2 in. wide, narrowed to point, channelled above. *fl.* white, tube greenish; tube 3 to 4 in. long, at first curved; segs. lanceolate, about as long as tube, ½ in. wide; filaments bright red, rather shorter than segs.; scape lateral, 1 ft. long or more; umbels 6- to 12-fld., pedicels none or very short. June, July. India. 1872. var. **el'egans,** bulb with longer neck than in type, *fl.* tube 1 in. shorter than segs. (B.M. 2592 as *C. elegans*); **venus'tum,** umbels about 30-fld.

**C. proce'rum.** A variety of *C. asiaticum*.

**C. purpuras'cens** (2). Bulb ovoid, about 2 in. thick. *l.* about 20, linear, 1½ to 3 ft. long, 1 in. wide, wavy. *fl.* white, tinged claret-red without; tube 5 to 6 in. long; segs. lanceolate, 2½ to 3 in. long, spreading; scape scarcely 1 ft. long, nearly cylindrical; umbel 5- to 9-fld. Summer. W. Africa. 1826. (B.M. 6525.) Stove.

**C. pusil'lum** (1). Bulb stoloniferous, cylindric, 4 in. long, ⅜ in. wide. *l.* 9 in. long, 1/16 in. wide, acute. *fl.* whitish, with a long slender tube and narrow linear segs., about 3 in. long; stamens and style 1 in. shorter than segs.; umbels 6-fld.; peduncles long. Nicobar Is.

**C. Rat'trayi** (3). Bulb large. 3 to 4 ft. h. *l.* ascending, dark green, much resembling *C. giganteum*. *fl.* white, fragrant, 6 to 7 in. across, segs. 3 to 3½ in. wide, inner rather narrower, tube shorter than segs.; umbel 6- or 7-fld. March. Albert Nyanza, Africa. 1904. (G.C. 38 (1905), 11.) Stove.

**C. rhodan'thum.** A synonym of *Ammocharis Tinneana*.

**C. Roozenia'num** (2). Habit of *C. erubescens*. *l.* spreading, acute. *fl.* white within, tube purple-crimson, slightly curved, longer and more slender than in *C. erubescens*; segs. crimson on back. Jamaica. 1894. (G.C. 15 (1894), 199.) Stove.

**C. Samuel'ii** (3). Near *C. Wimbushii*. *l.* 11 or 12, spreading, up to 4 ft. long, 2½ in. wide, long-acuminate, margin scabrous. *fl.* white, faintly flushed pink on keel, 4½ in. across, sessile, not scented; tube erect; stamens spreading. Cent. Africa. 1901. Greenhouse.

**C. Sanderia'num** (3). Bulb globose, 2 in. thick. *l.* ensiform, 1 to 1½ ft. long. *fl.* white with conspicuous reddish-crimson band down middle of segs.; segs. lanceolate, spreading-recurved; umbels 3- or 4-fld., pedicels absent. Sierra Leone. 1884.

**C. scab'rum** (3). Bulb large. *l.* strap-shaped, 3 to 5 ft. long, 2 to 2½ in. wide. *fl.* very fragrant, white with bright red on back of segs., tube greenish; tube 4 to 5 in. long; limb funnel-shaped, oblong-acute, 1 in. wide; scape 1 to 2 ft. long, flattish; umbel 6- to 8-fld. May. Africa? 1810. (B.M. 2180.) Stove. *C. submersum* is a form of this species.

**C. Schim'peri** (3). Bulb flat-round, 2½ in. thick, with yellow-grey scales and distinct neck. *l.* 8 to 10, linear, 3 ft. long, 2 in. wide, recurved, glabrous, green above, glaucous beneath. *fl.* white, tube reddish-green; tube cylindrical, 4 in. long; limb funnel-shaped, 4 in. long; segs. oblanceolate, acute; scape brownish, 2 ft. long; umbel few-fld. July. Mts. of Abyssinia. 1894. (B.M. 7417; G.F. 1309.) Half-hardy.

**C. Schmidt'ii.** A variety of *C. Moorei.*

**C. sin'icum.** A variety of *C. asiaticum.*

**C. specio'sum.** *See* **C. latifolium.**

**C. stric'tum** (2). Bulb ovoid, small, neck not distinct. *l.* strap-shaped, 1 ft. long, 2 to 2½ in. wide, sub-erect, pale green. *fl.* white with pale green tube; tube sub-erect, about 5 in. long; segs. lanceolate, 3 to 4 in. long, ½ in. wide; filaments red, shorter than segs.; scape green, about 2 ft. long; umbel about 4-fld., pedicels very short or none. September. S. America. (B.M. 2635.) Stove.

**C. suaveo'lens** (3). Bulb thick. *l.* many, spreading to erect. *fl.* very fragrant, white, tube greenish; tube 6 to 7 in. long, erect, rather curved; segs. white, ovate-oblong, apiculate, 3 to 4 in. long, 1¼ in. wide; scape 2 to 2½ ft. long; umbels 2- to 5-fld., pedicels absent. Ivory Coast. 1912. Stove.

**C. submer'sum.** *See* **C. scabrum.**

**C. sumatra'num** (1). Bulb ovoid, as large as in *C. asiaticum. l.* ensiform, sub-erect, 3 to 4 in. wide, narrowed to point, firm, toothed, dark green. *fl.* white, tube greenish; tube 3 to 4 in. long, erect; segs. linear, as long as tube; filaments bright red, shorter than segs.; scape much shorter than l.; umbel 10- to 20-fld., pedicels very short. July. *fr.* large. Sumatra. (B.R. 1049.)

**C. Tinnea'num.** A synonym of *Ammocharis heterostyla.*

**C. undula'tum** (2). Bulb ovoid, small, neck long. *l.* ensiform, 1½ ft. long, 1½ in. wide, sub-erect, firm, dark green. *fl.* white, tube greenish; tube curved at first, 7 to 8 in. long; segs. lanceolate, wavy, erecto-patent, 3 to 4 in. long; filaments bright red, 2 in. long; scape 1 ft. long; umbel 4-fld., pedicels very short or none. November. N. Brazil. (H.E.F. 200.) Stove.

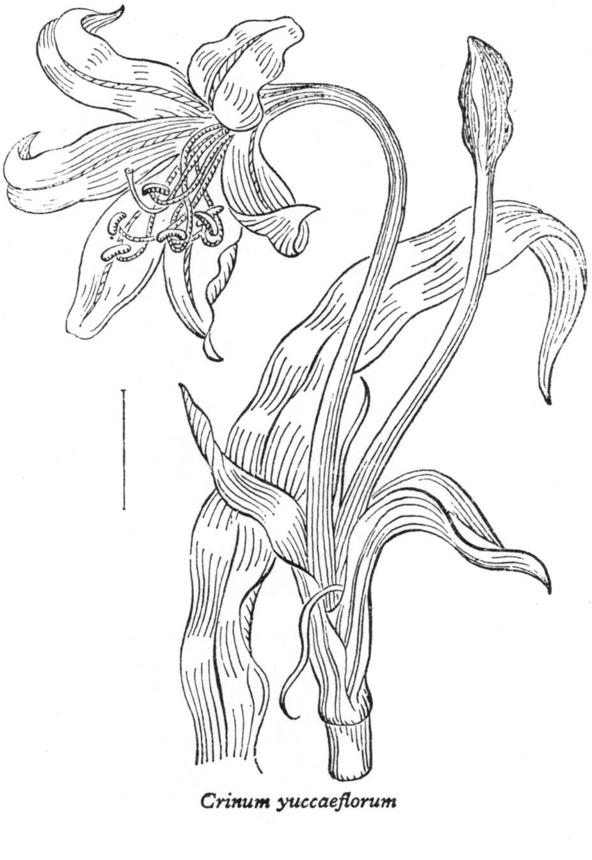

*Crinum yuccaeflorum*

**C. variab'ile** (3). Bulb ovoid, 3 to 4 in. thick, neck short. *l.* 10 to 12, linear, 1½ to 2 ft. long, 2 in. wide, green, weak. *fl.* white, flushed red at back, tube greenish; tube curved, 1½ to 2 in. long; segs. oblong, acute, 2½ to 3½ in. long; filaments red, 1 in. shorter than segs.; scape 1 to 1½ ft. long, erect, flattish; umbels 10- to 12-fld., pedicels ½ to 1 in. long. April. S. Africa. (B.R. 1844, 9 as *C. variable roseum*; B.R. 615 as *Amaryllis revoluta robustior.*) Greenhouse.

**C. Wimbush'ii** (3). Bulb globose, 3 in. thick, neck short, tunic loose, brittle. *l.* 11 or 12, 3 to 4 ft. long, 2½ in. wide, deeply channelled, slender-pointed. *fl.* white, tinged pink, fragrant, bell-shaped, nearly erect; tube 3 to 3½ in. long, somewhat curved; segs. ¾ to 1 in. wide; scape about 2 in. long; umbel 2- to 6-fld., pedicels ½ in. long. Lake Nyasa. 1898. Stove. Flowers much like those of *C. longiflorum.*

**C. Woodrow'i** (2). Bulb large, ovate, brown, neck almost wanting. *l.* broad, glaucous. *fl.* white, tube long; scape 2 ft. long; umbel 12-fld. Bombay. 1897. (B.M. 7597.)

**C. × Wors'leyi** (*C. Moorei* × *C. scabrum*). Intermediate between parents. Of garden origin. Not hardy.

**C. yemen'se.** *See* **C. latifolium.**

**C. yuccaeflo'rum** (3). Bulb small, globose, purplish. *l.* 10 to 12, rosette forming, linear, 1 to 1½ ft. long, about 1 in. wide, firm. *fl.* white, banded red at back, tube greenish; tube curved, 4 to 5 in. long; limb horizontal, 3 to 4 in. long; segs. oblong, acute, connivent; filaments 1 in. shorter than segs.; scape slender, 1 ft. long; umbel 1- or 2-fld., sessile. June. Sierra Leone. 1785. (B.M. 2121 and L.B.C. 668 as *C. Broussonetii.*) SYN. *C. yuccoides, Amaryllis spectabilis.* Stove.

**C. zeylan'icum** (3). Bulb globose, 6 in. thick. *l.* strap-shaped, 3 to 5 ft. long, 2 to 2½ in. wide. *fl.* white, with broad band of red at back and reddish or green tube, very fragrant; tube 3 to 4 in. long; limb horizontal, about 3 in. long; segs. 1 in. wide; scape 2 to 3 ft. long; umbel 10- to 20-fld. Early spring. Trop. Asia and Africa. 1771. (B.M. 1171; B.M. 1253 as *Amaryllis ornata.*) SYN. *C. Herbertianum.* Stove. var. **reduct'um,** *l.* ensiform, 1 to 1½ ft. long, 1⅓ to 1¾ in. wide, narrowed to tip, scape lateral, under 1 ft. long, umbel 4-fld., sessile. Zanzibar. 1884.

**CRIOC'ERIS.** A genus of beetles including the Asparagus beetle and the Lily beetle *under* **Lilium, Pests.**

***crispa'tus -a -um,*** finely curled or closely waved.

***cris'pus -a -um,*** curled; finely wavy, especially near margin.

***crista-gal'li,*** cocks-comb.

***crista'tus -a -um,*** crested; having tassel-like tips (in ferns).

***cristobalen'sis -is -e,*** of San Cristobal, Costa Rica.

***crite'rion,*** a standard for judging.

**CRITH'MUM** (*krithe*, barley; in allusion to the form of the seed). FAM. *Umbelliferae.* A genus of 1 glabrous, fleshy, perennial herb, somewhat woody at base, with 2-pinnate leaves. Leaflets oblong, linear, thick; petioles sheathing at base. Flowers small, white, fleeting. Fruit oblong-ovoid with a loose outer covering. A plant of seaside rocks not very easy to grow inland, requiring a sunny, warm, dry, well-drained spot and winter protection. Best increased by seed sown as soon as ripe, but may be divided.

**C. marit'imum.** Samphire. *fl.* white, in flat-topped umbels, *fr.* green or purplish. June to August. 9 in. h. Coasts of W. and S. Europe, including Britain. (E.B. 606.)

***croca'tus -a -um,*** saffron-yellow.

***croc'eus -a -um,*** yellow.

***cro'ci-,*** in compound words, signifying Crocus-like, as *crociflorus*, Crocus-flowered.

**CROCKS.** Pieces of broken pots, used for ensuring good drainage; hence crocking, placing a crock over the hole at the bottom of a pot, and generally others above it. The first crock must be placed so as to prevent soil washing through the drainage hole, and rough material is usually needed over the other crocks to keep fine soil from washing down among them.

***crocodi'liceps,*** crocodile's head.

**CROCOS'MIA** (*crocus*, saffron, *osme*, smell; the dried flowers when immersed in warm water smell strongly of saffron). FAM. *Iridaceae*. A genus of 2 species of herbaceous plants, natives of S. Africa, closely allied to Tritonia and frequently combined with it. Flowers large, stamens and styles as long as, or longer than, the perianth segments. Seeds few, large. Almost hardy over the country but in cold districts it is best to lift in November and store the corms in a frost-free place, not, however, so dry as to cause them to shrivel. Light, rich, sandy soil suits *C. aurea* best and it can be propagated by offsets or by seeds. Where it is suited the corms increase abundantly. Seeds should be sown as soon as ripe in pans in a cold house. A

**C. au'rea.*** Corms globose with offsets from clefts in the side, covered with a dry tunic. Stem cylindrical, 2 to 3 ft. h., usually branched with few l. *l.* at base, usually about 6, linear sword-shaped, sheathing at base, about 12 in. long. *fl.* golden-yellow with orange or brownish hairs, becoming reddish-yellow; the oblong segs. about 1½ in. long, nearly equal, spreading; tube curved, slender. S. Africa. 1846. (B.M. 4335; B.R. 33, 61.) SYN. *Tritonia aurea.* var. **flore ple'no**, *fl.* double; **imperia'lis**,* robust, *fl.* larger, brilliant, fiery orange-red, 1888; **macula'ta**, *fl.* orange, large, the 3 inner segs. with a dark reddish-brown spot near base. SE. Africa. 1888. *C. aurea* has crossed with *C. Pottsii* to produce *C. crocosmiiflora*.

**C. × crocosmiiflo'ra*** (*C. aurea × C. Pottsii*). *fl.* in a many-fld. panicle, erect, rachis zigzag; perianth funnel-shaped, about 1½ in. long, orange-scarlet; tube slender, curved; segs. spreading. July to winter. (R.H. 1882, p. 124.) SYN. *Montbretia crocosmiiflora*, *Tritonia crocosmiiflora*. Hardy.

The most popular of the plants of the group Tritonia to which Crocosmia belongs, the Montbretias of gardens, derivatives of *C. aurea*, introduced into England in 1846, crossed with *C. Pottsii*, introduced by Mr. Potts of Lasswade in 1877. The cross was first raised by Mr. Lemoine of Nancy in 1880 and since then many beautiful seedling forms have been raised, especially in England. These seedlings have to a large extent superseded *C. Pottsii*, having larger flowers with a considerable range of colouring within the limits of orange and yellow. The graceful form of the inflorescence and their value as cut-flowers, together with their bright colouring, has much recommended them. They are not all wholly to be depended upon as hardy, and while some will grow and survive on light soil and need division every third year, on heavy soils they are best lifted annually and planted in pots in frames and even started in gentle warmth in spring in pots, afterwards being planted out. Light, rich compost in a sunny position suits them. Seed should be sown, where new varieties are sought, as soon as ripe in sandy loam in autumn and kept in a frame or cool greenhouse, the seedlings being grown on singly in small pots.

**C. Pott'sii.*** Corm globose. Stem 3 to 4 ft. h. *l.* 4 to 6, linear, 2-ranked, 18 to 24 in. long, up to ¾ in. wide. *fl.* 12 to 20 in a loose 1-sided spike about 8 in. long, 2 in. wide when expanded; perianth bright yellow flushed brick-red outside, about 1¼ in. long, funnel-shaped; tube cylindrical at base, dilated abruptly at the middle; segs. oblong-obtuse, nearly equal. August. (B.M. 6722 as *Tritonia Pottsii*; Gn. 1880, 84 as *Montbretia Pottsii*.) Hardy.

**CRO'CUS** (a Chaldean name, applied by Theophrastus). FAM. *Iridaceae*. A genus of hardy bulbous plants. Scapes enveloped in a thin tubular sheath; perianth regular, of 6 segments nearly equal as a rule, and with a long slender tube. Stamens 3. Stigmas 3, often much divided. Leaves slender, developing after the blossoms have faded, or simultaneously with them. Corms fleshy, with sheathing, fibrous coats. The 80 species are distributed over Mid- and S. Europe, N. Africa, and W. Asia as far as Afghanistan. Generally represented in our gardens by about a dozen species, and the innumerable varieties of Dutch Crocuses, derived from *C. aureus* and *C. vernus*. A great many species are not distinct enough in general appearance to arrest the attention of the casual observer, but most are worthy of greater attention than is often bestowed upon them. For full account and descriptions of all the known species, the reader should consult the two books mentioned below.

Some of the species flower in the autumn as freely as nearly all the numerous cultivated varieties flower in spring. *C. speciosus* is one of the best. Those which flower from December to January are liable to be injured by severe frosts, and it is better to grow them so that they may be protected in very bad weather, as in a cold frame.

Propagation is by seed, for raising new varieties; and

the increase of the corms perpetuates species and forms. Each year, one or, in some instances, several young corms are formed either on the top or by the side of the old ones, the latter annually dying away. For increasing stock, these may be lifted and replanted singly, allowing sufficient room for each in its turn to develop new corms the following year. More would be obtained of varieties that increase rapidly, by this method, than if they were left crowded together. Some species increase very slowly, and these, with many that are scarce and valuable, are best left undisturbed, so long as they grow satisfactorily. The seed of the Crocus should be sown as soon as ripe, or early in spring, in pots or boxes, using a light, sandy soil, and afterwards placing them in a cold pit or frame, or in a well-drained site in the open. The seed germinates freely, and must be sown thinly, so as to allow the plants space to grow for two seasons in the seed-pan or bed, without lifting. They will need but little attention beyond being occasionally weeded and watered. After the second year, when the leaves die down, the corms should be shaken out and replanted. In the third or fourth year most of them will flower and any good ones may then be selected. It is an excellent plan to top-dress the seed-beds or pans after the first season with an inch or two of rich compost.

Many of the species will grow well in the rock garden, in soil that has a good proportion of small stones intermixed, thereby insuring thorough drainage. If planted deeply and permanently in such a position, dwarf-growing plants, such as mossy Saxifrages, may be placed above, and the Crocuses allowed to grow through when flowering. It is difficult to keep a collection separate and distinct if planted near each other. The corms, by their mode of propagation underground, gradually become removed to a considerable distance from where they were first placed; and, if other species are near, they soon become mixed. The remedy is to lift and replant, or make a limited inclosure for each with slates placed on edge in the ground. It is not necessary to lift often for any other purpose. As soon as the leaves are ripened and die away is the best time for lifting, if it is required. Sandy loam, with the addition of some leaf-soil and sharp grit or crushed stones, is a good compost; and it is preferable to prepare this and replant at once. A similar soil is needed and similar precautions should be taken when the Crocuses are grown in frames. Special precautions should be taken against mice. The ordinary varieties of spring-flowering Crocuses will grow and flower freely in almost any soil or position. They should be planted as early as possible in autumn. The margins of flower-beds, planted with other bulbs, or of borders running parallel with a walk, are positions, among innumerable others, that may be rendered attractive by a mass of differently coloured Crocuses. The corms can be planted regularly in a small trench about 3 in. deep and 3 in. apart. The leaves should be left alone after flowering is over until they ripen, and the corms need not be lifted unless the place is required for other plants in summer. They may be transplanted and allowed to ripen elsewhere, if the flowering quarters are needed.

*Cultivation in Pots.* Spring Crocuses are useful for flowering in pots. Place 5 or 6 corms in a 5-in. pot, or 4 in a smaller one, and bury them in ashes outside for a time until filled with roots, when they should be very gradually brought on in a cool pit or house. The Crocus will not flower if exposed to fire heat, nor must severe forcing be attempted. If placed in a light position, with a little higher temperature than that outside, each corm will produce several flowers earlier than those planted in the open. The individual flowers do not last long, but there is a succession which extends the season over a considerable period. The stronger-growing varieties may be grown in water if treated like Hyacinths.

The foliage of Crocuses may be destroyed by the Grey

Mould fungus *Botrytis cinerea*, but this is usually through overcrowding and may be avoided by separating the plants and dusting with copper-lime dust. Crocus corms may suffer from several rots, e.g. Hard Rot (*Septoria gladioli*) seen as hard shrunken patches, Dry Rot (*Sclerotinia gladioli*) causing coal-black patches with no shrinking, and Grey Bulb Rot (*Sclerotium tuliparum*). (*See* **Tulip Grey Bulb Rot.**) Most of these corm diseases require that an affected stock be examined by stripping off the scales and rejecting the infected corms before planting.

The classification proposed in the Monograph of *The Genus Crocus* by George Maw (1886) and followed since in all important contributions to the literature of the genus, e.g. in Mr. E. A. Bowles's *Handbook of Crocus and Colchicum* (1952), to both of which we are much indebted, has been followed here. **A**

DIVISION I. INVOLUCRATI. Species with a basal spathe springing at the base of the scape from the summit of the corm.

*Section I. Fibro-membranacei*, with a corm-tunic of membranous tissue, or of membranous tissue interspersed with nearly parallel fibres.

Autumn-flowering: *asturicus, byzantinus, Cambessedesii, Clusii, karduchorum, Kotschyanus, nudiflorus, ochroleucus, Salzmanni, Scharojani, serotinus, vallicola.*

Spring-flowering: *Imperati, Malyi, minimus, suaveolens, versicolor.*

*Section II. Reticulati*, with a corm-tunic of distinctly reticulated fibres.

Spring-flowering: *corsicus, etruscus, Heuffelianus, Tomasinianus, vernus.*

Autumn-flowering: *hadriaticus, longiflorus, medius, niveus, sativus.*

DIVISION II. NUDIFLORI. Species without a basal spathe.

*Section I. Reticulati*, with a corm-tunic of distinctly reticulated fibres.

Autumn-flowering: *cancellatus.*

Spring-flowering: *ancyrensis, carpetanus, Cvijicii, dalmaticus, gargaricus, reticulatus, Sieberi, stellaris, susianus, veluchensis* (see also *C. Sieheanus*).

*Section II. Fibro-membranacei*, with a corm-tunic of membranous tissue, or of membranous tissue interspersed with nearly parallel fibres.

Spring-flowering: Lilac or White: *alatavicus, hyemalis, nevadensis.*

Autumn-flowering: Lilac or White: *Boryi, caspius, laevigatus, Tournefortii.*

Spring-flowering: Yellow: *aureus, Balansae, Biliottii, candidus, graveolens, Korolkowi, Olivieri, Sieheanus, Suterianus, vitellinus.*

*Section III. Annulati.* Basal tunic of corm separating into annuli.

Spring-flowering: *Adami, aërius, biflorus, chrysanthus, Crewei, cyprius, Hartmannianus, Danfordiae, isauricus, Pestalozzae, tauri.*

Autumn-flowering: *pulchellus, speciosus.*

*Section IV. Intertexti*, with a corm-tunic of stranded or plaited fibres.

Spring-flowering: *Fleischeri.*

**C. Ad'ami.** Closely related to *C. biflorus* but with *fl.* either pale purple self (nearly blue) or with outer segs. feathered dark purple. February. Georgia. (B.M. 3868; M.C. 59. f., 2.)

**C. aë'rius.** *fl.* tube pale lilac, 3 in. long; throat yellow, glabrous; segs. bright lilac, obtuse, 1 to $1\frac{1}{2}$ in. long, outer feathered, blotched, or suffused darker purple. February, March. *l.* 3, just appearing with fl., 12 in. long, $\frac{1}{16}$ in. wide. *Corm* globose, $\frac{1}{2}$ to $\frac{3}{4}$ in. broad and high. Asia Minor. 1885. (B.M. 6852 B; M.C. 58.) var. **ma'jor,** *fl.* twice as large as in type. Has thinner tunic than *C. biflorus*, and is distinguished from *C. Biliottii* by the annulate tunic.

**C. alatav'icus.** *fl.* tube 4 in. long; throat yellow, unbearded; segs. white, buff, and sometimes freckled and feathered purple outside, $1\frac{1}{2}$ in. long, $\frac{1}{2}$ in. wide. February. *l.* 6 to 9 in. long, $\frac{1}{16}$ in. broad, ciliated. Ala Tau Mts., Turkestan. 1877. (M.C. 45.)

**C. ancyren'sis.** *fl.* tube orange or purple, about 3 in. long; throat unbearded; segs. rich orange, sometimes feathered, ovate-lanceolate, obtuse, $\frac{3}{4}$ to 1 in. long, $\frac{1}{3}$ in. broad. Jan., Feb. *l.* 3 or 4, 1 ft. long, glabrous, $\frac{1}{10}$ in. broad; sheathing ones about 4, $\frac{1}{2}$ to 3 in. long. *Corm* pyriform, $\frac{3}{4}$ in. broad, 1 in. h. Angora. 1879. (M.C. 38.) **A**

**C. astu'ricus.*** *fl.* tube 4 to 5 in. long; throat violet, bearded; segs. violet or purple, with a few darker lines towards the base, very variable, rarely white, $1\frac{1}{2}$ to $1\frac{3}{4}$ in. long, $\frac{1}{2}$ to $\frac{5}{8}$ in. broad. September to November. *l.* 4 or 5, just appearing with fl., about 1 ft. long, $\frac{3}{16}$ in. broad, glabrous; sheathing ones 4 or 5, $\frac{1}{2}$ to $2\frac{1}{2}$ in. long. *Corm* $\frac{2}{3}$ to $\frac{7}{8}$ in. broad, $\frac{1}{2}$ to $\frac{2}{3}$ in. h. Asturias and Sierra de Guadarrama, N. Spain. (M.C. 7.)

**C. au'reus.** Dutch Yellow Crocus. *fl.* tube $3\frac{1}{2}$ to 4 in. long; throat orange, glabrous; segs. bright orange, sometimes with a few grey lines towards base, $1\frac{1}{2}$ in. long, $\frac{1}{2}$ in. wide. February, March. *l.* about 6, with fl., 12 to 14 in. long, $\frac{1}{6}$ in. wide, slightly ciliated. *Corm* large. E. Europe (before 1597), naturalized in England. Long in cultivation. (B.M. 2986; M.C. 55.) In some forms the stigma is abortive, in the var. *sulphureus*, the stamens. var. **lac'teus,** *fl.* white with a yellowish shade, the latest variety to flower; **lacteus penicilla'tus,** *fl.* ivory-white with greenish-blue pencilling. (B.M. 2655.); **lutes'cens,** *fl.* throat apricot shading upwards to cream. (B.M. 3869.); **lu'teus stria'tus,** *fl.* with 3 distinct, black stripes on back of outer segs.; **sulphu'reus,** *fl.* paler, *l.* nar rower; **sulphu'reus stria'tus,** *fl.* paler with dark stripes. (B.M. 938.) A good doer; **sulphu'reus con'color,** *fl.* pale yellow without stripes. (B.M. 1384.)

**C. Balan'sae.** *fl.* tube 2 to $2\frac{1}{2}$ in. long; throat glabrous; segs. orange, $1\frac{1}{4}$ in. long, $\frac{1}{4}$ to $\frac{1}{3}$ in. broad, outer feathered bronze or suffused rich brown outside. March. *l.* before and with fl., about 10 in. long, $\frac{3}{16}$ in. broad, ciliated; sheathing ones about 3, $\frac{1}{2}$ to $2\frac{1}{2}$ in. long. *Corm* pyriform, $\frac{3}{4}$ in. broad and deep. W. Asia Minor. (M.C. 51.)

**C. banat'icus.** A synonym of *C. Heuffelianus*.

**C. biflo'rus.*** Cloth of Silver; Scotch Crocus. *fl.* tube 4 in. long; throat yellow, slightly bearded; segs. varying from white to lilac, $1\frac{1}{2}$ in. long, $\frac{1}{3}$ in. wide, outer buff feathered with 3 to 5 purple lines. February, March. *l.* 4 or 5, with fl., 10 in. long, $\frac{1}{12}$ in. wide, occasionally ciliate. *Corm* flattened, about $\frac{1}{2}$ in. broad. Italy eastwards to Persia mostly in lowland pastures. Long in cultivation. (M.C. 59; B.M. 845.) var. **argen'teus,** a synonym of var. *Parkinsonii*; **estria'tus,** *fl.* without feathering; **min'or,** *fl.* small, tinged blue; **Parkinson'ii,** *fl.* rounder and smaller than type, segs. white within, creamy-buff with 3 stripes outside, throat orange, stigmas scarlet; **Pestaloz'zae,** a synonym of *C. Pestalozzae*; **pusil'lus,** *fl.* small, starry, with a white ground colour; **Wel'denii,** *fl.* larger, white inside. Many colour forms of this exist, including **al'bus,** white outside, and **Alexan'dri,** deep purple with a white margin. (B.M. 7740.)

**C. Biliot'tii.** *fl.* tube about 3 in. long; throat glabrous; segs. rich purple, with a darker blotch at the base, about 1 in. long, $\frac{1}{3}$ in. broad. January to March. *l.* about 3, 10 in. long, $\frac{1}{8}$ in. broad, glabrous; sheathing ones 3 or 4, $\frac{1}{2}$ to 3 in. long. *Corm* $\frac{1}{3}$ to $\frac{1}{2}$ in. broad, $\frac{1}{2}$ in. h. Trebizond. (M.C. 56 B.) Like *C. aërius* but with a different corm tunic. var. **marathonis'ius,** a synonym of *C. niveus*.

**C. Bo'ryi.** *fl.* tube $2\frac{1}{2}$ in. long, yellow; throat orange, bearded; segs. creamy-white, yellow towards base, sometimes feathered purple, $1\frac{1}{2}$ in. long, $\frac{1}{2}$ in. wide; filaments orange, slightly papillose. November. *l.* 5 to 7, with fl., 15 to 18 in. long, $\frac{1}{10}$ in. broad, glabrous. *Corm* $\frac{3}{4}$ to 1 in. h. and broad. Greek Is. (M.C. 47 B; B.R. 33, 16.)

**C. byzanti'nus.** *fl.* outer segs. clear, rich purple, much larger than inner pale lilac; throat not bearded; anthers orange, shorter than stigmas, filaments lilac; stigmas purple, much cut. September, October. *l.* glabrous, vernal, $\frac{3}{8}$ in. wide, wider than in other species; sheathing l. shorter than proper spathe; proper spathe monophyllous, leafy. *Corm* small, oblate, tunic fibro-membranous. E. Carpathians. Before 1629. (B.M. 6141.) A white form is known and several named seedlings have been offered. SYN. *C. iridiflorus*.

**C. Cambessede'sii.** *fl.* tube $2\frac{1}{2}$ to 3 in. long; throat white within, unbearded; segs. vinous-lilac or white, $\frac{3}{4}$ in. long, $\frac{1}{8}$ in. broad, the outer buff outside, feathered purple; stigmas scarlet. September to March. *l.* 2 or 3, 5 to 6 in. long, $\frac{1}{20}$ in. broad, glabrous; sheathing ones about 4, $1\frac{1}{2}$ in. long. *Corm* pyriform, about $\frac{3}{8}$ in. broad and high. Balearic Is. (M.C. 13; B.R. 31, 37, f. 4.)

**C. cancella'tus.** *fl.* tube 4 to 5 in. long; throat yellow, unbearded; segs. varying from white to light purple, self- or purple-feathered, $1\frac{1}{2}$ to $1\frac{3}{4}$ in. long, $\frac{1}{2}$ in. broad; proper spathe 12 in. long. September to December. *l.* 4 or 5, just appearing with flowers, glabrous, 10 to 12 in. long, $\frac{1}{12}$ in. broad, keel prominent; sheathing ones about 4, $\frac{1}{2}$ to 3 or 4 in. long. N. Palestine to Armenia. (M.C. 31.) var. **cilic'icus,** *fl.* proper spathe, completely hidden by sheathing l., *fl.* bluish-lilac, stigmas much branched, yellow; **damascen'sis,** *fl.* dull white with lilac stripes, small, short, *l.* long at flowering time, ciliate; **Mazzia'ricus,** *fl.* white, with a bright golden-orange throat. (B.R. 33, 16, f. 5, 6.)

**C. can'didus.** *fl.* tube 2 to $2\frac{1}{2}$ in. long; throat orange, glabrous; segs. white, yellow, or orange, outer sometimes suffused or feathered purple outside, 1 to $1\frac{1}{4}$ in. long, $\frac{1}{3}$ in. wide; stigmas filiform, orange. March. *l.* 3 or 4, with fl., dark green, 20 to 22 in. long, $\frac{1}{4}$ in. wide, ciliate. *Corm* tunic strongly ribbed, $\frac{3}{8}$ to $\frac{3}{4}$ in. diam. Asia Minor. 1883. (M.C. 54.) var. **subfla'vus,** *fl.* with yellow ground colour. April.

**C. carpeta'nus.** *fl.* tube 3 in. long; throat white, unbearded; segs. varying from delicate vinous-lilac, darker on margins, to white, and suffused outside towards base with bluish veins, 1 to 1¼ in. long, ⅜ in. broad; stigmas lilac. February to April. *l.* about 4, 8 in. long, 1/10 in. broad, semi-cylindrical, without keel, ciliate; sheathing ones about 4, ½ to 3½ in. long. *Corm* tunic soft and thick. Spain, Portugal. 1879. (M.C. 41.)

**C. Cartwrightia'nus.** A variety of *C. sativus*.

**C. cas'pius.** *fl.* tube 2½ in. long, yellow; throat yellow; segs. white, yellowish towards base, 1 to 1½ in. long, ½ in. wide; stigmas unbranched, orange. October. *l.* 4 or 5, with fl. 1/16 in. wide. *Corm* ½ to ¾ in. wide, ¾ in. broad. Shores of Caspian Sea. 1902. (M.C. 46.) The flowers are occasionally tinged rosy-lilac (var. **lilaci'nus**).

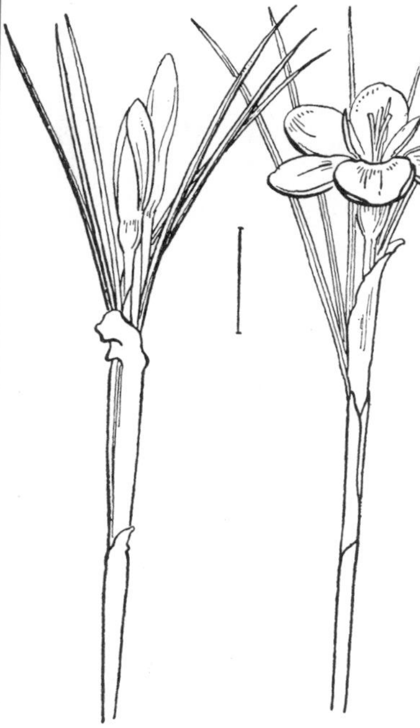

*Crocus chrysanthus*

**C. chrysan'thus.*** *fl.* tube 3 in. long; throat glabrous; segs. bright orange, outer often suffused or feathered bronze, 1 to 1¼ in. long, ½ in. wide; anthers orange, tipped black at base. February. *l.* 5 to 7, with fl. 10 in. long, 1/16 in. wide, keel ciliated. *Corm* ½ to ¾ in. broad and h.; tunic annulate. Greece, Asia Minor. (M.C. 62; B.M. 6162.) Very variable in colouring. var. **fusco-linea'tus** and **fusco-tinc'tus,** *fl.* striped or freckled dull grey or brown outside, anthers lined or suffused with smoky-brown. Some beautiful seedlings have been raised.

**C. Clu'sii.** *fl.* tube 3 to 4 in. long; throat white within, bearded; segs. light purple, darker towards the base, without feathering, 1½ in. long, ½ in. broad. September to December. *l.* 5 or 6, 9 to 10 in. long, 1/20 to 1/16 in. broad, glabrous, the margins with 3 prominent ridges; sheathing ones 3 or 4, the longest 2 to 3 in. long. *Corm* ¾ to ⅞ in. broad, about ⅝ in. h. W. Spain, Portugal. (M.C. 10.)

**C. cors'icus.** *fl.* tube 2 to 2½ in. long; throat white or lilac inside, not bearded; segs. pale purple, broadly lanceolate, about 1¼ in. long, ½ in. broad, outer buff and feathered purple outside. April. *l.* 3 or 4, with fl., 8 in. long, 1/10 in. broad; sheathing ones 2 to 4, ½ to 2½ in. long. *Corm* ½ to ¾ in. broad, barely ½ in. h. Corsica. 1843. (M.C. 21; B.R. 29, 21, two larger fl. as *C. insularis*.)

**C. Crew'ei.** *fl.* tube 2½ to 3 in. long; throat yellow, glabrous; segs. lilac, less than 1 in. long, outer tinged buff and with 3 to 5 lines of purple outside; anthers dark brown. February. *l.* 3 or 4, with fl., 12 in. long, 1/12 in. wide, with distinct, white band. *Corm* ovoid, ½ in. in diameter; tunics rigid. Greece. 1874. (B.M. 6168; M.C. 60.)

**C. Cvijic'ii.** *fl.* sulphur; throat bearded; segs. lanceolate, acute; stigmas dilated, 3-lobed. March. *l.* with *fl.* glabrous. *Corm* small, tunic finely reticulate-fibrose. N. Macedonia. 1937.

**C. cyp'rius.** *fl.* small, soft lavender with deep purple blotches at base of segs; throat orange; filaments bright scarlet. April. *l.* 3 or 4, with fl., ⅛ in. wide. *Corm* ½ in. diam., tunic soft, splitting into rings without teeth. Cyprus. (M.C. 57.)

**C. dalmat'icus.** *fl.* tube about 2 in. long; throat yellow, not bearded; segs. generally lilac, 1½ in. long, ⅜ to ½ in. broad, outer buff outside, with a few purple veins towards the base, or delicately feathered purple. February, March. *l.* 3 to 6, with fl., 8 to 9 in. long, ⅛ in. broad, glabrous, the keel convex; sheathing l. about 3, ½ to 2 in. long. *Corm* pyriform, ½ to ⅝ in. broad and h. Dalmatia. (M.C. 34.)

**C. damascen'sis.** A variety of *C. cancellatus*.

**C. Danford'iae.** *fl.* tube 2½ in. long; throat unbearded; segs. pale sulphur-yellow, about ¾ in. long, ⅜ in. broad, outer occasionally suffused brown without. February, March. *l.* 3 or 4, 12 to 14 in. long, 1/20 in. broad, ciliate; sheathing l. about 4, ½ to 3 in. long. *Corm* about ½ in. broad and h. Asia Minor. 1879. (M.C. 63.)

**C. Elwes'ii.** A variety of *C. sativus*.

**C. estria'tus.** A variety of *C. biflorus*.

**C. etrus'cus.** *fl.* tube striped lilac, 2 to 3 in. long; throat yellow, slightly bearded; segs. bright lilac-purple inside, 1 to 1½ in. long, the 3 outer cream, variously striped and feathered purple outside. March. *l.* 2 to 6, with fl., narrow-linear, with white band. *Corm* ½ to ¾ in. broad, rather less h. Italy. 1877. (B.M. 6362; M.C. 22.)

**C. Fleisch'eri.*** *fl.* tube about 3 in. long; throat pale yellow, not bearded; segs. white, linear-lanceolate, 1 to 1¼ in. long, barely ¼ in. broad, outer like tube veined rich purple outside. February. *l.* 4 or 5, with fl., 1 ft. long, 1/24 in. broad, glabrous; sheathing l. about 5, ½ to 3 or 4 in. long. *Corm* yellow, ½ to ¾ in. broad and h., tunic of finely woven strands, producing bulbils or cormlets at base. Asia Minor. (M.C. 66.)

**C. garga'ricus.** *fl.* tube about 2½ in. long; throat not bearded; segs. rich orange, about 1½ in. long, barely ½ in. broad; filaments orange, darker than anthers. Early spring. *l.* 3, 7 to 8 in. long, 1/10 in. broad, glabrous, margins revolute; sheathing l. 2 to 4, ½ to 2½ in. long. *Corm* ⅜ in. broad; forming stolons. Asia Minor. (M.C. 39.)

**C. graveo'lens.** *fl.* yellow, starry, markedly constricted in lower third, scent unpleasant; outer segs. paler than inner, often striped or feathered brown without. February. Asia Minor. Closely related to *C. vitellinus*.

**C. hadriat'icus.*** *fl.* tube 3 to 4 in. long; throat white or purple, bearded; segs. pure white, or purple towards base, ovate-lanceolate, 1½ in. long, ⅜ in. broad. October. *l.* 5 or 6, with fl., 1¼ ft. long, 1/12 in. broad, ciliated on margins and keel; sheathing l. 6 or 7, ½ to 3½ in. long. *Corm* about 1 in. broad and ¾ in. h. Albania, Ionian Is., &c. (M.C. 30, f. 1, 2.) var. **chrysobelon'icus,** throat of *fl.* yellow. (M.C. 30, f. 3.)

**C. Hartmannia'nus.** Related to *C. cyprius*, but more robust, *fl.* paler with purple markings carried nearly to tips of segs.; anthers dark, filaments scarlet. *Corm* tunic stiffer with fibrous teeth at base of rings. Mt. Inoodos, Cyprus. 1904.

**C. Haussknech'tii.** A variety of *C. sativus*.

**C. Heuffelia'nus.*** *fl.* tube violet, 3 in. long; throat white within, unbearded; segs. 1½ in. long, ⅝ in. broad, the inner rich, bright purple, with darker purple markings near the apex, paler than the outer, varying to white, or variegated purple and white. March. *l.* about 3, with fl. 1¼ ft. long, ⅜ in. broad, glabrous; sheathing ones about 4, ½ to 3 in. long. Hungary, &c. (M.C. 24; B.M. 6197 as *C. veluchensis*.) A plant is offered under this name, agreeing in essential characters with those of *C. Heuffelianus*, but with rosy-lilac ground colour, a yellow throat and filaments, and flowering rather later. Carpathians. 1903.

**C. hyema'lis.** *fl.* tube about 2 in. long; throat yellow, not bearded; segs. white, veined rich purple towards base, about 1¼ in. long and ⅓ in. broad; anthers orange. November to January. *l.* 4 to 7, with fl., 1¼ to 1½ in. long, ½ in. broad, glabrous; sheathing l. about 4, ½ to 2½ in. long. *Corm* ½ to ⅝ in. broad and h. Palestine and Syria. (M.C. 43, f. 1–7.) This form has not been seen recently. var. **Fox'ii,** *fl.* outer perianth segs. freckled and suffused purple outside, anthers black. (M.C. 43, f. 8, 9.)

**C. Impera'ti.*** *fl.* tube 3 to 4 in. long; throat orange, not beardless; segs. bright, pale purple, outer buff, feathered purple, 1½ in. long, ⅝ in. broad. January. *l.* before fl., linear, thick, recurved, with white line, sheathed for 2 or 3 in. at base. 3 to 6 in. h. Italy. (B.R. 1993; M.C. 14.) The sheath in one form (**monophyl'lus**) has 1 l., upright foliage and fl. earlier than the form with diphyllous sheath. There are many colour varieties, including white (**al'biflor,** pure white, **al'bus,** white with 3 stripes on outer segs., and another white, flushed lilac). The feathering varies in extent and intensity from year to year. A double var. (**flore ple'no**) is offered; **atropurpu'reus** (dark purple); **lilaci'nus** (lilac); **pal'lidus** (pale lilac); **purpu'reus** (purple); and **unico'lor** (lilac without stripes). This species rarely seeds in England.

**C. insula'ris.** A synonym of *C. corsicus*.

**C. iridiflo'rus.** A synonym of *C. byzantinus*.

**C. isaur'icus.** Intermediate between *C. biflorus* and *C. chrysanthus*. Asia Minor. 1907.

**C. karducho'rum.** *fl.* tube 2 to 3 in. long; segs. vinous-lilac, 1 to 1¼ in. long, 5/12 in. broad. September. *l.* vernal, glabrous, 1½ to 2 in. long, 1/20 in. broad, persistent till the next flowering; sheathing l. 4 or 5, about 1 in. long. *Corm* nearly spherical, ½ to ⅝ in. broad and h. Kurdistan. 1910. (M.C. 5.) The plant grown under this name is probably a form of *C. Kotschyanus*. The true plant does not appear to be in cultivation now.

A

**C. Korolkow'i.** *fl.* tube brownish, 3 in. long, glabrous; segs. bright yellow inside, 1 to $1\frac{1}{2}$ in. long, outer tinged with brown all over back; spathe valves 2, 1 in. long. March. *l.* 8 to 12, with fl., 12 in. long, $\frac{1}{12}$ in. wide, with distinct, white band. *Corm* about $\frac{3}{4}$ in. broad and h. Turkestan. 1885. (B.M. 6852 A; M.C. 56.)

**C. Kotschya'nus.*** *fl.* tube pale buff, $2\frac{1}{2}$ to 3 in. long; throat bright yellow, bearded; segs. rosy-lilac, about $1\frac{1}{2}$ in. long, $\frac{1}{2}$ in. broad, with 5 to 7 purple lines, and 2 semicircular, basal bright orange spots within. September, October. *l.* vernal, 1 ft. long, $\frac{1}{8}$ to $\frac{3}{16}$ in. broad, with a depressed, white band; sheathing l. 5 to 7, $\frac{1}{2}$ to 3 in. long. *Corm* oblate, 1 to $1\frac{1}{4}$ in. broad, $\frac{1}{2}$ to $\frac{5}{8}$ in. h. Cilicia, Lebanon. (M.C. 4 as *C. zonatus*; B.M. 9044.) Produces abundance of small corms.

**C. laeviga'tus.** *fl.* tube 2 in. long; throat glabrous, yellow; segs. varying from white to lilac, $1\frac{1}{4}$ to $1\frac{1}{2}$ in. long, $\frac{1}{2}$ in. broad, outer either self-buff outside, or more generally feathered or suffused rich purple. October to spring. *l.* 4 or 5, before fl., 9 to 10 in. long, $\frac{1}{10}$ to $\frac{1}{8}$ in. broad, glabrous; sheathing l. 3, $\frac{1}{2}$ to $2\frac{1}{2}$ in. long. *Corm* pyriform, $\frac{3}{4}$ in. broad and h.; tunic glabrous, hard and polished, very persistent. Greece. (M.C. 49; B.M. 9515.) var. **Fontenay'i,** *fl.* bright rosy-lilac with very fine, short violet lines at base of segs., buff outside. Greece.

**C. lagenaeflo'rus.** A synonym of *C. aureus*.

**C. Leicht'linii.** *fl.* small, greenish-yellow, fragrant; outer segs. 1 in. long, $\frac{1}{3}$ in. wide, with band of slate grey and a greenish-blue spot outside; throat orange, glabrous; anthers striped greenish-grey; stigmas scarlet. February. *l.* 6, with fl., narrow. *Corm* tunic with vandykes, moderately hard. Asia Minor. 1891.

**C. longiflo'rus.** *fl.* tube yellow, about 4 in. long; throat orange, slightly bearded; segs. uniform, pale vinous-lilac, yellow towards base, or veined or feathered purple outside, $1\frac{1}{2}$ in. long, $\frac{1}{2}$ to $\frac{5}{8}$ in. broad; scented. October and November. *l.* about 3, with fl., 8 to 9 in. long, $\frac{1}{8}$ in. broad; sheathing l. about 5, $\frac{1}{2}$ to 3 in. long. *Corm* nearly spherical, $\frac{1}{2}$ to $\frac{3}{4}$ in. wide. S. Italy, Sicily, &c. 1843. (B.R. 30, 3, f. 4; M.C. 28.) var. **meliten'sis,** *fl.* striped and feathered outside. Malta.

**C. maesi'acus.** A synonym of *C. aureus*.

**C. Mal'yi.** *fl.* tube yellow, about 3 in. long; throat orange, bearded; segs. white, bright orange towards the throat, occasionally suffused with vinous-purple outside throat, ovate-lanceolate, $1\frac{1}{2}$ to $1\frac{3}{4}$ in. long. March. *l.* 4 or 5, with fl., $1\frac{1}{2}$ ft. long, $\frac{1}{8}$ to $\frac{1}{6}$ in. broad, glabrous; sheathing l. 6 or 7, $\frac{1}{2}$ to 4 in. long. *Corm* oblate, $\frac{3}{4}$ in. broad, $\frac{1}{3}$ to $\frac{1}{2}$ in. h. Dalmatia. (B.M. 7590; M.C. 18.)

**C. marathonis'ius.** A synonym of *C. niveus*.

**C. me'dius.** *fl.* tube 4 to 5 in. long; throat nearly white, veined purple within, not bearded; segs. bright purple, veined near base with dark purple, ovate-lanceolate, 2 in. long, $\frac{3}{4}$ to $\frac{7}{8}$ in. broad, the inner somewhat shorter than the outer; stigmas much divided, bright scarlet. October, November. *l.* 2 or 3, vernal, 10 to 12 in. long, $\frac{3}{16}$ in. broad, the margins of keel and blade slightly ciliate; sheathing l. about 5, $\frac{1}{2}$ to 3 in. long. *Corm* a little broader than high, $\frac{3}{4}$ in. wide, much smaller in wild state. Riviera. 1843. (B.R. 31, 37, f. 5; F.M. 20; Gn. 30 (1886), 476; M.C. 27.) A white form is known.

**C. min'imus.** *fl.* tube $1\frac{1}{2}$ to 2 in. long; throat white or lilac, not bearded; segs. deep, rich purple, 1 to $1\frac{1}{4}$ in. long, $\frac{1}{3}$ in. broad, outer buff and feathered dark purple outside, occasionally white or self-purple. April. *l.* 3 or 4, before fl., 8 to 9 in. long, $\frac{1}{12}$ in. broad, glabrous; sheathing l. about 3, 1 to $2\frac{1}{2}$ in. long, including several scapes. *Corm* pyriform, fully $\frac{1}{2}$ in. broad and h. Corsica, Sardinia. Best increased by seed. (B.M. 6176; M.C. 19; B.R. 29, 21.) *C. minimus* of B.M. 2991 is a variety of *C. biflorus*.

**C. moab'iticus.** *fl.* white with purple stripes and tinged light violet; anthers yellow; stigmas entire, orange. October. *l.* numerous, narrow, glabrous. Palestine. 1912.

**C. nevaden'sis.** *fl.* starry; tube $2\frac{1}{2}$ to 3 in. long; throat pale yellow, bearded; segs. pale lilac or white, variously feathered or veined purple outside, 1 to $1\frac{1}{2}$ in. long, $\frac{1}{3}$ in. broad; stigmas frilled, white. January. *l.* 4 or 5, with fl., 1 ft. long, $\frac{1}{12}$ to $\frac{1}{10}$ in. broad, glabrous, channelled; sheathing l. about 4, $\frac{3}{4}$ to 4 in. long. *Corm* $\frac{3}{4}$ to $\frac{7}{8}$ in. broad, $\frac{1}{2}$ to $\frac{3}{4}$ in. h. Spain, Algeria. (M.C. 42; B.M. n.s. 439.)

**C. niv'eus.** *fl.* white, 2 in. or more long; throat orange; anthers yellow; stigmas scarlet. November. *l.* with fl. *Corm* tunic reticulated. Greece. SYN. *C. Boryi marathonisius, C. marathonisius.* **A**

**C. nubig'enus.** A variety of *C. biflorus*. **A**

**C. nudiflo'rus.*** *fl.* pale bright purple or violet; tube 3 to 10 in. long, and segs. $1\frac{1}{2}$ to 2 in. long; throat not hairy. Autumn. *l.* vernal, about $\frac{1}{8}$ in. broad. Forms long stolon-like shoots with corms at the ends. SW. Europe; naturalized in meadows about Nottingham, &c., in England. (M.C. 6; E.B. 1500; B.M. n.s. 169.)

**C. ochroleu'cus.** *fl.* tube pale buff, $3\frac{1}{2}$ in. long; throat orange, slightly bearded; segs. pale cream, suffused orange towards base, about $1\frac{1}{2}$ in. long and $\frac{1}{2}$ in. broad. Late autumn. *l.* 4 to 6, glabrous, before fl., 10 to 12 in. long, nearly $\frac{1}{8}$ in. broad; sheathing l. about 6, $\frac{1}{2}$ to $2\frac{1}{2}$ in. long. *Corm* oblate, 1 in. broad, $\frac{1}{2}$ in. h. N. Palestine, Syria. (B.M. 5297; M.C. 11.)

**C. Olivier'i.** *fl.* tube $1\frac{1}{2}$ to 2 in. long; throat glabrous; segs. bright orange, obtuse, 1 to $1\frac{1}{4}$ in. long, about $\frac{1}{3}$ in. broad. Spring. *l.* 3 or 4, with fl., 1 ft. long, $\frac{1}{8}$ in. broad, ciliated; sheathing l. about 4, $\frac{1}{2}$ to $3\frac{1}{2}$ in. long. *Corm* $\frac{1}{2}$ to $\frac{3}{4}$ in. broad and h., nearly spherical. Greece, &c. (B.M. 6031; M.C. 53.) The broad leaves distinguish this from *C. Suterianus*.

**C. Pallas'ii.** A variety of *C. sativus*.

**C. Pestaloz'zae.** *fl.* very small, white, throat yellow, outer segs. marked with grey at base outside; filaments stained black in lower half; stigmas filiform. *l.* as in *C. biflorus*. Greece, Turkey. SYN. *C. biflorus Pestalozzae*. The smallest species in cultivation.

**C. pulchel'lus.*** *fl.* tube 4 or 5 in. long; throat orange, glabrous; segs. bright bluish-lilac, yellow towards throat (sometimes white) with dark purple lines within, $1\frac{1}{2}$ in. long, $\frac{3}{4}$ in. wide; anthers white. September to November. *l.* 4 or 5, very short at flowering time, 10 in. long, $\frac{3}{16}$ in. broad. *Corm* about $\frac{1}{2}$ in. h., $\frac{3}{4}$ in. broad. Greece, Asia Minor, long in cultivation. (B.R. 30, 3; M.C. 65.)

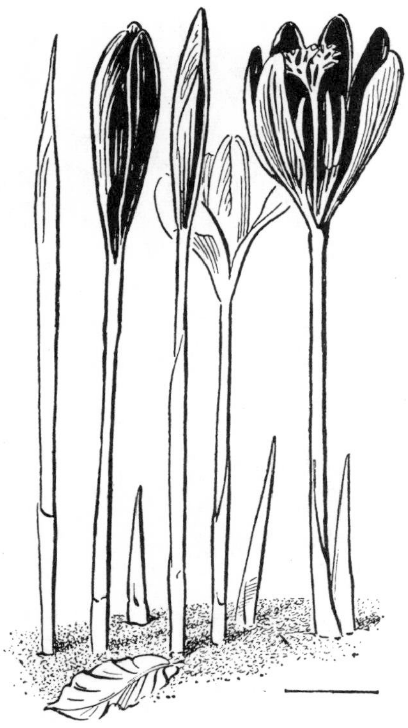

*Crocus nudiflorus*

**C. reticula'tus.** *fl.* tube $2\frac{1}{2}$ in. long; throat white or yellow, glabrous; segs. white to deep lilac, outer feathered purple outside, $1\frac{1}{2}$ in. long, $\frac{1}{3}$ in. wide, reflexed; anthers yellow. February, March. *l.* 3 or 4, with fl., 9 in. long, $\frac{1}{16}$ in. broad, glabrous. *Corm* $\frac{1}{2}$ in. broad and h. Hungary to S. Russia. (M.C. 35.) var. **micran'thus,** *fl.* under 1 in. long, anthers dark grey.

**C. Salzmanni.*** *fl.* tube 3 to 4 in. long; throat yellowish, bearded; segs. vinous-lilac rarely white, about 2 in. long and $\frac{5}{8}$ in. broad, outer feathered purple outside. October, November. *l.* 6 or 7, before fls., 1 to $1\frac{1}{2}$ ft. long, about $\frac{1}{6}$ in. broad, glabrous, the keel narrow and prominent; sheathing l. 3 or 4, $\frac{1}{2}$ to 2 in. long. *Corm* oblate, large, up to 2 in. wide. Tangier, Spain, &c. (B.M. 6000; M.C. 9; B.R. 4, f. 4.)

**C. sati'vus.** Saffron Crocus. *fl.* tube 4 in. long; throat purple, bearded; segs. 2 in. long and $\frac{3}{4}$ in. broad, bright lilac, purple towards the base, purple veined; stigmas long and drooping, entire, scarlet, the source of the saffron of commerce. September, October. *l.* 6 to 8, with fl., 15 to 18 in. long, $\frac{1}{12}$ in. wide, margins ciliate. (M.C. 29.) *Corm* rather large, globular, depressed. Italy to Kurdistan. It appears to have been cultivated in Palestine at the time of Solomon. Many forms have been named, among them the following which have received specific names. var. **Cartwrightia'nus,** *fl.* rosy-lilac, veined purple, segs. about 1 in. long, *corm* large, up to $1\frac{3}{4}$ in. diam. Greece. Much more free-flowering than the Saffron Crocus proper. White seedlings with purple veining occur; **Elwes'ii,** *fl.* lilac, obscurely veined purple, large; **Haussknech'tii,** *fl.* dull white to pale lilac with faint stripes. Persia; **Pallas'ii,** *fl.* rosy-lilac to white, throat yellow, small, stigmas shorter than stamens. Taurus, SE. Europe; **Thomas'ii,** *fl.* slender with pointed segs., stigmas shorter than stamens, *Corm* smaller than type. Italy. 1900.

**C. Scharoja'nii.** *fl.* orange; tube 4 to 5in. long; throat not bearded; segs. lanceolate, $1\frac{1}{2}$ to $1\frac{3}{4}$ in. long, $\frac{1}{2}$ in. broad, inner rather shorter than outer. July, August. *l.* 3, vernal, 10 in. long, glabrous, the keel as broad as the blade, without white band, often persistent till next flowering period; sheathing l. 3 or 4, $\frac{1}{2}$ to $1\frac{3}{4}$ in. long. *Corm* small, globose, $\frac{1}{2}$ in. broad, $\frac{1}{3}$ in. h. Caucasus. 1878. (M.C. 3; G.F. 578, f. 2, a-c.) **A**

**C. serot′inus.** *fl.* tube $2\frac{1}{2}$ to 3 in. long; throat white, bearded; segs. deep lilac, feathered outside with dark purple, $1\frac{3}{4}$ to 2 in. long, $\frac{1}{2}$ in. wide. November, December. *l.* 4 or 5, with fl. 10 to 12 in. long, $\frac{1}{10}$ in. wide. *Corm* 1 in. wide, $\frac{5}{8}$ in. h. Long known in gardens, but now uncommon. Europe, W. Asia. (M.C. 8.)

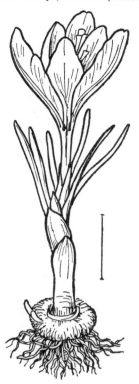

*Crocus serotinus*

**C. Sie′beri.** *fl.* tube 3 to 4 in., throat orange, not bearded; perianth a uniform bright lilac, with a rich golden base; segs. $1\frac{1}{2}$ to $1\frac{3}{4}$ in. long; anthers orange; stigmas broad, orange-scarlet. February, March. *l.* glabrous, 8 in. long, $\frac{1}{4}$ in. broad, with white central band, with fl. 2 to 3 in. h. *Corm* $\frac{2}{3}$ to 1 in. h. Greece, &c. (M.C. 33.) var. **heterochro′mus**, a synonym of var. *versicolor*; **vers′icolor**, *fl.* varying from white to purple, with white and purple stripings and featherings, and always with a rich golden base. Crete, Cyclades. (M.C. 33.) **A**

**C. Siehe′anus.** Resembles *C. ancyrensis* but corm with a smooth, shining tunic breaking up into numerous parallel fibres in lower part, not netted as in *C. ancyrensis*. Perhaps a hybrid *C. ancyrensis* × *C. chrysanthus*. Spring. Asia Minor. 1927. (B.M. 9583.)

**C. specio′sus.*** *fl.* tube 4 in. long; throat white; segs. bright lilac feathered with 3 main purple veins, 2 to $2\frac{1}{2}$ in. long, $\frac{3}{4}$ to 1 in. broad, the inner much wider than outer; anthers yellow. September, October. *l.* 3 or 4, very short at flowering time, 14 to 15 in. long, $\frac{1}{4}$ to $\frac{1}{3}$ in. wide, ciliate. *Corm* $\frac{3}{4}$ to $1\frac{1}{2}$ in. broad and h., with cormlets at base. S. Russia, Asia Minor, Persia. (M.C. 64.) var. **Aitch′isoni,*** *fl.* paler within and segs. up to 3 in. long, white in bud, late; **al′bus**, *fl.* white. Several variants have been raised, the one with purple veining on a white ground being very beautiful; **Ar′tabir**, *fl.* pale blue with dark feathering; **globo′sus**, *fl.* smaller, bluer, and later than type. *C. speciosus* varies considerably and some selected seedlings have been raised, e.g. **Cassio′pe**, a blue *fl.* variety with a yellowish base, and **Pol′lux**, pale blue.

**C. stella′ris.** *fl.* tube 2 to $2\frac{1}{2}$ in. long; throat not bearded; segs. bright orange, with 3 to 5 bronze lines without, $1\frac{1}{2}$ in. long, $\frac{1}{3}$ in. wide; pollen sterile. March. *l.* 4, with fl., 9 to 10 in. long, $\frac{1}{10}$ in. wide. *Corm* $\frac{1}{2}$ to $\frac{3}{4}$ in. broad and h. Unknown wild; probably a hybrid between *C. aureus* and *C. susianus*. Long cultivated. (M.C. 37.)

**C. suaveo′lens.** *fl.* tube 3 to 4 in. long; throat bright orange, not bearded; segs. lilac, narrow-lanceolate, acute, $1\frac{1}{2}$ in. long, $\frac{3}{8}$ in. broad, outer buff without, with 3 unbranched, purple lines. March. *l.* 4 or 5, with fl., 8 to 9 in. long, $\frac{1}{8}$ in. broad; sheathing l. 3 or 4, $\frac{1}{2}$ to $2\frac{1}{2}$ in. long. *Corm* oblate, $\frac{3}{4}$ in. broad, $\frac{1}{2}$ in. h. Rome. 1830. (B.M. 3864; M.C. 15; S.B.F.G. s. 2, 7.)

**C. susia′nus.*** Cloth of Gold Crocus. *fl.* tube $2\frac{1}{2}$ to 3 in.; throat orange, veined bronze; glabrous; segs. $1\frac{1}{2}$ in. long and $\frac{1}{2}$ in. broad,

acute, reflexed, deep orange, variously feathered outside, with deep brown, occasionally self orange, or evenly suffused with dull brown; anthers orange, twice length of orange filament; style divided into long, spreading, entire, orange-scarlet stigma. February. *l.* about 6, with fl., 10 in. long, $\frac{1}{16}$ in. wide; proper spathe diphyllous. *Corm* $\frac{3}{4}$ in. broad. 3 in. h. Crimea, Caucasus. Before 1597. (M.C. 36; B.M. 652.)

**C. Suteria′nus.** *fl.* tube 3 in. long; throat glabrous; segs. bright orange, brownish towards throat, 1 to $1\frac{1}{4}$ in. long, $\frac{1}{8}$ in. broad. January to March. *l.* about 3, with fl., 10 in. long, $\frac{1}{16}$ in. broad, ciliate; sheathing l. about 4, $\frac{1}{2}$ to 3 in. long, enclosing 3 or 4 scapes. *Corm* pyriform, $\frac{1}{2}$ to $\frac{3}{4}$ in. broad and h. Cent. Asia Minor. (M.C. 52; B.R. 33, 4 as *C. chrysanthus.*) Near *C. Olivieri* but with much narrower l.

**C. Suwarrowia′nus.** A variety of *C. vallicola.*

*Crocus speciosus*

**C. taur′i.** *fl.* tube 3 in. long; throat yellow, glabrous; segs. pale purple, unstriped, 1 to $1\frac{1}{4}$ in. long; anthers orange. *l.* 7 or 8, with fl., $\frac{1}{16}$ in. broad, white central band. *Corm* $\frac{3}{4}$ to 1 in. wide. February, March. Mts. of Cilicia and Lycia. 1892. (M.C. 61.) var. **melantho′rus**, *fl.* very small, globose, throat orange, segs. lilac, outer under 1 in. long, with dark red-purple median band, anthers deep black, stigmas entire, scarlet. February. *Corm* tunic hard, as in *C. biflorus.* Asia Minor. 1893. (Fl. & S. 2, 104.)

**C. Tomasinia′nus.*** *fl.* tube 3 to $3\frac{1}{2}$ in. long; throat white, bearded; segs. pale sapphire-lavender (occasionally marked with a darker blotch near the summit), 1 to $1\frac{1}{2}$ in. long, $\frac{1}{3}$ in. broad. March. *l.* 3 to 5, with fl., 9 to 10 in. long, $\frac{1}{8}$ in. broad, glabrous; sheathing l. about 4, $\frac{1}{2}$ to 3 in. long. *Corm* nearly spherical, barely $\frac{1}{2}$ in. wide. Dalmatia, &c. (M.C. 25.)

**C. Tournefor′tii.** *fl.* tube 2 in. long; throat glabrous, orange; segs. lilac, uniform, bright, with a few purple veins, $1\frac{1}{2}$ in. long, $\frac{1}{2}$ to $\frac{1}{2}$ in. wide; filaments orange, pubescent; anthers white, October, November. *l.* 4 to 6, with fl., 12 to 15 in. long, $\frac{1}{10}$ in. wide. *Corm* large, $\frac{3}{4}$ to 1 in. wide and h. Greek Archipelago. (M.C. 47; B.M. 5776 as *C. Orphanidis.*)

**C. vallic′ola.** *fl.* tube buff, about $3\frac{1}{2}$ in. long; throat bearded; segs. pale cream, veined internally with 5 to 7 purple lines, with 2 small orange spots towards throat, lanceolate, $1\frac{3}{4}$ to $2\frac{1}{2}$ in. long, apiculate; proper spathe monophyllous. August, September. *l.* 4 or 5, **vernal,**

10 to 11 in. long, ⅛ in. broad, glabrous, with an obscure, white band; sheathing l. 4 to 6, about 1½ in. long, shorter than proper spathe. *Corm* oblate, ½ to ¾ in. broad, ⅜ in. h. Caucasus, &c. 1880. (B.R. 33, 16, f. 3; M.C. 2; B.M. n.s. 424.)

**C. veluchen'sis.** *fl.* tube 2 to 2½ in. long; throat purple (not yellow), bearded; segs. uniform, clear purple, 1½ to 1¾ in. long, ½ in. broad; anthers yellow. March, April. *l.* 3, with fl., ⅛ in. wide. Greece. 1905. (M.C. 32.)

**C. vern'us.** *fl.* tube 3½ in., throat wide within, bearded; segs. ½ to 2 in. or more long, ¼ to 1 in. broad, varying from white to purple, self or variously feathered; stigmas fringed, orange or rarely pale. February to April. *l.* 3 or 4, with fl., 12 to 14 in. long, ⅛ in. broad, with white line. Europe. (M.C. 26.) A species showing great range of garden as well as wild varieties. var. **albiflo'rus,** *fl.* small, white. St. Gothard (M.C. 26 B, f. 6.); **leucorhyn'chus,** *fl.* pale lavender, segs. tipped white and suffused purple on backs (M.C. 26 B, f. 4); **leucostig'ma,** *fl.* blue-lilac, stigmas creamy-white. Early; **sic'ulus,** *fl.* very small. Sicily. (M.C. 26 B, f. 9.)

**C. vers'icolor.*** *fl.* tube 4 to 5 in. long, throat glabrous, white or yellowish; segs. about 1½ in. long, ⅛ in. wide, purple to white, all self, or feathered, or veined purple outside; stigmas orange, entire. *l.* 4 or 5, with fl., about ⅛ in. broad, and 8 or 9 in. long at maturity, sheathing l. shorter than proper spathe; proper spathe monophyllous. *Corm* pyriform, ¾ in. wide; tunic of parallel fibres. Maritime Alps. (B.M. 1110; M.C. 16.) A very variable species long in cultivation from which many named garden varieties have arisen. var. **pictura'tus,** *fl.* white with rich purple feathering.

**C. vitelli'nus.** *fl.* fragrant, tapering to tube; tube pale yellow, filiform, 2 in. long; segs. orange, occasionally feathered outside with bronze, about 1 in. long, ⅛ in. broad. November to March. *l.* 5 or 6, with fl., 10 to 12 in. long, glabrous, with white band. *Corm* pyriform, ½ to ¾ in. wide and h. Syria, Asia Minor. (B.M. 6416; M.C. 50.)

**C. Wel'deni.** A form of *C. biflorus.*

**C. zona'tus.** A synonym of *C. Kotschyanus.*

## CROCUS, AUTUMN. *See* **Colchicum.**

*Croe'sus,* from Croesus, king of Lydia, of boundless wealth.

## CROE'SUS septentrionalis. *See* **Nut sawfly.**

*crombezia'nus -a -um,* from the Villa Crombez, near Cannes.

## CRONAR'TIUM ribic'ola, causes the Rust disease of Black Currants. *See* **Currants, Black, Diseases.**

## CROPS AND CROPPING. *See* **Rotation Cropping.**

**CROSNES,** or Chinese Artichoke (*Stachys affinis*), the curious tuberous rhizomes of which bear a great resemblance to the larvae of an insect, are sometimes grown for use as a vegetable. They are produced in long strings and in some abundance. They can be grown in any ordinary garden soil, being planted in March in rows

about 12 in. apart, the tubers 6 in. apart in the rows, and merely kept free from weeds. They are quite hardy and should be dug as needed from October onwards. Exposure to air for any considerable time darkens them.

**CROSSAN'DRA** (*krossos*, fringe, *aner*, male; the anthers being fringed). FAM. *Acanthaceae.* A genus of about 12 species of evergreen, free-flowering shrubs, mostly natives of Trop. Africa and Madagascar but one in E. Indies. Leaves sub-entire, whorled. Flowers large in terminal 4-sided spikes with broad bracts and narrow bracteoles; corolla tube long, limb flat, 5-cleft. Easily grown in the stove in a compost of loam and peat and increased by cuttings at almost any season in sand with bottom heat. **A**

**C. fla'va.** Stem short, glabrous. *l.* obovate-lanceolate, about 9 in. long, glabrous, undulate, lower only stalked. *fl.* bright yellow, glabrous, tube much exserted, sharply bent about middle; bracts yellow-green, rather thin, large, round, keeled, very hairy, spine-pointed; spike cone-like, short. January. Trop. W. Africa. 1852. (B.M. 4710.)

*Crossandra subacaulis* (p. 583)

**C. guineen'sis.*** Stem 2 to 6 in. h., erect, rarely branched, red, furry. *l.* in 2 to 4 pairs, elliptic to obovate, 3 to 5 in. long, with pink reticulation, otherwise deep green, margin undulate. *fl.* pale lilac; cor. tube slender, incurved, ⅔ in. long, lobes ⅓ in., obovate; bracts lanceolate, ½ in. long, overlapping, green and leathery, spine pointed;

*Crosnes*

*Crossandra undulifolia* (p. 583)

spike solitary, many-fld., 4 in. long. Trop. W. Africa. 1877. (B.M. 6346.)

**C. mucrona'ta.** *l.* oblong-lanceolate. *fl.* in dense long-stalked spikes; cor. as in *C. nilotica* but rather smaller; bracts $\frac{5}{8}$ in. long, obovate, narrowed to base, apex rounded, mucronate. Trop. W. Africa.

**C. nilot'ica.** Stem 1 to 2 ft. h. Basal l. absent or small; stem l. elliptic, up to 4 in. long, narrowed at both ends, obtuse, base decurrent. *fl.* in dense spikes 1 to $2\frac{1}{2}$ in. long, bracts $\frac{1}{2}$ to $\frac{5}{8}$ in. long, softly hairy, not spiny; cor. brick-red or orange, tube $\frac{5}{8}$ to $\frac{3}{4}$ in. long, lobes $\frac{1}{2}$ in. long, obovate. British E. Africa, Mozambique. Var. **acumina'ta** has tip of bracts more acute.

**C. subacau'lis.** Almost stemless. *l.* crowded at base, narrowly obovate, up to 6 in. long, obtuse, almost sessile. Spikes about 4 in. long, usually much looser than in *C. nilotica*; bracts 5- to 9-nerved, almost plicate. *fl.* as in *C. nilotica.* Trop. E. Africa. (B.M. 9336.)

**C. undulifo'lia.*** Erect, 1 to 3 ft. h. *l.* ovate, slender-pointed, narrowed to base, margin wavy. *fl.* orange, tube about 1 in. long, linear-incurved, limb all on one side, 5-lobed, in linear axillary spikes about 4 in. long; bracts many, about $\frac{1}{2}$ in. long, elliptic, acute. E. Indies, &c. (B.M. 2186.)

**CROSSBRED.** A term usually applied to a plant raised by crossing two distinct varieties of a plant, but sometimes also to a hybrid between two species or the progeny of such a hybrid.

**CROSS-FERTILIZATION.** The fertilization of the egg-cells of a flower by pollen from another flower whether of another individual of the same species or of another species.

**CROSSING.** The act of placing the pollen of one species or variety of plant upon the stigma of another, related to, but distinct from it, with the object of obtaining a hybrid between the two. *See* **Hybridizing.** **A**

**CROSS-POLLINATION.** The placing of the pollen of one flower upon the stigma of another, whether of the same variety or species or of another. Cross-pollination may be effected artificially by man, or naturally by wind, insect, or other natural agent. It is normal in most plants but some, e.g. chickweed, peas, are normally self-pollinated, and in many where cross-pollination is normal, there is provision for self-pollination if cross-pollination does not occur. *See also* Supplt. and **Fertilization, Pollination** in Main Work.

**CROSSOSO'MA** (*krossai*, battlement or courses of steps, *soma*, body; in allusion to the aril). FAM. *Crossomataceae.* A genus of 4 glabrous shrubs with greyish bark, white or purplish flowers with many stamens, solitary near the ends of branches, arillate seeds in follicles, and alternate, oblong, entire leaves. A well-drained soil in a sunny spot is needed and the plants, which are increased by seed, are apt to be damaged in severe winters.

**C. Bigelov'ii.** Erect shrub to 4 ft., branches slender. *l.* mostly fascicled, grey-green, ovate-oblong or obovate, almost sessile, $\frac{1}{2}$ to $\frac{3}{4}$ in. long. *fl.* white or purplish, about $\frac{1}{2}$ in. across; pet. oval; stamens 15 to 20. *Follicles* usually 2, 2- to 5-seeded. April. South-west N. America.

**C. califor'nicum.** Shrub or small tree, 3 to 15 ft. *l.* alternate, oblong to obovate, $1\frac{1}{2}$ to $3\frac{1}{2}$ in. long, short-stalked. *fl.* solitary near ends of branches, numerous, about 1 in. across, white; pet. roundish, crinkled; stamens 40 to 50. May. Santa Catalina; Guadaloupe Is. **A**

**CROSSOSOMATA'CEAE.** Dicotyledons. A family of 1 genus, Crossosoma, with 2 species of shrubs in SW. N. America, closely allied to the Spiraea group of Rosaceae, but with kidney-shaped seeds rich in endosperm and with an aril.

***crossosteg'ius -a -um,*** with covered steps.

**CROSSWORT.** *See* **Crucianella.** **A**

**CROTALA'RIA** (*krotalon*, a castanet; the pods are inflated and when they are shaken the seeds rattle). FAM. *Leguminosae.* A genus of 250 to 300 species of shrubs, herbaceous plants or annuals, widely spread throughout the tropics and sub-tropics of both hemispheres. Leaves alternate, simple or 3-, 5-, or 7-foliolate, usually with stipules. Flowers papilionaceous, often showy, in terminal or nodal racemes. Fruit a turgid or inflated pod, few- to many-seeded. Easily grown in good loamy soil. The shrubby species can be increased by cuttings of youngish wood with a bell-glass over them; the annuals produce seed freely. **A**

*Crossosoma californicum*

**C. ageratifo'lia.** Shrub of 3 ft. with glabrous, green branches. *l.* 3-foliolate, stalks $1\frac{1}{4}$ to 4 in. long; lflets. ovate, 1 to $2\frac{3}{4}$ in. long, more or less wedge-shaped, shortly stalked. *fl.* very large, pale greenish-yellow, keel dull brownish-purple at tip; standard $1\frac{1}{2}$ in. long, $1\frac{1}{4}$ in. wide, ovate, clawed; wings $\frac{3}{4}$ to 1 in. long; stamens all joined below; racemes terminal, 8 to 14 in. long. November. Trop. E. Africa. 1912. (B.M. 8505.)

**C. ala'ta.** Sub-shrub 1 to 2 ft., shoots and l. silky downy. *l.* obovate to ovate-oblong, 2 to 3 in. long, rather thin, almost sessile. *fl.* pale yellow, in short, few-fld. racemes. *Pod* linear-oblong, long-stalked. India.

**C. cajanifo'lia.** Shrub 4 to 6 ft. *l.* 3-foliolate; lflets. oval-lanceolate, tapered to both ends, appressed-hairy beneath, glabrous above. *fl.* yellow, about $\frac{1}{2}$ in. long, crowded in sub-terminal racemes a few in. long. July. Cent. America. 1824. Greenhouse.

**C. capen'sis.** Evergreen shrub 5 to 10 ft.; shoots and l. soon glabrous. *l.* 3-foliolate; stalk 1 to 2 in. long; lflets. oval to obovate, $\frac{3}{4}$ to 2 in. long; stipules like small l. *fl.* fragrant, rich yellow, in terminal racemes 4 to 6 in. long, $2\frac{1}{2}$ in. wide; standard pet. roundish-cordate, 1 in. across, striped red-brown; wings small; keel strongly incurved. Autumn. S. Africa. 1774. (B.M. 7950.) Greenhouse.

**C. Cunningham'ii.** Softly downy, glaucous shrub, 2 to 4 ft.; shoots stout. *l.* simple, 3 to 4 in. long, $1\frac{1}{4}$ to 2 in. wide, oblong to ovate-oblong, both ends rounded. *fl.* yellow-green streaked with purple, in racemes up to 6 in. long by 4 in. wide; standard pet. $1\frac{1}{4}$ in. long, pointed, reflexed; keel $1\frac{1}{2}$ in. long, tapered to a narrow point. February. NW. and Cent. Australia. 1869. (B.M. 5770.) Greenhouse.

**C. Heynea'na.*** Shrub 1 to 2 ft. *l.* simple, 3 to 5 in. long, 1 to $1\frac{1}{2}$ in. wide, oval-lanceolate, pointed; stalk very short. *fl.* in axillary and terminal racemes, 3 or 4 in. long, 2 in. wide; standard pet. $\frac{3}{4}$ in. wide, white with blue streaks at the base; wings oblong, white and blue; keel white. March. India. 1868. (B.M. 5974.) Stove.

**C. jun'cea.** Sunn Hemp. Annual, 4 ft. or more h.; stems erect, silky-downy. *l.* simple, scarcely stalked, $1\frac{1}{2}$ to 4 in. long, linear-oblong, tapered at both ends, downy beneath. *fl.* rich yellow in a terminal raceme up to 1 ft. long; standard pet. $1\frac{1}{2}$ in. across, reflexed; Keel and wings $\frac{3}{4}$ in. long. August, September. Trop. Asia, Australia. 1700. (B.M. 490; 1933 as *C. fenestrata.*) Greenhouse.

**C. longirostra'ta.*** Semi-herbaceous shrub, 3 ft.; shoots glabrous. *l.* 3-foliolate; lflets. oval, often inclined to obovate, $\frac{1}{2}$ to 1 in. long, apex rounded, mucronulate, glabrous above, downy beneath. *fl.* almost entirely rich yellow, in terminal erect racemes up to 6 in. long by 2 in. wide; standard pet. 1 in. across. Winter. Mexico 1891. (B.M. 7306.) Greenhouse.

**C. purpu'rea.*** Shrub 3 to 5 ft.; shoots appressed-downy. *l.* 3-foliolate; lflets. 1 to 1½ in. long, ¼ to ½ in. wide, oval to obovate. *fl.* in erect, terminal, long-stalked racemes 2 to 3 in. long, 1½ in. wide; standard pet. ⅝ in. across, rich crimson-purple with a basal yellow spot; wings and keel similarly coloured. Spring, Summer. S. Africa. 1790. (B.M. 1913.) Greenhouse.

**C. semperflo'rens.** Shrub 3 to 4 ft.; shoots at first downy and angular. *l.* 2 to 4 in. long, 1½ to 2½ in. wide, downy on both surfaces, apex blunt, shortly stalked. *fl.* yellow, ¾ in. long, in lateral racemes of 6 to over 20 and up to 1 ft. or more long. Summer. India. 1816. Greenhouse.

**C. seric'ea.** Shrub 3 to 4 ft.; stems angular. *l.* obovate to oblong-lanceolate, 3 to 6 in. long, half as wide, cuneate, appressed-silky beneath. *fl.* purplish, ¾ in. long, in terminal and axillary racemes often 12 in long, carrying 20 to 40 fl. *Pod* 1 to 2 in. long on a stalk half its length, the cal. persisting at base. Trop. India. Stove.

**C. stric'ta.** Low erect shrub, 2 to 4 ft.; branches sulcate, thinly silky. *l.* with minute stipules, stalks 2 to 3 in. long; lflets. obovate-oblong, obtuse, 3 to 4 in. long. *fl.* yellow, striped red, glabrous, in 20- to 50-fld. racemes, axillary and terminal, 6 to 12 in. long. *Pod* deflexed, 1½ to 2 in. long. India.

**C. verruco'sa.*** Annual, 2 ft.; stems angular, slightly downy. *l.* 1½ to 3 in. long. ¾ to 2 in. wide, oval to obovate, cuneate, apex blunt or rounded. *fl.* blue and white, in erect, terminal, downy racemes of 4 to 8; standard pet. ¾ to 1 in. wide, darkly lined; wing and keel ¾ in. long. May, June. E. Indies. 1730. Stove. Seeds ripen in Autumn.

W. J. B.

***crotalophorioi'des,*** like a castanet bearer.

**CRO'TON** (*kroton*, a tick; the seeds being like a tick). FAM. *Euphorbiaceae.* A genus of over 600 species of trees and shrubs, rarely herbs, of varying aspect, distributed over the warmer parts of the world. Flowers monoecious or dioecious; male with cylindrical, 5-toothed calyx, 5 petals and 10 to 15 stamens, bent inwards in the bud; female with many-leaved calyx, usually no petals, and 3 2-fid styles. Capsule 3-celled. None of the species have any beauty to recommend them horticulturally but several are important economically, including *C. Cascarilla* and *C. Eluteria* which yield Cascarilla bark, used as a tonic, *C. Tiglium* which yields a powerful purgative drug expressed from the seeds and known as Croton Oil, and *C. lacciferus*, which yields a lac-resin used in varnish-making. The Crotons of gardens grown for their ornamental foliage belong to the genus Codiaeum.

**C. Cascaril'la.** Cascarilla. *l.* narrow-lanceolate, acuminate, green and glabrous above, pale and densely starry-hairy beneath, margin sometimes undulate. *fl.-spike* simple, monoecious. Bahamas.

**C. Eluter'ia.** Cascarilla. *l.* ovate-lanceolate, slender-pointed, somewhat cordate at base. *fl.* with pet. in both sexes. Bahamas. (B.M. 7575.)

**C. Tig'lium.** Croton-oil Plant. Small tree. *l.* ovate, slender-pointed, toothed, metallic green to bronze and orange, stalked. *Female fl.* without pet. SE. Asia.

**CROTON OIL.** *See* **Croton Tiglium.**

**A→**

**CROWBERRY.** *See* **Empetrum nigrum.**

**CROW'EA** (in honour of Dr. James Crow, 1750-1807, of Norwich, British botanist). FAM. *Rutaceae.* A genus of 4 species of evergreen shrubs all natives of Australia. Leaves alternate, simple, glandular dotted. Shoots mostly angular. Flowers axillary or terminal; solitary or rarely in pairs. Stamens 10. Croweas are useful decorative plants which need to be grown in a cool airy greenhouse free from draughts. Like all other hard-wooded plants they need great care in watering. The best soil for them is a compost of 2 parts peat and 1 of fibrous loam with a little sand added. They can be rooted from cuttings in sandy peat under a bell-glass in a cool greenhouse but grown from cuttings they rarely make good plants. If seed can be had it is much better to raise them from seed and failing that to graft on young stocks of *Correa alba.* To induce a bushy habit the young plants should be pinched once or twice.

J. C.

**C. angustifo'lia.*** Evergreen, glabrous shrub, 2 to 3 ft. *l.* linear, 1 to 2 in. long, either entire or sparsely toothed, $\frac{1}{10}$ to $\frac{3}{16}$ in. wide, pointed, stalkless. *fl.* pale rose or almost white, 1 in. wide, solitary or rarely 2 in the l.-axils; pet. narrow oblong; anthers yellow. March. W. Australia. (B.M. 7870.)

**C. latifo'lia.** A synonym of *C. saligna.*

*Crowea saligna*

**C. salig'na.*** Glabrous evergreen shrub of erect habit, 2 to 3 ft. *l.* mostly lanceolate, tapered to both ends, 1 to 2½ in. long, ¼ to ½ in. wide, but occasionally more, ovate or linear. *fl.* rich rosy-red, 1¼ to 1½ in. wide, solitary in the l.-axils; pet. spreading, ovate; anthers yellow. July. New S. Wales. 1790. (B.M. 989.) SYN. *C. latifolia.*

W. J. B.

**CROWFOOT.** *See* **Ranunculus.**

**CROWN.** *See* **Corona.**

**CROWN BARK.** *See* **Cinchona officinalis.**

**CROWN BEARD.** *See* **Verbesina.**

**CROWN GALL.** Besides outgrowths and swellings caused by insects on plants some galls are caused by *Bacterium tumefaciens* and as the galls are often near the ground level the name given to the disease is Crown Gall. It is now known that other parts of plants are liable to infection and galls are found both below ground on the roots and at times on the stems some feet above ground level. A wide range of plants has been found attacked by Crown Gall, including Apple, Pear, Peach, Plum, Loganberry, Raspberry, Blackberry, Rose, Beetroot, Hollyhock, Dahlia. The galls are irregular, rounded swellings, in size from a pea to a cricket ball or even larger, whitish and soft when young and brown and harder when old. On the roots many galls of all sizes may be seen at the same time or the base of the stem may be swollen up into one huge gall. The disease is more likely to spread on wet soils and the Bacterium is probably always a wound parasite, i.e. only able to infect through wounds. It is probably not so destructive as was first thought and in apple trees, for instance, trees with galls on the roots do not seem to be less vigorous nor is their crop reduced. Nevertheless, in a clean garden or nursery care should be taken not to plant galled stocks. Where the disease appears freshly planted trees should not have their roots injured or they should be dipped in a fungicide. This Crown Gall disease should not be confused with Leafy Gall or with the peculiar growths on Apples, &c., known as Burr Knots.

D. E. G.

A→

***Croya'nus,*** in honour of Count de Croy of Belgium, *c.* 1854.

**CRUCIANEL'LA** (diminutive of *crux*, cross, the leaves being placed crosswise). FAM. *Rubiaceae.* A genus of about 25 species of annual or usually perennial herbs, natives of the Mediterranean region; related to Phuopsis (which is often combined with it) but with 2 unequal style-arms, instead of a simple style with club-shaped or capitate tip. Leaves 4 to many in a whorl, linear or lanceolate. Flowers hermaphrodite, in spikes or clusters; corolla tubular, long, funnel-shaped. The perennial species which alone are worth growing are easily cultivated in ordinary soil, and readily raised from seed or by division in spring or autumn. Sunny places on the rock-garden suit them best.

**C. aegypti'aca** A synonym of *C. graeca* and *C. herbacea.*

**C. glau'ca.** Branched, nearly erect. *l.* 4 in a whorl, linear, mucronate, margins revolute, prickly. *fl.* yellow, in a loose spike; bracts ciliate. July. Persia. 1837.

**C. grae'ca.** Erect or decumbent annual. *l.* ovate or elliptic, upper linear, scabrid, margin revolute. *fl.* in long spikes; cor. longer than bracts. Greece. (F.G. 140 as *C. monspeliaca.*) *C. herbacea* has shorter spikes and fl.

**C. marit'ima.** Much branched from a woody base, procumbent, glaucous, glabrous. *l.* 4 in a whorl, lanceolate, stiff, mucronate. *fl.* cream, in interrupted bracteate spikes. July, August. 1640.

**C. stylo'sa.** A synonym of *Phuopsis stylosa.*

**C. suaveo'lens.** Erect, branched perennial. *l.* 6 or 8 in a whorl, linear, mucronate, margins prickly, revolute. *fl.* yellow, opposite, in dense spikes; bracts lanceolate, ciliate. July. W. Asia. 1838.

***crucia'tus -a -um,*** cross-shaped.

**CRUCIF'ERAE.** Dicotyledons. A family of over 200 genera with about 1,600 species of herbs, with a few shrubs and sub-shrubs, mainly in the temperate and colder regions of the world with a few in the tropics. Leaves usually alternate, sometimes pinnately lobed. Flowers perfect, usually in terminal racemes, regular; sepals 4; petals 4 (rarely absent), spreading to form a cross; stamens 6 (4 long, 2 short); stigmas 2; ovary superior, 2-celled (rarely 1-celled). Fruit a pod, usually dehiscent. The family contains no poisonous plant and many species are of importance as food, especially the genus Brassica, as preventives of scurvy (for many are rich in sulphur compounds), for the oil contained in the seeds (e.g. rape), or for the beauty or scent of their flowers. The genera treated here are Aethionema, Alyssoides, Alyssum, Anastatica, Arabis, Aubrieta, Barbarea, Berteroa, Biscutella, Brassica, Braya, Cakile, Cardamine, Cheiranthus, Chorispora, Cochlearia, Coluteocarpus, Crambe, Dentaria, Draba, Erysimum, Farsetia, Heliophila, Hesperis, Hutchinsia, Iberis, Ionopsidium, Isatis, Kernera, Lepidium, Lesquerella, Lobularia, Lunaria, Malcolmia, Matthiola, Megacarpaea, Moricandia, Morisia, Nasturtium, Noccaea, Notothlaspi, Orychophragmus, Parrya, Peltaria, Petrocallis, Ptilotrichum, Raphanus, Ricotia, Schivereckia, Schizopetalon, Schouwia, Selenia, Sinapis, Sobolewskia, Staehelina, Stanleya, Streptanthus, Tchihatchewia, Thlaspi, Vella, Vesicaria. Several diseases attack members of this family, most of them being of importance on Brassicas. *See* **Cabbage diseases.**

A

***cruciform,*** cross-like, as the petals of a flower of Cabbage or Wallflower.

***Cruckshanks'ii,*** in honour of Alexander Cruckshanks, who collected in the Andes, *c.* 1825–30.

**CRUEL PLANT.** *See* **Araujia sericofera, Cynanchum acuminatifolium.**

***cruen'tus -a -um,*** blood-coloured.

***crumena'tus -a -um,*** pouched.

***cru'ra,*** leg-shaped.

***crux-mal'tae,*** Maltese cross.

**CRYOPHY'TUM.** *See* **Mesembryanthemum.**

**CRYOSOPH'ILA** (*kryos*, cold, *phileo*, to love). FAM. *Palmaceae.* A genus of about 8 species of Trop. American trees with spineless trunks, except at the base where the aerial roots harden and become stiff spines pointing downwards, thus differing from Trithrinax; the palmate leaves also are divided to the base into stalkless segments; leaf stalk flat, slender, smooth; sheath short and fibrous. Inflorescence at first flattened. Flowers creamy-white; stamens free. These palms mostly need stove conditions with a minimum temperature of 60°, but *C. nana* will succeed in an intermediate house. The soil should be a good fibrous loam with considerable sand, the trees doing best if planted out. Propagation is by seed sown in spring in fresh peat with bottom heat.

**C. Chuc'o.** Stem 30 ft. h., about 5 in. thick, slender, flexuous. *l.* about 6 ft. across, divided to or beyond the middle into 15 to 20 lanceolate segs., dark green above, paler beneath. Brazil. SYN. *Thrinax Chuco.*

**C. nana.** Stem 30 to 40 ft. h. *l.* much divided in young plants, with fewer divisions in age, about 5 ft. across, deep green above, whitish beneath; l.-stalk 3 to 4 ft. long. *fl.* dark creamy-pink. Mexico. 1879. (B.M. 7302.) SYN. *Chamaerops stauracantha, Acanthorrhiza aculeata.*

**CRYPTAN'THA** (*cruptein*, hidden, *anthos*, flower). FAM. *Boraginaceae.* A genus of about 120 species of annual or perennial herbs, natives of Pacific America, with linear or lanceolate, rarely ovate leaves. Calyx divided to the base. Corolla usually cylindrical or funnel-shaped, lobes somewhat rounded; stamens 5, rarely 3, included. Nutlets 1 to 4, striate on the inner face. *C. barbigerum* is to be treated as other hardy annuals.

**C. barbig'erum.** Bristly annual, 12 to 15 in. h., branched at base. *l.* linear, $\frac{1}{2}$ to 2 in. long. *fl.* white, in branching scorpioid cymes; cor. tubular, $\frac{1}{8}$ in. across; cal. lobes linear, $\frac{1}{4}$ in. long. Summer, autumn. California. 1886. SYN. *Eritrichium barbigerum, Krynitzkia barbigera.*

**CRYPTAN'THUS** (*krypto*, to hide, *anthos*, flower; the flowers being buried among the bracts). FAM. *Bromeliaceae.* A genus of a dozen dwarf, more or less tufted, often stemless, herbaceous plants, natives of Brazil. Related to Bromelia but with petals joined by their margins. Flowers white or greenish-white in a dense head immersed in the centre of the leaf-rosette, which is of the same colour as the outer leaves. Leaves spreading, with stolons in the axils of the outermost. Treatment as for Billbergia.

**C. acau'lis.** Tufted, about 6 in. h., sometimes caulescent. *l.* narrowed above sheath, lanceolate, wavy, spiny, recurved, green above, white-scaly beneath. *fl.* white in a central subsessile cluster. (B.R. 1157 as *Tillandsia acaulis.*) In var. **dis'color** *l.* are shiny above; **pictura'tus,** *l.* variegated; **zebri'nus,** *l.* striped.

**C. Beuck'eri.** Dwarf, about 6 in. h. *l.* in an open rosette, elliptic, acute or acuminate, irregularly blotched green, rose and white above, covered with appressed scales beneath; stalked, margins spiny. *fl.* white in a small head. S. Brazil. 1883. (B.H. 1881, p. 342, t. 17.)

**C. bivitta'tus.** *l.* spreading, recurved, about 9 in. long, 1 to $1\frac{1}{2}$ in. wide, narrowed above sheath, rather undulate, sharply toothed at margin; dull brown beneath, green with 2 broad buff longitudinal bands above, which are dull red at base. *fl.* white, few. Brazil. 1859. (B.M. 5270 as *Billbergia bivittata.*) var. **atropurpu'reus** is smaller in all parts, *l.* constantly red.

**C. farino'sus.** Possibly a synonym of *Billbergia zebrina.*

**C. nit'idus.** A synonyn of *Catopsis nitida.*

**C. pu'milus.** A synonym of *C. acaulis.*

**C. undula'tus.** Closely related to *C. acaulis* but with cal. lobes much longer than tube, and *l.* only 2 in. long. Brazil. var. **ru'ber,** *l.* tinged reddish-brown. (Ref. B. 287 as var. *purpureus.*)

**C. zona'tus.** *l.* 10 to 15 in a short rosette, oblong-lanceolate, 6 to 9 in. long, $1\frac{1}{2}$ in. wide, with alternating green and ashen bands above, thinly white-scaly beneath, margins closely spiny. *fl.* white,

1½ in. long, in a small tuft in centre of rosette. Brazil. 1842. SYN. *Pholidophyllum zonatum, Tillandsia zonata, T. zebrina.* Var. **fus'cus,** *l.* deep red in winter, paler in summer.

***crypto-,*** in compound words, signifying hidden.

***cryptocar'pus -a -um,*** with hidden fruit.

**CRYPTOCHI'LUS** (*kryptos*, hidden, *cheilos* lip; the lip being partly hidden by the sepals). FAM. *Orchidaceae.* A genus containing 2 species of very interesting epiphytic orchids, allied to Eria, natives of the Himalaya. Flowers closely set in distichous spikes, shorter than their persistent bracts; sepals connate into a tube with divergent apices, concealing the narrow petals, the lip included, adnate to the foot of the column, narrow, erect; pollinia 8. Pseudobulbs crowded, 1 or 2-leaved. Leaves 4 to 6 in. high. Both species succeed well in the intermediate house with similar treatment to Erias.

**C. lu'tea.** *fl.* pale yellow, sub-globose; sep. obtuse; pet. and lip lanceolate; spike 2 to 4 in. long; scape 2 to 4 in. long, rather slender. Summer. *l.* 1 or 2, 3 to 5 in. long, linear-lanceolate, acute, petiolate or nearly sessile. *Pseudobulbs* oblong, 2 to 3 in. long. Sikkim Himalaya. 1882.

**C. Mei'rax.** A synonym of *Eria Meirax.*

**C. sanguin'ea.** *fl.* brilliant scarlet, disposed in a terminal erect raceme; sep. cohering in a tube 3-lobed at the top with dark-brownish margins; bracts rather shorter than fl. Summer. *Pseudobulbs* clustered, spheroidal, 1- to 3-leaved. Nepal. About 1837. (B.R. 24, 23; A.B.G.C. 8, 220.)

E. C.

**CRYPTOCOC'CUS fa'gi.** *See* **Fagus pests.**

***cryptoco'pis,*** hidden sword.

**CRYPTOCORY'NE** (*kryptos*, hidden, *koryne*, club; the spadix is completely hidden in the tube of the spathe). FAM. *Araceae.* A genus of about 40 species of rhizomatous herbs, natives of Trop. Asia and Malaya. Leaves cordate, elliptic, lanceolate or linear. Peduncle usually short. Spathe tube short or long, blade straight, folded, or twisted. Spadix very slender. Flowers unisexual, naked; stamens 1 or 2; carpels 1. The species need stove conditions, are mainly aquatic or marsh plants, and require treatment similar to that of the tender species of Arum.

**C. cilia'ta.** About 1 ft. h. *l.* oblong-lanceolate to linear-lanceolate, unequal-sided, 6 to 12 in. long, somewhat acute, deep green except for pale midrib; stalk 4 to 12 in. or more long. *Spathe* tube, lower part about ¾ in. long, narrow, upper about ½ in. long, very narrow, dirty green, limb ovate-oblong, about 2 in. long, densely fringed, throat yellow, rest purple. *fl.* fragrant. June. India, Malaya. 1823.

**C. Griffith'ii.** *l.* cordate-ovate, obtuse, about 2 in. long, 1½ in. wide, stalk slender, 4 to 6 in. long. *Spathe* tube, lower oblong-cylindrical, ½ in. long, upper about 1 in. long, rose; blade spreading, oblong-ovate to ovate-lanceolate, about 1 in. long with a cusp nearly ½ in. long, blood-red within. Malaya. (B.M. 7719.)

**C. retrospira'lis.** *rhiz.* vertical or oblique. *l.* linear-lanceolate, 4 to 12 in. long, ⅓ to ½ in. wide; stalk ½ to 2 in. long. *Spathe* tube, lower, ½ in. long, upper 4 in. long, about $\frac{1}{16}$ in. wide; blade linear-lanceolate, about 3 in. long, twisted. India, Malaya.

**C. spira'lis.** *l.* linear-lanceolate, 4 to 6 in. long, ⅓ to ½ in. wide. *Spathe* tube, lower obconic about ¾ in. long, upper ⅓ in. long; blade linear-lanceolate, 4 in. or more long, purple, rugose within, at first twisted, later straight. India. 1816. (B.M. 2220 and L.B.C. 525 as *Arum spirale.*)

**CRYPTOGAMAE.** Plants not Phanerogams (q.v.), i.e. which do not produce seeds. There are 3 great groups. Thallophyta, Bryophyta, and Pteridophyta; see under these titles.

**CRYPTOGRAM'MA** (from *kryptos*, hidden, and *gramme*, writing; in allusion to the concealed sori). Mountain Parsley Fern; Rock-Brake. FAM. *Polypodioceae.* A genus of 7 species of ferns nearly related to Pellaea and distinguished mainly by the dimorphic fronds. Sterile and fertile fronds usually different from the same root; sori terminal on the veins, at first separate, sub-globose, afterwards confluent, the continuous involucre formed of the changed margin of the frond, rolled over them till full maturity. *See also* **Ferns.**

The Mountain Parsley Fern is a deciduous plant, losing its fronds about the end of October and starting into growth again about the beginning of May. Its fertile fronds, considerably longer than the others, and produced as a second crop of foliage later in the season, are useful for bouquets and button-holes. The spores ripen and scatter themselves, in their native state, about September, after which the fronds soon die down, the barren ones remaining rather longer than the others.

Although usually found growing wild in exposed situations, the Mountain Parsley Fern grows well in a cool, moist, shady spot, and is adapted for a nook in a rock garden, where it should be planted in a well-drained place in a mixture of loam and peat in about equal parts, with the addition of bricks broken into small pieces; care should be taken that the compost is free from lime, which is injurious. It may be propagated by seedlings, but this is slow and tedious; it is readily increased by division of the crowns in the spring, just before growth begins. It will also grow luxuriantly in a cold frame, or for 2 or 3 years in the greenhouse, or under the shade of vines, where, however, it seldom lasts any longer. The plants should always be well established in pots before being turned out into the border or the rock-garden.

**C. acrostichoi'des.*** Larger and stronger than *C. crispa*; barren segs. thicker, more prominently veined, and not so deeply cut; fertile ⅜ to ½ in. long, $\frac{1}{12}$ in. broad; indusium spreading when mature. NW. America. (B.B. ed. 2, 1, 32.)

**C. Brunonia'na.** Habit of *C. crispa*, but fertile segs. oblong, about ¼ in. long, $\frac{1}{12}$ in. broad, indusium spreading when plant mature, and leaving a space free from fruit in the centre. (F.B.I. 164.)

**C. crisp'a.*** *sti.* tufted, slightly scaly towards base. *Fronds* 2 to 4 in. long, 1½ to 2 in. broad, oblong, 3- or 4-pinnate; ultimate segs. of barren frond obovate-cuneate, deeply pinnatifid, of fertile frond pod-shaped, ⅜ to ¼ in. long. Arctic and N. temperate regions (Great Britain). (H.B.F. 39.) SYN. *Allosorus crispus.*

**C. Stel'leri.** *sti.* 2 to 3 in. long, scattered, slender, straw-colour or pale brown. *Fronds* 2 to 4 in. long, 1 to 2 in. broad, ovate, 2- or 3-pinnatifid; pinnae deltoid-lanceolate, 1 to 2 in. long, cut to rachis; lower pinnules sometimes again slightly divided; ultimate segs. of barren frond obovate, slightly crenate; of fertile linear-oblong, terminal much larger than others. Indusia broad, continuous, membranous. N. America, N. India, &c. (H.S. 2, 133 B.) SYN. *Pellaea gracilis, P. Stelleri, Pteris gracilis, P. Stelleri.* Greenhouse.

**CRYPTOME'RIA** (*kryptos*, hidden, *meris* part; all parts of the flower being hidden). FAM. *Pinaceae.* Evergreen trees with reddish-brown, fibrous bark, shed in strips, usually whorled, or irregularly whorled, branches, and spreading or pendulous branchlets, which, after several years, are shed with the leaves. As with most other Conifers the juvenile and mature types of leaves greatly differ in character and in some varieties the juvenile type is persistent. Juvenile leaves spirally arranged, flattened, soft to the touch, ½ to 1 in. long; mature type stiff, harsh to the touch, spirally arranged, sickle-shaped and quadrangular in section, living 4 or 5 years. Male and female flowers on different parts of the same branch; male flowers in clusters from the leaf axils near the points of shoots, female near the points of short branches and first appearing as small rosettes of green leaves. Both are produced in autumn but do not expand until March. Cones solitary, terminating a short shoot, rather less than 1 in. wide, with numerous loose, wedge-shaped, prickly scales with from 3 to 6 seeds, bearing rudimentary wings, on each scale. It is not unusual to find a growing shoot prolonged from the apex of the cone. Only one species is known, a native of Japan and China. Cryptomerias are hardy in most parts of the country and grow to their largest dimensions in rich, deep, moist alluvial soils, in places sheltered from strong winds. Propagated by seeds, and the varieties by cuttings inserted in sandy soil in a cold close frame or under a handlight in autumn. The wood is fragrant, and is one of the most widely used timbers in Japan, where also the tree is one of the most important.

**C. el'egans.** A variety of *C. japonica.*

**C. japon'ica.*** Japanese Cedar. See generic description for l. and cones. Tree of 120 to 150 ft., girth 15 to 25 ft. Japan, China. 1842. (D.J.C. 181.) The following are the more important varieties, some of which are at times offered under Japanese names; var. **albovariega'ta,*** some of the shoots with white l., very dwarf. Rock-garden; **araucarioi'des,** branchlets long, slender, branching at the points into many secondary branchlets, *l.* short, rigid, curving inwards, dark green. Japan. 1885. SYN. var. *lycopodioides;* **Bandai-sugi,** dwarf, broadly conical, less stiff than var. *monstrosa,* remains green through winter. Rock-garden; **compac'ta,** dense, pyramidal bush; **crista'ta** has many of the secondary branches fasciated; **dacrydioi'des,** compact, with short, slender branches, and stiff, closely arranged l.; **el'egans,*** distinct by its plumose habit with the juvenile type of foliage, in summer *l.* green, becoming bronze or purplish in autumn until spring, branchlets usually short, densely arranged, with masses of secondary branchlets which tend to over-weight the branches, making it difficult to keep well developed trees erect. It is at its best in a young state. Cones rarely produced. 20 to 25 ft. h. Japan. 1861. SYN. *C. elegans;* **el'egans compac'ta** and **elegans na'na,** bushes with the juvenile type of leaves; **Fortu'nei,** *see* var. **sinensis; glau'ca,** habit of type but *l.* glaucous; **globo'sa na'na,** compact, roundish bush, up to 8 ft. h., slow growing. Rock-garden; **Lobb'ii,** differs from type by its denser and more erect branch system, more pyramidal habit, and shorter and darker green *l.* SYN. *C. viridis;* **Lobbii na'na,** a synonym of var. *pygmaea;* **lycopodioi'des,** *see* var. **araucarioides; monstro'sa,** has many branchlets fasciated; more singular than beautiful; **na'na,** a synonym of var. *pygmaea;* **pen'dula,** lateral branches long, slender, pendulous; **pun'gens,** *l.* short, straight, sharp pointed; **pyg'maea,** dwarf, compact bush. Rock-garden. SYN. var. *Lobbii nana,* var. *nana;* **selaginoi'des,** branches long, slender with branches tufted near tip; **sinen'sis,** the Chinese form of the species; more slender and more pendulous branchlets than the Japanese, and with rarely more than 2 seeds on each scale. SYN. var. *Fortunei;* **spira'lis,** a curious form with l. closely appressed in a dense spiral around the branchlets; **variega'ta,** has patches of shoots with yellow l. amongst the normal green; **Vilmorinia'na,** very dwarf, stunted, with sharp-pointed *l.* Rock garden.

**C. vi'ridis.** A synonym of *C. japonica Lobbii.*

W. D.

**CRYPTOPHORAN'THUS** (*kryptos,* hidden, *phoreo,* to bear, *anthos,* blossom; lip, petals, &c., concealed within the almost closed sepals). FAM. *Orchidaceae.* An epiphytic genus of about 10 species allied to Pleurothallis, differing by the formation of the sepals which, connate both at base and tip, leave a slit-like aperture on either side, 'windows' (hence the name 'Window-bearing Orchid') through which small insects can enter. Natives of Brazil and Trop. America. Temperatures, compost, &c., should be as for *Odontoglossum crispum.* Leaves rather leathery. Small pans which can be suspended are best, particularly as the flowers, produced from the junction of the stem and leaf, are sheltered by the leaf.

**C. atropurpu'reus.** *fl.* small, 2 to 4, ½ to ¾ in. long, dark violet. *l.* elliptic. 3 to 6 in. h. Cuba, Jamaica. 1836. (B.M. 4164 as *Masdevallia fenestrata.*)

**C. Daya'nus.*** *fl.* 2 to 3, 1 in. or more wide, yellow, irregularly spotted and marked with red-purple, yellow beneath. *l.* 4 in. long by 2 in. broad, somewhat heart-shaped. 3 to 8 in. h. The finest in the genus. Colombia. 1875. (B.M. 8740.)

**C. fenestra'tus.** *fl.* fasciculate, numerous, small, yellowish, spotted and shaded with purple. *l.* 3 to 4 in. long, 1 to 1½ in. broad. Brazil. 1882. SYN. *Pleurothallis fenestratus.*

**C. gracilen'tus.** *fl.* ⅓ to ½ in. long, dull purple. Allied to *C. atropurpureus. l.* narrow, about 5 in. long. Costa Rica. 1875. SYN. *Masdevallia gracilenta.*

**C. hypodis'cus.** Allied to *C. Dayanus,* but *fl.* smaller, dull purple with stiff whitish hairs on the nerves of the dorsal sep. *l.* long stalked. About 8 in. h. Colombia. 1878. SYN. *Masdevallia hypodiscus.*

**C. Lehmann'i.** *fl.* about 1 in. or less, greenish-yellow, lined with dull purple. 3 to 5 in. h. Allied to *C. Dayanus.* Brazil. 1899.

**C. macula'tus.** *fl.* fasciculate, ⅛ in. long, yellowish, densely spotted with crimson-brown, pubescent. *l.* 1 to 2 in. long, ¾ to 1¼ in. broad, spotted purple above. Dwarf so that fl. rest on ground. Brazil. 1887.

**C. minu'tus.** *fl.* ⅓ in. long, deep maroon purple. *l.* nearly orbicular, apiculate. Stem ½ in. h. Brazil. 1891?

**C. Moor'ei.** *fl.* ¾ in. long, dull red-purple with purple lines. *l.* broadly elliptical, 1½ in. long, purplish beneath. Habitat?

**C. oblongifo'lius.** *fl.* about 1 in. long, dull yellow, veined with maroon purple. *l.* elliptic-oblong, 1½ to 3 in. long. 3 to 5 in. h. Andes. 1894.

E. C.

**CRYPTORRHYN'CHUS lapath'i.** Willow Weevil. *See under* **Salix, Pests.**

*crytoso'rus -a -um,* with hidden sori.

*Cryptophoranthus Dayanus*

**CRYPTOSTE'GIA** (*kryptos,* hidden, *stego,* to cover; the scales in the throat of the flower cover the anthers). FAM. *Asclepiadaceae.* A genus of climbing evergreens easily grown in the stove-house in a mixture of loam and peat. Cuttings may be rooted in sand under a glass in heat.

**C. grandiflo'ra.*** *l.* opposite, elliptic, shining, tip blunt; stalk short. *fl.* large, reddish-purple, bell-funnel-shaped; tube with 5 narrow, 2-partite scales opposite to and covering the anthers. July. E. Indies. 1824.

**C. madagascarien'sis.** *fl.* pink. June. Madagascar. 1826.　　**A**

**CRYPTOSTEM'MA** (*kryptos,* hidden, *stemma,* crown). FAM. *Compositae.* A genus of 3 species of creeping or spreading hoary herbs, natives of S. Africa. Achenes hairy, the hairs hiding the scales of the pappus; receptacle honeycombed; involucral scales in many rows, overlapping. Seeds should be sown in gentle heat in early spring. The seedlings may, when large enough, be placed 2 or 3 in a pot and grown entirely in the greenhouse or be planted out in the border about mid-June.

**C. calendula'ceum.** Annual. *l.* lyrate, pinnatifid, 3-nerved, green and hispid above, white-hairy beneath. *fl.-heads* with many pale-yellow rays purplish beneath, sterile; disk. *fl.* greenish with black-purple border, 5-cleft; peduncles 1-fld., 2 or 3 together at ends of branches, red-hairy. May, June. Tender. (B.M. 2252.)

**C. Forbesia'num.** Stemless. *l.* pinnatipartite, lobes linear-lanceolate, entire, glabrous above, snow-white beneath, margin revolute. *fl.-heads* with yellow rays and dark disk. Summer.

**C. niv'eum.** Decumbent or creeping, branching, white-woolly. *l.* ovate, cordate or roundish; stalk long. *fl.-heads* yellow, solitary. SYN. *Microstephium niveum.*

**CRYPTOSTYL'IS** (*kryptos,* hidden, *stylos,* style). FAM. *Orchidaceae.* A small genus of terrestrial fleshy-rooted orchids of which 4 are known in Australia, and 2 or 3 in the E. Indies and Malaya. Flowers in loose racemes or spikes. Sepals and petals nearly equal, slender, convolute and appearing subulate when the flowers open. Lip uppermost, sessile with a broad base enclosing the column, above which it is contracted and expanded into an undivided blade. Column very short. Scapes leafless, simple, 2- or many-sheathed, bracts membranous, acute. Leaves few or solitary, on usually long, rigid petioles, oblong, narrow or broadly lance-shaped with prominent netted veins. The Australian species prefer a moist peaty soil, and a winter temperature of about 50° F., those from more tropical countries probably need a higher temperature. The genus is remarkable in that at least one of the Australian species, *C. leptochila*, is pollinated by the male of an ichneumon fly which, owing to shape or scent (perhaps both), mistakes the flowers for females of its species.

**C. arachni'tes.** *fl.* few or many in a loose spike; *pet.* dull green, linear, with the longer sep. spreading; lip yellowish, mottled and lined with purple, pubescent or cobwebby, erect, elliptic-ovate or lanceolate acute, greenish; scape 6 to 18 in. h., the base (and petioles) purple. *l.* long, petiolate, ovate, acuminate, striate nerved. Java. 1863. (B.M. 5381.) SYN. *Zosterostylis arachnites.*

**C. leptochi'la.** *fl.* 2 to 8, about 2 in. h.; sep. and pet. narrow, greenish; lip narrow, light or dark red with 2 rows of dark spots along the middle; margins incurved. Up to 18 in. h. (F.A.O. 1, pt. 3.)

**C. longifo'lia.** A synonym of *C. subulata.*

**C. subula'ta.** *fl.* 3 to 8, rather distant, over 1 in. broad; sep. yellowish-green, narrow; pet. the same colour, shorter; lip red, with reddish-brown markings, pointing upwards, margins reflexed, the short style hidden in the cucullate base. *l.* solitary?, lanceolate, on long stalks. 1 to 2 ft. h. Australia. 1885. Greenhouse. (F.A.O. 2.) SYN. *C. longifolia.*

E. C.

***crystall'inus -a -um,*** with crystal-like appearance.

***crystalloca'lyx,*** the calyx covered with glistening papillae.

**CTENAN'THE** (*kteis,* comb, *anthe,* flower; from the arrangement of the bracts). FAM. *Marantaceae.* A genus of about 12 Brazilian closely similar perennial herbs with long-stalked basal-, short-stalked stem-leaves, and the inflorescence with closely imbricate persistent green bracts. The green bracts and 2 petaloid staminodes serve to distinguish it from Stromanthe, where the bracts are coloured, the staminodes small or none. As in Stromanthe the leaves are inverted. For cultivation *see* **Calathea.**

KEY
1. *Lvs. irregularly spotted and striped yellow and green*     C. Lubbersiana
1. *Lvs. green above or striped white*     2
2. *Lvs. green on both sides*     3
2. *Lvs. red beneath*     4
3. *L.-stalk violet, very slender*     C. setosa
3. *L.-stalk green, stout*     C. compressa
4. *Lvs. rather leathery with white stripes along side-veins; sheath red, smooth*     C. Oppenheimiana
4. *Lvs. not leathery, white striped along side-veins; sheath strongly hairy*     C. Kummeriana

**C. compres'sa.** About 2 ft. h. *l.-stalk* about 5 in. long, its apical swelling appressed hairy; blade linear or somewhat ovate-oblong, slender pointed, up to 15 in. long, green on both sides. *fl.* white, in solitary or twin racemes. Brazil.

**C. Kummeria'na.** Stoloniferous herb about 15 in. h. *l.-stalk* about 2 in. long, its apical swelling downy; blade ovate or rather narrowly oblong, about 6 in. long, deep green above with white veins, purple beneath. *fl.* white in a solitary raceme. The peduncle densely red-hairy. Brazil.

**C. Lubbersia'na.** About 18 in. h. *l.-stalk* about 4 in. long, its apical swelling downy; blade linear-oblong, or linear, about 8 in. long, deep green with yellow variegation above, pale green beneath. *fl.* white. Brazil.

**C. Oppenheimia'na.** Strong herb about 3 ft. h. *l.-stalk* long, downy; blade unequal sided, lanceolate, long slender-pointed, about 15 in. long, leathery, deep green with pale ashy bands above, purple beneath. *fl.* in a usually solitary spike. Brazil. 1874. SYN. *Stromanthe Porteana Oppenheimiana, Calathea Oppenheimiana.*

**C. seto'sa.** Stoloniferous herb about 30 in. h. *l.-stalk* about 4 in. long, purple, its apical swelling downy; blade linear to lanceolate, about 15 in. long, green on both sides. *fl.* white with yellow throat, in a sessile or shortly stalked panicle. Brazil.

***ctenopet'alus -a -um,*** petals pinnatifid.

**CTENOPHRYN'IUM** (*kteis,* comb; from the arrangement of the bracts). FAM. *Marantaceae.* A genus of a single perennial Madagascar herb distinct from Phrynium by the dorsi-ventral comb-like arrangement of the bracts. For cultivation *see* **Calathea,** to which this is nearly related.

**C. unilatera'le.** About 2½ ft. h. Stem leafy. *l.-stalk* about 8 in. long, its apical swelling downy; blade lanceolate or linear-lanceolate about 12 in. long. *fl.* white; bracts yellow, reddish at base. Madagascar. Before 1872. (Ref. B. 312 as *Phrynium unilaterale.*) SYN. *Myrosma madagascariensis.*

**CUBA BAST.** The inner bark of *Hibiscus elatus.*

**CUBAN LILY.** *See* **Scilla peruviana.**

***cuba'nus -a -um,*** Cuban.

**CUBE ROOT.** *See* **Fish Poison Plants.**

***Cubeb'a,*** Arabic name.

**CUBEBS.** *See* **Piper Cubeba.**

***cuben'sis -is -e,*** Cuban.

***cubita'lis -is -e,*** the length of the fore-arm and hand.

**CUCKOO BUDS.** *See* **Ranunculus bulbosus.**

**CUCKOO FLOWER.** *See* **Cardamine pratensis.**

**CUCKOO PINT.** *See* **Arum maculatum.**

**CUCKOO SPIT.** Frothy fluid surrounding and exuded by the immature stage of the Frog-hopper (q.v.).

***cuculla'ris -is -e, cuculla'tus -a -um,*** cucullate; hood-like, having sides or apex curved inwards so as to resemble a hood.

**CUCULLI.** The curious appendages to the anthers which form the corona in Asclepiadaceae.

**CUCUMBER** (*Cucumis sativus*). The cucumber, believed to be a native of Africa and the warmer parts of Asia, has been grown extensively for some thousands of years, and reference to its forcing is made by Pliny. By nature it is a trailing plant with a hairy stem and large leaves at the ends of long petioles. The relatively coarse root system is made up of long thick white roots having thinner feeding roots chiefly towards the ends. These roots are unusually susceptible to attack by fungi and bacteria and are often in an advanced state of decay half-way through the crop. They are replaced by adventitious roots which break from the base of the stem above the original root system and so in commercial cultivation the beds are top dressed with soil and manure several times during the summer to encourage new root development and to nourish the surface roots.

The flowers, both male and female are produced in the axils of the leaves, singly or in clusters of 2 to 7. Male and female flowers rarely occur in the same axil. Cucumbers are allowed to develop on the lateral shoots or on any shoots which arise from them. Those growing on the main stem should be removed while they are young.

The English cucumber is parthenocarpic, and develops as a vegetative growth independently of fertilization. The long cucumber either smooth or spiny according to variety is seedless. To produce seeds the young female flower must be pollinated with pollen from a male flower. Accidental pollination by bees or large flies causes the cucumber fruit to swell at the end containing the seeds and spoils it for market purposes.

For successful cultivation the cucumber requires a good deal of heat and moisture and a rich open soil. Commercially it is grown in relatively low glasshouses, 100 to 200 ft. long and 13 to 15 ft. wide, in which the gutters are about 3 to 4 ft. and the ridge 8 to 9 ft. high. Houses 14 to 15 ft. wide are most suitable for they allow an early crop of tomatoes to be grown in pots standing in a double row down the centre. Further, the workers have greater freedom and can work in less cramped conditions than in the old 13-ft. wide house and so the work is done better. Commercial cucumber houses are provided with 4 rows of 4-in. hot-water pipes and a boiler sufficient to maintain a temperature of 70° F. when the outside temperature is 40° F. In small nurseries and in private gardens cucumbers are often grown on hotbeds in frames. They may also be grown on mounds or ridges in the open during the summer.

Cucumbers are not really satisfactory in unheated glasshouses. They can be grown in this way, but heavy crops should not be expected. In very small houses a few cucumber plants are sometimes grown alongside all kinds of other plants. This is not satisfactory, because to do well they need an air temperature around 70° F., which is much too high for the usual plants grown in very small houses. Cucumbers and tomatoes do not mix very well.

For the early cucumber crop seeds are sown towards the end of November and the young plants are planted out in beds about the middle of January. For the main crop seed is sown during the second half of December for planting out about the middle of February. A second crop may be planted out before the beginning of July, and in sunny districts a late crop may be planted out in August and carried through the autumn to the end of February.

Seeds are usually sown 45 to 50 in an ordinary tomato seed tray 14 in. × 9 in. × 3 in., filled with a compost of a good medium loam with an equal volume of an old cucumber bed and then sterilizing the mixture by means of steam. Where sterilization is impracticable mix 4 parts good turfy loam with 1 part well-decayed horse manure, choosing the strawy material in preference to the faecal matter. Germination of the seed in the boxes is assisted by resting them on staging in the propagating house, and maintaining a moist atmosphere of 65 to 70° F. at night. Quick germination is desirable and so 70° F. is advisable for the first 48 to 60 hrs. By this time germination should have taken place and then the temperature may be dropped to 65° F. The seedlings should be damped overhead with a fine spray of water twice a day, the ground beneath the staging and the pipes being damped at the same time. An alternative method of seed sowing is in small thumbs or direct into 3½-in. pots. If 3½-in. pots are used they are half-filled with compost and the seed is sown. Later, as the seedling grows above the pot, it is filled to the right height by top dressing with more compost.

The seedlings raised in boxes or in thumb pots are potted into 3½-in. pots (60's) when ready which is usually 10 days after sowing. As the roots and stem are brittle it is easy for them to be injured, but less risk occurs where the seeds were sown in thumb pots, for the roots are protected by the small ball of soil. Where seeds are sown direct into 3½-in. pots there is no risk of this kind of injury. When potting, therefore, care must be taken to start before the seedlings have become too leggy and also to see that the roots are not broken nor the stem cracked. Injury of this kind leads to infection by micro-organisms which may not be obvious at planting time but will kill the plants when they are coming into bearing, and so cause endless worry and trouble. When the plants in the 3½-in. pots have made sufficient root to hold the soil securely they must be transferred to 5- or 6-in. pots. The time for this varies with prevailing weather, but is usually 2 to 3 weeks after potting into 3½-in. pots. A few days after the final potting the plants are staked with thin wooden stakes 18 in. long and given a single loose raffia tie. Throughout the entire propagating season the plants must receive all the light possible, and every attempt must be made to produce good stocky plants. The temperature should not fall below 65° F. at night and during the day may rise to 75° or even 80° F. A moist atmosphere should be given during all bright days, but watering must be carefully done. Overwatering will cause yellowing of the foliage and death of the roots.

In commercial practice the beds are placed on the ground, but they can be made up on solid benches covered with some loose material such as gravel to provide drainage.

When cucumbers are grown year after year in the same houses, the soil in the house, upon which the new beds are placed every year, gradually deteriorates and becomes cucumber 'sick'. This can be prevented either by steam sterilization or by replacing the normal soil of the house with well-drained material such as gravel, sand, or even ashes to a depth of 6 to 10 in. If this is flooded thoroughly with water every year after removing the beds, the injurious influence is washed out and the material will last until it becomes silted up with soil from the beds above. Usually the method adopted to counteract soil sickness is steam sterilization. Winter work consists of steam sterilization of the soil in the house when necessary and failing that thorough cultivation by digging to a depth of 10 in., liming and watering as required.

The beds in which the young cucumber plants are to be planted are prepared from good turfy loam cut and stacked 2 to 3 months previously, and a certain quantity of long strawy horse manure. The usual mixture is 2 parts of loam to 1 part of stable manure, but some growers favour rather more manure in the mixture. Investigations carried out at the Cheshunt Research Station indicate that the beds should consist of 2 parts good turfy loam, 1 part of strawy horse manure, and 1 part of wheat or oat straw, especially when the soil is heavy. To make the beds cut turves 4 in. thick, if available, and lay them grass downwards on the ground covering a strip about 20 in. wide running the length of the house, as near to the outside of the house as possible, one on either side of the centre path. Then bring in 2 barrow loads of good strawy horse manure and 2 loads of broken soil to a pipe length (9 ft.). Mix them well together, cover the strip of turf, and mound up the bed with almost vertical sides. The manure must have been spread out in the open for 5 to 7 days, turning it at least twice to free it from ammonia gas, which otherwise would scorch the plants. The beds must be left in an open spongy condition, and must not be cold at planting time. The fires must be started and the beds allowed to warm up for 7 to 10 days before planting, or until the bed temperature has reached 65 to 70° F.

Having warmed up the houses and the beds, the young cucumber plants in 5- or 6-in. pots, are brought in and stood on the beds in their approximate positions, and left for some hours to accommodate themselves to the new conditions. Care must be taken to protect the plants from cold winds on their journey from the propagating house. The plants are planted 2 ft. apart along the top of the bed, making the hole sufficiently big to take the ball of soil and roots out of the pot without disturbing it in any way. This is pressed firmly but gently into the bed, leaving the top of the ball slightly below the level of the bed. The bed temperature must be at least 65° F. and preferably 70° F. at planting time. If colder than this the plants may stand on the beds in their pots 2 or 3 days to allow the beds to warm up.

The plants take 10 to 14 days before they are well rooted into the new soil, and 7 to 14 days later white roots will be found above the surface of the soil. These should be covered with a thin layer of clean or sterilized soil, and the following day bone-meal should be sprinkled over the surface of this soil, using 14 lb. to every 100 ft.

run of bed. Within a short time roots will grow through again to the surface. They must be covered again, preferably with a compost consisting of 2 parts turfy loam and 1 part horse manure, applying a layer about 1 in. thick. Before applying any top dressing the base of the plant should be protected by placing around it a handful of either soil or a mixture of soil and peat. Contact of the stem with manures and fertilizers may cause decay of the outer tissues and must be prevented. About 14 days after applying the compost, it should be covered with a thin layer of good strawy horse manure to a depth of about 1 in. Thick layers should be avoided. The manure must have been spread out in the open for 5 or 6 days and turned to get rid of any free ammonia. Despite these precautions, however, the manure must be well watered immediately it has been placed on the beds and it should be damped every day for the next 3 days, to prevent any evolution of gaseous ammonia from the surface. Should any signs of ammonia damage appear, the beds must be damped and a little ventilation given. Covering the roots and top dressing with manure is continued through the season about every 4 to 6 weeks. As the beds tend to become solid with the passage of time, it is a good plan to top dress them with straw covered with a layer of sterilized soil once or twice during the season. This helps to keep the bed open and promote good root action.

If the soil conditions are satisfactory the dressings of horse manure will supply all the food required by the crop, but if the plants seem to need a stimulant a mixture of 1 part sulphate of ammonia, 1 part nitrate of potash, 3 parts superphosphate, and 5 parts dried blood, at the rate of 2 oz. to the square yard will strengthen the growth. Should this mixture lead to excessively luxuriant leaf and stem growth, the amount of dried blood should be reduced accordingly.

The success of the crop depends upon maintaining reasonably strong vegetative growth of the laterals and rapid growth of the fruit. This requires a luxuriant clean root system which is only possible when the beds are maintained in an open well-aerated condition. This is maintained by the skilful use of the top dressing materials such as turfy soil, strawy horse-manure and straw itself. Fertilizers are of much less importance and on some nurseries are rarely used. The skilful grower will pay particular attention to the physical condition of his beds.

The optimum night temperature for cucumbers is 65 to 70° F., and during the day it can run up to 85° F. before giving any ventilation. Under such conditions the air must not be permitted to become too dry during the hours of daylight. For the first 3 days after planting the night temperature must, if possible, be kept at 70° F. to encourage the roots to push out rapidly into the new soil. After this the temperature must be regulated according to the weather. During a spell of dull weather, the night temperature should not rise above 65° F. and may even be reduced to 60° F. if the dull period is prolonged. During the summer the day temperature may reach 110° F. for a few hours or so. Ventilation must be given at 86° F. and every attempt made to prevent higher temperatures by shading and damping.

The cucumber needs large quantities of water and no part of the bed must be allowed to dry out, but it also requires well-aerated beds and therefore any waterlogging by watering excessively is bound to be injurious. It the bed has been made up correctly any water applied to the top will pass easily through the entire bed, and run out at the bottom. Therefore each watering should consist of just sufficient as will wet the drier parts of the bed and start to run away at the bottom. A little water frequently is better than heavy soakings at longer intervals. Cold water must be avoided for cucumber roots are easily chilled. The tender cucumber foliage benefits from a moist atmosphere, and it is good practice to damp the leaves, paths, and pipes to produce a steamy atmosphere

2 or 3 times each day. Under the usual method of cultivation the glass is shaded during the summer months, but shading should not be applied too soon. It is wise to wait until the plants show the need for some assistance of this kind. Early in April a light shade can be given, if necessary, increasing the intensity later. Flour and water is the best material to use for it is opaque in dry weather and translucent when wet.

Cucumbers are trained on wires running horizontally about 9 in. apart suspended about 12 in. from the roof bars. The object of training is to keep the wires furnished with the maximum amount of foliage, borne by laterals and sub-laterals which are spaced equidistantly, and which produce cucumbers at ever node. The main stem is grown vertically and is usually stopped at a height of about 4 ft. 6 in. to give the side branches or laterals a chance to develop properly. Later growth of the main stem is taken up to within 9 in. of the apex of the house. If the laterals produce fruit at the first and second nodes they are stopped at the second leaf beyond the second node. If the fruit is not produced the lateral should be allowed to grow on. If the third node produces fruit, the lateral is stopped at the second leaf beyond it. If it does not, it is cut back to the second node and two sub-laterals taken, one from each node. Too much pruning is often worse than too little, indeed if the laterals seem to be thin and weak, later in the season, it is a good plan to let them grow wild for a time. They will soon strengthen themselves and then the untidy growth can be cleaned up, cutting out all the useless laterals and tying in the strong fruiting shoots. As the shoots grow they are tied to the wires, taking care to release the young cucumbers which may be entangled in the wires.

Mr. Read of Hockley reports a novel method of training by which heavy crops of cucumbers of some varieties have been successfully secured. Hard-growing varieties do not respond. The plant is stopped at the second rough leaf and afterwards at every joint; no branches are allowed so that the plant presents the appearance of a cordon. This induces the appearance of clusters of 5 to 9 female flowers but no males at every joint. After cutting the first crop mossy-looking protuberances appear at the joints which develop into cucumbers. The fruits swell rapidly and are ready to cut in less than the customary 14 days from bloom to cutting. The original leaves continue in health throughout the summer and fruits are produced from top to bottom throughout the life of the plant. Fruits can often be cut in under 6 weeks from the date of sowing the seeds.

Cucumbers are cut off the laterals with a sharp knife leaving a very short piece of stalk attached to the neck. They should be pre-cooled before packing in trays or non-returnable boxes, using soft sweet hay and lining paper as packing material. 8 to 16 cucumbers are packed in the trays, 15 to 30 in the boxes.

FRAME CUCUMBERS. In private gardens cucumbers are often grown in frames. Hotbeds are prepared for the frames in the usual way, from stable manure and leaves. They are generally 3 to 4 ft. deep and are laid down about 3 ft. wider than the range of frames, which are stood directly upon them. The lights are put on and the frames ventilated for 2 or 3 days to allow the steam and gases to escape. Within the frames the hotbed is covered with about 6 in. of a mixture of good turfy loam and well-decayed horse manure, using 4 parts of the former to 1 part of the latter. The level of the soil should be about 12 in. from the glass. One plant is planted near the back of each Dutch light, training 3 shoots towards the south. The plants must be trimmed and stopped as they grow to space the shoots and allow ample room for development of the fruits. Shading should be applied to the glass as soon as the sun becomes too strong.

OUTDOOR CUCUMBERS. Cucumbers can be grown on ridges in the open, but the well-drained loamy types of soil are most suitable. Light sandy soils do not hold the water sufficiently unless reinforced with a good deal of organic material. Cucumbers should follow such crops as cabbage or potato which have been well manured. The best manure is horse manure which is usually ploughed in so that it lies in strips where the rows are to go, using about 15 lb. to the square yard. If the strips are 18 in. wide, 1 ton of manure is sufficient for a row about 300 yards long. Only well-rotted manure should be used, and it should be ploughed in about 6 in. deep. The soil above should be well cultivated and reinforced with a little bone-meal or super-phosphate. The rows of plants should be about 6 ft. apart. Seeds cannot be sown till all risk of frost has gone, which means the end of May. They are sown 6 in. apart in the rows and when the plants are up they should be thinned to 18 in. apart. An acre requires $1\frac{1}{2}$ to 2 lb. of seed. The crop must be well cultivated to keep down weeds and when the plants are growing strongly a complete fertilizer should be applied along the rows and mixed with the soil by hoeing. The mixture should be rich in phosphate and show an analysis of 4 per cent. nitrogen, 12 per cent. phosphoric acid, and 4 per cent. potash.

W. F. B.

*DISEASES.* It is essential to take early steps in cases of ill health of Cucumber plants, for under glasshouse conditions the spread of disease can be extremely rapid, especially in the moist atmosphere of a cucumber house. The roots of cucumbers may suffer from attack by the fungus *Verticillium albo-atrum*, causing Wilt, but this is not likely to be serious if the temperature is not below 77° F. Where the trouble is serious some form of soil sterilization is advisable, but in any case where an infected plant is removed the hole should be well watered with Cheshunt Compound before a fresh plant is planted. There is a disease at the base of the stem or even higher called Canker or Foot Rot, similar to that seen in Melons and likely to be serious, especially on young plants. This is caused by *Bacterium carotovorum* and is encouraged by very wet soil conditions around the base of the stem. The signs are soft rot of the tissues, which turn brown, and the trouble soon spreads. It is essential to avoid heavy, wet soil and many people plant out cucumbers on mounds so that surplus water is kept away from the base of the stem. Dusting the bases of the plants with copper-lime dust is a good practice where this disease is troublesome. The leaves of cucumbers may show pale areas which later turn dry and brown, the stems being to some extent affected also. This is Anthracnose, due to the fungus *Colletotrichum oligochaetum* which is very quick in spreading when the humidity is high. The plants should be sprayed with lime sulphur 1 part to 60 parts water plus a spreading agent, the badly affected leaves being first removed and burnt. If the attack is severe the house will need disinfecting by the cresylic acid treatment in the dormant season, in any case a good routine treatment. Mildew, *Erysiphe cichoracearum*, forms a powdery-white substance on the plants but is superficial and rarely harmful and is easily controlled by spraying with sulphur sprays. Leaf Blotch, due to *Cercospora Melonis*, is far more serious, appearing as pale round spots rapidly increasing and turning brown so that affected leaves soon wither. The variety Butcher's Disease Resister will not take this disease and some other varieties are more or less resistant. Gummosis, caused by *Cladosporium cucumerinum*, makes light brown spots on the leaves but may also attack the fruits causing small sunken spots from which a gummy liquid oozes. This in young fruits causes them to become curled and unshapely. Much can be done to reduce it by spraying with a sulphur spray, ventilating to reduce humidity, and removing affected fruits. There is a Virus disease of Cucumbers called Mosaic which exists in three forms:

viz. Green Mottle Mosaic with a mild mosaic of the leaves but very rarely any mottling of the fruit; Yellow Mosaic, a bright yellow mottling of the leaves, the fruit being marked with yellow or silver spots or streaks; and Yellow Mottle Mosaic with greenish-yellow mottling of the leaves and mottling of the fruit. The first two are found only on the Cucumber but the third affects certain other plants. To the gardener it is apparent that the last two kinds of mosaic are likely to spoil the fruit and plants are better destroyed but fruit may be obtained from plants showing Green Mottle. At all times growers should try to obtain cucumber seed from plants definitely free from any kind of mosaic.

D. E. G.

**CUCUMBER, BITTER.** *See* **Citrullus Colocynthis.**

**CUCUMBER, CALABASH.** *See* **Lagenaria vulgaris.**

**CUCUMBER, SQUIRTING.** *See* **Ecballium Elaterium.**

**CUCUMBER TREE.** *See* **Averrhoa Bilimbi, Magnolia acuminata,** *and* **M. Fraseri.**

*cucumerifo'lius -a -um,* with leaves like Cucumis.

**CUCU'MIS** (derivation?). FAM. *Cucurbitaceae.* A genus of about 30 species of tendril-climbing or trailing annuals or herbaceous perennials, mostly natives of Trop. Africa and Asia, a few in Australia and America, hairy or somewhat spiny. Leaves large, usually palmately lobed. Flowers monoecious; the males usually clustered; calyx tube turbinate or bell-shaped, 5-lobed, corolla more or less bell-shaped, deeply 5-lobed, stamens 3, free, sacks S- or U-shaped; the females solitary. Fruit a 3- to 6-celled many-seeded berry. The seeds of all species should be sown in heat in spring and the seedlings planted out when large enough to handle and danger of frost is past, or under glass as the case may be. *See also* **Cucumber, Melon.**

**C. Angu'ria.** Stem rather slender; tendrils simple. *l.* palmately lobed, sinuate, heart-shaped at base, roughly hairy. *fl.* usually solitary. June to August. *fr.* white, globose, 1 to 3 in. long, prickly. Trop. America? 1692. (B.M. 5817.) Fr. sometimes pickled.

**C. dipsa'ceus.** Habit and *l.* like *C. Melo. fl.* long-stalked. *fr.* oblong or nearly globose, 1 to 2 in. long, finally hard, dry, and densely covered with long hairs. Arabia, Africa. (R.H. 1860, 210.) Grown as ornamental gourd.

**C. Duda'im.** A variety of *C. Melo.*

**C. Me'lo.** Cantaloupe, Melon, Musk Melon. Annual. Stem trailing, rough-haired, tendrilled. *l.* roundish, or lobed, large, angular, sometimes toothed, stalked. *fl.* males clustered, peduncle short; female solitary; stigmas 3 or 4, shortly 2-lobed. July. *fr.* ovate or sub-globose, 8- to 12-furrowed, flesh sugary, yellow, red, or white. Asia. 1570. *See* Melon. A very variable species. *See* Monograph by Cogniaux in DC. *Monogr. Phaner.* 3. var. **agres'tis,** includes the Egyptian Cucumber, a wild form, a very hairy plant with 5-angled stem, elliptical *fr.* narrowed to both ends, hairy, about as large as a plum, inedible. SYN. *C. Melo Chate;* **cantalupen'sis,** rind usually hard, more or less warted or scaly, often deeply grooved. Cantaloupe. **Chi'to,** *l.* smaller than in Melon, *fr.* orange- or lemon-like in size and colour, not marked, flesh white or pale yellow, inedible except as pickle **Duda'im,** Canary Melon, Scented Cucumber, plant and *l.* smaller than type, *fr.* size and shape of orange, regular, smooth, marbled cinnamon-brown or red on yellow, very fragrant, but not edible. Persia; **flexuo'sus,** cal. very hairy, *fr.* white or yellow, long, cylindrical-club-shaped, sulcate, curved, green, 2 to 3 ft. long, 1 to 3 in. thick. E. Indies?; **reticula'tus,** rind more or less netted as a rule. Musk Melon.

**C. metulif'erus.** Hispid annual. *l.* somewhat 3-lobed, heart-shaped, stalked. *fr.* oblong-obtuse, spiny, about 4 in. long. S. Africa. A

**C. Sacleux'ii.** *l.* roundish, kidney-shaped, lobed, rough, greenish-grey. *fr.* ovoid, dark green with pale green stripes, 3 to 4 in. long. Zanzibar. 1890. Stove. Fr. may be pickled.

**C. sati'vus.** Common Cucumber. Stem rough, tendrilled. *l.* cordate, more or less 5-lobed, stalked, terminal lobe largest. *fl.* large, usually in threes. July to September. *fr.* usually long, smooth or prickly, usually shining. Habitat? Long cultivated in warm countries. *See* **Cucumber.** Variable. var. **sikkimen'sis,** *l.* large, 7- to 9-lobed, *fr.* reddish-brown, densely netted pale yellow, cylindrical-club-shaped. E. Himalaya. 1875.

**CUCUR′BITA** (ancient name). FAM. *Cucurbitaceae*. A genus of about 6 species of annuals (rarely perennials) with trailing or climbing tendrilled stems, natives of the warmer parts of Asia, Africa, and America. Leaves large, more or less palmately lobed. Flowers monoecious; corolla yellow, bell-shaped; male flower with hemispherical-bell-shaped calyx; stamens 3, one 1-celled, two 2-celled; female with obovate calyx narrowed towards top or bell-shaped. Fruit often very large, berry-like, many-seeded. Half-hardy. All may be grown as annuals. *See* **Gourds, Vegetable Marrow.** **A**

**C. Andrea′na.** Annual. Stem long, rooting at nodes. *l.* large, marbled with white. *fl.* yellow, about half the size of those of *C. Pepo. fr.* green with white and yellow markings, obovoid, about 8 in. long. Uruguay. 1896. (R.H. 1896, p. 8.) Greenhouse.

**C. ficifo′lia.** Perennial. Stem very long, stout, becoming rather woody. *l.* ovate or roundish, cordate at base, with 5 rounded lobes, pale green, sometimes marbled. *fl.* with short, bell-shaped cal. *fr.* large, up to 1 ft. long, roundish-ovoid, flesh white; rind striped white; seeds black, ovate. E. Asia. SYN. *C. melonosperma.* Ornamental, for trellises. var. **mexica′na,** seeds twice as large as in type. Mexico. 1890.

**C. foetidis′sima.** Perennial. Stem long, rooting at nodes, less prickly than most species. *l.* large, somewhat triangular, heart-shaped at base, with shallow crenations, grey-hairy. *fl.* much as in *C. Pepo. fr.* as large as an orange, nearly globose, smooth, green, splashed with yellow. Inedible. United States, Mexico. (R.H. 1851, 61.) SYN. *Cucumis perennis.* Ornamental Gourd.

**C. max′ima.** Pumpkin. Annual. Stem long, scarcely prickly. *l.* roundish or kidney-shaped, large, not or scarcely lobed. *fl.* with cal. tube obovate with a short neck; cor. tube nearly straight, lobes large and spreading. July. *fr.* deep yellow, red, or green, globose, often very large, flesh orange, sometimes hollow at maturity, its stalk smooth. Habitat? Widely cultivated. var. **sylves′tris,** *fr.* as large as a man's head. Himalaya. 1893. Perhaps the wild original of this long-cultivated plant.

**C. moscha′ta.** Annual. Stem long, tendrils often leafy. *l.* somewhat 5-lobed, rounded, obtuse, cordate at base, toothed. *fl.* with roundish-bell-shaped cal., short, throat much dilated, lobes often leaf-like; cor. tube widening towards top, lobes erect. May. *fr.* flattish-rounded, its stalk deeply ridged and widened next to fruit. Habitat? Known as Squash in America.

**C. Pep′o.** Pumpkin, Vegetable Marrow. Annual. Stem long, running, or very short, prickly (var. **conden′sa** of Bailey). *l.* large, 5-lobed, cordate at base, lobes obtuse, toothed. *fl.* large; cal. with neck beneath limb; cor. large with erect acute lobes. Summer. *fr.* very variable in size, shape, and colouring. 1570. Possibly native of Trop. America. var. **auran′tia,** *l.* 3-lobed, sharply toothed, *fr.* smooth, size, shape, and colour of an orange; **ovif′era,** *l.* 5-lobed, hairy, *fr.* ovate or obovate, greenish or yellowish. *See* **Vegetable Marrow.** This variety also includes grey, pear-shaped and nearly globose forms, and the name is sometimes restricted to a small, hard pear-shaped, inedible gourd, grown for ornament; **verruco′sa,** *l.* deeply 5-lobed, mid-lobe narrow at base, *fr.* roundish-elliptic, warted. Edible but usually grown as an ornamental gourd.

**C. peren′nis.** A synonym of *C. foetidissima.*

**CUCURBITA′CEAE.** Dicotyledons. A family of about 750 species of mostly tendril-climbing, sappy, annual herbs in about 87 genera scattered over the warmer parts of the earth with a few in temperate regions. Leaves alternate, usually lobed. Flowers mostly unisexual, regular (except stamens), usually in fives, sepals joined; petals joined; stamens very variable in form and arrangement; ovary inferior, 1- to 10-celled, but usually 3-celled, with 1 to many ovules in each cell. Fruit usually berry-like, sometimes with a hard outer skin (*pepo*). The morphological nature of the tendrils is often in dispute, but their sensitiveness is marked all through the family. Many genera contain plants of interesting, ornamental, or economic character. The genera dealt with here are Abobra, Alsomitra, Anguria, Benincasa, Bryonia, Ceratosanthes, Citrullus, Coccinia, Cucumis, Cucurbita, Cyclanthera, Ecballium, Echinocystis, Fevillea, Gurania, Gymnopetalum, Lagenaria, Luffa, Megarrhiza, Melothria, Momordica, Sechium, Sicana, Sicyos, Telfairea, Thladiantha, Trichosanthes, Zehneria.

*cucurbiti′nus -a -um,* Marrow-like.

**CUDRAN′IA** (*Cudrang,* the Malayan name). FAM. *Moraceae.* A genus of 5 or 6 species of deciduous and evergreen unisexual trees or shrubs from E. Asia,

Australia, and New Caledonia, closely akin to Maclura and the mulberries. Leaves alternate. Flowers minute, crowded in globose heads. Fruit fleshy. Unlike its near ally Maclura, *C. tricuspidata* has mostly 3-lobed (not entire) leaves, a fruit only 1 in. wide, and straight (not inflexed) stamens. For cultivation, *see* **Morus.**

**C. tricuspida′ta.** Silk-worm Thorn. Deciduous tree 20 ft. or more h., with thorny branches and glabrous young shoots. *l.* oval, ovate, or obovate, 1½ to 4 in. long, half as wide, either entire or 3-lobed at apex, dark green. *fl.* green, minute, crowded in globose, stalked clusters, ⅓ in. wide. *fr.* aggregated into an orange-shaped, hard, shining mass over 1 in. wide. China, Japan, Korea. (R.H. 1872, 56.) Of interest in providing food for the silk-worm; *fl.* of no beauty; *fr.* said to be edible. Very hardy. SYN. *C. triloba, Maclura tricuspidata.*

**C. trilo′ba.** A synonym of *C. tricuspidata.*

W. J. B.

*Cuffea′nus -a -um,* in honour of Lady Wheeler Cuffe, who collected in Shan States, Upper Burma.

**Cuje′te.** Brazilian name.

**CULCA′SIA** (from *Kulkas,* Arabic name for *Colocasia antiquorum*). FAM. *Araceae.* A genus of 15 species of creeping or climbing plants with slender stems and scattered evergreen leaves, natives of Trop. Africa. Spathes erect, small, rolled round the club-shaped spadix with the flowers on lower third female, in upper half male, all without perianth. For treatment *see* **Philodendron.**

**C. Mann′ii.** Stem 12 to 20 in. h. *l.* elliptic or elliptic-oblong, about 8 in. or more long, obtuse, rather leathery, bright green with intense green veins, paler beneath; stalk 3 or 4 in. long, sheathing in lower part. *Peduncle* about 2 in. long. *Spathe* oblong, 2 in. long, base convolute, expanded above, white within; spadix with few female fl. Cameroons. (B.M. 5760 as *Aglaonema Mannii.*)

**C. scan′dens.** Stem sub-shrubby, twining, up to 100 ft. h. in nature. *l.* more or less oblong-ovate, shortly slender-pointed, 4 to 10 in. long, rather thin, with pale main veins; stalk 2 to 3 in. long, sheathing. *Peduncle* about 3 in. long. *Spathe* 2 in. long, yellow-green. June. W. Africa. 1822.

**CULCI′TA** (Derivation?). FAM. *Cyatheaceae.* A genus of about 10 species allied to Dicksonia.

**C. du′bia.** *Fronds* ample, deltoid, 4-pinnatifid; pinnae oblong-lanceolate, 1 ft. or more long, 2 to 4 in. broad; pinnules close, lanceolate, stalked, with close oblong sessile segs. lower pinnatifid, upper entire. *Sori* minute, one to each final lobe. Australia. (H.S. 1, 24 c.)

**C. macrocar′pa.** *rhiz.* densely clothed with shining hairs. *Fronds* 1 to 1½ ft. long, 1 ft. broad, 3-pinnate; lower pinnules deltoid, divisions ovate, deeply cut with oblong-rhomboidal, unequal-sided, deeply toothed segs.; fertile fronds much contracted. *Sori* ₁/₁₆ in. across. Madeira and Azores. (L.F. 8, 39; B.C.F. 2, 176.) SYN. *Balantium Culcita, Dicksonia Culcita.* The dense woolly covering of the rhizomes has been used for stuffing cushions, &c. Greenhouse.

**CULM.** The straw or hollow stem of a grass.

*culminic′ola,* growing near the mountain top.

**A→**

*cultra′tus -a -um, cultriform′is -is -e,* shaped like a knife-blade.

**CULVER'S PHYSIC.** *See* **Veronica virginica.**

*cumanen′sis -is -e,* of Cumana, N. coast of S. America.

**CUMING′IA campanula′ta.** A synonym of *Conanthera Simsii.*

*Cuming′ii,* in honour of Hugh Cuming, 1791–1865, who collected in Malaya, Philippines, &c.

**CUNDURANGO.** *See* **Marsdenia Cundurango.**

*cunea′tus -a -um, cuneiformis -is -e,* wedge-shaped, having the broadest end uppermost, tapering to the base.

**CUNIL′A** (ancient Latin name). FAM. *Labiatae.* A genus of about 12 species of herbs or sub-shrubs, natives of N. America for the most part. Leaves large, toothed.

Flowers white or purplish, small; corolla 2-lipped, upper lip erect, flattish, usually notched, lower with 3 nearly equal lobes; calyx equally 5-toothed, hairy in throat. *C. mariana* grows well in loam and peat and may be increased by division.

**C. maria'na.** Dittany. Tufted, about 1 ft. h. Stem much branched. *l.* ovate, about 1 in. long, rounded or cordate at base, smooth, dotted, nearly sessile. *fl.* purplish, in stalked cymes; cal. striate. July to September. E. United States. (S.B.F.G. 243.)

**CUNNINGHAM'IA** (in honour of James Cunningham, who discovered *C. lanceolata*, about 1701 or 2 in Chusan). Fam. *Pinaceae*. A genus of evergreen trees with long, lanceolate leaves similar in shape to those of the Columbea group of Araucaria, and forming a connecting link between 2 divisions of the Family Pinaceae, the Araucarieae which includes the Araucarias, and the Taxodineae in which the Taxodiums and Sequoias are placed. Three species are known, 2 of which are in cultivation, the older one from China, the other from Formosa. The branch system is irregularly whorled but intermediate branches occur, and although the leaves are spirally arranged, a twist at the base of those on the lateral branchlets makes them appear to be on the sides and face of the shoot only. The leaves live for several years and after death may remain on the branches for a further lengthy period, many of them, eventually being shed with the branchlets. This often results in the trees presenting an untidy appearance. Neither species is very hardy and they can be grown out of doors only in the warmer parts of the country. They are amongst the few kinds of Conifers that have the power of renewal from stool shoots from cut down trees. Warm, rich soil and a sheltered position are necessary. Propagation is preferably by seeds, otherwise by cuttings of erect shoots. The botanist Zuccarini included the species of Athrotaxis in this genus.

**C. Kawaka'mii.** Not in cultivation. Formosa.

**C. Konish'ii.** Tree of 80 to 100 ft. with reddish-brown scented bark. *l.* spirally arranged, crowded, narrow-lanceolate, leathery, ¾ to 1⅓ in. long, shorter and stiffer on old trees, glaucous above, silvery beneath, tapering to a long, fine point, remaining green for 7 or 8 years. *Cones* ovate, ¾ to 1 in. long, scales spine-tipped; seeds 3 on each scale. Formosa. 1910.

**C. lanceola'ta.** Large tree up to 150 ft. with brown bark shed in long strips. *l.* lanceolate, curved, 1 to 2¾ in. long and up to ⅓ in. wide, leathery, green above, glaucous beneath, living about 5 years, turning reddish-brown in autumn, green in spring, narrowing to a long point. *Male fl.* in short catkins near the points of shoots; *female* small, enclosed by leafy bracts; both are formed in autumn and open in spring. *Cones* ovoid or rounded, nearly 1½ in. long and wide, of numerous pointed scales with 3 winged seeds on each scale. China. 1804. (B.M. 2743; D.J.C. 187, as *C. sinensis*.) The timber is light, fragrant, and durable. It is much used in China and is highly prized by the Chinese for coffins. var. **glau'ca** has more glaucous *l.* than the type.

**C. sinen'sis.** A synonym of *C. lanceolata*.

W. D.

**Cunningham'ii,** in honour of (1) Allan Cunningham, 1791–1839, (2) Richard Cunningham, 1793–1835, both employed at Kew. Allan travelled and botanized in S. America, Australia, and New Zealand and both were associated with the Botanic Garden at Sydney, New S. Wales.

**CUNO'NIA** (in honour of John Christian Cuno, 1708–80, of Amsterdam, who described his own garden in verse, in 1750). Fam. *Cunoniaceae*. A genus of 6 species, 5 in New Caledonia, 1 in S. Africa. Leaves unequally pinnate; leaflets serrate, leathery; stipules large, protecting the bud, caducous. Flowers in axillary, erect, cylindrical racemes up to 6 in. long; calyx 5-parted; petals 5, oblong; stamens 10. Fruit a 2-celled capsule. *C. capensis* is easily grown in sandy loam and peat in the cool greenhouse, and can be propagated by half-ripened cuttings in sandy soil under glass in gentle heat.

**C. capen'sis.** Large shrub or middle-sized tree; glabrous. *lflets.* 5 to 7, lanceolate, 2 to 4 in. long, toothed. *fl.* white; racemes spicate, opposite; pedicels numerous, in clusters. August. S. Africa. 1816. (L.B.C. 826; B.M. 8504.)

W. J. B.

**CUNO'NIA** of Miller is a synonym of Antholyza.

**CUNONIA'CEAE.** Dicotyledons. A family of about 120 species of shrubs and trees in 21 genera, natives of the south sub-tropical and warm temperate regions. Leaves opposite or whorled, leathery, evergreen, with stipules often united in pairs. Closely related to Saxifragaceae with small flowers, often without petals, but with the ovules in two ranks in the (usually) 2-celled ovary. Fruit usually a capsule, sometimes a drupe or nut. The genera dealt with here are Ackama, Acrophyllum, Aphanopetalum, Cunonia, Schizomeria, Weinmannia.

**CUP.** (1) The Corona of Narcissi, &c. (q.v.). (2) The concave involucre of a nut, as an Acorn. *See* **Cupula.**

**CUPA'NIA ed'ulis.** A synonym of *Blighia sapida*.

**CU'PHEA** (*kyphos*, curved, referring to the capsule). Fam. *Lythraceae*. A genus of about 90 species of herbs or sub-shrubs, natives of the warmer parts of America. Leaves opposite, rarely whorled, entire. Flowers usually drooping; calyx tubular, coloured; peduncles 1- or many-flowered, interpetiolar. Cupheas are easily grown in ordinary soils. The perennial species strike readily in March or April with brisk bottom heat, but are better grown from seed sown in January or February, the seedlings being grown on in rich soil, repotting as necessary, finally into 6-in. pots, feeding with liquid manure when the plants are filled with roots. *C. ignea* is particularly useful, propagated by cuttings, for greenhouse decoration or for small beds in the summer flower-garden. Greenhouse plants.

**C. aequipet'ala.** About 2 ft. h. *fl.* purple. June. Mexico. 1859. Syn. *C. ocimoides*.

**C. Commerson'ii.** 6 to 18 in. h., woody below. *l.* ovate- to narrow-lanceolate, wedge-shaped, nearly sessile. *fl.* with glandular-hairy cal. and pedicels, dorsal lobe of cal. largest; pet. obovate. Brazil. 1884.

**C. corda'ta.** Evergreen sub-shrub, branches clammy, about 18 in. h. *l.* in lower part, heart-shaped, acute, somewhat leathery; upper oblong. *fl.* scarlet, cal. and pedicels clammy; pet. 6, 2 upper large, nearly round, 4 lower small. June. Peru. 1842. (B.M. 4208; F.d.S. 7.)

**C. cya'nea.** Evergreen with clammy branches. *l.* ovate-oblong, acute, hairy. *fl.* in raceme; cal. scarlet at base, yellow above, slightly hispid, clammy; pet. and anthers violet-blue. Mexico. (B.R. 32, 14 as *C. strigillosa*; P.M. 11, 241, as *C. strigulosa*.)

**C. Hookeria'na.** Sub-shrub up to 3 ft. h. *l.* lanceolate. *fl.* in dense panicles, vermilion and orange, curved, cylindrical. Mexico. (R.H. 1877, 469.) Syn. *C. Roezlii*.

**C. ig'nea.*** Evergreen, about 12 in. h. *l.* lanceolate, nearly glabrous. *fl.* cal. bright scarlet, with a black and white expanded limb; pet. absent. Summer. Mexico. 1845. (F.d.S. 180 as *C. platycentra*.) var. **al'ba,** *fl.* white. 1848.

**C. jorullen'sis.** A synonym of *C. micropetala*.

**C. lanceola'ta.** Ascending annual, 18 in. h., clammy and hispid with brown hairs. *l.* oblong-lanceolate, obtuse, hairy. *fl.* bluish in a sub-secund spike-like raceme. Mexico. 1836. (B.M. 4362.)

**C. Llav'ea.** Stems many, hispid. *l.* ovate-lanceolate, strigose, nearly sessile. *fl.* purple; pet. 2, obovate, large. June. Mexico. 1830. (B.R. 1386.)

**C. Melvil'la.** Perennial herb, 2 to 3 ft. h. *l.* lanceolate, narrowed to both ends, sessile. *fl.* in a many-fld. terminal raceme; cal. long, red at base, green at apex. May. Guiana. 1823. (B.R. 852.)

**C. micropet'ala.*** Much-branched shrub, 1 ft. h. *l.* oblong-lanceolate, narrowed to both ends, rigid, scabrid. *fl.* secund, above the l.-axils; cal. scarlet, yellowish at apex, 12-toothed; pet. white; filaments red. July. Mexico. 1824. (B.M. 5232 as *C. jorullensis*.)

**C. minia'ta.*** Evergreen, up to 2 ft. h. *l.* ovate, slender-pointed, white-bristly. *fl.* solitary in l.-axils, pale vermilion; pedicels short. June to September. Mexico. 1843. (F.d.S. 65.)

**C. pineto'rum.** Evergreen, 18 in. h., branches ascending. *l.* ovate-lanceolate, strigose; nearly sessile. *fl.* crimson to deep purple, in a panicle. July. Mexico. 1850. (F.d.S. 527.)

**C. platycen′tra** of Lamarck. A synonym of *C. ignea*.

**C. procum′bens.** Procumbent annual. *l.* ovate-lanceolate; stalk short. *fl.* with purplish cal., rose pet., deflexed on solitary pedicels. June. Mexico. 1816. Warm house.

*Cuphea Llavea* (p. 593)

**C. verticilla′ta.** Perennial, hairy. *l.* 3 or 4 in a whorl, oblong, strigose. *fl.* violet, solitary or in pairs; cal. hairy, 10- to 16-toothed, coloured; pet. 5 to 8, unequal. Peru. (F.d.S. 510.) Stove.

*Cuphea micropetala* (p. 593)

**C. Zimapa′ni.** Evergreen, about 2 ft. h. *fl.* blackish-purple, purple. Autumn. Mexico. 1878. (B.M. 6412 as *C. lanceolata*.)

***cupressi′nus -a -um,*** Cypress-like.

**A→**

**CUPRES′SUS** (*kus*, to produce, and *parisos* equal; the growth of *C. sempervirens* is symmetrical). Cypress. FAM. *Pinaceae*. Ornamental evergreen trees from S. Europe, W. Asia, China, the Himalaya, and N. and Cent. America, usually pyramidal when young, spreading with age, but in some retaining a fastigiate or pyramidal habit throughout life. The branchlet systems either arise at varying angles, or less often are flattened as in Chamaecyparis. As in other genera of Conifers the juvenile and mature types of leaves are dissimilar. The juvenile type is soft, awl-shaped and often $\frac{1}{4}$ to $\frac{1}{3}$ in. or more long, the adult type scale-like and pressed close to the shoot. The flowers are monoecious, and the cones globular, of 6 to 10 peltate, woody, persistent scales, which may remain closed for several years after the seeds are ripe, eventually separating to free the seeds, which may number from 6 to 20 on each fertile scale. The cones usually take 18 months to mature. Nearly related to Chamaecyparis which is sometimes included in Cupressus: for distinctions *see* **Chamaecyparis.**

Some of the species are moderately hardy, but they should not be planted in the colder parts of the country, others are definitely tender and can be grown out of doors only in the most favoured localities. An unusually severe winter, such as that of 1939–40, may kill even the hardier species. They give the best results in the warmer and sheltered gardens of the south and west parts of England and Wales, the west coast of Scotland and in Ireland. Any good garden soil suits them, but it should be moderately deep and the position sheltered from violent winds. Propagation should be by seeds when possible. When the cones do not open naturally, they should be slightly heated, when the seeds will be released. They may be sown in light, friable soil in pots or boxes in a greenhouse, from January onwards, or in a bed in a cold frame in March. If seeds are not available, cuttings may be inserted in a frost-proof frame in September. Unless they are specially prepared by frequent transplanting, plants 5 or 6 ft. high do not move well and it is wise to place trees in their permanent places when not more than 2 ft. high. Some prefer to keep young plants in pots until they can be planted in permanent places, but when that is done they must not be left in the pots long enough for the roots to become badly entangled. When large plants are moved the work must be done with extreme care. They usually grow into shapely trees with little or no pruning.

*DISEASES.* Besides the usual root-rots peculiar to conifers, Cupressus trees may in the young state contract Crown Gall (q.v.) and also Stem Canker due to the fungus *Pestalozia Hartigii* which causes a swollen canker in the stems. Badly affected trees should be destroyed although in some instances the cankers can be cut out and the trees sprayed with Bordeaux mixture.

(D. E. G.)

*PESTS.* The aphis, *Cinara* (*Cupressobium*) *cupressi*, often occurs in vast numbers on the shoots and branches of *C. macrocarpa*. It is light brown or brownish-yellow and occurs from early spring to autumn, but is most numerous in April and May. Great quantities of honeydew are excreted, covering the foliage and shoots and providing a medium for the growth of Sooty Moulds, severely attacked trees looking as though dusted with soot. The infested trees lose vigour both as a result of the amount of sap that is abstracted and from the growth of moulds which hinder the normal functions of the leaves.

Watch should be kept on the plants from February onwards, and the infested shoots and branches should be well sprayed with nicotine-soap wash, taking care to wet both surfaces. The complete eradication of this pest in dense Cypress hedges is possible only by nicotine dust well blown into the hedge. Liquid sprays fail to penetrate into the hedge to a sufficient extent.

(G. F. W.)

**C. arizon′ica.** Tree of 70 ft. Branches erect and closely arranged, branchlets divided into irregularly disposed, quadrangular spray. *l.* scale-like with a disagreeable odour when bruised, in 4 ranks, closely overlapping, more or less glaucous, each with a depression on back. *Cones* globose, $\frac{1}{2}$ to $\frac{3}{4}$ in. wide, of 6 to 8 scales bearing 8 to 10 tubercled seeds on each fertile scale. Arizona to N. Mexico. 1882. Individual trees vary in hardiness. The following varieties are distinct. var. **boni'ta**, *l.* glaucous, with a large resin gland on back, and a less disagreeable odour. Syn. *C. glabra*; **bonita pyramid'alis**, dense pyramidal tree with very glaucous *l.*, moderately hardy and a popular garden tree; **con'ica**, of dense, conical habit, *l.* glaucous.

**C. Ba'keri.** A synonym of *C. Macnabiana.*

**C. Bentham'ii.** A variety of *C. lusitanica.*

**C. califor'nica.** A synonym of *C. Goveniana.*

**C. cashmeria'na.** Kashmir Cypress. Tree, 60 ft. or more h., pyramidal, with long, graceful, pendulous branchlets, flattened as in Chamaecyparis. *l.* scale-like with free tips, glaucous. *Cones* greenish-yellow with a glaucous covering, ½ in. wide, of 10 scales with about 10 winged seeds on each fertile scale. Kashmir? or, possibly, Tibet. One of the most beautiful of the Cypresses, but also one of the most tender. Syn. *C. funebris glauca, C. pendula.*

**C. Corneya'na.** A variety of *C. torulosa.*

**C. Coul'teri.** A synonym of *C. lusitanica.*

**C. dis'ticha.** A synonym of *Taxodium distichum.*

**C. Duclouxia'na.** Tree of 50 to 60 ft., allied to *C. sempervirens*, but with more slender and rather more glaucous branchlets. Although the branches of mature trees are said to be spreading, young trees are pyramidal and furnished with a mass of tiny branchlets. *l.* scale-like, bright green. *Cones* globose, ¾ to 1 in. wide, with usually 8 scales; seeds with tubercled coats. Yunnan, China. 1905.

**C. Duprezia'na.** A few trees remain, growing between Rhat and Djaret in the Sahara, probably the only survivors of a forest of the species. Apparently very near *C. sempervirens.*

**C. fastigia'ta.** A synonym of *C. sempervirens stricta.*

**C. filiform'is.** A synonym of *C. lusitanica flagellifera.*

**C. formosen'sis.** A synonym of *Chamaecyparis formosensis.*

**C. fune'bris.** Mourning Cypress, Chinese Weeping Cypress. Tree of 70 ft., closely allied to *C. cashmeriana* with similar flattened but not pendulous branchlets. *l.* grey-green, variable in shape, but small, scale-like, pointed, pressed close to shoot. *Cones* globose, ¼ to ½ in. wide, of 8 scales, with 3 to 5 winged seeds on each, the outer coat bearing resin tubercles. A connecting link between Cupressus and Chamaecyparis. Cent. China. 1848. One of the more tender species. var. **glau'ca**, a synonym of *C. cashmeriana.*

**C. glab'ra.** A synonym of *C. arizonica bonita.*

**C. glandulo'sa.** A synonym of *C. Macnabiana.*

**C. glau'ca.** A synonym of *C. lusitanica.*

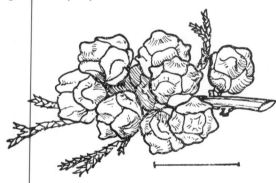

*Cupressus Goveniana*

**C. Govenia'na.** Californian Cypress. Tree of 50 ft. Branches and branchlets reddish-brown, final divisions quadrangular. *l.* fragrant when crushed, in 4 ranks, scale-like, pressed close to shoot. *Cones* globose, short-stalked, ¼ to ⅜ in. wide, with from 6 to 10 scales, and 10 to 12 winged, resin-tubercled seeds on each. California. 1848. (D.J.C. 199.) Syn. *C. californica.* Closely allied to *C. macrocarpa.* var. **attenua'ta**, has a looser branch system than type; **pen'dula**, branches pendulous and some with the juvenile type of *l.*; **pygmaea**, dwarf, suggestive of a depauperate form of the type. Syn. *C. pygmaea.*

**C. guadalupen'sis.** Tree from Guadalupe Islands, closely related to, and sometimes regarded as a variety of, *C. macrocarpa*, differing by its glaucous, rounder cones. Syn. *C. macrocarpa guadalupensis.*

**C. Hartweg'ii.** A synonym of *C. macrocarpa.*

**C. Hodgin'sii.** A synonym of *Fokienia Hodginsii.*

**C. horizonta'lis.** A variety of *C. sempervirens.*

**C. Knightia'na.** A variety of *C. lusitanica.*

**C. Lambertia'na.** A synonym of *C. macrocarpa.*

**C. Lawsonia'na.** A synonym of *Chamaecyparis Lawsoniana.*

**C. × Leyland'ii*** (*Chamaecyparis nootkatensis × Cupressus macrocarpa*). Pyramidal tree with cones and seeds intermediate between parents. Welshpool. 1888. **A**

**C. Lind'leyi.** A synonym of *C. lusitanica.*

**C. lusitan'ica.** Mexican Cypress, Cedar of Goa. Variable tree up to 100 ft. h., with, usually, pendulous or semi-pendulous branchlets, young plants often very glaucous. *l.* in 4 ranks, the juvenile state lasting longer than in most species, mature *l.* small, pointed, pressed close to the shoot, glaucous or grey-green, becoming greener as the tree ages. *Cones* ½ in. wide, glaucous at first, brown later; scales 6 to 8 with 8 to 10 winged, resin-tubercled seeds on each scale. Mexico, Guatemala. Introduced to Portugal at an early unknown date, and to England long afterwards. (D.J.C. 206.) Syn. *C. Coulteri, C. glauca, C. Lindleyi.* var. **argen'tea**, *l.* silvery; **Bentham'ii**, *cones* similar to type, but branchlets flattened and arranged in 2 opposite ranks in the same plane. Mexico. 1838. Syn. *C. Benthamii*; **flagellif'era**, branchlets long, slender, and pendulous, *l.* awl-shaped, *cones* up to ¾ in. wide. Syn. *C. filiformis*; **glau'ca pen'dula**, shoots pendulous, *l.* glaucous; **Knightia'na**, form of var. *Benthamii* with glaucous *l.* Syn. *C. Knightiana*; **majes'tica**, vigorous with glaucous *l.* **A**

**C. Macnabia'na.** Small tree about 40 ft. h., with spreading branches and slender irregularly arranged branchlets. *l.* scale-like with a small resin gland on back, pressed close to shoot, light green or glaucous, fragrant when bruised, blunt. *Cones* in clusters, globose, ½ to ¾ in. wide, often glaucous, of 6 to 8 conical scales, 10 to 12 seeds on each. California. 1854. Syn. *C. Bakeri, C. glandulosa, C. nevadensis.*

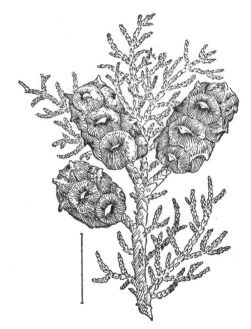

*Cupressus macrocarpa*

**C. macrocar'pa.** Monterey Cypress. Fast-growing tree, pyramidal when young, wide-spreading with age, about 70 ft. h., branchlets irregularly arranged, the final divisions a mass of small spray. *l.* scale-like, triangular, pressed close to shoot, blunt, bright green. *Cones* sub-globose, 1 to 1½ in. long, ¾ to 1 in. wide, brown, of 8 to 14 flattened scales, about 20 seeds on each, outer coat with small resin-tubercles. Monterey, California. 1838. (D.J.C. 209, 210.) Syn. *C. Hartwegii, C. Lambertiana.* The hardiest species in the British Isles, but killed in many places in the winter of 1939–40. It is widely planted on account of its rapid growth and its ability to withstand a salt-laden atmosphere near the sea. Used for hedges but not a good hedge plant, for if closely clipped it soon deteriorates and dies in patches. As, in a young state, branch growth is formed out of all proportion to roots, young trees should be supported by stakes. The following varieties are in cultivation: var. **Cripps'ii**, with short, stiff branches and silvery *l.* longer and sharper than those of type; **fastigia'ta**, stiff, narrow, fastigiate; **guadalupen'sis**, a synonym of *C. guadalupensis*; **Lebreton'ii**, delicate, with creamy-white variegation; **lu'tea**, very vigorous with golden *l.*; one of the best coloured-leaved Conifers; distributed in 1895; **variega'ta**, *l.* green and silver mixed on shoots, not a good garden tree.

**C. nepalen'sis.** A synonym of *C. torulosa.*

**C. nevaden'sis.** A synonym of *C. Macnabiana.*

**C. nootkaten'sis.** A synonym of *Chamaecyparis nootkatensis.*

**C. obtu'sa.** A synonym of *Chamaecyparis obtusa.*

**C. pen'dula.** A synonym of *C. cashmeriana.*

**C. pisif'era.** A synonym of *Chamaecyparis pisifera.*

**C. pyg'maea.** A variety of *C. Goveniana.*

**C. pyramid'alis.** A synonym of *C. sempervirens stricta.*

**C. Royl'ei.** A synonym of *C. sempervirens indica.*

**C. sempervi'rens.** Mediterranean Cypress. There are 2 principal forms of this tree, one stiff and erect, up to 100 or 150 ft. h., most frequent in cultivation, the other with spreading branches. Branchlets alternate, irregular, divided into fine, 4-angled spray. *l.* scale-like, in 4 ranks, pressed close to shoot, blunt. *Cones* sub-globose, short-stalked, 1 to 1¼ in. long, ¾ to 1 in. wide, 8 to 14 scales, with 8 to 20 non-tubercled seeds on each. Often difficult to distinguish from *C. macrocarpa*, but with relatively smaller l. and non-tubercled seeds. S. Europe, W. Asia, N. India. It is esteemed for formal gardening because of its stiff outline. The fragrant wood is popular in S. Europe for building and cabinet work. An essential oil is distilled from shoots and l. The following varieties are recognized: **flagellifor'mis**, with long, slender branchlets; **horizonta'lis**, with spreading branches; **in'dica**, stiff tree. SYN. *C. Roylei*; **stric'ta**, Italian Cypress, with a stiff, fastigiate habit. SYN. *C. fastigiata*; **thujaefo'lia**, of conical habit with 3-pinnate branchlets.

**C. thyoi'des.** A synonym of *Chamaecyparis thyoides.*

**C. torulo'sa.** Bhutan Cypress. Tree, up to 150 ft. h., pyramidal when young, with a wide-spreading crown at maturity. Branchlets pendulous at tip, irregular but flattened. *l.* in 4 ranks, scale-like, pressed close to shoot, pitted on back. *Cones* globose, ½ in. wide, green when young, brown later, of 8 to 10 scales with 6 to 8 winged seeds on each. W. Himalaya. 1824. (D.J.C. 225.) SYN. *C. nepalensis.* It occurs naturally on limestone formations. The fragrant wood is very resistant to decay and is of great value in India. var. **Corneya'na,** branches more irregularly arranged and more pendulous than type. SYN. *C. Corneyana.*

W. D.

*cu'preus -a -um,* copper-coloured.

**CUPULA,** the cup-like involucre enclosing or partly enclosing the nut in, e.g. Corylus and Quercus.

*cupula'ris -is -e,* shaped like a cup.

### CURARE POISON. *See* **Strychnos.**

*curassa'vicus -a -um,* of Curaçao, W. Indies.

**CURATEL'LA** (*curatus,* worked; the leaves are used in Guiana for polishing weapons). FAM. *Dilleniaceae.* A genus of 2 species of dwarf evergreen shrubs, natives of Trop. S. America. Leaves ovate, rough, stalks winged. Flowers white. *C. americana* needs a stove with a compost of loam and peat. Cuttings of ripe wood root freely in sand under glass, in heat.

**C. america'na.** About 10 ft. h., branches tortuous, bark thick, wrinkled, cracking, and falling off in large pieces. *l.* ovate, repand, somewhat toothed, very rough; stalk winged. *fl.* white on racemes from old wood. S. America.

*Cur'cas,* ancient Latin name for Jatropha.

**CURCULI'GO** (*curculio,* weevil; the ovary is beaked like a weevil). FAM. *Amaryllidaceae.* A genus of about 12 species of herbaceous, often very hairy, perennials with tuberous rhizomes, natives of Trop. America, Asia, Australia, Africa, and S. Africa. Leaves radical, often long-lanceolate, plicately veined, often very large. Flowers in spikes or racemes; segments of perianth 6, nearly equal, spreading; stamens 6, fixed at base of segments; carpels 3. Fruit more or less succulent. Ornamental leaved palm-like plants for the warm house, needing a compost of peat and loam in equal parts, used in moderate lumps with a fair amount of silver sand. Drainage must be perfect. Propagation by suckers from the base of the stem.

**C. den'sa.** Dwarf. *l.* oblong-ovate, acute, plicate, dark green with silvery lustre. India. 1885.

**C. recurva'ta.*** *l.* spreading, recurved, lanceolate, plicate, dark green; stalks long, erect. *fl.* yellow, in dense heads; scapes shorter than l.-stalks. E. Indies. (B.R. 770.) var. **stria'ta,*** *l.* with middle band of pure white, stalks white at back; **variega'ta,*** *l.* 2 ft. long, 6 in. wide, banded longitudinally with clear white, stalks 18 in. long. E. Indies.

*curculigoi'des,* Curculigo-like.

**CURCU'MA** (*kurkum,* Arabian name of a yellow colour). FAM. *Zingiberaceae.* A genus of about 40 species of moderate-sized perennial herbs with a thick rhizome and frequently tuberous roots. Leaves usually large, lanceolate or oblong, rarely narrow. Flower-spike dense, cone-like, bracts often forming a bright-coloured tuft at its summit. The spurred anthers distinguish it from all nearly related genera except Roscoea and Cautlea both of which have spike-like, not cone-like, inflorescences from which the flowers scarcely protrude. Most of species are natives of Tropical Asia but a few occur in Trop. Africa. All need warm greenhouse treatment and a compost of 2 parts of peat and 1 of loam, with a little sand. Propagation is best done by dividing the tubers in spring, when the plants should be repotted. The old soil should be shaken off the tubers, the pots well drained, and after repotting the plants should be put into a warm pit or frame with bottom heat, giving little water until growth begins. The young roots are soft and easily damaged by remaining too long in wet soil. After flowering the leaves begin to decay and water should then be gradually withheld, giving only enough to keep the tubers from shrivelling until the time for repotting comes. Turmeric, which is the powdered rhizome of some species, has stimulating properties and is used as a dye-stuff and as a condiment, other species yield E. Indian arrowroot, and *C. Zedoaria* is very similar in its properties to ginger. **A**

KEY

| | | |
|---|---|---|
| 1. | *Anthers not spurred at base* | 2 |
| 1. | *Anthers spurred at base* | 3 |
| 2. | *Fertile bracts green, sterile purple, or lilac* | C. petiolata |
| 2. | *All bracts orange-yellow* | C. Roscoeana |
| 3. | *Fl.-spikes vernal, preceding the leaves or appearing with them* | 4 |
| 3. | *Fl.-spikes autumnal, in centre of leaves* | 11 |
| 4. | *Cor.-lobes white or yellow* | 5 |
| 4. | *Cor.-lobes red* | 9 |
| 5. | *Rhizome small* | C. neilgherrensis |
| 5. | *Rhizome larger tuberous* | 6 |
| 6. | *Lvs. glabrous beneath* | 7 |
| 6. | *Lvs. downy beneath* | 8 |
| 7. | *Fertile bracts green, sterile pink tipped* | C. leucorrhiza |
| 7. | *Fertile bracts red at tip, sterile brilliant red* | C. Zedoaria |
| 8. | *Lvs. green* | C. elata |
| 8. | *Lvs. purple in middle* | C. latifolia |
| 9. | *Lvs. downy beneath* | C. aromatica |
| 9. | *Lvs. glabrous* | 10 |
| 10. | *Fertile bracts pale green, tubers white within* | C. rubescens |
| 10. | *Fertile bracts dark green tipped red, sterile, few, brilliant red* | C. ferruginea |
| 11. | *Rhizome small, plant slender* | C. albiflora |
| 11. | *Rhizome large* | 12 |
| 12. | *Rhizome white within* | C. australasica |
| 12. | *Rhizome pale yellow within* | C. Amada |
| 12. | *Rhizome deep yellow within* | C. longa |

**C. albiflo'ra.** *rhiz.* small. Stem 2 ft. h. *l.-stalk* about 3 in. long, blade oblong-lanceolate, acute, about 6 in. long, glabrous, deep green above, paler beneath. *fl.* in an elliptic spike, about 4 in. long, bracts green, somewhat zoned but not conspicuously coloured; cor. white. Ceylon. 1862. (B.M. 5909.)

**C. Ama'da.** Tuber large, yellow within, fragrant, roots not thickened, white within. Tufted, 2 to 3 ft. across. *l.-stalk* about 8 in. long; blade lanceolate, long-slender-pointed, up to 16 in. long, glabrous, green. *fl.* in a spike about 7 in. long; lower bracts striped green and white, upper sterile ones red, long, and narrow; cor. whitish-yellow. Autumn. India. 1819.

**C. aromat'ica.** Tuber large, yellow within, fragrant. Stem about 3 ft. h. *l.-stalk* about 2 ft. long; blade oblong, shortly slender-pointed, about 2 ft. long, slightly hairy beneath, often variegated with light green. *fl.* in a cylindrical spike about 12 in. long; lower bracts pale green, sterile bracts white more or less tinted red, narrow. April to June. India. 1804. (P.L. 96; B.M. 1546 as *C. Zedoaria*.)

**C. australas'ica.** *rhiz.* white within, scarcely aromatic. About 2½ ft. h. *l.-stalk* about 4 in. long; blade ovate-lanceolate to lanceolate, about 6 in. long, glabrous above. *fl.* in a spike about 6 in. long; fl.-bracts green, sterile bracts oblong-lanceolate, rose; cor. yellow. N. Australia. (B.M. 5620.)

**C. corda'ta.** A synonym of *C. petiolata.*

**C. ela'ta.** Tubers large, pale yellow within. Stem about 3 ft. h. or more. *l.* long-stalked, oblong, about 4 ft. long, green, glabrous above, somewhat hairy beneath. *fl.* in a large spike about 8 in. long; fl.-bracts dark green, sterile ones violet, acute; cor. and lip yellow. Burma.

**C. ferrugin'ea.** Tuber large, yellow within. l.-stalk long, reddish-brown, fragrant, blade oblong, slender-pointed, about 18 in. long, green at first, later tinged reddish-brown in middle. fl. few in a spike about 5 in. long, covered with red scales; fl.-bracts green with a red margin and stripes, upper bracts brilliant red; cor. red. Spring. India. 1819.

**C. latifo'lia.** Up to 12 ft. h. Tuber large, pale yellow within. l.-stalk long; blade oblong or oblong-lanceolate, up to 4 ft. long, green tinged purple in middle above, downy beneath. fl. in a cylindrical spike about 8 in. long; fl.-bracts green striped red at tip, sterile bracts brilliant red with white base, large and oblong; cor. white. Spring. India. 1820. The tallest of the genus.

**C. leucorrhi'za.** Tuber large, cylindrical or carrot-shaped, nearly white within. l. long-stalked, oblong, slender-pointed, about 2 ft. long, green and glabrous above. fl. in a cylindrical spike about 4 in. long; fl.-bracts green, sterile larger, narrower, flesh-coloured; cor. white. India. 1819.

**C. long'a.** Tuber large, elliptic or cylindrical, deep yellow and aromatic within. l.-stalk about 18 in. long; blade oblong or elliptic, slender-pointed, about 18 in. long, glabrous, green. fl. in a cylindrical spike about 8 in. long; fl.-bracts tipped white, sterile rose, lip deep yellow. India. 1759. (B.R. 88 b.) Widely cultivated in the tropics.

**C. neilgherren'sis.** rhiz. small, roots thickened irregularly. Only about 15 in. h. l.-stalk short; blade lanceolate or oblong, slender-pointed, cuspidate, about 10 in. long. fl. on a spike about 4 in. long; fl.-bracts pale yellow, green, sterile deep flesh-coloured; cor. yellow. Spring. Neilgherry Hills.

**C. petiola'ta.** rhiz. pale yellow within. l. 4 to 6, stalk up to 12 in. long; blade oblong, about 8 in. long, pale green beneath. fl. in a spike about 6 in. long; fl.-bracts pale or deep green, sometimes violet, sterile bracts deep violet or purple; cor. pale yellow. Malaya. 1869. (B.M. 5821; 4435 as C. cordata.)

**C. Roscoea'na.** rhiz. white within. l. 6 to 8, stalk up to 18 in. long; blade lanceolate, 6 to 12 in. long, glabrous above, with nerves dark green. fl. in a spike about 8 in. long; bracts orange; cor. yellow; lip deep yellow. August. Malaya. 1837. (B.M. 4667.)

**C. rubes'cens.** Tuber large, white within, aromatic. l.-stalk long, with a red wing; blade lanceolate, about 20 in. long, midrib red. fl. in a loose spike about 5 in. long; fl.-bracts pale green and red, sterile few, pale red; cor. tube yellow, lobes red. India. 1822.

**C. Zedoa'ria.** Tuber robust, white or yellow within, camphor-scented with a bitter-aromatic flavour. Stem about 2½ ft. h. l. 4 to 6, petioles long; blade oblong-lanceolate, slender-pointed, 10 to 24 in. long, glabrous above, purple-tinted in middle beneath. fl. in a spike, 3½ to 4 in. long; fl.-bracts green tinged red, sterile red or purple; cor. yellow. April to August. India. 1797. (C. Zedoaria of B.M. 1546 is C. aromatica.)

**CURD.** Garden name for the head of a Cauliflower or Broccoli.

**CURL BRUSH BEAN.** See **Pithecolobium.**

**curled.** See **crisped.**

**CURLED ROCK BRAKE.** See **Cryptogramma crispa.**

**CURLY DWARF.** A disease of Potato due to severe virus infection, the name being descriptive.

*Curnowia'nus -a -um,* in honour of Mr. Curnow who collected in Madagascar for Messrs. Low.

*Curran'ii,* in honour of Hugh McCullom Curran, b. 1875, of the Bureau of Forestry, Manila.

**CURRANTS, BLACK.** The Black Currant is derived from *Ribes nigrum*, a bush of wide distribution in Europe and Asia, occurring wild here and there in N. England. This fruit, which is grown in the British Isles perhaps more widely than elsewhere, is valued not only for cooking and preserving in the form of jam and jelly, but also for its medicinal properties and for dyeing. For these reasons it is more highly valued than either Red or White Currants. The Black Currant is best grown on deep sandy loams especially if well supplied with moisture and also well drained. Very heavy clays and chalky soils and thin dry soils with gravel subsoil suit it least, but with good supplies of organic manure given annually as a mulch or top-dressing it will give a fair crop on most soils. In planting frost-pockets should be avoided and also sites much exposed to high, cold winds, for it is partially dependent upon insects for pollination and these usually avoid windy sites.

The Black Currant is grown in the form of an open bush without a main stem and with its branches springing from near or below ground-level. Planting should be 5 ft. apart at least and somewhat more may well be allowed for very vigorous varieties on strong soil. As with other deciduous shrubs, planting is best done in October, but may be done at any time in winter when the weather is open and the soil in condition.

An open site is best and planting under trees is inadvisable, but if it is desired to make use of the space between when Plums are being planted Black Currants may be used for the purpose, cutting them out as soon as they begin to interfere with the growth or cultivation of the Plums. The heavy manuring called for by the Black Currants will not be detrimental to the Plums, and by the time the latter need most of the space the Black Currants will be near the end of their useful life which may be taken as 10 years. One or 2-year-old plants should be planted and cut back to 2 buds from the ground. If older bushes are planted cut back in the same way all but 3 or 4 shoots; these will be cut to the ground after fruiting.

Black Currants need liberal manuring. Farmyard manure or manure from the compost heap given as a top dressing annually in autumn or early spring is an essential for the production of heavy crops of large berries. Nitro-chalk or sulphate of ammonia at the rate of 1½ lb. to the sq. rod (say 2 cwt. to the acre) applied in late winter or early spring to bushes which have borne heavy crops will also be helpful.

Black Currants will fruit on spurs, but the fruit is smaller and less abundant than that formed on the strong shoots of the previous year. Pruning therefore is directed towards the production of such strong shoots annually from the base of the bush and consists in the removal, as soon after the fruit is picked as possible, of all the old wood. If too few new shoots have grown from the base, the old shoots are cut back to strong new laterals. These shoots are not shortened back.

Propagation is by cuttings taken from thoroughly healthy, heavy-cropping parents, particularly avoiding such as show any sign of the disease known as 'Reversion' (q.v.). Both hard-wood and soft-wood cuttings are employed. Hard-wood cuttings are made of the current years shoots, taken about 10 in. long as soon as the leaves have fallen and having the top inch or two of less-ripened wood removed. The cuttings are planted in an open spot in autumn (in spring only in case of need), taking out a trench and placing them about 9 in. apart against one side of it so that only 3 or 4 buds will be left above ground level when the trench is filled in and the ground firmed. In very heavy ground the soil about the cuttings should be lightened by the addition of sand. The rows should be 2 ft. apart. The ground must be kept free of weeds and the cuttings should be well-rooted and fit for planting in their permanent places in the following autumn, or if delayed cut back to 2 eyes above ground and left until the autumn after.

As a means of checking Big-bud, soft-wood cuttings made of the top 3 in. of young side growths in May, when they are most likely to be free from infection, are used. They are planted in a sandy compost in the cold frame or greenhouse, kept shaded and moist. Rooting soon occurs and the resulting plants are put out in autumn.

When stock is bought in recourse should be had to those certified by the Ministry of Agriculture, for to introduce infected stock may cause the spread of big-bud and reversion rapidly through the whole plantation.

Black Currants are self-fertile and all the varieties are interfertile, but in many instances the style is so long as to make pollination from the same flower most improbable and they are therefore dependent to a large extent upon insects to effect pollination. Wild bees and hive bees are the chief agents and a sheltered but not shaded position helps to ensure their presence. A common result of ineffective pollination is the dropping ('running-off') of many berries near the end of the truss, although they at first appear to have set. This is intimately connected with the varying structure of the flowers on the truss, for in many varieties the flowers towards the end of the truss have longer styles than those near its base.

Different varieties show differences in time of flowering and also in time of ripening, and by choice of variety ripening may be spread over six weeks at least, choosing varieties of the types of Boskoop Giant, Seabrook's Black, Victoria, Baldwin, and Daniel's September. The choice of varieties, however, within these types, must depend upon local conditions, for Black Currant varieties show great differences in cropping capacity in different localities and only local experience can be a sure guide.

The fruit should be picked when dry whenever possible. For preserving it is better to wait several dry days, but if for immediate use this is less important. As with other Currants and Raspberries birds are apt to take a heavy toll of Black Currants, and in private gardens protection with a fruit-cage (q.v.) is desirable.

The characters distinguishing one variety of Black Currant from another are not easy of definition, but Hatton, in the *Journal of Pomology*, 1 (1920) proposes the following classification into 4 groups the structural characters of which are largely correlated with behaviour.

GROUP I. FRENCH (such as Seabrook's Black). Bush large, much branched, compact; buds pink to purple, pointed, conical, of medium size; leaf late, slightly rugose, terminal lobe acute, sharply toothed, basal sinus very shallow; racemes 1 to 3, peduncle usually about 2 in. long or less, 6- to 10-flowered; truss rather short; fruit of medium size, very acid, with tough skin, mid-season.

GROUP II. BOSKOOP GIANT. Bush large to medium, spreading, sparsely branched; buds pink to purplish, blunt, broad compared with length, large; leaf early, very rugose, terminal lobe blunt, irregularly, often crenately toothed, basal sinus usually deep, blade almost at right angles with stalk; racemes frequently solitary, peduncle 2 to 4 in. long, 12- to 19-flowered, pedicels horizontal; calyx bronzy green; truss long; fruit very large, moderately sweet, skin tender; earliest group.

GROUP III. GOLIATH (Victoria comes here). Bush erect, of medium size, wood strong; buds small, often crowded, light green with slight tinge of pink, scales loose; leaf early, convex, very rugose, light green; terminal lobe irregular, tending to be 3-lobed, teeth very irregular, often blunt, basal sinus rather shallow; blade bent back; racemes 3 to 6, crowded, 8- to 11-flowered, peduncle often short, about 1½ in. long, basal pedicels long, apical ones short, often crowded; flowers rather small; calyx bright yellow; fruit medium to large in short trusses, sweet, skin rather tender; mid-season.

GROUP IV. BALDWIN. Bush dwarf, compact, wood weak; buds long, large, conical, often pointed, light green, almost whitish, protruding, scales loose and ragged; leaf, earliest to develop, often small, flat, slightly rugose, dark green, terminal lobe acute, lateral short, teeth regular, acute, basal sinus usually deep, blade twisted on stalk; racemes 2 or 3, 6- to 12-flowered, peduncle 1¼ to 2 in. long, pedicels short; flowers of medium size; calyx very pale yellow-green; fruit medium on trusses of medium length, somewhat acid, with very tough skin; season late, hanging very late.

Some of the newer varieties show characters intermediate between these groups as is to be expected and seedlings often appear in plantations, bearing characters very similar to those of their seed parent but differing in minute, though often important points, so that constant vigilance is necessary to keep stock true.

The fruits are normally deep purple-black, but green- and white-fruiting forms are known and a golden-leaved variety has been described. The Black Currant has been crossed with the Gooseberry (see *Journal R.H.S.* 24, p. 168).

*DISEASES.* AMERICAN GOOSEBERRY MILDEW disease occasionally attacks Black, Red, and White Currants. *See* **Gooseberry, American Mildew.**

BLACK PUSTULE caused by the fungus *Plowrightia ribesia* infects Currants, particularly Red Currants, and also Gooseberries, sometimes killing branches but occasionally the whole bush. Infection is through snags left after pruning and affected branches bear oval, black, wart-like pustules about 1 in. long. Infected branches must be cut out and burnt, and long snags should not be left, especially near the collar.

CLUSTER CUPS. *See* **Gooseberry, Cluster Cup Rust.**

CORAL SPOT. *See* **Coral Spot.**

EUROPEAN GOOSEBERRY MILDEW. *See* **Gooseberry, European Mildew.**

LEAF SPOTS. Currant foliage may be seriously harmed by a leaf spot due to attack by the fungus *Gloeosporium ribis*. These spots are dark brown and irregular in shape, being about $\frac{1}{12}$ in. across, but in wet seasons they increase and cause early defoliation (June, July) so weakening the bushes and shrivelling the fruit. On the fallen leaves the fungus further develops ascocarps which will release ascospores in spring. Baldwin and Boskoop Giant are the most susceptible varieties especially if heavily manured. Fallen leaves should be raked up and burnt or buried. In the nursery young bushes should be sprayed with Bordeaux mixture in May or June. Older bushes must be sprayed only after the fruit is picked. Another leaf spot due to *Mycosphaerella ribis* (*Septoria ribis*) is very similar but not very common and the remedial measures are the same as for the *Gloeosporium* leaf spot.

REVERSION is one of the most serious disorders in Black Currants. The symptoms are that the bushes begin to be barren although the flowers may appear earlier and be more brightly coloured than the normal ones. The greatest change is in the leaves which are smaller but relatively longer and narrower than the normal ones. The important symptom is that the veins which branch from the main central vein (sub-main-veins) in the top lobe of a reverted leaf are fewer than they should be. In a normal leaf 5 to 8 sub-mains are present in this top lobe but in a reverted one the number falls to 4 or fewer. There are fewer teeth on such a lobe and in severely affected bushes not only are the teeth few but even the lobes begin to be less distinct until the so-called Oak-leaf appearance may be reached. The time to look for Reversion is May or June selecting only strong growing shoots which are undamaged. There is a condition known as False Reversion in which the leaves on some shoots show the symptoms owing to the terminal bud being injured. In any case expert advice on Reversion is best before any drastic steps are taken. The disease is thought to be due to virus infection possibly transmitted by Big Bud mite. Cuttings must not be taken from reverted bushes, which should be grubbed up and burnt after fruit picking is over. Healthy bushes can safely be planted in the gaps. Cutting out individual reverted branches is useless.

SILVER LEAF. *See* **Silver Leaf Disease.**

RUST on Black Currant foliage is caused by the rust fungus *Cronartium ribicola* which forms light- and dark-brown spots on the undersurfaces of the leaves. These pustules contain the uredospore and teleutospore stage of the fungus which forms its third (aecidiospore) stage on the branches of 5-needled pines, especially the Weymouth Pine (*Pinus Strobus*). Other pines attacked are *P. Cembra, P. monticola*. The disease is usually not serious in this country as it appears late in the season on the older foliage when picking is finished, and such old branches can be pruned out and burnt after which the younger shoots may be sprayed with Bordeaux mixture. In those localities near infected 5-needled pines where the disease appears early, spraying with Bordeaux mixture up to the setting of the fruit and disposal of old leaves by burning or burying in the soil during the dormant season should be carried out.

(D. E. G.)

*PESTS*. APHIDES. Of the 6 species of Greenflies found on Currants as recorded by Massee (*The Pests of Fruits and Hops*, 1937) only 3 are generally distributed in this country, namely, the Currant and Lettuce Aphis, *Amphorophora sonchi*; the Lettuce Aphis, *Myzus lactucae*; and the Currant Aphis, *Capitophorus ribis*. All these species attack both Black, Red, and White Currants. The effect of their attack is that the foliage is partially or completely curled, new growth is stunted, and leaves and developing fruits become covered with honeydew and, later, with Sooty Moulds. All 3 species migrate to summer hosts, including Sowthistle, Lettuce, Dead Nettles, and other wild plants, and return to the Currant bushes to lay their eggs both in the bud-axils and beneath the loose bark of the stems.                    A

Thorough and forceful application of a 5 per cent. tar-distillate wash to every portion of the dormant bushes will give satisfactory control of all the Currant-infesting Aphides. Spraying the underside of the leaves in spring —mid- to late April—with nicotine and soap wash *before* leaf-curl occurs is recommended.

CAPSID BUG. See **Capsid Bug, Common Green.**

CURRANT GALL MITE, *Phytoptus ribis*, is responsible for the swollen buds on Black Currants, and is usually referred to as 'Big Bud'. This microscopic Gall Mite also attacks Red and White Currants and Gooseberry, the infested buds of which dry up and the shoots become 'blind'. The mites work their way into the buds of the current year's growth in June, and egg-laying soon begins. The immature mites speedily develop and feed on the tissues within the buds, which are seen to swell in late July. Feeding and reproduction inside the buds continue until the following April, and many hundreds of the mites may be found within a single bud. They migrate from the enlarged buds in spring over a period extending from late March to mid-April, and eventually find their way into the newly formed buds. Some of these mites are carried long distances by wind, on the feet of birds, attached to the bodies of pollinating insects, and even on the clothing of people walking among the infested bushes during the period of migration.

It is advisable to burn all very badly infested bushes owing to the number of useless buds present on the shoots. This pest may be controlled by thoroughly spraying the bushes in spring, when the first leaves are the size of a shilling or when the flower racemes are in the 'grape bud' stage, with 1 pint of lime sulphur to 2½ gallons of water. The concentration of lime sulphur should be reduced to 1 in 50 (1 pint to 6 gallons) for sulphur-shy varieties, e.g. Davidson's Eight and Victoria type. The importance of controlling this pest is not only because of the direct damage done to the buds but to the indirect effect of the mite in its role of carrier of the Virus disease known as 'Reversion'.

CURRANT CLEARWING, *Aegeria tipuliformis*, is a pest of Currants, chiefly Black. The tunnelled stems can be seen during pruning operations, though the first signs of attack are the wilting and yellowing of the foliage and the undeveloped fruit trusses to be seen during the growing season. The moths have clear wings almost devoid of scales, and fly about actively on sunny days among the bushes. The females lay their eggs on the stems in midsummer, and the young caterpillars immediately bore into the pith and begin to tunnel upwards towards the growing point. Feeding continues throughout the winter and early spring, when pupation takes place within the burrow near the entrance hole. It is not possible to prevent an attack of this pest, but it may be kept within bounds by pruning out during the winter shoots which, bent over, tend to snap off; cutting to a point below the larval tunnel and burning them.

CURRANT MOTH. *See* **Magpie Moth.**

CURRANT SAWFLY. *See* **Gooseberry Sawfly.**

CURRANT SCALE. *See* **Scale Insects.**

CURRANT SHOOT BORER, *Lampronia capitella*, is the name given to the caterpillar of a small moth which bores into the buds and stems of Currant bushes in spring causing the leaves to wilt and the buds to become 'blind' and die. It occurs chiefly in fruit plantations of Kent, Surrey, and Worcestershire. The small moth has a wing expanse of about ½ in., the fore-wings being brown and marked with a yellow band and 2 yellow spots near the tips. The female deposits her eggs in slits made in the fruits, and the young larvae feed for a time on the seeds. They then leave the fruits and spin small cocoons in crevices in the bark and there overwinter. They leave their cocoons in spring, and tunnel into the buds and shoots causing them to shrivel and die. When fully fed they pupate in the hollowed-out shoots and emerge as moths in April and May. The infested buds should be removed and the tunnelled shoots cut off and burned. In severe attacks it is necessary to spray the bushes thoroughly and forcibly with a 10 per cent. tar-distillate wash to destroy the hibernating caterpillars in their cocoons beneath the rind, in cracks, and elsewhere on the bushes.

(G. F. W.)

**CURRANTS, RED AND WHITE.** While the Black Currant has been derived from a single species, the varieties of the Red Currant have come either direct from or by the intercrossing of 3 species, *Ribes petraeum*, a species native to high mountains in Europe, N. Africa, and Siberia, *R. rubrum*, a native of Cent. and E. Europe eastwards through Asia to Manchuria, and *R. vulgare*, a native of W. Europe. Red Currants seem to have come first into cultivation in the fifteenth century and were probably introduced into British gardens in the first half of the sixteenth century, but the currants of that day judging by contemporary illustrations were no larger than those produced by the wild plants of *R. vulgare*. Soon after plants with larger fruits appeared. E. A. Bunyard considered that the earliest cultivated Red Currants were examples of *R. vulgare* while the larger fruited variety was a cross between *R. petraeum* and *R. vulgare*. *R. petraeum* itself is evident in such varieties as Prince Albert (Rivers' Late Red). The variety Raby Castle was introduced in 1820 and is a seedling of *R. rubrum*, though probably that species had been cultivated for a time before that. The really large-fruited varieties of the Fay's Prolific group, known as *macrocarpum*, of which many varieties were subsequently raised appear to have arisen from plants sent from Italy into France in 1840. They have many of the characters of *R. vulgare* but have larger, more leathery, leaves as well as larger fruits, and their thick shoots are apt to break out at the point of origin giving very ill-shaped bushes.

The White Currants have been derived from the Red and show the same characteristics of growth though they are often less vigorous than their red-fruited counterparts.

Red and White Currants are not particular as to soil so long as drainage is good and potash is sufficient. They benefit by a mulch of garden compost or its equivalent in spring and by annual dressings of sulphate of potash in autumn at the rate of 2 lb. to the square rod. Heavy dressings of nitrogenous manure should be avoided as they tend to make soft growth. The pruning of these currants is quite different from that required by the Black Currant for they produce their fruit on spurs on the old wood. The leaders should be pruned back in autumn to a sound bud (in some varieties, especially of the Fay's Prolific and other varieties of similar type, many buds are abortive; these varieties need special attention in pruning to a strong upward pointing bud). The lateral branches should be spurred back to leave 2 or 3 buds. Care should be taken to cut out branches attacked by the boring caterpillars of the Currant Clearwing Moth as well as all dead wood. Summer pruning should be carried out before the fruit is picked and should follow the same principles as in Apple-pruning. The centre of the bush should be kept open.

Propagation is by autumn cuttings treated like those of the Black Current except that, if it is desired to have bushes on a leg, as is preferable in gardens, the buds on the part of the cutting buried in the soil and about 5 inches above the soil should be removed and the cutting should be inserted much less deeply than with the Black Currant. They may, however, be grown without a distinct stem and this is often the practice in plantations. The spring plants are usually left until 2 years old before planting. The bushes should be planted 5 ft. apart each way; cordons 1 ft. apart. As these currants are self-fertile there is no need to mix varieties. They may be grown as cordons with 1, 2, or 3 stems trained against a trellis or wall, and if planted against a north wall and the fruit protected from birds it will remain fit for use until well into autumn. Whether as bush or cordon care should be taken to establish a firm system of branches before cropping the plants. They may be expected to have a useful life of 15 to 20 years.

The demand for Red Currants is much less than that for Black but they are useful as dessert fruits, for pies and preserves. Their juice mixed with other fruit in jam-making greatly assists setting. White Currants are used for dessert. Protection should be provided against birds which are very fond of both Red and White Currants and will quickly strip the bushes as soon as the fruit begins to ripen.

Earliest of Fourlands is the first variety to ripen and Wilson's Long Bunch the latest. Varieties recommended are listed in the Supplement.

Red and White Currant bushes may be attacked by the diseases common to Currants. The Honey Fungus *Armillaria mellea* may attack the roots (see **Honey fungus**) and the stem or collar may develop toadstool-like fructifications of *Collybia velutipes* or the bracket-like sporophores of *Fomes ribis* (see **Bracket fungi**). Both these fungi enter through wounds and old snags and emphasize the need to avoid injury at ground-level. Black Pustule disease (*Plowrightia ribesia*) has already been described under Black Currant (q.v.) as has the virus disease called Reversion, besides various leaf spots. Red Currants may be affected by diseases more common on Gooseberries such as American Gooseberry Mildew, European Gooseberry Mildew, and Rust or Clustercups, all of which are described under Gooseberry diseases. Perhaps the most common diseases of Red Currant bushes, especially old ones, are Coral Spot (*Nectria cinnabarina*) and Dieback (*Botrytis cinerea*). Both these cause sudden wilting and dying of branches or of the whole bush in summer and often when the bushes are full of fruit. The trouble is that one or other of the above fungi has entered the base of a branch or the collar and is killing the tissues there. For remedial treatments see **Coral Spot, Gooseberry Dieback.**

(D. E. G.)

*Cur'rori,* in honour of Dr. A. B. Curror who collected plants in W. Africa, *c.* 1834–44.

*cur'tidens,* having short teeth.

**CURTIS'IA** (in honour of Wm. Curtis, founder of the *Botanical Magazine*). FAM. *Cornaceae*. A monotypic genus, the parts of the flower-calyx, corolla, stamens, and fruit cells in fours. Greenhouse, needing sandy loam and peat. Cuttings of half-ripe wood can be rooted in sand under a light in gentle heat. *C. faginea* yields a valuable timber, heavy, close-grained, durable, and resembling a plain mahogany.

**C. fagi'nea.** Evergreen tree, 20 to 40 ft., sometimes 60 ft., shoots, l.-stalks, and infl. rusty downy. *l.* opposite, ovate, 2 to 3½ in. long, 1 to 2 in. wide, pointed, cuneate, coarsely toothed, shining green above, downy beneath. *fl.* minute, downy, numerous, in terminal panicles. *fr.* a bony nut with a thin, pure white covering, ⅓ to ½ in. long, globose. June, July. S. Africa. 1775.

W. J. B.

*Curtis'ii,* in honour of Chas. Curtis, 1853–1928, Asst. Supt. Gardens and Forests, Straits Settlements.

**CURTO'NUS** (*kurtos*, bent, *onos*, axis, from the zigzag axis of the flower spikes). FAM. *Iridaceae*. A genus of 1 species of S. African herb allied to Antholyza and at one time included in it, but with the stem ending in a paniculate inflorescence with pedunculate, many-flowered spikes on a zigzag axis, the bracts equal and many times shorter than the flowers. Leaves basal, broad. Flower tube abruptly narrowed about middle, lobes unequal, linear-oblong, upper longer than the other 5, concave; stamens about as long as upper lobe; ovules 8 to 10 in each cell. Cultivation as for Antholyza.

**C. panicula'tus.** Corms sub-globose. Stem 4 ft. h. *l.* basal, ensiform or lanceolate, 1 to 3 in. wide. *fl.* deep orange-red, in a panicle of several many-fld. spikes. August, September. Transvaal, Natal.

*cur'tus -a -um,* short.

**CURU'BA.** *See* **Sicana odorifera.**

*curva'tus -a -um, curvi-,* in compound words, curved.

**CUSCU'TA** (?). FAM. *Convolvulaceae*. Dodder. A genus of about 80 species of leafless twining parasites which send suckers (haustoria) into the tissues of the hosts over which they climb. Stems slender, often like fine copper wire. Flowers in clusters, rarely in spikes, bracteate; corolla urn- or bell-shaped with 5, rarely 4, lobes. In some species the flowers are very fragrant. The hardy species are apt to become pests on flax (*C. Epilinum*), clover (*C. trifolii*), or heaths and gorse (*C. Epithymum*), damaging the plants on which they feed. All the species can be readily grown by sowing their seeds with those of their hosts. The most ornamental and interesting species are: STOVE: *C. americana, C. Hookeri, C. odorata,* and *C. verrucosa.* GREENHOUSE: *C. australis, C. chilensis, C. monogyna,* and *C. reflexa.* HARDY: *C. Epilinum, C. Epithymum, C. macrocarpa,* and *C. trifolii,* the last four being natives of Britain.

**CUSHION PINK.** *See* **Silene acaulis.**

*Cusick'ii,* in honour of W. C. Cusick of Oregon.

**CUSP.** A short, acute point.

**CUSPA'RIA** (*Cusparé,* Venezuelan name for *Cusparia febrifuga,* the bark of which is used as a febrifuge). FAM. *Rutaceae.* A genus of about 20 species of usually small trees with erect unbranched stems and a crown of large leaves, natives of S. America. Flowers with petals more or less joined, sometimes forming a vase-like corolla. Related to Galipea. A compost of loam and leaf-mould with stove conditions suits them. Increase by seeds.

**C. heterophyl'la.** *l.* 3- to 5-foliolate, long-stalked; lflets. lanceolate, midrib slightly hairy. *fl.* in racemes above the l.-axils. Brazil.

**C. undula'ta.** *l.* palmately 5-foliolate, leathery. *fl.* white, about ¾ in. long, in axillary racemes shorter than l. Brazil? Before 1886.

**CUSPIDAR'IA.** Included in **Eschatogramme.**

A

**cuspida'tus -a -um, cuspidi-,** in compound words, cuspidate, suddenly narrowed to a projecting, often sharp, point.

**CUSSON'IA** (in honour of Peter Cusson, 1727–85, physician, Professor of Botany in the University of Montpelier). FAM. *Araliaceae.* A genus of about 20 species of evergreen small trees or shrubs with handsome foliage, all African. Leaves digitate with a long mainstalk; lflets. usually 5 to 9, sometimes more. Flowers small; petals 5 or 7, stamens of the same number. The following species require a greenhouse temperature (one of them, *C. paniculata,* is grown outside in Scilly) and show their best when planted in a border of good loamy soil.

**C. panicula'ta.** Evergreen shrub or small tree, 10 to 15 ft. *l.* digitate; *lflets.* 7 to 12, each 6 to 12 in. long, 1½ to 4 in. wide, coarsely pinnately lobed, the lobes ovate-lanceolate, spine-tipped, occasionally toothed but sometimes entire or merely serrate. *fl.* yellow, numerous in cylindrical spikes 1½ to 3 in. long combining to make panicles up to 1 ft. long. S. Africa.

**C. spica'ta.** Evergreen tree 10 to over 20 ft. *lflets.* usually 7 or 9, sometimes only 5, each 4 to 7 in. long, very variable in form, but mostly lanceolate, lobed or coarsely toothed, sometimes pinnate, sometimes nearly or quite entire; mainstalk 6 to 10 in. long. *fl.* densely set in cylindrical spikes 3 to 9 in. long, ¾ in. wide. S. Africa. 1789.

**C. thyrsiflo'ra.** Small evergreen tree, 6 to 12 ft. *lflets.* digitate, 5, obovate, not stalked, nearly or quite entire or sometimes 3-lobed, 1½ to 3½ in. long, 1 to 1½ in. wide, glabrous; mainstalk 3 to 6 in. long. *fl.* white, quite small, densely set in spikes 2 to 5 in. long, ½ to ¾ in. wide. S. Africa. 1795.

**C. umbellif'era.** Tree up to 30 ft. or more; bark resinous. *lflets.* 5, rarely 3, digitate, obovate, 3 to 6 in. long, 1 to 2½ in. wide, apex rounded and notched, glabrous; stalks 1 to·2 in. long; mainstalk 6 to 12 in. long. *fl.* green, small, in umbels forming collectively stalked, axillary panicles up to 8 in. long. S. Africa.

W. J. B.

**CUSTARD APPLE.** *See* **Annona reticulata.**

**CUTCH.** *See* **Acacia, Rhizophora.**

**CUT-FINGER.** *See* **Vinca major.**

**CUTHBERT'IA** (derivation?). FAM. *Commelinaceae.* A genus of 3 species of perennial herbs, natives of N. America, allied to Tradescantia but with minute instead of leaf-like bracts beneath the flower-clusters. Stems erect or spreading from a dense cluster of cord-like or fuzzy roots. Leaves narrow, long, flat, or half-round. Flowers in a simple cyme on a long peduncle with scale-like bracts; petals pink or purplish, equal; stamens 6, with downy filaments. Hardy in well-drained sandy soils with moisture below and containing leaf-mould; enduring some shade. For open sandy woods or rock-garden. **A**

**C. gramin'ea.** Densely tufted, 2 to 6 in. h. Stems slender. *l.* erect, filiform, awl-shaped. *fl.* ¾ to 1 in. across, pinkish; pet. entire. Spring, summer. SE. United States.

**Cuth'bertsonii,** in honour of Mr. Cuthbertson, leader of expedition into New Guinea, 1887.

**CUTICLE.** The outermost layer of the external wall of the epidermis of the shoots and leaves of land plants. This part of the cell-wall contains cutin, and becomes an elastic, extensible material scarcely permeable by water, and often including particles of wax, frequently on its surface where it forms the 'bloom'. This wax is readily wiped off.

**Cutsemia'nus -a -um,** in honour of Dr. Boddaert van Cutsem, botanist.

**CUTTING-BACK** or **CUTTING-IN.** The shortening of branches of trees and shrubs.

**CUTTINGS.** *See* **Propagation.**

**CUTWORMS.** *See* **Surface Caterpillars.**

**CYANAEOR'CHIS** (*kyanos,* blue, *Orchis*). FAM. *Orchidaceae.* A monotypic terrestrial genus of little horticultural value. The slender stems are 12 to 30 in. high with 3 to 5 grass-like, linear, coriaceous leaves, 6 to 15 in. long, sheathing the stem at the base. Peduncles 1- to 10-flowered are terminal; bracts narrow, pointed. Petals smaller than sepals; lip shortly clawed to the column foot, with comparatively large erect side lobes while the mid-lobe is ovate-tongue-shaped, papillose, 2-ribbed, recurved. Column without wings. Pollinia 4.

**C. arundin'ae.** *fl.* sep. ½ to 1 in. long, the dorsal about ⅓ broad; the lateral slightly broader; pet. inclined upwards, yellow, the outer surfaces shaded with green; lip yellow, side lobes striated with violet. Brazil. 1887. SYN. *Eulophia arundinae.*

**CYANAN'THUS** (*kyanos,* blue, *anthos,* flower). FAM. *Campanulaceae.* A genus of about 12 species of mostly bright-flowered alpine herbaceous perennials with procumbent stems, natives of Cent. and E. Asia. Flowers mostly solitary and terminal, blue or rarely yellow, usually bell-shaped; stamens 5, free from corolla or almost so; ovary superior, 3- to 5-celled. Fruit a capsule. Rock-garden or scree plants. The long, somewhat fleshy roots run far among damp leaf-mould and sand, or small loose stones, and require constant moisture but good drainage. Cuttings may be struck in spring or early summer in moist, sandy peat. Division may sometimes be done in spring but is always precarious.

**C. Delavay'i.** Decumbent, stems 5 to 8 in. long, branched from base, slender, hairy, leafy to apex. *l.* ⅓ in. long, reniform-angled, glabrous above, densely covered with bristly hairs beneath. *fl.* deep blue, about 1 in. long, cor. hairy within with exserted tuft of hair at throat; segs. spreading, ovate-lanceolate, somewhat shorter than tube. September. Yunnan. SYN. *C. barbatus.*

**C. inca'nus.** 3 to 4 in. h. *l.* oval, slightly lobed, softly hairy, hairs white. *fl.* soft azure-blue, 1 to 1½ in. long, ¾ to 1 in. across; segs. oblong, spreading, throat lined with soft, white hairs. August. Sikkim.

**C. in'teger.** Differs from *C. microphyllus* with which it has been confused, by the larger elliptic l. tapering to the stalk and covered with white hairs, and the funnel-shaped scarcely hairy corolla. Probably not yet introduced.

*Cyananthus lobatus*

**C. loba'tus.** About 4 in. h. *l.* small, fleshy, wedge-shaped, obovate, lobed. *fl.* bright purple-blue, about 1 in. across, funnel-shaped; segs. tongue-shaped, reflexed; throat with many soft, long, whitish hairs; cal. large, covered with short, blackish hairs. August, September. Himalaya. 1844. (B.M. 6485.)

**C. longiflo'rus.** Stems trailing, about 10 in. long, leafy, several from an erect rhizome, often with short branches, covered with stiff, brown hairs. *l.* lanceolate, often blunt, ⅓ to ⅔ in. long, margins revolute, densely white-silky beneath; stalks about ⅛ in. long. *fl.* deep blue-mauve, nearly 2 in. long; cor. tube cylindrical, about 1 in. long, lobes somewhat spreading, lanceolate-oblong with a tuft of whitish hairs near base within; fl. terminal or axillary, solitary. September. Yunnan. 1906. (B.M. 9387.)

**C. macroca'lyx.** Stems prostrate, or sub-erect, reddish-brown, about 5 in. long, from a woody rootstock. *l.* variously arranged, deltoid-ovate, about ⅖ in. long and nearly as wide, obtuse, yellowish-green, margin revolute; stalk winged. *fl.* terminal, sulphur- or greenish-yellow with or without short blue or purplish streaks along the tube; tube ⅗ to 1 in. long, cylindrical, lobes spreading, ovate-oblong, about ⅖ in. long with a tuft of long yellowish hairs at base; cal. bell-shaped, yellowish, becoming enlarged in fruit. Tibet, China. 1924. Moraine. Somewhat difficult. (B.M. 9562.)

*Cyananthus microphyllus*

**C. microphyl'lus.*** Stems tufted, trailing, or sub-erect, reddish, up to 12 in. long, from a woody rootstock. *l.* alternate, narrow-elliptic to ovate, ⅖ in. long, about ⅛ in. wide, rounded or cordate at base, dark green, entire, margins revolute; stalks very short, winged. *fl.* solitary, terminal, violet-blue; tube cylindrical, about ⅜ in. long, lobes spreading, about ½ in. long, ⅓ in. wide, narrow-obovate, acute, white hairy in lower half; cal. bell-shaped, hairy, hairs dark brown or blackish. Autumn. N. India, Nepal. 1900. (B.M. 9598.) SYN. *C. integer* of gardens. Rock-garden.

**C. neglec'tus.** Nearly related to *C. longiflorus* but cor. lobes shortly ovate, cal. lobes broadly triangular. Stems several, trailing, up to 10 in. long, branched, densely short-hairy. *l.* lanceolate, about ⅓ in. long, sparingly hairy above, silky-white beneath; stalks short. *fl.* solitary, blue; tube about ⅜ in. long; lobes slightly spreading, about ⅜ in. long, with a tuft of hairs near base of lobes. China. About 1930? (B.M. 8909.)

**C. Sherriff'ii.** Stems numerous from a stout, woody rootstock, slender, prostrate or ascending, up to 16 in. long. *l.* elliptic to deltoid-ovoid, blunt, entire, or nearly so, green and almost glabrous above, more or less greyish-hairy beneath; sessile or shortly stalked. *fl.* periwinkle-blue paler in throat, terminal; cal. shell-shaped, covered with grey or black hairs; cor. tube somewhat bell-shaped, about ¾ in. long, thickly bearded, lobes spreading or somewhat recurved, blunt. September. Bhutan and S. Tibet. 1937. (B.M. 9655.)

**A→**

**CYANEL'LA** (diminutive of *kyanos*, blue). FAM. *Amaryllidaceae.* A genus of about 6 species of herbs with rhizomes or tunicated bulbs, natives of S. Africa. Leaves mostly radical, lanceolate, or linear. Flowers in simple or branched racemes or solitary; segments 6, free or almost so, the lower 3 directed downwards; style and lowest stamen declinate. Fruit a capsule. For treatment of these not quite hardy bulbs *see* **Ixia.**

**C. capen'sis.** About 1 ft. h. Stem branched, the branches forked. *l.* lanceolate, wavy on margins. *fl.* purple in racemes. July, August. 1768. (B.M. 568.)

**C. lu'tea.** A synonym of *C. odoratissima.*

**C. odoratis'sima.** About 1 ft. h. Stem slightly branched. *l.* radical ensiform, straight, dark green, those of stem linear-lanceolate, slender-pointed. *fl.* deep rose fading to pale blush then yellow, fragrant, on long peduncles; anthers yellow, the 5 upper spotted. July, August. 1788. (B.R. 1111; B.M. 1252 as *C. lutea.*)

***cyan'eus -a -um, cyano-*** in compound words, blue.

**CYANIDING.** Fumigation with hydrocyanic acid gas. *See* **Fumigation.**

**CYANOPHYL'LUM.** Included in **Miconia.** *C. vittatum* is a synonym of *Clidemia vittata.*

**CYANO'TIS** (*kyanos*, blue, *ous*, ear; in allusion to the petals). FAM. *Commelinaceae.* A genus of about 35 species of herbs related to Tradescantia, distributed over the warmer parts of the globe. Leaves of various forms, small or of medium size, sheathing at base. Flowers nearly regular; segments 6, outer nearly equal, boat-shaped, joined at base; inner petal-like, joined by the claws. The plants need stove or greenhouse treatment, a rich loamy soil and good drainage. Propagation is by young cuttings put into sandy soil in brisk heat.

**C. barba'ta.** *l.* narrow. *fl.* dark blue; stamens with long, erect filaments densely covered with deep blue hairs. August. India, China, &c. Greenhouse perennial.

**C. kewen'sis.** Climber. *fl.* rose. Winter and spring. Malabar. 1874. (B.M. 6150 as *Erythrotis Beddomei.*) Stove perennial.

**C. nodiflo'ra.** About 9 in. h. *l.* strap-shaped, entire, ciliate. *fl.* purple. S. Africa. 1864. (B.M. 5471.)

**C. somalien'sis.** Branching, stem leafy. *l.* lanceolate to ovate, sheathing, hairy on both surfaces, long, ciliate, lateral shoots dorsi-ventral. Somaliland. Stove perennial.

**C. vitta'ta.** A synonym of *Zebrina pendula.*

**CYA'NUS.** Included in **Centaurea.**

**CYATH'EA** (*kyatheion*, a little cup; referring to the appearance of the sori on the back of the frond). FAM. *Cyatheaceae.* A genus of over 350 evergreen tree ferns native in tropical and sub-tropical regions. Fronds simple or pinnate, or decompoundly pinnate. Receptacle elevated, globose, or elongated; indusium globose, inferior, covering the whole sorus, finally breaking at the top and forming a more or less persistent cup, even or regular at the margin. Sori on a vein, or in the forking of a vein. Stem often spiny.

The genus contains some of the most beautiful of tree ferns with foliage equal in every respect to any Alsophila or Hemitelia, with which they are closely connected, while they offer a great variety in the size of their trunks. Those inhabiting temperate regions, such as *C. dealbata, C. medullaris,* are mostly stout and destitute of spines, whereas most of the tropical species are more slender and in many instances are densely armed with stout spines. To make good growth they require an abundance of water at the roots, and their trunks to be kept constantly moist. By these means only can Cyatheas be induced to produce fine heads of fronds, which last all the longer on the plants if they have gradually been inured to the sun during the summer. Like all other tree ferns, Cyatheas are satisfied with very little pot-room. The soil in which they should be potted, tubbed, or, better still, planted in the fernery, is a mixture of 3 parts fibrous peat, 1 of loam, and 1 of coarse silver-sand. All are easily grown, and, provided the moisture about the trunk and the roots be well attended to, there need be very little fear of failure in their cultivation. None among the numerous species known is in the habit of producing adventitious growths along the trunk or at the base, and none is known to be proliferous. The plants are therefore usually propagated from their spores, which are abundantly produced and germinate freely, making very showy young plants in the course of a couple of seasons.

*C. medullaris* is of very rapid growth; when planted in a conservatory where plenty of room can be allowed for its perfect development it makes a good-sized stem or trunk in a comparatively short time, and proves by far the most imposing of all known tree ferns which will succeed under cool treatment.

**C. aculea'ta.** A synonym of *Alsophila armata.*

**C. arbor'ea.*** *sti.* and rachis pale brown. *Fronds* large, 2-pinnate; secondary pinnae 5 to 8 in. long, sessile, oblong-lanceolate, deeply pinnatifid or again pinnate; pinnules oblong, sub-falcate, serrated. W. Indies. 1793. (B.H. 1864, 235.) SYN. *C. Grevilleana.* Unarmed or prickly. Stove.

**C. Beyrichia'na.** A synonym of *Hemitelia setosa.*

**C. borbon'ica.** *Fronds* glabrous, 2-pinnate; primary pinnae 8 to 18 in. long, oblong, acuminate, 2-pinnate and pinnatifid at apex; pinnules sessile, 1 to 1¼ in. long, oblong, sub-acute, entire or serrate. *Sori* copious near costa. Mauritius. (L.F. 8. 55.) SYN. *C. canaliculata.* Plant unarmed or indistinctly tuberculate. Stove.

**C. Brunonia'na.** *Fronds*, rachis of pinnae often free from prickles, of pinnules beneath more or less crisped-pubescent; veinlets 2- rarely 3-branched. Indusium membranous, reduced before sporangia ripen to a hemispheric cup or sub-patelliform scale. 10 to 40 ft. h. India. (F.B.I. 87.)

**C. Burk'ei.** A synonym of *C. Dregei*.

**C. canalicula'ta.** A synonym of *C. borbonica*.

**C. Cunningham'i.*** *cau.* 12 to 15 ft. long. *sti.* and main rachises straw-colour, asperous. *Fronds* rather leathery, flaccid, 3-pinnate; primary pinnae 1½ to 2 ft. long; secondary 3 to 5 in. long, oblong, acuminate, pinnatifid only at apex; lobes or ultimate pinnules 4 to 6 in. long, linear, obtuse, pinnatifid; lobules entire. *Sori* 1 to each lobe. Australia, New Zealand. 1860. (Gn. 5 (1874), 9.) Greenhouse.

*Cyathea dealbata*

**C. dealba'ta.*** *Fronds* 2- or 3-pinnate; pinnae oblong, acuminate, pure white beneath, deeply pinnatifid or pinnate at base; lobes oblong, acute, falcate, serrate. *Sori* copious, sometimes confined to lower half of lobes. New Zealand, &c. (L.F. 8, 58; B.C.F. 2, 79.) Unarmed or slightly asperous. Greenhouse.

**C. Dre'gei.** *Fronds* 2-pinnate; pinnules sessile, 2 to 3 in. long, glabrous, narrow-oblong, acuminate, deeply pinnatifid; lobes oblong-ovate, sub-falcate, obtuse, more or less serrate. (H.S. 1, 10, 17; F.S.A. (2) 6.) S. Africa. 1873. SYN. *C. Burkei*. Unarmed or only rough, with small tubercles at base of stipes. Stove.

**C. excel'sa.*** *Fronds* 2-pinnate, firm-membranaceous; primary pinnae 2 ft. long, 6 to 8 in. wide; pinnules 3 to 4 in. long, ½ in. wide, sessile, deeply pinnatifid, sub-pinnate at base; lobes oblong, obliquely sub-acute, serrate, scaleless. *Sori* in fork near costa. Mascarene Is. 1825. (L.F. 8, 56; H.S. 1, 12.) Unarmed. Greenhouse or stove.

**C. Grevillea'na.** A synonym of *C. arborea*.

**C. Hook'eri.** *cau.* 1½ in. thick. *sti.* short. *Fronds* firm-membranaceous, 2 to 3 ft. long, 4 to 5 in. wide, elongato-lanceolate, acuminate, pinnate, pinnatifid at apex; pinnae sub-linear-lanceolate, acuminate, sub-sessile, coarsely dentato-pinnatifid. *Sori* dorsal on veins or in lower axils. Ceylon. 1873. (F.S.I. 260.) Stove.

**C. insig'nis.*** *sti.* scaly. *Fronds* ample, coriaceous; primary pinnae 8 ft. long; secondary 7 to 8 in. long, elongato-oblong, finely acuminated, sessile, pinnatifid nearly to costa; lobes oblong-falcate, entire, margin slightly reflexed. *Sori* copious. Jamaica. (G.C. 1876, 6, Suppl. 3; B.C.F. 2, 83.) SYN. *C. princeps, Cibotium princeps*. Stove.

**C. inte'gra.*** *Fronds* firm-membranaceous, brownish-green, paler beneath; primary pinnae ample, 1½ ft. long; pinnules sessile or petiolate, 3 to 5 in. long, from a truncate base, oblong-acuminate, deeply pinnatifid, broad-oblong, sub-falcate, acute, serrate. *Sori* in 2 series between costule and margin. Amboyna, Philippine Is. (H.I.P. 638.) SYN. *C. petiolata*. Unarmed. Stove.

**C. Lindenia'na.** A synonym of *C. mexicana*.

**C. Mastersia'na.** *cau.* apparently not longer than 3 ft. *Fronds* 3 to 4 ft. long, the basal part densely spiny. Habitat not recorded. 1894.

**C. medul'laris.*** *cau.* tall. *Fronds* ample, 2- or 3-pinnate, leathery; secondary pinnae 5 to 6 in. long, about 1 in. broad, deeply pinnatifid or again pinnate; pinnules oblong or linear-oblong, obtuse, coarsely serrate in sterile, lobato-pinnatifid in fertile ones, with margins revolute. *Sori* 1 to each lobule of pinnule. Australia, New Zealand. (L.F. 8, 57; B.C.F. 2, 336.) Greenhouse.

**C. mexica'na.** *Fronds* 2-pinnate; pinnules smooth, spear-shaped, 3 to 4 in. long, cut into oblong, slightly sickle-shaped lobes. *Sori* chiefly in lower half of lobe, on back of a simple vein or at fork of a divided vein; thin, fragile. Mexico. SYN. *C. Lindeniana* (of gardens), *Alsophila Van Geertii*. Stove.

**C. microphyl'la.** *cau.* 4 ft. h. *sti.* and rachises rusty-tomentose. *Fronds* 2 to 3 ft. long, oblong-ovate, acuminate, 2-pinnate; primary pinnae sessile, broadly oblong, acuminate; secondary similar but smaller, crowded; pinnules scarcely ⅛ in. long, ovate-oblong, deeply pinnatifid; lobes entire. *Sori* solitary at base of veinlet; indusium globose. Andes of Peru and Ecuador. 1883. (H.S.C.F. 99; G.F. 51 (1902), 263.) Greenhouse.

**C. petiola'ta.** A form of *C. integra*.

**C. prin'ceps.** A synonym of *C. insignis*.

**C. pyg'maea.** *cau.* about 2 ft. h. *Fronds* soft, dark green, remarkable for the absence of the shiny appearance of most species of this genus. Habitat not recorded. 1894.

**C. sclerole'pis.** *sti.* greyish, rough with hard and sharp points, at base with firm, shining, brownish-black scales. *Fronds* smooth, rarely over 1 ft. long, 3-pinnate; pinnae less than 1 ft. long; pinnules sessile, 2 in. long, cut down into blunt, entire, sickle-shaped segs. *Sori* small, abundant; indusium parchment-like. New Caledonia. Stove.

**C. ser'ra.*** *sti.* thicker than a finger, muricate; scales dense, large, whitish. *Fronds* 2-pinnate; pinnules lanceolate, deeply pinnatifid, 6 to 8 in. long, lanceolate, acuminate; lobes linear-oblong, acute, serrate, falcate. *Sori* generally covering whole of lobes. W. Indies, Mexico, Ecuador. (H.S. 1, 9.) Stove.

**C. sinua'ta.** *cau.* slender, erect, 2 to 4 ft. long. *Fronds* simple, 2 to 3 ft. long, 1 to 2½ in. wide, elongato-lanceolate, sinuate at margin, acuminate, tapering into a short stipe. Ceylon. 1861. (B.C.F. 2, 90; H.G.F. 21.) SYN. *Schizocaena sinuata*. Stove.

**C. Smith'ii.** A synonym of *Hemitelia Smithii*.

**C. spinulo'sa.** *sti.* and main rachis strongly aculeate, often dark purple. *Fronds* glabrous, ample, somewhat flaccid; pinnules oblong, acuminate; lobes acute, serrulate, with small, bullate scales on costules beneath. *Sori* copious, close to costules; globose, very thin, membranous, soon breaking irregularly. India, Japan, &c. 1883. (H.S. 1, 12 c.) Stove.

**CYATHEA'CEAE.** A family of 7 genera with about 800 species of ferns with stout stems, mostly tree-like with a crown of leaves at the top of the stem which is covered with adventitious roots, found in the tropics and sub-tropics. The sori are either on the margins or on the backs of the fronds and may or may not have a cup-shaped indusium. The sporangia are stalked and have a complete annulus. All the genera are in cultivation, viz. Alsophila, Cibotium, Culcita, Cyathea, Dicksonia, Hemitelia, and Thyrsopteris.

**cyathiform,** shaped like a wine-glass.

**CYATHIUM.** The curious reduced inflorescence of Euphorbia consisting of a perianth-like organ of 5 leaves with 4 horn-like structures between them, a number of stamens each with a joint about half-way up the stalk, the oldest towards the middle of the inflorescence and in the middle a 3-carpelled pistil on a long stalk, the whole simulating a flower, but really consisting of an axis bearing a large number of unisexual flowers with no internodes developed.

**CYATHO'DES** (*kyathos*, a cup, *odous*, a tooth; in reference to the cup-shaped, 5-toothed disk). FAM. *Epacridaceae*. A genus of about 20 species of evergreen shrubs with small leaves. Flowers small, with numerous scales or bracts on their stalks; calyx·5-lobed; corolla tubular at the base with 5 spreading lobes at the mouth; stamens 5. Fruit a berry-like drupe, carrying 3 to 5 seeds. Natives of Australia, Tasmania, New Zealand, and some Pacific Islands. Cool greenhouse plants. Cultivation as for Epacris. In some catalogues the related Leucopogons have been erroneously placed under Cyathodes.

**C. acero'sa.** Closely branched shrub, erect, from 4 to 12 (occasionally 16) ft., but sometimes low and spreading. *l.* $\frac{1}{4}$ to $\frac{3}{8}$ in. long, about $\frac{1}{16}$ in. wide, bodkin-like, closely set, glaucous beneath; veins 3 to 7, parallel. *fl.* only $\frac{1}{10}$ in. long, whitish-green, solitary in upper l.-axils. *fr.* a globose drupe about $\frac{1}{3}$ in. wide, succulent, white or red. New Zealand, Victoria, Tasmania.

**C. empetrifo'lia.** Low, heath-like shrub, branches slender, wiry, downy. *l.* closely set, $\frac{1}{8}$ to $\frac{1}{5}$ in. long, linear, blunt, convex above, glaucous beneath, varying from glabrous to downy. *fl.* creamy-white, fragrant, axillary or terminal, solitary or 2 to 4 in a cluster; stalk clothed with overlapping bracts. *fr.* white, small, ovoid, $\frac{1}{10}$ in. long. New Zealand.

**C. glau'ca.** Shrub 2 to 6 ft., sometimes a small tree, even 30 to 40 ft. *l.* oblong-linear, $\frac{1}{2}$ to $1\frac{1}{2}$ in. long, glaucous beneath, mostly crowded at the end of each season's shoots. *fl.* white, scarcely stalked, $\frac{1}{4}$ to $\frac{1}{3}$ in. long; cal. ciliate; lobes of cor. hairy along middle. *fr.* pink, large, globose. Tasmania.

**C. robus'ta.** Shrub 5 to 12 ft. *l.* $\frac{1}{2}$ to $\frac{3}{4}$ in. long, $\frac{1}{8}$ to $\frac{1}{6}$ in. wide, linear-lanceolate to linear-oblong, 5- to 11-veined, margins recurved, apex bluntish. *fl.* $\frac{1}{8}$ in. long, axillary, solitary, stalks covered with overlapping bracts. *fr.* globose, $\frac{1}{3}$ to $\frac{1}{2}$ in. wide, white or red. Chatham Is. Akin to *C. acerosa* but with larger broader l. not spiny-pointed, and larger fr.

W. J. B.

***cyathoi'des,*** Cyathea-like.

**CYBISTE'TES** (*kubistetes*, a tumbler; in allusion to the umbel becoming detached when the fruit is ripe, and tumbled about by the wind). FAM. *Amaryllidaceae*. A genus of 1 species of bulbous plant in S. Africa (Cape Province). Related to Ammocharis. Bulb and foliage as in Ammocharis but flowers zygomorphic, stamens declinate, pedicels lengthening and the outer bending downwards in fruit; fruit strongly ribbed, seeds fleshy. Cultivation as for Brunsvigia. Bulbs cut lengthwise develop bulbs from basal disk (Duthie).

**C. longifo'lia.** 5 to 8 in. h. *l.* strap-shaped, often falcate, 3 to 16 in. long, $\frac{1}{2}$ in. wide, glabrous. *fl.* pale to dark pink, fragrant in 12- to 24-fld. umbel; tube $\frac{1}{3}$ to $\frac{2}{3}$ in. long, segs. $1\frac{1}{2}$ to $2\frac{1}{2}$ in. long, $\frac{1}{3}$ to $\frac{2}{3}$ in. wide, oblanceolate, gradually spreading from base; stamens declinate. S. Africa. 1774. (B.M. 1443 as *Brunsvigia falcata.*) SYN. *Amaryllis longifolia, A. falcata, Ammocharis falcata.*

**CYCADA'CEAE.** A family of about 75 species in 9 genera, the most primitive of flowering plants, allied to Coniferae, the only survivors of what was at one time an important part of the vegetation of the earth. They are now found only in tropical America, Australia, and Africa, with Cycas in tropical islands. In habit and appearance they are much like the tree ferns with short stout simple or little branched stems, except in Cycas, often much swollen, usually with a crown of pinnate or 2-pinnate leaves and covered below with scales. As in the Conifers the stem is thickened by the activity of the cambium but the secondary wood contains no vessels. The leaves are large with rigid, leathery leaflets springing from two grooves on the upper side of a stout rachis, and usually without a terminal leaflet; there are frequently stout spines near its base which is thickened and woody and often persists after the rest of the leaf falls. The flowers are dioecious and usually in terminal cones bearing a number of fertile leaves on the central axis. In the staminate cones the leaves are nail-shaped as in Equisetum, bearing pollen sacs upon its lower side; in the female cones the leaves or scales bear two ovules, except in Cycas where the place of the cone is taken by a whorl of brown woolly carpels bearing the large naked ovules in notches on their margins. The pollen is carried to the micropyle of the ovule by wind and on germination produces not a pollen tube as in normal flowering plants but antherozoids much as in ferns. Many species are ornamental in habit, and the long-lasting leaves of some are sought by florists for the making of various designs. A few are of economic value. The leaflets of Cycas have a midrib but no lateral veins, of Stangeria both a midrib and lateral veins, of Bowenia (with 2-pinnate leaves), Ceratozamia, Dioon, Encephalartos, Macrozamia, Microcycas, and Zamia, many parallel or wavy nerves running longitudinally.

***cycadoi'des,*** with the habit of Cycas.

**CY'CAS** (Greek name for a Palm). FAM. *Cycadaceae*. A genus of 8 species, some of them very variable, of evergreen perennials distributed over the tropics and sub-tropics. Trunk erect, cylindrical, sometimes much thickened at base. Leaves in a terminal crown, pinnatisect, large; leaflets circinnate, linear or linear-lanceolate, margin incurved or thickened. For floral characters *see* **Cycadaceae,** from other genera of which Cycas is distinguished by the form of the female inflorescence. Stove conditions are required, good drainage and strong loam and sharp sand for potting. Propagation by seeds or by suckers which are occasionally formed. *C. circinnalis* and *C. revoluta* are most commonly grown and are typical of the genus. They are both good for decorating stove, greenhouse, or conservatory, and also the sub-tropical garden in a warm, sheltered position from May to September.

KEY

| | |
|---|---|
| 1. *Lflets. linear, shining green above, margins thickened, revolute* | C. revoluta |
| 1. *Lflets. margins not distinctly thickened or revolute* | 2 |
| 2. *Stem cylindrical, erect; lflets. narrowed at tip* | 3 |
| 2. *Stem cylindrical, base often much thickened; lflets. linear-lanceolate* | 5 |
| 3. *Lflets. gradually narrowed to tip* | 4 |
| 3. *Lflets. abruptly spiny pointed* | C. media |
| 4. *Lflets. narrow linear-lanceolate,* $\frac{1}{5}$ *to* $\frac{3}{4}$ *in. wide* | C. circinnalis |
| 4. *Lflets. long lanceolate,* $\frac{2}{5}$ *to* $\frac{4}{5}$ *in. wide* | C. Rumphii |
| 5. *Lflets. linear-lanceolate* | C. siamensis |
| 5. *Lflets. forked* | C. Micholitzii |

**C. angula'ta.** A synonym of *C. media.*

**C. Beddo'mei.** A variety of *C. circinnalis.*

**C. Bellefont'ii.** A form of *C. circinnalis* with wavy l.-margins.

**C. circinna'lis.** Stem erect, cylindrical, growing slowly to 15 or even 40 ft. h., usually unbranched. *l.* 6 to 12 ft. long, green or glaucous green, covered with reddish-brown hair when young; stalk round in lower, triangular in upper part, 18 to 24 in. long, usually with short spines; lflets. 80 to 100, spreading, narrow linear-lanceolate, 6 to 14 in. long, curved, flat or somewhat wavy, margin scarcely thickened or revolute. E. Indies. 1800. (B.M. 2826, 2827.) var. **Beddo'mei,** stem only 2 to 3 in. h., densely leafy, *l.* about 3 ft. long, stalk about 6 in. long, lflets. narrow linear, spine-tipped. S. India. 1883. SYN. *C. Beddomei*; **Riuminia'na,** stem stout and eventually tall. *l.* bright green, erect except for spreading tips, lflets. 60 or more, narrow linear-lanceolate, not spine-tipped, 5 to 10 in. long. Philippine Is. 1864. (I.H. 405 as *C. Riuminiana*); **undula'ta,** *l.* margins undulate. SYN. *C. Bellefontii.*

**C. iner'mis.** A synonym of *C. revoluta.*

**C. me'dia.** Stem stout, cylindrical, eventually 10 to 15 ft. or even up to 30 ft. h., rarely branched at top. *l.* $1\frac{1}{2}$ to 5 ft. long or more, at first covered with rusty hair, finally glabrous; stalk usually flat above, convex beneath, often spiny, lflets. 20 to 120, more or less linear-lanceolate, $2\frac{1}{2}$ to 10 in. long, narrowed to a spine, flat, scarcely curved, margin more or less incurved. Australia, in warmer parts. 1874. (I.H. 1879, 378.) SYN. *C. angulata.*

**C. Micholitz'ii.** Stem cylindrical, 8 to 24 in. long, thickened at base, glabrous, reddish-brown. *l.* few, 6 to 10 ft. long, with short broad spines in lower part; lflets. about $1\frac{1}{2}$ in. apart, 8 to 12 in. long, linear-lanceolate, narrowed to a spine, glaucous when young, glabrous and deep green with margins more or less wavy in adult. Annam. 1905. (B.M. 8242.)

**C. Normanbya'na.** A variety of *C. Rumphii.*

**C. plu'ma.** A synonym of *C. circinnalis.*

**C. revolu'ta.** Stem 7 ft. or more h., sometimes branched above, stout, cylindrical, covered with l.-scars below, densely covered with l.-bases above. *l.* about 30 in. long; stalk more or less 4-angled; lflets. about 120, crowded, linear, the middle ones longest, 4 to 8 in. long, ending in an oblique brownish spine, margin thickened and revolute, shining green above, paler beneath. China, E. Indies. 1758. (B.M. 2963, 2964.) SYN. *C. inermis.*

**C. Rumph'ii.** Stem cylindrical, usually erect, about 25 ft. h. eventually, sometimes branched, grey, leafy above. *l.* 3 to 6 ft. long, stalk bluntly 3-angled, usually spiny; lflets. 50 to 100, lanceolate-linear, forked, slender-pointed, 8 to 12 in. long, rather thin, slightly curved, pale green. Java, Ceylon, &c. 1868. var. **Normanbya'na,** stem 8 to 12 in. h., thickened beneath soil surface, with a dense leafy crown, *l.* oblong-ovate; rachis and stalk angular, furry near base, lflets. very numerous, about 8 in. long, thinly leathery, pale green and shining above, dull beneath. New S. Wales, Queensland. 1875.

**C. siamen'sis.** Stem much thickened at base, cylindrical or ovoid above, 1 to 5 ft. h., covered with remains of dead l. *l.* 2 to 4 ft. h., at first hairy; stalk yellowish, grooved above, smooth beneath, somewhat spiny near base; lflets. 40 to 100 or more, short near base and apex of l., all decurrent, linear-lanceolate, 2 to 8 in. long with a projecting spine, margin somewhat incurved, shining or glaucous above, paler beneath, furry when young. Siam, China. 1878. (I.H. 433.)

**C. squamo'sa.** A synonym of *C. circinnalis.*

**C. undula'ta.** A variety of *C. circinnalis.*

**C. Wendland'ii.** A synonym of *C. circinnalis.*

**CYC'LAMEN** (*kyklos*, circular, from the spiral twisting of the peduncle of some species after flowering). FAM. *Primulaceae.* A genus of about 16 species of herbs with tuberous rootstocks, natives of the Mediterranean region. Leaves all radical, stalked, broad. Flowers solitary; calyx 5-partite; corolla tube short, lobes large, reflexed. Fruit a many-seeded capsule often drawn down to soil level after the flowers fade by the spiral twisting of the peduncle. The hardy species are excellent for naturalizing in well-drained places in woodland and will grow well, if care be taken to enrich the soil by an occasional dressing of bone-meal even in the shade of evergreen conifers. *C. neapolitanum* is particularly useful for this. It flowers in early autumn before the leaves appear, producing its flowers very freely, and the leaves, which are often prettily marked, persist well into the following year, forming a very pleasant carpet. It will seed itself provided mice, which are very fond of them, do not devour the seeds just before they are ripe. This and other hardy species are also good rock-garden plants, often thriving in sun, but not intolerant of some shade, though *C. libanoticum* needs a really warm place as do *C. africanum* and perhaps to a rather less extent *C. graecum,* nor do any of the species dislike lime, nor if the soil is really sweet, call for it. Collected corms will establish themselves though rather slowly, probably because the roots are bound to be injured in the collecting and new ones need to be formed, but the best way of increase is by the sowing of fresh seed—old seed germinates very slowly. *C. neapolitanum* and *C. coum* and indeed most species seed freely. *C. persicum,* the parent of all the well-known greenhouse forms, is a fine plant in its wild form for a warm corner where it will flower from late autumn to spring, but the wild form should be used, planted out while the corms are still small, in a warm and sheltered spot among bushes, and only in mild districts, for it will not long survive outdoors in our average climate. The seed of the hardy species may be sown in a warm well-drained place outdoors and the seedlings left until the corms are as big as large peas or a little more, then planted in their permanent quarters in June or July, or it may be sown in pans in a cold frame. The seed of *C. persicum,* than which there is scarcely a more decorative plant for flower under glass in winter and early spring, should be sown about mid-August. The light compost of loam, leaf-mould and sand in seed boxes or pans should be thoroughly watered and allowed to drain for some hours before the seed is sown. The seed should be spaced evenly over the surface, lightly pressed in, and then covered with a light compost. The boxes or pans should then be covered with a pane of glass and kept in a shaded place until germination occurs when they should be stood well up to the glass in a temperature of 55 to 60° F. When large enough to handle the seedlings should be pricked off into pans or boxes and early in the year moved into thumb pots, or they may be put straight into thumb pots from the seed pans. In spring they will need to be shifted into 3-in. pots and by mid-summer into their flowering pots, 5 or 6 in. according to requirements. The corms should be only half covered with soil, which, for the final potting, should consist of 3 parts good loam, 1 of well-decayed leaf-soil or peat, and enough coarse clean sand or old mortar-rubble to ensure porosity. If old mortar rubble is not available a sprinkling of powdered chalk should be added to the compost. Cyclamens enjoy a cool, moist atmosphere and should be stood on a cool bottom in low houses or pits where they can be kept well up to the roof-glass, and they should be shaded during bright weather. They can be grown in summer in cold frames and on dewy nights towards the end of summer the frame lights should be removed. About mid-September they must be housed in a cool, airy house or pit. When the pots are well-filled with roots the plants benefit by frequent watering with very dilute liquid manure or soot water. The winter temperature should be 45 to 50° F. and air should be given whenever possible. Cyclamens raised from seed sown in August should flower from November in the following year onwards until spring. The old plants can be grown on and if this is desired they must not be neglected when flowering is over but must be kept regularly watered until the leaves show signs of dying down; then water should be gradually withheld but at no time should they be subject to prolonged drying off. After a short rest they should be potted on into larger pots, or the old ball may be reduced so that they can be again potted into pots of the same size, or the corms may be shaken free of soil and planted out in a cold frame to be lifted and potted in autumn. Old plants flower freely but the flowers are usually smaller than those on young seedling plants.

The greenhouse Cyclamen provides an excellent example of what can be done by careful selection of variations and breeding within the range of a single species, for there is no evidence that any other species than *C. persicum* has played any part in its evolution. There is a great range of colour from pure white through various shades of pink, rose, purple, mauve, and salmon to crimson. In some varieties the leaves are beautifully marked with a silver-zone. The flowers are, as a rule, much larger, sometimes so much larger and coarser as to have lost the grace and poise of the original, but that is usually where breeders have sought mere size. Fimbriated petals are a feature of some varieties and this, combined with spreading wing-like corolla lobes, characterizes the Papilio section of continental origin, and there is also a variation to a raised feathered crest down the middle line of each petal. Careful breeding and seed-saving have secured that most of these variations come practically true from seed so that a desired type is now easy to ensure.

A
J. C.

*DISEASES.* There is a dwarfing disease of Cyclamen which is thought to be due to virus infection but this has not been elucidated. It would, however, be wise to destroy any stunted and deformed plants. Cyclamen may show Leaf Spot, due to the fungus *Cercosporella* sp., or Soft Rot, due to *Bacterium carotovorum* in the corm, but neither should be difficult to control and dusting with copper lime dust ought to check Soft Rot. A dangerous trouble is the Grey Mould fungus, *Botrytis cinerea,* which under moist conditions soon destroys foliage. It will not thrive if deprived of such moisture and every effort should be made to check it by removing all diseased leaves, &c., reducing moisture by proper ventilation, and if necessary dusting with copper lime dust.

(D. E. G.)

KEY

| | |
|---|---|
| 1. *Anther cone included within cor. tube* | 2 |
| 1. *Anther cone exserted beyond cor. tube* | C. Rohlfsianum |
| 2. *Cor. lobes not auricled* | 3 |
| 2. *Cor. lobes auricled* | 12 |
| 3. *Corm covered with a corky layer* | 4 |
| 3. *Corm covered all over with short hair* | 6 |
| 4. *Peduncle spirally twisted in fruit* | 5 |
| 4. *Peduncle not spirally twisted after flowering* | C. persicum |
| 5. *Cor. lobes rosy-violet, not spotted* | C. europaeum |
| 5. *Cor. lobes rosy-violet, base white with deep violet spots* | C. pseud-ibericum |

6. *Cor. lobes elongated* 7
6. *Cor. lobes ovate* 9
7. *Style exserted* C. repandum
7. *Style not exserted* 8
8. *Cor. lobes white, striped red* C. balearicum
8. *Cor. rose* C. cilicium
9. *Lvs. spotted with white* 10
9. *Lvs. green above, not spotted* C. coum
10. *Cor. lobes with round deep red spot at base* 11
10. *Cor. lobes with triangular spot* C. vernum
11. *Having 2 short deep red lines from basal spot running to cor. tube* C. alpinum
11. *Having one long line from basal spot running into cor. tube* C. hiemale
12. *Lobes of cal. lanceolate* 13
12. *Lobes of cal. ovate-lanceolate or triangular* 14
13. *Cal. lobes undulate on margin, 5-nerved; cor. lobes white or rose, basal spot deep carmine* C. libanoticum
13. *Cal. lobes irregularly toothed, nerves subsimple; fls. white* C. cyprium
13. *Cal. lobes entire, nerves branched; fls. rose* C. africanum
14. *Lvs. with horny margins, corms rooting below* C. graecum
14. *Lvs. not horny-margined, corms rooting above* C. neapolitanum

**C. africa'num.** *fl.* ¾ to 1 in. long, rose with a deep carmine spot at base of auricled, lanceolate, acute. cor. segs.; sep. lanceolate, acute, entire; anthers lemon yellow with violet lines at back. Autumn, winter. *Peduncles* about as long as leaves, spiral in fruit. *l.* late autumn, reniform, 6 to 8 in. wide, with wide basal sinus, margin undulate- or crenate-toothed. *Corm* large, flat-round, covered with cork, rooting all over. Algeria. (B.M. 5758; J.L. 419 as *C. venustum*; 420 as *C. subrotundum*;˙421 as *C. pachybolbon*; 422 as *C. algeriense*.) Rather tender; will live at base of south wall. A hybrid with *C. neapolitanum* has been recorded.

**C. alpi'num.** *fl.* bright carmine with a rounded or triangular blackish-purple spot at base of ovate-lanceolate, acuminate cor. segs., not auricled; sep. ovate-lanceolate, 5-nerved, nerves simple; anthers brownish-red at back; stigma tip red. Autumn. *l.* procumbent, before fl. appear, reniform, ¾ to 1¼ in. long, wider, deep green above with interrupted white zone, carmine beneath. *Corm* flattish, hairy, rooting from all parts below middle. Cilician Taurus up to snowline. 1892. (B.M. n.s. 437.)

**C. × Atkin'sii** (*C. coum × C. vernum*). *l.* uniform, rounded at apex, more or less shining deep green, with silvery white markings. Cor. lobes pale rose or white, lined or spotted red. Form of foliage that of *C. coum*, l.-colouring near *C. vernum*. Fertile. (Gn. 30 (1886), 433.)

**C. balea'ricum.** *fl.* white, rose at throat, about ¾ in. wide, fragrant; cor. lobes ovate, acute; style not exserted; long-stalked. Spring. *l.* glabrous, long-stalked, cordate-ovate, dull green with whitish spots, purple beneath, margin repand-dentate. *Corm* about ¾ in. across, flattish, hairy, rooting from centre of lower side. Balearic Is. (Willk. I. Fl. Hisp. 5; B.M. 8989.)

**C. cilic'ium.*** *fl.* pale rose with large rose spots at base of the oblong or oblong-obovate, acute cor. lobes, 2 to 2½ times as long as tube; sep. lanceolate, acute; anthers yellow; style scarcely exserted. Autumn. *Peduncle* 3 to 5 in. long, spiral in fruit. *l.* roundish-cordate, basal sinus short, lobes often overlapping, feebly toothed, with silvery zone above. *Corm* large, flattened, hairy, rooting from middle of underside. S. Asia Minor. 1872.

**C. Clu'sii.** A synonym of *C. europaeum*.

**C. coum.*** *fl.* carmine with deep carmine spots at somewhat constricted base, cor. lobes wide ovate, acute; sep. ovate-lanceolate; anthers yellow, papillose on back; style not exserted. Winter, spring. *Peduncles* somewhat longer than l., spiral in fruit. *l.* before fl., round or roundish reniform or obcordate, entire or slightly undulate crenate, dark green. *Corm* globose or flattish, roots from middle of underside only. E. Mediterranean to N. Persia. (B.M. 4; L.B.C. 108; J.L. 402 as *C. apiculatum*; 409 as *C. breviflorum*; 401 as *C. brevifrons*.) var. **al'bum**, white-fld.

**C.·cre'ticum.** See description in Supplement. (B.M. n.s. 450.)

**C. cyp'rium.** *fl.* white or pale rose with irregular carmine spot at auricled base; cor. lobes linear-lanceolate, somewhat twisted, subacute; sep. linear-lanceolate, entire; anthers yellow; ovary copper coloured. Autumn. Petiole, peduncle, cal. glandular; peduncle rolled in fruit. *l.* obcordate, basal sinus deep, open; lobate, dentate, lobes repand, terminal one acute. *Corm* 1½ to 2 in. across, covered with cork, rooting at one side below. Cyprus.

**C. europae'um.*** *fl.* carmine, deeply coloured near tube; cor. lobes oblong or ovate, about ¾ in. long, not auricled, twice as long as tube; sep. widely triangular, apiculate, toothed; anthers more or less spotted violet on back. Autumn or spring. *Peduncles* about equal l. or rather longer, spiral in fruit. *l.* almost evergreen, reniform or cordate, with rounded base, lobes meeting or overlapping, entire or crenate-toothed, with silver zone above. *Corm* globose or flattened, sometimes very large, covered with cork, rooting all over. Cent. and S. Europe to Transcaucasus. (B.R. 32, 56 as *C. littorale*; 1013 as *C. Clusii*; J.L. 410 as *C. cyclophyllum*; 411 as *C. umbratile*; 412 as *C. holochlorum* and *C. lilacinum*.) var. **al'bum** has white fragrant fl.; **denta'tum**, distinctly toothed l.; **verbanen'se viridifo'lium**, a green-leaved form.

**C. grae'cum.** *fl.* rose, deep carmine at auricled base; cor. lobes lanceolate or oblong-lanceolate, acute; sep. lanceolate, acuminate; anthers deep carmine. Autumn. *l.* large, obcordate, irregularly dentate on horny margin, autumnal, velvety green with whitish nerves and markings above, at first red, then generally green beneath. *Corm* globose or flattened, with longitudinally split corky covering, rooting from one place beneath, root fleshy. Greece, Macedonia, Crete. (J.R.H.S. 60 (1935) 213; J.L. 423 as *C. velutinum*.)

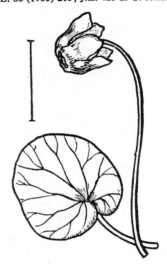

*Cyclamen coum*

**C. hederaefo'lium.** A synonym of *C. neapolitanum*.

**C. hiema'le.** *fl.* carmine with round deep red spot at base with 5 lines of colour passing to tube; cor. lobes roundish-oval; sep. lanceolate, 5-nerved. Winter. *l.* roundish reniform, dark green with silvery zone above. *Corm* flattish, hairy, rooting below. Cicilian Taurus.

**C. ibe'ricum.** A synonym of *C. vernum*.

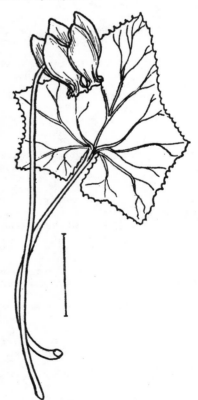

*Cyclamen neapolitanum* (p. 607)

**C. libanot'icum.*** *fl.* fragrant, white or pale to deep rose, with deep carmine T-shaped spot at base; cor. lobes wide ovate, entire; sep. oblong, acuminate, margin somewhat undulate with 5 somewhat branched nerves; style exserted. Spring. *Peduncles* spiral after fl. *l.* autumnal, obcordate, margin scarcely sinuate, rarely entire, sometimes sharply dentate or crenulate, opaque green with continuous white zone above, deep purple beneath. *Corm* globose, covered with cork, roots in tufts below. Lebanon. (G.C. 85 (1929), 283.)

**C. littora'le.** A synonym of *C. europaeum.*

**C. neapolita'num.*** *fl.* rose with deep carmine blotch at auricled base; cor. lobes ovate; sep. triangular to oblong, acute, more or less toothed; anthers brownish-red outside. July to November. *Peduncles* spiral in fruit. *l.* variable in form, size, and markings, usually obcordate, undulate-lobed, lobes obtuse, crenate or entire. *Corm* flattish, hemispherical below, covered with cork, rooting from upper part only. S. Europe, France to Greece, naturalized in Britain. (E.B. 548 as *C. europaeum;* B.M. 1001 as *C. hederaefolium;* J.L. 413 as *C. angulare;* 414 as *C. subhastatum;* 415 as *C. subaudum;* 416 as *C. insulare;* 417 as *C. albiflorum;* 418 as *C. oedirrhizum.*) var. **al'bum,** white fld.; **ro'seum,** rose-fld.

**C. per'sicum.*** *fl.* large, white or rose, deep carmine at scarcely contracted throat; cor. lobes oblong-lanceolate, $3\frac{1}{2}$ to 5 times as long as tube; sep. triangular or oblong-triangular, entire; anthers brownish-red at back. Winter, spring. *Peduncles* not spiral in fruit, longer than l. *l.* cordate-ovate, base angled, marked with more or less silver above, evergreen, crenate-toothed; petiole 2 to 6 in. long. *Corm* large, flattened, covered with cork, rooting only from middle below. E. Mediterranean. 1731. (B.M. 44; F.G. 185 as *C. latifolium;* J.L. 424 as *C. tomentosum;* 425 as *C. albidum.*) Tender.

**C. pseud-ibericum.** *fl.* very fragrant, purplish with white base with blackish-purple spot, throat scarcely contracted, surface glandular; sep. lanceolate with scarcely sinuate margin. Spring. *l.* obcordate, rounded, margin horny, crenulate, deep green above with silvery spots, deep purple beneath. Habitat? Nearly related to the most eastern forms of *C. europaeum.* (B.M. n.s. 417.)

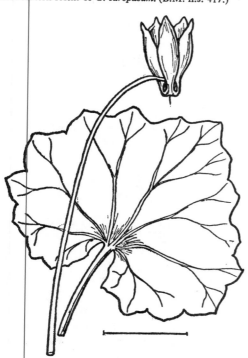

*Cyclamen repandum*

**C. repan'dum.*** *fl.* bright carmine, deepest near tube, throat constricted; cor. lobes oblong or linear-oblong, $3\frac{1}{2}$ to 5 times as long as tube, not auricled; sep. ovate, acuminate; style longer than tube. Spring. *Peduncle* spiral in fruit. *l.* soft, cordate with open sinus at base, undulate-lobed, lobes more or less mucronate, somewhat silvery above, reddish beneath. *Corm* about $\frac{3}{4}$ in. thick, globose or flattish, hairy, rooting only from centre below. Europe from S. France eastwards to Crete. (F.G. 186; J.L. 403 as *C. stenopetalum;* 404 as *C. spectabile;* 405 as *C. eucardium;* 406 as *C. lobospilum;* 407 as *C. ilicetorum;* 408 as *C. rarinaevum.*)

**C. Rohlfsia'num.** *fl.* fragrant, deep crimson, paler at apex on back; cor. lobes lanceolate, acuminate, somewhat auricled at base; sep. oblong-ovate, acuminate; style long exserted. Autumn. *Peduncle* spiral in fruit. *l.* rather earlier than fl., reniform, margin very irregularly dentate, sometimes distinctly lobed. *Corm* covered with

cork, rooting from centre below. Cyrenaica, N. Africa. (G.C. 85 (1929), 97, 98; B.M. n.s. 192.)

*Cyclamen vernum*

**C. vern'um.*** *fl.* carmine with large deep-coloured spot at base; cor. lobes more or less widely ovate, narrowed at base, acute; sep. lanceolate, acuminate, entire; anthers yellow. Winter, spring. *Peduncles* spiral in fruit. *l.* before fl., roundish reniform or obcordate, obtuse at apex, rarely mucronate, toothed, with silver zone or spots above. *Corm* 1 to $1\frac{1}{2}$ in. thick, velvety, globose or flattish, rooting from middle below. Transcaucasus, Syria to N. Persia. (J.L. 401 as *C. zonale;* B.M. n.s. 29.) SYN. *C. ibericum.* var. **al'bum,** white-fld.; **ru'brum,** red-fld. *See also* **C. × Atkinsii.**

**CYCLAMEN MITE.** *See* **Strawberry Mite.** in Suppl.

*cyclamin'eus,* Cyclamen-like.

**CYCLANTHA'CEAE.** Monocotyledons. A family of 45 species of Trop. American plants in 6 genera. It includes large perennial herbs with rhizomes, climbers, epiphytes, and small shrubs of palm-like habit. The monoecious flowers are variously alternated on a spadix at first enclosed in 2 to 6 sheaths; they are naked or with a short, thick bract; the staminate consist of 6 to many stamens; the pistillate have 2 or 4 carpels with many seeds, the ovary being sunk in the spadix. The genera dealt with are Carludovica, Cyclanthus, Ludovia.

**CYCLAN'THERA** (*kyklos,* circle, *anthera,* anther; from the arrangement of the anthers). FAM. *Cucurbitaceae.* A genus of over 30 species of herbaceous climbing perennials, natives of Trop. America, with simple or compound tendrils. Leaves entire, lobed, or 5- to 7-foliolate. Flowers yellow, greenish, or white, monoecious, sometimes 6-partite, usually very small; males in racemes; females solitary; stamens combined into a column with the anthers joined to form 2 ring-shaped loculi running round the top of the column. For cultivation of these stove plants *see* **Gourds.**

**C. explo'dens.** Climber; tendrils branched. *l.* 5-angled, $1\frac{1}{2}$ in. long, nearly as wide; basal sinus square, deep, apex acute. *fr.* helmet-shaped, prickly; opening suddenly to discharge seeds when ripe. August. Colombia.

**C. peda'ta.** Climbing Cucumber. Climbing to 15 to 18 ft., tendrils 2-fid. *l.* heart-shaped, pedately about 5-lobed; lobes mucronate, sharply toothed, sinus rounded. *Male* racemes axillary as long as l.; *female fl.* scarcely prickly. *fr.* glaucous-green, ovate, covered with soft prickles. Mexico.

**CYCLAN'THUS** (*kyklos,* circle; *anthos,* flower; from the arrangement of the flowers). FAM. *Cyclanthaceae.* A genus of 4 species of stemless perennial herbs with milky juice. Leaves clustered, large, forked into two at top; segments lanceolate, plicate; stalks long, terete, sheathing at base. Flowers scented, on a large cylindrical spadix with big bracts at base, the flowers on the sharpened edges of superimposed disks, every other disk bearing male flowers, or on two parallel spirals one bearing male the other female flowers. Fruit multiple. For cultivation of these stove plants *see* **Carludovica**.

**C. biparti'tus.** *l.* usually as described above; stalks 3 to 6 ft. h. *Spadix* straight, cylindrical; spathe yellow, 4-leaved, spreading; scape 2 ft. long. Guiana.

**C. crista'tus.** *l.* 3 ft. long, deeply 2-fid; lobes oblong, curved, connivent, acute, 4 to 5 in. wide. *Spadix* 7 to 8 in. long, 2 in. across when in fruit, oblong. Colombia.

**C. dis'color.** *l.* 2-fid; sep. lanceolate, tapered, more or less frilled at edges; streaked tawny-orange, when young. 1882.

**C. Godseffia'na.** *l.* rich green, oblong-ovate, narrowed to a sheathing base. Habitat? 1892.

*cy'clium,* round.

## CYCLOBOTH'RA. Included in **Calochortus**.

**CYCLO'DIUM** (*kyklos*, circle; in allusion to the joined veins). FAM. *Polypodiaceae*. Two species of ferns often included in Aspidium and closely related to Polystichum but with the veins pinnate and the opposite veinlets of adjacent groups joining. Natives of the tropics. For treatment *see* **Tectaria**.

**C. meniscioi'des.** *sti.* 1 to 2 ft. long, scaly below. *Fronds* 2 to 3 ft. long, 1 ft. or more broad, pinnate; barren pinnae sessile, 6 to 9 in. long, 1½ to 2 in. broad, oblong-acuminate, nearly entire; fertile pinnae much smaller. *Sori* in 2 close rows between primary veins. W. Indies to Ecuador. Stove. SYNS. *Aspidium confertum, A. meniscioides.*

*cycloglos'sus -a -um,* with a lip coiled in a circle.

*cyclolo'bus -a -um,* with circular lobes.

**CYCLOPEL'TIS** (*kyklos*, circle, *peltis*, a shield; from the form of the sori). FAM. *Polypodiaceae*. A genus of 6 species of ferns. For cultivation *see* **Tectaria**.

**C. semicorda'ta.** *sti.* scattered, 6 to 12 in. long. *Fronds* 2 to 3 ft. long, 8 to 12 in. broad, simply pinnate; pinnae spreading, 4 to 6 in. long, ½ to ¾ in. broad, nearly entire, acuminate, cordate, or truncate at base. *Sori* in 1 to 3 rows each side, inner close to midrib. Trop. America. (L.F. 6, 3; F.B.I. 35.) SYN. *Polystichum semicordatum.*

**CYCLOPH'ORUS** (*kyklos*, circle, *phora*, bearing; from the sori). FAM. *Polypodiaceae*. A genus of nearly a hundred species of ferns. The species described here are often placed under Polypodium, and for treatment see that genus.

**C. acrostichoi'des.** *rhiz.* woody, wide-creeping, scaly, black in centre. *sti.* 1 to 3 in. long, firm, erect. *Fronds* 1 to 2 ft. long, ½ to 1 in. broad, ligulate, gradually narrowed below, naked above, dirty-white-tomentose beneath. *Sori* bright-coloured, not immersed, small, close, covering whole upper part of frond. Ceylon, Queensland, &c. Greenhouse. (F.B.I. 81; B.C.F. 3, 93.) SYN. *Niphobolus acrostichoides.*

**C. america'nus.** *rhiz.* stout with large, spreading grey scales. *sti.* erect, 1 to 4 in. long. *Fronds* 1½ to 2 ft. long, ½ to ¾ in. wide, narrowed downwards, margin reflexed, tomentose, in age glabrous, bright green, pitted above. *Sori* large, in rows of 4 between midrib and margin. Ecuador.

**C. augusta'tus.** *rhiz.* stout, wide-creeping, clothed with whitish, linear, deciduous scales. *sti.* 2 to 4 in. long, strong, erect. *Fronds* 6 to 12 in. long, ½ to 1½ in. broad, ligulate, entire, very leathery; upper surface naked, the lower clothed with appressed, cottony, rusty tomentum. *Sori* large, prominent, in rows near margin of contracted upper part, sometimes confluent. N. India, Malaya, Polynesia. (H.G.F. 20.) SYN. *Niphobolus angustatus.* Greenhouse.

**C. Beddomea'nus.** *rhiz.* short-creeping, with rusty scales. *sti.* somewhat tufted, firm, erect, 1 to 6 in. long. *Fronds* 1½ to 2 ft. long, 1 to 3 in. broad, lower part gradually narrowed, acuminate, entire; tomentose beneath. *Sori* very small, in several rows between the transverse veinlets, continuous, occasionally covering whole frond except base. N. India, China. 1823. SYN. *Niphobolus costatus, Polypodium stigmosum.*

**C. flocculo'sus.** *rhiz.* short, clothed with bright brown scales. *sti.* firm, erect, 4 to 6 in. long, woolly upwards. *Fronds* entire, 6 to 18 in. long, 1 to 1½ in. broad, gradually narrowed to apex, leathery, densely clothed beneath with rusty-brown wool. *Sori* bright-coloured, in straight, diagonal rows from midrib to margin. N. India (at 5,000 ft.). Greenhouse. (F.B.I. 162.) SYN. *Niphobolus flocculosus.*

**C. Gard'neri.** *rhiz.* short-creeping; scales black, bordered brown. *sti.* 3 to 4 in. long, firm, naked. *Fronds* 1 to 1½ ft. long, 1 to 1½ in.

broad, narrowed gradually towards both ends, with entire edges; lower surface densely grey-tomentose. *Sori* in close rows of about 4 each between main veins. Ceylon. (H.E.F. 68.) SYN. *Niphobolus Gardneri.*

**C. hasta'tus.** *rhiz.* stout, woody. *sti.* firm, erect, 6 to 8 in. long. *Fronds* hastate, 2 to 4 in. each way, leathery, dark green above, densely matted beneath; central lobe broadly lanceolate, lateral spreading, much smaller, auricled at base. *Sori* minute, abundant, in rows of 3 or 4 between main veins, and 9 to 12 between midrib and margin. Japan, Korea. Greenhouse. SYN. *Niphobolus tricuspis, Polypodium tricuspe.*

**C. lanceola'tus.** *rhiz.* slender, firm, with linear, deciduous scales. *sti.* ¼ to 1 in. long, firm, erect. *Fronds* dimorphous; barren elliptical or spatulate, blunt; fertile, longer and narrower, 6 to 12 in. long, ¼ to ½ in. broad, naked above, white-tomentose beneath. *Sori* bright-coloured, small, immersed, occupying whole of contracted upper part of frond. Trop. Asia, Polynesia. 1824. (H.G.F. 19.) SYN. *Niphobolus adnascens, Polypodium adnascens.*

**C. Lin'gua.*** *rhiz.* wide-creeping with rusty scales. *sti.* 3 to 6 in. long, firm, erect. *Fronds* uniform, 4 to 8 in. long, 1 to 4 in. broad, often cuspidate, entire, base narrowed or rounded, matted with close, cottony, somewhat rusty down beneath. *Sori* in close rows of 4 to 6 each between main veins, rather large and prominent. N. India, Japan, &c. (L.F. 1, 122.) SYN. *Niphobolus Lingua.* var. **corymbif'erus** has fronds much divided at apex, forming a cluster. var. **heterac'tis** has broader, oblong-lanceolate fronds. N. India.

**C. penangia'nus.** *Fronds* almost stalkless, 1 to 1½ ft. long, 2 to 3 in. broad, entire, gradually narrowed towards base, sometimes wavy-edged, papery, hairy beneath. *Sori* in rows close together, only in upper part, short of margin. Burma, Java. (F.B.I. 121.) SYN. *Niphobolus penangianus.*

**C. rupes'tris.** The Australian form of *C. serpens* is sometimes distinguished under this name.

**C. ser'pens.** *rhiz.* firm, wide-creeping, clothed with scales. *sti.* firm, erect, ½ to 3 in. long. *Fronds* dimorphous; barren, round or elliptical; fertile, longer and narrower, 4 to 6 in. long, ½ to ¾ in. broad; tomentose beneath. *Sori* large, prominent, scattered, at length covering whole upper portion of the frond. New Zealand, New Caledonia, Norfolk Is. Greenhouse. (L.F. 1, 20.) SYN. *Polypodium rupestre, P. serpens, Niphobolus rupestris.*

**C. var'ians.** Allied to *C. lanceolatus* but with a creeping *rhiz.* and thick, fleshy *fronds*. Malaya, Polynesia.

*cyclophyl'lus -a -um,* with circular leaves.

**CYCLO'PIA** (*kuklos*, round-eyed; in reference perhaps to the blotch on the standard petal). FAM. *Leguminosae*. A genus of about 10 species of S. African shrubs. Leaves usually digitately 3-foliolate. Flowers yellow, axillary, usually solitary; petals about as long as calyx; standard nearly round, twisted at base, with a short recurved claw; wings oblong; keel incurved, with a blunt beak. Pods oblong, flat, compressed. Cool greenhouse conditions suit *C. genistoides*. Treatment as for Podalyria.

**C. genistoi'des.** Evergreen, usually glabrous, bushy shrub, 3 to 5 ft. *l.* stalkless, 3-foliolate; lflets. narrow-linear, margins strongly revolute, ½ to 1 in. long, very closely set, spreading. *fl.* papilionaceous, bright yellow, mostly solitary in the uppermost l.-axils; standard pet. ¾ in. across, obcordate with a purplish-brown stain at the base; wings and keel shorter. *Pod* flat, 1 in. long. June, July. S. Africa. (B.M. 1259 as *Ibbetsonia genistoides*; A.B.R. 427, as *Gompholobium maculatum*.)

W. J. B.

**CYCNOCH'ES** (*kyknos*, swan, and *auchen*, neck; referring to the long and gracefully curved column). Swan Neck. FAM. *Orchidaceae*. About 16 epiphytic species, natives of Trop. America, are included in this genus. Flowers large, produced from nearly the top of the bulb, unisexual; sepals sub-equal, free, spreading; petals similar, but rather broader; lip fleshy, continuous with the base of the column, spreading, contracted into a claw at the base, above lanceolate or orbicular, entire, or variously lobed, crested, or fringed. The female flowers are not known in all the species but are usually more fleshy, fewer in number, and of somewhat stellate form. The genus may be divided into two sections, one in which the male flowers, as in *C. chlorochilum* and *C. Loddigesii*, have an entire lip, the other in which the lip has its extremity divided into fingers. In all, the scape, few- or many-flowered, is arched or drooping. The apex of the curved column is usually rather swollen. Pollen masses 2.

Pseudobulbs thick and fleshy, 6 to 10 in. high, with 3 or 4 leaves on the top of each. For cultivation, see **Catasetum.**

**C. Amesia'num.** A synonym of *C. pentadactylon.*

**C. au'reum.*** *fl.* light yellow, in lor.g, closely set racemes; sep. and pet. comparatively broad, recurved; lip ending with 4 or 5 2-forked fingers on each margin. 1 ft. h. Cent. America. 1851. A remarkable and handsome species. (P.F.G. 75.) var. **San'der's,** *fl.* creamy-white shaded with green. Ecuador. 1939. (O.R. 1939, 241.)

**C. barba'tum.** A synonym of *Polycycnis barbata.*

**C. chlorochi'lum.*** *fl.* 4 to 6 in. across, very fragrant; sep. and pet. yellowish-green; lip lighter. June, July. 2 ft. h. Demerara. 1838. (W.O.A. 263.)

**C. Coo'peri.** *fl.* many, in drooping racemes, 1½ in. or more across; sep. and pet. greenish-yellow, nearly suffused with mahogany brown, lip whitish, broken into fingers. Resembles *C. pentadactylon* in habit. Female *fl.* chocolate-brown. Peru. 1913.

**C. densiflo'rum.*** *fl.* many, closely set, light green, spotted with brown, lip with the segs. white; female *fl.* larger, green with a white lip. Allied to *C. peruvianum.* Colombia. 1909. (B.M. 8268; O.R. 1909, 104.)

**C. Dian'ae.*** *fl.* green, heavily blotched with rosy-brown; lip green with 13 finger-like processes; column rosy-brown, the apex green, dotted with brown; female *fl.* large, green, the lip tipped white. Costa Rica. 1852.

**C. Egertonia'num.*** *fl.* dark purple; sep. and pet. membranaceous, recurved; disk of lip roundish, broken into clavate processes; column slender, very long; raceme pendulous, very long. Autumn. 2 ft. h. Mexico. 1835. (B.M. 4054 as *C. ventricosum Egertonianum*; 9260.)

**C. Forget'ii.** *fl.* sep. and pet. green, suffused with pale brown; lip dull glaucous green with broadly oblong, blunt processes to the lip. Allied to *C. Cooperi.* Peru. 1913.

**C. Haa'gii.** *fl.* 2 to 2½ in. broad, 5 to 7 in inclined racemes; sep. and pet. yellowish-green, brownish-green at back; lip entire, white or suffused with pale rose, sparsely spotted reddish-brown, cordate at base; column long, slender, speckled with reddish-purple below. October. *l.* lower 3 to 4 in. long, oblong-lanceolate; upper 6 to 8 in. long, recurved, lanceolate. Stem 6 in. h., 1 in. thick. Brazil. 1891. (B.M. 7502.)

**C. Loddiges'ii.*** *fl.* 4 in. across; sep. and pet. brownish-green, with darker spots, bearing some resemblance to the expanded wings of a swan; spikes 3- to 11-fld. Surinam. 1830. Very curious and desirable. (B.M. 4215; L.B.C. 2000; B.R. 1742.)

**C. macula'tum.*** *fl.* greenish-buff, thickly spotted with purple; lip whitish, fingers purple-spotted at base; numerously produced on a long raceme. *Pseudobulbs* very short. 1 ft. h. Mexico. 1839. (I.H. 20, 143.)

**C. muscif'erum.** A synonym of *Polycycnis muscifera.*

**C. pentadac'tylon.*** *fl.* sep. and pet. pale yellow, tinged green, with broad chocolate blotches; lip of the same colour, divided into 5 parts, like a man's hand. 1 ft. or more h. Brazil. 1841. Very curious, variable. (B.R. 29, 22.)

**C. peruvia'num.*** *fl.* in a drooping raceme; sep. and pet. pale green, spotted purplish-brown; lip white, cut into radiating, clavate processes. Peru. 1891. A curious species, allied to *C. ventricosum.* (L. 301.) var. **Tracy's** has shorter racemes and *fl.* more densely set.

**C. Pescator'ei.** A synonym of *Lueddemannia Pescatorei.*

**C. Rossia'num.** *fl.* males yellowish-green, with brown spots, 1½ in. across, in slender racemes; females bright green, solitary, twice as large as males. Habitat? 1891.

**C. stellif'erum.** *fl.* green, those on one spike much larger and totally different in appearance from the other, so that, seen separately, they would be taken as belonging to different genera; *fls.* on the shorter spike, with broad segs. and simple lip, are female, while the smaller and more numerous *fls.* on the long raceme, and which have a much-divided lip, are male. 1879. (G.C. 12 (1879), 493 as *C. Warscewiczii*; B.R. 32, 46 as *C. Egertonianum viride*.)

**C. ventrico'sum.** *fl.* very sweet-scented; sep. and pet. greenish-yellow, with an entire white lip. July, August. 2 ft. h. Guatemala. 1835. (B.M. 4054.) Allied to *C. chlorochilum.*

**C. versicol'or.*** *fl.* males 2 to 2½ in. wide, many, in pendulous racemes; sep. and pet. tawny-green with a velvety gloss and close-set, longitudinal, brown lines; lip creamy-white, spotted red in front of the 2 erect teeth in the apical part, entire; female *fl.* unknown. Brazil. 1888. Allied to *C. Haagii.*

**C. Warscewicz'ii.** Possibly the female-fld. form of *C. aureum,* but probably a distinct species.

E. C.

**CY'DIA.** See **Pea Moth.** A

**C. funebra'na.** See **Red Plum Maggot.** A

**C. pomonel'la.** See **Codling Moth.** A

**CYDIS'TA** (*kydistos*, most glorious; in reference to the flowers). FAM. *Bignoniaceae.* A genus of 2 species of climbing shrubs, natives of Trop. America and the W. Indies, related to Bignonia, but distinct by their unbranched tendrils, flowers in axillary or terminal panicles, with truncate calyx and without a disk. Leaves opposite, leaflets 2. Flowers bell- or funnel-shaped, cor.-lobes overlapping; stamens 4, included, anther lobes spreading. For cultivation see **Clytostoma.**

**C. aequinoctia'lis.** *lflets.* ovate to ovate-oblong, 3 to 4 in. long, obtuse, shining green. *fl.* white or pink with dark pink or purple veins, 2½ in. long. W. Indies, Brazil. SYN. *Bignonia aequinoctialis.*

**C. diversifo'lia.** Branches 4-angled, striped. *lflets.* roundish-ovate, more or less heart-shaped, glabrous, shining. *fl.* yellow, funnel-bell-shaped, in terminal panicles. Mexico. 1825. SYN. *Bignonia diversifolia.*

F. G. P.

**CYDO'NIA** (from Cydon in Crete). Quince. FAM. *Rosaceae.* A genus now reduced to this 1 species. (*See also* **Chaenomeles.**) Distinct from Chaenomeles by the free styles and entire leaves, like Docynia in its tomentose calyx and Chaenomeles in the numerous seeds in each cell of the fruit. See **Quince.**

**C. cathayen'sis.** A synonym of *Chaenomeles cathayensis.*

**C. japon'ica.** A synonym of *Chaenomeles lagenaria.*

**C. Maul'ei.** A synonym of *Chaenomeles japonica.*

**C. oblon'ga.** Quince. Deciduous tree up to 25 ft., young shoots woolly when young. *l.* broadly ovate to elliptic, 2 to 4½ in. long, grey-woolly beneath. *fl.* solitary, 5-petalled, 2 in. wide, white or pink; stamens 20; styles 5, free (united at base in Chaenomeles). May. *fr.* pear-shaped, yellow, 2½ to 4 in. long, fragrant and handsome. Native country doubtful; cultivated for many centuries in the Mediterranean region. 1573. An orchard tree, the fruit used for flavouring conserves. SYN. *C. vulgaris.* var. **lusitan'ica,** *fl.* pale rose, *fr.* larger; **maliform'is,** *fr.* apple-shaped. The Vranja Quince, from Vranja in Serbia, is probably the handsomest of all, the fr. being large, very fragrant, pale golden.

**C. Sargent'ii.** A synonym of *Chaenomeles japonica alpina.*

**C. sinen'sis.** A synonym of *Chaenomeles sinensis.*

W. J. B.

*cylin'dricus -a -um* (*cylindro-*, in compound words), cylindrical; long and round.

**CYLINDROPHYL'LUM.** See under **Mesembryanthemum calamiforme.**

**CYLIS'TA** (*kylix*, in allusion to the large calyx). FAM. *Leguminosae.* A genus of a single species of evergreen woody twiner, native of the E. Indies. Leaves pinnately 3-foliolate, leaflets rhomboid or ovate, acute, stipellate. Bracts large caducous. Flowers papilionaceous, yellow, in axillary racemes. Stove conditions are necessary with a compost of loam and peat. Cuttings may be rooted in sand in bottom heat under a glass.

**C. albiflo'ra.** A variety of *Rhynchosia cyanosperma.*

**C. scario'sa.** *fl.* pale yellow mixed with red; cal. very large, scarious, upper seg. emarginate, lower very large. 1806.

**CYMBALA'RIA.** Included in Linaria.

**CYMBIDIEL'LA** (from *Cymbidium*). FAM. *Orchidaceae.* A genus of 3 species, natives of Madagascar. Formerly included under Cymbidium, but strictly epiphytic and the flowers with labellum strongly 3-lobed, the side lobes rounded and erect, the front lobe recurved, large, obcordate or obovate, not tapered as in Cymbidium. The 2 species introduced should have at all times a warm, moist atmosphere. *C. Humblotii* is better on a raft. A compost of 2½ parts of cut Osmunda fibre to 1½ parts of Sphagnum moss may be used. *C. rhodochila* grows with and among *Platycerium madagascariense*; *C. Humblotii* on *Raphia madagascariensis.* The winter temperature should not be below 65° F.

**C. Humblot'ii.** *fl.* numerous, in arching panicles, green and black; pet. erect aligned with the dorsal sep.; lower sep. longer, falcately curved. *l.* Cymbidium-like, distichous. *rhiz.* stout, creeping. A large species. Madagascar. 1892. (O.R. 1918, front.) A

**C. rhodochi'la.** Differs from *C. Humblotii* by the *pseudobulbs* 2 to 5 in. h., set closely together. *fl.* 10 to 30, 3 to 4 in. across; sep. 1¾ in. long, light green; pet. shorter, erect, green, spotted with dark green-purple; lip with the side lobes green and spotted, front lobe 1½ in. broad, spreading, with reflexed sides, crimson red, disk with a yellow, purple-spotted band. *Spikes* arching, 24 to 30 in. long, elongating. Madagascar. 1900. (B.M. 7932–3 as *Cymbidium rhodochilum.*)

E. C.

***cymbidifo'lius -a -um,*** having leaves like a Cymbidium.

***cymbidioi'des,*** Cymbidium-like.

**CYMBID'IUM** (*kymbe*, a boat; there is a hollow recess in the lip). FAM. *Orchidaceae.* A genus of about 50 species, epiphytic, semi-epiphytic, and terrestrial, in N. India, Burma, Annam, and China, reaching Ceylon, Malaya, the Philippines, Australia, and Japan. Slight variations occur but the majority of the cultivated species and the hybrids have globose-conical or oval compressed pseudobulbs, in some very small, in others slenderly oval, compressed, inclined to be stem-like, all sheathed by the bases of the usually long and narrow leaves. The sepals and narrower petals are spreading, the lip 3-lobed, often very slightly, spurless. The spikes are produced from the axils of the lower leaves and may be 1-, few-, or many-flowered, erect lateral, arching or pendent. Two species included in the genus, *C. macrorhizon* and *C. nipponicum*, the first Himalayan, the second Japanese, are leafless and are said to be parasitic; not in cultivation.

Cyperorchis, often separated, is distinguished by the much narrower floral segments and the nearly straight lip the lateral lobes of which embrace the column, differences hardly sufficient to entitle to generic rank. A number of species have small, dull flowers, but others gain deserved popularity by the beauty and long lasting of their rather large flowers and their easy cultural requirements. A few are fragrant. The introduction of, among others, two particularly distinct and beautiful species, *C. insigne* and *C. erythrostylum*, since 1900 has through the hybridist raised Cymbidiums to high importance in horticulture. Hybrids have been intercrossed and now outnumber the species by hundreds; all have more or less large flowers on tall spikes with shades and variations of colour unknown in Nature.

Cultivation is easy. The hybrids largely derived from *C. Lowianum, C. grandiflorum, C. eburneum, C. insigne, C. erythrostylum*, and *C. Parishii* are all cool-growing and may fall to 45° F. with impunity in winter, rising to the sub-tropical by day in summer with shading; night air should be freely admitted on all suitable occasions and a moist atmosphere maintained; provided that water does not remain in the axils of the leaves through the night, syringing is beneficial. All may be potted in a compost of rough fibrous loam (that of a light nature is to be preferred), with a small amount of Sphagnum moss; if the loam is heavy, cut Osmunda fibre may be added and a larger proportion of finely broken crocks. Drainage is required but not to the extent given Cattleyas, &c. The roots are fleshy and extensive; repotting is required at least every second year. In repotting the removal of all dead roots is essential, and for convenience very long, healthy roots may be shortened. When grown into large plants, tubs of the desired size may take the place of pots. Though water must be given far less frequently in winter than in summer, especially when low temperatures obtain, it must never be withheld for long periods as, to a certain extent, Cymbidium roots are active throughout the year and the spikes are often perceptible in autumn but take some time to develop, December to May being the general flowering season. *C. Finlaysonianum, C. atropurpureum*, and plants from Ceylon or warm countries require the warm or intermediate house; *C. eburneum, C. Parishii, C. erythrostylum* should have a winter night temperature of 55° F.

Propagation may be by division of larger plants, though when space permits it is better to grow the plants on into specimens capable of producing several spikes. Healthy back pseudobulbs may be carefully removed, placed in extra heat for a time until a growth is well advanced, then given ordinary treatment. The old bulb should be removed after the development of the first small pseudobulb and second growth. Though their cultivation is simplified when a house is devoted to them alone, they are so accommodating that such restriction is by no means essential, though for the sake of other kinds a higher winter temperature of 50 to 55° F. must be maintained.

**C. affi'ne.** A synonym of *C. Mastersii affine.*

**C. albucaeflo'rum.** A synonym of *C. madidum.*

**C. aloifo'lium.** Distinct from *C. simulans* by spikes erect, mid-lobe of lip long, acute. S. India. Probably not in cultivation. *C. aloifolium* of gardens is a synonym of *C. simulans.*

**C. atropurpu'reum.** *fl.* about 25; sep. and broader pet. 1¼ in. long, deep velvety purple-red; lip with the side lobes suffused rose, the mid-lobe spreading, whitish, sparsely crimson-spotted (2 or 3 spots seem constant on the reflexed apex), disk with 2 raised, bright-yellow keels. *l.* fleshy, stiff, strap-shaped, 24 to 36 in. long. *Racemes* pendent. Allied to *C. Finlaysonianum.* Philippines. 1854. (B.M. 5710.)

**C. Ballia'num.** *fl.* 3 to 7, 3 in. or more across, on erect bract-clothed spikes; sep. and pet. white, slightly acuminate; disk of lip yellow; fragrant but not to the extent of *C. eburneum* to which it is allied. Winter, spring. Burma, Annam. 1895.

**C. bi'color.** *fl.* about 2 in. across, in arching or pendent racemes; sep. and pet. yellowish with a central purplish stripe, side lobes of the lip and the short, broad, obtuse front lobe and column purple. *l.* much as in *C. simulans.* Ceylon. 1837.

**C. canalicula'tum.*** *fl.* ½ to 1 in. across; sep. and pet. purplish-brown, edged with green; lip greenish-white, with a row of pink spots just within the white edge; racemes drooping, bearing numerous, very variable fl. April. *l.* 6 to 12 in. long, rigid, keeled. Stem short, compressed, almost pseudobulbless. NE. Australia. 1870. (B.M. 5851.) var. **Sparkes'ii,** *fl.* sep. and pet. intensely dark maroon, lip pink with a greenish base and crimson spots or suffused deep red, disk yellow. Queensland, Australia.

**C. chloran'thum.** *fl.* 2 in. across; sep. and pet. yellowish-green, with a few red spots at base; lip 3-lobed, side lobes red inside, incurved, mid-lobe yellowish-white, spotted red; column yellow, stained red; racemes 15 to 20 in. long, many-fld. May. *l.* ensiform, 15 to 20 in. long, recurved. Java. 1840. (B.M. 4907.) SYN. *C. sanguinolentum, C. variciferum.*

**C. cochlea're.** *fl.* 2 in. long; the narrow sep. and revolute pet. greenish-brown; lip yellowish, speckled with red, mid-lobe yellow, sub-orbicular. *Scape* 12 to 18 in. h. *l.* 18 to 30 in. long, ⅓ to ½ in. wide. Sikkim Himalaya. 1880.

**C. Coo'peri.** Considered a variety of *C.* × J. Davis, a hybrid between *C. insigne* and *C. Schroederi*, but imported with *C. insigne.* February. Annam. 1904.

**C. cyperifo'lium.** *fl.* 4 to 7, 2 in. across, distant, fragrant; sep. and pet. pale green and yellow, streaked red, acute; lip greenish or white, spotted red, narrow; scape shorter than l. Winter. *l.* 1 to 2 ft. long, ⅓ to ½ in. broad. Sub-trop. Himalaya, &c. 1895. (A.B.G.C. 8, 248.)

**C. Daya'num.*** *fl.* 3 in. across, yellowish-white, marked with wine-coloured streak on middle lines of the narrow sep. and pet., and a similar border and numerous small streaks on lip; racemes many-fld., pendulous. Autumn. *l.* about 2 ft. long, narrow. Annam, Assam. 1869. SYN. *C. Simonsianum.* (B.M. 7863.) var. **pulcher'rimum,** *fl.* waxy white, striped and flushed crimson, sep. and pet. narrow, acute, raceme slender, scape stout, *l.* grass-like. N. India. 1891.

**C. Devonia'num.*** *fl.* 1 to 1½ in. across, fleshy, close; sep. and pet. light brown, with dull mauve-purple streaks and blotches; lip white, with numerous dark-purple lines and blotches, the acute, reflexed, anterior part fine dark purple, almost rhomboid; racemes nodding, many-fld. Spring. *l.* lanceolate-oblong, acute, with long channelled petioles. India. 1837. (A.B.G.C. 8, 253; W.O.A. 170; B.M. 9327.)

**C. ebur'neum.*** *fl.* 3 to 4 in. across, deliciously fragrant, very handsome; sep. and pet. white or creamy-white, disk and keels of lip yellow; racemes erect, 1- or 2-fld. February. *l.* narrow, sword-shaped, distichous, bright light green. With age forms a stout stem-like pseudobulb, but, when young, it shows no sign of this. N. India, Burma. 1846. (B.M. 5126; B.R. 33, 67; A.B.G.C. 8, 262; W.O.A. 467.) There are 1 or 2 varieties. **Daya'num** has 2 purple spots on each side of the disk; **Philbrickia'num** has white fl., narrow sep. and pet., side lobes of lip distant from narrow mid-lobe, callus narrow, keel obscure. 1886. Habit of *C. Parishii.*

**C. el'egans.** *fl.* 20 to 40, not fully expanding, 1½ to 2 in. long; segs. narrow, straw yellow; lip with 2 orange lines on the disk, and sometimes marked with red. *Scapes* arching or nodding, clothed with sheaths; fl. closely set. *l.* narrow, numerous, 18 to 24 in. long. Nepal. 1840. (W.O.A. 430; A.B.G.C. 8, 259; B.M. 7007 as *Cyperorchis elegans.*)

**C. ensifo'lium.*** *fl.* about 2 in. across, greenish-yellow, very fragrant; sep. and pet. with some reddish-brown narrow lines; lip dotted, ovate, somewhat recurved; scape erect, about 12-fld. Late summer. *l.* ensiform, nerved. Assam, China, Japan. (B.M. 1751.) var. **estria'tum**, *fl.* segs. very narrow, sep. green with few red lines, pet. white with some purple lines, lip white, mid-lobe yellow with few brown spots, column white with purple blotches in front, *l.* over 1 ft. long, ¼ in. wide, with dark spots. Assam. 1887. (B.R. 1976.)

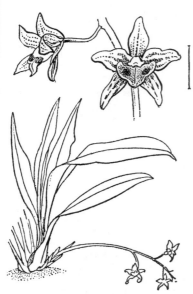

*Cymbidium Devonianum* (p. 610)

**C. erythrosty'lum.*** *fl.* 3 to 15, about 3 in. across; sep. and shorter pet. glistening white; lip with a rather short, broad mid-lobe, white, shaded yellow and lined with red; column crimson; racemes arching. *l.* 10 to 15 in. long, ½ in. wide. Beautiful and distinct. Annam. 1904. (B.M. 8131.)

**C. Finlaysonia'num.** *fl.* 2½ in. across; sep. and pet. yellow, shaded red, linear-lanceolate, side lobes of lip red, mid-lobe white, reddish-purple towards tip; disk yellow; raceme slender, pendent, 2 to 4 ft. long. Summer. *l.* 20 to 36 in. long, leathery. Malaya, Celebes, &c. (B.R. 26, 25.) SYN. *C. tricolor, C. Wallichii.*

**C. frag'rans.** A synonym of *C. sinense.*

**C. × Gammiea'num.** Probably a natural hybrid between *C. elegans* and *C. longifolium* (or possibly *C. giganteum*). Habit and fl. colour intermediate. Sikkim. 1890. (A.B.G.C. 257; O.R. 1936, 365.)

**C. Gib'sonii.** A synonym of *C. lancifolium.*

**C. gigan'teum.*** *fl.* 7 to 15, 3 to 4 in. across; sep. and pet. yellowish, striped with reddish-brown; lip stained with yellow and blotched with bright red, mid-lobe hairy; racemes arching. Autumn. The plant has distinct pseudobulbs, clothed with the broad sheathing bases of the long, sword-like *l.* N. India. 1837. SYN. *Iridorchis gigantea.* (B.M. 4844; L. 700; W.O.A. 284; A.B.G.C. 8, 255.) var. **margina'tum** has a white margin to the lip.

**C. grandiflo'rum.*** *fl.* 4 to 5 in. wide; sep. and pet. green; lip tomentose, straw-coloured, deep yellow at margins, round which are blotches of purple-red; racemes pendent-arched, 5 to 15 fl. *l.* 20 to 30 in. long, striped greenish-yellow at base. Sikkim Himalaya. 1866. (A.B.G.C. 8, 256; B.M. 5574 as *C. Hookerianum*.) SYN. *C. Griffithianum.* A fine cool-house species. var. **puncta'tum** has purplish dots on lower parts of segs. (L. 389.); **Tracya'num** is a large-fld. var. 1890. (J.H. 21 (1890), 535.)

**C. Griffithia'num.** A synonym of *C. grandiflorum.*

**C. Hookeria'num.** A synonym of *C. grandiflorum.*

**C. Humblot'ii.** A synonym of *Cymbidiella Humblotii.*

**C. Hut'tonii.** *fl.* 5 to 15, about 2 in. across, not expanding fully, yellowish-white, suffused and thickly spotted with dull purple, the pet. more so than lip, dull purple-green without; scapes arching or pendent, about 10 in. long. *Pseudobulbs* 2 to 5 in. h., ovoid, 2- or 3-phyllous. *l.* 12 to 15 in. long, broad, somewhat lanceolate. Java, Malaya. 1857. (B.M. 5676.) A very distinct species, so distinct that perhaps rightly it has been placed under Grammangis.

**C. I'Ansoni.*** *fl.* 7 to 12, 4 to 5½ in. across; sep. and pet. tawny-yellow, veined and suffused with purplish-brown; lip broad with a red-brown median line and striations and a suffusion of the same colour on its margin; disk and base of lip white. Winter, spring. Habit much as in *C. Lowianum.* Burma, Annam. 1900. SYN. *C. Mandaianum.*

**C. insig'ne.*** *fl.* 10 to 24, 3 to 4 in. across, rounded, whitish suffused with rose, the sep. and pet. bases thickly dotted with crimson; lip flushed, lined and dotted with rose-crimson on a white ground, disk yellow; spikes erect, 3 to 4 ft. h. February. *Pseudobulbs* somewhat globose. *l.* 20 to 36 in. h., ½ in. broad, glaucous green. A very variable but beautiful species of great value to the hybridist. Annam. 1904. (B.M. 8312.) var. **al'bum**, *fl.* pure white; **Bie'ri**,* *fl.* much larger and more richly coloured; **Glebelands var.**, *fl.* silver-white, lightly flushed rose-purple, spotted on lip and bases of petals; **rhodochi'lum**, sep. and pet. rose, lip ruby-red with deeper spots; **St. André**, lip deep red.

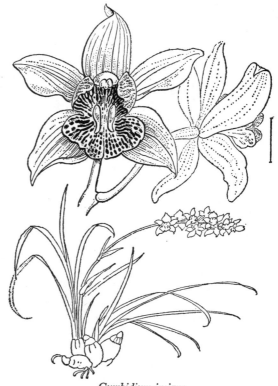

*Cymbidium insigne*

**C. Kan'ran.** *fl.* fragrant; sep. and pet. light green; sep. narrowly lanceolate, acuminate, 1½ in. long; pet. over 1 in., dotted with purple at base, lip yellowish-green with dark-purple marginal markings on side lobes and a longitudinal channel on disk. Allied to *C. ensifolium* but with shorter, narrower foliage. Variable. Japan. 1902.

**C. lancifo'lium.** *fl.* 1½ to 2 in. across; sep. white or greenish, lanceolate; pet. white, with a pink midrib, rather broader; lip white, spotted with reddish-purple, the side lobes narrow; scape nodding or erect, 6- to 8-fld. Autumn. *l.* 6 to 10 in. long, 1 to 2 in. broad, long-petiolate. *Pseudobulb* 2 to 6 in. long, fleshy, fusiform. Sub-trop. Himalaya. 1822. (L.B.C. 927; A.B.G.C. 8, 247.) SYN. *C. Gibsonii.*

**C. Leachia'num.*** *fl.* sep. and pet. ligulate, acute, whitish-ochre, with a brown line running nearly to the apex; lip brown except the whitish disk with 2 keels, 3-lobed; racemes loose. *l.* linear-lanceolate, acute. Formosa. 1878.

**C. longifo'lium.** *fl.* 9 to 20; sep. and pet. 1½ to 2 in. long, spreading, narrow, light green with interrupted brownish-red lines; lip tomentose, whitish with a central crimson line and a few crimson spots, side lobes comparatively large, mid-lobe acute, reflexed. Variable. *Spikes* 18 to 30 in. long, erect or arching. *Pseudobulbs* 2 to 3 in. long. *l.* 30 in. long, ½ in. wide, tapered. N. India. (A.B.G.C. 8, 254.)

**C. Lowia'num.*** *fl.* 15 to 40, 4 to 5 in. across; sep. and pet. green, with a few faint sepia-brown lines over the strongest nerves; lip whitish-yellow, front of mid-lobe widely bordered crimson-red. March. Burma. 1877. (W.O.A. 471.) var. **au'reum**, *fl.* yellow with orange blotch on lip. 1893; **con'color**, sep. and pet. greenish-yellow, light yellow replacing crimson border of lip; **flaveo'lum**, *fl.* pale yellow, large. 1897. (L. 572.); **superbis'simum**, *fl.* with front lobe of lip deep maroon-purple. 1893. (L. 392.); **vi'ride**, *fl.* greenish-yellow, lip without purple. 1892. (W.O.A. 527.)

**C. Mackin'noni.** Allied to *C. virescens.* *fl.* solitary, 2 in. across, nodding; sep. and pet. green; lip pale yellow blotched with purple. Himalaya. (A.B.G.C. 9, 115.)

**C. mad'idum.** *fl.* 1 in. across; sep. spreading, petals smaller and erect, both (as well as mid-lobe of lip) dull nankeen-yellow; side lobes of lip stained vinous-purple, erect; racemes pendulous, as long as l., many-fld. Autumn. *Pseudobulbs* 3 to 4 in. long. *l.* 18 to 36 in. long, leathery. Australia. 1840 and 1889. SYN. *C. albucae-florum.*

**C. Mas'tersii.*** *fl.* 3 to 10; segs. narrow, pure ivory-white, saving spots of pink on the lip which has a yellow disk; fragrant of almonds; racemes erect. Winter. Assam. 1841. Growth resembles *C. eburneum*, but l. longer, broader, more recurved, and destitute of the close sheathing base which is so striking in that plant. (L. 222; A.B.G.C. 8, 261; B.R. 31, 50.) SYN. *Cyperorchis Mastersii.* var. **affi'ne**, *fl.* slightly larger and with more purple on lip. SYN. *Cyperorchis affine;* **al'bum**, *fl.* white with yellow disk to lip. (R. 1, 66.)

**C. Munroia'num.** *fl.* fragrant; sep. and pet. straw-colour, dotted and streaked with red; lip barred with red with a yellow recurved tip; racemes erect. Allied to *C. ensifolium.* Sikkim. 1917. (A.B.G.C. 8, 249.)

**C. Parish'ii.*** A beautiful species allied to *C. eburneum.* *fl.* sep. and pet. ivory-white; lip with an orange middle zone, and an orange disk; side lobes and margins of lip with numerous purplish-violet spots, which give the chief charm to the flower. Back of column white, edges and front yellow, with some brownish-purple spots on foot. Summer. *Peduncle* erect, 2- or 3-fld. *l.* broader than in *C. eburneum*, acute. Burma. 1874. (W.O.A. 25; L. 717.) var. **San'derae**, *fl.* 3 to 6, similar to those of type but purple spots larger and sometimes confluent. Annam. 1904. SYN. *C. Sanderae.*

**C. pen'dulum.** *fl.* sep. and pet. brown; lip red, striped white with continuous keels; racemes long, drooping, from 1 to 2 ft. long, many-fld. July, August. *l.* erect, long, narrow, thick, leathery, dark green. Nepal. 1838. A large plant. (W.O.A. 437; L. 607.) SYN. *Epidendrum pendulum.* The name *C. pendulum* has also been applied to *C. simulans* and *C. Finlaysonianum.*

**C. pubes'cens.** *fl.* 1 to 1½ in. broad; sep. and pet. dark purple, margined with yellow or green, linear; lip pubescent, yellow, with a broad band of reddish-purple, or reddish-purple within margin of mid-lobe, side lobes acute; raceme short, pendulous, 6- to 10-fld., scape short, decurved. *l.* 1 to 2 ft. long, ½ in. broad, obtuse. Singapore, Borneo. 1838. (B.R. 37, 38.)

**C. pulcherrimum.** A variety of *C. Dayanum.*

**C. pu'milum.** *fl.* many, about 1 in. across; sep. and pet. light reddish-brown; lip white, dotted and lined with red-brown, disk and 2 keels bright yellow; mid-lobe reflexed. *l.* 9 to 12 in. long. Formosa. Spring. 1900.

**C. rhodochi'lum.** A synonym of *Cymbidiella rhodochila.*

**C. ro'seum.** *fl.* few, 2 in. across, on an arching scape; sep. and narrower pet. lanceolate, soft rose; lip shaped as in *C. giganteum*, whitish, spotted and marked deep rose. Winter. Java. 1935? Not to be confused with another species so named, an anomalous form from Annam.

**C. San'derae.** A synonym of *C. Parishii Sanderae.*

**C. San'deri.** A synonym of *C. insigne.*

**C. sanguinolen'tum.** A synonym of *C. chloranthum.*

**C. scep'trum.** A synonym of *Grammatophyllum speciosum.*

**C. Schroe'deri.** *fl.* up to 30, 3 in. across; sep. and pet. greenish-yellow, suffused, striped and dotted with red-brown; lip pubescent, light yellow, side lobes striped red-brown, mid-lobe with a central line and broad margin of red-brown. Feb. Annam. 1904.    **A**

**C. Simonsia'num.** A synonym of *C. Dayanum.*

**C. sim'ulans.** *fl.* 1½ to 2 in. across, yellowish with a central purplish stripe through the narrow sep. and pet.; lip with curved and interrupted keels, mid-lobe short, reflexed, obtuse, with purple stripes also present on the side lobes. *l.* stiff, fleshy, 12 to 20 in. long, obliquely 2-lobed at apex; racemes many-fld., decurved, shorter than l. Nepal, Sikkim, Assam, South China, Java, possibly Borneo. The name was applied on account of the confusion which existed between this species, *pendulum, bicolor*, and *aloifolium.* (L.B.C. 967 as *C. aloifolium*; B.M. 387 as *Epidendrum aloides*.) SYN. *C. pendulum, C. bicolor.*

**C. sinen'se.*** *fl.* very fragrant; sep. and pet. brown and purple; lip yellowish-green, spotted with purple; racemes tall, erect, many-fld. Autumn. China. 1793. (L.B.C. 37.) Allied to *C. ensifolium.*

**C. Sparkes'ii.** A variety of *C. canaliculatum.*

**C. sua've.** *fl.* fleshy, fragrant, ½ to 1 in. across, dull green faintly brown blotched or yellowish-green, or brownish externally, old gold within; sep. and pet. sub-equal; lip somewhat oblong, almost entire; racemes arching, 6 to 12 in. long, many-fld. *l.* narrow, coarsely grass-like. Very variable. Australia.

**C. suavis'simum.** *fl.* closely set; sep. spreading, ¾ in. long, broadly strap-shaped or oblong; pet. shorter, narrower, inclined upwards, deep brownish-red, margined green; lip whitish, spotted and blotched or entirely suffused with rose-purple, side lobes usually spotted, mid-lobe reflexed, crest with 2 yellow ridges; column brown-red above, margined yellow, yellowish beneath. Habit of *C. ensifolium* but l. broader and reddish at the base. *Spikes* ascending or arching, 30- to 50-fld. Very variable. Habitat unknown. 1928.

**C. tigri'num.** *fl.* 2 to 5, about 2 in. across; sep. and pet. greenish-yellow, spotted and lined with red; lip large, tapering to a point, middle portion white, striped with cross-bars of purple, sides of lip purple, disk hairy; spike arched. Summer. *l.* about 6 in. long. *Pseudobulbs* nearly round. Tenasserim. 1864. (B.M. 5457.)

**C. Tracya'num.*** *fl.* 5 to 15, 4 to 5 in. across, very fragrant; sep. and pet. yellowish, suffused and veined with interrupted lines of mahogany red; lip tomentose, creamy-white to yellow, spotted and striped red; scapes arching or nearly erect. Late autumn. Burma. 1890. (L. 154; B.M. n.s. 56.)

**C. tric'olor.** A synonym of *C. Finlaysonianum.*

**C. varicif'erum.** A synonym of *C. chloranthum.*

**C. vires'cens.** *fl.* solitary; sep. and pet. 1½ in. long, greenish; lip dull yellow with a few dull-red blotches. Japan. 1858. SYN. *C. Goringii.*

**C. Wallich'ii.** A synonym of *C. Finlaysonianum.*

**C. Wil'soni.** *fl.* 3½ in. across; sep. and pet. light green, tinged and spotted with red-brown; lip yellowish-white, spotted with red-brown near apex and on the hairy keels, side lobes lined red-brown. Winter, spring. Allied to *C. giganteum.* Yunnan. 1904.
                                                                    E. C.

**cymbiform,** boat-shaped.

**CYMBOPO'GON** (*kymbe*, cup; *pogon*, beard). FAM. *Gramineae.* A genus of about 40 species of perennial grasses mostly natives of the tropics of the old world. It is very nearly related to Andropogon and often treated as a section of that genus. It differs by having some of the lower pairs of spikelets in each spike staminate. The spike-like racemes are in pairs at the end of short branches of the inflorescence. The species are remarkable since several contain essential oils and some are cultivated for these products used in perfumery. The species mentioned below can be grown in pots in a warm house, where their scented foliage is an attraction. A full account is given of these grasses by Dr. Stapf in the *Kew Bulletin,* 1906.

**C. citra'tus.** Lemon Grass. Densely tufted. Habit much as *C. Schoenanthus* but *panicle* loose with slender branches, more or less nodding at ends, joints of rachis with rather spreading hairs. *Spikelets* not awned. Known only in cultivation in most tropical countries. The source of Lemon-grass oil. Much confused with *C. Schoenanthus.* (K.B. 1906, p. 297.) SYN. *Andropogon citratus.*

**C. Nar'dus.** Citronella Grass. Densely tufted. Habit much as *C. Schoenanthus*, but *panicles* large and very compound. *Spikelets* not awned. Known only in cultivation. Ceylon, Malaya, Java. The source of Oil of Citronella. SYN. *Andropogon Nardus.*

**C. Schoenanth'us.** Densely tufted. *l.* threadlike and flexuous, hard, rough-edged, basal sheaths close and thickened below. *Panicle* narrow, consisting of clusters of racemes, the joints long-haired all over, almost concealing the sessile spikelets. N. Africa to N. India. The source of Camel-grass oil. (H.I.P. 1871 as *Andropogon laniger.*)

**CYME.** A branched inflorescence with the central flower opening first as in Sedum.

**CYMINOS'MA oblongifo'lium.** A synonym of *Acronychia laevis.*

**cymo'sus -a -um,** see **CYME.**

**CYNANCH'UM** (*kynos*, dog, *ancho*, to strangle; some species are poisonous). FAM. *Asclepiadaceae.* A genus of about 25 species of twining herbs or sub-shrubs, natives of S. Europe, Africa, Asia, and Australia, related closely to Vincetonicum which is sometimes included here but distinct by the presence of a scale or ligule on each of the 5 parts of the crown. Leaves opposite, heart-shaped or hastate. Flowers small in cymose umbels; corolla nearly rotate, 5-parted, lobes oblong or roundish; corona membranous, forming a loose cup round the 5 anthers, with inner scales or lobes. Fruit of rather fleshy, smooth follicles. Easily grown in ordinary garden soil and readily increased by division in spring. The following are perennials. Pollination is effected by insects which are sometimes caught and held for a while.

**C. acuminatifo'lium.** Cruel Plant, Mosquito Plant. Erect or nearly so, or twining at tips. Stem angled, greyish. *l.* broadly ovate, slender-pointed, entire, grey-hairy beneath; stalk short. *fl.* in short clusters between l., white, small, in umbel-like cymes. Japan. Hardy.

**C. acu'tum.** 2 to 12 ft. climber. *l.* lanceolate, deeply heart-shaped at base. *fl.* white or rose, scented, in small axillary or terminal umbels. July. S. Europe. Hardy.

**C. formo'sum.** Glabrous twiner. *l.* ovate, elliptic-ovate, or oblong-ovate, 1¼ to 4 in. long, with a slender point, heart-shaped at base; stalk up to 1¼ in. long. *fl.* pale green in cymes 2½ to 3½ in. long; cor. lobes spreading or reflexed, about ¼ in. long; pedicels ½ to 2½ in. long. Peru. Greenhouse.

**C. nig'rum.** A synonym of *Vincetoxicum nigrum*.

**CYNA'RA** (*kynos*, dog; the spines of the involucre being likened to a dog's tooth). FAM. *Compositae*. A genus of about 12 species of large thistle-like perennial herbs, natives of the Mediterranean region and Canary Is. Leaves usually large, variously lobed or pinnatisect. Flower-heads large, violet, blue, or white; involucre broad or subglobose; bracts leathery in many series; receptacle fleshy, flat, densely bristly; pappus hairs in many series, feathery. The 2 species mentioned below are usually grown for their use as food but few plants are more stately or effective for planting at the back of borders or on the edge of shrubberies. For treatment *see* **Cardoon** and **Artichoke Globe.** *C. horrida* needs similar cultivation.

**C. Cardun'culus.** Cardoon. 5 ft. h. *l.* pinnatifid, spiny. *fl.-heads* purple; involucral scales ovate. August, September. S. Europe. 1658. (B.M. 3241.)

**C. hor'rida.** About 6 ft. h. *l.* pinnatifid, downy beneath, spiny; spines of base of l. and pinnae connate at base. *fl.-heads* purple. August, September. S. Europe. 1768. (S.F.G. 834.)

**C. Scol'ymus.** Globe Artichoke. 3 to 6 ft. h. *l.* long, nearly pinnatifid, somewhat spiny, white-cottony beneath. *fl.-heads* purple, very large, involucre of oval, obtuse, sometimes emarginate, downy scales. Autumn. 1548. The Globe Artichoke is nowhere found wild and is probably a derivative of *C. Cardunculus*.

**CYNIPID WASPS.** *See* **Gall Wasps.**

**CY'NIPS.** A genus of **Gall Wasps** (q.v.).

***cyno-,*** in compound words, signifying resemblance to a dog.

**CYNOCRAMBA'CEAE.** Dicotyledons. A family of 2 species of annual herbs forming the genus Thelygonum, the relationships of which are very obscure. The lower leaves are opposite, the upper have opposite to each a group of staminate flowers and in the leaf-axil a branch ending in female flowers. The perianth is of 2 to 5 leaves, stamens 10 to 30, the female flower has 1 carpel containing 1 seed. Fruit a drupe. *T. Cynocrambe* is used as spinach.

**CYNOCRAM'BE.** A synonym of Thelygonum.

**CYNOGLOS'SUM** (*kynos*, dog, *glossa*, tongue; from the form of the leaves). FAM. *Boraginaceae*. A genus of about 50 species of biennial or perennial (rarely annual) herbs distributed over the whole world except the arctic regions. Basal leaves long-stalked, upper alternate, inflorescence usually without bracts. Flowers in terminal secund racemes, sometimes forked; corolla funnel-shaped or sub-rotate, its throat closed by prominent scales. Related to Solenanthus but anthers scarcely reaching the throat of the corolla, not exserted. The Cynoglossums grow well in ordinary soil, well drained, and can be readily raised from seed. The species mentioned below are hardy except in very severe winters and are best sown where they are to flower.

**C. amab'ile.*** Biennial, with simple erect stem 1 to 2 ft. h., covered with long hair. *l.* lanceolate-oblong or lanceolate, variable in length, 2½ to 8 in. long, stalked, lateral nerves distinct, upper l. much smaller. *Racemes* numerous, terminal, and in upper l.-axils, forming a loose panicle. *fl.* beautiful blue, pink, or white, about ¼ in. long, funnel-bell-shaped. July, August. China, Tibet. (B.M. 9334.)

**C. appeni'num.** A synonym of *Solenanthus appeninus*.

**C. azu'reum.** A synonym of *Adelocaryum coelestinum*.

**C. cheirifo'lium.** Biennial with erect stem up to 18 in. h., densely white-hairy. *l.* lanceolate, 3 to 4 in. long, stalked, upper l. smaller, all white-hairy. *Racemes* many-fld., bracteate, forming a thyrsoid panicle. *fl.* at first rose, then purplish-violet, then blue, about ⅓ in. long, widely cylindrical, lobes shorter than tube. June, July. S. Europe. 1596.

**C. coelesti'num.** A synonym of *Adelocaryum coelestinum*.

**C. Colum'nae.** Densely hairy annual, 1 to 2½ ft. h., little-branched. *l.* elliptic to lanceolate, 1¼ to 2½ in. long, stalked, upper l. sessile, about as long as lower. *Racemes* forming a large panicle. *fl.* blue, about ¼ in. long, shortly and widely cylindrical. May. Italy, Balkans.

*Cynoglossum amabile*

**C. cre'ticum.** Densely hairy biennial, with usually solitary, erect, unbranched stems, 1 to 2 ft. h. *l.* elliptic or oblong, 4 to 6 in. long, with a stalk 2 to 5 in. long, finely hairy above, upper l. smaller, stem clasping. *Racemes* forming a large panicle. *fl.* pale violet to red, veined, shortly funnel-shaped. August. Mediterranean region, Canary Is. to Turkestan. 1658. SYN. *C. pictum*. *See also* **C. officinale bicolor.**

**C. denticula'tum.** Erect, branched, hispid annual, about 18 in. h. *l.* oblong, 2 to 3 in. long, acute, toothed. *fl.* in long, terminal and axillary racemes, blue, about ¼ in. long. Himalaya.

**C. Diosco'ridis.** Densely hairy biennial, 8 to 20 in. h. *l.* linear-lanceolate, about 8 in. long, stalked, upper sessile, stem-clasping. *Racemes* forming a loose panicle. *fl.* red or flesh-coloured with deeper veins, about ⅛ in. long, rather wider, bell-funnel-shaped. June. SW. Europe. 1820.

**C. furca'tum.** A synonym of *C. zeylanicum*.

**C. gran'de.** Perennial. Stem simple, erect, 12 to 30 in. h., glabrous or slightly hairy in lower part. *l.* ovate or elliptic, 6 to 12 in. long, slender-pointed, stalked, often densely hairy beneath. *Racemes* in a long interrupted terminal thyrse. *fl.* bright blue; cor. cylindrical, about ⅜ in. long, lobes as long as tube. Spring. Western N. America.

**C. nervo'sum.** Hairy, up to 2½ ft. h., erect, branched. *l.* narrow-lanceolate, about 8 in. long, acute, stalked, nerves in 6 or more pairs, strong, roughly hairy. *infl.* at first capitate, then lengthening. *fl.* blue, about ⅜ in. across. July. Himalaya. 1894. (B.M. 7513.)

**C. officina'le.** Biennial covered with hairs with swollen bases, 1 to 3 ft. h., stem usually solitary. *l.* broadly lanceolate about 10 in. long, long-stalked, upper sessile. *fl.* in a short dense panicle, later lengthening, dark purple, shortly and widely cylindrical, about ¼ in. long. June. Widely distributed in north temperate zone, including Britain. var. **bic'olor,** *fl.* white with purple throat scales, is probably a hybrid with *C. creticum*.

**C. pic'tum.** A synonym of *C. creticum*.

**C. virginia'num.** Hairy perennial with erect simple stem, 1 to 2½ ft. h., naked above. *l.* oval to oblong, 5 to 10 in. long, those on lower part of stem longer, stalked, uppermost sessile. *infl.* on long peduncles, umbellate before flowering. *fl.* pale blue, funnel-shaped-rotate, about ¼ in. long. July. Eastern N. America.

**C. zeylan'icum.** Biennial, hairy. Stem thick, branched, 1½ to 2½ ft. h. *l.* oblong or elliptic, up to 10 in. long, stalked, uppermost sessile, grey-green. *fl.* in large many-fld. panicles, clear blue, funnel-shaped. June, July. India. SYN. *C. furcatum*.

**CYNOMET'RA** (*kynos*, dog, *metra*, matrix; in allusion to shape and consistence of the pods). FAM. *Leguminosae*. A genus of about 40 species of evergreen trees, natives of the tropics of both hemispheres. Leaves with a single pair of leaflets. Flowers usually red, zygomorphic, arising from the main trunk of the tree. Pods brown, edible. Cultivation of these stove plants as for the related Copaifera.

**C. cauliflo'ra.** Tree of 30 to 40 ft. *lflets.* emarginate. *fl.* white, in clustered racemes from the trunk; racemes sometimes short and few-fld., sometimes long and many-fld. E. Indies. 1804.

**C. triniten'sis.** Tree of medium size with dense crown, branches ultimately pendulous, glabrous. *lflets.* 3 to 4 in. long, 1 to 2 in. broad. *fl.* red, 1 to 1½ in. across, in racemes; cal. with short tube; stamens short, anthers small. W. Indies. (H.I.P. 2443.)

F. G. P.

*Cy'nops*, ancient Greek name for a Plantain.

**CYNOR'CHIS** (*kynos*, dog, and *Orchis*). FAM. *Orchidaceae*. A genus of about 16 species of mostly terrestrial Orchids, allied to Habenaria, with fleshy or tuberous roots, natives of the Mascarene Is. and Trop. Africa. Flowers of medium size, rather small, shortly stalked; sepals subequal, concave, at length spreading; petals similar or smaller; lip continuous with the column, spreading, as long as the sepals, 3- to 5-cleft, produced in a spur; column very short with a dilated rostellum; raceme short or rarely elongated, rather loose. The majority require a warm house with a winter temperature when they are at rest of not less than 60° F. Compost should consist of loam fibre and sand with, particularly for the warm-growing species, finely broken crocks and Sphagnum moss. For the strictly deciduous species water is only occasionally required in the winter, sufficient to prevent the tubers from shrivelling. *C. purpurascens* and probably other species grow on trees among fern debris, &c., and must have a moist atmosphere throughout the year.

**C. compac'ta.** * *infl.* about 4 in. long. *fl.* 4 to 15, about ⅓ in. across, white with minute purple spots on the disk of the lip, the front lobe of which is 3-lobed; spur short, conical. *l.* somewhat oblong, developing fully after the flowering period. Natal. 1869. (B.M. 8053.) Cool house.

**C. el'egans.** *fl.* whitish, with a rosy tinge, in 3- to 7-fld. racemes; odd sep. gibbous, convex, abrupt; side sep. ligulate, longer than the odd sep.; lip with a small angle on each side at base, the lamina spotted or lined deep purple; scape slender. *l.* cuneate-oblong-lanceolate, acute, 2½ to 4 in. long, by ¾ in. wide, light green, striped and barred mauve-purple. Madagascar. 1888.

**C. grandiflo'ra.** *fl.* 1½ in. across; sep. and pet. greenish, spotted purple, small; lip bright rose-purple, large, 4-lobed, with a long spur; scapes erect, 1 ft. long, 1- or 2-fld. *l.* ensiform, annual, 3 to 5 in. long. Madagascar. 1893. (B.M. 7564.) var. **alba'ta,** *fl.* scented, lip white, purple at base; **purpu'rea,** *fl.* scentless, lip purple, spotted at base.

**C. × kewen'sis** (*C. Lowiana × C. purpurascens*). *fl.* dull purple-red. Of garden origin.

**C. Lowia'na.** *fl.* 3 to 7, distantly placed on erect spikes, 8 to 10 in. h.; lateral sep. oblong, obtuse, with the spur light green, or greenish-white; dorsal sep. shorter than lateral, convex-oblong like the ligulate, acute pet. purplish; lip 3-cleft, with 2 linear red blotches on disk, somewhat wedge-shaped, lilac-red; spur 1 in. long. *l.* 1 or 2, 4 in. or more long, ¾ in. wide, tapered. Usually fl. in spring. Madagascar. 1888. (O.R. 1911, 273; B.M. 7551 as *C. purpurascens*.)

**C. purpuras'cens.** *Infl.* umbellate, 10- to 25-fld.; sep. and pet. purple-rose, the dorsal sep. shaded green, ¼ in. long, the lateral twice as long; pet. purple-rose; lip spreading with a white disk, 3-cleft, the lobes comparatively broad, outline somewhat rounded; spur 1 in. or rather more. *l.* solitary or with a reduced second, 12 in. or more long, 2 to 3 in. wide. Epiphytic. Madagascar. 1894. (B.M. 7852; O.R. 1911, 272.)

**C. villo'sa.** *fl.* in dense oblong heads on erect racemes; purple shading to white on lip and lower parts of pet. Very hairy. Madagascar. 1901. (B.M. 7845.)

**CYNOSORCH'IS.** *See* **Cynorchis.**

**CYNOX'YLON.** Included in **Cornus.**

*Cyparis'sias*, ancient Greek name for a plant with a leaf like Cypress.

**CYPEL'LA** (*kypellon*, goblet or cup; from the form of the flowers). FAM. *Iridaceae*. A genus of about 8 species of small bulbous plants, natives of Trop. America, related to Marica but with terminal solitary or corymbose flowers, plicate leaves, and terete stems. Bulbs tunicated. Perianth segments free, outer obovate, spreading, inner much narrower, erect, recurved at tip. Fruit a capsule. Best lifted in autumn and planted in a warm spot in spring; if left out they must be well protected. Propagated by offsets or by seed sown as soon as ripe. Light sandy soil is best for them.

*Cypella Herbertii*

**C. Herbert'ii.** About 1 ft. h. *l.* lanceolate, tapering. *fl.* yellow, few, varying in shade to deep chrome; segs. ovate at tip, somewhat contracted in middle, spotted or barred deep yellow at base. July. Buenos Aires. 1823. (B.M. 2599 as *Tigridia Herbertii*.)

**C. peruvia'na.** Bulb ovoid, truncate. Stem *l.* linear, rather thin, glabrous; basal *l.* past at flowering time. *fl.* 2 or 3 in a solitary stalked cluster, fugacious, appearing successively from the spathe; bright yellow, spotted at base red-brown; stigma bright yellow, 2-fid, petaloid. Andes of Peru. (B.M. 6213.)

**C. plumb'ea.** 2 to 3 ft. h. Stem slender. *l.* distant, sword-shaped. *fl.* 3 or 4, lead-coloured, tinged yellow in centre, solitary, widely expanded, lasting only a few hours; stigma of short 2-lobed arms. Autumn. S. Brazil, Argentine. 1838. (B.M. 3710 as *Phalocallis plumbea*.)

**CYPERA'CEAE.** Monocotyledons. A family of about 2,600 species of grass-like herbs in 65 genera scattered over the whole globe, usually perennials with creeping rhizomes. The stems are usually solid, 3-sided, and with 3 ranks of leaves; the leaves narrow and sheathing at the base, the sheath being entire, thus easily marked off from the grasses. The flowers are usually without a perianth, enclosed in bracts (glumes), and arranged in a spikelet, these in turn in spikes or panicles. Stamens 3, carpels 3 or 2 with 1-celled ovary containing 1 ovule. The fruit is an achene. The family contains few plants of ornamental or economic value. The genera dealt with are Carex, Cyperus (including Papyrus), Eriophorum, Gahnea, Hypolytrum, Mapania, Mariscus, Scirpus.

*cyperi'nus -a -um, cyperoi'des,* Cyperus-like.

**CYPERORCH'IS.** Included in **Cymbidium.**

**CYPER'US** (ancient Greek name). FAM. *Cyperaceae*. A genus of over 400 species of mostly perennial rush- or grass-like herbs, widely distributed over the world in all climates except the cold. Leaves narrow, grass-like.

Flowers bi-sexual, enclosed in glumes; spikelets linear, compressed, in lateral or terminal bracteate heads or branched umbels or panicles; glumes many, distichous, almost all flower-bearing; bristles none; stamens 1 to 3; stigmas 2 or 3. Fruit a 3-angled or compressed nut. Some species are valuable as decorative plants, a few for margins of lakes and ponds, others for growing in pots. The latter may generally be grown in small pots in a compost of loam and sand with a little peat. All require plenty of water. Propagation is by division or by seed sown in gentle heat. *See also* **Mariscus,** sometimes included here.

**C. alternifo'lius.*** Perennial. Stems 1 to 2½ ft. h., numerous, erect, dark green, naked, crowned by many long, narrow l. *Spikelets* brown. Madagascar. Greenhouse. A good plant for table or room decoration in a 5-in. pot standing in shallow saucers of water. var. **grac'ilis,** about 18 in. h. with wiry, slender stems and narrower l. than type. 1893; **variega'tus,** *l.* and stems mottled and striped white, sometimes wholly white.

**C. antiquor'um.** A synonym of *C. Papyrus.*

**C. arista'tus.** Annual, about 6 in. h., slender. Mexico. 1893. Greenhouse.

**C. compres'sus.** Tufted, glabrous, green. Stems 4 to 16 in. long. *l.* linear, about as long as stem, $\frac{1}{8}$ to $\frac{1}{6}$ in. wide. *Spikelets* with densely over-lapping glumes, in short spikes of 3 to 10. Tropics, except Australia. 1870. Stove. var. **pectiniform'is,** stems 2 in. long or less.

**C. conges'tus,** Perennial. Tufted. Stems about 12 in. h. with few l. except at top. *l.* linear; l. of infl. long-linear, up to 9 in. long, much longer than infl. *Spikelets* brown, about 10, ½ in. long, stalked, in a rather close head. S. Africa, Australia, Mediterranean. SYN. *Mariscus congestus.* Nearly hardy.

**C. diffu'sus.*** Perennial, fibrous rooted. Stem solitary up to 3 ft. h. Basal l. many, as long as stem, $\frac{1}{4}$ to ½ in. wide; l. of infl. 4 to 15 in. long, longer than infl. *Spikelets* greenish-yellow to pale brown, ¼ to over ½ in. long, in a loose umbel; glumes striate, cuspidate. Tropics. 1874. Useful for table decoration. Needs a damp greenhouse. var. **variega'tus,** *l.* variegated white. SYN. *C. laxus* of gardens.

**C. erythrorhiz'os.** Annual 6 in. to 4 ft. h. Stem bluntly angled. *l.* linear, rough on margins, pale beneath. *Umbel* 3- to 12-rayed, sometimes compound, rays shorter than 3- to 10-lvd. involucre. *Spikelets* very many, 12- to 15-fld. narrow-linear, spreading, yellowish. July to September. N. America.

**C. esculen'tus.** Chufa. Stoloniferous perennial with long, lateral, very slender, tuber-bearing runners. *l.* and bracts long. *Spikelets* yellow or yellowish-brown, glumes plicate. S. Europe, India, &c. Half-hardy. Grown abroad for its edible, nut-flavoured tubers.

**C. flabellifor'mis.** Stoloniferous perennial with a stout rhizome. Stem stout, 2 to 4 ft. h. *l.* at top of stem, numerous, strongly plicate, up to 16 in. long. *Spikelets* very numerous, flat, shining, about ½ in. long; glumes firm, keeled, pale brown down middle, dark towards sides. Africa. Greenhouse.

**C. grac'ilis.** A variety of *C. alternifolius.*

**C. Has'pan.** Stems 12 to 18 in. long, 3-angled. *l.* linear, shorter than stem, often only sheaths. *Umbel* many-rayed, much divided, spreading, its filiform rays much longer than the 2-leaved involucre. *Spikelets* 3 to 5 in a cluster, about $\frac{1}{8}$ in. long, linear, 20- to 40-fld., light reddish-brown. July to September. Cosmop. Trop.

**C. lax'us.** A synonym of *C. diffusus.*

**C. long'us.*** Galingale. Stem solitary, erect, 3-angled, stiff, 2 to 4 ft. h. *l.* 2 or 3 in lower part of stem, grooved above or sharply keeled beneath, rough at edges, bright shining green above, paler beneath, sheaths reddish-brown at base. *Spikelets* linear, narrowed to each end in a loose umbellate panicle; glumes 3- to 5-nerved, erect, chestnut-red with green midrib. Europe, including England, N. America. (E.B. 1578.) Hardy perennial for margins of lakes, &c.

**C. natalen'sis.** A synonym of *Mariscus umbilensis.*

**C. Nuttal'lii.** Yellowish or glossy, up to about 15 in. h. Stem 3-angled, clustered. *l.* narrow-linear. *Umbel* sessile or of 3 to 6 rays. *Spikelets* many, spreading, linear-lanceolate, 12- to 20-fld., light brown. July to September. N. America.

**C. Papy'rus.** Papyrus. Egyptian Paper Reed. Perennial, stout. Stems about 10 ft. h., dark green, 3-angled, not jointed. *l.* in an umbel at top of stem, drooping. Egypt. 1803. SYN. *Papyrus antiquorum.* May be grown for sub-tropical bedding in shallow water in a warm position, otherwise stove treatment is necessary. The pith-like tissues of the larger flowering stems cut into strips, which, laid so that the edges overlap slightly and crossed by other strips similarly arranged, will unite under pressure, and were so treated by the ancient Egyptians to constitute the papyrus of antiquity.

**C. paramatten'sis.** A synonym of *C. congestus.*

**C. rotun'dus.** Nut Grass. Perennial with very slender tuber-bearing rhizomes. Stem 4 to 24 in h., bulbous at base, 3-angled. *l.* several, about $\frac{1}{6}$ in. wide, shorter than stem, rough on margins. *Bracts* 2 to 4, about as long as infl. *Spikelets* linear, ½ to 1 in. long, few in cluster, dull; glumes scarcely keeled, midrib green. Tropics and sub-tropics. Grown in warm countries for the edible tubers.

**C. umbilen'sis.** A synonym of *Mariscus umbilensis.*

**C. veg'etus.** Pale green, 2 to 4 ft. h. Stems stout, rough-angled above. *l.* broad, long, net-veined, margins rough. *Umbel* spreading, compound, many-rayed; involucre 4- to 6-lvd., much longer than umbel. *Spikelets* about 20 in cluster, $\frac{1}{6}$ to ½ in. long, pale green. July to September. SE. United States, Chile, &c.

**CYPHOKEN'TIA** (*kyphos*, tumour, *Kentia*; Kentia-like but having a lump on the side of the fruit). FAM. *Palmaceae.* A genus of 2 species of robust spineless Palms with terminal crowns of pinnately cut leaves, natives of New Caledonia. Leaves with long sword-shaped segments narrowed at the tip, margins at base recurved. Flowers arranged as in Cyphophoenix; spathe-valves 2, deciduous, with stout branching spadices. Fruit small, globose or elliptic. For cultivation, *see* **Areca.** A

**C. macrostach'ya.** *Spadix* with long, flexuose branches. *fr.* globose; stigma lateral; seeds sub-globose.

**C. robus'ta.** *Spadix* branches thick, cylindrical. *fr.* kidney-shaped; stigma not prominent above base; seeds reniform. 1878.

**CYPHOMAN'DRA** (*kyphos*, tumour, *aner*, man; the anthers form a hump). FAM. *Solanaceae.* A genus of about 30 species of spineless shrubs or trees, natives of S. America. Leaves entire, 3-lobed or deeply pinnately cut. Flowers in racemes, pedicellate; corolla deeply 5-lobed. Fruit an oblong or globose, usually large berry, many-seeded. *C. betacea* is sometimes grown as a curiosity for its edible fruit which has much the flavour of a Tomato. It needs a warm house and fruits in the second year from seed with compost, &c., as for the Tomato. It is particularly liable to attack by red spider-mite.

**C. beta'cea.** Tree Tomato. Erect, branching, up to 12 or 14 ft., shrubby. *l.* rather fleshy, cordate-ovate, entire, softly hairy. *fl.* purple in bud, then greenish-pink with a dark stripe on back of each seg., fragrant, in long pendulous racemes or clustered. *fr.* egg-shaped, reddish when ripe, 2-celled, about 2 in. long. S. Brazil. 1836. (B.M. 7682; 3684 as *Solanum fragrans.*)

**CYPHOPHOE'NIX** (*kyphos*, tumour, *Phoenix*; Phoenix-like Palms). FAM. *Palmaceae.* A genus of 2 species of stout, unarmed Palms with terminal crowns of pinnately cut leaves, natives of New Caledonia. Segments of leaves long sword-shaped, narrowed to tip, with thickened margins. Flowers monoecious on the same spadix, spirally arranged in threes, a female between 2 males; stamens 6; spadix stout, paniculately branched, branches long. Fruit of medium size, brown, long-ovoid or ellipsoid. Cultivation as for Areca. A

**C. el'egans.** *lflets.* alternate, rather distant, 3-nerved, scaly on midrib beneath, rachis convex beneath, keeled above. *Spadix* more or less spreading, or reflexed in age, branching simple. *fr.* oblong-elliptic, acute. SYN. *Kentia elegans.*

**C. fulci'ta.** Much as in *C. elegans* but stem covered with aerial roots at base. *fr.* ovoid, narrowed above. SYN. *Kentia fulcita.*

**CYPHOSPER'MA** (*kyphos*, tumour, *sperma*, seed; seed humped). FAM. *Palmaceae.* A genus of 2 species of spineless Palms with ringed stems, natives of New Caledonia. Leaves in a terminal crown, deeply pinnately cut; segments narrow sword-shaped, praemorsely toothed, margins thickened and recurved at base. Spadix branches many, somewhat distichous; bracts short. Flowers brownish, otherwise much as in Cyphophoenix. Fruit brown, small, globose, or cubic-ovoid. For cultivation *see* **Areca.** A

**C. Viellar'dii.** Stem of medium height. *l.* segs. leathery. SYN. *Kentia robusta, K. Viellardii.*

**CYPRESS.** *See* **Cupressus, Chamaecyparis.**

**CYPRESS, AFRICAN.** *See* **Widdringtonia.**

**CYPRESS APHIS.** *See* **Cupressus, Pests.**

**CYPRESS, DECIDUOUS.** *See* **Taxodium distichum.**

**CYPRESS, SWAMP.** *See* **Taxodium distichum.**

*Cypria'ni,* in honour of Pére Cypriani who collected plants in Hupeh, China, *c.* 1906.

*cyprifo'lius -a -um,* with a leaf like a Cyperus.

**CYPRIPE'DIUM** (*Kypris,* Venus, *pedilon,* slipper). Lady's Slipper. FAM. *Orchidaceae.* A genus of 90 to 100 species mostly natives of the N. Hemisphere, and one of the most interesting and important genera of the Orchid family, from both a botanical and a horticultural point of view. A characteristic of the vast majority of orchids is the possession of only one perfect stamen, the two lateral ones being abortive. To this rule Cypripedium forms an an exception, possessing as it does, two fertile lateral stamens, the central one (which is fertile in other orchids) being represented by a singular shield-like plate. The 3 stigmas, fused together, are easily seen. As a third stigma is present, the rostellum, a modification of this stigma, present in most orchids, is absent in the whole group. The large inflated pouch which is formed by the labellum suggested both English and Latin names. This pouch plays a considerable part in securing the fertilization of the flower.

Sir John Lubbock, speaking of *C. longifolium,* says: 'The opening into the slipper is small, and partly closed by the stigma and the shield-like body which lies between the two anthers. The result is that the opening into the slipper has a horseshoe-like form, and that bees or other insects which have once entered the slipper have some difficulty in getting out again. While endeavouring to do so, they can hardly fail to come in contact with the stigma, which lies under the shield-like representation of the middle anther. As the margins of the lip are inflected, the easiest exit is at the two ends of the horseshoes, and by one or other of these the insect generally escapes; in doing which, however, it almost inevitably comes in contact with, and carries off, some of the pollen from the corresponding anther. The pollen of this genus is immersed in a viscid fluid, by means of which it adheres first to the insect, and secondly to the stigma, while in most orchids it is the stigma that is viscid.'

The name Cypripedium has long been applied to a number of plants which in floral structure bear a strong resemblance to one another, particularly in the shape and structure of the labellum. Four different groups have been included under the name and at the International Horticultural Conference at Paris in 1932 it was decided for garden purposes to retain all the species under the one name Cypripedium. The characteristics of these groups are set out in what follows, and after each name in the descriptive list a number is given in brackets indicating the group to which the species belongs so that anyone may ascertain the alternative generic name.

*Group* 1. CYPRIPEDIUM in the restricted sense includes the hardy species with plicate leaves, persistent perianth, valvate sepals, 1-celled ovary with parietal placenta and fusiform seeds. The foliage is usually deciduous and often hairy. The species are widely distributed in Europe, temperate Asia and N. America, and Mexico. Though often growing in regions where severe frost is experienced, our inconsistent winters render them rather capricious except in favoured localities or positions made for them. The protection of snow given to so many in their own homes is absent here and the greater number of the mountain forms are better if grown in a cool frame or house, the roots being protected from frost. Out-doors a north-west or northerly aspect is often suitable as growth is then delayed in the spring till danger of frost is past. A mixture of rough loam, peat and a little leaf-mould, with the addition of sand and finely crushed crocks suits a number, others from limestone formations should have nodules of old mortar added. Protection should be given the rhizomes in the winter. Their scattered distribution and the close resemblance of many has caused confusion in their nomenclature. In this group the lip is often more globose than slipper-like. The N. American species, many of which extend to Asia, have been classified by Professor Oakes Ames as follows: under *C. acaule* are placed *C. humile, C. hirsutum.* Under *C. fasciculatum, C. pusillum, C. fasciculatum pusillum, C. Knightae.* Under *C. guttatum, C. Yatabeanum.* Under *C. parviflorum, C. luteum, C. bifidum, C. hirsutum parviflorum, C. bulbosum parviflorum.* Under *C. montanum, C. occidentale.* Under *C. parviflorum pubescens* are placed *C. Calceolus, C. flavescens, C. pubescens, C. parviflorum, C. hirsutum, C. veganum, C. bulbosum, C. bulbosum flavescens, C. pubescens Makasin, C. Calceolus hirsutus, C. Makasin.* Under *C. reginae, C. album, C. spectabile, C. canadense, C. hirsutum, C. reginae album, C. hirsutum album.*

*Group* 2. PAPHIOPEDILUM (the name applied by some to the species of the most popular section grown in our glasshouses), is distinguished from the Cypripedium group by their foliage which is conduplicate, leathery, and in several species mottled, and which persists longer than one season. The ovary is 1-celled, the seeds are fusiform and placed as in Cypripedium but the dorsal sepal is folded within the lateral ones in the bud, though when developed it is usually very much larger. Paphiopedilums are entirely old world ranging from Ceylon to Hong Kong, through Malaya, India, Borneo, New Guinea, Java, the Philippines. They have been extensively used by the hybridist; so numerous are the crosses that it is impossible to enumerate them in this work. Both species and hybrids are most useful as cut flowers. All the species have been used to produce hybrids, particularly *C. insigne, C. villosum, C. Boxallii, C. bellatulum, C. Fairieanum, C. callosum, C. Lawrenceanum,* and *C. Rothschildianum.* The hybrids themselves have been crossed with other hybrids and species and fresh crosses are still being effected. With such a wide distribution, temperatures must naturally vary. *C. insigne* is capable of withstanding a comparatively low temperature but better results are obtained if 55° F. is regarded as an approximate night temperature in winter, artificial heat being dispensed with in May till the end of September. A number of species *C. Spicerianum, C. villosum, C. Charlesworthii, C. Parishii,* &c., can be grown with it. *C. insigne* and many other green-leaved species should have a compost of 3 parts of loam fibre, 1 part of Sphagnum moss, and 1 part of Osmunda fibre well mixed with finely broken crocks. The species with mottled or tessellated foliage should have double the quantity of Osmunda fibre and Sphagnum and the loam, particularly with small plants, may be omitted. This compost is suitable for *C. Lowii, C. Haynaldianum* and the green-leaved species from New Guinea, Borneo, Malaya, and the Philippines, adding some loam fibre for large plants. The winter temperature broadly speaking for all the mottled-foliaged species and their hybrids and species from the countries just mentioned should be 65° F. at night; occasional slight falls seldom harm. Water must be given throughout the year, less frequently in winter than in summer, as root activity is more or less continuous. Throughout the summer months syringing is helpful but especially in winter water should not remain in the growths or in the bracts behind the flower buds during the night. Thrips will attack the foliage as will red spider-mite, and must be removed by sponging or fumigation. Shading is necessary throughout bright weather. Propagation may be effected by dividing large plants at the potting season—early spring. It is inadvisable to divide small plants with only 3 or 4 growths unless stock is specially required as, though such divisions grow readily, single-flowered plants are not as attractive as plants with several flowers. Usually hybrids derived from a warm-growing and a cooler-growing species are the better, especially while young, for the temperature suitable to the more tropical parent.

Group 3. PHRAGMIPEDILUM is the name applied by some to all the species familiarly known under cultivation as Selenipediums. All are natives of the New World and are characterized by conduplicate leaves, persisting for a considerable time, usually strap-shaped, tapered, narrower, and of a lighter green than those of Paphiopedilum. All the species produce several flowers more or less in succession on the spikes. The perianth is deciduous, the seeds fusiform, the ovary 3-celled and the sepals valvate. The species extend from Brazil to Peru. Their cultivation is the same as given to Paphiopedilums, a compost as for green-leaved Paphiopedilums, but the majority are suited in an intermediate house with a winter temperature falling not lower than 55° F. at night, for C. caricinum and C. Schlimii slightly below. Numerous hybrids in this section are recorded, usually as Selenipediums. Both hybrids and species resent, perhaps more than Paphiopedilums, drops in temperature when the foliage is wet and show the effect in brown patches on the leaves or decay of the young growths.

Group 4. SELENIPEDIUM. Species sometimes referred to Selenipedium are not in cultivation. Only 3 species are known, S. Chica, S. Isabelianum, and S. palmifolium; all are tall reed-like plants with terminal racemes of small flowers, the perianth of which is persistent, the sepals valvate, the seeds crustaceous and subglobose and the ovary 3-celled with axile placentas. Natives of Guiana, Brazil, and Cent. America.

No species of Cypripedium forms pseudobulbs, and with one or two exceptions in Paphiopedilum, they are terrestrial.

In the Paphiopedilum section, particularly in the later hybrids, the dorsal sepal is much larger than in the other sections. In all species with one exception in Group 1, the two lower sepals are reduced in size and connate, forming apparently but one segment. Individuals among Paphiopedilum hybrids sometimes revert and clearly show the 6 segments common to Orchid flowers. Both in Paphiopedilum and Phragmipedilum a few species have long attenuated petals.

C. acau'le* (1). *fl.* solitary, large; sep. and pet. greenish, shorter than the drooping lip, which is warm rose, blotched purple. May and June. *l.* twin, broad, light green, sparingly clothed with short soft downy hairs; from their centre arises the short scape. N. United States. 1786. (B.M. 192.) SYN. *C. humile.* A white-fld. variety occurs.

C. al'bum. A synonym of *C. reginae.*

C. ama'bile (2). *fl.* resembling those of *C. Bullenianum*; sep. greenish; pet. yellowish-green, brownish at base with small dark warts on upper margins; lip greenish, flushed with brown-red with darker dots. Borneo. 1894. Stove.

C. Appletonia'num (2). *fl.* dorsal sep. narrow, dark greenish, upper margins slightly involute; pet. narrow, spreading, flushed with magenta-purple on outer halves; lip slightly elongated, greenish-yellow, shaded purple; scapes slender, 12 to 18 in. h. *l.* much as in *C. callosum.* Siam. 1893. SYN. *C. Bullenianum Appletonianum.* Stove.

C. Ar'gus* (2). *fl.* white, rose, green, blackish-purple, and purple-brown; pet. ciliate and black-warted. March and April. *l.* handsomely tessellated with grey. 1 ft. h. Philippines. 1873. (B.M. 6175.) Stove. var. Moen'sii, segs. broader and spots on pet. larger than in type; superb'um, *fl.* larger and brighter.

C. arieti'num* (1). Ram's-head. *fl.* solitary; sep. and pet. greenish-brown; lip red and whitish-veined; lateral sep. free. May. Stems leafy, stiff, hairy, 7 to 10 in. h. N. United States, Canada. 1808. (B.M. 1569; L.B.C. 1240; S.B.F.G. 213.) A neat little hardy species.

C. barba'tum* (2). *fl.* solitary; dorsal sep. whitish, striped and flushed purple; pet. similar in colour, with several tufts of black hairs produced from purple, shining warts bordering upper edge of pet.; lip large, blackish-purple. Spring, summer. *l.* distichous, oblong, light green, curiously blotched and spotted with irregular very dark green markings. 1 ft. h. Malacca. 1838. (B.M. 4234.) Stove. var. biflo'rum, constantly 2-fld.; Cross'ii, *fl.* colour brighter, the purple stripes on dorsal sep. broader and brighter; Hook'erae a synonym of *C. Hookerae*; ni'grum, largest form, much darker than type; pulcher'rimum, *fl.* lighter with well-defined markings; super'bum, *fl.* handsome, lip very dark, dorsal

sep. purer white near tip, *l.* brightly variegated; War'neri, dorsal sep. large, white, striped near base, with a transverse band of wine-purple; pet. striped green above, white near base, rest purple, tip white, lip deep brownish-purple. March to May. India. (W.O.A. 3, 11.)

C. Bar'beyae. A synonym of *C. × ventricosum.*

C. bellat'ulum* (2). *fl.* white or whitish-yellow, beautifully spotted all over with purple-maroon, as much as 11 in. in circumference; staminode very long, oblong, 3-dentate at tip; lip ovate, sparsely spotted. *l.* 10 in. long, 3 in. wide, fleshy, closely set, tessellated. Burma. 1888. (L. 149.) This species may be regarded as the most popular of a section, the labellums of which are somewhat egg-shaped, the foliage leathery and set closely. All require careful watering in the winter. The species included are *C. bellatulum, C. Godefroyae, C. concolor, C. niveum,* and *C. Delenatii. C. Godefroyae, C. concolor,* and *C. niveum* should have a greater proportion of loam in their compost, with nodules of old mortar. var. al'bum, *fl.* pure white, foliage lighter green. Burma. 1895.

C. Boissieria'num* (3). *fl.* yellow, veined and reticulated with bright green, marked brownish-crimson on edges of sep. and in other places; sep. and pet. often margined white, 4 to 5 in. long, horizontally extended, edges erose; lip brownish. Peru. 1887. (G.C. 1 (1887), 143; R.X.O. 62). SYN. *C. Bungerothii. C. reticulatum* is a variety of it. (L. 10.) Intermediate house.

C. borea'le. A synonym of *C. Calceolus.*

C. Boxal'lii* (2). *fl.* upper sep. a beautiful fresh light green, with a white border, covered with brownish-black blotches; inferior sep. oblong-acute, shorter than lip, light green, with lines of very small reddish-brown spots; pet. broadly cuneate at base, dilated at apex, blunt, light green, with a dark, rather broad line from base to near apex with red-brown markings; lip forming a blunt conical pouch, greenish-yellow, with a dense row of cinnamon spots under mouth. *l.* green. *Peduncle* villose. India. 1877. (I.H. 345.) Often regarded as a variety of *C. villosum.* var. atra'tum, dorsal sep. green, heavily blotched with blackish-brown; lip and lateral pet. reddish-purple, irregularly mixed with light green, upper margin white. 1887. (R. 2, 8.) Winter temperature 55° F.

C. Bullenia'num (2). *fl.* somewhat smaller than in *C. Hookerae* (to which this species is allied); upper sep. with some blackish streaks at base; pet. narrow with 3 or 4 small, blackish warts on each margin, with the dilated tips violet-rose; lip green, shaded brown-purple. N. Borneo. 1862. (O.R. 1906, 17.)

C. Burbid'gei. A synonym of *C. × Petri.*

C. Calceo'lus* (1). *fl.* usually 2 or 3; sep. and pet. narrow, spreading, reddish-brown or maroon; labellum pale yellow. Summer. *l.* glabrous, dark green. 12 to 18 in. h. N. Asia and Europe (England). (E.B. 1490; L.B.C. 363.) Hardy.

C. califor'nicum (1). *fl.* 1 to 1¼ in. across; sep. pale brownish-yellow; pet. dull yellow; lip ¾ in. long, white, with a little pink, and obscurely spotted brown, obovoid-globose, hairy at base within. May. *l.* 3 to 4 in. long, acute. Stem 1 to 2 ft. h., leafy; 3- to 7-fld. California. 1888. (B.M. 7188.) Half-hardy.

C. callo'sum* (2). *fl.* 1 or 2, very large, remaining some weeks in perfection; dorsal sep. pure white, striped with dark chocolate-crimson, 2½ in. across; pet. greenish, deepening to purple, warted and ciliate, apices slightly up-curved; lip brown-purple. Winter to summer. *l.* oval-oblong, acute, 6 to 9 in. long, with blackish-green markings. Cochin China. 1885. (L. 73; R.H. 1888, 252.) Stove. In growth this plant resembles a strong *C. barbatum.* var. pulcher'rimum, *fl.* brighter and larger, dorsal sep. very broad; San'derae, *fl.* pale, dorsal sep. snow-white, with lines of emerald-green, remainder greenish-white. 1894; sublae've, a synonym of *C. × siamense.*

C. canaden'se. A synonym of *C. reginae.*

C. can'didum* (1). *fl.* solitary; sep. and pet. greenish-brown; lip white, sometimes veined. Early summer. 12 in. h. N America. 1826. Neat and pretty. (B.M. 5855.) Hardy.

C. carici'num* (3). *fl.* pale green, dorsal sep. with a whitish margin; pet. narrow, deflexed and twisted, 3 to 5 in. long, ends blotched with brown; lip black-dotted on inner margin, oblong; staminode bordered with black hairs; spike rising clear of *l.* 4- to 7-fld. *l.* stiff, narrow-channelled. 1 ft. h. or more. Peru. Plant like a sedge. (B.M. 5466.) SYN. *Selenipedium Pearcei.*

C. cauda'tum* (3). *fl.* dorsal sep. 5 to 6 in. long, tapered, creamy-white, tinged and veined green; pet. tail-like, often reaching 2½ ft. long, yellowish-green at base passing into reddish-brown; lip reddish-brown, the basal portion yellow, spotted with reddish-brown; scapes 1 to 1½ ft. h., 1- to 4-fld. April and May. *l.* ensiform, distichous, light green. Chiriqui, Peru. 1851. Very remarkable and variable. var. gigan'teum, sep. and pet. creamy-white with bright green veining, purplish on pet., pouch tinged brown. Peru. (L. 96.); Lin'deni, a remarkable variety in which the pouch usually has the form of a third ribbon-like pet., segs. mainly greenish-white but sometimes shading to yellow and brown. New Granada. 1850. SYN. *Uropedium Lindeni.* (B.H. 4, 31, 32; R.X.O. 15.); Luxembourg, sep. butter-yellow, veined green, pet. purplish, pouch greenish; ro'seum, *fl.* dark rose, mixed with yellow and green (I.H. 1886, 596.); Wal'lisii, *fl.* nearly white, slightly flushed and spotted rose; Warscewicz'ii, *fl.* brighter, pet. flushed with rose-purple, *l.* shorter and darker. Intermediate house.

**C. Chamberlainia'num** (2). *fl.* dorsal sep. small, greenish with suffused brown stripes, pubescent at back, margin undulate; pet. narrow, spreading, twisted at tip, very wavy, ciliate, spotted brown; lip much dotted pink on white; scapes 2 ft. h. producing fls. in succession. *l.* green, strap-shaped. New Guinea. 1892. (Gn. 43 (1893), 304.) Stove.

**C. Chantin'ii.** A synonym of *C. insigne Chantinii.*

**C. Charlesworth'ii*** (2). *fl.* dorsal sep. white, suffused with rosy-purple, 2 to 3 in. wide, lower greenish-white, 1 in. wide; pet. yellowish, tinged brown, 1½ in. long; pouch similarly coloured, somewhat like that of *C. insigne.* Late summer. Burma. 1893. Habit as *C. Spicerianum.* (L. 443; B.M. 7416; Gn. 47 (1895), 252; W.O.A. 508.) Winter temp. 55° F. **C. Fred Hardy** is probably an albino form of this.

**C. ciliola're** (2). *fl.* Much resembles *C. superbiens;* sep. and pet. having more numerous nerves and more hairy margins; pet. heavily warted black; lip dull purple; staminode low and broad; scapes 1 to 1¼ ft. h. Spring. *l.* narrow- or elliptic-oblong, 6 in. or more long, tessellated. Malaya, Philippines. 1882. (I.H. 1884, t. 530.) Stove.

**C. con'color** (2). *fl.* 1 or 2, yellowish, finely speckled with crimson. June. *l.* marbled with grey above, purplish beneath. Moulmein. 1865. (B.M. 5513.) var. **chlorophyl'lum** has *l.* free from marbling. 1886; **niv'eum**, a synonym of *C. niveum;* **Regnie'ri**, *fl.* 3 to 5, yellow with purple blotch on outside of sep., staminode ochre dotted purple with a white front margin. *l.* marbled. 1886; **San'derae**, *fl.* larger, more profusely spotted, scapes usually 3-fld.; **sulphuri'num**, *fl.* light sulphur with 2 dark yellow blotches. 1888; **tonquinen'se**, *fl.* larger than type. Tonkin. 1887. (L. 77.) SYN. *C. tonquinense.*

**C. cordig'erum** (1). sep. and pet. white, pale yellow or green; lip white with a few interior purple spots. Allied to *C. Calceolus.* Himalaya, Kashmir, Nepal, &c. 1825. (A.B.G.C. 9, 151; B.M. 9364.)

**C. × Craw'shawiae** (2). *fl.* large, dorsal sep. pure white, with a pale greenish spot at base; pet. lip, and lower sep. pale greenish-yellow. Summer. *l.* fleshy, bright green above, greyish beneath. Shan States. 1898. Allied to *C. Charlesworthii.* Possibly a natural hybrid.

**C. Cross'ii.** A variety of *C. barbatum.*

**C. Curtis'ii*** (2). Much like *C. ciliolare;* pet. narrower, with shorter cilia and smaller spots most numerous at tops of pet.; lip large, dull purplish-brown, with acute side angles. May, June. *l.* oblong or oval-oblong, 6 to 8 in. long, tessellated with deep and pale green. Sumatra. 1882. (L. 140; W.O.A. 122.) Stove. var. **San'derae**, the albino form, *fl.* white with green stripes on dorsal sep., pet., and the green-flushed lip. Sumatra. 1912. Stove.

**C. Czerwiakowia'num** (3). *fl.* yellow-green, lower sep. twice as long as lip. Ecuador. Possibly not in cultivation.

**C. Dallea'num** (3). *fl.* large; upper sep. 2½ in. long, red; pet. 5 in. long; lip deep glossy carmine-red, spotted within, oblong, smooth. *l.* lorate, acute, 1½ to 2 ft. long. Stems cylindrical, pubescent, 20 in. h. Habitat? 1895. (R.H. 1895, 548.)

**C. Daya'num** (2). *fl.* large; sep. whitish, veined green; pet. brownish, shading to dull rose, ciliate; lip purplish-brown. May, June. *l.* with very bright distinct variegation. Borneo. 1860. (F.d.S. 1527.) Stove.

**C. deb'ile** (1). *fl.* small, drooping; sep. and pet. light green; lip white, veined purple round the orifice. *l.* 2, cordate. Japan. (B.M. 8183.)

**C. Delena'tii*** (2). *fl.* 1 to 2, dorsal sep. rather small with the very broad pet. satiny-white, rose-flushed; lip large, somewhat globular, beautifully deep rose-flushed on a white ground; scapes 9 to 12 in. h. *l.* grey-tessellated, neat. Tonkin. About 1930. (O.R. 1933, 67.) **A**

**C. Dru'ryi*** (2). *fl.* sep. greenish-yellow, covered outside with numerous dark hairs, middle line broad, black; pet. narrow, bent a little downwards, each with a broad black line over middle; lip ochraceous, with numerous brown spots within. Spring and early summer. 6 in. h. India. 1877. General habit of *C. insigne,* but *l.* more acute and usually shorter, and *fl.* very different. (L. 6; I.H. 1877, 265.)

**C. Elliottia'num.** A synonym of *C. Rothschildianum.*

**C. ex'ul** (2). *fl.* dorsal sep. yellowish-white, greenish-yellow at base, irregularly spotted purple; pet. yellowish with purplish lines; lip as in *C. Druryi.* *l.* 7 to 10 in. long, 1 in. wide. Siam. 1892. (B.M. 7510.) var. **Imschootia'num**, *fl.* larger than in type, dorsal sep. having darker spots. 1892. (L. 327.) Winter temp. 55 to 60° F.

**C. Fairiea'num*** (2). *fl.* solitary, rather small, dorsal sep. large, white, beautifully veined with purple; pet. similar in colour and curiously curved at ends; lip inversely helmet-shaped, dull purple, suffused and lined dull brown and shaded green. August to October. *l.* 3 to 6 in. long, narrow, pale, green. 1 ft. h. Assam. *fl.* produced in great abundance, and last several weeks in full beauty if not sprinkled with water. (B.M. 5024; W.O.A. 70.) Best in a cool house. Winter temp. 55° F. Variable.

**C. fascicula'tum** (1). *fl.* 1 to 1½ in. across; sep. and pet. greenish, lanceolate, acute; lip greenish-yellow, with purplish-brown margin; spike 1- to 4-fld. *l.* twin, ovate or broadly elliptic. NW. America. 1888. (G. & F. 1888, i. 90, f. 16.) More interesting than beautiful. Hardy.

**C. fasciola'tum** (1). *fl.* solitary, large; lip much inflated, like the pet. red with darker striae or stripes along the nerves. W. China. 1894.

**C. flaves'cens.** A synonym of *C. pubescens.*

**C. Franchet'ii** (1). Allied to *C. macranthon,* but stem more villose, *fl.* smaller with a much inflated, almost globular pouch. China, Tibet. 1910. (O.R. 20, 358.)

**C. × Frankea'num** (2). Natural hybrid between *C. Curtisii* and *C. tonsum.* *fl.* greenish with golden to brownish-red shading; pouch large purplish-brown. *l.* more brightly tessellated than in *C. Curtisii.* Sumatra. 1908. Stove.

**C. Fred Hardy.** See *C. Charlesworthii.*

**C. glandulif'erum** of gardens. A synonym of *C. praestans.* True species probably not in cultivation.

**C. glaucophyl'lum** (2). Allied to *C. Chamberlainianum* and like that produces long, many-fld. spikes; dorsal sep. green, shaded with sepia; pouch slightly elongated, dull purplish; pet. hairy and strongly twisted. Winter. *l.* 9 to 12 in. long, 1½ to 2 in. broad, glaucous green, margins undulated. Java. 1900. (L. 811.) Stove. **A**

**C. Godefroy'ae*** (2). Allied to *C. bellatulum,* usually rather smaller in growth and fl. *fl.* resembling those of *C. bellatulum* but with a creamy-yellow ground with numerous blotches, spots, and reticulated markings of red-brown. Summer. *l.* leathery, tessellated, reddish beneath. Tonkin, Siam. 1876. (B.M. 6876; W.O.A. 177.) var. **leucochi'lum**, lip spotless. (L. 431.) Both type and variety are very variable.

**C. grac'ile.** A variety of *C. longifolium.*

**C. Gratrixia'num** (2). *fl.* not unlike those of *C. exul* but larger; dorsal sep. spotted with dark brown almost black, green near the base, apical portion and margins white. *l.* 6 to 9 in. long, broader than those of *C. exul.* Annam. 1904. (W.O.A. 524.) Winter temp. 55° F.

**C. gutta'tum*** (1). *fl.* beautiful snow-white, heavily blotched or marbled deep rosy-purple, rather small. June. *l.* twin, broadly-ovate, downy. 6 to 9 in. h. N. Russia, Siberia, N. America. 1829. Very charming in a shady position in rock-garden and border, in leaf-mould, moss, and sand; must be kept rather dry in winter. (B.M. 7746.)

**C. Hartweg'ii** (3). Very near to *C. longifolium* and often classed as a variety of that species, but distinct by its smooth green scapes, with 4 or 5 fl. bordered rose-pink, apical half of dorsal sep. stained rose. Ecuador. 1842. (R.X.O. 1, 27 as *Selenipedium Hartwegii.* See *C. longifolium Roezlii.* Intermediate house.

**C. Haynaldia'num** (2)*. *fl.* 3 to 6, large, segs. narrow; upper half of upper sep. faintly rose and white, lower greenish, beautifully blotched brown; lower sep. pale green, slightly spotted brown; pet. 3 to 4 in. long, horizontal, greenish, passing to dull purple; lip purple-tinged with a rounded base. Winter. Philippines. 1877. Stove. This species comes very close to *C. Lowii.*

**C. Hincksia'num.** A synonym of *C. longifolium Hincksianum.*

**C. hirsutis'simum** (2). *fl.* often 6 in. across, solitary, on erect hairy scapes; dorsal sep. green, shaded with purple and dotted with brown; pet. with upper basal margins crenulate, their apices dilated, magenta-purple; lip greenish, with a profusion of brown dots. March to May. *l.* pale green, about 10 in. long. 1 ft. h. Assam, India. (B.M. 4990.) Stove.

**C. hirsu'tum.** A synonym of *C. reginae.*

**C. Hook'erae*** (2). *fl.* of medium size, solitary, on very long scapes; sep. and pet. yellowish-brown, points of latter rich rosy-purple; pouch somewhat small, brown-purple, suffused with yellow beneath. Summer. *l.* broad, obtuse, tessellated. Borneo. 1868. (B.M. 5362.) Stove. Variable.

**C. hu'mile.** A synonym of *C. acaule.*

**C. insig'ne*** (2). *fl.* solitary, often 5 in. across; dorsal sep. broad, large, yellowish-green, faintly streaked with lines of reddish-brown, blotched brown, upper part pure white; lip large, tawny-yellow, paler within. Winter, lasting several weeks. *l.* long, strap-shaped, green, leathery. Nepal. 1819. (B.M. 3412; W.O.A. 155, 4; L.B.C. 1321.) Probably the most widely grown and most variable of all the species. Its season of flowering and the duration of the fl. render it of great service to the florist. Its vigorous constitution has been of immense value in the numerous hybrids derived from it. Though it will withstand low temperatures, better results are obtained when the winter night temperature is not allowed to fall below 50° F. Many varieties are known, among them var. **al'bens**, *fl.* yellow and white, almost without brown markings. 1893; **albomargina'tum**, dorsal sep. broadly margined white, spotted brown on green part, pet. tawny-yellow, with darker veins, lip pale brownish, yellow inside. India. (W.O.A. 232.); **au'reum**, colouring normal but with a golden glow. 1882; **biflo'rum**, scape constantly 2-fld.; **Bohnhoffia'num**, upper sep. red-brown near base banded above with yellowish-green passing into white; **Chantin'ii**, violet-purple spots on upper sep. and on the broad white apical margin. (R.H. 1878, 130; W.O.A. 278 as var. *punctatum violaceum.*); **Harefield Hall**, *fl.* exceptional in size, dorsal sep. yellowish, margined with white, boldly spotted with chocolate; **Mau'lei**, *fl.* brighter than type, dorsal sep. spotted dull purple, half snow-white; **monta'num**, a group of forms with richly marked *fl.* and shorter, narrower *l.*; **Moorea'num**, *fl.* 5 in. wide, dorsal sep. greenish-yellow, striped green, broadly margined white, with large purple spots, pet. pale yellowish-green flushed rosy-crimson, blotched at base, lip light bronze, spikes 18 to 20 in. long, *l.* 14 in. long. 1887. (W.O.A. 445.); **Oddity**, a curious form in which the 2 lateral pet. usually appear as labella clasping the true labellum. (O.R. 1895, 361.); **San'derae**, primrose-yellow with broad white area at apex and a few brown dots on dorsal sep.; **Sanderia'num**, *fl.* without the brown dots present in var. *Sanderae.* Other yellow vars. are **Dorothy, Ernestii, Laura Kimball, Luciani, Youngianum, William Millie Dow**.

**C. irapea'num\*** (1). *fl.* about 4 in. across; sep. and pet. uniform rich golden-yellow; lip same colour, stained inside reddish-brown, much inflated; spikes many-fld. June, July. *l.* broad, pale green, sheathing stem at base. 18 in. h. Mexico. 1844. (B.R. 32, 58.)

**C. japon'icum** (1). *fl.* solitary; sep. greenish, covered with red spots; pet. and lip white, stained and tinged crimson. June. *l.* large, twin, fan-like, veins radiating to margins. 6 in. to 1 ft. h. Japan. 1874. (G.C. 3 (1875), 625; B.M. 9520.) Hardy.

**C. javan'icum** (2). *fl.* 3 in. across vertically; sep. and pet. pale green, ciliolate, pet. blackish-dotted, one-third dull purple; lip brownish-green, nearly cylindrical, the infolded lobes spotted purple; scapes 1-, rarely 2-fld. *l.* elliptic-oblong, 6 to 8 in. long, mottled. E. Java. 1840. (F.d.S. 703.) var. **vi'rens**, a synonym of *C. virens*.

**C. kaieteu'rum**. A synonym of *C. Lindleyanum*.

**C. × Kimballia'num\*** (2). Probably a natural hybrid between *C. Rothschildianum* and *C. Dayanum. fl.* large, dorsal sep. yellowish-white lined with purple-brown; pet. 4 in. long, narrow, ciliate, coloured much as dorsal sep.; lip purplish. *l.* tessellated. Borneo.

**C. Klotzschia'num** (3). Habit of *C. caricinum*; dorsal sep. pale green tinted with rose; pet. pale rose, slightly twisted, 3 in. long; pouch pale green; scape 24 in. h., pubescent. Summer. British Guiana. 1840. (B.M. 7178.) Intermediate house.

**C. Knight'iae** (1). Sep. and pet. dark purple; lip greenish-yellow with the infolded margins purple. Wyoming. 1906.

**C. laeviga'tum**. A synonym of *C. philippinense*.

**C. Lawrencea'num\*** (2). *fl.* dorsal sep. very broad and round, 2 in. wide or more, white, with numerous dark purplish, shining stripes; lateral sep. very small, greenish-white, with dark purple spots; pet. narrow, green, dull purplish at tip, ciliate, brightly mottled, warted; lip very large. Summer. *l.* about 1 ft. long. Borneo. 1878. (B.M. 6432; W.O.A. 22.) Stove. Variable. var. **Hyea'num**, the albino of the species; green replaces the purple stripes on the dorsal sep. the remainder of which is white, pet. and pouch pale yellowish-green. Borneo. 1886. (L. 42.)

**C. × Leea'num**. A well-known garden hybrid found wild in Assam.

**C. Lin'deni**. A synonym of *C. caudatum Lindeni*.

**C. Lindleya'num** (3). *fl.* sep. pale green, with reddish-brown veins outside, pubescent, with crisped margins, dorsal sep. blotched at apex; pet. pale green, with brownish-crimson veins, 2½ in. long, falcately linear, margins recurved, ciliate; lip light olive-green, with brownish-crimson veins, densely dotted on side lobes; scape many-fld., pubescent, 36 to 40 in. long. Winter. *l.* bright dark green, 18 to 24 in. long, leathery, 2 to 2½ in. broad. Kaieteur Fall, British Guiana. 1885. SYN. *Selenipedium kaieteurum*. Winter temp. 60° F.

**C. × Littlea'num**. Probably a natural hybrid, intermediate between *C. Dayanum* and *C. Lawrenceanum* both in habit and *fl.* colour. Borneo. 1895. (O.R. 1895, f. 8.)

**C. longifo'lium** (3). *fl.* dorsal sep. yellowish-green, streaked purple, lower large; pet. green, with a red marginal band, bordered white, 4 to 5 in. long; lip green, suffused shining purplish-brown; spike erect, pubescent, 24 to 30 in. long, many-fld. *l.* distichous, long-ligulate, keeled, dark green, tapered, 18 to 24 in. long. Cent. America. 1869. (B.H. 1873, 65; B.M. 5970.) SYN. *C. Reichenbachii.* var. **colora'tum**, *fl.* sep. veined purple, pet. purplish. *l.* broader. 1873. A fine variety; **grac'ile**, smaller than type, with purplish-red pet.; **Hincksia'num**, *fl.* sep. whitish-green, with darker veins, pet. light greenish with deeper middle line and brown border at base, tails brown, lip green with small brown spots near base, long narrow. Darien. 1878. SYN. *C. Hincksianum*; **Roez'lii**, *fl.* very large, dorsal sep. yellowish-green, suffused rosy-purple on borders, lateral flesh-coloured; pet. green with red-purple border and tip, linear-lanceolate, spreading; lip large, greenish-yellow; scape 3 ft. long, *l.* bright green. Colombia. (B.M. 6217; I.H. 1873, 138.) SYN. *C. Roezlii.* Sometimes considered a synonym with *C. Hartwegii*.

**C. Low'ii\*** (2). *fl.* 2 to 6, dorsal sep. downy outside, pale green, yellowish, veined purple, shaded purple towards base; pet. long, basal half greenish, spotted purple, wholly purple towards ends; margins ciliate; lip large, smooth and shining, bluntly oblong, light brown suffused with purple; spike 20 to 30 in. long. Summer. *l.* oblong-ligulate, light green. Borneo. 1847. Curious. Allied to *C. Haynaldianum*. (W.O.A. 428.) Stove epiphyte.

**C. lu'teum** (1). Very near to *C. reginae* but with yellow, slightly smaller *fl.*, pouch red-spotted, much inflated. Tibet, Yunnan. 1869. (O.R. 1913, 80.) *C. luteum* of Rafinesque is *C. pubescens*.

**C. macran'thon\*** (1). *fl.* deep rich purple, solitary, large; sep. and pet. often 2½ in. long; lip much inflated, 1 to 1½ in. wide. May, June. *l.* medium-sized, bright green. 9 to 12 in. h. Tibet, Siberia. 1829. (B.M. 2938.) Hardy.

**C. manchu'ricum**. See **C. × ventricosum**.

**C. margarita'ceum** (1). *fl.* sep. and pet. deep purple, with rows of blackish-purple dots, shortly ciliate; lip dark brown, covered with small tubercles, slightly concave above, with a circular orifice formed by the short auricles overlapping each other; scape 1-fld. *l.* twin, glaucous green, spotted with purplish-brown. Yunnan, China. 1888.

**C. Mastersia'num\*** (2). *fl.* large; dorsal sep. green shading to white, yellow-bordered; pet. and lip copper, pet. ciliate and black-warted. Spring, summer. Malaya. 1879. Stove. (B.M. 7629.)

**C. microsac'cos** (1). sep. and pet. brown-purple; lip yellow, near to *C. Calceolus*, of which it may be a variety with broader *l.* Siberia. 1913.

**C. monta'num\*** (1). *fl.* brownish-purple, with a white lip, striped red inside; column yellow, spotted crimson. Summer. *l.* lanceolate, pubescent. About 1 ft. h. Oregon. 1883. (B.M. 7319.) SYN. *C. occidentale*. A beautiful little hardy Orchid. Variable.

**C. neoguinen'se**. A garden synonym of *C. praestans* and *C. Roths-childianum*.

**C. nig'ritum** (2). *fl.* near those of a dark variety of *C. barbatum*; dorsal sep. oblong, acute, lateral forming a very narrow body; pet. much narrower than dorsal sep. brownish-red with dark warts; lip brown-purple. Summer. *l.* as in *C. virens*. Borneo. 1882.

**C. niv'eum\*** (2). *fl.* 1 or 2, wholly pure soft snowy-white, save for cinnamon specks irregularly scattered over sep. and pet. Summer. *l.* leathery, dark green on upper side, irregularly blotched with lighter markings, under side dull vinous red. 6 in. h. Malaya. 1869. (B.M. 5922.) Stove. Variable.

**C. O'Brienia'num**. A synonym of *C. Appletonianum*.

**C. occidenta'le**. A synonym of *C. montanum*.

**C. papua'num** (2). *fl.* small; dorsal sep. 1 by ¼ in., green, with crimson-magenta veins, ciliolate; pet. oblong narrow, dull crimson, with deeper spots on the basal halves, tinged with greenish-yellow, margins ciliate; pouch dull crimson with greenish-yellow lobes. *l.* 3 to 4 in. long, acute, tessellated, green. New Guinea. 1915. (G.C. 58 (1915), 131.)

**C. pardi'num**. A variety of *C. venustum*.

**C. Parish'ii\*** (2). *fl.* sep. greenish-white; pet. much lengthened, from 4 to 5 in. long, pendulous, twisted, lower half purplish; lip 1½ in. long, purplish or yellowish-green; scape sometimes 2 ft. h.; 3- to 6-fld. Summer. *l.* distichous, leathery, and broad. 2 ft. h. Burma. 1869. (B.M. 5791; W.O.A. 86; L. 670.)

**C. parviflo'rum\*** (1). *fl.* comparatively small, fragrant; sep. and pet. glossy deep brown-purple, latter narrow and spiral; lip bright yellow, marked red, flattish from above. Summer. Stems leafy, 1½ to 2 ft. h. N. America. 1759. (B.M. 3024; L.B.C. 414; S.B.F.G. 80.) Hardy.

**C. Pearc'ei**. A synonym of *C. caricinum*.

**C. Perier'ae** (2). *fl.* white, spotted with pink on the pubescent dorsal sep. and pet. bases; dorsal sep. ovate, 1 in. h.; pet. oblong, 1½ in. long. Summer. *l.* 6 in. long, green, faintly mottled. Near *C. niveum.* May be a natural hybrid with that species as one parent. Laukawi. Stove.

**C. × Pet'ri\*** (2). *fl.* sep. white, with green veins; pet. light brownish, green at base, covered on whole border with long hairs; lip greenish-brown. Borneo. 1880. A natural hybrid between *C. Dayanum* and *C. virens.* SYN. *C. Burbidgei*.

**C. philippinen'se\*** (2). *fl.* sep. striped inside with purple; pet. 6 in. long, very much twisted, beautifully marked with chocolate, purple, and green; lip yellow; scape hairy, 3- or 4-fld. Spring. *l.* strap-shaped, long, thick, shining. Philippines. 1865. A very handsome stove species. (B.M. 5508.) SYN. *C. Roebelenii, C. laevigatum*.

**C. Poyntzia'num**. A synonym of *C. Appletonianum*.

**C. prae'stans\*** (2). *fl.* large; sep. nearly equal, dorsal whitish, striped purple; pet. greenish, suffused rose at base, spotted maroon along margins, linear-ligulate, much undulated at base; lip greenish-yellow, flushed red, shaped like that of *C. Stonei*, having a very long, channelled stalk; peduncle dark-hairy, 5-fld. Papua. 1884. (L. 102.) SYN. *C. neoguineum.* var. **Kimballia'num,\*** a fine variety with more definite markings and colour. (L. 249.) SYN. *C. Kimballianum*. Stove.

**C. pubes'cens\*** (1). *fl.* large; sep. and pet. yellowish-brown, marked with darker lines; lip pale yellow, flattened laterally; pet. narrow, spirally twisted, longer than the large showy lip. May, June. Stems 1½ to 2 ft. h., pubescent. N. America. 1790. Handsome hardy species, the root of which is employed as a nerve stimulant in the United States, and is considered equal to Valerian. The fresh plant sometimes causes the same symptoms of irritant poisoning as *Rhus Toxicodendron.* SYN. *C. flavescens*.

**C. purpura'tum** (2). Dorsal sep. white, shaded green, striped brown-purple; pet. purplish-red, warted, veined purple at base; lip brownish-purple. Dwarf, with tessellated *l.* Hong Kong. 1836. (B.R. 1991; B.M. 4901.) Stove.

**C. regin'ae\*** (1). *fl.* 1 to 3, large, rounder in outline than is usual, the pure white or rose-flushed sep. and pet. broadly ovate, not longer than lip; the large, beautiful, soft rich rose pouch, is very much inflated. June. *l.* bright and light green, soft white-downy. 1½ to 3 ft. h. N. United States. 1731. May be grown successfully either in a pot or the open border, thriving in the shady part of a Rhododendron bed. (L.B.C. 697; B.R. 1666; S.B.F.G. 240.) var. **al'bum,** pure white. 1897.

**C. Reichenbach'ii.** A synonym of *C. longifolium.*

**C. reticula'tum.** A variety of *C. Boissierianum.*

**C. Rob'insonii** (2). Allied to *C. Appletonianum* but smaller. *fl.* much as in that species but pet. dark purplish-red throughout; scape 6 to 9 in. Summer. *l.* 3 to 4 in. almost acute, brightly tessellated. Malaya. (B.M. 9155.) Stove.

**C. Roebelen'ii.** A synonym of *C. philippinense.*

**C. Roez'lii.** A synonym of *C. longifolium Roezlii.*

**C. Rothschildia'num\*** (2). *fl.* 2 to 5 or more, large, dorsal; sep. yellowish, with blackish longitudinal stripes, and white borders, cuneate-oblong, acute; pet. attenuated, horizontal, 5 to 6 in. long, yellowish-green, with dark lines, and dark blotches at base, ciliate; lip cinnamon-brown, mouth bordered ochre, almost leathery; staminode erect from a stout base, and bending down into a narrow, beak-like process. Summer. *l.* 12 to 24 in. long, from 2½ to 3 in. wide, glossy green, very strong. Papua. 1887. (B.M. 7102.) SYN. *C. Elliottianum.* A very fine species. Stove.

**C. Sanderia'num** (2). *fl.* 3 to 5; dorsal sep. large, yellowish-green, nerved purplish-brown; pet. purplish-brown, fading to yellowish, spotted and barred purplish-brown towards base, where are some purple bristles, linear, twisted, 1½ to 2 ft. long; lip greenish-bronze, in shape resembling that of *C. Stonei.* Summer. Malaya. 1886. (R. 3.) SYN. *C. Forstermannii.* A remarkable species. Stove.

**C. Sargentia'num** (3). Closely resembles *C. Lindleyanum* in fl. foliage, and habit; differs chiefly in having a pair of small, white tubercles on inner margin of side lobes of lip. Autumn. Brazil. 1893. (B.M. 7446.) Intermediate house.

**C. Schlim'ii\*** (3). *fl.* 2 in. across; sep. and pet. white, mottled, and striped dark rose; lip white, front of pouch suffused deep rose; stem hairy, longer than l., branching, 8-fld. *l.* ligulate, acute 8 in. long, light green. New Grenada. 1867. (B.M. 5614; R.X.O. i. 44). var. **albiflo'rum,** *fl.* sep. and pet. white, lip white, suffused with rose, more deeply coloured opposite the bright yellow column. Winter. 1875. (I.H. 1874, 183.) Robust, free-growing var. Winter temp. 55° F.

**C. Schomburgkia'num.** A synonym of *C. Klotzschianum.*

**C. × Ship'wayae** (2). Natural hybrid between *C. Dayanum* and *C. Hookerae.* Dorsal sep. green, passing into purple, tinged white; pet. greenish, with purplish spots and shading, ciliate; pouch brownish. Borneo. 1898. Stove.

**C. × siamen'se** (2). A natural hybrid between *C. callosum* and *C. Appletonianum.* *fl.* larger than those in *C. Appletonianum* with very similar colouring and shape but dorsal sep. much broader, faintly lined with purplish stripes. Siam. 1888. Stove.

**C. specio'sum** (1). Resembling *C. macranthon* but with white or pink-flushed fl. veined rose. Japan. (B.M. 8386.)

**C. spectab'ile.** A synonym of *C. reginae.*

**C. Spiceria'num\*** (2). *fl.* upper sep. white, with a central purple line; lateral sep. greenish; pet. pale green marked purple; lip greenish-purple, shining; top of the column white, spotted with violet. *l.* 4 to 9 in. long. Assam. (B.M. 6490; W.O.A. 119; L. 515, 516.) Winter temp. 55° F.

**C. Sto'nei\*** (2). *fl.* 3 to 5, sep. large, broad, china-white, striped and streaked red and purple without and sometimes within; shaded with ochreous yellow; pet. 4 or 5 in. long, narrow, yellow, blotched purple; lip dull, with reddish veins, large, pouch somewhat resembling a Turkish slipper; scape 1 to 2 ft. long. *l.* 1 ft. or more long, obtuse, leathery, dark shining green. Borneo. 1852. Stove. A handsome species. (B.M. 5349; W.O.A. 8; L. 281.) var. **can'didum,** ivory-white, pet. tinged rose, lip tinged lilac. Borneo. 1892. **platytae'nium,** dorsal sep. white, striped purple, pet. whitish outside, spotted and tinted yellow, deep crimson at tips, white blotched red-purple inside, nearly 1 in. wide. Sarawak. (W.S.O. 3, 14; W.O.A. 496.)

**C. sublae've.** A synonym of *C. Appletonianum.*

**C. super'biens\*** (2). *fl.* large; dorsal sep. whitish-green, erect; pet. large, broad, whitish, greenish at base, purplish at tip, spotted and warted, black, ciliolate; pouch very large, prominent, uniform rich brown; scape erect, 1-fld. Spring and summer. *l.* oblong, blunt at apex, beautifully mottled with dark green on yellowish-green, purple spotted beneath. Malacca. 1865. Stove. (W.S.O. 2, 12; W.O.A. 486; L. 261.) SYN. *C. Veitchianum.*

**C. tibet'icum** (1). *fl.* as large as those of *C. macranthon;* pouch more decidedly globose, blackish-purple, greenish at base; dorsal sep. and pet. greenish-white, lined and marked with reddish-purple. Summer. Tibet. 1892. (A.B.G.C. 8, 447; B.M. 8070.)

**C. tonquinen'se.** A variety of *C. concolor.*

**C. ton'sum** (2). *fl.* dorsal sep. whitish, with 21 green nerves, a small brown blotch on each border inside, and a green disk outside,

lower sep. half as long as lip; pet. oblong-ligulate, acute, nearly free from cilia, green, washed sepia, and spotted dark brown; lip greenish upper surface washed sepia. Autumn. *l.* brightly mottled. Sumatra. 1883. Stove.

**C. variega'tum.** A synonym of *C. guttatum.*

**C. vega'num** (1). *fl.* yellow, slightly fragrant. Allied to *C. parviflorum.*

**C. Veitchia'num.** A synonym of *C. superbiens.*

*Cypripedium speciosum*

**C. × ventrico'sum** (1). *fl.* dorsal sep. ovate, acute, 1½ in. long, yellow ground suffused with dark purple; pet. similar in colour; lip globose suffused and veined with dull purple. Natural hybrid (later also raised at home) between *C. macranthon* and *C. Calceolus.* W. Siberia. 1800. (S.B.F.G. s. 2, 1.) var. **al'bum,** *fl.* greenish-white. (B.M. 9117 as *C. manchuricum virescens.*)

**C. venus'tum** (2). *fl.* of medium size, solitary; dorsal sep. greenish-white with purplish stripes; pet. purple-tipped with purplish-hairy warts; lip yellowish with deep greenish veins purple-flushed. Winter. *l.* short, dark bluish-green, mottled and blotched pale green above, pale purple beneath. Nepal. 1816. Cool-house. (B.M. 2129; B.R. 788; L.B.C. 585; A.B.G.C. 8, 445.) var. **Measuresia'num,** *fl.* white and green. 1893. **pardi'num,** segs. white, striped green, and pet. blotched dark chocolate, lip yellowish, marked rose. 1869. The largest var. (G.C. 1 (1887), 382.) SYN. *C. pardinum.*

**C. Victo'riae-Ma'riae** (2). *fl.* 3 in. long; dorsal sep. cream or green-shaded, streaked red; pet. green, with broad purple-red margins and nerves, 2 in. long, narrow, twisted; lip purple-rose, green round mouth, 2 in. long, ¾ in. broad; scape 1½ ft. h. producing many fl. in succession. March. *l.* 1 ft. long, 1½ to 2 in. broad, emarginate. Sumatra. 1897. (L. 559; B.M. 7573 as *Paphiopedilum Victoriae-Mariae.*) Stove.

**C. villo'sum\*** (2). *fl.* solitary, often 5 in. across, glossy over whole surface, orange-red, mixed with light green and dark purple; dorsal sep. narrowly margined white; pet. yellow-brown, upper halves deeper than lower; lip large, protruding, bright light brown. May. *l.* light green, freckled on lower part with dark spots; scape 6 to 12 in. h., strongly villose. India. (I. H. 1857, 126; L. 132; W.S.O. 2, 30.) A fine cool-house species of great service to the hybridist. Several varieties occur, among them, **annamen'se,** *fl.* narrower than in type, dorsal sep. usually broadly white-margined, around a central suffusion of greenish-red-brown, scapes 12 to 14 in. h., strongly villose. Annam. 1904; **au'reum***, *fl.* 6 in. across, dorsal sep. bright yellow in upper part with broad white margin. Moulmein; **Box'allii**, a synonym of *C. Boxallii*; **Gor'tonii**, *fl.* purplish. 1893; **Measuresia'num**, approaches *C. Boxallii* in colour and might be regarded as a variety of that, dorsal sep. purple-black boldly spotted, white-margined, lip creamy-white shaded with rose-purple. 1893. **A**

C. vi'rens (2). *fl.* sep. and pet. deeper and brighter green than in *C. javanicum* (to which this species is closely allied); pet. spreading, reflexed beyond middle; lip deeper brown and glossier. N. Borneo. 1858. (R.X.O. ii. 162.) Syn. *C. javanicum virens.* Stove.

C. vitta'tum (3). *fl.* sep. pale green, dorsal only half as broad as lower, striped red; pet. brownish-red, lined green towards base, linear, arcuate-deflexed, undulate; lip brownish, inside green, spotted reddish-brown, shorter than lower sep., and half as long as pet.; scape 1 to 1½ ft. h., minutely puberulous, few-fld. *l.* 1 to 2 ft. long, linear-ligulate, acute, bright green, margined yellow. Brazil. 1876. (I.H. 1876, 238.) Syn. *C. Binotii.*

C. Volontea'num (2). *fl.* more brilliantly coloured and larger in all parts, *l.* shorter, narrower, and more rigid, otherwise closely resembling *C. Hookerae* of which it is probably a form. Borneo 1890. var. **gigan'teum**, *fl.* twice as large as in type. 1893. (J.H. 27 (1893), 27.)

C. Wal'lisii. A variety of *C. caudatum.*

C. Wardia'num (2). Dorsal sep. whitish, veined with green; pet. greenish, shading to pink, heavily spotted with chocolate, ciliate; lip greenish, shading to purple; segs. rather narrow. *l.* mottled, purple below. Superficially resembles *C. venustum.* Upper Burma. 1922. (B.M. 9481 as *Paphiopedilum Wardii.*) The specific name *Wardii* cannot be used when this plant is included in Cypripedium, it is already applied to a Cypripedium allied to *C. guttatum.* Stove.

C. Warneria'num. A variety of *C. barbatum.*

C. Warscewic'zii. A variety of *C. caudatum.*

C. Wil'sonii (1). Allied to *C. fasciolatum.* *fl.* larger; sep. and pet. striped with yellow and chocolate; lip globose, spotted with chocolate on a light yellow ground. China. 1906.

C. Yatabea'num (1). sep. and pet. yellow-green with a clavate-spatulate tip to the pet.; lip purplish. Allied to *C. guttatum.* Japan. 1899.

**A→**

E. C.

cy'ri, of Cyrum, African desert, near River Kara.

**CYRIL'LA** (in honour of Dominico Cyrillo, M.D., 1734–99, professor of botany at Naples). Fam. *Cyrillaceae.* A genus, of 1 species, a deciduous or evergreen shrub native of the southern part of N. America, W. Indies, and Brazil, with short-stalked smooth leaves and flowers in axillary racemes, each with 5 stamens shorter than the petals. Only the deciduous form is hardy in S. England. It grows well in sandy-peat or peaty-loam, and

*Cyrilla racemiflora*

as it flowers profusely in July or August is a valuable shrub then. In favourable circumstances the leaves colour well to orange and scarlet in late autumn. Cuttings root readily, placed in sand, under glass, with a small amount of bottom heat.

C. racemiflo'ra. Shrub of 4 to 6 ft. (deciduous from its northern limits and hardy, but evergreen, tree-like, and tender from the southern areas). *l.* oblanceolate, or obovate, 1½ to 4 in. long, shining green. *fl.* white, small, crowded on slender racemes 3 to 6 in. long, grouped at base of current year's growth. June to August. *fr.* a capsule. Eastern N. America to W. Indies. 1765. (B.M. 2456.)

**CYRILLA'CEAE.** Dicotyledons. A family of 3 genera in America with 8 species of shrubs or small trees with alternate, entire leaves without stipules. Flowers small, regular, in racemes, sepals and petals 5, imbricate; stamens 5 or 10, hypogynous; ovary superior, 2- to 4-celled. The genera included here are Cliftonia and Cyrilla.

**CYRTAN'DRA** (*kyrtos*, curved, *andros*, male; the two perfect stamens have curved filaments). Fam. *Gesneriaceae.* A genus of about 200 species of trees, shrubs, or sub-shrubs, natives of Malaya and the Pacific Is. Leaves in opposite, frequently unequal pairs, one sometimes absent. Flowers often whitish or yellowish, clustered or in heads or cymes in leaf-axils; calyx of 5-segments, sometimes free; corolla somewhat 2-lipped; perfect stamens 2; staminodes 2 or 3, small. Cultivation of following, which are of little horticultural value, as for Agalmyla.

C. pen'dula. Stem short, stout. *l.* elliptic or elliptic-lanceolate, acute, blotched grey above, stalks long. *fl.* sessile, on 3 to 5 removed peduncles about 6 in. long; cal. brownish, nearly 1 in. long; cor. pinkish-white, about 1½ in. long. Java. 1883.

C. Pritchard'ii. *l.* elliptic, 5 to 6 in. long, bluntly toothed, acute. *fl.* 3, on stalked axillary cymes, small, white. Fiji. 1887.

**CYRTAN'THERA.** *See* Jacobinia.

**CYRTAN'THUS** (*kyrtos*, curved, *anthos*, a flower; the flowers bend down from the summit of the scape). Fam. *Amaryllidaceae.* Including Gastronema and Monella. A genus of over 40 species of bulbs, natives of S. and E. Africa, mainly in the eastern part of S. Africa. Related to Crinum and distinct by its perianth tube being longer than the 6 lobes and its usually hollow scape. Flowers umbellate, usually more or less nodding. Three outer perianth lobes with incurved point or tuft of hairs, stamens inserted on perianth tube. Fruit an oblong capsule, seeds many, flattened, black. Leaves elongate, narrow, sometimes flexuose. Bulbs tunicated. A full descriptive list of the species is given by Mr. R. A. Dyer in *Herbertia*, 1939 (pp. 65–103), from which the accompanying key is adapted. Many other species are not yet in cultivation and would be worth introduction. Several of the species, such as *C. Mackenii* are swamp plants in their native localities, others grow in dry areas, and no doubt the main difficulty to be overcome in cultivating them is ignorance of the proper time to give or to withhold water. Flowering takes place at varying seasons for the different species so that each needs to be treated according to its peculiar character. Some species like *C. ochroleucus* and *C. sanguineus* have proved easy to maintain in cultivation. Most species are better kept growing through the year and annually repotted since offsets are often freely produced, but *C. sanguineus* should be dried off.

Intercrossing between the species of Cyrtanthus occurs freely and hybrids possibly occur naturally. *C. sanguineus* has given a good hybrid with *Vallota purpurea* which bears 3 or 4 large, loosely arranged flowers the colour of *Camellia reticulata.*

KEY

| | |
|---|---|
| 1. *Fl. several in an umbel, rarely 3 or less, not bell-shaped* | 2 |
| 1. *Fl. 1 or 2, rarely 3, upper part of perianth more or less bell-shaped* | 16 |
| 2. *Bulb large, 2 to 4 in. across* | C. obliquus |
| 2. *Bulb not 2 in. across* | 3 |

3. *Lvs.* 1 *in. or more wide; perianth lobes spreading* C. Huttonii
3. *Lvs. usually less than* 1 *in. wide* 4
4. *Fl. yellow, cream, or white* 5
4. *Fl. with red predominating* 8
5. *Fl. white* C. Mackenii
5. *Fl. yellow or cream* 6
6. *Lvs. produced after flowering begins* C. ochroleucus
6. *Lvs. well formed at flowering-time* 7
7. *Perianth tube up to* 1¾ *in. long, lobes somewhat reflexed* C. Mackenii Cooperi
7. *Perianth tube up to* 2½ *in. long, lobes spreading* C. Flanaganii
8. *Perianth tube inflated, l. spirally twisted* C. spiralis
8. *Perianth tube evenly dilated, not inflated* 9
9. *Perianth segs. not spreading or reflexed* 10
9. *Perianth segs. spreading or reflexed* 11
10. *Perianth* 1 *to* 1½ *in. long, lobes very short* C. parviflorus
10. *Perianth* 1½ *to* 2 *in. long, lobes* ¼ *in. long or more* C. Tuckii
11. *Inner perianth lobes rounded, under* ⅓ *in. long* 12
11. *Inner perianth lobes over* ⅝ *in. long* 14
12. *Perianth tube about* ½ *in. wide at throat; l.* ⅜ *to* ½ *in. wide* C. epiphyticus
12. *Perianth tube about* ½ *in. wide at throat; l. about* ⅓ *in. wide* 13
13. *Perianth lobes spreading* C. O'Brienii
13. *Perianth lobes more or less reflexed* C. Macowanii
14. *Perianth about* 2 *in. long, bright red, lobes* ⅝ *in. long* C. odorus
14. *Perianth* 2 *to* 3 *in. long, lobes about* ⅝ *in. long* 15
15. *Perianth lobes oblong-elliptic, rose scarlet* C. rhododactylus
15. *Perianth lobes ovate, red* C. angustifolius
16. *Fl. white or shell-pink, lobes with dark stripes* 17
16. *Fl. red or dark pink* 18
17. *Lvs. not twisted, perianth about* 2 *in. long* C. clavatus
17. *Lvs. spirally twisted, perianth about* 3½ *in. long or more* C. Smithiae
18. *Lvs. not over* ½ *in. wide, perianth* 2 *to* 3 *in. long* C. Galpinii
18. *Lvs.* ⅜ *to* ½ *in. wide, perianth* 3 *to* 4 *in. long* C. sanguineus

**C. angustifo'lius.** *fl.* 4 to 10, red, drooping, cylindrical, curved, nearly 2 in. long; perianth segs. spreading. May, June. *l.* 2 or 3, with fl., about 18 in. long, ⅓ to 1 in. wide when mature. 12 to 18 in. h. *Peduncle* stoutish. Cape Province. 1773. (B.M. 271; L.B.C. 368.)

**C. clava'tus.** *fl.* 1 to 3, white with 6 conspicuous red, red-brown, or green stripes down perianth; tube 1 to 1½ in. long, narrow at base, suddenly widened, about ½ in. wide at mouth; lobes spreading up to 1 in. long. May to August. *l.* 1 or 2, with fl., linear. 3 to 8 in. h. *Peduncle* slender. Cape Province. 1816. (B.R. 168 as *C. uniflorus*; B.M. 2291 as *Gastronema clavatum*.) *C. helictus* is very similar but has spirally twisted l.

**C. dendroph'ilus.** *See* **C. epiphyticus.**

**C. epiphyt'icus.** *fl.* 6 to 15, scarlet, 1½ in. long, trumpet-shaped, slightly curved; lobes more or less recurved, roundish. September. *l.* 2, with fl., linear, flat, 12 to 20 in. long, about ½ in. wide. 10 to 16 in. h. Natal. 1913. (B.M. 9252.) This species grows in moss on tree-trunks. Syn. *C. dendrophilus* of gardens.

**C. Flanagan'ii.** *fl.* 4 to 7, yellow, 2½ to 3 in. long, narrowly trumpet-shaped, about 2 in. wide at mouth, lobes ⅝ in. long, somewhat spreading. June. *l.* up to 4, with fl., narrow strap-shaped, somewhat falcate, about 12 in. long. 8 to 12 in. h. S. Africa. 1938. (F.P.S.A. 693.)

**C. Galpin'ii.** *fl.* 1 or 2, crimson to pink, 2 to 3½ in. long; tube narrow below, suddenly widened, and about ½ in. wide at throat; lobes about ¾ in. long. August. *l.* 1, usually after fl., linear, filiform at base, about 8 in. long. 8 in. h. Transvaal. 1892. (F.P.S.A. 343 as *C. Balenii*.)

**C. Hutton'ii.** *fl.* 12 to 20, nodding, orange-red to dark red, 1½ to 1¾ in. long; tube gradually widened to ⅓ in. at throat; lobes about ⅓ in. long, slightly spreading. May. *l.* 2 or 3, with fl., 20 to 24 in. long, up to 1½ in. wide, tapering. 14 to 18 in. h. *Peduncle* stout. Cape. 1864. (B.M. 7488; Gn. 50 (1896), 62.)

**C. lutes'cens.** A synonym of *C. ochroleucus*.

**C. Macken'ii.*** *fl.* 4 to 10, nearly erect, about 2 in. long, white (or yellowish in the slightly curved tube which is ⅓ in. wide at throat); lobes ⅓ in. long, spreading; fragrant. Spring. *l.* 2 to 6, with fl., linear, 8 to 12 in. long, ¼ in. wide. 12 in. h. Natal. 1868. (Gn. 17 (1880), 17.) var. **Coo'peri,** *fl.* cream or yellow. (B.M. 5374 as *C. lutescens*.)

**C. Macow'anii.** *fl.* 6 to 8, nodding, 1½ in. long, bright scarlet; tube curved, gradually widened to ⅓ in. at throat; lobes ¼ in. long, spreading. *l.* 1 to 3, with fl., linear, 6 to 12 in. long. 12 in. h. *Peduncle* slender, purplish. Cape Province. 1875. (B.H. 1885, 197.)

**C. obli'quus.** *fl.* 6 to 12, pendulous, 3 in. long, yellow, green, and red; tube widened to nearly 1 in. at throat; lobes 1 in. long, not spreading. May, June. *l.* 4 to 12, with fl., 4 to 12 in. long, 1½ to 2½ in. wide, twisted near top. 4 to 12 in. h., stout. Cape Province. 1774. (B.M. 1133; L.B.C. 947.)

**C. O'Brien'ii.** Closely related to *C. Macowanii* with bright pale scarlet *fl.* Natal. 1894.

**C. ochroleu'cus.*** *fl.* 2 to 4, more or less erect, pale yellow or yellowish-white, about 2 in. long, gradually widened to the throat which is about ¼ in. wide; lobes about ⅜ in. wide, spreading. February. *l.* produced after fl., linear or filiform. 6 to 12 in. h. Stem slender. Cape Province. 1836. Syn. *C. lutescens*. *See also* **C. Mackenii Cooperi.**

**C. odor'us.** *fl.* about 4, bright red, nodding, about 2 in. long, curved, narrow trumpet-shaped, gradually widened to ½ in. at throat; lobes ½ in. long, spreading; fragrant. July, August. *l.* 2 or 3, with fl., linear, 5 to 12 in. long. 6 in. h. S. Africa. 1818. (B.R. 503.)

**C. parviflo'rus.** *fl.* 6 to 12, bright red, about 1 in. long, nodding, about ⅛ in. wide at mouth; lobes not spreading. January. *l.* 3 to 6, with fl., linear, 12 in. long, straight; bright green. 12 in. h. S. Africa. (B.M. 7653.)

**C. rhododac'tylus.** *fl.* 6 to 8, rose-scarlet or lobes paler within, about 2 in. long, slightly curved, trumpet-shaped, ⅝ in. wide at throat; lobes ⅝ in. long, spreading. February. *l.* 2, with fl., linear, 6 to 12 in. long. 5 to 6 in. h. Stem purple at base. S. Africa. 1909. (B.M. 9175.)

**C. sanguin'eus.*** *fl.* 1 or 2, rarely 3, bright red, 3 to 4 in. long, much widened to an inch or more at throat; lobes 1½ in. long, spreading or recurved. August. *l.* 2 to 4, with fl., linear-lanceolate, narrowed at base, up to 16 in. long, keeled. About 12 in. h. S. Africa. 1860. (B.M. 5218; Gn. 37 (1890), 344.) Some variations in shade occur and there is both a green-leaved and a glaucous form (**glaucophyl'lus.**)

**C. Smith'iae.*** *fl.* 2 or 3, white or pale pink, striped red or red-brown on lobes, 3 to 4 in. long, almost horizontal, slightly curved, widened gradually to 1 in. at throat; lobes 1 in. long. *l.* 2 to 4, with fl., 6 to 12 in. long, spirally twisted. 10 to 12 in. h. S. Africa. 1876. Syn. *C. Smithianus*.

**C. spira'lis.** *fl.* 4 to 7, red, 1½ to 3 in. long, nodding, curved, about ⅝ in. wide at throat; lobes about ½ in. long, spreading. *l.* 2 or 3, produced after fl., linear, 6 to 8 in. long, spirally twisted. 10 in. h. S. Africa. 1815. (B.R. 167.)

**C. Tuck'ii.** *fl.* 10 to 15, 1½ to 2 in. long, yellowish at base, passing to blood-red above, nodding, curved, widening gradually to about ⅝ in. at throat, lobes not spreading, short. July. *l.* 2, with fl., linear, 12 to 18 in. long. 12 to 18 in. h. S. Africa. 1884. var. **transvaalen'sis** has *fl.* red throughout (F.P.S.A. 680); *fl.* of **viridiflor'us** have green lobes.

**C. uniflo'rus.** A synonym of *C. clavatus*.

***cyrto-***, in compound words, signifying curved.

**CYRTOCER'AS.** *See under* **Hoya multiflora.**

**CYRTOCHI'LUM.** Included in **Oncidium.**

**CYRTODEIR'A.** Included in **Episcia.**

**CYRTO'MIUM** (*kyrtos*, arched, from the habit of growth). Fam. *Polypodiaceae*. A genus of about 10 species of ferns, sometimes regarded as varieties of one; natives in SE. Asia, with once-pinnate rigid fronds with veins forming a network and small scattered sori, the indusia fixed by the depressed centre. *C. falcatum* and its varieties are among the most useful of decorative plants on account of their rapid growth, firm leathery fronds, and handsome appearance. They are good in rooms and other places where many plants are apt to suffer because of smoke or draughts. Their bold and shining evergreen foliage forms a good contrast too among other ferns in a cool fernery and they will grow well in an unheated house during the winter. A compost of about equal parts of fibrous loam, peat, and silver-sand suits them. They must not be potted hard, and if planted out must be in moderately loose soil. Abundant moisture is required during growth, as well as frequent syringing, but in winter water must be given sparingly. Propagation is by spores.

**C. falca'tum.*** *sti.* tufted, 6 to 12 in. long, densely scaly below. *Fronds* 1 to 2 ft. long, 6 to 9 in. broad, simply pinnate; pinnae numerous, lower stalked, ovate-acuminate, falcate, 3 to 5 in. long, 1 to 2 in. broad, entire or slightly undulated, upper side narrowed suddenly, sometimes auricled, lower rounded or obliquely truncate at base. *Sori* small, copious, scattered. Japan, China, India, Celebes, Hawaii. (F.S.A. (2) 32.) Syn. *Aspidium falcatum*. var. **caryotid'eum** has rather larger pinnae, sharply toothed, slightly lobed, sometimes auricled on both sides. Syn. *Cyrtomium caryotideum*; **Fen'somi** is a robust plant with broader pinnules. 1889; **Fortun'ei** has narrower pinnae, more opaque; **pen'dulum** also has narrower pinnae, fronds pendulous. Hardy in most places. Several other varieties have been named. These varieties are by some regarded as distinct species.

**CYRTOPE'RA.** Included in **Eulophia.**

**CYRTOPO'DIUM** (*kyrtos*, curved, *pous*, foot; referring to the form of the lip). FAM. *Orchidaceae*. A genus of terrestrial Orchids of about 30 species in Trop. America, varying from small plants with often simple spikes of little horticultural value to others of great size with large panicles of showy flowers produced with the young growths from the base of the pseudobulbs, which, small or large, are stoutly fusiform, set closely together, and carry long narrow more or less ribbed leaves contracted into a short stem-clasping petiole borne from the upper portion of the bulb; deciduous in some species. Peduncles usually clothed in large bracts. In some species the flower bracts assume the floral colouring but to a less degree. The species described below are all worth cultivating and represent the finest and showiest of the genus as far as it is known. The sepals free, spreading, nearly equal or the lateral sepals broader at base and more or less decurrent into the foot of the column; petals similar to the dorsal sepal, but rather broader and shorter; lip attached to the base of the column, the chin more or less prominent, the side lobes rather broad, mid-lobe rounded, entire, 2-lobed or crisped-toothed. Compost should be that advised for Cymbidium. While growing the tropical atmosphere of a warm house is required and water should be given freely. In autumn after the pseudobulbs are matured expose to more light and remove the plants to a light position with a temperature around 55° F. and water very infrequently; water may not be required throughout the winter. Repotting if necessary should be effected in early spring and the plants returned to warmer conditions. Cyrtopera, which is sometimes included with this genus, is now placed under Eulophia.

**C. Alic'iae.** *fl.* 1½ in. across; sep. and pet. green, with brown spots; lip white, with crimson spots, 3-lobed, crest yellow; scape tall, branched, many-fld. *l.* long, linear-lanceolate. *Pseudobulbs* about 12 in. long, fusiform. Brazil. 1893. (L. 371.)

**C. And'ersonii.*** *fl.* in many-fld. panicles; sep. and pet. about equal, yellow, with a faint green tinge; lip 3-lobed, rich yellow, side lobes large, erect, mid-lobe spatulate. Spring. *Pseudobulbs* 5 ft. h. Trop. America. (B.M. 1800; B.R. 27, 8; L.B.C. 121.) SYN. *C. flavum, Tylochilus flavus.* var. **cardiochi'lum,** *fl.* bright yellow, tinged green, nearly 2 in. across; front lobe of lip concave, round-cordate, raceme long, erect, forked at base. (W.O.A. 176.); **flaves'cens,** *fl.* yellow, lip broad kidney-shaped, scape 3 ft. h., *pseudobulbs* shorter than the type. Venezuela. 1895. (L. 84.)

**C. cardiochi'lum.** A variety of *C. Andersonii.*

**C. fla'vum.** A synonym of *C. Andersonii.*

**C. puncta'tum.*** *fl.* 1½ in. across, sep. and pet. wavy, yellowish, spotted brown; lip 3-lobed, clear yellow, side lobes incurved, red-chestnut, mid-lobe chestnut and yellow; bracts large, greenish-yellow, with purplish spots; panicle large, many-fld. April. Brazil. (B.M. 3507; L. 3441; W.O.A. 202.) More floriferous than *C. Andersonii.* Even when out of flower *C. Andersonii* and *C. punctatum* form two noble plants, with their fine long curved leaves. var. **Saintlegeria'num,** bracts and fls. brighter than in type. 1885. Paraguay; **splen'dens,** *fl.* small, many, in tall, branching racemes, fl. and upper bracts yellow, brown, and red. 1893.

**C. Saintlegeria'num.** A variety of *C. punctatum.*

**C. sanguin'eum.** A synonym of *Eulophia sanguinea.*

**C. vires'cens.** *fl.* pale primrose-yellow, blotched dark red, about 1 in. across; sep. ovate, acute; pet. rounded; lip fleshy, shortly clawed, side lobes dark red; raceme 1 to 2 ft. h., many-fld.; scape 2 to 4 ft. h. December. *l.* narrow-lanceolate, about 1 ft. long. *Pseudobulbs* tufted, 3 to 4 in. long, pale green, with narrow purple rings. Brazil. 1893. (B.M. 7396.)

**C. Wil'morei.** A synonym of *C. punctatum.*

**C. Wood'fordii.** A synonym of *Eulophia longifolia.*

E. C.

**CYRTOSPER'MA** (*kyrtos*, curved, *sperma*, seed; the seeds being sometimes reniform). FAM. *Araceae*. A genus of about a dozen species of tuberous or rhizomatous herbs, natives of the tropics. More or less robust plants with hastate or sagittate leaves, rarely somewhat lobed. Spathe ovate-lanceolate, persistent. Spadix, with stalk adnate to spathe or sessile, completely and densely covered by the hermaphrodite flowers. Flowers with 4 to 6 arching perianth segments, 4 to 6 stamens, and an ovoid ovary with one cell. Fruit a usually 1-seeded berry. Treatment as for Alocasia.

**C. fe'rox.** *l.-stalk* 10 to 30 in. long, very spiny, dark green with red spots; blade 10 to 24 in. long, hastate; lobes of equal length, narrow-lanceolate, sinus deep. *Peduncle* about as long as l.-stalk, dark green, prickly. *Spathe* 3 to 4 in. long, ovate-lanceolate or ovate, more or less long-pointed, smooth without, brownish-purple with yellowish veins, whitish within, finally more or less reflexed. Borneo. 1892. (I.H. 1892, 153.)

**C. Johnston'ii.** *l.-stalk* nearly 3 ft. long, olive-green with rosy spots and bands, and clusters of upward-pointing spines; blade 1½ to 2 ft. long, oblong-sagittate, olive-green; lobes nearly equal, sinus rectangular. Peduncle about 14 in. long, slender, spiny. *Spathe* about 6 in. long, ovate-lanceolate, brown or purplish-brown, leathery. Solomon Is. 1875. (B.M. 8567.) SYN. *Alocasia Johnstonii.*

**C. senegalen'se.** *l.-stalk* up to 6 ft. long, much exceeding blade, minutely spiny; blade 12 to 24 in. long, narrowly hastate; lobes nearly equal. *Peduncle* thick. *Spathe* 8 to 20 in. long, oblong-lanceolate or widely lanceolate, with a long slender point, twisted at apex, yellow-green without, dull purple with brownish-purple lines within. Trop. Africa. 1897. (B.M. 7617.)

**CYRTOSTACH'YS** (*kyrtos*, curved, *stachys*, spike; the spikes of flowers are curved). FAM. *Palmaceae*. A genus of 3 or 4 species of stately Malayan Palms, with tall, slender, spineless stem and pinnatisect leaves. Leaflets linear-lanceolate, somewhat obliquely 2-fid at tip. Spadix shortly stalked, branches somewhat flattened, alternate, sometimes drooping. Spathes 2, quickly falling. Flowers monoecious, in the same spadix; stamens 6, rarely 12 or 15. Fruit small, ovoid. For cultivation *see* **Areca.**

**C. Lak'ka.** *l.-stalk* not more than 4 in. long, green. *l.* arched, about 4 ft. long; lflets. about 20 in. long, 1¼ in. wide, green above, ashy-grey beneath; sheath red. *fr.* about ⅓ in. long. Borneo.

**C. Ren'da.** About 25 to 30 ft. h. *l.-stalk* dark brownish-red; lflets. linear-ensiform, grey beneath. *Spadix* drooping, 3 to 4 ft. long. Malaya.

**CYSTACAN'THUS.** Included in **Phlogacanthus.**

**CYSTAN'THE.** *See under* **Richea sprengelioides.**

**cysti-,** in compound words, signifying hollow or pouch-like.
A→

**CYSTOP'TERIS** (*kystis*, a bladder, *pteris*, a fern). Bladder Fern. FAM. *Polypodiaceae*. A genus of 18 elegant and graceful little hardy Ferns of delicate texture, allied to Microlepis and Woodsia. Indusium membranous, sub-orbicular, inserted by its broad base under the sorus, which, at first, it covers like a hood. Sori globose, on the back of the veins. Some species are indigenous to this country and well adapted for planting in the outdoor fernery, where shady and well-drained spots can be arranged for them. *C. montana* has underground creeping rhizomes, but all the other species produce their slender fronds in great abundance either from a closely tufted crown or from shortly decumbent rhizomes. On account of their delicate appearance, all are well adapted for pot-cultivation, either under glass, in a cold frame, or without glass protection, in a sheltered position. All lose their fronds early in the autumn and remain dormant until about April, during which period their crowns must not be allowed to get completely dry. When planted out, a compost of about equal parts fibrous peat, loam, and leaf-mould is the one which suits them best. For pots it is advisable to add to this mixture a small proportion of old, crumbled mortar or broken limestone, and also to pay special attention to the drainage.

The Bladder Ferns are usually propagated during March and April by division of the crowns, wherever more than one has formed; they are also easily raised from spores sown in autumn in a cold frame. *C. bulbifera*, however, is more readily increased by means of the bulbils produced along its rachises, which, having fallen to the ground, soon produce a few slender roots and send up some rudimentary fronds, producing perfectly developed foliage in the second year.

**C. alpi'na.** *sti.* 2 to 4 in. long. *Fronds* 4 to 8 in. long, 1 to 2 in. broad, oblong-lanceolate, 3-pinnatifid; main rachis winged above; largest pinnae deltoid, lanceolate, 1 to 1½ in. long, about ½ in. broad; pinnules ovate-rhomboidal; seg. slightly toothed. *Sori* small, 2 to 12 to a pinnule. European Mts. (Teesdale, England) and Asia Minor. (H.B.F. 24.) By some regarded as a sub-species (*regia*) of *C. fragilis.*

**C. bulbif'era.** *sti.* 4 to 6 in. long. *Fronds* 6 to 12 in. long, 3 to 4 in. broad at widest part, ovate-lanceolate, often much-elongated upwards, 2- or 3-pinnatifid; lower pinnules lanceolate, 2 to 3 in. long; segs. linear-oblong, slightly toothed. *Sori* 2 to 12 to a pinnule. N. America. 1638. Large fleshy bulblets form in axils of upper pinnae, which fall to the ground and become new plants.

**C. canarien'sis.** A synonym of *C. fragilis diaphana.*

**C. Dickiea'na.** A variety of *C. fragilis.*

**C. frag'ilis.*** *sti.* 2 to 4 in. long. *Fronds* 4 to 8 in. long, 1½ to 2 in. broad, ovate-lanceolate, 3-pinnatifid; largest pinnae 1 to 1½ in. long, ½ to ¾ in. broad; pinnules oblong-rhomboidal; segs. bluntly or sharply toothed. *Sori* 2 to 12 to a pinnule. Temperate regions. (H.B.F. 23.) This elegant little species is well adapted for growing in fern cases; it has numerous more or less distinct varieties, e.g. var. **denta'ta,** *fronds* 2-pinnate, bluntly toothed, *sori* close to margin, 6 in. h.; **Dickiea'na,** *fronds* 4 to 5 in. long, dark green, pinnae all bending down somewhat, and overlapping, pinnules slightly and bluntly toothed. Scotland.

**C. monta'na.** *sti.* slender, erect, 6 to 9 in. long. *Fronds* about 6 in. each way, deltoid, 4-pinnatifid; lowest pinnules deltoid-lanceolate, 1 to 1½ in. long, about ½ in. broad; segs. cut down to the rachis below; lobes oblong, deeply and sharply toothed. *Sori* small, 18 to 24 on lower segs. *rhiz.* wide creeping. Scotland (very rare), Mts. of N. Hemisphere. (H.B.F. 25.)

**C. re'gia.** A synonym of *C. alpina.*

**CYS'TOPUS can'didus** causes White Blister on Crucifers. *See* **Cabbage diseases.**

**CYSTORCH'IS.** *See* **Anoectochilus.**

***cythere'a,*** of the Greek island Kythera.

***cytisoi'des,*** Cytisus-like.

**CYT'ISUS** (possibly from Greek *kytisos*, a kind of clover). FAM. *Leguminosae.* A genus of deciduous and evergreen shrubs and small trees which, together with Genista and Spartium, is known as Broom. Cytisus, like Genista, is marked by alternate (usually), simple or 3-foliolate leaves; flowers pea-shaped, usually yellow, rarely white, whitish, or other coloured; calyx tubular or campanulate, 2-lipped, upper lip 2-lobed, lower 3-lobed. Pods neither thickened nor winged at their edges, 2- to many-seeded. The seeds show a wart-like eminence, the strophiole, near the hilum; it represents the seed-end of the funicle, i.e. the cord which ties the seed to the pod. Presence of the strophiole is the only reliable means of distinguishing Cytisus from Genista. Cultivation is simple in well-drained, friable soil in a sunny position but, as established plants transplant badly, those grown in pots should be used when planting out. The best specimens are raised from seed but cuttings are also used in propagation; grafting on Laburnum is employed, but chiefly in the making of standards.

KEY

| | | |
|---|---|---|
| 1. | *Evergreen or nearly so* | 2 |
| 1. | *Deciduous* | 8 |
| 2. | *Fl. yellow* | 3 |
| 2. | *Fl. white* | 6 |
| 3. | *Many lvs. almost or completely sessile* | 4 |
| 3. | *Lvs. distinctly stalked* | 5 |
| 4. | *Lflets. obovate-oblong, rounded at apex* | C. canariensis |
| 4. | *Lflets. lanceolate or linear* | C. linifolius |
| 5. | *Keel densely pubescent* | C. maderensis |
| 5. | *Keel almost smooth* | C. monspessulanus |
| 6. | *Lvs. pubescent beneath* | C. palmensis |
| 6. | *Lvs. silky-villous* | 7 |
| 7. | *Lvs. silky-villous on both surfaces* | C. Perezii |
| 7. | *Lvs. silky-villous beneath* | C. proliferus |
| 8. | *Fl. yellow, sometimes blotched or spotted brown* | 9 |
| 8. | *Fl. other than yellow* | 25 |
| 9. | *Fl. terminal* | 10 |
| 9. | *Fl. lateral* | 15 |
| 10. | *Fl. in racemes* | 11 |
| 10. | *Fl. in heads* | 13 |
| 11. | *Shrub over* 10 *ft. h.* | C. Battandieri |
| 11. | *Shrubs usually not more than* 6 *ft. h.* | 12 |
| 12. | *Pods smooth* | C. sessilifolius |
| 12. | *Pods hairy* | C. nigricans |
| 13. | *Adult lvs. smooth above, densely villous beneath* | C. supinus |
| 13. | *Lvs. appressed-pubescent* | 14 |
| 14. | *Lvs. hairy on both surfaces* | C. austriacus |
| 14. | *Lvs. almost smooth above, appressed-pubescent beneath* | C. Rochelii |
| 15. | *Lvs. simple* | 16 |
| 15. | *Lvs.* 3-*foliolate or both* 3-*foliolate and simple on same plant* | 18 |
| 16. | *Branches erect or nearly so* | C. purgans |
| 16. | *Branches prostrate or procumbent* | 17 |
| 17. | *Branches prostrate-decumbent* | C. decumbens |
| 17. | *Branches procumbent* | C. procumbents |
| 18. | *Lvs. all* 3-*foliolate* | 19 |
| 18. | *Lvs.* 3-*foliolate and simple* | 24 |
| 19. | *Pods smooth* | C. glabrescens |
| 19. | *Pods hairy or shaggy* | 20 |
| 20. | *Pods hairy at edges only* | C. ciliatus |
| 20. | *Pods hairy on both surfaces* | 21 |
| 21. | *Cal. campanulate* | C. Ardoinii |
| 21. | *Cal. tubular* | 22 |
| 22. | *Adult lvs. smooth above* | C. ratisbonensis |
| 22. | *Lvs. more or less hairy above* | 23 |
| 23. | *Shrub prostrate* | C. demissus |
| 23. | *Shrub from* 1 *to* 3 *ft. h.* | C. hirsutus |
| 24. | *Pod hairy at edges, smooth on surfaces* | C. scoparius |
| 24. | *Pod woolly all over* | C. grandiflorus |
| 25. | *Fl. purplish* | C. purpureus |
| 25. | *Fl. white or whitish* | 26 |
| 26. | *Fl. in loose terminal heads* | C. leucanthus |
| 26. | *Fl. lateral, from l.-axils* | 27 |
| 27. | *Fl. in clusters of* 4, 5, *or more; pods smooth* | C. supranubius |
| 27. | *Fl. solitary, in pairs or clusters of* 3; *pods downy* | C. albus |

**C. al'bus** (of Link).* White Spanish Broom. Deciduous, hardy, upright, and lovely shrub from 6 to 12 ft. h. with flexible, slender, ridged, downy young shoots. *l.* 3-foliolate at base of shoots, otherwise simple; lflets. linear-lanceolate, linear-oblong, or linear-obovate, minute or up to ½ in. long, sparsely silky-pubescent. *fl.* 1 to 3 in l.-axils; cor. white; cal. campanulate. May, June. *Pods* appressed-pubescent, about 1 in. long. Spain, Portugal, and NW. Africa. 1752. (B.M. 1438 as *C. leucanthus*, B.M. 8693.) SYN. *C. multiflorus, Genista alba, Spartium multiflorum.* var. **du'rus,** hardier than type. 1870; **incarna'tus,** *fl.* flushed pink (L.B.C. 1052.); **prae'cox,** said to flower earlier than type; **ro'seus,** similar to var. *incarnatus.*

**C. Andrea'nus.** A variety of *C. scoparius.*

**C. Ardoin'ii.** Deciduous, usually decumbent shrub from 4 to 8 in. h. with octagonal, hairy, slightly grooved young shoots. *l.* 3-foliolate, lflets. oblong or obovate, villous on both surfaces especially when young, $\frac{5}{16}$ in. long. *fl.* axillary, solitary or in clusters of up to 6 towards ends of branches; cor. golden-yellow; cal. villous, campanulate. April, May. *Pods* villous, up to 1 in. long. Maritime Alps. 1866. SYN. *Genista Ardoinii.* (M.F.M. 58.) Good species for rock-garden. var. **Sauzea'na** differs by its stouter stems, pentagonal young shoots, larger l., and sometimes pods hairy only at edges.

**C. austri'acus.** Deciduous shrub about 3 ft. h. with appressed-pubescent, rounded young shoots. *l.* 3-foliolate, lflets. elliptic-oblong or lanceolate, appressed-pubescent on both sides, ½ to 1½ in. long. Closely allied to *C. supinus* but differing by l. being appressed-pubescent. *fl.* in terminal heads; cor. bright yellow, standard silky-hairy without; cal. tubular, appressed-pubescent. July, August. *Pods* about 1½ in. long, appressed-pubescent. Cent. and SE. Europe, including Caucasus. 1741. (R.I.F.G. 22, 2078.) var. **Heuffel'ii,** branches more slender, *l.* linear-oblong or linear-obovate, ultimately smooth above. Hungary, Rumania. SYN. *C. Heuffelii, C. supinus Heuffelii.* (R.I.F.G. 22, 2078.)

**C. Battandier'i.*** Deciduous, vigorous, silvery shrub, 12 to 15 ft. h., with drooping, adsurgent branches. *l.* large, 3-foliolate with stalks up to 1½ in. long, lflets. almost sessile, soft, ovate, obovate, or broadly elliptical, blunt, or sub-acute at apex, tapering to base, silvery-pubescent especially beneath, 2 to 3½ in. long. *fl.* in plump, cylindrical racemes, 3 to 5 in. long, at end of lateral branchlets, fragrant; cor. bright yellow, standard about ½ in. wide; cal. tubular, silky-pubescent. May, June. *Pods* pubescent, about 2 in. long. NW. Africa. 1922. (B.M. 9528; G.C. 92 (1932), 21.) Hardy, at least in the south of England. Easily raised from seed. Fls. of mixed scents, all pleasant.

**C. × Bean'ii** (*C. Ardoinii* × *C. purgans*)? Deciduous, procumbent, intricately branched shrub up to 18 in. h. *l.* simple, linear-lanceolate, hairy, about ½ in. long. *fl.* axillary, solitary, in pairs or in groups of 3; cor. deep yellow; cal. campanulate, more or less hairy. May. Originated at Kew in 1900. (B.T.S. 1, 457; B.M. n.s. 366.)

**C. biflo'rus.** A synonym of *C. ratisbonensis* and *C. supinus ambiguus.*

**C. bisflo'rens,** a variety of *C. supinus.*

**C. canarien'sis.*** The 'Genista' of florists. Much-branched, half-hardy, evergreen shrub about 6 ft. h., with appressed-pubescent young shoots. *l.* 3-foliolate, lower shortly petiolate, upper sessile, lflets. obovate-oblong, rounded at apex, ¼ to ½ in. long, appressed silky-pubescent. *fl.* fragrant in short racemes at ends of young shoots; cor. bright yellow; cal. campanulate, appressed silky-pubescent. May to July. Canary Is. var. **ramosis'simus,** racemes shorter, more numerous, lflets. smaller, smooth above. (B.R. 3, 217.)

**C. can'dicans** (of Lamarck). A synonym of *C. monspessulanus*, and (of Holl) of *C. maderensis*.

**C. capita'tus.** A synonym of *C. supinus*.

**C. caraman'icus.** A synonym of *Laburnum caramanicus*.

**C. cilia'tus.** Closely resembles *C. hirsutus*, but *pods* hairy only at edges. SE. Europe. 1817. SYN. *C. hirsutus ciliatus*.

**C. × Dallimor'ei*** (*C. albus* × *C. scoparius Andreanus*). Deciduous shrub up to 8 ft. h. *l.* mostly 3-foliolate, lflets. elliptical, lanceolate, or oblanceolate, sessile, pointed, ciliate, at first appressed-pubescent. *fl.* axillary, solitary or in pairs; cor. pale mauvy-pink except crimson wings; cal. brown, hairy. *Pods* hairy at edges, about 1 in. long. May. Raised at Kew. 1900. (B.M. 8482.) Perhaps the most beautiful of all hybrid Brooms, but neither so vigorous nor so robust as the majority of them possibly due to the general practice of grafting it on Laburnum.

**C. dalmat'icus.** A synonym of *Genista germanica*.

**C. decum'bens.*** Deciduous, prostrate, decumbent shrub with hairy young shoots. *l.* simple, sessile, oblong or oblong-obovate, abruptly pointed, narrowing to base, hairy especially on lower surface and at edges, $\frac{1}{4}$ to $\frac{5}{8}$ in. long. *fl.* axillary, solitary, in pairs, or groups of 3; cor. bright shining yellow; cal. campanulate, hairy. May, June. *Pods* $\frac{3}{4}$ to 1 in. long, hairy. S. Europe (S. France to W. Balkans). 1775. SYN. *C. prostratus* (of Simonkai), *Genista prostrata, Spartium decumbens*. (B.M. 8230.) Uncommon in cultivation but perhaps the best of the prostrate species. Its eventual height of 3 or 4 in. is attained by the superimposition of its branches. Of the several plants called *C. prostratus*, this appears to be that most often described under that name.

**C. demis'sus.*** Deciduous, prostrate shrub, 2 to 3 in. h., with rounded, hairy shoots. *l.* 3-foliolate; lflets. oval or obovate, pointed or sub-acute, hairy especially on under surface and edges, $\frac{5}{16}$ to $\frac{5}{8}$ in. long. *fl.* axillary, solitary or in pairs; cor. relatively large, yellow usually stained reddish-brown in one or more of its parts; cal. tubular, hairy, usually reddish-brown. May, June. *Pods* about 1 in. long, hairy. SE. Europe, N. Asia Minor (Pontus); of recent introduction but known for at least a century. SYN. *C. hirsutus demissus, C. ponticus*. (J.R.H.S. 67, 90.) One of the most outstanding of the dwarf Brooms.

**C. elonga'tus.** A variety of *C. ratisbonensis*.

**C. frag'rans.** A synonym of *C. supranubius*.

**C. german'icus.** A synonym of *Genista germanica*.

**C. glabres'cens.** Deciduous, low, roundish, compact, and intricately branched shrub, usually about 1 ft. h. but occasionally 3 ft. *l.* long-stalked, 3-foliolate, lflets. oval or elliptic-oblong, blunt or sub-acute, appressed-pubescent on lower surface, about $\frac{3}{8}$ in. long. *fl.* axillary, solitary, in pairs, or groups of 3 or 4; cor. bright shining yellow; cal. campanulate, appressed-hairy. May, June. *Pod* smooth, 1 in. or more long. Cent. Europe; about 1890. (B.M. 8201 as *Genista glabrescens*.) SYN. *C. emeriflorus*. A beautiful plant but seldom seen in gardens. The strophiole on the seed of this species is very small and it is perhaps on this account that the shrub is sometimes included in Genista.

**C. grandiflo'rus** (of de Candolle). Deciduous shrub, up to 10 ft. h., shoots at first hairy, later smooth. *l.* sessile, hairy or smooth, the lower usually 3-foliolate with obovate or oblong-lanceolate lflets., upper simple, lanceolate, and, like lflets., up to $\frac{1}{2}$ in. long. *fl.* axillary, singly or in pairs; cor. bright yellow, large; cal. campanulate, smooth or slightly pubescent. May. *Pods* densely grey-woolly, about 1 in. long. Spain, Portugal. 1816. SYN. *C. affinis, Genista grandiflora, Spartium grandiflorum*. *C. grandiflorus* of gardens is a synonym of *C. scoparius pendulus*. Resembles *C. scoparius*. Rare in gardens but appears hardy.

**C. Heuffel'ii.** A variety of *C. austriacus*.

**C. × Hill'ieri** (*C. hirsutus hirsutissimus* × *C. versicolor*). Deciduous shrub with stout drooping branches. *fl.* large, axillary, yellow stained bronze. Of garden origin.

**C. hirsu'tus.** Deciduous shrub of variable size and habit and with hairy young shoots. The type is accepted as being from 1 to 3 ft. h. with erect or ascending and often flexuous branches. *l.* 3-foliolate, lflets. oval, obovate, or obovate-oblong, slightly hairy above, shaggy beneath, $\frac{3}{8}$ to $\frac{3}{4}$ in. long. *fl.* axillary in pairs or in groups of 3 or 4; cor. large, yellow often with brownish staining, especially on the standard; cal. tubular, hairy. May to July. *Pods* up to $1\frac{3}{4}$ in. long, shaggy. Cent. and SE. Europe from Germany and Maritime Alps to the Caucasus. Said to have been introduced about 200 years ago, now comparatively rare in cultivation. SYN. *C. prostratus hirsutus, C. triflorus* (of Lamarck), *Genista hirta*. (M.F.M. 28.) var. **hirsutis'simus,** upright shrub of about 4 ft., lflets. shaggy on both surfaces, *pods* more shaggy than in type. SE. Europe; **pu'milus,** up to 12 in. h. with prostrate, ascending, or erect stems, spreading branches, young shoots less hairy than in type, small ciliate lflets. smooth or sparsely hairy above, slightly pubescent beneath, *fl.* yellow, axillary, solitary or paired, cal. less hairy. Maritime Alps and NW. Italy. SYN. *Genista Notarisii*; **Scopol'ii,** prostrate shrub with tortuous branches, hairy young shoots, small, feebly pubescent above, hairy beneath, *fl.* in small groups from axils but often appearing to be almost terminal, cal. hairy, *pods* hairy. Maritime Alps, N. Italy, Hungary. SYN. *C. prostratus, C. hirsutus alpestris, Genista Scopolii*.

**C. hispan'icus.** A synonym of *Genista hispanica*.

**C. jun'ceus.** A synonym of *Spartium junceum*.

**C. × kewens'is*** (*C. albus* × *C. Ardoinii*). Deciduous, procumbent, and remarkably floriferous shrub eventually about 18 in. h. *l.* generally 3-foliolate, lflets. narrow-oblong, pubescent. *fl.* axillary, in pairs or groups of 3, cor. creamy-yellow. Raised at Kew. (Gn. 73, 228.) Well suited for rock-gardens and dry walls.

**C. leucan'thus.** Deciduous, spreading shrub, up to about 1 ft., with hairy, rounded shoots. *l.* 3-foliolate, lflets. oblong-obovate or elliptic, appressed-pubescent especially beneath and on edges, sometimes smooth above. *fl.* in dense terminal clusters; cor. creamy-white, prevented from opening fully by calyx, standard pubescent without; cal. tubular, hairy, about $\frac{1}{3}$ in. long. June to October. *Pod* flat, appressed-pubescent, $\frac{3}{4}$ in. long. SE. Europe. 1806. SYN *C. schipkaensis, C. leucanthus schipkaensis, C. albus* (of Hacquet, not Link).

**C. linifo'lius.** Half-hardy evergreen, or nearly evergreen, much-branched shrub from 8 to 20 in. h. with erect, nodular, and pubescent branches. *l.* sessile or nearly so, 3-foliolate, lflets. leathery, narrow-oblong to linear, tapered to base, blunt or pointed, more or less recurved, pubescent or smooth above, silky-pubescent beneath. *fl.* in short racemes terminating young shoots; cor. yellow, standard feebly pubescent; cal. bell-shaped, silky-pubescent. March to May. *Pod* irregularly linear-oblong, covered with brownish hairs. Spain to S. France, N. Africa, and Canary Is. (B.M. 442 as *Genista linifolia*.)

**C. maderen'sis.** Evergreen, half-hardy shrub or small tree, up to 20 ft. h. with stiff, nodular, ascending branches and brownish- or silvery-pubescent young shoots and pedicels. *l.* crowded, fairly long-stalked, trifoliolate, lflets. oblong-obovate or lanceolate, acute, silky-pubescent or smooth above, silky-pubescent beneath, $\frac{1}{4}$ to $\frac{3}{4}$ in. long. *fl.* fragrant, in fairly compact, 6- to 12-fld. racemes terminating young shoots; cor. large, bright yellow, standard smooth or nearly so, keel densely silky-pubescent; cal. campanulate, densely villous. May, June. *Pod* hairy, flat, about 1 in. long. Madeira. SYN. *C. candicans, Genista canariensis* (of Buchanan-Hamilton, not of Linnaeus) (of Holl, not of Lamarck). var. **magꞁifolio'sus,** *l.* larger than type, racemes elongated, 10- to 20-fld. Maaeira. (B.R. 26, 23 as *Genista bracteolata*.)

**C. monspessula'nus.** Montpelier Broom. Erect, much-branched, leafy shrub up to 10 ft. h. *l.* stalked, 3-foliolate, lflets. broadly obovate, obtuse-mucronulate, or notched, smooth above, hairy beneath, $\frac{1}{2}$ to $\frac{3}{4}$ in. long. *fl.* in small racemes or umbellate clusters of 3 to 9, terminating young shoots; cor. yellow, broadly oval, standard smooth, keel almost smooth; cal. bell-shaped, pubescent. April to June. *Pod* from $\frac{3}{4}$ to just over 1 in. long, hairy and scaly, straight, or slightly curved. S. Europe, Portugal to Dalmatia, Greece, W. Asia Minor, N. Africa. 1735. SYN. *C. candicans, C. pubescens, Genista candicans*. Evergreen in mild winters but of unreliable hardiness. Young shoots ridged and hairy. (B.M. 8685.)

**C. multiflo'rus.** A synonym of *C. albus*.

**C. nig'ricans.** Erect, deciduous shrub, 3 to 6 ft. h. with rounded, appressed-pubescent young shoots. *l.* long-stalked, 3-, rarely 5-foliolate, lflets. oblong-obovate, obovate, or oval, sparsely hairy beneath, smooth above, sub-acute, $\frac{1}{2}$ to 1 in. long. *fl.* 1 in. long, in terminal racemes; cor. yellow; cal. campanulate, hairy. July, August. *Pod* hairy, up to $1\frac{1}{2}$ in. long. Cent. and SE. Europe. 1730. (B.M. 8479.) SYN. *C. triflorus* (of l'Héritier, not of Lamarck). var. **elonga'tus,** fls. again in autumn at ends of fruiting branches. SYN. *C. nigricans Carlieri, C. nigricans longespicatus*. 1800.

**C. × Osborn'ii.** Seedling, possibly a hybrid, of *C. × Dallimorei*. *fl.* sulphur-yellow, late May and June. Originated at Kew.

**C. palmen'sis.** Tagasaste. Evergreen, half-hardy shrub of loose habit, 15 ft. or more in height when given support, with thin, pubescent shoots. *l.* 3-foliolate, lflets. lanceolate or oblanceolate, smooth above, pubescent beneath, $\frac{3}{4}$ to $1\frac{1}{2}$ in. long. *fl.* in axillary clusters of 2 to 4; pedicel densely pubescent; cor. white; cal. tubular, densely pubescent. February to April. *Pods* about $1\frac{1}{2}$ in. long. La Palma (Canary Is.). SYN. *C. proliferus palmensis*.

**C. Perez'ii.** Escabon de Canaria. White-fld., evergreen, half-hardy shrub closely related to and resembling *C. palmensis* but differing by its obovate lflets., silky-villous on both surfaces. Canary Is. (Grand Canary and Hierro).

**C. pilo'sa.** A synonym of *Genista pilosa*.

**C. × Porlock*** (*C. monspessulanus* × *C. racemosus*). Decorative evergreen, or partly evergreen, half-hardy shrub from 2 to 4 ft. h. with slightly grooved and white-hairy shoots. *l.* petiolate, 3-foliolate, lflets. obovate or oblanceolate, apex usually rounded or abruptly pointed, often mucronulate, sometimes notched, sparsely pubescent above, more densely on prominent mid-rib beneath, $\frac{1}{4}$ to $\frac{1}{2}$ in. or more long. *fl.* in racemes or clusters terminating young shoots, fragrant, freely borne; cor. bright yellow; cal. bell-shaped, pubescent. May to August. Raised by Mr. N. G. Hadden at Porlock, about 1900.

**C. × prae'cox** (*C. albus* × *C. purgans*). Warminster Broom. Bushy deciduous shrub, 3 to 5 ft. or more h., with shoots at first erect or ascending, eventually pendent. *l.* mostly simple, oblanceolate or almost linear, more or less pubescent, fall early, up to $\frac{3}{4}$ in. long. *fl.* axillary, solitary or in pairs, freely produced, having an acrid smell; cor. creamy-yellow. May. Originated with Messrs Wheeler of Warminster about 1867. G.C .29 (1901 ),41.)

**C. procum'bens.** Deciduous, procumbent, intricately branched very floriferous shrub, up to 2 ft. h. with appressed-pubescent young shoots. *l.* petiolate, simple, oblong-obovate or oval, blunt or sub-acute, appressed-pubescent beneath and edges, smooth or nearly so above, $\frac{1}{4}$ to $\frac{5}{8}$ in. long. *fl.* axillary, solitary, in pairs, or threes; cor. yellow, smooth; cal. campanulate, pubescent. May to July. *Pod* 1 in. or a little more in length. SE. Europe including Hungary. SYN. *Genista procumbens.* (B.R. 1150.) Closely related to *C. decumbens* but differing by its greater height, procumbent habit, stalked l., and appressed pubescence.

**C. prolif'erus.** Escabon. Loose, half-hardy, evergreen shrub up to 12 ft. h., with slender, pubescent shoots. *l.* 3-foliolate; lflets. oblanceolate or linear-lanceolate, slightly pubescent above, silky-villous beneath, up to 1$\frac{3}{4}$ in. long. *fl.* in axillary clusters of 3 to 7 near ends of young shoots; cor. white; cal. tubular, densely pubescent. April, May. *Pods* 1$\frac{1}{2}$ in. or more long, hairy. Canary Islands. Cultivated for over a century. (B.M. 1908.) Closely allied to *C. palmensis*, differing by l. hairy beneath.

**C. prostra'tus.** Name used variously for several species of Cytisus or Genista, which should be dropped.

**C. pubes'cens.** A synonym of *C. supinus.*

**C. pu'milus.** A synonym of *C. hirsutus pumilus.*

**C. purg'ans.** Deciduous, erect shrub from 8 in. to 3 or 4 ft. h.; shoots pubescent. *l.* sessile, simple, oblong or linear-lanceolate, pubescent, soon falling, $\frac{1}{4}$ to $\frac{1}{2}$ in. long. *fl.* axillary, singly or in pairs, vanilla-scented; cor. golden-yellow; cal. campanulate, pubescent. April to June. *Pod* up to 1 in. long, hairy. SE. France to Cent. Spain, N. Africa. 1750. SYN. *Genista purgans.*

**C. purpu'reus.** Purple Broom. Deciduous, procumbent, with flexuous branches, smooth or nearly so, usually 1$\frac{1}{2}$ to 2 ft. h. *l.* 3-foliolate; lflets. obovate, usually smooth but often ciliate, $\frac{1}{4}$ to 1 in. long. *fl.* axillary, solitary, in pairs, or groups of 3; cor. light or darkish-purple fairly large; cal. tubular, slightly pubescent. May, June. *Pod* smooth, up to 1$\frac{3}{8}$ in. long. Cent. and SE. Europe. 1792. (B.M.) 1176. var. **albo-car'neus,** *fl.* pale pink. Before 1840. SYN. *C. purpureus carneus*, *C. purpureus roseus*; **al'bus,** *fl.* white. Before 1838. SYN. *C. purpureus flore albo*; **atropurpu'reus,** *fl.* darkish-purple; **elonga'tus,** branches long, thin, drooping, *fl.* darkish. SYN. *C. purpureus pendulus.* Cultivated 1872; **erec'tus,** branches upright. Before 1840. *See also* **Laburnocy'tisus.**

**C. × racemo'sus*** (*C. canariensis* × *C. maderensis magnifoliosus*). Evergreen, half-hardy, bushy shrub usually about 6 ft. h., but up to 10 ft.; young shoots hairy. *l.* 3-foliolate; lflets. obovate, rounded at apex, smooth above, appressed silky-hairy beneath, $\frac{1}{4}$ to $\frac{3}{4}$ in. long. *fl.* in rather loose racemes, 2 to 4 in. long, terminating young shoots; cor. bright yellow; cal. campanulate, pubescent. March (or earlier) to May. SYN. *Genista formosa.* Often but wrongly named *C. fragrans* and *Genista fragrans.* Cultivated for about a century. var. **el'egans** is probably a hybrid of *C. × racemosus* rather than a variety of it. It has larger *fl.*, larger and greyer *l.*, and lflets. up to 2 in. long and is on the whole a finer plant than *C. × racemosus.* Propagated by grafting on *C. × racemosus.* SYN. *C. fragrans elegans*; **Everestia'nus,** dwarfer than type, *fl.* darker. (R.H. 1873, 390.) A popular florist's plant.

**C. ramenta'ceus.** A synonym of *Petteria ramentacea.*

**C. ratisbonen'sis.** Deciduous shrub up to 6 ft. h. with erect, appressed-pubescent shoots. *l.* 3-foliolate on $\frac{3}{4}$ in. stalks; lflets. oblong-obovate or elliptic-oblong, smooth above except when young, appressed-hairy beneath and on margins, $\frac{1}{4}$ to 1 in. or more long. *fl.* axillary, in pairs or small groups of 3 or 4 on year-old wood; cor. bright yellow; cal. tubular, appressed-hairy. May, June. *Pod* about 1 in. long, appressed-hairy. Cent. Europe to Caucasus, W. Siberia. About 1800. SYN. *C. hirsutus ratisbonensis*, *C. biflorus* (of l'Héritier). (B.M. 8661; B.R. 308 as *C. biflorus.*) var. **biflo'rus,** *l.* lanceolate or lanceolate-oblong, *fl.* paler, *pods,* silky-hairy. SE. Europe. 1750; **elonga'tus,** tomentose rather than pubescent shoots, lflets. hairy on both surfaces, obovate or oblong. S. France, Hungary, Balkans. SYN. *C. elongatus*, *C. hirsutus elongatus*, *Genista elongata*; **horniflo'rus,** *fl.* in Autumn on young shoots; **ruthen'icus** and **uralen'sis** are geographical vars.

**C. Rochel'ii.** Deciduous spreading shrub up to 3 ft. or more h. with appressed-pubescent young shoots. *l.* 3-foliolate; lflets. oblong-

lanceolate, almost smooth above, appressed-hairy below and on margins, up to 1$\frac{1}{4}$ in. long. *fl.* in terminal heads; cor. rather large, pale yellow, usually with brownish spots; cal. tubular, appressed hairy. June, July. *Pod* 1 in. or more long, villous. Cent. Europe. Cult. 1878. SYN. *C. leucanthus obscurus.* Closely related to *C. leucanthus.*

**C. schipkaen'sis.** A synonym of *C. leucanthus.*

**C. scopar'ius.** Common or Scots Broom. Deciduous, erect, rarely prostrate shrub, up to 8 ft. h. in the open but more in woodland, with pubescent young shoots. *l.* at lower end of shoots, usually 3-foliolate and petiolate with obovate or oblong-lanceolate lflets., upper sessile, simple, lanceolate; all appressed-pubescent when young, glabrous or sometimes slightly pubescent later, lflets. $\frac{1}{16}$ to $\frac{5}{8}$ in. long. *fl.* axillary, solitary or in pairs; cor. bright, shining yellow; cal. campanulate, smooth. May, June. *Pod* up to 2 in. long, hairy, especially at margins. W. Europe; common in Britain. Grown first as a medicinal plant. SYN. *Sarothamnus scoparius, Spartium scoparium.* (E.B. 329.) var. **al'bus,** *fl.* very pale or almost white. Before 1830. SYN. *C. scoparius ochroleucus, C. scoparius pallidus*; **Andrea'nus,** wing-petals typically crimson, remainder of the cor. yellow; other forms are often found, however, in which the *fl.* are irregularly marked with crimson, possibly the products of crossing the type with the variety. SYN. *C. Andreanus.* (R.H. 1886, 373.) The influence of this variety is seen in many popular hybrids such as **Daisy Hill splendens,** sulphur-yellow with crimson keel, **Firefly,** red-brown and yellow, **ful'gens,** orange-yellow and crimson, **Lord Lambourne,** crimson and yellow stained with rose; **flo're ple'no** has double *fl.* SYN. *C. scoparius plenus*; **Golden Sunlight** has brighter *fl.* than the type; **pen'dulus,** procumbent, up to 2 ft. h., with large *fl.* SYN. *C. grandiflorus* (of gardens), *C. prostratus* (of gardens). A useful shrub; **sulphu'reus.*** Moonlight Broom, dwarfer than type, spreading and somewhat drooping in habit, *fl.* sulphur-yellow.

**C. sessilifo'lius.** Deciduous, upright shrub, 6 ft. or more h., with smooth young shoots. *l.* 3-foliolate, usually sessile on flowering shoots but otherwise stalked; lflets. variable, commonly obovate, oval, or oblong-obovate, smooth, $\frac{5}{16}$ to $\frac{3}{4}$ in. long. *fl.* in short racemes terminating young shoots, cor. bright yellow; cal. bell-shaped, smooth. June. *Pod* smooth, about 1$\frac{3}{8}$ in. long. S. Europe, N. Africa; long cult. (B.M. 255.)

**C. supi'nus.** Deciduous, upright or procumbent shrub up to 3 ft. h. with round, hairy branches. *l.* 3-foliolate; lflets. obovate, elliptic, pointed, sparsely pubescent or almost smooth above, very hairy beneath, $\frac{1}{4}$ to 1 in. long. *fl.* in terminal heads about 2 in. wide, with occasionally, axillary *fl.* on year-old branches in spring; cor. bright yellow, standard silky-villous without; cal. tubular, hairy. June to August. *Pod* 1$\frac{1}{4}$ in. long, villous. Cent. and S. Europe. 1755. SYN. *C. gallicus, C. pubescens, Genista supina.* (L.B.C. 497 as *C. capitatus.*) var. **ambig'uus** with *fl.* axillary before the terminal heads. SYN. *C. biflorus*; **bisflo'rens,** racemes lateral along the branches in spring, habit and pods similar to those of *C. hirsutus.* SYN. *C. prostratus.*

**C. supranu'bius.** Teneriffe Broom. More or less erect, deciduous shrub, 8 ft. or more h., with rounded, semi-rigid young shoots sparsely pubescent at first but eventually smooth. *l.* shortly stalked, 3-foliolate; lflets. linear-lanceolate or narrow oblanceolate, more or less pubescent, $\frac{1}{4}$ to $\frac{1}{2}$ in. long, fall early, few, sometimes absent. *fl.* fragrant in axillary clusters of 3 to 6; cor. milky-white, stained pink, standard broadly obovate, notched; cal. bell-shaped, hairy. May, June. *Pod* 1 in. or more long, smooth. Canary Is., especially Teneriffe. About 1830. (B.M. 8509.) SYN. *C. fragrans, C. nubigenus, Genista fragrans, G. nubigenus, Spartocytisus supranubius.* Tender.

**C. triflo'rus.** A synonym of *C. hirsutus* and *C. nigricans.*

**C. uralen'sis.** A synonym of *C. ratisbonensis.*

**C. × ver'sicolor.** Hybrid of which *C. purpureus* is one parent and, either *C. hirsutus* or *C. ratisbonensis* the other. Upright or spreading deciduous shrub, 2 ft. or more h., with sparsely hairy shoots. *l.* 3-foliolate; lflets. obovate or oblong-obovate, smooth above, sparsely hairy beneath, up to 1 in. long. *fl.* axillary, solitary, in pairs, or groups of 3; cor. pale yellow and purple; cal. tubular, hairy. May, June. *Pod* villous. Of garden origin, about 1850.

**C. virga'ta.** A synonym of *Genista virgata.*

**C. Welde'nia.** A synonym of *Petteria ramentacea.*

# D

**DABOE'CIA** (adapted from the Irish name, St. Dabeoc's Heath). FAM. *Ericaceae*. A small genus of shrubs with 4-merous flowers, stamens 4, fruit a 4-celled, septicidal capsule. Allied to and resembling Erica, distinct by the deciduous corolla. Succeeds in lime-free loam and the other conditions suitable for Erica. Propagated by seed, cuttings, layers, and division.

**D. azor'ica.** Evergreen, heath-like shrub, 6 to 10 in. h., with glandular-hairy young shoots at first erect, later procumbent. *l.* ovate-lanceolate, sub-acute, callus-tipped, more recurved than in *D. cantabrica*, dark green and more or less glandular-hairy above, surface white-tomentose beneath, $\frac{3}{16}$ to $\frac{1}{4}$ in. long, about $\frac{1}{8}$ in. wide. *fl.* in upright, terminal, glandular-hairy racemes 4 to 8 in. long; cor. ruby-crimson, ovate-urceolate, $\frac{7}{16}$ in. long, with 4 short, broad, reflexed lobes; sep. ovate, glandular-ciliate, pointed, $\frac{1}{10}$ in. long. June, July. Azores. 1929. Plant forms a compact cushion, is hardier in youth than when aged and should be regarded as half-hardy in cold districts. (B.M. n.s. 46.)

**D. cantab'rica.** Evergreen, heath-like shrub 1 to 3 ft. h. with glandular-hairy young stems. *l.* oval to oblong-lanceolate, subacute, callus-tipped, sparsely glandular-bristly above, tomentose beneath, $\frac{1}{4}$ to $\frac{3}{8}$ in. long, $\frac{1}{16}$ to $\frac{1}{8}$ in. wide, recurved. *fl.* in erect, terminal, glandular-hairy racemes 3 to 6 in. long; cor. ovoid-urceolate, purple, rosy-purple or white, $\frac{2}{5}$ in. long with 4 small, reflexed lobes; sep. ovate, acute or acuminate, glandular-ciliate, less than half length of cor. June to September. SW. Europe, W. Ireland, Azores. In cult. 1800. SYN. *D. polifolia, Menziesia polifolia, Boretta cantabrica.* (Gn. 52 (1897), 344.) var. **al'ba,** *fl.* white, *l.* paler than in type. Connemara. About 1820 (S.B.F.G. 6, 276); **alba globo'sa,** a form with globular-urceolate white fl.; **atropurpu'rea,** *fl.* rich reddish-purple; **bi'color,** *fl.* of 3-colour forms on the same individual, some purple, some white, and some purple and white. SYN. var. *versicolor,* var. *striata;* **na'na,** dwarf, with smaller narrower l. (L.B.C. 1907 as *D. polifolia pygmaea.*) SYN. *Menziesia polifolia nana;* **ro'sea,** *fl.* pink. SYN. *Boretta cantabrica* var. *rosea.* Apt to be damaged in hard winters.

F. S.

*Daboecia cantabrica*

**DACRYD'IUM** (*dakrudion*, diminutive of *daku*, tear; resin drops are commonly exuded). FAM. *Taxaceae.* Ornamental evergreen trees, some with pendulous branches resembling the Cypresses, but more closely related to the Yew and to Podocarpus. There is a wide difference between the juvenile and adult types of foliage, and both forms often occur on the same tree. The juvenile type is soft and awl-shaped, that of mature branches is scale-like, densely arranged, thick, leathery, and overlapping. Male and female flowers are on different trees, the male in short spikes in the axils of the upper leaves, the female near, or at the tips of branchlets. The seed has a fleshy aril or receptacle. About 17 species, natives of New Zealand, Tasmania, New Caledonia, Australia, New Guinea, Malaya, the Philippine and Fiji Is., &c., constitute the genus. In this country 2 species, *D. cupressinum* and *D. Franklinii,* are moderately hardy but the others can only be grown under glass. A mixture of sandy loam and peat suits them. Propagation should be by seeds when possible, otherwise by cuttings taken in early autumn and inserted in sandy soil in a slightly warm propagating frame. Several are useful timber trees.

**D. araucarioi'des.** Tree of about 20 ft. Branches erect, in tiers, branchlets short and cylindrical. *l.* spirally arranged, mature type scale-like, overlapping, leathery, clasping shoot at base, free at tip. *Seeds* 1 to 3 with a fleshy aril. New Caledonia.

**D. Bidwill'ii.** Mountain Pine. Erect or prostrate closely branched shrub, 2 to 10 ft. h., sometimes spreading widely by naturally layered branches. *l.* of young plants linear $\frac{1}{4}$ to $\frac{1}{3}$ in. long, those of mature branches, scale-like, triangular, leathery, blunt. *Seeds* 1 to 2 partly enclosed by a fleshy aril. New Zealand.

**D. bifor'me.** Manoao. 15 to 40 ft. h. Branchlets quadrangular. *l.* on young plants Yew-like, $\frac{1}{8}$ to $\frac{3}{8}$ in. long, on old plants scale-like and overlapping, leathery, blunt. *Seeds* usually solitary. New Zealand.

**D. Colen'soi.** Westland Pine. 40 to 50 ft. h. Branchlets slender. *l.* of young plants linear, loosely arranged, $\frac{1}{4}$ to $\frac{1}{2}$ in. long, the mature type scale-like, densely arranged, leathery, blunt and usually incurved at apex. *Seeds* 1 to 2 together on a fleshy aril. New Zealand. The wood is used for furniture and cabinet work.

**D. cupressi'num.** Rimu. Pyramidal tree 60 to 100 ft. h., with Cupressus-like branchlets. Juvenile *l.* awl-shaped, up to $\frac{1}{4}$ in. long, mature *l.* scale-like, overlapping, pressed close to shoot, blunt. *Seeds* partly enclosed by a rather large aril. New Zealand. The wood is used for building, railway sleepers, furniture, and cabinet work. One of the hardiest species.

**D. ela'tum.** Tall tree of 40 to 60 ft. with spreading branches and pendulous branchlets. Juvenile *l.* awl-like, $\frac{1}{4}$ to $\frac{3}{8}$ in. long, mature scale-like, densely arranged, blunt. *Seeds* about the sides of branchlets. Malay States, Borneo, Fiji and Philippine Is. 1830.

**D. Franklin'ii.** Huon Pine. Decorative tree about 100 ft. h. with slender, pendulous branchlets, resembling a weeping Cypress. *l.* small, dark green, scale-like. *Seeds* small, with a fleshy aril. Tasmania. 1844. The fragrant, red wood is useful for furniture and cabinet work. One of the hardiest species and trees 30 ft. h. have been grown in Cornwall.

**D. interme'dium.** Yellow Silver Pine. 20 to 40 ft. h. Branches spreading. *l.* narrow, curved, pointed, $\frac{1}{8}$ to $\frac{1}{2}$ in. long, or, in the adult state, scale-like densely arranged, leathery, blunt. *Seeds* small. New Zealand.

**D. Kirk'ii.** 50 to 60 ft. h. Branches of young trees spreading, older trees erect. *l.* Yew-like, 1 to $1\frac{1}{2}$ in. long, or, mature, scale-like closely arranged, leathery. New Zealand.

**D. laxifo'lium.** Prostrate shrub a few inches high, but with branches several ft. long. *l.* on juvenile shoots $\frac{1}{4}$ in. long, adult l. scale-like. New Zealand.

**D. novo-guineen'se.** Small tree of 30 to 35 ft. with stiff, erect branches. Juvenile *l.* plumose, sharply pointed, curved at tip, adult scale-like, triangular. *Seeds* small with a red aril. Dutch New Guinea.

**D. taxoi'des.** A small tree up to 50 ft. h. or shrub with purple young shoots and alternate, slightly curved l. $\frac{1}{2}$ to $\frac{3}{4}$ in. long, narrowed and twisted at base. New Caledonia.

A→

W. D.

**DAC'TYLIS** (*daktylos*, finger; application doubtful). FAM. *Gramineae.* A monotypic genus found in all Europe, N. Africa, and part of Asia. A vigorous, coarse, tufted, flat-leaved grass. Panicles with few branches bearing crowded one-sided clusters of spikelets which are nearly sessile. *D. glomerata* will grow well on most good soils and is one of the few grasses that succeed under trees but it is too coarse for any but rough lawns. It is readily raised from seed. The varieties are propagated by division and are less coarse and smaller than the type.

**D. glomera'ta.** Cocksfoot. Perennial, densely tufted, coarse, grey-green. Stem 1 to 3 ft. h. *l.* about $\frac{3}{8}$ in. wide, sheath compressed, ligule about $\frac{1}{8}$ in. long, split. *infl.* as above. May, June. (E.B. 1788.) var. **au'rea,** *l.* yellow; **elegantis'sima,** more slender than type; **variega'ta,** striped silver and green smaller than type and useful for borders.

**dactylo-,** in compound words, signifying finger-like.

**DACTYLO'PIUS.** A genus of mealy-bugs now called Pseudococcus (*see* **Mealy bugs**).

**dactylop'terus -a -um,** finger-winged.

**DADDY LONG LEGS.** *See* **Crane Fly.**

**DAEDALACAN'THUS.** A synonym of Eranthemum.

**DAEM'IA** (the Arabic name). FAM. *Asclepiadaceae*. A genus of 6 species of evergreen twining plants, natives of Trop. Asia and Africa. Leaves opposite cordate. Flowers in umbels; corolla sub-rotate with a short tube; corona double, the outer annular, 5- or 10-lobed. Stove conditions are needed and a compost of fibrous peat and loam with a little sand. Firm side-shoots will root in sand with bottom heat.

**D. exten'sa.** *l.* roundish-cordate, acute, downy, base auricled. *fl.* ⅓ to ½ in. across, pale greenish-yellow, faintly tinged rose towards base, on long filiform, pedicels, reddish below middle. July. E. Indies. 1777. (B.M. 5704 as *Raphistemma ciliatum*.)

F. G. P.

**DAEMON'OROPS** (probably from *daemon*, a deity, and *ops*, like; alluding to the beauty of the trees.) FAM. *Palmaceae*. A genus of about 85 species of elegant slender spiny palms with pinnate leaves, natives of Trop. Asia, sometimes combined with Calamus from which it differs by the outer boat-shaped spathes which are deciduous at first, enclosing the inner spathes, and by the longer stalks of the flowers. For treatment, *see* **Calamus.**

**D. adsper'sus.** About 20 ft. long. Stem about as thick as that of wheat. *l.* pinnate; lflets. 6 to 8 in. long, narrow, deep green; stalks about 6 in. long, sheathing at base, with long, slender, black spines. Java. 1866.

**D. calicarp'us.** Erect or somewhat climbing, 1 in. thick. *l.* 6 to 8 ft. long, upper small with long points; lflets. numerous, 12 to 13 in. long, up to ½ in. wide, bristle-pointed, stalk 1 ft. long, with erect spines, base not swollen. *Male spadix* 6 to 16 in. long, much branched; *female* 4 to 8 in. long; outer spathe 12 to 16 in. long. *fr.* tawny, ⅜ in. wide. Malaya.

**D. Dra'co.** 20 to 30 ft. h. *l.* 4 to 6 ft. long, arching, pinnate; lflets. 12 to 18 in. long, narrow, slightly pendent, dark green; stalks sheathing at base, spines long, flat, black. India. 1819. One source of Dragon's blood.

**D. fis'sus.** *l.* pinnate, bright cinnamon when young; lflets. drooping, dark green with a few black hair-like bristles above; stalks with stout dark spines. Borneo.

**D. gran'dis.** *lflets.* linear-lanceolate, slender pointed, margins and keel sometimes slightly bristly; stalks swollen at base. *Spathe* rather thick; branches of spadix short, compact. Malacca.

**D. interme'dius.** 15 to 20 ft. long, ¾ in. thick. *l.* 4 to 6 ft. long; lflets. 18 to 20 in. long, 1 to 1¼ in. wide, linear-lanceolate, slender-pointed; stalks 1 ft. long with scattered spines. *spathe* 18 in. long, beak twice as long as body; spadix thyrsoid. Malaya.

**D. Jenkinsia'nus.** *l.* arching, 2 to 6 ft. long; lflets. 6 to 12 in. long, 1 in. wide, rich dark green; stalks slightly sheathing at base, spines long, flat. Sikkim.

**D. Lewisia'nus.** Climbing. Stem 1 in. thick. *lflets.* 13 to 15 in. long, up to 1 in. wide; stalk 1 ft. long, much swollen at base, with scattered, short, deflexed spines below and straight and hooked spines 1¼ in. long above. Sheath with one or more flat spines. *fr.* pale yellowish. Penang.

**D. long'ipes.** *l.* about 12 ft. long; lflets. linear-lanceolate, slender-pointed, 12 to 14 in. long, 1¼ in. wide; stalks convex below with long irregular spines. *Spathes* narrow-lanceolate, scurfy when young; Spadix very long, spikes 3 to 5 in. long. Malaya.

**D. melanochae'tes.** Erect, about 150 ft. h. *l.* 10 to 12 ft. long; lflets. long, narrow, drooping, very dark green with many cirrhi; stalks sheathing at base with very long sharp brown-tipped spines swollen at bases. *fr.* yellow-green. Malaya.

**D. palemban'icus.** Erect. *l.* broadly ovate, bright cinnamon-brown when young; lflets. many, narrow, 18 in. long, about ½ in. wide; stalks erect with stout spines on back. Sumatra. 1872.

**D. periacun'thus.** About 15 ft. h., like *D. palembanicus* but young *l.* nearly straw-coloured and stalks with numerous spines set in irregular rings. Sumatra. 1872.

**D. plumo'sus.** *l.* plume-like, 2 to 4 ft. long, very dark green; lflets. about 1 ft. long, less than 1 in. wide, tapering to a narrow point, drooping; stalks densely spiny, spines stout, black, white at base. India. 1870.

**D. verticilla'tus.** *l.* plume-like, lflets. long, broad, drooping; stalks with spines in whorls. Malacca.

**DAFFODIL.** *See* **Narcissus.**

*dahlemen'sis -is -e,* of the Botanic Garden, Dahlem, Berlin.

**DAH'LIA** (in honour of Dr. Andreas Dahl, Swedish botanist and pupil of Linnaeus). FAM. *Compositae*. A genus of perhaps a dozen species of stout, usually erect, Mexican herbaceous plants, sometimes woody at base. Roots tuberous. Stems branching at least at base. Leaves opposite, pinnate to 3-pinnate. Flower-heads long-stalked, large, with yellow disk and rays in a single series; ray-florets spreading, neuter or pistillate; disk-florets perfect; involucre of an inner series of thin scales slightly united at base and an outer of smaller somewhat leafy scales; receptacle flat with chaffy scales. Fruit oblong, flattened at back, rounded at apex and sometimes 2-toothed. The species mentioned below are scarcely ever seen in cultivation at the present day, the vast majority of the Dahlias grown being variations which have arisen in cultivation from the species originally introduced or derived from hybrids between a few of them. These varieties, which are of course, clonal varieties and do not come true from seed, number many thousands, and large numbers of named forms are in cultivation at the present time. A horticultural classification of these forms adopted by the National Dahlia Society and the Royal Horticultural Society is given below with a brief history of the introduction of the Dahlia, while lists of the best present-day varieties will be found in the current Supplement.

The cultivation of the species, except *D. excelsa* and *D. imperialis*, does not differ from that needed by the well-known garden forms and all can be dealt with together. Dahlias are gross feeders and need a deep rich soil if the flowers are to develop fully. It should be deeply dug, or rather double dug, in the autumn before planting in the spring and got into good condition by forking over in fine weather in winter to a depth of 3 or 4 in. The addition of manure, if required, should be made in autumn, never in spring near planting time, for this would tend to encourage rank growth at the expense of the flowers. Mulching with manure or garden compost, however, in hot weather is a great aid to the plants as it tends to prevent loss of water from the soil by evaporation and to keep the plants growing vegetatively after flowering begins. Watering may need to be resorted to if the weather is very dry, but is usually less necessary if the soil has been thoroughly dug and manured in autumn, and contains a reasonable amount of organic matter. A position fully exposed to light is necessary but shelter from high winds by surrounding shrubs is an advantage. Planting out should not be done before the beginning of June and the distance from plant to plant must be governed by the ultimate height of the variety. The Mignon varieties may be as close as 18 to 24 in., while 6 ft. apart will not be too much for the strong, tall varieties; for most varieties 3 ft. apart is enough. The plants should be staked as soon as planted; indeed many advise that the stakes should be put in first and the hole large enough to contain the roots made in front of the stake. Staking is essential for the stems are brittle and easily broken by a strong wind. A single stake may be used and the branches (usually 4 are permitted to grow from near the base) are looped in separately, not tied in a bundle to it. Alternately a separate stake may be used for each branch. Whichever method is used tying must not be neglected. When 6 in. high the top of the stem should be pinched out. If exhibition flowers are desired disbudding must be attended to, leaving the middle bud and removing also the two next below. The dwarf Pompon varieties are sometimes pegged down while the shoots are young but care must be taken to see that the shoots are not broken in the process. The flower-heads should be removed as soon as they are past their best. If allowed to remain flowering is checked and the season of value much shortened.

Propagation is by division of the rootstock or by cuttings. Buds are not produced on the tubers themselves and for each division care must be taken that a piece of the old stem bearing a bud is taken with the tuber. This is readily done if the old root is allowed to sprout before division is attempted. Cuttings root readily in spring. The rootstock which has been stored and kept dry in winter should be brought into heat at the end of January or in early February, the roots but not the crown being covered with soil or litter. Slight daily syringing will induce buds to develop and as soon as a shoot has 2 joints it may be removed as a cutting. The cuttings are placed singly in small pots of sandy loam with some leaf-soil or peat and plunged in a close frame on a hotbed or in the propagating house. Roots are soon formed and then the plants should be hardened, repotted, and moved to cooler conditions until the time for planting out. Cuttings will be produced in succession from the old roots and a considerable stock may thus be obtained. Seeds may be sown thinly in pans at the end of March and placed on a hotbed or in the propagating house, the seedlings being potted singly into small pots and grown in heat for a time, then hardened ready for planting out. The seedlings will not be quite true to the parental type and by this means new varieties may be raised. Some varieties do not produce tubers very freely and with these, in order to preserve them, grafting is sometimes resorted to in autumn. A shoot of 2 joints is taken, cut just below the bottom one, and a portion of the skin on one side is removed. A fleshy tuber of another variety is prepared by having a hole of the same size as the scion made in it to receive the scion which is then tied in. The raffia is then covered with clay and the whole potted and put under a hand-glass until the union has taken place. The plant must be kept growing slowly through the winter and cuttings taken in spring and rooted as described.

As soon as the tops of the plants are killed in autumn they should be cut down within a few inches of the ground and the roots lifted, the soil removed with a pointed stick, a label attached to each stem, and the whole stored in a dry, cool, frost-proof place. They need looking over occasionally to remove any part of the roots which may damp off.

The garden Dahlias are all half-hardy plants and the aerial parts are killed by the first frosts of autumn. The roots may at times survive in the ground through a very mild winter if the crown is protected by a covering of ashes, but in no part of the country is it safe to rely upon this. *D. excelsa* and *D. imperialis* rarely attain flowering time before autumn frosts and while they may be grown outdoors through the summer it is necessary to bring them into a warm house before frosts occur. They are interesting species but perhaps not worth the trouble and space their cultivation requires.

The garden varieties may be grown in the herbaceous border where they form a valuable addition to the plants flowering in August onwards, but perhaps they are most valuable in beds by themselves, where their varying colours and heights may be made use of with the greatest effect.

The Dahlia was introduced to Europe from Mexico to the Botanic Garden, Madrid, in 1789. There were 3 forms to which names were given, *D. pinnata* with double purple flowers, *D. rosea* with single rose flowers, and *D. coccinea* with single red flowers. From Spain these plants were introduced to France and in 1802 *D. coccinea* was obtained from France and flowered in 1803 at Chelsea, and in 1803 *D. rosea* flowered at Vauxhall. All 3 forms, however, had been sent to Kew from Madrid by the Marchioness of Bute in 1798, but both these and those obtained through France were subsequently lost. The plants from which the early garden Dahlias were derived originated in seed sent home from Madrid in 1804 by Lady Holland. It is said also that another stock was brought from France about 1815. These proved very variable when raised from seed and from them and from *D. Juarezii* the whole great range of garden varieties has

been derived. Numbers of varieties have been raised particularly in France, England, Germany, Holland, and America, partly by purposeful crossing, partly as chance seedlings, and the number is annually added to. Fashions have changed and new groups have been developed from time to time. The Show Dahlia of the nineteenth century, while still grown, is far less often seen than the large Decorative or Paeony-flowered varieties. The small Pompon varieties early became favourites and a few varieties of this type held their place for a century or so. They are still grown to a considerable extent especially for cutting. The introduction of the dwarf Coltness Gem about 1922 started a new race for bedding which has had a great vogue. Others with small more or less double flowers have been found not only useful for the garden but also for cutting, and of these, too, there are many varieties. The present grouping of these garden forms adopted by the National Dahlia Society and the Royal Horticultural Society is as follows:

CLASS I. SINGLE DAHLIAS.

(*a*) *Show Singles.* Flower-heads not exceeding 3 in. across, the 8 (only) rays smooth, somewhat recurved at tips, broad, overlapping to form a perfectly round flower.

*Show Single Dahlia.* Class I *a*

(*b*) *Singles.* Flower-heads with rays not so completely overlapping as in *a*, the tips separated.

*Single Dahlia.* Class I *b*

(*c*) *Mignon Dahlias.* Flower-heads as in *b*, but plants not exceeding 18 in. high.

CLASS II. ANEMONE-FLOWERED DAHLIAS.

Flower-heads with one or more series of flat ray-florets surrounding a dense group of tubular florets longer than the disk-florets in Class I and usually of a different colour from the rays.

*Anemone-flowered Dahlia.* Class II

### CLASS III. COLLARETTE DAHLIAS.

Flower-heads with one or more series of flat ray-florets as in Class I and above each series a ring of florets (the Collarette) only half the length of the rays and usually of a different colour.

(*a*) *Collarette Singles.* Flower-heads with a single series of rays and one collarette with a yellow disk.

*Collarette Dahlia.* Class III

(*b*) *Collarette Paeony-flowered.* Flower-heads with 2 or 3 series of rays and collars and a yellow disk.
(*c*) *Collarette Decorative.* Similar to *b* but fully double.

### CLASS IV. PAEONY-FLOWERED DAHLIAS

Flower-heads with 2 or 3 series of ray-florets and a central disk.

(*a*) *Large Paeony-flowered.* Flower-heads over 7 in. across.
(*b*) *Medium Paeony-flowered.* Flower-heads from 5 to 7 in. across.
(*c*) *Small Paeony-flowered.* Flower-heads less than 5 in. across.
(*d*) *Dwarf Paeony-flowered.* Plants not exceeding 30 in. high.

### CLASS V. FORMAL DECORATIVE Dahlias.

Flower-heads fully double, showing no disk. All florets regularly arranged, their margins usually slightly incurved, flattened towards tips which may be broadly pointed or rounded.

*Paeony-flowered Dahlia.* Class IV

Four subclasses *a, b, c, d,* corresponding with those under Class IV.

*Formal Decorative Dahlia.* Class V

### CLASS VI. INFORMAL DECORATIVE DAHLIAS.

Flower-heads fully double, showing no disk. Rays not regularly arranged, broad, more or less flat or slightly twisted, more or less acutely pointed.

Four sub-classes, *a, b, c, d,* corresponding with those under Class IV.

### CLASS VII. SHOW DAHLIAS.

Flower-heads fully double, over 3 in. across, almost globular, with central florets like the outer but smaller.

Florets with margins incurved, tubular or cup-shaped, short and blunt at mouth.

*Informal Decorative Dahlia.* Class VI

Fancy Dahlias form a sub-class here with florets tipped white or striped.

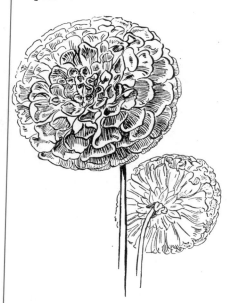

*Show Dahlia.* Class VII

**CLASS VIII. POMPON DAHLIAS.**

Flower-heads similar to those in Class VII but smaller. For show purposes the flower-heads must not exceed 2 in. across.

**CLASS IX. CACTUS DAHLIAS.**

Flower-heads fully double, margins of flowers revolute for not less than three-quarters of their length, the central florets forming a filbert-shaped group.

(*a*) *Large-flowered Cactus.* Flower-heads over 4½ in. across.

*Pompon Dahlia.* Class VIII

(*b*) *Small-flowered Cactus.* Flower-heads not over 4½ in. across.

(*c*) *Dwarf Cactus.* Plants not exceeding 30 in. h.

**CLASS X. SEMI-CACTUS DAHLIAS.**

Flower-heads fully double, florets broad at base, their margins revolute towards tip, slightly twisted for about half their length.

Three sub-classes, *a, b, c,* corresponding with those in Class IX.

**CLASS XI. STAR DAHLIAS.**

Flower-heads small, with 2 or 3 series of somewhat pointed rays, not or scarcely overlapping at their more or less recurving margins, forming a cup-shaped flower-head with a disk.

*DISEASES.* Dahlias are liable to suffer from several diseases. In the Virus group, Tomato Spotted Wilt (q.v.) shows as concentric rings or wavy lines on the leaves; Mosaic shows as mottling or vein banding of yellow; Ringspot appears as yellow or pale green rings or zig-zag markings; and Streak makes its appearance as brown spots or streaks on the stems and petioles. Although the effect on the plants is not rapid death but rather slow crippling and degeneration, affected plants should be destroyed so as to prevent the spread of the trouble and keep the stocks healthy. Much depends on growing the plants well—the virus symptoms are always more serious in badly grown plants or in those checked through drought, &c. In the fungus diseases Powdery Mildew, *Erysiphe polygoni,* may be a nuisance especially where the plants are massed closely together for effect, so causing moist conditions amongst the foliage. The same conditions will encourage Smut disease (*Entyloma dahliae*) which appears as small light spots first on the lower leaves and spreading upwards. As they increase in size the spots turn brown but always have a light marginal

*Cactus Dahlia.* Class IX

band giving a 'halo' effect. This spotting may be so severe as to cause defoliation. The Mignon types are the

*Semi-cactus Dahlia.* Class X

most susceptible, the others fairly so with the exception of Star and Pompon varieties which appear somewhat resistant. For Mildew and Smut picking off the first

affected leaves and spraying with Bordeaux mixture is advised. Wilt, *Verticillium dahliae* may attack the roots

*Star Dahlia.* Class XI

but is not very common. A word should be said about Dahlia tubers in storage which may be attacked by the fungus *Sclerotinia sclerotiorum.* This fungus destroys the tubers and forms a very fluffy white mass of fungus threads which soon produces the hard black resting bodies or sclerotia. This fungus often destroys carrots and similar vegetables in store. It will not thrive so well where moisture is absent so it is important to dry Dahlia tubers properly before storing and to see that the store is frost proof. Dusting with copper-lime dust is a good treatment for stored Dahlia tubers especially where the thick bases are difficult to dry thoroughly.

(D. E. G.)

*PESTS.* The chief insect enemies are Earwigs, the Tarnished Plant Bug, *Lygus pratensis*, and the Bean Aphis, *Aphis fabae.* Earwigs eat the leaves and flowers, and shelter during the day at the base of the plants, among the petals, and in bamboo support-canes, which should be cut close to a node to avoid this nuisance. They become active after dark and eat out holes in the foliage and cause the flowers to become ragged. The Tarnished Plant Bug or Bishop Bug may be as destructive to Dahlias as to Chrysanthemums. The adult bugs migrate to the plants from wild hosts in late July and August, insert their sucking mouth parts into the developing flower buds and young tender leaves causing the flowers to open malformed, and the leaves to be marked with rusty-brown spots which, later, tend to extend so that the leaves are ragged, deformed, and undersized. The Bean Aphis often occurs in vast masses on the young shoots, leaves, and flower buds during July, and causes considerable reduction in the vigour of the plants.

The control of these pests is dealt with under the heading of the particular pest (q.v.).

(G. F. W.)

The original types may be defined as follows, the specific limits, however, are often hard to define.

**D. coccin'ea.** Stem erect, about 3 ft. h., branching above base, glaucous, rather slender. *l.* pinnate or 2-pinnate; lflets. rather narrow-ovate, toothed. *fl.-heads* scarlet, orange or yellow; ray florets in wild form sterile, but in garden varieties often fertile. Mexico. 1798. (B.M. 762.) SYN. *D. Cervantesii, D. crocea.*

**D. excel'sa.** Erect, up to 20 ft. h. or more, branching at base, glaucous, more or less woody. *l.* 2-pinnate, 2½ ft. long; lflets. many, ovate, slender-pointed, toothed, not or scarcely hairy. *fl.-heads* erect, 4½ in. across; rays 8, pale purple; disk pinkish. Habitat? (G.C. 19 (1883), 80.) var. **anemonaeflo'ra,** disk-florets lilac or yellow; rays flat.

**D. grac'ilis.** Bushy, about 4 ft. h., stems slender. *l.* 2-pinnate, ternate, glabrous; lflets. small, ovate, coarsely toothed. *fl.* brilliant orange-scarlet; outer scales of involucre almost circular.

**D. imperia'lis.** 6 to 18 ft. h., usually branched only at base. Stem 4-angled, nodes swollen. *l.* 2- or 3-pinnate; lflets. ovate, narrowed to base, toothed, slightly hairy. *fl.-heads* nodding, 4 to 7 in. across, white with some tinge of red especially near base; rays lanceolate, acute, not toothed, sterile or pistillate. Mexico. (B.M. 5813.)

**D. Juare'zii.** Cactus Dahlia. Habit of *D. rosea*. *fl.-heads* bright scarlet; florets of irregular length, overlapping, rays long narrow, margins more or less recurved. 1864. (G.C. 12 (1879), 433.) Has been crossed with *D. rosea*, &c., and given rise to a distinct race of garden varieties with intermediates.

**D. Merck'ii.** 2 to 3 ft. h. Glabrous. Tubers more slender than in *D. rosea*. *l.* 2-pinnate; lflets. narrow; bracts linear. *fl.-heads* lilac; rays short, roundish, acute; peduncles branched, long, wiry, raising fl.-heads much above foliage. 1840. (B.R. 26, 29 as *D. glabrata*.)

**D. pinna'ta.** 2 to 3 ft. h. Glabrous. *l.* 5-foliolate, rachis winged; lflets. ovate, with roundish teeth, glaucous beneath; *fl.-heads* large, solitary; rays in more than 1 series in original plant, margins incurved, bluish-red. Mexico. 1798. (A.B.R. 408.)

**D. ro'sea.** 3 to 5 ft., erect, branching. *l.* pinnate, or sometimes 2-pinnate; lflets. broadly ovate, toothed. *fl.-heads* of various colours; margins of rays not recurved; florets cupped in double forms. Mexico. 1798. (B.M. 1885; B.R. 55 as *D. superflua*.) The chief parent of the garden Dahlia. Syn. *D. variabilis*.

**D. scapig'era.** 2 ft. h., nearly glabrous. Stem slender, striate. *l.* pinnate, rarely 2-pinnate; lflets. ovate to narrow-linear, toothed. *fl.-heads* about 2 in. across, of various colours; peduncles long, slender, glabrous, often in pairs or threes; disk yellow; rays ovate, 3-toothed at apex; outer involucral bracts rather spreading, not reflexed. 1838.

**D. superflu'a.** A synonym of *D. rosea*.

**D. variab'ilis.** A synonym of *D. rosea*. Several forms are often included under this name which was given by Desfontaines in 1829. Cavanilles' name, *D. rosea*, which covers much the same range dates from 1794.

**D. zimapan'ii.** A synonym of *Cosmos diversifolius*.

***dahu'ricus***, *see* ***dauricus***.

**DA'IS** (*dais*, a torch, in allusion to the form of the inflorescence). Fam. *Thymelaeaceae*. A genus of about 6 species of shrubs, natives of S. Africa and Madagascar. The following is the only species in cultivation and requires cool greenhouse treatment. Its bark is said to yield the strongest fibre known to the natives of Natal and by them to be used as a thread.

**D. cotinifo'lia.** Deciduous shrub up to 8 or 10 ft., occasionally a tree up to 20 ft. in a wild state. *l.* opposite or alternate, ovate, obovate or oblong, 1½ to 3 in. long by ¾ to 2 in. wide, cuneate, entire, glabrous; stalk ⅛ in. long. *fl.* in an erect umbel 1 to 3 in. across on a slender terminal stalk 1½ to 2 in. long; cor. ½ in. across with a slender tube ½ in. long and 5 spreading narrow lobes, pale lilac; stamens 10. June, July. S. Africa. 1776. (B.M. 147.)

W. J. B.

**DAISY.** *See* **Bellis.**

**DAISY GRUBBER.** A short implement with a claw for removing the roots of Daisies and other weeds from lawns. It has a handle and a flat portion bent to form a lever when pressed on the ground.

**DAISY, MICHAELMAS.** *See* **Aster.**

**DAISY, OX-EYE.** *See* **Chrysanthemum Leucanthemum.**

**DAISY, Swan River.** *See* **Brachycome iberidifolia.**

**DALBERG'IA** (in honour of Nicholas Dalberg, 1736–1820, Swedish botanist). Fam. *Leguminosae*. A genus of nearly 100 species of evergreen trees or climbing shrubs, natives of the tropics. Leaves alternate, unequally pinnate, rarely with 1 leaflet only; leaflets without stipels. Flowers papilionaceous, stamens united. Inflorescence cymose or paniculate, axillary or terminal. Pod indehiscent. They need stove conditions and a mixture of fibrous peat and turfy loam with some sand. Cuttings of firm young shoots will root in March in sand. Some species, like *D. latifolia* and *D. Sissoo*, yield valuable elastic and durable timber.

**D. Brown'ei.** Climber to 6 or 10 ft. h. *l.* ovate, somewhat cordate, acute, glabrous. *fl.* white, fragrant; peduncles axillary, 10-fld. sometimes downy. May. Jamaica. 1793. Syn. *Amerimnon Brownei*. Requires trellis or other support.

**D. cochinchinen'sis.** Tree up to 80 ft. h. *l.* 6 to 8 in. long; lflets. 7 to 9, ovate, acute, 1½ to 2½ in. long, glabrous, pale green above, more or less glaucous beneath; stipules ovate. *fl.* in loose axillary panicles up to 6 in. long, white; 9 stamens joined, 1 free or nearly so. *fr.* 2 to 3 in. long, glabrous. Cochin-China.

**D. latifo'lia.** Black Wood. Deciduous tree to 30 ft. *lflets.* roundish, emarginate. *fl.* white, in terminal panicles. May. *fr.* lanceolate. E. Indies. Wood extremely hard, dark; used for furniture, carving, fancywork, gun carriages, &c.

**D. seric'ea.** Tree. *l.* 8 to 10 in. long; lflets. usually 13 to 19, ovate, 1 to 1¾ in. long, slightly hairy above, hairy beneath; rachis silky-hairy. *fl.* in short, dense, axillary panicles, 1 to 2 in. long, white; stamens in 2 bundles of 5. *fr.* flat, brownish, indehiscent. Himalaya.

**D. Sis'soo.** Sissoo-tree. Tree of 30 ft. *lflets.* 5, alternate, obovate, abruptly slender-pointed, glabrous above, downy beneath. Bengal. 1820. Wood very hard; used for gun carriages, railway sleepers, boats, &c.

**D. strigulo'sum.** 6 to 10 ft. h., branches hairy, hairs light brown, dense, short. *l.* ovate, rather cordate, obtuse, appressed-hairy on both surfaces. *fl.* white in solitary, axillary racemes, 3 times as long as the l.-stalks. Trinidad. 1817. Syn. *Amerimnon strigulosum*.

F. G. P.

***D'Albertisii***, in honour of L. M. d'Albertis.

**DAL'EA** (in honour of Dr. Samuel Dale, 1659–1739. English botanist and author). Fam. *Leguminosae*. An American genus of considerable size but uncertain limits, being much confused with Parosela and Psoralea. Leaves unequally glandular; flowers in terminal spikes or heads. The species have no great horticultural value.

**D. alopecuroi'des.** Annual, 1 to 2 ft., branches glabrous. *lflets.* 15 to 41, narrow-oblong, cuneate, or oblanceolate, ⅛ to ½ in. long. *Spike* 1 to 3 in. long, cylindrical; standard white, keel and wings white tinged with rose or lilac. Summer. S. United States. Hardy.

**D. mutab'ilis.** Sub-shrub with a woody base, sending up glabrous stems 1 to 1½ ft. *l.* 1 to 2 in. long; lflets. 7 to 15, obovate, ⅛ to ⅜ in. long, ⅛ to ¼ in. wide, apex often notched. *fl.* in terminal downy spikes 2 to 3½ in. long; standard white, ⅝ in. long, with a slender claw; keel and wings white, tipped violet. October. Mexico. 1821. (B.M. 2486; H.E.F. 43 as *D. bicolor*.) Greenhouse.

W. J. B.

***dalecar'licus -a -um***, of Dalarne, Sweden.

**DALECHAMP'IA** (in honour of James Dalechamp, 1513–88, French physician, botanist, and philologist). Fam. *Euphorbiaceae*. A genus of about 60 species, spread over the tropics, a few being worth cultivation in the stove for the brilliantly coloured bracts. Related to Ricinus but with a complicated inflorescence. Stamens erect in bud, flower without petals. A compost of loam, peat, and leaf-mould suits them provided there is enough sand added to ensure thorough drainage. Propagation by cuttings.

**D. Roezlia'na.** Erect, branched, leafy. *l.* more or less cordate, 5 to 9 in. long, slender-pointed, short-stalked. *fl.* sweet-scented, on filiform angular pedicels 2 or 3 in. long, with 2 small ovate bracts at apex at base of 2 broadly ovate, slender-pointed, toothed, rosy-pink bracts, within these are other smaller bracts around and among the male and female fl., some of them thick and club-shaped, with a fringe of short, waxy-looking threads at the top. Mexico. 1867. (B.M. 5640.) var. **al'ba**, bracts white.

**D. scan'dens.** Climbing shrub. *l.* palmately 3- to 5-partite, more or less hairy; lobes entire; stipules ovate, narrow. *fl.* monoecious; ovary hairy. *fr.* hispid, 3-celled. Cent. America.

F. G. P.

***Dalhous'iae***, in honour of Countess Dalhousie, *née* Brown, 1786–1839, vice-reine of India.

**DALIBARD'A** (in honour of Thomas François Dalibard, 1703–79, French botanist). Fam. *Rosaceae*. A genus of a single species described below, differing from Rubus with which it has sometimes been united by its creeping habit, violet-like leaves, and fruit of a few dry achenes. It may be grown on the rock-garden in peaty soil in a rather sheltered place. Hardy.

**D. re'pens.** Tufted, creeping, hairy perennial. *l.* heart-shaped, about 1½ in. long, obtuse, wavy toothed, long-stalked. *fl.* white, 1 or 2 on each scape; sep. 5 or 6, 3 larger and toothed; pet. 5; stamens numerous; carpels 5 to 10. May, June. Eastern N. America. 1768. Syn. *Rubus Dalibarda*. Some fl. are cleistogamous as a rule.

**DALMATIAN INSECT POWDER.** *See* **Chrysanthemum cinerariifolium.**

***dalmat'icus -a -um.*** Of Dalmatia, eastern coast of Adriatic Sea.

***damasce'nus -a -um,*** of Damascus.

**DAMASK ROSE.** *See* **Rosa damascena.**

**DAMASK, VIOLET.** *See* **Hesperis matronalis.**

**DAMASON'IUM** (*damein*, to conquer; application obscure). FAM. *Alismataceae.* A genus of 2 species of aquatic herbs with radical, stalked, ovate to lanceolate leaves with a prominent midrib. Flowers white, in large panicles, segments 6, the 3 inner narrow, persistent, the 3 outer petal-like, deciduous. Differing from Alisma by the 6 to 8 spreading carpels, connate at base, forming a star-like fruit. Treatment as for Alisma.

**D. Alis'ma.** Perennial. *l.* sometimes floating, elliptical, 5-nerved; stalks long. *fl.* white, delicate; segs. with a yellow spot at base; scapes with a terminal umbel. June. W. and S. Europe. N. Africa, including Britain. (E.B. 144.) SYN. *D. stellatum, Actinocarpus Damasonium.*

**D. mi'nus.** Smaller in all parts. Australia. SYN. *D. australe, Actinocarpus minor.*

**D. stella'tum.** A synonym of *D. Alisma.*

**DAME'S VIOLET.** *See* **Hesperis matronalis.**

**DAMMAR, BLACK.** *See* **Canarium strictum** in Supplement.

**DAMMAR PINE.** *See* **Agathis.**

**DAMMARA.** *See* **Agathis.**

**DAMNACAN'THUS** (*damnas*, to conquer, *acanthos*, spine; in reference to the copious spines). FAM. *Rubiaceae.* A genus of 2 or 3 species of evergreen shrubs with opposite leaves and spines. Flowers small, axillary, in pairs; corolla funnel-shaped, hairy in the throat; stamens 4 or 5. Cool greenhouse shrubs requiring a good loamy compost. Propagated by cuttings.

**D. in'dicus.** Shrub 2 to 4 ft., shoots very slender, scurfy-downy, armed with needle-like, slender spines 1/2 to 3/4 in. long. *l.* opposite, ovate, 1/3 to 3/4 in. long, short-stalked, spine-tipped, mostly rounded at base, glabrous. *fl.* in axillary pairs, white, trumpet-shaped, 1/2 in. long with 5 short lobes. *fr.* red or scarlet, 1/8 to 1/4 in. wide, globose. China, Japan, Himalaya. 1868.

**D. ma'jor.** Shrub 3 to 4 ft., shoots scurfy, spines very slender, 1/4 to 5/8 in. long. *l.* broadly ovate or oval, 3/4 to 2 in. long, rounded to broadly tapered at base, glabrous. *fl.* white, fragrant; cor. 5/8 in. long, funnel-shaped with 5 short, pointed lobes. *fr.* red, 1/5 in. wide, seeds hard, white. Japan. 1868. Differs from *D. indicus* by its larger l. and smaller spines.

W. J. B.

**DAM'PIERA** (in honour of Capt. Wm. Dampier, R.N., the celebrated circumnavigator). FAM. *Goodeniaceae.* A genus of about 35 species of herbs and shrubs confined to Australia, distinguished by the auricled corolla lobes and united anthers. Leaves alternate; corolla tube slit; fruit small. Warm house.

**D. Brown'ii.** Tall evergreen shrub scurfy and hairy on most of its parts. *l.* roundish oval, 1/2 to 1 in. long (more in luxuriant specimens) coarsely wavy toothed or ovate-lanceolate and entire. *fl.* 5/8 to 3/4 in. wide, springing from the upper l.-axils often in threes; cor. purple or blue, clothed with dark hairs. July. Australia. 1824.

W. J. B.

**DAMPING DOWN.** The wetting of floors and walls of glass-houses, especially forcing houses. This operation is practised in most plant houses in summer and in tropical houses at all times. It has the effect of lowering the temperature since heat is absorbed by the water as it is converted into vapour, and of increasing the humidity of the air. Plants of tender growth bear more heat with less ventilation when damping down is well attended to, and undue transpiration from the leaves is prevented. It is thus a matter of great importance in maintaining healthy, free growth in most plants needing a high temperature. It is inadvisable to throw water over hot pipes, and is frequently undesirable, and often detrimental, to wet the foliage, especially when the sun is shining. Frequent watering around and beneath the plants may prove beneficial in dry weather in summer. The frequency of damping down must be governed by the kind of plants grown and by the conditions prevailing at the time.

**DAMPING OFF** is a term very loosely used to describe various kinds of plant ailments but is mainly intended to describe the attack by parasitic fungi on seedlings causing them to collapse and die.

Damping off in seedings, although usually due to the fungus *Pythium de baryanum,* may also be caused by other fungi such as *Rhizoctonia solani.* The trouble is encouraged by wet conditions and by overcrowding the seedlings, with the result that the fungus enters the stem near the ground level and by killing the cells causes them to collapse so that the seedling falls over. In *Pythium de baryanum* the fungus threads growing on the dying tissues form spores to spread the disease quickly, and also form oospores, i.e. resting spores that contaminate the soil for the next season. The remedy is to avoid overcrowding so that the seedlings are strong and to avoid very wet conditions which encourage the growth of the fungus. Attacks may be checked by watering with Cheshunt compound (*see* **Fungicides**), but where there is repeated trouble with damping off (e.g. in Tomato seedlings) it would be wise to use sterilized soil for seed raising and for the smaller pots and also to practise some sterilizing treatment on the pots and boxes. *See also* **Foot Rot.**

D. E. G.

**DAMSON** (*Prunus institiia*). The treatment of Damsons is that required by Plums (q.v.) generally, and they are propagated by budding on the same types of rootstocks. Usually grown as half-standards and often used as a wind-break, especially the compact pyramidal Farleigh Damson (also known as Crittenden's and Cluster). The typical damson has a somewhat astringent flavour, but some of the varieties grown under the name lack this distinction and may be regarded more as small plums. Most are blackish (black, blue-black, or red-black), oval, with yellowish-green firm flesh, and ripen from mid-September to October. One old variety, the White Damson, has whitish-yellow fruits with a few red dots. The following key includes most of the varieties commonly grown.

KEY

| | |
|---|---|
| 1. *Shoots smooth* | 2 |
| 1. *Shoots more or less downy* | 3 |
| 2. *Fruit large, roundish-oval, flat at base, tapering to stem, dark purplish-red with fine bloom; stone free* | Bradley's King Damson |
| 2. *Fruit medium size, roundish-oval, shoulder's sloping, blue-black; stone clinging* | Frogmore Damson |
| 3. *Growth upright, branches little spreading* | 4 |
| 3. *Growth more spreading making a round-headed tree* | 5 |
| 4. *Fruit small, black, bloomy, tapering to each end* | Farleigh Damson |
| 4. *Fruit of medium size, blue black* | Westmorland Damson |
| 5. *Fruit oval or roundish-oval* | 6 |
| 5. *Fruit small with sloping shoulders, blue-black. Flavour excellent* | Prune or Shropshire Damson |
| 6. *Fruit small, oval, flattish near stem, dark red-blue, slightly bloomy; stone clinging; without damson flavour; early* | Rivers Early Damson |
| 6. *Fruit large, oval, black with bloom, with damson flavour; late* | Merryweather Damson |

In addition to their value for pies and stewing, the Damsons make excellent preserves and are good for bottling.

**DA'NAË** (from Danaë, daughter of King Acrisius of Argos). FAM. *Liliaceae.* A genus of 1 species related to Ruscus but with perfect flowers in short terminal racemes of 4 to 6, perianth segments 6, joined. A plant for half-shady places in moist soil, hardy and excellent for cutting for its evergreen foliage. Increased by seed or division.

**D. racemo'sa.** Alexandrian Laurel. Branched, evergreen shrub, 2 to 4 ft. h., with alternate leaf-like cladodes in axils of minute scale l. *Cladodes* oblong-lanceolate, 1½ to 4 in. long, ¼ to 1½ in. wide, tapering to the unarmed point, bright green. *fl.* yellowish, small, short-stalked. *fr.* red, ¼ in. across, 1- or 2-seeded, not frequent in England. Asia Minor to Persia. 1713. SYN. *D. Laurus*, *Ruscus racemosus*.

**DANAE'A** (in honour of Pierre Martin Dana, 1736–1801; wrote on plants of Piedmont). FAM. *Marattiaceae*. A remarkable and distinct genus of about 30 species of ferns, natives of Trop. America. Rhizomes woody. Fronds pinnate, rarely simple, fleshy, leathery; pinnae usually jointed. Sori linear, occupying whole length of veins, crowded, covering whole under surface of the fertile pinnae. Sporangia sessile, in rows, opening by apical pores. The beauty of some of the species of Danaea renders it most desirable that the attempts made in the past to cultivate them should be repeated. Hitherto the plants imported have languished, and after a while usually died. They grow in nature in warm, constantly moist, and usually shady places, apparently in very porous soil of a light yellow colour and sandy texture. For general cultivation, see **Ferns**.

**D. ala'ta.** *sti.* of barren fronds 2 to 6 in. long. *Barren fronds* 1 to 1½ ft. long, 6 to 8 in. wide with 8 to 10 pinnae each side; central ones short-stalked, 3 to 5 in. long, ¼ in. wide, slender pointed, serrate, rounded at base. *Fertile fronds* on longer sti., pinnae more distinctly stalked, 1 to 3 in. long, acute or obtuse. W. Indies.

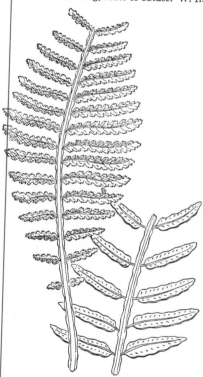

*Danaea crispa*

**D. cris'pa.** *Barren fronds* with about 18 sessile pinnae each side, rachis narrowly winged, wing undulate; pinnae narrow oblong, pinnatifid, lobes with 2 or 3 teeth at apex. *Fertile fronds* shorter; pinnae oblong-lanceolate, margins undulate, slightly recurved. Costa Rica.

**D. nodo'sa.** *sti.* 1½ to 2 in. long, erect, nodose. *Barren fronds* 3 to 4 ft. long, 1½ to 2 ft. wide; pinnae 10 to 15 pairs, upper sessile, lower short-stalked, slender pointed, entire, 6 to 12 in. long, 1 to 2 in. wide, base wedge-shaped or rounded, rather leathery. *Fertile fronds* 4 to 6 in. long, ½ to 1 in. wide. Trop. America.

*danaifo'lius -a -um,* with leaf like those of Danaë.

**DANCING GIRLS.** *See* **Mantisia saltatoria.**

**DANDELION** (*Taraxacum officinale*). Dandelion is grown for the blanched leaves for use in salad, seed being sown and the plants treated in the same way as Chicory, or the plants may be raised from root-cuttings. Blanching is effected in the same way as for Chicory. Care should be taken to remove flowers in summer to prevent the ripening and distribution of the seed since the dandelion may become such a troublesome weed both on lawns and on tilled ground.

**DANES' BLOOD.** Daneweed. Danewort. *See* **Sambucus Ebulus.**

*Danford'iae* in honour of Mrs. C. G. Danford who collected Crocuses, &c., in Asia Minor, 1876–9.

*danubia'lis -is -e,* of the neighbourhood of the Danube.

**DAPH'NE** (*Daphne*, the Bay-tree). FAM. *Thymelaeaceae*. A genus of about 35 species of evergreen and deciduous shrubs with alternate, rarely opposite, leaves nearly always entire. Inflorescence terminal or lateral usually in one or other form of group such as cluster, raceme, or fascicle. The flower is often coloured, usually fragrant, perfect and without petals, the 4- (rarely 5-) lobed calyx consisting of tube and limb taking their place; stamens 8 to 10, included; stigma usually capitate, sessile, or on a short style. Fruit a 1-seeded drupe, leathery or fleshy. Propagation from seed is successful for *D. Mezereum*, *D. pontica*, *D. Laureola*, and *D. alpina* at least. *D. japonica*, *D. odora*, *D. Bholua*, *D. Blagayana*, *D. Cneorum*, *D. arbuscula*, *D. petraea* and probably many others can be increased by layers and cuttings. Grafting may be used as a last resort, seedlings of *D. Laureola* being employed for evergreen species and those of *D. Mezereum* for deciduous. Several hybrids have occurred. The popular belief that European Daphnes prefer limy soil has little to support it. Some, like *D. Cneorum*, will thrive upon it in certain situations provided it is mixed with peat or leaf-mould. On the other hand, all Daphnes enjoy a cool, lime-free soil which must be friable and well-drained. Special individual requirements are mentioned below.

Of diseases a leaf spot rare in this country due to the fungus *Marssonina Daphnes* causes brown spots on the leaves, especially near the base of the main vein and results in defoliation. It should easily be checked by picking off badly infected leaves and spraying with Bordeaux mixture.

KEY (D. E. G.)

| | |
|---|---|
| 1. *Evergreen* | 2 |
| 1. *Deciduous* | 21 |
| 2. *Fl. in terminal heads or clusters only* | 3 |
| 2. *Fl. otherwise arranged* | 14 |
| 3. *Fl. red or purple* | 4 |
| 3. *Fl. white or tinged* | 12 |
| 4. *Fl. pink, rosy, or red* | 5 |
| 4. *Fl. purplish* | 8 |
| 5. *Shrubs erect* | 6 |
| 5. *Shrubs procumbent or prostrate* | 7 |
| 6. *Shrub of 2 to 3 ft.; lvs. silky beneath; fl. rosy-pink* | D. sericea |
| 6. *Shrub of 3 to 5 in.; fl. rosy* | D. petraea |
| 7. *Cal. tube about ⅛ in. long* | D. arbuscula |
| 7. *Cal. tube about ¹⁄₁₆ in. long* | D. Cneorum |
| 8. *Shrub prostrate; cal. tube striate* | D. striata |
| 8. *Shrub erect* | 9 |
| 9. *Lvs. tomentose beneath; shrub 2 to 3 ft. h.* | D. collina |
| 9. *Lvs. smooth* | 10 |
| 10. *Lvs. notched at apex; shrub 3 ft. h.* | D. retusa |
| 10. *Lvs. entire* | 11 |
| 11. *Cal. lobes pointed; shrub up to 6 ft. h.* | D. odora |
| 11. *Cal. lobes blunt; shrub of 4 ft. or more* | D. tangutica |
| 12. *Fl. white* | 13 |
| 12. *Fl. white or tinged with pink or purple; shrub of 18 to 24 in.; young shoots downy* | D. oleoides |
| 13. *Shrub about 1 ft. h.; young shoots smooth; fl. very fragrant* | D. Blagayana |
| 13. *Shrub of 10 ft. or more; fl. scentless* | D. papyracea |

14. *Fl. in terminal and lateral clusters* — 15
14. *Fl. all lateral* — 16
15. *Shrub of 7 to 8 ft.; cal. tube silky-downy* — D. Bholua
15. *Shrub of 4 to 6 ft.; cal. tube smooth* — D. japonica
16. *Fl. in racemes* — 17
16. *Fl. in clusters or smaller groups* — 18
17. *Shrub about 1 ft. h.; fl. pink* — D. glomerata
17. *Shrub about 5 ft. h.; racemes from upper part of previous year's growth; fl. yellowish-green* — D. Laureola
18. *Fl. in clusters* — 19
18. *Fl. in smaller groups* — 20
19. *White fl. in clusters of 6 or more near, or at, apex of shoot; shrub of 3 to 6 ft.* — D. acutiloba
19. *Yellow fl. in clusters or smaller groups* — D. jezoensis
20. *Greenish or yellowish-white fl., solitary, in pairs or threes from base of young shoots* — D. pontica
20. *Orange-yellow fl. in pairs, threes or fours towards ends of shoots* — D. aurantiaca
21. *Fl. white or nearly so* — 22
21. *Fl. other than white* — 27
22. *Fl. in terminal and lateral clusters* — 23
22. *Fl. in terminal clusters only* — 24
23. *Shrub of 2 to 4 ft.; lvs. under 2 in. long* — D. Gnidium
23. *Shrub of 9 ft. or more; lvs. up to 5 in. long* — D. Sureil
24. *Fl. in bracteate clusters* — D. Sophia
24. *Fl. in ebracteate clusters* — 25
25. *Lvs. pubescent* — D. alpina
25. *Lvs. smooth* — 26
26. *Cal. tube appressed-silky* — D. caucasica
26. *Cal. tube puberulent* — D. altaica
27. *Golden-yellow fl. in small terminal clusters* — D. Giraldii
27. *Fl. in lateral fascicles* — 28
28. *Lvs. silky-hairy beneath* — 29
28. *Lvs. smooth* — 30
29. *Ovary hairy on upper half* — D. Fortunei
29. *Ovary entirely hairy* — D. Genkwa
30. *Low, poorly branched shrub; fl. yellow, cal. lobes obtuse* — D. kamtschatica
30. *Branching shrubs; cal. lobes acute or nearly so* — 31
31. *Fl. pale to deep purple* — D. Mezereum
31. *Fl. greenish or yellowish-white* — D. Pseudo-mezereum

**D. acumina'ta.** A synonym of *D. oleoides*.

**D. acutilo'ba.** Smooth, evergreen shrub 3 to 6 ft. h., young shoots covered with more or less erect bristles. *l.* lanceolate or oblanceolate, tapered to both ends, 2 to 4 in. long, $\frac{1}{2}$ to 1 in. wide, smooth and leathery. *fl.* in pedunculate clusters of 6 or more near, sometimes at, ends of shoots, almost or quite scentless; cal. white, smooth, $\frac{5}{8}$ in. across; segs. narrowly elliptical. July. *fr.* red and showy. China: Hupeh and Szechwan. About 1908.

**D. alpi'na.** Deciduous, intricately branched shrub, 4 to 18 in. h., with erect, downy shoots. *l.* appearing before fl., lanceolate or oblanceolate, $\frac{1}{2}$ to 2 in. long, $\frac{1}{4}$ to $\frac{1}{2}$ in. wide, often crowded towards end of shoot, silky-pubescent, especially beneath. *fl.* fragrant, in terminal heads of 4 to 10; cal. white, tube downy without, lobes lanceolate, pointed. April, May. *fr.* ovoid, reddish. On limestone mountains, S. and Cent. Europe from N. Spain and Switzerland to the Balkans. 1759. SYN. *D. candida*, *Thymelaea alpina*.

**D. alta'ica.** Deciduous shrub from 1 to 3 ft. h., with smooth young shoots. *l.* oblanceolate or oblong, pointed or mucronulate, narrowing to base, 1$\frac{1}{2}$ to 2 in. long, $\frac{3}{8}$ to $\frac{1}{2}$ in. wide, smooth. *fl.* slightly fragrant, white, in terminal clusters of 3 to 6; cal. downy without, lobes reflexed. June. *fr.* globose-ovate, red. Siberia, Mongolia. About 1796. (B.M. 1875.)

**D. arbus'cula.** Evergreen, dwarf, procumbent shrub, branches spreading, young shoots ascending, reddish. *l.* crowded towards ends of branches, linear-oblanceolate, obtuse, about $\frac{3}{4}$ in. long, sometimes pubescent beneath. *fl.* in terminal clusters of 3 to 8; cal. rosy-pink, downy, tube $\frac{5}{8}$ in. long, limb about $\frac{3}{8}$ in. across, lobes ovate-oblong. June. Hungary. Resembles *D. Cneorum* to which it is allied, but cal. tube long and arrangement of leaves different. Enjoys light soil.

**D. auranti'aca.** Evergreen, rather straggly shrub of 3 to 5 ft., with smooth shoots. *l.* oval, obovate, or oblong, $\frac{3}{4}$ in. or more long, up to $\frac{3}{8}$ in. wide, pointed, tapered to base, recurved, smooth, somewhat glaucous beneath. *fl.* fragrant, in pairs, threes, or fours from axils towards ends of shoots; cal. orange-yellow, smooth, tube narrow, $\frac{1}{2}$ in. long, limb $\frac{7}{16}$ in. across with 4 broadly ovate lobes. May. SW. China: Lichiang Range. About 1910. Not often a success in cultivation possibly owing to the use of grafted plants. (B.M. 9313.)

**D. autumna'lis.** A synonym of *D. Mezereum grandiflora*.

**D. Bholu'a.** Evergreen, usually erect shrub of 7 to 8 ft., but usually less in cultivation. *l.* short-stalked, 2 to 4 in. long, $\frac{1}{2}$ to 1 in. wide, elliptic-lanceolate or oblanceolate, sub-acute or bluntly acuminate, slightly recurved, smooth, edges undulate and obscurely glandular-denticulate. *fl.* fragrant, short-stalked, in terminal and axillary clusters of 3 or more; cal. tube silky-downy, about $\frac{7}{16}$ in. long, purplish-pink; limb white faintly tinged pink, smooth, $\frac{3}{8}$ in. across, lobes ovate, blunt. January onwards. *fr.* ovoid, black. Nepal, Bhutan, Sikkim, NW. Assam. SYN. *D. papyrifera*, *D. cannabina*. Appears hardy, at least in the southern counties, though it may lose its leaves in winter. Until recently, the name *D. cannabina* covered 2 species, *D. Bholua* and *D. papyracea*. var. **glacia'lis**, deciduous, from 6 to 12 in. h. with purplish branches, *fl.* with or before *l.*

**D. Blagaya'na.*** Evergreen shrub 1 ft. or so in height with spreading branches which, if pegged down early in their second year and covered with a thin layer of soil, will throw out roots. *l.* crowded towards ends of shoots, sessile, oblong-obovate or obovate, 1 to 1$\frac{1}{2}$ in. long, $\frac{1}{2}$ to $\frac{3}{4}$ in. wide, tapered to base, blunt, smooth. *fl.* fragrant, in dense terminal heads of 20 or more; cal. creamy-white, tube silky-downy, up to $\frac{3}{4}$ in. long, limb $\frac{1}{2}$ in. across, lobes ovate. April, May. *fr.* rarely appears in gardens, said to be pinkish white. Styria and Carniola. 1875. (B.M. 7579.) Appreciates half-shade and pleasantly moist (but well-drained) lime-free soil.

**D. buxifo'lia.** A synonym of *D. oleoides*.

**D. cannabi'na.** A synonym of *D. Bholua* and *D. papyracea*.

**D. caucas'ica.** Deciduous shrub of 4 ft. or more. *l.* scattered, sessile, lanceolate or oblong, 1 to 1$\frac{3}{4}$ in. long, $\frac{1}{3}$ to $\frac{1}{2}$ in. wide, obtuse-mucronulate, crowded, narrowed to base, smooth. *fl.* fragrant in terminal heads or clusters of 2 to 20; cal. shining white, tube slender, silky-hairy, about $\frac{1}{3}$ in. long, limb $\frac{1}{3}$ in. across with ovate or oblong lobes. May, June. Caucasus, in cult. 1893. SYN. *D. salicifolia*, *D. euphorbioides*. (B.M. 7388.) Not of the first grade.

**D. Cneo'rum.*** Garland Flower. Low, evergreen, procumbent shrub. *l.* scattered, narrow-oblong to oblanceolate, $\frac{1}{3}$ to 1 in. long, up to $\frac{1}{4}$ in. wide, acute or blunt, rarely notched, recurved, smooth, glaucous beneath. *fl.* fragrant, in dense terminal clusters of 6 or many more; cal. pale pink to rosy red, tube downy, $\frac{7}{16}$ in. long, limb $\frac{3}{8}$ in. across, segs. ovate or oblong, obtuse or sub-acute. May, June. *fr.* ovoid-oblong, light orange at first, then brown. S. and Cent. Europe from Germany, France, and Spain to Cent. Russia and the Balkans. 1752. SYN. *D. odorata* (of Lamarck), *Thymelaea Cneorum*. (B.M. 313.) Probably the most popular Daphne. That it prefers a limy soil is doubtful but that it survives longer and is more robust on its own roots is incontestable. Neither it nor its varieties are difficult to raise from cuttings. These, when rooted, should not be potted more than once but planted out as soon as possible. var. **al'ba**, with white *fl.*, is exquisite but less vigorous than type; **exim'ia**, a fine, rich-coloured form, one-third larger in all parts. About 1934; **ma'jor**, resembles *eximia* but is inferior; **pyg'maea**, prostrate, very free-flowering, its parts one-third smaller than those of type. 1930. (N.F.S. 7, 275.); **Verlot'ii**, differs from type by looser clusters, narrower cal. lobes, longer cal. tube, and linear-oblong *l.* Dauphiny, Bavaria.

**D. colli'na.** Evergreen, branching shrub 2 to 3 ft. h., with silky-hairy young shoots. *l.* oblong-lanceolate or oblanceolate, $\frac{3}{4}$ to 1$\frac{1}{2}$ in. long, $\frac{1}{4}$ to $\frac{5}{8}$ in. wide, more or less blunt, smooth above, almost or quite tomentose beneath. *fl.* fragrant, in terminal heads of 10 to 15; rose or purplish-rose, densely silky-hairy without, cal. tube about $\frac{1}{2}$ in. long, limb $\frac{1}{2}$ in. across, lobes ovate, obtuse, often notched. May, June. Italy, Sicily, Crete, Asia Minor. 1752. SYN. *D. australis*. (B.M. 428.) A fine shrub but not reliably hardy. var. **neapolita'na**, a synonym of *D. × neapolitana*.

**D. Fionia'na** (of gardens). A synonym of *D. × neapolitana*.

*Daphne Fortunei*

**D. Fortun'ei.** Erect, deciduous shrub 2 to 3 ft. h., with clustered branches and downy shoots. *l.* shortly stalked, or rarely opposite, alternate, narrow oval or oblong, 1 to 1$\frac{1}{2}$ in. long, half as wide, obtuse or sub-acute, silky when young, pubescent on veins beneath. *fl.* in lateral clusters of 2 to 4 or sometimes at ends of shortest branches, cal. lilac, about $\frac{3}{4}$ in. long, tube slender, lobes ovate, obtuse, ovary hairy in upper half, smooth below. May, June. China. SYN. *D. Genkwa Fortunei*. (J.H.S. 2, t. 1.) Closely related to and resembling *D. Genkwa* but differing by its shorter petioles, larger *fl.*, and half-hairy ovary. Requires lime-free soil and appreciates half-shade.

**D. Gen'kwa.** Beautiful deciduous shrub, erect with slender branches, silky when young. *l.* usually opposite (rarely alternate), lanceolate, 1 to 2 in. long, about ½ in. wide, pointed, silky-downy in youth, silky-hairy on veins beneath, petiole about ⅛ in. long. *fl.* slightly fragrant, in lateral clusters of 3 to 7; cal. lilac, silky-hairy, about ½ in. long and wide, lobes spreading, acute; ovary hairy. April, May. China. (Largely cultivated in Japan.) 1843. (S.Z.J.F. 1, 75.) Much of the difficulty in its cultivation disappears if plants on their own roots are used and given a lime-free porous soil and half-shade. var. **Fortun'ei,** *see* **D. Fortunei**. (B.M. n.s. 360.)

**D. Girald'ii.** Beautiful deciduous, bushy shrub, 2 ft. or more h., smooth in all parts. *l.* crowded towards ends of branches, sessile, oblanceolate, 1½ to 2½ in. long, about ½ in. wide, acute or obtuse, mucronate, smooth. *fl.* slightly fragrant in terminal head of 3 to 8, cal. golden-yellow, smooth, $\frac{5}{16}$ in. long and about as much across, lobes spreading, acute. May. *fr.* ovoid, red. NW. China: Shensi, Kansu. 1911. (B.M. 8732.)

**D. glandulo'sa.** A synonym of *D. oleoides jasminea.*

**D. glomera'ta.** Lovely evergreen shrub 1 ft. or so in height. *l.* densely clustered towards ends of branches, obovate-oblong, lanceolate or oval lanceolate, 1 in. or more long, ⅓ to ½ in. wide, narrowing to base, acute or blunt, smooth, and shining. *fl.* in axillary, 2- to 6-fld. racemes, some of which are almost terminal, pale flesh-coloured, smooth, about ½ in. long and wide, cal. tube slender, lobes oblong. June, July. *fr.* pink. Asia Minor: Cappadocia, Caucasus, Transcaucasia, Armenia. Syn. *D. Mezereum* (of Güldenstaedt). Extremely rare in cultivation.

**D. Gnid'ium.** Erect, deciduous shrub, 2 to 4 ft. h., bark reddish-brown, young shoots white-downy. *l.* numerous, clothing the branches for all their length, erect and imbricate, lanceolate or linear-lanceolate, 1 to 2 in. long, ⅛ to $\frac{3}{16}$ in. wide, sharply pointed, smooth. *fl.* fragrant, in few-fld. terminal and sub-terminal clusters, pedicels white tomentose, cal. white or tinted rosy, ¼ to ⅓ in. long, silky, lobes ovate, obtuse. July to September. *fr.* small, ovoid, red. S. Europe, Asia Minor, N. Africa, and Canary Is. 1797. Syn. *D. paniculata.* (L.B.C. 150.)

**D. × Houttea'na** (*D. Laureola* × *D. Mezereum*). Purple-leaved Daphne. With the characters of both parents. Less than half-evergreen shrub, about 4 ft. h., with stout, erect branches. *l.* oblanceolate, tapering to base, smooth, purplish. *fl.* in short pedunculate lateral clusters of 2 to 5, lilac-violet. April. Syn. *D. Mezereum purpurea, D. Laureola purpurea* (of gardens). (F.d.S. 6, 592 as *D. Mezereum foliis atropurpureis.*)

**D. × hyb'rida** (*D. collina* × *D. odora*). Bushy, evergreen shrub, 3 to 4 ft. h. *l.* oval to elliptic-oblong, 1 to 3 in. or more long, smooth and shining above, smooth or slightly hairy on veins beneath. *fl.* fragrant, in terminal heads of 8 to 15; cal. pinkish-purple, hairy without. Almost continuous through the year but most freely in early summer. Syn. *D. Dauphinii, D. delphinii.* Hardier than is generally supposed. Its close growth renders it liable to be displaced by strong winds and it needs support by a stout stake.

**D. japon'ica.** Evergreen shrub, 4 to 6 ft. h., branches smooth, almost whorled. *l.* oblong or oblanceolate, 1½ to 3 in. or more long, ½ to ⅞ in. wide, obtuse, smooth, lustrous above. *fl.* fragrant, in axillary and terminal clusters of 8 to 12; cal. ½ in. long, ⅝ in. across, colour variable, generally pinkish-purple without, white within, smooth, lobes ovate, obtuse, or more or less acute. November onwards. Japan, China. 1866. Syn. *D. Mazeli, D. odora Mazeli, D. triflora.* (P.M.B. 8, 175.) Rare in cultivation. Resembles *D. odora*, hardier, but not quite hardy.

**D. jasmin'ea.** A variety of *D. oleoides.*

**D. jezoen'sis.** Upright, evergreen shrub about 2 ft. h. *l.* oblong-obovate, 1½ to 3 in. long, blunt, tapering towards base. *fl.* fragrant in axillary clusters, yellow, lobes ovate and pointed. March, April. Japan. Syn. *D. yezoensis* (a garden name).

**D. kamtschat'ica.** Low, upright, deciduous, sparsely branched shrub. *l.* oblong-lanceolate or oblong-obovate, somewhat acute. *fl.* in axillary fascicles; cal. yellow. NE. Asia.

**D. Laureo'la.** Spurge Laurel. Smooth, evergreen shrub, 2 to 4 (rarely 5) ft. h. *l.* oblong or obovate-lanceolate, 1½ to 5 in. long, ½ to 1½ in. wide, acute, tapered towards base, lustrous above. *fl.* fragrant, in pedunculate racemes of 5 to 10 from upper part of branches of previous year; cal. yellowish-green, smooth, ⅓ in. long, ¼ in. across. February, March. *fr.* ovoid, blue-black. Cent., S., and W. Europe including Britain, W. Asia. (Gn. 29, 602.) Syn. *D. multiflora.* More useful for its evergreen foliage than its flowers. var. **Phil'ippi,** sub-prostrate, evergreen shrub from 8 to 16 in. h. *fl.* fragrant, yellowish-green, often violet without, smaller than those of type. April and May. *l.* obovate, pointed, descending lower on branches. Pyrenees. Syn. *D. Philippi, D. pailhesiensis.* In cult. 1894.

**D. Mazel'i.** A synonym of *D. japonica.*

**D. Mezereum.*** Mezereon. Deciduous, more or less erect, rounded bush up to about 5 ft. h., young shoots appressed-hairy. *l.* commonly after fl., short-stalked, oblong, elliptical-lanceolate or oblanceolate, 1 to 3½ in. long, ¼ to ¾ in. wide, blunt or pointed, narrowing to base, at first ciliate, eventually smooth, pale grey-green beneath. *fl.* fragrant, sessile, in lateral pairs or threes, from pale lilac-pink to violet-red, ¼ in. long, ½ in. wide; tube slender, downy; lobes ovate. February to March or later. *fr.* sub-globose, scarlet. Europe, including Caucasus, Asia Minor, Siberia, a doubtful native of Britain. In cult. 1561. (Gn. 29, 602.) Syn. *Mezereum officinarum, Thymelaea praecox.* One of the finest and most easily cultivated Daphnes. Seen at its best, perhaps, in cottage gardens. var. **al'ba,** *fl.* white, *fr.* yellow. (Gn. 29, 602.); **grandiflo'ra,** *fl.* bright purple and larger. October to February. *fr.* scarlet. Syn. var. *autumnalis* (a garden name); **grandiflo'ra al'ba,** *fl.* white; **ple'na,** *fl* white, double. Syn. var. *fl. albo pleno* of gardens (Gn. 29, 602.) October to February. *fr.* yellowish-white.

**D. × neapolita'na.** Either a variety of *D. collina* or a natural hybrid between *D. collina* and *D. Cneorum* or, according to Bean, *D. oleoides* and *D. Cneorum.* Evergreen, erect, bushy shrub, from 2 to 3 ft. h., with hairy shoots. *l.* shortly petiolate, scattered, oblanceolate, ¾ to 1½ in. long, ⅛ to ¼ in. wide, blunt or sub-acute, smooth and shining above, glaucous beneath and hairy towards base. *fl.* in terminal clusters, rosy-lilac, white-downy, about ⅓ in. long and wide. March to June. (L.B.C. 719.) Syn. *D. collina neapolitana, D. Fioniana, D. Delahayana.* A very tolerant and robust plant and fond of lime in the soil. Of much the same distribution as *D. collina.*

**D. odo'ra.*** Evergreen shrub, up to 6 ft. h., branches smooth. *l.* narrowly oval or oblong, 1 to 3¼ in. long, ⅛ to ⅓ in. wide, pointed, tapered to both ends, smooth and shining. *fl.* fragrant, in crowded heads, reddish-purple or cal. tube white marked reddish-purple and limb at least margined purple, 1 in. long, ⅝ in. across, smooth or silky-downy; lobes spreading, cordate-ovate or oblong, pointed. January to March. China, Japan. 1771. Syn. *D. japonica* (of Paxton), *D. sinensis, D. indica* (of gardens). (B.M. 1587.) Not generally hardy.

**D. odora'ta.** A synonym of *D. Cneorum.*

**D. oleoi'des.** Erect, much branched, evergreen shrub, up to 3 ft. h., young shoots grey-pubescent. *l.* almost sessile, oblanceolate or lanceolate, ¾ to 1¼ in. long, about ¼ in. wide, pointed, mucronulate, tapering to base, at first silky beneath, later more or less pitted with glands, smooth above. *fl.* in terminal clusters of 3 to 6 or more, varying from white to purplish-rose, hairy without, about ½ in. long; lobes ovate or lanceolate, pointed. May, June. *fr.* red. S. Europe, N. Africa, Asia Minor, Afghanistan, and Himalaya. 1815. (F.G. 357 as *D. buxifolia.*) Syn. *D. glandulosa, D. acuminata* (of Bossier). var. **jasmin'ea,** *fl.* white, silky lobes lanceolate, acute. *l.* ½ to 1¼ in. long, downy on both surfaces or only beneath, or quite smooth. Spain, W. Asia. Syn. *D. glandulosa, D. lucida, D. buxifolia* (of Sibthorp and Smith).

**D. pailhesien'sis.** A synonym of *D. Laureola Philippi.*

**D. papyra'cea.** Erect, evergreen shrub, 10 ft. or more h., with bristly, downy young shoots and brown, papery bark. *l.* short-stalked, elliptical or oblanceolate, 4 to 6¼ in. long, ⅝ to 1½ in. wide, obtuse or obtuse-acuminate, smooth except at tip, slightly recurved. *fl.* scentless, in terminal clusters of about 12, white, softly hairy without, about $\frac{7}{16}$ in. long and ⅝ in. across; lobes spreading, elliptic-oblong, hairy at tips. January onwards. *fr.* red, inverted pear-shaped. N. India. Syn. *D. cannabina* (*see* **D. Bholua**), *D. odora* (of Don), *D. papyrifera.* Bark used in India as, or in the manufacture of, paper.

**D. papyrif'era.** A synonym of *D. papyracea* or of *Edgeworthia papyrifera.*

**D. petrae'a.*** Spreading, evergreen shrub of 3 to 6 in. h., young shoots slightly downy. *l.* crowded, sessile, narrowly spatulate or oblong, ¼ to ½ in. long, $\frac{1}{16}$ to $\frac{1}{12}$ in. wide, obtuse or sub-acute, leathery, smooth, shining above. *fl.* fragrant, in terminal clusters of 3 to 6, rose, about ⅜ in. long, ¼ to ⅓ in. across, white-downy without; tube striate; lobes oval, obtuse or acute. May, June. N. Italy, near Lake Garda. 1894. Syn. *D. rupestris.* Requires a moist soil and perfect drainage. Both it and its variety are usually grown in an alpine-house. var. **grandiflo'ra** (of gardens), rather larger with bigger *fl.*

**D. Phil'ippi.** A variety of *D. Laureola.*

**D. pont'ica.** Evergreen shrub, 3 to 5 ft. h., with smooth young shoots. *l.* obovate or obovate-oblong, 1 to 3 in. long, ½ to 1½ in. wide, pointed, tapered to base, smooth, glossy on upper surface. *fl.* fragrant, drooping, generally in pairs (rarely 1 or 3) on slender peduncles from base of young shoots, pale yellowish-white or greenish-yellow, about ⅜ in. long, tube slender, smooth; lobes spreading, lanceolate, acute. April. SE. Europe, Caucasus, Asia Minor. 1752. (B.M. 1282.) Well worth growing at the edge of woodland for its fragrant fl. and bright foliage. Likes moist, well-drained, lime-free soil and partial shade.

**D. Pseudo-meze'reum.** Deciduous, more or less decumbent shrub. *l.* oblanceolate, 2 to 3 in. long, ⅜ to ⅝ in. wide, blunt or pointed, tapering to a short stalk, smooth. *fl.* scentless, in lateral clusters with l., greenish or whitish-yellow, smooth, about ½ in. across; lobes ovate, blunt. March, April. *fr.* red. Cent. Japan. In cult. 1905.

**D. retu'sa.*** Evergreen, bushy shrub, about 3 ft. h., young shoots hairy. *l.* oblong-obovate or elliptical-oblong, 1 to 2¾ in. long, ½ to ⅞ in. wide, sub-acute or rounded, generally notched at apex, smooth, glossy above. *fl.* in crowded terminal clusters about 3 in. across, pinkish-purple without, white tinged purple within, ⅝ in. long, about ¾ in. across, smooth or nearly so. May, June. *fr.* red, broadly oval, ½ in. long. W. China. 1901. (B.M. 8430.) Much more tolerant of garden conditions than most Daphnes.

**D. salicifo'lia.** A synonym of *D. caucasica*.

**D. seric'ea.\*** Evergreen shrub 1 to 2 ft. h., young shoots puberulent or nearly glabrous. *l.* lanceolate or spatulate-lanceolate, ½ to 1½ in. long, pointed or sometimes blunt, smooth and shining above, silky-hairy or almost smooth beneath. *fl.* in terminal clusters of 3 to 8, rosy-pink, silky-hairy, ¾ in. long, ½ in. across; lobes broadly ovate, obtuse. May, June. E. Mediterranean. Syn. *D. oleifolia* (of Lamarck), *D. argentea*. Resembles *D. collina* but *l.* beneath and young shoots less hairy. A lovely plant better fitted for cool-house cultivation than for the open. Rare in cultivation.

*Daphne retusa* (p. 637)

**D. sinen'sis.** A synonym of *D. odora*.

**D. Soph'ia.** Deciduous shrub, under 1 ft. h., branches slender. *l.* sub-sessile, obovate-oblong, 1 to 3 in. long, ¼ to ¾ in. wide, mucronulate, narrowing to base, smooth and rather lustrous above, glaucous beneath. *fl.* fragrant, in terminal, bracteate clusters of 6 to 15, white or yellowish, about ½ in. long and ⅓ in. across; tube sprinkled with minute white hairs; lobes ovate, pointed. May, June. *fr.* cinnabar-red. Cent. Russia. In cult. 1895. Related to *D. altaica* and *D. caucasica*. Not a showy plant nor easy to establish.

**D. stria'ta.** Smooth, evergreen shrub, prostrate or nearly so, with smooth, spindly shoots. *l.* sessile, linear-lanceolate, obtuse and often mucronulate, narrowing to base, smooth, shining above. *fl.* in terminal clusters of 8 to 12, rosy or purplish-pink, smooth; tube slender, streaked pink; lobes ovate-lanceolate. May to July. W. France, Switzerland, Austria, N. Italy, Carpathians. (T.A.P.E. 60.) Closely related to *D. Cneorum* but differing by its low growth, weak, loose habit, and smooth, striated perianth tube. Difficult to cultivate. var. **al'ba**, *fl.* white, very rare both in nature and gardens. W. France.

**D. Su'reil.** Erect, deciduous or almost deciduous shrub, 7 or 9 ft. h. or more, young shoots densely white-downy; bark eventually almost smooth, brownish. *l.* lanceolate or oblong-lanceolate, 2 to 5 in. or more long, ⅝ to 1⅜ in. wide, narrowing to base, acuminate, smooth, or tomentose beneath in youth. *fl.* slightly fragrant, in rather loose terminal and lateral heads of 12 to 20, green paling to white, downy; tube ⅝ in. long; lobes triangular, acuminate. *fr.* ovoid, orange-red. Sikkim Himalaya, S. Assam. 1925. (B.M. 9297.) Rare in cultivation. Not considered hardy.

**D. tangu'tica.** Erect, rounded, evergreen shrub, up to 4 or 5 ft. h., young shoots stout, at first grey-bristly, eventually smooth. *l.* elliptical, oblong or oblanceolate, 1 to 3 in. long, ¼ to ¾ in. wide, tapered to base, notched, sub-acute or truncate, smooth, semi-lustrous above. *fl.* fragrant in terminal clusters 1½ to 2 in. across, rosy-purple without, white stained purple within, ⅝ in. long, ½ in. across; lobes ovate, blunt. March, April. *fr.* red, ovoid. Kansu. 1914. (B.M. 8855.) Closely related to *D. retusa* but with a downy stigma.

**D. × Thaum'a.** Low, sometimes almost prostrate, evergreen shrub. *l.* smooth, linear-lanceolate or oblanceolate. *fl.* of bright rosy-purple in terminal heads. S. Tyrol. About 1910. Natural hybrid, between *D. striata* and *D. petraea*, but leaning more to the former than the latter. (G.C. 52 (1912), 22.) Rare in nature, more so in gardens, and difficult to cultivate.

**D. Verlot'ii.** A variety of *D. Cneorum*.

F. S.

*daphniflo'rus -a -um,* with Daphne-like flowers.

**DAPHNIPHYL'LUM** (*Daphne,* and *phyllon,* leaf). Fam. *Euphorbiaceae*. A genus of about 25 species of evergreen shrubs or small trees, natives of Trop. Asia and the Malay Archipelago. Leaves alternate, long-stalked, entire, penni-nerved, usually glaucous beneath, without stipules. Flowers apetalous, dioecious, in axillary racemes; stamens of males 5 to 18; ovary 2-celled. Fruit a drupe, usually 1-seeded. Hardy near London

and grows well in moist shady places under ordinary treatment. Propagated by cuttings of fairly ripened wood in mild heat in July.

**D. glauces'cens** of gardens. A synonym of *D. macropodum*.

**D. hu'mile.** Wide-spreading, much branched shrub, 1 to 2 ft. h. *l.* elliptic or obovate, 2½ to 5 in. long, ¾ to 2 in. wide, shining green above, glaucous beneath. Yezo, Japan. 1879. Useful ground cover in half-shade. Syn. *D. jezoense*.

**D. macropo'dum.\*** Rounded bush, 8 to 12 ft. h., with stout, glaucous shoots, often reddish when young. *l.* oblong, 3 to 8 in. long, 1 to 3½ in. wide, slender pointed, dark green above, glaucous beneath, stalk often red. *fl.* inconspicuous in short racemes in axils of *l.* of previous year; stamens pink. May. Japan, Korea, China. 1879. (J.R.H.S. 27, 871.) Syn. *D. glaucescens* of garden. var. **variega'tum** has a broad cream margin to *l.*

*daphnoi'des,* Daphne-like.

**DARD.** A bud on an apple or pear tree which has not grown out beyond a certain point, surrounded by 2 or 3 leaves. It may develop into shoot if it receives too much sap, but usually with a steady supply of sap produces 2 more leaves and then a further 2 forming a loose rosette and becomes a spur carrying a fruit bud.

*Dar'dari,* in honour of M. Dardar of Bronvaux, Metz, in whose garden *Crataego-mespilus × Dardari* arose in 1895.

**DA'REA.** *See* **Asplenium.**

*darial'icus -a -um,* of Darial, Caucasus.

**DARLINGTON'IA** (in honour of Dr. William Darlington of Philadelphia, American botanist). Fam. *Sarraceniaceae*. A single species of herbaceous perennial, native of the mountains of Cent. California to S. Oregon where it grows on the edge of swamps, allied to Sarracenia, but lacking the curious umbrella-shaped summit of the style seen in that genus, but having somewhat similar pitchers in which insects are trapped and digested (*see* **Carniverous plants**). All the leaves are of the pitcher type, a radical rosette being formed annually from the end of the short perennial rhizome. The leaf is from 3 to 30 in. long and ½ to 3 in. wide, somewhat spirally twisted, hollow throughout its length, the two halves of the blade being represented by a sort of crest along one face of pitcher, the top of the pitcher being curved over so that the mouth of the pitcher is directed downward, and from the mouth depends a 2-lobed crimson and green appendage; the curved top is mottled with white translucent areas through which light passes, illuminating its interior which bears many honey glands. The honey secreted attracts many insects which alight on the smooth surface inside the hood and are prevented from passing out again by many downward directed hairs so that they soon fall to the lower part of the pitcher. A liquid is excreted by the interior walls of the pitcher which brings about the drowning and subsequent digestion of the captured insects. The products of digestion are absorbed by thin places in the pitcher walls and passed on for the benefit of the plant just as in Sarracenias and Nepenthes. Darlingtonia is hardy and will grow in a damp shady position in a compost of peat and chopped Sphagnum with plenty of sharp sand and small pieces of limestone, or better still charcoal, provided it is kept well supplied with water. It can also be grown in a cool greenhouse with the same conditions as Droseras, Dionaeas, and Sarracenias and must be given a shady position, a cool, moist atmosphere, and an even temperature best secured in a ventilated glass case in the house. The plants are best potted when least active, usually in early July, and repotting is needed every second year. The pots should be stood in saucers so that the soil never becomes dry, and the spaces between the pots filled with Sphagnum. Propagation is by division or by seed sown on a very even bed of living Sphagnum under a glass.

**D. califor'nica.** Rootstock horizontal. *l.* 5 to 8 in an annual terminal rosette, 3 to 30 in. long, hollow, slender at base, swelling upwards, top hood-like, with a large 2-lobed appendage from the mouth, bright green, upper part mottled white and with netted red-dish-pink veins. *fl.* 2 in. across, solitary inverted; sep. 5, whitish or pale green; pet. yellow-green, with dark red-brown veins, oblong; stamens 12 to 15. April, May. California. 1861. (B.M. 5920.)

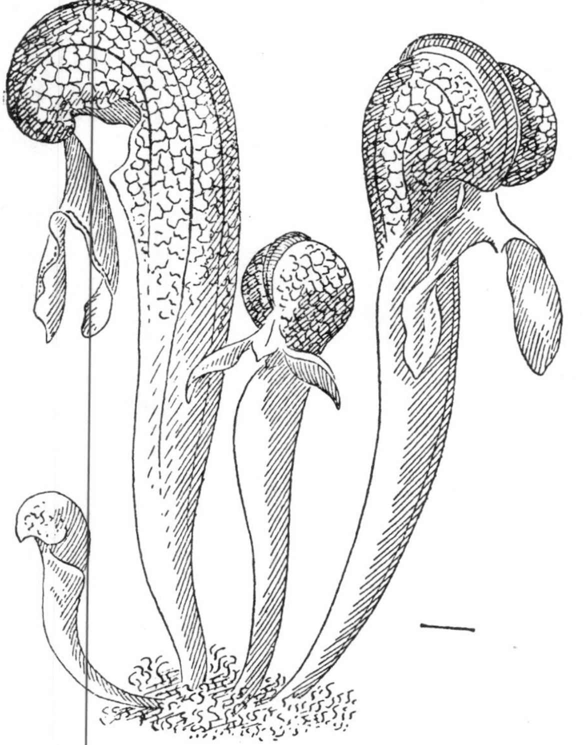

*Darlingtonia californica*

***D'Armandvil'lei,*** in honour of General-Major Jean Henri Isdibald Le Cocq d'Armandville, 1873– , Dutch army, who collected in New Guinea, &c.

**DARNEL.** *See* **Lolium temulentum.** A

***darwas'icus -a -um,*** of Darwas in Turkestan.

**DARWIN'IA** (in honour of Dr. Erasmus Darwin, 1731–1802, author of the poem *The Botanic Garden*). FAM. *Myrtaceae*. A genus of about 30 species of evergreen, mostly lowish shrubs confined to Australia. Leaves small, opposite or alternate, freely dotted with oil glands, entire. Flowers in terminal heads of a few to many which in one section of the genus (Genetyllis) are enclosed or hidden by a showy involucre of several bracts up to ¾ in. long. This section, by far the most ornamental, is represented in the following notes by *D. Hookeriana*, *D. macrostegia*, and *D. fimbriata*. The other species have their floral bracts reduced to similarity with the leaves, and the calyx and corolla become visible but are always small. They are cool greenhouse shrubs requiring about the same treatment as Cape heaths. The Genetyllis section remain long in flower.

KEY

1. *Fl.-heads nodding, surrounded by a coloured involucre* 2
1. *Fl.-heads with bracts almost like lvs.* 5
2. *Involucre longer than fl. and enclosing them* 3
2. *Involucre scarcely longer than fl., spreading* D. citriodora
3. *Lvs. and bracts entire* 4
3. *Lvs. and bracts ciliate* D. fimbriata
4. *Lvs. elliptic-oblong; inner bracts striate* D. macrostegia
4. *Lvs. linear-oblong; inner bracts one-coloured* D. Hookeriana
5. *Erect heath-like bush* 6
5. *Straggling or almost prostrate bush usually; lvs. ¼ to ½ in. long* D. taxifolia
6. *Lvs. under ¼ in. long; cal. glandular* D. diosmoides
6. *Lvs. ⅛ to ½ in. long; cal. smooth* D. fascicularis

**D. citriodo'ra.** Rounded, compact bush, 2 to 4 ft. and as much wide. *l.* lemon-scented, opposite or nearly so, narrow-oblong to ovate-lanceolate, blunt-ended, ¼ to ⅜ in. long. *fl.* usually in terminal heads surrounded by a white or reddish involucre of 4 bracts scarcely longer than the fl. W. Australia.

**D. diosmoi'des.** Shrub 2 to 3 ft. *l.* alternate, very crowded and heath-like, filiform, ⅛ to ¼ in. long. *fl.* up to 20 crowded in terminal globose heads under ½ in. across; cal. about ⅛ in. long; pet. white, only half as long. April. W. Australia. 1827.

**D. fascicula'ris.** Heath-like, much branched shrub 3 to 6 ft. *l.* very crowded, often at the end of the shoot, ⅛ to ½ in. long, narrow-linear, sharply pointed. *fl.* reddish-white, 6 to 12 together in terminal axillary heads; involucral bracts short and narrow; cal. tube ¼ in. long, 5-ribbed; stamens 10, with black globose anthers, alternating with 10 crimson-headed staminodes; stigma filiform, protruding ⅛ in. New S. Wales. 1820.

**D. fimbria'ta.*** Bushy shrub 1 to 2 ft. *l.* alternate, ⅙ to ⅕ in. long, oblong-oval, crowded, scarcely stalked, apex rounded, conspicuously furnished with tiny bristles. Involucre ¾ to 1 in. long, pink, fringed with bristle-like hairs, enclosing and hiding the true fl. June. W. Australia. 1860. (B.M. 5468 as *Genetyllis fimbriata.*) *D. squarrosa* of Turczaninov may be its correct name.

**D. Hookeria'na.*** Shrub 1½ to 2 ft., shoots slender. *l.* narrowly oblong, ⅛ to ⅜ in. long, $\frac{1}{12}$ to $\frac{3}{16}$ in. wide, apex rounded, very short-stalked, glabrous. Involucres tulip-shaped, drooping, 1¼ in. long; bracts rich pink, paling at margins, and concealing cal. and cor. April. W. Australia. (B.M. 4860 as *Genetyllis macrostegia.*)

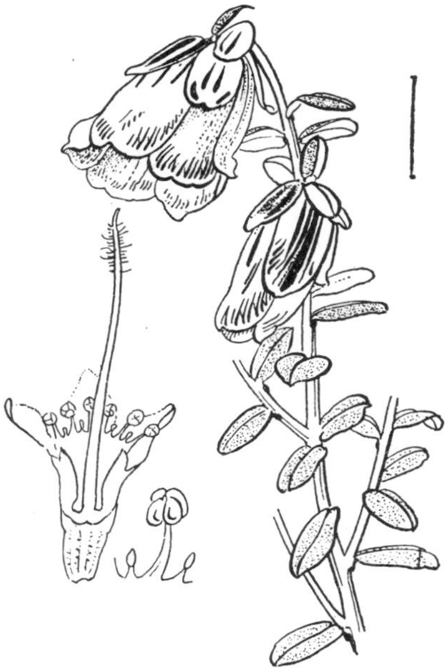

*Darwinia macrostegia*

**D. macroste'gia.*** Evergreen shrub, 2 to 3 ft. *l.* oval to oblong, ⅛ to ⅜ in. long, half as wide, apex rounded, margin recurved, very shortly stalked, dark green, dotted beneath. *fl.* terminal, several enclosed and hidden by a tulip-shaped involucre 1½ in. long, white, striped and stained pink and red. April. W. Australia. 1854. (B.M. 4858 as *Genetyllis tulipifera.*)

**D. squarro'sa.** *See* **D. fimbriata.**

**D. taxifo'lia.** Low, spreading shrub, rarely tree-like. *l.* ¼ to ⅝ in. long, linear, curved, pointed, yew-like. *fl.* 2 to 4, terminal, reddish-white, scarcely showing above uppermost l.; floral bracts about as long as fl.; cal. ⅛ in. long, 5-ribbed; pet. $\frac{1}{20}$ in. long. New S. Wales.

W. J. B.

***Darwin'ii,*** in honour of Charles Robert Darwin, 1809–82, the great British naturalist, author of *The Origin of species*, &c., grandson of Dr. Erasmus Darwin.

***dasy-,*** in compound words indicating thickly hairy, as *dasycaulon*, with a hairy stem, *dasypetalus*, with hairy petals.

**DASYCHIR'A pudibund'a.** *See* **Hop Dog.**

**DASYLI'RION** (*dasys*, thick, *lirion*, lily). FAM. *Liliaceae*. A genus of about 10 species of evergreen herbs allied to Nolina, natives of Texas and the Mexican highlands. Stems erect or ascending, thick and strong. Leaves long lanceolate, flat or concave, toothed. Inflorescence a very densely flowered panicle up to nearly 5 ft. long, with scape up to 10 or 12 ft. with spike-like branches. Flowers dioecious; bell-shaped. Fruit a 3-angled 1-celled capsule. Seed globose or ovate. A compost of 2 parts loam, 1 peat, and 1 sand suits these greenhouse plants which need perfect drainage and plenty of water in the summer months. Increased by seed. Dasylirions are excellent plants for subtropical bedding, their gracefully drooping leaves being ornamental at all times, and they are good also for conservatory and indoor decoration.

**D. acrot'richum.*** Trunk stout, simple. *fl.-stem* 6 to 10 ft. h. with a dense cylindrical panicle 4 to 5 ft. long. *l.* in a dense rosette, recurved, linear, 2 to 3 ft. long, under 1 in. wide, with a long fibrous tuft at tip, spines sharp, yellowish. *fl.* white. Mexico. 1851. (B.M. 5030.) SYN. *D. gracile*. var. **brevifo'lium,** *l.* shorter, scarcely over 2 ft. long, not pendulous.

**D. glaucophyl'lum.*** *fl.-stem* 10 to 12 ft. h. with a narrow panicle occupying 3 to 4 ft. *l.* in a dense rosette, 2 to 3 ft. long, about 3/4 in. wide, glaucous, teeth sharp, small. *fl.* white. Mexico. 1846. (B.M. 5041.) SYN. *D. glaucum*. var. **latifo'lium,** more robust and with wider *l.* than type.

**D. glau'cum.** A synonym of *D. glaucophyllum*.

**D. grac'ile.** A synonym of *D. acrotrichum*.

**D. graminifo'lium.** Trunk short. *fl.-stem* 8 to 9 ft. long with a narrow panicle. *l.* in a dense rosette, linear, 3 to 4 ft. long, about 1/2 in. wide, green, teeth 1/20 to 1/12 in. long. *fl.* white. Mexico. 1835.

**D. Hartwegia'num.** A synonym of *D. Hookeri*.

**D. Hook'eri.** Trunk a large tuber with l. springing in clusters from tubercles on surface. *fl.-stem* 3 ft. long with a dense panicle about 18 in. h. *l.* narrow, linear, 18 to 24 ft. long, 1/8 to 1/4 in. wide, pale glaucous green, toothed. *fl.* purplish. Mexico. 1846. (B.M. 5099 as *D. Hartwegianum*.)

**D. longis'simum.** Stem stout, about 3 ft. h. *fl.-stem* about 5 ft. h. in a dense, spike-like panicle. *l.* in a dense terminal tuft, slender, 4-angled, about 2 ft. long. *fl.* small. Texas. 1887. (G.F. 1887, p. 280, and B.M. 7749 as *D. quadrangulatum*.)

**D. quadrangula'tum.** A synonym of *D. longissimum*.

**D. serratifo'lium.** Stem stout. *fl.-stem* with a dense panicle 1 ft. long. *l.* 2 ft. long, nearly 1 in. wide, teeth 1/16 to 1/8 in. long. *fl.* white. Mexico.

**D. Wheel'eri.** Habit and stature as in *D. graminifolium*, panicles longer, flexuous, usually pendent. *l.* 1/2 to 3/4 in. wide; teeth tipped brown. Arizona, &c.

**DASYNEU'RA.** A genus of gall midges (Cecidomycidae). *See* **Arabis** and **Pear Midges.**

**DASYSCYPH'A calyci'na.** The fungus causing Larch Canker. *See* **Larix, Diseases.**

**DASYSTACH'YS** (*dasys*, thick, *stachys*, spike; referring to the dense raceme). FAM. *Liliaceae*. A genus of about 15 species of rhizomatous perennial herbs natives of Trop. Africa, with almost sessile leaves and short 3-lobed capsule, nearly related to Chlorophytum and sometimes included in it. Leaves radical, linear, or lanceolate. Flowers small, white; perianth bell-shaped, segments free; racemes densely many-flowered, usually simple, somewhat spike-like, bracts persistent. For treatment *see* **Chlorophytum.**

**D. drimiop'sis.** *l.* 3, linear, erect, glabrous, 12 to 18 in. long, 1/3 to 1/2 in. wide. *fl.* in a dense hairy raceme 3 to 6 in. long; perianth 1/8 in. long, segs. white, keeled brown; scape 3 to 12 in. long. Mozambique. 1898. (B.M. 7580.)

***dasyty'le,*** having thick scales.

**DATE PALM.** *See* **Phoenix dactylifera.**

**DATE PALM, PRICKLY.** *See* **Acanthophoenix.**

**DATE PLUM.** *See* **Diospyros Lotus.**

**DATE, WILD.** *See* **Phoenix sylvestris.**

**DATIS'CA** (derivation ?). FAM. *Datiscaceae*. A genus of 2 species of graceful perennial herbs needing good deep soil and propagated by division of well-established plants or by seeds. The value of *D. cannabina* lies in its fine foliage, and its stature fits it for growing as an isolated specimen, but both male and female plants should be grown as the fertilized female plant is the more graceful and remains green longer than the male. Hardy.

**D. cannabi'na.** 3 to 6 ft. h. *l.* pinnate, alternate; lflets. 7, about 2 in. long, 1/2 in. wide, toothed. *fl.* dioecious, yellow, in long, loose, axillary racemes. September. Crete, W. Asia. 1739. (F.G. 960.)

**DATISCA'CEAE.** Dicotyledons. A family of 4 herbs or trees in 3 genera, probably nearly related to Begonia, natives of tropical and temperate regions. Leaves without stipules. Flowers small, in racemes or spikes, regular, usually dioecious, sometimes without petals, in staminate flowers, sepals 3 to 9; petals 0 or 8; stamens 4 to 25; in pistillate flowers, sepals 3 to 8 united; petals 0; ovary inferior or 3 to 8 carpels, 1-celled with many ovules. Fruit a capsule. The only genus calling for mention is Datisca.

**DATU'RA** (?). FAM. *Solanaceae*. A genus of about 15 species of annuals, trees, and shrubs, distributed over the warm and temperate regions of the globe. Leaves usually large, entire or sinuately toothed. Flowers large, extra-axillary or from forks of branches, stalked; corolla funnel-shaped; stamens 5, equal or almost so; ovary 4-celled. Fruit a 4-valved capsule. The shrubby species are frequently known as Brugmansias, the annual species as Daturas. The annuals are readily raised from seed, the shrubby species from cuttings which should be about 6 in. long, placed in sandy soil, with bottom heat of about 60° F. Young shoots with a heel root freely. The annuals should be sown in a hotbed, the seedlings planted singly in small pots when large enough to handle, and later moved to their flowering quarters in the open border. A light sandy soil suits them best and they should have ample space to grow. *D. Stramonium* often sows itself and may become almost a weed. The shrubby species grow well against pillars or planted in beds or borders in the conservatory and allowed to grow into large bushes or dwarf trees. They bear severe pruning and may be cut to keep them to any form or size desired. The pruning is best done immediately after flowering or later in the autumn. These species are naturally evergreen but may be treated as deciduous, they enjoy moderate heat when in full growth but should be kept dry and quite cool in winter. In moderate-sized houses they should be grown in 12-in. pots as standards with a stem of 4 to 7 ft. and a head of three or more branches which will quickly form if the main stem is stopped. When once formed the shape may be maintained by cutting back the annual growths to where the leading branches originate. Old plants flower more freely than young ones. While flowering, manure water is useful in increasing the vigour of the plants and the number and size of the flowers. They are rather subject to attacks of Scale Insects on the leaves and stems and of Capsid Bugs (see notes on these pests). *D. sanguinea* and *D. suaveolens* are excellent for permanent planting in beds or groups indoors and *D. cornigera*, widely known as *D. Knightii*, does well planted in sheltered places outside in summer, and in favoured localities may be left permanently. **A**

**D. al'ba.** A variety of *D. fastuosa*.

**D. arbor'ea.** Angel's Trumpet. Shrub or small tree to 10 ft. *l.* elliptic-oblong to ovate-lanceolate, entire, hairy like the branches; stalk about 1 in. long. *fl.* white, 7 to 8 in. long with a terete tube and long lobes; cal. tubular, spathe-like; anthers distinct. August. Peru, Chile. 1813. (G.C. 11 (1879), 141.) SYN. *Brugmansia arborea*.

**D. ceratocau'la.** Annual of 2 to 3 ft. Stem terete, purplish, forked, hairy near base, branches horn-like. *l.* ovate-lanceolate, toothed, hoary beneath. *fl.* very large; tube green; limb white, tinged purple within, bluish outside, fragrant; opening in late afternoon until mid-morning. July. Trop. America. 1805. (B.M. 3352.)

**D. chloran'tha.*** Glabrous shrub. *l.* broadly ovate, almost triangular, wavy and sharply toothed on margin. *fl.* yellow, fragrant, pendulous on short, axillary peduncles; cal. tubular, teeth 5, very short, triangular; cor. funnel-shaped with a wide mouth. August to October. Origin unknown. 1845. Free-flowering. As originally known (see B.M. 5128) the flowers were double; the single form is referred to in Gard. Magazine, 1894. SYN. *D. humilis* var. **Golden Queen,** *fl.* deeper yellow.

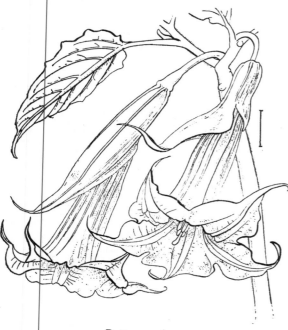

*Datura cornigera*

**D. cornig'era.*** Shrubby, about 10 ft. h., softly downy. Stem about 3 ft. long. *l.* mostly near ends of branches, ovate, slender-pointed, entire or angled, sometimes in pairs. *fl.* white or cream, large, drooping, funnel-shaped, striated, mouth spreading, 5-lobed, lobes ending in a long spreading or recurved point; cal. spurred. Summer. Mexico. (B.M. 4252.) SYN. *Brugmansia Knightii,* usually applied to the double form.

**D. cornuco'pia.** A synonym of *D. fastuosa.*

**D. fastuo'sa.** Downy or glabrous annual of 2 or 3 ft. or more. *l.* ovate-lanceolate, slender-pointed, acute, unequal at base, upper in unequal pairs, 7 to 8 in. long; stalks 1½ to 2½ in. long. *fl.* violet outside, whitish within, 6½ to 7 in. long, erect; cal. purple, angled, 2 in. long, 5-toothed. July. *fr.* spiny, globose. India. 1629. (Gn. 46 (1894), 224 as *D. cornucopia.*) var. **al'ba,** *fl.* white or nearly so. SYN. *D. alba;* **du'bia,** *fr.* without spines; **Huberia'na,** bushy, *fl.* of various colours, yellowish-blue or red. Perhaps a hybrid of *D. cornigera* with *D. chlorantha.*

**D. fe'rox.** Stem thick, glabrous, red at base, green or white-spotted above. *l.* rhombic-ovate, angled. *fl.* bluish-white, 1½ in. long, erect, limb angled; cal. striated. August. *fr.* unequally spiny, with 4 spines at top. S. Europe.

**D. Huberia'na.** See **D. fastuosa.**

**D. hu'milis.** A synonym of *D. chlorantha* and *D. fastuosa.*

**D. Me'tel.** Annual, hairy, 3 to 5 ft. h. *l.* cordate, entire or almost so. *fl.* white, 10 in. long, 4 in. across. June. *fr.* prickly, nodding. Tropics. 1596. (B.M. 1440.)

**D. meteloi'des.** Perennial, downy and glaucous, with slender, forked branches. *l.* unequally ovate, entire or almost so, acute at both ends, upper often in pairs, 2 to 2½ in. long; stalks swollen at base. *fl.* bluish-violet or white, 4 to 8 in. long, much like those of *D. Metel* but with longer tube, fragrant. Texas to California and Mexico. (F.d.S. 1266.) SYN. *D. Wrightii.* May be treated as annual.

**D. murica'ta.** Annual of 2 to 3 ft. *l.* ovate, repand, toothed, glabrous, unequal at base. *fl.* white, long. July. *fr.* muricate with strong short prickles. Trop. Asia. 1820.

**D. quercifo'lia.** Annual of 1 to 2 ft. *l.* pinnatifid with wavy margin, hairy on veins beneath. *fl.* violet. July. *fr.* with flattened prickles up to ½ in. long. Mexico. 1824.

**D. sanguin'ea.** Tree-like shrub, 4 to 8 ft. h., branches leafy near apex. *l.* alternate, ovate-oblong, about 7 in. long, margins wavy; lobes short, blunt, softly white-hairy; stalks stout. *fl.* orange-red, about 8 in. long, pendulous; cal. ovate, 5-angled, variegated, inflated, hairy. Peru. (S.B.F.G. 272 as *Brugmansia sanguinea.*)

**D. Stramo'nium.** Thorn Apple. Annual of about 2 ft. *l.* ovate, angular-toothed, wedge-shaped at base, smoothish, green. *fl.* white, funnel-shaped. July. *fr.* erect, with stout prickles. Widely distributed, including England. (E.B. 935.) The plant has medicinal value in treatment of asthma. var. **iner'mis,** capsule smooth.

**D. suaveo'lens.*** Angel's Trumpet. Tree-like shrub, 10 to 15 ft. h. *l.* ovate-oblong, 6 to 12 in. long, entire, smooth above, sometimes downy beneath, sometimes unequal at base. *fl.* white, pendulous, fragrant; cor. with 5 short lobes; cal. inflated, angled, with 5 small teeth; anthers crowded together. August. Brazil. The double form is more commonly grown.

**D. Tat'ula.** Similar to *D. Stramonium* but stem purple. *fl.* violet-purple or lavender. Prickles of capsule nearly equal. Tropics.

**D. Wright'ii.** A synonym of *D. meteloides.*

W. J. B.

**DAUBEN'YA** (in honour of Dr. Charles Daubeny, 1795–1867, Professor of Botany, &c., Oxford). FAM. *Liliaceae.* A genus of 3 species of bulbous plants with radical leaves, natives of S. Africa, related to Massonia but with equal perianth segments and stamens united into a ring. Inflorescence a very short-stalked, densely flowered, umbel about 2 in. across. Sandy loam and peat suits them and they can be increased by offsets. They need greenhouse treatment and to be kept quite dry while at rest.

**D. au'rea.** About 3 in. h. *l.* oblong, seated close to the earth. *fl.* yellow, tubular; limb 2-lipped. June. 1832. (B.R. 1813.)

**D. ful'va.** About 6 in. h. *fl.* dull reddish-yellow. June. 1836. (B.R. 25, 53.)

*daucifo'lius -a -um,* having leaves like a Carrot.

*daucoi'des,* carrot-like in some way.

**DAU'CUS** (*Daukos,* the ancient Greek name). FAM. *Umbelliferae.* A genus of about 60 species of annual, biennial, or perennial herbs, natives of Europe, N. Africa, and W. Asia. Leaves finely cut, segments small. Flowers in compound umbels usually with many rays, white or reddish; bracts many or none; outer flowers often rayed; petals notched, point inflexed. Fruit ovoid or oblong, spiny. The only species of horticultural value is *D. Carota,* the Carrot (q.v.).

**D. Caro'ta.** Carrot. 1 to 2 ft. h. *l.* pinnately much cut; segs. small, rather hairy. *fl.* white, in stalked umbels, outer rays incurved, middle flowers purplish; involucral bracts pinnatifid; bracteoles lanceolate. Summer. Europe, including Britain, eastwards to India. (E.B. 615.) Biennial.

*dau'ricus -a -um,* of Dauria, NE. Asia.

**DAVAL'LIA** (after E. Davall, 1763–98, Swiss botanist). FAM. *Polypodiaceae.* A genus of 36 ferns native of tropics of Old World, especially in Polynesia and SE. Asia with usually broad, somewhat leathery, deltoid, 3- or 4-pinnatifid fronds and sori near the margins of the fronds at the ends of veins with indusia of similar substance to the frond, half cup-shaped and attached by both sides and base. Sporangia stalked. Davallodes, Humata, Leucostegia, Microlepia, and Scyphularia are related genera, the species of which are sometimes included under Davallia. Several species have creeping, scaly rhizomes and when grown in pots or pans these species require to be raised a little above the rim of the pot, for the rhizomes must not be buried in the soil. Most species are averse to heavy or close soil, and thrive in a compost of 3 parts fibrous peat, 1 part chopped Sphagnum—or, better still, good leaf-mould—and 1 part silver-sand, with thorough drainage and an abundant supply of water at the roots during the growing season. During winter they must be watered sparingly, never allowing even deciduous kinds to become quite dry. The plants must not be syringed overhead; they are best kept near the glass. Propagation of species not producing rhizomes is by spores, sown in heat. Where Davallias like *trichomanoides, bullata,* and *Mariesii* are required in quantity they are best raised from spores. As soon as the seedlings have produced a rhizome 2 in. long, the latter is repeatedly pruned, which tends to make compact, bushy plants.

Many Davallias require special treatment. *D. bullata* is one of the most useful species in cultivation, succeeding equally well in stove or in greenhouse, and making a very fine specimen, whether grown in a shallow pan of good dimensions, on a pyramid of peat, or on a vertical piece of cork or tree-fern stem, where the rhizomes have plenty of room for extension. The hare's-foot fern (*D. canariensis*) is a very ornamental and interesting species, useful for pots and for planting on rockwork. Its popular name is derived from the fact that its prostrate stems, which are covered with pale-brown chaffy scales, have a very close resemblance to the feet of a hare. It succeeds well under greenhouse treatment, and is an excellent plant for rooms. *D. divaricata* is best accommodated on a projecting rock in the warm fernery. It is a shallow-rooting plant, requiring but a few inches of soil to develop itself to perfection, and on that account may easily be grown on the trunk of a dead tree-fern.

As basket plants, Davallias are in the first rank. Some of the best for baskets are *D. Mariesii*, *D. solida* and its forms (all of which like peat), *D. canariensis*, and *D. bullata*.

**D. brasilien'sis.** A synonym of *Ithycaulon inaequale*.

**D. bulla'ta.*** *rhiz.* creeping, stout, densely fibrillose. *sti.* strong, erect, 3 to 4 in. long. *Fronds* 8 to 12 in. long, 4 to 8 in. broad, deltoid, 4-pinnatifid; pinnules of lower pinnae lanceolate, 2 to 3 in. long, with deeply inciso-pinnatifid oblong-rhomboidal segs. *Sori* deeply half cup-shaped. Japan, China, Trop. Asia. (H.S. 1, 50 B.)

**D. canarien'sis.*** Hare's-foot fern. *rhiz.* creeping, densely scaly. *sti.* strong, erect, 4 to 6 in. long. *Fronds* 1 to 1½ ft. long, 9 to 12 in. broad, deltoid, 4-pinnatifid; pinnules of lower pinnae lanceolate-deltoid, 2 to 3 in. long, over 1 in. broad, with ovate-rhomboidal deeply inciso-pinnatifid segs. *Sori* occupying a whole ultimate division. W. Mediterranean. This fern derives its popular name from the peculiar form of the rootstock, which curves over the side of the pot in which it grows, and being covered with close brown hair, it much resembles a hare's foot. (H.S. 1, 56 A; B.C.F. 2, 122; L.B.C. 142.)

**D. cornicula'ta.** *Fronds* more leathery than in *D. denticulata*, more finely divided segs., very small sori, and sharp teeth protruded considerably beyond them. Malaya. Stove.

**D. deco'ra.** A synonym of *D. bullata?*

**D. decurr'ens.** Resembles *D. divaricata* but the rather leathery frond less divided, 1 to 2 ft. long, 9 to 15 in. wide. Philippine Is. (H.S. 1, 44.) SYN. *D. alata.* Greenhouse.

**D. denticula'ta.*** *rhiz.* stout, creeping, densely fibrous. *sti.* firm, erect, 4 to 8 in. long. *Fronds* 1 to 2 ft. long, 9 to 15 in. broad, deltoid, 3-pinnatifid; pinnules of lower pinnae 2 to 3 in. long, 1 in. broad, deltoid-lanceolate, cut to rachis on lower part with oblong-deltoid segs., slightly toothed. *Sori* several to a seg., marginal. Tropics of Old World. A variable plant. var. **ela'ta** has larger less leathery fronds, segs. narrower, more deeply and sharply cut. (H.S. 1, 55); **flac'cida** has finely cut foliage; var. **May'i** has larger fronds with broader pinnules than in type; **polydac'tyla** has widened much divided tips.

**D. dissec'ta.** A synonym of *D. trichomanoides.*

**D. divarica'ta.** *rhiz.* creeping, stout, scaly. *sti.* firm, erect, 6 to 12 in. long. *Fronds* 2 to 3 ft. long, 3-pinnatifid; lower pinnae often 12 in. long by 6 in. broad; segs. deltoid, or cut to rachis in lower part. *Sori* half cup-shaped. Trop. Asia. (H.S. 1, 59 A; F.B.I. 107 as *D. polyantha.*)

**D. el'egans.** A synonym of *D. denticulata.*

**D. fijien'sis.** See **D. solida.**

**D. foenicula'cea.** A synonym of *Loxoscaphe foeniculaceum.*

**D. illus'tris.** *rhiz.* stout, creeping, scaly. *sti.* reddish-brown. *Fronds* 2½ to 4 ft. long, arching; pinnae finely cut. A capital basket plant. 1899.

**D. Lorrain'ei.** *rhiz.* black-scaly. *sti.* 3 to 4 in. long. *Fronds* 6 to 12 in. long, deltoid, 4-pinnatifid; final lobes ligulate, with a sorus at base of inner side. Malacca. 1882.

**D. Maries'ii.*** A pretty dwarf evergreen species, with slender creeping rhizomes, well suited for the cool greenhouse. In general aspect much like *D. bullata.* Japan. 1879. (B.C.F. 2, 141.)

**D. Moorea'na.** A synonym of *Leucostegia pallida.*

**D. polyan'tha.** A synonym of *D. divaricata.*

**D. polypodioi'des.** A synonym of *Microlepia speluncae.*

**D. pyxida'ta.*** *rhiz.* stout, creeping, densely scaly. *sti.* strong, erect, 4 to 6 in. long. *Fronds* 9 to 18 in. long, 6 to 9 in. broad, deltoid,

3- to 4-pinnatifid; pinnules of lower pinnae lanceolate, 2 to 3 in. long, 1 in. broad, with deltoid or oblong segs. *Sori* deeply half cup-shaped in the teeth. New S. Wales. 1808. (H.S.F. 1, 55 c.)

**D. retu'sa.** A synonym of *Stenoloma retusum.*

**D. scab'ra.** A synonym of *Microlepia setosa.*

**D. sol'ida.*** *rhiz.* creeping, stout, densely scaly. *sti.* strong, erect, 4 to 6 in. long. *Fronds* 1 to 2 ft. long, 1 to 1½ ft. broad, deltoid, 3-pinnatifid; segs. ovate-rhomboidal, deeply toothed, narrower and sharper in fertile fronds. *Sori* nearly or quite marginal. Malaya, Polynesia, Queensland. 1844. (H.S.F. 42; F.B.I. 104.) *D. ornata* is a form with broad, slightly cut segs. var. **super'ba** is a particularly fine form; **fijien'sis,** *rhiz.* creeping, stout, densely fibrillose. *sti.* 6 to 9 in. long, erect, strong, *fronds* 1 to 1½ in. long, 6 to 12 in. broad, deltoid, 4-pinnatifid, pinnules of lower pinnae deltoid-lanceolate, lobes of seg. cut nearly to rachis into linear divisions, *sori* half cylindrical. Fiji. 1879. Of this several varieties have been named including **el'egans,** lighter green and less dense than the type, **ma'jor,** also light green, with broader segs. and more robust, **plumo'sa,** with very narrow segs. 1882.

**D. tenuifo'lia.** A synonym of *Stenoloma chussnum.*

**D. trichomano'ides.*** *rhiz.* wide-creeping, covered with pale-brown scales. *sti.* grey, naked, 3 to 6 in. long. *Fronds* 6 to 9 in. long, elongated-triangular, rather leathery, 4-pinnatifid; pinnae stalked, spear-shaped, lowest and largest 1½ to 2 in. broad; pinnules cut into strap-shaped segs. *Sori* with a horn projecting on both sides. Malaya. (G.F. 1909, 398 as *D. dissecta.*) Stove.

**DAVALLO'DES** (Davallia-like). FAM. *Polypodiaceae.* A genus of about 12 species, bearing great resemblance to Davallia. For cultivation *see* **Davallia.**

**D. borneen'se.** *rhiz.* wide-creeping, densely scaly. *sti.* firm, erect, naked, 6 in. long. *Fronds* lanceolate, 1 to 1½ ft. long, 4 to 6 in. broad; pinnae 2 to 3 in. long, about 1 in. broad, cut to a broadly winged rachis into narrow-oblong, notched lobes. *Sori* midway between midrib and margin; indusium persistent. Borneo. (B.C.F. 2, 478; H.C.F. 93.) SYN. *Lastrea borneensis, Nephrodium borneense.* Stove.

**D. hirsu'tum.** *rhiz.* creeping, densely covered with soft, brown hairs. *sti.* firm, erect, 3 to 4 in. long, hairy. *Fronds* 1 to 1½ ft. long, 6 to 9 in. broad, spear-shaped, 3-pinnatifid, thin and papery, rachis and under-surface softly hairy. *Sori* very small, 2 to 12 to a pinnule, near centre of teeth near the base. Luzon, Sumatra. (H.S. 60 A.) SYN. *Davallia ciliata, Microlepia ciliata, M. hirsuta.* Stove.

**D. membranulo'sum.** *rhiz.* wide-creeping, stout, densely clothed with pale brown scales. *sti.* 2 to 3 in. long. *Fronds* thin, papery, 6 to 9 in. long, 2 to 3 in. broad, once fully pinnate, lower pinnae cut into numerous sharply toothed, oblong segs. *Sori* 2 to 8 to a seg., oblique between mid-vein and margin. Yunnan, Tonkin, Himalaya. (H.S. 1, 53.) SYN. *Davallia* and *Leucostegia membranulosa.* Greenhouse.

*davallioi'des,* Davallia-like.

*Daveaua'nus -a -um,* in honour of Jules Daveau, 1852–1929, Director, Botanic Garden, Lisbon, &c.

*Da'vidi, Davidia'nus -a -um,* in honour of l'Abbé David, 1826–1900, French missionary, who collected many plants in China.

**DAVID'IA** (in honour of Pére Armand David, 1826–1900, French missionary in China, from 1862 to 1873, who collected many plants there). FAM. *Cornaceae.* A genus of 1 species, a deciduous tree with alternate slender-stalked, toothed leaves without stipules. Flowers without petals, in dense globose heads containing several male flowers each with 1 to 7 stamens, and one perfect flower with a 6- to 10-celled ovary. Fruit a drupe with a 3- to 5-seeded stone. At the base of the head of flowers are 2 (sometimes 3) large white or creamy-white bracts, the lower about 6 in. long, the upper about half that size, the whole inflorescence with its bracts being on a slender curved stalk about 3 in. long. It is to these enormous and conspicuous bracts that form a canopy over the flower-head that the tree owes its striking and remarkable appearance, not to the flowers themselves, giving it a character distinct from any other. The tree is a hardy one and will grow well in a moist loamy soil but does not thrive where the soil becomes very dry in summer. It can be propagated by cuttings of short side-shoots taken when the wood is becoming hard but before it ripens thoroughly. The exact place in natural classification which this tree occupies has been a matter for much discussion and by some it has been joined with

Nyssa in the family Nyssaceae. The smooth-leaved forms vars. *laeta* and *Vilmoriniana* mentioned below are distinct in appearance from the type and by some have been regarded as distinct species.

**D. involucra'ta.*** Tree up to about 60 ft. in the wild, with more or less ascending branches forming a shapely head; young shoots glaucous, eventually dark. *l.* broad-ovate, 3 to 6 in. long, slender-pointed, coarsely toothed, bright green above, white-felted beneath and with silky hair above; veins in about 8 pairs. *fl.-heads* about ¾ in. across; stamens red or black and white. Bracts 2, large, white. May. *fr.* pear-shaped, 1½ in. long, green with purplish bloom. W. China. 1905. var. **lae'ta**, like next except that *l.* are yellowish-green beneath; **Vilmorinia'na,*** *l.* smooth and glaucous beneath. 1897. (B.M. 8432.)

**D. lae'ta.** See above.

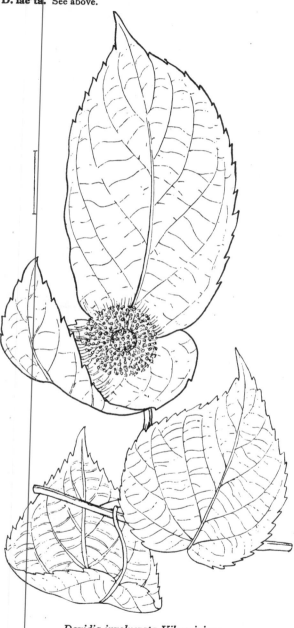

*Davidia involucrata Vilmoriniana*

**D. Vilmorinia'na.** See above.

## DAVID'S HARP. *See* **Polygonatum multiflorum.**

## DAVIDSON'IA (in honour of the discoverer who found it on a sugar plantation). FAM. *Saxifragaceae.* A genus of a single species of tree with unequally pinnate leaves

and flowers in a long-stalked clustered panicle. Calyx of 4 to 5 overlapping sepals; petals absent; stamens 8 to 10; styles 2, bristle-like. Fruit cylindrical-ovate with 1 pendent seed. To be grown in the stove in fibrous peat, loam, and sand.

**D. prur'iens.** Queensland Itch Tree. *l.* alternate, odd-pinnate, 2 ft. long, bright red with pungent hairs when young; lflets. 5 or 6 pairs, terminal, 9 in. long; stalks and rachis thickly covered with short stiff hairs, narrowly winged. NE. Australia. 1877.

F. G. P.

*Davidson'iae, Davidsonia'nus, -a -um,* in honour of Dr. and Mrs. W. H. Davidson of the Friends Mission at Changtu, Szechwan, China.

## DAVIES'IA (in honour of the Rev. Hugh Davies, 1739–1821, student of British botany). FAM. *Leguminosae.* A genus of about 63 species of evergreen or leafless shrubs, natives of Australia and Tasmania. Leaves alternate, entire, sometimes reduced to short prickles or teeth, sometimes entirely absent. Flowers small, usually in axillary racemes and orange-yellow or red; standard petal often stained with purple. Pod of curious triangular shape, 2-valved; seeds 1 or rarely 2. They require cool greenhouse conditions, and a compost of loam and peat with a little sand. Propagated by cuttings of firm young shoots in sand under a bell-glass, or by seeds sown in a slight hotbed in March.

KEY.

| | | |
|---|---|---|
| 1. *Shrub leafy* | | 2 |
| 1. *Shrub leafless, branches very thick cylindrical* | D. euphorbioides | |
| 2. *Shrub with spine-tipped shoots* | D. ulicina | |
| 2. *Shoots not spine-tipped* | | 3 |
| 3. *Fl. in umbels; lvs. deeply cordate* | D. cordata | |
| 3. *Fl. in racemes* | | 4 |
| 4. *Lvs. narrow* | | 5 |
| 4. *Lvs. ovate or ovate-lanceolate, 1 to 3 in. long* | D. latifolia | |
| 5. *Lvs. sharp-pointed, ½ to ¾ in. long* | D. umbellulata | |
| 5. *Lvs. hard-pointed, 1½ to 3 in. long* | D. corymbosa | |

**D. corda'ta.** Glabrous shrub 2 to 3 ft. *l.* 2 to 5½ in. long, ovate-lanceolate, very deeply cordate, pointed, sessile, basal lobes clasping stem. *fl.* in 1 to several axillary stalked clusters, each carrying 5 to 12 fl. with 2 or more large membranous bracts beneath each cluster; standard pet. ¼ in. wide, yellow, with a purple-brown stain; wings purple. May. W. Australia. (B.R. 1005.)

**D. corymbo'sa.*** Shrub, 2 to 5 ft., glabrous. *l.* linear to lanceolate, 2 to 5 in. long, 1/12 to ¼ in. wide, pointed, cuneate. *fl.* in stalked racemes, solitary or in pairs in the l.-axils and 1 to 1½ in. long; standard pet. ¼ in. wide, yellow, with dark blotch at base; wings short. May to July. Australia. 1804. (B.M. 1957 as *D. mimosoides.*)

*Daviesia ulicina* (p. 644)

**D. euphorbioi'des.** Erect, leafless shrub, glabrous, glaucous, shoots ⅜ in. thick, terete, upright like organ-pipes or some euphorbias or cacti, green and performing the functions of l. The place of the absent l. is taken by minute hooked scales. *fl.* several in short clusters. The only one introduced of a group of about 8 leafless species. W. Australia. A curiosity.

**D. latifo'lia.** Glabrous shrub, 2 to 6 ft. *l.* ovate-oblong, ovate-lanceolate, or obovate, apex pointed or blunt, 2 to 4 in. long, ¾ to 1½ in. wide, strongly veined. *fl.* in axillary, slender, cylindrical racemes 1 to 2½ in. long, orange-yellow; standard pet. ¼ in. wide, with a large dark stain in the centre. May. Australia, Tasmania. 1805. (B.M. 1757.)

**D. mimosoi'des.** A synonym of *D. corymbosa.*

**D. ulici'na.** Stiff, spiny shrub of several ft., shoots usually very downy, twigs ultimately spine-tipped. *l.* mostly about ¼ in. long, but sometimes ½ to ¾ in., varying from linear-lanceolate to broadly ovate or cordate, sessile, spine-tipped. *fl.* usually solitary (sometimes 2 to 4); standard pet. ⅜ in. wide, yellow, with a brownish-crimson stain; wings yellow. April, May. Australia, Tasmania. 1805. (L.B.C. 44.)

**D. umbellula'ta.** Shrub up to 6 ft., shoots very slender. *l.* linear-lanceolate, sharply pointed, ½ to 1¼ in. long, 1/12 to ⅛ in. wide. *fl.* in racemes ¾ to 1 in. long, borne in a long series of l.-axils, mostly at end of slender stalks, thus giving the infl. the appearance of an umbel; standard pet. and wings dark red at the base, margins yellow; keel dark crimson. April. New S. Wales, Queensland. 1816.

W. J. B.

***Davies'iae,*** in honour of Miss N. J. Davies who collected in California *c.* 1856.

***Davis'ii,*** in honour of Mr. Peter Davis who collected for Messrs. Veitch in Peru, *c.* 1875.

***davu'ricus.*** *See* ***dauricus.***

***Daw'ei,*** in honour of Mr. M. T. Dawe, 1880–1945, Director of Forestry Dept. Uganda, &c., *c.* 1905.

***Dawsonia'nus -a -um,*** in honour of Jackson T. Dawson, 1841–1916, of York, first Superintendent of the Arnold Arboretum.

***Daya'nus -a -um,*** in honour of John Day, 1824–88, who collected orchids in India, Ceylon, Brazil, &c.

**DAY-LILY.** *See* **Hemerocallis.**

**A→**

**DEADLY NIGHTSHADE.** *See* **Atropa Belladonna.**

**DEAD-NETTLE.** *See* **Lamium.**

**DEAL, WHITE.** Wood of *Picea Abies.*

**DEAL, YELLOW** or **RED.** Wood of *Pinus sylvestris* usually.

***dealba'tus -a -um,*** covered with opaque white powder.

**DEA'MIA** (in honour of Charles C. Deam who collected in Guatemala, &c., early in 20th cent.) Fam. *Cactaceae.* A genus of a single species, native of Mexico to Colombia. Plant pendent or climbing with long broadly 3-, or sometimes 5- to 8-winged, rooting joints. Spines of areoles numerous, needle-like, bristly when young. Flowers diurnal, very large, tube slender, long, throat funnel-shaped, inner segments yellowish-white. **A**

**D. testu'do.** Joints of stem 1¼ to 4 in. wide; ribs thin, wing-like, up to 1¼ in. h.; spines 10 or more to an areole, spreading. ⅖ to ⅘ in. long, brownish. *fl.* 10 to 11 in. long, with a long tube. (B.M. 5860 as *Cereus pterogonus.*)

***Dear'ei,*** in honour of Col. Deare of Englefield Green.

**DEATH'S HEAD HAWK MOTH.** *See* **Hawk Moths.**

***deb'ilis -is -e,*** weak.

**DEBREGEAS'IA** (in honour of Prosper Justin de Brégeas, 1807–?, who commanded the corvette *La Bonite,* on its voyage of discovery 1836–7). Fam. *Urticaceae.* A genus of about 5 species of shrubs or trees, natives of the warmer parts of Africa and Asia. Leaves alternate, toothed, 3-nerved; stipules 2-fid. Flowers monoecious or dioecious, in capitate, sessile, panicled or spicate clusters; males with 3 to 5 sepals, females with a fleshy receptacle and an ovoid perianth, orange-red and fleshy in fruit. The following species need greenhouse treatment and a compost of loam and peat. They may be increased by seed or by soft-wood cuttings under glass.

**D. ed'ulis.** Shrub about 6 ft. h., shoots at first appressed-hairy, finally glabrous. *l.* oblong-lanceolate to elliptic, slender-pointed, toothed, smooth above, whitish tomentose beneath. *fl.* in globose axillary clusters. *fr.* orange-red, globose. China, Japan.

**D. longifo'lia.** Shrub of 6 to 9 ft. *l.* linear to oblong-lanceolate, slender-pointed, toothed, rounded at base, 4 to 7 in. long, sometimes rough above, ashy- or white-hairy beneath. *fl.* in short, dichotomous cymes; sep. 4. *fr.* red or yellow, about as large as a pea, in short-stalked heads. SE. Asia. (R.H. 1896, f. 118 as *D. velutina.*)

**D. veluti'na.** A synonym of *D. longifolia.*

***deca-,*** in compound words, signifying 10.

**DECABELO'NE.** *See* **Tavaresia Barklyi.**

**DECAIS'NEA** (in honour of Joseph Decaisne, 1807–82, Director, Jardin des Plantes, Paris, an eminent French writer on plants). Fam. *Lardizabalaceae.* A genus of 2 upright deciduous shrubs with alternate, odd-pinnate leaves with entire leaflets. Flowers on slender stalks in long racemes at ends of lateral branches; sepals 6, lanceolate, petaloid, slender-pointed stamens 6 with filaments long and connate into a tube in staminate flowers, short and nearly free in pistillate; pistils 3, free. Fruits fleshy follicles with numerous seeds embedded in white pulp. *D. Fargesii* is hardy but liable to injury by late frosts; *D. insignis* needs protection. Both thrive in a moist loam and may be propagated by cuttings struck in a frame or by seeds.

**D. Farges'ii.** Deciduous shrub up to 10 or 12 ft. h. with several stout erect, smooth, pithy branches with large pointed buds. *l.* 2 to 3 ft. long; lflets. opposite in 6 to 12 pairs with an odd one, ovate, slender-pointed, 3 to 6 in. long, glaucous beneath, smooth or nearly so. *fl.* yellowish-green, paniculate, drooping; sep. erect, narrow-lanceolate, about 1¼ in. long. June. *fr.* dull blue, cylindrical, 3 to 4 in. long, ¾ in. thick, finely warted. W. China. 1897. (B.M. 7848.) The fr. is said to be eaten by the Chinese.

**D. insig'nis.** Habit and *fl.* similar to *D. Fargesii* but *fr.* golden yellow, edible. Himalaya. (B.M. 6731.) Tender.

***decan'drus -a -um,*** having 10 stamens.

**DECASCHIST'IA** (*deca,* 10, *schistos,* divided; in allusion to the 10 bracteoles and 10 parts of the pistil, &c.). Fam. *Malvaceae.* A genus of 4 or 5 species of shrubs found in India and Burma. Leaves lobed or entire. Flowers on short peduncles, axillary or clustered and terminal; sepals and petals 5, connate, the petals adnate at base to the staminal tube; bracteoles 10. For cultivation of this handsome shrub, *see* **Hibiscus.**

**D. ficifo'lia.*** *l.* 3-lobed, wedge-shaped at base, lobes toothed, hoary beneath. *fl.* coppery-red passing to yellow with red spot at base, 3 in. or more across. Burma. 1888. (G.C. 8 (1890), 629.)

**DECASPERM'UM** (*deca,* 10, *sperma,* seed; the seeds usually 8 to 10). Fam. *Myrtaceae.* A genus of shrubs or small trees, natives of E. Asia. Leaves opposite, pinnate veined. Flowers small in leafy racemes. *D. paniculatum* needs stove treatment, a compost of turfy loam with about one-third of dried cow manure and some sand, thorough drainage, and abundance of water while growing, but drier conditions when at rest. Cuttings of half-ripe shoots will root with bottom heat.

**D. frutico'sum.** Evergreen shrub or small tree, branches reddish. *l.* narrowly elliptic, 1 to 3½ in. long, ⅓ to 1½ in. wide, long-pointed, leathery. *fl.* white or greenish in short axillary panicles up to 3 in. long usually near ends of branches; bracts large, green, leaf-like. Burma, S. China. Young l. purplish to pink.

**D. panicula'tum.** Tweed River Cherry. Evergreen shrub of about 10 ft. *l.* oblong, slender-pointed. *fl.* white, in axillary racemes making a terminal leafy panicle. Moluccas. 1826. Syn. *Nelitris paniculata.*

F. G. P.

decem-, in compound words, signifying 10.

**DECE'MIUM** (decem, 10; from the 5 appendages between the 5 sepals). FAM. *Hydrophyllaceae*. A genus of a single species closely related to Hydrophyllum but with appendages to the calyx, and with a 1-seeded capsule much smaller than the calyx. For treatment see **Hydrophyllum.**

**D. appendicula'tum.** Biennial, little branched herb about 15 in. h., clammy-hairy above. *l.* at base much larger than those of stem, pinnate, up to 8 in. long with the stalk, upper palmately 5-lobed. *fl.* violet-blue, about ⅔ in. long, in long-stalked corymbose clusters. June, July. Eastern N. America. 1862. SYN. *Hydrophyllum appendiculatum.*

**DECIDUOUS CYPRESS.** See **Taxodium distichum.**

*decid'uus -a -um,* deciduous, falling off; not persisting beyond a season. Cf. **caducous.**

*decip'iens,* deceptive.

*declina'tus -a -um,* bent or curved downwards.

**DEC'ODON** (deca, 10, odon, tooth). FAM. *Lythraceae.* A genus of a single species, a perennial herb, native of swampy places in the E. United States, distinct from Lythrum by having 5 (or rarely 4) petals instead of 6, and 10 stamens instead of 6 or 12. Leaves opposite or whorled. Flowers in short-stalked clusters in upper leaf-axils. *D. verticillatus* is a hardy plant for swampy or moist places in the wild garden or margin of ponds.

**D. verticilla'tus.** Smooth or downy plant with 4- to 6-sided stems, 2 to 8 ft. long. *l.* lanceolate, nearly stalkless. *fl.* rose-purple; pet. wedge-shaped, ½ in. long; stamens 5 long, 5 short. E. United States. SYN. *Nesaea verticillata.*

*decompos'itus -a -um,* separated.

**decompound,** more than once compound.

*decor'ticans, decortica'tus -a -um,* shedding bark.

*decor'us -a -um,* handsome.

*decuma'nus -a -um,* very large, immense.

**DECUMA'RIA** (decimus, 10; from the number of parts in the flower). FAM. *Saxifragaceae.* A genus of 2 shrubs climbing by aerial roots with exfoliating bark, related to Hydrangea and Schizophragma but with all flowers perfect. Leaves more or less deciduous, opposite, without stipules, stalked. Flowers white, small, in terminal corymbs; sepals 7 to 10, minute; petals 7 to 10, valvate, more or less oblong; stamens 20 to 30; ovary inferior, 5- to 10-celled, with styles united. Fruit a capsule with numerous minute seeds. These climbers need a warm wall and are best in the favoured south-western counties. Propagated by cuttings of firm shoots in sand under glass.

**D. bar'bara.** Climber to 30 ft., shoots hairy. *l.* ovate, shortly pointed, 3 to 5 in. long, glabrous or slightly hairy at first, sometimes toothed towards tip. *fl.* white, ¼ in. across; corymb terminal, 2 or 3 in. across. June, July. *fr.* white, ribbed below, ⅓ in. long. SE. United States. 1785. (G.C. 46 (1909), 242.) Tender.

**D. sinen'sis.** Climber to 15 ft., shoots slightly hairy at first. *l.* sometimes evergreen, 1 to 3½ in. long, obovate or rounded, blunt, sometimes slightly toothed, glabrous except at base of stalk, dull green. *fl.* white, small; corymbs terminal or axillary, 1½ to 3½ in. h. and as wide. May. Cent. China. 1908. (B.M. 9429; H.I.P. 1741.) Variously described as fragrant and as having an unpleasant odour. Festoons cliffs in native habitat.

*decum'bens,* decumbent; lying on ground with ends ascending.

*decur'rens,* decurrent; running downwards; a leaf is decurrent when the blade tissues extend down the leaf-stalk or stem.

*decur'sivus -a -um,* running downwards.

*decurv'us -a -um,* curved downwards.

*decussa'tus -a -um,* decussate; at right angles.

**DEER GRASS.** See **Rhexia virginica.**

**DEERING'IA** (in honour of Karl Deering, d. 1749, Saxon physician practising in London, author of catalogue of British plants). FAM. *Amaranthaceae.* A genus of about 6 species of climbing herbs or sub-shrubs, natives of Australia, E. Indies, &c. Leaves alternate. Flowers sometimes dioecious, small, in terminal branching spikes; stamens 5, forming a ring. Fruit succulent, indehiscent. Stove temperature is needed and a compost of fibrous loam and peat.

**D. bacca'ta.** Climber to 10 to 12 ft., woody, glabrous. *l.* ovate or ovate-lanceolate, slender-pointed, entire. *fl.* greenish-white, in slender interrupted spikes up to 1 ft. long. *Berry* red. Australia, E. Indies, &c. (B.M. 2717 as *D. celosioides.*)

*defici'ens,* incomplete.

**definite,** constant, fixed or limited in number; stamens are said to be definite when they do not exceed 20; an inflorescence is definite when the main axis ends in a flower.

*deflex'us -a -um (deflexi-,* in compound words), bent downwards.

**defoliation,** the shedding of leaves.

*De'genii,* in honour of Dr. Arpád von Degen, 1866–1934, Director of Budapest Seed-testing Station.

*Degronia'nus -a -um,* in honour of M. Degron, Director of French posts, Yokohama, 1869.

**DEHERAIN'IA** (in honour of Pierre Paul Deherain, naturalist, Museum, Jardin des Plantes, Paris). FAM. *Myrsinaceae.* A genus of 2 species of shrubs natives of Mexico and Cuba. They need stove conditions and a rich sandy loam and fibrous peat compost. Ripened cuttings with a heel will root in sand under glass with bottom heat.

**D. smaragdi'na.** About 3 ft. h. *l.* oblong-lanceolate, toothed, hairy on veins. *fl.* green, about 2 in. wide, Primrose-like, in clusters beneath the foliage. Mexico. 1875. (B.M. 6373.)
F. G. P.

**dehiscence,** the opening of anthers or fruits to allow of discharge of contents.

*dehis'cens,* opening or gaping.

**DEILEPH'ILA el'penor.** Elephant Hawk Moth. See **Hawk Moths.**

**DEINAN'THE** (deinos, strange, anthos, flower; the flowers being large for the group). FAM. *Saxifragaceae.* A genus of 2 species of perennial herbs allied to Cardiandra but with opposite leaves and style with 1 to 5 branches, instead of 3 distinct. Hardy but needing cool, rich, well-drained peaty soil, sheltered from wind which would be likely to damage their glossy, rough leaves, where they will never suffer from drought. They are worth the trouble of supplying their needs for their handsome foliage and the beautiful white (in *D. bifida*) or pale clear violet flowers (in *D. caerulea*) which are produced in late summer. Propagation is by division of the creeping rhizome. Natives of E. Asia.

**D. bif'ida.** Habit of *D. caerulea* but about 8 in. h., *l.* crinkly, on stem, deeply divided at tip, rough and glossy. *fl.* white, stamens yellow; in terminal clusters among the *l.* Japan.

**D. caeru'lea.** Perennial herb, about 18 in. h. producing a solitary stem from the tip of the root-stock. *l.* about 4 at top of stem, ovate or broadly elliptic, sharply toothed. *fl.* in a terminal panicle, some sterile and small, the fertile more numerous, larger and nodding; pet. pale clear violet-blue; stamens blue. July. China. (B.M. 8373.)

**DELARB'REA** (in honour of M. Delarbre, 1722–1811, French naturalist). FAM. *Araliaceae.* A genus of 2 tall shrubs, natives of New Caledonia. Leaves alternate, odd pinnate, the leaflets sometimes deeply cut so as to be again compound, leathery, entire or slightly toothed, gracefully arched. Distinct from Aralia by their round, not angled, fruits and require the same treatment as that genus, with stove temperatures.

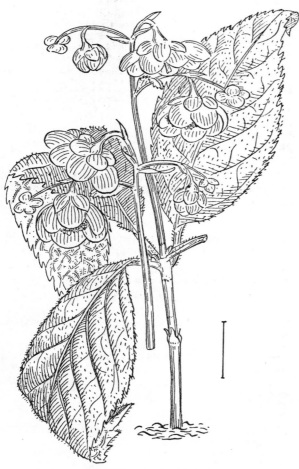

*Deinanthe caerulea* (p. 645)

**D. spectab'ilis.** Stem ash-grey with very dark brown warts. *lflets.* in 8 to 10 pairs, each lflet. entire, 3-lobed, or with 3 free segs. *fl.* small, in large umbellate clusters. New Caledonia. 1879. Syn. *Aralia concinna*, *A. spectabilis*.

**Delavay'i, Delavaya'nus -a -um,** in honour of l'Abbé Jean M. Delavay, 1834–95, who collected many plants in W. China.

**deleien'sis -is -e,** from the Delei Valley, Assam.

**DEL'IA antiq'ua. See Onion fly. D. bras'sicae.** *See* **Cabbage Root fly.**

**delicatis'simus -a -um,** very charming.

**delica'tus -a -um,** charming.

**delicio'sus -a -um,** of pleasant flavour.

**Deli'lei,** in honour of A. Raffeneau Delile, 1778–1850, French botanist.

**DELI'MA.** *See* **Tetracera.**

**A→**

**DELOSPER'MA.** Included in **Mesembryanthemum.** *D. crassuloides* is *M. crassulinum.*

**DELOSTO'MA** (*delos*, evident, *stoma*, mouth; from the wide mouth of the flower). Fam. *Bignoniaceae*. A genus of 6 or 7 species of Peruvian shrubs. Leaves opposite, simple, elliptic oblong. Flowers large, in few-flowered racemes; corolla with more or less incurved tube and 5 spreading lobes, somewhat 2-lipped; stamens, 4 fertile, the fifth thread-like, didynamous; ovary 2-celled. Fruit a capsule with many winged seeds. For cultivation, *see* **Clytostoma.**

**D. denta'tum.** Tree. *l.* elliptic, toothed, downy beneath. *fl.* bluish-white, large, about 2 in. across, bell-shaped, lobes spreading, round; racemes erect, 3- or 4-fld. October. Peru. (B.M. 5754.)

F. G. P.

*delphinen'sis -is -e,* of Dauphiné, France.

*delphinioi'des,* Delphinium-like.

**DELPHIN'IUM** (Greek name of 1 species used by Dioscorides). Fam. *Ranunculaceae*. A genus of about 200 species of annual, biennial, or perennial herbs, natives of Europe, Asia, N. America, and the mountains of Africa. Leaves digitately lobed. Flowers in racemes; sepals 5, coloured (mostly blue), deciduous; spur of one or both upper petals (in single flowers) enclosed in the spur of the upper sepals; stamens numerous, at first clustered then spreading outwards; carpels 1, 3, or rarely 5, free. Fruit a many-seeded follicle. Most Delphiniums are hardy though those from N. Africa, e.g. *D. candidum, D. macrocentron,* and *D. Wellbyi* need greenhouse treatment. Some, especially species from the Himalaya and W. China, are suitable for the rock-garden; others, among the taller perennials and the hybrids which constitute the group generally known in gardens as Delphiniums, are noble border plants which, though hardy, need care to keep them through wet and severe winters and special attention to secure the best results from their cultivation; still others are charming annuals both for the border and in pots for the cool greenhouse—these are the plants usually called Larkspurs in the garden. **A**

Well-grown Delphiniums should not suffer much from disease. One known as Leaf Blotch, due to *Bacterium delphinii*, shows as black spots and blotches on the leaves and is not easily checked by spraying. There is, however, great variation in susceptibility among modern varieties and it is best to discard those seen to be very susceptible. The common trouble with Delphiniums is Powdery Mildew, due to *Erysiphe polygoni*, which makes powdery white areas on the leaves and stems, and if severe may cripple the flower-spikes to some extent. Severe mildew attacks, even after first flowering, cripple the foliage and reduce the vigour of the plant for next spring, a fact of importance to nurserymen. This mildew is controlled by spraying with lime-sulphur, 1 part to 60 parts water, as soon as it is suspected, if not before. The trouble in Delphiniums known as Black Root Rot is not yet elucidated and the cause remains unknown. In this disease the roots of second year plants are blackened and dead and the plant slowly degenerates. Delphiniums are affected by one or two virus diseases which cause a chlorotic appearance of the leaves, with stunting in growth and distortion. Such plants should be lifted and destroyed.

(D. E. G.)

**D. Aja'cis.*** Larkspur. Glabrous or slightly hairy annual. Stem erect, 1 to 3 ft. h., branching, many-fld. *l.* 3-fid, upper deeply cut with linear segs. *fl.* in a loose spike-like raceme; bracts herbaceous, about as long as the ascending pedicels; sep. blue, rose or white; spur about as long as sep.; pet. 2, joined, 3-lobed, the middle lobe with basal marks said to resemble the letters AIA, whence the specific name from the Greek ΑΙΑΣ (Ajax). *fr.* softly hairy of 1 follicle. Summer. S. Europe, naturalized in England. A variable plant from which, and from *D. Consolida*, many of the annual Larkspurs of gardens have been derived; sometimes confused with the smooth-fruited *D. Consolida.* var. **mi'nus,** only 4 to 12 in. h. with smaller fl. and bright blue **sep.** much shorter than the spur. The following colour forms have been distinguished; **cyan'eum,** blue; **leucosep-**

**alum** (*album*), white; **purpu'reum**, purple; **rhodan'thum**, rose; **subcoerules'cens**, white with a blue tinge; **cyanopic'tum**, rose with blue dots or stripes; **cyanoleu'cum**, whitish with blue dots, the upper sep. violet-rose. Of the double-fld. forms with the same range of colours, there are **ranunculiflo'rum**, the Rocket Larkspurs, 2½ to 3 ft. h., and **hyacinthiflo'rum**, the Hyacinth-flowered Larkspurs, about 18 in. h.

**D. altis'simum.** Shaggy-hairy perennial about 3 ft. h. Stem slender, branching. *l.* palmately 5-partite, the divisions 3-lobed, toothed. *fl.* blue or purple in long branching racemes; spur straight or slightly incurved, as long as sep.; pet. 4, 2-lobed. August, September. *fr.* of 3 follicles, erect, seeds not winged or scaly. N. India.

**D. armeni'acum.** Perennial, 4 to 12 in. h., branched from base, appressed hairy. *l.* many-partite, segs. linear. *fl.* blue, spur up to 1 in. long; sep. somewhat hairy; pet. 3-lobed, pale blue; mid-lobe much shorter than lateral. August. Turkish Armenia.

**D. azu'reum.** A synonym of *D. carolinianum.*

**D. Bar'beyi.** Unbranched. *Lower l.* deeply 5-partite, lobes cut; *upper* 3-partite, segs. broadly lanceolate, entire, hairy above. *infl.* a simple raceme. *fl.* deep blue, spur straight, about ⅔ in. long; sep. glabrous, long slender-pointed with a flagellum; upper pet. dirty white, tipped blue, lower blue, 2-fid.; carpels glabrous. Colorado. Nearly related to *D. exaltatum.*

**D. bi'color.** Erect rather stout perennial of 6 to 12 in.; roots fascicled. *l.* small, thick, deeply cut, divisions cleft into linear obtuse segs; stalks dilated at base. Sep. blue, about ½ in. long; pet. 4, upper pale yellow or white, blue-veined, lower blue; spur about as long as sep.; racemes few-fld. May to August. NW. America. var. **grandiflo'rum**, *fl.* somewhat larger.

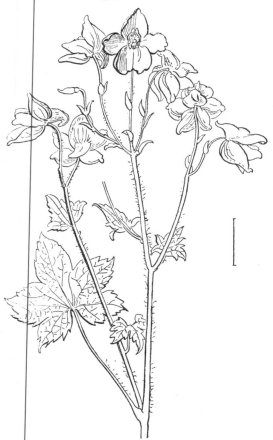

*Delphinium Brunonianum*

**D. Brunonia'num.** Erect, somewhat hairy perennial 10 to 18 in. h., leafy, foliage musk-scented. *Upper l.* 3-partite to almost entire; *lower l.* kidney-shaped, 5-lobed with wedge-shaped, toothed lobes. *Racemes* loose, branches curved, spreading. *fl.* large; sep. light blue shading to purple on margin; pet. 4, black, lower golden-bearded; spur very short. June, July. *fr.* of 3 to 5 hairy follicles; seed scarcely winged. Afghanistan to W. China. 1864. (B.M. 5461.) var. **al'bum**, *fl.* white.

**D. can'didum.** Dwarf, slightly hairy perennial, branches usually 3-fid. *l.* 5-lobed, 4 to 5 in. across; lobes usually 3-cut and toothed; lower stalks 8 to 15 in. long. *fl.* pure white, about 2½ in. across, slightly hairy, Primrose-scented; sep. roundish-ovate, up to 1 in.

across each with a thickish green spot at apex; spur slender, curved upwards, curved at tip, 1½ to 2 in. long; upper pet. glabrous, longer than stamens; lower 3-toothed, slightly hairy, shorter than stamens. July. Uganda. 1904. (B.M. 8170.) Greenhouse.

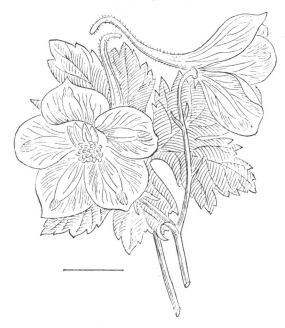

*Delphinium candidum*

**D. cardina'le.** Erect, sparsely hairy perennial, 2 to 3 ft. h. *Basal l.* 5-partite; lobes deeply 2- or 3-fid, usually entire, narrow at tip; *lower stem-l.* 3-partite; bracts linear-lanceolate, about as long as pedicels. *fl.* in long, many-fld. racemes; sep. bright red often with metallic lustre; pet. 4, yellowish; spur straight, about ¾ in. long, longer than sep. July, August. *fr.* of 3 spreading, recurved carpels, soon glabrous; seeds winged. California. (B.M. 4887.) Deep, rich, moist soil suits this species which will *fl.* in first year if sown early.

**D. cardiopet'alum.** *See* **D. verdunense.**

**D. carolinia'num.** Somewhat hairy perennial, 18 to 30 in. h., little branched. *l.* 3- to 5-partite, divisions 3- to 5-cleft into linear lobes. *fl.* azure-blue, sometimes white or whitish, in straight racemes; sep. often with brownish spot; pet. bearded. July. *fr.* of 3- to 5-follicles, oblong, erect. NW. America. var. **al'bum**, *fl.* ivory white, *l.* larger and with broader divisions. 1882; **vimin'eum**, 2 to 4 ft. h., *l.* with wider lobes, racemes looser. Texas. (B.M. 3593 and B.R. 1999 as *D. azureum.*)

**D. cashmeria'num.** Softly hairy perennial with erect stem 12 to 20 in. h. *Lower l.* heart-shaped, 5-lobed, long-stalked; *upper l.* almost sessile, short-stalked; lobes toothed, hairy on both sides; lower bract-l. 3-lobed, toothed, upper lanceolate, entire. *fl.* deep azure-blue in somewhat spreading corymbs; sep. about 1 in. long, hairy; pet. deep violet, upper smooth, lower weakly hairy; spur conical, much shorter than sep. June to October. *fr.* of 3 to 5 hairy follicles. Himalaya. 1875. (B.M. 6189.) var. **al'bum**, *fl.* white; **Walk'eri**, bracts broadly ovate, long-stalked. 1885. (B.M. 6830.)

**D. caucas'icum.** A synonym of *D. speciosum.*

**D. cheilan'thum.** Erect, simple or branched perennial, 2 to 3 ft. h. Stem leafy. *l.* 5-partite, divisions narrow, rhomboid, cut into lanceolate, acute lobes. *fl.* in racemes, dark blue, rarely whitish; sep. ovate, hairy outside; upper pet. smooth, bright yellow or blue, lower hairy, entire or 2-lobed; spur about ⅓ in. long, about as long as sep. June, July. *fr.* of 3 smooth or hairy follicles with 3-angled, winged seeds. Eastern Siberia, China. 1819. (B.R. 473.)

**D. chinen'se.** A synonym of *D. grandiflorum.*

**D. cilia'tum.** *See* **D. dictyocarpum.**

**D. Consol'ida.*** Annual or biennial, nearly or quite glabrous, 6 to 18 in. h. or up to 2½ or 3 ft. in gardens, with usually branching stem. *l.* 3-fid, the divisions 2- or 3-fid with linear segs., obtuse, or upper long-pointed; bracts much shorter than pedicels. Sep. blue, rarely rose or white, about ½ in. long; pet. 2, united, 3-lobed, blue or yellowish; spur straight, longer than sep. Summer. *fr.* erect, glabrous. Europe, including Britain. Here belong the Branching Larkspurs of which there are many colour forms; **pal'lidum**, *fl.* white; **al'bum**, *fl.* white, double; **versicol'or**, *fl.* smaller than in type, bluish-red, sprinkled white, plant robust with much cut l.; **azu'reum**, *fl.* sky blue; **caeru'leum**, *fl.* blue double; **purpu'reum**, *fl.* purple; **rhodosep'alum**, *fl.* rose [here would come the garden forms

**Exquisite Pink,** salmon pink; **La France,** pale salmon-pink; **Los Angeles,** bright rose on salmon; **Miss California,** deep salmon rose; **Rosamond,** deep bright-rose]; **viola'ceum,** *fl.* violet; **Coccin'eum,** robust, tall, *fl.* rosy scarlet; **imperia'le,** robust, *fl.* later and longer than type, often double, of various colours. *See also* **D. paniculatum.**

**D. corymbo'sum.** Hairy perennial about 2 ft. h., corymbosely branched with terminal 4- to 7-fld. racemes. *Lower l.* on ground; stem-l. palmate or 5-lobed, deeply 3-fid with narrow segs.; *upper l.* entire, linear. Sep. bright violet, greenish on back, hairy, hooded at tip; pet. almost black, about as long as sep., upper smooth, lower 2-lobed, ciliate. June, July. *Follicles* densely hairy. Turkestan. (G.F. 1059.)

**D. crassifo'lium.** A synonym of *D. speciosum.*

**D. cultra'tum.** Name proposed for the garden hybrids often offered under *D. hybridum,* a name belonging to an Asiatic species and used for other forms rather confusedly.

**D. dasycar'pum.** A synonym of *D. elatum.*

**D. deco'rum.** Slender perennial. Stem weak, 6 to 18 in. h., glabrous or nearly so. *l.* few, lower kidney-shaped, deeply 3- or 5-lobed, lobes variable; stalk dilated at base; upper small with 3 to 5 narrow lobes. *fl.* in a loose raceme or panicle; sep. blue, ½ in. long, upper pet. tinged yellow; spur as long as sep. Spring. *Follicles* 3, glabrous. California. 1881. (B.R. 26, 64.)

**D. Delavay'i.** Perennial. Stem tall, more or less branched, hairy. *l.* deeply 5-cut almost to base into broad-rhomboid lobes; stalk long, dilated at base; lower bracts with many narrow segs. *fl.* many in a narrow raceme; pedicels hairy; sep. blue, broadly ovate, about ⅝ in. long, hairy without; upper pet. glabrous, lower long-stalked, 2-lobed, long ciliate. October. *Follicles* 3, erect, sparsely bristly. W. China.

**D. denuda'tum.** Perennial with branching stems, 2 to 3 ft. h. *Basal l.* orbicular, 5- to 9-partite, 2 to 6 in. wide; segs. 2-pinnatifid; *stem-l.* few, upper 3-partite. *fl.* many in much-branched racemes, about 1 in. long; sep. yellow with blue margins; pet. pale blue. Himalaya. 1870.

**D. dictyocar'pum.** Habit of *D. elatum. l.* 3- to 7-lobed; lobes oblong, acute, deeply cut; stalk not dilated at base. *Raceme* loosely branched. *fl.* blue, spur straight, glabrous; pet. pale brownish or blue, lower 2-fid, bearded; carpels densely hairy; carpels 3 to 5. *Follicles* netted, ciliate on keel and margin. July. E. Russia. Sometimes regarded as a variety of *D. ciliatum.*

**D. ela'tum.** Robust perennial, 2 to 3 ft. h. or more. Stem smooth. *l.* palmately 5- to 7-partite, divisions with acute segs.; stalks not dilated at base; upper l. 3- to 5-partite, often entire; all sometimes hairy; bracts narrow linear, entire, shorter than pedicels. *fl.* in simple racemes sometimes branched at base, blue; sep. ovate, smooth; pet. brownish-violet, upper 2-lobed, with yellow beard; spur as long as sep. Summer. *Follicles* 3, smooth; seeds winged. Pyrenees to Mongolia. (F.d.S. 1287.) *See* **D. × Ruysii.**

**D. exalta'tum.** Almost glabrous perennial 2 to 4 ft. h. or more, rather fleshy. *Lower l.* 3- to 5-partite, with segs. 3-fid at apex; *upper l.* 3-partite with lanceolate segs.; stalks not or little widened at base. *infl.* branched at base. *fl.* blue; sep. oval, hairy without; pet. dirty yellow, lower 2-lobed, bearded; spur straight or somewhat bent, about as long as sep. Summer. *Follicles* 3, erect, hairy. Eastern N. America. 1758. (B.M. 1791.)

**D. fis'sum.** Close to *D. hybridum* but with terete usually softly hairy stem. *l.*-segs. with several apical teeth. *infl.* long, dense; pet. exserted, upper 2-lobed, lower 2-fid; seed oblong, narrow. Summer. SE. Europe.

**D. formo'sum.*** Perennial. Stem about 3 ft. h., thick, branched, hairy in lower part only. *l.* 5- to 7-partite; segs. toothed; bracts entire, lanceolate to linear. *Racemes* many-fld.; sep. purple-blue, about ¾ in. long; upper pet. with tuft of golden hairs at tip, lower 2-lobed, golden bearded; spur straight or slightly bent, scarcely as long as sep. August, September. *Follicles* 3, short-haired; seeds scaly. Caucasus, Asia Minor. (F.d.S. 1185.) A very hardy plant useful in borders or for naturalizing. Variable in gardens. var. **al'bum,** *fl.* white; **coelesti'num,** *fl.* pale blue.

**D. grandiflo'rum.*** Perennial with usually branched stem 1 to over 3 ft. h. *l.* palmately divided into many narrow linear segs.; uppermost bracts linear. *Racemes* many-fld., pedicels as long as fl. *fl.* large, blue, violet, or whitish; sep. about ¾ in. long, shortly hairy without; pet. yellowish or coloured as sep.; spur about as long as sep. July, August. *Follicles* 3, hairy; seeds 3-angled, winged. Siberia, Western N. America. (B.M. 1686.) var. **al'bum,** white; **Azure Fairy,** *fl.* pale blue; **Blue Butterfly,** *fl.* deep blue, with brown spot on each pet; **Blue Gem,** about 1 ft. h., deep bright blue; **chinen'se,** about 2 ft. h., *l.*-segs. about $\frac{1}{12}$ in. wide, *infl.* sometimes branched, *fl.* large. China. (L.B.C. 71.); double-fld. vars. both white and blue occur. *D. grandiflorum* may be treated as a hardy annual and used as a bedding plant.

**D. hyb'ridum.** Hairy perennial with a somewhat nodulose root and erect angled and furrowed stem 3 to 4 ft. h. *l.* 3- to 5-partite almost to base, the lobes often many and linear; stalk sheathing at base. *Racemes* long, pedicels scarcely as long as fl. *fl.* blue; sep. oval, white-hairy without, about ¾ in. long; pet. included, upper blue at tip, lower 2-lobed, bearded; spur straight, about ¾ in. long. May to July. *Follicles* 3, hairy; seeds scaly. S. Russia, Caucasus. 1794.

**D. imperia'le.** A variety of *D. Consolida.*

**D. laxiflo'rum.** A variety of *D. villosum.*

**D. likiangen'se.** Nearly glabrous perennial up to 15 in. h. *l.* nearly all radical, many-partite, dark glossy green above; segs. oblong; stalk dilated at base. *infl.* 3- to 5-fld. on an erect, stiff scape longer than l. *fl.* soft light blue, large, fragrant, spur straight, thick, ⅜ in. long; upper pet. glabrous, lower shortly 2-lobed, ciliate and bearded; carpels hairy. August. Yunnan. (G.C. 60 (1926), 128.) Border or Scree.

**D. linarioi'des.** Stem 4 to 6 in. long, velvety, somewhat prostrate, branched at base. *Lower l.* 3- or 4-fid, segs. linear; *upper* 3-partite to base; stalked. *Raceme* loosely branched, 3- or 4-fld. *fl.* blue, spur more or less incurved, hairy, shorter than sep.; pet. 3-lobed, obtuse; carpels hairy. Persia.

**D. Maackia'num.** Erect perennial to 3 ft., branched above, stem sometimes hairy. *l.* 3- to 5-partite, divisions toothed, base truncate or kidney-shaped, hairy on both sides; stalk dilated at base. *fl.* in loose panicles; sep. blue; pet. dark violet; spur twice as long as sep.; peduncles yellow hairy. July. *Follicles* often smooth; seeds scaly. Siberia.

**D. macrocen'tron.** Hairy perennial. Stems several, up to 6 ft. h., little branched. *l.* 3- to 7-lobed; segs. 3- to many-cut; stalk of lower l. 6 to 8 in. long, upper sessile. *fl.* blue and green, hairy, spur whitish, about 2 in. long, erect, broad, straight; sep. broad; pet. 4, narrower, blade oblong. July. Mt. Eglon, &c., Trop. Africa. 1906. (B.M. 8151.) Greenhouse.

**D. Menzies'ii.** Sparingly hairy perennial. Stem slender, 6 to 18 in. h. *l.* 3- to 5-partite, small, divisions cleft into linear or lanceolate segs.; stalk scarcely dilated at base. *fl.* blue, in conical racemes; sep. hairy without; upper pet. yellowish; spur as long as sep. April to June. *Follicles* 3, hairy as a rule; seeds black, winged on outer angles. California to Alaska. (B.R. 1192.)

**D. moscha'tum.** A synonym of *D. Brunonianum.*

**D. nudicau'le.** Smooth perennial, 12 to 18 in. h. Stem branched. *l.* few, rather fleshy, 1 to 3 in. wide, 3-partite; lower l. cut to middle, segs. rounded, often notched at apex, upper oblong, entire; stalks dilated at base. *fl.* in panicles; sep. red, obtuse; scarcely spreading; pet. yellow, nearly as long as sep., upper hairy at tip; lower 2-cleft, ciliate; spur stout, longer than sep. April to July. *Follicles* 3, spreading and recurved, soon glabrous; seeds with a narrow wing. California. 1869. (B.M. 5819.) var. **auranti'acum,** *fl.* orange; **Chamois,** *fl.* apricot; **Lemon Gem,** *fl.* clear yellow; **purpu'reum,** *fl.* purplish. *See also* **D. × Ruysii.**

**D. Nuttal'lii.** Perennial with erect stem, unbranched, leafy, 18 to 30 in. h. *l.* 3- to 5-partite, divisions cut into many linear-oblong segs., texture thin. *fl.* in long many-fld. racemes; sep. deep blue, ovate, rather hairy; pet. blue, or upper yellow, lower white-bearded; spur longer than sep. Summer. *Follicles* 3, hairy; seeds winged. Western N. America. 1892.

**D. panicula'tum.*** Macedonian or Siberian Larkspur. Annual or biennial. Much like *D. Consolida* but more branching and with stem 1½ to 4 or 5 ft. h. *l.* much cut with linear segs.; bracts linear, entire, much shorter than the pedicels which are smooth or with appressed hairs. *fl.* smaller; sep. blue-violet about ⅓ in. long; pet. 3-lobed; spur twice as long as sep. *Follicles* about twice as long as broad. June to October. S. Europe, Asia Minor. Forms with white, rose, or variegated fl. occur. (B.M. 9435 as *D. Consolida paniculatum.*) By some regarded as a subspecies of *D. Consolida,* but for garden purposes sufficiently distinct.

**D. peregri'num.** Perennial, smooth or hairy. Stem erect, 12 to 20 in. h., branches stiff. *Lower l.* 3- to 5-partite, divisions wedge-shaped, much cut into oblong to linear segs.; *upper* mostly entire. *fl.* in rather loose racemes; sep. blue, rarely white, hairy without; upper pet. blue, 2-lobed, lower yellowish; spur straight, up to twice as long as sep. June to November. *Follicles* 3, sometimes hairy; seeds scaly. Italy, eastwards to Asia Minor. 1629. (F.G. 506.)

**D. pic'tum.** Much like *D. Requienii* but bracteoles near base of the hairy pedicels; spur obtuse, 2-fid, about half as long as sep.; lower pet. broadly obovate. *Follicles* thicker, hairy. Corsica, Sardinia, Balearic Is. (S.B.F.G. 123.)

**D. Pylzow'ii.** Perennial. Stem silky hairy, leafy, about 12 in. h. *l.* much palmately cut; segs. oblong to linear, acute; stalk dilated at base. *fl.* 1 to 3, large, violet-blue; spur straight or curved at tip as long as the broadly ovate hairy sep.; pet. blackish violet, upper smooth, lower 2-fid, hairy. July, August. *Follicles* 5, densely silky. NW. China. (B.M. 8813.)

**D. Requien'ii.** Perennial. Stem softly hairy, 1 to 3 ft. h., little branched. *Lower l.* palmately 5- (rarely to 9-) partite, with 2- or 3-palmatifid divisions; segs. broadly lanceolate; *upper* 3-partite with oblong or lanceolate segs. *fl.* blue, in a loose spike-like raceme, with hairy, straight pedicels; sep. ovate, softly hairy; upper pet. pale yellowish, tinged blue near tip, lower roundish oblong, longer than sep.; spur bent. May, June. *Follicles* 3, ovate; seeds small. S. France. 1824.

**D. × Ruys'ii** (*D. elatum × D. nudicaule*). Of Belladonna type with pink fl. Raised at Moerheim Nurseries. Holland. (J.R.H.S. 60, f. 164.) Catalogued also as Pink Sensation.

**D. specio'sum.** Perennial. Stem simple, hairy, striped, 4 to 24 in. h. *l.* 5-partite, divisions much cut, hairy; bracts not longer than fl., upper lanceolate. *fl.* blue in a long raceme; pedicels densely hairy; sep. ½ to ⅔ in. long, hairy; pet. dark purple, upper smooth, lower golden-bearded, 2-lobed; spur about as long as sep. June to September. *Follicles* woolly. Caucasus to Himalaya. SYN. *D. caucasicum* of many authors. var. **glabra'tum**, similar in habit and fl. to *D. cashmerianum* but with larger infl. and spurs longer. Himalaya.

*Delphinium Pylzowii* (p. 648)

**D. Staphisag'ria.** Perennial or biennial, softly hairy, with thick stem 1 to 3 ft. h. *l.* palmately 5- to 9-partite; segs. entire, or 3-toothed at the broad apex. *fl.* in many-fld. raceme sometimes branched at base; upper bracts about as long as the thick pedicels which are about twice as long as fl.; sep. blue with greenish tinge, rarely pale or white, obtuse, hairy without; upper pet. whitish, exserted, lower obovate; spur obtuse. May to August. *Follicles* inflated, about ¾ in. long; seeds few. Mediterranean region, Canary Is. 1596. (F.G. 508.)

**D. sulphu'reum.** A synonym of *D. Zalil.*

**D. sutchuenen'se.** Erect perennial up to 30 in. h., glabrous, leafy. *l.* 3- to 5-sect; segs. oblong, narrowed to an entire base, somewhat stalked, 3-fid above, lobes acute; stalk slender, scarcely dilated at base. *infl.* branched, branches erect. *fl.* violet-blue, hairy without; spur horizontal or somewhat ascending, blunt, ⅔ in. long; lower pet. pale blue, 2-fid, beard yellow; carpels 3, silky hairy; pedicels slender, twice as long as fl. July. W. China.

**D. tangut'icum.** Perennial. Stem not branched, 4 to 6 in. h. *l.* subradical, hairy, palmately 3- to 5-partite, lobes acute, cut. *infl.* corymbose, 2- to 4-fld., bracts much cut. *fl.* large, blue, long-stalked; spur curved, hooked, up to 1 in. long; sep. downy without, up to 1 in. long; pet. dark brown, upper glabrous, lower nearly entire, margin within whitish; carpels 3, hairy at first. July. N. China.

**D. tatsienen'se.** Nearly related to *D. grandiflorum*. Hispid perennial, 20 in. h. or more. *l.* scabrid above, 3-partite to base; segs. pinnately cut, lobes long oblong, acute. *infl.* corymbose, many-fld. *fl.* violet-blue, spur awl-shaped, straight, twice as long as sep., up to 1 in. long; upper pet. dirty yellow, lower blue with orange beard; carpels 3, hairy. *Seeds* winged. July. Szechwan.

**D. tirolien'se.** Very near *D. villosum* but with softly hairy *l.*, ciliate bracts and lower pedicels, twice as long as *follicles*. July, August. Tirol.

**D. tricor'ne.** Perennial about 12 in. h. Stem fleshy. *l.* 3- to 5-partite, divisions 3- to 5-cleft, segs. linear, dying by midsummer. *fl.* blue, rarely whitish; upper pet. sometimes yellow with blue veins, lower white-beneath; spur as long as sep. May. *Follicles* 3 or 4, long, spreading, finally smooth. N. United States. 1806. (L.B.C. 306.)

**D. tris'te.** Perennial with simple or little branched leafy, hairy stem, about 2 ft. h. *l.* 3- to 5-partite, hairy on margin and nerves, divisions deeply cut. *fl.* dark violet with grey hairs in a loose, simple raceme; sep. ovate, about ½ in. long; pet. dark purple, upper sparsely hairy at tip, lower 2-lobed, bearded; spur as long as sep. Summer. *Follicles* densely hairy, about ½ in. long; seeds scaly. Siberia. 1819.

**D. trolliifo'lium.** Perennial. Stem more or less ascending, 2 to 5 ft. h., leafy. *l.* rather thin, large, 3- to 7-partite, kidney-shaped at base; lobes wedge-shaped, deeply cut. *fl.* blue in loose racemes up to 2 ft. l.; sep. about ¾ in. long; upper pet. white; spur as long as sep. April. *Follicles* smooth; seeds winged. Western N. America. 1889.

**D. verdunen'se.** Near *D. peregrinum* but with narrow lanceolate to linear l.-segs. *fl.* blue in a more or less dense raceme; spur straight or slightly bent, little longer than sep.; pet. blue, roundish-heart-shaped, shorter than claw, blue, not bearded. Pyrenees. SYN. *D. cardiopetalum, D. halteratum verdunense.*

**D. vesti'tum.** Perennial, 20 to 30 in. h.; unbranched, hairs spreading. *l.* cordate, 5- to 7-partite to middle, lobes wedge-shaped, coarsely toothed, hairy above. *Raceme* strict, long, many-fld. *fl.* pale blue, spur incurved, about as long as densely hairy sep.; pet. deep blue, upper densely hairy, lower 2-fid, bearded; carpels 3, hairy. *Seed* narrowly winged. August, September. N. India.

**D. villo'sum.** Robust perennial. *l.* 3- to 7- partite, slightly hairy on margin and veins beneath, divisions pinnately cut with lanceolate, acute segs.; upper l. 3-partite with narrow almost entire segs. *fl.* blue in a loose raceme; sep. about as long as spur, sometimes hairy; pet. brownish-purple, upper smooth, lower 2-lobed, yellow-bearded. Summer. *Follicles* hairy; seeds slightly winged. Russia, Siberia. var. **laxiflo'rum**, base of *l.* heart-shaped, infl. loose.

**D. vires'cens.** A synonym of *D. carolinianum.*

**D. vir'ide.** Biennial or winter annual, 24 in. h. Root rather stout. *l.* 3- to 5-partite, about 2 in. long, mostly basal, long-stalked, lobes cut, acute. *infl.* racemose, about 7-fld. *fl.* yellowish-green, spur long, stout; pet. short, deep purple. June. Sierra Madre, U.S.A.

**D. Wel'lbyi.** Erect, hairy perennial, little branched, branches usually 3-fld., 3 to 4 ft. h. *l.* palmately 5-partite, 2 to 2½ in. wide; segs. 3- to 7-lobed, lobes acute; stalk slender, up to 3 in. long. *fl.* blue, 2¼ in. across, hairy; sep. about ¾ in. long, spur ascending, 1½ to 2 in. long, gradually narrowed, scarcely acute; upper pet. oblong; lateral linear spatulate, entire; carpels 3, hairy. July. Abyssinia, 1898. (G.C. 88 (1930), 193.)

**D. yunnanen'se.** Perennial up to 30 in. h., somewhat branched. *l.* palmately 5- to 7-partite, segs. wedge-shaped, oblong-ovate, deeply cut and lobed. *fl.* deep blue, spur slender, about ⅔ in. long; upper pet. glabrous, pale brown, lower blue, apex 2-lobed with few blue hairs; carpels glabrous. *Seed* winged. August to October. Yunnan.

**D. Zal'il.** Erect perennial. Stem little or not branched, 1 to 2½ ft. h. becoming smooth. *l.* much cut into narrow segs., dark green. *fl.* about 1¼ in. across; pale yellow, in long racemes. May to August *Follicles* 3, ribbed; seeds scaly. Persia. 1892. (B.M. 7049.) SYN. *D. sulphureum.* The fls. are used in Persia, &c., for dyeing silk.

**deltoi'des, deltoi'deus -a -um,** deltoid; shaped like the Greek Δ.

**delum'bis -is -e,** weak.

**DEMAZER'IA.** *See* **Desmazeria.**

**demer'sus -a -um,** living under water.

**demis'sus -a -um,** hanging down.

**DENDRAGROS'TIS.** Now included in **Chusquea.**

**dendric'ola,** living on trees.

**dendrit'richus -a -um,** with branched hairs.

**DEN'DRIUM.** *See* **Leiophyllum.**

**DENDROBENTHAM'IA.** Included in **Cornus.**

**dendrobioi'des,** Dendrobium-like.

**DENDRO'BIUM** (*dendron*, a tree, *bios*, life; the species are epiphytes). Fam. *Orchidaceae*. A very large genus of over 900 species, exclusively old world, distributed through Ceylon, India, Burma, Malaya to the Philippines, China, Japan, &c. A few species are very fragrant, but the scent of some is objectionable. The species vary extremely in habit, some being little larger than the mosses among which they grow, while others are surpassed in stature by few of their family. In the majority of those cultivated the pseudobulbs are well developed. The flowers are characterized by 4 pollen masses and by nearly equal sepals and petals, the latter often the larger. The bases of the 2 lateral sepals are adnate to the column-foot, forming with it a more or less prominent 'chin'. The usually clawed base of the lip is in many species hidden by the connate portion of the lateral sepals and with them forms a second 'chin'. In many the 3-lobed lip, though its basal margins are convolute, or nearly so, over the column shows no distinct demarcation between the three lobes, the side lobes simply expanding it into a larger often nearly orbicular blade. In others the distinction is clearly shown, the side lobes descending abruptly into the mid-lobe, often somewhat tongue-shaped. In many the pseudobulbs are stem-like, often swollen at the nodes, and as in the familiar *D. nobile*, the flowers are produced in twos and threes from the nodes of the upper third or two-thirds. Others, e.g. *D. thyrsiflorum*, have stoutly clavate pseudobulbs and the inflorescence is more or less thyrse-like, produced from the apical part of the pseudobulb. Again, as in *D. Phalaenopsis*, a large number form more or less tall cylindrical stem-like pseudobulbs, tapered below, with often long many-flowered spikes growing from their apices. Closely allied are a number of Far Eastern species with hard pseudobulbs which in some reach a height of 3 ft. or more. Many of these are distinguished by rather narrow segments, the petals, often longer than the sepals and nearly erect, being spiralled. A few species separated at times under Sarcopodium are here included. A further group is characterized by the presence of short black hairs, particularly prevalent on the young growths and the bracts shielding the young flower buds. Among these, white is the prevailing colour, and the flowers are borne in twos or fours (sometimes more) from the upper part of the pseudobulbs. With the exception among cultivated species of many of the noded-stemmed species, chiefly Burmese and Indian, flowers are produced from both old and new pseudobulbs. In some the incipient inflorescences may remain as small rounded knob-like projections for several years. The foliage on many with noded-stems is deciduous or semi-deciduous, in some falling before the flowers are seen. In the Phalaenopsis group in particular the foliage is persistent and is more or less leathery. So diverse are the characters that the foregoing divisions must be taken in a very broad sense. It is impossible to give here a full detailed classification nor can a complete list of the species be given, but attempt has been made to give those which have been, or are, in cultivation, or worth growing. Many beautiful hybrids have been produced especially from *D. nobile* and its allies. Though known, hybrids between the different sections have so far been difficult to obtain. So beautiful are some of the species, however, that they alone are largely grown and do much to enhance orchid collections. With a genus so widely distributed and presenting so many diverse characters, cultivation must necessarily be adapted to the requirements of the species, the temperatures ruling in the localities whence they are imported governing to an extent the temperatures given in cultivation. All should have a compost of three parts of cut Osmunda fibre to one part of Sphagnum moss. Pots or pans should be used as small as possible, for no class of orchids resents over-potting to a greater extent. Repotting should be effected as the young growths and roots appear. Broadly speaking, the majority of the species, especially the Far Eastern, require while growing a buoyant moist atmosphere as near the tropical as possible. Shading is needed—heaviest while the growths are young. The hard-bulbed persistent-leaved species should have as little shading as possible—none in the autumn. Species from Burma and adjacent countries, the deciduous, semi-deciduous, and thick-leaved species, should be exposed to light in the autumn, and when the pseudobulbs are matured (denoted in the *nobile* section by the presence of a single leaf at the top of the stem, or by the yellowing and falling of the leaves of the deciduous species) given a cooler rest with only occasional, if any, waterings until growth appears in the spring. The winter temperature should at night be about 50° F. The hard-bulbed, thick-leaved Eastern species require more frequent waterings in the winter to compensate for the higher temperature needed by them—60 to 65° F. at night. The softer-stemmed species, e.g. *D. infundibulum*, require no decided rest; water must be given throughout the year, nor should the temperature, even in summer by natural heat, rise too high. They can often be accommodated in the Odontoglossum house, the cool house with its higher day temperature in summer with falls towards morning suiting many of the other Burmese and Indian species. When roots become active and growth begins water should be given freely and the syringe used with all, taking care that water is not allowed to stand in the young growths. Large plants may be propagated by division. With the noded-species (*D. nobile*, &c.) plump and firm back bulbs may be cut off, either cut in pieces including 2 nodes or laid entire on sand in a propagating case with bottom heat. Growths are often developed from these and may be potted as roots are seen, giving the newly potted plants extra heat for a time. In many, young growths appear on the pseudobulbs of growing plants and these may be removed as they root and potted in very small pots. In any case such growths should be removed as they tend to weaken the plant. The smaller growing species can be grown in pans and suspended near the glass; a few with straggling habit must be given rafts.

**D. acumina'tum.** Probably not in cultivation, the plants grown under the name being *D. Lyonii*. The 2 species are allied but *D. acuminatum* is said to have white and yellow fl. In general aspect the plant might pass as a luxuriant form of *D. cymbidioides. Pseudobulbs* lack the terminal 'horn' of *D. Lyonii.* Philippines. (J.R.H.S. 35, clxxiv.)

**D. adun'cum.** *fl.* white, tinged rose; tip of lip more or less hooked; small, appearing at different times of year. 2 ft. h. Manila. 1842. Evergreen, with a rather straggling habit. (B.M. 6784; B.R. 32, 15; A.B.G.C. 8, 67.)

**D. ae'mulum.** *fl.* white, fragrant, 1½ in. across, apical half of segs. sometimes stained pale yellow; sep. narrow-lanceolate; pet. linear; lip very short, 3-lobed, side lobes acute, spotted pink, mid-lobe reflexed; racemes terminal, lax, 5- to 7-fld. Spring. *Pseudobulbs* variable, 3 to 10 in. h., almost terete or resembling those of *D. Kingianum*, bearing at their summit 2 or 3 very leathery l. Australia. (B.M. 2906; F.A.O. i, pt. 2.)

**D. aggrega'tum.*** *fl.* 7 to 12, deep yellow, in arching racemes about 6 in. long; lip minutely pubescent. March to May. *Pseudobulbs* compressed, somewhat angled, wrinkled, 1-leaved. 3 to 4 in. h. N. India. 1837. (B.M. 3643; B.R. 1695; A.B.G.C. 8, 85.) Requires a decided rest. var. **ma'jus** has larger, brighter *fl.* about 2 in. across, and larger *pseudobulbs.*

**D. albosanguin'eum.*** *fl.* 2 or 3, soft creamy-white, about 4 in. across; pet. twice as broad as sep. with a few blood-red streaks at base; lip with 1 or 2 large reddish-crimson blotches at base. June. *Pseudobulbs* from a few inches to 1 ft. long, and nearly 1 in. thick. Moulmein. 1851. (B.M. 5130.)

**D. albovi'ride.** A synonym of *D. scabrilingue.*

**D. al'bum.** A synonym of *D. aqueum.*

**D. amboinen'se.** *fl.* in pairs; sep. and pet. creamy-white, spreading, nearly 3 in. long, linear-lanceolate; lip small, yellowish, marked with dark purple. Summer. *l.* terminal, oblong, acute. Stems jointed, 12 to 24 in. long, 4- to 6-angled above, bulbiform at the very base. Amboyna. 1856 and 1895. (B.M. 4937.) A very singular species.

**D. amethystoglos'sum.*** *fl.* ivory-white, except amethyst-purple front lobe of lip, crowded, about 1 in. across; sep. and pet. ovate-oblong, acute; lip elongated, linear-spatulate, apiculate, convex in middle, incurved at margins except towards tip; spur long, obtuse; column exposed; racemes 3 to 5 in. long, drooping, many-fld. January, February. *l.* sessile, oval-oblong, sub-acute. Stems 2 to 3 ft. h. and nearly 1 in. thick. Philippine Is. 1872. (B.M. 5968.) A handsome species.

**D. amoe'num.** *fl.* pure white, tipped violet-purple, scattered along the stems, violet-scented; throat yellow; lip white, slightly tinged magenta at base and often purple at tip. Summer. *Pseudobulbs* slender, 1 to 1½ ft. long, more or less pendulous. Himalaya. 1843. (B.M. 6199; A.B.G.C. 8, 69.)

**D. amp'lum.** Allied to and closely resembling *D. Coelogyne,* but with slightly smaller fl. *fl.* about 3½ in. long; sep. and pet. greenish, dotted brown; lip purple-brown. Sikkim. 1845. (A.B.G.C. 8, 89; W. Pl. R.A. 29.)

**D. an'ceps.** *fl.* greenish or yellowish, ½ in. long, axillary, very shortly stalked; mentum longer than sep.; lip cuneate-oblong, obscurely 3-lobed. *l.* 1 to 1½ in. long, lanceolate or ovate-lanceolate, acute evergreen. Stem 9 to 18 in. long, stout, flattened. India. (B.R. 1239; A.B.G.C. 8, 54; B.M. 3608; L.B.C. 1895 as *Aporum anceps.*)

**D. Andersonia'num.** A synonym of *D. undulatum.*

**D. An'dersonii.** A synonym of *D. Draconis.*

**D. anos'mum.** A synonym of *D. superbum anosmum.*

**D. Antelo'pe.** *fl.* yellowish; sep. ligulate-triangular, acute; pet. long, spiral, upright, sepia inside; lip striped and speckled mauve, side lobes marked with branched purple-red lines, partially enclosing column, the front lobe with a short, blunt apiculus. Moluccas. 1883. Habit of *D. undulatum.*

**D. antenna'tum.** *fl.* 3 to 10; sep. about ¾ in. long, whitish; pet. twice as long, narrow, greenish-yellow, once twisted; lip 3-lobed, side lobes erect, mid-lobe broadly ovate, greenish, marked with red-violet on either side of 5 whitish keels which eventually merge into one. *Pseudobulbs* 15 to 24 in. h., stiff, cylindrical; spikes arching, 12 in. or more long. New Guinea. (R.X.O. 3, 251.) Allied to *D. veratrifolium.*

*Dendrobium Aphrodite*

**D. Aphrodi'te.** *fl.* produced sparingly from the nodes of last matured growth; sep. and pet. whitish; lip bright orange, margined white, with 1 or 2 purplish blotches at base. July. *Pseudobulbs* 9 to 15 in. h., ½ in. through the very prominent nodes, which are a distinguishing feature. Moulmein. 1862. Erect, deciduous. (F.d.S. 1582; B.M. 5470 as *D. nodatum.*)

**D. a'queum.** *fl.* creamy-white, solitary or 2 together from nodes; lip recurved from middle, base oblong, ovate-rhomboid, obscurely 3-lobed, side lobes small, mid-lobe triangular; under side glabrous, upper very downy and striated, margin of mid-lobe fringed with soft cilia. November. *l.* distichous, ovate. Stem stout, jointed, compressed, striated, leafy (at the time of flowering). Bombay. 1842. (B.M. 4640; B.R. 29, 54.) Syn. *D. album.*

**D. Arachni'tes.*** *fl.* bright cinnabar-red, in twos or threes, sometimes solitary, 2½ in. across; sep. and pet. linear, acute; lip veined purple, shorter than other seg., sub-pandurate, convolute over column at base; column very short. *l.* linear-lanceolate, acute, 1½ to 2½ in. long. Stems terete, 2 to 3 in. long, tufted. Moulmein. 1874. Syn. *D. inversum.*

**D. Ash'worthiae.** A synonym of *D. Forbesii.*

**D. asperifo'lium.** Differs from *D. laevifolium* in that l. and other parts have a number of small wart-like protuberances on them; lip shape is also different. New Guinea.

**D. atropurpu'reum.** *fl.* yellowish or pink, about ½ in. long, sub-sessile in axillary, shortly stalked, bracteate heads; mentum as long as sep.; lip thick. *l.* 1 to 1½ in. long, variable. Stem 4 to 6 in. long. Tenasserim, &c.

**D. atroviola'ceum.*** *fl.* 7 to 15, nodding; sep. and pet. creamy-yellow, spotted deep purple; lip violet-purple inside, green outside, 3-lobed; spike terminal, erect. Spring. *Pseudobulbs* tapering downwards, with 2 or 3 stout, persistent, leathery l. near apex. New Guinea. 1890. (B.M. 7371; W.O.A. 444; L. 513; Add. 72.)

**D. Augus'tae-Victor'iae.** A synonym of *D. veratrifolium.*

**D. auranti'acum.** *fl.* golden-yellow, almost orange, with few faint crimson lines on side lobes of lip; solitary or in racemes of 2 or 3; sep. oblong; pet. broadly elliptic, almost as broad again as sep.; lip orbicular, pubescent, with minutely fimbriate margin, obscurely 3-lobed, the small side lobes rolled over the very short column; spur short, obtuse. *l.* from uppermost joints only, linear-lanceolate, 3 to 4 in. long. Stems terete, erect, 1 to 2 ft. h. Assam Bhutan. (A.B.G.C. 5, 21.) Syn. *D. chryseum.*

**D. au'reum.*** *fl.* pale yellow or brownish, in clusters of 4 to 6 from nodes of 2-year-old pseudobulbs, very fragrant; lip amber, disk of lip marked brown and purple. February. *Pseudobulbs* erect, 1 to 1½ ft. long, ¾ in. thick. India, Ceylon. 1837. (A.B.G.C. 8, 74; B.M. 4708 as *D. heterocarpum.*) var. **al'bum** has nearly white fl.; **Henshall'ii,** *pseudobulbs* longer and more slender than in type, more or less pendulous, lip whitish, disk brown and yellow with purple markings. (B.M. 4970.); **pal'lidum,** lip white except yellow stain at base, stems long and slender. (B.R. 25, 20.); **philippinen'se,** stems slender, pendulous, much longer than in type, *fl.* segs. longer and narrower. Philippines.

**D. Bancroftia'num.** A variety of *D. speciosum.*

**D. barbat'ulum.** *fl.* ivory-white, slightly tinged pink, small, closely set on short erect racemes. Summer. Stems slender, 12 to 15 in. long. W. India. 1844. (B.M. 5918.)

**D. barba'tum.** *fl.* white; lips lobed, edged with long, flexuous hairs; racemes terminal, short, 4- or 5-fld. *Pseudobulbs* with 6 or 7 lanceolate-linear l. Burma. 1897. Allied to *D. ciliatum.*

**D. Beck'leri.** *fl.* usually solitary; 1½ to 2 in. across; pet. and larger sep. narrow, tapered, white or greenish-white; lip somewhat rounded, white, often margined purple. *l.* cylindric, tapered, channelled, 2 to 6 in. long. Australia. (F.O.A. 1, pt. 7.) Habit much as in *D. teretifolium* but erect when young.

**D. bellat'ulum.** *fl.* 1 or 2, 1 to 2 in. across; sep. and pet. creamy-white; lip orange-red, bordered white. Variable. Summer. *Pseudobulbs* cylindrical, tapered, 2 to 3 in. h., black-haired. *l.* about 1 in. long. Annam. 1904. (B.M. 7985.) Cool house.

**D. Ben'soniae.*** *fl.* about 2 in. across, in twos or threes from nodes; sep. and pet. waxy-white; lip white, with orange centre, and 2 large velvety-black blotches near base. May, June. Burma. 1867. Erect, stiff-growing, deciduous, with pseudobulbs 1 to 1½ ft. long, and about ½ in. thick. (B.M. 5679, 8352 as *D. Dartoisianum*; L. 148.) var. **auranti'acum,** orange and brown. Moulmein. 1874; **xanthi'num,** white and yellow. 1878.

**D. bicamera'tum.** *fl.* yellow, with red speckles in stripes, ¼ in. broad, crowded on a short, sheathed peduncle; lip golden-yellow. Summer. *l.* linear-lanceolate, 3 to 4 in. long, obliquely 2-fid. Stem clavate, fusiform or elongate, and 1 to 1½ ft. long. Sikkim Himalaya. 1837. (Ref. B. 143; A.B.G.C. 8, 56.) Syn. *D. breviflorum.* Plant variable.

**D. bigib'bum.*** *fl.* rich rosy magenta, 1 to 2 in. across, with somewhat rounded pet.; lip with white crest; in 6- to 12-fld. arching spikes from top of 1-year and older pseudobulbs. September, October. *Pseudobulbs* 1 to 1½ ft. long, their upper part with 4 to 6 closely arranged l. 1 to 1½ in. long. Queensland. An erect stove evergreen species. (B.M. 4898; W.O.A. 38.) var. **albomargina'tum,** *fl.* white edged. 1892. (L. 317.); **Lady Colman,** *fl.* blush-white. Many varieties have appeared.

**D. bilocula're.** *fl.* copper-coloured, rather small; apex of lip golden-yellow, with one large brownish or purplish blotch each side of disk; raceme sub-erect. Summer. Burma. 1869. Tall and slender.

**D. Boxal'lii.** A synonym of *D. gratiosissimum.*

**D. bracteo'sum.** *fl.* small, purple, with an orange lip, marked reddish on front margins, in capitate masses; sep. triangular, keeled, spur about two-fifths length of free part of lateral sep., rather blunt; pet. narrower, oblong, acute; lip nearly spatulate, a little convex on upper sides, much thicker at base; bracts nearly as long as fl. *Pseudobulbs* stiff, 6 to 15 in. h. New Guinea. 1886. (L. 74; B.M. n.s. 389.) var. **al'bum,** sep. and pet. white, lip orange-red.

**D. breviflo'rum.** A synonym of *D. bicameratum.*

**D. brisbanen'se.** A synonym of *D. gracilicaule.*

**D. Bronck'hartii.*** *fl.* in thyrses similar to but longer than those of *D. Farmeri,* fl. larger, sep. and pet. flushed with dull rose-purple. *Pseudobulbs* up to 2 ft. h., obscurely 4-angled, more slender than those of *D. thyrsiflorum* to which the species is also allied, suffused with dark red. Annam. (B.M. 8252.) Handsome.

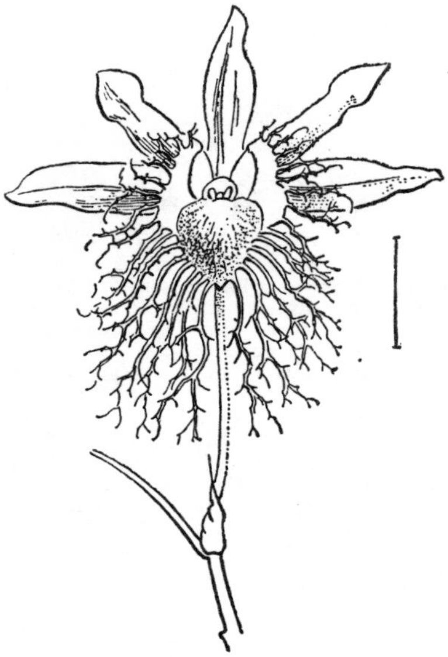

*Dendrobium Brymerianum*

**D. Brymeria'num.*** *fl.* 2 to 3 in. across, solitary, in pairs, or in short spikes of 3 or 4 from the upper part of the bulbs; sep. and pet. glossy yellow; lip yellow, with a very deep, branched, papillose fringe sometimes 2 in. wide. March, April. *l.* about 5 in. long and 1 in. broad, light green. *Pseudobulbs* 1 to 2 ft. h. with few l., tapered. Burma. 1875. A very remarkable and handsome evergreen species. (B.M. 6383; L. 183; W.O.A. 398.) var. **histrion'icum,** very inferior to the type, with shorter but comparatively stouter pseudobulbs, and smaller *fl.*, usually in pairs and cleistogamous. Siam, Burma.

**D. Bullenia'num.** *fl.* orange, striped red, ¾ in. long, densely clustered on the last matured growth. May, June. *Pseudobulbs* 9 to 15 in. h., about ½ in. thick. Philippines. 1874. Stove. Syn. *D. erythroxanthum.*

**D. Bulleria'num.** A synonym of *D. gratiosissimum.*

**D. bursig'erum.** Very near *D. secundum,* differing by the acuminate sep. and pet. and the cordate-hastate lip. Philippines. 1859.

**D. calamifor'me.** A synonym of *D. teretifolium.*

**D. Calceola'ria.** A variety of *D. moschatum.*

**D. Calceo'lus** var. **cu'preum.** A synonym of *D. moschatum cupreum.*

**D. cambridgea'num.** A synonym of *D. ochreatum.*

**D. canalicula'tum.** *fl.* sweet-scented, 15 to 20, about 1 in. across, scape about 1 ft. long; sep. and pet. narrow, yellowish-white; lip white, with a mauve disk. Autumn. *Pseudobulbs* short, stout. NE. Australia. 1865. A pretty little species, easily grown. (F.A.O. 1, pt. 3; B.M. 5537 as *D. Tattonianum.*)

**D. capil'lipes.** *fl.* 2 to 4, about 1½ in. across, in short erect racemes; pet. much wider than sep., bright golden yellow. Spring. *Pseudobulbs* 3 to 6 in. h., clustered, deciduous. Moulmein. (B.M. 7639.)

**D. capituliflo'rum.** *fl.* very numerous, in dense circular heads, small, white; column and disk of lip green. *Pseudobulbs* 2 to 6 in. h., stout, tapering, often red-tinted and purplish on the under surface of the lanceolate l. New Guinea. 1898.

**D. carinif'erum.** A synonym of *D. Williamsonii.* var. **Watt'ii,** a synonym of *D. Wattii.*

**D. chlor'ops.** *fl.* pale nankeen; base of lip pea-green, small, densely set. February to April. *Pseudobulbs* slender, tufted. Bombay. 1842. Syn. *D. barbatulum* of Wight.

**D. chlorop'terum.** *fl.* 5 to 9 in terminal racemes; sep. and pet. light green, streaked red outside, with broken lines of darker colour within; lip light reddish, with darker lines, front lobe with a light yellowish-green border, callus white; column whitish. Winter. *l.* narrow-oblong, 2-lobed at apex. *Pseudobulbs* fusiform. New Guinea. 1815. (J.B. 1878, 196.)

**D. chrysan'thum.*** *fl.* deep rich yellow, in twos and threes on new bulbs; lip fimbriate with a dark crimson blotch. September. *Pseudobulbs* from 3 to 6 ft. long, about ½ in. wide, pendulous. Nepal. 1828. (B.R. 1299.) A handsome deciduous species, most successfully grown in a basket, suspended from the roof. The var. **anophthal'mum** has no blotch on lip. 1883; **microphthal'mum** has short fimbriation and 2 or 4 pale brown blotches on lip. 1879.

**D. chry'seum.** A synonym of *D. aurantiacum.*

**D. chrysoceph'alum.** *fl.* deep golden-yellow, otherwise closely resembling *D. viridi-roseum*; racemes densely many-fld., capitate. Stems nearly terete, of a pleasing green. Habitat? 1892.

**D. chrysocre'pis.** *fl.* golden-yellow, with a deeper lip, 1½ in. across, solitary on short, slender peduncles from old, leafless stems; dorsal sep. and pet. similar, obovate, concave; lateral sep. ovate, more spreading; lip somewhat slipper-shaped, velvety, inner surface densely clothed with reddish hairs. March. *l.* 3 or more, elliptic-lanceolate, pointed, 2 to 3 in. long. Stems slender, 6 to 10 in. long, dilated above into flattened, leafy pseudobulbs. *rhiz.* branching. Moulmein. 1871. (B.M. 6007.)

**D. chryso'tis.** A synonym of *D. Hookerianum.*

**D. chrysotox'um.*** *fl.* 7 to 15, 2 in. across, from the leafy part of both old and young pseudobulbs; sep. and pet. yellow; lip deeper yellow, fringed; raceme arched, 6 to 12 in. long. March, April. *Pseudobulbs* club-shaped, 1 ft. long and 1½ in. thick, with 4 to 6 stout l. on the upper part. Moulmein. 1845. Strong, erect evergreen. (B.M. 5053; B.R. 33, 36.) var. **suavis'simum*** has 8 to 12 rich yellow *fl.* 2½ in. across, strongly hawthorn scented, lip with brown-purple blotch. June. Burma. 1873. (W.O.A. 13, G.N. 13. 1878, 166.) Syn. *D. suavissimum.*

**D. cilia'tum.** *fl.* 1 in. across, many, in pseudo-terminal and lateral racemes; sep. and pet. pale yellow-green, sep. linear-oblong, lower falcate, pet. linear, dilated at apex; lip deep yellow, streaked obliquely with reddish-brown disk, 3-lamellate, obscurely lobed, triangular, incurved at sides, front lobe ciliate. October, November. *l.* sessile, oval-oblong, gradually narrowing upwards, 3 in. long, deciduous. Stems tufted, 1 to 1½ ft. or more long. Moulmein. 1863. (B.M. 5430; W.O.A. 454.) Syn. *D. rupicola.* var. **annamen'se** has shorter, stouter *pseudobulbs* and whitish *fl.* with lip purplish at base; **bre've** has stout stems only 3 to 5 in. h.

**D. clava'tum.*** *fl.* 3 to 6, 2 or 3 in. across, bright yellow, with a maroon blotch in base of lip, in drooping spikes from tops of stems. Summer. *Pseudobulbs* 1 to 3 ft. h., ½ in. thick. *l.* 6 to 8 on upper part of stem. Assam. 1851. Erect evergreen. (B.M. 6993; A.B.G.C. 8, 60.) *D. clavatum* of Roxburgh is *D. densiflorum.*

**D. Coelog'yne.** *fl.* solitary, very large; sep. and pet. yellowish, mottled red; sep. 2½ in. long, acuminate; pet. narrower; lip deep dull purple, side lobes narrow, mid-lobe trapezoid-ovate. *l.* broadly elliptic-oblong, notched, 3 to 6 in. long, very leathery. *Pseudobulbs* very stout, 1½ to 2 in. long. *rhiz.* creeping. Requires a raft. Moulmein. 1894. (J.R.H.S. 34, cclxxi.)

**D. coerules'cens.** A synonym of *D. nobile.*

**D. compres'sum.** A synonym of *D. lamellatum.*

**D. Coop'eri.** *fl.* solitary from the leafless upper part of the old stem; sep. and slightly broader pet. almost equal, 1¼ in. long, ½ in. wide, elliptic, white, suffused green at base and there marked with purplish-red lines; claw of lip greenish with raised sides, blade heart-shaped with upturned sides, then gently reflexed, 1 in. long, ½ in. wide, obscurely 3-keeled; lower sep. extended into a blunt ventricose greenish-white mentum, faintly red-lined above, inclined towards ovary and nearly touching the small carinate bract which sheaths the pedicel; column short, stout, greenish with 2 frontal narrow reddish flanges 1½ in. from end of spur to tip of dorsal sepal. Stems slender, erect, 18 to 24 in. h. *l.* 2½ in. long, linear-lanceolate, amplexicaule. Habit near that of *D. Papilio.* Habitat? 1936.

**D. crassino'de.** A synonym of *D. pendulum.*

**D. crepida'tum.*** *fl.* from the last matured growth, 2 or 3 together, about 2 in. across, on somewhat long footstalks; sep. and pet. white, tipped with pink, sometimes flushed pink or rose throughout; lip stained yellow. March. *Pseudobulbs* 1 to 1½ ft. h. with white lines running their entire length. Assam. 1857. Handsome, deciduous. (B.M. 4993; A.B.G.C. 8, 66.) var. **al'bum,** *fl.* white except orange-yellow disk of lip, pedicels white.

**D. creta'ceum.** *fl.* chalky-white, usually solitary from the joints of leafless stems, rather small, downy; lip with a pale yellow disk, pencilled crimson; margin ciliate. May. *Pseudobulbs* 8 to 14 in. long, ½ in. thick, sub-pendulous. Deciduous. India. 1846. (B.M. 4686; B.R. 33, 62.)

**D. cruen'tum.** *fl.* from nodes, greenish, with a strongly marked cinnabar callus; sep. triangular, acuminate, the lateral ones with a nearly rectangular chin; pet. linear, acuminate; lip deeply 3-fid, side lobes falcate, erect, blood-red, mid-lobe ovate, apiculate; column broader at base than at 3-dentate tip. Summer. *l.* oblong, obtuse, 2-lobed, deciduous. *Pseudobulbs* 12 in. h., black-haired. Malaya. 1884. (W.O.A. 174.)

**D. crumena'tum.** *fl.* fugitive, solitary or in twos, white, 1 to 1½ in. long, many on the leafless ends of the often branched stem; mentum equalling lateral sep.; lip with a primrose disk and sometimes pink veins. Summer. *l.* 2 to 3 in. long, oblong, obtuse, notched. Stem 2 to 3 ft. h., stout, fusiform at base. Burma, Malaya. 1823. (B.M. 4013; B.R. 25, 22; L. 207.)

**D. crystalli'num.*** *fl.* about 2½ in. wide, freely produced from last matured growth; sep. and pet. white, tipped rose or purple; lip orange at base, tipped purple. Summer. *Pseudobulbs* 1 to 1½ ft. h., ½ in. wide. Deciduous. Burma. 1868. (B.M. 6319; W.O.A. 441.) Allied to *D. Bensoniae.*

**D. cuculla'tum.** A synonym of *D. Pierardii cucullatum.*

**D. cucumeri'num.** *fl.* sep. and pet. yellowish-white, streaked reddish-yellow, about ½ in. long, ⅛ in. wide; lip shorter. Summer. *l.* terminal, fleshy, above 1 in. long, thick ribbed, tubercled, resembling a little cucumber. *rhiz.* creeping, branched. New S. Wales. 1841. (B.M. 4619; B.R. 29, 37.) Requires a raft.

**D. cumula'tum.** *fl.* rosy-purple, suffused white, 1 in. across, in crowded, sub-globose corymbs; sep. and pet. oblong; lip obovate-oblong, longer and broader than pet., prolonged at base into a slightly curved, obtuse spur; rachis and pedicels deep reddish-purple. Autumn. *l.* oblong, acuminate, 3 to 4 in. long. Stems tufted, slender, pendulous, 1½ to 2 ft. long. Moulmein. 1867. (B.M. 5703; A.B.G.C. 8, 63.)

**D. cu'preum.** A variety of *D. moschatum.*

**D. Cur'tisii.** *fl.* magenta-rose, in short racemes. Stems tall, erect, slender, leafless; younger shoots with linear-lanceolate l. Borneo. 1882.

**D. cymbidioi'des.** *fl.* medium-sized, showy; sep. and pet. ochreous yellow, linear-oblong, spreading; lip white, blotched purple near base, much shorter than the sep. and pet., oblong-cordate, with 2 or 3 lines of tubercles on disk, side lobes short, incurved, mid-lobe ovate, obtuse; column short; peduncles terminal, erect, loosely racemose, 5- to 12-fld. *Pseudobulbs* ovate or oblong-ovate, angled, 2 in. long with 2 oblong, obtuse, leathery l. 3 to 6 in. long at top. Salak, Java. 1852. (B.M. 4755.) Should be grown on a raft.

**D. cymbifor'me.** *fl.* straw-yellow, a little whiter on pet., with about 5 purple stripes on each sep. and pet. (which are about ½ in. long), and similar lines at apex of flabellately dilated lip; raceme axillary, 2-fld. April. *l.* oblong-lanceolate, 2 to 2½ in. long. Stems terete, slender, 6 to 12 in. long. Sumatra. 1896.

**D. D'Albertis'ii.** *fl.* 5 to 20, odorous, distinctly spurred; sep. pure white; pet. greenish, narrow, erect, twisted, about 2 in. long; lip 3-lobed, side lobes oblong, erect, with purple lines, mid-lobe almost round, with purple veins; racemes erect. Summer. Stems square, tapering. New Guinea. A variable species, sometimes of considerable size.

**D. Dalhousiea'num.** A synonym of *D. pulchellum.*

**D. Dear'ei.*** *fl.* 5 to 15 in clusters from or near the tops of the erect pseudobulbs, white, 2½ in. across, on whitish pedicels; sep. lanceolate, acuminate, with recurved tips; pet. oval, nearly 3 times as broad as sep.; lip oblong, obtuse, obscurely 3-lobed, with a pale yellowish-green, transverse zone between the base and the margin. July, August. *Pseudobulbs* 1 to 2 ft. long or more, the upper part clothed with sessile, oval-oblong l. 2 in. long. Philippine Is. 1882. (W.O.A. 120.)

**D. delica'tum.** Resembles *D. Kingianum* but with taller, stronger bulbs, very variable. *fl.* larger and more numerous on taller spikes, whitish, peppered with brown-purple. Winter. Agrees with a hybrid raised between *D. speciosum* and *D. Kingianum*, but the variation is so great that imported plants may possibly be derived from further crosses between the hybrid and the parents. Australia.

**D. densiflo'rum.*** *fl.* rich clear yellow in numerous long dense pendulous trusses from near the top of the pseudobulbs old and new; lip orange, delicately fringed. April, May. *Pseudobulbs* somewhat club-shaped, 1 to 1½ ft. h. with several broad, oblong, deep green, shining, persistent l. in the upper part. India. 1829. (B.M. 3418; B.R. 1828; A.B.G.C. 8, 79; W.O.A. 303; L. 187.) var. **albolu'teum,** a synonym of *D. thyrsiflorum* and **Schroed'eri** of *D. Schroederi.*

**D. denu'dans.** *fl.* usually white with red veins on lip, sometimes yellowish with a green lip, ⅝ to 1 in. long; sep. and pet. slender; lip much shorter, tinged brown; raceme (with scape) 4 to 6 in. long, drooping, many-fld. *l.* 3 to 6 in. long. Stems 4 to 6 in. long, sub-erect, sheathed. Sub-tropical and temperate Himalaya. 1897. (B.M. 7548; A.B.G.C. 8, 62.)

**D. Devonia'num.*** *fl.* sep. and pet. soft creamy-white, tinged pink, pet. tipped purplish-magenta; lip white, margined purple and blotched rich orange at base, bordered all round with a delicate lace-like frill. Well-grown pseudobulbs often have 90 to 100 fls. about 2 in. across. March, April. *Pseudobulbs* 1 to 3 ft. long, ½ in. thick. India, Burma. 1837. (B.M. 4429; W.S.O. 2, 1.) SYN. *D. pictum.* A very beautiful pendulous deciduous species. It should be grown in a basket. var. **candid'ulum,** *fl.* pure white with yellow throat. 1876; **Elliottia'num,** sep. and pet. with much purple on their tips, whole fl. veined with rose. 1876; **rhodoneu'rum,** sep. and pet. streaked dark purple, lip large, round. Moulmein. 1868.

**D. dicu'phum.** *fl.* pink or purple, 7 to 20, raceme arching; sep. acuminate, ⅝ in. long; pet. rather longer and broader; lip nearly as long, the disk having 3 raised longitudinal lines; peduncle 6 to 12 in. long. *l.* few on the upper part of the stem, 3 to 6 in. long. *Pseudobulbs* slender, fusiform, cylindric, 6 to 12 in. long. N. Australia. 1895. Resembles a small *D. bigibbum.* var. **al'bum,** *fl.* pure white. N. Australia. 1939.

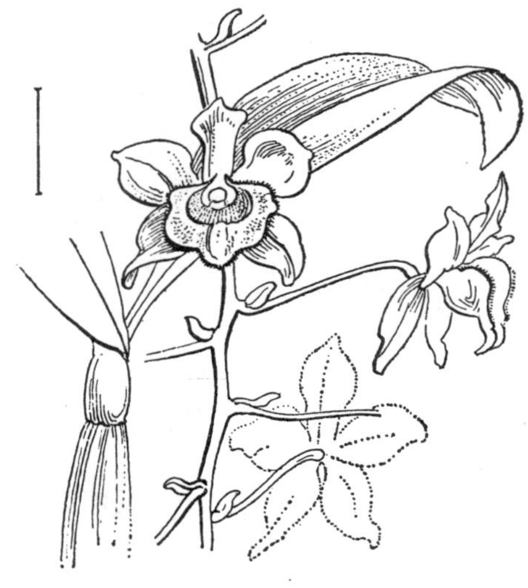

*Dendrobium densiflorum*

**D. dis'color.** A synonym of *D. undulatum.*

**D. dixan'thum.** *fl.* 2 to 5 from nodes, 1½ to 2 in. across, yellow; disk of lip darker. Spring. *Pseudobulbs* 1½ to 2 ft. h., ½ in. thick, slender, erect, stiff. Deciduous. Moulmein. 1864. (B.M. 5564.)

**D. Donnes'iae.** Possibly an exceptionally fine var. of *D. infundibulum* but possibly a natural hybrid between *D. formosum* and *D. infundibulum.* *fl.* larger, white with a chrome yellow basal blotch to lip. Spring. Stems stout, black-haired. Burma. 1895. (Gn. 48 (1895), 222.)

**D. Draco'nis.*** *fl.* white, moderate-sized, in twos from points of last matured growths; lip with orange or red base. May, June. *Pseudobulbs* 1 to 1½ ft. h., ½ in. thick, black-haired. Moulmein. 1862. (B.M. 5459 as *D. eburneum*; W.O.A. 103.) SYN. *D. Andersonii.*

**D. ebur'neum.** A synonym of *D. Draconis.*

**D. elonga'tum.** Allied to *D. cymbidioides.* *fl.* 6 to 10; sep. and narrower pet. whitish; lip nearly ochre-yellow throughout and with red-tinted asperities. Autumn. *Pseudobulbs* 1 to 1½ in. h., diphyllous. *rhiz.* ascending. Java.

**D. epidendrop'sis.** *fl.* about 15, thickly set on a drooping raceme, greenish-yellow; sep. ½ in. long; lip and chin larger. Stems slender, 18 in. h. *l.* narrow, 3 in. long. Summer. Philippines.

**D. eriaeflo'ra.** *fl.* many, small, greenish-white, in nodding racemes longer than l.; sep. and pet. narrow, lip shorter with long, pectinate side lobes. Stems 3 to 6 in. h. *l.* narrow, 1½ to 2½ in. long. Autumn. Burma. 1900?

**D. erythropo'gon.** *fl.* whitish-ochre and ochre, keels on the mid-lines well developed; pet. oblong, undulate; side lobes of lip white, edged crimson, blunt, rectangular, mid-lobe obcordate, toothed, with 7 thick, crimson keels on disk, the 2 outer ones having short, crimson hairs on each side; column nearly white, with 2 scarlet spots at base. Sunda Is. 1885. Allied to *D. Lowi.*

**D. erythroxan'thum.** A synonym of *D. Bullenianum.*

**D. Fair'faxii.** *fl.* white and green, purple on lip; racemes terminal, 4 in. long. *Pseudobulbs* 3 to 4 in. long. New Hebrides. 1889. A small plant.

**D. Fal'coneri.*** *fl.* solitary, about 4 in. across, handsome, from 1-year and older nodes; sep. and pet. white, tipped purple; lip same colour, with dark purple centre, margined orange. May. *l.* 3 in. long, ¼ in. broad. *Pseudobulbs* about 3 ft. long, very knotty, much-branched; nodes ½ in. thick, very close together. India. 1847. (B.M. 4944; L. 4.) Pendulous, requiring a raft or tilted basket. var. **albid'ulum,** *fl.* pure white but for a slight purple tinge at tips of segs. India. 1876. (B.H. 1874, 15.); **gigan'teum,** similar to type but larger, *l.* about 1 in. wide. (W.O.A. 257.)

**D. falcoros'trum.*** *fl.* very fragrant, 6 to 20 on terminal spikes as in *D. speciosum*; pet. and broader sep. white, tapered, ¾ in. long; lip shorter, white marked with crimson on side lobes, crest yellow. Spring. *Pseudobulbs* cylindrical-conical, 4 to 8 in. h. *l.* 2 to 6, persistent. Cool house. Australia. (F.O.A. 1, pt. 5.)

**D. Farm'eri.*** fl. about 1¾ in. across, in pendulous racemes as in D. densiflorum, but less closely set; pet. and sep. pale straw-colour with a delicate pink tinge, disk of lip golden-yellow. May. Habit of D. densiflorum but smaller. Pseudobulbs almost quill-like below, 4-angled and clavate with persistent dark-green l. above. (B.M. 4659; A.B.G.C. 8, 80.) var. albiflo'rum has almost pure white fl. and a downy orange lip. India. (B.H. 1860, 321.) Syn. D. Farmeri album; aureofla'vum, sep. and pet. bright yellow, lip golden. Moulmein. 1864. (B.M. 5451); au'reum, a dwarfer form, fl. clear yellow, lip orange-yellow. Moulmein. (W.O.A. 99.)

**D. fe'rox.** A synonym of D. macrophyllum.

**D. fimbria'tum.*** fl. about 2 in. across, deep rich orange; margin of lip beautifully bordered with a golden fringe; racemes pendulous, 6- or more fld., from the upper part of old and new pseudobulbs. March, April. Pseudobulbs 2 to 4 ft. high, with 30 to 40 l. 6 in. long, 1½ in. broad. India. 1823. (H.E.F. 71.) var. ocula'tum,* a very handsome variety, differing by its larger flowers with lips blotched in centre, deep blackish-purple or dark blood-colour. India. (B.M. 4160; A.B.G.C. 8, 82; W.S.O. 2, 19.) Syn. D. Paxtonii.

**D. Findlaya'num.*** fl. 1 to 3, 2 to 3 in. across, from upper nodes of the last-matured pseudobulbs; sep. and pet. white, sep. often flushed rose; lip tinged lilac with a large orange disk. January, February. Pseudobulbs 1 ft. or more h., semi-pendulous; remarkable for the large nodes, which are over ½ in. thick. Moulmein. 1877. (W.O.A. 92; B.M. 6438.)

**D. flaviflo'rum.** A synonym of D. aurantiacum.

**D. Forbes'ii.** fl. 6 to 12, 3 in. across; sep. and pet. white, slightly twisted, creamy-white; lip lined with purple on side lobes, mid-lobe crimson-purple; ovary hairy; spikes apical. Winter, Spring. Pseudobulbs 12 to 24 in., quill-like at base, then clavate. l. leathery. Allied to D. macrophyllum. New Guinea. 1886. (B.M. 7724 as D. Hodgkinsonii; 8141 as D. Ashworthiae.)

**D. formo'sum.*** fl. fragrant, white, about 4 in. across, of great substance, produced from the apex and the axils of l. nearest the apex of the pseudobulb; lip large, white, with an orange throat; spikes 3- 4- or 8-fld. Autumn. Pseudobulbs black-haired, 1 to 1½ ft. h., 1 in. thick with 8 to 10 leathery l. India. 1837. (B.R. 25, 64; A.B.G.C. 8, 65.) var. Berk'eleyi, fl. scentless, more funnel-shaped than in type, pet. narrower and shorter. Requires more heat and moisture in winter than type. Andaman Is. 1883. gigan'teum,* 6 in. across, lip 2 in. wide with bright golden blotch, stems up to 3 ft. long. Upper Burma. 1882. (L. 526; W.O.A. 308.)

**D. Free'manii.** A variety of D. lituiflorum.

**D. Friedricksia'num.** fl. light yellow, with darker yellow centre to lip and a dark-purple, semicircular blotch; lip rolled around column, oblong, with asperities on disk, and a clavate line in front of base; raceme 4-fld., slender. Stem rather thick, much-furrowed. Possibly a var. of D. signatum. Siam. 1887.

**D. fusca'tum.** A synonym of D. Gibsonii.

**D. fusifor'me.** Resembles D. speciosum of which it has been termed a variety. Racemes slender. fl. numerous, whitish or creamy-yellow with transverse purple lines on lip. Summer. Pseudobulbs fusiform, about 12 in. long. Queensland. 1885. Syn. D. speciosum fusiforme.

**D. Fytchia'num.*** fl. 10 to 15, in graceful racemes, 9 in. long, from the extremity of the upright stems; sep. and pet. white or rose-flushed; lip 3-lobed; lateral lobes small, oblong, incurved, purplish-rose. January. l. slender, linear, falling off before fls. expand. Moulmein. 1864. (B.M. 5444 as D. barbatulum); var. ro'seum, fl. about 1½ in. across, rose, lateral lobes of lip rich purple. (W.O.A. 336.)

**D. Gallicea'num.*** fl. white with yellow lip, resembling those of D. thyrsiflorum; pet. much broader than sep., slightly crisped on margins; lip very broadly cordate-ovate, fringed. Burma. 1890. (L. 241.) A beautiful plant.

**D. Gib'sonii.*** fl. 3 to 10, 2 to 3 in. across, rich orange on the upper parts of old and new pseudobulbs; lip bright yellow with two dark spots at base, fimbriate. Summer. 2 to 3 ft. h. Khasya. 1827. A pretty erect-growing evergreen species, closely resembling D. fimbriatum oculatum in habit, but with much larger fl. (B.M. 6226 as D. fuscatum.)

**D. glomera'tum.*** fl. somewhat tubular, in short, dense, axillary racemes, with large, imbricate bracts; sep. and pet. bright rose; lip orange. Summer. Stems 2 to 3 ft. long. Moluccas. 1894. (G.C. 60 (1916), 97.)

**D. glomeriflo'rum.** fl. pale rose, creamy-white at base of sep., in cluster of 5 or more, small. Moluccas. 1895. Allied to D. glomeratum.

**D. Gold'iei.*** fl. bright claret-purple, 2 in. across; segs. with undulated margins; spikes terminal, 12 to 30 in. long, many-fld. Allied to D. superbiens, with which it is imported, and sometimes regarded as a superior variety or hybrid. N. Australia. (Gn. 14 (1878), 244.)

**D. gracilicau'le.** fl. ¾ in. across, dingy yellow, spotted red; racemes short fls. almost clustered; spur short, broad. Stem 9 to 18 in. h. l. comparatively large. fl. resemble D. Kingianum in shape but are smaller. Australia. 1889. (B.M. 7042.) Syn. D. brisbanense. A variable species. var. Howea'num has cream fl. with rose or pink markings on lip. Lord Howe Is.

**D. gratiosis'simum.*** fl. scattered along the previous year's knotty growth, 2 in. across; sep. and pet. white or suffused rose, beautifully tipped rose; lip same colour with a large blotch of rich yellow. February, March. Pseudobulbs curved or pendulous, from 2 to 3 ft. long, and ½ in. through the nodes. Deciduous. Moulmein. (B.M. 5652 as D. Bullerianum.) Syn. D. Boxallii.

**D. Greatrixia'num.** fl. white; lip large, ovate, with a purplish blotch at base and apex. Slender. New Guinea.

**D. Griffthia'num.*** fl. very rich golden-yellow, in immense drooping spikes. May, June. Burma. 1838. One of the most beautiful of the yellow spring-flowering species, not unlike D. densiflorum, but in its smaller size nearer D. Farmeri. var. Guiber'tii* has larger, brighter fl., longer racemes, l. more leathery, stems less tufted and more abruptly narrowed below. (I.H. ser. 3, 258; R.H. 1876, 431 as D. Guibertii.)

**D. hainanen'se.** fl. not unlike those of D. crumenatum, white; lip stained yellow. l. terete. Hainan. 1893.

**D. hama'tum.** fl. 1½ in. wide, in terminal many-fld. racemes; sep. and pet. pale yellow with lines or purple dots; lip yellow, pandurate, with a purple stain on front lobe, its chin 1 in. long, hooked. l. oblong, acuminate, 5 in. long. Stems slender, 2 ft. long. Cochin China. 1894.

**D. Hanburya'num.** A synonym of D. lituiflorum.

**D. Harveya'num.** fl. deep chrome yellow, with 2 orange blotches on lip; chin short, emarginate; sep. triangular-lanceolate, acute; pet. oblong, acute, strongly fringed; lip round, with strong fringes, a rough surface, and an obscure callus at base; peduncle lateral, filiform, 3- to 9-fld. Spring. Pseudobulbs fusiform, 6 to 12 in. h. Burma. 1883. (G.C. 16 (1894), 593.)

**D. Hasselt'ii.** fl. pale purple; dorsal sep. lanceolate, lateral connate in a long chin; lip linear, acute. l. rigid, lanceolate, obliquely emarginate. Stems erect. Java, Sumatra. 1885. (I.H. 1885, 545.)

**D. hedyos'mum.** A synonym of D. scabrilingue.

**D. hercoglos'sum.** fl. similar to those of D. aduncum, but with a more oblique spur; sep. and pet. delicate mauve; lip white, with a mauve-purple, recurved tip, basal part cup-shaped, hairy inside, separated from the front by a transverse fringe of hairs. Stems slender, with lateral racemes at the top. Malacca. 1886. (B.M. 9428.)

**D. heterocar'pum.** A synonym of D. aureum.

**D. Heynea'num.*** fl. white, streaked violet, small, in spikes, from near top of the stems, at different times of the year. Bombay. 1838. A very pretty stove deciduous species, growing about 8 in. h.

**D. Hildebran'dii.** fl. 2 or 3 from the nodes, 3 in. across; sep. and pet. pale dull yellow, twisted; lip orange, short, roundish. Spring. l. 5 in. long, 1½ in. wide. Stems 15 to 30 in. h. Burma. 1894. (B.M. 7453.) Variable. Allied to D. signatum.

**D. Hill'ii.** A variety of D. speciosum.

**D. hirsu'tum.** A synonym of D. longicornu.

**D. histrion'icum.** A synonym of D. Brymerianum histrionicum.

**D. Hodg'kinsonii.** A synonym of D. Forbesii.

**D. Hookeria'num.** fl. about 3 in. across; sep. and pet. rich golden-yellow; lip buff-yellow, with 2 large purple blotches at base, fringed; racemes drooping, several springing from 1 bulb, 4- to 8-fld. Summer. Pseudobulbs 2 to 6 ft. long, ¼ in. thick, with dark, rather prominent nodes to every inch or two of the slender, rod-like stem. Himalaya, Assam. 1878. (B.M. 6013; W.O.A. 419; W.S.O. 3, 6. Syn. D. chrysotis.

**D. Hut'tonii.** A variety of D. superbum.

**D. Impe'ratrix.** A synonym of D. veratrifolium.

**D. Imthurn'ii.** Allied to D. veratrifolium. fl. white with purple stripes on side lobes of lip. New Hebrides. 1910? (B.M. 8452.)

**D. inaequa'le.** fl. solitary at alternate nodes on the outer face of the swollen upper part of the pseudobulb; sep. and pet. white, 1 in. long; lip sulphur yellow, base brown, with a raised tongue-like crest, side lobes striped lilac, front lobe small. Autumn. Pseudobulbs 4 to 8 in. h., 4-angled above, tapered below, diphyllous. New Guinea. 1899. (B.M. 7745.)

**D. inaudi'tum.** fl. 2 from base of leaf; sep. and pet. pale yellowish, 1½ in. long, narrow linear-lanceolate; lip pale ochreous, spotted brown, side lobes square, obtuse, mid-lobe lanceolate, acuminate. l. elliptic, obtuse. Pseudobulbs tufted, fusiform-ovate, narrowed at apex into a slender brownish l.-stalk 3 to 4 in. long. New Guinea. 1886. (L. 66.)

**D. infla'tum.** fl. white, about 1 in. long, with a yellow blotch on lip, in short, few-fld. racemes. l. 1 in. long. Stems slender, 6 in. long. Java. 1895.

**D. infundib'ulum.*** fl. pure ivory-white, large, often 4 in. across, in bunches of 2 or more from upper joints; lip with disk yellow extending into the tapering funnel-shaped spur about 1 in. long. May, June. Pseudobulbs erect, black-haired, 1 to 1½ ft. long, ½ in. thick, with 10 to 14 l. Moulmein. 1863. (B.M. 5446; L. 199; W.O.A. 448.) Cool or Odontoglossum house; requires water throughout winter. var. **carneopic'tum,** lip flesh-colour with a thick central line and a few streaks at sides. 1885; **Jamesia'num,** *see* **D. Jamesianum; ornatis'simum,** *fl.* large, waxy, lip with brown markings instead of yellow. 1883.

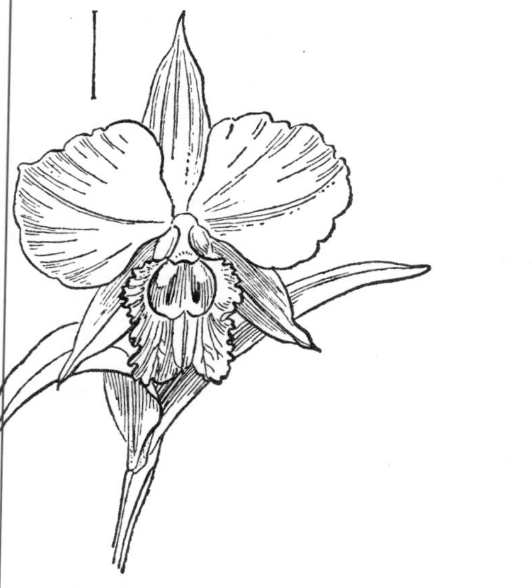

*Dendrobium infundibulum*

**D. interrup'tum.** *fl.* 3 or more on short peduncles; sep. and broader pet. ¾ in. long, narrowly triangular, acuminate, soft yellow striated at base with purple-brown; lip 1 in. long, 3-lobed, mid-lobe strongly reflexed, greenish in middle shading to pure white, margins frilled, purple-edged, side lobes white, pointed. *rhiz.* woody. Stems ascending, 2 ft. or more h. *l.* bulb-like, 2 to 5 in. long, ¼ in. wide, smooth, hard, their ends slightly tapered. Habit erect and pendent. Dutch E. Indies. 1925.

**D. inver'sum.** A synonym of *D. Arachnites.*

**D. iono'pus.** *fl.* deep yellow; sep. triangular, lateral elongating into a falcate chin; lip with a few purple and red blotches and with a red tinge, long-clawed, side lobes bluntly angled, mid-lobe rounded, emarginate; raceme short. Burma. 1882.

**D. Jamesia'num.*** Differs from *D. infundibulum* by its red instead of golden disk, its *pseudobulbs* slightly shorter and thicker, and its slightly more definite resting period. Moulmein. 1869. (W.O.A. 221.)

**D. japon'icum.** A synonym of *D. monile.*

**D. Jen'kinsii.** A synonym of *D. parciflorum.*

**D. Jennya'num.** *fl.* yellowish outside, brown and varnished inside, having untwisted segs. and a broad 3-lobed white and yellow lip; otherwise closely resembling *D. undulatum* except in size. Australia? 1896.

**D. Jerdonia'num.** *fl.* cinnabar-red, small, in small bunches from the last matured growth; lip dark purple. *Pseudobulbs* about 6 in. h. Nilgiri Hills. 1868. (B.M. 7741.)

**D. Johan'nis.** *fl.* 10 to 20, 1 to 1½ in. across, fragrant; sep. and pet. chocolate-brown, twisted; lip yellow with crimson pencillings. Autumn. *Pseudobulbs* 12 to 18 in. h. N. Australia. 1865. (B.M. 5540.) var. **semifus'cum,** sep. yellow, pet. brown, lip yellow with reddish-brown borders and lines on side lobes. 1883.

**D. John'soniae.*** *fl.* 5 to 10, 4 to 5 in. across; sep. and pet. white; sep. lanceolate, shorter than lip and the broader, acuminate pet.; lip white, side lobes arched over column, purple-marked, mid-lobe purple at base and on the furrowed callus; column white, bordered purple; racemes ascending. Summer. *l.* 2 or 3, oblong, sub-acute, leathery, 3 to 4 in. long. Stem erect, sub-cylindric, 9 to 18 in. h., 2- or 3-leaved. Papua. 1882. (J.H. 20 (1890), 177 as *D. MacFarlanei.*)

**D. Kingia'num.*** *fl.* violet-purple, about 1 in. across, spikes about 6 in. long, from leafy part of new and older bulbs. February. *Pseudobulbs* swollen at base, tapered, 2 to 12 in. h., crowded, with 3 to 6 l. Queensland, New S. Wales. 1843. (B.M. 4527.) Variable. *fl.* vary from white to purple. A pretty cool-house species. var. **al'bum** has pure white fl. and pseudobulbs about 6 in. long. 1888. (W.O.A. 332.)

**D. laevifo'lium.*** *fl.* 2 or 3, 1½ in. across; sep. and pet. sub-equal, clear rose-purple; lip yellow, reddish beneath, margins involute. Summer. *Pseudobulbs* 1 to 2 in. h., clothed with fibrous membrane. *l.* 2 to 3 in. long, smooth. New Guinea. 1920. (B.M. 9011.)

**D. lamella'tum.** *fl.* yellow, white, or pale pink, ¾ in. long, 3 to 5 in a short, drooping raceme; lip clawed, truncate. *l.* few, ovate, 1 to 1½ in. long. *Pseudobulbs* pyriform, 3 to 4 in. long, branched. Tenasserim. 1892. (B.R. 30, 53 as *D. compressum.*)

**D. lasian'thera.** *fl.* 20 to 35, 2½ in. across, spurred, in erect racemes; sep. 1¼ in. long, broadest at base, twisted, margins curled; pet. small, linear, erect, twisted; lip with broad, erect side lobes, yellowish-green without, dark red-violet within, bases greenish-yellow with red-violet stripes, mid-lobe heart-shaped, reddish, with 3 erect violet combs, crenate and yellowish at apex. *Pseudobulbs* up to 12 ft. long, stout. *l.* apical, leathery. New Guinea. 1932. (O.R. 1934, 205.) Syn. *D. Stuberi.*

**D. lasiogloss'um.** *fl.* 1½ to 2 in. across in twos and threes from the joints; sep. and pet. creamy-white; lip yellow in centre, side lobes streaked with purple, disk villous with orange hairs. Summer. *Pseudobulbs* 8 to 12 in. long. Burma. 1868. An erect slender-growing species, rather difficult to cultivate. (B.M. 5825.) Syn. *D. shillongense.*

**D. Leea'num.*** *fl.* 1½ to 3 in. across; sep. and pet. whitish, mottled warm rose-purple in upper half; lip very deep purple, tinged green at base of throat. Stems very tall, slightly compressed. New Guinea. 1891. Not unlike *D. superbiens* in habit and form of fl. and may be a natural hybrid between it or *D. undulatum* and *D. Phalaenopsis* var.

**D. leucolopho'tum.** *fl.* white, resembling *D. barbatulum,* but much larger; chin small, acute; sep. ligulate, acute; pet. much larger, oblong, acute; side lobes of lip triangular, rounded outside, mid-lobe linear-ligulate, acute; infl. lax, over 1 ft. long. *l.* oblong-ligulate, acuminate. Stems cylindrical, attenuate, many-leaved. Sunda Is. 1882. (L. 291.)

**D. Linawia'num.*** *fl.* pale rosy-lilac, nearly white in centre, produced freely in pairs; lip tipped crimson. Winter. 1 ft. h. or more. China. 1824. (W.O.A. 141; B.R. 1314; B.M. 4153, as *D. moniliforme.*) var. **maj'us,** *fl.* larger, richer-coloured.

**D. Lindleya'num.** A synonym of *D. nobile.*

**D. Lind'leyi.** A synonym of *D. aggregatum.*

**D. linea'le.** A synonym of *D. veratrifolium.*

**D. linearifo'lium.** *fl.* white; upper sep. small, oblong, acute, lateral with 2 mauve-purple lines; pet. very small, nearly rhombic; lip cuneate-dilated, 3-lobed with rhombic side lobes and a retuse mid-lobe, side lobes veined purplish-mauve. *l.* linear, 2-dentate, over 2 in. long. Stem thin, slender, with numerous branches. Java. 1883.

**D. linguiform'e.** *fl.* 3 to 20, about 1 in. across, white or creamy-white; sep. and pet. narrow, tapered; lip shorter; spikes 2 to 4 in. h. *l.* 1 in. long, leathery, furrowed when old. Habit of *D. cucumerinum.* Australia. 1800. (B.M. 5249.) Suitable for a raft.

**D. lituiflo'rum.*** *fl.* much like those of *D. nobile,* but smaller; sep. and pet. rosy-purple, acute; lip white, bordered purple, with dark purple centre, remarkable in being curved like a trumpet with the mouth upwards. April. *Pseudobulbs* 18 to 20 in. long, ½ in. thick, pendulous or sub-pendulous, joints about 1½ in. apart. Burma, Assam. 1856. (B.M. 6050; W.S.O. 2, 3.) var. **can'didum,** *fl.* pure white, with the faintest tinge of green on lip. 1880; **Freemanii,** lip deep-coloured, with zone of yellow, and erect, short, stiff pseudobulbs 12 in. long. Assam. 1878.

**D. Loddige'sii.** *fl.* solitary from nodes, 1½ in. across, rounded; sep. and pet. rose to rose-purple; lip orange banded by white, purple at tip, fringed. Spring. Stem 3 to 6 in. long, flattish. *rhiz.* creeping, branched. China. (L.B.C. 1935 as *D. pulchellum.*) Syn. *D. Siedelianum.* Should have a shallow pan or raft.

**D. longicor'nu.*** *fl.* white, many, from upper part of 2-year and older pseudobulbs, 3 to 6 together; lip with a yellow median line, fringed. May, June. *Pseudobulbs* 18 to 20 in. h., slender, black-haired. Allied to *D. infundibulum* but stem thinner and spur longer. (B.R. 1315; A.B.G.C. 64.) Cool house. India. var. **Watt'ii,** a synonym of *D. Wattii.*

**D. Low'i.** *fl.* 3 to 5, bright yellow with reddish veins and black hairs on upper part of lip; 1½ to 2 in. across; from upper nodes. Summer, autumn. *Pseudobulbs* 1 to 1½ ft. h., ¼ in. thick, black-haired. Borneo. 1862. (B.M. 5303.) var. **pleiot'richum** has no red veins on lip and has black hairs on basal lobes. 1885.

**D. luteo'lum.*** *fl.* primrose-yellow, with a little orange-crimson on lip, 1 to 2 in. across, in threes or fours from the upper nodes. March. *Pseudobulbs* 1 to 2½ ft. long, slender, usually erect. Moulmein. 1864. (B.M. 5441.) var. **chlorocen'trum,** *fl.* pale primrose with greenish, not yellow, hairs on disk of lip. 1883. (W.O.A. 322.)

**D. Lyon'ii.*** Habit of *D. acuminatum* but at the apex of the pseudobulbs is a small, sharp, tooth-like projection. *fl.* 3 in. or more across, chestnut-rose, nearly red, deepest on lip; sep. and pet. triangular, attenuated, less so than those of *D. acuminatum*; spikes long, arching, 10- to 25-fld. Philippines. (B.M. 9191.) A fine species. Heavy shading is detrimental.

**D. MacCarth'iae.*** *fl.* nearly 3 in. long and more across, in drooping 3- to 5-fld. racemes; sep. and pet. very pointed, rich rose-pink; lip rose-pink, veined rose, disk purple, throat whitish, purple-spotted. June. *Pseudobulbs* slender, 18 to 30 in. long, pendulous. Ceylon. 1854. (B.M. 4886; W.O.A. 319.) Difficult; requires a high temperature and moist atmosphere and should be rested in an intermediate temperature not below 60° F., during which it should not be allowed to become quite dry.

**D. MacFar'lanei.** A synonym of *D. Johnsoniae.*

**D. Macrae'i.** *fl.* 2 or 3, small, whitish; lip with 2 long wavy keels, front lobe pentagonal, side lobe running backwards. Summer. *Pseudobulbs* stout, compressed, 2 or 3 in. h., 1-leaved. India. 1885. (A.B.G.C. 8, 86.) SYN. *D. flabellum, D. pardalinum.*

**D. macran'thum.** A synonym of *D. superbum.*

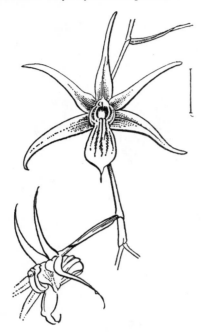

*Dendrobium Lyonii* (p. 655)

**D. macrophyl'lum.*** *fl.* 2 in. across, greenish-yellow, hairy outside, in long, terminal, erect racemes; lip 3-lobed, striped and spotted purple. Summer. *Pseudobulbs* clavate, 12 to 18 in. h. *l.* leathery, persistent. Philippines. 1838. (B.M. 5649.) SYN. *D. Veitchianum.* var. **al'bum,** *fl.* whitish. 1905. *D. macrophyllum* of Lindley is a synonym of *D. superbum.*

**D. macrostach'yum.** *fl.* greenish-yellow, fragrant, about 1½ in. across, 2 or 3 together; sep. and pet. recurved, sometimes tinged pink; lip veined purple. Autumn. *l.* 3 to 4 in. long. Stems 1 to 2 ft. long, pendulous, slender. Travancore, Ceylon. (B.R. 1865.)

**D. Madon'nae.** A synonym of *D. rhodostictum.*

**D. margina'tum.** A synonym of *D. cymbidioides* and *D. xanthophlebium.*

**D. marmora'tum.** *fl.* 1½ to 2 in. across, from nodes, white, tipped purple; lip purple in front, ciliate. May, June. Stem slender, erect, or subpendulous, 12 to 18 in. long. Deciduous. Burma. 1875. SYN. *D. transparens marmoratum.*

**D. × melanoph'thalmum** (*D. pendulum* × *D. Wardianum*). Burma. 1886. SYN. *D. crassinode Wardianum, D. Waltonii.*

**D. mesochlo'rum.** A synonym of *D. amoenum.*

**D. microglaph'ys.** *fl.* fragrant; small, ¾ in. long; sep. and pet. sub-connivent, white; lip purple at base, with 5 central purple lines and a yellowish tip. Borneo. 1865. Allied to *D. aduncum.*

**D. Mirbelia'num.** *fl.* 8 to 15 in an erect raceme over 1 ft. long; sep. and pet. greenish-yellow, with darker lines, narrow, acute; pet. 1¼ in. long; side lobes of lip enclosing the column, greenish-yellow with brown lines, the ovate, acute mid-lobe with a pale disk and borders veined brown. *l.* elliptic. Stems stout, 18 to 24 in. long. New Guinea. 1890. (L. 215.)

**D. mon'ile.*** *fl.* white, with a few purple spots on lip, fragrant, borne on upper part of previous year's leafless stems, in clusters of 2 or more. May. *Pseudobulbs* thin, about 10 in. h., clothed with narrow *l.* China, Japan. 1824. (B.M. 5482 as *D. japonicum.*) SYN. *D. moniliforme.*

**D. monophyll'um.** *fl.* 20 or fewer, small, bell-shaped, nodding, dull yellow, fragrant. *Pseudobulbs* 1 to 3 in. h., stout, furrowed, usually 1-, sometimes 2-leaved. *l.* lanceolate, stiff. Australia. (F.O.A. 1, pt. 6.)

**D. Moor'ei.** *fl.* pure white; sep. and pet. linear-lanceolate; lip similar but shorter, with a small, triangular lobe each side below middle; scapes filiform, with a terminal 6- to 10-fld. raceme. Stems terete, 4 to 6 in. long, with 3 to 5 oval-oblong leathery l. at their apex. Lord Howe Is. 1878. Tufted. (F.O.A. 1, pt. 7.)

**D. moscha'tum.** *fl.* yellowish-white, 3 to 4 in. across; tinged rose, lip concave or slipper-shaped, pale yellow, base darker, with a large blotch of deep blackish-purple each side; racemes from upper part of 1-year and older pseudobulbs, drooping, 8- to 14-fld. June. *Pseudobulbs* 3 to 5 ft. h., ½ in. thick. *l.* 20 to 30, large. India. 1828. (B.M. 3837; A.B.G.C. 8, 84.) var. **Calceola'ria,** *fl.* smaller and brighter. (H.E.F. 184.) SYN. *D. Calceolaria;* **cu'preum,** *fl.* apricot-yellow, lip usually slipper-shaped. (B.R. 1779; W.O.A. 165.) SYN. *D. Calceolus.* More or less musk-scented.

**D. moulmeinen'se.** A synonym of *D. infundibulum.*

**D. muta'bile.** *fl.* small, white or pinkish with orange mark on lip; spikes compactly 8- to 10-fld. May. *Pseudobulbs* slender, erect, 12 to 30 in. long. *l.* elliptic, obtuse, about 2 in. long. East Indies. 1844. (B.M. 5285; B.R. 33, 1 as *D. triadenium.*) SYN. *Callista mutabilis.*

**D. nitidis'simum.** Interesting, not beautiful. *Pseudobulbs* conical, 1½ to 2½ in. h., monophyllous. *l.* 3 to 5 in. long. The flowering growth is separate, elongating into a slender peduncle bearing a reduced *l.* at apex and a Cattleya-like spathe ¾ in. long from which the small solitary *fl.* less than 1 in. long is produced. Sep. and pet. narrow, yellowish, shaded with pink; lip yellowish with a pubescent disk and purple-spotted and bordered side lobes. New Ireland, New Guinea. 1875.

**D. niv'eum.** A synonym of *D. Johnsoniae.*

**D. no'bile.*** *fl.* large, very freely produced in twos and threes from nodes of 2-year-old pseudobulbs, fragrant, the scent varying at different times of the day; sep. and pet. white, tipped rosy-pink; lip white, rosy-pink in front, blotched deep velvety-crimson at base. January to April. *Pseudobulbs* 2 to 3 ft. h., 2 in. thick, with 10 to 16 bright green *l.* N. India, Assam, China. 1836. (A.B.G.C. 8, 71.) SYN. *D. coerulescens, D. Lindleyanum.* One of the oldest species in cultivation, one of the best known, one of the easiest grown, one of the cheapest in commerce, one of the most beautiful and variable. When growth is finished remove it to a cool house and keep it dry, or with just enough water to preserve the pseudobulbs from shrivelling. Among the many varieties the following are marked: **al'bum,** like var. *virginale* but without the primrose disk; **Ames'iae,** sep., pet., and margin of lip white, disk very dark; **Cooksonia'num,** mid-area of pet. very deep purple, their tips with purple borders, bases of pet. hastate, thickened in middle and velvety like the lip. 1865. (L. 340.); **el'egans,** *fl.* larger and more symmetrical than type, pet. broader, white at base, lip with pale sulphur zone around the maroon disk, tip rose-purple; **interme'dium,** sep. and pet. white, lip white with central crimson spot; **nobil'ius,*** *fl.* larger and of richer colour, sep. and pet. deep wine-purple, paler at base, the maroon disk of the lip shading to whitish. A very fine variety. (W.O.A. 214.); **pen'dulum,** *fl.* large, of richer colour than type, of pendulous habit; **Sanderia'num,** sep. and pet. purple, pet. white at base, disk of lip with a dark blotch surrounded by rosy-purple except for a small white area in front, veined purple with a white border in upper part. 1884. (R. 2, 58.); **virgina'le,** pure white except for a tinge of pale primrose on lip. 1897.

**D. noda'tum.** A synonym of *D. Aphrodite.*

**D. O'Brienia'num.** *fl.* 12 to 15, apple-green, on slender drooping spikes; upper sep. and narrower pet. ¼ in. long, lower sep. prolonged into a swollen spur ¾ in. long, their bases almost concealing the base of the lip which is raised and almost conceals the short, stout column. New Guinea. 1891.

**D. ochrea'tum.** *fl.* usually in pairs from the nodes, about 3 in. across, very thick; sep. and pet. bright orange; lip with a crimson blotch in centre. *Pseudobulbs* 10 to 15 in. long, nearly 1 in. thick, curved, knotted. Deciduous. N. India. 1837. (B.M. 4450 as *D. cambridgeanum.*) Cool house.

**D. Pal'pebrae.** *fl.* French white, with orange-yellow disk near base of lip, faintly hawthorn-scented; sep. oblong, narrower than the oval pet.; lip oblong, downy above, with 5 lines of reddish hairs near base; column yellowish; racemes ascending, 6- to 10-fld., from immediately below the l. Late summer. *l.* oblong-lanceolate, acute. Stems clavate, 4-angled, narrowed below, 7 to 9 in. long, with 3 to 5 *l.* near apex. Burma. 1849. (B.M. 8683.)

**D. Papil'io.** *fl.* large, solitary, fragrant, fugitive, pendent; sep. and pet. pale rose; lip yellow, veined, purple, long-stalked, wavy. *l.* linear, channelled to base. Stems thin and grass-like. Philippines. 1890. (O.R. 1927, 369.)

**D. parciflo'rum.*** *fl.* bright yellow, on short, erect spikes of 2 or 3 good-sized blossoms, from 2-year and older pseudobulbs. March, April. *Pseudobulbs* small, clustered, 1 in. long, ½ in. thick, with a solitary, thick, fleshy, dark green leaf, about 1½ in. long. N. India. 1838. (B.R. 25, 37; W.S.O. 2, 28, as *D. Jenkinsii.*)

**D. pardali'num.** A synonym of *D. Macraei.*

**D. Par'ishii.*** *fl.* purplish, fading into white towards centre, generally in twos; lip shorter than sep. and pet., very woolly, rose, with 2 purple blotches in front of column. May. *Pseudobulbs* stout, erect or curved, ½ in. in diameter. Scented like Rhubarb root. Moulmein. 1863. (B.M. 5488.) Requires a decided rest. var. **albens,** *fl.* white with crimson-purple blotch just within throat of lip. 1891.

**D. Parthe'nium.** *fl.* white, with purple blotch at base of lip; sep. lanceolate-triangular, with obscure keels; pet. oblong, obtuse, longer than sep.; racemes 2-fld. *l.* 1½ in. long. Stems thin. Borneo. 1885.

**D. Pax'tonii.** A synonym of *D. chrysanthum* and *D. fimbriatum oculatum.*

**D. pen'dulum.*** *fl.* 2 to 3 in. across, from matured growth, in twos to fours; sep. and pet. waxy-white, tipped rich purple; lip white, with orange blotch at base. February, March. *Pseudobulbs* 1 to 1½ ft. long. Burma. 1868. Remarkable for the enormously swollen joints of the stem, which are 1 in. in diameter, and about 1 in. apart. A pendulous deciduous species, best grown in a small basket. (B.M. 5766; W.O.A. 152.) var. **albiflo'rum,** *fl.* white with a lemon-yellow blotch in the lip base. (W.O.A. 458 as *D. crassinode albiflorum.*); **al'bum,** a synonym of var. *albiflorum*; **Barberia'num,** *fl.* much more richly coloured than the type with upper parts of sep. and pet. rich amethyst-purple.

**D. Phalaenop'sis.*** *fl.* about 3 in. across, spreading; sep. pale magenta, with reticulated nerves; pet. rose, much larger, rhomboid-orbicular, acute; lip dark purplish-red, side lobes rounded, mid-lobe tongue-shaped; raceme loosely 6- to 20-fld. September. *l.* alternate, distichous, 6 to 8 in. long. *Pseudobulbs* erect, stiff, 1 to 1½ ft. h. N. Australia. (B.M. 6817; L. 280; R. 42; W.O.A. 187.) var. **hololeu'cum,** *fl.* pure white; **Schroederia'num,** *fl.* larger, ranging from white to purple, spikes often 15- to 20-fld., *pseudobulbs* stout, 2 to 3 ft. h. New Guinea. 1890; the form **al'bum** is white except for a few purple lines in throat. 1894; form **Rothschildia'num** has *fl.* 4 in. across, sep. and pet. white, lip light pink with darker lines on disk. 1892; var. **Statteria'num,** *see* **D. Statterianum.** Many other vars. have been named.

**D. pic'tum.** A synonym of *D. Devonianum.*

**D. Pierard'ii.*** *fl.* often in threes from the nodes, creamy-white or delicate pink, on long, beautifully festooned stems; lip primrose, with a few purple lines near base. Winter. *Pseudobulbs* 2 to 8 ft. long, ½ in. thick, pendulous, deciduous. India. 1815. (B.M. 2584; B.R. 1756; L.B.C. 750; A.B.G.C. 8, 72.) var. **cuculla'tum,** *fl.* larger, lip more cucullate, stems shorter, stouter.

**D. platycau'lon.** *fl.* straw-coloured, over 1 in. long in short racemes, larger than in *D. lamellatum* which it resembles, and differing in shape of lip. Summer. *Pseudobulbs* flattened in upper part. Philippines. 1892.

**D. polycar'pum.** *fl.* yellowish, with purplish-red borders to side lobes; sep. ligulate-triangular; pet. longer, ligulate-spatulate; lip with roundish, angular side lobes, and a rounded, triangular, undulated mid-lobe; racemes many-fld., loose. Stems 3 ft. long. Sunda Is. 1883.

**D. × polyphle'bium.** Considered a natural hybrid, *D. Pierardii* × *D. rhodopterygium*, but possibly a variety of the latter which it much resembles, lip margins whitish, fringed. Burma.

**D. primuli'num.*** *fl.* in 2 rows along the stem; sep. and pet. small, pinkish-white; lip downy, very large, shell-shaped, yellowish, streaked red. February, March. *Pseudobulbs* 1 to 1½ ft. long, erect or pendulous, stout. Deciduous. Moulmein. 1864. (W.O.A. 286; L. 686; B.M. 5003 as *D. nobile pallidiflorum.*) var. **gigan'teum** is larger in all parts.

**D. profu'sum.** *fl.* sep. and pet. yellowish-green, purple near base, and with purple dots on the toothed pet.; sep. ligulate, acute; lip yellow, with a dark spot in middle, the blade pandurate, the front part very broad, toothed, and wavy; peduncles 7- to 9-fld. *l.* deciduous. Philippines. 1884.

**D. pulchel'lum.** *fl.* large, 3 to 5 in. across; sep. and pet. buff, shaded pale lemon; lip of same colour, spotted at base with two large blotches of dark, vinous crimson, and margined with rosy-pink; racemes drooping, produced from new and old pseudobulbs, 6- to 10-fld. April, May. *Pseudobulbs* stout, erect, 3 to 5 ft. h., about 1 in. thick, with purple lines running their entire length. India. 1837. (W.S.O. 1, 22 as *D. Dalhousieanum.*) A noble species, requiring considerable space. var. **lu'teum,** *fl.* light yellow, blotches on lip paler. *D. pulchellum* of Loddiges is *D. Loddigesii.*

**D. pu'milum.** *fl.* white, cream, or yellow, 1 in. long, solitary, shortly pedicellate; lip with dark spot at tip or veined red. *l.* ½ to ¾ in. long, orbicular to elliptic, obtuse. *Pseudobulbs* 1 to 1½ in. long. India. (A.B.G.C. 5, 5.) This name has also been used for *Geny-orchis pumila.*

**D. puncta'tum.** A synonym of *Dipodium punctatum.*

**D. punic'eum.** *fl.* rather small, almost tubular, rich rose-pink, crowded on short, lateral, apical spikes. *Pseudobulbs* 1 to 2 ft. h. August, September. Allied to *D. secundum* but with rather larger fl. not secund. New Guinea. 1897.

**D. purpu'reum.** *fl.* bright purple, campanulate, about ¾ in. long, in dense, spherical, sessile clusters, from the nodes of the old, leafless, spindle-shaped stems, 2 to 4 ft. long; bracts cordate. Summer. Moluccas. 1834. var. **candid'ulum,** pet. tip very bright green, ovary pure white, stalked. 1887. (L. 98.); **Mose'leyi,** *fl.* white, tipped green, segs. less acute than in type, bracts ovate, acuminate. Arn Is. 1884.

**D. pycnostach'yum.** *fl.* numerous, small, densely set in terminal spikes; sep. and pet. whitish, tapered; lip greenish. *Pseudobulbs* erect, tapered, 6 to 12 in. h., tufted. Deciduous. Burma.

**D. re'gium.** *fl.* 2 to 4 in. across; sep. and pet. rosy magenta; lip with a whitish base, a yellowish disk, and a deep rose-magenta tip. Habit of *D. nobile* but smaller. Summer. *l.* 3 to 4 in. long. Lower Hindustan. 1901. (B.M. 8003.)

**D. revolu'tum.** *fl.* solitary, axillary, ¾ in. long; sep. and pet. white, reflexed, turned up, lanceolate, acute, nearly equal; lip bright yellow, nearly quadrate, convex; disk with 3 furrows and red bands. July. *l.* numerous, distichous, 1 to 2 in. long, oblong, linear- or ovate-oblong, obtuse or retuse, half-amplexicaul. Stems tufted, 1 to 1½ ft. long. Malay Peninsula. 1882. (B.M. 6706.)

**D. rhodocen'trum.** *fl.* light rosy, from upper parts of the 2-year and older pseudobulbs, in hanging bunches of 6 to 12; sep., pet. and lip purple-tipped; lip white, base yellowish. Autumn. *Pseudobulbs* pendulous, 2 to 3 ft. long, ¼ in. thick. Burma. 1872.

**D. rhodoptery'gium.** *fl.* deep rose; lip streaked light purple, warted. May. *Pseudobulbs* 1 to 1½ ft. h., ½ in. thick. Burma. 1875. Resembling *D. Parishii*, but with much larger pseudobulbs. var. **Emeri'ci** has a white line down middle of lateral sep. and an amethyst bar across the lip blotch; the front border of the lip is at first white then straw-coloured; it has sometimes been placed under *D.* × *polyphlebium.*

**D. rhodostic'tum.** *fl.* 2 to 5, about 2 in. across; sep. and pet. pure white; side lobes of lip spotted, marked or margined with red. Winter. Habit of *D. atroviolaceum* but more slender. Papua. (B.M. 7900.) Syn. *D. Madonnae.*

**D. rhomb'eum.** A synonym of *D. aureum.*

**D. Rimann'i.** *fl.* equalling those of a good *D. speciosum*, in terminal, somewhat zigzag racemes; sep. and pet. yellow, sep. striped purple outside; lip white, with purple veins. *l.* oblong, 3½ in. long, very leathery. Stems cylindric-fusiform, leafy above. Moluccas. 1883.

**D. robus'tum.** *fl.* yellowish-green, with purple lines. Stems 2 ft. long. New Guinea. 1895. Closely allied to *D. Mirbelianum*, but with less acute seg. and smaller bracts.

**D. × Rolf'eae** (*D. nobile* × *D. primulinum*). Sikkim. 1890. Has also been raised artificially.

**D. Ruck'eri.** *fl.* greenish-yellow, almost white externally, fragrant; lip with brown marking on side lobes and a central villous line. Khasia, Bhutan. 1843. (B.R. 29, 60.) A pretty species, similar in habit to *D. luteolum.*

**D. rupic'ola.** A synonym of *D. ciliatum.*

**D. rutrif'erum.** *fl.* sep. rose, triangular, blunt, the lateral ones extended into a long pouch; pet. rose at base, whitish at the blunt end; lip ligulate-pandurate, with inflexed borders, thus saccate at apex, where the borders are denticulate; rachis rather short, with a capitate-umbellate infl. Stem furrowed, as thick as a goose-quill. Papua. 1887. (L. 119.)

**D. San'derae.*** Allied to *D. Dearei* but with larger clusters of flowers produced from both old and new bulbs; sep. and pet. pure white; lip white, shaded and striped with purple at base. *Pseudobulbs* up to 3 ft. h. Philippines. 1908. (O.R. 1909, f. 17.) var. **ma'jus,** *fl.* much larger than in type but fewer in cluster, pure white, throat only shaded with purple. Philippines. 1930. (B.M. 8351.) Several other vars. are known.

**D. Sanderia'num.*** *fl.* white, resembling those of *D. Dearei* but larger and with the mentum inflated into a short sac; lip broader and stained with purple at base. Stems continue to lengthen and produce fl. in twos and threes from the l.-axils. Borneo. 1894.

**D. sanguin'eum.** *fl.* solitary in upper axils, about 1 in. long; sep. and the broader pet. crimson, except at base in front, where they are marbled and spotted with crimson on a whitish ground; lip whitish, small, with purple lines and spots. Stems slender, about 3 ft. long. Labuan. 1895. (J.R.H.S. 22, clxxxii.)

**D. sanguinolen'tum.*** *fl.* in bunches of 6 or 8, from upper parts of old pseudobulbs; sep. and pet. amber, veined rose, with purple tips; lip large, with point heavily marked purple. Autumn. *Pseudobulbs* at first somewhat 4-sided, then tapered, 3 to 4 ft. h., with large dark-green l. Penang, &c. 1842. (B.R. 29, 6.)

**D. sarmento'sum.** *fl.* 1 in. across, fragrant, solitary or few, produced after the l.; sep. and pet. white; lip white, with a greenish blotch and a few lines of crimson at base. Stems very slender, 1½ ft. long, branched. Burma. 1897. (B.M. 7525.)

**D. scabrilin'gue.*** *fl.* 1 or 2 from apical nodes, 1½ in. across, fragrant like wallflowers, at first greenish, but soon changing to pure white, except the lip, which is shaded green and yellow, and striped orange on disk. Spring. *Pseudobulbs* 6 to 10 in. long, and about ⅓ in. thick, black haired. Burma. 1862. (B.M. 5515 as *D. hedyosmum.*) Syn. *D. alboviride.*

**D. Schroed'eri.*** Sep. and pet. white; lip orange-yellow. Habit of *D. Farmeri. infl.* as in *D. densiflorum* but more lax. Spring. Habitat?

**D. Schuetz'ii.*** Allied to *D. Dearei* and *D. Sanderae*, but with shorter, stouter, somewhat clavate pseudobulbs, 9 to 15 in. h. *fl.* 4 or more, large, pure white with a small emerald green disk to lip, and a few spots at its base. *fl.* much as in *D. formosum* but front lobe of lip nearly orbicular and with a distinct apiculus. Autumn. Philippines. 1910. (B.M. 8495.)

**D. sculp'tum.** *fl.* pure white, about 2 in. across, from the top of the matured growth, 3 or 4 on a spike; lip white, a square orange blotch on its centre, wrinkled at base. *Pseudobulbs* 1 to 1½ ft. long, ⅓ in. thick. Borneo. An erect stove evergreen. (R.X.O. 2, 146.)

**D. secun'dum.** *fl.* small, rosy-purple with a yellow lip, in dense 1-sided stiff racemes from the top of old and new pseudobulbs. Winter. *Pseudobulbs* 2 to 3 ft. h., stout. *l.* 3 to 4 in. long, 1 to 1½ in. wide. Malaya. 1829. (B.M. 4352; B.R. 1291.) var. **niv'eum** is white except for orange tip to lip, and has a shorter pseudobulb.

**D. sen'ile.** *fl.* bright golden-yellow, 1 to 1½ in. across, in short spikes of twos or threes from sides of last matured growth; lip with a few reddish stripes. Spring. *Pseudobulbs* 4 to 6 in. long, with the deciduous l. and the stems covered with white woolly hairs. Moulmein. 1865. (B.M. 5520.) Requires a decided rest and should never be syringed.

**D. shillongen'se.** A synonym of *D. lasioglossum*.

**D. Siedelia'num.** A synonym of *D. Loddigesii*.

**D. signa'tum.** *fl.* in pairs from nodes, 1½ to 2 in. across, chin very blunt-angled; sep. sulphur, ligulate, acute, reflexed; pet. white to lightest ochre, broader, acute, reflexed; lip shouldered at base, nearly square and narrow, suddenly enlarged, disk marked with a blotch and 4 lines of brown; column light green, with some mauve lines. *Pseudobulbs* 12 to 18 in. h. Spring. Siam. 1884. var. **al'bum,** sep. and pet. white, lip white with a central yellow suffusion marked by darker veins. Siam. 1939.

**D. Smil'liae.** *fl.* purplish-rose, small, in dense racemes 2 to 3 in. long from uppermost nodes. *l.* 2 to 4 in. long. Stems 1 to 2 ft. long, thick. Queensland. 1888. (F.A.O. i, pt. vii.)

**D. speciosis'simum.*** *fl.* pure white, 4 in. across, with a deep orange-red blotch on lip, resembling those of *D. formosum*. Summer. Stems 3 to 6 in. h. or more, black-haired, slender. Borneo. 1895.

**D. specio'sum.*** *fl.* wax-like, creamy or yellowish-white, fragrant, 1 in. long, many in a terminal raceme 1 to 1½ ft. long; sep. and pet. narrow; lip with red specks. Autumn. *Pseudobulbs* very stout, 6 to 15 in. long, conical, with 2 or 3 large, leathery, dark, shining l. Australia. 1824. (B.M. 3074; B.R. 1610.) When making its young growths, a little heat is necessary; but when these are mature, it should be removed to the open air for 2 or 3 months, giving only sufficient water to keep the sun from shrivelling it. Several varieties occur, among them: var. **Bancroftia'num,** smaller than type, *pseudobulbs* fusiform, brownish, furrowed, floral segs. narrower. Sometimes regarded as a distinct species; **Hill'ii,** sep. and pet. narrower and paler than in type, spikes longer and more slender, *pseudobulbs* about twice as long and half as thick. Remarkably floriferous. (W.O.A. 198; B.M. 5261 as *D. Hillii*.)

**D. spectab'ile.*** *fl.* 5 to 25, large, singularly formed, in upright spikes; sep. and pet. narrowed, twisted, pale yellow with irregular stripes of purple; sep. triangular, extended into a wavy tail, pet. narrower; lip white with crimson markings, yellow red-veined without, the side lobes erect, hood-like, mid-lobe elongated. Winter. New Guinea. (B.M. 7747.) SYN. *D. tigrinum, Latouria spectabilis*.

**D. Statteria'num.** Possibly a natural hybrid between *D. bigibbum* and *D. Phalaenopsis* (type) or a local form of the latter. Habit much as in *D. bigibbum*. *fl.* with rounded sep. and pet. dark purple; lip similar in colour. Autumn. N. Australia. 1889. (R. 2, 7. as *D. Phalaenopsis Statterianum*.)

**D. Stratio'tes.*** *fl.* 7 to 20 on erect spikes from tips of old and new pseudobulbs, of good size, very peculiar; sep. ivory-white, lanceolate, acuminate, rolled back; pet. pale green, longer than sep., narrow-linear, twisted, quite erect; lip cream, veined violet, 3-lobed, the front lobe ovate, acute; racemes numerous. *l.* rather short, oblong. *Pseudobulbs* stiff, erect, 2 to 3 ft. long. Sunda Is. 1886. (L. 43; B.M. n.s. 436.) Remarkable and handsome.

**D. strebloce'ras.** *fl.* sep. green, nerved brown on inner side at base, ligulate, acute, twisted, undulate; pet. dark cinnamon-brown, margined green, longer, linear, acute, twisted 4 times; lip green, brown, white, and mauve-purple, the side lobes oblique, oblong, truncate; column white, minutely spotted brown; infl. 8-fld. Sunda Is. 1887. (L. 621.) Allied to *D. Stratiotes*. var. **Rossia'num,** *fl.* white, pet. tinged green, lip and sep. at length yellowish. 1888. (L. 124.)

**D. Stu'beri.** A synonym of *D. lasianthera*.

**D. suavis'simum.** A synonym of *D. chrysotoxum suavissimum*.

**D. subclau'sum.** *fl.* brilliant orange, ¾ in. long, somewhat tubular, front part of lip infolded; racemes short, few-fld. Summer. *l.* about 1 in. long. Stems slender, 1½ ft. h. Moluccas. 1894.

**D. sulca'tum.** *fl.* 5 to 15 in a drooping raceme from the leafy joints; sep. and pet. amber; lip amber, with deep crimson markings. February. *Pseudobulbs* 6 to 9 in. h., swelling upwards, with 2 or 3 large l. in upper part. India. 1837. (B.M. 6962; B.R. 24, 65; A.B.G.C. 8, 78.)

**D. Sum'neri.** *fl.* pink, few, distant; sep. and pet. ½ in. long; lip shorter, claw much dilated from the base and expanded into broadly ovate lateral lobes; raceme (with peduncle) about 8 in. long. *l.* 3 to 4 in. long. Stems 1½ to 2 ft. long. Australia.

**D. super'biens.*** *fl.* 10 to 30, light or rich purple, sometimes claret, about 2 in. across; spikes erect or arching, from the upper part of old and new pseudobulbs; sep. and pet. undulate. Autumn. *Pseudobulbs* 1 to 3 ft. h. N. Australia. 1876. (W.O.A. 312; L. 294.) var. **Gold'iei,** *see* **D. Goldiei.**

**D. super'bum.*** *fl.* single or in pairs, rosy magenta, 4 in. or more across from the nodes; lip rich purple. April. *Pseudobulbs* 1½ to 4 ft. long, semi-deciduous, pendulous. Philippines. (W.O.A. 42; B.M. 3970 as *D. macranthum*.) The fl. have a strong scent of Turkey rhubarb. Should be grown in a basket. var. **anos'mum,** *fl.* often solitary, less strongly scented, stems shorter; **Burk'ei,** *fl.* white with a pale purple disk to lip; **Dear'ei,** *fl.* pure white; **gigan'teum,** *fl.* 5 to 7 in. across, sep. and pet. rose-purple; lip rose-purple with 2 purplish-red spots at base, *pseudobulbs* much shorter and thicker than in type. Manila. **Hut'tonii,** sep. and pet. pure white, lip downy, base purple inside, almost scentless. Malaya.

**D. sutepen'se.** *fl.* fragrant, 1½ in. across, fleshy, waxy-white; sep. and pet. sub-equal, tapered, 3-lobed, the front lobe somewhat reflexed with undulate slightly toothed margins, disk narrowly oblong, raised, side lobes erect, pointed, white, veined with orange; column greenish-white, spur nearly ½ in. long. Habit of *D. infundibulum* but stems quill-like, 9 to 15 in. h. Burma.

**D. Takahash'ii.** *fl.* white, about 2 in. across, in clusters of 2 to 4; dorsal sep. oblong-lanceolate, over 1 in. long not half as broad; lateral sep. broader at base; pet. 1½ in. long, 1 in. wide; lip with a rose-red, narrow claw; side lobes yellowish to rose-red, mid-lobe bright yellow, margined white, claw and bases of lower sep. produced into a slender rose-red spur. *Pseudobulbs* black-haired, erect, furrowed, 12 to 20 in. h. *l.* 3 in. long, 1 in. wide. S. Borneo. 1933. (O.R. 1934, 15.)

**D. Tattonia'num.** A synonym of *D. canaliculatum*.

**D. tauri'num.** *fl.* 2 to 3 in. across; sep. yellowish-green; the narrower pet. twice as long, deep purple, curling and spread out; lip white, margined and suffused pinkish-purple. Autumn. *Pseudobulbs* 3 to 5 ft. long. *l.* persistent. *fl.-spikes* 12 to 24 in. long, many-fld. Manila. 1837. (B.R. 29, 28; L. 621.) var. **amboinen'se,** sep. greenish-yellow tinged with bronze-brown, pet. and side lobes of lip purple-brown, mid-lobe greenish-yellow. Strong growing. Amboyna. 1896; **Col'manii,** sep. and pet. rose, lip margined rose. 1909. A variable species.

**D. teretifo'lium.** *fl.* 3 to 12, 1 to 2 in. across; segs. narrow white or creamy-white; lip red, undulate, with 3 undulate longitudinal lamellae. Autumn. *l.* 6 to 9 in. long or even much more, terete, from slender branched rhizomatous, pendulous stems, 1 to 10 ft. long. Australia. (B.M. 4711.) SYN. *D. calamiforme*. A variable species. var. **Fair'faxii,** *fl.* 1 to 3, white, bases of red-dotted lip and sep. suffused reddish-brown or purple. Australia. SYN. *D. Fairfaxii*.

**D. tetrag'onum.** *fl.* 3 to 5 in. across, fragrant; sep. yellow, spotted red, the dorsal one narrow, the lateral lanceolate, much broader at the base than the dorsal one; pet. white, streaked red, linear, shorter and narrower than sep., all tapered; lip white, transversely barred red, broadly ovate, apiculate, obscurely 3-lobed, with 2-lamellae between side lobes; raceme short, from apex of the acutely 4-angled pseudobulbs quill-like at base, 14 to 20 in. long. Australia. 1838. (B.M. 5956.) Suited to a raft as it grows inverted. Spring.

**D. thyrsiflo'rum.*** Habit of *D. densiflorum* but pseudobulbs usually taller, not so decidedly 4-angled. *fl.* in longer thyrses, 1½ to 2 in. across; sep. and pet. white or rose-flushed; lip pubescent; golden orange. Spring. A very fine species. Burma. 1864. (B.M. 5780.) SYN. *D. densiflorum albo-luteum*. var. **Walkeria'num,** *fl.* larger, thyrses longer. (W.S.O. 3, 21.)

**D. tigri'num.** A synonym of *D. spectabile*.

**D. Tofft'ii.** *fl.* 20 or more, white; pet. tinged violet, 1½ in. long, frequently curled; lip stained violet and with forked veins, disk 3 violet plates; column stained violet. July, August. *Pseudobulbs* somewhat compressed, 3 to 5 ft. h. Allied to *D. taurinum*. Queensland. 1890. (O.R. 1932, 135.)

**D. tor'tile.** *fl.* in twos or threes, 3 in. across, pale yellow, almost white, suffused purplish-rose; sep. and pet. long, slightly twisted. June. *Pseudobulbs* 1 to 1½ ft. h., tapered at base. Moulmein. 1847. (B.M. 4477.) Habit resembles *D. nobile*. var. **ro'seum,** sep. and pet. deep rose.

**D. transpar'ens.*** *fl.* transparent white, tinged purplish-rose towards tips, 1 to 1½ in. across, in pairs along stems; lip stained in middle with a blotch of deep crimson encircled by a yellow zone. March. *Pseudobulbs* 1 to 1½ ft., slender, erect or subpendulous, deciduous. Assam, &c. (B.M. 4663.) var. **al'bum,** *fl.* wholly white. 1888; **marmora'tum,** *see* **D. marmoratum.**

**D. Treacheria'num.** *fl.* 2 to 5, about 2 in. across, on terminal spikes 2 to 6 in. long; sep. narrow-lanceolate, the dorsal one straight, lateral striped with red; pet. like the dorsal sep.; sep. and pet. pale rose with whitish margins, forming a chin; lip crimson red, shorter than pet., 3-lobed, mid-lobe acute. Winter. *Pseudobulbs* brownish-green, stained red, 2 to 3 in. h., diphyllous. *l.* linear, 3 to 4 in. long. Borneo. 1880. (B.M. 6591; W.O.A. 288.)

**D. triade'nium.** A synonym of *D. mutabile*.

**D. triflo'rum.** *fl.* 2 to 6, sep. and pet. straw-yellow; lip 3-lobed, front lobe narrow, side lobes more or less dull purple. Allied to *D. cymbidioides* and often confused with it, but fl. slightly smaller, l. longer and narrower, *rhiz.* ascending. Sumatra, Java. 1899. (G.C. 37 (1896), 581 as *D. cymbidioides*.)

**D. trigono'pus.** *fl.* 2 to 4, in short racemes, 3 in. across, golden-yellow; sep. ligulate, acuminate, keeled; pet. broader and shorter; claw of lip rather long, dilated into a broad lamina, mid-lobe denticulate, nearly square side lobes, disk lined red, shaded green, column triangular-pandurate. *l.* thick, papery, dull green, rather rough, slightly hirsute at back. Burma. 1887. SYN. *D. velutinum*.

**D. undula'tum.** *fl.* 10 to 20, about 2 in. across, on apical spikes 1 to 2 ft. long; sep. and pet. dingy brown, usually bordered with yellow, very similar, about 1 in. long, very wavy; lip shorter than sep., side lobes large, mid-lobe small. Summer. *l.* 3 to 4 in. long, somewhat undulate. *Pseudobulbs* 2 to 4 ft. h., stout, forming large tufts. Australia. 1838. (B.R. 27, 52 as *D. discolor.*) SYN. *D. Andersonianum.*

**D. Veitchia'num.** A synonym of *D. macrophyllum.*

**D. veluti'num.** A synonym of *D. trigonopus.*

**D. veratrifo'lium.** *fl.* silvery-white shaded and marked with violet particularly on lip which has a yellow keel; many in a terminal, elongated raceme 1½ to 2 ft. long, up to 40-fld.; pet. spatulate, 1 in. or more long. *l.* oblong, persistent, leathery, amplexicaul. *Pseudobulbs* erect, stout, 3 to 7 ft. h. New Guinea. (R. 2, 95.) Variable. Related to *D. Mirbelianum.* SYN. *D. Augustae-Victoriae, D. Imperatrix, D. lineale.*

**D. versicol'or.** *fl.* at first greenish-yellow, afterwards changing to a good yellow, tinged with purple outside; pet. at first pale green, afterwards sulphur-yellow; lips passing from greenish to very pale yellow. Assam. 1895.

**D. vexab'ile.** *fl.* light sulphur-ochre, partly white; side lobes of lip with numerous narrow lines, mid-lobe sulphur, with an orange blotch each side of the tuft of hairs on the disk. 1878. Allied to *D. Ruckeri.*

**D. Victo'riae-regin'ae.*** *fl.* 1½ in. across in clusters of 3 to 7 from nodes; sep. and pet. whitish at base passing to purplish-blue; lip similar, tongue-shaped. Autumn. *rhiz.* ascending. *Pseudobulbs* erect, cylindric, reddish, 6 in. or more h. Philippines. 1897. (G.C. 22 (1897), f. 34; B.M. 9071.) A pretty distinct species succeeding in the Odontoglossum or cool house. Well adapted for growing on a tree-fern stem section.

**D. violaceo-flav'ens.** *fl.* about 20, 2 in. across, in racemes; sep. nearly oblong; pet. a little longer, somewhat spatulate, barely twisted; lip 3-lobed, side lobes broad, mid-lobe protruding; general colour cream-yellow with violet veins on lip. *Pseudobulbs* 9 to 16 ft. long. *l.* 10 in. or more long. Allied to *D. veratrifolium.* New Guinea. 1920.

**D. virgin'eum.** Resembles *D. infundibulum,* but *fl.* smaller, ivory-white, with 2 thickened, ligulate, reddish lines running from base to middle of lip. *l.* broader, apex 2-lobed. Burma. 1885.

**D. Wallichia'num.** A synonym of *D. nobile.*

**D. Wardia'num.*** *fl.* in twos or threes from nodes, about 3½ in. across, 30 to 40 to a pseudobulb; sep. and pet. white, upper part bright rich magenta, broad, thick, waxy, blunt at tips; lip large, white above, rich orange in lower part, with 2 deep spots of crimson-magenta. May. *Pseudobulbs* 2 to 4 ft. long, 1 in. thick, semi-erect or pendulous. Assam. 1863. (W.S.O. 1, 19; R. 1, 9; B.M. 5058 as *D. Falconeri* var.) During the growing season, it needs an abundant supply of water, with a good heat; but, when the growths are complete, it should be removed to a cooler atmosphere, and less water, as a matter of course, will suffice. var. **al'bum,** *fl.* pure white except yellow disk of lip; **can'didum,** a synonym of *album*; **gigan'teum,** *fl.* larger and of deeper colour. Burma. **Low'ii,** *fl.* much as in *giganteum.* Both *giganteum* and *Lowii* form longer, stouter pseudobulbs than the Assam type.

**D. Watt'ii.** Allied to *D. infundibulum* but stems more slender, about 12 in. h. *fl.* 2 or 3, about 2 in. across, white with a golden-yellow disk, papillose; spur about 1 in. long. Bengal. (B.M. 6715 as *D. cariniferum Wattii.*)

**D. Williamsia'num.*** *fl.* 5 to 12, 2 in. or more across, in terminal spikes 9 to 18 in. long; sep. and pet. ivory-white; dorsal sep. and pet. broad oblong, apiculate, lateral sep. triangular; lip purple, scoop-shaped, appressed to column. *Pseudobulbs* slender, 1 to 3 ft. h. New Guinea. 1886. (W.O.A. 252.) Allied to *D. Phalaenopsis.*

**D. Williamson'ii.*** *fl.* 1½ in. across, white, in clusters of 4 or more from one-year and older bulbs; sep. keeled, tinged with yellow at tips; lip orange, tipped white, with a cinnabar-red crest. April. *Pseudobulbs* erect, black-haired, 1 ft. long by ½ in. thick. Nearly deciduous. Burma. 1869. (B.M. 7974; A.B.G.C. 5, 9.) SYN. *D. cariniferum.*

**D. Woll'astonii.** *fl.* light cream-yellow with radiating carmine veins on side lobes of lip and a darker suffusion on the crenulate margins; sep. 1½ in. long, acuminate, lower white-haired without; pet. spatulate 1¾ in. long, with a longitudinal fold, 1¼ in. broad when flattened; mid-lobe of lip acuminate with sides infolded. Allied to *D. macrophyllum.* New Guinea. 1915.

**D. xanthophle'bium.*** *fl.* 1½ to 2 in. across; in pairs from the last matured and older pseudobulbs; sep. and pet. white; lip medium-sized, side lobes veined orange, mid-lobe downy, orange-yellow; margin white. *Pseudobulbs* slender, 1½ ft. h. Moulmein. 1864. (B.M. 5454 as *D. marginatum.*) Stove.

E. C.

**DENDROCAL'AMUS** (*dendron,* tree, *calamus,* ancient name for reed). FAM. *Gramineae.* A genus of about 16 species of mostly tropical bamboos, a few of which are cultivated in the largest hot-houses of botanic gardens. They have but little interest for cultivators in general and perhaps no species is grown out of doors at the present time in the British Isles.

**D. gigan'teus.** Evergreen tree and the giant of the bamboo tribe, 80 to 100 ft. h. Stems 8 to 10 in. diameter, thin-walled, with hairy joints, 12 to 16 in. apart. Largest *l.* 20 in. long, 3 to 4 in. wide, borne in heavy graceful masses towards the summit. Malay Peninsula, but cultivated in Burma, India, Ceylon, &c., where it makes a magnificent feature. (C.B. 85.)

**D. sikkimen'sis.** Evergreen tree, 50 to 60 ft., when fully grown. Stems 5 to 7 in. diameter with the joints up to 18 in. apart. *l.* oblong-lanceolate, 1½ to 2 in. wide, 6 to 10 in. long. NE. Himalaya. Has been grown in the Temperate House at Kew and out of doors at Castlewellen, Co. Down, in 1890. (G.C. 12 (1892), 674.)

W. J. B.

**DENDROCHI'LUM** (*dendron,* tree, *cheilos,* lip; the plant having lipped flowers and growing on trees). FAM. *Orchidaceae.* Including Acoridium and Platyclinis. Over 100 species are in the genus distributed in the East, Borneo, Java, the Philippines, &c., characterized by numerous small flowers in terminal, shortly pedicillate racemes; peduncle erect or nearly so; rachis as long and very often declinate; sepals narrow, spreading, petals similar, lip sessile or shortly clawed at the base of the column, almost equalling the sepals; column erect, semi-terete; pollen masses 4. Pseudobulbs small, clustered, or set on the rhizome at short intervals, with a single leaf contracted to a short footstalk. Most species are best in the warm house with a winter night temperature of 60 to 65° F., *D. Cobbianum, D. glumaceum,* and a few others, 55° F. The species enumerated here can be accommodated in pans suspended near the glass, or the stronger-growing in pots. Compost should consist of 3 parts of cut Osmunda fibre to 1 part of Sphagnum moss, with free drainage. When growth is in full vigour, water freely; when completed water should be given only as required, before the compost becomes really dry. Injury follows if the compost is kept consistently sodden or too dry. Repotting should be done in the spring at the first sign of activity. Propagation may be effected by then dividing large plants. All the species are more attractive with many inflorescences than when but a few can be produced; hence the plants should be grown into comparatively large size. In all the individual flowers are insignificant, but their great number, the grace of the inflorescence, and their often pleasant fragrance render the species mentioned attractive.

**D. abbrevia'tum.** *fl.* ½ in. across, green with a central brown suffusion on lip. *infl.* many-fld., arching. *Pseudobulbs* 1½ to 2 in. h. *l.* 9 to 14 in. long. Java.

**D. arachni'tes.** *fl.* 15 to 20, yellow tinged with green; sep. ½ in. long with the smaller pet. narrow-pointed. Habit dwarf. *Racemes* 4 to 5 in. long, laterally arched or lateral. Philippines.

**D. auranti'acum.** *fl.* very small, orange-red, fragrant. *rhiz.* creeping. *Pseudobulbs* at short intervals, 1½ in. h., cylindrical. *l.* 2½ to 5 in. long. Sunda Is.

**D. Cobbia'num.** Sep. and pet. sulphur; lip orange, flabellate; peduncle 6 to 12 in. long, raceme with a zigzag rachis nearly as long, many-fld. *l.* and *pseudobulbs* like those of *D. latifolium.* Philippines. 1881.

**D. cornu'tum.** *fl.* small, yellowish-green or cream; rachis arching, many-fld. *Pseudobulbs* 1½ to 2 in. h. *l.* 6 to 8 in., narrowly lanceolate. Java, Sumatra.

**D. cucumeri'num.*** *fl.* with a cucumber-like odour, light pellucid greenish-yellow, in a graceful distichous raceme; lip with toothed brown auricle each side of base running out into a narrow awn, mid-lobe obcuneate, retuse, apiculate, with two brown stripes on disk. *l.* shining. *Pseudobulbs* 1 in. or more h., cylindric-conical, at length furrowed, tufted. Philippines. 1885.

**D. filiform'e.*** *fl.* up to 100, yellow, fragrant, in slender, pendent racemes. *l.* linear-lanceolate, 5 to 7 in. long. *Pseudobulbs* small, conical. Manila. 1836. (I.H. 1878, 323.) Possibly the most attractive species.

**D. gluma'ceum.*** *fl.* white or creamy-white, very fragrant, sessile, in a linear-oblong, pendulous, elongated spike; peduncle curved. *l.* solitary, broad-lanceolate, rather obtuse, striated, tapering to a long petiole. *Pseudobulbs* crowded, younger ones with 2 or more large, often reddish, scales, within which is a much larger sheathing scale, 3 to 4 in. long, tinged red. Philippines. (B.M. 4853.) var. **val'ida** has much broader l.

**D. latifo'lium.** Habit much as in *D. Cobbianum* but larger. *fl.* yellowish-green with a reddish bract. Rachis drooping with many distichously arranged flowers. Philippines.

**D. longifo'lium.** Near to *D. abbreviatum* in habit. *fl.* about ½ in. across or less, greenish-yellow; sep. attenuated; lip centre tinged with sepia. Rachis drooping with many sweet-scented *fl.* loosely distichously set. *l.* as in *D. abbreviatum* but broader. Sunda Is., Malaya.

**D. ru'fum.** *fl.* reddish-brown; scapes 6 in. long, many-fld. *l.* linear, acute, 10 in. long. *Pseudobulbs* tufted, ovate, ½ in. long. Habitat? 1898. Allied to *D. uncatum.*

**D. unca'tum.** *fl.* pale green; sep. and pet. acute; racemes drooping, shorter than in *D. filiforme* which it otherwise resembles. Malaya. 1897.

E. C.

*dendroi'deus -a -um,* tree-like.

*dendrol'ogi,* of trees.

**DENDROLOGY.** Natural history of trees.

**DENDROM'ECON** (*dendron*, tree; *mekon*, Poppy). FAM. *Papaveraceae.* A genus of 2 or, according to some botanists, 20 shrubs closely allied to Romneya, differing by the entire leaves and yellow poppy-like flowers. Though *D. rigidum* can be grown successfully and is well worth growing against a very sunny wall it will not withstand a severe winter. The soil must be thoroughly drained and should be a light loam with mortar rubble. It is propagated by cuttings. Mr. Bean reco nmends cuttings of three joints made of well-ripened, firm summer shoots, placed singly in small thumb pots of very sandy soil in moderate heat.

**D. rig'idum.*** Glaucous evergreen shrub up to 10 ft. in the wild, usually much less in England; shoots smooth, slender. *l.* rigid, ovate or narrow-lanceolate, 1 to 3 in. long, entire. *fl.* bright yellow, 2 to 3 in. across, solitary stalked, fragrant. California. 1854. (B.M. 5134.)

*dendromorph'us -a -um,* tree-like.

**DENDROPA'NAX** (*dendron*, tree, *Panax*; tree Panax). FAM. *Araliaceae.* A genus of about 20 species of unarmed trees or shrubs, natives of Trop. Asia and America, China, and Japan. Leaves simple, entire, rarely 3- or 5-cleft. Flowers in solitary or paniculate umbels; petals and stamens 5. For treatment, *see* **Polyscias.**

**D. arbor'eus.** 12 to 20 ft. h. *l.* simple, elliptic, 4 to 6 in. long, obscurely toothed. *fl.* pale yellow in terminal, simple corymbs; peduncles 1 to 2 in. long. July. W. Indies. SYN. *Aralia arborea, Hedera arborea.* Stove.

**D. argen'teus.** Stem somewhat fleshy, spotted. *l.* alternate, oblong, about 1 ft. long, silvery-white above, with greenish veins, purplish beneath; stalks long, stout. Brazil. 1878. Stove.

**D. japon'icus.** Glabrous, evergreen shrub to 10 or 12 ft. h. or a small tree. *l.* variable in shape and size, often 3-lobed and up to 8 in. long on the young plant, rarely on adults, where they are usually oval, ovate, or rhomboid, 2 to 5 in. long, entire; stalks up to 5 in. long. *fl.* small in solitary, terminal umbels about 1 in. wide or in clusters of 3 to 5; peduncles long. August. *fr.* oval, black, ribbed, about ⅓ in. long. Japan, China, Korea. Hardy in favourable localities but usually needing a cool greenhouse. SYN. *Hedera japonica.*

F. G. P.

*dendroph'ilus -a -um,* tree-loving.

**DENDROPHYL'AX** (*dendron*, a tree, *phulax*, defender; in allusion to the habit of the plants). FAM. *Orchidaceae.* A small genus of epiphytic, leafless or very fugitive-leaved Orchids, natives of the W. Indies, allied to Angraecum. Flowers solitary or few in a raceme; sepals and petals sub-equal, free, spreading; lip sessile at the base of the column, the base produced into a long spur, the lateral lobes short, the middle one 2-lobed; column very short, broad; scapes slender, simple. Roots densely fascicled resembling those of a Phalaenopsis, produced from a central crown like the simple racemes. Pseudo-bulbs wanting. The 2 species described are closely allied but sufficiently distinct horticulturally.

*D. funalis* has by some authorities been transferred to the genus Polyrrhiza. Because of their habit the plants are best grown on rafts or pieces of board surfaced with a thin layer of Cattleya compost. Water should be very infrequently given while the roots are inactive. The plants should be exposed to light in the autumn. A warm, moist atmosphere is always necessary, in winter about 65° F. at night.

**D. Faw'cettii.** *fl.* 2 in. across, several on a scape varying from 2 to 24 in. long; sep. and pet. greenish-white, lanceolate, acute; lip white, with a slender spur 7 in. long. Roots long, green. 1888. Closely allied to *D. funalis.*

**D. funa'lis.** *fl.* sep. and pet. greenish; lip white, ⅔ in. broad, about half as long as the subulate-filiform, straight-descending white spur; scapes distantly sheathed, few-fld., 1 to 4 in. long. Roots often several feet long. 1846. (B.M. 4295 as *Angraecum funale.*)

E. C.

**DENDROS'ERIS** (*dendron*, a tree, *seris*, a kind of endive; referring to its habit and form of leaves). FAM. *Compositae.* A genus of 7 species of small trees confined to the Island of Juan Fernandez. They are interesting because arborescent forms are rare in Compositae, huge as the family is. Two species have been introduced, the following and another called *D. micrantha*, which is now probably lost. *D. macrophylla* requires a warm greenhouse, and a compost of loam, peat, and sand suits it.

**D. macrophyl'la.*** Small evergreen tree, 10 to 12 ft. *l.* usually in a tuft terminating the branch, up to 1 ft. long, oblong to roundish, cordate or rounded at the base, shallowly toothed or lobed; stalk 3 to 6 in. long, partially clasping stem. *fl.-heads* 2½ in. across, bright orange-yellow, suggesting a huge dandelion, borne comparatively few in leafy panicles 6 to 8 in. long; florets very numerous. May. 1875. (B.M. 6353.)

W. J. B.

*Dene'vei,* in honour of Herr T. A. de Neve, 1881– Superintendent of Plantations in W. Borneo, *c.* 1924.

*Den'hamii,* in honour of Capt. Denham, leader of expedition to the South Seas, *c.* 1853.

*Denisia'nus -a -um,* in honour of Fernand Denis, French amateur orchid-grower, *c.* 1899.

**DENITRIFICATION** is the change brought about by certain soil bacteria which leads to the reduction of nitrates to nitrites, ammonia, or gaseous nitrogen which, passing into the air is lost to crops, since nitrates alone are the source from which most plants obtain their nitrogen. This change occurs when the soil contains insufficient air for the supply of oxygen to these soil bacteria, as when the soil is waterlogged, and during wet periods in winter, the remedy being efficient drainage. The term has also been applied to reduction of available nitrogen and consequent reduction of crops after heavy applications of fresh animal manures or the burying of green crops in green-manuring, but this is a misapplication of the term for here the nitrates are made use of to build up the bodies of the bacteria which increase in great numbers after such applications. In this instance the nitrogen of the nitrates appears to be converted into protein nitrogen and exists as such in the bacteria and the protozoa that feed upon them. It will be reconverted into nitrates if soil conditions are favourable (*see* **Nitrification**) when the food of the bacteria which attack carbohydrates, including cellulose, begins to fail, and is therefore not lost. The immediate consequences of this rapid increase in soil bacteria calling for readily available nitrogen may be met by adding nitrates or sulphate of ammonia. *See also* **Compost manures.**

*Dennis'ae,* in honour of Mrs. Dennis of Murngal who collected and introduced plants from Victoria.

**DENNSTAED'TIA** (from August Wilhelm Dennstedt, *c.* 1818, German botanist). FAM. *Polypodiaceae.* A genus of about 70 species related to Dicksonia with which they are frequently grouped, differing in that the indusia are cup-shaped, not 2-valved. For treatment *see* **Dicksonia.**

**D. adiantoi'des.** *rhiz.* creeping. *Fronds* 2-pinnate; lower pinnae 1 to 2 ft. long, 6 to 12 in. broad; pinnules linear, cut nearly to rachis; segs. oblong-rhomboidal, blunt, with 2 to 4 bluntish lobes in each side. *Sori* 2 to 8 to a seg. W. Indies. 1828. Stove. (H.S. 1, 26 B.)

**D. anthriscifo'lia.** Allied to *D. rubiginosa* but with segs. larger and more divided. Mascarene Is.

**D. cicuta'ria.** *rhiz.* creeping. *Fronds* 2-pinnate; lower pinnae 1 to 1½ ft. long, 6 in. broad; pinnules linear-acuminate, deeply cut; segs. oblong-deltoid, deeply inciso-pinnatifid. *Sori* 2 to 12 to a seg. W. Indies. Stove. SYN. *Dicksonia cicutaria.*

**D. cornu'ta.\*** *Fronds* somewhat rigid, bright green, 3-pinnate; lower pinnae 1 to 1½ ft. long, 6 to 9 in. broad; pinnules long and narrow, lower segs. with sharply toothed lobes, about 1 in. long and ½ in. broad. *Sori* 2 to 12 to a seg. at bottom of notches of lobes; indusium cup-shaped, nearly circular. Andes of Ecuador and Peru. Stove. SYN. *Dicksonia apiifolia, D. tenera* (of gardens), *Patania apiifolia.*

**D. cunea'ta.** *Fronds* sub-deltoid, 4-pinnatifid; pinnae lanceolate, 6 to 12 in. long; pinnules close, short-stalked, lanceolate, ½ in. broad; segs. oblong-rhomboidal, inciso-pinnatifid. *Sori* at base of ultimate sinuses. Philippines. Stove. (H.S. 1, 28 c.)

**D. davallioi'des.** *Fronds* 3-pinnate; lower pinnae 6 to 9 in. long, 3 to 4 in. broad; pinnules linear-acuminate, cut to rachis; segs. oblong-rhomboid, deeply inciso-pinnatifid. *Sori* 2 to 8 to a seg. Australia. Greenhouse. (L.F. 8, 41.) var. **Young'ii** has large fronds minutely divided.

**D. dissec'ta.** Allied to *D. cicutaria* but with barren segs. more wedge-shaped and serrate. Trop. America.

**D. ero'sa.** Allied to *D. cicutaria* but with larger pinnules with shallow lobes, hairy. Peru.

**D. flac'cida.** *Fronds* 3-pinnate; lower pinnae 9 to 15 in. long, 6 in. broad; pinnules lanceolate, cut to rachis; lower segs. ovate-rhomboid, bluntish, cut to rachis 3 or 4 times on each side, lobes again toothed. *Sori* 2 to 8 to a seg. Aneiteum, &c. Very closely allied to *D. rubiginosa.* Stove.

**D. inci'sa.** Allied to *D. cicutaria* but fronds more divided. Guadeloupe, Brazil.

**D. Matthews'ii.\*** *Fronds* 2-pinnate; lower pinnae more than 1 ft. long, nearly 2 in. broad, deeply cut in lower part only; lobes blunt, entire, broadly oblong-rhomboid, unequal-sided, and decurrent downwards. *Sori* 2 to 6 to a seg. Peru. SYN. *D. concinna.*

**D. molucca'na.** *Fronds* 3-pinnate; lower pinnae 1 to 1½ ft. long, 9 to 18 in. broad; pinnules linear-lanceolate, cut to rachis; lower segs. oblong-rhomboid, deeply cut, with blunt, oblong-deltoid lobes. *Sori* 2 to 12 to a seg. Main and secondary rachises prickly. Malaya, Formosa, Fiji. Stove. (L.F. 8, 46.) *D. scandens* is related to this species.

**D. punctilob'ula.** *Fronds* 1 to 1½ ft. long, 6 to 9 in. broad, lanceolate, 2-pinnate; lower pinnae lanceolate, 4 to 6 in. long, deeply cut; pinnules ovate-rhomboid, about ½ in. long, deeply pinnatifid. *Sori* 2 to 12 to a pinnule. N. America. 1811. Hardy. Pleasantly fragrant. SYN. *Dicksonia pilosiuscula.*

**D. rubigino'sa.** *Fronds* 3-pinnate; lower pinnae 1 to 1½ ft. long, 6 to 9 in. broad; pinnules linear, cut to rachis; lower segs. deltoid, or oblong-rhomboid, deeply inciso-pinnatifid. *Sori* 2 to 12 to a seg. Trop. America. Stove. (H.S. 1, 27; L.F. 8, 45.)

**D. scab'ra.** *rhiz.* wide-creeping. *sti.* about 1 ft. long, rough, very hairy below. *Fronds* triangular or hastate, 2-pinnate, 20 to 30 in. long, 6 in. to 2 ft. broad; lower pinnae hastate, 4 to 8 in. long, pinnules quite distinct, lower ones cut nearly to stalk into pinnatifid segs., hairy beneath. *Sori* 2 to 6 to lower segs.; indusium cup-shaped. China, Trop. Asia. Stove. (H.S. 1, 28.) SYN. *Patania scabra, Sitolobium strigosum* (of gardens).

**D. scan'dens.** See *D. moluccana.*

**D. ten'era.** Allied to *D. cicutaria* but of a more membranous texture. Trop. America.

**dens-canis,** dog's tooth.

**dens'us -a -um** (in compound words *densi-*), close, crowded.

**DENTA'RIA** (*dens,* tooth; in allusion to the fang-like roots). FAM. *Cruciferae.* A genus of about 30 species of perennial herbs, related to Cardamine and sometimes included in it, but distinct by the leaves being mostly crowded towards the top of the stem and the reddish flowers. Natives of north temperate regions. Rootstocks creeping, scaly. Stem erect. Leaves stalked, rarely basal, those on middle of stem alternate or whorled, palmately or pinnately cut. Flowers in a terminal raceme, pedicels very slender. These hardy plants are mostly easily grown in rich, light, moist soils, and in a shady situation, and are propagated by seeds or by careful root-division; some species also produce bulbils. There are several pleasant dwarf species yet to be introduced suitable for woodland.

**D. bulbif'era.** 1½ to 2 ft. h. *Stem-l.* alternate, pinnate, uppermost simple or nearly so, mostly with bulbils in their axils. *fl.* purple, large, few. April. Europe, including England. (E.B. 107.)

**D. califor'nica.** 6 to 24 in. h. *Stem-l.* 2 to 4, usually short-stalked; segs. 3 to 5 (rarely simple or lobed), short-stalked, ovate to lanceolate or linear, sometimes toothed. *fl.* rose or white. California, Oregon.

**D. digita'ta.** About 18 in. h. *Stem-l.* many, alternate, palmately 5-cut, lobes oblong-lanceolate, acute, coarsely toothed. *fl.* rich purple. May. S. Europe. 1659. (L.B.C. 757.)

**D. diphyl'la.** Rootstock not tuberous. 6 to 12 in. h. *Stem-l.* 2, alternate, lobes 3, ovate-lanceolate, coarsely unequally toothed; stalks short. *fl.* white within, purple without. N. America. 1810. (B.M. 1465.)

**D. enneaphyl'la.** About 12 in. h. *Stem-l.* 3, in a whorl, pinnatisect; lobes 3, ovate-lanceolate, acute or acuminate, coarsely crenately toothed. *fl.* pale yellowish; stamens as long as cor. May. Italy, Hungary.

**D. glandulo'sa.** About 12 in. h. *l.* 3 in a whorl, stalked; segs. 3, ovate-lanceolate, slender-pointed, toothed, glandular in axils. *fl.* purplish. May. Hungary. 1815.

**D. integrifo'lia califor'nica.** A synonym of *D. californica.*

**D. interme'dia.** *rhiz.* as in *D. pinnata* but with very short scales, somewhat convex and recurved at margin. *l.* of *D. digitata* but a little longer, more or less acute and concave. Cent. Europe.

**D. × Killes'ii** (*D. digitata* × *D. polyphylla*). More robust than either parent. Alps. 1889.

**D. lacinia'ta.** About 12 in. h. *l.* 3 in a whorl, on short stalks; lobes or segs. 3, linear, entire, or deeply toothed or jagged. *fl.* rose or almost white, large. April. N. America. 1823.

**D. macrocar'pa.** 4 to 15 in. h. *l.* 1 to 3, palmately 3- to 5-cut, segs. linear to oblong, entire. *fl.* rose or purple. Western N. America.

**D. max'ima.** About 15 in. h. *Stem-l.* 2 or 3, usually alternate; segs. 3, ovate or oblong-ovate, coarsely toothed, short-stalked. *fl.* purplish or white. Eastern U.S. America.

**D. pinna'ta.** About 12 in. h. *Stem-l.* alternate, stalked, pinnate; segs. oblong, slender-pointed, toothed. *fl.* white, or pale purple, large. May. Switzerland, &c. 1683. (G.F. 623.)

**D. × pinnato-digita'ta** (*D. digitata* × *D. pinnata*). *l.* pinnate. *fl.* like those of *D. digitata.* Intermediate between parents. Jura Mts. 1889.

**D. polyphyl'la.** About 12 in. h. *l.* 3 in a whorl or alternate, stalked, pinnate; segs. 7 or 9, rather close, lanceolate, slender-pointed, toothed. Hungary. 1817. (G.F. 171.)

**D. tenel'la.** About 9 in. h. *l.* 2, alternate, sessile; segs. 3, linear-elliptic, entire. *fl.* purple, about as large as those of *Cardamine pratensis.* N. America. 1826.

**denta'tus -a -um,** dentate, toothed with teeth directed outwards.

**denticula'tus -a -um,** minutely dentate.

**denuda'tus -a -um,** with a hairy or downy surface becoming naked.

**DEODAR.** *See* **Cedrus Deodara.**

**deo'rum,** of the gods.

**DEPAR'IA.** The ferns at one time grouped under this name have been distributed over several genera. For *Deparia Moorei* see **Tectaria Moorei.**

**deparioi'des,** resembling Deparia.

**depaupera'tus -a -um,** imperfectly developed.

**depen'dens,** dependent, hanging down.

**DEP'PEA** (in honour of M. Deppe, d. 1828, who collected and sent home many plants from Mexico). FAM. *Rubiaceae.* A genus of about 12 species of Mexican shrubs. Leaves opposite, stalked, membranous, ovate or lanceolate. Flowers yellow, small, in cymes; corolla rotate or shortly funnel-shaped. *D. erythrorhiza* is a shrubby greenhouse plant with a woody root and reddish inner bark. For cultivation, *see* **Bouvardia.**

**D. erythrorhi'za.** Shrub 1 to 3 ft. *l.* elliptic, narrowed at both ends, rather hairy above and on margins; stipules triangular, deciduous. *fl.* yellow, cymes terminal and axillary, stalked.

**DEPRESSA'RIA.** A genus of Tineid moths, the caterpillars of which feed almost exclusively on Umbelliferae and Compositae. Parsnips grown for seed are frequently attacked by the larvae of *D. heracliana* which spin the flower-clusters together and feed upon the flowers and seeds. *D. depressella* and *D. nervosa* are similarly destructive to carrots.

G. F. W.

***depres'sus -a -um,*** depressed, flattened as though by downward pressure.

**DEPTFORD PINK** *See* **Dianthus Armeria.**

**DERMATOBOT'RYS** (*derma, dermatos*, skin or bark, *botrys*, a cluster; referring to the position and arrangement of the flowers). FAM. *Scrophulariaceae*. The only species is a small, epiphytic, deciduous shrub, with a long naked stem as thick as the wrist, and brown, nearly square branches. It requires greenhouse treatment with dry, airy atmospheric conditions. Although epiphytic it grows well in a pot in a well-drained compost of turfy loam, fibrous peat, and sand. Cuttings root readily in a close case or under a bell-glass.

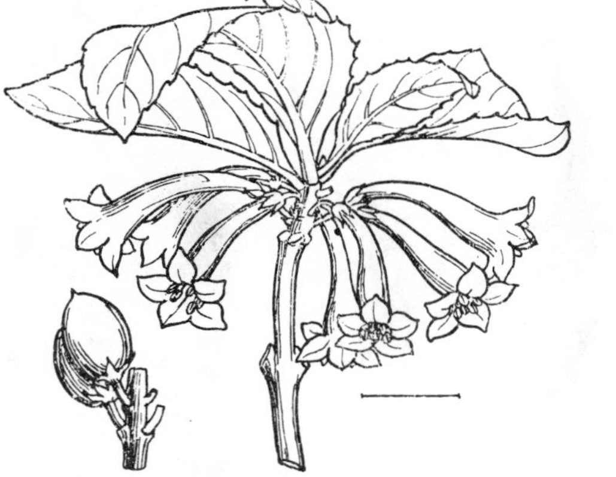

*Dermatobotrys Saundersii*

**D. Saunder'sii.** *l.* 2 to 6 in. long, rather fleshy, ovate or oblong, sub-acute, coarsely toothed. *fl.* 2 in. long, drooping in whorls below the new l.; cal. small, 5-parted; cor. pale red, tubular, gradually dilated from a slender base, the 5 short, spreading lobes, yellow within; anthers 5. Winter. Natal, Zululand. 1892. (B.M. 7369.)

**DERMATOGEN.** The superficial layer of cells at the growing point of root and stem which, by division, gives rise to the epidermis. In the stem the divisions of the cells of the dermatogen occur only at right angles to the external surface giving rise to a single layer of epidermal cells, while in the root there are also divisions parallel to the external surface resulting in a many-layered epidermis which is gradually shed except at the growing point where it persists as the root-cap.

**DERMATOPH'ORA.** Old name for the fungus *Rosellinia necatrix*. *See* **Vine Diseases, White Root Rot,** in Supplement.

**DER'RIS** (*derris*, a leathern covering, referring to the pod). FAM. *Leguminosae*. A genus of about 40 species of tall woody climbers, natives of the tropics related to Dalbergia and Lonchocarpus. Leaves unequally pinnate, the odd one distant, without stipels or tendrils. Flowers papilionaceous, violet, purple, or white (not yellow), standard rounded. Pod indehiscent, with 1 or more seeds. Need stove conditions, but of little horticultural merit. Of value as a source of an effective insecticide made from the powdered tuberous root. *See* **Fish-poison Plants.**

**D. ellip'tica.** Woody evergreen climber to over 50 ft., at first rusty-hairy. *l.* about 6 in. long, stalked; lflets. 11 to 13, elliptic-ovate, terminal obovate, 1¼ to 2½ in. long, hairy on veins. *fl.* in axillary racemes about 5 in. long, with 4 to 9 fl. at each node, pedicels about ½ in. long; standard white, tinged pink, nearly round, ½ in. long; wings pink, rather shorter; keel about ½ in. long. *Pod* about 1¾ in. long. Burma to New S. Wales. (B.M. 8530 as *D. oligosperma*.)

**descending,** directed downwards.

**DESCHAMP'SIA** (in honour of Dr. Deschamps, of St. Omer, naturalist on expedition in search of Lapeyrouse). FAM. *Gramineae*. A genus of about 20 species of perennial tufted grasses natives of the cooler parts of the N. Hemisphere. Stem slender. Panicle loose or narrow; spikelets shining, 2-flowered. The 2 species grown for ornament are raised from seed and succeed in any good ordinary soil in moist shady places. The dried inflorescences are useful for winter decoration. Allied to Aira and sometimes included in that genus.

**D. caespito'sa.** Making large dense tufts. Stem up to 3 ft. mostly smooth. *l.* flat, about ⅛ in. wide, nerves roughly hairy, ligule ⅓ in. long, acute. *Panicle* pyramidal, about 6 in. long, with horizontal slender branches, basal branches several; spikelets about ⅛ in. long. June, July. N. Hemisphere (including Britain), Tasmania, New Zealand. (E.B. 1730 as *Aira caespitosa*.)

**D. flexuo'sa.** Loosely tufted, about 18 in. h. Stem smooth. *l.* roundish, about $\frac{1}{25}$ in. long. *Panicle* about 6 in. long, ovate, with 2 basal branches; spikelets about ⅛ in. long. June, July. Widely distributed, including Britain. (E.B. 1732 as *Aira flexuosa*.)

***descis'cens,*** degenerate.

***deserto'rum,*** of the deserts.

**DESFONTAIN'EA** (in honour of R. L. Desfontaines, 1752–1833, French botanist). FAM. *Loganiaceae*. A monotypic genus in the Andes of Chile. An evergreen opposite-leaved shrub. Flower with 5-lobed calyx, corolla funnel-shaped with 5 shallow lobes, anthers almost sessile at base of corolla lobes. Fruit many-seeded. Hardy in favoured districts, especially in the west. Propagated by seed which is the best way, or by tip cuttings about 3 in. long in August in warm sand frame. Moist half-shade suits the young plants.

**D. spino'sa.** Evergreen shrub up to 10 ft. but usually smaller; branches pale, shining. *l.* holly-like, opposite, 1 to 2½ in. long, oval or ovate, shining dark green, margin spiny, stalk ⅛ in. long. *fl.* crimson-scarlet with 5 shallow yellow lobes; cor. 1½ in. long; cal. green, its oblong lobes ciliate. Summer. Chile, Peru. 1843. (B.M. 4781.) SYN. *D. Hookeri*.

**DESMAN'THUS** (*desme*, bundle, *anthos*, flower; the flowers are collected in bundles or spikes). FAM. *Leguminosae*. A genus of about 10 species of sub-shrubby herbs or shrubs, natives of sub-tropical N. America, one in Madagascar, related to Mimosa. Leaves 2-pinnate; leaflets small; stipules setaceous, persistent. Flowers all hermaphrodite; calyx bell-shaped, shortly dentate; petals free or slightly joined, valvate; stamens twice as many as petals, anthers without a gland. They need greenhouse treatment and a compost such as suits Mimosa.

**D. brachylo'bus.** Glabrous or nearly so. Stem erect, angled, striate. *lflets.* in 6 to 15 pairs, lower or all glandular. *fl.* small, greenish-white, with 5 pet., 5 stamens. *Pods* wide, falcate, 2- to 6-seeded. United States. Half-hardy.

**DESMAZE'RIA** (in honour of Jean Baptiste Joseph Henri Desmazières, 1796–1862, French botanist). FAM. *Gramineae*. A small genus of Mediterranean and S. African grasses with spike-like panicles of several densely arranged, flattened, many-flowered spikelets, without awns. *D. sicula* is useful for edging and the inflorescence (treated as is that of Briza) for winter ornament. Cultivation as for Briza. **A**

**D. sic'ula.** Annual, tufted, about 8 to 12 in. h. *Spikelets* about ½ in. long, in a nearly simple spike. Summer. Sicily.

***Desmetia'nus -a -um,*** in honour of M. De Smet, nurseryman of Ghent, Belgium.

**DESMO'DIUM** (*desmos*, band, the stamens being joined). FAM. *Leguminosae*. A genus of about 150 species of mostly suffruticose herbs or sub-shrubs distributed over all warm parts of the world, the N. American species being herbaceous perennials. Leaves 3-foliolate, pinnate, with 2 stipels at base of terminal and 1 at base of each lateral leaflet. Flowers papilionaceous, purple, blue, rose, or white in terminal (or lateral), usually loose, racemes; stamens joined; fruit a lomentum. Temperature requirements variable, soil well drained.

**D. canaden'se.** Erect herb, stem rather hairy and striate, 2 to 4 ft. h. *lflets.* 3, oblong-lanceolate, nearly glabrous. *fl.* red-purple. *infl.* racemose or paniculate. July. N. America. 1640. (B.M. 3553.) Hardy.

**D. gy'rans.** Telegraph Plant. Annual, 1 to 3 ft. h. *lflets.* 3, elliptic-oblong, terminal very large, lateral very small. *fl.* violet. *infl.* a many-branched panicle. July. E. Indies. 1795. Stove. At temperature above 72° F. in the day-time the lateral lflets. move steadily round in an elliptical orbit; at night the l. droop downwards. The meaning of the diurnal movement is not known.

**D. penduliflo'rum.** A synonym of *Lespedeza Thunbergii.*

**D. spica'tum.** Deciduous shrub up to 6 or 8 ft., laxly branched, shoots hairy, ribbed. *lflets.* 3, middle one roundish-obovate, up to 2 in. long; side ones smaller, obliquely ovate; all covered beneath with thick, soft, grey down. *fl.* rosy carmine, ⅝ in. long, in terminal spikes up to 6 in. long and in whorls of 6 or 8. September, October. *Pod* curved, 2 in. long, 4- to 6-seeded. China. 1896. (B.M. 8805 as *D. cinerascens.*) Hardy.

**D. tiliifo'lium.** Deciduous shrub sending up each season erect stems 3 to 5 ft. h. from a woody rootstock. *lflets.* 3, central one broadly obovate, 2 to 4 in. long, side ones ovate, smaller. Panicles 8 to 12 in. h. *fl.* ½ in. long, pale lilac to dark pink. August to October. *Pod* 2 to 3 in. long 6- to 9-seeded. Himalaya. 1879. Hardy.

W. J. B.

**DESMON'CUS** (*desmos*, band, *ogkus*, hook; the ribs of the leaves end in a hook-like tip). FAM. *Palmaceae.* A genus of about 65 species of climbing Palms with reed-like stems and hooks as in Calamus, all natives of Trop. America. Leaves pinnate, prickly. Flowers on a branched spike from the leaf-axils. When young these are handsome plants for table decoration; when too large for that purpose a pillar or rafter of the stove may be devoted to them to advantage and there they will provide pleasing shade. For treatment, *see* **Calamus.**

**D. hor'ridus.** Stem prickly. *l.* segs. in about 20 pairs, linear, slender-pointed; rachis prickly, covered with a blackish deciduous tomentum. *Spathe* covered with brown prickles. Trinidad.

**D. ma'jor.** A synonym of *D. horridus.*

**D. mi'tis.** Stem 3 to 5 ft., flexuous, unarmed. *l.* about 2 ft. long, loosely distichous, with a long sheath; segs. in 7 to 11 pairs, lanceolate, slender-pointed, opposite or alternate, about 5 in. long, 1¼ in. wide. *Spadix* slender. Brazil.

**D. orthacan'thos.** Stem and leaf sheaths prickly. *l.* with long sheaths; segs. elliptic-lanceolate, 6 in. long, 1¼ in. wide, sometimes with scattered prickles. *Spadix* about 1 ft. long, long-stalked; lower spathe long, smooth, upper armed with straight black prickles. Brazil.

**D. polyacan'thos.** *l.* remote, 3 to 4 ft. long with a very long sheath, tubercled or prickly near stalk; segs. in 7 to 15 pairs, broadly lanceolate, slender-pointed, about 6 in. long. *Spadix* 12 to 16 in. long; spathe double, inner densely prickly. Brazil.

***desquama'tus -a -um,*** without scales.

***Desvaux'ii,*** in honour of Étienne Émile Desvaux, 1830–54, writer on Chilean grasses and sedges.

***deter'gens,*** delaying.

***deton'sus -a -um,*** bare.

***detor'tus -a -um,*** twisted or bent aside.

***deus'tus -a -um,*** burned.

**DEUTEROMY'CES.** A name sometimes used for the Fungi Imperfecti (q.v.).

**DEUTZ'IA** (after Johann van der Deutz, 1743–88?, friend and patron of Thunberg, who founded the genus). FAM. *Saxifragaceae.* It consists of some 50 species of shrubs, those in cultivation all deciduous, the majority 5 to 8 ft. high. Most of them are natives of China, but others come from Japan, the Himalaya, Formosa, &c. Two species are found in Mexico. Bark usually brown and ultimately peeling. Leaves opposite, shortly stalked, finely toothed, pointed. Flowers mostly white, pink, or purplish, borne in corymbs or panicles (rarely racemes). Stamens 10, whose stalks are curiously flattened and winged, often forming a notch at the top in which the anthers are seated. Another feature of the Deutzias is their production on the leaves (and often on the flowers) of tiny, flattened, star-like hairs, the number of 'rays' on each hair varying from 3 to 10 and affording useful differentiating characters. As a strong lens is required for their proper examination they are omitted from the following descriptions.

Most of the species are quite hardy, but no group of shrubs suffers more than this from late spring frosts in low-lying localities. They like a good loamy soil and plenty of moisture. The best time for pruning them is just after the flowering season. It should consist in the removal of old, worn-out or overcrowded growths. No systematic shortening back can be done except at the expense of the following season's blossom. Some species, especially *D. gracilis*, are admirable for forcing early into bloom. Propagation is most readily accomplished by means of cuttings of half-ripened shoots put in gentle bottom heat in July or August, or by more fully ripened shoots under a handlight in a shady place.

The genus has been extensively hybridized and very many beautiful garden shrubs produced thereby.

KEY

| | | |
|---|---|---|
| 1. | *Margins of pet. touching only in bud* | 2 |
| 1. | *Margins of pet. overlapping in bud* | 24 |
| 2. | *Infl. 1- to 3-fld.* | D. grandiflora |
| 2. | *Infl. several-fld.* | 3 |
| 3. | *Infl. paniculate or racemose* | 4 |
| 3. | *Infl. corymbose or cymose* | 13 |
| 4. | *Filaments, or some of them, awl-shaped* | 5 |
| 4. | *Filaments winged, and toothed near top* | 8 |
| 5. | *Fl. pinkish outside* | D. × rosea |
| 5. | *Fl. white* | 6 |
| 6. | *Panicles wide and loose* | D. Sieboldiana |
| 6. | *Panicles narrow* | 7 |
| 7. | *Lvs. finely toothed, green beneath, l.-stalks ⅛ to ¼ in. long* | D. taiwanensis |
| 7. | *Lvs. often nearly entire, greyish beneath, l.-stalks ¼ to ⅝ in. long* | D. pulchra |
| 8. | *Lvs. glabrous beneath, or nearly so* | 9 |
| 8. | *Lvs. with starry hairs beneath* | 10 |
| 9. | *Fl. white* | D. gracilis |
| 9. | *Fl. pinkish outside* | D. × rosea |
| 10. | *Cal. teeth about as long as tube* | D. × magnifica |
| 10. | *Cal. teeth shorter than tube* | 11 |
| 11. | *Panicle broad and loose, lvs. sharply toothed* | D. Schneideriana |
| 11. | *Panicle narrow* | 12 |
| 12. | *Lvs. green beneath, teeth somewhat rounded* | D. scabra |
| 12. | *Lvs. white beneath, sharply serrate* | D. hypoleuca |
| 13. | *Fl. white* | 14 |
| 13. | *Fl. pinkish or purplish without* | 22 |
| 14. | *Cal. teeth shorter than tube* | 15 |
| 14. | *Cal. teeth as long as, or longer than, tube* | 17 |
| 15. | *Styles 3 or 4, equalling stamens, lvs. ½ to ¾ in. long, whitish beneath* | D. Monbeigii |
| 15. | *Styles shorter than stamens* | 16 |
| 16. | *Styles 3, lvs. ⅘ to 3 in. long* | D. setchuenensis |
| 16. | *Styles 4 or 5, lvs. ⅗ to 1 in. long, greyish beneath* | D. Rehderiana |
| 17. | *Inner filaments linear-oblong, longer than anthers* | D. glomeruliflora |
| 17. | *Inner filaments 2-toothed near apex* | 18 |
| 18. | *Corymb large, loose, pedicels about ⅜ in. long* | D. Vilmorinae |
| 18. | *Corymb dense, pedicels about ⅕ in. long* | 19 |
| 19. | *Margins of pet. reflexed* | D. reflexa |
| 19. | *Margins of pet. not reflexed* | 20 |
| 20. | *Lvs. wedge-shaped at base* | 21 |
| 20. | *Lvs. rounded at base* | D. staminea |
| 21. | *Veins of lvs. bristly beneath; shrub 12 to 15 ft.* | D. longifolia Farreri |
| 21. | *Lvs. with star-shaped hairs only beneath* | D. discolor |
| 22. | *Anthers at ends of filaments* | D. × elegantissima |
| 22. | *Anthers on face of filaments* | 23 |
| 23. | *Lvs. green beneath* | D. purpurascens |
| 23. | *Lvs. greyish or whitish beneath* | D. longifolia |
| 24. | *Lvs. softly hairy beneath with spreading hairs* | 25 |
| 24. | *Lvs. with star-shaped hairs or glabrous beneath* | 26 |
| 25. | *Filaments awl-shaped* | D. mollis |
| 25. | *Filaments abruptly contracted below tip* | D. Wilsonii |
| 26. | *Lvs. glabrous and glaucous beneath* | D. hypoglauca |
| 26. | *Lvs. green beneath* | 27 |
| 27. | *Infl. corymbose* | 28 |
| 27. | *Infl. paniculate* | 30 |
| 28. | *Shoots glabrous or nearly so, teeth of leaf rounded* | D. corymbosa |
| 28. | *Shoots with scattered hairs, teeth of leaf spreading* | 29 |
| 29. | *Lvs. wedge-shaped at base; fl. pinkish in bud, ⅓ in. across* | D. compacta |
| 29. | *Lvs. rounded at base; fl. white, ½ in. across* | D. parviflora |
| 30. | *Fls. white* | D. × Lemoinei |
| 30. | *Fl. pinkish outside* | 31 |
| 31. | *Fl. about ⅝ in. across, infl. many-fld.* | D. × multiflora |
| 31. | *Fl. about 1¼ in. across, infl. 7- to 15-fld.* | D. × kalmiiflora |

**D. al'bida.** A synonym of *D. longifolia Farreri.*

**D. compac'ta.** Shrub to 6 ft., shoots soon glabrous. *l.* 2½ in. long, 1 in. wide, lanceolate to ovate-lanceolate, usually rounded at base, apex long, tapered, minutely toothed, dark dull green above, grey-green beneath with minute starry hairs. *fl.* white, ⅓ in. wide, closely packed in clusters 2 in. across; pet. roundish; cal. lobes broadly ovate. July. China. 1905. (B.M. 8795.)

**D. corymbiflo'ra.** A variety of *D. setchuenensis.*

**D. corymbo'sa.** Vigorous shrub up to 9 ft. *l.* 2 to 5 in. long, ovate, long- and taper-pointed, base rounded or widely cuneate; minutely starry-scaly beneath. *fl.* fragrant, ⅝ in. wide, pure white, densely packed in a corymb or panicle 2 or 3 in. across; pet. roundish-ovate, overlapping; anthers large and conspicuous. June to August. Himalaya. 1830. (B.R. 26, 5.)

**D. crena'ta.** A synonym of *D. scabra.* var. **taiwanen'sis,** a synonym of *D. taiwanensis.*

**D. dis'color.** Shrub 4 to 6 ft. *l.* narrowly ovate-oblong, 1½ to 4½ in. long, rough and dull green above, grey beneath with minute starry scurf. Corymbs 3 in. across. *fl.* numerous, ½ to 1 in. wide, white; cal. lobes lanceolate, scurfy; pet. oval. June. China. 1901. var. **ma'jor,*** *fl.* fully 1 in. wide, rose-tinted especially outside (B.T.S. 1, 482), often confused with *D. longifolia,* but differs by having no simple hairs beneath the l.; **purpuras'cens,** a synonym of *D. purpurascens.*

**D. dumic'ola.** A synonym of *D. Rehderiana.*

**D. glomeruliflo'ra.** Shrub up to 6 ft. with arching branches, shoots starry-downy, finally peeling. *l.* 1½ to 3 in. long, slender-pointed, finely toothed, usually rounded at base, starry-downy above; softly downy beneath with both starry and simple hairs. *fl.* white, ¾ in. wide, densely borne in rounded clusters 2 in. across; pet. oval; cal. grey with down, teeth awl-shaped, purple. May, June. China. 1908.

**D. grac'ilis.** Shrub 3 or 4 ft. *l.* 1½ to 3 in. long, slender-pointed, sharply toothed, starry-downy above, glabrous or nearly so beneath. *fl.* pure white, ⅝ to ¾ in. wide, in erect racemes or panicles up to 3½ in. long; pet. obovate; cal. slightly scaly and with small triangular lobes. June. Japan. 1840. Much used for forcing early into fl. var. **au'rea,** *l.* yellow; **marmora'ta,** *l.* spotted yellow. (For hybrids *see* **D. × rosea.**)

**D. grandiflo'ra.** Shrub up to 6 ft., shoots grey with down. *l.* 1 to 2½ in. long, ovate, pointed, rough above, white beneath with close, starry down. *fl.* white, 1 to 1¼ in. wide, borne singly, in twos, or threes; pet. oblong; cal. with linear-lanceolate lobes. April, May. China. 1910. Blossoms earliest in the genus and has the largest but fewest fl.

**D. hypoglau'ca.*** Shrub up to 8 ft., stems erect, shoots glabrous. *l.* 1½ to 3 in. long, ovate to ovate-lanceolate, finely toothed, green and sprinkled with starry hairs above, glaucous and glabrous beneath. *fl.* ¾ in. wide, pure white, in a rounded cluster 3 or 4 in. wide; pet. obovate; cal. ⅛ in. long, cup-shaped and with 5 triangular lobes. June. China. 1910. Distinct by the glaucous l. glabrous beneath. (B.M. 9362.)

**D. hypoleu'ca.** Shrub 5 to 6 ft., shoots slender, starry-downy. *l.* 1½ to 3½ in. long, narrowly ovate-lanceolate, slender-pointed, inconspicuously toothed, covered with a white, very close down beneath. *fl.* white, ¾ in. wide, in erect panicles 2 to 3½ in. long. May. Japan. 1915. Akin to *D. scabra* but distinguished by the white under surface of the l.

**D. × kalmiiflo'ra** (*D. parviflora × D. purpurascens*). Graceful shrub, 5 or 6 ft., with arching branches. *l.* ovate-oblong to ovate-lanceolate, 1½ to 4 in. long, broadly cuneate at the base. *fl.* white inside, carmine outside, borne in clusters of up to 12. June.

**D. × Lemoin'ei** (*D. gracilis × D. parviflora*). Shrub up to 6 ft., shoots glabrous or nearly so. *l.* lanceolate, 1½ to 4 in. long, sharply toothed, long-pointed. *fl.* pure white, ⅝ in. wide, borne in erect pyramidal panicles, 2 to 4 in. h. May, June. Raised at Nancy. 1891. Valued for forcing into bloom early. **Boule de neige** belongs here with dense corymbs of larger fl.

**D. longifo'lia.** Shrub 6 to 8 ft. *l.* narrowly oval-lanceolate, 2 to 5 in. long, slender-pointed, finely toothed, whitish beneath with a felt of starry and simple hairs. Corymbs 2 to 3 in. long, and wide. *fl.* 1 in. across, pale purplish-rose in bud, becoming paler when open. June. China. 1905. (B.M. 8493.) var. **Far'reri,** *fl.* white, styles usually 4 or 5, distinct. China. 1914. (B.M. 9532.) SYN. *D. albida* of gardens, not of Batalin. The tallest of cultivated Deutzias; **Veitch'ii,*** *fl.* larger, rich rose.

**D. longipet'ala.** *See* **D. magnifica longipetala.**

**D. × magnif'ica*** (*D. scabra × D. Vilmorinae*). Shrub 6 to 8 ft. *l.* ovate-oblong, 1½ to 3½ in. long, rough above, greyish with starry down beneath. *fl.* packed in erect panicles 3 in. or more h., white, double. June, July. Raised at Nancy about 1906. var. **latiflo'ra,** *fl.* 1½ in. wide, single; **longipet'ala,** *fl.* single, pet. milk-white, long and narrow, fimbriate.

**D. mol'lis.** Shrub 5 to 6 ft., shoots red-brown, starry-downy when young. *l.* 2 to 4½ in. long, lanceolate, oval or broadly ovate, slenderly pointed, finely toothed, dull green and rough with starry hairs above, grey and softly felted beneath. Corymbs 2 to 3½ in. across. *fl.* white, ½ in. wide; pet. broadly obovate, with starry hairs outside. June. China. 1901. (B.M. 8559.) Distinct by the dense, soft down beneath the l.

**D. Monbeig'ii.** Shrub 4 to 6 ft.; shoots slender, red-brown, starry-scaly. *l.* ovate-lanceolate, ½ to 1 in. long, half or less than half as wide, quite minutely toothed, white and quite covered beneath with starry hairs, much more thinly above. *fl.* white in corymbs of 7 to 15; pet. ⅜ in. long, ⅛ in. wide; cal. with 5 triangular lobes. May, June. China. 1921. (J.R.H.S. 59, f. 151; B.M. n.s. 123.)

**D. parviflo'ra.** Erect shrub up to 6 ft. *l.* ovate to ovate-lanceolate, 2 to 4 in. long, sharply toothed, dull green sprinkled with minute starry down above, brighter green and almost glabrous beneath. *fl.* white, ½ in. wide, in corymbs 2 to 3 in. across. June. China. 1883. (G.C. 14 (1893), 153.)

**D. pul'chra.*** Shrub up to 8 ft. or more, shoots minutely scaly. *l.* 1½ to 4 in. long, half as wide, narrowly ovate to lanceolate, remotely and minutely toothed, scaly on both surfaces but much more densely beneath. *Panicle* 2 to 4 in. long (occasionally up to 7 in. by 2 in.). *fl.* pendulous, white, tinged pink; pet. narrowly oblong, pointed, nearly ½ in. long, ⅛ in. wide. May, June. Formosa. 1918. (B.M. 8962.) One of the very finest species.

**D. purpuras'cens.** Shrub 6 to 8 ft., branches slender. *l.* ovate to ovate-lanceolate, 2 to 4 in. long, slender-pointed, unevenly toothed, starry-scurfy on both surfaces. Corymbs rounded, 2 in. wide. *fl.* ¾ in. across, with the roundish-ovate pet. purplish outside, like the sep. and fl.-stalks. June. China. 1888. (B.M. 7708 as *D. discolor purpurascens.*)

**D. reflex'a.** Shrub 3 ft. or more, shoots glabrous. *l.* 2 to 4 in. long, oval-lanceolate, cuneate, slender-pointed, with simple hairs along midrib and veins. *fl.* white, ⅝ in. across, densely clustered in corymbose panicles 2½ in. wide; pet. reflexed at margins. May, June. China. 1901.

**D. Rehderia'na.** Shrub up to 6 ft. of close, bushy growth, shoots slender, densely covered with starry down. *l.* ½ to 1¼ in. long, half as wide, ovate to ovate-lanceolate, rounded at base, minutely toothed, dull green and rough above, starry-scaly on both surfaces. *fl.* white, 1 in. wide, borne 3 to 5 together at end of short axillary leafy twigs. April, May. China. 1913. SYN. *D. dumicola.* Resembles *D. Monbeigii* in its small l., but in that species they are tapered at the base and white beneath.

**D. × ro'sea** (*D. gracilis × D. purpurascens*). Compact shrub with arching branches. *l.* ovate-lanceolate to ovate-oblong, sharply toothed. *fl.* widely bell-shaped, ¾ in. wide, soft rose. Raised at Nancy about 1896. (B.M. n.s. 189.) var. **campanula'ta** has white *fl.* with purplish sep. and broader pet.; **carmin'ea,** *fl.* purplish outside, sep. purplish; **exim'ia,** *fl.* pinkish outside, sep. purplish; **grandiflo'ra,** large *fl.* glossy white, suffused pink (not to be confused with the few-fld. Chinese species).

**D. scab'ra.*** Shrub up to 8 or 10 ft. Stems erect, bark brown, peeling. *l.* 2 to 4 in. long, ovate to ovate-lanceolate, base rounded or cordate on barren shoots, starry-scurfy on both surfaces. *Panicles* erect, 3 to 6 in. long. *fl.* white or pinkish outside, ½ to ¾ in. wide; pet. oblong, pointed. June, July. Japan, China. 1822. (B.M. 3838.) SYN. *D. crenata.* var. **candidis'sima,** *fl.* double, pure white; **macroceph'ala,*** *panicles* very fine; **ple'na,** *fl.* double, suffused with rose-purple outside (**Pride of Rochester** belongs here); **puncta'ta,** *fl.* single, pure white, *l.* spotted white; **Wate'reri,*** *fl.* 1 in. wide, rosy outside.

**D. Schneideria'na.** Shrub 6 to 8 ft. *l.* 1½ to 4 in. long, ovate to lanceolate, slender-pointed, minutely and sharply toothed, sprinkled above with starry hairs, greyish-white beneath and with simple hairs near midrib and veins. *Panicles* 1½ to 2½ in. long. *fl.* white, ¾ in. across; pet. narrowly oblong; downy outside. June. China. 1907. Akin to *D. scabra* but with a broader, looser panicle.

**D. setchuenen'sis.** Shrub to 6 ft., year-old bark, brown, peeling. *l.* 2 to 3½ in. long, oval-lanceolate, finely toothed, starry-downy, especially beneath. Corymbs 2 to 3 in. across. *fl.* white, ½ in. wide, with ovate pet. and triangularly toothed persistent cal. June, July. China. 1895. var. **corymbiflo'ra,*** corymbs wider, up to 4 in.; *fl.* ⅝ in. across. (B.M. 8255.)

**D. Sieboldia'na.** Shrub 3 or 4 ft., shoots starry-downy. *l.* 1½ to 3 in. long, ⅝ to 1¼ in. wide, ovate or oval, sharply toothed, dull green, starry-downy on both surfaces. *Panicles* broadly pyramidal, 3 in. long, 2 in. across. *fl.* pure white, ½ in. wide; pet. ovate; cal. lobes triangular, pointed, downy. June. Japan. 1885. (B.T.S.I. 487.)

**D. stamin'ea.** Shrub 4 to 5 ft., shoots roughened with star-like scales. *l.* 1 to 2½ in. long, ½ to 1½ in. wide, ovate, long- and slender-pointed, mostly rounded at base, unevenly toothed, dull green and rough above, grey and densely scaly beneath. Corymbs 2 in. across. *fl.* ½ to ⅝ in. wide, white. June. Himalaya. 1841. (B.R. 33.13, and 26.5 as *D. corymbosa.*) Rather tender.

**D. taiwanen'sis.** Shrub up to 6 ft. or more, shoots slender, downy. *l.* 2 to 4 in. long, not quite half as wide, ovate to ovate-lanceolate, finely toothed. *Panicles* slender, 3 to 5 in. long. *fl.* white; pet. ⅜ in. long, ⅛ in. wide; cal. cup-shaped with short triangular teeth, scaly. June. Formosa. 1918. SYN. *D. crenata taiwanensis.*

**D. Vilmorin'ae.*** Shrub 6 to 8 ft., shoots scurfy at first, then brown and glossy. *l.* 2 to 5 in. long, oblong-lanceolate, base rounded, apex slender-pointed, closely grey-felted beneath and with simple hairs on veins. *fl.* white, 1 in. wide, in corymbose panicles 3 in. across. June. China. 1905. (R.H. 1905, 266, 267.)

**D. Wilson'ii.** Shrub 4 to 6 ft., shoots dark reddish-brown, bark soon peeling. *l.* 2 to 5 in. long, ovate-oblong to oblong-lanceolate, rough with starry hairs on both surfaces; bristly hairy on veins beneath. *fl.* white, 1 in. wide, in corymbose panicles 3 to 4 in.

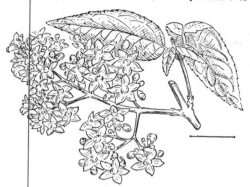

*Deutzia setchuenensis* (p. 664)

across. June. China. 1901. (B.M. 8083.) It has been suggested that it may be a natural hybrid (*D. discolor* × *D. mollis*).

W. J. B.

**Devansaya'nus -a -um,** in honour of M. A. de la Devansaye, amateur of Orchids, President of Horticultural Society of Maine et Loire, *c.* 1886.

**DEVIL-IN-THE-BUSH.** *See* **Nigella.**

**DEVIL'S APPLES.** *See* **Mandragora officinalis.**

**DEVIL'S BIT.** *See* **Scabiosa Succisa.** **A**

**DEVIL'S COACH HORSE** (*Ocypus olens*). This Rove Beetle is the largest British member of the family Staphylinidae, which possesses very short wing-cases resembling the shortened fore-wings of Earwigs. This beetle has the family habit of curling the end of its body

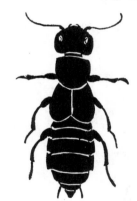

*Devil's Coach Horse Beetle*

over the back in a threatening manner, but is devoid of any sting. Both the grub, which is found in the ground, and the adult beetle feed on soil-inhabiting insects and similar creatures, and are beneficial. **A**

G. F. W.

**DEVIL'S FIG.** *See* **Argemone mexicana.**

**DEVIL'S HERB.** *See* **Plumbago scandens.**

**DEVIL'S LEAF.** *See* **Urtica spatulata.** **A**

**Devonien'sis -is -e,** in honour of Wm. G. Spencer Cavendish, Duke of Devonshire.

**Devosia'nus -a -um,** in honour of M. Devos, who collected for Messrs. Verschaffelt in Brazil.

**Devriesea'nus -a -um,** in honour of W. H. de Vriese, 1806–62, Dutch botanist.

**Devriesia'nus -a um,** in honour of Hugo de Vries, 1848–1935, Professor of Botany, Amsterdam.

**A→**

**DEWBERRY.** *See* **Rubus caesius.**

**DEXTRIN, DEXTROSE.** Dextrin ($C_6H_{10}O_5$) is one of the products of the action of diastase upon starch (*see* **Carbohydrates**), soluble but not crystallizable; dextrose ($C_6H_{12}O_6$) is formed by the action of an enzyme on cane-sugar, the other product being laevulose, another sugar, both soluble and crystallizable.

**DHAK.** *See* **Butea frondosa.**

**DHAL.** *See* **Cajanus.**

**di-, dis-,** a prefix indicating 2, as *dimorphus*, of 2 forms.

**dia-,** a prefix indicating through.

**diabol'icus -a -um,** slandrous or devilish.

**DIACAL'PE** (*dia*, through, *calpis*, an urn; in reference to the position of the sporangia). FAM. *Polypodiaceae.* A single species, native of Trop. Asia, constitutes this genus. Indusium inferior, globose, hard-membranous, entire, at length bursting irregularly at the top. Sporangia numerous, nearly sessile. Sori globose, receptacle small, scarcely elevated. *D. aspidioides* needs stove treatment. For cultivation, *see* **Ferns.**

**D. aspidioi'des.** *Fronds* 3-pinnate, rather thin, often hairy at first; pinnules oblong-cuneate, lobed, more or less decurrent. Trop. Asia. (B.C.F. 1, 180.)

**D. foenicula'cea.** A synonym of *Lithostegia foeniculacea.*

**DIACATT'LEYA.** Hybrids between Diacrium and Cattleya.

**diac'ritus -a -um,** distinguished.

**DIAC'RIUM** (*dia*, through, *akris*, a point; in allusion to the sheaths on the stalk). FAM. *Orchidaceae.* Of this genus, often included in Epidendrum but differing in the positions of the lip, 4 species have been described: they are epiphytic Orchids, natives of Mexico, Cent. America, and Guiana. Flowers showy, loosely racemose, shortly pedicellate; sepals sub-equal, free, spreading, rather thick, petaloid; petals somewhat similar; lip spreading from the base of the column, nearly equalling the sepals, the lateral lobes spreading or reflexed, the disk elevated between the lateral lobes, 2-horned above; column short and broad, slightly incurved; pollen masses 4; peduncle terminal, simple, with paleaceous sheaths. Cultivation should be as for Cattleyas, but the winter temperature should never fall below 60° F. Exposure to light is necessary in the autumn. As the pseudobulbs are hollow, of hard texture, and the leaves are leathery, light shading only should be used and a decided rest given.

**D. bicornu'tum.** *fl.* fragrant, 2 in. or more across; sep. and pet. pure white; the 3-lobed lip white, spotted with purple, crest yellow; spikes 9 to 18 in. long, terminal, 3- to 15-fld. *Pseudobulbs* 6 to 12 in. h., cylindric, stout, hollow, crowned with 3 or 4 leathery persistent *l.* 6 in. or more long. Trinidad, Brazil. 1833. (L. 296; W.O.A. 157; B.M. 3332 as *Epidendrum bicornutum.*)

**D. bigibbero'sum.** Very near to *D. bicornutum* but with smaller *fl.* Guatemala.

**D. indivi'sum.** Differs from *D. bicornutum*, of which it is sometimes considered a variety, by its smaller size and fl. which are often self-fertilizing and of short duration. Trinidad. 1864.

E. C.

**diadelphous,** having the stamens joined by their filaments so as to form 2 groups.

**diade'ma,** band or fillet.

**DIALAE'LIA.** Hybrids between Diacrium and Laelia.

**DIALAELIOCATT'LEYA.** Hybrids between Diacrium, Laelia, and Cattleya.

**DIALEURO'DES chittenden'i.** *See* **Rhododendron White-fly.**

*dialypeta'lus -a -um,* having corolla deeply cut or petals free.

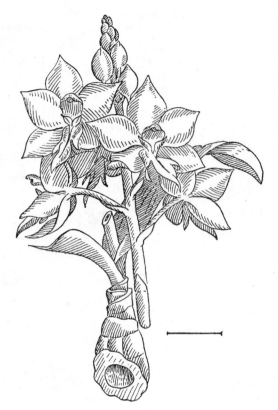

*Diacrium bicornutum* (p. 665)

**DIAMOND-BACK MOTH** (*Plutella maculipennis*). This moth has an almost world-wide distribution. Its worst attacks in this country are generally near the coast. The caterpillars cause considerable havoc to all the cultivated Crucifers, especially Cabbage, Swede, and Turnip, the leaves of which may be reduced to mere skeletons leaving only the mid-rib and main veins. It is abundant in hot, dry seasons, but rain has a deleterious effect upon the caterpillars. The small moths appear in May; the female lays her eggs singly or in groups of 2 to 5 on the underside of the leaves, often on Cruciferous weeds, e.g. Charlock. The young caterpillars may at first tunnel into the leaves, but soon feed on the surface. Later, they pupate in fragile silken cocoons, open at both ends, usually on the leaves of their food plant or upon dry leaves near by. The cycle from egg to adult moth is about a month, and there are two, and even a partial third, broods in a year. There are a number of natural enemies, including birds and hymenopterous parasites, which materially aid in checking the pest.

The most effective control is to dust young Brassicas with a nicotine dust, or mature plants with a nonpoisonous derris dust. Spraying is less effective owing to the difficulty of reaching the underside of the attacked leaves and of directing the wash into the hearts of the plants. **A**

G. F. W.

*Dia'nae,* from Diana, goddess of hunting.

*dian'drus -a -um,* having 2 stamens.

**DIANEL'LA** (diminutive of Diana). Fam. *Liliaceae.* A genus of about 12 species of herbaceous or sub-shrubby fibrous-rooted perennials, natives of E. Asia. Polynesia and Australia. Leaves 2-ranked, grass-like. Flowers in panicles on drooping pedicels; perianth 6-cleft; stamens 6, filaments thickened, anthers dehiscing by pores. Fruit a globose or oblong-ovate blue-berry with a few, black, shining seeds. Dianellas grow well in sheltered spots in the southern counties in a mixture of loam and peat. All succeed planted out in the conservatory or cool greenhouse. Readily propagated by division or by seeds sown in spring in gentle heat. **A**

*Dianella caerulea*

**D. caeru'lea.** About 2 ft. h. *Stem-l.* numerous, long, keel and edges rough. *fl.* blue; branches of panicle short. May. New S. Wales. (B.M. 505.)

**D. ensifo'lia.** A synonym of *D. nemorosa.*

**D. interme'dia.** Turutu. Free-growing. *l.* linear. *fl.* whitish in many-fld. much-branched panicles 10 to 18 in. long. *fr.* freely produced. New Zealand.

**D. lae'vis.\*** About 2 ft. h. *l.* bright green, glabrous, keeled, about 18 in. long. *fl.* bluish, in a loose panicle; outer segs. with 5, inner with 3 lines. Spring. New S. Wales. 1822. (B.R. 751 as *D. strumosa.*)

**D. longifo'lia.** A synonym of *D. revoluta.*

**D. revolu'ta.** *l.* crowded at base of stem, sheaths strongly keeled, inner l. rigid, 2 to 3 ft. long, margins revolute. *fl.* of deeper blue than *D. caerulea,* about ½ in. long in a looser more spreading panicle. Tasmania. 1823. (B.R. 1120 and 734 as *D. longifolia.*)

**D. tasman'ica.*** Up to 5 ft. h. *l.* broadly ensiform, rigid, 3 to 4 ft. long, margins revolute, spine-toothed. *fl.* pale blue, drooping, $\frac{1}{2}$ to $\frac{3}{4}$ in. across, in large, much branched, loose, many-fld. panicles; segs. reflexed. *Berries* deep blue, $\frac{1}{2}$ to $\frac{3}{4}$ in. long, broadly oblong, on slender pedicels, long-lasting. Tasmania. 1866. (B.M. 5551.) var. **variega'ta,** *l.* striped yellow.

**DIAN'THERA** (*dis*, two, *anthera*, anther; the anther-cells are separate). FAM. *Acanthaceae*. A genus of about 100 species of mostly tropical perennial herbs, sometimes almost woody at base, natives of usually wet places. Leaves opposite, mostly entire. Flowers usually purplish or whitish in axillary spikes, heads, or clusters; corolla tube slender, upper lip erect, lower 3-lobed and spreading; anther cells separated by a wide connective, the cells not parallel. Fruit a capsule, 2-celled, up to 4-seeded. For cultivation *see* **Justicia.**

**D. america'na.** Hardy aquatic herb, 1 to 3 ft. h., stem angled. *l.* narrow lanceolate, 3 to 4 in. long, tapered to base, nearly sessile. *fl.* pale violet or whitish, under $\frac{1}{2}$ in. long, in a close cluster, the peduncle usually longer than l. Summer. Canada, United States. (B.M. 2367 as *Justicia pedunculosa*.)

**D. cilia'ta.** Sub-shrubby, 2 ft. h. *l.* lanceolate, 2 to 3 in. long. *fl.* violet with white palate, in terminal and axillary clusters; cor. tube $\frac{3}{4}$ in. long, cylindric, upper lip small, recurved, lower $1\frac{1}{4}$ in. wide, flat, deeply 3-lobed; bracts awl shaped; ciliate. Winter. Panama, Venezuela, Chile. 1870. (B.M. 5888 as *Beloperone ciliata*.) Stove.

**D. nodo'sa.** Stems with swollen joints. *l.* ovate, slender-pointed, glabrous; stalk short. *fl.* large, pale crimson; cor. tube long, widened upwards, lobes long, upper erect, linear, lower deflexed, 3-lobed; racemes 2- or 3-fld., short, axillary. Brazil. (B.M. 2914 as *Justicia nodosa*.) A good pot plant. Stove.

**D. pectora'lis.** Herb of 1 to 3 ft., glabrous. *l.* lanceolate, 1 to 4 in. long, slender pointed. *fl.* about $\frac{1}{2}$ in. long, rose with variegated throat or pale blue, $\frac{1}{3}$ in. long in long, branched, usually 1-sided spikes. May. W. Indies. 1787. Stove.

**D. Pohlia'na.** A synonym of *Porphyrocoma lanceolata*.

**D. secun'da.** Herb. *l.* elliptic, slender-pointed. *fl.* pinkish-red, in terminal, 1-sided racemes, racemes loose, many-fld. W. Indies. 1793. (B.M. 2060; 1014 as *Justicia lucida*; 2487 as *J. geniculata*.)

**DIAN'THUS** (*dios*, divine, *anthos*, flower; Greek name given by Theophrastus in allusion to the fragrance, brilliance, and neatness of the flower of many species). FAM. *Caryophyllaceae*. A genus of about 300 species of annual or perennial herbs sometimes shrubby at base, natives of Europe, the Mediterranean region, Asia, and the mountains of Trop. and S. Africa. Stems usually thickened at the nodes. Leaves usually narrow, grasslike, often grey-green and rough on margin. Inflorescence terminal, solitary, panicled, or clustered. Flowers mostly red, rose, or white, rarely yellow; calyx cylindrical, 5-toothed, with 2 or 3 pairs of overlapping bracts at base, petals 5, narrowed to a claw, margin entire, toothed or fringed; stamens 10; styles 2. Fruit a many-seeded, 1-celled capsule, opening by 4 teeth. The following are hardy perennials unless otherwise specified. For cultivation *see also* **Carnation, Pink, Sweet William.** Many of the species are among the indispensable rock-plants needing gritty well-drained soil and sunny exposure. Several species are apt to intercross in the garden and others are extremely variable, especially under cultivation. **A**

Some species may show Anther Smut (*Ustilago antherarum*) which causes the anthers to swell and release a black sooty mass of spores on the centre of the flowers. Rust (*Uromyces caryophyllinus*) is rare on Dianthus species other than carnations but the rust of Sweet Williams (*Puccinia lychnidearum dianthi*) will attack some species. *See* **Carnation** and **Sweet William diseases.**

**D. acau'lis.** A synonym of *D. sylvestris frigidus*.

**D. aggrega'tus.** A variety of *D. barbatus*.

**D. × Allwoodii** (*D. Caryophyllus*, garden variety × *D. plumarius*). Seedlings of this cross vary much in height, from 4 to 30 in., in colour from white to purplish-pink, and in habit from that of a compact *D. plumarius* to the perpetual-flowering Carnation type. The name is usually applied to dwarf free-flowering forms of various colours. *See* **Pinks.** Raised by Messrs. Allwood of Wivelsfield, Sussex. (Gn. 81 (1917), 16.)

**D. alpest'ris.** A synonym of *D. furcatus*.

**D. alpi'nus.** Grass-green, mat-forming. Stem usually 1-fld., 4 in. long, leafy. *Lower l.* linear to lanceolate, stiff, glossy, glabrous, obtuse, $\frac{1}{12}$ to $\frac{1}{8}$ in. wide above middle; *stem-l.* as long as internodes. *fl.* 1 to $1\frac{1}{2}$ in. across, not scented, flesh-coloured to purplish-red with a ring of dark purple spots on a white ground, greenish-white without, bearded in throat; pet. obovate, often 3-toothed; cal. bell-shaped-cylindrical, about $\frac{1}{2}$ in. long, tinged red. June to August. Austrian Alps. 1759. (B.M. 1205.) Well-drained limy soil on rock-garden or moraine. var. **al'bus,** *fl.* white; **grandiflo'rus,** *fl.* larger.

*Dianthus alpinus*

**D. anatol'icus.** Dense mat-forming. Stems woody at base, branches many, erect, about 6 in. h., 1-, rarely 2- or 3-fld. on short straight pedicels. *l.* narrow-linear, slender-pointed, 3-nerved, margin scabrid; stem-l. short. *Scales* ovate, pale, dry, $\frac{1}{5}$ in. long, abruptly shortly mucronate; cal. $\frac{1}{2}$ in. long, narrowed upwards, teeth triangular-lanceolate, acute, ciliate; pet. pale rose, yellowish without, oblong-spatulate, toothed, obtuse. Summer. Asia Minor.

**D. annula'tus.** A variety of *D. plumarius*.

**D. aragonen'sis.** Glabrous, tufted perennial about 6 in. h. Stem 2-fld. *l.* narrow-linear, 1 in. long, strict, patent, flat, sheath equal in diameter. *fl.* lilac, pet. not touching, toothed, subrhomboid; cal. teeth lanceolate, slender-pointed; scales 6 to 8, lower oval, upper obovate, patent, half as long as cal. June. Aragon, Spain.

**D. arbor'eus.** Glaucous shrub of about 3 ft., smooth, branched, branches densely leafy near apex. *l.* linear, $1\frac{1}{2}$ in. long, acute, channelled above; l. on fl.-stem short. *fl.* in a close corymb; scales 12 to 20, overlapping, lower acute, upper obtuse, ciliate; cal. about $\frac{3}{4}$ in. long, teeth lanceolate, ciliate; pet. rose, deeper at base, obovate-rounded, toothed, slightly bearded. June. Greece, Crete. (F.G. 406.) Not dependably hardy.

**D. arbus'cula.** Shrubby, smooth, about 18 in. h. *l.* lanceolate. *fl.* rich purple-crimson, panicled, clustered, or solitary, single or double; pet. spotted at base, toothed. July. China. 1824. (B.R. 1086.) Greenhouse.

**D. arena'rius.** Mat-forming, grass- or rarely grey-green, barren shoots many. Stem erect, 8 to 18 in. h., usually 1-fld. *l.* linear, up to $1\frac{1}{2}$ in. long, $\frac{1}{20}$ in. wide, acute, margin scabrid. *fl.* white with a green spot and reddish beard, about 1 in. across, fragrant; pet. oblong to lanceolate, cut to about middle into very narrow lobes; cal. $\frac{1}{2}$ to 1 in. long, very slender, often tinged red. June to August. N. Europe. (B.M. 2038.) Does not resent some shade. Rock garden.

**D. a'ridus.** Glabrous perennial with diffuse stems. *l.* narrow linear, soft, slender-pointed. *fl.* showy, in loose clusters, whitish, green or purplish without; cal. teeth oblong-lanceolate with scarious margin, pet. obovate; scales 4, ovate, spreading, pale green. E. Rumelia.

**D. Arme'ria.** Deptford Pink. Annual. Stem erect, 12 to 18 in. h., with short rough hairs, especially above. *l.* linear-lanceolate to linear, lower obtuse, upper acute, shortly hairy. *fl.* in a dense up to 10-fld. head, small, purple to carmine, usually spotted white with purple spots and hairs in throat; cal. narrow-cylindrical, about 1 in. long, teeth acute. Summer. Europe, including Britain, W. Asia. (E.B 191.)

**D. × arvernen'sis** (*D. monspessulanus* × *D. sylvaticus*). Grey, mat-forming. Stems 12 to 20 in. h., smooth, branched above. *l.* broad-linear, narrowed to base; sheaths 2 or 3 times longer than broad. *fl.* large, purplish, solitary or 2 or 3; scales with a broad awn; cal. narrowed above. Cent. France. var. **fimbria'tus,** pet. fringed.

**D. × Atkinson'ii** (*D. chinensis* × ?). About 1 ft. h. *l.* flat, slender pointed. *fl.* $1\frac{1}{2}$ in. across, bright scarlet, edges of pet. strongly toothed. Raised by Mr. Atkinson of Bacton, *c.* 1844. (Gn. 25 (1844), 22.) Does not seed. Difficult of increase; best from cuttings of plants not flowered.

**D. atrorubens.** Related to *D. Carthusianorum*. Mat-forming. Stem stiffly erect, often stout, about 12 in. long. *l.* linear, 3-nerved. *fl.* in a cluster, mostly many-fld., dark to bright red; blade of pet. about half as long as claw. Summer. S. and E. Europe. 1802. (B.M. 1775.)

**D. Ba'keri.** *See* **D. gratianopolitanus, Baker's var.**

**D. Balbis'ii.** Related to *D. liburnicus*. Stems usually many, erect, up to 2 ft. long, 4-angled above, usually simple. *l.* linear to linear-lanceolate, 2 to 3 in. long, $\frac{1}{6}$ in. wide, long-pointed; sheath about $\frac{1}{3}$ in. wide. *fl.* sessile, in 2- to 6-fld. heads, bracts often as long as fl.; pet. purple to rose-red, spotted at base, much shorter than the oblong cal. June to August. Mediterranean region. (S.B.F.G. 23.)

**D. barba'tus.*** Sweet William. Green, prostrate at base, with both barren and flowering shoots. Stem erect, 12 to 24 in. long, thickened at nodes. *l.* broad-to oblong-lanceolate, about $\frac{3}{8}$ in. wide, midrib prominent, coarsely ciliate; bracts as long as or longer than fl. *fl.* clustered in many-fld. almost flat corymbs, $\frac{1}{4}$ to $\frac{1}{3}$ in. across; pet. reddish, striped and dotted white and red at base of blade, bearded in throat; cal. about $\frac{3}{8}$ in. long; sep. awned. S. and E. Europe. 1573. (B.M. 207.) var. **aggrega'tus,** rather roughly hairy, heads very dense, bracts longer than fl. (S.B.F.G. 8 as *D. aggregatus*.); **annula'tus,** cor. with ring of a second colour in middle. A very variable species especially in cultivation. *See* **Sweet William.**

**D. be'bius.** A variety of *D. strictus*.

**D. bi'color.** Stem branched, 1 to 2 ft. long. *l.* awl-shaped, lower hairy. *fl.* white above, lead-coloured beneath, solitary; pet. spreading, hairy. Summer. S. Russia. 1816.

**D. biflo'rus.** Related to *D. cinnabarinus* but with shorter ascending stems; clusters 1- or 2-fld.; scales smaller, appressed with somewhat spreading awns; pet. red or purplish-rose. S. Greece. (F.G. 393.) SYN. *D. cinnabarinus*.

**D. Bois'sieri.** Differs from *D. Caryophyllus* by scales 6, broadly ovate, and pet. limb small, included in cal. to middle. Stem 1 to 2 ft. h. *l.* 2 to 4 in. long, falcate, scarcely fleshy, margin toothed. *fl.* 1 or 2; cal. $1\frac{1}{4}$ in. long, teeth mucronate. June. S. Spain.

**D. brachyan'thus.** Densely tufted, glabrous, glaucous green, from a thick, perpendicular, root-like rhiz. Stem slender. *l.* rigid, linear, acute, plane, toothed. *fl.* pale rose, paler without, solitary, small; scales 4, one-third as long as cal., spreading in bud, roundish-ovate with a short mucro and wide scarious margin; sep. lanceolate, usually purplish; pet. rounded. July to September. Mts. of Spain. Variable in size.

**D. brev'icalyx.** A variety of *D. sylvestris*.

**D. brevicau'lis.** Related to *D. haematocalyx*; mat-forming, with shorter soft, obtuse *l.* and less swollen cal. *fl.* solitary, rosy mauve, yellowish beneath, toothed. High Mts. of Taurus.

**D. caes'ius.** A synonym of *D. gratianopolitanus*.

**D. × calalpi'nus*** (*D. alpinus* × *D. callizonus*). Intermediate.

**D. callizo'nus.** Loose mat-forming. Stem smooth, leafy, 2 to 4 in. long, single-fld. *l.* broadly linear, about $1\frac{1}{2}$ in. long, $\frac{1}{5}$ in. wide, acute, 3 to 5-veined. *fl.* pink with a purple white-dotted zone near base, about $1\frac{1}{2}$ in. across; pet. crenate; cal. cylindrical-obconic, about $\frac{3}{8}$ in. long, purple. June to August. Mts. of Cent. Europe. (B.M. 7223.) Rock-garden with well-drained soil of light limy loam in sun with sufficient water.

**D. capita'tus.** Blue-green. Stem up to 2 ft., almost cylindrical. *Basal l.* $\frac{1}{12}$ in. wide, somewhat scabrid; *stem-l.* flat, $\frac{1}{8}$ in. wide, 5- to 7-nerved, upper widened at base. *fl.* in dense, many-fld. heads; bracts ovate to broad-ovate, membranous, pale, abruptly narrowed to an awl-shaped point; scales ovate, pale, awn shorter than cal. teeth; cal. $\frac{2}{3}$ in. long, tinged red, teeth short; blade of pet. $\frac{1}{5}$ in. long, purple, toothed, bearded, about $\frac{1}{2}$ as long as claw. July to September. E. Europe, Transcaucasia.

**D. Carthusiano'rum.** Stem 12 to 20 in. long, smooth, 4-angled. *l.* linear, acute, margin scabrid; lower $\frac{1}{24}$ to $\frac{1}{16}$ in. wide, flat, upper $\frac{1}{12}$ in. wide, sheath long. *fl.* in usually many-fld. heads; bracts membranous to leathery, point awl-shaped; scales brown, scarious, ovate to obovate, obtuse, awned; cal. $\frac{3}{5}$ to $\frac{4}{5}$ in. long, purple; pet. bright purple, rarely white. Cent. Europe. (B.M. 2039.) A variable plant. var. **multiflo'rus,** dense and often branched with up to 30 stems about $2\frac{1}{2}$ ft. h., fl.-heads very close, up to 70-fld., sometimes white with forms **ro'seus** and **salmo'neus**; **saxige'nus,** 6 to 12 in. h., heads 2- to 6-fld., small. Carpathians.

**D. Caryophyl'lus.** Carnation. Glabrous and more or less glaucous, branched from the woody base, with densely leafy barren shoots and erect or ascending stems 1 to 3 ft. h., branched near top, cylindrical. *l.* linear-lanceolate, acute, scabrid on margin only.

*Dianthus callizonus*

*Dianthus Carthusianorum*

*fl.* solitary at ends of branches or in a cluster of up to 6, fragrant, 1 in. across (in garden forms much more; scales almost rhomboid, acute; blade of pet. obovate, not bearded, more or less notched, usually red, rarely bright (in garden forms of other colours). July, August. W. and S. France. The wild form of which the foregoing is a description varies little in nature but much under cultivation. *See* **Carnation.**

**D. caucas'icus.** A synonym of *D. Seguieri.*

**D. chinen'sis.** Chinese or Indian Pink. Glabrous annual or biennial. Stem erect or almost so, 12 to 18 in. h., smooth, branched above, solitary-fld. in wild, several-fld. in cultivated form. *l.* linear-lanceolate to broad-lanceolate, acute, short-stalked, finely ciliate. *Scales* from a broad base linear, awned, somewhat spreading, as long as cal., sometimes only half as long. Cal. of male fl. smaller than of perfect fl.; pet. bright to dull red or white, usually spotted, weakly bearded, mostly greenish without, toothed; stamens blue. June to September. E. Asia. 1716. (B.M. 25.) Variable in cultivation. *See* **Pinks.** var. **ignes'cens,** stem usually shorter, branches few, fl. many, limb of pet. scarlet. August. Manchuria.

**D. cinnabari'nus.** Woody at base. *l.* narrow-linear, acute, tips rigid. *fl.* in a head; pet. fiery red above, paler without, covered with sessile glands; stamens not exserted. Summer. Greece. 1888. Variable.

**D. cor'sicus.** A synonym of *D. Caryophyllus.*

**D. creta'ceus.** A synonym of *D. leptopetalus.*

**D. cret'icus.** A synonym of *D. arboreus.*

**D. crini'tus.** Mat-forming. Stems woody at base, many, erect, 4 to 12 in. h., 1- to 4-fld. *l.* linear-awl-shaped, rigid, acute. *Scales* 4, appressed, oblong, acute or abruptly cuspidate, about ¼ in. long. Cal. cylindrical, 1 to 1¼ in. long, teeth lanceolate, acute; pet. white, oblong, cut into many long segs. almost to base. Summer. Asia Minor to Persia. (F.G. 401.) Related to *D. fimbriatus* but with longer fl. more deeply fringed.

**D. cruen'tus.** Stem up to 2 ft. h., 4-angled, green. *Basal l.* 1/12 in. wide, downy, bristle-like when folded, sheath up to ½ in. long. *fl.* in a many-fld. head; bracts ovate to obcordate, leathery, brown, abruptly narrowed to a scabrid awn almost as long, membranous at margin; cal. ¾ in. long, purple; cor. about ½ in. across, bright blood-red, toothed, bearded. June, July. SE. Europe. (F.d.S. 488.)

*Dianthus cyri*

**D. cy'ri.** Annual with habit of *Tunica prolifera,* about 10 in. h., erect. *l.* rather broad, scabrid. *fl.* solitary; scales ovate, awn greenish, longer than cal.; cal. tube nerveless, teeth acute scarious; pet. small, oblong, rose, 5- or 6-toothed. Asia Minor to Afghanistan.

**D. deltoi'des.** Maiden Pink. Usually grass-green, branched at base with both fl. and barren shoots, fl.-stem usually branched above, 6 to 9 in. h., barren prostrate, 2 to 6 in. long. *l.* linear to linear-lanceolate, narrowed to wedge-shaped base; stem-l. up to ⅛ in. wide, 1-nerved, finely scabrid on margin and keel; sheath very short. *fl.* ½ to ¾ in. across, in succession on pedicels ½ to 1 in. long; scales elliptic, herbaceous, margin membranous, awn awl-shaped, half as long as cal. tube, outer narrower; cal. tube narrow, about ½ in. long, smooth, rarely faintly hairy, often tinged purple, teeth oblong-lanceolate, very acute, scarious; pet. obovate, purple to crimson-red with a dark stripe, bright spots, and a few long white hairs, rarely white; stamens blue. June to Autumn. Europe, including Britain. (E.B. 192.) A variable plant, var. **al'bus,** *fl.* white; **Brilliant,** *fl.* bright rose; **erec'tus,** stems erect, *fl.* very bright red; **glau'cus,** *l.* grey-green; **super'bus,** *fl.* dark purplish-red; **Wisley var.,** *l.* dark, *fl.* crimson with purple eye.

*Dianthus deltoides*

**D. dento'sus.** Amoor Pink. About 6 in. h. *l.* linear, rather broad, sometimes wavy, glaucous, tinged red. *fl.* violet-lilac, with a regular dark spot formed of purple streaks at base of each pet. forming a dark eye, over 1 in. across; pet. toothed, bearded. Summer. S. Russia.

**D. diuti'nus.** Blue-green, up to 20 in. h., stem 4-angled. *Basal l.* 3 in. long, bristle-like, about 1/20 in. wide, scabrid; *stem-l.* flat or somewhat folded, 1/24 to 1/12 in. wide. *fl.-head* 1- to 3-fld.; bracts obovate, brownish-white with membranous margin, shortly mucronate; scales wide obovate, bluish-white, margin membranous; cal. ¼ in. long, tinged blue-green or pale purple, about twice as long as scales; pet. rose-red, about ⅓ in. long, toothed, smooth. July. Serbia, S. Russia. (R.I.F.G. 251.)

**D. erina'ceus.** Forming a dense prickly cushion. 6 to 9 in. h. Branches covered with the persistent l. *l.* somewhat spreading, awl-shaped from a wide base, sharp-pointed, channelled above, keeled beneath, margins scabrid. *fl.-stems* short, 1- rarely 2-fld.; scales 8 to 10, oblong at base with a sharp awn longer than cal.; cal. about ¾ in. long, teeth awned, ciliate; pet. rose, bearded, toothed. June, July. Asia Minor.

**D. Fal'coneri.** 1 to 2 ft. h. from a shrubby base; branched, stout, rigid. *l.* channelled, 3 to 6 in. long, ⅛ in. wide, 1- to 3-nerved, toothed. *fl.* smaller than in *D. Caryophyllus*; scales in 2, rarely 3, pairs, broadly ovate with a long cusp, quarter to one-third as long as cal.; cal. strongly striate; pet. not bearded, finely toothed. W. Tibet.

**D. fimbria'tus.** *See* **D. orientalis.** The name *fimbriatus* has been applied to several species but the plant to which it is usually applied in England was earlier named *D. orientalis.*

**D. Fis'cheri.** A synonym of *D. Seguieri.*

**D. frag'rans.** Mat-forming with a woody rhizome. Stems many, erect, simple or little branched, 12 to 18 in. h. *l.* straight, narrow-linear, acute, 3- to 5-nerved, scabrid. *Scales* pale, ovate-oblong, narrowed to a long bristle; cal. teeth lanceolate; pet. white, tinged rose, obovate deeply cut into acute lobes. N. Caucasus. This name is often used for sweet-scented hybrids of mixed parentage. (B.M. 2067.)

**D. Freyn'ii.** Forming a dense bright green to grey-green mat about 2½ in. h. *Basal l.* ⅜ to 1 in. long, 1/24 to 1/12 in. wide, keeled, 3-nerved, obtuse, margin hairy. Stem 1-fld. with usually 2 pairs of l., their sheaths 1/12 to ⅛ in. long. *Scales* 2 to 4, ovate, narrowed to a spreading green mucro, outer tipped purple; cal. up to ½ in. long, many striped, purplish, teeth ovate, acute, ciliate; cor. up to ¾ in. across, bright rose; pet. wedge-shaped-obovate, more or less toothed, hairy, bearded. August. Hercegovina. 1893. Nearly related to *D. microlepis,* distinct by the scale-like stem-l.

**D. frig'idus.** A form of *D. sylvestris.*

**D. Frivaldskya'nus.** Mat-forming. Stems many, 6 to 9 in. h., terete, erect, slender, scabrid in lower part. *l.* straight, linear-awl-shaped, margin scabrid; sheath short. *fl.* 2 or 3 in a cluster; scales pale, hard, ovate, obtuse with a short spreading pointed mucro; cal. ⅝ in. long, striate below, teeth lanceolate, mucronate; pet. rose, scarcely bearded, toothed. Thrace.

**D. frutico'sus.** Shrubby with stout tortuous branches, glabrous. *l.* oblong-linear, about ¾ in. long, glaucous, obtuse. Flowering branches short, leafy, with a terminal corymb of fl. *Scales* 8 to 10, elliptic-obovate, acute, mucronate, one third as long as cal.; cal. teeth lanceolate, acute; pet. deep purple, roundish obovate, toothed, slightly bearded. Greece. (F.G. 407.)

**D. furca'tus.** Rather spreading, 6 to 8 in. h. but variable, more or less 4-angled. *Basal l.* up to 1/10 in. wide, often 5-nerved, finely ciliate. *fl.* usually 2, rarely 1 or 3; scales usually in 2 pairs, membranous, inner more or less abruptly narrowed to a point, reaching to about middle of cal. tube; cor. ⅝ to ¾ in. across, clear rose, not red; pet. rarely shortly hairy, usually almost entire, teeth when present short. June to August. S. Alps. SYN. *D. alpestris.* var. **Lereschii,** forming a dense mat similar to *Silene acaulis,* stems 1 to 1½ in. h., *fl.* always solitary, rosy-lilac with a thin blue ring about middle, deeply toothed. Graian Alps. (R.I.F.G. 265.)

**D. gal'licus.** Near *D. monspessulanus* but with thick, rigid, obtuse l. and obovate scales about as long as sep. Pale green or glaucous with creeping rhiz. and long, slender branches. *l.* linear, toothed with scabrid margin. *fl.* fragrant, rose to white, solitary. June, July. France.

**D. gel'idus.** Related to *D. gracilis* but less robust, *l.* broadened upwards, usually blunt with only 1 distinct vein, often bent outwards; sheath up to twice as long as width of stem. *Scales* 2 to 6, linear, reflexed at tip; cal. purplish; pet. larger, up to nearly ½ in. long. August. Carpathians. (G.C. 53 (1913), 247.)

**D. gigan'teus.** Grey-green, mat-forming. Stem up to 3 ft. h., 4-angled, usually simple. *Basal l.* 1/12 in. wide, 7- (or 5-) nerved, scabrid; *stem-l.* ⅛ in. wide, flat, slender-pointed, spreading; sheath 3 times as long as width of stem. *fl.* 10 to 12 in a dense head; bracts oblong, long-pointed, herbaceous; scales ovate-lanceolate to roundish-ovate, not awned, brown, rather shorter than cal.; cal. ¾ in. long, purplish, narrowed to apex; pet. oblong to obovate, about ⅓ in. long, purple-red. July, August. Carpathians, Balkan Mts. (S.B.F.G. 288.)

**D. gigantiaeform'is.** A variety of *D. Pontederae.*

**D. glacia'lis.** Habit of *D. alpinus,* grass-green, forming a very dense mat with both barren and flowering shoots. Stem very short, up to 4 in., 1- to 3-fld. with 1 or 2 pairs of l. *l.* narrower and longer than in *D. alpinus,* more linear, thickish, scarcely 1/12 in. wide, blunt, 1-nerved, margin finely scabrid; sheath very short. *fl.* nearly ¾ in. across, fragrant; scales ½ in. long, lanceolate, awn awl-shaped, longer than cal.; cal. ½ in. long, or more; pet. not flat as in *D. alpinus,* flesh-coloured, white at base, rarely wholly white, greenish on back, notched. July, August. Cent. Europe. (T.A.P.E. 12.) Rock-garden; should be kept dry in winter.

**D. glutino'sus.** Annual. Related to *D. tenuiflorus* but much more clammy, *l.* straighter, scales with a long awn, *fl.* always solitary, cal. longer and wide cylindrical. May. Greece, Asia Minor.

**D. grac'ilis.** Woody at base. Stems many, 4-angled, about 1 ft. h. *l.* linear, acute, scabrid. *fl.* solitary or 2 or 3 in a cluster; scales 4, pale, hard, with a long sharp awl-shaped tip; cal. about ¾ in. long, striate below, teeth lanceolate, mucronate; pet. rose, obovate, bearded, sharply toothed. Mt. Athos, Macedonia. (F.G. 404.)

**D. granit'icus.** Related to *D. hirtus,* but stem 4 to 16 in. h., slender, almost cylindrical, usually smooth, often branched above. *l.* less stiff, margin smooth, narrow-linear, slender-pointed, 3-nerved; stem-l. weak, spreading. *Scales* smaller, with almost straight awn, the smaller one-third as long as cal.; pet. broader oval, almost as long as claw. June to August. S. France.

*Dianthus gratianopolitanus*

**D. gratianopolita'nus.** Cheddar Pink. More or less blue-green, mat-forming, branched at base with up to 12 in. long, weak, very much branched, rooting, barren shoots forming a flattish cushion; fl.-stems erect or ascending, 3 to 12 in. h., simple, 1-, rarely 2-, fld. *l.* linear to linear-awl-shaped, stiff, usually not over 1 in. long, blunt, margin usually scabrid, sheath about twice as long as width of stem. *fl.* red to deep flesh-colour, rarely white, very fragrant, 1 in. or more across; scales in 2 pairs, herbaceous, blunt, outer elliptic, inner roundish-ovate with short point, about one-third as long as cal.; cal. smooth, about ½ in. long, tinged red, grooved, teeth ovate-oblong, scarious on margin, ciliate; pet. more or less toothed, bearded. May to July. Cent. Europe, including Britain. (E.B. 193 as *D. caesius.*) **Baker's var.,** *fl.* of deeper colour than type, *l.* larger. SYN. *D. Bakeri*; **flore ple'no,** of compact habit, *fl.* double; **monta'nus,** forming a very dense mat, *fl.* solitary, *l.* short and stiff. SYN. *D. pulchellus.*

**D. Grisebach'ii.** Allied to *D. viscidus* but glandular hairy, stems about 6 to 8 in. long, *fl.* 1 to 3, clustered, cal. clammy-hairy, scales appressed with a long bristle-like awn. Macedonia. (J.R.H.S. 39, 4.)

**D. haematoca'lyx.** Tufted with a woody base. Stems 6 to 9 in. h., 3- to 5-fld. *l.* linear, flat, acute, rigid, margin scabrid, the lower 1 to 2 in. long, about ⅛ in. wide. *Scales* 4, red, narrowed to a lanceolate herbaceous cusp, somewhat spreading, about as long as the cal.; cal. red, swollen, mealy, teeth pointed; pet. purple, yellow without, bearded, wedge-shaped, toothed. July. Greece. var. **alpi'nus,** *see* **D. pindicola; pruino'sus,** *see* **D. pruinosus.**

**D. hir'tus.** Mat-forming, woody at base, with short barren shoots from a l.-rosette. Stem thick, cylindrical, 6 to 9 in. h., coarsely hairy, usually simple. *l.* firm, linear, narrowed to point and forked, awl-shaped, scabrid on margin and back, 3- to 5-nerved; stem-l. erect. *fl.* rather small, 1 to 4; outer scales oval-lanceolate, inner oval, all widely membranous-margined with an erect awn about ¾ in. long; cal. teeth lanceolate, acute; pet. red, not touching, ovate, toothed, ciliate in throat. June to August. S. France. (R.I.F.G. 264.)

**D. hispan'icus.** Glabrous, sub-shrubby, tufted. Stem woody, many-angled. *l.* somewhat glaucous, 3-nerved, toothed. *fl.* solitary; scales 4, nearly equal, one-third as long as cal., elliptic or obovate-oblong with a wide scarious margin. *fl.* rose, throat naked; cal. purplish; anthers violet. June, July. Spain. var. **austra'lis,** stem slender, forked, often many-fld., *l.* flat, *fl.* small; **borea'lis,** 4 to 10 in. h., scarcely branched.

**D. Hoelt'zeri.** Tufted. *Radical l.* sub-spatulate; *stem-l.* linear, lanceolate, sheath as wide as l. *fl.* spotted rose or yellowish; scale 2, obovate-lanceolate, mucronulate, appressed, up to half length of cal.; pet. not contiguous, sometimes bearded. Turkestan. 1881. (G.F. 1032.)

**D. hungar'icus.** A synonym of *D. praecox*.

**D. × hyb'ridus** (*D. barbatus* × *D. chinensis*). Variable.

**D. inodo'rus.** *See* **D. sylvestris.**

**D. in'teger.** Habit of *D. strictus*, but stem 1-fld. *l.* linear-lanceolate. *fl.* small; scales scarious, acute, with herbaceous tip, about $\frac{1}{4}$ in. long; cal. $\frac{1}{2}$ in. long, tinged purple; pet. small, white, obovate or wedge-shaped, entire; fl. fragrant. June to August. Albania to Greece. (R.I.F.G. (6) 264.)

**D. Kitaibel'ii.** Mat-forming, glabrous, barren shoots prostrate, fl.-stems from the prostrate stems erect, 8 to 12 in. h., usually 1-fld. *l.* linear-lanceolate, short, about 1 in. long, stiff, acute, spreading; sheath twice as long as l.-width. *fl.* fragrant; scales 4, ovate to obovate, usually tinged reddish, abruptly narrowed to a point, one-third as long as cal.; cal. long-cylindrical, teeth lanceolate; pet. rose, smooth, not touching, throat not bearded, shortly fringed, about half as long as cal.; stamens yellowish. June. Roumania, Bulgaria, Thrace. (B.M. 1204 as *D. petraeus*.) var. **al'bus,** *fl.* white; **ocula'tus,** *fl.* white with rose ring; **ro'seus,** *fl.* larger than in type.

**D. Knapp'ii.** Habit of *D. liburnicus* but grey-green, forming a loose mat. Stem up to 15 in. h. *l.* finely downy, slightly scabrid; basal l. about $\frac{1}{24}$; stem-*l.* $\frac{1}{12}$ to $\frac{1}{8}$ in. wide, generally 3-nerved; sheath $\frac{1}{8}$ to $\frac{3}{5}$ in. long. *fl.* usually 4 in a head; bracts ovate, membranous; scales membranous, brownish-white, awned; cal. $\frac{3}{5}$ in. long pale green, narrowed to apex, teeth acute; pet. bright sulphur yellow, purple spotted near base. June. Hungary, Bosnia.

**D. latifo'lius.** A form of *D. × hybridus*. *See* **Pinks.**

**D. leptopet'alus.** Glabrous, about 6 in. h. Stems erect, dichotomously branched. *l.* rigid, narrow linear; sheath short. *fl.* solitary on long peduncles; scales obtuse, mucronate; cal. about 1 in. long with lanceolate, ciliate teeth; pet. yellowish-white, narrow oblong, entire, lead-coloured without. July, August. Macedonia, Caucasus. (B.M. 1739.) Fl. open in evening.

**D. Leresch'ii.** A variety of *D. furcatus*.

**D. libur'nicus.** 10 to 24 in. h., woody at base. Stem smooth, or hairy near base, 4-angled. *l.* bright green, linear-lanceolate to linear, $1\frac{1}{2}$ to $3\frac{1}{2}$ in. long, $\frac{1}{8}$ to $\frac{1}{5}$ in. wide, margin scabrid, lowest usually dead by fl.-time, sheath $\frac{1}{6}$ to $\frac{2}{5}$ in. long. *fl.-heads* 4- to 6-fld.; *fl.* sessile; bracts herbaceous, linear-lanceolate, often longer than fl.; scales greenish, oblong, awn of lower longer than cal., margin membranous; cal. green, $\frac{3}{4}$ in. long, distinctly striate; pet. purple to rose-red with darker spots forming a ring. Summer. Middle and E. Mediterranean region. 1817. (R.I.F.G. 249.) SYN. *D. Balbisii liburnicus*.

**D. microle'pis.** Dwarf and tufted, with habit of *D. glacialis*, but smaller in all parts. *l.* soft, linear, up to $\frac{4}{5}$ in. long, obtuse, 1-nerved, scabrid on margin. *fl.* minute, solitary, scarcely above foliage; scales 2, ovate-lanceolate, white at base, green above; cal. teeth short, lanceolate; pet. rose, obovate oblong, obtuse, crenate. Thrace. (J.R.H.S. 39, 4.)

**D. monspessul'anus.** Robust, woody at base 6 to 12 in. h., usually grass-green, somewhat glaucous, with habit of *D. superbus*, but more stiffly erect, with more fl. *l.* soft, not forming a distinct rosette, lower usually decayed by fl.-time. *Scales* awned, often as long as cal. or longer. *fl.* fragrant; pet. rose or white, obovate, deeply cut. May to August. SW. Europe. 1764. (R.I.F.G. 258.) var. **al'bus,** *fl.* white; **Sternberg'ii,** *see* **D. Sternbergii.**

**D. monta'nus.** A synonym of *D. aragonensis*.

**D. multiflo'rus.** A variety of *D. Carthusianorum*.

**D. Mussin'ii.** A synonym of *D. arenarius*.

**D. nardiform'is.** Glaucous, mat-forming. Stems numerous, about 4 in. h., erect, usually 1-fld. or with 2 or 3 on short branches. *l.* all straight and equal, not over 1 in. long, bristle-like, 3-angled, 2-grooved, indistinctly toothed, scabrid above; sheath very short. *Scales* 4 to 6, bright brown, almost papery, oblong-elliptic, reaching to middle of cal., awn spreading; cal. $\frac{3}{4}$ in. long, oblong-cylindrical, furrowed, teeth oblong-lanceolate to ovate, somewhat broadly margined; cor. rather large, bright purple; pet. roundish, bearded, slightly toothed. Summer. SE. Europe.

**D. neglec'tus.** Glabrous, forming a dense mat. Stem prostrate, branched at base, with short leafy barren shoots and angled fl.-stems 1 to 6 in. h. *l.* narrow-linear, stiff, almost flat; stem-l. usually longer than lower, margin scabrid; sheath very short. *fl.* solitary, rarely 2 or 3; scales up to 4, very unequal, larger outer with long straight point, inner with shorter point; cal. about $\frac{1}{2}$ in. long, broad, purplish, striate, teeth pale; pet. rose-red, rarely white, $1\frac{1}{4}$ in. across; pet. obovate, bearded, irregularly double-toothed. July, August. SW. Europe to Tirol. 1869. (G.C. 53 (1913), 255.) var. **Roys'ii,** larger in all parts.

**D. nit'idus.** Glabrous, with 1 to many stems, 6 to 24 in. h., erect, 1- to 3-fld., nodes large. *l.* somewhat fleshy, lower linear-oblanceolate, $1\frac{1}{4}$ to 2 in. long, $\frac{1}{5}$ in. wide; stem-l. smaller, linear, all obtuse, margins scabrid; sheath $\frac{1}{24}$ to $\frac{1}{5}$ in. long. *fl.* almost scentless, short-stalked; scales 4, somewhat herbaceous with membranous margin, ciliate, tinged red, inner ovate to obovate, longer than outer, all with long awl-shaped awn; cal. short, broadly cylindrical, about $\frac{1}{2}$ in. long, purplish, ciliate; pet. rose, sharply toothed. July, August. Cent. Europe. (R.I.F.G. 261.)

*Dianthus neglectus*

**D. Noea'nus.** Densely tufted. Stems 7 to 8 in. h., scarcely branched, with 2 to 5 fl. in a terminal cluster. *l.* rigid, spreading, linear-lanceolate, about $\frac{3}{4}$ in. long, sharp-pointed. *Scales* appressed, oblong, narrowed to a short mucro, about $\frac{1}{4}$ in. long; cal. about 1 in. long, straw-coloured, narrow tubular, teeth lanceolate; pet. white, glabrous, narrow wedge-shaped, cut half-way into linear lobes. Rumelia. Often offered as *Acanthophyllum spinosum*.

**D. orienta'lis.** Woody at base with many erect usually simple stems, 6 to 12 in. h. *l.* linear-awl-shaped, short, straight, somewhat channelled, margin scabrid. *fl.* solitary; scales 6 or 8, oblong, acute; cal. about 1 in. long, usually reddish, teeth narrow lanceolate; pet. rose, usually glabrous, oblong, pinnatifid. Summer. Caucasus to Persia. (B.M. 1069.) SYN. *D. fimbriatus*.

**D. pallidiflo'rus.** A synonym of *D. ramosissimus*.

**D. Pancic'ii.** About 16 in. h., obtusely 4-angled, green. *Basal l.* $\frac{1}{24}$ in. wide, flat, shining; *stem-l.* $\frac{1}{16}$ in. wide, shorter than the internodes. *fl.-heads* many-fld.; bracts ovate-lanceolate, blackish-purple, awned; scales obovate, blackish-purple, awn nearly as long as cal.; cal. $\frac{1}{3}$ in. long, blackish-purple; pet. $\frac{1}{8}$ in. long, bright rose, toothed. July, August. SE. Europe.

**D. papillo'sus.** A form of *D. sylvestris inodorus*.

**D. pelvifor'mis.** Stem about 16 in. h., weakly 4-angled, somewhat glaucous below. *Basal l.* bristle-like, $\frac{1}{24}$ in. wide; *stem-l.* flat, $\frac{1}{12}$ to $\frac{1}{5}$ in. wide, scabrid, folded at tip; sheath up to $\frac{1}{12}$ in. long. *fl.-heads* small, many-fld.; bracts broad, brown, tinged purple, rather shorter than cal., abruptly narrowed to awn, $\frac{1}{12}$ to $\frac{1}{8}$ in. long; scales obovate, truncate, shortly awned; cal. $\frac{1}{2}$ in. long, dark purple; pet. dark red, about $\frac{1}{8}$ in. long, sharply toothed. May to July. Serbia, Bulgaria. (G.C. 30 (1901), 97.)

**D. petrae'us.** A synonym of *D. Kitaibelii*

**D. pindic'ola.** Closely related to *D. haematocalyx*. Stems short, 1-fld., or *fl.* in a sessile tuft, *l.* very short, scales short and usually abruptly cuspidate. Greece. SYN. *D. haematocalyx alpinus*.

**D. pinifo'lius.** Tufted. Stem 8 to 16 in. h., 4-angled, somewhat scabrid. *l.* all bristle-like, scarcely $\frac{1}{24}$ in. wide, stiff, densely crowded, like *Nardus stricta*, 3-nerved, somewhat glaucous, scabrid, sheath $\frac{1}{12}$ to $\frac{1}{8}$ in. long. *fl.* in a dense many-fld. head; bracts leathery, yellowish, obovate-lanceolate, narrowed abruptly to a short awn; scales obovate, yellowish, awn $\frac{1}{12}$ to $\frac{1}{8}$ in. long; cal. pale, about $\frac{3}{4}$ in. long, teeth acute; pet. rose-red, oblong-ovate, $\frac{1}{6}$ in. long, sometimes weakly bearded. June. Greek Archipelago.

**D. pluma'rius.** Pink. Related to *D. gratianopolitanus* but stem 2-fld., pet. deeply cut to $\frac{1}{4}$ or $\frac{1}{3}$, winged margin of claw narrow, not broad as in *D. gratianopolitanus*. June, July. SE. Europe. 1629. (E.B. 195.) The origin of the Garden Pink which is a variety with smooth pet. and which has many forms. *See* **Pinks.** var. **annula'tus,** *fl.* white with dark crimson centre.

**D. Pontede'rae.** Grass-green, mat-forming. Stem 10 to 20 in. h., stiffly erect, 4-angled. *Basal l.* about $\frac{1}{16}$ in. wide, linear, grass-like, shining; *stem-l.* about $\frac{1}{12}$ in. wide, linear, acute, 5-nerved, margin somewhat scabrid; sheath about $\frac{2}{8}$ in. long. *fl.-head* with about 6, rarely up to 30 fl., dense; bracts scarious, ovate, brown, awn shorter than fl.; scales ovate-lanceolate, brown, dry, shortly or not awned; cal. narrowed upwards, brown, about $\frac{1}{2}$ in. long, striate, teeth awl-shaped; pet. $\frac{1}{8}$ to $\frac{1}{4}$ in. long, purple-red, bright red without, more or less toothed, hairy above. May, June. Serbia, Bulgaria. var. **gigantiifor'mis**, stem sharply 4-angled, fl. usually 2, with bracts as long as head, scales straw-coloured, inner lanceolate, acute, awnless, pet. with few sharp teeth. SYN. *D. gigantiaeformis*.

*Dianthus orientalis* (p. 671)

**D. prae'cox.** Glaucous to green, mat-forming, with 1 to many stems, 4 to rarely 12 in. h. Stems erect, 4-angled, 1- (rarely 2-) fld. *l.* linear, acute, finely toothed, 3-nerved; lower stem-l. somewhat spreading, $\frac{1}{2}$ to 2 in. long, about $\frac{1}{12}$ in. wide; sheath about $\frac{1}{8}$ in. long. *Scales* usually 4, glabrous, tinged purple, inner roundish to broadly elliptic, $\frac{1}{4}$ to $\frac{1}{3}$ in. long, outer smaller; cal. cylindrical, up to nearly 1 in. long, green or tinged purple with unequal ovate teeth, margin membranous, ciliate; pet. white, about $\frac{1}{2}$ in. long, rarely deeply cut, slightly bearded. May, June. W. Carpathians.

**D. pruino'sus.** Closely related to *D. haematocalyx*. Whole plant minutely pruinose. *l.* rigid, narrow, stems loosely branched, scales herbaceous nearly to base. Thessaly. SYN. *D. haematocalyx pruinosus*.

**D. pubes'cens.** Base woody, stems many, 6 to 9 in. h., decumbent, usually simple, whole plant glandular-hairy. *l.* linear, acute, 3-nerved. *fl.* solitary or 2; scales 2, pale, ovate-oblong, shortly awned; cal. slender, pale, glabrous, striate, teeth slender; pet. purple, papillose, yellowish without, oblong, coarsely toothed. June. Greece. (F.G. 397.)

**D. pulchel'lus.** A synonym of *D. gratianopolitanus montanus*.

**D. pu'milus.** Closely related to *D. gracilis*, but stems about 3 to 4 in. h., *l.* very short, scales more rigid and rather sharp-pointed. Macedonia.

**D. pun'gens.** This name is of doubtful application for a Spanish plant and is better dropped. It has been applied to several species.

**D. ramosis'simus.** Stems 1 to 2 ft. h. from a sub-shrubby base, many, slender, erect, loosely branching. *l.* narrow-linear, acute, 3-nerved. *fl.* solitary; scales 4, ovate with a membranous margin, abruptly cuspidate; cal. narrow, about $\frac{1}{2}$ in. long, teeth slender; pet. pale rose, oblong, acute, toothed. S. Russia. SYN. *D. pallidiflorus.*

**D. Requien'ii.** A synonym of *D. hispanicus.*

**D. Roys'ii.** A variety of *D. neglectus.*

**D. rupic'ola.** Glabrous, $2\frac{1}{2}$ in. h., stem terete below, 4-angled above, branched. *Radical l.* linear-lanceolate, 1 in. long, acute, recurved; *upper* linear, $1\frac{1}{2}$ in. long, patent, incurved. *fl.* in loose cymes, 3 to 5, clustered, showy on short peduncles; scales 8, obovate, mucronate, one-third as long as purple, 11-nerved cal.; pet. rose, contiguous; anthers red. Italy, N. Africa.

**D. scar'dicus.** Tufted from a naked procumbent base with stems 1 to 4 in. h., 1- or 2-fld. *l.* linear or linear-lanceolate, 1-nerved, obtuse, flaccid, ciliate near base. *Scales* 4, reddish, awl-shaped from an ovate-lanceolate base more than half as long as cal.; cal. about $\frac{1}{3}$ in. long, membranous, purple or blackish teeth ovate-lanceolate, ciliate, acute; pet. rose, obovate, bearded, toothed. Summer. Hungary. SYN. *D. nitidus* of Boissier.

*Dianthus Seguieri*

**D. Seguier'i.** Glabrous, mat-forming, creeping with barren and fl.-stems 8 to 15 in. h., rarely more, ascending, scabrid. *l.* rather firm, flat, linear, $\frac{1}{12}$ to $\frac{1}{8}$ in. wide, with long point, scarcely narrowed to base, glaucous or almost grass-green, margin scabrid; lower often longer and almost rosette-forming; sheath $\frac{1}{12}$ to $\frac{1}{8}$ in. long. *fl.* more or less clustered, rarely solitary or 2; scales oval-lanceolate to ovate, 2 or 3 times as long as broad, pale green, awl-shaped at tip; cal. striate, narrowed above, teeth dry, brown-purple; cor. ¾ to 1¼ in. across; pet. flesh-red to purple, whitish without, roundish, deeply toothed, bearded; fl. fragrant. July, August. Pyrenees, N. Italy. 1832. (S.B.F.G. 245 as *D. Fischeri*.)

**D. serot'inus.** Habit of *D. plumarius*, mat-forming, grey- or grass-green. Stem erect from an ascending base, 8 to 12 in. h., few-fld. *l.* stiff, narrow, linear-awl-shaped, about ½ in. wide, ciliate with stiff hairs; stem-l. ½ to 1 in. long, on young barren shoots glaucous. *Scales* 4 or 6, roundish-obovate, distinctly mucronate, up to ⅓ in. long; cal. about 1 in. long, narrowed above, teeth acute. *fl.* slightly fragrant, white; pet. about ¾ in. long with short broad lobes, slightly bearded. July to autumn. Russia, Roumania. var. **Stawkia'nus,** *l.* green, *fl.* rose.

**D. sinen'sis.** A synonym of *D. chinensis.*

**D. spiculifo'lius.** Grass-green, mat-forming. Stems many, about 6 in. h., cylindrical below, angled above, 1- to 2-fld. *Lower stem-l.* about 1 in. long, linear-awl-shaped, 3-nerved, about $\frac{1}{20}$ in. wide, finely toothed; sheaths about $\frac{1}{12}$ in. long. *Scales* 2 or 4, inner ovate-elliptic to obovate, acute or mucronate, margin membranous, glabrous, about one-fifth as long as cal.; cal. green, flushed purple, about 1 in. long, teeth acute, sparsely ciliate; pet. white or rose, nearly round, deeply cut, sparsely bearded. July, August. Carpathians.

**D. spino'sus.** A synonym of *Acanthophyllum spinosum.*

**D. squarro'sus.** Tufted, about 20 in. h. Stems slender, glabrous, spreading, few-fld. *l.* linear, about ¾ in. long, acute, recurved. *fl.* rose; cal. teeth slender-tipped; pet. pinnately cut, barbed. S. Russia, Siberia.

**D. Stawkia'nus.** A variety of *D. serotinus.*

**D. Sternberg'ii.** Habit of *D. arenarius*, glaucous. Stem creeping, 1-, rarely 2-fld., in mountains at lower elevations recemosely 2- to 4-fld. *l.* stiff; on barren shoots short, ascending. *Scales* abruptly narrowed to an acute green point, one-third to half as long as cal. *fl.* purplish to rose, fragrant. July, August. Tyrol to Montenegro. var. **Waldstein'ii,** 15 in. h. or more, 5- to 13-fld. in an umbel, *l.* longer, stiff, often leathery, usually sea-green.

**D. stric'tus.** Glabrous, mat-forming, barren shoots short, densely leafy, creeping. Stem straight, erect, 4-angled, 6 to 10 in. h.; loosely leafy, 1- rarely 2-fld. *l.* linear to linear-lanceolate, flat, acute, margin scabrid; stem-l. shorter; sheath short. *Scales* ovate, abruptly shortly awned, up to one-third as long as cal., margin membranous; cal. cylindrical, often narrowed upwards, about 1 in. long, teeth short, acute. *fl.* usually scentless, white; pet. usually not touching, ovate-oblong to oval-rhomboid, entire or slightly toothed. June, July. Dalmatia. (F.G. 403 ) var. **be'bius,** 1- to 2-fld., scales scarious on margin, up to half as long as cal., *fl.* slightly scented, larger, pet. triangular-obovate, sharply toothed. Syn. *D. bebius.*

**D. sua'vis.** A synonym of *D. gratianopolitanus.*

**D. subacau'lis.** Related to *D. furcatus*, dwarf, mat-forming, ½ to 3 in. h., woody at base, much branched with many barren rosettes. Stem erect, angled. *l.* short, stiff, narrow above, ciliate. *fl.* small to very small, rose; scales broadly ovate, all or the inner acute or mucronate, one-third to half as long as cal.; cal. about ⅓ in. long, broadly spindle-shaped, teeth broad, oval-lanceolate, blunt; pet. not touching, oval-oblong, entire or finely toothed, not bearded. June to August. Maritime Alps. (R.I.F.G. 261.)

**D. super'bus.** Usually green, woody at base, with both barren and fl. shoots. Stems 12 to 24 in. h., cylindrical, shining, smooth, usually branched above. *l.* $\frac{1}{12}$ to ⅜ in. wide, margin scabrid; lower blunt, upper acute; sheath about ⅛ in. long. *fl.* solitary at tips of up to 12 branches but usually about 6, 1½ in. across, fragrant; scales smooth, herbaceous with narrow membranous margin, acute or shortly awned, about ⅓ in. long; cal. narrowly cylindrical, 1 to 1¼ in. long, grass-green often spotted violet, teeth oblong-lanceolate, acute, often scarious; pet. bright lilac to pale rose-lilac, green-spotted at base, beard red, rarely wholly white, claw white or yellowish-green, lobed almost to base, lobes feathery. June to September. Europe, N. Asia to Japan. 1596. (B.M. 297.) Very variable. var. **specio'sus,** larger in all parts, with broader l. and more erect fl. which are twice as large as in type and often spotted black at base. Syn. *D. Wimmeri.*

**D. sylvat'icus.** Closely related to *D. Seguieri* but stem smooth, *l.* somewhat flaccid, broader linear to almost lanceolate, distinctly narrowed to base, the lower almost cylindrical there, point bluntish, outer *scales* ovate, not ciliate, one-third to half as long as the somewhat wider cal.; cal. teeth short, broad lanceolate. June to August. Jura, N. Alps.

**D. sylves'tris.** Grass-green, mat-forming with numerous, short, dense, barren shoots. Stems ascending or erect, 2 to 12 in. h., sometimes bluntly angled, 1- to many-fld. *Basal l.* 1 to 4 in. long, striate below, often stiff, narrow-linear, scabrid on margin; *stem-l.* mostly short, ovate, convex; sheaths ⅛ to ¼ in. long. *fl.* solitary, ¾ to 1⅛ in. across, usually scentless; scales mostly 4, broadly ovate, very blunt, scarcely ¼ in. long; cal. about 1 in. long, green, tinged deep violet, blue or red, teeth blunt; pet. usually rose, roundish wedge-shaped to triangular, more or less notched. June to August. S. Alps. 1816. (T.S.A.P. 8.) var. **al'bus,** *fl.* white; **brevica'lyx,** about 4 in. h., stem many-fld., *l.* very narrow, rolled, *fl.* pale rose, scentless, scales 4, pet. about ¼ in. wide. Bosnia; **inodo'rus,** plant large, up to 24 in. h., *l.* flat or rolled, *fl.* 1 to 5, weakly scented, larger, scales 2 only, pet. triangular, about ⅓ in. wide. Croatia; **papillo'sus,** pet. papillose. Dalmatia; **subacau'lis,** cushion-forming with very short stems and smaller fl. than in type. High Alps. Syn. *D. frigidus.*

**D. tenuiflo'rus.** Annual. Glandular hairy. Stem forked, loosely corymbose. *l.* linear, straight, basal obtuse, 3-nerved. *fl.* in a loose corymb, rarely solitary; scales awl-shaped from an ovate base; cal. narrow tubular, teeth awl-shaped; pet. purple, elliptic-oblong, bearded. July. Thrace.

**D. tergesti'nus.** Slightly glaucous. Stem about 12 in. h., branched, 4-angled. *l.* narrow-linear, stiff, blunt, finely toothed, lower about ½ in. long; stem-l. about ⅜ in. long; sheath short. *fl.* usually 2, scentless; scales 4, membranous, shining, truncate, narrowed abruptly to a green point, outer oval to roundish-oval, inner ovate, short; cal. scarcely narrowed above, teeth short, red; pet. bright rose to carmine, contiguous, obovate-wedge-shaped, almost entire; stamens violet. May, June. Dalmatia. (R.I.F.G. 266.)

**D. tymphres'teus.** Tufted, green clammy-hairy. Stem short, ascending. *l.* flaccid, linear, 3-nerved. *fl.* 1 to 3 in a cluster, bracts and scales pale, membranous, abruptly narrowed to an awn; cal. teeth acute; pet. rose, black-spotted in throat, obtuse, toothed. Greece.

**D. vagina'tus.** Near *D. Carthusianorum* and often regarded as a variety of that species with narrow *l.* up to about $\frac{1}{12}$ in. wide and rather weak stem about 15 in. h., *fl.* usually about 10 in head, sometimes more up to 30, dark purple. Cent. Alps. (R.I.F.G. 251.)

**D. Velenovs'kyi.** A synonym of *D. Pancicii.*

**D. virgin'eus.** Related to *D. sylvestris.* Loose mat-forming, rather glaucous, 2 to 4 in. h., barren shoots very short, fl. stem straight. *l.* 3-angled, linear-awl-shaped, scabrid at least on margin, upper bracts touching or overlapping. *fl.* fragrant; scales 4 or 6, leathery, striate, about a quarter as long as cal. with a very short triangular point; cal. narrow, long, narrowed upwards with membranous-margined lanceolate teeth; pet. not contiguous, oblong, toothed, not bearded. S. France. 1816. (B.M. 1740.)

**D. vis'cidus.** Tufted, many-stemmed, green, clammy-hairy. Stem 10 to 12 in., ascending. *l.* flaccid, linear, 3-nerved; sheath short. *fl.* 2 to 6 in a cluster, rarely solitary, bracts and scales oblong, pale, membranous, somewhat inflated, with a narrow awn; cal. teeth long-awned; pet. purple, wedge-shaped-oblong, bearded, slightly toothed. Summer. Greece. var. **parnas'sicus** differs by the scales, scarcely inflated and shorter.

**D. Waldstein'ii.** A variety of *D. Sternbergii.*

**D. Wim'meri.** A synonym of *D. superbus speciosus.*

**D. zona'tus.** Tufted from a woody base, about 12 in. h. Stems simple or stiffly branched. *l.* rigid, 5-nerved, slender-pointed. *fl.* usually with scarious bracts; scales 4, margin membranous, broader above, ovate, mucronate, usually one-third as long as cal. tube; cal. ¾ in. long, teeth lanceolate, mucronate; pet. rose with a purple zone at base, yellow without, sharply toothed. Spring. Moab.

**DIAPEN'SIA** (ancient Greek name, application ?). Fam. *Diapensiaceae.* A small genus of low, tufted, smooth, evergreen sub-shrubs characterized by a tubular corolla with 5 wide, spreading lobes, 5 broad, slightly overlapping calyx segments, 3-lobed stigma, and trilocular ovary. Cultivation of most species difficult. A soil of peaty, lime-free sand, or, perhaps better, of micaceous schist detritus is suggested together with partial shade. Propagation by cuttings or seed.

KEY

1. *Fl.-stalk about half elongated at flowering time; fl. invariably white* — D. lapponica
1. *Fl. subsessile, usually coloured (see* **D. Wardii***), stalk lengthens after fertilization* — 2
2. *Lvs. up to ⅜ in. long and often over ¼ in. wide* — D. Wardii
2. *Lvs. not over ¼ in. long, ⅛ in. wide* — 3
3. *Lvs. smooth, shining, and stomatose above* — D. himalaica
3. *Lvs. minutely papillose, dull, and without stomata above* — D. purpurea

**D. himala'ica.** Evergreen, creeping sub-shrub. *l.* petiolate, crowded below, sparser above, oval, lanceolate, narrow-oblong or spatulate, pointed, acuminate or notched at apex, $\frac{3}{16}$ to ¼ in. long and up to ⅛ in. wide. *fl.* terminal, solitary, and nearly sessile. cor. rosy purple, lilac, yellow, or white, tube ⅛ to ¼ in. long, lobes spreading. May to September in nature. A slender stalk, elongated after flowering from 1 to 2 in. long, supports the capsule. Upper Burma, SE. Tibet, NW. Yunnan on cold, wet, lime-free rocks at 11,000 to 16,000 ft. Syn. *D. acutifolia.* Seed has been sent to this country in recent years, but it is very doubtful whether this plant is in cultivation. var. **acutifo'lia,** *l.* acute or even acuminate, *fl.* white (**can'dida**) or rose-purple (**rubel'la**); **retu'sa,** *l.* notched at apex, *fl.* sulphur (**sulphu'rea**) or rose-purple (**viola'cea**).

**D. lappon'ica.** Evergreen, tufted, creeping sub-shrub up to 3 in. h. *l.* petiolate, crowded below, sparser above, spatulate, usually obtuse or rounded at apex, thick and leathery, slightly recurved, $\frac{1}{4}$ to $\frac{1}{2}$ in. long, about half as much wide. *fl.* solitary, terminal, stalks about 1 in. long at fl.-time, 2 in. or more when fr. is fully developed; cor. white, greenish within tube, $\frac{1}{4}$ to $\frac{1}{3}$ in. long, $\frac{1}{2}$ to $\frac{3}{4}$ in. across with broad, obtuse, spreading lobes; cal. about as long as cor. tube, lobes overlapping, obtuse and denticulate. April, May. N. America, NW. Asia, and N. Europe in alpine-arctic areas. 1801. SYN. *D. obtusifolia.* (B.M. 1108.) Difficult to cultivate in this country. var. **obova'ta** is the NE. Asia variant, *l.* obovate, shorter. N. Japan, Kamchatka, NE. Siberia. Much more amenable to British cultivation.

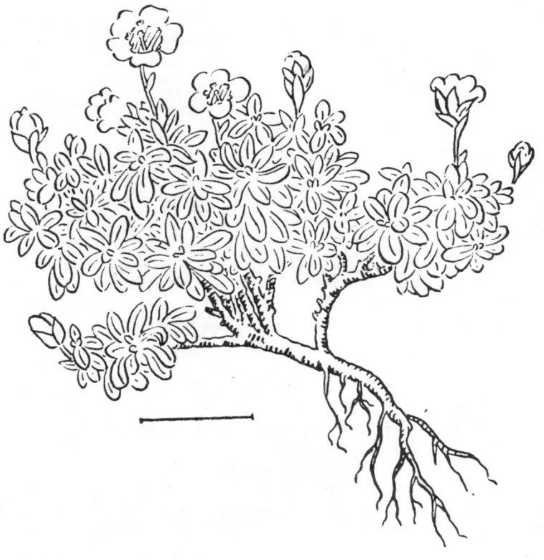

*Diapensia lapponica*

**D. purpu'rea.** Evergreen, cushion plant 1 to 8 in. h. *l.* petiolate, broadly oval, subacute or rounded at apex, dull, very finely papillose and without stomata above, $\frac{3}{16}$ in. long and $\frac{1}{8}$ in. wide. *fl.* terminal, solitary, sub-sessile, cor. usually rose or rosy purple, sometimes white or yellow, tube $\frac{1}{8}$ to $\frac{7}{16}$ in. long, terminated by 5 (rarely 4) broad, spreading lobes. May to August. The bright-red peduncle lengthens after flowering and is over 2 in. long and dark red by the time the capsule is ripe. Distribution as for *D. himalaica* but including Szechwan; both wet and dry situations amongst lime-free rocks at 9,000 to 15,000 ft. and in boggy alpine meadows. SYN. *D. Bulleyana, D. himalaica.* Probably not in cultivation. var. **al'bida,** *fl.* white or whitish; **Bulleya'na,** *fl.* yellow; **ro'sea,** *fl.* rosy or rosy purple.

**D. Ward'ii.** Evergreen, creeping, more or less prostrate sub-shrub. *l.* petiolate, ovate or oval, sub-acute or obtuse at apex, stomatose on both surfaces, up to $\frac{3}{8}$ in. long and often over $\frac{1}{4}$ in. wide. In all probability *fl.* are similar in position and arrangement to other Sino-Himalayan species; in cultivation reported to have had red-purple fl. Ripe capsule on a thin red stalk 2 to 3 in. long. SE. Tibet. Probably not now in cultivation.

**DIAPENSIA'CEAE.** Dicotyledons. A family of about 10 species of semi-shrubs or herbaceous perennials in 6 genera in Arctic and mountain regions of the N. hemisphere. Leaves simple, exstipulate. Flowers with 5 sepals, petals, and stamens; stamens adnate to corolla or monadelphous; ovary 3-celled; stigma 3-lobed. Fruit a capsule with several seeds; stigma 3-lobed. The genera dealt with are Diapensia, Galax, Pyxidanthera, Schizocodon, Shortia.

***diapensioi'des,*** Diapensia-like.

**DIAPHANAN'THE.** Included under **Angraecum.**

***diaph'anus -a -um,*** transparent.

***diapre'pes,*** distinguished.

**DIARTHRONOMY'IA sp.** *See* **Chrysanthemum midge.**

**DIAS'CIA** (*di*, two, *askos*, sac; referring to the 2 spurs). FAM. *Scrophulariaceae.* A genus of about 25 species of annual or perennial herbs, natives of S. Africa, with mostly opposite leaves. Flowers in terminal racemes or clusters; calyx 5-parted; corolla with 5 flat lobes, 2-lipped, 2-spurred; stamens 4, didynamous. Fruit a many-seeded capsule. *D. Barberae* is a half-hardy annual not particular as to soil so long as it is in good heart; *D. Aliciae* is a tender perennial which can be increased by cuttings and flowered outdoors in summer.

**D. Alic'iae.** Half-hardy perennial, up to $2\frac{1}{2}$ ft. h., with spreading branches. *l.* ovate, $1\frac{1}{4}$ to 2 in. long, toothed, with a narrowly winged stalk about $\frac{1}{2}$ in. long. *fl.* in a loose terminal raceme 2 to 10 in. long; cor. pale rose with darker blotches at the base of lips, greenish in pouch; limb about $\frac{2}{3}$ in. long, $\frac{1}{4}$ in. across; spurs about $\frac{1}{4}$ in. long. S. Africa. 1915. (B.M. 8782.)

**D. Bar'berae.** Half-hardy annual, erect, about 18 in. h. Stem square, glabrous. *l.* ovate, bluntly toothed. *fl.* several, rosy-pink with yellow, green-dotted throat, in a raceme; cor. about $\frac{2}{3}$ in. across. S. Africa. 1871. (B.M. 5933.) Makes a good pot plant. Variations have occurred in the colour of the fl.

**DIAS'PIS.** *See* **Scale Insects, Rose Scurfy Scale.**

**DIASTASE.** An enzyme which converts the insoluble carbohydrate starch into the soluble dextrin (q.v.) and the soluble crystallizable sugar maltose, thus enabling the store of food to be moved in the plant from cell to cell, wherever the demand may be.

**DIASTE'MA** (*dis*, two, *stemon*, stamen). FAM. *Gesneriaceae.* A genus of about 20 species of Trop. American herbs, usually dwarf, with creeping rhizomes, related to Isoloma. Leaves opposite, thin, stalked. Flowers pale violet, purplish, or white; corolla tube cylindrical, lobes 5, spreading; stamens affixed at base of tube, anthers cells short, nearly globular. For cultivation *see* **Gesneria.**

**D. Lehmann'ii.** Glandular herb with habit of *Isoloma picta.* *l.* ovate, crenate. *fl.* white, spotted and lined lilac; pedicels shorter than l. Colombia. 1889.

**D. ochroleu'cum.** Hairy, erect herb of 1 to 2 ft. Stem purplish. *l.* ovate, acute, deeply toothed, 3 to 4 in. long, $1\frac{1}{2}$ to 2 in. wide; stalk long. *fl.* white with yellow throat in terminal, many-fld. clusters. August. Colombia. 1844. (B.M. 4254.)

**D. quinquevul'nerum.** Dwarf, hairy herb; branches 4 to 5 in. long. *l.* ovate to ovate-elliptic, 3 to 4 in. long, 2 to $2\frac{1}{2}$ in. wide; long-stalked. *fl.* $\frac{3}{4}$ in. wide; cor. lobes white, throat with 5 rosy lilac spots; racemes terminal or axillary, loose, many-fld. August. Colombia. (F.d.S. 832.)

**DIBBER,** or **DIBBLE.** A useful implement in gardens, often made from a hard piece of wood, such as an old spade handle, and principally employed for planting out seedlings of small or medium size. Dibbers, when used on a large scale, are usually cased with a hollow, tapering point of steel. In heavy soils, the sides of the hole are liable to be pressed too close with the steel sheath, and the roots do not then penetrate them freely. On heavy soils planting with a trowel is to be preferred. Light soils give when the dibber is inserted, consequently they are best suited for its use. Two forms are in general use, one with a half right-angled bend above the pointed part, the other with a D- or T-handle at the top of the straight shaft.

**DIBBLING.** The process of planting with a dibber. Its chief advantages lie in economizing the plants, and rendering thinning almost unnecessary. Seedlings growing closely together should be dibbled out temporarily, until sufficiently strong for placing in permanent quarters by the same method. Dibbling has some disadvantages, the roots often being placed straight down instead of in the natural way in which they grow. It is, however, an expeditious mode, much practised with fast-growing plants that soon form new roots. The dibber is used not only for making the hole into which the roots are to be placed but also for pressing the soil against the roots. For this purpose the dibber is thrust into the soil at an angle about 2 in. from the plant held in the hole made for it and brought up to the perpendicular position. When the dibber is removed a hole for watering is left. A long dibber is often used for planting potatoes; it is large enough to make a hole for the set to drop in, and has a cross-handle, for the use of both hands, and a projecting piece of iron or wood which serves the double purpose of forming a tread and ensuring an equal depth to all the holes made. A similar dibber is useful in planting leeks. For inserting cuttings or young plants, small tapering pieces of wood are employed, even pointed match-sticks being useful for very small seedlings.

**dicallo'sus -a -um,** having 2 knobs.

**DICEN'TRA** (*dis*, two, *kentron*, spur; the flowers are 2-spurred). FAM. *Papaveraceae*. A genus of about 12 species of herbaceous perennials with tuberous, horizontal, or fibrous rootstocks. Leaves much cut, stalked. Flowers pink or yellow in terminal racemes; petals 4, the two outer equally spurred or gibbous at base. These handsome hardy perennials are easily grown in rich, light soil, *D. spectabilis* being the largest and most tender of them. Readily increased by division in early spring or by cutting the fleshy roots into short pieces and planting in sandy soil. *D. spectabilis* is an excellent plant for forcing in early spring but the forcing must be gentle, and the plants should be kept as near the glass as possible. The atmosphere should be moist and a temperature of 50 to 55° F. is ample. The roots for forcing should be lifted from the open border, potted in sandy loam in well-drained pots as soon as the foliage dies down, and put into a cold frame until brought in the house. If brought in in succession, flowering plants may be had from February to June. Plenty of water should be given when the plants are in full growth and occasional watering with manure water is a help. After flowering the plants should be put into the cold frame and planted out in the borders when severe frosts are past. The other species are useful for the rock-garden in sheltered corners. **A**

**D. canaden'sis.** About 6 in. h. *l.* glaucous; lobes linear. *fl.* white with blunt, short spurs; scape few-fld., naked; pedicels short. May. N. America. 1822. (B.M. 3031.)

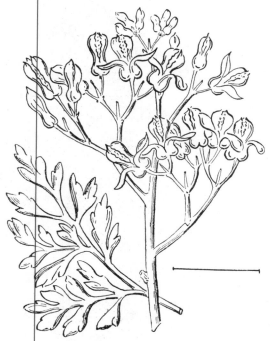

*Dicentra chrysantha*

**D. chrysan'tha.** 3 to 5 ft. h. *l.* very finely cut, glaucous, in a leafy tuft; stems rigid, leafy. *fl.* golden-yellow in erect racemes. Autumn. California. 1852. Dryish, well-drained position.

**D. Cuculla'ria.** Dutchman's Breeches. 3 to 5 in. h. *l.* 3-ternate, smooth, slender. *fl.* white with yellow tip; spur straight, acute; scape naked, raceme unbranched. May. United States. 1731. (F.d.S. 920.)

**D. exi'mia.** 9 to 18 in. h. *l.* 3 to 8 or more, with oblong lobes. *fl.* reddish-purple, drooping, oblong; spurs somewhat incurved, blunt, short; scape naked, racemes branched. United States. 1812. (B.R. 30 as *Fumaria eximia*.)

**D. formo'sa.*** Tufted and spreading with habit of *D. eximia*, up to 18 in. h. *l.-segs.* somewhat coarser. *fl.* pink or dull red, somewhat paler than in *D. eximia*; racemes somewhat branched on a naked scape. May, June. Western N. America. 1796. (B.M. 1335 as *Fumaria formosa*.) Tolerant of shade, and there long-flowering, if supplied with water.

**D. glau'ca.** See *D. oregana*.

**D. orega'na.*** Tufted, about 6 in. h. with stout rhizomes. *l.* much cut into coarsely toothed or lobed segs., silvery. *fl.* cream, tipped purple, with short, blunt spurs; nodding in a short raceme on a naked scape. Summer. Oregon. 1927 ? (J.R.H.S. 60, 488 as *D. glauca*.) Cool, well-drained position.

**D. peregri'na pusil'la.** About 3 in. h. *l.* 2-pinnatisect, segs. cut into linear acute divisions. *fl.* purplish; spurs 2, short, obtuse. Scape naked, 3- or 4-fld. Siberia, Japan.

**D. scan'dens.** Stem slender, flexuous, angled. *l.* much cut; segs. ¼ to 1 in. long, oval, oblong or orbicular. *fl.* ¾ to 1 in. long, yellow or purple, on slender, 8- to 12-fld., often leafy peduncles 2 to 3 in. long; pedicels ½ to 1 in. long. Summer. *Seeds* smooth, shining. Himalaya.

**D. specta'bilis.*** Bleeding Heart; Seal Flower. 18 to 24 in. h. Stem leafy. *l.* much cut, glaucous, long-stalked; segs. obovate-wedge-shaped, cut. *fl.* rosy crimson, nearly 1 in. long, in a graceful arching raceme; spurs blunt. ventricose, short. Spring, summer. Siberia, Japan. 1816. (B.M. 4458 as *Dielytra*.) var. **al'ba**, *fl.* white.

**D. thalictrifo'lia.** Much like *D. scandens* but seeds granular, and *fr.* broader, slow to open. Nepal, Bhotan. (S.B.F.G. s. 2, 127.)

**D. torulo'sa.** Annual climber. *l.* much cut. *fl.* golden-yellow. *fr.* red, seeds black on a white ground when ripe. August. Hardy annual, flowering earlier if sown under glass.

**dice'ras,** having 2 horns.

**DICH'AEA** (*dicha*, 2-ranked; leaves are in 2 rows). FAM. *Orchidaceae*. A genus of about 30 epiphytic Orchids, natives of the W. Indies and Trop. America. Allied to Maxillaria but without pseudobulbs. Flowers solitary, axillary, small, but well-flowered plants are not without attraction. Leaves small, ovate-oblong or linear, distichous. Stems tufted, often pendulous. The sepals and petals are free, the clawed lip is affixed to the base of the column and has an expanded blade, often concave, rounded in front, with the angles of the margins extended into a long, often filiform and recurved tooth. Pollinia 4. Their habit calls for a small raft or piece of board covered with a thin layer of Cattleya compost should be given the pendent-growing kinds. Hang in a moderately shaded, not gloomy, position where they can enjoy warmth and atmospheric moisture. Water must be given throughout the year. In some species the stems attain a length of 18 in. or more. By some a few of the species are included in the closely allied genus Epithecia (Dichaeopsis) which differs slightly in the foliage but is often included in Dichaea.

**D. Bradeor'um.** *fl.* fleshy, somewhat cup-shaped, ½ in. across; sep. broadly lanceolate, concave, pointed, flecked with red, greenish externally; pet. similar, smaller; lip concave, whitish beneath, marked deep purple above, the rounded front margin drawn to a short point, the outer corners lengthened like tendrils, ¼ in. long, inclined backward. Costa Rica. 1935 ?

**D. glau'ca.** *fl.* whitish, ½ in. long; lip sagittate-reniform, broadly clawed. June. Stem erect. *l.* linear-oblong, 1½ to 2 in. long, bluntly mucronate, glaucous beneath. Jamaica. 1837. SYN. *Epidendrum glaucum*, *Epithecia glauca*.

**D. pic'ta.*** *fl.* light leek-green, with purplish dots, axillary; lip unguiculate, sagittate, without a crest; fl.-stalks purplish; sep. cuneate-oblong, acute. *l.* distichous, numerous, linear-lanceolate, acuminate, oblique, nearly perpendicular, glaucous. Trinidad. 1870. An elegant species with erect stems.

**D. pu'mila.** *fl.* sep. and pet. about ¼ in. long, ovate-oblong, slightly concave, sep. slightly the broader, yellowish- or greenish-white, often faintly marked purple; lip clawed, the blade, slightly concave, thickly marked with purple. Stems 6 in. or more long, drooping. *l.* ¼ in. long, oblong, tapered, alternate. Brazil.

**D. vagina'ta.** *fl.* white, shaded green with a few brown markings, very small. Stems long and flattened, with small, close-set, distichous l. Mexico. 1885. Neat; suitable for a basket.

E. C.

**DICHASIUM.** A branch system, whether of the vegetative or the flowering part, in which 2 lateral branches grow with equal vigour and more vigorously than the axis from which they arise, as seen, e.g. in Lilac.

**A→**

**DICHIL'US** (*dis*, twice, *cheilos*, a lip; in allusion to the deeply cleft calyx). FAM. *Leguminosae.* A genus of 5 species of sub-shrubs, native of S. Africa. Leaves alternate. Flowers papilionaceous. *D. lebeckioides* needs greenhouse treatment like an Acacia and is propagated by seed.

**D. lebeckioi'des.** Semi-woody plant, 1½ to 2 ft., branches slender, graceful, thinly appressed-hairy. *l.* 3-foliolate; lflets. linear to oblanceolate, ¼ to ⅝ in. long, $\frac{1}{16}$ to ⅛ in. wide, appressed-hairy. *fl.* solitary or in small stalked clusters near tips of shoots, about ½ in. long; standard reddish-brown; wings and keel yellow. *Pod* 1 to 1½ in. long, ⅛ in. wide. 1825.

W. J. B.

**dichlamydeous,** having both calyx and corolla (cf. **monochlamydeous**). When calyx and corolla are similar the perianth is said to be homochlamydeous; when they differ, heterochlamydeous.

**dichogamous,** having stamens and pistil ripening at different times (*see* **protandrous, protogynous**).

**DICHO'NE** (possibly *di-* 2, *chone, choane;* funnel). FAM. *Iridaceae.* A genus of 3 species of herbs related to Tritonia and often included in it, natives of S. Africa, differing from Tritonia by the tube of the perianth cylindrical, not widened upwards. Flowers small, segments usually not overlapping, stamens and style much shorter than the perianth segments. For cultivation *see* **Tritonia.**

**D. scilla'ris.** About 1 ft. h. *l.* flat, narrow, grass-like. *fl.* reddish, varying to white, scentless; segs. regular; tube very slender, 2 or 3 times as long as spathe. May. S. Africa. (B.M. 542 as *Ixia scillaris*; B.M. 629 as *I. polystachya.*) SYN. *Tritonia scillaris.*

**D. undula'ta.** Very similar to *D. scillaris* but with much waved l. and larger fl. of a brighter colour. June. 1787. (B.M. 599 as *Ixia crispa.*) SYN. *Tritonia undulata.*

**DICHOPO'GON** (*dicha*, double, *pogon*, beard; from the 2 appendages of the anthers). FAM. *Liliaceae.* A genus of 2 S. Australian perennial herbs related to Anthericum, but with the inner perianth segments much broader than the outer. *D. strictus* needs a compost of sandy loam and peat, and may be increased by division of the rhizome or by the tubers on the root fibres.

**D. stric'tus.** Perennial with a short rhizome and clusters of root fibres often bearing fleshy tubers up to ¾ in. long. *l.* radical, grass-like with a shortly sheathing base, about 18 in. long, ¼ in. wide, channelled. *fls.* pale or dark purple, up to 1½ in. across; segs. spreading, outer elliptic-oblong, acute, inner twice as wide, in a raceme or panicle 3 to 8 in. long, on an erect scape, longer than the l., leafless or with leafy bracts below the infl. November. 1883. (B.M. 6746; G.F. 2, 37 as *D. undulatus.*)

**DICHOP'SIS Gut'ta.** *See* **Palaquium Gutta.**

**DICHORISAN'DRA** (*dis*, twice, *chorizo*, to part, *aner*, anther; the anthers are 2-valved). FAM. *Commelinaceae.* A genus of 27 species of Trop. American herbaceous perennials, with racemes of often beautiful flowers and frequently with ornamental foliage. Stems erect or ascending and often branched. Flowers with 3 green or coloured, almost equal, oblong or ovate sepals, 3 distinct petals, and 6 (rarely 5) perfect stamens on short, erect, naked filaments. The Dichorisandras need stove conditions and a compost of peat, loam, and leaf-mould in about equal parts with a little silver sand. In summer shading from direct sunlight and liberal watering are called for, but in winter much less water will be needed; they must, however, not be exposed to cold. Propagation is by divisions, cuttings, or seed.

**D. acau'lis.** Almost stemless. *l.* in a rosette, nearly sessile, lanceolate, glossy intense green with many short, longitudinal silvery white stripes above, violet-purple beneath. *fl.* deep violet-blue. Brazil. 1894. (I.H. 1894, t. 19.)

**D. albo-margina'ta.** Erect, glabrous, sometimes branched above, 2 to 3 ft. h. *l.* lanceolate, slender-pointed. *fl.* in a dense raceme 2 in. long; sep. white, blue, and puberulous without; pet. larger, rhomboid-ovate, blue, lower part white. Brazil. 1868. (G.F. 569.)

**D. angustifo'lia.** *l.* lanceolate, 4 to 6 in. long, acute, dark green with numerous transverse white streaks between the nerves, purple beneath. Ecuador. 1892. (I. H. 29, t. 158.)

**D. Gaudichaudia'na.** Branches 12 to 18 in. long, simple, hairy. *l.* obovate-lanceolate, 6 to 10 in. long, 2½ in. wide, with a short point, woolly hairy on margins; stalks ¼ in. long. *fl.* blue and yellow in a raceme 1½ to 2 in. long; bracts ovate-lanceolate. August. Brazil. 1847. (P.M.B. 15, 5.)

**D. grac'ilis.** Glabrous. Stem slender, little branched, 18 in. h. *l.* 6 in. long, 1½ in. wide, lanceolate, with a very long slender point. *fl.* blue; pet. obtuse; raceme 1½ in. long, downy. August. Brazil.

**D. leucophthal'mus.** Glabrous. Stems 2 or 3, erect, terete, 1 to 1½ ft. h. *l.* elliptic-lanceolate, sharply slender-pointed, somewhat narrowed below to the sheath, often recurved. *fl.* often 2 or 3 together on a branch of the prostrate peduncle, large; sep. oblong, spreading, somewhat dry; pet. 4 times as large as sep., blue-purple, white in lower half; anthers bright yellow. June. Brazil. (B.M. 4733.)

*Dichorisandra mosaica*

**D. mosa'ica.** Stems terete, chequered, surrounded at nodes by close, brownish sheaths, 1½ ft. h. *l.* ovate, acute, dark green, profusely pencilled and veined with zigzag transverse white lines above, reddish-purple beneath. *fl.* bright azure-blue, in a terminal truss. Autumn. Brazil. 1866. (F.d.S. 1711–12.) var. **gigan'tea,** about 2 ft. h., *l.* broadly ovate, 9 in. long, 5 in. wide, very deep green with light bars. 1892; **unda'ta,** very dwarf, *l.* broad ovate, dark green with longitudinal bands, alternately of green reflected with silver, and of green shaded to black, undulated or waved, above, uniform purple beneath. 1879. (F.d.S. 1763–4.)

**D. ovalifo'lia.** Branches 18 in. long. *l.* 5 in. long, 2¼ in. wide, sessile, oval, slender-pointed, glabrous, upper oblong-lanceolate. *fl.* purple; panicle 2½ in. long with spreading branches; bracts 2½ in. long. May. Panama, &c. 1846.

**D. oxypet'ala.** Stem oblique, sometimes forked, 2 ft. h. *l.* in upper part of stem only, elliptic, narrowed to both ends, entire, striate, slightly downy at base beneath. *fl.* segs. ovate, acute, spreading, veined reddish-purple with white spot at base; anthers linear-oblong, whitish at base. August. Brazil. 1810. (B.M. 2721.)

**D. pic'ta.** Branches short, about 6 in. h. *l.* broad-elliptic, about 4½ in. long, green with a broad brown stripe each side, edged with green. *fl.* purple-blue with a distinct white spot at base, about 1 in. across, in short terminal panicles. September. (B.M. 4760; L.B.C. 1667.)

**D. pubes'cens.** *l.* 3½ in. long, 1¼ in. wide, lanceolate or oblong-lanceolate, slender-pointed, sheath downy-hairy; stalk short. *fl.* blue; pet. elliptic with a short, sharp point; raceme 1½ to 4 in. long. Brazil. var. **taenien'sis,** *l.* lanceolate, slender-pointed, rich green striped white, *fl.* blue and white in short, terminal, spike-like panicles. Brazil. 1888. (G.C. 3 (1888), 557, f. 75.)

**D. Saunder'sii.** Stem slender, rarely branched, cylindrical, hairy, 2 ft. h. *l.* numerous, lanceolate, long-pointed, 5-nerved, dark green, margins recurved in lower part, pale beneath; sheaths green. *fl.* ¾ in. across; sep. oblong, white-tipped violet; pet. twice as large, obovate, rounded, violet except at white base. July. Brazil. 1873. (B.M. 6165.)

**D. thyrsiflo'ra.** About 4 ft. h. *l.* broad, sheathing, very dark green. *fl.* rich dark blue; anthers bright yellow; thyrse compact, often 6 to 7 in. long. Summer and autumn. Brazil. 1822. (B.R. 682.) A very handsome flowering plant.

**D. unda'ta.** A variety of *D. mosaica*.

F. G. P.

**DICHOTOMAN'THES** (*dichotomes*, to cut asunder, *anthos*, flower). FAM. *Rosaceae*. A genus of 1 species, a shrub or small tree, native of China, related to Cotoneaster but with a calyx persisting and enlarging after flowering and enveloping the fruit all but the tip, the fruit being a dry capsule ¼ in. long. Not hardy in exposed situations or severe winters when it is apt to be badly damaged. It grows well in ordinary soils and is usually safe against a wall.

**D. tristaniicarp'a.** Evergreen shrub or small tree, up to 20 ft. in nature, young shoots densely white-woolly. *l.* alternate, oval, tapered to both ends, entire; 1 to 4 in. long, up to 1½ in. wide, dark green and smooth above, silky-hairy beneath; stalk very short; stipules minute, deciduous. *fl.* white, ¼ in. across, in terminal corymbs about 2 in. across; cal. woolly without; stamens 15 to 20. June. China. 1917. (H.I.P. 2653.)

*dichot'omus -a -um,* dichotomous; repeatedly divided into 2 branches.

**DICHRO'A** (*dis*, 2, *chroa*, colour; in allusion to the 2 colours of the flowers). FAM. *Saxifragaceae*. A genus of 3 or 4 species of evergreen shrubs natives of E. Asia. *D. febrifuga* is the only one in cultivation and is easily grown in open, loamy soil and propagated by cuttings. As at present conceived, it is very widely spread. In Sumatra and similar climates the leaves are much larger. The flowers vary from blue to white. The plants at present in cultivation are Chinese and are only on the verge of hardiness, but can be grown in Cornwall in the open.

*Dichroa febrifuga*

**D. febrifu'ga.** Evergreen shrub 3 to 7 ft., shoots and infl. downy. *l.* opposite, lanceolate, 4 to 8 in. long, 1 to 3 in. wide, coarsely toothed. *fl.* pale blue to violet, in terminal rounded clusters 3 in. across; pet. 5, oval-lanceolate; stamens 10, spreading, bluish. June to August. *fr.* the size of peppercorns, deep blue. Himalaya, Malaya, China, Japan. 1829. (B.M. 3046 as *Adamia cyanea*.)

W. J. B.

*dichroan'thus -a -um,* with 2-coloured flowers.

*dichro'mus -a -um,* of 2 colours.

**DICHROSTACH'YS** (*dichroos*, 2-coloured, *stachys*, spike; the lower flowers of a spike differing in colour from those above). FAM. *Leguminosae*. A genus of 4 or 5 species of rigid shrubs in Trop. Africa and Asia, and one in Australia. Leaves 2-pinnate, leaflets usually small; stipules thorny. Flowers in upper part of spike hermaphrodite, yellow, in lower part neuter, either white, pink, or purple. Related to Mimosa and like that with stamens twice as many as petals, but having the anthers crowned with a gland while in bud. For treatment of these stove plants, *see* **Mimosa**.

**D. nu'tans.** *l.* Acacia-like, glabrous or downy; pinnae in 5 pairs. *fl.* in dense, drooping, axillary spikes, upper sulphur-coloured, lower rosy-lilac. *Pod* twisted. Cent. Africa.

**D. platycar'pa.** *l.* with 14 or more pairs of pinnae; lflets. in 26 to 30 pairs; glaucous green. *fl.* in drooping spikes, 1½ in. long, upper bright yellow, lower rose. Angola. 1866.

F. G. P.

**DICHROT'RICHUM** (*dichroos*, 2-coloured, *thria*, hair; the hair tufts at end of seed are 2-coloured in the original species). FAM. *Gesneriaceae*. Closely related to Aeschynanthus and needing the same treatment.

**D. ternate'um.** Of curious habit, climbing trees and rocks by means of abundant adventitious roots. *l.* opposite, unequal, the larger cordate. *fl.* crimson-red, tubular, in loose almost umbellate cymes. July. Moluccas. 1872. (B.H. 1871, 22.)

F. G. P.

*dichro'us -a -um,* of 2 colours.

**DICKSON'IA** (named after James Dickson, 1738–1822, a British nurseryman and botanist). FAM. *Cyatheaceae*. A genus of over 20 species mainly with tree-like stems and large much-divided leathery fronds. Sori are at the tips of veins just within the margin, the indusia being distinctly 2-valved, the outer valve being formed by the tip of a segment. Mostly natives of Polynesia, Australia, and New Zealand. Most species require cool treatment. Many of the tree-like species grow naturally in valleys and in deep, shady ravines, in countries where some of them occasionally have their fronds loaded with snow. *D. antarctica* thrives outside in sheltered spots in the warmer parts of England, Wales, and Ireland.

When grown in pots Dicksonias must have water to their roots all the year round. When not planted out, all tree-ferns grow best in pots or tubs with only 3 or 4 in. round the trunks. The best compost is fibrous loam, 2 parts; fibrous peat, 1 part; coarse silver sand, 1 part. In summer the trunks of Dicksonias should be thoroughly watered twice a day, the amount applied being reduced as the season advances, only enough being used to keep them moist during winter. They are propagated by spores but the related rhizomatous species may be divided in March and April. Several plants hitherto placed under Dicksonia should be sought under Cibotium and Dennstaedtia.

**D. antarc'tica.\*** *cau.* 30 to 35 ft. h. *sti.* under 1 ft. long, scaly. *Fronds* rhomboid, 3-pinnate, 5 to 6 ft. long, 2 to 3 ft. broad in centre; central pinnae 1 to 1½ ft. long, 4 to 5 in. broad; pinnules sessile, linear, ½ in. broad; segs. oblong. *Sori* 6 to 10 to lowest seg. Australia. 1786. (L.F. 8, 43; G.C. 50 (1911), 182.) Greenhouse.

**D. apiifo'lia.** A synonym of *Dennstaedtia cornuta*.

**D. arbores'cens.** *cau.* 10 ft. h. *Fronds* 2-pinnate; lower pinnae 1 to 1½ ft. long, 6 to 9 in. broad; pinnules linear, deeply cut; segs. ½ in. long, oblong. *Sori* 2 to 6 to a lobe, large, globose. St. Helena. 1824. (H.S. 22A.) Greenhouse.

**D. assam'ica.** A synonym of *Cibotium Barometz*.

**D. Berteroa'na.** A synonym of *D. Brackenbridgei*.

**D. Billardie'ri.** A synonym of *D. antarctica*.

**D. Blum'ei.** *Fronds* 2-pinnate; lower pinnae 1 to 1½ ft. long, 6 to 9 in. broad; pinnules linear, very deeply cut; segs. linear-oblong, deeply toothed, ½ in. long; fertile pinnules slightly contracted; main rachis clothed with a thick coat of shining yellowish-brown hairs at the base. Java. 1875. (I.H. 1875, 206 as *D. chrysotricha*.) Stove.

**D. Brackenbridg′ei.** *cau.* 6 to 15 ft. h. *Fronds* rhomboid, 3-pinnate; pinnae oblong-lanceolate, 1 to 1¼ ft. long, 5 to 6 in. broad; pinnules sessile, lanceolate, about 1 in. broad; segs. close, lanceolate, sterile sub-entire, fertile deeply pinnatifid. Juan Fernandez. 1880. (H.S. 1, 23A; Gn. 17 (1880), 499, as *D. Berteroana*.)

*Dicksonia Brackenbridgei*

**D. chrysot′richa.** A synonym of *D. Blumei*.

**D. Culci′ta.** A synonym of *Culcita macrocarpa*.

**D. fibro′sa.*** *sti.* very short, densely scaly. *Fronds* rhomboid, 3-pinnate, 3 to 4 ft. long; central pinnae lanceolate, 6 to 9 in. long; pinnules sessile, linear, 1 to 1½ in. long; segs. crowded, deltoid, falcate, deeply pinnatifid. *Sori* 4 to 6 to largest seg. New Zealand. (H.S. 23B.) Greenhouse.

**D. lana′ta.** *cau.* low. *sti.* about 1 ft. long. *Fronds* rhomboid, 3-pinnate, 3 to 4 ft. long; central pinnae oblong-lanceolate, about 1 ft. long; pinnules lanceolate, stalked, 1½ to 3 in. long, less than 1 in. broad. *Sori* crowded, 6 to 12 to largest seg. New Zealand. (H.S. 23C.) Greenhouse.

**D. La′thami.*** *Fronds* 3-pinnate, narrow-oblong, dark green, coriaceous, 14 to 15 ft. long; pinnae sessile, oblong-lanceolate, acuminate, 1½ to 2 ft. long, 6 to 8 in. broad, with close-set, sessile, lanceolate, acute pinnules; pinnulets oblong, obtuse, more or less lobed or crenulate. 1886. (G.C. 24 (1885), 689; J.H. 22 (1891), 513.) A noble, stove, evergreen Tree Fern, supposed to be a hybrid between *D. antarctica* and *D. arborescens*.

**D. magnif′ica.** A synonym of *D. Blumei*.

**D. princeps.** A synonym of *Cyathea insignis*.

**D. Sellowia′na.*** Arborescent. *Fronds* 6 to 8 ft. long, 2 to 3 ft. broad, lanceolate, 2-pinnate; lower pinnae 1 to 1¼ ft. long, 3 to 4 in. broad; pinnules linear, deeply cut; segs. ¼ in. long, close, oblong-deltoid. *Sori* 2 to 6 to a lobe. Brazil. 1871. (H.S. 22B; B.C.F. 2, 186.) Stove.

**D. spectab′ile.** A synonym of *Cibotium Wendlandii*.

**D. squarro′sa.*** *sti.* chestnut, 6 to 12 in. long, densely scaly. *Fronds* oblong-deltoid, 3-pinnate; pinnae oblong-lanceolate, 9 to 15 in. long, 4 to 6 in. broad; pinnules sub-sessile, linear, 2 to 3 in. long; segs. lanceolate. *Sori* 6 to 8 to lower segs. New Zealand. Arborescent. (Gn. 5 (1874), 301; G.F. 1874, 792.) Greenhouse.

**D. Young′iae.** Arborescent. *sti.* chestnut, 6 to 9 in. long, densely scaly. *Fronds* oblong-deltoid, 3-pinnate; pinnae oblong-lanceolate, 1 ft. long, 5 to 6 in. broad; pinnules sub-sessile, lanceolate, 2 to 3 in. long; segs. lanceolate, close. *Sori* 6 to 8 to lower segs. Australia. 1865. (G.C. 28 (1900), 72.) Greenhouse.

***dicksonioi′des,*** resembling Dicksonia.

**diclinous,** unisexual, having stamens in one flower, pistils in another.

**DICLIP′TERA** (*diklis,* double-doored, *pteron,* wing; the capsule is 2-winged). FAM. *Acanthaceae.* A genus of about 75 species of annual or perennial herbs, or sub-shrubs, natives of warm regions. Leaves opposite, entire, usually evergreen. Flowers in terminal or axillary clusters, with red, violet, or blue bracts; corolla tube slender, often widened above, lips narrow; stamens 2 affixed at the throat. For cultivation, *see* **Jacobinia.**

**D. Niederleinia′na.** Sub-shrub. *l.* oval, densely hairy, up to 3 in. long. *fl.* about 1¼ in. long, in crowded terminal panicles. Argentine. Greenhouse.

**D. Tweedia′na.** Stems numerous, perennial. *l.* oblong, narrowed to both ends. *fl.* bright scarlet, in compound heads; cor. tube 1½ in. long, slightly widened near throat, upper lip 2-, lower 3-fid. Autumn. Buenos Aires. 1874. (R.H. 1874, 171.)

**DICLY′TRA.** *See* **Dicentra.**

***dicoc′cus -a -um,*** having 2 nuts.

**dicotyledonous,** having 2 cotyledons.

**DICOTYLEDONS.** One of the 2 great classes of Angiosperms, the other being the Monocotyledons. It is characterized by the embryo having typically 2 cotyledons and by the vascular bundles possessing a cambium by which the wood (or xylem) is added to on the inside and the bast (or phloem) on the outside. The leaves are usually net-veined, and the parts of the flower usually in fours or fives, not threes.

**DICRANOSTIG′MA** (*dikranos,* 2-branched; *stigma*). FAM. *Papaveraceae.* A genus of 3 species of glaucous annual or perennial herbs with a woody root, natives of the Himalaya and W. China. Leaves mainly radical, pinnatifid, lobes distant, rhomboid, acute, sharply cut, the terminal 3-fid. Stems many, naked below, branched and with alternate leafy bracts above. Flowers orange or yellow; sepals 2, ovate; stamens many. Capsule narrowly cylindrical or linear. Related to Hunnemannia but with stigmas more or less distinctly 3-lobed. Hardy. Cultivation as for Chelidonium.

**D. Franchetia′num.*** Glaucous, mealy annual or biennial herb, 5 to 6 ft. h. *Radical l.* 6 to 8 in. long, 1½ in. wide, *cauline* 1 to 1½ in. long. Stems many, sparsely branched above. *fl.* terminal, orange, 1 in. across. Capsule linear, glabrous. Szechwan, Yunnan. (B.M. 9404.)

**D. lactucoi′des.** Herb, 1 to 2 ft. h., mealy. *Radical l.* 5 to 10 in. long, 1½ to 2 in. wide, *cauline* 2 in. or more long. Stems 3 or 4, slender, erectly branched above *fl.* terminal, orange, 1½ in. across. Capsule cylindrical, acute, softly hairy. Himalaya.

**D. leptopo′dum.** Glaucous herb. *Radical l.* 5 to 6 in. long, *cauline* ½ in. long. Stems many, much-branched. *fl.* terminal, yellow, about 1 in. across. Capsule narrow-cylindrical, glabrous. Kansu.

***dicranot′richus -a -um,*** having 2-pointed hairs.

**DICRYP′TA.** A synonym of Maxillaria.

**DICTAM′NUS** (from *Diktamnos,* old Greek name used by Hippocrates). FAM. *Rutaceae.* A genus of 1 or 2 species of perennial herbs, natives of Europe and Asia. Stem glandular in upper part, the glands producing a fragrant, very volatile, and inflammable oil. Leaves alternate, unequally pinnate, without stipules; leaflets in 4 to 6 pairs, toothed, full of pellucid dots. Flowers white or rose, showy, zygomorphic, in a long, terminal raceme. Easy grown in ordinary garden soil, best in a rather dry place, and best left undisturbed. On a hot still day the volatile oil may often be ignited by bringing a lighted match near the base of the inflorescence, flaming up for a short time and leaving the plant uninjured.

**D. al′bus.*** Burning Bush, Dittany, Fraxinella. About 18 in. h., scented of lemon peel when gently rubbed, of balsam when bruised. *lflets.* 4 to 6 pairs with an odd one, cordate at base, acute, finely toothed. *fl.* in a long, terminal raceme, white or pale purple. E. Europe, Asia. SYN. *D. Fraxinella.* var. **gigan′teus,** a large form (B.M. 8961 as var. *caucasicus*); **purpu′reus,** a large form with purplish *fl.* SYN. var. *ruber.*

**D. Fraxinel′la.** A synonym of *D. albus.*

**dictyo-**, in compound words, signifying netted, as *dictyocarpus*, with a netted fruit.

**DICTYOGLOS'SUM crinit'um.** A synonym of *Elaphoglossum crinitum.*

**DICTYOGRAM'MA japon'ica.** A synonym of *Coniogramme japonica.*

**DICTYOP'TERIS.** Included in **Polypodium.**

**DICTYOSPER'MA** (*diktyon*, net, *sperma*, seed; the raphe of the seed forms a loose network). FAM. *Palmaceae*. A genus of 1 species of slender, unarmed Palm native of Mauritius and the Seychelles, with a terminal crown of pinnate leaves, related to Areca, and requiring similar treatment. Leaflets with reflexed sides before unfolding. Flowers unisexual, often in threes with 1 female between 2 male flowers. **A**

**D. al'bum.** Slender, up to 30 ft. h. *l.* 4 to 8 ft. long, pinnate; stalks clothed with white tomentum; lflets. 2 ft. long, about 2 in. wide, bright green on both sides. Mauritius. 1842. SYN. *Areca alba.* var. **au'reum,** *lflets.* pendent, dark green, stalk yellow. Seychelles Is. 1868. SYN. *Areca aurea*, **furfura'ceum,** *lf.-stalk* and sheath covered with shaggy hair. Mauritius. SYN. *Areca furfuracea, A. pisifera;* **ru'brum,** main veins and l.-margins dark red, colour less noticeable in adult plants. Mauritius. SYN. *Areca rubra.*

**D. fibro'sum.** A synonym of *Vonitra fibrosa.*

**DICTYOXIPH'IUM** (*dictyon*, net, *xiphos*, sword; the sword-shaped fronds having netted veins). FAM. *Polypodiaceae*. A genus of 1 species allied to Lindsaya. Sori marginal, continuous; indusia like Lindsaya but outer valve obsolete. A compost of 2 parts peat or leaf-mould, 1 of rich fibrous loam, and 1 of sand best suits *D. panamense*. It must at all seasons be watered liberally. It does not like bright sunlight but should not be shaded heavily. Propagation by division of the crowns.

**D. panamen'se.** *Fronds* tufted, sessile, 2 to 3 ft. long, the barren 2 to 3 in., the fertile ½ to 1 in. wide, narrowed gradually from the middle downwards, entire. *Sori* in a continuous marginal line. Guatemala to Colombia. (L.F. 8, 69.) Warm house.

**DICYR'TA** (*dis*, twice, *kyrtos*, curved; the throat of the corolla has 2 tuberculated folds in the lower part). FAM. *Gesneriaceae*. A genus of 2 species of dwarf herbs, natives of Cent. America, nearly related to and sometimes combined with Achimenes, but having smaller flowers and diverging anther-cells. Leaves opposite, rather thin, hairy. Flowers white or pale lilac, often spotted, small; stamens fixed to bottom of corolla tube. For cultivation, *see* **Achimenes.** **A**

**D. can'dida.** About 18 in. h. *l.* ovate to ovate-lanceolate, about 4 in. long, slender-pointed, coarsely toothed, hairy, stalked. *fl.* 1 to 3 on an axillary peduncle, white with purple spots on lobes and throat and a yellowish decurved tube about ⅓ in. long. July. Guatemala. 1848. (J.R.H.S. 3, p. 317 as *Achimenes candida*.)

**Didier'i,** in honour of E. Didier, 1811?–89, student of the flora of Savoy.

**DIDIS'CUS** (*dis*, twice, *discus*, disk; from the form of the pistil). FAM. *Umbelliferae*. A genus containing one hardy annual or biennial herb closely related to Trachymene with which it is often combined, but differing by the distinct stipules and simple umbels. Leaves usually ternately divided, toothed. Flowers blue, calyx teeth minute, petals entire. The seed may be sown where the plants are to flower in any ordinary good garden soil or grown for greenhouse decoration in a 5-in. pot.

**D. caeru'leus.** Annual or biennial, 1 to 2 ft. h. *l.* once or twice 3-partite; segs. linear, toothed, acute; upper smaller. *fl.* blue, small, pet. unequal, numerous, in simple umbels 1 to 2 in. across; peduncle long; bracts numerous, linear. July. W. Australia. 1827. (B.M. 2875; B.R. 1225 as *Trachymene caerulea*.)

**DIDISSAN'DRA** (*di, dis*, twice two, *ander*, stamens). FAM. *Gesneriaceae*. A genus of about 20 species of perennial herbs with a thick woody rootstock. Leaves in a basal rosette, usually dense. Flowers in umbels (rarely solitary) on erect or ascending peduncles without bracts and usually numerous: calyx of 5 segments cut to base; corolla medium-sized or small with a cylindrical tube not inflated upwards and a 2-lipped limb, the upper lip shorter than the lower; tube hairy inside only, the hairs in 2 rows; anther cells divergent; after the anther cells burst they are drawn back by the spiral coiling of the

*Didiscus caeruleus*

filaments. These characters serve to distinguish this genus from the nearly related genera Ancylostemon, Briggsia, and Isometrum. Several species at one time placed in this genus are now under Briggsia and Corallodiscus. **A**

**D. lanugino'sa.** A synonym of *Corallodiscus lanuginosus.*

**D. muscic'ola.** *l.* radical, ovate-lanceolate or oblong, 3 to 4 in. long, toothed, densely ashy-hairy above. *Scape* 6 to 12 in. long, covered with brownish hairs. *fl.* bright orange, bell-shaped, over 1 in. long, somewhat constricted at mouth; lobes ciliate. W. China. Grows on moss-covered rocks.

**D. seric'ea.** Rootstock short, thick. l.-rosette up to 6 in. across. *l.* oblong- to lanceolate-ovate, blunt, about 2 in. long, leathery, densely silky-hairy above, with cinnamon-woolly hairs on veins beneath. *Peduncles* about 6 in. long, densely white- or cinnamon-hairy, many-fld., pedicels about ½ in. long. *fl.* blue with 2 interior lines of hair; cor. tube about ⅓ in. long; upper lip ¼ in. wide at base, ¼ in. long, 2-lobed; lower 3-lobed, about ⅛ in. wide. W. China. 1919.

**DIDYMOCAR'PUS** (*didymos*, twin, *karpos*, fruit; there being twin capsules). FAM. *Gesneriaceae*. A genus of about 80 species of perennial, often stemless herbs. natives of S. and E. Asia, Australia, and Madagascar. Leaves usually cordate, with rounded teeth, wrinkled, hairy. Flowers violet-blue or rarely yellow, in dichotomous umbels; corolla funnel-shaped, throat swollen. The plants require a stove temperature and a compost of peat, loam, and dried cow-dung with a little sand. They may be propagated by cuttings of young shoots as they begin growth, placed in sandy soil and with bottom heat. Chirita is nearly related to Didymocarpus and is sometimes combined with it. There are many species worthy of introduction in India.

**D. crini'tus.** Stem short, thick, erect, about 1 ft. h. *l.* alternate, 9 to 10 in. long, spatulate, acute, toothed, hairy, red. *fl.* white, tinged purple; tube incurved, swelling above; peduncles 2 to 5 in the l.-axils, each 1-fld. Malaya. (B.M. 4554.)

**D. cyan'eus.\*** Stemless herb. *l.* 3 to 6 in. long, ovate-elliptic to obovate, toothed, softly hairy. *fl.* deep blue, trumpet-shaped, 1½ in. long, 4 or 5 on a scape. Malaya. 1906. (B.M. 8204.)

**D. Humboldtia'nus.** Stemless herb. *fl.* pale lilac or light blue with yellow throat, in a loose long-peduncled 5- or 6-fld. infl. October. Ceylon. (B.M. 4757.) var. **primulaefo'lia,** stem 3 to 6 in. with 4 crowded wrinkled *l.* at top, *fl.* on twin, many-fld. peduncles, hairy. (B.M. 5161.) Requires intermediate temperature.

**D. lacuno'sus.** Almost stemless, hairy. *l.* crowded, oblong or obovate-cordate, toothed, with deep indentations. *fl.* deep blue, nodding, about 1½ in. long, on long, few-fld. peduncles. Malaya. 1892. (B.M. 7236.)

**D. malaya'nus.** Densely tufted, softly downy. *l.* spreading from root in unequal pairs, 2 to 3 in. long, broadly ovate. *fl.* pale straw with golden yellow lobes, 1 in. across, 2 in. long; scape 2½ to 3½ in. long. June. Malay. 1896. (B.M. 7526.)

**D. primulaefo'lia.** A variety of *D. Humboldtianus*.

**D. Wattia'nus.** About 3 in. h. *l.* oblong-elliptic, about 4 in. long, thick, rigid, deeply veined, dark green; stalked. *fl.* pale wine-colour, deeper near tip and in bud, 1 in. across, nearly 3 in. long; scape long, 3- or 4-fld. Spring. Siam. 1922. (G.C. 75 (1924), 89.)

**DIDYMOCHLAE'NA** (*didymos*, twin, *chlaina*, cloak; in reference to the indusia). FAM. *Polypodiaceae*. A genus of 2 species. Indusium elliptical, emarginate at base, attached to the linear receptacle, free all round edge. Sori elliptical, terminal on a veinlet, but distinctly within margin of frond. These ferns are easily grown but they frequently lose their pinnules, leaving the stalks naked, if they have suffered from want of water at the roots. Although then unsightly for a time they soon recover if given proper treatment. The plants should be potted in a mixture of 2 parts good fibrous peat and 1 of loam with a good amount of silver sand. The pots must be thoroughly drained. Propagated readily from spores which are freely produced.

**D. lunula'ta.** A synonym of *D. truncatula*.

**D. sinuo'sa.** A synonym of *D. truncatula*.

**D. truncat'ula.** Stem erect, somewhat tree-like. *Fronds* densely tufted, 4 to 6 ft. long, 2-pinnate; pinnules ¾ to 1 in. long, in shape and texture much resembling some Adiantums, dimidiate, nearly 4-sided, entire or slightly sinuate. *Sori* 2 to 6 to a pinnule. Tropics of Africa and America, Polynesia. (H.G.F. 17 as *D. lunulata*; F.S.A. (2) 24.) SYN. *Aspidium truncatulum*.

**DIDYMOGLOS'SUM.** *See* **Hymenophyllum.**

**DIDYMOSPER'MA** (*didymos*, twin, *sperma*, seed; the fruits are frequently 2-seeded). FAM. *Palmaceae*. A genus of about 6 species of unarmed Palms of moderate growth, natives of India and the E. Indies. Leaves pinnatisect, in a terminal crown; leaflets few, trapezoid, erose, 1-ribbed with flabellate veins. Flowers monoecious, sometimes on the same spadix; male with free or connate overlapping sepals; female with valvate petals; spadix produced among the leaves; spathes usually many. For treatment of these stove Palms, *see* **Areca.**

**D. nan'um.** Dwarf, robust. *l.* about 2 ft. long; stalk short, roundish; segs. alternate or nearly opposite, wedge-shaped at base, then oblique, variously lobed, toothed or spiny; terminal seg. irregular in shape, generally 2-lobed, green above, glaucous beneath. Assam. SYN. *Wallichia nana*.

**D. porphyrocar'pon.** *rhiz.* creeping underground. Stem slender, 3 to 6 ft. h. *l.* stalk 4 to 8 ft. long; segs. 9 to 17, wedge-shaped, somewhat panduriform, sinuate, 6 to 12 in. long, 2 to 5 in. wide, glaucous beneath. Java.

**D. trem'ulum.** Stem 3 to 4 ft. h. *l.* segs. long, flat, firm, linear, spiny-toothed, 2-fid at apex. Philippine Is.

*did'ymus -a -um, didymo-,* in compound words, twin.

**didynamous,** having 2 stamens long, 2 short.

**DIEBACK,** i.e. the death of young shoots of trees and shrubs which is often followed by death of the larger branches. It may be due to various factors. One of the commonest is poor soil conditions especially where waterlogging for long periods in winter and spring injures the roots. Another Dieback in cherries and plums is due to *Bacterial Canker*. In Gooseberry bushes dieback of the branches is caused by the fungus *Botrytis cinerea*. Several fungi are thus definitely able to cause dieback. Several others, e.g. *Cytospora* sp., are commonly found on dying twigs but act as weak parasites on tissues already injured and weakened by other causes and are not able to cause the trouble directly.

D. E. G.

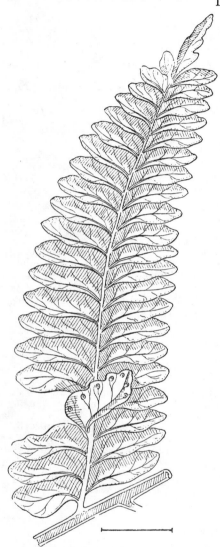

*Didymochlaena truncatula*, a single pinna

**DIEFFENBACH'IA** (in honour of Herr Dieffenbach, gardener in 1830 at Schönbrunn, Austria). FAM. *Araceae*. A genus of about 20 species of noble, erect, evergreen perennials, with often variegated foliage, natives of Trop. America. Stem fleshy, 6 to 8 ft. long. Leaves oblong with many veins diverging from midrib, usually green but sometimes irregularly marked with white or yellowish spots. Flowers monoecious on a spadix without appendix, males and females remote; spathe narrow, the boat-shaped blade rather shorter than the long convolute tube. The plants are poisonous and the very acrid sap causes intense pain. No part of the plant should, under any consideration, be placed in the mouth. Dieffenbachias need stove conditions. They may be propagated by suckers from the base which should be taken off and potted in small pots, or the tops with a considerable portion of the stem placed in a sand bed with bottom heat will send out strong roots in a week or two; the remainder of the old stems after the removal of the leaves may be cut into pieces 1 to 2 in. long, slightly dried, and planted in the propagating frame with bottom heat. Equal parts of good fibrous loam, peat, and leaf-mould, with a good sprinkling of sharp silver sand or clean river-sand, is the best compost. The species with small leaves may be planted 3 or 4 in a pot; the large-leaved species are best planted singly. The loam and peat should not be broken up too finely for good-sized plants, but should be used somewhat lumpy with sufficient drainage to allow the liberal waterings, required when the plants are in active growth, to pass freely. The plants should be syringed frequently and a brisk moist heat should be maintained except during the winter resting period when less moisture both in soil and air is required. The soil, however, should never be allowed to become quite dry as the plants are evergreen. Several of the following, though given specific names, are probably forms of other species, particularly *D. picta* and *D. Seguine.*

**D. amoe'na.** *l.* deep green, oblong, acute, marked with many long blotches of white and pale yellow, well defined on both surfaces. Trop. America. 1880.

**D. antioquien'sis.** A variety of *D. picta.*

**D. Barraquinia'na.** A variety of *D. Seguine.*

**D. Baus'ei.** A variety of *D. picta.*

*Dieffenbachia Bowmannii*, much reduced

**D. Bow'mannii.** *l.* very large, up to 2½ ft. long, 1 ft. wide, deep rich green, blotched with irregular parallel markings of light pea-green. Brazil. 1871. (I.H. 19, 105.)

**D. brasilien'sis.** A synonym of *D. picta.*

**D. Car'deri.** *l.* rich dark green, blotched and variegated, oblong-ovate, somewhat deflexed. Colombia. 1880.

**D. Chel'sonii.** *l.* dark satiny-green, midrib marked by a grey band with feathering one-third across blade, and with bright yellow-green spots about two-thirds across it. Colombia. 1877

**D. costa'ta.** *l.* deep velvety-green, midrib ivory-white, spotted with oblong ivory-white blotches, ovate, base blunt, margin undulate, apex acuminate, about 9 in. long. Colombia. 1860. SYN. *D. macrophylla.*

**D. delec'ta.** *l.* satiny-green with whitish variegation, elliptic-lanceolate, 8 to 10 in. long, spreading. Stem mottled green. Colombia. 1880.

**D. eburn'ea.*** Habit compact. Stem and l.-stalks stained pale cinnamon, ribbed ivory-white. *l.* light green with many white dots and spots, oblong-lanceolate. Brazil. 1868.

**D. Fournier'i.** *l.* blackish-green, spotted and blotched white, large, leathery. Colombia.

**D. impera'tor.** *l.* olive-green, curiously blotched, marbled and spotted pale yellow and white, ovate-lanceolate, 15 to 18 in. long, 5 in. wide. Colombia.

**D. imperia'lis.** *l.* dark-green with yellow spots; midrib greyish. S. America. (I.H. 1871, 85.)

**D. insig'nis.** *l.* dark green with irregular, angular, pale yellowish-green blotches, obliquely ovate, 6 in. or more wide, with a short slender point, stalks pale green. Colombia.

**D. Jen'manii.** *l.* pea-green with long oblique blotches parallel to main veins from middle almost to margin, with interspersed smaller blotches, oblong-lanceolate, long, and narrow. British Guiana. 1884. (G.F. 1884, 365.)

**D. latimacula'ta*.** *l.* dark glaucous green, barred white, and spotted and irregularly blotched yellowish-green, somewhat sagittate, acute. Brazil. 1871. var. **illus'tris,** *l.* banded yellow-green and grey on deep green. (I.H. 234.)

**D. Leopold'ii.** A synonym of *D. Seguine liturata.*

**D. maculo'sa.** *l.* blotched creamy-white. Colombia. 1876.

**D. magnif'ica.*** *l.* shining, sombre green with many white spots and blotches near secondary veins. Stems and short sheathing l.-stalks also variegated. Venezuela. (I.H. 482.)

**D. majes'tica.*** *l.* rich dark green with scattered bright-yellowish blotches and a feathery silver bar along the middle, oblong-ovate, slender-pointed, 12 in. or more long, 5 to 6 in. wide. Hab.? 1882.

**D. melea'gris.** *l.* dark green above, paler beneath, marked with a few white spots on both sides; stalks long, green with ivory-white markings. Ecuador. (I.H. 559.)

**D. nit'ida.** *l.* deep glossy green with angular yellowish-green blotches, oblong-lanceolate, slender-pointed. Colombia.

**D. nob'ilis.** A variety of *D. Seguine.*

**D. Parlato'rei marmo'rea.** *l.* deep green, blotched with greenish-white, long oblong, slender-pointed, midrib white. Colombia. 1878. (I.H. 201.)

**D. Pear'cei.** *l.* bright light green with many creamy-white spots and blotches and a creamy-white band on each side of the midrib, large, oblong-lanceolate. Ecuador.

**D. pic'ta.*** *l.* dark green, closely spotted and blotched with white and pale green, oblong, slender-pointed. Brazil. 1820. (L.B.C. 608 as *Caladium maculatum.*) SYN. *B. brasiliensis.* A variable species. var. **antioquien'sis,** *l.* deep green, blotched yellow. Colombia. 1875. (I.H. 192.); **Baus'ei,** *l.* yellowish-green, margined and irregularly spotted dark green, much spotted white, stalks white. (I.H. 338 as *D. Bausei.*); **Shut'tleworthii,** *l.* with a feathery white band along midrib. Colombia. 1878. (G.C. 10 (1878), 45 as *D. Shuttleworthii.*)

**D. prin'ceps.** *l.* dark green with a few scattered yellowish spots and a silver-grey band down middle, somewhat oblique, the narrower side cordate. Brazil. 1868.

**D. Regi'na.*** *l.* almost entirely greenish-white with pale green mottling and a narrow margin and a few streaky markings of deeper green, oblong-elliptic, rounded at base, shortly acuminate. S. America.

**D. Rex.*** *l.* closely placed on stem, very deep green, paler green near edge of narrower side, thickly covered to within ½ in. of margin with long, oblique, angular white blotches, with a few veins and suffusions of green, elliptic-lanceolate, unequal-sided. S. America. Free and vigorous of habit.

**D. Segui'ne.** Dumb Cane, Dumb Plant. About 6 ft. h. *l.* deep green with pellucid white spots, ovate-oblong, cuspidate, undulate. W. Indies. SYN. *D. grandis, Caladium Seguine.* The common name is derived from the effect of chewing any part of the plant which causes dumbness for several days. A variable species. var. **Barraquinia'na,*** *l.* bright light green, irregularly spotted white, 6 to 12 in. long, 3 to 6 in. wide, oblong-acuminate, midrib white, stalk shining clear ivory-white. Brazil. 1863. (I.H. 387 as *D. Verschaffeltii.*) SYN. *D. Barraquiniana, D. gigantea*; **litura'ta,*** *l.* deep lustrous satiny-green, with a broad, ivory-white midrib, bordered with a whitish band on each side. S. America. (G.C. 9 (1878), 441 as *D. Leopoldii.*) SYN. *D. liturata, D. Wallisii*; **nob'ilis,** *l.* deep rich green, with many white blotches and spots except at edges, marginal band broad, blade oblong-ovate, 18 in. long, 9 in. wide; stalk thick, channelled, pale green with transverse bands, up to 1 ft. long. Brazil. 1869. (G.C. 1873, 815.)

**D. Shut'tleworthii.** A variety of *D. picta.*

**D. splen'dens.** *l.* deep velvety bottle-green with whitish streaked blotches. Stem with faint dark and light green mottling. Colombia. 1880.

**D. trium'phans.** *l.* dark green with large irregular, angular, yellowish-green blotches, somewhat spreading, ovate-lanceolate, slender-pointed, about 12 in. long, 4 to 5 in. wide. Colombia.

**D. veluti'na.** *l.* satiny-green; stalks white. Colombia. 1877.

**D. Weir'ii.** *l.* bright green, thickly blotched and spotted pale yellow Brazil. 1866. Dwarf.

F. G. P.

A→

**DIEL'LIA** (?). FAM. *Polypodiaceae.* A genus of 6 species of ferns, related to Lindsaya with sorus not quite marginal, the outer valve of the indusium membranous, similar in shape to sorus. For cultivation *see* **Lindsaya.**

**D. falca'ta.** *sti.* 3 to 4 in. long, strong, erect, densely scaly. *Fronds* 1 to 1½ ft. long, 2 to 4 in. broad, lanceolate, simply pinnate; pinnae 1 to 2 in. long, ¼ to ⅜ in. broad, linear-lanceolate, falcate, acuminate, slightly undulate at margin, upper half rather broader and auricled at base, lower very short and blunt. *Sori* marginal, transversely oblong. Hawaii. SYN. *Lindsaya falcata.*

***Dielsia'nus -a -um,*** in honour of Professor Diels, 1874–1944, Director, Dahlem Botanic Gardens.

**DIELY'TRA.** A synonym of Dicentra.

**DIERA'MA** (*dierama*, funnel; from the shape of the perianth). FAM. *Iridaceae.* A genus of 2 to 4, or, according to some botanists, many species in S. Africa. (*See* J.R.H.S. 54, 194.) Corm large. Stem slender. Leaves long, linear, narrow, rigid, and grass-like. Flowers in a panicle on drooping branches. Perianth with short tube widening upwards and 6 nearly equal segments (not zygomorphic as in the related Sparaxis); filaments short, anthers linear; style filamentous, straight. The Dieramas are hardy or nearly so and succeed in deep, rich, moist, but well-drained soils. They should be placed where their graceful arching stems can be seen to advantage, as on the margin of a pond.

**D. pen'dulum.** *fl.* at ends of pendent branches, white or pink to purple; tube about $\frac{3}{8}$ in. long, segs. oblong, obtuse, about $\frac{4}{5}$ in. long; bracts brownish or with brown stripes. *l.* from base 5 or 6, very stiff, up to over 20 in. long. Stem wiry, 3 ft. long. June, July. S. Africa. (B.M. 1482; B.R. 1360 as *Sparaxis pendula.*) var. **al'bum,** *fl.* white; **ro'seum,** *fl.* rosy purple.

**D. pulcher'rimum.** Habit of *D. pendulum* but larger and stronger. *fl.* larger, bright purple or almost blood red; bracts much longer, almost white except at the brown base. *l.* broader and longer. Stem up to 6 ft. September, October. S. Africa to Transvaal. (B.M. 5555 as *Sparaxis pulcherrima.*) Several seedling forms have been named; **al'bum,** *fl.* white; **Heron,** *fl.* deep wine-red; **Kingfisher,** *fl.* pale pink; **Port Wine,** *fl.* deep wine-purple-red; **Skylark,** *fl.* purplish pansy-violet; **Windhover,** *fl.* bright rose-pink.

**DIERVIL'LA** (in honour of M. Dierville, a French surgeon who travelled in Canada 1699–1700 and introduced *D. Lonicera*). FAM. *Caprifoliaceae.* A genus of about 12 species including the Weigelas, natives of Eastern N. America and E. Asia, related to Lonicera but with a capsular fruit. Deciduous shrubs with opposite toothed leaves without stipules and generally showy flowers with a more or less funnel-shaped corolla, sometimes 2-lipped, 5 stamens, and a long, 2-celled, many-ovuled ovary below the calyx. Seeds small, often winged. The majority of the species are hardy and all grow best in a deep, rich, moist loam in a fairly sheltered place. They can be propagated by cuttings of half-ripe shoots in summer or by autumn cuttings or by suckers. The Chinese species are by far the most showy and from them a fine race of hardy shrubs has been raised by crossing and intercrossing; indeed, the original species are not frequently met with here, for these garden-raised plants surpass them in garden-value. All the Chinese species seem to have taken part in the parentage of this garden-raised race, viz. *D. coraeensis*, *D. floribunda*, *D. florida*, *D. hortensis*, *D. japonica*, and *D. praecox*, all of which have been, and sometimes are, called Weigela. Attempts are sometimes made in catalogues to assign these garden forms to one or other of the species and thus confusion of names has arisen. It would be better to call them all merely by their fancy name alone following Diervilla, for example, *Diervilla* Eva Rathke, *D.* Styriaca, and so on. A list of the best is given in the Appendix and they are not further referred to by name here. The annual removal cf shoots as soon as they have flowered in the species just named and their offspring is the best way of pruning to obtain good results. The flowers of many open pale and darken as they age and this should be borne in mind when comparing the descriptions of flowers. There are thus frequently flowers of different shades on the same bush. The American species are less showy, and as they flower on the current year's branches, they should be cut back before growth begins in spring.

KEY

| | | |
|---|---|---|
| 1. | *Fl. yellow* | 2 |
| 1. | *Fl. white, rose to crimson* | 5 |
| 2. | *Anthers connected, hairy* | D. Middendorfiana |
| 2. | *Anthers free* | 3 |
| 3. | *Shoots and lvs. hairy* | D. rivularis |
| 3. | *Shoots and lvs. not markedly hairy* | 4 |
| 4. | *Lvs. nearly sessile, branches 4-angled* | D. sessilifolia |
| 4. | *Lvs. stalked, branches nearly round* | D. Lonicera |
| 5. | *Sep. separate to base; seeds winged* | 6 |
| 5. | *Sep. joined; seeds not winged* | 9 |
| 6. | *Shoots and lvs. smooth, hairy only on veins beneath; ovary smooth* | D. coraeensis |
| 6. | *Shoots and lvs. more or less hairy* | 7 |
| 7. | *Fl. stalked, style not longer than cor.* | 8 |
| 7. | *Fl. sessile, style much longer than cor.; ovary hairy* | D. floribunda |
| 8. | *Fl.-stalk short; lvs. hairy, particularly on veins beneath* | D. japonica |
| 8. | *Fl.-stalk longer; lvs. densely grey, hairy beneath* | D. hortensis |
| 9. | *Lvs. glabrous above* | D. florida |
| 9. | *Lvs. pubescent above* | D. praecox |

**D. amab'ilis.** A synonym of *D. florida.*

**D. canaden'sis.** A synonym of *D. Lonicera.*

**D. coraeen'sis.** Shrub of 6 to 10 ft., young shoots smooth. *l.* 3, oval or obovate, 3 to 5 in. long, abruptly narrowed to a long point, usually hairy on veins beneath, stalk bristly. *fl.* usually in threes, terminal on short lateral twigs, pale rose deepening to carmine, bell-shaped, $1\frac{1}{4}$ in. long, $\frac{3}{4}$ in. wide at mouth, smooth. June. Japan. (F.d.S. 855 as *D. amabilis.*) SYN. *D. grandiflora.*

**D. floribun'da.** Shrub, 4 to 8 ft. h., shoots slender, hairy. *l.* ovate or oval, slender-pointed, 3 to 4 in. long, on fl.-shoots smaller, toothed, downy. *fl.* sessile, on short lateral shoots, terminal and axillary, funnel-shaped, 1 in. long, downy without, dark crimson; stamens as long as cor., style much longer, ovary hairy. June. Japan. 1860. (S.Z.F.J. 32.) One parent of the fine dark-fld. hybrids. var. **versico'lor,** *fl.* at first greenish-white, darkening to red or crimson. (S.Z.F.J. 33.)

*Diervilla florida*

**D. flo'rida.** Shrub, 6 or 7 ft. h., spreading; shoots with 2 rows of hairs. *l.* elliptic to elliptic-lanceolate, 2 to 4 in. long, slender-pointed, toothed except at base, hairy on veins beneath. *fl.* in threes or fours, terminal on short shoots, funnel-shaped, $1\frac{1}{4}$ in. long, narrowed below middle, deep rose without, paler to white within. May, June. China. 1845. (B.M. 4396.) SYN. *Weigela rosea*, *W. amabilis.* var. **al'ba,** *fl.* at first white, then pale pink. SYN. var. *candida.* Hardier than *D. hortensis.* *See also* **D. venusta**; **variega'ta,** *l.* edged pale yellow, *fl.* deep rose.

**D. grandiflo'ra.** A synonym of *D. coraeensis.*

**D. horten'sis.** Habit of *D. japonica* but less vigorous. Shoots downy, *l.* grey, pubescent beneath, fl.-stalks longer. Japan. 1870. (S.Z.F.J. 29, 30.) var. **niv'ea,** *fl.* white. 1864. Less hardy than other species, but a parent of many good varieties.

**D. japon'ica.** Shrub of 6 or 7 ft.; shoots glabrous or with 2 rows of hairs. *l.* oval to oblong-obovate, 2 to 4 in. long, slender-pointed, toothed, densely hairy beneath. *fl.* funnel-shaped, $1\frac{1}{4}$ in. long, whitish at first then carmine, often downy without. June. Japan. 1892.

**D. Lonic'era.** Shrub of 2 to 4 ft., spreading and suckering; shoots smooth. *l.* ovate or ovate-oblong, 2 to 5 in. long, tapering to a point, toothed, ciliate when young. *fl.* yellow, funnel-shaped, tube $\frac{1}{2}$ in. long, lobes narrow, in 3- to 5-fld. cymes at ends of current branches or solitary in l.-axils. June, July. Eastern N. America. 1734. (B.M. 1796.) SYN. *D. canadensis*, *D. trifida.*

**D. Middendorfia'na.** Shrub of 2 to 4 ft., young shoots with 2 rows of hairs. *l.* ovate-lanceolate, 2 to 3 in. long, wrinkled, slightly hairy at first. *fl.* sulphur-yellow, dotted orange on lower lobes, funnel-shaped, $1\frac{1}{4}$ to $1\frac{1}{2}$ in. long, 1 in. wide across mouth; cal. 2-lipped, ciliate. *infl.* a terminal cymose cluster. April, May. N. China, Manchuria, Japan. 1850. (B.M. 7876.) Spring tender.

**D. prae'cox.** Shrub of 5 or 6 ft., young shoots usually smooth. *l.* elliptic to obovate, 2 to 4 in. or more long, slender-pointed, toothed, hairy on both surfaces. *fl.* 3 to 5 on short, lateral shoots, rose, yellow in throat, 1½ in. long, funnel-shaped, abruptly narrowed below middle, hairy without. April; the earliest species in flower. Korea. 1894.

**D. rivula'ris.** Shrub of about 4 ft., young shoots round, shortly hairy. *l.* ovate to oblong-lanceolate, 1¼ to 3½ in. long, doubly serrate, downy on both surfaces. *fl.* lemon-yellow, in crowded terminal panicles; cor. ½ in. long, tube narrow with lobes of about equal length. July, August. *fr.* ¼ in. long. SE. United States, 1902.

**D. sessilifo'lia.** Habit of *D. rivularis* but young shoots 4-angled, downy at corners, *l.* sessile and smooth except on midrib, *fl.* sulphur-yellow, in crowded terminal panicles 3 in. across and smaller axillary ones, *fr.* ½ in. long. SE. United States. 1902.

**D. venus'ta.*** Allied to *D. florida* but with smaller *l.* mostly obovate, 1½ to 2½ in. long, usually nearly smooth, *fl.* in dense clusters with small l. at base, rosy pink, 1½ in. long, gradually narrowed. May. Korea. 1905. (B.M. 9080.) SYN. *D. florida venusta.*

**DIE'TES.** Included in **Moraea.**

*difform'is -is -e,* of unusual form.

*diffu'sis -is -e,* diffuse, spreading.

*Digbya'nus -a -um,* in honour of Edward St. Vincent Digby, of Minterne Abbey, amateur grower of Orchids, *c.* 1846.

**DIGGING.** Digging is one of the most important operations in horticulture, having for its purpose, among other things, the admission of air to the soil, and exposure of as great a part of it to air as possible to contact with the atmosphere and to the action of the weather; the pulverization of the soil to enable roots to penetrate it more easily; and the mixing in of manures. For the first of these purposes some degree of moisture in the soil is an advantage: for the other two dry weather is generally more favourable.

Single digging results in the moving of the top spit only; double digging or bastard trenching results in the moving of the soil to the depth of two or more spits but retains the spits in their original position; trenching results in the moving of the soil two or more spits deep and bringing the subsoil to the surface, burying the top spit.

The chief digging implement is the spade, though in some circumstances, for instance, where the soil is very stony, the digging-fork may be used. In digging, the workman should stand nearly upright; he should insert his spade vertically and drive it in to its full depth; lifting the spit he should turn it from the direction in which he is standing so that what was at the bottom is now fully exposed to the air. A competent digger will be able to reverse the position of his hands on the spade and proceed either way with equal ease.

All vegetable ground which carries annual crops needs digging at least once a year. For single digging a trench is opened at one end of the plot to its full width, a full spit deep, and 9 in. to 1 ft. wide, the soil removed being taken to near the place where it is intended to finish. A wide plot is best dug in two or more strips. Digging then proceeds, preserving an even depth and a reasonably straight and open trench throughout. No attempt should be made to take a greater bulk of soil on the spade than can be lifted cleanly and turned completely over (on heavy soil the width of the spit should not exceed 9 in.), and it will often be found well to make a shallow cut at right angles to the trench before each insertion of the spade as an aid to the clean removal of the spit.

Ground occupied with summer crops is best dug in the autumn, manure being added then and distributed evenly through the soil. The spits should not be broken by the spade but be left rough for full exposure to the weather. Digging is best done when the surface is fairly dry: it should not be attempted when it is covered with snow or when frozen, though in frosty weather the surface may be protected from freezing by a cover of litter upon it to be dug in, and the work then may not be greatly hindered. Light sandy soils may be worked at times when it would be unwise to tread on a clayey soil.

Double-digging is the best means of deepening a soil and of making it more able to carry crops through a dry season. It may well be a routine operation on vegetable ground, or on herbaceous borders, every third year. To carry it out, a trench is made as in single digging, but 2 ft. or 2 ft. 6 in. wide. The bottom of this trench is then broken up with the spade or digging-fork and manure added, not in such a way as to make a sandwich but well mixed with the soil and subsoil. This being done, the top spit from the next 2 ft. or 18 in. is thrown on to the broken-up subsoil of the first trench and the bottom of the second trench so exposed is broken up. The work then proceeds until the last trench after its bottom is broken up is filled with the soil removed in making the first trench. If the ground to be double-dug is in grass the turf should be pared off and buried face down at the top of the subsoil, cutting it up with the spade.

Trenching, or full trenching as it is sometimes called, is rarely wise unless the ground to be dealt with is of similar texture and appearance to a great depth as it may be in many old gardens, for the subsoil is often infertile and devoid of beneficial bacteria, and may be heavy, cold, intractable clay or even contain incompletely oxidized and poisonous salts. In many old gardens, however, it may be done without danger. The first trench is made as in double-digging, the next spit of subsoil below it is also removed and placed in a separate heap. The top spit of the next section is then put into the bottom of the trench so made and the subsoil from this section is put on top of it and the work proceeds in this manner until the last trench is filled with the soil taken out of the first.

Both double-digging (bastard-trenching) and trenching are sometimes carried to a depth of 3 or 4 spits, but it is doubtful whether the labour involved is repaid by increases in the resulting crop, save in exceptional instances.

If, in carrying out any of these operations, hard pan is met with, it should be broken up and, if need be, removed.

Ridging is a variant of digging, the surface being thrown into ridges running the way of the slope if there be one, instead of being left merely rough. This results in a greater amount of surface being exposed to the action of the weather with the advantages that this confers.

All the foregoing are autumn operations. In spring- and summer-digging the spits are broken up with the spade as they are turned over and the surface left relatively level and smooth.

The effect of the weather in winter, especially of frost, acting on the rough clods is such that they are easily broken down in spring with the rake and a fine tilth obtained suitable for the sowing of small seeds. In summer the same result can generally be obtained by the action of a shower on the finer surface left then.

In dealing with larger areas the spade is replaced with the plough and the cultivators of various types which do the work more expeditiously and at less cost, but usually much less efficiently.

*digitaliflo'rus -a -um,* Foxglove-like.

**DIGITA'LIS** (*digitus,* finger; from the form of the flower). FAM. *Scrophulariaceae.* A genus of about 20 species of biennial or perennial herbs, natives of Europe, N. Africa, and W. Asia. Leaves in radical rosettes and also on stem. Flowers showy, purple, yellowish-brownish, or white, in long terminal, often secund, racemes, sometimes branched; corolla tubular; limb obliquely 4-lobed, upper segment shorter than the lower, all overlapping in bud. Growing easily in ordinary garden soil, especially when it contains much organic matter, as that of a wood. Seed should be sown in April or May and the seedlings should be planted out 6 to 8 in. apart when large enough to handle. The perennial species may also be increased by division. **A**

**D. ambig'ua.** Hairy perennial, 2 to 3 ft. h. *l.* ovate-lanceolate, toothed, sessile, veiny, downy beneath. *fl.* yellowish, netted with brown, about 2 in. long; lower bracts as long as *fl.* July, August. Europe. 1596. (B.R. 64). SYN. *D. grandiflora, D. ochroleuca.* var. **fusces'cens,** *fl.* brownish; perhaps a hybrid between *D. lutea* and *D. purpurea.*

**D. au'rea.** A synonym of *D. ferruginea.*

**D. chinen'sis.** A synonym of *Adenosma grandiflorum.*

**D. du'bia.** Perennial, 6 to 9 in. h. *l.* glabrous above, downy beneath; radical *l.* lanceolate, flat on ground, toothed; stem-*l.* entire. *fl.* purplish, much spotted within, large; throat dilated; racemes few-fld. June. Spain. 1789. (B.M. 2160 as *D. minor.*)

**D. ferrugin'ea.** Biennial, 4 to 6 ft. h. with a glabrous, densely leafy stem. *l.* glabrous or ciliate. *fl.* in long, dense, pyramidal racemes; rusty-red, netted within, downy without; lip ovate, entire, bearded. July. Europe. 1597. (B.M. 1828.) SYN. *D. aurea.*

**D. gloxiniiflo'ra** or **D. gloxinioi'des.** A variety of *D. purpurea.*

**D. grandiflo'ra.** A synonym of *D. ambigua.*

**D. laeviga'ta.** Perennial, 2 to 3 ft. h. *l.* linear-lanceolate; radical *l.* obovate-lanceolate, slightly toothed; upper recurved. *fl.* scattered, glabrous, brownish, netted; lip white, ciliate. July. Europe. 1816. (B.M. 5999.)

**D. lana'ta.** Perennial, 2 to 3 ft. h. *l.* deep green, oblong, ciliate. *fl.* in dense, many-fld. racemes with bracts shorter than *fl.*; greyish, downy, netted; lip white or purplish, naked. July, August. E. Europe. 1789. (B.M. 1159.)

**D. lu'tea.** Glabrous perennial, about 2 ft. h. *l.* oblong or lanceolate, toothed. *fl.* in many-fld., 1-sided racemes, yellow to white, glabrous; cal. segs. lanceolate, acute. July. Europe. (B.R. 251.)

**D. × me'dia** (*D. ambigua × D. lutea*). Habit of *D. ambigua.* *fl.* yellowish; anthers spotted rose; upper *l.* on stem rounded at base. S. Europe.

**D. min'or.** A synonym of *D. dubia.*

**D. obscu'ra.** Sub-shrubby perennial. *l.* linear-lanceolate, entire, smooth. *fl.* nodding, yellow veined with red within, reddish without; cor. tube cylindrical, somewhat flattened, upper lip short, 2-lobed, recurved, lower 3-lobed, mid-lobe ovate, twice as long as side lobes. July, August. Spain. (B.M. 2157.)

**D. ochroleu'ca.** A synonym of *D. ambigua.*

**D. orienta'lis.** Perennial. Nearly related to *D. lanata* but raceme lax, *fl.* paler, less ferruginous netting within, none without, upper lip and side lobes rounded, not pointed, lower *l.* much longer and narrower. July, August. Levant. (B.M. 2253.)

**D. parviflo'ra.** Perennial. Erect, unbranched. *Basal l.* obovate; *stem-l.* oblong-lanceolate, deflexed. *fl.* small, brownish-purple, in a dense cylindrical raceme, lowest almost hidden by bracts; cor. hairy; anthers not spotted. July. S. Europe.

**D. purpu'rea.*** Foxglove. Biennial up to 5 ft. h. *l.* oblong, rugose, crenate, forming a large radical rosette in first year. *fl.* purple, varying to white, with dark purple spots edged white within, large, in a dense raceme, sometimes branched at base. Summer. W. Europe, including Britain. (E.B. 952.) Variable. Useful in damp, semi-shaded places as well as in borders. var. **al'ba,** *fl.* white; **campanula'ta,** raceme with the terminal *fl.* monstrous, open cup-shaped with many segs.; **gloxinioi'des,*** a large-fld. strain of varying colouring and amount of spotting; **monstro'sa,** *fl.* peloric, more or less double.

**D. × purpu'reo-ambig'ua** (*D. ambigua × D. purpurea*). Intermediate between parents.

**D. sibir'ica.** Habit of *D. ambigua.* *l.* downy, ovate-lanceolate, lower *l.* toothed, upper entire. *fl.* yellowish tube swollen at base, hairy; cal. segs. linear, hairy. Siberia.

**D. Thaps'i.** Perennial, 2 to 4 ft. h., hairy, much like *D. purpurea.* *l.* ovate-lanceolate or oblong, rugose, crenate, wavy, decurrent. *fl.* purple with a paler throat with red spots; cal. segs. raceme loose, ovate or oblong. June to September. Spain. 1752. (B.M. 2194 as *D. tomentosa.*)

**DIGITA'RIA.** Included in *Panicum.*

*digita'tus -a -um,* digitate, fingered; shaped like an open hand with divisions arising from one point.

*digy'nus -a -um,* having 2 carpels.

*dilata'tus -a -um,* dilated; widened.

**DILL** (*Peucedanum graveolens*). A sweet herb of which the young leaves are sometimes used in flavouring soups and sauces, and with fish and pickled cucumbers. Dill vinegar, made by steeping the seeds for some days in vinegar, is also sometimes used, and the seeds are used abroad for flavouring preserves and cakes, and in pickling cucumbers. The seeds are a source of a medicinal oil. Dill is an annual easily grown. It should be sown in March or April in drills 10 in. apart and thinned to 8 in. in the rows, subsequently keeping the ground clear of weeds. As soon as the lowest fruits are ripe the stems should be cut, preferably in dry weather in early morning or late evening, shaking as little as possible, so as to avoid loss. Ripening is done as a rule in small stacks and after threshing the seed is laid out to dry thoroughly.

**DILLE'NIA** (in honour of John James Dillenius, 1684–1747, professor of Botany at Oxford, author of *Hortus Elthamensis*). FAM. *Dilleniaceae.* A genus of about 40 species of beautiful evergreen trees, natives of Trop. Asia to Australia. Leaves large, with conspicuous pinnate parallel venation. Flowers showy, solitary or clustered; sepals and petals 5, spreading; stamens many, free or more or less joined at base, anthers linear, opening by 2 slits; carpels 5 to 20, ovules many. Fruit fleshy, enclosed in the enlarged calyx. Dillenias need stove conditions and plenty of room to grow. A light sandy loam suits them. Cuttings root readily, taking half-ripe wood, and giving bottom heat. Seeds can sometimes be imported and they germinate readily.

**D. in'dica.** Handsome tree to 40 ft. but usually a bush in cultivation under glass. *l.* elliptic-oblong, simply toothed, 6 to 12 in. long, bright light green. *fl.* white, 9 in. across, stamens yellow; peduncles lateral, 1-fld. E. India. 1800. (B.M. 5016.) SYN. *D. speciosa.*

**D. pentagy'na.** Tree to 20 ft. *l.* oblong, hairy on veins beneath. *fl.* yellow; pet. ovate-oblong, acute; peduncles 1-fld. along naked branches of preceding year. March. India. 1803.

**D. scabrel'la.** Spreading tree. *l.* elliptical, acute, 1 ft. long, hairy, with bristly teeth. *fl.* yellow, fragrant; pet. orbicular; peduncles clustered in l.-axils. Assam. 1820.

F. G. P.

**DILLENIA'CEAE.** Dicotyledons. A family of about 200 species, belonging to 12 genera of trees or shrubs, often climbing (rarely herbs), mostly in the tropics. Leaves nearly always alternate, simple, rarely stipulate. Flowers sometimes unisexual, regular, hypogynous; sepals up to 5, sometimes many, imbricate, persistent; petals 5 (rarely 2 to 7), deciduous; stamens usually over 10; carpels usually several, free or connate, rarely one; ovules many. Fruit variable. The genera dealt with are Acrotrema, Curatella, Dillenia, Hibbertia, Tetracera.

**DILLWYN'IA** (in honour of Lewis Weston Dillwyn, a notable student of the British *Confervae*, 1778–1855). FAM. *Leguminosae.* A genus of about 12 species of evergreen shrubs, natives of Australia and Tasmania. Leaves alternate, all linear or even filiform and mostly under 1 in. long. Flowers papilionaceous, few in axillary or terminal clusters or racemes, yellow, orange, and red. Cool greenhouse plants. Treatment as for Chorizema.

KEY

| | |
|---|---|
| 1. *Fl. mostly in terminal racemes or clusters* | 2 |
| 1. *Fl. all axillary. Lvs. not keeled* | D. floribunda |
| 2. *Lvs. not prominently keeled* | 3 |
| 2. *Lvs. with an evident keel, spine-tipped* | D. juniperina |
| 3. *Fl. in long-stalked racemes, keel nearly as long as wings, acute* | D. hispida |
| 3. *Fl. usually in short racemes, keel much shorter than wings, obtuse* | D. ericifolia |

**D. ericifo'lia.** Evergreen heath-like shrub, 2 to 3 ft., shoots erect, slender. *l.* very densely set, linear, pointed; usually between ¼ and ½ in. long, sometimes up to 1 in. *fl.* in terminal clusters of 6 to 8; standard pet. ½ in. across, 2-lobed, rich yellow, with a starry crimson blotch; wing short, similarly coloured. May. Australia, Tasmania. (B.M. 944.)

**D. floribun'da.*** Evergreen shrub, 5 to 6 ft., shoots stiffly erect, glabrous to hairy. *l.* crowded, ⅛ to ½ in. long, narrowly linear, warty. *fl.* all axillary, 1 to 3 in each axil, forming densely cylindrical leafy spikes 1 to 4 in. long; standard pet. and wings yellow with starry red stains. Spring. Australia, Tasmania. 1796. (B.M. 1545 as *D. ericifolia*, which is distinguished by its terminal infl.)

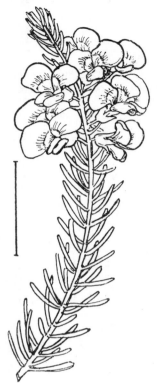

*Dillwynia floribunda*

**D. glycinifo'lia.** Shrub with weak, slender, procumbent or somewhat climbing branches. *l.* linear, acuminate, somewhat hairy beneath, margins revolute; stalk short; stipules setaceous. *fl.* with 2-lobed, erect, orange standard, wings rose, obtuse, keel white shorter than wings; ovary hairy. SW. Australia. 1831. (B.R. 1514.)

**D. hisp'ida.** Evergreen shrub 4 to 8 ft., shoots scabrid, varying from hairy to (rarely) glabrous. *l.* heath-like, filiform, ¼ to ½ in. long, blunt, terete, usually very hairy. *fl.* in slender-stalked clusters or racemes of 3 to 8, standing out well from the l.; standard pet. broad, red or yellow, wings and keel shorter, crimson. Victoria, S. Australia. SYN. *D. scabra.*

**D. juniperi'na.** Evergreen shrub, 2 to 3 ft., shoots slender, hairy. *l.* heath-like, filiform, ¼ to ½ in. long, keeled, prickly pointed. *fl.* scarcely stalked, in terminal clusters of 4 to 9; standard pet. orange, red at base, wings and keel red. March. Australia. (L.B.C. 401.)

**D. scab'ra.** A synonym of *D. hispida.*

W. J. B.

**DI'LOBA caeruleoceph'ala.** *See* **Figure of Eight Moth.**

**DILO'PHUS feb'rilis.** *See* **Fever Fly.**

*dilu'tus -a -um,* diluted.

**dimerous,** having parts in twos.

*dimidia'tus -a -um,* divided into 2 dissimilar parts.

**DIMORPHAN'THUS mandshur'icus.** *See* **Aralia elata.**

**dimorphism,** having 2 forms of leaf, flower, or other organ on the same plant or in the same species.

**DIMORPHORCH'IS** (in allusion to the different-coloured and slightly different-shaped flower on the same spike). A generic name applied by Mr. Rolfe to the plant described here as *Aracnanthe Lowii*, as that and *A. Rohaniana* hardly agree with Vandopsis in which they have been placed by some authorities.

E. C.

**DIMORPHOTHE'CA** (*dis*, 2, *morphe*, shape, *theca*, fruit; the achenes being of 2 forms). FAM. *Compositae.* A genus of about 20 species of herbs or sub-shrubs, natives of S. Africa, often with clammy hairs. Leaves alternate, variously cut, rarely entire, often rough to the touch. Flower-heads radiate, terminal, solitary, the ray-florets female, disk-florets variable but usually outer perfect, inner abortive. Involucre in a single series of linear, slender-pointed scales. Achenes without pappus, straight, those of the ray-florets 3-cornered, warted or sharply toothed, rarely smooth; of disk-florets flattened with 2 thickened wings wider than the seed. The Dimorphothecas are only half-hardy, and suitable for cultivation outdoors in summer, or in the cool greenhouse in winter. They grow freely in well-drained loam. The annual species should be sown in heat under glass in spring and planted out at the end of May; the perennials are easily raised from cuttings. The flowers open in sunny weather or in mid-morning, closing in afternoon in most instances.

KEY

| | | |
|---|---|---|
| 1. *Ray-florets white or purple, or white above, purple beneath* | | 2 |
| 1. *Ray-florets yellow or orange* | | 6 |
| 2. *Annual* | | D. pluvialis |
| 2. *Perennial* | | 3 |
| 3. *Stems short, simple, tufted, ending in peduncles* | D. nudicaulis | |
| 3. *Shrubby or sub-shrubby* | | 4 |
| 4. *Disk-florets all similar* | | 5 |
| 4. *Disk-florets of 2 forms, outer bearded, inner flat-topped, closed* | | D. Barberiae |
| 5. *Lvs. entire* | | D. Ecklonis |
| 5. *Lvs. toothed* | | D. Tragus |
| 6. *Annual* | | 7 |
| 6. *Perennial* | | 9 |
| 7. *Lvs. pinnate* | | D. pinnata |
| 7. *Lvs. oblong. Plant branched from base, spreading* | | 8 |
| 8. *Lvs. sinuate, glabrous or nearly so* | | D. sinuata |
| 8. *Lvs. glandular-scabrous* | | D. calendulacea |
| 9. *Lvs. linear-oblong, obtuse, entire* | | D. aurantiaca |
| 9. *Lvs. oblong, sharply cut* | | D. chrysanthemifolia |

**D. an'nua.** A synonym of *D. pluvialis.*

**D. auranti'aca.*** Perennial and shrubby in the wild but usually grown as an annual. Stems spreading, branches many about 9 in. h. terminating in a solitary fl.-head. *l.* 2 to 3 in. long, linear-oblong or spatulate, downy at first, entire. *fl.-heads* 2 to 2½ in. across, bright orange; disk golden-brown tipped with metallic blue. Summer, autumn. Little Namaqualand. 1774. (B.M. 408 and B.R. 28 as *Calendula Tragus.* SYN. *Castalis Tragus.* Half-hardy but may be sown outside in April in light soils. Hybrids of varying shades have been raised, yellow, salmon-apricot, and orange. *D. aurantiaca* of gardens is *D. calendulacea* and *D. sinuata.*

**D. Barber'iae.** Straggling sub-shrub, downy. *l.* oblong-lanceolate, 3 to 4 in. long, upper shorter. *fl.-heads* on long stalks; ray-florets about 1 in. long, bright purple above, dull purple beneath; disk-florets with bearded bluntish lobes, inner not opening. SYN. *Osteospermum Barberiae.* Caffraria. 1862. (B.M. 5337.) Greenhouse.

**D. calendula'cea.** Free-branching annual, glandular-downy, branches from base leafy. *l.* oblong or linear-oblong, sinuate-toothed, obtuse. *fl.-heads* on short terminal stalks; ray-florets, orange-yellow, about 1¼ in. long; scales of involucre black-dotted. Namaqualand. (F.P.S.A. 246.) Half-hardy. SYN. *D. aurantiaca* of gardens. A pale yellow, var., **Lemon Queen** is offered.

**D. chrysanthemifo'lia.** Shrubby, about 2 ft. h., erect, branches simple, leafy. *l.* obovate-oblong, 2 to 3 in. long, sharply cut, lobes often toothed. *fl.-heads* large; ray-florets yellow, 1¼ to 1½ in. long, opening about 11 a.m., closing about 3 p.m. April to July. Cape Province. 1790. (B.M. 2218 and B.R. 40 as *Calendula chrysanthemifolia.*) Half-hardy.

**D. Ecklo'nis.*** Robust sub-shrub 2 ft. or more h., branched near top, leafy. *l.* linear-lanceolate or lanceolate, entire or nearly so, 2 to 3 in. long. *fl.-heads* 2½ to 3 in. across, on stalks 5 to 8 in. long; ray-florets white above, purple beneath, with a conspicuous blue-violet ring round disk; disk metallic violet-blue. S. Africa. 1897. (B.M. 7535.) Half-hardy. SYN. *Osteospermum Ecklonis.*

**D. nudicau'lis.** Stems many from the thick, woody rootstock, short, simple, densely leafy, terminating in a scape-like peduncle about 1 ft. long. *l.* very variable in form and toothing. *fl.-heads* large; ray-florets about 1 in. long, white above, purple beneath; disk purple. Table Mt., &c. var. **graminifo'lia.** *l.* narrow-linear, entire or nearly so. (B.M. 5252 as *Calendula graminifolia.*) Half-hardy.

**D. pinna'ta.** Clammy, downy annual, 6 to 12 in. h., with many branched stems. *l.* ½ to 1 in. long, pinnately cut into linear obtuse lobes, usually entire. *fl.-heads* large, ray-florets about 1 in. long, orange-yellow or pinkish buff on peduncles 1 to 2 in. long. S. Africa. Half-hardy. SYN. *Osteospermum pinnatum.*

**D. pluvia'lis.*** Erect or spreading annual about 12 in. h. *l.* narrow-oblong or obovate-oblong, 1 to 3 in. long, hairy, tapered to the base, bluntly toothed. *fl.-heads* about 2 to 2½ in. across; ray-florets, white above, purple beneath, minutely 3-toothed, disk golden-brown tipped with metallic blue. June to August. W. S. Africa. 1752. (S.B.F.G. 39 as *Calendula hybrida.*) Syn. *D. annua.* var. **ring'ens**, *fl.-heads* with conspicuous blue-violet zone round disk; **ringens fl. pl.**, remaining open, outer rays white, inner rays (of disk) half length of outer, dirty creamy-white, stained blue. Hardy.

**D. sinua'ta.** Much like *D. calendulacea* but much less downy, *l.* more entire, involucral scales glabrous, not black-dotted, *fl.-heads* smaller. S. Africa. (F.P.S.A. 205; J.R.H.S. 34, cxxiv as *D. aurantiaca.*) Crosses with *D. pluvialis.*

**D. specta'bilis.** Perennial. *fl.-heads* rich wine-colour, disk deeper, on long peduncles. Not freely produced. (F.P.S.A. 57.)

**D. Tra'gus.** Rigid sub-shrub 12 to 18 in. h., robust. *l.* linear-lanceolate or narrow-oblong, 1 to 2 in. long, slenderly pointed, sparsely toothed. *fl.-heads* white, purple beneath on peduncles scarcely 2 in. long; ray-florets about 1 in. long. May, June. S. Africa. 1774. Syn. *Osteospermum pulchrum.* Nearly hardy.

*dimorph'us -a -um,* **dimorphous,** occurring in 2 forms.

*dina'ricus -a -um,* of the Dinaric Alps.

**DINE'MA.** *See under* **Epidendrum polybulbon.**

*dio'don,* having 2 teeth.

**dioecious,** having female flowers on one individual, males on another.

*dioi'cus -a -um,* dioecious.

**DIONAE'A** (one of the names of Venus). Fam. *Droseraceae.* A single species of herbaceous perennial, native of Carolina, where it occurs in damp mossy places on moist sandy lands over a rather narrow strip of country. It is one of the insectivorous plants (q.v.), trapping flies by its leaves which close when either one of the three bristles present in the centre of each lobe is lightly touched twice or the leaf-blade more heavily knocked; the flies are subsequently digested. It can be raised from seed under a bell-glass sown on moist sandy soil mixed with chopped Sphagnum, or by division in early spring. It can be grown in a pot with a mixture of fine silver sand and peat with living Sphagnum around the plant. The pots should be stood in about an inch of water so that the tips of the roots are always in moist surroundings. In sunny exposures the leaves become red except for a margin of green but in the shade they are entirely green.

**D. muscip'ula.** Venus's Fly-trap. Stem short, underground, covered with the swollen bases of *l*. *l*. 4 to 8 in. in a basal rosette, each 1 to 5 in. long, with the lower part a flattened, winged petiole, the upper an oblong blade the 2 halves of which are bent upwards, the margins furnished with long teeth close together like those of a comb; the middle part of each half is covered with reddish digestive glands and on each half also 3 long hairs jointed at the base, the sensitive trigger hairs. *fl.* in an umbel, white, ¾ to 1 in. across; peduncle 3 to 6 in. h. July, August. Carolina. 1768. (B.M. 785.)

**DIONY'SIA** (from Dionysos, the Greek Bacchus). Fam. *Primulaceae.* A genus of about 20 species of tufted sub-shrubs or forming dense cushions, natives of Persia. Leaves small, overlapping, rarely large. Flowers solitary, often sessile, or in umbels of 1 to 3, heterostyled; corolla salver-shaped, tube 4 to 6 times as long as calyx, without scales in throat, tube swollen in middle or at throat; anthers sessile. Fruit a roundish capsule dehiscing by 5 valves to base; seeds 1 to 4. Perennials for the alpine house, needing treatment similar to that given *Silene acaulis* or the Androsaces of the Aretia section. Four species have recently been introduced and grown with some success, but watering needs to be done with great care.

**D. bryoi'des.** Densely tufted, branches ½ to 1¼ in. long, crowded, forming a cylindrical column 1/12 to ⅛ in. thick. *l.* densely overlapping, obovate, cucullate, 1-nerved, densely covered with pellucid glands. *fl.* violet, tube twice as long as cal., lobes small, ovate. SW. Persia. (J.R.H.S. 73, 292.)

**D. curviflo'ra.** Cushion forming, branches hard, erect, densely crowded, column-like. *l.* hard, minute, densely overlapping, obovate or lingulate, obtuse, leathery at tip and there shortly pinnately veined, ciliate, without glands, becoming reddish-brown. *fl.* yellow; cor.-tube about ⅓ in. long, very slender, 5 times as long as cal. Persia.

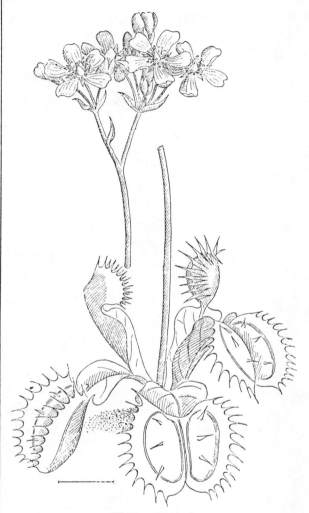

*Dionaea muscipula*

**D. Michaux'ii.** Tufted, forming a dense cushion; branches erect. *l.* densely overlapping, flat, nerves fan-wise, ovate-spatulate or angled, thick, velvety-hairy, entire, obtuse. *fl.* yellow, solitary, sessile; cor. hairy, tube 4 or 5 times as long as cal., dilated in middle, lobes wedge-shaped-ovate, entire. SW. Persia.

**D. oreodox'a.** Shrubby, loosely tufted. Stem branched; branches long, without *l.* at base, densely leafy above. *l.* near tip of stem green, loosely overlapping, forming an almost globose group, shortly hairy or almost glabrous, rather thin, obtuse, crenately toothed, margin usually resolute. *fl.* yellow, 1 or 2, nearly sessile; cor. lobes obovate, tube 5 times as long as cal. SE. Persia.

**DIO'ON** (*dis,* 2, *oon,* egg; the seeds are borne in pairs). Fam. *Cycadaceae.* A singular genus of 4 or 5 Mexican species, all noble plants in a collection grown for the ornamental foliage of its constituents. Leaves pinnate with numerous nerves running longitudinally. They require warm greenhouse conditions and grow well in a compost of good loam and river sand. They are raised from seed, which is very large.

**D. ed'ule.** Stem about 3 ft. round. 3 ft. h. *l.* 3 to 6 ft. long, 6 to 7 in. wide, very firm, glaucous green, entire, tapering towards base where clothed with short white woolly hairs. 1844. (B.M. 6184.) The seeds as large as a chestnut are powdered by the natives and formed into a kind of arrowroot.

**D. spinulo'sum.** Very similar to *D. edule* in general appearance but with lflets. armed with marginal spiny teeth up to ⅛ in. long. Much taller in a wild state, being up to 50 ft. h., being one of the tallest of Cycads, but extremely slow in growth.

W. J. B.

**DIOSCOR'EA** (in honour of the Greek Pedanios Dioscorides, native of Anazauba, Cilicia, first century A.D., author of a book on medicinal herbs which was the foundation of all botanical knowledge until modern times). Fam. *Dioscoreaceae*. A genus of about 200 species of herbaceous twining plants with broad, cordate or angular, 3- to 7-veined, reticulate, rarely lobed, frequently handsome leaves Roots large, tuberous. Flowers monoecious or dioecious; male flowers with 6 stamens with connate filaments (3 stamens only fertile); ovary inferior. Fruit a capsule with winged seeds. In winter Dioscoreas should be kept in a cool (not cold) place, either in pots or in some perfectly dry sand. The soil should be light and rich, a compost of turfy loam and well-decomposed manure suiting them well. They need much root room and plenty of water during growth, the supply being gradually lessened as the shoots begin to die down. Propagation is by division of the tubers while they are at rest, never while in growth. Several species are grown in warm countries for their edible tubers which are used like potatoes. Among these the yam (*D. Batatas*) is the best known. It is hardy in this country but the great depth to which the tubers descend makes them very difficult to dig. Some of the Latin names which have appeared in catalogues and lists have no botanical standing and usually apply apparently to some form of the *D. discolor–D. multicolor* group grown for their handsome leaves. The name *D. sativa* used for cultivated yams covers, apparently, several distinct species and is better dropped.

**D. ala'ta.** Tubers large to very large. Stem 4-winged or -angled. *l.* opposite, oblong or ovate, deeply heart-shaped at base, glabrous, 7- (rarely 9-) nerved, the outer pair united. Staminate spikes branched, pistillate simple. *fl.* distant. *fr.* a leathery capsule. India and South Sea Is. Widely grown in tropics, the tubers sometimes weigh 100 lb. and reach 6 to 8 ft. in length; edible. Warm house.

**D. argyrae'a.** *l.* green, heart-shaped, about 5 in. wide, 7-nerved, with angular patches of silvery-grey along nerves. Colombia. Probably a form of *D. discolor*. Stove.

**D. Bata'tas.** Chinese Yam. Tubers 2 to 3 ft. long, deep in ground. Stem smooth, green or purplish, 6 to 10 ft. h. or more. *l.* deep green, with small axillary tubers, glossy, opposite, heart-shaped at base, slender-pointed, 7- to 9-nerved; stalk short. *fl.* white, very small, cinnamon-scented, in axillary racemes. Philippines. (F.d.S. 971.) Hardy. var. **Decaisnea'na,** tubers short, potato-like. (R.H. 1865, 110 as *D. Decaisneana.*)

**D. bulbif'era.** Air Potato. Root-tubers small or absent, aerial axillary tubers often large up to several lb. Stem tall. *l.* alternate, ovate-heart-shaped, cuspidate, 7- to 9-nerved; stalk longer than blade. *fl.* greenish, in drooping axillary racemes. E. Indies. 1692. (G.C. 8 (1877), 48.) Tubers edible.

**D. cauca'sica.** *rhiz.* thick, horizontal. Stem smooth. *Upper l.* nearly opposite, *lower* in whorls of 3 to 5, sometimes entire and ovate-heart-shaped, sometimes with wavy margin and lobed. *fl.* small, greenish, in l.-axils. Caucasus. 1894. Climber for warm, shady nooks.

**D. crini'ta.** Stem hairy, slender. *l.* long-stalked; lflets. 5, 2 to 3 in. long, stalked, elliptic-lanceolate or oblanceolate, with a long, bristly mucro. *fl.* white; racemes numerous, drooping, in l.-axils, 2 to 3½ in. long, forming a terminal panicle. September. Natal. 1884. (B.M. 6804.) Useful pot plant trained on a balloon trellis.

**D. Decaisnea'na.** A variety of *D. Batatas.*

**D. dis'color.** Root tuberous. *l.* large, heart-shaped, cuspidate, marked with several shades of green, with a white band along midrib, purplish beneath. *fl.* greenish, inconspicuous. S. America. Warm house.

**D. elephan'tipes.** Elephant's Foot; Hottentot Bread; Tortoiseplant. Stem annual, up to 10 ft. from a large corrugated tuber. *l.* broadly ovate-heart-shaped, or kidney-shaped, shortly mucronate, 7- to 9-nerved. *fl.* greenish-yellow, sometimes with dark spots, pedicels rather long; racemes axillary, male sometimes branched, up to 1½ in. long, female simple about 1 in. long. S. Africa. 1774. (B.R. 921 as *Testudinaria elephantipes*; B.M. 1347 as *Tamus elephantipes*.) Greenhouse.

**D. Farges'ii.** Tubers aerial, spherical; root tubers edible, globular. *l.* 3- to 5-partite or of 3 to 5 lflets., digitate, lflets. ovate to ovallanceolate, slender-pointed. *Female fl.* oblong, sessile, in a very long raceme. W. China. (R.H. 1900, p. 685.) Hardy.

**D. illustra'ta.** *l.* satiny-green with fine transverse whitish lines between the nerves, an irregular middle band of silvery-grey and a few angular patches of the same near the nerves, about 6 in. long, heart-shaped at base, purple beneath. Brazil. 1873. (G.C. 1873, 1870.) Probably a form of *D. discolor.*

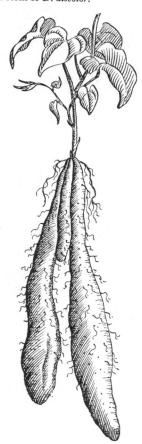

*Dioscorea Batatas*

**D. multico'lor.*** Near *D. discolor*. *l.* rich green, spotted and variegated with pale green, especially near veins, heart-shaped, 3 to 5 in. long, up to 3 in. wide, pale purple beneath. Brazil. 1868. (I.H. 1871, 53.) Variable in colouring; var. **chrysophyl'la,** *l.* olivebrown variegated with yellow; **Eldora'do,** *l.* satiny-green with median band and irregular blotches of silver-grey; **melanoleu'ca,** *l.* deep green with median silvery band and blotches along veins; **metal'lica,** *l.* bronzy-green, median band copper.

**D. pyrena'ica.** A synonym of *Bordera pyrenaica.*

**D. racemo'sa.** Roots tuberous. Stem 8 ft. h. *l.* scattered, cordateovate, 9-nerved, slender-pointed, glandular at base. *fl.* yellow and purple; male raceme axillary, solitary. Cent. America. 1850. Syn. *Helmia racemosa.*

**D. retu'sa.** Stem slender, twining, finely hairy. *l.* digitate, alternate; lflets. 5 to 7, stalked, obovate, about 2 in. long, retuse, green, shining. *fl.* dull yellowish in drooping, many-fld., slender, axillary racemes. S. Africa. 1870. (G.C. 15 (1881), 511.) Greenhouse.

**D. vitta'ta.** *l.* large, heart-shaped, variegated red and white on both sides or flushed claret beneath. (B.M. 6409.) Warm house.

**DIOSCOREA'CEAE.** Monocotyledons. A family of about 220 climbing herbs or shrubs in 9 genera, natives chiefly of tropical climates but with a few representatives in temperate regions. Rootstock tuberous or rhizomatous. Leaves alternate, net-veined, often arrow-shaped. Flowers small, in racemes or spikes; usually dioecious; perianth tubular, 6-cleft; stamens 6, 3 sometimes reduced to staminodes; ovary inferior, usually 3-celled, with 2 ovules in each cell, occasionally 1-celled. Fruit a capsule or berry. The tubers of some, e.g. species of Dioscorea (Yam), are used as food. The peculiar habit of some renders them attractive. Genera dealt with are Bordera, Dioscorea, and Tamus.

**DIOS'MA** (*dios*, divine, *osme*, smell, in allusion to the pleasant fragrance of the crushed leaves). FAM. *Rutaceae*. A genus of about 12 species of evergreen, heath-like shrubs, natives of S. Africa. Leaves alternate or opposite, very small, channelled. Flowers terminal, white or reddish; petals without a claw; stamens 5 or 10, all fertile; capsule in 5 sections. Many figures in the older botanical publications labelled 'Diosma' belong really to Agathosma or Barosma (which see for distinctions and cultivation).

**D. cupressi'na.** Heather-like, twiggy, evergreen shrub, 1 to 2 ft. *l.* opposite, overlapping, often appressed closely to the stems, ovate-lanceolate, $\frac{1}{12}$ to $\frac{1}{8}$ in. long, glandular-dotted beneath. *fl.* solitary or 2 to 4, small, white. November. S. Africa. (L.B.C. 303.)

**D. ericoi'des.** Shrub 1 to 2 ft., very twiggy; shoots quite glabrous. *l.* alternate, about $\frac{1}{8}$ in. long, oblong, keeled beneath, glabrous, appressed at base, recurved at the blunt end, glandular-dotted beneath. *fl.* in twos or threes forming a terminal cluster. S. Africa. This is the true *D. ericoides* of Linnaeus, but the name has also been used for *D. aspathaloides*, *D. vulgaris*, and, in the B.M., for its var. *longifolia*.

**D. oppositifo'lia.** A synonym of *D. vulgaris* or *Coleonema pulchrum*.

**D. vulgar'is.** Shrub, 2 ft. and upwards. *l.* opposite or alternate, erect, linear, $\frac{1}{8}$ to 1 in. long, ciliate, keeled, and with 2 rows of glandular dots beneath. *fl.* white or reddish, $\frac{1}{4}$ in. wide, borne in terminal clusters and in the uppermost l.-axils. March to September. Cultivated at Chelsea in 1756. SYN. *D. oppositifolia.* var. **longifo'lia,** *l.* longer, glabrous, *fl.* white (B.M. 2332 as *D. ericoides*); **ru'bra,** *fl.* reddish. (B.R. 563 as *D. rubra*.)

W. J. B.

**DIOSPHAE'RA.** Included in **Trachelium.** *D. dubia* is a synonym of *T. rumelicum*.

**DIOSPY'ROS** (Greek *Dios*, Jove; *pyros*, grain, in allusion to the edible fruits). FAM. *Ebenaceae*. A large genus (about 200 species) of evergreen and deciduous trees and shrubs, mostly unisexual. Leaves alternate, simple, entire. The few species in cultivation have little beauty of flowers but are interesting and shapely trees. *D. Ebenum*, the best Ebony tree, requires a stove temperature. The other three described below are hardy, but *D. Kaki* requires a south wall to ripen its fruits. The female tree does not require its flowers to be pollinated to produce fruits, but these are then seedless. Propagated by seed except the varieties of *D. Kaki* which are grafted on seedlings.

**D. arma'ta.** Tree, deciduous in hard winters, to 20 ft. with rounded head, much-branched; shoots downy, sometimes ending in a thorn. *l.* $\frac{1}{2}$ to 2$\frac{1}{2}$ in. long, $\frac{1}{4}$ to 1$\frac{1}{4}$ in. wide, entire, roundish to oval, midrib and l. beneath, minutely downy, speckled with transparent dots; stalk $\frac{1}{8}$ in. long. *fr.* yellow, roundish, $\frac{3}{4}$ in. wide, bristly. Cent. China. 1904. Perhaps tender in severe winters.

**D. Ebe'num.** Ebony. A large tree, shoots glabrous. *l.* oblong or oval, blunt-ended, 2 to 7 in. long, $\frac{3}{4}$ to 2$\frac{1}{2}$ in. wide, glabrous, thinly leathery; stalk $\frac{1}{6}$ to $\frac{1}{3}$ in. long. *Male fl.* 3 to 15 together; *females* solitary. *fr.* sub-globose, $\frac{1}{2}$ in. long; or globose and $\frac{3}{4}$ to 1 in. wide. India, Ceylon. Heart wood jet-black, sometimes streaked with yellow or brown, very heavy and strong. The best of many kinds of ebony.

**D. Kak'i.** Kakee or Chinese Persimmon. Deciduous tree, 20 to 40 ft. *l.* oval, 3 to 8 in. long, half as wide, shining green above. *fl.* yellowish-white, 1$\frac{1}{2}$ in. wide. *fr.* 3 in. wide, depressed globose, yellow. China, Japan. 1796. (B.M. 8127.) Much cultivated in China and Japan for its fr., also in S. Europe where several vars. are grown differing in the size and shape of the fr. var. **auran'tium,** *fr.* pale orange-yellow, apple-shaped. (R.H. 1887, 349.); **costa'ta,** *fr.* large, orange-shaped with 4 furrows, orange-yellow; **ellip'tica,** *fr.* oval, orange-yellow; **Mazel'ii,** *l.* oval to sub-cordate, *fr.* orange-shaped with 8 furrows, orange-yellow. A plant on a south wall at Kew produced several scores of fr. in the autumn of 1937, but none ripened. Under glass it fruits freely.

**D. Lo'tus.** Date Plum. Deciduous round-headed tree up to 60 ft., but rarely more than 20 ft. in cultivation. *l.* oval to oblong, 2 to 5 in. long, 1 to 2 in. wide, dark glossy green above, downy beneath, stalk $\frac{1}{4}$ to $\frac{1}{2}$ in. long. *fr.* orange-shaped, $\frac{1}{3}$ to $\frac{1}{2}$ in. across, yellow or purplish. China, Japan, W. Asia, Himalaya. 1597.

**D. virginia'na.** Persimmon. Deciduous round-topped tree, 45 to 100 ft., bark very rugged. *l.* oval to ovate, 1$\frac{1}{2}$ to 5 in. long, $\frac{3}{4}$ to 2 in. wide, pointed, dark shining green above, pale beneath, glabrous except on midrib; stalk $\frac{1}{3}$ to 1 in. long. *Male fl.* $\frac{2}{3}$ in. long, 1 to 3 in l.-axils; cor. bell-shaped with 4 recurved lobes; *females* solitary, larger. *fr.* 1 to 1$\frac{1}{2}$ in. wide, orange-shaped, yellow with a red cheek. N. America. 1699. (S.S. 252–3.)

**DIOS'TEA.** *See* **Baillonia.**

**DIO'TIS** (*dis*, 2, *otos*, ear; the corolla lobes are ear-shaped). FAM. *Compositae*. A genus of a single species of perennial cottony herb, hardy and useful as an edging or rock-plant. Readily increased by cuttings or seeds. Related to Achillea and needing a hot, sunny spot in well-drained soil. Liable, like many woolly plants, to damage in wet winters.

**D. candidis'sima.** Cotton-weed. 6 to 12 in. h. from a creeping woody rootstock. *l.* alternate, oblong, entire or toothed, densely covered with white felted wool. *fl.-heads* yellow, discoid, sub-globose. S. England, Mediterranean region, Canary Is. (E.B. 725 as *D. maritima*.)

**D. marit'ima.** A synonym of *D. candidissima.*

**DIPCA'DI** (oriental name for a species of Muscari). FAM. *Liliaceae*. A genus of about 30 species of bulbous plants of middle size with the habit of Hyacinthus, natives of S. Europe, Trop. and S. Africa, and the E. Indies. Flowers erect or spreading in a loose raceme; segments joined, lobes 2 or 3 times as long as tube, outer spreading, inner more erect. They need a light sandy loam and leaf-mould, and must be kept dry during winter. Propagated by offsets in spring. SYN. Uropetalum.

**D. Balfour'ii.** About 2 ft. h. *l.* 3 or 4, ensiform, nearly erect, about 12 in. long, 1 in. wide. *fl.* greenish-yellow, nearly 1 in. long in a loose 10- to 12-fld. raceme 6 to 9 in. long; scape green, terete, 2 to 3 ft. long. September. Socotra. 1880.

**D. glau'cum.** 2 to 3 ft. h., glaucous. *l.* erect, lorate, lanceolate, flat, sheathing at base. *fl.* tawny-green, bloomy without, nearly 1 in. long, tubular-bell-shaped; segs. oblong, obtuse; raceme long, many-fld. *fl.* irregularly scattered; pedicels straight, 2 or 3 times as long as fl.; scape erect. August. S. Africa. 1814. (B.R. 156 as *Uropetalon glaucum*.)

**D. serot'inum.** About 9 in. h. *l.* linear, channelled, nearly as long as scape. *fl.* brownish, nodding, on a many-fld. raceme, tubular-bell-shaped; segs. joined in lower quarter, linear-oblong, equal, outer acute, inner blunter; scape flexuose. June. Spain. (B.M. 859 as *Scilla serotina*.) var. **ful'vum,** *fl.* pink. (B.M. 1185 as *Scilla serotina fulva*.)

**D. tacazzea'num.** 6 to 9 in. h. *l.* 2 or 3, linear, flat, 3 to 4 in. long. *fl.* green, drooping, $\frac{1}{2}$ in. long, in a loose 6- to 12-fld. raceme; scape slender. Nile region. 1892. (G.F. 1892, 611, f. 127 as *Uropetalum tacazzeanum*.)

**D. umbona'tum.** Close to *D. Welwitschii* but with a smaller bulb of different shape, larger bracts, more numerous and shorter fl., with an ovary of different shape. S. Africa. 1865. (Ref. B. 17 as *Uropetalum umbonatum*.)

**D. Welwits'chii.** About 1 ft. h. *l.* linear, as long as scape, $\frac{1}{8}$ in. wide, sheathing at base, flat upwards, recurved, fleshy, glaucous. *fl.* green, nodding at first, later nearly erect, inner segs. connate, outer reflexed in upper third; raceme 4- to 6-fl., 3 to 4 in. long, secund; scape erect, slender, glaucous. Angola. 1867. (Ref. B. 16 as *Uropetalum Welwitschii*.)

**DIPEL'TA** (*dis*, twice, *pelte*, shield; referring to the form of the bracts). FAM. *Caprifoliaceae*. A genus of 4 deciduous shrubs from Central and W. China, related to Abelia but with the 4- (not 3-) celled ovary (only 2 cells fertile) enclosed between 2 large bracts; corolla 2-lipped. Fruit a capsule enclosed by the persistent bracts. The shrubs have a general resemblance to Diervilla, grow well in an open loam, and are readily increased by cuttings.

**D. floribun'da.** Shrub of 6 ft. (up to 15 ft. wild) with peeling bark, young shoots glandular-hairy. *l.* ovate to elliptic-lanceolate, 2 to 4 in. long, usually entire, long-pointed, stalked. *fl.* 1 to 6 on nodding stalks in l.-axils and terminal, fragrant; cor. tubular-bell-shaped, 1$\frac{1}{4}$ in. long, pale pink, orange in throat; largest bracts $\frac{3}{4}$ to 1 in. wide when fruit is mature. May, June. Cent. China. 1902. (B.M. 8310.)

**D. ventrico'sa.** Shrub of 6 ft. (up to 15 ft. wild), young shoots downy. *l.* elliptic to lanceolate, 2 to 5$\frac{1}{2}$ in. long, slender-pointed, usually glandular-toothed, hairy on veins beneath. *fl.* 1 to 4 on nodding stalks, axillary or terminal; cor. 1 in. long, swollen at base on one side, deep rose, paler outside, orange in throat; largest bracts about $\frac{4}{5}$ in. long in fruit. May, June. W. China. 1904. **A**

**D. yunnanen'sis.** Habit of last, young shoots angled, downy. *l.* ovate-lanceolate, slender-pointed, entire, 2$\frac{1}{2}$ to 5 in. long, downy on midrib beneath. *fl.* 1 to 4, at ends of short shoots; cor. $\frac{3}{4}$ to 1 in. long, with tubular base and spreading rounded lobes deeper than in *D. floribunda*, creamy-white flushed rose. May. Yunnan. 1910.

*diphroca'lyx,* having a calyx like a chariot board.

**DIPHYLLEI'A** (*dis*, 2, *phyllon*, leaf; the leaf is usually deeply 2-lobed). Fam. *Podophyllaceae*. A genus of 2 herbaceous perennials, one N. American, the other Japanese. Rhizome thick, creeping, knotty, producing a very large, umbrella-like radical leaf, deeply 2-cleft,

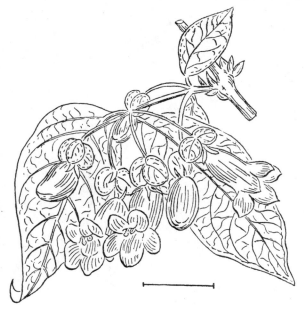

*Dipelta ventricosa* (p. 688)

and a flowering stem bearing 2 smaller similar alternate leaves. Flowers in a terminal cyme; sepals 6, very quickly falling; petals 6; stamens 6. Berry globose, few-seeded. A plant for moist peaty soils. Propagated by division in spring. Hardy.

*Diphylleia cymosa*

**D. cymo'sa.** Umbrella Leaf. About 1 to 3 ft. *l.* peltate, 1 to 2 ft. across, 2-cleft, each division 5- to 7-lobed, lobes toothed; stem-*l.* smaller. *fl.* white, in loose terminal heads. Summer. Berries blue. SE. United States. 1812. (B.M. 1666.) Dwarfer in dry soils.

**diphyl'lus -a -um,** having 2 leaves.

**DIPHY'SA** (*dis*, twice, *physa*, bladder; the pod has a large membranous bladder on each side). Fam. *Legu-*

*minosae*. A genus of about 10 species of evergreen trees or shrubs, natives of Mexico and Cent. America, often glandular. Flowers papilionaceous. Fruit a pod. Sandy loam and fibrous peat suits *D. carthagenensis* which needs stove conditions and can be propagated by cuttings of young shoots in sand with mild bottom heat.

**D. carthagenen'sis.** Small unarmed tree 6 to 10 ft. h. *l.* unequally pinnate; lflets. in 5 pairs. *fl.* yellow; peduncles axillary, 2- or 3-fld. Carthagena. 1827.

**DIP'IDAX** (*dis*, 2, *pidax*, spring). Fam. *Liliaceae*. A genus of 2 species of bulbous plants, natives of S. Africa, related to Wurmbea. Leaves few, radical. Flowers in terminal spikes without bracts; segs. with a honey gland on both sides near the base. Fruit a 3-lobed capsule. Treatment as for Androcymbium. Greenhouse.

**D. trique'trum.** Bulb roundish. *l.* sheathing at base, half-round, narrowed to tip, grooved above. *fl.* whitish, with 2 dark crimson nectaries at base of outer segs. S. Africa. (B.M. 558 as *Melanthium junceum*.) Syn. *D. roseum*.

**DIP'LACUS.** *See under* **Mimulus glutinosus.**

**DIPLADE'NIA** (*diploos*, double, *aden*, gland; there are 2 glands on the ovary). Fam. *Apocynaceae*. A genus of about 40 species of very ornamental evergreen twiners, all natives of Trop. America. Leaves opposite, entire. Flowers showy, usually in terminal or axillary racemes, rose or purple, rarely red or white; calyx 5-parted, corolla funnel- or almost salver-shaped, with 5 spreading, twisted lobes. When in flower and well grown Dipladenias are among the most beautiful of stove plants. The large flowers of some of the species and hybrids are unrivalled for brilliancy of colour, especially if the plants have free root run in a properly prepared border, but they may also be grown with rewarding effect in large pots. They are propagated by cuttings of young shoots formed when the plants begin to grow in spring. These, or single eyes (pieces of stem with 2 leaves and about an inch of stem below them), should be inserted in a compost of equal parts of sand and peat, covered with a bell-glass, and placed in brisk bottom heat. They soon root and the young plants may then be moved into separate pots and grown on, shifting as is necessary. Their future cultivation consists chiefly in giving plenty of heat and moisture early in the season and in thoroughly ripening the main growths in autumn for the succeeding year. The compost should consist of fibrous peat broken up roughly for use with sufficient silver sand to ensure good drainage. The drainage must be good for Dipladenias soon show the bad effects of a waterlogged soil. Young plants should be grown on without stopping and should be supported by a stake. If they are to be grown permanently in a pot, when of sufficient size the shoot should be placed on a trellis, best made of galvanized wire, in the form of a cone or a globe. If they are to be grown to train on the roof of the house they should be grown upright until sufficiently large to plant out. A little bottom heat is an advantage. The plants flower freely on the wood of the current year all the latter part of the summer. When flowering is over the wood that has flowered should be nearly all pruned away unless required to form a main shoot to cover the trellis or roof space. Dipladenias should be kept warm and moderately dry while at rest in winter, gradually giving more water when it is desired to start them in spring. Plenty of heat and frequent syringing in early summer will encourage the production of good flowering wood and occasional watering with weak manure-water will benefit plants in pots filled with roots. Watch should be kept to suppress insect attacks on their first appearance.

**D. acumina'ta.** Glabrous climber. *l.* ovate or elliptic, shortly pointed, short-stalked. *fl.* deep rose, streaked deeper red at throat, 4 in. across, panicle many-fld. July. Brazil. 1854. (B.M. 4828.)

**D. × amab'ilis\*** (*D. crassinoda* × *D. splendens*). About 10 ft. h. *l.* oblong-acute, short-stalked. *fl.* rosy-crimson, 4 to 5 in. across, in clusters; pet. round, stiff. May to September.

**D. × amoe'na** (*D. amabilis* × *D. splendens*). *l.* oblong-acuminate. *fl.* pink, suffused rose, resembling *D. splendens* but much finer, very free; pet. round, stiff, not r·flexed.

**D. atropurpu'rea.** Glabrous climber. *l.* ovate, acute, about 2 in. long; stalks ½ in. long. *fl.* deep velvety-maroon, tube 2 in. long; peduncles 2-fld., axillary, rather longer than l. July. Brazil. 1814. (B.R. 29, 27 as *Echites atropurpurea*.) var. **Clark'ei**, *l.* rather smaller, *fl.* intense crimson, shaded velvety-black, 2¼ in. across, tube paler veined crimson. 1892.

**D. bolivien'sis.** Small with slender stems. *l.* oblong, slender-pointed. *fl.* 2 in. across, white with yellow throat, in 3- or 4-fld. racemes. Bolivia. 1866. (B.M. 5783.)

**D. × Brearleya'na.\*** *l.* oblong, acute, dark green. *fl.* opening pink, becoming rich crimson, very large. Very free-flowering.

**D. × caris'sima.** *fl.* 5 in. across, soft, delicate blush pink, throat open, marked opposite middle of each seg. by radiating bright rose lines.

**D. crassino'da.** About 10 ft. h. *l.* oblong-lanceolate. *fl.* rose, of a beautiful shade. Brazil. (B.R. 30, 64 as *D. Martiana*.) var. **Hout-tea'na**, *fl.* with orange throat.

**D. × delec'ta.** *fl.* of good form and substance, rosy-pink, mouth deep rose, shaded violet, throat shaded yellow.

**D. × diade'ma.** *fl.* large, of good form, soft rose-pink suffused rose, mouth encircled deep rose.

*Dipladenia eximia*

**D. exim'ia.** Very slender glabrous twiner. *l.* elliptic or orbicular, nearly 2 in. long. *fl.* rich rose-red, 2½ in. across, in cymose racemes. Brazil. 1889. (B.M. 7720.)

**D. fla'va.** *See* Urechites suberecta.

**D. Har'risii.** A synonym of *Odontadenia speciosa*.

**D. illus'tris.** Climber, glabrous or downy. *l.* oblong or rounded, obtuse or subacute, rounded or somewhat cordate at base. *fl.* rose-red, 3 to 3½ in. across, 4 to 8 in a terminal raceme; cor. lobes ovate, obtuse; filaments very short. July. Brazil. 1891. (B.M. 7156, the glabrous form.)

**D. × insig'nis.** Stout with large l. *fl.* rose-purple, large.

**D. Martia'na.** A synonym of *D. crassinoda*.

**D. × nob'ilis.** Vigorous. *fl.* rosy-purple changing to orange-red, large.

**D. × orna'ta.** *fl.* rich crimson suffused violet, large.

**D. pastor'um tenuifo'lia.** *l.* very narrow, 2 to 3 in. long, 1-nerved, margins recurved. *fl.* rose; peduncles axillary, slender, as long as l. May, June. Brazil. 1896. (B.M. 7725.) SYN. *D. polymorpha tenuifolia*.

**D. × Regi'na.** *fl.* blush at first, becoming delicate flesh colour, throat suffused rose. May.

**D. × rosa'cea.** *fl.* soft rosy pink, flushed and bordered deeper, throat yellow with bright rose ring at mouth.

**D. San'deri.** *l.* thick, oblong, 2 in. long, slender-pointed; stalks ½ in. long. *fl.* rose, 3 in. across. Brazil. 1896. Allied to *D. eximia*.

*Dipladenia splendens*

**D. splen'dens.** Tuberous-rooted, herbaceous twiner with flexuous stems. *l.* broad, *fl.* white, suffused pink; spikes lengthening for months, 1 fl. opening at a time. Brazil. 1841. (B.M. 3976 as *Echites splendens*.) var. **profu'sa**, *fl.* rich carmine, 5 in. across, abundant in bunches from l.-axils; **Wil'liamsii**, *fl.* with deep pink throat, fls. more freely than type.

**D. urophyl'la.** About 3 ft. h., glabrous. *l.* oblong-ovate, narrowed to a long point; stalk rather long. *fl.* salmon-yellow, 4 to 6 in a loose, nodding raceme; cor. tube narrow at base, then bell-shaped, lobes spreading. Brazil. 1847. (B.M. 4414.)

F. G. P.

**DIPLARRHE'NA** (*diploos*, double, *arrhena*, male; there being 2 perfect stamens). FAM. *Iridaceae*. A genus of 2 closely related species allied to Libertia but with zygomorphic flowers, one outer perianth segment larger, and one stamen without an anther. The plants have short rhizomes and long linear leaves in a tuft from the base of the stem with large flowers in a terminal cluster. Treatment as for Libertia but tender.

**D. latifo'lia.** Closely related to *D. Moraea* but stronger and larger. *l.* almost 3 ft. long, nearly 1 in. wide. *fl.* 5 or 6, lilac and yellow; bracts larger. Tasmania.

**D. Morae'a.** *l.* narrow, about 20 in. long. *fl.* 2 or 3, white; outer segs. reflexed, roundish, inner shorter, narrower, and erect. Tasmania, S. Australia. 1873.

*diplazioi'des*, resembling Diplazium.

**DIPLAZIOP'SIS** (like *Diplazium*). FAM. *Polypodiaceae*. A genus of 2 E. Asiatic species, differing from Asplenium by the dehiscence of the indusium which, at first the same shape as the sorus and completely enclosing it, dehisces by splitting in an irregular line down the middle. The soil must be fairly rich but light for the fleshy roots; a mixture of equal parts of fibrous peat, leaf-mould, turfy loam, and silver sand. Potting should not be hard and drainage must be perfect. Exposure to direct sun must be avoided otherwise the bright green of the fronds is lost. Water in abundance is needed in summer but only sufficient to prevent shrivelling in winter. Propagation by spores.

**D. javan'ica.** *Fronds* often 1 to 2 ft. long, 6 in. to 1 ft. broad; pinnae 3 to 6 in. long, 1 in. broad, entire. *Sori* on front vein of first fork only. China, Japan, N. India to Java. (F.S.I. 139.) SYN. *Allantodia Brunoniana.*

**DIPLA'ZIUM** (*diplazios*, double, referring to the double indusia). FAM. *Polypodiaceae*. About 380 species of ferns closely related to Asplenium and often included in that genus, differing by the sori and indusia or some of them extending both sides of the free veins. For cultivation *see* **Asplenium.**

**D. arbores'cens.** *cau.* oblique. *sti.* 1 to 2 ft. long. *Fronds* 3 to 4 ft. long, 2 to 3 ft. broad, deltoid, 3-pinnatifid, with numerous pinnae, lower 12 to 18 in. long, 4 to 6 in. broad; pinnules 3 in. long, about ½ in. wide, acuminate, cut two-thirds of the way to rachis into nearly entire lobes, ¼ in. deep, ⅛ in. broad. Lower *sori* ⅛ in. long. Mauritius, &c. 1826. Stove.

**D. bantamen'se.** *sti.* 6 to 12 in. long, firm, erect, nearly naked. *Fronds* 9 to 18 in. long, with a large terminal pinna and 1 to 4 pairs lateral 6 to 8 in. long, 1½ to 2 in. broad, narrowed at both ends, nearly entire. *Sori* slender, irregular, nearly touching margin and midrib. Trop. Asia. (F.B.I. 69.) SYN. *Asplenium fraxinifolium.* Greenhouse.

**D. Beddom'ei.** *cau.* erect. *sti.* 1 to 1½ ft. long. *Fronds* deltoid, 1½ to 2 ft. long, 3-pinnatifid; lower pinnae distant, oblong-lanceolate, 6 to 8 in. long, 1½ to 2 in. broad, rachis winged to base; pinnules ligulate-oblong, ⅜ in. broad, sessile, cut into shallow, close, oblong blunt lobes. *Sori* ⅛ in., medial in a single row in pinnules. Ceylon. SYN. *Asplenium Schkuhrii.* Stove.

**D. Campbell'ii.** *rhiz.* small, erect, with a few pale brown scales. *sti.* tufted, erect, rather strong, 4 to 6 in. long. *Fronds* erect, with 1 or 2 pairs of contiguous, spreading, lateral pinnae, and a slightly larger terminal one, lanceolate, acuminate, 3 to 5 in. long, 1¼ in. broad, shortly decurrent on rachis. Guiana. 1885. Stove.

**D. celtidif'olium.** *sti.* strong, erect, 1 ft. or more in length, brownish, scaly below. *Fronds* 2 to 4 ft. long, 9 to 18 in. broad, pinnatifid at apex, pinnate below; pinnae numerous, lower distinctly stalked, 6 to 9 in. long, 1½ to 2 in. broad, acuminate, sub-entire or slightly toothed or lobed. *Sori* beginning at midrib and falling short of edge. Trop. America. Stove.

**D. cordifo'lium.** *sti.* firm, erect, 6 to 12 in. long, scaly below. *Fronds* leathery, of an extraordinary shape, being entire, cordate at base, long-acuminate. *Sori* extending from midrib to margin. Philippine and Malay Is. (F.B I. 331.) SYN. *Anisogonium cordifolium.* Stove.

**D. costa'le.** *sti.* 1 ft. or more long, tufted, stout, erect. *Fronds* large, apex pinnatifid, lower part pinnate; pinnae often 1 ft. long, 3 in. broad, cut half or two-thirds of way to rachis into blunt, slightly incise-serrate lobes. *Sori* many, broad, falling very short of margin. W. Indies to Peru. Stove.

**D. cultrifo'lium.*** *sti.* 4 to 6 in. long. *Fronds* 6 to 12 in. long, 4 to 6 in. broad, 2-pinnate, deltoid-ovate, with a lobed terminal point and 6 to 10 pinnae on each side, 3 to 4 in. long, ½ to ¾ in. broad, acute, broadly toothed, sometimes lobed below nearly or quite to rachis, base nearly at a right angle on upper, but obliquely truncate on lower side. *Sori* falling short both of margin and midrib. Trop. America. 1820. Stove.

**D. Cuming'ii.** *sti.* 2 to 6 in. long. *Fronds* varying in shape, from simple oblong-lanceolate, 6 to 9 in. long, 2 to 3 in. broad, acuminate, entire, to ternate or pinnate, with a large terminal and 3 pairs of lateral pinnae, each like the entire frond of the simple state, leathery. Isle of Luzon. SYN. *Anisogonium alismaefolium.* Stove.

**D. dilata'tum.** *sti.* strong, erect, smooth, 1 ft. or more long, clothed at base with dark-brown scales. *Fronds* 3 to 4 ft. long, 1 to 1½ ft. broad; pinnae about 12 on each side, largest 1 ft. long and 4 in. broad; pinnules numerous, coriaceous, 2 in. long, ½ in. broad, truncate at base, slightly toothed. *Sori* linear, about ⅛ in. long. Asia, Polynesia. SYN. *D. latifolium.* Greenhouse. Almost arborescent.

**D. esculen'tum.*** *cau.* sub-arborescent. *sti.* 1 to 2 ft. long. *Fronds* 4 to 6 ft. long, pinnate or 2-pinnate; lower pinnae 12 to 18 in. long, 6 to 8 in. broad; pinnules 3 to 6 in. long, about 1 in. broad, acuminate, more or less deeply lobed; base narrowed suddenly, often auricled; lines of *sori* often on all lateral veinlets. India, &c. 1822. SYN. *Anisogonium esculentum.* Stove.

**D. Franco'nis.*** *sti.* tufted, 1 ft. long. *Fronds* 1 to 2 ft. long, 9 to 15 in. broad, deltoid, with numerous pinnae on each side, lower 6 to 8 in. long, acuminate, cut in lower half into distinct pinnules, 1½ to 2 in. long, ½ in. broad, lanceolate, unequal-sided, edge cut half-way down below into oblong sharply toothed lobes; lower side obliquely truncate. *Sori* in parallel rows, not reaching margin. Mexico to Ecuador. (B.C.F. 1, 579.) Stove.

**D. grandifo'lium.** *sti.* 1 ft. or more long. *Fronds* 2 to 3 ft. long, 9 to 12 in. broad, deltoid-lanceolate, point pinnatifid, with 12 to 20 pinnae on each side; lower 2 in. or more apart, distinctly stalked, 4 to 6 in. long, 1 to 1½ in. broad, acuminate; edge slightly toothed, and sometimes broadly lobed below, base equally rounded on both sides. *Sori* irregular, falling slightly short of both midrib and margin. Trop. America. 1793. Stove.

**D. heterophle'bium.** *sti.* 1 ft. long, grey, scaly. *Fronds* thinly herbaceous, 1 to 1½ ft. long, 8 to 9 in. broad, with 6 to 8 pairs of pinnae below the pinnatifid apex; lowest pinnae 2 in. or more apart, 3 to 4 in. long, 1 to 1¼ in. broad, acute, cordate, dark green, undulate, naked; rachis villous; veins pinnate. *Sori* not reaching margin. E. Himalaya. (F.B.I. 329.) SYN. *Anisogonium heterophlebium.*

**D. hi'ans.** *sti.* 1 to 1½ ft. long, slightly scaly. *Fronds* 3 to 4 ft. long, 2 to 3 ft. broad; pinnae thin, papery, dark green, lower 1 ft. or more long, 4 to 6 in. broad; pinnules numerous, lanceolate, with blunt lobes reaching nearly to rachis. *Sori* short, oblong, only lower double. W. Indies, Ecuador. Almost arborescent. Stove.

**D. japon'icum.** *rhiz.* slender, creeping. *sti.* straw-colour. *Fronds* 9 to 15 in. long, 4 to 6 in. broad; pinnae 8 to 10, papery, bright green, cut in lower part into close, oblong, slightly toothed lobes. *Sori* reaching two-thirds of way to edge on both margins. Japan, China, Trop. Asia. Greenhouse.

**D. Klotzs'chii.** *sti.* strong, upright, dark brown, scaly at base. *Fronds* 3 to 5 ft. long, 9 to 18 in. broad; pinnae 6 to 9 in. long, 3 to 4 in. broad, deep green, papery; pinnules 2 to 3 in. long, divided into slightly toothed lobes. Jamacia. Venezuela. Stove.

**D. lan'ceum** *sti.* scattered, 4 to 6 in. long. *Fronds* 6 to 9 in. long, ¾ to 1 in. broad, narrowed gradually upwards and downwards, entire or slightly undulate. *Sori* linear, irregular, reaching nearly to margins, but not to midrib. Himalaya, &c. SYN. *Asplenium subsinuatum.* Greenhouse.

**D. Lasiop'teris.** *See* **D. Petersenii.**

**D. latifo'lium.** A synonym of *D. dilatatum.*

**D. Lech'leri.** *sti.* stout, upright, 2 to 3 ft. long, scaly towards base. *Fronds* 3 ft. long, 2 ft. broad at the base; pinnae very leathery, 1 ft. long, 3 in. broad, slightly toothed, tapering to a sharp point, rounded at base. *Sori* beginning at midrib, but falling short of margin. Trop. America. Stove.

**D. lu'cidum.** A synonym of *Asplenium tenerum.*

**D. margina'tum.** *sti.* 2 to 3 ft. long, strong, erect, woody, about ½ in. thick at base. *Fronds* simply pinnate, 4 to 6 ft. long; pinnae in several opposite pairs, lowest to 2 ft. long, 3 to 4 in. broad, entire, base often cordate. *Sori* long, linear, confined to free veins. Trop. America. (L.F. 5, 53.) SYN. *Asplenium marginatum, Hemidictyum marginatum.* Stove.

**D. melanocau'lon.*** *sti.* 1 to 2 ft. long. *Fronds* 2 to 3 ft. long, 9 to 18 in. broad; lower pinnae 4 to 9 in. long, 4 to 6 in. broad; pinnules lanceolate, 2 to 3 in. long, ¾ in. broad, cut two-thirds of way to rachis into linear-oblong, falcate, inciso-crenate lobes. *Sori* short, oblong, free of midrib and margin. Fiji. Stove.

**D. Meyenia'num.** *sti.* smooth, angular. *Fronds* ample, 3-pinnatifid; lower pinnae 9 to 12 in. long, 4 to 6 in. broad; pinnules 3 to 4 in. long, 1 in. or more broad, cut below to distinctly winged rachis into deeply crenate, blunt, oblong lobes, ⅓ in. deep, ¼ in. broad. *Sori* many, nearly all diplazioid, and filling when mature nearly the whole surface of lobes. Hawaii. 1877. SYN. *Asplenium Arnottii, A. diplazioides, Diplazium Arnottii.* Greenhouse.

**D. nigropalea'ceum.** *cau.* decumbent. *sti.* 1 to 1½ ft. long, ½ in. thick, thickly clothed with nearly black scales. *Fronds* thick, 2 to 3 ft. long and nearly as broad; lower pinnae 1 to 1½ ft. long, 6 to 8 in. broad; pinnules numerous, spreading, 3 to 4 in. long, 1 in. broad, cut half or two-thirds to rachis into inciso-crenate lobes ¼ in. broad; rachis slightly zigzag. *Sori* lower, ¼ in. long. St. Helena. SYN. *D. Loddigesii.* Greenhouse.

**D. Petersen'ii.** *rhiz.* wide-creeping. *sti.* 6 to 9 in. long, erect, dark, villous. *Fronds* herbaceous, 1¼ to 1½ ft. long, 6 to 8 in. broad, with 8 to 10 pinnae on each side below the pinnatifid apex; largest pinnae 3 to 4 in. long, 1 to 1¼ in. broad, lower lobes cut nearly or quite to rachis, ⅜ to ½ in. deep, obtuse, the dark rachis and dark green fronds villous. *Sori* lower ones ⅛ in. long. China, India, Java. SYN. *D. decussatum* (of gardens). *D. Lasiopteris* is a form of this. Stove.

**D. plantaginifo'lium.** *sti.* tufted, 6 to 9 in. long. *Fronds* 6 to 9 in. long, 2 to 3 in. broad, simple, acuminate, base rounded, slightly undulate-dentate upwards, sometimes lobed towards base. *Sori* slender, linear, sometimes nearly touching both edge and midrib. Trop. America. 1819. (L.B.C.1588.) SYN. *D. plantagineum.* Stove.

**D. polypodioi'des.** *cau.* erect, nearly arborescent. *sti.* stout, green, 1 ft. or more in length. *Fronds* 4 ft. long, 2 ft. broad; pinnae 8 or 9 on each side, 1 ft. long, 6 in. broad, thin, papery, bright green; pinnules numerous, cut into narrow-oblong, slightly toothed lobes. *Sori* falling short of margin. N. India, Malaya to Trop. Australia. (F.B.I. 293.) Greenhouse.

**D. prolif'erum.** *sti.* 1 to 2 ft. long. *Fronds* 2 to 4 ft. long, simply pinnate, with numerous pinnae on each side, 6 to 12 in. long, 1 to 2 in. broad, often proliferous in axils, nearly entire. *Sori* reaching nearly to margin, double. Polynesia, Malaya, Trop. Africa. SYN. *Anisogonium decussatum, Callipteris prolifera.* Stove.

**D. Shepherd'ii.** *sti.* tufted, 12 in. long. *Fronds* 12 to 18 in. long, 6 to 9 in. wide; lower pinnae stalked, 4 to 6 in. long, 1 to 1½ in. wide, acuminate, lobed above, ¼ in. broad, somewhat toothed. *Sori* linear, not reaching margin. Trop. America. SYN. *Asplenium Shepherdii.* Stove.

**D. specio'sum.** *rhiz.* wide-creeping. *sti.* erect, straw-colour, 1 ft. or more long. *Fronds* 1 to 2 ft. long, 8 to 12 in. broad; pinnae thin but firm, 4 to 6 in. long, ¾ to 1 in. broad, conspicuously lobed, slightly toothed, somewhat cuneate at base. *Sori* slender, reaching nearly to margin. Philippine and Malayan Is. (B.C.F. 1, 647.) Stove.

**D. stria'tum.** *cau.* erect. *sti.* firm, erect, 1 to 1½ in. long, hardly scaly below. *Fronds* 2 to 3 ft. long, 9 to 15 in. broad, pinnatifid at apex; pinnae 6 to 8 in. long, 1¼ in. broad, cut half or two-thirds to rachis into slightly toothed, oblong lobes. *Sori* about ½ in. long, close to mid-vein of fertile segs. Trop. America. Nearly arborescent. SYN. *D. crenulatum.* Stove.

**D. sylvat'icum.** *cau.* decumbent. *sti.* 1 ft. long. *Fronds* 1 to 2 ft. long, 4 to 8 in. broad, ovate-lanceolate, with numerous spreading pinnae, largest 3 to 4 in. long, ½ to ¾ in. broad, acuminate; broadly and briefly lobed; base narrowed suddenly on both sides. *Sori* in long slender lines, reaching nearly to margin. India, &c. Stove.

**D. Thwaites'ii.*** *rhiz.* wide-creeping, stout. *sti.* 6 in. long, slender, densely clothed with strong white woolly hairs. *Fronds* 1 ft. or more long, 4 to 6 in. broad, with 8 to 10 distinct pinnae below pinnatifid apex, largest 3 in. long, ⅝ in. broad, cut two-thirds of way to rachis in oblong crenulated lobes, ¼ in. deep, ⅛ in. across. *Sori* reaching half-way to margin, the lowest about 1/16 in. long. Ceylon. (H.S.C.F. 45.) Stove.

**D. tomento'sum.** *sti.* 6 to 9 in. long, erect, brown-tomentose, at length glossy. *Fronds* 6 to 12 in. long, 3 to 4 in. broad, ovate-lanceolate; pinnae numerous, closely placed, lanceolate, lower pair deflexed, next horizontal, 2 to 3 in. long, ½ in. broad, acute, cut down regularly into oblong-falcate lobes ⅛ in. broad; rachis finely tomentose. *Sori* linear, touching margin but not midrib. E. Indies, &c. Stove.

**D. unilo'bum.** *sti.* 6 to 9 in. long, slender. *Fronds* herbaceous, 6 to 9 in. long, 3 to 4 in. broad, pinnatifid at apex, pinnate below; pinnae mostly simple, oblong, auricled, lowest stalked, 2 in. long, 1 in. broad, toothed, cut nearly or quite to rachis into spatulate pinnules. *Sori* reaching from midrib nearly to margin. Cuba. SYN. *D. semihastatum.* Stove.

**D. zeyla'nicum.*** *sti.* scattered, 4 to 8 in. long. *Fronds* 6 to 12 in. long, 1 to 2 in. broad, acuminate, apex slightly lobed, lower two-thirds more deeply, at base quite down to rachis; lobes blunt, ¼ to ½ in. across. *Sori* linear, 2 to 3 lines long. Ceylon. (B.C.F. 1, 666.) Stove.

**DIPLOCAR'PON.** A genus of fungi including *D. rosae*, the cause of Black-spot disease of Roses. *See* **Rose diseases.**

**DIPLOCLIS'IA** (*diploos*, double, *clisia*, enclosure; in reference to the double calyx). FAM. *Menispermaceae.* A small genus closely akin to Cocculus differing in the structure of the fruit.

**D. affin'is.** Deciduous, glabrous climber, 20 to 30 ft. *l.* roundish-rhomboid, broadly tapered to both ends, blunt, almost entire, 1¾ to 3 in. long, 5-nerved; stalk as long as blade. *fl.* yellow, ¼ in. wide, in axillary clusters of 6 to 12 terminating a stalk 1 to 2 in. long. May. *fr.* obliquely obovate, ⅓ in. long, blue-black. China. 1907. SYN. *Cocculus affinis.*

W. J. B.

**DIPLOCYATH'A** (*diploos*, double, *kyathos*, a cup; referring to the shape of the flowers). FAM. *Asclepiadaceae.* Stems short, 4-angled, toothed, branching freely at the base and decumbent. Flowers from near the base, similar in structure to Stapelia (q.v.) but with a curious tube in the throat with a recurved rim covered with stiff purple hairs; corolla 3 in. across, densely papillate on the inside, greyish near the tube, yellowish towards the lobes which are fringed with vibratile white hairs. For cultivation *see* **Stapelia.**

**D. cilia'ta.** The only species. S. Africa. SYN. *Stapelia ciliata.* (W. & S. 710–15.)

V. H.

**DIPLOGLOT'TIS** (*diploos*, double, *glottis*, tongue; the inner scale of the petals is double). FAM. *Sapindaceae.*

*D. Cunninghamii* is the only species. It is cultivated like the closely allied species of Blighia, in subtropical conditions in a compost of peat and loam. Cuttings of ripe shoots will root in sand under a glass.

**D. Cunningham'ii.** Tree of 30 or 40 ft., shoots, l.-stalks and infl. densely reddish-downy. *l.* pinnate, 1 to 2 ft. long; lflets. 8 to 12, oval-oblong to ovate-lanceolate, 6 to 8 (sometimes up to 12) in. long, glabrous above, strongly veined beneath. *fl.* greenish-yellow, small, in terminal pyramidal panicles 1 ft. or more long. May. Queensland, Victoria. 1825. A fine-foliaged tree but fitted only for lofty structures. (B.M. 4470 as *Cupania Cunninghamii.*)

**DIPLOLAE'NA** (*diploos*, double, *chlaina*, a cloak; alluding to the double involucre of the flower-heads). FAM. *Rutaceae.* A genus of 4 species of evergreen shrubs, confined to Australia, with alternate leaves and flowers in dense heads arranged as in the Compositae. Bentham suggested that the 2 following species together with the remaining 2—*microcephala* with small heads and *angustifolia* with narrow linear leaves—run so much into each other that they may come to be regarded as merely varieties. Greenhouse with a compost of sandy peat and a little fibrous loam. Propagated by cuttings of firm young shoots.

**D. Dampier'i.** Shrub 5 or 6 ft., shoots closely downy. *l.* oblong-obovate, base cuneate, apex rounded, minutely notched, ½ to 2 in. long, ¼ to ⅝ in wide, glabrous above, entire. *fl.* in crowded, solitary, drooping heads, 1 to 1½ in. across; surrounded by two series of bracts; pet. hidden, the chief feature being a mass of stamens, 1 in. long, red, hairy. April. W. Australia. (B.M. 4059.)

**D. grandiflo'ra.** Shrub up to 8 ft., very closely akin to *D. Dampieri*, shoots hoary with close down. *l.* larger, 1 to 2 in. long, and broader, oblong, ovate or oval, hoary on both sides. *fl.-heads* as in *D. Dampieri* but rather larger; pet. linear, ciliate, concealed. April. W. Australia.

W. J. B.

**DIPLOME'RIS** (*diploos*, double, *meris*, a part). FAM. *Orchidaceae.* A small genus of about 4 species of terrestrial orchids, *D. hirsuta* from central Himalayas, Sikkim, *D. pulchella* from Khasia, *D. Boxallii* from lower Burma, and *D. chinensis* from the Tientai Mts. All are dwarf. From a small tuber 1 to 3 leaves are developed, lying more or less on the ground. The flowers are comparatively large and attractive; the 2 cells of the anther are widely separated by a broad connective so much so that the appearance is that of 2 anthers. *D. hirsuta*, the only species in cultivation, requires a compost of loam fibre 2 parts, Sphagnum moss 1 part, and cut Osmunda 1 part, with an addition of finely crushed crocks or coarse sand. Water may be required in winter, after the leaves fall, but only to compensate for the artificial heat used to maintain a night temperature of 55 to 60° F. Owing to the position of the principal leaf, water should be given by immersing the small pan or pot up to the rim until the compost is wetted. The summer temperature can reach the tropical, but careful shading is required. *D. pulchella* would probably require similar treatment but the other species are said to grow in damp places.

**D. hirsu'ta.** *l.* light green, 4 in. long, 1½ in. broad, hairy on both surfaces, with a similarly shaped but very much smaller leaf opposite; between them rises the slender, green, hairy scape, terminating in 1 or 2 beautiful fl. Sep. lanceolate, narrow, keeled, pure white, hidden by the pet. and lip; pet. almost orbicular, 1 in. across, pure white; lip short-clawed, 1½ in. broad, 1 in. long, with a central raised lamina; lip base contracted into a curved greenish spur, 2 in. long, funnel-like at first, then cylindrical; shaded yellow and green around stigma, dilated rostellum and base of lip. Nepal. 1832. (B.M. 9113.) SYN. *Diplochilus hirsutus.*

E. C.

**DIPLOPAP'PUS.** *See* **Aster, Cassinia.**

**DIPLOPEL'TIS** (*diploos*, double, *pelte*, a shield; in allusion to the double fruit). FAM. *Sapindaceae.* Four species of shrubs or undershrubs confined to Australia. Leaves alternate; sepals 5; petals 4 (the place of the fifth vacant); stamens 8; fruit a 2- or 3-celled capsule. *D. Huegelii* may be grown in a compost of loam, peat, and sand. Greenhouse. Increased by cuttings.

**D. Huegel'ii.** Shrub 1½ to 3 ft., shoots terete, grey with down or softly hairy. *l.* varying from oblong-linear and entire to narrowly obovate and irregularly deeply lobed, 1 to 2 in. long, scarcely stalked, downy. *fl.* in terminal glandular-downy panicles 2 to 6 in. long; male and female usually on the same raceme; cor. about ½ in. across; pet. 4, roundish, pink. April, May. W. Australia. 1837. (B.R. 25, 69.)

W. J. B.

**DIPLOPO'DA.** *See* **Millepedes.**

**DIPLOPRO'RA** (*diploos*, double, *prora*, front). FAM. *Orchidaceae.* A genus of a single species of epiphytic Orchid allied to Vanda and needing similar treatment to the more tender species of that genus.

**D. Champion'ii.** *fl.* 5 or 6, ½ to ¾ in. across; sep. and pet. nearly equal, ovate, yellow; lip white and purplish, 3-lobed, connate with base of column, side lobes roundish quadrate, streaked red, base curved, boat-shaped, mid-lobe narrowed to a bicaudate tip, callus large; column short, papillose. Stem short. *l.* 3 to 4 in. long, ½ in. or more wide. India, Burma, Hongkong. Before 1900. SYN. *Cottonia Championii, Vanda bicaudata.*

**DIPLO'RA** (*diploos*, double, *lora*, thongs; in allusion to the strap-shaped valves of the indusium). FAM. *Polypodiaceae.* A genus of 4 species of ferns in the E. Indies and Philippine Is. For treatment *see* **Asplenium.**

**D. integrifo'lia.** *rhiz.* widely creeping, green, woody. *sti.* naked, greenish, scarcely 1 in. long, jointed at base. *Fronds* 9 to 10 in. long, rarely over ½ in. wide, entire, linear-ligulate, parchment-like, narrowed to both ends. *Sori* conspicuous, ½ to ½ in. long, 50 to 60 on each side of midrib. Solomon Is. (H.I.P. 1651.) Stove.

**D. longifo'lia pinna'ta.** *sti.* compressed, greyish. *Fronds* 2 to 4 ft. long, with an entire terminal pinna, 4 to 6 in. long, 1½ to 2 in. wide, proliferous at the point, and 1 to 6 pairs of similar lateral ones; veins usually once forked. *Sori* ½ to ¾ in. long, ₁⁄₁₂ in. wide. Philippines. SYN. *Scolopendrium pinnatum.* Greenhouse.

**diplostemonous,** having twice as many stamens as petals, the outer opposite the sepals (cf. obdiplostemonous, outer stamens opposite petals).

**DIPLOTHEM'IUM** (*diploos*, double; *thema*, sheath). FAM. *Palmaceae.* A genus of 5 species of Brazilian palms, almost stemless, or with a short, ringed trunk. Leaves in a terminal crown, pinnatisect with crowded narrow, slender-pointed segments, glaucous or silvery beneath with a prominent midrib and margins recurved at base; stalk concave above; sheath fibrous, open. Flowers monoecious, rather large and showy, cream or yellow. Fruit small, ovoid or obovoid. A compost of 2 parts rich loam, 1 of peat, and 1 of sand suits these very handsome stove palms which, if properly hardened, are excellent for sub-tropical bedding. Increased by seed.

**D. caudes'cens.** Wax Palm. Stem about 10 ft. h. or more. *l.* 2 to 6 ft. long, segs. 70 to 90 each side, 1½ to 2 ft. long, about 1 in. wide, obtuse, waxy-white beneath. Brazil. 1847. SYN. *Ceroxylon riveum.*

**D. littora'le.** Stemless or nearly so. *l.* about 3 ft. long, almost straight; segs. 50 or more each side, rigid, linear, in groups of 2 or 4. *fl.* bright yellow; spadices 2 to 3 ft. long, outer spathe 3 to 4 in. long, inner 18 to 24 in. long, hairy. Spring. Brazil. (B.M. 4681.)

**D. marit'imum.** About 10 ft. h. *l.* somewhat ovate in outline; segs. close, 10 to 12 in. long, about 1 in. wide; deep green above, silvery-green beneath. Brazil. 1823.

**DIPLYCO'SIA** (*diploos*, double, *kos*, covering; the two connate bracteoles form a second covering to the flower). FAM. *Ericaceae.* A genus of 10 species of evergreen shrubs, natives of India and Malaya, closely related to Gaultheria whose anthers have 2 horns on their back, absent in Diplycosia. For cultivation *see* **Gaultheria.**

**D. dis'color.** Shrub a few ft. h., of spreading habit. *l.* 1 to 2 in. long, ¾ to 1½ in. wide, ovate to oval, pointed, toothed, base cuneate, glabrous, 3-veined, silvery-white beneath; stalk ⅛ in. long. *fl.* crowded in axillary downy racemes shorter than the l.; cor. ovoid, ¼ in. long, white, mouth red within; limb small, pink, 5-lobed. *fr.* a blue-black berry. Bhutan. 1856. (B.M. 5034 as *Gaultheria discolor.*)

W. J. B.

**DIPO'DIUM** (*dis*, twice, *pous*, a foot; in allusion to the caudicles on the pollen masses). FAM. *Orchidaceae.* A genus of about 12 species of terrestrial or semi-epi-

phytic orchids, distributed in Malaya, the Pacific Is., and Australia. The flowers are characterized by sub-equal sepals and petals, usually spreading. The lip base appressed to the column base is slightly gibbous or shortly saccate at the base, 3-lobed, the mid-lobe the largest. Pollen masses 2. Leaves narrow, tapered, distichous. In some species foliage is absent. Racemes simple with numerous flowers. Only occasionally in cultivation. *D. punctatum* should have a compost of sandy loam with a little leaf-mould. *D. paludosum* and *D. pictum* succeed better in a Cattleya compost with about one-third of loam-fibre. All must have free drainage. Temperature depends largely on their native habitat. The leafy species should not fall below 60° F. in winter, the leafless may be grown in a moderately cool house.

**D. Hamiltonia'num.** Very near to, and by some considered, a variety of *D. punctatum.* Distinct by its pale green flowers with darker blotches. Australia.

**D. paludo'sum.** *fl.* creamy-white, blotched purple, sweet-scented, 1½ in. across, 10 to 12 in a raceme; sep. and pet. somewhat reflexed; lip lanceolate, acute, with a villous ridge from the base to the cuspidate tip, side lobes reduced to small teeth. *l.* ensiform, 10 in. long. Stem 1 to 3 ft. h.; peduncle 1 to 2 ft. h. Malacca (in swamps). 1888. (B.M. 7464; W.O.A. 422.)

**D. pic'tum.** *fl.* larger than those of *D. punctatum,* yellow thickly spotted with dark red on the outer surfaces paler on the inner. *Infl.* racemose or panicled. *l.* light green, tapered. Climbing, ascending, moisture-loving. Java. 1849. (B.M. 7951.) SYN. *D. rosea, Wailesia picta, W. rosea.*

*Dipodium punctatum*

**D. puncta'tum.** *fl.* 20 to 50, about 1 in. or more across, fleshy; sep. and pet. broadly ligulate, white with deep rose-red spots; lip with erect side lobes, mid-lobe somewhat heart-shaped, slightly convex, puberulous, red-streaked. Roots thick, fleshy. Flower stem 2 to 3 ft. h., sheathed with bract-like, reddish-brown scales. Australia. 1822. (B.R. 1980.) Very variable.

**D. ro'sea.** A synonym of *D. pictum.*

**D. scan'dens.** *fl.* 6 to 8, 1½ in. across, whitish, the pet. shading to yellow apically and like the sep. flecked with violet-red; peduncles 12 to 15 in. long. Apparently begins life as a terrestrial plant then attaches itself to a tree by short roots, the lower part dying off. Java.

E. C.

**Dippelia'nus -a -um,** in honour of Herr Dippel, 1827–1914, author of *Handbuch der Laubholzkunde.*

**DIP'RION** sp. *See* **Pine Sawflies.**

**DIPSACACEAE.** Dicotyledons. A family of about 160 species of herbs or sub-shrubs in about 8 genera, mostly natives of the Mediterranean region. Leaves opposite, sometimes connate, without stipules. Flowers in cymes or heads, the outer flowers being irregular as in many Compositae and some Cruciferae. Sepals and petals 4 or 5, joined, stamens 4, free, on the corolla tube; ovary inferior of 2 carpels, 1-celled, with one ovule. Fruit an achene. There are many ornamental plants in this family and *Dipsacus Fullonum* provides the fullers' teasel. Genera dealt with are Cephalaria, Dipsacus, Morina, Pterocephalus, Scabiosa.

**DIP'SACUS** (Greek name used by Dioscorides). FAM. *Dipsacaceae.* A genus of 12 species of erect, hairy or prickly biennial herbs, natives of Europe, Asia, and N. Africa. Leaves opposite, usually connate at base, toothed or jagged. Flower-heads terminal, oblong-ovate or roundish; flowers opening first in a ring round the middle of the head. Plants for the wild garden, growing well in almost any soil and easily raised from seed.

**D. Fullo'num.** Fullers' Teasel. Similar to *D. sylvestris* but with hooked bracts. Known only in cultivation. The dried fl.-heads are used for teasing or raising the nap of cloth.

**D. lacinia'tus.** Stem prickly, 3 to 5 ft. h. *l.* connate at base, lobed and jagged. *fl.-heads* ovoid; fl. whitish; anthers reddish; bracts slightly erect, stiffish, usually shorter than the head. July. Europe, Siberia. 1683.

**D. sylves'tris.** Common Teasel. Stem prickly, about 6 ft. h. *l.* connate at base, ovate-lanceolate, slender-pointed, toothed. *fl.-heads* ovate-oblong; fl. pale lilac; bracts inflexed, weak, not hooked, longer than the head. Europe, including Britain. (E.B. 674.) The cup formed by the connate bases of the l. catches and holds water, some of which is probably absorbed by the plant.

**DIP'TERA.** A very large Order of Insects, including the 2-winged flies. *See* **Insects.**

**DIPTERACAN'THUS.** *See* **Ruellia.**

**DIP'TERIS** (*di*, 2, *pteris*, fern; referring to the form of the fronds). FAM. *Polypodiaceae.* A genus of 8 species of ferns often included in Polypodium with fronds in 2 fan-shaped halves, deeply lobed, the areolae fine, abundant, irregular, the free veinlets spreading in various directions. Sori in a single row. For cultivation, *see* **Polypodium.**

**D. Lobbia'na.** *Fronds* 1 ft. long and broad; main lobes reaching base, 3 or 4 times forked; ultimate segs. linear, entire, leathery, dark brownish-green above, tawny beneath. *Sori* in a single row on each side of, and near, midrib. Borneo, &c. (F.B.I. 233.) SYN. *Polypodium Lobbianum, P. bifurcatum.*

**DIPTEROCARPA'CEAE.** Dicotyledons. A family of about 320 species of evergreen trees in 16 genera, mostly Indian. Leaves alternate, leathery, entire, stipulate. Flowers regular, with parts in fives, often sweet-scented; inflorescence racemose. Stamens 5, 10, 15, or more; ovary superior, 3-celled. Fruit a 1-seeded nut enclosed in the persistent calyx, some sepals of which grow out to form wings aiding in the wind-distribution of the seeds. Many species are valuable timber trees. *See* **Dryobalanops.**

**DIPTERO'NIA** (*dis*, 2, *pteron*, winged; from the form of the samara). FAM. *Aceraceae.* A genus of 2 Chinese deciduous trees related to Acer but with the fruit winged all round. Leaves opposite, odd pinnate. *D. sinensis* is an ornamental tree, hardy and growing well in a loamy soil, and distinct in its handsome foliage. It can be propagated by cuttings or by layers.

**D. sinen'sis.** Tree up to 25 ft. or a large bush with densely hairy buds. *l.* 8 to 12 in. long with 7 to 13 leaflets; leaflets ovate to lanceolate, short-stalked, coarsely and irregularly toothed. *fl.* greenish-white, very small, in glabrous, erect, pyramidal panicles, 6 to 12 in. long. June. *fr.* in large clusters, each one with 2 flat-winged samaras, ¾ to 1 in. long. China.

*dip'terus -a -um,* having 2 wings.

**DIP'TERYX** (*dis*, 2, *pteryx*, wing; the upper lobes of the calyx resemble 2 wings). FAM. *Leguminosae.* A genus of 8 Trop. American evergreen trees. Of no horticultural value in this country, but *D. odorata* furnishes the Tonka or Tonquin Beans used in perfumery, snuff, &c. The fruit is 1-seeded (the Bean) and indehiscent.

**D. odora'ta.** Tonquin Bean. Evergreen tree to 60 ft. *l.* alternate; lflets 5 or 6, alternate; stalks winged. *fl.* purple with violet blotches in terminal panicles. Guiana. 1799.

*dipyre'nus -a -um,* having 2 kernels.

**DIR'CA** (*dirke*, fountain; the plants grow in moist places). FAM. *Thymaeleaceae.* A genus of 2 N. American deciduous, much-branched shrubs. Leaves alternate, thin, stalk enclosing the bud at its base. Flowers without petals, in clusters of 3 or 4 in last year's leaf-axils, before the leaves appear; stamens 8, exserted; ovary glabrous, style exserted. Fruit a yellowish drupe, 1-seeded. The early flowers are apt to be cut by late frosts, but *D. palustris* thrives in moist peaty soil and is readily increased by seed or by layers.

**D. palus'tris.** Leather-wood. Shrub of 3 to 6 ft. with flexible shoots and very tough smooth bark. *l.* oval or obovate, 1½ to 3 in. long, entire, pale green above, rather glaucous beneath and hairy there when young. *fl.* yellowish. Eastern N. America. 1750. (B.R. 292.) The flexible tough shoots have been used as tying material and for basket-making; the bark for making ropes.

**DI'SA** (derivation?). FAM. *Orchidaceae.* A terrestrial genus of 120 species, chiefly African, mostly in the southern and central areas, but extending into Madagascar and the Bourbon Isles. Flowers variously disposed, large or small; sepals much larger than the petals, the dorsal one erect, hooded, and having a spur in the majority of the species; petals small, polymorphous; lip small, spurless, linear, acute, projecting forward; column short, rather thick; bracts usually shorter than the flowers. Stems sometimes tall and leafy, sometimes slender and few-leaved or with the leaves usually narrow and lanceolate, arranged in a rosette form, sometimes reduced to sheathing bracts on the flower stems. The roots are more or less tuberous. The value of this lovely genus has been considerably increased by the raising of several beautiful hybrids. These hybrids have proved far more amenable to cultivation than the imported species, and are often found to thrive where failure has followed attempts to grow the species. For cut-flowers these hybrid Disas are most useful. *D. uniflora* and the hybrids derived from it, the most popular and useful, require a cool, moist, airy, rather shaded position and must never be allowed to become really dry. A compost of 3 parts of finely shredded sifted Osmunda fibre, 2 parts of Sphagnum moss and a half-part of decayed oak-leaves with a little sand and finely crushed crock is suitable but position seems more important than compost. Moderately deep pans in which several plants can be placed may be used and it is an advantage to plunge the pans in a bed of Sphagnum moss. The plants resent artificial heat which should only be used when danger from frost is feared. A winter temperature of 45 to 50° F. is sufficient as the plants are then resting, though not absolutely quiescent, and the compost must be kept moist. When growing a moist atmosphere produced by frequent dampings and light sprayings is essential. The spraying will tend to minimize the danger from thrips which seem to have a special fondness for the leaves and flowers and, as strong fumigations quickly injure the plants, are difficult to keep under control. It is often advisable to place fine-meshed muslin over the ventilators to prevent their ingress. Occasional spraying with very weak nicotine solutions is helpful. Under suitable conditions offsets are rapidly formed and should be potted early in the spring of each year; the smaller growths can be placed in shallow boxes or large pans about 3 in. apart as they will not flower, or only weakly, the first year. The larger tubers should be placed 4 to 6 in. apart, or singly in a 5-in. pot. Drainage must be free. Species from the warmer parts of Africa are not as amenable to cultivation, possibly because the natural conditions to which they have adapted themselves are not thoroughly known. It is probable that they may require a higher temperature and more decided rest as do some of the more definitely deciduous and tubered S. African forms. Many of the species were originally described under Orchis and Satyrium but the specific names remain in the majority.

**D. barba'ta.** *fl.* 2 to 7, 1 in. across, white or blush-white; edges of the lip fringed. 1 to 2 ft. h. *l.* very narrow. S. Africa. (B.I.O. 3, 51.) SYN. *Herschelia barbata.*

**D. Coop'eri.** *fl.* strongly clove-scented; dorsal sep. narrowed into a long horn, whitish suffused carmine, lateral pink, reflexed; pet. dolabriform, retuse; lip greenish-yellow, broadly ovate; bracts large, tipped with chestnut-red at apex; spike robust, 12 to 24 in. h., many-fld. February. *l.* narrowed to petioles. Natal. (B.M. 7256; B.I.O. 2, 65.)

**D. cornu'ta.*** *fl.* green, white, and purple, moderately large; spikes 4 to 6 in. or more long, many-fld.; pet. small, oblong, decurved, and falcate, with a broad auricle at base; lip small, spatulate, green, with a large black velvety spot. December. *l.* lanceolate, erect or erecto-patent, acuminate, lower sheathing at base, and there marked with red spots, uppermost sessile. Stem 12 to 18 in. h., green, spotted red, leafy to summit. S. Africa. 1843. (B.M. 4091; B.I.O. 2, 81.)

*Disa crassicornis*

**D. crassicorn'is.*** *fl.* 2 in. across, white, blotched inside, pale purple; upper sep. (hood) conical, with an oblique mouth, acute above, slightly curved, undulate; lateral sep. decurved, oblong-lanceolate, with a short recurved point behind the tip; pet. broadly obovate; lip narrowly tongue-shaped, with a revolute tip, glabrous, smooth. August. *l.* lanceolate, long-acuminate, concave. Stems 1 to 3 ft. h., robust, leafy, several-fld. S. Africa. 1880. (B.I.O. 3, 66, 67; B.M. 6529 as *D. megaceras.*) SYN. *D. macrantha* of gardens.

**D. erubes'cens.** *fl.* 5 to 8, large; upper sep. obovate-spatulate, somewhat concave, 1¼ in. long, rich orange spotted with crimson; lateral sep. about ¾ in. long, spreading, oblong, scarlet paling towards base; pet. erect, auriculate at base, extending upwards into a linear lobe with a broader diverging apex, coloured like the dorsal sep.; lip linear, ½ in. long; spur linear, ¼ in. long, dull crimson. Trop. Africa. 1895.

**D. fal'lax.** A synonym of *D. incarnata.*

**D. graminifo'lia.** *fl.* bright azure-blue; dorsal sep. having an acute, erect helmet, and a short spur; the lateral sep. obtuse; lip obtuse, toothed at apex, alternately striped white and reddish-violet on disk; column tipped reddish-violet; scape erect, 5- to 8-fld., with numerous bracts. *l.* few, cylindrical, filiform, appearing after fl. 1½ ft. h. S. Africa. 1825. (W.O.A. 399; B.I.O. 1, 37.) SYN. *Herschelia coelestis, H. graminifolia.*

**D. grandiflo'ra.** A synonym of *D. uniflora.*

**D. incarna'ta.** *fl.* 7 to 15, orange-red (but probably varying), 1 in. across; spur of dorsal sep. as long as blade; pet. dimidiate-ovate; lip narrow-linear, deflexed; bracts spathe-like; spike rather dense. April. *l.* elongated-linear. Stem 12 to 24 in. h., leafy. Madagascar. 1892. (B.M. 7243.) SYN. *D. fallax.*

**D. lac'era.** *fl.* blue or white; upper sep. helmet-shaped, with a short spur, the side ones somewhat boat-shaped; lip abruptly hooked at apex, fringed at apex only, or nearly or quite entire. Stems 10 to 12 in. h., leafless. *l.* linear-filiform. S. Africa. 1826. (B.I.O. 3, 52.) var. **multif'ida.** *fl.* violet outside, blue within; lip more or less fringed from base to apex. 1888. (B.M. 7066.)

**D. lu'gens.** *fl.* 4 to 12; dorsal sep. greenish-lilac or purple with darker veins; pet. purple; lip green, broken into a mass of hair-like segs. S. Africa. 1897. (B.I.O. 2, 76; B.M. 8415.)

**D. natalen'sis.** A synonym of *D. polygonoides.*

**D. nervo'sa.*** *fl.* bright rose, in racemes, on erect scapes 2 ft. h.; segs. spreading; spur straight, about 1 in. long. *l.* strap-shaped. Natal. 1894. (B.I.O. 1, 84; 3, 62.) Handsome.

**D. polygonoi'des.*** *fl.* orange-yellow, or light red or scarlet; spikes very many-fld.; dorsal sep. erect, oblong, sub-acute, concave cymbiform, spurred at base behind; pet. much smaller than sep., erect, partially concealed by upper sep., linear-oblong, tip obtuse, incurved; lip tongue-shaped, smooth, flat or convex, obtuse or sub-acute, slightly constricted above base. September. *l.* linear-lanceolate, or almost strap-shaped, gradually narrowed to the acuminate point, nearly flat. Stem tall, stout. 1 to 2 ft. h. Natal. 1879. (B.M. 6532; B.I.O. 2, 84.) SYN. *D. natalensis.*

**D. pul'chra.** *fl.* pale lilac and purple, 2 in. across; spur, including base of perianth tube, 2 in. long; raceme erect, 6 in. long. Stems 2 ft. long, leafy. Tubers large. S. Africa. 1896. (B.I.O. 3, 63.)

**D. racemo'sa.*** *fl.* 6 to 12, 1½ to 2 in. across, light purple-rose, shading to white; middle sep. rhombic, lateral oblong; pet. cuneate-triangular, serrate on upper margin, with inflexed apex; lip rhombic-lanceolate, narrow, small; infl. 15 to 24 in. h. 1887. (B.M. 7021; W.O.A. 356; B.I.O. 2, 85.) SYN. *D. secunda.*

**D. sagitta'lis.** *fl.* pale lilac, with red streaks on pet. and lip, about ⅜ in. long, in a somewhat corymb-like raceme. May. *l.* radical, 2 to 4 in. long, oblanceolate, bright green. Stems 6 to 8 in. h., dark brown. Tuber fusiform. S. Africa. (B.M. 7403; B.I.O. 1, 32.)

**D. secun'da.** A synonym of *D. racemosa.*

**D. spathula'ta.** *fl.* 1 to 4, about 1 in. across; upper sep. greenish, shaded with violet; lip olive-green, claw long. S. Africa. (B.I.O. 3, 53.) SYN. *D. propinqua, D. tripartita.* var. **atropurpu'rea,** *fl.* rich purplish-lake, solitary on slender pedicels 3 to 6 in. h.; upper sep. hooded with a very short knob-like spur, lateral elliptic-lanceolate, acute; pet. auricled at base, 2-fid at apex; lip with a claw ¼ in. long, blade cordate, acuminate, undulate with 2 or 3 teeth each side. *l.* linear. S. Africa. 1885. (B.I.O. 3, 54; B.M. 6891 as *D. atropurpurea.*)

**D. tripetaloi'des.*** *fl.* creamy-white, flushed pale pink and dotted crimson, 1 in. across, 15 to 30 in a rather loose raceme; dorsal sep. roundish helmet-shaped, lateral sep. rather large; pet. falcate; lip linear-oblong; scape erect, clothed below with large bracts. *l.* rosulate, lanceolate, acuminate, shining, leathery. S. Africa. 1889. (B.M. 7206; W.O.A. 462.) var. **aura'ta,** *fl.* bright golden yellow. (B.I.O. 1, 30.)

**D. uniflo'ra.*** *fl.* 1 to 7, about 4 in. across; lower sep. scarlet, upper paler, veined crimson, shaded yellow; lip small, tongue-like. June, July. *l.* stem-clasping, alternate, dark green, shining. Stems 2 to 3 ft. h. Table Mt. 1825. (B.I.O. 2, 63; B.M. 4073 and B.R. 926 as *D. grandiflora.*) var. **Barrell'ii,** *fl.* orange-scarlet, lip pale with crimson veins. 1874. (Gn. 21 (1882), 114.); **super'ba,** *fl.* bright scarlet and crimson, veined pink, over 4 in. across. June, July. Stems 1½ to 2 ft. h., 2- to 8-fld. (W.S.O. 1, 36.)

E. C.

**DISAN'THUS** (*dis*, twice, *anthos*, flower; the flowers being in pairs). FAM. *Hamamelidaceae.* A monotypic genus. A deciduous shrub with entire, palmately veined, long-stalked alternate leaves with small stipules which fall away very quickly. Flowers in short-stalked pairs back to back, in leaf-axils; calyx 5-parted; petals 5, narrow-lanceolate, spreading; stamens 5; ovary superior. Fruit a capsule, 2-lobed at apex, with several glossy black seeds. A peaty soil such as heaths flourish in suits it. Cuttings root readily.

**D. cercidifo'lia.** Shrub of 8 to 15 ft. with slender, spreading glabrous shoots dotted with pale lenticels. *l.* roundish-ovate, more or less cordate, 2 to 4 in. across, dull bluish-green, somewhat leathery, glabrous; stalk 1 to 2 in. long. *fl.* dark purple, ¾ in. across; cal. hairy; pet. linear. October. Japan. 1892. (B.M. 8716.) Remarkable for the autumn colour of its l. which become claret red with orange tints. *fl.* insignificant.

**DISBUDDING.** The removal of superfluous buds, flowers, or shoots, in the early stages of growth in order to divert the sap into those which are stronger, and required to remain either for the production of branches, flowers, or fruits of superior quality. It is very largely practised with fruit-trees under glass that have to be kept within a limited space, and where the crop of fruit

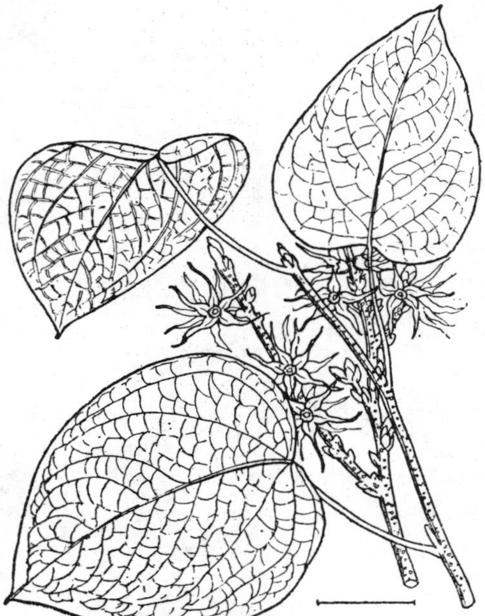

*Disanthus cercidifolia* (p. 695)

and continued vigour of the trees are annually matters of very great importance. The branches of Figs, Peaches, and Vines, amongst many others, are each year so full of young shoots in spring, or at other seasons, when started into growth, that if all were allowed to remain, the result would be a dense thicket of useless branches. Disbudding should always be performed with judgement, and only by those who understand it, as irreparable damage may easily be caused by the inexperienced. The operation should be begun as soon as the young buds or shoots are large enough to pinch out with the finger and thumb, and the process should be spread over a period, rather than remove too much at a time. Many plants may, with advantage, be disbudded occasionally to thin the branches, for admitting more light and air, or for inducing a more compact habit. Disbudding of flowers, where crowded, if carefully performed when in an early stage, may also be recommended in some instances, e.g. with Chrysanthemums, Carnations, Roses for exhibition, and so on.

**DISCA'RIA** (*diskos*; the disk of the flower is large and fleshy). FAM. *Rhamnaceae*. A genus of about 12 species of spiny shrubs, natives of S. America, Australia, and New Zealand, related to Colletia and readily distinguished by the 2 distinct lines connecting the stipules which are not present in Colletia. The spines (reduced branches) are slender and opposite, the leaves opposite or clustered and small, flowers small, 4- or 5-parted (petals sometimes absent), solitary or clustered, disk below the calyx often with wavy margin, stigma 3-lobed. Fruit dividing into three when ripe. No special soil is required but the plants should have a sheltered sunny position in a well-drained site, and in some parts of the country even the hardiest require a wall; *D. serratifolia*, however, succeeds in the open near London. Propagation by July cuttings in a close frame.

**D. austra'lis.** Almost leafless, downy shrub, 2 ft. h.; branchlets simple, spiny. *l.* few, obovate, minute, entire. *fl.* yellow in short, many-fld. racemes, from below the spines. May. Australia. 1824. Greenhouse.

**D. dis'color.** Deciduous spiny shrub, 4 to 6 ft. h. and about 8 ft. wide, nearly or quite smooth. *l.* elliptic, $\frac{1}{8}$ to $\frac{3}{4}$ in. long, sometimes notched at the blunt tip, entire or with shallow teeth. *fl.* 2 or 3 in axillary clusters, short-stalked; cal. white, $\frac{3}{16}$ in. long; pet. absent. May, June. Argentina, Patagonia. 1927. (H.I.P. 538 as *Colletia discolor.*)

**D. longispi'na.** Closely related to *D. serratifolia*, but less hardy, with small obovate *l.* up to $\frac{1}{2}$ in. long, slender spines about 2 in. long, and *fl.* yellowish-white in crowded axillary clusters. Uruguay.

**D. serratifo'lia.*** Deciduous spiny shrub up to 14 ft. with pendulous branches, spines in pairs, stiff, sharp, about $\frac{3}{4}$ in. long. *l.* ovate-oblong, $\frac{1}{2}$ to 1 in. long, with rounded teeth, smooth, shining green. *fl.* greenish-white; cal. tubular, $\frac{1}{8}$ in. across; pet. absent; in crowded clusters on short shoots; fragrant. June. Chile, Patagonia. 1842.

**D. Touma'tou.** Wild Irishman. Deciduous shrub or a small tree in New Zealand, with long, slender, very spiny branches. *Spines* opposite, almost at right angles to shoot, 1 to over $1\frac{1}{2}$ in. long, green, stiff, and sharp. *l.* (absent on old plants) opposite, or in clusters beneath spines, $\frac{1}{2}$ to $\frac{3}{4}$ in. long, often obovate but variable in size, shape, and toothing. *fl.* greenish-white; pet. absent; cal. $\frac{1}{8}$ in. across; in very many-fld. clusters. May. New Zealand. 1875. Needs a wall.

**DISCHID'IA** (*dischides*, twice cleft; the segments of the corona are 2-fid). FAM. *Asclepiadaceae*. A genus of about 50 species of evergreen perennial epiphytic trailers, rooting at the joints, natives of Malaya, E. Indies, and Trop. Australia. Leaves opposite, roundish, thick, fleshy, sometimes formed into pitchers, and in some species myrmecophilous. The leaves, including the pitchers, are covered with wax. Flowers white or red, small, more or less in umbels. Related to Hoya with erect pollinia, 2 in each anther, erect. For cultivation, *see* **Hoya.**

**D. benghalen'sis.** *l.* oblong-lanceolate, 2-edged, flat. *fl.* small, urn-shaped; umbels few-fld. from alternate axils; peduncles short. September. India. 1818. (B.M. 2916.)

**D. hirsu'ta.** Slender, papillose, more or less downy. *l.* broad ovate, acute, fleshy, nerves in 2 or 3 pairs. *fl.* blood-red, $\frac{1}{3}$ in. long, throat with 2 rows of hairs. India, Java. 1896. (B.M. 7853.)

**D. nummula'ria.** Succulent, more or less mealy white, about 6 in. h. *l.* nearly round, thick, fleshy, about $\frac{1}{2}$ in. wide; stalks very short. *fl.* very small, lobes narrow; in small clusters. August. Queensland.

**D. Rafflesia'na.** Stem stout. *l.* much like *D. hirsuta* but not papillose, changing into oblong pitchers, 2 to 5 in. long, obtuse, fleshy, the cavity filled with rootlets from adjoining node. *fl.* yellowish, fleshy, $\frac{1}{8}$ in. long. Malaya. (F.d.S. 1592–3.)

**DISCHIS'MA** (*dis.* twice, *scheizen*, split). FAM. *Selaginaceae*. A genus of about 12 species of small, branched shrubs and herbs, natives of S. Africa with habit of Hebenstreitia. Leaves alternate or lowest opposite, usually narrow and toothed. Flowers in dense terminal spikes or heads, the bracts sometimes leaf-like. Treatment as for Hebenstreitia.

**D. arena'rium.** Annual, decumbent, 1 to 6 in. h., somewhat hairy. *l.* sessile, linear or narrow-lanceolate, $\frac{1}{4}$ to $\frac{1}{2}$ in. long, sub-acute, sometimes toothed near tip, glabrous. *fl.* yellowish-white, $\frac{1}{8}$ in. long, in ovoid or oblong spikes about $\frac{1}{2}$ in. long. S. Africa.

**D. spica'tum.** Annual 3 to 6 in. h., branched from base. Stem densely hairy. *l.* linear, $\frac{1}{2}$ to 2 in. long, blunt, entire, glabrous. *fl.* many in dense spikes 1 to 4 in. long, white; tube slender, $\frac{1}{2}$ in. long, lobes $\frac{1}{16}$ in. long. S. Africa.

***disciflo'rus -a -um,*** having disk-like flowers.

***discig'erus -a -um,*** bearing a disk.

***disco-,*** in compound words, signifying a disk.

***discoi'deus -a -um,*** discoid, disk-like; in Compositae, a flower-head without ray-florets.

***dis'color,*** of different colours.

**DISEASES.** Disease in plants includes any disturbance of the normal life processes resulting in (1) abnormal growth, (2) temporary or permanent check to development, or (3) premature death of part or all of the plant. Apart from attacks by animals, including insects, slugs, and so on, the causes of disease fall into two classes: (a) *Parasitic* diseases due to the attacks of parasites such as Bacteria, Fungi, Viruses, or even certain flowering plants such as mistletoe (*see* **Parasites**). (b) *Non-parasitic* diseases or *Functional* disorders which result from adverse conditions in the environment. The largest group of parasitic diseases is caused by fungi (q.v.) but the as yet imperfectly understood virus diseases continue to grow in importance as more is discovered about them. Fungus diseases (q.v.) are spread by means of the spores the fungi produce, while virus diseases (q.v.) are generally spread by insects which feed on the virus-diseased foliage and transmit the infected sap when they pass on to a healthy plant. Non-parasitic troubles (q.v.) are brought about by unsuitable conditions of soil, temperature, or wrong methods of cultivation. It will be seen that one great difference between the two kinds of disease is that the parasitic type is infectious while the non-parasitic is not, but it must be remembered that where conditions likely to cause a non-parasitic disease prevail, all the plants are likely, sooner or later, to be affected. It is also certain that many parasitic attacks are made possible by adverse environmental conditions: in other words, a healthy plant is more able to resist these attacks than an unhealthy one.

There can be no hard-and-fast distinction between the symptoms seen in plants affected by parasitic as compared with non-parasitic diseases. Even with parasitic diseases the parasite is almost always microscopic and we have to judge the trouble by the symptoms shown by infected plants. These symptoms usually give some clue to the trouble otherwise expert advice should be sought. Some of the symptoms associated with the presence of parasites are yellowing, silvering, browning, shrivelling, spotting, and shot-holing of leaves; wilting, blackening, stunting, or dwarfing of the plant; dropping of leaves, flowers, or fruits; cankers, blisters, or pustules on shoots; bleeding, gumming, and dieback of branches; malformations such as hard or soft galls or warts, witches' brooms, and other proliferations; dry or soft rot in root crops, fruits, buds, corms, bulbs, and rhizomes; or even mummification of fruits such as apples, plums, and peaches while still on the tree. In some instances the disease symptoms are seen only on one part of a plant while in others all the plant is affected. The symptoms need not necessarily appear on the part where the fungus has gained a footing. In most instances they do and the unhealthy signs appear near where the parasitic fungus enters and remains localized, but in some diseases the parasite may be at work far away from where the disease symptoms show, for example, the Silver Leaf Fungus in the main stem causes silvering in the leaves and in Michaelmas Daisy Wilt the fungus in the collar causes browning of the leaves. In each of these the disturbance in the leaves is due to a toxic substance made by the fungus parasite and carried in the sap to the leaves. The nature of a disease is, therefore, based on a judgement of the symptoms, but so great is the number of known plant ailments that some symptoms are common to many different diseases. It becomes necessary in some instances for experts to get additional evidence by dissection of the affected tissues so as to identify the parasite, or in non-parasitic troubles to carry out experiments to discover the environmental condition which is adversely affecting the plant. *See also* **Resistance**. For detailed information on diseases of various kinds the following books may be consulted: *Diseases of Fruit and Hops*, by Dr. H. Wormald; *Diseases of Glasshouse Plants*, by Dr. W. E. Bewley; and *Diseases of Bulbs*, Ministry of Agriculture, Bulletin No. 117, as well as the several plants and diseases described under their appropriate headings in this work.

D. E. G.

**DISEL'MA** (*di*, 2, *selma*, upper deck; alluding to the 2 fertile scales). FAM. *Pinaceae*. A monotypic genus allied to and once combined with Fitzroya. Male and female flowers on different plants, the small cones consisting of 2 pairs of scales, the upper pair only fertile.

**D. Arch'eri.** Bush or small tree 5 to 20 ft. h. with erect branches which may become spreading with age. *l.* scale-like, closely arranged and overlapping, blunt. *Seeds* 2 in each cone, small, 3-winged. Tasmania. Very rare in cultivation. SYN. *Fitzroya Archeri.*

W. D.

**DISK.** A growth from the receptacle of the flower, around or at the base of the ovary; the tubular flowers in a rayed-flower-head in the Compositae; the middle part of the lip of an orchid flower.

**DISOCAC'TUS** (*dis*, twice, *cactus*; so called because the perianth leaves of the inner and outer series were equal in number in the type species). FAM. *Cactaceae*. Epiphytic plants with cylindrical stems from which arise flattened branches with small areoles on the margins. Flowers diurnal, borne near the tips of the branches, tube short. Fruit round or ovoid, smooth. A

**D. biform'is.** Stems long, branches flat, narrow, with serrated margins. *fl.* magenta, small. Honduras. (B.M. 6156; B.R. 31, 9; B.R.C. 4, t. 32.) SYN. *Phyllocactus biformis.*

V. H.

*dis'par,* unequal.

**DISPE'RIS** (*dis*, 2, *peris*, pouch; referring to the form of the sepals). FAM. *Orchidaceae*. A genus of about 50 species of terrestrial orchids needing stove or greenhouse cultivation, usually small and slender, natives of the E. Indies, Trop. and S. Africa, Mascarene Is., Ceylon, and N. India. Flowers solitary or racemose; dorsal sepal erect, hooded or spurred, lateral sepals spreading or oblique, free or more or less united; petals united to the dorsal sepal, falcate, usually constricted in the middle and obliquely acute or lobed at the apex; lip adnate to the face of the column, long-clawed above it, variously curved within the hood; column erect, very stout. The granular pollinia become spirally revolute after withdrawal in many of the species. Leaves one or few, alternate, or a single opposite pair. Tubers ovoid. For cultivation *see* **Habenaria**, but with a greater amount of leaf-mould in the compost. Not strikingly beautiful.

**D. capen'sis.** *fl.* 1 or sometimes 2; lateral sep. ⅜ in. long, spreading, lanceolate, obtusely saccate, ending in a bristle; upper sep. hooded, produced into an erect, filiform, tubular appendage; lip linear at base, then lanceolate, tapering into a decurved tip. Variable in colour—rosy, lilac, yellow, or greenish. *l.* 2, distant, sheathing at base, narrow. 9 to 12 in. or more h. S. Africa. (B.I.O. 1, 89.)

**D. Fannin'iae.** *fl.* pure white, tinged purple, with raised purple dots on pet., 1 to 4 in a leafy spike; bracts like l. but smaller. *l.* 2 to 2⅓ in. long, cordate-amplexicaul, tapering to an acute point. Stem 5 to 15 in. long, weak, with 3 or 4 l. S. Africa. 1869. (B.I.O. 3, 92.)

E. C.

*disperm'us -a -um,* having 2 seeds.

*disper'sus -a -um,* scattered.

**DISPHY'MA.** Included under **Mesembryanthemum.**

**DISPOR'UM** (from the usually 2-seeded fruits). FAM. *Liliaceae*. A genus of about 20 species of perennial herbs, natives of N. America and the mountains of Trop. Asia, allied to Tricyrtis, differing by the fruit which is a few-seeded berry. Leaves alternate, sessile or shortly stalked, ovate or lanceolate on spreading, creeping, or erect stems from an underground rhizome, sparingly branched. Flowers solitary or clustered at the tips of the branches. Disporums grow in moist peaty or woodland soil in partial shade. They may be propagated by seeds or by dividing in spring before active growth begins.

**D. ful'vum.** A synonym of *D. pullum.*

**D. Hook'eri.** Stem 1 to 2 ft. h. *l.* ovate, usually deeply cordate, rough on margins and on veins beneath. *fl.* greenish; segs. spreading, ½ in. long, base narrow; stamens about as long as segs.; peduncles 1- to 6-fld. *fr.* red. California.

**D. lanugino'sum.** Stem about 1 ft. h. with 2 or 3 branches. *l.* ovate-lanceolate, with a long slender point, 3-ribbed, veins netted, smooth above, downy beneath. *fl.* yellow and green; peduncles 2-fld. May. S. Carolina. 1758. (B.M. 1490 as *Uvularia lanuginosa.*)

**D. Leschenaultia'num.** 1 to 2 ft. *l.* rather rigid, 1 to 4 in. long, 1 to 2 in. wide, narrowed to stalks, elliptic-lanceolate to almost round, shortly or slenderly pointed. *fl.* white, ½ to ¾ in. across, somewhat bell-shaped; 2 to 5 in clusters in upper l.-axils. *fr.* blue. S. India, Ceylon. (B.M. 6935.) Tender. var. **variega'tum,** *l.* streaked white and grey, *fl.* greenish-white, small, *fr.* black.

**D. Menzies'ii.** 1 to 3 ft. h. *l.* ovate to ovate-lanceolate, with a narrow slender point, rounded or somewhat cordate at base, more or less woolly downy. *fl.* greenish, in clusters up to 5; segs. nearly erect, ½ to 1 in. long, stamens one-third shorter than segs. California.

**D. orega'num.** *l.* ovate to oblong-lanceolate, slender-pointed, woolly. *fl.* greenish, about ¼ in. long, segs. spreading. NW. America.

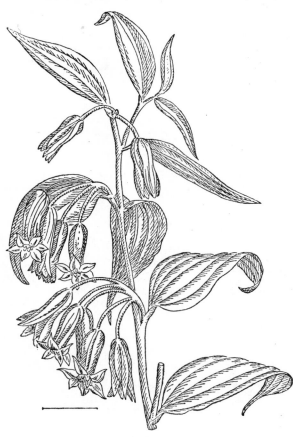

*Disporum pullum*

**D. pul'lum.** Stem 1½ ft. h., angled, branches 2 or 3. *l.* ovate-lanceolate, slender-pointed, shortly stalked. *fl.* white to deep purple, nodding, bell-shaped, longer than pedicels; stamens one-third shorter than segs. India, China, E. Indies. 1801. (B.M. 916 as *Uvularia chinensis.*) SYN. *D. fulvum.* var. **brun'neum,** *fl.* brownish-pink with segs. spreading at mouth. China. 1917 (B.M. 8807); **parviflo'rum,** *fl.* smaller than in type.

**D. ses'sile.** *l.* sessile. *fl.* white, often solitary or few. Japan. SYN. *Uvularia sessile.* A variegated form of this is known.

**D. trachycar'pum.** Somewhat branched, hairy at first. *l.* ovate to oblong-lanceolate, 2 to 4 in. long, acute, rounded or somewhat heart-shaped at base. *fl.* 1 to 3 in clusters, greenish-white, narrowly bell-shaped. NW. America.

**dissec'tus -a -um,** dissected, cut into many deep lobes.

**dissim'ilis -is -e,** unlike.

**DISSO'TIS** (*dissoi,* of 2 kinds; in reference to the anthers). FAM. *Melastomataceae.* A genus of about 60 species of herbs or small shrubs, usually hairy, natives of Trop. and S. Africa. Leaves ovate or oblong, 3- or 5-nerved. Flowers rose, purple, or violet, usually large, solitary or in heads or panicles; calyx-lobes 4 or 5, often bristly; petals 4 or 5, obovate; stamens 8 or 10, very unequal. For treatment *see* **Melastoma.**

**D. canes'cens.** A synonym of *D. incana.*

**D. grandiflo'ra.** Perennial of 1 to 2 ft. with a woody, tuberous base, branches few, twiggy, 4-angled, hispid. *l.* few, elliptic-oblong or lanceolate, 2 to 3½ in. long, narrowed to both ends, 3-nerved, toothed, sparingly hairy on both sides; stalk short. *fl.* purplish, 2 to 3 in. across, in few-fld. terminal racemes; pet. broadly triangular; anthers of long stamens shorter than the 2-spurred connective, of shorter stamens much shorter; style long, slender. Sierra Leone, Senegambia.

**D. inca'na.** Shrub of 2 to 3 ft. Stem purple, 4-angled. *l.* linear or linear-oblong, 2 to 3 in. long, ½ to ½ in. wide, sub-sessile, leathery, obtuse, entire. *fl.* rose-purple, 1 to 1½ in. across, in leafy, crowded, almost terminal panicles; pedicels short. June. Trop. and S. Africa. 1838. (B.M. 3790 as *Osbeckia canescens.*) SYN. *D. canescens.* Stove or greenhouse.

**D. Irvingia'na.** Annual of 1 to 3 ft. Stem erect, 4-angled. *l.* linear-oblong or oblong-lanceolate, 2 to 3 in. long, ½ to ⅝ in. wide, acute, 3-nerved. *fl.* reddish-purple, 1 to 1½ in. across, solitary or 2 to 5 in axillary and terminal cymes, freely produced; pet. obovate. Upper Guinea. 1859. (B.M. 5149.) Stove.

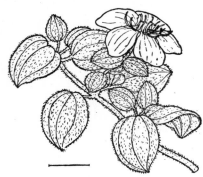

*Dissotis Mahonii*

**D. plumo'sa.** Perennial, woody below, branches slender, procumbent, 4-angled, rooting, bristly at nodes. *l.* broadly ovate, ½ to 1½ in. long. *fl.* solitary, purple; pet. very broadly ovate; anthers of long stamens not longer than connective, appendage 2-lobed. Sierra Leone &c. *D. Mahonii* scarcely differs.

F. G. P.

**distach'yus -a -um,** with 2 branches.

**dis'tans,** widely separated.

**DISTEGAN'THUS** (*distegos,* 2 stories, *anthos,* flower; the corolla being above the receptacle). FAM. *Bromeliaceae.* A genus of a single herbaceous species, native of Guiana, with a slender rhizome and shoots of 2 kinds, one with a rosette of well-developed foliage leaves, the other bearing flowers with small bracts only. Related to Aregelia. For treatment of this stove plant, *see* **Billbergia.**

**D. basilatera'lis.** *rhiz.* wide-creeping. *l.* 6 to 10 in rosette, cordate-oblong, acute, 6 to 12 in. long, white-scaly beneath, deeply channelled; stalks 2 to 3 in. long. *fl.* in several dense oblong spikes, about 3 in. long, on separate shoots from rhizome; pet. bright yellow, the oblong blade ½ in. longer than cal. French Guiana. 1846. (F.d.S. 227.)

**D. scarlati'na.** A synonym of *Bromelia scarlatina.*

**dis'tichus -a -um,** 2-ranked.

**DISTIC'TIS** (*di,* twice, *stiktos,* spotted; the much-flattened seeds look like 2 rows of spots in the capsule). FAM. *Bignoniaceae.* A genus of 7 or 8 species of climbing shrubs, often very hairy, natives of Trop. America and the W. Indies. Leaves 3-foliolate or the terminal leaflet transformed to a tendril; leaflets entire, stalked. Flowers similar to those of Pithecoctenium but capsule smooth, oblong, curved. Branches not angled. Stove plants.

**D. lactiflor'a.** Branches striate. Tendrils 3-fid. *lflets.* cordate, ovate, 2 in. long, glabrous. *fl.* milk-white, 1¼ in. long, long-hairy without; racemes twin with a stalked bract at base of each pedicel. April, July. Santa Cruz. 1823. SYN. *Bignonia lactiflora.*

F. G. P.

*distillato'rius -a -um,* shedding drops.

**distinct,** having its similar parts not united, as petals distinct.

*distor'tus -a -um,* mis-shapen, of grotesque form.

**distribution,** area occupied by any particular group of plants in nature.

**DISTY'LIUM** (*dis,* 2, *stylos,* style; having 2 styles). FAM. *Hamamelidaceae.* A genus of 6 species of evergreen shrubs or trees related to Sycopsis, but with flowers in slender racemes, stamens 2 to 8, calyx without a tube, sometimes absent. Fruit a capsule, cells one-seeded. Leaves alternate, leathery, thick, ovate or oblong-lanceolate; stipules lanceolate, caducous. Natives of China, Japan, and N. India. *D. racemosum* grows best in mild localities and in a sandy soil. Propagated by cuttings.

**D. racemo'sum.** Evergreen shrub of 3 or 4 ft. (a tree in Japan) with smooth shoots. *l.* elliptic to obovate, 1½ to 3 in. long. *fl.* in stellately downy racemes, ¾ to 1½ in. long; anthers red. March, April. Japan. 1876. (B.M. 9501.) var. **variega'tum,** *l.* bordered yellowish-white.

**DITA BARK.** *See* **Alstonia scholaris.**

A→

**DITTANY.** *See* **Cunila mariana** and **Dictamnus.**

**DITTANY OF AMORGOS.** *See* **Origanum Tourne-fortii.**

**DITTANY OF CRETE.** *See* **Origanum Dictamnus.**

**DIUR'IS** (*dis,* double, *oura,* tail; in allusion to the 2 tail-like sepals). FAM. *Orchidaceae.* This genus of terrestrial orchids, containing about 30 species, all of them interesting and some very beautiful, is almost unknown in our gardens, and the species as yet introduced are very rare. The genus is very largely Australian. Flowers 1, 2, or several in a terminal raceme, often rather large, usually yellow but a few species are white or lilac; many have brown markings conspicuous from the antennae-like lateral sepals, either parallel or crossed, the upper sepal shorter and broader, often rounded, the petals broad and spreading, usually slenderly clawed; lip 3-lobed, the mid-lobe often rounded and spreading. The lower sepals are green in many and in some only equal the other segments in length. Tubers entire. For cultivation *see* **Pterostylis.**

**D. al'ba.** *fl.* 1 to 6, white, rose, green, brownish-purple. August. 1 ft. h. *l.* 2 or 3. New S. Wales. 1875. (B.M. 6201.)

**D. au'rea.** *fl.* 2 to 6, yellow; marked with light brown especially on the rather large lip, the side lobes of which are broadly falcate and the mid-lobe somewhat ovate; lower sep. broadened at apex. Variable. 6 to 24 in. h. *l.* 2 to 4. Queensland, New S. Wales.

**D. cunea'ta.** *fl.* few, pale lilac with darker markings, 1½ to 2 in. across; latera sep. long; pet. wedge-shaped, not clawed, mid-lobe of lip scallop-shaped; about 12 in. *l.* solitary. New S. Wales.

**D. curvifo'lia.** A synonym of *D. maculata.*

**D. elonga'ta.** A synonym of *D. punctata.*

**D. lilaci'na.** A synonym of *D. punctata.*

**D. longifo'lia.** *fl.* 2 to 5, yellow and purple-brown; dorsal sep. broadly ovate, lateral sep. long, narrow; pet. spatulate; lip 3-lobed, mid-lobe comparatively small, oblong to wedge-shape. 12 to 18 in. h. *l.* radical, narrow. Variable. Australia, Tasmania. 1907. (F.O.A. 2.)

**D. macula'ta.** *fl.* 2 to 10, yellow, spotted or blotched brown or purple, sometimes almost entirely dark-coloured except the yellow centre of the pet., under ⅓ in. long; dorsal sep. erect, rigid, embracing the column at base, ovate-oblong, very open at top; lateral sep. at length recurved, narrow, rarely exceeding pet.; pet. ovate, on a long, rigid, dark claw; lip shorter than dorsal sep., 3-lobed from above base, side lobes large and about as long as the broad mid-lobe. March. *l.* narrow. Australia. 1825. A rather small, slender species, usually under 1 ft. h. (B.M. 3156; F.O.A. 1, pt. 2.) SYN. *D, curvifolia, D. pardina.*

**D. pardi'na.** A synonym of *D. maculata.*

**D. puncta'ta.** *fl.* 1 to 10, pale or dark lilac or purplish, often dotted; dorsal sep. broadly ovate-oblong; lateral deflexed, very narrow, 2 to 3 in. long; pet. broadly elliptical-oblong; lip about as

*Diuris punctata*

long as dorsal sep., 3-lobed from base. *l.* usually two, linear, 3 to 6 in. long, with 2 empty sheathing bracts above them. Stems 1 to 2 ft. h., or more. A very variable plant. Australia. (F.O.A. 1, pt. 4 as *D. elongata.*) SYN. *D. lilacina.*

**D. tric'olor.** *fl.* 2 to 8; 1 in. or more across, yellow, marked with purple or purplish-brown; lower sep. green; lip somewhat oblong with large purplish side lobes. Up to 18 in. h. *l.* 2. Australia. (F.O.A. 2.)

E. C.

**diurnal,** of flowers which open during the day but close at night (cf. nocturnal).

*diuti'nus -a -um,* long-lasting.

*divarica'tus -a -um,* divaricate, widely spreading, growing in a straggling manner.

*diven'sis,* of Deva, the Roman name of Chester, England.

*diver'gens,* divergent, spreading outwards from a centre.

*diversi-,* in compound words, indicating different, as *diversiformis,* of different shapes.

**DIVI-DIVI,** pods of *Caesalpinia coriaria,* imported from W. Indies and S. America for tanning.

**division,** see **Propagation.**

*di'vus -a -um,* belonging to the gods.

**DIZYGOTHE'CA** (*di,* 2, *zygos,* yoke, *theka,* case; the anthers have double the usual number of cells). FAM. *Araliaceae.* A genus of 3 or 4 species of shrubs or small trees without spines. Leaves always digitate but varying in form with age, usually long-stalked. Flowers 5-parted, ovary cells 10. Many names occur in horticultural literature of plants which should probably be referred to this genus, but the floral characters of many of them are unknown and they cannot be referred with certainty to the proper wild species. For treatment *see* **Trevesia.** All the following have been offered under Aralia.

**D. elegantis'sima.** Stem straight, erect. *l.* digitate, on long dark green stalks mottled with white; lflets. 7 to 10, filiform, pendulous. New Hebrides. 1873. Adult form unknown. Excellent for table decoration. SYN. *Aralia elegantissima.*

**D. Kerchovea'na.** Stem slender. *l.* digitate, almost circular in outline; lflets. 9 to 11, spreading, elliptic-lanceolate, toothed or wavy on margins, deep glossy green except for a pale midrib. South Sea Is. 1881. Adult form unknown. SYN. *Aralia Kerchoveana.*

**D. leptophyl'la.** *l.* digitate; lflets. 7 or more, stalked, somewhat pendent, dark green. Australasia. 1862. Adult form unknown. SYN. *Aralia leptophylla.*

**D. long'ipes.** *l.* digitate; lflets. oblong-lanceolate, slender-pointed, margins wavy. N. Australia. SYN. *Aralia longipes.*

**D. Nilsson'ii.** A synonym of *D. Vieillardii.*

**D. Osya'na.** Resembling *D. leptophylla* but with lflets. deeply 2-fid at tips, bright green, veins and l.-tips chocolate-brown. South Sea Is. 1870.

**D. quercifo'lia.** *l.* opposite, 3-foliolate; lflets. deeply sinuate; stalks about 3 in. long, light shining green. New Britain.

**D. Regi'nae.** *Lflets.* very narrow, glabrous, plane, drooping; stalks olive, pink, and brown. New Hebrides. (I.H. 26, 337.) A graceful plant.

**D. rotun'da.** Stems erect, brownish-green with long pale lenticels. *l.* sometimes reduced to a single orbicular lflet., heart-shaped at base, margined with white-tipped teeth; sometimes 3-foliolate, especially in older plants, with lflets. roundish, toothed, middle lflet. about twice as large as the other two. Polynesia. 1882.

**D. terna'ta.** Slender. *l.* opposite, ternate; lflets. oblong-lanceolate, deeply toothed or only sinuate at margins, light green. New Britain. 1879.

**D. Veitch'ii.** Erect, stem slender. *l.* digitate on long, slender stalks; lflets. about 11, filiform, glossy green above, dark red beneath, margins wavy. N. Caledonia. SYN. *Aralia Veitchii.* var. **gracil'lima,** lflets. still narrower, midrib white. (Gn. 39 (1891), 565.) SYN. *Aralia gracillima.*

**D. Vieillard'ii.** Tree of 9 to 10 ft., glabrous, unbranched, and unarmed. *l.* alternate, digitate, long-stalked; lflets. oblong, 9 to 13 in. long, up to 3½ in. wide, blunt, somewhat sinuate, glabrous, with long petiolules. *fl.* greenish-yellow, ⅜ in. across, in a terminal umbel about 18 in. across; anthers white. *Berry* dark violet. New Caledonia. 1880.

***Doch'na,*** Arabian plant-name.

**DOCK.** *See* **Rumex.**

**DOCKWEED, TROPICAL.** *See* **Pistia Stratiotes. A**

**DOCYN'IA** (anagram of Cydonia). FAM. *Rosaceae.* Five species wild in China, India, and Annam, closely related to Cydonia which differs in its styles being free (united at the base in Docynia). Flowers in clusters of 2 to 5; petals 5, stamens 30 to 50, styles 5, calyx very woolly, persisting at the top of the fruit. Only suitable for the milder localities.

**D. Delavay'i.** Evergreen, rounded tree up to 35 ft., sometimes spiny; shoots downy. *l.* oval-lanceolate, entire, up to 3 in. long, white-felted beneath. *fl.* 1¼ in. wide, white, rose-tinted outside. April, May. *fr.* quite apple-like, 1½ in. wide, yellowish. China. Succeeds on the Riviera. (R.H. 1918, 133, tt. 45–7.)

**D. docynioi'des.** Evergreen tree up to 30 ft., shoots downy. *l.* very variable, some entire and elliptic-lanceolate, others deeply lobed like a hawthorn, 1½ to 3½ in. long, at first softly felted beneath. *fl.* 1 in. wide, scarcely stalked, creamy-white; cal. felted. May. *fr.* sub-globose to ellipsoid, 1 to 1½ in. long, edible. China. 1903.

***Dodar'tii,*** in honour of D. Dodart, 1634–1707, botanist of Paris.

**DODDER.** *See* **Cuscuta.**

**DODECATH'EON** (*dodeka*, 12, *theoi*, gods). FAM. *Primulaceae.* A genus of about 30 species of usually glabrous herbs, natives of N. America, mostly in the mountains of the west. Leaves in a basal rosette, linear or spatulate, narrowed to a more or less winged petiole. Flowers on a tall scape in few- to many-flowered umbels, nodding, white, rose, or purple; all parts in fives (rarely fours), the calyx and corolla lobes reflexed much as in Cyclamen; related to Soldanella and Primula but in these the corolla is not reflexed. Petals long, narrow; stamens inserted at throat of corolla, exserted. Fruit a many-seeded capsule which opens at the apex by 5 valves or teeth. Many of the species are very ornamental and well adapted for sheltered places on the rock-garden, and some of them for borders, preferring moist, moderately rich, well-drained soil and some shade or at least not full exposure to the summer sun. They are also useful for the cold greenhouse, and for this purpose the plants should be taken up in November, potted into 6-in. pots, and kept in a cold frame until March: they will not stand forcing. After flowering they should be plunged in a bed of sand or coal ashes for the summer under a north wall. They may be raised from seed like Primulas or divided in spring or autumn, the latter being the better. **A**

KEY

| | | |
|---|---|---|
| 1. | *Filaments without a tube, or if tube present not exserted* | 2 |
| 1. | *Tube of filaments exserted* | 7 |
| 2. | *Lvs. narrowed to a winged petiole* | 3 |
| 2. | *Lvs. with a distinct petiole* | D. latilobum |
| 3. | *The wide connective deep purple, distinct from the brownish-yellow anthers* | D. Meadia |
| 3. | *Connective and anthers of same colour* | 4 |
| 4. | *Capsule shorter than cal.; lvs. linear-lanceolate, light green* | 5 |
| 4. | *Capsule longer than cal.; lvs. ovate-lanceolate to ovate-oblong, deep green* | 6 |
| 5. | *Umbel many-fld.; plant* 1 *ft. or more h.* | D. Jeffreyi |
| 5. | *Umbel few-fld.; plant rarely* 1 *ft. h.* | D. alpinum |
| 6. | *Capsule much longer than cal.; lvs. ovate or ovate-lanceolate* | D. integrifolium |
| 6. | *Capsule little longer than cal.; lvs. oblong-ovate; stamens usually* 4 | D. tetrandrum |
| 7. | *Tube of filaments yellow* | 8 |
| 7. | *Tube of filaments deep purple* | 10 |
| 8. | *Anthers with yellow margin* | 9 |
| 8. | *Anthers wholly purple* | D. radicatum |
| 9. | *Umbel many-fld.* | D. Cusickii |
| 9. | *Umbel few-fld.* | D. pauciflorum |
| 10. | *Anthers deep purple* | D. cruciatum |
| 10. | *Anthers spotted with yellow* | 11 |
| 11. | *Connective deep purple* | D. Hendersonii |
| 11. | *Connective yellow* | D. Clevelandii |

**D. alpi'num.** Glabrous, slender herb, about 12 in. h., with short, thick rhizome and fleshy roots. *l.* linear-oblong, 3 to 6 in. long, acute. *fl.* 2 to 5 in an umbel; cor. lobes 4, deep reddish-purple, tube recurved, yellow, throat with a purple ring; anthers deep purple. California.

**D. Cleveland'ii.** Glabrous herb, 12 to 18 in. h. *l.* spatulate-ovate, rather fleshy, pale green, 1½ to 2½ in. long, irregularly toothed. *fl.* 2 to 10 in an umbel; cor. purple, yellow at base with deep purple spots in the throat; tube of filaments deep purple, anthers purple. California. 1890.

**D. crucia'tum.** Deep green, glabrous herb, up to 15 in. h. *l.* widely ovate, up to 3 in. long, entire, blunt. *fl.* 4 to 7 in an umbel, deep reddish-purple. Western N. America, 1869. (B.M. 5871 as *D. Meadia frigidum.*) Stones around its roots assist it.

**D. Cusick'ii.** Characters of *pauciflorum* but *l.* more or less clammy, sometimes toothed, *fl.* numerous in the umbel, staminal tube shorter. Western N. America.

**D. frig'idum.** Glabrous, 2 to 10 in. h., from a brown rhizome. *l.* more or less widely ovate, narrowed to a stalk, up to 2 in. long, toothed or nearly entire. *fl.* 2 or 3 in an umbel, violet; cor. lobes oblong-linear, about ⅝ in. long, stamens included. July, August. Both sides of Behring Straits.

**D. Henderson'ii.** Deep green, glabrous herb, about 12 in. h. *l.* oblong-ovate, up to 3 in. long, rather fleshy, more or less irregularly toothed. Cor. violet, lobes about ½ in. long; anthers yellow-margined. California.

**D. integrifo'lium.** Glabrous herb, up to 10 in. h., with short thick rhizome and numerous fleshy roots. *l.* obovate to spatulate, about 5 in. long or more. *fl.* 3 to 10 in an umbel, purplish. Similar to *D. Meadia* but distinct by its fleshy bracts. British Columbia.

**D. Jeff'reyi.** Slightly clammy, up to 24 in. h., rhizome vertical, thick, densely covered with fleshy roots. *l.* oblanceolate, about 12 in. long, erect, entire. *fl.* many, in an umbel, deep reddish-purple; cor. lobes about 1 in. long, oblong; stamens deep purple. California. 1887. Distinct by its large leaves, but *see also* **D. tetrandrum.**

**D. latilo'bum.** Very slender, glabrous herb, up to 12 in. h., with oblique rhizome and fleshy roots. *l.* more or less oblong, including the distinct petiole about 8 in. long. *fl.* 2 to 4 in an umbel, yellowish-white; anther reddish-purple. Western N. America.

**D. macrocar'pum.** Glabrous herb, 8 to 12 in. h. Stem short, flattish-globose. *l.* membranous, not glandular, pale green, entire or nearly so, lanceolate-spatulate, 4 to 8 in. long; stalk broadly winged. *fl.* 3 to 8 in an umbel, purplish-lilac; cor. lobes linear, tube yellow, recurved; anthers purplish-lilac. *fr.* large, cylindrical. Alaska.

*Dodecatheon Meadia*

**D. Mead'ia.** Glabrous herb, up to 24 in. h. *l.* ovate-oblong or oblong-linear, about 6 in. long, somewhat toothed, blunt. *fl.* 10 to 20 in an umbel, rose with a white base; anthers reddish-yellow, connective purple. Eastern N. America. 1744. (B.M. 12.) *fl.* variable in colour and size, e.g. vars. **al'bum** and **viola'ceum**, and var. **grandiflo'rum.**

**D. pauciflo'rum.** Glabrous herb, about 8 in. h., with a short, almost globose, rhizome. *l.* lanceolate-spatulate, about 3 in. long, sometimes slightly toothed. *fl.* 1 to 7 in an umbel, pale lilac, with a recurved yellow tube and a deep-purple wavy ring in the throat; anthers purple. Western N. America. 1829. (B.M. 3622 as *D. integrifolium.*)

**D. radica'tum.** Glabrous herb with a slender, rather long rhizome with many roots and rooting from the base of the stem. *l.* 3 to 5, oblong-spatulate, about 4 in. long. *fl.* 3 to 5 in an umbel, rose or red; stamens purple. Colorado.

**D. tetrand'rum.** Glabrous, with the habit and roots of *D. Jeffreyi* with even larger *l.* *fl.* purple with a ring of yellow spots, cor. lobes and stamens usually 4. Western N. America.

*dodentra'lis -is -e,* a span (9 in.) across.

**DODO'NAEA** (in honour of Rembert Dodaens (Dodonaeus), *c.* 1518–85, royal physician and writer on plants). FAM. *Sapindaceae.* A genus of about 50 species of trees and shrubs, mostly Australian, with a few in Hawaii, N. America, and Africa. Leaves alternate, simple or pinnate, without stipules, sometimes glandular, and producing a resin- or varnish-like exudation. Flowers small, often dioecious, solitary or in racemes or panicles; sepals 5 or fewer; petals absent; stamens 5 to 10, filaments very short; ovary 3- to 6-celled with 2 ovules in each cell. Fruit a capsule winged on back of each valve. Tender plants needing warm greenhouse or stove conditions with no special requirements as to soil, &c.

**D. cunea'ta.** Much-branched, usually clammy shrub. *l.* obovate or wedge-shaped, under 1 in. long, sometimes toothed at the blunt apex, margin usually entire or nearly so; stalk short. *fl.* in short, almost simple, racemes and in few-fld. axillary clusters; sep. ovate-oblong. *Capsule* narrowly winged. Australia.

**D. multiju'ga.** Large, hairy shrub. *l.* pinnate; lflets. 15 to 30, oblong to lanceolate, under ¼ in. long, blunt, margin toothed or lobed at apex, recurved, rachis dilated. *fl.* few in loose racemes, pedicels slender; sep. lanceolate, acute, rather large. *Capsule* with broad, rounded wings. Australia.

**D. triquet'ra.** Erect shrub with flattish or angular branches. *l.* oval-elliptic to oblong-lanceolate, up to 4 in. long, slender-pointed, entire or nearly so. *fl.* in short, oblong, compact panicles or racemes, inconspicuous. *Capsule* as in *D. viscosa.* Java.

**D. visco'sa.** Akeake. Shrub to 15 ft. *l.* linear to oblong, wedge-shaped at base, entire, with resinous dots on both surfaces. *fl.* greenish, in short terminal or axillary racemes, sep. ovate. *Capsule* about ¼ in. long, broadly 3-winged. Australia, S. Africa, N. America.

**DOG BANE.** *See* **Apocynum.**

**DOG DAISY.** *See* **Chrysanthemum Leucanthemum.**

**DOG ROSE.** *See* **Rosa canina.**

**DOG'S CABBAGE.** *See* **Thelygonum.**

**DOG'S MERCURY.** *See* **Mercurialis perennis.**

**DOG'S TOOTH VIOLET.** *See* **Erythronium.**

**DOGWOOD.** *See* **Cornus sanguinea.**

**DOGWOOD, JAMAICA.** *See* **Piscidia.**

**DOGWOOD, SWAMP.** *See* **Cornus Amomum.**

**DOGWOOD, VICTORIAN.** *See* **Prostanthera.**

*dolabra'tus -a -um, dolabriform'is -is -e,* hatchet-shaped.

**DOLICHAN'DRA** (*dolichos*, long, *andros*, man, in allusion to the exserted anthers). FAM. *Bignoniaceae.* A genus of tall climbing shrubs, natives of Trop. America, differing from Macfadyena, to which it is closely related, by the slightly exserted stamens and scarcely diverging anther lobes. Leaves with 2 leaflets and often a 3-fid tendril. Flowers showy; corolla tube long and rather broad, with 5 rounded lobes; stamens 4. *D. cynanchoides* needs a stove or warm greenhouse and should be planted in the border for covering the back wall or for training up the rafter, but roots should be restricted to restrain excessive growth. It can be grown also in large pots with a compost of rough fibrous loam and rough peat, 2 parts to 1, 1 of leaf-soil, and 1 of sand. Cuttings should be about 3 joints long of strong shoots taken in spring and put in sand in a close frame for a short time.

**D. cynanchoi'des.** *l.* opposite; lflets. 2, oblong; tendril 3-fid. *fl.* red, 1 to 3 on a peduncle at tips of branches; cal. spathe-like, cut to middle. S. Brazil, Argentine. 1891. SYN. *Macfadyena Dolichandra, Spathodea Dolichandra.*

F. G. P.

**DOLICHANDRO′NE** (*dolichos*, long, *andros*, man; in reference to the anthers). FAM. *Bignoniaceae*. A genus of about 12 species of trees or shrubs natives of the hotter parts of Asia, Africa, and Austria. Leaves opposite, pinnate; leaflets sometimes toothed. Flowers in terminal racemes or panicles; calyx spathe-like as in Spathodea. Fruit a long, narrow capsule. Treatment as for Spathodea.

**D. Hildebrandt′ii.** Shrub. *l.* of 2 or 3 pairs of oblong, acute, glabrous lflets. *fl.* yellow; cor. 3 times as long as cal.; panicles axillary, many-fld. Nairobi.

**D. hirsu′ta.** Twigs densely hairy. *l.* of 2 or 3 pairs of oblong, obtuse lflets., hairy on both surfaces. *fl.* few in axillary panicles. Lower Zambesi.

**D. obtusifo′lia.** Shrub or small tree. *l.* of 7 to 9 pairs of oblong, obtuse lflets., hairy on both surfaces. *fl.* yellow in dense thyrsoid panicles. E. Africa.

F. G. P.

*dolicho-*, in compound words, signifying long.

**DOLICHODE′RIA.** *See* **Achimenes tubiflora.**

**DOL′ICHOS** (*dolichos*, long; referring to the stems). FAM. *Leguminosae*. A genus of about 30 species of usually twining herbs or sub-shrubs widely distributed over the warmer parts of the world. Leaves pinnately 3-foliolate; leaflets stipulate; stipules acute. Flowers papilionaceous, solitary or clustered in leaf-axils, or in stalked racemes. Closely related to Phaseolus. Easily grown in ordinary soil, with temperature according to habitat and duration. Cuttings of the perennial species root readily in sand.

**D. bicornu′tus.** *l.* on long stalks. *fl.* white and purple; peduncles long. Summer. Japan. Half-hardy.

**D. biflo′rus.** *fl.* purple and white, differing from *D. Lablab* by the upper lip of cal. 2-toothed, and by having only a ring or brush of hairs just beneath stigma. *Seed* small. India. Often grown for fodder in India. Greenhouse.

**D. gigan′teus.** A variety of *D. Lablab*.

**D. Lab′lab.** Hyacinth Bean. *lflets.* broadly ovate, rounded below, with a short point at apex, often crinkly. *fl.* purple or white, 2 to 4 in l.-axils in erect racemes. July to September. *Seed* about ⅔ in. long, ⅓ in. wide, black, brown, or grey, white in the white-fld. forms. *Pods* 2 to 3 in. long, flat, smooth. Tropics. (B.M. 896; B.R. 830; S.B.F.G. 2, 236 as *Lablavia vulgaris*.) SYN. *Lablab vulgaris*. An ornamental, vigorous climbing annual, the pods and seeds of which are eaten in the tropics. var. **gigan′teus,** white-fld., strong grower. SYN. *D. giganteus*.

**D. ligno′sus.** Australian Pea. Woody, evergreen twiner, rather hairy. *lflets.* ovate, acute, smooth, glaucous beneath. *fl.* rose, keel purplish, in umbels. July. Seed smaller than in *D. Lablab*. (B.M. 380.) Greenhouse.

**D. lupiniflo′rus.** Herb, about 3 ft. h., covered with appressed hairs. Stem angular, about 3 ft. h. *l.* long-stalked; 3-foliolate; lflets. oblong, 1½ to 2 in. long. *fl.* violet-purple, in many-fld. terminal racemes 10 in. long. February, March. E. Africa. Greenhouse.

**D. sesquipeda′lis.** A synonym of *Vigna Catjang*.

**D. simplicifo′lius.** Base of stem woody, thick, tuberous, stems herbaceous, erect, simple. *l.* simple, lanceolate, 6 in. long, short-stalked. *fl.* pink, ½ in. long, clusters in l.-axils, as long as pedicels. April. Trop. Africa. 1892. (B.M. 7318.)

F. G. P.

**DOLICHOTHE′LE** (*dolichos*, long, *thele*, a nipple, referring to the elongated tubercles). FAM. *Cactaceae*. Plants round, soft in texture, not milky; tubercles long, not grooved. Flowers borne in the axils of old tubercles, very large with a long tube, differing from the small flowers of Mammillaria. Fruit round, green or red, smooth. For cultivation *see* **Cactus** (terrestrial).

**D. longimam′ma.** Plants solitary or in clusters; tubercles elongated, glaucous; axils hairy or naked; radial spines 6 to 12, slender, spreading, 1 in. long, pale; centrals 1 to 3, similar but with dark tips. *fl.* large, lemon-yellow. Mexico. (B.R.C. 4, f. 61.) SYN. *Mammillaria longimamma*.

**D. melaleu′ca.** A synonym of *D. longimamma*.

**D. sphae′rica.** Plants low, growing in large clusters with a large thickened root; tubercles soft, like *D. longimamma* but shorter; spines 12 to 15, pale; central spine solitary. *fl.* yellow. Texas and Mexico. (B.R.C. 4, t. 1; f. 60.)

**D. uberiform′is.** Plants round; tubercles long, bright green; axils naked; spines 4 or 5, all radial, horn-coloured or reddish. *fl.* yellow. Mexico. (B.R.C. 4, f. 62.)

V. H.

*Dolichothele sphaerica*

A→

**DOLLAR SPOT.** A disease of lawn grasses. *See* **Turf Diseases.**

*dolomit′icus -a -um,* preferring dolomitic rock.

**DOLPHIN.** Black-fly of Broad Beans. ·*See* **Aphis.**

*domatiif′erus -a -um,* bearing or providing a house.

**DOMBEY′A** (in honour of Joseph Dombey, French botanist of eighteenth century, who accompanied Ruiz and Pavon in Chile and Peru). FAM. *Sterculiaceae*. A genus of about 100 species of ornamental evergreen trees or shrubs, natives of Trop. Africa and the Mascarene Is. Leaves often cordate, palmately veined, frequently lobed. Flowers axillary or terminal, few or many in cymes; petals flat, persistent; anthers 10 to 20; ovules 2 in each cell. A compost of sandy loam and turfy peat suits these fine stove plants which can be propagated by cuttings of firm young shoots in April. Several fine hybrids have been raised.

**D. acutang′ula.** About 10 ft. h. *l.* cordate, slender-pointed, with 3 to 5 shallow broad, or deep narrow palmate lobes, toothed. *fl.* red, large, crowded. Mauritius. 1820. (B.M. 2905, form with l. not lobed.) SYN. *Astrapaea tiliifolia*.

**D. Burges′siae.** About 10 ft. h. *l.* 6 to 9 in. long, cordate, with 2 deep cuts and 2 shallow ones, downy, bright green. *fl.* large, pet. spreading, white with rose tinge at base and on veins, rounded; clusters corymbose. August to December. S. Africa. 1865. (B.M. 5487.)

**D. calan′tha.** *l.* 1 ft. across, 3- to 5-lobed, coarsely toothed, cordate at base, downy above, hairy beneath, long-stalked. *fl.* rose, 1½ in. across. Trop. Africa. 1907. (B.M. 8424.)

**D. × Cayeux′ii** (*D. Mastersii* × *D. Wallichii*). Stems bristly hairy. *l.* cordate, acute, toothed, dark green, netted; stalks 4 to 6 in. long. *fl.* pink, finely veined, in axillary, pendent, many-fld. umbels. 1897. The first hybrid Dombeya raised.

**D. Dregea′na.** Shrub or small tree, shoots glabrous. *l.* cordate, angled or 3-lobed, acute, toothed, starry-downy; stalks long, hairy. *fl.* rose, about 1 in. across, in 2- to 4-fld. umbels; involucral lflets. broadly ovate. S. Africa.

**D. Master′sii.** *l.* cordate-ovate, toothed, velvety. *fl.* white with slight rose tinge, sweet-scented, in axillary corymbs. Trop. Africa. 1867. (B.M. 5639.)

**D. nairoben'sis.** Shrub or tree, shoots becoming glabrous. *l.* ovate-cordate, slender-pointed, somewhat 3-lobed, irregularly roundish-toothed, hairy beneath *fl.* in few-fld. umbels; peduncles long, pedicels hispid; pet. ½ in. long, obtuse. E. Africa.

**D. natalen'sis.** *l.* cordate, acute, Poplar-like, the narrow involucral *l.* awl-shaped, toothed, starry-downy. *fl.* large, white, sweet-scented, in umbels of 4 to 8. Natal. 1850.

*Dombeya Burgessiae* (p. 702)

**D. popul'nea.** 10 to 20 ft. h. *l.* cordate, slender-pointed, smooth, teeth few. *fl.* white in a terminal 2-fid corymb; peduncles short. June. Mauritius. 1822. SYN. *Assonia populnea.*

**D. spectab'ilis.** *l.* cordate, oblong or roundish, acute, wavy, rough above with rusty or whitish down beneath; stalks downy. *fl.* white, ¾ in. across, in many-fld. axillary and terminal cymes. Trop. Africa. 1842.

**D. viburniflo'ra.** 12 to 15 ft. h., branches and l.-stalks covered with spreading hairs. *l.* heart-shaped, 3-lobed, toothed, green above, pale downy beneath. *fl.* small, white, numerous; pet. narrow. February, March. Comorin Is. (B.M. 4568.)

**D. visco'sa.** 10 to 15 ft. h. but may be kept smaller by careful pruning. *l.* cordate, roundish with 5 angles, angles slender-pointed, margins serrate; stalks long. *fl.* sweet-scented of honey, white; pet. deep crimson at base; the young head of fl. enveloped by bracts, (one to each fl.) which fall as the fl. expands, the globose head being 4 in. or more across. Madagascar. 1823. (B.M. 4544.) SYN. *Astrapaea viscosa.*

**D. Wallich'ii.** Up to 30 ft. h. *l.* large, cordate, angularly lobed, stipules leafy, ovate, slender-pointed. *fl.* scarlet in drooping umbels; peduncles long, hairy. July. Madagascar. 1820. SYN. *Astrapaea Wallichii.*

F. G. P.

*domes'ticus -a -um,* frequently used as house plant.

*domingen'sis -is -e,* of St. Dominica, W. Indies.

## DO'NAX. *See* **Arundo.**

*Doncklaer'i,* in honour of M. Doncklaer, Director, Botanic Garden, Ghent, *c.* 1841.

## DON'DIA. *See* **Hacquetia.**

*Donia'nus -a -um,* in honour of (1) David Don, 1799–1841, Librarian, Linnean Society; (2) his brother, George Don, 1798–1856, who collected for the Royal Horticultural Society in Brazil, &c.; (3) their father, G. Don, 1764–1814, Keeper, Botanic Garden, Edinburgh.

**DOOD'IA** (in honour of Samuel Doody, 1656–1706, a London apothecary and botanist, Keeper of Chelsea Botanic Garden, 1691). FAM. *Polypodiaceae.* Eleven species of ferns, natives of the islands from Ceylon to New Zealand. Fronds pinnate or pinnatifid. Indusia membranous, the same shape as the sorus. Sori oblong or slightly curved, superficial, in one or more rows, parallel with and between the midribs and margins of the pinnae. With the exception of *D. maxima* they are small but decorative ferns, particularly useful for fern-cases and edgings of window-boxes filled with larger species. *D. caudata* is the most useful species but *D. media* is a pretty species for greenhouses. Although some Doodias grow more luxuriantly in a stove temperature, none actually requires great heat and the cool and intermediate houses are suitable for all of them. They are useful, too, as undergrowth in cool houses devoted to Palms and various flowering plants. Insects seldom attack them and they bear fumigating and syringing well, though they can do without the latter. They should be potted in a compost of 3 parts peat and 1 of silver sand, with a little chopped Sphagnum. The drainage, especially when they are grown in pots, must be good and they do not like exposure to full sun. They are propagated by spores or by division of the crowns in spring.

**D. as'pera.** *sti.* 2 to 4 in. long, rough. *Fronds* 16 to 18 in. long, 2 to 4 in. wide, oblong-lanceolate with many spreading linear pinnae each side, 1 to 2 in. long, ⅓ in. wide, strongly toothed, base dilated. *Sori* oblong, in 2 rows. Temperate Australia. 1818. (H.E.F. 1, 8.) var. **corymbif'era,** tip of frond densely crested; **multif'ida,** arching fronds divided at tip, claret-coloured when young.

**D. blechnoi'des.** A synonym of *D. maxima.*

**D. cauda'ta.** *sti.* 4 to 6 in. long, erect. *Fronds* 6 to 12 in. long, 1½ to 2 in. wide, lanceolate with spreading linear pinnae each side about 1 in. long, point of frond often entire. Australia, New Caledonia, New Zealand. 1820. (H.E.F. 1, 25.) var. **con'fluens** has long narrow linear fronds undivided in upper part, sinuate-pinnatifid in lower part. New Caledonia. SYN. *D. linearis;* **Harry-a'na** is larger with firmer fronds.

**D. di'ves.** *sti.* 6 to 12 in. long, slender, erect, smooth, scaly towards base. *Sterile fronds* 1 ft. long, 3 to 5 in. wide, oblong-lanceolate with spreading oblong-linear pinnae on each side, 2 to 3 in. long, ⅓ in. wide, margin undulate, serrate. *Fertile fronds* longer, with narrow linear pinnae. *Sori* linear-oblong. Ceylon. (F.S.I. 222.)

**D. linea'ris.** A synonym of *D. caudata confluens.*

**D. lunula'ta.** A synonym of *D. media.*

**D. max'ima.** *sti.* 3 to 4 in. long, erect. *Fronds* 15 in. long, 6 in. wide, oblong-lanceolate with many spreading linear pinnae each side, about 3 in. long, ⅓ in. wide, sharply toothed, bases dilated. New S. Wales. 1835. (L.F. 4, 32.) SYN. *D. blechnoides.*

**D. me'dia.** *sti.* 4 to 6 in. long, erect, smooth. *Fronds* 12 to 18 in. long, 1½ to 4 in. wide, with spreading linear pinnae each side, 1 to 2 in. long, about ⅓ in. wide, toothed; upper dilated and connate at base, those below middle free and gradually smaller. *Sori* short, oblong, distant. (B.C.F. 2, 204.) SYN. *D. lunulata.* There are several varieties including **Brackenbridg'ei** with firm fronds, rather fewer, more distant obtuse pinnae, and dense sori in 2 irregular rows. Fiji; **connex'a** with larger, softer, and more papery fronds, the pinnae up to 3 in. long or more; **durius'cula** with firm caudate fronds, the middle pinnae about ½ in. long, oblong, obtuse, and the sori in a single series with 6 to 10 pairs. New Caledonia; **Kunthia'na,** fronds rather firm, pinnae close, blunt, sharply toothed, sori in one series. Sandwich Is.; **Mil'nei,** fronds firm, dark green, pinnae close, 4 to 5 in. long, sharply toothed, sori in two rows. Kermadec Is.

**D. rupes'tris.** A synonym of *D. caudata.*

## DOOM PALM. *See* **Hyphaene thebaica.**

## DOORWAY. *See* **Archway.**

**DOR BEETLE,** *Geotrupes stercorarius,* one of the Dung Beetles which flies about in a heavy and clumsy manner with a loud droning noise on warm summer evenings. It is about 1 in. long, black, dark violet, or metallic blue. It constructs burrows about 1 to 1½ ft. deep in the soil below a patch of dung, portions of which are carried down to serve as food for the grubs. The Dung Beetles are thus harmless in gardens.

G. F. W

**DORE'MA** (*dorema*, gift; the plant produces gum ammoniac). FAM. *Umbelliferae*. A genus of 2 species of perennial herbs, natives of Persia and Baluchistan, usually glabrous or inflorescence finely hairy, glaucous. Leaves pinnately much-divided, lobes wide, entire, usually decurved. Flowers yellow or white, in a simple umbel, branches long in a large panicle; pedicels usually short; involucral bracts none. Fruit ovate, flattish. Hardy plants easily grown from seed in ordinary soil.

**D. Ammonia'cum.** About 7 ft. h. *l.* large, somewhat 2-pinnate, 2 ft. long, lower lflets. distinct, upper confluent, deeply pinnatifid; stalked. *fl.* white; peduncles terete, woolly. June. Persia. 1831.

**DORI'TIS** (*doru*, a lance; the lip being lance-shaped). FAM. *Orchidaceae*. A monotypic genus founded by Lindley on dried specimens of the plant later described by Reichenbach f. and known in gardens as *Phalaenopsis Esmeralda*. It differs from true Phalaenopsis by 2 linear appendages to a long slender claw of the lip which furthermore is deflexed and has a raised ridge from the base of the side lobes to the tip of the mid-lobe. The plant too develops a distinct stem on which the leaves are carried at evident intervals. Other plants, included under Doritis, hardly agree with *D. Esmeralda* and are placed under Kingiella, a name proposed by Mr. Rolfe. Compost should be as for Phalaenopsis but may include a rather larger proportion of Osmunda fibre. Small pots are suitable. The winter temperature should not fall below 60° F.

**D. pulcher'rima.*** *fl.* about 1 in. across, variable in colour; sep. and pet. oval-oblong, light or dark-amethyst; lip 3-lobed, usually deep purple, the lateral lobes roundish, erect, sometimes shading to orange or brown-red, mid-lobe oblong, acute; peduncles erect, sometimes branched, 15 to 30 in. h., many-fld. *l.* broadly elliptic-oblong, 5 to 8 in. long, thick, often purplish beneath. Cochin China, Burma, Malaya, &c. 1874. (W.O.A. 321; B.M. 7196 as *Phalaenopsis Esmeralda*.) SYN. *P. antennifera, P. Regnieriana, P. Buyssoniana*. A pretty, variable species.

**D. taenia'lis.** A synonym of *Kingiella taenialis*.

**D. Wight'ii.** A synonym of *Kingiella decumbens*.

E. C.

A→

*Dormania'nus -a -um*, in honour of Charles Dorman of Sydenham, amateur orchid-grower, *c.* 1880.

**DORMANT BUD.** A bud which, though formed normally when the branch bearing it was first developed, remains, perhaps for years, undeveloped.

*doronicoi'des*, Doronicum-like.

**DORON'ICUM** (*Doronigi*, the Arabic name). FAM. *Compositae*. A genus of about 25 species of perennial herbs, natives of Europe and temperate Asia. Leaves alternate, basal leaves stalked, stem leaves distant, often stem-clasping. Flower-heads yellow, radiate; involucral bracts in 2 or 3 series, nearly equal; disk-florets perfect, with pappus hairs in many series; ray-florets usually female only, without pappus or with 1 to 3 hairs. Doronicums are hardy and thrive in ordinary garden soils. While they are somewhat coarse they are useful for their early flowering habit. They are easily propagated by division.

**D. alta'icum.** About 1 ft. h. *Radical l.* obovate-spatulate, narrowed to the stalk; *stem-l.* obovate, stem-clasping, all toothed. *fl.-heads* large. July. Siberia. 1783.

**D. austria'cum.** 12 to 18 in. h., somewhat hairy. *l.* toothed; radical l. heart-shaped, stalked; lower stem-l. ovate-spatulate, suddenly narrowed at base; upper lanceolate, heart-shaped, stem-clasping. *fl.-heads* large, 1 to 5 on stem. Spring. Europe. 1816.

**D. carpeta'num.** Stoloniferous, with tuber-like rhizome; hairy. Stem stout, leafy, 2- to many-headed. *l.* ovate-heart-shaped, more or less crenate or nearly entire, basal sinus large; stalk long; upper l. smaller, stalk shorter or none. *fl.-heads* 1 to 2 in. across; rays yellow, large; involucral bracts medium, narrow-lanceolate. N. and Cent. Spain.

**D. caucas'icum.** About 12 in. h., almost glabrous. *Radical l.* kidney-shaped, deeply toothed; *stem-l.* ovate, acute, toothed, base broadly clasping. *fl.-heads* about 2 in. across, solitary. Europe, Asia. (B.M. 3143.) var. **magnif'icum**, *fl.-heads* larger.

**D. Clu'sii.** About 1 ft. h. *l.* softly hairy; radical l. oblong, obtuse, entire or nearly so, narrowed to the stalk; stem-l. sessile, half stem-clasping, lanceolate, toothed in lower half. *fl.-heads* solitary; peduncle thickened towards top, covered with long hairs. Summer. Swiss and Austrian Alps. 1819. SYN. *Arnica Clusii, Aronicum Clusii*.

**D. Colum'nae.** A synonym of *D. cordatum*.

**D. corda'tum.** 5 in. or so h., glabrous. Rootstock very fibrous. *l.* heart-kidney-shaped, upper ovate-lanceolate, stem-clasping. *fl.-heads* solitary. Spring. Mts. of SE. Europe and W. Asia. SYN. *D. Columnae, D. cordifolium*.

**D. cordifo'lium.** A synonym of *D. cordatum*.

**D. cors'icum.** 2 to 3 ft. h., branched at top, erect, striate, glabrous or nearly so below, glandular-hairy above. *l.* ovate-lanceolate or lanceolate, stem-clasping, toothed, glabrous or nearly so; stem-l. sessile. *fl.-heads* yellow, large on 3 to 8 long peduncles in a terminal corymb. July, August. Corsica. SYN. *Aronicum corsicum*.

**D. Fal'coneri.** Stout, 12 to 18 in. h. Stem nearly smooth above. *l.* obovate or spatulate, obscurely toothed, 5 to 6 in. long. *fl.-heads* 2 to 3 in. across, rays very many, longer than bracts. Kashmir, Tibet.

**D. glacia'le.** About 6 in. h. Hairy. Stem erect, simple, leafy, from a blackish rhizome. *Basal l.* oblong, obtuse, narrowed to a wide stalk; *stem-l.* lanceolate, more or less stem-clasping, remote. *fl.-heads* 1½ to 2 in. across s. July. Alps and Carpathians.

**D. grandiflo'rum.** 6 to 12 in. h. *l.* pale green, toothed; radical l. broadly ovate, long-stalked; stem-l. stem-clasping. *fl.-heads* large; stems 1- to 3-fld. S. Europe. 1710. SYN. *Arnica scorpioides, A. Aronicum, Aronicum scorpioides*.

**D. Hook'eri.** Stout, 1 to 2 ft. h. *Radical l.* soon withering; *upper* oblong to elliptical-lanceolate, entire or irregularly toothed, 4 to 6 in. long. *fl.-heads* 1 or 2, 2½ in. across, rays as long as involucral bracts. Sikkim.

**D. macrophyl'lum.** Rootstock ending abruptly, with long fibrils, not stoloniferous. Stem tall, corymbosely branched above. *Lower l.* deeply heart-shaped, coarsely toothed, long-stalked, intermediate with dilated auricles; *upper* sessile, stem-clasping. *fl.-heads* large, rays 1 in. or more long; involucre papillose and glandular; scales oblong-lanceolate. Persia.

**D. magnif'icum.** A variety of *D. caucasicum*.

**D. Orphan'idis.** Tall, somewhat hairy below, glandular above. *Lower l.* from a cordate base, ovate-oblong, acute, crenate; *upper* sessile or stem-clasping and narrower. *fl.-heads* yellow, large, 2½ times as wide as disk, rays hairy at base; involucre glandular, bracts lanceolate, slender, half as long as rays. Achenes hairy. July. Greece.

**D. Pardalianch'es.** Great Leopard's Bane. Rootstock tuberous. Stem 18 to 36 in. h. *l.* cordate, toothed; basal l. heart-shaped, long-stalked; stem-l. few, ovate, upper stem-clasping. *fl.-heads* often 3 to 5 to the stem. Spring. Europe, including Britain. (E.B. 762.) Reputed to be poisonous.

**D. plantagin'eum.** Rootstock fibrous. Stem 2 to 3 ft. h. *l.* toothed; lower ovate or slightly heart-shaped, stalked; upper sessile except lowest which has a winged stalk. *fl.-heads* usually solitary. Spring. W. Europe, including Britain. (E.B. 762.) var. **excel'sum**, 5 ft. or more h., stem stout, somewhat roughly hairy, sometimes with 1 or 2 branches. *fl.-heads* 3 to 4 in. across. SYN. *Harpur Crewe's* var.

**DOROTHEAN'THUS.** Included under **Mesembryanthemum**.

**dorsal**, on the back, or growing on the back; or, applied to the leaf, the lower surface.

**dorsifixed**, of an anther, when the filament is continued to the back where the connective joins the anther lobes (cf. **basifixed** with filament at base of anther).

**dorsiventral**, having two distinct faces.

**DORSTEN'IA** (in honour of Theodore Dorsten, 1492–1552, German botanist). FAM. *Moraceae*. A genus of about 50 species of herbaceous plants, sometimes with a woody rootstock, natives of America and Africa with one in India. Interesting though not showy plants from the arrangement of the monoecious flowers, small and inconspicuous, crowded on a flat, simple or lobed receptacle bearing both male and female flowers. (Cf. **Ficus**.) Leaves radical or alternate, entire or lobed, sometimes of ornamental form or decorated with simple markings. Habit neat and compact. Easily grown in a rather damp stove. Increased by division before growth begins or by seeds sown on a hotbed in March or April.

**D. argen'tata.** Erect with a downy purple stem. *l.* elliptic or oblong-lanceolate, 3 to 5 in. long, dark green at margins with a broad silvery median band of varying width. S. Brazil. 1869. (B.M. 5795.)

**D. arifo'lia.** *l.* heart-arrow-shaped, undulate, crenate or lobed. *Receptacle* green, nearly round. Brazil. (B.M. 2476.)

**D. Bar'teri.** About 2 ft. h., more or less hairy. Rootstock creeping. *l.* obovate to elliptic, 5½ to 7 in. long, up to 3 in. wide, entire or wavy; stalk short. *Receptacle* orbicular, 1 to 1¾ in. wide, with a wide membranous margin and many unequal arms; more or less flat. Guinea.

**D. Bowmann'ii.** About 6 in. h. Stem leafy. *l.* lanceolate, 3 to 5 in. long, up to 1½ in. wide, faintly toothed, bright green and smooth above, white along midrib and lower half of main veins. *Receptacle* round, irregularly lobed, purple beneath. Rio de Janeiro. 1872. (Ref. B. 303.)

**D. Contrajer'va.** *rhiz.* creeping. *l.* almost radical, heart-shaped at base, spear-shaped, with rounded teeth, deep green, blotched white. *Receptacle* quadrate, green. Mexico, &c. (B.M. 2017 as *D. Houstonii*; I.H. 362 as *D. maculata.*)

**D. convex'a.** Ascending, 1 ft. or more h., shortly hairy. *l.* obovate-elliptic, shortly pointed, sometimes somewhat cordate, 1½ to 5 in. long, glabrous, undulate. *Receptacle* solitary in upper l.-axils, convex, up to 1½ in. long with many fleshy, linear, greenish-yellow. Congo.

**D. ela'ta.** Sub-shrub to 3 ft. h. *l.* elliptic, over 4 in. long, leathery, base cordate; stalk short; stipules large. *infl.* peltate, 1½ in. across, obtusely 4-angled; petiole about 4 in. long. Organ Mts.

**D. Lu'jae.** Densely hairy herb. *l.* obovate, 4 to 5 in. long, narrowed to stalk. *infl.* solitary in upper l.-axils, stalk about 1 in. long; receptacle polygonal to orbicular, ¾ in. wide, with a narrow margin fringed by numerous bract arms of different lengths. Congo.

**D. macula'ta.** A synonym of *D. Contrajerva.*

**D. Mann'ii.** 6 to 10 in. h. Erect, with rather flexuous stem swollen at nodes from which l. have fallen, densely hairy. *l.* elliptic or obovate, acute, narrowed to a rounded or heart-shaped base, dark green above, pale beneath, entire or nearly so, glabrous and opaque. *Receptacle* on stem at scars of old l.; peduncles orbicular, about 1 in. across, green, convex, very hairy on back, margined by 10 to 15 slender, stiff, unequal processes. November. W. Trop. Africa. 1863. (B.M. 5908.)

**D. psilu'rus.** Up to 2½ ft., erect, from a creeping, knotted, fleshy rhiz., rather succulent, laxly lvd. below, densely above. *l.* variable, ovate-elliptic or obovate, more or less cut at apex or 3- to many-lobed, 4 to 6 in. long, slightly hairy above, hairy on veins beneath; long-stalked. *infl.* solitary, long-stalked, vertical; receptacle linear-lanceolate, green, up to 1½ in. long, with a tapering appendage up to 3½ in. long. Trop. Africa.

**D. tubici'na.** Root large, woody, sub-fusiform, descending, truncate, powerfully aromatic. About 3 in. h. *l.* heart-shaped, oblong, toothed net-veined; stalk about as long as blade. *fl.* numerous in a wineglass-shaped receptacle with incurved margin and granular scales; anthers purplish, 2-lobed. Trinidad. 1817. (B.M. 2804.)

**D. Wal'leri.** Allied to *D. Mannii.* *l.* ovate, 2 to 5 in. long, fleshy. *Receptacle* green, star-shaped, nearly 1 in. wide with 5 tails 2 in. long. Nyasaland. 1893.

**D. yambuyaen'sis.** Erect hispidly hairy herb, 12 to 18 in. h. *l.* elliptic-lanceolate, 3 to 6 in. long, abruptly long-pointed, irregularly toothed, shining green above, pale and dull beneath. *Receptacle* green, angularly round, about ¾ in. across with a narrowly winged margin and many marginal processes ⅛ to 4 in. long, the longer often pinnatisect. Belgian Congo. 1910. (B.M. 8616.)

***Dortman'na***, in honour of Herr Dortmann, *c.* 1640.

**DORYAN'THES** (*dory*, spear, *anthos*, flower; the flower-stem is frequently 12 to 20 ft. long). FAM. *Amaryllidaceae.* A genus of 3 species similar to Cordyline and Dracaena in habit, related to Fourcroya and Beschorneria and differing from the last by the spreading perianth almost without a tube; the filaments are attached to the base of the segments where they are thickened but less markedly than in Fourcroya. Leaves lanceolate forming a basal rosette; stem-leaves small. The species need greenhouse conditions but can be accommodated only in large houses, and the plants must attain a considerable size before flowers are produced. A compost of loam and leaf-soil in equal parts suits them. Suckers may be potted into small pots and potted on as necessary.

**D. excel'sa.** 8 to 16 ft. h. *l.* 50 to 100, lanceolate, up to 6 ft. long, 4 in. wide, with a much shorter point than in *D. Palmeri.* *fl.* brilliant scarlet, each as large as that of *Lilium candidum*, in a globose head at the top of a bracteate stem. Summer. New S. Wales. 1800. (B.M. 1685.)

**D. Guilfoy'lei.** Closely related to *D. Palmeri.* *l.* 9 ft. long, 8 in. wide. *fl.* crimson, numerous, clustered, in a spike, on a stem about 16 ft. h. Queensland. 1893. (Gn. 44 (1893), 69.)

**D. Palm'eri.** 8 to 16 ft. h. *l.* 100 or more in a dense rosette, broadly lanceolate, about 6 ft. long, 6 in. wide, arching gracefully, with a long, slender, cylindrical, finally brownish point. *fl.* red, lighter in centre, large, funnel-shaped, in a pyramidal spike 12 to 18 in. long, 10 to 12 in. wide, many-fld., bracts leafy. Queensland. (B.M. 6665.)

**DORYC'NIUM** (old Greek name). FAM. *Leguminosae.* A genus of about 12 species of sub-shrubs or herbs. Leaves 3-foliolate with a pair of leaf-like stipules adjoining. Flowers papilionaceous, white or pink, in axillary, stalked clusters. Mediterranean region and Canary Is. Easily cultivated in light loamy soil and propagated by seeds.

**D. herba'ceum.** Erect herb to 18 in. *lflets.* and stipules obovate, blunt. *fl.* white; peduncles long. July. S. Europe, Asia Minor. 1802.

**D. hirsu'tum.** Semi-herbaceous; the erect, hairy, branching stems springing from a woody base and dying back every winter. *l.* of apparently 5 scarcely stalked lflets., which are obovate, ¾ to 1 in. long, hairy. *fl.* white, ¾ in. long, borne from June to September, in heads 1½ in. wide of 6 to 10. *Pod* ½ in. long, the very hairy cal. persisting at the base. S. Europe. 1683. SYN. *Cytisus Lotus.*

**D. latifo'lium.** Hairy, erect sub-shrub, 1 to 2 ft. h. *lflets.* and stipules obovate-mucronate; l. sessile. *fl.* white, in many-fld. umbels, bracteate. June. E. Europe. 1818.

**D. rec'tum.** Sub-shrub, hairy, erect, about 2 ft. h. *l.* stalked; lflets. obovate-mucronate. *fl.* rose, small, in many-fld. umbels without bracts. June. Mediterranean region. 1640.

**D. suffrutico'sum.** Deciduous sub-shrub 2 to 3 ft., shoots slender, springing from a woody base. *l.* stalkless, apparently 5-foliolate; lflets. linear-obovate, ¼ to ⅜ in. long, grey-silky. *fl.* pinkish-white, ¼ in. long, in numerous rounded clusters each 10- to 12-fld. and springing from the terminal l.-axils. June to September. *Pod* rounded, 1-seeded. S. Europe. 1640.

W. J. B.

**DORYOP'TERIS** (*dory*, spear, *pteris*, fern; from the shape of the fronds). FAM. *Polypodiaceae.* A genus of about 40 species of ferns with small fronds, sagittate or more or less pedate, veins forming a network with free veinlets, often included in Pteris with the sori along the margins of the pinnae. *D. pedata palmata* reproduces by bulbils borne at the top of the stalk, just at the junction with the leafy portion; the bulbils if pegged down on the ground without being severed from the parent plant quickly makes young plants, but the quickest way to propagate it is by spores which are freely produced. For treatment *see* **Pteris.**

**D. con'color.*** *sti.* 6 to 9 in. long, erect, wiry, brownish-black, slightly scaly towards base. *Fronds* 2 to 4 in. each way, deltoid, cut nearly to rachis into 3 or 4 pinnae each side, lowest pair much largest with pinnules on lower side much larger than others, deeply lobed, with linear-oblong segs. *Sori* in broad, marginal lines. Tropics. Greenhouse. (F.S.A. (2) 104; B.C.F. 3, 59.) SYN. *Pellaea geraniifolia, Pteris geraniifolia.*

**D. lu'dens.*** *rhiz.* wide-creeping. *Fronds* dimorphous; barren on slender, black stipes 3 to 4 in. long, varying from triangular with 2 slightly deflexed basal lobes to hastate, with entire margins; fertile on stipes often 1 ft. long, 4 to 6 in. each way, cut into 5 narrow-lanceolate lobes, all or some (except terminal) sometimes forked. *Sori* in a continuous line round margin. India, Philippine Is. (G.C. 15 (1894), 783; B.C.F. 3, 283.) SYN. *Pteris ludens.*

**D. nob'ilis** (noble).* *sti.* naked, wiry, 1 ft. or more long. *Fronds* very leathery; first-produced one cordate; later hastate and finally somewhat palmate, with terminal and upper lateral pinnae, lower lateral divided into 2 to 4 lanceolate pinnules on lower side, all having a broad band of white in centre. *Sori* in a continuous line from base to apex. Brazil. A very handsome species. SYN. *Pteris elegans, P. nobilis, Litobrochia elegans.* var. **Duval'i** has stout palmate fronds. 1897; **variega'ta,** robust, well marked with silver. 1894.

**D. peda'ta.*** *sti.* blackish, those of barren fronds 3 to 4 in. long. *Fronds,* barren 1 to 2 in. each way, with an almost entire, triangular apex, and a bluntly divided, lateral lobe each side; fertile 4 to 6 in. each way, cut nearly to rachis into several pinnae each side, upper linear and entire, 1 to 1½ in. long, lowest pair much larger than others with several pinnules on under side, lowest are again pinnatifid; costa dark. *Sori* reaching tips of segs. Trop. America. (B.M. 3247.) SYN. *Pteris pedata.* var. **palma'ta,*** *sti.* 1 ft. or more long, erect, chestnut-brown. *Fronds* 4 to 9 in. each way; barren with a broad, undivided centre, and five or more triangular lobes, terminal the largest, lowest deflexed, sinuses rounded; fertile fronds cut to a broadly winged centre into linear lobes, upper entire, lower again cut on lower side, longest entire ones 3 to 4 in. long, ¼ to ⅜ in. broad; costa black. Trop. America. 1821. (H.G.F. 22; L.B.C. 1299.) SYN. *Pteris palmata.*

**D. sagittifo'lia.*** *sti.* 4 to 6 in. long, erect, blackish. *Fronds* 4 to 6 in. long, 2 to 3 in. broad, hastate-lanceolate or sub-triangular, basal lobes triangular, acuminate, directed downwards, margins entire, midrib blackish. *Sori* continued all round margin. Venezuela to Brazil. (B.C.F. 3, 293.) SYN. *Pteris sagittifolia.*

**D. triphyl'la.** *sti.* 2 to 3 in. long, slender, wiry. *Fronds* digitate, ¾ in. each way; segs. 3 to 5, nearly equal, linear-oblong. *Sori* in close rows along margins of segs. Brazil, Argentina. 1824. Stove. (B.C.F. 2, 26.) SYN. *Cassebeera triphylla.*

**DORYPH'ORA** (*dory,* spear, *phoros,* bearing; the anthers having spear-like appendages). FAM. *Monimiaceae.* A single species of aromatic tree of irregular growth, glabrous, except young shoots and inflorescence which are hoary-tomentose. Closely related to Atherosperma and requiring similar cultural treatment.

**D. Sas'safras.** Large tree. *l.* ovate, elliptic or oblong-lanceolate, 2 to 4 in. long, slender-pointed, narrowed at base, coarsely toothed, pinnately and reticulately veined beneath; stalked. *fl.* hermaphrodite, ¼ in. long; 3 together on short, axillary peduncles; perianth segs. 6, in 2 rows; connective of anthers produced into a long, linear-awl-shaped appendage. New S. Wales. 1895. (B.M. n.s. 30.)

**DORYPH'ORA decemlinea'ta.** Old name for **Colorado Beetle** (q.v.).

**DOSSIN'IA.** Included in **Anoectochilus.**

**DOSSINIMA'RIA.** FAM. *Orchidaceae.* Hybrids between species of the genera Dossinia and Haemaria when these are kept distinct.

***Dosua,*** from *Dosi-swa,* native name of *Indigofera Dosua.*

**DOT MOTH,** *Mamestra persicariae,* is closely related to *M. brassicae,* Cabbage Moth (q.v.), but is a far more general feeder. The moth has dark brownish fore-wings with a brownish centred white kidney-shaped spot towards the upper margin, and greyish brown hind wings. It is on the wing in July and August. The caterpillars are green or brown with a double series of oblique dark-olive-green or brown marks along the body, which terminates in a slight hump. They feed from August to October on a great variety of plants, both annual and perennial, cultivated and wild, and often abound in gardens where they are found attacking the foliage of *Anemone hupehensis,* Chrysanthemums, Dahlias, Lupins, Marigolds, Brassicas and Lettuce, Gooseberry and many others. When fully fed they descend to the soil and there pupate, the moths emerging the following summer. Slight attacks may be controlled by handpicking the caterpillars at night from the attacked leaves with the aid of a torch, but in severe infestations it is necessary to spray the plants lightly with arsenate of lead or D.D.T. emulsion.

G. F. W.

**DOUBLE COCO-NUT.** *See* **Lodoicea.**

**DOUBLE FLOWERS.** The term 'double' is applied in two ways: (1) a flower is said to be double when the petals are much increased in number, (2) a flower-head is said to be double when the normal disk-florets are replaced by ray-florets or the disk-florets themselves are greatly enlarged. Both kinds of doubling are common in garden flowers and both occur to some extent in nature. The root cause of the tendency to doubling is unknown but it is constitutional, though generous treatment undoubtedly leads to fuller development of doubling where the tendency exists, and poor cultivation often reduces the development to a great extent. The doubling of a flower may result from the transformation of stamens and carpels or some of these organs into petals, to the repeated development of sepals and petals on the floral axis instead of the formation of stamens and carpels (well seen in the double Stock and double *Cardamine pratensis* so that no seeds are formed by these plants), or to the branching or multiplication of the petals themselves leaving the stamens and carpels more or less unaltered. No method of causing doubling of flowers is known, but repeated selection and breeding from plants

in which the tendency to doubling, seen, for instance, in the partial change of a stamen into a petal, may in time result in the establishment of a double race. Dr. M. T. Masters's account of doubling in Vegetable Teratology (Ray Society) may be consulted by readers interested in the morphology of doubling, and De Vries's Mutation Theory may be consulted on fluctuating variation which not infrequently occurs especially in 'double' Compositae.

**DOUBLE TONGUE.** *See* **Ruscus Hypophyllum.**

**doubly serrated,** or **double-toothed,** the teeth of a leaf themselves toothed.

**DOUCIN STOCK.** *See* **Rootstocks.**       **A**

**DOUGLAS FIR.** *See* **Pseudotsuga taxifolia.**

**DOUGLAS'IA** (in honour of David Douglas, 1798–1834, a zealous collector for the Royal Horticultural Society in NW. America who came to an untimely end in the Sandwich Is.). FAM. *Primulaceae.* A genus of 6 tufted or stoloniferous evergreen herbs closely related to Androsace but with a long-tubed flower, the few seeds in the capsule marking it off from Primula and the scales at the throat of the corolla from Dionysia. Five of the species are N. American and have rose or pinkish flowers, the other, *D. Vitaliana,* with yellow flowers, is confined to the mountains of Cent. Europe and Spain. The leaves are more or less crowded, small, and usually narrow, the inflorescence a scape with 1 to 7 flowers usually in a bracteate umbel. The Douglasias need a sandy peat with leaf-mould and much grit and broken stone to avoid any risk of stagnant moisture, though *D. Vitaliana* will grow in a rather more loamy soil than best suits the others. Propagation is by seed.

KEY

| | | |
|---|---|---|
| 1. *Fl. rose or pink* | | 2 |
| 1. *Fl. yellow* | | D. Vitaliana |
| 2. *Adult lvs. leathery, usually glabrous, oblong* | | D. laevigata |
| 2. *Adult lvs. hairy at margin, usually narrow* | | 3 |
| 3. *Adult lvs. minutely downy on margin* | | 4 |
| 3. *Adult lvs. with starry down* | | 5 |
| 4. *Densely tufted, the leafy shoots very close* | | D. montana |
| 4. *More loosely tufted, the leafy shoots distinct* | | D. arctica |
| 5. *Lvs. linear-tongue-shaped* | | D. nivalis |
| 5. *Lvs. oblong-lanceolate, toothed near apex* | | D. dentata |

**D. arc'tica.** Closely related to *D. montana* but less densely tufted, with 1-fld. scapes. Arctic N. America.

**D. denta'ta.** Rather loosely tufted with somewhat lax l.-rosettes. *l.* ashy-green, spatulate, about ⅔ in. long, irregularly and bluntly toothed near tip. *fl.* violet, ¼ in. across; scape 2- to 6-fld., ½ to 1½ in. h. Cascade Mts.

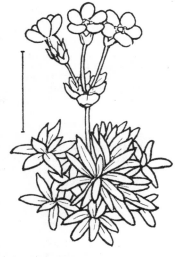

*Douglasia laevigata* (p. 707)

**D. laeviga'ta.** Densely leafy tufted perennial. *l.* glabrous, greyish-green, oblong-lanceolate to lanceolate, about ⅜ in. long. *fl.* rose, ⅓ in. across; scape 2- to 4-fld., 1 to 1½ in. h. Spring and autumn. Cascade Mts. 1886. (B.M. 6996.)

**D. monta'na.** Tufted with *l.* closely overlapping. *l.* linear-strap-shaped, glabrous except for downy margin. *fl.* rose; scape 1- or 2- (rarely 3-) fld., sometimes scarcely longer than *l.* Montana, Wyoming.

**D. niva'lis.** Rather loosely tufted with hairy shoots. *l.* in loose rosettes, linear-tongue-shaped, stellately hairy, about ⅜ in. long. *fl.* flesh-pink; scape 3- to 7-fld., scarcely longer than *l.* April. British Columbia. 1827. (B.R. 1886.)

**D Vitalia'na.** Tufted with numerous stems, brown in lower leafless part. *l.* narrow-linear, overlapping, entire, about ½ in. long, margins starry-hairy. *fl.* yellow, about ⅓ in. across, shortly stalked, at apex of shoots. Spring. Mts. of Spain and Cent. Europe. (L.B.C. 166 as *Aretia Vitaliana*.) SYN. *Androsace Vitaliana, Primula Vitaliana, Vitaliana primulaeflora, Gregoria Vitaliana.*

## DOUM PALM. *See* **Hyphaene thebaica.**

## DOVE FLOWER. *See* **Peristeria elata.**

## DOVE WOOD. *See* **Alchornea ilicifolia**

## DOVYA'LIS. *See* **Aberia.** *D. hebecarpa = A. Gardneri.*

*Dowia'nus -a -um,* in honour of J. M. Dow, *c.* 1866.

**DOWNIN'GIA** (in honour of Andrew Jackson Downing, 1815–52, American pomologist and landscape gardener). FAM. *Campanulaceae.* A genus of about 8 species of annual herbs, mostly Californian. Leaves small, linear-lanceolate. Flowers 2-lipped, upper lobes much narrower than lower; stamens joined into a tube free of corolla. Fruit a many-seeded, long, linear capsule crowned by the linear calyx lobes, dehiscing for entire length by 1 to 3 valves. Seed is best sown under glass in March, the seedlings being thinned or pricked out and then planted out in May in the open. *D. pulchella* is useful for hanging baskets. Sometimes erroneously listed under Clintonia.

**D. el'egans.** About 6 in. h. *l.* sessile, ovate to lanceolate. *fl.* blue with a large white streak at base, solitary, axillary; the 2 lobes of upper lip parallel, lanceolate, lower mainly white with 2 green or yellowish spots; throat often spotted purple and lined yellow. Summer. California. 1827. (B.R. 1241.)

*Downingia pulchella*

**D. pulchel'la.** 6 to 10 in. h., sometimes rather straggling. *l.* oblong-ovate to linear, ½ in. long. *fl.* deep blue with yellowish blotch with white border on lower lip; throat marked violet and yellow; lobes of upper lip spreading, oblong-lanceolate. Summer. California. 1827. (B.R. 1909.)

**downy,** covered with soft, short hairs.

**DOWNY MILDEWS.** Fungi, which show a characteristic production of aerial conidiophores in loose white tufts or downy patches on leaves, generally on the under surface. To the naked eye these spore-producing areas often look mealy white or furry but a hand lens shows them up well. The Downy Mildews are all members of the large group Phycomycetes, having hyphae which first penetrate deeply into plant tissues and later produce the spores. In the diseased tissues the resting stage (oospore) is formed which on decay of the infected plant is released and will contaminate the soil. The habit of the Downy Mildew fungi is thus very different from that of the Powdery or True Mildews (*see* **Erysiphaceae**) which have a whiter appearance and in which the fungal threads are superficial and live entirely on the surface of the plants. Downy Mildews are therefore in general more difficult to control than most Powdery Mildews (q.v.). An example of a common Downy Mildew is Onion Mildew (*Peronospora destructor*).

D. E. G.

**-doxa,** in compound words implying glory, as *adoxa* without glory, *chionodoxa*, glory of the snow.

**DOXAN'THA** (*doxa*, glory, *anthos*, flower). FAM. *Bignoniaceae.* A genus of a single evergreen climbing shrub, native of United States of America. Related to Bignonia. Calyx rotate, bell-shaped, 5-toothed. Corolla bell-shaped or funnel-shaped, lobes flat, tube curved; stamens included; disk saucer-shaped. Fruit a linear capsule with rather leathery narrow valves. Cuttings of short-jointed lateral growths will root in sand under a glass in heat. They need careful watering till rooted. A vigorous greenhouse climber, hardy in favoured places.

**D. capreola'ta.** Vigorous climber to 40 ft. *l.* ending in a branched tendril with small disks at tips; lflets. oblong, cordate, entire, stalked. *fl.* yellow-red, paler within, 2 in. long, tubular with a stout limb; in short stalk 2- to 5-fld. cymes. April to August. Southern U.S. America. (B.M. 864 as *Bignonia capreolata.*) var. **atrosanguin'ea,** *l.* longer and narrower, *fl.* dark purple, lobes short, triangular-ovate. (B.M. 6501.)

F. G. P.

**DRA'BA** (name used by the Greek Dioscorides for *Lepidium Draba*). FAM. *Cruciferae.* A genus of over 250 species of spring-flowering annual, biennial, or perennial herbs, rarely suffraticose, usually dwarf, tufted or cushion-forming, found in cold regions including the north circumpolar, and the high mountains of Europe, Asia, and America. More or less hairy, with simple leaves, those at the base of the stem stalked and forming a rosette, those on the stem (when present) sessile. Flowers often minute, but of medium size and showy in several species; racemes on naked or bracteate scapes, usually yellow or white, occasionally lemon, lilac, violet, orange, or reddish. Fruit usually short, ovoid or lanceolate, sometimes oblong or linear, many-seeded, dehiscent. A somewhat neglected but very useful set of plants for the rock-garden, moraine, and alpine house, growing well in light open soil and in a sunny space. Like many high-alpines the choicer species may need protection from excessive wet in winter. The annual and biennial species can be readily raised from seed and the annual species will often become in effect biennial if sown in late summer. The perennial species may be propagated by division of the roots or by removing shoots or rosettes in August. The most important sections of the perennial species are Aizopsis with rosettes of rigid spine-pointed leaves growing closely in a cushion, nearly all yellow-flowered, Chrysodraba with soft-foliage without bristly points or teeth, generally forming spreading mats, all yellow-flowered, and Leucodraba also mat-forming, with white or sulphur flowers. Several other sections of less importance are recognized. (See the account by O. E. Schulze in *Das Pflanzenreich*, Heft 89, pp. 1–343. The following key is adapted from this account.) All the species described are perennial unless otherwise stated.

KEY

1. *Fl.-stems leafless*                                                    2
1. *Fl.-stems more or less leafy*                                          34
2. *Lvs. stiff, narrow (Sect. Aizopsis)*                                   3
2. *Lvs. soft, wider, rarely somewhat stiff (Sect. Chrysodraba)* 25

| | |
|---|---|
| 3. *Branches marked with old l.-scars below, never rooting* | 4 |
| 3. *Branches covered with remains of old lvs. below, rooting, making with l.-rosette a columnar growth. Stamens shorter than pet.* | 19 |
| 4. *Lvs. in a dense rosette, linear. Stem erect* | 5 |
| 4. *Lvs. in a loose rosette, spatulate. Stem decumbent with fibrous scales below* | D. Sauteri |
| 5. *Stamens about as long as pet.* | 6 |
| 5. *Stamens distinctly shorter than pet.* | 11 |
| 6. *Lvs. of rosette narrow-linear, up to $\frac{1}{16}$ in. wide. Fr. in short raceme* | 7 |
| 6. *Lvs. of rosette wide-linear, $\frac{1}{16}$ to $\frac{1}{10}$ in. wide. Fr. in long raceme* | 10 |
| 7. *Fr. flattish, walls thin. Sep. smooth without* | 8 |
| 7. *Fr. swollen, walls firm. Sep. hairy without* | 9 |
| 8. *Style of fr. thin, somewhat curved* | D. aizoides |
| 8. *Style of fr. thick, straight* | D. Hoppeana |
| 9. *Lvs. of rosette up to $\frac{1}{4}$ in. long. Scape usually smooth* | D. longirostra |
| 9. *Lvs. of rosette up to $\frac{3}{8}$ in. long. Scape softly hairy* | D. cuspidata |
| 10. *Slender, up to $2\frac{1}{2}$ in. h. in fr. Lvs. rough-ciliate. Pet. $\frac{1}{8}$ in. long* | D. scardica |
| 10. *Robust, up to 5 in. h. in fr. Lvs. pectinate-ciliate and rough-hairy. Pet. $\frac{1}{4}$ in. long* | D. athoa |
| 11. *Scape smooth* | 12 |
| 11. *Scape hairy* | 15 |
| 12. *Fr. more or less flat. Lvs. pectinate-ciliate* | 13 |
| 12. *Fr. swollen at base. Lvs. often with few cilia* | D. Haynaldii |
| 13. *Lvs. tongue-shaped, up to $\frac{3}{4}$ in. long, $\frac{1}{8}$ in. wide* | D. Aizoon |
| 13. *Lvs. linear, up to $\frac{1}{16}$ in. wide* | 14 |
| 14. *Fr. in a long raceme, fr. pedicels $\frac{1}{4}$ to $\frac{1}{2}$ in. long* | D. Lacaitae |
| 14. *Fr. in a crowded raceme, fr. pedicels $\frac{1}{8}$ to $\frac{3}{8}$ in. long* | D. compacta |
| 15. *Fr. covered with starry hairs* | D. cretica |
| 15. *Hairs of fr. not starry* | 16 |
| 16. *Fl. white or rarely pale sulphur* | D. Dedeana |
| 16. *Fl. yellow* | 17 |
| 17. *Scape with woolly hairs* | D. parnassica |
| 17. *Scape with bristly hairs* | 18 |
| 18. *Fr. swollen at base, hairs rather long* | D. hispanica |
| 18. *Fr. flattish, rough with shor hairs* | D. Loiseleurii |
| 19. *Lvs. obtuse or rounded at tip* | 20 |
| 19. *Lvs. acute, spine-tipped* | 24 |
| 20. *Lvs. of medium size, $\frac{1}{8}$ to $\frac{1}{2}$ in. long, not strikingly imbricate* | 21 |
| 20. *Lvs. very small, $\frac{1}{16}$ to $\frac{1}{12}$ in. long, densely imbricate* | D. bryoides |
| 21. *Fr. distinctly narrowed to style* | D. oxycarpa |
| 21. *Fr. broad at top* | 22 |
| 22. *All lvs. pectinate-ciliate, bristles $\frac{1}{25}$ in. long* | D. olympica |
| 22. *Lvs. of short branches pectinate-ciliate, bristles $\frac{1}{12}$ in. long* | 23 |
| 23. *Scape more or less downy. Ovules few* | D. bruniifolia |
| 23. *Scape glabrous. Ovules many (about 32)* | D. rigida |
| 24. *Lvs. wide-lanceolate, glabrous, bristles small* | D. scabra |
| 24. *Lvs. narrow-linear, pectinate-ciliate, bristly* | D. Hystrix |
| 25. *Branches with the dense persistent lvs. making a long column* | 26 |
| 25. *Branches not strikingly columnar* | 30 |
| 26. *Lower part of stem covered with imbricate scales with persistent nerves of old lvs.* | D. polytricha |
| 26. *Whole of lvs. long persisting* | 27 |
| 27. *Plant white-hairy, lower part of branches scarcely scaly* | 28 |
| 27. *Plant grey-hairy, lower part of branches fibrous-scaly* | D. vesicaria |
| 28. *Fl. 8 to 20. Lvs. $\frac{1}{4}$ to $\frac{3}{4}$ in. long* | D. rosularis |
| 28. *Fl. 1 to 8. Lvs. $\frac{1}{8}$ to $\frac{1}{4}$ in. long* | 29 |
| 29. *Fl. 1 to 3* | D. acaulis |
| 29. *Fl. 5 to 8* | D. cappadocica |
| 30. *Lvs. toothed, distinctly stalked* | D. hispida |
| 30. *Lvs. entire, scarcely stalked* | 31 |
| 31. *Branches long creeping* | D. sibirica |
| 31. *Branches crowded* | 32 |
| 32. *Pet. about $\frac{1}{4}$ in. long. Fl. large* | D. elegans |
| 32. *Pet. $\frac{1}{8}$ in. long or less* | 33 |
| 33. *Lvs. thin or rather stiff, more or less downy* | D. alpina |
| 33. *Lvs. fleshy, glabrous or almost so, sparingly ciliate* | D. ochroleuca |
| 34. *Stems woody below (Sect. Calodraba)* | 35 |
| 34. *Stems herbaceous, fl. white (Sect. Leucodraba)* | 36 |
| 35. *Fl. white* | D. Gilliesii |
| 35. *Fl. purplish-violet* | D. violacea |
| 36. *Plant very small; lvs. rarely over $\frac{3}{8}$ in. long; lvs. on peduncles 0 to 3* | 37 |
| 36. *Plant larger; lvs. $\frac{3}{8}$ to $\frac{4}{5}$ in. long; lvs. on peduncles many* | 45 |
| 37. *Style of fr. $\frac{1}{25}$ to $\frac{1}{12}$ in. long* | D. austriaca |
| 37. *Style of fr. very short* | 38 |
| 38. *Fr. acute* | 39 |
| 38. *Fr. rounded or obtuse at apex* | 42 |
| 39. *Fr. clustered* | D. altaica |
| 39. *Fr. in a long raceme* | 40 |
| 40. *Hairs on lower lvs. unbranched* | 41 |
| 40. *Hairs on lower lvs. branched or starry* | D. carinthiaca |
| 41. *Lower l.-margins distinctly ciliate* | D. norvegica |
| 41. *Lower l.-margin and upper surface with simple hairs* | D. rupestris |

| | |
|---|---|
| 42. *Lvs. thin, densely starry-hairy* | D. tomentosa |
| 42. *Lvs. fleshy, thinly hairy, hairs simple or forked* | 43 |
| 43. *Stigma not wider than style, hairs simple or forked* | 44 |
| 43. *Stigma wider than style, hairs irregularly branched* | D. lactea |
| 44. *Stem-l. toothed* | D. Kotschyi |
| 44. *Stem-l. entire* | D. fladnizensis |
| 45. *Fr. elliptical* | 46 |
| 45. *Fr. oblong or linear* | D. cinerea |
| 46. *Peduncles smooth or minutely stellately downy* | 47 |
| 46. *Peduncles covered with simple, forked, or stellate hairs* | 49 |
| 47. *Fr. acute at apex* | 48 |
| 47. *Fr. blunt at apex* | D. pycnosperma |
| 48. *Plant large, up to 10 in. h.* | D. hirta |
| 48. *Plant small, 2 to 4 in. h.; lvs. stem-clasping* | D. subamplexicaulis |
| 49. *Lvs. rough with stiff starry hairs* | D. borealis |
| 49. *Lvs. hairy* | 50 |
| 50. *Fr. glabrous* | D. incana |
| 50. *Fr. hairy* | D. magellanica |

**D. acau'lis.** Habit of *Androsace helvetica*, forming a semi-globose cushion about 4 in. across, stems crowded, clothed with dead l. below. *l.* in rosette soft, entire, $\frac{1}{8}$ to $\frac{1}{4}$ in. long, covered with fine white stellate hairs above, margins ciliate. *fl.* 1 to 3 on a very short scape; pet. yellow, $\frac{1}{8}$ in. long; sep. yellowish. April. Cilician Taurus.

**D. Adams'ii.** A variety of *D. alpina*.

**D. aizoi'des.** Tufted, stems more or less crowded, thickened here and there with remains of old l. *l.* in a rosette about $1\frac{1}{4}$ in. wide, narrow-linear, rigid, more or less incurved, bristle-tipped, margins distantly ciliate. *fl.* 4 to 18, yellow, on glabrous, shining, erect scapes, 2 to 4 in. long. April. *fr.* elliptic, flattish, glabrous. Mts. of Middle Europe, including Britain. (E.B. 138.) A very variable plant.

**D. Ai'zoon.** Habit of *D. aizoides* but plant more robust, l.-rosettes larger. *l.* linear-lanceolate, margin pectinate-ciliate. *fl.* sulphur-yellow, 10 to 15 in a raceme, smaller than in *D. aizoides*, on a naked, smooth scape up to 6 in. h. *fr.* elliptic, flattish, bristle-haired at margin. Alps eastwards, Carpathians. 1819. var. **compac'ta**, a synonym of *D. compacta*.

**D. al'gida.** A variety of *D. alpina*.

**D. alpi'na.** Tufted. *l.* in a dense rosette, elliptic-lanceolate, acute, soft, covered with branched hairs, margin ciliate. *fl.* 4 to 10, at first corymbose, on downy stems up to 4 in. long, yellow pet. about $\frac{1}{8}$ in. long. N. Europe, Iceland. Arctic regions. 1816. Shows many varieties, among them var. **Adams'ii**, hispidly hairy, *fr.* hairy. Syn. *D. Adamsii*; **al'gida**, *l.* obovate-oblong, less hairy than type, Siberia, Greenland, Alaska, &c. Syn. *D. algida*; **glacia'lis**, *fl.* sulphur-yellow, *l.* sparsely ciliate. Syn. *D. glacialis*.

**D. alta'ica.** Tufted, stems crowded, nerves of dead l. persisting. *l.* in a rosette about 1 in. wide, at top of branches, linear-lanceolate, $\frac{1}{4}$ to $\frac{3}{8}$ in. long, entire, or with 1 or 2 teeth, ciliate. *fl.* 8 to 15, white, crowded on short pedicels, small, about $\frac{1}{4}$ in. across. N. Asia. Himalaya.

**D. androsa'cea.** A synonym of *D. lactea*.

**D. arma'ta.** A synonym of *D. longirostra erioscapa*.

**D. atho'a.** Generally like *D. Aizoon*. Dwarf but robust forming a rather wide clump. *l.* wide-linear, up to $\frac{3}{4}$ in. long, densely ciliate. *fl.* 8 to 20, yellow; pet. longer than in *D. Aizoon*. *fr.* oblong-elliptic. Greece.

**D. au'rea** of gardens. A synonym of *D. olympica*.

**D. austri'aca.** Tufted, many-stemmed. Tufts about 3 in. wide. Stems clothed below with whitish fibres. *l.* in rosette narrowly obovate, obtuse, entire or with 1 or 2 teeth; stem-l. wide-ovate, acute; all hairy above and ciliate. *fl.* 8 to 12, in a close corymb at first; pet. white, about $\frac{1}{8}$ in. long; scape up to 4 in. long, hairy in lower part. *fr.* oblong or ovoid, flattish, smooth. Austria. Syn. *D. stellata*.

**D. Bertolon'ii.** A synonym of *D. longirostra erioscapa*.

**D. borea'lis.** Stems more or less crowded, covered with nerves of dead l. below, l.-rosette at top up to 3 in. wide. *l.* narrowly obovate-spatulate, obtuse, $\frac{1}{4}$ to 1 in. long, entire or with 1 or 2 teeth, stellately hairy above; stem-l. shorter and wider. *fl.* 8 to 12, at first crowded in a corymb, on the somewhat leafy 2 to 8 in. h. stem, white; pet. about $\frac{1}{8}$ in. long. *fr.* on a nodding hairy stem, wide-oblong or oval, flattish. Arctic.

**D. bruniifo'lia.** Tufted, rather loose, up to 4 in. wide. Stems densely leafy at tops. *l.* linear, obtuse, about $\frac{1}{3}$ in. long, keeled, margin bristly, pale green. *fl.* 8 to 16 in a loose corymb, golden-yellow; pet. $\frac{1}{8}$ in. long; scape $1\frac{1}{2}$ to 4 in. long, hairy. March. *fr.* small, ovoid, hairy. Caucasus. 1825. Syn. *D. olympica bruniifolia*. var. **diversifo'lia** has rather longer oblong-ovoid *fr.* Armenia; **globif'era**, smaller in all parts, about $1\frac{1}{2}$ in. h., *l.* $\frac{1}{6}$ to $\frac{1}{4}$ in. long. Armenia; **natol'ica** has denser, shorter *l.* about $\frac{1}{8}$ in. long.

**D. bryoi'des.** Dense cushion about 2 in. h., 3 in. wide. Stems erect, covered with dead l. below, pale or violet l. of last year in middle, green l. at tip, columnar. *l.* small, oblong, rigid, $\frac{1}{16}$ to $\frac{1}{12}$ in. long. *fl.* 3 to 6, on a thread-like scape up to 2 in. long, golden-yellow, about $\frac{1}{8}$ in. long. *fr.* oblong-ovoid, more or less flattened. Caucasus. var. **imbrica'ta**, smaller, only about 1 in. across. Syn. *D. imbricata*; **squarro'sa**, looser with *l.* about $\frac{1}{8}$ in. long.

**D. calyco'sa.** A synonym of *D. cappadocica.*

**D. cantab'rica.** A variety of *D. Dedeana.*

**D. cappado'cica.** Close to *D. acaulis* but *l.* larger, fl. 5 to 8, smaller, scape up to 2 in. long. Asia Minor.

**D. carinthi'aca.** Tufted or many-stemmed, tufts about 1½ in. wide. Stems with nerves of dead l. below. *l.* in a close rosette above, lanceolate, acute, rarely with one tooth, about ⅜ in. long, hairy above, ciliate; stem-l. shorter, often 1- or 2-toothed. *fl.* 4 to 18 at first in a corymb, white, 1/12 to ⅛ in. long. *fr.* oblong-elliptic, compressed. Pyrenees, Alps, Carpathians. A variable plant. SYN. *D. Johannis, D. nivalis.*

**D. cilia'ta** of gardens. A synonym of *Arabis Scopoliana.*

**D. ciner'ea.** Tufted, about 1 in. wide. *l.* of rosette densely arranged, narrow-lanceolate, obtuse, sometimes faintly 1-toothed, shortly ciliate, stem-l. oblong-ovate, acute. *fl.* 15 to 20, white, at first forming a head; pet. about ⅛ in. long; peduncle slender, erect, shortly hairy, about 1 in. or more long. *fr.* oblong or linear. Arctic regions. 1820.

**D. compac'ta.** Tufts minute, about 1 in. wide, up to 2 in. h. at flowering. *fl.* 5 to 20, small, pale yellow; pet. about ⅛ in. long, scape slender, glabrous. *fr.* flattish, elliptic. SE. Europe. SYN. *D. Aizoon compacta.*

**D. contor'ta.** A synonym of *D. incana pyrenaea.*

**D. cors'ica.** A synonym of *D. Loiseleurii.*

**D. cre'tica.** Densely tufted, minute, about ¾ in. h. at flowering, and as much across. *l.* oblong, obtuse, ciliate, about ¼ in. long. *fl.* 3 to 6, in a dense corymb, pale yellow, pet. about ⅙ in. long; scape hairy. *fr.* oblong-elliptic. Crete.

**D. cuspida'ta.** Densely tufted. *l.* linear, obtuse, glossy, about ⅓ to ½ in. long, bristle-tipped. *fl.* 5 to 12, in a loose raceme, yellow; pet. ⅓ in. long; scape pilose. *fr.* narrowly ovoid, densely hairy. Crimea. Closely akin to *D. aizoides.*

**D. Dedea'na.** Cushions about 2½ in. wide. Rosettes dense. *l.* wide-linear, ⅕ in. long, blunt, margin pectinate-ciliate, bristle-pointed. *fl.* 3 to 10, in a crowded corymb, white, pale violet at base; pet. about ⅕ in. long; scape up to 3 in. h., hairy. *fr.* oboid, flattish, hairy. Pyrenees. var. **cantab'rica** has pale sulphur *fl.* SYN. *D. cantabrica*; **Maw'ii** has smaller *l.* and 3 to 5 *fl.* on a much shorter scape; **Zapat'eri** has longer, narrower, acute *l.* up to ⅓ in. long, and a looser raceme of fl. *See also D.* × *Salomonii.*

**D. dicranoi'des.** A synonym of *D. rigida.*

**D. diversifo'lia.** A variety of *D. bruniifolia.*

**D. Doerf'leri.** A synonym of *Schivereckia Doerfleri.*

**D. el'egans.** Tufts small, up to 1½ in. wide. *l.* oblong, obtuse, entire, about ⅓ in. long, stiffly hairy. *fl.* 8 to 25 in a corymb, golden yellow; pet. about ⅕ in. long, scape naked, up to 3½ in. long, smooth or downy at base. Asia Minor.

**D. fladnizen'sis.** Tufts up to 2 in. wide. *l.* close, oblong, usually entire, about ¼ in. long, stiffly hairy on margin. *fl.* 2 to 12, crowded, greenish-white; pet. about 1/12 in. long; scape usually leafless, up to 2½ in. long. Mts. of Europe and Cent. Asia. SYN. *D. helvetica.* A variable species.

**D. gi'gas.** A synonym of *Arabis carduchorum.*

**D. Gillies'ii.** Tufts up to 5 in. wide. *l.* oblong-spatulate, obtuse, entire or almost so, up to 1½ in. long; stem-l. oblong-elliptic, all densely hairy and somewhat ciliate. *fl.* 10 to 25 in a close corymb at first, white; pet. about ¼ in. long. 2 to 12 in. h. Chile. (B.M. 7913 = var. **rosula'ta** with hairy *fr.*)

**D. glacia'lis.** A variety of *D. alpina.*

**D. globif'era.** A variety of *D. bruniifolia.*

**D. Haynald'ii.** Near *D. compacta* but with *fr.* inflated at base, 3 to 8 *fl.* rather larger than in *D. compacta*, on slightly longer scapes. Carpathians.

**D. helvet'ica.** A synonym of *D. fladnizensis.*

**D. hir'ta.** Tufts about 2 in. across. *l.* long-lasting, narrow-lanceolate, acute, sometimes 1- or 2-toothed near tip, downy, sparsely ciliate; stem-l. oblong-ovate, ½ to ¾ in. long. *fl.* 8 to 20, at first in a corymb, whitish; pet. about ⅕ in. long; scape up to 9 in. h., nodding at top in fl., somewhat downy. *fr.* ovate-lanceolate, compressed, smooth. N. Europe, Greenland. A variable species.

**D. hispan'ica.** Densely tufted. Stems closely leafy in upper part. *l.* linear, acute, keeled beneath, roughly hairy above, margin pectinate-ciliate. *fl.* 6 to 15 in a close corymb at first, pale yellow; pet. about ⅓ in. long; scape naked, up to 2 in. long, rough-haired. *fr.* oblong-elliptic, somewhat inflated at base, rough-hairy. Spain.

**D. his'pida.** Tufts very small, ½ to 1½ in. wide. Stems with few fibrous scales below, rosette dense. *l.* obovate, more or less obtuse, thin, rough with stiff hairs, margin with 1 to 3 teeth, ciliate. *fl.* 10 to 45, in a congested corymb, golden yellow; pet. ¼ in. long; scapes smooth, or hairy below, glossy, up to 6 in. h. *fr.* oblong, flattish, smooth. Caucasus. 1838.

**D. Hoppea'na.** Densely tufted, scarcely 1 in. h. *l.* linear, mucronate, margin bristly, ⅛ to ⅓ in. long. *fl.* 2 to 9, at first in a head, pale yellow scarcely emerging from foliage; pet. about ⅛ in. long; scape smooth. *fr.* narrowly ovoid, smooth. European Alps. SYN. *D. Zahlbruckneriana.*

**D. Hys'trix.** Densely tufted. Stems spiny with remains of old l. below. *Rosette-l.* narrowly linear, stiff, acute, keeled, bristles white, margin pectinate-ciliate. *fl.* 12 to 25 in a close corymb, pale yellow; pet. about ¼ in. long; scapes about 1½ in. long, erect, downy. *fr.* lanceolate, pale green, more or less bristly. Afghanistan.

**D. imbrica'ta.** A variety of *D. bryoides.*

**D. inca'na.** Biennial or perennial. *l.* lanceolate, obtuse, slightly hairy, sometimes toothed, ⅔ to 1 in. long, dying at flowering time, stem-l. shorter and wider. *fl.* 10 to 40 in a dense hairy raceme, white; pet. about ⅕ in. long. *fr.* lanceolate or oblong. Arctic, northern and cool regions (including Scotland—var. **confu'sa** with downy *fr.*). A variable species.

**D. Johan'nis.** A synonym of *D. carinthiaca.*

**D. Kotsch'yi.** Tufts about 1 in. wide. *l.* oblanceolate or elliptic, obtuse, often toothed, stem-l. ovate, acute, all thin, downy, sometimes smooth. *fl.* 6 to 15 in a close corymb, white; pet. about ⅙ in. long; scape hairy, up to 1½ in. long. *fr.* elliptic or oblong, glabrous or ciliate. European Alps.

**D. Lacait'ae.** Densely tufted, tufts about 1½ in. wide. *l.* widely linear, obtuse, bristly, ciliate, ⅙ to ⅓ in. long. *fl.* 6 to 18, in a corymb, yellowish-white; pet. ⅙ in. long; scape slender, glabrous, up to 3 in. h. *fr.* oblong-elliptic, rough. Greece.

**D. lac'tea.** Loosely tufted. *l.* narrow, lanceolate-linear, ciliate, downy. *fl.* white; pet. about ⅐ in. long; scape glabrous. *fr.* oblong-ovoid. Very close to *D. fladnizensis.* SYN. *D. androsacea, D. lapponica.*

**D. lappon'ica.** A synonym of *D. lactea.*

**D. lax'a.** A variety of *D. norvegica.*

**D. Loiseleur'ii.** Habit of *D. hispanica*, but *l.* wide-linear, obtuse, bristly ciliate, about ¼ in. long, *fl.* 5 to 10, pet. about ⅕ in. long, *fr.* ovoid, somewhat swollen. Corsica.

**D. longiros'tra.** Near *D. aizoides* but smaller with usually 2 to 6 *fl.* on a scape ½ to 1½ in. h., *fr.* ovoid, rather swollen, and bristly with a long beak. Italy. var. **eriosca'pa,** stem hairy.

**D. magellan'ica.** Habit of *D. incana* but with smaller stem *l.* and longer pedicels; scape erect. Antarctic region.

**D. Maw'ii.** A variety of *D. Dedeana.*

**D. natol'ica.** A variety of *D. bruniifolia.*

**D. niva'lis** of gardens. A synonym of *D. carinthiaca.*

**D. norveg'ica.** Tufts under 1 in. wide, congested. Stem covered with fibrous scales below, rosette usually close. *l.* oblong-lanceolate, acute, entire or nearly so, ⅕ to ½ in. long, hairy and ciliate; stem-l. ovate, toothed. *fl.* 5 to 15 in raceme, white; pet. ⅛ in. long; scape up to 6 in. h. *fr.* oblong-elliptic, flattened, smooth. NW. Europe, Greenland. SYN. *D. scandinavica.*

**D. ochroleu'ca.** Loosely matted. *l.* oblanceolate or oblong-spatulate, ⅕ to ¾ in. long, entire or almost so, softly ciliate. *fl.* in a close cluster on glabrous scapes up to 3 in. long, yellowish-white. *fr.* oblong-ovoid, smooth. N. and Cent. Asia. Close to *D. alpina.*

**D. olym'pica.** Mat-forming. *l.* crowded, imbricate, stiff, linear, obtuse, ¼ in. long, densely pectinate-ciliate. *fl.* 5 to 12 in a close corymb on hairy scapes up to 2 in. long, golden-yellow; pet. ¼ in. long. *fr.* ovoid, swollen, bristly. Bithynica. var. **bruniifo'lia,** a synonym of *D. bruniifolia.*

**D. oxycar'pa.** Tufts small, dense, about 1½ in. wide about 1 in. h. or less at flowering time. *l.* wide-linear or oblong-obtuse, ⅕ to ⅓ in. long, bristly ciliate, densely bristly on branch l. *fl.* 5 to 12 in a close corymb on a roughly hairy slender scape, yellow. *fr.* ovoid, swollen, with spreading hairs. Lebanon.

**D. parnas'sica.** Tufts dense, about 1½ in. wide. *l.* wide-linear, obtuse, ¼ to ⅖ in. long, bristly ciliate. *fl.* 6 to 22 in a close corymb, yellow; pet. about ¼ in. long; scape up to 2 in. long, hairy. *fr.* ovoid, somewhat swollen at base, bristly. Greece.

**D. polytrich'a.** Tufts dense, dwarf. *l.* soft, oblong, obtuse, about ⅕ in. long, entire, white-hairy. *fl.* 4 to 10, at first corymbose, yellow; pet. ⅕ in. long, obovate; scapes numerous, up to 1½ in. long, with spreading hairs. *fr.* ovoid, swollen. Armenia.

**D. pycnosperm'a.** Mat-forming, tufts up to 6 in. wide. *l.* ⅓ to 1¼ in. long, obovate, obtuse, entire or almost so, densely downy above; stem-l. ovate or oblong. *fl.* 8 to 22, in a loose raceme, white; scape hairy. *fr.* minute, ovoid, somewhat swollen, smooth. Canada. SYN. *D. canadensis pycnosperma.*

**D. pyrena'ica.** A synonym of *Petrocallis pyrenaica.*

**D. re'pens.** A synonym of *D. sibirica.*

**D. rig'ida.** Tufts about 3 in. across. *l.* wide-linear or oblong-elliptic, obtuse, stiff, spreading with tip more or less inflexed, bristly. *fl.* 5 to 20, at first in a dense corymb, golden yellow, on smooth scapes 1 to 3 in. h.; pet. ¼ in. long, obovate. *fr.* oblong-elliptic, flattish, smooth. Armenia. SYN. *D. dicranoides.* var. **bryoi'des, a** synonym of *D. bryoides.*

**D. rosula'ris.** Tufts minute, up to 1½ in. wide. Stems covered below with dead l. *l.* soft, oblong, obtuse, entire, about ½ in. long, downy. *fl.* 8 to 20 in a rather loose raceme, yellow; pet. about ⅛ in. long; scape up to 4 in. long, stout, softly hairy. *fr.* ovoid, swollen, hairy. Armenia. var. **veluti'na,** more compact with shorter *l.* and scape, whitish-hairy.

**D. rupes'tris.** Tufts rather loose, up to 3 in. wide. *l.* thin, linear-lanceolate, hairy. *fl.* 3 to 10, white; pet. 1/10 in. long on slender hairy scapes. *fr.* oblong, small, hairy. Sub-arctic Europe, including Scotland.

**D.× Salo'mon'i** (*D. bruniifolia× D. Dedeana*). Similar in habit to *D. Dedeana* but with white *fl.* Sterile.

**D. Sau'teri.** Loosely tufted. Stems decumbent, covered in lower part with fibrous remains of old l. *l.* in loose rosette, spatulate-linear or oblong, 1/6 to 1/3 in. long, rounded at tip, shining, pectinate-ciliate. *fl.* 3 to 5, in loose corymb, on smooth, thread-like scapes about 1/4 to 1/2 in. long, yellow; pet. 1/8 in. long. *fr.* wide-oval, flattish, smooth. Alps.

**D. scab'ra.** Tufts up to 8 in. wide. Stems showing scars of old l. below with l.-rosettes above. *l.* lanceolate, acute and spine-pointed, 1/4 to 2/3 in. long, glossy, glabrous except for ciliate margin and nerves. *fl.* 5 to 10, golden yellow, on a glabrous, thread-like, glossy scape about 2 in. h.; pet. 1/8 in. long. *fr.* more or less ovoid, smooth. Caucasus. 1897. Allied to *D. Hystrix*.

**D. scandinav'ica.** A synonym of *D. norvegica*.

**D. scar'dica.** Allied to *D. aizoides*, but tufts smaller and plant more slender, densely rough-haired. *fl.* 4 to 10; pet. about 1/4 in. long; scape very short. Albania.

**D. sibir'ica.** Soft and bright green with more or less prostrate stems. *l.* more or less congested, oblong-lanceolate, acute, entire, hairy, becoming purplish at flowering time. *fl.* 8 to 20, yellow, in a loose corymb at first; pet. about 1/4 in. long. *fr.* oblong-elliptic. Russia, Siberia. Greenland.

**D. stella'ta.** A synonym of *D. austriaca*.

**D. subamplexicau'lis.** Allied to *D. hirta*, but smaller. Tufts very close, about 3/4 in. wide. *fl.* smaller, pet. about 1/8 in. long. Altai.

**D.× Thomas'ii** (*D. austriaca × D. incana*). Habit of *Schivereckia podolica*. Loosely tufted up to 5 in. h. in fl., hairy. *l.* in a loose rosette, about 3/4 in. long, lanceolate, more or less acute, toothed; stem-l. smaller. *fl.* 8 to 20, in a dense raceme, white; pet. about 1/4 in. long. Austria.

**D. tomento'sa.** Loosely matted. Stems flaccid, thick. *l.* elliptic or obovate, entire; stem-l. widely ovate; sometimes toothed; all thickly hairy. *fl.* 3 to 14 in a dense raceme; scape about 3 in. h.; pet. white or pale yellowish, 1/8 in. long. *fr.* wide-elliptic, hairy. Alps of Europe.

**D.× Traunstein'eri** (*D. carinthiaca × D. dubia*). *l.* more hairy than in *D. carinthiaca*, pet. about 1/8 in. long. Occurs with parents.

**D. tridenta'ta.** A synonym of *D. hispida*.

**D. velutin'a.** A synonym of *D. rosularis velutina*.

**D. vesica'ria.** Densely tufted. Allied to *D. acaulis*. Tufts about 3½ in. wide. Stems distinctly covered with remains of old l. in base; plant greyish (not whitish-hairy); scapes many, 3- to 10-fld.; pet. 1/8 in. long. *fr.* swollen, ovoid, hairy. Lebanon.

**D. viola'cea.** Sub-shrubby. Stem branched up to 6 in. h., erect, hairy. *l.* crowded, more or less imbricate, sessile, obovate or elliptic, about 1/4 in. long, whitish-hairy. *fl.* 4 to 15, in, at first, a crowded raceme, violet; pet. 1/4 in. long. *fr.* lanceolate, hairy. Andes. 1867. (B.M. 5650.)

**D. Zahlbruckneria'na.** A synonym of *D. Hoppeana*.

**D. Zapat'eri.** A variety of *D. Dedeana*.

**DRACAE'NA** (*drakaina*, female dragon; the colouring matter, dragon's blood, can be obtained from *D. Draco*). FAM. *Liliaceae*. A genus of about 40 species of tree- or shrub-like plants without creeping rootstocks, widely distributed over the tropics of the Old World. Leaves lanceolate or oblanceolate, often arching. Flowers generally in panicles, rarely in dense sessile heads or oblong spikes, whitish. Related to Cordyline, but the species of that genus always have a creeping rootstock, the inflorescence has 3 large bracts at its base (none in Dracaena) and the cells of the ovary contain 6 to 15 ovules (only one in Dracaena). The flowers of Cordyline are generally smaller than those of Dracaena. In spite of these differences there has been, and still is, much confusion in the nomenclature of the plants of the 2 genera. This is no doubt partly due to the plants being grown in the main for their ornamental foliage. Although the Dracaenas and the large group of plants grown as such, but which properly belong to Cordyline, belong essentially to the stove, they will keep in good condition in the greenhouse through the summer. Many of them are well suited for room and table decoration, especially those with narrow recurved leaves, and useful sizes for this purpose can soon be obtained if stove treatment with plenty of light is given. A compost of loam and lumpy peat in equal proportions with a little sand suits them well. They need a moderate amount of pot room in comparison with the size of the plants, but 5- or 6-in. pots are large enough for plants 12 to 18 in. high, and such plants must be potted on into pots proportionately large if larger specimens are desired. Plenty of heat and moisture are needed when the plants are young to ensure vigorous and rapid growth, but syringing much in winter is inadvisable as the lodging of water in the leaf-axils at that season is liable to be injurious. Plenty of light is also needed to ensure the full development of colouring in the leaves.

Plants of this group are readily propagated by cutting up the stems of old plants into pieces 1 to 2 in. long, and placing them, at any season, in peat-fibre, or light soil, in a propagating house with bottom heat. Almost every bud on the firm wood that has been cut in pieces will develop into a young plant if thus treated, and the tops of the old plants will strike as cuttings while the fleshy base of the stem may also sometimes be removed and used for propagation.

Many garden-raised forms have been given Latin names as though they were species, and a number of these really belong to Cordyline, especially to *C. terminalis*. The heights given below are those of mature plants growing wild. Many are very ornamental while small, as already noted. Syn. *Terminalis*.

J. C.

**D. arbo'rea.** Tree-like, to 40 ft. h. *l.* lorate, many, 1½ to 3 ft. long, 2 to 3 in. wide in middle. *fl.* greenish, 3/4 in. long. May. N. Guinea. 1800.

**D. bi'color.** Trunk about 5 ft. h. *l.* close, upper slightly ascending, oblong, 4 to 6 in. long, 2 to 3 in. wide, deltoid, cuspidate at tip, narrowed to a 1- to 3-in. stalk at base; lower oblong-lanceolate, 1 to 1½ ft. long, 4 to 5 in. wide. *fl.* white, tinged red, in a dense, globose, terminal, short-stalked spike; bracts large, brown. Fernando Po, &c. (B.M. 5248.)

**D. concin'na.*** About 6 ft. h., compact. *l.* narrow, sombre green, with purplish-red margins, narrowed to a green, purple-tinged stalk. Mauritius. 1870. (G.F. 1864, 441.)

**D. cylin'drica.** Trunk erect, unbranched, about 5 ft. h. *l.* linear-lanceolate, or obovate-lanceolate, bright green, spreading. *fl.* white, small, in a terminal, sessile, cylindrical spike. W. Trop. Africa. (B.M. 5846.)

**D. deremen'sis.** Branched, 9 to 15 ft. h. *l.* 18 in. long, 2 in. wide, narrowed to a broad, stalk-like base. *fl.* dark red without, white within, in a large infl.; perianth about 1/2 in. long; scent unpleasant. Africa. (J.R.H.S. 37, cxxxix.)

**D. Dra'co.*** Dragon-tree. Tree-like, 40 to 60 ft. h., branched. *l.* in a terminal, crowded head, linear-lanceolate, 18 to 24 in. long, 1½ to 1¾ in. wide, erect or the outer recurved, entire, glaucous. *fl.* greenish-white, very small, in a large panicle. Canary Is. 1640. (B.M. 4571.) Decorative as young plants for the conservatory or for sub-tropical bedding. The famous Dragon-tree of Oratava, one of the oldest of known trees, measured 70 ft. in height and 15 ft. in diameter at the base of the trunk.

**D. ellip'tica.** About 2½ ft. h. Stem 2 to 3 ft. long, terete. *l.* usually spreading, elliptic-lanceolate, acute, mucronate, rather leathery, glossy, marked with close parallel longitudinal lines; stalk grooved, dilated, clasping at base. *fl.* greenish-yellow, sometimes solitary, usually in clusters of 3. March. India, Java, &c. SYN. *Sanseviera javanica*. var. **macula'ta**, *l.* blotched with yellow. (B.M. 4787.)

**D. frag'rans.*** Tree-like, 20 ft. or more h., sometimes branched. *l.* oblanceolate, lax, spreading or recurved, 1½ to 3 ft. long, 2½ to 4 in. wide, acute, green, glossy, sessile. *fl.* clustered, yellow, fragrant, about 1/2 in. long. *fr.* orange-red. Guinea. 1768. (B.M. 1081.) Leaves variable. var. **Linden'ii**, *l.* recurved, deep green with a median longitudinal stripe of yellow and pale yellow. 1879. SYN. *D. Lindenii*; **Massangea'na**, *l.* broad-lanceolate with a median whitish stripe. (B.H. 1881, 61.) SYN. *D. Massangeana*.

**D. Godseffia'na.*** Slender, rather spreading. *l.* opposite or in whorls of 3, oblong or obovate, spreading, 3 to 4 in. long, 1½ to 2 in. wide, firm, green with numerous bright cream spots; at some nodes l. scale-like, small. *fl.* in a short-stalked raceme. *fr.* greenish-yellow or red, nearly 1 in. wide. Congo. 1893. (B.M. 7584.)

**D. Goldiea'na.** Stem slender, unbranched, erect. *l.* rather distant, cordate-ovate, 7 to 8 in. long, 4 to 5 in. wide, spreading, midrib yellowish-green, blade glossy green with alternate transverse bands (sometimes forked) of silver-green; stalks erect, 2 to 3 in. long, deeply grooved; l. sometimes tinged pink when young. W. Trop. Africa. 1872. (B.M. 6630.)

**D. Hookeria'na.** Trunk 3 to 6 ft. h., sometimes branched, leafy near top. *l.* crowded, ensiform, 2 to 2½ ft. long, 1½ to 2 in. wide, outer reflexed, all gradually narrowed to a long point, pale green bordered white. *fl.* greenish, 1 to 1¼ in. long; filaments filiform. *fr.* orange. S. Africa. (B.M. 4279 as *Cordyline Rumphii.*) var. **latifo′lia,** *l.* 2 to 3 in. wide in middle, narrowed to base. (Ref. B. 353.) Of garden origin; **variega′ta,** *l.* variegated.

**D. kewen′sis.** *l.* broad-lanceolate, acute, dark green; stalk red, half as long as blade. New Caledonia. Probably a Cordyline.

**D. margina′ta.** Trunk 4 to 5 ft. h., 1 in. thick, branched. *l.* in a dense terminal rosette, ensiform, 12 to 15 in. long, ¾ in. wide, spread, rigid, green, margined, and veined red. Madagascar.

**D. marmora′ta.** *l.* crowded, lanceolate, recurved, plicate, bright green much marbled white; sessile. *fl.* greenish-white, less than 1 in. long, in an erect, narrow panicle, 18 to 24 in. long. Spring. Malaya. 1882. (B.M. 7078.) Perhaps a form of *D. arborea.*

**D. phrynioi′des.*** Dwarf. *l.* broad-ovate, long-pointed, 6 to 8 in. long, leathery, very dark green, spotted yellow above, paler beneath; stalked. Fernando Po. 1863. (B.M. 5352.) Needs a moist stove.

**D. Sanderia′na.*** Slender, branched at base. *l.* distant, narrow-lanceolate, 7 to 10 in. long, ½ to 1½ in. wide, spreading or recurved, green broadly margined white; stalk 1 to 3 in. long, rather wide. Congo. 1892. (G.C. 13 (1893), f. 65.)

**D. Smithii.** Closely related to *D. fragrans.* Stem up to 15 ft. h., nearly smooth, cylindric. *l.* in a terminal spreading crown, 3 to 4 ft. long, somewhat recurved, not waved, narrow-ensiform, widest beyond middle, bright green, striped; midrib prominent beneath. *fl.* in crowded clusters on the panicle, pale yellow, ½ in. long. Winter, early spring. Trop. Africa. 1850. (B.M. 6169.)

**D. umbraculif′era.** Tree-like, 3 to 10 ft. h., unbranched. *l.* very crowded, 2 to 3½ ft. long, 1½ to 2 in. wide, horizontal with ends somewhat recurved, scarcely narrowed to the wavy base, midrib distinct on both sides. *fl.* white, tinged red, 2 in. long; filaments filiform. Mauritius. 1778. (L.B.C. 289.) A curious flat-topped plant.

*Dra′co,* dragon.

**DRACOCEPH′ALUM** (*drakon,* dragon, *kephale,* head; from the form of the corolla). Fam. *Labiatae.* A genus of about 40 species of annual or perennial herbs, related to Lallemantia and Physostegia, natives of Europe and temperate Asia. Leaves opposite, entire, toothed or palmatifid. Flowers in a terminal spike of many-flowered whorls; bracts usually leafy; corolla usually large with a very wide throat and a 2-lipped limb. Hardy border plants with showy flowers, growing best in a cool situation. The perennial species are increased by root division or by cuttings of the young shoots in April or May; the annuals by seeds sown in the open in April. The following are perennial unless otherwise stated.

**A**

**D. alpi′num.** Dwarf, related to *D. nutans.* *l.* widely and shortly ovate, with rounded teeth. *fl.* small, blue, pendulous. Altai Mts., Songaria. Rock-garden.

**D. altaien′se.** A synonym of *D. grandiflorum.*

**D. argunen′se.** Erect, stems rather hairy, 12 to 18 in. h. *l.* linear-lanceolate, 1¼ to 3 in. long, entire, ciliate, minutely gland-dotted beneath, nearly sessile. *fl.* blue, 1½ in. long or more, downy; in a terminal panicle. July. Dahuria. 1822. (B.M. 8384; L.B.C. 797.) Related to *D. Ruyschianum.*

**D. austri′acum.** Erect, stem rather hairy, about 18 in. h. *l.* 3- or 5-cleft; segs. linear with revolute margins. *fl.* blue, over 1½ in. long; bracts hispid, whorls 6- to 10-fld. in an interrupted spike. July. Europe. 1597.

**D. botryoi′des.** Stem procumbent, hairy. *l.* roundish-ovate, truncate or cuneate at base, deeply pinnatifid, hairy above; stalked. *fl.* in a head or oblong spike, purplish, about 1½ times as long as cal., hairy; bracts deeply cut. Caucasus.

**D. bulla′tum.** Stem ascending, 3 to 10 in. long, purplish, covered with grey hairs. *Basal l.* long-stalked; all ovate-elliptical from a cordate base, about 2 in. long, somewhat leathery, almost glabrous, purplish beneath; *upper* more or less sessile. *fl.* bright deep blue, 1¼ to 1½ in. long, in a dense raceme up to 3½ in. long. Yunnan, China. (B.M. 9657.) Rock-garden.

**D. calophyl′lum.** Tufted, 6 to 18 in. h., rarely more, loosely branched, stems softly hairy. *l.* deeply pinnatifid, segs. of lower *l.* 7 to 9, linear, narrowly recurved, about ¾ to 1¼ in. long, whitish on back. *fl.* bright purplish-blue in short dense spike-like racemes about 4 in. long, sometimes longer; cal. 15-nerved, dull purple; cor. with long tube, widened to a pouch, hairy within. Szechwan, Yunnan. 1918. Near *D. Forrestii* but with longer internodes and less leafy. Rock-garden. (B.M. 8892.)

**D. canes′cens.** A synonym of *Lallemantia canescens.*

**D. For′restii.** Stem 12 to 20 in. h., slender, simple, densely leafy, more or less covered with white hairs. *l.* pinnatisect with 2 or 3 pairs of segs. or 3-partite, segs. linear, up to ⅝ in. long, glabrous above, hairy beneath. *fl.* deep purple-blue, outside densely white-

hairy, with 10 to 30 2- to 4-fld. whorls in a dense spike-like raceme. W. China. 1916. Border or rock-garden.

**D. grandiflo′rum.** Erect, 6 to 9 in. h. *Radical l.* oblong, crowded, obtuse, cordate at base, long-stalked; *stem-l.* ovate, short-stalked. *fl.* blue, nearly 2 in. long in oblong spikes about 3 in. long; bracts roundish, hairy. July. Siberia. 1759. (G.F. 855 as *D. altaiense*; B.M. 1009.) Rock-garden.

**D. Hemsleya′num.** Erect, tufted perennial, about 18 in. h. Stem hairy, branched, very leafy. *l.* oblong or elliptic oblong, up to 2 in. long, and ½ in. wide, entire, sessile. *fl.* in a loose spike about 8 in. long; the cymes 3- to 7-fld., pedicels very short; purplish-blue, 1 to 1¼ in. long, about ⅓ in. wide at mouth; anthers glabrous. June. 1935. (B.M. 9547.)

**D. heterophyl′lum.** Dwarfer than *D. Moldavica.* Stem ascending. *l.* roundish, kidney-shaped, blunt, with rounded teeth, base cordate, rugose; stalked; upper *l.* oblong. *fl.* in a dense spike, bluish; cor. hairy. Cent. Asia.

**D. ibe′ricum.** A synonym of *Lallemantia iberica.*

**D. imber′be.** About 6 in h., *fl.* branches erect. *Radical l.* long-stalked; *stem-l.* few, short-stalked; all reniform, deeply crenate. *fl.* lilac-blue, about 1 in. long; lips nearly equal; bracts wedge-shaped, deeply cut, glabrous. Siberia. 1883. (G.F. 1080, f. 4, 5.)

**D. integrifo′lium.** Shrubby, erect, glabrous or minutely hairy. *l.* ovate-lanceolate or oblong, acute, muticous, almost entire; stalk very short. *fl.* in an interrupted somewhat secund spike, purplish; cor. about twice as long as cal.; bracts oblong, bristly toothed. Altai Mts.

**D. Isabel′lae.** Stem 12 to 20 in. h., covered with dense, white, crisped hair. *l.* cut to base into 5 to 7 linear segs., lower segs. ⅔ to ⅘ in. long, nearly entire. *fl.* deep purple-blue, 1½ in. long, in 4- to 6-fld. whorls making a close, spike-like raceme 3½ to 4 in. long. W. China. 1914. Rock-garden. (B.M. 8952.)

**D. japon′icum.*** Habit of *D. Ruyschianum,* about 2 ft. h. *fl.* white, mid-lobe of cor. with a blue border and white spots. Japan. 1879.

**D. Moldav′ica.** Annual. Stem erect, branched, about 18 in. h. *l.* lanceolate, deeply crenate, stalked. *fl.* blue or white in distinct whorls forming a long raceme; bracts narrow. July. E. Siberia. 1596.

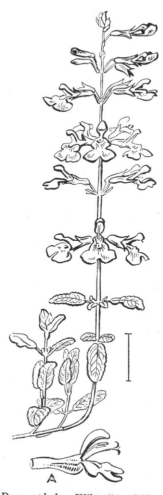

*Dracocephalum Wilsonii* (p. 712)

**D. nu'tans.** Stems erect, about 12 in. h. *l.* ovate, crenate, stalked. *fl.* blue in many-fld. distinct whorls on a long drooping raceme; bracts oblong-lanceolate. July. E. Russia. 1731. (B.R. 841.) Rock-garden.

**D. pelta'tum.** A synonym of *Lallemantia peltata*.

**D. peregri'num.** Decumbent with ascending branches. *l.* lanceolate, usually with a few teeth, glabrous; stalked short. *fl.* blue in few-fld. distinct whorls, forming a secund panicle about 18 in. long. July. Siberia. 1759. (B.M. 1084.)

**D. Ruprech'tii.** Of neat habit, about 18 in. h. *l.* ovate-lanceolate, variously cut and toothed. *fl.* rose-purple or lilac, about 1 in. long, in axillary clusters. Turkestan. 1880. (G.F. 1018.)

**D. Ruyschia'num.** Stem erect, finely downy, 2 ft. h. *l.* linear-lanceolate, 1 to 1½ in. long, entire, margins revolute; nearly sessile. *fl.* purplish, 1 in. long; whorls generally 6-fld., approximate, forming a spike. June. Europe. 1699. var. **japon'icum**, a synonym of *D. japonicum*.

**D. sibi'ricum.** 15 to 40 in. h. *l.* oblong-lanceolate, 2 to 3½ in. long, toothed, dark green and minutely hairy above, with minute golden glands beneath; stalks ⅛ to ⅝ in. long. *fl.* bluish or lavender-violet, 1 to 1¼ in. long, hairy without, tube straight; cal. about ⅔ in. long; infl. 5 to 10 in. long, with up to 12 whorls clearly separated from one another, each often many-fld. S. Siberia, Mongolia, Kansu. 1760. (B.M. 9646.) Syn. *D. Stewartianum* of gardens, *Nepeta macrantha*, *N. Stewartianum*. Border.

**D. specio'sum.** A synonym of *D. Wallichii*. The N. American plant offered under this name is *Physostegia virginiana*.

**D. Stewartia'num** of gardens. A synonym of *D. sibiricum*. The true *D. Stewartianum* has a curved cor. and the floral whorls crowded in the upper part of the infl.

**D. tangu'ticum.** Aromatic herb, 6 to 16 in. h. *l.* as in *D. Isabellae*. *fl.* deep blue, smaller than in *D. Forrestii*. China. Rock-garden.

**D. tenuiflo'rum.** Very similar to *D. sibiricum* but *fl.* ½ to ⅔ in. long, *l.* bluntly toothed, 2¼ to 4 in. long. Yunnan.

**D. Veitch'ii.** Habit of *D. sibiricum*. *l.* toothed or nearly entire and sessile or very shortly stalked. *fl.* about 1 to 1¼ in. long, tube straight, upper whorls very close, bracts linear or subulate. Szech-wan, Kansu. 1905. Syn. *Nepeta Veitchii*. Border.

**D. virginia'num.** A synonym of *Physostegia virginiana*.

**D. Wallich'ii.** About 18 in. h. *Radical l.* broadly heart-shaped, stalks long; *stem-l.* few, stalks short; all wrinkled and green on both sides, hairy beneath. *fl.* pinkish-blue, smaller than in *D. bullatum*, lip with darker spots; whorls 2 to 4, dense, more or less 1-sided. June. Himalaya. 1877. (B.M. 6281.)

**D. Wil'sonii.** Habit of *D. sibiricum* but *l.* blunt, regularly crenate, upper sessile or nearly so. *fl.* about 1 in. long; cor. tube much curved; whorls as in *D. Veitchii*; bracts lanceolate to elliptic. Szech-wan, Yunnan. 1905. Syn. *Nepeta Wilsonii*. Border.

**DRACONTIOI'DES** (Dracontium-like). Fam. *Araceae*. A genus of a single species of marsh herb, native of Brazil, related to Urospatha but with the ovary 2-celled with 1, not 2, ovule in each, and the spathe long and lanceolate, spirally contorted near apex. Seed smooth, not warted. For treatment *see* **Urospatha**.

**D. descis'cens.** *rhiz.* spongy. *l.-stalk* more than double as long as blade, up to 2 ft., spotted purple; blade, about 10 in. long, sagittate, lower lobes rather longer than upper, oblong-lanceolate. *Peduncle* up to nearly 3 ft. long. *Spathe* about 4 in. long, convolute below, gaping above, with a long slender point, brownish-violet outside with pale stripes, purple within with deeper stripes; spadix about 1½ in. long. Brazil. 1860.

**DRACON'TIUM** (ancient Greek name for a plant with 'serpent' or 'dragon' colouring). Fam. *Araceae*. A genus of 10 species of tuberous Andean herbs with gigantic solitary leaves on long stalks. Leaves deeply 3-partite, the divisions again cut. Peduncle at flowering time short, lengthening later. Spathe oblong, cuspidate, hooded, persistent, glaucous green or green or reddish-brown without, usually reddish-purple within. Spadix short-stalked, densely many-flowered, much shorter than spathe. Flowers hermaphrodite, with 4 to 8 perianth segments, and usually 4 to 6 stamens, rarely 9 to 12. Fruit a berry with 2 to 5 one-seeded cells. For treatment *see* **Amorphophallus**. The foliage of these plants is very striking but the flowers usually have a fetid odour.

**D. as'perum.** *l.-stalk* up to 10 ft. long, mottled with livid-green and brownish or lilac spots and bands; blade 3-partite, 3 ft. across; the middle lobes 2-partite, and all irregularly and unequally pinna-tipartite; ultimate segs. oblong or oblong-lanceolate. *Peduncle* 4 in. or more long. *Spathe* 4 to 6 in. long, incurved at tip, firmly leathery, persistent, brownish-green without, dark violet within, hooded. Brazil. 1869. (Ref. B. 382; I.H. 1865, 424 as *Amorphophallus nivosus*; G.C. 1870, 344 as *D. elatum*.)

**D. Card'eri.** *l.-stalk* slender, about 3 ft. long, irregularly spotted brown on dull flesh-colour; blade 3-partite, often twice dichotomous, segs. oblong, rachis irregularly winged. *Peduncle* slender, up to 6 ft. long, smooth. *Spathe* lanceolate, 12 in. long, lurid green without, midrib red-brown, reddish-purple within. Colombia. 1877. (B.M. 6523.)

**D. ela'tum.** A synonym of *D. asperum*.

**D. foecun'dum.** Tuber surrounded by numerous tubercles, rising just above ground. *l.-stalk* about 6 ft. long, mottled grey; blade 4 to 5 ft. across, 3-partite; lobes pinnately divided; segs. mostly lanceolate or ovate-lanceolate. *Peduncle* rough, greyish-purple, 2 to 3 ft. long. *Spathe* oblong-lanceolate, boat-shaped, midrib brown, deep purple within. British Guiana. 1880. (B.M. 6808.)

**D. gi'gas.** Tuber as large as a man's head. *l.-stalk* 10 to 12 ft. long, spiny, shining metallic pale green, mottled brown; blade 9 ft. across, umbrella-like, deep green above, paler beneath, 3-partite; lobes 2-pinnate; ultimate segs. obliquely ovate or ovate-oblong. *Peduncle* 16 to 20 in. long with variegated sheath at base. *Spathe* about 2 ft. long, erect, convolute above middle, deep violet, brownish-red within. Nicaragua. 1869. (B.M. 6048 as *Godwinia gigas*.)

**D. polyphyl'lum.** *l.-stalk* 3 ft. or more long, livid purple with greenish-white; blade about 30 in. long, green, paler beneath, 3-partite, and again much divided; ultimate segs. usually obliquely oblong, acute. *Peduncle* very short in flower, afterwards lengthening. *Spathe* deep violet, oblong, cuspidate, about 6 in. long. Guiana. 1759. (B.R. 700.)

*dracontoceph'alus -a -um,* dragon's head.

**DRACOPHYL'LUM** (*drakon*, a dragon, *phyllon*, a leaf; the leaves resemble those of the Dragon Tree, *Dracaena Draco*). Fam. *Epacridaceae*. A genus of over 30 species of evergreen shrubs or (rarely) small trees, most abundantly represented in New Zealand, but also found wild in temperate Australia and New Caledonia. Leaves curiously resembling those of some monocotyledonous plants in clasping the stems, often lanceolate, pointed, or grass-like. Flowers in terminal racemes or spikes; corolla cylindrical or bell-shaped, with a limb of 5 spreading lobes; anthers 5, stalkless, at the mouth of the corolla. Cool greenhouse shrubs that like a peaty soil and treatment similar to that of Epacris. Some half a dozen species are grown in the open in Scilly.

**D. capita'tum.*** Shrub 2 to 4 ft. sparsely branched. *l.* ⅓ to 1 in. long, ⅛ in. wide, linear-lanceolate, slender-pointed, bases entirely covering shoots. *fl.* closely packed in heads 1 in. wide, terminating a stalk 3 or 4 in. h.; cor. pure white, tubular, with a limb ⅓ in. wide of 5 obovate lobes. April to June. W. Australia. (B.M. 3624.)

**D. grac'ile.*** Slender, sometimes straggling shrub, 3 to 4 ft., shoots slender. *l.* ⅓ to ½ in. long, narrowly lanceolate, much recurved, pointed. *fl.* closely packed in an ovoid head about 1 in. long, nearly as wide, at the summit of a slender stalk 2 to 4 in. long; very fragrant; cor. pure white, tubular, the limb ⅓ in. across the 5 obovate lobes. June. W. Australia. 1826. (B.M. 2678.)

**D. paludo'sum.** Shrub up to 6 ft. often flowering at a few in. h. *l.* 1 to 1½ in. long, crowded towards top of branches; base sheathing, ⅛ to ⅓ in. wide; margins ciliate. *fl.* white about ¼ in. long, in short spike-like racemes of 3 to 6. Chatham Is. (J.R.H.S. 37, 60.) Syn. *D. scoparium paludosum*.

**D. scopa'rium paludo'sum.** A synonym of *D. paludosum*.

**D. secund'um.*** Shrub 1 to 2 ft. *l.* 2 to 4 in. long, linear-lanceolate, tapering from base to a long slender point, bases clasping and hiding stem. *fl.* on slender cylindrical spikes up to 6 in. long, ⅓ to 1 in. wide; cor. white, tubular, ⅓ to ½ in. long, ⅓ in. wide, with a limb of 5 tiny triangular lobes. April. New S. Wales. 1823. (B.M. 3264.)

W. J. B.

**DRACUN'CULUS** (name used by Pliny for a plant with a curved rhizome). Fam. *Araceae*. A genus of 2 species related to Arum with which it has often been combined, but with the ovules attached at the base and apex of the ovary not on its walls and the leaves pedate; from Helicodiceros the contiguous position of the male and female flowers on the spadix distinguish it, in Helicodiceros they are separated by rudimentary flowers. For cultivation *see* **Arum**.

**D. canarien'sis.** *l.-segs.* long-lanceolate, middle ones about 5 to 6 in. long, pale green; stalk 12 to 16 in. long, striate, sheath with greenish-purple spots. *Peduncle* 16 to 20 in. long, spotted. *Spathe* narrow, pale green; tube oblong, about 2 in. long; blade 8 to 12 in. long, lanceolate. Appendix of spadix like a mouse-tail, yellow, 8 to 9 in. long. Madeira, Canary Is.

**D. vulga'ris.** Tuber about 2 in. across. *l.-segs.* 13 to 15, bright green, middle ones 6 to 8 in. long, about 2 in. wide; stalk 8 to 12 in. long. *Peduncle* not spotted, 12 in. or more long. *Spathe* tube 2¼ to 3 in. long, purplish-white, except the mouth which is striped purple; blade widely ovate-oblong, purple, deeper at margin, 8 to 12 in. long. Appendix of spadix about 3 in. long with a purple club-like end. Mediterranean region. (G.C. 47 (1910), 198.) Syn. *Arum Dracunculus.* var. **cre'ticus,** peduncle densely spotted, *spathe* tube white, spotted dark purple at mouth, blade dark purple. Greece, Crete. Syn. *D. creticus.*

**DRAGON, GREEN.** *See* **Arisaema Dracontium.**

**DRAGON-ROOT.** *See* **Arisaema Dracontium** and **A. triphyllum.**

**DRAGON TREE.** *See* **Dracaena Draco.**

**DRAGONFLIES** (Order *Odonata*) are predaceous insects with strongly developed biting mouthparts and with large and prominent eyes. The immature stages (nymphs or naiads) are aquatic and have a characteristic prehensile lower lip which is used for seizing prey. They feed on insects, fish fry, and other aquatic animals.

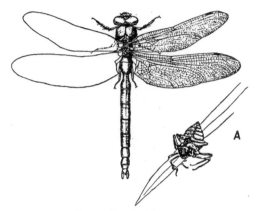

*Dragonfly. A. Nymph*

Dragonflies abound in the neighbourhood of ponds, streams, canals, rivers, and lakes, and are noted for the beauty and brilliancy of their colouring and, in the larger species, for their swift flight. There are over forty British species which have been described and figured by Lucas (*British Dragonflies*, 1900), who has also described and figured the immature stages (*Aquatic (Naiad) Stage of British Dragonflies*, Ray Soc., 1930). There are two Sub-orders, namely, the *Anisoptera*, which include the strongly built, swift-flying insects whose wings are held open in repose; and the *Zygoptera*, which include the weak, slender-bodied, feeble-flying insects whose wings are held closed over the body when at rest. The eggs may be either dropped into the water during flight or attached loosely to the leaves of water plants. The name given to these insects in some districts is 'Horse-stingers', but no sting is present, though the habit of the insect in bending its body down and round the fingers on handling may suggest that the insertion of a sting is imminent. The food habits of these insects should render them free from molestation for, as 'hawks' of the insect world, they capture and devour many kinds of insects. The presence of their ravenous nymphs in fish hatcheries may necessitate measures to destroy them in such situations.

G. F. W.

**DRAGON'S BLOOD.** The resin that exudes from the *Dracaena Draco* and some other plants.

**DRAGON'S HEAD.** *See* **Dracocephalum.**

**DRAINAGE.** Efficient drainage is one of the most important points in connexion with the cultivation of garden crops. Few plants will succeed in an undrained soil which soon becomes sour and waterlogged, whether in a pot or in the open ground.

In draining, first it should be ascertained whether there is a permanent accumulation of water just under the soil or whether it is surface water only that will need to be conducted away. Land somewhat light on the surface with a gravelly sub-soil will generally be sufficiently porous to let all such water pass away naturally, but heavy soils with a sub-soil of clay require an efficient system of drainage to render them fit for cultivation.

Water collecting underneath the surface is the most troublesome. If this can be removed, the surface water will naturally follow and this will be succeeded by fresh air drawn into the soil.

For conducting away water a main drain of sufficient size to take water from all of its branches along its course should first be laid. A means of outlet lower than any part of the land to be drained is, of course, essential and the main drain should proceed so far as possible in a straight line and with an even gradient from the highest point to the point of outfall. A fall of one in a hundred is desirable, although many drains have to be laid and work satisfactorily with less fall.

Branches 10 to 20 ft. apart according to the nature of the ground should be arranged to meet the main drain at an angle not wider than 60 degrees. No two branches should meet the main drain at the same point but should run in alternately from each side. Not less than 4-in. diameter pipes should be used for the main drain with 3-in. pipes for the branches, socket pipes being fixed in the main drain for the reception of the branches. The requisite depth for drains varies with the different soils, the fall of the ground and the purpose for which it is used, but for general garden purposes the pipes should be kept not less than 3 ft. below the surface. For lawns, pipes may often with advantage be laid within 18 in. of the surface but where the soil has a tendency to dry out readily, the laying of pipes too near the surface may cause browning of the turf over the line of the pipes during dry spells.

For land drainage glazed and common earthenware pipes are both largely used. The former are the more expensive but are the stronger and best suited for mains. They should be fitted together closely and if passing near trees the joints should be cemented to prevent the entry of tree roots. Another type of pipe now extensively used is that having thick walls of porous concrete similar in composition to that of a breeze block. This adds considerably to their draining capacity.

Draining, to be effective, must be systematically carried out and levels properly calculated and set out by means of level pegs and boning rods. The main drain should be laid first and work begun at the higher end, proceeding with a regular fall towards the outlet. Where the trenches are very deep it may be necessary to shore up the sides with timber, and tools specially employed for draining should be used. Before filling in with soil over the pipes a covering of clinker, or broken stones will greatly assist the percolation of water and help to keep the pipes free from obstruction. Heather or brushwood may also be used.

The provision of drainage for plants in pots and boxes is no less important. This is usually carried out by placing crocks over the holes in the bottom of the container and covering with a layer of porus material such as moss, decayed leaves. *See* under **Planting,** Suppl.

**DRA'KAEA** (named in honour of Miss Drake, botanical artist for the Botanical Register). Fam. *Orchidaceae.* A genus comprising 7 or 8 species of extremely curious Australian terrestrial Orchids. The term hammer orchids has been applied to them owing to the hammer-like appearance of the lip which is delicately poised on a slender, hinged, comparatively long claw, the blade, which in some species is hairy, moving with every breeze; resembling an insect. All are small and require similar treatment to Caleana to which they are allied.

**D. elas'tica.** *fl.* solitary; sep. and pet. ½ in. long, linear, reflexed; dorsal sep. longer and erect; lip upturned at the tip, solid and fleshy, the basal part of claw marked with light and dark bands, general colour reddish-purple. Stem 6 in. or more h. *l.* solitary, basal, heart-shaped, ½ in. wide. (G.C. 9 (1878), 213.)

**D. glyptopo'don.** Habit much as in *D. elastica.* Lip hairy at base, the shape so curious that it has been likened to a miniature Glyptopodon. (F.O.A. 2, pt., 29.)

**D. irrita'bilis.** *fl.* 10 to 20, small yellowish-green with red or purplish markings; terminal lobe hammer-shaped with a tuft of hairs. 6 to 12 in. h. *l.* 2 to 4, lanceolate, 1 to 3 in. long. (R.X.O. 2, 189.) Syn. *Spiculaea irritabilis.*

**D. Jeanen'sis.** Similar to *D. elastica. fl.* bright reddish-brown; terminal lobe densely covered with branching hairs.

E. C.

**drawn,** of spindly growth with thin stem and long internodes, the result of overcrowding leading to obstruction of light and check to transpiration, or of growing too far from the glass in a greenhouse or frame, or of having too great an amount of water and heat in relation to the intensity of light. A drawn condition is to be avoided as likely to lead to weakness, and is only to be encouraged when material for propagation of a plant difficult to root is required.

**DREG'EA.** A synonym of Wattakaka.

*Dreg'ei, Dregea'nus -a -um,* in honour of Johann Franz Drege, 1794–1881, German botanist who collected in S. Africa.

*Drenow'skyi,* in honour of M. Drenowsky who discovered *Fritillaria Drenowskyi.*

**DREPANIUM.** A cymose inflorescence with the lateral branches on the same side of the main axis and in a straight line, as seen in Juncus.

*drepa'nus -a -um (drepano-* in compound words), sickle-shaped.

**DRESSING.** (1) An old term for digging and general care of the garden. (2) The addition of manure, lime, &c., to the soil. If applied to the surface without digging or hoeing in, the material is termed a top-dressing.

**DRILL.** A shallow trench in which seeds are sown. It may be flat at the bottom and about 6 in. wide as is often made for sowing peas and broad beans, but is more often V-shaped. The depth of the drill must depend upon the size of the seed, the nature of the soil, and the season of the year. The depth of sowing should be such that the seed is covered to at least twice its diameter when the drill is filled and more if there is either risk of the soil becoming really dry around the seeds or of severe frost reaching them when germination occurs, thus in light soils sowing may, and often should, be deeper than in heavy ones and in very early spring deeper than somewhat later in the year. It is important that the drills should be straight and a uniform distance apart, and most important that they should be of equal depth throughout. A common fault is to have a curve in the middle owing to a slack garden line, and another is to have them more shallow at the end than in the middle, or of uneven depth owing to the use of the hoe to dig the soil out instead of to draw it out in forming the drill.

**DRIM'IA** (*drimys,* acrid; the juice of the roots is sufficiently acrid as to cause inflammation when applied to the skin). Fam. *Liliaceae.* A genus of about 15 species of bulbous plants, natives of S. and Trop. Africa, related to Scilla, but with compressed or angular seeds and connate perianth segments. Leaves lanceolate or narrow-

lanceolate. Flowers in a long raceme, somewhat spreading; perianth segments rather longer than the tube, spreading or reflexed. The Drimias need greenhouse protection and grow well in sandy loam and peat, being kept dry or almost so during the resting season, but none is of any great horticultural merit.

**D. ano'mala.** *l.* usually 1, sometimes 2, 18 to 24 in. long, ⅓ in. thick, rather fleshy. *fl.* yellowish, in a rather loose 30- to 40-fld. raceme, on a slender, terete, pale glaucous-green scape, 18 in. long. S. Africa. 1862. (Ref. B. 178 as *Ornithogalum anomalum.*)

**D. Co'leae.** *fl.* small, greenish; anthers purple. (B.M. 7565.)

**DRIMIOP'SIS** (*Drimia* and *opsis,* like). Fam. *Liliaceae.* A genus of about 5 species of bulbous plants closely related to Scilla and Ornithogalum, natives of S. and Trop. Africa. Leaves 2 to 4, oblong, sometimes distinctly keeled, often spotted. Flowers small, up to 30 or more, greenish-white, in a spike. Treatment as for Drimia.

**D. Kirk'ii.** Bulb globose, up to 1½ in. across, tunic thin, whitish. *l.* with fl., lanceolate, 12 in. long, narrowed to base, acute, pale green with dark green blotches above, paler beneath. *fl.* white, about ¼ in. long; segs. oblong, blunt, hooded at tip; spike 3 or 4 in. long, scape 12 in. July. Zanzibar. 1871. (B.M. 6276.)

**D. macula'ta.** Bulb globose, upper half scaly. *l.* cordate-ovate, more or less fleshy, acute, bright green above blotched deep green. *fl.* 12 to 20, lowest loose, white at first, becoming greenish-white; scape 8 to 12 in. long. S. Africa. 1851. (Ref. B. 191.)

**DRIM'YS** (*drimys,* acrid, from the taste of the bark). Fam. *Magnoliaceae.* A genus of 5 species, 1 S. American, 2 Australasian, 1 from New Zealand, 1 from Borneo. Evergreen rather tender shrubs (or trees) with alternate leaves, entire and glabrous, aromatic bark, and axillary and terminal flowers. *D. Winteri* grows freely in warm sandy loam against a wall if the winters are not too severe, but is then apt to cut back severely. It needs a little management in training and the shortening of its long branches. *D. aromatica* grows well outdoors in the south-west. Propagation is by cuttings of half-ripe shoots, under a glass in a cold frame, or by layers.

**D. aromat'ica.** Up to 15 ft. h. *l.* oblong or oblanceolate, blunt, light green with distinct transparent dots, veinless beneath. *fl.* in axillary and terminal clusters, white, ½ in. across, dioecious; sep. 3, very concave; pet. 6 or sometimes 8. April. *fr.* globose, sub-didymous. Tasmania. 1843. (B.R. 1845, 43 as *Tasmannia aromatica.*) Every part of plant highly aromatic and pungent. Fruit has occasionally been used as pepper.

**D. colora'ta.** Pepper Tree. Small tree up to 10 ft., branches stiff. *l.* of medium size, blotched red and purple, glaucous beneath. *fr.* a black berry. New Zealand. Syn. *Wintera colorata.* Tender.

**D. Winteri.** Winter's Bark. Up to 25 ft. h., young shoots reddish. *l.* oblong, 5 to 10 in. long, blunt, glaucous beneath. *fl.* milk-white, 1¼ in. across, fragrant of Jasmine; in clusters of 7 or 8 in long-stalked umbels; pet. 8 to 12, linear, spreading. S. America. 1827. (B.M. 4800.) Syn. *Wintera aromatica.*

**DRIVE.** A way for wheeled vehicles within the garden or estate for giving access from the road and connecting the house, garage, stables, or other important features. Where practicable a drive should extend to the kitchen garden in order to facilitate the delivery of manure, soil, &c.

In planning a drive, convenience must be the first consideration. It should be reasonably direct and safe at its junction with the road. It must also provide adequate turning and parking accommodation. (*See also* **Avenue.**)

For a forecourt giving full turning space a diameter of 60 ft. is necessary but with a small modern house this is often impracticable and even if there is room for a forecourt it is liable to dwarf the house and absorb valuable gardening space.

The following are possible treatments: (1) Straight drive to the garage only with a footpath to front door. (2) Two entrances and semicircular drive. (3) Single drive with a dead end for backing and turning.

For a single track the width of a drive should be 8 to 9 ft., for a double track 13 to 15 ft. Minimum radius for forecourt or bend 27 ft

Drives are usually made by rolling down successive layers of hardcore, coarse gravel, and top surfacing, after the ground has first been excavated to the required depth. On clayey or water-retentive soils it is advisable to lay a bed of clinker or ashes before the hardcore is put down, while on sites where the ground is exceptionally boggy layers of brushwood or heather will tend to prevent the hardcore from being swallowed up.

In constructing a drive it should be made with a camber, the centre after consolidation being 2 to 3 inches higher than the sides. Catch-pits should be arranged leading into drains at all places at which water is likely to collect. (*See* **Catch-pit**.)

A usual composition for a drive for light traffic is as follows: 6 to 8 in. of hardcore, 2 in. coarse gravel, and 1 in. fine hoggin (measured after rolling).

Hardcore should be free from rubbish and may consist of broken bricks, stone, or chalk, according to what is obtainable in the locality.

Coarse gravel, clinker, smaller broken stone, or granite is next laid, and finally the top surfacing material, which may consist, of fine hoggin; or pea shingle, clean small gravel or stone chippings bound with bituminous emulsion or tar. Various bituminous preparations are on the market which may be applied cold and at almost any time of year. After a firm and even surface has been obtained the bituminous liquid is poured over the surface from a can with special spreader and the shingle or clippings rolled into it. To obtain a completely waterproof surface, a second and for preference a third dressing should be applied at a few weeks interval. For length of life a tar-bound surface is superior but this needs to be carried out during dry summer weather and is hardly the job for the amateur.

Where gravel alone is used for the final surface it should be of a binding nature such as Farnham gravel. It must not be laid too thickly (about 1½ in. being sufficient) and should be watered in. Time must be allowed for it to dry out, during which all traffic must be kept off the drive.

Recently concrete roads and drives have become popular being clean, permanent, free from weeds and reasonably cheap. This type of drive, however, should not be attempted except under expert supervision, and is best entrusted to firms who specialize in this work.

J. E. G. W.

**DRONE FLIES** (Dipterous family *Syrphidae*), are larger and less conspicuously coloured than Hover Flies (q.v.). Their larvae are known as 'Rat-tailed Maggots' being provided with a long, flexible, telescopic breathing process at the end of the body, and are found in liquid mud, manure tanks, and dirty gutters. The adult flies are often confused with Hive Bees, which they closely resemble. The flies, like Hover Flies, visit flowers for pollen and nectar, and are useful pollinating agents in orchards.

G. F. W.

**DROPSY.** *See* **Oedema**.

**DROPWORT.** *See* **Filipendula hexapetala**.

**DROSAN'THEMUM.** *See* **Mesembryanthemum**.

**DROS'ERA** (*droseros*, dewy; from the gland-tipped hairs on the foliage). Fam. *Droseraceae*. A genus of about 80 species of annual or perennial usually glandular herbs, sometimes bulbous, of small growth but often beautiful, and interesting from their carnivorous habits; sometimes climbing. Leaves with reddish, sensitive glandular hairs, discharging from their tips a viscid fluid which retains and digests insects and other small creatures, the digested parts of which are absorbed by the leaves. When an insect comes into contact with the leaf the sensitive hairs curve inwards and entrap it,

the leaf spreading open again after digestion is complete. Flowers usually in scorpioid cymes, rarely solitary. Most species grow in boggy places, but the Australian species and some others grow in dry ground, remaining dormant for the greater part of the year until they are revived with the first rains. Droseras are easily grown in a mixture of peat and Sphagnum moss with good drainage and full exposure to light. They are best treated as greenhouse plants, the pots standing in a saucer of water. Propagation is by seed but *D. binata* which is the most frequently grown of the exotic species, while it may be increased by root division, is best raised from root cuttings. Pieces of the roots ½ to 1 in. long, are laid on the surface of shallow earthenware pans of sandy peat and covered to the depth of ½ in. with the same mixture. They are placed under a bell-glass in a damp, warm propagating house. In about 14 days swellings begin to form on the detached roots which increase in length until they reach the top of the soil usually in about 5 weeks. When 2 in. high they may be potted singly in the same mixture with some chopped Sphagnum added in small pots, and will if carefully treated soon make good plants. The tuber-forming species should be given a period of rest.

A

**D. an'glica.** Similar to *D. longifolia* but with longer, narrower l., the blade about 1 in. long, and larger fl. Europe, including Britain. (E.B. 183.) Hardy.

**D. bina'ta.** Perennial. About 6 in. h. *l.* all radical, deeply cut into 2 linear lobes, stalk long. *fl.* white, large, in a dichotomous raceme. June to September. Australia. 1823. (B.M. 3082.) Syn. *D. dichotoma*.

**D. capen'sis.** Perennial. About 6 in. h. *l.* nearly radical, linear-oblong, blunt, tapered to base; stalk glabrous, shorter than blade. *fl.* purple on an ascending, rather hairy scape, longer than l. June, July. S. Africa. 1875. (B.M. 6583.)

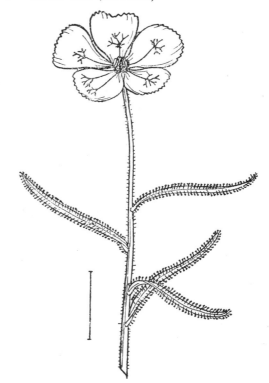

*Drosera cistiflora*

**D. cistiflo'ra.** Perennial, 6 to 12 in. h. *l.* 2 to 4 in. long, ⅛ in. wide. *fl.* scarlet, violet or white, nearly 2 in. across, 1 to 3 at end of stem; pet. wedge-shaped, obovate, outer margin erose, rounded, truncate or retuse. S. Africa. 1889. (B.M. 7100.)

**D. dichot'oma.** *See* **D. binata**.

**D. filiform'is.** Perennial. About 12 in. h. *l.* filiform, very long, from a bulb-like base; stalks woolly at base, much shorter than blade. *fl.* purple, large, on erect scapes scarcely as long as l. N. America. (B.M. 3540.)

**D. interme'dia.** A synonym of *D. longifolia.*

**D. linea'ris.** Perennial. *l.* linear, blunt, 2 to 3 in. long, scarcely ⅛ in. wide; stalk erect, naked, as long as blade. *fl.* white or purple. July. N. America. 1818. Hardy.

**D. longifo'lia.** Much like *D. rotundifolia* but *l.* much more erect, not half as broad as long, gradually narrowed to stalk. scape shorter, and less slender. Europe, including Britain. (E.B. 184.) Hardy.

**D. paucifo'ra.** Perennial. About 3 in. h. *l.* ovate-oblong, tapered to stalk. *fl.* white, 1 or 2 on a glandular-hairy scape. July, August. S. Africa. 1821.

**D. pelta'ta.** Annual, about 1 ft. h. *l.* scattered along stem, forming minute, flattened cups, the stalks attached to the bottom of the cups. *fl.* pink, in racemes. Australia. (G.C. 19 (1883), 436.) var. **folio'sa,** *fl.* white; **grac'ilis,** *fl.* pink.

**D. rotundifo'lia.** Annual, about 4 in. h. *l.* orbicular; stalk hairy, longer than blade. *fl.* white, on scapes 4 or 5 times as long as l. July, August. N. Hemisphere, including Britain. (E.B. 182.)

**D. spathula'ta.** Perennial. About 3 in. h. *l.* oblong-spatulate, somewhat narrowed to stalk. *fl.* purple, almost sessile, in short racemes; cal. and top of scape glandular. July. Australia. (G.C. 16 (1881), 852.)

**DROSERA'CEAE.** Dicotyledons. A family of about 90 species in 6 genera some of which are found in all parts of the world and all of which catch and digest insects—for details see the different genera. Plants herbaceous, usually perennial with radical rosettes of leaves. Flowers in circinni, rarely in racemes or solitary, perfect, regular, with parts in fives or fours. Sepals joined, petals free; ovary superior of 2, 3, or 5 united carpels. Fruit a capsule, usually with many seeds. Genera dealt with are Aldrovanda, Dionaea, Drosera, Drosophyllum.

**DROSOPHYL'LUM** (*drosos,* dew, *phyllon,* leaf; the leaves are beset with stalked glands each bearing a dew-like drop of a glutinous fluid by which insects are captured). Fam. *Droseraceae.* A genus of a single species of sub-shrubby carnivorous plant, native of SW. Europe and N. Africa. It needs greenhouse treatment and light sandy loam; good light and a fairly dry atmosphere suit it.

**D. lusita'nicum.** *Stem* 2 to 3 in. h., thick, woody, leafy at top. *l.* long-linear, narrowed to point, circinate, and revolute (a very exceptional and perhaps unique condition) in vernation. *fl.* yellow, large, in a corymb at the top of a leafy stem up to 12 in. long. Summer. 1869. (B.M. 5796.) The hairs are rigid, not motile as in Drosera.

**Drum'mondii,** in honour of (1) James Drummond, 1784–1863, Curator, Botanic Garden, Cork, d. W. Australia; (2) James Larson Drummond, 1783–1853, M.D., founder of Botanic Garden, Belfast; (3) James Ramsay Drummond, 1851–1921, Indian Civil Service; (4) Thomas Drummond, d. 1835 at Havana, brother of James, succeeded G. Don in the Forfar Nursery, collected in N. America, &c.

**drupa'ceus -a -um,** having stone fruit.

**DRUPE.** Fruit with a fleshy pericarp and a hard kernel; a 'stone fruit', e.g. cherry, plum.

**DRUPEL.** A small drupe, as the individual parts of a blackberry which is an aeterio of drupels.

**DRY ROT.** A term used to describe the condition of a dry spongy rot which occurs in many plants attacked by disease fungi, e.g. Gladiolus Dry Rot, Swede Dry Rot. Perhaps the best known is the disease due to the fungus *Merulius lacrymans* causing the dry rot of wood which attacks worked timber in houses and other buildings. This fungus is called the Dry Rot fungus although occasionally other fungi may do the same sort of damage. *M. lacrymans* may also appear on logs in timber yards but not on tree-stumps. Infection is more probable on badly seasoned wood or where ventilation is defective. The hardest kinds of wood may be attacked, even teak.

The fungus mycelium is at first superficial on the wood, then the threads penetrate and the wood eventually begins to crumble. A good deal of the mycelium remains superficial and under suitable conditions hangs as white flocculent masses with drops of water exuding, so suggesting the specific name *lacrymans,* i.e. weeping. Later the mass will become grey. The fructifications arise on the surface of the wood either as circular disks or more or less bracket-like, often large yellowish-brown and fleshy, with a white margin. The fungus exhibits two kinds of growth. One is of very fine threads which penetrate the wood and feed on it, and the other coarser with the threads usually woven into cord-like strands, white when fresh but becoming black with age and in thickness from that of a thread up to ¼ in. Thin sheets or thick pads of this growth may also be developed. These types of growth enable the fungus to spread over the surfaces or to run great distances and so to attack other wood away from the original point, and infection may thus spread through a building from cellar to roof, causing very great destruction with the collapse of woodwork or even parts of the building. It most frequently begins in cellars or under floors where the space is badly ventilated. Infected material previous to building should be burnt, well-seasoned wood only should be used, protected from wet during building and afterwards by proper ventilation. Good ventilation will prevent dry rot and the fungus will not establish itself where there is free circulation of air. For the protection of wood, painting with creosote is effective but its odour may be objected to in a house. Where the disease is found it is necessary to remove all the fungus both at the source and also any growths which may have extended to other places. Walls may need flaming and woodwork washing with formalin or a solution of mercuric bichloride. New wood can be so treated especially at the ends and ventilation must be improved. Dry rot in houses is sometimes caused by the fungus *Poria vaporaria* which can be distinguished from *Merulius lacrymans* by the fact that the cord-like strands remain white and even when old are tough, not brittle.

D. E. G.

*dryadifo'lius -a -um,* Dryas-leaved.

**DRYAND'RA** (in honour of Jonas Dryander, a Swedish botanist, 1746–1810). Fam. *Proteaceae.* A genus of about 50 species of evergreen shrubs confined to W. Australia. Leaves alternate, almost always more or less pinnately toothed or lobed. Flowers orange or yellow, densely packed in terminal or lateral heads surrounded at the base by an involucre of numerous overlapping bracts. Perianth slender, erect, the tubular base dividing above into four narrowly linear segments which broaden at the top and become concave where the stalkless anther is attacked; style erect, slender, often overtopping the anthers. A beautiful, once popular, but now neglected genus requiring cool greenhouse conditions like Banksias. A few species are grown outside in Scilly.

**D. arma'ta.**\* Shrub 2 to 4 ft., shoots downy. *l.* 1½ to 3 in. long, ½ in. wide, often crowded in terminal clusters, deeply pinnately cut into triangular or lanceolate, sharply pointed lobes. *fl.* yellow, crowded in terminal, broadly ovoid or globose heads 1 in. across; perianth 1 in. long, more or less downy. W. Australia. 1803. (B.M. 3236.)

**D. calophyl'la.**\* Low shrub with a short stem, erect or prostrate and clothed, like stalk and midrib of l., with bright orange-red hairs. *l.* often more than 1 ft. long, 2 in. wide, cut almost to the midrib into ovate-oblong lobes ½ to ⅝ in. wide. *fl.* golden-yellow, closely packed in a stalkless terminal head 2 to 3 in. across; perianth 1¼ in. long, tube silky, the 4 narrowly linear segs. shaggy. May. W. Australia. 1803. (B.M. 7642.)

**D. cardua'cea.** Shrub 4 to 12 ft. *l.* stalkless, 1 to 3 in. long, ½ to ¾ in. wide, lanceolate to linear-lanceolate, coarsely spine-toothed or pinnately lobed, dark green and glabrous above, white with close down beneath. *fl.* yellow, in terminal heads 1 in. across; perianth ¾ in. long, silky hairy. Spring. Queensland. (B.M. 4317 (narrow-leaved form).)

**D. floribun'da ma'jor.** Shrub 4 to 8 ft., shoots silky-hairy. *l.* stalkless, 1½ to 3 in. long, 1 in. wide, obovate, coarsely, prickly toothed. *fl.* yellow, numerous in terminal heads 1½ in. wide; perianth nearly 1 in. long, the tubular lower part silky. May. W. Australia. 1803. (B.M. 1581.) The typical form has l. often under 1 in. long.

**D. formo'sa.** Shrub 8 to 15 ft., shoots downy and hairy. *l.* 4 to 8 in. long, ⅜ to ⅝ in. wide, divided to midrib on both margins into triangular lobes, downy underneath. *fl.* yellow-orange, fragrant, in heads, 2½ in. across; perianth 1¼ to 1½ in. long, base glabrous, silky above, segs. densely villous. May. W. Australia. (B.M. 4102.)

**D. longifo'lia.*** Tall shrub, shoots downy. *l.* 6 to 12 in. long, ⅓ to ½ in. wide, pinnately and regularly lobed; lobes triangular, pointed, ½ in. wide, lower surface grey-downy. *fl.* yellow, crowded in a terminal head 1½ to 2 in. wide and h.; perianth 1½ in. long, the 4 slender segs. downy. February. W. Australia. 1805. (B.M. 1582.)

**D. nervo'sa.** A synonym of *D. pteridifolia.*

**D. nob'ilis.** Shrub 6 or 7 ft. Stems stout, woolly. *l.* 5 to 9 in. long, ½ to ¾ in. wide, pinnately cut almost to midrib into roughly triangular lobes recurved at the pointed apex, glabrous above, white with down beneath. *fl.* yellow, in heads 2 to 3 in. across; perianth 1½ in. long, downy; style 2 in. long. May. W. Australia. (B.M. 4633.)

**D. pteridifo'lia.*** Low shrub a few ft. h., shoots thick, densely downy. *l.* 8 to 12 in. long, pinnately and deeply lobed; lobes 1 to 2 in. long, linear to lanceolate, pointed, rusty downy beneath. *fl.* orange, closely packed in terminal heads 2½ in. across, set in a cluster of numerous rusty-downy bracts; perianth 1¼ in. long, loosely hairy. September. W. Australia. (B.M. 3500; B.M. 3063 as *D. nervosa.*)

W. J. B.

**DRY'AS** (Greek, a wood nymph). FAM. *Rosaceae.* A genus of 3 species of prostrate, evergreen, sub-shrubs in high mountains and cold regions of the N. Hemisphere, allied to Potentilla but with undivided leaves and flowers with 8 to 10 sepals and petals. Leaves alternate, with stipules adnate to petioles. Flowers solitary, white or yellowish-white, sepals persistent, stamens and carpels many, free. Fruits, achenes with persistent feathery style as in the related Cowania and Fallugia. Ordinary soil suits it, and in nature *D. octopetala* frequently grows on limestone rocks. Propagation is easy by August cuttings placed in sand, or by division of the already layered branches which root well into a sandy soil, or by seed. Seedlings take 2 or 3 years to reach flowering size and need to be moved carefully so as to avoid damage to the root. *D. octopetala* is an excellent plant for the rock garden, making, if left alone after planting as it should be, a wide mat of good foliage and flowering freely.

**D. Drum'mondii.** Similar to *D. octopetala*, but with crenate-dentate *l.* usually wedge-shaped at base on longer stalks, nodding, bell-shaped, yellowish *fl.*, and *fr.* with a style over 1½ in. long. Northern N. America. 1800. (B.M. 2972.)

**D. integrifo'lia.** A variety of *D. octopetala.*

**D. lana'ta.** A variety of *D. octopetala.*

**D. octopet'ala.** Mountain Avens. Trailing, mat-forming evergreen. *l.* elliptic-oblong, obtuse, deeply crenate, about 1 in. long, deep green above, white tomentose beneath, stalks about ⅜ in. long. *fl.* upright, white, about 1½ in. across, on hairy stalks 1½ to 5 in. long. June. *fr.* with feathery style 1 in. long. N. Europe, including Britain, N. America. (E.B. 459.) A variable plant. var. **integrifo'lia,** *l.* entire or scarcely toothed with revolute margins, *fl.* rather smaller than in type. SYN. *D. integrifolia, D. tenella*; **lana'ta,** smaller than type, covered with fine greyish down; **mi'nor,** with all parts about half as large as in type.

**D. × Suenderman'nii** (*D. Drummondii* × *D. octopetala*). *l.* and habit as in *D. octopetala*; *fl.* slightly nodding, yellowish in bud, opening white. 1919.

**D. tenel'la.** A synonym of *D. octopetala integrifolia.*

**D. tomento'sa.** *l.* obovate or elliptic, hairy on both sides. *fl.* yellow, sepals without glands. Rocky Mts., Canada.

**DRYMA'RIA** (*drymos*, wood; from the habitat). FAM. *Caryophyllaceae.* A genus of about 30 species of spreading, rarely erect herbs, natives of S. America, Asia, Africa, and Australia. Leaves opposite, broad or narrow. Flowers small, solitary or in cymes; sepals 5; petals deeply cut, white, usually shorter than sepals; stamens 5 or fewer. Seeds many. Of little horticultural value. Seed should be sown outdoors in spring on rather rich soil where the plant is to flower.

**D. corda'ta.** Annual or perennial to sub-shrubby, 8 to 24 in. h., glabrous. *l.* small, roundish ovate, acute, sometimes heart-shaped at base; stalk short. *fl.* small in a forked cyme, sep. and pet. about ⅛ in. long, smooth. June to August. Tropics.

**DRYMO'DA** (*drymodes*, woody; the plants are epiphytic). FAM. *Orchidaceae.* A genus of 2 species. *D. picta* is one of the smallest and most curious of orchids. It may be grown in a warm house on pieces of hard wood with the bark attached.

**D. pic'ta.** *fl.* solitary on a slender scape 1 to 1½ in. long, ⅝ in. long from the small, acute, yellow-green dorsal sep. to the purple lip, lateral sep. yellow-green with purple bands forming wings at the tip of a long, curved, green, purple-spotted stalk which projects from the base of the column; the column has 2 long, yellow, purple-spotted wings. *Pseudobulbs* clustered, discoid, dull green, with a minute central swelling from which springs a very short-lived l. Burma. 1871. (B.M. 5904.)

E. C.

**DRYMOGLOS'SUM** (*drymos*, wood, *glossum*, tongue; growing on trees and with tongue-shaped fronds). FAM. *Polypodiaceae.* A genus of 6 species of small creeping ferns with dimorphous fronds. Sori as in Taenitis. They are easily grown in the stove in a mixture of 2 parts leaf-mould, one of Sphagnum and one of peat with a little silver sand and some will grow luxuriantly on cork bark for several years. The slender rhizomes adhere firmly to bark, especially if it is so placed as to be permanently moist. The ferns like strong light but moisture on the fronds is harmful. Propagation is usually effected by dividing the rhizomes. *D. heterophyllum* is very effective when grown on a piece of dead Tree-fern.

**D. carno'sum.** *rhiz.* wide-creeping, filiform. Barren *fronds* suborbicular or elliptical, 1 to 2 in. long, ¾ in. wide; fertile linear-spatulate, 2 to 3 in. long, ⅓ in. wide, both narrowed to base. *Sori* in a line mid-way between margin and midrib, at first covered with stalked, peltate scales. Himalaya, China. (F.B.I. 55.) var. **sub-corda'tum** has smaller *fronds* (barren roundish, almost sessile), thinner texture and *sori* nearer midrib. China, Japan.

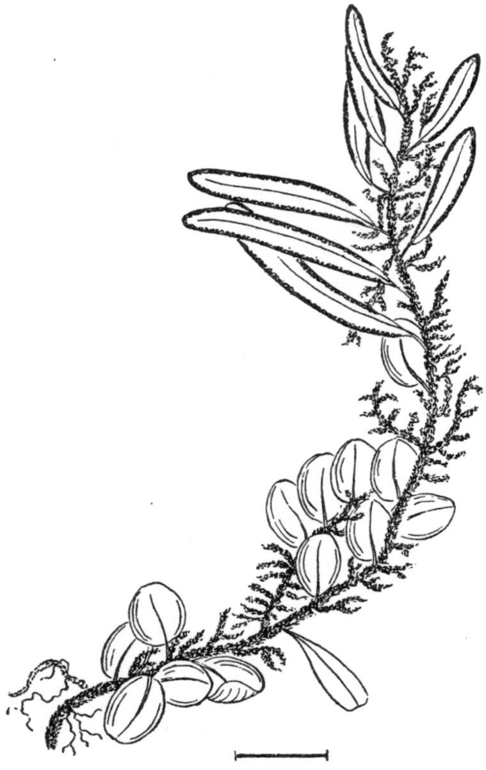

*Drymoglossum heterophyllum*

**D. heterophyl'lum.** *rhiz.* creeping, filiform. Barren *fronds* roundish, ½ to 2 in. long, ½ to ¾ in. wide; fertile linear-oblong, 2 to

4 in. long, ⅛ to ¼ in. wide; both narrowed to base. *Sori* in a broad continuous submarginal line; sporangia mixed with stellate hairs. Trop. Asia. 1828. (H.G.F. 46 as *D. piloselloides.*) SYN. *D. spatulatum.*

**D. piloselloi'des.** A synonym of *D. heterophyllum.*

**D. rig'idum.** Barren *fronds* 1 to 1¼ in. long, half as wide, obovate, entire, with thickened edges, on firm erect stems 1 in. long; fertile 4 to 5 in. long, ⅛ in. wide, narrowed into a stalk about as long as the frond. *Sori* in a deep groove between midrib and margin. Borneo. (H.C.F. 96.)

**D. spatula'tum.** A synonym of *D. heterophyllum.*

**DRYMO'NIA** (*drymos*, an oak wood; the plants growing on trees). FAM. *Gesneriaceae.* A genus of about 15 species, natives of Trop. America, shrubs with prostrate, rooting, or climbing stems. Leaves opposite, thickish, toothed, stalked. Flowers whitish or yellowish, on short axillary peduncles, often solitary, mostly large; calyx large, oblique, 5-parted; corolla tube swollen, declined, gibbous at base, lobes 5, spreading, almost equal, stamens 4, perfect. Closely allied to Episcia. For cultivation *see* **Besleria.**

**D. bi'color.** A synonym of *D. serrulata.*

**D. marmora'ta.** Erect or climbing with more or less 4-angled stems. *l.* large, 6 in. long, 3½ in. wide, dark green, parts between the veins convex, glistening grey, purplish beneath; stalks long, reddish. *fl.* creamy-white; cor. lobes sharply toothed; cal. rose. Guiana? (B.M. 6763.)

**D. serrula'ta.** Climbing shrub. *l.* oblong, narrowed at both ends, hairy, toothed. *fl.* yellowish; cal. large, green. W. Indies. 1806. (B.R. 24, 4 as *D. bicolor.*)

**D. Turrial'vae.** Tall sub-shrub. *l.* broadly ovate, bullate, metallic in colouring. *fl.* white, large, drooping in axillary racemes, lower cor. lobe toothed, lip-like; cal. dull red. Costa Rica.

**DRYMOPHLOE'US** (*drymos*, oak wood, *phloios*, bark). FAM. *Palmaceae.* A genus of about 12 species of spineless palms with slender ringed trunks and pinnate leaves, natives of New Guinea, Australia, and the Pacific Is. Leaves terminal, regularly pinnatisect, segments wedge-shaped-oblong or linear, rather thin, 3- to many-nerved, margins recurved at base; rachis 3-sided, scaly, sheath long. Flowers monoecious in branched panicles; spadices springing from trunk beneath the leaf-crown; spathe 2 or many, the lower 2-crested. *D. appendiculatus* flowers when only a few feet high and is suitable for pot-cultivation in the stove-house, fruiting regularly every year. For cultivation *see* **Archontophoenix.**

**D. appendicula'ta.** 20 to 30 ft. h. Stem 3 to 4 in. thick. *l.-segs.* cuneate-oblong, irregularly toothed at apex, terminal one larger, fan-shaped. *fr.* olive-shaped, reddish, maturing in about 6 months. Moluccas. (B.M. 7202.)

**D. olivaeform'is** of gardens. A synonym of *D. appendiculatus.*

**DRYNA'RIA** (*dryad*, a wood nymph; the fronds much like oak leaves). FAM. *Polypodiaceae.* Over 20 species of ferns often included in Polypodium, differing from the species grouped under Aglaomorpha by the dimorphic fronds. The distribution of the genus is in E. Trop. Asia, E. Indies to Australia. Mostly epiphytic with short, thick, fleshy rhizomes and rigid fronds, the fertile fronds being mostly pinnate or pinnatifid. Sori round, small, numerous, sometimes confluent between the veins. For treatment *see* **Polypodium.**

**D. mol'lis.*** *rhiz.* stout, creeping, clothed with bright rusty-brown scales. *Fronds*, barren, 4 to 6 in. long, 2 in. broad, cut three-quarters of way to rachis into blunt lobes, papery; fertile 1½ to 2 ft. long, 6 to 8 in. broad, distinctly stalked, with blunt, entire lobes 2 in. long, and ½ in. broad, reaching nearly or quite to rachis. *Sori* in a single row on each side of, and close to, midrib. Himalayas, China. (B.C.F. 3, 204.) SYN. *Polypodium rivale.*

**D. propin'qua.** *rhiz.* wide-creeping, woody, with bright ferruginous scales. *Fronds* dimorphous; barren, 4 to 9 in. long, 3 to 4 in. broad, cut half or three-quarters of way into acute or bluntish lobes; fertile 1½ to 3 ft. long, often 1 ft. broad, with a distinct stem, and lobes 4 to 6 in. long, ½ to ¾ in. broad, reaching nearly or quite to rachis. *Sori* in a row near midrib, at junction of several veinlets. *Areolae* many. India, &c. (L.F. 2, 57.) SYN. *Polypodium propinquum.*

**D. quercifo'lia.*** *rhiz.* stout, with bright brown scales, nearly ½ in. long. *Fronds* dimorphous; barren 3 to 12 in. long, 2 to 6 in. broad, sessile, brown, rigid, bluntly lobed often half-way down; fertile on long stalks, 2 to 3 ft. long, 1 ft. or more broad, cut nearly to rachis into erecto-patent, entire lobes, 6 to 9 in. long, ½ to 1½ in. broad; main veins distinct to margin, with 4 to 6 quadrangular areoles between them with each 2 large sori and many lesser areoles between midrib and margin. India, Queensland, Fiji. 1824. (L.F. 2, 10.) SYN. *Polypodium quercifolium.*

**D. rigid'ula.** *rhiz.* wide-creeping, stout, with glossy-brown scales. *Fronds* dimorphous; barren sessile, 6 to 9 in. long, 3 to 4 in. broad, cut about half-way to the rachis into blunt lobes; fertile 2 to 4 ft. long, 1 to 1½ ft. broad, long-stalked, pinnate; pinnae 6 to 12 in. long, ¼ to ⅜ in. broad, 1 in. or more apart, narrowed or stalked at base, acuminate, inciso-crenate. *Sori* in a single row half-way between midrib and margin. *Areolae* many. Queensland, &c. (H.G.F. 5.) SYN. *Polypodium diversifolium, P. rigidulum.*

**DRYOBALAN'OPS** (*drys*, tree, *balanos*, acorns, *ops*, like). FAM. *Dipterocarpaceae.* A large evergreen tree, native of Sumatra. Stove conditions are necessary. *D. aromatica* furnishes the liquid Camphor-oil and crystalline solid, Sumatra or Barus Camphor, and is greatly prized by the Chinese.

**D. aromat'ica.** Tree up to 100 ft. *l.* elliptic, bluntly slender-pointed, entire, leathery, shining. *fl.* yellow, in panicles. SYN. *D. Camphora.*

**DRYOP'TERIS** (*dryad*, a wood-nymph, *pteris*, fern). FAM. *Polypodiaceae.* A very large genus of over 1,200 species which differ widely in size, texture, and the degree of cutting of the fronds, and in the nature of the veining. The sori are sub-globose, on the back or at the ends of the veins, the indusia cordate-reniform attached by the sinus. The genus is world-wide in distribution, several species being British. It includes many species remarkable for their decorative qualities, and some unequalled for their hardiness and power of endurance. Plants of all dimensions are found amongst them, from the tiny *D. sancta*, with fronds only a few inches long, to the majestic *D. villosa* or the beautiful and massive *D. Boryana*, both with very handsome fronds from 4 to 6 ft. and even 8 ft. in length. Whatever their size, however, most of the species are easily grown.

They grow well in a mixture of loam and peat, which, for the most robust, should be in about equal proportions, with a small amount of cow-manure previously dried and well mixed together, and a sprinkling of silver-sand; for the smaller and slower-growing species, less loam and more sand should be used. Most of them, especially the strong-growing kinds, are quite indifferent as to shading; a little sunshine acts as a strengthening agent, making the foliage last much longer during the winter than they otherwise do. They all require a good supply of water at the roots all the year round, but principally during the growing season. Although they do not actually suffer from occasional waterings overhead, it is very doubtful if they derive any benefit therefrom; the foliage of many kinds, being of soft texture, soon becomes spotted and loses its beauty if allowed to remain wet for any length of time. The plants must not be kept close; confinement leads to attacks of thrips and to browning of the mature foliage. The only way to avoid such unhealthy appearances is to grow the plants in well-ventilated houses, where moisture cannot condense on their foliage.

The species of Dryopteris are easily and rapidly propagated by spores, which are abundantly produced and germinate very freely; the species with creeping rhizomes may also be increased by division which is most successful during March and April.

The beautiful *D. cristata* is one of the rarest of British plants. Owing to its native places being boggy it is somewhat difficult to grow successfully for any length of time. As an outdoor fern, if planted in peaty soil near water, it will flourish as well as in its native habitat; but in less favourable situations it will become weaker every year, until finally, in 2 or 3 years, it dies.

*D. decomposita* is comparatively easy to grow, and is a most desirable plant. It is usually of medium growth, exceedingly useful for table-decoration, and also for growing in the rockery in front of taller kinds, as it is of a neat and compact habit. Its near relative *D. glabella* is well adapted for pots, or for planting in nooks in the rockery where there is but little soil or space at disposal. It is also a capital plant for fern-cases, as generally seen in dwelling-rooms, where it grows luxuriantly, its tender, soft green colour forming a striking contrast with plants of a darker hue. The beauty of this variety is readily destroyed by watering or syringing overhead, which causes the fronds, young or old, to assume a brownish, sickly appearance.

*D. erythrosora* is a highly decorative species, in many respects distinct, and deserves to be cultivated on a large scale. It has proved perfectly hardy even in London, having stood, without any protection whatever, our hardest winters; but under such treatment it becomes deciduous. When treated as a cool indoor plant its magnificent fronds, of a beautiful bronzy hue in a young state, but turning with age to a dark shining green, remain on the plant all the year round, and make it a very useful species for winter decoration. The whole plant is rendered exceedingly attractive by the bright red indusia, which contrast pleasantly with the dark glossy green of the upper surface of the frond. It is easily propagated from spores.

*D. Filix-mas*, when planted in naturally sheltered places, becomes almost evergreen, most useful for the rockery and shrubbery. Like many other ferns, it looks much handsomer when planted out, especially upon an irregular surface, in clumps of 6 or 8 strong plants each, with a few pieces of stone or rock, which greatly add to their appearance, laid in between and among them. The male fern is not, however, in any way fastidious, and will grow luxuriantly either in pots or planted out, in almost any soil, provided that during its growing season it receive a good supply of water at the roots; but it prefers a light and sandy loam to a stiff clay, and although it will bear exposure to the sun, yet it flourishes much better in a shady situation. It is readily propagated from spores, which are usually ripe about midsummer; and also from division of the crowns, which is a much slower process.

*D. hispida* is particularly adapted for growing in a fern-case in the dwelling-room, where, in company of Todeas and other filmy ferns, it will be found to thrive admirably; indeed, it is a plant rather difficult to manage in the open house, unless a close and shady corner can be devoted to it. Either as a pot plant or planted out it forms a beautiful and interesting object.

*D. parasitica* is an accommodating plant, succeeding in either stove or greenhouse. It does well grown in a pot or planted out in the rockery, where it forms a capital background, showing off to advantage other and choicer Ferns, and in which position it soon multiplies, as it is readily propagated from spores. Several varieties have been produced under cultivation, the most distinct being var. *corymbifera*. When given cool or intermediate treatment it is never, to our knowledge, attacked by any insect; it is only when grown in too warm a house that the plant is seen covered with Mealy Bug, which pest is only eradicated with great difficulty, as the texture of the fronds is very soft, and they do not bear fumigating or dipping in any insecticide.

Though generally considered as an evergreen greenhouse species, *D. Sieboldii* is sufficiently hardy to withstand the severity of an English climate, as it is reported to have withstood very severe winters.

*D. spinulosa* is well adapted for the moist parts of the Fernery or the shady parts of the shrubbery, where, through its bold, free habit, it is rendered very distinct and decorative. The plant will bear a moderate degree of exposure, though it prefers shade; but, whichever situation it may occupy, a good supply of water at its roots is necessary all the year round.

*D. triphylla* is one of the smallest species of this genus and can be grown in a fern case where it does well. *D. angustifolia*, *D. gigantea*, *D. reticulata*, *D. serrata*, and *D. Thwaitesii*, at one time grouped under Meniscium, are all swamp-growers and thus useful for planting on the margins of pools.

Many species now placed in Dryopteris have been called Nephrodium.

**D. abort'iva.** *sti.* tufted, 6 to 12 in. long, firm, erect. *Fronds* 1 to 2 ft. long, 6 to 8 in. broad; central pinnae 3 to 4 in. long, $\frac{5}{8}$ to $\frac{7}{8}$ in. broad, cut about one-third of the way down into close, entire, truncate lobes, $\frac{1}{8}$ in. broad; lower pinnae distant, and reduced suddenly to auricles. *Sori* medial. Malaya.

**D. aem'ula.*** Hay-scented Buckler Fern. *sti.* tufted, 1 ft. long, densely scaly below. *Fronds* lanceolate-deltoid, 1 to $1\frac{1}{2}$ ft. long, 6 to 10 in. broad, lowest pinnae much the largest; lowest pinnules larger than others, ovate-lanceolate, cut down to rachis below into deeply pinnatifid lobes, with aristate teeth; under-surface glandular. *Indusium* not gland-ciliated. W. Europe (Britain), Madeira, and Azores. (H.B.F. 20; B.C.F. 2, 467.) Syn. *Nephrodium Foenisecii*, *Lastrea recurva*. Hardy, smelling like hay when dried.

**D. africa'na.** *rhiz.* decumbent. *sti.* 6 to 12 in. long, slightly scaly below. *Fronds* soft, 1 to $1\frac{1}{2}$ ft. long, 6 to 10 in. broad, 2-pinnatifid; pinnae sessile, lanceolate, 3 to 5 in. long, about 1 in. broad, with blunt, undivided lobes reaching about half-way down. *Sori* narrow-oblong, simple, sometimes very profuse. S. Africa, India, &c. A strong-growing species. (L.F. 1, 12.) Syn. *Gymnogramma Totta*, *Leptogramme Totta*.

**D. amboinen'sis.** *sti.* tufted, 6 to 8 in. long, nearly naked. *Fronds* 2 ft. or more long, 8 to 12 in. broad; pinnae spreading, 3 to 4 in. long, $\frac{1}{2}$ to $\frac{5}{8}$ in. broad, cut about a quarter down into bluntish, slightly falcate lobes; lower pinnae shorter, deflexed. *Sori* in rows close to midrib; sporangia naked. Philippines, &c.

**D. am'pla.** *sti.* densely hairy at base. *Fronds* 2 to 5 ft. long, 2- or 3-pinnatifid; pinnules 9 to 12 in. long, lanceolate; ultimate segs. oblong, blunt, slightly indented. *Sori* large, in one row on each side of mid-vein, eventually covering whole under-side of the frond. Trop. America. (B.C.F. 3, 100.) Syn. *Phegopteris ampla*, *Polypodium amplum*, *P. lachnopodium*.

**D. angustifo'lia.** *sti.* sub-tufted, 6 to 18 in. long, firm, erect, slightly pubescent. *Fronds* $1\frac{1}{2}$ to 2 ft. long, 1 ft. broad; pinnae spreading, 4 to 6 in. long, $\frac{1}{4}$ to $\frac{3}{4}$ in. broad, gradually narrowed to a long acuminate point, sub-entire, cuneate, lower ones often stalked; fertile pinnae much narrower than the barren; rachis pubescent. *Areolae* 4 to 6 between midrib and margin. Trop. America. Syn. *Meniscium angustifolium*.

**D. arbus'cula.*** *sti.* tufted, 4 to 8 in. long. *Fronds* 1 to $1\frac{1}{2}$ ft. long, 6 to 8 in. broad; pinnae close, numerous, 3 to 4 in. long, $\frac{3}{8}$ to $\frac{1}{2}$ in. broad, cut down a quarter or less into blunt lobes, several of lower pairs short and distant. *Sori* in close rows. Mascarene Is., Ceylon, &c. (B.C.F. 2, 472.) Syn. *Nephrodium Hookeri*.

**D. asper'ula.** *sti.* brownish, firm, terete, pubescent. *Fronds* $1\frac{1}{2}$ to 2 ft. long, 1 ft. or more broad; lower pinnae 6 to 9 in. long, $\frac{1}{2}$ in. broad, unequal-sided, cut to rachis below into oblong, pinnatifid segs. villous. *Sori* copious, one to each ultimate lobe. Philippines. 1842. Syn. *Phegopteris asperula*, *Polypodium asperulum*.

**D. biseria'lis.** *sti.* slightly scaly, 1 to 2 ft. long. *Fronds* much-divided, 2 to 3 ft. long, 1 ft. or more wide; lowest pinnae 6 to 8 in. long, cut to rachis into oblong-lanceolate pinnules; lobes of pinnules thin, papery. *Sori* in pairs on lower lobes. Andes of Peru and Ecuador. Syn. *Phegopteris biserialis*, *Polypodium biseriale*.

**D. Borya'na.** *sti.* 2 to 3 ft. long, straw-colour or brownish, scaly. *Fronds* 6 to 8 ft. long, 2 to 3 ft. broad; lower pinnae 1 to $1\frac{1}{2}$ ft. long, 6 in. broad; pinnules lanceolate, 3 to 4 in. long, cut to a winged rachis into blunt, spreading, more or less toothed lobes $\frac{1}{8}$ to $\frac{1}{4}$ in. broad; rachis and under-side naked. *Sori* in rows near midrib. N. India, Japan, China. (F.S.I. 97.) Syn. *Nephrodium divisum*, *Lastrea Boryana*. Greenhouse.

**D. Brunonia'na.** *sti.* tufted, black, 4 to 6 in. long, densely dark brown scaly. *Fronds* 1 to $1\frac{1}{2}$ ft. long, seldom more than 4 in. broad; pinnae close, unequal, oblong-lanceolate, blunt, cut half-way to rachis into sharply toothed, blunt lobes. *Sori* abundant, midway between margin and midrib. Himalayas (at 12,000 ft.). (H.S. 4, 251.) Syn. *Lastrea Brunoniana*. Greenhouse.

**D. calcara'ta.** *sti.* densely tufted, straw-colour, villous above. *Fronds* 1 ft. long, 3 to 6 in. broad; pinnae spreading, 2 to 4 in. long, $\frac{3}{8}$ to $\frac{3}{4}$ in. broad, cut down two-thirds or more to rachis into oblique, sub-falcate, linear-oblong, acute or blunt lobes; rachis villous. *Sori* medial; indusium glabrous, persistent. China, India, Malaya. Syn. *Lastrea calcarata*.

**D. ca'na.** *sti.* densely tufted, 6 to 8 in. long, slender, finely villous. *Fronds* 8 to 12 in. long, 3 to 4 in. broad; central pinnae 2 in. long, $\frac{1}{2}$ in. broad, gradually narrowed from base to apex, cut nearly to rachis into close, slightly crenate lobes $\frac{1}{8}$ in. broad; lower pinnae distant, gradually smaller. *Sori* sub-marginal; indusium thin, fugacious. Sikkim. (F.B.I. 357.) Syn. *Lastrea cana*.

**D. chrysolo'ba.** *sti.* tufted, 4 to 6 in. long, slender, villose, scaly below. *Fronds* 6 to 9 in. long, 3 to 4 in. broad; pinnae $1\frac{1}{2}$ to 2 in. long, $\frac{5}{8}$ in. broad, cut nearly to rachis into close, blunt, entire lobes, $\frac{1}{8}$ in. broad, lowest pair deflexed and slightly stalked. *Sori* near apex. Brazil, Colombia. 1840. SYN. *Lastrea chrysoloba.*

**D. crena'ta.** *sti.* 1 to $1\frac{1}{2}$ ft. long, densely scaly at base. *Fronds* 9 to 18 in. long, deltoid; lowest pinnae much largest, deltoid, 6 to 9 in. long, 3 to 4 in. broad; pinnules lanceolate, often imbricate, with ovate or oblong pinnatifid segs. with blunt rounded lobes. *Sori* many; indusium large, pale, villous. Trop. Asia, Abyssinia. (H.S. 4, 240; B.C.F. 2, 553.) SYN. *Nephrodium eriocarpum, N. hirsutum, N. odoratum.*

**D. crista'ta.** Resembles *D. Filix-mas*, but fronds less erect, pinnae less regular; segs. broader, thinner, more wedge-shaped on lower side, much more toothed, lower ones sometimes almost pinnatifid, the plant then approaching *D. spinulosa*, from which it differs in the much narrower fronds, with segs. much broader and much less divided. *Sori* large, as in *D. Filix-mas*, with conspicuous indusium. Europe (Britain), W. Siberia, N. America. (H.G.F. 17; B.C.F. 2, 486.) SYNS. *Aspidium cristatum, Lastrea cristata.* var. **Clintonia'na** and **flo'rida** are vigorous forms, the latter with thickish, broadly lanceolate *fronds*, 1 to 2 ft. h., the barren fronds shorter. Hybrids with *D. marginalis* and *D. spinulosa* are known. The latter (SYN. *Aspidium uliginosum*) has broader *fronds* than *D. cristata* with smaller and more numerous pinnules, more acute and more deeply cut, sharply toothed at tips, *sori* covering lower surface. Hardier than type.

**D. cyatheifo'lia.** *sti.* 1 to $1\frac{1}{2}$ ft. long, firm, naked, straw-colour. *Fronds* $1\frac{1}{2}$ to 2 ft. long, 1 ft. or more broad; pinnae 6 to 9 in. long, 2 in. or more broad, cut down to a broadly winged rachis into falcate, entire lobes, $\frac{1}{4}$ to $\frac{3}{8}$ in. broad, lowest pair rather smaller and deflexed. *Sori* about the centre of veinlets. Mascarene Is. SYN. *Polypodium cyatheifolium, P. Sieberianum.*

**D. cyatheoi'des.*** *sti.* 1 to 2 ft. long, naked. *Fronds* 2 to 3 ft. long, 1 ft. or more broad; pinnae close, spreading, 4 to 6 in. long, $\frac{3}{4}$ to 1 in. broad, apex acuminate, margin irregular, with acute forward-pointing teeth $\frac{1}{12}$ to $\frac{1}{24}$ in. long, lowest pair not shorter than the next. *Sori* usually one on each veinlet, close to main vein. Sandwich Is. and Sumatra. (H.S.F. iv. 241A.) Greenhouse.

**D. decompos'ita.*** *rhiz.* wide-creeping. *sti.* 1 to $1\frac{1}{2}$ ft. long, scaly at base. *Fronds* 1 to 2 ft. long, 1 ft. or more broad, ovate-lanceolate or deltoid; lower pinnae much the largest, deltoid, 4 to 9 in. long, 2 to 4 in. broad; pinnules lanceolate, more or less deeply pinnatifid; segs. unequal-sided, ovate-rhomboidal, deeply pinnatifid, with toothed lobes. *Sori* rather large, midway between midrib and margin. Australia to Fiji. 1825. (B.C.F. 2, 492.) SYN. *Lastrea decomposita.* Greenhouse. var. **nephrodioi'des** has rather firm and shining *fronds* up to 3 ft. long, 4-pinnate, lower pinnae stalked, pinnules deltoid, 4 in. long, *sori* marginal, globose, sessile.

**D. decursivo-pinna'ta.*** *sti.* tufted, 3 to 4 in. long, scaly. *Fronds* 1 ft. or more long, 3 to 4 in. broad; pinnae linear, 1 to 2 in. long, $\frac{1}{4}$ in. broad, margin more or less pinnatifid, bases connected by a broad lobed wing, lower one gradually reduced and sometimes distinct; indusium minute, fugacious. E. Asia. SYN. *Lastrea decurrens.* Hardy.

**D. decussa'ta.** *sti.* 2 to 3 ft. long, stout, erect, polished upwards, scaly at base, sometimes slightly muricate. *Fronds* 3 to 4 ft. or more long, 1 to $1\frac{1}{2}$ ft. broad; pinnae 8 to 12 in. long, 1 to $1\frac{1}{2}$ in. broad, cut nearly or quite to rachis into close, spreading, entire, blunt lobes, with a large, subulate gland at base beneath. *Sori* in rows near midrib. Trop. America. (L.F. 2, 54.) SYN. *Phegopteris decussata, Polypodium decussatum.*

**D. deflex'a.*** *sti.* 6 to 12 in. long, stout, densely scaly. *Fronds* 1 to 2 ft. long, 6 to 10 in. broad; pinnae 3 to 5 in. long, $\frac{3}{4}$ to 1 in. broad, cut to a narrowly winged rachis into blunt, entire, falcate lobes, broad. *Sori* close to midrib. Brazil. (H.S. 4, 245.) SYN. *Nephrodium Raddianum, Lastrea vestita.*

**D. deltoid'ea.*** *sti.* tufted, 3 to 6 in. long, densely scaly. *Fronds* 1 to 2 ft. long, 4 to 8 in. broad; pinnae of lower third or quarter suddenly dwarfed, the larger 2 to 4 in. long, $\frac{3}{4}$ to 1 in. broad, cut two-thirds of way down into close entire lobes, $\frac{1}{8}$ in. broad. *Sori* nearer margin than midrib; indusium fugacious. W. Indies. (F.S.I. 118.) SYN. *Lastrea deltoidea.*

**D. denticula'ta.** *sti.* tufted, 1 ft. or more long, densely scaly at base, naked above. *Fronds* triangular, coriaceous, 1 to 2 ft. long, 8 to 12 in. broad; lowest pinnae much the largest; lowest pinnules largest, lanceolate, segs. cut into spatulate lobes, spiny. *Sori* scattered over whole under-surface. Trop. America.

**D. deparioi'des.** *sti.* firm, 1 ft. or more long, slightly scaly below. *Fronds* oblong-lanceolate, $1\frac{1}{2}$ to 2 ft. long; lower pinnae 4 to 6 in. long, lanceolate; pinnules unequal-sided, stalked, triangular, their broad, blunt, nearly quadrangular lobes distinctly toothed. *Sori* terminal in the teeth (as in a Deparia). S. India. (F.S.I. 104.) SYN. *Lastrea deparioides.* Greenhouse. var. **Thwaites'ii** has the *sori* marginal. SYN. *Nephrodium Thwaitesii.*

**D. Dia'nae.** *sti.* 1 ft. or more long, stout, with deciduous scales. *Fronds* 2 to 3 ft. long, 1 to $1\frac{1}{2}$ ft. broad; lower pinnae not reduced, 6 to 9 in. long, $1\frac{1}{2}$ to 2 in. broad, cut to a broadly winged rachis into oblong, entire or crenate blunt lobes; under-surface finely villous. *Sori* small, copious, distant from midrib. St. Helena. SYN. *Polypodium Dianae, P. molle, Phegopteris mollis.*

**D. diplazioides.** *sti.* 3 to 4 in. long, scaly below. *Fronds* soft, $1\frac{1}{2}$ to 2 ft. long, 2-pinnatifid; central pinnae 3 to 4 in. long, $\frac{3}{4}$ to 1 in. broad, cut about two-thirds of way into blunt, entire lobes, lower gradually smaller. *Sori* oblong, often reaching from midrib to edge. Mexico, W. Indies. SYN. *Gymnogramma diplazioides, G. Linkiana, G. rupestris, Leptogramme diplazioides.*

**D. dissec'ta.** *sti.* tufted, 1 ft. or more long, rather slender. *Fronds* 1 to 5 ft. long, 1 to 3 ft. broad, deltoid; lower pinnae varying from simply pinnatifid, with broad, blunt lobes, to 1 ft. long, with similar pinnatifid pinnules, centre usually uncut for a breadth of $\frac{1}{4}$ to $\frac{1}{2}$ in., and the uncut bluntish or acute ultimate divisions as broad. *Sori* copious, generally sub-marginal. Malaya to Madagascar. (B.C.F. 2, 503; H.S. 4, 261.) SYN. *Nephrodium membranifolium, Lastrea dissecta.*

**D. effu'sa.*** *rhiz.* short-creeping, woody. *sti.* 2 ft. or more in length, scaly below. *Fronds* pale green, decompound, 4 ft. long, 2 ft. broad, 4- or 5-pinnatifid; lower pinnae longest, 1 to $1\frac{1}{2}$ ft. long, often 1 ft. broad; pinnules lanceolate, closely set; segs. lanceolate, unequal-sided, lower cut to midrib into pinnatifid lobes. *Sori* scattered over under-surface, usually without indusium. Trop. America. SYN. *Polypodium divergens, P. effusum.*

**D. ela'ta.** *sti.* $1\frac{1}{2}$ ft. long, naked, greyish, sharply angled. *Fronds* 4 ft. long, 1 to $1\frac{1}{2}$ ft. broad; pinnae numerous, lowest short and very distant, largest 8 to 9 in. long, 1 in. broad, cut half-way to rachis into slightly toothed, oblong lobes; veins about 9 on each side, conspicuous above, with a sorus on each midway to margin. Guinea, Fernando Po. SYN. *Nephrodium venulosum.*

**D. erythroso'ra.*** *sti.* tufted, 6 to 9 in. long, more or less densely scaly. *Fronds* 1 to $1\frac{1}{2}$ ft. long, 8 to 12 in. broad, ovate-lanceolate; pinnae lanceolate, lowest largest, 5 to 6 in. long, $1\frac{1}{2}$ in. broad, cut to rachis below into oblong bluntish pinnules, 2 or 3 in. broad, slightly, sometimes spinosely, toothed. *Sori* in rows of 6 to 9 to a pinnule near midrib; indusium $\frac{1}{24}$ in. broad, flat, bright red when young. Japan, China. Hardy. SYN. *Lastrea erythrosora.* (H.S. 4, 253.) var. **prolif'ica** has rigid, deltoid, 2-pinnate, deep-green *fronds* with buds in the axils of segs. and on margin; pinnae rather distant, obliquely ovate-lanceolate; pinnules unequal, usually linear, acute, somewhat foliate, *sori*, large, reniform, over entire back of frond; indusia prominent. Japan. 1883.

**D. exten'sa.** *sti.* 1 to 2 ft. long. *Fronds* 2 to 4 ft. long, 1 to $1\frac{1}{2}$ ft. broad; pinnae 6 to 9 in. long, $\frac{5}{8}$ to $\frac{3}{4}$ in. broad, cut about two-thirds down to rachis into linear-oblong lobes; lower pinnae scarcely shorter than the rest. *Sori* in rows, nearly terminal in the veins, and not confined to lobes. Ceylon, Philippines, &c. (H.S. 4, 240.)

**D. Fil'ix-mas.** Male Fern.* *sti.* tufted, 6 in. or more, long, more or less densely scaly. *Fronds* 2 to 3 ft. long, 8 to 12 in. broad; pinnae lanceolate, 4 to 6 in. long, $\frac{3}{4}$ to $1\frac{1}{4}$ in. broad, cut down very nearly to the rachis into close, blunt, regular, sub-entire lobes, $1\frac{1}{2}$ to 2 lines broad, lower ones rather shorter than the others; involucre large, convex. Cosmopolitan. (H.B.F. 15.) SYN. *Lastrea Filix-mas.* Of this very widely distributed hardy species a very large number of forms have been described and grown, most of which will be found in detail in works on British Ferns.

**D. florida'na.*** *sti.* 6 in. or more long, with a few scales. *Fronds* $1\frac{1}{2}$ to 2 ft. long, 6 to 8 in. broad, oblong-lanceolate; fertile pinnae only on upper half, close, lanceolate, 3 to 4 in. long, 1 to $1\frac{1}{4}$ in. broad, cut down to a narrowly winged rachis into oblong, slightly crenate, blunt pinnules, their own breadth between them, and 2 rows of sori reaching from midrib nearly to margin; barren pinnae broader (lower rather reduced, and sub-deltoid), not so deeply cut, pinnules close. S. United States. Hardy.

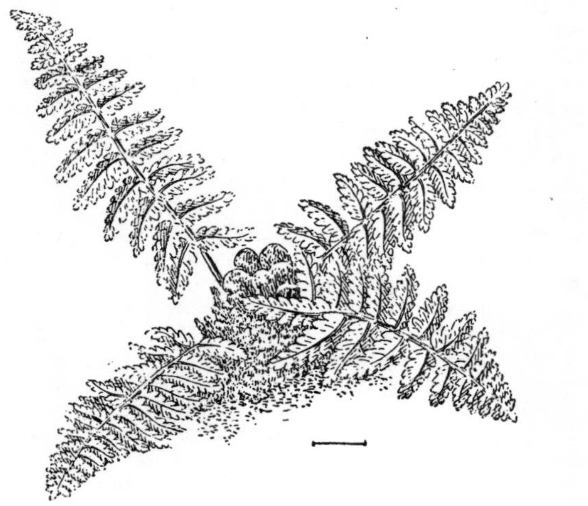

*Dryopteris fragrans*

**D. frag'rans.*** *sti.* densely tufted, very short, scaly. *Fronds* 6 to 9 in. long, $1\frac{1}{2}$ to 2 in. broad, oblong-lanceolate; pinnae $\frac{3}{4}$ in. long,

¼ to ⅜ in. broad, cut nearly to rachis below into oblong, toothed or pinnatifid lobes; lower pinnae reduced gradually. *Sori* in lower part of pinnules; indusium very large and membranous. Caucasus, N. Asia, Japan, Arctic America. 1820. (B.C.F. 2, 523.) Hardy.

**D. Ghiesbregh'tii.** *sti.* 1 ft. or more long, firm, erect, densely villous. *Fronds* 1 to 1½ ft. long, with a terminal pinna 6 to 9 in. long, 1½ to 2 in. broad, margin slightly lobed, with 3 to 6 similar pinnae on each side; rachis and frond densely villous below, slightly above. *Sori* in dense rows close to main vein. Mexico, Guatemala.

**D. gigan'tea.** *sti.* 1 ft. long, dark brown, slightly pubescent. *Fronds* simple, 1½ to 2 ft. long, 4 in. broad, elongate-oblong, narrowed rather suddenly at both ends, slightly repand. *Areolae* 30 to 40 between midrib and margin. Colombia, Peru.

**D. glabel'la.** Allied to *D. decomposita* but *rhiz.* short, *fronds* more finely cut, with more copious spinulose teeth, villous only on rachis above, glossy, lobes not imbricate. New Zealand, Australia, Polynesia. Syn. *Lastrea glabella.*

**D. glandulo'sa.*** *sti.* smooth, slightly scaly when young. *Fronds* glabrous, pinnate, 2 to 3 ft. long; pinnae distant, ovate-lanceolate, shortly petiolate, sub-cordate at base, crenate; lower ones almost opposite, upper alternate. *Sori* small, reniform. India, &c. (F.B.I. 132.)

**D. Goldiea'na.*** *sti.* tufted, 1 ft. long, scaly below. *Fronds* 2 to 3 ft. long, 1 ft. or more broad, ovate-deltoid; lower pinnae 6 to 9 in. long, 2 in. broad, cut nearly to rachis into linear-lanceolate, sub-falcate, slightly toothed lobes. *Sori* in rows near midrib. Eastern America. (B.C.F. 2, 527.) Hardy.

**D. gongylo'des.** *sti.* 1 to 1½ ft. long, naked. *Fronds* 2 ft. or more long, 6 to 8 in. broad; pinnae 4 to 5 in. long, ½ in. broad, edge cut from one-third to half-way down into spreading, triangular, acute lobes; lower pinnae not smaller. *Sori* near tip, principally in lobes; sporangia naked. Florida and W. Indies to Brazil, &c. (F.S.A. (2) 13.) Syn. *Nephrodium unitum.*

**D. grac'ilis.*** *sti.* short, glossy, scaly, about 4 in. long. *Fronds* very handsome, 2 to 4 ft. long, 1 ft. or more wide, soft, bipinnatifid; central pinnae 4 to 8 in. long, 1 to 1½ in. broad, cut nearly to midrib into slightly falcate lobes. *Sori* nearer margin than midrib. Jamaica, Guadeloupe. (H.S. 5, 292; B.C.F. 2, 251.) Syn. *Gymnogramma gracilis, Leptogramme gracilis.*

**D. gran'dis.** Trunk somewhat arborescent. *sti.* 2 ft. or more long, strong, glabrous, angular. *Fronds* 4 to 6 ft. or more long; pinnae lanceolate, 6 to 9 in. long, 2 in. broad, with entire, oblong-falcate lobes, ¼ to ⅜ in. broad, reaching down three-quarters of way to midrib. Brazil. Syn. *Polypodium macropterum.*

**D. Grisebach'ii.** Allied to *D. setigera*, differing principally in its larger size and in its stipes densely clothed at base with scales fully 1 in. long, leaving distinct tubercles when they fall. Cuba, Jamaica.

**D. hexagonop'tera.** *rhiz.* wide-creeping. *sti.* 1 to 1½ ft. long, slender, glossy, straw-colour. *Fronds* 8 to 12 in. long, nearly as broad, deltoid; lower pinnae 4 to 6 in. long, lowest pair deflexed, often 2 in. broad; pinnules reaching nearly to rachis, those of lower side 1 to 1½ in. long, pinnatifid half-way down with broad, blunt lobes; under side slightly villous. *Sori* marginal. NE. United States. 1811. Hardy. Syn. *Phegopteris hexagonoptera.*

**D. hir'tipes.** *sti.* tufted, 1 ft. or more long, densely scaly. *Fronds* 2 to 3 ft. long, 8 to 16 in. broad; pinnae 4 to 8 in. long, about ¾ in. broad, with broad blunt lobes reaching from a quarter to a third down, lower not reduced. *Sori* medial. China, Japan, Malaya. Syn. *Lastrea atrata.* (H.S. 4, 249; B.C.F. 2, 531.) Hardy, in general habit resembling *D. Filix-mas.*

**D. hir'tula.** *sti.* tufted, 3 to 4 in. long, densely scaly. *Fronds* oblong-lanceolate, 6 to 9 in. long, 3-pinnatifid, parchment-like, scaly on both sides, but especially below. *Sori* in a row on each side of, and close to, the midvein. Brazil. Syn. *Phegopteris hirsuta, Polypodium hirsutum.*

**D. his'pida.*** *rhiz.* stout, creeping. *sti.* 1 to 1½ ft. long, densely scaly. *Fronds* 1 to 1½ ft. long, 8 to 12 in. broad, sub-deltoid; pinnae lanceolate, lowest deltoid; lowest pinnules larger than others, which are lanceolate, with lanceolate segs. cut to a winged rachis into small, oblong or linear, sharply toothed lobes. *Sori* copious. New Zealand, Australia. Syn. *Nephrodium hispidum.*

**D. Hopea'na.** *sti.* 1 to 1¼ in. long, grey, glossy, naked. *Fronds* oblong-lanceolate, 1 ft. long, 6 to 7 in. broad, 2-pinnatifid; pinnae distant, sessile, caudate, lower 3 to 4 in. long, ⅝ to ¾ in. broad, cut to a narrow wing into ligulate-falcate, entire lobes ⅛ in. broad; tip of frond like one of pinnae; rachis grey, slightly pubescent. *Sori* crowded close to midrib; indusium firm, persistent. Polynesia. 1883. Syn. *Lastrea Hopeana.*

**D. inaequa'lis.*** *sti.* 1 ft. or more long, with a dense tuft of reddish-brown scales at base. *Fronds* 1 to 2 ft. long, 8 to 12 in. broad, ovate-deltoid; pinnae 6 to 8 in. long, 2 to 3 in. broad, lower rather shorter and broader; pinnules lanceolate cut nearly to rachis into oblong spinose-serrated segs. *Sori* in 2 rows near the midrib; indusium firm, naked. S. Africa. Greenhouse. (F.S.A. (6) 18.)

**D. inci'sa.** *sti.* tufted, 2 to 4 in. long, scaly below. *Fronds* narrow-oblong, 1 ft. or more long, ¾ to 1½ in. broad, leathery, finely hairy below, gradually narrowed towards base, with triangular or lanceolate lobes often not reaching more than one-third to rachis. *Sori* nearly marginal; indusium very fugacious. W. Indies, Colombia.

**D. interrup'ta.*** *sti.* 1 to 2 ft. long, slender, slightly scaly below. *Fronds* 2 to 4 ft. long, 1 ft. or more broad; pinnae spreading, 4 to 8 in. long, ¾ in. broad, acuminate, edge cut one-third or half-way down into oblong or subtriangular lobes. *Sori* marginal, and confined to lobes. Trop. Asia, &c. Syn. *Nephrodium pteroides.*

**D. invis'a.** *rhiz.* stout, wide-creeping. *sti.* 1 ft. or more long, stout, villose. *Fronds* 1½ to 2 ft. long, 8 to 12 in. broad; pinnae numerous, 4 or 5 in. long, ½ in. broad, cut about one-third down into sharp, triangular, falcate lobes; lower pinnae distant, dwarf. *Sori* in rows close to midrib; sporangia setose. Polynesia. 1830. Syn. *Lastrea invisa.*

**D. Jenman'i.** *sti.* stout, scaly, erect. *Fronds* 2-pinnate, about 2 ft. long, 9 to 12 in. broad, densely pellucid-dotted. Jamaica. 1887. Syn. *Lastrea Jenmani.*

**D. Khasia'na.** *sti.* 1 ft. or more long, naked, densely scaly at base. *Fronds* 2 to 3 ft. long, 8 to 12 in. broad; pinnae 4 to 6 in. long, ½ in. broad, sharply inciso-serrated to a depth of $\frac{1}{24}$ to $\frac{1}{12}$ in.; indusium fugacious. N. India, China. Syn. *Nephrodium cuspidatum.*

**D. lanugino'sa.*** *sti.* 3 to 4 ft. long, pubescent. *Fronds* 4 to 6 ft. long, 2 to 3 ft. broad; lower pinnae 1 to 1½ ft. long, oblong-lanceolate, with close, lanceolate pinnules, or sub-deltoid, some of pinnules of lower side compound; segs. oblong, bluntish, about ½ in. long, ¼ in. broad, more or less deeply pinnatifid. *Sori* copious; indusium firm. S. Africa, &c. Greenhouse. (F.S.A. (2) 21.) Syn. *Nephrodium catopteron.*

**D. lep'ida.** *sti.* green, setose on margins of groove down face. *Fronds* ovate, acuminate; pinnae alternate, very shortly stalked, lanceolate, acuminate, pinnatifid, central longest, glabrous, with hairy midribs and setose margins. *Sori* near midrib on each side, with inflated, roundish-reniform, lead-coloured, hairy indusia. 1886. (B.C.F. 2, 537.) Syn. *Lastrea lepida.*

**D. Lindig'ii.** *cau.* erect, with dull brown scales. *sti.* 2 to 3 in. long, slender, naked, straw-colour. *Fronds* 8 to 12 in. long, 2 in. broad; pinnae 1 in. long, ¼ in. broad, lanceolate, acuminate, cut to rachis into linear-oblong, pointed lobes; lower pinnae deflexed, gradually smaller, slightly hairy. *Sori* nearer midrib than margin. Peru to Colombia. 1830. Syn. *Phegopteris deflexa, Polypodium deflexum.*

**D. Linnaea'na.*** Oak Fern. *rhiz.* slender, wide-creeping. *sti.* 6 to 12 in. long, slender, straw-colour, scaly below, naked upwards. *Fronds* 6 to 10 in. each way, deltoid; lower pinnae much the largest; pinnules lanceolate, only lowest free, oblong, slightly crenate. *Sori* sub-marginal. N. Hemisphere (Britain). (H.B.F. 4.) Syn. *Thelypteris Dryopteris*; var. **Robertia'na** (Herb-Robert scented) has a thicker *rhiz.*, is more rigid, and finely glandular. (H.B.F 5.)

**D. lu'cida.** *rhiz.* short-creeping, with a few small, brown basal scales. *sti.* contiguous, 1 to 3 in. long. *Fronds* oblong-lanceolate, 2-pinnatifid, glabrous, 1 to 1¼ ft. long, 5 to 6 in. broad; pinnae 12 to 20 pairs, sessile, linear, pinnatifid. *Sori* apical on veins. Madagascar. 1877. Habit of *D. sophoroides.*

**D. margina'lis.** *sti.* tufted, 6 to 12 in. long, with large concolorous scales at base. *Fronds* 18 to 24 in. long, 6 to 8 in. broad, oblong-lanceolate, 2-pinnate; pinnae 3 to 4 in. long, 1 to 1½ in. broad; pinnules ovate-oblong, blunt, nearly entire. *Sori* marginal. E. United States. 1772. (B.C.F. 2, 542.) Hardy. var. **el'egans** has most of pinnules twice as large as in type, and all pinnatifid.

**D. Maximowicz'ii.** *sti.* light brown, glossy, scaly, 6 to 8 in. long. *Fronds* smooth, deltoid, 4-pinnatifid, about 1 ft. each way; lowest pinnae largest, long-stalked, on the lower side; lowest pinnules and segs. deltoid, stalked, cuneate at base; ultimate lobes unequal-sided, toothed. *Sori* small, just below final notches; indusium persistent. Japan. Syn. *Lastrea Maximowiczii.* Greenhouse.

**D. megal'odus.** Allied to *D. tetragona* with pinnae 1½ and lobes ¼ in. broad, lobes sub-falcate.

**D. megaphyl'la.** *sti.* tufted, stout, 8 to 12 in. long, villose. *Fronds* 2 to 4 ft. long, 1 to 1½ ft. broad; pinnae numerous, spreading, 6 to 9 in. long, 1 to 1½ in. broad, acuminate, edge cut above a quarter of the way down to midrib into oblong, falcate lobes, lower pinnae dwarf, distant. *Sori* medial; sporangia setose. India, Malaya. Syn. *Nephrodium articulatum, N. pennigerum.*

**D. moulmeinen'sis.** *sti.* firm, erect, naked, 2 ft. or more in length. *Fronds* pinnate, 3 to 4 ft. long, 1½ to 2 ft. broad; pinnae numerous sometimes 1 ft. long, acute, leathery, glabrous. *Sori* in 2 rows. China-India, Fiji, Celebes. (F.B.I. 3 as *Goniopteris lineata.*) Syn. *G. multilineata.*

**D. noveboracen'sis.** *rhiz.* slender, wide-creeping. *sti.* 1 ft. long, straw-colour. *Fronds* 1 to 2 ft. long, 4 to 6 in. broad; pinnae spreading, 2 to 3 in. long, ½ in. broad, cut very nearly to rachis into linear-oblong lobes, those of barren frond broadest; lower pinnae small, deflexed. *Sori* soon confluent in rows near the flat edge. E. United States. 1812. Hardy.

**D. oligocar'pa.** *sti.* tufted, 4 to 6 in. long, slender, slightly pubescent. *Fronds* 1½ to 2 ft. long, 6 to 8 in. broad, oblong-lanceolate; pinnae 3 to 4 in. long, ½ to ⅝ in. broad, cut nearly to rachis into spreading, entire, blunt lobes, ⅛ in. broad, lower not enlarged, and lower pinnae smaller gradually. *Sori* medial; indusium fugacious. W. Indies to Brazil. Syn. *Nephrodium Kaulfussii.*

**D. orbicula'ris.** *sti.* 1 ft. or more long, naked. *Fronds* 2 to 3 ft. long; pinnae 6 to 8 in. long, 1 in. broad, cut to a broadly winged rachis into nearly close, spreading, entire, linear-oblong lobes ⅛ in. broad. *Sori* nearer margin than midrib. Malaya. Stove. Syn. *Aspidium Hookeri, Cyclodium Hookeri.*

**D. orega'na.** *rhiz.* creeping, slightly scaly. *Fronds* pale green, 1½ to 3 in. long, including the short stipes; divisions of the pinnae in fertile fronds generally folded together early in the day, opening in afternoon. *Sori* close to margins covered with a minute hairy indusium. California, Oregon. Greenhouse.

**D. Oreop'teris.** Mountain Buckler Fern. *sti.* short, tufted. *Fronds* 1½ to 2 ft. long, 6 to 8 in. broad; pinnae 3 to 4 in. long, 1 in. broad at base, cut to a broadly winged rachis into close, blunt, oblong lobes; lower pinnae distant, and gradually dwarfed to auricles. *Sori* in rows near margin. Europe (Britain), Madeira, Japan. (H.B.F. 14.) SYN. *Lastrea montana.* Hardy. The following are the more important varieties: var. **Barnes'ii** with much narrower *fronds*; **coron'ans,** apices of *fronds* and pinnae crisped; **crista'ta,** *fronds* nearly as large as in type, tasselled at tips of fronds and pinnae; **Nowellia'na,** *fronds* 1 to 1½ ft. long, 4 to 5 in. wide, with narrow pinnae, lobes very short, erose; **trunca'ta,** pinnae truncate.

**D. Ota'ria.** *sti.* 6 to 12 in. long. *Fronds* 1 ft. or morel ong, with a linear-oblong terminal pinna, 4 to 6 in. long, 1 to 1½ in. broad, apex acuminate, margin with finely serrated lanceolate lobes reaching a quarter or a third of the way down, and from 3 to 6 distant spreading similar lateral ones on each side, lower stalked. *Sori* one on each veinlet. Philippines, Assam, Ceylon. (H.S. 4, 238.) SYN. *Nephrodium aristatum.*

**D. oyamen'sis.*** *rhiz.* wide-creeping and freely branching. *sti.* slender, wiry, 3 to 4 in. long. *Fronds* thin, pale green, 5 to 6 in. long, 2½ to 3 in. broad, cut half-way to rachis into oblong, undulated lobes, lower pair more deeply cut and deflexed. *Sori* numerous, black, scattered over the under-surface. Japan. 1878. (Gn. 17 (1880), 397.) SYN. *Polypodium Krameri.* Hardy.

**D. palus'tris.** *sti.* 1 ft. or more long, naked. *Fronds* 2 to 3 ft. long, 8 to 12 in. broad; pinnae close, erecto-patent, 4 to 6 in. long, ¾ in. broad, cut nearly to rachis into linear-oblong, entire, slightly falcate lobes, ⅛ in. broad. *Sori* filling most of space between midrib and margin; indusium small, ciliated. Brazil.

**D. parasit'ica.*** *sti.* tufted, 1 ft. or more long, rather slender, hairy. *Fronds* 1 to 2 ft. long, 8 to 12 in. broad; pinnae spreading, 4 to 6 in. long, ¾ in. broad, cut about half-way to midrib into scarcely falcate, blunt lobes; lower pinnae distant, and rather shorter than others. *Sori* distant from midrib; sporangia naked. Tropics and subtropics. 1820. (F.S.A. (2) 11.) A well-known and very variable species, of which the following are varieties: var. **corymbif'era,** erect, *fronds* branching, 1 to 2 ft. long, apices of fronds and pinnae crested; **gran'diceps,** *fronds* with large crest.

**D. Parish'ii.** *sti.* slender, naked, 6 to 9 in. long. *Fronds* deltoid, 6 to 8 in. each way; lower pinnae much the largest; pinnules oblong-lanceolate, 1½ to 2 in. long, cut nearly to rachis into close, crenate parchment-like lobes. *Sori* in rows not far from midrib. Burma. (H.S. 4, 260.) SYN. *Lastrea Parishii.*

**D. pa'tens.*** *rhiz.* oblique. *sti.* 1 ft. or more long, naked or slightly pubescent. *Fronds* 2 to 3 ft. long, 8 to 12 in. broad; pinnae 4 to 9 in. long, ½ to ¾ in. broad, cut about three-quarters of the space to rachis into linear-oblong, subfalcate lobes. *Sori* nearer margins than midrib; indusium persistent. Tropics, &c. var. **crista'ta** has much-divided tips; **invi'sa** has stout creeping *rhiz.*, *fronds* up to 4 ft. long, with narrower, more acute lobes. Trop. America. SYN. *Lastrea Sloanei.* Stove.

**D. pennig'era.** *sti.* 6 to 12 in. long, tufted, slightly scaly. *Fronds* 1½ to 2 ft. long, 8 to 12 in. broad; pinnae 4 to 6 in. long, nearly 1 in. broad, cut half-way into slightly crenate, blunt, falcate lobes, about ⅛ in. broad; lower pinnae gradually reduced. *Sori* in rows near midrib. New Zealand. 1835. SYN. *Goniopteris pennigera.* Greenhouse.

**D. Phegop'teris.*** Beech Polypody. *rhiz.* wide-creeping, slender. *sti.* slender, 6 to 9 in. long, naked, except towards base. *Fronds* 6 to 9 in. long, 4 to 6 in. broad, almost deltoid, slightly hairy beneath; lower pinnae 2 to 3 in. long, ½ to ¾ in. broad, cut three-quarters of the way to rachis into close, entire or slightly toothed, blunt lobes, ⅛ in. broad, lowest pair deflexed. *Sori* nearer margin than midrib. N. Hemisphere (Britain). (H.B.F. 3.) **A**

**D. podophyl'la.** *sti.* tufted, 1 ft. long, naked upwards. *Fronds* 1 to 1½ ft. long, 8 to 12 in. broad; pinnae 4 to 8 on each side, erecto-patent, 4 to 6 in. long, 8 to 12 in. broad, nearly entire, or with shallow, broad, blunt lobes; veins pinnate in the lobes, having 2 to 4 veinlets on a side, with sometimes a sorus on each, distant from main vein. S. China. Greenhouse, or nearly hardy.

**D. Poitea'na.** *sti.* 1 to 2 ft. long, erect, naked or pubescent. *Fronds* 1 to 2 ft. long, 1 ft. or more broad, with an oblong-lanceolate, terminal pinna, 6 to 8 in. long and 1½ to 2 in. broad, edge a little bluntly lobed or nearly entire, and 2 or 4 opposite pairs of similar ones. *Sori* in rows near main veins. Cuba, &c. 1823. SYN. *Goniopteris crenata, Polypodium crenatum.*

**D. prolif'era.** *rhiz.* stout, creeping. *sti.* 2 to 8 in. long, spreading. *Fronds* 1 to 2 ft. or more long, 6 to 12 in. broad, erect or decumbent, often elongated and rooting at tip and much branched from the axils; pinnae 4 to 6 in. long, ½ to ¾ in. broad, broadest at base, truncate or cordate, margin bluntly lobed; under side and rachis sometimes slightly pubescent. *Sori* medial, oval, sometimes confluent. India, China, &c. 1820. (L.F. 2, 18; F.S.A. (2) 14.) SYN. *Goniopteris prolifera, Polypodium proliferum.*

**D. pubes'cens.** *sti.* 6 to 18 in. long, slender, villous. *Fronds* 6 to 18 in. long, deltoid; lower pinnae much the largest; pinnules lanceolate; lower segs. usually free, oblong-rhomboidal, unequal-sided. *Sori* small, distant from midrib. W. Indies. SYN. *Phegopteris villosa.*

**D. rece'dens.** *sti.* erect, 1 ft. long, woolly scaly. *Fronds* 1½ to 2 ft. long, 1 ft. or more broad, deltoid; lower pinnae 6 to 12 in. long, 3 to 6 in. broad, pinnules often 6 in. long, 2 in. broad, and divided into distinct 1-sided, lanceolate segs. and close, slightly toothed lobes, smooth above, woolly beneath. *Sori* 6 to 8, round margins of larger lobes. S. India, Philippines. (H.S. 4, 265.) SYN. *Lastrea recedens.*

**D. refrac'ta.** *sti.* tufted, 1 ft. long. *Fronds* erect, 1 to 1½ ft. long, 6 to 9 in. broad; pinnae shorter upwards, lower deflexed, 4 to 5 in. long, ¾ in. broad, lowest pairs much deflexed; lobes broad, blunt, reaching about a quarter of way to midrib. *Sori* medial; indusium minute, fugacious. Brazil to Argentine. 1837. (H.S. 4, 252.)

**D. rep'tans.** *sti.* 1 to 8 in. long, slender, wiry. *Fronds* 4 to 12 in. long, 1 to 3 in. broad, spreading, often decumbent and rooting; pinnae ½ to 1½ in. long, about ½ in. broad, entire or bluntly lobed, often auricled at base, lower stalked; under-side and rachis sometimes slightly hairy. Florida to Brazil. Very variable. SYN. *Polypodium reptans.* var. **asplenioi'des** is more erect and larger.

**D. reticula'ta.** *sti.* tufted, 1 to 3 ft. long, stout. *Fronds* pinnate, 2 to 4 ft. long, 1 ft. or more broad; pinnae 6 to 12 in. long, 1 to 4 in. broad, acuminate, entire or sub-repand, base rounded or cuneate. *Areolae* 8 to 12 between midrib and margin. Mexico to Peru. 1793.

**D. Richards'ii.** *Fronds* oblong-lanceolate, 2-pinnatifid, 1¼ to 1½ ft. long, 8 to 9 in. broad; pinnae moderately close, patent, ligulate-caudate, ¾ in. broad, cut to a narrow wing into close, ligulate, slightly repand, blunt lobes, $\frac{1}{10}$ in. wide; lowest pinnae not reduced, their lowest lobes on both sides slightly so. *Sori* medial; indusium firm, persistent, slightly pilose. New Caledonia. SYN. *Lastrea Richardsii.* Greenhouse. var. **multif'ida** is a crested form reproducing true from spores. (B.C.F. 2, 563.)

**D. Rodigasia'num.*** *Fronds* spreading, lanceolate, 3 to 4 ft. long; pinnae sessile, linear-lanceolate, pinnatifid. Samoa. 1882. (I.H. 1882, t. 442.)

**D. rufes'cens.** *rhiz.* short-creeping. *sti.* 1 to 1½ ft. long, erect, firm, naked. *Fronds* length of stipes, 9 to 12 in. broad, almost deltoid; lower pinnae largest, deltoid, 6 to 8 in. long, 3 to 4 in. broad; pinnules lanceolate, unequal-sided, bluntly lobed, lowest nearly down to rachis. *Sori* medial. Ceylon, Java, Queensland, &c. (F.S.I. 236.) SYN. *Phegopteris rufescens, Polypodium rufescens.*

**D. sagitta'ta.** *sti.* tufted, 1 to 2 in. long, wiry, deciduously scaly. *Fronds* 6 to 9 in. long, 1½ to 2 in. broad; pinnae blunt, entire, ⅓ in. broad, with a sharp, distinct auricle on both sides at base, those of lower half of frond gradually reduced. *Sori* below middle of veinlets. W. Indies. (L.F. 2, 55.) SYN. *Phegopteris hastaefolia, Polypodium hastaefolium.*

**D. sanc'ta.** *sti.* densely tufted, slender, 2 to 3 in. long, naked upwards. *Fronds* 6 to 9 in. long, 1 to 2 in. broad, lanceolate; pinnae distant, ½ to 1 in. long, 1½ to 3 in. broad, bluntish, more or less deeply pinnatifid; lobes sometimes close and linear-oblong, sometimes distinct, linear or spatulate. *Sori* minute; indusium very fugacious. W. Indies, Guatemala. SYN. *Lastrea sancta.*

**D. scabro'sa.** *sti.* slender, 1½ to 2 ft. long, clothed with straw-coloured scales. *Fronds* 1½ to 2 ft. long, 1 to 1½ ft. broad; pinnae 6 to 9 in. long, 3 to 5 in. broad; pinnules of lower side largest, with lanceolate segs. cut nearly to rachis into soft, toothed, ligulate lobes. *Sori* small, usually one at base of each lobe. Nilgiri Hills. (F.S.I. 169.) SYN. *Lastrea scabrosa, Polypodium nigrocarpum.* Greenhouse.

**D. Ser'ra.** *rhiz.* wide-creeping. *sti.* firm, glossy, 1 ft. or more long. *Fronds* slender, 2 to 3 ft. long, 1 or more wide, broadly lanceolate; pinnae spreading, 6 to 9 in. long, seldom ½ in. broad, cut about half-way to midrib into sickle-shaped, acute lobes, leathery, pale green. *Sori* in 2 rows a little apart from midrib; indusia hairy. Cuba, Mexico, &c.

**D. serra'ta.** *sti.* 1 to 3 ft. long, stout. *Fronds* pinnate, 3 to 4 ft. or more long, 1 ft. or more broad; pinnae 1 to 3 in. apart, 6 to 12 in. long, ½ to 2 in. broad, oblong-lanceolate, acuminate, base cordate or cuneate, finely toothed. *Areolae* 12 to 20 between midrib and margin. Mexico to Peru. SYN. *Meniscium palustre, M. serratum.*

**D. setig'era.** *rhiz.* creeping. *sti.* 1 to 2 ft. long, scaly at base, hairy. *Fronds* 1 to 3 ft. long; lowest pinnae largest, 8 to 12 in. long, 4 to 6 in. broad; pinnules narrow-lanceolate, cut to rachis into soft, close, deeply cleft, pale green lobes, covered with white hairs. *Sori* small, 8 to 12 to a lobe. Trop. Asia. 1840. SYN. *C. tenericaulis, Lastrea setigera, Polypodium trichodes.* Greenhouse. In var. **crista'ta** the fronds are more or less crested.

**D. Siebold'ii.*** *cau.* tufted, scaly. *sti.* 6 to 12 in. long, scaly below. *Fronds* with an entire or slightly toothed, lanceolate-oblong, terminal pinna, 8 to 12 in. long, and 1½ to 2 in. broad, and 2 to 4 pairs, lowest shortly stalked. *Sori* large, copious, scattered. Japan, China. SYN. *Pycnopteris Sieboldii.* Greenhouse, or nearly hardy. A variegated form (**variega'ta**) is sometimes grown.

**D. sim'plex.** A synonym of *D. triphylla.*

**D. simula'ta.** Close to *D. Thelypteris* but with longer *sti.*, larger *sori*, and less convolute margins. E. United States. 1886. SYN. *Aspidium simulatum.* (G. & F. 1896, 484, f. 69.)

**D. sophoroi'des.** *sti.* 1 ft. or more long, slender, pubescent. *Fronds* 1 to 2 ft. long, 6 to 9 in. broad; pinnae spreading, 4 to 6 in. long, ½ to ¾ in. broad, acuminate, cut one-third the way down into oblong-triangular, subfalcate lobes. Japan, China, Formosa. Greenhouse.

**D. spar'sa.** *sti.* tufted, 6 to 12 in. long, scaly only at base. *Fronds* 1 to 2 ft. long, 8 to 12 in. broad, ovate-lanceolate; lowest pinnae largest, 4 to 6 in. long, 1½ to 2 in. broad; lowest pinnules sometimes compound, others lanceolate, unequal-sided, pinnatifid, with oblong, blunt lobes. *Sori* usually one to each lobe, near midrib; indusium naked, flat, 1/16 in. wide. N. India to Mauritius. (H.S. 4, 262.) SYN. *Nephrodium purpurascens, N. undulatum.* Greenhouse. var. **grac'ilis** has short, slender, conspicuously scaly *sti.* and lanceolate, 2-pinnatifid *fronds,* 3 to 4 in. long.

**D. spinulo'sa.*** Buckler Fern. *sti.* tufted, about 1 ft. long, scaly. *Fronds* 1 to 1½ ft. long, 6 to 8 in. broad, oblong-lanceolate; lower pinnae sub-deltoid, 3 to 4 in. long, 1½ to 2 in. broad, lowest pair about equal to next; pinnules ovate-lanceolate, largest about 1 in. long, ½ in. broad, cut down to rachis below into close oblong lobes, with many aristate teeth; indusium not gland-ciliate. Europe (Britain), Africa, NE. Asia, and N. America. (H.B.F. 18.) Hardy. The following are important varieties: var. **Boot'ii,** *fronds* deep green, slightly scaly beneath, disposed in a circle or crown 3 ft. h. including the chaffy, rusty-scaly stipes; pinnae lanceolate, distant; lowest pinnules ½ in. long, ¼ in. broad, cut one-third to half-way to rachis. N. America, &c.; **dilata'ta,*** scales denser and narrower than in type, centre dark brown, *fronds* ovate-lanceolate or sub-deltoid, larger and more deeply cut, darker, pinnae closer, under-surface often finely glandular, indusium gland-ciliate. SYN. *Lastrea dilatata*; **interme'dia,** *fronds* broader than in type (often 22 in. long and 9 in. broad) and more finely cut, pinnae more spreading, lowest nearly 3 in. apart. N. America; **lepido'ta,** rachises chestnut-brown, scaly, *fronds* sub-deltoid, lower pinnae deltoid, 5 to 6 in. each way, lowest pinnules much the largest, often 3 in. long, 2 in. broad, its segs. cut down to rachis below, with lobes again deeply pinnatifid; **remo'ta,** *fronds* oblong-lanceolate, about 2 ft. long, 6 in. broad, pinnae lanceolate, close, pinnules ovate-oblong, only lowest free, largest about 1 in. long, ½ in. broad, cut half-way down to rachis or more, spinulose teeth few, under-side and indusium not glandular.

**D. squamisti'pes.** *sti.* tufted, about 1 ft. long. *Fronds* broadly lanceolate, 1½ to 2 ft. long, 8 to 10 in. broad; pinnae 3 to 5 in. long, ¾ to 1 in. broad, cut nearly to midrib into narrow-oblong, falcate lobes of a soft, paper texture; lower pinnae having a small gland at base. *Sori* close to midrib. E. Himalayas. SYN. *Polypodium appendiculatum.*

**D. Standish'ii.*** *sti.* 4 to 6 in. long, straw-colour, scaly at base. *Fronds* 12 to 18 in. long, 6 to 9 in. broad, ovate-deltoid, 3-pinnate; lower pinnae largest, with pinnules on lower side prolonged, lanceolate, imbricate with small, distinct, bluntly lobed segs. *Sori* in 2 rows, very copious. Japan, China. SYN. *Lastrea Standishii, Polystichum laserpitiifolium.* Greenhouse.

**D. stegnogrammoi'des.** *cau.* sub-arborescent. *sti.* 1½ to 2 ft. long, erect, firm, pubescent upwards. *Fronds* 2 to 3 ft. long, 1 ft. or more broad; pinnae 6 to 9 in. long, 1½ in. broad, bluntly lobed about a quarter way down, acuminate; rachis and veins beneath slightly hairy. *Sori* in rows near midrib. Hawaii. SYN. *Polypodium stegnogrammoides, Goniopteris stegnogrammoides.*

**D. stria'ta.** *sti.* 1 ft. or more long, naked or nearly so. *Fronds* 2 to 3 ft. long, 8 to 12 in. broad; pinnae 4 to 6 in. long, ¾ to 1 in. broad, cut two-thirds of the way to rachis into linear-oblong, slightly falcate lobes; lower pinnae not much smaller than rest. *Sori* small, in close rows about midway between the midrib and margin. Guinea Coast. SYN. *Nephrodium pallidivenium.*

**D. subtripinna'ta.** *cau.* decumbent. *sti.* about 6 in. long, slender, scaly. *Fronds* 1 to 1½ ft. long, 6 to 9 in. broad; pinnae few, lowest much the largest, 5 to 6 in. long, 3 to 4 in. broad; lowest pinnules much longer than others, which are lanceolate, with distinct, oblong-deltoid, deeply pinnatifid lower segs., nearly glabrous. *Sori* copious, distant from midrib. N. China and Japan. SYN. *Nephrodium chinense.* Greenhouse.

**D. tetrag'ona.** *sti.* 1 to 2 ft. long, erect, naked or slightly villous. *Fronds* 1 to 3 ft. long, 1 ft. or more broad; pinnae 6 to 8 in. long, ½ to 1 in. broad, numerous, spreading, lowest narrowed at base, sometimes stalked, cut a quarter to half-way into blunt lobes; rachis and under-side sometimes slightly hairy. *Sori* in rows near midrib. Florida to Peru. 1843. SYN. *Goniopteris tetragona, Polypodium androgynum, P. tetragonum.*

**D. Thelyp'teris.** *rhiz.* slender, wide-creeping. *sti.* about 1 ft. long, slender. *Fronds* 1 to 2 ft. long, 4 to 6 in. broad; pinnae spreading, 2 to 3 in. long, ½ in. broad, cut nearly to rachis into entire, spreading, linear-oblong lobes, those of barren frond broadest; lower pinnae equalling others. *Sori* small, not confluent, in rows near recurved edge. Europe (Britain), Asia, Africa, N. America, New Zealand, &c. (H.B.F. 13.) Hardy.

**D. Thwaites'ii.** *rhiz.* firm, wide-creeping. *sti.* 9 to 12 in. long, pale straw-colour, nearly naked. *Fronds* 8 to 10 in. long, 4 to 5 in. broad, sub-deltoid, acuminate, crenato-pinnatifid; below apex several blunt, linear-oblong, sub-entire pinnae, lowest largest, distinctly stalked, 2 to 3 in. long, ¾ in. broad, edge bluntly (not deeply) lobed; base narrowed suddenly. *Areolae* and *sori* 4 or 5 in lower pinnae between midrib and margin. Ceylon, S. India. (F.S.I. 223.) SYN. *Meniscium Thwaitesii.*

**D. triphyl'la.** *rhiz.* firm, wide-creeping. *sti.* slender, pale straw-coloured, of barren fronds 4 to 6 in., of fertile 1 ft. or more, long. *Fronds,* simple, 6 to 9 in. long, cordate, or with an oblong-lanceolate terminal pinna, 4 to 6 in. long, 1 to 1½ in. broad, base cuneate or rounded, edge repand, and 1 or 2 similar but smaller ones on each side, fertile ones smaller than barren. *Areolae* 8 to 12 between mid-rib and margin. China, N. India to Malaya, and Queensland. 1828. (F.S.I. 56.) SYN. *Meniscium simplex, M. triphyllum.*

**D. trunca'ta** (truncate). *sti.* tufted, stout, erect, 2 ft. long, naked or slightly villous. *Fronds* 2 to 4 ft. long, 1 to 1½ ft. broad; pinnae 6 to 9 in. long, 1 in. broad, cut down one-third or more of the distance to the rachis into blunt, spreading, oblong lobes; lower pinnae small. *Sori* 1 on each veinlet, near the main vein. N. India, Australia, &c. 1869. SYN. (H.S. 4, 241 as *Nephrodium abruptum*; F.B.I. 130 as *N. eusorum.*) Greenhouse.

**D. unidenta'ta.** *sti.* 1 ft. long, tufted, with dark brown scales. *Fronds* 2 to 3 ft. long, 1 ft. or more broad, deltoid; lower pinnae largest, deltoid, 6 to 9 in. long, 4 to 5 in. broad; pinnules lanceolate, lower segs. distinct, ovate-oblong, deeply pinnatifid, with slightly toothed lobes. *Sori* sub-marginal. Hawaii. SYN. *Phegopteris unidentata, Polypodium unidentatum.*

**D. urophyl'la.** *rhiz.* creeping. *sti.* 2 ft. or more in length, stout, erect. *Fronds* 2 to 4 ft. or more long 1 to 1½ ft. broad, with a terminal pinna and usually several on each side, which are sometimes 1 ft. long and more than 2 in. broad, entire or slightly lobed. *Sori* in 2 close rows, or sometimes in 1 row. India, Australia, &c. SYN. *Goniopteris urophylla, Polypodium urophyllum.*

**D. va'ria.*** *rhiz.* sub-creeping. *sti.* 6 to 12 in. long, densely fibrillose below. *Fronds* 12 to 18 in. long, 9 to 12 in. broad, lanceolate-deltoid; lower pinnae much largest, sub-deltoid, unequal-sided, 4 to 6 in. long, 3 to 4 in. broad; pinnules lanceolate, imbricate, with oblong, blunt, slightly toothed segs. *Sori* principally in 2 rows near midrib. Japan. SYN. *Lastrea varia, Polystichum varium.* Greenhouse.

**D. veluti'na.** *sti.* 1 ft. or more long, bright brown, villous upwards, scaly at base. *Fronds* 1 to 1½ ft. long, nearly as broad, deltoid, pubescent; lower pinnae much the largest, deltoid; lowest pinnules largest, cut to rachis below into pinnatifid, oblong lobes; rachis densely villous. *Sori* small, copious; indusium glandular-ciliate. New Zealand. SYN. *Lastrea velutina.* Greenhouse.

**D. venus'ta.*** *sti.* tufted, 1 ft. or more long, naked. *Fronds* 2 ft. or more long, 1 ft. broad; pinnae numerous, spreading, 6 in. long, 1 in. broad, with blunt, oblong lobes, reaching half-way down. *Sori* principally in lobes close to margin. Jamaica. (G.C. 1855, 677.)

**D. vi'lis.** *sti.* 1 to 2 ft. long, densely fibrillose at base. *Fronds* 2 to 3 ft. long, 1 to 1½ ft. broad, sub-deltoid; lower pinnae lanceolate, often 1 ft. long, soft, 4 to 5 in. broad; pinnules close, lanceolate, having distinct oblong-lanceolate segs., with ligulate sub-entire lobes, about 1 in. broad. *Sori* small, copious, nearer midrib than margin, indusium thin, fugacious. N. India, Japan, Java. SYN. *Nephrodium intermedium, N. setosum.* Greenhouse.

**D. Villar'sii.*** *sti.* tufted, 6 in. long, densely scaly below. *Fronds* 1 to 1½ ft. long, 4 to 6 in. broad, oblong-lanceolate; largest pinnae 2 to 3 in. long, 1 to 1½ in. broad, pinnules of lower half free, ovate-rhomboidal, cut nearly to rachis below. *Sori* close to midrib; indusium firm, prominent, fringed with glands. Europe (Britain), Asia Minor, N. America. (H.B.F. 16.) SYN. *Nephrodium rigidum.* Hardy.

**D. villo'sa.*** *sti.* tufted, 2 to 3 ft. or more long, stout, usually villous, and densely scaly. *Fronds* 4 to 6 ft. or more long, 2 to 3 ft. or more broad; pinnae often 2 ft. long, 1 ft. broad; pinnules lanceolate, cut to rachis into close, oblong, pinnatifid segs.; largest entire lobes ¾ in. long, ½ in. broad. *Sori* copious; indusium flat, 1/20 in. broad, often suppressed. Trop. America. 1793. (H.S.F. iv. 264.)

**D. vivip'ara.** *sti.* 1 to 2 ft. long, tufted, slender, naked. *Fronds* 1 to 2 ft. long, 6 to 9 in. broad; pinnae 3 to 5 in. long, ¾ to 1 in. broad, acuminate, lower narrowed at base, nearly entire. *Sori* in contiguous rows. S. Brazil, &c. SYN. *Polypodium diversifolium, P. fraxinifolium.*

**D. Vogel'li.** *sti.* 1 ft. or more long, firm. *Fronds* 6 to 18 in. each way; lower pinnae much largest, with pinnules on lower side much larger than others, which are 1 to 3 in. broad, often cut nearly to rachis below into broad, oblong lobes. *Sori* medial. Trop. America. SYN. *Lastrea pilosissima, Nephrodium subquinquefidum.*

**D. Webbia'na.** *sti.* scattered, 1 to 2 ft. long, densely scaly below. *Fronds* 18 to 24 in. long, 1 ft. or more broad, sub-deltoid; lower pinnae much largest, long-stalked; pinnules lanceolate; segs. very unequal-sided, pinnatifid, with rounded mucronate lobes, obliquely truncate at base below. *Sori* large, copious. Madeira. SYN. *Polystichum frondosum.* Greenhouse.

**DRYP'IS** (name used by Theophrastus, from *drypto,* to tear, on account of the strongly spiny leaves). FAM. *Caryophyllaceae.* A genus of 1 half-shrubby perennial with much-branched stem and narrow, almost spiny, leaves, native of S. Europe. Related to Silene but with its capsule dehiscing irregularly instead of by teeth. Inflorescence terminal, densely branched. Flowers small; calyx with 5 teeth; petals 5, deeply lobed;

stamens 5; styles 3. Hardy in very sunny, well-drained places on the rock-garden. Propagated by cuttings or by seed sown in a sandy compost. The seedlings should be put into their permanent place early and need some care to establish.

**D. spino'sa.** Glabrous, tufted, sub-shrubby perennial, with spreading stems 3 to 6 in. h., and numerous, 4-sided branches. *l.* opposite, awl-shaped, about ⅓ in. long, with sharp points, bright glossy green. *fl.* pale pink or white, about ⅓ in. across, in dense corymbs, pedicels short. June, July. 1775. (B.M. 2216.)

*dschischungaensis -is -e,* of Dschischungari, Kaiser Wilhemsland.

*dua'lis -is -e,* double.

**dubbing,** term, rare, for clipping or trimming hedges.

*Dubernardia'nus -a -um,* in honour of Père Dubernard of the French Mission at Tseku, China, *c.* 1906.

*du'bius -a -um,* uncertain.

**DUBOIS'IA** (in honour of Louis Dubois, French botanical author). FAM. *Solanaceae.* Three species of small trees or shrubs. Leaves alternate, entire. Flowers small, in terminal panicles; corolla lobes 5, broad; stamens 4, didynamous, the 5th uppermost one a minute rudiment. Seeds few in an indehiscent berry. Greenhouse. Sandy loam suits them and they can be propagated by cuttings under a bell-glass.

**D. myoporoi'des.** Quite glabrous small tree or tall shrub, 20 to 25 ft. *l.* oblong-lanceolate to obovate-oblong, 2 to 4 in. long, cuneate. *fl.* white or pale lilac, in terminal pyramidal panicles 4 in. long; cal. 5-toothed; cor. ⅛ in. long, with 5 short, blunt lobes. *fr.* a globose berry. Australia, New Caledonia. A preparation from this tree is used by oculists for dilating the pupil of the eye.

W. J. B.

**DUCKMEAT, DUCKWEED.** See **Lemna.**

**DUCK'S FOOT.** See **Podophyllum.**

**DUCKWEED.** See **Dockweed,** p. 700.

*Duclouxia'nus -a -um,* in honour of Monsignor Fr. Ducloux, 1864–?, who collected in Yunnan *c.* 1900.

**DUD'LEYA.** Included in **Echeveria.**

*Duf'fii,* in honour of Sir Mountstuart Elphinstone Grant Duff, 1829–1906, Governor of Madras, amateur botanist.

**DUHAMEL'IA.** A synonym of Hamelia.

**DULCAMA'RA.** See **Solanum Dulcamara.**

*dul'cis -is -e,* sweet.

**DULICH'IUM** (*Doulichion,* an island in the Ionian Sea). FAM. *Cyperaceae.* A genus of a single species of grass-like perennial with terete, hollow stems, and 2-ranked spikelets on axillary peduncles. Flowers with a perianth of 6 to 9 barbed bristles, 3 stamens, and a 2-cleft persistent style. Fruit a linear-oblong, flat achene. Hardy bog-plant of no special beauty.

**D. arundina'ceum.** Stems leafy at top, 16 to 24 in. h. *Lower l.* reduced to sheaths. N. America.

*duma'lis -is -e,* compact.

**DUMA'SIA** (in honour of Jean B. Dumas, 1800–84, professor of Pharmacy and Chemistry in Paris). FAM. *Leguminosae.* A genus of some 8 or 10 species of evergreen climbers found in Trop. and Temperate Asia and Africa, related to Glycine. Flowers papilionaceous, middle-sized, in racemes, calyx tube swollen at base; standard spurred at both sides at base, wings and keel adherent with small blades and very long claws; stamens diadelphous. Pod linear, falcate, and torulose. The compost should be peat, loam, and sand.

**D. villo'sa.** Climber twining over shrubs. Stems very slender, clothed with grey or reddish hairs. *l.* 3-foliolate, mainstalk 1 to 2 in. long; lflets. ovate, blunt, 1 to 3 in. long, about half as wide, hairy beneath. *fl.* up to 40 in axillary, downy racemes 2 to 6 in. long; cor. bright yellow or reddish-purple; standard pet. ⅓ to ¾ in. long, reflexed, notched. August to October. India, Ceylon. 1824. (B.R. 961 as *D. pubescens.*) Greenhouse.

W. J. B.

**DUMB CANE.** See **Dieffenbachia Seguine.**

*dumeto'rum,* of bushy places.

*Dumortier'i,* in honour of B. C. Dumortier, 1797–1878, of Belgium.

*dumo'sus -a -um,* compact, bushy.

**DUMPY LEVEL.** An instrument somewhat similar to a theodolite consisting of a telescope to which a level is attached, mounted on a tripod.

It is used in conjunction with a levelling-staff marked in hundredths of a foot, for finding out accurately differences of level at various points in the ground. From levels taken, sections may be drawn out, and from these the most economical way of carrying out levelling operations, terracing, &c. may be determined.

The dumpy level is equally useful for the setting out of level pegs as, for example, for tennis courts or for fixing the weir at the margin of a pond.

J. E. G. W.

*Dunalia'nus -a -um,* in honour of M. F. Dunal, 1789–1856, botanist of Montpellier.

*dunen'sis -is -e,* of the sand dunes.

**DUNG BEETLES.** This name is given to certain groups of Beetles belonging to the Coleopterous family Scarabaeidae, and includes the Dor Beetle (q.v.) and Scarabs. Both the adults and their grubs live in or near, and feed on, dung, while some feed on dead animal matter. Some species live in burrows beneath dung heaps, the beetles packing the burrows with manure upon which their grubs feed. Others, e.g. the sacred Scarab beetles of the ancient Egyptians, collect dung, form it into balls, and roll them along the ground and bury them after laying an egg in the dung-mass. Their grubs resemble those of Chafers, being soft and white, with curved bodies and with the lower portion of the body swollen. The common Dung Beetles in this country belong to the genera Aphodius and Geotrupes, and are useful scavengers.

G. F. W.

*du'plex,* double.

**DURAMEN.** Heart-wood; the part of the timber of a tree which becomes hardened by matter deposited in it.

**DURANT'A** (in honour of Castor Durantes, physician and botanist in Rome, who died about 1590). FAM. *Verbenaceae.* A genus of about 10 species of Trop. American trees and shrubs. Leaves evergreen, opposite or whorled, entire or toothed. Flowers rather small, in long terminal or short axillary racemes; corolla tube cylindrical, limb spreading, 5-lobed; stamens 4, didynamous. Fruit an 8-seeded juicy drupe enclosed in the enlarged calyx. The Durantas need stove conditions and a compost of peat and loam in equal parts. They can be propagated by cuttings in heat in early spring.

**D. Ellis'ii.** A synonym of *D. Plumieri.*

**D. Lorentz'ii.** Spineless shrub with 4-angled branches. *l.* small, ovate or elliptic, blunt, leathery, toothed. *fl.* white in terminal interrupted racemes. Argentine.

**D. Mutis'ii.** Shoots somewhat angular, sometimes spiny. *l.* opposite, or ternate, ovate or oblong-elliptic, 2 to 4 in. long, leathery, sometimes coarsely toothed, shining above, pale and opaque beneath; stalk short. *fl.* violet, drooping in terminal and axillary racemes. Colombia.

**D. Plumier'i.** Shrub, 6 to 15 ft. h., sometimes spiny, shoots 4-angled. *l.* variable, oblong-lanceolate, usually entire. *fl.* lilac-blue, very numerous in racemes towards ends of branches. *fr.* yellow, up to ½ in. across, enclosed in the twisted yellow cal. August. Mexico, W. Indies, &c. (B.M. 1759 as *D. Ellisii*; B.R. 244.)

*Dur'hamii,* in honour of F. R. Durham, Secretary Royal Horticultural Society 1925–46, who introduced *Astragalus Durhamii.*

**DURIAN.** The fruit of *Durio zibethinus.*

**DU'RIO** (*Duryon*, Malayan name of the fruit). FAM. *Bombacaceae.* A genus of 7 species of large evergreen trees, natives of Indo-Malaya. *D. zibethinus* needs stove treatment and will grow in a compost of peat, loam, and leaf-mould. Cuttings of firm young shoots root readily in spring in sand under a glass with bottom heat. Its fruit is ranked among the most delicious of Indian fruits by those who have overcome its disagreeable smell of civet and turpentine, or, according to some, of rotting onions. It is oval or globular, larger than a coco-nut, and reaches up to 8 or 10 in. in length. The shell is hard and prickly and covers a creamy pulp and seeds. The pulp is eaten and the seeds also are eaten after roasting like chestnuts. When unripe the fruit may be salted and pickled but its strong smell is against its use in Europe.

**D. zibethi'nus.** Evergreen tree up to 80 ft. *l.* oblong, slender-pointed, rounded at base, lurid-silvery beneath and there covered with brown scales. *fl.* white. *fr.* see above. Malaya, E. Indies. 1825.

*durius'culus -a -um,* rather hard.

*durobriven'sis -is -e,* of Rochester, Kent, or United States.

*du'rus -a -um,* hard.

*Durvillea'nus -a -um,* in honour of J. S. C. Dumont D'Urville, 1790–1842, French Naval Officer.

**DUSTING.** Dusting is a method of applying fungicides in powder form. The powder is in a very finely divided state so as to give a good cover on the foliage. The substances used are sulphur in the form of Flowers of Sulphur and Green Sulphur, Copper compounds mixed with some other substance such as lime to give a copper-lime dust, Derris, Nicotine, &c. The dusts are put on with various forms of dusting machines ranging from small hand bellows or powder blowers, to large manual or engine-driven rotary fan blowers delivering the dust through adjustable pipes. In Canada and the United States even aeroplanes are used for large-scale dusting. Where but few plants are to be treated, the dust can be put into a muslin bag tied to the end of a stick and beaten with another stick. Dusting should be done when the foliage is damp as after dew in the early morning. Dusting is easier to carry out than spraying but whether it is more efficient against disease is a matter of opinion and of circumstance. Although easier and cheaper than spraying, dusting requires to be done much oftener. *See* **Fungicides, Insecticides.**

D. E. G.

**DUTCH RUSHES.** *See* **Equisetum.**

**DUTCHMAN'S BREECHES.** *See* **Dicentra Cucullaria.**

**DUTCHMAN'S PIPE.** *See* **Aristolochia.**

*Duthiea'nus -a -um,* in honour of John Firminger Duthie, 1845–1922, Superintendent, Botanic Garden, Saharanpur.

**DUVA'LIA** (named after H. A. Duval, 1777–1814, author of *Enumeratio Plantarum Succulentarum in Horto Alenconio*). FAM. *Asclepiadaceae.* Stems very short, decumbent or erect, often subterranean, rising at the tip, 4- to 6-angled, with spreading teeth. Flowers from near the base of the stem, resembling those of Stapelia

(q.v.) with a fleshy disk in the centre; lobes usually folded back along the centre line. All the species come from Africa.

**D. Corderoy'i.** Stems short, with 6 angles divided into sharp-pointed tubercles, green or purplish in the sun. *fl.* 2 to 4 together near the base of the stem; cor. lobes folded back, at least at the tip, smooth, ciliate towards the base, dark purple; inner disk covered with long, soft, purple hairs. S. Africa. (W. & S. 738–44; B.M. 6082 as *Stapelia Corderoyi*.)

**D. el'egans.** Stems less than 2 in. long, stout, somewhat tuberculate, green to purplish. *fl.* rather flat, dark purple-brown, shining, with long, soft, purple hairs all over the inner surface; disk not obvious. Cape Province. (W. & S. 733–4; B.M. 1184 as *Stapelia elegans*.)

**D. modes'ta.** Stems very short and stout, somewhat tuberculate. *fl.* dark purple-brown; lobes folded back towards tip, spreading at base, with fine purple hairs on lower half; disk smooth. S. Africa. (W. & S. 752–6 and Pl. 21.)

**D. poli'ta.** Stems rather elongated, lax, and decumbent. *fl.* rich chocolate-brown, somewhat shining on the lower part of the lobes which are spreading, not folded back; disk paler, spotted. S. Africa. (W. & S. 745–51 and Pl. 20; B.M. 6245.)

**D. reclina'ta.** Stems longer and more slender, 4- to 5-angled, slightly tuberculate. *fl.* dark chocolate-brown, somewhat shining, disk paler; lobes folded back to the base, hairy along edge. S. Africa. (W. & S. 774–8.)

V. H.

**DUVA'UA.** *See* **Schinus dependens.**

**DUVERNO'IA** (in honour of J. G. Duvernoy, a pupil of Tournefort). FAM. *Acanthaceae.* A genus of about 15 species of herbs or shrubs related to Adhatoda. Flowers solitary or in short spikes; calyx short, 4-toothed, the back lobe toothed or partite; corolla tube short, limb 2-lipped, upper lip helmet-shaped, 2-toothed, lower flat. Treatment as for Adhatoda.

**D. Dewev'rei.** Tufted herb about 2 ft. h. *l.* oblong, stalked. *fl.* in a short panicle; cor. about ½ in. long, upper lip white with red stripes; lower greenish-white. Congo.

**DWALE.** *See* **Atropa Belladonna.**

**DWARF BAMBOO.** *See* **Arundinaria vagans.**

**DWARF FAN PALM.** *See* **Chamaerops humilis.**

**DWARF PALMETTO.** *See* **Sabal minor.**

A→

**dwarf shoots,** short shoots which take no part in the extension of growth of a tree and bear no buds destined to do so, but which, as in the pines, bear the foliage leaves, or, as in apples, pears, and cherries, form 'spurs' on which most of the flowers are produced.

*Dybow'skii,* in honour of a French inspector-general of Colonial Agriculture (about 1908).

**DYCK'IA** (in honour of Prince Salm-Dyck, German botanist, and author of a splendid work on succulent plants). FAM. *Bromeliaceae.* A genus of about 80 species of S. American stemless, herbaceous, rhizomatous perennials with thick, rigid, spiny leaves in a rosette, and usually yellow or orange flowers in spikes, racemes, or panicles on an erect, well-developed scape. Fruit a hard, shiny, 3-angled capsule. Related to Puya but with petals joined. They are best grown with Agaves, and thrive well in a mixture of 2 parts loam, and 1 part vegetable mould, to which a little sand should be added. Perfect drainage is essential, and water must be liberally applied during summer; but in winter a very small quantity will suffice. Propagated by suckers. Mostly greenhouse plants but a few nearly hardy.

**D. altis'sima.** *fl.* many, in an ample panicle, with sometimes 10 to 12 branches, the lower ones 1 ft. long; pet. bright yellow, twice as long as cal.; peduncle stout, not longer than the *l. l.* sometimes 100 in a dense rosette, ensiform, acuminate, 1½ ft. long, 1 in. broad, with copious strong brown spines. 3 ft. h. Brazil. 1840. SYN. *D. gigantea, D. laxiflora, D. princeps,* and *D. ramosa* (of gardens).

**D. argen'tea** of Baker. A synonym of *Hechtia argentea.*

**D. brevifo′lia.** *fl.* yellow, many in a spike about 1 ft. long; shorter than sharp-pointed bracts. *l.* about 30 in a dense rosette, central erect, outer recurved with lines of whitish scales; when fully mature, about 8 in. long, 18 in. h. Brazil. 1869. (Ref. B. 236.)

**D. Desmetia′na.** A synonym of *Hechtia Desmetiana*.

**D. frig′ida.** *fl.* orange-yellow, very numerous, about ½ in. long, many in a branched spike, covered with pale down. February. *l.* tufted, linear-lanceolate, spine-toothed, recurved, up to 3 ft. long, pale or glaucescent below. Brazil. 1877. (B.M. 6294.) SYN. *Pourretia frigida*.

**D. gemella′ria.** Differs from *D. sulphurea* by the laxly arranged erect *fl.*, and its greater size. 3 ft. h.

**D. gigan′tea.** A garden synonym of *D. altissima*.

**D. laxiflo′ra.** A garden synonym of *D. altissima*.

**D. leptostach′ya.** *fl.* 20 to 25 in a simple, erect spike 6 to 9 in. long; sep. reddish, densely pruinose; pet. bright scarlet, ¾ in. long, ½ in. broad; peduncle slender, 3 ft. long. Summer. *l.* 15 to 18 in a dense rosette, lanceolate, acuminate, falcate, rigid, 1¼ to 1¾ ft. long, 1 to 1½ in. broad, semicircular at back, marginal spines brown. Brazil. 1867.

**D. prin′ceps.** A synonym of *D. altissima*.

**D. ramo′sa.** A synonym of *D. altissima*.

**D. rega′lis.** A synonym of *D. frigida*.

**D. remotiflo′ra.** *fl.* deep orange, nearly 1 in. long, in a loose spike; infl. brownish, hairy, bracts patent. *l.* lanceolate, narrow, recurved, about 9 in. long, sharply spiny. 3 ft. h. Uruguay, Argentine. 1832. (B.M. 3449, B.R. 1782.) SYN. *D. rariflora* of some. In warm, sheltered situations this species may prove hardy.

**D. sulphu′rea.** *fl.* many, ascending, in a lax, simple raceme 1½ ft. long; pet. pale sulphur-yellow, longer than sep.; peduncle 1 ft. or more. *l.* 30 to 40 in a dense rosette, 8 in. long, ¾ in. to 1 in. broad, gradually narrowed to a pungent tip, marginal spines minute with pale scaly lines beneath. 18 in. h. Montevideo. 1873. SYN. *D. gemellaria* (of gardens).

**Dy′erae,** in honour of Lady Thistleton-Dyer (*née* Hooker), 1854–1945, who introduced several alpine plants.

## DYER'S GREENWEED. *See* **Genista tinctoria.**

## DYER'S ROCKET or WELD. *See* **Reseda Luteola.**

## DYER'S YELLOW WEED. *See* **Reseda Luteola.**

**Dykes′ii,** in honour of William Rickatson Dykes, 1877–1925, author of *The Genus Iris*, Secretary, Royal Horticultural Society, 1920–5.

**DYP′SIS** (*dupto*, to dip). FAM. *Palmaceae*. A genus of about 21 species of palms, sometimes included in Areca. Slender-stemmed, small, unarmed palms, natives of Madagascar. Leaves terminal, entire, 2-fid or pinnatisect. Spadix long, loosely flowered. Fruit small, oblong or ovoid. Seeds germinate easily. Cultivation as for Chamaedorea.

**D. madagascarien′sis.** A synonym of *Chrysalidocarpus madagascariensis*.

**D. pinnat′ifrons.** Only grown as young plants. Characters as genus. SYN. *Areca gracilis*.

**D. Thouarsia′na.** A synonym of *Vonitra fibrosa*.

**DYSCHORIS′TE** (*dys*, poorly, *choriste*, divided; the stigma is almost entire). FAM. *Acanthaceae*. A genus of about 60 annual or perennial plants allied to Ruellia, natives of the tropics. Leaves opposite, usually entire, small. Flowers mostly axillary, solitary or clustered in small, rather lax cymes; corolla more or less 2-lipped, tube inflated above, linear below; stamens 4, pointed or spurred at base; style hairy. Capsule 4-seeded. For treatment *see* **Ruellia.**

**D. Hildebrandt′ii.** Dwarf, free-flowering, with peculiar odour. *l.* elliptic, 1 in. long, silvery, scarcely toothed, short-stalked. *fl.* pale purple, 1⅓ in. long, 2-lipped; cal. about ½ in. long, glandular-downy; cymes axillary, 3- to 10-fld. Trop. Africa. (B.M. 7973.) Stove. A good pot plant. SYN. *Calophanes Hildebrandtii*.

**D. oblongifo′lia.** Dwarf perennial. Stem 4-angled. *l.* oblong to spatulate, entire, short-stalked. *fl.* solitary in l.-axils; azure with purple spots on lower lip; cor. funnel-shaped, ventricose, nearly bell-shaped, lobes rounded, nearly equal; cal. segs. short. N. America. (S.B.F.G. 181 as *Calophanes oblongifolia*.) Hardy or nearly so. Border plant.

*dysente′ricus -a -um,* causing dysentery.

**DYSO′DIA** (*dusodes*, evil-smelling, which applies to some species). FAM. *Compositae*. A genus of about 20 species of small shrubs and herbs, natives of California, Mexico, and Cent. America. Leaves more or less pin-natifid. Flower-heads with a bell-shaped or almost hemispherical involucre with a single series of rigid, rather thin bracts; ray-florets female, disk florets fertile. Ordinary well-drained loam and a greenhouse tempera-ture suit them, and they can be propagated by seeds sown in spring, by division of the roots, or by cuttings.

**D. Coop′eri.** Perennial with many herbaceous stems from a thick woody rootstock; about 14 in. h.; rather roughly hairy. *l.* alternate, obovate to oblong, ½ to 1 in. long, spiny toothed, tip often with oil-gland, base with 2. *fl.-heads* golden; ray-fl. 12 to 16, about ⅓ in. long; peduncles dilated upwards; bracts with 1 to 3 oblong oil-glands. *Pappus* about ⅓ in. long. Colorado to Arizona.

**D. grandiflo′ra.** Herbaceous perennial, 1 to 2 ft. h. *l.* opposite, ovate, slender-pointed, sharply toothed. *fl.-heads* rich deep orange. (B.M. 5310 as *Comaclinium aurantiacum*.) SYN. *Clomenocoma montana*.

**D. pubes′cens.** Shrub up to 1½ ft. h. *l.* pinnatifid; segs. linear, acute, hairy. *fl.-heads* golden, solitary on peduncle. November. Mexico. 1828. (B.R. as *Boebera incana*.)

**DYSOX′YLUM** (*dusodes*, evil-smelling, *xylon*, wood). FAM. *Meliaceae*. A genus of 100 species of trees, often with fetid odour, natives of Trop. Asia, E. Indies, Australia, and New Zealand. Leaves pinnate; leaflets entire, often oblique. Flowers of medium size; sepals and petals 4 or 5, the latter sometimes joined to the staminal tube; disk tubular enclosing the ovary within the staminal tube. Fruit a 1- to 5-celled capsule. Stove.

**D. Lessertia′num.** Tree, glabrous save for young shoots and infl. *l.* scarcely oblique at base; lflets. 4 to 10, elliptic or lanceolate. *fl.* in a loose panicle, 3 to 4 in. long; pet. usually 5, glabrous; cal. cup-shaped, shortly toothed; staminal tube 8- to 10-toothed, glabrous without; ovule 1 in each cell. New S. Wales.

**DYSSOCHRO′MA** (*dysoos*, sickly, *chroma*, colour; from the lurid colour of the flowers). FAM. *Solanaceae*. A genus of 2 species of climbing sub-shrubs or small trees natives of Brazil, sometimes included under Solandra but differing by the large, 5-cleft calyx with acute, lanceolate, equal segments, and by the 5 straight stamens the same length as the straight style. Leaves somewhat leathery, narrowed to both ends, entire. Flowers large, pendulous, on often solitary peduncles at the end of short nodose branchlets; cor. funnel-shaped, limb-plicate, deeply 5-lobed. For treatment of *D. viridi-flora see* **Solandra.**

**D. exim′ia.** Shrub. *l.* oval, firm, glossy, entire with a short, slender point. *fl.* green, in pairs, about 6 in. long, drooping; funnel-bell-shaped. Habitat? (B.M. 5092 as *Juanulloa eximia*.)

**D. viridiflo′ra.** Deciduous shrub of 2 to 3 ft. *l.* elliptical-oblong, narrowed to both ends, slender-pointed, glabrous. *fl.* green, ter-minal, solitary, stalked; cor. drooping, segs. long, revolute. May to July. Brazil. 1815. (B.M. 1948 as *Solandra viridiflora*.)

F. G. P.

# E

*e-* in compound words implying without, as *estriatus*, without lines.

**EAGLE FERN.** *See* **Pteridium Aquilinum.**

**EAGLE'S CLAW MAPLE.** *See* **Acer plantanoides laciniatum.**

**eared,** auriculate; having ears or appendages.

**EAR'INA** (*earinos*, the spring; spring-flowering). FAM. *Orchidaceae.* A genus of about 7 species of tufted epiphytic orchids from the Pacific Is. and New Zealand. They have small flowers crowded together in sessile terminal heads or spikes; the lateral sepals and foot of the column form a chin. Compost, temperature, &c., should be as for Odontoglossum.

**E. suave'olens.** *fl.* small, numerous, very fragrant, whitish. Stems slender, erect, 4 to 8 in. h., sheathed with the bases of narrow leathery l. 2 to 2½ in. long. New Zealand. (Laing & Blackwell, Pl. N. Zea. 117.)

E. C.

**EARTHING-UP.** Drawing, or applying additional, soil around the stems of plants. The plan is especially employed for plants needing more space for the development of leaves than for their roots and particularly for those, like Tomatoes, which root readily from the base of the stem; or for excluding light from some part of the plants so that they do not become green there, such as the leaf-stalks of Celery, the leaf-bases of Leeks, and the tubers of Potatoes; or for preserving the stems of plants from frost.

**EARTH-NUT.** *See* **Arachis hypogaea.**

**EARTHWORMS.** The importance of Earthworms is very considerable for their burrowings aid in the aeration and drainage of the soil, their habit of drawing fallen leaves into their burrows results in the production of humus, and their excrement in the form of 'worm-casts' has a beneficial manurial effect on vegetation. Earthworms are hermaphrodite, but the eggs, which are enclosed in a cocoon resembling a swollen wheat grain, are fertilized by the sperm cells of another worm. There are a number of species, *Lumbricus terrestris* being one of the most abundant in garden soils. Measures must be taken to reduce the population of Earthworms in lawns, bowling- and golf-greens, and on tennis courts where the presence of numerous worm-casts is objectionable. There are a number of preparations, both poisonous (colloidal lead arsenate, copper sulphate, and corrosive sublimate) and non-poisonous (lime-water, mowrah meal, and potassium permanganate), available for the purpose. An effective dressing is to dissolve ½ to 1 oz. of potassium permanganate crystals in 1 gallon of water, and to apply it to 1 sq. yd. of turf with the aid of a fine-rose watering-can. The worms soon come to the surface, when they may be swept up.

G. F. W.

**EARWIGS,** which belong to the Order *Dermaptera*, are characterized by the shortened leathery fore-wings covering the beautiful folded pair of flying wings and by a pair of forceps at the end of the body. While there are a number of indigenous and a few exotic species established in this country, it is only the Common or European Earwig, *Forficula auricularia*, that is generally known. The sexes are readily determined from the shape of the forceps—those of the male being rounded and calliper-like, and of the female straight with the inner sides touching from base to tip. This Earwig overwinters in the adult stage beneath bark, grease-bands, in rubbish, and elsewhere. The female lays her eggs in spring in a nest formed in the soil or beneath a stone and watches over them and even over the newly hatched nymphs, which resemble their parents but are pale and wingless. Considerable damage is done by these insects, which are active at night, to the blooms and foliage of Chrysanthemum, Dahlia, Heliotrope, Helianthus, and to many hardy Annuals, to ripening fruits (especially Peach and Nectarine), and to the blossoms of fruit-trees which are made ragged by their gnawing. They hide away during the daytime in curled leaves, bamboo-canes, amongst the petals, and elsewhere.

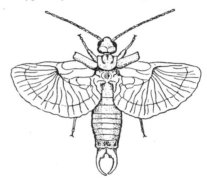

*Earwig with expanded wings*

All dead and curled leaves should be removed from the base of herbaceous plants, old seed-pods, and plant refuse, which provide shelters for the pests. They may be trapped by providing shelters in the form of plant pots stuffed with straw inverted over canes and placed among the attacked plants, in sponges, rolled pieces of sacking, corrugated paper, split Bamboo canes, and the dried stems of Broad Beans or similar hollow stems. The application of a poison bait is necessary for the reduction of a plague of Earwigs, one formula being: bran, 4 lb.; black treacle, 1 pint; sodium fluoride, ½ lb.; and water, 1 gallon. Dissolve the treacle in a little water and add to the sodium fluoride solution, which should then be mixed with the bran to form a moist, but not wet, mash. Apply the bait thinly towards evening on to the staging and floors of infested houses and to the ground between the plants in open borders. **A**

G. F. W.

**EAST INDIAN ARROWROOT.** *See* **Curcuma, Tacca.**

**EAST INDIAN ROSEWOOD.** *See* **Dalbergia.**

*Eat'onii,* in honour of Amos Eaton (1776–1842).

**EAU DE CRÉOLE.** *See* **Mammea americana.**

**EBENA'CEAE.** Dicotyledons. A family of about 320 trees and shrubs in 5 genera, natives mostly of the tropics, especially SE. Asia. Leaves usually alternate, entire, without stipules. Flowers axillary, usually solitary or in small cymes, regular, usually dioecious, parts 3 to 7; sepals joined; petals joined; stamens attached to base of corolla tube, as many or double as many as petals, or numerous, represented by staminodes as a rule in the female flowers; ovary superior, 2- to 16-celled. Fruit usually a berry with rather few seeds. Some of the species yield valuable timber, the very hard heart-wood of several constituting the ebony of commerce. The genera dealt with here are Euclea, Maba, and Royena.

***ebena'ceus -a -um,*** ebony-like.

***ebenoi'des,*** like Ebenus.

***eb'enus -a -um,*** ebony-black.

**EB'ENUS** (*ebenos*, used by Hippocrates for a leguminous plant). FAM. *Leguminosae*. A genus of over a dozen species of herbs or sub-shrubs, natives of the Mediterranean region and Asia Minor, one species in Beluchistan. Leaves alternate, pinnate, with 3 to 11 leaflets. Flowers papilionaceous, crowded in rounded heads or spikes; the prominently exposed, subulate calyx-lobes make a conspicuous feature of the inflorescence. Pod compressed, 1- or rarely 2-seeded. *E. cretica* and *E. Monbretii* are suitable for a sunny place on the rock-garden.

**E. cre'tica.** Evergreen shrub, 1 to 2 ft., younger parts densely furnished with silky hairs. *l.* of 3 or 5 lflets. which are linear-oblong, ¾ to 1½ in. long, pointed, cuneate. *fl.* purplish-red, closely packed in axillary cylindrical spikes 2 to 3 in. long on slender stalks up to 3 in. long; standard obcordate, ½ in. wide, streaked with dark lines; lobes of cal. ⅝ in. long, slender, ciliate, well exposed. June, July. Grecian Archipelago. 1737. (B.M. 1092 as *Anthyllis cretica.*)

**E. Monbret'ii.** Sub-shrub, base woody. Stems 4 to 10 in., erect, herbaceous, densely downy. *l.* pinnate, with 3½ or 4½ pairs of lflets., which are oblong-elliptical to obovate; ⅓ to ¾ in. long, tawny-downy. *fl.* purple, closely packed in globose or ovoid heads about 1 in. wide, the stalk 3 or 4 in. long; standard 7/16 in. wide, lobes of cal. ½ to ⅝ in. long, linear, feathered, conspicuously exposed. Orient.

**E. Sibthorp'ii.** Herbaceous, 1 to 2 ft. Stems erect, slender, appressed-downy. *l.* pinnate with 9 to 13 lflets., which are ⅓ to ¾ in. long, linear-oblong, pointed, stalkless; appressed silvery-hairy. *fl.* purplish, in compact, spherical heads 1 to 1½ in. across terminating stalks 4 to 6 in. long; standard erect, infolded; lobes of cal. linear, ciliate, exposed. Greece. (F.G. 740.) SYN. *E. pinnata.*

W. J. B.

**EBONY.** *See* **Diospyros Ebenus, Maba.**

***ebractea'tus -a -um,*** without bracts.

***ebur'neus -a -um,*** ivory-white.

***Ec'ae,*** in honour of Mrs. E. C. Aitchison. *See* ***Aitchisonii.***

**ECBAL'LIUM** (*ekballein*, to cast out, the seeds being violently ejected from the ripe fruit). FAM. *Cucurbitaceae*. A single trailing annual native of the Mediterranean region constitutes this genus. Related to Cucumis and distinct from Momordica by the absence of the scales which close the base of the calyx in that genus. The fruits are very turgid when ripe and squirt out their seeds through the hole left where it falls from the stalk, or may do so at the slightest touch. The watery juice of the fruit yields a powerful purgative, Elaterium. For cultivation, *see* **Gourds.**

**E. Elate'rium.** Squirting Cucumber. Roughly hairy trailer, somewhat grey, without tendrils. *l.* cordate, more or less 3-lobed, stalks long. *fl.* yellow, staminate in axillary racemes, stamens free or nearly so, pollen sacs curved. June. *fr.* green, prickly, oblong. Middle and E. Mediterranean. 1548. (B.M. 1914.)

**ECCREMOCAR'PUS** (*ekkremes*, pendent; *karpos*, fruit). FAM. *Bignoniaceae*. A genus of 3 or 4 evergreen climbers, natives of Chile and Peru, with shrubby stems. Leaves opposite, 2-pinnatisect, ending in a branched tendril. Flowers yellow, red, or golden, tubular; corolla shortly 5-lobed or 2-lipped; stamens 4, included. Fruit a 1-celled, many-seeded capsule; seeds orbicular with a broad wing. *E. scaber* is hardy in sheltered situations in the southern counties and farther north in mild winters. Where it is liable to be killed in winter it can be treated as a half-hardy annual and raised annually from seed. It will grow in any ordinary light fertile soil. Seeds should be sown in February in gentle heat, potted on and planted out in May, and flowers will be produced in the latter part of the same year.

**E. longiflo'rus.** *l.* abruptly 2- or 3-pinnate; lflets. oval, entire, sessile. *fl.* yellow with a green limb, tube a little curved; peduncles many-fld., opposite l. July. Peru. 1825. Greenhouse.

**E. sca'ber.*** Stems, angular, ribbed, 10 to 15 ft. h. *l.* abruptly 2-pinnate; lflets. alternate, obliquely cordate, ovate, serrate or entire. *fl.* scarlet or deep orange-red, 1 in. long; throat swollen; racemes opposite l., secund, many-fld. Chile. 1824. Useful for covering walls, trellises, and pillars. (B.R. 939.) var. **au'reus** has clear golden *fl.*; **ru'ber** has orange-red *fl.* SYN. *Calampelis scaber.*

**ECHEVE'RIA** (in honour of Atanasio Echeverria or Echevarria, one of the botanical draughtsmen employed on *Flora Mexicana*, 1858). FAM. *Crassulaceae*. The genus contains about 150 species, all occurring in America, especially Mexico, Texas, and California; they were at one time included in Cotyledon (q.v.) but form a very distinct group. American botanists have further subdivided this genus into Dudleya, Oliveranthus, Stylophyllum, and Urbinia; these names are sometimes found in catalogues. The leaves are always in rosettes and vary greatly in form and texture, being often beautifully coloured and sometimes covered with hairs like plush. The lateral inflorescence bears flowers which are bell-shaped but pinched in towards the mouth; the colouring is usually scarlet, yellow, or white. The Echeverias hybridize very freely, not only amongst themselves but also with the Pachyphytums, the result of this union being known as Pachyveria. For cultivation, *see* **Cotyledon.**

**E. adun'ca.** A synonym of *Pachyphytum Hookeri.*

*Echeveria agavoides*

**E. agavoi'des.** *l.* in a close rosette, triangular, wide at base, fleshy, pale green with sharp brown tips. *fl.* reddish-yellow. Mexico. SYN. *Cotyledon agavoides, Urbinia agavoides.* (F.d.S. 2003, Ref. B.I. 67, as *Cotyledon agavoides.*)

**E. amoe'na.** Rosettes small, stemless, forming clumps. *l.* narrow, loosely arranged, bluish. *fl.* pink. Mexico. *l.* are easily detached and plantlets readily develop at their base.

**E. arizon'ica.** A synonym of *Sedum Weinbergii.*

**E. atropurpu'rea.** Shrubby. *l.* crowded in rosettes at top of stems, broad and not very thick, dark purple with a glaucous bloom. *fl.* red. Mexico. SYN. *Cotyledon atropurpurea.*

**E. austra'lis.** Shrubby, branching. *l.* spatulate, in a loose rosette, bluish-green tinged with pink. *fl.* pink, freely produced. Costa Rica.

**E. Braun'tonii.** *l.* spatulate, up to 8 in. long, ⅗ in. wide, acute, very grey above. *infl.* 12 to 24 in. long, with 3 or 4 branches 4 to 8 in. long. *fl.* pale greenish-yellow, about ½ in. long. S. California. SYN. *Dudleya Brauntonii.*

**E. caespito'sa.** *l.* up to 3 in. long, ¾ in. wide, tapering gradually, grey-green. *fl.* yellow. California. SYN. *Cotyledon caespitosa, Dudleya caespitosa.*

**E. califor'nica.** A synonym of *Echeveria Cotyledon.*

**E. can'dida.** Rosettes on short stems. *l.* linear, pointed, mealy white. *fl.* white. California. SYN. *Dudleya candida.*

**E. carnicol'or.** Rosettes small, stemless, making offsets. *l.* very fleshy, flat above, convex below, pink with a metallic tinge. *fl.* orange-red, freely produced. Mexico. SYN. *Cotyledon carnicolor.*

**E. coccin'ea.** Stems stout, branching chiefly from base, 1⅓ to 2½ ft. h. *l.* narrow, up to 3 in. long, green covered with fine soft hairs. *fl.* orange-red. Mexico. (B.M. 2572.) SYN. *Cotyledon coccinea.*

**E. Corderoy'i.** Rosettes stemless, with many *l.*, similar to *E. agavoidea. fl.* red with yellow tips. N. Mexico. SYN. *Cotyledon Corderoyi, Urbinia Corderoyi.*

**E. Cotyle'don.** Rosettes short-stemmed. *l.* linear, 3 to 4 in. long, widest at base, covered with dense white meal. *fl.* whitish-yellow in loose, branched racemes. California. SYN. *Cotyledon californica, Dudleya Cotyledon.*

**E. cultra'ta.** Rosettes stemless. *l.* 3 to 4 in. long, ½ in. wide, sharply pointed, green. *fl.* yellow. Lower California. SYN. *Dudleya cultrata.*

**E. Derenberg'ii.** *l.* in rosettes, wide, fleshy but not very thick, rounded above, grey with a reddish edge and red spiny tip. *fl.* orange with red keels. Mexico.

**E. Desmetia'na.** A synonym of *E. Peacockii.*

**E. ed'ulis.** Stems low, branching, terminating in close rosettes. *l.* cylindrical, 4 to 6 in. long, ¼ in. wide, fleshy, soft, and brittle, with a white waxy coating. *fl.* yellowish-white. California. SYN. *Cotyledon edulis, Stylophyllum edulis.*

**E. el'egans.** Stem up to 12 in. h., branching. Rosettes close. *l.* wide, concave, alabaster white with a translucent green edge. *fl.* pink with yellow tips. Mexico. SYN. *Cotyledon elegans.*

**E. farino'sa.** Stem low, much branched, branches ending in close rosettes of linear, pointed *l.*, widest at base, covered with dense white meal. *fl.* yellow, not often produced. California. SYN. *Cotyledon farinosa, Dudleya farinosa.*

**E. ful'gens.** Stem low, little branched, rosettes loose. *l.* rounded with a wavy edge, bluish-green. *fl.* brilliant scarlet. Mexico. SYN. *E. retusa.*

**E. gibbiflo'ra.** Shrubby with loose rosettes terminating branches. *l.* not very thick, 5 to 8 in. long, 3 to 5 in. wide, grey-green flushed with red or purple, surface waxy. *fl.* scarlet, in a freely branched infl. Mexico. SYN. *Cotyledon gibbiflora.* var. **caruncula'ta,** similar to type but with curious blister-like outgrowths on the surface of *l.*; **metal'lica,** similar to type but *l.* bronze with a fine red edge.

**E. glau'ca.** Rosettes compact, about 4 in. across, making offsets. *l.* ¾ in. wide at base, rounded with a short tip, thin, blue-grey with reddish margins. *fl.* bright red, yellow at tips. Mexico. SYN. *E. secunda glauca.* Formerly much used for bedding.

**E. grandiflo'ra.** Stem thick. *l.* in a rosette, rather thin, 4 to 6 in. long, 1 in. wide or less at base, tapering gradually to a point, greyish-white. *fl.* greenish-yellow turning pink. California. SYN. *Cotyledon grandiflora, Dudleya grandiflora.*

**E. Green'ei.** Stem short. *l.* in a rosette, 2 to 3 in. long, ¾ in. wide at base, tapering, thick, greyish-white. *fl.* yellowish. Santa Cruz. SYN. *Dudleya Greenei.*

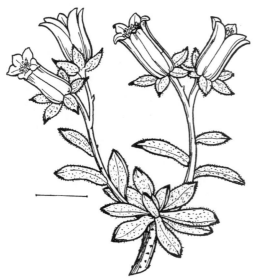

*Echeveria Harmsii*

**E. Harms'ii.** Stems 12 to 18 in. h. *l.* in rosettes, linear, pointed, I in. long, covered with fine soft hairs. *fl.* large, 1 in. long, red with yellow tips. Mexico. (B.M. 7993.) SYN. *Cotyledon elegans, Oliveranthus elegans, E. elegans.*

**E. leucot'richa.** Stem short, branching. *l.* in a loose rosette, lanceolate; whole plant covered with thick hairs like plush, red-brown on stems, silvery on *l.* with red-brown at their tips. *fl.* orange-red. Mexico.

**E. linguaefo'lia.** Stem thick, 8 to 16 in. h. *l.* in a loose rosette, ovate, blunt, thick, pale green. *fl.* straw-yellow. Mexico. SYN. *Cotyledon linguaefolia.*

**E. metallica.** A synonym of *E. gibbiflora metallica.*

**E. multicau'lis.** Stem woody, branched. *l.* in open rosettes, small, spatulate, dark green with conspicuous scarlet edges. *fl.* scarlet. Mexico.

**E. nodulo'sa.** Stem up to 8 in. h. *l.* in rosettes at tips of branches, 2 to 3 in. long, dull green with a red edge. *fl.* straw-coloured, tinged red. Cent. Mexico. SYN. *Cotyledon nodulosa.*

**E. nu'da.** Stem 6 to 8 in. h. *l.* in rosettes, 2 in. long, 1 in. wide, green. *fl.* pale yellow. Mexico. SYN. *Cotyledon nuda.*

**E. Peacock'ii.** Stem short. Rosettes close. *l.* 2 in. long, 1½ in. wide, bluish-white with a red edge. *fl.* scarlet. Mexico. SYN. *E. Desmetiana.*

**E. perel'egans.** A synonym of *E. elegans.*

**E. pubes'cens.** Shrubby. Stems stout, 20 to 30 in. h. *l.* up to 3 in. long, green, covered with soft white hairs. *fl.* red. Mexico. SYN. *Cotyledon pubescens.*

**E. pulverulen'ta.** Stem 2 ft. h. *l.* spatulate, 6 in. long, 2 to 3 in. wide, covered with white meal. *fl.* reddish-yellow. California. SYN. *Cotyledon pulverulenta, Dudleya pulverulenta.*

**E. pulvina'ta.** Stem low, branching. Rosettes loose. *l.* 1½ to 2 in. long, 1 in. wide, thick; whole plant covered with white hairs which are sometimes crimson along edges of *l. fl.* scarlet. Mexico. (B.M. 7918.)

**E. pu'mila.** Rosettes very compact. *l.* 1½ in. long, ½ in. wide, pale glaucous green, sometimes reddish. *fl.* yellow, red at base only. Mexico. SYN. *Cotyledon pumila.*

**E. Purpus'ii.** *fl.* scarlet, otherwise similar to *E. pulverulenta.* California. (B.M. 7713.) SYN. *Cotyledon Purpusii, Dudleya Purpusii.*

**E. retu'sa.** A synonym of *E. fulgens.*

**E. retu'sa hyb'rida.*** Stemless. *l.* in a rosette, large, spatulate, glaucous green, margin red. *fl.* crimson, in terminal cymes on lateral branches. *infl.* 2 ft. h. Winter. Free-flowering hybrid of uncertain parentage, suitable for house or conservatory decoration.

**E. ro'sea.** Stem short, branched. *Upper l.* in a rosette; *lower* more distant, 2 to 3 in. long, ¾ in. wide, reddish. *fl.* yellow with pink *cal.* Mexico. SYN. *Cotyledon rosea.*

**E. secun'da.** Stem up to 12 in. Rosette close. *l.* 1½ in. long, 1 in. wide, pale green, becoming red. *fl.* reddish-yellow. Mexico. SYN. *Cotyledon secunda.* var. **glauca,** a synonym of *E. glauca.*

**E. seto'sa.** Rosettes stemless, making offsets freely. *l.* convex on both sides, narrow, green, covered closely with white bristles. *fl.* red with yellow tips. Mexico. (B.M. 8748.)

**E. vis'cida.** Rosettes almost stemless. *l.* cylindrical, 3 to 4 in. long, ¼ in. wide, green, very sticky. *fl.* pinkish. California. SYN. *Stylophyllum viscidum.*

V. H.

**ECHID'NIUM** (*echis*, viper; related to Dracontium). FAM. *Araceae.* A genus of 2 species of tuberous American herbs, natives of Guiana, related to Dracontium but with the ovary 1-celled with 2 ovules instead of 2- to 5-celled with 1 ovule in each cell. Treatment as for Caladium.

**E. Regelia'num.** *l.-stalk*, 18 to 36 in. long, irregularly variegated brownish-green and brown; blade about 18 in. wide, 3-partite, ultimate segs. ovate or oblong-ovate. *Peduncle* about 2 in. long, brownish. *Spathe* scarcely 4 in. long, oblong-ovate, deep purple, shining within. Trop. America. 1864. (G.F. 1866, 503 as *E. Spruceanum.*)

**ECHIDNOP'SIS** (*echidne*, a viper, *opsis*, like; referring to the stems). FAM. *Asclepiadaceae.* Leafless, succulent plants with cylindrical stems, branching chiefly from the base, divided into very low tubercles with a leaf-scar but no spine in the centre of each. Flowers small, hardly distinguishable from Caralluma. **A**

**E. cereiform'is.** Stems slender, erect or becoming prostrate. *fl.* in clusters near the tip, yellow; outer corona absent. N. Africa, along the Red Sea. (W. & S. 1050; B.M. 5930.) There is a darker *fl.* form sometimes confused with *E. Dammanniana.*

**E. Dammannia'na.** Stems similar to *E. cereiformis. fl.* dark purple-brown on the lobes, yellow with dark dots inside; outer corona present. Eritrea.

V. H.

**ECHINA'CEA** (*echinos*, hedgehog; scales of receptacle prickly). FAM. *Compositae.* A genus of 2 species of perennial herbs, natives of the United States, very closely related to Rudbeckia and often included there but with rose or purple rays. Hardy plants for the herbaceous border, best in a deep rich loam with plenty of leaf-mould. Readily propagated by division or seed.

**E. angustifo'lia.** 2 to 4 ft. h. Stem hairy below. *l.* lanceolate, 4 to 6 in. long, ½ in. wide, hairy. *fl.-heads* light purple or rose, 4 to 6 in. across; rays drooping. Summer. United States. 1861. (B.M. 5281.) SYN. *Rudbeckia angustifolia.*

**E. purpu'rea.*** 3 to 4 ft. h. Stem smooth. *Radical l.* ovate-lanceolate; *stem-l.* narrower, narrowed to base; all roughish, faintly toothed. *fl.-heads* about 4 in. across, solitary on a long, thick, rigid peduncle; rays reddish-purple, passing to grey-green at tips; disk orange. Summer. United States. 1799. (A. 114; B.M. 2 as *Rudbeckia purpurea.*) var. **interme'dia,** ray-*fl.* more spreading than in type; **na'na,** dwarf, rays long, narrow; **seroti'na,** *fl.* in autumn, roughly hairy. (L.B.C. 1539.) Fl. last well and are useful for cutting.

*echina'tus -a -um,* covered with prickles like a hedgehog.

## ECHINOCAC'TUS (*echinos,* a hedgehog; referring to the prickly form). FAM. *Cactaceae.* Large plants, round or cylindric, ribbed, the crown of the plant densely woolly; areoles very spiny. Flowers from the top of the plant, usually yellow, rarely pink; tube short, stout with numerous scales. Fruit very woolly, thin-skinned, ovoid. As at present recognized, the genus Echinocactus contains only about 9 species, all from N. America; formerly a much larger number were included but they have now been divided amongst 28 genera (*see under* **Cactus**). Plants previously known as Echinocacti will be found in the list of synonyms below. **A**

**E. gran'dis.** Plants large, cylindric, dull green, with broad horizontal bands when young; ribs rather thin, especially in old plants; spines stout, banded, 6 or 7, long and straight. *fl.* yellow, about 2 in. long. Mexico. Young plants are very different from old ones.

**E. Gru'son'ii.** Plants solitary, globose, depressed, very large; ribs 21 to 37, thin and high; spines golden yellow when young, paler with age; radial spines 8 to 10, centrals 4, up to 2 in. long. *fl.* 1½ to 2 in. long, yellowish; cultivated plants are seldom large enough to flower. Mexico. (B.R.C. 3, f. 182–4.)

*Echinocactus horizonthalonius*

**E. horizonthalo'nius.** Solitary, globular or depressed, becoming short-cylindric, glaucous; ribs about 8, low, rounded; spines 6 to 9, curved, very stout, flattened, annulate and pinkish; one central spine stouter than the radials. *fl.* pale pink. Texas, New Mexico, Arizona, Mexico. (B.R.C. 3, t. 20.)

**E. in'gens.** Large globular plants, glaucous, very woolly at the top; ribs about 8 when young, far more numerous in age; areoles distant, with much yellow wool; spines stout, brown. *fl.* yellow, small. Mexico. (B.R.C. 3, f. 185–6.)

**E. Palm'eri.** Plants large, ribs 12 to 26 in old plants; radial spines 5 to 8, pale and weak; centrals 4, up to 3 in. long, stout, annulate, yellow with a brown swollen base. *fl.* yellow, rather small. Mexico. (B.R.C. 3, f. 188–9.) SYN. *Echinocactus saltillensis* of gardens.

**E. polyceph'alus.** Plants forming large clumps, each head globose; ribs 13 to 21, high; areoles large; spines 7 to 15, reddish, awl-shaped, flattened, the radials up to 2 in. long, the 4 centrals stouter and up to 4 in. *fl.* yellow, small. Nevada, Utah, Arizona, California, Sonora. (B.R.C. 3, f. 191.)

**E. Visna'ga.** Very large plants up to 3 ft. h., glaucous green, with masses of tawny wool on the top; ribs 15 to 40, acute; areoles large, almost touching; four radial spines only, stout, up to 2 in. long. *fl.* yellow, large. Mexico. (B.M. 4559.)

Species formerly classed as Echinocactus: **E. brevihama'tus,** see *Ancistrocactus brevihamatus*; **E. centete'rius,** see *Malacocarpus mammillarioides*; **E. concin'nus,** see *Malacocarpus concinnus*; **E. coptonog'onus,** see *Echinofossulocactus coptonogonus*; **E. cornig'erus,** see *Ferocactus latispinus*; **E. coryno'des,** see *Malacocarpus erinaceus*; **E. Cum'ingii,** see *Lobivia Cumingii*; **E. Diguet'ii,** see *Ferocactus Diguetii*; **E. durangen'sis,** see *Echinomastus durangensis*; **E. Echid'ne,** see *Ferocactus Echidne*; **E. Emor'yi,** see *Ferocactus Covillei*; **E. gibbo'sus,** see *Gymnocalycium gibbosum*; **E. glau'cus,** see *Sclerocactus Whipplei*; **E. Haselberg'ii,** see *Malacocarpus Haselbergii*; **E. Joad'ii,** see *Malacocarpus concinnus*; **E. John'sonii,** see *Ferocactus Johnsonii*; **E. latispi'nus,** see *Ferocactus latispinus*; **E. Lecon'tei,** see *Ferocactus Lecontei*; **E. Leea'nus,** see *Gymnocalycium Leeanum*; **E. longihama'tus,** see *Ferocactus hamatacanthus*; **E. Mackiea'nus,** see *Gymnocalycium gibbosum*; **E. mammulo'sus,** see *Malacocarpus mammulosus*; **E. multiflo'rus,** see *Gymnocalycium multiflorum*; **E. obvalla'tus,** see *Echinofossulocactus obvallatus*; **E. Orcut'tii,** see *Ferocactus Orcuttii*; **E. orna'tus,** see *Astrophytum ornatum*; **E. Ot'tonis,** see *Malacocarpus Ottonis*; **E. pectinif'erus,** see *Echinocereus pectinatus*; **E. penin'sulae,** see *Ferocactus peninsulae*; **E. Pent'landii,** see *Lobivia Pentlandii*; **E. Pfeif'feri,** see *Ferocactus glaucescens*; **E. polyancis'trus,** see *Sclerocactus polyancistrus*; **E. Pott'sii,** see *Thelocactus Pottsii*; **E. rhodophthal'mus,** see *Thelocactus bicolor*; **E. Schilinzkya'nus,** see *Frailea Schilinzkyanus*; **E. sco'pa,** see *Malacocarpus scopa*; **E. sen'ilis,** see *Neoporteria nidus*; **E. sinua'tus,** see *Ferocactus hamatacanthus*; **E. spira'lis,** see *Ferocactus nobilis*; **E. tenuispi'nus,** see *Malacocarpus Ottonis*; **E. texen'sis,** see *Homalocephala texensis*; **E. tubiflo'rus,** see *Echinopsis tubiflora*; **E. turbiniform'is,** see *Strombocactus disciformis*; **E. uncina'tus,** see *Ferocactus uncinatus*; **E. virides'cens,** see *Ferocactus viridescens*; **E. Williams'ii,** see *Lophophora Williamsii*; **E. Wisliz'eni,** see *Ferocactus Wislizeni.*

V. H.

*echinocar'pus -a -um,* prickly fruited.

## ECHINOCE'REUS (*echinos,* hedgehog; on account of the spiny fruit by which Echinocereus differs from Cereus). FAM. *Cactaceae.* Usually low plants, solitary or often in clumps; stems 1-jointed, round or cylindrical, ribbed; areoles with spines, Flowers always from old areoles on the side, not top, of the plant, usually large, diurnal; scarlet, crimson, or purple, rarely yellow; tube and ovary spiny. Fruit spiny, often edible. These plants used to be classed with the Cerei but are distinguished by the spiny fruit and usually much shorter stems. For cultivation *see under* **Cactus** (terrestrial).

**E. amoe'nus.** Often considered a variety of *E. pulchellus.*

**E. Blanck'ii.** Stems procumbent, joints slender; ribs 5 to 7, strongly tuberculate; areoles fairly close; radial spines 6 to 8, short; central one longer, all brownish. *fl.* purple, 2 to 3 in. Mexico and Texas. (B.R.C. 3, t. 3; R.H. 1865, 92.) SYN. *Cereus Blanckii.*

**E. Brandeg'eei.** Always in clumps; stems long, erect; ribs strongly tuberculate; spines yellow, turning to grey; radials about 12, spreading; centrals 4, much stouter. *fl.* purple. Lower California. (B.R.C. 3, f. 41.)

**E. caespito'sus.** A synonym of *E. Reichenbachii.*

**E. chloran'thus.** Stems cylindric, usually solitary; ribs about 13, nearly hidden by spines; one central spine, very long. *fl.* greenish-yellow. Texas, Mexico. (B.R.C. 3, t. 2.)

**E. cineras'cens.** Stems erect, branching freely from the base; ribs about 12, low; areoles scattered; spines pale, radials 10, centrals 3 or 4. *fl.* purple, tube short. Mexico. SYN. *E. cirrhiferus.*

**E. coccin'eus.** Usually in large clumps; stems up to 20 in. h. and 2 in. across; ribs 8 to 11, tuberculate; spines numerous, white or yellowish. *fl.* crimson. Mexico, Arizona, Colorado. (B.R.C. 3, t. 2.) SYN. *E. phoeniceus.*

**E. dasyacan'thus.** Plants solitary, cylindrical; ribs 15 to 21, low; areoles almost touching; radial spines spreading, pinkish, centrals stouter. *fl.* often very large, yellow, tinged red. Texas, New Mexico. (B.R.C. 3, f. 19.)

**E. Da'visii.** The smallest species, stems round or oval, less than 2 in. long; radial spines 9 to 12, pale, spreading; centrals absent. *fl.* greenish. Texas.

**E. Delae'tii.** Stems branching from the base, cylindrical; ribs indistinct; spines replaced by long, bristly, curly hairs completely hiding the plant. *fl.* pink. Mexico. (B.R.C. 3, f. 1.)

**E. du'bius.** Growing in clumps; stems of a flabby texture; ribs 7 to 9, broad; spines numerous, centrals longer and curved. *fl.* pale purple. Texas. (B.R.C. 3, f. 48.)

**E. Engelman'ii.** Forming large clumps; stems cylindrical, erect; ribs 11 to 14; 10 radial spines, spreading; 5 or 6 very stout, curved centrals, sometimes flattened, all yellowish-brown. *fl.* purple, variable in size. SW. United States. (B.R.C. 3, t. 5.) SYN. *Cereus Engelmanii.*

**E. enneacan'thus.** Forming clumps; stems long, prostrate; ribs prominent, rather soft in texture; spines yellowish, the central one longer. *fl.* bright red, wide-opened. Mexico, Texas. (B.R.C. 3, f. 49.)

**E. Fend'leri.** Forming clumps; ribs prominent, strongly tuberculate; spines very variable, about 6, fairly stout, dark. *fl.* deep purple, very large, freely produced. Texas, Arizona, Mexico. (B.M. 6533; B.R.C. 3, t. 4.) SYN. *Cereus Fendleri.*

**E. Fitch'ii.** Plants short, stems cylindrical; ribs 10 to 12, low; areoles close; spines white, about 20, very short, pale, and spreading. *fl.* pink, wide-opened. Texas. (B.R.C. 3, t. 3.)

**E. Hem'pelii.** Stems solitary, erect, ribs 10, strongly tuberculate; spines 6, white with brown tips. *fl.* large, violet. Mexico. (B.R.C. 3, f. 42.)

**E. Knippelia'nus.** A small plant with 5 to 7 prominent ribs; areoles minute, spines 1 to 3, very small, yellow. *fl.* small, pinkish. Mexico. (B.R.C. 3, f. 38.)

**E. mamilla'tus.** Forming clumps, stems cylindrical; ribs 20 to 25, strongly tuberculate; spines numerous, white. *fl.* unknown. Lower California. (B.R.C. 3, f. 54.)

**E. marit'imus.** Forming very large clumps; stems round or short cylindrical; ribs 8 to 10; areoles close; radial spines about 10, centrals 4, all long, stiff and yellow. *fl.* yellow. Lower California. (B.R.C. 3, t. 2.)

**E. Merk'eri.** Forming clumps; joints short, roundish; ribs 8 or 9; spines glassy white. *fl.* purple. Mexico. (B.R.C. 3, f. 43.)

**E. mojaven'sis.** Forming large clumps; stems round or oblong; ribs 8 to 13; spines slender, spreading, whitish. *fl.* crimson, rather narrow. California, Nevada, Utah, Arizona. (B.M. 7705.)

**E. octacan'thus.** Forming clumps; stems ovoid; ribs 7 to 9, somewhat tuberculate; areoles close; spines greyish-brown, stiff. *fl.* red, remaining open for several days. Texas. (Gn. 13 (1878), 291 as *Cereus Roemeri*.)

**E. pectina'tus.** Plants solitary, cylindrical, almost hidden by the interlocking spines; ribs 20 to 22; areoles close; radial spines 30, in 2 series, short, white or pink, in bands of colour round the plant; several central spines. *fl.* purplish. Mexico. (B.M. 4190.)

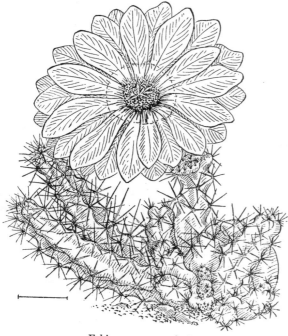

*Echinocereus pentalophus*

**E. pentaloph'us.** Stems procumbent; ribs 4 to 6, with low tubercles; radial spines 4 or 5, very short, white; one central spine. *fl.* reddish-violet. Mexico, Texas. (B.R.C. 3, t. 3; B.M. 7205.) SYN. *E. procumbens.* Grows well and flowers freely.

**E. pulchel'lus.** Small plants; stem top-shaped, branching from the base; ribs 12, divided into low tubercles; spines few, small, straight. *fl.* pale pink. Mexico. (B.R.C. 3, f. 39.)

**E. Reichenbach'ii.** Stems solitary or in clumps; ribs 12 to 19; areoles close; spines 20 to 30, white or brown, closely pressed to the plant. *fl.* light purple, fragrant. Texas, Mexico. (B.M. 6669.) SYN. *E. caespitosus.*

**E. rigidis'simus.** Rainbow Cactus. Similar to *E. pectinatus* and sometimes regarded as a variety of it.

**E. Salm-Dyckia'nus.** Stems decumbent, elongated; ribs 7 to 9, low; spines 8 or 9, short and yellowish. *fl.* orange. Mexico. (B.R.C. 3, f. 3.)

**E. scopulo'rum.** Similar to *E. Reichenbachii.* (B.R.C. 3, f. 31.)

**E. stramin'eus.** Forming large clumps; stem ovoid, ribs 13; spines straw-coloured, numerous, spreading; centrals 3 or 4, up to 4 in. long. *fl.* purple, large. Texas, New Mexico. (B.R.C. 3, f. 51–3.)

**E. subiner'mis.** Plants usually solitary; ribs 5 to 8, broad, spines very small; some areoles spineless. *fl.* yellow. Mexico. (B.R.C. 3, f. 15.)

**E. triglochida'tus.** Forming clumps; stems erect, stout, short; ribs 5 to 8; spines yellowish, 3 to 8 about an inch long, spreading. *fl.* scarlet. Texas, New Mexico, Colorado. (B.R.C. 3, f. 6, 7.) SYN. *E. paucispinus.*

**E. viridiflo'rus.** Similar to *E. chloranthus* but with larger *fl.*, shorter stems, and shorter central spines. (B.R.C. 3, t. 2.)

V. H.

**ECHINOCYS'TIS** (*echinos*, hedgehog, *kystis*, bladder; in reference to the prickly fruit). FAM. *Cucurbitaceae.* A genus of about 25 species of American annual or perennial herbs, prostrate or climbing, sometimes tuberous rooted. Leaves palmately 5- to 7-angled. Flowers white, mostly small, monoecious; staminate in racemes or panicles, pistillate solitary in same leaf-axil. Fruit dry or berry-like, with long spines. *E. lobata* is a half-hardy annual growing very rapidly in rich soil, needing a good deal of water.

**E. faba'cea.** Tendril climber, 20 to 30 ft. long. *l.* deeply 5- to 7-lobed. *fl.* greenish-white. *fr.* about 2 in. long, globose or ovoid, densely spiny; seed about 1 in. long, margined by a narrow groove or dark line. S. California.

**E. loba'ta.** Tendril climber, very rapid in growth, tendrils branched. *l.* thin, deeply 5-lobed, lobes triangular, toothed. *fl.* greenish-white, small; staminate panicles longer than l. July to September. *fr.* about 2 in. long, weakly prickly; seed ¾ in. long. N. America. (R.H. 1895, f. 1.)

**E. macrocarp'a.** Tendril climber, 10 to 20 ft. long. *l.* deeply lobed, 3 to 8 in. across. *fl.* greenish-white, saucer-shaped. *fr.* broadly oblong, 3 to 4 in. long, densely spiny; spines very unequal, ¼ to 1 in. or more long. S. California.

**ECHINOFOSSULOCAC'TUS** (*echinos*, hedgehog, *fossula*, groove; from the form of the plant). FAM. *Cactaceae.* This genus is sometimes known as Stenocactus. Plants generally small, usually solitary, globular; ribs very numerous, often very thin and wavy; areoles very distant; spines numerous, sometimes flattened. Flowers small, with a very short tube. Fruit round or oval with a few papery scales. All are natives of Mexico. For cultivation *see under* **Cactus** (terrestrial).

**E. alba'tus.** Plants depressed globose, glaucous; ribs about 35; radial spines 10, bristly; centrals 4, flat and annulate. *fl.* white. Mexico.

**E. coptonog'onus.** Plants depressed, sometimes forming clusters; glaucous green; ribs stout, only 10 to 14; young areoles very woolly, spines 3 to 5, stout, incurved, flattened. *fl.* purple and white. Mexico. SYN. *Echinocactus coptonogonus.*

**E. crispa'tus.** Plants egg-shaped; ribs about 25, very wavy and thin; spines 10 or 11, unequal, not very long. *fl.* small, purplish. Mexico. (B.R.C. 3, f. 123.) SYN. *Echinocactus crispatus.*

**E. gladia'tus.** Plants egg-shaped, depressed at the top; glaucous; ribs 14 to 22, rounded; spines 10, some ascending, up to 2 in. long, covering the crown. *fl.* unknown. Mexico. (B.R.C. 3, f. 126.)

**E. hasta'tus.** Plants depressed-globose, pale green; ribs 35, slightly indented; radial spines 5 or 6, very short, straight, the upper ones flattened; one long central projecting at right angles. *fl.* white, the largest of the genus. Mexico.

**E. lamello'sus.** Plants short-cylindric; ribs about 30, flattened and wavy; areoles very distant; spines 5 to 6, white with brown tips. *fl.* red. Mexico.

**E. Lloyd′ii.** Plants round, crowned with overtopping spines; ribs very numerous, thin, wavy; radial spines 10 to 15, white, spreading, very short; centrals 3, much longer, incurved, middle one up to 4 in., flattened, papery. *fl.* small, whitish. Mexico. (B.R.C. 3, f. 118.)

**E. multicosta′tus.** Globose plants, 2 to 4 in. in diameter, with more than 100 very thin, wavy ribs with 1 or 2 areoles on each; spines 6 to 9, the 3 upper erect, up to 3 in. long, thin, flexible, the lower spreading, awl-shaped, quite short. *fl.* whitish. Mexico.

**E. obvalla′tus.** Plants globose, depressed; ribs about 25, rather thin; spines about 8, half long and ascending, the other half hardly spreading, a quarter as long. *fl.* very large, pink. Mexico. (B.R.C. 3, f. 122.)

**E. pentacan′thus.** Plants depressed-globose, glaucous; ribs about 25 or more; areoles few on each rib; spines 5, unequal, flattened, 3 erect, the lower 2 much shorter. *fl.* large, violet. Mexico.

**E. phyllacan′thus.** Plants depressed-globose, dull green; ribs 30 to 35, thin, wavy; areoles few on each rib; spines 5 to 9, upper spine erect or curving over the top of the plant, flattened, annulate, others short, weak, spreading. *fl.* yellowish, small. Mexico. (B.R.C. 3, f. 124.)

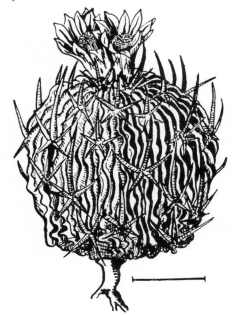

*Echinofossulocactus violaciflorus*

**E. violaciflo′rus.** Plants round, becoming columnar; ribs about 35, thin, indented; spines about 7, the 3 upper curving over the top of the plant, up to 2 in. long, broad and flattened; lower short, awl-shaped, incurved. *fl.* violet with a white stripe down each pet. Mexico. (B.R.C. 3, t. 23; f. 121.)

**E. Wippermann′ii.** Plants egg-shaped; ribs 35 to 40, flattened, wavy; areoles close, hairy when young; radial spines 18 to 22, bristle-like, white, short; centrals 3 or 4, erect, up to 2 in., awl-shaped, black. *fl.* dull yellow. Mexico.

**E. zacatecasen′sis.** Plants globular, pale green; ribs about 55, very thin; radial spines 10 to 12, spreading, slender, white; centrals 3, middle one flattened, curving over the top, flattened but not annulate. *fl.* white, tinged lavender. Mexico. (B.R.C. 3, f. 119.)

V. H.

**ECHINOMAS′TUS** (*echinos*, a hedgehog, *mastos*, breast; referring to the spiny tubercles). FAM. *Cactaceae*. Small, roundish, tuberculate plants, resembling Mammillaria but the flowers are borne on the tips of the tubercles. Fruit small, scaly, and dry. **A**

**E. durangen′sis.** Stem ovoid, 3 or 4 in. h.; ribs 18 to 21, tuberculate; radial spines 15 to 20, incurved, white with black tips; centrals 3 or 4, rather longer. *fl.* purplish. Mexico.

**E. intertex′tus.** Plants small, round with 13 acute ribs divided into tubercles; spines red with darker tips, numerous, short, almost hiding the plant. *fl.* whitish. Texas, Arizona, Mexico. (B.R.C. 3, f. 156.)

**E. Macdowell′ii.** Plants round, covered with interlocking spines; ribs 20 to 25, tuberculate; radial spines 15 to 20, white; centrals 3 or 4, darker, up to 2 in. long. *fl.* pink. Mexico. (B.R.C. 3, f. 158.)

**E. Trolliet′i.** A synonym of *E. unguispinus*.

**E. unguispi′nus.** Plants round or becoming cylindric; bluish-green; spines almost hiding the plants, most of them being erect and curving over the crown; radials up to 25, white with darker tips; centrals 4 to 8, stouter, reddish. *fl.* reddish. Mexico. (B.R.C. 3, f. 155.)

V. H.

**ECHINOPA′NAX** (*echinos*, hedgehog, *Panax*). FAM. *Araliaceae*. A genus of 1 species with the characters set out below. It needs a moist, cool soil and is propagated by seeds or by suckers. Naturally very hardy but liable to be cut back by spring frosts through starting into growth early. Said to grow in dense shade in nature.

**E. hor′ridus.** Deciduous shrub up to 10 ft., shoots, l.-stalks, and infl. densely covered with needle-like spines. *l.* alternate, 6 to 10 in. wide, palmately 5- or 7-lobed; lobes ovate, sharply toothed. *fl.* pale green, crowded in globose umbels making a panicle 3 or 4 in. long. June. *fr.* roundish-oval, ⅓ in. long, red. Japan, N. America. 1828. (B.M. 8572.) SYN. *Fatsia horrida*.

**ECHIN′OPS** (*echinos*, hedgehog, *ops*, resemblance). FAM. *Compositae*. Globe Thistle. A genus of about 75 species of herbaceous plants, natives of Spain eastwards to India and Abyssinia. Usually white-woolly, rather coarse in growth, biennial or perennial, thistle-like, with large globose heads of flowers. Flower-heads usually blue or white, composed of numerous 1-flowered heads each with its own involucre, the whole with an outer involucre of linear scales; pappus of many small scales, forming a crown. Easily grown and hardy in ordinary garden soil and useful for the large herbaceous border or for planting in the wild garden. Increased by seed sown in April, or the perennial species by division.

**E. bannat′icus.** Perennial, 2 to 3 ft. h., slightly branching. *l.* rather rough, hairy above, downy beneath; radical l. almost pinnate, upper pinnatifid, spiny. *fl.* blue. Hungary. 1832. (R.H. 1858, p. 519.)

**E. commuta′tus.** Perennial, 5 to 7 ft. h. *l.* pinnatifid, roughly hairy above, downy beneath, margins with small spines. *fl.* whitish. Summer. Austria, &c. 1817.

**E. exalta′tus.** Biennial, tall. Stem simple, erect, glandular-hairy. *l.* pinnatifid. *fl.* blue. Russia. (B.M. 2457 as *E. strictus*.)

**E. gigan′teus.** Perennial. Stem 6 to 16 ft., erect, branched; branches cottony, striped or ribbed. *l.* obovate, deeply pinnately, cut, somewhat bristly above, whitish hairy beneath, about 12 in. long, 6 in. wide, teeth spiny. *fl.-heads* globose. Abyssinia.

**E. Gmel′inii.** Somewhat branched perennial, hairy at base, cobwebby above. *Stem-l.* entire, green and glabrous above. *fl.-heads* whitish, pappus bristles free. E. Mongolia. *See also* **E. latifolius.**

**E. grae′cus.** Perennial, hairy, not glandular. Stem dwarf branched. *l.* pinnatisect with narrow-lanceolate spiny lobes. *fl.* blue, heads small. May to August. Greece.

**E. hor′ridus.** Stem cobwebby and with long brownish hair. *l.* rough above, white-tomentose beneath, simple or 2-pinnatipartite, spiny. Caucasus.

**E. hu′milis.** Perennial, 3 to 4 ft. h. *l.* at base wavy-margined, almost spineless, on stem entire, cobwebby above, hairy beneath. *fl.* blue, heads large. September. Asia.

**E. latifo′lius.** Stout perennial, brownish hairy at base. *Lower l.* deeply pinnatifid, lobes entire, acute, densely cobwebby above. *fl.-heads* bluish; involucral bracts long-bristled. Pappus bristles connate below. Siberia, Mongolia. SYN. *E. Gmelinii* of some.

**E. panicula′tus.** A synonym of *E. sphaerocephalus*.

**E. Ri′tro.** Perennial, about 3 ft. h. *l.* pinnatifid, not spiny, cobwebby above, downy beneath. *fl.* blue. Summer. S. Europe. 1570. (B.M. 932.) var. **na′na**, dwarfer; **tenuifo′lius**, taller, *l.* leathery, lobes spiny, dull green above, cottony beneath, *fl.* blue. E. Europe, W. Asia. 1816. SYN. *E. ruthenicus*.

**E. ruthen′icus.** A synonym of *E. Ritro tenuifolius*.

**E. sphaeroceph′alus.** Perennial, 5 to 7 ft. h., erect, branched, glandular-hairy. *l.* sinuate-pinnatifid, scarcely spiny, green above, felted white or grey beneath. *fl.* silvery-grey. Summer. Europe, W. Asia. (B.R. 356 as *E. paniculatus*.) var. **al′bidus**, *fl.* paler.

**E. stric′tus.** A synonym of *E. exaltatus*.

**E. Tournefort′ii.** Perennial, 3 to 4 ft. h. Stem branched, velvety. *l.* deeply divided into 5 linear segs., rough above, white-hairy beneath, spiny. *fl.* pale blue; involucral bracts free, bristly. September. S. Europe. (B.M. 8217.)

**E. visco′sus.** Clammy hairy perennial. Stem tall, branched. *l.* pinnately cut, the lobes lanceolate, spiny, green above, ashy-grey beneath. *fl.-heads* pale blue. June to August. Greece, E. Mediterranean.

**ECHINOP'SIS** (*echinos*, hedgehog, *opsis*, like; the round spiny plants resembling hedgehogs). FAM. *Cactaceae*. Stems usually low, round or short cylindric, solitary or clustered, ribbed. Flowers from old areoles, large with a very long, hairy tube, usually white, occasionally pink, often fragrant. Fruit round or ovoid, fleshy. These plants are easily grown, do not require a high temperature, and can usually be propagated by offsets. A certain amount of hybridization was done some 50 years ago and the older species have not been re-imported to any great extent, so that many of the specimens in cultivation are hybrids, generally with *E. Eyriesii* as one parent. For cultivation *see* **Cactus**.

**E. au'rea.** A synonym of *Lobivia aurea*.

**E. Eyries'ii.** Plants round or short cylindric; ribs 11 to 18, not tuberculate, rather thin; areoles with whitish wool; spines 14 to 18, very short. *fl.* 10 in. long, white. Brazil, Uruguay, Argentina. (B.M. 3411; B.R. 1707.) SYN. *Echinocactus Eyriesii*.

**E. Huot'tii.** Stem cylindrical, making offsets; ribs 9 to 11, rounded; radial spines 10, slender, spreading; centrals 1 to 4, straight. *fl.* large, white. Bolivia.

**E. leucan'tha.** Stems round or oblong, large; ribs 12 to 14, compressed; areoles close; radial spines 8, curved, central spine 1, often up to 4 in. long. *fl.* large, white. Argentina. (B.M. 4567; B.R. 26, 13; B.R.C. 3, t. 7.)

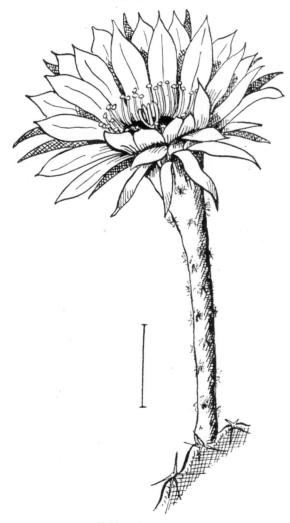

*Echinopsis multiplex*

**E. mul'tiplex.** Plants globular, making many offsets at the base; ribs 13 to 15, broad at base, acute; areoles large; spines brown, awl-shaped; radials 5 to 15, centrals 2 to 5. *fl.* 8 in. long, pale pink, fragrant. S. Brazil. (B.M. 3789; B.R.C. 3, t. 6.)

**E. obrepan'da.** Plants round, depressed; ribs 17 or 18, prominent, thin, wavy; areoles sunk in the ribs; spines rigid, brown; radials 10, spreading, recurved, short; one central, erect, up to 1 in. long. *fl.* large, white or purplish. Bolivia. (B.M. 4521, 4687.) SYN. *Echinopsis cristata*.

**E. oxyg'ona.** Plants round, making offsets; ribs 14, rounded; spines about 14, short and stout, 1½ in. long. *fl.* pink, 12 in. long. S. Brazil. (B.M. 4162.)

**E. Pent'landii.** A synonym of *Lobivia Pentlandii*.

**E. tubiflo'ra.** Plants solitary or with offsets; ribs 12, prominent, wavy; areoles with white wool; spines black, short. *fl.* white, large. Argentina. (B.M. 3627.)

**E. turbina'ta.** Plants round; ribs 13 to 14; spines several, short. *fl.* white, strongly scented. Argentina. (B.R.C. 3, t. 6.)

V. H.

**echinosep'alus -a -um,** having prickly sepals.

**ECHINOSTACH'YS Pinelia'na.** A synonym of *Aechmea Pineliana*.

**echioi'des,** Echium-like.

**ECHI'TES** *echis*, viper; in allusion either to its poisonous properties or to its twining habit). FAM. *Apocynaceae*. A genus of about 40 species of often handsome twining shrubs, all natives of Trop. America, closely related to Dipladenia from which it differs by the 5-lobed disk or the glandular or scaled calyx. Leaves opposite; interpetiolar cilia glandular. Flowers subcorymbose; calyx small, 5-lobed, with many glands at the base inside or with 5 scales opposite the lobes; corolla salver-shaped, throat and tube naked, segments unequal; stigma appendage like a reversed cup or with 5 lobes; peduncles interpetiolar. For cultivation *see* **Dipladenia**.

**E. Andrews'ii.** *l.* oval or oblong, 1½ to 2 in. long, mucronate, acute or rounded at base, margins revolute. *fl.* yellow, 2 in. long, cor. bell-shaped, tube scarcely longer than the lobes; anthers tapered to a long, bristle-like awn. July, August. S. Florida, W. Indies. 1759. (B.M. 1064 as *E. suberecta*.)

**E. atropurpu'rea.** A synonym of *Dipladenia atropurpurea*.

**E. francis'cea.** A synonym of *E. varia*.

**E. nu'tans.** A synonym of *Prestonia venosa*.

**E. rubroveno'sa.** *l.* emerald-green netted with brilliant bright red or golden-yellow. S. America. 1867. (F.d.S. 1728.) Foliage very striking.

**E. stella'ris.** About 6 ft. h., branches downy. *l.* ovate-oblong, glabrous above, downy beneath. *fl.* rose, yellow; in 10- to 12-fld. racemes; pedicels somewhat hispid. September. Brazil. 1831. (B.R. 1664.) Stem cuttings are sometimes difficult to root but root-cuttings are reliable.

**E. sulphu'rea.** Free-growing creeper. Habit of *E. varia*. *fl.* sulphur with red tube and rose eye. Brazil. (B.M. 4547 as *E. franciscea pallidiflora*.) Useful either as a pot-plant supported by neat stakes or a wire trellis, or planted in the border against a wall or pillar.

**E. umbella'ta.** *l.* roundish-ovate, mucronate, 2½ in. long. *fl.* white or pale yellow, tube green, villous within, silky without, large; umbels few-fld. July. W. Indies. 1733.

**E. var'ia.** *l.* dark green. *fl.* purplish-red, large; umbels 6-to 8-fld.; peduncles short. September. Brazil. 1845. (B.R. 33, 24 as *E. franciscea*.)

F. G. P.

**ECH'IUM** (*Echion*, ancient Greek name used by Dioscorides). FAM. *Boraginaceae*. A genus of perhaps 40 species of shrubs and herbs, chiefly natives of the Mediterranean region and the Canary Is. Leaves alternate, usually scabrid, hispid or whitish-hairy. Flowers in 1-sided spikes, simple or forked; flowers tubular to trumpet-shaped with a dilated throat without appendages; corolla lobes 5, unequal; stamens 5, inserted below the middle of the tube, unequal, exserted; style 2-fid at tip. Fruit of 4 nutlets. All the species are easily grown in good garden soil but if too rich they are apt to be very leafy. The herbaceous species are usually easily raised from seed. The larger species are not dependably hardy in any but mild districts, but there they make noble and striking plants for the border or planted in the wild garden.

**E. al'bicans.** Perennial of 6 to 18 in., clothed with hoary, appressed, bristly hairs. *l.* in a dense tuft, linear-lanceolate, narrowed to base. *fl.* at first rose, then violet, about 1 in. long in a branching spike. Spain. (G.C. 15 (1881), 301.) Hardy.

**E. Bourgea'num.** Biennial, stout, with leafy stem up to 8 ft. or more h. *l.* long-linear, silvery-hairy, drooping. *fl.* rose, in a large pyramidal infl. of many spikes. May. Canary Is. (G.C. 53 (1913), 25.) Greenhouse. **A**

*Echium callithyrsum*

**E. callithyr'sum.** Woody, robust, bristly hairy. *l.* strongly nerved. *fl.* pale red to bluish-violet in large branching spikes. May. Canary Is. Greenhouse.

**E. can'dicans.** Biennial with branched stem, 2 to 4 ft. h. *l.* lanceolate, covered with silky, silvery hair. *fl.* blue, downy without, in conical, terminal, rather loose panicles. May. Madeira. 1777. (B.M. 6868.) Greenhouse.

**E. coeles'te.** Monocarpic. Stem up to 30 in. h., simple. *l.* lanceolate, acute, grey-green, stiffly hairy, lower up to 4½ in. long, upper shorter. *fl.* very numerous in a dense erect panicle, 1-sexual; cor. sky-blue with whitish tube, about ⅓ in. across; stamens scarcely exserted. Palma, Canary Is. 1919. Temperate house plant. **A**

**E. cre'ticum.** Annual, diffuse herb, 6 to 18 in. h., branched at base, bristly hairy. *l.* oblong-lanceolate. *fl.* reddish-violet, in many-fld. axillary and terminal spikes. S. Europe. 1683. Hardy.

**E. fastuos'um.** Branched perennial of 2 to 4 ft., long-haired above. *l.* oblong-lanceolate, long-pointed, veiny, covered with soft white hair, ciliate. *fl.* deep blue, bell-shaped, in a large, ovate, dense thyrsoid panicle; spikelets stalked, simple. April to August. Canary Is. 1779. (R.H. 1876, 10.) Greenhouse evergreen.

**E. lusitan'icum.** Erect perennial, branched in upper part. *l.* lanceolate, lower narrowed at base. *fl.* bluish with violet veins, tube white; spikelets simple, erect-spreading. Portugal.

**E. Perez'ii.** Related to *E. Wildpretii* but with *l.* decurrent to base, looser infl. and longer style-arms. *fl.* pale rose, regular, about ⅓ in. long with spreading lobes deflexed on margin; stamens long exserted, spreading, filaments red. Palma, Canary Is. 1911. (B.M. 8617; K.B. 1914, p. 266, 267.)

**E. plantagin'eum.*** Annual or biennial of 3 ft. h., hairy, erect, or spreading. *Lower l.* ovate or oblong, upper cordate-lanceolate. *fl.* rich purplish-violet, showy; cor. 4 times as long as cal.; spikes many in a long panicle. June. Mediterranean region. 1658. Syn. *E. violaceum.*

**E. ru'brum.*** Biennial, 1 to 2 ft. h., erect, unbranched, hairy. *l.* linear-lanceolate, slender-pointed. *fl.* reddish-violet, in a long, spike-like panicle; cor. 4 times as long as cal. May. Hungary, &c. (B.M. 1822.)

**E. sim'plex.** Biennial, 8 to 10 ft. h. Stem woody, unbranched. *l.* large, ovate-lanceolate. (G.C. 53 (1913), 20.)

**E. vulga're.** Biennial, 2 to 4 ft. h., often unbranched, warted. *l.* linear-lanceolate, bristly, hairy. *fl.* purple in bud, then violet-blue, downy without; in long spike-like racemes, spikelets spreading, simple. Europe, including Britain. (E.B. 1095.)

**E. Wildpre'tii.*** Biennial, softly hairy, 2 to 3 ft. h., unbranched. *l.* narrow-linear-lanceolate; bracts longer than cymes. *fl.* pale red with long-exserted stamens, in a large terminal thyrae. Summer. Canary Is. (B.M. 7847.) Greenhouse. Hardy only in favoured districts. **A**

***Ecklo'nis, Ecklonia'nus -a -um,*** in honour of Christian Friedrich Ecklon, apothecary, *b.* N. Schleswig, 1795, *d.* S. Africa, 1868, student of S. African flora.

***eclec'teum,*** worthy to be chosen.

**ECOLOGY,** the study of the habits and life of plants in relation to their environment.

***ecornu'tus -a -um,*** without spurs.

**EDAN'THE** (Derivation?) Fam. *Palmaceae.* Characters as below. **A**

**E. Tepejilo'te.** Stem about 10 ft. h., about 1½ in. thick, ringed. *l.* 4 ft. long, pinnate; lflets. 20 to 30, 7-nerved, close, alternate, narrow-lanceolate, 13 to 15 in. long, 1½ in. wide, deep rich green, pendent; rachis channelled above. *fl.* yellow. Mexico. 1860. (B.M. 6030 as *Chamaedorea Tepejilote.*)

**EDÉLWEISS.** *See* **Leontopodium alpinum.**

***edenta'tus -a -um,*** without teeth.

***Edgaria'nus -a -um,*** in honour of the Rev. J. H. Edgar of the Tibetan Missions.

**EDGEWORTH'IA** (in honour of M. P. Edgeworth, 1812–81, of the E. India Co.'s Service and a botanist). Fam. *Thymelaeaceae.* A genus of 2 or 3 species of shrubs allied to Daphne, natives of E. Asia. From Daphne, Edgeworthia is known by its annular disk with very short lobes and from Wikstroemeria by the lobed disk of the latter. Leaves alternate, entire, crowded at ends of branches. Flowers in dense, stalked, axillary heads, the calyx very hairy without, 4-lobed, petals absent. Fruit a dry drupe. A compost of 2 parts sandy loam and 1 of turfy peat suits these greenhouse plants which need good drainage and plenty of moisture in summer. Propagation is by cuttings in sand under a bell-glass in spring.

**E. chrysan'tha.** A synonym of *E. papyrifera.*

**E. Gard'neri.** Very similar to *E. papyrifera* but *l.* evergreen, and hairs on outside of cal. shorter and less silky. Nepal, Sikkim. (B.M. 7180.) Less hardy than *E. papyrifera.*

**E. papyrif'era.** Deciduous shrub, 4 to 6 ft. h., shoots silky-hairy at first, very tough. *l.* alternate, narrow-oval, 3 to 5½ in. long, entire, dark green above, grey-green beneath. *fl.* rich yellow coloured outside with white silky hairs, 40 or 50 together in a close terminal head, 1 to 2 in. across, fragrant; cal. tubular, lobes 4; stamens 8 in 2 rows. China. 1845. (B.R. 33, 48 as *E. chrysantha.*) Long cultivated in Japan and used in paper-making. Hardy only in favoured districts.

**EDGING.** This term is applied to dwarf plants, turf, or material of any description used in gardens for dividing beds, borders, &c., from the walks, thus preventing the mixing up of soil and gravel. It also refers to an outside line of dwarf plants bordering a flower-bed.

In the pleasure garden a strip of turf is commonly

used to form an edging between walks and borders. This is frequently made too narrow which gives a mean effect as well as being difficult to mow and keep in good order. At least 2 ft. width of grass should be allowed. Where the walk consists of paving-stone or brick-paving an edging is not essential but will usually improve the effect.

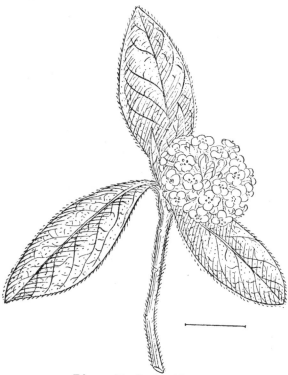

*Edgeworthia Gardneri* (p. 734)

Alternatively, an edging to paths may be formed by the use of dwarf shrubs kept well trimmed, such as box, dwarf heaths, lavender or lavender-cotton (Santolina), or by compact-growing herbaceous perennials such as *Armeria maritima*, London Pride, &c. It is impossible to plant an edging of this type properly if the ground is not previously well levelled, firmly trodden, and raked. Level pegs and a line should be used.

For the kitchen garden, box edging, though once very popular, is undesirable owing to the fact that it harbours slugs and other pests, and a clean and permanent edging may be formed by short lengths of paving-stone set on edge 6 in. in the ground and 2 in. above the path level. Tiles, frost-resistant bricks, and concrete slabs may also be employed in similar fashion. If the kitchen garden paths are of concrete no further edging will be required.

For ornamental edging of flower-beds or borders the following are but a few of the many plants suitable— Ageratum, Alyssum, dwarf Antirrhinum, Aubretia, Calceolaria, *Campanula carpatica*, Double Daisies, Echiverias, Forget-me-not, Gazania, *Gentiana acaulis*, Lavender, Lobelia, London Pride, French Marigolds, Nemesia, Nepeta, dwarf Petunias, Phacelia, *Phlox subulata*, Pinks, Polyanthus, Violas.

J. E. G. W.

**EDGING-IRON** or **VERGE-CUTTER.** A crescent-shaped tool, made of steel, with a socket in which is inserted a straight wooden handle. This tool is very useful for cutting turf verges by the sides of walks, flower-beds, &c., since it is well under the guidance of the hand and can be used both for curved and straight lines.

**EDIBLE FERN** of Tasmania. *See* **Pteridium aquilinum esculentum.**

*edinen'sis -is -e,* of Edinburgh.

*E'dithae,* in honour of Mrs. Hance, who collected *Agathosma Edithae.*

**EDRAIAN'THUS** (*edraios,* sessile, *anthos,* flower). Fam. *Campanulaceae.* A genus of a few tufted perennial herbs very closely related to Wahlenbergia from which it is distinguished by having the flowers in clusters at the top of the peduncle instead of solitary as in Wahlenbergia. All are natives of the Mediterranean region, and are hardy. The stout roots grow to a considerable length, and a well-drained, good deep soil is needed for them on the rock-garden. The compost should be a mixture of three parts friable loam to two parts limestone chips, and it is well to provide a foot depth of this with well-drained soil beneath in a sunny open place. Propagation is by seed. All may sometimes be found under Wahlenbergia, and some species of Wahlenbergia may be listed under Edraianthus.

A

KEY
1. *Fl. white*
1. *Fl. blue or purple*    E. niveus
2. *Plant glabrous, stem erect*    2
2. *Plant more or less hairy, stem often ascending*    E. serbicus
3. *Stem nearly glabrous; lvs. entire*    3
3. *Stem hairy; lvs. usually toothed*    E. caudatus
4. *Cal. with minute teeth alternate with its lobes*    4
4. *Cal. without alternate small teeth*    E. Kitaibelii
5. *Lvs. with bristly margins*    5
5. *Lvs. sometimes bristly above, downy elsewhere*    E. tenuifolius    E. graminifolius

**E. carici'nus.** A synonym of *E. graminifolius.*

**E. cauda'tus.** Tufted. *Lower l.* in a rosette; *upper* linear-lanceolate, entire, acute, stem-clasping, 1 to 2 in. long, those below the fl.-head about ⅓ length of fl. Stems ascending or erect, about 3 in. long, nearly glabrous. *fl.* 6 to 10 in a head; cor. violet-blue, funnel-shaped, 5-cleft. Summer. Dalmatia. Syn. *E. dalmaticus.*

**E. croat'icus.** Very similar to *E. graminifolius* but *l.* glabrous except for a fringe of hair near base. Dalmatia.

**E. dalmat'icus.** A synonym of *E. caudatus.*

**E. graminifo'lius.** Habit of *E. caudatus. Lower l.* linear to linear-spatulate, ½ to 1½ in. long, downy, sometimes bristly above, entire or slightly toothed; *upper* few, erect, 1 in. or more long, those beneath the fl.-head ovate with a long, slender point. Stems downy, 3 in. long. *fl.* 3 to 6 in a cluster; cor. purple, large, rather narrowly bell-shaped. May to July. Dalmatia. Very variable. The forms, e.g. **austra'lis, ela'tus, pusil'lus,** and **sic'ulus,** are not well defined and raised from seed pass into one another. *See also* **E. caricinus, E. croaticus,** and **E. tenuifolius.**

**E. Kitaibel'ii.** Larger and more robust than *E. graminifolius,* with bright- (not grey-) green *l.* all distantly toothed, purplish hairy stems about 6 in. h. and bluish-purple *fl.,* the cal. with small reflexed teeth alternating with its lobes. Summer. Croatia. (B.M. 6188.)

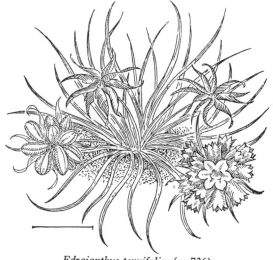

*Edraianthus tenuifolius* (p. 736)

**E. niv'eus.** Habit of *E. graminifolius*; *l.* long, narrow, hairy at tips. Stems and bracts purple. Cal. reddish; cor. pure white, large. Bosnia. 1883.

**E. ser'bicus.** Habit of *E. graminifolius* but erect, up to about 8 in. h., glabrous. *fl.* purple, with or without the alternate cal. teeth seen in *E. Kitaibelii*. Serbia, Bulgaria.

**E. tenuifo'lius.** Closely allied to *E. graminifolius* but less desirable. *l.* bristly on margins. Stems hairy, purplish, 3 to 6 in. h. *fl.* 6 to 10 in a cluster, violet-blue with a white base. Summer. Dalmatia. 1879. (B.M. 6482.)

A→

*edu'lis -is -e,* an article of food.

*Edward'ii,* in honour of Edward Klaboch.

**EDWARD'SIA.** *See* **Sophora.**

*Edwardsia'nus -a -um,* in honour of George Edwardes, Governor of Labuan, c. 1859.

**EEL FERN.** *See* **Elaphoglossum Herminieri.**

**EEL GRASS.** *See* **Vallisneria spiralis, Zostera.** A

**EELWORMS.** These minute, often microscopic, worm-like creatures belong to a class—the *Nemathelminthes* or Roundworms—which is far removed zoologically from other worms, e.g. Earthworms (q.v.). The body of Eelworms is generally elongate, worm-like, but tapering towards each end, though the head end, in which is the mouth, is somewhat blunt. The sexes are distinct and similar in appearance except in the genus *Heterodera* (Potato and Root-knot Eelworms) where the gravid females become swollen and sac-like and are termed 'cysts'. A great number of species are important parasites of crops, including those that give rise to galls on shoots (e.g. Bulb and Stem Eelworm), and on roots (Root-knot Eelworm); others invade buds (Currant Eelworm), leaves (Chrysanthemum and Fern Eelworms), and stems (Coco-nut Eelworm). Other species are feebly parasitic or saprophytic (free-living). Free-living eelworms are widely distributed in soils, and invade the tissues of plants damaged by other organisms thereby extending the initial injury. These secondary invaders occur only in dead and decaying organic matter and play their part in the ultimate destruction of the damaged plants. The more important plant-parasitic species are considered under their respective headings (*see* **Stem, Chrysanthemum, Fern, Potato-Root,** and **Root-knot Eelworms**). A

G. F. W.

*effu'sus -a -um,* effuse; spread out.

**EGENOL'FIA** (in honour of Christian Egenoloph, 1502–55, author of a German book on Herbs). FAM. *Polypodiaceae.* A genus of 10 species related to Polybotrya from which it differs by the presence of a seta in the angle between the ultimate pinnules. For cultivation *see* **Acrostichum.**

**E. appendicula'ta.*** *rhiz.* firm, woody. *Barren fronds* 6 to 18 in. long, 4 to 8 in. broad, simply pinnate. *sti.* 3 to 6 in. long, erect, naked, or slightly scaly; pinnae 2 to 4 in. long, ⅜ to ¾ in. broad, edge varying from sub-entire to cut half-way down to midrib of blunt lobes, upper side often auricled, lower obliquely truncate, dark green. *Fertile fronds* narrower, on longer spike, pinnae roundish or oblong, often distinctly stalked. Trop. Asia. 1824. Stove. (H.E.F. 2, 108.) SYN. *Acrostichum appendiculatum.*

**EGER'IA den'sa.** A synonym of *Elodea densa.*

**EGG PLANT.** *See* **Aubergine, Solanum Melongena esculentum.**

*Egg'eri,* in honour of G. Egger, who collected in NW. Persia, c. 1930.

**EGG-KILLING WASHES.** Sprays capable of destroying the eggs of insects, of which Carbolineum was the first to be used widely. *See* **Insecticides.**

*Eglante'ria,* from French name, Eglanties.

**EGLANTINE.** *See* **Lonicera Periclymenum** and, more commonly, the Sweet Brier, **Rosa Eglanteria.**

**EGYPTIAN BEAN.** *See* **Nelumbo nucifera.**

**EGYPTIAN LOTUS.** *See* **Nymphaea Lotus.**

**EGYPTIAN PAPER REED.** *See* **Cyperus Papyrus.**

**EGYPTIAN ROSE.** *See* **Scabiosa atropurpurea** and **Knautia arvensis** in Supplement.

**EGYPTIAN THORN.** *See* **Acacia arabica.**

*Ehrenberg'ii,* in honour of Karl August Ehrenberg, 1801–49, German collector in St. Thomas 1827–8, Port-au-Prince 1828–31, Mexico 1831–40; younger brother of the Berlin merchant Christian Gottfried Ehrenberg.

**EHRET'IA** (in honour of G. D. Ehret, German botanical artist, 1708–70, brother-in-law of Philip Miller). FAM. *Boraginaceae.* A genus of about 50 species of deciduous and evergreen trees or shrubs widely distributed in the warmer regions of E. Asia, America, Africa, Australia; few in temperate parts. Leaves alternate. Flowers small, usually white, in mostly terminal panicles; calyx and corolla 5-lobed, stamens 5. Fruit a globose drupe.

KEY

| | |
|---|---|
| 1. *Lvs. and shoots glabrous* | E. acuminata |
| 1. *Lvs. more or less hairy or bristly* | 2 |
| 2. *Lvs. with short bristles above and beneath* | E. Dicksoni |
| 2. *Lvs. with tufts of hair in vein-axils beneath* | E. thyrsiflora |

**E. acumina'ta.** Tree 20 to 30 ft. or a shrub, shoots and l. glabrous. *l.* oval or oblong, short-pointed, usually cuneate, 3 to 6 in. long, toothed. *fl.* ⅓ in. wide, white, crowded densely in panicles which are terminal and from upper l.-axils. Trop. Asia, Australia. A subtropical species very much confused in botanical literature with *E. thyrsiflora* which is hardy and not a native of Australia.

**E. Dick'soni.** Deciduous tree up to 30 ft. *l.* oval to roundish, 4 to 7 in. long, rounded to broadly cuneate at base, short-pointed, rough with small bristles on both surfaces. *fl.* fragrant in flattish panicles up to 4 in. long and wide; cor. ⅔ in. across, white. *fr.* roundish, beaked, ½ in. wide, yellowish. China, Formosa. 1900. (R.H. 1914, 174–5.) Long erroneously grown as *E. macrophylla.*

**E. serra'ta** of gardens. A synonym of *E. thyrsiflora.* The Bot. Reg. plate 1097 under this name probably represents *E. acuminata.*

**E. thyrsiflo'ra.** Deciduous tree, 20 to 40 ft., shoots soon glabrous. *l.* oval, ovate, or slightly obovate, 3 to 7 in. long, half as wide, short-pointed, toothed, tufted in vein-axils beneath. *fl.* fragrant, in terminal panicles up to 6 in. long; cor. white, ¼ in. wide, with oblong lobes; stamens well exposed. August. *fr.* a globose drupe, ⅛ in. wide, orange then black. China, Japan. About 1880. Hardy. Has long been grown erroneously as *E. acuminata* and *E. serrata.* (B.M. n.s. 440.)

W. J. B.

*Ehrhar'tii,* in honour of J. Fr. Ehrhart of Switzerland, 1742–95.

**EICHHORN'IA** (in honour of J. A. F. Eichhorn, 1779–1856, an eminent Prussian). FAM. *Pontederiaceae.* A genus of 6 species of aquatic plants, natives of S. America and Trop. Africa. Leaves floating or emerging, obovate, rounded, cordate, or rarely emarginate. Inflorescence sessile or stalked in a leafy sheath; perianth funnel-shaped, the limb erecto-patent, more or less oblique; stamens 6, affixed at varying heights in tube, declinate. Two or three species of this genus are among the most beautiful of plants for the stove Lily tank, particularly *E. azurea* and *E. speciosa.* *E. azurea* is very vigorous and needs restriction by shortening back the stems occasionally and replanting the young growths. *E. speciosa* unfortunately is backward in flowering in cultivation. It increases rapidly and is variable in habit. Grown as a floating aquatic or close to the glass its leaf-stalks are short and much inflated but when rooted in soil or at a distance from the light this inflation is much less marked, the petioles being then cylindrical and much longer. Flowers are more certain when the growths of this

species become crowded and the roots matted. It should be given the sunniest position in shallow water with a little loam to root in. In its native habitat it increases so rapidly as to impede navigation and is used as fodder on Mexican ranches. When grown as a floating plant the long, purplish roots hang down 10 or 12 in. into the water and are extensively used in goldfish breeding. The plant is somewhat difficult to winter but may be preserved by potting the roots (giving good drainage) tightly together and storing the receptacle in dim light and free from frost.
A

**E. azu'rea.** Stem as thick as the thumb, floating and rooting, green, smooth, flexuous. *l.* rounded-cordate to trapezoid or rhomboid, but variable to broadly oblate or cordate, 3 to 8 in. across, rounded-retuse or sub-acute; petioles of variable length, not inflated. *fl.* scattered or crowded in pairs along a stout, hairy, sessile rachis; perianth bright pale blue, funnel-shaped, hairy without. July. Brazil. 1879. (B.M. 6487.) SYN. *Pontederia azurea.*

**E. cras'sipes.** A synonym of *E. speciosa.*

**E. Martia'na.** Stems often several from a root, up to 12 to 18 in. h., erect, terete, soft, herbaceous, sheathed below by the bases of the radical l. and a few, long scale l. *Radical l.* long-stalked; all cordate, entire, striate; basal sinus deep, narrow. *fl.* 10 to 12 in a compound spike; perianth petaloid, 2-lipped; lower lip of 3 purple segs., upper 3 smaller, blue with a 2-lobed central white spot and yellowish disk. Summer. S. America. (B.M. 5020 as *E. tricolor.*) SYN. *E. paniculata.*

**E. panicula'ta.** A synonym of *E. Martiana.*

**E. specio'sa.** Water Hyacinth. *rhiz.* thick. *l.* large, fleshy, orbicular, acute; stalk much thickened at base. *fl.* funnel-shaped, about 1½ in. long, of 6 ovate-oblong violet segs.; racemes many-fld.; fl.-stalks thick; spathe terminal, recurved. Summer. America. 1879. (B.M. 2932 as *Pontederia azurea.*) SYN. *E. crassipes.* var. **au'rea,** *fl.* yellow.

***Eich'leri, Eichleria'nus -a -um,*** in honour of Wilhelm Eichler of Baku who sent *Tulipa Eichleri* to Regel about 1873.
A

**EL SPIRITO SANTO.** *See* **Peristeria elata.**

**ELAEAGNA'CEAE.** Dicotyledons. A family of about 45 species in 3 genera of trees or shrubs more or less covered with minute silvery or brown scurfy scales. Leaves alternate or opposite, entire, without stipules. Flowers white or yellow, regular, 1- or 2-sexual, axillary, clustered or cymose, without petals; calyx lobes 4, rarely 2 or 6, valvate; stamens as many or twice as many, inserted on the tube; ovary superior, 1-celled, 1-seeded. The calyx tube becomes fleshy as a rule and encloses the dry fruit which thus appears like a drupe. The genera are all worthy of representation in the garden and are Elaeagnus, Hippophae, and Shepherdia.

**ELAEAG'NUS** (*elaia*, olive, *agnos*, Greek name of *Vitex Agnus-castus*; Theophrastus's Elaeagnus was a willow). FAM. *Elaeagnaceae*. A genus of about 40 species of shrubs or trees, often spiny. Leaves alternate (by which it is easily distinguished from Shepherdia in which they are opposite), short-stalked, entire, covered like other parts of the plant with brown or silvery scales, sometimes very closely. Flowers axillary, solitary or clustered, perfect (thus differing from Hippophae in which they are dioecious), with a bell-shaped or tubular 4-lobed calyx, and 4 stamens on very short stalks. In some species the drupe-like fruit is edible, as, for instance, *E. angustifolia*, *E. argentea*, and especially *E. multiflora*. The fruits of the last make a good jelly, rather rough to the palate, suitable for use with game. The silvery foliage of *E. angustifolia* and *E. argentea* and silver reverse of other species, the fragrant flowers of some, the handsome fruits which some produce abundantly, the fine evergreen foliage of others make this genus a valuable one in the garden. The species are generally hardy, do best in a soil only moderately rich, and are propagated by seeds when obtainable (as they are with most deciduous species), or by cuttings of the evergreen variegated varieties. Grafting of the latter on seedlings of deciduous species is sometimes practised but is less desirable than cuttings. *E. argentea* produces suckers by which it may be propagated. Few shrubs better resist drought or do so well on a dry bank, none gives better and brighter colour in winter than *E. pungens aureo-variegata*, but, like all the group, it should be planted in a sunny place.

Considerable confusion exists regarding the names of the different forms of Elaeagnus in nurseries and their catalogues, many unnecessary names (synonyms) being used and specific names being transposed. For instance, varieties of the evergreen *E. pungens* appear in catalogues as varieties of the deciduous *E. multiflora*. *E. argentea* is frequently still confused with the opposite-leaved *Shepherdia argentea* as it was a hundred years ago, and so on, and further confusion arises by the use of varietal names in place of specific which still occurs, as, for instance, *E. Simonii* instead of *E. pungens Simonii*.

KEY

1. *Lvs. deciduous* 2
1. *Lvs. evergreen* 6
2. *Mature lvs. silvery on both sides* E. argentea
2. *Mature lvs. greenish above, silvery beneath* 3
3. *Young shoots with silvery scales* 4
3. *Young shoots with reddish-brown or brown scales* 5
4. *Young shoots both downy and scaly; bush often spineless* E. orientalis
4. *Young shoots not downy; bush spiny* E. angustifolia
5. *Lvs. about half as wide as long, with reddish-brown mingled with silvery scales beneath* E. multiflora
5. *Lvs. about one-third as wide as long, usually without brown scales beneath* E. umbellata
6. *Shoots silvery white* E. macrophylla
6. *Shoots brown scaly* 7
7. *Spreading spiny shrub; lvs. dull with white and brown scales beneath, wavy at margins* E. pungens
7. *Rambling spineless shrub, lvs. shining with yellow and brown scales beneath* E. glabra
7. *Moderately spiny; lvs. not wavy at margins, brown scaly beneath* E. × reflexa

**E. angustifo'lia.** Oleaster. Deciduous shrub or tree to 15 or 20 ft., branches spiny, when young covered with glistening, silvery scales. *l.* narrow-oblong or lanceolate, 1½ to 3½ in. long, ⅜ to ⅝ in. wide, dull green above, scaly beneath. *fl.* 1 to 3 in l.-axils, yellow within, silvery without, ⅜ in. long, tube bell-shaped, as long, segs. spreading; fragrant. June. *fr.* oval, ½ in. long, yellowish with silvery scales, mealy, sweet. S. Europe, W. Asia. 16th cent. (B.R. 1156; L.B.C. 1339.) Apt to be cut back in very severe winters.

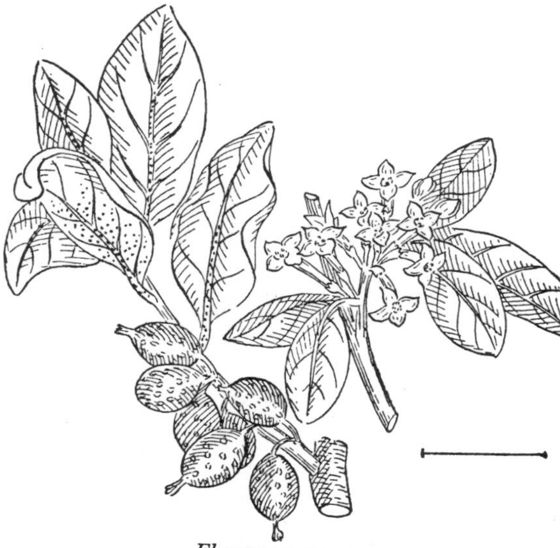

*Elaeagnus argentea*

**E. argen'tea.** Deciduous shrub, 6 to 10 ft., erect, young shoots covered with glistening, brown scales. *l.* oval to narrow-ovate, 1½ to 2½ in. long, half as wide, glistening silvery on both sides. *fl.* about 3 in l.-axils, drooping, yellow within, silvery without, ½ in. long, tube narrow; fragrant; very profuse. May. *fr.* roundish, ⅜ in. long, silvery, flesh dry, mealy. South to Cent. United States. 1813. (B.M. 8369.)

**E. ed'ulis.** A synonym of *E. multiflora.*

**E. glab'ra.** Evergreen shrub of rambling or climbing habit, up to 15 ft., usually not spiny, young shoots shining brown. *l.* elliptic-ovate, or elliptic-lanceolate, 1½ to 4 in. long, pointed, shining, with yellow and brown scales beneath. *fl.* white within, brown scaly without, funnel-shaped, tube narrow, twice as long as segs.; fragrant. October, November. Japan, Cent. China. 1880. Unlike *E. pungens* no variegated forms are cultivated.

**E. long'ipes.** A synonym of *E. multiflora.*

**E. macrophyl'la.** Evergreen shrub, up to about 10 ft. h., wider than high, rounded, not spiny, young shoots silvery-white. *l.* ovate to broad-oval, 2 to 4½ in. long, at first silvery, then shining green above, silvery lustrous beneath. *fl.* 4 to 6 in. l.-axils, nodding, ½ in. long, with silvery and brown scales without, bell-shaped, tube narrowed above ovary, as long as segs., fragrant. October, November. *fr.* oval, ⅝ in. long, red, scaly. Korea, Japan. 1879. (B.M. 7638.)

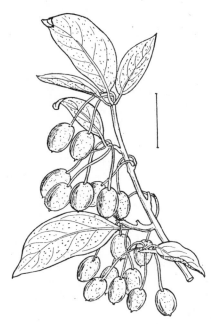

*Elaeagnus multiflora*

**E. multiflo'ra.** Deciduous shrub (occasionally retaining some l.) 6 to 10 ft. h. and as wide, young branches covered with red-brown scales. *l.* oval to ovate, 1½ to 2½ in. long, about half as wide, green with tufted hairs above at first, silvery beneath with scattered larger reddish-brown scales. *fl.* in l.-axils, yellowish-white, ½ in. long, tube bell-shaped, about as long as segs., distinctly constricted above ovary; fragrant. April, May, with new shoots. *fr.* ⅔ in. long, oblong, red, scaly, pendulous, stalks up to 1 in. long, of pleasant acid flavour. China, Japan. 1873. (B.M. 7341; Add. 155.) Variable. var. **cris'pa** is often spiny with *l.* often crisped at margin, and *fr.* stalks about as long as fr. Japan; **ova'ta** has 1 to 3 *fl.* in l.-axils in July, August, and smaller *fr.* on stalks about ½ in. long.

**E. orienta'lis.** Differs from *E. angustifolia* in having less spiny branches, young shoots downy as well as scaly, more oval l. with tufts of down beneath. E. Mediterranean. 1739.

**E. pun'gens.** Evergreen up to 15 ft., dense, spreading, spiny, young shoots covered with brown scales. *l.* oval or oblong, 1½ to 4 in. long, less than half as wide, margins wavy, leathery, dull beneath with white and scattered brown scales. *fl.* 1 to 3 in l.-axils, silvery-white, pendulous, ½ in. long, tube longer than segs., contracted above ovary; fragrant. October, November. *fr.* uncommon, oval, ½ in. long, at first brown, then red. Japan. 1830. Variable in colouring. var. **au'rea** has *l.* margined rich yellow; **aureo-variega'ta** has large *l.* up to 4½ in. long, with a central deep yellow patch sometimes occupying nearly all the l., a fine shrub for winter effect. SYN. var. *maculata*; **Frederi'ci** has smaller, narrower *l.* with cream or pale-yellow middle blotch and a narrow green margin; **Simon'ii** has rather large *l.* very silvery beneath; **tric'olor,** *l.* variegated with yellow and pinkish-white; **variega'ta,** *l.* margined pale yellow.

**E. × reflex'a.** Hybrid of *E. glabra × E. pungens* with long branches only slightly spiny, *l.* evergreen, not wavy at margins, ovate-anceolate, shining green above, reddish-brown, scaly beneath.

**E. umbella'ta.** Deciduous shrub (sometimes partly evergreen), up to 12 or 18 ft. h., wide-spreading, often spiny, young shoots covered with brownish scales. *l.* narrow-oval, 2 to 4 in. long, about

one-third as wide, silvery beneath. *fl.* 1 to 3 in l.-axils, creamy-white within, silvery without, ½ in. long, funnel-shaped, tube much longer than segs. gradually narrowed towards base. May, June. *fr.* round, ¼ to ⅓ in. wide, silvery at first, then red, short-stalked. Himalaya, China, Japan. 1829. Variable. var. **parvifo'lia** has young shoots, silvery, *l.* with starry down above when young, silvery and scaly beneath. Himalaya. 1843. (B.R. 29, 51.)

**ELAE'IS** (*Elaia*, the olive; oil is obtained from the fruit as from olives). FAM. *Palmaceae.* A genus of 1 species of tropical palm, native of W. Africa (*E. guineensis*), related to Cocos but with 1- to 3-seeded fruits with 3 pores above the middle. Leaves pinnate; segments sword-shaped, slender-pointed, recurved at base; stalks short and thick, sometimes spiny-margined. Spadix short, thick. Fruit bright red in large obovate clusters. The fruits of *E. guineensis* yield the palm oil used for lubricating, and in making candles and soap. It is slow growing but ornamental in the young state and needs stove treatment with a night temperature of about 65° F. and plenty of water. It is best in a sandy soil.

**E. guineen'sis.** Oil Palm. Erect, 20 to 30 ft. h. Stem stout, deeply ringed, not spiny. *l.* 10 to 15 ft. long, dark green, stalk spiny-toothed; lflets. 50 to 60, linear-lanceolate, acute. Guinea. 1730.

**E. melanococ'ca.** A synonym of *Corozo oleifera.*

**ELAEOCARPA'CEAE.** Dicotyledons. A family of about 150 species in 7 genera, natives of the tropics and S. Hemisphere, related to Tiliaceae. Trees and shrubs with alternate or opposite simple leaves with stipules. Flowers in racemes or panicles or clustered; parts in 4 or 5, but petals occasionally absent, free or joined; stamens many, free, sometimes on an androphore, anthers usually opening by 2 pores at tip; ovary sessile, usually 2- to many-celled. Fruit a capsule or drupe. The genera dealt with here are Aristotelia, Crinodendron, Elaeocarpus, Sloanea, and Vallea.

**ELAEOCAR'PUS** (*Elaia*, an olive, *carpos*, fruit; from the round fruit enclosing a nut with a rugged shell). FAM. *Elaeocarpaceae.* A genus of about 60 species of handsome evergreen trees or shrubs. Leaves rarely opposite, entire or toothed. Flowers small, usually fragrant, in racemes; petals 5, toothed or fringed. A mixture of peat and loam suits these stove or greenhouse trees. Cuttings of nearly ripe shoots with leaves intact, placed in sandy soil with bottom heat, and seed sown in a hotbed both afford means of propagation. A

**E. cya'neus.** Tree to 15 ft. *l.* oblong-lanceolate, toothed, with prominent netted veins. *fl.* creamy-white, fringed; in close-fld. axillary racemes shorter than l. July. *Drupe* blue. Australia. 1803. (B.M. 1737; B.R. 657.) SYN. *E. reticulatus.* Greenhouse.

**E. denta'tus.** *l.* oblong, leathery, silky beneath, narrowed to the stalk. *fl.* straw-coloured; pet. 3-lobed; raceme axillary. New Zealand. 1883. Greenhouse.

**E. ganit'rus.** Bead Tree of India. *l.* oblong. *fl.* creamy-white. *fr.* brown, round, warty. India, Malaya. The fr. used for beads, heads of ornamental pins, and other decorations.

**E. grandiflo'rus.*** About 7 ft. h. *l.* broad-lanceolate, mostly towards tops of branches, 3 to 6 in. long, entire or toothed, leathery, deep green above, paler beneath, tapered to stalk. *fl.* white or pale yellow, more or less silky, racemes few, 2- to 5-fld., drooping, usually among upper l.-clusters, pedicels red, longer than l.-stalk. Summer. Java. 1852. (B.M. 4680 as *Monocera grandiflora.*)

**E. obova'tus.** Evergreen tree, 60 to 80 ft. h. *l.* obovate. *fl.* white. Australia. SYN. *E. parviflorus.*

**E. oppositifo'lius.** About 20 ft. h. *l.* opposite, elliptic-oblong, with a few mucronate teeth. *fl.* white on 3-fld. terminal peduncles. June. Amboyna. 1818. SYN. *Aceratium oppositifolium.* Stove.

**E. prunifo'lius.** Erect, much branched shrub, 5 to 6 ft. h. *l.* elliptic, obtuse, margins undulate, crenulate, nearly glabrous. *fl.* white, nodding, in axillary racemes towards ends of branches in clusters of 6 to 10; infl. thickly hairy. India.

**E. serra'tus.** Tree to 50 ft. *l.* elliptic-oblong, toothed, slender-pointed, glandular in axils of veins beneath. *fl.* white, purplish in bud, fragrant; racemes axillary or lateral, drooping. March to October. *Drupe* globose. E. Indies, Malaya. 1774. Stove.

F. G. P.

## ELAEODEN'DRON

**ELAEODEN'DRON** (*Elaia*, olive, *dendron*, tree; from the olive-like fruit with oily seeds). FAM. *Celastraceae*. A genus of about 40 species of tropical trees and shrubs, mostly African or Indian. Leaves small, laurel-like, opposite. Flowers small, in axillary clusters. Ornamental foliage plants, decorative in the young state. For treatment, see **Elaeocarpus**.

**E. austra'le.** Tree of 30 to 40 ft. *l.* ovate to oblong-lanceolate, holly-like in texture, more or less obtuse, entire or with wide rounded teeth, netted beneath. *fl.* 4-parted. *fr.* about ½ in. long, red, ovoid or globose. Australia.

**E. capen'se.** Cape Phillyrea. Up to 18 ft. h., with spreading, drooping branches. *l.* lanceolate-elliptical, somewhat unequal-sided, leathery, distantly spine-toothed, slightly revolute on margins, dark green above, paler and often rusty beneath. *fl.* green, inconspicuous, in axillary cymes. *fr.* about ½ in. long, fleshy, yellow, oval. S. Africa. 1828. (B.M. 3835.) Greenhouse. Handsome in *fr.*

**E. glau'cum.** Evergreen shrub to 6 ft. *l.* acute or long-pointed, with rounded teeth or nearly entire, rather leathery. *fl.* greenish-yellow, small, in axillary panicles nearly as long as *l.* India, &c. Stove.

**E. laurifo'lium.** Glabrous shrub or small tree. *l.* oblong to elliptic, 2 to 5 in. long. *fl.* greenish-yellow, axillary in clusters of 3 to 5, nearly sessile. S. Africa.

**E. orienta'le.** Juvenile *l.* slender, passing gradually to the adult stage with obovate, blunt *l.* about 2½ in. long, wedge-shaped at base, with rounded teeth. *fl.* yellow-green, in close axillary cymes shorter than *l. fr.* as large as an olive, oblong. Madagascar, Mauritius. Warm house. Graceful and handsome, especially when young. SYN. *Aralia Chabrieri*.

**E. sphaerophyl'lum.** Branching, leafy shrub. *l.* elliptic, ¾ to 1½ in. long, blunt or slightly emarginate, rounded or heart-shaped at base, finely toothed, sometimes velvety beneath. S. Africa. 1891. Greenhouse.

F. G. P.

## ELAPHOGLOS'SUM

**ELAPHOGLOS'SUM** (*elaphos*, a stag, *glossa*, a tongue; from the shape of the fronds). FAM. *Polypodiaceae*. Over 400 species of ferns with simple fronds, free veins and sori spread over the whole surface of the fertile fronds or the fertile pinnae, almost entirely tropical in distribution. For cultivation see **Acrostichum**. *E. crinitum* is a somewhat special case. Its popular name, Elephant's Ear, is by no means inappropriate for the fronds are in shape not unlike an elephant's ear. It does best in a mixture of two parts peat and one part chopped and partly decayed Sphagnum, but care must be taken with the watering for if too much water is given the fleshy fronds become covered with oily-looking circular spots which gradually spread and completely destroy it. Platyceriums similarly over-watered show similar symptoms. If these symptoms appear the whole of the soil should be removed from the roots by washing and then re-pot in a smaller pot. After this is done very little water should be given and even when in good health, unless the plants are in a very warm house, water should be given only when they begin to flag. *E. scolopendrifolium* does not like root-disturbance and is best when pot-bound provided watering is carefully done.

**E. apo'dum.*** *cau.* thick, woody, scales dense, linear, brown, crisped. *sti.* tufted, very short, or obsolete. *Barren fronds* 1 ft. or more long, 1½ to 2 in. broad, apex acuminate, lower part narrowed very gradually, edge and midrib densely fringed with soft, short, brown hairs. *Fertile fronds* much smaller than the barren. W. Indies to Peru. 1824. Stove.

**E. appendicula'tum.** A synonym of *Egenolfia appendiculata*.

**E. Aubert'ii.** *rhiz.* woody, short-creeping, prostrate, densely scaly. *Barren fronds* 1 ft. or more in length, borne on stems 4 to 6 in. long, clothed with squarrose, linear, brown scales. *Fertile fronds* 2 to 3 in. long, suddenly narrowed at base, borne on stems 6 to 9 in. long. Fernando Po, S. Africa, Trop. America. A distinct species, resembling *E. petiolatum*. (Ferns of South Africa by T. R. Sim (2nd ed.) (2), 152; B.C.F. 1, 186, as *Acrostichum Aubertii*.)

**E. barba'tum.** A synonym of *E. scolopendrifolium*.

**E. Burchell'ii.** *rhiz.* short, woody, with small, dark brown scales. *sti.* 8 to 12 in. long, erect, nearly naked. *Barren fronds* 1 to 2 ft. long, ¾ to 1¼ in. broad, point very acute, lower part very gradually narrowed, naked and glossy on both sides. *Fertile fronds* much smaller. Brazil.

**E. cauda'tum.** A synonym of *E. petiolosum*.

**E. confor'me.** *rhiz.* wide creeping, scaly. *sti.* 1 to 12 in. long, firm, erect, stramineous, naked or slightly scaly. *Fronds* 2 to 9 in. long, ½ to 2 in. broad, acute or bluntish, base cuneate or spatulate, edge entire; barren fronds narrower than fertile one. Tropics. (L.F. 7, 44; *Ferns of South Africa* by T. R. Sim (2nd ed.) (2), 147.) SYN. *Acrostichum conforme*. A variable species. Stove.

**E. crassiner've.** A variety of *E. latifolium*.

**E. crini'tum.** Elephant's Ear Fern.* *cau.* woody, erect. *sti.* of barren fronds 4 to 8 in. long, densely clothed with long scales. *Barren fronds* 9 to 18 in. long, 4 to 9 in. wide, broadly oblong, subcoriaceous; apex blunt, base rounded, edge entire, ciliated; both sides with scattered scales like those of stipes. *Fertile fronds* similar, but much smaller, the stipes longer. W. Indies, &c. 1793. (B.C.F. 1, 196, as *Acrostichum crinitum*.) SYN. *Chrysodium* and *Hymenodium crinitum*. Stove.

**E. decora'tum.** *cau.* stout, with bright brown scales ¾ in. long. *Barren fronds* 1 ft. or more long, 3 to 4 in. broad, coriaceous, bright green, acute, rounded at base, edges densely fringed with squarrose, brown scales. *Fertile fronds* nearly as large as barren. W. Indies, &c.

**E. foenicula'ceum.** A synonym of *Rhipidopteris foeniculacea*.

**E. furca'tum.** *sti.* densely tufted, 2 to 4 in. long, slender, stramineous, naked. *Fronds* 3 to 4 in. long, about ½ in. broad, pinnate; lower pinnae of fertile fronds 2- or 3-cleft, with linear divisions; of barren pinnae broader, and not so deep. St. Helena. SYN. *Polybotrya bifurcata*. Greenhouse.

**E. Herminie'ri.*** *rhiz.* stout, creeping. *sti.* very short, or none. *Barren fronds* 1½ to 3 ft. long, 1 to 1½ in. broad, simple, acuminate, the lower part narrowed gradually. *Fertile fronds* short-stalked, 3 to 4 in. long, 1 to 1½ in. broad. Trop. America. 1871. Stove.

**E. heteromorph'um.** *rhiz.* slender, wide creeping, scaly. *sti.* 1 to 3 in. long, slender, slightly scaly. *Barren fronds* 1½ to 2 in. long, ¾ to 1 in. broad, simple, bluntish, base rounded, both surfaces with scattered linear dark castaneous scales. *Fertile fronds* much smaller, stipes much longer. Colombia, Ecuador. Stove.

**E. hir'tum.*** *rhiz.* woody, densely scaly. *sti.* 2 to 4 in. long, densely clothed with pale or dark scales. *Barren fronds* 6 to 12 in. long, about 1 in. broad, simple, acute, base narrowed gradually; both sides matted, edge densely ciliate with reddish scales. *Fertile fronds* as long, but much narrower, stipes much longer. Tropics. Stove or greenhouse. (L.F. 7, 48.) SYN. *Acrostichum paleaceum, A. squamosum*.

**E. hyb'ridum.** *rhiz.* woody, densely clothed with dark chestnut-brown, crisped scales. *sti.* firm, erect, scaly, 6 to 9 in. long. *Barren fronds* 6 to 12 in. long, about 2 in. broad, acuminate, rounded at base, sub-coriaceous, scaly at edges. *Fertile fronds* much smaller. Trop. Africa. (Ferns of South Africa by T. R. Sim (2nd ed.) (2), 151.) SYN. *Acrostichum Lindbergii*. The var. **melan'opus** has blackish or dark chestnut scales, *sti.* 2 to 3 in. long, *fronds* rather smaller. Venezuela. SYN. *E. melanopus*.

**E. Langsdorf'fii.** A synonym of *E. muscosum*.

**E. latifo'lium.*** *rhiz.* thick, woody, creeping, scaly. *sti.* 6 to 12 in. long, firm, erect, naked, or scaly. *Barren fronds* 9 to 18 in. long, 2 to 4 in. broad, simple, acute, gradually narrowed below, entire; texture leathery. *Fertile fronds* considerably narrower than barren. Trop. America. Stove. A variable species.

**E. Lindberg'ii.** A synonym of *E. hybridum*.

**E. Lin'gua.** Differs from *E. latifolium*. *rhiz.* firm, wide-creeping or long-trailing, covered with small, ovate, dark brown scales. *Fronds* coriaceous, suddenly narrowed at base. Trop. America.

**E. mag'num.** *rhiz.* sub-erect, basal paleae small, nearly black. *sti.* tufted, those of barren fronds 3 to 4 in. long. *Barren fronds* 2 to 3 ft. long, 1½ to 2 in. broad, narrowed gradually to both ends, paleae of upper surface numerous, minute, whitish, those of under-side ferruginous. British Guiana. 1880.

**E. melan'opus.** A variety of *E. hybridum*.

**E. musco'sum.*** *rhiz.* woody, densely scaly. *sti.* 4 to 6 in. long, firm, clothed with large pale brown scales. *Barren fronds* 6 to 12 in. long, 1 to 1½ in. broad, simple, narrowed at both ends; upper surface slightly scaly; lower quite hidden by imbricated brownish scales; barren fronds much smaller than fertile, stipes longer. Trop. America. (B.C.F. 1, 211.) SYN. *Acrostichum Langsdorffii*. Greenhouse.

**E. nervo'sum.*** *cau.* woody, erect. *sti.* tufted, 2 to 6 in. long, firm, erect, scaly. *Barren fronds* 4 to 8 in. long, 1 to 1½ in. broad, simple, both ends narrowed, entire. *Fertile fronds* much narrower, on longer stipes. St. Helena. Greenhouse. SYN. *Aconiopteris subdiaphana, Acrostichum subdiaphanum*.

**E. pelta'tum.** A synonym of *Rhipidopteris peltata*.

**E. petiola'tum.*** *rhiz.* woody, creeping, densely scaly. *sti.* 3 to 6 in. long, firm, erect, scaly, often viscous. *Barren fronds* 6 to 12 in. long, ½ to 1 in. broad, simple, acute, lower part narrowed gradually; both surfaces more or less scaly, and minutely scaly. *Fertile fronds* smaller, with longer stipes. Tropics. 1826. (Ferns of South Africa by T. R. Sim (2nd ed.) (2), 149.) SYN. *Acrostichum viscosum, A. Blumeanum?* Very variable in form. Stove.

**E. petiolo'sum.** *rhiz.* woody, wide scandent. *sti.* woody, erect, scaly at base. *Fronds* 2-pinnate, or 3-pinnatifid, 2 to 4 ft. long, 1 to

3 ft. broad, deltoid; upper barren pinnae lanceolate, pinnatifid, longest sometimes 18 in. long, and 6 to 10 in. broad; pinnules with long falcate lobes reaching half-way to midrib, both surfaces naked; fertile pinnules very narrow, and dangling, continuous or beaded. W. Indies, Mexico, &c. Stove. (H.I.P. 3, 215.) SYN. *Polybotrya* and *Acrostichum caudatum*.

**E. plica'tum.*** *rhiz.* thick, woody, very scaly. *sti.* 1 to 3 in. long, firm, scaly throughout. *Barren fronds* 3 to 6 in. long, about ½ in. broad, simple, usually blunt, base cuneate or rather rounded, both surfaces and midrib very scaly. *A. Dombeyanum*, of garden origin, is a varietal form of this, of which there are several others. Mexico to Peru.

**E. Plumie'ri.** A variety of *E. villosum*.

**E. scolopendrifo'lium.*** *rhiz.* woody, creeping, scaly. *sti.* 4 to 12 in. long, firm, erect, densely clothed with blackish scales. *Barren fronds* often 1 ft. long, 1½ to 3 in. broad, simple, acute, the base narrowed gradually; edge and midrib scaly. *Fertile fronds* much smaller than the barren ones. Trop. America. (L.F. 7, 45.) SYN. *Acrostichum barbatum*. Stove. var. **Preston'ii** has the barren fronds densely fringed with persistent brown scales (Brazil).

**E. sim'plex.** *rhiz.* woody, creeping, scaly. *sti.* 1 to 4 in. long, firm, erect, naked. *Barren fronds* 4 to 12 in. long, about 1½ in. broad, very acute, the lower part narrowed very gradually. *Fertile fronds* narrower, with longer stipes. Trop. America, Trop. Africa, Madagascar. 1798. (L.B.C. 709.) SYN. *E. brasiliense*. Stove.

**E. spathula'tum.** *sti.* tufted, 1 to 2 in. long, firm, erect, scaly. *Barren fronds* ½ to 4 in. long, ¼ to ½ in. broad, leathery, obovate-spatulate, blunt, tapering narrowly or gradually at base; both surfaces and margins copiously scaly. *Fertile fronds* smaller, with longer stipes. Trop. America, S. Africa, Ceylon. (*Ferns of South Africa* by T. R. Sim (2nd ed.) (2), 150.) SYN. *Acrostichum piloselloides*. Stove.

**E. tomento'sum.** *rhiz.* woody, with dense, black, fibrillose scales. *sti.* 3 to 5 in. long, rigid, erect, densely ciliate, scaly, upper scales white. *Barren fronds* 1 ft. or more in length, 1 to 1¼ in. broad, bluntish at apex, lower part gradually narrowed, thick but flaccid, both sides matted with scales. *Fertile fronds* narrower, on stems 1 ft. or more in length. Réunion.

**E. undula'tum.** A variety of *E. villosum*.

**E. villo'sum.*** *rhiz.* woody, densely scaly. *sti.* 2 to 4 in. long, slender, densely clothed with scales. *Barren fronds* 6 to 9 in. long, 1 to 1½ in. broad, acute, lower part narrowed gradually; both surfaces scaly, edge more or less ciliate. *Fertile fronds* much smaller. Trop. America. (L.F. 7, 54 as *Acrostichum villosum*.) Stove. var. **undula'tum** has *fronds* wavy at edges.

**E. visco'sum.** A synonym of *E. petiolatum*.

***elas'ticus -a -um,*** elastic.

***Elate'rium,*** driving away. *See* **Ecballium Elaterium.**

***Elati'nes,*** from the old German plant name, Elatine.

***ela'tior,*** taller.

***ela'tus -a -um,*** tall.

***Elbert'ii,*** in honour of J. Elbert, 1878–1915, who collected in Celebes, &c.

**ELDER.** *See* **Sambucus.**

***eleagrifo'lius -a -um,*** with leaves like the wild olive.

**ELECAMPANE.** *See* **Inula Helenium.**

**A→**

***el'egans,*** graceful.

***elegantis'simus -a -um,*** very graceful.

***elegan'tulus -a -um,*** somewhat graceful.

***Elemeetia'nus -a -um,*** in honour of M. Jonghe van Elemeet, amateur of succulents, *c.* 1864.

**ELEMI.** Stimulant gum resins derived from various plants.

**ELEMI, AMERICAN.** *See* **Bursera Simaruba.**

**ELEMI, MANILA.** *See* **Canarinum commune.**

**ELEPHANT APPLE.** *See* **Feronia.**

**ELEPHANT BEETLE.** *See* **Strawberry Blossom Weevil.**

**ELEPHANT HAWK-MOTH.** *See* **Hawk Moths.**

**ELEPHANT'S EAR.** *See* **Begonia.**

**ELEPHANT'S FOOT.** *See* **Dioscorea elephantipes.**

***elephan'tipes,*** like an elephant's foot.

***el'ephas,*** elephant.

**ELETTA'RIA** (native name in Malabar). FAM. *Zingiberaceae*. A genus of 2 Indian perennial herbs allied to Amomum but with flowers few in loose spikes arising from the creeping rhizome, the connective without appendages and the lip yellow and blue. Leaves in 2 ranks, few. *E. Cardamomum* is one of the chief sources of the Cardomoms of commerce. For cultivation *see* **Maranta.**

**E. Cardamo'mum.** *rhiz.* thick. Stems many, up to 10 ft. h. *l.* linear-lanceolate, slender-pointed, about 2 ft. long, softly downy beneath; nearly sessile. *fl.* in a spreading almost prostrate, panicle up to 2 ft. long, small; cor. white, about ⅝ in. long; lip about as long, blue with white stripes and a yellow margin. India.

**ELEUSI'NE** (from Eleusis, the Greek town where was the Temple of Ceres). FAM. *Gramineae*. A genus of about 6 species of annual tropical grasses of rather coarse growth, some of which are grown for grain in Africa and India, one or two being useful for drying for winter decoration. Spikes 1-sided, dense, grouped at top of stem; spikelets with several flowers in 2 rows on one side of the rachis, awnless. The following can be grown in ordinary soil in the open during summer.

**E. barcinonen'sis.** A synonym of *E. tristachya*.

**E. coraca'na.** Similar to *E. indica* but stouter, with shorter, broader spikes. SE. Asia.

**E. in'dica.** 8 to 18 in. h., tufted, erect. Stem smooth. *l.* about 12 in. long, usually blunt, sheath smooth, ligule usually under $\frac{1}{25}$ in. long. *Spikes* 3 to 5, up to 4 in. long, straight or slightly bent. July, August. Tropics.

**E. oligostach'ya.** A synonym of *E. tristachya*.

**E. tristach'ya.** Dwarfer than *E. indica* with narrower *l. Spikes* usually 3, 1 to 1½ in. long. SYN. *E. barcinonensis*, *E. oligostachya*.

**ELEUTHERI'NE** (*eleutheros*, free; in reference to the free filaments). FAM. *Iridaceae*. A genus of 1 or 2 species of S. American bulbous plants needing stove conditions and treatment otherwise like that of Ixia.

**E. anom'ala.** Probably identical with *E. plicata*.

**E. plica'ta.** *l.* 1 or 2, linear, 1 to 1½ ft. long, plicate. *fl.* in several stalked clusters, with a short linear l. at base of each; perianth white, ¾ in. across, free, fugitive; stamens 6, attached at base of segs., filaments short, free; peduncles 6 to 12 in. long. April. Trop. America. (B.R. 1843, 57 as *E. anomala*; B.M. 655 as *Marica plicata*.) SYN. *Keitia natalensis*, *Sisyrinchium palmifolium*.

**ELEUTHEROCOC'CUS.** Included in **Acanthopanax.**

**ELEUTHEROPET'ALUM** (*eleutheros*, free, *petalon*, petal; the parts of the perianth being free of one another). FAM. *Palmaceae*. A genus of 2 species often included in Chamaedorea (q.v.)

**E. Ernesti-Augus'ti.** Stem of 3 to 4 ft. h., reed-like, rooting at base. *l.* simple, 2 ft. long, 1 ft. wide, deeply 2-fid at apex, coarsely serrate, rich dark green. *fl.-spikes* bright orange-scarlet, very ornamental, 8 to 9 in. long, the simple branches 6 to 8 in. long. Colombia. (B.M. 4831, 4837 as *Chamaedorea Ernesti-Augusti*.) SYN. *Chamaedorea simplicifrons*, *Geonoma latifrons*.

**E. Sartor'ii.** Stem 8 to 14 ft. h. *l.* pinnate, 3 to 3½ ft. long, sheath, stalk and rachis white beneath; lflets. 12 in. long, 1½ to 2 in. wide, alternate, falcately curved, slender-pointed, narrowed to base. *Spadix* from among or just below l., bright red. Mexico. SYN. *Chamaedorea Sartorii*.

***E'leyi,*** in honour of Charles Eley of East Bergholt, amateur gardener, who raised *Malus × Eleyi*.

**ELICHRYSUM.** *See* **Helichrysum.**

**ELISE'NA** (in honour of Princess Élise, sister of Napoleon). FAM. *Amaryllidaceae*. A genus of 3 or 4 very closely related species of S. American bulbous plants, nearly related to Hymenocallis. Bulb tunicated. Leaves lorate. Flowers few in an umbel on a long, solid, leafless peduncle; white; perianth tube short, broadly funnel-shaped, segments long, narrow, equal; stamens as long as perianth. Ornamental greenhouse plants requiring the same treatment as Hymenocallis. *E. longipetala* may be grown successfully against the outside wall of a heated house in some districts.

**E. longipet'ala.** *fl.* white; segs. linear, about 3 in. long, undulate, recurved at the point, corona 1¼ in. deep; umbel about 6-fld.; scape 3 ft. h., 2-edged. Lima. 1837. (B.M. 3873.) A hybrid of this species with *Hymenocallis calathina* (SYN. *H. × festalis, Ismene × festalis*) can be grown under the same conditions.

**Eli'shae,** in honour of the wife of G. Elisha of Canonbury Park, who grew Mesembryanthemums.

**ELIS'MA** (variant of Alisma). FAM. *Alismataceae.* A genus of a single aquatic herb distinguished from Alisma by the flowers being solitary or almost so from the nodes and the leaves floating. Native of W. Europe, including Britain. Easily grown.

**E. na'tans.** Root fibrous. *Radical l.* 2 to 8 in. long, submerged, narrow, pellucid; *floating l.* oblong, ½ to 1 in. long, with long petioles, arising from the floating, rooting stem. *fl.* white, ⅓ in. across, the claw yellow, usually solitary on peduncles 2 to 3 in. long. (E.B. 1441.) SYN. *Alisma natans.*

**Elizabeth'ae,** in honour of Queen Elizabeth of Roumania (Carmen Sylva).

**ELK NUT.** *See* **Pyrularia pubera.**

**ELK'S HORN FERN.** *See* **Platycerium.**

**Ellacombia'nus -a -um,** in honour of Canon H. N. Ellacombe, 1822–1916, Rector of Bitton.

**ELLEAN'THUS** (*eilo*, I shut in, *anthos*, a flower; the flowers are enclosed by bracts). FAM. *Orchidaceae.* A genus of pretty stove terrestrial orchids. Flowers in terminal spikes, or closely set heads, with a bract often ciliate and usually taller behind each flower; sepals free, erect; petals often narrower than the sepals, the side lobes of the lip erect or broadly rounded, their margins often incurved; column erect, semi-terete or two-winged in the middle. Pollen masses 8. Leaves sessile, plicate, ovate-lanceolate or linear. About 50 species have been described, but few have been in cultivation. All are natives of Trop. America. The genus is allied to Sobralia and includes short and tall species. They require the same cultural conditions, compost, &c., as Sobralias.

**E. Carava'ta.** *fl.* small, numerous, yellow, with a short, rosy, twisted ovary; sep. concave, acute, ⅓ in. long; pet. about the same, narrower; lip slightly longer, somewhat obovate, base concave, front margin rounded; spike elongato-capitate, very compact. November. *l.* distant, with long, sheathing bases, lanceolate, rigid, 5 to 8 in. long, gradually and finely acuminate. Stem 1 to 2 ft. h., erect, slender, terete, hispid, like the foliage and the ¾ to 1 in. long rosy bracts. Guiana. 1858. (B.M. 5141 as *Evelyna Caravata*.) SYN. *Sobralia Caravata.*

**E. kermesi'na.** *fl.* bright carmine. January. 6 in. h. Mariquita. 1843.

**E. xanthoco'mus.** *fl.* yellow, in erect racemes. May. *l.* lanceolate, acuminate, vaginate. 1 ft. h., erect. Peru. 1872. (B.M. 6016.)

E. C.

**ELLIOT'TIA** (in honour of Stephen Elliott, 1771–1830, an American botanist). FAM. *Ericaceae.* A monotypic genus characterized by an irregularly rotate corolla of 4 separate petals, a feature which distinguishes it from the allied genera, Tripetaleia and Cladothamnus. Requires well-drained, lime-free loam and prefers open woodland. Propagated by separation of suckers.

**E. racem'osa.** Deciduous shrub or small tree up to 20 ft. *l.* alternate, oval to elliptic-oblanceolate, narrowing to both ends, acute at tip, 2 to 5 in. long, ¾ to 1¾ in. wide, mucronate, smooth above, slightly hairy beneath. *fl.* in an erect, terminal raceme or panicle 4 to 10 in. long; pet. white, oblong, rounded at tip, ciliate, decurved, ¼ to ⅜ in. long; cal. lobes 3 to 4, rounded or triangular, very short. July, August. *fr.* a 4- to 5-celled sub-globose capsule. SE. United States. 1894. (B.M. 8413.) SYN. *Tripetaleia racemosa.* Extremely rare both in nature and gardens.

F. S.

**Elliot'tii,** in honour of (1) Prof. G. F. Scott-Elliott, botanist to Sierra Leone Boundary Commission, traveller in Madagascar, &c. (2) Capt. Elliott of Farnboro' Park, Hants, who, *c.* 1895, grew rare plants there.

**ellip'ticus -a -um,** elliptical, about twice as long as wide.

A

**Ellis'ii, Ellisia'nus -a -um,** in honour of the Hon. Chas. Ellis of Frensham Hall, Surrey, who grew uncommon plants there.

**Ellwangeria'nus -a -um,** in honour of George Ellwanger, 1816–1906, of Würtemberg, and of the great Mt. Hope Nursery, Rochester, New York.

**ELM.** *See* **Ulmus.**

**ELM BARK BEETLE,** *Scolytus destructor,* and the smaller species, *S. multistriatus,* are serious pests of Elm trees both directly by tunnelling beneath the bark and killing the branches and main stem, and indirectly by transmitting the injurious Elm fungus, *Graphium ulmi* (Dutch Elm Disease). The mother-galleries are longitudinal with the galleries of the grubs radiating from the parent gallery. The beetle has a black head and thorax with pitchy-red or brown wing-covers. There are 2 generations a year, the first egg-laying beginning in April and May with the new brood of beetles appearing in late July and August, and the second in late summer which results in grubs that overwinter within the thick bark.

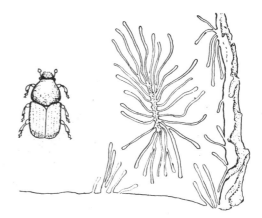

*Elm bark beetle and its galleries*

Unfavourable conditions for the trees favour an attack, and trees that either have an unhealthy root system as a result of drought or waterlogged soil, are subjected to fungus attack, or lack vigour from one cause or another, are rendered more liable to infestations. All dead and dying branches should be removed and burned. The placing of trap-branches or logs on the ground near Elm trees from April to July will attract the beetles which, together with their grubs, may be destroyed by barking the attacked traps in late July.

G. F. W.

**eloba'tus -a -um,** without lobes.

**ELO'DEA** (*elodes*, growing in watery places). FAM. *Hydrocharidaceae.* A small genus of aquatic plants, natives of S. America, closely related to Anacharis (q.v. for treatment) with which it is often combined but which occurs wild only in N. America and Africa.

**E. callitrichoi'des.** A synonym of *Anacharis callitrichoides.*

**E. canaden'sis.** A synonym of *Anacharis canadensis.*

**E. cris'pa.** A synonym of *Anacharis crispa.*

**E. den'sa.** Stems stout, ascending. *l.* dark green. S. America. A good oxygenator for the aquarium and useful also in outdoor pools. SYN. *Egeria densa.*

**elonga'tus -a -um,** lengthened out.

**ELSHOLTZ'IA** (after John Sigismund Elsholtz, 1623–88, German physician and naturalist). FAM. *Labiatae*. A genus of about 36 species of aromatic herbs or sub-shrubs, rarely genuinely woody, mostly natives of India and China but one is European, another Abyssinian. Leaves opposite, toothed; flowers in crowded whorls forming 1-sided spikes and, collectively, large terminal panicles; calyx tubular or bell-shaped, 5-toothed; corolla 2-lipped, lower lip 3-lobed, upper undivided; stamens 4, exserted. *E. Stauntonii* grows well in good loam in the sun and is readily propagated by green cuttings in summer.

**E. Staunton'ii.** Semi-woody plant about 5 ft., dying back considerably in winter but sending up each spring new crops of erect downy shoots. *l.* aromatic, lanceolate, 2 to 6 in. long, ½ to 1½ in. wide, pale and densely glandular beneath. *Spikes* cylindrical, axillary, 4 to 8 in. long, 1 in. wide, forming large terminal panicles; *fl.* small, purplish-pink. Autumn. N. China. 1909. (B.M. 8460.)

W. J. B.

**Elute'ria,** from Elutheria, name used by Petiver in 1747 for *Croton Eluteria*.

**Elwes'ii, Elwesia'nus -a -um,** in honour of Henry John Elwes, 1846–1922, traveller, naturalist, amateur gardener, author of *Genus Lilium* and, with Dr. A. Henry, of *The Trees of Great Britain*.

**ELY'MUS** (Greek name for a kind of millet). Lyme Grass. FAM. *Gramineae*. A genus of about 25 species of erect perennial grasses distributed over the temperate regions of the world. Leaves flat or rolled, with terminal bristly spikes somewhat like rye. Spikelets 2- to 6-flowered. *E. arenarius* has long rhizomes and is an excellent sand-binding grass. Several other species are ornamental. Sandy soil suits *E. arenarius* well, but it is apt to spread widely. It and others can be grown in ordinary soil, and are hardy.

**E. arena'rius.** Stout blue-green perennial, 4 ft. or more h. Rootstock wide-creeping. *l.* flat, except when dry, about 20 in. long, ¼ in. wide, rough above, sheath smooth, ligule short. *Spike* stiffly erect, 6 to 12 in. long; spikelets about 1 in. long, awnless. May to July. Cool temperate N. Hemisphere. (E.B. 1819.)

**E. canaden'sis.** Stout dark green perennial, about 2½ ft. h. Stem erect, smooth. *l.* flat, rough, 6 to 12 in. long, ⅜ in. wide. *Spikes* about 6 in. long; spikelets ¾ in. long, very stiff, awned. July, August. N. America. var. **glaucifo'lius,** pale and glaucous, awns slender.

**E. glaucifo'lius.** A variety of *E. canadensis*.

**E. glauc'us.** Blue-green, densely tufted perennial, about 3 ft. h. Stem erect. *l.* very short, smooth. *Spikes* long; spikelets hairy, short awned. Turkestan.

**E. Hys'trix.** *See* Hystrix.

**emargina'tus -a -um,** having a small notch at the end as though a piece had been removed.

**emasculate,** to remove the anthers of a flower before the pollen is ripe.

**emas'culus -a -um,** without functional stamens.

**EMBE'LIA** (Cingalese name of 1 species). FAM. *Myrsinaceae*. A genus of about 60 species of mostly climbing shrubs or trees natives of the Old World tropics. Allied to Ardisia with their chief beauty in the fruits and foliage. Leaves entire or toothed, stalks often narrowly winged or glandular. Flowers white or greenish-yellow, small, often dioecious. Fruit small, globose, 1- (rarely 2-) seeded. A compost of loam and peat is needed for these stove-plants, which can be propagated by cuttings of half-ripe shoots.

**E. Ri'bes.** *fl.* green and white. *fr.* pungent, edible. Trop. Asia. 1886. Known in E. Indies as currants.

**E. robus'ta.** Large glabrous straggling shrub to about 20 ft. h. *l.* obovate-oblong, elliptic or obovate, more or less toothed, rustydowny or rarely glabrous beneath, netted. India. 1823.

F. G. P.

**EMBOTH'RIUM** (*en* in, *bothrion*, a little pit; referring to the anthers). FAM. *Proteaceae*. A genus of 3 or 4 species of evergreen shrubs or trees natives of S. America. They like a peaty soil but succeed also in open sandy loam quite free from chalk or lime.

*Embothrium coccineum longifolium*

**E. coccin'eum.*** Evergreen suckering tree, 40 to 50 ft. in Cornwall, but also flowering as a shrub a few ft. h. *l.* 2½ to 4½ in. long, ¾ to 1½ in. wide, ovate-lanceolate to narrowly oval, entire, glabrous, dark glossy-green. *fl.* crimson-scarlet, in axillary and terminal racemes 3 to 4 in. long and wide; cor. with a tube 1 to 1½ in. long separating into 4 recurving, twisted, linear lobes enclosing the anthers and exposing the long protruding style; stalk ½ to 1 in. long; stigma yellow. May, June. Chile. 1846. (B.M. 4856.) var. **longifo'lium,** *l.* longer and narrower. Tierra del Fuego. The typical form is only seen at its best in such places as Cornwall, but the var., which may be identical with *E. lanceolatum* of Ruiz and Pavon, is decidedly hardier and has been successfully grown in S. Surrey, Sussex, &c.

**EMBRYO.** The rudimentary plant within the seed: sometimes the embryo occupies the whole seed, as in the pea, and the seed is said to be exalbuminous; sometimes it lies beside, or is embedded in, a mass of food material (the endosperm) as in the maize or the ash, and the seed is then said to be albuminous.

**EMBRYO-SAC.** The large cell in the ovule in which the embryo is formed by the development of the fertilized egg-cell or oospore, and in which also the endosperm is developed.

**Emeric'ii,** in honour of Emeric Berkley.

**Em'ersonii,** in honour of Dr. Emerson who collected, *c.* 1829, in Ceylon.

**E'merus,** from the Greek name of a plant.

**emet'icus -a -um,** causing vomiting.

**EMIL'IA** (probably a commemorative name). Fam. *Compositae*. A genus very closely allied to Senecio and Cacalia including about 12 species of annual or perennial herbs, natives of India, Polynesia, and Trop. Africa. Like Cacalia the flower-heads are without ray-florets. Lower leaves crowded, stalked, upper few, stem-clasping. Flower-heads on long peduncles, solitary or in a loose corymb, orange or scarlet, rather small; florets 5-toothed, all with stamens and pistil; involucre simple, cup-shaped, without outer scales. Achenes with 5 ciliate and acute angles. *E. flammea* is an easily grown hardy annual. It may be sown in heat in early spring or in the open in April.

**E. flam'mea.** Tassel Flower. Annual, erect, 1 to 2 ft. h. *l.* lanceolate-oblong, glabrous or slightly hairy, entire or toothed, upper large, oblong or ovate-oblong. *fl.*-heads in corymbose clusters, terminal, small, scarlet, longer than involucral scales. July to October. Trop. America. (B.M. 564 as *Cacalia coccinea*.) var. **au'rea**, orange-scarlet; **lu'tea**, golden-yellow. Syn. *Cacalia lutea*.

**E. sagitta'ta.** A synonym of *E. flammea*.

**E. sonchifo'lia.** Similar to *E. flammea* but with involucral scales nearly as long as florets. Syn. *Cacalia sonchifolia*.

**em'inens,** prominent, outstanding.

**Emin'ii,** in honour of Emin Schnitzer, 1840–92; (Emin Pasha), physician, of Egypt and the Congo.

**EMIN'IUM** (ancient name used by Dioscorides). Fam. *Araceae*. A genus of 4 species of tuberous herbs, natives of W. Asia, the tuber producing 2 or 3 long-stalked leaves and a short peduncle. Leaves rather thick, linear or hastate or pedatisect, all the segments joined at the base, the lateral ones spirally twisted round the midrib. Spathe, tubular below, blade oblong or ovate-oblong, erect; spadix free, slender, shorter than the spathe. Related to Sauromatum but with awl-shaped (not club-shaped) rudimentary flowers between the males and females. *E. Alberti* is hardy on a sunny border in well-drained sandy loam and may be increased by seed or by small tuber offsets.

**E. Al'berti.** Tuber flattish. *l.-sheaths* pale green or purplish; blade pedatisect; segs. narrow, 2½ to 5 in. long, the lateral ones narrow linear, 1 to 1½ in. long. *Peduncle* 4 to 6 in. long, usually thickened upwards and wrinkled near top. *Spathe* 6 to 8 in. long, pale green or variegated with purple without, tube swollen below, about 1¾ in. long, spathe double as long, ovate-oblong, dark purple within, covered with white hairs. May. Very fetid. Bokhara. 1884. (B.M. 6969.)

**EMMENAN'THE** (*emmenos*, enduring, *anthos*, flower; the corolla persists). Fam. *Hydrophyllaceae*. A genus of about 5 species of annual herbs, natives of Western N. America with alternate pinnatifid leaves and yellowish bell-shaped flowers with 5 to 10 broad spreading corolla lobes, the calyx segments 10 to 12. Cultivation as for other hardy annuals.

**E. penduliflor'a.** Bushy, somewhat clammy annual, 9 to 12 in. h. *l.* pinnatifid with numerous short, somewhat cut or toothed lobes. *fl.* cream or yellow, about ½ in. long, numerous in short rather loose racemes; cor. bell-shaped not unlike Lily of the Valley, persistent and retaining its shape; cal. teeth broader downwards; seeds coarsely pitted. California. 1892. (G.C. 11 (1892), 339, f. 49.)

**EMMENOP'TERYS** (*emmenos*, enduring, *pterys*, wing; in allusion to the large, wing-like calyx-lobe). Fam. *Rubiaceae*. Two species of trees found in China, Siam, and Burma. Leaves opposite, entire, stalked, thinly leathery; stipules caducous. Flowers in a terminal, many-flowered cyme, yellow or white.

**E. Hen'ryi.** Deciduous tree, 30 to 80 ft., shoots glabrous. *l.* opposite, oval or ovate, the largest up to 8 in. by 4 in., usually smaller, veins and midrib downy beneath. *fl.* in terminal, pyramidal panicles 6 to 8 in. long; cor. white, 1 in. wide, funnel-shaped, with 5 spreading lobes; cal. usually ¼ in. long, but in a proportion of the fl. one lobe becomes stalked, wing-like, as much as 2 in. long and 1½ in. wide, white. June, July. *fr.* a spindle-shaped capsule 1 to 1½ in. long. *Seeds* winged. China. 1907. Evidently very beautiful and quite hardy, but has not yet flowered in cultivation. Increased by cuttings.

W. J. B.

**emo'di,** of Mt. Emodus, N. India.

**Em'oryi,** in honour of Lt.-Col. W. H. Emory, in charge of U.S. and Mexican boundary survey.

**EMPETRA'CEAE.** Dicotyledons. A family of only 7 species in 3 genera found in arctic and north temperate regions and in America south to the Andes. Its members are small, evergreen, heath-like shrubs with crowded linear leaves and small regular flowers without petals, either solitary as in Empetrum or in terminal heads as in Corema. Sepals 2 or 3; stamens 2 to 4; ovary superior 2- to 9-celled and styles 2 to 9. Fruit a berry in Empetrum, dry in Corema.

**empetrifo'lius -a -um,** with Empetrum-like foliage.

**EMPET'RUM** (old Greek name for a plant, used by Dioscorides, from *en*, upon, *petros*, a rock). Fam. *Empetraceae*. A genus of 1 or a few species found on moors in the North Temperate Zone and in the Andes. For characters see **Empetraceae**. Hardy plants for the rock-garden on moist peaty soil. Easily propagated by cuttings in summer in sand under a handlight. The flowers are usually dioecious but occasionally both stamens and pistil occur in the same flower (var. *hermaphroditum*).

**E. ni'grum.** Crowberry, 6 to 12 in. h. *l.* linear-oblong. *fl.* small, sessile; sep. rounded, concave; pet. pink, reflexed; filaments very long; anthers red. May. *fr.* a brownish-black, globose berry, resembling that of Juniper, edible. (E.B. 1251.) var. **ru'brum**, *l.* with woolly margins, *fl.* brownish-purple, axillary, drupered. Chile, Tierra del Fuegia. (B.R. 1783.)

**E. scot'icum.** A synonym of *E. nigrum*.

**EMPHYT'US cinc'tus.** See **Sawflies (Rose)**.

**EMPLEU'RUM** (from *en*, in, *pleuron*, the pleura or membrane which envelops the lungs; seeds attached to a kind of leathery membrane). Fam. *Rutaceae*. Greenhouse treatment as for Boronia.

**E. serrula'tum.** Evergreen, entirely glabrous, very leafy shrub 2 to 6 ft., shoots slender, angled, erect, yellowish. *l.* linear 1 to 2 in. long, ⅛ in. wide, erect, apex pointed, base cuneate, minutely toothed. *fl.* unisexual, axillary, solitary or in pairs; cal. ¹⁄₁₂ in. long; cor. absent; males with 4 stamens with yellow anthers, females without stamens. June, July. S. Africa. 1774.

W. J. B.

**ENARG'IA.** See **Luzuriaga marginata**.

**ENCARS'IA formo'sa.** See **White-fly parasite**.

**ENCE'LIA** (*eychelion*, a little eel; from the form of the seeds). Fam. *Compositae*. About 20 species of branched hairy herbs, natives of W. America, sometimes shrubby at base. Leaves opposite or upper rarely alternate, entire, toothed or lobed. Flower-heads yellow or purplish, of moderate size; ray-florets spreading, entire or shortly toothed; involucral bracts in 2 or 3 series; peduncles long, terminal or somewhat panicled. *E. canescens* needs greenhouse treatment and a loamy soil and may be propagated by cuttings under glass, care being taken not to over-water.

**E. canes'cens.** Sub-shrub about 18 in. h. *l.* broadly ovate, obtuse, entire, softly grey-hairy. *fl.*-heads orange, involucre hairy, ciliate. July. Peru. 1786. (B.R. 909.) Syn. *Pallasia halimifolia*.

**ENCENO OAK.** See **Quercus agrifolia**.

**ENCEPHALAR'TOS** (*en*, within, *kephale*, the head, and *artos*, bread; the inner parts of the trunk are farinaceous). Fam. *Cycadaceae*. A genus of about 24 species, natives of S. and Trop. Africa. Stems varying from underground to 30 ft. high and from 6 to 24 in. in diameter, usually unbranched, covered with scales and the scars of fallen leaves. Leaves clustered at the top, pinnate; leaflets stiff and leathery, linear to ovate-lanceolate, mostly more or less spiny-toothed. Cones dioecious; males stalked, cylindrical; scales densely arranged in spirals; females usually wider and heavier. Handsome stately plants, those from S. Africa thriving in a greenhouse temperature, those from Trop. Africa intermediate or stove. They require a good loamy soil and are only suitable for roomy structures owing to the unyielding stiffness of their often widely spreading leaves. Their growth is slow except when given a high temperature, and during growth they take a good deal of water and should also be freely syringed, but at other times little water is needed.

KEY

1. *Veins of lflets. prominent, margin black, revolute* — 2
1. *Veins of lflets. striate* — 3
2. *Lflets. rigid* — E. cycadifolius
2. *Lflets. less rigid* — E. Friderici-Guilielmii
3. *Veins of lflets. prominent, margins somewhat recurved* — 4
3. *Veins of lflets. slender* — 9
4. *Lflets. short, twisted at base, lanceolate* — E. caffer
4. *Lflets. long or lanceolate, narrowed at base* — 5
5. *Tip of lflets. acute, entire or spinose-lobed* — 6
5. *Lflets. not spinose-lobed* — 7
6. *Lflets. ⅓ to ⅗ in. wide with terminal straight or curved spines* — E. horridus
6. *Lflets. broader, with short, sharp point* — E. latifrons
6. *Lflets. oblong-oval with large triangular teeth or lobes* — E. kosiensis
7. *Lflets. narrow-lanceolate* — 8
7. *Lflets. broad-lanceolate, mucronate* — E. Altensteinii
8. *Lflets. often with 1 to 3 large teeth* — E. longifolius
8. *Lflets. often with 1 or 2 teeth, margin plane* — E. Lehmannii
9. *Deep-rooting; lflets. long-lanceolate with large somewhat spiny teeth, veins prominent* — E. Laurentianus
9. *Veins slender, striate* — 10
10. *Lflets. linear-lanceolate, toothed, widest in lower third* — E. villosus
10. *Lflets. lanceolate* — 11
11. *Lflets. widest in middle* — E. Hildebrandtii
11. *Lflets. widest in lower third* — 12
12. *Lflets. shining green* — E. Woodii
12. *Lflets. deep green* — E. gratus

**E. Altenstein'ii.*** Stem ultimately about 16 by 2½ ft. in girth. *l.* 5 ft. long; lflets. very numerous, 6 in. long, 1 in. wide, linear-oblong, with 3 to 5 spiny teeth on each margin. *Male cone* 12 to 15 in. long, 4 in. wide, cylindrical; *female* broadly oval, sessile, up to 1½ ft. tall by 10 in. wide. S. Africa. 1835. (B.M. 7162–3.) Syn. *E. regalis, E. Vromii.*

**E. brachyphyl'lus.** A synonym of *E. caffer.*

**E. caf'fer.** Kaffir Bread. Stemless or nearly so, 1 ft. in diameter, woolly. *l.* about 14 in a crown, up to 2 ft. long; lflets. numerous, crowded, middle ones 2 to 4 in. long, ⅓ in. wide, much smaller at the base, entire or with 1 or 2 teeth near the apex. *Male cones* solitary to 3 together, 8 to 12 in. long, 2 to 3 in. wide; *females* oblong or oval, 6 in. long by 4 in. wide; scales with orange margins. S. Africa. Syn. *E. brachyphyllus.*

**E. cycadifo'lius.** Stem up to 10 ft., densely woolly. *l.* up to 5 in. long, mainstalk very woolly when young; lflets. entire, up to 120 pairs, usually overlapping, 3 to 6 in. long, ⅛ to ⅙ in. wide, margins thickened, veins 8 or 9. *Male cone* cylindric, 8 to 10 in. long, about 3 in. wide, densely covered with brown wool; *females* several, oblong-oval, 10 in. long, half as wide, densely woolly. S. Africa. 1876.

**E. elonga'tus.** A synonym of *E. Lehmannii.*

**E. Friderici-Guilielm'ii.** Stem 6 ft. *l.* up to 3 ft. long, mainstalk at first woolly; lflets. numerous, the longest about 4 in., narrowly linear, margins recurved, entire but very sharply pointed, woolly when young. *Male cones* cylindric, 9 in. long by 3 in. wide, densely woolly; *females* broadly oblong-ellipsoid, about 15 in. long by 9 in., scales woolly, brownish. S. Africa. 1867. (I.H. 567 as *E. Ghellinckii.*) Distinct by its very narrow lflets. with recurved margins.

**E. Ghellinck'ii.** A synonym of *E. Friderici-Guilielmii.*

**E. gra'tus.** Stem globose to oval, 1½ to 2 ft., sometimes 4 ft. h., 1½ ft. in diameter. *l.* 4 to 5 ft. long; lflets. ovate-lanceolate, curved, in 30 to 70 pairs, 6 to 10 in. long, 1⅕ in. wide, 1- to 4-toothed on lower margin. *Male cone* stalked, narrowly ovate to cylindric, 9 to 12 in. long, 3 to 4 in. wide; *females* 1½ to 2 ft. long, 6 to 8 in. wide, greenish-yellow. Trop. Africa. 1903.

**E. Hildebrandt'ii.** Stem cylindric, varying from short to 20 ft. by 1 ft. in diameter. *l.* up to 9 ft. long, mainstalk woolly when young; lflets. in 50 to 70 pairs, linear-lanceolate, up to 9 in. long, ⅔ to 1 in. wide, with usually 2 or 3 spines on each margin. *Male cone* 8 to 18 in. long, 2½ to 4 in. wide; *females* cylindric up to 2 ft. long, 7 in. wide. Trop. E. Africa. 1877. (B.M. 8592–3.)

**E. hor'ridus.** Stem very short or subterranean. *l.* glaucous, recurved at the end, up to about 2 ft. long; lflets. up to 4 in. long, 2 in. wide, obliquely ovate-lanceolate, spinily lobed. *Male cone* cylindric, stalked, 1 ft. long by 2½ in. in diameter; *female* broadly oblong-ovoid, 15 in. long by 6 to 8 in. wide, top rather triangular. S. Africa. 1800. (The Cycad figured B.M. 5371, as *E. horridus* var. *trispinosus*, is now referred to *E. Lehmannii.*)

**E. kosien'sis.** Stem up to 4 ft. h. in cultivation, but stemless or nearly so in nature. *l.* about 3 ft. long; lflets. in about 20 pairs, closely set or overlapping, oblong-oval, 3 to 6 in. long, 1½ to 2 in. wide, margins continuously and formidably armed with large triangular teeth or lobes. *Cones* bright red. S. Africa.

**E. lanugino'sus.** A synonym of *E. horridus.*

**E. lati'frons.*** Stem up to 8 ft. by 4 ft. in girth. *l.* 2 to 3 ft. long, recurved towards the top; lflets. in about 30 pairs, the middle and largest ones 5 in. long by 2 in. wide, ovate to ovate-lanceolate, overlapping, coarsely 3- or 4-toothed or lobed, spine-tipped. *Male cones*, 1 to 3, brownish-yellow, 2 ft. long, 6 in. wide; *females* 22 in. long by 10 in. wide, up to 60 lb. weight. Habitat ?

**E. Laurentia'nus.** Stem up to 30 ft. or more and 2 ft. in diameter in its wild state. *l.* sometimes over 20 ft. long; the middle lflets. up to 16 in. long and 2 in. wide, linear-lanceolate, margins spiny-toothed. (Plants at present in cultivation are much smaller.) *Male cones* long-stalked, 10 in. long; *females* about as long, red. Trop. Africa. (G.C. 35 (1904), 370.)

**E. Lehmann'ii.** Stem up to 9 ft. *l.* very glaucous, up to 3 ft. long; lflets. 8 in. long, ⅔ in. wide in the middle, smaller towards both ends, sometimes entire, sometimes with 1 or 2 spiny lobes or teeth usually on the lower side, point spiny. *Male cones* slender cylindric, yellow, 9 in. long by 2 in. wide; *female* up to 18 in. long by 12 in. broad, reddish-brown. S. Africa. (B.M. 5371 as *E. horridus trispinosus.*) Syn. *E. elongatus.*

**E. longifo'lius.** Stem 12 ft. and upwards, 3½ ft. girth. *l.* arched, recurved near the apex, 3 to 4 ft. long; lflets. in 40 or more pairs, up to 7 in. long by 1 in. wide, usually entire. *Male cones* 1 to 2 ft. long, 4 to 8 in. wide, apex of scales hooked; *female* up to 2 ft. long, 12 to 14 in. wide, weighing up to 90 lb. S. Africa. (B.M. 4903 as *E. caffer.*)

**E. rega'lis.** A synonym of *E. Altensteinii.*

**E. Verschaffelt'ii.** A synonym of *E. caffer.*

**E. villo'sus.** Stem subterranean or very short, densely woolly. *l.* usually few, erect then spreading, slightly arched, 5 to 9 ft. long; lflets. in 60 to 90 pairs, densely woolly when young, varying from mere spines at the base, up to 8 in. long and ¾ to 1 in. wide, linear-lanceolate, armed with scattered spine-tipped teeth. *Male cone* pale yellow, slender, cylindric, 12 to 24 in. long; *female* greenish-orange to apricot-coloured, 1½ ft. long by 7 in. wide. S. Africa. 1866. (B.M. 6654.)

**E. Vrom'ii.** A synonym of *E. Altensteinii.*

**E. Wood'ii.*** Stem ultimately up to 18 ft. *l.* 5 or 6 ft. long, arching; lower lflets. ovate, spinily lobed, the lowest reduced to mere prickles; at and above the middle they are linear-lanceolate, up to 8 in. long and 1½ in. wide armed with a few spiny teeth, the uppermost ones often quite entire. *Male cones* slender, cylindric, up to 4 ft. long; *females* not known. S. Africa. 1906.

W. J. B.

**ENCHANTER'S NIGHTSHADE.** *See* **Circaea. A**

**ENCHYTRAEID WORMS,** also known as Aster and Pot Worms, are nearly related to Earthworms, having their bodies segmented. They are small white worms which often occur in vast numbers in leaf-mould, compost heaps, and similar situations where there is an abundance of moist, decaying, organic matter. They are frequent in plant-pots having been introduced with

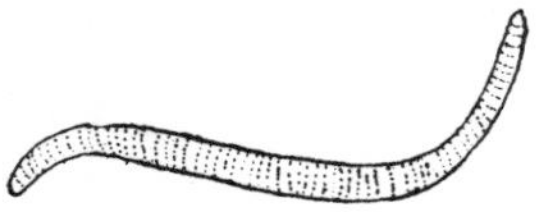

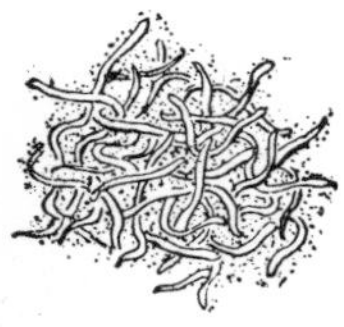

*Enchytraeid Worms*

leaf-mould, and are found clustered round the roots of Perennial Asters and many other plants being attracted by moisture and decaying roots. They are seldom directly destructive to living plants unless there is a scarcity of their natural food—humus and decayed organic matter generally—when they are known to injure the fleshy stems of Celery and the roots of plants and will invade, also, plant-tissues damaged mechanically or by soil pests and extend the initial injury. White worms are sometimes taken to be eelworms but eelworms cannot be seen with the naked eye.

G. F. W.

**ENCYC'LIA.** *See under* **Epidendrum odoratissimum.**

**endemic,** growing naturally in a region (cf. exotic). **A**

*Enderia'nus -a -um,* from the name of the captain of a small Chinese boat, *c.* 1889, trading off New Guinea.

**ENDIVE** (*Cichorium Endivia*) is a hardy annual grown for the use of its leaves as a salad before the flower-stems appear. It has been cultivated for this purpose in England since the early part of the sixteenth century but is often omitted from gardens though it is a valuable salad plant when lettuce is less easy to obtain. It may be had with care at almost any season but its chief value is in autumn and winter when it is most easily obtained, since early summer sowings are very apt to run to seed. For autumn and winter crops the first sowing of a curled-leaved variety should be made on good soil (rich light soil is best for this crop) such as has carried a crop of early Potatoes or Peas in early or middle July in drills about 15 in. apart. The seed should be sown thinly and the seedlings thinned to about 1 ft. apart when large enough to handle, filling in any blank spaces. It may be sown more thickly for transplanting but transplanted seedlings are later and more apt to run to seed. A second sowing should be made in early August and a third in the middle or at the latter end of that month. For these later sowings the hardier broad-leaved or Batavian Endive may be used, but the finely cut varieties find the greatest favour. If early supplies are needed, a first sowing may be made on a warm border or in a frame in April and successional sowings as soon as the previous one is well up. Care must be taken to keep the plants moist in dry weather so as to encourage quick growth and discourage running to flower. The latest sowings will give plants which may need to be lifted to blanch in a protected place, and it is probably best to transplant these as soon as large enough to handle as the root-system formed by transplanted seedlings will be better suited for lifting than if allowed to grow without transplanting.

As soon as the plants are nearly full-grown blanching should begin. The curled-leaved varieties blanche more quickly than the broad-leaved, and in early autumn blanching takes from 10 to 14 days. The blanched plants do not keep well and so no great number should be blanched at once, a small quantity being covered at frequent intervals. For blanching thoroughly, and the plants are of little use without, light must be excluded. Tying-up is sometimes sufficient, but generally inverted flower-pots with the bottom hole covered up are better where small quantities are concerned; or boards placed at right angles over the rows and covered with mats; or frames with the glass darkened may be used. For the later supplies, the full-grown plants should be tied and lifted with a good ball of soil about the end of October when quite dry and planted in moist soil as closely as possible in frames, or failing this, in a dry shed. When the frames are filled, the ties are removed and the lights put on, raised a little at the corner to ensure ventilation. Blanching of these stored plants is done by covering batches successively with hay and at this season about 3 weeks of exclusion of light will be needed. The lights should be covered with mats in severe weather. All these operations of covering for blanching and transplanting must be done when the plants are dry and any dead or damaged leaves must be removed before the plants are covered. Decay soon sets in if the foliage becomes wet after covering.

The 2 classes of Endive are distinguished by the foliage, the curled Endives having narrow, much-cut leaves, the broad-leaved larger leaves not curled. The former is the more tender and closer growing. Within each group there are several varieties, and if seed is saved the best plants should be selected for the purpose. Birds are very fond of the seed, and must be kept off the plants as soon as seed begins to form.

**ENDIVE, WILD.** *See* **Chicory.**

**endiv'ia,** Italian name derived from *Intibum*, Latin name for chicory.

*Endlicheria'nus -a -um,* in honour of S. L. Endlicher, 1804–49, director, Botanic Garden, Vienna.

**ENDOCARP.** The inner layer of the fruit wall (pericarp), often different in texture from the rest, as in 'stone fruits', like the plum where the endocarp forms the 'stone'.

**ENDOGENS.** An old term for Monocotyledons.

**ENDOPHYL'LUM sempervi'vi.** *See* **Sempervivum Rust.**

**endophytic,** growing inside another plant, as do many parasitic fungi.

**ENDOSPERM.** Food stored in seeds outside the embryo but formed inside the embryo-sac. Cf. Perisperm.

*Endres'ii,* in honour of Señor Endres, who, *c.* 1868–73, collected plants in Costa Rica.

*Endres'sii,* in honour of P. A. C. Endress, 1806–31, of Würtemberg, who collected, *c.* 1831, in the Pyrenees.

**ENDY'MION.** A synonym of Scilla. **A**

*ener'vis -is -e,* without evident veins.

**ENGELMAN'NIA** (in honour of Georg Engelmann, 1809–84, physician of St. Louis, who wrote on American plants). FAM. *Compositae.* A genus of a single species of erect, hairy, perennial herb, native of the prairies of N. America, hardy and growing in any ordinary good garden soil. Increased by seed or division.

**E. pinnatif'ida.** Hardy perennial to 2 ft. *l.* oblong, 2 to 5 in. long, sinuate-pinnatifid to below middle; lobes toothed, entire or lobulate. *fl.-heads* golden-yellow, 1 to 2 in. across in corymbose panicles; ray-fl. 8 to 10, female; disk-fl. hermaphrodite but sterile; involucral bracts in several series. (B.M. 6577.)

*Eng'leri,* in honour of Dr. Adolph Engler, 1844–1930, Director, Botanic Garden, Dahlem.

**ENKIAN'THUS** (*enkuos,* swollen, *anthos,* flower; presumably alluding to pouching of the base of the corolla in certain species). FAM. *Ericaceae.* A genus of deciduous or, rarely, partially evergreen shrubs with whorled branches, alternate leaves, 5-merous flowers, campanulate or urceolate corollas, 10 stamens and loculicidal-capsular fruit. Thrives in lime-free loam. Propagation by seed and cuttings. Foliage brilliant in autumn colouring. Tolerant of light shade.

KEY

| | | |
|---|---|---|
| 1. *Base of cor. saccate* | | 2 |
| 1. *Base of cor. not saccate* | | 4 |
| 2. *Fl. urceolate* | | E. perulatus |
| 2. *Fl. campanulate* | | 3 |
| 3. *Fl. pink* | | E. quinqueflorus |
| 3. *Fl. white* | | E. serrulatus |
| 4. *Lvs. smooth* | | E. chinensis |
| 4. *Lvs. more or less hairy* | | 5 |
| 5. *Lvs. hairy on midrib and veins of lower surface; cor. fringed* | | E. cernuus |
| 5. *Lvs. more or less hairy on both surfaces* | | 6 |

6. *Cor. urceolate* E. subsessilis
6. *Cor. campanulate* 7
7. *Style and ovary smooth* E. campanulatus
7. *Style and ovary downy* E. himalaicus

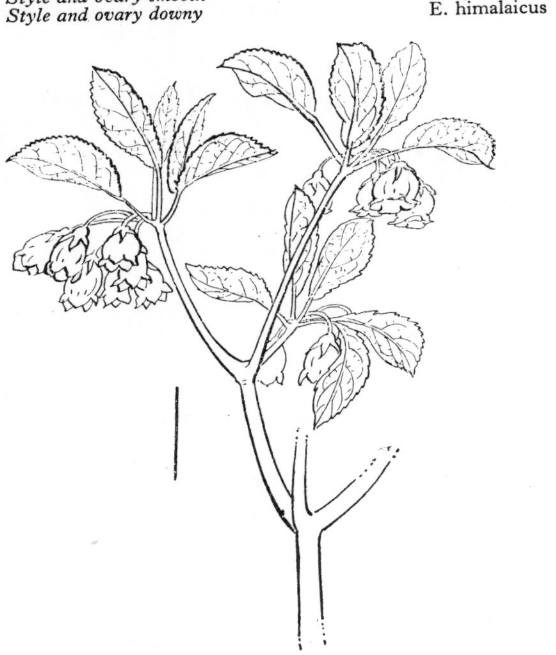

*Enkianthus campanulatus*

**E. campanula'tus.*** Deciduous shrub, branches whorled, young shoots smooth, red. *l.* usually clustered at ends of shoots, elliptic or obovate, pointed, serrate, 1 to $2\frac{1}{2}$ in. long, half as wide, sparsely hairy above and on veins beneath, brilliant red in autumn. *fl.* in terminal, sometimes sub-umbellate, pendulous racemes; cor. open-campanulate, pale yellow with red lines, $\frac{1}{2}$ in. or more across with 5 rounded lobes; cal. lobes lanceolate, acute, $\frac{1}{8}$ in. long. May. Japan. 1880. Syn. *Andromeda campanulata.* (B.T.S. 1. 512.) var. **albiflo'rus,** *fl.* whitish. Syn. *E. pallidiflorus*; **Palibin'ii,** *fl.* rich red, hairs on and near the lower part of the midrib reddish. (B.M. 7059.) The following names belong to varieties of *E. campanulatus: E. ferrugineus, E. latiflorus, E. pendulus, E. recurvus,* and *E. tectus.*

**E. cernuus.*** Deciduous shrub of 5 to 8 ft. or more with smooth young shoots. *l.* elliptic, oblong, or elliptic-obovate, pointed or blunt, crenate, $\frac{3}{4}$ to $1\frac{1}{2}$ in. long, $\frac{5}{8}$ to 1 in. wide, sparsely pubescent on midrib and veins beneath. *fl.* nodding in 10- to 12-fld. pubescent racemes; cor. white, campanulate, $\frac{5}{16}$ in. wide, shortly frilled; cal. lobes ovate-lanceolate, ciliate. May. Japan. In cult. 1900. Syn. *E. Meisteria, Meisteria cernua.* var. **ru'bens,** *l.* shorter, broader, *fl.* rich red. A very beautiful plant.

**E. chinen'sis.** Closely resembles *E. himalaicus* but has smooth *fl.-stalks* and smooth or nearly smooth *l.*; cor. lobes reflexed, not erect. Cent. and W. China. 1900. (B.M. 9413.) Syn. *E. Rosthornii.*

**E. himala'icus.** Deciduous shrub or small tree up to 20 ft. or more h. *l.* clustered at ends of shoots, oval, obovate, or oblong-lanceolate, finely serrate, sparsely hairy on both surfaces and having appressed hairs on midrib beneath, 1 to 3 in. long, $\frac{1}{2}$ to $1\frac{3}{4}$ in. wide. *fl.* pendent, clustered on downy stalks, in terminal, often umbel-like, racemes; cor. yellow-red with deeper markings, open campanulate, $\frac{5}{8}$ in. across with triangular lobes; cal. lobes triangular, pointed, $\frac{1}{12}$ in. long. May, June. Himalaya. 1878. W. China. 1908. Syn. *E. deflexus, E. sulcatus, Rhodora deflexa.* (B.M. 6460.) The Himalayan type is not reliably hardy.

**E. perula'tus.*** Deciduous shrub 6 ft. or more h. with smooth, reddish young shoots. *l.* clustered towards ends of shoots, oval or obovate, finely serrate, acutely pointed, $\frac{3}{4}$ to 2 in. long by nearly half as wide, more or less downy on midrib and veins beneath. Pendulous *fl.* in umbellate, terminal clusters; cor. white, globose-urceolate, pouched at base, about $\frac{1}{3}$ in. long and wide with rounded, recurved lobes; cal. lobes narrowly triangular, $\frac{1}{12}$ in. long. May. Japan. 1870. (B.M. 5822 as *E. japonicus.*) Syn. *Andromeda perulata.*

**E. quinqueflor'us.*** Deciduous or sub-evergreen shrub 4 to 6 ft. h. in cultivation; young shoots smooth. *l.* red when young, afterwards dark green above, paler beneath; narrowly elliptical or obovate-elliptical, acute, entire smooth, leathery, 2 to 4 in. long, $\frac{3}{4}$ to $1\frac{1}{2}$ in. wide. *fl.* pendulous, on pink stalks, in terminal, umbellate clusters; cor. pink or pink and white, open-campanulate, saccate, about $\frac{9}{16}$ in. wide with short, rounded, reflexed lobes; cal. lobes triangular, acute, minutely ciliate. May. SE. China, Hong-Kong. About 1810. (B.M. 1649.) Syn. *E. reticulatus, E. uniflorus, Melidora pellucida.*

**E. serrula'tus.** Closely resembles *E. himalaicus* but is constantly deciduous. *l.* serrate. *fl.* pure white. Shrub or small tree up to 20 ft. h. Cent. and W. China. 1900. Syn. *E. quinqueflorus serrulatus.*

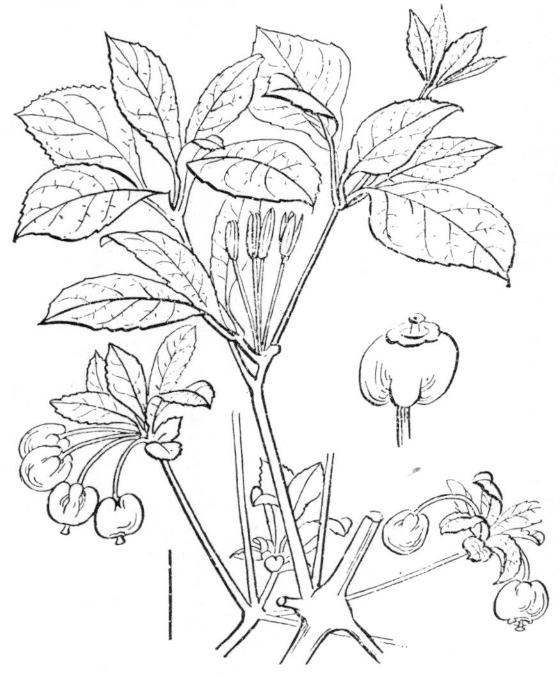

*Enkianthus perulatus*

**E. subses'silis.** Deciduous, branching shrub 4 to 10 ft. h. with smooth young shoots. *l.* clustered at ends of shoots, oval or obovate, acute, tapering downwards, finely serrate, $\frac{3}{4}$ to $1\frac{1}{2}$ in. long, half as wide, pubescent on midrib especially beneath. *fl.* in terminal, pubescent, pendent racemes $1\frac{1}{2}$ to $2\frac{1}{2}$ in. long; cor. white, globose-urceolate, $\frac{3}{16}$ in. long with short recurved lobes; cal. lobes ovate, pointed, about $\frac{1}{16}$ in. long. May. Japan. 1892. Syn. *E. nikoensis, Andromeda subsessilis.* (S.T.S. 1, 25.)

F. S.

***enneaphyl'lus -a -um,*** having nine leaflets.

***ensa'tus -a -um,*** sword-like.

***Ense'te,*** Abyssinian name of Musa.

***ensifo'lius -a -um,*** having straight, sword-shaped leaves.

***ensiform'is -is -e,*** quite straight with an acute point like the blade of a sword or the leaf of an Iris.

**ENTA'DA** (the Malabar name of one species). Fam. *Leguminosae.* A genus of about 15 species of climbing shrubs, natives of the tropics. Stems unarmed. Leaves 2-pinnate. Flowers white or yellow, sometimes unisexual, sessile or nearly so, in a dense spike; calyx bell-shaped; petals 5; stamens 10, free, shortly exserted. The pods, which are jointed, sometimes reach a length of several feet. For treatment, *see* **Mimosa.**

**E. polystach'ya.** *Lflets.* in 6 to 8 pairs, oblong, blunt. *fl.* in terminal panicles. *Pod* oblong, straight, often 1 ft. long. W. Indies. 1816.

**E. scan'dens.** Sword Bean. Woody climber. *l.* long-lanceolate, rigid, often ending in a tendril; pinnae stalked, mostly 4; lflets. oblong or obovate, 1 to 2 in. long, rigidly leathery. *fl.* about $1\frac{1}{2}$ in. long; pet. lanceolate, rigid, at length separate; spikes long, slender, solitary axillary, or in terminal panicles. *Pod* 2 to 4 ft. long, 3 to 4 in. wide. E. and W. Indies, &c. The large, handsome brown or purple seeds are called Gala in India and are used by natives for washing their hair, and in the making of trinkets and small receptacles.

F. G. P.

**ENTE'LEA** (*enteles,* perfect; stamens all fertile). Fam. *Tiliaceae.* Monotypic genus. This is a handsome shrub or tree, easily grown in loamy soil and propagated by cuttings. Cool greenhouse.

**E. arbores'cens.** Evergreen, 8 to 20 ft., shoots, l., and inflor. all covered with short, soft, stellate hairs. *l.* alternate, 4 to 9 in. long, cordate, pointed, doubly toothed, obscurely 3-lobed; stalk 4 to 8 in. long. *fl.* white, 1 in. wide, in erect or terminal open cymes 3 to 5 in. across; sep. 4 or 5, roundish-ovate, margins crumpled; stamens numerous, making a yellow circular patch in the centre of the fl. *fr.* globose, developing a ball-like mass of rigid, slender bristles ½ to ¾ in. long. May. New Zealand. 1820. (B.M. 2480.) Wood one of the lightest known, its specific gravity much less than that of cork.

W. J. B.

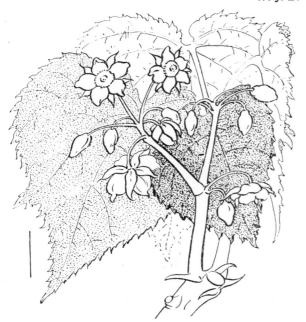

*Entelea arborescens*

**entomoph'ilus -a -um,** insect-loving. An entomophilous flower is one that by means of attractive colour, odour, or nectar attracts insects which carry its pollen from one flower to another.

**ENTRANCES.** The approach or entrance to a garden or important glasshouse should be the subject of careful attention in the laying out of grounds and should at all times be kept in good order and clear from obstruction. Forecourts, if made of gravel, should be frequently swept and rolled. *See* **Avenues, Drives.**

**ENTYLO'MA.** A genus of Smut Fungi, some of which attack garden plants, e.g. *E. Calendulae* on Calendulas, *E. Dahliae* on Dahlias (q.v.).

**ENVIRONMENT.** Surroundings, including other plants as well as soil, water, air, &c.; the conditions under which a plant grows.

**Eny'sii,** in honour of J. D. Enys, 1837–1912, who introduced *Carmichaelia Enysii,* &c., to Cornish (and British) gardens.

**A→**

**EOME'CON** (*heos,* Aurora, eastern, *mekon,* poppy; from its habitat). FAM. *Papaveraceae.* A genus of a single E. Chinese species of herbaceous perennial widely spreading by its rhizome. Sap reddish-orange. Leaves many, tufted, cordate, palmately veined. Scape, producing a panicle of short-lived flowers. Sepals 2, joined, deciduous; petals 4, roundish-elliptic; stamens numerous; style 2-lobed. Nearly hardy. Cultivation as for Hylomecon.

**E. chionan'thum.** Glabrous herb. *l.* cordate-reniform to cordate-sagittate, rather blunt, about 4 in. wide, margin somewhat waved, dull beneath, rather fleshy. *Scape* 8 to 16 in. h. from the l.-sheath. *fl.* white, about 1½ in. wide, on erect pedicels. E. China. (B.M. 6871.)

**EPACRIDA'CEAE.** Dicotyledons. A family of mostly small shrubs resembling Heaths in habit, containing 21 genera and about 430 species almost confined to Australia and Tasmania but with some species in India, New Zealand, and S. America. Leaves usually alternate, narrow, entire, rigid, sessile and often sheathing the stem. Flowers usually in terminal racemes or spikes, perfect and regular; sepals 5, free; petals 5, joined; stamens 5, sometimes hypognous, usually epipetalous; anthers without appendages (cf. Ericaceae); ovary superior, 5-celled. Fruit a capsule or stony drupe with 1 to many seeds in each cell. The genera dealt with here are Acrotriche, Andersonia, Astroloma, Brachyloma, Conostephium, Cosmea, Cyathodes, Dracophyllum, Dracunculus, Epacris, Leucopogon, Lissanthe, Lysinema, Melichrus, Monotoca, Richea, Rupicola, Sprengelia, Styphelia, Trochocarpa.

**EPAC'RIS** (from *epi,* upon, *akros,* summit; in allusion to the species growing on the tops of hills in their wild state). FAM. *Epacridaceae.* A genus of some 40 species of evergreen shrubs confined to Australia and Tasmania except for 2 species endemic in New Zealand. Leaves alternate, always small and crowded, usually short-stalked or sessile, and sharply pointed. Flowers solitary in the leaf-axils; the base of the corolla tubular or rarely bell-shaped, divided into 5 short lobes at the mouth; anthers inserted in the throat of the corolla tube; stigma sunk in a deep depression at the top of the ovary.

The Epacrises are most useful winter-flowering plants, but none is sufficiently hardy to be grown entirely outdoors. The flowers last better than those of Heaths when cut and the plants are as a rule more easily propagated by cuttings treated in the same way as those of Heaths. They are, too, easily raised from seed sown in a compost of fine peat and sand. The chief thing to aim at in their cultivation is to obtain a few strong shoots and get them thoroughly ripened in autumn to flower in the following winter and spring. The erect-growing species should be pruned hard back about March after flowering and kept rather close until new growth begins. When the new shoots are ½ in. long any repotting needed should be attended to at once, using a compost of fibrous peat and about one-sixth silver sand. Efficient drainage should be provided and the new soil made firm around the ball which should not be broken, nor should the roots be disturbed in the process. The newly potted plants should not be watered for a few days, but should be lightly syringed overhead. As the plants progress more air and sunlight should be given until, about the end of July, they may be plunged outdoors in ashes or kept in a cool airy greenhouse. Watering, as with all similar plants, must be carefully performed at all times. A cool greenhouse where frost is excluded is suitable for them in winter, but they will bear with impunity more heat and moisture at this season than do the majority of Heaths. A few are naturally of pendent habit and these do not require severe pruning, but the long shoots should be trained to stakes or to a balloon-shaped framework by which means large specimens may be grown. A number of beautiful garden forms have been raised from seed, often improvements upon their parents, and with care all these beautiful and useful plants may be grown on for several years with advantage.

J. C.

**E. acumina'ta.** Shrub, 2 to 4 ft. h., of erect, bushy shape. *l.* ⅓ to ½ in. long, scarcely stalked, ovate, usually sharply pointed, concave, base clasping stem. *fl.* white, few, solitary in uppermost l.-axils; sep. ¼ in. long, ciliate; cor. tube about the same length, lobes blunt, scarcely as long. Tasmania. SYN. *E. mucronulata* (of Hooker f. not R. Brown).

**E. grandiflo'ra.** A synonym of *E. longiflora.*

**E. impres'sa.*** Shrub 3 to 5 ft. erect, loosely branched, shoots usually more or less downy. *l.* stalkless, linear-lanceolate to ovate-lanceolate, ¼ to ½ in. long, sharply pointed, rounded at base. *fl.* pure white to different shades of red; cor. tube ½ to ¾ in. long with 5 short triangular lobes. Australia, Tasmania. 1825. (B.M. 3407; B.M. 3253 as *E. nivalis.*) var. **ceraeflo'ra,** *fl.* short, white. (B.M. 3243 as *E. ceraeflora.*); **grandiflo'ra,*** *l.* larger, thicker, less sharply pointed; *fl.* longer, deep purple-red; **ova'ta,** *l.* small, ovate, sometimes sub-cordate.

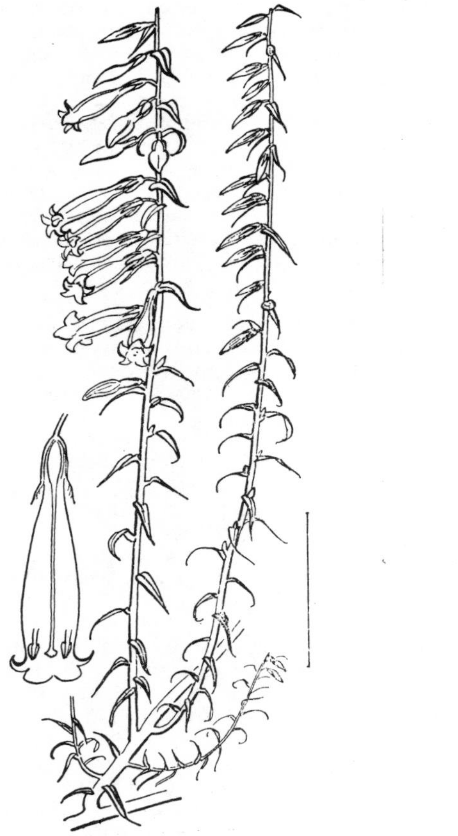

*Epacris impressa*

**E. lanugino'sa.** Erect shrub up to 3 ft. h., shoots usually downy. *l.* $\frac{1}{4}$ to $\frac{1}{2}$ in. long, lanceolate to linear-lanceolate, shortly and stiffly pointed. *fl.* white, borne numerously in uppermost l.-axils of shoots and forming a terminal head or a slender, leafy spike; sep. and cor. tube $\frac{1}{4}$ to $\frac{1}{3}$ in. long, the cor. lobes $\frac{1}{6}$ to $\frac{1}{4}$ in. across. Victoria, Tasmania.

**E. longiflor'a.*** Shrub 4 to 5 ft., shoots usually downy. *l.* closely set, scarcely stalked, $\frac{1}{4}$ to $\frac{5}{8}$ in. long, ovate to ovate-lanceolate, rounded to cordate at base, sharply pointed. *fl.* $\frac{3}{4}$ to 1 in. long, tubular, rosy-crimson excepting the 5-lobed limb which is white and $\frac{1}{4}$ to $\frac{3}{8}$ in. across. May. New S. Wales. 1803. (B.M. 982 as *E. grandiflora*; B.R. 31, 5 as *E. miniata.*)

**E. microphyl'la.** Erect shrub with slender, hairy shoots. *l.* broadly ovate, cordate, $\frac{1}{6}$ to $\frac{1}{4}$ in. long, shortly pointed, concave, base partly clasping stem. *fl.* fragrant, white, $\frac{1}{4}$ in. wide, forming cylindrical leafy spikes $1\frac{1}{2}$ to 4 in. long. May. Australia, Tasmania. (B.M. 3658; 1170 as *E. pulchella.*)

**E. minia'ta.** A synonym of *E. longiflora.*

**E. mucronula'ta.** A synonym of *E. acuminata.*

**E. niva'lis.** A synonym of *E. impressa.*

**E. obtusifo'lia.*** Erect shrub, 1 to 3 ft., shoots usually downy. *l,* oblong-lanceolate, $\frac{1}{4}$ to $\frac{1}{2}$ in. long, tapered to a very short stalk, apex thick and blunt, glabrous. *fl.* sweetly scented, waxy yellowish-white, $\frac{3}{8}$ in. across the spreading lobes; tube of cor. almost bell-shaped; anthers and stigmas reddish. Queensland, New S. Wales. 1804. (L.B.C. 292.)

**E. onosmaeflo'ra.** A synonym of *E. purpurascens.*

**E. paludo'sa.** Shrub, usually a few ft. h. but sometimes tall, rigid; shoots usually downy. *l.* linear-lanceolate, $\frac{3}{8}$ to $\frac{5}{8}$ in. long, $\frac{1}{12}$ in. wide, tapered to both ends. *fl.* white, axillary, often crowded towards top of shoots to form a head-like cluster; tube of cor. $\frac{1}{2}$ in. long, the 5-lobed limb $\frac{1}{4}$ in. across. New S.Wales, Victoria. (L.B.C. 1226.)

**E. pulchel'la.** Small erect shrub, shoots long, slender, minutely downy. *l.* scarcely stalked, ovate, cordate, sharply pointed, about $\frac{1}{4}$ in. long, the base concave. *fl.* white or reddish, $\frac{1}{4}$ in. long, not so wide, very shortly stalked. May. New S. Wales. 1804. *E. pulchella* of B.M. 1170 is *E. microphylla.*

**E. pun'gens** of B.M. 844 and 1199 is *E. purpurascens.*

**E. purpuras'cens.*** Shrub, erect, stiff, a few ft. h. *l.* very closely set, ovate, $\frac{1}{2}$ to $\frac{5}{8}$ in. long, base rounded or cordate and clasping stem, long and sharply pointed, concave. *fl.* white, more or less suffused with reddish-purple; tube of cor. $\frac{3}{8}$ in. long, $\frac{1}{2}$ in. across the pointed lobes. March, April. New S. Wales. 1803. (B.M. 844 and 1199 as *E. pungens*; 3168 as *E. onosmaeflora.*)

**E. reclina'ta.** Shrub of low, straggling habit, shoots downy. *l.* $\frac{1}{6}$ to $\frac{1}{4}$ in. long, very closely set, ovate to ovate-lanceolate, pointed, base rounded to cordate, glossy green. *fl.* varying from deep or pale pink to white; tube of cor. cylindrical, $\frac{1}{3}$ to $\frac{1}{2}$ in. long, lobes $\frac{1}{8}$ in. long. May. New S. Wales.

**E. rig'ida.** Shrub, erect, stiff, bushy, 1 to 3 ft. h. *l.* scarcely stalked, $\frac{1}{12}$ to $\frac{1}{8}$ in. long, ovate to ovate-oblong, sometimes $\frac{1}{4}$ in. long and narrower, very blunt and, owing to prominence of midrib underneath, very thick. *fl.* white; sep. $\frac{1}{12}$ to $\frac{1}{8}$ in. long; tube of cor. about the same, the blunt lobes rather longer. New S. Wales.

**E. serpyllifo'lia.** Shrub up to 3 ft. varying from bushy to prostrate and often under 1 ft. h. *l.* ovate, $\frac{1}{8}$ to $\frac{1}{5}$ in. long, pointed. *fl.* white, crowded in the uppermost l.-axils to form short, leafy heads or sometimes in lower ones also to form cylindrical spikes; tube of cor. $\frac{1}{8}$ to $\frac{1}{6}$ in. long, lobes shorter. Victoria, Tasmania.

W. J. B.

***epeiropho'rus -a -um,*** like a garden spider.

**EPHED'RA** (Greek name used by Pliny for the Horsetail, Hippuris). FAM. *Gnetaceae.* A genus of about 30 species of low evergreen trailing (or rarely climbing) shrubs, natives of S. Europe, N. Africa, temperate and Trop. Asia, and extra-Trop. America. Leaves small and scale-like; stems with numerous slender, jointed branches. Flowers dioecious in slender catkins, usually in dense axillary clusters, small; male with 2- or 4-lobed perianth and 2 to 8 stamens united into a column; female with an urn-shaped perianth enclosing a naked ovule. The bracts of the female catkins of some species become fleshy and form a berry-like syncarpous fruit which makes the plant attractive. The hardy Ephedras are best accommodated in well-drained places in the rock-garden. They need little water and can be increased by seeds, suckers, or layers. Many, as may be concluded from their habitat, are tender.

**E. altis'sima.** Glaucous green climbing shrub of 12 to 24 ft., branches almost terete, opposite, ternate or solitary. *fl.* pale yellow. *fr.* red, oval. N. Africa. 1899. (B.M. 7670.)

**E. andi'na.** Related to *E. nevadensis.* Low-spreading shrub. *l.* about $\frac{2}{5}$ in. long. Chile. 1896. (B.M. n.s. 142.)

**E. distach'ya.** Upright, slender, rigid branches from a procumbent base, dark green. *l.* scale-like, about $\frac{1}{12}$ in. long. *Female catkins* 2-fld. *fr.* globose, red, $\frac{1}{4}$ in. long. S. Europe, N. Asia. 1570. var. **helvet'ica,** habit of type but integument twisted; **monostach'ya,** prostrate or almost so; male spikes solitary. SYN. *E. monostachya.*

**E. frag'ilis.** Upright, but sometimes prostrate or climbing. Branches fragile, dark green, about $\frac{1}{6}$ in. thick. *l.* scale-like. *Male spikes* clustered; *female* solitary. *fr.* red, $\frac{1}{3}$ in. long. Mediterranean region.

**E. Gerardia'na.** Low shrub, about 2 in. h., branches dark green, finely striate, *Male spikes* 1 or 2, sessile, globose; *female* solitary. *fr.* globose, $\frac{1}{4}$ in. long. Himalaya, SW. China. 1896.

**E. helvet'ica.** A variety of *E. distachya.*

**E. interme'dia.** Upright, densely branched, or prostrate and ascending; branches yellowish-green or glaucous. *l.* 2, rarely 3 or 4, scale-like, scarious. *fl.* sometimes monoecious; male spikes clustered; female solitary, stalked. *fr.* $\frac{1}{4}$ in. long, red. Cent. Asia. 1902.

**E. ma'jor.** Usually upright, up to 6 ft. h., densely branched; branches dark green. *l.* scale-like, about $\frac{1}{8}$ in. long, scarious. *Male spikes* 1 to 3, roundish; *female* 1 to 3, 1-fld. on short stalks. *fr.* red, $\frac{1}{4}$ in. long. Mediterranean region to N. India. 1750. SYN. *E. nebrodensis.*

**E. monostach'ya.** A variety of *E. distachya.*

**E. nebroden'sis.** A synonym of *E. major.*

**E. nevaden'sis.** Pale or bluish-green, branchlets spreading to about 3 ft. *l.* about $\frac{1}{8}$ in. long. *Catkins* solitary or few; male 6- to 8-fld., ovate; female 2-fld. *fr.* dry with ovate bracts. SW. United States.

**E. proce'ra.** Erect dioecious shrub, 3 to 5 ft. h., twigs green, clustered, stiff, very slender, finely ribbed, smooth, more or less glaucous, old bark grey. *l.* opposite, scale-like, about $\frac{1}{8}$ in. long, brown, scarious. *Catkins* solitary or few; male 4- to 8-fld., roundish; female long-ovoid. *fr.* roundish, up to $\frac{2}{5}$ in. long, red or rarely yellow, fleshy. Greece to Afghanistan. SYN. *E. nebrodensis procera.* **A**

**E. sikkimen'sis.** Closely related to *E. Gerardiana.* Upright, robust. Branches about 6 in. long. N. India. 1915.

**E. trifur'ca.** Pale green, erect, rigid, 2 to 4 ft. h. *l.* in threes, connate, about ⅓ in. long. *Catkins* solitary; female 1-fld. *fr.* dry, bracts roundish, their margins transparent. Arizona, Colorado. 1899.

**E. vi'ridis.** Dioecious, bright green, branchlets fastigiate, broom-like. *l.* in pairs. *Catkins* stalked. *fr.* 2-seeded, bracts in 3 pairs, sessile, eventually ivory-white. SW. United States. 1930 ? (B.M. 9366.)

**E. vulgar'is.** A synonym of *E. distachya*.

**ephemeral,** lasting but one day, as do flowers of, e.g. Helianthus, Hemerocallis, and Tradescantia.

*ephe'sius -a -um,* of Ephesus, Asia Minor.

**EPHIP'PIUM.** Included in **Bulbophyllum.**

*epi-,* prefix in words derived from Greek, signifying upon.

**EPICARP.** The outside layer of the fruit-wall (pericarp), sometimes different in texture from the rest, as in the vegetable Marrow.

**EPICAT'TLEYA.** Fam. *Orchidaceae.* Hybrids between species of Cattleya and Epidendrum.

**EPICHIL.** The upper part of the 3-parted lip of some orchids. *See* **mesochil, hypochil.**

**EPICOTYL.** The part of the stem above the cotyledons (cf. **hypocotyl**).

**EPICRAN'THES.** A synonym of Monomeria.

**EPIDEN'DRUM** (*epi*, upon, *dendron*, tree; the plants are usually epiphytes). Fam. *Orchidaceae.* Several groups of this genus are often given generic rank but they differ in minor points only from Epidendrum. Diacrium has been included but owing chiefly to the distinct character of its pseudobulbs is now considered distinct. The genus contains about 1,000 species, mainly epiphytic, but a few appear to have adapted themselves to terrestrial conditions. They are distributed chiefly from the W. Indies to S. Brazil, from the Pacific to the Atlantic, extending as far north as the U.S.A. and to an approximately corresponding limit in S. America. With such a wide distribution great variations in both floral and vegetative characters are naturally present. Many species are inconspicuous, often of dull colours, but the family also contains a number with brightly coloured flowers freely produced. With few exceptions the inflorescences are terminal; they may be spicate, racemose, corymbose or nearly so, paniculate, or of but a solitary flower. Sepals free, equal or nearly so, usually spreading or reflexed; petals similar, often slightly narrower; lip clawed, the claw parallel to the column, wholly or partly connate to the column edges, appressed to it in a few species; its blade may be entire or deeply divided, the divisions in some species fringed; disk sometimes with 2 calli or with raised laminae or ribs; column usually narrow and semi-terete, often with 2 small wings or auricles and a fimbriated margin to the clinandrium. Pollinia 4.

Equal diversity is exhibited in the plants. Decided pseudobulbs of various shapes, globose, pyriform, clavate, spindle, &c., are found, while the so-called true Epidendrums have cylindric reed-like, often slender, stems of various heights with few or many distichous or alternate leaves.

The following list, though by no means exhaustive, includes the majority of the known species with attractive flowers and a few which owe their charm either to fragrance or their curious floral shape. Hybrids have been obtained between Epidendrum, Cattleya, Laelia, Sophronitis, Brassavola, and Diacrium, and the genus is also allied to Broughtonia, Lanium, Isochilus, and Hexisia. Hormidium and Lanium were placed under Epidendrum by Dr. Lindley, but are now considered distinct and kept separate here.

Many sections of the genus have been proposed by various botanists but some of them have little bearing on the horticultural value or treatment of the plants and a full list is therefore not attempted here. The groups Barkeria and Nanodes are well-marked horticulturally.

The group **Barkeria** includes *E. Barkeriola*, *E. chinense*, *E. cyclostellum*, *E. elegans*, *E. Lindleyanum*, *E. melanocaulon*, *E. Skinneri*, *E. spectabile*, and *E. Vannerianum*. Distinguished by compressed or quill-like pseudobulbs sheathed with parchment-like membrane, clustered or at intervals on a creeping rhizome. The column is winged (petaloid), and the lip only shortly adnate to the column. Rafts are necessary for the species with long rhizomes. All are impatient of artificial heat. In a dull summer they may be grown in the intermediate house near the glass, but usually succeed well in the cool-house. The leaves, usually few, are deciduous or nearly so, and exposure to light in the autumn is required to ensure ripening of the stems. In winter, water is seldom if ever required; the night temperature should be around 50° F.

**Nanodes** includes *E. congestum*, *E. discolor*, *E. Lambeauianum*, *E. Mantinianum*, *E. Mathewsii*, *E. Medusae*, *E. Porpax*, and *E. Schlechterianum*, all of which have short stems, erect or arched, with fleshy, almost succulent, leaves, the bases of which sheath the stems. The flowers are terminal, curious if not attractive. *E. Medusae*, the best known in this group, does well in the Odontoglossum house. A moist atmosphere is required for it throughout the year. As for its sister but smaller species, they should have a winter night temperature around 55° F.

Of the other species the majority have pseudobulbs, sometimes globose with 2 or 3 thick strap-shaped leaves, sometimes taller but with not more than three leaves. The greater number are suited to the intermediate house, the small-growing in pans, the larger in pots. A decided rest should be given to all with hard pseudobulbs and leaves, and a winter night temperature around 55° F. Occasional falls in temperature are harmless.

Most of the rest have leafy stems, reed-like or comparatively stout, and usually a terminal inflorescence; in *E. Stamfordianum* and *E. Rosseauae* the inflorescence is produced from the rhizome near the base of the last-made pseudobulb on a rudimentary growth. The majority of this group should be given a place in the intermediate house. Pots are necessary, as in many the stems attain a height of 3 to 5 ft. or more. Water is required throughout the year.

Compost as advised for Cattleyas suits all Epidendrums but a slightly larger proportion of Sphagnum moss should be given to the smaller-growing plants. A very high temperature is unnecessary, but those with leafy stems are not averse to a higher winter temperature. Discrimination must be made as to resting, &c., but the hints given under Orchidaceae should be sufficient with study of the plants. In the bulbed section of Epidendrum propagation can only be effected by division as suggested under Cattleya. Some of the stemmed species will, after the flower-stems have been cut back by a third or half their length, produce young growths which can be removed and potted as soon as roots are seen, or larger plants may be divided.

**E. acicula're.** A synonym of *E. bractescens*.

**E. Acland'iae.** A synonym of *Cattleya Aclandiae*.

**E. adve'num.** *fl.* 2 in. across; sep. and pet. yellowish, tessellated brown, narrowed at base; lip yellow to white with central purple streaks; spikes 2 to 4 ft. long, shortly branched. *Pseudobulbs* 3 to 4 in. h., stout, cylindrical, diphyllous. *l.* 12 to 14 in. long, leathery. Brazil. 1872. (B.M. 7792 as *E. osmanthum*, L. 333 as *E. Capartianum*.) Variable.

**E. ae'mulum.** A synonym of *E. fragrans*.

**E. aeridifor'me.** A synonym of *E. Harrisoniae*.

**E. ala'tum.*** *fl.* 2 to 3 in. across, pale yellow, shaded with brown-purple, fragrant, in straggling panicles, remaining nearly 6 weeks in beauty; lip striped purple. June, July. *Pseudobulbs* 3 in. h. or more, globose-conical. *l.* 12 to 18 in. long, leathery. Guatemala. (B.M. 3898 as *E. calocheilum.*) *E. alatum* of Lindley is *E. ambiguum*.

**E. alcifor'me.** A synonym of *E. falcatum*.

**E. Alleman'ii.** *fl.* 3 to 5, fragrant; sep. 1 in. long, narrow; pet. slightly shorter, slightly broader, whitish or greenish-white, faintly flushed rose; lip broadly heart-shaped, acuminate, slightly convex. *Pseudobulbs* ovoid, compressed, 2 to 3 in. h., diphyllous. *l.* 3 to 5 in. long, 1¼ to 1¾ in. wide. *Peduncle* short, stout. Brazil. 1877.

**E. aloifo'lium.** A synonym of *E. Parkinsonianum*.

**E. ama'bile.** A synonym of *E. dichromum amabile*.

**E. ambig'uum.*** *fl.* small, fragrant, numerous; sep. and clawed narrow pet. pale yellowish-green, curved inwards; lip straw-yellow spotted and streaked red. Habit much as in *E. aromaticum* to which it is allied. Cent. America. 1846. (B.R. 33, 53 as *E. alatum.*)

**E. amethystoglos'sum.** A synonym of *Cattleya amethystoglossa*.

*Epidendrum arachnoglossum*

**E. arachnoglos'sum.*** *fl.* 1 to 1¼ in. across, reddish-purple, in a short, roundish raceme; sep. and pet. acute, recurved; side lobes of lip roundish, pectinate, mid-lobe cuneate, deeply 2-lobed, crest orange; column violet, club-shaped. *l.* distichous, alternate, glabrous, sessile, oblong-lanceolate, obtuse, fleshy. Stems tufted, 3 to 5 ft. h., erect. Colombia. 1883. (R.H. 1882, 554.) var. **can'didum,*** *fl.* wholly white, or faintly flushed rose, except the orange lateral calli of lip. 1886.

**E. aromat'icum.*** *fl.* numerous, fragrant, about 1 in. across; sep. and pet. very pale yellow; lip whitish, streaked red, 3-lobed, side lobes appressed to column except at apex; scape 2 to 3 ft., branching. *l.* 9 to 12 in. long, linear, rigid. *Pseudobulbs* 2 to 3 in. h., 2- or 3-leaved. Guatemala. 1835. (Ref. B. 2, 89.)

**E. atropurpu'reum.*** *fl.* 5 to 15, 2 to 3 in. across; sep. and pet. dark rose or purple, greenish at tips, incurved; lip rose with a dark crimson-purple blotch in centre. May, June. *Pseudobulbs* ovate, 2 to 3 in. h., diphyllous. *l.* 12 to 15 in. long, leathery. Brazil. 1836. Succeeds in a shallow pan. (W.O.A. 149.) var. **al'bum** has a white lip; **Randia'num** has greenish-brown sep. and pet. with paler margin and a white lip with a central red-purple rayed blotch, *pseudobulbs* and *l.* often reddish. 1886. (L. 49; B.M. 3534 as *E. macrochilum.*) Syn. *E. Randianum*; **ro'seum** has smaller *fl.* than *album*, sep. and pet. deep purplish-brown, lip rose with a purple blotch. (I.H. 1868, 541.)

**E. atroru'bens.*** *fl.* 1 in. across; sep. and pet. very dark reddish-purple; lip lighter, free, 3-lobed; scape 4 ft. loosely paniculate. October. *Pseudobulbs* globose, 2 in. h. *l.* linear-oblong, 8 in. long, obtuse. Mexico. 1876.

**E. auranti'acum.** A synonym of *Cattleya aurantiaca*.

**E. au'reum.** A synonym of *Cattleya aurantiaca*.

**E. auriculig'erum.** *fl.* sep. and pet. long, straight; lip auricled at base, mid-lobe triangular, acuminate, with 2 long keels, swollen between auricles. 1888. Allied to *E. Brassavolae*.

**E. auri'tum.** *fl.* 1 in. across, with apple scent; sep. and pet. light yellow, pet. much shorter; lip deeper yellow, with purple stain at base; peduncles 3- to 5-fld. *l.* 6 in. long, narrow-ligulate. *Pseudobulbs* compressed, 1½ to 3 in. long, 1- or 2-leaved. Guatemala. 1839.

**E. Barkerio'la.*** *fl.* 4 to 7, sep. and pet. light rose; lip white, with a deep purple blotch and some short purple lines on disk, where there are 2 raised lines, pandurate or obovate; raceme 1-sided. *l.* lanceolate, acute, narrow. Stems 2 to 3 in. h. Mexico. 1884.

**E. basila're.** A synonym of *E. Stamfordianum*.

**E. bicamera'tum.** *fl.* ¾ in. across, numerous, fragrant; sep. and pet. yellowish or tawny-brown; lip white, ochre at base. Mexico. 1871. Habit of *E. vitellinum*. Syn. *E. Karwinskii, E. squalidum*.

**E. bic'olor.** A synonym of *Cattleya bicolor*.

**E. bicornu'tum.** A synonym of *Diacrium bicornutum*.

**E. bitubercula'tum.** Allied to *E. Schomburgkii* but smaller and more slender, with rose-purple *fl.*; calli at base of lip yellow. Habitat? 1892.

**E. bractea'tum.** *fl.* 1 or 2 about 1 in. across on slender scapes; sep. and pet. yellowish-green, spotted brown-purple; lip purple shading to white, side lobes greenish-yellow. *Pseudobulbs* clustered, small, monophyllous. *l.* 4 to 5 in. long, rigid. Brazil. 1877. Syn. *E. pusillum*.

**E. bracteola'tum.** A synonym of *E. radiatum*.

**E. bractes'cens.** *fl.* 3 to 7, on slender erect peduncles 4 to 6 in. h.; sep. and pet. ¾ to 1 in. long, narrow, brownish-green; lip clawed, roundly oval, whitish to light rose, veined lilac, side lobes with deeper coloured erect tips. *Pseudobulbs* small, clustered. *l.* 2 or 3, linear, 4 to 8 in. long. Mexico. 1840. (B.M. 4572 as *E. linearifolium.*). Syn. *E. aciculare*.

**E. Brassav'olae.*** *fl.* 10 to 30, 4 in. across, on erect spikes; sep. and pet. yellowish-brown, narrow, tapered; lip ovate, straw-coloured at base, apex purple, sweet-scented in evening. *Pseudobulbs* pyriform, 4 to 8 in. h., diphyllous. *l.* 6 to 10 in. long. Guatemala. 1867. (B.M. 5664.)

**E. calama'rium.** *fl.* small, 2 to 4, yellowish-green, shaded brown, *Pseudobulbs* somewhat conical, diphyllous. 3 to 5 in. h. Brazil. Variable.

**E. calochei'lum.** A synonym of *E. alatum*.

**E. campylosta'lix.** *fl.* 10 to 20 or more, on erect spikes; sep. and narrower pet. ¾ in. long, inclined forward, vinous-red-purple with yellowish lines, glaucous beneath; lip ¾ in. long, mid-lobe white, broadly oval; column dark red; extending from beneath it on the lip are 3 raised white keels. *Pseudobulbs* compressed, oblong to orbicular, 1½ to 2½ in. h., monophyllous. *l.* broadly lanceolate, contracted at base, channelled, thick, glaucous green. Costa Rica. 1889. (B.M. 9243; Ref. B. 2, 86.)

**E. Candol'lei.*** Closely allied to *E. aromaticum*. *fl.* 1½ in. across; sep. and pet. yellowish-brown; lip white or yellowish-white with rose-red nerves, nearly round, shortly pointed. Mexico. (B.M. 3765 as *E. cepiforme.*)

**E. Capartia'num.** A synonym of *E. advenum*.

**E. carolinia'num.** A synonym of *E. nocturnum*.

**E. Cat'illus.** *fl.* numerous; sep. and pet. narrow, obovate-lanceolate, acute, cinnabar-red; lip vermilion, 3-lobed, side lobes toothed on outer margins, mid-lobe narrow, triangular, toothed, disk carinate, callus large, obovate, yellowish; ovaries and pedicels red. Stems tall. *l.* oblong, acute, channelled, their bases sheathing the stems which develop into long stout scaly peduncles with erect racemes. New Granada. (I.H. 1874, 162.)

**E. cepifor'me.** A synonym of *E. Candollei*.

**E. chinen'se.** *fl.* numerous, less than 1 in. across, rose-red. *infl.* often branched. Stems spindle-shaped. *l.* narrowly lanceolate. Costa Rica, Guatemala. Syn. *E. nonchinense, Boughtonia chinensis*.

**E. chione'um.** *fl.* fragrant, ¾ in. wide, fleshy, pure white, in nodding many-fld. racemes 2 in. or more long; dorsal sep. oblong; pet. oblong, spatulate; lateral sep. sub-falcate; lip 3-lobed, side lobes concave, mid-lobe squarely obovate. Stems 2 ft. or more h. *l.* leathery, 1¼ to 1¾ in. long, oblong-ligulate, acute. New Granada. 1845. (G.C. 29 (1901), 70 as *E. Claesianum.*)

**E. chloranth'um.** A synonym of *E. chloroleucum*.

**E. chloroleu'cum.** *fl.* ¾ in. across; sep. and pet. spreading, clear green; lip 3-lobed, side lobes narrow, the white mid-lobe somewhat heart-shaped with crenulate margins and a short apiculus; spikes erect, 10 or more-fld. *Pseudobulbs* clustered, ovately conical, 1 to 2 in. h., diphyllous. *l.* 6 to 8 in. long, ½ to 1 in. wide. Brazil. 1837. (B.M. 3557.)

**E. Christya'num.** *fl.* greenish and brown, in an erect raceme; sep. oblong, apiculate; pet. spatulate; side lobes of lip sub-quadrate, mid-lobe triangular, apiculate; column 3-fid. *l.* ligulate, acute. *Pseudobulbs* long-pyriform, 2-leaved. Bolivia. 1884.

**E. cilia're.*** *fl.* fragrant, 4 to 8 in a raceme, each with a long bract at base; sep. and pet. greenish-yellow, linear, acute; lip white, 3-parted, side lobes pectinately incised, mid-lobe setaceous, much longer. Winter. *Pseudobulbs* oblong, compressed, 4 to 7 in. h., 1- or 2-leaved. *l.* 6 to 9 in. long. Trop. America. 1790. (B.R. 784; L.B.C. 9.) Syn. *E. viscidum*. One of the first epiphytic orchids to be cultivated in England. var. **cuspida'tum** has larger, yellower *fl.* with the mid-lobe of lip linear-lanceolate and equal to side lobes. 1844. (B.R. 783 and L.B.C. 10 as *E. cuspidatum*; B.M. 463 as *E. ciliare.*)

**E. cinnabari'num.*** *fl.* orange-red, 1½ to 2 in. across, few or many on a tall scape; lip toothed, disk yellow, tuberclad. May to July. 4 ft. h. or more. Brazil. 1837. (B.R. 28, 25.)

**E. Claesia'num.** A synonym of *E. chioneum.*

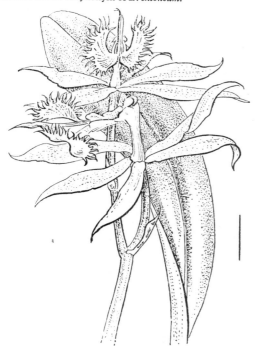

*Epidendrum ciliare cuspidatum* (p. 750)

**E. clava'tum.** *fl.* 4 to 10, 1½ to 2 in. across; sep. greenish with revolute margins; pet. narrow, greenish, faintly tinged red; lip and column pure white; lip 3-lobed, mid-lobe expanded into a triangle, side lobes wing-like, similar to but smaller than the lips of *E. nocturnum* and *E. Parkinsonianum. Pseudobulbs* slender clavate; 3 to 6 in. h. *l.* 2 (sometimes 1 or 3), channelled, tapered, up to 10 in. long, 1 in. wide. Brazil, Costa Rica. 1834. (B.R. 1870.)

**E. cnemidoph'orum.*** *fl.* light yellow, spotted red-brown inside, pure white at back; sep. oblong, obtuse; pet. linear; lip white, shaded rose, deeply divided; spike terminal, about 1 ft. long. *l.* about 8 in. long, glossy, acuminate. 4 to 6 ft. h. Guatemala. 1867. (B.M. 5656.) A stately plant, with drooping racemes.

**E. cochlea'tum.** *fl.* 3 to 4 in. across; sep. and pet. greenish-white, attenuate; lip sub-orbicular or fan-like, somewhat resembling a shell, deep maroon-purple beneath, yellowish-green above, with a large maroon-purple blotch each side; calli 3, white; racemes 4- to 7-fld. *l.* acute, 6 in. long. *Pseudobulbs* 3 to 4 in. h., pyriform, compressed, usually 2-leaved. W. Indies, Cent. America. 1787. (B.M. 572; L.B.C. 22; B.R. 28, 50 as *E. lancifolium.*) Said to have been the first epiphytic Orchid to flower in this country.

**E. confu'sum.** A synonym of *E. pentotis.*

**E. conges'tum.** Dwarf. Near to *E. Mathewsii. fl.* pale green; lip darker; column suffused and mottled red-purple. Costa Rica. 1911.

**E. Cooperia'num.*** *fl.* 10 to 25, 2 in. wide, fleshy, brownish-yellow; lip broad, rosy-purple; racemes terminal, drooping. *l.* lanceolate, acute. Stems stout, 2 to 3 ft. h. Brazil. 1866. (B.M. 5654.)

**E. coria'ceum.** A synonym of *E. variegatum coriaceum.*

**E. coriifo'lium.** *fl.* greenish or red-tinged, fleshy; upper sep. ovate, lateral sep. slightly larger, keeled; pet. narrow; lip about ¾ in. across. Stems 6 to 9 in. h., clasped by the bases of fleshy, ligulate, keeled l. 2-lobed at their tips. *infl.* up to 15-fld., remarkable for the presence of imbricated, fleshy deep-green bracts which partially conceal the lower sep. Cent. America, Brazil, Ecuador. 1851. (B.M. 9477.)

**E. crassifo'lium.** A synonym of *E. ellipticum* and *E. elongatum.*

**E. crassila'bium.** A synonym of *E. variegatum.*

**E. crinif'erum.** *fl.* 3 to 7; sep. and narrower pet. yellowish-green with cinnamon blotches and bars; lip white, hairy. Stems about 15 in. long. *l.* narrow, 4 in. long. Costa Rica. 1871. (B.M. 6094.)

**E. cristobalen'se.** *fl.* ¾ in. across; sep. and pet. tawny yellow, fleshy; lip shield-like, olive-green, thickened. *Peduncle* erect, rachis abruptly curved downward, sometimes 30 in. long, many-fld. *Pseudobulbs* stem-like, 12 to 18 in. h. *l.* 5 or 6 on upper parts of stem, 3 to 4 in. long, tapered. Costa Rica. 1918. (B.M. 8996.)

**E. cuspida'tum.** A synonym of *E. ciliare cuspidatum.*

**E. cyclotel'lum.** *fl.* 3 to 7, about 2 in. h.; sep. and pet. purplish-rose; lip similar but with a whitish disk. *Spikes* 6 to 9 in. h. Stems quill-like, 3 to 5 in. h. *l.* 3 in. long on upper half of stem, deciduous or nearly so. Guatemala. 1880. (W.O.A. 148 as *Barkeria cyclotella.*)

**E. cycnostach'ys.** A synonym of *E. Stamfordianum.*

**E. cycnosta'lix.** A synonym of *E. Stamfordianum.*

**E. decip'iens.** A synonym of *E. fulgens.*

**E. densiflo'rum.** A synonym of *E. polyanthum densiflorum. See also* **E. floribundum.**

**E. dichro'mum.*** *fl.* light rose, about 2 in. across in large panicles, 2 to 3 ft. h.; lip 3-lobed, rich crimson. *Pseudobulbs* short and stout, with 2 or 3 dark-green leathery l., 6 to 12 in. or more in length. Pernambuco. 1865. Cool-house. var. **ama'bile**, sep. and pet. almost white at base, lip deep crimson bordered white (W.O.A. 452; L. 699; B.M. 5491); **stria'tum** has white sep. and pet. with radiating deep-purple lines.

**E. diffor'me.** *fl.* several, green, 1¾ to 2 in. across; pet. and broader sep. narrow; lip deeper green, over 1 in. wide, broadly reniform. *infl.* umbellate. Stems erect or arched, 4 to 12 in. h. *l.* distichous, amplexicaul, 2 to 3 in. long, ½ to 1 in. wide. W. Indies to Brazil. 1760. (B.R. 80 and B.M. 2030 as *E. umbellatum.*) Variable.

**E. diffu'sum.*** *fl.* ½ in. across, numerous, greenish-white with narrow segs. *infl.* a large panicle. Stems reed-like, 12 in. or more long. *l.* 1½ in. or more long, leathery. W. Indies. 1816. (B.M. 3565; L.B.C. 846.) SYN. *Seraphyta diffusa, S. multiflora.*

**E. dio'tum.** *fl.* over 1 in. across, very sweetly scented; sep. and pet. cinnamon-brown with wavy edges; lip yellow, streaked deep brown, thick and fleshy; scape twice as long as l., many-fld. *l.* about 1 ft. long, spreading. *Pseudobulbs* long, 1-leaved. Guatemala.

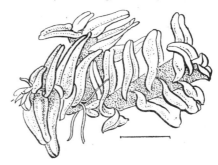

*Epidendrum discolor*

**E. dis'color.** *fl.* solitary, purplish-green, about ⅔ in. across or more; lip rounded, ½ in. wide, slightly shorter. *l.* stiff, greenish or flushed brown-purple, small, ovate-oblong, amplexicaul, closely set on the prostrate or semi-erect stems which are 2 to 3 in. long. Brazil. 1832. (B.R. 1541 as *Nanodes discolor.*)

**E. dolo'sum.** A synonym of *Cattleya dolosa.*

**E. ebur'neum.** *fl.* sep. and pet. yellowish-green; lip very large, ivory-white, with yellow callosities; raceme terminal, 4- to 6-fld. Stems slender, 20 to 30 in. h. *l.* alternate, large, deep green. Panama. 1867. (B.M. 5643.)

**E. el'egans.*** *fl.* 3 to 7, 2 in. across; sep. and pet. dark rose; lip deep crimson, base and sometimes margins paler or whitish. Stems 8 to 15 in. h. *l.* narrow, 2 to 2½ in. long. Mexico. 1836. (B.M. 4784 as *Barkeria elegans.*) Variable. var. **nobil'ior**, *fl.* larger, with a blackish-purple blotch on lip. 1886.

**E. ellip'ticum.** *fl.* rose-magenta, ¾ in. across; lip paler than sep. and pet., disk very pale or yellowish, deeply 3-lobed, outer margins of side lobes dentate; raceme corymbiform, elongating. Stems 2 to 3 ft. long. *l.* leathery, stiff, 1½ to 3 in. long, ½ to 1 in. wide. Brazil. 1826. (L.B.C. 1276; B.M. 3543 as *E. crassifolium.*) *E. ellipticum* of Reichb. f. is *E. elongatum.*

**E. Ellis'ii.** *fl.* rose, with a yellowish crest on lip; in short racemes. *l.* 4 in. long. Stems 1½ ft. h. (J.R.H.S. 17, civ.) Colombia. 1894.

**E. elonga'tum.** *fl.* bright rose, differing from *E. ellipticum* by its brighter colour, the longer, thinner, more acute l. and taller stems. *Peduncles* up to 2 ft. long. Brazil, Cent America. 1798. (B.M. 611; L.B.C. 986.)

**E. Endres'ii.*** *fl.* 10 to 20, about 1 in. across; sep. white, tipped violet or green, upper cuneate-oblong, acute, lateral, triangular; pet. white, or coloured like sep.; lip white blotched mauve or spotted violet, base convolute over column, then forming 2 auricles, mid-lobe cuneate-obreniform. Stems usually 6 to 12 in. h., warted, with small, fleshy, distichous l. Costa Rica. 1883. (B.M. 7855.)

**E. erubes'cens.*** *fl.* in large panicles; sep. and pet. delicate mauve, broad; lip rather darker, yellow at base. *Pseudobulbs* fusiform, 2-leaved. Mexico. 1837. This very desirable greenhouse species is somewhat difficult to grow, but it has been found to thrive in a cool house. Should be placed on a raft.

**E. evec'tum.\*** *fl.* racemes loose, sub-cylindric, many-fld., on 18 in. peduncles; perianth bright rose-purple; sep. and pet. narrow-obovate, obtuse; lip adnate to column, rather longer than sep., 3-lobed nearly to base, lobes all deeply cut and fringed. Stems 2 to 3 ft. h. or more. *l.* sessile, oblong-lanceolate, obtuse, emarginate, leathery; sheaths rather short. Colombia. (B.M. 5902.)

**E. falca'tum.** A synonym of *E. Parkinsonianum*, but possibly the right name.

**E. falsiloq'uum.** *fl.* paniculate; sep. and pet. whitish-ochre; lip white, with 3 linear, acute, depressed, mauve keels; calli white. *l.* linear, acuminate. Habitat ? 1885. Allied to *E. verrucosum*. By some regarded as a var. of *E. paniculatum.*

**E. flav'idum.** A synonym of *E. leucochilum.*

**E. floribun'dum.** *fl.* about 1 in. across, many, in a loose panicle; sep. oblong-lanceolate, greenish; pet. narrow with dilated apex, greenish-white; lip greenish-white, sometimes spotted red, 3-lobed, side lobes rounded, mid-lobe with 2 divergent lobules; disk with 3 keels and 2 tubercles. Variable. Brazil. 1830? (B.M. 3637; 3791 as *E. densiflorum.*)

**E. formo'sum.** A synonym of *E. alatum.*

**E. frag'rans.\*** *fl.* very fragrant, 2 in. across, inverted; sep. and pet. creamy-white; lip white, streaked purple, sub-orbicular, with a fleshy callus at base; peduncles short, few-fld. *l.* lanceolate, 8 to 12 in. long. *Pseudobulbs* 3 to 4 in. h., compressed, usually oval, variable, 1- or 2-leaved. Trop. America. 1778. (B.M. 1669; L.B.C. 1039; B.R. 1898 as *E. aemulum.*) var. **megalan'thum**, *see* **E. pentotis.**

**E. Frederici-Guiliel'mi.\*** *fl.* in large terminal panicles; sep. and pet. dark purple, about 1 in. long, lanceolate; lip 3-lobed; apex of column and disk pure white. Stems rather stout, 2 to 5 ft. h. *l.* distichous, 6 to 8 in. long, 1 to 2 in. broad, dark green. Peru. 1871. (I.H. 1871, 48.) A fine species.

**E. ful'gens.\*** *fl.* rather small, in crowded heads, brilliant orange-scarlet; front lobe of lip small, denticulate-fimbriate, almost confluent with the rounded denticulate side lobes. Habit near that of *E. radicans* but the stems do not root and l. usually longer. Brazil, Guiana. 1829. Very variable. *E. fulgens* of Focke is *E. Schomburgkii.*

**E. gluma'ceum.** *fl.* 1½ in. across, inverted, fragrant; sep. and pet. white striped with pale rose inside, white outside, tapered, spreading; lip stained and streaked rose in centre, margined white, acuminate; peduncles racemose. *l.* 6 to 8 in. long. *Pseudobulbs* pyriform, 4 to 6 in. h., 2-leaved. Pernambuco. 1837. (B.R. 26, 6.)

**E. glutino'sum.** A synonym of *E. odoratissimum.*

**E. Godseffia'num.** A synonym of *E. advenum.*

**E. Gra'hamii.** A synonym of *E. phoeniceum.*

**E. granulo'sum.** A synonym of *Cattleya granulosa.*

**E. Hanbur'ii.** *fl.* 2 in. across, numerous, spike branching, erect, 2 ft. h.; sep. and pet. deep, dull purplish-brown; lip rose, veined crimson. Spring. *Pseudobulbs* and *l.* much as in *E. atropurpureum.* Mexico. 1843. (G.F. 398.)

**E. Harriso'niae.** *fl.* 7 to 15, fleshy; sep. and narrower pet. ¾ in. long, inclined backwards with reflexed tips, dull green, flushed brown-red on their reverse; lip 3-partite, white flushed on the basal divisions with purplish-brown, the front part reflexed strongly with age. Stems 3 ft. or more h. *l.* fleshy 3½ to 5 in. long by 1 in. broad. *Peduncle* erect or arched. Brazil. 1833. (B.M. 3209.)

**E. Harrisonia'num.** A synonym of *Cattleya Harrisoniana.*

**E. Hart'ii.** *fl.* whitish-yellow, small, in branched, terminal panicles. *l.* linear, 4 in. long. Stems 8 in. long. Trinidad. 1894. Allied to *E. purum.*

**E. hasta'tum.** *fl.* 6 or 7, with brownish-green sep. and pet. lined purple, and a pure white lip. 1896. Colombia. A pretty little species.

**E. ibaguense.\*** *fl.* in a dense, almost globose head; sep. and pet. orange; lip yellow, obcordate, side lobes cordate, rounded at tip and fringed. *l.* very fleshy, amplexicaul, oblong, obtuse, 3 to 4 in. long. Stems 2 to 4 ft. h., slender. Colombia, Peru. 1867.

**E. Impera'tor.** A synonym of *E. Catillus* and *E. leucochilum.*

**E. Imschootia'num.** *fl.* 6 to 14; sep. oblong, ¾ in. long, spreading, greenish, tinged purple; pet. narrower, light green; lip 3-lobed, lobes entire, oblong, sub-obtuse, white, tinged green on margins. Stems about 3 ft. h. *l.* short, leathery. Origin? 1893.

**E. indivi'sum.** A synonym of *Diacrium bicornutum.*

**E. inver'sum.** *fl.* 5 to 9, inverted, pale straw-coloured, or white lined light rose, with purple streaks or flush on lip, and sometimes with a few purple spots at base of other segs., crowded, fragrant; calli bright yellow; peduncles racemose, erect. *l.* 4 to 6 in. long. *Pseudobulbs* fusiform, 3 or 4 in. h., 2-leaved. Minas Geraes. 1839. Near to *E. glumaceum.*

**E. ionocen'trum.** *fl.* sep. and pet. lemon, spotted with greenish-brown, lanceolate, acuminate; lip white, violet or purple in centre; raceme 20- to 24-fld. *Pseudobulbs* broad. Otherwise like *E. Brassavolae.* Trop. America.

**E. ionophle'bium.\*** Distinct from but allied to *E. radiatum*. *fl.* 3 to 7 on short, stout peduncles, long-lasting, very fragrant; lip broad, concave, heart-shaped, pointed, white with violet-purple lines; sep. and pet. white. *Pseudobulbs* stoutly pyriform, 2 in. or more h., diphyllous. *l.* 9 to 14 in. long, 1 to 1¼ in. wide. Costa Rica.

**E. ionos'mum.\*** *fl.* 3 to 10, fragrant, 1½ in. across; sep. and pet. greenish-brown, bordered pale yellow, obovate; lip 3-lobed, yellow streaked red, side lobes erect, mid-lobe emarginate; peduncles racemose. *l.* oblong-lanceolate, 3 to 6 in. long. *Pseudobulbs* globose, 2- or 3-leaved. British Guiana. About 1838.

**E. Karwin'skii.** A synonym of *E. bicameratum.*

**E. Kienas'tii.** *fl.* about 2 in. across; sep. and pet. very light rose, with darker purple veins; sep. lanceolate; pet. cuneate at base; lip 3-lobed, shortly clawed, white, side lobes cuneate-ligulate, 2-toothed outside, disk purplish; raceme several-fld. *Pseudobulbs* fusiform, cylindric. *l.* usually 2, 6 in. long, ½ to 1 in. broad. Mexico.

**E. lactiflo'rum.** A synonym of *E. falcatum.*

**E. Lambeaua'num.** *fl.* solitary, about 1 in. across, on a short erect peduncle; sep. and ascending pet. whitish; lip orbicular, claret with a lighter margin, not fringed. Allied to but slightly more robust than *E. Mathewsii.* Brazil. Before 1908.

**E. lamella'tum.** A synonym of *E. stenopetalum.*

**E. lancifo'lium.** A synonym of *E. cochleatum* and *E. radiatum.*

**E. lan'ipes.** Differs from *E. purum* by pedicels and ovaries densely tomentose. *fl.* yellowish. Brazil, Venezuela, &c. 1853.

**E. Lankes'teri.** A synonym of *E. Schlechterianum.*

**E. latera'le.** A synonym of *E. Rosseauae.*

**E. latifo'lium.** A synonym of *E. nocturnum.*

**E. latilab'rum.** *fl.* 3 or 4, about 2 in. across, green; front lobe of lip with 2 comparatively large spreading lobes. Stems erect or sub-erect, fleshy, 6 to 9 in. h. *l.* 1 to 3 in. long, ½ to 1½ in. wide. Near to *E. difforme.* Brazil. 1841. (G.C. 25 (1899), 98 as *E. umbellatum.*)

**E. Lauchea'num.** *fl.* small; sep. and pet. dull brown-red; lip thick, rigid, green or yellowish-green; peduncle slender, erect, 5 to 9 in. h.; rachis pendent, often much longer than the peduncle, with up to 100 fl. Stems stoutly quill-like, 4 to 9 in. h. *l.* 2 to 4, 3 to 4 in. long, barely ½ in. wide. Brazil. 1889.

**E. leucochi'lum.** *fl.* 5 to 9, 2 to 3 in. across, yellowing with age; sep. and pet. light greenish, reflexed; lip ivory-white, 3-lobed; peduncles from a compressed sheath. Stems as thick as a cedar pencil, 1¼ ft. to 2½ ft. h. *l.* 3 to 5, leathery. *rhiz.* stout, woody. Colombia, Venezuela. 1842. SYN. *E. flavidum*, *E. Imperator* of gardens.

**E. Lilias'trum.** A synonym of *Sobralia Liliastrum.*

**E. Lindleya'num.\*** *fl.* 3 to 10, about 2 in. across; sep. and pet. rose-purple; lip white with a deep purple blotch at the tip, often spotted purple; spike 12 to 24 in. h. Stems 9 to 15 in. h. *l.* elliptic-oblong, acute. Variable. Costa Rica, Mexico. 1842. (B.M. 6098.) var. **Cen'terae**, a larger-fld. variety, *fl.* purple-lilac, the front portion of the more acute lip much deeper, the column purple blotched. (Gn. 27 (1885), 396.); var. **cyclotellum**, *see* **E. cyclotellum.**

**E. linea're.** A synonym of *Isochilus linearis.*

**E. linea'tum.** A synonym of *E. fragrans.*

**E. Loefgren'ii.** *fl.* usually 4, not ½ in. across, whitish or greenish-white, fleshy. Stems pendulous 9 to 15 in. long, clothed with glaucous-green leaves minutely dotted purple-red, keeled, broadly lanceolate when flattened, but sheathing the stem, gradually larger upwards, the uppermost 2 enclosing the infl. Brazil. 1938.

**E. longipet'alum.** A synonym of *E. alatum.*

**E. luteo'lum.** A synonym of *Cattleya luteola.*

**E. macrochi'lum.** A synonym of *E. atropurpureum.*

**E. macula'tum.** A synonym of *E. prismatocarpum.*

**E. Mantinia'num.** *fl.* pale whitish-green, large, solitary, with purplish-brown dots on veins of sep. and pet. which are often flushed rose, lip 3-lobed, dotted or flushed purple-violet, side lobes large. Stem 3 or 4. *l.* about 2 in. long, 1 in. wide, glaucous green. Brazil. 1892. (I.H. 1892, 150.)

**E. Mathew'sii.** *fl.* sep. and pet. stained purplish outside, small, nearly transparent, lateral sep. connate half-way up; lip deep, dull blood-purple, shining, orbicular, 2-fid at apex, convex above, concave beneath, completely concealing the lateral sep. *l.* distichous, rigid, fleshy. Stems 2 in. h. Peru. 1886. SYN. *Nanodes Mathewsii.*

**E. Medu'sae.** *fl.* 2 to 3 in. across, usually in pairs, fleshy; sep. and pet. greenish, shaded brown; sep. linear-oblong, keeled behind; pet. margins slightly revolute; lip 2 in. across, rounded, dark purple-red, strongly fringed. Stems pendulous, fleshy, 4 to 12 in. long. *l.* fleshy, glaucous green, broadly lanceolate, 2 to 3 in. long, sheathing at base. Ecuador. 1867. (B.M. 5723 as *Nanodes Medusae.*) Should be grown in the Odontoglossum house.

**E. melanocau'lon.\*** *fl.* 1½ in. across, the narrowly elliptic sep. and broader pet. rose-lilac; lip almost square, deeper in colour, disk greenish. Stems dark, about 12 in. h. *l.* narrow, pointed. Mexico, Costa Rica. 1848. SYN. *Barkeria melanocaulon.*

**E. Moorea'num.** A variety of *E. oncidioides.*

**E. Mo'seni.** A synonym of *E. fulgens.*

**E. myrianth'um.*** *fl.* 1 in. long, bright rosy-purple, in enormous panicles. Autumn. *l.* distichous, linear-oblong or lanceolate. Stems 3 to 4 ft. h. Guatemala. 1866. (B.M. 5556.) This free-flowering species grows best in a cool-house.

**E. nemora'le.*** *fl.* 3 to 4 in. across, freely produced in large arching panicles; sep. and pet. delicate mauve or rosy-lilac, narrow-lanceolate; lip striped violet, mid-lobe 1½ in. long, 1 in. wide, tapered. July. *Pseudobulbs* 2 to 3 in. h., sub-globose, 2-leaved. Mexico. 1840. (B.M. 4606; L. 155; B.R. 30, 51 as *E. verrucosum.*) Cool-house. var. **ma'jus,** *fl.* panicles sometimes 3 ft. long; sep. and pet. delicate rosy-mauve; lip white in centre, with 3 short red lines, bordered deep rose. (W.S.O. 1, 13.)

**E. nigromacula'tum.** A synonym of *E. prismatocarpum.*

**E. noctur'num.** *fl.* often solitary but up to 10, fragrant chiefly at night; sep. and pet. pale ochre-yellow or greenish-white, 3 to 4 in. across; lip white, 3-lobed, with 2 yellow calli at base of the narrow, pointed mid-lobe, side lobes wing-like. Stems stoutish, compressed, 1 to 2½ ft. long. *l.* linear or oblong-lanceolate, 6 to 8 in. long. Trop. America. Before 1816. (B.M. 3298; L.B.C. 713; B.R. 1961 as var. *latifolium.*) Very variable in size, number of fl., and fragrance.

**E. nu'tans.** *fl.* 20 to 50, 1 in. across; sep. and narrower pet. soft green; lip white, tinged with green, mid-lobe spreading, rounded, deeply 3-cleft with its central division often again divided. *infl.* a drooping, branched panicle. *fl.* closely set, fragrant, especially at night. Stems 18 to 30 in. long. *l.* 6 to 7 in. long, 1 to 1½ in. wide, tapered. W. Indies, Brazil, &c. 1793. (L.B.C. 645; B.R. 17, less good.)

**E. odoratis'simum.** *fl.* small, about ¾ in. across, rather fleshy, greenish or yellowish-green, often lightly flushed or marked with purple; mid-lobe of lip sub-orbicular, apiculate, wrinkled with a fold on each side of the raised callus. *infl.* erect with a few short, usually 4-fld. branches. *Pseudobulbs* ovoid, tapered, 1 to 2½ in. h., 2- or 3-phyllous. *l.* 8 to 15 in. long, ½ to 1 in. broad. Brazil. 1827. Only grown for sweet fragrance of fl. (B.R. 1415; B.M. 3013 as *Encyclia patens.*)

**E. oncidioi'des.*** *fl.* about 1½ in. across, yellow, blotched brown, very fragrant; sep. and pet. obovate, unguiculate; lip white or yellowish, flushed or lined reddish-purple, 3-lobed, side lobes narrow, obtuse, flat, much shorter than the roundish, cuspidate mid-lobe, disk 3-keeled; panicle long, loose. *l.* 2 or 3, 2 ft. long, 1½ in. wide. *Pseudobulbs* oblong-fusiform, 4 to 8 in. h. Brazil. 1833. (B.R. 1623; I.H. 1887, 28.) A stately species. var. **granit'icum,** lip white, flushed rose at base; smaller in all parts than type, widely distributed. SYN. *E. graniticum*; **Moorea'num,** *fl.* very fragrant, sep. and pet. light green, lip deep purple with light-green margin, panicle lax, *l.* linear, 1 ft. long, *pseudobulbs* smaller than in type and more globose. (B.M. 9179 as *E. Mooreanum.*)

**E. organen'se.** *fl.* 3 to 7, small, on short spikes; sep. and pet. yellow-brown; sep. streaked purple-brown behind; lip heart-shaped, white with purple lines round crest. Brazil. 1891. Habit of *E. polybulbon,* but slightly larger. Forms a pretty cushion-like plant.

**E. osman'thum.** A synonym of *E. advenum.*

**E. pachysep'alum.** A synonym of *E. variegatum.*

**E. palea'ceum.** Perhaps the correct name of *E. auritum.*

**E. pallidiflo'rum.** *fl.* pale yellow, 1 in. across, usually with purple streaks at apex of column and on side lobes of lip; peduncles many-fld. *l.* linear-oblong, 5 to 7 in. long. Stems terete, 1 to 1½ ft. h. W. Indies. 1828. (B.M. 2980.)

**E. pamplonen'se.** A synonym of *E. variegatum.*

**E. panicula'tum.*** *fl.* ¾ in. across, fragrant, purple or lilac-purple, with some yellow at tip of column; very numerous, in a densely branched, drooping panicle, upwards of 1 ft. long; sep. spatulate-ligulate; pet. almost filiform; lip deeply 4-lobed. *l.* 5 to 7 in. long, lanceolate-acuminate. Stems tall, reedy, 2 to 6 ft. h. Colombia. 1868. (B.M. 5731.) One of the finest of the paniculate Epidendrums. *See also* **E. falsiloquum.**

**E. Parkinsonia'num.** *fl.* usually 1 or 2, 4 in. or more across; sep. and pet. similar, narrowly lanceolate, acute, 2½ in. long, creamy-white or yellowish-green; lip similarly coloured or white, 3-lobed, side lobes sub-rhomboid, wing-like, mid-lobe narrowly triangular-acicular. *rhiz.* stout, branching. *Pseudobulbs* stout, hardly ½ in. long with a single pendent, very fleshy, narrow-tapered l., 6 to 12 in. long. Mexico. 1837. (B.M. 3778.) The pendulous habit necessitates a raft. *See* **E. falcatum.**

**E. pa'tens.** *fl.* 1½ in. across, yellowish-green, changing to white; sep. and pet. similar, oblong, acute, with revolute margins; lip 3-lobed, mid-lobe again partially divided. Stems 1 to 3 ft. long. *l.* oblong-lanceolate, leathery, 4 to 6 in. long, on the upper parts of the stems only. *Racemes* pendulous, often branched. W. Indies, Guatemala. 1831. (L.B.C. 1537.) *E. patens* of Hooker is *E. odoratissimum.*

**E. payten'se.*** *fl.* brilliant scarlet-vermilion, with some orange on lip, which is also marked with darker spots. *l.* short, very strong, oblong, acute, tinted purplish-brown. Stems stiff, with purplish-brown sheaths. Colombia, Peru. 1885.

**E. pento'tis.*** *fl.* usually 2 or 4, 3 to 4 in. across, creamy-white or yellowish, very fragrant; sep. and pet. nearly equal, tapered; lip cochleate, with radiating purple lines; peduncles short. *Pseudobulbs* erect, somewhat fusiform, compressed, 6 to 12 in. h., 2-phyllous. *l.* 6 to 12 in. long, about 1 in. wide. Brazil. 1877.

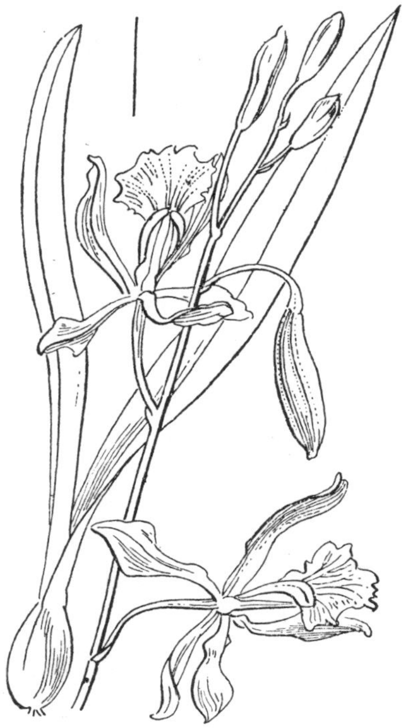

*Epidendrum phoeniceum.* Leaves much reduced

**E. phoenic'eum.*** *fl.* sep. and pet. deep purple, mottled green; lip clear bright violet, veined and stained with crimson. Summer. *Pseudobulbs* stout, ovoid, 2-phyllous, 3 in. long. *l.* 6 to 9 in. long, narrow. Cuba. 1840. (B.M. 3885 as *E. Grahamii.*) Allied to *E. atropurpureum.* A handsome, large-fld. species, with branching panicles, 2 to 3 ft. h.

**E. plica'tum.*** *fl.* several, about 2 in. across; sep. and narrower pet. narrow at base then widening and becoming shortly acuminate; sep. yellowish-green, more or less shaded maroon chiefly at the tips and on back; pet. usually more brightly coloured; lip 3-lobed, the magenta-rose lateral lobes oblong-lanceolate, extended beyond the column; mid-lobe broadly heart-shaped, crimped, crimson-rose, base whitish. *Pseudobulbs* ovate, 2-phyllous. Cuba. 1847 or earlier. (B.R. 33, 35.) A handsome variable species.

**E. polyan'thum.*** *fl.* orange or salmon-colour, with a strong scent of cowslips; sep. ovate-lanceolate, acute, striated; pet. linear, reflexed; lip 3-lobed, 3-ribbed, lateral lobes sub-cuneate, retuse, mid-lobe retuse; scape branched. Stems 18 in. or more long. *l.* distichous, ovate-lanceolate, acute. Mexico. 1841. (Ref. B. 2, 112.) var. **as'perum** has ovaries and rachis warty. 1885.

**E. polybul'bon.** *fl.* 1 in. across; sep. and pet. tawny or light yellow with brown centre; lip white, with a short claw; peduncles 1-fld. *l.* ovate-oblong, 1 to 1½ in. long. *Pseudobulbs* produced from a branching rhiz. at intervals of about 1 in., ovoid, ½ in. long. W. Indies, &c. 1841. (L.B.C. 1230; B.M. 4067 as *Dinema polybulbon.*) var. **luteoal'bum** has sep. and pet. yellow, lip white.

**E. Por'pax.** Allied to *E. Mathewsii.* Stems 2 in. h., terminating in a solitary *fl.* with a broad purple lip, and paler sep. and pet. *l.* fleshy ½ in. long, oblong. Nicaragua, Costa Rica. 1855.

**E. prismatocar'pum.*** *fl.* 10 to 20, about 2 in. across, fragrant, on erect racemes; sep. and pet. yellow-green, spotted dark purple or black; lip lilac-purple, bordered white; all segs. shortly pointed. June. *Pseudobulbs* flask-shaped, 10 to 12 in. h., 2-phyllous. *l.* 10 to 12 in. long. Cent. America. 1862. (B.M. 5336; L. 200; W.S.O. 1, 9.)

**E. Pseudepiden'drum.** *fl.* 2½ in. across, raceme terminal, few-fld.; perianth bright green, except lip and upper part of column which are orange-vermilion; lip sub-orbicular, end recurved; margin erose, obscurely lobed. July. Stems 2 to 3 ft. h., leafy at top. *l.* distichous, sub-erect, narrow linear-oblong, acuminate, leathery, deep green; back keeled; margins recurved. Cent. America. 1871. (B.M. 5929.) var. **aura'tum** has disk of lip crimson, borders deep orange. 1885. A fine variety.

**E. pugioniform'e.*** *fl.* large, usually 2 in a sub-sessile, terminal raceme; sep. and pet. at first greenish, then yellowish; lip at first white, afterwards yellow, 3-lobed, cordate at base. *l.* 4 to 6 in. long, narrow-lanceolate-oblong. Mexico. 1890. Allied to *E. leucochilum*.

**E. pu'milum.** Closely resembling *E. Endresii* but usually smaller. Variable. Sep. and pet. pale green or yellowish; lip white with a purple or violet blotch on the cleft mid-lobe and a yellow crest. Costa Rica. 1890. (B.M. 9170.)

**E. punctula'tum.** *fl.* stellate, in a slender panicle; sep. and pet. brown inside, green outside, lanceolate, acute; lip sulphur, with minute dots, 3-fid, side lobes square, mid-lobe sessile, ovate, acute, mid-nerves thickened; column brown and green; border of the anther-bed white, spotted brown. *Pseudobulb* and *l.* much as in *E. vitellinum*. Mexico. 1885.

**E. pu'rum.** *fl.* numerous, white or greenish-white, ¾ in. h., fragrant, in a slender, nodding panicle; sep. narrow-lanceolate; pet. filiform; scape terminal. Spring and summer. Stems erect, 12 to 20 in. h. *l.* narrow, obtuse, about 6 in. long, light green, persistent. Caracas. 1842.

**E. pusil'lum.** A synonym of *E. bracteatum*.

**E. radia'tum.*** *fl.* 1½ in. across; sep. and pet. cream, reflexed; lip white, with radiating bright-purple lines, concave, shell-like; racemes 7- or more fld. *l.* linear-ligulate, 10 to 15 in. long. Stems shortly fusiform, stalked, 3 to 5 in. long, 2- or 3-leaved. *rhiz.* woody. Mexico. 1841. (B.R. 30, 45.) Allied to *E. fragrans*.

**E. radi'cans.** *fl.* 1 to 1½ in. across, bright orange-red, remaining in beauty for a considerable time, clustered on long racemes; lip deeply 3-lobed, side lobes rounded, denticulate, mid-lobe cuneate, fimbriate. Guatemala. 1836. (W.O.A. 161.) SYN. *E. rhizophorum.* A pretty scandent species, sometimes reaching 10 ft. in height, and requiring the support of a stake. Stem rooting.

**E. Randia'num.** A variety of *E. atropurpureum*.

**E. ranif'erum.** *fl.* few or many, 2 in. h., less in width; sep. with revolute margins; sep. and pet. greenish-yellow, spotted red; lip ½ in. wide in 6 divisions, basal lobes wing-like with toothed outer margins, intermediate and front lobes narrower, yellow, flecked red. Mexico, Guiana, Brazil, Demerara, &c. 1839. (B.R. 28, 42.) A very variable species, particularly as regards the shape of the lip, number of lobes, &c. Some forms are fragrant. Habit much as in *E. leucochilum*.

**E. replica'tum.** *fl.* sep. and pet. yellowish-brown, bordered yellow; lip white, streaked and veined rosy-pink, 3-lobed, sides of front lobe turned downwards; racemes terminal, 1 to 1½ ft. long, many-fld. Summer. *l.* long, strap-shaped, persistent. *Pseudobulbs* oblong-ovate, 2-leaved. Colombia. 1881.

**E. rhizoph'orum.** A synonym of *E. radicans*.

**E. rig'idum.** *fl.* small, greenish-yellow, arranged distichously on a flattened bracteate rachis, 2 to 4 in. long or more; bracts green, keeled, partially corticealing the fl. Stems 2 to 9 in. h. *l.* 1 to 3 in. long, ⅓ to 1 in. broad. Brazil, W. Indies, &c. 1760. (H.I.P. 314.) A curious widely distributed sp. occasionally seen in cultivation.

**E. Rosseau'ae.** *fl.* few, about 1 in. across, green; lateral sep. slightly concave, broader than the dorsal; pet. linear-lanceolate; lip uppermost, 3-lobed, its claw confluent with the column. *Pseudobulbs* cylindrical, 2 to 3 in. h., monophyllous. *l.* 3 in. long, 1 in. wide. *Spike* 1 to 2 in. long, produced from rudimentary growths as in *E. Stamfordianum*. Costa Rica. 1910. SYN. *E. laterale*.

**E. sanguin'eum.** A synonym of *Broughtonia sanguinea*.

**E. scep'trum.*** *fl.* 12 to 30, about 1 in. across; sep. and pet. golden-yellow, spotted dark purple; sep. lanceolate, pet. obovate; lip white at base, profusely marked bright purple; racemes 1 to 2 ft. long. September, October. *l.* 3 or 4, long, thin, lorate. *Pseudobulbs* slightly compressed, 1 ft. h. or more. Venezuela, Colombia. 1843. (B.M. 7169.)

**E. Schilleria'num.** A synonym of *Cattleya Schilleriana*.

**E. Schlechteria'num.** *fl.* in pairs, ½ in. across, almost translucent greenish-yellow, pink tinged; lip entire, acute, fleshy, column purplish. Growths clustered, 1 to 2 in. h. *l.* small, fleshy, channelled. Panama. Before 1926. SYN. *E. Lankesteri*.

**E. Schomburgk'ii.*** *fl.* rich vermilion-scarlet; sep. and pet. linear-lanceolate, ⅞ in. long; lip deeply 3-lobed, strongly keeled, 2-callose at base, side lobes broadly semi-ovate, rounded and lacerated, front lobe cuneate, gradually widening upwards, edge denticulate, apex shortly cuspidate; raceme loosely corymbiform. Stems 15 to 30 in. h. *l.* distichous, oblong, obtuse, fleshy. Brazil, Demerara, &c. (B.R. 24, 53.) A handsome species. var. **conflu'ens,** a synonym of *E. fulgens*.

**E. Schumannia'num.*** *fl.* sep. and pet. equal, soft yellow, sparsely spotted red; margins of sep. revolute; lip with mid-lobe cuneate, front part expanded into 2 rounded lobes, flushed rose-pink, yellow and thickly spotted red at base; column with 2 light purple, toothed wings hooding the apex. *infl.* erect, branched, many-fld. Stems 2 ft. or more. *l.* 2½ in. long, 1 in. wide. Costa Rica. 1837?

**E. secun'dum.** A synonym of *E. elongatum*.

**E. sellig'erum.*** *fl.* fragrant, 1½ in. across; sep. and pet. brown with a pale margin, spatulate, concave; lip with side lobes white, the crisped mid-lobe light purple; disk saddle-like; peduncles 3 to 4 ft. long, many-fld., paniculate. *Pseudobulbs* ovoid, 3 to 4 in. long, stout, 2-leaved. Mexico, Guatemala. 1836. (R.X.O. 3, 233.)

**E. Skin'neri.*** *fl.* 15 to 30, over 1 in. across, deep rose; spikes 15 to 20 in. h. Variable in colour, number, and size of fl. Stems erect, slender, about 12 in. h. *l.* narrowly lanceolate, fleshy, 2 to 3 in. long. Mexico, Guatemala. 1835. (B.M. 3951; B.R. 1881.) SYN. *Barkeria Skinneri.* var. **super'ba,** stronger growing than type, *fl.* darker, *infl.* often branched. Guatemala. 1863. (W.S.O. 38.)

*Epidendrum Schomburgkii*

**E. Sophroni'tis.** *fl.* dull yellow-green, mottled dull violet-purple. May, June. *l.* 2 or 3 at tip of pseudobulb, 2 to 3 in. long, spreading, oblong-lanceolate, acute, thick-leathery, keeled, clothed on both surfaces with a pale glaucous green waxy secretion; margins purple. *Pseudobulbs* ovoid, green. Peru. 1867. (B.M. 6314.) One of the most singular species of the genus.

**E. specta'bile.*** *fl.* 5 to 10, 2 to 3 in. h.; the linear-lanceolate sep. and broader pet. rose-lilac; lip paler, spotted purple with 3 to 5 raised lines. July. Stems 3 to 6 in. h. *l.* 2 to 4, 3 to 4 in. long, oblong-lanceolate. Mexico, Guatemala. 1842. (B.M. 4094 as *Barkeria spectabilis*.)

**E. spondia'dum.** *fl.* sep. and pet. reddish-green, shading to dull purple, acute or acuminate; lip dark, margined pale green; peduncle few-fld. The Spondias, Costa Rica. 1893. (B.M. 7273.) In general appearance resembling *E. variegatum*.

**E. Sprucea'num.** A synonym of *E. nocturnum*.

**E. Stamfordia'num.*** *fl.* numerous, fragrant, 1½ in. long; sep. and narrower pet. lanceolate, yellow, spotted red; lip 3-lobed, side lobes spreading, pale yellow, 1 in. across, front lobe clawed, spreading, oblong, yellow, margin fimbriate, disk purple. Variable in colour. *Pseudobulbs* fusiform, 9 to 12 in. h., slender below, 2- or 3-leaved. *l.* 6 to 9 in. long, 1½ to 2½ in. wide. Guatemala, Brazil, &c. 1837. (B.M. 4759.) The many-fld. often branched infl. is produced against the base of the latest-made pseudobulb on a rudimentary growth. var. **Leea'num,** sep. and pet. ochre within, covered with purple hieroglyphic markings, lip light rose, purple spotted within, broad. 1887; **Wallac'ei,** purple spotting dense, mid-lobe of lip obcordate, entire, very narrow, *infl.* shorter than in type. Bogota. 1887.

**E. stenopet'alum.** *fl.* 5 to 7 or more, 1¾ in. across, rose or lilac; lip darker with a whitish disk, broadly ovate, entire, adhering to the column to half-way. W. Indies, Cent. America. 1887. (B.M. 3410.) SYN. *E. lamellatum, Isochilus elegans*.

**E. subpa'tens.** *fl.* 20 to 34; sep. and pet. green, narrow; lip cream with reflexed side lobes. Stems comparatively slender, 2 to 3 ft. h. Costa Rica. 1935. Remarkable for the length of the pendulous infl.

**E. syringothyr'sis.*** *fl.* dark purple, with a little orange and yellow on lip and column, densely 70- to 80-fld. in thyrse-like panicles. *l.* distichous, about 6 in. long, light green. Stems slender, 3 to 5 ft.h. Bolivia. 1866. Stove. (B.M. 6145.) Much resembles Lilac in form and colour.

**E. tampen'se.** *fl.* about 1¼ in. across, several on a slender scape; sep. and pet. yellowish-brown, cuneate-linear; lip white, with more or less confluent purple lines. *l.* linear, 6 in. long. *Pseudobulbs* small, ovoid. Florida. 1888.

**E. tibici'nis.** A synonym of *Schomburgkia tibicinis*.

**E. tovaren'se.** *fl.* milk-white; sep. and pet. linear-spatulate; side lobes of lip almost quadrate, mid-lobe emarginate; peduncle 6 to 8 in. long, few-fld. *l.* oval-oblong, 4 to 5 in. long. Stems erect, 9 to 12 in. h., as thick as the little finger. Tovar, Venezuela. 1850.

*Epidendrum spectabile* (p. 754)

**E. trachychi'lum.** *fl.* very leathery, in a dense, much-branched panicle; sep. and pet. olive-brown, sep. oblong, spreading; pet. somewhat conformed; lip deep yellow, studded with red warts, white and spotted pink on callus, brilliant green with red warts on lower lobes. *l.* straight, ensiform, much shorter than scape. *Pseudobulbs* elongated, 2-leaved. Mexico. 1885. (G.F. 1885, 1205.)

**E. tri'color.** *fl.* clear yellow, small, numerous, with a cucumber-like odour. *l.* 4 in. long. *Pseudobulbs* about 5 in. h. Venezuela. 1893. Allied to *E. purum*.

**E. tri'dens.** A synonym of *E. nocturnum*.

**E. umbella'tum.** A synonym of *E. difforme*.

**E. Uroskin'neri.** A synonym of *E. prismatocarpum*.

**E. Vanneria'num.** *fl.* rosy-purple, similar to those of *E. Lindleyanum*, with a small whitish disk on the lip; lip rounded, acute, much like that of *E. Skinneri*. 1885. A fine plant intermediate in character between the species named. Probably not now in cultivation.

**E. variega'tum.** *fl.* fragrant about 1 in. across; sep. and pet. pale yellow, or yellowish-green blotched with purplish-brown; lip rose or white spotted rose, very short, cordate, acute; racemes longer than l., many-fld. *l.* oblong-lanceolate, 6 to 9 in. long. *Pseudobulbs* fusiform, 6 to 9 in. h., 2- or 3-leaved. S. America, &c. 1832. (B.M. 3151; B.R. 25, 11.) var. **coria'ceum** is spotted reddish-brown, lip paler than sep. and pet., *l.* broader, shorter and more leathery, stems shorter and thicker than in type. (B.M. 3595 as *E. coriaceum*.)

**E. veno'sum.** *fl.* 4 or 5, nearly 2 in. across; sep. and pet. light green; lip snow-white, with dark purplish lines on side lobes. *Pseudobulbs* fusiform. *l.* narrow. Mexico. Before 1855. SYN. *E. Wendlandianum*. Cool-house.

**E. verruco'sum.*** *infl.* simple but usually assuming a diffused paniculate shape. *fl.* often over 100, about ½ in. across; sep. and pet. creamy-white, light yellow or greenish; lip yellow, longer than the sep.; mid-lobe deeply cleft. Stems 1 to 5 ft. h. *l.* lanceolate, 2½ to 5 in. long, l.-sheaths minutely warted or smooth. Jamaica. 1825. (L.B.C. 1084.) A fine species.

**E. vesica'tum.** *fl.* small, about 4, greenish to greenish-white. *l.* glaucous green, thick, sharply folded inwards at the midrib, almost amplexicaul, the lower scale-like, gradually larger above, the upper pair 2 to 4 in. long, ¾ to 1½ in. wide, forming a cup in which the fl. are set. Stems 6 to 10 in. long, ascending or pendulous. Brazil. 1838. (J.R.H.S. 33, 387.) A curious but not showy species.

**E. viola'ceum.** A synonym of *Cattleya Loddigesii*.

**E. viscid'um.** A synonym of *E. ciliare*.

**E. vitelli'num.*** *fl.* bright orange-red, about 2 in. across, lip small, bright yellow; spike erect, 10- to 30-fld., sometimes branched. Autumn. *Pseudobulbs* ovoid, 1 to 3 in. h., 2-phyllous. *l.* 6 to 9 in. long, glaucous. Mexico. 1840. (B.M. 4107; B.R. 26, 35; L. 196.) Cool-house. var. **flore ple'no** has regular *fl.* with 12 segs. 1890; **gigan'teum,** *see* var. **majus; ma'jus,*** *fl.* segs. broader than in type, sep. and pet. bright cinnabar-orange, lip and column yellow. Spring. *infl.* from matured pseudobulb, often branched. (W.O.A. 4.)

**E. Wallis'ii.*** *fl.* 2 to 5, about 1½ to 2 in. across, scented; sep. and pet. golden-yellow, spotted carmine-crimson, ligulate-oblong; lip white, with radiating, tubercled lines of magenta-purple, broad, cuneately flabellate; racemes short. October, November. *l.* distichous. Stems 2 to 4 ft. h., spotted brownish-purple, leafy. Colombia. 1874. (W.O.A. 74; L. 341.) Cool or Odontoglossum house.

**E. Wendlandia'num.** A synonym of *E. venosum*.

**E. xanthi'num.*** *fl.* yellow, sometimes tinted orange, in a dense head, on a peduncle 1 ft. or more long; sep. and pet. acute; lip 3-lobed, fringed. *l.* oblong-lanceolate, 3 to 4 in. long. Stems 1½ to 3 ft. long, as thick as a goose-quill, leafy throughout. Minas Geraes. About 1839. (B.M. 7586.)

**E. xipheroi'des.** *fl.* 1½ in. across, few in a slender raceme; sep. and pet. green, with purple lines; lip broadly oblong; margins undulate, yellow, with a thick, white callus. *l.* linear, thick, 8 in. long, ½ in. wide. *Pseudobulbs* stout, 3 in. h., pear-shaped, 2-leaved. *l.* about 8 in. long, barely ½ in. wide. Brazil. 1896.

E. C.

**EPIDERMIS.** The superficial layer of cells covering almost all parts of plants, usually of one layer and without chlorophyll grains, but in some plants, natives as a rule of very leafy places, chlorophyll grains are present in the epidermis, as they are in the guard-cells of the stomata.

**EPIDIAC'RIUM.** FAM. *Orchidaceae*. Hybrids between species of Diacrium and Epidendrum.

**EPIGAE'A** (*epi*, upon, *gaea*, the earth; in allusion to its creeping growth). FAM. *Ericaceae*. A genus of 2 species of evergreen, creeping shrubs with 5-merous flowers, 10 stamens, 5-lobed stigma and 5-valved, loculicidal, mealy glutinous capsules; corolla tubular with more or less spreading limb, white or rosy. Requires open, lime-free, humous soil and shade from direct sunlight. Propagated from seed, cuttings, and layers. Allied to and resembling Orphanidesia (q.v. for points of distinction). **A**

**E. asiat'ica.*** Creeping, evergreen shrub with bristly, rooting stems; increases in height by superimposition of branches. More tolerant of cultivation than *E. repens*. *l.* ovate to oblong-ovate, pointed, cordate or abruptly tapering to base, ciliate, more or less bristly both sides, 1½ to 3 in. long, half as wide, rugose. *fl.* in short terminal and, more rarely, axillary racemes; cor. about ⅓ in. across, 5-lobed, rose-pink; cal. lobes ovate, acute, about half length of cor. April, May. Japan. About 1930. (B.M. 9222.)

**E. × Aurora** (*E. asiatica* × *E. repens*). Intermediate between parents. *l.* 1 to 2 in. long. *fl.* pink with more or less spreading lobes.

**E. re'pens.*** May flower; Trailing Arbutus. Prostrate, evergreen shrub with hairy, rooting stems. Requires more shade than *E. asiatica*. *l.* ovate, oblong-ovate or sub-orbicular, blunt or pointed, base rounded or sub-cordate, sparsely bristly on both sides or rarely almost smooth, ciliate, undulate, ¾ to 3 in. long, ½ to 2 in. wide. *fl.* in terminal, rarely axillary, racemose clusters; cor. white, pinkish or rosy, ½ to ⅝ in. across, 5-lobed, elusively fragrant; cal. lobes ovate to lanceolate, about one-third length of cor. tube. April, May. N. America, Newfoundland to Saskatchewan southwards to Michigan, Kentucky, and Florida. 1736. (L.B.C. 160.)

F. S.

*epigae'us -a -um,* growing close to the ground, growing on land not water.

**epigeal,** having the cotyledons raised above the ground-level on germination of the seed (cf. hypogeal in Supplement).

**epigynous,** growing upon the ovary; the sepals, petals, and stamens spring from above the ovary of the flower.

**EPILAE'LIA.** FAM. *Orchidaceae*. Hybrids between species of Epidendrum and Laelia.

*epili'thes,* of stony ground.

**EPILO'BIUM** (*epi*, upon, *lobos*, pod; the petals, &c., surmount the pod-like ovary). FAM. *Oenotheraceae*. A genus of about 60 species of perennial herbs or sub-shrubs, natives of cold and temperate climate. Leaves opposite or scattered irregularly. Flowers axillary, solitary, or in terminal spikes; calyx 4-parted, deciduous; petals 4, obovate or obcordate, erect or spreading, stamens 8, alternately long and short. Fruit a capsule with numerous seeds furnished with silky hairs by the aid of which they are distributed by winds. A few species are of horticultural value but most are apt to spread rapidly and become a nuisance, although often beautiful. This applies not only to the 2 handsome native species *E. angustifolium* and *E. hirsutum* but also to some of the dwarf species for the rock-garden. They thrive generally in any good garden soil. *E. angustifolium* is best restricted to open woodland in wild gardening and *E. hirsutum* to the margins of streams or lakes. Several small-flowered British species are apt to become weeds and though not very deep-rooting need care to eradicate them especially if they have been once allowed to seed. **A**

**E. alpi'num.** Perennial, stoloniferous, slightly hairy. Stem ascending, 3 to 9 in. h., slender, with 2 lines of hair. *l.* elliptic-oblong, $\frac{1}{2}$ to $\frac{2}{3}$ in. long. *fl.* rose-purple, about $\frac{1}{4}$ in. across, drooping. July. N. Hemisphere, including Britain. (E.B. 507.) var. **al'bum,** *fl.* white.

**E. alsinefo'lium.** Tufted, stoloniferous. Stem 4 to 12 in. long, ascending. *l.* ovate to ovate-lanceolate, 1 to 2 in. long, toothed, glabrous, shining. *fl.* few, bright rose-purple, $\frac{1}{3}$ in. across. July. N. Hemisphere, including Britain. (E.B. 505.) Rock-garden.

**E. angustifo'lium.*** French Willow; Rose-bay. Perennial of 3 to 6 ft., erect, scarcely branched. *l.* lanceolate, undulate, sessile, about 4 to 5 in. long. *fl.* rose in long terminal racemes. July. N. Hemisphere, including Britain. (E.B. 495.) var. **al'bum,** *fl.* white; a fine pale-pink form is also known.

**E. bre'vipes.** *l.* glossy, reddish, thick. *fl.* small, pinkish. N. Zealand. Rock-garden.

**E. Dodo'naei.*** Perennial, about 12 in. h., erect, branched at apex. *l.* linear, scarcely toothed, glossy. *fl.* large, deep rose, crowded near ends of branches. June to August. Europe. 1800. Rock or border plant. SYN. *E. Fleischeri, E. Halleri.*

**E. glabel'lum.** Erect perennial of 6 to 12 in. h. or decumbent. *l.* in scattered pairs, $\frac{1}{3}$ to $\frac{2}{3}$ in. long, oblong, ovate or lanceolate-oblong, bluntly toothed, sometimes glossy, sessile or almost so. *fl.* pink, $\frac{1}{6}$ to $\frac{1}{3}$ in. across in upper axils. July, August. New Zealand.

**E. hirsu'tum.** Codlins and Cream. Softly downy perennial, 3 to 5 ft. h., clammy. *Lower l.* opposite; *upper* alternate, ovate-lanceolate, hairy, half stem-clasping. *fl.* pale pink, large, in leafy corymbs. July. Europe, including Britain. Moist places. (E.B. 497.) var. **al'bum,** *fl.* white. Apt to spread.

*Epilobium latifolium*

**E. latifo'lium.** 8 to 16 in. h., branching from base. *l.* ovate-lanceolate, thickish, up to 2 in. long; sessile or almost so. *fl.* pink, about 2 in. across, in a short infl., pet. entire, bracts leafy. July. Siberia, NW. America.

**E. lu'teum.** Slender, about 12 in. h., glabrous below. *l.* ovate-lanceolate, 2 to 3 in. long, glandular-toothed. *fl.* pale yellow, about $1\frac{1}{4}$ in. across; pet. notched; infl. few-fld. July. Western N. America.

**E. macro'pus.** Aquatic species. *fl.* large. New Zealand.

**E. nummularifo'lium.** Prostrate perennial with branches 2 to 6 in. long, sometimes downy. *l.* many, opposite, orbicular or oblong, $\frac{1}{8}$ to $\frac{1}{3}$ in. long, blunt, sometimes convex; often sessile. *fl.* small, pink or whitish, on slender axillary peduncles, $\frac{1}{4}$ to 4 in. long. June to September. New Zealand. Invasive.

**E. obcordatum.*** Creeping, about 3 in. h., branches about 6 in. long. *l.* opposite, ovate, $\frac{1}{3}$ to $\frac{2}{3}$ in. long, glaucous, dull green. *fl.* large, bright rose-purple. June to August. Sierra Nevada, California. Rock-garden in sun, in well-drained deep sandy soil or moraine. Hardy but needing care in winter, best frequently propagated and kept in frame in winter.

**E. peduncula're.** Prostrate, small perennial. *l.* rather crowded. orbicular or oblong, $\frac{1}{8}$ to $\frac{1}{3}$ in. long, blunt, sometimes stalked. *fl.* pink or whitish, small; on slender axillary peduncles up to 4 in. long. New Zealand. Invasive.

**E. rosmarinifo'lium.*** Erect perennial up to 2 ft. h., branched near middle. *l.* linear, slightly toothed. *fl.* bright pink, crowded near ends of branches. June to September. Europe, including Britain. 1775. (E.B. 494.) Border or rock-garden.

**EPIME'DIUM** (name used by Dioscorides). FAM. *Berberidaceae.* A genus of about 20 species distributed over the North Temperate regions of the Old World. Herbs with creeping perennial rhizomes and annual stems. Leaves stalked, compound; leaflets usually spiny-toothed. Flowers regular; sepals 8, outer pairs unequal, inner 4 petaloid; petals 4, flat or forming pouches or spurs; stamens 4; ovary one-celled, ovules many. Fruit a capsule. Epimediums are ornamental hardy plants, tolerant of semi-shade and at their best in a compost of peat and loam in equal parts. Propagation by division in July or August. Useful plants for the rock and wild gardens.

**E. alpi'num.*** 6 to 9 in. h., with a long-creeping rhizome. *l.* 2-ternate; lflets. cordate-ovate, long-pointed, spinose. *fl.* 12 to 20 in a loose panicle; outer sep. greyish, speckled red; inner dark crimson; pet. yellow, slipper-shaped, $\frac{1}{6}$ in. long. S. and Cent. Europe, naturalized in Britain. 1597. (E.B. 52.) var. **ru'brum,** a synonym of *E.* × *rubrum.*

**E. col'chicum.** A synonym of *E. pinnatum colchicum.*

**E. diphyl'lum.** *rhiz.* short. The dwarfest species, 4 to 8 in. h. *lflets.* 2, cordate-ovate, stalk 2 to 3 in. long. *fl.* many, small, white; peduncles with 4 to 6 drooping fl. in a very loose panicle; pet. not spurred, $\frac{1}{4}$ in. long. April, May. Japan. 1830. (B.M. 3448; L.B.C. 1858.) SYN. *Aceranthus diphyllus.*

**E. grandiflo'rum.*** 8 to 15 in. h. *rhiz.* long, $\frac{1}{5}$ in. thick. *l.* 2- or 3-ternate, about 1 ft. long; lflets. cordate-ovate, 2 to 3 in. long, acute, margins spiny-toothed. *fl.* white, pale yellow, deep rose to violet, in a short, close 6 to 16-fld. raceme; spur of pet. deflexed, $\frac{1}{2}$ in. long. Early spring to summer. Japan, Manchuria. 1830. (B.R. 1906 as *E. macranthum.*) One of the finest species. var. **Rose Queen,** *l.* crimson carmine, spurs tipped white; **viola'ceum,** rather dwarfer, *fl.* with light violet pet. scarcely longer than inner sep. (B.M. 3751 as *E. violaceum.*)

**E. hexan'drum.** A synonym of *Vancouveria hexandra.*

**E. macran'thum.** A synonym of *E. grandiflorum.*

**E. Musschia'num.** A synonym of *E.* × *Youngianum.*

**E.** × **perralchicum.** A group of plants varying between *E. pinnatum colchicum* and *E. Perralderianum* among which they arose at Wisley.

**E. Perralderia'num.** *rhiz.* creeping. *lflets.* 3, cordate-ovate, 2 to 3 in. long, bright green or tinted red-brown, spinose. *fl.* bright yellow, $\frac{3}{5}$ to 1 in. across when expanded, in a simple loose raceme about as long as the peduncle, 12- to 25-fld.; outer sep. minute, oblong, deciduous; inner obovate, spreading horizontally; pet. small, blade bright yellow, erect, toothed, spur brown, ligulate, bent upwards and nearly as long. Algeria. 1867. (B.M. 6509.)

**E. pinna'tum.*** 8 to 12 in. h. *rhiz.* long. *l.* all radical, 12 to 18 in. long, 2-ternate (lflets. sometimes 5 to 11), hairy at first; lflets. ovate, acute, spinose-toothed, stalked. *fl.* bright yellow; pet. very small with very short brownish-purple spurs; racemes 6 in. long, loose, 12- to 30-fld.; peduncles about 6 in. long. Summer. Persia. 1849. var. **col'chicum,** 10 to 16 in. h., *l.* 3- to 5-foliolate, larger and less spinose than in type, often evergreen, *fl.* yellow, spur brown or yellow, $\frac{1}{12}$ in. long. Transcaucasia, Georgia. (B.M. 4456 as *E. pinnatum.*) SYN. *E. colchicum.*

**E. pubig'erum.** 3 to 30 in. h. *rhiz.* short and thick. *l.* usually 2-ternate; lflets. ovate to roundish, cordate at base, somewhat spinose, hairy beneath; flowering-stem with one 2-ternate *l.* *fl.* pale yellow ⅓ to ½ in. across; inner sep. pale rose or white, ⅜ in. long; inner pet. shorter, slipper-like; racemes 12 to 30-fld. May. Transcaucasia, Balkans, Asia Minor. 1887. (H.I.P. 3116.)

**E. × ru'brum\*** (probably *E. alpinum × E. grandiflorum*). *rhiz.* long, thin. Habit of *E. alpinum* but more robust. *l.* varying from 2-ternate to almost 3-ternate; lflets. up to 20, often tinged red when young. *fl.* ⅔ to 1 in. across, in a loose 20- to 30-fld. panicle; outer sep. greyish, oblong, soon falling; inner bright crimson, oblong-lanceolate, convex at back, spreading horizontally in the open fl.; pet. pale yellow or tinted red with a small but distinct blade. Origin? 1854. (B.M. 5671 as *E. alpinum rubrum.*)

**E. sagitta'tum.** 10 to 20 in. h. *rhiz.* short. *l.* 3-foliolate or rarely 2-ternate, 1½ to 2 ft. long; lflets. cordate-ovate or hastate, very firm, 2 to 6 in. long, sometimes densely hairy beneath, margin fringed with horny teeth; stalks 12 in. long; stem-l. 2, 3-foliolate. *fl.* many, ⅓ in. across; inner sep. white; pet. brownish-yellow. China. 1856. Syn. *E. sinense.*

**E. sinen'se.** A synonym of *E. sagittatum.*

**E. × versico'lor** (*E. grandiflorum × E. pinnatum colchicum*). *l.* red when young, usually 2-ternate but varying to 3-ternate or 5- or 3-foliolate, spiny-toothed. *fl.* similar to those of *E. grandiflorum,* ⅓ in. across; inner sep. old rose; pet. yellow, with red-tinged spurs; racemes 10- to 20-fld. var. **neosulphu'reum,** like var. *sulphureum* but usually with 3 lflets., *l.* brownish when young, and spurs slightly shorter than inner sep. Wisley; **sulphu'reum,** stem often leafy, *fl.* pale yellow, pendulous, spur longer than in *E. pinnatum.* (G.F. 86, 53.) Syn. *E. ochroleucum, E. sulphureum.*

**E. × warleyen'se** (probably *E. alpinum × E. pinnatum colchicum*). 8 to 22 in. h. *rhiz.* long. Stem leafless or with 1 l. *l.* 9- or 5- (rarely 3-) foliate, green when young; lflets. cordate, spiny-toothed, finely hairy beneath. *fl.* ⅔ in. across; outer sep. coppery-red; pet. shorter than sep., yellow, with blunt, sometimes red-streaked spurs; in 10- to 30-fld. racemes. April, May. Warley Garden.

*Epimedium × Youngianum*

**E. × Youngia'num\*** (probably *E. diphyllum × E. grandiflorum*). 6 to 12 in. h. lflets. 9. *fl.* white, tinged greenish, ⅜ to ½ in. across, few, bell-shaped, nodding; pet. spurless or with a short slender spur. April. Japan? (B.M. 3745 as *E. Musschianum.*) var. **niv'eum,** lflets. 2, 3, 6, or 9 on the same plant, habit compact, about 6 in. h., *fl.* white, with or without spurs on the same plant. May, June. (G.F. 86, p. 53 as *E. Musschianum.*) Syn. *E. niveum, E. macranthum niveum;* **ro'seum,** 4 to 12 in. h., *l.* 2-, 6-, or 7-foliolate, *fl.* purplish-mauve, racemes 4- to 12-fld. Syn. *E. lilacinum, E. roseum.*

**EPIPAC'TIS** (name of a plant mentioned by Dioscorides). Fam. *Orchidaceae.* A small genus of terrestrial orchids natives of Europe, N. America, and temperate Asia, hardy in England. Flowers purple, brown, or white in a loose raceme; petals and sepals spreading or connivent; lip contracted in the middle, mid-lobe broad with two basal tubercles. Pollen masses 2. Stem-leaf, root-stock creeping. Plants for shady woods in friable loam, not objecting to lime. *E. palustris* grows in boggy places. Not difficult to cultivate; propagated by division.

**E. atroru'bens.** *fl.* reddish-brown; front of lip broader than long, somewhat cuspidate. June, July. *Lower l.* 1½ to 2 in. long, 1 in. wide, ovate, acute. 18 in. h. (E.B. 1481.)

**E. falcata.** A synonym of *Cephalanthera falcata.*

**E. gigan'tea.** *fl.* sep. yellowish- or greenish-brown; pet. and lip striped red; raceme lax, pubescent. *Lower l.* oval; *upper* ensiform. N. America, Mexico. (B.M. 7690.)

**E. latifo'lia.** *fl.* greenish variously marked with yellow, white, or purple; front of lip broader than long, somewhat pointed. July, August. *Lower l.* 4 to 5 in. long, 2 to 3 in. wide. 2 to 3 ft. h. Stem not tufted. (L.B.C. 982; E.B. 1480.) A form devoid of chlorophyll has occurred wild.

**E. palus'tris.** *fl.* whitish, tinged with crimson, slightly drooping, few, in a loose ovate spike. July. *l.* lanceolate, stem-clasping. About 12 in. h. Europe (Britain), Siberia. (E.B. 1482; L.B.C. 156.)

**E. purpura'ta.** *fl.* more or less violet-purple; front of lip as broad as long. July, August. *Lower l.* 3 to 4 in. long, 1½ to 2 in. wide. 2 to 3 ft. h. Stem more or less tufted. (E.B. supp. 2775.)

**epipetalous,** growing on petals, usually used concerning stamens.

**EPIPHRONI'TIS.** Fam. *Orchidaceae.* Hybrids between species of Sophronitis and Epidendrum.

**epiphyllous,** growing upon a leaf.

**EPIPHYL'LUM** (*epi,* upon, *phyllos,* a leaf, as it was supposed that the flowers were borne on leaves, really flattened stems). Fam. *Cactaceae.* There has been some confusion in the application of this name, which is the correct one for the plants previously called Phyllocacti; the species heretofore known as Epiphyllum are now under Zygocactus and Schlumbergera. Plants usually epiphytic; branches flattened and leaf-like, sometimes 3-angled; areoles are very small, borne along the margins in the crenations; spines generally wanting in adult plants but freely produced in young seedlings. Flowers usually very large and showy, generally diurnal, some species nocturnal; flower tube long. Fruit round or oblong, red or purple, eventually splitting to expose the pulpy interior; sometimes edible. About 16 species are

*Epiphyllum Ackermannii* (p. 758)

recognized but a number of hybrids are in cultivation. These plants are easily grown but, like most of the epiphytic cacti, they require more water and a richer soil than the desert types (*see* **Cactus**). They are propagated by cuttings which root easily, or by seeds.　　　**A**

**E. Ackerman'nii.\*** Stems weak, flat and thin with crenate margins; a few weak spines especially on young growths. *fl.* very large, crimson. Possibly Mexico but it is now thought probable that the plant is of hybrid origin; it is the parent of many hybrids. (B.R. 1331; B.M. 3598, as *Cereus Ackermannii*.) SYN. *Phyllocactus Ackermannii*.

**E. angu'liger.** Branches flattened, rather fleshy, with deeply toothed margins; areoles small. *fl.* white. Mexico. (B.M. 5100.) SYN. *Phyllocactus anguliger*.

**E. crena'tum.** Stems glaucous, flat and broad, with large deep crenations, midrib thick, often rooting from tip. *fl.* large, cream to yellow, very fragrant, remaining open several days. Honduras, Guatemala. (B.R. 30, 31.) SYN. *Phyllocactus crenatus*. The parent of many hybrids.

**E. Gaert'neri.** A synonym of *Schlumbergera Gaertneri*.

**E. Hook'eri.** Stems long, broad but rather thin, crenate, pale green. *fl.* white with a very slender tube, not scented. Tobago, Trinidad, Venezuela. (B.M. 2692; B.R.C. 4, t. 19.) SYN. *Phyllocactus Hookeri*.

**E. oxypet'alum.\*** Plants much branched; stems flat, thin and broad, crenate. *fl.* opening in the evening, fragrant, white with reddish outer perianth l. Mexico, Guatemala, Venezuela, Brazil. (B.M. 3813.) SYN. *Phyllocactus oxypetalus*, *P. grandis*, *P. latifrons*.

**E. Phyllan'thus.** Stems flat or 3-angled, thin, bright green with a purple margin, crenate. *fl.* slender, white, perhaps nocturnal. Panama, Bolivia, Peru, Brazil. (B.R.C. 4, f. 194–5.) SYN. *Phyllocactus Phyllanthus*.

**E. trunca'tum.** A synonym of *Zygocactus truncatus*.

V. H.

**EPIPHYTE** (*epi*, upon, *phyton*, a plant). A plant growing upon another but deriving no nourishment from it. Many lichens, mosses, and ferns provide examples in temperate regions, and in the warmer parts of the world, in addition, many species of Orchidaceae, Bromeliaceae and Araceae, Gentianaceae, some Cacti and Rhododendrons, &c., are epiphytic. (*Cf.* **Parasitic plant.**) Many of these have roots of a peculiar structure enabling them to condense and absorb moisture from the atmosphere, or leaf structures preventing dangerous loss of water. Their peculiar powers and habit of growth have earned for several the name of Air Plant. They are naturally most abundant where the atmosphere is humid and the temperature uniformly high, as in luxuriant tropical forests.

*epiphyt'icus -a -um,* growing upon a plant, but not a parasite.

**EPIPREM'NUM** (*epi*, upon, *premnon*, trunk; epiphytes on tree trunks). FAM. *Araceae*. A genus of about 8 species of climbing plants, natives of Malaya and the Pacific Is. Leaves ovate, ovate-cordate, or lanceolate, often large, entire or pinnatifid; stalk sheathing at base. Spathe thick, boat-shaped; spadix included, thick, cylindrical, dense-flowered. Needing stove conditions and general treatment as for Monstera.　　　**A**

**E. gigan'teum.** Tall climber to 90 ft. *l.-stalk* up to 2 ft. long, bent at junction with oblong or long-oblong, thick, leathery, obtuse, cordate blade 1 to 2 ft. long. *Spathe* sub-cylindric, shortly cuspidate, 6 to 12 in. long, green or purple, yellow within. SW. Malaya, Siam.

**E. mirab'ile.** Tonga Plant. Climber. *l.* pinnatisect, large, dark green. *infl.* large, resembling those of Monstera. Fiji. The l. in young plants are small and entire.

**EPIS'CIA** (*episkios*, shaded; from their natural habitat). FAM. *Gesneriaceae*. A genus of about 30 species of herbaceous perennials, natives of Trop. America, many of them with very beautiful foliage, related to Cyrtandra, Columnea, &c. Leaves opposite, stalked. Flowers often showy, axillary, solitary or in small cymes; calyx 5-parted, segments some toothed; corolla tube funnel-shaped with 5 rounded, spreading lobes. The species like *E. chontalensis, E. cupreata, E. fulgida* make very beautiful basket plants or may be grown as pyramids or mounds in warm

houses. With care they may be grown in moss and if a soil compost is used it must contain plenty of sand, small crocks and nodules of charcoal, with ample drainage. Cuttings may be rooted in sand under a close frame. For general cultivation, *see* **Gesneria**. Several species at one time included will be found under Nautilocalyx.　　　**A**

**E. bi'color.** Procumbent, 3 in. h. *l.* large, hairy, ovate-cordate, somewhat glossy, coarsely nerved; stalks short, hairy. *fl.* white, spotted within and bordered purple, tube rather short; peduncles slender, hairy. Colombia. (B.M. 4390.)

**E. bracts'cens.** A synonym of *Nautilocalyx bracteatus*.

**E. chontalen'sis.\*** About 6 in. h. *l.* ovate to ovate-oblong, acute, sub-cordate at base, light green above, pale purple beneath. *fl.* whitish or pale lilac with yellow centre, about 2 in. across, tube whitish; solitary in l.-axils. November, December. Nicaragua. 1867. (B.M. 5925.)

**E. cilio'sa.** Prostrate and rooting. *l.* about 12 in. long. *fl.* clustered in l.-axils; cal. lobes awl-shaped, purple; cor. 1 in. long, yellowish, somewhat bell-shaped. Trop. America.

**E. cuprea'ta.\*** Creeping, downy, about 6 in. h. *l.* elliptic, toothed, wrinkled, with a broad band of red and silver down middle. *fl.* scarlet, solitary; cal. spotted within; cor. lobes toothed, ciliate. Colombia. 1846. var. **metal'lica**, *fl.* orange-scarlet. 1869; **viridifo'lia**, *fl.* much larger than in type, *l.* green. 1860. (B.M. 5192 as *Cyrtodeira cupreata*.)

**E. den'sa.** Stem short. *l.* few, crowded, ovate-oblong, 6 to 10 in. long, bright blood-red beneath; stalks stout, 3 to 4 in. long. *fl.* pale straw-coloured, clustered, in very short racemes; cor. tube 2 in. long, hairy, lobes short. Guiana. 1895. (B.M. 7481.)

**E. erythro'pus.** Stem short, stout. *l.* oblanceolate, teeth irregular, bright green above, reddish beneath; stalk and midrib stout, and like the arched nerves, blood-red. *fl.* pale flesh-colour, spotted orange-purple in the yellow throat and tube; cor. lobes rounded; peduncles clustered in l.-axils, slender, 1 to 2 in. long. Colombia. 1874. (B.M. 6219.)

**E. ful'gida.\*** About 6 in. h. *l.* 3 to 5 in. long, elliptic or elliptic-ovate, acute, with roundish teeth, wrinkled, dark emerald-green, paler along midrib, inclined to coppery. *fl.* vermilion, about 2 in. long, 1 in. across, hairy, tube nearly straight; solitary in l.-axils; peduncles stout, 1 to 2 in. long. July. Colombia. 1873. (B.M. 6136.)

**E. glab'ra.** A synonym of *Paradrymonia glabra*.

**E. Lucia'ni.** Stem thick. *l.* ovate, fleshy, deep green above with paler nerves, reddish beneath; stalk short. *fl.* pale scarlet, reddish, hairy without, salver-shaped, tube wide, straight, narrowed above, lobes rounded; sep. linear-lanceolate, as long as tube; in clusters in l.-axils. Colombia. 1876. (I.H. 1876, 236.)

**E. macula'ta.** Trailing. Stem fleshy. *l.* ovate, 3 to 6 in. long, somewhat recurved, paler beneath. *fl.* yellow, spotted brown, 2 in. long, one lobed folder over tube as though to form a lid; in axillary dense cymes. September. British Guiana. 1890. (B.M. 7131.)

**E. melittifo'lia.** Erect, about 1 ft. h. *l.* large, nearly elliptic, acute, coarsely doubly rounded-toothed, dark green, glossy, wrinkled above, pale beneath. *fl.* crimson, tube curved downwards, base spurred, lobes spreading, rounded; peduncles usually few-fld. April, May. Dominica, Brazil. 1853. (B.M. 4720.)

**E. pic'ta.** A synonym of *Nautilocalyx pictus*.

**E. puncta'ta.** Creeping, hairy, fleshy. *fl.* yellow with many purple dots, rather large, solitary. Guatemala. 1843. (B.M. 4089 as *Drymonia punctata*.)

**E. tessella'ta.** A synonym of *Nautilocalyx bullatus*.

**E. villos'a.** A synonym of *Nautilocalyx villosus*.

*Episcopi,* in honour of Bishop Hannington of Uganda.

**EPISTEPH'IUM** (*epi*, upon, *stephas*, a crown; at the base of the perianth there is a small-toothed calyculus). FAM. *Orchidaceae*. A genus of half a dozen species of beautiful terrestrial Orchids, allied to Sobralia, natives of southern Trop. America. The flowers are in terminal racemes, seldom axillary. The sepals and petals are sub-similar. The lip is shortly clawed at base, then spreading, its base often partially enclosing the column base. The foliage is not plicate as in Sobralias but of thicker texture, leathery in some, often ribbed and veined. Roots fleshy, fibrous, underground. The only species introduced thrives in good fibrous loam and sand; perfect drainage and copious supplies of water are essential elements in its cultivation. Propagated by division.

**E. Williams'ii.** *fl.* 6 to 8, bright reddish-purple, large; sep. 1 in. or more longer and slightly narrcwer than pet., lip shape not unlike that of *Cattleya labiata*, 1 in. or more wide and long, with a whitish disk and yellow hairy crest, front margin deeply 2-fid, often deep mauve; spike terminal 6- to 8-fld. *l.* very dark, shining. Stem about 1 ft. h. Bahia. 1864. (B.M. 5845.)

E. C.

**EPITHELAN'THA** (*epi*, upon, *thele*, nipple, *anthos*, flower; flowers are borne on tubercles). FAM. *Cactaceae*. A genus of a single species of very small round plants, solitary or in clusters; tubercles small and low, in spiral rows; areoles with numerous stiff white spines lying close to the plant, those on the young areoles covering the crown of the plant. Flowers from the tips of young tubercles (in Mammillaria, they are borne in the axils of the tubercles), very small, pale pink. Fruit club-shaped, red, projecting from the woolly crown when ripe, which takes a year. For cultivation *see* **Cactus** (terrestrial).

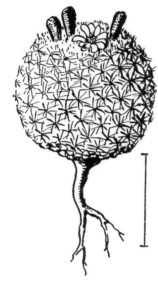

*Epithelantha micromeris*

**E. microme'ris.*** Texas and Mexico. (B.R.C. 3, f. 102.) SYN. *Mammillaria micromeris*. Very attractive plants but they grow very slowly. var. **Greg'gii** is larger but does not appear to differ in any other way.

V. H.

**Epithym'um,** parasitic on thyme.

**Epresmesnilia'nus -a -um,** in honour of Count Eprésmesnil.

**equa'lis -is -e,** equal.

**eques'tris -is -e,** pertaining to the horse or like the rider of a horse.

**equi'nus -a -um,** of horses.

**EQUISETA'CEAE.** A family allied to ferns and lycopods but belonging to a distinct class with only one surviving genus, Equisetum (q.v.).

**EQUISE'TUM** (*equus*, a horse, *seta*, a hair). Horsetail. FAM. *Equisetaceae*. The only genus in the family at the present day numbering about 24 species most numerous in temperate northern regions but also found in the tropics where some species reach a large size. Allied to the ferns. The rootstock is generally a creeping rhizome; stems erect, hollow, grooved, jointed with a sheath at each joint, often with whorls of branches at the joints. Spores all alike in sporangia on lower surface of peltate, whorled leaves in a cone-like spike terminal on the main stem as a rule, but occasionally on lateral branches. In *E. arvense* the fertile branches appear before the barren in early spring and have no chlorophyll. The spores germinate on the surface of the ground, producing prothallia which bear either antheridia or archegonia (rarely both) and the latter bear the young plants. Equisetums all grow in moist soil and sometimes cover large areas.

*E. arvense* is a persistent weed where the water table is rather high, only to be kept in check by continual hoeing, or by spraying thoroughly when in full growth with sodium chlorate (8 oz. to 1 gallon water). A few species are ornamental and worth growing in wet, rather shady spots, but *E. limosum* and *E. palustre* have no beauty to recommend them and should be introduced to pond margins, &c., with diffidence.

The dry stems of *E. arvense*, *E. hyemale*, and *E. sylvaticum* are used for polishing wood and metal, owing their value for this to the silicon deposited in the cell walls. *E. hyemale* is the Dutch Rush.

**E. max'imum.** Sterile stems 3 to 6 ft. h., 20- to 40-grooved, branches 4-angled, whorled, sub-erect, sheaths very short. Fertile stems about 1 ft. h. with large close loose sheaths; teeth 2-ribbed. Cones 2 to 3 in. long. N. Hemisphere, including Britain. (E.B. 1888.) SYN. *E. Telmateia*. A fine plant for damp shady places.

**E. scorpioi'des.** Forming a dense turf. Stems about 6 in. long, usually unbranched, bright green; sheaths shortly tubular, black or with black rim. N. Europe, Asia, America.

**E. sylvat'icum.** Stems 1 to 2 ft. h. nearly smooth, 10- to 18-grooved, branches divided, recurved; stem-sheaths lax, teeth long, obtuse; teeth of branch sheaths 3-ribbed at tip. Cones ¾ to 1 in. long. N. Hemisphere, including Britain. (E.B. 1891.)

**E. Telmate'ia.** A synonym of *E. maximum*.

**equitant,** having the base of the leaf folded so as to enclose the opposite leaf next above it, and that in its turn in the same state, as leaves of Iris.

**ERAGROS'TIS** (*eros*, love, *agrostis*, grass). Love Grass. FAM. *Gramineae*. A genus of about 100 species of mostly annual grasses with spreading panicles of small several-flowered, compressed spikelets occurring in the warm and temperate regions of the world. The light spreading inflorescences are useful for the border, and for winter decoration if gathered before they are too old. For treatment, &c., see **Briza**.

**E. abessin'ica.** Similar to *E. pilosa* but up to 3 ft. h., branches of panicle more spreading, fruit somewhat larger. The Teff of Abyssinia, where the seeds are used for bread.

**E. abyssin'ica.** A synonym of *E. abessinica*.

**E. aegyp'tica.** Bluish-green, strong-growing annual about 18 in. h. *l.* ⅛ in. wide, rough above, sheath smooth, ligule of long hairs. *Panicle* up to 10 in. long, broad, with 2 or 3 basal branches, branches rather stiff; spikelets mostly green. August. NE. Africa.

**E. ama'bilis.** Erect or spreading annual, 1 to 2 ft. h. *Panicle* small, 4 to 6 in. long, oblong, rather compact; spikelets purple, about ¼ in. long. August. India. SYN. *E. plumosa*.

**E. el'egans.** A synonym of *E. interrupta*.

**E. grandiflo'ra.** Perennial, about 3 ft. h. *l.* 12 to 16 in. long, about ⅛ in. wide, narrowed to a fine point, rough above and on margin, sheath smooth, hairy at mouth. *Panicle* large, branches slender, 5 or 6 in. long; spikelets 10- to 20-fld., about ¾ in. long. Texas. 1894.

**E. interrupt'a.** Erect annual, 1 to 2 ft. h. *Panicle* many-flowered, about 12 in. long, rather narrow, branches ascending. Brazil. SYN. *E. elegans.*

**E. max'ima.** Erect annual, strong-growing, 2 to 3 ft. h. *l.* rather broad, cordate at base. *Panicle* about 8 in. long and as wide, branches very slender, spreading; spikelets oblong, ⅓ to ½ in. long. Madagascar.

**E. namaquen'sis.** A synonym of *E. interrupta* or *E. pilosa*.

**E. obtu'sa.** Densely tufted perennial. Stems zigzag, wiry, 6 to 18 in. long, glabrous. *l.* linear, bristle-pointed, 2 to 5 in. long, glabrous or nearly so; ligule of short hairs. *Panicle* erect, ovoid to oblong, 2 to 4 in. long, rather lax, branches capillary; spikelets more or less nodding, broadly ovate-oblong, laterally compressed, whitish or grey, 8- to 20-fld. S. Africa. SYN. *Briza geniculata*.

**E. pappo'sa.** Perennial, tufted, glaucous, 6 in. to 2 ft. h. *l.* rolled inwards, rigid, rather sharp-pointed, sheath glabrous with clusters of hairs at base. *Panicle* 4 to 8 in. long, loose and spreading with very thin flexuous branches; spikelets long-stalked, 5- to 8-fld., 2 to 3 in. long, blackish-purple. S. Spain. SYN. *E. verticillata*.

**E. pectina'cea.** Perennial.

**E. pellu'cida.** A synonym of *E. pilosa*.

**E. pilo'sa.** Annual, tufted, 6 to 12 in. h. *l.* about ⅛ in. wide, ligule of white hairs. *Panicle* 5 to 6 in. long, oblong, finally very loose, broadly pyramidal, with branches (3 or 4 at base); spikelets about ¼ in. long, dark violet. August to October. All warm countries. SYN. *E. namaquensis, E. pellucida*.

**E. plumo'sa.** A synonym of *E. amabilis*.

**E. suaveo'lens.** Annual spreading, 1 to 2 ft. h., much like *E. abessinica* but with a less spreading *panicle* and more compact spikelets. W. Asia.

**ERAN'NIS aescular'ia.** See **March Moth.**     **A**

**ERAN'THEMUM** (*erranos*, lovely, *anthemon*, flower). FAM. *Acanthaceae*. A genus of about 15 species of erect shrubs or sub-shrubs, natives of SE. Asia. Leaves entire or nearly so. Flowers in bracteate spikes (or panicles); bracts usually longer than the deeply 5-cut calyx; corolla tube slender, curved, limb 5-lobed, lobes spreading, stamens 2, included, attached in throat. Fruit a few-seeded capsule. All the species mentioned below were placed in a genus Daedalacanthus and are frequently still so called. Most plants referred to as Eranthemum belong to Pseuderanthemum. Propagation by cuttings put in at any time from March to June; the young shoots root readily in peaty soil in a close frame with a bottom heat of 70° F. When rooted the cuttings should be potted singly into 3-in. pots in a compost of equal parts of leaf-mould, peat and loam, lightened by a little sand. In this with bottom heat they root and grow rapidly and should be potted on and stood near the glass to keep them from becoming drawn and to encourage free-flowering. They need abundance of water in warm weather. They should be cut back after flowering and potted into a size larger pot for flowering in the next year. A side shelf in the stove suits them. They are apt to be attacked by scale insects and constant attention should be given to reduce this attack. Several species become leggy with age and propagation should therefore be frequent and the young plants should be pinched to induce branching. Those grown for their ornamental foliage, indicated below, show it to the best advantage in young plants.

**E. Anderson'ii.** A synonym of *Pseuderanthemum acutissimum*.

**E. bi'color.** A synonym of *Pseuderanthemum asperum*.

**E. coccin'eum.** A synonym of *Odontonema strictum*.

**E. Coop'eri.** A synonym of *Pseuderanthemum sinuatum*.

**E. crenulat'um grandiflor'um.** A synonym of *Pseuderanthemum Parishii*.

**E. el'egans.** A synonym of *Pseuderanthemum acuminatissimum*.

**E. gracil'limum.** A synonym of *Pseuderanthemum malaccense*.

**E. ig'neum.** A synonym of *Xantheranthemum igneum*.

**E. macrophyl'lum.** About 3 ft. h. *l.* elliptic-lanceolate, slender-pointed, 5 to 9 in. long, sometimes toothed. *fl.* very pale blue, 1¼ in. long, ¾ in. wide, in long, narrow, interrupted spikes; bracts elliptic overlapping. Burma. (B.M. 6686 as *Daedalacanthus macrophyllus*.)

**E. nervo'sum.** A synonym of *E. pulchellum*.

**E. nigres'cens.** A synonym of *Pseuderanthemum atropurpureum*.

**E. ni'grum.** A synonym of *Pseuderanthemum atropurpureum*.

**E. pulchel'lum.*** Glabrous or nearly so. *l.* elliptic, narrowed to both ends, sometimes with rounded teeth. *fl.* dark blue, 1¼ in. long; cal. whitish; spikes 1 to 3 in. long, often in panicles; bracts ½ in. long, entire, elliptic. Winter. India. (B.M. 1358 as *Justicia nervosa*). SYN. *Daedalacanthus nervosus*, *D. pulchellum*.

**E. ro'seum.** *fl.* rose, 1 to 1½ in. long, in linear spikes, rarely loosely arranged, 5 to 6 in. long; bracts obovate, glandular-hairy, tips recurved. S. India. SYN. *Daedalacanthus roseus*.

**E. strict'um.** *fl.* blue, in linear, interrupted spikes forming a large, terminal panicle; bracts narrow, elliptic, obtuse. N. India. (B.M. 3068; B.R. 867.) SYN. *Daedalacanthus strictus*.

**E. Watt'ii.** Rather straggling when old. Related to *E. nervosum* but smaller. *fl.* deep rich purple in panicles. Autumn. N. India. (B.M. 8239; J.R.H.S. 27 (1902), ccxxix as *Daedalacanthus parvus*.) SYN. *Daedalacanthus Wattii*.

**ERAN'THIS** (*er*, spring, *anthos*, flower; from its early flowering). FAM. *Ranunculaceae*. Winter Aconite. About 7 species of dwarf herbaceous perennials with tuberous rootstocks and short-lived aerial organs. Stem short, leaves forming a rosette almost like a calyx beneath the flower; sepals petal-like, yellow; nectaries shorter than sepals as in Helleborus; carpels long-stalked. Fruit a many-seeded follicle. The winter aconites are best in woodland soil or among shrubs where they may be left undisturbed and will naturalize themselves. They so quickly lose their foliage that even among deciduous trees and shrubs they are in sunny places through all their green existence. Fresh plantings should be made in summer or early autumn for they succeed better then than if planting is delayed. Propagation is by division of the tubers or by seed which will germinate freely when shed around the old plants and which otherwise should be sown in the open as soon as ripe.

**E. cilic'ica.** Of similar habit to *E. hyemalis* but stouter in all parts with a shorter stem (about 2½ in. h.), stem-l. with more numerous lobes and carpels longer than stamens. February, March. Greece, Asia Minor to Syria. 1892.

**E. hyema'lis.*** About 4 in. h. *Basal l.* and *l.* on non-flowering plants stalked, roundish, 7-partite; *l.* on fl.-stem 5 to 8, broad-linear, rounded at tip. *fl.* solitary, sessile, bright yellow; sep. 5 to 8, oblong. February, March. W. Europe. (B.M. 3; E.B. 43.) Varying in size with the locality, small in dry, large in moist shady places.

**E. pinnatif'ida.** *Basal* and *involucral l.* pinnatifid. *fl.* stalked, white, carpels scarcely stalked. Japan.

**E. sibir'ica.** Habit of *E. hyemalis*, but sep. 5, oval. Capsule stalked, ovate-oblong, seed globose, slightly flattened. E. Siberia.

*Eranthis × Tubergenii*

**E. × Tubergeni** (*E. cilicica × E. hyemalis*). *fl.* larger than in *E. hyemalis*, shining golden yellow. *Involucral l.* intermediate between parents. Raised in Haarlem. 1923. (B.M. n.s. 196.)

**ERCIL'LA** (in honour of Don Alonso de Ercilla, 1533–95, of Madrid). FAM. *Phytolaccaceae*. A genus of 2 species of evergreen climbers, natives of Peru and Chile. Leaves stalked, alternate, entire, rather leathery and thick. Flowers small. *E. spicata* is a rapidly growing climber with aerial roots by which it clings to a wall like ivy. It is liable to be damaged by very severe winters but otherwise makes a good, though not especially beautiful, cover for a wall. Propagated by seed or by cuttings of young shoots taken in July and put in sand on a warm border.

**E. spica'ta.** Tall climber. *l.* roundish-ovate, about 2 in. long. *fl.* in dense sessile racemes, purplish. *fr.* a berry. Chile. 1840. SYN. *Bridgesia spicata*.

**ERDIS'IA** (in honour of E. C. Erdis, a member of the Yale University Peruvian Expedition, 1914). FAM. *Cactaceae*. Stems much branched at the base, partly subterranean; ribs few, areoles spiny; flowers small with a small tube. For cultivation *see under* **Cactus** (terrestrial).

**E. spiniflo'ra.** Underground stem slender, branches club-shaped, 6-ribbed, spines slender. *fl.* purple, about 2 in. long. Chile. SYN. *Cereus hypogaeus*, *Echinocereus clavatus*.

**E. squarro'sa.** Stems with 8 or 9 ribs, areoles fairly close, spines yellow, very unequal. *fl.* scarlet, borne towards ends of branches. Peru. (B.R.C. 2, f. 154–5.) SYN. *Cereus squarrosus*.

V. H.

**erecto-patent,** between upright and spreading.

***erec'tus -a -um,*** upright.

**ERE'MIA** (*eremos*, solitary; the cells of the fruit are 1-seeded). FAM. *Ericaceae*. A genus of about 30 species of much-branched, heath-like evergreen shrubs, natives of S. Africa, needing the same treatment as the tender species of Erica.

**E. Tot'ta.** About 2 ft. h. *l.* spreading, small, bristly. *fl.* small, red, clustered; cor. urn-shaped, lobes 4, small. June. 1812.

***e'remit,*** solitary.

**EREMOPH'ILA** (*eremos*, solitary, *philes*, to love; allusion doubtful). FAM. *Myoporaceae*. A genus of some 60 species of trees and shrubs, confined in a wild state to Australia. Leaves alternate; flowers axillary; calyx 5-parted or 5-lobed; corolla tubular at the base, constricted above the ovary, the limb oblique or 2-lipped and 5-lobed. Fruit a dry or succulent drupe, subtended by the calyx. Greenhouse. Propagated by cuttings.

**E. Brown'ii.** Evergreen shrub 8 to 15 ft., shoots, l. and fl. mostly downy. *l.* lanceolate, pointed, cuneate, $\frac{3}{4}$ to 2 in. long, rarely toothed. *fl.* solitary, axillary; cal. $\frac{3}{8}$ in. long, slenderly 5-lobed; cor. 1 in. long, mixed yellow or red or entirely one or the other, base tubular with a limb of 4 short, erect lobes and 1 much larger and decurved. April, June. Australia. 1803. (B.M. 1942 as *Stenochilus glaber*; 2930 as *S. viscosus*.)

**E. macula'ta.** Evergreen shrub, 4 to 8 ft., shoots rigid, downy. *l.* erect, lanceolate, linear, or oblanceolate, $\frac{3}{4}$ to $1\frac{1}{4}$ in. long, entire, nearly sessile, downy when young. *fl.* solitary, axillary; cal. segs. pointed, $\frac{1}{8}$ in. long; cor. 1 to $1\frac{1}{2}$ in. long, red, spotted yellow, hairy inside, 4 upper lobes erect, short, lower one strap-shaped, $\frac{1}{2}$ in. long, rolled inwards; fl.-stalk very slender, curved, $\frac{3}{4}$ in. long. Australia. (B.R. 647 as *Stenochilus maculatus*.)

**E. Mitchel'li.** Tall shrub or tree, 10 to 30 ft., aromatic. *l.* linear-lanceolate, entire, 1 to 2 in. long, $\frac{1}{8}$ to $\frac{1}{6}$ in. wide, tapered to a hooked point, glabrous. *fl.* white or purplish, solitary or in pairs; cal. lobes oblong; cor. woolly inside, $\frac{3}{4}$ in. long, with 5 rounded lobes, the lower one the largest and slightly reflexed. Australia.

W. J. B.

**EREMOSTACH'YS** (*eremos*, solitary, *stachys*, spike; from the nearly simple stems). FAM. *Labiatae*. A genus of about 50 species of perennial herbs, natives of W. and Cent. Asia. Leaves pinnate or pinnatifid. Calyx 5-toothed; corolla tube included, upper lip long, hooded, somewhat compressed, narrowed at base. *E. laciniata* is an easily grown hardy perennial.

**E. lacinia'ta.** Stem nearly simple, 12 to 18 in. h. *l.* pinnatisect; segs. lanceolate or linear, deeply pinnatifid; radical l. 6 in. long. *fl.* yellow, in whorls of 10 to 20, upper whorls close. July. Levant. 1731. (B.R. 31, 52.) var. **nu'da,** plant glabrous.

**E. super'ba.** About 2 ft. h., erect, unbranched. *l.* in a basal rosette, pinnatisect, the segs. lobed. *fl.* deep primrose, in woolly heads 6 in. long, 4 in. wide, showy. Summer. W. Himalaya.

**EREMU'RUS** (*eremos*, solitary, *oura*, tail; referring to the flower-spike). FAM. *Liliaceae*. A genus of about 30 species of stately herbaceous perennials with short, frequently thick rootstocks, natives of the steppes of W. and Cent. Asia, particularly Persia and Turkestan. Leaves radical, linear, long. Scape naked, with a long, often very long, unbranched, densely flowered raceme of white or yellow flowers sometimes tinged rose. Flowers of narrow spreading segments somewhat joined at base. These magnificent plants are all fairly hardy but are apt to be damaged by spring frosts followed by warm sun and cutting winds; protection by a covering of dry leaves or bracken at this season is a wise measure. A thoroughly drained, very rich, light sandy loam is the best soil for them; they do not succeed in close, damp soils in which their fleshy roots cannot run freely, nor do they do well in shade. A warm sunny position protected from wind should be given them as far as possible. They are best planted in August or September, and in lifting them great care should be taken that the long roots, which are very brittle, are not injured. The tuber and its roots should be buried about 6 in. deep, the tuber resting upon and surrounded by coarse sand. They should be left in the same position for 2 or 3 years, giving each spring a good mulch of well-decayed manure, which, however, should not be allowed to cover the crown of the plant lest damping-off should occur. Seedlings take about 6 years to attain flowering size, but the crowns split in 2 or 3 if growth is vigorous, as it should be if these directions are followed, and these can be carefully separated when the leaves have died down and thus afford a means of increase. Some of the species are variable and hybrids have been raised, some of them having been given names of Latin form, and these are unlikely to come true. Mr. Beamish, whose experience as given in *Flora and Sylva* is epitomized above, suggests planting with a background of conifers whose dark-green foliage makes an excellent foil for the fine spikes of such species of *E. himalaicus* and *E. robustus* and their hybrids. Several good seedlings have been raised of recent years by Col. F. C. Stern of Highdown, Goring-by-Sea.

**E. Aitchison'ii.*** 3 to 5 ft. h. Closely allied to *E. robustus*, with dense spikes of pale reddish *fl.* June. Afghanistan.

**E. auranti'acus.** Closely related to *E. Bungei* but with less keeled *l.*, root-fibres tapering upwards, *fl.* orange. Turkestan.

**E. buchar'icus.** About 3 ft. h. *l.* 3-angled, glaucous, with small teeth pointing backward on keel and margins. *fl.* white, about 1 in. across, segs. with a brownish-red median line; racemes long, rather loose. Bokhara. 1890. (G.F. 1890, 1315, f. 1.)

**E. Bun'gei.*** About 1 ft. h. or more. *l.* linear, 1 ft. long, under $\frac{1}{2}$ in. wide, firm, glabrous, minutely ciliate. *fl.* bright yellow, $\frac{1}{2}$ in. long; pedicels erecto-patent; racemes oblong, dense, 4 to 5 in. long; scape terete, glabrous. June. Persia. 1885. (G.F. 1168 a.) var. **Highdown Gold,** *fl.* golden yellow; **magnif'icus,** *fl.* larger and brighter yellow than type; **sulphu'reus,** raceme dense, *fl.* large, clear yellow, probably the same as var. *citrinus* of gardens.

**E. Elwes'ii.*** Up to 6 to 9 ft. h. *l.* 3 ft. long, fleshy. *fl.* pink, very numerous on spike, stalked. May. 1897. Origin ? Related to *E. robustus* but earlier; by some thought to be *E. himalaicus* × *E. robustus* but crosses between these species have not reproduced it. var. **al'bus,** *fl.* white.

**E. himala'icus.** $1\frac{1}{2}$ to 2 ft. h. *l.* strap-shaped, acute, about 1 ft. long, glabrous, entire. *fl.* white, starry, in dense racemes. Himalaya. 1881. (G.C. 16 (1881), 49.)

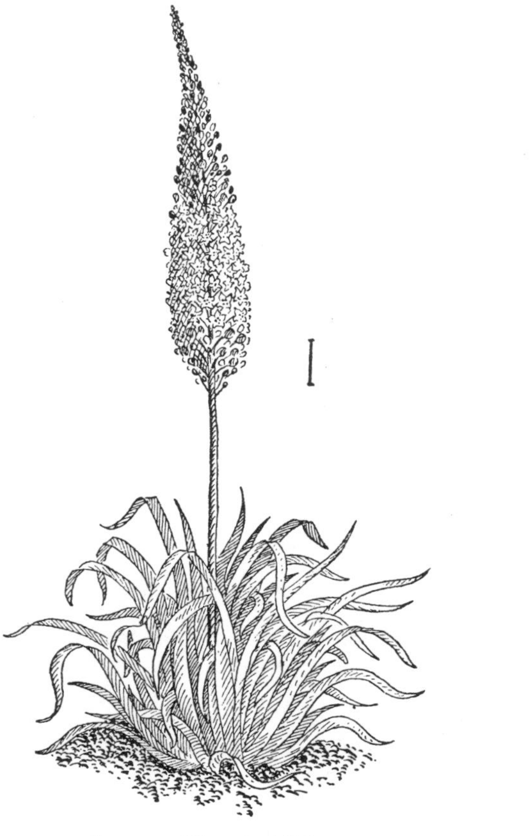

*Eremurus Olgae* (p. 762)

**E. × himrob** (*E. himalaicus × E. robustus*). *Spike* long. *fl.* light blush-pink. May. SYN. *E. robustus superbus.*

**E. inderien'sis.** 3 to 4 ft. h. *fl.* in a dense raceme; pedicels equal, not jointed, more or less erecto-patent; outer sep. 3-nerved at base, inner 1-nerved; all involute only at apex. Turkestan.

**E. Kaufmannia'nus.** 3 to 4 ft. h. *l.* hairy above. *fl.* in a dense raceme; more or less bell-shaped; segs. all 1-nerved; pedicels as long as the slender, incurved, ciliate bracts. Turkestan.

**E. Korolkow'ii.** 3 to 4 ft. h. *l.* ligulate linear, glaucous; *fl.* bright rose, as large as in *E. robustus*. June. Turkestan.

**E. lactiflo'rus.** Habit of *E. robustus, fl.* milk-white. Turkestan.

**E. Ol'gae.** *l.* linear, scabrid, recurved. *fl.* white, starry, stamens long; raceme long, dense. July. Turkestan. 1881. (G.F. 1048.)

**E. robus'tus.*** 8 or 9 ft. h. *l.* 2½ to 4 ft. long, 4 in. wide, bright green. *fl.* peach-coloured, in a long, many-fld. raceme. June. Turkestan. 1874. (B.M. 6726.) vars. **al'bus** and **Elwesian'us,** *see* **E. Elwesii;** **super'bus,** *see* **E. × himrob.**

**E. × Shelford*** (*E. Bungei × E. Olgae*). Free-flowering with *fl.* of various colours, orange-buff in type, pink shaded orange in **Isobel,** pale yellow in **Moonlight,** bright pink in **Rosalind,** white in **White Beauty.** June.

**E. spectab'ilis.** 2 ft. h. *l.* linear-strap-shaped, slightly channelled, and keeled, glaucous. *fl.* sulphur, slightly tinged orange, in a many-fld. long raceme. Siberia. 1800. (B.M. 4870.)

**E. × Tubergen'ii** (*E. Bungei × E. himalaicus*). *fl.* pale yellow; spikes 18 in. long, many-fld. May.

**E. turkestan'icus.** About 4 ft. h. *l.* broad-linear, slender-pointed. *fl.* reddish-brown, segs. margined white; stamens much exserted; raceme very long and dense. Turkestan. 1881. (G.F. 997.)

**E. × War'ei** (*E. Bungei × E. Olgae*). Up to 8 ft. h. *fl.* small, shaded orange; spikes slender. June. Said to be a natural hybrid from Turkestan. 1900.

**EREP'SIA.** Included under **Mesembryanthemum.**

**E'RIA** (*erion*, wool; flowers, pedicels, &c., are often woolly). FAM. *Orchidaceae.* A large, very varied genus of epiphytic orchids with probably over 400 species, distributed through the East from Ceylon to Java. Though closely allied to Dendrobium, differing from that genus by the presence of 8 pollen masses, the genus contains comparatively few species of any floral merit. From their free-flowering qualities, however, though the individual flowers are small, a number are attractive. The flowers resemble those of Dendrobium in shape. The sepals are usually free, the lateral sometimes connate, their bases, with the elongated column foot, forming a more or less decided short or comparatively long chin; the lip attached to the column foot is usually 3-lobed and has raised lines or crests on its disk. The flowers may be solitary, few, or densely set on spikes, axillary, lateral, sub-terminal, or in a few species from the base of the pseudobulb. The pseudobulbs vary from small, almost minute, to stems 2 ft. high; one section can hardly be said to have pseudobulbs, fleshy leafy stems taking their place. As in Dendrobium the leaves of some are persistent, of others deciduous. The cultivation and compost are that given to Dendrobiums and, as with that polymorphic genus, treatment must, to a great extent, depend on the characters of the plants. Those from Java, Malaya, and the Philippines require a higher winter temperature (65 to 70° F.) than the N. Indian and Upper Burmese species for which suitable temperatures will be found in the Cattleya house. The hard-bulbed or deciduous species require a decided rest; the softer-stemmed species must have water and a moist atmosphere throughout the year. Species with straggling habit, i.e. the pseudobulbs set at distances on the rhizome, must be given rafts or baskets, but in many the pseudobulbs are set very closely together and for these and all small-growing species small pans or pots should be used.

**E. acerva'ta.** *fl.* yellowish, small, numerous, crowded, on spikes 2 to 3 in. long. *Pseudobulbs* 1 to 3 in. h., clustered, compressed. Himalaya, Burma. 1851. (A.B.G.C. 8, 170.)

**E. acuminatis'sima.** Very near to *E. Cooperi* and by some considered the correct name of that plant.

**E. aeridostach'ya.** Allied to *E. paniculata. fl.* many, small, deep brownish, in racemes 10 to 15 in. long; sep. broader than long; pet. narrow; lip sessile. *l.* 6 to 12 in. long, acute, fleshy, leathery. Malaya.

**E. a'mica.** *fl.* small; sep. and pet. with 5 reddish nerves; lip fleshy, side lobes with a red-brown band and blotch at base of the yellow mid-lobe. *Pseudobulbs* 2 to 6 in. h., 2- or 3-leaved. Assam. 1867. (R.X.O. 2, 168; B.M. 9453.) Variable.

**E. armenia'ca.** Closely allied to *E. ornata.* The habit is the same, but the bracts are shorter and apricot rather than orange, the keels on the lip violet, and the mid-lobe ochre-brown. Possibly *E. ornata* is a superior variety. Philippines. 1835. (B.R. 27, 42.)

**E. bambusifo'lia.** *fl.* small, grey-white, striped with red; lip 3-lobed, veined and suffused with red as are 5 raised keels on the lip. *infl.* brown-hairy; panicle terminal, 6 to 10 in. long. Stems stout, 2 to 3 ft. h. *l.* bamboo-like. Sikkim. 1858. (A.B.G.C. 8, 163.)

**E. barba'ta.** A synonym of *Eriodes barbata.*

**E. bi'color.** *fl.* pure white, with pubescent, purple ovaries and rachis, in 1-sided racemes; bracts white. *l.* 5 to 7, cuneate-lanceolate, stiff, 4 to 5 in. long. Stems 4 to 5 in. long, very tumid at base. Ceylon. 1888. A pretty species.

**E. bigib'ba.** *fl.* sep. and pet. light reddish, lanceolate, the sep. with green median nerves; lip whitish, with small, purple dashes at base, transversely 3-fid; column yellowish-white, purple at base inside. *l.* long, petiolate, on a tumid foot. Borneo. 1884.

**E. bractes'cens.** *fl.* several, ⅜ in. across, white; lip 3-lobed with 3 keels, base purplish, mid-lobe whitish; spike 4 to 6 in. long; bracts comparatively large, greenish-white. *Pseudobulbs* cylindric, tapered, 2- or 3-leaved. *l.* elliptical, 4 to 5 in. long. Malacca, Java. 1839. (B.R. 30, 29; A.B.G.C. 8, 166.)

**E. carina'ta.** *fl.* sep. light yellowish-green, 1 in. long, keeled at back; pet. yellowish-green; lip deep dull yellow, veined crimson, narrow-oblong, obtuse, with small, rounded lateral lobes; racemes terminal, 2- or 3-fld. *l.* linear-lanceolate, acute, 8 to 9 in. long. *Pseudobulbs* ovoid, smooth. Hong Kong. 1886. (A.B.G.C. 8, 179.) SYN. *E. Fordii.*

**E. cinnabari'na.** *fl.* rich cinnabar-orange, about 1 in. across; bracts lanceolate; racemes 4 in. long, about 6-fld. *l.* 6 in. long. *Pseudobulbs* 1 in. long. Borneo. 1894. (L. 448.)

**E. clavicau'lis.** *fl.* white; lip bordered pink. India. 1837. (A.B.G.C. 5, 31.)

**E. convallarioi'des.** *fl.* white, small; racemes dense, oblong, drooping, on short peduncles. August. *l.* oblong-lanceolate. *Pseudobulbs* 2 to 8 in. long, compressed, densely and loosely sheathed. India, Nepal. 1839. (B.R. 27, 62; A.B.G.C. 161.)

**E. Coop'eri.** *fl.* numerous, small, densely set, on an erect or arching softly hairy scape, 12 in. or more long; lateral sep. with yellowish border, their bases forming a yellow-tipped 'chin', softly hairy; upper sep. and pet. dark red; lip pale pinkish-red, claw short, white. Stem terete, about 4 in. h. *l.* several, sheathing, about 12 in. long, ½ to ¾ in. wide, acute. Summer. Java? 1928.

**E. corona'ria.** *fl.* 3 to 5, very fragrant; about 1 in. or more across; sep. and pet. creamy-white, lip 3-lobed, side lobes erect, white, streaked with red-purple, mid-lobe reflexed, yellow, margined white and crimson-brown; scapes terminal. Stems tufted, quill-like, 3 to 6 in. h., crowned with 2 large opposite l. 4 to 8 in. long, 1 to 1½ in. broad, fleshy. Himalaya. 1841. (A.B.G.C. 8, 172; B.R. 28, 21 as *Trichosma suavis*.) Requires Odontoglossum house temperature and treatment.

**E. crista'ta.** *fl.* sep. and pet. pure white; lip yellow, somewhat darker on disk and margins of side lobes; column white, with a yellow anther-case. Moulmein. 1882. A pretty species.

**E. Elwes'ii.** A synonym of *Porpax Elwesii.*

**E. extinctor'ia.** *fl.* solitary, about ½ in. across, white, spurred; lip with rose blotch; spur about ¼ in., stout, retuse; peduncle 2 to 3 in. long, slender. *Pseudobulbs* small, flattened, wrinkled, clustered. *l.* solitary, small, deciduous. Burma. 1871. (B.M. 5910.) SYN. *Dendrobium extinctorium.*

**E. fe'rox.** *fl.* large, usually in fours on a flexuous drooping peduncle; sep. red-haired without; lip broad, whitish, or yellowish tinged with red on basal margins, blade 2-lobed. Stems 1 to 3 ft., leafy, arching or pendulous. *l.* lanceolate, 2 to 3 in. long, covered with short brown-red hairs. Malaya, Java.

**E. floribun'da.** *fl.* white, or tinged red, small but very numerous, in curved racemes not infrequently 6 to 8 in. long. Summer. *l.* lanceolate-acuminate. Stems fleshy, stout or terete, 10 to 18 in. long. Singapore, Borneo, Burma. 1842. (B.R. 30, 20.) Variable.

**E. Ford'ii.** A synonym of *E. carinata.*

**E. globif'era.** *fl.* solitary, inverted; densely tomentose; sep. and broader pet. ¾ in. long, cream to white with pink lines; lip 3-lobed, side lobes lined with pink, mid-lobe tapered, reflexed, with 2 yellow marginal callosities. *Pseudobulbs* small, almost globular, monophyllous. *l.* 3 to 5 in. long, nearly ½ in. wide. Annam. 1904. A quaint but attractive species. (B.M. n.s. 83.)

**E. hyacinthoi'des.** Near to *E. rhynchostyloides* in habit. *fl.* white with a brown spot on the side lobe of lip, numerous, closely set on spikes, 6 to 9 in. long, fragrant. Java. 1825. (B.M. 8229.)

**E. javan'ica.** *fl.* 12 to 30, white or creamy-white, stellate, in a long curved raceme, 12 to 15 in. long, fragrant; sep. and pet. nearly equal, linear-lanceolate, spreading, lip lanceolate, 3-lobed, almost parallel with column. April. *Pseudobulbs* stout, 3 to 4 in. h. *l.* 2, 12 to 18 in. long, broad-lanceolate, petiolate, with 5 longitudinal ribs. Java. 1837. (B.R. 904; B.M. 3605 as *E. rugosa*.) SYN. *E. stellata, E. vaginata, Dendrobium javanicum, Tainia stellata.*

**E. latebractea'ta.** *fl.* 6 to 10, creamy-white; lip with rose side lobes, yellow mid-lobe, front margin 3-lobed; racemes 4 in. long; bracts yellow. *l.* 2 or 3, 2 to 4 in. long. *Pseudobulbs* stout, 1 to 3½ in. h. Borneo. 1895. (B.M. 7605.)

**E. Lauchea'na.** A synonym of *E. rhodoptera.*

**E. lineolig'era.** *fl.* white, very thin; sep. and pet. acute, curved; lip cuneate-dilated, 3-fid, side lobes triangular, very short, mid-lobe projecting, triangular, undulated, with purple lines each side; raceme ascending, with orange bracts. *l.* rather thick, cuneate-oblong-lanceolate. *Pseudobulbs* fusiform. Siam. 1885.

**E. margina'ta.** *fl.* 1 in. across; sep. and pet. white, flushed pink; lip pale yellow, margined red; bracts yellow, large; scape ½ in. long, 2-fld. *l.* and stem each 3 in. or more long, the latter clavate. Burma. 1889. (B.M. 7238.)

**E. Mei'rax.** A synonym of *Porpax Elwesii* and *P. Meirax.*

**E. monostach'ya.** *fl.* small; sep. and pet. greenish-yellow; lip with a small front lobe and 2 angular calli; *infl.* a simple raceme. Habit of *E. paniculata.* Java. 1885.

**E. muscic'ola.** *fl.* yellowish-green, very small, racemose. *l.* about ⅓ in. long. *Pseudobulbs* globose, crowded. Ceylon, Burma. 1887. A very small species. (A.B.G.C. 159.)

**E. myristicifor'mis.** *fl.* white, medium size, sweet-scented; racemes erect, shorter than l.; bracts about as long as pedicel, oblong, acuminate, white, reflexed; lip spurred, 3-lobed; disk with 2 orange glands. September. *Pseudobulbs* clustered, oblong, green; the old bulbs remain, and are shaped like nutmegs. *l.* 2, lanceolate-spatulate. Moulmein. 1863. (B.M. 5415.)

**E. obe'sa.** *fl.* white, scarcely tinged pale pink; racemes arising from the leafless pseudobulbs, 3 to 4 in. long; labellum oblong, obscurely 3-lobed. February. *Pseudobulbs* oblong-oval, tapering at each end, 2 to 3 in. long and 1 in. thick, compressed, clustered. *l.* 2, terminal. Malaya. 1863. (B.M. 5391.)

**E. orna'ta.\*** *fl.* long-lasting, ¾ in. h., with reddish-brown hairs without; sep. greenish; pet. narrower, yellowish, flushed red at tip; lip 3-lobed, side lobes whitish, mid-lobe orange tinted or flushed red, margins crenulate; spike 12 to 15 in. long, arching, many-fld.; bracts 1 in. long, ½ in. wide, cinnabar-orange. *Pseudobulbs* broadly oval, at intervals on a stout rhizome. *l.* 2 or 3, leathery, about 8 in. long, bases contracted into a short, stout petiole. Philippines. (B.M. 8642.) *See* **E. armeniaca.** A distinct, handsome species.

**E. panicula'ta.** *fl.* many, small, greenish-yellow; sep. softly hairy; pet. and lip tinged lavender, blotched brownish; lip 3-lobed with a comparatively large mealy callus; racemes terminal, rather long, clustered in twos or threes. Stem 12 to 24 in. h. *l.* long, narrow, tapered. Summer. N. India. (A.B.G.C. 7, 174.) The plant so named by Reichenbach is the allied *E. monostachya.*

**E. pan'nea.** *fl.* 1 to 3, about ½ in. across; sep. and pet. whitish; lip orange-red. *l.* 2 to 8 in. h., terete, channelled, usually in fives, arranged fan-like, imbricate at base, at intervals on a creeping rhizome, white tomentose. Burma and the East. (A.B.G.C. 8, 176.) Curious and pretty. Should be grown on a raft.

**E. rhodop'tera.** *fl.* sep. whitish-ochre, as well as pedicels, ovaries, and bracts; pet. purple; lip 3-fid, side lobes purple, produced, the mid-lobe ligulate, retuse; raceme elongated. *l.* linear-ligulate, acute. Stems cylindrical, 6 to 8 in. long. Philippines. 1882. (B.M. 8296.) SYN. *E. Laucheana.* Allied to *E. bractescens.*

**E. rhynchostyloi'des.\*** *fl.* small, white, flushed rose, column purple; often 200 to 300 densely set in lateral or ascending spikes, 8 to 12 in. long. *Pseudobulbs* clustered, stout, 4 to 6 in. h. or more. *l.* 4 to 5, 12 to 18 in. long, narrow. Java. 1908. (B.M. 8234.) A fine species.

**E. Riman'ni.** *fl.* pellucid pale yellow, front lobe of lip golden-yellow, with 2 purple spots; raceme nodding, dense, with a few reddish hairs. *l.* cuneate-oblong, acute, very leathery, light green, nerves dark. *Pseudobulbs* pyriform, about 3 in. long. Burma. 1885.

**E. ro'sea.** *fl.* 2 or more, not spreading; sep. ¾ in. long, broadly triangular, keeled behind, whitish; pet. smaller, flushed rose; lip white, side lobes crimson. *Pseudobulbs* clustered, nearly globular, monophyllous. *l.* fleshy, 8 in. long, 2 in. wide; peduncle erect, from the young growth. N. India, China, &c. 1824. (B.R. 978; L.B.C. 1817.)

**E. rugo'sa.** A synonym of *E. javanica.*

**E. stella'ta.** A synonym of *E. javanica.*

**E. striola'ta.** *fl.* sep. and pet. light ochre, linear-ligulate, acute, sep. with 3 stripes and pet. with 1 stripe of reddish-purple; lip ligulate, with very blunt side lobes, and 3 conspicuous, partly crenulate, yellow keels; raceme dense-fld., rachis slightly hairy. *l.* cuneate-oblong, acute, very fleshy. Papua. 1888. (I.H. 1888, 48.)

**E. sua'vis.** A synonym of *E. coronaria.*

**E. tomento'sa.** Very near to *E. ornata* but worthless in comparison. *fl.* dull brown, bracts small, dull brownish-yellow. Burma. (B.M. 8662.)

**E. vagina'ta.** A synonym of *E. javanica.*

**E. veluti'na.** *fl.* whitish, solitary or few in short axillary spikes, Stems slender, 1 to 2 ft. h. *l.* 2 to 3 in. long, softly brown-villous. Burma. 1840.

**E. vesti'ta.** *fl.* 10 to 25, reddish-brown without, white within, of medium size; racemes pendulous, flexuous, 12 in. long. *l.* leathery, lanceolate, 3 to 4 in. long. Stems more or less pendulous, 18 to 24 in. long. Whole plant with soft reddish-brown hairs. Indian Archipelago. 1840. (B.R. 31, 2; B.M. 5807.) SYN. *Dendrobium vestitum.*

E. C.

**ERIAN'THUS** (*erion*, wool, *anthos*, flower; alluding to the silvery-hairy appearance of the inflorescence). Plume Grass. FAM. *Gramineae.* A genus of about 17 species of perennial reed-like grasses in the tropics and warm temperate zones. Tall perennials with rather narrow leaves and large panicles of crowded spikes, the spikelets in pairs, one sessile, the other stalked as in Andropogon, clothed with long hairs, especially about the base, the whole forming a handsome plume. *E. Ravennae* is hardy but apt to flower only in warm summers. In light soil, however, it forms dense tufts and is a stately plant. It needs a sunny, well-drained position.

**E. Raven'nae.** Stout perennial of tufted habit. Stem 3 or 4 ft. h. *l.* about ½ in. wide, almost round with a firm point, forwards rough on both sides, and often with a whitish median stripe. *Panicle* up to 2 ft. long, the basal spikes up to 8 in. long, almost erect; spikes beset with long hairs especially at base. August to October. S. Europe.

**ERI'CA** (*Erica* of Pliny, is altered from *Ereike* of Theophrastus). Heath. FAM. *Ericaceae.* A genus of evergreen shrubs and a few trees, confined to Africa and Europe. Of over 500 species, about 470 are natives of S. Africa, some 6 or 8 of Trop. Africa, the remainder of S. Europe, N. Africa, and the Atlantic Islands. One species is wild in Ireland. In stature they range from shrubs a few in. high to trees (rarely) up to 20 ft. Leaves linear to narrowly oblong or lanceolate, most frequently in whorls of 3 or 4, sometimes of 6, sometimes in pairs, occasionally scattered, ranging between ⅛ to ⅝ in. in length. Flowers either solitary in the leaf-axils or in terminal umbels, often forming collectively leafy pseudo-racemes several in. long; calyx of 4 sepals, rarely merely 4-lobed or toothed; corolla varying in shape between tubular and bell-shaped and in size from ⅛ to 1¼ in. long, often more or less inflated towards the base; stamens normally 8 with the anthers enclosed or slightly protruding, but in a few species exserted as much as ¼ in.; capsule globose, conical or cylindrical; seeds very numerous, minute.

Towards the end of the eighteenth century and the earlier part of the nineteenth, when Masson, Niven, and others were assiduously exploring in S. Africa, 'Cape heaths' were very popular. In 1811, for instance, 186 species were cultivated at Kew. But as time went on many were displaced by more easily grown plants and there is now less than half that number to be found in British gardens. The 'Cape heaths' are almost invariably beautiful, often supremely so.

The Cape heaths need greenhouse conditions and probably no class of plants requires more careful and skilled treatment than the hard-wooded section of the genus. Those now usually seen belong to the species with softer growth or are garden hybrids. They include *E. campanulata, E. canaliculata, E. × Cavendishiana, E. gracilis* and its white variety *alba, E. hyemalis, E. persoluta* and its variety *alba, E. perspicua, E. regerminans, E. ventricosa* and its varieties, and *E. Willmorei.* These are grown in quantity by a few growers for market, their flowering season extending from autumn to spring. Even in the hands of these specialists their cultivation often presents difficulties and at times considerable losses occur from no apparent reason, though careless potting or watering is frequently a contributory cause.

Seed is freely produced (but crossing frequently occurs and many beautiful hybrids have been raised in the past) and seedlings are easily raised. The seed is very fine and should be sown on the surface of the fine sandy peat compost and just covered with a sprinkling of sand. The pot should be covered with a piece of glass and kept shaded until the seed germinates. The seed-pots should be well drained and the compost made fairly firm, watered, and allowed to drain for several hours before the seed is sown. Any subsequent watering required should be effected by standing the pots in a vessel of rain-water. Spring is the best time for sowing since the young plants should then be well-established in thumb-pots before the winter. The seedlings should be potted-off singly into thumb-pots as soon as large enough to handle, and kept close and shaded until they are established, and then gradually accustomed to more light and air. As they grow the points of the leading shoots should be pinched out to induce a bushy growth. In the following spring they will need potting-on into larger pots.

The soft-wooded species and hybrids and the hardy species are readily increased by cuttings and are mostly so grown; the hard-wooded species are much more difficult and take longer to root. The soft-wooded species start growth early in the year and cuttings of these are ready to take earlier than those of the hard-wooded species. Cuttings should be about 1 in. long and taken from twiggy lateral shoots towards the base of the plants. They should have the lower leaves carefully removed and should be inserted rather closely in the pots which should be two-thirds filled with crocks, the remaining one-third with fine sandy peat with a layer of silver sand on the surface. After being well watered the pots of cuttings should be stood under bell-glasses or in a close frame in a temperature of about 60° F. The glasses will require to be wiped every day, and a sharp look-out must be kept for any cuttings which damp-off and they must be at once removed. When rooted and growth has begun more light and air should be given and when hardened they should be stood well up to the roof glass. The tips of the young plant should be stopped and the young plants either left in the cutting-pots until the following spring or potted-up singly.

The soil used for heaths should be a good brown fibrous peat with about one-third part of fine silver sand. For the hard-wooded species a mixture of this and hard heath peat is best. Thorough drainage is essential at all times. The young plants should never be allowed to become pot-bound and in repotting the roots should be disturbed as little as possible. The best time for re-potting is as soon as growth begins in spring, or for the late-flowering species early autumn. The new compost should be added a little at a time and be rammed very firm, and particular care should be taken not to bury the stem of the plant. After repotting the plants should be given less air until established in the new compost.

Heaths suffer very quickly from fire-heat and close, stuffy atmospheric conditions, and should have plenty of air without draughts. Short of freezing they do not suffer seriously from low temperatures; nevertheless, it is not advisable to subject them for long to a temperature lower than 35 to 40° F. during winter. No more fire-heat should be used than is necessary to maintain this condition with a buoyant atmosphere. Close conditions are apt to lead to attacks of mildew, which can be checked by giving more air and dusting with flowers of sulphur.

After flowering the shoots of the softer species should be cut hard back and the plants kept on the dry side until new growth begins when they should be repotted if necessary. At no time, however, should they be allowed to dry out. With the hard-wooded species, beyond the removal of dead flowers, little or no pruning is necessary, and quite large plants may be grown in comparatively small pots for a number of years.

The best type of house is a low span-roofed one standing north and south and having top, side, and bottom ventilators on both sides.

Careful watering is necessary at all times and wherever possible rain-water should be used. If this is not available, water that has been exposed in an open tank may be substituted occasionally. Except clear soot-water, it is unwise to use any manure.

J. C.

Cultivated Heaths are sometimes subject to Wilt caused by the fungus *Phytophthora cinnamomi* which is also suspected of attacking Calceolarias, Schizanthus, and other plants. The signs are wilting and greying of the foliage which finally turns brown and dry owing to the roots being attacked by the parasite. In nurseries diseased plants should be destroyed, water tanks disinfected, and ashes, pots, &c., disinfected with formaldehyde or other disinfectant. Another trouble which occasionally occurs is the attack on hardy Heaths by the parasitic flowering plant Dodder. Where severe infestation occurs the eradication of the parasite is a difficult problem but the affected patches should be burnt over before the Dodder seeds, after which the Heaths should be able to grow away free from the parasite.

D. E. G.

The hardy species prosper in open situations in rather light, lime-free loam which should not be enriched in any way. Those from the Mediterranean region are more tolerant of drought than others, and *E. carnea* and its varieties are tolerant of a more calcareous soil than other species. To ensure compact growth and to prolong life annual clipping-over after flowering is advisable, but the clipping should not be too severe. Propagation is by seed, cuttings, layers, and division.

KEY TO HARDY SPECIES

| | | |
|---|---|---|
| 1. *Lvs. ciliate or glandular-ciliate* | | 2 |
| 1. *Lvs. not ciliate* | | 6 |
| 2. *Cilia terminate in glands* | | 3 |
| 2. *Cilia plain* | | 4 |
| 3. *Dwarf plant, lvs. in 3's, fl. pink* | | E. ciliaris |
| 3. *Tall plant, lvs. in 4's, fl. purplish-red* | | E. australis |
| 4. *Lvs. in 3's* | | E. cinerea |
| 4. *Lvs. in 4's* | | 5 |
| 5. *Fl. pink* | | E. Tetralix |
| 5. *Fl. yellow* | | E. Pageana |
| 6. *Anthers included* | | 7 |
| 6. *Anthers exserted* | | 10 |
| 7. *Young wood smooth* | | E. scoparia |
| 7. *Young wood downy or hairy* | | 8 |
| 8. *Fl. pink* | | E. terminalis |
| 8. *Fl. white* | | 9 |
| 9. *Stigma white* | | E. arborea |
| 9. *Stigma pink* | | E. lusitanica |
| 10. *Shrubs to over 6 ft. h.* | | 11 |
| 10. *Shrubs under 4 ft. h.* | | 12 |
| 11. *Lvs. in 3's, fl. open-campanulate* | | E. canaliculata |
| 11. *Lvs. in 4's, fl. ovoid-urceolate* | | E. mediterranea |
| 12. *Fl. in terminal umbels* | | E. umbellata |
| 12. *Fl. in racemes* | | 13 |
| 13. *Racemes 1-sided* | | E. carnea |
| 13. *Racemes columnar* | | 14 |
| 14. *Anther lobes united almost to apex* | | E. multiflora |
| 14. *Anther lobes separated to base* | | E. vagans |

**E. abieti'na.** Shrub 2 ft. and upwards. *l.* in fours, linear, pointed, $\frac{1}{4}$ to $\frac{3}{8}$ in. long. *fl.* solitary in a dense leafy raceme towards tip of shoot; sep. linear from a broadly ovate base; cor. rich yellow, tubular, $\frac{3}{4}$ to 1 in. long, $\frac{1}{4}$ in. across mouth; lobes of limb recurved. May to August. S. Africa. 1790. (A.H. 228 as *E. Patersonia major*.)

**E. Aiton'ia.** A synonym of *E. jasminiflora*.

**E. al'bens.** Erect, glabrous shrub, 1 to 1$\frac{1}{2}$ ft. *l.* in threes, $\frac{1}{8}$ to $\frac{1}{4}$ in. long, erect, rather thinly disposed, pointed, minutely ciliate. *fl.* axillary, solitary, very shortly stalked, forming collectively a slender leafy raceme 1$\frac{1}{2}$ to 3 in. long; cor. white, $\frac{1}{8}$ in. long, ovoid-urn-shaped, much narrowed at mouth; lobes minute, ultimately connivent. April to July. S. Africa. (A.H. 2.)

**E. alopecuroi'des.** A synonym of *E. nudiflora*.

**E. amoe'na.** Shrub 1 to 2 ft. *l.* in fours or sixes, linear, hairy, blunt, $\frac{1}{8}$ to $\frac{1}{4}$ in. long. *fl.* axillary, each on a stalk $\frac{1}{4}$ in. long; cor. purplish-red, glabrous, $\frac{1}{8}$ to $\frac{1}{4}$ in. long, broadly bell-shaped, lobes erect. March to July. S. Africa. (A.H. 36 as *E. plumosa*.)

**E. ampulla'cea.** Shrub $1\frac{1}{2}$ ft., shoots glabrous. *l.* in fours, often distinctly recurved, narrowly ovate-lanceolate, ciliate, $\frac{1}{8}$ to $\frac{1}{3}$ in. long. *fl.* in terminal clusters of usually 4; cor. flask-shaped, 1 to $1\frac{1}{4}$ in. long, $\frac{1}{3}$ in. wide at inflated base, pale rose with darker veins, viscous, purple near the contracted mouth; $\frac{1}{4}$ in. across lobes. June to August. S. Africa. 1780. (B.M. 303.)

**E. andromedaefo'lia.** A synonym of *E. holosericea.*

**E. arbo'rea.** Tree Heath. Tall shrub or small tree up to 20 ft. h. Young shoots hairy. *l.* closely packed in whorls of 3, linear, $\frac{1}{8}$ to $\frac{1}{4}$ in. long, smooth, grooved beneath. *fl.* towards end of lateral twigs, the whole forming a panicle-like infl. 9 to 18 in. long, fragrant; cor. globular-bell-shaped, greyish-white, $\frac{1}{8}$ in. long, lobes more or less spreading; cal. about $\frac{1}{16}$ in. long, lobes ovate; stigma flattish, white; stamens included. March, April. S. Europe, N. Africa, Caucasus. 1658. (Moggridge, Fl. Men. 59.) Hardy only in milder parts of British Is. and liable even there to be severely cut in hard winters. var. **alpi'na,*** dwarfer, more erect, and much hardier than type, *l.* brighter green. Mts. of Cuenca, W. Spain. 1899.

**E. arista'ta.** Erect, glabrous shrub, 1 to 2 ft. *l.* in fours, strongly recurved, densely set, $\frac{1}{4}$ to $\frac{1}{3}$ in. long, narrowly oblong, bristle-pointed, ciliate. *fl.* in terminal umbels of 4; cor. $1\frac{1}{4}$ in. long, flask-shaped, rich rosy-red with 8 darker veins and darker at mouth; $\frac{1}{4}$ in. across the broad, shallow lobes. Spring, autumn. S. Africa. 1801. (B.M. 1249.)

**E. austra'lis.*** Spanish Heath. Upright shrub of rather open habit, up to 8 ft. h. with hairy young shoots. *l.* in fours, linear, glandular-ciliate especially in youth, about $\frac{1}{4}$ in. long. *fl.* in terminal umbel-like clusters on previous year's twigs; cor. purplish-red, cylindrical, about $\frac{1}{4}$ in. long with recurved lobes; cal. less than $\frac{1}{8}$ in. long, slightly hairy; anthers exserted. April to June. Spain, Portugal. 1769. (B.M. 8045.) Hardier than *E. arborea* but liable to serious injury in hard winters. var. **Mr. Robert,*** hardier and more compact than type, *fl.* large, white. Named in honour of Lt. Robert Williams who found it at Algeciras.

**E. bac'cans.** Erect, quite glabrous shrub, 3 to 5 ft. *l.* in fours, narrowly linear, $\frac{1}{3}$ in. or less long. *fl.* mostly in terminal fours; stalk $\frac{1}{4}$ in. long; cor. globose, $\frac{1}{4}$ in. wide, constricted beneath the 4 short lobes, reddish-purple; sep. lanceolate, pointed, nearly as long as cor. tube and of same colour. April to July. S. Africa. 1774. (B.M. 358.)

**E. Banks'ia.** Low, almost procumbent shrub, 6 to 12 in., shoots grey-downy. *l.* in threes, broadly linear, closely packed, $\frac{1}{6}$ to $\frac{1}{3}$ in. long, pointed. *fl.* nearly sessile, often in pairs or threes; sep. $\frac{1}{2}$ in. long, ovate-lanceolate; cor. rosy, white, or yellowish, tubular, $\frac{3}{4}$ in. long; anthers exserted by $\frac{1}{2}$ in. Spring. S. Africa. 1787. (A.H. 105.)

**E. Bauer'a.** A synonym of *E. Bowieana.*

**E. Beaumont'ia.** A synonym of *E. odorata.*

**E. Bergia'na.** A synonym of *E. turrigera.*

**E. bi'bax.** Shrub 1 to 2 ft., shoots slightly downy. *l.* in threes or fours, erect, $\frac{1}{8}$ to $\frac{1}{3}$ in. long. *fl.* solitary arranged in whorls of 6 to 8 forming a leafy raceme; cor. $\frac{3}{4}$ in. long, tubular, broadest and $\frac{3}{16}$ in. wide near the mouth, pale yellow, downy. Autumn. S. Africa. (A.H. 23, as *E. flammea.*)

**E. bi'color.** A synonym of *E. dichrus.*

**E. Blandfordia'na.*** Shrub 1 to 2 ft., shoots stout, downy. *l.* in fours, $\frac{1}{8}$ to $\frac{1}{4}$ in. long, narrowly linear, keeled. *fl.* terminal, usually solitary or in pairs but also in fours; cor. yellow, ovoid-campanulate, $\frac{3}{8}$ in. long, swollen towards base; lobes rounded, spreading. Spring. S. Africa. 1803. (B M. 1793.)

**E. Bowiea'na.** Shrub with long, virgate branches. *l.* in fours, crowded, grooved, glabrous, $\frac{1}{4}$ in. or less long. *fl.* in a leafy raceme towards the end of the shoots; cor. tubular, but somewhat bellied, $\frac{7}{8}$ in. long, contracted at the mouth to 4 short, erect lobes, white changing to rose. August to October. S. Africa. 1822. (A.H. 252 as *E. Bauera*; B.M. n.s. 222 as *E. Bauera.*)

**E. caf'fra.** A synonym of *E. subdivaricata* and *E. urceolaris.*

**E. calyci'na.** A synonym of *E. corifolia.*

**E. campanula'ta.** Shrub 1 to 2 ft., shoots very slender. *l.* usually in threes but sometimes in fours or in pairs, narrowly linear, pointed, keeled, glabrous, $\frac{1}{8}$ to $\frac{1}{4}$ in. long. *fl.* usually solitary, but sometimes in threes or fours at end of short lateral twigs; cor. bell-shaped, $\frac{1}{4}$ in. across mouth, bright yellow, sometimes cream; cal. yellow. June to August. S. Africa. 1791. (A.H. 55.)

**E. canalicula'ta.** Erect shrub with densely hairy young shoots. *l.* usually in threes, linear, much recurved, $\frac{1}{8}$ to $\frac{1}{4}$ in. long. *fl.* clustered towards ends of twigs, together forming a panicle-like infl. at end of branch; cor. open-bell-shaped, white or pinkish, $\frac{1}{8}$ in. long and wide with shallow lobes; cal. nearly as long as cor., lobes ovate, acute; anthers exserted. March to May. S. Africa. 1802. (L.B.C. 867 as *E. melanthera*, an erroneous name.) Only suitable for milder counties and even there liable to damage or death in severe winters.

**E. car'nea.*** Low, spreading, decumbent shrub up to 12 in. h. with smooth young wood. *l.* usually in fours, linear, up to $\frac{5}{16}$ in. long. *fl.* in terminal, leafy, 1-sided racemes 1 to 3 in. long; cor. ovoid-urn-shaped, rosy-red, about $\frac{1}{4}$ in. long; cal. pink, over $\frac{1}{8}$ in. long, lobes oblong-lanceolate; anthers exserted, dark red. December to April. Cent. and S. Europe. 1763. (B.M. 11 as *E. herbacea*, a name often applied to var. *alba.*) A species with many varieties in fl.-colour, all tolerant of lime. var. **al'ba,** *fl.* white, January to April; **Eileen Porter,** *fl.* pink, fl.-period long; **James Backhouse,** *fl.* pale pink, late spring; **King George,** *fl.* dark red, early spring; **Queen Mary,** *fl.* rich pink, January, February; **Springwood Pink,** *fl.* pink, otherwise much like **Springwood White,** *fl.* white, large, growth very vigorous, spreading rapidly, the best white variety. February, March; **Vivel'lii,** *fl.* dark crimson-red, *l.* dark, February, March.

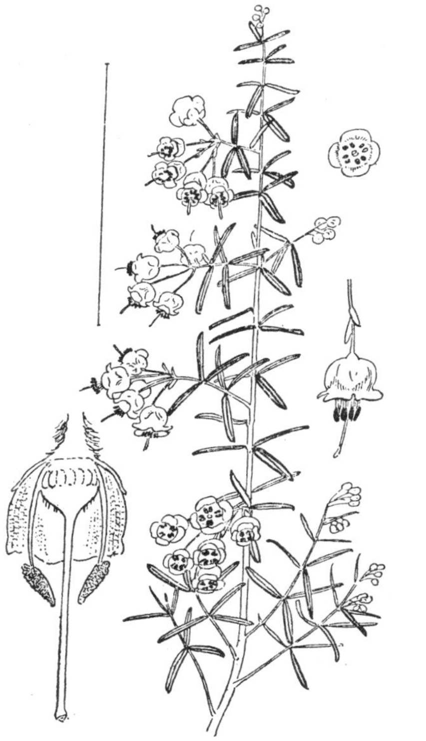

*Erica canaliculata*

**E. × Cavendishia'na*** (*E. abietina* × *E. depressa*). Raised by Mr. W. H. Story at Isleworth about 1842. From *E. abietina* it inherits the lovely rich yellow of its fl. which are about $\frac{7}{8}$ in. long, and $\frac{3}{8}$ in. across the rounded lobes of the cor. *l.* $\frac{3}{8}$ in. long, awl-shaped. $1\frac{1}{2}$ to 2 ft. h. May, July. (P.M.B. 13, 3.)

**E. cerinthoi'des.** Shrub 2 to 3 ft., branches virgate, erect. *l.* 4 to 6 in a whorl, about $\frac{1}{2}$ in. long, linear, distinctly ciliate. *fl.* in a close terminal cluster, 2 to $2\frac{1}{2}$ in. across; cor. tubular, slightly bellied, 1 to $1\frac{1}{4}$ in. long, rich crimson, sometimes rosy, mouth constricted, bracts and sep. glandular-ciliate. May to October. S. Africa. 1774. (B.M. 220.)

**E. Chamisson'is.*** Shrub 1 to $2\frac{1}{2}$ ft., shoots downy. *l.* in threes, very crowded, $\frac{1}{4}$ to $\frac{1}{3}$ in. long. *fl.* solitary to 4 at the end of short, lateral twigs forming cylindrical leafy racemes up to 6 in. long; cor. broadly bell-shaped, fully open at the mouth, rose-coloured, $\frac{1}{4}$ in. across. April. S. Africa. 1872. (B.M. 6108.)

**E. cilia'ris.*** Dorset Heath. Procumbent shrub 12 in. or more h., with ascending, glandular-downy shoots. *l.* in threes, ovate, $\frac{1}{8}$ in. long, glandular-ciliate; anthers included. *fl.* in threes in a terminal raceme 1 to 5 in. long; cor. bright pink, urn-shaped, about $\frac{3}{8}$ in. long with short, rounded lobes; cal. lobes lanceolate, glandular-ciliate; anthers included. July to November. *fr.* a smooth capsule. SW. Europe, including Cornwall, Dorset, and W. Ireland. 1773. (B.M. 484.) var. **al'ba,** *fl.* white, rather small but freely produced; **globo'sa,** *fl.* rich pink, broadly ovate; **Mawea'na,** *fl.* larger, slightly darker than in type, growth more upright, less hardy. Portugal. 1872. (B.M. 8443.) Syn. *E. Maweana*; **Stoborough,*** *fl.* fine white, better than var. *alba*. This species resents dry soil.

**E. ciner'ea.*** Scotch or Bell Heather. Branching shrub 9 to 24 in. h. with downy young wood. *l.* usually in threes, linear, strongly recurved, $\frac{3}{16}$ in. long, minutely bristly ciliate. *fl.* in terminal umbels or racemes; cor. ovoid-urn-shaped, rosy-purple, $\frac{1}{4}$ in. long with short lobes; cal. $\frac{1}{12}$ in. long; lobes narrow-lanceolate, rosy-purple. June to September. W. Europe, including Britain. (E.B. 891.) var. **al'ba**, 9 to 12 in. h., *fl.* white, in long racemes, June to August; **Apple Blossom,** 12 in. h., *fl.* shell-pink, freely produced, June to August; **atroru'bens,** 6 in. h., *fl.* bright red, July, August, not vigorous; **C. D. Eason,** 9 in. h., *fl.* bright pink, June, July; **coccin'ea,** 6 in. h., *fl.* ruby-red, June, July.

**E. colo'rans.*** Shrub 1½ to 3 ft., shoots downy. *l.* in fours, ⅛ to ¼ in. long, ciliate. *fl.* in slender, tapering racemes below the end of the shoot, built up of clusters of up to 4, terminating short side shoots; cor. white, then rosy, tubular-campanulate, ⅜ in. long, swollen towards the top. April to June. S. Africa. 1817. (A.H. 209.)

**E. concin'na.** Shrub 3 to 5 ft. *l.* in whorls of 4 to 6, imbricate, ⅛ to ¼ in. long. *fl.* clustered below the end of the shoots; cor. ⅝ in. long, tubular, downy, pale rose, ¼ in. across the mouth. October to December. S. Africa. (A.H. 58.) SYN. *E. verticillata.*

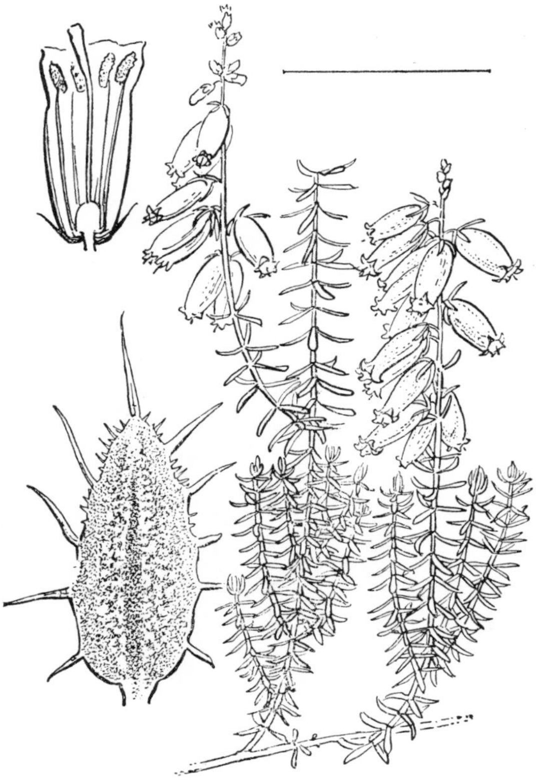

*Erica ciliaris* (p. 765)

**E. conspic'ua.** Shrub 2 to 3 ft., shoots usually downy, developing numerous short side twigs. *l.* in fours, usually downy, 1/10 to ¼ in. long. *fl.* solitary or 2 to 4 together; cor. 1 to 1½ in. long, slenderly funnel-shaped, rosy-red or yellow, ½ in. across the rolled-back lobes. June to August. S. Africa. (A.H. 12 (yellow); A.H. 222 as *E. longiflora.*)

**E. corifo'lia.** Shrub 1 to 2 ft. *l.* usually in threes, sometimes in pairs, ⅛ to ⅓ in. long, erect or even appressed to the stem. *fl.* in terminal clusters, 1 to 1¼ in. wide, stalk ⅛ to ⅙ in. long; sep. sometimes rosy or white, about as long as the cor. which is ovoid-urn-shaped, ⅙ to ⅓ in. long, bright red to white; lobes ovate, spreading. August, September. S. Africa. (A.H. 8 as *E. calycina.*)

**E. corona'ta.** A synonym of *E. fascicularis.*

**E. costa'ta.** A synonym of *E. versicolor.*

**E. cruen'ta.** Shrub 2 to 3 ft. *l.* in threes, linear, ⅙ to ⅓ in. long. *fl.* axillary, racemosely arranged in twos or threes towards the end of the shoot; stalk ¼ in. long; cor. 1 in. long, ¼ in. wide near the mouth, but tapering downwards, blood-red; lobes small, erect. August to October. S. Africa. (A.H. 110.)

**E. curviflo'ra.** Shrub 2 to 5 ft. *l.* in fours, linear, keeled, ⅛ to ⅓ in. long, ciliate. *fl.* solitary and terminal on short, lateral shoots forming collectively a loose raceme several in. long; cor. 1 to 1¼ in. long, curved, downy, red, orange, or yellow, ⅜ in. across the recurved lobes. March to June. S. Africa. (A.H. 16; A.H. 27 as *E. ignescens.*) var. **sulphu'rea,** the form with yellow fl. (B.M. 1984 as *E. sulphurea.*)

**E. curviros'tris.** Shrub 1 to 1½ ft., shoots hairy. *l.* in threes, ⅛ to ¼ in. long, broadly linear, keeled, glabrous. *fl.* in threes or in umbels; cor. white to rosy-red, rather bell-shaped to hemispherical, ⅛ in. long, widening upwards, lobes sometimes nearly as long as the tube. Spring, summer. S. Africa. (L.B.C. 1662 as *E. declinata.*)

**E. cyathiform'is.** A synonym of *E. persoluta laevis.*

**E. × darleyen'sis*** (*E. carnea* × *E. mediterranea*). Vigorous, quick-growing, spreading shrub about 2 ft. h., young wood smooth. *l.* usually in fours, linear, ¼ to ½ in. long, margins strongly recurved. *fl.* in terminal, leafy racemes 3 to 6 in. long; cor. pale pink, urn-shaped, 3/16 to ¼ in. long; cal. lobes three-quarters as long as cor., ovate-lanceolate, pale greenish-white or tinged pink. November to May. Spontaneous garden hybrid. SYN. *E. hybrida, E. mediterranea hybrida.* One of the most valuable of hardy heaths. (Gn. 54 (1898), 262.)

**E. decip'iens.** Shrub 1 to 2 ft., shoots grey-downy. *l.* in threes, linear, grooved, glabrous, ⅙ to ⅓ in. long. *fl.* in threes; cor. narrowly cup-shaped becoming ovoid, constricted slightly below the mouth, white, sometimes rosy-tinted, ⅙ in. long, lobes erect. S. Africa.

**E. declina'ta.** A synonym of *E. curvirostris.*

**E. demis'sa.** Dwarf shrub, young shoots downy. *l.* in threes, linear to narrow-oblong, lustrous, ciliate, ⅛ to ¼ in. long. *fl.* terminal on stalks up to ⅙ in. long; sep. lanceolate; cor. ⅛ in. long, narrowly cup-shaped to ovoid. S. Africa.

**E. densifo'lia.** Shrub 2 to 3 ft., shoots downy. *l.* in threes, ⅛ to ¼ in. long. *fl.* solitary, axillary, set on the branch in a raceme 3 in. or more long; cor. 1 to 1¼ in. long, curved, narrowly funnel-shaped, deep red, throat and lobes greenish-yellow; lobes erect. August to October. S. Africa. (A.H. 149 as *E. Uhria.*) var. **pilo'sa,** parts more downy; cor. paler red and very much more downy outside. (A.H. 150 as *E. Uhria pilosa.*)

**E. depres'sa.** Rigid, low shrub, 6 to 12 in. *l.* in threes, ¼ to ⅓ in. long, very crowded. *fl.* in terminal twos or threes; cor. white, bell-shaped, ¼ in. long and nearly as wide. July to September. S. Africa. 1789. (A.H. 145 as *E. rupestris.*) The *E. depressa* of A.H. 17, with rich yellow fl., is *E. nana.*

**E. diaph'ana.** A synonym of *E. transparens.*

**E. dich'rus.** Erect shrub, 3 to 5 ft., shoots downy. *l.* in fours, erect, linear, grooved, ciliate when young, ¼ to ½ in. long. *fl.* 2 to 4 terminating short, lateral twigs, erect; cor. ¾ to 1 in. long, viscous, tubular, red below, yellow or greenish at the top; lobes erect. February to April. S. Africa. (A.H. 54 as *E. bicolor.*)

**E. dis'color.** Shrub 2 to 3 ft., shoots downy. *l.* in threes, ⅛ to ⅓ in. long, linear, lustrous. *fl.* in twos or threes on short, lateral twigs; cor. narrowly funnel-shaped, ¾ in. long, lower part rosy-red, limb with its small, erect lobes yellowish-white or greenish. November to April. S. Africa. (A.H. 160.)

**E. el'egans.*** Shrub about 2 ft. *l.* in threes, glaucous, ⅓ to ½ in. long, incurved, upper ones petaloid, pink. *fl.* in terminal umbels of about 8; sep. roundish-ovate, ¼ in. wide, pointed, red; cor. pink, bottle-shaped, bellied at base, ½ in. long, contracted at mouth; lobes short, greenish. May. S. Africa. 1799. (A.H. 111.) SYN. *E. glauca elegans.*

**E. exsurg'ens.** Shrub 1½ to 3 ft. *l.* in fours, ½ to ¾ in. long, linear, pointed. *fl.* axillary, forming a cluster of horizontal whorls below the tips of shoots; cor. orange-yellow in the type, funnel-shaped, widening towards mouth, ¾ to 1 in. long; limb ½ in. across; lobes recurved. June to September. S. Africa. 1792. (A.H. 20.) var. **mi'nor,** *l.* in sixes, *fl.* smaller, darker coloured. (A.H. 21.)

**E. exu'dans.** A synonym of *E. glandulosa rubra.*

**E. × Fairea'na.*** Shrub with oblong-lanceolate *l.* fringed with long white hairs. *fl.* in terminal clusters of about 8; cor. rich rose, flask-shaped, 1 in. long, 3/16 in. wide at the swollen base; limb white, ¼ in. wide; lobes rounded. Hybrid. (R.H. 1880, 467.)

**E. fascicula'ris.** Shrub 2 to 6 ft., shoots densely packed with *l.* in sixes or scattered, blunt, glabrous, ½ to ⅝ in. long. *fl.* 10 to 20 in an umbel crowning the shoots; stalk ¼ to ⅓ in. long; cor. tubular, 1 to 1⅓ in. long, rosy below, paler above; lobes and top of cor. green. February to April. S. Africa. (A.H. 109 as *E. coronata.*) var. **imperia'lis,** cor. inflated towards base, ⅜ in. wide there. (A.H. 266 as *E. imperialis.*)

**E. fastigia'ta.*** Shrub 1 to 1½ ft. *l.* in fours, awl-shaped, ¼ to ⅓ in. long. *fl.* sessile, usually in terminal fours; cor. narrowly cylindrical, about ½ in. long, red or rosy; limb ⅜ in. wide; lobes flat and spreading, white, dark at centre; attractive. June to August. S. Africa. (B.M. 2084; A.H. 273 as *E. mundula.*) The *E. fastigiata* of A.H. 62 is *E. Walkeria.*

**E. formo'sa.** Shrub, 1 to 2 ft., shoots slender, downy. *l.* in threes, rather 3-cornered, narrowly oblong, ⅛ to 3/16 in. long, glabrous or slightly ciliate. *fl.* in threes terminating short, lateral shoots; cor. globose to cup-shaped, 3/16 in. wide, white; lobes recurved. May to July. S. Africa. (A.H. 265 as *E. grandinosa.*)

**E. gemmif'era.** A synonym of *E. Massonii minor.*

**E. glandulo'sa.** Shrub, 2 to 3 ft., all the parts more or less glandular-hairy. *l.* in fours, linear, blunt, ⅙ to ½ in. long. *fl.* usually in fours forming umbels, sometimes isolated, sometimes in whorls; cor. white, ¾ in. long, tubular but tapering downwards. March to June. S. Africa. (A.H. 183.) var. **ru'bra,** *fl.* red. (A.H. 216 as *E. exudans.*)

**E. glau'ca.** Shrub 2 to 3 ft., shoots glabrous. *l.* in threes, glaucous, ¼ to ½ in. long, upper ones sub-petaloid. *fl.* in terminal clusters of 4 to 7, nodding; sep. oval to ovate, ¼ in. long, 3/16 in. wide, red; cor. ovoid, contracted towards mouth, ⅓ to ½ in. long, purple. May to July. S Africa. (B.M. 580.) Distinct by its glaucous l. and coloured (petaloid) bracts and cal.

**E. glomiflo'ra.** Shrub 1 to 2 ft., shoots hairy. *l.* in threes, awl-shaped-linear, furrowed beneath, blunt, up to ¼ in. long. *fl.* nodding, in terminal threes on short, leafy twigs; cor. ovoid, ⅜ in. long, ¼ in. wide, narrow-necked, white, tinged pink; lobes short, erect. July to September. S. Africa. (A.H. 283 as *E. reflexa.*)

**E. glumaeflo'ra.** Erect shrub about 1 ft., shoots very downy. *l.* linear-awl-shaped, grooved, glabrous, ⅛ to ¼ in. long. *fl.* nodding, on short, lateral twigs; stalk downy, ⅛ in. long; cor. cup-shaped to ovoid, ⅛ to ¼ in. long, white. S. Africa.

**E. grac'ilis.** Shrub 1 to 1½ ft., shoots slender, downy. *l.* in fours, erect or incurved, slender, ⅛ to $\frac{3}{16}$ in. long, glabrous. *fl.* in terminal clusters of 4 or more on side shoots; cor. globose, somewhat constricted at the mouth, rose, ⅛ to ⅙ in. wide; lobes small. September to December. S. Africa. 1774. (A.H. 68.) var. **al'ba,** *fl.* white.

**E. grandiflo'ra.*** Shrub 3 to 5 ft. *l.* mostly in sixes, sometimes scattered, linear, ¾ in. long, glabrous. *fl.* axillary, solitary, clustered below but often near the end of the shoot; cor. 1 to 1⅙ in. long, trumpet-shaped, $\frac{3}{16}$ in. wide at the mouth, narrowing downwards, orange-red; lobes shallow, curled back. May to September. S. Africa. 1785. (B.M. 189.)

**E. Haroldia'na.** Shrub 1½ to 2 ft., shoots glabrous. *l.* in threes, linear-awl-shaped, usually ⅛ to ⅜ in. long, deeply grooved beneath, glaucous. *fl.* in a terminal cluster of about 6; cor. white, ⅝ in. long, tubular, narrowing upwards; lobes recurved. January. S. Africa. 1915. (B.M. 8835.)

**E. hebeca'lyx.** Erect shrub. *l.* in threes, linear to linear-lanceolate, downy, ⅛ to ¼ in. long. *fl.* in threes usually on stalks ¼ in. long; sep. softly downy; cor. tubular but widening towards mouth, glabrous, viscous, 1 to 1¼ in. long. S. Africa.

**E. Hibbert'ia.** Shrub 1 to 1½ ft., shoots downy. *l.* in sixes, crowded, linear, blunt, ¼ to ½ in. long. *fl.* in whorls of 6 to 10 near the tips of the branches; cor. 1¼ in. long, curved-tubular, ⅛ to ¼ in. wide, very viscous, rich red but green at the mouth and short, erect lobes. July to September. S. Africa. 1800. (A.H. 118.)

**E. hirtiflo'ra.** Shrub 1 to 2 ft., shoots hairy. *l.* in fours, blunt, hairy, linear, up to ⅙ in. long. *fl.* in nodding clusters of 4 to 7 terminating short, leafy twigs; cor. roundish-ovoid, ⅛ to ⅙ in. long, contracted at mouth, pale purple. Autumn, winter. S. Africa. (B.M. 481.)

**E. holoseric'ea.** Shrub 1 to 3 ft. *l.* in threes, ⅛ to ⅜ in. long, pointed, awl-shaped, incurved, downy or glabrous. *fl.* usually in threes, axillary, wholly rosy-red; sep. ovate, pointed, overlapping, ¼ in. wide, coloured like cor. which is ovoid, ¼ in. wide; lobes erect. March to May. S. Africa. 1803. (A.H. 151 as *E. andromedaeflora.*) var. **triumph'ans** is believed to be a garden hybrid. (B.M. 2322; L.B.C. 257 as *E. triumphans.*)

**E. hyema'lis.*** This, the most popular of S. African heaths, is of unknown origin. It began to attract notice about 1845 and may have come in from S. Africa unknowingly, or, more probably, it may be a hybrid or seedling variation raised in Britain. Erect in growth, it produces in winter tall, tapering racemes of tubular, rose-tinted white fl., each about ¾ in. long. (G. and F. 5, 137.) The nearest species to it is *E. perspicua*, but this blooms in summer.

**E. ignes'cens.** A synonym of *E. curviflora*.

**E. imperia'lis.** A synonym of *E. fascicularis imperialis*.

**E. Irbya'na.*** Erect, glabrous shrub, 1 to 2 ft. *l.* in threes, linear-subulate, pointed, ⅛ to ⅜ in. long. *fl.* in umbels of 6 to 10, terminal; sep. lanceolate, viscous, ¼ to ⅓ in. long, deep red; cor. pinkish-white, ⅛ to ¾ in. long, flask-shaped, narrowed towards the mouth; limb ¼ in. across. June to August. S. Africa. (A.H. 219.)

**E. jasminifl'ora.*** Erect, thinly branched shrub, ½ to 2 ft. *l.* in threes, linear, blunt, ¼ to ⅓ in. long. *fl.* terminal, usually in threes; cor. white, or pale rose, with red stripes, slenderly tubular, 1 to 1⅛ in. long, ⅞ in. across the expanded, broadly ovate lobes. Summer. S. Africa. (B.M. 429 as *E. Aitonia.*) Probably the largest fld. of the heaths.

**E. laev'is.** A synonym of *E. persoluta laevis*.

**E. × Lambertia'na*** (? *E. physodes* × ?). Shrub 2 to 3 ft. *l.* mostly in threes, linear, blunt, thick, furrowed beneath. *fl.* 1 to 3, terminating short, leafy twigs near top of branch; stalk ¼ to ½ in. long; sep. broadly lanceolate, coloured; cor. ⅓ in. long, pitcher-shaped, clammy; lobes small, rounded. Summer. (A.H. 171.)

**E. lanugino'sa.** Dense shrub about 1 ft., shoots glabrous. *l.* in threes, linear, ½ to 1 in. long, ciliate when young. *fl.* in threes but often solitary; stalk downy, ⅙ in. long; cor. broadly ovoid, swollen at base, ⅙ in. wide; lobes rounded, rosy-white together with bracts and cal. October to January. S. Africa. (A.H. 122.)

**E. longiflo'ra.** A synonym of *E. conspicua*.

**E. lusitan'ica.** Portuguese Heath. Erect, branching shrub up to 12 ft. h. with hairy young wood. *l.* scattered, linear, about ¼ in. long, pale green. *fl.* in clusters towards ends of lateral twigs, forming a leafy panicle; cor. white, cylindrical, $\frac{3}{16}$ in. long; lobes sub-erect, rather acute; cal. lobes white, roughly rhomboidal, acute; stigma and anthers pink; stamens included. March to May or earlier. SW. Europe. About 1800. (B.M. 8018.) Syn. *E. codonodes.* Less hardy than *E. australis* but hardier than *E. arborea*.

**E. Mackay'i.** A variety of *E. Tetralix*.

**E. mammo'sa.** Shrub up to 4 ft. *l.* in fours or scattered, linear, ¼ to ⅜ in. long. *fl.* pendulous, in a dense cluster 2 to 2½ in. long; cor. ½ to ¾ in. long, tubular but narrowed towards the mouth, reddish-purple, scarlet, or white. July to October. S. Africa. (A.H. 124 (purple) and A.H. 48 (scarlet) as *E. verticillata.*) var. **pallida,** *fl.* of the paler type. (L.B.C. 951.)

**E. Masson'ii.*** Shrub 1 to 3 ft. *l.* in fours or sixes, very densely crowded, narrowly oblong, retuse, ⅛ to $\frac{3}{16}$ in. long, ciliate-hairy. *fl.* in sub-terminal umbels of 10 or 12; cor. 1¼ in. long, $\frac{3}{16}$ in. wide, contracted below mouth, very viscid, red or orange at base, paling upwards; lobes small, erect, greenish. Summer. S. Africa. 1789. (B.M. 356.) var. **minor,** cor. shorter, less inflated. (B.M. 2266 as *E. gemmifera.*)

**E. mediterra'nea.*** Dense, upright shrub, 4 to 10 ft. h., young shoots smooth. *l.* in fours, linear, about ¼ in. long. *fl.* in leafy racemes at ends of branches; cor. pink, ovoid-urn-shaped, ¼ in. long; cal. lobes oblong-lanceolate, just over half as long as cor. March to May. SW. Europe, including Galway. 1648. (B.T.S. 1, 523.) Syn. *E. carnea occidentalis*. var. **al'ba,** *fl.* white, dwarfer and less robust than type, February to April; **Brightness,** *fl.* bright red, dwarf and more tender than type, March to May; **hiber'nica,** *l.* rather glaucous, dwarfer and less floriferous than type, February to April. Syn. var. *glauca*; **na'na,** cushion-like, 1 to 1½ ft. h., not very free-flowering, March, April; **ru'bra,*** *fl.* red, April to June; **superb'a,** *fl.* rather large, pinkish, April to June. For *E. mediterranea hybrida* see **E. × darleyensis.**

**E. melan'thera.** Compact shrub, 1 to 2 ft., shoots downy. *l.* ⅛ to ⅙ in. long, linear to ovate-lanceolate, grooved. *fl.* on downy stalks $\frac{1}{12}$ to ⅛ in. long; cor. pale or bright red, obconic to funnel-shaped, ⅛ in. long; lobes rounded; anthers black. S. Africa. Probably not in cultivation; the plant figured L.B.C. 867, and until lately grown under this name, is *E. canaliculata*, q.v.

**E. muco'sa.** Shrub 1½ to 4 ft., entirely glabrous. *l.* in fours, up to ¼ in. long, linear to linear-oblong, thick, rigid, blunt. *fl.* in terminal umbels of 3 to 6, stalks up to ¼ in. long; sep. narrowly ovate to lanceolate, clammy, ⅛ in. long, coloured; cor. dull red or purple, urn-shaped, ⅛ in. long, very clammy; lobes erect. Summer. S. Africa. (A.H. 174.)

**E. multiflo'ra.** Ascending shrub, 12 to 18 in. h. in cultivation, but sometimes almost like a small tree in nature. Young shoots smooth. *l.* in whorls of 4 or 5, linear, ¼ to ⅜ in. long, slightly hairy at base. *fl.* in erect, terminal racemes 2 to 4 in. long; cor. ovate-urn-shaped, pink, about ⅙ in. long, lobes narrow, acute; cal. one-third as long as cor., lobes white, oblong-lanceolate; stamens exserted. November to February. S. Europe, Algeria. 1731. (Moggridge, Fl. Men. 59.) Syn. *E. peduncularis*. Resembles *E. vagans* but less hardy, *fl.* larger, anther-lobes different.

**E. mun'dula.** A synonym of *E. fastigiata*.

**E. nidula'ria.** Shrub with slender, reddish, downy shoots. *l.* in fours, linear-oblong, blunt, ⅛ in. long. *fl.* in clusters of 6 to 8; cor. urn-shaped to bell-shaped, ⅛ to ⅙ in. long, white, scarcely constricted at mouth, finely downy; lobes erect. S. Africa. (L.B.C. 764.)

**E. nudiflo'ra.** Shrub 1 to 1½ ft., shoots hairy. *l.* in threes, linear, ⅛ to ⅙ in. long, glabrous above, bristly below, ciliate. *fl.* axillary making short terminal racemes; stalks slender, downy, ⅛ to ⅙ in. long; cor. bell-shaped, not contracted at mouth, bright red, purplish-red, rarely pale rose. September, October. S. Africa. 1810. (L.B.C. 874 as *E. alopecuroides.*)

**E. odora'ta.*** Shrub 1 ft., shoots glabrous. *l.* in threes, linear, thick, keeled, ⅛ to ⅙ in. long, ciliate. *fl.* fragrant, in terminal clusters of 3 or 6 or indefinite; stalks slender, ½ to 1 in. long; cor. bell-shaped, white, tinged purple, about ⅙ in. long and wide; lobes shallow, spreading. May to July. S. Africa. 1784. (B.M. 1399; A.H. 253 as *E. Beaumontia.*)

**E. Pagea'na.** Erect shrub 1 ft. or more h., young shoots downy. *l.* in whorls of 4, linear, sub-acute, about ¼ in. long, ciliate, downy at first. *fl.* terminal and lateral, the whole forming an irregular panicle; cor. bell-shaped, rich yellow, ¼ in. long or more, ¼ in. across; lobes 4, broad, rounded; cal. lobes ovate-lanceolate, ciliate, pale green, short; anthers included; stigma dark brown. March, April. S. Africa. About 1920. (B.M. 9133.) Syn. *E. campanulata*.

**E. Parment'ieri.** A synonym of *E. pellucida*.

**E. parviflo'ra.** Shrub 1 to 3 ft., shoots hairy. *l.* in fours, linear, grooved, more or less hairy, ⅛ to ¼ in. long. *fl.* clustered, 3 to 6, terminal on short side twigs making, collectively, slender racemes 6 or 8 in. long; cor. urn-shaped, ⅛ in. long, red or pink, downy; lobes erect. November to April. S. Africa. (B.M. 480 as *E. pubescens.*) var. **his'pida,** cor. broader, ovary bristly.

**E. Paterson'ia.** A synonym of *E. abietina*.

**E. peduncula'ta.** A synonym of *E. pilulifera*.

**E. pellu'cida.*** Shrub about 1 ft. *l.* in fours, incurved, linear, closely set, ⅛ to ⅓ in. long. *fl.* in fours, often in dense masses, terminating short side shoots; cor. bright rose, about ½ in. long, tubular, rather inflated. June to August. S. Africa. 1810. (L.B.C. 197 as *E. Parmentieri.*)

**E. penicilla'ta.** A synonym of *E. Plukenetii*.

**E. persolu'ta.** Shrub 1 to 3 ft., shoots downy. *l.* $\frac{1}{8}$ to $\frac{1}{4}$ in. long, glabrous or slightly downy. *fl.* in fours, terminating short, lateral twigs, making collectively leafy racemes 4 to 7 in. long; cor. cup-shaped, $\frac{1}{6}$ in. wide, rosy-red. March to May. S. Africa. 1774. var. **al'ba,** *fl.* white; **lae'vis,** *fl.* white, cor. more open. (A.H. 221 as *E. laevis.*) SYN. *E. cyathiformis.*

**E. perspic'ua.*** Shrub 2 ft. or more. *l.* in threes or fours, narrow-linear, downy or glabrous, $\frac{1}{8}$ to $\frac{1}{4}$ in. long. *fl.* 1 to 3, terminating short twigs forming a panicle $2\frac{1}{2}$ in. wide and several in. long; cor. tubular, $\frac{3}{4}$ to 1 in. long, $\frac{1}{4}$ in. wide at mouth, pale rose or almost white at upper part, deeper rose or purplish towards base. May to August. S. Africa. 1800. (A.H. 230.) May have some part in the origin of *E. hyemalis.*

**E. Petiv'eri.** Shrub 2 to 3 ft. *l.* in threes, $\frac{1}{8}$ to $\frac{1}{3}$ in. long, densely set. *fl.* solitary, in twos or threes terminating short shoots, nodding; cor. narrowly conical-tubular, greenish-yellow, orange or reddish, up to $\frac{3}{4}$ in. long, narrowed at mouth; anthers exserted by $\frac{1}{4}$ in. August to October. S. Africa. 1774. SYN. *E. Sebana.* var. **auran'tia,** *fl.* orange. (A.H. 83.); **lut'ea,** *fl.* yellow. (A.H. 84.); **spica'ta,** *fl.* scarlet; cor. incurved inwards. (A.H. 190.); **vi'ridis,** *fl.* pale green (A.H. 85). All these varieties are placed as such under *E. Sebana* by Andrews.

**E. Pezi'za.** Shrub 1 to $1\frac{1}{2}$ ft., shoots downy. *l.* in threes, linear, blunt, lustrous, $\frac{1}{8}$ to $\frac{1}{6}$ in. long. *fl.* mostly in threes, copiously produced; stalks downy, $\frac{1}{8}$ in. long; cor. white, $\frac{1}{8}$ in. long, cup-shaped to obconic, not contracted at mouth, densely downy. S. Africa. (L.B.C. 265.)

**E. physo'des.** Shrub $1\frac{1}{2}$ to $2\frac{1}{2}$ ft., shoots and fl.-stalks downy. *l.* in fours or sometimes threes, linear, 3-angled, keeled, shining, $\frac{1}{4}$ in. long. *fl.* in terminal twos, threes, or fours, nodding; cor ovoid-globose, much-narrowed or almost closed at mouth, $\frac{1}{4}$ to $\frac{1}{3}$ in. long, very clammy, white; lobes small, erect. Spring. S. Africa. 1788. (A.H. 34.)

**E. pilulif'era.** Shrub 1 to 2 ft. *l.* in fours or scattered, crowded, erect, downy, ciliate, $\frac{1}{4}$ to $\frac{1}{2}$ in. long. *fl.* in terminal umbels of 4 to 8, each on a glabrous stalk up to $\frac{1}{2}$ in. long; sep. red; cor. globose-bell-shaped, $\frac{1}{4}$ in. long, nearly as wide, soft pinkish-purple; lobes short, erect. March to June. S. Africa. (A.H. 229 as *E. pedunculata.*)

**E. Plukenet'ii.** Shrub 1 to 2 ft., glabrous. *l.* in threes, $\frac{1}{2}$ to $\frac{3}{4}$ in. long, dense and overlapping, *fl.* solitary on a curving stalk $\frac{3}{8}$ in. long, pendulous; cal. $\frac{3}{8}$ in. long; sep. narrow-lanceolate, pointed; cor. tubular, narrowing towards mouth, $\frac{1}{2}$ to $\frac{3}{4}$ in. long, purplish-red; stamens exserted $\frac{1}{2}$ in. May to August. S. Africa. (A.H. 186; 135 as *E. penicillata.*)

**E. plumo'sa.** A synonym of *E. amoena.*

**E. prae'stans.** A synonym of *E. Walkeria praestans.*

**E. primuloi'des.*** Shrub 1 to $1\frac{1}{2}$ ft., young shoots downy. *l.* in fives or sometimes fours, very crowded, incurved, $\frac{1}{8}$ to $\frac{1}{4}$ in. long, pointed. *fl.* in terminal clusters of usually 4 or 5, scarcely stalked; cor. cylindrical-ovoid, $\frac{1}{3}$ in. long, swollen towards base, bright red, narrowed to mouth; limb $\frac{3}{8}$ in. across, white, the most showy part. Summer. S. Africa. 1802. (A.H. 233.)

**E. propen'dens.** Shrub 1 to $1\frac{1}{2}$ ft., young shoots downy. *l.* in fours, linear, ciliate, $\frac{1}{8}$ to $\frac{1}{6}$ in. long. *fl.* terminal, nodding, solitary to fours; cal. $\frac{1}{8}$ in. long, coloured; cor. bell-shaped, pale red, $\frac{1}{3}$ in. long, downy; lobes erect or spreading. Spring. S. Africa. (B.M. 2140.)

**E. pubes'cens.** A synonym of *E. parviflora.*

**E. pusil'la.** Shrub 1 to 2 ft., shoots downy and hairy. *l.* in fours, $\frac{1}{8}$ to $\frac{1}{5}$ in. long, slenderly linear. *fl.* in fours; stalk hairy, $\frac{1}{10}$ in. long; cor. small, bell-shaped to obconic, widening to mouth, hairy, pale rose; lobes half to as long as the tube. S. Africa. (L.B.C. 1844 as *E. villosiuscula.*)

**E. pyramida'lis.** Shrub 1 to 2 ft. *l.* in fours, erect, linear, $\frac{1}{4}$ to $\frac{1}{3}$ in. long. *fl.* in fours terminating short, leafy, lateral twigs, forming as a whole a pyramidal panicle 5 or 6 in. long; cor. broadly funnel-shaped, $\frac{3}{8}$ in. long, rosy-red; lobes almost erect. September to March. S. Africa. 1787. (A.H. 142.)

**E. quadrangula'ris.** Shrub 1 to $1\frac{1}{2}$ ft., shoots minutely downy. *l.* in fours, linear, ciliate when young, up to $\frac{1}{8}$ in. long. *fl.* in fours, small but abundant, stalk slender, $\frac{1}{12}$ in. long; cor. broadly cup-shaped to inversely conical, $\frac{1}{8}$ in. long, white to rosy; lobes erect. S. Africa. *E. quadrangularis* of A.H. 280, is quite different, probably a hybrid.

**E. racemif'era.** A synonym of *E. regerminans.*

**E. ramenta'cea.*** Shrub 1 to 2 ft. *l.* in fours, linear, very slender, $\frac{1}{6}$ to $\frac{1}{4}$ in. long, erect. *fl.* in terminal umbels, scent musk-like; stalk red, $\frac{1}{8}$ in. long, bracts and sep. red or reddish; cor. globose or rather ovoid, $\frac{1}{8}$ to $\frac{1}{6}$ in. long, crimson; lobes short, erect, darker. August to October. S. Africa. 1786. (A.H. 143.)

**E. reflex'a.** A synonym of *E. glomiflora.*

**E. reger'minans.** Shrub 1 to 2 ft. *l.* in threes, fours, or sixes, erect, $\frac{1}{4}$ to $\frac{1}{2}$ in. long, slender. *fl.* crowded in dense, cylindrical, spike-like racemes 2 to 5 in. long, $\frac{5}{8}$ in. wide, near end of shoot; cor. globose inclined to ovoid, $\frac{1}{8}$ in. long, pale rosy to bright red; lobes very short, slightly reflexed. April to June. S. Africa. (A.H. 188 as *E. racemifera.*)

**E. re'gia.*** Straggling, slender-stemmed shrub, 2 to 3 ft. *l.* in sixes, erect, $\frac{1}{4}$ to $\frac{1}{2}$ in. long, glabrous or slightly downy. *fl.* drooping, crowded in a group surrounding the stem below top of shoot; cor. tubular, contracted at mouth, $\frac{3}{4}$ in. long, $\frac{1}{6}$ in. wide, clammy, crimson. S. Africa. var. **variega'ta,** cor. white or pink at base, changing upwards to purple-red and sometimes green. Known locally as Elim Heath.

**E. retor'ta.** Shrub 1 to $1\frac{1}{2}$ ft., densely leafy. *l.* in fours, $\frac{1}{8}$ to $\frac{3}{16}$ in. long, narrowly ovate-lanceolate, decurved, thick and stiff, ciliate, terminated by a long bristle. *fl.* in erect terminal clusters of 4 to 8; cor. flask-shaped, $\frac{3}{4}$ in. long, $\frac{1}{4}$ in. wide at base, pink except below mouth where it is crimson. June to August. S. Africa. (B.M. 362; L.B.C. 1105 as *E. eximia.*)

**E. ru'bens.** Glabrous shrub, 12 in. or more. *l.* in fours, erect, dense, and overlapping, $\frac{1}{6}$ to $\frac{1}{4}$ in. long. *fl.* in terminal, nodding clusters of 3 to 8; cor. globose-ovoid, about $\frac{1}{6}$ in. long, rich red; lobes erect. June to August. S. Africa. 1798. (A.H. 43.)

**E. rubroca'lyx.*** Shrub 1 to 2 ft. *l.* in fours, $\frac{1}{8}$ to $\frac{1}{4}$ in. long, linear. *fl.* in pairs to fours, terminal on lateral twigs; cal. reddish-purple; cor. tubular, $\frac{1}{2}$ in. long, white; lobes erect, pointed. Spring to summer. S. Africa. (A.H. 285.) Probably a natural hybrid.

**E. Savil'eana.** Shrub about 1 ft., shoots downy. *l.* in fours, linear, ciliate, up to $\frac{1}{4}$ in. long. *fl.* axillary, solitary, forming leafy racemes 1 to 2 in. long; cor. ovoid-globose, $\frac{3}{16}$ in. wide, purplish-red. April to August. S. Africa. 1800. (A.H. 238.)

**E. scabrius'cula.** Shrub 2 to 3 ft., shoots glandular-bristly. *l.* in fours, $\frac{1}{8}$ to $\frac{1}{6}$ in. long, margins revolute, blunt, glandular-bristly. *fl.* in fours or clusters; stalks $\frac{1}{8}$ in. long, hairy; sep. oblong to lanceolate, coloured, downy; cor. pale rose, $\frac{1}{8}$ in. long, ovoid to urn-shaped; lobes short, erect. S. Africa. (L.B.C. 517.) **A**

**E. scopa'ria.** Besom Heath. More or less erect shrub or small tree to 15 ft. Young wood smooth. *l.* in scattered whorls of 3 or 4, linear, $\frac{1}{4}$ in. long, acute. *fl.* insignificant, in terminal leafy racemes; cor. globose-urn-shaped, greenish, $\frac{1}{12}$ in. long; cal. about half as long as cor., lobes ovate; anthers included. May, June. W. Mediterranean region, Madeira. 1770. (Moggridge, Fl. Men. 59.) var. **pu'mila,** rarely over 18 in. h.

**E. Seba'na.** A synonym of *E. Petiveri.*

**E. sessiliflo'ra.** Shrub $1\frac{1}{2}$ to 2 ft., erect, densely leafy. *l.* in fours, linear-awl-shaped, $\frac{1}{4}$ to $\frac{1}{3}$ in. long. *fl.* sessile in the axils of the topmost l., yellowish-green, forming a rounded cluster 2 or 3 in. across; cor. about 1 in. long, slightly curved and funnel-shaped, $\frac{3}{16}$ in. wide at top, tapering downwards; lobes rounded, $\frac{1}{10}$ in. wide. May to July. S. Africa. (B.M. 8868.)

**E. Shannonia'na.*** Shrub 1 to 2 ft., shoots glabrous, densely leafy. *l.* in threes, awl-shaped, bristle-tipped, ciliate, $\frac{1}{2}$ to $\frac{3}{4}$ in. long. *fl.* in terminal umbels of 6 to 9; stalk $\frac{1}{2}$ to $\frac{5}{8}$ in. long; sep. linear-lanceolate, $\frac{1}{3}$ in. long, red; cor. $1\frac{1}{4}$ in. long, $\frac{3}{8}$ in. wide at the swollen base, viscous, white, tinged red, narrowed to the greenish neck, nearly $\frac{1}{2}$ in. wide across the broadly ovate lobes. June to September. S. Africa. 1828. (A.H 239; B M. 4069.)

**E. sit'iens.** Shrub 1 to 2 ft. erect, shoots more or less downy. *l.* in fours or threes, $\frac{1}{8}$ to $\frac{1}{3}$ in. long, linear, pointed, sometimes ciliate. *fl.* in fours, sometimes in threes or solitary; sep. lanceolate, inflated, $\frac{1}{4}$ to $\frac{1}{3}$ in. long, white to red. S. Africa.

**E. Solan'dra.** Shrub 6 to 12 in., shoots downy or hairy. *l.* in fours, linear, grooved, up to $\frac{1}{5}$ in. long, densely bristly, hairy beneath. *fl.* crowded in hemispherical terminal heads, $\frac{1}{4}$ to $\frac{1}{2}$ in. across; sep. bristly hairy; cor. ovoid, $\frac{1}{8}$ to $\frac{1}{6}$ in. long, pink. February to April. S. Africa. (A.H. 89.)

**E. specio'sa.** Shrub 2 to 4 ft. *l.* in threes, linear to narrow-lanceolate, $\frac{1}{6}$ to $\frac{1}{2}$ in. long, grooved, often ciliate. *fl.* in terminal clusters of 2 to 4; cor. curved-tubular, 1 in. long, $\frac{1}{4}$ in. wide, viscous, bright red, greenish towards top; lobes small, recurved. June to August. S. Africa. 1800. (A.H. 192.)

**E. × Spenceria'na** (*E. depressa* × *E. hybrida*). Shrub 1 to $1\frac{1}{2}$ ft. *l.* very densely set, linear-awl-shaped, $\frac{1}{6}$ to $\frac{1}{4}$ in. long. *fl.* in terminal clusters; cor. white, 1 in. long, tubular, tapering slightly towards base; limb $\frac{1}{4}$ in. across; lobes rounded. June. (F.d.S. 2323.)

**E. stric'ta.** A synonym of *E. terminalis.*

**E. Stuar'tii** (*E. mediterranea* × *E. Tetralix Mackayi*). Shrub of 9 to 12 in. *fl.* pink, rather narrowly urn-shaped. June to September. W. Galway. 1890.

**E. subdivarica'ta.** Shrub 1 to 3 ft., shoots usually hairy. *l.* in fours, linear, $\frac{1}{6}$ in. long. *fl.* fragrant, in fours terminating very short twigs, forming collectively slender, leafy racemes 2 to 4 in. long; cor. white, bell-shaped, not contracted at mouth, $\frac{1}{8}$ in. long. Winter. S. Africa. 1802. SYN. *E. caffra.*

**E. subula'ta.** Erect shrub, 1 to $2\frac{1}{2}$ ft., shoots downy and hairy. *l.* $\frac{1}{3}$ to $\frac{2}{3}$ in. long, sharply pointed, incurved, glabrous. *fl.* terminal, in fours or numerous in clusters $\frac{1}{2}$ in. across; bracts and sep. bristle-tipped; cor. tubular-bell-shaped, pale rose, $\frac{1}{6}$ to $\frac{3}{16}$ in. long; lobes shallow, erect. S. Africa.

**E. sulphu'rea.** A synonym of *E. curviflora sulphurea.*

**E. taxifo'lia.*** Shrub about 1 ft. *l.* in threes, linear, 3-sided, pointed, $\frac{1}{3}$ to $\frac{1}{2}$ in. long. *fl.* in terminal umbels or clusters, sometimes axillary; bracts, sep. and cor. wholly pink; sep. ovate to obovate, pointed, $\frac{1}{4}$ to $\frac{3}{8}$ in. long; cor. roundish-ovoid, $\frac{1}{4}$ to $\frac{3}{8}$ in. long. Autumn. S. Africa. (A.H. 93.)

**E. termina'lis.*** Corsican Heath. Erect, bushy shrub, 4 to 8 ft. h., young shoots downy. *l.* usually in whorls of 4, linear, $\frac{1}{4}$ in. long, sub-acute, finely ciliate. *fl.* in terminal umbels of 4 to 8; cor. cylindrical-urn-shaped, rosy-pink, $\frac{3}{16}$ to $\frac{1}{4}$ in. long, lobes recurved; cal. about half as long as cor., lobes ovate-acuminate, brownish; anthers included. June to November. W. Mediterranean region. 1765. (B.M. 8063.) SYN. *E. corsica, E. ramulosa, E. stricta.*

**E. Tet'ralix.** Cross-leaved Heath. Rather spreading shrub 12 to 20 in. h., young shoots ascending, downy. *l.* in whorls of 4, oblong-ovate, $\frac{1}{8}$ in. long, glaucous beneath, ciliate. *fl.* from terminal l.-axils in umbel-like clusters; cor. cylindrical-urn-shaped, rosy-pink, about $\frac{1}{4}$ in. long, lobes short, recurved; cal. lobes ovate-lanceolate, downy, ciliate; anthers included. June to October. *fr.* a downy capsule. N. and W. Europe, including Britain. (E.B. 889.) Like *E. ciliaris* this resents dry soil. var. **al'ba,** *fl.* white; **Mackay'i,** *l.* less recurved, *fl.* darker, shorter, and wider than in type, capsule smooth. W. Ireland, NW. Spain. 1833. SYN. *E. Mackaiana.* Probably a hybrid (*E. ciliaris* × *E. Tetralix*); **Martine'sii,** *fl.* pink, stems and *l.* whitish-downy giving a grey appearance to the plant. SYN. var. *canescens,* var. *tomentosa*; **E. mol'lis,** *fl.* white, otherwise like var. *Martinesii*; **ple'na,** *fl.* double. SYN. var. *fl. pleno, E. Crawfurdii*; **Silver Bells,*** *fl.* silvery-pink, plant only 6 in. h.

**E. Thunberg'ii.*** Shrub 6 to 18 in. *l.* in threes, erect, linear, $\frac{1}{8}$ to $\frac{1}{4}$ in. long. *fl.* in terminal umbels of 1 to 3; stalk slender, $\frac{1}{4}$ to $\frac{1}{2}$ in. long; cor. globose at base which is small and largely hidden by sep. constricted above; limb cup-shaped, $\frac{3}{8}$ in. across; lobes large, rounded, rich red, making much the chief feature of the fl. May. S. Africa. 1794. (B.M. 1214.)

**E. × translu'cens** (*E. tubiflora* × *E. ventricosa*). Shrub $1\frac{1}{2}$ to 2 ft., shoots very slender. *l.* in threes and fours, linear, erect, $\frac{1}{8}$ to $\frac{1}{4}$ in. long, 3-sided, glabrous. *fl.* mostly in threes terminating short side twigs; cor. deep rose, tubular, downy, $\frac{5}{8}$ to $\frac{3}{4}$ in. long; lobes shallow, recurved. June to August. (A.H. 295.)

**E. transpar'ens.** Shrub 2 to 5 ft., shoots slightly downy. *l.* in threes, linear, grooved, $\frac{1}{8}$ to $\frac{1}{3}$ in. long. *fl.* mostly in terminal threes, nodding; cor. 1 in. long, $\frac{1}{8}$ in. wide, tubular, very viscous, tube pink; lobes erect, green. Winter, spring. (A.H. 296.) SYN. *E. diaphana.*

**E. trium'phans.** Figured in L.B.C. 257 under this name and in B.M. 2322 as *E. andromedaeflora triumphans,* this Heath is now considered to be a coloured var. of *E. holosericea* or perhaps a hybrid. *fl.* white, axillary; cor. ovoid, $\frac{1}{3}$ in. long, $\frac{1}{4}$ in. wide; cal. coloured like cor. June, July.

**E. turrig'era.** Shrub 1 to 3 ft., shoots hairy. *l.* $\frac{1}{8}$ to $\frac{1}{4}$ in. long, linear, furrowed, sometimes rough and hairy, ciliate. *fl.* in terminal fours on lateral twigs; cor. globose to broadly ovoid, $\frac{3}{16}$ in. wide, deep pink; stalk $\frac{1}{8}$ to $\frac{1}{4}$ in. long, red. Spring to summer. S. Africa. 1787. (L.B.C. 939 as *E. Bergiana*; A.H. 41 as *E. quadriflora.*)

**E. umbella'ta.** Shrub of 1 to 3 ft. with erect or tortuous branches, young shoots downy. *l.* usually in threes, linear, about $\frac{1}{8}$ in. long, obtuse. *fl.* in umbels of 3 to 6 at ends of shoots; cor. ovoid-globose-urn-shaped, pink or red, about $\frac{1}{8}$ in. long, lobes broad; cal. half as long as cor., lobes linear-oblong; anthers exserted, 2-partite to middle. May, June. Spain, Portugal, Morocco. Not reliably hardy, but will endure any but very severe winters in S. and W. Britain.

**E. urceola'ris.** Shrub 4 to 12 ft., erect, shoots downy. *l.* in threes, $\frac{1}{4}$ to $\frac{1}{2}$ in. long, linear to linear-lanceolate, pointed, grey-downy. *fl.* in terminal threes or in umbels of 6 or more; cor. white or yellowish-white, tubular-ovoid, contracted towards the mouth, $\frac{1}{4}$ in. long, $\frac{1}{12}$ in. wide, downy; lobes erect. June to August. S. Africa. (L.B.C. 1894.)

**E. va'gans.*** Cornish Heath. Straggling shrub 1 to 3 ft. h., young wood glabrous. *l.* in whorls of 4 or 5, linear, about $\frac{3}{8}$ in. long, blunt or almost so, margin strongly recurved. *fl.* in erect, terminal, cylindrical racemes 3 to 8 in. long; cor. globose-urn-shaped, purplish-pink, about $\frac{1}{8}$ in. long; lobes broad, scarcely recurved; cal. about one-third as long as cor., lobes ovate, whitish; anthers exserted, 2-partite to base. July to November. SW. Europe, including Cornwall. (E.B. 893.) Liable to suffer in very severe winters; less hardy than *E. mediterranea.* var. **al'ba,** *fl.* white, in dense, terminal racemes, not very attractive; **grandiflo'ra,** *fl.* pinkish, rather larger than in type; racemes long; **Lyonesse,*** *fl.* white, in long racemes; **Mrs. Maxwell,*** similar to *St. Keverne* but racemes longer; **Mullion,** compact, *fl.* rose. Cornwall; **ru'bra,** more erect and *fl.* darker than in type; **St. Keverne,** dwarfer than type, *fl.* bell-shaped, rose. Cornwall. SYN. var. *kevernensis.*

**E. × Veitch'ii*** (*E. arborea* × *E. lusitanica*). Intermediate between parents. Shrub of 3 to 6 ft. with upright-spreading, feathery branches. *fl.* in a leafy panicle; cor. more or less ovoid, white, about $\frac{1}{8}$ in. long; stigma pink, flattened. February to April. Of garden origin. 1905. (G.C. 37 (1905), 228.)

**E. ventrico'sa.*** Shrub 2 to 6 ft. *l.* in fours, densely set, $\frac{1}{2}$ to $\frac{5}{8}$ in. long, ciliate, linear-awl-shaped. *fl.* erect, packed in terminal umbels; stalks downy, $\frac{1}{4}$ to $\frac{1}{3}$ in. long; cor. $\frac{1}{2}$ to $\frac{3}{4}$ in. long, ovoid, bellied towards base, narrowed to mouth, white to rosy, shining as if glazed; lobes small, reflexed. June to September. S. Africa. 1787. (B.M. 350.) Numerous vars. of this popular Heath have been raised; **al'ba,** china-white; **breviflo'ra,** cor. rosy-red, short, stout; **car'nea,** flesh-coloured; **coccin'ea mi'nor,*** cor. white, slender; lobes bright red, reflexed; **grandiflo'ra,*** *fl.* rosy-purple, over 1 in. long; **splen'dens,** cor. nearly 1 in. long; neck and limb rosy-purple and white; **tric'olor,** tube of cor. blush; neck carmine; lobes white.

**E. ver'sicolor.*** Shrub 2 to 4 ft. *l.* in threes, $\frac{1}{3}$ to $\frac{1}{3}$ in. long, linear, sometimes downy and ciliate. *fl.* in terminal clusters of 3 on short, leafy shoots; sep. lanceolate, coloured, $\frac{1}{4}$ in. long; cor. tubular, $\frac{3}{4}$ to 1 in. long, red below, the top and lobes greenish-yellow. Autumn to spring. S. Africa. (A.H. 47; A.H. 13 as *E. costata.*)

**E. verticilla'ta.** A synonym of *E. concinna* and *E. mammosa.*

**E. vesti'ta.*** Shrub 2 to 3 ft. *l.* in sixes, very densely set, erect, linear, pointed, glabrous, $\frac{1}{2}$ to $1\frac{1}{3}$ in. long. *fl.* axillary, in whorls crowded at 1 or 2 in. below the end of the shoots; cor. 1 in. long, tubular, downy, white, yellow, rosy, or crimson; lobes erect. May to September. S. Africa. 1789. var. **al'ba,** cor. pure white. (A.H. 47.); **car'nea,** cor. flesh-colour. (A.H. 246.); **coccin'ea,*** cor. scarlet. (A.H. 199.); **incarna'ta,** cor. delicate pink, over 1 in. long. (A.H. 97.); **lu'tea,** cor. pale yellow. (A.H. 247.); **ro'sea,** cor. rosy-red. (A.H. 98.)

**E. villosius'cula.** A synonym of *E. pusilla.*

**E. viridiflo'ra.*** Shrub 3 to 4 ft., shoots stout. *l.* spreading, linear, $\frac{1}{4}$ to $\frac{1}{3}$ in. long, pointed, glabrous. *fl.* in nodding clusters of threes terminating short, leafy shoots; cor. green, 1 to $1\frac{1}{8}$ in. long, tubular but tapering slightly to both ends and forming a neck; lobes ovate-oblong, $\frac{3}{16}$ in. long. June to August. S. Africa. (A.H. 299.)

**E. viridipurpu'rea.** Shrub 1 to 2 ft., shoots downy. *l.* in fours, linear, blunt, sometimes ciliate, $\frac{1}{8}$ to $\frac{1}{4}$ in. long. *fl.* in fours clustered at end of short twigs, fragrant; sep. usually rosy; cor. bell-shaped, purplish-red, $\frac{1}{8}$ in. long and wide; lobes spreading. S. Africa. 1774. (B.M. 342 as *E. persoluta*; A.H. 235 as *E. regerminans.*)

**E. Walker'ia.** Shrub 1 to $1\frac{1}{2}$ ft. *l.* in fours, linear, $\frac{1}{8}$ in. long. *fl.* in terminal fours, scarcely stalked, erect; cor. flask-shaped, rosy or red, $\frac{1}{4}$ to $\frac{1}{3}$ in. long; limb $\frac{1}{4}$ in. wide; lobes spreading. February to June. S. Africa. (A.H. 50; A.H. 62 as *E. fastigiata.*) var. **prae'stans,** cor. white, lobes larger. (A.H. 232 as *E. praestans.*)

**E. × Wat'sonii** (*E. ciliaris* × *E. Tetralix*). *l.* usually in whorls of 4. *fl.* urn-shaped as in *E. ciliaris,* but racemess horter; cor. rosy, stamens included. Nr. Truro, Cornwall.

**E. × Williams'ii** (*E. Tetralix* × *E. vagans*). *fl.* rosy, urn-shaped, in terminal umbels; stamens included. Lizard, Cornwall. 1910.

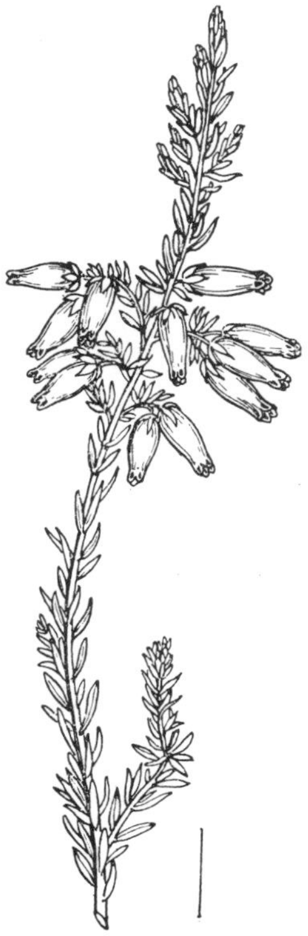

*Erica × Willmorei*

**E. × Willmor'ei.*** Shrub up to 2 ft. *l.* in threes, $\frac{1}{8}$ to $\frac{1}{4}$ in. long, linear, densely set, channelled. *fl.* axillary, crowded, forming leafy racemes 6 in. or more long and 2 in. wide; cor. deep pink, tipped white, tubular, about 1 in. long, $\frac{1}{4}$ in. wide at mouth, tapering slightly downwards. Hybrid of unrecorded parentage. Raised about 1835. (G.C. 19 (1896), 200.)

## ERICA'CEAE.

**ERICA'CEAE.** Dicotyledons. A family of about 70 genera with 1,500 species in cold and temperate regions and on high mountains in the tropics. Shrubs or small trees often evergreen with usually alternate (sometimes opposite or whorled) leaves without stipules. Flowers perfect, regular or almost so, variously arranged; calyx 4- or 5-parted, persistent; corolla 4- or 5-parted (petals rarely distinct) or urceolate; stamens 5 or 10, at base of a hypogynous disk, anthers opening by apical pores (rarely slits); ovary superior or inferior, 2- to 5-celled, ovules many. Fruit a capsule, rarely a berry or drupe. The family contains many highly decorative plants and almost all its members fail to flourish in any but acid soils and are among the most marked of mycorrhizal plants. The genera treated in this book are Agapetes, Agarista, Agauria, Andromeda, Arbutus, Arcterica, Arctostaphylos, Befaria, Blaeria, Bruckenthalia, Bryanthus, Calluna, Cassiope, Cavendishia, Chamaedaphne, Chiogenes, Cladothamnus, Comarostaphylos, Daboecia, Diplocosia, Elliottia, Enkianthus, Epigaea, Eremia, Erica, Ericinella, Eurygania, Gaultheria, Gaylussacia, Gonocalyx, Kalmia, Kalmiopsis, Ledum, Leiophyllum, Leucothoe, Loiseleuria, Lyonia, Macleania, Menziesia, Orphanidesia, Oxydendron, Pentapera, Pentapterygium, Pernettya, Phyllodoce, × Phyllothamnus, Pieris, Psammisia, Pterospora, Rhododendron, Rhodothamnus, Sympieza, Themistoclesia, Thibaudia, Tripetaleia, Tsusiophyllum, Vaccinium, Wittsteinia, Zenobia.

**ERICINELL'A** (diminutive of Erica). FAM. *Ericaceae*. A genus of some 4 species of evergreen shrubs closely related to Erica (which differs in having 8 stamens). Natives of Trop. and S. Africa and Madagascar. The following species, a graceful, pretty shrub, should be treated like a Cape Heath. Two S. African species, *E. multiflora* and *E. passerinoides*, are not yet introduced.

**E. Mann'ii.** Heath-like shrub 4 to 12 ft., shoots erect, downy. *l.* in whorls of 3 or 4, 1/8 in. long, linear, margins revolute, very densely set, glabrous. *fl.* in terminal clusters of 3 or 4, nodding; cor. red, nearly globose, 1/10 in. long, with 4 short, ciliate lobes; stamens 4 or 5, included in the cor., style exserted. July. Cameroon Mts., Upper Guinea, up to 10,000 ft. alt. 1861. (B.M. 5569.)

W. J. B.

***erici'nus -a -um,*** heath-like.

***ericoi'des,*** heath-like.

***Ericsson'ii,*** in honour of Mr. Ericsson, traveller for Messrs. Sander of St. Albans, *c.* 1893, collected in Malaya.

**ERIG'ERON** (*Eriogron*, name given by Theophrastus to a Composite). FAM. *Compositae*. A genus of about 150 species of annual, biennial, or perennial herbs, resembling Aster but with ray-florets in several series. Most species are hardy but 1 or 2 from warmer regions, like *E. mucronatus*, may be liable to winter damage in some districts, and of these cuttings should be made in autumn and put into a cold frame. Most of the species are best placed in front of the herbaceous border or on the rock-garden, and several provide excellent material for cut-flowers. The larger perennial species can be grown readily in almost any garden soil which is reasonably moist and well drained. Propagation is by seed sown in early summer outdoors and by division in autumn, or better in spring. Two introduced annual species, *E. acer* and *E. canadensis*, have become widely spread weeds which should be rigorously kept down as they harbour pests such as the tarnished plant-bug which does very considerable damage to many cultivated plants.

**E. a'cer.** See above.

**E. alpi'nus.** Perennial, hispid, hairy, 6 to 8 in. h., with a short root-stock. *l.* radical, oblong-lanceolate, those on stem few, linear-oblong. *fl.-heads* 1 to 3, 3/4 in. across, on a stout peduncle; ray-florets numerous, purple, rays very slender; disk-florets yellow. July, August. Pappus reddish. Widely distributed in alpine and arctic regions, including Britain. (E.B. 775.) Rock-garden.

**E. at'ticus.** Perennial, downy, erect, about 12 in. h., branched near top. *l.* lanceolate, roughly hairy, sessile. *fl.-heads* solitary or in corymbs; ray-florets many, purple. Europe. 1804. (B.R. 583; L.B.C. 1390 as *E. Villarsii*.)

**E. auranti'acus.** Orange Daisy. Herbaceous, more or less velvety perennial about 1 ft. h. *l.* oblong, entire, the upper lanceolate, sessile. *fl.-heads* about 2 in. across, solitary, on a stout, erect peduncle; ray-florets bright orange. Summer. Turkestan. 1879. A paler form is var. **sulphu'reus.** Border.

**E. au'reus.** Perennial, about 3 in. h., hairy. *Basal l.* spatulate, entire, stalked; *stem-l.* narrower, sessile. *fl.-heads* solitary, 1/2 to 3/4 in. across, ray-florets deep-yellow, rather broad. Western N. America. Rock-garden.

**E. bellidifo'lius.** Rather weedy perennial making new l.-rosettes on offsets from rhiz., about 2 ft. h. *l.* radical, broadly spatulate or obovate, 2 to 3 in. long, stem-l. oblong, stem-clasping. *fl.-heads* on long stems, corymbose, clear blue. Spring. Eastern N. America. 1790. (B.M. 2402.) Damp border.

**E. canaden'sis.** See above.

**E. caucas'icus.** A synonym of *E. pulchellus*.

**E. compos'itus.*** Grey-tufted perennial. *l.* hairy, often clammy, divided into 3 lobes each again deeply cut into 3 linear segs. *fl.-heads* solitary, large, rays white or pale blue; peduncles leafless or almost so, 3 to 4 in. long. Western N. America. Moraine or well-drained corner. Seed sometimes produces plants with rayless heads (var. **discoi'deus**). SYN. *E. multifidus*.

**E. Coul'teri.** Perennial about 15 in. h., branching. *l.* obovate or oblong, usually softly hairy. *fl.-heads* solitary or rarely 2 or 3 on a branch, about 2 1/2 in. across; ray-florets white or mauve-tinged, narrow. July. Rocky Mts. (G.C. 30 (1901), 99.)

**E. diver'gens.** Annual or biennial with spreading branches, 6 to 15 in. h., covered with grey hairs. *Lower l.* spatulate or oblanceolate, 1 to 2 in. long, mostly stalked, sometimes lobed; *upper* narrower, sessile. *fl.-heads* up to 1 in. across, usually many, on slender peduncles; rays purplish-violet, about 100, sometimes nearly white. April to September. W. United States. Differs from *E. philadelphicus* by its double, not single, pappus.

**E. ela'tior.** A variety of *E. grandiflorus*.

**E. erioceph'alus.** A synonym of *E. uniflorus*.

**E. flagella'ris.** Perennial with slender stems 4 to 8 in. h., naked above, spreading by stolons. *Basal l.* oblong or spatulate; *upper* smaller. *fl.-heads* solitary, 1/2 to 3/4 in. across; ray-florets very many, pink or white. Brit. Columbia. Rock-garden.

**E. folio'sus confin'is.*** Perennial herb, more orless woody at base. Stems numerous, decumbent then ascending, 8 to 16 in. h., with very short shoots bearing a tuft of l. in axils of upper l. *l.* narrow-linear up to 1 3/4 in. long, more or less reflexed, glabrous or minutely hairy (densely hairy in nature). *fl.-heads* bright mauve, 1 1/4 in. across, on long peduncles; ray-florets sterile; disk orange-yellow, about 3/8 in. wide. Summer. California, Oregon. (B.M. 9572.) *E. foliosus* is a very variable species, the variety *confinis* coming from its highest altitudinal range. Rock-garden.

**E. frig'idus.** Tufted, ashy-grey perennial, 1 to 2 in. h. *l.* spatulate-lanceolate, narrowed to stalk, entire. *fl.-heads* about 2/3 in. across; rays in 2 or 3 series, lilac; involucral bracts densely hairy. July to September. Sierra Nevada, Spain. Rock-garden, alpine house.

**E. glabel'lus.** Nearly glabrous perennial 6 to 18 in. h. *l.* in lower part spatulate, stalked, upper oblong-lanceolate, acute, sessile or stem-clasping; all ciliate. *fl.-heads* large, 1 to 7 on the leafless summit of the stout stems; ray-florets numerous, purple or white, very narrow; disk-florets yellow. June. N. United States. (B.M. 2923.) Borders. var. **mol'lis,** downy, rays rose.

**E. glau'cus.** Glaucous (or green in cultivation), herbaceous perennial 6 to 12 in. h. *l.* clammy; radical with winged stalks; stem-l. sessile, entire. *fl.-heads* solitary; ray-florets purple, rather wide. July to September. Western N. America. 1812. (B.R. 10.) Border or rock-garden.

**E. grandiflo'rus.** Herbaceous perennial 4 to 8 in. h. *Radical l.* obovate-spatulate; *stem-l.* oblong to lanceolate. *fl.-heads* solitary, large; ray-florets purple or whitish. July. Rocky Mts. 1819. var. **ela'tior,** leafy, up to 2 ft. h. Borders.

**E. × hyb'ridus** (*E. atticus* × *E. aurantiacus*). *fl.-heads* of varying shades of apricot. (I.H. 1896, p. 301.)

**E. hyssopifo'lium.** Perennial, paniculately branched. *l.* linear, entire, glabrous, ciliate. *fl.-heads* solitary on naked peduncles; rays lilac, much longer than bracts of involucre. E. United States. Borders.

**E. interme'dius.** A synonym of *E. speciosus*.

**E. leiom'erus.** Tufted perennial, about 4 in. h., glabrous. *l.* mainly radical, spatulate, up to 1 in. long. *fl.-heads* violet, about 3/4 in. across; rays about 40, linear. Rocky Mts. Rock-garden. A

**E. macran'thus.*** Hardy perennial, leafy to summit, about 2 ft. h. *l.* lanceolate to ovate, obtuse, variably hairy, sometimes almost glabrous; stem-l. about 1 in. long. *fl.-heads* blue or purple with yellow eye, rays very numerous, about 3/4 in. long. July, August. Rocky Mts. SYN. *Aster mesa-grande*. Borders.

**E. mesa-gran'dis.** A synonym of *E. macranthus*.

**E. mucrona'tus.** Spreading by underground rhiz., branched, about 6 in. h. *l.* lanceolate, narrowed to base, ciliate, sometimes lobed or toothed in upper half. *fl.-heads* stalked, numerous; ray-florets white above, purplish beneath, about ¼ in. long. Summer, autumn. Mexico. Sometimes damaged in severe winters but rarely killed. Rock-garden, wall-garden. Apt to spread rapidly.

*Erigeron leiomerus* (p. 770)

**E. multif'idus.** A synonym of *E. compositus*.

**E. multiradia'tus.** Perennial 6 to 24 in. h. *l.* oblong, toothed, narrowed to a long stalk. *fl.-heads* solitary, about 2 in. across, surrounded by numerous overlapping linear leaves; ray-florets purplish or pinkish; disk yellow. Summer. N. India. 1880. (B.M. 6530.) Borders.

**E. neomexica'nus.** Annual or perennial, 12 to 18 in. h., bushy; stems much-branched, rather hairy, striate. *l.* oblong, slightly pinnately lobed, lobes obovate, obtuse, terminal lobe toothed, lobes of stem-l. narrower. *fl.-heads* solitary, about 1¼ in. across; ray-florets white, linear. New Mexico, Arizona. 1901. Borders.

**E. philadelph'icus.** Perennial about 2 ft. h., slender, branched, roughly hairy. *l.* spatulate or oblong, narrowed to a winged stalk, midrib whitish, upper stem-clasping or cordate. *fl.-heads* rather small in corymbs; ray-florets very numerous, narrow, pale reddish-purple or flesh-coloured. June to August. N. America. 1778. Hardy. Borders. *See* **E. divergens**.

**E. pulchel'lus.** Perennial about 1 ft. h. *Radical l.* spatulate; *stem-l.* clasping, ligulate. *fl.-heads* about 1 in. across, sometimes in some numbers; ray-florets rosy-purple. Caucasus. 1821. SYN. *E. caucasicus. E. pulchellus* of Michaux is *E. bellidifolius*. Borders or rock-garden.

**E. Royl'ei.** Allied to *E. alpinus*; about 6 in. h. *l.* oblong-spatulate, smooth, ciliate. *fl.-heads* 2 in. across in a loose corymb; ray-florets bluish-purple. Summer. Himalaya.

**E. salsugino'sus.** Perennial to 20 in. h., more or less downy. *l.* lanceolate to broadly lanceolate, up to 4 in. long, long-stalked, margins hairy; upper l. sessile. *fl.-heads* one to several, 1½ to about 2 in. across; rays 30 to 50, rather broad, violet or white; disk rather small. Western N. America. Borders.

**E. specio'sus.*** Perennial about 18 in. h., robust. Stem leafy, round, striate, smooth, more or less erect. *l.* spatulate, narrowed to a stalk, upper oblong, ciliate. *fl.-heads* about 2 in. across, in corymbs; ray-florets violet. Summer, autumn. Western N. America. (B.R. 1577 and B.M. 3606 as *Stenactis speciosa*.) Several varieties of this handsome border plant have been raised. var. **ma'jor** has broader rays of brighter colour; **superb'us** has more numerous, paler *fl.* than type, 1889; **Quakeress**, *fl.* more rosy than in type, plant more slender, probably a hybrid of *E. speciosus*.

**E. trif'idus.** Closely related to *E. compositus* but with somewhat fleshy l. and hairy all over. *fl.-heads* white or pale lilac. Rocky Mts. Rock-garden.

**E. uniflo'rus.** Perennial, about 4 in. h., tufted, clothed with white or purplish woolly hairs. *Lower l.* spatulate to oblanceolate-oblong, ½ to 1½ in. long; *stem-l.* narrower. *fl.-heads* usually solitary; rays whitish or purplish, rather short; involucral bracts dark purple, densely woolly. Western N. America. SYN. *E. eriocephalus*. Rock-garden.

**E. Villar'sii.** A synonym of *E. atticus*.

# ERINA'CEA (*erinaceus*, a hedgehog). FAM. *Leguminosae*.

A monotypic genus, branches evergreen, with 2 to 4 papilionaceous flowers on the terminal part of a short peduncle arising from the uppermost leaf-axil; calyx persistent, tubular, swollen, and 5-toothed; petals narrow with short claws which, on the wings and keel, are adherent to the staminal tube; standard ovate. Prefers a sunny, well-drained position and should be planted out of pots. Somewhat slow in flowering. Propagate by seeds and cuttings.

*Erigeron uniflorus*

*Erinacea pungens*

**E. pung'ens.*** Hedgehog Broom, Branch Thorn. Dome-like shrub up to 1 ft. or a little more h., densely intricately branched, branches rigid, spine-tipped, smooth or nearly so, young shoots silky-hairy. *l.* few, fall quickly, simple, opposite or upper alternate, shortly petiolate, linear-oblong, or linear-spatulate, silky-pubescent, ¼ to ½ in. long. *fl.* violet-blue, about 1 in. long; cal. membranous, silky-hairy, with 5 short, lanceolate-acuminate teeth. May (or earlier), June. *Pod* just over ¾ in. long, linear-oblong, silky-hairy, pointed. Spain, France (E. Pyrenees), Algeria, Tunisia. 1759. (B.M. 676 as *Anthyllis Erinacea*).

A

F. S.

**ERINOSE.** Excessive hairiness arising from irritation set up by certain Mites, e.g. the Greenhouse Red Spider, but more generally by Gall Mites. Erinose often follows an attack of Red Spider on Cinerarias, Pelargoniums, and Vines. A number of Gall Mites give rise to this condition so that the underside of the entire leaf or restricted areas between the veins become covered with a mat of fine hairs, e.g. the Walnut Leaf Gall Mite, *Phytoptus tristriatus erineus*, produces erinose on the leaves of Walnut.

G. F. W.

**ERI'NUS** (*Erinos*, a plant mentioned by Dioscorides). FAM. *Scrophulariaceae*. A genus of about 8 species, mostly natives of S. Africa. Tufted alpine plants with characters generally as below. They are best grown in stony or gritty peat and loam or on brick walls and are easily established by sowing the seed in crevices and crannies. When the plants are developed, the seeds are self-sown and seedlings therefrom withstand winter conditions better than do those from seed which has been stored. The plants may also be divided.

**E. alpi'nus.** Tufted, 5 to 6 in. h. *l.* spatulate, deeply toothed, hairy. *fl.* purple or white, alternate, in simple racemes, terminal, more or less corymbose. March to June. Mts. of W. Europe, naturalized in Britain. 1739. (B.M. 310.) var. **al'bus**, *fl.* white; **carmi'neus**, *fl.* carmine; **hirsu'tus**, more hairy than type.

**erio-** in compound words, signifying woolly, as *eriocarpus*, woolly fruited.

**ERIOBOT'RYA** (*erion*, wool, *botrys*, cluster). FAM. *Rosaceae*. A genus of about 10 species in E. Asia. Related to Photinia but with the carpels wholly connate, and styles 5, distinct. *E. japonica* is well worth growing for its noble foliage but while hardy in Cornwall it needs the shelter of a wall in most parts. It will grow well in any ordinary well-drained garden soil.

**E. japon'ica.** Japanese Loquat. Evergreen tree, 20 to 30 ft., young shoots thick and woolly. *l.* 6 to 12 in. long, 3 to 6 in. wide, stout, strongly ribbed, toothed, dark glossy green above, undersurface and very short stalk woolly. *fl.* yellowish-white, fragrant, ¾ in. wide, closely packed on stiff, terminal, woolly panicles 3 to 6 in. long. *fr.* pear-shaped, 1½ in. long, yellow, edible. China. September. 1787. (B.R. 365 as *Mespilus japonica*.) SYN. *Photinia japonica*. The fr. rarely ripens in Britain but does so freely in S. Europe. Well worth growing for its noble foliage. There is a variegated form.

W. J. B.

**ERIOCAM'PA.** A genus of sawflies, now known as Caliroa. *See under* **Sawflies.** A

**ERIOCAULA'CEAE.** Monocotyledons. A family of about 500 species in 6 genera, found in the warmer parts of the world, especially S. America, with a few in temperate regions, for the most part plants of damp sandy soil or marshes. Generally herbs with long linear leaves and a tall scape with a head of minute flowers, usually perennial. Flowers with a dry perianth, frequently in a single series of 2 or 3; stamens 3 or 6; carpels 2 or 3; ovary 2- or 3-celled. Of little horticultural importance. Eriocaulon (q.v.) is occasionally offered.

**ERIOCAU'LON** (*erion*, wool, *kaulos*, stem; some species have woolly scapes). FAM. *Eriocaulaceae*. A genus of about 180 species of aquatic or marsh plants, mostly tropical or sub-tropical. Distinguished in its family by the male flowers being chiefly in the centre of the head, each with 4 or 6 stamens, and the outer perianth segments almost spatulate. *E. septangulare* is sometimes offered. It grows in lakes in Skye and the west of Ireland.

**E. septangula're.** Rootstock creeping, roots white. Stem very short, leafy. *l.* 2 to 4 in. long, translucent green. *Scape* 6 to 24 in. long, twisted. *fl.-head* ½ to ¾ in. across; *fl.* minute, brownish. N. America, Scotland, Ireland. (E.B. 1546.)

**ERIOCEPH'ALUS** (*erion*, wool, *kephale*, head; the heads become woolly after flowering). FAM. *Compositae*.

A genus of about 20 species of much-branched, rigid, evergreen, scented shrubs, natives of S. Africa, usually silky or silvery. Leaves small, often clustered, entire or rarely 3-lobed at tip. Flower-heads in racemes, umbels, or solitary, homogamous, sub-globose; ray-florets in one series whitish; disk yellow or purple; involucral bracts in 2 series, outer of 4 or 5 bracts, inner bell-shaped, densely woolly. These shrubs need greenhouse conditions and a compost of sandy loam with a little peat. They may be propagated by cuttings of young shoots in sand under a glass.

**E. africa'nus.** *l.* opposite or tufted, linear or 3-fid, ½ to 1 in. long, silky-hairy, thickish, obtuse, channelled. *fl.-heads* white, in terminal umbels. January to March. 1731. (B.M. 833.)

**ERIOCEREUS.** *See* **Harrisia.**

**ERIOCHI'LUS** (*erion*, wool, *cheilos*, a lip; the disk of the lip is hairy). FAM. *Orchidaceae*. A genus of about 6 species of pretty terrestrial orchids, allied to Caladenia, natives of Australia. The species are interesting but small. The flowers have the upper sepal erect, the petals similar; the lower sepals are longer and clawed; lip entire, clawed, shorter than the lower sepals; pollinia 4. Leaf solitary at the base or higher up the stem. They thrive in a compost of light turfy loam, peat, and sand, in equal parts, and may be increased by division. Greenhouse.

**E. autumna'lis.** *fl.* pink, solitary, or 2 or 3 rather distant; lip about half as long as lateral sep., with an erect, concave, narrow claw. October. *l.* radical, ovate, acute, usually dying before flowering. 6 in. h. 1823. (F.A.O. 2.) SYN. *Epipactis cucullata*. Slender.

**E. dilata'tus.** *fl.* resembling *E. autumnalis*, 1 to 5; lip much shorter, claw erect, with slightly prominent rounded side lobes. May. *l.* linear-lanceolate, sessile, stem-clasping. 6 to 12 in. h. Variable.

**E. multiflo'rus.** Closely resembles *E. dilatatus* of which it is probably a variety, but *fl.* more numerous and rather smaller, 12 in. or more h. March.

**E. sca'ber.** *fl.* pink, 1 to 3; sep. and pet. rather shorter and broader than in *E. autumnalis*; lip with small, erect, rounded side lobes, mid-lobe round. September. *l.* radical, ovate or cordate, usually persisting at base of fl.-stem. (F.A.O. 2.) Closely allied to *E. autumnalis*.

E. C.

**ERIOC'NEMA marmora'tum.** *See* **Bertolonia marmorata.**

**ERIOCO'MA frag'rans.** A synonym of *Montanoa tomentosa*.

**ERIODEN'DRON.** A synonym of Ceiba.

**ERIO'DES** (resembling *Eria*). FAM. *Orchidaceae*. A monotypic genus founded on the plant better known in gardens as *Eria barbata* and *Tainia barbata*. It differs from both these genera by its mobile lip. Treatment and temperatures should be as for the deciduous Calanthes but the compost should consist of 2 parts of cut Osmunda fibre, 1 of Sphagnum moss, 1 of loam fibre. The rest-period must not be so decided nor should the plant be removed from its pot.

**E. barba'ta.** *fl.* inverted, over 1 in. across if spread out; the narrow, tapered sep. and pet. are reflexed, the mobile lip strongly recurved; prevailing colour yellow, flushed with red-brown; lip brighter than other segs., column sharply angled; pollinia 8. A feature is the presence of an irregular line of flat brown hairs on one side of the pedicels. *Pseudobulbs* pyramidal, 2 to 4 in. h., wrinkled. *l.* narrowly lanceolate, plicate, 12 in. long or more, often deciduous. *Spikes* lax, erect, tomentose, 18 to 24 in. h. Khasia, Shillong. 1857. (Ref. B. 2, 114.) SYN. *Tainiopsis barbata*.

**ERIOGO'NUM** (*erion*, wool, *gonu*, joint; stems downy at nodes). FAM. *Polygonaceae*. A genus of about 140 species of annual or perennial herbs or sub-shrubs, natives of Western N. America for the most part. Most species are densely woolly. Leaves radical, alternate or whorled, entire, without stipules. Flowers perfect, small, in a head, cluster, or umbel with an involucre; perianth 6-parted; stamens 9 from base of perianth; styles 3. Fruit an achene, mostly 3-angled. Rich loamy peaty soil suits them and full sun. Raised from seed sown in sandy soil in heat, or by division. Like many woolly plants these are liable to suffer from winter wet unless protected by a glass cover of some kind. They are rarely seen in cultivation but as they flower in summer when the flowering of many rock plants is over, while not very brilliant, they might well be grown more frequently. Many of the species are weedy and only a few are here described as likely to be of value and interest.

**E. arbores'cens.** Shrub several ft. h., much branched; branches leafy at tips. *l.* linear or oblong, ½ to 1¼ in. long, strongly revolute, white-hairy beneath, glabrous above. *fl.* in a compound cyme, rose, densely covered with white hair at base of cal.; peduncles stout, involucres in capitate clusters. California.

**E. auricula'tum.** A variety of *E. nudum.*

**E. Ba'keri.** A variety of *E. Jamesii.*

**E. compos'itum.** Perennial about 1 ft. h. *l.* oblong-ovate, usually cordate, 1 to 3 in. long, densely hairy beneath, greener above. *fl.* dull white or rose, glabrous, narrowed to base; heads on stout, naked peduncles, 6 to 18 in. long. Washington, California. (B.R. 1774.)

**E. corymbo'sum.** Perennial about 1 ft. h. *l.* ovate to oblong-lanceolate. *fl.* white to deep rose, rarely yellow, in broad, stiff umbels, involucral l. mostly sessile. Western N. America. (G.C. 8 (1890), 525.)

**E. Doug'lasii.** Small, sub-shrub, prostrate or nearly so, with erect peduncles. *l.* oblong to spatulate, not revolute. *fl.* cream in round heads; perianth hairy, tapering to base; involucral lobes reflexed. Washington to Colorado. Perhaps not yet introduced.

**E. effu'sum.** Low shrub with spreading, leafy branches, hairy. *l.* scattered, narrow, 1 to 1½ in. long. *fl.* white or pink, segs. spreading, shortly top-shaped at base; involucre narrow bell-shaped. *infl.* a diffuse cyme. Rocky Mts. Very variable.

**E. fla'vum.** Hairy, 4 to 8 in. h. with a woody, somewhat woolly base. *l.* obovate to oblanceolate, greenish above. *fl.* light yellow, densely hairy below; in an umbel, pedicels about ½ in. long, usually with several involucres of leafy bracts. Rocky Mts., Brit. Columbia southwards.

**E. James'ii.** Tufted or matted, sub-erect from a woody base. *l.* in a basal rosette, spatulate or ovate, margins undulate, densely hairy beneath; stalks hairy. *fl.* white, cream, or yellow, hairy, inner segs. longer than outer; cymes once or more divided. Colorado to New Mexico. A variable species. var. **Ba'keri,** stem shorter, branches slender, *l.* elliptic-lanceolate, thin, loose, *fl.* yellow, hairy, with a stalk-like base, involucre turbinate, peduncle several times forked.

**E. latifo'lium.** *See* **E. nudum.**

**E. Lobb'ii.** Prostrate. Stem stout, densely leafy, in lower part crowded with old l.-bases, crowned above with a tuft of silvery-white l. *l.* roundish to ovate, ½ to 1½ in. long, narrowed to a wide stalk. *fl.* in simple umbels, white becoming pinkish, not stalk-like at base; involucre broadly bell-shaped, ¼ to ½ in. long. California.

**E. microthe'cum.** Stem rather woody from a shrubby base. *l.* alternate, shortly stalked. *fl.* yellow or pale, small, obtuse at base; involucre bell- or top-shaped, variable in size; peduncle up to 4 in. long, much forked. Arizona to California. Very variable. Stem darker and more woody than in *E. effusum.*

**E. niv'eum.** Erect or ascending, with few branches; whole plant dense white-hairy. *l.* oblong-ovate, about ½ in. long, stalked. *fl.* white or rose, glabrous; in compound umbels; involucres mostly solitary; outer perianth segs. broader than inner. British Columbia to California.

**E. nu'dum.** Tufted perennial up to 6 ft. h. Stems up to 4 in. h., more or less hairy. *l.* ovate-elliptic to oblong, 1¼ to 3 in. long, but very variable in size, margins wavy and more or less toothed, densely white lorate beneath, deep green above; stalked. *fl.* cream to pink, rarely yellowish, in spherical clusters up to ¾ in. across in a forking panicle with leafless branches, up to 6 ft. h. July. California. 1935. A variable plant. var. **auricula'tum,** *stem-l.* usually longer than in type, long-stalked; *infl.* much divided, its branches and peduncles usually hollow. (B.M. 9571.) SYN. *E. auriculatum, E. latifolium auriculatum.*

**E. ovalifo'lium.** Densely white-hairy, stem short, closely branched. *l.* elliptic to orbicular, ¼ to ¾ in. long, narrowed to stalk. *fl.* white or yellow, about ⅛ in. long in close simple umbels; peduncles 2 to 8 in. h.; involucres bell-shaped. British Columbia to California. var. **purpu'reum,** *fl.* rose to purple. (G.C. 7 (1890), 260.)

**E. racemo'sum.** Sparingly branched. *l.* at base ovate to elliptical or roundish, white beneath; as long as stalk. *fl.* white to pink, turbinate; segs. all alike, spreading. *infl.* spike-like, sometimes branched. Utah to New Mexico. (G.C. 8 (1890), 528.)

**E. saxat'ile.** Erect perennial. Stem 2 to 5 in. long, woody, densely leafy. *l.* wide, upturned, leathery, densely white-hairy, roundish to round-ovate, ¼ to 1 in. long, stalk short. *Scape* 3 in. to 2 ft. long, panicled above. *fl.* white to pale yellowish, narrowed to stalk-like base as long as segs.; filaments hairy at base; involucres downy, ⅛ to ⅛ in. long. S. California.

**E. specio'sum.** A synonym of *E. umbellatum.*

**E. sphaeroceph'alum.** Erect perennial, much branched. *l.* linear or linear-spatulate, often revolute. *fl.* soft bright yellow, narrow below, involucral lobes reflexed; sep. hairy. Washington to California.

**E. subalpi'num.** Much like *E. umbellatum* but *fl.* cream becoming rose in age, peduncles stouter, 12 to 16 in. h. Rocky Mts., British Columbia. SYN. *E. umbellatum major.*

**E. thymoi'des.** Shrubby, dwarf. *l.* linear, revolute. *fl.* very pale yellow, buds pink; involucral bracts erect; otherwise much like *E. Douglasii.* Washington, Oregon.

**E. umbella'tum.** Much branched with short spreading or prostrate shoots. *l.* spatulate to obovate, downy or nearly glabrous above, white-hairy beneath. *fl.* yellow in a simple umbel; peduncle 3 to 12 in. long; pedicels up to 1 in. long; involucral bracts leafy, lobes reflexed. British Columbia. Somewhat variable.

**ERIOLO'BUS.** A section of Malus sometimes kept as a separate genus. It is distinguished by the fruits not having a sunken calyx at the summit and by their having grit-cells as in pears. The following species will be found under Malus: *trilobatus, Tschonoskii, yunnanensis.*

**ERIOPH'ORUM** (*erion,* wool, *phoreo,* to bear; the heads are cottony). Cotton Grass. FAM. *Cyperaceae.* A genus of about a dozen perennial herbs natives of bogs in Northern temperate and arctic regions, related to Scirpus but with the hypogynous bristles lengthening greatly beyond the spikelets as flowering proceeds, giving rise to silky-cottony tufts. Plants for the margins of pools or boggy places; very conspicuous in summer.

**E. alpi'num.** Rootstock creeping. Stem 6 to 10 in. long, very slender, rigid. *l.* short, very slender, rough, channelled, keeled. *Spikelet* solitary, terminal, bristles 4 to 6, crumpled, about 1¼ in. long. N. Hemisphere. (E.B. 1603.) Sometimes included in Scirpus as *S. Hudsonianus.*

**E. angustifo'lium.** A synonym of *E. polystachion.*

**E. Chamisson'is.** 8 to 24 in. h. Stems rather soft, not tufted. *l.* slender, channelled, upper reduced to inflated sheaths. *Spikelet* solitary; bristles tawny, up to nearly 2 in. long. Western N. America. var. **al'bidum** has white bristles.

**E. latifo'lium.** Like *E. polystachion* but tufted with hollow 3-angled stems, and cymes with rough branches. N. Hemisphere.

**E. polystach'ion.** Rootstock long, stems not tufted, solid, 6 to 18 in. h., leafy. *l.* chiefly radical, channelled, 3-angled above middle. *Heads* variable in number in lateral drooping cymes with smooth branches; bristles 1½ to 2 in. long. N. Hemisphere. (E.B. 1605.)

**E. vagina'tum.** Tufted, 6 to 10 in. h. Stems glabrous. *l.* filiform, 3-angled, very short. *Spikelet* solitary, terminal; bristles very numerous. N. Hemisphere. (E.B. 1604.)

**ERIOPHYL'LUM** (*erion,* wool, *phyllon,* leaf; from the woolly leaf). FAM. *Compositae.* A genus of about 12 species of mostly woolly perennial herbs, rarely sub-shrubs, natives of Western N. America. Leaves alternate or partly opposite. Flower-heads with yellow rays or none, stalked; involucral bracts obtuse, woolly, joined below; disk-florets with a short tube; receptacle not chaffy. Pappus none. Achenes glabrous. For borders and the rock-garden in well-drained soil. Propagated by seed and by division. Quite hardy.

**E. caespito'sum.** A synonym of *E. lanatum.*

**E. confertifo'lium.** 1 to 2 ft. h., white woolly. Stem erect, slender, naked near summit. *l.* small, wedge-shaped, 1- or 2-pinnate, 3- to 7-partite; segs. narrow-linear. *fl.-heads* in a compact, cymose cluster; rays 4 or 5, yellow; involucral bracts about 5, oval or ovoid-oblong. California. Borders.

**E. lana'tum.** Tufted, 6 to 12 in. h. *l.* deeply cut, but sometimes ligulate and entire. *fl.-heads* yellow, solitary, produced in great numbers; rays usually short. Summer. N. America. (B.R. 1167 as *E. caespitosum.*) SYN. *Bahia lanata.* Rock-garden.

**ERIOP'SIS** (resembling *Eria*). FAM. *Orchidaceae.* A genus of about 7 species of very ornamental epiphytic orchids, natives of N. Brazil, Guiana, and Colombia. Flowers showy, pedicellate; sepals equal, spreading, free, or the lateral ones connate with the foot of the column in a very short chin; petals similar to the sepals; lip affixed to the foot of the column, shortly incumbent, at length erect, the lateral lobes broad, erect, loosely en-folding the column, the middle one small, spreading, entire or 2-lobed; column rather long, incurved; pollen masses 2. The long arching flower-spikes are produced from the base of the pseudobulbs and the inflorescence is attractive by reason of its grace and the number of flowers, though individually the flowers are not large. Leaves usually 2, long, large. A compost of 3 parts of finely cut Osmunda fibre mixed with 1 part of Sphagnum moss suits them. Pans which can be suspended are preferable to pots, as though water may be freely given when the plants are in full growth it must pass quickly away, and in winter must be given to compensate for the fire heat used. Shade the plants when growths are young but as they grow gradually expose to more and more light.

**E. bilo'ba.** *fl.* 20 to 30, about 1 in. across; sep. and pet. oblong, dark yellow, shaded brown round margins; lip 3-lobed, disk white, spotted dark brown; spike 1 to 3 ft. long, curved or drooping. *l.* broad-lanceolate, 8 to 12 in. long, about 2 in. wide, in twos or threes at apices of pseudobulbs. *Pseudobulbs* about 5 in. h., conical, dark brown. British Guiana, Brazil. 1845. (B.R. 33, 18.) SYN. *E. Schomburgkii.*

**E. Hel'enae.** *fl.* resembling those of *E. biloba,* but spikes 1½ to 3 ft. long, many-fld.; sep. and pet. yellow, marked and flushed red; lip whitish, spotted and flecked red or purple, front lobe small, rounded. *l.* 3 to 5, linear-lanceolate, 15 to 20 in. long, 1¼ in. wide. *Pseudobulbs* 16 in. h. Peru. 1897. (B.M. 8462.)

**E. rutidobul'bon.** Similar to *E. biloba,* but with larger, more deeply coloured *fl. Spike* 15 to 30 in. long. Colombia. 1847. (B.M. 4437; W.O.A. 377; L. 739.)

**E. Schomburgk'ii.** A synonym of *E. biloba.*

**E. Spru'cei.** *fl.* sep. and pet. light yellow, pet. with red borders; side lobes of lip whitish, dotted red, nearly round, mid-lobe lemon-yellow, spotted mauve at base of its broad stalk, elliptic, disk white, with 2 acute horns on middle; raceme long, cylindrical. *l.* lanceolate, acute, 2-ligulate, 18 to 24 in. long, about 2 in. wide. Amazons. 1884.

**E. Werck'lei.** Little known, near *E. rutidobulbon* but possibly distinct. Sarapiqui. (O.R. 1943, 9.)

E. C.

**ERIOSE'MA** (*erion,* wool, *sema,* standard; the standard is covered with silky hair). FAM. *Leguminosae.* A genus of about 40 species of herbs and shrubs distributed over S. America and Trop. and S. Africa, 1 species widely ranged over Asia and Australia. Leaves digitate, 3-foliolate. Flowers yellow or violet, papilionaceous, in axillary racemes or clusters. The Eriosema need stove conditions and a compost of peat and loam. Propagation by seed or cuttings.

**E. grandiflo'rum.** 1 to 2 ft. h. with angular branches. *lflets.* oblong-elliptic, mucronate; the short stalks and veins beneath covered with reddish, silky down. *fl.* in a panicle; cor. covered with soft hairs. N. Mexico.

**E. viola'ceum.** About 4 ft. h. *lflets.* oblong-linear, acute, greenish and velvety above, rusty-hairy beneath. *fl.* violet, in many-fld. axillary and terminal racemes. July, August. Trop. S. America, Trinidad. 1820.

**ERIOSO'MA lanig'erum.** *See* **Woolly Aphis.**

**ERIOSPERM'UM** (*erion,* wool, *sperma,* seed; the seeds are densely woolly). FAM. *Liliaceae.* A genus of about 30 species of tuberous herbs natives of Trop. and S. Africa. Leaves 1 to 3, ovate, lanceolate or linear, rather thick, produced after the flowers, radical. Scape sometimes with a small leaf. Flowers whitish or yellowish, rarely purple, in a simple raceme; perianth segments distinct; pedicels solitary. Fruit a 3-angled capsule with a few densely woolly oblong seeds. Cultivation as for Bulbine. Few species are of horticultural value.

**E Bellenden'ii.** About 12 in. h. *l.* roundish, slender-pointed, cucullate at base. *fl.* light-blue. June to August. S. Africa. 1800. (B.M. 1382 as *E. latifolium.*)

**E. Macken'ii.** *l.* ovate-oblong, obtuse, glabrous, smooth, nerveless. *fl.* bright golden-yellow; scape slender, cylindric, glabrous. July. Natal. 1871. (B.M. 5955 as *Bulbine Mackenii.*)

**E. prolif'erum.** About 9 in. h. *l.* proliferous, filiform, undivided, sessile. *fl.* white and green. June to August. S. Africa. 1821.

**E. pubes'cens.** About 12 in. h. *l.* sub-cordate, acute, cucullate, downy. *fl.* white and green. June. S. Africa. 1820. (B.R. 578.)

**ERIOSTEM'ON** (*erion,* wool, *stemon,* stamen; the stamens being woolly). FAM. *Rutaceae.* A genus of about 30 species of evergreen shrubs, natives of Australia outside the tropics, with one in New Caledonia. Leaves alternate, simple, entire, full of pellucid dots. Flowers solitary in the leaf-axils, bracteate, white or pale pink, long-lasting in a cool atmosphere. Handsome and useful hard-wooded plants, flowering, in healthy plants, very freely in winter and early spring. A suitable compost is fibrous peat, not broken too fine, a little loam, and silver sand. The soil should be rammed tolerably firm, but care should be taken not to bury the stem. They are best kept rather close while growth is being made, afterwards admitting more air, and finally putting outside in a sunny place from July to the end of September, in order to ensure thorough ripening. The plants are naturally of bushy habit but may be trained as pyramids if desired; little pruning save shortening of a few long growths is necessary to induce symmetrical growth. Thorough drainage and careful watering are at all times essential. Eriostemons will flower earlier in winter if given a temperature of 55° F. but grow quite healthily and flower freely somewhat later in a house from which the frost is merely excluded. Old plants becoming unhealthy should be pruned back hard in spring, the balls of soil should be reduced, and they should be replanted in fresh soil in pots of a smaller size. Propagation may be by cuttings taken in early spring, put into sand under a glass with gentle heat, hardened, and potted off singly into small pots, moving on into larger sizes very gradually; or grafting on small stocks of *Correa alba.* By good cultivation decorative plants are soon developed.

**E. buxifo'lius.** Shrub of 1 to 2 ft., branches round, hairy. *l.* cordate-ovate or obovate, small, usually mucronate, glands prominent. *fl.* pink or rose, almost sessile in l.-axils. April to June. 1822. (B.M. 4101.)

**E. interme'dius.** About 3 ft. h. *l.* obovate. *fl.* white, tinged rose-pink, large, solitary in l.-axils. April. Habitat? (B.M. 4439.)

**E. linearifo'lius.** A synonym of *Geijera parviflora.*

**E. myoporoi'des.** 1 to 2 ft. h. *l.* linear-lanceolate, entire, smooth, glandular, mucronate. *fl.* rose; in threes in l.-axils. Early spring. 1824. (B.M. 3180.)

**E. neriifo'lius.** A synonym of *E. myoporoides.*

**E. obova'lis.** Shrub of 2 to 3 ft. *l.* obcordate, obovate, or oblong-spatulate, blunt or truncate, usually under ½ in. long, narrowed at base, often stalked. *fl.* rather smaller than in *E. buxifolius,* solitary in l.-axils. New S. Wales, &c. A double-fld. form (**flore ple'no**) is known.

**E. salicifo'lius.** Shrub of 2 to 3 ft., branches 3-angled. *l.* linear-lanceolate, entire, smooth. *fl.* pink, almost sessile in l.-axils. July. 1822. (B.M. 2854.)

**E. sca'ber.** Shrub of 18 in. *l.* linear, entire, dark green, mucronate. *fl.* white, tinged pink, rather small, on short peduncles. March to June. 1840. (P.M.B. 13, 127.)

**ERIOSY'CE** (*erion,* wool, *sykos,* a fig; from the woolly fruit). FAM. *Cactaceae.* Very large plants with numerous ribs; flowers from the crown, the tube longer than the free perianth segments; fruit dry, very woolly, spiny above, opening by a basal pore. For cultivation *see under* **Cactus** (terrestrial).

**E. ceratis'tes.** Plants up to 3 ft. h., very woolly at the top; ribs 21 to 25; spines 11 to 20, straight or curved, 1 to 1½ in. long, yellow. *fl.* yellowish-red, small. Chile. (B.R.C. 3, f.186.) SYN. *Echinocactus ceratistes, E. Sandillon.*

**E. korethroi'des.** Large plant; ribs 12 to 20, spiral, low; spines 12 to 20, needle-like, spreading horizontally, up to 1½ in. long; centrals 4, flattened. *fl.* pale red. Argentina.

**E. Sandil'lon.** A synonym of *E. ceratistes.*

V. H.

**ERITHA'LIS** (a plant name used by Pliny, signifying very luxuriant). FAM. *Rubiaceae.* A genus of 5 species of evergreen shrubs, natives of Florida and the W. Indies. Leaves opposite, stalked, leathery, elliptic, obovate or lanceolate. Flowers in terminal, erect, stalked panicles, very rarely solitary; calyx truncate or 5- to 10-toothed: corolla salver-shaped or rotate, with 5 to 10 lobes. Sandy fibrous loam with a little peat suits these stove plants. Propagation by cuttings of side shoots during spring or summer, put into sand under a bell-glass with a little heat.

**E. frutico'sa.** Shrub of 10 to 15 ft. *l.* obovate or spatulate-lanceolate; stipules broad, short, mucronate, sheathing, persistent. *fl.* small, white, fragrant; peduncles axillary, panicled. July. Jamaica. 1793. SYN. *E. odorifera.*

**ERITRICH'IUM** (*erion*, wool, *trichos*, hair; plants woolly). FAM. *Boraginaceae.* A genus of 8 species of dwarf, tufted, perennial herbs inhabiting the higher parts of the mountains of the N. Hemisphere. Leaves alternate. Inflorescence axillary or terminal, short; calyx cut to base; corolla sub-rotate or funnel-shaped with spreading lobes, usually with swellings at the throat; stamens included. Nutlets 4, ovoid or half-pyramidal. The brilliant blue *E. nanum* is not a success in cultivation. It can with care be kept alive in the alpine-house in thoroughly drained but moist soil, and with especial care in watering, particularly in winter, and will sometimes produce a few flowers, but it is at best only a caricature of its native brilliance. *E. rupestre* is somewhat easier.

**E. barbig'erum.** A synonym of *Cryptantha barbigera.*

**E. Hook'eri.** Hairy, tufted, about ½ in. h. *l.* spatulate, densely hairy at tip. *fl.* blue, among the upper l.; sep. spatulate, densely hairy near tip; cor. tubular, about ¼ in. long, ¼ in. across. N. India, W. China. SYN. *Myosotis Hookeri.*

**E. na'num.** Densely tufted perennial covered with long silky hairs, usually very dwarf, rarely up to 6 in. h. *l.* linear or oblong, about ⅓ in. long, sessile. *fl.* blue, rarely white, about ¼ in. across; cor. bell-shaped-rotate. June to August. High Mts. of N. Hemisphere. 1869. (B.M. 5853.) SYN. *E. terglouense.*

**E. nippon'icum.** A synonym of *Hackelia nipponica.*

**E. nothoful'vum.** A synonym of *Plagiobothrys nothofulvus.*

**E. rupes'tre.** Tufted, more or less densely strigose. Stems up to 12 in. h. or more. *l.* variable, linear to narrowly oblanceolate, up to 4 in. long, lower more or less stalked. *infl.* many-fld., blue, bell-shaped-rotate, about ½ in. across. Mts. of Asia. var. **pectinat'a** has linear-oblong basal l., stem-l. ashy. SYN. *E. strictum.*

**E. stric'tum.** A synonym of *E. rupestre pectinatum.*

**ERLANG'EA** (of the University of Erlangen, Bavaria). FAM. *Compositae.* A genus of about 40 species of herbs or shrubs, nearly all natives of Africa, closely related to Vernonia in which many of the species were at one time included, differing in its small achenes with the pappus reduced to a few short hairs which are very soon lost. For cultivation *see* **Eupatorium.** **A**

**E. aggrega'ta.** Perennial herb with softly woolly erect stem. *l.* ovate-lanceolate, 3½ to 5 in. long, rather acute, toothed, downy, thin, stalked. *fl.* in densely clustered terminal and axillary heads on softly downy main peduncles up to 1¼ in. long; heads sessile, about 8-fld.; fl. blue, flushed rose; involucral bracts green with scarious margins. Midwinter. Angola. 1915. (B.M. 8755.) Greenhouse.

**E. tomento'sa.** Shrub at 3½ ft. h. with densely white hairy shoots, branches furrowed. *l.* oblong, somewhat wedge-shaped at base, acute, 2 to 5 in. long, double-toothed, hairy especially beneath where the veins are prominent; stalked. *fl.-heads* lilac, bell-shaped, about ⅜ in. wide, in loose corymbose panicles about 6 in. across. Winter, spring. E. Africa. 1907. (B.M. 8269.) Greenhouse.

***Erman'i,*** in honour of G. A. Erman, 1806–77, of Berlin, who travelled and collected widely.

**ERMINE MOTHS.** *Yponomeuta*, a genus belonging to the super-family *Tineina*, consists of small moths with white or greyish wings, the fore-wings being generally spotted with black. Their caterpillars live in dense webs chiefly on fruit-trees and shrubs. There are several British species, the most destructive being the Small Apple Ermine, *Y. malinella*; the Small Ermine, *Y. padella*; the Willow Ermine, *Y. rorella*; the Spindle Ermine, *Y. cognatella*; and *Y. vigintipunctata*, which occurs on *Sedum Telephium* both in the wild state and in gardens.

Some confusion still exists between *Y. malinella* and *Y. padella*. Some authorities consider that there exist only biologic races of the one or the other. The spotted caterpillars are very harmful to Apple-trees and Hawthorn hedges, which may be completely defoliated during June and July. They live in colonies in conspicuous webs or nests, which are formed during May by the young caterpillars which have overwintered beneath the egg-case. Pupation takes place in July within the web, and the adult moths emerge in July and August. The eggs are laid on the shoots in small circular patches.

The Willow Ermine is occasionally responsible for the defoliation of *Salix alba* and other Willows, and a severe outbreak occurred in Suffolk in June 1937 when the stems and surrounding vegetation were entirely covered with dense sheets of webbing.

The Spindle Ermine is destructive to Euonymus, including hedges of *E. japonicus* and many ornamental species during June and July. The moths and their caterpillars closely resemble those of the fruit-infesting Ermines, and they have similar habits.

The Sedum Ermine is occasionally abundant during August on clumps of *Sedum Telephium* in herbaceous borders. The attacked plants are rendered unsightly with webbing and the autumn blooms are ruined.

Control measures against the fruit-infesting species include spraying with a 10 per cent. tar-distillate wash in December to destroy the hibernating caterpillars, the spraying of the foliage of Apple-trees before or after blossoming with arsenate of lead, and the collection or burning out of the caterpillar 'nests' in June.

It is not desirable to spray Euonymus hedges with an arsenical poison owing to the danger to children who are inclined to pull the leaves and place them in their mouths. The 'nests' may be collected and destroyed, or the attacked hedge dusted with a Derris dust.

Outbreaks of the Sedum Ermine may be checked by dusting the infested plants in August with nicotine or derris dust.

G. F. W.

***ermin'eus -a -um,*** of the colour of ermine. **A →**

***erodioi'des,*** Erodium-like.

**ERO'DIUM** (*erodius*, heron; the carpels resemble the head and beak of a heron). FAM. *Geraniaceae.* A genus of about 50 species of herbs and sub-shrubs, natives of Europe, temperate Asia, N. and rarely S. Africa, and Australia; closely related to Geranium but with 5 fertile stamens and 5 staminodes. Leaves alternate or opposite and unequal, stipulate. Flowers regular or nearly so, in umbels or rarely solitary on axillary peduncles. Ovary, fruit, and seed as in Geranium but the tails of the carpels spirally twisted and usually hairy within. The awn is very hygroscopic. When the fruit is ripe it splits into 1-seeded parts each with its awn; these fall to the ground often with the sharp end downwards and the awn may catch against surrounding objects; if the air becomes damp it untwists and so lengthens, pushing the fruit into the soil; as the air dries the awn again curls and this whole process may be repeated several times. Erodiums are plants of sunny, well-drained places and given similar positions on the rock-garden in good deep limy soil, or soil at least not acid, they are most valuable plants both for their foliage and flowers. Some species are dioecious and of these both male and female plants must be grown in order to obtain good seed. Seeds readily germinate and the plants may also be propagated by cutting. Some species cross freely in the garden and natural hybrids are also known. The following species are perennial unless otherwise stated.

**E. absinthoi'des.** Hairy, tufted, of varying height. *rhiz.* thick. *l.* oblong, 2-pinnatisect; segs. lanceolate or oblong, those of stem few and often simple. *fl.* in loose heads, large, violet, pink, or white; peduncles glandular. Summer. SE. Europe, Asia Minor. Variable in the length of the stem (which may be long and leafy or short and scape-like), in the hairy covering (which may be green or grey), and in the veins of the sep. which are more or less ciliate. var. **amanum,** *l.* 2 to 2½ in. long, dwarfer and more slender than type, hairy with short white hairs *fl.* large. white. N. Syria. SYN. *E. amanus*;

**ciner'eum,** taller, grey-hairy, l.-segs. narrow, acute. Armenia; **Sibthorpia'num,** *l.* almost silky at first, becoming smooth, densely tufted, segs. rather narrow, stems 6 in. h., *fl.* rosy lilac. Greece. SYN. *E. olympicum.*

**E. alpi'num.** Sparsely grey-hairy. *l.* tufted, 2-pinnatifid, narrow-oblong; segs. rather broad, toothed. *Scapes* ½ to 6 in. long. *fl.* in a loose umbel, 2 to 10, purplish-violet, without spots, ½ in. across. May. Mts. of S. Italy. 1814. (F.G. 653.)

**E. ama'num.** A synonym of *E. absinthoides amanum.*

**E. carvifo'lium.** 6 to 10 in. h. *l.* 2-pinnatisect; midrib softly white-hairy beneath. *fl.* red, ½ in. across, 8 to 10 in umbel. Spring. Mts. of Cent. Spain.

**E. cedro'rum.** Whole plant glandular-hairy, much branched at base; stems decumbent, leafy. *Lower l.* oblong, 2-pinnatisect; segs. linear-wedge-shaped, deeply cut. *fl.* white or purple, about 1 in. across; pet. obovate, upper 2 smaller; dioecious. Summer. Cicilian Taurus. SYN. *E. Kotschyanum.*

**E. chamaedryoi'des.** Densely tufted, 1 to 3 in. h., rootstock stout, deeply rooting. *l.* small, cordate, with roundish teeth, obtuse, dark green. *fl.* white faintly veined pink, solitary, on peduncles about ½ in. long. Summer. Majorca. 1783. var. **ro'seum,** *fl.* rose. Needs a deep rich well-drained soil in a sunny spot and in all but favoured localities some winter protection. SYN. *E. Reichardii.*

**E. cheilanthifo'lium.** Densely hoary, glandular, tufted, stemless. *l.* oblong-lanceolate, 2-pinnatisect; segs. minute, oblong, obtuse. *fl.* blush pink. Summer. Mts. of S. Spain, Morocco. There is often confusion between this and *E. trichomanefolium.*

**E. chrysan'thum.** Silky, silvery, tufted, with a thick rootstock and many branches from base. *l.* 2-pinnatisect; segs. rather wide, obtuse. *fl.* sulphur-yellow on short, rarely leafy scapes; pet. twice as long as sep. Summer. Greece. 1897. (F.G. 652 as *E. absinthoides.*) Dioecious. *See* **E. Crispii.**

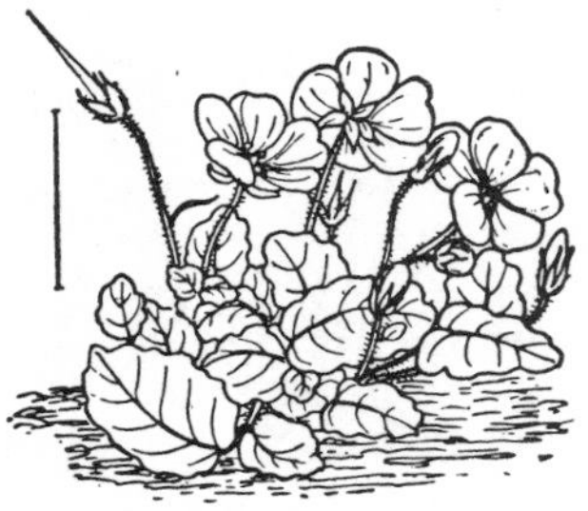

*Erodium corsicum*

**E. cor'sicum.** Mat-forming, silvery-downy, stems much branched. *l.* scalloped, crumpled. *fl.* rosy pink with deeper veins; pet. equal. Summer. Corsica, Sardinia. (B.M. 8888.) Needs a sunny spot.

**E. Crisp'ii.** A form of *E. chrysanthum* with perhaps slightly larger fl.

**E. daucoi'des.** Hairy, 2 to 4 in. h. *l.* many, lanceolate to triangular; lflets. pinnatisect, lobes linear-lanceolate, stalks longer than blades. *fl.* rose; pet. obovate, more or less rounded; peduncles 3 to 5 in. long, about 4-fld. Summer. Spain.

**E. grui'num.** Annual or biennial. Stem short. *Lowest l.* undivided; *upper* ovate-heart-shaped, deeply 3- or 5-lobed, acute, toothed. *fl.* on peduncles longer than l., large, violet with a deeper eye. *fr.* with a remarkable beak 3 to 4 in. long. Spring. Sicily. (F.G. 656.)

**E. Guicciar'dii.** Tufted, densely silky, with many stems. *l.* oblong, 2-pinnatisect; segs. linear, acute. Stems forked, leafy. *fl.* rose; pet. obovate, twice as long as sep.; peduncles 5- to 7-fld. July, August. N. Greece.

**E. Gusson'ei.** More or less decumbent, up to 10 in. h. from a woody base, hairy. *Basal l.* many, soon deciduous, stalked; *upper* sessile, ovate-heart-shaped, 1½ to 2 in. long, deeply lobed, base widely heart-shaped, lobes obtuse. *fl.* 8 to 14, on peduncle up to 6 in. long; pet. equal, not spotted, with deeply coloured veins, about ½ in. long, about ⅘ in. across. May, June. *fr.* beak 2 to 2½ in. long. S. Italy. (B.M. 2445.)

**E. gutta'tum.** Woody at base, 3 to 6 in. h. *l.* many, radical, ovate- to long-heart-shaped, slightly lobed, with rounded teeth. *fl.* white, 2 upper pet. with a dark spot at base, all pet. broadly obovate, rounded; peduncles about 5 in. long. SW. Europe.

**E. × hyb'ridum** (*E. daucoides × E. Manescavi*). *l.* finer and more fern-like than in *E. Manescavi* with smaller and paler fl., otherwise much like *E. Manescavi.*

**E. hymeno'des.** Softly hairy, with erect stem about 12 in. h., branched, shrubby at base. *l.* more or less 3-lobed, blunt, deeply toothed. *fl.* pink on many-fld. peduncles; upper pet. with brown spot at base. Spring, summer. Atlas Mts. 1789. (B.M. 1174.)

**E. Jacquinia'num.** Annual or biennial. Related to *E. cicutarium* but with *l.* 2- or 3-pinnatisect, segs. linear-lanceolate, acute, beaks of fr. longer. Mediterranean region. SYN. *E. Salzmanii. See* **E. × sebaceum.**

**E. × Kolbia'num** (*E. macradenum × E. supracanum*). *l.* more lax than in *E. supracanum. fl.* white to soft shell-pink with faint veins. Raised by Mr. Sundermann.

**E. leucan'thum.** Sub-shrubby, up to 6 in. h., from a dark vertical rhiz. Stem more or less erect, glandular-hairy. *Basal l.* many, up to 2 in. long, including stalk; *stem-l.* sessile; oblong or triangular, 2- or 3-pinnatisect, segs. filiform, acute. *fl.* 2 to 5 on a peduncle up to 2 in. long, white, about ⅖ in. across; pet. equal, not spotted. June. Asia Minor.

**E. × linda'vicum** (*E. absinthoides amanum × E. chrysanthum*). *l.* with rather broad segs. *fl.* rather dull yellow. Raised by Mr. Sundermann.

**E. macrade'num.** Tufted, 2 to 6 in. h., stemless, strongly scented. *l.* glandular-hairy, pinnate; segs. 2-pinnatifid; lobes lanceolate-linear. *fl.* pale violet, veined; pet. acute, the 2 broadest with dark purple spot at base; peduncles many-fld. June, July. Pyrenees. 1798. (B.M. 5665.) var. **ro'seum,** *fl.* rose.

**E. malacoi'des.** Annual or biennial, 4 to 16 in. h., softly hairy. *Basal l.* many, much shorter than stem-l., ovate-cordate, up to 1½ in. long, sometimes lobed. *fl.* on filiform pedicels with pale involucral bracts; pet. small, equal, unspotted. July. Mediterranean to S. Africa, naturalized in N. and S. America. (F.G. 658.) Very variable.

**E. Manesca'vi.** Stemless. 10 to 24 in. h. *l.* lanceolate to ovate-lanceolate, 6 in. or more long; segs. ovate, short-stalked, toothed or pinnatifid. *fl.* up to 2 in. across, purplish-red, spots on 2 upper pet. slightly darker. Pyrenees. Summer. (Gn. 55 (1899), 292.) Border plant.

**E. Moure'tii.** Closely related to *E. gruinum* but distinctly glandular-hairy and *fl.* white or rose with dark purple blotches at base of 2 upper pet., and with purple veins. *fl.-stem* leafy. Morocco. 1928. (B.M. 9268.)

**E. olym'picum.** A synonym of *E. absinthoides Sibthorpianum.*

**E. pelargoniiflo'rum.** Woody at base, 1 ft. or more h., branched. *Basal l.* many, ovate-heart-shaped, somewhat lobed, with rounded teeth. *fl.* white, 2 upper pet. spotted purple; peduncles about 5 in. long; umbels 8- to 10-fld. Summer. Anatolia. (B.M. 5206.)

**E. petrae'um.** Stems 2 to 6 in. h., weakly ascending, 2- to 4-fld. *l.* radical, many, softly hairy, 3 to 6 in. long, pinnate; segs. 2-pinnatifid; lobes lanceolate-linear. June. S. France, Spain. 1640.

**E. Reichard'ii.** A synonym of *E. chamaedryoides.*

**E. roma'num.** Stemless, 6 to 9 in. h., silvery-hairy. *l.* pinnate; lflets. ovate, deeply cut. *fl.* bright pink; peduncles about 6 in. long; umbels about 6-fld. Spring. Mediterranean region. 1724. (B.M. 377; F.G. 654.)

**E. × seba'ceum** (*E. cicutarium × E. romanum*). Much like *E. Jacquinianum.* France.

**E. serot'inum.** Perennial up to 16 in. h., densely whitish hairy. *l.* fern-like, up to about 3 in. long. *fl.* 3 to 10 on a peduncle, deep violet; pet. equal, obovate, as long as cal. Caucasus. (S.B.F.G. 312.)

**E. Sibthorpia'num.** A variety of *E. absinthoides.*

**E. supraca'num.** Stemless. *l.* many, about 2 in. long, silvery-hairy above, green beneath, ovate or oblong, 2-pinnatisect; lobes sometimes cut. *fl.* white, veined red, without spots; pet. obovate, rounded; peduncles 4 to 6 in. h. Summer. Pyrenees.

**E. tordilioi'des.** A synonym of *E. gruinum.*

**E. trichomanefo'lium.** Habit of *E. supracanum* but *l.* green, downy; lflets. oblong-linear. *fl.* pink or white, veined; pet. blunt, a little longer than sep.; peduncles about 6 in. long. 3- to 7-fld. Summer. Lebanon, Hermon.

**E. × Willkommia'num** (*E. cheilanthifolium × E. macradenum*). Intermediate between parents, the *l.* larger and more hairy than in *E. cheilanthifolium.*

***ero'sus -a -um,*** jagged as if gnawed or bitten off irregularly.

**ERPE'TION reniform'e.** A synonym of *Viola hederacea.*

***errabun'dus -a -um,*** wandering.

***errat'icus -a -um,*** differing from the typical.

***Erskinea'nus -a -um,*** in honour of Sir James Elphinstone Erskine, 1838–1911, naval commander, explored in New Guinea.

***erubes'cens,*** blushing, becoming red.

**ERU'CA** (ancient Latin name for *Eruca sativa*). FAM. *Cruciferae.* A genus of 5 species in the Mediterranean region. Annual or perennial herbs with usually pinnatifid leaves and racemes of moderate-sized usually yellow flowers with brownish or violet veins, or sometimes violet. Fruit swollen, 4-sided, sub-elliptic, about $\frac{1}{2}$ to 1 in. long with a rough beak; seeds 15 to 30, brown. *E. sativa* is an annual grown for its seed which is rich in oil, and sometimes for use as a salad. It is easily raised from seed sown in spring in the open.

**E. sativ'a.** Annual, rarely branched at base. *Lower l.* stalked, pinnatipartite with terminal lobe nearly round, obtuse; *upper* sessile, shorter, terminal lobe acute; all fleshy, toothed, hairy on main veins beneath. *fl.* 15 to 50 in a raceme; *pet.* at first yellow then whitish, veins dull brownish. Now widely distributed in warm regions. A variable plant.

*erucas'trum,* Eruca-like.

*erusifo'lius -a -um,* with Eruca-like foliage.

**A →**

**ERV'UM.** Included in Vicia. *E. gracile = V. unijuga.*

**ERYCI'NA** (a name of Venus, from Mt. Eryx in Sicily, where she had a temple). FAM. *Orchidaceae.* A genus of a singular species of small Oncidium-like orchid, differing from that genus in the structure of the equally 3-lobed lip and in the short, thick, wingless column; rostellum long, sigmoid. Treatment as for Oncidium.  **A**

**E. echina'ta.** *fl.* 5 to 9, $\frac{2}{3}$ in. across; *pet.* greenish-yellow; *lip* yellowish, large, flat; racemes axillary from base of the small pseudobulb, decurved. April. *l.* 2, 2 to 4 in. long, ovate-oblong, with a few brown stripes. Stems tufted, 2 to 3 in. h., with imbricate scales below and *l.* above, terminating in a small pseudobulb. Mexico. 1892. (B.M. 7389.) SYN. *Oncidium echinatum.*

E. C.

**ERYNG'IUM** (*eringion*, name used by Theophrastus). FAM. *Umbelliferae.* A genus of over 100 species of herbaceous, spiny plants, usually perennial, natives of temperate and sub-tropical regions, especially in S. America. Leaves more or less sheathing at base. Flowers in dense oblong or roundish heads, lowest bracts usually longest, forming an involucre, sometimes strikingly coloured. Many species are very handsome, either because of their bright bluish inflorescences, the colour often extending to the stems, or by their striking foliage. They grow best in light, sandy soil and must have good drainage. Several are well fitted for borders, a few for the rock-garden, others for the shrub-garden or as isolated plants on lawns. Propagation by seeds, careful division, or by root-cuttings.

**E. agavifo'lium.** Up. to 6 ft. h., stem branched above. *Radical l.* ensiform, up to 5 ft. long, coarsely-spine-toothed. *fl.-heads* cylindrical, about 2 in. long, 1 in. thick; involucre of 10 to 16 bracts, long, ovate below and gradually narrowed upwards, scarcely or not spiny. January to March. Argentine.

**E. alpi'num.*** 1$\frac{1}{2}$ to 2 ft. h. *Basal* and lower *stem-l.* deeply heart-shaped, toothed, long-stalked; *upper* palmately lobed, finely toothed; involucral l. 10 to 20, little longer than fl.-head, rather soft. *fl.* in oblong heads, the upper part of plant and fl. beautiful blue. Europe. 1597. (B.M. 922.) Hardy.

**E. amethysti'num.*** 1 to 2 ft. h. Stems smoothish, corymbosely branched at apex. *Basal l.* pinnatifid; lobes cut, somewhat pinnatifid; involucral l. 7 or 8, lanceolate, with a few teeth at base, much longer than fl.-head. *fl.* in globose heads, amethyst. July, August. Europe. 1648. Hardy.

**E. aquat' cum.** A synonym of *E. yuccaefolium.*

**E. Bourga'ti.** 1 to 2 ft. h. Stems a little branched at apex. *Basal l.* orbicular, 3-partite; lobes pinnatifid or forked, entire between the divisions; involucral l. 10 to 12, lanceolate, spiny, erect, much longer than fl.-head. *fl.* in ovate heads, bluish. June to August. Pyrenees. 1731. Hardy.

**E. bromeliifo'lium.** 3 to 4 ft. h. *Basal l.* broadly lanceolate-linear, with large, awl-shaped teeth, shorter than breadth of l.; veins parallel; involucral l. 10, lanceolate, longer than fl.-heads. *fl.* in round heads, white. July. Mexico. Half-hardy.

**E. caeru'leum.*** 2 to 3 ft. h. Stems forked, forming a spreading corymb. *Basal l.* ovate-heart-shaped, 3-lobed or 3-sect; *stem-l.* rigid, palmate or almost pinnate, sessile; involucral l. 5, awl-shaped, 2 or 3 times as long as the fl.-head. *fl.* blue. July. Orient. 1816. Hardy.

**E. campes'tre.** 1 to 2 ft. h. Stem paniculately branched. *Basal l.* nearly 3-nate; sep. pinnatifid, lobes ovate; *stem-l.* auricled; involucral l. linear-lanceolate, longer than fl.-heads. *fl.* in roundish heads, blue. July, August. Europe, including Britain, N. Asia. (E.B. 570.)

*Eryngium amethystinum*

**E. Carli'nae.** *Radical l.* lanceolate, deeply spine-toothed, acute; *stem-l.* pinnatifid, lobes deeply cut. Stem many-headed. *fl.-heads* blue; involucral l. yellowish above, 7 to 9, ovate-lanceolate, deeply toothed. Mexico.

**E. cornicula'tum.** Erect. *Radical l.* ovate or elliptic, small, somewhat toothed near tip; *stem-l.* spatulate, incised, spiny, lobes subulate. *fl.-heads* numerous in a terminal infl.; involucre of 5 or 6, unequal, subulate scales. Portugal.

**E. cre'ticum.** Stem much branched above, branches spreading. *Stem-l.* palmately cleft, lobes lanceolate, spiny, finely toothed at base; involucral l. 5, longer than fl.-head. *fl.* in a long, somewhat rounded head, amethyst blue. Summer. Crete, &c. Hardy.

**E. dichot'omum.** 1 to 2 ft. h. *Basal l.* oblong, cordate, toothed, stalked; *stem-l.* palmately partite, spreading, lobes spiny; involucral l. lanceolate, much longer than fl.-head. *fl.* in globose heads, blue. July, August. S. Europe. 1820. Hardy.

**E. ebractea'tum.** Perennial. Stem trichotomous. *l.* sword-shaped, nearly entire. *fl.-heads* small, cylindric, about $\frac{1}{2}$ in. long, without involucre. Paraguay to Argentine.

**E. gigan'teum.** 3 to 4 ft. h. Stem forked. *Basal l.* deeply heart-shaped, crenately toothed, long-stalked; *stem-l.* stem-clasping, deeply lobed, toothed; involucral l. 8 or 9, large, longer than fl.-heads. *fl.* in ovate heads, blue. July, August. Caucasus. 1820. (Gn. 79 (1915), 395.) Hardy.

**E. glacia'le.** 3 to 6 ft. h. *Basal l.* spatulate-wedge-shaped, 3-sect, with long, rigid spines; segs. 3-lobed; *stem-l.* deeply much cut, nearly sessile; involucral l. 6 to 8, 3 times as long as fl.-heads. *fl.* in roundish heads, blue. Summer. Spain. SYN. *E. asperifolium.* Hardy.

**E. Heldreich'ii.** Habit and l. of *E. Bourgati* but involucral l. longer, keeled, margin entire, not spiny. Stem much branched, pale green or bluish in upper part. *fl.-heads* in 3- to 5-parted corymbs. Summer. Syria, Antilebanon.

**E. Lassaux'ii.** 6 to 9 ft. h., slightly leafy. *l.* 2$\frac{1}{2}$ to 3 ft. long, narrow, forming a strong tufted growth. *fl.* in small heads, reddish-purple, in a loose branched panicle. Summer. S. America. (R.H. 1874, 375.)

**E. Leavenworth'ii.** *Stem-l.* palmately 7- to 9-partite, about 2 in. long; segs. spreading, spiny. *fl.-heads* 1$\frac{1}{2}$ in. long, nearly 1 in. across, crowned with a leafy tuft, fl. bright violet-purple. Arkansas, &c.

**E. marit'imum.** Sea Holly. 12 to 18 in. h. *Basal l.* roundish heart-shape, spine-toothed; *upper* stem-clasping, palmately lobed; all whitish-glaucous, leathery; involucral l. 5 to 7, ovate, longer than fl.-heads. *fl.* very pale blue, in roundish heads. July to October. Europe, including Britain. (E.B. 569.) Hardy.

**E. × Oliveria'num*** (*E. giganteum* × ?). ? 3 to 12 ft. h. Involucral *l.* 10 to 12, longer than fl.-heads, with about 6 teeth each side. *fl.* blue. E. Mediterranean. (Gn. 27 (1885), 238.) Hardy.

**E. palmatum.** Green perennial, erect, glabrous, little branched. *Lower l.* palmately 3- to 7-parted, segs. oblong, wedge-shaped, spiny, 2- or 3-lobed at tip, segs. of upper l. narrower. Involucral bracts twice as long as bluish head. Serbia.

**E. pandanifo'lium.*** 10 to 15 ft. h. *Basal l.* 4 to 6 ft. long, concave, slender-pointed, spiny, glaucous. *fl.* in small globose heads, purplish; involucre scarcely developed; panicles very large, forked. Summer. Monte Video. (G.C. 5 (1876), 76.) Half-hardy.

**E. pla'num.*** About 2 ft. h. *Lower l.* oval, heart-shaped, entire; *upper* 5-partite, toothed; involucral l. 6 to 8, lanceolate, equal to or longer than fl.-heads. *fl.* in roundish heads, blue. July, August. E. Europe. 1596. Hardy.

**E. ser'bicum.** Perennial. *Lower l.* laciniate, segs. 7 to 5, linear, grassy, undivided, long-spiny; *upper* dilated at base, spiny-ciliate. *fl.-heads* in subraceme corymbs; involucral l. lanceolate, spine-tipped, upper 1½ times as long as fl.-heads. S. Macedonia.

**E. Ser'ra.** 4 to 6 ft. h. *Basal l.* in a spreading rosette, sometimes deeply pinnatifid, sometimes merely spine-margined, 1 to 2 ft. long, 4 in. wide, nearly flat. *fl.* white, in small globose heads. Autumn. Brazil. 1872. Half-hardy.

**E. Spinal'ba.** Stem thick, nearly simple. *Basal l.* 3- to 5-parted, lobes deeply toothed or forked; involucral l. 9 or 10, pinnatifid, very rigid. *fl.* whitish, in an ovate-cylindrical head. Summer. Europe. Hardy.

**E. tripar'titum.** Perennial. *Radical l.* glabrous, 3-lobed, obovate-oblong-wedge-shaped, coarsely toothed, subspiny; *stem-l.* subsessile, 3- to 5-parted, lobes lanceolate, coarsely toothed. *fl.-heads* ovate, globose; involucral l. twice as long as fl.-heads, outer 3-cusped, inner undivided. Summer. Origin?

**E. trique'trum.** About 12 in. h. *Basal l.* heart-shaped, 3-lobed, lobes spine-toothed; stalked; *stem-l.* 3- to 5-partite; involucral l. 3 or 4, spine-pointed, keeled, longer than fl.-heads. *fl.* in rounded heads, blue; peduncles triquetrous. July. Sicily, &c. 1824. Hardy.

**E. yuccaefo'lium.** 2 to 3 ft. h. *Lower l.* broad linear, remotely finely spiny; veins parallel; *upper* lanceolate, toothed; involucral l. 8 or 9, shorter than fl.-heads. *fl.* in globose heads, white or very pale blue. July to September. N. America. 1699. (B.R. 372.) Syn. *E. aquaticum.* Hardy.

**ERYS'IMUM** (old Greek name used by Hippocrates, from *eryo*, to draw; some species produce blisters). FAM. *Cruciferae.* A genus of about 80 species of annual, biennial, or perennial more or less hoary herbs, natives of the N. Temperate zone. Hairs branched. Leaves variable, usually oblong-linear, entire or toothed. Racemes long or corymbose, terminal, many-flowered; sepals unequal; nectaries lateral and 2 median. Fruit a long siliqua. Closely related to Cheiranthus, in which some species are sometimes included. Comparatively few species are of horticultural value and these are easily grown in ordinary soil and are for the most part showy border or rock-garden plants. Propagated by seed or (perennials) by division or, if desired, by cuttings.

**E. alpi'num.** Perennial, about 6 in. h. Stem simple, straight. *l.* lanceolate, starry-hairy, teeth distant. *fl.* fragrant, sulphur. May. *fr.* short, stalked. Scandinavia. 1823. Syn. *Cheiranthus alpinus.* Variable. var. **Moonlight,** fl. soft yellow, buds dark. A hybrid between *Cheiranthus* × *Allionii* (q.v.) and *E. alpinum*; **Pamela Pershouse** has deep golden fl. about 1 in. across. Rock-garden or border.

**E. arkansa'num.** Biennial. Stem simple, 1½ to 3 ft. h. *l.* oblong-lanceolate, runcinate, toothed, narrowed at base, about 2 in. long. *fl.* yellow, as large as a Wallflower. Summer. *fr.* about 2 in. long. Arkansas, Texas. var. **Golden Gem,** fl. deeper yellow.

**E. as'perum.** Biennial about 8 in. h. *l.* linear-oblong, lower runcinate, toothed, rough, greyish with appressed forked hairs. *fl.* yellow with white claws. July. California, Texas. 1824. var. **perenne,** perennial.

**E. au'reum.** Annual or biennial, 2 to 3 ft. h. *l.* lanceolate, slender pointed, toothed, hairy, green. *fl.* golden, somewhat scented, stalked, larger than in *E. repandum.* Caucasus.

**E. capita'tum.** Biennial or perennial, 1 to 2 ft. h., erect, downy, sometimes branched. *l.* oblong, oblanceolate or linear, entire or repandly toothed. *fl.* cream or pale yellow; pet. 1 in. long, rounded. W. United States. There is much confusion concerning these species and this may be, like *E. arkansanum* merely a form of *E. asperum.* Syn. *Cheiranthus capitatus.*

**E. du'bium.** Perennial. Stems decumbent, branched. *l.* oblong-lanceolate, somewhat toothed, smooth or with 2-branched hairs. *fl.* pale yellow, scarcely scented; pet. obovate. April to July. Jura. 1819. Syn. *E. ochroleucum, Cheiranthus ochroleucus.* var. **helvet'icum,** about 1 ft. h., stems ascending, *l.* narrower, entire or toothed, fl. yellow. Rhaetian Alps. 1819. Syn. *E. helveticum.* See **Cheiranthus × Allionii.**

**E. hieraciifo'lium.** Erect, 1½ to 3 ft. h. Stem branched above in a terminal raceme, hairy. *l.* oblong-lanceolate, sinuately toothed, covered with 3-fid hairs above. *fl.* of medium size, yellow, corymbose. *infl.* lengthening after fl. June, July. S. Europe.

**E. Kotschya'num.** Densely tufted, 2 to 3 in. h., pale green. *l.* narrow linear, about ½ in. long, densely crowded, toothed or sometimes entire. *fl.* large, orange-yellow. June, July. Asia Minor. Rock-garden.

**E. linifo'lium.*** Evergreen, with many ascending slender, simple stems, 5 to 15 in. long, from a root-like rhiz. *Basal l.* oblong, narrowed to a long stalk, repand-toothed, others narrower, linear-lanceolate, entire, acute. *fl.* in a dense raceme; sep. purplish; pet. purple or violet; anthers greenish. May to July. Spain. Syn. *Cheiranthus linifolius.* Rock-garden.

**E. mura'le.** Biennial or perennial. Tufted, 6 to 8 in. h. *l.* deep green, linear. *fl.* golden-yellow. Europe. This, like *E. helveticum*, may be a form of *E. dubium* (q.v.).

**E. ochroleu'cum.** A synonym of *E. dubium.*

**E. pachycar'pum.** Robust, 18 to 24 in. h. Stem erect, angled. *l.* lanceolate, sinuate, toothed, stalked. *fl.* bright orange-yellow; pet. obovate-spatulate. Summer. Sikkim, Himalaya.

**E. Perofskia'num.*** Annual. About 1 ft. h. *l.* erect. *fl.* reddish-orange. Summer (or spring if sown in September). Afghanistan, Caucasus. 1838. (B.M. 3757.) Border.

**E. pulchel'lum.** A synonym of *E. rupestre.*

**E. pu'milum.*** Tufted perennial of 1 to 3 in. *l.* mostly basal, linear-lanceolate, greyish-green, somewhat toothed. *fl.* large, pale yellow, fragrant. July, August. European Alps. 1823. (L.B.C. 899.) Rock-garden or scree.

**E. purpu'reum.** Ash-grey perennial with herbaceous ascending branches from a sub-shrubby procumbent stem; 3 to 6 in. h. *l.* narrow-linear; lower runcinate-pinnatipartite, upper toothed or entire. *fl.* purple, of medium size, about ½ in. long, shortly pedicellate. Asia Minor. Rock-garden.

**E. repan'dum.** Annual with somewhat hairy, linear-lanceolate, repandly toothed *l.* and small yellow *fl.* E. Europe to NW. India, N. Africa. (R.I.F.G. 4384.)

**E. rupes'tre.*** Perennial, forming compact tufts. Stems up to 1 ft. h. *l.* spatulate, slightly toothed, hairy, upper oblong. *fl.* sulphur, rather small. Spring. Asia Minor. 1880. The forms of this variable species are ill-defined. It may be only 3 in. h. and the l. vary much in toothing. var. **auranti'acum** has golden-yellow fl.

**E. sylves'tre** var. **pu'milum.** See **E. pumilum.**

**E. thyrsoi'deum.** Silvery biennial. Stem short. *l.* densely crowded, narrow linear, entire, acute. *fl.* yellow, as large as a Wallflower. Asia Minor.

**ERYSIPHA'CEAE.** A family of fungi which comprises the true or powdery mildews (q.v.). They are nearly all white and are surface parasites growing on the outside of leaves, stems, &c., obtaining food by sinking haustoria (suckers) into the epidermal cells of the host plant. Although superficial they can have a serious smothering effect. The white growth rapidly produces spores to spread the disease. This white stage at one time was given generic rank and called Oidium. It is now known that most of the species form perithecia for overwintering and are therefore Ascomycetes. Many species are highly parasitic, causing Apple mildew, Chrysanthemum mildew, Rose mildew, &c.

D. E. G.

**ERYS'IPHE polyg'oni.** In the genus Erysiphe this species is parasitic on many plants showing a high degree of specialization and having a number of biologic forms (q.v.). A common disease caused by it is Pea Mildew.

D. E. G.

**ERYTHE'A** (a Greek mythological name, one of the Hesperides). FAM. *Palmaceae.* A genus of about 8 species of tall, usually unarmed, Palms with erect stems ringed at base and a terminal crown of fan-shaped leaves, the upper part of trunk hidden by dead leaf-bases, natives of Mexico and Lower California. Leaves plicate, filiferous, stalks stout, in some species with marginal spines. Sheaths and inflorescence densely hairy, thick, leathery. Spadices long, usually panicled, with thick branches. Flowers pale. Fruit globose or ovoid. Greenhouse conditions suit these Palms with a night temperature of 55 to 60° F., and light, rich soil with abundance of water. Nearly related to Brahea.

**E. arma'ta.** Blue Palm. Tall, slender, up to 40 ft. h. *l.* large, glaucous; segs. 30 to 40, somewhat torn at tips, slightly filiferous; stalk spiny-margined. *fl.* on a pendent spadix up to 18 ft. long, somewhat branched. *fr.* reddish-brown. Lower California. 1887. (G.C. 20 (1896), 425.) SYN. *Brahea glauca.*

**E. ed'ulis.** Guadeloupe Palm. Slender, up to 50 ft. h., 15 in. thick, with thick, corky bark. *l.* about 3 ft. long; segs. 70 to 80, torn at apex, filiferous; stalk about 1 in. wide, not spiny. *fl.* on branched spadices, 5 to 6 ft. long. *fr.* black, shining, in large clusters weighing up to 40 or 50 lb. California. (G.C. 22 (1897), 157.) SYN. *Brahea edulis.*

**E. Roez'lii.** Closely related to *E. armata* but with smaller fruits.

**ERYTHRAE'A.** A synonym of Centaurium.

***erythrae'us -a -um*** (in compound words, ***erythro-***), red.

**ERYTHRI'NA** (*erythros*, red; from the flower colour). FAM. *Leguminosae.* A genus of about 30 species of usually shrubs and trees, mostly tropical with some in S. Africa. Leaves 3-foliolate, large. Flowers coral-red, in dense racemes, large, papilionaceous, usually produced before the leaves (sometimes terminal on the shoots of the year); calyx split, spathe-like, 2-lipped; petals very unequal, standard large; upper stamen sometimes free, sometimes connate with others half-way up filaments; anthers uniform. Fruit a linear, turgid, torulose pod. A strong loamy soil suits all species with abundant water except during rest, and exposure to bright sun. The woody-stemmed species should be kept growing in a warm house through summer and in September water should be gradually withheld so that wood may ripen, the leaves fall, and the plants go to rest for winter. They should be repotted or top-dressed in early spring, placed in a high temperature in a moist atmosphere and given plenty of water at the roots, treatment that should cause them to produce their large racemes of gorgeous flowers. Any pruning should be delayed until after flowering. The herbaceous-stemmed species, *E. Crista-galli* and *E. herbacea*, produce annual shoots from a stout root-stock, and flower in autumn. These species should be started in heat in spring unless planted outdoors. As growth proceeds a lower temperature will suffice and when fear of frost is past they may be placed outdoors for the summer. Young shoots with a heel may be planted in sandy soil in spring and with a little bottom heat serve to increase stock. After flowering the shoots die and the plants should then be put under the staging in a cool house, kept dry and at rest until the following spring. Erythrinas planted outdoors need a covering of leaves to protect the rootstocks from frost. **A**

**E. × Bidwill'ii** (*E. Crista-galli* × *E. herbacea*). *infl.* axillary and terminal on annual shoots. Of garden origin. (B.R. 33, 9.)

**E. caf'fra.** 30 to 60 ft. h. *l.* rhomboid, narrowed to an obtuse point; stalk longer than blade, prickly. *fl.* brilliant scarlet fading to purple, in a somewhat verticillate spike; peduncles axillary, longer than l., erect, rounded, with white, linear warts. S. Africa. (B.M. 2431.) SYN. *E. Humeana.*

**E. Coralloden'dron.** Coral-tree. Stem woody, 6 to 12 ft. h., prickly. *lflets.* broad, rhomboid-ovate, acute; stalks not prickly. *fl.* deep scarlet, in long racemes, appearing after l.-fall. May, June. W. Indies, S. United States. 1690. SYN. *E. spinosa.*

**E. Cris'ta-gal'li.*** Common Coral-tree. Stems 6 to 8 ft. h. *lflets.* oval or ovate, more or less glaucous, leathery, rather blunt; stalks prickly, glandular. *fl.* bright deep scarlet, in large terminal racemes. May to July. Brazil. 1771. (B.M. 2161.) SYN. *E. laurifolia.* Variable. *See* **E. × Bidwillii.** Nearly hardy.

**E. ful'gens.** Shrub of 2 to 3 ft. h., spiny. *l.* ternate, not spiny; lflets. triangular, about 1½ in. long. *fl.* brilliant scarlet, narrow, about 1½ in. long, in a terminal cluster of about 12; cal. truncate. India.

**E. herba'cea.** 2 to 3 ft. h. with annual herbaceous branches, not prickly. *lflets.* ovate or somewhat hastate. *fl.* deep scarlet, distant; racemes long. June to September. Carolina. 1724. (B.M. 877.) *See* **E. × Bidwillii.**

**E. in'dica.*** Tree of 20 to 30 ft. Stem erect, prickly, spines black. *lflets.* broadly ovate, acute, smooth; stalks not prickly. *fl.* scarlet. Trop. Asia, Australia. 1814. var. **al'ba,** *fl.* white; **marmora'ta,** *l.* large, broad, with white spots and blotches, 1879; **Parcel'lii,** *l.* variegated yellow, sometimes along midrib and veins.

**E. insig'nis.** Somewhat prickly tree. *l.* ovate, hairy at first. *fl.* scarlet, in short, dense racemes. Habitat ?

**E. pulcher'rima.** Tree up to 30 ft., branches slightly prickly. *l.* glabrous, 3-foliolate; stalk 2¼ to 4½ in. long, thickened at base, channelled above, prickly; lateral lflets. oblong-ovate, 2½ to 3¾ in. long, terminal rather larger, elliptic or obovate, with usually 1 or 2 prickles on midrib beneath near base. *fl.* in 3-fld. axillary cluster, pedicels about 1½ in. long; cor. red, standard elliptic-obovate, over 2 in. long, 1⅓ in. wide, wing pet. narrow, ⅜ in. long, keel 1⅜ in. long. Argentine? (B.M. 8532.) Stove.

**E. Vespertil'is.** *lflets.* ob-triangular with front deeply hollowed. *fl.* numerous, drooping, in erect racemes; standard ovate, nearly 1½ in. long. W. Australia. 1885. Warm greenhouse.

**ERYTHROCHAE'TE palmatif'ida.** A synonym of *Ligularia japonica.*

**ERYTHROCHI'TON** (*erythros*, red, *chiton*, tunic; the calyx is red). FAM. *Rutaceae.* A genus of 3 species of evergreen trees, natives of Brazil, Guiana, Colombia. Leaves alternate, 2-foliolate, towards tip of stem, very long. Flowers showy, racemose or clustered; calyx large, red; corolla white or pink, tube straight or curved, lobes spreading, almost equal. *E. brasiliensis* needs stove conditions and a compost of loam and leaf-mould. Increased by seed or cuttings.

**E. brasilien'sis.** About 10 ft. h. Axillary branches almost leafless, fl. at tips. *l.* alternate, simple, lanceolate, very long, entire, smooth; stalked. *fl.* large in axils of bracts, 2 to 4 or more in cluster, on short, bracteolate pedicels; cal. red; cor. white. July. Brazil. 1842. (B.M. 4742.)

**ERYTHRO'DES.** Included in **Anoectochilus.**

**ERYTHRONEU'RA pallid'ifrons.** *See* **Glasshouse leaf-hopper.**

**ERYTHRO'NIUM** (*erythros*, red, the colour of the flowers in the European species). FAM. *Liliaceae.* A genus of about 20 species of very ornamental, hardy, bulbous plants, of which one species is dispersed through Europe, Asiatic Russia to Japan, and the rest are N. American. Leaves radical, ovate, ovate-lanceolate or, in *E. montanum*, cordate, in many species mottled and very ornamental. Flowers usually on a scape, one to many, pendulous; perianth segments 6, erect or reflexed. They succeed in almost any light soil, but prefer a mixture of loam and peat. Propagated by offsets, which are produced freely when the plants do well. The best time for replanting is immediately the leaves die away after flowering. Erythroniums have a better effect when planted in groups than if placed in very small quantities separately; the bulbs should be inserted about 3 in. deep. If left untouched afterwards, an annual top-dressing of good soil will be advantageous. The flowers generally appear in March and April, and are very attractive.

For the rock-garden, the front of mixed borders, and for naturalizing, these charming little plants, with their Cyclamen-like flowers and often elegantly marbled foliage, are well adapted. As pot-plants they are likewise useful. A partially shaded situation and a loam and peat soil suit them well, and they should be planted about 3 in. deep in autumn, and covered with sand. Several species have recently been distinguished in N. America and await introduction.

A good account of the cultivation of Erythroniums is in *Flora and Sylva*, vol. i, p. 250.

KEY

| | |
|---|---|
| 1. *Lvs. not mottled* | 2 |
| 1. *Lvs. mottled* | 6 |
| 2. *Fl. solitary* | 3 |
| 2.* *Fl. typically 2 to many* | 4 |
| 3. *Fl. lavender* | E. mesochoreum |
| 3. *Fl. rose or pink* | E. propullans |
| 3. *Fl. bright yellow* | E. parviflorum |

4. *Lvs. with cordate base* — E. montanum
4. *Lvs. not cordate* — 5
5. *Fl. large, yellow or white* — E. grandiflorum
5. *Fl. medium, pure yellow, lvs. large* — E. tuolumnense
5. *Segs. less than 1 in. long* — 7
6. *Fl. solitary* — 9
6.* *Fl. typically 2 to 9* —
7. *Fl. yellow* — 8
7. *Fl. rose, pink, or white* —
8. *Lvs. narrow* — E. albidum†
8. *Lvs. oval-acuminate* — E. Dens-canis
9. *Infl. a sessile umbel* — E. multiscapoideum
9. *Infl. not an umbel* — 10
10. *Stigma 3-lobed* — 11
10. *Stigma entire* — 13
11. *Filaments not dilated* — E. californicum
11. *Filaments dilated below* — 12
12. *Fl. cream with yellow base* — E. oregonum
12. *Fl. creamy-white, tinged purple* — E. revolutum
13. *Segs. without auricles at base* — E. Howellii
13. *Fl. white with yellow base* — E. citrinum
13. *Fl. pale purple with deeper base* — E. Hendersonii

\* Weak or immature plants may have but one flower.
† Leaves occasionally without mottling.

**E. al′bidum.** Corm ovoid, stoloniferous. Stem 6 to 9 in. long. *l.* oblong-lanceolate, 4 to 6 in. long, sometimes slightly mottled. *fl.* white or bluish-white, solitary; segs. 1 to 1½ in. long, not auricled, recurved. Ontario to Texas. 1824. (B.B. ed. 2, 1, 506.)

**E. america′num.** 4 to 8 in. h. *l.* elliptic-lanceolate, recurved at tip, generally dotted and marbled violet and white. *fl.* bright yellow, about 1 in. across, solitary; segs. spreading, oblong-lanceolate, obtuse. Eastern N. America. (B.M. 1113; B.B. ed. 2, 1, 506.) Several vars. have been named, including var. **bractea′tum** with longer bracts.

**E. californ′icum.** 8 to 18 in. h. *l.* obovate-lanceolate, mottled; stalk long. *fl.* creamy-white with orange base, 1 or 2 to many; filaments not dilated, anthers white. April, May. Mts. of NW. California, before 1904. (G.C. 65 (1919), 242.) Often grown as *E. giganteum.*

**E. citri′num.** 4 to 8 in. h. *l.* obovate-lanceolate, mottled; stalk margined. *fl.* 1 to 9, usually 3, white with yellow near auricled base of segs.; stigma short, entire. Oregon. Confused in catalogues with *E. tuolumnense.*

**E. Dens-ca′nis.** Dog's-tooth Violet. 6 in. h. *l.* broadly oval, base rounded, slender-pointed, blotched purple-brown and white; stalked. *fl.* purplish-rose, about 2 in. across, solitary, drooping. March, April. Europe, Asia to Japan. 1596. (B.M. 5; S.B.F.G. 4, 71.) Varying in colour and habit. var. **al′bum,** *fl.* white; **japon′icum,** *fl.* violet-purple with black spot at base of segs. Japan; **longiflo′rum,** similar to var. *majus;* **ma′jus,** *fl.* larger; **sibir′icum,** more robust, *fl.* deep rose-purple banded purplish-crimson near base of segs., eye yellow. Altai Mts.

**E. gigan′teum.** A synonym of *E. oregonum,* and confused with *E. californicum* (q.v.).

**E. grandiflo′rum.** *l.* oblong-lanceolate, 3 to 6 in. long, crowded, not mottled; stalks broad, usually short. *fl.* bright yellow with orange base, solitary or in a 2- to 6-fld. raceme; segs. lanceolate, slender-pointed, 1 to 2 in. long, much recurved; anthers yellow. NW. America. var. **can′didum,** *fl.* white. SYN. var. *albiflorum;* **gigan′teum,** a synonym of *E. oregonum;* **Nuttallia′num,** anthers red. (B.R. 1786.)

**E. Hartweg′ii.** A synonym of *E. multiscapoideum.*

**E. Hen′dersonii.** *l.* 2, opposite, oblong, spotted purplish-brown, dull green, narrowed to a long, channelled base. *fl.* pale lilac, spotted dark purple at base, bell-shaped, about 2 in. across, drooping, faintly scented; segs. reflexed from half-way; peduncle 6 to 8 in. long, 1- or 2-fld. April. Oregon. 1887. (B.M. 7017.)

**E. How′ellii.** 6 to 8 in. h. *l.* obovate-lanceolate, mottled; stalk broadly margined. *fl.* 1 to 4, pale yellow with a deep orange spot at base of each seg.; inner segs. not auricled; stamens white; peduncle slender. Oregon.

**E. John′sonii.** A synonym of *E. revolutum Johnsonii.*

**E. mesocho′reum.** *l.* linear-lanceolate, green. *fl.* lavender, 1 to 2 in. long, solitary; segs. not recurved. March. Kansas, Iowa. (B.B. ed. 2, 1, 507.)

**E. monta′num.** 6 to 8 in. h. *l.* cordate at base, scarcely mottled. *fl.* white with orange base, fading to pinkish, 1- to many-fld.; anthers yellow. June. Mts. of Brit. Columbia, Oregon, Washington. Starts into growth too late for successful cultivation. (J.R.H.S. 41, 21.)

**E. multiscapoi′deum.** *l.* marbled dull purple above. *fl.* cream-yellow with orange base, fading to pale pink, 1 to 3 or 4 on long pedicels from a sessile umbel. Spring. Mt. near Sacramento. 1898. (B.M. 7583 as *E. Hartwegii.*) SYN. *Fritillaria multiscapoideum.*

**E. Nuttallia′num.** A synonym of *E. grandiflorum Nuttallianum.*

**E. oreg′onum.** About 16 in. h. *l.* obovate-lanceolate, mottled light-brown and white; stalk broadly margined. *fl.* creamy-yellow with yellow base, often with a greenish-brown spot above, generally

few-fld. (1 to 6) on a stout scape; filaments dilated below, anthers white. April, May. Brit. Columbia, Oregon, Washington. 1868. SYN. *E. revolutum Watsonii.* Fl. variable in colour. var. **albiflo′rum,** *fl.* white with a greenish tinge, pet. slender. (B.M. 5714 as *E. giganteum.*)

**E. parviflo′rum.** 4 to 10 in. h. *l.* oblong, narrowed to both ends, green. *fl.* bright yellow with greenish base, usually solitary, anthers creamy-white. April. Cent. Rocky Mts.

**E. propul′lans.** Bulb small, ovoid, stoloniferous. *l.* oblong-lanceolate, 2 to 3 in. long, slightly spotted. *fl.* rose-purple, yellow at base, solitary; segs. ½ in. long; stigma undivided; peduncle 2 to 3 in. long. May. Minnesota, Ontario. (B.B. ed. 2, 1, 507.)

**E. purpuras′cens.** Bulb 1 to 2 in. long. *l.* large, more or less oblong, often undulate, tinged purple. *fl.* 4 to 12 in a sub-umbellate raceme, light yellow, tinged purple, deep orange at base, small; segs. under 1 in. long. May. Sierra Nevada. (Gn. 20 (1881), 186.)

**E. revolu′tum.** 10 to 12 in. h. *l.* faintly mottled white and brown. *fl.* 1 or 2, rarely more, cream, usually tinged purple with age; segs. with prominent auricles; filaments dilated at base. May. California, Oregon. var. **Bolan′deri,** *fl.* white, rarely becoming purple. SYN. *E. Smithii;* **Pink Beauty,** *fl.* pink, *l.* darkly mottled; **John′sonii,** *fl.* deep rose. (Gn. 51 (1897), 136.)

**E. sibir′icum.** A synonym of *E. Dens-canis sibiricum.*

**E. Smith′ii.** A synonym of *E. revolutum Bolanderi.*

**E. tuolumnen′se.** 10 to 12 in. h. *l.* not mottled, lustrous, bright yellow-green, broad lanceolate, 8 to 12 in. long, petiole clasping. *fl.* deep yellow with pale yellow base, running to nearly white below, 1- or many-fld.; segs. broadly lanceolate, generally rounded at apex, 1¼ in. long, auricles not marked; anthers yellow. Spring. California. Often confused with *E. citrinum,* which has mottled leaves and white fls.

**ERYTHROPHLOE′UM** (*erythros,* red, *phloios,* bark; red sap is exuded when the tree is cut). FAM. *Leguminosae.* Red-water tree. A genus of 3 or 4 species of unarmed evergreen trees. Leaves 2-pinnate. Flowers small, almost sessile, in long, cylindrical spikes, forming a terminal panicle; petals 5, small, slightly overlapping; stamens 10, free. Stove. For treatment *see* **Acacia.**

**E. guineen′se.** 40 to 100 ft. h. *lflets.* opposite, oval, oblique, roundish to lanceolate, repand, entire, slender-pointed. *fl.* pale yellow. Sierra Leone. Bark very poisonous.

**E. Labouche′rii.** Tall tree, glabrous. Pinnae opposite, in 2 or 3 pairs. *lflets.* 4 to 9, alternate, oblique, obovate or orbicular, obtuse or retuse. *fl.* in dense spikes 1 to 3 in. long; pet. longer than cal. with woolly edges; stamens more than twice as long as pet., in 2 rows. N. Australia.

**ERYTHRORHIPSA′LIS** (*erythros,* red, *Rhipsalis;* the fruit is red). FAM. *Cactaceae.* A single species of epiphyte with slender, pendent, cylindrical stems; branches forked or in whorls; areoles scattered, bearing several bristles. Flowers terminal, white or pink, diurnal. Fruit red, bristly. For cultivation *see* **Cactus.**

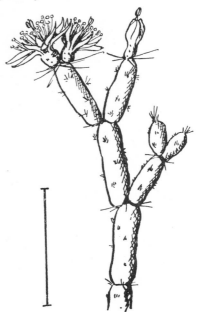

*Erythrorhipsalis pilocarpa*

**E. pilocar'pa.** Brazil. Syn. *Rhipsalis pilocarpa.* (B.R.C. 4, t. 21.)

V. H.

## ERYTHROXYLA'CEAE.
Dicotyledons. A family of about 100 species of tropical woody plants in 2 genera. Leaves alternate, simple, with stipules. Flowers regular, perfect, heterostyled in many instances. Sepals and petals 5, free; stamens 10 united at base; ovary 1-celled with 1 or 2 ovules. Fruit a drupe. The only genus calling for mention is Erythroxylon.

## ERYTHROX'YLON
(*erythros*, red, *xylon*, wood; some of the species have red wood). Fam. *Erythroxylaceae.* A genus of about 90 species of shrubs or small trees of little or no value in horticulture. Leaves alternate, entire. Flowers small, mostly in axillary fascicles; sepals and petals 5 or 6, stamens 10 or 12. Fruit a 1-seeded drupe. *E. Coca* has no horticultural or ornamental value but is of interest as the source of the drug 'cocaine' now famous for its ruinous effects on the minds and bodies of those who take it habitually. Its leaves have been used as a stimulating masticatory by the S. Americans for centuries past. For this purpose it is cultivated over very large areas. Peru alone has produced 15 million lb. of dried leaves annually. So long has it been cultivated that its real native area is not known, nor is its original wild form. It needs greenhouse treatment in England.

**E. Co'ca.** Evergreen shrub or small tree, shoots glabrous. *l.* narrowly oval, inclined to obovate, 2 to 3 in. long, $\frac{3}{4}$ to $1\frac{1}{2}$ in. wide. *fl.* few in axillary, scarcely stalked clusters, greenish-white or yellowish, $\frac{3}{8}$ in. wide. April. S. America. (B.M. 7334.)

W. J. B.

## ESCALLO'NIA
(in honour of Señor Escallon, Spanish traveller in S. America). Fam. *Saxifragaceae.* A genus of between 50 and 60 species of shrubs or small trees, the great majority (all but one of cultivated species) evergreen. Natives of S. America, mostly Chile. Leaves alternate, very rarely entire, shortly stalked or sessile. Flowers from $\frac{1}{3}$ to $\frac{1}{2}$ in. wide, borne in terminal panicles or racemes; calyx mostly top-shaped or funnel-shaped, 5-lobed; petals 5, with long slender claws forming a kind of imitation tube (except in *E. virgata*) and a short spreading limb.

The majority of the species are rather tender, and although mostly hardy in the open air in Sussex and Hants, and thence westward, require wall protection farther north. The hardiest are *E. virgata* and the hybrids raised from it. Easily propagated by late summer cuttings placed in gentle heat.

Several beautiful hybrid Escallonias have been raised with *E. virgata* as one parent. *E. × langleyensis* is described below and *E. × edinensis* (*virgata × rubra*) is very similar. From *E. virgata, E. × langleyensis, E. macrantha,* and *E. pterocladon* a fine group has been raised including *Balfouri*, blush-tinted white; *C. F. Ball*, carmine red; *Donard Seedling*, white; *Donard Brilliance*, dark crimson; *Donard Gem* and *Slieve Donard*, pink; *Donard Beauty*, rich rosy pink; *newryensis* (*pterocladon × langleyensis*).

**E. × Balfour'i.** See above.

**E. × C. F. Ball.** See above.

**E. × Donard Beauty, Donard Brilliance, Donard Gem, Donard Seedling.** See above.

**E. × edinen'sis.** See above.

**E. × exonien'sis\*** (*E. pterocladon × E. rubra*). Evergreen shrub 12 to 20 ft., shoots downy, glandular. *l.* $\frac{1}{2}$ to $1\frac{1}{2}$ in. long, scarcely half as wide, nearly glabrous. *fl.* white or pink-tinted, in panicles $1\frac{1}{2}$ to 3 in. long. June to October. One of the hardiest.

**E. floribun'da.** Evergreen shrub up to 10 ft. or a small tree, shoots glabrous, rather viscid. *l.* $1\frac{1}{2}$ to 4 in. long, $\frac{1}{2}$ to 1 in. wide, obovate or narrowly oval, apex rounded or notched, minutely toothed or entire, glabrous and resinously dotted beneath. *fl.* pure white, $\frac{1}{2}$ in. across, fragrant, borne in terminal panicles, the largest up to 9 in. by 5 in. July, August. S. America. Much confused with *E. montevidensis* (q.v.).

**E. Fonk'ii.** Evergreen shrub up to 5 ft., often wider than h., quite glabrous, shoots angled. *l.* stalkless, obovate to oblanceolate, $\frac{1}{2}$ to $1\frac{1}{4}$ in. long, glossy green on both sides. *Panicles* columnar, up to 4 in. long. *fl.* $\frac{1}{3}$ in. long, varying from crimson to dark red, almost maroon. Chile. 1926.

**E. illini'ta.** Evergreen shrub up to 10 ft. or more, shoots glandular, resinous. *l.* obovate or oval, $\frac{3}{4}$ to $2\frac{1}{2}$ in. long, base cuneate, apex rounded or shortly pointed, glabrous but resinous when young; stalk $\frac{1}{8}$ to $1\frac{1}{4}$ in. long. *Panicle* 3 or 4 in. long, cylindrical, resinous. *fl.* white $\frac{1}{3}$ in. wide, claws $\frac{1}{4}$ in. long; cal. green with 5 linear lobes. June to August. Chile. 1830. (B.R. 1900.) Odour somewhat like a pig-sty.

**E. × Ing'ramii** (*E. macrantha × E. punctata?*). With considerable resemblance to *E. macrantha* this differs by its *l.* being smaller and of narrower shape; *fl.* smaller and paler. Evergreen, up to 12 ft.

**E. × Iv'eyi\*** (*E. × exoniensis × E. montevidensis*). Sturdy, rounded, evergreen shrub, probably 10 or 12 ft. h. eventually, shoots angled and slightly hairy. *l.* glittering, very dark green, oval, 1 to $2\frac{1}{2}$ in. long, glabrous. *fl.* white, $\frac{1}{2}$ in. wide, packed in terminal panicles 5 or 6 in. h., 3 or 4 in. wide. July, August. Caerhays, Cornwall. (B.T.S. 3, 150.)

**E. × langleyen'sis\*** (*E. punctata × E. virgata*). Elegant, semi-evergreen shrub up to 10 ft. with long, slender, gracefully arching shoots. *l.* stalkless, $\frac{1}{2}$ to 1 in. long, half as wide, obovate to narrowly oval, with minute resin glands beneath. *fl.* rosy carmine, $\frac{1}{2}$ in. wide, in racemes of about 6, terminating short twigs. 1893. (B.T.S. 1, 528.)

**E. leucan'tha.\*** Tree up to 35 ft. or a tall shrub (about half as h. in S. England), shoots downy, angular. *l.* obovate to oblanceolate, $\frac{1}{2}$ to 1 in. long, finely toothed. *Racemes* $1\frac{1}{2}$ to 2 in. long, terminal on short, leafy, lateral shoots, the whole forming magnificent panicles up to 1 ft. long and 3 to 7 in. wide, *fl.* pure white, stalks downy. July, Chile. 1927.

*Escallonia macrantha*

**E. macran'tha.\*** Densely leafy, rounded, evergreen bush, 6 to 10 ft., shoots glandular, downy. *l.* broadly oval to obovate, 1 to 3 in. long, doubly toothed, dark shining green above, resinous-glandular beneath. *Racemes* terminal, 2 to 4 in. long, sometimes paniculate. *fl.* bright rosy-crimson, $\frac{5}{8}$ in. long and wide; cal. and fl.-stalk clammy. June to September. Island of Chiloe. 1848. (B.M. 4473.) Admirable evergreen in the south coast towns, where it makes excellent hedges. var. **duplicato-serra'ta** differs in the longer, more irregular (often double) toothing, *l.* not so rich a green, *fl.* pink to dull red; **sanguin'ea**, *fl.* deep red.

**E. monteviden'sis.\*** Evergreen shrub or small tree, closely akin to *E. floribunda. l.* narrowly oval, $1\frac{1}{2}$ to 3 in. long, very finely toothed. *fl.* white, in flattish, rounded panicles; lobes of cal. more pointed than in *E. floribunda* and with minute glandular teeth; style twice as long as cal. lobes. S. Brazil. (B.M. 6404 as *E. floribunda.*) The true *E. floribunda* has the style about as long as the cal. lobes.

**E. × newryen'sis.** See above.

**E. organen'sis.** Evergreen shrub of sturdy habit, 4 to 6 ft., shoots stout, angled, glabrous, slightly resinous. *l.* up to 3 in. long, narrowly obovate or oval, sharply toothed, glabrous. *Panicles* terminal, short, rounded, $1\frac{1}{2}$ to 3 in. wide. *fl.* clear rosy-red, $\frac{1}{3}$ to $\frac{1}{2}$ in. across; stalk glandular; cal. with 5 linear lobes. Organ Mts. of Brazil. 1844. (B.M. 4274.)

**E. Philippia'na.** A synonym of *E. virgata.*

**E. pterocla'don.** Evergreen bushy shrub, 8 to 10 ft., shoots downy, angled. *l.* narrowly obovate, $\frac{1}{3}$ to 1 in. long, $\frac{1}{8}$ to $\frac{1}{4}$ in. wide, toothed, cuneate, shining dark green. *Racemes* $1\frac{1}{2}$ to 3 in. long, terminating short leafy shoots. *fl.* fragrant; white, $\frac{1}{3}$ in. long; pet. with a short limb; cal. glabrous. June to August. Patagonia. 1847. (B.M. 4827.)

**E. pulverulen'ta.** Evergreen shrub up to 10 or 12 ft., shoots downy, angled, viscid. *l.* 2 to 4 in. long, oblong, the base cuneate, apex rounded, toothed, bristly hairy. *Racemes* erect, cylindrical, 4 to 9 in. long, 1 in .wide. *fl.* white, $\frac{1}{3}$ to $\frac{1}{2}$ in. wide, densely crowded. July to Sept. Chile. (S.B.F.G. s. 2, 310.) Distinct by its long, slender raceme.

**E. puncta'ta.** Evergreen shrub of bushy form, up to 10 ft., shoots downy and clammy with gland-tipped bristles. *l.* obovate to oval, $\frac{3}{4}$ to 2 in. long, tapered to both ends, toothed, glabrous above, specked with resinous dots beneath. *fl.* rich crimson, $\frac{1}{3}$ to $\frac{1}{2}$ in. long, in terminal rounded panicles 2 in. long and wide; fl.-stalk and cal. covered with glands. July, August. Chile. (B.M. 6599 as *E. rubra punctata.*) Akin to *E. rubra* but much more glandular and with more richly tinted fl.

**E. revolu'ta.** Evergreen shrub up to 20 ft., shoots angled, grey-felted. *l.* $\frac{3}{4}$ to 2 in. long, obovate, unevenly toothed, apex rounded to pointed, both surfaces grey-downy. *fl.* white, borne in terminal racemes $1\frac{1}{2}$ to 3 in. long; pet. $\frac{5}{8}$ in. long; cal. and fl.-stalks grey-downy. July to September. Chile. 1887. (B.M. 6949.)

**E. ru'bra.** Evergreen shrub up to 15 ft., shoots reddish, downy, viscid, and glandular. *l.* obovate to lanceolate, 1 to 2 in. long, tapering to both ends, with stalked glands towards the base. *Panicles* loose, terminal, 1 to 3 in. long. *fl.* red, $\frac{1}{3}$ in. wide, $\frac{1}{2}$ in. long. July, August. Chile. 1827. var. **al'ba,** *fl.* white; **puncta'ta,** a synonym of *E. punctata*; **pyg'maea,** very dwarf, dense, and compact, 1 to 2 ft.

**E. Sellowia'na.** Evergreen shrub 10 to 20 ft., shoots slender, glabrous. *l.* stalkless, oblanceolate, 1 to $2\frac{1}{2}$ in. long, apex shortly pointed to rounded, toothed at the terminal half only, resinous-glandular beneath. *fl.* white, $\frac{1}{3}$ in. across, densely borne in terminal panicles 1 to $2\frac{1}{2}$ in. long; cal. lobes triangular, glabrous. Brazil.

**E. virga'ta.*** Deciduous shrub 4 to 6 ft. *l.* obovate, $\frac{1}{2}$ to $\frac{3}{4}$ in. long, finely toothed, the base cuneate, glabrous. *fl.* pure white, $\frac{1}{3}$ to $\frac{1}{2}$ in. across, borne in the l.-axils of short shoots and forming leafy racemes up to 2 in. long; pet. roundish obovate, scarcely clawed. June, July. Chile. 1866. (B.T.S. 1, 530.) Syn. *E. Philippiana.* The hardiest species.

**E. visco'sa.** Evergreen shrub up to 10 ft., shoots clammy with resinous glands. *l.* obovate, 1 to 3 in. long, finely toothed, the base cuneate, apex rounded or shortly pointed, glossy green and resinous on both surfaces. *Panicle* 5 or 6 in. long, its branches 1- to 4-fld. *fl.* white, $\frac{1}{3}$ in. wide, pendulous. June to August. Chile. Akin to *E. illinita*, but distinct by its 1-sided panicles and even stronger pig-sty-like odour.

W. J. B.

**ESCHALOT.** *See* **Shallot.**

**ESCHATOGRAM'ME** (*eschatos*, farthest, *gramma*, line; from the position of the sori). Fam. *Polypodiaceae.* A genus of 4 species of fern with compound fronds with sori linear, continuous, or interrupted, sub-marginal, without indusia. Soil should be 2 parts peat to 1 of loam. They should have a moist atmosphere. Propagation is usually by division of the crowns.

**E. furca'ta.** *rhiz.* somewhat creeping, densely tomentose. *Fronds* 6 to 18 in. long, once or twice dichotomously forked or sub-pinnatifid; lobes linear, erecto-patent, acuminate, entire, 4 to 8 in. long, $\frac{1}{4}$ to $\frac{1}{2}$ in. broad, leathery, minutely scaly below. *Sori* sub-marginal, continuous, or interrupted. Trop. America. 1824. Syn. *Cuspidaria furcata, Pteropsis furcata, Taenitis furcata.*

**ESCHSCHOLZ'IA** (in honour of Johann Friedrich Eschscholz, 1793–1831, physician and naturalist who accompanied Kotzebus round the world). Fam. *Papaveraceae.* A genus of 4 or 5 species (40 or more according to some, 123 to other botanists) of annual or perennial glabrous and glaucous herbs, natives of NW. America. Leaves much cut into narrow segments. Flowers showy; petals 4; sepals coherent forming a cap which is pushed off as the flower opens. Fruit a long, many-seeded capsule. The Eschscholtzias include some of the most brilliant of hardy annuals, easily grown in ordinary garden soil and flowering over a long period. Seed may be sown in spring or autumn in the places where the plants are to flower. The species are very variable in colour and to the varieties of *E. californica* especially many names of Latin form have been given.

**E. caespito'sa.*** Annual of close, compact habit, about 6 in. h., much branched near the base. *l.* segs. almost thread-like. *fl.* yellow, about 1 in. across. California. (B.M. 4812 as *E. tenuifolia.*)

**E. californ'ica.*** Californian Poppy. Annual, 12 to 18 in. h. *l.* 3-pinnatifid; segs. linear. *fl.* large, about 2 in. across, bright yellow in typical form. Summer. NW. America. 1790. (B.M. 2887.) Extremely variable. One of the marked forms introduced by Douglas from Monterey as *E. crocea* (B.M. 3495) has deep rich orange flowers. From the type and the var. *crocea* have sprung a great range of colour forms to many of which distinctive names have been given, examples only of which are quoted here. The forms, carefully saved, come true or almost true from seed. **al'ba,** *fl.* creamy-white, single; **alba flore ple'no,** *fl.* creamy-white, semi-double; **canicula'ta,** pet. fluted, colour various; **Doug'lasii,** more slender, early in fl., *fl.* pure yellow. Among the colours found are *Pale Lemon*, e.g. **Sulphur Yellow, Sunlight**; *Apricot*, e.g. **Chrome Queen**; *Orange with a paler reverse*, e.g. **Orange Queen, Aurantí'aca, Crocea,** with semi-double races; *Orange with red-tinged reverse*, e.g. **Mandarin**; *Orange with red reverse*, e.g. **Geisha** with the semi-double **Toreador**; *Orange-scarlet*, e.g. **Fireflame,** *single*, **Flambeau,** semi-double; *Scarlet*, e.g. **Mikado**; *Crimson-scarlet*, e.g. **Dazzler**; *Cream, pink-tinged reverse*, e.g. **Ramona white**; *Pink-tinged Cream with pale rose reverse*, e.g. **Rosea**; *Salmon-apricot, with rosy-red reverse*, e.g. **Eastern Queen**; *Pinkish-apricot*, e.g. **Salmon**; *Rose*, e.g. **Carmine King** single, **Enchantress,** semi-double; *Carmine*, e.g. **Crimson Carmine**; *Purplish-carmine*, e.g. **Rajah**; *Rosy-purple*, e.g. **Mauve Beauty.**

**E. cuculla'ta.** *l.* when young strongly incurved. *fl.* lemon-yellow with a basal orange spot, rather small, on long spreading branches. N. California. 1894.

**E. Doug'lasii.** A variety of *E. californica.*

**E. marit'ima.** A pale-yellow *fl.* with orange-blotch at base. *l.* greyish-white. Otherwise as in *E. californica.* 1894.

***Eschweileria'nus -a -um,*** in honour of F. G. Eschweiler, 1796–1834, lecturer in natural history, Regensburg.

**ESCOBA'RIA** (in honour of two distinguished Mexicans, Romulo and Numa Escobar). Fam. *Cactaceae.* Plants which generally grow in clusters; the tubercles are grooved and persist as woody knobs at the base of old plants after the spines have fallen. Flowers small, borne in the groove on young tubercles. Fruitnaked, red, round, with the withered flower remaining attached. **A**

**E. dasyacan'tha.** Plants round or elongated, in clusters; radial spines 20 or more, white, bristle-like; centrals 9, stouter and longer, reddish, nearly 1 in. long. *fl.* pink. Texas, New Mexico, Mexico. (B.R.C. 4, t. 7.) Syn. *Mammillaria dasyacantha.*

**E. Run'yonii.** Plants round, in large clusters of 100 heads or more; radial spines numerous, slender, stout, white; centrals 5 to 7, brown with darker tips. *fl.* very small, pale purple. Mexico. (B.R.C. 4, t. 6.)

**E. Sneed'ii.** Plants small, branching at the base and higher up the stem; stems hidden by the short white spines. *fl.* small, pink. Texas. (B.R.C. 4, f. 54.)

**E. strobiliform'is.** A synonym of *E. tuberculosa.*

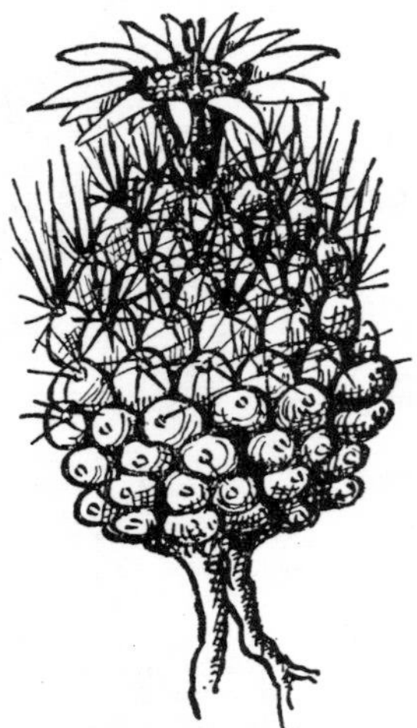

*Escobaria tuberculosa* (p. 783)

**E. tuberculo'sa.** Plants cylindric, usually in clumps; radial spines up to 30, slender, white; several stouter centrals, brown to black. *fl.* pale pink. Texas, New Mexico, Mexico. (B.R.C. 4, f. 51.) Syn. *Mammillaria tuberculosa, M. strobiliformis.*

V. H.

**ESCON'TRIA** (in honour of Don Blas Escontria, a distinguished Mexican). Fam. *Cactaceae*. A single species of tree-like cactus, branching freely from a short trunk; branches thick with few, prominent ribs; areoles elliptical; spines light coloured, one of the centrals very long. Flowers small, yellow, campanulate; fruit purple, fleshy, edible.

**E. Chiotil'la.** Mexico. (B.R.C. 2, t. 10.) Syn. *Cereus Chiotilla.* The ripe fruits are sold as chiotilla or tuna. It is best raised from seed; cuttings do not root easily.

V. H.

*esculen'tus -a -um,* fit for food.

**ESMERAL'DA.** See **Arachnan'the.**

**ESPALIER.** A term applied to a mode of training fruit-trees in the open ground, either as permanent features or preparatory to placing them on walls or on a trellis inside a house. Many methods are employed, some of a temporary, and others of a permanent, character. For a single tree a row of stakes about 5 ft. high, driven in the ground, 9 in. apart, is suitable. A narrow strip of wood is generally laid on the tops of the stakes, and a nail driven into each, to hold them firmly. Fruit-trees trained as Espaliers, to separate borders running parallel to walks from the inside garden, sometimes have strained wires fixed for the purpose. Another mode is to have end posts, to which are secured top and bottom rails, with vertical strips of wood nailed to them. The trees may be trained to any desired shape as Espaliers, in the same way as if they were on walls, but the commonest form has a tier of horizontal branches on each side of the main stem, and the method of training is usually applied to apples or pears that fruit mainly on spurs. Full exposure to light on both sides is obtained by proper thinning; but the advantages of a wall regarding the protection afforded cannot, of course, be similarly secured.

In addition to their value in producing fruit, espaliers may well serve to form the sides of an ornamental walk, also to act as a screen for hiding views of the vegetable garden from main walks. They will need to be trained on posts and wires.

Pleasing effects may be obtained by training the trees to form an archway over a path. Plenty of headroom must be allowed.

J. E. G. W.

**ESPARTO GRASS.** See **Stipa tenacissima.** Leaves of other grasses, e.g. *Aspelodesma tenax* and *Lygeum Spartum* are used like Esparto in paper-making.

**ESPELE'TIA** (in honour of Don José de Espeleta, a Viceroy of New Grenada). Fam. *Compositae*. A genus of about 30 species of remarkable American woolly leaved plants with the habit of Aloe. Leaves alternate or rarely opposite, entire, lanceolate or linear, woolly covering white or rust-coloured. Flower-heads yellow, sometimes over 1 in. across, in corymbs. Belonging to the Helianthus section of the family. They can be grown in sandy peat in a dry and airy part of the greenhouse. During damp weather in winter only enough water should be given to keep the soil moist and care should be taken that the woolly leaves are not wetted. They may be propagated by cuttings in light sandy compost, standing the pots on the open bench.

J. C.

**E. argen'tea.** Shrub with an underground or short, erect stem. *l.* densely packed in a terminal spreading cluster, 10 to 18 in. long, strap-shaped, ½ to 1½ in. wide, covered with silvery, silky, appressed down. *infl.* erect, 1½ to 4 ft. h., silvery-hairy. *fl.-heads* 1½ in. wide in a terminal head or corymb; ray-florets very numerous, yellow, 3-toothed; disk ⅝ in. across, brownish. Summer. Colombia. (B.M. 4480.)

**E. grandiflo'ra.** Stem 3 to 10 ft., clothed with old deflexed *l. l.* elliptic-oblong, 12 to 20 in. long, 1½ to 3 in. wide, clothed densely on both surfaces with grey or rust-coloured wool. *fl.-heads* 1 to 1½ in. wide, in terminal panicles up to 2 ft. h., made up of close clusters of 6 to 15 heads; ray-florets golden yellow. Colombia.

**E. neriifo'lia.** Shrub 6 to 12 ft., branches stout, covered at first with yellowish wool. *l.* oblong, 6 to 20 in. long, 1¼ to 3 in. wide, covered beneath with pale yellow, close down. *infl.* woolly, much branched into a corymb 6 to 12 in. across. *fl.-heads* ⅜ in. wide; ray-florets 15 to 20, yellow. Venezuela.

W. J. B.

**ESPOSTO'A** (in honour of Nicholas E. Esposto, a keen botanist of Lima, Peru). Fam. *Cactaceae*. Columnar plants, ribbed, producing a pseudo-cephalium like Cephalocereus; flowers small, nearly hidden in the wool, pinkish; fruit smooth, with pure white, juicy flesh, edible. For cultivation *see under* **Cactus** (terrestrial).

**E. Dautwitz'ii.** Probably a variety of *E. lanata*; hair less thick so that the plant body shows through. Peru. Syn. *Cereus sericatus, Pilocereus Dautwitzii.*

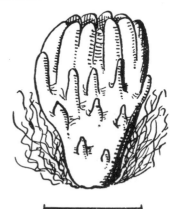

*Espostoa lanata.* Flower

**E. lana'ta.** Stems erect, branching at the top, with numerous low ribs; areoles close, with much pale silky hair entirely covering the plant; spines yellow, glassy. *fl.* white. Ecuador, Peru. (B.R.C. 2, f. 87-91.) Syn. *Pilocereus lanatus.*

V. H.

*Estra'dae,* in honour of Doña Estrada, of Colombia, amateur grower of orchids.

*etaerio,* an aggregate of fruits as in the Mulberry. **A**

*Eth'elae,* in honour of Mrs. Ethel Beringfield.

**ETHU'LIA** (derivation?). Fam. *Compositae*. A genus of 2 species of branching herbs, one a native of Java, the other of India, Trop. Africa, &c. Leaves alternate, toothed. Flower-heads rather small, homogamous and corymbose; involucral bracts in many series; receptacle flat, naked; florets tubular. Half-hardy, growing well in any fairly good soil; increased by seed.

**E. conyzoi'des.** Erect, leafy annual. *l.* elliptic-lanceolate, slender-pointed, 2 to 5 in. long, narrowed to base, coarsely toothed in upper part, gland-dotted. *fl.-heads* purplish or reddish, very numerous; peduncles short or long. India, &c. (B.R. 695.) Syn. *E. angustifolia.*

**A →**

**ETIOLATION.** See **Blanching.**

*etrus'cus -a -um,* of Etrusca, Italy.

*Et'tae,* in honour of Miss Etta Stainbank of S. Africa.

*eu-,* prefixed to Greek words signifies good or well-marked.

**EUADE'NIA** (*eu*, well, *aden*, gland; the base of the gynophore terminates with 5 spherical knobs). Fam. *Capparidaceae*. A genus of 2 or 3 species of Trop. African herbs or sub-shrubs. Flowers with 4 free sepals; 4 linear petals; 5 free or almost free stamens. *E. eminens* needs stove conditions and a well-drained loam. Cuttings strike readily in bottom heat.

**E. em'inens.** *l.* alternate, 3-foliolate, glabrous. *fl.* in a candelabrum-like infl.; pet. 4, sulphur, 2 dorsal 4 in. long, erect, narrowly linear-awl-shaped, narrowed to a long claw, 2 lower smaller, pointing forward; sep. 4, green, lanceolate, slender pointed, ½ in. long. W. Trop. Africa. 1880. (B.M. 6578.)

**EUAN'THE Sanderia'na.** A synonym of *Vanda Sanderiana*.

**EUCALYP'TUS** (*eu*, well, *kalypto*, to cover as with a lid; limb of calyx covers the stamens before expansion, and afterwards falls off in one piece, in the shape of a lid or cover, known as the *operculum*). Gum-tree. FAM. *Myrtaceae*. A genus of 500 or more species of tall evergreen trees, with very few exceptions natives of Australia, where they constitute a large portion of the forest vegetation. Peduncles axillary, 1-flowered, or bearing an umbel of from 3 to 15 flowers; sometimes terminal; calyx tube turbinate or campanulate, the base adnate to the ovary, the apex truncate, entire or remotely toothed; stamens numerous, in several series, free. Leaves quite entire, coriaceous, usually opposite in the juvenile state, alternate in the adult, quite glabrous except in a very few of the species. The beauty of the flowers is due entirely to the stamens, which are very numerous and, in some species, richly coloured. It is worthy of remark that the Gum Trees, though among the largest trees in the world, have very small, or even minute, seeds. In their native country the Eucalypti form extensive forests, and grow very fast, some of them reaching an immense height and having trunks in the same proportion. Their heights, however, as estimated in the early days after their discovery, were much exaggerated, some specimens being estimated at over 400 or even 500 ft. In 1888 a reward of £120 was offered to anyone who could point out a tree of 400 ft. But the tallest tree that could then be found (*E. amygdalina regnans*) by scientific measurement was only 326 ft. The timber is extremely durable, and is largely used by Australian ship-builders, implement-makers, engineers, &c. None of the species attain a size in this country sufficiently large for use as timber, as they are not hardy enough to withstand a severe winter outside except in the mildest localities. Several succeed on a south wall with protection in winter, and all are useful decorative greenhouse plants. They are called Gum Trees in consequence of the quantity of gum that exudes from their trunks. *E. globulus*, the Blue Gum, one of the most valuable timber trees of the Southern hemisphere, is also largely cultivated in many parts of the world, especially in the Mediterranean region and in malarious districts in Italy. Further, it is the species grown more than others in this country for its value in sub-tropical gardening, the leaves being of a distinct glaucous hue, and quite different from those of any other plant similarly employed. Eucalypti are only raised from imported seeds, which generally vegetate freely. They should be sown thinly in pots or pans of light sandy soil, and placed in a little heat. *E. globulus*, when intended to be used for sub-tropical bedding or for a group on a lawn, is best sown in August and grown on through the winter for use the following season. By this method much larger and better plants may be obtained than when sowing is deferred till spring. It is best to raise new plants each year, as lifted ones do not regain their beauty of the preceding season, and they cannot be depended on to stand outside, at least, not in many places. Being fast-growing plants, considerable space must be allowed when they become established, either in the open ground or in pots. A rather rich soil, composed of loam and decayed manure, with the addition of some charcoal, to keep it open, is most suitable. *E. citriodora* is very useful for growing in small pots for the conservatory, its scented leaves rendering it a general favourite. Comparatively few of the species are grown outdoors in Britain, but *E. coccifera*, *E. Gunnii*, *E. Macarthuri*, *E. viminalis* are more or less hardy in mild districts. *E. Gunnii* has maintained and reproduced itself for many years in Essex.

In a recent work, published in Sydney (1934), W. F. Blakely describes 500 species and 138 varieties, and writes that a large number still await discovery.

**E. amygdali'na.** Tall shrub or slender tree. *Juvenile l.* opposite, sessile or shortly stalked, linear to narrowly lanceolate; *adult l.* alternate, stalked, narrowly curved and lanceolate, 3 to 5 in. long, ⅓ to ⅝ in. wide. *fl.* 5 to 12 in stalked, axillary umbels, each fl. ¼ in. across; stamens white; anthers yellow. Australia, Tasmania. 1820. (B.M. 3260; B.R. 947, as *E. longifolia*.) var. **reg'nans,** the largest of the Eucalypti, sometimes exceeding 300 ft. SYN. *E. regnans*.

**E. calophyl'la.*** Medium-sized to large tree. *Juvenile l.* opposite, stalked, peltate, oval to oval-lanceolate, 3 to 6 in. long, 2 to 4 in. wide, usually abundant on old trees; *adult l.* stalked, longer but narrower. *infl.* terminal, 9 in. across. *fl.* in umbels of 3 to 7, each fl. about 2 in. wide; stamens white or pale yellow; anthers yellow. *fr.* 1½ to 2 in. broad, urn-shaped. W. Australia. (B.M. 4036 as *E. splachnicarpon*.)

**E. citriodo'ra.** Tall shrub or tree of moderate size. *Juvenile l.* opposite, stalked, oblong to oblong-lanceolate, 3 to 6 or more in. long, scarcely half as wide; *adult l.* alternate, narrowly to broadly lanceolate; strongly lemon-scented. *infl.* a terminal corymb of 3- to 5-fld. umbels. Queensland. Valued for the charming fragrance of its l. Sometimes regarded as a variety of *E. maculata*.

**E. coccif'era.*** Tree up to 60 or 70 ft. *Juvenile l.* opposite, sessile, ¾ to 1½ in. long, roundish or oval, glaucous; *adult l.* alternate, narrow-oblong or lanceolate, 2 to 4 in. long, ½ to ¾ in. wide; stalk up to 1 in. long. *fl.* 3 to 7 in axillary, stalked umbels; stamens yellow, in clusters ⅝ in. across. *fr.* top-shaped. Tasmania. (B.M. 4637.) One of the hardier species. var. **viridifo'lia,** *l.* dark green, narrower than in type. (B.M. 9511.)

**E. corda'ta.** Tree up to 50 ft., sometimes a shrub. *l.* all opposite, sessile, cordate, vividly glaucous, 1½ to 3½ in. long, 1 to 2¼ in. wide. *fl.* in umbels of 3, the yellow stamen-clusters ¾ to 1 in. across. November, December. *fr.* cup-shaped. Tasmania. (B.M. 7835.) One of the few that retain the opposite and sessile form of l. permanently. Young plants are used in tropical bedding.

**E. coria'cea.** A synonym of *E. pauciflora*.

**E. cornu'ta.*** Tall shrub or small to moderately sized tree. *Juvenile l.* opposite, stalked, orbicular to broadly lanceolate, dark green, 1½ to 3 in. long; *adult l.* 3 to 4 in. long, alternate, leathery, oval-lanceolate. *fl.* in a globose head 4 to 6 in. across, the operculum (or lid over the undeveloped stamens) 1 to 1½ in. long, horn-shaped, beaked, rich red; stamens yellow, forming a dense crown 3 to 4 in. across. *fr.* crowded in a ball-like mass 3 in. across, on a thick stalk 2 in. long. W. Australia.

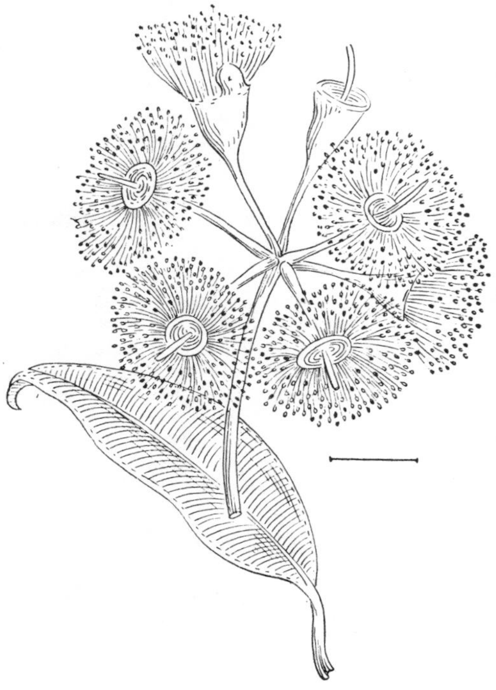

*Eucalyptus ficifolia*

**E. ficifo'lia.*** Red gum. Tree up to 30 ft. *Juvenile l.* opposite stalked, ovate to ovate-lanceolate, 3 to 4 in. long; *adult l.* alternate ovate-lanceolate, up to 6 in. long, slender pointed; margin and midrib yellow. *infl.* a terminal corymb 6 to 7 in. across; each *fl.* 2 in. wide, stamens scarlet, anthers dark red. August. *fr.* 1½ in. long, 1 in. wide, urn-shaped. SW. Australia. (B.M. 7697.) Probably the richest coloured species.

**E. glob'ulus.** Blue Gum. Tree exceeding 200 ft. in a wild state, 120 ft. in Cornwall; young shoots and l. glaucous white. *Juvenile l.* opposite, 3 to 6 in. long, 1½ to 3 in. wide, cordate-ovate, the base stem clasping; *adult l.* alternate, stalked, dark shining green, lanceolate-falcate, long pointed, 6 to 12 in. long, 1 to 1¾ in. wide. *fl.* axillary, 1 to 3, closely sessile. Tasmania, Victoria. Popular in its glaucous juvenile state for sub-tropical bedding. An antiseptic oil is obtained from the l.

**E. Gun'nii.*** Cider Gum. Tree up to 100 ft., shoots glaucous white. *Juvenile l.* opposite, orbicular, up to 2½ in. wide, cordate, sessile or short-stalked, glaucous; *adult l.* alternate, stalked, greenish, lanceolate, up to 4 in. long. *fl.* white in umbels of 3, each ⅝ in. across. October to December. Tasmania, S. Australia. (B.T.S. i. 534.) Syn. *E. whittingehamensis.* Variable species in regard to shape of l. Has lived quite uninjured in the open at Kew since 1896 and is now 50 ft. h. A

**E. leucox'ylon.*** Iron bark. Tree 50 to 100 ft. *Juvenile l.* opposite, sessile or short-stalked, roundish to broadly lanceolate, rather glaucous, 1½ to 3 in. long, half to nearly as wide; *adult l.* broadly lanceolate, 3 to 6 in. long, ½ to 1½ in. wide. *fl.* ½ to ¾ in. wide, in umbels of 3, axillary, white, pink, or crimson. S. Australia. (Gn. 39 (1891), 316.)

**E. longifo'lia.** A synonym of *E. amygdalina.*

**E. Macarth'uri.** Tree with rough woolly bark. *Juvenile l.* ovate, slender-pointed, opposite, bright green; *adult l.* alternate, narrow, lanceolate, often falcate, thick, veins pinnate, not prominent, about 4 in. long. *Buds* small, in 5- to 8-fld. axillary umbels, stalks short, flattened, or sessile. *fr.* very small, nearly hemispherical, with a well-defined rim. New S. Wales. Hardy.

**E. macrocarp'a.*** Shrub 6 to 10 ft., of stout habit; glaucous white all over; stem 4-angled. *l.* opposite, sessile, broadly cordate-ovate, stem-clasping at base, slender-pointed, 2 to 6 in. long, thick and rigid. *fl.* axillary, solitary on a very short thick stalk, 2½ in. across; stamens rich red, anthers yellow. *fr.* 2 to 3½ in. wide, hemispherical. W. Australia. 1842. (B.M. 4333.)

**E. Maid'enii.** Tree 120 to 150 ft., young shoots quadrangular. *Juvenile l.* opposite, glaucous, sessile, often stem-clasping, ovate-cordate to ovate-lanceolate, 6 in. long, 4½ in. wide; *adult l.* stalked, alternate, dark shining green, 8 in. long, 1 in. wide. *fl.* sessile or nearly so, in umbels of 3 to 7 or more, white; peduncle compressed or angular. New S. Wales, Victoria.

**E. multiflo'ra.** Spreading tree, 100 ft. and upwards. *Juvenile l.* opposite, stalked, broadly lanceolate to oval-lanceolate, up to 4 in. long and 3 in. wide; *adult l.* alternate, stalked, smooth and shining, 4 to 7 in. long, 1½ to 3 in. wide. *fl.* in axillary or sub-terminal umbels of 5 to 12, each fl. ¾ to 1 in. across, white. New S. Wales. Syn. *E. robusta.*

**E. obli'qua.** Tree 100 to 300 ft., but flowering when small. *Juvenile l.* opposite, broadly lanceolate, 2 to 3½ in. long; *adult l.* alternate, very obliquely lanceolate, 4 to 8 in. long, 1 to 1⅓ in. wide. *fl.* in lateral umbels of 7 to 16, each fl. ¾ in. across, white, anthers yellow. *fr.* pear-shaped, ⅓ in. wide, in globose clusters. Tasmania, Australia. The bark peels off in large concave slabs used by the aboriginals for roofing, and for making rude canoes, with the help of mud, for crossing rivers.

**E. pauciflo'ra.** Small to large tree up to 100 ft. *Juvenile l.* opposite, shortly stalked, roundish to broadly lanceolate, glaucous, 4 to 7½ in. long, 4 to 6 in. wide; *adult l.* alternate, longer-stalked, 3 to 8 in. long, ¾ to 1½ in. wide, shining. *fl.* white, in umbels of 5 to 12, each fl. ⅝ in. wide. Australia, Tasmania. Syn. *E. coriacea.*

**E. polyan'themos.** Tree up to 40 or 50 ft., low branching. *Juvenile l.* opposite, stalked, orbicular, glaucous, 1½ to 4 in. across; *adult l.* alternate, longer-stalked, orbicular or narrow- to broad-lanceolate, up to 6 in. long. *infl.* an umbel of 3 to 6 small white fl., or numerous in a terminal panicle. Victoria, New S. Wales. Syn. *E. populnea.*

**E. Preissia'na.** Shrub 8 to 15 ft. *Juvenile l.* opposite, sessile or shortly stalked, oblong, ovate or oval, stout, 3 or 4 in. long; *adult l.* oblong to broadly lanceolate, up to 4½ in. long, 2 in. wide, stalked. *fl.* in axillary, thick-stalked umbels of 3, yellow, 1½ in. wide. W. Australia. (B.M. 4266.)

**E. pulverulen'ta.** Small tree up to 30 ft., bark peeling. *Juvenile l.* 2½ in. long, nearly as wide, very glaucous, opposite, sessile, ovate to roundish-oval or kidney-shaped, base cordate, entire; *adult l.* not very different. *fl.* in axillary umbels of three, each fl. 1¼ in. across, white. *fr.* very glaucous, ⅜ in. wide. New S. Wales. (B.M. 2087; L.B.C. 328 as *E. cordata.*) Closely akin to *E. cordata*, which has slightly crenate l. and less tapered fr.

**E. resinif'era.** Tree 80 to 100 ft. *Juvenile l.* opposite, narrow-lanceolate, short-stalked, 1¾ to 2¼ in. long; *adult l.* alternate, 4 to 7 in. long, 1 to 1½ in. wide, long- and slender-pointed, stalk ⅝ in. long. *fl* in axillary umbels of 6 to 10, each fl. ⅝ in. wide, white. July. *fr.* ovoid to hemispherical, ¼ in. wide. New S. Wales, Queensland.

**E. robus'ta.** A synonym of *E. multiflora.*

**E. Siderox'ylon.** Tree 50 to 100 ft., bark usually jet-black. *Juvenile l.* opposite, linear to broadly oblong, shortly stalked, 1½ to 3 in. long, ⅙ to ⅝ in. wide; *adult l.* alternate, longer stalked, broadly lanceolate, up to 4½ in. long, ⅘ in. wide. *fl.* in umbels of 3 to 7, each fl. 1 in. across; stamens creamy-white to deep rosy-red. *fr.* ovoid to pear-shaped, ⅜ in. wide. Victoria, New S. Wales, Queensland.

**E. Sieberia'na.** Tree. *Juvenile l.* glaucous on both sides, venation with midrib; *adult l.* more or less falcate, smooth, shining, leathery, somewhat peppermint scented when crushed. *fl.-buds* clavate, operculum hemispherical, or slightly umbonate. *fl.* white. *fr.* pear-shaped with a dark rim. July. SE. Australia, Tasmania.

**E. Smith'ii.** Tree of medium size to 150 ft. *Juvenile l.* opposite, sessile to stem-clasping, glaucous, narrowly lanceolate, 1⅓ in. to 3 in. long, ⅜ to ⅓ in. wide; *adult l.* up to 7 in. long, ⅔ in. wide, alternate, narrow-lanceolate, stalked. *fl.* on axillary peduncles in umbels of 5 to 9, each ½ in. wide. Victoria, New S. Wales.

**E. splachnicarp'a.** A synonym of *E. calophylla.*

**E. Staigeria'na.*** Medium-sized tree. *Juvenile l.* opposite, shortly stalked, oblong to lanceolate, 1½ to 2½ in. long, ¾ to 1 in. wide, glaucous, lemon-scented; *adult l.* alternate, longer-stalked, glaucous, 3 to 4 in. long, ½ to 1 in. wide. *infl.* in axillary umbels or terminal panicles, umbels of 3 to 6 fl. which are ⅓ in. across. October. N. Queensland. Equal to *E. citriodora* for the scent of the l.

**E. strict'a.** Shrub with numerous stems, or a small tree 12 to 20 ft. *Juvenile l.* opposite, shortly stalked, narrowly lanceolate, 1⅝ to 2¼ in. long, ½ to ¾ in. wide; *adult l.* alternate, 3 to 3½ in. long, ¼ to ⅜ in. wide. *fl.* 4 to 8 in axillary umbels, each fl. ½ in. across, yellowish. New S. Wales. 1885.

**E. tetrag'ona.** Shrub or a tree up to 25 ft., wholly glaucous, shoots mostly 4-angled or even winged. *l.* opposite in both juvenile and adult states, the latter sometimes alternate, longer-stalked and larger, being 3 to 5 in. long, scarcely half as wide, ovate-lanceolate, pointed, red-margined. *fl.* 3 in stout peduncled axillary umbels, each fl. ¾ in. across; stamens white, anthers yellow. W. Australia. 1824. (S.F.A. 21 as *Eudesmia tetragona*).

**E. urnig'era.** Tree 25 to over 50 ft. *Juvenile l.* opposite, orbicular to ovate, 1 to 1¾ in. wide, cordate, very glaucous; *adult l.* alternate, ovate to lanceolate, 3 to 6 in. long, dark glossy green. *fl.* 3 in a stalked axillary umbel, pedicels terete, the yellow or whitish stamens in a ring ¾ in. across. *fr.* urn-shaped. Tasmania. (G.C. 3 (1888), 460.)

**E. vernico'sa.** Bushy shrub or small tree, 6 to 12 ft., shoots 4-angled. *l.* opposite or rarely alternate, oval-lanceolate, thick, leathery, ¾ to 2 in. long, ½ to 1 in. wide, green and shining above, resinous on both surfaces; stalk ¼ to ⅜ in. long (stalkless in juvenile plants). *fl.* honey-scented, stamens yellow-white; peduncles very short, thick, more or less flattened, each with 1 to 3 sessile fl. *fr.* hemispherical, ⅓ in. wide. Tasmania. Quite hardy.

**E. vimina'lis.** Tree 50 to 150 ft., branches slender, pendulous. *Juvenile l.* opposite, pale green, sessile, often stem-clasping, 2 to 4 in. long, ½ to 1⅓ in. wide; *adult l.* alternate, stalked, lanceolate, acuminate, 4 to 8 in. long, ¾ to 1½ in. wide. *fl.* in axillary umbels of 3 (sometimes 6 to 8) each fl. ⅝ in. wide, white. *fr.* globose to top-shaped, ¼ in. wide. Tasmania, Australia. (G.C. 4 (1888), 597.)

W. J. B.

**EUCHAE'TIS** (*eu*, well, *chaite*, hair; the petals are bearded within). Fam. *Rutaceae.* A genus of 4 or 5 species of evergreen heath-like shrubs, natives of SW. Africa. Leaves opposite, rarely alternate, 3-angled or keeled, rarely concave, glabrous or ciliate. Flowers at tips of branches, capitate or almost solitary, shortly pedicellate, 5-merous; petals oblong, clawed, hairy within; ovary small, deeply immersed in the disk. For treatment, *see* **Barosma.**

**E. glomera'ta.** Shrub of about 2 ft. *l.* scattered, lanceolate, small, keeled, margin pellucid and ciliate. *fl.* white, clustered at tips of branches; peduncles very short, bracteate. May. S. Africa. 1818.

***euchai'tes,*** having beautiful hair.

**EUCHARID'IUM** (*eucharis*, pleasing; from the appearance of the plant). Fam. *Oenotheraceae.* A genus of 3 species of annual herbs related to Clarkia and sometimes included in it, differing by the calyx tube much extended beyond the ovary, and the stamens 4 (not 8) without basal appendages, opposite sepals. Petals 4. Treatment as Clarkia, seed being sown in spring or autumn in the open border.

**E. Brew'eri.** 1 to 2 ft. h., branching. *l.* ovate-oblong or linear, about 1 in. long, entire. *fl.* pink with white centre, fragrant, numerous, in l.-axils; pet. 3-lobed, middle lobe very long and narrowed to base. Summer. California.

**E. concin'num.*** 1 to 2 ft. h., not or slightly branched. *l.* oblong, small, entire, stalked. *fl.* rose, about 1 in. across; cal. tube very slender, 1 in. or more long; pet. 3-lobed, middle lobe little longer than others. Summer. California. 1787. (B.M. 3589; B.R. 1962.)

**E. grandiflo'rum.** Related to last but much branched from base, *fl.* larger, irregular, 3 upper pet. close, lower separate and declined with its middle lobe long-clawed. California. var. **al'ba,** *fl.* white.

**EU'CHARIS** (Greek manufactured name, implying very graceful). FAM. *Amaryllidaceae.* A genus of about 8 species of beautiful, fragrant, bulbous plants, natives of Colombia. Bulb tunicated. Leaves oblong, stalked. Flowers white, showy, few in an umbel; perianth tube cylindrical, straight or curved, lobes equal, rather broad, spreading; stamens shorter than lobes; bracts many, narrow, the outer 2 or 3 broader, forming an involucre. The 3 species *E. candida, E. grandiflora,* and *E. Sanderi* are among the most popular stove bulbous plants, needing a temperature of 65 to 70° F., rising to 80° F. in summer, with plenty of water except for a short time in autumn, but they must never be dried off completely. The best compost for them is 2 parts of good turfy loam to 1 of leaf-soil and cow manure with some charcoal to keep it open. A free root run should be given and the plants may be planted out in beds beneath which hot-water pipes are placed, or they may be grown in pots. Ten-inch pots are suitable and in these 6 strong bulbs of the species mentioned may be planted; for the other smaller species 6 bulbs to a 6-in. pot would be suitable. Spring is the best time to plant. All dead and decaying matter should be removed from the bulbs before potting and it is best not to cover the bulbs at first, but watering carefully, with a temperature of 70° F., allow them to start into growth before the bulbs are completely covered. If potted in good soil in the first instance the plants will need only top-dressing annually until they begin to get over-crowded. Liquid cow-manure should be given when the scapes appear. Generally 2 crops of flowers may be had within the year, and occasionally 3 are produced, but this should not be encouraged as it weakens the bulbs. Propagation is by offsets which can be removed from the parent bulb in spring and potted singly in 6-in. pots. This operation must be done with care since the plants resent root disturbance. Seeds are sometimes produced and they should be sown as soon as ripe in a warm house. Failure is liable to follow over-flower production, anything more than slight reduction in the water-supply in autumn, and inattention to the attacks of pests. The Eucharis or Bulb Mite is particularly dangerous and much loss will be likely to follow attacks of Mealy Bug and of Red Spider Mite. They should all be dealt with with great promptitude.

**E. amazon'ica.** A synonym of *E. grandiflora.*

**E. Bakeria'na.** *l.* 4 or 5, elliptic, 10 to 18 in. long, very dark green, veins many, rather obscure, stalks stout. *fl.* as in *E. grandiflora* but corona of *E. candida,* 2½ in. across; umbels 4- to 6-fld.; scape 10 to 18 in. long. January, May. Colombia. 1890. (B.M. 7144; G.C. 7 (1890), f. 61.)

**E. × burfordien'sis** (*E. Mastersii × E. × Stevensii*). *l.* as in *E. Mastersii, fl.* bell-shaped, 3 in. across, 2 in. long. 1899. (G.C. 26 (1899), 247.)

**E. can'dida.*** Bulb as large as hen's egg, neck long. *l.* solitary, broadly elliptic, slender pointed; stalk 12 in. long, flattish. *fl.* white, drooping, 3 in. across; corona very prominent with 6 pointed segs. to which anthers are attached; umbel 6- to 8-fld.; scape 2 ft. long. Colombia. 1851. (F.d.S. 788.) The name has been applied in gardens to *E. subedentata.*

**E. × elemeta'na** (*E. grandiflora × E. Sanderi*). Of freer growth than *E. Sanderi.* (G.C. 26 (1899), 345.)

**E. grandiflo'ra.*** Bulb ovate, neck long. *l.* several, broadly ovate, 8 in. long, slender-pointed, channelled, slightly waved and plaited; stalk 10 in. long. *fl.* white, drooping, 4 to 5 in. across; corona tinged green; umbels 3- to 6-fld.; scapes 2 ft. long. Colombia. 1854. (B.M. 4971.) SYN. *E. amazonica, E. candida grandiflora.* var. **frag'rans,** more fragrant than type, umbel 6-fld., *l.* small; **Low'ii,** *see* **E. Lowii; Moor'ei,** *l.* much smaller than type, roundish, *fl* smaller, corona white within with a yellow line where filament runs down, teeth between filaments large, acute. 1888.

**E. Leh'mannii.** Closely related to *E. candida. l.* 2, elliptic-oblong. *fl.* white, 1½ in. across; umbel 4-fld.; corona deeply 12-toothed. Popayan. 1889. (G.F. 1889, 1300.)

**E. × Low'ii** (Possibly *E. grandiflora × E. Sanderi*). Bulb globose, neck stout. *l.* ovate-cordate, 9 in. long, 7 in. wide; stalk 12 in. long. *fl.* white; tube funnel-shaped, 2½ in. long, limb 5 in. across; segs. elliptic, slightly concave, acute; corona stained green; umbel 2- to 5-fld.; scape 2 ft. long. Peru. 1912. (B.M. 8646.)

**E. Mas'tersii.** Bulb 1½ to 2 in. thick. *l.* oblong, 8 to 10 in. long, 4 to 5 in. wide; stalked. *fl.* nearly sessile, white; tube 2 to 2½ in. long, limb 3 in. across; segs. ovate, much overlapping; corona striped green; umbel 2-fld.; scape under 1 ft. long. February. Colombia. 1885. (B.M. 6831 A; G.C. 26 (1899), 241.)

**E. San'deri.*** Habit and l. of *E. grandiflora. fl.* white, about 3 in. across; filaments and tube within yellow, corona absent; umbel 3- to 7-fld.; scape 18 in. long. Colombia. (B.M. 6676.) var. **multiflo'ra,** *fl.* 5 or 6, much smaller than in type, filaments green. Colombia. 1885. (B.M. 6831 B.)

**E. × Stev'ensii** (*E. candida × E. Sanderi*). *l.* 12 to 14 in. long, 5 to 6 in. wide. *fl.* white, 3 to 3½ in. across; corona tinged yellow without; umbels about 7-fld. 1883. (G.C. 26 (1899), 243.)

**E. subedenta'ta.** *l.* ovate-oblong. *fl.* white, funnel-shaped, in an umbel; scape 18 in. h. Winter. Colombia. 1876. (B.M. 6289 as *Caliphruria subedentata.*)

***euchlo'rus -a -um,*** of a beautiful green.

**EUCHREST'A** (*euchrestos,* useful; in allusion to the medicinal qualities of the seeds). FAM. *Leguminosae.* A genus of 4 species of shrubs, natives of E. Asia. Leaves alternate with 3 to 7 leaflets pinnately arranged. Flowers papilionaceous; standard oblong; wings narrow-oblong, free. Pod ovoid, indehiscent. Ordinary soil suits them.

**E. Horsfield'ii formosa'na.** Shrub lately collected in Formosa but perhaps not yet introduced. Differs from *E. japonica* by the *l.* having 5 or 7 lflets. which are ovate-lanceolate, pointed, 2 to 4 in. long. *fl.* ⅝ in. long, both cal. and cor. waxy-white, densely borne on erect racemes 3 to 4 in. long. It may prove hardy in the warmer counties. The type is tropical and native of Java, Siam, &c., its lflets. are up to 7 in. long by 3 in. wide.

**E. japon'ica.** Shrub 1 to 2 ft., young shoots downy. *l.* 3-foliolate, mainstalk 1 to 2 in. long; lflets. obovate or oval, rounded at one or both ends, 2 to 4 in. long, soft with fine down when young. *Racemes* erect, terminal and axillary, 3 to 5 in. long. *fl.* white, standard, wings and keel all about ½ in. long. *Pod* purple-black, oblong, ⅝ in. long, ⅜ in. wide. Japan. 1862. (G.F. 1865, 487.) Greenhouse.

W. J. B.

***euchro'mus -a -um,*** well-coloured.

**EU'CLEA** (*eukleia,* good fame; in allusion to the value and beauty of the ebony-like wood). FAM. *Ebenaceae.* A genus of about 20 species of evergreen shrubs or small trees. They have no beauty of flower and deserve mention mainly for their wood value. Greenhouse and loamy soil.

**E. polyan'dra.** Shrub 3 to 7 ft. *l.* alternate or nearly opposite, 1 to 3 in. long, half as wide, oval, entire. *fl.* small, dioecious, fragrant, white; the *males* in axillary racemes, ½ to 1½ in. long, of 3 to 9; *female infl.* of 3 to 5, much smaller. S. Africa. 1774.

**E. pseudeb'enus.** Small tree, with a trunk 1 ft. or more diam., or a shrub. *l.* alternate, entire, linear, leathery, 1 to 2½ in. long, 1/10 to ¼ in. wide, tapered to both ends. *Male racemes* ¼ to ½ in. long, with 3 to 7 fl.; *female racemes* with 1 to 3 fl. which are white and about ⅛ in. long. S. Africa. Tree valuable on account of the beauty and usefulness of its wood which is jet-black, hard, and durable.

W. J. B.

**EUCNI'DE** (*eu,* good, *knide,* nettle; from the nettle-like hairs). FAM. *Loasaceae.* A small genus of N. American annual or biennial herbs related to and often included in Mentzelia but with stinging hairs. Leaves alternate or lower opposite, cordate or ovate, more or less lobed. Flowers yellow or white; calyx tube oblong, limb 5-lobed; petals 5, united at base; stamens many, filaments filiform. Fruit a 1-celled capsule. For cultivation *see* **Mentzelia.**

**E. bartonioi'des.** Annual, about 1 ft. h. Stems flexuous, succulent, almost translucent. *l.* ovate, acute, lobed and toothed. *fl.* sulphur, almost white without, solitary, terminal, opening in sunshine; pet. ovate or obovate, slightly toothed; pedicels long. Summer. Western United States. (B.M. 4491 as *Microsperma bartonioides.*) SYN. *Mentzelia bartonioides.*

**E. u'rens.** Branching annual about 18 in. h. *l.* oblong, deeply cut, pinnatifid or almost pinnate, hairy, stalked. *fl.* bright lemon, variegated white and green in centre, about 1 in. across, freely produced. July. Lima. 1830. (B.M. 3057 as *Loasa hispida*.) SYN. *Loasa urens.*

*Eucnide bartonioides* (p. 786)

**EUCODO'NIA.** Included in **Achimenes.**

**EUCO'MIS** (*eukomes*, beautiful headed, from the crown of leaves on the flower-spike). FAM. *Liliaceae.* A genus of about 10 species of bulbous plants related to Scilla and Ornithogalum natives of S. and Trop. Africa. Bulb tunicated. Basal leaves oblong or lorate. Flowers greenish, in a dense raceme on a leafless scape crowned with a tuft of large, lanceolate leaves; perianth persistent, segments 6, almost equal; stamens 6, shorter than the perianth. Any rich, well-drained soil suits these plants which can be increased by offsets. *E. punctata* and other species from the south of Africa need greenhouse treatment in most parts of the country but in favoured districts may be left out over winter; *E. zambesiaca* needs warm house conditions. They make good pot-plants. A light, rich soil is best for them when planted out and they should be planted about 5 or 6 in. deep in autumn and protected in winter by a light covering of litter. Potting should also be done in autumn, giving little water in winter.

KEY

| | |
|---|---|
| 1. *Scape clavate* | 2 |
| 1. *Scape cylindrical* | 4 |
| 2. *Crown of scape with 12 to 20 l.* | 3 |
| 2. *Crown of scape with 20 to 30 l.* | E. robusta |
| 3. *Lvs. purplish at back, broad-lanceolate* | E. nana |
| 3. *Lvs. green, lingulate* | E. regia |
| 4. *Pedicels short* | 5 |
| 4. *Pedicels long* | 6 |
| 5. *Lvs. undulate at margin* | E. autumnalis |
| 5. *Lvs. not undulate at margin* | E. zambesiaca |
| 6. *Segs. green or greenish-white* | 7 |
| 6. *Segs. green margined purple* | E. bicolor |
| 7. *Lvs. not spotted* | 8 |
| 7. *Lvs. spotted purple* | E. comosa |
| 8. *Raceme about 1 ft. long* | E. pallidiflora |
| 8. *Raceme 2 to 3 in. long* | E. amaryllidifolia |

**E. amaryllidifo'lia.** Bulb ovoid. *l.* with *fl.*, sub-erect, lorate-ligulate, narrowed to base, fleshy, unspotted, channelled on face in lower half. *fl.* green in an oblong, dense raceme 2 to 3 in. long; *segs.* oblong; scape cylindrical, terete, under 1 ft. long. August. S. Africa. 1878.

**E. autumna'lis.** Bulb globose, 2 to 3 in. across. *l.* ovate-oblong, up to 2 ft. long, 2 to 3 in. wide, spreading, thin, not spotted, margins wavy. *fl.* green, ½ in. long, in a dense raceme about 6 in. long, pedicels short; scape about 1 ft. long, cylindrical; crown of 12 to 30 crisped l. March, April. S. Africa. 1760. (B.M. 1083 as *E. undulata*.)

**E. bi'color.** Bulb globose. Growth robust. *l.* oblong, unspotted, crisped on margin, sub-erect. *fl.* pale green in a dense oblong raceme, 3 to 4 in. long; *segs.* with a distinct purple edge; scape terete, ¼ in. thick. Natal. 1878. (B.M. 6816.)

**E. clava'ta.** A synonym of *E. regia.*

**E. como'sa.** Bulb 2 to 3 in. thick. *l.* lanceolate, spreading, up to 2 ft. long, 2 to 3 in. wide, channelled, not undulate at margin, spotted purple beneath. *fl.* green, ½ in. long, in a loose, cylindrical raceme up to 1 ft. long; ovary brown; scape 2 ft. long, cylindrical, spotted purple. July. S. Africa. 1783. (B.M. 913 as *E. punctata*.) var. **stria'ta**, *l.* striped brown beneath. 1790. (B.M. 1539.)

**E. na'na.** Bulb 2 in. thick. *l.* broad lanceolate, about 2 ft. long, obtuse, firm, purplish near base at back. *fl.* greenish-brown, nearly sessile on a short scape thickened upwards, spotted purple, raceme 3 to 4 in. long, dense; *segs.* oblong. S. Africa. 1774. (B.M. 1495.) A purple-scaped form has been called *E. purpureocaulis.* (A.B.R. 369.)

**E. pallidiflo'ra.** *l.* 5 or 6 to a stem, oblanceolate, over 2 ft. long, 4 to 5 in. wide. *fl.* greenish-white, 1¼ in. across, in a raceme about 1 ft. long, with about 30 l. in crown; *segs.* oblong, acute; scape 1½ to 2 ft. long, cylindrical. S. Africa. 1887.

**E. puncta'ta.** A synonym of *E. comosa.*

**E. re'gia.** Bulb globose, 2 to 3 in. thick. *l.* 6 to 8, lingulate, 12 to 18 in. long, 3 to 4 in. wide, obtuse. *fl.* green in a dense raceme 3 to 6 in. long; *segs.* obtuse; scape 3 to 6 in. long, thickened upwards; crown of 12 to 20 crisped l. S. Africa. 1702. (Ref. B. 238 as *E. clavata*.)

**E. robus'ta.** Bulb large. *l.* 2 ft. long, 2 in. wide, acute, very thick, crisped on margins. *fl.* green, ⅛ to ¼ in. long, in a dense, oblong raceme 6 to 8 in. long; scape very short; crown of 20 to 30 l. S. Africa. 1894.

**E. undula'ta.** A synonym of *E. autumnalis.*

**E. zambesi'aca.** Much like *E. punctata* but with shorter pedicels, a longer, denser raceme, firmer *l.*, and an unspotted scape. E. Trop. Africa. 1886. Stove.

**EUCOM'MIA** (*eu*, well, *kommi*, gum; in allusion to the quantity of rubber contained in all parts). For characters see **Eucommiaceae.**

**E. ulmoi'des.** Tree up to about 40 ft., perhaps taller. *l.* ovate, long pointed, 3 to 8 in. long, slightly hairy when young, becoming smooth above. *fl.* inconspicuous. April. China. 1900. A perfectly hardy tree, the bark of which is regarded as tonic by the Chinese, but interesting in this country solely because it is the only hardy tree producing rubber, in insufficient quantity, however, to be of commercial value. If leaves are torn gently across, the threads of rubber remain and can be easily seen, and are indeed strong enough to support the broken end of the leaf. Male plants are commonest here and perhaps the only form yet raised. They are easily propagated by cuttings of half-ripe wood in gentle heat and the young plants grow rapidly in ordinary soil without protection.

**EUCOMMIA'CEAE.** Dicotyledons. A family of a single deciduous tree (*Eucommia ulmoides*) in Cent. China, perhaps related to the Hamamelidaceae. Leaves alternate, stalked, toothed, without stipules. Flowers dioecious, inconspicuous, without perianth, in axils of bracts at base of young shoots; staminate flowers stalked with 4 to 10 linear anthers almost sessile; pistillate with 2 carpels, only one of which develops, stalked. Fruit stalked, flat, 1-seeded, winged nutlet, notched above.

**EUCRO'SIA** (*eu*, good, *krossos*, fringe; alluding to the beautiful fringe formed by the staminal cup). FAM. *Amaryllidaceae.* A genus of a single bulbous perennial, rare and beautiful, differing from Callipsyche by the many leaves from the bulb (not 2) and the stamens joined at the base to the rudimentary corona. For treatment see **Pancratium.**

**E. bi'color.** About 1 ft. h. *fl.* orange, ringent, nodding; in umbels. April. Peru. (B.M. 2490.)

**EUCRYPH'IA** (*eu*, well, *kryphios*, covered; in allusion to the cap formed by the sepals cohering at their tips). FAM. *Eucryphiaceae.* The only genus. Four species of trees and shrubs mostly evergreen, 2 natives of Chile, 1 of Australia, and 1 of Tasmania. Two have simple leaves, 2 are pinnate-leaved; there are also 2 hybrids which have both types of leaf. Leaves opposite, leathery, entire or toothed. Flowers white, axillary, solitary, produced near the end of the shoots; sepals 4, cohering at the apex; petals 4; stamens very numerous. Fruit a woody capsule separating into 5 to 18 carpels; seeds winged.

*E. glutinosa* is the only species with a claim to be hardy

in our average climate; the others are cool greenhouse plants or only suited for the warmer counties. They succeed in any free, open, loamy soil but *E. glutinosa* and possibly others dislike chalk. Propagation is by layers and cuttings. **A**

**E. Billardier'i.** A synonym of *E. lucida*.

**E. cordifo'lia.*** Evergreen tree 40 to 80 ft., shoots downy. *l.* simple, cordate-oblong, 1½ to 3 in. long, 1 to 1¾ in. wide, wavy-margined, softly downy and pale beneath. *fl.* milk-white, solitary in the l.-axils clustered near the apex of the shoot, 2½ in. across; pet. roundish-obovate. August. Chile. 1851. (B.M. 8209.) Hardy only from Sussex southwards and westwards. Succeeds in limy soil.

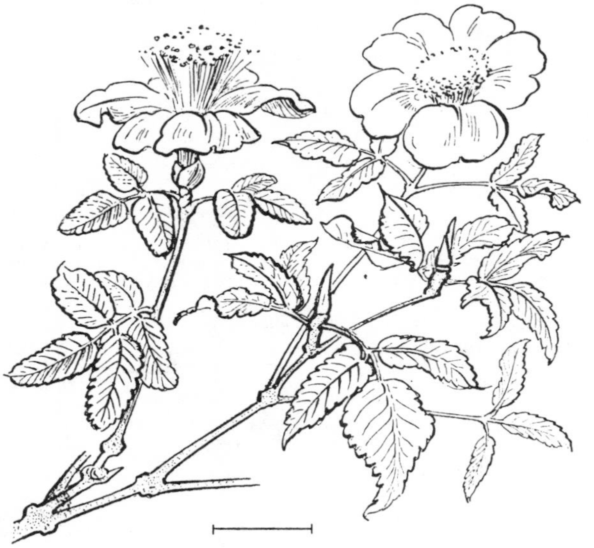

*Eucryphia glutinosa*

**E. glutino'sa.*** Deciduous or partly evergreen shrub or tree, up to 15 ft., shoots erect, downy when young. *l.* pinnate; lflets. 3 or 5, oval to ovate, ¾ to 2½ in. long, regularly toothed, dark shining green. *fl.* single or paired at the end of the shoots, 2½ in. across; pet. 4, white, obovate; anthers yellow. *fr.* a woody, pear-shaped capsule ⅝ to 1 in. long. Chile. 1859. (B.M. 7067 as *E. pinnatifolia*.) Seedlings from home-saved seed often give a proportion of double-flowered plants. The hardiest species; does not like chalk.

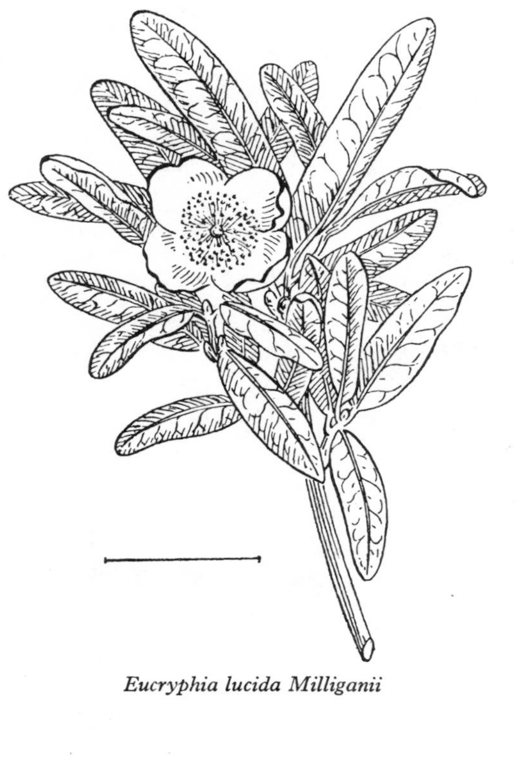

*Eucryphia lucida Milliganii*

**E. × interme'dia.** Name proposed for hybrids between *E. glutinosa* and *E. lucida*.

**E. lu'cida.** Slender evergreen tree, 20 to 80 ft., shoots downy. *l.* simple, oblong, 1 to 3 in. long, ⅜ to ⅝ in. wide, entire, apex rounded, deep shining green above, glaucous beneath, resinous; stalk ⅛ in. long. *fl.* fragrant, pure white, 1½ to 2 in. across, axillary. June, July. Tasmania. SYN. *E. Billardieri*. Tender. var. **Milligan'ii**, shrubby mountain form, with smaller *fl.* and *l.*, the latter sometimes only ½ to ¾ in. long, succeeds in chalky soil. (B.M. 7200.) SYN. *E. Milliganii*.

**E. Moor'ei.** Small or medium-sized evergreen tree, shoots and common l.-stalk hairy. *l.* pinnate, 3 to 5 in. long; lflets. 5 to 13, narrowly oblong, entire, 1 to 4 in. long, ¼ to ⅝ in. wide, mucronate, lustrous dark green above, hairy and glaucous beneath. *fl.* 1 in. wide, pure white, axillary, solitary; pet. obovate; stamens white. Autumn. New S. Wales. 1915. (B.M. 9411.) Tender.

**E. × Nymansay.*** Vigorous evergreen tree of medium size and erect habit. *l.* simple to pinnate the latter of 3 or 5 leaflets which are 1½ to 3½ in. long, 1 to 1½ in. wide, toothed, dark lustrous green. *fl.* white, 2½ in. wide across, pet. obovate, overlapping; anthers yellow. August. A chance hybrid between *E. cordifolia* and *E. glutinosa* raised at Nymans, Sussex, about 1915. (G.C. 80 (1926), 177.) Rather hardier than *E. cordifolia*; succeeds in chalky soil.

**E. × nymansen'sis.** Name proposed for hybrids between *E. cordifolia* and *E. glutinosa*.

**E. pinnatifo'lia.** A synonym of *E. glutinosa*.

**E. × Rostrev'or*** (*E. glutinosa* × *E. lucida*). Small evergreen or partly evergreen tree, probably 30 to 40 ft. *l.* either simple and from 1 to 2½ in. long, oblong-ovate or pinnate with lflets. ½ to 1½ in. long; entire or more or less toothed. *fl.* white, 2 in. across. Raised at Rostrevor, Co. Down.

**EUCRYPHIA'CEAE.** Dicotyledons. A family of but 1 genus with a few species in Chile and Australia. Evergreen or deciduous trees or shrubs with opposite leaves, simple or pinnate. Flowers perfect, white, axillary, usually large; sepals 4, imbricate, connate at tips, separating at base as flower opens; petals 4, convolute; stamens numerous, on the long floral axis below the 5- to 18-celled ovary. Fruit a dehiscent capsule separating into 5 to 18 several-seeded divisions; seeds winged. The only genus, Eucryphia, has been placed in several different families but fits well into none.

**EUGE'NIA** (in honour of Prince Eugene of Savoy, 1663–1736, a promoter of botany). FAM. *Myrtaceae*. A genus of very large size but variable, owing to the different conception of its limits taken by various authorities. For instance, Acmena, Jambosa, and Syzygium (included here) are often kept separate. Bentham calculated that over 700 species had been included under Eugenia, but probably less than 30 are in cultivation. They inhabit tropical and temperate regions, being most abundant in E. Asia and S. America, but found also in Africa and Australia, not in Europe.

Evergreen trees up to 120 ft. down to shrubs a few feet high. Leaves opposite, very rarely alternate, often dotted with oil-glands. Calyx lobes 4 or 5; petals 4 or 5, in some species very small and falling away in one piece, in others free and spreading; stamens very numerous and frequently the most attractive part of the flower. Fruit a berry or drupe, often juicy and edible, sometimes dry with a tough rind. Easily cultivated in a loamy soil and propagated by cuttings or seeds.

**E. apicula'ta.** A synonym of *Myrtus Luma*.

**E. aromat'ica.** Clove Tree. Tree of medium size, entirely glabrous. *l.* 3 to 5 in. long, 1 to 2 in. wide, oval-lanceolate, slenderly tapered to both ends. *fl.* yellow, 1 in. long, in terminal, short, trichotomously divided panicles; pet. 4, at first compressed into globular shape; stamens in a cluster ⅝ in. wide. *fr.* an elliptical purple berry, 1 in. long. Moluccas. 1797. (B.M. 2749–50 as *Caryophyllus aromaticus*.) Now cultivated in many tropical countries. The cloves of commerce are the dried, unexpanded flowers of this tree.

**E. austra'lis.** A synonym of *E. myrtifolia*.

**E. brachyan'dra.** Tall, quite glabrous tree, shoots 4-angled. *l.* 4 to 7 in. long, ¾ to 2 in. wide, oblong-lanceolate, pointed, cuneate, thin, and leathery; stalk ¼ in. long. *fl.* of no beauty, in small, compact, terminal clusters; pet. 5 or 6, very minute; stamens very short. *fr.* globuse, ¾ to 1 in. wide, reddish. New S. Wales (where it is known as 'Red Apple'). Queensland. 1873. SYN. *Acmena brachyandra*.

**E. brasilien'sis.*** Small tree. *l.* 3 to 5 in. long, 1 to 2 in. wide, oblong-ovate to obovate. *fl.* pure white, 1 in. wide, borne in several terminal racemes, each 3 or 4 in. long, leafy at the end and carrying 2, 4, or 6 fl. with several pairs of membranous scales; pet. 4 or 5, obovate, ½ in. long; stamens shorter. April. *fr.* globose, white, red, or black-violet, ½ to ¾ in. wide. Brazil. (B.M. 4526.) Stove.

**E. buxifo'lia.** Small tree or shrub, shoots and l. glabrous. *l.* elliptic to obovate, ½ to 1½ in. long, ⅙ to ½ in. wide, base cuneate, apex blunt. *fl.* ¼ in. long, 3 to 7 in axillary clusters; sep. and pet. very small; stamens erect, white with yellow anthers. July, August. *fr.* globose, shining, orange-coloured to black, ½ in. wide, fragrant. Chile. (Add. 257.) Cool greenhouse.

**E. cauliflo'ra.** *fl.* and *fr.* in clusters on old wood down to ground. fr. about ¾ in. wide, purple. Brazil.

**E. cotinifo'lia orbicula'ta.** A synonym of *E. orbiculata*.

**E. cyanocar'pa.** Shrub or small tree, up to 20 ft. *l.* elliptic-lanceolate to elliptic, 2 to 4 in. long, 1 to 1¼ in. wide, base cuneate, apex slender-pointed, glabrous. *fl.* few in loose panicles, creamy-white; pet. very small; stamens spreading ⅜ in. long. *fr.* globose, nearly ½ in. wide, violet (colour very unusual). Australia. (B.M. 9602.) Cool greenhouse.

**E. ed'ulis.** All young parts covered with rusty down. *l.* lanceolate-oblong, slender-pointed. *fr.* orange or yellow, downy, as large as an apple. Brazil, Argentine.

**E. ellip'tica.** A synonym of *E. Smithii*.

**E. ferrugin'ea.** Shrub or small tree, shoots slender, erect, downy. *l.* densely set, oblong or elliptic, rounded at both ends, ¼ to ½ in. long, 1/12 to ⅙ in. wide, rusty-coloured and conspicuously dotted beneath; midrib not perceptible above. *fl.* white, ¼ in. wide, solitary in the terminal l.-axils of short side twigs. *fr.* 3/16 in. long, oblong-ovoid, rusty-downy. Chile. 1860.

**E. Gar'beri.** Tree 50 to 60 ft., of compact, narrow shape. *l.* ovate-oblong to roundish-ovate, abruptly narrowed to a slender point, pale red when young, very lustrous green later, 1½ to 3 in. long, ⅓ to 1½ in. wide. *fl.* minute, produced in axillary clusters in autumn. *fr.* ¼ to ⅓ in. long, bright scarlet, globose-ovoid. Florida. (G. and F. 1889, 29.) Said by Sargent to be the largest myrtaceous tree in N. America and one of the most beautiful of Floridan trees.

**E. Jambola'na.** Tall, glabrous shrub or tree. *l.* oval-oblong, 4 to 6 in. long, half as wide. *fl.* red, small, fragrant, borne in rounded heads forming collectively pyramidal panicles up to 8 by 5 in., pet. falling away in one piece; stamens very numerous. August. *fr.* purple-black, oblong to roundish, ¾ to 1¼ in. long, 1-seeded. Australia, Trop. Asia. 1796. SYN. *Syzygium Cumini*. Much grown for its edible fr. in the warmer countries.

**E. Jam'bos.*** Rose Apple. Tree, 20 to 40 ft., glabrous. *l.* lanceolate, 4 to 8 in. long, 1 to 2 in. wide, pointed, base cuneate, dark glossy green, stalk very short. *fl.* few in terminal clusters, white; stamens long and numerous giving a diam. of 2½ to 3 in. June. *fr.* ovoid, 1½ in. long, 1¼ in. wide, yellowish-white, fragrant, used in confectionery. E. Indies. 1696. (B.M. 3356 as *Jambosa vulgaris*.) SYN. *Syzygium Jambos*.

**E. javan'ica.** Glabrous tree 20 to 30 ft. *l.* ovate-oblong to oblong-lanceolate, base rounded, apex blunt, 4 to 8 in. long, 2 to 3½ in. wide. *fl.* white, ¼ in. across, 1 to 3 on a slender stalk 2 to 3 in. long. *fr.* ⅝ to ¾ in. diam., ovoid-globose, glossy-white. Malaya. SYN. *Syzygium samarangense*.

**E. malaccen'sis.*** Shrub 6 to 8 ft. or a small tree. *l.* 6 to 12 in. long, 2½ to 4 in. wide, oblong to ovate-oblong, shining on both surfaces. *fl.* closely set in clusters 3 in. long and wide springing from the year-old wood; stamens rich crimson, very numerous, forming a cluster 1 in. wide; anthers yellow. June. *fr.* edible, as large as a hen's egg, rose to dark purple. Malaya. (B.M. 4408 as *Jambosa malaccensis*.) SYN. *Syzygium malaccense*. Stove.

**E. Ma'to.** *l.* ovate, 1½ in. long, obtuse. *fl.* solitary in l.-axils, peduncles much shorter than l. *fr.* about 1 in. wide, ribbed, orange. Argentine.

**E. Michel'ii.** A synonym of *E. uniflora*.

**E. microphyl'la.** Bushy, myrtle-like shrub, 2 to 8 ft., or a small tree 15 to 18 ft., shoots slender, glabrous. *l.* ⅓ to 1¼ in. long, oval and ovate-lanceolate to obovate, base cuneate, apex blunt, glabrous. *fl.* white, small, clustered at or near end of shoots. *fr.* pea-shaped, purple-black, edible. SE. China, Hong Kong. Warm greenhouse. SYN. *E. sinensis*, *Syzygium microphyllum*.

**E. myriophyl'la.** Downy on all young parts. *l.* mostly ternate, narrow-linear, ¾ to 1½ in. long. *fl.* solitary, peduncles shorter than l. Brazil.

**E. myrtifo'lia.** Glabrous shrub. *l.* narrowly oval to obovate, mostly pointed, cuneate, 1 to 3 in. long, about half as wide. *fl.* terminal on leading shoot and on short, lateral twigs in clusters of 3 to 15, the numerous white stamens with yellow anthers giving each fl. a breadth of ¾ to 1 in. July. *fr.* red, ⅓ in. wide, ovoid or nearly globular. Australia. Hardy in Scilly. (B.M. 2230; B.R. 627.) SYN. *E. australis*.

**E. orbicula'ta.** Stiff, glabrous shrub, 6 to 8 ft. *l.* nearly sessile, oval, orbicular, or broadly obovate, ¾ to 2½ in. long, thick and leathery. *fl.* ½ in. wide, in dense, axillary clusters which have stalks ½ to 1 in. long; pet. 4, orbicular-concave, yellowish-white; stamens very numerous, ¼ in. long, anthers yellow. November. Bourbon, Mauritius. 1824. (B.M. 4558 as *Myrtus orbiculata*.) SYN. *E. cotinifolia orbiculata*.

**E. ova'ta.** Small tree, shoots and fl.-stalks reddish, downy. *l.* densely set, ovate, ½ to ¾ in. long, base rounded, apex pointed, pale dotted and hairy on the midrib beneath. *fl.* white, ⅓ in. wide, solitary, axillary, but very abundant, forming dense, leafy, cylindrical panicles. Chile. Cool greenhouse. SYN. *Acmena ovata*.

**E. Pitang'a.** Low shrub, all young parts covered with reddish down. *l.* elliptic-oblong from an acute base, 1½ to 3 in. long. *fr.* about ½ in. wide, red, almost round. *fl.* solitary, axillary. Brazil, Argentine.

**E. pung'ens.** All young parts hairy. *l.* elliptic-oblong, 2 to 3 in. long, ¾ to 1 in. wide, spine-tipped. *fl.* solitary in l.-axils, peduncles much shorter than l. *fr.* small, downy, flattish-round. Brazil.

**E. rubicun'da.** Large shrub or small tree. *l.* 2 to 4 in. long, one-third to half as wide, narrow-oblong, tapered to both ends, leathery, transparently dotted. *fl.* in terminal corymbs 2 to 3 in. across, minute. *fr.* ovoid, ⅝ in. long, ½ in. wide. India.

**E. Sello'i.** Shrub. *l.* distichous, oval or obovate-oblong, leathery, slender-pointed; stalk short. *fl.* axillary or lateral, solitary; sep. and pet. 4; sep. leafy; stamens many. *fr.* yellow, oblong, about 1½ in. long, with a pleasant aromatic flavour and pine-apple odour. Brazil. 1884. (R.H. 1884, 348 as *Phyllocalyx edulis*.) Greenhouse.

**E. sinen'sis.** A synonym of *E. microphylla*.

**E. Smith'ii.** Glabrous tree 80 to 100 ft. *l.* ovate to ovate-oblong or oblong-lanceolate, tapered to both ends, 1½ to 3½ in. long, one-third to half as wide; stalks short. *fl.* small, white, in terminal corymbs, 2 to 4 in. across; stamens only 1/12 in. long. May to July. *fr.* ¼ to ½ in. diam., globular, white acquiring a pinkish tinge, or purple. Australia. 1790. (B.M. 1872 as *E. elliptica*; B.M. 5450 as *Acmena floribunda*.) SYN. *Acmena Smithii*.

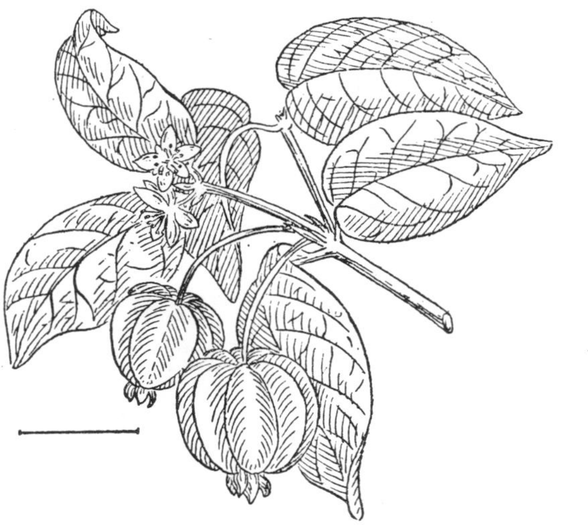

*Eugenia uniflora*

**E. uniflo'ra.*** Glabrous shrub or small tree. *l.* ovate to oval, base rounded, apex tapered but blunt, 2 to 2½ in. long, 1 to 1½ in. wide. *fl.* solitary, white, ½ in. wide; sep. and pet. 4; stamens short, anthers yellow. *fr.* ovoid-globose, red, 1 to 1¼ in. wide, with 8 deep longitudinal grooves, edible; these fluted fr. are very distinctive. Tropical S. America. (B.M. 8599.) SYN. *E. Michelii*.

**E. Ventena'tii.** Shrub or small tree, entirely glabrous. *l.* oblong-lanceolate, 3 to 5 in. long, ½ to 1½ in. wide, tapered to both ends. *fl.* ¼ in. wide, in loose, leafy, terminal and axillary panicles; pet. 4, very small; stamens ⅙ in. long, white. *fr.* globose, up to ⅜ in. wide, red New S. Wales, Queensland.

**E. xalapen'sis.** Tree up to 45 ft., shoots glabrous. *l.* sometimes alternate, ovate to ovate-oblong, 2 to 5 in. long, ¾ to 2 in. wide, base rounded to cuneate, apex tapered but blunt, glabrous; stalk ¼ in. longer. *fl.* small, white, several in almost sessile axillary clusters; pedicel ¼ in. long. *fr.* black, globose or ovoid, ⅜ in. long. Mexico.

**E. Zey'heri.** Glabrous shrub or small tree, 10 to 15 ft., branches grey-white. *l.* ¾ to 1½ in. long, ⅓ to ¾ in. wide, oblong, ovate, elliptic or obovate, tapered to both ends, apex blunt. *fl.* ⅓ in. wide, in numerous axillary clusters of 3 to 12 or solitary; pet. 4 or 5, white or pinkish. *fr.* globose, ⅓ to ½ in. diam., purplish or bright red. S. Africa. Greenhouse.

W. J. B.

**EULA'LIA** of gardens. *See* **Miscanthus.**

**EULOPH'IA** (*eulophos*, handsome-crested; the handsome labellum has elevated ridges). FAM. *Orchidaceae*. A genus of chiefly terrestrial orchids, about 200 species, distributed in Africa, Madagascar, Malaya, Ceylon, India, China, &c., and also represented in America. Flower scapes simple or branched, few- or many-flowered usually from the base of the pseudobulbs; sepals and petals nearly equal, lip pouched or spurred, entire or 3-lobed, bearded or crested in the middle; pollen masses 2. The rhizomes are tuberous or produce pseudobulbs; the leaves grass-like, lanceolate, plaited (exceptions occur). The genus on the whole has little to recommend it horticulturally. *E. guineensis* and its var. *purpurata* still remain the most beautiful species in cultivation. The compost should be that advised for terrestrial Phaius. Many species require a decided rest in winter. A number are deciduous or nearly so and these require very infrequent waterings in the winter, if any. Effort should be made to mature the plants in autumn by exposure to light particularly the deciduous species, but the plants must not be subjected to too great a fall from their growing temperature. While the leaves are young the syringe should not be used on them. Temperatures must vary according to their native locality. The species from W. Africa and Madagascar should be kept at 65 or 70° F. on winter nights. Many of the S. African forms and those from Burma, India, &c., are suited in the intermediate house. No new species of any great floral merit have been added to our collections this century.

**E. al'ta.** Sep. greenish-yellow, 4/5 in. long; pet. shorter, slightly broader; lip lilac flushed with purple, deeply 3-lobed, apex of mid-lobe emarginate. *Spike* erect, 4½ ft. h. or more, many-fld. *Pseudobulbs* ovoid-globose, about 3 in. h. *l.* 3 ft. long or more, 1½ to 3 in. wide. Brazil, U.S.A., W. Indies, &c. 1767. A widely distributed, variable species.

**E. bel'la.** A synonym of *Lissochilus milanjianus*.

**E. bi'color.** A synonym of *E. Zeyheri*.

**E. campes'tris.** *fl.* many, sub-secund; sep. yellow or green, striped pink, ½ to ⅔ in. long; pet. narrower; lip as long as sep., mid-lobe usually purple; scape 6 to 18 in. long, stout or slender, from a deformed tuber. Plains of India. (A.B.G.C. 8, 241.)

**E. congoen'sis.** A synonym of *E. guineensis*.

**E. deflex'a.** *fl.* 2 in. across, in a lax raceme; sep. and pet. purple and lilac; lip fringed white; scape 2 ft. h. *l.* lanceolate, about 1 ft. long. Natal. 1895.

**E. Dregea'na.** *fl.* on spikes, chocolate; lip white. S. Africa. (I.O.A. 2, 9.)

**E. epidendroi'des.** *fl.* 1½ to 2 in. across; sep. and pet. whitish; lip violet-crested; spur short. *Pseudobulbs* oval, 2 to 3 in. h. *l.* narrow. *Spikes* 2 ft. h. Spring. Ceylon, India. 1866. (B.M. 5579 as *E. virens*.)

**E. euglos'sa.** *fl.* sep. and pet. green, lanceolate, acuminate, nearly equal, spreading; lip 3-fid, side lobes semi-ovate, acute, greenish-yellow, mid-lobe semi-oblong, acute, somewhat crisp, white, with purple streaks on base; spur clavate, green. *l.* cuneate-oblong, acute, 1 ft. long. Old Calabar. 1866. (B.M. 5561.) A curious plant, requiring plenty of heat to flower it successfully.

**E. explana'ta.** *fl.* purple and yellowish, spreading, ⅔ to ¾ in. across; lip sessile; spur broad; scape 4 to 8 in. long, 10- to 12-fld. *l.* very young at flowering, surrounded at base by broad sheaths. Nepal. (A.B.G.C. 9, 108.)

**E. gigan'tea.** A synonym of *Lissochilus giganteus*.

**E. guineen'sis.*** *fl.* 6 to 12, about 2½ in. across, whitish-pink; sep. and pet. narrow, acuminate; lip side lobes small, mid-lobe large, somewhat cordate, whitish, flushed and streaked rose-crimson. May to November. *Pseudobulbs* 1 to 2 in. h. *l.* 2 or 3, broad-lanceolate, plicate, 12 to 18 in. long. *Spike* 18 to 30 in. long. Sierra Leone. 1822. (B.M. 2467; B.R. 686; L.B.C. 818; L. 486 as *E. congoensis*.) This and its variety *purpurata* are very handsome and the most beautiful under cultivation in the genus. var. **purpura'ta*** has dark dull-purple sep. and pet. and a rose-purple lip, *pseudobulbs* 2- or 3-leaved. W. Trop. Africa. 1883. (W.O.A. 89.)

**E. lu'rida.** *fl.* small, numerous, yellowish-brown, on branching panicles, 6 to 15 in. long. *Pseudobulbs* 2 to 3 in. h., Cymbidium-like. Aerial roots freely produced. *l.* 4 to 5, 6 to 9 in. long. W. Trop. Africa, Madagascar. 1834? SYN. *Eulophiopsis lurida*. (B.R. 1821.)

**E. macrostach'ya.** *fl.* shortly pedicellate, 1 in. across; lateral sep. erecto-patent; lip very concave, golden-yellow, with red-purple stripes on disk, broader than long, shallowly 3-lobed. January. *l.* about 2, from top of pseudobulb, oblong-lanceolate, acuminate, contracted into a petiole, membranous, plaited, about 3-ribbed. *Pseudobulbs* elongate, conical, striate. Ceylon. 1837. (B.M. 6246; B.R. 1972.) Desirable on account of its flowering period.

**E. megistophyl'la.** *fl.* greenish-yellow, lined brownish-red, panicled; sep. lanceolate, narrower than pet.; lip 4-lobed, lobes obtuse; spur very short, cylindrical; sheath ample, ochreous, oblong, acute. *l.* over 1 ft. long and 9 in. broad, petiolate, cuneate-oblong, acute. Comoro Is. 1885. (Gn. 35 (1889), 62.) A striking species.

**E. nu'da.** *fl.* rosy lilac, green, or purple, rather large; sep. 1 in. long, linear-oblong; pet. many-nerved; raceme elongated, many-fld.; scape stout, 1 to 3 ft. long. *l.* 10 to 14 in. long, elliptic-lanceolate. *Pseudobulbs* tuber-like, usually underground. Trop. Himalaya, China. 1891. (B.M. 8057; A.B.G.C. 8, 243.)

**E. pul'chra.** Resembles *E. Saundersiana* and *E. macrostachya* in habit. *fl.* yellowish-green; sep. and pet. marked and lip spotted with purple. Madagascar, Bourbon Is. var. **diver'gens** is purple-spotted with oblong-linear sep. and pet. and lip with 2 divergent lobes. Isle of Bourbon. 1884.

**E. Saundersia'na.** *fl.* about 1 in. across, greenish-yellow, pet. and lip with a few broad, black lines, the centre of sep. black; lip 4-lobed; racemes 4 to 6 in. long, many-fld.; scapes erect, 1 to 2 ft. h. *Pseudobulbs* 6 to 9 in. h., slender, pear-shaped, 2-leaved. *l.* petiolate, elliptic-oblong, 5 to 9 in. long. Trop. Africa. Before 1864. (R.X.O. 2, 173.)

**E. scrip'ta.** *fl.* green, brown, and yellow, about 1 in. across; sep. and pet. linear-oblong; lip 3-parted; spur very short; scape radical, branched. *l.* linear-lorate, somewhat distichous. Stem fleshy, oblong. Madagascar, &c. 1872. SYN. *Eulophiopsis scripta*.

**E. streptopet'ala.** A synonym of *Lissochilus streptopetalus*.

**E. Wendlandia'na.** *fl.* in a raceme 16 in. long; sep. pale green, linear; pet. white; lip green, with falcate lateral lobes. *Pseudobulbs* 2½ in. long. *l.* 3 or 4 at the summit of the pseudobulbs, 2 ft. long, lanceolate, acute. Madagascar. 1897.

**E. Zey'heri.** *fl.* pale yellow, dark purple on side lobes and base of lip, crowded at top of scape; sep. about 1½ in. long. April. *l.* as long as scape, narrow-lanceolate, acuminate. 1 to 1½ ft. h. Natal, &c. (B.M. 7330.) SYN. *E. bicolor*.

E. C.

**EULOPHID'IUM** (resembling *Eulophia*). FAM. *Orchidaceae*. A genus of about 5 species of which 4 are in Africa and Madagascar and 1 in Brazil. The genus has been separated from Eulophia and the species are readily distinguished by the leathery texture of the persistent single leaf carried by the small pseudobulb. Though probably more epiphytic than Eulophias the following species should have similar compost and similar treatment, but may be grown in small pans and suspended near the glass. Winter night temperature should be around 60° F.

**E. Ledien'ii.** *fl.* 6 to 12, nearly 1 in. across; sep. brownish; the slightly shorter pet. whitish; lip somewhat fiddle-shaped, yellowish-white flecked with red; spikes erect, 12 in. long. *Pseudobulbs* oval, about 1 in. h. *l.* 5 to 6 in. long, 1½ in. wide, tapered, shortly conduplicate at base, green tessellated grey-green. W. Africa.

**E. macula'tum.** Very similar to *E. Ledienii*, but segs. sometimes spotted rose and lip whitish with purplish bases to side lobes and purplish blotches on mid-lobe. *l.* 6 to 12 in. long, more brightly blotched than in *E. Ledienii*. Brazil. 1821. (B.R. 618 as *Angraecum maculatum*; L.B.C. 496 as *Limodorum maculatum*.)

E. C.

**EULOPHIEL'LA** (a diminutive of *Eulophia*). FAM. *Orchidaceae*. An epiphytic genus of 2 or 3 species, natives of Madagascar. The genus is grouped between Eulophia and Cyrtopodium, but horticulturally is widely apart. It is characterized by ringed pseudobulbs, somewhat conical, springing at intervals from a stout, creeping rhizome. The showy flowers on erect or laterally inclined spikes are produced from the base of the pseudobulbs and have rounded, rather fleshy segments; the 3-lobed lip is without spur or sac. The column is prolonged into a short foot. A tropical atmosphere is required throughout the year. The winter temperature should not fall below 65° F. at night. Water and a moist atmosphere are required throughout the year, but the plants must not be kept unduly wet at the root, particularly in winter. A compost of 2 parts of perfectly clean Osmunda fibre mixed with 1 part of picked Sphagnum moss should be used. *E. Elizabethae* may be grown in a shallow basket, but the other stronger species with stouter, more rambling rhizomes should have rafts or troughs which can be lengthened as the plants grow. Propagation is by division of the rhizome. Shading is required, but a gloomy position should be avoided. A beautiful hybrid, *E.* × *Rolfei* (*E. Elizabethae* × *E. Roempleriana*) is possibly more amenable to cultivation than its parents, and is now perhaps more largely grown.

**E. Elizabeth'ae.*** *fl.* up to 40, white flushed pale pink, back of sep., ovary, and scape dull purple, 2 to 2¼ in. across; sep. orbicular, larger than pet.; lip jointed to column, disk smaller, golden-yellow with several bristles, near base of lip is a deep-orange semi-circular callus with two divergent white keels each with an orange-tipped tooth; scape and rachis 24 to 30 in. long. April. *l.* linear-lanceolate, about 2 ft. long. *rhiz.* creeping, rooting, with annulate pseudobulbs 4 to 6 in. h., the scars with 1 in.-long brown fibres. (B.M. 7387.)

**E. Peetersia'na.** A synonym of *E. Roempleriana.*

**E. Roempleria'na.*** *fl.* 20 to 25, purple-rose, 2¾ to 4 in. across; sep. and pet. rounded; lip white in middle with broad-oblong side lobes, front lobe smaller, 2-lobed, disk with 3-lobed callus at base from which radiate nerves, the middle ones enlarged into narrow triangular lamellae; scapes 3 to 5 ft. long. Stronger growing than *E. Elizabethae* with stouter yellowish-white rhiz. *l.* 3 to 4 ft. long, 3 to 3½ in. wide. (B.M. 7612, 7613 as *E. Peetersiana.*) SYN. *Grammatophyllum Roemplerianum.*

E. C.

**EULOPHIOP'SIS.** Included in **Eulophia.**

**EU'MERUS** sp. *See* **Small Bulb-flies.**

**EUNO'MIA** (*eu*, well, *nomos*, order; leaves opposite, seeds twin). FAM. *Cruciferae.* A genus of 2 species of evergreen sub-shrubs, natives of Mts. of Asia Minor. Leaves opposite, sessile or stem-clasping, rather thick, entire Flowers pink, in short racemes. Half-hardy, needing well-drained soil. Propagated by cuttings under a glass in summer, or by seeds in spring. Alpine house or cool greenhouse.

**E. oppositifo'lia.** Stem decumbent, branched, 6 to 12 in. h. *l.* almost orbicular, glabrous. *fl.* in 10- to 12-fld. terminal racemes. June. 1827.

**EUON'YMUS** (the ancient Greek name). FAM. *Celastraceae.* A genus of about 120 species of shrubs or small trees, occasionally creeping or climbing by rootlets, natives of Europe, Asia, N. and Cent. America, and Australia. Related to Celastrus but with usually opposite, not alternate, leaves, stems upright or climbing by rootlets, not twining, and fruit a 4- or 5- (not 3-)celled capsule. Branches usually 4-angled; leaves stalked, usually glabrous; flowers with 4 or 5 parts, in axillary cymes; fruits usually lobed or winged. The species of Euonymus have no beauty of flower but many of them are extremely fine in fruit and have good autumn colouring. The pendulous fruits are brightly coloured and as they ripen split to reveal the usually orange outer coverings (aril) of the seeds (1 or 2 in each cell), adding to the brightness of the bush after most of its foliage has fallen. Most of the species in cultivation are quite hardy and succeed in a well-drained loam soil, not objecting to lime. Propagation of the deciduous species is by seed sown in gentle heat in early spring (or outdoors but then takes somewhat longer), by layers or by cuttings in sand. The evergreen species root readily at any time of year with a little bottom heat. *E. japonicus* makes a good evergreen hedge (though liable to attack by the caterpillars of the lesser ermine moth and by mildew) near the sea, standing clipping well, and acting as a wind screen in a very efficient fashion in such places as the Isles of Scilly where the small fields are often protected by it. Cattle thrive on the clippings. All the evergreen species grow well in light, permanent shade and *E. americanus* and *E. atropurpureus* require shade from bright midday sun. *E. japonicus* has sometimes been grown as a standard grafted on *E. europaeus.* The stock should have a good stem so that it can be grafted at about 3 ft. high and it should be established in pots prior to grafting in February. When grafted the plants should be laid on their sides or stood in deep pits in a moist atmosphere at 60° F. until union has taken place when a little air can be given and the syringe used freely over the tops. In a few weeks the grafted plants should be stood out in a sunny place and by the end of the season will have formed good heads and be ready for planting out from the pots. *E. radicans* in its juvenile state is prostrate and rooting. It makes in both its green and variegated forms an excellent wall-plant growing up to 20 ft. high. It can be used in the same places as ivy and for most of the same purposes. Its miniature form *E. radicans kewensis*, with leaves about half as long and wide, will also climb.

A

KEY

| | | |
|---|---|---|
| 1. | *Lvs. evergreen, more or less* | 2 |
| 1. | *Lvs. deciduous* | 10 |
| 2. | *Fr. spiny* | E. Wilsonii |
| 2. | *Fr. not prickly or spiny* | 3 |
| 3. | *Fr. winged or angled* | 4 |
| 3. | *Fr. smooth, more or less round* | 7 |
| 4. | *Young lvs. shining red; shoots waxy; fr. winged* | E. pendulus |
| 4. | *Young lvs. green* | 5 |
| 5. | *Lvs. scarcely toothed; fr. pear-shaped, yellowish* | E. Sargentianus |
| 5. | *Lvs. finely toothed* | 6 |
| 6. | *Fl. ½ in. across; pet. purple-veined* | E. tingens |
| 6. | *Fl. 1 in. across; pet. greenish or yellowish-white* | E. grandiflorus |
| 7. | *Shrub climbing* | E. radicans |
| 7. | *Shrub not climbing* | 8 |
| 8. | *Lvs. slenderly long-pointed* | E. semipersistens |
| 8. | *Lvs. spiny* | E. ilicifolius |
| 8. | *Lvs. obtuse or acute* | 9 |
| 9. | *Lvs. rather thin, half-evergreen, lower branches rooting* | E. radicans |
| 9. | *Lvs. leathery, evergreen; branches upright* | E. japonicus |
| 9. | *Lvs. thin, tender* | E. chinensis |
| 9. | *Lvs. thin; branches spreading* | E. kiautschovicus |
| 10. | *Lvs. alternate, linear* | E. nanus |
| 10. | *Lvs. opposite* | 11 |
| 11. | *Shoots with corky wings* | 12 |
| 11. | *Shoots not winged* | 13 |
| 12. | *Lvs. strongly veined beneath; stalk ¼ to ½ in. long; fr. not lobed to base* | E. phellomanus |
| 12. | *Lvs. not strongly veined; stalk $\frac{1}{12}$ in. long; fr. very deeply lobed* | E. alatus |
| 13. | *Young shoots warted* | E. verrucosus |
| 13. | *Young shoots smooth* | 14 |
| 14. | *Fr. with prickly warts; pet. 5* | 15 |
| 14. | *Fr. not prickly* | 16 |
| 15. | *Shrub more or less upright in growth* | E. americanus |
| 15. | *Prostrate or nearly so* | E. obovatus |
| 16. | *Fr. winged or ribbed* | 17 |
| 16. | *Fr. obtusely lobed at most* | 24 |
| 17. | *Fr. angled* | 18 |
| 17. | *Fr. distinctly winged* | 19 |
| 18. | *Fr. conical at top, angles distinct; lvs. 3 to 5 in. long* | E. planipes |
| 18. | *Fr. globose, ribs slender; lvs. 1½ to 3½ in. long* | E. oxyphyllus |
| 19. | *Fr. usually 5-winged* | E. latifolius |
| 19. | *Fr. usually 4-winged* | 20 |
| 20. | *Lvs. linear, small* | E. oresbius |
| 20. | *Lvs. ovate or oblong* | 21 |
| 21. | *Wings of fr. ½ in. long or more* | 22 |
| 21. | *Wings of fr. ¼ to ⅓ in. long* | 23 |
| 22. | *Fl. green; fr. pink* | E. macropterus |
| 22. | *Fl. yellow; fr. red* | E. sanguineus |
| 23. | *Lvs. 1½ to 4 in. long, fimbriate* | E. fimbriatus |
| 23. | *Lvs. 3½ to 5½ in. long* | E. macropterus |
| 24. | *Anthers yellow* | 25 |
| 24. | *Anthers purple* | 27 |
| 25. | *Lvs. 1 to 2 in. long, toothed* | E. Semenovii |
| 25. | *Lvs. 1½ to 4 in. long* | 26 |
| 26. | *Lvs. crenate-serrate; fr. roundish* | E. europaeus |
| 26. | *Lvs. irregularly toothed; fr. turbinate* | E. Hamiltonianus |
| 27. | *Lvs. downy beneath; fl. purple* | E. atropurpureus |
| 27. | *Fl. yellowish-white* | 28 |
| 28. | *Lvs. broadest above middle* | E. yedoensis |
| 28. | *Lvs. broader at or below middle* | 29 |
| 29. | *Lvs. roughly hairy on midrib beneath, 3 to 4 in. long or more* | E. lanceifolius |
| 29. | *Lvs. quite smooth* | 30 |
| 30. | *Lvs. abruptly long-pointed, broadly rounded at base* | E. Bungeanus |
| 30. | *Lvs. gradually narrowed to long point, tapered at base* | E. Maackii |

**E. ala'tus.*** Winged Spindle tree. Deciduous shrub 6 to 9 ft., of stiff, open growth; branches with 2 thin, corky wings ¼ to ½ in. wide. *l.* narrowly oval or obovate, 1 to 3 in. long, ½ to 1¼ in. wide, tapered to both ends, finely toothed, dark green. *fl.* 1 to 3 in a cyme, ¼ in. wide, yellowish. *fr.* purplish, of normally 4 ovoid lobes, frequently only 2 or 1. Autumn foliage rich rosy scarlet. China, Japan. 1860. (B.M. 8823.) var. **ap'terus,** shoots not or only slightly winged. SYN. *E. subtriflorus.*

**E. america'nus.** Strawberry Bush. Deciduous, glabrous shrub, 6 or 7 ft. *l.* narrowly oval to lanceolate, 1 to $3\frac{1}{2}$ in. long, $\frac{1}{2}$ to $1\frac{1}{4}$ in. wide, cuneate, slightly toothed; stalk $\frac{1}{12}$ in. long. *fl.* 1 to 3 on a slender stalk, greenish-purple, $\frac{1}{3}$ in. wide; pet. 5, rounded. June. *fr.* $\frac{1}{2}$ to $\frac{3}{4}$ in. across, 3- to 5-lobed, deep pink, prickly warted. E. United States. 1683. (L.B.C. 1322.) var. **angustifo'lius,** *l.* 4 or 5 times longer than wide.

**E. atropurpu'reus.** Deciduous shrub, 6 to 10 ft., or a tree up to 20 ft. *l.* oval to ovate, 2 to 5 in. long, pointed, finely toothed, downy beneath. *fl.* $\frac{1}{3}$ in. broad, dark purple, 7 to 15 in branched cymes 1 to 2 in. long. June. *fr.* deeply 4-lobed, crimson, $\frac{5}{8}$ in. wide; seed-coat scarlet. Cent. United States. 1756. (S.S. 53.) Autumn colour pale yellow.

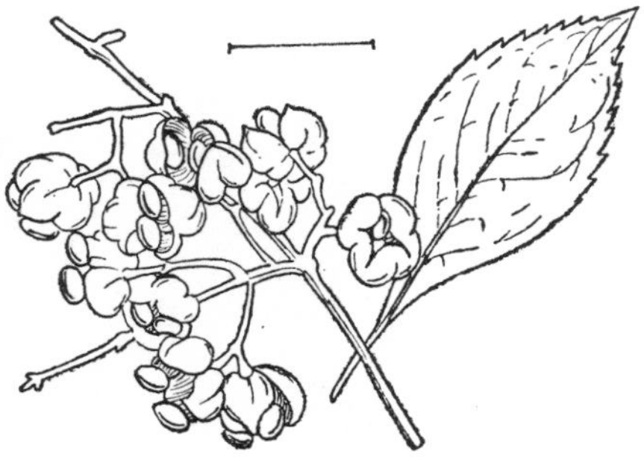

*Euonymus Bungeanus*

**E. Bungea'nus.** Deciduous shrub or small tree, glabrous, up to 20 ft., shoots slender. *l.* oval to ovate, $1\frac{1}{2}$ to 4 in. long, half as wide, slender-pointed, toothed; l.-stalk slender, up to 1 in. long. *fl.* $\frac{1}{3}$ in. across, yellowish, in cymes 1 to 2 in. long. *fr.* deeply 4-lobed, $\frac{1}{2}$ in. wide, yellowish, tinged pink. N. China. 1883. (B.M. 8656.) Distinct by its long l.-stalk.

**E. chinen'sis.** Evergreen shrub. *l.* obovate, obscurely toothed, less leathery than in *E. japonicus. fl.* few in axillary cymes. China. 1824. Tender and not specially ornamental.

**E. europae'us.*** Common Spindle tree. Deciduous, glabrous shrub, or a tree up to 25 ft. *l.* narrowly oval, ovate, or obovate, 1 to $3\frac{1}{2}$ in. long, pointed, cuneate, minutely toothed. *fl.* $\frac{1}{2}$ in. wide, greenish-white, in cymes of 3, 5, or more. *fr.* pinkish-red, $\frac{1}{2}$ to $\frac{3}{4}$ in. wide, 4-lobed; seed-coat orange. Europe (Britain). (E.B. 317.) var. **al'bus,** *fr.* white; **aldenhamen'sis,** *fr.* large, brilliant pink, on longer stalks; **aucubaefo'lius,** *l.* blotched yellow; **interme'dius,*** *l.* larger and more broadly ovate, *fr.* bright red, large; **purpu'reus,** young shoots and *l.* purple.

**E. fimbria'tus.** Related to *E. sanguineus* but *l.* elliptic to oblong-ovate, up to 4 in. long, abruptly narrowed to a point, finely and doubly toothed and fimbriate, rather thick, *fl.* small, in cymes about $\frac{3}{4}$ in. across, *fr.* with long, pointed wings. Himalaya. 1920.

**E. grandiflo'rus.*** Deciduous, glabrous shrub or small tree, 25 ft. or more. *l.* linear-lanceolate, narrowly oval, 2 to $4\frac{1}{2}$ in. long, $\frac{5}{8}$ to $1\frac{1}{4}$ in. wide, acuminate and cuneate in the cultivated form (**salicifo'lius**) but in other forms obovate and broadly ovate, dark bright green, finely toothed. *fl.* greenish or yellowish, in cymes 2 in. long of 3 to 9. *fr.* 4-lobed, $\frac{5}{8}$ in. wide, pale pink. N. India to W. China. 1867. (B.M. 9183. var. *salicifolius.*)

**E. Hamiltonia'nus.** Small tree related to *E. europaeus. l.* lanceolate-oblong, $2\frac{1}{2}$ to 4 in. long, irregularly toothed. *fr.* turbinate, 4-lobed, pink. Himalaya. 1825.

**E. ilicifo'lius.** Evergreen shrub, 6 to 9 ft., glabrous, young shoots angled. *l.* holly-like, $1\frac{1}{4}$ to 3 in. long, 1 to 2 in. wide, leathery, oval, margins spiny; stalk up to $\frac{1}{4}$ in. long, pale and strongly veined beneath. *fl.* small, dull olive-green, in short cymes of mostly 3. *fr.* sub-globose, $\frac{1}{4}$ to $\frac{1}{2}$ in. wide, not lobed, grey-white; seed-coat scarlet. W. China. 1930. Tender.

**E. japon'icus.*** Evergreen, glabrous shrub or small tree, 10 to 15, sometimes 25 ft. *l.* obovate to narrowly oval, 1 to $2\frac{1}{2}$ in. long, $\frac{3}{4}$ to 2 in. wide, cuneate, apex blunt or rounded, leathery, dark bright green, shallow-toothed. *fl.* $\frac{1}{3}$ in. wide, greenish-white, 5 to 12 in cymes up to 2 in. long. *fr.* $\frac{1}{3}$ in. wide, pinkish, not lobed; seed-coat orange. Japan. 1804. (B.R. 30, 6.) var. **albo-margina'tus,** *l.* yellow, white-margined; **au'reus,** *l.* almost wholly yellow, fastigiate, habit columnar; **macrophyl'lus,** *l.* oval, 3 in. long; **microphyl'lus,** *l.* oblong-lanceolate, $\frac{1}{2}$ to 1 in. long, $\frac{1}{8}$ to $\frac{1}{3}$ in. wide; **ovatus-au'reus,** *l.* broadly margined with rich yellow; **pyramida'tus,** of erect, slender shape, very compact. There are many other forms that have been raised in nurseries with only slight colour differences.

**E. kiautschov'icus.** Evergreen, glabrous, spreading shrub up to 10 ft. *l.* broadly oval to ovate, 2 to $3\frac{1}{2}$ in. long, $\frac{3}{4}$ to 2 in. wide, cuneate, crenate. *fl.* greenish-white, $\frac{1}{3}$ in. wide, numerous in loose cymes $1\frac{1}{2}$ to $3\frac{1}{2}$ in. across. *fr.* $\frac{3}{8}$ in. wide, pink, not lobed; seed-coat orange-red. China. 1860. (Add. 158 as *E. patens.*)

**E. lanceifo'lius.*** Deciduous or semi-evergreen tree up to 30 ft. or a shrub. *l.* oval-oblong to lanceolate-oblong, 3 to 5 in. long, 1 to 3 in. wide, cuneate, pointed, faintly toothed. *fl.* whitish, $\frac{1}{2}$ in. wide, in cymes of 7 to 15. May, June. *fr.* 4-lobed, pink, $\frac{1}{2}$ in. wide; seed-coat scarlet. China. 1908.

**E. latifo'lius.*** Deciduous, glabrous tree, 10 to 20 ft. *l.* oval, oblong, or obovate, 3 to 5 in. long, half as wide, pointed, finely toothed; stalk $\frac{1}{4}$ in. long. *fl.* greenish, $\frac{3}{8}$ in. across, 7 to 15 on slender-stalked cymes, 2 to 3 in. long. *fr.* pendulous, $\frac{3}{4}$ in. broad, 5- (sometimes 4-) winged, rich rosy red; seed-coat orange. Europe. 1730. (B.M. 2384.)

**E. Maack'ii.** Glabrous shrub or small tree. *l.* narrowly oval, cuneate, slender-pointed, 2 to $3\frac{1}{2}$ in. long, $\frac{3}{4}$ to 1 in. wide, finely toothed. *fl.* yellowish, $\frac{3}{8}$ in. wide, in small cymes 1 to $1\frac{1}{2}$ in. long; pet. narrowly oblong; anthers purple. June. *fr.* $\frac{1}{3}$ in. broad, 4-lobed, pink; seed-coat orange. N. China to Korea. 1876.

**E. macrop'terus.** Deciduous, glabrous shrub, 10 ft. or more, habit spreading. *l.* obovate or oval, cuneate, slender-pointed, finely toothed, $2\frac{1}{2}$ to 5 in. long, 1 to $1\frac{3}{4}$ in. wide, dark glossy green. *fl.* small, green, numerous in cymes 1 to 2 in. long. May. *fr.* $\frac{7}{8}$ in. wide, pink, with 4 wings each $\frac{1}{4}$ in. long, thin; seed-coat deep red. NE. Asia. 1905. SYN. *E. ussuriensis.*

**E. na'nus.*** Low, deciduous or partly evergreen, glabrous shrub, of spreading growth, 2 to 6 ft., shoots angled. *l.* alternate, opposite or whorled, linear to narrow-oblong, revolute, $\frac{3}{4}$ to $1\frac{1}{2}$ in. long, $\frac{1}{12}$ to $\frac{3}{16}$ in. wide, entire or slightly toothed. *fl.* $\frac{1}{6}$ to $\frac{1}{4}$ in. wide, 4-parted, brown-purple, 1 to 3 on a slender stalk. May. *fr.* 4-lobed, pink to rose-red, $\frac{1}{2}$ in. long. Caucasus to China. 1830. (B.M. 9308.) var. **Koopman'nii,** of sturdier habit, *l.* broader and not revolute. Thian-shan and Altai Mts.

**E. obova'tus.** Deciduous, glabrous shrub, prostrate, self-rooting, rarely more than 1 ft. h. *l.* obovate, 1 to $2\frac{1}{2}$ in. long, $\frac{1}{2}$ to $1\frac{1}{2}$ in. wide, obscurely toothed, cuneate. *fl.* $\frac{1}{4}$ in. wide, greenish-purple, 1 or 3 on a slender stalk; pet. 5, rounded. *fr.* usually 3-lobed, $\frac{1}{2}$ to $\frac{3}{4}$ in. wide, crimson, warty. Eastern N. America. 1820. (G. and F. 9, 385.)

**E. ores'bius.*** Deciduous, glabrous shrub, 5 to 6 ft., shoots square. *l.* linear to oblanceolate, apex rounded, base cuneate, $\frac{1}{2}$ to $\frac{7}{8}$ in. long, $\frac{1}{16}$ to $\frac{1}{8}$ in. wide. *fl.* green, small, solitary or in threes. June. *fr.* $\frac{1}{2}$ in. across, rich rosy red, with 4 winged lobes; stalk $\frac{1}{4}$ to $\frac{1}{2}$ in. long; seed-coat scarlet. W. China. 1913.

**E. oxyphyl'lus.** Deciduous, glabrous, small tree up to 25 ft., or a shrub. *l.* ovate to ovate-oblong, $1\frac{1}{2}$ to $3\frac{1}{2}$ in. long, about half as wide, pointed, toothed. *fl.* greenish-purple, $\frac{3}{8}$ in. across, in loose cymes 2 to 4 in. long. *fr.* sub-globose, slightly 5-ribbed (not winged), $\frac{1}{2}$ in. wide before opening to show the scarlet-coated seeds. Japan, Korea. 1895. (B.M. 8639.)

**E. pa'tens.** A synonym of *E. kiautschovicus.*

**E. pen'dulus.*** Small evergreen tree. Shoots glabrous, waxy. *l.* narrowly oval to lanceolate, 2 to 5 in. long, $\frac{3}{4}$ to $1\frac{1}{2}$ in. wide, shining red when young, deeply regularly toothed. *fl.* small, greenish, in cymes $1\frac{1}{2}$ in. long. May. *fr.* $\frac{1}{2}$ in. wide, 4-winged; seed-coat orange. Himalaya. 1850. (F.d.S. 1851, 71 and L.P.F.G. ii. 55, as *E. fimbriatus,* a distinct sp.) Only hardy in the south-west.

**E. phelloma'nus.** Deciduous, glabrous shrub, 6 to 15 ft., shoots conspicuously corky-winged. *l.* oval to obovate, slender-pointed, base cuneate to rounded, shallowly toothed, 2 to $4\frac{1}{2}$ in. long, one-third as broad, strongly net-reined beneath. *fl.* 3 to 7 in cymes less than 1 in. long. *fr.* 4-lobed, rosy red, $\frac{1}{2}$ in. wide; seed-coat deep red. N. and W. China. 1928.

**E. plan'ipes.*** Deciduous glabrous shrub or small tree, 10 to 20 ft., winter buds $\frac{3}{8}$ to $\frac{1}{2}$ in. long, slender-pointed. *l.* obovate, 3 to 5 in. long, toothed, pointed. *fl.* numerous in loose cymes up to 3 in. long. *fr.* rosy red, 5-angled, scarcely winged, conical at the top. Japan. 1895.

**E. radi'cans.** Evergreen, glabrous shrub creeping or climbing 20 ft. or more, shoots minutely warty, rooting. *l.* oval to ovate, shallowly toothed, $\frac{1}{2}$ to $1\frac{1}{4}$ in. long in the creeping state but up to $2\frac{1}{2}$ in. long in the adult or flowering state when the growths become more erect and bushy and have fl. and fr. similar to those of *E. japonica.* Japan. 1863. vars. **Carrier'ei** and **veg'etus** shrubby and fr.-bearing; **colora'tus,** purple in autumn; **min'imus*** (*kewensis*), a dainty close-creeping or climbing form, *l.* ovate, $\frac{1}{4}$ to $\frac{5}{8}$ in. long, pale-veined; **variega'tus** (including **Silver Queen**), *l.* edged white. The affinities of *radicans* and *japonicus* are confusing.

**E. sanguin'eus.** Deciduous, glabrous shrub or small tree up to 20 ft., young shoots reddish. *l.* reddish at first, ovate, oval, or obovate, $1\frac{1}{2}$ to $4\frac{1}{2}$ in. long, half as wide, base broadly cuneate to rounded, slender-pointed. *fl.* purplish, in 3- to 15-fld. cymes up to 4 in. wide. *fr.* red, 4- (rarely 5-) lobed with wings $\frac{1}{3}$ in. wide; lobes indistinct. China. 1900.

**E. Sargentia'nus.** Evergreen, glabrous shrub, 10 or 12 ft. *l.* oval-lanceolate to oblong-obovate, slender-pointed, cuneate, 2 to $4\frac{1}{2}$ in. long, $\frac{3}{4}$ to $1\frac{1}{2}$ in. wide. *fl.* in 3 or 4 times divided cymes. *fr.* $\frac{5}{8}$ in. long, pear-shaped, 4-angled, yellowish, on a slender stalk up to 2 in. long. W. China. 1908.

**E. Semeno'vii.** Small shrub related to *E. europaeus*. *l.* lanceolate, up to 1¾ in. long, toothed. *infl.* usually 3-fld. Turkestan. 1910.

**E. semipersis'tens.** Close to *E. Bungeanus* but *l.* half-evergreen, elliptic, hanging until severe frost occurs. *fr.* turbinate, pink, not freely produced. China.

**E. subtriflo'rus.** A synonym of *E. alatus apterus*.

**E. ting'ens.** Evergreen, glabrous shrub or small tree 20 to 25 ft., shoots angled. *l.* narrowly oval to lanceolate, tapered to both ends, 1½ to 3 in. long, ⅝ to 1¼ in. wide, dark glossy green. *fl.* ½ in. across in branched cymes 1 to 1½ in. wide, creamy-white marbled or veined with deep purple. May. *fr.* ½ to ⅝ in. wide, 4- or 5-angled, deep pink; seed-coat scarlet. Himalaya, W. China. 1849.

**E. ussurien'sis.** A synonym of *E. macropterus*.

**E. verruco'sus.** Warted Spindle tree. Deciduous shrub, 6 to 8 ft., shoots densely covered with conspicuous warts. *l.* ovate to ovate-lanceolate, 1 to 2½ in. long, ½ to 1 in. wide, finely toothed, slender-pointed. *fl.* purplish-brown, ¼ in. wide, usually 3 on a cyme. *fr.* deeply 4-lobed, ½ in. across, yellowish. E. Europe, W. Asia. 1763.

**E. Wil'sonii.** Evergreen shrub up to 20 ft., of scandent habit. *l.* 3 to 6 in. long, one-third as wide, slender-pointed, cuneate, shallowly toothed, conspicuously veined beneath; stalk ¼ to ½ in. long. *fl.* yellowish-green, numerous in loose cymes 2 to 3 in. across. *fr.* 4-lobed, set with awl-shaped spines ⅕ in. long; seed-coat yellow. W. China. 1904. (G.C. 72 (1922), 49.)

**E. yedoen'sis.*** Deciduous small tree, 10 ft. or more. *l.* obovate to oval, tapered to both ends, 2 to 5 in. long, 1½ to 3 in. wide, glabrous, minutely toothed, strongly veined beneath. *fl.* ½ in. wide, numerous in cymes up to 1 in. long. *fr.* deeply 4-lobed, ½ in. wide, pale pink, seed-coat orange. Japan. 1865. (S.T.S. i. 62.) Autumn foliage brilliant red.

W. J. B.

**EUO'SMA albiflo'ra.** A synonym of *Logania floribunda*.

**EUPATO'RIUM** (name used by Pliny and Dioscorides; from Mithridates Eupator, king of Pontus, who found one species to be an antidote against poison). FAM. *Compositae*. A genus of over 400 species of herbs and shrubs, mostly American, but represented also in the Old World. Leaves usually opposite, sometimes toothed, rarely deeply cut. Flower-heads purplish, bluish, or white in terminal corymbs; receptacle naked; pappus rough; involucral bracts overlapping, in 2 or 3 series; flowers all tubular, 5-fid. Some, though comparatively few, species are very ornamental. Among them are some useful for the wild garden and for the border, easily grown in ordinary garden soil, and increased by division. *E. atrorubens*, *E. ianthinum*, and *E. macrophyllum*, often called Hebecliniums, need a warm greenhouse (50 to 55° F., drooping if exposed to cold) and make distinct and useful winter-flowering plants, *E. ianthinum* being less vigorous than the other two. They may be raised from cuttings of young shoots made in spring and rooted with heat in a close frame. When rooted the plants should be grown on through the summer without being stopped and will then produce in the following winter a large terminal head of flowers. If pruned back after flowering and repotted each year large bushy plants may be grown in time. The species suited for cool greenhouse cultivation are readily increased by cuttings inserted in spring. *E. micranthum* is somewhat shrubby and may be grown for several years if pruned in a little after flowering. It is useful for greenhouse decoration in early autumn and winter and for cut-flowers. *E. riparium* and *E. glandulosum* carry on the flowering time. They grow rapidly and are best propagated every year. A frame where plenty of air can be admitted is suitable for them during summer and a house where frost is excluded is warm enough in winter. If attempts to grow them in heat are made they become weak and drawn. *E. riparium* is slender and best results are obtained by planting 3 plants in an 8-in. pot, tying the shoots to small stakes. A rich compost of loam, leaf-soil, sand, and dried cow-manure in almost equal parts. Plenty of water is necessary at all seasons and artificial or liquid manure may be used with advantage when the flower-heads appear.

**E. adenoph'orum.** A synonym of *E. macrophyllum*.

**E. ageratoi'des.** Herbaceous, 1 to 4 ft. h., branching. *l.* opposite, ovate or somewhat cordate, coarsely toothed, stalked. *fl.-heads* pure white, numerous; corymbs compound, 12- to 25-fld. Summer. N. America. 1640. Hardy.

**E. aromat'icum.** 3 to 4 ft. h., robust. *l.* opposite, rounded, toothed, stalk usually very short. *fl.-heads* white; corymbs loose, 8- to 20-fld. Late summer. N. America. 1739. Hardy, variable.

**E. atroru'bens.*** *l.* large, opposite, more or less ovate, toothed, covered with reddish hairs. *fl.-heads* reddish with lilac shading, numerous. Autumn, winter. Mexico. 1862. (I.H. 1862, 310 as *Hebeclinium atrorubens*; B.M. 8227 as *E. Raffillii*.) Greenhouse.

**E. cannabi'num.*** Hemp Agrimony. Herbaceous, 2 to 4 ft. h., erect, nearly unbranched, downy. *l.* 3- to 5-foliolate; lflets. lanceolate, toothed. *fl.-heads* reddish-purple in terminal, close coryrmbs. July. Asia, Europe (including Britain). (E.B. 785.) Hardy. var. **ple'num**, *fl.* double. Moist places.

**E. coelesti'num.** Herbaceous perennial, about 30 in. h. Somewhat hairy. *l.* opposite, triangular-ovate, shortly stalked, rather thin, coarsely toothed. *fl.-heads* Ageratum-like in compact clusters, light blue to violet. August, September. E. United States. Hardy.

**E. glandulo'sum.** Sub-shrub, 3 to 6 ft. h., much-branched, clammy, glandular-hairy. *l.* opposite, rather thin, rhomboid-ovate or triangular, up to 9 in. long, smaller above, coarsely toothed. *fl.-heads* numerous, white, in ternately branched corymbose panicles, fragrant, about ½ in. across. Winter, spring. Mexico. 1826. (B.M. 8139; B.R. 1723.) SYN. *E. adenophorum*, *E. trapezoideum*. Greenhouse.

**E. glechonophyl'lum.** Perennial. *l.* opposite, ovate-lanceolate, slender-pointed, toothed, stalk up to 1 in. long. *fl.-heads* pink, in corymbs. Chile. 1831. Greenhouse.

**E. grandiflo'rum.** A synonym of *Brickellia grandiflora*.

**E. ianthi'num.*** 3 ft. h. *l.* large, ovate, deeply toothed, soft. *fl.-heads* purple, in very large terminal corymbs. Winter. Mexico. 1849. (B.M. 4574 as *Hebeclinium ianthinum*.) Warm greenhouse.

**E. japon'icum.** Closely resembling *E. cannabinum* but fl. white. Japan and Formosa. 1889.

**E. Kirilow'ii.** A synonym of *E. Lindleyanum*.

**E. Lasseaux'ii.** A synonym of *Ageratum Lasseauxii*.

**E. Lindleya'num.** Herbaceous, 2 to 3 ft. h., hairy. *l.* in whorls of 4, lanceolate, deeply and irregularly toothed. *fl.-heads* white in numerous corymbs. N. China. (G.F. 850 as *E. Kirilowii*.) Hardy.

**E. macrophyl'lum.*** About 4 ft. h., more robust than *E. ianthinum*. *l.* large, cordate, dark green. *fl.-heads* reddish-lilac, in large corymbs, very freely produced. Autumn, winter. Trop. America. (R.H. 1866, 42 as *Hebeclinium macrophyllum*.) Warm greenhouse.

**E. micran'thum.*** Up to 8 ft. h., but usually less, bushy, evergreen, shoots slender, often purplish. *l.* opposite, elliptic to elliptic-lanceolate, 2 to 4 in. long, faintly toothed towards the point, narrowed to the rather short stalk. *fl.-heads* white, sometimes tinged rose, fragrant, in flattish corymbs up to 8 in. across; peduncles and bracts hairy. September to November. Mexico. 1867. (G.C. 38 (1905), 229.) SYN. *E. Weinmannianum*. Hardy in south-western counties. Greenhouse elsewhere.

**E. petiola're.** A synonym of *E. Purpusii*.

**E. pro'bum.** Clammy hairy perennial with woody base. *l.* opposite, triangular-ovate, ½ to 1½ in. long, acute, rounded or more or less heart-shaped at base, bluntly toothed; stalks ½ to 1 in. long. *fl.-heads* white, about ½ in. across, 2 to 4 on a branch in a flat-topped corymb. Winter. Peru. 1870. (G.C. 7 (1890), 321.) Greenhouse.

**E. purpu'reum.** 3 to 9 ft. h. *l.* 3 to 6 in a whorl, more or almost ovate or lanceolate, slender-pointed, rough, unequally toothed, downy beneath. *fl.-heads* purplish; corymbs with 5 to 9 heads. Autumn. N. America. 1640. Hardy.

**E. Purpu'sii.** Tender herb. Stem weak, branched, sometimes clammy-hairy. *l.* roundish-ovate, heart-shaped at base, narrowed to apex, bluntly, coarsely toothed. *fl.-heads* white, becoming pinkish-lilac, ½ in. across; peduncles slender. California. (G.C. 35 (1904), 163 as *E. petiolare*.)

**E. Raf'fillii.** A synonym of *E. atrorubens*.

**E. ripa'rium.*** *l.* oblong-lanceolate, deeply toothed. *fl.-heads* white, numerous in a terminal panicle of corymbs. April. Mexico. 1867. (G.F. 525.) Greenhouse.

**E. serrula'tum.** Branches terete. *l.* opposite, lingulate-lanceolate, 2½ in. long, ⅓ to ½ in. wide, toothed; stalk short. *fl.-heads* rosy lilac, oblong, many in a corymb. Brazil. 1894. (R.H. 1894, 304.) Greenhouse.

**E. verna'le.** Sub-shrub of about 3 ft., young stems hairy. *l.* opposite, ovate, about 4 in. long, acute, unequally coarsely toothed, more or less cordate at base, shining and with scattered hairs above, white-hairy on veins beneath. *fl.-heads* white, in a loose, more or less pyramidal corymb. February, March. Mexico. (G.F. 1873, 750.)

**E. verticilla'tum.** A synonym of *E. purpureum*.

**E. Weinmannia'num.** A synonym of *E. micranthum*.

*Euphe'miae,* in honour of Euphemia, wife of Professor Morren of Belgium, *c.* 1872.

*euphle'bius -a -um,* well-veined.

**EUPHORB'IA** (name given by Dioscorides to this plant; said by Pliny to have been given in honour of Euphorbus, physician to King Juba of Mauritania). FAM. *Euphorbiaceae.* A very large genus containing probably 1,000 species, differing widely in habit and including annual and perennial herbs, shrubs, and trees, many being succulent. They are widely distributed throughout the world, 12 species being natives of the British Isles. The succulent species mostly occur in Africa, the more interesting species from the collector's point of view being found in S. and SW. Africa. The plants are characterized by a milky latex which exudes freely when they are damaged; it is often poisonous though some kinds are used medicinally by natives. The floral arrangement is characteristic; the flowers are reduced, the male to a single stamen, the female to a long-stalked ovary; these are aggregated together within a series of bracts fused to form an involucre which is surrounded by 2 or more real bracts, the whole inflorescence being called a cyathium. Cyathia may contain both male and female flowers, or they may be unisexual. In most instances the bracts are green or yellow, but in some, e.g. *E. fulgens, E. pulcherrima,* and *E. splendens,* they are brilliantly coloured and the whole inflorescence looks like a single flower. In the herbaceous species the leaves are normal but in the succulent species they may be much reduced or absent, the stem being green and swollen and, in many, armed with spines. The spines of Euphorbias are of two types: (1) they may be the remains of peduncles which have become woody after bearing flowers, or the woody peduncles of cyathia which normally abort, when a sharp tip is developed; (2) pairs of spines are formed which probably represent metamorphosed stipules; these are generally mounted on horny sections of the tubercles known as spine-shields. Horticulturally the herbaceous types are useful in the border or rock-garden where they do well in rather dry places. *E. fulgens* and *E. pulcherrima* (Poinsettia) are useful for greenhouse decoration or for cut flowers; the former wants rather warmer treatment than the latter and both object to sudden changes of temperature. They can be propagated by cuttings taken annually and will strike readily in heat; if single sprays or heads are required for cutting, they can be grown on unstopped; if plants are to be used for decoration they should be stopped to induce a branching habit. They want plenty of light and water when growing, but after flowering should be kept much drier. The soil should be rich, consisting of good loam and old cow-manure.

None of the succulent Euphorbias are hardy but few require high temperatures: 45 to 50° F. in winter is sufficient, but both soil and air must be dry during the resting period. When growing they require a fair amount of water and plenty of light and ventilation. The soil should be well drained, with plenty of coarse sand and broken brick, but not too poor; a good loam should be used and bone-meal may be included. Most of the succulent species can be increased by cuttings which should be dried for a week or two before being put in sand (or sand and peat-moss) in heat; they may take some time to form roots. The lateral branches which arise from central heads, as in *E. Caput-Medusae,* will strike but will continue to grow in length only, without forming the characteristic 'head'. Euphorbias can also be raised from seed but in collections there is always a risk of this being hybridized. If seed is wanted, the capsules should be protected when nearly ripe as they are explosive and the seed may be shot several feet. **A**

**E. abyssin'ica.** Succulent, spiny tree up to 30 ft. h. Stems 5- to 8-angled, jointed, joints 4 to 12 in. long, angles winged, sinuate;

sides very concave with swollen veins; spines in pairs, spreading, short and stout. *fl.* inconspicuous. Abyssinia and Eritrea.

**E. aggrega'ta.** Similar to *E. pulvinata* but smaller; spines modified peduncles, reddish-purple when young. Cape Province.

**E. alcicor'nis.** Spiny, succulent shrub up to 2 ft. h. Stem bluntly 5-angled, angles with small tubercles which later flatten out; spines in pairs, thin, short. *l.* hardly longer than the spines, tapering. Madagascar.

**E. antiquo'rum.** Spiny, succulent shrub up to 10 ft. h. Stem 4- to 5-angled; branches 3-angled, jointed, angles sinuate, sides flat or concave; spines in pairs, small, distant. *fl.* inconspicuous. India. 1688.

**E. antisyphilit'ica.** Spineless, succulent shrub up to 3 ft. h. Stems erect, very slender, cylindrical, leafless, branching from the base. *fl.* small, with 5 white bracts, closely resembling a single fl. Mexico.

**E. aphyl'la.** Low, branching, spineless shrub; branches cylindrical, jointed, curved outwards and upwards, grey-green with round l.-scars. *l.* linear, blunt. *fl.* small. Canary Is.

**E. atropurpu'rea.** Spineless, branching shrub. Stems finger-thick, succulent, becoming woody. *l.* grey-green, up to 2 in. long, covering the young shoots. *fl.* in branched cymes with purple bracts. Teneriffe. (B.M. 3321.)

**E. balsamif'era.** Spineless, branching shrub with bare grey stems and rosettes of small, narrow, lanceolate l. at the apex. *fl.* inconspicuous. Canary Is. 1779.

**E. Beaumieria'na.** Very similar to *E. Echinus* but distinguished by the greater number of angles (9 to 10) of the stem. Morocco.

**E. biglandulo'sa.** Perennial, about 2 ft. h., glaucous, glabrous, with many ascending or erect, simple, leafy stems from a thick rhizome. *l.* thick, lanceolate, acute, sometimes almost spine-tipped. Rays of umbel many, 2-fid, short; involucre sub-globose, lobes ovate, ciliate, glands oblong. February, March. Greece. Larger than *E. Myrsinites.* Hardy.

**E. Boj'eri.** .Similar to *E. splendens* but stems and spines thinner, *l.* smaller, more leathery, grey-green, and floral bracts only half the size. Madagascar. 1836. (B.M. 3527.)

**E. bubali'na.** Succulent shrub up to 3 ft. h., spineless but with persistent woody peduncles. Stem simple or branched, stout; curved grooves from each l.-scar divide the surface into low tubercles. *l.* at the apex, 2 to 3 in. long, ¼ in. wide. *fl.* in long-stalked umbels, bracts green with red edges. Cape Province. 1860. (F.P.S.A. 285.)

**E. bupleurifo'lia.** Spineless, dwarf plant, globose or cylindrical, 2 to 3 in. across, tuberculate, rarely branched; tubercles prominent, spirally arranged, with a l.-scar at the apex. *l.* deciduous, in a tuft at the top, spatulate-lanceolate, 2 to 3 in. long. *fl.* pale green, on long peduncles. Cape Province. 1791. (B.M. 3476; F.P.S.A. 650.)

**E. canalicula'ta.** A synonym of *Pedilanthus tithymaloides.*

**E. canarien'sis.** Spiny, succulent shrub up to 18 ft. h. Branches chiefly from base, erect, 5- (or 4-)angled, flat-sided; spines in pairs, small, spreading. *fl.* small, yellow. Canary Is. 1697. (DC. Pl. Gr. 140.)

**E. Caput-Medu'sae.** Dwarf, spineless, succulent. Main stem globose, partly buried, bearing except in the central area, a large number of erect, clavate, tuberculate branches up to 8 to 12 in. h. (longer if not given a sunny position). *l.* very small, soon deciduous. *fl.* small, solitary, almost sessile. Cape Province. (B.M. 8673; DC. Pl. Gr. 150.)

**E. cereiform'is.** Unisexual, spiny, succulent shrub. Branches from base and above, erect, with 9 to 15 angles formed by small, tooth-like tubercles. Spines modified sterile peduncles. *fl.* inconspicuous. 1731. Common in cultivation but now unknown wild.

**E. clandesti'na.** Spineless, dwarf, succulent; rarely branched. Stem up to 2 ft. h., cylindrical, covered with spirally arranged prominent tubercles. *l.* linear, 2 to 3 in. long, very narrow, fleshy, on the upper part of the stem. *fl.* inconspicuous, sessile. Cape Province.

**E. cla'va.** Spineless, succulent shrub up to 3 ft. h. Main stem clavate, cylindrical, with spirally arranged tubercles. *l.* towards the apex, linear, long, deciduous. *fl.* solitary on long peduncles which persist but do not form spines. Cape Province. 1700.

**E. coerules'cens.** Spiny, succulent shrub, branching from the base and spreading by rhizomes; branches 4- to 5-angled, markedly constricted. Spines in pairs, spine-shields forming a conspicuous horny edge; young growth glaucous blue. *fl.* canary yellow, small, numerous. Cape Province. 1823. Used as fodder.

**E. Cyparis'sias.** Cypress Spurge. Perennial herb with slender stems up to 1 ft. h. *l.* linear, crowded. *fl.* small, greenish-yellow. Europe. (E.B. 1262.) Hardy. Spreads by underground shoots; rather invasive.

**E. Echi'nus.** Succulent, spiny shrub. Stems 6-angled, flat between angles, bright green with paler markings; angles almost straight. Spines in pairs, ¼ in. long, close together, red turning grey. *fl.* inconspicuous. S. Morocco.

**E. ellip'tica.** A synonym of *E. silenifolia.*

**E. enneag'ona.** Probably a synonym of *E. heptagona*.

**E. enop'la.** Unisexual, spiny, succulent shrub, up to 3 ft. h. Branches at base and above, 6- to 7-angled, glaucous green, purple at apex; angles straight, scarcely tuberculate. Spines modified peduncles, very numerous, straight or curved, ascending, dark red, later black. *fl.* small, clustered at the tops of the branches. Cape Province.

*Euphorbia epithymoides*

**E. epithymoi'des.** Perennial herb. Stems 1 ft. h., forming a hemispherical clump. *l.* narrow, oblong, dark green. *fl.* surrounded by yellow l. Europe. (B.M. 2258.) Syn. *E. polychroma*. Hardy.

**E. esculen'ta.** Very similar in habit to *E. inermis*. Cape Province. (F.P.S.A. 209.)

**E. fe'rox.** Habit of *E. aggregata* and *E. pulvinata*, but forming less regular cushions; spines more strongly developed, sometimes curved. Cape Province.

**E. Fournier'i.** Shrub. Stem slightly angular; branches in whorls. *l.* roundish, ovate, 1 ft. long, green, with whitish veins and red petioles. *fl.* white, small. Madagascar. Not truly succulent but young plants have a fleshy, 5-angled stem.

**E. ful'gens.*** Leafy shrub with slender branches. *fl.* in small clusters along the branches, conspicuous by their scarlet bracts. Mexico. 1836. Syn. *E. jacquinaeflora*. (B.M. 3673.) Used as decorative plants or as cut flowers. Warm house.

**E. globo'sa.** Spineless, dwarf, succulent plant consisting of a top-shaped main stem and globose or sub-globose, tuberculate branches produced irregularly; fl. branches clavate. *fl.* shortly pedunculate and then bisexual, or with long, branched peduncles and then usually male. Cape Province. 1820. (B.M. 2624; F.P.S.A. 647.)

**E. gor'gonis.** Very similar to *E. pugniformis* and sometimes combined with it but branches stouter and more rigid, main stem usually smaller and more deeply embedded in soil. Cape Province.

**E. grandicor'nis.** Spiny, succulent shrub up to 3 ft. Branches from ground, deeply constricted into short segs., 3-angled, angles wing-like, wavy; spine-shields united into a continuous, grey, horny margin; spines in pairs, divergent, up to 3 in. long. *fl.* small, yellow. *fr.* red. Zululand. 1876. (F.P.S.A. 642.)

**E. gran'didens.** Spiny, succulent tree up to 40 ft. h., with cylindrical main trunk. Secondary branches in whorls near upper ends, 3-angled, angles rather deeply sinuate, tuberculate; spines in pairs up to 1 in. long. *fl.* small, yellowish-green. Cape Province. 1820.

**E. heptag'ona.** Unisexual, spiny, succulent shrub up to 3 ft. h., freely branched; 7- to 10-angled, angles slightly tuberculate, divided by broad, triangular grooves. Spines modified sterile peduncles, brown, up to 1 in. long. *fl.* inconspicuous. Cape Province. 1731. (F.P.S.A. 390.)

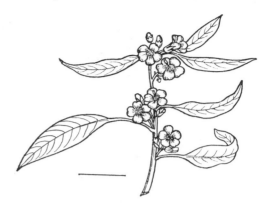

*Euphorbia fulgens*

**E. Hermentia'na.** Succulent, spiny shrub or tree with erect branches. Stem 3- to 4-angled, constricted; angles compressed, sides concave, green, with whitish lines running from margin. Similar to *E. lactea* but branches wider, angles almost wing-like, tubercles close. W. Africa.

**E. heterophyl'la.** Annual up to 3 ft. h. *l.* ovate or panduriform, dark green, sometimes variegated, petiolate. *fl.* small, surrounded by bracts scarlet at the base. July to Spetember. N. and S. America. 1889. Hardy.

**E. hor'rida.** Similar to *E. polygona* but the pedunculate spines more numerous, sometimes several from one flowering eye. Cape Province.

**E. iner'mis.** Dwarf, spineless, succulent plant with tuberous roots; main stem distinct, low, broad, tuberculate with 2 to 3 series of ascending, tuberculate branches round the crown. *l.* very small, soon deciduous. *fl.* inconspicuous. Cape Province. (B.M. 1494.) Syn. *E. serpentina*, *E. viperina*. Branches become long and weak under damp, shady conditions.

**E. in'gens.** Spiny, succulent tree up to 30 ft. Trunk branching and rebranching, branches erect, all attaining the same general level. Trunk 3- (to 4-)angled; fl. branches 4-angled, constricted into segs.; angles wing-like; crenate, spines in pairs, small or absent. *fl.* small, numerous. Natal. (F.P.S.A. 522.)

**E. jacquinaeflo'ra.** A synonym of *E. fulgens*.

**E. lac'tea.** Spiny, succulent shrub or tree. Stem 3- to 4-angled, angles sinuate, sides flat, dark green with milk-white lines running from depressions in angles to centre; spines short, thick. India. Often confused with *E. Hermentiana*.

**E. Lath'yrus.*** Caper Spurge. Annual or biennial. Stem 3 ft. h. *l.* linear, 3 to 4 in. long. *fl.* in small, long-stalked umbels; bracts large, green. Europe. Hardy.

**E. Ledien'ii.** Closely allied to *E. coerulescens* but fl. more freely produced, stem taller and more slender, constrictions less distinct, spines less stout. Cape Province. 1866. (B.M. 8275.) Probably poisonous, not used as fodder.

**E. ligno'sa.** Dwarf, spiny shrub, branching freely to form a hemispherical clump up to 3 ft. across. Branches succulent when young, becoming woody with sharp tips. *fl.* sessile, not often produced in cultivation. SW. Africa.

**E. mammilla'ris.** Unisexual, dwarf, succulent. Main stem about 8 in. h. (or more in cultivation), branching freely. Stems cylindrical, 7- to 17-angled, angles tuberculately tessellated. Spines consisting of persistent peduncles, in whorled bands up the stem. *fl.* numerous, at top of stem, small, on peduncles ¾ in. long. Cape Province. 1759.

**E. margina'ta.*** Annual up to 2 ft. h., much branched. *l.* ovate or oblong, 1 to 3 in. long, the upper ones white-margined or entirely white. *fl.* with large white bracts. September. N. America. 1811. (B.M. 1747.) Hardy. Used as button-hole plant; long lasting.

**E. melofor'mis.** Unisexual, dwarf, spineless, succulent plant. Tap-root long; main stem sub-globose, depressed, usually 8-angled, angles prominent, tubercles not much raised; glossy green, sometimes banded lighter green or purple. In age producing similar branches from base. *fl.* very small on long-branched, persistent peduncles. Cape Province. 1774. (DC. Pl. Gr. 139.)

**E. micran'tha.** Similar to *E. squarrosa* but with 4-angled stems and very slender spines. Cape Province.

**E. Montei'ri.** Succulent, spineless shrub. Stem up to 15 or more in. h., 2 in. thick, simple, tuberculate. *l.* long and narrow, glaucous green, produced up the first few inches of the flowering branches. *fl.* in long-peduncled, umbel-like cymes, bracts green. Angola. (B.M. 5534; F.P.S.A. 218.)

**E. Muir'ii.** Dwarf, succulent plant with main stem buried in ground and tuberculate branches produced from below ground-level; secondary branches more or less in whorls. *l.* very small. Cape Province. (F.P.S.A. 528.)

**E. mul'ticeps.** Dwarf, spiny, succulent plant with a cone-shaped, fleshy, main stem bearing tuberculate branches decreasing in size upwards, clavate, so close that only upper ends are visible. Spines modified sterile peduncles. *fl.* inconspicuous. Cape Province. 1905.

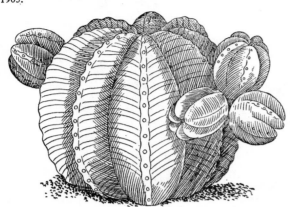

*Euphorbia meloformis* (p. 795)

**E. Myrsini'tes.** Perennial herb. *l.* fleshy, sessile, concave, light glaucous green in close spirals along the prostrate stems. *fl.* yellow. S. Europe. Hardy.

**E. neriifo'lia.** Spineless, succulent tree up to 20 ft. h. Stem 5-angled, later round; branches in whorls with spirally arranged tubercles. *l.* large, up to 6 in. long, obovate, narrowing to a short petiole, leathery, pale green, deciduous. India. 1690. (DC. Pl. Gr. 46.)

**E. obe'sa.** Unisexual, spineless, dwarf, succulent. Stem un-branched, globose or short cylindrical, up to 8 in. h., 3½ in. thick, usually 8-angled, angles not prominent except at apex, flattened towards base, minutely tuberculate; surface faintly grooved, grey-green with numerous, dull purple, transverse lines. *l.* rudimentary, soon deciduous. *fl.* very small. Cape Province. (B.M. 7888; F.P.S.A. 788.)

**E. officina'rum.** Spiny, succulent shrub with 9- to 13- (generally 11-)angled stem; angles straight with grey, horny edge. Spines short, unequal in length, pointing downwards. *fl.* inconspicuous. N. Africa. (DC. Pl. Gr. 77.)

**E. ornitho'pus.** Similar to *E. tridentata* but differing by the cyathia in cymes. Cape Province. The very prominent, finger-like glands resemble a bird's foot.

**E. pas'sa.** A synonym of *E. Woodii.*

**E. pilo'sa.** Perennial. Stems 18 in. h., from a thick rootstock, pilose. *l.* oblong. Europe and N. Asia. Hardy. var. **ma'jor,** *l.* golden yellow.

**E. polyceph'ala.** Spineless, dwarf, succulent plant, main stem a continuation of the tuberous root. Branches very short, closely packed, forming a slightly convex, cushion-like mass. *fl.* in-conspicuous. Cape Province.

**E. polychro'ma.** A synonym of *E. epithymoides.*

**E. polyg'ona.** Unisexual, succulent shrub, spiny or sometimes spineless, branching freely and irregularly from the base. Stems stout, 7-angled when young, up to 20-angled later; angles very prominent, wavy, with deep grooves between; spines pedunculate, more robust and numerous on male plants. *fl.* dull purple. Cape Province. 1790. (F.P.S.A. 645.) This and *E. horrida* are the only natural hosts of the red-berried Misletoe, *Viscum minimum.*

**E. procum'bens.** Name should be discarded. Plants so called are usually *E. Woodii* or *E. pugniformis.*

**E. pseudocac'tus.** Spiny, succulent shrub. Main stem mostly buried in the ground, producing many semi-erect branches, forming clumps up to 3 ft. h. Branches 4- or 5-angled, irregularly constricted into segs.; angles tuberculate, spines in pairs, spine-shields united to form a horny edge; stems dark green, usually with yellowish V-shaped markings. *fl.* small, yellow. Natal. (F.P.S.A. 778.)

**E. pteroneu'ra.** Spineless, succulent shrub. Stems as thick as a pencil, with 5 to 6 angles formed by low ridges decurrent from the l. bases. *l.* with short petioles, oblanceolate, blunt, 1 to 2 in. long, soon deciduous. *fl.* numerous. Habitat? Perhaps Mexico.

**E. pugniform'is.** Spineless, dwarf, succulent plant consisting of a short, much-thickened, tuberculate main stem, depressed in centre; from the shoulders arise in 2 or 3 series short, stout, tuberculate branches, spreading, ascending, crowned with very small deciduous l. *fl.* inconspicuous. Cape Province.

**E. pulcher'rima.** Poinsettia. Deciduous shrub, 2 to 10 ft. h., branched. *l.* ovate-elliptical to lanceolate, entire, toothed or lobed. *fl.* yellow, bracts vermilion. Mexico. 1834. (B.M. 3493 as *Poinsettia pulcherrima.*) var. **al'ba,** bracts white, not so vigorous; **plenis'sima,** bracts in double series, vermilion. Used as decorative plants or as cut flowers. Warm house.

**E. pulvina'ta.** Unisexual, spiny, dwarf, succulent plant forming a dense, cushion-like mass, up to 5 ft. across. Stems globose, later cylindrical, 7- to 10-angled, angles acute, crenate, tuberculate. *l.* rudimentary, deciduous. *fl.* inconspicuous; peduncles persisting as spines. Cape Province.

**E. Re'gis-Jubae.** Spineless, branching shrub or small tree. *l.* linear, shorter than peduncles. *fl.* in a branched cyme. Canary Is.

**E. serpenti'na.** A synonym of *E. inermis.*

**E. silenifo'lia.** Unisexual, spineless, succulent, with a long tuberous root and very short stem. *l.* lanceolate, petiolate, a number produced annually, falling in dry season. *fl.* in pedunculate umbels. Cape Province. Syn. *E. elliptica,* a well-known name but not the earliest.

**E. Sipolos'i.** Spineless, succulent shrub with erect, leafless, jointed branches. Joints sharply 4-angled, about 4 in. long, with concave sides, grey-green with reddish angles. *fl.* small, terminal or lateral. Brazil. 1892.

*Euphorbia splendens*

**E. splen'dens.\*** Crown of Thorns. Spiny, succulent shrub up to 3 ft. h. Stems brown, irregularly branched, with long, straight, tapering spines. *l.* few, chiefly at tips of branches, obovate, narrowing to short stalk, thin, bright green. *fl.* in branching cymes with clammy red peduncles, the pair of bracts round, scarlet. Madagascar. 1828. (B.M. 2902.) Warm house.            **A**

**E. squarro'sa.** Similar to *E. stellata* but stouter, branches less prostrate, 3-angled, without variegated markings and with tubercles more prominent. Cape Province. 1823. (F.P.S.A. 789.)

**E. stellaespi'na.** Unisexual, spiny, succulent, up to 20 in. h., branching from base. Stems 10- to 16-angled, with deep grooves between angles. Spines modified fertile peduncles, stout, forming a whorl of 3 to 5 sharp spine branches at apex. *l.* rudimentary, deciduous. *fl.* inconspicuous. Cape Province. 1822. (F.P.S.A. 344.)

**E. stella'ta.** Dwarf, spiny, succulent, with large tuberous stem buried in ground except the apex from which radiate prostrate branches up to 6 in. long, with 2 spine-bearing angles; convex above, concave below, green variegated with white on upper side. Spines in pairs from tubercles along angles. *fl.* yellow, very small. Cape Province. 1794.

**E. Susan'nae.** Unisexual, dwarf, spineless, succulent. Main stem with a long tap-root. Branches from base make a close ring round the main stem. Stems angled, with elongated triangular tubercles. *l.* rudimentary, deciduous. Cape Province.

**E. tetrag'ona.** Spiny, succulent tree up to 40 ft. h. Main stem slightly 6- to 8-angled; branches usually in whorls at upper ends, 4- to 5-angled, with concave or flat sides; angles slightly tubercled; spines in pairs, small, divergent. *fl.* inconspicuous. Cape Province. 1823.

**E. Tirucal'li.** Unisexual, spineless, succulent tree, up to 30 ft. h. Ultimate branches in brush-like masses, slender, round, pale green. *l.* small, soon falling. *fl.* clustered at tips of branches, small. Trop. and S. Africa. 1690. Very early introduced into India where it was first described from cultivated plants.

**E. tridenta'ta.** Dwarf, spineless, succulent. Main stem a continuation of the tuberous root, producing rhizomes below ground; branching at base. Branches cylindrical, tuberculate. *l.* small, soon deciduous. *fl.* small, conspicuous by the white, finger-like glands. Cape Province. (DC. Pl. Gr. 144; F.P.S.A. 197.)

**E. val'ida.** Closely resembling *E. meloformis* and by some considered a natural hybrid between that and *E. obesa*, but the species do not occur in the same districts. *E. valida* has surface markings like *E. obesa* but long, persistent peduncles like *E. meloformis*; it rarely branches. Cape Province. (F.P.S.A. 526, 527.)

**E. variega'ta.** A synonym of *E. marginata*.

**E. viperi'na.** A synonym of *E. inermis*. (B.M. 7971.)

**E. viro'sa.** Spiny, succulent shrub up to 5 ft. h. Main stem partly buried in ground, bearing a large number of ascending branches, 5- to 8-angled, constricted at irregular intervals; angles tubercled, spines in pairs, spine-shields united into continuous horny bands. *fl.* inconspicuous. Cape Province.

**E. Wilman'ae.** Spineless, dwarf, succulent plant, mostly subterranean; stems above ground only a few in. h., stumpy, clavate, tubercles. Cape Province.

**E. Wood'ii.** For long confused with *E. pugniformis*, both being known as *E. procumbens*. *E. Woodii* is larger than *E. pugniformis*, more closely resembling *E. Caput-Medusae*. Natal. 1862. (F.P.S.A. 723.)

**E. Wulfen'ii.** Perennial. Stems up to 4 ft. h., forming a clump densely covered with linear, bluish-green, hairy *l.* *fl.* surrounded by yellow bracts. Europe. Hardy.

**E. xylophylloi'des.** Spineless, succulent shrub or tree with round stems up to 6 ft. h.; branches in irregular whorls, compressed, 2-angled, tapering at each end, with small roundish *l.* which soon fall. Madagascar.

V. H.

## EUPHORBIA'CEAE.
Dicotyledons. A family of over 210 genera with about 4,500 species of shrubs or herbs, often with milky juice, found in all but Arctic climates. Leaves opposite or alternate, simple, often stipulate. Flowers 1-sexual, bracteate or involucrate; sepals and petals usually free, or latter or more rarely both, absent; staminate flowers with 1 to many stamens; pistillate with hypogynous disk, ovary usually 3-celled (rarely 1- or 2- or 4- to 20-celled), ovules 1 or 2 in each cell. Fruit usually a 3-celled dehiscent capsule, rarely berry- or drupe-like. The genera dealt with here are Acalypha, Alchornea, Aleurites, Andrachne, Breynia, Cluytia, Codiaeum, Croton, Dalechampia, Daphniphyllum, Euphorbia, Fluggia, Hevea, Himalanthus, Hippomane, Hura, Jatropha, Macaranga, Mallotus, Manihot, Omphalia, Phyllanthus, Poranthera, Ricinus, Sapium, Securingea, Synadenium, Toxicodendron.

## EUPHO'RIA (*eu*, well, *phora*, carrying; the fruit carries well).
FAM. *Sapindaceae*. A genus of about 6 species of trees, natives of S. Asia allied to Litchi but with petals and a deeply lobed 5-partite imbricate calyx. Leaves pinnate. Flowers regular; petals spatulate or lanceolate, hairy within; stamens usually 8. Fruit globose or elliptic, more or less warted, about 1 in. across. Stove plants needing good well-drained turfy loam, and occasional watering with liquid manure. Propagated by seed or by cuttings of half-ripe wood.

**E. Longan'a.** Longyen. Linkeng. Evergreen tree, 30 to 40 ft. h. *l.* alternate; lflets. in 2 to 5 pairs, rather obtuse at both ends, up to 12 in. long, entire. *fl.* white, about ¼ in. across, in terminal or axillary panicles. May. *fr.* globose, almost smooth, yellowish-brown; pulp (the aril) white, sweet, sub-acid. India. 1786. (B.M. 4096; B.R. 1729.) SYN. *Nephelium Longana*.

## EUPHRA'SIA (*euphraino*, to cheer; supposed to cure blindness).
FAM. *Scrophulariaceae*. A large genus of semi-parasitic dwarf herbs widely distributed, usually growing among grasses to the roots of which they are attached. Leaves opposite, toothed or more or less deeply cut. Flowers small, white, yellow, or purple in dense, 1-sided or interrupted spikes; 2-lipped, upper lip broad, spreading, lower spreading, 3-lobed. Of little horticultural value. Seeds should be sown among thin grass and in a moist, but not marshy, soil.

**E. lu'tea.** Annual, downy. *l.* linear-lanceolate, lower only remotely toothed. *fl.* golden yellow, downy, cor. ciliate; stamens longer than cor., anthers glabrous, free. On limestone. Europe. A variety is known with lemon fl.

**E. monta'na.** Annual. Dwarf form of *E. officinalis*.

**E. officina'lis.** Eyebright. Annual, 1 to 10 in. h. Stems wiry, erect, branched. *fl.* very small, white or lilac, purple-veined, mid-lobe yellow. May to September. Very variable. N. parts of Old World, including Britain. (E.B. 991.)

*euphrat'icus -a -um,* of the R. Euphrates.

*euphu'es,* well grown.

*eupo'dus -a -um,* long-stalked.

## EUPOMAT'IA (*eu*, well, *poma*, a lid; in allusion to the conical lid which covers the flower-bud).
FAM. *Annonaceae*. Two species of evergreen shrubs or small trees natives of Australia and New Guinea. Leaves alternate, entire; flowers solitary, terminal or lateral (not truly axillary). The chief feature of the flower is made by numerous petal-like imperfect stamens (staminodes) which come between the anther-bearing stamens and the stigma so that fertilization has to be effected by insect agency. Cool greenhouse plants. Compost sandy peat and fibrous loam.

**E. Bennet'tii.*** Glabrous evergreen shrub, 1 to 4 ft. h. *l.* oblanceolate, 3 to 5 in. long, ¾ in to 1½ in. wide, pointed, cuneate. *fl.* solitary, 1 to 1½ in. wide, terminal on a short stalk. Staminodes pet.-like, yellow very numerous and arranged in many series, outer stained with orange or blood-red. *fr.* ¾ in. across, succulent. Queensland. (B.M. 4848 as *E. laurina*.)

**E. lauri'na.** Evergreen glabrous shrub or tree up to 15 ft. h. *l.* dark glossy green, oval-oblong, often inclined to narrowly obovate, 3 to 6 in. long, 1 to 2 in. wide. *fl.* solitary, nearly axillary, shortly stalked, 1 in. across, buds purplish, the pet.-like staminodes numerous, greenish-yellow. Queensland, New S. Wales. 1824. An American expedition to New Guinea (1925–6) found a Eupomatia there which is probably a form of this species, but its largest *l.* are 9 by 3 in. and its fl. are described as white.

W. J. B.

*eupris'tus -a -um,* comely.

## EUPRITCHARD'IA (*eu*, handsome, *Pritchardia*, in honour of W. T. Pritchard, author of *Polynesian Reminiscences*).
FAM. *Palmaceae*. SYN. *Pritchardia*. A genus of about 6 species of unarmed Palms, natives of the Friendly and Sandwich Islands. Leaves large, in a terminal crown, often white furfuraceous, orbicular or wedge-shaped at base, not deeply plicate-multifid; segments narrow, 2-fid at tip, induplicate; petioles concave; sheaths short. Flowers rather large, hermaphrodite, calyx and corolla 3-partite, stamens 6; spathe large, affixed to peduncle, often silvery-furfuraceous; spadices long-pedunculate, about 3 ft. long, branchlets ascending. These ornamental Palms need stove treatment with a compost of 2 parts peat and 1 of loam and sand. They need plentiful water-supply. Propagation by seeds. A

**E. Gaudichau'dii.** Trunk low. *l.* roundish-flabellate, wedge-shaped at base, rachis extended near middle, plicate, divided about one-third down into about 20 linear-lanceolate segs., 2-fid at tips, leathery-membranous; scaly beneath, about 12-nerved; petiole quite smooth. Sandwich Is. 1879. (I.H. 352 as *Pritchardia macrocarpa*.)

**E. Mart'ii.** Smaller than *E. Gaudichaudii*. *l.* dark-green, flabelliform, plicate; petioles smooth, unarmed, enclosed at base in a few rough, brown fibres. *Seeds* very small. Sandwich Is.

**E. pacif'ica.*** About 10 ft. h. *l.* rich dark green, large, flabelliform, palmatisect, plicate, covered with white down when young; petioles covered with white scaly tomentum, flat above, rounded below, enclosed at base in a few coarse brown fibres, quite unarmed. Pacific Is. 1870. (F.d.S. 2262–3, I.H. 161.)

**E. Thurston'ii.*** Tall. *l.* flabelliform, palmatisect, large, in a dense crown. *fl.* in compact panicles at tips of slender stems; stems longer than *l.*, growing from *l.*-axils. Fiji. (G.F. 1887, 486–9.)

## EUPTE'LEA (*eu*, handsome, *ptelea*, elm; referring to the fruit).
FAM. *Trochodendraceae*. A genus of 3 species of slender deciduous trees or shrubs in E. Asia. Buds large, dark shining brown. Leaves alternate, conspicuously toothed, long-stalked. Flowers without sepals or petals

in clusters along shoots before the leaves; stamens many with red anthers; carpels many developing into 1- to 4-seeded, stalked, winged, wedge-shaped samaras. Foliage reddish at first and colouring well to yellow and red in autumn. Propagated by layers or seed. Soil as for Magnolias.

**E. Davidia'na.** A synonym of *E. Franchetii* and *E. pleiosperma.*

**E. Franchet'ii.** Tree up to 40 ft. h., branches greyish-brown. *l.* roundish-ovate, 2 to 4 in. long, abruptly slender-pointed, slightly hairy beneath, stalk up to 2 in. long. *Samara* 1- to 3-seeded. Cent. China. 1896. Syn. *E. Davidiana.*

**E. pleiosper'ma.** *l.* glaucous beneath, *fr.* larger, otherwise very similar to *E. Franchetii.* W. China, Himalaya. Syn. *E. Davidiana.*

**E. polyan'dra.** Similar to *E. Franchetii* but with branches reddish-brown, *l.* broadly ovate, 3 to 6 in. long with teeth more irregular, slightly hairy on veins beneath, and with carpels 1-seeded on stalks ultimately about ½ in. long. Japan. 1877.

**A→**

***europae'us -a -um,*** European.

**EURO'TIA** (from *euros*, mould; in reference to the grey-white downy character). Fam. *Chenopodiaceae.* A genus of 4 species natives of Cent. Asia, S. Europe, and N. America. Perennial herbs or low shrubs. Leaves alternate, entire, narrow. Flowers unisexual; males with a 4-parted perianth and 4 exserted stamens; females without a perianth but coming in the axils of a pair of united silky-hairy brackets; styles 2. Their only garden merit is in the white foliage. They need a sunny spot and are best in a light soil.

**E. ceratoi'des.** Deciduous shrub, 3 or 4 ft. h., more in width, grey-white with starry down at first. *l.* ¾ to 2 in. long, ¼ to ½ in. wide, downy especially beneath. *fl.* packed in spikes ½ to 1½ in. long terminating short twigs and forming collectively a panicle 1 to 2 ft. long; males grey and very woolly, anthers yellow; females axillary, scarcely visible. July. Caucasus to China. 1780.

**E. lana'ta.** Erect shrub, up to 3 ft. h., grey-white with starry down. *l.* linear to linear-lanceolate, rather lavender-like, ½ to 2 in. long, ⅛ to ⅓ in. wide, margins recurved. *fl.* densely packed in axillary heads 1 in. wide, forming terminal leafy spikes. June, July. Differs from *E. ceratoides* by the revolute-margined l. which retain their whiteness. NW. America, in dry regions. 1894. (B.B. ed. 2, 20.)

W. J. B.

***eury-,*** in compound words, signifying broad.

**EU'RYA** (origin uncertain). Fam. *Theaceae.* A genus of about 50 species of evergreen, unisexual trees and shrubs, natives of E. Asia. Leaves short-stalked, alternate. Sepals and petals 5; stamens numerous, shorter than the petals. Fruit a many-seeded berry. Easily propagated by cuttings in gentle heat.

This genus is very much confused in gardens with Cleyera; they differ botanically as follows: *Eurya*, petals united at the base, anthers glabrous. *Cleyera*, petals free or scarcely united, anthers hairy.

**E. japon'ica.** Glabrous evergreen, varying from a small, neat shrub to a tree of 30 ft. *l.* 1½ to 3 in. long, oval or obovate, toothed, apex tapered but blunt, base cuneate, glossy dark green, rather leathery; stalk very short. *fl.* 1 to 3, axillary, white, ⅛ in. wide. *fr.* globose, black, ⅙ in. wide. Japan, Korea, &c. By some authorities its habitat is extended to India, Ceylon, and Fiji. The dwarf form grown in Britain is quite hardy, but it has been 7 ft. h. in Ireland. Syn. *E. pusilla, E. Sieboldii.* var. **variega'ta,** a synonym of *Cleyera Fortunei.*

**E. latifo'lia variega'ta.** A synonym of *E. japonica variegata.*

**E. ochna'cea.** A synonym of *Cleyera ochnacea.*

**EURYA'LE** (*Euryale*, one of the mythological Gorgons, is represented with fierce thorny locks; the plant is thorny). Fam. *Nymphaeaceae.* A genus of a single species of large annual aquatic herb, second only in size to *Victoria regia.* Leaves circular, about 2 ft. across, veins prominent, spiny, rich purple beneath, upper surface, olive-green, puckered, spiny. Fruit a berry 2 to 4 in. across; seeds varying from the size of a Cherry to that of a Pea, much eaten in India when roasted. Treatment as for the stove species of Nymphaea. The seeds ripen on the plant and germinate at once unless kept dry.

**E. fe'rox.** *l.* large, peltate, spiny. *fl.* deep violet; peduncles and cal. covered with stiff prickles. September. E. Indies. 1809. (B.M. 1447.)

**EURYB'IA.** Included in **Olearia.**

**EURYCENT'RUM.** *See* **Anoectochilus.**

**EURYCHO'NE.** Included in **Angraecum.**

**EURYC'LES** (*eurys*, broad, *kleio*, close up; the cup is often imperfect). Fam. *Amaryllidaceae.* A genus of 2 species of plants with tunicated bulbs, closely related to Pancratium. Leaves broad, stalked, with lax, arching veins. Flowers white, many in an umbel, stamens inserted at throat of tube, shorter than the nearly equal, ascending segments; filaments margined in lower half, united into a more or less distinct cup. *E. sylvestris* needs stove treatment, *E. Cunninghamii* will grow well in a warm greenhouse. When growth is completed the plants should not be watered for a few weeks so that the bulbs may rest and ripen.

**E. amboinen'sis.** A synonym of *E. sylvestris.*

**E. Cunningham'ii.*** Brisbane Lily. About 1 ft. h. *l.* ovate. *fl.* less crowded in the umbel than in *E. sylvestris*; stigma 3-lobed; corona two-thirds as long as perianth lobes. Queensland. (B.M. 3399.)

**E. sylves'tris.** 1 to 2 ft. h. *l.* very broad, cordate. *fl.* in a many-fld. umbel; scape stout; perianth tube cylindric, segs. equal; stigma simple; corona not one-quarter as long as perianth lobes. March. Amboina. 1759. (B.M. 1419 as *Pancratium amboinense.*) Syn. *E. amboinensis, E. australasica, Pancratium australasicum.*

**EURYGAN'IA** (from the wife of Oedipus). Fam. *Ericaceae.* A genus of about 12 species of evergreen shrubs with pendent branches, natives of the S. American Andes. Leaves alternate, thickly leathery, persistent, entire or almost so; short-stalked. Flowers rather large, in axillary racemes or corymbs, rarely solitary, nodding or pendulous; calyx 5-lobed or -toothed; corolla tubular or conical-tubular, 5-lobed. Cultivation of these ornamental greenhouse plants as for Thibaudia to which they are allied.

**E. ova'ta.** Stem stout, branches long, rambling, cylindric, green. *l.* ovate, acute, toothed, 1 to 1½ in. long. *fl.* in very spreading axillary corymbs 4 to 5 in. across; peduncle short; cal. deep red; cor. red with white mouth, urn-shaped. July. 1873. (B.M. 6393.)

**EU'RYOPS** (*euryops*, having large eyes; in allusion to the conspicuous flowers of some species). Fam. *Compositae.* A genus of about 60 species of evergreen shrubs, natives of Africa. Leaves alternate, crowded, entire to pinnately divided. Flower-heads yellow, solitary, terminal or axillary on erect, naked stalks. Light-loving shrubs requiring greenhouse treatment in most places. Some species, such as *E. Athanasiae, E. pectinatus,* and *E. virgineus,* are hardy in S. Cornwall and the Scilly Is.

**E. abrotanifo'lius.** Evergreen shrub, 2 to 3 ft. *l.* densely crowded, 1 to 2 in. long, pinnately lobed, the lobes about 11 or 13, filiform, ¼ to ¾ in. long. *fl.-heads* 1½ to 2 in. across, terminal on slender stalks 2 to 6 in. long; ray-florets 14 to 18, golden yellow, oblong-ovate; disk ¾ in. across. January to March. S. Africa. 1692. (B.R. 108 and L.B.C. 1698 as *Othonna abrotanifolia.*) Resembles Southern-wood in l.

**E. Athana'siae.** Evergreen, glabrous shrub, 2 to 4 ft. *l.* pinnately lobed, 2 to 6 in. long, lobes in 4 to 7 pairs, filiform, often only $\frac{1}{16}$ in. wide. *fl.-heads* 2 to 3½ in. across, on a terminal, erect, terete, pale stalk 6 to 12 in. h.; ray-florets yellow, strap-shaped, disposed rather thinly round the broad-based involucre. S. Africa. Hardy in the Scilly Is.

**E. pectina'tus.*** Evergreen shrub, 2 to 3 ft., shoots and l. grey-white with fine down. *l.* 2 to 3 in. long, ½ to 1 in. wide, deeply lobed, lobes 16 to 20, ½ to ¾ in. long, ⅛ in. wide, often notched or toothed at the end. *fl.-heads* 1½ in. across on a stalk 3 to 6 in. long, rich yellow; ray-florets 12 or 14, ⅛ to ¼ in. wide. May, June. S. Africa. 1731. (B.M. 306 as *Othonna pectinata.*)

**E. virgin'eus.*** Evergreen shrub, 1 to 2 ft., shoots erect, glabrous. *l.* densely set, ¼ to ½ in. long, ⅛ in. wide, deeply bluntly 3- or 5-lobed, leathery, glabrous. *fl.-heads* ⅝ in. across, solitary, axillary on a slender stalk 1 in. long, numerous towards the end of the shoot; ray-florets 6, yellow, narrow-oblong. March, April. S. Africa. 1821. (B.M. 8291; L.B.C. 728 as *Othonna flabellifolia.*) Charming in Cornwall.

W. J. B.

**EUSCAPH'IS** (Greek *eu*, good, *scaphis*, vessel; in allusion to the characters of the seed-pod). FAM. *Staphyleaceae*. Monotypic genus closely akin to Staphylea whose inflated pods make it very distinct. *E. japonica* will grow in ordinary soil and is propagated by cuttings or seeds.

**E. japon'ica.** Deciduous shrub or small tree, glabrous, shoots stout, pithy. *l.* opposite, 6 to 10 in. long; lflets. 7 to 11, ovate to ovate-lanceolate, 2 to 4 in. long, slender-pointed, finely toothed, very shortly stalked. *fl.* greenish or yellowish, ¼ in. wide; parts in fives in terminal long-stalked panicles 3 to 7 in. wide. *fr.* consisting of 3 reddish pods splitting vertically and yielding 1 to 3 dark blue seeds. May. China, Japan. 1890. SYN. *E. staphyleoides*. Not very hardy.

W. J. B.

*eustach'yus -a -um,* having a long truss of flowers.

**EUSTEPH'IA** (*eu*, well, *stephos*, crown; in allusion to the appearance of the circle of stamens). FAM. *Amaryllidaceae*. A genus of 2 or 3 species of Peruvian bulbous plants closely related to Phaedranassa. Distinct from Urceolina by its short perianth tube, and from Phaedranassa and Eucrosia by its sessile leaves and winged filaments. Bulb tunicated. Leaves linear or narrow-lanceolate, radical. Scape somewhat flattened; umbel many-flowered, more or less drooping. Flowers red and green; perianth narrowly funnel-shaped, tube short, lobes long, erect; filaments winged, ending in spreading setae; ovary 3-celled, ovules many. For cultivation *see* **Phaedranassa.**

**E. coccin'ea.** *l.* narrow-lanceolate, 1 ft. or more long, about ¼ in. wide, slender-pointed, bright green. *fl.* 1¼ in. long; segs. pale on margins, keeled green in upper fourth, rest bright red; umbel few-fld., pedicels ½ to ¾ in. long; scape slender. Andes. SYN. *Phaedranassa rubro-viridis*.

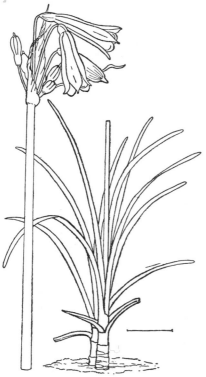

*Eustephia Pamiana*

**E. Pamia'na.** Bulb ovoid, about 3 in. long, 2½ in. wide, with a stout collar, dark brown. *l.* about 6, linear, 14 in. long, about ¼ in. wide, sheaths streaked red. *fl.* about 1¼ in. long, nodding, greenish without with red tips and purplish-red below middle, inner segs. dark red in upper part; umbel 6-fld., pedicels red or purple, 1¼ in. long; scape cylindrical, 12 to 16 in. long. April. Argentine. 1926. (B.M. 9164.)

**EUSTO'MA** (*eustomos*, of beautiful countenance). FAM. *Gentianaceae*. A genus of 2 species. Leaves opposite, sessile or stem-clasping. Flowers white, purplish, or blue, pedunculate; corolla tube short, broadly bell-shaped, deeply 5- or 6-cleft, lobes oblong or obovate, twisted; stamens 5 or 6. Both species are elegant little plants, closely allied to Lisianthus. *E. Russellianum* is a beautiful but difficult plant, best treated as a biennial, sowing the seeds in June in a light compost in a cool house, covering them very lightly. When fit to handle the seedlings should be put in thumb-pots and afterwards into 3-in. pots in which they should be wintered. The aim should be to get a good rosette of leaves for the winter. During winter the young plants should be kept well up to the roof-glass in a low pit or airy greenhouse with a temperature of 50 to 55° F., giving water very carefully. Early in the year they should be moved into larger pots using a compost of 3 parts good turfy loam to 1 of leaf-soil, with enough sand to ensure good drainage. The plants will remain in flower for a long time in 5- or 6-in. pots in a cool greenhouse, or they can be successfully used in the open if put out just as they are coming into flower.

J. C.

**E. exalta'tum.** A synonym of *E. silenifolium.*

*Eustoma Russellianum*

**E. Russellia'num.*** Annual or biennial. Stem terete, 1 to 2 ft. h. *l.* ovate to lanceolate-oblong. *fl.* lavender-purple, corymbose. July. Nebraska to Texas. 1804. (B.M. 3626.)

**E. silenifo'lium.** Herbaceous perennial, 2 ft. h. *l.* spatulate. *fl.* purple, corymbose; cor. funnel-shaped, contracted above the apex, segs. crenate. July. S. United States. 1804. (B.R. 31, 13.) SYN. *E. exaltatum.* Greenhouse.

**EUSTREPH'US** (*eu*, well, *strepho*, to twine; from the habit of the plant). FAM. *Liliaceae*. A genus of a single species. For treatment *see* **Dianella.**

**E. latifo'lius.** Stems much branched, weak, flexuous, not twining, often climbing to a great height. *l.* sessile or nearly so, broadly ovate-lanceolate to narrow-linear, tapered to a point, 2 to 4 in. long, firm, nerves fine, prominent. *fl.* pale purple; pedicels 2 to 6 together, filiform, rigid, ½ to ¾ in. long, jointed beneath fl., persistent. June. New S. Wales. (B.M. 1245.) SYN. *E. Brownii.*

**EUTAX'IA** (*eutaxia*, modesty; in allusion to the character of the plants). FAM. *Leguminosae*. A genus of 8 species of evergreen shrubs confined to Australia.

Leaves small, opposite. Flowers axillary, solitary or 2 to 4 together; standard petal, not markedly notched. Pods ovate. Cool greenhouse shrubs (E. myrtifolia is grown in the open in Scilly) requiring the same treatment as Chorizema.

**E. empetrifo'lia.** Glabrous shrub. 2 to 4 ft., diffuse in growth, stiffly and intricately branched, young shoots very slender. *l.* oval-oblong to linear, $\frac{1}{12}$ to $\frac{1}{4}$ in. long, without a midrib. *fl.* 1 or 2 in l.-axils, each on a stalk up to $\frac{1}{4}$ in. long; standard $\frac{1}{4}$ to $\frac{1}{3}$ in. long, yellow and red; wings yellow; keel red. Australia. 1803. SYN. *Sclerothamnus microphyllus.*

**E. myrtifo'lia.*** Evergreen glabrous shrub, 2 to 5 ft., shoots angular. *l.* obovate-oblong to narrowly oblong and oblanceolate, $\frac{1}{8}$ to $\frac{1}{4}$ in. long, $\frac{1}{12}$ to $\frac{3}{16}$ in. wide, sharply pointed, tapered to a scarcely stalked base. *fl.* axillary, 2 to 4 together; standard $\frac{1}{4}$ in. across, yellow, streaked with red; keel dark orange. May. *Pod* ovate, $\frac{1}{4}$ in. long. W. Australia. (B.M. 1274 as *Dillwynia obovata.*)
W. J. B.

**EUTER'PE** (the name of one of the 9 Muses). FAM. *Palmaceae.* A genus of about 60 species of graceful Trop. American unarmed palms allied to Areca with tall, erect stems and a terminal crown of large pinnatisect leaves. Leaves with narrow linear-lanceolate segments, gradually tapering to a slender point, rather thin, plaited, the thick margins recurved at the base; stalk and rachis convex on back, concave above, stalk long; sheaths very long, entire. Spadix long, paniculately branched, the branches erect in flower; flowers small, white; spathes 2, the lower shorter, split at apex. Fruit purple, about $\frac{1}{4}$ in. across. A good turfy loam with a little stable manure suits them and they need a night temperature of about 65° F. and abundant moisture. They grow rapidly and root freely. They do not sucker and must be raised from seed. *E. edulis* has an edible fruit from which also a nutritious drink (assai) is prepared by soaking it in water. *E. montana,* the mountain cabbage palm, and *E. oleracea,* the cabbage palm, yield a food prepared by pickling it or used fresh in the terminal bud and the soft parts of the stem.

**E. ed'ulis.** Assai Palm. Stem 60 to 90 ft. h., 8 in. thick, flexuous. *l.* 10 to 15, spreading; blade 6 to 9 ft., stalk $1\frac{1}{2}$ ft. long; lflets. lanceolate, densely crowded, 30 to 36 in. long, often drooping; rachis and nerves scaly beneath. Brazil.

**E. monta'na.** A synonym of *Prestoea montana.*

**E. olerac'ea.** Cabbage Palm. Stem 60 to 100 ft. h., about 1 ft. thick, narrower above. *l.* arched and spreading, 4 to 6 ft. long; segs. linear-lanceolate, glabrous, upper about 2 ft. long, 1 in. wide. *Spadix* hairy. Brazil.

**EUTO'CA.** *See* **Phacelia.**

*euxanthi'nus -a -um,* beautiful yellow.

*evanes'cens,* quickly disappearing.

**EVANS'IA.** Included in **Iris.**

*Evansia'nus -a -um,* in honour of Thomas Evans of Stepney, *c.* 1810.

*evec'tus -a -um,* lifted up.

**EVELYN'A.** *See* **Elleanthus Caravata.**

**EVENING PRIMROSE.** *See* **Oenothera biennis.**

*eve'nius -a -um,* occurring.

*Everet'tii,* in honour of (1) A. H. Everett, English traveller in Celebes; (2) Harry Day Everett, 1880–1908, who collected in Manila.

**EVERGREEN.** A plant which retains its foliage green for at least a full year; foliage so retained. Opposed to deciduous. A plant whose foliage remains only one full year is sometimes distinguished as winter-green.

**EVERGREEN BEECH.** *See* **Nothofagus.**

**EVERGREEN LABURNUM.** *See* **Piptanthus laburnifolius.**

**EVERGREEN OAK.** *See* **Quercus Ilex.**

**EVERLASTING MOUNTAIN.** *See* **Antennaria dioica.**

**EVERLASTING PEA.** *See* **Lathyrus sylvestris platyphyllus.**

**EVERLASTINGS.** Flower-heads with coloured bracts that retain much of their showy character after being cut and dried. Many of them are among the most ornamental plants, either for cultivation in pots or in the open ground. The principal genera concerned are Acroclinium, Ammobium, Helichrysum, Helipterum, Rhodanthe, Waitzia, and Xeranthemum. The name is more particularly used for the many highly coloured varieties of *Helichrysum bracteatum* which are called Immortelles by the French, and are more largely used by them than in this country. To obtain them in the best condition, they should be gathered on a dry day when each flower-head is sufficiently open to show the inside of the bracts without exposing the centre of the head. If examined with sufficient frequency the whole stock may be secured in this condition. They should be hung, head downwards, in a cool shed and allowed to remain until dry. The individual flower-heads may be wired, and used with good effect, amongst dried ornamental grasses in winter, either in tall glasses or vases. The French use large quantities for memorial wreaths and crosses. If properly gathered and dried, many species will keep good, except for some loss of colour, for two or three years, but it is better to grow a fresh stock every year.

**EVE'S CUSHION.** *See* **Saxifraga hypnoides.**

**EVETE'RIA buolia'na.** *See* **Pinus, Pests.**

**EVO'DIA** (*euodia,* sweet scent; in allusion to fragrance of the leaves). FAM. *Rutaceae.* Deciduous or evergreen trees or shrubs (all cultivated species are deciduous), natives of E. and S. Asia and Australia. About 50 species are known. Leaves opposite, pinnate (sometimes simple); leaflets decreasing in size downwards; buds exposed. Flowers small, unisexual, in terminal or axillary panicles or corymbs, the parts in fours or fives. Fruit of 4 or 5 pods, sometimes with a beak or curved hook. Seeds oval or globose. The nearly related Phellodendron, with which Evodia is often confused, can be distinguished by its leaf-buds being completely hidden by the base of the leaf-stalk. Evodias are easily grown in good loam; propagated by seed.

KEY

| | |
|---|---|
| 1. *Lflets.* 5 to 13 | 2 |
| 1. *Lflets.* 7 to 17 | 7 |
| 2. *Lvs.* glabrous or quickly so | 3 |
| 2. *Lvs.* more or less hairy at least beneath | 4 |
| 3. *Lflets.* 2 to 9 in. long, ovate-oblong | E. fraxinifolia |
| 3. *Lflets.* $2\frac{1}{2}$ to 5 in. long, ovate to ovate-lanceolate | E. Henryi |
| 4. *Lflets.* with tufts of hair in vein-axils beneath only | E. hupehensis |
| 4. *Lvs.* downy on veins beneath | 5 |
| 5. *Lvs.* downy on both surfaces | E. velutina |
| 5. *Lvs.* hairy on midrib and veins | 6 |
| 6. *Lflets.* shortly pointed, wedge-shaped at base | E. Bodinieri |
| 6. *Lflets.* slender-pointed, often cordate at base | E. Daniellii |
| 7. *Lvs.* glaucous beneath, white downy at base of midrib only | E. glauca |
| 7. *Lvs.* downy beneath | E. officinalis |

**E. Bodinier'i.** Shrub to 10 ft., shoots downy. *lflets.* 5 to 13, oval, ovate, or oblong, $1\frac{1}{2}$ to 4 in. long, cuneate, shortly and bluntly pointed, downy on midrib above, more so beneath on both midrib and veins; mainstalk downy. *inflor.* 4 to 8 in. wide, flattish to rounded, downy to velvety. August. *fr.* reddish, not beaked; seeds black, shining, globose, $\frac{1}{10}$ in. wide. China. 1910. Tender.

**E. Daniell'ii.** Small tree, shoots at first downy. *l.* 9 to 15 in. long; lflets. ovate-cordate to ovate-oblong, slender-pointed, 2 to 5 in. long, broadly cuneate to slightly cordate at the base. *fl.* $\frac{1}{4}$ in. long, dull white, in flattish clusters 4 to 7 in. across; stalks downy. June. *fr.* $\frac{1}{4}$ in. long, shortly beaked, shining black, the size of medium gun-shot. China, Korea. 1907.

**E. fraxinifo'lia.** Tree 30 to 50 ft., scented like Caraway when bruised. *l.* 12 to 18 in. long; lflets. 5 to 11, ovate-oblong, 2 to 9 in. long, 1 to $3\frac{1}{2}$ in. wide, entire or faintly toothed, pointed, cuneate, glabrous; stalk $\frac{1}{3}$ to $\frac{1}{8}$ in. long. *inflor.* a flattish rounded panicle 6 in. wide; fl. greenish-yellow. *fr.* red, $\frac{1}{2}$ in. wide; seed dark brown. Himalaya. SYN. *Tetradium trichotomum.*

**E. glau'ca.** Tree up to 50 ft. *l.* 6 to 10 in. long; lflets. 5 to 17, oval-lanceolate, oblique at the base, slender-pointed, indistinctly toothed or entire, glabrous and dark green above, very glaucous beneath, white-downy at the base of the midrib only. *fl.* in broad, flattish clusters up to 8 in. across. *fr.* $\frac{1}{5}$ in. long. China. 1907.

**E. Hen'ryi.** Tree 20 to 30 ft., shoots at first downy. *l.* 6 to 12 in. long; lflets. 5 to 9, ovate to ovate-lanceolate, very shallowly toothed, 2 to 4 in. long, soon glabrous on both sides, pale and slightly glaucous beneath. *fl.* in flattish clusters 2 to 3 in. wide, pinkish-white. July. *fr.* reddish-brown, $\frac{1}{4}$ in. wide, with a slender beak. China. 1908.

**E. hupehens'is.** Tree up to 60 ft., shoots glabrous. *lflets.* 5 to 9, narrowly ovate, $2\frac{1}{2}$ to 5 in. long, very slenderly pointed, shallowly toothed or entire, glabrous except for small axil-tufts beneath. *fl.* $\frac{1}{4}$ in. long, whitish, in broad, pyramidal, downy clusters 4 to 7 in. across. August. *fr.* reddish-brown, with a slender hooked beak, glandular beneath; seeds black. China. 1908. (G.C. 12 (1949), 99 as *E. halselensis.*)

**E. officina'lis.** Shrub or small tree, 15 to 20 ft., shoots at first downy. *lflets.* 7 to 15, ovate to oval-ovate, 2 to $3\frac{1}{2}$ in. long, pointed, cuneate, glabrous above except on the midrib, downy beneath. *fl.* in downy-stalked clusters 3 to $4\frac{1}{2}$ in. wide. July. *fr.* reddish, warty, $\frac{1}{4}$ in. long; seeds nearly globose, shining blue. China. 1907.

**E. veluti'na.** Tree 40 to 50 ft., shoots velvety. *l.* up to 10 in. long; lflets. 7 to 11, oblong-lanceolate, 2 to 4 in. long, 1 to $1\frac{1}{2}$ in. wide, long-pointed, base obliquely rounded, dull green and downy above, velvety beneath. *fl.* yellowish-white, small, and very numerous, borne in terminal and axillary compound umbels 6 to 7 in. across. August. *fr.* purplish-brown, hairy, $\frac{1}{8}$ in. wide; seeds shining, black. China. 1908. Distinct by its velvetiness.

W. J. B.

**EVOL'VULUS** (*evolvo*, to untwist; to distinguish from Convolvulus, many of which twine). FAM. *Convolvulaceae.* A genus of about 70 species, mostly American, but distributed over the tropics. Annual or perennial, prostrate or creeping, rarely erect, herbs. Leaves entire. Peduncles axillary, 1- or few-flowered; corollas subrotate, bell-shaped or funnel-shaped, plicate. The species need stove conditions but few are of horticultural merit.

**E. purpuro-caeru'leus.** Perennial. Stem woody in lower part, 18 in. h. *l.* small, lanceolate, acute, entire. *fl.* purplish-blue at ends of leafy branches, stalked; cor. rotate, rich ultramarine blue, centre white with a purple line up the middle of each lobe. July, August. (B.M. 4202.)

**EVOT'OMYS glareo'lus.** *See* **Voles.**

***Ewer'sii,*** in honour of J. P. G. Ewers, Russian botanist, who studied the Altai flora, *c.* 1829.

***ex-,*** in compound words, signifying without, or outside, as exstipulate, without stipules, extrorse, turned towards outside.

***exacoi'des,*** Exacum-like.

**EX'ACUM** (name used by Pliny, from *ex*, out, *ago*, to arrive; in allusion to its supposed expulsive power). FAM. *Gentianaceae.* A genus of about 20 species of erect, annual, biennial, or perennial herbs, natives of India, E. Asia, Malay Archipelago, and Socotra. Leaves opposite, sessile. Flowers terminal and axillary; corolla 5-partite, salver-shaped or nearly rotate, with a globose or ventricose tube. The Exacums are pretty greenhouse or stove plants. They grow best in a compost of equal parts of peat and turfy loam with enough sand to ensure free drainage, for watering must at all times be done with care. Although they may be flowered from seed sown early in the year, the best results are obtained when the seed is sown towards the end of August or at the beginning of September, wintering the plants in 3-in. pots in a house with a temperature of about 60° F. Potted on at the beginning of the year good specimens can be grown in 4- or 5-in. pots.

A

J. C.

**E. affi'ne.** Compact, 6 in. h., free-flowering biennial. *l.* broadly ovate, stalked. *fl.* bluish lilac, fragrant; stamens yellow. Summer and autumn. Socotra. (G.C. 21 (1884), 605.) Warm greenhouse.

**E. macran'thum.** Biennial, about 18 in. h. *l.* large, glabrous, glossy. *fl.* deep rich blue-purple, 2 in. across; stamens large, bright yellow; corymbs terminal and axillary. Ceylon. 1853. (B.M. 4771.) Perhaps a variety of *E. zeylanicum.* Stove.

**E. zeyla'nicum.** Biennial, 1 to 2 ft. h., branches 4-angled. *l.* ovate-lanceolate, slender-pointed, nearly sessile. *fl.* a beautiful violet; pet. obovate; in a corymb-like panicle. Ceylon. 1848. (B.M. 4423.)

**exalbuminous,** without albumen, applied to a seed without a store of food outside the embryo, as, e.g., the pea and bean.

***exalta'tus -a -um,*** lofty.

***exara'tus -a -um,*** engraved.

**EXARRHE'NA.** *See under* **Myosotis macrantha.**

***exaspera'tus -a -um,*** rough.

***excava'tus -a -um,*** hollowed.

***exce'dens,*** lengthened.

***excel'sus -a -um,*** very tall.

***exci'sus -a -um,*** cut out.

***excortica'tus -a -um,*** without a bark or cortex.

***excur'rens,*** excurrent, having a projecting tip, as the point of a vein, beyond the leaf-margin.

**exfoliating,** peeling off in thin layers, as the bark of the birch or plane.

***exig'uus -a -um,*** very small.

***exil'is -is -e,*** slender, thin.

***exim'ius -a -um,*** excellent for beauty or size.

***exo-,*** in compound words, implying outside.

**EXOAS'CUS.** An old generic name, now *Taphrina.* *See* **Peach Leaf Curl.**

**EXOBASID'IUM.** A genus of Basidiomycetous fungi, some of which cause the formation of galls in plants, e.g. Rhododendrons (q.v.).

**EXOCARP.** The outer layer of the pericarp.

**EXOCHOR'DA** (*exo*, external, *chorde*, cord; referring to fibres outside the placenta). FAM. *Rosaceae.* Four species of N. Asiatic deciduous shrubs of great beauty. Leaves alternate. Flowers white, 1 to $1\frac{1}{2}$ in. across, borne in terminal racemes of 4 to 12; sepals 5, short; petals 5, spreading, obovate, narrowed at the base to a claw; stamens 15 to 30. Fruit consisting of 5 bony, 2-edged divisions (carpels) adhering round a central axis but spreading star-fashion. All the species are hardy and succeed in any reasonably good soil; they like a sunny position. Propagated by seed or layering, occasionally by sucker growths.

KEY

1. *Stamens 15; pedicels of lower fl.* $\frac{1}{2}$ *in. long; pet. abruptly narrowed below* — E. racemosa
1. *Stamens 20 to 30; all fl. sessile or very short-stalked* — 2
2. *Stamens about 20; habit upright* — E. × macrantha
2. *Stamens usually more than 20; pet. gradually narrowed below* — 3
3. *Stamens 20 to 30; lvs. without stipules; habit spreading* — E. Giraldii
3. *Stamens 25* — 4
4. *Lvs. sharply serrate,* $1\frac{1}{2}$ *to 3 in. long, hairy beneath when young* — E. serratifolia
4. *Lvs. mostly entire,* $1\frac{1}{2}$ *to* $3\frac{1}{2}$ *in. long, glabrous, stipulate* — E. Korolkowii

**E. Al'berti.** A synonym of *E. Korolkowii.*

**E. Giral'dii.*** Shrub 10 ft., shoots glabrous, pink, as are the l.-stalks and veins. *l.* ovate to oblong, pointed, mostly entire, $1\frac{1}{2}$ to $2\frac{1}{2}$ in. long; stalk $\frac{1}{2}$ to 1 in. long. *fl.* white, $1\frac{3}{4}$ in. across, borne in erect racemes of 6 to 8; pet. obovate, gradually narrowed to base; stamens 20 to 30. May. NW. China. 1907. (B.T.S. 1. 548.) var. **Wil'sonii,** habit more erect, *l.* oval to oblong, occasionally toothed, *fl.* 2 in. wide, stamens 20 to 25. Cent. China. 1907.

**E. grandiflo'ra.** A synonym of *E. racemosa.*

**E. Korolkow'ii.** Glabrous shrub, 10 to 15 ft. *l.* obovate, 1½ to 3½ in. long, about half as wide, entire or toothed towards apex, tapered gradually at base to a stalk about ½ in. long. *fl.* white, 1½ in. wide, in erect, 5- to 8-fld. racemes; stamens in 5 groups of 5 each. May. Turkestan. 1881. SYN. *E. Alberti.*

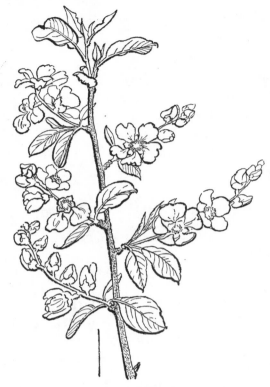

*Exochorda × macrantha*

**E. × macran'tha** (*E. Korolkowii × E. racemosa*). Its hybridity is shown in the grouping of the stamens which are in batches of 3, 4, or 5. Very floriferous, the racemes bearing 6 to 10 fl., each 1¼ in. wide. Raised by Lemoine of Nancy. 1900. (B.T.S. 1. 549.)

**E. racemo'sa.*** Rounded bushy shrub, 10 or 12 ft., shoots slender, glabrous. *l.* narrowly obovate to oval or oblong, 1½ to 3 in. long, ⅓ as wide, shortly pointed, entire or toothed towards the apex, glabrous. *fl.* white, 1¼ to 1½ in. wide, on erect racemes of 6 to 10; pet. rounded but abruptly narrowed to a claw at the base; stamens 15, in 5 groups of 3. May. China. 1849. (B.M. 4795 as *Spiraea grandiflora*.) SYN. *E. grandiflora.* Very handsome.

**E. serratifo'lia.** Shrub 4 to 6 ft. *l.* obovate-oblong to oval, 1½ to 3 in. long, up to 2 in. wide, sharply toothed in terminal half, slightly downy beneath when young; stalk up to ¾ in. long. *fl.* 1½ to 2 in. wide, crowded on erect racemes of 6 to 12; pet. narrowly oblong-obovate, notched at end; stamens 25. Manchuria, Korea. 1918. *l.* largest and most strongly toothed in the genus.

W. J. B.

**EXOGENS,** an old term, now nearly obsolete, for plants whose stem is thickened by the activity of a ring of cambium, including the Coniferae and Dicotyledons.

**EXOGO'NIUM.** See under **Ipomoea Purga.**

*exonien'sis -is -e,* of Exeter.

**EXOSTEM'MA** (*exo,* without, *stemma,* crown; the stamens are exserted). FAM. *Rubiaceae.* A genus of about 40 species of evergreen shrubs and trees, natives of Trop. America and the W. Indies. Leaves ovate or lanceolate, sometimes almost sessile. Flowers white, axillary, solitary or in terminal few- or many-flowered panicles; corolla tube long, limb 5-lobed, salver-shaped. For treatment of these stove plants, see **Cinchona.**

**E. caribae'um.** Tree of about 20 ft. *l.* ovate-lanceolate, narrowed to apex. *fl.* white, fragrant, as long as l., solitary in l.-axils. June. W. Indies. 1780. (S.S. 226.)

**E. longiflo'rum.** Tree of about 20 ft. *l.* linear-lanceolate, narrowed to both ends. *fl.* white, 5 in. long before opening, on very short axillary pedicels. June. St. Domingo. 1820. (B.M. 4186.)

**E. subcorda'tum.** Shrub of 6 to 9 ft., branches round, at first downy. *l.* ovate to ovate-lanceolate, 2 to 3 in. long, slightly cordate at base, slender-pointed, rather leathery, margins revolute. *fl.* in a loose terminal corymb, white; cor. tube narrow-cylindrical, about ¾ in. long, lobes linear, obtuse, about 1 in. long; stamens about 1 in. long, exserted, anthers yellow. Autumn. St. Domingo. 1903. (B.M. 8274.)

**exotic,** introduced from other countries; not native. Compare endemic.

*explo'dens,* bursting suddenly.

*exsca'pus -a -um,* without a stem.

*exsec'tus -a -um,* cut out.

*exser'tus -a -um,* exserted, projecting beyond other organs.

**exstipulate,** without stipules.

*ex'sul, ex'ul,* out of the land, banished.

*exten'sus -a -um,* wide.

*extra-,* in compound words, implying outside, beyond.

**extra-axillary,** growing from above or below the axils of leaves or branches (*see* **adnate**).

**extra-tropical,** living in regions outside the tropics.

**extrorse,** facing outwards away from the axis.

*exu'dans,* exuding.

**EXUDATIONS.** Substances which ooze from injured plant tissues. This often happens in plants affected with certain diseases, especially in stone fruit trees, but it also happens in healthy tissues through injury of some kind. In stone fruits the exudate usually consists of some form of gumlike substance which will probably harden (*see* **Gummosis**). Escape of sap through injury to trees such as Walnut, &c., or the milky juice called latex which flows from such herbs as Dandelion, &c., when wounded, may be described as exudation. Slime-flux is also to be included here, and is distinguished by its frothy or slimy consistence caused by the growth of species of Saccharomyces (yeast), Torula, Endomyces, and similar small organisms which bring about fermentation in the exudation. The slime-flux is usually white in Oak, red in Hornbeam, brown in Apple, Horse-chestnut, Elm, Birch, &c., and sometimes black in Beech. It usually has its origin in a wound, which may heal over and the flux break out again nearby. This rarely causes death.

D. E. G.

**EYE.** An undeveloped bud; the centre of a flower; a stem-cutting with a single lateral bud, often used in propagating the vine (q.v.).

**EYEBRIGHT.** See **Euphrasia officinalis.**

**EYED HAWK MOTH,** *Smerinthus ocellatus,* is generally distributed through southern England, but is scarcer and more local elsewhere in the British Isles. The large handsome moths, on the hind wings of which are a pair of prominent bluish eye-spots, are on the wing during June and July. The yellowish-green eggs are laid, generally singly, on leaves or on the stalks of their food plants, chiefly Apple and Willow. The caterpillars are greenish, dotted with white spots, with 7 violet-tinged, oblique, lateral stripes, and a bluish horn at the end of the body. They feed so voraciously that they soon strip the shoots completely of their leaves. When fully fed they go down into the soil and pupate in an earthern cell. There may be two broods a year, the first appearing in May, the second in August.

This pest may generally be controlled by handpicking the young caterpillars from bush, maiden, and cordon Apples. Severe attacks may be checked by lightly spraying the foliage with arsenate of lead.

**Eyries'ii,** in honour of Alexander Eyries of Havre, France, who brought *Echinopsis Eyriesii* from Uruguay in 1830.

**EYSENHARDT'IA** (in honour of C. W. Eysenhardt, M.D., Professor in the University of Königsberg, Prussia). FAM. *Leguminosae.* A genus of 2 species of evergreen shrubs, natives of Mexico and Texas. Leaves unequally pinnate with numerous small leaflets. Flowers white, small, in dense spicate racemes. These half-hardy plants need a compost of loam and peat. Young cuttings will root in sandy soil under a bell-glass.

**E. amorphoi'des.** Shrub of 4 to 6 ft. *lflets.* numerous, stipellate, glandular. *fl.* pale yellow in terminal, cylindrical racemes. June. Mexico. 1838.

# F

**FA'BA vulga'ris.** *See* **Vicia Faba.**

**faba'ceus -a -um,** bean-like.

**Fa'beri,** in honour of the Rev. Ernst Faber, 1839–99, of the Rhenish Missionary Society, who collected on Mt. Omei, China.

**FABIA'NA** (in honour of Francisco Fabian y Fuero, 1719–1801, of Valencia, a Spanish promoter of plant study). FAM. *Solanaceae.* A genus of about 20 species of S. American shrubs, botanically like Cestrum with all its stamens fertile, but differing in having, like Nicotiana, a capsular fruit. The two species in cultivation are heath-like shrubs with small, evergreen leaves crowded on short lateral shoots and many tubular flowers. They are unfortunately rather tender. They do best in a light soil in a sunny, sheltered position and are readily increased by late summer cuttings in slight heat.

**F. imbrica'ta.*** Heath-like shrub, 3 to 6 ft. h., at first erect, then spreading to about 6 ft. across; young shoots downy; branches slender, bearing many short twigs densely covered with triangular l. about ¹⁄₁₆ in. long, each ending in a solitary white fl. Cor. tubular, about ¼ in. long, narrowed to base, with 5 short, rounded, reflexed lobes. June. Chile. 1838. (B.R. 25, 59.) var. **viola'cea.** *See* **F. violacea.**

**F. viola'cea.*** Shrub of generally similar habit to *F. imbricata* but more spreading when young, somewhat hardier, and growing more quickly. *fl.* variable from pale mauve to bluish lilac. Chile. 1854.

**FABRAE'A.** A genus of fungi, of which some, e.g. *F. maculata,* cause disease in plants. *See* **Quince Leaf Blight.**

**FABRIC'IA.** Included under **Leptospermum.** *See* **L. laevigatum.**

**face'tum,** elegant.

**FADYEN'IA** (in honour of James MacFadyen, 1800–50, who wrote a flora of Jamaica). FAM. *Polypodiaceae.* A genus of 1 species, native of the W. Indies. Sori near the midrib, at the ends of free veinlets, oblong, in 2 series. Indusium large, somewhat kidney-shaped, attached by the middle, free round margin. *F. Hookeri* is a peculiar little fern quite distinct in appearance from every other. It is often found difficult to manage but it succeeds in a compost of 3 parts fibrous peat and 1 part sand with abundant moisture at the roots in a stove-house. Given these conditions it will spread widely through the rooting of the proliferous tips of its barren fronds, the young plants thus produced, while still attached to the parent, reproducing all the characters of a mature plant.

**F. Hook'eri.** *Fronds* entire, dimorphous; barren, ¾ to 1 in. wide, long, rooting at tip; fertile ligulate, narrowed below, 6 to 9 in. long, about ¼ in. wide. 1843. (L.F. 6, 2; B.C.F. 2, 416.) SYN. *F. prolifera.*

**FAGA'CEAE.** Dicotyledons. A family of 6 genera with about 400 species of trees (rarely shrubs) in temperate and sub-tropical regions of the world. Leaves alternate, simple, stalked, sometimes lobed, with pinnate veining, stipulate. Flowers monoecious, usually axillary on young shoots; perianth 4- to 7-lobed; staminate spikes slender, each bract with 1 flower, stamens as many or twice as many as perianth lobes, rarely more; pistillate, flowers solitary or in threes, ovary inferior with 3 styles, ovules 6 but only 1 develops. Fruit a nut (1, 2, or 3) partly enclosed by an involucre or cup. Seeds often large. All 6 genera, Castanea, Castanopsis, Fagus, Lithocarpus, Nothofagus, and Quercus, are represented in British gardens, and many of the species are very ornamental.

**FAGEL'IA** (in honour of Caspar Fagelius, horticulturist). FAM. *Leguminosae.* A monotypic genus in S. Africa. A sub-shrubby 3-foliolate twining plant, with a sharply 5-cleft calyx cut beyond the middle, keel longer than wings, very blunt and swollen pod constricted between the seeds. Cool greenhouse; can be trained up pillars or rafters; propagated by seed.

**F. bituminos'a.** Twining shrub about 10 ft., shoots and fl.-stalks covered with clammy hairs. *l.* 3-foliolate; lflets. rhombic-ovate, 1 to 1½ in. long, ¾ to 1 in. wide, mucronate, hairy especially beneath on the veins. *fl.* in axillary racemes borne towards the top of a stalk 6 in. long; cor. ¾ in. long; standard and wings yellow, apex of keel dark violet-purple. April onwards. *Pod* shaggily hairy, swollen, 2 in. long, about 6-seeded. S. Africa. 1774. (B.R. 261 as *Glycine bituminosa.*)

W. J. B.

**FAGO'NIA** (in honour of Monsignor Fagon, 1638–1718, consulting physician to Louis XIV of France). FAM. *Zygophyllaceae.* (A genus of about 3 species of annual or perennial herbs, branched, sometimes prostrate. Leaves opposite, sometimes 3-foliolate, leaflets mucronate, stipules somewhat spiny. Flowers solitary; sepals and petals 5; stamens 10. Fruit a 5-angled nut with a single seed. *F. cretica* needs only ordinary soil and is best in the greenhouse, seeds being sown in autumn.

**F. cre'tica.** Annual. More or less procumbent; branches about 12 in. long. *l.* 3-foliolate; segs. lanceolate, acute, about ¾ in. long. *fl.* purple, about 1¼ in. across, in axils of upper l. June to August. Spain, Portugal, N. Africa, Canary Is. 1739. (B.M. 241.)

**FAGOPY'RUM** (*phago*, to eat, *pyros*, wheat; the seeds being edible). FAM. *Polygonaceae.* A genus of 2 species, natives of Asia. Leaves cordate or lanceolate on an erect branching stem. Perianth 5-partite, not increasing in size after flowering. Seed mealy. For cultivation *see* **Buckwheat.** The seed is used in England for pheasant and poultry food, but abroad for human food.

**F. sagitta'tum.** Common Buckwheat. About 3 to 5 ft. h., branched. *fl.* pinkish-white. July. Cent. Asia, naturalized elsewhere. SYN. *F. esculentum.*

**FAGRAE'A** (in honour of Jonas Theodore Fagraeus, 1729–97, physician and botanist). FAM. *Loganiaceae*. A genus of about 30 species of trees and shrubs. Leaves opposite, large, broad, leathery. Flowers showy; corolla funnel-shaped, lobes 5 (rarely 6 or 7), overlapping. Compost should be of loam, peat, and sand. Stove conditions are called for. Cuttings of young shoots, about April, root readily in sand, with heat under a bell-glass.

**F. auricula'ta.** Epiphytic shrub. *l.* cuneate-oblong, broad, acute, veiny; interpetiolar stipules 2-lobed, recurved. *fl.* yellow, very large, in threes, terminal. Java. SYN. *F. imperialis*.

**F. frag'rans.** Tree of 25 to 30 ft. *l.* elliptic, 4 in. long, 1¼ in. wide, acute; stalks ¼ to ¾ in. long, often connate. *fl.* in compound corymbs in axils towards ends of branches, often 50- to 100-fld., but sometimes much smaller; cor. tube ½ in. long, narrowly funnel-shaped below; pedicels ⅙ in. long. India.

**F. obova'ta.** About 12 ft. h. *l.* 5 to 6 in. long, thick, stalks glandular-ciliate, connected by interpetiolar stipules. *fl.* white, smaller than in *F. zeylanica*, fragrant, in threes, terminal. Ceylon. 1816. (B.M. 4205.)

**F. zeylan'ica.** Shrub of 12 ft., erect, branches somewhat 4-angled. *l.* crowded, obovate-oblong, obtuse. *fl.* white, large, in few-fld. terminal umbels. Ceylon. 1816. (B.M. 6080.)

F. G. P.

***Faguetia'nus -a -um,*** in honour of A. Faguet, ?–1900, of Paris, artist.

**FA'GUS** (ancient Latin name). FAM. *Fagaceae*. Deciduous trees with smooth grey trunks. Leaves alternate, parallel-veined, usually thin and shining green. Flowers unisexual; males in slender-stalked heads; calyx 4- to 7-lobed; stamens 8 to 16; females in pairs or threes, styles 3. Fruit a triangular nut with sharp edges, enclosed in a 4-lobed husk. Of the cultivated species 2 are European, 1 N. American, 2 Japanese, and 3 Chinese; very homogeneous.

The beeches are very hardy, handsome trees, and most, if not all, are valuable for limy soils; they are ill-adapted for heavy, wet soils. Common beech is easily raised from seeds, enormous crops of which frequently occur, but the foreign species rarely if ever ripen their nuts with us. They, as well as its own numerous garden varieties, are grafted on *F. sylvatica*. Beech timber is not adapted for exposure out of doors, but is valued for indoor use such as kitchen utensils, tools, and especially for kitchen chairs, the manufacture of which has long been an established industry in the Chilterns. (*See also* **Nothofagus.**)

*DISEASES*. A common disease of beech and other tree seedlings, especially in forest nurseries, is 'damping off' caused by the fungus *Phytophthora fagi*. This trouble is more severe in damp and shady places, and it may be necessary to sterilize the seed-beds with weak formalin (1 part in 300 parts water) or commercial sulphuric acid, 1 fluid ounce to half a gallon of water. Beeches may be attacked when growing by Canker due to *Nectria galligena* or *N. coccinea* or by Silver Leaf (*Stereum purpureum*). Less serious parasites, which probably are purely wound parasites, are the large Bracket fungi, represented by such fungi as *Fomes fomentarius*, *F. igniarius*, *Polyporus applanatus*, or even the well-known Jew's Ear fungus, which is somewhat smaller. Such Bracket fungi are usually seen on old or weakened trees attacking the wood. (For details see separate articles.)

(D. E. G.)

*PESTS*. Beech trees are liable to attack by a number of insect pests, among the more important being the Woolly Beech Aphis, *Phyllaphis fagi*, the Felted Beech Coccus or Scale, *Cryptococcus fagi*, and the Beech leaf-miner, *Orchestes fagi*.

The Woolly Beech Aphis, *Phyllaphis fagi*, is a widely distributed pest of Beech trees and hedges, and also attacks the Copper Beech, becoming very abundant in certain years especially in the home counties. The Aphides, whose bodies are covered with a quantity of white, flocculent, waxy, wool-like material, live on the underside of the leaves during May and June. Their feeding causes the leaves to turn brown and shrivel, but seldom to fall off. The yellowish eggs are laid on the leaves and young shoots in autumn, and hatch in April when the young yellowish-green insects shelter in the unfolding leaves. They soon become covered with white woolly threads, and dense white masses appear on the lower leaf surface. Considerable injury is done by this pest, and control measures against it are necessary. The underside of the leaves should be drenched with nicotine and soap wash, or the foliage dusted with nicotine dust. The latter method is more effective for checking an attack on hedge plants, owing to the greater penetration possible into the closely planted bushes.

Felted Beech Coccus, *Cryptococcus fagi* (Homopterous family *Coccidae*), produces masses of white waxy wool material but no hard scale. It is confined to Beech and is found upon trees of all ages, favouring the Common more than the Copper Beech, and living in colonies in the bark fissures of the trunk and main branches. The male is unknown. The female scale insect is very small, legless, and oval. Egg-laying begins in June. The young scales are active and wander about for a time, but eventually settle down to a sedentary existence. They insert their sucking mouthparts into the tissues and abstract the sap. Though healthy trees are attacked little damage is done; but the pest increases when the host plant is unhealthy as a result of root trouble arising from drought or waterlogged soil. This Coccus must be considered as a secondary rather than a primary cause of ill health in Beech trees. A severe attack brings in its train a number of fungus diseases which may eventually destroy the tree. It is not possible to eradicate this pest on tall standing trees, but the trunks and larger branches of specimen trees should be sprayed during the winter with tar-distillate wash, or during the spring with white oil and nicotine emulsion, directing the wash with considerable force into the bark crevices to ensure the thorough wetting of the insects. Painting the trunks with tar-distillate with a stiff brush should be done where there is danger of the wash falling on plants growing beneath the affected trees.

The Beech Leaf-miner, *Orchestes fagi*, is a Weevil whose grub attacks the leaves of Beech, producing blotch-like mines which in some years are so numerous that the trees have a scorched appearance at some distance. The Weevil is about ⅛ in. long, dark grey or black, and is on the foliage in early spring. The female deposits a single egg near the mid-rib, and the grub feeds on the tissues between the upper and lower leaf surfaces. When fully fed the grub pupates in its mine, and the winter is passed in the adult stage in the soil or in rubbish at the base of hedges and elsewhere. The attacked leaves on specimen trees should be handcrushed to destroy the mining grubs or removed and burned at the first sign of mines.

(G. F. W.)

KEY

1. *Lvs. green beneath; stalk of husk stout, up to 1 in. long, downy* 2
1. *Lvs. glaucous or glossy beneath; stalk of husk slender, 1 to 3 in. long, glabrous or almost so* 5
2. *Lvs. with 9 to 15 pairs of veins, coarsely toothed* F. grandifolia
2. *Lvs. with 5 to 10 pairs of veins, usually wavy-margined or scarcely toothed* 3
3. *Bristles at base of husk awl-shaped* F. sylvatica
3. *Bristles at base of husk linear or spatulate* 4
4. *Lvs. broadest below middle, up to 4 in. long* F. Sieboldii
4. *Lvs. broadest above middle, up to 6 in. long* F. orientalis
5. *Husks about as long as nuts* 6
5. *Husks shorter than nuts* 7
6. *Lvs. downy beneath; l.-stalks ½ to 1⅛ in. long* F. longipetiolata
6. *Lvs. glabrous beneath; l.-stalks ¼ to ½ in. long* F. Engleriana
7. *Lvs. with 9 to 14 pairs of veins; nuts half-exposed* F. japonica
7. *Lvs. with 8 to 12 pairs of veins, glossy beneath; nuts partly exposed* F. lucida

**F. america'na.** A synonym of *F. grandifolia*.

**F. antarc'tica.** A synonym of *Nothofagus antarctica*.

**F. betuloi'des.** A synonym of *Nothofagus betuloides.*

**F. cliffortioi'des.** A synonym of *Nothofagus cliffortioides.*

**F. Cunningham'ii.** A synonym of *Nothofagus Cunninghamii.*

**F. Dom'beyi.** A synonym of *Nothofagus Dombeyi.*

**F. Engleria'na.** Tree 20 to 50, rarely 70 ft. h., divided into several stems at the base, nearly glabrous. *l.* 2 to 4 in. long, oval to ovate, pointed, the base cuneate to rounded; veins in 10 to 14 pairs; stalk ¼ to ½ in. long. *Husk* ⅝ in. long, covered with downy often spoon-shaped bracts; stalk 1½ to 2½ in. long. China. 1911. Distinct by the long and slender-stalked husk, and the divided stems.

**F. ferrugin'ea.** A synonym of *F. grandifolia.*

**F. fus'ca.** A synonym of *Nothofagus fusca.*

*Fagus grandifolia*

**F. grandifo'lia.** American Beech. Wide-spreading tree 70 to 80 ft. or more, suckering. *l.* 2 to 5 in. long, ovate-oblong, coarsely toothed, broadly cuneate, taper-pointed, soon glabrous above, downy on the midrib and in the vein-axils beneath; veins in 9 to 15 pairs; stalk ⅓ to ½ in. long. *Husk* downy, prickly, ¾ in. long. N. America. 1766. (G. and F. 8, 125.) Not a success in Britain. Easily distinguished from common beech by the longer narrower l. with nearly twice as many veins. SYN. *F. americana, F. ferruginea.* var. **pubes'cens,** softly downy beneath.

**F. japon'ica.** Japanese Beech. Tree 70 to 80 ft. h., often with several stems, shoots glabrous. ! . 2 to 4 in. long, oval to ovate, short-pointed, base rounded to broadly cuneate, margins wavy, rather glaucous beneath; veins in 9 to 14 pairs; stalk ⅓ to ½ in. long. *Nut* triangular, ½ in. long, lower half only enclosed in the husk, upper half-exposed. Japan. 1907.

**F. longipetiola'ta.** Tree to 80 ft., shoots glabrous. *l.* 2½ to 5½ in. long, ovate, slender-pointed, base broadly cuneate, margin sparsely toothed or merely wavy, downy beneath; veins in 9 to 13 pairs; stalk ½ to 1⅛ in. long. *Husk* up to 1 in. long, its bristles slender and curled; stalk 1½ to 2¼ in. long. China. 1911. Distinct by its long-stalked l. and husks.

**F. lu'cida.** Tree to 30 ft. h., shoots soon glabrous. *l.* 2 to 3½ in. long, ovate to elliptic-ovate, pointed, base broadly cuneate, glossy green on both surfaces, the 8 to 12 pairs of veins running out to indentations of the wavy margins to form small teeth there. *Husk* ⅓ in. long, downy; nut slightly exposed. China. 1911.

**F. macrophyl'la.** A synonym of *F. orientalis.*

**F. Menzies'ii.** A synonym of *Nothofagus Menziesii.*

**F. Moor'ei.** A synonym of *Nothofagus Moorei.*

**F. obli'qua.** A synonym of *Nothofagus obliqua.*

**F. orienta'lis.** Tree 100 ft. or more, trunk very pale grey, shoots silky-hairy. *l.* 2½ to 6 in. long, broadly obovate to roundish-ovate, shortly pointed, base cuneate to rounded; margins wavy; veins in 7 to 10 pairs, silky-hairy beneath; stalk ¼ to ½ in. long. *Husk* ⅝ in. long, obovoid, lower bristles spatulate; stalk up to 1¼ in. long. Europe. 1910. Largest leaved of beeches. SYN. *F. macrophylla.* The 'Prince George of Crete' Beech belongs here.

**F. proce'ra.** A synonym of *Nothofagus procera.*

**F. Siebo'ldii.** Tree to 100 ft. *l.* 2 to 4 in. long, ovate to obovate, pointed, base tapered to slightly cordate; margins wavy, ciliate; veins in 7 to 10 pairs; stalk ¼ to ⅓ in. long. *Husk* ¾ in. long, woody, downy, covered with bristles, the lower ones of which are ½ in. long and spatulate; stalk stout, ½ in. long. Japan. 1892.

**F. Solan'deri.** A synonym of *Nothofagus Solanderi.*

**F. sylva'tica.*** Common Beech. Tree up to 100, sometimes 140 ft., trunk up to 6 ft. or more in diameter. *l.* 2 to 3½ in. long, oval to roundish-ovate, pointed, the margin wavy or obscurely toothed; veins in 5 to 9 pairs, silky-hairy at first; stalk ¼ to ½ in. long. *Husk* ¾ in. long, its downy stalk ½ in. long. Europe (Britain). (E.B. 1291.) var. **conglomera'ta,** dwarf bush, *l.* contorted; **cu'prea,** Copper Beech, *l.* coppery-red; **fastigia'ta,*** Dawyck Beech, of very fastigiate growth; **grandidenta'ta,** *l.* coarsely toothed; **hetero-phyl'la,*** Fern-leaved Beech (including **asplenifo'lia, inci'sa, lacinia'ta,** and **salicifo'lia**), *l.* variously shaped from linear to deeply pinnatifid; **latifo'lia** and **macrophyl'la,** synonyms of *F. orientalis*; **miltonen'sis,** leading shoot erect, branches pendulous; **pen'dula,*** Weeping Beech, limbs wide-spreading, often horizontal, with quite pendulous branches; **purpu'rea,*** Purple Beech, *l.* pale red in spring, deep purple later, including **purpu'rea pen'dula,** a weeping form; **rotundifo'lia,*** *l.* round, cordate, ½ to 1¼ in. wide, small, dainty, erect tree; **tric'olor,** *l.* purplish, edged and striped with rose and pinkish-white; **variega'ta,** *l.* striped with white or yellow; **Zlat'ia,** *l.* yellow at first, gradually becoming pale green. 1892.

W. J. B.

**FAIR MAIDS OF FRANCE.** *See* **Ranunculus aconitifolius, Saxifraga granulata.**

**FAIR MAIDS OF KENT.** *See* **Ranunculus aconitifolius.**

***fairfield'ii,*** from the Fairfield Nursery, New Zealand.

**FAIRY RINGS.** Green circles or parts of circles produced by the growth of certain fungi in meadows, on lawns, &c. On the outer and inner edges of the ring the grass is generally darker green, but the middle band where the fungi are growing contains very weak and brown dead grass. Various ideas are held regarding the origin of these differences, but one commonly held is that the outer band receives stimulation by additional nitrogen made available by the fungus growing outwards, and the inner band is richer in nitrogen due to decomposition of the fungus mycelium, while the death of the middle band may be due to dryness at the roots because the fungus mycelium prevents water percolating through the soil. The species of fungi generally found in British fairy rings is *Marasmius oreades* (q.v.), but species of *Tricholoma* and other capped-fungi sometimes form the rings. More than one crop of the fungus fruits may arise in the same year. Methods for their eradication are watering with Bordeaux mixture or with sulphate of iron, 1 lb. to 1 gallon of water, repeating in a week or 10 days at half this strength. Such treatments must be given when the soil is already moist either through a shower of rain or from previous watering.

D. E. G.

***falca'tus -a -um, falci-,*** in compound words, sickle-shaped.

***falcifor'mis -is -e,*** sickle-shaped.

***falcinel'lus -a -um,*** like a little scythe.

***Fal'coneri,*** in honour of (1) Dr. Hugh Falconer, 1808–65, Superintendent, Botanic Garden, Saharanpur; (2) William Falconer, 1850–1928, gardener at Harvard, United States.

**FALK'IA** (in honour of John Peter Falk, 1730–74, Swedish botanist, Professor at St. Petersburg). FAM. *Convolvulaceae.* A genus of 3 or 4 species of herbaceous plants, natives of S. Africa. Leaves heart-shaped, ovate, orbicular or reniform. Flowers rather small, solitary, on short stalks; sepals 5; corolla broadly bell-shaped,

5-angled or -lobed. *F. repens* is a pretty little evergreen creeper for the greenhouse, growing in any light compost, and increased by cuttings under a hand-glass in April or by division.

**F. re'pens.** Stem decumbent, rooting, branches filiform. *l.* scattered, cordate-ovate, obtuse, entire, stalked. *fl.* red with a paler throat, stalks scarcely longer than l. May. S. Africa. 1774. (B.M. 2228.)

*fal'lax,* false.

*Fallowia'nus -a -um,* in honour of George Fallow, 1890–1915, gardener in Botanic Garden, Edinburgh, killed in Egypt.

**FALLOWING.** Cultivating but leaving uncropped for a year. It is not an advisable measure in a garden and can only be excused when the ground is too foul with perennial weeds to give any prospect of a crop of any kind, even one that permits of constant cultivation. Not only does fallowing mean the loss of a year's crops, but the residues of previous crops which go a good way towards providing humus and nitrogenous compounds will be diminished by the action of bacteria encouraged by the constant stirring of the soil and the solvent action of the rain which can fall uninterruptedly upon it. Whenever possible foul land should be utilized for a cleaning crop, such as potatoes or turnips.

**FALLU'GIA** (in honour of Virgilio Fallugi, a Florentine botanist who wrote about the end of the 17th century). FAM. *Rosaceae.* A genus of 1 deciduous shrub related to Potentilla but with many persistent feathery styles, white flowers, glandular, pinnatifid leaves, and a calyx with bracts at the base by which it may be distinguished from Cowania. It needs a very sunny place in well-drained soil, and in most parts of England would be best either at the foot of a south wall or in a sunny spot in the temperate house.

**F. paradox'a.** Shrub of 2 to 4 ft., slender, branched freely near base, shoots white with down. *l.* clustered, alternate, ⅛ to ¾ in. long, 3- to 5-lobed, stalked, lobes linear, obtuse, with recurved margins, pale beneath, downy. *fl.* solitary or few on a short raceme at or near the ends of shoots, white, 1 to 1¼ in. across; cal. teeth pointed, with 5 small bracts alternating with them. June to August. *fr.* with persistent feathery style in handsome heads 1½ in. across. New Mexico to Utah. 1877. (B.M. 6660.)

**false,** similar in appearance only.

**FALSE ACACIA.** *See* **Robinia Pseudacacia.**

**FALSE ASPHODEL.** *See* **Tofieldia.**

**FALSE BOX.** *See* **Schaefferia frutescens.**

**FALSE DITTANY.** *See* **Dictamnus albus.**

**FALSE HELLEBORE.** *See* **Veratrum.**

**FALSE JALAP.** *See* **Mirabilis Jalapa.**

**FALSE JASMINE.** *See* **Gelsemium sempervirens.**

**FALSE SILVER-LEAF.** Silvery appearance of foliage usually owing to presence of air between the epidermis and the palisade tissue due to some other cause than attacks of the fungus *Stereum purpureum.* *See* **Silver-leaf Disease.**

*falx,* sickle.

**FAME FLOWER.** *See* **Talinum teretifolium.**

**FAMILY.** A group of plants more comprehensive than a genus, e.g. Cactaceae, Cactus family; Liliaceae, Lily family. The names of Families always terminate in -aceae, except Compositae, Labiatae, and Gramineae.

A→

**FAN PALM.** *See* **Chamaerops, Corypha,** and **Sabal.**

**fan-shaped,** (1) arranged like the ribs of a fan, as a trained peach-tree; (2) plaited like a fan, as the leaves of Chamaerops and Livistona; flabellate.

**FARADAY'A** (in honour of Michael Faraday, 1794–1867, the celebrated chemist). FAM. *Verbenaceae.* A genus of about 6 species of climbing shrubs, allied to Clerodendron, natives of Australia and the S. Pacific Is. Leaves opposite, entire, leathery, smooth. Flowers white, showy, in terminal loosely corymbose panicles or sessile at the nodes; corolla 4-cleft, one lobe larger than others, lobes spread, tube exserted from calyx, enlarged above; stamens 4, long exserted; ovary 4-lobed and celled. Fruit a drupe. They need warm conditions and a rich loamy soil with plenty of root-room, the branches spreading close to the glass in as light a position as the stove affords.

**F. papua'na.** *l.* large, bullate. *fl.* salver-shaped in corymbose panicles. Java. 1884.

**F. splen'dida.** Tall, woody climber. *l.* ovate, 6 to 12 in. long, slender-pointed, rounded or cordate at base, prominently nerved; stalks 1 to 2 in. long. *fl.* large, in a terminal corymbose panicle; cal. segs. about ¾ in. long; cor. tube over 1 in. long, lobes flat, about ¾ in. long. *fr.* size, colour, and shape of a hen's egg, with an acrid kernel. Queensland. 1879. (B.M. 7187.)

F. G. P.

**FARA'MEA** (native name in Guiana). FAM. *Rubiaceae.* A genus of about 100 species of Trop. American plants with opposite, usually oblong or lanceolate leaves. Flowers in a terminal inflorescence, white; calyx cup-shaped or almost tubular; corolla tubular or funnel-shaped, its lobes spreading or recurved; stamens 4, with pollen grains of two forms. *F. odoratissima* is an ornamental, fragrant, evergreen shrub needing stove conditions, a compost of fibrous peat and loam with a little silver sand and some lumps of charcoal. Cuttings made in spring will root in heat.

**F. odoratis'sima.** Shrub of 6 ft. *l.* oval-oblong, narrowed to base, abruptly slender-pointed. *fl.* white, about ½ in. across, in terminal corymbs. W. Indies. 1793.

*farc'tus -a -um,* not hollow.

*farfar'a,* mealy.

**FARFU'GIUM.** *See under* **Ligularia tussilaginea.**

*Farges'ii,* in honour of Père Paul Farges, 1844–1912, of the French Foreign Missions, Szechwan.

*farina'ceus -a -um,* farinaceous, mealy, like flour.

*farino'sus -a -um,* covered with meal.

*farleyen'sis -is -e,* of Farley Hill, Barbados.

*Farm'eri,* in honour of W. G. Farmer, c. 1840.

**FARMYARD AND STABLE MANURE.** Once the main means of improving the fertility of the soil, this mixture of the excreta of farm animal and litter is now rarely available for use in the garden, and its place must be taken mainly by the material from the compost heap and by green manuring, both of which help to maintain the humus content of the soil which was one of the important functions of farmyard manure, the other being the return of much of the mineral and nitrogenous matter contained in the food of animals and in the litter, which would otherwise have been lost. The value of farmyard manure depended upon the nature of the materials of which it was formed, the conditions of its formation, and the way it was kept and treated before it was applied to the soil. The excreta of farm animals are of varying manurial value, that of horse and sheep standing highest and yielding hotter, more rapidly fermenting material than dung from oxen and cows, and lastly pigs. The nature of the litter used, straw, bracken, peat-moss, saw-dust, also causes variation in the value of the farmyard or stable manure, as well as the age and condition of the animals. The use of farmyard manure as a source of heat in the construction of hotbeds was also an important factor in the raising of early crops, and in the making of mushroom beds, the substitutes for which are not yet entirely satisfactory. *See* **Heating, Manures.**

**Farnesia′nus -a -um,** in honour of Odoardo Farnese of Rome, *c.* 1611.

**Farquharia′nus -a -um,** in honour of General William Farquhar, 1770–1839, of Singapore.

**Far′reri,** in honour of Reginald J. Farrer, 1880–1920, English author and plant-hunter.

**FARSE′TIA** (in honour of Philip Farseti, a Venetian botanist). FAM. *Cruciferae.* A genus of about 20 species of branching herbs or sub-shrubs, more or less hoary or downy, natives of the Mediterranean region eastwards to N. India. Leaves entire, opposite, often hoary. Flowers in racemes or spikes. Hardy or half-hardy plants needing hot, rather dry places on the rock-garden or in the flower-border with thorough drainage; of value mainly for their hoary foliage. For pots a compost of sandy loam and peat is most suitable. All are easily increased by seed.

**F. aegyp′tica.** Shrubby, erect, much-branched, about 1 ft. h. *l.* linear, hoary. *fl.* white. June, July. N. Africa. 1788. Half-hardy.

**F. clypea′ta.** Erect herb, 1 to 2 ft. h. *l.* oblong, repand. *fl.* yellow. June. S. Europe. 1596. Hardy.

**F. eriocar′pa.** Erect sub-shrub. *l.* oblong. *fl.-head* yellowish. *fr.* densely silky hairy. Asia Minor. Hardy.

**F. lunarioides.** Sub-shrubby; branches ascending, about 1 ft. h. *l.* oblong-obovate, hoary. *fl.* yellow; sep. whitish. June. Grecian Is. 1731. (B.M. 3087.) Hardy.

**FASCIATION.** A condition due to the failure of lateral shoots to separate normally from the main axis, producing flattened stems, sometimes several inches wide, and, where the leaves are normally opposite, often spirally contorted as well. This condition is common in most plants but usually affects only a few individuals or only some shoots of an individual plant. It sometimes affects all parts of the plant as in some Sedums and in the Stag's-horn Ash (*Fraxinus excelsior* var.), and can then be carried on by cuttings or grafts, and is occasionally hereditary as in the Garden Cockscomb (Celosia). The conditions inducing fasciation are not known, for none of the suggested causes, e.g. heavy feeding, attacks of bacteria, mutilation of the principal axes, and so on can be relied upon to produce the phenomenon. Something closely akin to stem fasciation may be seen in the monstrous terminal flowers of some varieties of the common Foxglove (*Digitalis purpurea*) and in twin apples. The condition is rarely seen in conifers, though not unknown in the group, e.g. in *Cryptomeria japonica fasciata.*

**fascia′tus -a -um,** bound together.

**FASCICULA′RIA** (*fasciculus,* a little bundle; referring to the habit of growth). FAM. *Bromeliaceae.* A genus of 5 Chilean stemless herbaceous perennial plants with densely fasciculate rosettes of narrow, linear, spiny leaves and blue flowers immersed in the centre of the leaf-rosette. Related to Bromelia and Cryptanthus but petals and filaments free and ligulate at base. Treatment as for Billbergia but rather more hardy.

**F. bi′color.** *fl.* pale blue, about 1¼ in. long, in heads of 30 or 40 surrounded by ivory bracts longer than the *fl.,* and serrate on margins. *l.* numerous, brownish below, about 18 in. long, ⅜ in. wide, inner shorter, crimson. Chile. 1851. (B.H. 1873, 229, t. 14 as *Bromelia bicolor.*) SYN. *Rhodostachys bicolor.*

**F. Kirchoffia′na.** Differs from *F. pitcairniifolia* by its fewer smaller *fl.* 1⅛ in. long, *l.* about 30, about 1 ft. long, ⅝ in. wide. Probably Chile; only known in cultivation.

**F. litora′lis.** *fl.* about 1⅜ in. long. *infl.* surrounded by densely scaly, lacinate-spiny bracts longer than the *fl.* September to November. *l.* about 18 in. long, green above, densely covered with pale scales beneath. Chile. 1873.

**F. pitcairniifo′lia.*** *fl.* blue, 1⅜ in. or more long, in dense, many-fld. head, in centre of rosette, which is here bright red, and bracts shorter than *fl. l.* numerous, about 3 ft. long, rather paler below than above. Chile. 1866. (B.M. 8087 as *Rhodostachys pitcairnii-folia* and B.H. 1876, 161, t. 10–11 as *Billbergia Joinvillei.*) Nearly hardy.

**fascicula′ris -is -e,** clustered or grouped in bundles.

**fascicula′tus -a -um,** clustered or grouped in bundles.

**fastigia′tus -a -um,** fastigiate, having erect branches, often forming a column.

**fastuo′sus -a -um,** proud, tall.

**✕FATSHED′ERA** (bigeneric hybrid between Fatsia and Hedera). FAM. *Araliaceae.*

✕**F. Liz′ei** (*Fatsia japonica Moseri* ♀✕*Hedera hibernica*). Evergreen shrub of loose sprawling growth, shoots stout, ⅜ in. thick, warty. *l.* 4 to 10 in. wide, palmately and deeply 5-lobed, dark lustrous green, leathery; stalk about as long as blade. *fl.* pale green, in globose umbels 1 in. wide, making a terminal panicle 8 to 10 in. long, 4 in. wide. October, November. France. 1910. (R.H. 1924, 179; B.M. 9402.) Quite hardy and vigorous, should be useful for shady places. Easily increased by cuttings.

W. J. B.

**FATS′IA** (adaptation of the Japanese name for *F. japonica*). FAM. *Araliaceae.* A genus of 2 species of evergreen shrubs akin to Aralia, differing by the petals being separate or only touching, instead of overlapping as in Aralia.

**F. hor′rida.** A synonym of *Echinopanax horrida.*

**F. japon′ica.*** Evergreen shrub 8 to 15 ft., of spreading habit, shoots ¾ in. diameter. *l.* 6 to 16 in. wide, the deeply palmate lobes 7 or 9, rarely 11, oblong-lanceolate, pointed, toothed, dark shining green, leathery, glabrous; stalk 3 to 12 in. long. *fl.* milky-white, in globose, long-stalked umbels 1 to 1½ in. wide, forming a branching panicle 9 to 18 in. long. October, November. *fr.* black, globose, ⅓ in. wide. Japan. 1838. (B.M. 8638.) SYN. *Aralia japonica, A. Sieboldii.* Valuable late-flowering evergreen, hardy in our average climate if given a sheltered, shady spot. Increased by cuttings. var. **Mo′seri,** *l.* larger, habit more compact; **variega′ta,** lobes of *l.* white at the ends.

**F. papyrif′era.** Shrub or small tree 10 to 25 ft., shoots ½ in. thick, nearly filled with white pith from which Chinese rice-paper is made. *l.,* branches, and *infl.* covered with loose floss. *l.* up to 1 ft. long, much wider, 5- or 7-lobed, toothed; stalk 10 to 20 in. long. *fl.* white, in globose umbels ⅝ in. wide, very numerous, in a terminal panicle 3 ft. long. October. China, Formosa. (B.M. 4897.) Cool greenhouse. May be used for sub-tropical bedding in a well-sheltered spot. SYN. *Aralia papyrifera, Tetrapanax papyriferus.*

W. J. B.

**fat′uus -a -um,** not good.

**FAUCA′RIA** (*fauces,* throat; the gaping leaves resembling an open mouth). FAM. *Aizoaceae* (Mesembryanthemum). Dwarf, almost stemless, succulent plants with opposite leaves united at the base; the leaves are flat above, very convex on the under side or keeled, spatulate or lanceolate; they are characterized by the long slender teeth which interlock in young growths, but when the leaves have separated they give the appearance of a gaping jaw, hence the old names of Tiger's Chaps, Cat's Chaps, &c. The flowers are large, yellow, without stalks and generally open in the afternoon. This genus comes from the Karroo, S. Africa. Cultivation as for Mesembryanthemums (2); these plants grow chiefly in autumn and then they need most water.

**F. feli′na.** Similar to *F. tigrina* but distinguished by the more slender *l.,* less conspicuous white dots, and fewer teeth. 1730. SYN. *Mesembryanthemum felinum.* (M.A.S. 5. 2; D.C. Pl. Gr. 152.)

**F. lupi′na.** Similar to *F. tigrina. fl.* smaller. *l.* more spreading and with 7 to 9 teeth tapering to fine hairs. 1824. SYN. *Mesembryanthemum lupinum.* (M.A.S. 5. 3.)

**F. tigri′na.** Several pairs of *l.* to each growth, at right angles to each other, almost stemless, branching from the base. *l.* broad at base, 1½ to 2 in. long, 1 in. broad, face flat, back concave and keeled, with 9 or 10 stout recurved teeth which taper to fine hairs along the edge; grey-green with conspicuous white dots below, keel and teeth horny, white or tinged pink. *fl.* 2 in. across, yellow. 1790. SYN. *Mesembryanthemum tigrinum.* (M.A.S. 5. 1; N.E. Br. 211.)

**F. tuberculo′sa.** *l.* very thick, short, and wide, with about 3 stout teeth on the edge, upper side covered with white, tooth-like tubercles, dark green. *fl.* 1½ in. across, yellow. SYN. *Mesembryanthemum tuberculosum.* (B.M. 8674.)

V. H.

**Fauconnet′tii,** in honour of Dr. Charles Fauconnet, 1811–75, of Geneva.

**Faur'ei,** in honour of (1) the Abbé Faure of Grenoble, Director of the Seminary there, 1874–90; (2) Abbé Urbain Faure, 1847–1915, French missionary in Japan.

**FAUX.** The orifice or throat of the calyx or corolla.

**faveolate,** favose, pitted or excavated, like the cells of a honeycomb.

*favig'erus -a -um,* bearing honey-glands.

**FEABERRY.** A local name for Gooseberry.

**FEATHER GRASS.** *See* **Stipa pennata.**

**feather-veined,** having veins making an acute angle with the midrib; pinnate-veined.

**febrifugal, febrifuge,** having a moderating effect upon fevers.

*fecun'dus -a -um,* fruitful.

**FED'IA** (derivation?). FAM. *Valerianaceae.* Horn of Plenty. A genus of a single species of annual herb, native of the Mediterranean region, closely related to Valerianella. Glabrous. Leaves entire or toothed. Flowers red or white. *F. Cornucopiae* is best sown in pots in March, the seedlings being planted out thickly at the latter end of April in any good garden soil; or seed may be sown in the open towards the end of April.

**F. Cornuco'piae.** About 6 in. h. Stem purplish. *l.* ovate-oblong, toothed, lower stalked, upper sessile. *fl.* red, the clusters forming a corymb, peduncle thick, hollow. July. S. Europe, &c. 1796. (B.R. as *Valerianella Cornucopiae.*) var. **candidis'sima,** *fl.* white; **floribun'da ple'na,** tufted, *fl.* reddish-pink, double, very freely produced. 1886. (G.F. 1218.)

*Fedtschenkoa'nus -a -um,* in honour of Madame Olga Fedtschenko or Dr. Boris Fedtschenko, Russian botanists.

*Fe'ei,* in honour of A. L. A. Fée, 1789–1874, botanist of Strassburg.

**FEIJO'A** (in honour of Don da Silva Feijoa, a botanist of San Sebastian). FAM. *Myrtaceae.* Monotypic genus, distinguished from its allies by the opposite punctate leaves, berry fruit, and stamens straightish in bud, not incurved as in most related genera. *F. Sellowiana* is not quite hardy in our average climate but quite happy on a sunny wall. In Cornwall it is a tree over 20 ft. high, fully in the open. Succeeds in any reasonably good soil, even chalky. Propagated by cuttings.

**F. Sellowia'na.*** Evergreen shrub or small tree, shoots whitish-felted. *l.* opposite, oblong, 1½ to 3 in. long, mostly rounded at the base and blunt at the apex, dark shining green, whitish-felted beneath. *fl.* solitary, axillary, 1½ in. across, in 1 or 2 pairs at the base of the current year's shoots; sep. 4, recurved, roundish-oblong, felted; pet. 4, roundish-oval, concave, red in the centre, white at the margin; stamens numerous, erect, crimson, ¾ in. long; anthers yellow. July. *fr.* an ovoid berry, 2 in. long, with a pleasant rich guava-like flavour. Brazil. 1898. (B.M. 7620.) A form with variegated l. (var. **variega'ta**) is known.

W. J. B.

*fejeen'sis -is -e,* of Fiji Is.

**FELI'CIA** (in honour of Herr Felix, a German official). FAM. *Compositae.* A genus of perhaps 50 species of dwarf sub-shrubs or rarely annual herbs, mostly natives of S. Africa with some in Abyssinia, closely related to Aster. Leaves alternate, entire or toothed. Flower-heads radiate; ray-florets blue or white, disk yellow; involucre hemispherical or broadly bell-shaped, its scales in two to many series, narrow, overlapping with scarious margins. Bristles of pappus in one series only. The shrubby species are best grown in a cool greenhouse in sandy peat, propagated by cuttings struck in sandy soil under a propagating-glass. They, especially *F. amelloides,* make pretty pot-plants and may be planted out for summer flowering. The annual species are best treated as half-hardy annuals.

A

**F. abyssin'ica.** Tufted, much-branched shrub, 4 to 12 in. h. *l.* close, alternate, linear, ½ to ⅝ in. long, entire or minutely bristly serrate; sessile. *fl.-heads* lilac, solitary, terminal; peduncles 1 to 2 in. long. Trop. Africa. 1896. Half-hardy.

**F. amelloi'des.*** Blue Daisy; Blue Marguerite. 1 to 2 ft. h., bushy. *l.* opposite, roundish-ovate. *fl.-heads* sky-blue, large. Summer. S. Africa. 1753. (B.M. 249. A variegated form is known and a var. **monstro'sa** with fl.-heads twice as large as in the type. SYN. *Agathaea coelestis, Aster rotundifolius.*) Perennial.

**F. Bergeria'na.** Kingfisher Daisy. Annual about 4 in. h. *l.* grass-like. *fl.* bright blue, about ½ in. across. S. Africa. Half-hardy.

**F. echina'ta.** 1 to 2 ft. h., leafy. *l.* oblong-lanceolate, spine-tipped, ¾ in. long, ciliate, sessile. *fl.-heads* lilac, about 1¼ to 1½ in. across; disk yellow, involucral bracts oblong-lanceolate with pellucid margin, densely ciliate. S. Africa. 1904. SYN. *Aster echinatus.* Half-hardy. Needs cutting back to prevent sprawling habit and induce flowering. (B.M. 8049.)

**F. fra'gilis.*** Annual or biennial, slender, about 4 in. h. *l.* narrow-linear, usually bristly ciliate, hard-tipped. *fl.-heads* pale violet-blue, disk yellow, about ½ in. across. July to September. S. Africa. 1759 (B.M. 33 as *Aster tenella.*) SYN. *F. tenella.* Half-hardy.

**F. frutico'sa.** A synonym of *Aster fruticosus.*

**F. petiola'ta.** A synonym of *Aster petiolatus.*

**F. reflexa.** A synonym of *Aster reflexus.*

**F. rotundifo'lia.** A synonym of *Aster rotundifolius.*

**female,** term applied to a plant or flower having pistils but no functional stamens. Such flowers may be found on the same plant as staminate flowers, when the species is said to be monoecious, or on a different plant, when it is said to be dioecious.

**FENCING.** An essential preliminary to the construction of a garden in an open site is to make provision for fencing it in against cattle and other animals.

A height of not less than 4 ft. is usually desirable and a simple fence may consist of wire strained on iron pillars or on stout wooden posts treated with preservative. Another simple type of fencing is cleft chestnut paling.

If rabbits are prevalent any open type of fencing must be supplemented by wire-netting not less than 3 ft. 6 in. out of the ground with 6 in. buried in the ground and turned outwards so as to counteract burrowing.

Still more permanent is the chain-link type of fencing. Where a close screen is considered necessary either for privacy or for protection from wind, a close-boarded fence may be employed. As an alternative, hurdles of woven hazel or willow wired to stout posts may well be used, or for more formal effect panels of inter-woven oak laths in conjunction with sawn oak posts. The view of an expanse of fencing is seldom attractive and an endeavour should be made to cover it as quickly as possible, either by planting climbers such as Pyracantha, Honeysuckles, Loganberries, &c., against the fence, or where space permits by planting an ornamental border of trees and shrubs to serve as a screen. Although this may take away from the area left for gardening, the general effect of screening the hard lines of the boundary will be to increase the apparent size of the plot.

J. E. G. W.

**FEND'LERA** (in honour of August Fendler, 1813–83, one of the first botanists to collect in New Mexico and Venezuela). FAM. *Saxifragaceae.* A genus of 3 species of shrubs, natives of Colorado to Mexico. Deciduous with striped branches. Leaves almost sessile, opposite, entire, 1- to 3-veined, without stipules. Flowers 1 to 3 on short lateral branches, stalked; sepals and petals 4, stamens 8; ovary half-superior, 4-celled. Fruit a 4-valved many-seeded capsule longer than the persistent calyx. *F. rupicola* needs a very sunny position and will grow in ordinary soil. A south wall is needed in most districts. It can be propagated by cuttings of rather soft wood in gentle heat.

**F. rupic'ola.** Deciduous shrub to 6 or 8 ft., rather straggling, shoots ribbed, downy. *l.* lanceolate, ½ to 1½ in. long, with 3 prominent veins, rough-bristly above, hairy beneath, almost sessile. *fl.* white or tinted rose, ¾ to 1¼ in. across, usually solitary, rarely 3 on short lateral shoots with small clustered l.; pet. hairy without; cal. downy. May, June. SW. United States. 1879. (B.M. 7924.)

*fenestra'lis -is -e,* pierced with holes like windows.

**FENESTRA'RIA.** Included in **Mesembryanthe-mum.** *See under* **M. rhopalophyllum.**

*fenestra'tus -a -um, see fenestralis.*

**FENNEL** (*Foeniculum vulgare*) is grown for the use of its leaves in fish sauces and for garnishing, and after blanching for salads. In Italy the young tender stems are used in soups or eaten raw in salad, and the peeled stems cut just before the flowers open are eaten dressed with vinegar and pepper. The seeds are used in flavouring and an oil is distilled from them. Fennel is easy to grow and will do well in almost any soil in an open situation. The seed should be sown in April and thinned out to about 1 ft. apart, or the seedlings may be transplanted. Though the plants will often live much longer it is best to renew the bed every 3 years or so, and unless the seeds are desired the flowering stems should be removed to encourage the production of fresh leaves. The type has given rise to variations, the most important of which are the Finnochio or Florence Fennel (*F. vulgare* var. *dulce*), a dwarfer plant with very large leaf bases which may be grown about 8 in. apart and is better for a richer soil and calls for considerable quantities of water, and the Carosella of S. Italy (var. *piperitum*) which is the variety of which the young stems are eaten raw. Finnochio is cooked in stock and has a flavour somewhat like celery but sweeter, and a pleasant aroma.

**FENNEL FLOWER.** *See* **Nigella.**

**FENNEL, GIANT.** *See* **Ferula.**

*fen'nicus -a -um,* Finnish.

**FENUGREEK.** *See* **Trigonella Foenum-graecum.**

**FENZ'LIA.** Included in **Gilia.** *See* **G. dianthoides.**

*Fenzlia'nus -a -um, Fenzlii,* in honour of E. Fenzl, 1808–79, director Botanic Garden, Vienna.

*-fer, -ferus -a -um,* in compound words, implying bearing, as conifer, bearing cones.

A→

*Ferdinan'di-Coburg'i, Ferdinan'di-re'gis,* in honour of King Ferdinand of Bulgaria, student of alpine plants.

*Ferguson'ii,* in honour of W. Ferguson, 1820?–1887, who collected in Ceylon.

**FERNANDEZ'IA.** Included in **Lockhartia.**

*Fernandezia'nus -a -um,* in honour of George Garcias Fernandez, Spanish botanist.

**FERN-BALL.** *See* **Fern cultivation.**

**FERNEL'IA** (in honour of Jean François Fernel, 1497–1558, physician to Henri II, of France). FAM. *Rubiaceae.* A genus of 4 species of small evergreen trees or shrubs, natives of the Mascarene Is., with much the habit of Box. Leaves small, opposite, obovate-oblong or nearly round, leathery. Flowers small, usually solitary, sometimes in pairs, on very short axillary pedicels. Fruit a berry. For cultivation *see* **Rondeletia.**

**F. buxifo'lia.** Shrub of 1 to 3 ft. *l.* obovate to oblong, about ½ in. long, ¼ to ⅓ in. wide. *fl.* whitish; cor. lobes obtuse. *Berry* red, obovate, about as large as a pea, with the awl-shaped cal. lobes at apex. Mauritius. 1816.

**FERNS.** Ferns have of late years lost much of the popularity they once enjoyed, but their great, if quiet, beauty, the extreme diversity of their forms, and the wide range of conditions under which they thrive recommend them to lovers of beautiful and interesting plants. Somewhere about 10,000 different species of Ferns have been distinguished and among them are many that can be grown with ease even in the exacting conditions of a living-room, while there are others that challenge the skill of the most devoted gardener to keep them alive, let alone to give them the conditions they need for their full development. They have an extremely wide range in nature: they exist in profusion in the Tropics, and are found in greater or less abundance thence to the Arctic Regions as far north as Greenland and south to the regions of the Antarctic, wherever vascular plants can find a footing, and they are found from sea-level to very high altitudes. A very large number of ferns are shade- and moisture-loving but by no means all, for there are many that grow, like our own *Asplenium Ruta-muraria, A. Trichomanes,* and *Ceterach officinarum* in the most exposed and sunny places and show the characters of the flowering plants that inhabit similar situations in their habit of growth and in the structure of their leaves; some few indeed develop succulence so that they might be grown with Cacti, as, for instance, *Drymoglossum carnosum* of northern India and *Cyclophorus adnascens* of Trop. Asia and Polynesia, while many, including the Tree Ferns, store water in their stem tissues. Epiphytes, too, are well represented among the ferns, especially in the tropics, but they occur even in our own country where the air is sufficiently moist, *Polypodium vulgare* being the commonest example here. Among these epiphytes the species of Platycerium are especially interesting from the adaptive nature of their fronds.

The minute size of their spores as well as the adaptability of some species has enabled certain ferns to become very widely distributed over the world; thus the common Bracken (*Pteridium aquilinum*) is found in all temperate countries and in many parts of the tropics as well, the Royal Fern (*Osmunda regalis*) all over Europe, in India, E. Asia, Eastern N. America, Mexico, and the W. Indies southwards to Uruguay, S. Africa and adjacent islands, and Madagascar, and the beautiful Maidenhair (*Adiantum Capillus-Veneris*) found here and there in England occurs not only in W. Europe but also in W. and S. Africa, temperate Asia, Ceylon, Polynesia, Queensland, the W. United States, and southwards to Colombia and the Amazon. These are only a few of the many examples that might be given of species very widely distributed over the surface of the earth, but on the other hand special features often appear to mark the ferns of different parts of the world. Thus, the ferns of N. America are, to a considerable extent, deciduous, as, for example, the Ostrich Fern, *Matteuccia Struthiopteris,* several Osmundas, *Onoclea sensibilis, Adiantum pedatum, Dennstaedtia punctilobula,* and the tiny *Pellaea Breweri.* On the contrary, the greater part of the hardy and half-hardy ferns from Japan are evergreen, for instance, *Cyrtomium falcatum, Dryopteris hirtipes, D. varium, Polystichum tsussimense,* the Japanese form of *P. lobatum,* all have a peculiarly glossy appearance and thick texture such as few ferns of other regions show. The Tree Ferns found in the E. and W. Indies and in S. America, with few exceptions, have comparatively slender stems, whereas the stems of those native of New Zealand, Australia, and Tasmania are comparatively thick as in *Dicksonia antarctica,* in the silver Tree Fern, *Cyathea dealbata,* and *C. medullaris,* and some others. British Ferns seem to have developed a propensity to produce crisped, crested, and depauperate forms of the original species, both evergreen and deciduous, in a degree unapproached by those of any other country. These forms cannot be attributed to the influence of cultivation for a great majority of them have been found growing wild and have been brought into and increased in gardens where they have retained their peculiar characters. *Nephrolepis exaltata* provides a striking example of the production of variations under cultivation, and a few exotic ferns have produced crested forms after being introduced into this country as may be seen in some of the Adiantums, and in species of Gymnogramme and Pteris.

As in many other groups of plants the variation in stature exhibited by members of the family is immense. Some of the gigantic Tree Ferns reach to 50 ft. in height, and there are many ferns that never exceed a few inches; while the fronds themselves are often but an inch long or even less, in other instances they may attain to 15 ft. In habit, too, the contrast is great for there are many that are of a bushy and symmetrical form while there are others that spread widely by means of rhizomes, or twine round other plants or climb by their long stems to the tops of tall trees.

In addition to the great diversity of form shown by the fronds, sometimes entire, sometimes finely and variously divided, though they are for the most part uniformly green, yet here too there is considerable diversity. The common Hard Fern, *Blechnum Spicant*, and the Prickly Shield Fern, *Polystichum aculeatum*, have a particularly dark shade of green which contrasts markedly with the soft pea-green of the Oak Fern, *Dryopteris Linnaeana*, and *Adiantum trapeziforme*. *Polypodium aureum* and *P. glaucophyllum* have a peculiar blue tint which they retain throughout their lives. Though quite green when mature, many ferns develop brilliant bronzy tints in the young fronds, and this is particularly noticeable in the Adiantums, as in *A. macrophyllum*, *A. monochlamys* var. *Veitchii*, *A. rubellum*, and *A. tinctum* which turn from a delicate pink to bright magenta and finally to the soft glaucous green tint that characterizes the mature growth. *A. tenerum Farleyense* is perhaps even more striking. The same changes of colour are to be seen in the hardy *A. pedatum*, in *Blechnum occidentale*, in *Doodia aspera multifida* and *D. media*, *Didymochlaena truncatula*, the dwarf *Blechnum L'Herminieri*, and the large *Davallia divaricata*, as well as in many other species both small and great, and as the evergreen species are growing for the greater part of the year, this variation of colouring is to be seen at all seasons. One type of colour variety is not very common in ferns, the spotted variegation that so often occurs in the leaves of flowering plants, but there are a few that show white stripes on the leaves that are pleasing, and there are, as well, the gold and silver ferns such as Cheilanthes that add another variety of colouring to beauty of form.

PROPAGATION. The most general plan of propagation of ferns is by spores, but with many species this is at best difficult, and with some it is impossible to obtain them, or to raise plants from them if they are obtained, but most Adiantums and many species of Pteris are easily raised in immense numbers from spores. All ferns that form several crowns may be increased by division, and those with creeping rhizomes, like Davallias, are easily propagated by layering the points or by removing pieces that have formed roots. A few—Aspleniums particularly—produce small bulbils along the upper portion and at the end of the fronds which will eventually form plants if removed and planted. The increase of Filmy Ferns is usually a delicate operation, for plants imported from their native habitats, with every care in transit, frequently die before they have become established even though they may arrive in good condition. They may, however, be propagated by carefully made divisions of such plants as do become established and grow well. Tree Ferns are usually imported and a large proportion generally succeed. Young plants may be raised from spores when obtainable but it takes many years for them to grow to the size of imported plants. The spores of many of the Tree Ferns germinate freely enough, but, under cultivation, seldom advance beyond the prothallus stage.

*Spores.* The fronds from which spores are to be taken should be carefully examined at frequent intervals when they begin to ripen, so as to obtain the spores at the proper time. When the sori being to turn brown the fronds should be cut and allowed to dry in closed paper bags. The sooner they are sown after being shed the better, and they may be sown at any time in the year, though spring is perhaps the best. They should be sown in pots or pans that have been half-filled with crocks and then filled to within half an inch of the top with a mixture of finely sifted loam and very small pieces of crushed brick. The use of sterilized soil, crocks, &c., is an advantage. An even surface should be secured by pressing firmly with another pot. The soil should then be watered and allowed to drain before the extremely minute spores are sown very thinly over the surface; the pots should then be covered with pieces of glass and stood in water in a close frame in a propagating house, being shaded at all times during sunshine but not in dull weather. Laying pieces of paper on the outside of the frame and removing them when not required is a convenient method of shading. When the spores have grown sufficiently to be visible as very minute plants (the prothallus)—the time taken varies considerably with different ferns—they should be very carefully pricked off into pots of similar soil, filled this time to the top. Very small patches should be taken on a stick having a tiny notch cut at the end, and they should be merely pressed into the soil about an inch apart. Adiantums are frequently ready to prick out in a month or 6 weeks from the time of sowing. After pricking out, the pots should be placed in a similar frame and kept close until the small plants are established. No water should be given overhead until the little plants have been pricked off some time and have formed fronds. Sufficient will be supplied by the pots having been stood in water and the moisture inside the frame, which will usually not be one with bottom heat. If conditions are suitable, the young ferns will grow fast in spring and summer and will soon require to be potted on. The next shift will be singly into small pots, or Adiantums may be treated as though each little group were one plant and will make decorative plants in a shorter time. The whole operation is an exceedingly delicate one, and requires considerable care and attention to accomplish successfully. Not rarely, after the spores germinate, most of the young plants are eventually found to belong to another species or genus than that which was intentionally sown. Fern spores are so light that a breath of wind will waft them about and this may account for the presence of the commoner one which might well overgrow the one desired, or good spores of the one desired might not have been present at all. The treatment outlined is suitable for both stove and greenhouse ferns, and the same method with a lower temperature will also suit the hardy species. Young plants should be moved on before the pots become very full of roots, for if the plants are allowed to become starved in the early stages it is a long time before they recover.

*Divisions, &c.* The best time for dividing ferns, or for increasing by means of the creeping rhizomes, is just before growth begins in February or early spring. The plants should not be divided too severely—if a large number of small plants is required, if at all possible, they should be raised from spores. Rhizomes should be pegged to a piece of peat or on the surface of a small pot of soil and allowed to root before they are detached. The insertion of the little bulbils in pots of soil in a close frame will soon increase the stock of the species that produce them.

SOIL, POTS, ETC. FOR FERNS. Nearly all ferns require much water in summer, and rarely need to be dry at the roots at any season; efficient drainage is, therefore, a very important thing. Anything approaching a sour or a waterlogged soil is detrimental, and may be fatal; even to ferns not quickly injured in other ways. Success in the cultivation of established ferns depends more upon this, with careful watering and attention to temperature, atmospheric moisture, and proper shade, than on any soil in which they may be grown. Adiantums, for instance, will succeed either in loam or peat alone, the texture of the fronds being firmer in the former, and this is the only apparent difference. A large amount of peat was at one time thought necessary for all ferns, but sweet leaf-soil, where it can be obtained, can be used with greater advantage to the plants. Soft sandstone, mixed with the soil, tends to keep it porous, and suits some species better than others; charcoal may be used freely for all. The different habits of the plants will frequently suggest the best type of soil to use for them. A compost of loam with an equal quantity of leaf-soil and peat combined and sufficient charcoal, small pieces of crocks or sharp sand to keep the whole open, may be used successfully for all Tree Ferns and established plants of Adiantum, Aspidium, Asplenium, many species of Blechnum, Davallia, Dryopteris, Gymnogramme, Pteris, and any others of similar habit. Davallias and other ferns that have slender rhizomes must be fixed to something upon which they can grow. A good plan is to place an inverted pot or a piece of Tree Fern stem in the middle of a pan and build a small mound on top with lumps of peat, loam, and Sphagnum, fixing the rhizomes to the surface with small pegs. Epiphytic ferns, of which Platycerium is a well-known and distinct example, often succeed admirably if fastened with a little moss and peat to a block of wood, and suspended in the stove. They should be kept rather dry in winter. The composts for *young* plants should be passed through a sieve. Small pots are best, and have also an advantage in appearance, and any deficiency in the quantity of food contained in the soil may be made good by manure water during the growing season.

HARDY FERNS. There are many places in gardens where few flowering plants thrive and some of these are well adapted for the cultivation of ferns. Whenever practicable the Hardy Fernery should be in a naturally moist and cool spot, and strong light being usually objectionable, the neighbourhood of tall deciduous trees should be preferred over all other places, for there the plants would be little exposed to the sun and protected from strong winds. A north aspect is the most suitable, the plants then having full light without being spoilt by the sun. The Hardy Fernery should be constructed of stone, in the form of a rock-garden, either on the level ground or as a ravine more or less deep, or the roots and stumps of felled trees may be made to serve instead of stones. In whatever way the Fernery is arranged drainage is most important, and ample means should be provided for the escape of surplus moisture. It should be borne in mind in building the outdoor Fernery that the requirements and comfort of the plants are more important than the appearance of the rockwork and that provision must be made to guard against the disastrous effects of high winds. Besides the neighbouring trees, judicious grouping in masses of the larger and more robust species may be made to provide shelter for the smaller and more tender ferns.

In planting the Hardy Fernery, the distribution of the evergreen and the deciduous species should be carefully considered, and the plants arranged in such a way that never at any time shall there be a bare appearance, and that the whole shall be covered with foliage even in the resting season. The N. American and Japanese species that are available greatly add to the diversity of size and habit exhibited by the British species and their numerous varieties.

The planting of the Hardy Fernery may be safely undertaken at any time from October to March, but if the situation is tolerably sheltered it is better to plant in autumn, as root action in most hardy ferns begins long before there is any visible sign of growth in the foliage. Plants moved in the autumn will, if kept sufficiently moist during winter, make a quantity of fresh roots upon which

the new growth is mostly dependent. If, however, the site is exposed, it is better to defer the planting till the spring just before vegetation begins, say about the end of March, for the plants are then in full vigour. Special attention to the nature of the plants employed in planting the Fernery is indispensable, and of much greater consequence than the preparation of the material in which they are to grow and which for general purposes consists of 2 parts of fibrous turf, 1 part of half-decayed leaf-mould, and 1 part of coarse silver sand.

When the Hardy Fernery is once established, very little attention is required to keep it in good order. The whole work in connexion with it is limited to occasional waterings during the summer, while during the winter a slight covering of leaves or other light material placed over the plants will enable the more tender sorts to withstand the rigours of our most severe winters. The species of Osmunda which are among the most decorative of the hardy ferns should be planted in a partial bog or by the side of water to give the best effect. *Dryopteris Thelypteris* enjoys a similar situation.

In the following lists an attempt has been made to indicate the size to which ferns hardy in this country may be expected to grow, by a dagger (†) those best in an airy, exposed (though of course not very dry) situation, and by the sign (‖) those needing more than ordinary moisture at the roots. All the others do well in naturally moist and shady places. For all it is necessary to provide protection from high winds such as neighbouring trees will give and in general a north aspect is best for them, for there the light will be good and the strong rays of midsummer sun will not be felt.

FOR OUTDOOR FERNERIES. Growing from 4 to 12 in. high: *Asplenium Adiantum-nigrum*, *A. Ruta-muraria†*, *A. Trichomanes†*, *A. viride*, *Athyrium Filix-foemina crispum* and other dwarf vars., *Blechnum amabile*, *B. pennamarina*, *B. Spicant* and vars., *Ceterach officinarum†*, *Cryptogramma acrostichioides*, *C. crispa*, *Cystopteris bulbifera*, *C. fragilis*, *C. montana†*, *Dryopteris Filix-mas crispa*, *D. hexagonoptera*, *D. Linnaeana*, *D. oregana*, *D. Phegopteris*, *D. Robertiana*, *D. Villarsii*, *Phyllitis Scolopendrium‖* vars., *Polypodium vulgare†* vars. *cornubiense* and *elegantissimum*, *Polystichum aculeatum angulare* vars. *Bayliae* and *parvissimum*, *P. Lonchitis*, *Woodsia ilvensis*, *W. obtusa*, *Woodwardia radicans angustifolia*.

Growing from 1 to 2 ft. high: *Asplenium acrostichoides*, *A. alpestre*, *A. alpestre flexile*, *Athyrium filix-foemina* (many varieties), *Dennstaedtia punctiloba*, *Dryopteris aemula*, *D. cristata†*, *D. Filix-mas Crouchii*, *D. Filix-mas fluctuosa*, *D. marginalis*, *D. novaeboracensis*, *D. oreopteris†*, *D. spinulosa dilatata* vars., *D. spinulosa intermedia*, *D. Thelypteris‖*, *D. Villarsii arguta*, *Phyllitis Scolopendrium‖* vars., *Polypodium vulgare auritum*, *P. vulgare cambricum*, *P. vulgare crenatum*, *P. vulgare semilacerum*, *Polystichum acrostichoides*, *P. aculeatum*, *P. aculeatum angulare* vars., *Woodwardia radicans‖*.

Growing from 2 ft. high upwards: *Athyrium filix-foemina* (many vars.), *Blechnum chilense*, *Dryopteris cristata Clintoniana*, *D. erythrosora*, *D. Filix-mas* (many vars.), *D. Goldieana*, *D. spinulosa Boothii*, *D. spinulosa dilatata* (vars.), *Matteuccia Struthiopteris‖*, *Onoclea sensibilis‖*, *Osmunda cinnamomea‖*, *O. Claytoniana‖*, *O. gracilis‖*, *O. regalis‖*, *Polystichum aculeatum angulare* (vars.), *P. munitum*, *Pteridium aquilinum*.

STOVE FERNS. That tropical ferns require great heat at all times with constant heavy shading in summer and but little air at that season as well is altogether a mistake. If attempts are made to grow them under these conditions the result is invariably weak, elongated fronds that are at once subject to the attacks of insects, and are rarely strong enough to stand any change to which it may be necessary to subject them. Blinds on rollers that can be let down and removed as desired should be used. Ferns like both shade and moisture but both may be given in excess, especially in the winter when all should be at rest. Growing and resting periods are as necessary for ferns as for other plants. The general arrangement of ferns in the stove greatly depends upon the structure and space at command. Adiantums, Davallias and their kin, Gymnogrammes, and Platyceriums are examples of ferns for the lighter places in the house where only thin shade is given in sunny weather. Acrostichums and their kin, Aspleniums, Dryopteris, Pteris, and Tectarias are ferns that succeed in darker and more shady positions. Tree Ferns produce a fine effect where there is sufficient height, but if planted out they soon require much more room than it is possible to give in the majority of stoves. By growing them in tubs, and plunging them, a more suitable appearance is presented, the restriction of the roots checking the rate of growth of the fronds. Any repotting necessary should be done before growth begins, for, if deferred, many of the young fronds will be crippled. For stove ferns a growing period of 8 months should be allowed, from February to September inclusive. The other 4 months should be a resting period when a night temperature of 50 to 55° F. will be sufficient, with a minimum rise by day of 5° more. A drier atmosphere must also be maintained and less water supplied to the roots, avoiding extremes in both directions. When growth begins in spring the minimum night and day temperatures may be gradually raised until, in summer, the minimum temperature will rarely fall below 60 or 65° F. at night. Air should be carefully admitted and plenty of water supplied to the roots and among the pots, with a view to the production of fronds of moderate growth and good substance—conditions not to be secured by a close atmosphere and very high temperature. Light syringings may be given occasionally to most stove ferns in summer, but too much has a tendency to weaken many of the fronds. Adiantums, Gymnogrammes, and generally speaking all ferns with powdery or hairy fronds should not be syringed at any time. The whole beauty of ferns consists in the full development of the fronds; if these are to remain in good condition until the new ones of the following year appear, it is important to keep the plants properly watered and to give them the treatment in summer calculated to produce a moderate amount of sturdy growth that, in autumn, should be thoroughly ripened by the admission of sun and air to the house in which the ferns are grown. If blinds or rollers are used for shading they will have to pass over the ventilators in the roof. This has an advantage both in breaking the force of the wind and preventing undue evaporation of moisture from the inside. If the blinds are found to fit too closely blocks can easily be fixed to the rafters at the top to keep the shading a little open.

GREENHOUSE FERNS. A large number of ferns, often grown and treated as stove plants, succeed equally but do not grow so quickly, in a greenhouse temperature, either alone or in combination with flowering plants. The majority of ferns succeed in comparatively small pots, and are consequently well suited for mixing with other occupants of the side stages. The stronger-growing ones may be planted out in permanent beds or among other plants, such as Camellias, where not too much crowded, the partial shade and moisture suiting the ferns admirably. Nearly all Adiantums do well under greenhouse treatment in summer but need warmer quarters in winter. Many species of Dryopteris and of Pteris, especially *P. longifolia*, *P. serrulata* and its varieties, and *P. tremula*, do better planted in a cool structure than anywhere else. *Blechnum gibbum* and other species are among the most beautiful of coolhouse ferns, and the same may be said of *Asplenium bulbiferum* and others from Australia and New Zealand, *Davallia canariensis*, *Nephrolepsis exaltata* and its very numerous vars., *Onychium japonicum*, *Woodwardia radicans*, and many others. *Todea barbara* is well

adapted for planting out in a position where considerable space can be given for its large fronds to develop; it may also be grown in pots in any cool house, or even in a sheltered position outdoors with protection in frosty weather. The genus Gleichenia contains many beautiful species that do not require much heat, excepting 2 or 3 from tropical countries. If grown in large pans and tied out with neat stakes, beautiful specimens may be obtained by greenhouse treatment. These are propagated by layering the slender rhizomes, or by separating rather large pieces from the parent plant and planting separately. The shade needful for ordinary greenhouse flowering plants in summer will suit the ferns, plenty of moisture being given at the roots at that season and also overhead except to Adiantums.

FERNS SUITABLE FOR BASKETS. Hanging baskets, in either the stove or greenhouse, are at all times an attraction, and the graceful habit of many ferns constitutes them excellent subjects for use in this way. Baskets made in different sizes, of stout galvanized wire, may be suspended from the roof, and if carefully watered the plants will usually succeed extremely well. Many ferns may be so seen to better advantage, especially those with long and drooping fronds, than when growing in pots and placed on the stage. Some of the fast-growing Selaginellas are also useful to plant with basket ferns, for covering the soil or hanging down. Adiantums will be found very good for this purpose, especially *A. caudatum*, *A. cuneatum*, *A. gracillimum*, and *A. Moorei*. The following also will be useful: *Anogramma schizophylla*, *Asplenium Belangeri*, *A. longissimum*, and *A. viviparum*; *Davallia dissecta* and *D. pallida*; *Nephrolepis acuminata* and *N. exaltata*; and there are many others of similar habit and usefulness. Nearly all of those mentioned will grow well in the cool house in summer.

FILMY FERNS constitute a distinct class, requiring different treatment from any other members of the family. Very few do well in an open house as sufficient atmospheric moisture cannot be obtained. On the whole they do not need much heat, and will often grow stronger and keep in better health when grown in close cases in a cool Fernery, than when in similar cases in a stove. Filmy Ferns should never be watered overhead, but the stones and moss amongst which they are generally grown must be kept continually moist by having water poured on from the small spout of a can. This, when evaporating inside the close case, becomes condensed on the extremely numerous divisions of the fronds seen in the majority of the species, and its continued presence there invariably indicates good health and the frequency with which it will be necessary to give water. Pieces of rough fibrous peat and loam, with charcoal and Sphagnum, are most suitable for Filmy Ferns. Nearly all that grow in soil succeed better when planted amongst stones, while those that form rhizomes should be placed on blocks of peat, dead pieces of Tree Fern, &c. They must always be shaded from sunshine, and not much light is needed at any time. The difficulty generally experienced is in establishing the plants; when once they begin to grow and increase, their treatment is, in most instances, simple enough. Hymenophyllum, Leptopteris, and Trichomanes are three of the principal genera. *Leptopteris superba* is a vigorous species having large fronds of a filmy texture; *L. hymenophylloides* is of smaller growth but very desirable: both are beautiful and more easily grown than the majority of the plants in this section.

WARDIAN CASES. Ferns used for decorating Wardian Cases must include only those that are of small or moderate growth, the space inside the case being very limited. The system admits of more moisture being kept around the plants than is possible in an ordinary room where the arrangements for heating tend to dry the air. It is always important in changing plants in these cases that have become unhealthy to substitute others from a cool house, for if insufficiently hardened the young fronds soon wither and die. Ample drainage must be provided and if pots are used they should be covered with living Sphagnum. Ferns in Wardian Cases keep fresh for a long time if they are properly looked after and are then very attractive. Cases of somewhat similar construction can be used in cool houses for small collections of Filmy Ferns.

TREE FERNS. Considerable space and lofty houses are necessary for growing Tree Ferns so as to show their true characters. In Ferneries of limited size, where a few are cultivated, it is best to restrict their root growth by planting in large tubs or pots, and this allows of their being rearranged from time to time when they begin to overgrow neighbouring plants. In very large conservatories, a few permanent specimens planted out in well-drained borders succeed better than in any other positions, and always present a majestic appearance unexcelled by any other plant that can be similarly employed. *Alsophila australis, A. excelsa, Cyathea dealbata, C. medullaris* (probably the tallest growing of all cultivated ferns), and *Dicksonia antarctica* are the best for growing in greenhouses. All these may be used in subtropical gardening outside in summer in shady, sheltered places. There are many Tree Ferns that need stove conditions: all are beautiful and worth growing in large heated structures. They all, especially Alsophilas, delight in plenty of atmospheric moisture and shade. The stems of newly imported Tree Ferns should, on their arrival, be covered with damp moss or canvas, and be kept moist by syringing until the new fronds appear. The time this takes varies according to the condition in which they arrive and the season. When the head of fronds is established the covering may be removed from the stem, but frequent syringing in summer is of the highest importance as by far the greater part of the stems of many is literally a mass of roots requiring a quantity of water. Tree Ferns in poor health may often be greatly improved by covering the stem from base to fronds with Sphagnum to the depth of an inch and tying it on. If kept moist the roots soon fill the moss and the stem is thus considerably enlarged. Tree Ferns that are dead on arrival can be utilized by covering with epiphytic or other small ferns for stove or greenhouse decoration, the top being scooped out and a free-growing species with a pendent habit planted therein in soil, others being fastened on the side with blocks of peat and some thin wire.

REPOTTING FERNS is an operation of great importance. The principal points to be observed are that they should on no account be over-potted, and that special care should be taken to prevent the roots of the plants being torn away or broken off. Over-potting is a frequent cause of loss of ferns. Although a hard-and-fast rule as to the dimensions of the pots to be used cannot be laid down, it is well to remember that by far the better plan is to repot several times as becomes necessary, giving a slightly larger pot every time, than to put plants into much larger pots with the object of saving labour, or the trouble of repotting in a month or two. Through successive pottings the plants derive from each additional supply of soil the full nutritive properties it possesses, while over-potting frequently leads to the soil becoming sour and so to ill health. Healthy, well-rooted plants may be safely repotted as follows: from 3-in. pots to 4½-in.; from 4½-in. to 6-in.; from 6-in. to 8-in.; from 8-in. to 10-in.; from 10-in. to 13-in.; and so on. Ferns require repotting the less frequently the larger they become and the larger the pots are in which they are growing; they should be repotted more or less frequently according to their nature and their power of growth. Ferns make their hardiest and most luxuriant growth when the inside surface of the pots is covered with a network of roots.

If proper attention is given to ferns after repotting the operation may be done at any time of year, but generally it is better to begin in the warm house in early February, and in the cool house in early March. It is always advisable to have the repotting done as the plants start into new growth. The operation may be continued through the spring and summer but it is better to stop about the middle of September, as very little growth is made after that time, and the addition of new soil, even if not injurious, is of little use, for its nutritive properties will be lost before the spring through the frequent waterings that will be necessary before growth begins again. It is not advisable to put into larger pots plants with their roots matted in a hard mass until they have been loosened as much as can be done with safety. When the roots have filled the bottom of the pot and have become thickly matted among the crocks, it is best to repot without disturbing them, leaving the crocks in, for it is certain that if for the sake of removing the crocks the roots are torn away, the plants will be deprived of a considerable part of their feeders and will suffer accordingly. Large plants should be examined and repotted if they require it, but there is no necessity to do it every year: indeed, it is often advisable not to do it, although young plants benefit by being repotted several times in a year because in the growing season they make new roots very rapidly.

On account of the extremely sensitive nature of the roots of ferns they should preferably be potted in old pots; these should, of course, be clean and dry, so as to prevent, whenever the plants are repotted, the breaking of their roots, which is bound to happen if the plants have been previously potted in wet or dirty pots to the sides of which the roots will be found to adhere strongly. When new pots have to be used it is advisable to have them put into water in which they should remain until they are thoroughly soaked, and then be well dried before using; pots fresh from the kiln absorb a great quantity of water and when they have not been previously soaked it frequently happens that the first two or three waterings, instead of being of benefit to the plants, only serve to soak the pots, while the balls of soil which the latter contain become so dry that it is often most difficult afterwards to get them moist.

Great care must always be taken that the plants when repotted are sufficiently moist at the roots. When a fern has suffered from lack of water at the roots, the effect is shown by the shrivelling of the fronds, the older ones being usually affected first. In most plants, whether of a herbaceous or of a woody nature, the temporary flagging of the foliage can be repaired by an ordinary watering or at most by a thorough soaking, but such treatment has no apparent effect upon most ferns, and few, indeed, are the species whose fronds, having once flagged, regain their full elasticity by the application of water either to their roots or over their foliage. Notholaenas and Cheilanthes seem to show the least effects of dryness at their roots.

It will be found greatly to the benefit of ferns in pots that they should stand on a solid, cool, moist bottom, and the ordinary stage or shelf cannot give the best results. The most suitable standing for most ferns is a solid bed of ashes, or one of sand, covered with a layer of coal cinders, which will remain sweet for an indefinite time. Wherever practicable the houses in which it is intended to grow ferns in pots should be low, sunk 15 or 18 in. below the surface of the ground and provided with solid beds, bricked on their vertical face. The walks should be of either coarse gravel or of the natural earth, if of a sandy nature, simply covered with a layer 2 or 3 in. thick of coal-cinders, these being the most porous and at the same time the best moisture-retaining materials that can be used in a house in which the air must be constantly moist.

GROWING FERNS IN PANS. Like the hanging basket, the shallow pan will offer to certain species advantages that they could not obtain if grown in the ordinary flower-pot. The shallow pan is especially useful for the cultivation of the ferns with rhizomes. These organs in some instances prefer to be underground, but in most they run over the surface of the soil to which they should be carefully fastened down by means of small wooden pegs, which are useful until the rhizomes have rooted sufficiently to retain their position, when the pegs can be dispensed with. As the plants grow and the rhizomes spread, they are apt to reach over the sides of the pans; for the good of the plants this should be prevented, and it is easily done by carefully turning them inside the pans and pegging them securely on to the soil. Under these conditions the rhizomes produce fresh roots all along their length and add to the strength of the plant, whereas when they extend over the sides of the pan and out of the damp soil and moss they seldom form roots and have to be supported by the plant instead of helping it, and the results are not satisfactory. When put into use, the pans, like the pots, must be clean and dry. Drainage is essential; the holes should be covered with large crocks, which should be covered with either moss or rough peat, and this in its turn with a layer of very rough compost, higher in the middle than at the sides; then the pan should be filled with finer material until there is sufficient depth to plant the ferns. The principal thing is to have the work firmly done and when the rhizomes are well pegged down and the pans are watered, very little attention will be needed for some time. A greater surface in a pan of the same dimensions may be obtained by raising the compost in the centre of the pan and forming a cone resting on rough pieces of peat, all made secure by being skewered together. This method is particularly suitable for Davallias, and with a little extra care these mounds need never become dry.

FERNS ON CORK. Virgin cork may be used in many ways, as, for instance, in making artificial tree-trunks of various sizes, by firmly binding or tying pieces of cork bark together, leaving little spaces here and there so that the hollow parts may be filled with a compost of a type suitable for the ferns that are to occupy them. Many ferns will grow under these conditions but Davallias, Nephrolepis, and Platyceriums especially thrive.

FERN BALLS. A terra-cotta bottle, made of specially porous material, and usually known as a Madeira Fern bottle, is procured and covered with a layer of clay an inch thick, which is fastened to it and held in position by copper wire worked across in all directions. Quite tiny seedlings of *Adiantum Capillus-Veneris* are then planted in the clay and the bottle is filled with water, and hung up. The water soon percolates through the clay and keeps the plants moist. There is no need to give water direct to the plants—the bottle only requires to be replenished occasionally, and by this means a pleasing ball of green foliage is produced, lasting in perfection so long as the bottle is not allowed to become dry.

FERNS FOR SPECIAL PURPOSES. The lists of ferns which follow give a selection of those best suited for special purposes. The kinds which grow best under warm treatment are distinguished by an asterisk (*); those succeeding under ordinary greenhouse conditions have no special mark; those that are hardy are indicated by a dagger (†).

1. Tree Ferns. *Alsophila excelsa, A. glauca*\*, *A. villosa*\*, *Blechnum cycadoides, B. discolor, B. gibbum, Brainea insignis*\*, *Cibotium Barometz, C. regalis*\*, *C. Schiedei*\*, *Cyathea arborea*\*, *C. australis, C. Cooperi, C. dealbata, C. Dregei*\*, *C. insignis*\*, *C. medullaris, C. Rebeccae, Dicksonia antarctica, D. Blumei, D. fibrosa, D. squarrosa, Hemitelia Smithii.*

2. Other very large Ferns, not tree-like. *Acrostichum aureum*\*, *Adiantum polyphyllum*\*, *A. tenerum*\*, *A. trapeziforme*\*, *Aglaomorpha Heracleum*\*, *Angiopteris evecta*\*, *Asplenium longissimum*\*, *A. Nidus*\*, *Blechnum brasiliense*\*, *Culcita macrocarpa, Davallia divaricata, Dennstaedtia adiantoides, D. davallioides Youngii, Didymochlaena*

*truncatula*\*, *Hemitelia capensis, Marattia alata*\*, *M. Cooperi*\*, *M. salicina*\*, *Microlepis hirta cristata*\*, *M. platyphylla, Nephrolepis acuminata* and vars.\*, *N. hirsutula tripinnatifida*\*, *Polybotrya cervina, Polypodium aureum, P. subauriculatum*\*, *P. verrucosum*\*, *Pteris Drinkwateri, P. moluccana*\*, *P. tremula* and vars., *Todea barbara, Woodwardia radicans* and vars.

3. Small-growing Ferns. *Actiniopteris australis, Adiantum Capillus-Veneris fissum, A. Legrandii, A. Luddemannianum, A. mundulum, A. Pacottii, A. reniforme, Asplenium flabelliforme, A. fontanum, A. incisum, A. monanthemum, A. Rutamuraria, A. Trichomanes, A. viviparum, Ceterach officinarum, Cryptogramma Stelleri, Davallia parvula, Dryopteris fragrans, D. sancta, Elaphoglossum peltatum, Fadyena Hookeri, Humata repens, Pellaea Breweri, P. Bridgesii, Polypodium lycopodioides, P. piloselloides, P. vaccinifolium, Woodsia glabella, W. alpina, W. oregana, W. scopulina.*

4. Ferns with Coloured or Tinted Fronds. *Adiantum colpodes, A. cyclosorum*\*, *A. hispidulum, A. lunulatum*\*, *A. macrophyllum* and vars.\*, *A. monochlamys*\*, *A. peruvianum*\*, *A. polyphyllum*\*, *A. rhodophyllum*\*, *A. rubellum*\*, *A. tetraphyllum gracile*\*, *A. tinctum, Blechnum L'Heritieri*\*, *B. meridense, B. microsorum gracile, B. occidentale, Brainea insignis*\*, *Davallia divaricata*\*, *Didymochlaena truncatula*\*, *Dryopteris corusca*†, *D. erythrosora*† and var. *monstrosa*†, *D. squamaestipes, D. varia*†, *Osmunda regalis palustris, Pellaea*, nearly all species glaucous, *Polypodium aureum* and var. *areolatum, P. glaucophyllum, Pteris biaurita* vars., *Stenoloma chusanum Veitchianum*\*, *S. retusum*\*, *Woodwardia radicans orientalis.*

5. Variegated Ferns. *Adiantum cuneatum variegatum, A. macrophyllum striatum, Aneimia phyllitidis tessellata, Athyrium Goeringianum pictum*†, *Coniogramme japonica variegata, Doryopteris pedata palmata nobilis*\*, *Phyllitis Scolopendrium variegatum*†, *Polypodium aristatum variegatum, P. vulgare variegatum, Pteridium aquilinum variegatum, Pteris biaurita quadriaurita argyreia* and *tricolor, P. biaurita variegata, P. cretica albo-variegata, P. cretica Mayii, P. ensiformis Victoriae* and *cristata.*

6. Crested Ferns. *Adiantum Capillus-Veneris Luddemannianum, A. cuneatum grandiceps* and *verscillense, A. excisum multifidum, Asplenium Adiantum-nigrum grandiceps*†, *A. marinum ramosum*†, *A. Trichomanes* (several forms)†, *Athyrium Filix-foemina* (numerous forms)†, *Blechnum Spicant* (several forms)†, *Cyclophorus Lingua corymbifera, Davallia denticulata polydactyla*\*, *D. Mariesii cristata, Doodia aspera multifida*\*, *Dryopteris Filix-mas* (numerous forms)†, *D. patens cristata, D. Richardsii multifida, D. spinulosa polydactyla*†, *Microlepis hirta cristata*\*, *Nephrolepis acuminata furcans*\*, *N. Daffii*\*, *Osmunda regalis corymbifera* and *cristata*†, *Phyllitis Scolopendrium* (numerous forms)†, *Pityrogramma chrysophylla grandiceps, P. pulchella Parsonsii* and *Wettenhalliana, Polypodium vulgare* (several forms)†, *Polystichum angulare* (numerous forms)†, *Pteridium aquilinum grandiceps*†, *Pteris cretica* (several forms), *P. serrulata* (several forms), *P. tremula grandiceps* and *Smithiana, Woodwardia radicans cristata.*

7. Gold and Silver Ferns. *Adiantum scabrum, A. sulphureum, A. Williamsii, Alsophila quadripinnata, Cheilanthes argentea, C. Clevelandii, C. Eatonii, C. farinosa, C. tomentosa, Cyathea dealbata, Notholaena Eckloniana, N. hypoleuca, N. Newberryi, N. sinuata, N. sulphurea*\*, *N. trichomanoides*\*, *N. vellea, Pityrogramma calomelanos* (several silver forms), *P. chrysophylla* (several golden forms)\*, *P. triangularis, Onychium siliculosum*\*, *Trismeria trifoliolata*\*.

8. Filmy or Transparent Ferns. *Hymenophyllum aeruginosum, H. asplenioides, H. australe, H. caudiculatum, H. ciliatum, H. cruentum, H. demissum, H. dicranotrichum, H. dilatatum, H. Forsterianum, H. hirsutum, H. pectinatum, H. peltatum*†, *H. pulcherrimum, H. scabrum, H. tunbrid-*

genset†, *Leptopteris Fraseri*, *L. hymenophylloides*, *L. intermedia*, *L. pellucida*, *L. superba*, *Trichomanes capillaceum*, *T. exsectum*, *T. humile*, *T. parvulum*, *T. pyxidiferum*, *T. radicans* and vars., *T. reniforme*, *T. tenerum*, *T. venosum*. All these succeed with cool treatment.

9. Ferns of Drooping Habit. *Adiantum caudatum\**, *A. concinnum\**, *A. dolabriforme*, *A. Moorei\**, *A. philippinense*, *Asplenium caudatum*, *A. flabellifolium*, *A. flaccidum*, *A. longissimum*, *A. oceanicum*, *A. Sandersonii*, *Davallia pulchra*, *D. solida\**, *D. trichomanoides*, *Dryopteris squamaestipes*, *Lindsaya repens\**, *Nephrolepis acuminata\** and var. *furcans\**, *N. acuta*, *N. cordifolia* and var. *pluma*, *N. Duffii\**, *N. exaltata*, *Pityrogramma schizophylla* and var. *gloriosa*, *Polypodium lachnopus*, *P. Paradiseae*, *P. subauriculatum*, *P. subpetiolatum*, *P. verrucosum\**, *Pteris moluccana\**, *Stenoloma chusanum Veitchianum\**, *S. retusum\**, *Woodwardia radicans cristata* and *orientalis*.

10. Climbing Ferns. *Lygodium circinnatum\**, *L. japonicum*, *L. palmatum*, *L. polymorphum\**, *L. polystachyum\**, *L. scandens*, *L. volubile\**.

11. Ferns of Wandering Habit (Rhizomatous). *Cyclophorus Lingua*, *Davallia denticulata\**, *D. divaricata*, *D. hymenophylloides*, *D. immersa*, *D. Mariesii*, *D. pulchra*, *D. pyxidata*, *D. solida*, *Dennstaedtia adiantoides*, *D. cicutaria*, *D. davalloides Youngii\**, *Dryopteris hexagonoptera†*, *D. Linnaeana†*, *D. Phegopteris†*, *Elaphoglossum peltatum\**, *Gleichenias*, *Humata Griffithiana\**, *H. repens*, *H. Tyermannii*, *Hymenophyllums*, *Leptolepia novae-zelandiae*, *Leucostegia pallida\**, *Microlepia marginata*, *M. pilosa*, *Nephrolepis* (all species), *Odontosoria aculeata\**, *Oleandra articulata\**, *O. nodosa\**, *O. Wallichii*, *Polybotrya cervina\**, *P. osmundacea\**, *P. scandens\**, *Polypodium aureum* and var. *sporadocarpum\**, *P. Billardieri*, *P. glaucophyllum\**, *P. lachnopus*, *P. Paradiseae\**, *P. piloselloides*, *P. pustulatum*, *P. repens\**, *P. Schneideri\**, *P. subauriculatum\**, *P. subpetiolatum\**, *P. vaccinifolium\**, *P. verrucosum\**, *P. vulgare* and vars.†, *Polystichum adiantiforme*, *Pteris moluccana\**, *P. scaberula*, *Scyphularia pentaphylla\**, *Stenochlaena palustris*, *Trichomanes* (most species), *Woodwardia radicans angustifolia*.

12. Ferns of Curious Forms. *Actiniopteris australis\**, *Adiantum reniforme\** and var. *asarifolium\**, *Aneimia* (all species), *Angiopteris evecta*, *Asplenium Nidus* and var. *australasicum\**, *A. palmatum*, *Botrychium Lunaria†*, *Ceratopteris thalictroides\**, *Coniogramme fraxinea*, *Doryopteris concolor*, *D. ludens\**, *D. pedata palmata*, *D. sagittifolia*, *Elaphoglossum crinitum\**, *E. peltatum\**, *Fadyena Hookeri*, *Gymnopteris Muelleri*, *Helminthostachys zeylanica\**, *Hemionitis arifolia*, *H. palmata*, *Llavea cordifolia*, *Lygodium* (all species), *Marattia* (all species)\**, *Platycerium* (all species)\**, *Polypodium fossum\**, *P. Xiphias*, *Schizaea* (all species)\**, *Schizoloma reniforme\**, *Taenitis* (all species)\**, *Trichomanes reniforme\**, *Trismeria trifoliata*, *Vittaria* (all species)\**.

13. Viviparous and Proliferous Ferns. *Adiantum caudatum\** and var. *hirsutum\**, *A. dolabriforme\**, *A. philippinense\**, *Asplenium attenuatum*, *A. bulbiferum* and vars., *A. caudatum\**, *A. Colensoi\**, *A. compressum\**, *A. dimorphum*, *A. flabellifolium*, *A. flaccidum*, *A. longissimum*, *A. monanthemum*, *A. oceanicum*, *A. Sandersonii\**, *A. viviparum\** and var. *nobile\**, *Camptosorus rhizophyllum*, *Ceratopteris thalictroides\**, *Cystopteris bulbifera*, *Diplazium proliferum*, *Doryopteris pedata palmata*, *Dryopteris effusa*, *D. erythrosora*, *D. refracta*, *D. vivipara*, *Fadyena Hookeri\**, *Hemionitis arifolia\**, *H. palmata\**, *Hypolepis Bergiana*, *Nephrolepis* (nearly all species), *Phyllitis Scolopendrium* vars. *densum†*, *proliferum†*, and *Wardii†*, *Platycerium bicornutum*, *P. Stemmaria\**, *P. Willinckii\**, *Polystichum angulare proliferum* and vars., *P. viviparum*, *Trichomanes pinnatum\**, *Woodwardia radicans*.

14. Ferns for Hanging Baskets in Warm Fernery. *Adiantum caudatum*, *A. concinnum*, *A. cuneatum grandiceps*, *A. dolabriforme*, *A. fragantissimum*, *A. gracillimum*, *A. Moorei*, *A. peruvianum*, *A. tenerum farleyense*, *A.*

*Williamsii*, *Asplenium caudatum*, *A. longissimum*, *Blechnum glandulosum*, *Davallia denticulata*, *D. solida* and vars., *D. trichomanoides*, *Humata Griffithiana*, *Leucostegia pallida*, *Microlepia cristata*, *Nephrolepis acuminata furcans*, *N. exaltata*, *N. pectinata*, *Pityrogramma* (all species), *Platycerium bicornutum*, *Polypodium subauriculatum*, *Scyphularia pentaphylla*, *Stenoloma chusanum Veitchianum*.

15. Ferns for growing on Cork Blocks in Warm Fernery. *Adiantum diaphanum*, *A. dolabriforme*, *A. philippinense*, *Asplenium nobile*, *Davallia bullata* and all species with running rhizomes, *Nephrolepis cordifolia compacta*, *N. pectinata*, *Oleandra nodosa*, *Pellaea flexuosa*, *Platycerium grande*, *P. Hilli*, *P. Stemmaria*, *P. Willinckii*, *Polypodium Phymatodes cristatum*, *P. stigmaticum*, *Stenochlaena palustris*.

16. Ferns for Hanging Baskets in Cool Fernery. *Adiantum assimile*, *A. venustum*, *Asplenium flaccidum*, *Davallia bullata*, *D. Mariesii* and var. *cristata*, *Dryopteris effusa*, *Hypolepis distans*, *H. tenuis*, *Leptolepia novae-zelandiae*, *Leucostegia immersa*, *Nephrolepis cordifolia pluma*, *Pellaea ternifolia*, *Platycerium bicornutum*, *Polypodium pustulatum*, *Polystichum lepidocaulon*, *Pteris multifida* and vars., *Woodwardia radicans*.

17. Ferns for growing on Cork blocks in Cool Fernery. *Adiantum Capillus-Veneris* and vars., *A. colpodes elegans*, *Asplenium flabellifolium*, *Davallia bullata*, *D. Mariesii*, *D. Mariesii cristata*, *Hypolepis distans*, *Pellaea rotundifolia*, *P. ternifolia*, *Platycerium bicornutum*, *Polypodium lycopodioides*, *P. polypodioides*, *P. pustulatum*, *P. triangulare laxum*.

18. Ferns for planting on Walls in the Warm Fernery. *Adiantum aemulum*, *A. caudatum*, *A. cuneatum* and vars., *A. fragrantissimum*, *A. hispidulum*, *A. peruvianum*, *A. tenerum*, *Asplenium flaccidum*, *A. planicaule*, *Blechnum glandulosum*, *Davallia bullata*, *D. denticulata*, *D. solida* and vars., *D. trichomanoides*, *Dryopteris squamaestipes*, *Humata Tyermannii*, *Leucostegia immersa*, *L. pallida*, *Lindsaya repens*, *Nephrolepis* (all species), *Osmunda regalis palustris*, *Pellaea ternifolia*, *Polypodium Billardieri*, *P. Catherinae*, *P. glaucophyllum*, *P. subauriculatum*, *Polystichum echinatum*, *Scyphularia pentaphylla*, *Stenoloma palustre*, *Tectaria Ridleyana*.

19. Ferns for planting on Walls in the Cool Fernery. *Adiantum aethiopicum*, *A. affine*, *A. assimile*, *A. Capillus-Veneris*, *A. colpodes*, *A. cuneatum* and vars., *A. formosum*, *A. fulvum*, *A. hispidulum*, *A. tinctum Wagneri*, *A. venustum*, *A. Williamsii*, *Asplenium flaccidum*, *A. incisum*, *Blechnum occidentale*, *Cyclophorus Lingua*, *Davallia bullata*, *D. Mariesii*, *Diplazium Thwaitesii*, *Doodia caudata*, *Hypolepis distans*, *H. repens*, *Leptolepia novae-zelandiae*, *Leucostegia immersa*, *L. pallida*, *Nephrolepis cordifolia*, *Onychium japonicum*, *Polypodium triangulare laxum*, *Pteris adiantifolia*, *P. longifolia*, *P. multifida* and vars.

20. Ferns suitable for Dwelling-rooms. *Asplenium bulbiferum* and var. *laxum pumilum*, *A. Colensoi*, *A. fragrans foeniculaceum*, *A. Nidus*, *Cyrtomium falcatum* and var. *Fortunei*, *Davallia canariensis*, *Dryopteris Filix-mas cristata*, *D. hirtipes*, *Nephrolepis cordifolia*, *N. exaltata* and vars., *Osmunda regalis palustris*, *Pellaea viridis*, *Platycerium bicornutum*, *Polypodium aureum*, *Polystichum adiantiforme*, *P. aristatum variegatum*, *P. discretum*, *Pteris cretica* and vars. *Mayi* and *Wimsettii*, *P. longifolia*, *P. multifida* and vars., *P. tremula*, *Todea barbara*.

21. Ferns suitable for Ordinary Fern Cases. *Adiantum affine*, *A. Capillus-Veneris* and vars., *A. diaphanum*, *A. hispidulum*, *A. reniforme*, *Asplenium fragrans*, *A. lineatum inaequale*, *A. lunulatum*, *A. monanthemum*, *A. palmatum*, *Blechnum penna-marina*, *Cyclopteris Lingua*, *Davallia bullata*, *D. canariensis*, *Diplazium zeylanicum*, *Doodia cordata*, *Leptolepia novae-zelandiae*, *Onychium japonicum*, *Phyllitis Scolopendrium* vars., *Polypodium Billardieri*, *P. lycopodioides*, *P. Scouleri*, *Polystichum*

*lobatum setosum*, *Pteris cretica* and vars., *P. multifida* and vars., *Stenoloma chusanum strictum*.

22. Ferns for Cutting. *Adiantum aemulum*, *A. Capillus-Veneris*, *A. cuneatum*, *A. fragrantissimum**, *A. gracillimum*, *A. Moorei**, *A. Pacottii*, *A. tenerum** and var. *farleyense**, *A. tinctum Wagneri*, *Asplenium Adiantumnigrum*†, *Davallia bullata*, *D. dissecta** and var. *elegans**, *D. solida fijiensis**, *Humata Griffithiana**, *H. Tyermannii*, *Leucostegia immersa*, *Odontosoria chinensis* and var. *Veitchiana**, *Onychium japonicum*, *Osmunda regalis palustris*, *Polystichum aculeatum angulare** and vars., *Pteris cretica* and vars., *P. multifida* and vars., *Tectaria Ridleyana*.

*PESTS*. Fern Eelworm, *Aphelenchoides fragariae*, is a common glasshouse pest attacking Adiantum, Asplenium, Begonia, Coleus, Gloxinia, and Pteris. Fern fronds infected by this pest become blotched with brown and black areas, which are sharply defined. Begonia leaves become pinkish-yellow and transparent, the infection usually beginning along the leaf-margins. Gloxinia foliage shows small yellowish areas, which extend and become brown, while the leaf-margins tend to curl inwards. The microscopic eelworms live and breed within the leaf-tissues which they invade through the stomata, and move about on the outside of the plants in a film of moisture. Infected plants are greatly disfigured, and become weak and stunted.

All discoloured, dry, and shrivelled leaves should be removed and burned to prevent the eelworms from being carried down to the soil. Overcrowding of susceptible plants should be avoided to prevent the pests from spreading by way of the leaves. Young ferns may be subjected to the warm-water treatment by immersing them for 20 minutes in water at a constant temperature of 110° F. The pots, crocks, soil, and staging in and upon which infected plants have been grown should be sterilized with boiling water to prevent infection being carried in them.

Fern Mite, *Tarsonemus tepidariorum*, is a pest chiefly of *Asplenium bulbiferum*, in the still curled fronds of which the minute Mites congregate. They feed by piercing the tissues with their stylet-like mouthparts and abstracting the sap causing minute brown spots to appear on the fronds which ultimately shrivel. In light infestations the fronds become distorted, swollen, and stunted. The microscopic, pearly white, oval eggs are laid on the upper side of the fronds while still curled and between the leaf-bases. The newly hatched, glistening white, 6-legged mites run about over the fronds and, later, become 8-legged. There are several overlapping generations a year, their activity being greatest in late spring and summer.

Propagation of these ferns should be made only from mite-free plants, and care must be taken to avoid infestation by quarantining newly acquired plants. Dusting the fronds with finely divided sulphur dust is effective, while slow fumigation with Grade 16 naphthalene (*see* **Insecticides**) may be carried out. The immersion of young ferns in warm water at a constant temperature of 110° F. for 20 minutes is advisable in severe outbreaks, together with the sterilization of the pots, crocks, and soil.

(G. F. W.)

**FEROCAC'TUS** (*ferus*, wild; referring to the strongly developed spines). FAM. *Cactaceae*. Round or cylindric, usually large; ribs thick and prominent; spines well developed, some hooked. Flowers with a very short, scaly tube. Fruit oval, dry, dehiscing by a basal pore. All come from N. America. **A**

**F. acantho'des.** Round, but cylindrical with age; ribs up to 27; areoles large with dense, brown felt, close; spines pink or red; radial spines weak, bristle-like; centrals awl-shaped, spreading, flattened, twisted, annulate but never hooked, up to 5 in. long.

*fl.* yellow. California, Lower California, Nevada. (G.C. 8 (1890), 167; B.R.C. 3, t. 15; f. 134–7.) SYN. *Echinocactus acanthodes*, *E. cylindraceus*.

**F. Covil'lei.** Large plants, ribs 22 to 32, thin, somewhat tuberculate; areoles distant; radial spines 5 to 8, spreading, awl-shaped, long, annulate, straight or curved backwards; central spine hooked, flattened or 3-angled. *fl.* red, tipped with yellow. Sonora. (G.C. 35 (1904), 181; B.R.C. 3, f. 138–9.)

**F. crassihama'tus.** Plants globose, glaucous; ribs 13, prominent, very wavy; areoles large; radial spines 8, upper one straight, lower 2 or 3 hooked; central spines 5, longer and stouter, usually red, 1 hooked. *fl.* small, purple. Mexico. (B.R.C. 3, f. 151.) SYN. *Echinocactus Mathssonii*.

**F. Echid'ne.** Globose depressed, green; ribs 13, sharp; areoles distant, oval; radial spines 7, nearly 1 in. long, yellow; central spine solitary, longer. *fl.* lemon-yellow. Mexico. (B.R.C. 3, f. 144.) SYN. *Echinocactus Echidne*.

**F. flavovi'rens.** Large plants forming clumps; ribs 13, high, somewhat wavy; areoles large, grey, woolly; spines pale brown, long and stout, 4 centrals much longer than the radials. *fl.* ? Mexico. (B.R.C. 3, t. 13.)

**F. Ford'ii.** Globose, greyish-green plants; ribs about 21; radial spines whitish, spreading, very slender; centrals 4, 1 flattened, hooked, much stouter and longer. *fl.* pink. Lower California. (B.R.C. 3, f. 132.)

**F. glauces'cens.** Large, round plants, glaucous; ribs 11 to 15, flattened, sharp; areoles close; radial spines 6, straight, about 1 in. long, yellow becoming darker; central spine solitary, similar. *fl.* yellow. Mexico.

**F. hamatacan'thus.** Plants round or elongated; areoles large, radial spines about 12, slender, 2 to 3 in. long; central spines 4, longer, angled, 1 hooked. *fl.* large, yellow, sometimes scarlet within. Texas, New Mexico, Mexico. (B.R.C. 3, t. 16.) SYN. *Brittonia Davisii*, *Echinocactus longihamatus*.

**F. hor'ridus.** Large, globose plants; ribs broad, 13, not tuberculate; areoles fairly close; radial spines 8 to 12, spreading, slender, white; centrals 6 to 8, all reddish and straight except one which may be up to 6 in. long, flattened and hooked. *fl.* ? Lower California.

**F. John'sonii.** Stems elongated, often hidden under a mass of spines; ribs 17 to 21, low, tuberculate; spines reddish, radials 10 to 14; centrals 4 to 8, stouter, curved. *fl.* red to pink. Arizona, California, Utah, Nevada. (B.R.C. 3, f. 150.)

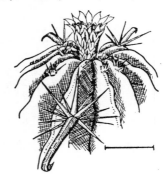

*Ferocactus latispinus*

**F. latispi'nus.** Plants round, depressed, large; ribs 15 to 23, prominent; radial spines 6 to 10, slender, annulate, white to pink; centrals 4 or more, stouter, highly coloured, straight except 1 which is flattened or hooked. *fl.* pink to purple. Mexico. (B.R.C. 3, t. 13, 16.)

**F. Lecon'tei.** Plants round, becoming cylindric, large, rather slender; ribs 20 to 30; some of the radial spines bristly; the others and the centrals flattened, pressed against the plant, most of them ascending, rarely hooked, red and white. *fl.* yellow or red. Arizona.

**F. macrodis'cus.** Plants globose or short-cylindric, large; ribs 16 or more, edge sharp, depressed at the areoles; spines yellow, curved backwards; radials 6 to 8; centrals 4, stouter and flatter. *fl.* dark red to purple. Mexico. (B.R.C. 3, f. 147.)

**F. Mathsson'ii.** A synonym of *F. crassihamatus*.

**F. melocactiform'is.** Plants cylindric, large, bluish-green; ribs 24, spines 10 to 12, curved, yellow becoming brown, unequal, about 1 in. long; centrals 3 or 4, one much stouter and longer, annulate. *fl.* bright yellow. Mexico. (B.R.C. 3, f. 146.) SYN. *Echinocactus electracanthus*.

**F. nob'ilis.** Plants round, ribs 15; radial spines straight, spreading; central spine solitary, erect, 3 in. long, flattened and hooked. *fl.* reddish. Mexico.

**F. Orcutt'ii.** Plants solitary or in clusters, large; ribs 13 to 30, spiralled, tuberculate; areoles close; spines reddish, all annulate, angled or flat. *fl.* dull crimson. Lower California.

**F. penin'sulae.** Plants club-shaped or cylindric, very large; ribs 12 to 20, prominent; spines red with yellow tips; radial spines straight, annulate; centrals 4, much stouter and longer, 1 hooked. *fl.* reddish-violet. Lower California.

**F. rectispi'nus.** Plants round or cylindric when old; radial spines 8 to 12, upper 3 stouter, curved; 1 central 4 to 5 in. long, straight, annulate, never hooked. *fl.* yellowish Lower California. (B.R.C. 3, t. 14.)

**F. robus'tus.** Forming large clumps; ribs 8, prominent in young plants, indistinct when old; radial spines about 10, very fine; centrals about 6, flattened, annulate, over 2 in. long. *fl.* yellowish. Mexico. (B.R.C. 3, f. 143.)

**F. Staines'ii.** Plants solitary or forming clusters; ribs 13 to 20, compressed, wavy; radials about 10, very fine; centrals about 6, flattened, annulate, over 2 in. long. *fl.* yellow. Mexico. (R.H. 1845, 1.)

**F. Townsendia'nus.** Plants short cylindric; ribs about 16, often spiralled; radial spines 14 to 16, long but very slender; centrals awl-shaped, curved, 1 hooked. *fl.* reddish-yellow. San Josef Island, Gulf of California. (B.R.C. 3, t. 12.)

**F. uncina'tus.** Plants short cylindric, glaucous; ribs about 13, strongly tuberculate; flowering areoles elongated, the *fl.* arising from the end opposite the spines and hence almost in the axils of the tubercles; some radial spines straight, others hooked; 1 central, up to 5 in. long, hooked. *fl.* reddish-brown. Texas, Mexico. (B.R.C. 3, f. 153.)

**F. virides'cens.** Plants round, becoming cylindric; ribs 13 to 21, rounded; spines red, becoming grey; radials 9 to 20, spreading, short; centrals 4, lower one stouter and flattened. *fl.* yellowish-green. Coast of Lower California. (B.R.C. 3, t. 14; G.C. 7 (1877), 172.)

**F. Wislizen'ii.** Globose plants much elongated in age; ribs about 25; areoles large; spines variable; radials very slender; centrals several, white to red, annulate, awl-shaped, 1 flattened and hooked. *fl.* yellow or red. Texas, New Mexico, Arizona. (B.R.C. 3, t. 1, 12.)

V. H.

**FERON'IA** (nymph who presided over woods and groves in Roman mythology). FAM. *Rutaceae.* A genus of a single species of spiny evergreen tree allied to Citrus, with characters given below. *F. Limonia* needs a mixture of rich loam and peat with a little sand, and stove treatment. Cuttings taken in spring or summer of ripe young shoots and placed in sandy soil under glass with bottom heat will root. The wood is used in India and the tree produces a gum used like gum arabic. The fruit has a hard, compact, woody shell, the seeds being embedded in an acid, edible pulp which is used for making jelly and, with other ingredients, a kind of chutney by the natives of India. It has also been used in Java as a substitute for soap.

**F. Limo'nia.** Elephant's Apple or Wood Apple. Tree to 30 ft. *l.* unequally pinnate; lflets. 5 or 7, obovate, crenulate, shining, sessile; rachis margined, jointed; spines long, straight axillary. *fl.* white, small, anthers reddish; panicles terminal or axillary. *fr.* as large as an apple, rind greyish. Coromandel. 1804. SYN. *F. elephantum, Limonia acidissima, Schinus Limonia.*

F. G. P.

*fe'rox,* very prickly.

**FERRA'RIA** (in honour of Giovanni Battista Ferrari, 1584–1655, Italian botanist). FAM. *Iridaceae.* A genus of 7 species of dwarf bulbous plants natives of S. Africa and Angola, related to Homeria, with curiously spotted evanescent flowers. Stem branched about 6 in. high, with many small ovate-lanceolate, stem-clasping leaves. Basal leaves few, broadly linear, long, stiff. Pedicels short. Flowers large, purple or green; perianth regular, spreading, segments ovate-lanceolate; stamens oblong-awl-shaped, joined by their filaments; stigmas petaloid, fringed. Hardy if planted 6 in. deep in a warm, sunny situation. Increased by seeds and offsets.

**F. anthero'sa.** A synonym of *F. Ferrariola.*

**F. atra'ta.** *fl.* dark reddish-purple, fringed brownish-green. (L.B.C. 1356.)

**F. divarica'ta.** *l.* more or less glaucous, linear, acute. Stem branched at top. *fl.* brown. May to July. 1825. (S.B.F.G. 192.)

**F. Ferrario'la.** Stem simple. *l.* ensiform, lower narrow. *fl.* greenish-brown. March to July. 1800. (B.M. 751 as *F. antherosa.*) SYN. *F. viridiflora.*

**F. obtusifo'lia.** Stem branched, many-fld. *l.* obtuse, keeled on both sides. *fl.* brown. May to July. 1825. (S.B.F.G. 148.)

**F. puncta'ta.** A synonym of *F. undulata.*

**F. uncina'ta.** Stem branched, shorter than l. *l.* linear, striated, hooked at tip. *fl.* brown; spathe 2-fld.; perianth segs. involute at tip. May to July. 1825. (S.B.F.G. 161.)

**F. undula'ta.** Stem branched. *l.* wavy; inner half as wide as outer. *fl.* greenish-brown. March, April. 1755. (B.M. 144.) SYN. *Tigridia undulata.*

**F. viridiflo'ra.** A synonym of *F. Ferrariola.*

**F. Welwits'chii.** Stem branched below middle. *Stem-l.* linear, 3 to 4 in. long. *fl.* bright yellow; segs. 1 in. long, dotted brown; peduncles long, erect. July. 1871.

*Ferrari'ola,* a diminutive of Ferraria.

*fer'reus -a -um,* iron-hard.

*ferrieren'sis -is -e,* of the Ferrières nursery, France.

*ferrugin'eus -a -um,* rust-coloured.

*fer'tilis -is -e,* fertile; producing numerous seeds.

**FERTILIZATION.** The process of fusion of male and female reproductive cells (gametes). The term is often misapplied to pollination (q.v.). Pollination is a necessary preliminary to fertilization in flowering plants but must not be confused with it. Fertilization is effected by the pollen-tube making its way to the female organ (the ovule), its tip finally coming into close contact with the egg-apparatus. A small amount of protoplasm with a nucleus (the male cell) is extruded from the tube into the oosphere where it fuses with the nucleated female cell, protoplasm with protoplasm, nucleus with nucleus. This is the process of fertilization and it results in the fertilized female cell surrounding itself by a cell-wall (constituting the oospore) and beginning to divide to form the embryo. If the pollen has come from the same plant and is effective self-fertilization occurs, if from another plant cross-fertilization results. If the cross-fertilization is effected by pollen from a different species the resulting embryo will be a hybrid, but the pollen produced by a plant is often incapable of fertilizing the egg-cell of the same plant (incompatibility), and fertilization results only when pollen from another plant of the same (or where hybridization is concerned of a related plant of another) species is available. **A**

A→

**FE'RULA** (old Latin name). FAM. *Umbelliferae.* A genus of about 80 species of noble herbaceous perennials, natives of the Mediterranean region and Cent. and W. Asia. Tall with thick roots. Leaves very greatly divided, the ultimate segments usually linear. Umbels of many rays, lateral umbels usually opposite or in whorls; flowers small, yellow or yellowish-white. The Giant Fennels (not to be confused with the true Fennels which belong to the genus Foeniculum) call for no special soil, but they should be planted in their permanent situations while young as they do not move well. Some grow for many years before they have stored enough food to enable them to flower. They are hardy and make fine foliage plants for the large herbaceous border and on the banks of ponds, or in clumps on a grassy bank, or on the side of a shrubbery. All the species mentioned are worth growing but perhaps the best are *F. communis* and its form *gigantea* of gardens, and *F. tingitana.* The growth in early spring is particularly valuable, starting early, and being quite hardy. Seed is easily raised outdoors, and should be sown as soon as gathered. Gum ammoniac comes from *F. communis brevifolia,* gum asafoetida from *F. Asafoetida* and *F. Narthex,* gum galbanum from *F. galbaniflua,* and is obtained by notching the roots; all these gums have reputed medicinal value.

**F. Asafoe'tida.** 6 to 12 ft. h. Stem stout, branched. *Radical l.* 18 in. long, stalked; *stem-l.* with a broad sheath; segs. oblong-lanceolate, blunt, 1 to 2 in. long. *fl.* greenish-yellow; umbels stalked. July. SW. Asia. 1855. (G.C. 32 (1902), 443.)

**F. commu'nis.*** 8 to 15 ft. h. *l.* green, sheaths of upper l. very large; segs. very narrow-linear, flaccid. *fl.* yellow; central umbel nearly sessile; lateral (male) stalked; involucre absent. June. Mediterranean region. 1597. (F.G. 279 as *F. nodiflora.*) var. **brevifo'lia,** *l.* segs. shorter than in type. (B.M. 8157.) SYN. *F. brevifolia, F. Linkii.* The source of gum ammoniac.

**F. Ferula'go.** 6 to 8 ft. h., glabrous and green. *l.* pinnatifid; segs. linear, forking, cuspidate. *fl.* yellow in a large, 5- to 10-rayed, terminal umbel; involucral l. many, oblong-lanceolate, margined white, reflexed. June, July. Spain to Caucasus. SYN. *F. nodiflora, F. galbanifera.*

**F. galbanif'era.** A synonym of *F. F rulago.*

**F. galbaniflu'a.** Perennial. Stem tall, thick, terete, naked above. *l.* ashy-hairy, 4-pinnatisect, primary and secondary divisions long-stalked; segs. small, crowded, linear or setaceous, entire or 3-fid; stem-l. reduced to sheaths. *fl.* yellow, in 6- to 12-rayed umbels without involucels; stalks short, thick; pet. glabrous. *fr.* oblong or elliptic. Persia. Gum galbanum exudes from the lower part of the stem and the base of the l.-stalks.

**F. glau'ca.** Stem 6 to 8 ft. h., branched. *l.* glaucous beneath; segs. linear, long, flat. *fl.* yellow; central umbel pedunculate, lateral made on longer peduncles; involucre wanting. June. S. Europe. 1596. (G.C. 32 (1902), 141, 142.) SYN. *F. neapolitana.*

**F. Jaeschkea'na.** Stem, l., and infl. as in *F. Narthex* but *l.* closely singly or doubly crenate or almost toothed. *fl.* yellowish-white. Cent. Asia. 1878. (G.F. 1878, 944, as *F. foetidissima.*)

**F. Link'ii.** A synonym of *F. communis brevifolia.*

**F. Nar'thex.** 5 to 8 ft. h. *Lower l.* 1 to 2 ft. long, ovate, the secondary and tertiary pinnae decurrent, entire or irregularly crenate, hairy when young; *stem-l.* with large sheath. *fl.* yellowish, umbels simple or nearly so. July. SW. Asia. (SYN. *Narthex asafoetida*; B.M. 5168 as *Narthex asafoetida.*) A source of gum asafoetida.

**F. neapolita'na.** A synonym of *F. glauca.*

**F. orienta'lis.** 3 to 5 ft. h., branches more or less verticillate in upper part. *Lower l.* about 18 in. long, ovate in outline, much cut in fine segs.; *upper l.* a short, inflated sheath. *fl.* pale yellow in short 10- to 15-rayed umbels; involucre and involucels absent. Summer. Asia Minor.

**F. per'sica.** Stem glaucous, 3 to 6 ft. h. *lflets.* rather remote, often decurrently pinnate; segs. linear-lanceolate, dilated and cut at tips. *fl.* yellow; involucral bracts absent. Persia. (B.M. 2096.)

**F. Sum'bul.** Sumbul Plant. About 9 ft. h. *l.* finely cut. *fl.* in umbels forming a pyramidal panicle. Turkestan. 1872. (B.M. 6196.) Sap of root milky, fetid, and musky. Used as substitute for musk in Russia and as a remedy against cholera.

**F. tingita'na.*** 6 to 8 ft. h., branched. *l.* shining; segs. oblong-lanceolate, deeply toothed; upper petiole large, sheathing. *fl.* yellow; terminal umbel shortly pedunculate, lateral few, male on longer peduncles; involucre absent. June. N. Africa. 1680. (B.M. 7267.)

***ferula'ceus -a -um,*** Ferula- or fennel-like.

**FERULA'GO.** Included in **Ferula.**

***fe'rus -a -um,*** wild.

***-ferus -a -um,*** suffix implying bearing or possessing.

***fer'vidus -a -um,*** glowing.

**FESCUE GRASS.** *See* **Festuca.**

***festa'lis -is -e, festi'vus -a -um,*** agreeable, bright, gay.

**FESTU'CA** (Latin name for a grass stem). FAM. *Gramineae.* A genus of about 100 species of annual or perennial grasses, natives of the cooler parts of the world. Usually small or middle-sized plants with narrow leaves, spikelets usually few in a panicle (rarely a spike), 2- or more-flowered, glumes rounded, acute or awned from tip. Some species are important constituents of pastures and lawns and a few are cultivated for ornament. *F. ovina glauca* is excellent for edging. The fine-leaved species, *F. ovina* and its relatives, are most important for the Lawn, &c. *See* **Lawns.**

**F. alpin'a.** Closely related to *F. ovina.* Densely tufted perennial 3 or 4 in. h. *l.* bright green, 3-nerved, filiform, about $\frac{1}{8}$ in. wide, sheath brownish-red. *Panicle* about 1 in. long, oblong-linear; spikelets curved. July, August. Alps of Europe.

**F. clava'ta.** A synonym of *F. incrassata.*

**F. Cri'num-ursi.** A synonym of *F. Eskia.*

**F. durius'cula.** Less densely tufted than *F. ovina*, stoloniferus. *l.* flat, sheaths downy. *Panicle* open; spikelets many-fld. June, July. Cool regions.

**F. Esk'ia.** Perennial. Very densely tufted with a creeping rootstock, $\frac{3}{4}$ to $1\frac{1}{4}$ ft. h. *l.* thick, nearly cylindrical, sharp-pointed, glaucous; ligule long. *Panicle* $1\frac{1}{2}$ to 2 in. long, narrow; spikelets 5- to 11-fld., $\frac{1}{6}$ to $\frac{1}{3}$ in. long, shortly awned. June to August. Pyrenees.

**F. glacia'lis.** Closely related to *F. ovina.* Densely tufted perennial, up to 6 in. h. *l.* 5-nerved, filiform, obtuse, smooth like the sheath, remaining long after death. *Panicle* very short, thick, clustered; spikelets often violet, usually awned. July, August. Mts. of Cent. Europe and Spain.

**F. glau'ca.** A synonym of *F. ovina glauca.*

**F. incrassa'ta.** Annual, tufted, erect, about 6 in. h. *l.* rough above, flat, about $\frac{1}{12}$ in. wide, short, sheath smooth, ligule long. *Panicle* stiff, about $2\frac{1}{2}$ in. long; spikelets about $\frac{3}{8}$ in. long, awned. June. Algeria, Tunis.

**F. nigres'cens.** A form of *F. rubra.*

**F. ovi'na.** Sheep's Fescue. Densely tufted perennial. *l.* filiform or upper flat, ligule 2-lobed. *Panicle* somewhat one-sided; spikelets 3 to 12, purplish, sometimes awned. All cool climates. var. **glau'ca,** about 9 in. h.; *l.* all filiform, about $\frac{1}{32}$ in. thick, usually 9-nerved, rigid, blue-green; spikelets awned; **tenuifo'lia,** *l.* thinner and softer than in var. *glauca*, green, spikelets not awned.

**F. puncto'ria.** Perennial. About 1 ft. h. *l.* rigid, recurved, rolled, without keel, sharp-pointed, sheath longer than blade. *Panicle* small, erect, glabrous. Greece.

**F. rig'ida.** Annual. Rigid, purplish, smooth, 3 to 6 in. h. *l.* more or less setaceous, ligule oblong. *Panicle* erect, $1\frac{1}{2}$ to 2 in. long with distichous branches. W. Europe.

**F. ru'bra.** Creeping dark-green perennial, loosely tufted, about 15 in. h. *l.* flat or rolled, obtuse, lower sheaths hairy. *Panicle* rather large, spreading to one side; spikelets often reddish, shortly awned. June, July. Cool regions.

**F. stipoi'des.** A synonym of *F. incrassata.*

**F. valesi'aca.** Closely related to *F. ovina.* Densely tufted with a slender stem 6 to 9 in. h. *l.* filiform, about $\frac{1}{40}$ in. thick, usually 5-nerved, more or less rough, sheath smooth. *Panicle* oblong, about 3 in. long; spikelets small, awned. Alps.

**F. vir'idis.** A synonym of *F. rubra.*

***festucoi'des,*** Festuca-like.

***fes'tus -a -um,*** hallowed, suitable for festivals.

***fe'tidus -a -um,*** stinking.

***Feuilleta'ui,*** in honour of W. K. H. Feuilletau de Bruyn, b. 1886, of the Netherlands army, who collected in Sumatra, &c.

**FEVER FLY,** *Dilophus febrilis*, belonging to the Family *Bibionidae*, is closely related to the St. Mark's Fly (q.v.). The small black flies appear towards the end of April and in May, and are frequent visitors to the blossoms of hardy fruits, especially Apple, Pear, and Cherry. The female fly lays several hundred eggs on or beneath the surface in lawns, heaps of decaying grass mowings, and in compost and leaf-mould heaps. The legless maggots, which closely resemble those of the St. Mark's Fly, live in colonies, often several inches in width, and feed on grass roots and decaying vegetation. Pupation takes place in an earthern cell a few inches below soil level. The flies of the second brood appear towards the end of August and in September when eggs are again deposited in similar places to those of the first brood. The second-brood maggots, together with some of the first brood, continue to feed throughout the winter, except when the weather is very severe, and pupate in the following April.

The maggots may be destroyed by watering infested turf with liquid derris, or by dressing the turf with $1\frac{1}{2}$ oz. of arsenate of lead powder to each square yard, followed by watering, using 1 gallon to the square yard, to wash the poison into the soil.

G. F. W.

**FEVERFEW.** *See* **Chrysanthemum Parthenium, Matricaria Chamomilla.**

**FEVERWORT.** *See* **Triosteum perfoliatum.**

**FEVIL'LEA** (in honour of Louis Feuillée, 1660–1732, traveller and botanist). FAM. *Cucurbitaceae.* A genus of 6 species of climbing shrubs, natives of Trop. America. Leaves stalked, rather thin, cordate, angled or palmately lobed; tendrils simple or 2-fid. Flowers dioecious, about 1 in. across, in panicles; pedicels slender. Fruit large. *F. Moorei* is a very vigorous evergreen climber for the stove house, growing well in sandy loam. Propagated by cuttings of young wood in summer.

**F. Moor'ei.** Slender, glabrous climber. *l.* alternate, broadly ovate, 3 to 5 in. long, slender-pointed, shining, base rounded. Male *fl.* pale brick-red; cor. lobes round or broadest near outer edge, wavy at margins. Female? Guiana. (B.M. 6356.)

F. G. P.

**FIBRE.** The thread-like tissues found in flowering plants and ferns generally; any substance, the constituent parts of which may be separated into, or used to form, threads for textile fabrics or the like.

**FIBRE, CARAGUATA.** *See* **Eryngium pandanifolium.**

**FIBRE, PIASSABA.** *See* **Attalea funifera.**

**fibrillose,** covered with little fibres.

***fibro'sus -a -um,*** fibrous, composed of or furnished with fibres.

**FICA'RIA.** Included in **Ranunculus.**

***ficarioi'des,*** Ficaria-like.

***ficifo'lius -a -um,*** with fig-like leaves.

***ficoi'des,*** fig-like.

***ficto-,*** in compound words, signifying false, as *fictolacteum,* false *lacteum,* applied to a species wrongly identified with *lacteum.*

**FI'CUS** (old Latin name). FAM. *Moraceae.* Fig. A genus of over 600 species distributed in all warmer regions of the world. Trees or shrubs. Flowers monoecious growing on the inner surface of a hollow, globular or pear-shaped, fleshy receptacle having at the tip an orifice closed by small scales. The flowers in the upper part are male, in the lower female. Many species are ornamental plants easily grown and readily propagated by cuttings or eyes (in the evergreen species having a leaf attached) inserted in a close frame inside a propagating house in early spring. *F. elastica* is one of the most ornamental and stands confinement in rooms exceedingly well, the chief requirements being a light but draught-free position. The leaves should be sponged frequently to remove dust likely to accumulate upon them, using tepid water. If necessary repotting should be done in April using sandy loam with a little leaf-soil and small pots in comparison with the size of the plant. Small plants are most attractive when kept to a single stem, but they may be grown on into tall branched plants if desired by keeping for several years and pinching out the points. *F. elastica* is also useful for stove and greenhouse decoration and for sub-tropical gardening outside. Shoots 1 ft. long may be used for cuttings and if furnished with leaves soon root and form plants much quicker than eyes. *F. Chauvieri* is a fine species forming a large bush even when grown in a comparatively small pot. It succeeds in a greenhouse and also outside in summer. The soil should be as already mentioned and, in common with other species, plenty of syringing and occasional sponging will keep the leaves clean, and almost any amount of water may be given at the roots. *F. pumila* (often called *F. repens* or *F. stipulata*) is one of the best climbers for covering conservatory walls, especially on those facing north. It clings close forming a dense mat of small, somewhat heart-shaped leaves. Occasionally it fruits, the fruiting branches having an entirely different habit, standing out from the wall instead of lying flat and close, the leaves too being different—much larger, elliptic-oblong, narrowed at the base, and with much longer stalks. Other species suitable for covering walls are *F. falcata* and *F. radicans,* like *F. pumila,* presenting a lively green appearance. For the cultivation of *F. Carica, see* **Fig.**

Several species produce lac by the punctures of a small insect and several, including *F. elastica,* yield caoutchouc, obtained by notching the stems.

Many species form aerial roots by which the branches maintain connexion with the ground even though the lower portion of the original stem may have died, as frequently happens in nature in such species as *F. Benjamina* which begins life by climbing other trees, clasping their trunks with aerial roots which eventually thicken and throttle the tree which has acted as a support. The death of the original part converts *F. Benjamina* into an epiphyte. Long aerial roots from the branches are a feature, too, of the remarkable Banyan Tree (*F. benghalensis*); they not only add to the power of collecting food materials but also act as supports and enable the tree to extend itself over an enormous area, and practically indefinitely. SYN. Urostigma. **A**

**F. acumina'ta.** A synonym of *F. parietalis.*

**F. au'rea.** Tree, said to attain 60 ft. *l.* oblong, 3 to 4 in. long, entire, smooth, bluntly narrowed at both ends; stalk stout. *fr.* orange-yellow, globose. S. Florida. Greenhouse.

**F. barba'ta.** A synonym of *F. villosa.*

**F. Bar'teri.** Shrub or small tree. *l.* narrow, 6 to 14 in. long, 1½ in. wide or less, bright green above, paler beneath, stalked. *fr.* orange, almost globose, in axillary clusters of 2 or 3, edible. S. Nigeria. Stove.

**F. Belling'eri.** Tall, glabrous tree. *l.* ovate, 5 to 6 in. long, leathery, dark green and glossy above, paler beneath; stalk 2 to 3 in. long. *fr.* 1¼ to 1¾ in. wide, warty. New S. Wales. Greenhouse.

**F. benghalen'sis.** Banyan. Large tree (see above). *l.* ovate to elliptic, 4 to 8 in. long, sometimes minutely downy beneath. *fr.* in pairs as large as a cherry, sessile. India and Trop. Africa. Stove.

**F. Benjami'na.** Tree, quite glabrous, with slender drooping branches. *l.* ovate or oblong-ovate, slender-pointed, 2 to 4 in. long, entire, rather leathery with many parallel veins. *fr.* solitary or in pairs, globose, about ½ in. wide. Trop. Asia. var. **como'sa,** stem 1 ft. wide, with many slender branches, the leathery, shining l. with a pellucid edge in masses near their ends. India. (B.M. 3305 as *F. comosa.*) Greenhouse.

**F. Bras'sii.** Erect. Stems and l.-stalks rusty-hairy. *l.* somewhat fiddle-shaped, deep green. Sierra Leone. Greenhouse or sub-tropical bedding. 1824.

**F. brevifo'lia.** Evergreen tree of 10 to 30 ft., often epiphytic in nature. *l.* ovate, rarely obovate, 1½ to 4 in. long, acute, broad at base, slightly leathery. *fr.* yellow at first, then bright red, nearly globose, about ½ in. wide. Florida.

**F. Cannon'ii.** About 7 ft. h. *l.* sometimes simple and cordate, sometimes lobed, glossy, rich bronzy crimson tinted purple above, bright red beneath; stalks and midrib bright red. Society Is. 1877. (F.d.S. 11, 131.) SYN. *Artocarpus Cannonii.* Stove.

**F. capen'sis.** Shrub or small tree. *l.* ovate or ovate-oblong, narrowed to obtuse apex, rounded or sub-emarginate at base, deeply toothed in upper part, glabrous; stalk rather short. S. Africa. 1816. (F.S.A. 1, 24, 25.) SYN. *Sycomorus capensis.* Greenhouse.

**F. Car'ica.** Common Fig. Tree or large shrub, 15 to 30 ft. h. Deciduous. *l.* more or less 3-lobed, palmately veined, rough above, downy beneath; stipulate. *fr.* of various shapes and colours. W. Asia. 1548. *See* **Fig.**

**F. Cavron'ii.** Shrub. *l.* wedge-shaped-obovate, 18 in. long, 9 in. wide, obtuse, dark green with yellowish-white midrib above, rusty beneath. Brazil. 1887. Stove.

**F. Chauvie'ri.** Erect. *l.* oval-obtuse, broader than in *F. elastica,* dark shining green, margin waved, veins pale yellow. *fr.* red or orange. Habitat? Greenhouse.

**F. como'sa.** A variety of *F. Benjamina.*

**F. dealba'ta.** A synonym of *Coussapoa dealbata.*

**F. diversifo'lia.** Mistletoe Fig. Glabrous shrub or small tree. *l.* broadly obovate, 1 to 3 in. long, narrowed to a short stalk, bright green with light-brown specks above, pale green beneath. *fr.* axillary, solitary or occasionally in pairs, dull yellow or reddish. India, Malaya. (G.C. 16 (1881), 247.) Greenhouse. SYN. *F. lutescens.*

**F. ebur'nea.** Free-growing. *l.* oblong-ovate, about 15 in. long, 9 in. wide, bright shining green, midrib and main veins ivory-white; stalked. India. 1869. Warm house.

**F. elas'tica.** Indiarubber Plant. Up to 100 ft. in nature, but best as a small, erect plant up to 8 ft. *l.* oblong to elliptic, with an abrupt, dull point, 6 to 18 in. long, 3 to 6 in. wide, leathery, veins transversely parallel at almost right angles to midrib, dark, bright shining green above, yellowish-green beneath; young l. enclosed in a rosy sheath. *fr.* in pairs, at naked nodes, greenish-yellow. Trop. Asia. 1815. (G.C. 2 (1874), 358.) A fine plant for rooms and for sub-tropical gardening. var. **foliis aureo-margina'tis,** *l.* golden, for 1 in. at margin, especially in autumn; **variega'ta,** *l.* variegated with creamy-white and yellow.

**F. erec'ta.** Shrub or small tree, very variable in all parts. *l.* entire or more or less lobed or toothed. *fr.* solitary or in pairs, glabrous or roughly hairy, globose and sessile or pear-shaped and stalked. India, China, Japan. var. **Siebold'ii,** *l.* linear or oblong-lanceolate, 6 to 8 in. long, slender-pointed, entire or slightly lobed on one side, *fr.* yellow and red. Japan, Sikkim, &c. (B.M. 7550.) SYN. *F. Sieboldii.* Greenhouse.

**F. falca'ta.** Dainty evergreen creeper. Stems slender, with light-brown hairs. *l.* oblong, more or less angled or rhomboid, ½ to 1 in. long, not tapered at base, blunt, midrib towards one side, pale beneath, stalk short; stipules small. Malaya. Good for covering walls of warm greenhouse, stumps or stems of palms.

**F. glomera'ta.** Cluster Fig. Slender downy tree. *l.* elliptic, 6 to 8 in. long, 2 in. wide, slender-pointed, thin, with metallic lustre; stalks long. *fr.* in clusters on naked branches, reddish, 1¼ in. thick. Australia. 1869. SYN. *F. vesca.*

**F. in'dica.** Pagoda Tree. Glabrous tree, except stipules downy. *l.* 4 to 7 in. long, veins in 4 to 7 pairs, not prominent. *fr.* sessile, globose, yellow-red, ⅓ in. thick, in crowded pairs. Trop. Asia, Malaya. Similar to the Banyan. *F. benghalensis,* but without aerial roots. Warm house.

**F. infecto'ria.** Glabrous tree, often deciduous. *l.* 2½ to 3 in. long, veins in 5 to 7 pairs, not prominent. *fl.* sessile, globose, ¼ in. thick, whitish, flushed and dotted, in axillary pairs. Trop. Asia, Malaya. Warm house.

**F. Krish'nae.** Krishna Bor. Small tree. *l.* cup-shaped with upper surface outside, limb of cup irregular, containing midrib with 4 or 5 lateral nerves. *fr.* axillary, solitary or in pairs, about ½ in. wide, yellow, sessile. India. 1902. (B.M. 8092.) Warm house.

**F. lutes'cens.** A synonym of *F. diversifolia.*

**F. macrophyl'la.** Australian Banyan, Moreton Bay Fig. Tree. *l.* ovate-oblong, entire, heart-shaped at base, 4 to 10 in. long, 3 to 4 in. wide, glossy, veins evident, stalks 1 to 2 in. long. *fr.* globose, nearly 1 in. thick, axillary, in threes or fours. Queensland, New S. Wales. 1869. Greenhouse.

**F. Neu'mannii.** Glabrous tree with nearly straight branches. *l.* long-oblong, 12 in. long, 1½ in. wide, acute, rounded or heart-shaped at base, 3-nerved, entire; stalks 3 to 4 in. long. Habitat? Stove.

**F. nymphaeifo'lia.** Glabrous tree. *l.* roundish, 1 ft. long, 8 in. wide, deeply heart-shaped at base, mucronate at apex, 5-nerved, dark green above, whitish beneath; stalks about 8 in. long. Trop. America. Stove.

**F. pandura'ta.** Shrub or tree. *l.* fiddle-shaped, often 12 in. long, emarginate at apex, heart-shaped at the narrow base, glossy green, veins prominent, whitish. Habitat? 1903. (G.C. 33 (1903), 284.)

**F. Parcel'lii.** Variegated shrub. *l.* oblong, slender-pointed, toothed, bright green, irregularly blotched dark green and ivory-white. Pacific Is. (F.d.S. 2273–4.)

**F. parieta'lis.** 5 to 6 ft. h. *l.* elliptical, 4 to 5 in. long, somewhat leathery, green and glabrous above, downy with veins prominent beneath; stalked. *fr.* solitary, axillary, pendent, bright orange, mealy and warted, stalk longer than fr. Asia. (B.M. 3282.) Stove.

**F. Portea'na.** Small tree or shrub. *l.* oblong, acute, 2 ft. long, 1 ft. wide, with 2 lateral lobes, pendent, glabrous, dark green. Mexico. 1862. Cool house.

**F. Pseudo-Car'ica.** Somewhat like fig of commerce but l. more deeply lobed, 3- or occasionally 5-nerved. *fr.* axillary, round, and said to contain much sugar. Abyssinia.

**F. pu'mila.*** Climber. *l.* small, ovate-heart-shaped, veiny, dark green. Fruiting branches stiff, erect, with thick, much larger l. 2 to 4 in. long, elliptic to oblong, entire; stalks long. China, Japan. 1721. (B.M. 6657.) SYN. *F. repens, F. scandens, F. stipulata.* A handsome, small-leaved plant attaching itself to walls, &c., by roots like Ivy. Almost hardy, frequent in greenhouses and occasionally grown outdoors in favoured parts of the country. var. **min'ima,** very slender form with smaller l. SYN. *F. minima, F. stipulata minima;* **variega'ta,** vigorous, tufted, *l.* margined creamy-white. 1897. Type and varieties make attractive basket plants.

**F. quercifo'lia.** Shrub. *l.* 2 to 5 in. long, like those of the common oak, veins in 5 to 7 pairs; stalks ½ to 1 in. long. *fr.* axillary, egg- or pear-shaped, in pairs. Burma, Malaya. (L.B.C. 1540.) SYN. *F. heterophylla.*

**F. radi'cans.*** Evergreen trailer. *l.* oblong-lanceolate, 2 in. long, slender-pointed, base rounded or notched, entire, glabrous except veins; stipules awl-shaped, about as long as l.-stalks. Habitat? var. **variega'ta,** *l.* variegated with creamy-white. 1897. Good basket plants. Greenhouse.

**F. religio'sa.** Peepul or Bo Tree of the Hindus. About 25 ft. h. or in cultivation a compact bush. *l.* nearly heart-shaped, tip drawn out into a tail; stalk 3 to 4 in. long; stipules minute. *fr.* dark purple, sessile, in axillary pairs. E. Indies. 1731. Stove.

**F. re'pens.** A synonym of *F. pumila.*

**F. Roxburgh'ii.** Tree to 20 ft. *l.* roundish-heart-shaped, 5 to 15 in. long, veins in 5 to 7 pairs, prominent, downy on veins beneath. *fr.* clustered (8 to 12) on short cauline branches, 2 in. across. India. 1840. (R.H. 1872, 385.) Greenhouse.

**F. rubigino'sa.** Small tree with numerous spreading branches. *l.* elliptic, 3 to 4 in. long, leathery, at first covered with reddish down, then glabrous except on veins beneath. *fr.* greenish-brown, warted, nearly round, about ½ in. across. Australia. 1789. (B.M. 2939.) Makes roots like the Banyan in Australia. Stove.

**F. scan'dens.** A synonym of *F. pumila.*

**F. stipula'ta.** A synonym of *F. pumila.*

**F. Sycomo'rus.** Sycomore Fig. Mulberry Fig. Tree. *l.* ovate, heart-shaped at base, entire. 8- to 10-nerved, nearly glabrous; stalks (and shoots) slightly hairy. *fr.* small, abundant, edible. Egypt, Syria. The Sycomore of the Bible. SYN. *Sycomorus antiquorum.* Greenhouse.

**F. villo'sa.** Creeping and rooting like Ivy. *l.* heart-shaped, about 3 in. long, leathery, dark green, tip long, edges brown-hairy. *fr.* stalked, in axillary clusters. Malaya. 1832. SYN. *F. barbata.* Excellent for covering walls of stoves.

F. G. P.

***-fid; -fidus -a -um,*** in compound words, signifying cleft, as pinnatifid, *pinnatifidus,* cleft in a pinnate manner.

**fiddle-shaped,** obovate with 1 or 2 deep indentations on each side; panduriform.

**FIDDLE-WOOD.** *See* **Citharexylum quadrangulare.**

***Fiebrig'ii,*** in honour of Dr. C. Fiebrig (*c.* 1904), director of Museum and Garden at Asuncion, Paraguay.

**FIELD MICE** include the Short-tailed *Microtus hirtus* and the Long-tailed *Apodemus sylvaticus,* both of which are extremely common and invade gardens from pastures, commons, hedge banks, and ditch-sides. Both are vegetarians, feeding on seeds, bulbs, roots, the bark of trees, and shrubs which are partially or completely girdled at or just below ground-level, and low-growing fruits of Tomatoes and other plants. They have a number of natural enemies, including the Weasel and such beneficial birds of prey as Owls, Hawks, and Magpies, all of which should be protected to act as a natural check on their increase.

Measures for reducing their numbers in gardens include trapping by jam-jars half-filled with water and buried to their rims in the ground in beds of bulbs and other attacked plants, or by break-back or figure-of-4 traps baited with small bulbs, corms, or nuts; gassing their runs in dry ditch-sides; and the use of poison baits containing barium carbonate. A good hunting cat kept in a glasshouse will soon clear these rodents.

G. F. W.

**FIELD'IA** (in honour of Baron Field, 1786–1846, once Judge of the Supreme Court, New S. Wales). FAM. *Gesneriaceae.* A genus of a single species of straggling, shrubby habit, native of New S. Wales. It is evergreen and grows well in the greenhouse in a compost of peat and loam, to which a little sand and pieces of charcoal have been added. Firm side shoots with their leaves left on will root in sandy soil under glass.

**F. austra'lis.** Straggling, rooting at nodes. *l.* simple, opposite, ovate-lanceolate, coarsely toothed, acute; internodes long. *fl.* yellow, drooping, long, tubular, solitary on axillary peduncles. 1826. (B.M. 5089.)

**FIELDIA** of Gaudichaud. *See* **Stauropsis lissochiloides.**

**FIG** (*Ficus Carica*). The Fig is a native of W. Asia, its wild habitat probably extending from Syria and E. Persia to Afghanistan. It has been grown for its fruit from remote antiquity and early spread widely through the north warm temperate and sub-tropical regions to China, where, according to Bretschneider, it was grown

**Fig** ( 821 ) **Fig**

at least as early as the latter half of the 14th century. It was probably early introduced into Britain and subsequently lost, like the Vine, to be reintroduced later. According to Pliny it was largely cultivated by the Romans who grew at least 6 varieties prior to the Christian era. The reintroduction to Britain was apparently due to Cardinal Pole, when he brought, in 1525, several trees from Italy and planted them in the garden of the Archbishop's Palace of Lambeth. Another celebrated tree was introduced from Aleppo by Dr. Pocock in 1648 and planted in the garden of the Regius Professor of Hebrew, at Christ Church, Oxford, where it was severely damaged by fire in 1809 but survived by means of branches from the root, and was producing fine fruit still in 1833. In Britain, if unprotected, the tree is apt to be cut to the ground in severe winters and the points of the shoots may be destroyed by frosts less severe, but even if cut to the ground it becomes re-established by means of suckers. In the milder districts, such as Sussex and the southern counties generally, it may be grown as a standard or half-standard tree, but it is not likely to succeed as such farther inland. A warm situation with well-drained soil is necessary for success and generally a wall with a south or south-west aspect is best, but in districts with a hot summer, where very sharp frosts rarely occur, it may be grown as an espalier, for it can then be easily protected in occasional very severe weather.

For trees in the open a well-drained medium to light loam is suitable; heavy wet soil leads to excessively vigorous growth with poor fruit development. For standard or half-standard trees in the open the soil should be deeply dug and a good quantity of lime rubble should be mixed with it. For trees planted against a wall or in the greenhouse special borders should be made and, as it is best to restrict the root-run in order to secure short-jointed growth and heavy cropping, the bottom of the border, 2½ ft. down, should be of lime rubble or chalk beaten down hard. This will restrict the roots without impeding the drainage. The border should not be very wide, not over 3 ft. at the most, and should be beside a hard path. If this be impossible then some means of confining the roots should be adopted such as a narrow wall underground, otherwise root-pruning will be necessary. The soil for the border should be a mixture of good medium loam and brick rubbish. A good mulch of manure may be spread over the roots in spring, rather to conserve moisture than to provide nitrogen, and, if necessary, a dressing of bone-meal may be given also in spring, but rich manures should be avoided as they tend to encourage too vigorous growth. Plenty of water is needed during the growing season and the border should be regularly soaked while the crop is swelling, reducing the quantity as the fruits near ripening.

In very severe weather the stem and branches may need protection. This may be given by means of Spruce branches, fern, thatched hurdles, or canvas, or the branches may be loosened from their support, collected into bundles, and covered with a thick coat of straw or mats, but this protection will not be needed in the south of the country and should not be given elsewhere unless really needed. If given it should be gradually removed in spring.

The Fig produces 2 or, in some climates, 3 crops in the year and the fruit crop thus extended is an important article of food in the East, both in a fresh and in a dried state. Dried figs are also exported in great quantities from the countries where favourable conditions for the production of 3 crops occur. The fresh fruit remains in good condition for a very short time and this, combined with its extremely tender skin, renders it among the most difficult of fruits to pack to travel any great distance, and it is thus not in any general favour as an article of commerce in this country.

The fruits are produced, 1 or 2 together, in the axils of the leaves and are formed along the shoot as growth proceeds. They come to maturity, if at all, only on new or recently ripened wood and it is therefore important to preserve the points of the shoots from frost damage and in pruning. At the same time overcrowding of shoots and overcropping must be avoided. Growth rarely begins in this country before May and then both new shoots and embryo fruits on the wood of the previous year start at the same time. Fruits will start to form along the new growths and in suitable climates these would form the second crop of the year, but in this country the summers are too short for them to reach maturity. We have to depend upon the youngest of these second crop fruits for the crop of the following season. Any that are sufficiently advanced in early autumn to show the shape of a fig are useless, but if they be carefully pinched off, others may form later by the side and remain dormant along with those formed nearer the tips of the shoots ready to start into growth in the following season.

Winter pruning is therefore not much required except to keep the branches thinned, and much of this should be done in summer along with the pinching of the strongest shoots so as to leave only those required for fruiting. Heavy pruning frequently results in the growth of soft, unproductive wood, especially if the trees are in rich soil. New shoots should be encouraged near the main branches to replace any that become bare or exceed the limits of space available.

Badly placed shoots should be suppressed as they appear each spring, and vigorous young shoots should be shortened to 5 or 6 leaves from the base in summer.

The branches should be trained either fan-wise or horizontally if the trees are grown on walls or as espaliers. Suckers are often freely produced and if trained up at about 15 in. apart will in course of time produce fruit, but this is not advisable as better wood can be obtained from healthy branches.

Pollination is not necessary for the production of ripe figs save in the Turkish or Smyrna Fig where it is effected by the small gall-wasp, Blastophaga, see **Caprification.** For the structure of the inflorescence which constitutes the edible fig, see **Ficus.**

In outdoor figs the crop matures in August and September and is at its best when it shows a 'tear in its eye' and a slight cracking of the skin. They are best left on the trees as long as possible to secure full flavour, but if they have to be packed for travelling they must be picked while dry and still firm, early in the day. In packing each should be wrapped carefully in soft paper and then folded separately in a vine leaf. They should then be packed as firmly as possible with such soft fruits in a single layer in square punnets, and these should be fitted into a shallow box so that the chance of moving them will be reduced to a minimum.

Trees under glass will produce 2 crops a year and possibly 3 if temperature and other conditions are right: the first crop should ripen in late March and April, the second in June, the third in August if the house is started in December with a temperature of 65 to 70° F., gradually increasing to 80° F., for figs require a higher temperature to start them into growth than any other fruit tree generally forced. It is usually better, however, to forgo the earliest crop and start the house in February with a temperature of 55 to 60° F., rising with sun-heat to 80° F. in summer, thereby securing 2 crops without unduly forcing the trees. The air must be kept moist by damping down the paths and syringing the trees with tepid water until the fruit begins to ripen, when a somewhat drier atmosphere should be maintained. Large quantities of water are necessary in summer and it should not be used at a lower temperature than that of the soil in which the trees are growing. Disbudding, pinching, and pruning should be attended to as for outdoor figs. After the first crop is gathered the trees should be watered

Fig ( 822 ) Figure

freely to encourage fresh growth. As the second crop and the leaves ripen water should be gradually withheld, and when all the leaves have dropped the trees must be kept cool and the soil only a little moist until they are required to start again in the next season.

Figs may also be successfully grown in pots and the season extended by bringing the plants into the warm house in succession. They are best grown without shading and in pots no larger than is necessary for their roots, 9- or 10-in. pots being usually large enough. The compost should be good turfy calcareous loam with plenty of mortar rubble, broken to the size of a large pea, thoroughly mixed with it. Drainage should be ample, and the potting of those intended for early forcing should be in September, and those for later crops in January. Repotting is not usually necessary every year and when it is done the roots should be reduced so that the tree may usually go into a pot no larger than it previously occupied. Top-dressing is an important process where repotting is not deemed necessary, the old soil being removed to the depth of 3 or 4 in. (taking care of the roots in doing this) and replaced by fresh compost, laying the roots carefully in as filling proceeds and making all firm. Firm potting should always be the rule with figs. Top-dressing may also be desirable during the growing season, building up a ring of moist soil round the edge of the pot leaving the stem clear. It will be found that the roots soon invade this addition. Temperatures and other attention will be the same as that for trees planted out. For the resting season the trees may be stood pot to pot in a house from which frost is excluded.

Propagation is easily effected by cuttings, layers, and suckers, and in special instances by seed (for the raising of new varieties) and by grafting with scions removed in autumn and inserted soon after the stock begins to grow in spring. Where seed raising is attempted the seed should be carefully cleaned from the pulp, stored until January, and then sown in heat, growing the seedlings on as quickly as possible.

The common methods, and the best for increasing stock, are by cuttings and layers. Cuttings should be short-jointed shoots of the previous year, 6 to 9 in. long, preferably with a heel, put into pots of sandy compost and placed in bottom heat in early spring. Rooting soon takes place and if grown on in heat good plants are soon secured. It is, in fact, possible to secure fruit in the first year from plants raised from cuttings put in at the beginning of January. Layers may be rooted quite successfully in one season and then detached from the parent, good-sized branches being used. Suckers make less satisfactory plants as the wood is soft.

A large number of varieties of figs are known, differing in vigour of growth, in season of ripening, in colour of skin and flesh, in flavour of fruit, and in amenability to different methods of cultivation. Among the best for British gardens are the following:

**d'Agen.** Fruit of medium size, roundish-turbinate, green, tinged brownish, deep brown or chocolate round the very flat crown with a mixture of green, covered with blue bloom. Cracking with white netting when ripe. Eye open, with dark or reddish-brown iris. Flesh very dark blood-red, thick, syrupy, of excellent flavour. Season late. For general cultivation.

**Black Ischia,** or **Early Forcing.** Fruit medium, roundish-obovate; skin nearly black when ripe; flesh deep red, richly flavoured. Early and prolific. Pots.

**Bourjassotte Grise.** Fruit medium to large, round, with flattened crown, pale green; skin suffused with purple; flesh red, with a thick, sweet juice. One of the richest-flavoured varieties, free bearer, and excellent for pots. SYN. *Grizzly Bourjasotte.*

**Brown Turkey.** Fruit large, short, pear-shaped, with a thick stalk; skin brown, with sometimes a purplish tinge; flesh tinged red in the middle, rich and sugary. One of the best grown either for forcing or outside as standards or on walls. It has numerous synonyms, including Blue Burgundy, Brown Naples, Common Purple, Italian, Large Blue, Lee's Perpetual, Purple, &c.

**Brunswick.** Fruit pear-shaped, very large, with short, thick stalk; skin greenish-yellow, tinged with brown; flesh reddish near the middle, yellowish outside, rich and sweet. Hardier than most, not suitable for forcing. Walls outdoors. It has large, deeply divided l.

**Col di Signora Bianca.** Fruit medium, pear-shaped, with a long neck; skin thick, yellowish-white when ripe; flesh dark blood-red, syrupy and delicious. This is considered one of the finest figs in cultivation, but is very late. Pots.

**Negro Largo.** Fruit pear-shaped, ribbed, very large and long; skin black; flesh pale red, tender, juicy, and richly flavoured. A variety of good habit when restricted at the root; one of the best for pots.

**Pingo de Mel.** Fruit large, pear-shaped; skin pale green; flesh yellowish, very juicy, of good flavour. A variety of the highest merit for early forcing in pots, and an enormous cropper, with a strong, vigorous habit.

**St. John's.** Fruit large; skin pale green; flesh white, firm, juicy, and of excellent flavour. A valuable early variety, producing splendid crops in pots. Sometimes regarded as the same as Pingo de Mel, but is distinct, the fruit of St. John's being more pear-shaped.

**Violette de Bordeaux.** Fruit small, pear-shaped, with shallow ribs, neck absent or very short, deep violet to violet-black, with much bloom. Eye closed, yellow. Stalk long, arching. Flesh pinkish-buff, of fair flavour. Pots.

**Violette Sepor.** Fruit large; skin reddish-brown; flesh dark, of first-class flavour. An abundant bearer and good grower, forcing well in pots or planted out.

**White Ischia.** Fruit small; skin greenish-yellow, thin and delicate; flesh dark red, juicy, sweet, and rich. Small-growing and a great bearer, well adapted for pots and forcing.

**White Marseilles.** Fruit large, almost round, and slightly ribbed, with a short thick neck; skin thin, pale green, nearly white when ripe; flesh almost transparent, sweet, and rich. One of the hardiest varieties, and also suitable for forcing. Walls. It has several synonyms, including Figue Blanche, Ford's Seedling, White Genoa, White Naples, &c.

Of diseases the fig may suffer from the attack of the Coral Spot fungus (q.v.). It may also show serious Canker of the branches caused by *Phomopsis cinerescens*, and such cankered branches must be carefully removed. The fungus is a wound parasite so that where it is giving trouble wounds should be protected with paint. Fig Mosaic, a virus disease, is not a serious trouble. Some leaves show yellowish-green spots or blotches scattered anywhere on the surface, while others show pale-green spots or bands usually near the large veins and often with reddish-brown margins, but the leaves are not deformed. The fruit is rarely affected. Although the effects are not severe in this country it is more virulent in California and trees showing the symptoms should not be used for propagation. (D. E. G.)

Scale insects, Mealy bugs, and Red-spider Mites sometimes prove troublesome but the measures suggested for dealing with these pests will keep them in check.

A→

**FIG, HOTTENTOT.** *See* **Mesembryanthemum edule.**

**FIG, INDIAN.** *See* **Opuntia.**

**FIG MARIGOLD.** *See* **Mesembryanthemum tricolor.**

A→

**FIG, MULBERRY.** *See* **Ficus Sycomorus.**

A→

*Fi'go,* native name in Cochin China.

**FIGURE-OF-8 MOTH,** *Diloba caeruleocephala*, is so named from the marking of a figure 8 on the fore-wing. The bluish-grey caterpillars eat the leaves of Hawthorn, Blackthorn (Sloe), Apple, Cherry, and Plum during May, June, and July. The moths are on the wing from late September to November, and the eggs are laid singly or in small groups on the spurs, shoots, and branches. The fully fed caterpillars spin their cocoons on the trees and on neighbouring fences, posts, and support-stakes.

This pest is readily controlled by the application of arsenate of lead in spring.

G. F. W.

**FIGWORT.** *See* **Scrophularia.**

*fijien'sis -is -e,* of the Fiji Is.

**FILAMENT.** The stalk of a stamen connecting the anther with the receptacle or corolla.

*filamento'sus -a -um,* thread-like.

*fila'rius -a -um,* thread-like.

**FILBERT.** Long varieties of the Hazel Nut, *Corylus maxima*, covered with the long husk. The name is probably derived from St. Philibert whose day, 22 August, falls in the ripening period of the nut. Cf. **Cob-nut.**

*fili-,* in compound words, signifying thread-like, as *filicaulis*, with very slender stems.

**FILICI'NEAE.** One of the 3 divisions of the great group Pteridophyta, the other 2 being the Equisetineae and the Lycopodineae. The Filicineae usually have a monoecious prothallus (except in the Marsiliaceae and Salviniaceae), a stem with few or no branches, leaves large and branched, numerous sporangia on either the ordinary foliage leaves or on modified ones, mostly collected into groups called sori, and, except in the 2 families already mentioned, spores all of 1 kind. The characters distinguishing the families comprised in the Filicineae will be found under their proper headings: Cyatheaceae, Gleicheniaceae, Hymenophyllaceae, Marattiaceae, Marsiliaceae, Ophioglossiaceae, Osmundaceae, Polypodiaceae, Salviniaceae, Schizaeaceae.

*filici'nus -a -um, filici-,* in compound words, fern-like.

**FILIC'IUM** (*filix*, a fern; the foliage is fern-like). FAM. *Sapindaceae*. A genus of 3 African and 1 Singalese species with the characters set out below. A warm house is required for this beautiful tree which grows well in an open sandy loam.

**F. decip'iens.** Medium-sized evergreen tree. *l.* unequally pinnate, fern-like, ordinarily 10 to 15 in. long by 3½ to 7 in. wide, occasionally larger; lflets. 13 to 25, alternate or opposite, stalkless, 3 to 6 in. long, ½ to 1⅛ in. wide, narrowly oblong to oblanceolate, the spaces on the rachis between them conspicuously winged, dark bright green. *Panicles* slender, axillary, up to 9 in. long; *fl.* very small, 1-sexual; cal. 5-lobed, pet. 5, yellowish-white; stamens 5. *fr.* a fleshy drupe ¼ to ⅜ in. wide, globose. India, Ceylon. Cultivated extensively in tropical countries for its attractive foliage. SYN. *Pteridophyllum decipiens.*

W. J. B.

*filiform'is -is -e,* filiform, thread-like.

**FILIPEN'DULA** (*filum*, thread, *pendulus*, hanging; in reference to root tubers hanging on the fibrous roots of *F. hexapetala*). FAM. *Rosaceae*. A small genus for long included in Spiraea and frequently known by that name still, and by some put into a genus Ulmaria with similar limits. The species are hardy herbaceous perennials with pinnate or palmately lobed leaves and numerous flowers in terminal corymbs on leafy stems, sometimes 6 to 8 ft. high. The flowers have usually 5 sepals and petals, 20 to 40 stamens, and 5 to 15 1-seeded indehiscent carpels. The genus is found in N. Asia, Himalaya, Europe, and N. America, mostly in moist places but *F. hexapetala* also on rather dry, chalky hills. *F. hexapetala* is therefore capable of growing on rather dry borders; the other species are also good border plants if the soil moisture can be maintained in summer, but better still by water, and they will put up with partial shade. All are early summer-flowering plants. Propagation by division or by seeds sown in pans or boxes preferably in the autumn of the year of ripening in the cool greenhouse or cold frame.

The species of Astilbe bear considerable resemblance to Filipendula both in foliage and flower, but differ in floral details. The related *Spiraea Aruncus* is to be found under Aruncus.

KEY
1. Lflets. numerous, small, almost all alike, pinnately lobed — F. hexapetala
1. Lflets. few, terminal much the largest, palmately 3- to 5-lobed — 2
2. Lateral lflets. 3- to 5-lobed — 3
2. Lateral lflets. few or none, ovate — 4
3. Lvs. glabrous — F. rubra
3. Lvs. tomentose beneath — F. palmata
4. Plant 4 to 10 ft. h. — F. camtschatica
4. Plant 12 to 24 in. h. — 5
5. Carpels 5, ciliate; lateral lflets. none or few — 6
5. Carpels about 10; lateral lflets. present, ovate — F. Ulmaria
6. Lvs. glabrous — F. purpurea
6. Lvs. tomentose beneath — F. vestita

**F. camtschat'ica.** 4 to 10 ft. h. *l.* terminal lflet. very large, 3- to 5-lobed, doubly serrate; lateral lflets. often absent; stipules large. *fl.* white, fragrant, larger than in *F. Ulmaria*, corymbose. July. Manchuria, Kamtchatka. 1889. (Gn. 66 (1904), 174 as *Spiraea gigantea*.) Some variation in flower colour is found, for example **carnea, elegantissima rosea, rosea.**

**F. hexapet'ala.** Dropwort. 2 to 3 ft. h. Rootstock with many tubers. *l.* pinnate, glabrous, 4 to 10 in. long; lflets. many, sessile, 1 in. long. *fl.* white, often tinged red outside, ¾ in. wide, often with 6 sep. and pet. in loose panicles on slender peduncles. June, July. Europe, including Britain, Asia. (E.B. 416.) SYN. *Spiraea Filipendula.* A double form (**flore ple'no***) is common. var. **grandiflo'ra** has rather larger *fl.* The foliage is ferny and beautiful.

**F. palma'ta.*** 2 to 3 ft. h. *l.* with large 7- to 9-lobed terminal lflet. and 3- to 5-lobed lateral lobes, white hairy beneath or glabrous; stipules large. *fl.* pale pink becoming white. July. Siberia, Kamtchatka. 1823. SYN. *Spiraea digitata.* The plant offered as *Spiraea palmata* is frequently *F. purpurea.*

**F. purpu'rea.*** 1 to 4 ft. h. *l.* with large 5- to 7-lobed terminal lflet., doubly serrate and acuminate; lateral lflets. few or none; stipules narrow. *fl.* carmine or deep pink in large paniculate cymes, peduncles and stems crimson. June to August. Japan. 1823. (B.M. 5726; Gn. 17 (1880), 36.) SYN. *Spiraea palmata.* A very fine and effective plant of which some varieties are grown: **al'ba** has white *fl.* and lighter green *l.*; **purpuras'cens** has purple-tinted *l.*

**F. ru'bra.*** Queen of the Prairie. 2 to 8 ft. h. *l.* with a very large 7- to 9-lobed terminal lflet., lobes incised and toothed; lower *l.* with 3- to 5-lobed lateral lflets.; pubescent only on veins beneath, green on both surfaces; stipules reniform. *fl.* deep peach in a large somewhat clustered panicle. June. E. United States. 1765. (B.B. ed. 2, 2, 249.) SYN. *Spiraea lobata, S. venusta.* var. **al'bicans** has whitish or light pink *fl.*; **magnif'ica** is a fine form; **venus'ta*** has deep-pink or carmine *fl.*

**F. Ulma'ria.** Meadow Sweet, Queen of the Meadows. 2 to 4 ft. h. Stem erect, furrowed. *l.* with 3- to 5-lobed terminal lflet., 2 to 4 in. long, and smaller ovate lateral lflets.; glabrous above, white tomentose beneath; stipules leafy, half-ovate, toothed. *fl.* white; in dense, very compound cymes, 2 to 6 in. across, pubescent. June to August. Asia, Europe, including Britain. (E.B. 415.) SYN. *Spiraea Ulmaria.* var. **au'rea** has yellow variegated *l.*; **floreple'no** has double *fl.*

**F. vesti'ta.** 12 to 18 in. h. *l.* hoary beneath. *fl.* white, ¼ in. across, in many-fld., much-branched, oblong cymes. June. Otherwise like *F. camtschatica*. Himalaya. 1838. (B.R. 27, 4 as *Spiraea kamtschatica himalensis*.) SYN. *Spiraea vestita.*

*Filix,* fern.

**FILMY FERNS.** *See* **Ferns, Hymenophyllaceae.**

*fimbria'tus -a -um, fimbri-,* in compound words, fimbriate, fringed.

*Findlaya'nus -a -um,* in honour of James Findlay, who collected in Siam.

**FINGER AND TOE DISEASE.** *See* **Cabbage, Finger and Toe.**

**FINIAL.** An ornamental finish to the top of a pier or apex of a gable; e.g. gate piers are often embellished with stone baskets of fruit or flowers, balls, pine-apples, vases, urns, &c.

*finiti'mus -a -um,* adjacent.

*Finlaysonia'nus -a -um,* in honour of G. Finlayson, 1790–1823, who collected in Siam.

**FINNOCHIO.** *See* **Fennel.**

**FIORIN GRASS.** *See* **Agrostis alba.**

A

**FIR.** A name used somewhat indiscriminately for several kinds of coniferous trees. It is best associated with the Silver Firs, species of Abies, alone.

**FIR, DOUGLAS.** *See* **Pseudotsuga taxifolia.**

**FIR, SCOTS.** *See* **Pinus sylvestris.**

**FIR, SPRUCE.** *See* **Picea.**

**FIR, UMBRELLA.** *See* **Sciadopitys verticillata.**

**FIRE PINK.** *See* **Silene virginica.**

**FIRE THORN.** *See* **Pyracantha coccinea.**

**FIRE TREE.** *See* **Nuytsia floribunda.**

**FIRMIA′NA** (in honour of Karl Joseph von Firmian, 1716–82, Governor of Lombardy). FAM. *Sterculiaceae.* A genus of about 10 Asiatic and 1 African species. Deciduous trees with deciduous, alternate, palmately lobed leaves, flowers 5-parted, 1-sexual; sepals coloured, petals none, carpels distinct at base but joined above with a single style. Fruit opening long before seeds mature, then like 5 leathery leaves with seeds on the edges near the base. *F. simplex* is a tree for the milder parts of the country where it can develop its fine foliage without damage, or for the greenhouse. A good sandy loam suits it.

**F. sim′plex.** Tree up to 60 ft. with smooth bark. *l.* with 3 or 5 lobes, cordate, 6 to 8 in. long but on vigorous shoots up to 12 in. and as wide, glabrous or with stellate down especially in l.-axils beneath; stalk long. *fl.* in terminal panicles 10 to 20 in. long, 6 to 9 in. wide, yellowish-green; segs. ⅓ in. long; stamens 15, united into a column. July. China, cult. in Japan. 1757. SYN. *Sterculia Mariesii, S. platanifolia.*

*firm′us -a -um,* firm, strong.

**FIRST OF MAY.** *See* **Saxifraga granulata.**

*Fisch′eri,* in honour of (1) Friedrich Ernst Ludwig von Fischer (1782–1854), Director Botanic Garden, St. Petersburg; (2) Walter Fischer, *c.* 1914, who collected Cacti for Dr. Rose.

**FISCHER′IA** (in honour of Dr. Fischer of the Botanic Garden, Leningrad). FAM. *Asclepiadaceae.* A genus of about 12 species of twining shrubs or sub-shrubs, natives of the warmer parts of S. America. Leaves opposite. Flowers white or red in umbel-like cymes or short racemes. Related to and often confused with Gonolobus. Stove conditions and a compost of peat and loam suit it.

**F. Martia′na.** Climber to 30 ft. Stems hairy, hairs becoming red. *l.* oblong-cordate; stalks short, hairy. *fl.* white and green; cor. lobes fleshy, rounded; umbels many-fld.; peduncles long. May, June. Brazil. 1845. (B.M. 4472 as *Gonolobus Martianus.*)

F. G. P.

**FISH-BONE THISTLE.** *See* **Cnicus Casabonae.**

**FISH-POISON PLANTS.** A considerable number of tropical leguminous plants are known to possess fish-poisoning properties, and have been used from early times for catching fish. The crushed roots, stems, or leaves are thrown into lagoons and streams, the effect being to stupefy the fish which float to the surface insensible and are collected. Many such plants possess medicinal properties, and have been used, also, for destroying human and animal parasites. Within comparatively recent years many species of plants belonging to the genera *Derris* (Tuba root), *Lonchocarpus* (Cube root and Haiari), *Milletia, Mundulea,* and *Tephrosia,* have been found to possess insecticidal properties with the outstanding advantage that in normal concentrations they are non-poisonous to man and domestic animals. The main sources of supply of these plants are in the tropical regions of SE. Asia, Australasia, Africa, and America. The main active principle present is Rotenone, though others, including Deguelin and Tephrosin, occur and exert a poisonous effect on insects. As these plants are poisonous to fish, the preparations containing them must not find their way into ponds or water-courses.

A full account of these plants, together with their chemistry, countries of origin, and related matter, is given in a bulletin, entitled *A Survey of Insecticide Materials of Vegetable Origin,* published in 1940 by the Imperial Institute, South Kensington.

G. F. W.

*fis′sus -a -um, fissi-,* in compound words, cleft.

**FISTULI′NA hepat′ica.** *See* **Beef-steak Fungus.**

*fistulo′sus -a -um,* fistular; hollow like a pipe.

*Fitch′ii,* in honour of W. R. Fitch who collected Cacti with Dr. Rose in the W. Indies and Texas, 1913.

*Fittia′nus -a -um,* in honour of W. A. Fitt, gardener to Mr. Williams at Werrington Park.

**FITTON′IA** (in honour of Elizabeth and Sarah Mary Fitton, authors of *Conversations on Botany*). FAM. *Acanthaceae.* A genus of 3 species of evergreen perennials with beautifully marked leaves, natives of Peru. They are easily grown in the stove in a compost of loam, peat, and silver sand in shady places provided they are given ample supplies of water. The leaves are cordate and veined red or white. The flowers are small and solitary in the bracts of a terminal spike; they are negligible horticulturally and are best pinched off as soon as they appear. They may be grown on peat-covered shady walls or under other plants so long as they are able to get enough water, or under the greenhouse benches along with other tropical shade-loving plants.

**F. argyroneu′ra.** Dwarf. *l.* bright green, beautifully netted with white veins, oval, about 4 in. long, nearly 3 in. wide. 1867. (F.d.S. 1664.)

**F. gigan′tea.** Erect sub-shrub, about 18 in. h., branched. *l.* broadly ovate, sub-cordate, veined carmine-red. *fl.* pale red; bracts large. 1869. (G.F. 629.)

**F. Verschaffelt′ii.** Dwarf, trailing. *l.* larger than in *F. gigantea,* dark green, netted with deep red. (F.d.S. 1581.) var. **Pearc′ei,** *l.* 3 to 4 in. long, 2 to 3 in. wide, light bright green with light bright-carmine veins.

*Fitzal′ani,* in honour of E. F. A. Fitzalan, 1830–1911, who explored in Australia.

**FITZROY′A** (in honour of Capt. R. Fitzroy, R.N., 1805–65, commander in the Beagle expedition). FAM. *Pinaceae.* A monotypic genus distinguished from other closely related conifers by the cones which are composed of 9 scales in 3 alternating whorls, the lowest whorl sterile, the second sterile or bearing single seeds on the scales, the top whorl fertile, each scale with 2 to 6, 2- or 3-winged seeds. *F. cupressoides* is a very beautiful tree in cultivation but not very hardy. Plant in good light soil containing a little peat. Propagate by cuttings taken in August and inserted in sandy soil in a close frame, or by imported seed.

**F. Arch′eri.** A synonym of *Diselma Archeri.*

**F. cupressoi′des.**＊ A large Cupressus-like evergreen tree, 80 to 100 ft. h., with reddish bark shed in strips, and long, slender, pendulous branchlets. *l.* small, scale-like, in whorls of 3, overlapping, the lower part clasping the shoot, the upper part free, dark green, but with a single broken band of grey stomata beneath and 2 unbroken bands above, persisting several years. *fl.* usually dioecious, occasionally monoecious or hermaphrodite. *Cones* ¼ to ⅓ in. wide. Chile, N. Patagonia. 1849. (D.J.C. 226, 228; B.M. 4616 as *F. patagonica.*) Wood reddish, fragrant.

**F. patagon′ica.** A synonym of *F. cupressoides.*

W. D.

**FIVE FINGERS.** *See* **Syngonium auritum.**

*flabella′tus -a -um,* like an open fan.

*flabellifor′mis -is -e,* plaited like a fan.

*flac'cidus -a -um,* feeble, weak.

**FLACOURT'IA** (in honour of Étienne de Flacourt, 1607–61, a director of the French E. India Co.). FAM. *Flacourtiaceae.* A genus of about 12 species of trees and shrubs, often spiny, natives of Trop. Africa and Asia. Leaves toothed, shortly stalked. Flowers small, in racemes or clusters; sepals 4 or 5, scale-like; petals absent; stamens many; styles 2 to many. Fruit a 1-seeded berry with a hard endocarp. The species need stove conditions.

**F. Cataphrac'ta.** Small tree with compound spines, glabrous, branches dotted. *l.* oblong to oblong-lanceolate, 2 to 4 in. long, stalk short. *fl.* very small, $\frac{1}{10}$ to $\frac{1}{8}$ in. across, dioecious; in irregular glabrous racemes. *fr.* size of small plum, purple, very acid. India.

**FLACOURTIA'CEAE.** Dicotyledons. A family of trees and shrubs, mostly tropical, containing about 500 species in 70 genera. The usually alternate leaves are mostly pinnate-veined. Flowers usually in cymes, regular, occasionally 1-sexual. Sepals and petals 4 or 5 (rarely 2 to 6), stamens numerous, hypogynous or perigynous; ovary superior, 1-celled, with 3 to 5 parietal placentae, ovules numerous. Fruit usually a capsule or berry. The genera dealt with here are Aberia, Azara, Berberidopsis, Bonnetia, Flacourtia, Idesia, Oncoba, Poliothyrsis, Ryania, Xylosma.

*flagellarifor'mis -is -e,* long, thin, and supple, like the runner of a Strawberry.

*flagella'ris -a -um,* having long, thin shoots.

*flagellif'erus -a -um,* bearing long, thin, or supple shoots.

*Flahault'ii,* in honour of Charles Flahault, Professor of Botany, Montpelier, c. 1852.

**FLAKES.** A class of Carnations with pure ground marked with splashes of one colour. (Cf. **Bizarres.**)

**FLAMBOYANTE.** *See* **Poinciana regia.**

**FLAME FLOWER.** *See* **Kniphofia aloides.**

A→

**FLAME TREE.** *See* **Sterculia acerifolia.**

**FLAMINGO FLOWER.** *See* **Anthurium Scherzerianum.**

*flam'meus -a -um,* fiery-red.

**FLAT PEA.** *See* **Platylobium.**

*flav'ens, flavi-,* in compound words, yellowish.

*flaveo'lus -a -um,* yellowish.

**FLAVE'RIA** (*flavus,* yellow; plant used in Chile to dye yellow). FAM. *Compositae.* A genus of about 7 species of herbs, 1 Australian, the others American. Leaves opposite, narrow, entire or toothed. Flower-heads yellow, narrow, sessile, secund, in dense cymes. *F. contrayerba* needs a greenhouse and sandy loam, the seeds being sown in heat.

**F. contrayerb'a.** About 18 in. h. *l.* stalked, lanceolate, 3-nerved, toothed. *fl.-heads* yellow, terminal. July to September. Peru. 1794. (B.M. 2400.)

*flaves'cens,* pale yellow.

*flav'idus -a -um,* yellowish.

*fla'vus -a -um,* nearly pure yellow.

**FLAX.** *See* **Linum.**

**FLAX, NEW ZEALAND.** *See* **Phormium.**

**FLEABANE.** *See* **Conyza, Erigeron.** A

**FLEA-BEETLES** belong chiefly, but not exclusively, to a group of Chrysomelid Beetles of the genus Phyllotreta. They include *Psylliodes affinis* and *P. chrysocephala,* the Potato and the Cabbage-stem Flea-Beetle respectively. The active, jumping, metallic Phyllotreta beetles are familiar to all who grow Cabbages and related plants, often under the names Turnip Fly, Turnip Flea, or Jacks. They are on occasion destructive to ornamental Crucifers, e.g. Alyssum, Draba, and Iberis. The chief damage is done to the cotyledons (seed-leaves) above and even below ground-level, and the beetles feed later on the older leaves. Severe injury occurs to the seedlings, especially to Turnips, during a dry period in May and June. The beetles vary in size and colour according to the species, but they are usually bluish or black with or without a yellow stripe down each wing-case. Their small size makes them inconspicuous, but the effect of their feeding soon becomes apparent for the seed-leaves become spotted with minute holes, and quickly wither. The older leaves become netted and lace-like, but older plants withstand an attack better than the developing seedlings. The beetles, as a rule, overwinter in rubbish, in hedge bottoms, wood-piles, at the base of hay- and straw-ricks, and beneath the bark of trees. They become active in spring, and feed at first on Brassica crops left over winter, and on wild cruciferous weeds, e.g. Charlock and Shepherd's Purse. They fly freely on warm days, and migrate to germinating Cabbage, Radish, Swede, and Turnip. The female beetles lay their eggs from early June to mid-August either in the soil or on the leaves according to the habits of the particular species. The grubs feed either on the roots or mine the leaves of their food plants, but little injury is done during this stage of the beetle's life-cycle. When fully grown, the larvae pupate in the soil and emerge as adult beetles in a short time, and severe injury may be done to summer- and autumn-sown crops of turnips by the second-brood adults, which later hibernate until spring when feeding recommences.

Clean cultivation both as regards the destruction of cruciferous weeds in the neighbourhood of the vegetable garden, and the clearing out of rubbish from hedge bottoms, shrubberies, and similar sites, will tend to reduce their attacks. The soil of seed-beds should be in fine tilth, and the young plants provided with sufficiently rich soil to encourage rapid growth so that the plants grow away from any check received. Regular hoeing between rows of seedling Brassicas during drought is advisable to conserve the soil moisture and thus avoid any check to the developing plants. Dusting the seedlings as soon as the cotyledons appear above ground with soot, lime and soot, or basic slag will provide some measure of relief from attack, but a more effective check is possible by the use of D.D.T. preparations (q.v.).

G. F. W.

*Flei'scheri,* in honour of M. Fleischer, 1861–1930, of Mentone.

**FLEMING'IA** (in honour of John Fleming, 1747–1829, President, Medical Board of Bengal). FAM. *Leguminosae.* A genus of about 20 species of shrubs and sub-shrubs, natives of Trop. Asia and Africa. Erect, prostrate, or climbing with digitately 3-foliolate or rarely simple leaves, with striate stipules. Flowers usually in crowded racemes or panicles, sometimes solitary, papilionaceous; standard obovate, auricled at base; wings obliquely obovate, often adherent to the keel; stamens 9, connate, 1 free. Pods short, oblique, swollen. Flemingias need a warm greenhouse and light sandy soil. They are best raised from seed.

**F. conges'ta.** Erect shrub of 5 to 6 ft. *lflets.* oblong or broadly lanceolate, lateral 2-, terminal 3-nerved. *fl.* purple; cal. silky-hairy; racemes axillary. *Pods* 2-seeded. Summer. India.

**F. strobilif'era.** Erect shrub of 5 to 6 ft. *l.* simple, oblong, sub-acute, rounded at base, sometimes silky beneath. *fl.* purple; cal. hairy, its teeth lanceolate; racemes zigzag, 3 to 6 in. long; bracts long, almost hiding the fl. Summer. India. (B.R. 617.)

F. G. P.

**fleshy,** thick but not fibrous; with a firm or rather firm pulp.

*Fletcheria'nus -a -um,* in honour of the Rev. J. C. B. Fletcher of Mundham Vicarage, Chichester, amateur grower of Orchids, &c.

**FLEUR DE LIS.** *See* **Iris.**

*flex'ilis -is -e,* capable of being bent.

*flexuo'sus -a -um,* zigzag, with a bending or wavy direction.

**FLINDER'SIA** (in honour of Capt. M. Flinders, 1774–1814, who, in company with the famous botanist Robert Brown, explored the Australian coast). FAM. *Meliaceae.* A genus of 6 species of evergreen trees with pinnate leaves, natives of Australia and the Moluccas. Flowers small, in terminal panicles, the parts in fives. Greenhouse; loamy soil.

**F. austra'lis.** Evergreen tree of 60 to 100 ft. with a trunk 3 to 4 ft. in diameter. *l.* pinnate, 6 to 12 in. long; lflets. 11 to 13, reduced to 3, 5, or 7 near the infl., narrowly oval to lanceolate, 2 to 4 in. long, 1 to 2 in. wide, glabrous, dotted with transparent glands. *fl.* white, small, numerous, in panicles 1 to 4 in. long near the end of the shoots. *fr.* an oval cone, 2 to 3 in. long, woody, covered with large, pyramidal, pointed tubercles. New S. Wales, Queensland. 1828. One of the most valuable of Australian timber-trees.

W. J. B.

*floccig'erus -a -um,* woolly.

*flocco'sus -a -um,* covered with close woolly hairs which fall away in little tufts.

*flocculo'sus -a -um,* somewhat woolly.

**FLORA.** (1) The whole of the plants that grow in a particular region or locality; (2) a book that describes them.

**floral,** of or belonging to a flower; near a flower.

**FLORAL ENVELOPES.** The calyx and corolla or perianth of a flower.

*flo're ple'no,* having double flowers.

*florenti'nus -a -um,* of Florence, Italy.

**FLORESCENCE.** Flowering; the opening of the blossoms.

**FLORETS.** Little flowers, especially those in heads as of the Compositae, and in the inflorescences of grasses and sedges.

*floribun'dus -a -um,* flowering freely.

A→

**FLORIDA RIBBON FERN.** *See* **Vittaria lineata.**

*florida'nus -a -um,* of Florida, N. America.

*flor'idus -a -um,* flowery.

*florif'erus -a -um,* floriferous, flower-bearing; producing many flowers.

*Florin'dae,* in honour of Florinda Norman Thompson.

**FLORIST.** Cultivator of flowers; maker of floral designs.

**FLORISTS' FLOWERS.** Usually greenhouse or hardy plants of which a great number of garden-raised forms exist, derived from a small number of species of each of the genera included, e.g. Aster, Auricula, Begonia, Callistephus, Carnation, Chrysanthemum, Cyclamen, Dahlia, Delphinium, Fuchsia, Gladiolus, Hyacinth, Iris, Narcissus, Pansy, Pelargonium, Pink, Polyanthus, Pyrethrum, Rose, Tulip, Viola. Many other kinds might be cited and in all the aim of florists has been not only to raise new varieties, but to set a standard of perfection at which to aim and to exclude varieties which fail to conform to the standard set. In many instances and at various times the standards set have been very rigid, such as only a few cultivators could reach (and to attain the standards not only the qualities of the variety but the skill of the cultivator had to combine), with the not-infrequent result that the cultivation of a particular type of florists' flower has eventually been restricted to a very few enthusiasts and the plant itself has quite undeservedly fallen out of public favour. On the other hand, florists have conferred a great benefit on horticulture generally by seeking new combinations of characters and seizing upon new and desirable variations when they occur and propagating them. Practically all florists' varieties must be propagated vegetatively, for raised from seed they vary, sometimes only slightly, from the original, but sufficiently to put them out of court as an example of the named variety, in other words, they are clonal varieties and must be treated as such.

*florulen'tus -a -um,* flowery.

*-florus -a -um,* as a suffix signifying -flowered, as *multiflorus,* many-flowered, *sparsiflorus,* few-flowered.

*flos,* flower, as in *flos-Jovis,* Jove's flower.

**FLOWER.** The special organ of reproduction in the higher plants (Spermaphytes) consisting essentially of one or more stamens or carpels usually with protecting envelopes. In the normal flower there are four distinct parts, the outer calyx of sepals, the corolla of petals, the androecium of stamens, the gynoecium or pistil of carpels. Any of these may be absent and the parts of which each is composed varies from 1 upwards, but is usually constant for each species and often for all the species in a genus or a family. The number and arrangement of these parts forms an important basis for classification as it is to a great extent an indication of natural relationship; indeed, the Linaean classification was based upon this.

Where the flower contains only stamens without pistils as in some flowers of, e.g., Cucumber, Melon, Vegetable Marrow, it is often said to be 'barren' or 'blind' since it produces no fruit. Their function is to provide the pollen which fertilizes the ovules in the second type of flower which these plants bear. The ray florets of many Compositae have neither stamens or pistils, they are 'neuter flowers' whose sole function is that of attracting the insects necessary for effective pollination (q.v.). Of the same nature are the neuter flowers of some species of Viburnum.

**FLOWER BUD.** *See* **Bud.**

**FLOWER-DE-LUCE.** Old name for Iris.

**FLOWER FENCE.** *See* **Poinciana.** A

**FLOWER OF A DAY.** *See* **Hemerocallis, Tradescantia virginiana.**

**FLOWER OF JOVE.** *See* **Lychnis Flos-Jovis.**

**FLOWER OF THE WEST WIND.** *See* **Zephyranthes.**

**FLOWER-POTS.** *See* **Pots, Potting.** A

**FLOWER STAGES.** *See* **Stages.**

**FLOWERING ASH.** *See* **Fraxinus Ornus.**

**FLOWERING-BOX.** *See* **Vaccinium Vitis-idaea.**

**FLOWERING CURRANT.** *See* **Ribes sanguineum.**

**FLOWERING RUSH.** *See* **Butomus umbellatus.**

**FLUE.** Channels for the passage of heated air were once generally in use for the heating of greenhouses before hot-water heating was employed, being constructed of bricks covered with large flat tiles or slates with a piece of sheet iron over each joint, or of large pipes properly connected. Fire-bricks were used near the furnace, the flue being then led round the front part of the house and either returning along the back or terminating in a chimney at the end, taking care that there was a gentle rise from the furnace until the chimney was reached and that all corners were turned by a curve. The danger of fumes escaping through cracks in the flue or through imperfect joints had to be carefully guarded against.

**FLUED WALLS** were at one time built with the idea of giving more heat than the sun provided to Peaches and Nectarines. The need of such means was done away with through the cheapening of glass.

**FLUELLEN.** An old name for **Veronica officinalis. A**

**FLUG'GEA** (in honour of John Fluegge, German cryptogamic botanist, c. 1810). FAM. *Euphorbiaceae*. A genus of about 6 species of tropical shrubs. Leaves entire, obovate to ovate. Flowers apetalous; males in axillary clusters with a rudimentary pistil; females solitary with a lobed disk. Fruit a small berry. The genus is closely related to Phyllanthus and requires the same cultivation in a moist stove.

**F. leucopy'rus.** *l.* alternate, round to ovate, entire, glabrous; spines whitish, strong and numerous, 2 to 3 in. long. *fl.* inconspicuous. *Berries* white, attractive, edible. E. Indies. 1825.

*flu'itans,* floating in water.

*fluminen'sis -is -e,* growing in running water.

*fluvia'lis -is -e,* growing in a stream.

**FLY HONEYSUCKLE.** See **Lonicera Xylosteum.**

**FLY ORCHID.** See **Ophrys insectifera.** **A**

**FLY TRAP, AMERICAN.** See **Apocynum androsaemifolium.**

**FLY TRAP, VENUS'S.** See **Dionaea muscipula.**

**FLYWORT.** See **Catasetum,** Section MYANTHUS.

**FOAM FLOWER.** See **Tiarella cordifolia.**

*foecun'dus -a -um,* very fruitful.

*foemi'na,* female.

*foenicula'ceus -a -um,* fennel-like.

**FOENIC'ULUM** (the old Latin name). FAM. *Umbelliferae*. A genus of 3 or 4 species of often tall perennial or biennial herbs. Leaves pinnate, much cut into fine segments. Flowers yellow in compound umbels without an involucre; petals entire, inflexed at tip, but not pointed. Fruit variable in size, more or less oval. For cultivation see **Fennel.**

**F. vulga're.** Sweet Fennel. Short-lived perennial with stout, erect, branching stems 4 to 5 ft. h. *l.* 3 or 4 times pinnate with very narrow linear or awl-shaped segs. *fl.* yellow in rather large umbels. Late summer and autumn. S. Europe, naturalized in Britain especially on calcareous soils near the sea. (E.B. 601.) SYN. *F. officinale.* var. **dul'ce,** smaller than type with stem compressed, not round, at base, and smaller umbels; **piperi'tum,** about 2 ft. h. with very large *l.*-sheaths.

*Foerster'i,* in honour of Friedrich Förster, 1865–1918, of Baden, botanist.

*Foersterman'ni,* in honour of J. F. Föstermann, who collected, c. 1885, for Messrs. Sander in Assam, &c.

*foe'tens,* stinking.

**FOETID'IA** (*foetidus,* in allusion to the unpleasant smell of the wood). FAM. *Myrtaceae*. A genus of 4 species of trees endemic in the Mascarene Isles, with alternate, entire leaves. *F. mauritiana* needs stove treatment and a loamy soil.

**F. mauritia'na.** Evergreen tree, 20 to 40 ft., quite glabrous. *l.* sessile, crowded near end of shoot, obovate to oblanceolate, 3 to 6 in. long, 1 to 2½ in. wide, leathery. *fl.* solitary, axillary, on a stalk 1 to 1½ in. long; pet. none; cal. tube obconic, divided into 4 leathery, spreading lobes about 1 in. long, lanceolate; stamens very numerous. *fl.* obconic, woody, crowned by the cal. whose lobes have become enlarged, reflexed, persistent, with a flat, square disk ½ in. wide at the top. Mauritius. 1827.

W. J. B.

*foetidus -a -um,* stinking.

**FOGG'ING-OFF.** *See* **Damping-off.**

**FOKIEN'IA** (named after Fokien Province in China). FAM. *Pinaceae*. A small genus intermediate between Libocedrus and Cupressus.

**F. Hodgins'ii.** About 110 ft. h. with habit rather similar to Libocedrus, branchlet systems flattened and arranged in one plane. In adult trees in whorls of 4, the lower part clasping the shoot, but spreading towards tip and giving the shoot a jointed appearance, green with white stomata, tip a triangular point, l. on young trees larger with more prominent points. *Cones* resembling those of Chamaecyparis, ripening in second year, about 1 in. long and nearly as wide, of 12 to 16 scales with 2 seeds with 2 unequal wings on each fertile scale. Fokien, E. China. 1909. (D.J.C. 229.) SYN. *Cupressus Hodginsii.* Not hardy in the British Is. but succeeds in a cold greenhouse.

W. D.

**FOLIA JABORANDI.** Leaves of *Pilocarpus pennatifolius.*

**foliaceous,** leaf-like.

**FOLIATION.** The process of producing leaves.

*folia'tus -a -um,* leafy.

*foliola'tus -a -um,* in compound words preceded by a numerical prefix, implying composed of *n* leaflets.

**FOLIOLE.** Leaflet.

*folio'sus -a -um,* leafy.

*-folius -a -um,* in compound words, signifying -leaved, as *asplenifolius,* having leaves like an Asplenium.

**FOLLICLE.** A fruit consisting of a single carpel, dehiscing along the ventral suture only. (Cf. **Legume.**)

*follicula'ris -is -e,* having follicles.

**FO'MES.** A genus of large fungi belonging to the Basidiomycetes, growing on tree-trunks and branches, sometimes on fruit-trees, e.g. *F. pomaceus* on plums and cherries. They are woody and often hoof-shaped, and share with other fungi having fruits of similar form the common name of Bracket-fungi (q.v.).

D. E. G.

**FONTANE'SIA** (in honour of M. René Louiche Desfontaines, 1750–1833, author of *Flora Atlantica*). FAM. *Oleaceae*. A genus of 2 Asiatic deciduous shrubs of no great distinction, with 4-angled shoots and opposite, short-stalked leaves. Flowers in small axillary and terminal panicles, small, with 4 free petals shorter than the 2 stamens; ovary superior, 2-celled. Fruit a samara, winged all round. They are quite hardy, grow well in ordinary soil, and resemble Privet but with rough bark and slender branches. They would probably make a hedge as does *F. Fortunei* in China. Increased by cuttings under a glass in autumn.

**F. Fortu'nei.** Shrub of 12 ft. with slender, upright shoots. *l.* lanceolate, 1½ to 4½ in. long, entire, long-pointed, glossy green above, paler beneath. *fl.* creamy-yellow in axillary and terminal panicles. China. 1845.

**F. phyllyraeoi'des.** More densely branched and spreading than *F. Fortunei*, 5 to 6 ft. h. *l.* lanceolate, ¾ to 3 in. long, minutely toothed. *fl.* as in *F. Fortunei*. Syria. 1787. (L.B.C. 1308.) var. **na'na,** slower in growth and more compact.

*fonta'nus -a -um,* of a spring or fountain.

**FOOD-OF-THE-GODS.** An exudant from the notched roots of *Ferula Narthex* and *F. Asafoetida*. A Persian condiment and medicinal stimulant.

**FOOT ROT.** A very general term used to describe various diseases of herbaceous plants which, though due to different fungi, all show typically as a blackening and rotting of the base of the plant. Examples are Tomato Foot-rot seen in young tomato plants in pots and due to the fungus *Phytophthora cryptogea*. The same fungus causes similar trouble in Asters, Petunias, Wallflowers, &c. Various species of the fungus Fusarium cause similar symptoms in the Foot-rot diseases of Carnations, Dwarf Beans, and Peas. Many other plants, especially when young, are liable to these foot-rots due to various fungi either living in the soil or carried on the seed.    **A**
D. E. G.

**FOOTSTALK.** The stalk of a leaf or flower.

*Forbes'ii, Forbesia'nus -a -um,* in honour of (1) Professor Forbes, 1815–54, Professor of Botany, Edinburgh, who collected in Norway and the Levant; (2) James Forbes, gardener to the Duke of Bedford, Woburn Abbey, author of several books on garden plants between 1825 and 1850; (3) John Forbes who sent plants to England from Africa, *c.* 1825; (4) H. O. Forbes, author of *A Naturalist's Wanderings in the Eastern Archipelago*, and introducer of plants from New Guinea, *c.* 1886.

**FORCING.** Hastening the maturity of plants by artificial means is one of the important operations of gardening, calling for considerable care and skill both in the preliminaries and in the carrying out of the final stages. It has to be carried out mainly in the winter and early spring when outside temperatures are low and very variable and the amount of light very limited. While temperatures indoors can be raised by artificial means it is not yet possible to provide entirely suitable artificial light though some success has been obtained in this direction. (*See* **Light.**) Two types of plants are forced, perennials and annuals. The former are less dependent upon light during the forcing process than the latter and, indeed, the forcing of some perennials is independent upon light. The crops of forced Asparagus, Chicory, Rhubarb, Seakale, and a few other things are obtained in the entire absence of light, and for success dependence has to be placed upon the proper development of the plants before the process begins, and the process itself consists in the regulation of the heat and water-supplies. The plants themselves feed upon the food stored in previous months. At the other end of the scale are the annuals such as Lettuces, French Beans, Tomatoes, Stocks, Salpiglossis, which must have light to make food as they go on, though some of these also have a period when the light is good to prepare for their final effort in the duller days. The majority of the plants it is desired to force fall between these two extremes and need both to be carefully prepared before the process begins and to be treated in such a way that temperature and water-supply are regulated in relation not only to the stage of growth but also to the amount of available light. Notes will be found upon most of the plants normally forced under their appropriate headings but some general principles must be observed. Plants to be forced usually have their flowers already formed within the bud scales ready for development as soon as the necessary heat and moisture are provided, and an important consideration is that they shall have been grown so that this development has occurred. Many plants are injured by the forcing process so that they are not fit for forcing in the succeeding year, but they generally recover in the course of 2 seasons if planted out and cultivated with care. In the early stages of forcing heat should be applied as gradually as possible, beginning with a little warmer, closer atmosphere than that of the resting period. 50 to 55° F. by artificial heat will suit a large number of plants to start with, but this is too high for some. Most plants will bear more heat after the buds swell and begin to grow than they will previously. The value of sunshine cannot be over-estimated and light should be admitted to the fullest extent in winter when the sun will seldom be strong enough to injure the most tender foliage. It is inadvisable to maintain a temperature on dull days equal to that of bright days for the result would be to encourage weak, drawn growths which would droop immediately with the return of bright sun. Almost any position in heated houses may be used for plants and vegetables which are rendered useless by forcing and are to be destroyed after the crop is taken, but with Vines, Peaches, and so on under glass the greatest care is necessary, not only to conduct forcing so as to gain a crop in the following season but also to avoid doing anything that may prove injurious to the well-being of the trees afterwards.

Certain special treatments can be applied successfully as an immediate preliminary to forcing, the most important being Etherization (q.v.) and the Warm Bath method (q.v.), but not all plants respond to these treatments. Retarding in a cold chamber enables certain plants, e.g. Lily of the Valley, to be had at any season. In addition to vegetables, fruit-trees, and strawberries, the following are among the plants often forced; Almonds, Double Peaches, Astilbes, Azaleas, Japanese Cherries, *Clethra alnifolia*, Deutzias, Dicentra, Forsythias, Helleborus, Kalmias, Lilacs, Philadelphus, Pieris, Polygonatum, *Prunus triloba* and other plums, *Rhodora canadensis*, Spiraeas, Staphylea, Viburnum, Wisteria, Zenobia, and bulbs of many kinds.

**FORCING HOUSE.** For the provision of forced flowers in a garden a span-roofed house about 30 ft. long, 16 ft. wide, and 9 ft. high with a central stage and side beds with bottom heat provides the best accommodation. If it has a glass partition and separate valves in the heating pipes a greater range of temperatures can be secured. The house should be in a sheltered but not shaded position, and should have plenty of heat at command. Stronger and more equable bottom heat is obtained when the pipes pass through a shallow water-tank beneath the plunging material. Air temperature with a minimum of 50° F. for starting and rising to perhaps 65° F. after growth begins should be possible, and while ventilators should be available they must be used with great care. Interchange of air goes on continually through the laps of the glass when there is a considerable difference in temperature between the air in the house and that outside, and the ventilators are usually needed when forcing only on account of tender foliage and flowers. Usually all possible sun-heat should be retained in the winter and early spring and light syringings may be given on bright days using water at the same temperature as the house. Fire-heat should be cut down in the daytime as soon as the sunshine is strong enough to give sufficient warmth without it.

*Ford'ii,* in honour of (1) Charles Ford, I.S.O., 1844–1927, Superintendent of Hong Kong Botanic Garden; (2) Lyman M. Ford of San Diego, California.

**FORE-RIGHT SHOOTS.** *See* **Breast-wood.**

**FOREST OAK** of Australia. *See* **Casuarina.**

**FORESTIER'A** (after Chas. Le Forestier, a French physician and naturalist). FAM. *Oleaceae.* SYN. *Adelia, Borya.* A genus of about 20 species, mostly deciduous, privet-like. Leaves opposite, short-stalked. Flowers small, of no beauty, greenish, 1-sexual, or 2-sexual, sometimes dioecious; petals absent. Fruit a black or purple drupe, oval or oblong, ¼ to ½ in. long.

The cultivated species are of privet-like appearance and without floral attractions; they succeed in ordinary soil and are easily propagated by cuttings.

**F. acumina'ta.** Deciduous, glabrous shrub, 6 to 10 ft., sometimes a small tree 20 to 30 ft., shoots sometimes spine-tipped. *l.* lanceolate to oval-lanceolate, 1½ to 3 in. long, ½ to ¾ in. wide, tapered to both ends, shallowly toothed towards apex. *Male fl.* in small stalkless clusters; *female* in small panicles; both minute, greenish. *fr.* cylindrical, ½ in. long, purple. United States. 1812.

**F. ligustri'na.** Deciduous shrub up to 10 ft., widely bushy, shoots downy. *l.* oval or obovate, ¾ to 2 in. long, shallowly toothed except near base, downy beneath; stalk ¼ in. long. *fl.* green, inconspicuous; males in dense stalkless clusters; females fewer. *fr.* ⅓ in. long, ovoid, blue-black. SE. United States. 1812.

**F. neo-mexica'na.** Deciduous, glabrous shrub up to 10 ft., shoots sometimes spine-tipped. *l.* obovate to oblanceolate, bluntish at apex, ½ to 1¾ in. long, ¼ to 1 in. wide; stalk ⅛ to ¼ in. long. *fl.* clustered, small, inconspicuous. *fr.* blue-black, ovoid, ¼ in. long. SW. United States. 1925.

**FORFIC'ULA auricula'ria.** *See* **Earwigs.**

***Forgetia'nus -a -um,*** in honour of Louis Forget, Breton collector for Messrs. Sanders of St. Albans for 23 years in S. and Cent. America; introduced many Orchids, &c., d. 1915.

**FORGET-ME-NOT.** *See* **Myosotis palustris.**

**FORK.** This implement is made in various shapes and sizes to suit different purposes. Two pronged forks are best for light litter and for mixing manure, and so on. The 4- or 5-pronged forks are most serviceable for digging and are usually more useful for levelling down soil than the spade. This type of fork is indispensable for removing earth from the roots of trees and shrubs when transplanting, as if worked from the stem outwards, the soil is loosened, and the roots uninjured in the process. For digging the fork is less useful than the spade as it does not so thoroughly remove the earth from the bottom of the spit, but, nevertheless, the fork can often be used when it is impossible to use the spade. The flat-tined form is especially useful for lifting crops such as Potatoes. It should be borne in mind that the quality of the steel is most important for if of poor quality the tines may bend when they meet any resistance, or may easily snap. Forks for loading leaves and light manure are made with 4 or 5 long, somewhat curved, tines, and are very useful when large quantities have to be moved. Worn-down forks with the tines bent at right angles about 4 in. from the handle make good scarifiers.

Hand-forks are useful for planting out, plunging, and so on; the best form is made with 3 flat prongs and a handle of the same length like that of a trowel. Workers in the rock-garden often find a fork made from an old kitchen fork with two prongs very useful for working among the plants.

**FORMALDEHYDE** is a colourless gas known only in dilute solution and as a gas at high temperatures. It is probably an intermediate product in the photosynthesis of sugar and starch in the chlorophyll-containing cells of plants. Its chemical composition is H.CHO. It is soluble in water and in this form it is used in horticulture as a fungicide and sterilizing agent for the treatment of soil. The commercial solution is known as Formalin. Formalin contains about 40 per cent. of Formaldehyde, and has a very penetrating, suffocating odour and a neutral reaction. It is a powerful disinfectant and its fumes are deadly to plant life. It can therefore be used only in dilute solutions and with special precautions. *See* **Fungicides.**

**FORMALIN.** *See* **Formaldehyde.**

***Formanekia'nus -a -um,*** in honour of Dr. Eduard Formanek, Professor of botany, Brünn, d. 1900, collected in Athos, &c.

***formica'rius -a -um,*** pertaining to ants.

***-formis -is -e,*** in compound words, implying shape, as *multiformis*, many-shaped.

***formosa'nus -a -um,*** of Formosa.

***formo'sus -a -um,*** beautiful.

***fornica'tus -a -um,*** arched.

**FORREST'IA** (in honour of Peter Forrest, 17th-century botanist). FAM. *Commelinaceae.* A genus of about 7 species of herbaceous perennials, 1 in Trop. Africa, the rest in India and Malaya. Stem creeping, rooting below. Leaves broad with a tubular sheath persisting after the fall of the blade. Flowers crowded in almost sessile axillary panicles; sepals and petals nearly equal; stamens 6. Requiring stove conditions and treatment like Commelina.

**F. Hook'eri.** Stem creeping, 1 to 3 ft. long, 3 ft. h. *l.* obovate-lanceolate, somewhat fleshy, finely pointed, more or less hairy, purple beneath, finally smooth and green above; tapered to base, sheath large, striated, often very hairy. *fl.* in dense sessile clusters from lower sheaths and often from those from which the blade has fallen; sep. purplish, boat-shaped; pet. paler, almost white, ovate, acute. Malaya. 1864. (B.M. 5425 as *F. hispida.*) SYN. *Pollia purpurea.*

***Forrest'ii,*** in honour of George Forrest, 1873–1932, who collected in China.

**FORSELLES'IA.** *See* **Glossopetalon.**

***Forskal'ii,*** in honour of Peter Forskål, 1732–61, of Helsinfors, who collected in SW. Arabia.

***Forsten'i,*** in honour of E. A. Forsten, 1811–43, explorer in E. Indies.

***Forst'eri, Forsteria'nus -a -um,*** in honour of J. R. Forster, 1729–98, of Halle, and his son J. G. A. Forster, 1754–94.

**FORSYTH'IA** (in honour of William Forsyth, 1737–1804, superintendent of the Royal Gardens, Kensington, author of book on fruit-growing). FAM. *Oleaceae.* A genus of about 6 species of deciduous shrubs from E. Asia, 1 in SE. Europe. Winter buds with several scales, often superposed. Leaves opposite, simple or 3-partite or 3-foliolate. Flowers yellow, 1 to 6 from lateral buds on previous year's wood, before foliage. Calyx and corolla 4-lobed, corolla tube short, stamens 2, longer or shorter than style. Forsythias grow well in ordinary garden soils so long as the drainage is good but are best if it is rich; their early-flowering habit and floriferousness make them valuable shrubs for any garden. *F. suspensa* in some forms is rather a straggling grower and will scramble up neighbouring trees, even pines, and can be well used for trailing down steep banks, being rooted at the top of the bank. *F. suspensa Fortunei* may have the stems that have flowered cut back hard each spring as soon as the flowering is over, but other species need little or no pruning. Cuttings of bare wood about 12 in. long put into a sheltered border outside in October usually root readily, and so do the tips of shoots cut in late June to about 5 or 6 in. long if put into a warm sand frame.

KEY

1. *Branches hollow except at nodes. Lvs. often 3-foliolate* F. suspensa
1. *Branches at least partly with chambered pith* 2

2. *Mature branches dark grey, green, or brown* 3
2. *Mature branches yellowish. Lvs. ovate or broadly ovate* F. ovata
3. *Lvs. usually toothed above middle* 4
3. *Lvs. mostly entire, 2 to 3 in. long. Mature shoots green* F. europaea
4. *Lvs. on strong shoots often 3-partite. Shoots with or without lamellate pith* F. × intermedia
4. *Lvs. not, or very rarely, 3-partite* 5
5. *Lvs. 2 to 5 in. long. Mature shoots dark grey. Fl. pale yellow* F. Giraldiana
5. *Lvs. 3 to 6 in. long. Mature shoots green. Fl. bright yellow with greenish tinge* F. viridissima

**F. europae'a.** 6 ft. h., erect, rather lank. *l.* ovate, 2 to 3 in. long, glabrous, entire or toothed. *fl.* yellow, large, sometimes in pairs; cor. lobes 7/8 in. long, 3/8 in. wide, rather spreading; cal. lobes shorter than cor. tube, spreading or reflexed. February, March. SE. Europe. 1899. Both long- and short-styled forms occur. (B.M. 8039.)

**F. Fortu'nei.** A synonym of *F. suspensa Fortunei.*

**F. Giraldia'na.** *l.* elliptic to oblong, 2 to 5 in. long, broadly wedge-shaped, entire or toothed, sometimes hairy beneath. *fl.* rather pale yellow, lobes 3/4 in. long; cal. lobes deeply cut. February. NW. China. 1910. An erect shrub of rather thin growth, shoots dark grey. (B.M. 9662.)

**F. × interme'dia.*** Of stiffer habit and more compact than *F. suspensa*, flowering between that and *F. viridissima*, with l. sometimes 3-foliolate, more tapering at base than in *F. suspensa*. Cal. shorter than cor. tube; cor. lobes about 1/2 in. long. March. A hybrid of *F. suspensa* and *F. viridissima*. var. **densiflo'ra,** *fl.* crowded, rather pale, with flattish, rather spreading lobes, style long; **primuli'na,** *fl.* pale yellow, revolute, style short; **spectab'ilis,*** *fl.* crowded, bright yellow, lobes longer, style long; **vitelli'na,** erect, vigorous, deep bright yellow, style long. SYN. *F. vitellina.*

**F. ova'ta.** 3 or 4 ft. h., somewhat spreading, shoots yellowish-brown. *l.* ovate to almost orbicular, acute or acuminate, 2 to 4 in. long, entire or coarsely toothed. *fl.* butter-yellow; cor. lobes 1/4 to 1/2 in. long, spreading, tube longer than rounded cal. lobes. February, March. Korea. 1919. (B.M. 9437.)

**F. Siebold'ii.** A synonym of *F. suspensa Sieboldii.*

**F. spectab'ilis.** A synonym of *F. × intermedia spectabilis.*

**F. suspen'sa.*** Golden Bell. 8 to 10 ft. h. (or if on wall or depending down a bank much longer). *l.* 2 to 4 in. long, wedge-shaped at base, or more rarely 3-partite or 3-foliolate and tapering, coarsely toothed, acute. *fl.* golden-yellow, from 1 to 6 in a cluster; cor. lobes 3/4 in. long, spreading; cal. lobes as long as cor. tube. March, April. E. China. 1850. Branches slender, angled, hollow, except at nodes. (B.M. 4995.) Several varieties are known; **atrocau'lis** has dark-purplish young shoots, pale-lemon fl.; **decip'iens** has long-stalked deep-yellow fl., singly borne, and long styles; **pal'lida** has pale-yellow fl., solitary; **pubes'cens** has shortly hairy young branches and leaves. All these are forms of the stiffer-stemmed var. **Fortu'nei,*** with arching branches best suited for open positions. There is also a golden variegated form of this (**variegata aurea**). var. **Siebold'ii** has slender pendent branches which often root at the tip and is better for covering arbours and steep banks.

**F. viridis'sima.*** 5 to 8 ft. h., stiff, erect, smooth when young. *l.* elliptic-oblong to lanceolate, 3 to 6 in. long, acute, entire or toothed in upper part. *fl.* bright yellow, solitary or in clusters of 3; cor. lobes about 1/2 in. long, revolute; tube twice as long as cal. lobes. April. E. China. 1844. (B.M. 4587.) var. **korea'na** is more spreading in habit with larger and brighter fl. A golden variegated form (**variega'ta**) is offered.

**F. vitelli'na.** A variety of *F. × intermedia.*

**FORTHRIGHT.** The name given to the main walks in Elizabethan gardens which followed the main axial lines leading out from the mansion, thus giving a sense of connexion between house and garden. The same principles are adopted in formal design of to-day.

***for'tis -is -e,*** strong.

***fortuna'tus -a -um,*** favourite of fortune, rich.

**FORTUNEA'RIA** (in honour of Robert Fortune, 1812–80, famous plant-collector for the Royal Horticultural Society in China, &c., 1843–61, who introduced the tea-plant to India). FAM. *Hamamelidaceae.* A genus of a single species related to Corylopsis but leaves with much-branched (not straight) veins, and unequal teeth, flowers with very narrow (not broad) minute petals, and stamens with very short filaments. Cultivation as for Hamamelis.

**F. sinen'sis.** Deciduous shrub, 20 to 25 ft., young parts densely starry-downy. *l.* obovate, shortly pointed, base rounded, 3 to 6 in. long, half as wide; stalk 1/8 to 1/3 in. long. *fl.* green, 1/8 in. wide, in terminal racemes which are wholly male or wholly bisexual, the latter 1 to 2 in. long; cal. 5-lobed, pet. 5. *fr.* a woody 2-valved capsule 1/2 in. long. February. China. 1910. Vigorous and very hardy but with little to recommend it except its botanical interest.

***Fortu'nei, Fortuni.*** *See* **Fortuneara.**

A→

***Fosteria'nus -a -um,*** in honour of Prof. Sir Michael Foster, F.R.S., physician of Shelford, Cambridge, amateur of Irises.

**FOTHERGIL'LA** (in honour of Dr. John Fothergill, 1712–80, who grew many American plants at Stratford, Essex). FAM. *Hamamelidaceae.* A genus of 4 species of deciduous shrubs, natives of south-eastern N. America, with alternate, stalked, coarsely toothed, stipulate leaves; flowers without petals, in terminal heads or spikes without basal bracts; calyx 5- to 7-toothed; stamens about 24 with white filaments thickened towards top. The ornamental character of the 'bottle-brush' spikes of flowers which open before the leaves appear lies in the white filaments; the crimson or orange-yellow autumn colouring of the foliage especially of *F. major* and *F. monticola* itself makes them worthy of a place in our gardens where they grow best in a moist (but well-drained) peaty sandy loam. They do not object to some shade, and can be raised from seed, often taking 2 years to germinate, or by layers, or by cuttings of firm wood with a slight heel in gentle heat in July.

KEY

1. *Lvs. 1 to 2 in. long, stellate-hairy above; growth low* F. Gardeni
1. *Lvs. 2 to 4 in. long, smooth or almost as above; growth taller* 2
2. *Lvs. glaucous beneath* F. major
2. *Lvs. green and less hairy beneath* F. monticola

**F. alnifo'lia.** A synonym of *F. Gardeni.*

**F. Gar'deni.*** Shrub of 2 or 3 ft., shoots slender, rather spreading, covered with white stellate hairs. *l.* oval or obovate, 1 to 2 1/2 in. long, unequally toothed above middle, somewhat downy above, downy beneath. *fl.* in cylindrical terminal spikes, 1 1/2 in. long, 1 in. wide, fragrant. April, May. Foliage crimson in autumn. Varieties have been named according to the form of the leaf, **acu'ta** or **obtu'sa** (B.M. 1341), or the time of flowering, e.g. **serot'ina** (late).

**F. ma'jor.*** Shrub of 6 to 8 ft. with fairly erect shoots at first covered with white stellate down. *l.* roundish-oval or broad-ovate, 2 to 4 in. long, often almost entire dark glossy green above, glaucous beneath with stellate down on veins at least. *fl.* in erect cylindrical spikes, 1 to 2 in. long, fragrant. May. Alleghany Mts. 1780. (B.M. 1342; L.B.C. 1520.) SYN. *F. alnifolia major.*

**F. montic'ola.*** Very similar to *F. major* but growth more spreading. *l.* green not glaucous and less downy beneath, and sometimes redder in its autumn colouring, while the fr. is without the red markings inside seen in *F. major*. SE. N. America. 1910.

**FOUNTAIN.** A pleasing garden feature consisting of a spray or spout of water thrown into the air and caught in a basin. The water may be conducted by pipes from a natural source or from the main. Usually a sufficient force is obtainable from the action of gravity or from the pressure of the water-main, but for throwing a jet to any considerable height the pressure may have to be supplemented by mechanical means as, for example, by the use of a motor

Simple, inexpensive fountains are now available for use in small gardens driven by an electric motor which pumps up the same water over and over again.

The water forming the fountain may be delivered from nozzles in the centre or at the sides of the basin. Alternately it may be arranged to come from a figure such as a bird, frog, or mermaid. In a wall fountain the water usually issues from a mask on the wall and drops into a basin at the foot.

For details of the construction of fountain basins *see under* **Water Plants.**

**FOUNTAIN PLANT.** *See* **Amarantus salicifolius.**

**FOUQUIE'RA** (in honour of Peter Edward Fouquier, M.D., French physician). FAM. *Fouquieraceae.* A genus of about 5 species of glabrous, spinous shrubs, natives of Mexico. Leaves clustered or almost solitary in the axils of the spines which are modified leaves, small, obovate, entire, rather fleshy. Flowers showy, in thyrsoid or shorter and looser panicles; sepals 5, free; corolla 5-merous, tubular, lobes spreading, overlapping, hypogynous; stamens 10 or more, in one or two series. The plants need a loamy soil with fibrous peat and may be increased by cuttings in heat under a bell-glass. A minimum temperature of 50° F., partial shade, and a fair amount of water while in growth with little during the winter months.

**F. columna'ris.** Stems pyramidal, succulent, deeply wrinkled, with thin, straggling branches, beset with scattered, slender spines, having a tuft of small, fleshy *l.* in the axil of each. *fl.* in panicles. (G.C. 26 (1899), p. 277, f. 94.) **A**

**F. formo'sa.** 6 to 10 ft. h. *l.* oblong, scattered, rather fleshy. *fl.* scarlet, 1 in. long, in terminal erect spikes; cor. tube cylindrical, somewhat curved; limb reflexed spirally. (Add. 8.) **A**

**F. spino'sa.** About 15 ft. h. *l.* mostly in clusters, obovate-oblong, membranous. *fl.* scarlet, stalked, in a corymbose panicle; stamens 10. SYN. *Idria columnaria.* **A**

**F. splen'dens.** 6 to 18 ft. h., somewhat branched at base, branches up to 1 in. thick, nearly straight, spiny, at length ash-grey. *l.* obovate to oblong-lanceolate, narrowed to a short stalk; l. of short branches clustered, smaller; including stalk ¾ to 1¼ in. long. *fl.* red, tube straight, about ½ in. long, lobes nearly round, more or less recurved, 2 to 2½ in. long; stamens 15; panicles 4 to 6 in. long, narrow, usually many-fld. SW. United States, Mexico. (B.M. 8318.)

**FOUQUIERA'CEAE.** Dicotyledons. A family of a single genus, Fouquiera, with about 5 species, natives of Mexico, related to Tamaricaceae but with petals joined, 10 or 15 stamens, and fruits with 4 to 6 oily seeds, long-haired or winged. **A**

**FOUR O'CLOCK.** *See* **Mirabilis Jalapa.**

**FOURCROY'A.** *See* **Furcraea.**

*Fournie'ri,* in honour of Eug. P. N. Fournier, 1834–84, of Paris, physician.

*foveola'tus -a -um,* foveolate, having small pits or depressions.

**FOXBANE.** *See* **Aconitum Vulparia.**

**FOXGLOVE.** *See* **Digitalis.**

**FOXGLOVE, MEXICAN.** *See* **Tetranema mexicana.**

*Fox'ii,* in honour of Walter Fox, 1858–?, gardener at Singapore.

**FOXTAIL GRASS.** *See* **Alopecurus pratensis.**

**FOXTAIL PINE.** *See* **Pinus Balfouriana.**

**FRAGA'RIA** (*Fraga*, the old Latin name, from *fragrans,* fragrant in reference to the perfume of the fruit). FAM. *Rosaceae.* A genus of about 12 species of perennial herbs with runners, natives of north temperate regions, the Andes, Sandwich Is., and Bourbon. Leaves 3-foliolate, pinnate, or 1-foliolate. Flowers white or yellow (pinkish flowering varieties of several species are recorded), honeyed, often polygamous. Achenes many, very small, embedded on the surface of the large convex fleshy receptacle. Most of the following are hardy and can be grown in the same way as the Strawberry which is a derivative of some of them. *F. indica* is often grown on the rock-garden. *See* **Strawberry.**

**F. alpi'na.** A synonym of *F. vesca semperflorens.*

**F. californ'ica.** Perhaps related to *F. moschata.* l. few, stalk silky-hairy, slender, long; lflets. sessile, broadly rounded, coarsely toothed. *fl.* white, about ⅝ in. across, on scapes 2 to 4 in. h. *fr.* nearly hemispherical; rather small; achenes in shallow pits. SW. United States.

**F. chiloen'sis.** About 1 ft. h. *lflets.* obovate, blunt, toothed, leathery, wrinkled, silky beneath. *fl.* white; sep. erect; peduncles thick, silky. April, May. *fr.* rose, flesh-white, pendulous. S. America. 1727. var. **grandiflo'ra,** Pine Strawberry, *lflets.* glaucous, leathery, broadly crenated, hairy beneath, *fl.* white, sep. reflexed, peduncles thick. April, May. *fr.* red. 1759.

**F. Daltonia'na.** Small. Stems red; runners very slender. *lflets.* distinctly stalked, hairy or glabrous, teeth few. *fl.* white, solitary; cal. lobes and bracts toothed. May, June. *fr.* bright scarlet, about 1 in. long, ½ in. wide; flavourless. N. India. SYN. *F. sikkimensis.* Rock-garden.

**F. ela'tior.** A synonym of *F. moschata.*

**F. in'dica.*** Trailing. *l.* 3-foliolate; lflets. wedge-shaped-ovate, deep green, crenated. *fl.* golden-yellow; cal. 10-parted, outer 5 forming an epicalyx, large, leafy; cal. 10-parted, outer 5 peduncles axillary, solitary, 1-fld. May to October. *fr.* red, insipid, numerous. India, Japan. 1805. (A.B.R. 479.) SYN. *Duchesnea fragarioides, D. indica.* Rock-garden, alpine house.

**F. moscha'ta.** About 1 ft. h. *lflets.* plicate, rather leathery, green. *fl.* white; sep. at length reflexed. April, May. *fr.* with a firm receptacle adhering little to the cal. Europe, probably naturalized in Britain. (E.B. 439.) SYN. *F. elatior.* A curious form, known as the Plymouth Strawberry, occurs in which the carpels are replaced by small leafy growths. It has long been known but is uncommon.

**F. ves'ca.** Wild Strawberry. 6 to 12 in. h. *lflets.* plicate, thin, hairy beneath. *fl.* white; sep. at length reflexed. April, May. *fr.* pendulous. Britain, &c. (E.B. 438.) var. **monophyl'la,** about 6 in. h., *l.* simple, teeth crenate. *fl.* white. May. *fr.* small, round, pendulous, receptacle long, red. Europe. 1773. (B.M. 63); **semperflor'ens,** Alpine Strawberry, up to 10 in. h., vigorous, *fl.* from May to November, small, *fr.* more or less oblong or roundish, red or white.

**F. virginia'na.** Scarlet Strawberry. About 1 ft. h. *fl.* white; peduncles and pedicels as long as l. April. *fr.* deep red when ripe; receptacle very tumid, pendulous. N. America. 1629.

**F. vi'ridis.** More or less dioecious. Rootstock little branched. Stem weak, 3 to 6 in. h. *l.* hairy, stipules narrow, brownish. *fl.* about 4, small, yellowish-white; outer sep. about equal to inner. May, June. *fr.* red, cal. appressed or erect. Europe, N. Asia.

*fragarioi'des,* Strawberry-like.

*frag'ilis -is -e,* brittle.

*frag'rans,* sweet-scented.

*fragrantis'simus -a -um,* very fragrant.

**FRAIL'EA** (in honour of Manuel Fraile, for many years in charge of the Cactus collection in the United States Department of Agriculture, Washington). FAM. *Cactaceae.* Small plants, with ribs divided into tubercles and somewhat resembling a Mammillaria, but the flowers are very different; they are borne on the tubercles and are usually cleistogamous; fruit small, round, scaly, and bristly. For cultivation *see under* **Cactus** (terrestrial).

**F. cataphrac'ta.** Little round plants, less than 1 in. wide, depressed at top; ribs low, tubercles flattened above; radial spines 5 to 9, whitish, minute; no centrals. *fl.* ?. Paraguay. SYN. *Echinocactus cataphractus.*

**F. Grahlia'na.** Plants small, often in clusters; ribs low; spines curved backwards, very short. *fl.* yellowish. Paraguay. SYN. *Echinocactus Grahlianus.*

**F. Knippelia'na.** Small cylindrical plants; ribs tuberculate; spines yellowish. *fl.* yellow, rarely opening. Paraguay. SYN. *Echinocactus Knippelianus.*

**F. pulcher'rima.** A synonym of *Malacocarpus pulcherrimus.*

**F. pyg'mea.** Small plants, often in clusters, tuberculate; spines white, bristle-like. *fl.* yellow, pinkish outside, rarely opening. Uruguay, Argentina. SYN. *Echinocactus pygmaeus.*

**F. Schlinzkya'na.** Little round plants, flattened above, ribs indistinct but strongly tuberculate; radial spines more or less reflexed, one central stouter than the radials. *fl.* yellow, rarely opening. Paraguay, Argentina. SYN. *Echinocactus Schlinzkyanus.*

V. H.

**FRAMES, GARDEN.** Frames are low portable or permanent structures with readily removable glass covers known as lights. They are most useful in the garden for a great variety of purposes, especially in spring and early summer when quantities of plants have to be brought on for transplanting. They are also employed in forcing by placing on a hotbed of fermenting material or heated by hot-water pipes or soil electric cables, supplemented by a covering of litter or mats when there is severe frost. Melons, cucumbers, and winter-flowering greenhouse plants may be grown in them during the summer and in winter they may be useful for storing plants that require protection from frosts, for blanching endive, and so on. They are also very useful for raising cuttings at almost all seasons and are an indispensable adjunct to the alpine house and large rock-garden. Especially in recent years they have been brought into further service for the raising of salads and early vegetables. This is a development or rather an adaptation of the French gardening system which was much advocated for use in this country in the early part of the present century. Both portable and permanent frames may be made use of, the former being better adapted to the requirements where a hotbed or the type of compost used in French-gardening is concerned.

Frames are of various sizes, determined largely by convenience of working. The box of the frame may, if permanent, be constructed of brick, concrete, or wood, or even, in case of need, of turves, the front being lower than the back so that greater exposure to the sun may be secured and rain may be rapidly shed from the surface. The important points to bear in mind are that the greatest possible amount of light should be available for the plants; that the plants should be as near as possible to the glass to ensure sturdy and robust growth; that the box itself should not provide shelter for pests; that drip from the lights should be avoided by proper glazing; that the lights should be readily moved from place to place by one man and opened without difficulty and danger of breakage for all necessary work, best carried out from the back of the frame when the lights are in use, and for ventilation; that the lights are of uniform size and interchangeable.

Permanent frames are sometimes made with a span roof or with a three-quarter span, and for certain purposes these have advantages, provided due care is taken to avoid drip from the ridge, but usually a lean-to type of light is found sufficient. For portable frames the lean-to type only need be considered, though a span-roofed type of cloche of the dimensions of a frame is coming into use. The permanent frame range may be as long as is desired but the portable type should not exceed the length necessary for 3 lights, unless the box is so constructed that it can be taken to pieces and readily reassembled. The size of the frame is determined by the lights and 3 main types of lights are in use, the English, French, and Dutch. There is no standard-size for the English light which is usually of substantial construction with styles about 2½ in. wide and about 2 in. thick, wooden sash-bars, and 3 or 4 rows of glass; its length may be 4 to 6 ft. and width about 4 ft. The box will be 9 or 10 in. high in front and 12 to 14 in. high at the back, but may be more or less according to the purpose for which it is used. The lights are arranged on runners and a handle is provided at the back so that they can be lifted to allow for watering, &c., or for ventilation. If the box is of wood it will usually be 1¼ in. thick. All wooden parts must be thoroughly painted or coated with Stockholm tar applied hot or some other wood-preservative which should be renewed annually. Neither coal-tar nor any preparation containing creosote should be used as the fumes are injurious and may be set free whenever the weather is hot. French lights are constructed with narrower styles and with T-iron sash-bars, admitting more light and being somewhat less heavy. They have 4 rows of glass as a rule and rest on movable cross-bars and on the sides of the frame instead of runners. The Dutch light consists of the wooden frame and a single sheet of glass, thus admitting all possible light.

The box of the portable frame may be made of wood 1 in. thick. It should take 3 lights placed so that they touch each other, and there should be stops in front of the box so that the lights do not slip when lifted at the back by the handle placed for the purpose. For the cultivation of salads the depth in front may be 7 in. and at the back 9 in. When the plants grow so as to be in danger of touching the glass the whole box is raised an inch or two by means of hooks, the space so created being filled with manure, taking care that the legs at each corner are adequately supported. For taller plants medium to deep frames are necessary though the shallow frame may be utilized for these in the early stages of growth, the depth being increased when necessary by means of another frame of the same size made to fit on top of the first and carrying the same lights.

If the lights are made of small panes, four rows of panes each 12 in. by 10 in. will be convenient, ½ in. overlap being allowed. This gives 16 panes to each light and the light will measure 3 ft. 11 in. wide and 4 ft. 3 in. long over all. The panes should be set in putty and the top panes will need putty along the top edge to prevent drip. The only advantage of this type of light over the Dutch light, where the glass pane measures 62 in. long and 35 in. across, is that the cost of making good breakages is less.

In dealing with the cultivation of plants, directions for the use of frames and for the best type of compost are given, but the following notes will show how continuous use may be made of them for the growing of salads and vegetables. It is important to note, however, that certain varieties of each vegetable are better suited for cultivation in frames than others, and indeed some varieties of certain kinds cannot be grown successfully in frames where intensive methods are adopted.

Where a hotbed of fermenting manure or leaves is used in early February alternate rows of Carrot (Early Horn or Nantes) and Radish (French Breakfast) may be sown, or Lettuces from seed sown in October and wintered under glass may be planted between the rows of Carrots, using Early French Frame or Early Paris. The Radishes and Carrots will be ready for use by mid-March and their place may be taken by Cauliflowers raised from seed sown under glass in September or January. The Carrots will be ready to clear by the end of May or in early June and bush Marrow plants may take their place. In mid-June the Cauliflowers should be ready to cut, leaving the Marrows to fill the frame. Each light should accommodate 9 Cauliflowers and 2 Marrows. The crops will need plenty of water from early April onwards. In mid-June the lights can be dispensed with entirely. Care must, of course, be used in making up the hotbed (see **Hotbeds**) and in keeping the frames lined and protected by mats, &c., in frosty weather. Planting should not be undertaken till the frame temperature has dropped to about 68° F. and all fumes of ammonia have escaped. Many variations in cropping are possible, e.g. Dwarf Beans may be sown when the Lettuces and Radishes are cleared at the end of March, or Frame Turnips such as White Milan may be sown at the same time. The same crops may be grown without a hotbed and will mature about a fortnight or 3 weeks later. Other crops that can be grown to maturity in the frame without a hotbed are Parsley and Onions for pulling green, sown in August, ready in April, Lettuces such as May King sown in September, ready in May, Spinach sown in January, ready in April, Beetroots sown in March, ready in June. In the south during the hottest part of the year in rich soil with scrim shading and plenty of moisture, Lettuces, Mustard and Cress, Spinach, Radishes, Turnips, crops which often fail in the open, may be grown to perfection.

For deeper frames Potatoes, Cauliflowers, Marrows, Frame Cucumbers, Tomatoes, Self-blanching Celery, and Melons may be grown, while with suitable treatment headed Broccoli may be protected in cold districts from November to February, Endive blanched, and Asparagus, Chicory, Mint, Rhubarb, and Seakale may be forwarded from November to March.

In cold districts many vegetables may be raised in frames and ultimately planted out, but the soil should not be too rich for these plants. They include Broad Beans, Brussels Sprouts, Cabbages, Cauliflowers, Celery, Celeriac, Ridge Cucumbers, Dwarf Beans, Leeks, Lettuces, Onions, Peas, Runner Beans, Sweet Corn, and Tomatoes.

The imperative need for cleanliness, especially in the removal of dead leaves and moribund plants, ventilation without draughts, protection from frost in severe weather, prompt treatment for pests such as slugs and woodlice, careful attention to the preparation of seed-beds, and to watering cannot be too much emphasized.

**Franchet'ii,** in honour of Adrien Franchet, 1834–1900, French botanist.

**FRANCIS'CEA.** A synonym of Brunfelsia.

*francis'ceus -a -um,* of the neighbourhood of the River Francisco, Brazil.

**Francisci-Ferdinand'ii,** in honour of the Archduke Franz Ferdinand of Austria, President, Austro-Hungarian Dendrological Society, 1913.

**FRANCO'A** (in honour of F. Franco, M.D., of Valentia, who encouraged the study of botany in the 16th century). FAM. *Saxifragaceae.* A genus of 2 or 3 species of perennial herbs with radical leaves and flowers in spikes or racemes on naked scapes, natives of Chile. Plants covered with simple hairs or glands. Leaves lyrate, much in shape like those of a turnip, net-veined. Flowers 4-merous; ovary 4-celled. Hardy or half-hardy. Best raised from seed sown in February or March in well-drained pans of sandy peat, covered with glass and kept at about 50° F. The seedlings should be pricked out when large enough to handle into pans or boxes at about 2 in. apart, potted into 4-in. pots in April or May, and grown on in a cool greenhouse or frame, or planted out in a well-drained but moderately moist, sunny place. They may also be divided. Flowers last well cut.

**F. appendicula'ta.** About 2 ft. h. *l.* lyrate, stalked. *fl.* in a compact raceme on a nearly simple scape; pet. pale red, each with a deeper spot near the base. July. 1830. (B.M. 3178; L.B.C. 1864 as *F. sonchifolia.*)

**F. glabra'ta.** Like *F. ramosa* but somewhat dwarfer.

**F. ramo'sa.** Caulescent, 2 to 3 ft. h. *l.* lyrate, usually decurrent, stalk short. *fl.* in a much-branched, loosely arranged panicle; white; sep. and panicle branches smooth. July, August. 1831. (B.M. 3824.) Hybrids with *F. appendiculata* having larger fl. than in parents have been reported. (G.F. 1911, p. 128, coloured plate.)

**F. sonchifo'lia.** Bridal Wreath. About 2 ft. h. *l.* usually decurrent below the auricles at the base; stalk short. *fl.* in a loose raceme; pet. pink with a darker spot near base. July. 1830. (B.M. 3309; S.B.F.G. 169.)

**FRANGIPANI PLANT.** *See* **Plumeria acutifolia, P. rubra.**

**FRAN'GULA.** Included in **Rhamnus.**

**FRANKE'NIA** (in honour of John Frankenius, 1590–1661, Professor of Botany, Upsala, Sweden, author of a list of Swedish plants, *Speculum Botanicon,* 1638). FAM. *Frankeniaceae.* Sea Heath. A genus of about 40 species of small, usually prostrate, heath-like, evergreen sub-shrubs or perennial herbs, natives of sea-coasts in temperate and sub-tropical regions. Leaves small, inrolled, opposite, hairy, without stipules. Flowers small, terminal or from forks of branches; calyx tubular, gamosepalous, persistent; petals overlapping, free; stamens 4 to 6 or more, hypogynous; ovary with parietal placenta. Fruit a capsule. Several species are good carpeters for the rock-garden or for borders in light sandy soil. Propagation by division. The following are hardy unless otherwise noted.

**F. ericifo'lia.** Trailing. *l.* linear, margins revolute, glabrous above, velvety-mealy beneath. *fl.* red, in terminal clusters; pet. toothed. July. Canary Is. 1816.

**F. hirsu'ta.** More or less erect. Stems velvety, about 6 in. h. *l.* clustered, linear, ciliate near base, otherwise glabrous, margins revolute. *fl.* rose, in terminal corymbs. June, July. SW. Europe, &c. 1823.

**F. lae'vis.*** Stems prostrate, rooting. *l.* clustered, linear, ciliate at base, otherwise glabrous, margins revolute. *fl.* flesh-coloured, solitary at ends of shoots and in forks of branches. July. Britain, &c. (E.B. 190.)

**F. pulverulen'ta.** Prostrate annual. *l.* obovate, retuse, mealy beneath. *fl.* rose in fastigiate terminal clusters; cal. glabrous. E. Mediterranean, S. Africa on seashores. (F.G. 344.)

**F. thymifo'lia.** Densely tufted, grey-hairy, with numerous stems 2 to 6 in. long, finally decumbent. *l.* downy, small, thick, rigid, triangular, oblong, blunt. *fl.* many, rose. Spain. SYN. *F. Reuteri.*

**FRANKENIA'CEAE.** Dicotyledons. A family of about 64 species of herbs or sub-shrubs occurring in salt soils in temperate and tropical regions, falling into 4 genera. Leaves opposite, with rolled margins, without stipules. Flowers perfect, regular, small. Sepals and petals 4 to 7; stamens usually 6 in 2 whorls, slightly united at base; ovary superior, 1-celled, with usually 3 parietal placentas. The only genus calling for treatment here is Frankenia.

**FRANKINCENSE.** A gum-resin obtained by notching the stems of *Boswellia Carteri.*

**FRANKINCENSE PINE.** *See* **Pinus Taeda.**

**Franklin'iae,** in honour of Lady Franklin, wife of Sir John Franklin, Governor of Tasmania.

**FRANSER'IA** (in honour of Dr. Ant. Franser, a Spanish botanist). FAM. *Compositae.* A genus of about 10 species of annual or perennial herbs, natives of N. America, Peru, and Chile. Leaves alternate, toothed or cut or once or more pinnatisect. Flower-heads small, unisexual, monoecious, nodding, sessile or on short pedicels, in simple, leafless spikes or racemes at the tips of the branches or in panicles. Sandy loam suits the half-hardy *F. artemisioides.* Propagation by seeds.

**F. artemisioi'des.** 5 to 6 ft. h., woody at least at base. *l.* 2-pinnatifid, toothed, greenish above, whitish-hairy beneath; stalks winged. *fl.-heads* in spikes. July. Peru. 1759.

**Fransonia'nus -a -um,** in honour of Marchesa Isabella Fransoni.

**Franssenia'nus -a -um,** in honour of A. Franssen Herderschee, 1872–1932, of the Netherlands army, who collected in Surinam, &c.

**Franzosin'ii,** in honour of Signor Franzosini, amateur horticulturist of Intra, Lake Maggiore.

**FRA'SERA** (in honour of John Fraser, 1750–1811, nurseryman of Chelsea, collector of N. American plants). FAM. *Gentianaceae.* A genus of about 7 species of N. American perennial herbs. Leaves opposite or whorled. Flowers axillary, forming a dense panicle, stalked; corolla rotate, 4-cleft. Differing botanically from Swertia by the presence of a style. They need a moist but well-drained place and a stony, peaty soil. Increased by seeds or division.

**F. america'na.** Biennial. Erect, leafy. *l.* oblong-spatulate to lanceolate. *fl.* greenish-yellow, in a crowded terminal cyme; lobes recurved. June. NW. America. SYN. *Halenia deflexa.*

**F. carolinen'sis.** *l.* opposite or nearly so, oblong, on 4-angled stems 3 to 4 ft. h. *fl.* yellowish, whorled, on short 1-fld. pedicels. July. Carolina. 1795. SYN. *F. Walteri.*

**F. Par'ryi.** Glabrous, up to 3 ft. h. Stem simple, erect, stout, terete. *l.* lanceolate or linear-lanceolate, opposite or rarely ternate. *fl.* white or greenish-white with a few, short, purple linear markings; sep. ovate; pit of pet. lunate, solitary, with fringed margins. S. California. 1875. (B.M. 8891.) Alpine house.

**F. pulverulen'ta.** About 9 in. h., spreading. *fl.* greenish with purple markings. United States. Rock-garden.

**F. specio'sa.*** 2 to 5 ft. h., stout. Stem simple below, minutely downy. *l.* oblong-lanceolate, 9- to 13-nerved, 5 to 11 in. long. *fl.* greenish-white dotted purple, lobes ovate with fringed appendages at base, glands 2 to each lobe; panicle 1 to 2 ft. long, narrow. California, Washington.

*frater'nus -a -um,* brotherly; thus nearly related.

***Fraxinel'la,*** diminutive of Fraxinus; like a small Ash.

***fraxin'eus -a -um,*** ash-like.

**FRAXI'NUS** (Old Latin name for the Ash). FAM. *Oleaceae.* A genus of some 60 species of deciduous trees and a few shrubs scattered over the cool temperate parts of the N. Hemisphere. Leaves normally opposite, occasionally in whorls of 3, unequally pinnate; leaflets from 3 to 13, rarely solitary, stalked or sessile. Flowers perfect or unisexual; calyx 4-lobed or absent; petals 2 to 6, but usually 4 unless altogether absent. Fruit 1-seeded, developing at the end a narrow flattened wing usually ¾ to 1½ in. long.

The genus is divided into two sections according to the composition of the individual flower: (1) Ornus ('flowering ashes') flowers with linear petals, white or whitish, borne in panicles; (2) Fraxinaster, flowers without petals but with a calyx, or without either petals or calyx. *F. Ornus* is the typical species of the first group; *F. excelsior* of the second.

The ashes, with a few exceptions, are very hardy even in exposed positions. They grow best in a deep loam and are quite happy if it is rather on the heavy side. Propagated by seed; the garden varieties by grafting.

The common ash is sometimes attacked by the powdery mildew of the Hazel (*Phyllactinia corylea*) but the most serious attacks by fungi are those upon the branches and stems. Canker due to *Nectria coccinea* is not infrequent on the branches and the Beef Steak Fungus and several species of Bracket Fungi, such as *Fomes igniarius* and *Polyporus hispidus* occur in the trunks. See notes on these.

*Hylesinus fraxini*, the Ash Bark Beetle, is common in Ash throughout the country. The galleries are distinct, the mother-gallery being 2-armed and horizontal with the arms of about equal length, the short larval galleries running at right angles to the parent gallery with the pupal chambers at their ends within the sapwood. An attack reduces the vigour of the trees, while the indirect effect of this pest is that rosette-like galls arise near the feeding tunnels of the beetles allowing the invasion of fungal organisms into the damaged tissues. Ash sticks intended for walking-sticks are disfigured by the grubs whose tunnellings weaken the stem. The burying of such sticks in sand until the wood is seasoned will prevent an attack. There are two other species of *Hylesinus* which attack Ash in this country, namely, the large *H. crenatus*, and the smaller and rarer *H. oleiperda*.

KEY

1. *Fl. in terminal panicles on leafy shoots* 2
1. *Fl. from leafless axillary buds, appearing before lvs.* 11
2. *Cor. present* 3
2. *Cor. absent* 10
3. *Lowest pair of lflets. not or scarcely smaller than others* 4
3. *Lowest pair of lflets. usually much smaller than others* 5
4. *Lflets. hairy on base of midrib beneath, stalked, usually 5 to 7, 1½ to 3 in. long* F. Ornus
4. *Lflets. glabrous, usually 5, 1 to 1¾ in. long* F. Bungeana
5. *Lflets. sessile* 6
5. *Lflets. stalked* 7
6. *L.-stalk not much enlarged at base; lflets. 7 to 9, 3½ to 6½ in. long* F. Paxiana
6. *L.-stalk much enlarged at base; lflets. 5 to 9, variable in size, up to 9 in. long* F. Spaethiana
7. *Lflets. 3 or 5, 1 to 3½ in. long, glabrous* F. Mariesii
7. *Lflets. hairy on base of midrib beneath at least* 8
8. *L.-stalk and rachis grooved above; hairy on midrib and veins* 9
8. *L.-stalk and veins not or slightly grooved above; hairy on midrib only* F. longicuspis
9. *Lflets. 5 to 9, 2 to 5 in. long* F. pubinervis
9. *Lflets. 7 to 9, 3 to 6 in. long* F. floribunda
10. *Lflets. usually 7, terminal 3 to 5 in., lowest 1½ to 3 in. long* F. chinensis
10. *Lflets. 5, terminal 3 to 7 in. long, lower successively smaller* F. rhyncophylla
11. *Cor. absent* 12
11. *Cor. of 2 pet.* F. dipetala
12. *Cal. persistent on fruit; anthers linear* 13
12. *Cal. wanting; anthers cordate* 26
13. *Rachis of lvs. winged; lflets. 5 to 11, ⅜ to 1¾ in long.* 14
13. *Rachis of lvs. not winged* 15
14. *Shoots minutely downy; lflets. ¾ to 1¾ in. long* F. xanthoxyloides
14. *Shoots glabrous; lflets. scarcely exceeding 1 in. long* F. dimorpha
15. *Fr. lanceolate or oblanceolate, not or scarcely winged in lower part; fl. dioecious* 16
15. *Fr. obovate or elliptic to oblong-elliptic, compressed, winged to base* 25
16. *Wing of fr. terminal, not or scarcely decurrent; lflets. slender-stalked, papillose beneath* 17
16. *Wing of fr. decurrent to about middle, body margined* 19
17. *Lvs. and shoots glabrous* 18
17. *Lvs. and shoots hairy* F. biltmoreana
18. *Lflets. 5 to 9 (usually 7), 4 to 6 in. long* F. americana
18. *Lflets. 5 to 7, 1½ to 4 in. long* F. texensis
19. *Fr. 1 to 3 in. long, wing much exceeding body; lflets. 5 to 9* 20
19. *Fr. ½ to ¾ in. long, wing not longer than body; lflets. 3 to 7, sessile* F. velutina
20. *Lflets. stalked* 21
20. *Lflets. sessile* 24
21. *Fr. 2 to 3 in. long; lvs. and shoots hairy* F. tomentosa
21. *Fr. 1 to 2½ in. long; lvs. and shoots hairy or not* 22
22. *Lflets. 5 to 9, 3 to 6 in. long, oblong-lanceolate to lanceolate* 23
22. *Lflets. 3 or usually 5, terminal 3 to 4 in. long, oblanceolate, soon glabrous* F. Berlandieriana
23. *Shoots and l.-stalks densely hairy; lflets. 3 to 6 in. long* F. pennsylvanica
23. *Shoots glabrous; lflets. 7 to 9, 2 to 5 in. long* F. lanceolata
24. *L.-stalks not dilated at base; lvs. and shoots hairy* F. oregona
24. *L.-stalks much dilated at base; shoots glabrous* F. platypoda
25. *Shoots terete; lflets. 5 or 7, 2 to 5 in. long* F. caroliniana
25. *Shoots 4-angled; lflets. 1, rarely 2 or 3, 1 to 2½ in. long* F. anomala
26. *Shoots 4-angled, often winged; lflets. 5 to 11* F. quadrangulata
26. *Shoots terete or nearly so* 27
27. *Rachis at base of lflets. densely hairy* 28
27. *Rachis not conspicuously hairy at base of lflets.* 29
28. *Lflets. sessile, nearly rounded at base* F. nigra
28. *Lflets. narrowed to a very short stalk* F. mandshurica
29. *Lflets. sessile or nearly so* 30
29. *Lflets. distinctly stalked, 1 to 3 in. long* F. potamophila
30. *Lflets. glabrous, or at most hairy on midrib beneath* 31
30. *Lflets. hairy on both sides at least at first* F. holotricha
31. *Lflets. 7 to 13* 32
31. *Lflets. 3 or 5, rarely 7, 1½ to 4 in. long* F. syriaca
32. *Winter buds black or nearly so* F. excelsior
32. *Winter buds brown* 33
33. *Lflets. roundish-ovate to obovate, 7 to 13, 1 to 3 in. long* F. rotundifolia
33. *Lflets. lanceolate to narrow-oblong* 34
34. *Lflets. 7 to 13* 35
34. *Lflets. 7 or 9, rarely 5, hairy on midrib beneath* F. oxycarpa
35. *Lflets. glabrous* 36
35. *Lflets. 9 to 13, 1 to 3 in. long, downy on midrib beneath* F. Elonza
36. *Lflets. 7 to 13, 1½ to 3 in. long, lanceolate* F. angustifolia
36. *Lflets. 9 to 11, ovate-lanceolate, 2 to 3½ in. long, terminal to 5 in. long* F. obliqua

**F. al'ba.** A synonym of *F. americana.*

**F. america'na.*** White Ash. Tree 70 to 120 ft., shoots glossy, glabrous. *l.* 8 to 15 in. long; lflets. stalked, mostly 7, occasionally 5 or 9, lanceolate or oblanceolate, 4 to 6 in. long, entire or toothed near the slender apex, glabrous above, glaucous and glabrous (or nearly so) beneath. *fl.* without pet. *fr.* 1 to 2 in. long, the wing oblanceolate. N. America. 1724. (E.H. 4, 246.) SYN. *F. alba.* var. **ascidia'ta,** *l.* funnel-shaped at the base. (G.C. 70 (1921), 335.); **juglandifo'lia,** *lflets.* 6 to 9 in. long by 2 to 3 in. wide; **microcarp'a,** *fr.* only ½ in. long.

**F. angustifo'lia.*** Tree 60 to 90 ft., shoots and l. glabrous. *l.* 6 to 10 in. long; lflets. 7 to 13, stalkless, lanceolate, cuneate, 1½ to 3 in. long, slenderly pointed, coarsely toothed. *fr.* 1 to 1¼ in. long. S. Europe, N. Africa. 1800. (E.H. 4. 245.) Very elegant tree. var. **austra'lis,** mainstalk of l. hairy. 1890; **lentiscifo'lia,** *lflets.* more spreading and farther apart; **monophyl'la,** *lflets.* solitary, occasionally in twos or threes, lanceolate, 2 to 5 in. long, coarsely and sharply toothed. SYN. *F. Veltheimii.*

**F. anom'ala.** Utah Ash. Tree 18 to 20 ft., shoots slender, square, slightly winged, glabrous. *l.* reduced to 1, rarely 2 or 3, lflets., which are ovate, roundish, scarcely toothed, 1 to 2½ in. long, ¾ to 1¾ in. wide, soon glabrous. *fr.* obovate, ½ in. long; wing rounded, ⅓ in. wide, surrounding the seed. SW. United States. 1893. (S.S. 6. 266.) Distinct by its simple l. and 4-angular shoots.

**F. Berlandieria'na.** Tree rarely over 30 ft., shoots glabrous. *l.* 3 to 7 in. long; lflets. 3, more usually 5, the terminal one oblanceolate, 3 to 4 in. long; lower ones smaller, more oval; all coarsely toothed towards the slender apex, soon glabrous or nearly so. *fr.* 1 to 1½ in. long. Texas and Mexico. 1897. (S.S. 6. 273.)

**F. biltmorea'na.** Closely akin to *F. americana* but a smaller tree (50 to 80 ft.). Differs by the densely downy shoots, lflets. more or less downy beneath, and wing of fr. notched at end. E. United States. 1800. (E.H. 4. 247.)

**F. Bungea'na.*** Shrub or small tree up to 15 ft., winter buds black, shoots minutely downy. *l.* 4 to 6 in. long; lflets. usually 5, stalked, oval to obovate, 1 to 1¾ in. long, half as wide, cuneate, short-pointed, glabrous. *fl.* white in panicles 2½ in. wide. May. *fr.* 1 in. long, narrow-oblong, often notched at the end. N. China. 1881. (G. & F. 7. 5.) Pretty in fl., charming for a small garden.

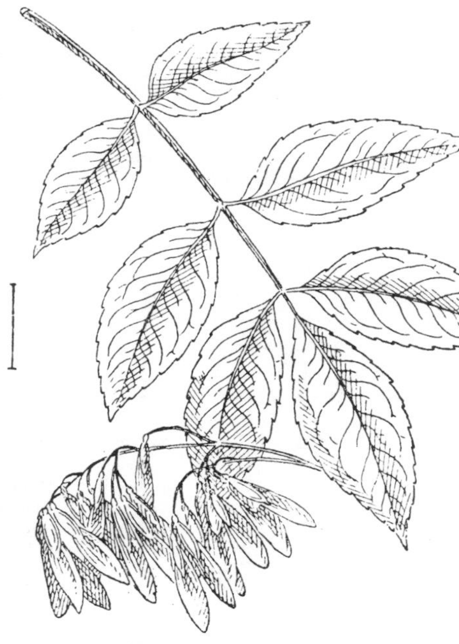

*Fraxinus americana* (p. 834)

**F. carolinia'na.** Water Ash. Tree rarely more than 45 ft., shoots usually glabrous. *l.* 5 to 12 in. long; lflets. 5 or 7, stalked, oval, 2 to 5 in. long, glabrous above, usually hairy along midrib and veins. *fr.* elliptic to obovate, up to 2 in. long and ⅞ in. wide. SE. United States. 1783. (S.S. 274–5.) Remarkable for the broad wing of fr.

**F. chinen'sis.** Tree 40 to 50 ft., buds blackish, downy, shoots glabrous. *l.* 5 to 8 in. long; lflets. usually 7, variable in shape and size; terminal one 3 to 5 in. long, obovate, lowest pair 1½ to 3 in. long, oval; all shallow-toothed, downy on veins beneath. *fl.* white, in large loose panicles 6 in. long. May. *fr.* oblanceolate, 1¼ in. long. China. 1891. The wax insect lives on this tree. var. **rhyncophyl'la,** a synonym of *F. rhyncophylla.*

**F. dimor'pha.** Shrub or small tree, 20 ft., shoots glabrous. *l.* 1½ to 3 in. long; lflets. 5 to 11, ovate, ⅜ to 1½ in. long, ⅛ to ½ in. wide, distinctly toothed, glabrous except at base of midrib. *fr.* 1½ in. long. N. Africa. Syn. *F. xanthoxyloides dimorpha.* var. **dumo'sa,** dwarfer and always shrubby, densely twiggy; lflets. smaller, ¼ to ⅝ in. long. Interesting dwarf ashes with small l.

**F. dipet'ala.** Shrub 10 to 18 ft., shoots 4-angled, glabrous. *l.* 2 to 5 in. long; lflets. usually 5, obovate or oval, cuneate, bluntish at apex, ½ to 1¼ in. long, glabrous. *fl.* bisexual, creamy-white, ⅓ in. long, in axillary panicles 2 to 4 in. long; pet. 2. *fr.* 1 in. long, oblanceolate, apex notched. California. 1879. (S.S. 6. 261.) Attractive in fl. but rather tender.

**F. Elon'za.** Small tree; shoots greyish, warted. *l.* up to 11 in. long; lflets. 9 to 13, ovate, oval, or lanceolate, cuneate, sharply toothed, 1 to 3 in. long, ½ to 1 in. wide, stalkless, glabrous above, downy on midrib beneath. *fr.* 1¼ in. long. Of unknown origin; cultivated in 1864.

**F. excel'sior.** Common Ash. Tree 100 to 140 ft., of rounded shape; buds black, shoots glabrous. *l.* 10 to 12 in. long; lflets. 7 to 11, oblong-lanceolate, 2 to 4½ in. long, midrib downy beneath. *fr.* numerous, in pendent clusters, 1½ in. long, apex often notched. Europe (Britain), Asia Minor. (E.H. 4. 239–44.) One of the noblest and most valuable of our timber trees. var. **angustifo'lia,** *lflets.* ⅛ to ⅝ in. wide; **argenteo-variega'ta,** *lflets.* margined with white; **asplenifo'lia,** *lflets.* ⅛ to ¼ in. wide: a curiosity; **au'rea,** younger branches yellow; **aurea pen'dula,** weeping form of var. *aurea*; **concaviifo'lia,** *lflets.* small, boat-shaped; **crisp'a,** stunted bush, *l.* only 2 to 3 in. long; **globo'sa,** dwarf, rounded bush; **glomera'ta,** *lflets.* up to 15, short and broad, closely set on the common stalk; **heterophyl'la,** 1-leaved Ash, *lflet.* single, rarely 3, oval to ovate, up to 6 in. or more long, comes partially true from seed; sub-var. **lacina'ta** has jagged, deeply cut l.; **laciniata pen'dula,** weeping; **pen'dula,** Weeping Ash, branches very pendulous, widely spreading and often ungainly; **pendula Wentworth'ii,** trunk erect, only branches pendulous; **Transon'ii,** *lflets.* yellow; **verticilla'ta,** *l.* often in threes instead of pairs.

**F. floribun'da.** Tree up to 120 ft., shoots glabrous. *l.* 10 to 15 in. long; lflets. 7 or 9, stalked, oblong, cuneate, pointed, 3 to 6 in. long, sharply toothed, downy on midrib and veins beneath. *fl.* white, in terminal panicles 8 to 12 in. long. Himalaya. 1822, 1876. Fine tree, but suitable only for the milder counties.

**F. holot'richa.** Small tree; shoots, l.-stalks, and both surfaces of l. densely downy. *l.* 6 to 10 in. long; lflets. 9 to 13, ovate to lanceolate, 1½ to 3 in. long, ¼ to ½ in. wide, fairly even in size, sharply toothed. E. Balkans. 1909. Distinct by its numerous, narrow, completely downy lflets.

**F. lanceola'ta.** Green Ash. Tree 60 to 70 ft., closely akin to *F. pennsylvanica* and chiefly distinguishable by its bright green glabrous shoots and more sharply toothed lflets. which number 7 or 9, are lanceolate and green on both surfaces; midrib downy. E. United States. 1824. (S.S. 6. 272.) Syn. *F. pennsylvanica lanceolata.*

**F. longicus'pis.** Tree 20 to 30 ft. or more, shoots slender, 4-sided, glabrous. *l.* 4 to 6 in. long; lflets. usually 5, ovate to obovate, cuneate, abruptly slender-pointed, 1½ to 4 in. long, downy only at base of midrib beneath. *fl.* white, in panicles 3 to 5 in. long. May. *fr.* narrow-oblong, oblanceolate, 1¼ in. long. Japan. 1894. Elegant but rare tree; autumn colour purple. var. **Sieboldia'na,** *lflets.* up to 3 in. long, longer-pointed.

**F. mandshu'rica.** Tree often 100 ft., shoots 4-sided, glabrous. *l.* 8 to 15 in. long; lflets. 9 or 11, stalkless, oblong-ovate to oblong-lanceolate, sharply toothed, 2 to 4½ in. long, with scattered bristles above and (more densely) on the midrib and veins beneath. *fr.* 1 to 1½ in. long. NE. Asia. A noble tree, but of no value where late spring frosts prevail.

**F. Maries'ii.*** Small tree up to 20 ft., shoots and buds grey, downy. *l.* 3 to 7 in. long; lflets. 3 or 5, oval or ovate, pointed, 1 to 3½ in. long, half as wide, glabrous. *fl.* creamy-white, in loose, broad panicles, 3 to 6 in. long. June. *fr.* ½ to 1¼ in. long, oblanceolate, deep purple in July. China. 1878. (B.M. 6678.) Very attractive both in fl. and fr.

**F. nig'ra.** Black Ash. Tree 80 to 90 ft., shoots glabrous. *lflets.* 7 to 11, stalkless, oblong to oblong-lanceolate, 3 to 5 in. long, slender-pointed, minutely toothed; midrib downy beneath. *fr.* 1 to 1½ in. long. N. America. 1800. (S.S. 6. 264–5.) Syn. *F. sambucifolia.* Inhabits damp places. Not a success in Britain.

**F. obli'qua.** Small tree, quite glabrous, shoots warty. *l.* 9 to 12 in. long; lflets. 9 or 11, the pairs ovate-lanceolate, 2 to 3½ in. long, terminal one up to 5 in. long, coarsely toothed. *fr.* 1 in. long. W. Asia. 1830.

**F. orego'na.** Tree 70 to 80 ft., shoots more or less downy, usually densely so. *l.* 6 to 14 in. long; lflets. mostly 5 or 7, ovate to oblong, 3 to 6 in. long, mostly stalkless, entire or obscurely toothed, thinly downy above, densely so beneath. *fr.* 1½ to 2 in. long, oblanceolate. Western N. America. 1870. (S.S. 6. 276.)

**F. Or'nus.*** Manna Ash. Tree 50 to 65 ft., buds grey. *l.* 5 to 8 in. long; lflets. usually 5 or 7, ovate or oblong (terminal one obovate), 1½ to 3 in. long, cuneate, abruptly pointed, shallowly toothed, glabrous except on the midrib beneath. *fl.* heavily scented, dullish white, in panicles 3 or 4 in. long. May. *fr.* narrow-oblong, 1 in. long. S. Europe, Asia Minor. 1710. (B.T.S. 1. 572.) Manna is obtained from its sap.

**F. oxycar'pa.** Tree closely akin to *F. angustifolia*, with usually 7 or 9 lflets. of similar size and shape, glabrous except along midrib and lower veins, which are always downy. *fr.* narrowly obovate to lanceolate, 1½ in. long. S. Europe to Persia and Asia Minor. 1815. Syn. *F. oxyphylla.* var. **parvifo'lia,** a synonym of *F. rotundifolia.*

**F. parvifo'lia.** A synonym of *F. rotundifolia.*

**F. Paxia'na.** Tree 40 to 60 ft., buds ½ in. long, rusty-downy. *l.* 10 to 13 in. long; lflets. 7 or 9, ovate to lanceolate, slender-pointed, bluntly toothed, glabrous, 3½ to 6½ in. long, basal pair much the smallest. *fl.* creamy-white, thinly disposed in pyramidal panicles 8 in. long; pet. ⅛ in. long. June. *fr.* 1 to 1¼ in. long. China. 1901. (B.M. 9024.)

**F. pennsylvan'ica.** Red Ash. Tree 40 to 60 ft., shoots densely downy. *l.* up to 1 ft. long; lflets. 7 or 9, oblong-lanceolate, narrowly oval, cuneate, slenderly pointed, obscurely toothed or entire, 3 to 6 in. long, downy beneath. *fr.* 1 to 2½ in. long. Eastern N. America. 1783. (S.S. 6. 271.) Syn. *F. pubescens.* var. **aucubaefo'lia,** *lflets.* mottled with yellow; **lanceola'ta,** a synonym of *F. lanceolata.*

**F. platypo'da.** Tree 60 to 70 ft., shoots glabrous. *l.* 6 to 10 in. long; lflets. 7 to 11, oval, oblong, or lanceolate, 2 to 4 in. long, finely toothed, glabrous above, with a conspicuous patch of down at base of midrib beneath; mainstalk conspicuously dilated at base. *fr.* oblong, slender-pointed, 2 in. long. China. 1909. (H.I.P. 1929.)

**F. potamoph'ila.** Tree 30 to 35 ft., shoots glabrous. *l.* 4 to 12 in. long; lflets. mostly 9 or 11, broadly oval, triangularly toothed, 1 to 3 in. long, conspicuously stalked, glabrous. *fr.* oval-oblong, 1⅜ in. long. Turkestan. 1891. Very rare elegant tree.

**F. profun'da.** A synonym of *F. tomentosa.*

**F. pubes'cens.** A synonym of *F. pennsylvanica.*

**F. pubiner'vis.** Tree 45 ft. or more; shoots glabrous. *l.* 1 ft. or more long; lflets. 5 to 9, narrowly ovate to oblong, slenderly pointed, broadly cuneate to rounded at base, toothed, 2 to 5 in. long, hairy along midrib and veins beneath. *fr.* oblanceolate, 1½ in. long. Japan. 1907.

**F. quadrangula'ta.** Blue Ash. Tree 60 to 70 (sometimes over 100) ft., shoots square, 4-winged, glabrous. *l.* 7 to 14 in. long; lflets. 5 to 11, ovate to lanceolate, slender-pointed, sharply toothed, 3 to 5 in. long, 1 to 2 in. wide, downy on midrib and veins beneath. *fr.* 1 to 2 in. long, oblong, notched at apex. N. America. 1823. (S.S. 6. 263.) Distinct by its square shoots and notched fr.

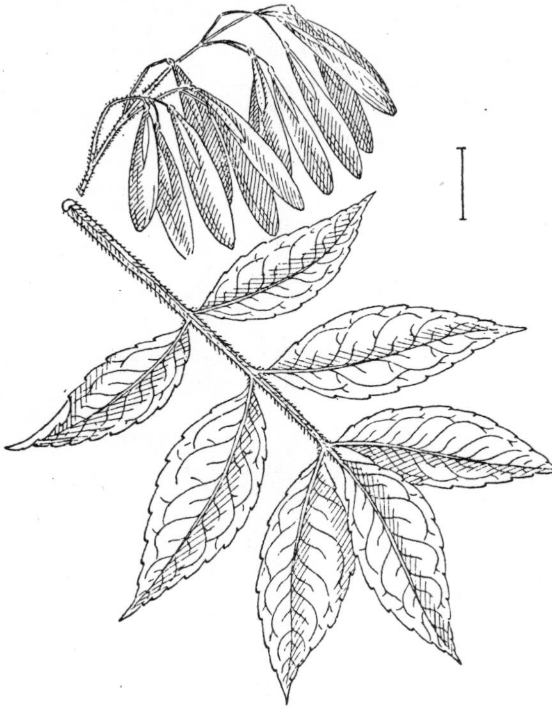

*Fraxinus pennsylvanica* (p. 835)

**F. rhyncophyl'la.** Tree up to 80 ft., shoots glabrous. *l.* 6 to 12 in. long; lflets. 5, oblong, ovate or obovate, shortly pointed, coarsely and bluntly toothed; terminal one 3 to 7 in. long, 1 to 3 in. wide, lower pairs successively smaller; midrib and veins downy beneath. *fl.* in a panicle 3 to 6 in. long, white. June. *fr.* oblanceolate, 1½ in. long. China, Japan, Korea. 1881. (G. & F. 6, 485.) Notable for its large terminal lflets. Syn. *F. chinensis rhyncophylla.*

**F. rotundifo'lia.** Small tree or shrub; buds black, shoots glabrous. *l.* 5 to 8 in. long; lflets. 7 to 13, roundish-ovate to oval or obovate, 1 to 2 in. long, half as wide, toothed, downy along midrib beneath. *fr.* oblong, 1¼ in. long. S. Europe, Asia Minor. 1750. Syn. *F. parvifolia, F. oxycarpa parvifolia.*

**F. sambucifo'lia.** A synonym of *F. nigra.*

**F. Spaethia'na.*** Tree of medium size; shoots shining, grey, glabrous. *l* up to 1½ ft. long; lflets. 5 to 9, oblong or narrowly obovate, variable in size, largest 6 to 9 in. long, one-third as wide, coarsely round-toothed, mainstalk very much enlarged at base and distinctive. *fl.* in terminal panicles. *fr.* 1½ in. long, oblanceolate. Japan. 1873. Handsome and distinct tree.

**F. syri'aca.** Syrian Ash. Small tree, shoots glabrous. *l.* 4 to 8 in. long, mostly in threes, usually very crowded on shoots, leaving twigs rough with their scars when fallen; lflets. usually 3 or 5, lanceolate, 1½ to 4 in. long, ½ to 1¼ in. wide, sharply toothed, glabrous. *fr.* narrowly obovate, 1½ in. long. W. and Cent. Asia.

**F. texen'sis.** Texan Ash. Tree up to 50 ft., shoots glabrous. *l.* 6 to 10 in. long; lflets. 5 or 7, oval, ovate or slightly obovate, 1½ to 4 in. long, round-toothed towards apex. *fr.* as in *F. americana* but only ½ to 1¼ in. long. Texas. 1901. (S.S. 6. 270.) Closely akin to *F. americana* but a smaller tree, lflets. blunter-toothed.

**F. tomento'sa.** Pumpkin Ash. Tree 50 to 120 ft., shoots, l.-stalks, and fl.-stalks densely downy. *l.* 10 to 18 in. long; lflets. usually 7, oblong-lanceolate or ovate, slender-pointed, 3 to 9 in. long, 1¼ to 3½ in. wide, almost or quite entire, downy beneath. *fr.* 2½ in. long, extending down sides of seed. E. United States. 1913. Syn. *F. profunda.*

**F. Veltheim'ii.** A synonym of *F. angustifolia monophylla.*

**F. veluti'na.** Tree 30 to 50 ft., shoots densely clothed like the l. with velvety down. *l.* 4 to 6 in. long; lflets. 3 or 5, stalkless or nearly so, oval to ovate, 1½ to 2 in. long, toothed towards apex. *fr.* ⅓ to ¾ in. long, wing oblong-obovate. SW. United States, Mexico. var. **Tou'meyi,** tree usually 20 to 30 ft.; *lflets.* 5 or 7, lanceolate, taper-pointed, up to 3 in. long. 1891.

**F. xanthoxyloi'des.** Tree up to 25 ft., more often a shrub; shoots minutely downy. *lflets.* 7 to 11, oval to oblong, ¾ to 1¾ in. long, pointed, bluntly toothed, slightly downy beneath. *fr.* narrow-oblong, apex often notched. Himalaya, Afghanistan. 1870. Akin to *F. dimorpha,* but l. more downy and comparatively longer and narrower. var. **dimor'pha,** a synonym of *F. dimorpha.*

W. J. B.

***Frederi'ci,*** in honour of Dr. Friedrich Welwitsch.

**free,** separate, not joined to one another.

**free-central,** *see* **Placenta.**

**FREE'SIA** (in honour of Friedrich Heinrich Theodor Freese, d. 1876, a pupil of Ecklon who named the genus). Fam. *Iridaceae.* A genus of perhaps 4 species of medium-sized herbs related to Tritonia. Corm with a loosely netted tunic. Stem branched. Inflorescence a 1-sided spike with short bracts 2- or 3-toothed at apex. Flowers yellow or pink to purple, scented; perianth zygomorphic, cylindrical in lower part widening to a funnel-shaped throat with short, oblong, unequal, little-spreading segments; stamens included, filaments slender; style slender with deeply 2-fid stigmas. Freesias are easily raised from seed sown as soon as ripe in pots of light sandy soil in a sunny position in a cool frame. Air should be given when the seedlings appear but care must be taken to avoid draughts, which are liable to injure them. The seedlings do not transplant well and it is best to sow thinly in 5-in. pots and thin out to 6 or 8 strong plants which will give space for flowering, which they should do in the following spring. Another method is to sow seed early in March and to keep the seedlings growing steadily in a cool pit; these should flower the following November. Corms for flowering the following year should be potted during August and September in a compost of 3 parts medium loam to 1 of leaf-soil, with enough sand to keep the whole open and porous. The smaller corms should be planted in separate pans from the larger ones, or planted out in cold frames to grow on to flowering size. The pots of corms of flowering size should be stood in cold frames from which frost can be excluded, and kept shaded until growths appear. Water should not be required until growth begins when plenty of air should be given on every possible occasion. As they are required they should be removed in successive batches to a cool greenhouse or pit, keeping them well up to the roof glass to ensure sturdy growth. They must have support in good time, for if the shoots are allowed to fall over they receive a check from which they never recover. Freesias will bear mild forcing for special purposes, but forcing is always at the expense of quality. Failure to grow Freesias well is generally due to neglect after flowering, the time in fact when they require good cultivation to build up and mature good flowering corms for the next season. The plants after flowering should be given a cold frame or pit, keeping them watered regularly and fed until the foliage shows signs of dying down. When that occurs water should be gradually withheld afterwards exposing the pots to all possible sun under the frame lights.

The elegant habit and delicate fragrance of their flowers has made Freesias very popular and of recent years, following the introduction of the pink-flowered *F. Armstrongii* to Kew in 1898 (which crossed with *F. refracta Leichtlinii* gave *F.* × *kewensis*), a very beautiful race of Freesias with coloured flowers has been obtained, in the development of which on the Continent, Dr. Ragioneri of Florence and Messrs. van Tubergen of Haarlem, and in England Mr. F. N. Chapman, the Rev. Joseph Jacob, and Mr. G. H. Dalrymple have played the chief part. There is now a wide range of colours over pink, rose, purple, lavender, yellow, and pure white. Selected varieties are mentioned in the Supplement.

The season of flowering may be prolonged by importing corms from S. Africa immediately after they have died down there and at once potting them up for a cool house.

Freesias, if grown well, should not suffer much from disease. The corms are subject to certain diseases which are better known on Gladioli. These are Dry Rot, due to *Sclerotinia Gladioli* which on Freesias causes sunken chocolate-brown lesions and patches, the latter becoming dead black. If this or any similar trouble is seen to be prevalent on the corms the stock should be strictly examined by stripping off the scales at planting time, and being careful not to use soil for the compost that may contain debris from a Gladiolus crop. Wilt caused by various species of the genus Fusarium shows in the yellowing of the leaf tips and blades, and sometimes by a browning and death of the bases of the outer leaves. The fungus lives on the corms and can be detected when it causes reddish spots or patches especially near the root plate but often involving the whole corm. The treatment must be the same as for Dry Rot, and all the corms should be stripped before planting, only healthy ones being planted in clean compost. The only other Freesia trouble is a Virus disease called Mosaic in which the leaves show small yellow areas which then turn paper white. These may be so abundant as almost to cover the leaf—the flower stems also show brown marks and the flowers may be distorted with spots appearing on the petals. It is necessary to take up such affected plants and burn them and this should be done thoroughly if the stock is to be saved. In addition fumigation to destroy insect carriers must be done. (D.E.G.)

**F. Armstrong'ii.** Like *F. refracta* but fl. pink. Humansdorp, S. Africa. 1898.

**F. Leichtlin'ii.** A variety of *F. refracta*.

**F. refrac'ta.** Corm ovate, of middle size with a firm tunic. Stem about 18 in. h., zigzag. *l.* 5 or 6, linear, much shorter than stem. *fl.* greenish-yellow or yellow with a few violet lines, about 1¼ in. long, 2-lipped; segs. about ⅔ in. long. Spring. S. Africa. 1816. (B.R. 135 as *Tritonia refracta*.) var. **al'ba**, *fl.* pure white; **Leicht'linii**, *fl.* larger than in type, bright pale yellow with deep yellow blotch (G.F. 808); **odora'ta**, *l.* broader and less stiff than in type, *infl.* with fewer branches and fl., *fl.* more regular, bright yellow; **xanthospi'la**, perianth tube abruptly widened above.

**Freestone Peaches and Nectarines.** Varieties of Peaches and Nectarines in which the flesh of the fruits parts readily from the stone (cf. **Clingstone**).

## FREMON'TIA

(in honour of Col. John Charles Fremont, 1813–90, explorer in western N. America). FAM. *Sterculiaceae*. A genus of 2 species of deciduous shrubs or small trees with cordate hairy leaves, natives of California and Mexico. Flowers with a coloured calyx, no petals, and a short staminal tube. They are handsome plants best in a sandy loam. A west or north wall suits them but they are not dependably hardy elsewhere. Increased by cuttings in spring, inserted under a handglass, or by seeds. They do not transplant well and young plants should, therefore, be grown in pots until they are put into their permanent quarters. Flowers are frequently produced by shoots which have overtopped the wall rather than by those on the face of the wall. Care should be taken to prevent damage to the bark of the stems by frost or by swaying movements, for they rarely survive the cracking of the bark.

**F. californ'ica.** 15 to 30 ft. h., young shoots covered with rich brown tomentum. *l.* heart-shaped, 2 to 4 in. long, 3- to 7-lobed, hairy beneath. *fl.* bright yellow, about 2 in. across, solitary on short peduncles opposite *l.* April. California. 1851. (B.M. 5591; J.R.H.S. 38, 204.)

**F. mexica'na.** Habit of *F. californica* but *l.* usually 5-lobed, more densely downy. *fl.* 2½ to 4 in. across, orange-yellow. Lower California. 1926. (B.M. 9269.) Less hairy than *F. californica*, growing rapidly and flowering well when young.

## FREYCINE'TIA

(in honour of Admiral Freycinet, 1779–1842, the French circumnavigator). FAM. *Pandanaceae*. A genus of about 60 species of usually climbing perennials which usually retain the bases of the leaves in rings around them, rooting from their slender stems, natives of Trop. SE. Asia, N. Australia, and the Pacific Is., distinguished from Pandanus by the many ovules in the 1-celled ovaries. They need stove temperatures, and are useful for clothing pillars, &c., which must be covered with Sphagnum or fibrous peat, kept moist, into which the roots may grow. The soil should be a well-drained, sandy loam. Propagation is by offsets.

*Fremontia mexicana*

**F. angustifo'lia.** Climbing stem about ⅛ in. thick. *l.* narrow-linear, 8 to 12 in. long, minutely toothed. *fl.* on 3 to 5 spadices, ¾ to 1 in. long. *fr.* white. E. Indies, Malaya.

**F. Banks'ii.** Kiekie. Tall climber, stem about ½ in. thick. *l.* narrow-linear, about 2 to 3 ft. long, 1 in. wide, minutely spiny on margin. *fl.* in solitary spadix about 3½ in. long, bracts white or pale lilac, fleshy. *fr.* brown, edible. New Zealand. (B.M. 6028.)

**F. Cumingia'na.** A synonym of *F. luzonensis*.

**F. gramin'ea.** Climbing. *l.* shorter than in *F. angustifolia*, spiny on margin. Amboyna.

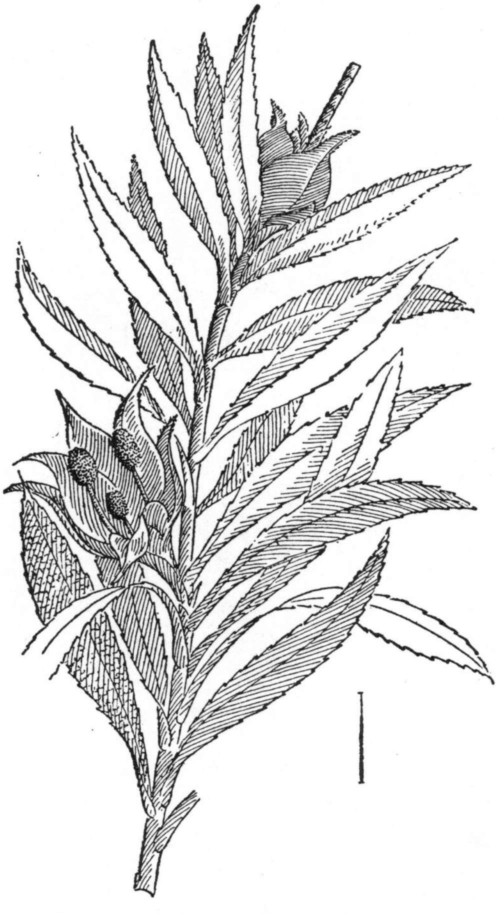

*Freycinetia luzonensis*

**F. luzonen'sis.** Climbing stem about $\frac{1}{8}$ in thick. *l.* 4 to 6 in. long, usually spiny on margin and back of midrib, horizontally spreading (not arching). Philippines. SYN. *F. Cumingiana.*

**FREYLIN'IA** (in honour of L. Freylin, compiler of a catalogue of plants growing in the garden of Buttigliera, Marengo, N. Italy. 1810). FAM. *Scrophulariaceae.* An African genus of about 4 species of evergreen shrubs. Leaves entire, varying from opposite to alternate. Flowers in terminal panicles or racemes. Calyx 5-lobed, persistent; lobes ovate. Corolla cylindrical, with a 5-lobed limb. The two species mentioned are hardy in the south-west counties and in similar climates, but need a cool greenhouse elsewhere. Easily cultivated in warm, loamy soil.

**F. cestroi'des.** Shrub of dense, leafy growth up to 12 ft. or more, young shoots slightly downy, angled. *l.* opposite linear, tapering to both ends, 2 to 5 in. long. $\frac{1}{8}$ to $\frac{3}{8}$ in. wide, glabrous. *fl.* fragrant in terminal pyramidal panicles 4 to 10 in. h.; cor. $\frac{1}{2}$ in. long, tubular with the limb $\frac{1}{4}$ in. wide, creamy-white, yellow inside. November. S. Africa. 1774. Hardy in S. Devon, Isle of Wight, &c. (Add. 77 as *F. lanceolata.*) SYN. *F. oppositifolia.*

**F. undula'ta.** Shrub up to 6 ft. *l.* opposite, verticillate or alternate, $\frac{1}{4}$ to 1 in. long, densely set, ovate to ovate-lanceolate, pointed, broad at the base. *fl.* in terminal racemes 3 to 6 in. long; cor. pale purple or lilac, $\frac{3}{4}$ in. long, slenderly tubular; limb $\frac{1}{4}$ to $\frac{1}{3}$ in. across, lobes rounded. June. S. Africa. 1774. (B.M. 1556.) SYN. *F. rigida, Capraria undulata.*

W. J. B.

***Freynia'nus -a -um,*** in honour of Joseph Freyn, 1845–1903, of Prague, Austrian botanist.

***Friderici-Augus'ti,*** in honour of Friedrich August II of Bavaria, 1797–1854.

**FRIDERIC'IA** (in honour of Frederick III, King of Bavaria). FAM. *Bignoniaceae.* A genus of 2 or 3 species of tall, climbing shrubs, natives of Brazil, closely related to Bignonia. Leaves opposite, 3-foliolate. Flowers scarlet or yellowish-red in a large panicle. For treatment of these stove plants *see* **Clytostoma.**

**F. Guiliel'ma.** *lflets.* ovate-oblong, acute at base, shortly pointed at apex, glabrous. *fl.* 7 in a compact, terminal panicle; cal. and cor. often 6-cleft. Bahia.

F. G. P.

***Friedri'chae,*** in honour of Fraulein Margarete Friedrich of Warmbad, S. Africa.

***Friesea'nus -a -um, Fries'ii,*** in honour of Elias Magnus Fries, M.D., 1798–1874, celebrated Swedish cryptogamic botanist.

**FRIE'SIA.** Included in **Aristotelia.**

***Friesia'nus -a -um,*** in honour of Thore Magnus Fries, 1832–1913, son of E. M. Fries, who explored in Spitzenberg, &c.

***frig'idus -a -um,*** cold.

**FRINGE FLOWER.** *See* **Schizanthus.**

**FRINGE LILY.** *See* **Thysanotus.**

**FRINGE TREE.** *See* **Chionanthus.**

**FRINGED VIOLET.** *See* **Thysanotus.**

***fris'icus -a -um,*** Friesian.

**FRITILLA'RIA** (*fritillus*, a dice-box). Fritillary. FAM. *Liliaceae.* A genus of over 80 species of bulbous plants distributed over the temperate regions of the N. Hemisphere, related to Lilium, Notholirion, and Tulipa, with nodding bell-shaped flowers with a roundish or oblong nectary at the base of each (or at least the inner) perianth segment. The bulbs of the old-world species are for the most part tunicated, while those of the N. American species are scaly. The stems are unbranched, erect, and leafy, the leaves sometimes in whorls, narrow and sessile, the flowers solitary or few at or near the top of the stem. Perianth segments 6, nearly equal, sometimes tessellated; stamens 6 on slender filaments with linear basifixed anthers; ovary 3-celled. Fruit a capsule with numerous seeds.

All the species are spring-flowering and most of them are hardy, though a few need some protection for their early spring growth. Save for the species of E. Europe, Fritillaries do not take very readily to cultivation in British gardens though most of them do well in various places. The species of the Balkan, Greek, and Asia Minor floras do best in the alpine house, but the taller ones like *F. libanotica* and *F. persica* will do well in a narrow border outside a greenhouse, while the species of Turkestan and California seem better suited in a cold frame. A frame for these plants should be well-drained and filled with well-worked loam, the bulbs being planted in lines. The soil of the frame is allowed to become quite firm and must not be turned over, the only movement allowed being that imposed on the surface by the removal of weeds. Probably the best results are obtained by planting seedlings which have been raised in pots and pricked out in their second year after germination, or bulbils which can be sown direct in the frame. These plants will at first produce only a single leaf and in that state will not flower, but when established may be expected to flower annually and should not be disturbed. As soon as the leaves die down the frame light should be put on, and remain so that the soil is baked throughout the summer and autumn. Growth begins in early spring and the soil can then be soaked with rain, the light being left off except in very severe weather. Some species, like *F. caucasica, F. pallidiflora, F. pluriflora,* and *F. recurva* may be grown successfully outdoors in a bed of river sand and leaf-mould about 2 ft. deep. *F. imperialis* and its relatives seem to grow best in heavy soil where the surface is rarely disturbed either by hoeing or forking. The bulbs should be planted in July, covered with 4 or 5 in. of soil and left undisturbed except for the firming of the soil about them when the spikes are developed. They are seen at their best as a rule in old gardens and cottage gardens where the Madonna Lily and the Mezereum flourish undisturbed. *F. camschatcensis* does well in gritty, stony soil. *F. Meleagris* is useful almost everywhere in the sun or in light shade, and though it does not increase freely by offsets, when planted in the grass will persist there and if allowed to seed will often spread in this way.

Seeds are freely produced by several species. The seeds should be sown as soon as ripe in pots or pans of sandy soil. It usually germinates within 6 months, about the time growth of the old plants starts in spring, and the seedlings should remain undisturbed until the second year. The young bulbs often find their way to the bottom of the pots and may need to be searched for among the crocks. The flowering stage is reached in from 4 to 6 years from the time of seed sowing. An alternative method of propagation is by bulb-offsets which can be removed when the bulbs are being lifted and planted in lines in prepared soil. These will yield flowering plants more quickly than seeds. Some species, including *F. lanceolata, F. camschatcensis, F. mutica, F. pinetorum, F. recurva*, most of them woodland plants, on light loamy soil produce numerous offsets looking like grains of rice, often densely covering the flattish or cone-shaped fleshy bulb, by which they can be propagated. Others like *F. agrestis, F. pluriflora, F. Purdyi, F. liliacea* have bulbs composed of thick scales by which they can be increased if the scales are carefully detached and planted in sandy compost with the apex just above the level of the soil.

Krause has divided the genus (see *Pflanzenfamilien* 15A, ed. 2, pp. 332–5 (1930)) into sections as follows:

1. EUFRITILLARIA. Stem 1-, rarely 2- or more-, flowered, anthers basifixed, style arms spreading.
    Typical species are *F. cirrhosa, F. Meleagris*, and *F. pyrenaica*.
2. PETILIUM. Stem many-flowered with bracts in a terminal tuft.
    Typical species: *F. imperialis*.
3. THERESIA. Flowers in racemes, anthers small, basifixed, style undivided or with very short arms.
    Typical species: *F. Karelinii*.
4. AMBLIRION. Stems 1-flowered, anthers dorsifixed, erect, not versatile, style undivided.
    Typical species: *F. pudica*.
5. LILIORHIZA. Bulbs many-scaled, anthers dorsi-fixed, more or less versatile, styles shortly 3-fid.
    Typical species: *F. biflora, F. camschatcensis, F. Sewerzowii*.

**F. acmopet′ala.\*** *Bulb* depressed, mainly of 2 fleshy scales. Stem 12 to 18 in. h. *l.* 6 or 7, scattered from below middle of stem to from 1 to 3 in. below fl., about 3 in. long, linear, green. *fl.* 1, rarely 2, about 1½ in. long, 1 in. across, outer segs. green or olive-green without, streaked brown-purple, yellowish and shining within, inner segs. purple or brownish-green without, greenish and polished within, sometimes with a transverse brown-purple band across top, nectary deep green, oblong to subulate. Syria, Cilicia. 1874. (B.M. 9148.) Rock-garden.

**F. agres′tis.** *Bulb* of 4 or 5 thick scales, united only at base. Stem 12 to 20 in. h. *l.* 8 to 12 on lower half of stem, scattered, or lowest whorled, oblong-lanceolate. *fl.* 3 to 8, about 1¼ in. long, ¾ in. across, dull or yellowish-green with a green band running nearly to apex of each seg.; nectary distinct. Scent very unpleasant. California. Border; clay loam.

**F. arme′na.** *See* **F. caucasica.**

**F. askabaden′sis.\*** *Bulb* large, scaly. Stem 24 to 30 in. h. *l.* bright green, alternate below, whorled above, 4 to 6 in. long. *fl.* 5 to 8, grouped as in *F. imperialis*, but smaller and greenish-yellow. Transcaspia. 1902. (B.M. 7850.) Border.

**F. atropurpu′rea.** *Bulb* thick-scaled. Stem 6 to 18 in. h. *l.* 7 to 14 in upper half of stem, alternate or whorled, narrow-linear, 4

to 6 in. long. *fl.* 1 to 4, rarely more, open bell-shaped, about ¾ in. long, purple-brown, mottled yellowish-green; style cleft three-quarters of length. California, Oregon, &c. (B.B. ed. 2, i, 505.)

**F. au′rea.** *See* **F. latifolia.**

**F. biflo′ra.** Mission Bells. *Bulb* as in *F. agrestis*. Stem 4 to 10 in. h. *l.* 2 to 7, scattered, or whorled below, oblong- to ovate-lanceolate, 2 to 4 in. long. *fl.* 2 to 4, rarely more, dark brown or greenish-purple with a greenish band on each seg. reaching nearly to tip; style cleft to about middle. S. California.

**F. Burneti.** A variety of *F. tubiformis*.

**F. camschatcensis.\*** *Bulb* small, scaly. Stem 6 to 18 in. h. *l.* 10 to 15, above middle of stem, lower whorled, lanceolate, 2 to 4 in. long. *fl.* 1 to 3, 1¼ to 1¾ in. long, livid wine-purple, not tessellated, bell-shaped. Siberia, Alaska. (Gn. 25 (1884), 232; B.M. n.s. 63.) Moraine or rock-garden.

*Fritillaria Elwesii* (p. 840)

**F. caucas′ica.\*** *Bulb* about ½ in. across. Stem 6 to 12 in. h. *l.* 2 to 4, in upper part of stem, elliptic to elliptic-lanceolate, scattered. *fl.* solitary, ⅞ to 1 in. long, tulip-shaped, rusty brown-purple within, not chequered, dark glaucous blue without with streaks of purple, inner segs. with glaucous blue band down back. Caucasus. 1872. (B.M. 5969 as *F. tulipifolia*; B.M. n.s. 227 as *F. Pinardii*.) *F. armena* (B.M. 6365) with dark purple *fl.* belongs here.

**F. caussolen′sis.** A synonym of *F. nigra*.

**F. chitralen′sis.** Closely allied to *F. imperialis* with smaller butter-yellow fl. *See* **F. imperialis chitralensis.**

**F. cirrho′sa.** 12 to 18 in. h. *l.* 8 to 10, narrow-linear, lowest opposite, about middle of stem, 1 to 3 in. long, upper in twos or threes, uppermost close to fl., with tendril-like tips. Himalaya.

**F. citri′na.\*** 12 in. h. *l.* about 20, scattered, linear, 2 to 2½ in. long, ¼ in. wide. *fl.* 3, about 1 in. long, oblong, pale yellow, not chequered, tinged green without; nectary brownish, not prominent. Greece, Taurus. (G.F. 1893, 729; B.M. 9560.)

**F. coccin′ea.** A variety of *F. recurva*.

**F. contor′ta.** A variety of *F. Meleagris*.

**F. crassifolia.** *Bulb* flat-round, ½ to ¾ in. wide. Stem 4 to 6 in. h. *l.* 5 or 6, in upper part of stem, oblong-spatulate, 2 to 3 in. long, ½ to ¾ in. wide. *fl.* solitary, ¾ to 1 in. long, deep wine-purple, nectary small, wide. Armenia, Palestine .&c

**F. dasyphyl'la.** About 6 in. h. *l.* rather fleshy, scattered or sometimes opposite, lowest more or less oblong, others lanceolate or linear. *fl.* 1 or 2, broadly funnel-shaped, $\frac{3}{4}$ in. long, purplish without, yellow within, not chequered; nectary oblong, small, green. Asia Minor. 1875. (B.M. 6321.)

**F. delphinen'sis.** A synonym of *F. tubiformis*.

**F. dis'color.** A synonym of *F. Sewerzowii*.

**F. Drenov'skii.** *Bulb* small, ovoid. Stem slender, 8 to 12 in. h. *l.* linear, bluish-green scattered. *fl.* 1 to 3, up to 1 in. long, conical, purple-brown with light yellow median line, lemon-yellow veined purple within. (L.Y.B. 1932, 94; B.M. 9625.) Bulgaria, S. Macedonia. **A**

**F. Egg'eri.** *fl.* small, bell-shaped, yellowish-green flushed brown without. Asia Minor.

**F. Ehrhart'ii,** 6 to 12 in. h. *l.* in middle of stem, lower opposite, upper scattered, narrow-linear. *fl.* 1 to 5, of medium size, obconic, ashy-brown without, greenish-yellow within. Syra Is. (B.M. 9635.)

**F. Elwes'ii.*** 12 to 18 in. h. *l.* scattered, linear, 4 to 5 in. long. *fl.* solitary, bell-shaped, about 1 in. long, green, suffused purple on back and at tips, not chequered. Asia Minor. (B.M. 6321 as *F. acmopetala*.)

**F. glau'ca.*** *Bulb* small with many bulblets. Stem 3 to 6 in. h. *l.* 2 to 4, scattered, oblong-lanceolate, glaucous. *fl.* 1 to 3, about $\frac{3}{4}$ in. long, purple with greenish-yellow markings; nectaries large, oblong. Oregon.

**F. glaucovi'ridis.** 15 in. h. or more. *l.* 9 or 10, mostly scattered, oblong-lanceolate to linear, up to 4 in. long. *fl.* 1 or 2, about 1 in. long, glaucous green without, yellowish-green within, not chequered; nectary linear. Cilicia. 1930. (B.M. 9462.)

**F. grac'ilis.** Stem 12 to 18 in. h. *l.* narrow-linear-lanceolate, grey green, upper in threes. *fl.* solitary, about $1\frac{1}{2}$ in. long, widely bell-shaped; bright purplish with brown and yellow chequering and green median stripe. Dalmatia. (B.M. 9500.)

**F. grae'ca.*** Stem 3 to 9 in. h. *l.* 4 to 8, scattered, lanceolate, 2 to 4 in. long, upper linear. *fl.* usually solitary, bell-shaped, about $\frac{3}{4}$ in. long, lurid wine-purple, without chequering but with green median line; nectary small, wide. Greece. (B.M. 5052.)

**F. imperia'lis.*** Crown Imperial. *Bulb* large, round, scaly. Stem 3 to 4 ft. h. *l.* partly scattered, upper whorled, 5 to 6 in. long. *fl.* many in a terminal umbel among 8 to 20 erect, linear l. 2 in. or more long, yellow or bronze, without chequering; nectary large. W. Himalaya, before 1590. Many varieties have been grown including **Aurora,** *fl.* bronzy crimson; **max'ima lu'tea,** *fl.* large, yellow; **maxima ru'bra,** *fl.* large, red; and many others of garden origin, though few that have had a long existence; those mentioned are among the more vigorous. var. **chitralen'sis** from the Chitral Valley is less vigorous with clear butter-yellow fl.; **Raddea'na** is dwarf with straw-coloured fl.; **inodo'ra** lacks the foxy odour which renders the type objectionable to many, fl. yellow or bronze. Bokara. (G.F. 1884, 1165 as *F. imperialis inodora purpurea*.) Varieties with double fl. and with variegated l. have been raised and one with a supplementary whorl of fl.

**F. involucra'ta.** *Bulb* globose, $\frac{1}{2}$ in. thick. Stem 12 in. or more h. *l.* 6 to 9, above middle of stem, lower opposite, upper in threes, linear, 2 to 4 in. long. *fl.* solitary, 1 to $1\frac{1}{2}$ in. long, narrow bell-shaped, purple with yellow chequering; nectary, small, oblong. Maritime Alps. (M.F.M. 36.)

**F. kamtschatcen'sis.** A synonym of *F. camschatcensis*.

**F. karadaghen'sis.*** *Bulb* nearly round, $\frac{3}{4}$ in. across. Stem purplish below. *l.* 6 to 14, linear-lanceolate, 2 to $3\frac{1}{2}$ in. long, scattered. *fl.* 1 to 3, bell-shaped, $\frac{3}{4}$ to 1 in. long, greenish-yellow with a broad greenish-median stripe, suffused with dark purple; nectary ovate. Persia. 1928. (B.M. 9303.)

**F. Karelin'ii.*** *Bulb* globose, about 1 in. across with few scales. *l.* 4 to 6, lanceolate or linear, lowest sometimes opposite, upper linear, alternate, largest about $2\frac{1}{2}$ in. long. *fl.* 2 to 12, rather close, bell-shaped, not quite 1 in. long, rose-purple with a few darker spots; nectary yellowish-green. Cent. Asia. (B.M. 6406.) Syn. *Rhinopetalum Karelinii*.

**F. lanceola'ta.*** *Bulb* of few scales or solid with many small bulblets. Stem 18 to 24 in. or more h. *l.* 6 to 10 in 2 or 3 whorls in upper part of stem, ovate-lanceolate, 2 to 4 in. long. *fl.* 1 to 4 or more, deep bowl-shaped, 1 to $1\frac{1}{2}$ in. long, dark purple mottled greenish-yellow; nectary large, ovate-lanceolate, deep green. NW. America. A variable species.

**F. latifo'lia.*** *Bulb* small. Stem 6 to 12 in. h. *l.* 6 to 10, lower scattered, upper in threes, 3 to 4 in. long, $\frac{1}{2}$ to 1 in. wide, lanceolate. *fl.* usually 1, squarish-bell-shaped, about $1\frac{1}{2}$ in. long and wide, purplish chequered greenish, or yellowish. Caucasus. (B.M. 853, 1207, 1538 as *F. lutea*; 7374 as *F. aurea*.) A variable plant in colour. Includes *F. aurea* with bright-yellow fl. with reddish chequering and *F. lutea* with yellow fl. veined and chequered purple.

**F. libanot'ica.** *Bulb* up to over 2 in. long. Stem glaucous, 2 to 3 ft. h. *l.* up to 30, scattered, lanceolate, up to 6 in. long, pale glaucous green. *fl.* 12 to 25, bowl-shaped, about $\frac{1}{2}$ in. deep, 1 in. wide; segs. greenish, flushed rose-purple on back, inner dull rose with darker veins inside; nectary oblong, greenish. Palestine, Syria. (B.M. 9108.)

**F. lilia'cea.*** Stem rather stout, 3 to 12 in. h. *l.* on stem few in lower half, sometimes in twos or threes, linear-oblong or linear; basal l. $1\frac{1}{4}$ to $4\frac{1}{2}$ in. long, linear to oblong-lanceolate. *fl.* 1 to 5, about $\frac{3}{4}$ in. long, dull white, open bell-shaped; nectary greenish with purple dots. California. (B.M. 9541.)

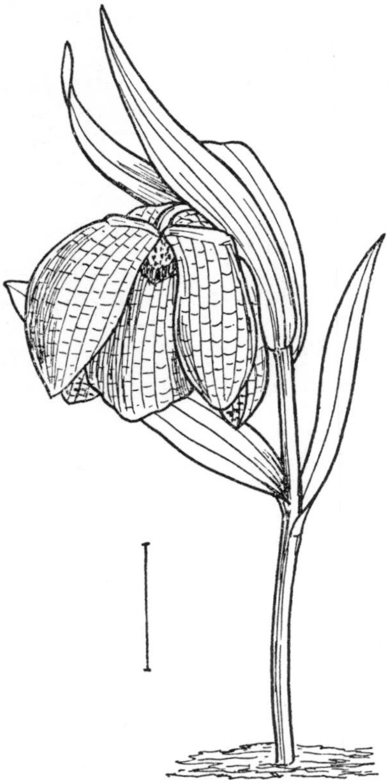

*Fritillaria latifolia*

**F. lusitan'ica.** *Bulb* small, whitish. Stem 8 to 16 in. h. *l.* 7 to 9, linear, scattered near the top of stem, $1\frac{1}{2}$ to $3\frac{1}{2}$ in. long, glaucous. *fl.* solitary, 1 to $1\frac{1}{2}$ in. long, reddish-brown, yellow chequered with brown within; nectary small. SW. Spain, Portugal.

**F. lu'tea.** *See* **F. latifolia.**

**F. macran'dra.** About 6 in. h. *l.* scattered, oblong-lanceolate to linear, lower $\frac{1}{2}$ to 1 in. wide. *fl.* 1, rarely 2, about $\frac{3}{4}$ in. long, bell-shaped, lurid purple outside, upper part and inside greenish-yellow, veined and chequered purple. Greece. Syn. *F. rhodocanakis*.

**F. macrophyl'la.** A synonym of *Notholirion Thomsonii*.

**F. Meleag'ris.*** Snake's Head. *Bulb* $\frac{1}{3}$ to $\frac{1}{2}$ in. across. Stem 9 to 15 in. h. *l.* 4 to 5, about middle of stem, scattered, 3 to 6 in. long, $\frac{1}{8}$ to $\frac{1}{4}$ in. wide, more or less glaucous. *fl.* usually solitary, $1\frac{1}{4}$ to $1\frac{1}{2}$ in. long, purple with white chequering or white with green veins; nectary linear, $\frac{1}{2}$ in. long, green. Europe, including Britain. (E.B. 1519.) Considerable variations in colour occur, among them var. **al'ba,** *fl.* white with green veining (Gn. 32 (1887), 536); **Aphrodi'te, a** good white; **Ar'temis,** *fl.* grey-purple with pronounced chequering; **contor'ta,** a curious form with the bell contracted and the segs. joined in the lower part, making a narrow fl. about 2 in. long; **erec'ta,** *fl.* upright; **fl. ple'no,** *fl.* double, purple. Any soil, best in light soil with plenty of humus.

**F. messanen'sis.*** *Bulb* globose, $\frac{1}{3}$ to $\frac{2}{3}$ in. thick. Stem 6 to 25 in. h. *l.* 7 to 12 in middle and upper part, linear, tapering, lower opposite, uppermost usually in a whorl, 2 to 4 in. long, entire, somewhat glaucous. *fl.* 1, or rarely 2, more or less nodding, bell-shaped, 1 to $1\frac{3}{4}$ in. long, purplish, with broad, green, middle band at back, brownish-purple with narrow darker stripes and green midband, sometimes tessellated; nectaries rather large, elliptic to lanceolate. Spring. Sicily, Crete, Greece. 1939. (B.M. 9659.)

**F. monta'na.** A synonym of *F. nigra*.

**F. multiflo'ra.** *Bulb* with numerous bulblets. Stem 15 to 30 in. h. *l.* in upper part of stem, scattered, whorled or upper scattered, linear-lanceolate, $2\frac{1}{2}$ to 4 in. long, pale green. *fl.* 4 to 10. $\frac{1}{3}$ to $\frac{1}{2}$ in. long, bell-shaped, purplish or greenish-white, sometimes faintly mottled. California. Syn. *F. parviflora*.

**F. mu'tica.** *Bulb* with many bulblets. Stem 16 to 30 in. h. *l.* in 2 or 3 whorls about middle of stem, with a few scattered, linear-lanceolate, 1½ to 4 in. long. *fl.* up to 10 on a long raceme, 1 to 1½ in. long, bowl-shaped, greenish-yellow with bronzy-purple blotches; nectary prominent, purple. California. var. **grac′ilis**, *fl.* narrower, about ¾ in. long. SYN. *F. lanceolata gracilis.*

**F. neglec′ta.** Allied to *F. gracilis*, but *fl.* longer, purple tinged green with green median vein, chequered purple. Dalmatia, E. Adriatic. (R.I.F.G. 445, f. 981, 982 as *F. messanensis*; f. 982 shows the form sometimes called *illyrica.*)

**F. nig′ra.\*** *Bulb* white. Stem 6 to 12 in. h. *l.* narrow-linear, almost grass-like, upper in twos and threes. *fl.* solitary, rarely 2, about 1 in. long, narrow-bell-shaped, dull purple or greenish-yellow with purple flush, or chequering without, yellow and purple chequered within; nectary small, ovate. Italy eastwards to Caucasus. (R.I.F.G. 443 as *F. tenella*; 444 as *F. montana.*) A variable species in colouring. SYN. *F. caussolensis.*

**F. obli′qua.** 12 to 15 in. h. *l.* about middle of stem, scattered, lower oblong, about 1 in. wide, upper linear, somewhat twisted. *fl.* 1 to 5, about ½ in. long, obconical, black-purple inside and out; nectary greenish, linear. Greece. (B.M. 857.)

**F. Olivie′ri.** 12 to 18 in. h. *l.* 7 to 10, scattered, lower lanceolate, 3 to 3½ in. long, upper linear. *fl.* solitary, about 1½ in. long, bell-shaped, deep purplish, without chequering; nectary oblong. Persia. (B.M. 9104.)

**F. oranen′sis.** *Bulb* about ¾ in. thick. Stem 6 to 8 in. h. *l.* 8 to 10, generally scattered, lower lanceolate, upper linear to linear-lanceolate, 2 to 4 in. long. *fl.* solitary, 1½ in. long, wide-bell-shaped, dark livid-purple with green median band, greenish inside, veined purple, rarely chequered; nectary oblong. N. Africa. (B.M. 9066.)

**F. pallidiflo′ra.\*** *Bulb* about ¾ in. thick. Stem 6 to 15 in. h. *l.* 8 to 25, lowest oblong, opposite, others scattered, lanceolate, 2 to 3 in. long, glaucous. *fl.* 1 to 6 in axils of upper l., about 1½ in. long, broadly bell-shaped, cream-white, tinged green outside, dotted reddish-purple within; nectary small, green. S. Siberia. (B.M. 6725.)

**F. parviflo′ra.** A synonym of *F. multiflora.*

**F. per′sica.\*** About 3 ft. h. *fl.* deep violet-blue, rather small, bell-shaped, slightly scented. Persia. (B.M. 1537.) var. **mi′nor**, *fl.* smaller, stamens somewhat exserted. (B.M. 962.)

**F. Pinard′ii.** A variety of *F. caucasica.*

**F. pineto′rum.** *Bulb* with many bulblets. Stem 4 to 12 in. h. *l.* few or many, scattered, narrow-linear, 2 to 6 in. long, glaucous. *fl.* 1 to 3, about ⅜ in. long, erect or nearly so, dull purple mottled greenish-yellow; nectaries obscure. California.

**F. pluriflo′ra.\*** *Bulb* with few scales, up to 1 in. long, yellowish. Stem 6 to 12 in. h. *l.* 4 to 10, mostly at base, oblong-lanceolate, 3 to 4 in. long. *fl.* 1 to 7, 1 to 1½ in. long, pink-purple. California. (B.M. 7631.)

**F. pon′tica.** About 18 in. h. *l.* in upper part of stem, lower opposite or scattered, upper in a whorl of 3 near fl., lanceolate, 2 to 3 in. long. *fl.* solitary, 1⅜ in. long, bell-shaped, green, purple near tip, outer with more green than inner segs.; nectary small. SE. Europe, Asia Minor. (B.M. 8865.)

**F. pu′dica.\*** *Bulb* with 2 or 3 fleshy scales and many bulblets, Stem 3 to 8 in. h. *l.* 3 to 8, scattered or occasionally whorled, linear, 2 to 4 in. long. *fl.* 1 or 2, bell-shaped, ⅝ to 1 in. long, golden-yellow or orange with purple tinge; nectaries not prominent. Western N. America. (G.F. 1871, 679; Gn. 13 (1878), 598; B.M. 9617.)

**F. Pur′dyi.** 4 to 9 in. h. *l.* in lower part ovate to oblong, upper linear, 1½ to 2½ in. long. *fl.* 1 to 7, white, shaded pink, chequered purple. California. Related to *F. liliacea.*

**F. pyrena′ica.** *Bulb* about ½ in. thick. Stem 12 to 18 in. h. *l.* 6 to 10, scattered, upper linear, lower wider, glaucous. *fl.* generally solitary, 1¼ to 1½ in. long, wine-purple with dull-green spots, shining green within, chequered red-purple, ill-smelling; nectary green, oblong. Pyrenees. (B.M. 664.)

**F. recurv′a.\*** *Bulb* large, flattish, with many bulblets. Stem 18 to 30 in. h. *l.* in twos or threes near middle of stem, linear to linear-lanceolate, ⅛ to ½ in. wide. *fl.* 3 to 6, more or less funnel-shaped, 1 to 1½ in. long, scarlet, chequered yellow, the scarlet darkening with age; segs. recurved at tips; nectary oblong. California. 1870. (B.M. 6264, 9353; Gn. 18 (1880), 458.) var. **coccin′ea**, *fl.* brighter scarlet, tips less recurved.

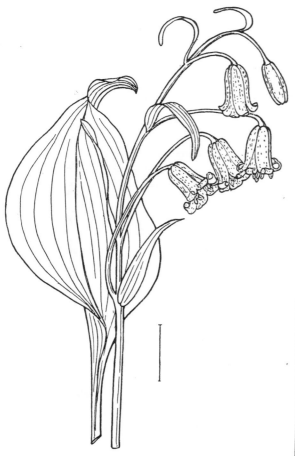

*Fritillaria recurva*

*Fritillaria Walujewii* (p. 842)

**F. rhodoca'nakis.** A synonym of *F. macrandra.*

**F. Roy'lei.** *Bulb* flattish-round, $\frac{1}{2}$ to $\frac{3}{4}$ in. wide. Stem 12 to 24 in. h. *l.* in upper part of stem, lower opposite, upper whorled, lanceolate. *fl.* 1 to 3, 1$\frac{1}{4}$ to 2 in. long, yellowish-greenish-purple, chequered purple within; nectary wider than long. Himalaya. (H.I.P. 860.) Habit of *F. verticillata* but l. without tendrils.

**F. ru'bra.** A form of *F. caucasica.*

**F. ruthen'ica.** *Bulb* small, globose. Stem slender, 12 to 24 in. h. *l.* 6 to 20, narrow-linear, 4 to 5 in. long, $\frac{1}{8}$ to $\frac{1}{4}$ in. wide, upper some distance below fl., with terminal tendril. *fl.* 1 to 3, wide-bell-shaped, 1 to 1$\frac{1}{4}$ in. long, dark purple with obscure chequering; nectary oblong. Caucasus. 1826. (S.B.F.G. s. 2, 343.)

**F. Sewerzow'ii.** *Bulb* about 1 in. thick. Stem 12 in. h. or more, glaucous. *l.* 5 or 6 below infl., opposite or nearly so, oblong, blunt, 4 to 5 in. long, upper similar but scattered and gradually shorter. *fl.* 4 to 12, singly in upper axils, funnel-shaped about 1 in. long, lurid purple, greenish at base. Turkestan. 1874. (B.M. 6371.) SYN. *F. discolor.*

**F. Sibthorpia'na.** 5 to 10 in. h. *l.* in lower part sometimes opposite, 3 to 4 in. long, up to $\frac{1}{4}$ in. wide, upper linear-lanceolate. *fl.* solitary, $\frac{1}{2}$ to $\frac{3}{4}$ in. long, obconic, yellow flushed red; nectary oblong, linear, deep green. Greece. (B.M. 6365, right-hand fig. as *F. armena*; B.M. n.s. 129.)

**F. tenel'la.** A synonym of *F. nigra.*

**F. tubiform'is.*** 6 to 12 in. h. *l.* 4 to 6, about middle of stem, 2 to 3 in. long, upper linear, lower oblanceolate. *fl.* usually solitary, 1$\frac{1}{4}$ to 1$\frac{1}{2}$ in. long, purplish, obscurely chequered with yellow, squarish-bell-shaped. Maritime Alps. var. **Burnet'i**, *fl.* smaller, deeper in colour; **Moggridge'i**, *fl.* yellow with some brown chequering. (Gn. 18 (1880), 132; M.F.M. 25 as *F. delphinensis*.),

**F. Tunta'sia.** About 12 in. h. Stem thick, 2- to 4-fld., naked below. *l.* many, linear-lanceolate or linear, spreading. *fl.* obconic, nodding, deep purple; segs. oblong, obtuse; filaments glabrous; style entire. March, April. Greek Is.

**F. verticilla'ta.** *Bulb* round, $\frac{3}{4}$ in. thick. Stem 12 to 18 in. h. *l.* 20 to 40, all opposite or whorled, linear-lanceolate, upper with tendril tips. *fl.* 1, rarely 2 to 5, 1 to 1$\frac{1}{4}$ in. long, wide-bell-shaped, white or yellowish with green base and some purple spotting. Altai Mts. (B.M. 3083 as *F. leucantha.*) var. **Thunberg'ii**, a synonym of *Uvularia cirrhosa.*

**F. Walujew'ii.** Stem 15 in. h. *l.* lanceolate, slender pointed in whorls of 3 or 4 or lower ones opposite, upper with a long, cirrhose point. *fl.* solitary or up to 3, nodding, large, bell-shaped, white, shaded grey without, pink and chocolate with white spots within. Spring. Turkestan. (Gn. 52 (1897), 242.)

### FRITILLARY. *See* Fritillaria.

*Frivaldskya'nus -a -um,* in honour of Emmerich Frivaldsky von Frivald, 1799–1870, director of the Hungarian National Museum.

*Frobelia'nus -a -um,* in honour of Messrs. Frobel, nurserymen of Zurich, *c.* 1874.

**FROELICH'IA** (in honour of Jos. Al. Froelich, German physician and botanist, 1796–1841). FAM. *Amaranthaceae.* A genus of about 10 species of annual or perennial herbs, natives of the warmer parts of America. Leaves opposite, ovate, linear-oblong, or spatulate. Flowers hermaphrodite, bracteate, in spikes or racemes. Grow in sandy loam and leaf-mould. Propagated by seeds sown in heat in spring.

**F. florida'na.** Erect, 6 in. to 3 ft. h. *l.* linear to oblong; bracts blackish, shorter than cal. *fl.* white, woolly, in oblong or ovate spikes. S. United States. (B.M. 2603 as *Oplotheca floridana.*)

### FROG ORCHIS. *See* Habenaria viridis.

### FROGBIT. *See* Hydrocharis Morsus-ranae.

### FROGBIT, AMERICAN. *See* Limnobium Spongia.

**FROG-HOPPERS,** the adults of the Hemipterous family *Cercopidae,* their nymphs or larvae being called 'Cuckoo-spit insects'. Three genera occur in Britain; *Philaenus spumarius* is the Common Frog-hopper and Cuckoo-spit insect of garden plants; *Aphrophora alni* and *A. salicis* are found on Alders and Willows respectively; and *Tomaspis sanguinae* is the most striking Frog-hopper owing to the blood-red and black-banded forewings: its nymphs occur on the roots of Grasses, Bracken, and occasionally, Mint. The Common Frog-hopper is a general feeder, its larval form (the Cuckoo-spit insect) attacks a great variety of cultivated plants (especially Rose, Lavender, and many herbaceous plants), and wild plants such as Dock, Sheep's Sorrel, and Grasses. The larva is pale yellowish-green and is surrounded by a frothy or spittle-like exudation. It sucks the sap of its food plant causing the leaves to wilt and the shoots to become distorted. The adult is an active, jumping, sucking insect about $\frac{1}{4}$ in. long, broad, with the wings completely covering the body. It varies from pale yellowish to dark brown. Plants such as Chrysanthemums should be examined for this pest before they are brought into houses for flowering, especially if they have been on weedy standing-grounds. The destruction of weeds in headlands, hedgebanks, and fruit plantations is desirable for such herbage provides both harbourage for the over-wintering adults and breeding-places. Infested plants should be dusted with nicotine dust, or syringed forcibly with clear water to remove the froth and then sprayed with nicotine soap-wash.

G. F. W.

**FROND.** A leaf of a palm or fern.

*frondo'sus -a -um,* leafy.

**FROST.** Frost occurs when the temperature falls to the point at which pure, still water changes from the liquid to the solid state. Like most substances, as the temperature of water falls its volume contracts, but unlike most substances contraction ceases shortly before the freezing-point is reached, and when freezing actually occurs the volume suddenly increases. To this peculiarity the beneficial effect upon soil is due, and to it also are due some of the injuries which freezing causes to plants. *See* **Heat, Temperature, Thermometer.** The action of freezing upon the soil is due to the change in volume of the water between the soil particles. The sudden and irresistible expansion of the water between the particles, when it freezes, pushes them apart and thus breaks down clods into small crumbs and enables, after thawing, a fine surface tilth to be produced, suitable for the sowing of fine seeds.

**FROST-GRAPE.** *See* **Vitis cordifolia.**

A→

**FRUCTIFICATION.** All the parts composing the fruit of a plant.

*fructu-,* in compound words, signifying fruit, as *fructu-luteo,* yellow fruited.

**FRUIT.** The act of fertilization of the egg-cell in flowering plants results in growth changes in parts of the flower, and sometimes of the inflorescence, which are not directly concerned in the act. The parts so affected constitute the fruit. If only the walls of the carpels are affected the result is often called a true fruit; if, however, any other parts are also involved—perianth, receptacle, or other part of the inflorescence—the result is often known botanically as a false fruit or pseudocarp.

The true fruit may be, when ripe, dry or succulent.

If the walls are dry and do not split open (i.e. dehisce) to liberate the seed and the fruit is one-seeded it may be an **achene**, a **caryopsis, cypsela,** or **nut.**

If many-seeded and indehiscent (schizocarps) the fruit usually breaks into one-seeded parts (mericarps) and may be called a **carcerule.** Such fruits are often winged and constitute a **samara.**

Dry fruit which open on maturity to liberate the seed are usually many-seeded. The fruit may be a **capsule, follicle, legume,** or **siliqua,** or, if it dehisces transversely, a **pyxidium.**

Succulent fruits may be either a **berry** or a **drupe.**

False fruits are of many types including the **pome** (e.g. Apple, Hawthorn), the Strawberry, where the receptacle is greatly enlarged and succulent, the Fig, where the receptacle is the succulent part, and the Pineapple, Mulberry, and Vaccinium, where the perianth becomes succulent. *See* **sorosis, syconus.**

See also **aeterio** and **lomentum** for special types of fruit.

Occasionally the bracts enlarge and form a cover for one or more fruits (*see* **cupule**) or a wing as in the Lime (Tilia).

For the special characters of these fruits see separate headings.

**FRUIT-BARK BEETLE,** *Scolytus rugulosus,* attacks a number of fruit-trees, especially Apple and Plum. The small black beetles, about $\frac{1}{10}$ in. long, bore into the stems and main branches, which are seen to be riddled with 'shot-holes'—the emergence holes of the adults. The eggs are deposited along the sides of the burrows made by the adult beetles beneath the bark, and the white legless grubs tunnel outwards from the main parent gallery. They pupate in a wide chamber at the end of the tunnel, and eventually emerge through holes made in the bark.

This and allied species of Bark Beetles appear to attack trees that are not in full vigour either as a result of un-favourable soil conditions, fungus attack, or of water-logging or prolonged drought, faulty pruning, and similar causes of ill health. It is advisable to remove and burn all dead and dying branches, and to destroy the entire trees if found to be heavily infested. The application of a 10 per cent. tar-distillate wash in March or April to the trunks of attacked standard and half-standard fruit-trees tends to drive the beetles from their galleries soon after the wash is applied, and they are destroyed as they come into contact with the winter wash. Care must be taken to avoid spraying the buds, young shoots, and developing foliage at this late time of application.

G. F. W.

**FRUIT BORDERS.** *See* **Borders, Fruit.**

**FRUIT CAGES.** *See* **Birds.**

**FRUIT-FLIES.** A group of 2-winged insects belonging to the family *Trypaneidae* (*Trypetidae*), whose maggots tunnel in fruits. The wings of these flies are charac-teristically marbled. The most important species are (i) the Mediterranean Fruit-Fly, *Ceratitis capitata,* which attacks a wide range of succulent fruits, including Citrus, Peach, and Vine, in the Mediterranean region, S. Africa, and elsewhere; (ii) the Cherry Fruit-Fly, *Rhagoletis cerasi,* which infests both wild and cultivated Cherries in France and Germany, and against which pest there is legislation in force to exclude from this country Cherries from certain zones in Europe; and (iii) the Olive Fly, *Dacus oleae,* which is a pest of cultivated Olives in Spain, southern France, Italy, Greece, Turkey, and Palestine. The Celery Fly (q.v.) is a member of this family. The only British species of fruit-flies of note are the Barberry and the Rose-Hip Flies (q.v.).

G. F. W.

**FRUIT GATHERING.** Notes as to the best time and method of harvesting particular kinds are given in the articles dealing with the separate fruits, but there are some general principles that apply to all or nearly all of those grown in this country. Careless picking and hand-ling of fruits leads to much loss and often to damage to the trees themselves. Ripe or nearly ripe fruits are very easily bruised and spoilt. None suffer more than ripe Peaches and Nectarines which are liable to damage by even slight pressure; ripe Pears are nearly as easily bruised. Handling them with finger and thumb is very apt to result in breaking some of the cells within, gorged as they are with sugary sap, and once this is done the death of neighbouring cells and rot soon follow. When

the skin of a fruit is only slightly damaged as by the pressure of a finger-nail the wound, scarcely visible though it may be, is sufficiently large to admit the inva-sion of fungi which soon bring about rot all through the fruit; the brown-rots of fruit often spread in the store through this kind of damage, just as they spread on the tree itself when the fruits are damaged by birds, insects, wind, or hail. Damage to the trees by the breaking of boughs by careless placing of ladders, or by scrambling among them in picking, not infrequently results in wounds apt to permit the entrance of such fungi as *Stereum purpureum,* causing silver-leaf. The 'pulling' of fruit often results in either the pulling out of the stalk of the fruit, making a wound from which rotting starts, or the breaking off of the spur on which the fruit was borne, thus robbing the tree of the fruit-buds for the future. The term 'pulling of fruit', as well as the practice, should be banished from the fruit-garden. Shaking trees to cause the fruit to fall, throwing the gathered fruit into the receptacle intended to hold it, tipping the fruits out from one receptacle to another, all cause bruising and other damage and should not be permitted. Careful handling at all stages of the harvesting process and sub-sequently should be insisted upon, and this even for the harder fruits as well as the more delicate. Care is needed also in the choice of receptacles into which the gathered fruit is placed, for if, for example, unlined wicker-baskets are used, there is danger of the fruit being scratched.

There is a stage with the larger fruits at which the stalk parts readily from the shoot from which it springs, so that taking the fruit gently in the palm of the hand and lifting it causes it to part readily from the tree. At this stage the fruit should be gathered, and by this method. Some fruits will, at this stage, be ripe for use, many varieties of Apples and Pears will, however, be still im-mature, and will need to be stored for a longer or shorter time. The ideal would be to leave them upon the tree until they were fully ripe, but this is impracticable since storm, frost, and various enemies would almost certainly destroy them. The longer such varieties can be left on the tree the better. Fruit picked in an immature state shrivels and loses or never attains its flavour, and spoils before its proper season of use comes round, whereas if allowed to become as ripe as circumstances permit, and properly stored, its season of usefulness is greatly pro-longed. The normal season for Britain's premier dessert Apple, Cox's Orange Pippin, is November to February, but if picking is delayed until well into October it will keep in a useful condition in a good ordinary store until May.

On the other hand, nothing is gained by allowing fully ripe fruits to remain on the tree; they lose both flavour and texture rapidly, while careful storage may help to retain both for a while. Fruits should therefore be picked as soon as ripe and used at their proper season.

Some fruits are picked before maturity. Green Goose-berries, cooking Apples and Pears, are picked for use as soon as large enough, and cooking Plums as soon as they begin to colour, but all these should be used within a short time of harvesting for they quickly deteriorate.

Not all the fruits on a plant mature on the same day and picking should be spread over a time so that it takes place at the best time. The successional pickings must depend upon the kind of fruit and the weather; in Rasp-berries, Strawberries, and dessert Plums, as well as other choice dessert fruits, maturity is quickly reached when once the changes towards ripening begin and daily attention may be necessary to secure the fruits at their best.

When fruit is gathered, any that is damaged should be kept separate from the sound fruit and excluded from the store. Diseased and useless fruits should not be allowed to remain on the trees nor cast upon the ground but, with other fallen fruit which cannot be used, collected and destroyed. Such fruits left in proximity to the trees are a source of infection in the following year and may lead to considerable loss.

An implement is made somewhat like the standard tree pruner with a small bag or net attached to receive the fruit when severed from the tree. It is convenient for use where fruits are beyond the reach of the hand or when a ladder would be likely to damage the tree, and is made in various lengths to suit requirements. No implement, however, equals the hand for fruit-gathering.

The time at which fruits should be picked is not always easy to judge. The falling of fruit is not usually a good guide though with some fruits, e.g. early Apples that ripen over a rather long period, the falling of some fruits may be a warning that the time for picking is at hand. The dropping of fruit may, however, be due to a variety of causes. In most of the larger fruits there is a period—sometimes called the June drop—when many fruits fall off, sometimes owing to imperfect fertilization or some other cause interfering with the due development of the seeds such as insufficient water-supply and so on. Fruits attacked by insects such as Codlin Moth, or Apple Sawfly, usually fall early. Gales may cause much fruit to fall before it is fit to pick. If, however, well-grown sound fruits fall in still weather it is usually a sign that picking should be attended to, to be confirmed by hand test already mentioned.

No exact dates can be given for the picking of any particular fruit for the dates will vary according to locality, stock used for grafting, and weather as well as variety. Speaking generally the colour of the pips of Apples and Pears is some guide for they become brown or black when ripe, but even this is less reliable than the hand test. There is, however, a general successional order for the picking of varieties which will be a guide in each locality.

Colour is also a guide in some fruits and colour combined with a slight softening of the flesh, easily detected by a gentle hand, in others such as Peaches, Nectarines, and Plums. No fruits should be gathered when wet, still less put into store in that condition.

Taking the fruits usually grown alphabetically, Apple picking may begin in July with the variety Gladstone or with such early cooking varieties as the early Codlins. All these early Apples should be used as soon as they are picked, for the ripening goes on so rapidly that they quickly deteriorate and with the possible exception of Hunt's Early none of the early dessert varieties retains its flavour for more than a few days. The latest varieties may hang until the end of October, or beginning of November, when all have to be cleared on account of the weather.

Cherries are best picked with the stalk attached when coloured and while the flesh is still firm.

Currants are ready when all the berries on a branch are fully coloured and should be picked on the bunch. They will usually hang safely on the bush, provided it is protected from birds, for a week or two without deterioration and keep better there than if picked.

Gooseberries, apart from those picked while green for cooking, proclaim their time for picking by their colour and a slight softening of the flesh. They reach their full flavour only when quite ripe.

Peaches and Nectarines ripen their fruits successionally and the hand test is the best criterion of time to pick—mere inspection with the eye may be deceptive. Great care in handling is essential.

Pears, like apples and peaches, are ready to gather when the stalk parts easily from the stem as the fruit is gently lifted. The earliest must be used at once, only the later varieties going into store.

Plums and Gages must ripen on the tree when for dessert use—colour and a softening of the flesh are the tests to apply and the choicest may well be left until they begin to shrivel. They are best picked with the stalk.

Damsons and Bullace are ready for picking when fully coloured but still firm-fleshed. Plums attacked by the Plum Sawfly are usually the first to colour and may deceive as to the condition of the rest. Even allowing for this, ripening is not simultaneous over the whole tree.

Raspberries, Loganberries, and Blackberries should be gathered when fully ripe only. With them all ripening goes on over a considerable period and almost daily inspection is necessary.

Strawberries similarly ripen over a considerable time and must be gathered when fully coloured and beginning to soften.

**FRUIT PROTECTORS.** Choice dessert fruits in the open are open to attacks by birds and insects and, apart from methods of dealing with such pests as Wasps and Earwigs, protection of some sort is often desirable. Paper or muslin bags or sleeves large enough to enclose the fruits without pressure, tied so as to prevent the fruit from falling, are useful for the purpose. They may be large enough to enclose bunches of grapes or if of muslin to enclose branches of currants or gooseberries, or may be used only for single fruits of Apple, Pear, or the stone-fruits. A useful type of protector against birds for Apples and Pears is made of celluloid cones which can be slipped over the fruit and clasp the stalk. Birds cannot stand upon them and the chances of pecking are therefore greatly reduced. *See also* **Birds**—**Fruit Cages.**

In places where Apricots, Peaches, &c. on walls are liable to damage by frost a good method of protecting them is the provision of a temporary glass structure over and in front of the trees. A permanent framework is fixed to stout brackets projecting from the top of the wall and glazed on a system that permits the glass to be removed in summer. The glass may be carried down to the ground in front of the trees or only the top for about 18 in. from the wall, may be glazed and the front provided with netting or some other material which will preserve the flowers from frost, suspended from the front of the glazed portion.

Temporary netting may also be necessary as the fruit ripens, especially for cherries, which are often severely damaged by birds.

**FRUIT ROOM.** *See* **Storing.**

**FRUIT SPUR.** A short branch bearing one or more buds containing embryo flowers. Some trees and shrubs produce all or most of their flowers from short lateral branches usually of the preceding or earlier years.

**FRUIT-TREE RED SPIDER** (*Oligonychus ulmi*). This is a comparatively recent pest, and little was heard of it prior to 1923. Its increase in orchards during recent years is stated to be due to modern methods of pest control, for it has become abundant only since the advent of tar-oil winter washes. These washes are not toxic to the eggs of the Mite, but destroy its natural enemies, chiefly the small Anthocorid Bugs, which suck the eggs and attack the mites in spring thus keeping the pest in check. This Mite, which occurs also in Canada and the United States, where it is known as the European Red Mite (with the synonym *Paratetranychus pilosus*), attacks a number of fruit-trees and bushes, especially Apple, Pear, and Plum. The adult mite is just visible to the naked eye, yellowish-green to reddish-purple in colour, and covered with a number of spines. The female lays her minute, globular, red eggs on the spurs, shoots, branches, and stem of the trees in September and October. The eggs hatch towards the end of April and in early May into 6-legged mites, which pierce the leaves and abstract the sap causing the foliage to become pale and chlorotic. After several moults, the mites become 8-legged and fully grown. The summer eggs are deposited on the underside of the leaves, and hatch in a few days. Several summer broods may occur in a favourable season, and there is considerable overlapping, so that all stages—eggs, immature and adult mites—are found on the foliage at the same time. The winter eggs are laid in autumn when their colour renders them easily visible.

Tar-oil washes have no effect on the eggs of this Mite, but the application of D.N.O.C. or a thiocyanate-petroleum emulsion has given good, but not consistent, results. The most effective control is obtained with lime-sulphur applied either as a post-blossom spray (strength 1 to 50) on Plums and Damsons, or as a pre-blossom spray (strength 1 to 100) on Apples and Pears. The latter fruits may, however, require both a pre- and post-blossom spray if the attack is severe. Some varieties of Apples (e.g. Stirling Castle) and Gooseberries (e.g. Golden Drop and Leveller) are sulphur-shy, and require a 1 per cent. summer white-oil emulsion. A spreader should be added to the lime-sulphur to increase its wetting powers, and the wash must be applied thoroughly and directed to the undersurface of the leaves so that the mites are wetted by the liquid. **A**
G. F. W.

*frumenta'ceus -a -um,* grain-bearing.

*frutes'cens:* **frutescent** (*frutex,* shrub). Shrubby.

*fru'ticans, frutico'sus -a -um:* **fruticose.** Shrubby.

*fruticic'olus -a -um,* growing in bushy places.

*fruticulo'sus -a -um:* **fruticulose.** Dwarf shrubby.

**FUCHS'IA** (in honour of Leonard Fuchs, 1501–66, a German botanist who published a book of very beautiful woodcuts of plants). FAM. *Oenotheraceae.* A genus of about 100 species of shrubs or small trees, natives of Cent. and S. America and New Zealand. Leaves opposite or whorled, rarely alternate, entire or toothed. Flowers solitary in the leaf-axils, often forming a racemose inflorescence, usually drooping on slender pedicels; calyx-tube globose or tubular from above the ovary, with 4 usually spreading or reflexed segments; petals 4 (rarely none), free, erect, spreading or reflexed; stamens 8 (rarely 4). Fruit a berry with usually several seeds.

Fuchsias are very valuable for greenhouse and window decoration, for bedding out in summer, for planting vases, for hanging baskets and, where hardy varieties are concerned, for the flower-garden and decorative wild planting. Trained on the rafters or pillars of the green-house the hanging flowers of Fuchsias make in summer and autumn an exceedingly beautiful feature. Fuchsias can be raised from seed, but the named varieties must be propagated by cuttings. Seeds usually ripen well in summer, and if required for sowing should be washed free of the pulp surrounding them and afterwards dried. They may be sown at once or kept until early in the following year. Cuttings are obtained from the points of young growing shoots that are free from flowers and they root readily at any season, but the best are produced by old plants started in early spring and these may be grown very rapidly in the summer following.

At one time, large specimens several years old were common in gardens. After flowering they were stood outdoors to ripen the wood and in autumn, after being partially pruned back, they were stored dry for the winter in a frost-free building. Early in the year they were pruned back and started into growth in a temperature of 55 to 60° F. When growth had started they were turned out of their pots, the old balls reduced, and repotted in fresh compost in pots of the same size or larger. Plants 6 to 8 ft. high can, however, be produced in less than twelve months, but strong-growing varieties must be selected for the purpose. To achieve this, cuttings should be taken in September. When well-rooted they

should be potted singly in 4-in. pots and kept, during the winter, well up to the roof glass in a temperature of 55 to 60° F. Early in the following year they should be moved into larger pots, moving them on as they require it until they are in the flowering-size pots which will vary from 12 in. up to 18 in. in diameter. If given plenty of root-room they remain much longer in flower. The leading shoot should not be stopped and should be secured to a neat stake, the laterals should be stopped at every second leaf until about 6 weeks before they are required to flower. During the growing period Fuchsias enjoy a cool, moist atmosphere, and slight shade when the sun is bright. They should be freely syringed in the morning and late afternoon, and liquid manure or a fertilizer may be used with advantage as soon as the pots are full of roots. Fuchsias succeed in any good loam with the addition of leaf-soil and sand. A 5-in. pot of fine bone-meal should be added to every bushel of the mixture. Where Fuchsias are wanted for greenhouse stages, good plants can be grown in 6-in. pots and for these it is as well to stop both leading and lateral shoots several times. Some varieties are of trailing habit and these are excellent for hanging baskets.

Stock plants, and those required for growing another year, should be ripened outdoors and stored in a frost-free, cool, dry place as soon as frosty nights occur. They should not be repotted until growth begins in spring. Tender varieties grown in the open air should be at least a year old when planted, and they may be lifted in autumn and treated in the same way. Hardy varieties in districts where they are liable to be damaged in winter are safer if covered with a mound of ashes after being cut down in autumn. Those grown on rafters or pillars in a greenhouse are best planted out and allowed to grow freely, needing only an occasional thinning out of shoots. They should be kept rather dry at the roots in winter and be pruned back to 2 eyes at the base of each shoot. **A**
J. C.

**F. alpes'tris.** Scrambling, up to 20 ft. h. with round, densely downy shoots. *l.* opposite (not ternate), oblong-lanceolate, slender-pointed, downy above and beneath, margins slightly revolute and somewhat toothed. *fl.* pale crimson; *pet.* broadly wedge-shaped, obtuse, deep purple. Organ Mts., Brazil. 1842. (B.M. 3999.) Greenhouse.

**F. ampli'ata.** Shrub of 3 to 5 ft. *l.* usually in threes, drooping, elliptic-oblong, 2 to 3 in. long, acute at both ends, toothed, glabrous, sometimes downy beneath; stalks about ½ in. long. *fl.* scarlet, solitary or 2 or 3 in axillary clusters; *cal.* lobes ovate-lanceolate, slender-pointed; *pet.* shorter than cal lobes, obtuse. June. Ecuador. 1877. (B.M. 6839.) Greenhouse.

**F. arbores'cens.** Small tree or tall shrub. *l.* elliptical, narrowed to both ends, entire. *fl.* rose, including pedicels, erect, in many-fld. terminal panicles; tube short to globose; *cal.* lobes and *pet.* of about equal length. October to February. Mexico. (B.M. 2620.) SYN. *F. amoena, F. syringaeflora.* Greenhouse.

**F. bacilla'ris.** Compact, low shrub, branches reddish. *l.* opposite or in threes, lanceolate or ovate-lanceolate, entire or slightly toothed, small, nearly sessile. *fl.* numerous in a terminal leafy thyrse; *pet.* deep rose, obcordate, spreading, with a blunt mucro at the retuse apex. Summer. Mexico. (B.M. 4506.) Greenhouse.

**F. bolivia'na.** Compact branched shrub, 2 to 4 ft. h. *l.* large, elliptic-ovate, more or less acute, toothed. *fl.* rich crimson, 2 to 3 in. long, tube trumpet-shaped; in profuse drooping clusters; *cal.-* lobes and *pet.* nearly equal, more or less acute; *cal.* lobes spreading, *pet.* erect; filaments red. Bolivia. (R.H. 1876, 150.) Much like *F. corymbiflora.* Greenhouse.

**F. coccin'ea.** Bushy shrub up to 3 ft. with slender downy branches. *l.* small, ovate, broad at base, obtuse, toothed, downy white beneath, smooth above; stalks short, hairy. *fl.* graceful; *sep.* scarlet, purple at base, oblong, acute; *pet.* violet, obovate, clasping stamens. Summer. Brazil? (B.M. 5740.) This name was at one time usurped by *F. magellanica* which is less graceful in all its forms and glabrous or nearly so.

**F. Colens'oi.** Shrub with long, straggling branches, sometimes several ft. long and unbranched. *l.* alternate, ½ to 2 in. long, ovate to roundish-ovate, rounded or cordate at base, thin, entire or nearly so; stalk often long. *fl.* somewhat shorter than those of *F. excorticata;* *pet.* small. Summer. New Zealand. Hardy in mild districts only.

**F. con'ica.** A variety of *F. magellanica.*

**F. coralli'na. See F. magellanica.**

**F. cordifo'lia.** Bush to 5 ft. *l.* opposite or in threes, slender-pointed, toothed, nearly smooth. *fl.* scarlet and green; cal. downy, its tube longer than the ovate pet.; pedicels solitary in the l.-axils. August, September. Mexico. 1840. (B.R. 27, 70.) Greenhouse.

**F. corymbiflo'ra.** Shrub of 4 to 6 ft., stem weak, somewhat 4-angled, reddish, needing support as on rafters. *l.* large, opposite, oblong-lanceolate, downy, almost entire, midrib rose. *fl.* deep red, in long corymbs; cal. tube 3 to 4 in. long, nearly uniformly cylindrical, its lobes lanceolate, acute; pet. oblong-lanceolate, about as long as cal. lobes. Summer. Peru. (B.M. 4000; Gn. 11 (1877), 70 as *F. boliviana.*) var. **al'ba**, cal. tube and lobes white or nearly so. Greenhouse.

**F. dis'color.** A variety of *F. magellanica.*

**F. × Dominia'na** (*F. serratifolia × F. spectabilis*). *fl.* long, drooping, red. (F.d.S. 1004.) Raised by Messrs. Veitch.

**F. excortica'ta.** Shrub or small tree to 40 ft. in the wild, with loose, papery bark and brittle branches. *l.* alternate, ovate-lanceolate to lanceolate, 2 to 5 in. long, slender-pointed, entire or nearly so, thin, pale and silvery beneath. *fl.* ¾ to 1¼ in. long, solitary, axillary, pendulous, on long, slender pedicels; cal. tube contracted above base then funnel-shaped, with spreading lobes; pet. small. Spring. New Zealand. (B.R. 857.) Hardy in mild districts.

**F. × exonien'sis** (*F. cordifolia × F. magellanica globosa*). *fl.* 2½–3 in. long, sep. scarlet, lanceolate, long-pointed, somewhat spreading; pet. purple, blunt. Of garden origin. 1842.

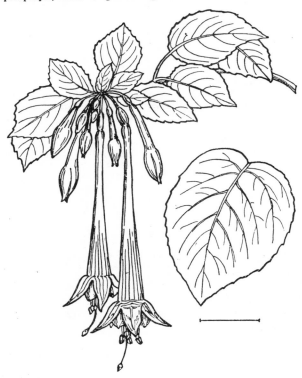

*Fuchsia fulgens*

**F. ful'gens.** Shrub of 4 to 6 ft. with somewhat succulent, often reddish stems. *l.* opposite, large, ovate-cordate, acute, toothed, glabrous. *fl.* scarlet, in drooping terminal leafy clusters; cal. tube 2 to 3 in. long, cylindrical, its lobes rather short, only slightly spreading, greenish at tips; pet. shorter than the ovate-lanceolate, acute sep., rather acute. Summer. Mexico. (B.M. 3801.) Greenhouse. A parent of the ordinary type of greenhouse Fuchsia.

**F. globo'sa.** A variety of *F. magellanica.*

**F. grac'ilis.** A variety of *F. magellanica.*

**F. macran'tha.** About 3 ft. h., downy. *l.* ovate-acute, entire. *fl.* pinkish-red, 4 to 6 in. long, in large drooping clusters; pet. absent. April to June. Peru, Columbia. 1844. (B.M. 4233.) Greenhouse.

**F. macrostem'ma.** A synonym of *F. magellanica.*

**F. magellan'ica.*** Shrub of 6 to 12 ft. h., shoots smooth. *l.* opposite or in whorls of 3, lanceolate-ovate, acute, toothed, stalk short. *fl.* nodding, axillary, with scarlet cal., tube oblong, little longer than ovary, lobes oblong-lanceolate; pet. bluish, shorter than cal. lobes, obovate, spreading; stamens much exserted. Summer, autumn. Peru south to Terre del Fuego. 1823. (B.M. 97 as *F. coccinea.*) A variable plant to which belong nearly all the hardiest Fuchsias. Syn. *F. macrostemma.* var. **con'ica**, 3 to 6 ft. h., *l.* 3 or 4 in a whorl,

ovate, flat, stalks downy. *fl.* small, with scarlet cal., the tube conical, widest at base, as long as the lobes, pet. dark purple, erect. Chile. 1824. (B.R. 1062.); **dis'color**, dwarfer, compact, *l.* rather small, wavy at the toothed margin, *fl.* small, numerous, cal. red, tube slender, lobes narrow, rather longer than tube, spreading, pet. purple, obtuse, shorter than sep. August. Falkland Is. (B.R. 1805.); **globo'sa,** 5 to 6 ft. h., *l.* opposite, ovate, *fl.* small and short,

*Fuchsia magellanica*

buds nearly globular, the tips of the sep. long-joined, cal. purplish-red, tube very short, pet. reddish-purple, half as long as sep., erect. Summer. Chile. A variegated form is known. (B.M. 3364.); **grac'ilis**, 6 to 10 ft. h., shoots finely downy, *l.* opposite, glabrous, remotely toothed, stalk long, cal. scarlet, segs. oblong, acute, longer than purple pet., pet. erect, retuse. Mexico. 1823. A variegated form occurs. (B.R. 847; B.M. 2507 as *F. decussata.*); **pu'mila**, dwarf, compact shrub, *l.* lanceolate, ⅓ to ¾ in. long, stalks, veins, shoots, pedicels red, *fl.* about ¾ in. long, cal. red, pet. purple; **riccarton'ii**, 6 to 10 ft. h., spreading, *fl.* red of var. *globosa* type of which this is said to be a seedling. 1830. Perhaps the hardiest Fuchsia.

**F. microphyl'la.** Bush about 2 ft. h. with downy shoots. *l.* opposite, small, elliptic-oblong, somewhat acute, toothed, smooth. *fl.* small, axillary; cal. tube scarlet, funnel-shaped, lobes ovate, slender-pointed; pet. deep red, retuse, toothed. Autumn. Mexico. 1828. (B.R. 1269.) Greenhouse.

**F. parviflo'ra.** Prostrate shrub, shoots downy. *l.* opposite, oval to obovate, ½ to 1¼ in. long, stalk slender. *fl.* drooping; cal. pink, tube ⅓ to ½ in. long; pet. purple. Mexico. 1824. (B.R. 1048.) Hardy only in very mild districts.

**F. × penduliflo'ra.** Very near *F. fulgens* of which it is said to be a hybrid; *fl.* rich crimson shaded maroon. (J.H. 3, 51 (1905), 301.) Greenhouse.

**F. procum'bens.** Slender, branched, prostrate plant, shoots up to several ft. long. *l.* alternate, roundish, ¼ to ¾ in. long, cordate at base, on slender long stalks. *fl.* erect, ½ to ¾ in. long; cal. tube pale orange, lobes purple at tips, green at base, sharply reflexed; pet. absent; stamens exserted. Berry bright red, ¾ in. long, glaucous. (B.M. 6139.) New Zealand. Fairly hardy and a good basket plant. The persistent berries add to the beauty of the plant.

**F. serratifo'lia.** Bush of 6 to 8 ft., branches reddish, furrowed. *l.* in whorls of 3 or 4, narrow-oblong, acute, glandular-toothed. *fl.* drooping; cal. tube about 1½ in. long, somewhat swollen at base, pinkish-red, rather hairy; pet. scarlet, ovate-oblong, shorter than sep. Summer. Peru. 1844. (B.M. 4174.) Greenhouse.

**F. simplicicau'lis.** *l.* on main stem in threes, 4 to 5 in. long, on fl.-shoots much smaller, ovate to lanceolate, entire, stalk short or absent. *fl.* in drooping clusters, numerous, crimson; cal. tube long, slender; *pet.* ovate, acute, shorter than sep. October. Peru. 1858. (B.M. 5096.) Greenhouse.

**F. specio'sa.** A name sometimes used to include the numerous greenhouse hybrid Fuchsias, probably derived for the most part from crosses between *F. fulgens* and *F. magellanica*, but certainly of very mixed parentage.

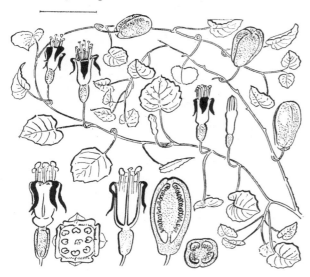

*Fuchsia procumbens* (p. 846)

**F. splen'dens.** Much branched shrub up to 6 ft. *l.* ovate-cordate, pale green, toothed. *fl.* drooping, rather short, about 1½ in. long, scarlet, tipped green, base swollen, compressed above; stamens much exserted. June. Mexico. 1841. (B.M. 4082; B.R. 28, 67.) Greenhouse.

**F. × super'ba** (*F. fulgens × F. magellanica globosa*). *fl.* 3½ to 4 in. long; sep. lanceolate, slender-pointed, deep red tipped green; pet. long, blunt, purplish-red. Of garden origin. 1840.

**F. syringaeflo'ra.** A synonym of *F. arborescens*.

**F. thymifo'lia.** Shrub of 4 to 6 ft. *l.* opposite or nearly so, small, ovate or roundish-ovate, obtuse, nearly entire, downy above, smooth beneath. *fl.* red; cal. funnel-shaped with oblong-acute lobes; pet. obovate-oblong, undulated. Summer. Mexico. 1827. (B.R. 1284.)

**F. triphyl'la.** Shrub of 1 to 2 ft., downy. *l.* often in threes, oblanceolate, 1½ to 3 in. long, purplish beneath, toothed. *fl.* in terminal racemes, nodding, 1½ in. long, the cinnabar-red tube enlarging upwards; pet. very short; stamens 4, not exserted. W. Indies. 1872. (B.M. 6795.) Greenhouse.

**F. venus'ta.** Shrub of about 3 ft., downy. *l.* in twos or threes, elliptic, acute, entire, glabrous. *fl.* forming a terminal raceme; cal. tube 2 in. long, purplish-red, narrow-trumpet-shaped, lobes ovate-lanceolate, slender-pointed; pet. about as long as cal. lobes, scarlet, oblong-lanceolate, undulate at margin, acute. Colombia. (J.H. 3, 49 (1904), 243.) Greenhouse.

**FUCHSIA, CALIFORNIAN.** See *Zauschneria californica*.

*fuchsioi'des,* Fuchsia-like.

*fuciform'is -is -e,* seaweed-like; resembling the Bladder-wrack (Fucus).

*fucoi'des,* resembling the Bladder-wrack (Fucus).

**FUEL AND FURNACES.** See **Heating.**

**fugacious,** lasting a very short time.

*fu'gax,* fleeting.

**FUGO'SIA.** See **Cienfugosia.**

*ful'gens,* shining, often applied to scarlet flowers.

*ful'gidus -a -um,* shining.

**fuliginous,** dirty brown, verging upon black.

**FULLERS' HERB.** *See* **Saponaria officinalis.**

**FULLERS' TEAZEL.** *See* **Dipsacus Fullonum.**

*Fullo'num,* of the cloth-fullers.

*ful'vus -a -um,* fulvous, tawny.

**FUMA'GO.** A genus of saprophytic fungi forming a black growth on the surface of leaves, &c., living on honeydew.

**FUMA'NA** (from *fumus*, smoke; in allusion to the greyness of leaf and shoot). Fam. *Cistaceae*. A genus of 9 species of shrubs or sub-shrubs closely related to Helianthemum, differing chiefly in the outer stamens being sterile and the ovules anatropous. Natives of the Mediterranean region, Cent. Europe, and W. Asia. For cultivation *see under* **Helianthemum.**

**F. laev'ipes.** Much branched sub-shrub, tufted, glabrous, shoots very thin. *l.* bristle-like, revolute, with short leafy clusters in l.-axils. *fl.* lemon-yellow in 5- to 10-fld. cymes. N. Africa, Mediterranean Is.

**F. nudifo'lia.** Low sub-shrub, heath-like, of tufted, contorted growth, 6 to 9 in. h., stems often procumbent, downy. *l.* linear, ¼ to 1 in. long, 1/16 to 1/12 in. wide, alternate. *fl.* ½ in. across, yellow, borne near the end of the shoot. Europe, W. Asia. 1752. (S.C. 16.) Syn. *Cistus nudifolius, Helianthemum Fumana*.

**F. procum'bens.** A synonym of *F. nudifolia*.

W. J. B.

**FUMA'RIA** (*fumus*, smoke; a poetical name is Smoke of the Earth). Fam. *Papaveraceae*. A genus of about 20 species of mostly annual herbs without milky juice, natives of temperate regions of the Old World. Usually much branched, often climbing, with leaves divided into narrow segments. Flowers small, in racemes; petals 4, erect, conniving, the posterior gibbous or spurred at base, anterior flat, inner 2 narrow, joined at tip. Weedy plants 4 species of which occur, 3 as weeds of cultivated ground, in Britain, but otherwise of no horticultural importance.

A→

*fumarioi'des,* Fumaria-like.

*fu'midus -a -um,* smoke-coloured.

A→

**FUMIGATION.** A method of destroying insects such as Thrips, Aphides, White Fly, and Mealy Bug, Mites, such as Red-spider Mites, and Begonia Mites, Fungi causing mildew, and various pests that inhabit soil, by distributing poisonous vapour through the air about the organism aimed at. For application of the method to certain soil pests, *see* **Carbon disulphide, Formaldehyde.** The chief value of the method lies in the treatment of glasshouse pests, and the choice of material for use must depend upon the organism aimed at, and the nature of the plants grown. The chief materials used are **Hydrocyanic acid gas, Nicotine, Tetrachlorethane,** for insects and mites, and **Sulphur** for fungi. Notes on the use and value of each will be found under the respective headings.

In fumigating, care must be taken to distribute the vapour evenly through the house, to use no more of the fumigant than is necessary, and to safeguard the lives of those having possible access to the house treated. A dull, still evening is best for fumigating a house or frame, and the leaves of the plants should, if possible, be dry at the time. If heat is necessary to bring about vaporization of the material used, care must be taken to see that the material does not flame, otherwise damage to foliage is bound to occur, and, similarly, if sunshine falls on a house filled with the vapour, tender plants are bound to be scorched. Some plants will not stand even minute traces of poisonous vapour without injury, while other varieties of the same species can be fumigated without danger. A

**FUMITORY.** See **Fumaria.**

*fumo'sus -a -um,* smoky.

**FUNCK'IA.** A synonym of Hosta.

*Funck'ii,* in honour of Christian Heinrich Funck, apothecary of Gefrels, Tirol.

*fu'nebris -is -e,* funereal.

**FUNERAL CYPRESS.** *See* **Cupressus funebris.**

**FUNGI.** The Fungi form one of the great groups into which the Vegetable Kingdom is divided. They share with the Bacteria and the Myxomycetes the peculiarity of possessing no chlorophyll, and therefore depend upon living or dead organic matter for the supplies of carbon necessary in building their bodies, and as a source of energy. The chlorophyll-containing plants to which they are most nearly related are the Algae, with which in structure and methods of increase they have much in common, but they are, of course, independent of light which the Algae must have.

The vegetative body of a fungus usually consists of fine tubes or threads called hyphae, and these together constitute the mycelium of the fungus. The wall of the hyphae is sometimes coloured and may be very dark, the contents are protoplasm and reserve food, especially oil-drops. Some fungi show red, brown, blue, or green colouring, especially in the fructification, but these pigments play no part, as does the chlorophyll in Algae and other green plants, in manufacturing food. The hyphae often become woven and intertwined, and then, especially when the fructification is being formed, they produce a solid mass which may be soft, corky, leathery, or even (in Bracket Fungi, q.v.) woody, but no matter what the size, form, and texture, it consists only of interwoven threads.

Fungi are reproduced by spores, not seeds, and, unlike seeds, the spores are simple structures containing no embryo. They may be 1-celled or consist of several cells due to the formation of cross walls, or even longitudinal walls which again divide the cells. On germination, each cell of a multi-celled spore behaves independently of the others. The spores may be oval, elliptical, spherical or spindle-shaped, straight or curved; there is great variation in form, size, and colour. Most fungi are able to produce spores by cutting off ('abstricting') the tips of the hyphae, and such spores are called conidia, the hypha producing them being a conidiophore. The stage of a fungus forming conidia is usually known as the 'imperfect stage', for many fungi produce other complex fructifications, in or on which a special type of spore is produced, and the production of this fructification is the 'perfect stage' of the fungus. The form and structure of this perfect fructification, and the size and shape of the spores it produces, are the chief characters by which fungi are classified into such classes as Ascomycetes, Basidiomycetes, Phycomycetes (q.v.). The possession of 2 reproductive stages, the imperfect and the perfect, has led to many fungi receiving two names, one given to the conidial stage, the other to the perfect stage, and these stages are often so unlike that only after careful study of the life-cycle of the organism has the identity been established. Thus the fungus which causes Apple Scab disease was long known by its conidial stage and called *Fusicladium dendriticum,* but later it was observed to form fruit-bodies of the type known as perithecia (q.v.) on fallen apple leaves with ascospores inside them. This perfect stage of the fungus was known as *Venturia inaequalis,* belonging to the Class Ascomycetes, and by it the fungus is properly known, for the correct name to use for a fungus is that of its perfect stage.

As already stated Fungi have to obtain their food from tissues already built up by other organisms. According to the manner in which this is accomplished they are divided into Saprophytes, which live upon the dead remains of plants and animals, and Parasites, which prey upon living tissues. The organism attacked by a parasite is called the host and some parasitic fungi will live only upon a particular kind of plant, or even only upon a particular part of that plant. Most parasitic fungi must live only on their host plant or remain dormant : such are called Obligate Parasites. Others, called Facultative Parasites, can live and grow on dead tissues for a time until the proper living host becomes available.

A fungus absorbs its food directly through the walls of its threads or hyphae. The hyphae of some parasitic fungi creep between the cells of the host and are said to have intercellular hyphae; those which penetrate into the cells of the host are said to be intracellular. As they grow the hyphae produce ferments (enzymes) which soften the cell walls of the host and so assist penetration; they may also produce toxic substances which kill the protoplasm of the cell of the host which the fungus then absorbs. Sometimes cells invaded by parasitic fungi are stimulated to grow abnormally, and so enlarge and produce the condition known as hypertrophy, such as is seen in Finger and Toe disease caused by a Myxomycete, and in the Witches' Brooms and Galls seen in some diseases.

Fungi, like all living things, require warmth and moisture for good growth. Generally speaking moisture is very important, and warm, damp air encourages the growth and spread of disease and other fungi. The Saprophytes do not harm living plants, and, in general, play a useful part in nature by hastening the process of decay of vegetable (or even animal) remains. Some are, however, a nuisance because they attack and grow on stored products such as jam, bread, tobacco, wood, fruits, and fabrics. They are not very dangerous to human beings but such diseases as 'Ringworm' and 'Thrush' are due to fungus parasites, and in tropical countries more serious ones are known. Birds and animals may be affected by fungi, but in Great Britain such ailments are not abundant.

Use is made of some species of fungi in industry, e.g. various species of Penicillium and others are essential in producing certain kinds of cheese. Some of the larger fleshy fructifications of fungi are eaten as food, the best known being the common Mushroom (*Psalliota campestris,* q.v.), and related species in the Basidiomycetes, and in the Ascomycetes, the Truffle (*Tuber melanospermum*), Morel (*Morchella esculenta*), and others are highly esteemed for table use. These edible parts consist of the fructifications, and the fungus which produces each one has a vegetative body consisting of a mass of fine threads living in the soil and extracting nourishment from it, ramifying in all directions in search of food before sending up the fructification. In parasitic fungi the mycelium ramifies through the cells of the host plant to obtain its food, thus injuring that part of the plant. Threads are then sent up to the surface to produce spores at their tips or to become aggregated and form a fruit-body containing them. When released under suitable conditions the spores may alight on other plants where they germinate. The germ-tube penetrates leaf, stem, &c., and soon branches to grow into a new mycelium. To check this infection by disease fungi we adopt various measures, the chief of which is spraying with fungicides (q.v.). An important agent in assisting the spread of disease spores is wind, but rain, insects, and birds may play a part and some fungus spores are ejected violently into the air from the fructification in which they were produced. Diseases may also be spread by materials such as infected cuttings, bulbs, corms, tubers, and even by tools, boxes, &c., used in growing them. Some spores have very thick, resistant walls (chlamydospores) and some fungi form bodies known as sclerotia in which the hyphae weave themselves into a dense, compact mass, brown, grey, or black, which becomes very solid and hard and will withstand very adverse conditions until in favourable weather it can germinate. Obviously these types of spores are dangerous as they contaminate the soil which it may become necessary to sterilize (see **Soil sterilization**). In some, e.g. the Honey Fungus (q.v.), *Armillaria mellea*, the hyphae are woven into compact, cord-like strands known as rhizomorphs which travel long distances in search of food from other plants or plant debris.

The invasion of the host plant by the parasitic fungus spore may occur by direct penetration through the epidermal wall, or, more commonly, by the easier method of entering through a stoma or a wound. Sometimes the host plant may make an attempt to form a barrier of corky tissue to prevent the invasion of the fungus and sometimes this is done successfully (see **Diseases**).

Although Bacteria do not possess the vegetative body of fine, branched threads, those which attack plants are generally included as a special group with the Fungi in most systems of classification dealing with parasitic diseases of plants, and so also are the allied plants which do not form mycelia but in the vegetative state possess only an amoeboid type of body (see **Bacteria, Myxomycetes**).

**FUNGI, EDIBLE.** Many species of British Fungi may be eaten : a few are good to eat, though their food value, reckoned in calories, is not great but they have a value also as appetizers. The average composition of edible fungi is: water 80 to 90 per cent., Protein Nitrogen, partly indigestible, 2 to 5 per cent., Sugars 5 per cent., Cellulose 1 per cent., Fat 1 per cent., Mineral matter, mostly potassium salts and phosphates, $\frac{1}{2}$ to 1 per cent. The following are mentioned among the most esteemed British species : Mushrooms—*Psalliota arvensis, P. campestris, P. pratensis*; Parasol Fungus—*Lepiota procera*; Inky Caps—*Coprinus atromentarius, C. comatus*; Fairy-ring Champignon—*Marasmius oreades*; Chantarelle—*Cantharellus cibrarius*; *Tricholoma personatum*; Pennybun Fungus—*Boletus edulis*; Beefsteak Fungus—*Fistulina hepatica*; Puffballs—*Bovista* and *Lycoperdon*; *Melanogaster variegatus*; Truffle—*Tuber aestivum*; *Sparassis crispa*; Morel—*Morchella*. Most of these are readily recognized but care must be exercised in collecting them lest poisonous species are gathered in error. For full descriptions, books dealing especially with the larger Fungi should be consulted and the distinguishing characters carefully compared, for there is no other safe criterion by which poisonous species can be differentiated from edible ones. It is to be remembered also that the effect of some of these fungi is not the same upon all people.

**FUNGI IMPERFECTI.** Whereas most fungi produce a more or less complex type of fruit-body in the later (perfect) stage of their life-cycle (see e.g. **Ascomycetes**) as well as an earlier (imperfect) stage, there are some where no second, or perfect, stage is known. These plants are classified as Fungi Imperfecti or Deuteromycetes.

**FUNGICIDES** are chemical substances used to pervent or check the attack of fungus diseases on plants. Their application depends in the main on the following: (1) The substance used must kill the parasitic fungus or prevent the germination of its spores. (2) It must be applied at the right time, and for this we need to know as much as possible about the habits and life-history of the parasite. Fungicides can be applied in liquid or in powder form and as they are usually poisonous some care with regard to animals must be used or for the application of some sprays the operator himself may need protecting goggles and gloves. Fungicidal treatment can be very effective when dealing with such fungi as Powdery Mildews which grow on the surface of plants (see **Powdery Mildews**), but where the parasite penetrates deeply into the host tissues (see **Fungi**) the application

of sprays is mainly intended to protect those plants which are still unaffected. Resting spores often make it necessary to carry out some form of soil sterilization, and one method of doing this is by using chemicals in solution, brief mention of which will be made here. Against the winter spores of some fungi, too, sprays called winter washes are used in strong solution as the trees (e.g. fruit-trees) are dormant at the time. The substances found most useful are (1) copper salts and (2) sulphur, either alone or as one of its compounds. Different strengths of spray are used for different plants so as to avoid injury to the foliage. The substances used must cover the tissues well to get the maximum protection, and to help sprays to spread a substance called a 'spreader' is often added. This also helps the spray to adhere to the foliage and may sometimes be referred to as a 'sticker'. The aim is to get a thin film of the fungicide all over the surfaces of leaves and stems. Both upper and lower leaf surfaces must be treated. Most spreaders now sold are suitable for mixing with any spray, but older ones sometimes set up a chemical action in the spray, e.g. soft soap cannot be used with Bordeaux mixture or any other spray that contains lime. For details of how to spray or dust see **Spraying, Spraying Apparatus, Dusting,** &c.

Among the more useful sprays may be mentioned:
*BORDEAUX MIXTURE* (4-4-40). Many formulae are employed but the usual standard one is: For 40 gal. dissolve 4 lb. copper sulphate (bluestone) in about 5 gal. water in a wooden vessel. This is best done by suspending it in a muslin bag in the water over-night. Slake 4 lb. quicklime in another vessel adding the water gradually until the liquid known as 'milk of lime' is obtained. When cold strain this through a coarse cloth into the copper sulphate solution and constantly stir when a flocculent blue liquid will result. Make the whole up to 40 gal. with water and use fresh, for this spray does not keep. If the spray is still acid it will injure foliage, so test for this by dipping a clean bright piece of steel or iron such as a clean wire nail into the spray for a minute or two. If the spray is correct it will remain bright, otherwise add some more milk of lime. Plants already injured by aphis may be slightly injured by Bordeaux spraying. Grape Vines, Potatoes, and Tomatoes are very resistant to Bordeaux spraying, but certain plants with very sensitive foliage may suffer leaf-scorch from it. For these and for delicate fruit-trees after flowering use 'excess Bordeaux' with the formula: copper sulphate 3 lb., lime 10 lb., water 50 gal. Saponin and various other spreaders can be used with Bordeaux mixture. If hydrated lime is used instead of quicklime the weights should be, copper sulphate 4 lb., hydrated lime 5 lb., water 40 gal. The hydrated lime can be stirred directly into the water and is easier to handle.
*BURGUNDY MIXTURE* is made like Bordeaux mixture but washing soda is used instead of lime. The formula is: copper sulphate 4 lb., washing soda 5 lb., water 40 gal. It is an easy spray to prepare but is worse for scorching and should not be used on fruit-trees in leaf. Saponin can be used as a spreader and the test can be made with a clean steel or iron nail as for Bordeaux. This spray is very efficient for peaches and nectarines affected by Leaf Curl disease. See **Peach Leaf Curl.**
*COLLOIDAL COPPER.* The name given to some trade preparations which are intended for use instead of home-made Bordeaux mixture and similar copper-containing fungicides. In general these made-up sprays are not so effective as freshly made Bordeaux mixture.
*AMMONIACAL COPPER CARBONATE.* A very suitable spray for delicate foliage, e.g. Peaches, which will not stain fruit. Formula: copper carbonate 5 oz., strong ammonia 3 pints, water 50 gal. Make the copper carbonate into a thin paste with water, then 1 pint of the ammonia diluted with water to 1 gal. should be

added and the mixture well shaken, allowed to settle, and the blue fluid poured off. Repeat this process with further quantities of diluted ammonia until all the residue has been dissolved, when water should be added to the blue fluid to make up to 50 gal. This fungicide does not keep well, and is not much used at the present day. It can be purchased ready for dilution.

*CHESHUNT COMPOUND.* Produced by the Cheshunt Research Station, this substance is of great value in the prevention of 'damping off' disease in seedlings (apart from those caused by *Rhizoctonia* sp.). It consists of finely powdered copper sulphate 2 parts and finely powdered ammonium carbonate 11 parts. These 2 substances are well mixed and kept in a tightly stoppered vessel (not of tin or zinc) for 24 hours. It is used as wanted at the rate of 1 oz. to 2 gal. water and is watered over the affected plants. It will not injure them but will check damping off fungi. It is easier to dissolve first in a little hot water, then make up to 2 gal. with cold.

*CUPROUS OXIDE* has recently been introduced as a powder dressing for seeds and for preventing 'damping off' in seedlings as well as so-called 'pre-emergence rotting' of the seeds. Its use on seedlings requires the addition of water to form a fluid for spraying the seedlings or for dipping them into before transplanting. It is, however, injurious to certain seeds, e.g. Brassicae, Compositae, and Malvaceae, and should be used with care.

*COPPER LIME DUST* is for use as a dusting powder and has been called by other names such as Bordeaux Dust. Similar preparations exist under such names as Colloidal Copper Dust, &c. It is used in some instances instead of spraying against diseases like Potato Blight, but it is also very useful against Rhizome Rot of Iris (q.v.), and it can also be used for rubbing on wounded surfaces after cutting out diseased parts of the stem as in Melon Canker and the Grey Mould fungus in Tomato stems. *See* **Melon Canker,** and **Tomato Grey Mould.**

*COPPER SULPHATE.* Copper sulphate alone is used at a strength of 1 lb. to 20 gal. water as a dormant spray or winter wash (q.v.) for killing fungus spores and clearing lichens from the bark of trees. In this operation a little milk of lime added will show which parts have been sprayed or missed. This treatment is hardly necessary on fruit-trees which are usually kept clean by the ordinary routine spraying of lime sulphur (against apple scab) and the tar-oil washes used against insects.

*COPPER CARBONATE* is not very soluble in water and is mainly used in powder form as a seed dressing, and has been tried as a soil disinfectant, being raked into the soil. This practice is not recommended, as an excess will retard growth. As a seed dressing its use is mainly against Smut and Bunt diseases in cereals, the seed being dusted with powdered copper carbonate about 2 oz. to the bushel of grain before sowing.

*SULPHUR* is used alone either as a dust or as a spray. It is not very easily mixed with water, but when moistened with certain chemicals it becomes wettable so we are able to get sulphur in spray form. There are thus many sulphur sprays containing finely divided sulphur particles in water, now sold under such names as Aqueous Sulphur, Colloidal Sulphur, Wettable Sulphur, &c. In powder form it is used as a dust in the form of flowers of sulphur, green sulphur, black sulphur, &c., and is considered one of the best fungicides against Powdery Mildews. In greenhouses it can be used when the houses are vacant, being burnt as flowers of sulphur, 1 lb. for every 1,000 cub. ft., mixed with some wood shavings, but this cannot be done when plants are in the house. Against mildew on plants, e.g. Chrysanthemum Mildew (q.v.), flowers of sulphur can be used by being vaporized, which means it is not burnt but heated in a special apparatus called a sulphur vaporizer. The sulphur in this process vaporizes and then condenses in a thin film all over the foliage. When whitewashing walls, &c., in greenhouses it is a good plan to put some handfuls of flowers of sulphur in the whitewash. Against Grape Vine Mildew it is also a good plan to paint the vines when dormant with a mixture of flowers of sulphur and soft soap.

*LIME SULPHUR* is made by boiling together lime and sulphur, but good commercial brands of specific gravity 1·3 are now on the market. For use, this concentrated solution is simply diluted with water 1 part to 29, 1 part to 59, or 1 part to 99 as the case requires. Lead arsenate or nicotine can be added if required to lime-sulphur sprays for controlling insects. Lime sulphur is one of the most useful sprays we have and is extensively used in the control of Apple Scab, and has also been found useful against Mildews on some ornamental plants (*see* **Delphinium**). At 1 part in 29 parts water, lime sulphur can be used as a winter wash (q.v.).

*LIVER OF SULPHUR* was at one time popular for use against Mildews, but has been largely replaced by lime sulphur and other sulphur sprays. It is used at a strength of 1 lb. to 25 gal. water with a spreader added.

*AMMONIUM POLYSULPHIDE* was at one time used for late application against American Gooseberry Mildew as it does not spot the fruit. It is now largely replaced by other sprays such as lime sulphur or, for varieties that are 'sulphur-shy' by washing soda and soft soap. *See* **Gooseberry, American Mildew.**

*WASHING SODA* is still used as a spray in some instances, e.g. against American Gooseberry Mildew, where washing soda is useful for late sprayings as it does not spot the fruit. The formula is 2 lb. washing soda and 1 lb. soft soap to 10 gal. of water. Washing soda in hot water is also useful for scrubbing shelves, &c., in fruit stores where the use of a more powerful disinfectant is not wise owing to the possibility of the fruit taking up an odour.

*SULPHURIC ACID* has been found valuable for treating nursery beds of conifers against 'damping off', and it also kills weed seeds. The beds are watered immediately after the seed is sown with a solution of 1 oz. commercial sulphuric acid to 4½ pints of water, an amount sufficient to treat 3 sq. ft. of bed. Afterwards the beds need watering during germination to prevent any excess acid (*see* **Fagus diseases**). Sulphuric acid may be used to destroy the remains of potato foliage quickly when attacked by blight at the end of the season (*see* **Potato blight**).

*CARBOLIC ACID* is an old-fashioned remedy for Rose Mildew against which it is used as a spray, 1 dessert spoonful to the gal. of water plus 2 oz. soft soap.

*CRESYLIC ACID.* Commercial (straw-coloured) 98 per cent. cresylic acid is used for disinfecting empty greenhouses as follows. Dissolve 8 lb. pure potash soft soap in 1 gal. straw-coloured cresylic acid in a bucket over a brisk fire: this takes about 10 minutes. Then from this emulsion make a spray by putting 1 gal. of the emulsion to 39 gal. of water. With ventilators open apply this by forcibly spraying glass, woodwork, all crevices, &c., and then do the ventilators from the outside. The operator should wear gloves and goggles. The floor of the house should be sprayed as well. Close the ventilators and doors for some days, then open to air and do not plant until the vapour has disappeared (say 2 weeks). For a house 13 ft. wide and 8 ft. to the ridge the amount of *spray* required is about 1 gal. for every yard run of the house, but if the soil is done thoroughly as well it will need 1 gal. for every foot run. It is said, however, that cresylic acid is of little value as a soil fungicide as it penetrates the soil very feebly. Soil may be partially sterilized by watering with cresylic acid directly mixed with water, 1 gal. to 39 gal., covered with sacks for 2 days and then aired. Such treated soil may need to be left a month before using.

*FORMALIN* (*see also* Formaldehyde). A solution of formaldehyde in water to which a little methyl alcohol has been added is termed Formalin. It is used at varying strengths as desired for horticultural work, in sterilizing soil, disinfecting boxes, pots, garden tools, frames, &c., and for treating fungus-contaminated seed. It is a very efficient soil fungicide and is usually used at 2 per cent., i.e. 1 gal. to 49 gal. water. For soil sterilization this is watered on the forked-up soil at the rate of about 3 gal. to the square yard, then covered with wet sacks or tarpaulin for 48 hours, but planting must not be done until the vapour has gone (usually about 2 weeks after uncovering). Soil can be put up in 9-in. layers, each being watered as above and the complete heap covered in similar fashion. Pots, boxes, tools, &c., can be stacked and watered with formalin, then covered for 24 hours. For some seed-borne diseases the seeds are also sterilized with formalin. *See* **Celery Leaf Spot.**

*POTASSIUM PERMANGANATE* was once a very popular remedy against 'damping off' and is still used in some places, the soil being watered before sowing with 1 oz. to 4 gal. of water, or even 1 oz. to 2 gal. of water where the disease is severe. For watering cuttings after insertion use 1 oz. to 4 gal. of water. Its effects are very fleeting and freshly made solutions must be used.

*CAUSTIC SODA WASH* is used at the rate of 1 lb. to 10 gal. of water for cleansing trees and shrubs of growths such as algae and lichens and for killing fungus spores. It is used in winter (January), and the operator should wear goggles and gloves. It has now been largely replaced by such sprays as strong lime sulphur (1 to 29) or tar-oil washes.

*MERCURIC CHLORIDE* (Corrosive Sublimate) has been used in many ways as a fungicide, but as it is a deadly poison it must be handled with great care. A well-known use is against Finger and Toe disease in Brassicas (*see* **Cabbage, Finger and Toe disease**). It is generally used at a dilution of 1 in 1,000 or 1 in 2,000, i.e. 1 oz. to 6 gal. or 12 gal. water. Against certain diseases of turf, e.g. Snow Mould (*Fusarium nivale*), it has been used as a dry powder mixed with sand. It will control damping off in young plants caused by the fungus *Rhizoctonia solani* which Cheshunt Compound (q.v.) will not. With Tomato seedlings, however, injury may be caused and the strength for these is 1 in 2,000.

*MERCUROUS CHLORIDE* (Calomel) has been found successful in controlling Brown Patch of Turf (*Rhizoctonia* sp.) either used dry or in liquid form as above. Like corrosive sublimate its chief disadvantage is that it is not easily soluble in water. As a dust, calomel may be used successfully for the control of Finger and Toe in Brassicas. Dry calomel is mixed with a carrier such as sand or dry soil and the mixture is sprinkled either directly into dibble holes or broadcast in a shallow drill. Allow about 1 oz. of calomel for every 50 plants, and use as much soil or sand as convenient.

*ORGANIC MERCURY COMPOUNDS.* There are many of these fungicides now being offered. Most are proprietary articles and their composition may alter from time to time, but they are usually effective as substitutes for calomel and corrosive sublimate in controlling turf diseases, &c. Some are sold as seed-dressings against rotting or damping off diseases in peas, &c.

*ZINC OXIDE* is sometimes used against 'damping off', and also for treatment of seeds and soil before sowing, in rather similar fashion to cuprous oxide.

A→

A→             D. E. G.

**FUNGUS GNATS.** Small flies belonging to the Dipterous family *Mycetophilidae*, and chiefly to the genus *Sciara*, which accounts for the alternative name of Sciarid Flies. The adults are gnat- or midge-like, small, slender-bodied, 2-winged flies, generally dark grey or black with long antennae. They may be seen swarming and running over rubbish heaps, glasshouse borders, seed-boxes, Orchid-pots, and Mushroom-beds where the odour of manure and fungi attract them. The maggots are worm-like, white, slender, legless, with conspicuous black heads. The pupae are contained in slight, parchment-like cocoons in the soil and in plant refuse. The life-cycle is comparatively short, and several overlapping generations occur in the year. The maggots prefer dead and decaying organic matter and fungi, including the stems and caps of cultivated Mushrooms, which become riddled with holes. They attack, however, seedlings and cuttings of a variety of plants to which they are attracted chiefly by the presence of leaf-mould in the compost. One species, *Sciara pectoralis*—the Moss or Orchid Fly—is destructive to the roots and pseudobulbs of certain Orchids though primarily a feeder on decaying Sphagnum Moss. The maggots of other Mycetophilids, including *Pnyxia scabiei*, are occasionally destructive in Cucumber houses where they attack the roots and the lower portions of the stems, especially in borders that have been allowed to become dry.

Manure and leaf-mould known to be infested with Sciarid maggots should be steam-sterilized prior to its incorporation in potting composts. The ventilators and doors of Mushroom houses should be fitted with screens of muslin or wire-gauze to exclude the flies. Infested Mushroom-beds may be watered at weekly intervals with 1 fluid oz. of nicotine to 5 gal. of water for each 100 sq. yds. Cucumber beds and other glasshouse borders which have been allowed to dry out should be thoroughly soaked with water to destroy the maggots. Mushroom-beds may be dusted at intervals with pyrethrum powder to destroy the flies as they run over the casing-soil. Periodic light fumigations of infested propagating pits and Mushroom houses with either nicotine vapour or hydrocyanic acid gas will reduce the population of the flies. The placing of *Pinguicula* plants on the staging among Orchids attacked by the Moss Fly is a simple method of reducing the number of Sciarids, which are trapped as they alight on the sticky leaves of this insectivorous plant.     **A**

          G. F. W.

*funicula'tus -a -um,* resembling thin cord.

**FUNK'IA.** A synonym of Hosta.

A→

*fur'cans, furca'tus -a -um,* forked.

**FURCRAE'A** (in honour of A. T. Fourcroy, 1755–1809, a celebrated French chemist). FAM. *Amaryllidaceae.* A genus of about 17 species of striking plants allied to Agave, but with the perianth segments spreading horizontally, all natives of S. America. Leaves in a dense rosette, usually rigid, tipped and edged with spines. Flowers in a loose panicle, often replaced by bulbils; perianth rotate, tube short, cylindrical, segments oblong, nearly equal, spreading; filaments erect. Greenhouse or stove plants needing treatment like Agave. They may be increased by bulbils. The leaves of *F. gigantea* yield an excellent fibre.

**F. albispi'na.** *l.* 15 to 20, 12 to 18 in. long, 2 in. wide; marginal prickles greenish-white, deltoid. *fl.* white, tinged green, solitary, pendulous; inner segs. ½ in. long; panicle rhomboid, central branches 6 to 8 in. long; peduncle 5 ft. long. November. Cent. America? 1892.

**F. Bedinghaus'ii.** Stem about 3 ft. long. *l.* 30 to 40, lanceolate, 3 ft. long, margin minutely toothed. *fl.* greenish; scape 12 to 15 ft. long; branches drooping. Mexico. 1860. (B.M. 7170.) SYN. *Yucca argyrophylla.*

**F. cuben'sis.** *l.* 25 to 30, bright green, rigid, channelled and smooth on face, usually scabrid on back, tip a minute, brown, scarcely spiny point, margin with regular hooked, brown prickles. Trop. America. 1879. var. **iner'mis,** *l.* less rigid, almost without teeth. Trop. America. (B.M. 6543.) See also **F. Lindenii.**

**F. el'egans.** Stemless. *l.* 40 to 50, 6½ to 8 ft. long, narrow-lanceolate, channelled in upper third, tip a straight spine nearly ⅞ in. long, marginal spines curving forwards, dull green with purplish margins above, scabrid beneath. *Scape* and panicle up to 25 ft. h., branching, branches up to 5½ ft. long, many-fld. *fl.* pale green within, 2½ in. across, lobes and tube at first purple then brownish without. Mexico. 1868. (B.M. 8461.)

**F. flavo-vi'ridis.** *l.* more or less spreading, somewhat tortuose, lanceolate, spiny at tip and on margin. *Scape* 12 to 14 ft. h. with a long, loose panicle; perianth pale yellowish-green. Mexico. 1846. (B.M. 5163.)

**F. foe'tida.** Stem about 3 to 4 ft. h. *l.* 40 to 50, lanceolate, 4 to 6 ft. long; margin almost entire. *Scape* 30 to 40 ft. h. *fl.* milk-white within, greenish without. S. America. 1690. (B.M. 2250.) Syn. *F. gigantea.*

**F. gigan'tea.** A synonym of *F. foetida.*

**F. Linden'ii.** A form of *F. cubensis* with variegated *l.*

**F. longae'va.*** Stem about 3 to 4 ft. in cultivation but sometimes up to 40 or 50 ft. *l.* many, in a dense rosette, lanceolate, 4 to 5 ft. long. *fl.* whitish on a branched scape 30 to 40 ft. long, the branches spreading, compound. Mexico. 1833. (B.M. 5519; J.R.H.S. 69, 356.) Hardy in Scilly Is.

**F. pubes'cens.** Stemless. *l.* about 30, lanceolate, rigid, not wavy, 2 ft. long, 2½ in. wide, spine tipped, medium-sized spines on margins. *fl.* greenish-white, over 1 in. long, up to ⅜ in. across; scape rather longer than l., the panicle 5 times as long as scape. Trop. America. 1892. (B.M. 7250; B.M. 6160 as *F. undulata.*)

**F. pugionifor'mis.** A synonym of *F. elegans.*

**F. Sello'a.** Stemless or almost so. *l.* 30 to 40 in a dense rosette, lanceolate, 3 to 4 ft. long, margins with upcurved brown spines about ¼ in. long. *fl.* white, tinged green; scape 15 to 16 ft. long; panicle 3 ft. broad. Guatemala. 1865. (B.M. 6148.)

**F. stric'ta.** *l.* about 30 in rosette, lanceolate, 2 to 2½ ft. long, 2 to 2½ in. wide, bright green, deeply channelled, spines large, distant. *fl.* about 1 in. long; scape with panicle 8 to 9 ft. long. Trop. America. 1868.

**F. Watsonia'na.** *l.* tufted, spreading, about 2½ ft. long, convolute at first, blue-green with bands of cream, margins undulate, spines minute, distant. Trop. America. (G.C. 23 (1898), 242, f. 90.)

***furfura'ceus -a -um,*** scaly, mealy, scurfy.

***fu'riens,*** exciting madness.

**FURNACES.** *See* **Heating.**

**FURZE.** *See* **Ulex europaeus.**

**FUSA'RIUM.** A large genus of Fungi, many of which are very harmful parasites of plants. *See* **Carnation, Stem Rot,** due to *F. culmorum*; **Potato, Dry Rot,** due to *F. caeruleum*; **Turf diseases** under Fusarium Patch due to *F. nivale.*

***fusces'cens,*** slightly fuscous.

***fus'cus -a -um, fusci-*** or ***fusco-,*** in compound words, fuscous, dark-coloured.

**FUSICLA'DIUM.** A genus of Fungi, many of which are parasites of plants. Several at one time placed here have been found to be the conidial stage of species of Venturia, *see* e.g. **Apple, Scab,** due to *V. inaequalis*; **Pear, Scab,** due to *V. pirina.*

***fusiform'is -is -e,*** spindle-shaped, like the root of a Carrot.

**FUSTIC.** *See* **Chlorophora tinctoria.**

**FUSTIC, YOUNG.** *See* **Rhus Cotinus.**

***fu'tilis -is -e,*** useless.

# G

***gadita'nus -a -um,*** of Cadiz, Spain, from its ancient name Gades.

***Gaert'neri,*** in honour of J. Gärtner, 1732–91, physician of Stuttgart.

**GA'GEA** (in honour of Sir Thomas Gage, 1781–1820, of Hengrave Hall, Suffolk, who botanized in Suffolk, Ireland, and Portugal). Fam. *Liliaceae.* A genus of 30 to 40 species of small bulbous plants, natives of Europe, temperate Asia, and N. Africa, allied to Lloydia but with flowers of medium size, shining golden-yellow within, greenish-yellow without, with 6, free, persistent segments, arranged in a terminal, bracteate umbel. Leaves radical, linear. The species closely resemble one another. For cultivation, *see* **Ornithogalum.**

**G. arven'sis.** *l.* radical 2, lanceolate, obtuse, channelled, recurved; stem-l. narrower, opposite. *fl.* 5 to 10 in a corymbiform raceme; segs. about ⅜ in. long, blunt. March, April. Mediterranean region. Syn. *G. stellaris.*

**G. fistulo'sa.** *l.* radical, 1 or 2, linear, 1/10 in. wide, tubular, half cylindric; stem-l. almost opposite, broader, uppermost half length of fourth. *fl.* 1 to 5 in umbel, on stalks up to 4 times as long as fl., thickly hairy; segs. elliptic-lanceolate, obtuse; stamens scarcely half as long as segs. May, June. Tyrol. Syn. *G. Liottardii.*

**G. Liottard'ii.** A synonym of *G. fistulosa.*

**G. lu'tea.** A synonym of *G. sylvatica.*

**G. praten'sis.** About 4 in. h. *l.* radical, solitary, glaucous, revolute, linear-lanceolate, acute; stem-l. opposite, linear, acute, glaucous, sharply keeled, hairy and long, ciliate. *fl.* 1 to 5 in umbels, large; segs. about ½ in. long, obtuse, pale yellow; pedicels very long, smooth. March. Europe. (S.B.F.G. 177 as *G. glauca.*) Syn. *G. stenopetala.*

**G. stenopet'ala.** A synonym of *G. pratensis.*

**G. sylvat'ica.** Stem slender, rarely 6 in. h., smooth. *l.* radical, 1, rarely 2, broad-linear, about ⅓ in. wide, pointed and curved like tulip l.; stem-l. lanceolate, the fourth shorter than infl. *fl.* 1 to 7, almost umbellate, longest stalk twice length of fl.; segs. about ⅝ in. long, yellow with green back, spreading, about ⅝ in. long, narrow-oblong, obtuse; stamens about half as long. Spring. Europe, including England, Russian Asia except extreme north. (E.B. 1822.) Syn. *G. lutea.*

**GAGNEBI'NA** (in honour of P. Gagnebin, botanical writer of 17th century). Fam. *Leguminosae.* A monotypic genus closely related to Mimosa. Shrub, evergreen, unarmed. For treatment *see* **Mimosa.**

**G. tamarisci'na.** About 6 ft. h. *l.* with about 20 pairs of pinnae, each pinna with about 30 pairs of lflets. *fl.* yellow, in spikes crowded into a racemose corymb near top of branch. Mauritius. 1824. Syn. *G. axillaris.*

F. G. P.

***Gagnepain'ii,*** in honour of Fr. Gagnepain, b. 1866, botanist of the Muséum National of Paris.

**GAHN'IA** (in honour of H. Gahn, 1747–1816, Swedish botanist). Fam. *Cyperaceae.* A genus of about 40 species of perennial herbs, natives of Australia, N. Zealand, SE. Asia, and the Pacific Is., many making huge tussocks. Leaves usually long, terete, with a long, awl-shaped point. Spikelets blackish or brown, often 2-flowered; glumes many; hypogynous bristles none; stamens 3 or 6; panicle large and loose, or narrow and spike-like. Nut reddish-brown, whitish or black, ovoid or somewhat fusiform. For treatment *see* **Cyperus.** The seeds of some species are decorative and can be used as beads for ornamental work.

**G. as'pera.** *l.* lanceolate, bright green, channelled, wavy. *fl.*, spikelets whitish-yellow. *infl.* terminal, New S. Wales, Queensland. Of Arundo-like habit. Stove.

**G. xanthocar'pa.** Stems numerous, stout, densely tufted, often 1 in. thick, 5 to 7 ft. h. *l.* very long, scabrid on margins and veins. *fl.,* spikelets brown, densely crowded, lower fl. male, upper perfect. *Seeds* yellow when immature, becoming black when fully ripe. New Zealand, Lord Hower Is. (G.C. 1873, 1668.) Greenhouse.

F. G. P.

**GAILLARD'IA** (in honour of Gaillard de Marentonneau, a French patron of botany). FAM. *Compositae.* Blanket Flower. A genus of about 12 species of annual or perennial herbaceous plants, natives of America, especially in the west, related to Helenium but having a number of bristles or awl-shaped growths among the flowers on the receptacle. Leaves alternate, usually more or less toothed and rough. Flowers in solitary, usually showy heads, the ray-florets yellow and red, 3- to 5-toothed, always neutral, the disk-florets purple and fertile. Involucre broad, bracts in 2 or 3 series, hairy. The annual species may be sown in any good friable soil in March where they are to flower, and both *G. amblyodon* and the various forms of *G. pulchella* are very useful. They may also be raised from cuttings taken in autumn, and these make excellent plants if wintered in a cold frame. The perennial forms in cultivation are derived from *G. aristata.* They are fine border-plants planted in good light and well-drained soil in full sun, but are not reliably hardy in wet or cold localities. They should be planted in spring. These perennials do not breed true from seed and are best propagated by cuttings taken in August or September and rooted and wintered under glass. Root cuttings are also used in spring, choosing the fine roots from which to make the cuttings. The plants may also be divided in autumn. The Gaillardias have a long period of flowering, beginning in early summer and continuing until late autumn, and withstand hot, dry weather better than most. They are useful also for cutting, lasting well in water. *G. aristata* is normally yellow-rayed, but in cultivation varieties have arisen with varying amounts of red on the rays, especially near the base, and others with 'double' flowers with a very narrow disk, or with yellow disk-florets instead of purple. A number of names of Latin form have been given to these varieties, but all have their origin in *G. aristata.* The flowers of *G. pulchella* and its varieties are so similar to those of *G. aristata,* as indeed is its growth which is usually less tall, that they can be distinguished only with difficulty, though *G. aristata,* which flowers the first year from seed, is perennial and *G. pulchella* annual, the flowers of the larger varieties of *G. aristata* may be 5 in. across, however, and those of *G. pulchella* are usually much smaller.

**G. amblyo'don.** Annual, erect, to 3 ft., leafy, hairy. *l.* oblong to spatulate, sessile, somewhat stem-clasping, entire or nearly so. *fl.-heads* 2 in. across, on long stalks; ray-florets numerous, brownish-red or maroon throughout. August. Texas. 1873. (B.M. 6081.) This species has varied little.

**G. arista'ta.** Perennial, erect, to 2 ft. *l.* lanceolate or oblong, entire or coarsely and remotely toothed. *fl.-heads* 3 to 4 in. (or in garden-raised varieties more) across; ray-florets yellow (or in cultivated varieties more or less red), usually 3-lobed; styles of disk-florets red, prominent. June to November. Western N. America. 1812. (B.M. 2940; B.R. 1186.) The parent of the perennial border Gaillardias, known in gardens as *G. grandiflora, G. gigantea, G. hybrida, G. maxima, G. perennis grandiflora,* &c.

**G. bi'color.** A synonym of *G. pulchella.*

**G. lanceola'ta.** Annual or biennial, 1 to 2 ft. h., loosely branching, ashy-grey, branches spreading. *l.* spatulate to elliptic, $\frac{1}{2}$ to 3 in. long, acute, entire or nearly so. *fl.-heads* with yellow rays $\frac{1}{2}$ to $\frac{3}{4}$ in. long, 3-cleft; disk purplish or purplish-brown; involucral bracts oblong to lanceolate, acute. Spring, summer. Southern U.S.A.

**G. pic'ta.** A variety of *G. pulchella.*

**G. pulchel'la.*** Annual, erect, 1 to 2 ft. h., branching, softly hairy. *l.* oblong, lanceolate or spatulate, nearly sessile, sparingly and coarsely toothed, especially the lower ones. *fl.-heads* 2 in. across or more; ray-florets yellow with crimson base. July to October. Arizona, Louisiana, &c. (B.M. 1602 as *G. bicolor.*) This has given rise to many colour variations. var. **Lorenzia'na** has the ray and sometimes the disk-florets developed into tubular, funnel-shaped fl. with 3 to 5 lobes and is of various colours in reds and yellows (SYN. *G. fistulosa, G. tubulosa*); **pic'ta** is of the form of the type but the *fl.-heads* are larger and the plant taller (B.M. 3368 as *G. bicolor Drummondii* and 3551 as *G. bicolor Drummondii integer-*

rima). Of both forms there are many named races (see Journ. R.H.S. 55, 141).

**GALA.** See **Entada scandens.**

*galacifo'lius -a -um,* Galax-leaved.

*galacti'nus -a -um,* milky.

**GALACTI'TES** (gala, galaktos, milk; the veins of the leaves are milk-white). FAM. *Compositae.* A genus of erect annual or biennial herbs allied to Cnicus, but with the outer florets of the flower-head larger than those of the disk and sterile as in Centaurea. There are 3 species, natives of the Mediterranean region. Leaves pinnatifid with spine-pointed segments, spotted white above, covered with cottony-down beneath. Ordinary garden soil suits these hardy plants which can be raised from seed sown in the border in March or April.

**G. tomento'sa.** About 18 in. h. *fl.-heads* purple, pedunculate. July. 1738.

**GALACTODEN'DRON.** See under **Brosimum Galactodendron.**

**GALAN'GA.** See **Alpinia.** Ancient name of an aromatic plant belonging to the Zingiberaceae.

**GALANGALE.** An alternative spelling for **Galingale** (q.v.).

*galanthifo'lius -a -um,* having leaves like the Snowdrop.

**GALAN'THUS** (gala, milk; anthos, flower). FAM. *Amaryllidaceae.* A genus of about 15 species of bulbous plants, mostly natives of the eastern Mediterranean region, related to Leucojum from which it is distinguished by the inner perianth segments being much smaller than the outer. Flower white with green or yellow markings, usually solitary, drooping; spathe usually simple; perianth-tube absent, outer segments oblong-spatulate, inner much shorter, obovate, emarginate; stamens epigynous; filaments very short. Leaves 2 or 3, lorate. Bulb tunicated. The bulbs should be planted as early as possible in autumn, 2 or 3 inches deep, and are best among shrubs or in grass. *G. Elwesii* is best in a warm, sunny place. The autumn-flowering forms of *G. nivalis* (Olgae, Rachelae, &c.) are best accommodated on the rock-garden in a sheltered place. Once planted, Snowdrops should remain undisturbed for some years, unless it is desired to propagate them. For pots, about 8 bulbs may be put into a 5-in. pot and, after potting, plunged in ashes until well rooted, then taken into a cool house or frame to flower in January. They will not put up with forcing. Propagation may be effected by dividing the clumps, after the foliage has died down, and replanting immediately, or by sowing the seed as soon as it is ripe, either in a cold frame or in the open. The seed will germinate in early spring. Hybrids occur from time to time in gardens combining the features of their parents, *G. plicatus* being a frequent component. For an excellent account of the Snowdrops by Mr. E. A. Bowles, see Journ. R.H.S. 43, 28.

Snowdrops are occasionally attacked by the fungus *Botrytis galanthina* which affects the young shoots so early that they appear through the soil enveloped in the grey masses of fungus-growth covering them. This may appear in patches, and all the affected shoots and leaves usually rot away while the bulb is often destroyed as well. This fungus forms black sclerotia of pinhead size on bulbs that may be slightly attacked and these carry the disease. Mild weather is said to favour this Grey Mould and it is probably introduced to a garden on infected bulbs, so that any brought into the garden should be very carefully examined. At first sign of the trouble, the affected clumps should be removed and burnt. Old leaves should be collected and destroyed where the attack has occurred.

A

(D. E. G.)

KEY

| | |
|---|---|
| 1. *Lvs. flat with a single furrow on upper side* | 2 |
| 1. *Lvs. more or less plicate at the margins* | 6 |
| 2. *Lvs. flat in bud-stage, more or less blue-green* | 3 |
| 2. *Lvs. rolled in bud-stage, grass-green* | 4 |
| 3. *Lvs. ⅜ in. broad* | G. nivalis |
| 3. *Lvs. broader, grey-green, inner fl. segs. with basal green spot* | G. Elwesii |
| 4. *With green spot at base of inner segs.* | G. Fosteri |
| 4. *Without green spot at base of inner segs.* | 5 |
| 5. *Lvs. less than ½ in. wide, strongly keeled* | G. cilicicus |
| 5. *Lvs. over ¾ in. wide or more, channelled* | G. latifolius |
| 5. *Lvs. much bent outwards, fls. much marked with green, late* | G. Ikariae |
| 6. *Lvs. glaucous green* | G. byzantinus |
| 6. *Lvs. deep green* | G. plicatus |

**G. Al'leni.*** A fine form of *G. latifolius*.

**G. byzanti'nus.*** *fl.* outer segs. up to 1¼ in. long; inner with both apical and basal green markings, sometimes wholly green. November to January. *l.* plicate at margin, but glaucous and paler green than *G. plicatus*. 6 to 8 in. h. Broussa. 1893. (J.R.H.S. 43, 33; Gn. 80 (1916), 64.)

**G. caucas'icus.** *See* **G. nivalis.**

**G. cilic'icus.** *fl.* outer segs. up to 1¼ in. long; inner half as long, without basal green splotch. November to March. *l.* flat, narrow-linear, less than ½ in. wide, bright green, simply keeled. 5 to 6 in. h. Cilician Taurus. 1896. (G.C. 23 (1898), 79; Gn. 73 (1909), 88.)

**G. Elwes'ii.*** *fl.* outer segs. about 1¼ in. long, ⅜ in. wide; inner marked with green at base and apex, sometimes almost throughout. January, February. *l.* wide, concave, glaucous. 6 to 10 in. h. Asia Minor. 1875. (J.R.H.S. 43, 33; B.M. 6166.) This species shows much variation in season, size, and markings, forms with green-tipped outer segs. and others without the basal green blotch of the inner segs. or with the 2 blotches confluent being known. var. **globo'sus** has a round *fl.* with wide outer segs. and frequently 2 fl. from the spathe.

**G. Fos'teri.** *fl.* as in *G. Elwesii*, about 1¼ in. long. February. *l.* bright green, deeply concave, shining, about 1 in. wide. Asia Minor. 1899. (J.R.H.S. 43, 33.)

**G. × grandiflo'rus.** A name given to large-fld. hybrids between *G. nivalis* and *G. plicatus*.

**G. Ika'riae.** *fl.* large, marked as in *G. nivalis*; inner segs. quadrate with crisped edges. March, April. *l.* bright green, margins not recurved, ½ to ¾ in. wide, much spreading. 7 to 8 in. h. Nikaria. 1893. (Gn. 49 (1896), 330; B.M. 9474.)

**G. Impera'ti.** *See under* **G. nivalis.**

**G. latifo'lius.** *fl.* about ¾ in. long; inner segs. with a small green patch at apex; anthers narrowed suddenly. February, March. *l.* bright green, channelled, ¾ to 1 in. wide, somewhat arching. Caucasus. 1868. (J.R.H.S. 43, 33; G.C. 7 (1890), 269; B.M. 9669.) **G. Al'lenii** of gardens is a large variety of this. 1883; **rizehen'sis,** *l.* narrow, otherwise as type. Rizeh. 1933. (J.R.H.S. 43, 33.)

**G. niva'lis.*** Common Snowdrop. *fl.* about 1 in. long; inner segs. streaked green within, and with apical green spot. February, March. *l.* usually 2, linear, about ⅜ in. wide, glaucous, keeled. 3 to 8 in. h. France eastwards to Caucasus. (E.B. 1507; Gn. 11 (1877), 194; 34 (1888), 58.) Like most plants with a wide range, this shows considerable variation and many good forms have also been raised in gardens, some being crosses with other species. Variations from the type in colour are seen in **Scharlok'ii** with green-tipped outer segs. and 2 long, green spathe-valves; plant yellow-green. 1868. (J.R.H.S. 43, 33.); **vi'ridans** with inner segs. green with a white margin; **vires'cens,** like *viridans*, but with outer segs. also striped green; **pic'tus** with outer segs. with a green spot; **lutes'cens** with yellow ovary and inner segs. yellow-tipped; **al'bus,** inner segs. with a very small green tip only; **viridap'icis,** outer segs. green-tipped. Varieties in form mostly less desirable than the type have been described, including **poculifor'mis** with inner segs. almost as large as outer and almost or entirely white. (J.R.H.S. 43, 32.) Autumn or winter flowering varieties with a central white stripe have been found in SE. Europe; **corcyren'sis,** a dwarf small-fld. plant. December Corfu; **El'sae,** plant larger and more robust with larger fl., November to March, Mt. Athos, 1886; **Rachel'ae,** still larger and more robust with wider leaves, October, November, Mt. Hymettus, 1886; **Ol'gae,** *fl.* about 1 in. long, green of inner segs. gradually fading. October, Mt. Taygetus, 1888; **Impera'ti*** is a marked form with larger *fl.*, often 1½ in. long and wider *l.* than the type. Outer segs. generally spatulate, narrowed to an almost stalked base, Italy, Balkans. Green markings usually large and leaf margins more or less rolled. (J.R.H.S. 43, 32; Gn. 11 (1877), 194.); **At'kinsii** is probably a seedling form of this; **caucas'icus*** has a rounder *fl.* with broader outer segs. about 1 in. long, narrowed at the base; bulb often 2-fld. The **'Straffan Snowdrop'** and **'Allen's Seedling'** (J.R.H.S. 43, 32) belong here. Caucasus, 1856; **max'imus, Melvil'lei, Magnet,** and **Galatea** (J.R.H.S. 43, 32) are other good forms; **fl. plena** has double *fl.*

**G. octobren'sis.** *See* **G. nivalis Olgae.**

**G. Ol'gae.** *See* **G. nivalis Olgae.**

**G. plica'tus.** *fl.* about 1 in. long, similar to *G. nivalis*. March, April. *l.* about 1 in. wide with a fold along each margin. 6 in. h. Crimea, Dobrudscha. 1818. (B.M. 2162; B.R. 545; L.B.C. 1823; Gn. 11 (1877), 194.) A variable species. var. **max'imus,** *fl.* about 1½ in. long, *l.* 1½ in. wide. (J.R.H.S. 43, 33.)

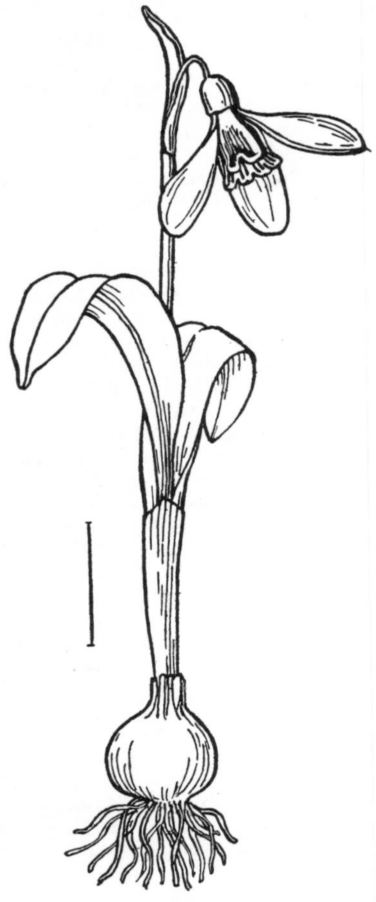

*Galanthus Ikariae*

**GALAPEE TREE.** *See* **Sciadophyllum Brownii.**

**GALATEL'LA.** Included in **Aster.**

***galat'icus -a -um,*** of Galatia, near Angora.

**GA'LAX** (*galaktos*, milk; meaning obscure). FAM. *Diapensiaceae*. A genus of a single stemless herb, native of Eastern N. America. Leaves roundish heart-shaped, many, evergreen. Flowers in a dense, spike-like raceme; calyx persistent; petals 5, oblong-spatulate; stamens united into a 10-toothed tube, the 5 teeth alternating with the petals bearing anthers, the others petaloid; ovary 3-celled, many-ovuled; style short. Fruit a capsule. Hardy, and best in peaty woodland soil among shrubs, as ground cover for Rhododendrons and the like, or in the rock-garden with some shade and moisture. The leaves, bronzy in winter, are used widely for decoration in America. Propagated by division.

**G. aphyl'la.** Evergreen, tufted, perennial herb, with a thick matted, creeping root-stock. *l.* roundish-cordate, 1 to 3 in. across, shining green, becoming bronze in exposed places in winter, veins palmate, netted; stalks long, slender. *fl.* white, about ⅛ in. across, in a dense, spike-like raceme on a naked scape, 12 to 24 in. h. June, July. Eastern N. America. 1756. (B.M. 754.)

**GALAX'IA** (*galaktos*, milk; in reference to the sap). FAM. *Iridaceae*. A genus of 2 species of bulbous plants, natives of S. Africa. Leaves linear or rather broad, sheathing at base; almost stemless. Flowers solitary; perianth funnel-shaped, tube slender, terete, segments 6, equal, oblong-wedge-shaped, spreading; stamens inserted at throat of perianth-tube, filaments connate in a cylindrical tube. Greenhouse plants, or, in warm districts, for sheltered places outdoors with winter protection. Sandy peat with a little fibrous loam suits them, and they may be propagated by offsets.

**G. gramin'ea.** *l.* linear, filiform, dilated at base. *fl.* light yellow, spathe 1-valved, 1-fld. July. 1795. (B.M. 1292.)

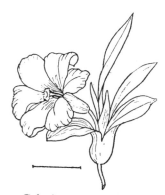

*Galaxia ovata grandiflora*

**G. ova'ta.** *l.* oblong. *fl.* dark yellow, 1 in. across; spathe 1-fld., 1-valved. May to September. 1799. var. **grandiflo'ra**, *fl.* 1½ in. across. (B.M. 1208.)

*galbaniflu'us -a -um,* producing a yellowish exudation.

**GALBANUM, GUM.** A product of resinous species of Ferula (q.v.).

*galbi'nus -a -um,* greenish-yellow.

*Ga'le,* from the English common name.

**GALE, SWEET.** *See* **Myrica Gale.**

**GALEA.** Helmet or hood, usually applied to a sepal or petal.

**GALEAN'DRA** (*galea,* helmet, *andros* stamen; the stamen is crested). FAM. *Orchidaceae.* A genus of about 20 species of terrestrial or epiphytic orchids, natives of Trop. America, from Brazil to Mexico; having slender, erect, fleshy, jointed stems, from the tops of which the flower-spikes are produced, just after the growth is finished. Leaves from the upper parts of the stems, narrow-lanceolate, 2-ranked, sheathing. Flowers of medium size, conspicuous, but not brilliantly coloured, shortly pedicellate, usually in nodding racemes. Sepals and petals free, similar, rather narrow, lip affixed to the column base, produced into a spur often broad and somewhat funnel-shaped, 3-lobed, the lateral lobes large, often convolute over the column and forming a tube; pollinia 2. While growing, the plants need a moist atmosphere and a nearly tropical temperature, but when growth is completed the intermediate house with a winter temperature never less than 55° F. will suit them. Water may be required at intervals as the necessary rest must not be severe. When growth first begins it is inadvisable to water too frequently, but as growth and root action increase, water more and more frequently until after the flowering period, then gradually decrease. Red-spider Mites will attack the foliage, but if atmospheric conditions are right are seldom harmful. If their presence is suspected, light fumigations should be given. The same applies to thrips which feed in the young plicate leaves and in the flowers. The syringe should not be used until the foliage is expanded. Shading is required, but not too heavy; after flowering expose to more light. Compost should consist of 3 parts of Osmunda fibre,

1 part of Sphagnum moss, and 1 part or more of loam fibre. Good drainage is essential. Propagation can be made by the division of plants, but they are unfortunately generally too small.

**G. Bateman'ii.** *fl.* several, 2 to 2½ in. across; sep. and pet. greenish-brown, narrow; lip somewhat funnel-shaped, reddish-violet, bordered with white, front margin deeply cleft. *Pseudobulbs* 4 to 6 in. h. *l.* narrow, 6 to 8 in. long, deciduous. Mexico, Guatemala. 1838. (B.R. 26, 49; L. 729; W.O.A. 267.)

*Galeandra Baueri*

**G. Bau'eri.*** *fl.* 12 to 16, about 2 in. h.; sep. and pet. narrow, yellowish flushed with purple or brown; lip yellowish lined or flushed with purple on the front lobe, which has an undulated margin; spur 1 to 1½ in. long. Stems 15 to 24 in. h. *l.* 6 to 10 in. long. Brazil. 1840. var. **lu'tea** has yellow *fl.,* lip lined purple, margins wavy. (B.M. 4701.)

**G. Beyrich'ii.** *fl.* 7 to 12, sep. and pet. about 1 in. long, greenish; lip greenish-white lined and margined purple; raceme erect, bracteate. A terrestrial species with globose-conical pseudobulbs 1 to 2 in. h., produced after the fl. *l.* 12 in. long, 1 to 1½ in. broad, the lower part contracted into a petiole. Brazil. 1849.

**G. Claes'ii.** *fl.* about 2 in. across, 6 to 8 in a drooping raceme about 9 in. long; sep. and pet. purplish-brown; lip purplish-rose, often with white margin. *l.* bluish-green. *Pseudobulbs* slender, 10 to 15 in. long. Brazil. 1893. (L. 391.) Allied to *G. villosa.*

**G. crista'ta.** A synonym of *G. Baueri.*

**G. d'Escagnollea'na.** A synonym of *G. lacustris.*

**G. Devonia'na.*** *fl.* 3 to 7, about 4 in. across on pendent terminal racemes; sep. and pet. brownish-purple margined yellow; lip white, pencilled purplish-violet. At various seasons, long-lasting. 2 ft. or more h. S. America. (B.M. 4610; W.S.O. 1, 37.) var. **Delphi'na**, more slender than type. Venezuela. 1887.

**G. flaveo'la.** *fl.* 8 or 9; sep. and pet. yellowish, tinged sepia, lanceolate, acuminate; lip yellow, dotted purple; anther tip with black anchor-like process. *l.* linear-lanceolate, acuminate, ½ in. wide, uppermost smaller. Over 9 in. h. Venezuela, Brazil. 1887. (L. 90.)

**G. Harveya'na.** *fl.* sep. and pet. sepia or greenish-brown; lip light yellow, with a tuft of hair on front part of disk. Allied to *G. Devoniana.* Trop. America.

**G. lacus'tris.** *fl.* 2 to 6; sep. and pet. brownish-ochre or greenish-white, purple flushed, lip white and sulphur, mid-lobe marked with dark purple; spur funnel-shaped. *Pseudobulbs* fusiform, 6 to 8 in. h. *l.* narrow-lanceolate, acuminate. Para. 1887. (I.H. 1887, 22.)

**G. lagoen'sis.*** Sep. and pet. narrow, dull or greenish-purple; upper sep. over 1 in. long, lateral sep. slightly longer; lip pale yellow, centre of mid-lobe deep purple. 24 to 30 in. h. *l.* 12 to 15 in. long, narrow. Brazil. 1894.

**G. mi'nax.** *fl.* yellowish-copper, whitish, purple. June. Colombia. 1874.

**G. niva'lis.*** *fl.* about 2 in. long, in nodding racemes with narrow, reflexed, rich olive segs.; lip large, funnel-shaped, white with central violet blotch. *Pseudobulbs* somewhat conical, 4 to 12 in. h. *l.* 4 to 9 in. long, narrow. (G.C. 12 (1892), 431; I.H. 1885, 555.)

**G. villo'sa.** *fl.* 4 to 6, 1½ in. or more across; sep. and pet. brownish; lip white, front margin deep violet; villous on disk and on face of column; spur whitish, ascending, 1 in. long; peduncle often with 2 branches. *Pseudobulbs* 6 to 9 in. h. *l.* as long. Brazil. 1877.

E. C.

*galea'tus -a -um,* galeate, helmet-shaped.

**GALE'GA** (*gala,* milk; said to increase the flow of milk). FAM. *Leguminosae.* Goats' Rue. A genus of 3 erect, bushy perennial herbs with smooth stems, natives of S. Europe and W. Asia. Leaves unequally pinnate, leaflets entire, stipulate. Flowers white or blue in axillary and terminal racemes, differing from those of the nearly related Tephrosia and Wisteria by the stamens being in one closed cylinder round the ovary. The Galegas are vigorous perennials standing well without support and flourishing in rich deep loam in the sun where they may remain in one position without deterioration for many years. They will grow in almost any soil, but repay good treatment. They can be divided, and good pieces replanted where they are to flower, or raised from seed sown in the open in spring. *G. officinalis* has been grown as a fodder plant.

**G. officina'lis.** Bright green herbaceous perennial, 3 to 4 ft. h. *l.* short-stalked; lflets. 11 to 17, oblong to lanceolate, obtuse; stipules free, large, pointed. *fl.* in stalked racemes much longer than the l., blue or white. Summer, autumn. S. Europe, Asia Minor. 1568. Many coloured varieties have occurred. var. **africa'na** has broader stipules, elliptic *l.*, and longer racemes; **al'ba,** *fl.* pure white, 3½ to 4 ft. h.; **albiflo'ra,** *fl.* white, 2 to 3 ft. h. SYN. *G. persica alba*; **bi'color,** *fl.* white and blue; **compac'ta,** *fl.* lilac, 3 ft. h.; **car'nea,** *fl.* flesh-coloured; **car'nea ple'na,** *fl.* pinkish, double; **Hart'landii,** *fl.* large, racemes 6 to 7 in. long, wings and keel white, tinged lilac, standard bluish-lilac, tinged pale purple at base; **ro'sea,** similar to var. *carnea*.

**G. orienta'lis.** Habit much as *G. officinalis* but stem hairy, *l.*flets. 11 or 13, large, ovate-oblong, acute, almost smooth; stipules broad-ovate, *infl.* loose, cal. hairy, cor. bluish-violet. Caucasus. 1810. This species creeps underground and has a more flexuose stem than *G. officinalis.* (B.M. 2192.)

**G. per'sica.** A synonym of *G. officinalis albiflora.*

**G. tric'olor.** A synonym of *G. officinalis.*

*galegiform'is -is -e,* Galega-like.

*Galen'i,* in honour of Claudius Galenus, 131–200.

**GALEOB'DOLON.** Included in **Lamium.** Ancient Latin name.

**GALEOT'TIA** (in honour of Galeotti, an Italian botanical explorer). FAM. *Orchidaceae.* An epiphytic genus of 2 species, allied to Zygopetalum and Batemannia but differing slightly from both, chiefly in the pectinate edges of the lip. The presence of pseudobulbs and the 2- to 5-flowered inflorescence are also distinguish it from the Huntleya section of Zygopetalum, and the characters of the lateral sepals further separate it from Batemannia. Cultivation as for Batemannia.

**G. fimbria'ta.\*** *fl.* 2 to 5; sep. and pet. about 2 in. long, greenish-yellow with brown stripes; lip whitish, streaked violet with a violet-streaked callosity; column white with a yellowish face. *Pseudobulbs* 2 to 2½ in. h., diphyllous. *l.* 12 in. long by 2 in. or more broad; scapes arched. Colombia, Ocana. SYN. *Batemannia fimbriata.* (G.C. 1856, 660.)

**G. grandiflo'ra.\*** *fl.* 3 to 5, 3 in. across; sep. and pet. broad-lanceolate, acuminate, light green with 5 or more longitudinal brown lines; lip broadly ovate, side lobes white with pectinate margins, front lobe reflexed, dentate, white with 10 or 12 raised reddish-purple lines, crest semicircular, large, orange-yellow, ridged and furrowed, ridges reddish and with projecting teeth in front. *Pseudobulbs* 2 to 3 in h., diphyllous. *l.* broad-lanceolate, 12 in. long. Peru, Costa Rica. 1865. (B.M. 5567 as *Batemannia grandiflora.*)

E. C.

*galericula'tus -a -um,* helmet-shaped.

**GALERUCEL'LA.** See **Water-lily Beetle, Willow-leaf Beetle.** A

**GALINGALE.** See **Cyperus longus.**

*galioi'des,* Galium-like.

**GALIP'EA** (native name of one species). FAM. *Rutaceae.* A genus of about 6 species of S. American evergreen trees or shrubs related to Cusparia. Leaves evergreen, alternate, stalked, 1- to 7-foliolate; leaflets usually entire, with many pellucid dots. Flowers in simple or compound, axillary or terminal racemes. They need stove conditions and treatment as for Erythrochiton.

**G. macrophyl'la.** Shrub of about 2 ft. *l.* 1-foliolate, elliptic, glabrous, blunt, somewhat leathery, 6 to 12 in. long. *fl.* pale rose or white in an interrupted spike or raceme. Brazil. (B.M. 4948.)

**G. odoratis'sima.** Shrub of about 2 ft. *l.* obovate, broad, blunt, deep green. *fl.* white, very fragrant, in short, almost sessile, many-fld. axillary spikes. Rio Janeiro. (B.R. 1420.)

**G. trifolia'ta.** Shrub of about 6 ft. *l.* 3-foliolate, smooth. *fl.* greenish, small, in corymbs. September. Guiana.

**GA'LIUM** (*gala*, milk; the flowers of *G. verum* having been used to curdle milk for cheese-making). FAM. *Rubiaceae.* A genus of about 220 species mostly weedy, dispersed over the temperate regions and occurring on mountains in the tropics. Several S. European species have been offered for the rock-garden, but they are not dependably hardy, and, though with some value for the purpose if they were, cannot be recommended. *G. Aparine*, Cleavers, Goose-grass, is a persistent weed, especially in soil rich in decaying leaves and *G. verum*, Yellow Bedstraw, Lady's Bedstraw, may be troublesome by its running habit if introduced into the rock-garden or on a bank.

**GALL MIDGES.** These minute, fragile, 2-winged insects (FAM. *Cecidomyidae*) possess characteristic long antennae (feelers) with bead-like segments. Their legless larvae are oval, and vary in colour, being white, yellow, orange, brown, or red. The habits of Gall Midges are diverse, a few species being true parasites, some are predators, others live in decaying organic matter, but the greater number produce galls on plants. It is not uncommon to find the orange-coloured larvae of certain species browsing on the spores of rust-infected leaves of Antirrhinums, and others devouring the larvae ('scales') of White Fly and of Scale insects. The best-known species is the Hessian Fly, *Mayetiola destructor*, a destructive pest of Wheat. A considerable number of Gall Midges are important pests of horticultural plants, including those that malform fruits (e.g. Pear Midge, *Contarinia pyrivora*); cause the margins of leaves to curl (e.g. Pear Leaf-curling Midge, *Dasyneura pyri*); produce 'blindness' in buds (e.g. Swede Midge, *Contarinia nasturtii*); give rise to stem galls (e.g. Raspberry-Stem-Gall Midge, *Lasioptera rubi*); raise pimple-like galls on leaves and buds (e.g. Chrysanthemum Midge, *Diarthronomyia chrysanthemi*); cause proliferation of buds (e.g. Violet Midge, *Dasyneura affinis*); produce an abnormal swelling of the terminal shoots (e.g. Arabis Midge, *Dasyneura arabis*); and so on. The measures of control against these several Gall Midges differ according to the life-cycle and type of injury inflicted on the host-plants, and are considered under their respective headings.

G. F. W.

**GALL MITES.** These Mites (FAM. *Phytoptidae*, ORDER *Acarina*) are too small to see with the naked eye. They are of considerable importance owing to their plant-feeding habits. Their bodies are white, semi-transparent, segmented, and provided with a varying number of spines or bristles. Two pairs of legs are situated near the head, and the end of the body terminates in a clasper or sucker-like organ that enables the Mite to cling to the plant. While the bristles may aid in locomotion, a Gall Mite may be seen moving about in a manner similar to the Looper caterpillar of a Geometrid Moth, i.e. by bending the body forward so that the legs grip the plant when the anal clasper is drawn up to a position near the legs, after which the body is stretched out and the legs grip elsewhere. A large number of species occur in the British Is., some attacking buds (see **Currant-Gall** and **Nut-Gall Mites**), some the leaves (see **Pear-Leaf Blister** and **Plum-Gall Mites**), and some the fruit (see **Blackberry Mite**), while other species give rise to 'Pimple' and 'Nail' Galls on Maple and Lime leaves.

G. F. W.

**GALL WASPS.** Minute, 4-winged insects belonging to the Hymenopterous family *Cynipidae.* Most species cause gall formations, but some are inquilines, i.e. they live as 'guests' in galls made by other species, and a few are parasitic. Their legless, soft-bodied maggots live within the galls formed by the host-plant as a result of the stimulus induced by their presence. The Oak is the chief host for Cynipids, over 80 per cent. of the known species being confined to this genus, among them those which form such familiar galls as the 'Marble' and the 'Oak Apple'. The life-cycle of many Gall Wasps is very complicated, the sexual generation, in which both males and females occur, gives rise to an entirely different kind of gall from that produced by the asexual generation of females only. The galls vary considerably in shape, size, colour, and consistency, and such terms as button, Currant, and spangle will enable one to visualize the more common galls on Oak leaves. About 7 per cent. of the species of Cynipids are confined to the Rosaceae, including the familiar Robin's Pincushion or Bedeguar Gall (q.v.).

Leaf-galls arising from Gall Wasp infestations appear to have little or no deleterious effect on the general health of the host-plant, and their presence does not warrant any expenditure in labour and spray material.

G. F. W.

*gal′licus -a -um*, French.

**GALLOTANNIN.** A glucoside ($C_{24}H_{28}O_{22}$) occurring in oak-bark, yielding glucose on decomposition.

**GALLS.** Excrescences of various kinds on various parts of plants resulting from the laying of eggs in the tissues of the plant by insects or from the presence of bacteria or fungi. *See* **Gall Midges, Gall Mites, Gall Wasps, Crown Gall, Leafy Gall,** &c.

**GALPHIM′IA** (anagram of Malpighia). FAM. *Malpighiaceae*. A genus of about 15 species of handsome evergreen shrubs or sub-shrubs, natives of Cent. America and Brazil, closely related to Thryallis with which it is sometimes combined. Leaves opposite, small, glandular. Flowers yellow or reddish in terminal racemes; petals toothed. Fruit a 3-parted capsule. Stove conditions are needed and a compost of peat and loam. Cuttings of ripe wood will root in heat in sand under a bell-glass.

**G. brasilien′sis.** Shrub. *l.* ovate or lanceolate, about 1 in. long, glabrous, grey-green beneath. *fl.* yellow, small, in short, loose panicles; *pet.* ovate-lanceolate, obtuse, scarcely twice as long as sep. Winter. Brazil.

**G. glandulo′sa.** Shrub of 3 to 4 ft. *l.* oval-lanceolate, smooth, with 2 large glands at top of stalk. *fl.* yellow; *pet.* oblong. April. Mexico. 1824.

**G. glau′ca.** Shrub. *l.* ovate, obtuse, glabrous, grey-green beneath, with a single tooth each side near base. *fl.* yellow. Mexico. (B.H. 8, 45.) SYN. *G. nitida.*

**G. hirsu′ta.** Shrub to 6 ft. *l.* ovate, nearly 2 in. long, acute, hairy on both sides, stalks short. *fl.* yellow, in rather long panicles. Mexico.

F. G. P.

*Gal′pinii*, in honour of Ernest E. Galpin of Barberton, S. Africa, who collected many plants, *c.* 1890.

**GALTON′IA** (in honour of Francis Galton, 1822–1911, who travelled in and wrote of SW. Africa and advocated the fingerprint method of identification). FAM. *Liliaceae*. A genus of 3 species of beautiful bulbous plants, natives of S. Africa, closely related to Hyacinthus. Leaves few, radical, linear, flat. Flowers white, showy, nodding, in a long, loose raceme; perianth-tube rather broad, rounded at base, lobes as long as or longer than the tube, spreading; stamens 6, shorter than the lobes; scape simple, leafless. Fruit a capsule, seeds few. They are well adapted for growing in clumps in borders, being hardy, and for conservatory decoration. *G. candicans* will thrive outside in a sunny position in well-drained soil,

light and rich. The bulbs may be planted in autumn or spring, the latter being best. They should be buried about 6 or 7 in. deep. Once planted they should not be frequently transplanted. Potted up for the conservatory or the greenhouse they are excellent and may be had in flower either early or late in the year. Bulbs so treated should, however, be returned to the borders.

*Galtonia candicans*

**G. can′dicans.** * Bulb large, round. *l.* lorate-lanceolate, sub-erect, 2½ ft. long. *fl.* pure white, about 1½ in. long, fragrant, drooping, funnel-shaped; raceme about 1 ft. long, about 15-fld.; scape erect, glaucous, about 4 ft. h. Summer. (R.H. 1882, 32.) SYN. *Hyacinthus candicans.*

**G. clava′ta.** *l.* 6 to 8, sessile, lanceolate, glabrous, glaucous green, 2 ft. long. *fl.* scentless; tube clavate, about 1 in. long; lobes ½ in. long, oblong, obtuse; scape 2 ft. h.; raceme lax. Autumn. 1879. (B.M. 6885.)

**G. prin′ceps.** Closely related to *G. candicans* but less attractive, with shorter, broader racemes and smaller greenish *fl.* with spreading segs. (B.M. 8533.) A hybrid has been raised between *G. candicans* and *G. princeps.* It is of no great merit.

**GAMASID MITES.** *See* **Mites.**

*Gambelia′nus -a -um*, in honour of Gamble.

**GAMBOGE.** *See* **Garcinia Cambogia.**

**GAMETES.** The sexual reproductive cells of pollen and ovule.

**GAMETOPHYTE.** The generation of plants bearing the gametes, i.e. the germinated pollen grains and the contents of the embryo sac in the ovules in flowering plants, the prothallus in ferns and their allies.

**GAMMA MOTH.** *See* **Silver-Y Moth.**

**GAMOGY′NE** (*games*, to unite, *gyne*, female; the ovaries are united). FAM. *Araceae*. A genus of about 2 species of small, erect herbs, 10 to 12 in. high, in Malaya. The spathes are attractively coloured and the leaves thick and tapering. Closely related to Piptospatha but with truncate anthers and united ovaries. They need a very moist warm atmosphere and a rich sandy loam mixed with fibrous peat and leaf-mould. Propagation is by division and by seed.

**G. Burbidg'ei.** *l.* narrow. *Spathe* pale red; stigmas greenish-yellow, with neuter organs between male and female portions of the spadix. Borneo.

**G. pul'chra.** *l.* sub-erect, lanceolate, acute, stalk channelled. *Spathe* bright crimson, stigmas red; spadix with neuter organs at base; peduncle reddish-brown. Malaya. 1905. (B.M. 8330.)

F. G. P.

**GAMOLE'PIS** (*games*, to unite, *lepis*, a scale; the involucral bracts being united). FAM. *Compositae*. A genus of about 12 species of shrubs or rarely herbs, natives of S. Africa, differing from Euryops by the absence of a pappus and by the appendaged anthers. *G. Tagetes* requires the treatment of ordinary half-hardy annuals; the other species are cultivated like Othonna.

**G. an'nua.** A synonym of *G. Tagetes*.

**G. euryopoi'des.** Erect, leafy shrub, about 2 ft. h., quite glabrous. *l.* crowded 3-fid to the middle or entire; lobes linear, thickish, 1 to 1½ in. long. *fl.-heads* yellow; peduncle 2 to 4 in. long. Similar to *Euryops abrotanifolius*, but achenes strongly ribbed and furrowed and without pappus. S. Africa. 1863. (B.M. 6249.) Greenhouse.

**G. Tage'tes.** Slender branching annual, 3 to 10 in. h. with wiry flexuous branches. *l.* with 5 to 7 lobes each side, 1 to 1½ in. long; lobes linear, entire or lobulate. *fl.-heads* bright yellow; peduncles 2 to 4 in. long, solitary at ends of branches; free-flowering. SYN. *G. annua*. A useful edging plant.

**gamopetalous,** with petals more or less joined to form a cup or tube.

**gamophyllous,** with perianth pieces more or less joined.

**gamosepalous,** with sepals more or less joined.

*gandaven'sis -is -e,* of Ghent, Belgium.

*ganget'icus -a -um,* of the region of the R. Ganges, India.

*ganit'rus,* from the Malayan name, *ganitri*.

**GANYM'EDE.** Included in **Narcissus**.

**GAR'CIA** (?). FAM. *Euphorbiaceae*. A genus of a single species of tree, native of West Indies, Cent. America, and Colombia. Needs stove conditions. A

**G. nu'tans.** Free *l.* alternate, large, membranous, entire. *fl.* unisexual, with 8 to 12 narrow silky pet. in few-fld., short stalked clusters at tips of branches; stamens numerous; ovary 3-celled.

**GARCIN'IA** (in honour of Laurent Garcin, M.D., 1683–1751, French botanist and traveller in India, author of many botanical memoirs). FAM. *Guttiferae*. A genus of about 180 species of evergreen trees, many of them producing valuable fruit, natives of Trop. Africa, Asia, and Polynesia. Leaves usually leathery. Flowers polygamous, usually solitary at ends of branches; sepals and petals 4 or 5, sepals valvate, petals overlapping. Fruit often delicious and refreshing. Garcinias need stove conditions and a compost of loam and peat. Cuttings of ripe shoots in sand under glass with heat afford means of propagation.

**G. Cambo'gia.** Gamboge. Tree of about 40 ft. with opposite, spreading branches. *l.* elliptic, 5 in. long, tapering to both ends. *fl.* yellow. November. *fr.* about 2 in. across, drooping, on peduncles about 1 in. long. E. Indies. 1822. Resin obtained by notching the stem is the Gamboge of commerce.

**G. cochinchinen'sis.** Shrub. Branches 4-angled. *l.* ovate-oblong, sub-acute. *fl.* whitish, in close clusters on short peduncles; stamens in many bundles. *fr.* a pear-shaped, yellowish-red berry. China, India.

**G. corn'ea.** Tree of about 20 ft. *l.* opposite, oblong. *fl.* pale yellow, scentless. January, February. *Berry* nearly round, as large as a medlar, covered with a dark-purple dry bark. E. Indies. 1823.

**G. Cow'a.** Tree of about 60 ft. *l.* broadly lanceolate. *fl.* yellow. February. *fr.* edible, but not so palatable as in some species. Chittagong. 1822. Yields an inferior Gamboge.

**G. dul'cis.** Tree of 20 ft. *l.* opposite, oblong, slender-pointed, 6 in. or more long, entire, bright glossy green above, paler beneath. *fl.* creamy-white, in clusters; pet. incurved so that fl. is globular; peduncles about as long as fl. February. *fr.* bright yellow, smooth, as large as an apple, pulp yellow, palatable. Moluccas. 1820. (B.M. 3088 as *Xanthochymus dulcis*.)

**G. Gibb'siae.** Tree of about 20 ft. *l.* elliptic with many lateral veins almost at right angles with midrib. *fl.* white, becoming brown, in apparently terminal clusters; stamens many, anthers nearly sessile. Queensland.

**G. Han'buryi.** Tree up to 60 ft. *l.* ovate-oblong, 7 in. long, 4 in. wide. *fl.* axillary; male sometimes in groups of 3 to 6; female much larger. *fr.* spherical, larger than in *G. Morella*. Cochin-China, &c. Produces Gamboge.

**G. Livingston'ei.** Small tree with short branches, glabrous. *l.* oblong, elliptic, blunt, macronulate, leathery, margin undulate, pinnately nerved; stalk very short. *fl.* pale green, fragrant of vanilla, axillary, solitary or in 2- to 5-fld. clusters; sep. 4; pet. 5, rounded; staminodes free, in 2 series. *fr.* as large as a walnut. Zambesia. Fr. eaten by natives.

**G. Mangosta'na.** Mangosteen. Tree of 20 ft. *l.* elliptic-oblong, slender-pointed, 7 to 8 in. long. *fl.* red, like a single rose; pet. 4, roundish, thick at base. *fr.* round, as large as an orange, with a rind of the same thickness, the edible segs. similarly arranged. Malaya. 1789. (B.M. 4847.) The fr. is greatly esteemed.

**G. Morel'la.** Tree to 50 ft. *l.* oblong-elliptic, tapering to both ends. *fl.* yellowish; staminate fl. axillary, in clusters of 3, sep. very small; pistillate fl. much larger, solitary, with about 12 staminodes. *fr.* similar in size and shape to a Morello cherry. SE. Asia. Yields Ceylon Gamboge.

**G. ovalifo'lia.** Tree of medium size. . roundish to lanceolate, 3¼ to 8½ in. long, obtuse. *fl.* white, up to ⅓ in. across, males and females often in 1 cluster but females usually clustered, males in a spike. Summer. *fr.* as large as a walnut, deep green. India. SYN. *Xanthochymus ovalifolius*.

**G. Xanthochy'mus.** Tree to 40 ft. with straight trunk. *l.* linear-oblong or oblong-lanceolate, 9 to 18 in. long, shining. *fl.* white; males ¾ in. across, in axillary clusters of 4 to 8; hermaphrodite ones like males. Summer. *fr.* dark yellow, as large as an apple, globose, pointed. India. (J.R.H.S. 34, f. 103.) SYN. *Xanthochymus pictorius*. Yields a large quantity of indifferent Gamboge.

F. G. P.

**GARDEN BALSAM.** *See* **Dianthera pectoralis.** A

**GARDEN CHAFER.** *See* **Chafers.**

**GARDEN CRESS.** *See* **Cress, Garden,** and **Mustard.**

**GARDEN FRAMES.** *See* **Frames.**

**GARDEN HOUSES.** A garden house has many uses in a garden and may serve as a shady or a sunny sitting place, a place for watching such games as lawn tennis, or from which to bathe, or for storing garden furniture. Unless, however, it is of a pleasing design and in keeping with its surroundings it may be an eyesore and spoil otherwise attractive garden views. Where it is used as a sitting place it is equally desirable to arrange that as attractive a picture as possible is presented to anyone using the house.

When the garden house is very near to, or intimately connected with, the house proper its design and materials of construction should approximate those of the house, while in less formal parts of the garden it may well be of a very simple design, perhaps carried out in sawn oak, with a roof of wooden shingles or thatch. (*See* **Gazebo**.)

J. E. G. W.

**GARDEN PEBBLE MOTH,** *Pionea forficalis*, is widely distributed over the British Is. and frequently a pest of Brassicas, especially Cabbage and Cauliflower. The egg clusters are laid on the leaves in early June, and the yellowish-green, later dark-green, caterpillars feed chiefly on the under-side of the leaves and beneath silken shelters in the hearts of the plants. They pupate in silken cocoons in the surface soil under their food plants. The second brood occurs in August and September, and the damage is then more severe owing to the larvae penetrating deep into the centre of the plants.

Spraying both leaf-surfaces of young plants with D.D.T. (q.v.) will give satisfactory control of this pest, but dusting with nicotine powder is essential to control the second brood of caterpillars as they are protected from liquid sprays in the hearts of the plants. It is of great importance to take measures against the first brood to lessen injury by the second generation of caterpillars.

G. F. W.

## GARDEN SWIFT MOTH. *See* **Swift Moths.**

## GARDENER.
In a broad sense, anyone who cultivates a garden. In the restricted sense, one who has been trained in horticulture for a number of years, passing through the different grades of student or apprentice, journeyman, and foreman. Such a man or woman must possess plenty of tact, ability to manage a staff, be well educated, and above all, be thoroughly practical with a sufficient knowledge of the scientific principles on which horticultural practice is based to appreciate and apply the results of horticultural experiment and research.

## GARDENER'S GARTERS. *See* **Phalaris arundinacea variegata.**

## GARDE′NIA
(in honour of Dr. Alexander Garden, 1730–91, Charlestown, Carolina, correspondent of Linnaeus). FAM. *Rubiaceae*. A genus of about 60 species of evergreen shrubs, rarely trees, natives of Trop. Asia and Trop. and S. Africa. Closely related to Randia in which the ovary is 2-celled, whereas in Gardenia it is 1-celled. Leaves opposite or rarely in whorls. Flowers white, yellow, or violet, usually solitary, terminal or axillary, usually fragrant; corolla salver- or funnel-shaped, its tube much longer than the calyx, the segments of the limb twisted in bud, afterwards spreading. *G. jasminoides*, especially in its double forms, is grown for its pure white, strongly fragrant flowers for cutting, and at one time was much more valued than at present as a decorative stove shrub although its habit of producing its flowers in succession renders it less striking than it would be if they came more together. Old plants are far less satisfactory than young ones and they are best thrown away after 2 or 3 years. Propagation is readily effected by strong, healthy cuttings taken preferably with a heel from the points of side shoots when half- or fully ripened. Cuttings may be made at any time when suitable growths are to be found, but those taken in January are best since the resulting plants have a long period of growth before flowering in the succeeding winter. They should be placed singly in small pots of sandy peat unless large numbers have to be dealt with when several may be put into a larger pot. The pots should be plunged in bottom heat of about 75° F. in a close frame in the propagating house and allowed to remain there until the cuttings are rooted.

Gardenias are not difficult to grow provided they have plenty of heat and moisture while growing and are kept free from insects. The temperature from March to September should be 60 to 85° F., but during winter 50 to 60° F. with less moisture will suffice. These conditions encourage the growth of strong, healthy shoots which, after ripening, and the resting of the plants, will produce large numbers of flowers from the points. The best soil consists of equal parts of fibrous loam, sandy peat, and well-rotted dung. When the young plants are rooted they should be hardened from the frame to the open house and potted on by liberal shifts as becomes necessary, using a lumpy compost. Where bottom heat is not available a hotbed of fermenting material may be made in the house for plunging the pots, the house being heated by pipes in the ordinary way, but the bed must not be allowed to become too hot. Almost any amount of water may be applied to the roots in summer and they should be freely syringed morning and evening, except when the plants are in flower. Very large plants may be grown under this treatment in one season and if a succession of cuttings is taken so as to have plants in different stages of growth the supply of flowers may be prolonged. When the season's growth is completed a lower temperature and more air should be given. Gardenias may be grown planted out in beds over hot-water pipes, but to grow them in large pots gives greater freedom and enables the plants to be moved for the destruction of insects and for the seasonal rest. Gardenias are even more subject to attacks by parasites than are most plants in the warm house. Mealy Bugs, Green Flies, and Red-spider Mites are particularly liable to attack them and should be watched for and dealt with immediately.

The chief fungus attack is Stem Canker, caused by the fungus *Phomopsis gardeniae*. Cuttings can be affected by swollen cankers at soil-level, but older plants are more usually attacked and the cankers are then present on the stems up to a foot above ground-level. The canker fungus almost always enters through snags left after cutting the flowers. There is no reason to fear the disease, but if it occurs, clean cuttings should be obtained from an uninfected stock and kept apart from the old plants which should be sprayed with Bordeaux mixture the infected parts being continually cut out.

(D. E. G.)

**G. amoe′na.** Spiny shrub of 3 to 5 ft. *l.* oval, acute, glabrous; stalk short; spines axillary, short, straight. *fl.* white; lobes partly purple outside, solitary, almost terminal, sessile; tube greenish, long, terete. June. China. (B.M. 1904.) Stove.

**G. citriodo′ra.** A synonym of *Mitriostigma axillare*.

**G. Devonia′na.** Unarmed shrub. *l.* oblong, slender-pointed, about 5 in. long, undulate, downy at first, especially beneath; stalk short. *fl.* white, becoming cream, 5 in. across; segs. obtuse, revolute, oblique; tube slender, green, with a bell-shaped throat. Sierra Leone. 1846. (B.R. 32, 63.) Stove.

**G. flo′rida.** A synonym of *G. jasminoides*.

**G. globo′sa.** Much-branched unarmed shrub. *l.* broadly lanceolate, 2 to 4 in. long, slender-pointed, glabrous; stalk short. *fl.* white, 1½ in. across, fragrant, solitary at ends of branches; cor. tube bell-shaped, limb deeply 5-lobed, lobes spreading acute, throat hairy. June. Natal. 1852. (B.M. 4791.) Greenhouse.

**G. grandiflo′ra.** Unarmed shrub or tree. *l.* lanceolate, shining. *fl.* white, large, solitary, sessile; cal. segs. reflexed, falcate; cor. salver-shaped; segs. 6. *fr.* yellow, glabrous. Cochin-China. Greenhouse.

**G. jasminoi′des.** Unarmed shrub, erect, or rooting from stem, 1 to 6 ft. h. *l.* lanceolate to elliptic, narrowed to both ends. *fl.* white, salver-shaped, solitary, almost terminal. June to August or later. China, Japan. 1754. Stove. A variable plant. (B.M. 3349 as *G. florida*; B.M. 1842 as *G. radicans*, branches spreading.) var. **flo′rida,** *fl.* double (B.M. 2627); **Fortunia′na,** *l.* bright shining green, *fl.* larger than in type. China (B.R. 32, 43); **ma′jor,** *fl.* large but smaller than in var. *florida*, very free-flowering; **variega′ta,** *l.* margined white (known in both the erect and spreading forms); **Veitchia′na,** winter-flowering.

**G. nit′ida.** Shrub of about 3 ft. *l.* opposite or ternate, oblong-lanceolate, wavy. *fl.* white, terminal, solitary; cal. 7-parted; cor. tube narrow, segs. 7, reflexed. October, November. Sierra Leone. 1844. (B.M. 4343.) Stove.

**G. radi′cans.** A form of *G. jasminoides*.

**G. Rothman′nia.** Shrub of 10 ft. *l.* oblong, stipules awl-shaped. *fl.* yellow and purple, sep. awl-shaped, rounded; tube smooth, dilated, short. July. S. Africa. 1774. (B.M. 690.) Greenhouse.

**G. spatulifo′lia.** Tree of 15 to 18 ft., branches glabrous. *l.* obovate-spatulate, 1½ to 3½ in. long, blunt. *fl.* pale yellow, becoming deep yellow, cor. tube 2 to 3 in. long, lobes 6 or 7, rarely 9, 1 to 2 in. long, glabrous. Trop. S. Africa. Related to *G. Thunbergia*. Stove.

**G. Stanleya′na.** A synonym of *Randia maculata*.

**G. Thunber′gia.** Unarmed shrub of 4 to 7 ft. *l.* elliptic, acute, glabrous, opposite or in whorls of 4 or 5. *fl.* white, large, solitary, terminal; cor. segs. 8. January to March. S. Africa. (B.M. 1004.) Greenhouse.

*gardeniiflo′rus* -a -um, Gardenia-flowered.

*Gard′neri, Gardneria′nus* -a -um, in honour of the Hon. Edward Gardner, political resident in Nepal, *c.* 1817, correspondent of Calcutta Botanic Garden; or of G. Gardner, 1812–49, Scotch traveller in Brazil, and superintendent, Botanic Garden, Peradeniya.

**GARDO'QUIA** (in honour of Don Diego Gardoqui, Minister of Finance under Charles IV of Spain, who favoured the expedition of Ruiz and Pavon to S. America and promoted the publication of a Flora of Peru). FAM. *Labiatae*. A genus of about 30 species of evergreen shrubs or sub-shrubs all from S. America, allied to Melissa and Calamintha. Leaves opposite; calyx 13-nerved, 5-toothed; corolla tubular or slenderly funnel-shaped, with the upper lip slightly 2-lobed, lower one more deeply 3-lobed; stamens 4. Cool greenhouse plants which thrive in a compost of peat, loam, and sand, and are easily propagated by cuttings of half-ripened wood. Rare in cultivation.

**G. Gillies'ii.** Very leafy, sub-shrubby plant, usually under 1 ft. *l.* linear-oblong to linear-obovate, entire, apex rounded; ⅓ to ½ in. long, ¹⁄₁₀ in. wide. *fl.* axillary, solitary, forming leafy racemes; cor. ⅝ in. long, funnel-shaped, lilac; limb ¼ in. across, oblique. June to September. Chile, near Valparaiso. 1820. (B.R. 1812.)

**G. Hook'eri.** A synonym of *Calamintha coccinea*.

*Gardoquia multiflora*

**G. multiflo'ra.** Erect, glabrous shrub, 1 to 2 ft. h. *l.* ovate, 1 to 2 in. long, obscurely toothed, minutely dotted beneath; stalk ¼ in. long, lemon-scented when bruised. *fl.* in pendulous, axillary, stalked clusters of 3 to 5, collectively forming handsome leafy panicles 4 to 6 in. long; cor. tubular, purplish-red, about 1 in. long, widening upwards to a limb ½ in. across; anthers exposed, lilac. Summer. Chile. 1820. (B.M. 3772.)

W. J. B.

***gargan'icus -a -um,*** of Mt. Gargano, S. Italy.

**GARLAND FLOWER.** A common name for Hedychium, used also for *Daphne Cneorum*.

**GARLIC** (*Allium sativum*). Wild perhaps only in the Kirghiz Desert of Cent. Asia, garlic has been cultivated in countries bordering the Mediterranean from remote antiquity and is still used in those countries to a much greater extent than here. It has certainly been grown here since the sixteenth century, and probably long before, but in the present day most people find it sufficient to rub the dish, intended to contain the material it is desired to flavour, with a 'clove of garlic', that is, with one of the small divisions of the Garlic bulb. Its flavour is

too pungent to our taste to warrant more. The quantity called for is therefore very small, but at the same time it should be included in the herb-garden. The 'cloves' should be planted at the end of February on well-dug ground raked to a fine tilth, using a dibber and just covering the bulbs, which should be 9 in. apart in the rows and a foot between the rows. A rather light soil is best. Keep clean of weeds and lift the crop when the foliage dies down in late summer, drying thoroughly in the sun. When dry, remove the dead leaves and store the bulbs in a cool shed in the same way as shallots. A few bulbs may be planted in autumn if a supply of fresh garlic is desired early in the year.

*Garlic bulbs*

**GARLIC PEAR.** *See* **Crataeva gynandra.**

**GARNET BERRY.** *See* **Ribes rubrum.**

***garrexia'nus -a -um,*** of Garessio, Liguria, Italy.

**GAR'RYA** (in honour of Nicholas Garry, of the Hudson's Bay Company, who helped David Douglas on his plant-collecting expeditions). FAM. *Garryaceae*. For characters of this, the only genus in the family, *see* **Garryaceae**. Only 1 species, *G. elliptica*, and the hybrid *G.* × *Thuretii*, can be regarded as really hardy in our gardens, and they are best in most places against a south or west wall, but a sunny dry bank with a slope to south or west with protection on north and east suits them well in many places. The chief value of these shrubs lies in their silvery-grey catkins, the flowers themselves having little beauty. *G. elliptica* have pendent male catkins about 6 in. long, or longer, in mild districts, from November to February; the female catkins are rarely over 3 in. long, often less. As these shrubs transplant badly they should be grown in pots until put into their permanent places. They should never be cut back in summer. The best time is immediately they have done flowering and before new growth begins, as they are then given the full growing season in which to make and mature their wood. Shorten some of the breast-wood and remove the worn-out growths altogether, to encourage and make room for young, vigorous shoots. When grown in bush form keep the middle of the plants well thinned, so that the air can pass freely amongst the branches, for it is at the points of the previous season's matured shoots that the catkins are borne during winter.

Propagation is by seed, or better (since the sex of the shrub is known) by cuttings of half-woody shoots in sandy loam in gentle heat in August.

KEY

1. Lvs. 5 or 6 in. long
1. Lvs. up to 4 in. long ................................ **G. macrophylla**
2. Mature lvs. smooth, tapering at ends ........................ 2
2. Mature lvs. smooth, tapering at ends ........ **G. Fremontii**
2. Mature lvs. hairy beneath ................................ 3
3. Lvs. dark green above, margin wavy, catkins simple .................................. **G. elliptica**
3. Lvs. glossy green above, male catkins branched **G. Fadyenii**

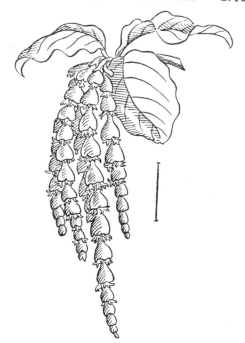

*Garrya elliptica*

**G. ellip′tica.** Shrub of 6 to 12 ft. or more, bushy, quick-growing, young shoots downy. *l.* oval to roundish, 1½ to 3 in. long, rounded at both ends, dark green above, grey-woolly beneath, wavy at margin. *Male catkins* 3 to 6 in. (to 12 in.), *female* 1½ to 3 in. long, silver-grey, pendent, clustered near ends of shoots. November to February. California, Oregon. 1828. (B.R. 1686; B.M. n.s. 220.)

**G. Fadyen′ii.** Shrub to 15 ft. *l.* elliptic to oblong, mucronate, glossy above, more or less hairy beneath, 2 to 4 in. long. *Male catkins* branched, pendent; *female* simple. Spring. Jamaica, Cuba. Tender. (H.I.P. 333.)

**G. flaves′cens.** Shrub to 8 ft. *l.* elliptic, 1 to 2 in. long, silky downy beneath. *Catkins* dense, about 1 in. long. SW. America.

**G. Fremon′tii.** Shrub to 13 ft. *l.* leathery, obovate to oval, tapering at both ends, dark glossy green, with appressed hairs on both surfaces at first. *Catkins* clustered, 2 to 4 in. long, grey-woolly. April, May. California. Oregon. 1842. (G.C. 35 (1904), 44.) Fairly hardy in some places.

**G. macrophyl′la.** Shrub or small tree to 12 ft., robust; young wood grey-downy. *l.* oblong, 5 to 6 in. long, dark glossy green, smooth above, grey-downy beneath. *Male catkins* 1 to 3 in. long. May, June. Mexico. 1846. The largest leaved species. Needs a wall.

**G.×Thuret′ii.** A hybrid between *G. elliptica* ♂ and *G. Fadyenii* ♀, intermediate between the parents. 1862. (R.H. 1879, 154.)

**G. Wright′ii.** Shrub to 10 ft. *l.* elliptic or elliptic-ovate, 1 to 2 in. long, acute or mucronate, glabrous or nearly so beneath. *Catkins* slender, about 2 in. long. *fr.* glabrous, nearly sessile. SW. America.

**GARRYA′CEAE.** Dicotyledons. A family of 1 genus (Garrya) of about 15 species of evergreen trees and shrubs, natives of W. United States and Mexico, and 1 (*G. Fadyeni*) in the W. Indies. Leaves opposite, stalked, entire, without stipules. Flowers dioecious, without petals, in axillary or terminal catkins, staminate flowers with 4 stamens; pistillate without sepals, ovary 1-celled, with 2 ovules and 2 styles. Fruit a round, rather dry, 2-seeded berry.

**GARU′GA** (native E. Indian name). Fam. *Burseraceae*. A genus of about 10 species of tropical trees, natives of Asia, America, and Australia (1). Leaves opposite, hairy, unequally pinnate; leaflets almost sessile, toothed. Flowers yellowish, large, in panicles. Fruit a drupe with up to 5 stones. For cultivation see **Boswellia**.

**G. pinna′ta.** Deciduous tree to 60 ft. *l.* about 1 ft. long, hairy; lflets. oblong-lanceolate, bluntly toothed. *fl.* small, in a very large panicle. *Drupe* black, about as large as a gooseberry, fleshy, with rough taste. E. Indies. 1808. Fr. pickled or sometimes eaten raw. Wood soft.

F. G. P.

**GARUL′EUM** (?) Fam. *Compositae*. A genus of 3 species of sub-shrubs, natives of S. Africa with alternate, pinnatifid leaves, the lobes toothed. Flower-heads monoecious, rayed, terminal; ray-florets blue, strap-shaped; disk-florets yellow, tubular; receptacle convex, naked; involucral bracts in 2 series. For cultivation of these greenhouse plants see **Lagenophora**, a nearly related genus.

**G. visco′sum.** Minutely velvety sub-shrub 1 to 2 ft. h. *l.* deeply pinnately cleft, 1 to 1½ in. long, ¾ in. wide. *fl.-heads* stalked, rays sky-blue, stalks glandular and downy. 1774. Syn. *G. pinnatifidum*.

A→

**GAS-LIME.** At one time in the process of purifying coal-gas before it was distributed to the public, it was passed through lime, the lime being largely converted into calcium sulphate, and retaining various poisonous substances. The resulting material was known as gas-lime and though, since the lime was now in the form of sulphate and was thus of little value as a substitute for slaked or hydrated lime or chalk, it had a great reputation as an insecticide, being used (after exposure to air to ensure the oxidizing of the various deleterious substances) at the rate of 30 or 40 bushels to the acre for this purpose, and as a specific against Club-root of Brassicas. Lime is rarely used for the purifying of gas nowadays and gas-lime is, therefore, rarely available.

A→

*Gasparrin′ii,* in honour of Guglielmo Gasparrini, 1804–66, Professor of Botany and Director Botanic Garden, Naples.

**GASTE′RIA** (*gaster*, belly; referring to the swollen base of the flower tube). Fam. *Liliaceae*. A genus of about 40 species, closely allied to Aloe, distinct by the form of the flowers. The plants are generally stemless; the leaves, much thickened or succulent, are normally arranged in 2 ranks, but occasionally in a rosette. The inflorescence is simple or branched, 2 to 3 ft. long, with the small flowers hanging some distance apart, not crowded into spikes; the flowers are about 1 to 2 in. long, the base of the curved tube swollen, the limb not spreading. The Gasterias are all natives of S. Africa. For cultivation see **Aloe**.

**G. acinacifo′lia.** *l.* in 2 ranks, 14 in. long, 2 in. wide, 3-edged, dark green with scattered, pale dots. *fl.* orange, not much inflated, long-stalked. *infl.* up to 4 ft., branched. (B.M. 2369 and S.-D. 29. 11, as *Aloe acinacifolia*.)

**G. carina′ta.** *l.* in a rosette, spreading, 5 to 6 in. long, 2 in. wide, thick, grooved, acute, dull green with coarse white tubercles. *fl.* small, much swollen. *infl.* 2 to 3 ft., branched. (B.M. 1331 and S.-D. 29. 29, as *Aloe carinata*.)

**G. Ling′ua.** *l.* in 2 ranks 8 to 10 in. long, 2 in. wide, concave, 2-edged, blunt, green banded with paler dots. *fl.* scarlet. *infl.* 3 ft. h., unbranched. (B.M. 1322 and S.-D. 29. 33, as *Aloe Lingua*.) Syn. *G. disticha*.

**G. macula'ta.** *l.* in 2 ranks, twisted spirally, 6 in. long, 2 in. or less wide, blunt, margin rough, glossy dark green with large, pale, confluent blotches. *fl.* scarlet. *infl.* 3 to 4 ft. h., branched. (B.M. 765 and S.-D. 29. 1, as *Aloe maculata.*)

**G. nig'ricans.** *l.* in 2 ranks, oblong, abruptly mucronate, 5 to 8 in. long, 2 in. wide, dark green or purple with bands of pale-green blotches. *fl.* pinkish. *infl.* 3 to 4 ft., branched. (S.-D. 29. 7, as *Aloe nigricans.*)

**G. planifo'lia.** *l.* in 2 ranks, slender, 6 to 10 in. long, ¾ in. wide, abruptly mucronate, edge roughened, green with white blotches, margin pink. *fl.* suddenly inflated. *infl.* 6 ft. h., unbranched.

**G. pul'chra.** *l.* in an open spiral, 8 in. long, 1 in. wide, acute, margin slightly roughened, glossy dark green with confluent blotches. *fl.* scarlet. *infl.* 3 ft. h., branched. (S.-D. 29. 2, as *Aloe pulchra.*)

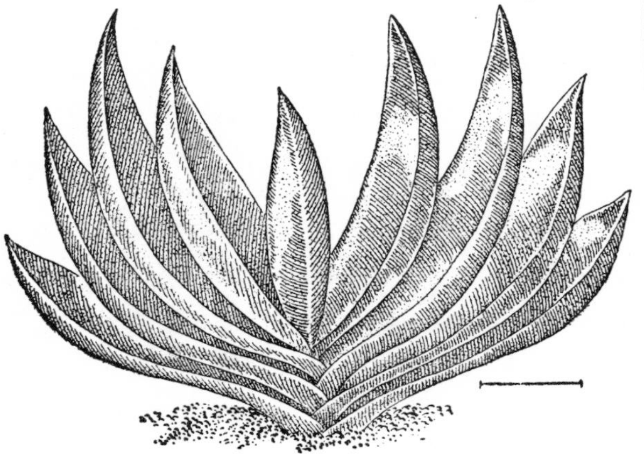

*Gasteria verrucosa*

**G. verruco'sa.** Tufted. *l.* in 2 ranks, 6 in. long, ½ in. wide, concave, 3-sided, dull grey, the surface rough with crowded white tubercles. *fl.* small. *infl.* 2 ft. h., unbranched. (B.M. 837 and S.-D. 29. 25, as *Aloe verrucosa.*) There are several varieties and hybrids of this species.

V. H.

**GASTEROMYCE'TES.** One of the 2 sub-orders of the class of fungi known as Basidiomycetes. In the Gasteromycetes the spore-bearing surface or hymenium (q.v.) remains entirely enclosed inside a membrane or peridium until the spores are mature.

D. E. G.

***Gas'toni,*** in honour of Pastor P. Gaston who collected *Lithospermum Gastoni* in 1839 in the Pyrenees.

**GASTON'IA.** *See* **Polyscias** and **Trevesia.**

**GASTROCHIL'US** (*gaster*, belly, *cheilos*, lip; in reference to the swollen lip). FAM. *Zingiberaceae.* A genus of 13 perennial herbs, natives of India and the E. Indies, with thickened, usually creeping, rhizomes, and tuberous roots. Leaves usually large, lanceolate or oblong with a slender point. Allied to Kaempferia but the connective of the anther without appendages, the filament short, and the lip usually concave. Stove conditions are required, a sandy-loam compost, good drainage, and ample water when growing. Propagated by division as new growth begins.

**A**

KEY

| | |
|---|---|
| 1. *Lvs.* 1 *or* 2 *from each branch of creeping rhizome* | G. alboluteus |
| 1. *Lvs. many* | 2 |
| 2. *Fl. in an exserted terminal spike* | G. pulcherrimus |
| 2. *Fl. in a short spike included in a sheath, stemless* | 3 |
| 3. *Lvs. glabrous beneath, cordate at base* | G. longiflorus |
| 3. *Lvs. downy beneath* | G. Curtisii |

**G. albolu'teus.** Slender, stemless herb about 8 in. h. with stalked l. in pairs. *l.* blade oblong, about 4 in. long, dark green with white midrib above, pale green beneath. *fl.* 2 or 3 from middle of foliage; cor. tube white, 1½ in. long, lobes white, ½ in. long; lip elliptic ¾ in. long, flat, white with yellow middle line and purple veins. July. Andaman Is. 1894.

**G. Curtis'ii.** *rhiz.* fleshy. Stemless. *l.* usually 4; l.-stalk about 5 in. long; sheath red; blade about 10 in. long, oblong, smooth, shining green above, downy beneath. *fl.* many in a short spike, bracts white; cor. white, its tube over 2 in. long, dilated at throat, lobes 1 in. long, lanceolate; lip oblong, yellow with red spots at sides. Malaya. 1894. (B.M. 7363.)

**G. Jenkins'ii.** A variety of *G. longiflorus.*

**G. longiflo'rus.** Stemless with many fleshy roots. *l.* 4 or 5; l.-stalk about 4 in. long; blade oblong, shortly pointed, about 12 in. long, green above, purple beneath. *fl.* on many 1- or 2-fld. spikes from base; bracts membranous; cor. white, tube up to 2½ in. long, slender, often shorter, lobes 1 in. long; lip half as long, concave, rose tinted. July. India, Assam, Burma. 1843. var. **Jenkins'ii,** *fl.* larger, lip whiter, tipped red. (B.M. 4010 as *G. Jenkinsii.*)

**G. pulcher'rimus.** Stem up to 15 in. h. *rhiz.* fleshy, creeping. *l.* 4 or 5, shortly stalked, oblong, about 6 in. long, pale green beneath. *fl.* many in terminal spikes; cor. white, tube about ¾ in. long, lobes ½ in. long; lip obovate, 1 in. long, red. August. Burma. 1828. (B.M. 3930.)

**GASTROLOB'IUM** (*gaster*, belly, *lobus*, a pod; in reference to the inflated pods). FAM. *Leguminosae.* A genus of about 36 species of evergreen shrubs confined to W. Australia. Leaves mostly opposite or in threes or fours, rarely scattered, simple; stipules short, bristle-like or prickle-like. Flowers in terminal and axillary racemes, papilionaceous; standard orange or yellow; keel mostly purplish-red. Pod short, ovoid or nearly globular. Greenhouse shrubs requiring the same treatment as Australian Acacias.

KEY

| | |
|---|---|
| 1. *Lvs. 3-lobed, lobes spine-tipped* | G. trilobum |
| 1. *Lvs. not lobed* | 2 |
| 2. *Lvs. broad* | 3 |
| 2. *Lvs. narrow or wedge-shaped, emarginate* | 4 |
| 3. *Lvs. undulate* | G. villosum |
| 3. *Lvs. ovate-lanceolate-elliptic, spine-pointed* | G. calycinum |
| 4. *Lvs. flat, margins slightly recurved, about ½ in. long. Racemes cylindrical* | G. velutinum |
| 4. *Infl. almost umbellate* | G. bilobum |

**G. bilo'bum.** Shrub 3 to 8 ft., shoots angular, usually downy. *l.* in threes or fours at each joint, obovate or obcordate, 2-lobed at the apex, minutely mucronate, ¾ to 1¾ in. long, often minutely downy beneath. *fl.* in a terminal head, 1 to 1½ in. long, scarcely so wide, standard ½ in. wide, 2-lobed, yellow like the wings; keel dark red-purple. March to May. W. Australia. 1803. (B.M. 2212.)

**G. calyci'num.** Erect, quite glabrous shrub. *l.* in pairs or threes, ovate-lanceolate to lanceolate or oblong-oval, spine-tipped, 1 to 2 in. long, ¼ to ¾ in. wide, stiff, leathery. *fl.* few in pairs or threes forming racemes up to 4 in. long; standard ¾ in. across, orange; keel purple-red. W. Australia. Fl. large for the genus.

**G. retu'sum.** A synonym of *Oxylobium virgatum.*

**G. trilo'bum.** Quite glabrous, much-branched shrub, shoots angular. *l.* ¾ to 1 in. long, very rigid, rhomboidal to ovate but deeply triangularly lobed; sometimes short and broad, always spine-tipped, often glaucous. *fl.* few in loose, short, axillary racemes ¾ to 1 in. long; standard ⅓ in. long, orange-yellow, keel purple-red. W. Australia.

**G. veluti'num.** Shrub 3 to 4 ft., shoots angular, minutely downy. *l.* in threes or fours, obovate to obcordate or narrowly cuneate, mostly notched at end, ½ to ¾ in. long, downy beneath, scarcely stalked. *fl.* in terminal leafy panicles 2 to 5 in. long; stalk and cal. softly downy; standard ½ in. across, orange-red, keel red-purple. April. W. Australia.

**G. villo'sum.** Shrub 2 to 4 ft., with erect stems softly downy and hairy. *l.* opposite, oblong-ovate, ¾ to 2 in. long, margins wavy, base truncate or cordate. *fl.* in terminal and axillary racemes 4 to 6 in. long, 1½ in. wide; standards ½ in. wide, 2-lobed, orange-red, wings and keel purplish-red. May. W. Australia. (B.R. 33, 45.)

W. J. B.

**GASTRONE'MA.** Included in **Cyrtanthus.**

**GASTROPACH'A quercifo'lia.** *See* **Lappet Moth.**

**GATES.** Care and attention to the designing of garden gates and gateways will be well repaid. They should be made of a size and importance in scale with their surroundings. Their width should approximate that of the drive or walk leading to and from the gate. For wheeled traffic they may be from 8 to 12 ft. wide, and for foot traffic 3 to 6 ft.

If privacy is not necessary the wrought-iron gate is attractive, but where it is desirable to shut out the view beyond, a well-built gate of seasoned oak is to be recommended. For making a satisfactory job, gate-posts should be set in concrete and, if of wood, they should be treated with preservative such as creosote or solignum before being set in the ground. The preservative should extend several inches above the ground-level.

J. E. G. W.

***Gates'ii,*** in honour of Rev. F. S. Gates of the American Mission in Armenia, *c.* 1888.

**GAUDICHAUD'IA** (in honour of Charles Gaudichaud-Beaupré, naturalist, on Freycinet's voyage round the world, 1817–20). FAM. *Malpighiaceae.* A genus of about 12 species of mostly twining shrubs, natives of Mexico and adjacent S. America. Leaves opposite, entire. Flowers yellow, of 2 forms, in one petals perigynous, roundish, spreading; in the other absent or almost so. For cultivation *see* **Galphimia.**

**G. cynanchoi'des.** About 10 ft. h. *l.* stalked. *fl.* yellow, crowded in terminal or axillary racemes. Mexico. 1824.

F. G. P.

***Gaudin'ii,*** in honour of J. Fr. G. Ph. Gaudin, 1766–1833, student of the Swiss flora.

**GAULTHER'IA** (in honour of Dr. Gaultier who, about the middle of the 18th century, was well known as a physician and botanist in Quebec). FAM. *Ericaceae.* A genus of evergreen shrubs having alternate or rarely opposite leaves, 5- (rarely 4-)merous, campanulate or urceolate flowers, with 10 stamens. The fruit is a loculicidal capsule which is commonly, but not invariably, enclosed by and coalescent with the calyx which is enlarged and fleshy. In the following descriptions the term 'fruit' is applied to the berry-like structure formed by capsule and accrescent calyx or, in those species in which the calyx remains dry and unaltered, to the capsule alone. Gaultheria resembles Pernettya, Chiogenes, and Vaccinium, but is distinguished from them by the essentially capsular nature of the fruit; in the related genera the fruit is a berry.

Gaultherias vary from low and compact to large shrubs, and are grown for the attractiveness of their evergreen foliage and the beauty of their flowers and fruit. They thrive in lime-free, friable, humus soil and half-shade, and are easily propagated by seed, cuttings, layers, and, when available, offsets. The hardy species in cultivation are natives of N. America, the Magellan region, Himalaya, E. Asia, Australia, Tasmania, and New Zealand.

KEY.

| | | |
|---|---|---|
| 1. | *Cal. unchanged in fruit* | 2 |
| 1. | *Cal. fleshy in fruit* | 4 |
| 2. | *Lvs. opposite* | G. oppositifolia |
| 2. | *Lvs. alternate* | 3 |
| 3. | *Fl. in racemes* | G. rupestris |
| 3. | *Fl. solitary* | G. Wardii |
| 4. | *Fl. campanulate* | 5 |
| 4. | *Fl. urceolate* | 13 |
| 5. | *Fl. in racemes* | G. yunnanensis |
| 5. | *Fl. solitary* | 6 |
| 6. | *Lvs. under* 1 *in. long* | 7 |
| 6. | *Lvs.* 2 *to* 7 *in. long* | G. codonantha |
| 7. | *Lvs. thin and soft* | 8 |
| 7. | *Lvs. firm and leathery* | 9 |
| 8. | *Cal. only slightly shorter than cor.* | G. humifusa |
| 8. | *Cal. half as long as cor.* | G. ovatifolia |
| 9. | *Leaf surfaces hairy* | G. microphylla |
| 9. | *Leaf surfaces smooth or nearly so* | 10 |
| 10. | *Shrub up to* 1 *ft. h. with rigid stems* | G. depressa |
| 10. | *Shrubs of* 4 *to* 6 *in. h. with flexible stems* | 11 |
| 11. | *Lvs. under* ½ *in. long* | G. thymifolia |
| 11. | *Lvs.* ½ *in. or more long* | 12 |
| 12. | *Fr. fig-shaped* | G. sinensis |
| 12. | *Fr. broadly oval* | G. trichophylla |
| 13. | *Parts of fl. in* 4*'s* | G. tetramera |
| 13. | *Parts of fl. in* 5*'s* | 14 |
| 14. | *Fl. in racemes* | 15 |
| 14. | *Fl. solitary* | 24 |
| 15. | *Fr. blue or blue-black* | 16 |
| 15. | *Fr. white or pink* | 21 |
| 16. | *Shrubs not more than* 3 *ft. h.* | 17 |
| 16. | *Shrubs more than* 3 *ft. h.* | 18 |
| 17. | *Procumbent shrub. Fr. lapis-lazuli blue* | G. Veitchiana |
| 17. | *Low shrub with erect stems. Fr. blue-black* | G. pyrolifolia |
| 18. | *Lvs. cordate or rounded at base* | 19 |
| 18. | *Lvs. tapering to base* | 20 |
| 19. | *Lvs. cordate. Fr. purple-black* | G. Shallon |
| 19. | *Lvs. rounded at base. Fr. lapis-lazuli blue* | G. Hookeri |
| 20. | *Rachis, pedicels, and cal. waxy white, young shoots bristly and round. Fr. blue* | G. Forrestii |
| 20. | *Rachis, &c., of no striking colour, young shoots smooth and angular. Fr. blue* | G. fragrantissima |
| 21. | *Lvs. oval to obovate* | 22 |
| 21. | *Lvs. narrow or lanceolate* | 23 |
| 22. | *Ovary silky-downy. Fr. white* | G. cuneata |
| 22. | *Ovary smooth. Fr. white or pinkish* | G. Miqueliana |
| 23. | *Shrub of* 4 *to* 6 *in. h. with wiry stems. Fr. white or pink* | G. Merrilliana |
| 23. | *Erect shrub,* 2 *ft. or more h. Lvs. lanceolate. Fr. white* | G. hispida |
| 24. | *Alternate lvs. arranged normally* | 25 |
| 24. | *Alternate lvs. arranged unusually* | 26 |
| 25. | *Fr. hairy* | G. adenothrix |
| 25. | *Fr. smooth* | G. antipoda |
| 26. | *Lvs. in* 2 *opposite rows* | G. nummularioides |
| 26. | *Lvs. clustered at ends of shoots* | G. procumbens |

**G. aden'othrix.** Dwarf, procumbent shrub with zigzag branches. *l.* ovate to oval, pointed or blunt, slightly serrate towards tip, bristly at margin, leathery, upper surface reticulate, ½ to 1¼ in. long, ¼ to ⅞ in. wide. *fl.* solitary, on pendent stalks from upper l.-axils; cor. broadly ovoid-urceolate, white, $\frac{5}{16}$ in. long, ¼ in. across mouth; cal. fleshy in fr., lobes acute, hairy, red or green. May. *fr.* globose, bright red, hairy, ¼ in. wide. Japan. 1915. (N.F.S. 10, 204.) SYN. *Diplycosia adenothrix.*

**G. antarc'tica.** A synonym of *G. microphylla.* **A**

**G. antip'oda.** Prostrate or upright shrub from a few in. to 4 ft. or more h. *l.* rounded to obovate and oblong-lanceolate, ⅓ to ⅜ in. long, acute or obtuse, serrate, thick and leathery; blades smooth, petioles hairy. *fl.* solitary from upper l.-axils; cor. white, cylindrical-urceolate, $\frac{1}{10}$ to ⅛ in. long; cal. fleshy in fr., rarely unchanged, lobes oblong-ovate, acute. June, July. *fr.* red or white, globose, about ½ in. across. New Zealand, N. and S. Islands. 1820. SYN. *G. epiphyta, G. erecta.*

**G. codonan'tha.** Straggling bush to 8 ft., branches densely bristly hairy. *l.* 2-ranked, ovate to lanceolate, 2 to 7 in. long, ¾ to 6 in. wide, acute, sparsely to irregularly toothed, in older l. smooth above, densely bristly hairy beneath. *fl.* cream in bud, greenish-white when expanded, sometimes tinged red without, ⅔ to ¾ in. across, in 4- to 7-fld. axillary corymbose racemes. November. *fr.* deep purple-black, flattish-globose, nearly ¾ in. across. Assam. 1928. (B.M. 9456.) Temperate house.

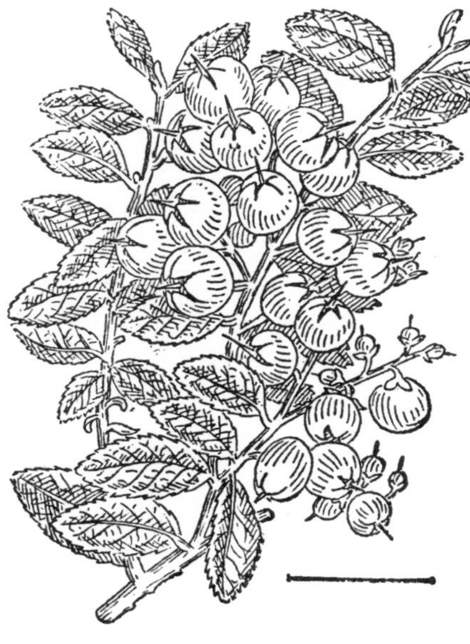

*Gaultheria cuneata*

**G. cunea'ta.** Fairly compact, tufted shrub 1 ft. or more h. with very downy young shoots. *l.* oval to obovate, glandular-serrate, tapered to both ends, acute, leathery, ½ to 1¼ in. long, ¼ to ½ in. wide. *fl.* in short racemes from upper l.-axils; cor. white, ovoid-urceolate, ¼ in. long; cal. fleshy in fr., lobes small, white, triangular-ovate, ovary silky-downy. June. *fr.* white, globose, ⅜ in. wide. W. China. 1900. (B.M. 8829.) SYN. *G. pyroloides cuneata.*

**G. depress'a.** Cushion-like shrub up to 1 ft. h., branches procumbent, rooting, brown-bristly when young. *l.* oval to broadly obovate, blunt or sub-acute, bristly serrate, especially when young, $\frac{1}{8}$ to $\frac{1}{3}$ in. long, $\frac{1}{8}$ to $\frac{3}{16}$ in. wide, thick, leathery, bronzy in autumn. *fl.* solitary from l.-axils, especially near ends of branchlets; cor. white or stained pink, bell-shaped, about $\frac{1}{8}$ in. long; cal. fleshy in fr., lobes ovate, acute. May. *fr.* globose, scarlet, $\frac{1}{2}$ to $\frac{2}{3}$ in. across. New Zealand. Recently introduced. SYN. *G. antipoda depressa.* (J.L.S. Bot. 49, 624.)

**G.×fagifol'ia.** (Natural hybrid, *G. antipoda*×*G. oppositifolia.*) Intermediate between parents. Shrub varying much in height ($1\frac{1}{2}$ to 8 ft.) and habit (from low and spreading to nearly erect). *l.* alternate or sometimes opposite, oblong to ovate-oblong, acute or sub-acute, usually cordate, bristly serrate, finely reticulate, smooth, $\frac{1}{2}$ to 1 in. long, leathery. *fl.* in axillary and terminal racemes or panicles; cor. white, ovoid-bell-shaped, about $\frac{1}{6}$ in. long; cal. remaining dry and unaltered. New Zealand, N. Island. Of recent introduction.

**G. Forrest'ii.** Spreading shrub $1\frac{1}{2}$ to $4\frac{1}{2}$ ft. or more h. with bristly young wood. A very attractive plant owing much of its beauty to the white rachis, fl.-stalks, and calyces. *l.* narrowly oval to oblong or oblanceolate, usually pointed, bristly serrate, smooth and dark green above, paler beneath, dotted with bristles; when young, these fall leaving brownish spots 2 to $3\frac{1}{2}$ in. long, $\frac{1}{2}$ to $1\frac{3}{8}$ in. wide, tough and leathery. *fl.* in white-stalked axillary racemes; cor. white, widely urceolate, about $\frac{3}{16}$ in. long; cal. white, fleshy in fr., lobes ovate. May. *fr.* blue, ovoid or globose, $\frac{1}{4}$ to $\frac{3}{8}$ in. long. Yunnan. About 1908. (G.C. 82 (1927), 285.)

**G. fragrantiss'ima.** Shrub of 4 ft. upwards or a small tree. *l.* ovate, oval, obovate, or lanceolate, acute, 2 to 4 in. long, $\frac{3}{4}$ to 2 in. wide, tipped with a glandular mucro, bristly serrate, smooth above, dotted below with sites of earlier bristles. *fl.* in racemes from upper l.-axils, fragrant; cor. white or pinkish, ovoid- to globose-urceolate, about $\frac{3}{16}$ in. long; cal. fleshy in fr., lobes ovate, pointed. April, May. *fr.* usually dark violet-blue, rounded, $\frac{1}{4}$ to $\frac{3}{8}$ in. wide. Himalaya, Khasia Hills and Mts. of Burma, Ceylon, and S. India. 1850. (B.M. 5984.) SYN. *G. fragrans, G. Leschenaultii, G. ovalifolia, G. punctata, Andromeda flexuosa.* Suitable only for mild districts.

**G. fu'riens.** A synonym of *Pernettya furiens.*

**G. his'pida.** Snow-berry. Upright-spreading shrub 2 to 3 ft. or more h. *l.* ovate-lanceolate to oblong, sharp-pointed, sparsely and shortly bristly above, more markedly so beneath, bristly serrate, $1\frac{1}{4}$ to $2\frac{1}{2}$ in. long, $\frac{1}{4}$ to $\frac{5}{8}$ in. wide, leathery, reticulate. *fl.* in short, compact racemes from upper l.-axils; cor. white, campanulate-urceolate, $\frac{3}{16}$ in. long, $\frac{1}{8}$ in. across mouth; cal. fleshy in fr., lobes white, ovate, acute. May, June. *fr.* globose, pure white, $\frac{3}{8}$ in. across. Australia (Victoria) and Tasmania. Known since 1810 but only recently introduced. (N.F.S. 2, 187.)

**G. Hook'eri.** Upright-spreading shrub 3 to 6 ft. h. *l.* ovate, oval, or obovate, bristly serrate, tipped with glandular mucro, smooth above, sparingly bristly on veins below, 2 to $4\frac{1}{2}$ in. long, $\frac{3}{4}$ to $1\frac{3}{4}$ in. wide, reticulate, leathery. *fl.* in terminal and axillary racemes; cor. pink, ovoid-urceolate, $\frac{1}{6}$ to $\frac{1}{4}$ in. long; cal. fleshy in fr., lobes ovate-acuminate. March, April. *fr.* light violet, top-shaped, $\frac{5}{16}$ to $\frac{7}{16}$ in. long and wide. E. Himalaya. Closely allied to *G. Veitchiana.* Not reliably hardy except in milder areas.

**G. humifu'sa.** Tufted, creeping shrub 3 to 4 in. h. with zigzag branches. *l.* oval or rounded, blunt or sub-acute, thin, bristly serrate, $\frac{3}{8}$ to $\frac{7}{8}$ in. long, $\frac{3}{16}$ to $\frac{1}{2}$ in. wide. *fl.* solitary in l.-axils; cor. white or pinkish, campanulate, $\frac{3}{16}$ in. long; cal. fleshy in fr., lobes ovate, only slightly shorter than cor. July. *fr.* scarlet, depressed-globose, $\frac{1}{4}$ in. across. Western N. America. 1830. (Fl. Boreali-Americana, t. 129 as *G. Myrsinites.*) Closely allied to *G. ovatifolia.* Quite hardy but difficult to keep; likes considerable shade and a soil slightly on the moist side.

**G. laxiflo'ra.** A synonym of *G. yunnanensis.*

**G. Merrillia'na.** Wiry-stemmed shrub 4 to 6 in. h. *l.* lanceolate to narrow-oblong-obovate, pointed, slightly glandular-serrate, leathery, $\frac{5}{16}$ to $\frac{9}{16}$ in. long, $\frac{1}{8}$ to $\frac{3}{16}$ in. wide. *fl.* in racemes from upper l.-axils; cor. white, ovate-urceolate, $\frac{1}{4}$ in. long, $\frac{3}{16}$ in. across at widest part; cal. pinkish-white, fleshy in fr., lobes smooth, triangular, acute. May. *fr.* white or pink, thin-walled, globose, $\frac{5}{16}$ in. across. Formosa. Recently introduced.

**G. microphyl'la.** Low, sprawling shrub a few in. h., with hairy shoots. *l.* ovate, oval, or oblong, pointed, obscurely serrate, more or less hairy, leathery, $\frac{1}{4}$ in. long, $\frac{1}{8}$ in. wide. *fl.* solitary from upper l.-axils, few; cor. white, campanulate, $\frac{1}{8}$ to $\frac{3}{16}$ in. long; cal. fleshy in fr., lobes triangular, acute. Spring. *fr.* pear-shaped, top-shaped, or depressed-globose, white, or rosy-pink, $\frac{1}{4}$ to $\frac{5}{16}$ in. wide. Falkland Is., Magellan region. Long known but extremely rare in gardens. (Fl. Falkland Is. 40.) SYN. *G. antarctica, Arbutus microphylla, A. serpyllifolia, Pernettya serpyllifolia.* **A**

**G. Miquelia'na.** Diffuse shrub about 1 ft. h. with obscurely downy young wood. *l.* oval to obovate, rounded, blunt or sub-acute, glandular-serrate, dotted with brown glands beneath, otherwise smooth, $\frac{7}{8}$ to $1\frac{1}{2}$ in. long, $\frac{7}{16}$ to $\frac{3}{4}$ in. wide. *fl.* in racemes from the terminal 2 or 3 l.-axils; cor. white, globular-urceolate, about $\frac{3}{16}$ in. long; cal. white, fleshy in fruit; lobes triangular; ovary smooth. May, June. *fr.* white or flushed pink, rounded, $\frac{1}{4}$ to $\frac{7}{16}$ in. wide. Japan. 1892. SYN. *G. pyroloides* in part. The latter name was given to 2 distinct species, *G. pyrolifolia* and *G. Miqueliana,* and is now abandoned. Closely resembles *G. cuneata* but distinguished by its smooth ovary. **A**

**G. nummularioi'des.** Prostrate rather than procumbent shrub with long, slender, bristly, densely leafy, and interwoven stems. *l.* in opposite rows, ovate or oval, $\frac{3}{8}$ to $\frac{1}{2}$ in. long, about $\frac{2}{3}$ as much wide, acute, tipped with glandular mucro, bristly serrate, smooth, dull green above, pale, shining, more or less bristly beneath. *fl.* solitary, axillary, pendent, hidden beneath l.; cor. white, pink, or brownish-red, conical-urceolate, $\frac{7}{32}$ in. long, rather wider at base; cal. fleshy in fruit, lobes ovate-triangular. July, August. *fr.* blue-black, oval, $\frac{1}{4}$ in. or more long. Himalaya and Khasia Hills. About 1850. SYN. *G. Nummularia, G. nummularifolia, G. repens, Pernettya repens.* (Royle Ill. B.H., 63.)

**G. oppositifo'lia.** Erect-spreading shrub 3 to 4 ft. h. in gardens, up to 10 ft. in nature. *l.* usually opposite, oblong or ovate-lanceolate, pointed or obtuse, cordate, bristly serrate, smooth or more or less minutely bristly, especially beneath, 1 to $2\frac{1}{2}$ in. long, $\frac{3}{4}$ to $1\frac{5}{8}$ in. wide. *fl.* in upper axillary and terminal racemes, the latter usually paniculate; cor. white, campanulate, about $\frac{1}{6}$ in. long; cal. unaltered in fr., lobes ovate, acute. May to July. *fr.* depressed-globose, brown, about $\frac{1}{6}$ in. across. New Zealand, N. Island. Recently introduced. SYN. *G. multibracteolata, Brossaea oppositifolia.* (I.N.Z.Fl. 123.) Not reliably hardy nor particularly attractive.

**G. ovatifo'lia.** Trailing shrub with ascending branches, 6 to 12 in. h. *l.* broadly ovate to nearly round, truncate or sub-cordate at base, acute or blunt at apex, thin, bristly serrulate $\frac{1}{2}$ to 1 in. long, $\frac{1}{3}$ to $\frac{5}{8}$ in. wide. *fl.* solitary in l.-axils; cor. white or pinkish, campanulate, $\frac{3}{16}$ in. long; cal. fleshy in fr., lobes half as long as cor., lanceolate, acute. June. *fr.* scarlet, depressed-globose, $\frac{5}{16}$ in. wide. Western N. America. 1890. Resembles *G. humifusa* but distinguished by the short cal. Prefers a rather moist soil and considerable shade, but not a satisfactory plant in, at least, S. England.

**G. perplex'a.** A synonym of *Pernettya macrostigma.*

**G. procum'bens.** Creeping or Spicy Wintergreen Checkerberry. Creeping shrub with ascending shoots, 3 to 6 in. h. *l.* clustered towards end of shoot, elliptical to elliptical-obovate, usually cuneate at base, acute and glandular-mucronate at apex, bristly serrate, especially towards apex, minutely downy on midrib and at base above, and at base of midrib beneath, $\frac{3}{4}$ to $1\frac{1}{2}$ in. long, $\frac{1}{2}$ to $\frac{7}{8}$ in. wide. *fl.* terminal and axillary, solitary or, more rarely, in short racemes; cor. white or stained pink, conical-urceolate, $\frac{3}{16}$ in. long; cal. fleshy in fr., white or pinkish, lobes broadly ovate, acute. July, August. *fr.* red, globose, $\frac{1}{4}$ to $\frac{5}{16}$ in. wide. Eastern N. America. 1762. (B.M. 1966.) One of the most useful, decorative, vigorous, and hardy species.

**G. pyrolifo'lia.** Tufted, more or less erect shrub 4 to 8 in. h. *l.* clustered towards ends of shoots, oval, obovate, or sub-orbicular, rounded or obtuse at apex, cuneate at base, bluntly mucronulate, finely bristly serrate, firm, leathery, $\frac{3}{8}$ to $1\frac{1}{2}$ in. long, $\frac{1}{4}$ to 1 in. wide. *fl.* in axillary racemes from upper l.-axils; cor. white or pinkish, ovoid-urceolate, $\frac{1}{8}$ in. long; cal. fleshy in fr., lobes ovate, pointed. May. *fr.* blue-black, globose, about $\frac{1}{4}$ in. wide. E. Himalaya. Recently introduced. SYN. *G. pyroloides* in part.

**G. pyroloi'des.** A synonym of *G. Miqueliana* and *G. pyrolifolia.*

**G. rupes'tris.** Erect or more or less procumbent shrub showing great variation in habit and foliage, 8 to 12 in. h. in gardens, but up to 3 to 4 ft. in nature. *l.* oblong or lanceolate, blunt or sub-acute, bristly serrulate, $\frac{3}{8}$ to 1 in. long, $\frac{1}{8}$ to $\frac{1}{3}$ in. wide. *fl.* in upper axillary and terminal racemes; cor. ovoid-campanulate, white, $\frac{1}{8}$ in. long; cal. unaltered in fr., lobes ovate. June, July. *fr.* brownish, depressed-globose, $\frac{5}{32}$ in. across. New Zealand, N. and S. Islands. Of recent introduction. SYN. *Andromeda rupestris.* Not very hardy.

**G. Shal'lon,** Salal, Shallon. Thicket-forming shrub 2 to 4 ft. or more h. *l.* broadly ovate, cordate, pointed, thick, leathery, shortly and closely bristly serrate, finely reticulate, $2\frac{1}{4}$ to 4 in. long, $1\frac{1}{2}$ to $3\frac{1}{2}$ in. wide. *fl.* in axillary and terminal 2- to 4-in. racemes; cor. pinkish-white, ovoid-urceolate, about $\frac{3}{8}$ in. long; cal. fleshy in fr., lobes white, ovate-triangular, acute. May, June. *fr.* purple-black, obconic, sparsely glandular-hairy, about $\frac{3}{8}$ in. across and $\frac{3}{8}$ in. long. Western N. America from Alaska to S. California. 1826. (B.M. 2843.) Spreads rapidly.

**G. sinen'sis.** Compact or more or less procumbent shrub 4 to 6 in. h., young wood beset with small, rusty, appressed bristles. *l.* oblong to obovate-oblong, $\frac{3}{8}$ to $\frac{9}{16}$ in. long by about $\frac{3}{16}$ in. wide; tip blunt, callous, minutely bristly serrate, smooth except for a few minute bristles on midrib beneath. *fl.* solitary from l.-axils towards end of shoot; cor. white, open-campanulate, $\frac{1}{4}$ in. long, $\frac{1}{4}$ in. across mouth, lobes $\frac{1}{16}$ in. long; cal. fleshy in fr., lobes ovate, pointed. April, May. *fr.* usually blue, sometimes white or pink, top-shaped, $\frac{3}{8}$ in. or more wide. Upper Burma and neighbouring parts of Yunnan and Tibet. Of recent introduction. (A.G.S.B. 37, 208.)

**G. tetram'era.** Erect shrub with spreading or more or less decumbent branches, 1 to 2 ft. h., rarely up to $4\frac{1}{2}$ ft. *l.* broadly oval, oval-lanceolate, or oblanceolate, rounded or sub-acute at apex with a short, blunt mucro, $1\frac{1}{4}$ to $2\frac{1}{2}$ in. long, $\frac{5}{8}$ to 1 in. wide, bristly serrulate, leathery, smooth above, dotted with bristles beneath. *fl.* in axillary racemes; usually 4- (or very rarely 5-)merous; cor. greenish-white, ovoid-urceolate, about $\frac{3}{16}$ in. long; cal. fleshy in fr., lobes ovate, acute. May. *fr.* blue, rounded, about $\frac{1}{4}$ in. wide. W. China and Tibet. Of recent introduction. The parts of the fl. in fours sets this apart from other species herein described. **A**

**G. thibet'ica** of gardens. A synonym of *G. thymifolia.*

**G. thymifo'lia.** Evergreen, close-growing shrub 4 to 6 in. h. with slender, minutely bristly stems. *l.* shortly stalked, oblanceolate, tapering gradually to base and more abruptly to the rather sub-acute apex, obscurely bristly toothed in upper half slightly recurved, smooth and shining above, smooth, dull, paler below, $\frac{7}{16}$ to $\frac{3}{4}$ in. long, $\frac{3}{16}$ to $\frac{1}{4}$ in. wide. *fl.* solitary from l.-axils towards ends of shoots; cor. white or reddish, short, campanulate; cal. fleshy in fr., lobes lanceolate, obtuse. June. *fr.* blue or ? reddish. Upper Burma between 1920 and 1926. SYN. *G. thibetica* of gardens. Attractive but not always reliable in cultivation. Closely allied to *G. trichophylla.*

*Gaultheria Shallon* (p. 864)

**G. trichophyl'la.** Cushion-forming shrub 3 to 4 in. h. with wiry, bristly stems. *l.* elliptical, or ovate-elliptical, sub-acute, $\frac{3}{8}$ to $\frac{1}{2}$ in. long, about $\frac{1}{4}$ in. wide, smooth on both surfaces, bristly serrulate. *fl.* solitary from l.-axils; cor. red, pink, or nearly white, campanulate, $\frac{1}{4}$ in. long; cal. fleshy in fr., lobes ovate-oblong. May. *fr.* lapis-lazuli blue, broadly oval, $\frac{3}{8}$ to $\frac{1}{2}$ in. long about $\frac{1}{4}$ in. wide. Himalaya, W. China. 1897. (Royle Ill. B.H., 63.)

**G. Veitchia'na.** Dense, procumbent shrub 1 to 3 ft. h. with bristly shoots. *l.* oval or obovate, tapered to or rounded at base, tipped at the nearly acute apex with a glandular mucro, reticulate, smooth above, dotted with glands and bristly on veins beneath, especially in youth, bristly serrate, 2 to 3 in. long, $\frac{7}{8}$ to $1\frac{1}{2}$ in. wide, firm, leathery. *fl.* in dense axillary and terminal clusters; cor. white, ovoid-urceolate, $\frac{1}{8}$ to $\frac{1}{4}$ in. long; cal. fleshy in fr., lobes lanceolate. May. *fr.* rounded darkish blue, $\frac{1}{4}$ in. wide. Cent. China (Hupeh). 1908. (B.T.S. 1, 582; B.M. 9174.) SYN. *G. fragrantissima hirsuta.*

**G. Ward'ii.** Rather lanky shrub of 3 ft. or more with somewhat arching shoots, generally bristly. *l.* oblong to ovate-lanceolate, pointed, rounded, or sub-cordate at base, bristly serrate, coarsely hairy on both surfaces, especially beneath, veins deeply impressed

*Gaultheria yunnanensis*

above and prominent beneath. *fl.* in short, compact racemes from upper l.-axils; cor. white, urceolate, about $\frac{1}{4}$ in. long; cal. remaining unaltered in fr., lobes hairy, ovate-lanceolate. May, June. *fr.* blue, globose, $\frac{1}{4}$ in. across. SE. Tibet. About 1925. (B.M. 9516.) Top growth apt to be cut down in a severe winter even in S. England.

**G. yunnanen'sis.** Loosely branching, rather pendulous shrub 3 to 5 ft. h. *l.* oblong, oval, ovate, or lanceolate, sub-acute, acute, or acuminate, cordate, finely serrate, reticulate, leathery, smooth except for a few glandular bristles beneath, $1\frac{7}{8}$ to $3\frac{1}{2}$ in. long, $\frac{5}{8}$ to $1\frac{1}{8}$ in. wide, turning reddish in autumn. *fl.* in slender axillary and terminal racemes and sometimes also solitary from axils; cor. greenish-white and brown marked or banded, open-campanulate, $\frac{3}{16}$ in. long, $\frac{1}{4}$ in. across mouth, lobes about half as long, ovate, recurved; cal. fleshy in fr., lobes ovate, ciliate. May onwards. *fr.* globose-depressed, black, $\frac{3}{16}$ to $\frac{6}{16}$ in. across. W. China. Of recent introduction. (J.R.H.S. 65, figs. 96, 97.) SYN. *G. laxiflora, Pieris Vaccinium, Vaccinium yunnanense.* Liable to be severely cut in hard winters.

**A→**

F. S.

**GAU'RA** (*gauros*, superb). FAM. *Oenotheraceae.* A genus of about 25 species of annual or perennial herbs, rarely shrubs, natives of the warmer parts of N. America. Leaves alternate, simple. Flowers in terminal, spiral racemes, white or rose; calyx with a long tube and 4 reflexed lobes; petals clawed, unequal; stamens 8. Fruit 3- or 4-ribbed, 1-celled, 1- to 4-seeded. Few of the species are very showy since there are few flowers open at once, but *G. Lindheimeri* is a slender, graceful plant which continues in flower for a long time, and *G. coccinea* has showy flowers. They prefer a light soil, are hardy, and should be raised from seed sown early in spring outdoors and moved to their flowering quarters in a sunny border as soon as large enough.

**G. bien'nis.** 4 to 6 ft. h. *l.* lanceolate-oblong, acute, toothed. *fl.* at first white, then reddish; pet. obovate, ascending, spreading; sep. tipped purple; raceme long. August to October. 1762. (B.M. 389.)

**G. coccin'ea.*** Much-branched perennial, about 1 ft. h., fairly erect. *l.* lanceolate to linear, toothed or entire. *fl.* rose, becoming scarlet, in spikes. Cent. N. America.

**G. Lindheim'eri.*** Branched perennial, 3 to 4 ft. h. *l.* lanceolate or spatulate, toothed, margins recurved. *fl.* rosy-white in a loose spike. Texas, Louisiana. 1850. (R.H. 1907, 373.)

**G. parviflo'ra.** Annual, 1 to $1\frac{1}{2}$ ft. h. *l.* oblong, slender-pointed, slightly toothed, ciliate, velvety at first. *fl.* very small, yellow, crowded on the long spikes. 1835. (B.M. 3506.)

**GAUS'SIA** (?). FAM. *Palmaceae.* A genus of 2 species of W. Indian Palms with slender unarmed stems, thickened below, and heads of pinnate leaves. Allied to Chamaedorea and requiring the same treatment. **A**

**G. prin'ceps.** Stem up to 20 ft. *l.* pinnatisect; segs. narrow-linear, crowded, sometimes 2-fid. *fl.* monoecious, very small on filiform branches. *Spadix* long-stalked. *fr.* small, purple or red. Cuba.

*Gautier'i,* in honour of P. H. Gauttier, 1772–?, shipmaster after whom the Gauttier Mt. in New Guinea were named.

**GAY'A.** *See under* **Hoheria Lyallii.**

*Gaya'nus, -a -um* in honour of Jacques Gay, 1776–1864, botanist of Paris.

*Gay'i,* in honour of Jacques or Claude Gay, writers on plants of Chile and Peru.

**GAYLUSSA'CIA** (in honour of J. L. Gay-Lussac, 1778–1850, celebrated French chemist). Huckleberry. FAM. *Ericaceae.* A genus of about 40 shrubs with alternate leaves, 5-merous flowers in axillary racemes; corolla cylindrical-campanulate or urceolate; ovary inferior, 10-celled; fruit a berry-like drupe containing 10 1-seeded nutlets and crowned by the persistent calyx lobes. The position of the ovary indicates its close relationship with Vaccinium, but the character of the fruit distinguishes it. Requires lime-free, humus, well-drained loam and is propagated from seed, cuttings, and layers. The genus is confined to America.

KEY

| | |
|---|---|
| 1. *Lvs. evergreen* | G. brachycera |
| 1. *Lvs. deciduous* | 2 |
| 2. *Lvs. glaucescent beneath* | G. frondosa |
| 2. *Lvs. green or greenish beneath* | 3 |
| 3. *Cor. urceolate* | G. baccata |
| 3. *Cor. campanulate* | 4 |
| 4. *Hairs glandular* | G. dumosa |
| 4. *Hairs not glandular* | G. ursina |

**G. bacca'ta.** Black Huckleberry. Deciduous, more or less erect shrub of about 3 ft. h. with resinous young shoots. *l.* oval to obovate, blunt or sub-acute, mucronulate, resinous-glandular beneath, 1 to 2 in. long, $\frac{1}{2}$ to $\frac{3}{4}$ in. wide. *fl.* nodding in more or less drooping racemes; cor. red, ovoid-urceolate, $\frac{3}{16}$ in. long, the 5 lobes erect or spreading; cal. lobes ovate to lanceolate. May, June. *fr.* rounded, about $\frac{5}{16}$ in. across, black, shining, and edible. Eastern N. America; 1772. (B.M. 1288 as *Vaccinium resinosum.*) var. **glaucocarp'a** has blue, bloomy fr., larger than in type; **leucocarp'a** has white or pink, rather transparent fr. SYN. *G. resinosa, Andromeda baccata.*

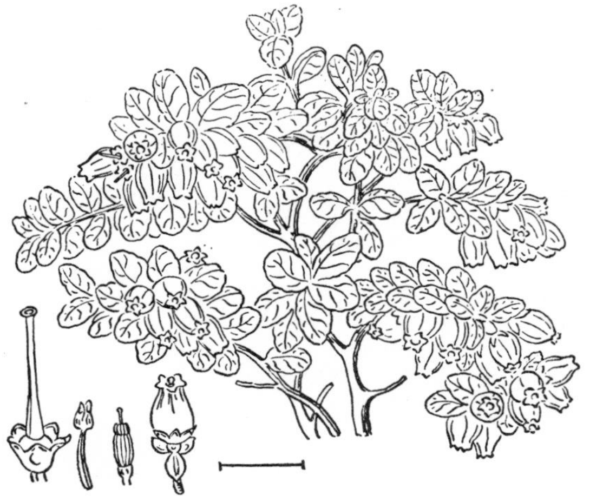

*Gaylussacia brachycera*

**G. brachyce'ra.** Box Huckleberry. Mat-forming evergreen shrub, 6 to 18 in. h. with ascending, roughly triangular or winged, downy young wood. *l.* ovate, oval, or oblong, $\frac{5}{16}$ to 1 in. long, about half as wide, smooth, slightly revolute, shortly mucronate, shallowly dentate-glandular, leathery, crowded. *fl.* in short racemes from near ends of branchlets; cor. white, striped and tipped red, cylindrical-urceolate, $\frac{1}{5}$ in. long with short, triangular, almost erect lobes; cal. lobes short, triangular, acute. *fr.* bluish, sub-globose to pear-shaped, up to $\frac{1}{3}$ in. long, edible. Eastern U.S.A. 1796. (B.M. 928 as *Vaccinium buxifolium.*) SYN. *Buxella brachycera, Vaccinium brachycerum.*

**G. dumo'sa.** Dwarf Huckleberry, Bushy Whortleberry. Branching deciduous shrub 1 ft. or more h. with glandular-hairy young shoots. *l.* oval to obovate, sub-acute or pointed, entire, mucronate, firm, more or less glandular-pubescent, $\frac{3}{4}$ to $1\frac{1}{2}$ in. long, $\frac{1}{4}$ to $\frac{3}{4}$ in. wide.

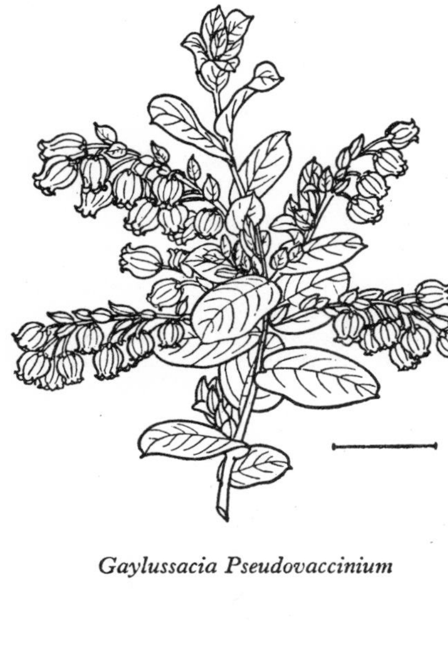

*Gaylussacia Pseudovaccinium*

*fl.* pendent, in short, loose, axillary racemes; cor. white or faintly pink-stained, campanulate, about $\frac{1}{4}$ in. long with rather long, almost erect lobes; cal. lobes glandular-downy, triangular, margined with red. June. *fr.* globose, black, up to $\frac{5}{16}$ in. wide. Eastern N. America. 1774. (B.M. 1106 as *Vaccinium dumosum.*) SYN. *Lasiococcus dumosus, Vaccinium hirtellum.*

**G. frondo'sa.** Dangleberry, Blue Tangle. Spreading-erect deciduous shrub, 2 to 6 ft. h. with almost smooth young wood. *l.* oval to obovate, obtuse or notched at apex, 1 to $2\frac{1}{2}$ in. long, half as wide, downy, dotted with resin-glands and glaucescent beneath. *fl.* in loose, axillary racemes; cor. white or greenish-purple, campanulate, $\frac{1}{8}$ to $\frac{1}{4}$ in. long with recurved lobes; cal. lobes shortly and broadly triangular. June, July. *fr.* bright blue, rounded, edible, about $\frac{3}{8}$ in. wide. Eastern U.S.A. 1761. SYN. *Decachaena frondosa, Vaccinium frondosum.* (B.B. ed. 2, 2, 695.)

**G. Pseudovaccin'ium.** Evergreen shrub about 2 ft. h. *l.* elliptic-lanceolate, slightly toothed near tip, somewhat ciliate at base. *fl.* in erect, axillary, somewhat 1-sided racemes, crimson; cor. urceolate. April, May. Brazil. 1842. (P.M.B. 14, 102.)

**G. resino'sa.** A synonym of *G. baccata.*

**G. ursi'na.** Bear Huckleberry, Buckberry. Somewhat loose, deciduous shrub 2 to 6 ft, h. with slightly hairy young wood. *l.* oval, oblong, or obovate pointed, thin, slightly pubescent on both sides, $1\frac{1}{2}$ to 4 in. long, $\frac{3}{4}$ to $1\frac{1}{2}$ in. wide. *fl.* in rather short, loose axillary racemes; cor. whitish or reddish, campanulate, about $\frac{3}{16}$ in. long with recurved lobes; cal. resinous with broad, pointed lobes. May, June. *fr.* globose, black, about $\frac{7}{16}$ in. across, edible. South-eastern U.S.A. 1891. SYN. *Decachaena ursina, Vaccinium ursinum.*

F. S.

**GAZAN'IA** (possibly in honour of Theodore of Gaza, 1398–1478, who translated the botanical works of Theophrastus into Latin). FAM. *Compositae.* Treasure Flower. A genus of about 24 species of S. African, usually perennial, herbs. Leaves crowded at the base of the plant or scattered, variable in shape on the same plant. Flower-heads often large and very showy; ray-florets neuter, yellow or orange, dark-brown or iridescent at base; disk dark, florets 5-toothed, perfect; peduncle leafless, 1-flowered; involucral bracts in 2 to several rows, connate into a cup, toothed round apex. Achenes hairy, pappus 2-rowed, very delicate. Gazanias are easily grown in a cool greenhouse or outdoors in summer, a compost of loam and peat suiting them well. The showy flowers, usually freely produced, unfortunately close in the afternoon. Propagation is easy by cuttings in July and August, taking the side shoots from the base of the plant, putting into sandy soil in a close frame; spring cuttings are not easily dealt with. The plants must be wintered under glass except in favoured districts and hardened off before putting out in June. They make good dry-wall plants and also flower well in pots or pans. Many hybrids have been raised between species of the genus, *G.* × *splendens*, one of the best known, being probably of hybrid origin. *G. bracteata, G. Pavonia, G. rigens,* and *G. uniflora* have also been crossed and given rise to a race of handsome plants, some of which have been named, and all of which respond to treatment like the parents and are propagated by similar cuttings. A good account is in *Flora and Sylva,* vol. 3 (1905), p. 139.

**G. × hyb'rida** (*G. longiscapa* × *G. nivea*). Intermediate between parents.

**G. longisca'pa.** Rootstock woody, with short branches. *l.* crowded at ends of the short branches, very variable, lanceolate and entire or pinnatisect with linear lobes, white-woolly beneath, smooth above, margins reflexed, cartilaginous-ciliate. *fl.-heads* on glabrous peduncles longer than l., golden yellow; involucre glabrous. Natal. (B.M. 9354.) SYN. *Gazaniopsis stenophylla.* May be treated as a hardy annual.

**G. monta'na.** Prostrate perennial. *l.* entire, erect, bright green, silvery beneath. *fl.-heads* pale yellow with ring of deep yellow; disk golden; rays rosy-violet without. 1899. var. **al'ba,** *fl.* pure white. Best in pots.

**G. niv'ea.** Stems $\frac{1}{2}$ in. long, very leafy, from a thick, woody rhizome. *l.* crowded, pinnatisect with short segs., 1 to $1\frac{1}{2}$ in. long, hoary on both sides. *fl.-heads* with hairy involucre; peduncles not longer than l.

**G. Pavo'nia.** Woody at base with short branches. *l.* oblong, usually pinnatifid, sometimes entire, lanceolate, 3 to 9 in. long, rough and green above, white-hairy beneath. *fl.-heads* large, handsome; rays bright orange with black or eyed spot at base; involucral scales short, not slender-pointed. July. 1864. (B.R. 35; F.P.S.A. 69.)

**G. pinna'ta.** Perennial. *l.* radical, very variable, usually pinnatipartite, 3 to 8 in. long, usually rough above, white beneath. *fl.-heads* about 3 in. or more across; rays orange, spotted at base; involucral bracts slender-pointed; peduncles scarcely longer than l. Cape Province. 1881. var. **scab'ra,** *l.* very roughly hairy above.

**G. pyg'maea.** Rootstock woody with many short branches. *l.* radical, linear-spatulate, obtuse, 2 to 3 in. long, rigid, tapered to a ciliate stalk. *fl.-heads* small; rays about 12, white, purplish beneath; peduncles shorter than l. (B.M. 7455; F.P.S.A. 64.)

**G. rig'ens.** Stems 6 to 12 in. long, diffuse, numbrous. *l.* entire or sometimes pinnatifid, 4 to 5 in. long, tapered to base, green and smooth above, white (except midrib) beneath, margins reflexed. *fl.-heads* large and showy; rays 1½ in. long, orange with black, eye-spotted spot at base; involucre glabrous; peduncles 4 to 8 in. long. June onwards. 1755. Habitat unknown. (B.M. 90 as *Gorteria rigens.*)

**G. scab'ra.** A variety of *G. pinnata.*

**G.× splen'dens.*** Habit of *G. uniflora* but more compact. *l.* linear-spatulate, silky-white beneath. *fl.-heads* over 3 in. across; ray-florets bright orange, with a black and white spot without brown at base. Of hybrid origin. (I.H. 1860, 235.)

**G. uniflo'ra.** Stems spreading from base, 6 to 12 in. long, leafy. *l.* very variable in form and hairiness. *fl.-heads* rather small; rays yellow, not spotted; involucre woolly. July, August. 1816. (B.M. 2270; L.B.C. 795.)

**GAZANIOP'SIS stenophyl'la.** A synonym of *Gazania longiscapa.*

**GAZEBO.** A garden house in a commanding position, usually in the form of a temple.

**GEAN.** *See* **Prunus Avium.**

**GEAS'TER.** A genus of fungi (Basidiomycetes), sometimes called Earth Stars, growing on the ground in meadows and sandy woods, shaped like a ball. The outer layer of this ball splits downwards into several segments or lobes which, when opened out, give the star-like effect.

D. E. G.

*gebel'ius -a -um,* of Gebel-cher.

*Geertia'nus -a -um,* in honour of Auguste van Geert of Ghent, author of *Iconography of Indian Azaleas,* 1882.

**GEI'JERA** (?). Fam. *Rutaceae.* A genus of about 3 species of small evergreen, Australian trees with simple, alternate leaves and small, yellowish-white flowers in short terminal panicles. Calyx 5-cleft, persistent; petals 5, deciduous; stamens 5, awl-shaped; ovary flattish, 5-lobed; styles united, short, with a capitate 5-lobed stigma. Fruit of 1 or 2 separate obtuse carpels. Greenhouse plant needing treatment similar to Citrus.

**G. parviflo'ra.** Small tree with often pendulous branches. *l.* linear, 3 to 6 in. long, rarely over ¼ in. wide, glabrous. New S. Wales.

**GEIS'SOIS** (*geisson* tile; the seeds are arranged like tiles on a roof). Fam. *Saxifragaceae.* A genus of about 4 species of evergreen trees, natives of Pacific Is. and Australia. Leaves opposite, leathery, digitate with 3 or 5 entire or toothed leaflets, stalked and stipulate. Flowers showy, purple, in simple, axillary racemes; calyx 4- or 5-parted; petals absent; stamens 10 to 20. *G. racemosa* needs stove temperature, and a very sandy loam with some peat.

**G. racemo'sa.** Handsome tree to 20 ft. flowering on old wood. *lflets.* 5, elliptic, obtuse, entire; stipules oblong, ribbed. *fl.* crimson. New Caledonia. 1851. (I.H. 1880, 385.)

**GEISSOME'RIA** (*geisson,* tile, *meris,* part; the bracts overlap like the tiles of a roof). Fam. *Acanthaceae.* A genus of about 10 species of evergreen shrubs, one native of Jamaica, the others of Brazil and Guiana. Leaves oval or oblong, entire. Flowers red, often velvety, long, in racemes or panicles; calyx 5-parted; corolla tubular, widened upwards. Stove temperatures are required and a compost of loam and peat with some sand and rotten cow manure. Cuttings of rather firm shoots will strike in sand with bottom heat.

**G. coccin'ea.** Glabrous, about 3 ft. h. *l.* oblong, leathery, entire. *fl.* scarlet, whitish in mouth; cor. tube 1¼ in. long, lobes small, rounded, equal; spikes solitary in l.-axils or ternate if terminal. August. Jamaica. 1842. (B.M. 4158 as *Salpixantha coccinea.*)

**G. longiflo'ra.** About 3 ft. h. *l.* ovate-lanceolate, tapered at base, wavy, smooth above, silky-downy beneath; sessile. *fl.* dull scarlet, velvety; cor. tube arching, smooth within; upper seg. rounded, notched, lower bearded; spike leafy at base. October. Brazil. (B.R. 1045.)

**G. nit'ida.** Shrubby, glabrous. *l.* oblong, acute, shining. *fl.* purplish-red, glabrous, 1½ in. long, somewhat 2-lipped; spike simple or racemose at base. Brazil.

**GEISSORHI'ZA** (*geisson,* tile, *rhiza,* root; from the tunics of the corm, which is covered by them like a roof with tiles). Fam. *Iridaceae.* A genus of about 24 species of herbs with corms, natives of S. Africa with one in Madagascar. Leaves narrow, thread- or sword-like. Flowers Ixia-like; perianth funnel-shaped, tube short, limb 6-partite, segments nearly equal; stamens inserted at throat, free, filaments filiform. For cultivation *see* **Galaxia.**

**G. exci'sa.** About 6 in. h. *Radical l.* ovate-oblong. *fl.* white. April, May. 1789. (B.M. 584 as *Ixia excisa.*)

**G. gran'dis.** Stout, stem leafy. *Radical l.* linear-ensiform, obtuse, strongly ribbed near base. *fl.* inclined; perianth-segs. pale straw-coloured with blood-red midrib, elliptic-obovate, obtuse; spike 6- to 8-fld. 1868. (B.M. 5877.)

**G. hir'ta.** *l.* hairy. *fl.* bright red; perianth-tube very short; segs. without basal blotch; spike loosely 2- to 6-fld.

**G. hu'milis.** About 1 ft. h. *Radical l.* bristle-like. *fl.* sulphur; spike few-fld. June, July. 1809. (B.M. 1255 as *G. setacea.*)

**G. inflex'a.** About 18 in. h. *l.* ensiform, acute, falcate, or obliquely bent. *fl.* large, tube very short, narrow at base; segs. bright yellow with an obcordate, dark-purple, velvety spot at base of each. May. (S.B.F.G. 138 as *G. vaginata.*)

**G. Rochen'sis.** Smooth up to about 9 in. *Radical l.* linear, acute. *fl.* blue, with crimson spot in centre; solitary at end of stem or branches. May. 1790. (B.M. 598 as *Ixia Rochensis.*) var. **spatha'maea,** more robust. *fl.* several in a spike.

**G. secun'da.** Hairy, about 1 ft. h. *Radical l.* linear-acute. *fl.* white. May. 1795. (B.M. 1105 as *Ixia secunda.*)

**G. vagina'ta.** A synonym of *G. inflexa.*

**GEITONOPLE'SIUM** (*geiton,* neighbour, *plesion,* near; the genus being nearly related to Eustrephus, also Australian). Fam. *Liliaceae.* A genus of 1 or 2 species differing from Eustrephus only by the inflorescence and the entire (not fringed) inner segments of the perianth. For treatment of this greenhouse climber *see* **Dianella.**

**G. cymo'sum.** Woody perennial, climbing by twining. *l.* linear to ovate, 2 to 3 in. long. *fl.* purplish-green, ⅓ in. long, drooping, in loose terminal cymes, sometimes short and few-fld., sometimes in an oblong panicle, 3 to 4 in. long consisting of several cymes. Queensland to Victoria. 1832. (B.M. 3131.)

**GELASI'NE** (*gelasinos,* a smiling dimple). Fam. *Iridaceae.* A genus of 2 Trop. American herbs. Rootstock a corm, leaves plicate. Flowers blue, fugitive, several in a spathe; stamens inserted at base of the very short perianth-tube, united at top of filaments into a cylindrical column; segments of perianth equal, obovate. Hardy. Treatment as for Romulea.

**G. azu'rea.** About 1 ft. h. *l.* plicate, 1½ to 2 ft. long. *fl.* blue, dotted black and white at base of segs.; spathe many-fld., shorter than peduncles; peduncles closely clasped by 3 or 4 bracts. 1838. (B.M. 3779.)

*gel'idus -a -um,* of icy regions.

**GELSEM'IUM** (*Gelsomino,* Italian name of Jasmine). Fam. *Loganiaceae.* A genus of 2 evergreen species of glabrous, twining shrubs, one N. American, the other native of E. Asia. Leaves opposite or whorled, entire. Flowers yellow, showy, axillary, 1 or few, fragrant, funnel-shaped with 5 short, over-lapping lobes; style slender, 4-cleft. Fruit with flattened, winged seeds. *G. sempervirens* is a tender shrub needing rich loamy soil; it may be propagated by cuttings under a bell-glass.

**G. sempervi'rens.** False Jasmine. Twining evergreen shrub with slender stem up to 20 ft. long. *l.* oblong or ovate-lanceolate, 1¼ to 2 in. long, shining. *fl.* deep yellow, over 1 in. long, on very short axillary peduncles; in one form the anthers, in another, the stigmas are exserted. April to June. Southern U.S.A. 1840. (B.M. 7851.)

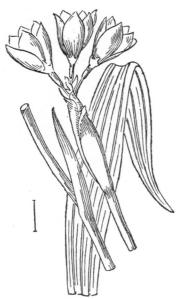

*Gelasine azurea* (p. 867)

*gemina'tus -a -um,* united in pairs.

*geminiflo'rus -a -um,* with twin flowers, i.e. with 2 flowers growing together as in some honeysuckles.

**GEMMAE.** Buds usually deciduous and capable of propagating the species.

*gemma'tus -a -um,* jewelled.

*gemmif'erus -a -um,* bearing buds.

**A→**

**GENERA.** Pl. of genus (q.v.).

*Genestieria'nus -a -um,* in honour of Père Annet Genestier, 1858–?, of the French Tibetan Mission, who assisted botanical explorers in early 20th century.

**GENET'YLLIS.** Included in **Darwinia.**

*geneven'sis -is -e,* of Geneva.

*genicula'tus -a -um,* bent abruptly, like a knee.

**GENIP TREE.** See **Melicocca bijuga.**

**GENI'PA** (Genipaps, the name of one species in Guiana). Fam. *Rubiaceae.* A genus of about 8 species of evergreen shrubs or small trees, natives of Trop. America and the W. Indies, closely related to Randia and Gardenia. From Gardenia it differs by the 2- instead of 1-celled ovary, and from Randia by the petals having tufts of hair in the throat and at the base, and the style being acute, while in Randia the petals are hairy at the throat or at the base, not both, and the style is not acute. Leaves opposite, obovate or lanceolate, leathery, shining. Flowers at first white then yellow. Fruit succulent, edible, with a rather thick rind, crowned by the calyx and tapering to each end. Cultivation as for Gardenia.

**G. america'na.** Genipap Fruit. Tree of 20 to 30 ft. *l.* oblong-lanceolate, 5 to 10 in. long, glabrous. *fl.* white, about 1 in. across, silky; in axillary corymbs. *fr.* greenish-white, large, full of dark-purple juice, pulp rather acrid. W. Indies. 1779. The fruit is used in Trop. America as a preserve called Genipot, and for making marmalade.

**G. Caru'to.** About 20 ft. h. *l.* obovate, glabrous above, velvety beneath. *fl.* white, tube silky; in terminal clusters of 2 or 3. W. Indies.

**G. clusiifo'lia.** Shrub of 4 to 10 ft. *l.* obovate, up to 4 in. long, glabrous. *fl.* white, tube as long as glabrous lobes. *Berry* ovoid. W. Indies.

**G. Mer'ianae.** About 20 ft. h. *l.* oblong-ovate. *fl.* crowded near ends of branches, sessile or almost so. *Berry* hairy, umbilicate; pulp edible. Guiana. 1800.

**G. oblongifo'lia.** About 20 ft. h. *l.* oblong-ovate, obtuse, downy on veins beneath, margins rather revolute. *fl.* crowded at tops of branches on short pedicels. *fr.* as large as a peach. Peru. 1821. Seeds and pulps used by Indians as a dye.

F. G. P.

**GENIPAP.** *See* **Genipa americana.**

**GENIS'TA** (Latin name used by Virgil). Fam. *Leguminosae.* A genus of deciduous or almost leafless shrubs and small trees; many have an evergreen appearance owing to the fresh green colour of their shoots and younger branches. Some are unarmed, others have apical spines or simple or compound spines on the branches. The flowers, usually in terminal or sub-terminal racemes, sometimes in terminal heads, rarely in lateral clusters, are yellow, rarely white, and similar in construction to those of the closely allied genus Cytisus (for distinction from which *see* **Cytisus**). Leaves usually alternate, rarely opposite, simple or 3-foliolate; in some species both forms are present on the same shoots. Cultivation is simple in well-drained, light soil in sunny positions, but transplanting of established plants is hazardous. Pot-plants should, if possible, always be used when planting. Propagation is best from seed but is often done by means of cuttings in sandy soil. Unless otherwise indicated, the species described below are hardy. For *G. fragrans* of gardens, see *Cytisus × racemosus.*

KEY
| | |
|---|---|
| 1. *Fl. white* | 2 |
| 1. *Fl. yellow* | 3 |
| 2. *Pods wrinkled* | G. monosperma |
| 2. *Pods inflated* | G. Raetam |
| 3. *Branches or tips of shoots spiny* | 4 |
| 3. *Branches and shoots unarmed* | 15 |
| 4. *Lvs. opposite* | G. horrida |
| 4. *Lvs. alternate* | 5 |
| 5. *Basal lvs. 3-foliolate, remainder simple* | 6 |
| 5. *Lvs. all simple* | 7 |
| 6. *Shrub up to 9 ft. h.* | G. ferox |
| 6. *Shrub of 8 to 24 in. h.* | G. corsica |
| 7. *Lvs. smooth* | 8 |
| 7. *Lvs. hairy or pubescent* | 10 |
| 8. *Pods densely white-hairy at edges* | G. berberidea |
| 8. *Pods smooth* | 9 |
| 9. *Pods swollen, nearly cylindrical* | G. anglica |
| 9. *Pods flat* | G. lydia |
| 10. *Shrub up to 7 ft. h.* | G. Scorpius |
| 10. *Shrubs not more than 3½ ft. h.* | 11 |
| 11. *Fl. in terminal heads* | G. hispanica |
| 11. *Fl. in lateral clusters or in racemes* | 12 |
| 12. *Fl. lateral, solitary or in small clusters* | G. aspalathoides |
| 12. *Fl. in terminal racemes* | 13 |
| 13. *Lvs. minutely stipulate* | G. murcica |
| 13. *Lvs. without stipules* | 14 |
| 14. *Shrub erect or ascending, up to 2 ft. h.* | G. germanica |
| 14. *Shrub diffuse, 4 to 6 in. h.* | G. dalmatica |
| 15. *Stems triangular or winged* | 16 |
| 15. *Stems roughly rounded* | 19 |
| 16. *Stems triangular* | 17 |
| 16. *Stems winged* | 18 |
| 17. *Basal lvs. 3-foliolate, remainder simple* | G. triquetra |
| 17. *Lvs. all simple* | G. januensis |
| 18. *Fl. in terminal racemes* | G. sagittalis |
| 18. *Fl. in terminal and lateral clusters* | G. delphinensis |
| 19. *Lvs. 3-foliolate* | 20 |
| 19. *Lvs. 3-foliolate and simple or all simple* | 21 |
| 20. *Lvs. opposite; fl. in terminal heads* | G. radiata |
| 20. *Lvs. alternate; fl. in terminal racemes* | G. nyssana |
| 21. *Basal lvs. 3-foliolate, remainder simple* | G. ephedroides |
| 21. *Lvs. all simple* | 22 |
| 22. *Shrubs over 6 ft. h.* | 23 |
| 22. *Shrubs less than 4 ft. h.* | 25 |
| 23. *Shoots smooth or nearly so; lvs. few and insignificant* | G. aethnensis |
| 23. *Shoots pubescent; lvs. plentiful and obvious* | 24 |
| 24. *Lvs. loosely folded lengthwise* | G. cinerea |
| 24. *Lvs. not folded but slightly incurved* | G. virgata |

25. *Very low or prostrate shrubs* 26
25. *Shrubs between 1 and 4 ft. h.* 30
26. *Lvs. smooth* G. micrantha
26. *Lvs. hairy or pubescent on one or both surfaces* 27
27. *Lvs. hairy or pubescent on lower surface only* 28
27. *Lvs. hairy or pubescent on both surfaces* 29
28. *Hairs silky; shrub procumbent* G. sericea
28. *Hairs silvery-silky; lvs. much folded; shrub erect* G. teretifolia
29. *Hairs whitish, long and shaggy* G. albida
29. *Hairs silky and spreading, not shaggy* G. pulchella
30. *Cor. quite smooth* G. tinctoria
30. *Standard and keel of cor. hairy or pubescent* 31
31. *Lvs. flat* G. ramosissima
31. *Lvs. more or less folded* G. pilosa

*Genista aethnensis*

**G. aethnen'sis.*** Mt. Etna Broom. Handsome shrub, 15 ft. or more h., with drooping branches. *l.* few, simple, alternate, linear, silky-pubescent, about $\frac{1}{2}$ in. long. *fl.* in loose, terminal, leafy racemes; cor. golden-yellow, about $\frac{1}{3}$ in. across, somewhat silky; cal. slightly pubescent, campanulate. July. *Pod* pubescent when young, $\frac{1}{2}$ in. long with decurved, pointed apex. Sicily. (B.M. 2674.) SYN. *Spartium aethnense.* The weight of the branches often necessitates support.

**G. al'bida.** White Genista. Procumbent, thickly branched dwarf shrub 8 to 12 in. h. *l.* simple, alternate, linear or lanceolate, whitish-villous. *fl.* in short, terminal, leafy racemes; cor. yellow, silky-pubescent; cal. silky villous. June. *Pods* oblanceolate, acuminate at apex, hairy, about $\frac{3}{8}$ in. long. Bessarabia, Syria, Palestine. (R.I.F.G. 22, t. 36.) Allied to *G. pilosa.* Half-hardy.

**G. Andrea'na.** *See* **Cytisus scoparius.**

**G. ang'lica.** Petty Whin. Spiny, somewhat procumbent, smooth shrub up to 2 ft. h. *l.* alternate, simple, linear-oblong or elliptic, pointed, smooth, $\frac{1}{4}$ in. or a little more long. *fl.* in short, terminal, leafy, few-fld. racemes; cor. yellow, standard smooth and oval; cal. smooth. May to July. *Pods* elliptic-oblong, smooth, $\frac{1}{2}$ in. long. W. Europe from Portugal to Sweden; common on moorlands in Britain. (E.B. 326.) The Planta Genista of the Plantagenets. var. **subiner'mis,** more or less prostrate with feeble, few, or scarcely any spines.

**G. anxan'tica.** A variety of *G. tinctoria.*

**G. aspalathoi'des.** Dense, erect or sub-prostrate, spiny bush, 4 to 12 in. h., resembling Erinacea, with nodular branches and smooth old wood; young shoots silky-hairy. *l.* alternate, simple, linear-lanceolate, elliptical, or oval-obovate, almost leathery, folded longitudinally, appressed-pubescent, fall early, about $\frac{1}{4}$ in. long. *fl.* 1 to 4 at nodes on year-old branches; cor. pale yellow, standard and keel pubescent; cal. silky-pubescent. June. *Pod* oblong-lanceolate, grey-silky-hairy, about $\frac{1}{2}$ in. long. SW. Europe, NW. Africa. Recently introduced. SYN. *G. Lobelii, Spartium erinaceoides.*

**G. berberid'ea.** Tall shrub with wand-like branches, usually spiny, internodes very short. *l.* alternate, simple, lanceolate, sharply pointed, smooth, stipules at first bristly but later hard and sub-spinous. *fl.* in terminal racemes on branchlets; cor. yellow, standard falls early, keel obtuse and hairy without; cal. pilose. July. *Pod* obliquely rhomboid-lanceolate, densely white-pilose at edges, $\frac{1}{3}$ to nearly $\frac{1}{2}$ in. long. Spain (Galicia). Not reliably hardy.

**G. Boissier'i.** A synonym of *G. horrida eriocalyx.*

**G. can'dicans.** A synonym of *Cytisus monspessulanus.*

**G. ciner'ea.*** Unarmed shrub, 10 ft. or more h., with spreading, somewhat drooping branches and silky-pubescent young shoots. *l.* alternate or fasciculate, simple, sessile or nearly so, loosely folded lengthwise, oblong, elliptical, or lanceolate-linear, silky-pubescent below, about $\frac{1}{2}$ in. long. *fl.* in loose, leafy, terminal racemes; cor. yellow, standard notched, keel hairy; cal. silky-hairy. June, July. *Pod* linear-oblong, silky, $\frac{1}{2}$ to $\frac{3}{4}$ in. long. Spain to Italy, Tunisia, Algeria. (B.M. 8086.) SYN. *Cytisus cinereus, Spartium cinereum, Genista ramosissima* (of Boissier). Whole plant greyish; one of the most floriferous and beautiful of the taller Brooms.

**G. cor'sica.** Erect, much branched, spiny bush from 8 to 24 in. h., branches striate and interwoven. *l.* alternate, 3-foliolate at base of branchlets, otherwise simple; lflets. oval-oblong, stipules spiny. *fl.* in lateral clusters of 2 to 6, rarely solitary; cor. yellow, standard and keel smooth; cal. ciliate. March to June. *Pod* irregularly linear, smooth, compressed. Corsica, Sardinia. SYN. *Spartium corsicum.* Not reliably hardy.

**G. dalmat'ica.*** Dalmatian Broom. Very floriferous, compact, spiny bush up to 6 in. h. with hairy branches. *l.* alternate, simple, linear to linear-lanceolate, acute, pubescent, $\frac{1}{4}$ to $\frac{3}{8}$ in. long. *fl.* closely set in terminal racemes up to $1\frac{1}{2}$ in. long; cor. bright yellow, standard ovate; cal. hairy. *Pod* rounded, flat, hairy, about $\frac{1}{2}$ in. long. W. Balkans. About 1893. (B.M. 8075.) SYN. *G. sylvestris pungens.* Excellent for well-drained ledges in rock-gardens.

**G. delphinen'sis.*** Tiny prostrate-decumbent shrub, 1 or 2 in. h., with winged branches; wings membranous, pubescent, green, and usually narrowed at nodes. *l.* few, simple, alternate, oval-elliptic or ovate, acutely pointed, pubescent (especially at first), shortly petiolate, $\frac{1}{8}$ to $\frac{3}{16}$ in. long. *fl.* in clusters of 2, 3, or more, terminal or axillary; cor. relatively large, bright yellow, standard more or less pubescent; cal. silky-hairy. July, August. *Pod* linear-oblong, compressed, hairy. S. France. Of recent introduction. (J.R.H.S. 67, 90.) SYN. *G. sagittalis delphinensis, G. tetragona.* Might be a miniature of *G. sagittalis* except for the axillary fl.-clusters. One of the best rock-garden species.

**G. ephedroi'des.** Erect or slightly pendulous Ephedra-like shrub, 1 to $3\frac{1}{2}$ ft. h., with slightly pointed, slender, grooved, pubescent shoots. *l.* few, alternate, shortly stalked, basal 3-foliolate; lflets. linear or linear-oblong, silky-hairy, $\frac{1}{4}$ in. long. *fl.* fragrant, in loose terminal racemes; cor. yellow, small, standard and keel hairy; cal. silky-hairy. May, June. *Pods* oval, compressed, hairy, apiculate, $\frac{3}{8}$ in. long. Corsica, Sardinia. SYN. *G. gymnoptera, Spartium gymnoptera.* Not absolutely hardy.

**G. fe'rox.** Erect shrub up to 9 ft. h., older branches with large spines, young ones spiny at tips. *l.* sessile, basal only 3-foliolate; lflets. oblong to obovate, downy or nearly smooth, stipules tiny spines. Fragrant *fl.* in leafy racemes at ends of lateral branchlets; cor. yellow, smooth; cal. shortly pubescent. May, June. *Pods* linear, finely pointed, silky-hairy. NW. Africa. (B.R. 368.) SYN. *Spartium ferox.* Half-hardy.

**G. frag'rans.** A synonym of *Cytisus × racemosus.* A

**G. german'ica.** 1 to 2 ft. h. or more with erect, branching stems; older branches armed with usually compound spines, branchlets spineless, hairy. *l.* simple, ovate-lanceolate, shortly petiolate, hairy, $\frac{1}{2}$ to $\frac{3}{4}$ in. long. *fl.* in 1- to 2-in. leafy racemes at ends of young shoots; cor. yellow, downy, standard shorter than keel, cal. hairy. June, July. *Pods* oblong, compressed, hairy, $\frac{3}{8}$ in. long. Cent. and W. Europe. In cult. 1588, probably as a medicinal plant. (R.I.F.G. 22, f. 35.) SYN. *Cytisus dalmaticus* (of Visiani), *Scorpius spinosus.* Not in the first rank of Brooms. var. **iner'mis,** completely unarmed and, in a way, resembles *G. tinctoria.*

**G. glabres'cens.** A synonym of *Cytisus glabrescens.* The seed of this plant carries a very small strophiole but one, however, sufficient to stamp the species as a Cytisus.

**G. grandiflo'ra.** A synonym of *Cytisus grandiflora* (of de Candolle).

**G. hispan'ica.*** Spanish Gorse. Much-branched, very spiny shrub 1 to $3\frac{1}{2}$ ft. h. with ascending branches, branchlets densely covered with long white hairs. *l.* simple, about $\frac{1}{4}$ in. long, hairy, lower oblong-lanceolate and bluntish, upper linear-lanceolate, acute. *fl.* in clusters terminating erect, leafy shoots; cor. bright golden-yellow, standard smooth, keel pubescent; cal. hairy. June, July. *Pods* oblong, more or less pubescent, acute. SW. Europe. 1759. (B.M. 8528.) SYN. *Spartium Scorpius, S. spinosum.* One of the most brilliant garden shrubs when in flower, shapely and compact in its early years, but in age inclined to open out at the top and become straggling and untidy. Liable to damage in very severe winters.

**G. hor'rida.** Very spiny, compact shrub, seldom more than 2 ft. h., with smooth young shoots. *l.* opposite, small, 3-foliolate, lflets. linear-lanceolate, silky, ⅛ to ⅓ in. long. *fl.* in small terminal heads; cor. yellow, standard smooth, keel silky; cal. almost bell-shaped, yellowish, hairy. July to September. *Pods* oval-oblong, silky-tomentose, 1 in. or more long. Spain, where it is widely distributed, France (N. Pyrenees). 1821. (G.C. 53 (1913), 140. SYN. *G. erinacea, Spartium horridum.* Not absolutely hardy. var. **erioca'lyx,** cal. woolly hairy or reddish tomentose, outer surface of standard and keel silky or reddish tomentose. Spain. SYN. *G. Boissieri.*

**G. humifu'sa.** A synonym of *G. micrantha, G. pilosa, G. Villarsii,* and *G. tinctoria littoralis.*

**G. januen'sis.*** Genoa Broom. Procumbent shrub, shoots erect or ascending about 1 ft. h., 3-angled, slightly winged with translucent membrane. Dwarf Broom, up to 2 or 3 ft. across, growing quickly. *l.* simple, usually clustered at base of flowering shoots, lanceolate to oblong, shortly apiculate or sub-acute, obscurely ciliolate, otherwise smooth, ½ to 1 in. long. *fl.* in leafy racemes at ends of erect branchlets; cor. bright yellow, smooth; cal. smooth. May, June. *Pods* smooth, about 1 in. long. SE. Europe, about 1840, but lost until recently reintroduced. (B.M. 9574.) SYN. *G. scariosa, G. triangularis, G. triquetra* (of Waldstein). Apt to be badly cut in a severe winter.

**G. jun'cea.** A synonym of *Spartium junceum.*

**G. Lobel'ii.** A synonym of *G. aspalathoides.*

**G. lyd'ia.** About 2 ft. h., unarmed except for spine-tipped flowering shoots. *l.* simple, linear-elliptical or linear-obovate, sub-acute or pointed, smooth, about ⅜ in. long. *fl.* in sub-terminal racemes on apical, spine-tipped shoots; cor. bright yellow, smooth; cal. tubular, smooth. May, June. *Pods* smooth, flat, linear, about 1 in. long. E. and SE. Europe, Syria. Recent. SYN. *G. spathulata.* Hardy in S. England.

**G. micran'tha.** Smooth, unarmed dwarf shrub, 4 to 12 in. h., branches erect or ascending, shoots narrow, and graceful. *l.* sessile, simple, linear-lanceolate, mucronate, smooth, shining with persistent awl-shaped stipules. Fragrant *fl.* in loose terminal racemes of 5 to 20 on branchlets; cor. yellow, smooth, standard ovate-cordate, keel short; cal. short-campanulate, smooth. July, August. *Pods* oblong, acuminate, upper margin ciliate. Spain. SYN. *G. humifusa* (of Boutelow), *G. odoratissima, G. tenella.* Allied to *G. tinctoria.* Not reliably hardy.

**G. monosper'ma.** Half-hardy, loose, unarmed shrub 2 to 4 ft. h. in cultivation, up to 10 ft. in nature, branches slender, drooping, silky when young. *Lower l.* obovate or linear-lanceolate; *upper* linear-obovate, all simple, rarely 3-foliolate, silky, falling early, ¼ to ¾ in. long, sparse. Very fragrant *fl.* in short, lateral racemes from wood of current year; cor. white, silky-pubescent without; cal. purplish, shortly campanulate. Early spring. *Pod* knife-shaped or ovate, mucronate, slightly wrinkled, brownish-yellow. S. Spain, Portugal, NW. Africa. 1690. (B.M. 683.) SYN. *Retama monosperma, Spartium monospermum.*

**G. murc'ica.** Much-branched, spiny shrub of 4 to 16 in. h., erect or almost prostrate, Erinacea-like, older branches tortuous and bare, young ones at first silky-pubescent, terminating in spines. *l.* usually simple, small, linear-oblong, silky-pubescent, fall early, stipules denticulate or almost wanting. *fl.* in sub-terminal racemes on spine-tipped branchlets; cor. yellow, standard widely ovate, smooth without, keel silky-pubescent; cal. campanulate, silky. May, June. *Pod* linear, silky. W. Spain (Murcia and Valentia). Half-hardy.

**G. nyssa'na.*** Nissa Broom. Erect, unarmed, pubescent shrub with rounded, silky-hairy young shoots. *l.* 3-foliolate; lflets. linear or lanceolate, acute, silky-hairy, ¾ to 1 in. long. *fl.* in terminal, leafy racemes up to 8 in. long; cor. yellow, standard and keel pubescent; cal. pubescent. June, July. *Pod* broadly oblong, pointed, about ⅜ in. long. Cent. Balkans. 1889.

**G. ova'ta.** A synonym of *G. tinctoria ovata.*

**G. pilo'sa.*** Low procumbent or prostrate shrub from 3 to 20 in. h., with erect or ascending, silky-hairy young shoots, eventually forming an intricate mass of interwoven, rooting branches. *Lower l.* clustered; *upper* alternate, all simple, elliptical-oblong or obovate, obtuse, almost smooth above, hairy beneath, often folded lengthwise, stipulate, ¼ to ½ in. long. *fl.* in terminal racemes on branchlets; cor. rather small, yellow, standard and keel silky-pubescent without; cal. appressed-silky. May to July. *Pod* linear-oblong, compressed, hairy, up to 1 in. long. S. Europe including SW. England. Cult. 1790. (E.B. 327.) SYN. *G. repens, G. humifusa* (of Thore), *Cytisus pilosus, Spartium pilosum.*

**G. procum'bens.** A synonym of *Cytisus procumbens.*

**G. prostra'ta.** A synonym of *Cytisus decumbens.*

**G. pulchel'la** (of Grenier and Godron, not of Visconti). A synonym of *G. Villarsii.*

**G. radia'ta.** More or less rounded, densely branched, unarmed shrub about 3 ft. h. with evergreen, pubescent shoots. *l.* opposite, shortly petiolate, 3-foliolate; lflets. linear, silky-hairy, ¼ to ½ in. long. *fl.* in terminal heads of 2 to 7; cor. yellow, standard pubescent, keel hairy; cal. silky-hairy. May to July. *Pods* curved, acuminate, ovate, silky-hairy, about $\frac{5}{16}$ in. long. SE. France, Cent. and E. Europe. About 1750. (B.M. 2260.) SYN. *Cytisus radiatus, Spartium radiatum.*

**G. Raet'am.** White Broom, Juniper Bush. Graceful, half-hardy shrub, 3 to 10 ft. h., with wand-like branches and shoots, the latter appressed-pubescent. *l.* sparse, mostly simple, more or less pubescent, linear, $\frac{3}{16}$ in. long. *fl.* in subsessile, lateral clusters from shoots of current year; cor. white; cal. small, shortly campanulate, more or less pubescent. March, April. *Pod* inflated, sharply and obliquely beaked, ⅜ in. long. Syria, Palestine. SYN. *Retama Raetam.*

**G. ramosis'sima** (of Poiret). Shrub, 2 or 3 ft. h., with tomentose shoots. *l.* oblong, obovate, or oval, obtuse where near fl., lanceolate and acute on shoots of the year; all simple, flat, smooth above, hairy beneath. *fl.* usually in pairs from shoots of previous year; cor. yellow, standard notched and silky-hairy without, keel silky-hairy; cal. grey-tomentose. April, May. *Pod* linear-oblong, acuminate, silky-hairy. Spain, Algeria. (Fl. Atl. 2, t. 178 as *Spartium ramosissimum.*) Half-hardy. *G. ramosissima* of Boissier is *G. cinerea.*

**G. re'pens.** A synonym of *G. pilosa.*

**G. sagittal'is.*** Deciduous, prostrate shrub with winged and occasionally rooting evergreen branches, wings hairy and usually narrowed at nodes giving the stems a jointed appearance. Very robust. *l.* simple, shortly petiolate, oval, ovate, or lanceolate, acute, hairy, especially in youth, ¼ to ½ in. long. *fl.* in erect, terminal racemes; cor. yellow, smooth, large; cal. silky-hairy. June, July. *Pod* linear-oblong, compressed, apiculate, about ¾ in. long. Cent. and SE. Europe, France. Cult. 1588, probably as a medicinal plant. (T.S.A.P., 15.) SYN. *Cytisus sagittalis, Spartium sagittale.* Has no objection to partial shade and capable of considerable spread.

**G. scopa'ria.** A synonym of *Cytisus scoparius.*

**G. Scor'pius.** Much-branched, very spiny shrub up to 7 ft. h. *l.* simple, lanceolate or linear-lanceolate, shortly petiolate, feebly pubescent on lower surface, stipules small and spine-like. *fl.* usually in axillary clusters, rarely solitary or in pairs, from upper part of young spine-bearing branches forming a raceme; cor. golden-yellow, standard and keel smooth; cal. smooth, lips almost equal, teeth of upper sharply pointed, triangular, of lower linear. May to July. *Pod* broadly linear, smooth, more or less curved. Portugal, Spain, Balearic Is., SE. France. (S.B.F.G. s. 2, 63.) SYN. *Spartium Scorpium, S. spinosum.* Half-hardy.

**G. seric'ea.** Low decumbent shrub, 6 to 9 in. h., with ascending, appressed-pubescent young shoots. *l.* simple, narrowly oblong or elliptical, blunt or sub-acute, silky-hairy at edges and on lower surface, ¼ to ⅓ in. long. *fl.* in sub-racemose, terminal clusters; cor. yellow, standard and keel silky-hairy; cal. silky-hairy. May, June. *Pod* silky-hairy, about ⅜ in. long. NE. Adriatic, especially near Trieste.

**G. sibir'ica.** A synonym of *G. tinctoria elongata.*

**G. spathula'ta.** A synonym of *G. lydia.*

**G. teretifo'lia.** Low, dense, erect shrub about 1 ft. h. with silky-puberulent young shoots. *l.* simple, lower clustered, upper alternate, obovate-lanceolate or lanceolate, silky-hairy beneath, much folded longitudinally, about ¼ in. long. *fl.* in short racemes terminating branchlets; cor. yellow, standard slightly notched, silky without, keel silky, obtuse; cal. very short, tubular-campanulate, silvery-hairy. June. N. Spain. Not reliably hardy.

**G. tincto'ria.** Dyer's Greenweed. Waxen Woad. Erect, ascending or procumbent shrub from a few in. to over 3 ft. h. with slender, smooth, downy or hairy young shoots. *l.* simple, oval to linear-lanceolate, acute or obtuse, smooth or more or less pubescent or hairy especially beneath and on margins up to 1 in. long. *fl.* in terminal, leafy racemes, erect or sub-erect, forming a panicle; cor. yellow, smooth; cal. smooth, pubescent or hairy. June to late summer. *Pods* linear, slightly arched, more or less abruptly pointed, smooth, up to 1 in. long. Europe, including Britain, W. and N. Asia. (E.B. 328.) SYN. *G. inermis, Spartium tinctorium, Cytisus tinctorius.* var. **ela'tior,** glabrous, *l.* longer and a little wider than in type, *fl.* large, *pods* smooth. Very robust. Italy. 1818. SYN. *G. anxantica, G. tinctoria anxantica*; **elonga'ta,** hairy, more vigorous than type, erect, up to 6 ft., branches long, slender, very leafy, *l.* up to 1¾ in. long, lanceolate, pointed. SYN. *G. elata, G. sibirica*; **elongata fl. pl.** has double fl. SYN. *G. sibirica fl. pl.*; **hirsu'ta,** branches and *l.* hairy but *pod* almost smooth. SYN. *G. pubescens*; **man'tica,** procumbent, hairy or bristly, 18 in. or more h. Italy. 1816. (R.I.F.G. 22, f. 37.) SYN. *G. mantica, G. tinctoria humilior*; **ova'ta,** hairy, ascending or erect, about 20 in. h., *l.* ovate or lanceolate, *pods* usually villous. Cent. and S. Europe. 1819. SYN. *G. ovata.*

**G. triangular'is.** A synonym of *G. januensis.*

**G. triquet'ra** (of l'Héritier, not of Waldstein). Procumbent shrub with sparsely pubescent, 3-angled stems. *l.* usually 3-foliolate at base of shoots, simple above; lflets. oval, lanceolate, or oblong-obovate, acute or obtuse, sparsely pubescent. *fl.* in leafless terminal racemes of 3 to 8; cor. bright yellow, standard broad; cal. sparsely pubescent. May, June. Unknown wild and by some presumed to be a hybrid. 1770. Now exceedingly rare if still cultivated. (B.M. 314.) *G. triquetra* of Waldstein and Kitaibel is *G. januensis.*

**G. Villars'ii.*** Dense low shrub with prostrate, tortuous, rooting branches, at first ascending or spreading and very hairy. *l.* simple, subsessile, lower clustered, upper alternate, linear-lanceolate, hairy, ⅛ to $\frac{5}{16}$ in. long. *fl.* in short, leafy racemes at ends of branchlets, sometimes reduced to 1 fl.; cor. yellow, silky-hairy; cal. very hairy.

June, July. *Pod* oblong, compressed, hairy, about ⅓ in. long. SE. France, W. Balkans. (J.R.H.S. 67, 90.) Syn. *G. humifusa* (of Villars), *G. pulchella*, *G. Villarsiana*, *Cytisus Villarsii*. In nature, in poor and dry situations, the branchlets are sometimes spine-tipped, greyish-green owing to the hairiness of the young shoots and l. Excellent plant for sunny ledges in rock-gardens.

**G. virga′ta.** Madeira Broom. Tall, graceful shrub, 6 to 12 ft. h. with both erect and spreading, slightly pendent shoots, keeping l. a long time. *l.* simple, short-stalked or sessile, shape very variable but generally narrower towards ends of shoots, on the lower part of latter elliptical or obovate, obtuse, sub-acute, or rarely mucronate, on upper part narrowly oblong or lanceolate, more or less acute or mucronate, all silky-pubescent, especially beneath, and from ½ to ¾ in. long. *fl.* in shortish terminal racemes; cor. yellow, standard somewhat rounded and, with the keel, silky-pubescent; cal. campanulate, silky-pubescent. June, July. *Pods* oblong or elliptical, acute, often mucronate, silky-hairy, about ¾ in. long. Madeira. 1777. (B.R. 30, 11.) Syn. *Cytisus virgatus*.

F. S.

## GENTIAN. *See* Gentiana.

**GENTIAN′A** (in honour of Gentius, a King of Illyrica in ancient days, who is said to have been the discoverer of the medicinal value of Gentian root). Fam. *Gentianaceae*. A genus of about 400 species of annual or perennial, (rarely biennial) often tufted herbs, distributed over the temperate and alpine regions of the world, especially in Europe and Asia, where they often form a brilliant feature of the mountain flora, N. and S. America, and New Zealand. Their distribution is a guarantee that the great majority are hardy. They vary a great deal in stature. Leaves opposite, often sessile. Flowers of various colours, especially blues, purples, violet, mauve, and occasionally yellow, predominate in Europe and Asia; whites in New Zealand; while bright colours, including red and something approaching scarlet, occur in S. America. The flowers may be solitary or clustered, terminal or axillary, sessile or stalked, erect or inclined, rarely nodding; calyx of 4 or 5 sepals, the tube sometimes split on one side; corolla usually funnel- or bell-shaped, sometimes tubular or club-shaped, lobes 4 or 5 to 7; stamens 4 or 5; ovary 2-celled. Fruit a capsule with many ovules. A few species are half-hardy climbers, often kept separate as a distinct genus, Crawfurdia, but structurally so similar to Gentiana, that they are included here. These (see synonyms) may be grown in the cold greenhouse or seedlings raised in gentle heat may be planted out at the foot of a south wall. The great majority of Gentians are moisture-loving plants from high mountains where they have full exposure to sun, and a continuous supply of underground water in summer, and are, in many instances, covered with snow for several months in the winter. It is not surprising, therefore, that with few exceptions their cultivation in this country is far from easy, and especially in eastern and southern districts. In the north and west, where cooler, damper conditions prevail, their cultivation is an easier matter. The number of Gentians which can be grown without any difficulty in all parts of the country is small; it includes *G. acaulis*, *G. gracilipes*, *G. lagodechiana*, *G. septemfida*, and, where some shade and moisture are available, *G. asclepiadea* and *G. Pneumonanthe*. *G. sino-ornata* can be easily grown if soil conditions are suitable, but it will refuse to grow at all if there is any trace of lime in the soil; in a light soil of sand and peat or leaf-soil it will flourish with no more trouble than to give it water in spring and early summer when it is growing. Many of the species which are particularly desirable can, however, be grown with comparative ease, not only in northern and western districts, but in many other localities where sharp drainage and an ample supply of water can be provided.　　　**A**

Gentians may be used to beautify many parts of the garden; those which are easily grown, and can be left to look after themselves without special care or attention, such as *G. acaulis*, *G. septemfida*, and some few others, may be grown in drifts or groups in beds, or may be used as an edging to beds or borders, where they will form an attractive feature in spring and summer. Dwarf Gentians of the *G. ornata* and *G. sino-ornata* types and their hybrids are admirably suited for planting in the lower, moister parts of the rock-garden, in the south with a north exposure, or where they can have shade from trees or shrubs in the hottest part of the day, while in the north a more open exposure will meet their requirements, but Gentians other than the woodland species should never be planted under trees where there is drip from the leaves and branches. Even in southern and eastern districts some of the Gentians require fuller exposure to sun than others, and experience alone can decide how full that exposure must be for different species in varying localities. There is no doubt, however, that *G. acaulis* and the many species to which it is closely related, *G. alpina*, *G. Loderi*, and probably *G. cachemirica*, are among those which should have an open, sunny position in the garden. Other species, such as the stately *G. lutea*, the British *G. Pneumonanthe*, and its variety from the Styrian Alps, can be effectively used for planting by the water-side, while in the woodland and in semi-shady spots *G. asclepiadea* in many shades of blue and in its white form will look after itself and quickly become naturalized. The introduction of such plants as *G. Farreri*, *G. ornata*, *G. sino-ornata*, and *G. Veitchiorum*, and the many fine hybrids which have been produced from them, of which *G.×Macaulayi* is a good example, has enabled the rock-garden to produce a wealth of colour in the late summer and autumn which was entirely unknown in the first 20 years of the present century. In preparing places for Gentians in the rock-garden a light soil and thorough drainage should be the main considerations, though it must always be remembered that Gentians should never be allowed to get dry at the root, and that all of them benefit from an ample supply of water in spring and summer.

Propagation may be effected by seed, by cuttings, and by division of the plants. Most of the Gentians set and ripen their seed in this country, and propagation from seed is the general method of increasing a stock of plants, but it is not always the most satisfactory method. Within a few years of their introduction to this country several of the species seem to lose both the habit and characteristics of their species and the form and colour of their flowers, to such an extent that the plants as originally introduced are being lost to cultivation. Where plants do not come true from seed, propagation by cuttings or by division of the plants will always be advisable if possible.

The raising of Gentians from seed is not a difficult matter but it requires a good deal of care and attention. The seed should be sown thinly in pots or pans as soon as it is ripe, and should be only just covered; old seed is very slow in germinating and seedlings may not appear for a year or more. The soil in the pots must be light and porous, and the drainage must be perfect; a useful mixture would consist of equal parts of finely sifted loam, sharp sand, and peat or leaf-mould. It is a good plan to sink the pots in sand or sifted ashes up to the rim, cover them with a light to protect them from heavy rain, and shade them from the sun; if this is done they will require no further attention until the winter when the light and shading may be taken off, and the pots fully exposed to frost and snow. With the return of milder weather the pots should be removed to a greenhouse or cold frame as the seedlings appear. Watering and shading will then require attention for the seedlings should never be exposed to the sun or allowed to get dry. When they are big enough to handle with ease the seedlings may be pricked off into pans or boxes, and again in light soil, and, if there are only a few, they may be put singly in small pots, but this must be done with care as Gentian seedlings resent disturbance of their roots. If the seedlings are not big enough to handle before the end of June it is better to leave them in the seed-pot until the following spring when they will be more likely to stand the move.

In recent years propagation of Gentians by cuttings in spring has been taken in hand by some specialists and by a few nurserymen and amateurs, but is far from being a general practice. It requires skill, care, and attention for several months though it is a quick and useful method of increasing a stock of plants. It cannot be adopted for all Gentians, but only where the plants form a series of shoots from the base such as those in the *G. septemfida* and *G. ornata* groups. When the young growths are an inch or two in length they are cut off just above the crown of the plant and inserted in sharp sand or other suitable medium in a frame or greenhouse where they must be kept moist and shaded from the sun. When well rooted the cuttings should be potted off singly in light soil and will require care for some time in watering and shading until they have grown and can be hardened off. For some years gardeners have propagated a few of the Gentians from cuttings taken in July and August when, for instance, it has been desired to increase a well-coloured form of a plant such as *G. Farreri*, which cannot be relied on to reproduce itself true from seed.

Gentians which have fibrous roots and which form a number of shoots from the base can be propagated by division of the plants; those which have a single root stock and a central rosette of leaves do not admit of propagation in this way. *G. acaulis* and the several species to which it is akin are the easiest to deal with and can be divided without much risk of damage to the plants, but it must always be remembered that, as before-mentioned, all Gentians are very sensitive of root disturbance, and division should be done as carefully and expeditiously as possible. Early spring, when the plants are starting into growth, is the best time for dividing them, and for transplanting them, but, when once planted, a Gentian with a tap root should not be moved unless it is really necessary. *G. sino-ornata* is a good example of the class of plant which can be easily divided, and in the same class there are many others including *G. Farreri*, *G. ornata*, *G. prolata*, *G. Veitchiorum*, and the numerous hybrids of all of them. The plants are lifted in the spring when they are starting into growth and the soil carefully shaken away from the roots, when it will be found that each of the basal shoots has a root system to itself which can easily be separated from the others and replanted.

(C. T. M.)

Gentians are not likely to suffer from many fungus attacks, but occasionally leaf-spots occur, the chief being Rust, *Puccinia gentianae*, causing light- and dark-brown pustules on the leaves and stems. Destruction of all affected leaves or badly affected plants should soon eliminate it as all stages are on the Gentian. There is a yellowing and Stem Rot of Gentians, especially *G. sino-ornata*, which is caused by various fungi, but usually the plants are first weakened by dry conditions. Mulching with peat-mould or fine leaf-mould is advisable on light soils to ensure constant moisture at the root.

(D. E. G.)

**G. acau'lis.*** Perennial of 2 to 4 in., tufted, fl.-stem unbranched. *Basal l.* narrow-ovate to spatulate, ¾ to 1½ in. long, half as wide, glossy green, narrowed to base; *stem-l.* smaller, wider. *fl.* solitary, terminal, deep blue, with deeper markings in tube, 2 in. long or more, funnel-bell-shaped; cor. lobes ovate, spreading, acute; plicae irregularly triangular; cal. ½ in. long, funnel-shaped, lobes ¼ in. long, ovate, acute, narrowed at base. May, June. Europe. (Gen. 14.) SYN. *G. Gentianella* of gardens. Variable with many colour forms. var. **al'ba,** *fl.* white; **alpi'na,** a synonym of *G. alpina*; **azu'rea,** *fl.* paler blue; **dinar'ica,** a synonym of *G. dinarica*; **gigan'tea,** *fl.* larger than type; **grandiflo'ra, Kochia'na, latifo'lia,** and **vulga'ris,** synonyms of *G. Kochiana*.

**G. adscend'ens.** A synonym of *G. decumbens*.

**G. af'finis.** Erect or sub-erect perennial about 12 in. h. *l.* in many pairs, ½ to 1½ in. long, thick, lower obovate to oblong, blunt, upper narrower, more acute. *fl.* few together, terminal and in upper l.-axils, blue or purplish-blue, 1 to 1½ in. long, tubular to funnel-shaped; cal. ¼ to ½ in. long, rarely split, the longer lobes unequal, linear-lanceolate, equalling the tube, the shorter awl-shaped; cor. lobes ovate, slightly spreading; plicae ovate, 2- or 3-cleft. August, September. N. America. (B.B. 2, 615.) Differs from *G. oregana* by the narrower cal. lobes, narrower l., and narrower funnel-shaped cor. var. **Bigelov'ii,** *see* **G. Bigelovii**; **Forwood'ii,** *see* **G. Forwoodii**; **ma'jor,** upper part of stem long, *fl.* larger.

**G. al'ba.** Perennial of 1 to 2 ft. Stem thick, erect. *l.* on stem only, ovate to oblong-lanceolate, 3 to 4 in. long, ¾ to 1 in. wide, cordate at base, pointed, entire. *fl.* in terminal and axillary clusters, sessile or nearly so, whitish, tinged yellowish-green, 1¼ in. long, club- or bell-shaped; cor. lobes ovate; plicae half length of lobes, irregularly toothed; cal. ¼ to ½ in. long, bell-shaped, the ovate or heart-shaped lobes shorter than tube, acute, reflexed. Autumn. N. America. (B.M. 1551 as *G. ochroleuca*.) SYN. *G. flavida*.

*Gentiana algida*

**G. al'gida.** Perennial of 4 to 8 in. Stems erect, simple. *l.* at base narrow-spatulate, 3 in. long, thick, blunt, entire, on stem in 2 or 3 pairs, shorter, lanceolate. *fl.* 1 to 3, terminal and axillary, stalked, whitish, spotted and lined blue, 1½ to 1¾ in. long, narrowly obconic; cor. lobes ⅕ to ¼ in. long, erect, triangular, acute; plicae irregular, sometimes toothed; cal. ½ in. long, cylindric, tinged purple, lobes ¼ to ½ in. long, unequal, linear. August. Siberia. 1808. (G.F. 1006.) Distinct from *G. frigida* by the size of the cal. and the ovate unequal cal. lobes. SYN. *G. frigida algida*. var. **Igarash'ii,** cor. white, lined blue. Japan.

**G. alpi'na.*** Perennial of 2 to 5 in. Stems erect, simple. *l.* at base broadly elliptic, ½ to ¾ in. long, leathery; on stem ⅓ in. long, narrower. *fl.* solitary, terminal, deep blue, deeper in throat, spotted green, 1 to 1¾ in. long, funnel-shaped; cor. lobes rounded; plicae irregular, triangular; cal. ¼ to ½ in. long, bell-shaped, lobes ⅛ in. long, ovate from a wide base. July. European Alps. 1854. (R.I.F.G. xvii, 1053, f. 1, 2 as *G. acaulis alpina*.) Distinct from *G. acaulis* by the size and shape of the cal. lobes and by the funnel-shaped cor.

**G. alta'ica.** Perennial of 2 to 3 in. Stems erect, simple. *Basal l.* in a lax rosette, linear to linear-lanceolate, 1 in. long, pointed, margins rough; *stem-l.* ½ in. long, overlapping. *fl.* solitary, terminal, deep blue, paler in throat, 1½ in. long, funnel-shaped; lobes rounded, ovate; plicae half as long as cor. lobes, toothed; cal. about ½ in. long, lobes ¼ in. long, unequal, lanceolate, acute. May, June. Asia. (Gen. 19.) *l.* more tapered than in *G. pyrenaica* and cor. of different shape.

**G. ambig'ua.** *G. brachyphylla* × *G. verna*.

**G. amoe'na.** Tufted perennial, 1 to 2 in. h. *l.* broadly obovate, ¼ to ½ in. long, overlapping, truncate, and nicked at tip, entire. *fl.* solitary, sessile among l., pale to deep blue, tinged purple on lobes, with whitish bands, ½ to ¾ in. long, bell-shaped; lobes ovate; plicae triangular, entire; cal. ¼ in. long, tubular, lobes slightly shorter than tube, truncate, nicked at tip. Autumn. Himalaya. (Gen. 18.) var. **ma'jor,** larger than type, *l.* ½ to 1 in. long, *fl.* 1½ to 2½ in. long. 1938; **pal'lida,** *fl.* pale blue, 1 to 1¼ in. long, widely bell-shaped. (Gen. 17.)

**G. Andrew'sii.** Perennial with leafy erect stem 1 to 2 ft. h. *l.* lanceolate to ovate, 2 to $3\frac{1}{2}$ in. long, deep green, tinged purple; lower l. shorter. *fl.* in terminal heads and in upper axils, deep blue, white on lobes, $1\frac{1}{2}$ in. long, club-shaped, the mouth closed; lobes ovate; plicae larger than lobes, many-cleft; cal. $\frac{1}{2}$ in. long, lobes shorter than tube, linear-obovate, recurved. Summer. N. America. 1776. (B.M. 6421.) var. **al'ba,** not so tall, *fl.* white or whitish.

**G. angulo'sa.*** Tufted perennial. Stem erect, simple, 2 to 5 in. h. *l.* in rosette, ovate-oblong to oblong-lanceolate, $\frac{3}{4}$ to 1 in. long; on stem ovate, shorter. *fl.* solitary, sessile or nearly so, deep lilac, $\frac{3}{4}$ to 1 in. across, saucer-shaped; lobes broadly ovate; plicae 2-fid, small; cal. tubular, prominently winged, $\frac{1}{2}$ to $\frac{3}{4}$ in. long; lobes $\frac{1}{4}$ in. long, lanceolate, acute. May, June. Caucasus, Siberia. 1808. (Gen. 16.) Larger than *G. verna* and distinct by the prominently winged cal.

**G. angustifo'lia.*** Slender-stemmed perennial, 2 to 4 in. h., tufted and stoloniferous. Stems simple, erect. *Basal l.* broadest in middle, 2 in. long, $\frac{1}{8}$ to $\frac{1}{3}$ as wide; *stem-l.* 1 in. long, broader. *fl.* solitary, stalked, terminal, deep sky-blue, paler within, 2 in. long, funnel-shaped; lobes ovate, acute; plicae irregular, blunt; cal. $\frac{1}{2}$ in. long, bell-shaped; lobes $\frac{1}{4}$ in. long, ovate-oblong, narrowed at base, acute, standing at right angles to cal. tube. July. European Alps. 1852. (R.I.F.G. xvii, 1200, f. 3 as *G. sabauda.*) Taller and more slender than *G. acaulis* with different cal. lobes. *G. angustifolia* of Michaux is *G. Porphyrio.*

**G. arvernen'sis.** A synonym of *G. Pneumonanthe depressa.*

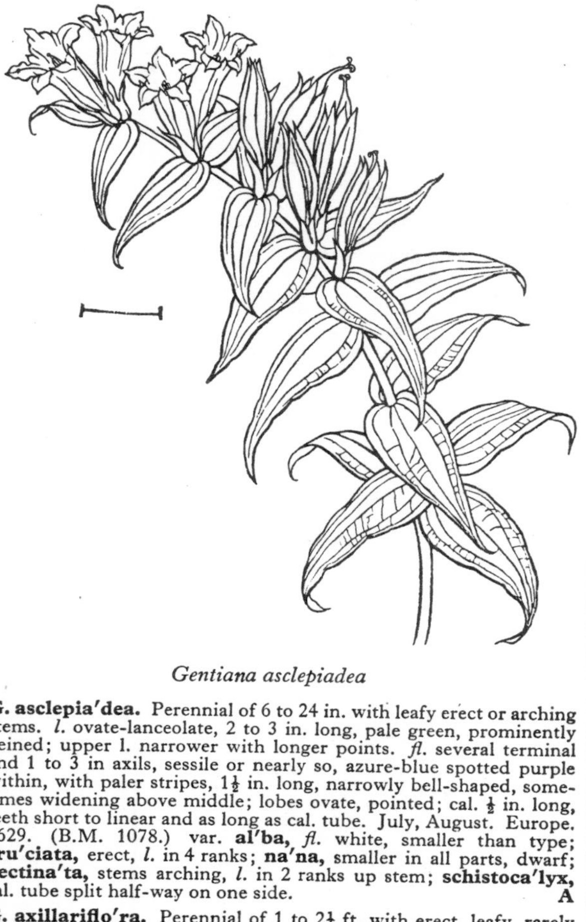

*Gentiana asclepiadea*

**G. asclepia'dea.** Perennial of 6 to 24 in. with leafy erect or arching stems. *l.* ovate-lanceolate, 2 to 3 in. long, pale green, prominently veined; upper l. narrower with longer points. *fl.* several terminal and 1 to 3 in axils, sessile or nearly so, azure-blue spotted purple within, with paler stripes, $1\frac{1}{2}$ in. long, narrowly bell-shaped, sometimes widening above middle; lobes ovate, pointed; cal. $\frac{1}{2}$ in. long, teeth short to linear and as long as cal. tube. July, August. Europe. 1629. (B.M. 1078.) var. **al'ba,** *fl.* white, smaller than type; **cru'ciata,** erect, *l.* in 4 ranks; **na'na,** smaller in all parts, dwarf; **pectina'ta,** stems arching, *l.* in 2 ranks up stem; **schistoca'lyx,** cal. tube split half-way on one side. **A**

**G. axillariflo'ra.** Perennial of 1 to $2\frac{1}{2}$ ft. with erect, leafy, rarely branched stems. *l.* ovate to ovate-lanceolate, narrower in upper part of stem, 2 to 4 in. long. *fl.* forming a raceme, sessile or nearly so, mauve-blue, 2 in. long; lobes ovate, nearly erect; plicae triangular, short; cal. $\frac{1}{2}$ to $\frac{3}{4}$ in. long, tubular; lobes $\frac{1}{4}$ in. long, linear, wide apart. September. Japan. Distinct from *G. scabra* by the racemose infl.

**G. barbella'ta.** Erect, branched at base, 4 to 6 in. h. *Basal l.* spatulate, $1\frac{1}{2}$ to 2 in. long, thick, fleshy; *stem-l.* linear. *fl.* terminal on short stalks, bright blue, $1\frac{1}{4}$ to $1\frac{1}{2}$ in. long, funnel-shaped, lobes 4, oblong, toothed at tips, fringed at sides; cal. $\frac{1}{2}$ in. long, lobes 4, outer linear-lanceolate, inner ovate-lanceolate. N. America.

**G. bavar'ica.** Tufted perennial, 2 to 6 in. h. Stem erect. *Basal l.* obovate to spatulate, $\frac{1}{4}$ to $\frac{1}{3}$ in. long, thick, lowest smallest, rounded at tip, entire; on stem rounded. *fl.* deep blue, saucer-shaped, $\frac{1}{2}$ to $\frac{3}{4}$ in. across; lobes obovate, blunt, plicae 2-lobed; cal. $\frac{1}{4}$ to $\frac{1}{2}$ in. long, funnel-shaped, angled or slightly winged, lobes lanceolate, $\frac{1}{4}$ in. long. July, August. Cent. Europe. 1775. (Gen. 22.) SYN. *G. rotundifolia.* Differs from *G. verna* and *G. Rostanii* by the rounded l. and from *G. verna* by the thick l. smallest near root. Swampy soil in full sun.

*Gentiana bavarica*

**G. bellidifo'lia.** Branching perennial, 1 to 6 in. h. Stem erect. *l.* dark brownish-green, rosettes loose, spatulate to linear-spatulate, 1 to $1\frac{1}{2}$ in. long, fleshy, tip rounded, on stem in 2 or 3 pairs, linear obovate, sessile, recurved at margin. *fl.* in terminal umbels, stalked, white, $\frac{3}{4}$ in. across, open bell-shaped, lobes 3 times as long as tube, oblong-obovate, tips rounded; plicae very small; cal. small, bell-shaped, lobes $\frac{1}{4}$ in. long, linear-oblong to elliptic-ovate. July, August. New Zealand. (Gen. 23.) Smaller and with fewer fl. in umbel than in *G. patula.*

**G.×Bernard'ii** (*G. sino-ornata*×*G. Veitchiorum*). Habit and *l.* intermediate between parents. *fl.* solitary, terminal on branched stems, deep purple-blue, deepest within and on plicae, 2 to $2\frac{1}{2}$ in. long, funnel-shaped, lobes broadly triangular; plicae small; cal. tube $\frac{1}{2}$ to $\frac{3}{4}$ in. long, lobes about as long as tube, lanceolate. August, September. Of garden origin. (Gen. 6.) Differs from *G. sino-ornata* by the shape of the cor. tube, colour, and broader cor. lobes, from *G. Veitchiorum* by the cal. tube and lobes being of equal length, and the erect fl.

**G. Bigelov'ii.** Erect, leafy perennial, 12 to 15 in. h. *l.* oblong to obovate, upper narrower, 1 to 2 in. long, blunt. *fl.* in a raceme, sessile or nearly so, mauve-blue to violet, $\frac{3}{4}$ to 1 in. long, funnel-shaped to cylindrical, lobes broadly ovate, acute; plicae half as long as lobes, erect, 2-cleft; cal. tubular, $\frac{1}{3}$ to $\frac{1}{2}$ in. long, tinged purple, lobes as long or nearly as long as tube, linear, pointed. August. Rocky Mts., Colorado to Arizona. (B.M. 6874.) More erect than *G. affinis* with more cylindric and shorter cor. and racemose infl. SYN. *G. affinis Bigelovii.*

**G. bisetae'a.** Erect or ascending perennial, 12 to 15 in. h. *l.* ovate to oblong, upper lanceolate, $\frac{3}{4}$ to 1 in. long. *fl.* solitary, stalked, blue to purplish-blue, 1 to $1\frac{1}{4}$ in. long, bell-shaped; lobes oblong, acute; plicae 2- to 3-cleft, long, hair-like; cal. long, lobes $\frac{1}{3}$ in. long, lanceolate, acute. July, August. Oregon.

**G. Boissier'i.** Prostrate or decumbent perennial, 6 in. long. *l.* in many pairs, broadly ovate, $\frac{1}{3}$ to $\frac{1}{2}$ in. long. *fl.* solitary, terminal, blue, 1 to $1\frac{1}{2}$ in. long, nearly club-shaped; lobes ovate; plicae short, 2- to 4-cleft; cal. $\frac{1}{3}$ to $\frac{1}{2}$ in. long, sometimes split, $\frac{1}{4}$ in. long, elliptic to linear. August. Asia Minor.

**G. bomareoi'des.** Climber of 4 to 8 ft. *l.* broadly ovate to heart-shaped, 2 to 3 in. long, markedly veined; stalk long. *fl.* 2 or 3 in l.-axils, purple-blue, lined, $1\frac{1}{4}$ in. long; lobes short, triangular; plicae short; cal. tube less than $\frac{1}{2}$ in. long, tubular, lobes erect, as long as tube, ovate, nearly touching. October. NE. Burma.

**G. Bor'yi.** Tufted, creeping, stems branched, 1 to $1\frac{1}{2}$ in. h. *l.* ovate to orbicular, under $\frac{1}{4}$ in. long, fleshy, blunt. *fl.* solitary, terminal, pale blue, white inside, purplish-brown without, $\frac{1}{2}$ in. long; lobes rounded; plicae white, toothed; cal. bell-shaped, $\frac{1}{4}$ in. long, lobes shorter, erect, lanceolate. Spain.

**G. brachyphyl'la.*** Tufted, erect perennial, 2 to 3 in. h. *l.* rhomboid, all $\frac{1}{4}$ in. long, thick, overlapping, slightly glaucous, margins rough. *fl.* solitary, terminal, deep blue, saucer-shaped, $\frac{3}{4}$ in. across, lobes lanceolate to ovate-lanceolate, blunt; plicae 2-lobed, very short; cal. $\frac{1}{2}$ in. long, tubular, angled or slightly winged, lobes one-third as long as tube, triangular. Europe. (Gen. 21.) High alpine form of *G. verna,* with overlapping l. of equal size and more slender cal. and cor.

**G. bracteo'sa.** Erect, leafy perennial about 1 ft. h. *l.* elliptic to broad-ovate, over 1 in. long, uppermost rounder at apex. *fl.* in heads with upper pairs of l. forming an involucre; purplish-blue,

1½ in. long, widely funnel-shaped; cal. ½ in. long, split on one side, lobes one-third as long as tube; cor. lobes broadly ovate, pointed. August. N. America. Differs from *G. Parryi* by the narrower l. and ovate, not obovate, cor. lobes.

**G. brev'idens** of Regel is *G. tibetica*; of Franchet, *G. triflora*.

**G. Buerg'eri.** A variety of *G. scabra*.

**G. Bulleya'na.** Climber to 20 ft. *l.* broad-ovate to heart-shaped, 1 to 3 in. long, long-pointed. *fl.* axillary, solitary, pale bluish-purple, deeper within, 2 in. long, bell- to wide-funnel-shaped, lobes triangular; plicae rounded, short; cal. ⅓ to ¾ in. long, entire, lobes about ¼ in. long, leafy connate. October. Burma. SYN. *Crawfurdia Bulleyana*.

**G. Bungea'na.** A variety of *G. scabra*.

**G. Bur'seri.** Erect, unbranched perennial, 2 to 3 ft. h. *Basal l.* elliptic-ovate, 6 to 10 in. long, stalked; on stem rounder, 2 to 3 in. long, sessile. *fl.* terminal and in whorls in axils, yellow, greenish-yellow at base, 1½ in. long, narrow-bell-shaped; lobes 5 to 7, oblong, not widened in middle; plicae large, entire, triangular; cal. ½ in. long, papery, split to base, lobes none or very small. July. Europe. 1820. (R.I.F.G. xvii, 1055, f. 1.) Differs from *G. punctata* by the split cal. tubes and minute cal. lobes, and from *G. purpurea* by the colour of cor. and lobes not widened in middle. var. **Villars'ii**, cor. deeply spotted, lobes broader, rounder, plicae more abrupt. (R.I.F.G. xvii, 1055, f. 2.)

**G. cachemir'ica.*** Prostrate, branched perennial. Stems 6 to 10 in. long. *Basal l.* narrow ovate, 1 to 2 in. long, of stem roundish-ovate to ovate, blunt, glaucous. *fl.* solitary or few, terminal, pale blue, tubular-bell-shaped, over 1 in. long, lobes roundish-ovate; plicae toothed or fringed; cal. tubular, ½ in. long, lobes shorter, linear-oblong, acute. W. Himalaya. 1929. (Gen. 27, 28.) Stems longer and cal. narrower than in *G. Loderi*.

**G. calyco'sa.*** Erect or ascending perennial. Stems branched, 6 to 12 in. long. *l.* broadly ovate to heart-shaped, ½ to 1½ in. long, blunt. *fl.* solitary or rarely few, terminal with pair of l. just below; dark blue, paler in throat, spotted green, bell-shaped, 1½ in. long; lobes ovate, blunt, rather erect; plicae triangular, many-cleft, acute; cal. ⅛ to ½ in. long, lobes broadly ovate to heart-shaped. Autumn. N. America. 1888. (Gen. 26.) var. **montic'ola**, a synonym of *G. monticola*; **stric'ta**, dwarfer, more erect, with smaller fl.

**G. campanulifor'mis.** Tufted perennial. Stems erect, 4 to 6 in. h. *l.* narrow-spatulate, 1 to 1½ in. long, those of stem in 1 or 2 pairs. *fl.* solitary or rarely 2, long-stalked, blue, open bell-shaped, lobes obovate; cal. short, bell-shaped, cut almost to base, lobes ⅓ to ½ in. long, ovate to lanceolate. Andes of Peru. 1932.

**G. campes'tris.** Annual or biennial, erect, 2 to 12 in. long, very variable. *Basal l.* oblanceolate to spatulate, ½ to 1½ in. long, of stem lanceolate to ovate, longer than basal. *fl.* terminal, stalked, 4-parted, violet-blue to white, ¾ to 1 in. long, salver-shaped, throat hairy, lobes oblong-lanceolate; plicae absent; cal. ⅓ in. long, obconic, lobes twice length of tube, unequal, 2 broadly lanceolate, 2 lanceolate. Europe, including Britain. (E.B. 919.)

**G.×Carol'ii** (*G. Farreri*?×*G. Lawrencei*). Habit, *l.* and weak growth resembling *G. Lawrencei*. *fl.* solitary on branched stems, pale blue, striped without and within, about 2 in. long, narrowly funnel-shaped to tubular; lobes oblong; plicae pointed, often split; cal. ⅓ in. long, lobes ¾ to 1 in. long, linear. September. Of garden origin.

**G. Cates'baei** of Andrews is *G. Andrewsii*; of Walter, *G. Saponaria*; of Elliott, *G. Elliottii*.

**G. cephalan'tha.*** Leafy perennial. Stems sub-erect or decumbent, branched, 12 to 15 in. long. *Basal l.* oblong-lanceolate to lanceolate, 4 to 6 in. long, on stem oblong-lanceolate, all glaucous beneath. *fl.* clustered at and near top, 6 to 10, pale to mauve blue, funnel- to bell-shaped, ¾ to 1 in. long, lobes broad-ovate, acute; plicae under half length of cor. lobes, unequal, 2-fid; cal. ¼ in. long, 2 lobes large, leafy, 3 short, linear. September. SW. China. (B.M. 9468.) Differs from *G. rigescens* by branching habit, softer, narrower l., and clustered fls.

**G. ceri'na.** Stems stout, numerous, much branched, more or less prostrate at base, 4 to 14 in. h. *Lower l.* obovate or oblong-spatulate, ½ to 1½ in. long, obtuse, thick, smooth, shining; upper smaller with shorter stalks. *fl.* white with reddish-purple veining, crowded in corymbs at tips of branches; cor. ¾ in. long, deeply lobed, lobes blunt, oblong; cal. lobes ⅜ in. long, oblong-spatulate, obtuse, tip usually recurved; tube ⅛ in. long. August, September. New Zealand.

**G.×Charpentier'i.** *G. lutea*×*G. punctata*.

**G. cilia'ta.** Annual. Stem erect, simple or branched, 6 to 24 in. h. *Basal l.* oblanceolate; *stem-l.* oblong-lanceolate to linear. *fl.* solitary, terminal, long-stalked, blue, 1½ to 2 in. long, funnel-shaped; lobes 4, ovate, margin long-fringed; cal. ½ in. long, lobes 4, ½ to ¾ in. long, inner broader than outer. September. Europe. (B.M. 639.)

**G. Clu'sii.*** Perennial with loose l.-rosette, erect, simple stem, 1 to 4 in. h. *Basal l.* elliptic to elliptic-lanceolate, broadest at or beyond middle, stiff, leathery; of stem ovate-lanceolate, acute. *fl.* solitary, terminal, stalked, deep blue, throat paler, spotted olive-green, 2 to 2½ in. long, funnel-bell-shaped; lobes rounded; plicae irregular, rounded; cal. ½ in. long, bell-shaped, lobes half length of tube, tapered to point, not contracted at base, close to tube, margins rough. June. Europe. 1888. SYN. *G. acaulis vulgaris*. var. **Cos'tei**, taller, *l.* broader and softer, cal. lobes larger. SYN. *G. Costei*; **Rochel'lii**, *l.* narrower; **undulatifo'lia**, *l.* wavy on margin.

**G. confu'sa.** Climber to about 2 ft. *l.* narrowly heart-shaped to sagittate, 1½ to 2 in. long, markedly veined. *fl.* greenish-yellow, stalked, in axillary pairs or rarely threes, 1 to 1½ in. long, widely funnel-shaped; lobes triangular; plicae short, pointed; cal. tube funnel-shaped, ⅛ in. long, lobes ⅛ in. long, linear, widely separated. September, October. Himalaya. SYN. *Crawfurdia affinis*.

**G. cordifo'lia.** A variety of *G. septemfida*.

**G. corymbif'era.*** Compact, branched perennial. Stems erect, stout, almost bare, 6 to 18 in. h. *Basal l.* oblong-spatulate to lanceolate-spatulate, 2 to 4 in. long, blunt, on stem linear-oblong, all purplish-brown. *fl.* several in a compact corymb, white, ¾ to 1 in. across, bell-shaped; lobes broad-oblong, blunt; cal. short, open bell-shaped, lobes about as long as tube, lanceolate, deltoid, acute. August. New Zealand. (Gen. 29.)

**G. Cos'tei.** A form of *G. Clusii*.

**G. crassicau'lis.** Coarse perennial of 1 to 2 ft., stem thick, hollow, erect, leafy. *l.* at base elliptic-ovate, up to 12 in. long, 2 to 3 in. wide, on stem smaller, broader, sessile. *fl.* in heads with pair of l. just below, greenish-white with spots, ½ to ¾ in. long; lobes erect, ovate, plicae small, triangular; cal. about ¼ in. long, papery, split on one side, lobes 5, minute. July. W. China. 1906.

**G. crawfurdioi'des.** Semi-climber of 1 to 2 ft. *l.* broadly ovate, long-pointed, base rounded; stalk short. *fl.* deep purple-maroon, terminal, solitary; cor. tube funnel-shaped, 1½ to 2 in. long, lobes triangular, short; plicae large, rounded; cal. tube ¾ in. long, split half-way, lobes unequal, linear, about ¼ in. long. September. SE. Tibet.

**G. crucia'ta.** Leafy, erect or sub-erect perennial, 6 to 18 in. h. *Basal l.* ovate to ovate-lanceolate, 5 to 8 in. long, margin rough, on stem larger upwards, ovate to ovate-lanceolate. 2 to 3 in. long. *fl.* in terminal and axillary clusters with a pair of l. just beneath, azure-blue, ¾ to 1 in. long, club-shaped; lobes 4 or 5, ovate, acute; plicae 2-fid, half as long as cor. lobes; cal. ¼ in. long, bell-shaped, lobes 4, linear, teeth-shaped. Summer. Europe, Asia. 1854. (R.I.F.G. xvii, 1052.) Differs from *G. phlogifolia* by the short cal. lobes and the shorter and narrower cor. lobes and l. var. **depres'sa**, dwarfer, 1- to 4-fld., stems prostrate or procumbent.

**G. curviflo'ra.** 8 to 12 in. h., erect. *l.* ovate to heart-shaped, ½ to 1 in. long, almost sessile. *fl.* reddish-violet, terminal, solitary; cor. tube funnel-shaped, 1½ to 2 in. long, curved, lobes about ¼ in. long, plicae short, abrupt; cal. tube ½ in. long, split almost to base, lobes spatulate, ¼ in. long. China.

**G. dahu'rica.** Erect or ascending perennial. Stems branched, 6 to 8 in. long. *Basal l.* narrow-lanceolate, 6 to 8 in. long, blunt, on stem in 2 or 3 pairs, shorter, narrower, more acute. *fl.* deep blue, paler in throat, 1 to 1½ in. long; lobes ovate, acute; plicae triangular, nicked or cleft; cal. about ⅓ in. long, lobes shorter, unequal. August. Asia Minor, China. SYN. *G. Kurroo brevidens*. Differs from *G. gracilipes* by the fl. being sessile or nearly so, and from *G. decumbens* by the cal. tube not split. (B.M. 8911.)

**G.×Dav'idi** (*G. Lawrencei*×*G. prolata*?). Habit and *l.* near *G. prolata*. *fl.* pale sky-blue, solitary, terminal on branched stems, stalked; cor. tube narrowly funnel-shaped, 1½ to 1¾ in. long, lobes long-triangular; plicae short, acute; cal. tube ½ in. long, lobes slightly longer. September. Of garden origin. Differs from *G. Lawrencei* by its equal cal. tube and lobes, and from *G. prolata* by the larger, more open cor.

**G. decum'bens.** Perennial with ascending stems 6 to 9 in. long sometimes branched near tip. *Basal l.* linear-lanceolate, 3 to 5 in. long; *stem-l.* in 2 to 3 pairs, oblong to oblong-lanceolate, 1 to 1½ in. long. *fl.* 1 to 3, terminal and axillary, sessile or nearly so, deep blue to purplish-blue, 1 to 1¼ in. long, bell-shaped; lobes ovate, acute; plicae entire, short; cal. ½ in. long, papery, split down one side, lobes 2 to 5, linear or tooth-like. August. Asia. 1803. (B.M. 723 as *G. adscendens*.) var. **Geb'leri**, taller, *l.* broader, cal. lobes none; **mongol'ica**, cor. more tubular, lobes long, acute, plicae 2-fid; **Olivie'ri glomera'ta**, *see* **G. tianschanica Olivieri**; **Pallas'ii**, *l*, narrower, cor. lobes blunt, cal. lobes always 5. The name *G. decumbens* has been used for *G. tianschanica*.

**G. dendrolo'gi.** Erect or ascending perennial, 6 to 14 in. h., branching near top. *Basal l.* lanceolate to linear, 4 to 10 in. long; *stem-l.* in 4 or 5 pairs, broader, 2 to 4 in. long, blunt. *fl.* in small sessile terminal or stalked axillary clusters, white or whitish, 1 to 1½ in. long, cylindric; lobes ovate, rather blunt; plicae short, abrupt; cal. ½ to ⅝ in. long, split almost to base, lobes 5, short, slender. July. W. China. Differs from *G. Fetisovii* by the 5 distinct cal. lobes, and from *G. macrophylla* by fl. colour and larger size.

**G. depres'sa.** Tufted perennial with many barren and fl.-shoots, stoloniferous, 1 to 1½ in. h. *l.* on barren shoots ½ in. long, obovate, overlapping, on fl.-stems ⅜ in. long, ovate-oblong, all somewhat glaucous, margins rough. *fl.* solitary, sessile in tuft, pale to greenish-blue with white on plicae, over 1½ in. long, widely bell-shaped; lobes sub-erect, broadly ovate, rounded; plicae as long as cor. lobes; cal. ½ in. long, tubular, lobes about ¼ in. long, erect, ovate, acute. September. Himalaya. (J.R.H.S., 62, 48; B.M. n.s. 230.) Differs from *G. amoena* by the ovate l. and cal. lobes. Difficult to grow and fl.

**G. deton'sa.** Annual, erect, much branched, 18 to 24 in. h. *Basal l.* broad-ovate to spatulate, 1 to 1½ in. long; *stem-l.* linear to lanceolate, 1 to 2 in. long. *fl.* terminal on branched stems, long-stalked, pale blue to bluish-purple, 1½ in. long, funnel-shaped; lobes 4, ovate; cal. ½ in. long, keeled, lobes 4, slightly longer than tube, broadly lanceolate. August, September. China, &c. SYN. *Gentianella detonsa.*

*Gentiana detonsa*

**G.×Devonhall*** (*G. Farreri*×*G. ornata*). Tufted with decumbent stems. *Basal l.* ½ to ¾ in. long; *stem-l.* ½ to 1 in. long, linear. *fl.* pale blue, paler and spotted green within, solitary, terminal; cor. tube 2 in. long, wide funnel-shaped, lobes triangular; plicae short; cal. tube ½ in. long, lobes about ¾ in. long, linear. August, September. Of garden origin. (J.R.H.S. 61, f. 146.) Differs from *G. Farreri* by its colour and by the shorter fl. and l. and wider cor. tube, from *G. ornata* by its larger growth, and longer, more funnel-shaped cor. of a deeper blue.

**G.×digen'ea** (*G. Clusii*×*G. Kochiana*).

**G. dina'rica.*** Tufted perennial with erect, simple stems 1 to 5 in. h. *Basal l.* broadly elliptic, 1½ in. long, broadest in middle, acute, on stem smaller, elliptic-lanceolate. *fl.* solitary, terminal, deep blue, unspotted, 2 in. long, funnel-bell-shaped; lobes heart-shaped, with long tapering points; plicae irregular, broadly triangular; cal. ½ in. long, bell-shaped, lobes ¼ to ⅓ in. long, lanceolate, narrowed at base, acute, widely spaced. S. Europe. 1887. (G.C. 85 (1929), 475.)

**G. Douglasia'na.** Erect annual, 2 to 10 in. h., branched from base. *Basal l.* broadly elliptic, ⅓ to ½ in. long, rounded; *stem-l.* heart-shaped. *fl.* solitary or few together, terminal, sessile or nearly so, whitish, ⅓ in. long, bell-shaped; lobes oblong; plicae short, sometimes 2-lobed; cal. ⅛ to ⅙ in. long, lobes very short, lanceolate. June. NW. America.

**G. dschunga'rica.** Leafy, branched, ascending or nearly erect perennial, 6 to 9 in. h. *l.* lanceolate, ½ to ¾ in. long, veins marked, margins rough. *fl.* in terminal and axillary heads, deep blue to purple-blue, 1½ in. long, tubular-funnel-shaped; lobes broad, blunt; plicae toothed or fringed; cal. ½ in. long, sometimes split on one side, lobes ¼ to ⅓ in. long, linear. August. Turkestan.

**G.×Edi'na** (*G. ornata*×*G. prolata*). Habit of *G. ornata. fl.* single, terminal on branched stems, deep sky-blue, lined and spotted on tube, 1¼ to 1½ in. long, funnel-shaped; lobes narrow triangular; plicae short, blunt; cal. about ½ in. long, lobes ½ in. long, lanceolate. August, September. Of garden origin. 1941. Differs from *G. prolata* by the wider, more open cor. of deeper blue, from *G. ornata* by the branched stems, funnel-shaped cor., and several fl. on a stem.

**G. Elwes'ii.** Annual or perennial, loosely tufted. Stem erect, 6 to 15 in. h. *Basal l.* 1 to 2 in. long, elliptic to ovate, blunt, smaller and rounder on stem. *fl.* in heads with upper l. beneath, pale blue, paler between lobes, 1 to 1¼ in. long, tubular, inflated in middle, closed at mouth; lobes erect, ovate, blunt; plicae short, triangular; cal. about ⅓ in. long, lobes unequal, pointed, recurved. Autumn, Himalaya. (Gen. 30.) Differs from *G. sikkimensis* by its taller, less tufted habit and more tubular closed cor.

**G. exacoi'des.** Slender, erect, branched perennial, 8 to 14 in. h. *Basal l.* lanceolate, 2 to 4 in. long, acute, shorter on stem. *fl.* 2 to 4, terminal, long-stalked, violet, white at base, 1 to 1½ in. long; tube short, obconic to bell-shaped, lobes oblong, obovate, rounded; cal. ½ in. long, bell-shaped, lobes ¾ to 1 in. long. March. Peru. 1932. (A.G.S.B. 3 (1935), 222.)

**G. exci'sa.** A synonym of *G. Kochiana.*

**G. Far'reri.*** Prostrate perennial. Stems ascending at tips, leafy, branched, up to 8 in. long. *Basal l.* 1½ in. long; *stem-l.* ½ to 1½ in. long, all linear-lanceolate, with a long point recurved at tip. *fl.* terminal, solitary, stalked, Cambridge blue, greenish-white at base, banded and spotted greenish-blue, 2 to 2½ in. long, narrow-funnel-shaped; cal. about ½ in. long, narrow-funnel-shaped, tinged red at base, lobes twice as long as tube, linear, pointed, spreading, slightly recurved at tips; cor. lobes broadly ovate, recurving, abruptly pointed; plicae abrupt, sometimes ragged. August. NW. China, Tibet. (B.M. 8874, 8875.) Differs from *G. Lawrencei* by its more robust habit, and from *G. sino-ornata* by its paler colour with cal. lobes twice as long as tube.

**G. fascicula'ris.** Climber to over 8 ft. *l.* narrow-ovate, rounded at base, long-pointed, 2 to 3 in. long. *fl.* terminal and axillary, pale bluish-lilac, 1¼ to 1½ in. long, funnel-shaped; lobes blunt, short; plicae blunt; cal. ½ in. long, entire, lobes shorter, linear. September. Himalaya. (B.M. 4838 as *Crawfurdia fasciculata.*)

**G. Favra'tii.** Tufted perennial, 3 in. h., with barren and fertile shoots. *l.* ¼ to ⅓ in. long, smallest at top of stem, broadly ovate, widest in upper third, glaucous, not overlapping, tip blunt. *fl.* solitary, terminal, deep blue, ¾ in. across, saucer-shaped; lobes rounded, often wider than long; plicae 2-fid; cal. ⅕ to ¼ in. long, triangular, acute. July. Europe, Asia. Differs from *G. brachyphylla* by the blunt-rounded l. and broad cor. lobes. SYN. *G. verna Hinterhuberi, G. verna obtusifolia.*

**G. Fetisov'ii.** Erect perennial with simple stems. *Basal l.* narrow-lanceolate, over 6i n. long; *stem-l.* in 2 or 3 pairs, smaller. *fl.* in a head, sessile, purplish-blue, 1 to 1½ in. long, tubular-bell-shaped; lobes ovate, acute, recurved; plicae short, abrupt; cal. ½ in. long, split almost to base, lobes usually of 3 small teeth, often none. August. China. (G.F. 1069.) var. **al'ba,** smaller, *fl.* whitish.

**G. fil'ipes.** Annual, 2 to 3 in. h., erect, sometimes branched from base. *l.* mostly on stem, oblong to obovate-spatulate, ⅙ to ⅓ in. long. *fl.* solitary, terminal, white, ⅓ in. across, lobes ovate, about as long as tube; cal. ⅛ in. long, lobes broad, ovate. Summer. New Zealand.

**G. flac'cida.** Annual, 2 to 6 in. h., erect, sometimes branched. *Basal l.* oblong to oblong-spatulate, 1 in. long, thin; *stem-l.* ½ in. long. *fl.* white, ¾ in. across, solitary, terminal; cor. lobes 4, blunt; cal. small, lobes oblong-lanceolate, acute. July. New Zealand.

**G. flav'ida.** A synonym of *G. alba.*

**G. formosa'na.** Annual or biennial, erect, 2 to 4 in. h., tufted at base. *Basal l.* linear to linear-lanceolate, ¾ in. long; *stem-l.* slightly longer. *fl.* 1 to 3, terminal, pale pink, ½ to ¾ in. long, tubular-bell-shaped, lobes rounded; plicae acute, entire; cor. ¼ to ½ in. long, tubular, lobes linear, equalling tube. August. Japan. 1905.

**G. Fortun'ei.** A variety of *G. scabra.*

**G. Forwood'ii.** Erect or ascending, leafy perennial of 6 to 12 in., rarely branched. *l.* oblong to ovate, ½ to 1¼ in. long, thick, narrowed to tip. *fl.* 1 to 3 at apex, sessile, and solitary, stalked in upper l.-axils, 1 to 1¼ in. long, narrow, tubular, mouth open, lobes obovate, blunt; plicae 2-cleft, lanceolate, shorter than cor. lobes; cal. ⅓ to ½ in. long, purplish-brown, split on one side, lobes none or minute. Summer. N. America. SYN. *G. affinis Forwoodii.* Differs from *G. affinis* by the thick l., split cal. tube, and minute cal. lobes

**G. Freynia'na.*** Leafy perennial. Stems ascending, 6 to 12 in. h. *l.* linear-lanceolate, ½ to 1 in. long, blunt. *fl.* usually solitary, terminal, sessile, purplish-blue, ¾ to 1¼ in. long, bell- to club-shaped; lobes ovate, acute; plicae one-third as long as cor. lobes, 2-fid, acute; cal. ¼ to ½ in. long, tubular, split down one side, lobes linear, acute, margins rough. Autumn. Asia Minor. Differs from *G. septemfida* by the 2-fid, not fringed, plicae. SYN. *G. septemfida Freyniana.*

**G. frig'ida.** Ascending or erect perennial 5 to 6 in. h. *Basal l.* linear to linear-oblong, 2 to 3 in. long, ⅛ in. wide, blunt; *stem-l.* in 2 or 3 pairs, half as long, linear, pale green, thick. *fl.* solitary, terminal, sessile, yellowish, spotted and lined blue, bell-shaped; lobes short, ovate, blunt; plicae entire, acute, less than half as long as cor. lobes; cal. ½ to ¾ in. long, tubular, lobes shorter than tube, linear to lanceolate, acute. Europe. (R.I.F.G. xvii, 1050, f. 4.) SYN. *G. algida frigida.*

**G. Froelich'ii.*** Tufted perennial, 1 to 2 in. h. *l.* of loose rosettes, linear-oblong to spatulate, 1 to 1½ in. long, thick, revolute; stem-l. in 1 or 2 pairs, ovate, acute. *fl.* solitary, terminal, water-blue, 1 to 1½ in. long, narrow-bell-shaped; lobes erect, ovate, abruptly pointed; plicae entire, triangular, less than half cor. lobes; cal. ½ in. long, lobes equalling tube, lanceolate, twisted, set wide apart. Summer. Europe. (Gen. 34.)

**G. Geb'leri.** A variety of *G. decumbens.*

**G. gel'ida.** Ascending leafy perennial. Stem simple or shortly branched near tip, 12 in. long. *l.* ovate- to linear-lanceolate, 1 to 1½ in. long, largest near top of stem, rounded or blunt at tip. *fl.* few together, terminal and axillary, yellow to white, 1 in. long, club- or bell-shaped; lobes broadly ovate, blunt; plicae entire or toothed; cal. ½ in. long, sometimes slightly split, lobes ¼ to ½ in. long, unequal, linear, margin rough. Summer. Asia Minor, Caucasus. 1807. Differs from *G. septemfida* by the yellow cor.

**G. Gentianel'la** of gardens. *See* **G. acaulis.**

**G. Georg'ei.** Perennial. Stems ascending from basal rosette, 3 to 4 in. long. *Basal l.* ovate-oblong, 1 to 2½ in. long, overlapping, forming a cross, on stem narrower, ¾ to 1 in. long, all often tinged purple, margins rough. *fl.* solitary, terminal, sessile, deep purplish-blue, green-lined without, paler in throat, spotted, 2 to 2½ in. long, open-funnel-shaped; lobes broadly triangular, almost as broad as long; plicae at least half as long as lobes, triangular, entire; cal. ¾ to 1 in. long, papery, funnel-shaped, tinged purple, lobes ⅛ to ⅜ in. long, unequal, ovate, margins rough. July. W. China. (Gen. 35.) Differs from *G. Szechenyii* by the broader cal. and cor. lobes and plicae.

**G. Gibbs'ii.** Densely branched, 2 to 5 in. h., erect. *Basal l.* ovate-spatulate, ½ to ¾ in. long, thick; *stem-l.* linear-oblong, ⅓ to ½ in. long. *fl.* white with purplish veins, freely produced at ends of branches; cor. narrow bell-shaped, ½ to ¾ in. long, cut almost to base, lobes 4, ovate-lanceolate, apiculate; cal. about ½ in. long, lobes 4, narrow awl-shaped, acute. July. N. Zealand.

**G. gilvo-stria'ta.*** Tufted perennial with prostrate barren and decumbent fl.-shoots. *Basal l.* oblanceolate, ¼ in. long, blunt; *stem-l.* obovate-spatulate, up to ½ in. long, clustered below fl., uppermost largest, all slightly glaucous. *fl.* solitary, terminal, nearly sessile, sea-blue, paler within, spotted purplish-blue with brownish-purple bands without, 1½ in. long, funnel-shaped; lobes broadly ovate, almost as wide as long; plicae broadly ovate, blunt; cal. about ½ in. long, tubular, tinged purple, lobes ⅛ in. long, roundish to spatulate. Autumn. Upper Burma, Tibet. (Gen. 37.) Differs from *G. stragulata* by the smaller l. and open-funnel-shaped cor.

**G. glau'ca.** Tufted perennial with many erect barren and fl.-shoots 4 in. h. *Basal l.* ovate to obovate, ⅓ to ½ in. long, fleshy, on stem smaller, obovate to spatulate. *fl.* 1 to 3 together, terminal and sessile, axillary and stalked, pale blue, whitish within, ¾ in. long, club-shaped; lobes ovate, blunt; plicae ovate, entire or 2-fid, blunt; cal. about ¼ in. long, lobes ⅛ in. long, equal, triangular. E. Asia, N. America. (Gen. 38.) Differs from *G. venusta* by the few fl. together, broader cal. lobes, and cor. three times as long as cal.

**G. × Glendevon** (*G. ornata* × *G. sino-ornata*). Habit and *l.* of *G. ornata.* *fl.* deep blue, markedly lined and spotted, single, terminal on branched stems; cor. tube narrowly bell-shaped, 1½ to 1¾ in. long, lobes broadly triangular; plicae very small; cal. tube about ½ in. long, lobes longer with recurved tips. August, September. Of garden origin. Differs from *G. ornata* by its larger growth and fl. and deeper blue of cor., from *G. sino-ornata* by its smaller, more compact habit and shorter fl.

**G. gracilifo'lia.** 4 to 6 in. h., decumbent and much branched from base. *Basal l.* narrow-linear to linear-spatulate, ⅜ in. long, thick, shining; *stem-l.* shorter. *fl.* white, ½ in. across, bell-shaped, 2 to 4 together at ends of branches; cor.-lobes long, oblong-obovate; blunt; cal. divided ⅔, lobes linear-lanceolate. Summer. N. Zealand. (C.I.N.Z. 137.)

**G. gracil'ipes.*** Decumbent perennial, stem 10 in. long. *Basal l.* narrow-lanceolate, 6 in. long; *stem-l.* shorter, in 2 to 4 pairs. *fl.* solitary, terminal, long-stalked, deep purplish-blue, greenish outside tube, 1½ in. long; lobes ovate, triangular, blunt; plicae entire, triangular, half as long as cor. lobes; cal. about ½ in. long, split nearly to base, lobes 3 to 5, triangular, acute. August. Kansu. (B.M. 8630.) SYN. *G. Purdomii* of gardens. Differs from *G. dahurica* by the long pedicels.

**G. grandiflo'ra.** A synonym of *G. altaica.*

**G. gran'dis.** Annual or biennial. *l.* broad lanceolate to narrow-ovate, up to 3 in. long, on a branching stem up to 18 in. h. *fl.* long-stalked, solitary, terminal on branches, blue, up to 3 in. long, widely funnel-shaped; lobes 4, fringed at base, broad-ovate; cal. tube keeled, lobes 4, long-lanceolate, 1½ in. long. September. China. SYN. *Gentianella grandis.*

**G. Grisebach'ii.** Annual, 3 to 14 in. h., stem slender, more or less decumbent. *Basal l.* few, spatulate, ½ to 1 in. long, thin; *stem-l.* smaller, oblong to ovate-oblong. *fl.* white, ½ in. across, bell-shaped, solitary at ends of branches; cor. lobes as long as tube, narrow oblong to ovate, acute; cal. short, angled, lobes narrow, acute. June, July. New Zealand. (H.I.P. 636.)

**G. Grombczews'kii.** Perennial, loosely tufted. Stem ascending or erect, 12 to 16 in. long. *Basal l.* oblong-lanceolate, 6 to 12 in. long, on stem 2 to 4 in. long in a few pairs. *fl.* sessile in a head, yellowish, ¾ to 1 in. long, tubular-funnel-shaped; lobes ovate-oblong, blunt; plicae nearly as long as cor. lobes, lanceolate, entire or cleft; cal. ¼ to ⅓ in. long, split on one side, lobes many times shorter than tube, tooth-like or awl-shaped. August. Asia.

**G. Hel'eni.** Climber of 6 to 20 ft. *l.* broadly ovate, 1½ to 3 in. long, slender-pointed. *fl.* 2 or 3, axillary, pedicels long; cor. bright pink to purple-rose, 2½ in. long, widely funnel-shaped; plicae triangular; cal. tube ½ to ¾ in. long, narrow-tubular, lobes broadly triangular, recurved. November, December. SW. China. SE. Tibet. (G.C. 47 (1910), 44.) SYN. *Crawfurdia Trailliana.*

**G. × hexa-Farreri** (*G. Farreri* × *G. hexaphylla*). More compact than *G. Farreri.* *l.* very variable, ½ to ¾ in. long, oblong to lanceolate. *fl.* deep blue, lined within and without, single, terminal; cor. tube bell-shaped, 1¾ in. long, lobes 5 to 6, triangular, mucronate; cal. tube ½ in. long, lobes 5 or 6, slightly longer than tube, broadly lanceolate. August. Of garden origin. (Gen. 3.) Differs from *G. Farreri* by the l. not in pairs, fl. more bell-shaped, cor. lobes mucronate, and from *G. hexaphylla* by the larger fl., l. 2 to 4 in a whorl (not 6).

**G. hexaphyl'la.*** Tufted perennial without basal rosette. Stems many, fl.-stems prostrate, or decumbent, 4 to 6 in. long, sterile, stems erect. *l.* in whorls of 6, linear, pointed, ¼ to ½ in. long, progressively longer upwards. *fl.* solitary, terminal, erect, pale blue spotted green with broad blue bands without, 1½ to 1¾ in. long, funnel-shaped; cal. ¼ in. long, entire, lobes 6, as long as tube, linear; cor. lobes 6, broadly ovate, long-pointed; plicae about half as long as lobes, triangular, margin nicked. July, August. Kansu, E. Tibet. (Gen. 40.) Differs from its allies by the 6-merous cal. and cor. and the whorls of 6 l.

**G. Ho'pei** of gardens. A synonym of *G. trichotoma.*

**G. Igarash'ii.** Erect perennial, 4 in. h., with a loose basal l.-rosette. *Basal l.* linear-lanceolate to linear-spatulate, 2 to 2½ in. long, thick, margins revolute; *stem-l.* in 2 or 3 pairs, broader, 1 to 1½ in. long. *fl.* 1 to 3, terminal, blue with deeper markings, 1½ to 2 in. long, bell-shaped; cal. tubular-obconic, ⅓ in. long, lobes ¼ to ½ in. long, unequal, oblong to ovate-oblong, thick, reflexed, margins revolute; cor. lobes triangular, rounded, broader than long, plicae abrupt, 2-fid. July. Japan. (A.F.J. 79.) Differs from *G. algida* by size of fl., shape of cal. lobes, and revolute margins of l. and cal. lobes.

**G. imbrica'ta.** A synonym of *G. terglouensis.*

**G. interme'dia.** *See* **G. ochroleuca.**

**G. interrup'ta.** Erect, leafy perennial, 12 to 24 in. h., lower internodes short, upper long. *l.* ovate to oblong, lower ¾ to 1 in. long, upper 1 to 1½ in. long. *fl.* terminal and axillary, upper sessile, lower long-stalked, purplish-blue, ¾ to 1¼ in. long, funnel-shaped; cal. ⅓ in. long, tubular, lobes ⅛ in. long, linear to awl-shaped; cor. lobes obovate; plicae 2-fid. August. Colorado. Differs from allies by its long fl.-stalks and long tops of stems. *G. interrupta* of Sims is *G. ochroleuca.*

**G. × Inverleith** (*G. Farreri* × *G. Veitchiorum*). Habit of *G. Veitchiorum* but *l.* narrower and longer on procumbent stems up to 9 in. long. *fl.* stalked, solitary at ends of branches, deep Cambridge blue, 2¼ to 2½ in. long, funnel-shaped, lobes broadly triangular; plicae short, sometimes 2-fid; cal. ½ to ¾ in. long, lobes of same length, recurved. September. Of garden origin. Differs from *G. Veitchiorum* by its narrow, recurved l., wider cor., and cal. tube with lobes of equal length, and from *G. Farreri* by the deeper colour of the fl., broad-triangular cor. lobes, and cal. tube and lobes being of equal length.

**G. iochro'a.** 1 to 2 ft. h., erect. *l.* broadly ovate to orbicular, 1 to 1½ in. long. *fl.* purple-rose, solitary, terminal and axillary; cor. tube funnel-shaped, widened above cal., 1½ in. long, lobes broadly triangular; plicae nearly as large as lobes; cal. tube about ½ in. long, lobes erect, linear, shorter than tube. August. SE. Tibet.

**G. japon'ica.** A synonym of *G. trinervis.*

**G. Kaufmannia'na.** Decumbent or ascending perennial, 6 to 8 in. long. *Basal l.* oblong-lanceolate, 2 to 4 in. long, thick, blunt; *stem-l.* broader. *fl.* 1 to 3, terminal, stalked, blue, 1½ to 2 in. long, tubular-funnel-shaped; cal. ½ in. long, tubular, lobes ⅛ to ½ in. long, oblong-linear, blunt; cor. lobes ovate-oblong, rounded; plicae short, entire or toothed. July, August. Asia. Distinct from *G. Kurroo* by the blunt ovate-oblong cor. lobes and short plicae.

**G. Kawaka'mii.** Perennial with straggling, eafy, sub-erect barren stems, 3 to 6 in. h. *l.* ⅜ to ¾ in. long, broad-ovate to lanceolate-ovate, recurved. *fl.* 6 to 7 together, violet-purple, ¾ in. long; lobes obovate, blunt; plicae triangular, acute, many-cleft, turned inward closing throat; cal. ⅜ in. long, lobes broadly ovate, acute, reflexed. Summer. Japan. Differs from *G. nipponica* by the stouter, more erect growth and the plicae closing cor. throat.

**G. Kesselring'ii.** Erect or sub-erect perennial. Stems 8 to 10 in. long, thick. *Basal l.* lanceolate to linear-lanceolate, 3 to 5 in. long; *stem-l.* lanceolate to broad-lanceolate. *fl.* in a head, uppermost pairs of l. forming an involucre, whitish to cream, spotted purple, $\frac{3}{4}$ to 1 in. long, tubular; cal. $\frac{1}{2}$ in. long, tubular, lobes $\frac{1}{4}$ in. long, oblong-lanceolate, sharp; cor. lobes ovate; plicae 2-fid, long-pointed. July, August. Turkestan. 1882. (G.F. 1087, f. 3, 4.) SYN. *G. Walujewi Kesselringii.*

**G. King'donii.** Weak, slender climber with purplish stems. *l.* ovate, long-pointed, $1\frac{1}{2}$ to 3 in. long; stalks short. *fl.* solitary, terminal or axillary, purple, 1 to $1\frac{1}{2}$ in. long, broadly bell-shaped; lobes broad, apiculate; cal. $\frac{1}{2}$ in. long, partly split, purplish, lobes small, triangular, recurved. October. SE. Tibet. SYN. *Crawfurdia Wardii.*

**G. Kochia'na.** Perennial of 2 to 4 in. Stems erect from a basal tuft, unbranched. *Basal l.* broad-elliptic, 1 to $1\frac{1}{2}$ in. long, half as wide, soft, flaccid, rounded, widest in upper third; *stem-l.* smaller. *fl.* solitary, terminal, dark azure-blue, spotted and marked green within, 2 to $2\frac{1}{2}$ in. long, funnel-bell-shaped, lobes broad, roundish, blunt, spreading; cal. $\frac{3}{4}$ to 1 in. long, bell-shaped, lobes $\frac{1}{3}$ to $\frac{1}{2}$ in. long, broadly spatulate, wide apart, narrowed at base, abruptly pointed. June, July. Europe. (B.M. 52.) SYN. *G. acaulis* vars. q.v., *G. excisa*, *G. latifolia*. Differs from allies by the broad, soft l. and broad, spreading cal. lobes.

**G. Kur'roo.** Sub-erect perennial, 4 to 8 in. long, from a basal rosette. *Basal l.* lanceolate, 4 to 6 in. long, $\frac{1}{2}$ in. wide, blunt; *stem-l.* in 2 or 3 pairs, narrow-linear, 3 to 4 in. long. *fl.* one (rarely 2), terminal, stalked on a branched infl., deep blue, paler in throat, spotted green and white, over $1\frac{1}{2}$ in. long, narrow funnel-shaped; cal. about $\frac{1}{2}$ in. long, almost tubular, lobes linear, as long as or longer than tube, acute; cor. lobes broad-ovate, acute; plicae quarter length of lobes, triangular, toothed. August, September. Himalaya. (Gen. 41.) Distinct by its entire cal., broadly ovate cor. lobes, and large fl. var. **brev'idens,** *see* **G. dahurica.**

**G. lagodechia'na.*** Prostrate, leafy perennial. Stems 9 to 15 in. long. *l.* ovate to heart-shaped, $\frac{1}{2}$ to 1 in. long, blunt. *fl.* solitary, terminal sessile, axillary stalked, deep blue, paler without, spotted green, $1\frac{1}{2}$ in. long, tubular-funnel-shaped, narrowed at base; lobes broad-ovate to heart-shaped, pointed; plicae half as long as cor. lobes, many-cleft, pointed; cal. $\frac{1}{2}$ in. long, narrowed at base, lobes $\frac{1}{4}$ in. long, broadly lanceolate, contracted at base. Autumn. E. Caucasus. Differs from *G. septemfida* by the branched 1-fld. stems, short cal. tube with long lobes contracted at base. SYN. *G. septemfida lagodechiana.*

**G. latifo'lia.** A synonym of *G. Kochiana.*

**G. Lawren'cei.*** Leafy perennial with prostrate stems 4 to 6 in. long, from a central rosette. *Basal l.* narrow-linear, 1 to $1\frac{1}{2}$ in. long, acute, slightly recurved, pale green; *stem-l.* shorter. *fl.* solitary, long-stalked, torquoise-blue, paling towards whitish base, banded blue outside; cor. tube, $1\frac{1}{2}$ to 2 in. long, lobes triangular, ragged; cal. about $\frac{1}{2}$ in. long, tubular, lobes twice as long as tube, linear, acute. July. Siberia. (B.M. 8140.) Smaller than *G. Farreri* with more tubular cor. and more triangular cor. lobes.

**G. lhas'sica.** Decumbent perennial with simple stems 3 to 4 in. long. *Basal l.* lanceolate, 3 in. long, blunt; *stem-l.* in many pairs, $\frac{3}{4}$ to 1 in. long, narrow-elliptic. *fl.* solitary, terminal, sessile, deep cornflower blue to lilac with purplish-brown bands without, narrow-bell-shaped, 1 in. long; lobes round-ovate; plicae ovate; cal. $\frac{1}{3}$ to $\frac{1}{2}$ in. long, tubular-funnel-shaped, purplish, lobes $\frac{1}{8}$ to $\frac{1}{4}$ in. long, unequal, narrow-ovate. September. Tibet. (A.G.S.B. 11 (1943), 79.)

**G. linea'ris.** Leafy, erect or ascending, unbranched perennial, 12 to 18 in. h. *l.* linear- to narrow-lanceolate, 1 to 3 in. long, $\frac{1}{4}$ to $\frac{1}{3}$ in. wide. *fl.* 1 to 5 in a terminal cluster within uppermost pairs of l., blue to purplish-blue, 1 to $1\frac{1}{2}$ in. long, narrow-funnel-shaped; cal. $\frac{1}{2}$ in. long, tubular, lobes shorter, linear; cor. lobes erect, round-ovate; plicae triangular, entire, sharp, much shorter than cor. lobes. August. W. America. (B.B. 2, 617.) Differs from *G. Saponaria* by the open fl., entire plicae, and linear l.

**G. linea'ta.** Tufted, erect, 2 to 3 in. h. *l.* linear to linear-spatulate, $\frac{1}{2}$ to $\frac{3}{4}$ in. long, acute, gradually narrowed to flat stalk. *fl.* white, $\frac{1}{4}$ to $\frac{1}{2}$ in. long, narrow bell-shaped, solitary, terminal; cor.-lobes $\frac{1}{4}$ to $\frac{1}{3}$ in. long, ovate, acute; cal. lobes $\frac{1}{10}$ in. long, awl-shaped. July, August. New Zealand.

**G. Lo'deri.*** Compact, prostrate perennial. Stems 4 to 6 in. long. *l.* in many pairs, $\frac{1}{2}$ in. long, broad-elliptic, blunt to rounded, thick, slightly glaucous, margins rough, stalk very short. *fl.* solitary, terminal, pale blue, 1 to $1\frac{1}{4}$ in. long, tubular-bell-shaped; cal. $\frac{1}{3}$ to $\frac{1}{2}$ in. long, bell-shaped, lobes shorter than tube, broadly spatulate, recurved; cor. lobes broadly ovate, pointed; plicae regular, many-cleft. July, August. Kashmir. (Gen. 42, 43.) Distinct from *G. cachemirica* by the broadly spatulate cal. lobes and more compact habit.

**G. lu'tea.*** Erect, unbranched, leafy perennial, 4 to 6 ft. h. *Basal l.* 12 in. long, broadly ovate, stalked, 5- to 7-nerved; *stem-l.* ovate, smaller, sessile. *fl.* more or less whorled, pale yellow veined or spotted, 1 in. long, wheel-shaped; cal. $\frac{1}{2}$ to $\frac{3}{4}$ in. long, split on one side, without lobes; cor. lobes 3 to 7, reaching almost to base, oblong; plicae wanting. July, August. Europe. (Gen. 91.) Furnishes the Gentian-root of commerce. Distinct by its height, deeply cut wheel-shaped cor., and absence of plicae. var. **symphyan'dra,** stamens forming a tube, stigma not recurved.

**G. luteovir'idis.** Climber of 4 to 6 ft. *l.* ovate, $1\frac{1}{2}$ to $2\frac{1}{2}$ in. long, long-pointed, base rounded. *fl.* in axillary pairs, greenish-yellow, $1\frac{1}{2}$ in. long, narrow-funnel-shaped, lobes ovate; plicae triangular, short; cal. $\frac{1}{2}$ in. long, lobes $\frac{1}{2}$ in. long, linear. October. China, Himalaya. (B.M. 6539 as *Crawfurdia luteoviridis.*) SYN. *C. japonica luteoviridis.* The correct name of this species is *G. volubilis.*

**G. × Macau'layi*** (*G. Farreri* × *G. sino-ornata*). *l.* as in *G. Farreri. fl.* deep blue, terminal, solitary, shortly stalked; cor. tube widely funnel-shaped, about $2\frac{1}{2}$ in. long, lobes broadly triangular; plicae short and abrupt; cal. tube $\frac{1}{2}$ in. long, lobes about 1 in. long. September, October. Of garden origin. (Gen. 7.) var. **Wells'ii,** *fl.* paler. Differs from *G. Farreri* by the shorter pedicels, and cor. tube and lobes wider and of deeper colour, from *G. sino-ornata* by its narrower l. and cal. lobes twice as long as tube.

**G. Macoun'ii.** Annual. Erect, stems branched, about 12 in. h. *Basal l.* spatulate, 1 in. long; *stem-l.* narrower. *fl.* stalked, at tips of branches, deep purplish-blue, 1 to $1\frac{1}{2}$ in. long, funnel-shaped, lobes 4, broadly obovate, tip toothed, sides fringed; cal. $\frac{1}{3}$ to $\frac{1}{2}$ in. long, lobes 4, slender-pointed, inner ovate, outer linear-lanceolate. August. N. America.

**G. Makino'i.** Erect, unbranched perennial, 1 to $1\frac{1}{2}$ ft. or more h., leafy without basal rosette. *l.* in many pairs, largest towards top of stem, lanceolate-ovate, 1 to 2 in. long, thick, slightly glaucous, margins smooth. *fl.* clustered at top of stem and in upper l.-axils, pale blue, heavily spotted, $1\frac{1}{2}$ in. long, tubular-bell-shaped; cal. $\frac{1}{2}$ in. long, lobes unequal, 2 long, 3 short; cor. lobes ovate, abruptly pointed, sub-erect; plicae short, entire, abrupt. August, September. Japan. (Gen. 46.) Distinct among its allies by the unequal cal. lobes.

**G. membrana'cea.** Climber to 9 ft. *l.* lanceolate, $1\frac{1}{2}$ to 3 in. long, long-pointed, base rounded. *fl.* in axillary pairs, pale purple, $1\frac{1}{2}$ in. long, narrow-funnel-shaped; lobes triangular; plicae abrupt; cal. $\frac{1}{2}$ in. long, split down one side, lobes about $\frac{1}{2}$ in. long, unequal, linear, long-pointed. NE. Upper Burma.

**G. Menzies'ii.** Erect, with leafy stems 9 to 12 in. h. *l.* oblong-elliptic, up to 1 in. long, largest near apex of stem, lowest mere scales. *fl.* bluish-purple, solitary or rarely 2 or 3, terminal; cor. club-shaped with slightly open mouth, 1 to $1\frac{1}{4}$ in. long, lobes heart-shaped; plicae toothed; cal. $\frac{1}{3}$ in. long, split on one side, lobes small teeth. September. NW. America. (J.R.H.S. 57, 188.) Much like *G. sceptrum* but cal. tube split and lobes very small.

**G. microdon'ta.** Perennial, erect or nearly so, unbranched, 2 ft. h. *Basal l.* and l. of sterile shoots spatulate, 4 to 6 in. long; *stem-l.* ovate-oblong, about 2 in. long, all narrowed to base with smooth margins. *fl.* deep azure, $\frac{3}{4}$ to 1 in. long, tubular; cal. $\frac{1}{2}$ in. long, usually slightly split on one side, lobes shorter than tube, linear to delta-shaped, pointed; cor. lobes ovate; plicae irregular, ovate. July, August. W. China. (Gen. 44.) Differs from *G. rigescens* by the slender stems, narrower l., and larger fl.

**G. monta'na.** Erect perennial. Stem branching near apex, 10 to 24 in. h., purplish. *Basal l.* broadly obovate to spatulate, $1\frac{1}{2}$ in. long, $\frac{3}{4}$ in. wide above middle; *stem-l.* ovate-oblong. *fl.* in a terminal corymb or umbel, white, often veined with purple, $\frac{3}{4}$ to 1 in. across; cal. divided three-quarters of length, lobes lanceolate, acute; cor. lobes obovate. Summer. Australia, New Zealand. var. **saxo'sa,** *see* **G. saxosa.**

**G. montic'ola.** Perennial, erect or nearly so, 4 in h. Stem leafy. *l.* broad-ovate to cordate, about 1 in. long. *fl.* solitary, terminal, between uppermost pair of l., deep blue, 1 to $1\frac{1}{4}$ in. long; cal. $\frac{1}{3}$ in. long, bell-shaped, lobes ovate, leafy, slightly exceeding tube; cor. lobes broad-ovate; plicae lanceolate, much shorter than lobes, toothed. August. N. America. SYN. *G. calycosa monticola.*

**G. Moorcroftia'na.** Annual of 4 to 12 in., branching from root. *l.* oblong to elliptic, 1 to $1\frac{1}{2}$ in. long, upper often lanceolate. *fl.* blue to pink, solitary at tips of branches or in leafy cymes; cor. $\frac{1}{2}$ to 1 in. long, lobes 4 to 5, ovate; cal. tube $\frac{1}{4}$ in. long, lobes linear. Summer. Himalaya. (B.M. 6727.)

**G. Newber'ryi.** Erect, tufty perennial, 2 in. h., with loose basal rosettes. *Basal l.* obovate to spatulate, 1 to $1\frac{1}{4}$ in. long; *stem-l.* shorter and narrower. *fl.* 1 (rarely 2), terminal, pale blue (almost white) to deep blue with 5 brownish-green bands outside cor. tube, 1 to $1\frac{1}{2}$ in. long; cal. $\frac{1}{2}$ in. long, tubular, lobes shorter than tube, ovate-lanceolate, acute; cor. lobes ovate, acute; plicae slender, 2- to many-cleft, much shorter than cor. lobes. August, September. N. America. (Gen. 47.)

**G. nikoen'sis.** A synonym of *G. algida.*

**G. nippon'ica.** Branched perennial without basal rosette, stems straggling, leafy, 2 to 5 in. long. *Lower l.* ovate to ovate-lanceolate, $\frac{1}{2}$ in. long; *upper* smaller, narrower, all thick with recurved margins. *fl.* 1 to 5, but usually 2 or 3, terminal, purplish-blue, $\frac{1}{2}$ to $\frac{3}{4}$ in. long, funnel-shaped; cal. $\frac{1}{3}$ in. long, ribbed but not winged, lobes shorter than tube, lanceolate, pointed, recurved; cor. lobes ovate to nearly obovate, blunt; plicae about half as long as cor. lobes, triangular, entire. August. Japan. (A.F.J. 81.)

**G. niva'lis.** Annual, 1 to 6 in. h. *Basal l.* obovate, blunt; *stem-l.* ovate, acute. *fl.* solitary, deep blue, $\frac{3}{4}$ in. long; cal. $\frac{1}{2}$ in. long, ribbed, lobes equalling tube, lanceolate; cor. lobes ovate, acute; plicae white, 2-fid. July. Europe. (E.B. 916.)

**G. Nopcs'ae.** A variety of *G. Pneumonanthe.*

**G. nubige'na.** Erect perennial. Stem simple, 3 to 6 in. h. from a basal rosette. *Basal l.* spatulate to oblong-linear, 1 to 2 in. long, blunt; *stem-l.* in several pairs, shorter, broader, all thick and fleshy with smooth margins. *fl.* 1 to 3, terminal on short pedicels, yellowish-white with blue on lobes and blue bands outside cor. tube, 1½ to 1¾ in. long, funnel-shaped; cal. ½ in. long, tubular, lobes ⅕ to ¼ in. long, oblong, blunt, widely separated; cor. lobes erect, broadly ovate with short points; plicae irregular, triangular, entire. August, September. Himalaya. (Gen. 49.) Larger and with more numerous l. than *G. frigida*; cal. lobes shorter and cor. lobes blunter than in *G. algida*. Syn. *G. algida nubigena*. var. **parviflo'ra,** *fl.* solitary, stalked, deep blue, less than 1 in. long. Himalaya. Syn. *G. algida parviflora*.

**G. ochroleu'ca.** Stout, leafy, often branched perennial, 6 to 12 in. h. *l.* oblong to obovate, 1 to 3 in. long. *fl.* clustered at top of stem and in upper l.-axils, greenish-white, often tinged purple, 1½ in. long; cal. ⅓ to ½ in. long, funnel-shaped, lobes longer than tube, unequal, linear; cor. lobes triangular, acute; plicae sometimes toothed. September. N. America. (B.M. 2303 as *G. intermedia*.) Syn. *G. villosa*.

**G. Olivier'i.** Erect perennial, about 9 in. h., with basal rosette. *Basal l.* spatulate, 4 in. long, ½ in. wide; *stem-l.* in 1 or 2 pairs, shorter, more ovate. *fl.* in a terminal umbel, deep blue, 1 to 1¼ in. long, bell-shaped; cal. ¼ in. long, lobes at least as long as tube, narrow, erect, acute; cor. lobes narrow-oblong; plicae triangular, 2-fid. July. Asia Minor. (Gen. 53.) Distinct by its umbellate infl., and entire cal. with lobes as long as tube. *G. Olivieri* of Clarke is *G. tianschanica*.

**G. orega'na.** Leafy, erect or ascending perennial, 12 to 15 in. h., without basal rosette. *l.* broad-ovate to oblong, ¾ to 1¼ in. long, pointed, margins rough. *fl.* more or less in a raceme, purplish-blue, 1 to 1¼ in. long, broadly bell-shaped; cal. ⅓ to ½ in. long, lobes equal to or shorter than tube, oblong to ovate; cor. lobes ovate, acute; plicae triangular, 2-fid, acute. August. N. America. Distinct from *G. affinis* by the broader cal. lobes about as long as the cal. tube and the bell-shaped cor.

**G. oreodox'a.** Prostrate perennial. Stems 4 in. long. *Basal l.* few or none; *stem-l.* linear-lanceolate, recurved, ¼ to ¾ in. long. *fl.* solitary, terminal, sessile, blue, spotted yellowish-white, 1 to 1¼ in. long, obconic; cal. ¼ in. long, cylindric-bell-shaped, lobes equalling tube or longer, linear, recurved, acute; cor. lobes ovate, acute; plicae nicked or toothed. August, September. NW. China. (G.C. 97 (1935), 323 as *G. lhaguensis*.)

**G. Or'fordii.** Usually erect, leafy perennial, 1 to 2 ft. h. *l.* longest in upper part of stem, linear-lanceolate, 1 to 3 in. long. *fl.* many, terminal, stalked, blue, paler within throat, speckled, 1 to 1¼ in. long, bell-shaped; cal. ¼ to ½ in. long, lobes longer than tube, linear-lanceolate, acute; cor. lobes broadly ovate, pointed; plicae sometimes 2-fid. October. N. America. Perhaps only a var. of *G. sceptrum*.

**G. orna'ta.*** Perennial with rosette and prostrate, leafy stems 4 in. long, ascending at tips. *Basal l.* 1 in. long; *stem-l.* ½ in. long, all narrow-linear, acute. *fl.* solitary, terminal, sessile, pale blue, 1 to 1½ in. long, widely bell-shaped; cal. ½ in. long, bell-shaped, lobes slightly shorter than tube, narrow-linear, acute; cor. lobes broadly triangular or ovate; plicae much shorter than lobes, ragged. August. Nepal. (B.M. 9416.) Differs from allies by the short, wide bell-shaped cor. var. **congestifo'lia,** *l.* shorter and broader, *fl.* more tubular, cal. lobes spreading. Nepal. (Gen. 52.)

**G. Pallas'ii.** A variety of *G. decumbens*.

**G. pannon'ica.** Stout perennial, 1 to 2 ft. h. with erect, unbranched stem from a basal rosette. *Basal l.* broadly elliptic; 6 to 8 in. long, long-stalked; *stem-l.* ovate to lanceolate, 3 to 4 in. long, the uppermost narrower. *fl.* clustered, terminal and axillary, sessile, brownish-purple heavily spotted with darker shade, 1¼ to 1½ in. long, bell-shaped; cal. ½ in. long, bell-shaped, thick, lobes 5 to 7, unequal, shorter than tube, reflexed; cor. lobes broadly ovate; plicae short, blunt. July. Europe. (Gen. 48.) Differs from allies by the reflexed cal. lobes, entire cal. tube, and fl. colour.

**G. Par'ryi.** Perennial with leafy, erect or ascending stem, about 12 in. h. *l.* broadly ovate, 1½ in. long, rounded at base, thick, margins rough. *fl.* in heads, with involucre of uppermost l., purplish-blue, 1½ in. long, obconic to bell-shaped; cal. about ½ in. long, sometimes slightly split, lobes ¼ to ½ in. long, narrow spatulate to linear; cor. lobes erect, obovate, acute; plicae half as long as lobes, 2-fid. August, September. N. America. (Gen. 57.) Differs from *G. bracteosa* and *G. calycosa* by the erect, obovate cor. lobes and linear cal. lobes.

**G. pat'ula.** Erect, branching perennial, 6 to 18 in. h. *Basal l.* oblong-spatulate, 3 in. long, thick; *stem-l.* narrower and smaller. *fl.* many in an umbel or cyme, terminal, white, 1 in. across, deeply cut; cal. divided three-quarters way down, lobes linear-oblong, acute; cor. lobes broad-oblong, rounded at tips. July, August. New Zealand. Differs from *G. bellidifolia* by the more robust habit and larger fl.

**G. phlogifo'lia.** Perennial. Stem erect or nearly so, leafy, 12 to 18 in. h. *Basal l.* 3½ to 4 in. long, oblong-lanceolate; *stem-l.* shorter, lanceolate, acute, margins rough. *fl.* in terminal heads with a few in upper l.-axils, blue, ½ to ¾ in. long, bell-shaped; cal. ¼ in. long, lobes 4 or 5, unequal linear-lanceolate; cor. lobes 4 or 5, rounded-ovate; plicae ovate, entire. July. Europe, Asia. Syn. *G. cruciata phlogifolia*. Differs from *G. cruciata* by the unequal cal. lobes and rounded cor. lobes.

**G. phylloca'lyx.** Annual or biennial, rarely perennial. Stem erect, unbranched, 1 to 6 in. h. *Basal l.* broadly obovate, ½ to 1 in. long; *stem-l.* ¼ to ½ in. long. *fl.* terminal, 1 (rarely up to 4), enclosed by topmost l., pale to deep blue, 1 to 1¼ in. long, tubular, inflated in middle; cal. ⅕ to ¼ in. long, unequal, larger leafy; cor. lobes ovate; plicae irregular, toothed. August, September. Himalaya, China, Tibet. (Gen. 55.) Differs from allies by the form of the cal.

**G. Pneumonan'the.*** Perennial. Stems simple, slender, leafy, 6 to 12 in. h. *l.* linear-spatulate to linear, 1 to 1½ in. long, the smaller towards base, blunt, margins smooth. *fl.* terminal, axillary, stalked, deep to purplish-blue, paler towards base, banded and spotted green, 1½ to 2 in. long, funnel-shaped; cal. ⅓ to ½ in. long, bell-shaped, lobes linear, long-pointed, about as long as tube; cor. lobes ovate, acute; plicae short, triangular, entire. August. N. Hemisphere. (B.M. 1101.) Variable in fl.-colour and size and shape of l. var. **al'ba,*** fl. white, smaller; **depres'sa,** prostrate or ascending, stems 6 to 9 in. long, *fl.* deep blue, spotted green. Syn. *G. arvernensis*; **Styrian form,*** taller, more robust, erect, *fl.* paler; **Nopcsae,** *l.* ovate-lanceolate, rounded at base, *fl.* 2 or 3 together, sessile, cal. lobes broader.

**G. Porphyr'io.** Perennial. Stem erect or ascending, simple, slender, 12 to 15 in. h. *l.* in few pairs, narrow-spatulate to linear near apex of stem 1½ to 2½ in. long, thick. *fl.* solitary, terminal, long-stalked, bright blue, 1½ to 2 in. long, funnel-shaped; cal. ½ in. long, tubular, lobes exceeding tube, linear to narrow-linear; cor. lobes ovate, narrowed at base, acute; plicae less than half length of lobes, many-cleft. August, September. N. America. (B.B. 2, 618.) Differs from allies by the long-stalked, brilliant blue, solitary fl.

**G. prola'ta.*** Prostrate perennial. Stems 6 in. long, branched near apex. *l.* elliptic-lanceolate to oblong, ¼ to ½ in. long, longest towards apex, short-pointed. *fl.* solitary, terminal, sessile, purplish-blue, banded yellowish-white, 1 to 1½ in. long, almost tubular, slightly wider above; cal. ½ in. long, tubular, reddish, lobes oblong, half as long as tube, acute; cor. lobes erect, broadly triangular, pointed; plicae short, toothed. July. Sikkim, Bhutan. (B.M. 9311.) Differs from allies by the narrower l. and erect cal. lobes.

**G. prostra'ta.** Annual with stem simple or branched from base, 3 to 6 in. h. *l.* small, ovate-spatulate to linear-spatulate. *fl.* solitary, terminal, nodding, azure, ½ in. long; cal. tubular, lobes erect, narrowly ovate; cor. lobes ovate, acute; plicae, triangular, 2-fid. Summer. N. Hemisphere. (R.I.F.G. xvii, 1049.) A variable species.

**G. Przewals'kii.*** Tufted perennial with erect fertile and sterile shoots, 6 to 9 in. h. *Basal l.* narrow-spatulate, 3 in. long; *stem-l.* oblong-lanceolate, all margins rough. *fl.* in a loose terminal head, stalked, whitish, blue on lobes, tinged and streaked blue, club-shaped to obconic, 2 in. long; cal. ½ to ¾ in. long, cylindric, lobes ¼ to ⅓ in. long, erect, unequal, linear; cor. lobes erect, broadly deltoid; plicae short, broadly triangular, 2-fid or nicked. July, August. W. China, NE. Tibet. (Gen. 61.) Syn. *G. algida Przewalskii*. Differs from *G. algida* by the more club-shaped cor.

**G. pseudo-Pneumonan'the.** A synonym of *G. linearis*.

**G. pube'rula.** Erect, unbranched perennial with leafy, usually angled stems, 9 to 12 in. h. *l.* ovate-lanceolate to linear-lanceolate near base, oblong above, 1 to 2 in. long, margins rough. *fl.* terminal and axillary, sessile in a raceme-like infl., blue to purplish-blue, 1½ in. long, narrow-bell-shaped, slightly constricted at mouth; cal. ½ to ⅓ in. long, tubular, lobes as long as tube, spreading, entire, equal; cor. lobes ovate to obovate, spreading; plicae triangular, 2- to many-cleft. August. N. America. (B.B. 2, 615.) Differs from *G. affinis* by the spreading cor. lobes and equal cal. lobes.

**G. pu'mila.** Tufted perennial, with erect, unbranched stems, 2 to 3 in. h. *Lower l.* about ½ in. long, the lowest slightly the largest; *upper l.* ¼ in. long, all linear, acute, not narrowed at base, margins sometimes rough. *fl.* solitary, terminal, deep azure, over ½ in. long, saucer-shaped; cal. ¼ in. long, tubular, narrowly winged, lobes shorter, linear-lanceolate, spreading, acute; cor. lobes half as long as tube, ovate-lanceolate, acute, often nicked on margin; plicae very small, 2-fid. July, August. Europe. (R.I.F.G. xvii, 1048.) Differs from *G. verna* by the narrower l. not narrowed at base and the more pointed cor. lobes.

**G. puncta'ta.** Perennial with erect, unbranched, ridged stems, 1 to 2 ft. h. *Basal l.* elliptic, 4 in. long, shortly pointed, stalked; *stem-l.* narrower, sessile or short-stalked. *fl.* terminal and axillary in whorls, sessile, pale yellow, spotted purple, 1½ in. long, bell-shaped; cal. ⅓ to ½ in. long, rarely split, lobes 2 to 7, small, unequal, distant, erect, elliptic; cor. lobes 6 to 8, ovate, rounded; plicae short. June, July. Europe. (R.I.F.G. xvii, 1056.) *See* **G. Burseri** and **G. purpurea.**

**G. Pur'domii** of gardens. *See* **G. gracilipes.**

**G. purpu'rea.** Perennial with unbranched, erect, hollow stem, 1 to 2 ft. h., from a loose rosette. *Basal l.* ovate-oblong, 8 in. long, 2 in. wide, long-stalked, margins smooth; *stem-l.* sessile or nearly so. *infl.* as in *G. punctata*. *fl.* purplish-red, yellowish at base of tube, striped and spotted green, 1¼ to 1½ in. long, open-bell-shaped; cal. ½ to ¾ in. long, papery, split on one side, lobes small, tooth-like, or absent; cor. lobes 5 to 8, obovate-rounded, widest in middle; plicae short, abrupt. July, August. Europe. (R.I.F.G. xvii, 1054.)

Distinct by the split cal., fl. colour, cor. lobes widest in the middle var. **na'na,** *l.* 4 to 6 in. long, *fl.* 3 or 4; **camtschat'ica,** *l.* 2 in. long lanceolate with long, tapering point, stem 2 ft. h. Kamtschatka.

*Gentiana pumila* (p. 878)

**G. pyrena'ica.** Tufted perennial with sterile and fertile stems 3 in. h. *Lower l* crowded, all ¼ to ½ in. long, linear-lanceolate, shortly pointed, margins rough. *fl.* solitary, terminal, violet-blue within, pale greenish-blue without, 1 to 1¼ in. long, narrowly obconic; cal. ⅓ in. long, angled, lobes ⅛ in. long, ovate-lanceolate, erect, blunt; cor. lobes ovate, rounded; plicae rounded, nicked, almost as long as lobes. May, June. Europe, Asia. (B.M. 5742.) Differs from *G. altaica* by the shorter cor.

**G. quinqueflo'ra.** Much-branched annual, 12 to 24 in. h. *l.* broadly ovate, ¾ to 1½ in. long, base cordate. *fl.* 3 to 5 clustered at ends of branches, purplish-blue, ½ to ¾ in. long, club-shaped; cal. ⅛ in. long, lobes ⅛ to ½ in. long, lanceolate; cor. lobes ovate, without plicae. N. America. (B.M. 3496.) Distinct from allies by its broad ovate-cordate l.

**G. quinquefo'lia.** A synonym of *G. quinqueflora.*

**G. Regel'ii.** A synonym of *G. tianschanica.*

**G. riges'cens.** Perennial with erect, unbranched stems, 15 in. h., tinged purple. *Basal l.* small, orbicular; *stem-l.* larger upwards, oblong-ovate, ¾ to 2 in. long, blunt, 3-nerved, thick. *fl.* in terminal heads with a few in upper l.-axils, purplish-rose to purplish-blue, dotted green, 1 to 1½ in. long, tubular-funnel-shaped; cal. ¼ to ½ in. long, bell-shaped, lobes ½ to ¾ in. long, unequal, linear to oblong-lanceolate; cor. lobes broadly ovate, abruptly slender-pointed; plicae irregular, short-ovate, entire. September. China. (B.M. 8974.) Distinct from *G. cephalantha* by the erect, unbranched stem, thick, blunt, oval l., and infl. without whorl of l. at base.

**G. robus'ta.** Erect perennial about 12 in. h. *Basal l.* linear, 12 in. long, ⅓ in. wide, acute; *stem-l.* linear-lanceolate, 2 in. long or more. *fl.* clustered at and near top of stem, sessile, white or whitish, 1¼ in. long, tubular-bell-shaped; cal. ⅝ in. long, split to base, lobes linear, acute, short; cor. lobes ovate-triangular; plicae triangular, about half as long as lobes. August. S. Tibet. (H.I.P. 1439.) Syn. *G. tibetica robusta.* Distinct from *G. tibetica* by the split cal. and narrower l.

**G. Rochel'lii.** A form of *G. Clusii.*

**G. Romanzov'ii.** Erect perennial, 4 to 8 in. h. *Basal l.* linear-lanceolate to narrow-lanceolate, about 4 in. long; *stem-l.* in 2 or 3 pairs, broader, 1 to 1½ in. long. *fl.* 1 or 2 (rarely 3), terminal, yellowish-white, tinged blue, spotted purple, ¾ to 1½ in. long, obconic to bell-shaped; cal. ½ in. long, lobes ¼ in. long, linear-oblong, blunt; cor. lobes triangular, acute; plicae triangular, blunt, entire. August. N. America. (A.G.S.B. 5 (1937), 127.) Syn. *G. algida Romanzovii, G. frigida Romanzovii.* Dwarfer and with fewer *fl.* than in *G. algida*, cal. entire with short lobes.

**G. Rosta'nii.** Tufted perennial with erect stems 4 to 6 in. h. *Basal l.* linear-lanceolate to linear, over ½ in. long, equal, overlapping; *stem-l.* in few pairs, smaller. *fl.* solitary, terminal, deep blue, ¾ in. across, saucer-shaped, cal. ½ in. long, tubular-funnel-shaped, angled but not winged, lobes ⅕ to ¼ in. long, lanceolate, acute; cor. lobes obovate, blunt to round; plicae short, 2-fid. June, July. Europe. Syn. *G. bavarica elongata, G. bavarica Rostanii.* Differs from *G. bavarica* by the smaller fl. with narrower cor. lobes and the narrow l.

**G. Sabau'da.** A synonym of *G. angustifolia.*

**G. Sapona'ria.** Erect perennial with leafy stems 1 to 2½ ft. h. *l.* ovate-lanceolate to oblong, 1½ to 2½ in. long, margins rough. *fl.* clustered at and near top of stem, blue, 1 to 2 in. long, club-shaped; cal. ⅓ to ½ in. long, lobes leafy, slightly longer than tube, oblong-obovate to linear-oblong; cor. lobes ovate, blunt to rounded; plicae nearly as long as lobes, unequal, 2- to many-cleft. August, September. N. America. (B.M. 1039.) Syn. *G. Catesbaei.* Differs from *G. Andrewsii* by the plicae shorter than cor. lobes. var. **al'ba,** dwarfer, *fl.* white.

**G. saxo'sa.*** Tufted perennial with erect stems 6 in. h. *l.* spatulate to linear-spatulate, ¾ to 1½ in. long, fleshy, deep green, tinged brown-purple. *fl.* solitary or in 5-fld. cymes, terminal, white often veined purple, ¾ to 1 in. across; cal. about one-third as long as cor., divided three-quarters of length, lobes linear to linear-spatulate, tips recurved; cor. lobes oblong, blunt. July to September. New Zealand. (Gen. 60.) Differs from allies by the larger fl. and spatulate, fleshy l.

**G. scab'ra.*** Erect or sub-erect leafy perennial about 12 in. h. *l.* in many pairs, topmost equalling internodes, sessile, ovate, acute, margin and midrib rough. *fl.* several in clusters, terminal, and, in topmost axils, sessile, purplish-blue, 1 to 1¼ in. long, bell-shaped, broadly ovate, wide at middle, acute; plicae entire, rarely toothed; cal. about ½ in. long, tubular, purplish, lobes linear-oblong. August. Manchuria, N. China. (G.C. 47 (1910), supp. t.) var. **angustifo'lia,** *l.* lanceolate, acute; **Buerg'eri,*** 12 to 18 in. h., *fl.* blue, narrowly bell-shaped, plicae 2-fid or toothed, cal. linear-lanceolate; **Bungea'na,*** *l.* broad-ovate, *fl.* blue, spotted white, cal. lobes erect; **Fortun'ei,** more slender, stem sub-erect or ascending, *fl.* blue, heavily spotted white, cal. lobes linear, *l.* ovate to ovate-lanceolate. (B.M. 4776 as *G. Fortunei*); **saxat'ilis,*** slender, prostrate, stems 6 to 12 in. long, *l.* lanceolate to linear, *fl.* purplish-blue, tubular-funnel-shaped, plicae toothed. (G.C. 102 (1937), 273.) (Syn. *G. Kirishimo-Rindo.*)

**G. scarlati'na.** About 4 in. h., branched. *Basal l.* lanceolate, 1 to 1¼ in. long, fleshy; *stem-l.* much smaller. *fl.* scarlet, terminal; cor. ½ to ⅝ in. long, obconic to open-bell-shaped, lobes obovate, acute; cal. ¼ in. long, bell-shaped, tube short, lobes lanceolate, acute. April. Peru. (G.C. 99 (1936), 135.)

**G. scep'trum.** Perennial with leafy stem, erect or nearly so, 1½ to 3 ft. h. *l.* narrow-oblong, 1½ to 3 in. long, blunt, margins smooth. *fl.* clustered at and near top of stem, 2 or 3 together, dull bluish-purple, spotted, 1½ to 2 in. long, club- to bell-shaped; cal. ⅓ in. long, lobes leafy, narrow-lanceolate, unequal; cor. lobes broadly ovate, erect, rounded; plicae triangular, entire. August. N. America. (Gen. 73, 74.) Distinct from allies by the erect cor. lobes, entire cal. tube, and leafy cal. lobes. var. **hu'milis,** dwarf, with solitary *fl.* and 2- or 3-cleft plicae.

**G. schistoca'lyx.** A variety of *G. asclepiadea.*

**G. semiala'ta.** Stems erect, 8 to 12 in. h., branched. *l.* broadly ovate to heart-shaped, ½ to 1½ in. long, long-pointed, stalked. *fl.* violet, sessile at tip of branch; cor. tube funnel-shaped, 2½ in. long, lobes triangular; plicae toothed; cal. tube about ½ in. long, tubular, lobes ovate to spatulate. October. China.

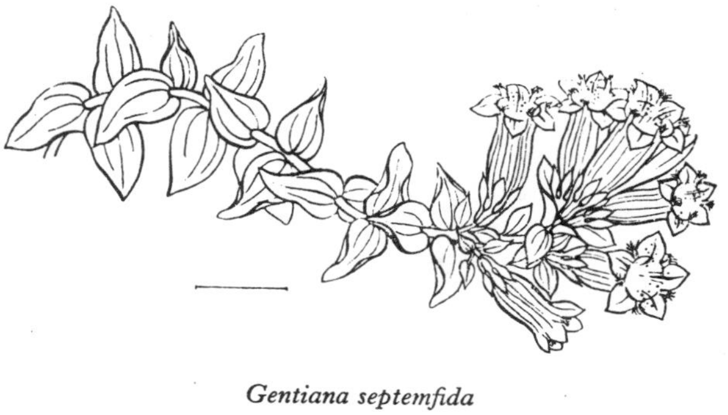

*Gentiana septemfida*

**G. septem'fida.*** Erect or ascending perennial. Stems several, simple, leafy, 6 to 12 in. long. *l.* ovate, 1 to 1½ in. long, acute. *fl.* few in cluster, terminal, deep blue to deep purplish-blue with paler spots within, 1 to 1¾ in. long, narrow- to wide-bell-shaped, lobes ovate, acute; plicae nearly as long as lobes, many cleft; cal. ½ in. long, tubular, lobes linear, equalling tube. Summer. Asia Minor to Persia. Variable with many forms. var. **cordifo'lia,*** decumbent, shorter than type, *l.* broader, round or heart-shaped, *fl.* solitary or few. Syn. *G. cordifolia, G. septemfida procumbens.* **A**

**G. serot'ina.** Annual or biennial, 6 to 9 in. h., erect, sometimes branched from base. *Basal l.* few, linear-spatulate, 1½ in. long, thick, tinged purple-brown; *upper l.* narrowly triangular. *fl.* white, ¾ in. across, 3 to 5 in a terminal umbel; cor. lobes 4, obovate, obtuse, shortly mucronate; cal. ¼ in. long, lobes ⅛ in. long, awl-shaped. April, May. New Zealand.

**G. setig'era.** Stout perennial with ascending stems, 12 in. long. *Basal l.* broad-ovate, 2 in. long, blunt, thick, on stem shorter, oblong to narrow-oblong, in 2 or 3 pairs. *fl.* usually 4 in terminal cluster, stalked, purplish-blue, 1½ in. long, broadly bell-shaped; lobes spreading, almost cordate; plicae slightly shorter than cor. lobes, finely cut; cal. ½ in. long, lobes as long as tube, broadly ovate. Summer. California. (Gen. 72.)

**G. setulifo'lia.** Creeping perennial with short, almost prostrate, barren, and erect fl.-stems, 4 to 6 in. h. *l.* 7 in a whorl, linear, ¼ to ½ in. long, stiff, acute, ciliate, sessile. *fl.* solitary, sessile, sea-blue, tube with darker stripes on whitish ground, 1½ to 1¾ in. long, funnel-bell-shaped; lobes 7, ovate, acute; plicae short, toothed; cal. purplish, ⅜ in. long, lobes 7, linear, acute, ciliate. Burma, Tibet. (Gen. 76.)

**G. sikkimen'sis.** Tufted with sterile and fl.-shoots up to 8 in. long. *l.* roundish to elliptic. *fl.* blue, in heads, surrounded by topmost l.; cor. club-shaped, 1 in. long, lobes short, ovate, blunt; plicae irregular, 2-fid, short; cal. tube ¼ in. long, split down one side, lobes unequal, narrowly triangular. July, August. China, Himalaya. (Gen. 69.)

**G. sikokia'na.** Slender, erect perennial, 8 to 12 in. h. *l.* in many pairs, elliptic, up to 3 in. long, acute, with a cartilaginous margin, lower ones stalked. *fl.* usually 3 together, terminal and in topmost l.-axils purplish-blue, spotted white, 1½ in. long, funnel-shaped; cal. ½ in. long, lobes round to heart-shaped, spreading; cor. lobes broadly ovate; plicae triangular, entire. July, August. Japan. (A.J.F. 47.) Differs from allies by the rounded to heart-shaped cal. lobes.

*Gentiana sino-ornata*

**G. sino-orna'ta.*** Prostrate perennial. Stems ascending at tips, often tinged purple. *l.* linear-lanceolate, ½ to 1½ in. long, acute. *fl.* solitary, terminal, usually sessile, deep blue, paler at base, banded purplish-blue, 2½ in. long, funnel-shaped; cal. about ½ in. long, tubular, lobes twice as long as tube, lanceolate, stiff, acute; cor. lobes broadly ovate, acute; plicae broadly triangular, entire or nicked. September, October. W. China, Tibet. (B.M. 9241.) Distinct from *G. Farreri* by the deeper blue colouring, the blue throat of cor. tube and the linear-lanceolate l. var. **prae'cox,** *fl.* stalked, cor. tubular-funnel-shaped. August, September.

**G. siphonan'tha.** Perennial, erect or ascending, 8 to 12 in. h. *Basal l.* linear-lanceolate, 9 in. long, acute; *stem-l.* linear-lanceolate to lanceolate, 4 to 6 in. long, longest at base of stem. *fl.* in heads, terminal and in topmost axils, sessile, blue to purplish-blue, ¾ to 1 in. long, tubular-funnel-shaped; cal. ½ in. long, sometimes partly split on one side, lobes unequal, awl-shaped; cor. lobes erect, ovate-oblong, acute; plicae entire, narrow awl-shaped. July, August. W. China, Tibet. var. **latifo'lia,** *l.* broader, over 1 in. wide, *fl.* stalked.

**G. specio'sa.** Climber to 6 ft. *l.* narrow- to broad-ovate, 1½ to 4 in. long. *fl.* terminal or axillary in twos and threes, blue-violet, 1½ in. long, wide-funnel-shaped; lobes broad triangular; cal. ½ in. long, lobes about ½ in. long, broad-ovate, slightly recurved. September. Himalaya. Syn. *Crawfurdia speciosa.*

**G. squarro'sa.** Annual, 1 to 4 in. h. *l.* acute, silvery. *fl.* terminal, blue. NE. Asia, Himalaya.

**G.×stevenagen'sis** (*G. sino-ornata*×*G. Veitchiorum*). Habit and *l.* intermediate between parents. *fl.* deep purple-blue, lined and spotted greenish-yellow within, shortly stalked, terminal on branched stems; cor. tube 2 to 2½ in. long; plicae narrow, acute; cal. tube over ½ in. long, teeth equal or longer, broadly lanceolate. September. Of garden origin (A.G.S.B. (1942), 207.) Syn. *G.* × *Wellsiana.* Differs from *G. sino-ornata* by the branched stems, narrower cor. tube, and deeper colour, and from *G. Veitchiorum* by the erect fl. with cal. tube and lobes of about equal length.

**G. stictan'tha.** Perennial with stems 8 to 10 in. long, erect or nearly so. *Basal l.* narrow-lanceolate, 4 to 6 in. long, on stem 1½ to 2½ in. long. *fl.* in loose heads, yellowish-white, spotted and streaked violet-blue, 1 to 1¼ in. long, narrow-funnel-shaped; lobes ovate, acute; plicae very short, blunt; cal. ⅓ to ½ in. long, purple tinged, partly split on one side, lobes triangular, acute, recurved. Autumn. SE. Tibet. (Gen. 68.)

**G. stragula'ta.*** Tufted perennial. Stems decumbent, 2 to 3 in. long. *Basal l.* obovate, ½ to ⅝ in. long, stalked, on stem ovate, ½ in. long, tips rounded. *fl.* 1 to 3 in cluster, terminal sessile, axillary stalked, purplish-blue without, throat purple, tubular, throat narrowed, 2 in. long; lobes triangular, spotted at base; plicae 2-fid or nicked, whitish; cal. ¾ to 1 in. long, tubular, purple-tinged, lobes equal, leafy, broadly ovate. W. China. (B.M. 8897.)

*Gentiana stragulata*

**G. stramin'ea.** Stout perennial with ascending stems 10 to 12 in. long. *Basal l.* 9, linear-lanceolate to lanceolate, 9 in. long, on stem in few pairs only, linear-oblong, 2 to 3 in. long, acute. *fl.* in sub-terminal racemes, stalked, greenish-white to straw-colour, 1¼ in. long, narrowly obconic; lobes ovate, acute; plicae one-third length of cor. lobe, 2-fid or toothed; cal. ½ to ¾ in. long, whitish, papery, split on one side, lobes 2 or 3, awl-shaped. July. W. China. (Gen. 75.)

**G. styloph'ora.** Perennial 4 to 6 ft. h. *Basal l.* elliptic, 12 in. long, 4 in. wide, stalked; *stem-l.* 4 to 6 in. long, sessile. *fl.* few, stalked, straw-yellow, 1½ to 2½ in. long, wide-funnel- to bell-shaped; cal. ⅓ to ¾ in. long, wide-funnel-shaped, lobes ovate; cor. lobes cut almost to base, broadly ovate; plicae inconspicuous. July, August. Himalaya. (Gen. 78, 79.) Differs from *G. lutea* by the more open, larger fl., not verticillate.

**G. symphyan'dra.** A variety of *G. lutea.*

**G. tenel'la.** Annual 1 to 6 in. h. *l.* ovate, ¼ in. long. *fl.* solitary, terminal, pale blue, ¼ to ½ in. long; cal. small, cup-shaped. June, July. Northern regions. Syn. *G. glacialis.*

**G. tenuifo'lia.** Annual, 12 to 16 in. h., stem simple, slender. *Basal l.* 3 to 5 in. long, oblong-obovate to obovate-spatulate, thin; *stem-l.* narrow, somewhat triangular, subacute. *fl.* white, ½ in. long, in many-fld. umbels; cor. lobes 4, ⅓ in. long, acute; cal. ½ in. long, teeth ¼ in. long, linear-awl-shaped. July, August. New Zealand.

**G. tereticau'lis.** Annual, 9 to 18 in. h., stem simple, erect. *Basal l.* few, narrow-oblong-ovate, 1¾ in. long, thin; *stem-l.* shorter, ovate-wedge-shaped. *fl.* white, ¾ in. long, 4 to 7 in an umbel; cor. lobes ½ in. long, obovate; cal. ¼ in. long, lobes ⅛ in. long, linear-awl-shaped. July. New Zealand.

**G. tergesti'na.** Perennial with an erect, unbranched stem 1 to 4 in. h. *Basal l.* linear-lanceolate, ½ to 2 in. long, one-fourth as wide, widest near base, leathery; *stem-l.* smaller. *fl.* solitary, terminal, deep azure-blue, ¾ to 1 in. across, saucer-shaped; cor. lobes ovate; plicae acute; cal. ¾ to 1 in. long, tubular, tinged purple, winged, the wings widest in middle, lobes ½ in. long, lanceolate, acute, scabrid on margin. April, May. Europe. Differs from *G. angulosa* by the narrower l. and less winged cal. tube; from *G. verna* by the longer fl., opening earlier. It is the *G. angulosa* of Reichenbach.

**G. terglouen'sis.** Perennial with an erect, unbranched stem 1 to 1½ in. h. *Basal l.* ⅛ to ¼ in. long, ovate, the smallest at base, overlapping; *stem-l.* slightly larger, all scabrid on margin with dry tips. *fl.* solitary, terminal, sessile, deep azure-blue, ½ to ¾ in. across, saucer-shaped; cor. lobes rounded, emarginate; plicae 2-fid; cal. ½ in. long, tubular, strongly angled (not winged), lobes ⅛ in. long, lanceolate, acute. July, August. Europe. Syn. *G. imbricata.* Differs from its allies by the overlapping l., the smallest at base with dry tips and by the sessile fl.

**G. Thunberg'ii.** Annual 1 to 4 in. h. *Basal l.* broad-ovate to round, ¼ to ½ in. long, on stem lanceolate. *fl.* solitary, stalked, blue, ½ to ¾ in. long, funnel-shaped; lobes ovate, erect; plicae toothed or entire; cal. ¼ in. long, tubular, lobes erect, lanceolate. Japan.

**G. tianschan'ica.** Erect or semi-decumbent perennial, stems 10 in. long. *Basal l.* linear-lanceolate, over 3 in. long, blunt, margins rough; *stem-l.* in 2 to 4 pairs, oblong, 1 to 2 in. long. *fl.* clustered at and near top of stem, stalked, deep blue to purplish-blue, ¾ to 1 in. long, tubular-funnel-shaped; cal. ⅓ to ½ in. long, split half down or more, lobes unequal, ⅛ to ½ in. long, linear, margins rough; cor. lobes ovate-oblong, acute, narrowed to base; plicae triangular, entire or 2-fid. August. Himalaya. (G.F. (1882) 1087, f. 1, 2 as *G. decumbens.*) Syn. *G. Regelii.* There are several vars. of this species, of which var. **glomera'ta** with narrower cal. lobes is in cultivation. Differs from allies by the split cal. which is not papery, the stalked fl., and cor. lobes not narrowed at base.

**G. tibet'ica.** Robust perennial, 24 in. h. from a basal rosette. *Basal l.* lanceolate, up to 12 in. long, 3 in. wide; *stem-l.* narrower, bases forming a tube round the stem, uppermost enclosing infl. *fl.* many, crowded at and near top of stem, greenish-white, 1 to 1¼ in. long, tubular-funnel-shaped; cal. about ½ in. long, papery, tubular-bell-shaped, lobes minute; cor. lobes triangular-ovate; plicae short, triangular. July, August. Himalaya. (H.I.P. 1441.) Of no garden value though often offered. Leaf wider than in *G. robusta.*

**G. Town'sonii.** 6 to 18 in. h., stem usually simple, erect. *Basal l.* ovate-lanceolate, 1 to 1½ in. long, blunt, fleshy; *stem-l.* smaller. *fl.* white, 1 in. across, 5 to 12 in terminal cymes or umbels; cor. lobes long, broadly oblong, rounded at tip; cal. ½ in. long, lobes ⅜ in. long, lanceolate, acute. August. New Zealand. (C.I.N.Z. 139.)

**G. trichot'oma.*** Erect, branched perennial, 12 to 24 in. h. *Basal l.* linear-lanceolate to lanceolate, 4 in. long, ½ in. wide; *stem-l.* lanceolate to spatulate. *fl.* usually in threes in uppermost nodes forming a loose raceme, deep clear blue, 1 to 1½ in. long, club-shaped to cylindric; cal. ½ in. long, purplish, tubular, lobes unequal, linear, short; cor. lobes ovate, obtuse; plicae irregular, triangular, toothed. July. W. China. (Gen. 80.) SYN. *G. Hopei* of gardens. Variable in size and colour, ranging from clear blue to whitish with purple lines outside cor. Differs from its allies by its short cal., unequal cal. lobes, narrow cor., and fl. in threes. (B.M. 9638.) var. **albes'cens,** *fl.* white or whitish, plant smaller; **brevicau'lis,** dwarf, not over 4 in. h., stems simple.

**G. triflo'ra.** Perennial, stem erect, branched, slender, leafy, 9 to 15 in. h. *l.* narrow-lanceolate, 1 to 2 in. long, increasing in size from base upwards, blunt, margins smooth, slightly reflexed, not forming a tube around stem. *fl.* in a spike, topmost fl. sessile; deep blue to purplish-blue with whitish bands without, 1¼ to 1½ in. long, narrow-bell-shaped; cal. ½ in. long, sometimes slightly split, tinged purple, lobes ⅛ to ½ in. long, unequal, 3 large, 2 small, narrow-lanceolate, acute, margins smooth; cor. lobes erect, broadly ovate, blunt; plicae abrupt, small. August, September. Asia. Differs from allies by slender stems, narrow l., unequal cal. lobes, slightly split cal., and short, undeveloped plicae.

**G. trinerv'is.** Weak climber to about 4 ft. *l.* broad-ovate, 2 to 3½ in. long, rounded at base, long-pointed. *fl.* 2 or 3 together, axillary, stalked, purplish, 1½ in. long, funnel-shaped; lobes broad triangular; plicae short, abrupt; cal. ⅛ to ⅜ in. long, lobes broadly lanceolate, longer than tube. Autumn. Japan, China, Himalaya. (G.C. 85 (1929), 28.) SYN. *Crawfurdia japonica, C. trinervis, Golownina japonica.*

**G. tubiflo'ra.** Tufted, leafy perennial. Stem erect, 1 to 2 in. h. *Basal l.* about ½ in. long, spatulate to oblong; *stem-l.* narrower. *fl.* solitary, terminal, sessile, deep blue, about 1 in. long, tubular; cal. about ½ in. long, lobes erect, short, narrow-ovate; cor. lobes erect, triangular to ovate; plicae short, entire. August, September. Himalaya. (Gen. 77.)

**G. tubulo'sa.** Small annual about 6 in. h. *l.* narrow-oblong to oblong-lanceolate, acute. *fl.* solitary or 3, blue, ¾ to 1 in. long; cal. ¼ to ½ in. long, tubular, lobes linear-lanceolate; cor. lobes broadly oblong to obovate, rounded. July, August. Argentine.

**G. undulatifo'lia.** A form of *G. Clusii.*

**G. utriculo'sa.** Annual. Stem erect, 4 to 12 in. h. *Basal l.* ovate to roundish; *stem-l.* ovate-spatulate, recurved at tip. *fl.* solitary, terminal, deep blue, 1 in. across, wheel-shaped; cal. ¼ to ½ in. long, broadly winged, lobes about half as long as tube; cor. lobes broadly ovate; plicae 2-fid. July, August. Europe. (R.I.F.G. xvii, 1049.)

**G. Veitchio'rum.*** Perennial with stems usually flat on ground fl.-stems up to 5 in. long. *Basal l.* linear-oblong, 1 to 1½ in. long, thick; *stem-l.* much shorter, all acute. *fl.* solitary, terminal, deep royal-blue with broad bands of greenish-yellow without, about 2 in. long, wide-funnel-shaped; cal. ¾ to 1 in. long, funnel-shaped, lobes ovate-lanceolate to lanceolate, acute, half as long as tube; cor. lobes broadly triangular, spreading; plicae short, broad. August. W. Szechwan, E. Tibet. (B.M. 8883.) Differs from allies by its deep-blue colouring, wide-funnel-shaped cor., cal. lobes half as long as tube, and broader, thicker l. var. **coeles'tis,** *fl.* paler with larger, more acute plicae.

**G. venus'ta.** Tufted perennial with erect, unbranched fl.-stems 4 in. h. and prostrate sterile stems. *l.* of fl.-stems round-ovate to broad-spatulate, ½ in. long; of sterile stems spatulate, about ¼ in. long. *fl.* solitary or few together, terminal, sessile, blue with yellow on tube, about 1 in. long, tubular; cal. ¼ in. long, lobes as long, oblong, acute, with wide folds between them; cor. lobes roundish-ovate; plicae irregularly toothed or nicked. August, September. Himalaya. (Gen. 82.) Differs from allies by cal. tube and lobes equally long, l. broadly ovate or spatulate.

**G. ver'na.*** Tufted perennial to 4 in. h. with unbranched, erect stems. *Basal l.* elliptic-lanceolate, ½ to ¾ in. long, one-third to half as wide, widest in middle, acute, narrowed to base; *stem-l.* ovate to spatulate, smaller. *fl.* solitary, terminal, deep azure-blue, saucer- or wheel-shaped, ¾ in. across; lobes ovate, rounded, plicae 2-fid, tipped white; cal. ½ in. long, tubular, scarcely angled or winged, lobes ⅛ to ¼ in. long, lanceolate, acute. May, June. Europe, including Britain, Asia. (Gen. 83.) Variable with many colour forms. var. **aesti'va, ala'ta,** and **angulo'sa,** synonyms of *G. angulosa*; **al'ba,** *fl.* white; **azu'rea,** *fl.* pale blue; **coeles'tis,** *fl.* sky-blue; **grandiflo'ra,** *fl.* large; **Favra'tii** and **obtusifo'lia,** synonyms of *G. Favratii*; **oschte'nica,** *fl.* yellow; **viola'cea,** *fl.* purplish-blue.

**G. Victori'nii.** Biennial with erect stems of 4 to 16 in. *l.* 1 to 4 in. long, lower spatulate, upper linear-lanceolate, fleshy. *fl.* deep blue, terminal on long peduncles; cor. ¾ to 1¼ in. long, funnel-shaped, lobes 4, oblong to obovate, fringed; cal. tube cleft to middle, lobes 4, ½ to ⅝ in. long, 2 shorter ovate, longer lanceolate. August. Canada. (Rhodora 25, 139.)

**G. Villar'sii.** A variety of *G. Burseri.*

**G. villo'sa.** A synonym of *G. ochroleuca.*

**G. volu'bilis.** The proper name of *G. luteoviridis,* q.v.

**G. vulgar'is.** A synonym of *G. Clusii.*

**G. Wallichia'na.** A variety of *G. tianschanica.*

**G. Wal'tonii.** Sub-erect or decumbent perennial. Stems 8 to 16 in. long. *Basal l.* linear-lanceolate, 6 to 8 in. long; *stem-l.* linear to linear-lanceolate, 1½ to 2½ in. long. *fl.* at apex sessile, in uppermost l.-axils shortly stalked, deep sky-blue to purplish-blue, narrowly bell-shaped, 1 to 1¾ in. long; cal. ½ to ⅝ in. long, split on one side, lobes ¼ to ½ in. long, unequal, larger leafy, ovate, acute, smaller, narrower, margins rough. Tibet. (J.R.H.S. 66, f. 53, 55.) Distinct from *G. decumbens* by the larger leafy cal. lobes, from *G. dahurica* by the bell-shaped cor., and from *G. gracilipes* by the sessile and shortly stalked fl.

**G. Walujew'i.** Coarse perennial with erect or sub-erect stems 12 in. h. *Basal l.* ovate-lanceolate, 4 to 6 in. long, blunt; *stem-l.* 1½ to 2 in. long, broader. *fl.* in sessile heads, white to yellowish-white, spotted blue, 1 to 1¼ in. long, cylindrical; cal. ⅛ in. long, tubular, lobes oblanceolate, acute; cor. lobes elliptic-lanceolate, acute; plicae lanceolate, entire or toothed. E. Turkestan. (G.F. 1884, 1140.) Of no garden value.

**G.×Wellsia'na.** A synonym of *G.×stevenagensis.*

**G. Weschniakow'ii.** A synonym of *G. Olivieri.*

**G. wutaien'sis.** Semi-prostrate perennial. Stems 6 to 8 in. long. *Basal l.* strap-shaped, 4 to 6 in. long; *stem-l.* lanceolate to linear-lanceolate, about 2 in. long. *fl.* densely clustered at and near top of stem, sessile, deep blue, paler below, ¾ to 1 in. long, tubular-bell-shaped; cal. ¼ to ½ in. long, split to base, purplish, lobes linear, very short; cor. lobes ovate to rounded; plicae triangular, acute, entire. July. China. Differs from *G. siphonantha* by the stalked ovary and shorter plicae.

**G. Zolling'eri.** Annual or biennial. Stems erect, at most slightly branched, without basal l. *l.* ovate to ovate-oblong, acute, margins scabrid. *fl.* 1 to 3, terminal, sessile or almost so, blue or purplish-blue, ¾ to 1 in. long; cor. funnel-shaped, lobes ovate, acute; plicae triangular, entire or 2-fid, acute; cal. ½ in. long, tubular, lobes ¼ in. long, erect, lanceolate, acute, margins scabrid. Japan. SYN. *G. Thunbergii* of Sieb. and Zucc.

D. W.

**GENTIANA'CEAE.** Dicotyledons. A family of about 900 species of mostly annual and perennial herbs of mostly temperate regions in over 60 genera. A large number are alpine or Arctic plants, but some grow in salt soils, in marshes, or are aquatics or epiphytes. Leaves mostly glabrous, entire, opposite, without stipules. Flowers often showy, regular, perfect; sepals usually 5 or 4, joined, overlapping; petals 5 or 4, joined, corolla bell- or funnel- or salver-shaped; stamens 5 or 4, epipetalous; ovary superior, usually 1-celled, carpels 2, united. Fruit a capsule with many seeds, rarely a berry. Seeds small. The family contains a few plants of medicinal value and many are ornamental. Genera dealt with are Cansora, Chironia, Chlora, Coutoubea, Erythraea, Eustoma, Exacum, Frasera, Gentiana, Halenia, Ixanthus, Leianthus, Limnanthemum, Lisianthus, Menyanthes, Orphium, Sabbatia, Sebaea, Swertia, Tachiadenus, Villarsia.

**GENTIANEL'LA.** *See* **Gentiana.**

**gentianoi'des,** Gentian-like.

***Gentilia'nus -a -um,*** in honour of M. Louis Gentil, Curator, Botanic Garden, Brussels, in early part of 20th century.

***genui'nus -a -um,*** natural, true.

**GENUS.** A group of species with common structural characters which may be supposed to have derived in the remote past from a common ancestor. The main characters upon which reliance is placed in defining genera are found in the flower, fruit, and seed. *See* **Classification.** The number of species in a genus may be large as in, e.g. Senecio, or it may be only one so much structurally isolated from its nearest relative as to stand by itself. The name of the genus is, in designating a plant, placed first and invariably has a capital initial letter.

**GENYOR'CHIS** (*genu,* knee, *orchis*). FAM. *Orchidaceae.* A small epiphytic genus of 3 species differing from Polystachya in that the inflorescence is basal, not terminal, and the pollen is much as in Monomeria. Treatment as for Bulbophyllum.

**G. pu'mila.** Habit of a creeping Bulbophyllum. *fl.* 5 to 15, very small, whitish, lip flecked with red; column with purple checks; pet. rudimentary. *Pseudobulbs* ¼ in. or a little more h., diphyllous. *l.* ¼ to ¾ in. long. Sierra Leone, French Congo. 1806. SYN. *Bulbophyllum pumilum, B. apetalum, Polystachya bulbophylloides.*

E. C.

**geocarp'us -a -um,** with fruit ripening on or in the earth.

**GEODOR'UM** (*ge*, the earth, *doron*, a gift). FAM. *Orchidaceae.* A small genus of about 9 species of terrestrial orchids, natives of E. India, Burma, Papua, Australia, and Malaya. Scapes terminating in a nodding spike of flowers, which in some are pale green, the lip white, veined with purple or yellow lines; and in others bluish, with a yellow spot on the lip. The sepals and petals are free, nearly equal. The lip is ventricose, obscurely 3-lobed or entire, shortly spurred or pouched at its base, more or less parallel with the column. The column is not produced into a foot. Pollen masses 2. Leaves radical, lance-shaped or elliptical, plicate, sheathing at the base, often deciduous. The species thrive in a compost as given to Phaius, in a hot, damp stove, but require to be rested after the leaves have withered. The tuberous rootstock should be placed just below the surface of the compost. The leafless flowering scapes spring from the base of new growths.

**G. can'didum.*** *fl.* white, ascending or erect, inodorous, less spreading than usual; pet. almost orbicular; lip very broad, shell-shaped, marked red and yellow, narrowed upwards from the 2-crested base. Burma. Variable.

**G. citri'num.** *fl.* yellow, close; spike arched; lip somewhat spurred at base, blunt and entire at end; scape shorter than l. Autumn. *l.* lanceolate. 1 ft. h. Burma. 1800. (B.M. 2195.)

**G. dilata'tum.** *fl.* whitish-flesh-colour, crowded; almost bell-shaped, nodding; racemes many-fld., sparsely imbricate. Summer. *l.* 6 in. long, 3 to 4 in. broad, erect, lanceolate; scape *l.* short. 6 to 12 in. h. India. 1800. (B.R. 675; L.B.C. 1797.)

**G. Duperrea'num.*** *fl.* 9 to 15 in a spike; sep. and pet. white, linear-oblong; lip white, with purple veins, concave. *l.* 3 or 4, oblong-lanceolate. Cochin China. 1883.

**G. fuca'tum.** *fl.* sub-campanulate; sep. pink, linear-oblong, acute; lip ovate, concave, emarginate, entire; scapes radical, erect, clothed, recurved at apex. July. *l.* oblong-lanceolate, acute, plicate, 1 ft. h. Ceylon. 1832. (B.R. 1687.)

**G. pic'tum.** *fl.* numerous, about 1 in. across, dull rose-purple or pink, shaded with brown or white; lip shell-shaped or ovate, dark rose with darker veins and markings; racemes densely set with fl., often curved. New Guinea, N. Australia, &c. A variable species.

E. C.

**GEOFFRAE'A** (in honour of Dr. M. E. F. Geoffrey of Paris, 1672–1731, author of a *Materia Medica*). FAM. *Leguminosae.* Bastard Cabbage Tree. A genus of 4 species of Trop. American evergreen trees. Leaves alternate, unequally pinnate, with alternate or nearly opposite leaflets. Stems sometimes spiny. Flowers yellow, often evil-smelling, papilionaceous, in racemes. Seeds edible. Geoffraeas need stove conditions and a compost of peat and loam. They can be propagated by cuttings of ripe shoots.

**G. spinulo'sa.** Tree without spines, branches with spongy bark. *lflets.* ovate, obtuse, downy, netted beneath; stalks winged. *fl.* in a spreading panicle. Brazil.

**G. super'ba.** Tree about 24 ft. h. *l.* Tamarind-like, shining and downy above, glaucous and paler beneath. *fl.* in simple racemes as long as l. *fr.* as large as, and of same shape as, a walnut, rind greenish-yellow, downy; pulp fleshy; seed solitary enclosed in a hard shell. Brazil.

F. G. P.

**GEOMETER MOTHS** (FAM. *Geometridae*) are slenderly built moths with comparatively large wings, which are extended horizontally when the insect is at rest on tree-trunks, palings, and walls. The females of some genera have greatly reduced wings (*see* **Winter Moth**) or are completely wingless (*see* **Mottled Umber** and **March Moths**). Their caterpillars are termed 'Loopers' owing to their method of walking provided as they are

with 3 pairs of true (thoracic) legs and only 2 pairs of abdominal sucker-feet.

G. F. W.

*Geometer or Looper Caterpillar*

**GEO'NOMA** (*geònomos*, skilled in agriculture, 'for this tree puts forth buds at the apex of its stem which become new trees'—Wittstein). FAM. *Palmaceae.* A genus of about 100 species of slender, unarmed palms, with ringed, reed-like stems, and crowns of entire leaves, sometimes 2-lobed at apex, or pinnatisect. They are natives of the mountains of S. and Cent. America, related to Chamaedorea, with flowers monoecious on each simple or branched, often coloured spadix. Spathes 2, often falling before flowers open. They need a night temperature of about 60° F. and a good loamy or peaty compost, well drained and abundantly supplied with water. Being natives of tropical forests where they help to form the undergrowth they must not be exposed to too bright sun. Many grow well when plunged in a tank. They are ornamental in the young state but will not long survive the conditions imposed by use as decoration in a dwelling-house, though occasional use in this way is not detrimental. Many species have been introduced and the following includes only a small number of those which have been grown here from time to time. Propagation is by seed or by suckers.

**G. acau'lis.** Stemless. *l.* 8 to 12 or more, pinnatifid, in a close cluster, 3 to 4 ft. long; lflets. about 13, lanceolate, the lowest only about ¼ in. wide, upper 1 to 4 in. wide or more. *Spadix* stiff, nearly 2 ft. long, with its thick stalk. Brazil. 1823.

**G. Card'eri.** A synonym of *Prestoea Carderi.*

**G. el'egans.** Stem slender, reed-like, 6 to 10 ft. long. *l.* up to 2½ ft. long with a short stalk; lflets. 3 to 7, of varying width, the terminal broad, 2-fid; pink when young. *Spadix* about 10 in. long. Cent. Brazil.

**G. grac'ilis.** Habit of *Cocos Weddeliana*, covered at first with scurfy brown scales. *l.* pinnate, arching; segs. about 1 ft. long, all except the terminal about ¾ in. wide, dark green. *Spadix* long, drooping. *fl.* yellow. Brazil. 1874. (B.M. 7963.) SYN. *G. Riedeliana.*

**G. Pohlia'na.** Stem slender, 10 to 15 ft. h. *l.* very numerous, 5 to 7 ft. long; lflets. linear-lanceolate, more or less falcate, very unequal in width, 16 to 20 in. long. *Spadix* short. Trop. Brazil.

**G. Schottia'na.** Stem slender, up to 15 ft. h., about 1 in. thick. *l.* 1 to 3 ft. long, pinnate, arching; segs. many, about 10 in. long, ¾ in. wide, equal, very long-pointed. *Spadix* about 10 in. long, its stalk 1 ft. Brazil. 1820.

**G. Spixia'na.** Stem slender, 6 to 9 ft. h. *l.* simple, 2-lobed, about 4 ft. long, in a dense cluster. *Spadix* 1 to 1½ ft. long, panicled. Brazil. 1824.

**G. Swartz'ii.** Stem 50 to 60 ft. h. *lflets.* linear, slender-pointed, green, glabrous. Cuba. SYN. *Calyptronoma Swartzii.*               A

**GEOPH'ILA** (*ge*, the earth, *phileo*, to love; plant is dwarf). FAM. *Rubiaceae.* A genus of 12 to 14 species of slender, creeping perennials, differing from Psychotria by their small size. *G. picta* will grow in the stove in a compost of sandy, fibrous peat, leaf-soil, and loam, well drained, and may be increased by seed or division.

**G. pic'ta.** *l.* ovate-oblong, 2 in. long, dull green with pink midrib and hairs. British Guiana. 1896.

**GEOPH'ILUS. See Centipedes.**

**Georg'ei,** in honour of George Forrest.

**geor'gicus -a -um,** of Georgia, S. Russia.

**GEORGI'NA.** A synonym of Dahlia.

A→

**GEOTROPISM,** the turning, usually of the root, towards the earth.

**GEOT′RUPES stercorar′ius.** *See* **Dor Beetle.**

**GERANIA′CEAE.** Dicotyledons. A family of about 500 species, mostly herbs of temperate or sub-tropical regions, in 11 genera. Leaves usually more or less deeply lobed, with or without stipules. Flowers often showy, perfect, usually regular; sepals 5, free, persistent; petals 5, usually free; stamens 5, 10, or 15, joined at base; ovary superior; carpels joined, 2 to 5; ovules 2 to many in each cell; style long with 5 stigmas. Fruit a schizocarp splitting off from the central 'beak', the persistent style. Many ornamental plants are contained in the family, and a few are of economic value. Genera dealt with are Balbisia, Biebersteinia, Erodium, Geranium, Monsonia, Pelargonium, Sarcocaulon.

*geranioi′des,* Geranium-like.

**GERA′NIUM** (*Geranion*, old Greek name used by Dioscorides, from *geranos*, crane, in allusion to the long beak of the carpels). FAM. *Geraniaceae.* Crane's-bill. A genus of about 160 species of herbs or rarely sub-shrubs, mostly perennial, distributed over the temperate regions of the world. Leaves opposite or alternate, usually more or less palmately, rarely pinnately, lobed or dissected. Flowers in cymes, often in pairs; petals usually 5, overlapping, equal; stamens 10, rarely 5. When ripe the carpels separate explosively, the awns twisting so as to carry the carpels outwards and upwards; at the same time, in many species, the carpels open and fling the seeds out. Geraniums will grow in almost any soil, but usually require a well-drained one; many are good plants for the rock-garden, and several good for the flower-border. Some species produce seed so freely as to make the plants rather shabby and need the developing fruits to be removed in good time. Propagation is easy in most by division or by seeds. The great range of Scarlet, Fancy, Scented, and Show Geraniums of the garden belong, not to this genus, but to Pelargonium. The following are perennial unless otherwise described.

**G. aconitifo′lium.*** 9 to 24 in. h. *l.* 2 to 2½ in. across, 3- to 9-parted; segs. narrow, acute or obtuse; upper *l.* sessile, palmately lobed. *fl.* white, black-veined, 1 to 1¼ in. across; sep. long, awned; pet. spreading, ovate, rounded at tip. May, June. S. Europe. 1775. SYN. *G. rivulare.* Rock-garden.

**G. alba′num.** About 1 ft. h. Stems weak, long, thin, somewhat straggling. *l.* kidney-shaped, 7-lobed; lobes 3-fid; segs. 3-toothed. *fl.* purple, pet. emarginate; peduncles 2-fld., long, hispid. May. Tauria, &c. 1820. SYN. *G. cristatum.* Rock-garden.

**G. albiflo′rum.** Stems many, 12 to 18 in. h. from a woody base. *Basal l.* 7-lobed, lobes deeply cut into ovate-oblong segs., hairy above, long-stalked; *stem-l.* 3- to 5-lobed, acute, with short stalks. *fl.* white or flesh-coloured; cal. purple at base; peduncles 2-fld. May to July. Altai Mts.

**G. anemonifo′lium.*** Shrubby at base, 1 to 2 ft. h. *l.* smooth, rather large, palmately 5-cleft; segs. 2-pinnate, upper segs. 3-partite; *l.* often near top of stem. *fl.* large, purplish-red; peduncles 2-fld., opposite, erect, smooth. May, June. Madeira, Teneriffe. 1778. (B.M. 206.) Needs winter protection in all but favoured districts.

**G. angula′tum.** A variety of *G. sylvaticum.*

**G. argen′teum.*** About 3 in. h. *l.* almost all radical, hoary or silky on both surfaces, 5- to 7-parted; lobes 3-fid; segs. linear. *fl.* pink, with darker veins, large; pet. emarginate; peduncles almost radical, 2-fld. June, July. N. Italy. 1699. var. **ro′seum,*** *fl.* somewhat darker. Rock-garden. Should be planted as rather small seedlings.

**G. arme′num.** A synonym of *G. psilostemon.*

**G. asphodeloi′des.** About 6 in. h. *l.* 5-lobed; lobes 3-fid; radical *l.* long-stalked, very downy. *fl.* usually purplish-violet, few; pet. obovate, often truncate, twice as long as the acute, downy sep. Summer. S. Europe, Asia Minor. 1828. (F.G. 661.)

**G. atlan′ticum.** 12 to 18 in. h. *l.* roundish, cut nearly to base into 5 or 7 narrow-obovate or wedge-shaped lobes; lobes 3-fid or pinnatifid, toothed. *fl.* pale purple with red veins, 1½ in. across; pet. obcordate, 3 or 4 times as long as sep.; peduncles 2-fld., hairy. June. Algiers. 1878.

**G. bohem′icum.** Annual, hairy, rather sprawling. *l.* 5-lobed; lobes wedge-shaped-ovate, deeply toothed. *fl.* pinkish, small; pet. emarginate; sep. with long awn; peduncles 2-fld. Bohemia, Silesia.

**G. caeru′leum.** Probably a form of *G. pratense.* The name has been used for several different things.

**G. caf′frum.** Stems spreading often 1 to 2 ft. long, making a tangled growth about 9 in. h., naked below, grey-glandular-hairy in upper part. *l.* 1 to 3 in. wide, 3- to 5-lobed, acutely and irregularly toothed, green above, minutely hairy, paler beneath. *fl.* pale lilac or white; pet. obovate, emarginate at apex, much longer than sep.; peduncles 2-fld., pedicels long, slender. June. S. Africa. (Ref. B. 147.)

*Geranium argenteum*

**G. canarien′se.** A synonym of *G. anemonifolium.*

**G. ciner′eum.*** About 6 in. h., almost stemless. *l.* glaucous, hairy, 5- to 7-lobed; lobes wedge-shaped, 3-fid. *fl.* pale purplish-pink with darker veins, rather larger than in *G. argenteum;* pet. emarginate; peduncles 2-fld. June. Pyrenees. var. **al′bum,*** a good white-fld. form; **ro′seum,** *fl.* deep rose with crimson veins; **subcaules′cens,*** stem short, *fl.* larger, carmine, bright. Balkans. SYN. *G. subcaulescens.*

**G. colli′num.** Stem diffuse, decumbent, hairy. *l.* 5- to 7-lobed; lobes 3-fid, deeply toothed. *fl.* purplish-violet; pet. roundish, entire, hairy at base, scarcely exceeding cal.; peduncles (2-fld., long), and cal. covered with clammy hairs. May. E. Europe. 1815. SYN. *G. Londesii.* var. **al′bum,** *fl.* white.

**G. crista′tum.** A synonym of *G. albanum.*

**G. dahu′ricum.** Stem erect, about 18 in. h., smooth, bare at base. *l.* opposite, 3- to 5-lobed; lobes cut, acute. *fl.* purple; pet. entire, bearded at base; peduncles 2-fld., 3 times as long as *l.* June. Dahuria. 1820.

**A→**

**G. Endres′sii.*** Up to about 12 in. h., spreading, nearly evergreen. *l.* opposite, lower 5-, upper 3-lobed; lobes acute, toothed; stalked. *fl.* light rose, faintly veined darker; pet. oblong-ovate, entire, fringed at base; filaments densely hairy; peduncles 2-fld., axillary. Summer, autumn. Pyrenees. Border, among shrubs, rock-garden. Apt to cross with *G. striatum* and yield seedlings with intermediate veined fl.

**G. erioste′mon.** Stem erect, 6 to 36 in. h., slightly angled, forked. *l.* 5-lobed; lobes ovate, deeply toothed; lower *l.* alternate, long-stalked; upper opposite, sessile. *fl.* pale to muddy violet; pet. entire, bearded at base; stamens white, purple towards apex. June. Nepal, W. China. 1822. (S.G. 197.) SYN. *G. platyanthum.*

**G. Far′reri.** A synonym of *G. napuligerum.*

**G. Fremont′ii.** Stem erect, 12 to 24 in. h. *l.* nearly round, 5- to 7-lobed; lobes 3-toothed or crenate, somewhat hairy. *fl.* pale rose-purple, 1 to 1½ in. across; pet. obovate, densely hairy towards base; sep. oblong, 3-nerved; peduncles 2-fld. Summer. Rocky Mts. Border-plant.

**G. grandiflo′rum.*** Stem erect, 10 to 16 in. h., branched. *l.* roundish, 5-lobed; lobes irregularly toothed; long-stalked. *fl.* blue, red-veined with a red-purple eye, large, clustered at top of peduncle. July. Sikkim. A good border-plant. var. **alpi′num,** dwarfer with larger *fl.*

**G. Grevillea′num.** Creeping with thick fl.-stem, glandular-hairy. *l.* kidney-shaped; 5-lobed, hairy; lobes deeply toothed; stalk long. *fl.* pale rose, sometimes with large, purple spots, up to 2 in. across; pet. obovate, somewhat hairy at base; sep. oblong-ovate. Summer. Himalaya. Rock-garden.

**G. gymnocau′lon.** A synonym of *G. ibericum brachytrichum.*

**G. iber'icum.*** Tufted, about 12 in. h. *l.* roundish-heart-shaped, *l.* deeply 5- to 7-lobed, woolly; lobes pinnately cut; segs. toothed. *fl.* blue to violet, about 1 in. across, in open panicles; pet. obcordate, sometimes somewhat 3-fid. Summer. 1802. Caucasus. (B.M. 1386.) var. **al'bum,** *fl.* white; **brachyt'richum,** hairs on upper part of stem and peduncles crisped, short. SYN. *G. gymnocaulon*; **platypet'alum,** a synonym of *G. platypetalum.*

**G. inci'sum.** About 12 in. h., leafy, branched. Stem thick below. *l.* much and finely cut, silky-hairy. *fl.* purple, about 1 in. across, the hairs stiff, white; sep. oblong-lanceolate, mucronate; pedicels glandular-hairy. Summer. Oregon. Borders.

**G. interme'dium.** Erect, branched, shaggy hairy. *l.* 5-lobed, long-stalked; lobes 3-fid, segs. rounded. *fl.* purple, small; pet. entire. Chile.

**G. lancastrien'se.** A variety of *G. sanguineum.*

**G. liv'idum.** A variety of *G. phaeum.*

**G. Londes'ii.** A synonym of *G. collinum.*

**G. Low'ei.** Related to *G. anemonifolium* but annual or biennial without a stem and somewhat hardier. *l.* 3 to 12 in. across, 5-lobed; lobes deeply cut. *fl.* pink, in large clusters; peduncles thick, up to 12 in. or more long. Summer, autumn. Madeira. Borders. The l. sometimes turn crimson in autumn.

**G. macrorrhi'zum.** Roots large. Stem woody at base, forked, hairy. About 18 in. h. *l.* smooth, 5-lobed; lobes toothed at apex. *fl.* deep red or bright purple; pet. entire, somewhat reflexed; cal. globose, inflated. May to July. S. Europe. 1576. (B.M. 2420.)

**G. macula'tum.** About 18 in. h. Stem erect, rath r angular, forked, hairy. *l.* 3- to 5-lobed, lobes deeply toothed, lower long-stalked; upper opposite, sessile. *fl.* lilac to rose-purple, 1 to 1½ in. across, more or less in umbels; pet. obovate, entire, woolly at base. N. America. 1732. var. **al'bum,** *fl.* pale lilac or white; **ple'num,** *fl.* double, darker. Borders in damp soil.

**G. malviflo'rum.** Root tuberous. Stem usually one up to 18 in. h. *l.* 5- to 9-lobed; lobes finely cut, hairy. *fl.* rose-purple, large; pet. obcordate, often emarginate; sep. ovate-oblong, hairy, about half as long as pet.; peduncles and pedicels densely hairy. Mediterranean region. (B.M. 6452, as *G. atlanticum.*)

**G. Meebold'ii.** A synonym of *G. grandiflorum.*

*Geranium napuligerum*

**G napulig'erum** Tufted. *rhiz.* short with fleshy, cylindrical roots. Stems up to 6 in. long, usually more or less decumbent, slender, finely downy. *l.* opposite, kidney-shaped, about 1 in. across, 3- to 5-fid, segs. obovate-wedge-shaped, coarsely toothed or 3-lobed, bright green; stipules purple; stalks of lower l. long. *fl.* pale rose or lilac, about 1½ in. across; pet. roundish, the short claw bearded, sep. oblong, with a hyaline margin, apiculate; peduncles 2 to 4 in. long, 2-fld., pedicels 1 to 1½ in. long. June. Kansu, Szechwan, China. 1917. (B.M. 9092.) Rock-garden or Alpine-house. SYN. *G. Farreri.*

**G. nepalen'se.** Stem rather slender, up to 18 in. long, spreading or ascending. *l.* ovate-rhomboid, deeply 5-lobed, hairy; lobes almost spine-toothed. *fl.* rose-purple, rather small, numerous; pet. broadly obovate; sep. lanceolate, slender-pointed. June to August. Mts. of Asia. Rock-garden.

**G. nodo'sum.** Stem somewhat 4-angled. *l.* in lower part 5-, upper 3-lobed; lobes oblong, slender-pointed, toothed. *fl.* purplish-red, veined; pet. emarginate. Summer. Europe, naturalized here and there in Britain. (E.B. 295.)

**G. ornithopo'dum.** Much branched, diffuse, 4 to 5 ft. h. Stems densely hairy, hairs soft, white, short, decurved. *l.* roundish, hairy, especially beneath, 5-lobed, lobes pinnatifid, sessile. *fl.* white, veined red; peduncles 2-fld., pedicels slender, densely downy, drooping. S. Africa. 1872. (Ref. B. 290.) Half-hardy.

**G. palus'tre.** Stem decumbent, sprawling, covered with spreading, somewhat stiff hairs. *l.* 5- to 7-lobed, lobes deeply toothed. *fl.* magenta-purple on long, hairy, declining pedicels; pet. entire; stamens awl-shaped, glabrous. France eastwards to Asia.

**G. phae'um.** Mourning Widow. About 2 ft. h., erect, stem short-haired, glandular above. *l.* 5- to 9-lobed, lobes deeply toothed, often with purple spots at bases of lobes. *fl.* almost black with a white spot at base of each pet.; spreading, obovate, unequally notched; peduncles 1- or 2-fld. May, June. Cent. and W. Europe, naturalized in Britain. (E.B. 294.) Will put up with shade. Borders and woodland. Colour of fl. variable. var. **liv'idum,** *fl.* greyish-mauve. SYN. *G. lividum.*

**G. platyan'thum.** A synonym of *G. eriostemon.*

**G. platypet'alum.*** Related to *G. ibericum.* 1 to 2 ft. h. *l.* fringed. *fl.* deep violet with reddish veins, over 1 in. across; pet. emarginate. Georgia.

**G. polyan'thes.** *rhiz.* oblique, ½ in. thick. Stem more or less erect, hairy above. *Basal l.* with stalk 4 to 7 times as long as blade, hairy, kidney-shaped, 7- to 9-partite; lobes 2- or 3-toothed, apex rounded. *fl.* red, in umbels. August. NW. Himalaya.

**G. praten'se.** Meadow Crane's bill. Erect, up to 3 or 4 ft. h., branched above, hairs reflexed. *l.* roundish, 3 to 6 in. wide, 7-9-parted, lobes cut, coarsely toothed, lower long-stalked. *fl.* blue, often red-veined, 1½ in. across, peduncles many-fld.; peduncles somewhat corymbose, many-fld. June to September. N. Europe, including Britain. (E.B. 297.) Colour of fl. varies. var. **al'bum,** *fl.* white; **bi'color,** *see* var. **striatum**; **ple'num,** *fl.* fully double, of various shades; **stria'tum,** *fl.* sometimes white, sometimes blue, sometimes half and half, sometimes striped. Borders. Moist grassy places.

**G. prostra'tum.** A variety of *G. sanguineum.*

**G. psiloste'mon.*** About 3 ft. h. *Lower l.* 6 to 8 in. wide, broadly heart-shaped, 5-lobed; lobes cut, acute, deeply toothed; *upper l.* triangular. *fl.* magenta-red with black spot at base, about 1½ in. across; pet. obovate, retuse; peduncles long. Summer. Armenia. (R.H. 1891, 350, as *G. armenum.*)

**G. Pylzowia'num.** *rhiz.* filiform, tubercles pea-like. Stem slender, erect, about 1 ft. h. *l.* about 2 in. wide, pedately 5-partite; lobes 3-lobed. *fl.* purple, 1½ in. across; peduncles 3- or 4-fld. Kansu. Nearly related to *G. napuligerum.*

**G. reflex'um.** Stem cylindrical, erect. *l.* alternate, 5- to 7-lobed, sharply toothed, upper sessile. *fl.* deep red-purple; pet. reflexed, irregularly toothed at apex; stamens glabrous; peduncles 2-fld. Italy, France.

**G. Renard'ii.** Clump-forming, 6 to 12 in. h., 12 in. across. *l.* palmately 5-lobed; lobes rounded, dark olive green above, veins prominent. *fl.* white with violet-purple centre, flat; peduncles 2-fld. Caucasus. 1935. Needs full sun in well-drained soil.

**G. Richardson'ii.** About 18 in. h., tinged red when young. *l.* thin, 3- to 5-lobed; terminal lobe of upper l. longer than lateral. *fl.* white, sometimes streaked pink, large; pet. with long white hairs within; pedicels glandular-pubescent. Colorado, W. United States.

**G. rivula're.** A synonym of *G. aconitifolium.*

**G. Robertia'num.** Herb Robert. Annual, 6 to 9 in. h. *l.* roundish-ovate, 3- to 5-lobed; lobes 3-fid; segs. pinnatifid. *fl.* crimson, often streaked, about ½ in. across; peduncles slender, 2-fld. June to October. N. Hemisphere including Britain. (E.B. 305.) Often turns red in autumn. var. **al'bum,*** *fl.* white. Of this there are 2 forms 1 with green, the other with red stems.

**G. sanguin'eum.** Erect or diffuse, branched, 12 to 24 in. h. *l.* opposite, 5- to 7-lobed; lobes 3-fid; segs. linear. *fl.* crimson to blood-red, about 1½ in. across; pet. notched; peduncles 1-fld., much longer than l.-stalks. Summer. Europe, including Britain, W. Asia. (E.B. 293.) Rock-garden. var. **al'bum,** *fl.* white; **lancastrien'se,*** much dwarfer, spreading, *fl.* flesh-coloured, veined purplish; **prostra'tum,** habit of var. *lancastriense, fl.* of type.

**G. sessiliflo'rum.** Tap-rooted. *l.* almost radical, 5- to 7-lobed, thick, stalks long. *fl.* white and purple, mostly sessile. Australia, New Zealand. 1894.

**G. Shikokia'num.** Erect, 2 ft. or more h. *l.* long-stalked, kidney-shaped, 5- to 7- to many-partite; segs. wedge-shaped, acute, 2- or 3-cut, covered with appressed hairs; stipules large, membranous. *fl.* rose-purple, large; peduncles longer than l., hairy. August. Japan.

**G. stria'tum.** Stem round, decumbent. *Lower l.* 5-, *upper* 3-lobed; lobes ovate, acute, deeply toothed. *fl.* pink, veined more deeply; pet. emarginate. May to October. S. Europe, naturalized here and there in Britain. 1629. (B.M. 55.) Apt to cross with *G. Endressii* when growing near.

**G. subcaules'cens.** A variety of *G. cinereum.*

**G. sylvat'icum.** About 2 ft. h. Rootstock creeping. Stem round, erect, branched above, hairy and glandular in upper part. *l.* roundish, deeply 7-lobed, 3 to 5 in. across; lobes cut and toothed; lower l. stalked, upper sessile. *fl.* bluish-purple to rose, ½ to ¾ in. across; pet. notched, bearded on claw, sep. awned; peduncles 2-fld., in terminal cymes. June, July. Europe, including Britain, W. Asia, Siberia. (E.B. 296.) var. **al'bum,**\* *fl.* white; **angula'tum,**\* *fl.* 1½ in. across; **ro'seum** and **Wan'neri,** *fl.* rose.

**G. Travers'ii.** Loose mat-forming. *l.* roundish, deeply lobed. *fl.* white, about ¾ in. across. New Zealand. (J.R.H.S. 37, 65.) var. **el'egans,**\* *fl.* pink, about 1 in. across. Chatham Is. Needs a warm, sunny, sheltered place on the rock-garden.

**G. tubero'sum.** Root tuberous. About 9 in. h. Stem naked below. *l.* many-lobed; lobes linear, pinnatifid, toothed. *fl.* purplish-violet, large, numerous; pet. deeply notched. May. S. Europe. 1596. (S. Ger. 155.) var. **Charles'ii,** *fl.* rose, 1 to 1½ in. across. Afghanistan. 1835 (B.M. 6910.) Rock-garden.

*Geranium Wallichianum*

**G. Wallichia'num.** Stem decumbent, purplish, covered with silky hairs. *l.* 5-lobed; lobes broadly wedge-shaped, deeply toothed, silky-hairy. *fl.* purple, large; pet. emarginate. August, September. Temperate Himalaya. 1820. (B.M. 2377.) Rock-garden. **Buxton's var.,**\* *fl.* violet-blue, about 1¼ in. across, with a white eye. Should have a sheltered place.

**G. Webbia'num.** Habit of *G. argenteum* but less silvery. *fl.* white with almost black veins. India? Not reliably hardy.

**G. Wlassovia'num.** *rhiz.* oblique-vertical, somewhat woody. Stem up to 30 in. h., hairy above. *l.* long-stalked, roundish kidney-shaped, 3- to 5-cut at tips. *fl.* purple-violet, about 1½ in. across; pet. entire, nerves deeply coloured; peduncles 2-fld., densely hairy. Siberia, Manchuria. Nearly related to *G. palustre.*

**G. yedoen'se.** *rhiz.* short, robust, covered with thickened fibres. *l.* stalk about 4 in. long, palmately 5- to 7-partite, lobes ovate-rhomboid, deeply toothed in upper part. *fl.* deep violet; pet. obovate, entire; peduncles as long as l. Japan. Nearly related to *G. pratense.*

**GERAR'DIA** (in honour of John Gerard, 1545–1612, author of the 'Herbal' published in 1597, and cultivator of many exotic plants in Holborn). FAM. *Scrophulariaceae.* A genus of about 30 species of erect, branching, annual or perennial herbs, natives of N. and S. America. Leaves usually opposite, uppermost with flowers in axils. Flowers showy, in terminal racemes; calyx bell-shaped, 5-toothed or -cleft nearly to middle; corolla rose-purple or yellow, rarely white, tube broad, limb spreading, the 5 lobes rounded; stamens 4. The species are not readily established in gardens as they are either root-parasites or saprophytes. They need a friable soil, rich in decaying vegetable matter, and a warm sheltered situation. Seed readily germinates.

**G. glutino'sa.** A synonym of *Adenosma grandiflorum.*

**G. pedicula'ria.** Perennial, 2 to 3 ft. h. *l.* pinnatifid, with coarse teeth. *fl.* citron-yellow to deep yellow, sometimes tinged red. U.S.A. (G.C. 1872, 43.) Smaller and more branched than *G. quercifolia,* with fewer, smaller fl. about 1 in. long.

**G. purpu'rea.** Annual with spreading branches, 1 to 2 ft. h. *l.* usually spreading, narrow-linear, scabrid or smooth except margins. *fl.* purple, up to 1 in. long, pedicels shorter than cal. July. U.S.A. 1772. (B.M. 2048 shows var. *paupercula* as *G. purpurea.*) Variable.

**G. quercifo'lia.** Perennial, 3 to 6 ft. h. *Lower l.* large, pinnatifid; *upper* oblong-lanceolate, pinnatifid or entire. *fl.* yellow, nearly 2 in. long, tubular-bell-shaped; cal. large, somewhat inflated. July, August. U.S.A. 1812.

**G. tenuifo'lia.** Perennial, much branched, about 18 in. h. *l.* linear, acute, 1/16 to 1/8 in. wide, light green. *fl.* pale violet, Penstemon-like, ½ in. long, pedicels slightly longer than l. June to August. Mexico. 1894.

*Gerardia'nus -a -um,* in honour of P. Gerard who sent new plants to Dr. Nathaniel Wallich.

**GERASCAN'THUS,** an old generic name for part of the present genus Cordia.

**GER'BERA** (in honour of Traugott Gerber, a German naturalist who travelled in Russia, *d.* 1743). FAM. *Compositae.* A genus of about 40 species of African and Asiatic herbs, with very short stems, mostly inhabiting temperate and mountainous regions. Leaves radical, entire or pinnati-lobed, sometimes leathery. Scapes 1-flowered. Flower-heads sometimes very showy, yellow, orange, or scarlet, the rays often coppery or red outside, in 1 or 2 rows, the inner series when present, very short and sub-tubular, outer 2-lipped with the outer lip ligulate, 3-toothed, inner minute; disk-florets also somewhat 2-lipped; involucral scales oblong or lanceolate, closely overlapping. Achenes beaked; pappus of rough bristles in 2 or more rows. The best species, *G. Jamesonii,* grows best in a good free loam, but some have reported good success by growing in sand watered periodically with liquid manure. It is a deep-rooting plant disliking transplanting, and should be planted as soon as possible in a warm, sunny, sheltered place. It is hardy only in very favoured localities except at the foot of a warm south wall, especially if heated on the other side, as that of a stove. It can be grown in pots in a house suitable for Gazania, but must not be over-potted nor overwatered. Seed is set as a rule only after cross-pollination from another plant. It should be sown in gentle heat early in the year, the plants being planted out or potted at the end of May. They usually flower in the second, but are not at their best until the third year. Side shoots (not freely produced) taken off with a heel may be struck with bottom heat. The plant is variable in colouring and crossing with *G. viridifolia* has resulted in the production of white and pink flowers and some hybrid forms have been named. (See, for instance, *Journ. R.H.S.,* vol. 40, p. 261–2.)

Gerberas may show Leaf Spots caused by various leaf-spotting fungi, e.g. Ascochyta and Septoria, but these should not be serious. A more serious trouble is Foot Rot, *Phytophthora parasitica,* causing blackening of the base of the plant and probably due in great measure to overwatering or unsuitable, such as heavy, soil. Steps should be taken to avoid such conditions and to provide a well-drained soil for these plants.

(D. E. G.)

**G. asplenifo'lia.** Fern-like. *l.* narrow, 4 to 6 in. long, more or less deeply pinnately lobed, leathery, glossy above; lobes roundish, concave, terminal not larger than others; margins revolute. *fl.-heads* purple on a hairy scape. Cape Province.

**G. auranti'aca.** *l.* lanceolate to oblong, acute, 5 to 6 in. long, 1 to 2 in. wide, entire or toothed, finally smooth, rather thin. *fl.-heads* orange, 2½ in. across, anthers yellow. Transvaal, Natal. (B.M. 8079.)

**G. Jameson'ii.\*** Barberton Daisy. Hairy throughout. Base woody. *l.* runcinate, 5 to 10 in. long, 2 to 3 in. wide, stalks 6 to 8 in. long. *fl.-heads* 3 to 4 in. across, nearly erect on scapes 10 to 18 in. long; ray-florets about 30 in one series, yellow, bright orange, or flame-coloured above in wild forms, but varying to pink and white in cultivation. Spring, summer. Transvaal, Natal. 1887. (B.M. 7087.)

**G. Kunzea'na.** A Himalayan species sometimes offered but without merit as the flowers scarcely open.

**G. viridifo'lia.** Crown of rootstock silky. *l.* elliptic or oblong, obtuse, 1½ to 2½ in. wide, entire or toothed, green on both sides, smooth or nearly so; stalks short. *fl.-heads* dirty white, small. 1896.

**GERMAN CATCHFLY.** *See* **Viscaria vulgaris.**

**GERMAN IVY.** *See* **Senecio mikanioides.**

**GERMANDER.** Common name for *Teucrium Chamaedrys.*

**german'icus -a -um,** of Germany.

**GERMEN,** obsolete name for the ovary.

**GERMINATION.** The growth of the embryo in the seed and its emergence as a young plant. (In seed testing the emergence of the radicle is regarded as germination.) The factors necessary for inducing germination are the presence of sufficient water, oxygen, and a certain temperature. The temperature necessary to start germination varies with the species. Light has some influence, favourable in some plants, detrimental in others, while other plants are unaffected by it. There are 3 stages in germination. First the absorption of water by the seed through the testa, and especially through the micropyle, next the solution of reserve foods in the seed by means of enzymes so that they can be moved from place to place and used by the embryo as a source of energy for growth, and thirdly, the expansion of the embryo partly by absorption of water and partly by growth leading to the rupture of the testa and the emergence of the young plant into the open. *See* **Seed-sowing** in Suppl.

**Germinya'nus -a -um,** in honour of Count Adrien de Germiny, of Gonville, France, amateur of Orchids, *c.* 1890.

**Gersen'ii,** in honour of G. J. Gersen, 1826–?, who collected in India, Celebes, &c.

**GES'NERA.** *See* **Gesneria.**

**GESNE'RIA** (in honour of Conrad Gesner of Zurich, 1516–65, a famous student of botany and natural history). Fam. *Gesneriaceae.* A genus of about 50 species of S. American perennials, mostly natives of Brazil, closely related to Naegelia, but having an interrupted, not ring-like, disk at the base of the corolla. Mostly tuberous-rooted (the tuberous-rooted species are sometimes separated as a genus Corytholoma), and herbaceous with opposite leaves. Flowers usually showy, in a terminal thyrse with bracts at base of peduncles; tube of corolla often long, sometimes swollen, often curved and pouched at base; lobes regular or 2-lipped. The Gesnerias being tropical, need stove conditions and a compost of peat and leaf-soil with a little loam and sand which should be pressed only moderately firm when potting. The tubers may be grown either 1 in a 5-in. or about

5 in a 6-in. pot, covered with 1 in. of soil and kept rather dry until growth begins, when the amount of water given may be increased as roots develop. Thorough drainage is essential. Shade from bright sun is necessary in summer, and care must be taken to keep the leaves clean, for which reason syringing should not be done after the leaves are developed or if it is then only pure rain-water should be used for the purpose, for any other water will leave a deposit as it evaporates, impairing the beauty of the foliage. The plants succeed best on a moist bottom such as a bed of ashes, in a house kept at about 65° F. by night in summer, and not below 55° F. in winter. The season of flowering may be prolonged by successive potting and starting of tubers from March to midsummer. When flowering is over water should be gradually withheld until finally, when the leaves are dead, no water should be given, the pots and their contents being stored in a dry part of the house until starting time in the next season. Thrips are frequently very troublesome on the young leaves and should be carefully watched for and immediately destroyed by fumigation. Sponging is sometimes attempted, but the leaves are very brittle and easily broken. If it can be avoided these plants should not be placed in a house where thrips or other insects are present. A collar rot due to a species of Fusarium sometimes attacks Gesnerias and the fungus is encouraged by very moist soil conditions near the base of the stem, often the result of imperfect drainage. Gesnerias are also liable to the virus disease known as Spotted Wilt—see under Tomato Spotted Wilt.

Propagation is by the increase of the tubers; by the minute seeds; by cuttings of the shoots in peat taken soon after growth starts, or by detached mature leaves.

**G. aggrega'ta.** About 2 ft. h. with rounded branches. *l.* oblong-ovate, crenate. *fl.* 2 to 4 in *l.*-axils on 1-fld. peduncles; dull red, small, cylindrical. August. Brazil. 1816. (B.M. 2725; B.R. 329.)

**G. allagophyl'la.** Erect, hairy. *l.* opposite or ternate, linear-oblong or spatulate, about 4 in. long, crenate. *fl.* pale red in a terminal spike 6 to 8 in. long; cor. tube cylindrical, ⅔ in. long, hairy, lobes equal. Brazil. 1834. (B.R. 1767.)

**G. Blas'sii.\*** Pendent, up to 6 ft. long, stems woolly. *l.* ovate-cordate, slender-pointed, crenate, nerves reddish beneath. *fl.* scarlet, in drooping panicles from upper *l.*-axils. Brazil. (F.d.S. 1140–1 as *Dircaea Blassii.*)

**G. bulbo'sa.** Tuber large. Erect, up to 2 ft. *l.* ovate-cordate, toothed, fleshy; stalks short. *fl.* scarlet; tube narrow, widened above; lobes unequal, upper long; in terminal many-fld. panicles. Summer. Brazil. (B.R. 343.)

**G. cardina'lis.\*** Tuber large. Procumbent, velvety; stem round. *l.* large, cordate, blunt, crenate; lower ovate-elliptic, upper rounder. *fl.* large, bright red, velvety, in cymes on long peduncles. Habitat? 1850. (Gn. 42 (1892), 232; B.M. 8167.) SYN. *G. macrantha* of gardens.

**G. cochlear'is.** About 1 ft. h. *l.* cordate-ovate, concave, wrinkled, hairy; stalks long. *fl.* scarlet in simple terminal racemes; cor. tube swollen at base. June to August. Brazil. 1837. (B.M. 3787.)

**G. Coop'eri.** Tuber large. Erect, downy, 2 to 3 ft. h. *l.* cordate, 3 in. long, dark green, white-downy, toothed. *fl.* bright scarlet, densely spotted within, 3 in. long, in a terminal panicle. May. Brazil. 1829. (B.M. 3041 as *G. bulbosa.*)

**G. Donkelaeria'na.\*** Tubers large, 1 to 2 ft. h. *l.* nearly heart-shaped, about 8 in. wide, green, tinged purple and red. *fl.* bright vermilion, about 2 in. long, in terminal heads. June. Summer. Colombia. 1858. (B.M. 5070.)

**G. ellip'tica.** About 1 ft. h. *l.* opposite, elliptic, wrinkled, toothed, lower only stalked. *fl.* yellow; limb obliquely 2-lipped; terminal peduncles racemose, axillary solitary. May. Colombia. (B.M. 4242.)

**G. × exonien'sis** (? parentage: probably a Naegelia, to which it is closely allied, is one). *l.* dark, rich velvety, covered with minute red hairs. *fl.* deep orange-scarlet, throat yellow; produced in close masses about 1 ft. through. Winter. Of garden origin.

**G. faucia'lis.** Herbaceous perennial. *l.* cordate-oblong, 2 in. long, acute, wrinkled, hairy. *fl.* brick-red, about 3 in. long in a terminal raceme; cor. hairy, 2-lipped, upper lip 2-lobed, narrowed to base, lower smaller, revolute, throat wide. Brazil. 1834. (B.M. 3659; B.R. 1785.)

**G. laterit'ia.** About 2 ft. h. *l.* ovate-heart-shaped, lower 6 in. long, 5 in. wide. *fl.* much like those of *G. cardinalis,* scarlet, 1½ in. long, somewhat club-shaped, downy, in umbellate racemes. June. Brazil. 1834. (B.R. 1950.)

**G. latifo'lia.** About 3 ft. h., growth coarse. *l.* large, roundish-ovate, crenulate. *fl.* red, in axillary cymes. Brazil. (B.R. 1202 as *G. macrostachya*.)

**G. Leopold'ii.** Dwarf, compact. Allied to *G. cardinalis*. *fl.* bright red, tubular, throat oblique, lobes rounded; stamens violet; panicle terminal, umbel-like. Brazil. 1898. (F.d.S. 704; Gn. 53 (1898), 542.) Free-flowering.

**G. Lind'leyi.** Tall. *l.* broadly ovate, deep velvety green and red. *fl.* rosy-pink, lower part and limb yellow, freckled red, in a terminal raceme. Brazil. 1825. (B.M. 3602.)

**G. macropo'da.** Tuber sub-globose, perennial. Stems 1 or 2, annual, unbranched bearing 1 or 2 pairs of l. *l.* nearly round, 3 to 5 in. across, cordate at base, toothed, glandular-hairy above, hairy on veins beneath; stalks short. *fl.* in axillary, 5- to 7-fld. cymes, cinnabar-red, drooping; cor. tube nearly cylindrical, 1 in. or more long, limb 2-lipped, upper lip 2-, lower 3-lobed and blotched purple. April. S. Brazil. 1906. (B.M. 8228 as *Corytholoma macropodum*.)

**G. magnif'ica.** Tuber large. *l.* ovate-heart-shaped, downy; stalks short. *fl.* scarlet, cal. small, covered with red hairs; cor. 3 in. long, downy; panicles terminal, large. Brazil. (B.M. 3886 as *G. bulbosa*.)

**G. × naegelioi'des.** A garden hybrid with many varieties from white to plum-colour.

**G. × reful'gens.** Hybrid of *G. × exoniensis* type, 1 to 1½ ft. h. *l.* broad-ovate, toothed, cordate at base, downy. *fl.* deep rich red. Summer. Of garden origin.

**G. ru'tila.** Tall, hairy, round, erect, 2 to 3 ft. h. *l.* oblong, hairy, coarsely crenate, stalked. *fl.* scarlet, solitary in l.-axils, erect with hairy pedicels shorter than l., tube 2 in. long, yellow within, straight, only slightly swollen, limb oblique, segs. erect, upper longest. Brazil. 1827. (B.R. 1158.)

**G. Scep'trum.** About 3 ft. h. *l.* ternate, heart-shaped; teeth obtuse. *fl.* white, long-tubular, in long thyrses. Summer. Brazil. var. **ig'nea,** *fl.* reddish-yellow. (B.M. 3576.)

**G. Sut'tonii.** Branched, 1½ to 2 ft. h. *Lower l.* heart-shaped, hairy, stalked; *upper l.* ovate, mostly sessile. *fl.* scarlet, downy, 1¼ in. long, peduncles solitary, 1-fld. July. Brazil. 1833. (B.R. 1637.)

**G. tubero'sa.** *rhiz.* horizontal. Stem of 6 in. *l.* mostly near base, broad-ovate, covered with short blood-red hairs. *fl.* scarlet; tube curved; peduncles from base of rhizome. Brazil. 1834. (B.M. 3664.)

**GESNERIA'CEAE.** Dicotyledons. A family of about 1,100 species of mostly herbs, but with a few trees or shrubs, in about 85 genera in tropical and sub-tropical countries. Leaves opposite, simple, without stipules. Flowers often large, showy, perfect, zygomorphic; calyx with 5 very short teeth; corolla usually distinctly 2-lipped, but nearly regular in Ramondia, &c.; stamens 4, didynamous, or 2, with sometimes 2 or 3 staminodes, anthers often connivent in pairs or all drawn close together; pistil of 2 joined carpels superior or more or less inferior, ovules many. Fruit a capsule with many small seeds. Many species are tuberous or propagate themselves by rhizomes; a few are root climbers and among them are some epiphytic species with water-storage organs. None is of economic value but many are very decorative. Genera dealt with are: Acanthonema, Achimenes, Aeschynanthus, Agalmyla, Alloplectus, Ancylostemon, Asteranthera, Baea, Besleria, Briggsia, Campanaea, Chirita, Codonanthe, Columnea, Conandron, Cyrtandra, Diastema, Dichrotrichum, Dicyrta, Didissandra, Didymocarpus, Drymonia, Episcia, Fieldia, Gesneria, × Gloxinera, Gloxinia, Haberlea, Houttea, Hypocyrta, Isoloma, Isometrum, Jankaea, Jerdonia, Klugia, Koellikeria, Lietzia, Lysionotus, Mitraria, Monopyle, Naegelia, Nautilocalyx, Nematanthus, Niphaea, Oreocharis, Ornithoboea, Paliavana, Paradrymonia, Pentaraphia, Petrocosmea, Phinaea, Primulina, Ramondia, Rhabdothamnus, Rhytidophyllum, Saintpaulia, Sarmienta, Sinningia, Stauranthera, Streptocarpus, Trichantha, Tussacia.

**GETHYL'LIS** (an old Greek name, diminutive of *gethuon*, leek). FAM. *Amaryllidaceae*. A genus of about 9 species of dwarf bulbous perennials allied to Sternbergia, natives of S. Africa. Habit Crocus-like. Leaves linear. Flowers white, very fragrant; perianth-tube long, cylindrical, lobes 6, regular and spreading; scapes short, 1-flowered. Sandy loam and peat suits these greenhouse plants which may be increased by offsets or by seeds.

**G. af'ra.** *l.* 12 to 20, linear, twisted, glabrous, strongly ribbed. Perianth-tube 3 to 4 in. long; segs. 1½ to 2 in. long. August. 1820. (B.R. 1016.)

**G. ciliar'is.** 6 in. h. *l.* linear, spirally twisted, ciliate. Perianth segs. ovate-oblong. June, July. 1788. (E.S.A. 4, 35.)

**G. lanceola'ta.** A synonym of *Apodolirion lanceolatum*.

**G. spiral'is.** About 9 in. h. *l.* linear, spirally twisted, smooth. Perianth segs. ovate-oblong. June, July. 1780. (B.M. 1088.)

**G. villo'sa.** About 9 in. h. *l.* filiform, spirally twisted, hairy. Perianth segs. ovate-oblong. June, July. 1787.

**Gettlef'fii,** in honour of Mr. G. F. Gettleffi of Louis Trichardt, Transvaal, *c.* 1911.

**GE'UM** (old Latin name used by Pliny). FAM. *Rosaceae*. A genus of about 36 species of perennial herbs widely distributed over the world, especially in temperate and cold regions. Leaves variously cut, the terminal lobe always largest, and usually 3-toothed. Inflorescence arising from leaf-axils of radical rosette, flowers solitary or in loose panicles, yellow, red, or white; sepals 5, overlapping in the bud and larger than the lobes of the epicalyx; petals 5; stamens numerous. Fruit an achene terminated by the usually hairy style which is sometimes bent or twisted into a hook. Geums are usually easily grown in any moderately good soil if it is well drained, and provide both border- and rock-plants. Propagated by seed and division. The named forms of hybrids and garden varieties must always be increased by division; unfortunately attempts are often made to raise them from seed which is usually freely produced with the result that variations occur, usually inferior to the originally named plant. Furthermore, crossing readily occurs between the species and many plants of hybrid origin are in gardens. **A**

At least 2 species of Sawflies occur upon Geums, the leaf-feeder, *Blennocampa geniculata*, and the leaf-miner, *Metallus gei*. The former appears in May, and the dark-green larvae are found towards the end of May and in June feeding on the under-side of the leaves and, occasionally, completely skeletonizing the foliage of plants in herbaceous borders. The latter is double-brooded, the larval mines being abundant in June and July, and from August to early October. Several larvae may occur in a single leaf when the mines become fused until the entire leaf is eaten out into a single large mine. As both species frequently occur in great numbers on herbaceous borders in the south of England, it is necessary to dust the leaves when the larvae are seen with nicotine dust, which will give a more effective control than a liquid spray. The mined leaves should be removed and burned and the leaves sprayed with nicotine-soap wash.

(G. F. W.)

**G. al'bum.** Smooth or downy, about 2 ft. h. Stem slender, branches spreading. *Basal l.* pinnate; *upper* 3-partite, lobed or toothed. *fl.* white. Spring. *fr.* bristly hairy; style hooked. N. America. Border.

**G. alep'icum.** Hairy. About 2 ft. h., larger in all parts than *G. urbanum*. *Lower basal l.* with small, irregularly cut terminal lobe and lateral lflets.; *upper* with large, cordate, broadly rounded, 3-toothed terminal lobe. *fl.* yellow; pet. often longer than cal. June to September. *fr.* long-awned, almost smooth. Europe, N. America. 1778. SYN. *G. strictum*. Border.

**G. atrococcin'eum.** See *G. chiloense atrosanguineum*.

**G. au'reum.** A synonym of *G. montanum grandiflorum*.

**G. × Boris'ii** (*G. bulgaricum × G. reptans*). *fl.* bright orange. Bulgaria.

**G. bulgar'icum.** Hairy and with short glandular hairs, about 12 to 18 in. h. *l.* with very large cordate-reniform terminal lobe, with jagged teeth and often with small, scattered, 3-toothed lateral lobes. *fl.* bright yellow, nodding; pet. obovate, about as long as cal. Summer. *fr.* with long, feathery plume. Bulgaria. Border.

**G. calthifo'lium.** Slender, hairy, 4 to 12 in. h. *Basal l.* with a large roundish-heart-shaped, slightly lobed, crenate terminal lobe, and few small lateral lobes; *stem-l.* few. *fl.* yellow, solitary or few, over 1 in. across. Summer. *fr.* styles feathery. NW. America. Rock-garden.

**G. chiloen'se.** Hairy and glandular, 1 to 2 ft. h. *Basal l.* with large, cordate, lobed, crenate terminal lobe, lateral lobes small, about 1 in. long; *stem-l.* 3-parted, deeply cut. *fl.* large, scarlet, sometimes copper-coloured in erect panicles. Summer. *fr.* styles feathery. Chiloé. 1826. Borders. (B.R. 1088 and L.B.C. 1527 as *G. coccineum.*) This is the *G. coccineum* of gardens, the true *G. coccineum* of SE. Europe and Asia Minor being very rarely seen. var. **atrosanguin'eum,** *fl.* coppery-red, usually seen in the double-fld. form **fl. pleno; fl. pleno,** *fl.* scarlet, double. **Mrs. Bradshaw,** is a fine form of this; **grandiflo'rum,** see **G. × Ewenii; minia'tum,** *fl.* lighter red than in type.

**G. cilia'tum.** A synonym of *G. triflorum.*

**G. coccin'eum.** Shortly hairy, erect, 6 to 15 in. h. Stem usually solitary. *Basal l.* interruptedly lobed, side lobes obovate, terminal lobe much larger, almost kidney-shaped, sharply toothed; *stem-l.* not lobed, with 3 to 5 large teeth, short-stalked. *fl.* usually 2 to 4, about 1¼ in. across, brick-red; *pet.* as long as cal. June to October. *fr.* styles feathery. Greece, Asia Minor. Border. (F.G. 485; B.M. n.s. 212.) This, the true *G. coccineum*, is rarely seen, being confused with *G. chiloense.*

**G. ela'tum.** Stem very slender, 2 or 3 times forked, rarely simple. *Basal l.* pinnatisect, narrow, gradually widened to the rounded tip; *stem-l.* small; stipules large. *fl.* golden-yellow, erect; *pet.* sometimes 2-lobed; peduncles long, slender. Himalaya. 1880. (B.M. 6568.) Rock-garden.

**G. × Ewen'ii.** Said to be a hybrid, probably with *G. chiloense* as a parent. 18 to 24 in. h. *fl.* orange and terra-cotta. April to October. Border.

**G. × Heldreich'ii.*** Said to be a hybrid, probably with *G. montanum* as a parent. 9 to 12 in. h. *fl.* large, orange-red. June to October. 1896. Various forms are offered as varieties of this, e.g. **lu'teum,** *fl.* deep yellow; **magnif'icum, splen'dens,** and **superb'um,** *fl.* 1½ to 2 in. across. May to October. *See also* **G. montanum.**

**G. heterocarp'um.** Softly hairy, with spreading branches. *Basal l.* interruptedly pinnate with large cordate-reniform terminal lobe and much smaller ovate side lobes; *stem-l.* smaller, simple, or with 1 pair of side lobes. *infl.* spreading, many-fld. *fl.* pale yellow; *pet.* shorter than the lanceolate, toothed sep. May to July. *fr.* styles straight, hairy. Mediterranean region. Rock-garden.

**G. × hyb'ridum.** A synonym of *G. × Ewenii*, but often used indiscriminately for seedlings not conformable to *G. chiloense, G. montanum*, and *G. rivale.*

**G. × Jank'ae** (*G. coccineum × G. rivale*). Intermediate between parents. Rhodope Mts. 1895.

**G. japon'icum.** Robust, hairy, 1 to 2 ft. h. or more. Stems erect. *Basal l.* long-stalked, side lobes small, ovate, end lobe very large, cordate-reniform, 3- to 5-lobed; *stem-l.* roundish, coarsely toothed. *fl.* rather large, yellow. *fr.* style hairy above. June, July. E. Asia, N. America. SYN. *G. macrophyllum.* Border.

**G. × Kolbia'num.** A synonym of *G. × rhaeticum.*

**G. macrophyl'lum.** A synonym of *G. japonicum.* A variety of *G. reptans* is sometimes so named.

**G. magellan'icum.** A synonym of *G. parviflorum.*

**G. mol'le.** Related to *G. aleppicum.* Thickly, softly hairy, about 12 in. h. *Basal l.* with a very large cordate or cordate-reniform terminal lobe and 2 or 3 small side lobes; *stem-l.* coarsely toothed *fl.* yellow, smaller than in *G. aleppicum* with short, ovate, acute sep. Spain to Serbia. Border.

**G. monta'num.*** Softly hairy, 6 to 12 in. h. Stems usually 1-fld. *Rosette-l.* interruptedly lobed with large, broad, roundish or reniform end lobe, and much smaller ovate or cordate side lobes; *stem-l.* small, often deeply cut. *fl.* erect, golden-yellow, 1¼ to 1½ in. across; *pet.* longer than sep. Spring. *fr.* styles feathery. S. Europe. Rock-garden. var. **auranti'acum,** *fl.* rich orange; **grandiflo'rum,** *fl.* deep golden-yellow. *See* **G. × Heldreichii** which is sometimes, with the varieties named under it, included here. *See also* **G. × rhaeticum, G. × tirolense.**

**G. parviflo'rum.** Hairy, more or less erect perennial, 4 to 18 in. h. *l.* mainly radical, 2 to 5 in. long; terminal lobe large, ¾ to 2 in. across; roundish-kidney-shaped, faintly 3- to 5-lobed, crenate, hairy on both sides; lateral lflets. in 4 to 8 pairs, all very small, deeply cut. *fl.* white, ½ in. across in a loose, few-fld. panicle; pedicels long, slender; *pet.* longer than sep. New Zealand, S. America. Rock-garden.

**G. pyrena'icum.** Hairy, 1½ ft. h. Stem erect, simple, 1 to 4-fld. *l.* interruptedly lobed, longer than in *G. montanum*; lower lflets. small, toothed. *fl.* yellow, nodding. Pyrenees. 1804. Rock-garden.

**G. rep'tans.*** About 8 in. h., erect, simple, with creeping sterile stems. *Basal l.* interruptedly pinnatifid, larger lobes obovate-wedge-shaped deeply toothed at tip, smaller ones ovate, entire or 3-toothed. *fl.* yellow; about 1½ in. across, erect; *pet.* longer than cal. July, August. European Alps, mostly on limestone. (Gn. 29 (1886), 479.) var. **macrophyl'lum,** *l.* very large. *See* **G. × rhaeticum.** Rock-garden but not easy.

**G. × rhae'ticum** (*G. montanum × G. reptans*). 6 to 8 in. h. Stems numerous. *Basal l.* interruptedly pinnate, 3 to 5 in. long, terminal lobe large, heart-shaped, lobed, side lobes ovate, entire or 3-toothed; *stem-l.* few, small, pinnate. *fl.* golden-yellow, 1 in. across. Summer. Monte Rosa. 1886. (G.F. 1229.) SYN. *G. × Kolbianum, Sieversia rhaetica.* Rock-garden.

**G. riva'le.** Water Avens. Roughly hairy; rootstock thick, brown. Stem more or less erect, branched above, 8 to 12 in. h., tinged red in upper part. *Basal l.* interruptedly pinnate, terminal and upper pair of lobes large, obovate, toothed; *stem-l.* 3-lobed. *fl.* reddish, nodding, about 1¼ in. across; *pet.* scarcely longer than cal.; cal. lobes not reflexed. May, June. *fr.* styles hairy, not feathery, bent. N. Hemisphere, including Britain. (E.B. 459.) Damp places. var. **grandiflo'rum,** *fl.* larger than in type; **Leonard's var.,*** *fl.* pinkish with orange tints; **superb'um,** a large-fld. form. *G. rivale* has crossed with several other species in nature, *see*, e.g. **G. × Jankae, G. × tirolense.**

**G. Ros'sii.*** Somewhat hairy above, *l.* deeply cleft. *fl.* yellow, about 1½ in. across. Summer. *fr.* style straight, not hairy. Alaska.

**G. strict'um.** A synonym of *G. aleppicum.*

**G. × tirolen'se** (*G. montanum × G. rivale*). Stem erect or ascending, almost always branched, 2- or more flowered. *Basal l.* interruptedly pinnate with very large roundish or cordate-kidney-shaped terminal lobe, and much smaller ovate side lobes; *stem-l.* entire, deeply toothed. *fl.* more or less nodding, rarely nearly erect, yellow. Summer. *fr.* styles bent, hairy. Carpathians, Bosnia. Rock-gardens.

**G. triflo'rum.** Hairy, 8 to 20 in. h. *Basal l.* interruptedly pinnate; *lflets.* much toothed and cut; *stem-l.* few, small. *fl.* on long peduncles, often 3 in infl., cream or purple-tinged or white with purplish-red margin; cal. and peduncles purplish to dark purple; *pet.* oblong, not spreading, about as long as cal. July. *fr.* styles feathery. N. America, east of Cascade Mts. (B.M. 2858 as *Sieversia triflora.*) Border.

**G. uniflo'rum.*** Forms wide patches. Rootstock woody, clothed with remains of old l., creeping. *l.* radical, 1 to 3 in. long; terminal lflet. ¾ to 1 in. wide, oblong- or rounded-kidney-shaped, slightly lobed, deeply crenate, ciliate, lateral lflets. in 1 or 2 pairs, minute, deeply toothed. *fl.* solitary, white, ¾ to 1½ in. across on a slender scape 3 to 6 in. h.; *pet.* roundish. S. Island, New Zealand. (C.I.N.Z. 38.) Moist places on rock-garden.

**G. versipatel'la.** Perennial, 18 in. h. Stem slender. *Basal l.* lyrate, 3 to 4 in. long, hairy; terminal lobe rounded or kidney-shaped; *stem-l.* few, about 1½ in. long. *fl.* 1 to 3, white, nodding; *pet.* obovate. Nepal. 1930. (B.M. 9344.)

**G. virginia'num.** Throat-root. 1 to 3 ft. h. *Basal l.* long-stalked, variously cut; *stem-l.* nearly sessile. *fl.* white; *pet.* wedge-shaped to obovate, about as long as cal. June to August. N. America. Border.

**GEVUI'NA** (native name). FAM. *Proteaceae.* The only species is a handsome evergreen tree succeeding in a peat and loam soil, hardy only in mild localities, and often requiring sheltered situations there. Propagated by cuttings, in sand under a glass.

**G. Avella'na.*** Chilean Nut; Chile Hazel. A tree of 40 ft. in its native country, usually much less here. *l.* alternate, unequally pinnate or 2-pinnate, 6 to 16 in. long, 4 to 10 in. wide; lflets. 3 to 15, each with 1 to 5 divisions, variable in size, ovate, sharply toothed, acute, leathery, shining green. *fl.* white to yellowish-white, sometimes tinged red, tube cylindrical, limb ovoid, recurved; stamens exserted; racemes axillary, about 4 in. long. June. *fr.* a nut at first cherry-red, finally black, about as large as a hazel-nut, seed edible. Chile. 1826. (B.M. 9161 as *Guevina Avellana.*)

**GHERKIN,** small-fruited variety of Cucumber, *Cucumis sativa.* Cultivation as for outdoor Cucumbers. Used mainly for pickling.

**GHIESBREGH'TIA.** A synonym of Calanthe.

**GHOST SWIFT MOTH.** *See* **Swift Moths.**

**GIANT FENNEL.** *See* **Ferula communis.**

**GIANT SUGAR PINE.** *See* **Pinus Lambertiana.**

**GIBBAE'UM** (*gibba*, hump; one leaf of each pair prolonged into a hump). FAM. *Aizoaceae* (Mesembryanthemum). Dwarf, usually stemless, succulent plants from the Karroo, S. Africa, forming small clumps; each growth consists of 2 leaves united for a good part of their length, forming an ovoid or roundish body; it is not uncommon for one leaf to be appreciably longer than the other so that, in profile, the growth resembles a shark's head; the leaves spread open when the new growth is forming and ultimately dry up; they are usually glaucous green. The flowers are short stalked, white or mauve, and produced in autumn or spring. For cultivation *see* **Mesembryanthemum** (2).

**G. al'bum.** Stemless, forming clumps; 2 unequal *l.* forming an ovate body about 1 in. long, and ¾ in. wide, green, covered with fine white hairs. *fl.* 1 in. across, white or pink. (N.E. Br. 218.)

**G. dis'par.** Stemless, forming clumps; the 2 uneven *l.* lying close together at first, gaping later, grey-green with velvety hairs. *fl.* ¼ in. across, mauve.

**G. gem'inum.** Stems short, branching, forming clumps. *l.* united at base, very unequal, longest ¾ in. long, ¼ in. thick, pale grey-green. *fl.* ½ in. across, magenta. (N.E. Br. 216.)

**G. Heath'ii.** Stemless, forming clumps; plant bodies almost round, 1 in. h., the 2 *l.* equal, hemispherical, remaining close together, whitish-green. *fl.* 1½ in. across, white or pink. SYN. *Mesembryanthemum Heathii, Rimaria Heathii.* (N.E. Br. 288.)

**G. veluti'num.** Almost stemless. *l.* widespread, unequal, the longer 2 in. long, 1 in. wide at base, tapering, face slightly concave, back obliquely keeled, bluish-green with velvety hairs. *fl.* 1½ in. across, white. SYN. *Mesembryanthemum velutinum.*

V.H.

*gibbero'sus -a -um,* hump-backed.

*Gibbs'iae,* in honour of Lilian Suzette Gibbs, 1870–1925, of London, who collected in S. Africa, Fiji, Java, &c.

*Gibbs'ii,* in honour of the Hon. Vicary Gibbs of Aldenham (1853?–1933), a lover and collector of trees.

*gib'bus -a -um* (*gibbi-* in compound words), gibbous; swollen on one side.

*gibralta'ricus -a -um,* of Gibraltar.

**GIBRALTAR MINT.** *See* **Mentha Pulegium gibraltarica.**

*Gib'soni,* in honour of (1) gardener to the Duke of Devonshire who introduced *Cymbidium Gibsoni*; (2) a member of Lugard's E. African expedition, 1892.

*gigan'teus -a -um,* unusually tall or large.

*gig'as,* giant.

*Gilgia'nus -a -um,* in honour of E. Gilga of the University Botanical Museum, Berlin, 1867–1933.

**GILI'A** (in honour of Philipp Salvador Gil, a Spanish botanist of 18th century). FAM. *Polemoniaceae.* A genus of over 100 species of annual, biennial, or perennial herbs, very rarely sub-shrubs, mostly natives of western N. America, with a few in the Andes of S. America. Flowers usually in dense heads; calyx tubular or bell-shaped, its 5 teeth equal; corolla funnel-, bell-, or salver-shaped, or rotate, 5-lobed; stamens 5, on the corolla; usually at one level (cf. Phlox), filaments usually glabrous; ovary superior, 3-celled. Distinct from Navarretia by the equal calyx teeth. Many Gilias are very attractive plants for beds and edgings. The annual species are readily raised from seed sown in the open in March or April where the plants are to remain. A rather light soil and an open situation suits them best, and attention should be paid to the heights they attain.

KEY

| | |
|---|---|
| 1. *Cor. rotate* | |
| 1. *Cor. funnel- or salver-shaped* | G. Parryae |
| 2. *Lvs., at least the upper, alternate* | 2 |
| 2. *Lvs. opposite (except sometimes upper* | 3 |
| 3. *Annual species* | 11 |
| 3. *Biennial or perennial species* | 4 |
| 4. *Cor. 3-coloured; cal. teeth equalling tube* | 10 |
| 4. *Cor. self- or 2-coloured; cal. teeth shorter than tube* | G. tricolor |
| 5. *Cor. tube ⅔ to 1 in. long* | 5 |
| 5. *Cor. tube up to about 2 in. long* | G. tenuiflora |
| 6. *Infl. after flowering a dense head* | 6 |
| 6. *Infl. after flowering rather spreading or globular* | 7 |
| 7. *All or the lower fl. distinctly stalked* | 9 |
| 7. *All fl. sessile or nearly so* | G. multicaulis |
| 8. *Cor. tube ovate, about ½ in. long* | 8 |
| 8. *Cor. tube linear or oblong, about ⅓ in. long* | G. achilleifolia |
| 9. *Cor. twice as long as cal.* | G. capitata |
| 9. *Cor. little longer than cal.; throat little shorter than tube* | G. inconspicua |
| 10. *Fl. fragrant; seeds mulcilaginous when wet* | G. laciniata |
| 10. *Fl. scentless. Seeds not mulcilaginous when wet* | G. aggregata |
| 11. *Perennial* | G. rubra |
| 11. *Annual* | 12 |
| 12. *Stamens attached to throat of cor., cor. ½ to ¾ in. long; lvs. spine-tipped* | 16 |
| | 13 |

| | |
|---|---|
| 12. *Stamens attached to middle of cor. tube, cor. over 1 in. long* | G. californica |
| 13. *Lvs. all opposite* | G. Watsonii |
| 13. *Upper lvs. sometimes alternate* | 14 |
| 14. *Cor. of 2 colours* | G. Veatchii |
| 14. *Cor. self-coloured* | 15 |
| 15. *Cal. tube deeply waved between teeth* | G. pungens |
| 15. *Cal. tube truncate between teeth* | G. lilacina |
| 16. *Cor. funnel-shaped* | 17 |
| 16. *Cor. salver-shaped* | 18 |
| 17. *Lvs. entire* | G. dianthoides |
| 17. *Lvs. palmately cut; stamens hairy* | G. liniflora |
| 18. *Stamens attached at top of cor. tube, exserted* | 19 |
| 18. *Stamens attached in middle of cor. tube included* | G. dichotoma |
| 19. *Cor. lobes as long as tube* | G. densiflora |
| 19. *Cor. lobes shorter than tube* | 20 |
| 20. *Throat of cor. funnel-shaped* | 21 |
| 20. *Throat of cor. not, or scarcely, dilated* | G. lutea, G. × hybrida |
| 21. *Throat dark-coloured at base* | G. androsacea, G. × hybrida |
| 21. *Throat not dark-coloured at base* | G. longituba |

**G. abrotanifo'lia.** A variety of *G. achilleifolia.*

**G. achilleifo'lia.** Stout branched annual, 2 to 3 ft. *l.* small with short, narrow lobes. *fl.* purplish-blue, large, funnel-shaped, in many-fld. heads, later *fl.* scattered. August. California. 1833. (B.M. 5939.) var. **abrotanifo'lia,** dwarfer; *l.* 3-pinnately lobes, lobes very narrow, curved backwards, *fl.* blue. Various colour forms of the type are offered—**al'ba, ro'sea,** and a large-fld. form, **ma'jor.**

**G. aggrega'ta.** Half-hardy biennial much like *G. rubra,* but generally dwarfer with a slender hairy stem and fiery-red fragrant *fl.* with cor. lobes reflexed. Western N. America. The cor. varies in colour from red or rose, to red with yellowish spots, yellow, or white and there is considerable variety in the form of the flower and in the arrangement of the stamens. (S.B.F.G. s. 2, 218.)

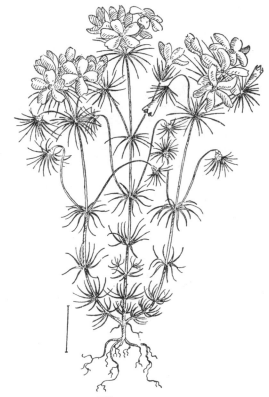

*Gilia androsacea*

**G. androsa'cea.** Annual with erect stem 12 to 18 in. h., much like *G. densiflora* but with cor. tube very slender and much longer than cal., 1 in. long, lobes entire, lilac, pink, or nearly white with yellow or dark throat. August. *l.* with 5 to 7 slender lobes, more or less spine-tipped. California. (T.H.S. 2, 18; B.R. 1710; B.M. 3491, all as *Leptosiphon androsaceus.*) var. **rosa'ceus** is a variety of the nearly related *G. longituba.*

**G. Brandege'i.** A synonym of *Polemonium Brandegei.*

**G. californ'ica.** Low, spreading, much branched, half-hardy sub-shrub. *l.* very crowded, soon widely spreading, alternate, digitate, with 3 to 7 stiff, very narrow, hairy segs. *fl.* rosy-lilac, 1½ in. across, cor. lobes broadly cuneate-obovate, margins often minutely toothed. W. California. 1854. (B.M. 4872 as *Leptodactylon californicum.*) A beautiful but tender perennial.

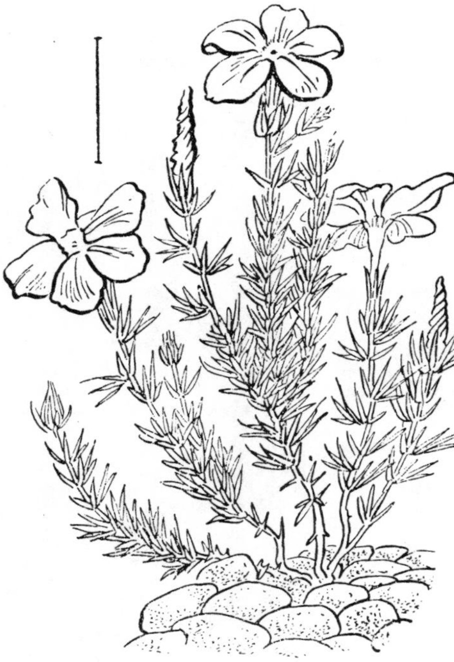

*Gilia californica*

**G. capita'ta.** Annual, 1 to 2 ft. *l.* 2-pinnatifid; segs. linear, unequally cut. *fl.* blue, ½ in. long, sessile, in dense heads on long peduncles. Summer. NW. America. 1826. (B.M. 2698; B.R. 1170.) var. **al'ba,** *fl.* white; **maj'or,** *fl.* larger.

**G. coccin'ea.** A synonym of *Collomia biflora.*

**G. coronopifo'lia.** A synonym of *G. rubra.*

**G. densiflo'ra.** Annual, erect, stem hairy, 1 to 2 ft. *l.* opposite, very finely cut. *fl.* in rather close heads, lilac or white, ⅛ to ⅜ in. long; cor. lobes spreading, obtuse, dentate, about as long as tube. June. California. (T.H.S. 2, 18; B.R. 1725; B.M. 3578 as *Leptosiphon densiflorus.*)

**G. dianthoi'des.** Annual, tufted, 2 to 5 in. h. *l.* narrow-linear, opposite, hairy. *fl.* 1 to 1½ in. long; cor. lilac or purplish, usually with darker or yellowish throat, lobes flat, toothed or fringed. July. California. 1855. (B.M. 4876.) SYN. *Fenzlia dianthoides.* var. **al'ba,** *fl.* white.

**G. dichot'oma.** Annual, glabrous, erect, 5 to 12 in. h. with forking branches, leafy. *l.* usually palmately 3- to 5- lobed; segs. filiform, entire. *fl.* terminal, solitary or twin, and solitary in l.-axils, white or purple, about 1 in. long; cor. lobes wide-ovate. Summer. California. 1833. SYN. *Linanthus dichotomus.*

**G. × hyb'rida.** Diffusely branched annual with slender, often purplish branches, 3 to 6 in. *l.* as in *G. lutea* between which and *G. androsacea* this may be a hybrid. *fl.* as in *G. lutea* but cor. tube red or upper part yellow, throat bell-shaped, purple or brown or yellow in upper part, lobes lilac or violet. California. Long in cultivation. SYN. *Leptosiphon hybridus.*

**G. inconspic'ua.** A synonym of *G. parviflora.*

**G. lacinia'ta.** Annual similar to *G. capitata* but smaller and more compact. *l.* pinnatifid; segs. narrow-oblong, margin wavy. *fl.* purplish on axillary 1- to 3-fld. peduncles. July. S. America. 1831.

**G. lilaci'na.** Perennial with many erect clammy stems, 4 to 5 in. *l.* alternate, palmately 3-lobed; segs. spine-pointed. *fl.* terminal, solitary or in small groups, lilac, ¾ in. long, funnel-shaped. Nevada.

**G. liniflo'ra.** Tufted annual, 10 to 20 in. *Lower l.* opposite, all sessile, palmately 3- to 7-cut. *fl.* white or tinged pink, large, solitary on long peduncles. Summer. Western N. America. 1833. (B.M. 5895.)

**G. longitu'ba.** Much like *G. androsacea*, but dwarfer and more spreading. *fl.* yellow, white, or purplish about ½ in. wide, up to 2 in. long, in dense-fld. involucrate heads. Summer. California. var. **rosa'cea,** *fl.* 1 to 1½ in. long, rose, purplish, &c. (B.M. 5863 as *Leptosiphon parviflorus rosaceus.*) SYN. *Leptosiphon roseus.*

**G. lu'tea.** Annual, branching from base, branches slender, ascending, 3 to 12 in. h. *l.* 5- to 7-parted; segs. narrow, ciliate. *fl.* yellow or orange, more deeply coloured in throat, 1 to 1½ in. long, in heads. Summer. California, Mexico. (B.M. 4735.) var. **au'rea,** *fl.* golden; **micran'tha,** *fl.* about 1 in. long.

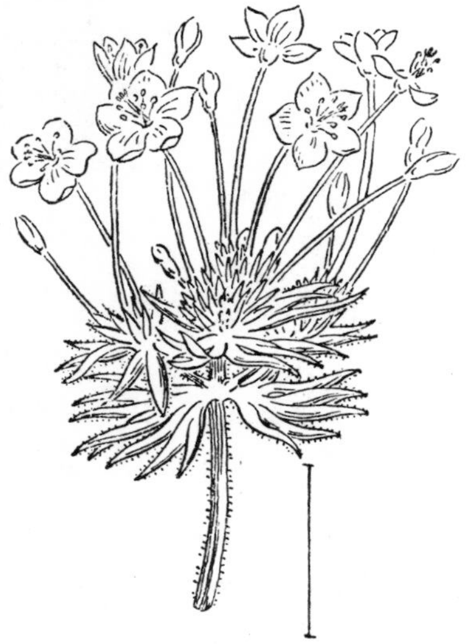

*Gilia lutea*

**G. micran'tha.** A variety of *G. lutea*, but confused with *G. longituba.*

**G. multicau'lis.** Allied to *G. achilleifolia* but usually dwarfer. *l.* 2- or 3-pinnatisect, with narrow lobes, downy. *fl.* blue or purple in terminal cymes, 3- to many-fld. Summer. California. 1833. (B.M. 3440 and B.R. 1682 as *G. achilleifolia.*)

**G. Par'ryae.** Hairy dwarf annual, 1½ to 2½ in. h. with slender branches. *Lower l.* opposite, palmately 3- to 7-parted; segs. shortly spine-pointed. *fl.* in umbels, crowded, purple-yellow, or white, with dark throat, about ½ in. long, tube funnel-shaped, throat with arched crests. Summer. S. California. var. **modes'ta,** throat of cor. without crests. SYN. *Linanthus Parryae.*

**G. parviflo'ra.** Annual, little branched, 9 to 12 in., with numerous radical and smaller stem-l. *l.* pinnatifid or 2-pinnatifid, variable. *fl.* in loose terminal corymbs, stalked, white or purple, cor. not twice as long as cal. August. Western N. America. (B.M. 2883 as *G. inconspicua.*)

**G. pung'ens.** Perennial resembling a dwarf mat-forming Phlox, 3 to 8 in., base woody, shoots hairy at first. *l.* palmately 3- to 5-lobed; lobes up to ½ in. long, slender. *fl.* white, pink, or yellow, solitary in l.-axils or clustered, ¾ to 1 in. long, funnel-shaped, tube twice as long as lobes. Western N. America. Variable in size.

**G. ru'bra.** Unbranched leafy biennial, up to 6 ft. h. *l.* pinnate, 1 in. long, lobes needle-like. *fl.* many, scarlet or pink, dotted and yellowish-white within, 1½ in. long, trumpet-shaped, lobes spreading. N. America. (B.R. 1691 as *G. coronopifolia.*)

**G. tenuiflo'ra.** Annual with erect or ascending stems from a basal cluster of l., up to 2 ft. *l.* ½ to 2 in. long, variously cut; segs. narrow. *fl.* clustered or paniculate; cor. ½ to 1¼ in. long, pink, red, or blue, throat yellow, narrow-tubular-funnel-shaped; stamens exserted. Summer. California, Nevada. (B.R. 1888.) SYN. *G. arenaria, G. splendens.* var. **Dav'yi,** segs. of lower l. short or toothlike, cor. distinctly dilated at throat.

**G. tric'olor.** Diffuse, twiggy annual, 2 to 2½ ft., rather hairy. *l.* pinnatifid or 2-pinnatifid; segs. very slender. *fl.* in few-fld. corymbs; cor. funnel-shaped, tube yellow, throat yellow spotted dark purple, lobes rose or purple. June. Western N. America. 1833. (T.H.S. 2, 18; B.R. 1704; B.M. 3463.) Variable in colour. var. **niva'lis,** *fl.* white. SYN. *G. nivalis, Snow Queen*; **ro'sea,** *fl.* rose; **ro'sea splen'dens,** larger than type; **ru'bra,** *fl.* reddish.

**G. Veatch'ii.** Bushy sub-shrub, clammy, fragrant, 12 to 20 in. *l.* rigid, spine-pointed, ½ in. long. *fl.* yellowish within, brownish-purple without. California.

**G. Wat'sonii.** Sub-shrub with erect stem, glandular-hairy. *l.* palmately cut; segs. 3 to 7, spine-pointed. *fl.* terminal, solitary, white with yellow throat, about ¾ in. long, salver-shaped. Utah.

**GILL,** a radiating plate on the lower surface of the cap of a fungus of the family Agaricaceae on which the spores are borne, as in the common mushroom.

**GILLEN'IA** (in honour of Arnoldus Gillenius, a German botanist of the 17th century). FAM. *Rosaceae*. A genus of 2 species of perennial herbs, natives of the Cent. and S. United States. Erect, 2 to 4 ft. high. Leaves nearly sessile, 3-foliolate, stipulate; leaflets stalked, toothed. Flowers in loose panicles; petals strap-shaped, unequal, ⅓ to ¾ in. long; stamens 10 to 20, very short; ovaries 5, hairy, finally distinct. Fruit a 2- to 4-seeded follicle. Gillenias are hardy, easily grown plants for rather moist peaty soil in partial shade, easily increased by division in spring.

**G. stipula'cea.** A synonym of *G. stipulata*.

**G. stipula'ta.** 1 to 2 ft. h. *l.* lanceolate, deeply toothed, stipules broad, leaflike. *fl.* white.

**G. trifolia'ta.*** Up to 4 ft. *l.* toothed, stipules linear, slender-pointed, entire. *fl.* red to white, in panicles; cal. persisting and becoming red after pet. fall. June. 1713. (B.M. 489 as *Spiraea trifoliata*.)

**GILLIES'IA** (in honour of Dr. Gillies of Mendoza, Chile, *c.* 1829). FAM. *Liliaceae*. A genus of 3 or 4 species of bulbous herbs, natives of Chile. Leaves few, radical, linear. Flowers greenish in terminal umbels; perianth segments 6, of which 2 are sometimes united; filaments united into a tube split on one side, fertile anthers 3. Scape simple, leafless. *G. graminea* needs a warm border with some protection in winter and a compost of loam and peat. Propagation by offsets.

**G. gramin'ea.** *l.* linear, channelled, about 1 ft. long. *fl.* small, green, drooping, in a few-fld. spreading umbel; spathe greenish, 2-valved, erect, persistent; scapes weak, terete, decumbent. September. Chile. 1825. (B.M. 2716; B.R. 992; L.B.C. 1755.)

**GILLIFLOWER** from French *Giroflée*. Sometimes written Gillyflower or Gilloflower. Originally given in Italy to flowers of the Pink tribe, especially to the Carnation (the Clove Gilliflower, *Dianthus Caryophyllus*), but later in England to Stocks (Matthiola) and Wallflower (Cheiranthus). The Gilliflower of Chaucer, Spenser, and Shakespeare was the Carnation.

*gil'vus -a -um, gilvo-* in compound words, pale yellow.

**GINGELLY OIL PLANT.** See **Sesamum indicum.**

**GINGER.** The dried rhizomes of *Zingiber officinale*, imported from E. and W. Africa and China and used both as a condiment and as a preserve.

**GINGER, WILD.** See **Asarum.**

**GINGERBREAD PALM.** See **Hyphaene thebaica.**

**GINGERBREAD PLUM.** See **Parinarium macrophyllum.**

**GINGILI.** See **Gingelly Oil Plant.**

**GIN'KGO** (the Chinese name). Maidenhair tree. FAM. *Ginkgoaceae*. A monotypic genus, a fine deciduous tree, unknown in a wild state, perhaps the most ancient of existing flowering plants, the remaining representative of a widespread and otherwise extinct race. It succeeds best in a rather dry loam. Though quite hardy it should not be planted in bleak, exposed places especially in ill-drained soils. Fruits have been borne in a few places in England but most of the old trees are males and propagation is usually by imported seed which should be sown in a cold frame or in the open in a sheltered situation. Where practicable layers may also be used, and grafting is the best method for the named varieties. Grafting is done in spring on ordinary seedlings in a warm house, the scions being occasionally syringed overhead, but care must be taken not to give too much water. The grafts must be shielded from direct sun until union is effected.

**G. bilo'ba.*** Deciduous tree of 80 to 100 ft. with whorled branches. *l.* fan-shaped, cleft about half-way and irregularly notched, thickened at margin, veins evident, parallel. *fl.* Spring (see **Ginkgoaceae**). *fr.* yellow, with fleshy outer covering, kernel edible, sweet. N.

China. 1874. (D.J.C. 544.) Several varieties have occurred including **fastigia'ta** with stiff, erect branches; **lacinia'ta,** *l.* more deeply cut than in type; **pen'dula,** with weeping branches; **varie-ga'ta,** with poorly marked yellowish stripes.

**GINKGOA'CEAE.** A family of very ancient lineage only one species of which now remains in existence, a resinous tree with deciduous, fan-shaped, parallel-veined leaves, dioecious flowers, the staminate with the anthers in stalked pairs on a slender stem, the female on long stalks, usually with 2 ovules without an ovary, and a drupe-like fruit with a fleshy outer and a hard inner coat. The pollen grains produce motile sperm-cells as in the Cycadaceae. *See* **Ginkgo.**

*Ginna'la,* native name.

**GINSENG.** The root of *Panax quinquefolius*, a most important drug plant in China.

**GIPSIES' ROSE.** *See* **Knautia arvensis** in Suppl.

**GIPSY MOTH,** *Lymantria dispar*, does extensive damage to forest, park, and street trees in the Eastern United States of America; it was accidentally introduced from Europe about 1868. It has there become one of the chief pests of broad-leaved trees which it completely defoliates. Many parasitic and predaceous species of insects have been collected in Europe over a number of years and released in the Eastern States to reduce the population of this pernicious pest.

G. F. W.

*Giral'dii,* in honour of Pére Giuseppe Girald, Italian missionary in Shensi, China, *c.* 1897.

**GITHA'GO.** *See* **Agrostemma.**　　A

**GITHOP'SIS** (*Githago, opsis*; like). FAM. *Campanulaceae*. A genus of a single annual herb with scattered, narrow leaves, native of California. Flowers bell-shaped; stamens free of corolla and of one another; ovary inferior; stigmas 3-lobed. Fruit a capsule. *G. specularioides* is half-hardy and much like Venus's Looking Glass. Cultivation as for other annuals.

**G. specularioi'des.** Sometimes hairy, 2 to 10 in. h. *l.* sessile, small, linear-oblong, coarsely toothed. *fl.* blue, erect, solitary at ends of branches. *fr.* on a short, stout peduncle. California. 1894. (G.C. 16 (1894), 245.)

*Gizel'lae,* in honour of Gizella von Borbas, wife of the author of a monograph of Hungarian Roses.

*glabel'lus -a -um,* somewhat smooth.

*gla'ber -bra -brum, glabri-,* in compound words, glabrous, smooth-skinned, destitute of hairs.

*glaber'rimus -a -um,* very smooth.

*glabra'tus -a -um,* smooth.

*glabres'cens,* becoming glabrous.

*glabrius'culus -a -um,* somewhat smooth.

*glacia'lis -is -e,* of the ice.

**GLADE.** A long, open stretch between high planting, usually comprising a grass walk of varying width and margined by informal plantations of herbaceous plants backed by ornamental trees and shrubs.

J. E. G. W.

*gladia'tus -a -um,* sword-like.

**GLAD'IOLUS** (name used by Pliny, diminutive of *gladius*, sword, from the shape of the leaves). FAM. *Iridaceae*. A genus of over 150 species of perennial herbs with base of stem swollen into a corm and usually 2 or 3 sword-shaped lateral leaves, natives of Europe, Mediterranean region, tropical and S. Africa, and the Mascarene

Islands. Inflorescence a spike, often 1-sided; perianth zygomorphic with a tube more or less curved, segments as long as, or longer than the tube (in Homoglossum and Antholyza perianth segments shorter than tube). Fruit a 3-celled capsule, seeds many, winged. Many of the species have great beauty and are well worth cultivating in pots in cool-houses, or in mixed flower-borders in summer, but they have been superseded by the numerous and beautiful hybrids the raising of which was begun early in the history of the introduction of the genus to gardens, first in France and soon after in England, while many have in later years been raised in Germany, Holland, and N. America. Propagation is easy by seeds which are usually freely produced, germinate freely, and yield seedlings which, if grown on carefully, will flower in the second year, and sometimes in the first; and by the numerous large and small bulbils (usually called 'spawn') which are produced around the old corms or at the ends of short underground shoots from the base of the newly formed corm. Seed should be sown in early March in large pans or pots where the seedlings may be thinned, if necessary, and allowed to remain for the first season. The pans should be given a little heat at first. As the seedlings appear more light and air should be given and the seedlings should be gradually hardened off to stand outside during summer. They should be carefully attended to while growing and thoroughly ripened in autumn, the young corms being stored like the larger ones. The seedlings of hybrids naturally differ from their parents and for the increase of special plants recourse must be had to the small corms they form which should be separated and planted 4 to 6 in. apart in a warm border about mid-March. They will, if grown on carefully, attain flowering size for the next year. **A**

To grow Gladioli well the best situation is a sunny one with light, sandy soil, or if heavy, one lightened by the addition of river-sand spread thickly over the surface and forked in. The ground should be double dug, and well-decayed compost forked into both top and bottom spit in October. This treatment should be given to the whole bed, not merely to the lines where the plants are to be planted. During winter and early spring when the soil is dry the surface should be lightly forked. Fresh manure should not be used at planting time, but a dressing of bone-meal or steamed bone-flour may be given with advantage. Planting may begin in the first week in March, drills being drawn 14 or 15 in. apart and the corms set about 8 to 12 in. apart so that the tops are about 4 in. below the surface. Dry sand should be put beneath and around the corms and if the ground is wet the drills should be filled up with dry soil, otherwise the soil drawn out should be used. For succession fresh plantings should be made at fortnightly intervals until the end of May. The ground should be cultivated with the Dutch hoe as soon as the plants appear and at intervals during the summer, not only for the destruction of weeds. Staking should be attended to before the flowering season begins, a measure especially necessary in exposed and windy sites. Watering may be necessary in hot weather and a mulch of short litter will be found very helpful.

The foliage of Gladioli remains green till very late in the autumn, but the corms (except for the S. European species which may remain in the soil through the winter) should be lifted from the middle to the end of October before the onset of severe weather. They should be forked out of the ground, shaken free of soil, taking care to preserve the 'spawn', cutting off the stalk close to the crown, and spreading the corms out in an airy place to dry. When well dried they should be stored in bags (being labelled) or boxes in a frost-free place until planting time. Damp and close conditions leading to heating must be carefully avoided. It is better to store the large and small corms separately.

Large-flowered Gladioli may be grown in pots for summer and autumn flowering in the greenhouse. One large corm is sufficient for a 7-in. pot and successional planting will extend the flowering season, the plants being grown at first in a frame or in a sheltered position outdoors. The small-flowered Gladioli of the G. × Colvillei type and many of the smaller species are also excellent for pot cultivation. The Colvillei type may be gently forced and had in flower in April and May. The small corms may be planted 5 in a 5- or 6-in. pot in autumn and treated like other autumn-planted bulbs, being covered with ashes on a standing ground outside until roots are well developed or they may be placed in a cold frame. When roots are formed the pots should be brought successionally into a house with a temperature of 55° F. Each strong corm will produce 2 or more scapes and when these appear a somewhat higher temperature may be given. Full light should be allowed and plenty of water during the growing time. Later plantings will develop well in the cold frame.

Gladioli are very useful for cutting. The spike should be cut when the first 4 to 6 flowers have opened. The remainder will open in water. Like most flowers when cut Gladioli look best with their own foliage.

New varieties are raised from seed and flowers selected for seed-formation should be cross-pollinated. The anthers should be removed from the selected seed-bearing flowers before they are half-open (this may be done with the fingers). When the flowers are fully expanded the pollen from the flower selected as the male parent should be taken when that flower has fully expanded and deposited on the stigma of the seed-bearer; this should be done on successive days as the flowers develop until all the flowers on the spike have been pollinated.

J. C.

As already noted garden-raised hybrids have gained great favour among Gladiolus growers. The earliest of the hybrids which became well known, if not the first raised, was G. × Colvillii, named after the nurseryman of Chelsea and figured in *Sweet's British Flower Garden*, t. 155, in 1823. It was the result of a cross between G. cardinalis and G. tristis and was the forerunner of a race of early-flowering Gladioli useful both for forcing and for the flower-border, Ackermannii and The Bride being particularly well known and still grown. New varieties of this group continue to appear and are now often grouped under the name G. nanus. Of the large-flowered, usually taller and stouter hybrids G. × gandavensis was sent out by Messrs. Van Houtte in 1841, and the parentage given was G. cardinalis × G. psittacinus, though Dean Herbert considered it to be G. oppositiflorus × G. psittacinus. Later G. × brenchleyensis with light-red flowers and G. × citrinus of gardens with yellow flowers of the same parentage gained much popularity. Selection and crossing among the seedlings of this race did much to secure variety and improvement at the hands of M. Souchet of Fontainebleau in France, and later, in Germany, Max Leichtlin, working on the same race originated the very robust plants with almost erect, very large flowers produced earlier in the season than those of G. × gandavensis which became known as G. × Childsii. Meanwhile M. Lemoine of Nancy raised and introduced in 1878 another race by crossing G. × gandavensis with G. purpureo-auratus, calling it G. × Lemoinei. In this the flowers were more or less open bell-shaped with broad, highly coloured segments of good substance, the upper ones projecting forward or forming a hood. Later, in 1889, there came from the same source G. × nanceianus, resulting from the crossing of plants of the Lemoinei race with G. Saundersii, giving a very robust type of plant with open flowers having the uppermost segment long and erect, the 2 lateral next to it spreading widely and sometimes giving the open flower a diameter of over 6 in. Messrs. Froebel of Zurich by crossing the parents of *G. × Lemoinei* introduced a number of good varieties and one under the name of *G. × turicensis* (*G. × gandavensis × G. Saundersii superbus*) with purplish-crimson flowers marked on the lower segments with white, and having a well-formed spike. More recently, while European raisers including Herr Pfitzer of Stuttgart and Dutch and British raisers have not been idle, American raisers have been very active and various races have resulted from their efforts of which among others are those sometimes offered as *G. hybridus princeps* originated by Mr. W. W. Van Fleet by crossing *G. × Childsii* with *G. cruentus*, producing, like the latter (the seed parent), scarlet-crimson flowers with white and cream feathering on the lower segments of the large, round, flat flowers about 6 in. across, the Groff hybrids put out by Mr. Groff of Canada, a very fine race of the *gandavensis* type and originating in the varieties of that type, and the ruffled type in which the segments have markedly wavy margins, a feature not unknown among wild species but greatly developed by Mr. Kunderd of Indiana, who has, among other species, brought *G. Quartinianus* into the race of garden-raised Gladioli. A new impetus was given to hybridizing by the introduction of *G. primulinus* in 1879. It gave a race of very refined, hooded flowers, of soft colours, and has carried its characters into the large-flowered type increasing the range of variety and adding interest and beauty to the garden. The identity of the species from the Victoria Falls of the Zambesii, to which this remark applies, has recently been questioned on the ground that the true *G. primulinus* is a native of Tanganyika, and the name *G. nebulicola* has been proposed for it.

The various crossings that have been made, bringing in a considerable number of species of varying characters, have resulted in plants impossible to place in one species or another since they often combine the characteristics of several, and for garden purposes an artificial classification is best adopted. The great number fall into the following more or less arbitrary groups.

EARLY-FLOWERING VARIETIES (treated like *G. × Colvillii*). *Nanus.* Dwarf, rather slender plants. Flowering April and May.

*Herald Gladioli.* About 36 in. high. Stems strong, rigid, erect. Flowering very early, often before the Nanus types. Need protection from frost. Flowers large.

*Gladiolus × Tubergeni.* About 30 in. high. Leaves thin, spikes loose, graceful. Flowering mid-June. Flowers of type of *G. × Colvillii*, but larger.

SUMMER- AND AUTUMN-FLOWERING VARIETIES (planted in spring, lifted in autumn). *Primulinus Types.* Mostly 36 to 56 in. high. Stems rather slender. Spikes rather loose or close, simple or branched. Flowers usually 10 to 14, usually $2\frac{1}{2}$ to $3\frac{1}{2}$ in. across, upper segment horizontal or hooded.

The flower colours may be grouped into: (1) white; (2) yellow; (3) yellow shaded pink; (4) orange; (5) pale pink on white; (6) pink on cream; (7) apricot; (8) pink on yellow; (9) salmon; (10) cerise; (11) orange-scarlet; (12) scarlet; (13) crimson; (14) purple.

PRIMULINUS GRANDIFLORUS TYPES. Mostly 40 to 56 in. high. Stems usually strong. Spikes often branched, usually close. Flowers usually 12 to 18, $3\frac{1}{2}$ to $4\frac{1}{2}$ in. across, upper segment horizontal or hooded.

The flower colours may be grouped into: (1) yellow; (2) cream shaded pink; (3) apricot and pink; (4) yellow and pink; (5) orange and salmon; (6) pink on cream; (7) salmon on cream; (8) salmon; (9) old rose; (10) cerise on cream; (11) cherry-red; (12) orange-scarlet; (13) scarlet; (14) crimson; (15) purple.

LARGE-FLOWERED TYPES. Mostly $3\frac{1}{2}$ to $4\frac{1}{2}$ ft. high. Stem stout. Spikes usually close, sometimes branched. Flowers 14 to 20, 4 to 6 open at a time, mostly $3\frac{3}{4}$ to $4\frac{1}{2}$ in.

or more across, upper segments often erect, sometimes hooded.

The flower colours may be grouped into: (1) white; (2) white with pink markings; (3) white flushed pink; (4) white blotched red; (5) yellow; (6) yellow blotched red; (7) pink on white; (8) pink on cream; (9) rose-pink; (10) rose; (11) orange-pink; (12) salmon-orange; (13) apricot and salmon; (14) old rose and ash; (15) salmon-pink; (16) salmon; (17) salmon-cerise; (18) cerise; (19) rosy-scarlet; (20) orange-scarlet; (21) scarlet; (22) crimson; (23) maroon; (24) lavender; (25) lilac; (26) lavender-blue; (27) mauve shaded red; (28) purple; (29) reddish-purple; (30) claret; (31) violet.

A selection of varieties in the different classes will be found in the Supplement.

*DISEASES.* Most fungus diseases of Gladiolus persist on the corms and are thus transmitted from season to season. The best known is dry rot, due to *Sclerotinia gladioli*, seen in the early yellowing of the foliage, and as black spots and blotches on the corms which in severe attacks turn into coal-black mummified objects. Leaf spot or Hard Rot, due to *Septoria gladioli*, causes spotting of the leaves and later hard, black, sunken patches on the corms. Neck Rot and Scab, due to *Bacterium marginatum*, causes soft rot at the base of the leaves and distinct, round, sunken craters with definite margins on the corms. In all these diseases the remedy must include stripping the tunics from the corms and rejecting infected ones before planting on clean ground. The corms may also be attacked by leafy gall (q.v.). In storage dampness must be avoided or the corms may be seriously damaged by green mould, *Penicillium gladioli*, or core rot, *Botrytis* sp., which affects and rots the central core after destroying the root plate. Less important diseases are smut, *Urocystis gladioli*, producing sooty black streaks on the leaves, and flower spot, *Botrytis cinerea*, which may spoil the flowers in very hot weather. A virus disease also causes irregularities in the colouring of the flowers.

(D. E. G.)

**A**

**G. Ad′lami.** 12 to 18 in. h. *l.* ensiform, 12 to 18 in. long, 1 in. wide in middle, ribs distant. *fl.* greenish-yellow, 5 or 6 in a dense, simple, erect spike; tube nearly straight, 1 in. long; segs. oblong, acute, 2 spotted with red towards tip. S. Africa. 1889. SYN. *G. sulphureus* of Baker.

**G. ala′tus.** Corm small, globose. Stem up to 12 in. h. *l.* 3 or 4, rather narrow-linear, stiff. *fl.* on 3- to 6-fld., loose, zigzag spike, large, carmine-red, tube strongly bent, segs. obovate, upper long, lower yellow at base, both inner lower segs. almost rolled together; stamens almost as long as upper seg. May. S. Africa. (B.M. 586.) *G. namaquensis* of B.M. 592 appears to be a dark-colour form of this and var. *algoensis* of B.M. 2608 a brighter form. *G. alatus* has been crossed with *G. vittatus*.

**G. anatoli′cus.** Related to *G. illyricus* and sometimes listed as a variety of that species, differing by the shorter upper lip and narrower lower segs., filaments scarcely longer than anthers. Spring. Syria.

**G. angus′tus.** Corm globose, rather small. Stem about 18 in. h. *l.* 3 or 4, linear, flat, up to $\frac{1}{4}$ in. wide, lower 12 in. or more long. *fl.* 2 to 6 in a loose spike, white, tinged red without; tube narrow, $1\frac{1}{2}$ to 2 in. long; segs. oblong, the 3 lower smaller with a heart-shaped, purple mark in centre; stamens scarcely half as long as segs. June. S. Africa. 1756. (B.M. 602.) SYN. *G. trimaculatus*.

**G. atroviola′ceus.** 2 to 3 ft. h. *l.* 3, narrow-linear, 6 to 12 in. long, veins parallel. *fl.* dark purple or violet, in a short, 1-sided, densely 5- to 7-fld. spike; segs. oblong-spatulate; anthers at least as long as filaments. Spring. Syria. 1889.

**G. auranti′acus.** About 3 ft. h. *l.* 4 to 6, ensiform, 12 to 18 in. long, $\frac{1}{4}$ to $\frac{1}{2}$ in. wide. *fl.* bright orange-yellow, or tinged red, in a loose spike up to 1 ft. long, tube curved, 2 in. long, suddenly dilated in middle, upper segs. 1 to $1\frac{1}{2}$ in. long, 3 lower shorter. Summer. S. Africa. var. **rubro-tinc′tus,** *fl.* orange-yellow, thickly dotted red. 1894.

**G. blan′dus.** Corm of medium size. Stem 12 to 18 in. h. *l.* usually 4, smooth. *fl.* white or reddish- or rose-tinged, in 4- to 8-fld. loose spikes, tube bent, segs. rather large, outer usually tinged rose, upper unicolorous, lower narrower and usually with a reddish-blue spot in centre. June. S. Africa. 1774. (B.M. 625.) Colour variable. var. **al′bidus,** *fl.* white. (B.M. 648 as *G. blandus niveus*); **car′neus,** robust, *fl.* purplish-white, with broader segs. (B.M. 645 as var. *purpureo-albescens*; A.B.R. 188 as *G. campanulatus*); **excel′sus,**

more robust than type, *l.* longer, perianth-tube longer. (B.M. 1665.); **Morton'ius,** robust *fl.* white with fine rose stripes, perianth tube very long, slightly curved, segs. broad, somewhat crisped. (B.M. 3680 as *G. Mortonius.*) Hybrids with *G. cardinalis, G. floribundus, G. grandis, G. hirsutus, G. recurvus,* and *G. tristis,* have been raised. **A**

**G. brachyan'drus.** About 2 ft. h. *l.* 4 or 5, near base of stem, strongly nerved and margined, only about 3 in. long, ⅓ in. wide. *fl.* bright pale scarlet, 2 to 2½ in. long; tube ½ in. long; segs. oblong, acute; spike about 12 in. long, 8- to 10-fld. July. Trop. Africa. 1879. (B.M. 6463.)

**G. × brenchleyen'sis** (*G. cardinalis* × *G. psittacinus*). *See* **G. × gandavensis.**

**G. byzanti'nus.** Related to *G. illyricus.* Stem robust, about 2 ft. h. *l.* narrower, deep green. *fl.* red in rather loose, 6- to 10-fld. spikes, weakly 1-sided; tube short; 3 upper segs. inclined together, lower bent down, middle broad, anther as long as filament. June. Mediterranean region, Corsica eastwards. 1629. (B.M. 874.) For a hybrid with *C. cardinalis, see* **G. × Victorialis.**

**G. callis'tus.** Slender, about 18 in. h. *fl.* pale pink, in long, rather loose spikes, segs. widely spreading. S. Africa. 1930.

**G. cardina'lis.*** Corm large. Stem stout, up to 3 ft. h. *l.* rather wide, somewhat glaucous, many-nerved, ensiform. *fl.* scarlet; tube almost straight; upper segs. oblong-spatulate, up to 2 in. long, acute, lower shorter and narrow, with a broad, whitish stripe; stamens at least half as long as segs. July, August. S. Africa. 1789. (B.M. 135.) Has given rise to many garden forms and hybrids with *G. blandus, G. brachyandrus, G. floribundus, G. hirsutus, G. oppositiflorus, G. psittacinus, G. purpureo-auratus, G. Saundersii,* and *G. tristis.*

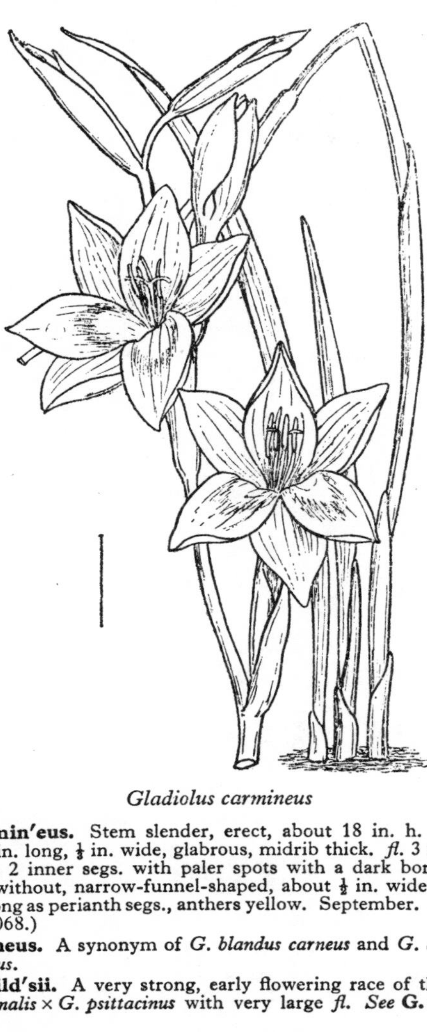

*Gladiolus carmineus*

**G. carmin'eus.** Stem slender, erect, about 18 in. h. *l.* linear, about 8 in. long, ⅓ in. wide, glabrous, midrib thick. *fl.* 3 in. across, carmine, 2 inner segs. with paler spots with a dark border; tube whitish without, narrow-funnel-shaped, about ½ in. wide; stamens half as long as perianth segs., anthers yellow. September. S. Africa. (B.M. 8068.)

**G. car'neus.** A synonym of *G. blandus carneus* and *G. cuspidatus ventricosus.*

**G. × Child'sii.** A very strong, early flowering race of the hybrid *G. cardinalis* × *G. psittacinus* with very large *fl. See* **G. × gandavensis.**

**G. × citri'nus.** A form of *G. × gandavensis* (q.v.) with yellow *fl.* (F.d.S. 539.)

**G. × Colvil'lii** (*G. cardinalis* × *G. tristis*). About 18 in. h. Stem somewhat flexuose, leafy, glaucous. *l.* narrow-ensiform, acute, strongly nerved. *fl.* bright red in a few-fld. spike; segs. oblong, acute with a lanceolate bright-yellow spot on 3 lower. July. 1823. Of garden origin. (S.B.F.G. 155.) var. **al'bus,** *fl.* snow-white. SYN. The Bride.

**G. commu'nis.** Corm ovate, about ⅘ in. thick. Stem 12 to 24 in. h. or more. *l.* 3 to 5, up to ⅝ in. wide, acute, nerves not very strong. *fl.* bright rose or white, rather large, in a 1-sided, 6- to 8-fld. spike; tube bent, reddish-brown; segs. close, forming a somewhat bell-shaped perianth; filaments somewhat longer than anthers. May to July. Mediterranean region. 1596. (B.M. 86.) var. **car'neus,** a synonym of *G. pallidus.*

**G. Coo'peri.** Closely allied to *G. psittacinus. fl.* with large red-striped yellow upper, and smaller, clustered, yellow lower segs. Natal. (B.M. 6202.)

**G. crispiflo'rus.** A variety of *G. imbricatus.*

**G. cruen'tus.** 2 to 3 ft. h. *l.* linear-ensiform, 12 to 18 in. long. *fl.* brilliant scarlet, yellow-white speckled red at base of limb, broadly bell-shaped, about 4 in. across, lateral segs. marked white; spike dense-fld., 6 to 10 in. long. September. Natal. 1868. (B.M. 5810.) A parent of some large-fld. hybrids.

**G. cuspida'tus.*** Corm globose, large, with very fine parallel-veined tunic. About 20 in. h. *l.* 3 or 4, broad, almost as long as stem. *fl.* white to bright purple in a 4- to 8-fld., loose, 1-sided spike; tube about 3 in. long, widened upwards; segs. about 2 in. long, narrow, crisped, lower 3 with a yellow spot; stamens half as long as segs. May, June. S. Africa. 1759. (B.M. 582.) var. **ventrico'sus,** *fl.* purple-rose with purple central spots, less upright and with shorter tube. (B.M. 591 as *G. carneus.*) Has been crossed with *C. cardinalis.*

**G. deb'ilis.** Corm flat-round. Stem slender, weak, about 16 in. long. *l.* usually 3, sheath bluish, tip rigid. *fl.* 1 to 3, white or whitish; tube almost straight, widened upwards; segs. oblong, blunt, with a blood-red spot at base of lower segs. April, May. S. Africa. 1820. (B.M. 2585.)

**G. dracoceph'alus.** Stem stout, terete, 16 to 18 in. h. *l.* pale green, 6 to 12 in. long, 1 to 1½ in. wide. *fl.* yellowish with close, dull red-purple lines, about 2 in. long and 2 in. across; lower segs. bright green, spotted purple; spikes erect, 5- to 7-fld. August. Natal. 1871. (B.M. 5884.)

**G. du'bius.** A synonym of *G. segetum.*

**G. Eck'lonii.** Corm large, globose. Stem 1½ to 3 ft. h., robust. *l.* 4 to 6, ensiform; lower 12 in. long, nerves thick. *fl.* white, minutely closely spotted red, 6 to 12 in a loose spike; tube long, bent; upper segs. ovate to oblong, about 1 in. long, 3 lower smaller, 2 with a yellow central spot. Autumn. S. Africa. 1862. (B.M. 6335.) **A →**

**G. floribun'dus.** Corm globose, of medium size, tunic thin. Stem about 18 in. h. *l.* broad, strongly nerved. *fl.* 4 to 12 in a loose spike, almost upright, large, white; tube slightly bent; segs. spatulate-obovate, blunt, mucronate, striped purple in middle, sometimes weakly crisped; stamens about half as long as segs. May. S. Africa. 1788. (B.M. 610.) Plants in gardens under this name are frequently hybrids (*G. cardinalis* × *G. oppositiflorus*).

**G. × gandaven'sis** (*G. cardinalis* × *G. psittacinus,* or, according to Herbert, *G. oppositiflorus* × *G. psittacinus*). *fl.* bright rich crimson with yellow markings; upper segs. curving forward. Late summer. Of garden origin. 1844. *See* **G. × brenchleyensis, G. × Childsii, G. × citrinus.** Crossed with *G. floribundus* this gave *G. × Wilmoreanus.*

**G. grac'ilis.** Corm globose. Stem very slender, weak, about 2 ft. long. *l.* usually 3, almost cylindrical, stiff. *fl.* 2 to 6 in a loose, 1-sided spike, bright blue with a curved tube and very shortly pointed to blunt segs., the lower narrow with many pale spots at base. April, May. S. Africa. 1800. (B.M. 562.)

**G. gran'dis.** Corm usually small. *l.* usually flat. *fl.* 2 to 6, white with a purple middle stripe or purple-brown stripes and spots, so numerous that segs. appear purple. May, June. S. Africa, naturalized in Spain. 1749. (B.M. 1042 as *G. versicolor.*) Extremely variable in fl.-colour, and size, height, and l.-width. Related to *G. tristis,* and sometimes regarded as a variety of that species.

**G. hasta'tus.** A synonym of **G. vomerculus.**

**G. hirsu'tus.** Corm globose, of medium size. Stem robust, 12 to 18 in. h. *l.* 4 or 5, strongly nerved, shortly hairy on sheath. *fl.* 3 to 6, in a very loose, 1-sided spike. *fl.* rose-red; tube curved; segs. obovate, mucronate, spotted white, or lower white with pale-red stripes; stamens over half as long as segs. April to June. S. Africa. 1795. (B.M. 574 as var. *roseus.*) Related to *G. blandus.*

**G. illyr'icus.** Corm globose, large. Stem 12 to 20 in. h. *l.* 2 or 3, rather narrow, all acute. *fl.* 3 to 6, in a very loose, 1-sided spike, rather large, bright purple; tube weakly curved; segs. oblong-rhomboid, blunt, somewhat mucronate, upper wider and larger than lower; anthers shorter than filaments. May. Mediterranean region, England. (E.B. 1493.) var. **Reu'teri** is a more slender race in Spain and Portugal.

**G. imbrica'tus.** Corm globose or ovate, nearly 1 in. thick. Stem 1 to 2 ft. h. *l.* usually 2 or 3, linear, loosely veined, up to ½ in. wide, lower usually blunt. *fl.* 4 to 10 in a dense, 1-sided spike, dark purple; tube decidedly bent; segs. nearly equal, obovate, narrowed to base; filaments longer than anthers. June, July. E. Europe. 1820. (R.I.F.G. 9, 350.) Somewhat variable in size, l.-width, and infl. var. **crispiflo'rus,** *fl.* smaller with margin of segs. crisped. S. Russia. SYN. *G. crispiflorus*; **galicien'sis,** plant smaller, in all parts, *l.* about ⅓ in. wide, *fl.* 3 or 4, more erect, small, tube less curved. Galicia, Siebenburg.

**G. Kirk'ii.** 3 ft. h. Stem terete. *l.* 5 or 6, linear, glabrous, firm, strongly veined, slightly glaucous, 12 to 18 in. long, ⅓ to ½ in. wide. *fl.* pale pink without spots; tube ½ in. long; segs. 1 in. long, cuspidate; spike loose, 6 to 12 in. long. E. Africa. 1890.

**G. Kotschya'nus.** Dwarf. *l.* 3, linear, 6 to 8 in. long. *fl.* light violet, about 1½ in. long; segs. nearly regular, lower rather paler with a dark, median stripe; scape loosely few-fld., 1 to 2 ft. long. Afghanistan, Persia. 1886. (B.M. 6897.)

**G. lacca'tus.** Corm globose. Stem weak, up to 18 in. long. *l.* usually 3, sheath long, hairy, blade ciliate. *fl.* 2 to 4, in a loose, 1-sided spike, bright red to lilac; tube curved, widened upwards; segs. obovate, blunt, upper narrowed at base, lower narrower, spotted with pale spots at base. April, May. SW. Africa. (B.M. 823 as *G. hirsutus villosiusculus.*)

**G. Leicht'linii.** 2 ft. h. *l.* 4, bright green, 12 in. long. *fl.* bright red, in a dense, 1-sided spike; tube curved, 1¼ in. long; upper segs. connivent, lower 3 much smaller, red at tip, yellow towards base. S. Africa. 1889.

**G. × Lemoin'ei** ((*G. cardinalis* × *G. psittacinus*) × *G. purpureo-auratus*). *fl.* bright yellow or red with large purple-brown markings at base of the 3 flat lower segs. Raised by Messrs. Lemoine. Crossed with *G. Saundersii*, the race *G.* × *nanceanus* (q.v.) resulted.

**G. Ludwig'ii calva'tus.** A synonym of *G. sericeo-villosus calvatus.*

**G. × massilien'sis** (*G.* × *gandavensis* × *G. psittacinus*). A race of garden varieties, introduced 1894.

**G. Masonior'um.** Related to *G. Quartinianus. l.* about 24 in. long, over ⅓ in. wide, narrowed to a long point, hairy, midrib prominent. *fl.* in a rather loose glabrous spike about 1 ft. long; cream, pale yellow in throat, greenish in tube; tube narrowly funnel-shaped, ¾ in. long, curved, lobes about 1¼ in. long, 5 upper nearly equal, lower narrower; anthers cream; spathes green, outer about 1⅜ in. long, inner somewhat shorter. Spring. Tembuland. 1913. (B.M. 8548.)

**G. Mel'leri.*** Corm about ¾ in. across. *l.* few, linear, 12 in. long, ⅓ in. wide, glabrous. *fl.* on a slender, rigid scape about 2 ft. long; red; tube about ⅝ in. long, narrowly funnel-shaped, slightly curved; lobes oblong-wedge-shaped, upper about 1½ in. long, lower 1 in. long, narrower than upper; spathes tinged red, outer 1½ in. long, inner ⅞ in. long. October. E. Trop. Africa. 1913. (B.M. 8626.)

**G. Mil'leri.** Related to *G. undulatus*, but usually taller and more robust, *l.* usually only 3 or 4, broader and with fewer nerves, shorter than stem. *fl.* usually only 3 or 4, larger, bright yellow with a narrow, purple middle stripe; segs. broad-oblong. April, May. S. Africa. (B.M. 632.)

**G. Morton'ius.** A variety of *G. blandus.*

**G. × nanceia'nus.** A race of hybrids between *G.* × *Lemoinei* × *G. Saundersii.*

**G. natalen'sis.** A synonym of *G. psittacinus.*

**G. nubic'ola.** *See* Introduction.

**G. ochroleu'cus.** A synonym of *G. sericeo-villosus calvatus.*

**G. oppositiflo'rus.*** 3 to 4 ft. h., often branched. *l.* at base about 4, 1 to 1½ ft. long, ¾ to 1 in. broad. *fl.* in a many- (30- to 40-)fld., dense, distichous spike, white with a violet middle stripe and a few side lines. June. Caffraria. 1892. (B.M. 7292.) A hybrid has been raised with *G. cardinalis, see* **G. ramosus.**

**G. orchidiflo'rus.** Related to *G. alatus*, upper fl.-segs. greenish with a reddish-brown middle spot, lower yellow at base with a reddish-brown margin, greenish in upper part. SW. Africa. (A.B.R. 241; B.M. 688 as *G. viperatus.*)

**G. pal'lidus.** Closely related to *G. communis* but with rose-purple fl. S. Africa. (B.M. 1575.)

**G. palus'tris.** Corm ovate, up to ⅝ in. thick, tunic pale brown. Stem slender, 12 to 20 in. h., somewhat stiff. *l.* usually not over ⅜ in. wide, nerves distant, few. *fl.* in a loose, 1-sided spike, of medium size; tube strongly curved; segs. obovate, blunt, purple-red. June, July. Mid-Italy, Balkans.

**G. Papil'io.*** Up to 6 ft. h., vigorous. *l.* 2 to 3 ft. long, narrow-ensiform, striped. *fl.* in a loose spike over 1 ft. long; tube rather short; segs. broadly obovate, blunt or slightly acute, yellow, margin violet to bright purple, somewhat bell-shaped, 3 lower with a bright blood-red spot tinged golden-yellow. Summer. S. Africa. 1866. (B.M. 5565.)

**G. primuli'nus.*** 1½ ft. long. *l.* from base 3, ensiform, strongly ribbed, lowest 1 ft. long, ¾ in. wide. *fl.* primrose-red, 4 or 5 in a loose spike; tube much curved, 1 in. long, upper much overlapping forming a hood, 1½ in. long, lower smaller. SE. Trop. Africa. 1889. (B.M. 8080.) Tender. The introduction of this species which has been largely used in hybridizing has led to an entirely new race with hooded fl. *See* note in Introduction.

**G. psittaci'nus.*** Corm large, flattish-globose. Stem up to about 3 ft. h. *l.* usually up to 4, stiff, firm, lower up to 12 ft. h. *fl.* in a 10- to 12-fld. spike, 1-sided, large; tube curved; segs. broad, obovate, blunt, bright red with a yellow middle, red-spotted, the 3 lower much narrower. Autumn. SE. Africa. (B.M. 3032; L.B.C. 1756 as *G. natalensis.*) Hybrids with *G. cardinalis, G. floribundus, G. purpureo-auratus*, and *G. Saundersii.* var. **Coop'eri,** *see* **G. Cooperi.**

**G. × pudibun'dus** (*G. blandus* × *G. cardinalis*). 2 to 3 ft. h. *fl.* rose, large, about 10 in a spike; anthers purple. Of garden origin. (S.B.F.G. s. 2, 176.)

**G. puncta'tus.** A synonym of *G. recurvus.*

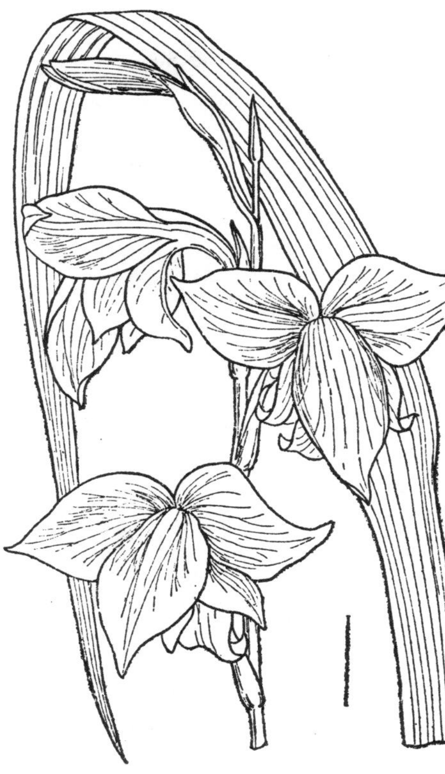

*Gladiolus primulinus*

**G. purpureo-aura'tus.*** 3 to 4 ft. h. *l.* much shorter than stem, stiff, acute. *fl.* in simple or branched spike, almost in 2 ranks; tube short, broadly bell-shaped; segs. broadly obovate, rounded with a short point, overlapping, bright yellow, on inner and the 2 lower segs. a purple spot in middle. August, September. Natal. 1872. (B.M. 5944.) One of the parents of large-fld. garden hybrids.

**G. Quartinia'nus.** 3 to 4 ft. h. *l.* linear-ensiform, 1 ft. or more long, stiff, nerves prominent. *fl.* yellow, flushed and spotted scarlet, in 6-fld. spikes. August. Trop. Africa. 1883. (B.M. 6739.) A variable plant. Enters into some of the large-fld. garden hybrids.

**G. × ramo'sus** (*G. cardinalis* × *G. oppositiflorus*). *fl.* broadly funnel-shaped, usually bright red with darker spots at base of 3 lower segs., generally earlier than *G.* × *gandavensis.* Often known in gardens as *G. floribundus.* Of garden origin. 1839.

**G. recur'vus.*** Corm tunic white, mottled purplish-brown. Stem 1 to 3 ft. h., slender, erect. *l.* 3, outer as long as stem. *fl.* 2 to 6, yellow, thickly dotted blue, eventually blue, violet-scented; tube long, strongly curved. April, May. 1758. (B.M. 578.) Syn. *G. punctatus.* Has been crossed with *G. blandus* and *G. tristis.*

**G. Saun'dersii.*** About 3 ft. h. *l.* 2 to 3 ft. long, ½ to ¾ in. wide, gradually pointed, stiff, strongly nerved. *fl.* 6 to 12 in a loose, rather irregular spike, bright carmine-rose, 3 to 3½ in. across; tube bent; segs. oblong-obovate, mucronate, uppermost straight, upper laterals rather reflexed, 3 lower connivent, white with small red dots below middle; anthers yellow. Autumn. S. Africa. 1870. (B.M. 5873.) Has been crossed with **G. × gandavensis** in German gardens.

**G. seg'etum.** Corm globose or rarely ovate, about 1 in. thick. Stem about 2 ft. h., stout. *l.* about ½ in. wide, tapering to a point, nerves few, firm. *fl.* in 2 rows, many. in a rather loose, rather 1-sided spike, of moderate size, rosy-purple; tube short, little curved; upper segs. broad and long, separate from lateral, lower with a long white spot. April, May. S. Europe. 1596. (B.M. 719.) Syn. *G. dubius.*

**G. sericeo-villo'sus.** Up to about 3 ft. h., stout, thickly hairy, *l.* up to over 12 in. long, striped. *fl.* somewhat bell-shaped, greenish-yellow, tinged pale yellowish-brown, in many-fld. spikes with shaggy spathes; segs. about equal, ovate. Late summer. S. Africa. 1864. (B.M. 5427.) var. **calva'tus,** stem and spathes smooth, upper and lower segs. rather unequal. (B.M. 6291 as *G. ochroleucus.*) Syn. *G. Ludwigii calvatus.*

**G. Stanford'iae.** Corm flattish-round, about ½ in. across. *l.* about 8, about 4 basal, linear-lanceolate, longest up to 2 ft. long, about ⅛ in. wide, glabrous, gradually acute. *Spike* unbranched, about 12-fld. *fl.* about 2 in. long, delicate pink on white; lower segs. with a yellowish-white area, lower lateral segs. shorter than mid-lobe; tube short; upper seg. not hooded, somewhat acute. S. Africa. 1936. (B.M. 9522; n.s. 357. f. symmetranthus.)

**G. trichonemifo'lius.** Corm globose. Stem very weak and slender, about 16 in. long. *l.* usually 3, almost cylindrical, stiff. *fl.* 1 to 3, in a very loose spike, bright yellow; tube scarcely curved; segs. oblong with a rather slender point, the 3 lower with a purple spot or lines at base. May. S. Africa. 1810. (B.M. 1483.)

**G. tris'tis.** Corm globose, of medium size with strong tunic. Stem about 18 in. h. *l.* 3, more or less cylindrical, strongly 3- to 5-ribbed. *fl.* 3 or 4, 2 to 3 in. long, in a very loose, strongly 1-sided spike, fragrant, yellowish-white, outer usually tinged red; tube rather long, curved; segs. oblong-lanceolate, almost equal, bent. July. Natal. 1745. (B.M. 272.) The amount of spotting varies. var. **con'color,** *fl.* wholly whitish or usually pale yellow. *See* **G. grandis** which is nearly related. Hybrids between this and *G. blandus, G. cardinalis, G. primulinus,* and *G. recurvus* occur, mostly of the Nanus type.

**G. undula'tus.** Corm of middle size. Stem about 1 ft. long. *l.* usually 4 or 5, rather wide, about as long as stem. *fl.* 4 to 7, in a rather loose, zigzag spike, often much bent, bright or milky-yellow with broad middle stripe on the oblong-spatulate segs., their margin somewhat crisped; tube nearly straight; stamens about half as long as segs.; anthers purple. S. Africa. 1790? (B.M. 647.)

**G. × Victoria'lis** (*G. byzantinus* × *G. cardinalis*). *fl.* somewhat fragrant, bright pale crimson, in a spike (sometimes forked) about 12 in. long. Of garden origin. 1893.

**G. vin'ulus.** A synonym of *G. vittatus.*

**G. vitta'tus.** Corm globose. Stem 12 t 15 in. h. *l.* ensiform, about ⅜ in. wide. *fl.* 3 to 6 in a loose spike, pink or whitish; tube slightly curved; segs. oblong, obtuse, margins more or less crisped, lower or all with a red or lilac middle stripe; stamens half as long as segs., anthers purple. April, May. SW. Africa. 1760. (B.M. 538 as *G. undulatus* var.) SYN. *G. vinulus.*

**G. vomer'culus.** Much like *G. angustus* but l.-sheath spotted purple. *fl.* usually only 2 or 3, lilac to white, with short tube, the 2 inner lower segs. with red and blue arrow-shaped spots. April, May. S. Africa. 1812. (B.M. 1564 as *G. hastatus.*)

**G. watsonioi'des.** A synonym of *Homoglossum watsonioides.*

**G. Watson'ius.** A synonym of *Homoglossum revolutum.*

A →

**GLADWYN.** *See* **Iris foetidissima.**

**GLAND.** An apparatus secreting some substance such as oil, chalk, sugar; it may consist of a single cell, often terminating a hair, or may be more complex as in the chalk-glands of many Saxifrages or in nectaries, or may be internal, like those showing as pellucid dots in many leaves, such as those of Rutaceae.

**GLANDULAR.** Covered with hairs having glands at their tips.

***glandulo'sus -a -um,*** bearing glands.

***glareo'sus -a -um,*** of gravelly places.

**GLASS.** The quality and thickness of Glass are important considerations in the construction of houses for horticultural purposes. Since the value of light for plants has been more fully recognized, the old system of very small panes has been entirely superseded. Various sorts of Glass have been tried at different times, but none is found to equal good sheets of not less than 21 oz. or 24 oz. to the square foot. It is not advisable to have the panes more than 3 ft. long for any plant structure, on account of the expense of repairs should breakage occur. Opaque corrugated Sheet-glass, and rough or unpolished Plate-glass have each been tried for plant houses, but have been found unsuitable on account of admitting insufficient light in dull weather, and also as not affording the requisite shade for tender plants in summer without additional covering being applied. Green-tinted Glass is sometimes used where a subdued light is desirable, such as a house devoted to ferns, but even this does not prevent the necessity of giving other shade in addition on bright summer days. Glass specially prepared to pass the violet rays has given no definite advantage and is apt soon to fail in this respect unless kept scrupulously clean. Glass weighing only 16 oz. to the square foot should not be used for glazing any framework that is exposed to hail or snow storms and other rough weather. Curvilinear roofs require specially bent Glass for certain parts, which, however, costs nearly double the price of the ordinary kind, and consequently renders repairs to such structures considerably more expensive. If Glass is of bad quality, e.g. of uneven thickness, or contains bubbles, injury by burning of the tender foliage of plants beneath is almost certain. This is caused by the defects in the Glass acting as lenses, and so resulting in uneven distribution of the heat rays.

**GLASS CASES** may range from the small bell-glass, or hand-glass of rectangular shape, to the long Cases covering many feet or yards of wall, under which are planted some of the choicer kinds of hardy fruits, such as Peaches, Nectarines, Cherries, Pears, &c. Small bell-glasses are employed for growing delicate plants that require protection from rapid loss of water, both in hot-houses and outside. Large Cases are used for filmy Ferns, and the Wardian Case is useful for plants in rooms, as well as for its original purpose of protecting delicate, exotic plants during transport. Whether such Cases are in hot-houses or in rooms, fresh air should be admitted daily to sweeten the internal atmosphere, and to allow moisture to escape. The glass may need wiping to remove superfluous water and avoid drip and a removable glass cap is often advantageous in small hand-glasses used in propagation. Glass Cases employed for fruit-growing against walls are not heated artificially, but much may be done by closing the Case early with a good sun heat—bottling the natural heat, as it were. By means of Glass Cases, excellent crops of fruit are annually obtained from walls that would otherwise fail through climatic conditions.

**GLASSHOUSE.** A glass or mainly glass structure large enough for a man to work in, and used for growing plants. The term includes Conservatory, and cold, cool, and heated structures. *See* **Greenhouse.**

**GLASSHOUSE LEAF-HOPPER,** *Erythroneura pallidifrons,* is responsible for the irregular whitish or bleached and mottled areas seen on the upper surface of attacked leaves of many glasshouse plants, especially Fuchsia, Geranium, Heliotrope, forced Mint, Primulas, Tomato, and Verbena. The adult hoppers are slender, delicate, pale-yellowish insects, about ⅛ in. long, with pale, iridescent wings extending beyond the tip of the body, and with dark spots on the head, thorax, and wings. The minute eggs are inserted into the veins on the underside of the leaves. The nymphs are small, white, and almost transparent, at first somewhat sluggish, but soon become active running over the leaves and moving from plant to plant. They feed on the lower surface pushing their sucking mouthparts deeply into the tissues and, by abstracting the sap, give rise to the typical mottled areas on the upper leaf-surface. They pass through 5 stages, the wing-buds becoming visible during the third nymphal stage. The moult-skins are white and persist on the leaves, anchored by the mouth stylets, and this has given the name of 'Ghost Fly or Insect' to this pest. Breeding is continuous under glasshouse conditions, and all stages occur on the plants at the same time.

Clean cultivation and weed destruction in and around glasshouses is advisable as the pest persists on many wild hosts, e.g. Chickweed. Handcrushing the nymphs on the leaves is an effective measure of dealing with light attacks. Dusting the foliage with nicotine dust gives the best control for this pest is somewhat tolerant of fumigants, including hydrocyanic acid gas, nicotine, and tetrachlorethane.

G. F. W.

**GLASSINESS.** *See* **Water Core** of Apples.

**GLASSWORT.** *See* **Salicornia.**

*glastifo'lius -a -um,* having leaves like woad (Isatis), from an old name of woad.

**GLASTONBURY THORN.** *See* **Crataegus mono-gyna praecox.**

*glauces'cens,* somewhat blue- or sea-green.

**GLAUCID'IUM** (derivation?). FAM. *Podophyllaceae.* A genus on a single species of perennial herb, native of Japan, with an unbranched herbaceous stem with 2 or 3 leaves and a large solitary terminal flower. Sepals 4, petaloid; petals none; stamens very numerous; carpels 2, united in the lower one-third. Fruit dry, about 2 in. across, compressed, dehiscing on 3 outer edges, seeds many, about ½ in. long, broadly winged. This beautiful herbaceous perennial needs soil of woodland type, and a half-shady position. It would probably succeed in cool positions in the open but being still rare is usually grown in the cold frame or the alpine house.

*Glaucidium palmatum*

**G. palma'tum.*** 4 to 15 in. h. from a short, thick rhizome. *l.* usually 2, from upper part of stem, palmately 5- to 7-lobed, 4 to 12 in. wide, somewhat hairy when young; base cordate; lobes more or less rhomboid-ovate, middle ones 3-fid at apex, slender-pointed, sharply toothed. *fl.* 1, rarely 2, pale mauve, the petaloid sep. up to 2 in. long, 1½ in. wide. April, May. Japan. (B.M. 9432.)

**GLAUC'IUM** (*glaukos,* greyish-green, from the colour of the leaves). FAM. *Papaveraceae.* A genus of perhaps 12 species of glaucous annual, biennial, or perennial herbs, mostly natives of the Mediterranean region, one on sandy sea-coasts of Britain. Leaves lobed or dissected. Flowers large, yellow or crimson, solitary. Fruit a long, many-seeded, siliqua-like capsule. Glauciums are easily

grown in any good garden soil and make better plants there than in the sandy soil of the sea-shore. Seeds should be sown in April or May in the open ground and the seedlings should be moved to their flowering quarters as soon as large enough to handle.

**G. cornicula'tum.** Annual. About 9 in. h. *l.* oblong, pinnatifid, hairy. *fl.* crimson with a black spot at base of each pet. June. Europe. (E.B. 65.) SYN. *G. phoeniceum, G. rubrum.*

**G. fla'vum.*** Horned Poppy, see Poppy. Sometimes perennial. Glaucous. 1 to 2 ft. h. or more. *Radical l.* many, stalked, pinnatifid, hairy. *fl.* bright yellow, large. June to August. *Pod* nearly 1 ft. long. Europe, including Britain. N. Africa, W. Asia. (E.B. 66 as *G. luteum.*) var. **tric'olor,** *fl.* particoloured.

**G. leiocar'pum.** Velvety perennial. *l.* with wavy, toothed margin, much-divided; upper *l.* lobed. *fl.* yellow, rather small; sep. papillose. Mediterranean region.

**G. lu'teum.** A synonym of *G. flavum.*

**G. phoenic'eum.** A synonym of *G. corniculatum.*

**G. ru'brum.** A synonym of *G. corniculatum.*

**G. squamig'erum.** *Radical l.* lyrate, pinnatifid; *stem-l.* few, minute, sessile. *fl.* yellow, 1½ in. across. June. *Pod* scaly. Altai Mts. (G.F. 972.)

*glau'cus -a -um,* (*glauci-* or *glauco-* in compound words), grey with waxy bloom (*glaucifolius, glaucophyllus,* having grey or bluish-green leaves).

*Glaziov'ii,* in honour of A. F. M. Glaziou, 1828–1906, French Director of the Imperial Gardens, Rio de Janeiro, in latter half of 19th century.

**GLECHO'MA.** Included in **Nepeta.**

**GLEDITS'CHIA** (in honour of J. Gottlieb Gleditsch, once director of Berlin Botanical Garden, d. 1786). FAM. *Leguminosae.* A genus of about 12 species of trees mostly armed with simple or branched spines which are much the larger on young trees. Leaves alternate, pinnate or 2-pinnate; leaflets up to 32 on a single leaf. Flowers uni-sexual or bisexual, mostly green and without beauty; calyx lobes and petals 3 to 5, petals of nearly equal size and shape, stamens 6 to 10. Pod thin, flattened, 1- to many-seeded. In some of the species the pods are lined inside with a sweetish pulp in which the seeds are imbedded and to which the genus owes its popular name of 'Honey locust'.

Ornamental trees with graceful foliage which often turns a fine yellow in autumn. Easily grown in loamy soil and withstanding drought well. Propagated by seeds. Some species are rather tender, but *G. caspica,* *G. japonica,* and *G. triacanthos* are perfectly hardy.

**G. aquat'ica.** Water Locust. Tree up to 60 ft., much smaller in Britain, spines about 4 in. long, branched. *l.* up to 8 in. long, pinnate or 2-pinnate; lflets. 12 to 14, narrowly ovate-oblong, 1 to 1½ in. long, margins wavy, slightly ciliate, glossy and glabrous except on the fl.-stalks. *fl.* in racemes 3 or 4 in. long. *Pod* 1⅔ in. long, 1 in. wide, seeds usually solitary. SE. United States. 1723. (S.S. 3, 127–8.) SYN. *G. monosperma.*

**G. cas'pica.** Tree 30 to 40 ft., trunk armed with spines 6 in. or more long. *l.* 6 to 10 in. long, simply or doubly pinnate; lflets. up to 20, ovate or oval, 1 to 2 in. long, bristle-tipped, shining green and glabrous except on the midrib and l.-stalk. *fl.* green, densely packed in racemes 2 to 4 in. long. *Pod* 8 in. long, 1¼ in. wide, curved. N. Persia. 1822.

**G. hor'rida.** A synonym of *G. japonica* and *G. sinensis.*

**G. japon'ica.** Tree 60 to 70 ft., trunk armed with branched spines, shoots purplish-brown, glabrous. *l.* 8 to 12 in. long, simply or doubly pinnate; lflets. 14 to 24, ovate to lanceolate, ¾ to 1½ in. long. *Pod* 10 to 12 in. long, twisted. Japan. 1894. (B.T.S. 3, 178.) SYN. *G. horrida.*

**G. macracan'tha.** Tree 40 to 50 ft. *l.* pinnate; lflets. 6 to 12 ovate-oblong or obovate, largest 2 to 3 in. long, half as wide, glabrous except on midrib and l.-stalk. *fl.* in downy racemes. *Pod* 6 to 12 in. long. China. 1800.

**G. monosper'ma.** A synonym of *G. aquatica.*

**G. sinen'sis.** Tree up to 45 ft., armed with branched spines. *l.* pinnate, 5 to 8 in. long; lflets. 8 to 16, ovate or ovate-lanceolate obliquely tapered at base, 1 to 3 in. long, downy on midrib above. *fl.* in downy racemes. *Pod* 5 to 10 in. long, dark purplish-brown, scarcely curved. China. 1774. SYN. *G. horrida.*

**G. × texa′na** (*G. aquatica* × *G. triacanthos*). Tree 100 to 120 ft., spines slender, branched. *l.* 6 to 7 in. long; lflets. 12 to 22, ½ to 1 in. long, oblong-ovate, dark green and glossy; midrib and stalks downy. *Male fl.* in racemes 3 to 4 in. long. *Pods* 4 to 5 in. long, 1 in. wide, pointed not curved, with no pulp. Texas. 1900. (S.S. 13, 627.)

**G. triacan′thos.\*** Honey Locust. Tree up to 140 ft., half as h. in Britain, usually with simple or branched spines 3 to 12 in. long (some as much as 7-branched). *l.* pinnate or 2-pinnate, 4 to 8 in. long; lflets. 20 to 32, oblong-lanceolate, ½ to 1½ in. long. *fl.* green; males in downy racemes 2 in. long, females few. July. *Pods* up to 12 or 18 in. long, scimitar-shaped, twisted, remaining on tree through winter. N. America. 1700. (S.S. 3, 125–6.) var. **Bujot′ii**, elegant, branches pendulous, *lflets.* narrow; **iner′mis**, unarmed; **na′na**, bush or small sturdy tree.

*Glehn′ii*, in honour of Peter von Glehn, 1835–76, Conservator, Botanical Garden, Leningrad. F. Schmidt's assistant on the Eastern Asiatic expedition, 1861.

**GLEICHE′NIA** (in honour of W. F. Gleichen, 1717–83, a German botanist). FAM. *Gleicheniaceae*. A genus of about 120 species widely dispersed throughout the world mainly in its warmer parts. The caudex is mostly creeping, fronds rarely unbranched, generally dichotomously divided; pinnae deeply pinnatifid, with the segments small and concave. Sori of few (usually 2 to 4) sessile sporangia on a lower exterior veinlet. For general cultivation, see **Ferns**.

For most species cool treatment is the most suitable, and with very few exceptions they fare best in a house where during the winter the temperature falls as low as 45° F. Most, if not all, the failures experienced in the early attempts at cultivating these plants may be traced to growing them in too much heat—treatment which causes them to make stunted growths, generally full of thrips and scale. The house should at most be what is usually called intermediate; it should also be light and well ventilated. Bright light is indispensable in growing Gleichenias; they will even benefit by a little sunshine during morning and afternoon. Light, in fact, is of such importance that if a plant in perfect health be placed under, say, Tree Ferns, or under any other plant that will permanently shade it, it will soon go back, and show by its spindly growth that it does not at all appreciate the presence of neighbours taller than itself. Success cannot reasonably be expected unless these plants are in a perfect state of cleanliness.

The species have in the section *Eugleichenia* rhizomes of a particularly slender and naturally hard nature. They are very shallow rooters, and when not planted out should be grown in rough, sandy peat, in pans. Their rootlets being short and exceedingly brittle, it is necessary that the rhizomes from which they are produced should receive special attention at the hands of the cultivator; and as they have a particular objection to being buried underground, they must be carefully kept on the surface by being pegged on the potting material, which must be made firm, if not altogether hard. It is therefore indispensable that the plants should have abundance of pot-room, so as to give the rhizomes every facility for spreading. The pans should be well drained, as stagnant moisture at the roots is injurious.

Not only do the plants belonging to the *Mertensia* section differ from the others by their general appearance, but they have rhizomes of a totally different nature, being fleshy, brittle, much stouter, and usually root deeply into the ground of their own accord. For these, a mixture of 2 parts fibrous peat, 1 part fibrous loam, and 1 part of sand is preferable to the sandy peat recommended for the first-named section. They require a quantity of water at the roots, though stagnant moisture must carefully be avoided. Plants of both sections are better for being at all times kept dry over-head. One of the most distinct species in the *Mertensia* section is *G. pubescens*, which has a peculiar cobwebby underside to its handsome frond.

One of the principal causes of the scarcity of Gleiche-nias is their slow propagation, as, with the exception of seedlings of *G. circinnata semivestita* and *G. c. speluncae* of commerce, and of *G. rupestris*, at various times raised by Messrs. J. Veitch, increase has been limited to the division of clumps, an operation very tedious, extremely hazardous, and seldom attended with complete success. We have never heard of seedlings of plants belonging to the *Mertensia* section being raised in this country, and that, together with the fact that the importations direct from their various habitats seldom give entire satisfaction, is probably the reason why they are so rare.

**G. acutifo′lia.** A synonym of *G. quadripartita*.

**G. alpi′na.** Related to *G. dicarpa* but generally smaller and more compact, rachis and young shoots with rusty woolly scales. SYN. (H.S. 1, 2 as *G. hecistophylla*.)

**G. bifurca′ta.** A synonym of *G. laevigata*.

**G. circinna′ta.\*** *Fronds*, lobes of pinnae ovate or sub-rotund, more or less glaucous beneath, margins slightly recurved; branches and rachis glabrous, or more or less pubescent. *Capsules* 3 or 4, superficial. Australia, New Zealand, Malacca. Greenhouse. (F.B. I, 177.) SYN. *G. microphylla*. var. **Mendel′li**, has perfectly flat lobes, silvery beneath, and is much more robust; **semivesti′ta** has rachises and young fronds very palaeaceo-pubescent. (H.S. 1, 2); **spelun′cae** has numerous pendent fronds with segs. curved inwards; silvery-glaucous beneath, pale green above. Australia. (L.F. 8, 49.)

**G. cryptocar′pa.** *Fronds* proliferous, leathery, deep yellow or yellow-brown when dry; branches dichotomously flabelliform; pinnae broad-lanceolate, sub-erect, and compact, 4 to 5 in. long, 1 in. broad, pectinate-pinnatifid; segs. narrow-linear, strongly veined, margins revolute, concealing the sori. *Capsules* 1 to 4 in a sorus. Chile, Falkland Is. 1865. (H.S. 1, 6.) Greenhouse.

**G. Cunningham′ii.** *Fronds* often proliferous, leathery; branches dichotomously flabelliform, glaucous beneath, hairy; pinnae linear-lanceolate, acuminate, 4 to 6 in. long, ½ to 1 in. broad; segs. linear, acute. *Capsules* 2 to 4 in a sorus. New Zealand. (H.S. 1, 6B.) Greenhouse.

**G. dicar′pa.\*** *Fronds*, lobes of pinnae round, sub-hemispherical, very arching. *Capsules* 2, concealed within almost slipper-shaped lobes, and mixed with rusty paleaceous hairs, which often extend to rachis. Australia. (H.S.1, 1c; R.H. 1861, 210.) Variable. Greenhouse. var. **longipinna′ta**, *fronds* longer than in type, growth exceedingly graceful.

**G. dichot′oma.** A synonym of *G. linearis*.

**G. excel′sa.** A synonym of *G. glauca*.

**G. ferrugin′ea.** A synonym of *G. linearis*.

**G. flabella′ta.** *Fronds* very proliferous; branches dichotomously flabelliform; pinnae ascending, about 6 in. long, 1 to 2 in. broad, lanceolate; segs. linear. Australia, New Zealand. 1823. (L.F. 8, 50.) Greenhouse.

**G. flagellar′is.** A synonym of *G. laevigata*.

**G. furca′ta.** A synonym of *G. pubescens*.

**G. glau′ca.\*** *sti.* stout, forked; branches very long; pinnae numerous, 4 to 8 in. long, 1 to 2 in. broad, deeply pinnatifid; segs. linear, acuminate, or oblong. China, Japan. SYN. *G. Bancroftii*, *G. excelsa*, *G. longissima*. (H.S. 1, 3B.)

**G. hecistophyl′la.** A synonym of *G. alpina*.

**G. Hermann′ii.** A synonym of *G. linearis*.

**G. laeviga′ta.\*** *Fronds*, branches glabrous, repeatedly dichotomous, copiously foliaceous, glabrous, often glaucous beneath, somewhat leathery; pinnae erecto-patent or divaricating, extremely variable, broad or narrow, or linear-lanceolate, 5 in. to 1 ft. or more long; segs. ½ to 2 in. or more long, linear, sometimes rusty-tomentose at base beneath. *Capsules* 2 to 4. Mauritius and Bourbon, Madagascar; abundant in Java and Malay Is. SYN. *G. bifurcata*, *G. bracteata*, *G. flagellaris*. Stove.

**G. linea′ris.\*** *sti.* zigzag, repeatedly 2- or 3-chotomous, ultimate branches bearing a pair of forked pinnae, about 8 in. long and 2 in. wide; segs. never decurrent, glaucous beneath. Tropics. (B.C.F. 2, 221; L.F. 8, 51.) SYN. *G. dichotoma*, *G. ferruginea*, *G. Hermannii*, *G. rufinervis*. Stove.

**G. longis′sima.** A synonym of *G. glauca*.

**G. Matthew′sii.** A synonym of *G. pubescens*.

**G. Mendel′li.** A form of *G. circinnata*.

**G. microphyl′la.** A synonym of *G. circinnata*.

**G. pectina′ta.\*** *sti.* zigzag, branched; branches bearing 1 to 3 pairs of forked divaricating pinnae; segs. never decurrent, frequently glaucous beneath. *Sori* of 8 to 10 capsules. Trop. America. 1824. Stove.

**G. pubes′cens.\*** *sti.* and rachises often woolly; branches of frond repeatedly dichotomous, leafy; pinnae 5 in. to 2 ft. long, 1 in. broad, pectinate-pinnatifid clothed with cobwebby pubescence; segs. spreading, linear. *Capsules* 2 to 5. Trop. America. (B.C.F. 2, 227; H.S. 1, 7.) SYN. *G. furcata*, *G. longipinnata*, *G. Matthewsii*, *G. tomentosa*. These are often kept as distinct species. Stove.

**G. quadriparti'ta.** *Fronds* coriaceous, black when dry, rufous-brown beneath, not proliferous, only once-forked; each branch dichotomously flabelliform; pinnae lanceolate, acuminate, falcately curved, pectinate-pinnatifid, 4 to 6 in. long, 1 to 1½ in. broad; lobes narrow-linear, sub-falcate, sharply acute, margins a little recurved. *Capsules* 1 to 3 in a sorus. Antarctic America. (H.S. 1, 8 as *G. acutifolia*.) Greenhouse.

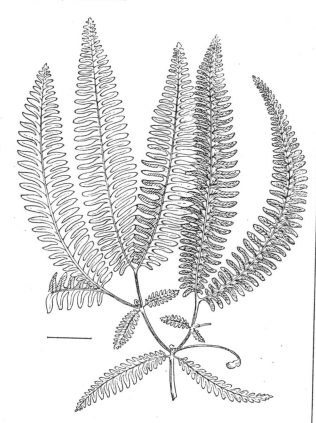

*Gleichenia linearis* (p. 898)

**G. rufiner'vis.** A synonym of *G. linearis*.

**G. rupes'tris.*** *Fronds* 2 to 6 ft. long; lobes of pinnae rounded or obtusely sub-quadrangular, leathery; margins thickened and re-curved, sub-glaucous beneath. *Sori* of 3 or 4 capsules, superficial. Australia. 1860. (H.S. 1, 1; L.F. 8, 53.) Greenhouse. Perhaps only a variety of *G. circinnata*. var. **glauces'cens**, *sti.* reddish-purple, *fronds* glaucous, much thicker than in type.

**G. semivesti'ta.** A variety of *G. circinnata*.

**G. spelun'cae.** A variety of *G. circinnata*.

**GLEICHENIA'CEAE.** A family of about 120 species of ferns 1 of which is placed in the genus Stromato-pteris, the remainder in Gleichenia. Mostly tropical or sub-tropical but a few in the temperate parts of the S. Hemisphere. The principal characteristics of these small ferns are the creeping rhizomes, dichotomously branched leaves, and the naked sori of 2 to 8 sessile sporangia each with a complete transverse annulus and splitting lengthwise. *See* **Gleichenia.**

**A→**

**glisch'rus** -a -um, sticky, clammy.

**globa'tus** -a -um, collected into a ball.

**GLOB'BA** (*Galoba*, native name in Amboina). Fam. *Zingiberaceae*. A genus of about 75 species of perennial herbs, natives of SE. Asia, with slender rhizomes and fibrous roots, related to Mantisia but with the lateral staminodes elliptic and flowers white, rose, or yellow, not purple or violet. Rather small plants for the family with almost sessile, lanceolate or oblong, slender-pointed leaves, and terminal panicles of flowers with slender corolla tubes and staminodes similar to the petals. Glob-bas are easily grown in loam and peat in the moist stove and increased by division as new growth begins.

**G. albo-bractea'ta.** Slender, about 2½ ft. h. *l.* oblong or oblong-lanceolate, 4 to 5 in. long, softly downy beneath. *fl.* in a loose panicle; bracts white, 1 to 2½ in. long; cal. white; cor. yellow. Sumatra. 1882.

**G. atrosanguin'ea.** Slender, arching, 1½ to 3 ft. h. *l.* oblong-lanceolate, slender-pointed, 6 to 8 in. long, deep green, glabrous above, more or less downy beneath, margin yellowish. *Panicle* about 2½ in. long; bracts red; cor. yellow, tube about 1 in. long. Borneo. 1881. (B.M. 6626.) Continuous flowering.

**G. Schomburgk'ii.** Erect, about 20 in. h. *l.* oblong-lanceolate or lanceolate, slender-pointed, about 5 in. long. *Panicle* nodding, about 3 in. long; bracts pale green, lower bearing bulbils. *fl.* 4 or 5 on each branch; cor. yellow, tube ⅔ in. long, lip yellow with red spots at base, 2-fid. August. Siam, &c. 1864. (B.M. 6298.)

**G. sessiliflo'ra.** Slender, about 18 in. h. *l.* oblong-lanceolate, slender-pointed, about 6 in. long, minutely downy beneath. *Panicle* narrowly pyramidal, about 6 in. long; lower bracts bearing bulbils. *fl.* yellow; cor. tube about ¾ in. long, lip 2-fid. August. Burma. 1807. (B.M. 1428.)

**G. Winit'ii.** Erect, up to 3 ft. h. *rhiz.* short, fleshy. *Lowest l.* reduced to sheaths tightly clasping stem; sheaths up to 14 in. long, smooth, ligule oblong; stalks slender up to 4 in. long; blades oblong, basal lobes overlapping, up to 8 in. long, finely pointed, hairy on back. *fl.* in a loose, drooping glabrous, spreading panicle up to 6 in. long; upper bracts 1 to 1½ in. long, rose-purple to magenta; cor. yellow with a curved, slender tube ½ in. long. Autumn. Siam. 1925. (B.M. 9314.)

**GLOBE AMARANTH.** *See* **Gomphrena globosa.**

**GLOBE FLOWER.** *See* **Trollius.**

**GLOBE MALLOW.** *See* **Sphaeralcea.**

**GLOBE THISTLE.** *See* **Echinops.**

**globo'sus** -a- um, **globi-,** in compound words, round or spherical.

**GLOBULA'RIA** (*globulus*, a small round head, from the form of the flower-head). Fam. *Globulariaceae*. A genus of about 18 species of dwarf perennial herbs, sub-shrubs, or shrubs, natives of the Mediterranean region. Leaves radical or alternate, leathery, entire or with a few sharp teeth. Flowers usually blue or white in a rounded head with a many-leaved involucre. Globularias are plants for the rock-garden, the dwarfer species being especially valuable. They are plants for a sunny dry spot in light limy soil, and except where indicated are hardy if given these conditions. Propagation by seed or by division.

**G. Aly'pum.** Stem shrubby, up to 2 ft. h. *l.* alternate, lanceolate, 3-toothed at tip. *fl.-heads* pale blue, at ends of branches. August, September. S. Europe. 1840. (Fl. Ment. 34.) Greenhouse.

**G. bellidifo'lia.** Densely tufted, very leafy. *l.* ¼ to ⅞ in. long, scarcely 1/12 in. wide, wedge-shaped, crenulate, obtuse. *Scape* short or none, heads ⅓ to ½ in. across. *fl.* blue; lower lip of cor. usually 3-fid to one-third; cal. densely hairy. S. Europe. Syn. *G. cordifolia nana.*

**G. cordifo'lia.** Mat-forming with woody, prostrate, much-branched stems. *l.* in rosettes, obovate-wedge-shaped, emarginate, dark evergreen. *fl.-heads* blue, small, globular, terminal; peduncles about 2 in. long. June to August. Europe, W. Asia. 1633. (S.B.F.G. 34.) var. **al'ba,** *fl.* white; **na'na,** see *G. bellidifo'lia*; **ro'sea,** *fl.* rose.

**G. incanes'cens.** Sub-shrubby. *l.* sparse, glaucous; lower *l.* widely obovate-spatulate; *l.* of *fl.*-shoots small, oval or lanceolate. *fl.* violet-blue; upper lip of cor. entire or scarcely divided. Italy.

**G. majorcen'sis.** Allied to *G. vulgaris* but larger in all parts and with *l.* more or less toothed. Balearic Is. Syn. *G. vulgaris major.*

**G. na'na.** Stem creeping, woody, prostrate. About 1 in. h. *l.* radical, narrow obcordate-wedge-shaped, small, fleshy. *fl.-heads* bluish, globular, nearly ½ in. across. Summer. S. Europe. 1824.

**G. nudicau'lis.** About 6 in. h. with herbaceous stems. *l.* radical, oblong, blunt, with rounded teeth. *fl.-heads* blue, larger than in *G. cordifolia*, on naked peduncles about 6 in. long. Summer. S. Europe. 1629. Syn. *G. alpina.* Will tolerate some shade.

**G. orienta'lis.** Glabrous perennial, with tortuous, spreading, ascending branches from a woody base. *l.* 1-nerved; lower oblong or obovate spatulate, narrowed to stalk; upper narrower, sessile. *fl.-heads* blue, 5 to 7 in a loose spike on fragile, sparsely leafy shoots; involucral bracts obovate, 3-nerved. Summer. N. Syria.

**G. pyg'maea.** A garden synonym of *G. bellidifolia.*

**G. sty'gia.** Stems slender, prostrate, rooting, leafy. *l.* roundish-ovate, wedge-shaped at base, obtuse, leathery, glabrous. *fl.-heads*, like *l.*, larger than in *G. cordifolia*; scape short; involucral *l.* oblong-lanceolate, ciliate; cal. segs. lanceolate, awl-shaped, white-ciliate; cor. blue, upper lip 2-lobed, segs. narrow-lanceolate, lower 3-lobed, long-linear. June, July. Greece.

**G. trichosan'tha.** 6 to 8 in. h., somewhat glaucous, with herbaceous leafy stems. *Basal l.* spatulate, sometimes 3-toothed at apex; *stem-l.* linear, with a small abrupt point. *fl.-heads* light blue, large. Summer. Asia Minor.

**G. vulga'ris.** Blue Daisy. Stem erect, 6 to 12 in. h. *Basal l.* spatulate, emarginate or shortly 3-toothed; *stem-l.* small, lanceolate. *fl.-heads* bright blue, dense, terminal with an involucre of 9 to 12 overlapping bracts. Summer. Europe. 1640. (B.M. 2256.) var. **al'ba,** *fl.* white; **ma'jor,** *see* **G. majorcensis.**

**G. Willkomm'ii.** Glabrous, green, about 1 in. h. *l.* obovate or oblong, obtuse or emarginate, narrowed to stalk. *Scape* erect or ascending, ½ to 1 in. long; involucral *l.* ovate-lanceolate, 3-nerved; cor. blue, bell-shaped, tube exserted, bristly, funnel-shaped; upper lip short, 2-lobed to base, lower twice as long, deeply 3-partite, segs. linear. April to June. Mid and S. Europe.

**GLOBULARIA'CEAE.** A family of 3 genera with about 20 species of herbs and shrubs in the Mediterranean region as far south as Socotra and west to the Cape Verde Is. Leaves alternate, simple, without stipules. Flowers in heads with an involucre; calyx 5-parted, sometimes 2-lipped; corolla 2-lipped with overlapping lobes; stamens 4, didynamous, exserted; ovary superior, 1-celled, 1-ovuled. Fruit enclosed in the persistent calyx, dry. Globularia is the only genus of horticultural interest.

*globula'ris -is -e,* spherical.

**GLOBU'LEA.** Included in **Crassula.**

*globulif'erus -a -um,* globe-bearing.

*globuligem'ma,* having round buds.

**GLOBULIN.** A protein reserve food which forms an important part of Aleuron (q.v.). It is insoluble in water but dissolves in solutions of neutral salts such as common salt, and coagulates on boiling. It occurs in crystal-like bodies in potato tubers and is found, e.g. in Castor-oil beans and Brazil nuts.

*globulo'sus -a -um,* small and spherical.

*glochidia'tus -a -um,* having glochids.

**GLOCHIDIUM** (*pl.* **glochidia**), glochid, a short, barbed, easily detachable bristle which occurs in the areole of some Cacti, e.g. Opuntia.

**GLOEO'DES.** A genus of Fungi Imperfecti, one of which, *G. pomigera,* causes black blotches on apples and pears. *See* **Sooty Blotch.**

**GLOEOSPOR'IUM.** A genus of Fungi Imperfecti, several species of which are parasitic. *See* **Apple Diseases, Apple Rots.**

*glomera'tus -a -um,* collected into roundish heaps or heads.

**GLOMEREL'LA.** A genus of Fungi in the class Ascomycetes, some species of which cause disease in plants, e.g. *Glomerella cingulata,* causing Bitter Rot in apples and Ripe Rot in Grapes. *See* **Apple** and **Vine Diseases.**

**GLOMERULE.** A head-like cyme.

**GLONER'IA.** Included in **Psychotria.**

**GLORIO'SA** (*gloriosus,* full of glory). Fam. *Liliaceae.* Creeping or climbing Lily. A genus comprising 3 species of very ornamental bulbous plants natives of Africa and Trop. Asia, related to Sandersonia and Littonia, climbing by means of tendrils at leaf-tips. Flowers showy, on long pedicels in leaf-axils, with spreading or reflexed segments, generally undulate at margin. Propagation is effected by seeds and by offsets. Seeds are best inserted singly, in small pots, in January, using a light sandy soil, and plunging in bottom heat. Offsets should be carefully removed from old bulbs when starting them in spring, as the roots are very brittle, and are easily injured if division is attempted at other times. Good drainage is essential, and an open soil, composed of loam and peat in about equal proportions, is recommended. The bulbs should be carefully repotted in February, and then started in a temperature of about 70° F. Plenty of heat and moisture are necessary in summer; but, as the growth ripens, water should be gradually withheld. During winter, the soil must be kept quite dry, and the pots laid on their sides in a warm place. Exposure to cold, when at rest, should be avoided. *G. superba* is probably the species which will grow with the least artificial heat; indeed, it is said sometimes to be half-hardy. (*See* J.R.H.S. 69, 338.) The winter treatment applies alike to seedlings and established bulbs. Gloriosas are frequently very slow-growing and are impatient of root disturbance on account of their brittleness. The seasons of growth and complete rest in a warm place are most important.

**G. abyssin'ica.** *fl.* from upper axils; perianth segs. reflexed, not crisped, 2 to 3 in. long, ¾ to 1 in. broad; pedicels 3 to 4 in. long. *l.* oblong, acuminate, sometimes tendrilled at tip, 5 to 6 in. long, 1½ in. broad; upper alternate. Stem erect, 1½ to 2 ft. long, simple or branched. Trop. Africa. 1894.

**G. Carson'ii.** *fl.* red with yellow towards centre; segs. about 2½ in. long, ½ in. wide, margins waved. *infl.* many-fld. in a loose cyme. August. *l.* stem-clasping, 4 to 5 in. long with terminal tendril. 3 ft. h. Cent. Africa. 1904. (F. & S. 2, 355.)

**G. Leopold'ii.** *See* **G. simplex.**

**G. Plant'ii.** *See* **G. simplex.**

**G. Rothschildia'na.** *fl.* crimson, axillary, peduncles 3 to 4 in. long; segs. at first yellow at base finally ruby-red, over 3½ in. long. Summer. *l.* oblong-acuminate, 5 in. long, terminating in a tendril. (F. & S. 2, 248.) var. **citri'na** has *fl.* citron yellow and claret-purple. (G.C. 38 (1905), 211.)

**G. sim'plex.** *fl.* deep orange and yellow; perianth segs. spatulate, margins not crisped, slightly undulated. 4 ft. h. Mozambique. 1823. (B.M. 4938.) *G. Plantii* is the form with reddish-yellow fl. (F.d.S. 863 as *Methonica virescens Plantii*.) var. **grandiflo'ra** (*Methonica grandiflora,* B.M. 5216) is a Trop. African form, with much larger yellow fl. than the type. **G. Leopold'ii** is very similar but with segs. inrolled. (R.H. 1903, 548.)

**G. super'ba.\*** *fl.* deep rich orange and red; perianth segs. narrow, deeply undulate and crisped, reflexed. Summer. 6 ft. h. Trop. Asia, Africa. 1690. (B.R. 77; Gn. 38 (1890), 576.)

**G. vires'cens.** A synonym of *G. simplex.*

**GLORY OF THE SNOW.** *See* **Chionodoxa.**

**GLORY PEA.** *See* **Clianthus.**

*glosso-, -glossus -a -um,* in compound words, signifies tongue-shaped.

**GLOSSO'DIA** (*glossa,* a tongue, *eidos,* like; there is a tongue-like appendage within the flower). Fam. *Orchidaceae.* A genus comprising about 5 species of terrestrial orchids, limited to Australia. Flowers purple or blue, rarely white, erect, 1 or 2 on an erect scape, leafless except an empty sheathing bract at or below the middle and a similar one under each pedicel; lip sessile, undivided, not fringed. Leaf solitary, oblong or lanceolate, from within a scarious sheath close to the ground. Glossodias thrive in sandy loam and peat, and require but little water when dormant. Propagation by division if the plants increase. All are figured in Fitzgerald, *Australian Orchids,* vol. 2, t. 33 and 37.

**G. Bruno'nis.** *fl.* 1 to 3, about 1 in. across; sep. and pet. spreading, purple above, whitish with purple spots beneath; lip white, small, narrow, tapered, recurved; column with a concave hood-like wing. *l.* 1 to 3 in. long, lanceolate.

**G. emargina'ta.** *fl.* usually solitary, 1½ in. across; sep. and pet. rose-pink; lip red with 3 longitudinal ridges and orange-yellow, purple-tipped, callus-like appendages at its base. Habit much as in *G. Brunonis.*

**G. interme'dia.** *fl.* solitary, about 1 in. across, lilac-purple; sep. and pet. ovate-lanceolate, blunt, glossy; lip linear with 2 enlargements towards the end. *l.* oblong, 2 to 3 in. long.

**G. ma'jor.** *fl.* about 2 in. across, blue; sep. and pet. oblong-lanceolate, obtuse, not blotched; lip ovate, broadest in middle, disk with 2 white hairy cushions, upper half lanceolate, blue, glabrous. June. *l.* oblong or lanceolate, 2 to 4 in. long. Tuber ovoid. 1810. SYN. *Caladenia major.* (B.M. n.s. 441.)

**G. mi'nor.** *fl.* under 1 in. across, violet or blue; sep. and pet. oblong-lanceolate; lip about one-third length of sep., broad, the 2 hairy cushions smaller, the spreading upper half triangular, acute, flat, glabrous. June. *l.* lanceolate, hairy, the small sheathing bract usually green. 1810. SYN. *Caladenia minor.*

E. C.

**GLOSSOPET'ALON** (*glossa*, a tongue, *petalon*, a petal; in reference to the shape of the petals). FAM. *Celastraceae.* A genus of 3 or 4 species of N. American shrubs with often spine-tipped twigs. Leaves alternate, entire, small. Flowers axillary, often solitary, small; sepals and petals 4 to 6; stamens twice as many. Being of more botanical than horticultural interest, they are but little known in cultivation. They should be quite hardy in a well-drained loamy soil and a sunny spot. SYN. *Forsellesia.*

**G. meionand'rum.** Deciduous shrub up to 3 ft., shoots yellowish-grey. *l.* grey-green, up to ⅝ in. long, cuneate-oblong or oblanceolate. *fl.* white; pet. narrowly linear, ¼ in. long; stamens 5 to 7. May. *Pod* ovoid, flattened. NW. America. (G.F. 1894, p. 239, f. 52.)

**G. spines'cens.** Deciduous, spinescent shrub 1 to 4 ft., intricately branched, glabrous or nearly so. *l.* ⅛ to ⅜ in. long, 1/12 to ⅛ in. wide, linear, oblanceolate, glaucous. *fl.* solitary, axillary, ⅓ in. wide; pet. filiform, usually 5; stamens twice as many. April. *Pod* ⅛ in. long with 1 or 2 brown seeds. Western N. America.

W. J. B.

**GLOTTIPHYL'LUM** (*glottis*, tongue, *phyllon*, leaf; referring to the tongue-shaped leaves). FAM. *Aizoaceae* (Mesembryanthemum). Dwarf, succulent plants with very short branching stems; the leaves are united in pairs, arranged in 2 ranks, 2 or 3 pairs forming a growth; each leaf is tongue-shaped, very thick with soft flesh, and easily broken; the colour is generally translucent bright green. The flowers are large and yellow, on very short stalks and are produced from July onwards. This genus is found on the Karroo, S. Africa. For cultivation *see* **Mesembryanthemum.** These plants do not need to be dried so completely as some types. Glottiphyllums hybridize very easily and many of the plants in cultivation are not true species; they set seed freely and this readily germinates, but propagation by division or cuttings is the only method if true species are required.

**G. depres'sum.** Stemless, 3 or 4 pairs of l. to a growth, closely packed in two ranks, lying on the ground, 4 in. long, 1 in. wide, keeled, green. *fl.* 1 in. across, on short stalks, yellow. SYN. *Mesembryanthemum depressum.* (S.-D. 8, 7; B.M. 1866.)

**G. frag'rans.** *l.* very crowded, tongue-shaped, 2½ to 3 in. long, 1 in. broad, blunt. *fl.* 4 in. across, sessile, bright yellow, scented. SYN. *Mesembryanthemum fragrans.* (S.-D. 8, 2; N.E.Br. 226.) A

**G. la'tum.** Stemless. *l.* tongue-shaped, curved downwards, thicker at tip, 3½ in. long, 1 in. wide, dark green. *fl.* 2½ in. across, yellow. SYN. *Mesembryanthemum linguiforme latum.* (S.-D. 8, 8B.)

**G. linguifor'me.** Stemless, growths prostrate. *l.* crowded, tongue-shaped, 2½ in. long, 1½ in. wide, rounded at tip, glossy green. *fl.* 2 to 3 in. across, yellow. SYN. *Mesembryanthemum linguiforme.* (S.-D. 8, 8; N.E.Br. 230.) The true form is very rare in cultivation.

**G. praepin'gue.** *l.* spreading, then curved inwards, 3 in. long, ½ in. wide, semi-cylindrical, bright green. *fl.* 2 in. across, yellow. 1792. SYN. *Mesembryanthemum praepingue.* (S.-D. 7, 5.)

V. H.

***-glottis,*** in compound words signifying a tongue, e.g. *platyglottis*, wide-tongued.

**GLOW-WORM** (*Lampyris noctiluca*). A species of beetle found in gardens, mossy heaths, hedgerows, and commons in many parts of Britain, especially in the south. The female is wingless and grub-like without wing-cases and produces a bright light; the male is fully winged and gives a feebler light. The mature beetle eats little or nothing but the larvae are carnivorous, feeding upon slugs and snails which they seize with their sharp, sickle-shaped jaws.

G. F. W.

**GLOXINER'A.** FAM. *Gesneriaceae* Hybrids between Gesneria and Gloxinia.

**Brilliant** (*Gesneria* sp. × *Gloxinia Radiance*) has foliage intermediate between the parents and rich carmine-crimson fl. with the cor. horizontal, as large as a Gloxinia. Raised by Messrs. J. Veitch of Chelsea. (G. C. 18 (1895) 144, f. 22.)

**GLOXIN'IA** (in honour of Benjamin Peter Gloxin, a botanical writer (1785) of Colmar). FAM. *Gesneriaceae.* A genus of 6 species of erect S. America perennial herbs with knobbed roots, not tuberous. Leaves opposite, stalked. Flowers of various colours, variegated with spots, solitary or a few together in the leaf-axils, large, nodding; disk at base of corolla annular, not of 5 distinct glands as in Sinningia. The Gloxinias are stove plants needing much the same treatment as the Gloxinias of the florist, which belong to the genus Sinningia (see next article). They can be propagated by seed, by the knobbed roots, or by leaf-cuttings. For species sometimes under Plectonema *see* **Achimenes.**

**G. fimbria'ta.** A synonym of *Achimenes fimbriata.*

**G. glab'ra.** A synonym of *Achimenes glabrata.*

**G. macula'ta.** Stem simple, spotted, about 1 ft. h. *l.* at base cordate, obtuse, doubly toothed, shining above, reddish beneath. *fl.* large, purplish-blue, downy, solitary on axillary peduncles. June to October. S. America. 1739. (B.M. 1191.) Much grown in tropical gardens, requiring considerable heat and moisture—a variable plant. var. **insig'nis,** *fl.* lilac and crimson; **pallidiflo'ra,** stem not spotted, *fl.* pale blue. 1844. (B.M. 4213.)

**G. specio'sa.** A synonym of *Sinningia speciosa.*

**GLOXINIA** of florists (*Sinningia speciosa* and hybrids). For the characters of the plant from which the florists' Gloxinia has developed *see* **Sinningia speciosa.** While it is possible that *S. guttata*, which was early (1844) reported to have been crossed with *S. speciosa*, may have played some part in the production of the present-day Gloxinia there is little doubt that the deep bells with their great variety of colouring, varied shape and markings, large size, erect poise, and freedom have been secured by seizing upon and raising seed from variations that have occurred in the main in the progeny of *S. speciosa*, which, in the original form (*see* B.M. 1937), had purple flowers, drooping and much smaller than those of the present-day florists' Gloxinia. The form called Fyfiana appeared about 1860 and had erect flowers (forms with pink flowers, pale blue flowers, and white with blue dots near the throat, all with erect flowers are mentioned soon after) but the flowers were small. In 1866 Mr. van Houtte sent out a variety named for his wife Gloxinia Mina. It had brilliant carmine-red flowers edged with white, but the flowers were drooping. This was crossed with the offspring of Fyfiana and a series of erect-flowered plants with a great variety of colours appeared in the nurseries of M. Duval as a result. Meanwhile M. J. Vallerand crossed a pale lilac *S. speciosa* dotted with dark violet with the erect-flowered race and obtained a race of finely spotted and marked flowers, and from another source, possibly M. Rossiaud, came a race subsequently called *G. crassifolia.* This race had rounded, very velvety, thick leaves, plump, short buds, large solid flowers very wide open at the mouth, with some range of colour from dark blue through rose to a white ground marked with blue spots, but with a narrow tube. Selection through many generations has improved these types and many have taken a part in the process—those mentioned were among the early workers who laid the foundations of what is now one of the most brilliant, varied, decorative, and floriferous of stove plants, plants, too, that by successive potting may be had in flower over the greater part of the year; they are always attractive in the warm greenhouse and in summer when in flower prove useful also for the cool greenhouse. The variations include intense rich crimson and pure white, with varying shades of blue and purple, or delicately spotted and pencilled internally if seed is procured from a good source. The various colours come true from seed.

Gloxinias if needed in large numbers should be raised annually from seed, and they can be raised from cuttings of the stems or leaves. The very small seeds should be sown early in February in well-drained pots or small pans of finely sifted soil, composed of peat, leaf-mould, and sand in about equal amounts. After watering well and standing to drain for a few hours the seeds are sown thinly and evenly, given only a very thin covering of soil, placed in a temperature of about 70° F., and kept shaded. Careful watch must be kept to prevent damping off. As soon as the seedlings are large enough they should be pricked off about 1 in. apart into pots of similar soil, and in due course potted singly in small pots. Such seedlings sown early and grown on without a check in a shaded place with a moist warm atmosphere will form good plants and flower the same season. Stem cuttings are best taken when the old tubers are started in spring; they strike readily then in a close frame and make good plants for flowering in the following summer. Leaf cuttings may be made when the leaves are mature. They are inserted in the sandy compost with a small piece of the leaf-stalk attached, and at the base of this a tuber will be formed for flowering in the next year. Another more rapid method is to cut the midrib of each mature leaf used, at distances of about 1 in. apart and peg it down flat on a pan of light soil. Tubers will eventually form at all the firmer parts of the midribs where the cuts were made and they may be collected from the soil when the other parts of the leaf decay.

Summer is the natural flowering time of Gloxinias and they should be started into growth in February, or earlier. Some of the tubers may be kept back for succession to be followed by seedlings in early autumn, thus securing a long period of display. The tubers should be taken from the dry soil in which they have been stored, placed in small pots, and stood in a temperature of about 65° F. The best soil for them is partly decayed leaf-mould and lumpy peat in equal parts with a little sand or charcoal. Loam is sometimes used but if watering is attended to it is not needed. The pots should be well drained and nearly filled, the tubers being pressed in and just covered with soil. No water is required until growth begins except a little syringing round the pots to prevent the soil becoming too dry. When growing the plants need plenty of water and are benefited by thorough syringings with tepid water morning and evening in summer. Before the pots are filled with roots if the plants appear to be strong they should be shifted into their flowering pots, 5 to 8 in. being needed according to their vigour. A light position shaded from direct sunshine will then ensure sturdy growth which eventually results in flowers of good substance. Air should be given carefully and the leaves should be handled cautiously for they are very brittle. Artificial manure or manure water is of benefit when the flowers appear, but it should not be allowed to reach the foliage. The flowers last longer if the plants are given a lower temperature and more air at flowering time. After flowering, as the leaves ripen, less water should be given, and when they die away the tubers should be stored in a warm, dry place.

J. C.

Gloxinias may be affected by Foot Rot (*Phytophthora parasitica*) which causes blackening of the base of the stem. This disease is encouraged by too moist conditions and these should be avoided by careful watering and care in preparation of the compost so as to provide good drainage. Watering with Cheshunt Compound when the plants are well established in the pots is a safeguard. Gloxinias may also be affected by the Virus disease known as Spotted Wilt, which appears as large brown circular rings on the leaves and can hardly fail to be seen early in its development. Affected plants ought to be removed at once and insects kept down by fumigation.

D. E. G.

*gloxinioi'des*, Gloxinia-like.

**GLUCOSE.** Sugar ($C_6H_{12}O_6$), including grape-sugar, occurring as a reserve in many fruits. It is soluble in water and crystallizable.

**GLUCOSIDES.** Substances, mainly complex chemical compounds of C, H, and O, like coniferin in the wood of conifers and salicin in willow bark, or containing nitrogen like amygdalin in the seeds of many Rosaceous plants, which, on decomposition by an enzyme such as emulsin, yield glucose.

*gluma'ceus -a -um*, like, or furnished with, glumes.

**GLUMES.** Chaffy bracts enclosing the flowers of grasses and sedges.

*glutino'sus -a -um*, sticky, gluey.

**GLYCE'RIA** (*glykys*, sweet; leaves and roots of some species are sweet). FAM. *Gramineae*. A genus of about 16 species of medium-sized perennial grasses mostly of marshy places in the cooler parts of the N. Hemisphere, one in Australia. Closely related to Festuca but the spikelets many-flowered and the convex glumes not nerved to the tip as in Festuca, and awnless. Propagated by division and useful for the waterside.

**G. aquat'ica variega'ta.** Creeping, about 3 ft. h. Stems stout, smooth, striate. *l.* flat, 1 to 2 in. wide, striped with white, sheaths smooth, ligule short. *Panicle* much branched, 6 to 12 in. long; spikelets ¼ in. long. N. Hemisphere. **G. fo'liis variega'tis** is a synonym.

**G. specta'bilis.** A synonym of *G. aquatica*.

**GLYCI'NE** (*glykys*, sweet; leaves and roots of some species are sweet). FAM. *Leguminosae*. A genus of about 40 species of mostly twining plants, natives of the warmer parts of Asia, Africa, and Australia. At one time Glycine was made to include a large number of plants now distributed over other genera, including Apios, Kennedya, Wisteria, and so on. As now understood it is nearly related to Dolichos, Phaseolus, and Vigna. The plants are conspicuously reddish-brown-hairy throughout. Leaflets 3, large and thin as in Phaseolus. Flowers papilionaceous, small; corolla slightly longer than calyx, petals about equal in length; stamens in one bundle. Pods jointed or constricted between the seeds. *G. Soja*, the Soy bean, is a plant of great importance in China, Japan, and the United States of America, being used directly or indirectly both for human and for cattle food and for the production of oil for which purpose large quantities of the seeds have been imported into this country. It has also been used as a substitute for coffee. Though some varieties of this very variable plant will in favourable seasons ripen a good crop of seed here, as a rule little success has followed attempts to grow it, for it needs a hot summer to perfect and ripen a remunerative crop. A well-drained sandy soil in a dry and sunny district would offer the best chance of growing it successfully if a good growing season, a hot summer and a dry autumn, could be ensured. It is about as hardy as the Scarlet Runner bean which gives a lead as to the time of sowing.

**G. his'pida.** A synonym of *G. Soja*.

**G. sinen'sis.** A synonym of *Wisteria sinensis*.

**G. Soj'a.** Soy Bean. Annual, erect, roughly hairy, 1½ to 2 ft. h. *l.* 3-foliolate, stalked; lflets. ovate-elliptical, thin, entire. *fl.* violet on short, axillary racemes. *Pods* up to 3 in. long, ⅜ in. wide, roughly hairy, constricted between seeds, pendent, 3- or 4-seeded;

seeds about $\frac{1}{4}$ in. thick, smooth, nearly rounded, black, brown, yellow, green, or white. E. Asia. 1790. SYN. *Dolichos Soja, Soja hispida.*

***glycinoi'des,*** Glycine-like.

***glyco-*** or ***glycy-*** in compound words, signifying sweet.

**GLYCOS'MIS** (*glykys*, sweet, *osme*, smell; leaves and flowers are fragrant). FAM. *Rutaceae.* A genus of 5 species of unarmed trees or shrubs, natives of the tropics. Leaves evergreen, unequally pinnate or of 1 leaflet; leaflets alternate, entire, or toothed, dark green above, pale beneath. Flowers small, fragrant, in terminal or, more commonly, axillary panicles, white, 5-merous; calyx downy. Fruit small, pulp fleshy, seeds large. The species need stove conditions and rich loamy soil. Cuttings may be struck in sand in heat.

**G. arbo'rea.** Tree to 20 ft. *lflets.* 5, long, faintly toothed. *fl.* May to August. E. Indies. 1796.

**G. citrifo'lia.** Shrub to 6 ft. *lflets.* 1 or 3, ovate-oblong, slender-pointed. *fl.* on axillary peduncles shorter than l.-stalk. Continuous. China.

**G. pentaphyl'la.** Shrub. *lflets.* usually 5, elliptical, entire, dark green, glossy. *fl.* summer. *fr.* a translucent, pinkish berry, 2- or 3-celled. India, Malaya, Philippines. 1790. SYN. *Limonia pentaphylla.*

F. G. P.

**GLYCYRRHI'ZA** (*glykys*, sweet, *rhiza*, root). FAM. *Leguminosae.* A genus of about 12 species of perennial herbs, natives of the Mediterranean region, Trop. Asia, W. and S. America. Leaves odd-pinnate, with rarely as few as 3 leaflets, minutely glandular or toothed. Flowers papilionaceous in axillary racemes or spikes, which are stalked or sessile. *G. glabra* is widely grown in S. Europe for its long, perpendicular, sweet roots which are the source of Liquorice, used widely by druggists and confectioners, in the manufacture of tobacco, and in the preparation of cooling drinks, as well as by brewers. It is hardy, and needs a deep mellow soil, moist, rich, and free from stones to grow the roots well, but is rather a coarse grower. Propagation is by division of the roots, each piece of which should have 1 or more buds. The other species mentioned below are not particularly valuable horticulturally, but are hardy.

**G. echina'ta.** Clammy herb, about 3 ft. h. *lflets.* oval-lanceolate, mucronate, glabrous; stipules oblong-lanceolate. *fl.* purple, racemes about half as long as l. June, July. S. Europe. (B.M. 2154.)

**G. foe'tida.** Perennial with creeping rootstock. Stem erect, 1 to 2 ft. h. *lflets.* 9 to 11, greyish, lower obcordate, upper ovate-lanceolate, $\frac{1}{2}$ in. long. *fl.* crowded, in axillary spikes, pale yellow. Spring. N. Africa. Scent unpleasant.

**G. glab'ra.** Herb of 3 to 4 ft., perennial. *lflets.* ovate, rather retuse, and beneath, like the branches, somewhat clammy. *fl.* pale blue, distant, the stalked racemes rather shorter than l. Summer, autumn. Mediterranean region. 1562. (F.G. 709.)

**G. lepido'ta.** Perennial, 2 to 3 ft. h., root creeping. *lflets.* 15 to 19, oblong-lanceolate, acute, scaly, covered with glandular dots beneath. *fl.* whitish, in dense, stalked spikes shorter than l. July, August. N. America. 1817. (B.M. 2150.)

A→

**GLYPH'AEA** (*glyphe*, carving; the fruits are marked as though carved). FAM. *Tiliaceae.* A genus of 2 Trop. African shrubs with simple, 3-ribbed toothed leaves, and yellow flowers in small axillary or terminal cymes. For cultivation *see* **Apeiba.**

**G. grewioi'des.** *l.* oblong or ovate, 4 to 6 in. long, glabrous, rather thin, rounded or obliquely heart-shaped at base, slender-pointed, sharply irregularly toothed. *fl.* bright yellow, $1\frac{1}{2}$ in. across, in 3- or 4-fld. downy cymes, hairs starry. September. Trop. Africa. 1866. (B.M. 5610 as *G. Monteiroi.*)

F. G. P.

**GLYPHOSPER'MA** (*glyphe*, carving, *sperma*, seed; from the markings on the seed). FAM. *Liliaceae.* Herb, native of N. Mexico, closely related to Anthericum, with clusters of fleshy, fibrous roots, and slender, grass-like, soft, bright green leaves. Dry sandy soil suits it, and it is hardy, given protection from excessive moisture in winter. Propagated by division.

**G. Palm'eri.** Perennial herb. *l.* linear, 12 to 18 in. h., channelled. *fl.* white, starry, $\frac{3}{4}$ in. across, in panicles. Summer. N. Mexico. 1884. (B.M. 6717.)

**GLYPTOSTRO'BUS** (*glyptus*, carved, *strobus*, cone; in allusion to markings on the cone). FAM. *Pinaceae.* A monotypic genus, characters as species.

**G. pen'silis.** Chinese deciduous cypress. Deciduous tree allied to Taxodium, differing by its pear-shaped cones, borne on short stalks. Branchlets of two kinds, persistent with buds in the l.-axils, and deciduous without buds, falling with l. in autumn. *l.* on permanent shoots, spirally arranged, scale-like, overlapping; on deciduous shoots in 3 ranks, $\frac{1}{3}$ to $\frac{1}{2}$ in. long, soft and pointed, bright green in summer, rich brown in autumn. *Male and female fl.* on the same tree; male in tassel-like clusters, female very small, developing into pear-shaped cones up to $\frac{3}{4}$ in. long on stalks $\frac{1}{2}$ to $\frac{3}{4}$ in. long. *Scales* thin; seeds oval or oblong with a single well-developed wing. Canton, S. China, in damp ground. (G.C. 66 (1919), 258.) SYN. *G. heterophyllus, G. sinensis, Taxodium heterophyllum, Thuja pensilis.* Interesting tree rarely hardy in the British Is.

W. D.

**GMELI'NA** (in honour of J. Gottlieb Gmelin, 1709–55, German naturalist and traveller). FAM. *Verbenaceae.* A genus of 8 or 10 species of evergreen or deciduous trees or shrubs, natives of India, E. Asia, and N. Australia. Leaves opposite, entire, toothed or lobed. Flowers large, irregular, blue, pale violet, or yellow in downy panicles; calyx bell-shaped, shortly 5-toothed or entire; corolla limb oblique, 5- (or 4-)lobed. The species need stove conditions and rich fibrous loam. They can be struck from cuttings of firm young shoots in sand, in heat.

**G. arbo'rea.** Tree to 20 ft. or more. *l.* cordate-ovate, sometimes 3-lobed, up to 9 in. long, 6 in. wide, downy beneath. *fl.* deep tawny-yellow within, paler and downy without; in many-fld. thyrse. June to August. E. Indies. 1824. (B.M. 4395 as *G. Rheedii.*)

**G. asiat'ica.** Shrub, sometimes spiny. *l.* ovate or obovate, $\frac{1}{2}$ to $1\frac{1}{2}$ in. long, sometimes lobed. *fl.* yellow, in racemose clusters. India, Ceylon. 1792.

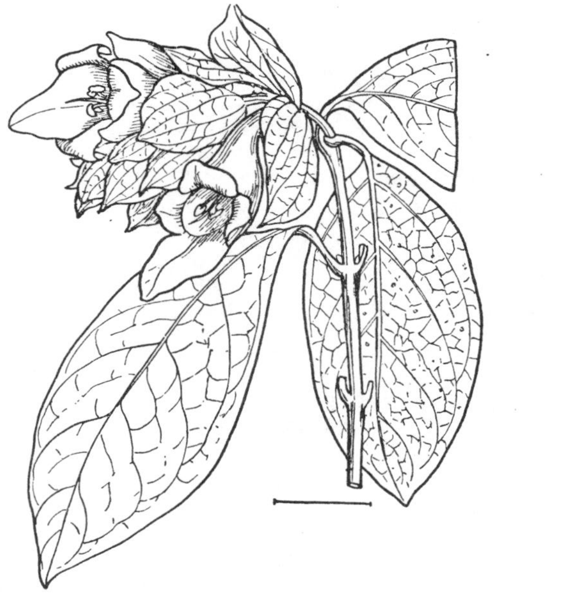

*Gmelina Hystrix*

**G. Hys'trix.** Spiny climbing shrub with habit of Bougainvillaea. *l.* elliptic, or oblong, 3 in. long, glaucous beneath. *fl.* yellow, irregularly bell-shaped, 3 in. long, 2 in. across, smooth without, in short, dense, terminal spikes with large reddish-purple bracts. E. Indies. 1894. (B.M. 7391.)

F. G. P.

**GNAPHA'LIUM** (*gnaphalon*, soft down; several species are covered with woolly hairs). FAM. *Compositae.* A genus of about 120 species of herbs or sub-shrubs widely distributed over the world, having entire, alternate, usually sessile leaves and small heads of yellow or white flowers in corymbs or clustered; involucral bracts appressed and scarious; receptacle flat, naked; ray-florets tubular, perfect. Some species are annual weeds, a few worth growing in the garden, and several sometimes known as Gnaphalium, to be sought here under Helichrysum or Leontopodium. In addition to those mentioned below some of the New Zealand species might be worth introducing for their trailing habit and small 'everlasting' flowers. *G. trinerve* is already here and *G. keriense* and *G. Lyallii* would probably be equally good in moist ground, *G. Traversii* and *G. subrigidum* on somewhat drier spots, and *G. Mackayi* making small circular patches with white leaves, all, of course, for the rock-garden or alpine house.

**G. decur'rens.** Hardy perennial, 2 to 3 ft. h. *l.* strongly scented, lanceolate or linear, white beneath. *fl.-heads* white in clusters. July, August. N. America. (Gn. 19 (1881), 99.)

**G. japon'icum.** Annual about 1 ft. h. *l.* silvery, lower lanceolate, narrowed to base; upper sessile, linear. Cosmopolitan. The fl. should not be allowed to open. Useful as an edging, especially on poor soils.

**G. Leontopo'dium.** A synonym of *Leontopodium alpinum*.

**G. margarita'ceum.** A synonym of *Antennaria margaritacea*.

**G. triner've.*** Sprawling shrub with slender prostrate stems, 1 to 2 ft. long. *l.* $\frac{1}{2}$ to 1 in. long, $\frac{1}{6}$ to $\frac{3}{8}$ in. wide, obovate-oblong to oblanceolate, glabrous above, white with silvery down beneath; obscurely 3-veined. *fl.-heads* in terminal corymbs of 3 to 10 on erect stems a few in. h., measuring with the pure white, involucral bracts $\frac{1}{2}$ to $\frac{3}{4}$ in. wide. New Zealand.

W. J. B.

**GNETA'CEAE.** A family of trees or shrubs, mainly tropical but reaching temperate parts of the N. Hemisphere, with 3 genera and about 45 species but few of which are cultivated. Erect, climbing and prostrate plants are included. Leaves opposite, sometimes large but often only scales. Flowers usually dioecious with a 2- or 4-parted perianth; stamens 2 to 8; female flowers consisting of an ovule with 1 or 2 skins but without an ovary. Fruit fleshy or winged. Of the 3 genera only species of Ephedra are in cultivation in English gardens. The curious *Welwitschia mirabilis* with 2 leaves continually lengthening at the base and wearing away at the apex belongs here; concerning it information may be sought in books on S. African plants. The 2 genera dealt with are Ephedra and Welwitschia.

**GNID'IA** (ancient Greek name for the Laurel, from Gnidus, a town in Crete). FAM. *Thymelaeaceae*. A genus of 60 or 70 species of evergreen shrubs confined to Africa, almost entirely to the south. Leaves opposite or alternate, usually small. Flowers nearly always in terminal clusters, yellow or white or occasionally red or violet. Calyx cylindrical, 4-lobed; petals 4, 8, or 12, smaller than the calyx lobes. Fruit small, dry, enclosed in the persistent base of the calyx. The few species introduced require a cool greenhouse temperature; one species is grown in the open in Scilly. Treatment needed is similar to that for Pimelea.

KEY

| | |
|---|---|
| 1. *Pet.* 4 | 2 |
| 1. *Pet.* 8 | 4 |
| 2. *Pet. fleshy* | 3 |
| 2. *Pet. membranous* | G. subulata |
| 3. *Lvs. alternate* | G. pinifolia |
| 3. *Lvs. opposite* | G. oppositifolia |
| 4. *Lvs. glabrous* | G. polystachya |
| 4. *Lvs. hairy* | G. denudata |

**G. carina'ta.** A synonym for *G. polystachya*.

**G. denuda'ta.** Shrub 4 to 12 ft., shoots densely hairy. *l.* opposite, stalkless, ovate-oblong, $\frac{1}{2}$ to $\frac{3}{4}$ in. long, downy on both surfaces. *fl.* in terminal clusters of about 6 on short lateral shoots; cal. pale yellow, its tube $\frac{3}{4}$ in. long, hairy, lobes $\frac{1}{6}$ in. long; pet. 8, quite tiny. Spring. S. Africa. 1820. (B.R. 757; B.M. 2761, but wrongly as *G. tomentosa*, which has alternate l.)

**G. juniperifo'lia.** A synonym of *G. subulata*.

**G. oppositifo'lia.** Shrub up to 12 ft., shoots slender, spreading, glabrous. *l.* ovate to ovate-lanceolate, $\frac{1}{2}$ in. long, $\frac{1}{6}$ in. wide, glabrous. *fl.* pale yellow, hairy, 4 to 6 in terminal clusters; cal. tube $\frac{2}{3}$ in. long, with obovate lobes $\frac{1}{8}$ in. long; pet. $\frac{1}{12}$ in. long. May to July. S. Africa. 1783. (B.M. 1902.)

**G. pinifo'lia.** Shrub 2 ft. or more, erect or fastigiate, shoots glabrous. *l.* alternate, rather crowded, $\frac{1}{2}$ to $\frac{3}{4}$ in. long, $\frac{1}{24}$ in. wide, linear, glabrous. *fl.* fragrant in the evening, white, numerous in terminal clusters 1 to $1\frac{1}{2}$ in. wide; cal. tube $\frac{1}{2}$ in. long, its lobes oblong or obovate, $\frac{1}{6}$ in. long; pet. 4, densely hairy, $\frac{1}{10}$ in. long. Spring, summer. S. Africa. 1760. (B.M. 2016.) var. **orchroleu'ca** shoots more slender, cal. purple at base, pet. longer. (B.R. 624.)

**G. polystach'ya.*** Graceful shrub, 4 to 6 ft., stems appressed hairy. *l.* $\frac{1}{4}$ to $\frac{1}{2}$ in. long, $\frac{1}{16}$ in. wide, closely set, alternate, linear, glabrous. *fl.* densely packed in terminal rounded clusters 1 in. wide; cal. yellow, its tube hairy, $\frac{1}{3}$ to $\frac{1}{2}$ in. long, limb $\frac{1}{4}$ in. wide, lobes ovate; pet. 8, very small. S. Africa. Spring. (B.M. 8001.) SYN. *G. carinata*.

**G. sim'plex.** A synonym of *G. polystachya*.

**G. subula'ta.** Shrub 1 to 2 ft., shoots downy at first. *l.* alternate, stalkless, densely set, up to $\frac{1}{2}$ in. long, linear-subulate, glabrous. *fl.* entirely yellow, in terminal pairs or threes; cal. tube $\frac{1}{3}$ in. long, slenderly funnel-shaped, glabrous; lobes ovate, $\frac{1}{8}$ in. long; pet. 4, nearly as long. July, August, S. Africa. 1786. (B.M. 812 as *G. simplex*.) SYN. *G. juniperifolia*.

**G. tomento'sa** of B.M. 2761 is *G. denudata*.

W. J. B.

**GOAT MOTH** (*Cossus cossus*) is one of the largest British Moths. Its caterpillar is a wood-borer found attacking fruit (Apple, Cherry, Pear, and Plum) and forest trees (Elm, Oak, Poplar, and Willow). The large brown moths are on the wing in June and July, and the female lays her eggs on the trunks. The young caterpillars bore straight into the bark, and spend 3 or 4 years tunnelling in all directions in the wood. The young larva is bright pink, but later becomes dark red with yellowish sides. The mature caterpillars, which are 3 to 4 in. long, pupate near the entrance to the burrows in a cocoon formed of silk, wood chips, and excrement. The foliage of attacked trees flags and turns yellow, and a close examination of the trunks will reveal the entrance holes to the larval burrows. The name of the moth is derived from the disagreeable goat-like odour of its larva. It is a pest chiefly of old and neglected trees, and careful attention paid to fruit and broad-leaved specimen trees will prevent extensive injury being done by this Moth.

It is desirable to fell and to split up the timber of old and heavily attacked trees, thus destroying any 'nursery' of the pest. The caterpillars may be destroyed either by pushing a pointed wire along their burrows and spearing them, or by inserting some crystals of sodium cyanide or cotton-wool soaked in carbon disulphide (highly inflammable) into the mouths of the tunnels and blocking the entrance with clay or putty to prevent escape of the fumes.

G. F. W.

**GOAT WILLOW.** *See* **Salix Caprea.**

**GOAT'S BEARD.** *See* **Aruncus sylvester, Tragopogon pratensis.**

**GOAT'S FOOT.** *See* **Oxalis caprina.**

**GOAT'S RUE.** *See* **Galega officinalis.**

**GOAT'S THORN, GREAT.** *See* **Astragalus Tragacantha.**

**A→**

***Godefroy'ae,*** in honour of M. Godefroy-Leboeuf, who collected in the Congo Free State *c.* 1903.

**GODE'TIA** (in honour of C. H. Godet, 1797–1879, a Swiss botanist). FAM. *Oenotheraceae*. A genus of 20 species of annual plants related to Oenothera (in which genus they have sometimes been included) with showy flowers in leafy racemes or spikes. The calyx tube is obconic or funnel-shaped, sepals 4, petals 4, large, stamens 8, ovary 4-celled, inferior, many-seeded. Though closely related to Oenothera, the Godetias are not difficult to distinguish for in Oenotheras the anthers are versatile but not in Godetias in which they resemble Clarkias. From Clarkia the genus is distinct by its sessile, not clawed, petals. Further the Godetias have a distinct value in gardens as summer-flowering annuals growing well in ordinary good soil, better if somewhat moist, and they are therefore kept separate here from Oenothera. The garden forms are derived mainly from 2 species, *G. amoena* giving rise to the taller varieties including those listed under *G. rubicunda* and *G. Schaminii*, *G. grandiflora* to most of the dwarfer varieties often listed as *G. Whitneyi*. The distinct variety known as Lavender is probably derived from *G. viminea*. Like many other annuals Godetias may be sown in the open in September.

**G. amoe′na.*** About 2 ft. h., slender, branches at first spreading, then erect. *l.* linear to lanceolate, ½ to 2½ in. long. *fl.* lilac-crimson or reddish-pink, satiny, 1 to 2 in. across, in a loose spike or panicle. Western N. America. 1818. Variable both in nature and in the garden. var. **Lind′leyi**, *fl.* crimson with large central blotch of deep crimson. (B.M. 2832 as *Oenothera Lindleyana*.); **rubicun′da**, *fl.* lilac-crimson. (B.R. 1856.); **Schamin′ii**, taller, up to 3 ft. 6 in., *fl.* usually semi-double, whitish, pink with crimson base, rose-purple, or carmine, stamens 8 to 12. (Gn. 70 (1906), 203.); **vino′sa**, *fl.* white (B.R. 1880), all originally regarded as distinct species belong here. Many colour-forms have received distinct names.

**G. decum′bens.** Stems ascending, flattened, whitish-hairy. Ovary white-woolly. Oregon. (B.M. 2889; B.R. 1221.) Not now known wild.

**G. grandiflo′ra.*** 9 to 12 in. h., bushy, stem rather stout. *l.* oblong, narrowed to both ends. *fl.* 3 to 5 in. across, satiny, rose-red with a deeper suffused blotch in middle, but varying much in colour from white to crimson, base of pet. white or pale; stamens 8, crimson. California. 1867. (B.R. 28, 61; B.M..5867 as *Oenothera Whitneyi*.) Very variable in colour and somewhat in height, races of similar colouring having been selected for height. **Lady Albemarle**, dark crimson, **Duchess of Albany**, white, **Sybil Sherwood**, bright salmon pink, **Wild Rose**, pale rose with carmine flush, are good varieties illustrating the colour range. **Azaleiflora plena** has double fl.

**G. Lind′leyi.** *See* **G. amoena Lindleyi.**

**G. quadrivul′nera.** Erect, slender, downy. *l.* linear to obovate, upper lanceolate. *fl.* lilac or pale crimson, about 1 in. across; ovary woolly. Western N. America. (B.R. 1119 as *Oenothera quadrivulnera*.)

**G. Romanzov′ii.** Erect, glaucous, white hairy in youth. *l.* lanceolate-oblong, mucronate. *fl.* violet, margins of pet. crenulate. NW. America. 1817. (B.R. 562.)

**G. rubicun′da.** *See* **G. amoena rubicunda.**

**G. Schamin′ii.** *See* **G. amoena Schaminii.**

**G. vimin′ea.*** About 2 ft. h., slender. *fl.* lavender; pet. deep purple at base; stamens deep purple. Western America. 1826.

**G. vino′sa.** *See* **G. amoena vinosa.**

**A→**

**GODOY′A** (in honour of E. Godoy, 1764–1839, Spanish statesman who concluded peace between France and Spain, a patron of Botany). Fam. *Ochnaceae*. A genus of about 2 species of Peruvian and Colombian trees. Leaves alternate, leathery, thick, marked with numerous transverse veins. Flowers in terminal and axillary racemes or panicles; calyx twin. A compost of peat and loam with stove conditions is needed. Propagated by cuttings in sand, under glass, with strong bottom heat.

**G. gemmiflo′ra.** A synonym of *Blastemanthus gemmiflorus*.

**G. splen′dida.** About 10 ft. h., compact. *l.* pinnate, large. *fl.* pure white, fragrant, in spikes of 10 to 15. Colombia. 1869.

F. G. P.

***Godron′ii*,** in honour of D. A. Godron, 1807–80, of Nancy, French botanist.

**GOD′S EYE.** *See* **Veronica Chamaedrys.**

***Godseffia′nus -a -um*,** in honour of Joseph Godseff, 1846?–1921?, who collected widely for Messrs. Sander of St. Albans.

***goegoeen′sis -is -e*,** of Goegoe, Sumatra.

***goen′sis*,** of Goa, India.

**GOETHE′A** (in honour of J. W. Goethe, 1749–1832, German poet and botanist). Fam. *Malvaceae*. A genus of 2 species of evergreen shrubs, natives of Brazil. Leaves alternate, sometimes remotely toothed; axillary buds many, some later becoming flowers. Flowers showy, the epicalyx brightly coloured, in cymes from the leafless

stems or solitary and axillary; styles twice as many as carpels. Closely related to Pavonia and needing the same treatment.

**G. cauliflo′ra.** A synonym of *G. strictiflora*.

**G. Mackoya′na.** About 2 ft. h. *l.* elliptical, dull green, short-stalked; stipules leafy, lanceolate. *fl.* with a 5-leaved epicalyx of large, cordate, oval-acute, crimson bracts. 1873. (B.M. 6427.) Syn. *Pavonia Makoyana*.

**G. multiflo′ra.** A synonym of *Pavonia multiflora*.

**G. semperflor′ens.** A synonym of *Pavonia semperflorens*.

**G. strictiflor′a.** About 18 in. h. *l.* ovate, large. *fl.* clustered, axillary; bracts yellowish-white, tinged red. August. 1852. (B.M. 4677.) Syn. *G. cauliflora*.

F. G. P.

**GOLD CUP.** *See* **Ranunculus bulbosus.**

**GOLD FERN.** *See* **Pityrogramma.**

**GOLD KNOTS.** *See* **Ranunculus acris.**

**GOLD-TAIL MOTH** (*Euproctis similis*). The striking black, red-lined caterpillars of this moth often abound on fruit-trees, especially Apple, Cherry, Pear, Plum, and Nut. The white-winged moths have a tuft of yellowish or orange hairs at the end of the body, and are on the wing in late July and August. The caterpillars feed for a time in autumn and then seek over-wintering quarters in the dark and there spin small silk cocoons. They recommence feeding on the leaves in spring, and are fully fed by late June when they spin greyish cocoons between the leaves and there pupate. This pest is most abundant on old trees and in neglected orchards where routine winter spraying is not carried out. A 10 per cent. tar-distillate wash destroys the over-wintering caterpillars provided they are wetted by the wash and are not too deeply bedded in the bark or protected beneath grease bands.

G. F. W.

**GOLD THREAD.** The slender yellow roots of *Coptis trifolia*, used in Canada and Siberia for dyeing skins and wool.

**GOLDEN APPLE.** *See* **Poncirus** and **Spondias lutea.**

**GOLDEN BALL.** *See* **Trollius.**

**GOLDEN CHAIN.** *See* **Laburnum anagyroides.**

**GOLDEN FEATHER.** *See* **Chrysanthemum Parthenium aureum.**

**GOLDEN HAIR.** *See* **Chrysocoma.**

**GOLDEN LARCH.** *See* **Pseudolarix amabilis.**

**GOLDEN MAIDENHAIR.** *See* **Polypodium vulgare.**

**GOLDEN PLUSIA MOTH** (*Plusia moneta*) is a pest of Delphinium and Monkshood (*Aconitum*), the buds, flowers, and seed-vessels of which are eaten by the caterpillars during late April, May, and June. The female moth lays her eggs amongst the buds or on the petals of the open blooms. The white-dotted, greenish caterpillars hide among the flower-buds, which are spun together, or in turned-down young tender leaves. They over-winter in the hollow stems of their food plants both above and below ground level, and ascend the shoots in spring and make their 'nests' in the tips of the shoots and later feed openly on the leaves. When fully grown, they spin conspicuous yellowish cocoons on the under-side of the leaves and in the leaf-axils.

The twisted leaves and spun flower-heads should be handpicked during May and June, and the cocoons collected and destroyed. Dusting with nicotine dust on the attacked shoots is an effective measure of control.

The hollow stems of herbaceous plants should be cut down as low as possible in autumn to prevent the caterpillars from seeking shelter in the snags.

G. F. W.

**GOLDEN ROD.** *See* **Solidago.**

**GOLDEN SEAL.** *See* **Hydrastis canadensis.**

**GOLDEN SHOWER.** *See* **Cassia Fistula.**

**GOLDEN THISTLE.** *See* **Scolymus hispanicus** and **Protea scolymocephala.**

**GOLDEN WILLOW.** *See* **Salix vitellina.**

**GOLDFUS'SIA.** Included in **Strobilanthes.**

***Goldiea'nus -a -um,*** in honour of the Rev. Hugh Goldie, of the United Presbyterian Mission, W. Africa, who collected *c.* 1870.

**GOLDILOCKS.** *See* **Aster Linosyris.**

**GOMBO.** *See* **Hibiscus esculentus.**

***gomeren'sis -is -e,*** of Gomera, Canary Is.

**GOME'SA** (in honour of Bernardino Gomez, surgeon in the Portuguese Navy, who wrote on the plants of Brazil in 1803). FAM. *Orchidaceae.* A genus of 10 species of epiphytic Orchids, natives of Brazil, with the habit of small Odontoglossums. Flowers numerous, pale yellow or greenish, inconspicuous but usually fragrant, produced in winter and early spring; margins of the narrow segments often undulate; sepals and petals similar, the lateral sepals often connate or partially so; lip affixed at the base of the column, continuous, incurved-erect or erect from the base, at length reflexed, spurless; column erect, semi-terete; raceme often many-flowered; scape axillary often arched. Pseudobulbs terminating in 1 or 2 leaves which are broadly petiolate. The species introduced require similar treatment to *Odontoglossum crispum*, but should have a winter temperature not below 55° F.

**G. Bar'keri.*** *fl.* ¾ in. h., light yellowish-green, with some red spots on the lip and an orange line round the stigma; sep. undulate, lateral connate to middle; scape loosely racemose, many-fld. *l.* 5 to 7 in. long. *Pseudobulbs* 3 to 4 in. long, 2-lvd. 1836. (B.M. 3497 as *Rodriguezia Barkeri.*) SYN. *Odontoglossum Barkeri.*

**G. cris'pa.*** *fl.* sea-green, edged yellowish, primrose-scented; sep. and pet. undulate-crisped; raceme elongated. *l.* oblong-lanceolate, spreading, undulated. *Pseudobulbs* elongated, compressed, 2 to 4 in. h., 1 in. wide, 2-lvd. *l.* 6 to 10 in. long, 1 to 1½ in. wide. 1839. (B.R. 26, 54 as *Rodriguezia crispa.*) SYN. *Odontoglossum crispatulum.*

**G. folio'sa.*** *fl.* buff-yellow, very fragrant, ¾ in. across; lateral sep. connate at base; lip reflexed, with 2 white keels on disk; raceme longer than l. *l.* 8 to 15 in. long, ¾ to 1¼ in. wide. *Pseudobulbs* much compressed, 2 to 3 in. long, 2-lvd. 1825. (B.M. 2746 as *Pleurothallis foliosa.*) SYN. *Odontoglossum foliosum.*

**G. Glaziov'ii.** A synonym of *G. scandens.*

**G. planifo'lia.*** *fl.* light greenish-yellow, very fragrant; lateral sep. connate nearly to tips; lip reflexed, with 2 oblong tubercles on disk; raceme longer than l. *l.* 4 to 8 in. long, recurved. *Pseudobulbs* about 2 in. long, 2-lvd. 1822. (L.B.C. 660 as *G. recurva*; B.M. 3504 as *Rodriguezia planifolia.*) SYN. *Odontoglossum planifolium.*

**G. recur'va.** *fl.* light greenish yellow, fragrant, ¾ in. long; lateral sep. connate into an oblong blade deeply 2-fid at apex; lip having 2 short, raised plates at base; raceme as long as or longer than l., arching. *l.* 8 to 12 in. long. *Pseudobulbs* 2 to 3 in. long, 2- or 3-lvd. 1815. (B.M. 1748.) SYN. *Odontoglossum recurvum, Rodriguezia recurva.*

**G. scan'dens.** *fl.* small, yellowish-white; lip with greenish or white keels; lateral sep. connate for half their length then divergent. *Pseudobulbs* elliptic-oblong, compressed, 1 to 2 in. h., borne at intervals of 2 to 4 in. on a stout ascending rhizome, monophyllous. *l.* 3 to 5 in. long. Brazil. 1902. SYN. *G. Glaziovii.* Requires the temperature of the intermediate house and is better suited with a raft than a pot or pan.

**G. ses'silis.** *fl.* small, greenish, not fragrant; sep. linear-ligulate, the lateral connate to their slightly reflexed tips; lip with a 2-lobed crest. *Pseudobulbs* clustered, ovoid or oblong, dark green, 1½ to 2 in. h., about 1 in. broad, diphyllous. *l.* 6 to 8 in. long, ¾ to 1 in. wide. Brazil.

**G. Theodo'rea.** A synonym of *Theodorea gomezoides.*

E. C.

**GOMPH'IA.** A synonym of Ouratea.

**GOMPHOCAR'PUS.** Included in **Asclepias.**

**GOMPHOLO'BIUM** (*gomphos*, club, *lobos*, pod; in reference to the club-shaped seed-pod). FAM. *Leguminosae.* A genus of about 30 species of evergreen shrubs confined to Australia. Leaves usually 3-foliolate, digitate or pinnate, rarely simple; the terminal leaflet is sessile between the uppermost pair. Flowers papilionaceous, mostly yellow, but also red or purplish; standard usually large and handsome. Beautiful cool-greenhouse shrubs now much neglected. They are not so easily cultivated as many Australian plants. Perfect drainage and care against over-watering are important.

**G. barbig'erum.** A synonym of *G. latifolium.*

**G. capita'tum.** Shrub 2 to 3 ft., shoots and inflor. white-hairy. *l.* pinnate with 3 to 11, usually 5 or 7, lflets., filiform, ⅓ to ¾ in. long, margins revolute. *fl.* in dense, terminal, leafy clusters 1 to 1½ in. across; cal. very hairy; standard ⅝ in. long, reniform, yellow; wings and keel much smaller. July. W. Australia. 1830. (B.R. 1563.)

**G. fimbria'tum.** A synonym of *G. latifolium.*

**G. grandiflo'rum.*** Glabrous shrub, 3 ft. *lflets.* in threes, narrow-linear, ½ to 1¼ in. long, ⅙ in. wide, pointed. *fl.* solitary or in twos or threes, terminal on short axillary shoots; standard 1½ in. wide, ¾ in. deep, rich yellow, deeply notched; wings much smaller. June. New S. Wales, Victoria. 1803. (B.R. 484; A.B.R. 427 as *G. maculatum.*) Hardy in Scilly Is.

**G. Hen'dersonii.** A synonym of *Burtonia Hendersonii.*

**G. Knightia'num.** Glabrous, low shrub, shoots very slender. *l.* pinnate; lflets. 3 to 15, linear to linear-oblong, but usually obovate on the lower part of the shoot; variable in size, narrow ones up to 1⅓ in. long, the obovate ones up to ¾ in. long and ½ in. wide, wrinkled above. *fl.* in terminal clusters of 6 to 10; standard ⅜ in. wide, pinkish-purple with a yellow spot at base. July, August. W. Australia. (B.R. 1468.)

**G. latifo'lium.*** Tall, glabrous, erect shrub. *lflets.* 3 on a very short stalk, linear-lanceolate to oblanceolate, 1 to 2 in. long, ⅛ to ⅙ in. wide, glaucous beneath, apex pointed to notched. *fl.* solitary in the upper l.-axils, rich yellow; standard reniform up to 1½ in. across; wings up to 1 in. long. June. Queensland, New S. Wales. 1824. (B.M. 4171 as *G. barbigerum*; S.E.B. 58 as *G. fimbriatum.*)

**G. macula'tum.** A synonym of *G. grandiflorum*, and *Cyclopia genistoides.*

**G. margina'tum.** Shrub 1 to 1½ ft., shoots slender, glabrous. *lflets.* 3 (rarely 1) on a stalk ⅛ in. long, obovate, oblanceolate or narrow-oblong, ½ to ¾ in. long, ⅛ to ¼ in. wide, mucronate, glaucous, glabrous. *fl.* yellow, from solitary to few in loose terminal racemes; standard ⅜ in. wide. W. Australia. 1820. (B.R. 1490.)

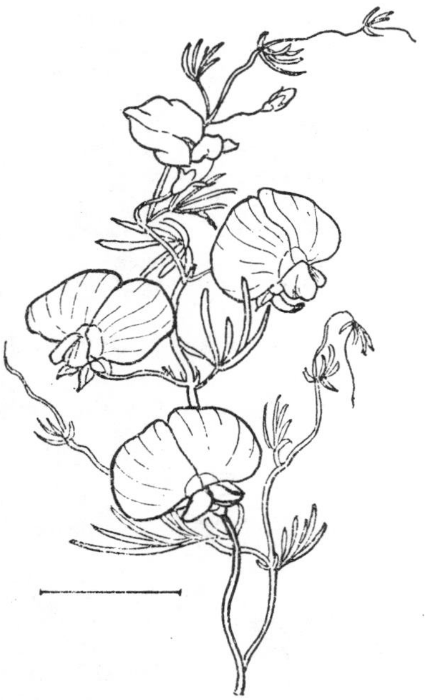

*Gompholobium polymorphum* (p. 907)

**G. polymorph'um.** Shrub or undershrub, very variable in habit and l., sometimes twining, glabrous. *l.* with 3 or 5 (rarely 7 or 9) lflets., digitate, linear to oblanceolate, ⅓ to 1 in. long. *fl.* solitary or few, axillary or terminal, from orange-yellow to bright crimson; standard ⅓ to 1 in. across. June. W. Australia. 1809. (B.M. 1533; B.R. 1574 as *G. venulosum*; B.M. 4179 as *G. versicolor*.) Hardy in Scilly Is.

**G. tomento'sum.** Shrub 1 to 3 ft., shoots hairy. *l.* pinnate; lflets. 5 or 7, sometimes 3 or 11, filiform, ⅛ to ¾ in. long, downy. *fl.* few, yellow, terminal, in compact clusters or solitary; standard ½ in. wide; cal. ⅓ in. long, shaggy. May to August. W. Australia. 1830. (B.R. 1474.) Near *G. capitatum* but with twice as many ovules in each ovary.

**G. venulo'sum.** A synonym of *G. polymorphum*.

**G. venus'tum.\*** Shrub 1 to 2 ft., shoots slender, flexuose, glabrous. *l.* pinnate, ½ to 1 in. long; lflets. 11 to 21, ⅛ to ¾ in. long, closely revolute, filiform, warty. *fl.* rose-purple, in a terminal cluster of 12 to 20, the stalk slender, 1½ to 3 in. long; standard ⅝ in. across, roundish-reniform, stained yellow at the base. July. W. Australia. (B.M. 4258.) Grown out of doors in Scilly Is.

**G. versico'lor.** A synonym of *G. polymorphum*.

W. J. B.

**GOMPHRE'NA** (derived from *Gromphaena*, a name used by Pliny for a kind of Amaranth). FAM. *Amaranthaceae*. A genus of about 70 species of half-hardy annual, biennial, or perennial herbs, natives of Trop. America and Australia with 1 species widely distributed in Asia and Trop. Africa. Leaves opposite, entire, sessile or almost so. Flower-heads usually sessile and solitary at the tips of branches. Two or 3 species have been introduced, but *G. globosa* is the only one now in cultivation and the varieties of it once distinguished are now rarely offered separately. It may be grown in ordinary soil treated like other half-hardy annuals or as a pot-plant for summer flowering in greenhouses and conservatories. Its flower-heads are 'everlasting' and, if cut just before reaching maturity, will retain their colour for a long time. Cultivation as for Celosia.

**G. globo'sa.\*** About 12 in. h. (taller under glass). *l.* oblong, hairy. *fl.-heads* of various colours from white through yellow to purple. Summer. India. 1714. (B.M. 2815.) var. **na'na,\*** about 5 in. h., fl. fine dark red.

**GONATAN'THUS** (*gonu*, knee, *anthos*, flower; the spathe being bent). FAM. *Araceae*. A genus of 2 species of tuberous Himalayan herbs allied to Colocasia, but the spadix without an appendix and the ovules attached at base of ovary. Stove perennials treated like Caladium.

**G. pu'milus.** Tuber small, creeping, slender-branched. *l.* ovate or oblong-ovate, acute, base cordate, 3 to 8 in. long, thinly leathery, dark green above, grey-green or reddish-violet beneath; l.-stalk 10 to 16 in. long. *Spathe* rich golden-yellow, 6 to 8 in. long, about 1 in. wide. *fl.* fragrant. Himalaya. (B.M. 5275 as *G. sarmentosus*.)

**G. sarmento'sus.** A synonym of *G. pumilus*.

**GONATO'PUS** (*gonu*, knee, *pous*, foot; the leaf-stalk has a 'knee' about the middle). FAM. *Araceae*. A genus of 2 species of Trop. E. African herbs allied to Zamioculcas but 3- or 4-pinnate leaves, long peduncles, and the upper flowers with rudimentary ovaries, the lower destitute of staminodes. For treatment *see* **Zamioculcas**.

**G. Boivin'ii.** Tuber flattish, about 6 in. across. *l.* solitary, 3- or 4-pinnate, pinnae remote; lflets. lanceolate, slender-pointed, about 4 in. long, 1½ in. wide; stalk 3 ft. long (including the rachis), spotted blackish-brown. *Peduncle* about 12 in. long, slender, spotted like l.-stalk. *Spathe* tube sub-globose, blade lanceolate about 5 in. long, dirty yellowish without, pale straw within; spadix as long as spathe, yellowish-white. Zanzibar, &c. 1873. (B.M. 6026.) SYN. *Zamioculcas Boivinii*.

*Gondoui'ni*, in honour of M. Gondouin, gardener at St.-Cloud, nr. Paris (*c.* 1863).

**GON'GORA** (in honour of D. Antonio Cabellero of Gongora, once Viceroy of New Granada, and a patron of Mutis). Including Acropera. FAM. *Orchidaceae*. A singular genus of about 25 species of evergreen, epiphytic orchids, natives of Trop. America. The species are easily grown and the majority are worth attention from the quaint appearance of the flowers which has gained for the genus the name of 'Punch and Judy orchids'. The

flowers are borne in drooping racemes often long and many-flowered. Considerable variation occurs in the flowers of the different species. Usually the pedicel is so curved that the labellum is uppermost. Generally all the segments are narrow; the upper sepal, often remote and reduced in size, is partially adnate to the column; the usually larger lateral sepals are free, spreading or reflexed, their bases adnate to the foot of the column; the pointed petals, often smaller than the upper sepal and often horn-like, are adnate to the column base. The clawed lip is continuous with the foot of the column and usually parallel with it but may be ascending; it is usually tapered and fleshy, the fleshy side lobes erect, horned or bristled, the mid-lobe very varied, fleshy, often apparently squeezed into complicated folds. A figure is

*Lip of Gongora grossa*

necessary to understand the shape. Often it is compressed laterally and pinched almost to contortion, terminating in a point, or a long apiculus, or may be blunt. In many the short, slender claw, abruptly expands into a flanged or rounded body the sides of which each finish in a horn- or bristle-like process; similar bristles may or may not be present near the base. Between the front horns and epichil (front lobe) is often a very short, narrow connexion, really a continuation of the main part of the lip but almost separate because of a deep sinus on either side. This connexion (which expands abruptly into the fleshy epichil) is often triangular in shape, and so compressed laterally as to form a second triangle in profile, more or less long-apiculate, the apiculus straight, waved, or hooked. So many variations occur that the foregoing can only be taken as broadly descriptive. The column is produced into a foot. Pollinia 2. The pseudobulbs are somewhat oblong, usually pale yellowish-green, and strongly ribbed and bear 2 broadly lanceolate plicately veined leaves, their bases contracted into short petioles. Out of flower the larger-ribbed pseudobulbs and the smoother texture of the leaves distinguish the genus from Stanhopeas. In common with Stanhopeas, Gongoras often develop numerous erect, aerial roots. Acropera was only kept separate by reason of the galeate dorsal sepal and the somewhat saccate mid-lobe of the lip. Compost should be as that for Stanhopeas and their cultural requirements are the same. Though the flower-spikes are arching, rather than pendulous, baskets are preferable to pots or pans. If pots or pans are used the compost should be elevated so that the plant is brought slightly above the pot rim, so as to allow the inflorescence to hang over the edge. A rest is required in winter, frequency of the waterings being governed by the artificial heat used.

**G. armeni'aca.*** *fl.* sep. rich yellow, slightly spotted or barred red; pet. very small; lip ochre-yellow, fleshy, somewhat saccate, pointed; raceme lax, 12- to 20-fld., pendulous, 12 in. or more long. Summer. *Pseudobulbs* oval, 2 in. h. *l.* 2, 12 to 15 in. long, 2½ to 4 in. wide, light green. Nicaragua. 1850. (B.M. 5501 as *Acropera aurantiaca.*)

**G. atropurpu'rea.*** *fl.* dark purple; lower sep nearly 1 in. long; pet. ½ in. long; lip fleshy, base tapered, compressed, epichil vertically compressed, sub-saggitate with a recurved point, variable; raceme long, many-fld. *Pseudobulbs* ribbed, 2 or 3 in. h. Brazil, Guiana, Venezuela, Trinidad. 1824. (B.M. 3220.)

**G. auranti'aca.** *fl.* bright vermilion-orange, distant in a nodding spike, long-lasting. Autumn and early spring. Evergreen. Colombia.

**G. bufo'nia.*** *fl.* nodding, rosy or purplish on a whitish ground; upper sep. 1 in. long, lower slightly longer sub-falcate, all with revolute margins; pet. small; lip fleshy; the epichil compressed, its apex acuminate, hooked. Habit, &c., as in *G. atropurpurea.* Brazil. 1841. (B.R. 27, 2.)

**G. Charlesworth'ii.** A synonym of *G. scaphephorus.*

**G. Charon'tis.** *fl.* sep. and pet. yellow, spotted brown; lip white, apex and wings rich yellowish, spotted crimson, as is the white column; spike many-fld., hairy. *Pseudobulbs* large, rounded. Colombia. 1877. Allied to *G. scaphephorus* but with smaller fl.

**G. flaveo'la.** *fl.* light ochre-yellow, spotted brown, distant; lip with a sigmoid claw, and median bristle and very small horns to the basal part (hypochil); peduncle angulate; raceme many-fld. 1886.

**G. galea'ta.*** *fl.* strongly scented like Wallflowers; sep. and pet. pale tawny-yellow, upper sep. strongly hooded; lip brownish-red; racemes drooping, freely produced, ovaries curving inwards. Summer. *Pseudobulbs* ovate, clustered, 1 to 2 in. h. *l.* 4 to 8 in. long. Mexico. 1828. (B.M. 3563 as *Acropera Loddigesii*; L.B.C. 1645 as *Maxillaria galeata.*) Allied to *G. armeniaca.* var. **purpu'rea,** *fl.* sep. dark purple, pet. deep yellow, lip dotted black. 1890.

**G. gratulabun'da.*** *fl.* yellow, profusely dotted dull red; sep. revolute-margined, the dorsal erect, lateral reflexed; raceme loosely many-fld. *l.* oblanceolate, caudate-acuminate. *Pseudobulbs* oblong, strongly and acutely ribbed. Colombia. 1857. (B.M. 7224.)

**G. gros'sa.** *fl.* whitish or yellowish, much spotted with dark purple. Ecuador. Allied to *G. atropurpurea*, differing by a tooth inside, a small, terete, acuminate body between the horns, and a broader and stouter lip. (B.M. 8562.)

**G. Jenisch'ii.** A synonym of *G. odoratissima.*

**G. leucochi'la.*** Resembling *G. bufonia* in habit. Dorsal sep. and pet. lilac-purple spotted dark brown; lateral sep. lilac-purple and spotted brown passing to white; lip white with 4 horn-like appendages, the basal ones short and flat, the anterior pair long, acuminate. *Pseudobulbs* ovate, strongly ribbed. *l.* elliptic-lanceolate 5-ribbed. Guatemala. (F.d.S. 1845, 87.)

**G. Loddige'sii.** A synonym of *G. galeata.*

**G. macran'tha.** A synonym of *Coryanthes macrantha.*

**G. macula'ta.** A synonym of *G. quinquenervis.*

**G. maculata tric'olor.** A synonym of *G. tricolor.*

**G. nigri'ta.*** *fl.* with long curved pedicels, fragrant, dark brown; lower sep. 1 in. long with revolute margins; pet. small; lip fleshy, stiff, the mesochil horns almost straight, the sinus between them and the epichil deeply cut; epichil terminating in a recurved apiculus. *Pseudobulbs* 3 to 3½ in. h. *l.* 15 to 20 in. long. *infl.* 2 to 3 ft. long. Brazil, Trinidad, &c. 1839. var. **al'ba,** *fl.* pure white, probably an albino of this species. Trinidad.

**G. odoratis'sima.** *fl.* clear yellow, mottled and blotched reddish-brown; lip continuous with column foot, base clawed, arched and compressed laterally with 2 petaloid processes at back, upper part long-oval, acute, sides folded face to face; racemes drooping. *l.* broadly lanceolate. Venezuela. (F.d.S. 229.) SYN. *G. Jenischii.*

**G. portento'sa.*** *fl.* 1½ to 2 in. long; sep. pale flesh-coloured or yellowish; pet. and lip speckled with small violet-purple spots, fleshy, the bristle-like horns inclined backwards; raceme long, many-fld. April. Ecuador. 1869. (B.M. 6284.) var. **ro'sea,** sep. and pet. bright rose-purple, with small purplish spots, lip citron-yellow and brown, large and thick. Colombia. 1896.

**G. quinquener'vis.*** *fl.* fragrant, yellowish, spotted and striped with brownish-purple or red; upper sep. about 1 in. long, lateral sep. 1 in. or more long with revolute margins; pet. small; lip compressed laterally; peduncle 15 to 24 in. long. *Pseudobulbs* 2 to 3 in. h. *l.* 12 to 15 in. long, 2 to 4 in. wide. A very variable species. Brazil, Peru, Guiana, &c. 1798. (L. 208; B.M. 3687 and B.R. 1616 as *Gongora maculata.*)

**G. Sanderia'na.** *fl.* yellowish with rose spots; raceme about 6-fld. *l.* 10 in. long, 2 in. wide. *Pseudobulbs* conical, 5 in. long. Peru. 1896. Allied to *G. portentosa.*

**G. scapheph'orus.*** *fl.* fragrant, whitish, blotched and marked with purple-brown; lip shaded yellow and purple-barred towards its base; dorsal sep. ½ in. long by ¼ in. wide; pet. small; side lobes of lip terminated by a slender bristle ½ in. long; mid-lobe acuminate; scapes arching. *Pseudobulbs* 2 to 3 in. h. *l.* broadly lanceolate, 12 in. long, over 2 in. wide. Peru. 1854.

**G. Siedelia'na.** Allied to *G. galeata* and resembling that species in habit. *fl.* deep yellow; sep. heavily marked with transverse brown bars; lip with a few bars of the same colour. Mexico. 1852. (R.X.O. 1, 20.)

**G. Tracya'na.** Allied to *G. scaphephorus* but with smaller fl. with greenish-yellow sep. and pet. and a white lip all spotted with brown. Ecuador. 1911.

**G. tric'olor.*** *fl.* sep. deep bright yellow, blotched sienna-brown, the dorsal lanceolate, affixed half-way up back of column, lateral obliquely triangular; pet. pale yellow, lightly spotted; hypochil white, oblong, convex, 2-horned at base, epichil stained on sides with cinnamon; racemes stout, drooping. *Pseudobulbs* thickly ribbed. Peru. (B.M. 7530; B.R. 33, 69 as *G. maculata tricolor.*)

**G. trunca'ta.** *fl.* whitish or straw-coloured, freckled brownish-purple; dorsal sep. obovate, carinate, lateral roundish-oblong, very blunt; pet. small; lip clear yellow, curved, hypochil compressed in middle and bearing 2 awns in front, epichil ovate, channelled; pedicels mottled purple. Mexico. (B.R. 31, 56.) Habit of *G. atropurpurea.*

E. C.

***gongylo'des,*** roundish.

**GONIO'MA** (*gonia*, angle; the corona is angled near the top). FAM. *Apocynaceae.* A small genus allied to Tabernaemontana but having the ovules in 2 series instead of many. Needs only ordinary good soil and a cool greenhouse. Cuttings root under a hand-light with a little bottom heat, or the plants may be raised from seed.

**G. Kamas'si.** Evergreen shrub with l. opposite or in threes, oblong-lanceolate, entire, leathery. *fl.* small, yellowish, salver-shaped, tube wide at middle and angled, constricted at top, hairy within in upper half, lobes one-third as long as tube, twisted to right in bud; corymbs terminal, 8- to 10-fld. S. Africa. SYN. *Tabernaemontana Camassi.* Yields the hard Kamassi wood of S. Africa.

**GONIOPHLE'BIUM appendicula'tum.** *See* **Polypodium plesiosorum; G. brasilien'se.** *See* **P. triseriale.**

**GONIOP'TERIS.** *See* **Dryopteris.**

**GONIOSCYPH'A** (*gonia*, angle, *skyphe*, cup; in allusion to the form of the perianth). FAM. *Liliaceae. G. eucomoides* is the only species. It needs similar treatment to Eucharis.

**G. eucomoi'des.** Rootstock short, fleshy. *l.* in a basal rosette, elliptical, 1 ft. long, about 5 in. wide, acute. *fl.* dull green, bell-shaped, lobes 6, nearly round, blunt, in a dense cylindrical spike on the leafless scape which terminates in a crown of fine awl-shaped bracts like those among the fl. Bhotan. 1886.

**GONOCA'LYX** (*gonos*, an angle, *kalyx*; in allusion to the angled calyx). FAM. *Ericaceae.* A genus of 3 species of S. American, compact, evergreen shrubs, sometimes epiphytic. Leaves alternate, leathery. The following species requires greenhouse conditions and should be given a lime-free, largely peaty soil and treatment generally similar to that given to the more tender Azaleas.

**G. pul'cher.** Shrub with glabrous shoots, at first purplish and angled. *l.* ⅝ to 1⅛ in. long, roundish-ovate, apex rounded with a minute point, minutely crenulate, glabrous, at first rosy-purple. *fl.* axillary, solitary or in pairs; cor. cylindric ¾ in. long, ⅛ in. wide, bright rose paling towards the erect, 5-toothed limb. Andes of Colombia. 1853.

W. J. B.

**GONOLO'BUS** (*gonia*, angle, *lobos*, pod; in some species the fruits are angled). FAM. *Asclepiadaceae.* A genus of about 70 species of prostrate or twining shrubs or sub-shrubs, natives of Trop. and N. America. Leaves opposite, often cordate. Flowers usually dark, in racemes or corymbs, the peduncles interpetiolar; corolla rotate or reflexed, 5-lobed. The greenhouse species grow well in a compost of peat and loam with ordinary treatment, the hardy ones need light sandy soil in a warm, dryish place. Propagation is by division or seed.

**G. carolinen'sis.** Deciduous, hairy climber. *l.* ovate-cordate, slender-pointed; stalks long. *fl.* purplish; cor. segs. oval-oblong, blunt. *infl.* umbellate. June, July. Carolina. 1824. (S.B.F.G. 1.) Greenhouse.

**G. diadema'tus.** *l.* oblong to elliptical-lanceolate, cordate. *fl.* green; corona at bottom of tube. Autumn. Mexico. 1812. (B.R. 252.)

**G. ed'ulis.** Guayota. Rusty-hairy, twining shrub. *l.* ovate-oblong, deeply cordate. *fl.* white; cor. densely bearded within; peduncles short, 3- to 5-fld. *fr.* as large as a swan's egg, edible. Costa Rica. Warm-house.

**G. his'pidus.** About 4 ft. h., bristly hairy. *l.* cordate-ovate, acute. *fl.* brown; cor. leathery, tubercled inside at base. *infl.* umbellate. July. Brazil. 1837. (B.M. 3786.) Syn. *Fischeria hispida.* Warm-house.

**G. laev'is.** Herbaceous perennial. *l.* oblong, deeply cordate, abruptly slender-pointed. *fl.* green; cor. long-conical in bud, not twisted, lobes narrow-lanceolate, blunt, glabrous within. June. N. America. 1806. Hardy. var. **macrophyl'la** has wider *l.*, the basal lobes touching or overlapping.

**G. ni'ger.** Evergreen. *l.* ovate-cordate, acute. *fl.* very dark purple to black; in few-fld. racemes. October. Mexico. 1825. (B.M. 2799.) Syn. *Cynanchum nigrum.* Stove.

**G. obli'quus.** Herbaceous perennial. *l.* rounded- to ovate-cordate, abruptly slender-pointed. *fl.* crimson-purple within, dull or greenish and minutely downy without; oblong-conical in bud. *infl.* umbellate. Summer. N. America. 1809. (B.M. 1273 as *Cynanchum discolor.*) Hardy.

**G. subero'sus.** Herbaceous perennial. *l.* cordate, slender-pointed, sometimes hairy. *fl.* with broadly conical cor., abruptly slender-pointed, twisted in bud; lobes ovate or triangular-lanceolate, acute, thickish and firm; umbels 3- to 9-fld., shorter than petiole. Summer. N. America. 1732. Hardy.

F. G. P.

**Gooch'iae,** in honour of Mr. P. B. Webb's mother.

## GOOD KING HENRY (*Chenopodium Bonus-Henricus*).

Sometimes called All-good or Mercury. This has long been grown in England for its shoots used as a substitute for Asparagus and for its leaves used like Spinach, though for the latter purpose the Spinach Beet has practically superseded it. It is a perennial and to grow it well needs a deep, rich, rather dry soil. The best way to start a plantation is to sow seeds in drills 9 in. apart, hoeing out the seedlings which are not needed so as to leave the plants 9 in. apart. As soon as the growths have ripened off a dressing of 4 or 5 in. deep of leaf-soil should be spread over the bed. In the spring of the next year a few shoots may be cut, but to cut severely would impoverish the plants; in succeeding years a full crop may be cut. The young shoots of well-grown plants should be as thick as the little finger and they should be cut below the surface of the soil as is Asparagus. The leaves may be gathered for use as Spinach, but the gathering should be light lest the plants are denuded of leaves to their detriment. Cutting may begin in April and be continued until June. During the season of most active growth the plants will be much benefited by applications of manure water.

## GOODE'NIA (in honour of Dr. Samuel Goodenough,

1743–1827, Bishop of Carlisle, author of a monograph of the genus Carex). Fam. *Goodeniaceae.* A genus of about 80 species of herbs or sub-shrubs, rarely shrubs, natives of Australia. Leaves alternate or radical. Flowers yellow, purplish, or blue in axillary panicles or terminal racemes or panicles. A compost of peat and loam suits these greenhouse plants which are readily rooted from cuttings inserted under a bell-glass in spring.

**G. grandiflo'ra.** Herb, 3 to 4 ft. h. *l.* ovate-lanceolate to ovate, truncate or cordate, toothed, stalked. *fl.* yellow, glabrous or slightly hairy without, more or less streaked purple; peduncles axillary, 1-fld. July. (B.M. 890; B.R. 31, 29.)

**G. ova'ta.** Erect, 2 to 4 ft. h., shrub or sub-shrub, often clammy. *l.* ovate to broadly lanceolate, lower often roundish-cordate, 1 to 2 in. long, toothed, stalked. *fl.* yellow, glabrous without; peduncles often many-fld., twin or forked near base. July. (A.B.R. 68.)

**G. radi'cans.** A synonym of *Selliera radicans.*

**G. stellig'era.** Erect herb 12 to 18 in. h., stem almost leafless. Radical *l.* linear, blunt, rather thick, entire; *stem-l.* very few, shorter. *fl.* yellow, sessile or nearly so, in clusters of 2 or 3, upper solitary, woolly without; in a long, interrupted spike. June. 1823.

## GOODENIA'CEAE. Dicotyledons. A family of about

250 species of herbs, sub-shrubs, or rarely shrubs falling into 12 genera. Leaves alternate or radical, very rarely irregularly opposite, entire, toothed or rarely pinnatifid. Flowers hermaphrodite, 5-merous, usually regular; stamens free; carpels 2, 1- to many-seeded, usually inferior. Fruit a capsule, rarely a drupe or nut. The family is almost confined to Australia, a few species of 1 genus (Scaevola) occurring in New Zealand, the Pacific Is., and the coasts of Trop. and Sub-trop. Africa, Asia, and America, and 1 species of another genus extending to the coast of China. The genera included here are Brunonia, with flowers in a head, Dampira, Goodenia, Leschenaultia, Scaevola, Selliera, Velleia, all with flowers loosely arranged.

## GOODENOV'IA. A synonym of Goodenia.

## GOOD'IA (in honour of Peter Good, botanical collector

in Australia, where he died in 1804). Fam. *Leguminosae.* Two species of evergreen shrubs natives of Australia and Tasmania. Leaves alternate, of 3 entire, obovate leaflets. Pods, thin, flat. Cool greenhouse shrubs easily grown either in pots or planted out; propagated by cuttings. *G. lotifolia* is grown in the open in Scilly Is.

**G. lotifo'lia.*** Evergreen shrub 4 to 8 ft., shoots sometimes minutely downy and glaucous. *l.* of 3 lflets. which are obovate, round-ended, cuneate, ½ to ¾ in. long. *fl.* in axillary and terminal racemes of 10 to 20 and 2 to 4 in. long; standard pet. ½ in. wide, deeply notched, yellow with a reddish-purple, basal stain; wings similarly coloured. April to July. Australia, Tasmania. 1802. (B.M. 958.)

**G. pubes'cens.** Shrub up to 4 ft., similar in growth to *G. lotifolia* but with the shoots, *l.*, and *infl.* softly downy. *l.* smaller, mostly ½ to ½ in. long. *fl.* in racemes 1 to 2 in. long, similarly coloured but smaller. Australia, Tasmania. 1803. (B.M. 1310.)

W. J. B.

## GOOD'YERA (in honour of John Goodyer, 1597?–

1650, of Mapledurham, British botanist, who assisted Johnson in his edition of *Gerard's Herbal*). Fam. *Orchidaceae.* As first constituted by R. Brown the genus consisted of terrestrial orchids with more or less fleshy roots, flowers in spikes, often pubescent, rising from a basal rosette with the dorsal sepal and petals formed into a helmet, the lip ventricose or concave, entire, spurless, free or connate to the column. The genus is widely distributed through the East to Japan and is represented in Britain by *G. repens*, a species with less brilliant foliage than many others. In the original genus are some of the most beautiful of the Anoectochilus group, and as they require the same treatment under cultivation, they are included under that heading in this work. Revisions have been made of the genus and of the species described in the previous volumes of this work, some are now placed in Haemaria and Macodes (*see* **Anoectochilus**), while *G. pubescens*, *G. repens*, and *G. tessellata* have been transferred to Epipactis in a recent revision. Another authority has retained them in the genus with other species which have an entire or almost entire, more or less concave lip. The species given below are suitable for the cool greenhouse or, as with *G. repens*, a select position in the outdoor garden. A somewhat shady site and a well-drained compost of peat, leaf-mould, and sand or pieces of soft sandstone.

**G. japon'ica.** *l.* stout, oblong-ovate, velvety-green, tinged olive-brown; midrib broadly striped silvery-white, suffused with rosy-pink when young. Japan. (B.H. 369.)

**G. macran'tha.** *fl.* pale rose, large, 2 or 3, terminal. June. *l.* ovate, acute, bordered yellow, dark green in middle, reticulated with pale green. Japan. 1867. Nearly hardy. (G.C. 1867, 1022.) Syn. *G. picta.*

**G. Menzies'ii.** *l.* elliptic, 1½ to 3 in. long, dark green with a whitish central stripe and veins. 12 in. h. N. America. Syn. *G. decipiens, Spiranthes decipiens, Epipactis decipiens.*

**G. pic'ta.** A synonym of *G. macrantha.*

**G. pubes'cens.** *l.* 4 to 6 in a rosette broadly elliptical, dark velvety-green, silver-veined. *fl.* whitish-yellow. N. America. 1802. (L.B.C. 1; S.B.F.G. s. 2, 47.) A pretty species varying in height, suitable for a cool fernery or favourable position out of doors. Requires a shady place and a compost, well drained but moist, of peat, sand, and leaf-mould.

**G. re'pens.** *l.* evergreen, deep green, occasionally marbled or marked, 1 in. or more long. *fl.* small, yellow to white; spike much as in Spiranthes. N. temperate zone, including Britain. (L.B.C. 1987.) Has been grown in a mixture of pine-needles and sand; requires shade; rhizome creeping.

**G. tessella'ta.** Though figured as a var. of *G. pubescens* this has been accorded specific rank. *G. pubescens* has globular fl. while the lip of *G. tessellata* is only slightly saccate and its elongated tip is almost straight. It is very variable, the leaves varying in shape and length from less than 1 to more than 2 in., from ovate to narrowly lanceolate; the tessellation also varies greatly. E. United States. 1824. (B.M. 2540 as *G. pubescens minor.*)

**G. veluti'na.** *fl.* white, shaded rose or salmon; spike about 10-fld. *l.* ovate, acute, deep velvety purplish-green, with white mid-vein. Japan. 1867. Nearly hardy. (G.F. 533.)

E. C.

## GOORA NUT. *See* **Cola acuminata.**

## GOOSEBERRY (*Ribes Grossularia*).

The Gooseberry occurs wild in various parts of Europe, including Britain, where it is widely distributed though perhaps truly wild only in the north. It has been cultivated here certainly since the time of Henry VIII and is more popular in this country than in any more southerly lands. It is hardy but the young leaves and fruits are apt to suffer from late spring frosts occurring after a spell of mild weather. The best-flavoured fruits are produced in the cooler parts of the country where they are less liable to be ripened prematurely by scorching sun and dry atmospheric conditions. The competitive growing of very large fruits fostered by the Gooseberry Clubs which were a common vogue in the middle of the nineteenth century, especially in Cheshire, Lancashire, and the neighbouring counties, has fallen into desuetude, but the large varieties, since they usually attain a usable size earlier than the smaller and often more highly flavoured varieties, are still of value for there is a considerable demand for half-grown green berries for cooking, bottling, and preserving, while the ripe fruits may be had by choice of varieties and variation in planting sites from early August (or in some districts late July) to late autumn.

The best soil is a deep loam well drained, or a deep alluvial soil. But any garden soil may be made suitable for growing gooseberries though heavy soils are apt to encourage soft, coarse growth liable to disease, and light gravelly soils need heavy dressings of manure before planting is undertaken. Regular applications of organic matter are required to keep the bushes fruitful but too much nitrogen available at one time is apt to induce too soft growth. No fruit is more susceptible to potash deficiency, shown especially by the death of the leaf-margins and early leaf fall, and a dressing of sulphate of potash at the rate of ¼ lb. to the sq. yd. should be given in late winter each year. The useful life of gooseberry bushes is about 20 years and may at times be much more. The commonest and best form of bush is that with a leg of about 6 in. Occasionally bushes with several stems from the ground-level are grown but these are more difficult to keep clear of weeds and the ripening berries are more apt to become fouled by splashings from the soil. Gooseberries may also be grown as single, double, or treble cordons or trained on a north wall to provide an autumn crop of dessert berries. For the summer crop in hot districts the bush form is by far the best, for the branches help to protect the fruits hanging beneath them from scorching sun. The later bushes planted on a north border usually escape injury from spring frosts as they come later into flower. In northern districts cordons have much to recommend them, but varieties with a pendent habit are best as bushes.

Bushes should be planted 5 or 6 ft. apart each way, cordons 1 ft. apart.

Propagation is usually by cuttings of sturdy shoots taken as soon as growth is ripe in October. The cuttings are about 10 in. long, the top 1 in. or so of the less ripe tips and all the buds except the uppermost 4 or 5 being removed to prevent sucker-growths from developing. To plant the cuttings take out a trench deep enough to leave a few inches of the bare stem above ground-level, the cuttings being placed against the side of the trench 9 to 12 in. apart, the trenches being 2 ft. apart. In heavy soil some sand should be placed around the lower part of the cuttings before the trench is filled and the soil well firmed. The ground should be kept clean by hoeing through the summer and by autumn the young bushes should be ready for planting in their permanent quarters.

An alternative method of propagation is by layering, branches large or small being pegged down in summer and covered with light soil. Bushes so raised are less symmetrical than those raised from cuttings, and less easy to prevent from suckering. Suckers may also be used for propagating, but plants so raised themselves sucker and so are objectionable for it is difficult to remove the buds from the underground parts of layers and suckers.

If at planting time 3 shoots can be obtained these shoots should be cut back to 3 or 4 buds. The next summer 2 shoots should be secured from each and the laterals kept stopped for forming spurs; the main branches are cut back to about 1 ft. in the autumn. When the bush is so formed routine pruning will be to keep the branches evenly and widely spaced around an open centre. Inward-growing shoots are cut back so that the centre of the bush is not crowded. This will tend to good health and facilitate picking. Varieties with weak spreading and pendent growth should have the lower drooping branches cut back up to half-way to an upward-pointing bud and upward-growing leaders should be retained. Careless, Cousen's Seedling, and Leveller are examples of varieties needing this treatment. Varieties of erect growth like Whinham's Industry should be pruned to an outward-growing bud. In all strong, well-ripened shoots of the previous summer should be retained to replace older branches, for the best fruit is borne on the young growths, and all diseased branches and suckers should be cut clean out. Where birds are troublesome by destroying buds pruning may be deferred until January or February, otherwise it should be done soon after the fruit is picked.

Fan training may be adopted for north walls, new shoots being laid in to replace part of the old each year. With cordons fruiting is, of course, restricted to spurs.

Fruit is usually picked in stages, those picked first being used for cooking green and the picking aimed at an even distribution of the fruit over the bush, next the fruit from the centre and low branches being picked, leaving the best-placed fruits on the outer branches to ripen. Birds may be troublesome as ripening occurs, especially in dry seasons, and means of protection must be adopted.

Special measures were taken by the members of Gooseberry Clubs whose object was to grow the largest berry, taking no account of flavour. To attain this end only large-fruited varieties were grown in specially prepared rich, moist soil kept well watered. The fruit was severely thinned out and under those retained saucers full of water were placed so that a moist atmosphere was maintained about the berries at all times. The weights of berries exhibited at the Club meetings were recorded and the annual lists published show that the berries obtained were very much larger than those produced by the ordinary methods of cultivation. These clubs, like those devoted to, for instance, the cultivation of the Pansy and the Auricula, were a pleasant feature of village and town life where they flourished, providing a hobby which called for no little skill and unremitting care, and promoting friendly intercourse between the folk who were brought together in healthy rivalry, though they added little to the bulk of food produced and nothing to its culinary value. It is to be regretted that such clubs have almost entirely died out, but perhaps in times of greater stability and greater leisure they may be revived and the benefits they confer upon a local community may be regained.

The gooseberries of N. America, derived from the N. American *Ribes Cynosbati*, are not usually successfully grown in this country and indeed do not usually compare favourably with our gooseberry which does not succeed in N. America.

Large numbers of varieties have been raised (the Index to the J.R.H.S., 1838–1935, gives over 400 varietal names) and in many instances it has been found that local conditions are more favourable to some varieties than to others. Local preferences therefore should be taken into consideration, though not necessarily allowed to say the last word, in the selection of varieties to plant. Lists of varieties of general value and for special purposes will be found in the Supplement.

The varieties are usually classified primarily according to the colour of the skin of the fruit; red, yellow, green, or white; then by their relative hairiness, size, shape, and flavour and by the habit of the bush.

Speaking generally, the largest-fruited varieties are less well flavoured than the smaller. Some of the red-skinned varieties are more or less acid but in this class are late-keeping varieties valuable for dessert in autumn and it includes the variety London which produces the largest berries. The amber and yellow varieties include the highest-flavoured fruits and they usually ripen early, the variety Leveller being a favourite early dessert variety among market growers in some districts (e.g. Sussex) because of its good appearance, abundant bearing, and large size. Most of the varieties in this class have thin skins as have the green-fruited varieties which also differ in size, some rich-flavoured varieties of small size among them. The varieties with white skin are more rarely grown though Careless is a well-known market variety of handsome appearance and very fertile.

Hybrids have been raised between the Black Currant and the Gooseberry and though interesting are not of great horticultural merit. *See* **Black Currant.** **A**

*DISEASES.* Most gooseberry diseases are also seen on currants but do not affect the latter to the same extent. Some which affect currants more severely are already dealt with under that heading. Gooseberry roots may be attacked by the Honey Fungus, causing death, but a more serious Dieback is due to the Grey Mould fungus *Botrytis cinerea*. The margins of the leaves of affected branches turn yellow then almost white, but the chief symptom is the death of the bush branch by branch, the leaves turning brown and withering. The fruit on affected branches in wet weather may show soft rot and have a boiled appearance. The trouble is due to the fungus having started in a wound or pruning snag and then penetrated into the branch and killed it. If this occurs at the collar the whole bush will die. Affected branches should be cut out well below the affected part or where all the bush has gone it must be grubbed out and burnt. Diseased material of this sort should not be left lying about near gooseberry plantations and large wounds made in removing branches should be painted over.

The most serious gooseberry disease is probably AMERICAN GOOSEBERRY MILDEW (due to *Sphaerotheca-mors-uvae*), which is easily recognized by the fungus growth on leaves, stems, and berries, at first white then turning dark brown. It is also occasionally seen on currant bushes. The berries are covered by the felted coating and are rendered unsightly as well as reduced in size. The affected shoots twist and curl at their ends and are stunted. In the white stage the fungus is releasing its summer spores (conidia) to spread the infection and later the brown felt contains small black perithecia for over-wintering. Remedial measures include giving the bushes plenty of room and pruning so as to encourage free air circulation between the branches. Heavy dressings of nitrogenous fertilizers are inadvisable as they encourage soft growth which is more easily attacked. The affected shoots must be cut off at the tips about the end of August; these being burnt will destroy a good deal of the over-wintering stage of the fungus. The bushes must be sprayed with a spray containing washing soda 2 lb., soft soap 1 lb., water 10 gall. Lime sulphur, 1 part in 60 parts of water, can be used as the bushes come into flower, again after the first fruit has set, and a third time 3 weeks later, but some varieties are shy of sulphur and may suffer defoliation. Among sulphur-shy varieties are Early Sulphur, Yellow Rough, and Leveller, but others may suffer if the spray is put on in hot weather, so that sulphur of any kind must be used with caution.

EUROPEAN GOOSEBERRY MILDEW (due to *Microsphaera grossulariae*) appears as a white, delicate mould on the upper surfaces of the leaves especially in shady places and where the bushes are crowded. It is easily distinguished from American Mildew as it is very rarely seen to attack the fruit and it is seldom serious. Crowded bushes should be pruned hard to let in the light and air and in some cases a dusting with green sulphur dust may be necessary.

The LEAF SPOT due to *Gloeosporium ribis* attacks gooseberries as well as currants and is dealt with under Currant Leaf Spot.

The CURRANT RUST *Cronartium ribicola* (q.v.) may occur on gooseberries but is rare. The Rust fungus *Puccinia Pringsheimiana*, however, often attacks gooseberries. It is rarely serious but its bright-red or orange-coloured patches on the leaves, stems, and especially berries fill the grower with apprehension. These orange patches are the Cluster Cups or Aecidial stage of the fungus and the other 2 stages are formed on Sedges (*Carex* sp.) from which the infection comes in spring. Sedges should therefore be eradicated if growing near gooseberry plantations. Infected fruits, leaves, &c., should be removed and burnt, and in serious cases the bushes should be sprayed with Bordeaux mixture about a fortnight before the bushes start to flower.

GOOSEBERRY LEAF SCORCH is a non-parasitic trouble due to unsuitable conditions in the soil which results in the margins of the leaves turning brown. Severe defoliation may occur later. This is similar to Apple Leaf Scorch (q.v.) and can usually be corrected by giving a dressing of sulphate of potash at the rate of 1½ oz. to the sq. yard.

(D. E. G.)

*PESTS.* GOOSEBERRY MOTH. *See* **Magpie Moth.**

GOOSEBERRY SAWFLY, *Pteronidea ribesii*, is the most widely distributed and destructive of the 3 species of Sawflies that attack cultivated Ribes, the others being *Pteronidea leucotrochus* and *Pristiphora pallipes*, but the control in each case is the same. The adult sawfly is on the wing in April and May, and the pearly white or greenish eggs are laid in rows along the main veins on the underside of the leaves—as many as 20 or 30 eggs being laid on 1 leaf. The caterpillars have a black head and a green- and black-spotted body with 3 orange-yellow areas near the head and at the end of the body. There are 3 generations a year, the first in April and May, the second in June, and the third in September. The very young larvae congregate together and bite out small holes in the leaves, later separating and then devouring the entire leaf except the midrib and main veins. When fully grown they descend to the soil and spin cocoons in which they pupate. In small gardens the young caterpillars may be removed by hand or shaken off the bushes on to sheets of paper or sacking spread beneath the bushes. Spraying against the first-brood caterpillars with arsenate of lead is advisable, but it is necessary to substitute a non-poisonous Derris wash or Pyrethrum extract when the fruit is forming.

GOOSEBERRY RED SPIDER MITE, *Bryobia praetiosa*, is widely distributed in this country, and is frequently abundant and destructive during late April and May, especially in hot, dry periods. The leaves of attacked bushes become discoloured and fall prematurely, while the fruit is undersized and poor in quality. The rusty-red or greyish mites are just visible to the naked eye, and may be distinguished from other fruit-infesting Red Spiders by the presence of the very long front legs, the other 3 pairs being normal in size. These mites invade Gooseberry plantations in spring, arriving from their hibernating quarters in sheds, outhouses, cracks in wooden posts and brickwork, or in ivy-covered walls. They feed only on sunny, warm days and abstract the sap from the leaves, causing them to become bleached. Old bushes should be sprayed in December with a 5 per cent. tar-distillate wash to destroy any mites that may be sheltering beneath the bark. Infested bushes should be sprayed immediately after flowering with 2 per cent. lime sulphur or, in sulphur-shy varieties (e.g. Keen's Seedling and Leveller), with a 2 per cent. white-oil emulsion.

(G. F. W.)

**GOOSEBERRY, CAPE.** *See* **Physalis peruviana.**

**GOOSEBERRY-TOMATO.** *See* **Physalis peruviana.**

**GOOSEFOOT.** *See* **Chenopodium.**

**GOR'DIUS.** *See* **Horse-hair worms.**

**GORDON'IA** (in honour of James Gordon, nurseryman at Mile End, d. 1781). FAM. *Theaceae.* A genus of about 20 species of evergreen or deciduous trees and shrubs, 2 natives of SE. United States, the others of tropical or warm temperate Asia. Leaves alternate, entire or toothed. Flowers solitary, axillary; sepals and petals 5 (sometimes more); stamens numerous, making with the anthers a conspicuous centre to the blossom. Fruit a 3- to 6-celled, woody capsule. The Gordonias succeed in a lime-free, open, sandy loam, or in a peaty soil and under conditions that suit the less hardy Rhododendrons. Propagated by cuttings or layers.

KEY

| | |
|---|---|
| 1. *Lvs. deciduous* | G. altamaha |
| 1. *Lvs. evergreen* | 2 |
| 2. *Fl. nearly sessile* | G. axillaris |
| 2. *Fl. on slender 2- to 3-in. stalks* | G. Lasianthus |

**G. altamah'a.** Deciduous shrub or small tree, 20 to 30 ft., shoots densely silky. *l.* obovate-oblong, 4 to 8 in. long, 1½ to 3½ in. wide, cuneate, short-stalked, toothed, dark, lustrous green, downy beneath. *fl.* short-stalked, solitary, axillary, cup-shaped, 2 to 3½ in. across, white; pet. obovate, wavy-toothed. August, September. *fr.* a globose, woody capsule, ¾ in. wide. Georgia, United States. 1774. Not seen in a wild state since 1790. (S.S. 22.) SYN. *G. pubescens, Franklinia alatamaha.* Very rare. Autumn colours rich. Requires same treatment as Himalayan rhododendrons.

**G. anom'ala.** A synonym of *G. axillaris.*

**G. axillar'is.*** Evergreen shrub or small tree (occasionally 30 to 40 ft.), shoots glabrous. *l.* 2½ to 7 in. long, ¾ to 2½ in. wide, oblanceolate to oblong, glabrous, dark, shining green, entire or toothed. *fl.* creamy-white, 3 to 5 in. across, solitary on very short stalks in the terminal l.-axils; stamens very numerous, orange-yellow. November to May. *fr.* oblong 1½ to 1⅓ in. long, woody. China, Formosa. 1818. (B.M. 4019 as *Polyspora axillaris.*) SYN. *G. anomala.* Hardy only in Cornwall and similar climates.

**G. chrysan'dra.** Tall leafy evergreen shrub. *l.* obovate-lanceolate, 2½ to 5 in. long, leathery, slightly toothed; stalk short. *fl.* white, 3 to 4 in. across, solitary on ends of short shoots; stamens numerous, yellow, rather shorter than the crenate pet. January, February. Yunnan. 1931. Cool greenhouse.

**G. Lasian'thus.** Evergreen tree occasionally 60 to 70 ft., down to a shrub. *l.* leathery, obovate-lanceolate, pointed, cuneate, shallowly toothed. *fl.* white on slender stalks 2 to 3 in. long, solitary, 2½ to 3 in. across, borne in axils of 2 or 3 terminal l., cal. velvety outside, ½ in. long; pet. concave, with uneven margins, silky at back; anthers yellow. July, August. *fr.* conical, woody, 1¼ in. long. SE. United States. 1768. (B.M. 668.) Cool greenhouse or south-west counties.

*Gordonia axillaris*

*Gordonia chrysandra*

**G. pubes'cens.** A synonym of *G. altamaha.*

W. J. B.

*Gordonia'nus -a -um,* in honour of George Gordon, 1806–79, gardener in R.H.S. Gardens, Chiswick.

**GORGOGLOS'SUM** (*Gorgon, glossum,* tongue). FAM. *Orchidaceae.* A small epiphytic genus distinguished from Sievekingia by the deeply fringed petals and lip. Treatment as for Stanhopeas. A small pan can be used in the place of a basket.

**G. Reichenbachia'num.** *fl.* about 5, 2 in. across; sep. yellowish-green; pet. greenish or yellow, fringed orange-yellow; lip 3-lobed, greenish-yellow thickly flecked with purple-red and fringed with deep-yellow hairs; scape pendulous. *Pseudobulbs* about 1 in. h., monophyllous. *l.* plicate, 6 in. long, 1⅓ in. broad. Colombia, Cauca. 1896. (B.M. 7576 as *Sievekingia Reichenbachiana.*)

*gorgon'eus -a -um,* from the mythological Gorgon.

**GORMA'NIA.** Included in **Sedum.**

**GORNUTI PALM.** See **Arenga.**

**GORSE.** See **Ulex europaeus.**

**GORTE'RIA** (in honour of David Gorter, Dutch botanist, author of *Flora Belgica*). FAM. *Compositae*. A genus of about 4 species of hispid annuals, natives of S. Africa. Leaves alternate, rough and bristly above, white beneath, one-nerved. Flower-heads solitary or in corymbs; ray-florets ligulate, neuter; disk-florets 5-toothed, some marginal ones fertile, central sterile. Involucral scales in many series, finally forming a closed structure somewhat resembling a bulb through which the root fibres pierce when the seed germinates. The hard spiny scales become attached to the coats of animals and are so distributed. A hot sunny place in well-drained soil is needed for *G. diffusa*.

**G. diffu'sa.** Diffuse, 6 to 8 in. h., 12 in. or more across. *l.* entire or pinnatifid, upper ones sessile, entire or toothed; *fl.-heads* with rich orange rays marked irregularly with brown, shining greenish-blue without; involucral scales narrow-awl-shaped, ciliate, nearly as long as rays. S. Africa.

*gossypi'nus -a -um,* like the Cotton Plant.

**GOSSY'PIUM** (ancient Latin name used by Pliny). FAM. *Malvaceae*. A genus of 30 or more species of perennial herbs or shrubs distributed over the tropics of the Old and New Worlds. Leaves 3- to 9-lobed, rarely entire. Flowers white, yellow, or purple, usually large and showy; calyx truncate or shortly 5-fid. Fruit a 3- or 5-celled capsule, bursting when ripe, and exposing the numerous seeds covered with cottony down. Gossypiums grow well in a light, rich soil in the stove. They can be propagated by seed sown in heat in spring, the seedlings when large enough to handle being planted singly in small pots and moved into larger ones as required. They can also be raised from cuttings in sand with bottom heat in a close frame. The genus is exceedingly important as to it belong the plants yielding the cotton of commerce. Of these there are a number of botanical types, some of them with several forms or varieties, often known by native names.

**G. arbor'eum.** Tree Cotton. Shrub or low tree, rarely herbaceous. *l.* deeply palmately 5- to 7-lobed; lobes linear-oblong, mucronate, nearly glabrous. *fl.* purple, rarely white; pet. spreading. Plains of India. 1694.

**GOTHIC MOTH** (*Naenia typica*) is occasionally a pest of Azaleas and Chrysanthemums under glass, but it has a variety of food plants, including Apple, Blackthorn (Sloe), Willow, and low herbage. The moths are on the wing during July and August, the colour of the fore-wings being brown with light markings and whitish veins, and the hind-wings greyish-brown. The eggs are laid in clusters on the leaves, and the young caterpillars feed in colonies on the upper leaf-tissue and produce a skeletonizing effect. When older, they disperse and feed on the entire leaf-tissue. Their colour varies from brownish-grey to greenish-grey with darker lines along the body. They develop slowly during the winter, pupate in the soil in the following spring, and emerge as moths in summer. Plants that are brought into glasshouses are often found to be attacked, especially if they have been plunged in weedy beds. Spraying the foliage lightly with arsenate of lead will effect a control. The plants may be shaken over sheets of paper, canvas, or sacking to dislodge the larvae sheltering among the foliage, while hand-picking the egg clusters and the young caterpillars will prevent further injury.

G. F. W.

*goth'icus -a -um,* of the country of the Goths, Germany.

*Gotoa'nus -a -um,* in honour of Sukichi Goto, of the University, Tokyo.

A

*Gouldia'nus -a -um,* in honour of John Gould Veitch, 1839–70, of the firm of James Veitch & Sons, Chelsea.

**GOURDS.** Most of the plants known as Gourds belong to the genus Cucurbita (q.v.) of which 2 species in cultivation, *C. ficifolia* and *C. foetidissma*, are perennial, the others annual. The 3 annual species most commonly grown are *C. maxima, C. moschata,* and *C. Pepo,* all hardy enough to succeed outside in warm situations from May to autumn, and the ornamental Gourds usually grown in this country are mainly varieties of these. Other ornamental Cucurbitaceae not belonging to this genus will be found under their proper headings. Many of these varieties are vigorous trailing plants that may be used for covering bare walls, hedges, and unsightly fences and so on. They all need rich soil and do best when a considerable quantity of manure is placed beneath the soil in which they are planted. They all need much water during the summer but the drainage must be good. Seed should be sown in gentle heat in April and the young plants should be grown on under glass, hardened off, and then planted outside about the end of May. Protection should be given by hand-lights until fear of frost is past and the plants established. Supports must be provided, such as trellis or branches, strong enough to support the weight of fruit where otherwise bare surfaces are to be covered. The fruits of all these are edible but, with the exception of the Vegetable Marrows, they are grown more for ornament than for the value of their fruit for eating, though the young fruits may be cooked as vegetables. Where the fruits of the very large varieties can be ripened before the onset of frost, they may be cut, hung in a dry, airy place, and kept for several months. The flesh is usually scooped or cut out after they have been kept some time and used in soups and stews, or baked either alone or with apples in pies. The varieties of *C. maxima* have large broad leaves and the fruits have stalks without furrows. Here belong the Turk's Cap and Large Yellow Gourds; the latter has been grown with individual fruits up to 200 lb. in weight. The varieties of *C. moschata* known as Squashes in America have deeply 5-lobed leaves, the fruit stalk furrowed and widened next the fruit, and rough seeds. The varieties of *C. Pepo* (which includes the Vegetable Marrow, q.v.) have 5-lobed roughly hairy leaves, and slender, deeply furrowed fruit-stalks. They include the Custard, Crook-neck, and Orange Gourds.

The Gourds readily intercross and, unless they are isolated, are difficult to keep true.

Varieties are very numerous and only a few which have been well tried for the purposes indicated are mentioned here.

*For poles, fences, and trellis*: White Egg, Apple, Orange, Lemon, Ostrich Egg, White, Green, Warted and Bicolor Pear, Striped Onion, Golden Ball; all varieties of *C. Pepo*.

*For arbours*: Red, Green, White and Striped Turk's Cap, Melopepo, and Stradella. Musk Gourd (*C. moschata*). Malabar Gourd (*C. ficifolia* a perennial with non-edible fruits).

*For a pergola*: any of the above and the Flat Corsican and Yokohama Gourds.

*For winter culinary use*: Golden Crookneck, Red Étampes, Ohio Squash, Patagonian Squash, Golden Hubbard Squash, Scalloped White Bush, Golden Oblong Pumpkin.

In addition to the foregoing Cucurbitas varieties of *Lagenaria vulgaris* (q.v.) may be used for similar purposes, e.g., Miniature Bottle Gourd, Warted Bottle Gourd, Siphon, Spoon, Dipper, and Club.

For gourds for indoor cultivation the following genera should be referred to: Benincasa, Coccinia, Cyclanthera, Lagenaria, Luffa, Momordica, Sicana, Telfairia, Trichosanthes.

***gouria'nus -a -um,*** of the old state of Gour, Bengal.

**GOUR'LIEA** (in honour of Mr. Gourlie who botanized in Mendoza, d. about 1882). FAM. *Leguminosae*. A genus of a single spinescent shrub, native of Argentina, with small, equally pinnate leaves of 6 to 8 leaflets and yellow paplionaceous flowers. Needs greenhouse conditions and calls for no special soil.

**G. decor'ticans.** Spiny shrub of 16 to 20 ft., glabrous. *l.* in clusters of 2 to 4; lflets. oblong, about ¼ in. long. *fl.* golden yellow with red veins except on keel, in short axillary, spiny corymbose clusters. September, October.

**GOUT WEED.** *See* **Aegopodium Podagraria.** A

**GOVEN'IA** (in honour of J. R. Gowen, of Highclere, Secretary, Royal Horticultural Society, 1845–50, raiser of some fine hybrid Rhododendrons). FAM. *Orchidaceae*. A genus of 20 or more species of terrestrial orchids, natives of Trop. America. Flowers usually white or cream, but in some yellow, with or without blood-red spots; sepals and petals nearly equal; the narrower petals connivent with the upper sepals form a hood; the lower sepals are larger and diverge but are connate at the base forming with the column foot a short chin; lip much shorter, tongue-like, without spur, entire, and joined to the base of the column. The rhizomes are tuberous, the growths stem-like, formed by the bracts and sheathing bases of the leaves. The base of the stem is in some species surrounded by a large bladder-shaped bract which, flask-like, holds water conducted into it by the leaves. In cultivation these bracts should be refilled with water as required. In some species are evident pseudobulbs much as in some Phaius, in others the bases are hardly thickened. Compost, cultivation, and temperatures should be as for *Phaius grandifolius* but the winter night temperature should not fall below 55° F.

**G. Andrieux'ii.*** *fl.* yellowish, white at base; lip white, spotted purplish-red in front, above yellow, barred with brown. Mexico. 1884.

**G. delicio'sa.*** *fl.* 6 to 8, white, marked with small purple bars inside; lip nearly elliptic, apiculate, with dark-brown spots in front. Stem about 18 in. long. *l.* about 9 in. long, lanceolate-plicate. Mexico. 1884. (W.O.A. 210.)

**G. fascia'ta.** A synonym of *G. tingens*.

**G. Gard'neri.*** *fl.* 8 to 15, white, spotted rose, finally refracted; raceme elongated; sep. and pet. ovate, bluntish; lip ovate, acute, naked, marked with 5-marginal spots; scape bluntly tetragonal, sheathed in middle. *l.* 10 in. long, over 2 in. wide. 2 ft. h. Brazil. 1837. (B.M. 3660.)

**G. lagenoph'ora.*** *fl.* 40 to 50; segs. about ½ in. long; dorsal sep. yellow, forming a hood with the purplish pet.; sep. light yellow; crescent-shaped, converging at tips; lip shorter, light yellow with 2 brown lines on disk and 3 brown spots near apex. *Pseudobulbs* ovoid-globose. *l.* 3, nearly 1 ft. long, 1½ to 3½ in. wide, their petioles included in a large flask-like semi-transparent, purplish sheath, 6 in. h. Mexico. 1839. (B.M. 8794.) Allied to *G. utriculata*.

**G. sulphu'rea.** *fl.* rather large; sep. light sulphur, lateral rather broader than the cuneate-lanceolate dorsal; pet. white on disk, sulphur on margin, with numerous broken purple lines; lip white, spotted dark brown at apex, cordate-oblong. *l.* scarcely 2 in. broad, cuneate-lanceolate, acuminate. *Pseudobulbs* onion-like. Paraguay. 1885. A curious species.

**G. super'ba.*** *fl.* numerous, hardly 1 in. long, golden-yellow to orange; pet. broader than sep. and reddish within; lip small, blue-grey, 5 ft. h. *l.* 2 ft. long. Mexico. 1834. (B.R. 1795; L.B.C. 1709.)

**G. tin'gens.** *fl.* 8 to 15; sep. pale yellow; pet. with transverse purple lines; lip whitish or pale yellow with a reddish base and marked red near apex. *Pseudobulbs* 3 to 5 in. h. *l.* 10 to 15 in. long. Mexico, Guatemala, Brazil. 1842. (B.M. 8768; B.R. 31, 67 as *G. fasciata*.)

**G. utricula'ta.** *fl.* white; racemes elongated, many-fld.; sep. and pet. curved, acuminate; lip oblong, ovate, acute, marked red. September. *l.* twin, broad-oblong, plicate. *Pseudobulbs* ovate, enclosed in a large, membranous, oblong, pellucid, striated sheath. 1½ ft. h. Jamaica. 1843. (B.M. 4151.)

E. C.

**GRABOWS'KIA** (in honour of N. Grabowsky of Ohlaf, Silesia, an apothecary and botanical author, 1792–1842). FAM. *Solanaceae*. A genus of about 5 species of shrubs from S. America, related to Lycium. Leaves alternate; parts of the flower in fives; fruit a 2-seeded berry. Perhaps of more botanical than horticultural interest, the following 2 shrubs are valued in warmer, sunnier climates than ours for the landscape effect of their very glaucous foliage. Both require wall protection with us except in the mildest counties.

**G. boerhaaviifo'lia.** Deciduous shrub, 6 to 10 ft., shoots glabrous, armed with a spine in each l.-axil, ¼ in. long. *l.* glaucous, fleshy, roundish, 1 to 1½ in. long, roundish to broadly obovate, cuneate, glabrous. *fl.* either solitary and axillary or terminal and racemose; cor. ⅜ in. long and wide, pale blue. May. Brazil, Peru. 1780. (B.R. 1985.)

**G. duplica'ta.** Deciduous shrub up to 10 ft. with a sharp spine in the l.-axils. *l.* broadly ovate to roundish, ¾ to 2 in. long, often about as much wide, very glaucous, wavy. *fl.* few in axillary clusters; cal. short, 5-lobed; cor. greenish-white, ½ in. across, lobes ovate; stamens 5, hairy towards the base; anthers yellow. July. Brazil. 1840. (B.M. 3841.)

W. J. B.

**GRACILA'RIA.** *See* **Rhododendron,** PESTS, Azalea leaf-miner; **Syringa,** Lilac leaf-miner.

***grac'ilis -is -e,*** slender.

***gracil'limus -a -um,*** very slender.

***Graebneria'nus -a -um,*** in honour of Dr. K. O. R. P. P. Graebner, 1871–1933, of the Berlin Botanic Gardens.

***grae'cus -a -um,*** Grecian.

***Graël'lsii,*** in honour of Mariano de la Paz Graells, Professor of Zoology, Madrid, *c.* 1854–9.

**GRAFT.** A small shoot or scion of a plant or tree, inserted, for purposes of propagation, on another plant, the stock, which supports it and provides it with water and plant nutrients derived from the soil. A modification of grafting is budding (q.v.) where the scion consists only of a bud of the desired variety.

**GRAFT-HYBRID.** A plant derived from both the stock and the scion which have grown up together, forming a chimera (Supplement). Graft hybrids are not common but are well illustrated in Laburnum+Adami and Crataego-Mespilus+Aisnieri (q.v.). They are distinguished by the sign + from true hybrids (sign ×).

**GRAFTING.** Grafting is the operation of combining a shoot, the scion, of one plant with a rooted portion, the stock, of another so that the two may grow together and form one plant. It differs from budding (q.v.) in its general application only in that in budding the undeveloped shoot, a bud, is used as the scion, instead of a developed shoot.

The art of grafting has been known and practised from remote ages, while budding is a comparatively recent development. It is not an art confined to any particular region, for Greeks and Romans wrote about it, albeit not always with understanding, and the Chinese practised it, though they knew nothing of budding until that knowledge was introduced in modern times from the west. Some of the old writers seem to have thought grafting might be applied to almost anything with beneficial results, an idea not altogether dead to-day, for even in this century we have been assured that pears were growing upon willow-trees as the result of grafting, and of other improbable occurrences. Doubtless grafting originated from observation of natural growths. It is by no means uncommon to find in untended woods 2 branches which have come in contact growing together where they met and where the bark of one has been abraided by the other, so making a natural graft; but somewhat similar observations were sometimes carried to an erroneous conclusion, as when the seeds of one tree had been caught and germinated in a cleft or hollow in another of a different kind, and grown to maturity there. The erroneous conclusion has been come to then that oaks have been grafted successfully upon beeches, the apple on the plane, the strawberry tree upon the walnut, and so on. True grafting in none of these is likely, for it is essential that scion and stock shall have natural affinity either as varieties of the same species, species of the same genus, genera of the same family. It is not possible to predict with certainty by studying relationship of scion and stock that grafting will be successful between them, but it can be said that the nearer the relationship, as a rule, the greater the probability of success. The second essential for successful grafting is that the cambiums of scion and stock shall be placed and maintained in intimate contact, for then only can union occur. Wood and pith and outer bark of the original parts do not unite and only the new tissues formed by the growth and interlocking of the cells of the cambium bring about the union and complete it, and even then the particular characteristics of the cells of scion and of the stock are retained unchanged in the parts subsequently developing from them. Provided these two essentials are complied with the methods of grafting may be varied almost indefinitely. Rather over a hundred varieties of the operation have been described and illustrated in old books, not a few of them over-elaborations of what is, after all, a simple process if the structure of the parts of the plant involved is clearly understood and the simple facts of its life-processes appreciated.

The objects of grafting are, in the main, the same as those of budding. By grafting or budding it is possible to multiply many plants true to type which either do not form seeds at all, or if seeds are formed they are difficult to germinate or do not reproduce the characters of the plant that bore them true to type. Many plants that do not layer or root from cuttings readily may also be so increased. Thus it is a means of propagating the plant and rendering propagation more easy.

The growth developed from the scion may be profoundly modified by the stock, not so much in the characteristics which distinguish it as a particular variety—flavour, colour, season, form of flower or fruit, and keeping qualities are indeed little affected—but by rendering it more compact in growth, i.e. dwarfer, more fruitful, and so on. In some instances, though in a small area this is less likely than in a large one, by providing a particular kind of root the plant is enabled to grow better on certain soils or withstand greater variations in soil temperature, or even to avoid the results of the attacks of pests such as Phylloxera on the Vine and Woolly Aphis on Apple.

Grafting affords a means of overcoming the results of girdling of stems by rodents or even of saving trees damaged by heavy frosts at the collar, as bridge-grafting can be practised. It also gives a better opportunity of using the framework of old but healthy trees as a basis for fresh growth or for repairing injuries. Neither of these results can be obtained by budding.

There is often a prejudice against the planting of grafted plants and in some instances this is justified. It is not always possible to find stocks which will keep pace with the growth of the scion and ugly stems may be produced as a result, nor is it always possible to find stocks which will give a permanent union or such good anchorage as roots developed direct from the variety it is desired to grow. Further, as the stock retains all its original characters, shoots growing directly from it, whether above or below ground, will reproduce the characters of the stock, not those of the scion, and unless they are promptly removed will often grow and smother the scion growth. This is sometimes regarded as reversion but is, of course, nothing of the kind. The scion does not revert because it is grafted on an inferior variety though it may well become submerged as is often seen in Lilacs, Rhododendrons, and Roses which have been neglected for a few years, and even sometimes in Apples, Pears,

and Plums. The effect of incompatible unions is often seen in Japanese Cherries grafted on unsuitable stocks and in the sudden death of grafted Clematises. None of these results follow where cuttings or layers have been used to multiply the variety nor where it has been possible to use compatible stocks, but apart from this the advantages of budding and grafting far outweigh the disadvantages where large numbers of a particular variety have to be produced at a reasonable cost.

A special case of incompatible grafting is met with in pears. Some varieties will not succeed if grafted direct on to a desired stock, but the difficulty can be overcome by double-grafting. Scions of some other variety of pear are grafted on the stock and the variety it is desired to grow is grafted in turn upon that. In the result the plant obtained is composed of three different individuals, the base of the stem and the roots being, e.g. quince, the piece of stem immediately above it of one variety, the remainder of the tree of another.

In rare instances, in addition to some effect upon the rate of growth of the stock, the scion may produce visible effects upon the stock itself. The most marked effect is seen where certain types of variegation are concerned. Shoots produced on the stock, i.e. below the point of union, show variegation similar to that possessed by the scion grafted upon the stock. This is not always found, but is well seen in, for example, *Abutilon striatum Thompsonii* and other Malvaceous plants and in the Golden-leaved variety of the common Laburnum.

A special application of grafting is that where dioecious plants are concerned. It is sometimes possible to graft upon the plants of one sex scions of the other sex, thus rendering the production of fruits and seeds more likely and on a single plant, instead of having to grow 2 occupying double the space. Occasionally this method of promoting more certain pollination has been used where space is precious with self-sterile varieties of fruit-trees, some branches of which have been grafted with another variety providing pollen capable of bringing about fertilization. In these instances a pollen carrier is of course still necessary but the closer proximity of the flowers of the two varieties makes pollination more probable.

The necessary closeness of relationship between stock and scion cannot be stated with any degree of exactitude. Successful grafting of a scion of one genus upon a stock of another has been reported as follows: CONIFERAE. Athrotaxis on Cryptomeria; Chamaecyparis nootkatensis on Thuja orientalis. ROSACEAE. Cotoneaster on Crataegus; Pear on Crataegus Oxyacantha; Raphiolepis on Crataegus; Amelanchier on Crataegus; Raphiolepis on Pyracantha coccinea; Photinia on Cydonia; Pear on Cydonia; Crataegus on Cydonia; Eriobotrya on Cydonia; Chaenomeles lagenaria on Cydonia; Rosa Wichuraiana on Rubus; Amelanchier on Sorbus Aucuparia; Eriobotrya on Raphiolepis. CORNACEAE. Aucuba on Garrya; Garrya on Aucuba. OLEACEAE. Chionanthus on Fraxinus; Olea on Ligustrum; Phillyrea on Ligustrum; Osmanthus on Ligustrum; Lilac on Ligustrum; Lilac on Phillyrea; Ligustrum on Phillyrea; Osmanthus on Phillyrea; Ligustrum on Lilac; Phillyrea on Olea; Phillyrea on Osmanthus. LEGUMINOSAE. Genista on Laburnum; Cytisus on Laburnum. MAGNOLIACEAE. Magnolia on Liriodendron. RUTACEAE. Choisya on Skimmia. ELAEAGNACEAE. Elaeagnus on Hippophae. ERICACEAE. Kalmia on Rhododendron. FAGACEAE. Castanea on Quercus Robur. SOLANACEAE. Tomato on Potato. Thus in 11 families grafting of a plant of one genus on to a species of another genus has been found possible. At times grafting of 2 species within a single genus has proved impossible and even the grafting of one variety on another variety of the same species has in some instances met with scant success. M. Daniel has claimed that success has followed in a number of instances his attempts to graft plants of widely different families, obtaining sound and durable unions. Among them are Haricot Beans on Ricinus, Sunflower on Melon, Cabbage on Tomato, Chrysanthemum on Tomato, Coleus on Iresine, Aster on Phlox, Coleus on Tomato, Maple on Ash. He also successfully grafted Vanilla on itself, white Lily on itself, and Philodendron on itself. However, he offers no evidence for the grafting of a monocotyledon on any other genus. M. Daniel's conclusion is that generic affinities are of less importance than similarity of size, vigour, and vegetative habit or anatomical characters between the scion and the stock, analogy of tissue, and similarity of alimentary needs. His supposition was that such grafts might affect the character of the seed produced by the resulting plants. It cannot be said that such results followed and all or most subsequent experience leads to the conclusion that the essential varietal characters of the scion are not altered by the stock upon which it is grafted, although there may be modifications in the rate of growth, extent of flower and fruit production, and occasionally possibly to susceptibility to diseases due to parasitic attacks or physiological derangement. Some, perhaps all, of these effects of stock on scion can be explained by changes in the amount of water made available to the scion by the stock, rather than by postulating any genetic change. There can be no question that similar anatomical characters, analogous tissue, and similar alimentary requirements render successful grafting more probable, and that these are more likely to be found between plants of close affinity than between those of widely different relationship; nor is there any question that similarity of size, vigour, and vegetative habit and, it may be added, age render the operation of grafting easier and more certain.

There is a rather prevalent idea that grafting is a means of producing hybrids, but this is very rare and occurs only when the grafting or budding is so done that the resulting plant consists of a central core of tissue of the scion covered with an external layer of the stock. *See* **Graft Hybrids.** Even then the cells produced retain the characters of the individual from which they are derived, those from the stock, the characters of the stock, those from the scion, the characters of the scion. If seeds are produced they do not give rise to hybrid offspring.

It will be realized that the amount of water that can be passed on to the scion from the stock will be almost negligible until new tissue has been produced by the cambium and the new vessels of the wood along which the ascending sap-current passes are continuous from stock to scion. Upon this fact almost all the technique of grafting, other than the 2 essentials already laid down, depends. The scion should make as little demand upon the water-supply from the stock as possible and all precautions should be taken to prevent loss of water from the stock. Thus the scion should be less advanced in growth than the stock; the stock should be ready to supply the demands upon it as soon as the scion begins growth; the wounds made where the 2 are in contact should be well covered to prevent bleeding or evaporation from their surfaces, and if the scion is leafy, such measures as are possible to check transpiration must be adopted. There is thus an important difference in treatment of leafless and leafy plants after grafting—the latter must be kept close and in a humid atmosphere; the former may usually be exposed fully to the air.

The stocks appropriate to the different plants propagated by grafting are mentioned under their descriptions.

The operation of grafting should be performed, as a rule, when the stock, at least, is active, and therefore between the time when the sap begins to rise in spring and before it ceases in autumn, avoiding the middle of summer and very hot weather. There are exceptions to this but it applies generally to the grafting of deciduous woody plants. The operation is usually carried out for all woody plants, both deciduous and evergreen, in early spring. It is of course essential that both stock and scion should be healthy and free from parasites.

For all the usual methods of grafting the stock should be established in the soil or in pots. Scions of deciduous trees and shrubs are prepared by cutting ripened shoots of the current year in late autumn when the leaves have fallen, tying them in bundles, and after labelling them, heeling them in, preferably under a north wall to ensure same retardation of growth.

For grafting outdoors calm moist weather is most suitable. All cuts should be made with a keen knife, clean and regular, and the operation should be carried out as expeditiously as possible. As soon as the cut surfaces are fitted together they should be tied firmly with soft woolly string, raffia, or rubber tape so that they cannot move. As an additional precaution a stake may be used to which both stock and scion should be tied. The graft should be at once covered with grafting clay or wax (*see* **Grafting Wax**). Where tender plants are concerned, and with evergreen trees and shrubs, close frames or cool houses are needed for protection until union is effected, but no artificial heat is needed for hardy plants. Under glass a close, moist atmosphere and shade can be given and no waxing is then usually necessary. The tie should remain until union is certain and the grafted stem begins to swell. If rubber tape has been used it will give and save labour in removing wax and tie.

The chief variations in methods of grafting are as follows, the best, in any instances, depending upon the size and variety of the plant to be grafted.

WHIP AND TONGUE-GRAFTING. This is the best method for grafting when the stock and scion are of approximately the same diameter. The stock would be 1 or 2 years old, firmly rooted, with stems about $\frac{1}{2}$ in. thick or little more.

The stock is first trimmed of all side growths near the base and cut down to within 4 or 5 in. of the ground, not lower. It is then prepared to receive the scion by making a sloping upward cut beginning $1\frac{1}{2}$ to 2 in. below the top and removing a tapering wedge-shaped piece. A second cut is then made vertically downwards, beginning near the top and cutting down nearly to the level where the first cut began. A common fault is to begin the first cut too near the top, leaving too short a slope for safe tying.

The scion is prepared from a stout 1-year-old shoot which has been heeled in, taking a piece from the middle containing 4 good buds, the lowest bud being about $\frac{3}{4}$ in. above the end. In this also 2 cuts are made to correspond with those made in the stock. The first cut is a sloping one beginning about 2 in. from the lower end on the side opposite to the lowest bud. The second is a straight upward cut beginning near the lower end of the first cut and extending to the same depth as the corresponding vertical cut in the stock, making a tongue.

The scion is then fitted on to the stock so that the cambiums of stock and scion correspond at least on one side, the tongue of the scion fitting into the cleft in the stock and keeping it firmly in position.

Any growths that appear from the stock must be removed and when the tie is taken off a stake to support the graft should be placed in position and the scion tied to it, for at first there will be danger of it being knocked or blown out.

SPLICE-GRAFTING is essentially similar except that no tongue is made and the fixing of scion on stock is less secure. It is, however, more convenient for thin stems where a practicable tongue is difficult to make.

NOTCH-GRAFTING. Where the stock is considerably thicker than the scion notch-grafting may be done. The preparation of stock and scion up to the making of the cut is as for whip and tongue-grafting, but instead of the sloping cut the side of the stock is cut so as to remove a wedge of bark and wood about 2 in. long gradually tapered from the top of the stock to the lower end, and the base of the scion is cut to fit. Tying and subsequent treatment as before.

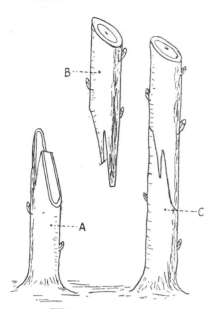

*Whip and Tongue graft*
A, stock prepared. B, scion prepared
C, scion inserted on stock

SADDLE-GRAFTING is suitable for plants where stock and scion are of the same diameter but it is usually used only for such plants as Rhododendrons. The *top* of the stock is cut on both sides so as to leave the top wedge-shaped. The base of the scion is slit through the middle and shaped so that it will fit closely on the wedge and is then bound in place. It is important that the scion should not be split farther than the end of the stock will reach, and a narrow-bladed knife will be necessary to make the cut in the scion clean and not too deep.

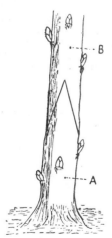

*Saddle graft*
A, stock. B, scion

CLEFT-GRAFTING is the converse of saddle-grafting and is rarely used, for the splitting of the stock is almost certain to extend farther than the scion reaches and insecure unions are produced at the best, while if the stock is, as is usual where this method is adopted, much wider than the scion, the wood of the stock does not unite and there is danger of decay through the entrance of fungi, &c.

WEDGE-GRAFTING is a refinement upon this for special purposes.

*Wedge graft*
A, stock. B, scion

Where wide stocks are to be grafted a much safer and in every way preferable method is CROWN or RIND-GRAFTING. This is of much value where healthy old trees are top-grafted to change them from one variety to another, or where repair to a broken limb is to be effected, or to provide flowers for pollination. To prepare an old tree for top-grafting the 5 or 6 main branches are cut back in January or February to within 2 or 2½ ft. of the main stem ready for grafting in April or early

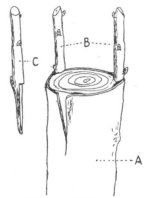

*Crown or Rind graft*
A, stock prepared for grafting
B, scions inserted
C, prepared scion

May. It is bad practice to cut off the whole head of the tree. If the tree is a very large one 2 or 3 small branches may be left, but otherwise all the branches except the chosen 5 or 6 should be cut clean away. Those left should have clean bark and be strong enough to carry a new head of branches. Each of them is treated as though it were a separate stock and will need if less than 4 in. thick, 1 scion, if thicker, 2, 1 on each side. In April, or as soon as the tree shows signs of growth, 2 in. is sawn off the end of each stump, the cut being made smooth and level with the knife. The bark is then slit with the point of a knife beginning at the top and going through the bark to the hard wood but no farther, making the slit 3 in. or so long. The bark is slightly lifted, beginning at the top, and the scion which has been simply cut with a sloping cut about 2 in. long is slipped gently in so that the cambium is in contact with that of the stock. The graft is tied with raffia and the whole cut surface covered with clay or wax to prevent drying up and the entry of fungus spores. Any growth, other than that from the scions, where the whole tree is top-grafted, must be removed.

FRAME-WORK GRAFTING. An alternative to top-grafting is frame-work grafting, which it is claimed does not lay the tree open to subsequent fungus attacks to anything like the extent the methods of top-grafting are apt to do. Another advantage is that the trees come into bearing in the second year after frame-work grafting, providing the number of scions inserted is sufficient to avoid very vigorous growth. Frame-work grafting is no new thing, for Thomas Andrew Knight described it in 1813 (see *Transactions of the Horticultural Society*), but it has recently been revived and advocated as an economic method of using healthy old trees to bear better varieties. Several different systems have been used. In one the branches are headed back (or 'de-horned') by about 3 ft. and all small lateral branches and fruit spurs are cut back to about 2 in. long, weak branches and unhealthy spurs being removed altogether. All those left are grafted by whip-and-tongue or rind-grafts according to size, and where none are left scions are inserted in the branch itself, using the inverted-L graft (see below). It has been observed that where the three types of graft were used not all developed equally and this has led to the removal of all lateral growths entirely and to the use of the inverted-L graft alone, the best results following the insertion of scions at a distance of 8 in. apart along each branch, placing them so that on subsequent growth they will not interfere with one another. The INVERTED-L GRAFT is so called from the form of the incision made in the bark; the lower cut is made between 1 and 1½ in. long

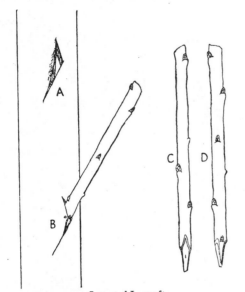

*Inverted L graft*
A, L cut in bark of stock, top cut bevelled
B, scion inserted and tacked
C, D, scions prepared for inserting, front and back

through the bark to the wood, the upper cut is shorter and made at an obtuse angle with the first, reaching to the cambium, somewhat bevelled so that the bark can be slightly raised from the top cut and the scion slipped in as in a rind-graft. The scion is prepared by making a long sloping cut as for a whip graft; a thin layer of bark is then cut from the other side but somewhat to the side and a very thin strip trimmed from the sides. The preparation of the scion should be completed before the cut is made in the branch to receive it and better results follow the use of scions containing 6 to 8 buds than the usual 4-bud type. The scion is inserted so that the trimmed side rests against the edge of bark made by the longer, lower cut and that the thin base of the scion is in no way damaged. The scion is fixed in position by driving a

thin, flat-headed nail ⅝ in. long straight through the raised bark and the base of the scion into the wood of the limb. The wound is then sealed with grafting wax which is also used to seal the cut end at the top of the scion. It is obvious that a large number of scions will be needed to furnish even a medium-sized tree, but it is claimed that the re-formed trees come so rapidly into bearing that the time and skill needed to carry out the operation are amply compensated for.

Other methods of inserting the scions have been used, e.g. the CHISEL-GRAFT, a type of cleft-graft, the incision being made with a thin-bladed chisel ⅝ in. wide making an oblique cut through the bark penetrating a short distance into the wood. Into this cleft a wedge-shaped scion is tapped by a mallet and the wound sealed with grafting-wax. The V-GRAFT is made by making a small V-shaped incision in the bark and a wedge-shaped scion

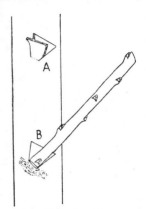

*V bark graft*
A, first cut and bark of stock lifted
B, scion inserted, flap of bark cut off

is pushed down behind the raised lip of the V. When the scion has been pushed in, the flap of bark that has been raised is neatly cut off and the wounds waxed. This requires no tacking.

The AWL-GRAFT is somewhat similar, the incision in the bark being made with a sacking-needle or the bent point of a small screwdriver. The scion is cut to a wedge-form by two sloping cuts about 1 in. long and inserted behind the needle, which is then removed and the scion pushed in until the whole wedge is out of sight. The wound is then waxed.

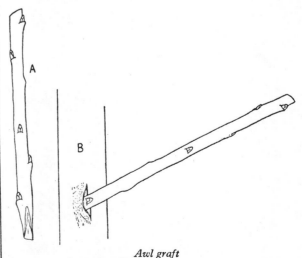

*Awl graft*
A, prepared scion
B, bark lifted by awl and scion inserted

STUB-GRAFTING is a further method used on cut-back spurs and laterals and being a cleft-graft can be carried out before the bark rises freely in spring. The best-placed spurs and laterals up to a diameter of 1 in. are retained and in these an oblique cleft is cut near the base, starting on the top-side and cutting about half-way through. The cut is made to gape by bending down the lateral and a scion, made wedge-shaped at the base by two sloping cuts on opposite sides, one about 1 in. long, the other ½ in. long, is slipped in. When released the lateral springs back and grips the scion which is held firmly and needs only waxing.

In all these methods of frame-grafting only growths from the scions must be permitted to develop and the tree may need going over several times to ensure this.

A full account of this type of grafting is published from East Malling, Kent, by the Imperial Bureau of Horticulture and Plantation Crops.

INARCHING, or grafting by approach, is practically veneer grafting with both stock and scion in leaf and still on their own roots, the scion being usually rooted in a pot. It may be done at any time while the sap is flowing. A piece of bark down to the cambium is removed from both the parts intended for joining and they are then carefully fitted together and secured by bandaging and tying. When the union is complete the unwanted parts of stock and scion are very carefully and gradually cut away. Inarching is a convenient way of grafting vines and nuts and is used where other methods are usually unsuccessful.

BRIDGE-GRAFTING. Where the bark of a tree has been badly damaged by rodents or goats, even possibly completely removed, or killed near the ground by severe frost, the injured part may be bridged over by grafting and the life of the tree preserved. The edges of the damaged bark are carefully trimmed and healthy shoots of the previous year are cut of such a length that when a splice-cut is made at each end it can be slipped under the bark of the tree above and below the injury as in crown-grafting. Two or more bridging shoots should be inserted according to the diameter of the stem to be treated and the whole covered with grafting clay, which may also be wrapped with sacking to prevent drying up. The buds should be removed from the bridging shoots.

SIDE-GRAFTING is a method employed for inserting scions without beheading the stock. It is useful for propagating plants and for supplying a branch in any part of a tree. There are two systems: (1) The scion is placed under the bark using either a 'shooting bud', that is, one beginning to grow, or a dormant bud. Side-grafting with a shooting bud is done in a branch of the previous year as soon as the sap-flow begins in April; if a dormant bud is to be used the scion is put into a shoot of the current year about August or September to develop in the following season. The scion is prepared for an upright stem of the stock by making a long cut as for splice-grafting at the lower end, taking care that the surface is left smooth throughout and that the scion is thin at the point. An incision is made in the stock, down to, but not beyond, the cambium, and the scion inserted much in the same way as in budding, tied, and covered with wax. In horizontal branches of the stock a notch may be cut and part of the bark raised nearer the main stem, the scion being cut to fit, inserted, tied, and waxed as usual. (2) The scion is inserted in the young wood, an oblique or vertical cleft being made in the stock to receive it. This is especially adapted for evergreens and is performed under glass either in February or at the latter part of summer.

VENEER-GRAFTING is especially used for evergreen trees and shrubs and may be done either in spring or autumn, spring being the best time. The scion should be well ripened and the stock in an active state. The scion should not have its upper leaves removed and should be cut at the base with an even splice-cut about 1 in. long. A piece of the bark down to the cambium should be cut exactly the same size and shape, fitted, and tied with a cotton or woollen bandage and, waxed or not, placed in a close frame. The top of the stock should be gradually removed when the parts are united.

HERBACEOUS GRAFTING. Shoots of herbaceous dicotyledons can be grafted using the same methods as for woody stems but keeping the plants quite close after the operation and giving the temperature required by the plants for active growth. In practice it is rarely necessary; it is used for grafting dwarf Cacti on tall ones, but principally for grafting resinous trees such as Pines. The best time for grafting Pines by this method is in May, when the young shoots are beginning to grow, or at a time when growth has stopped and is beginning to harden. Stock and scion should be of similar texture. The stock must be cut off just below the terminal buds and nearly all the leaves must be removed from the point left. This is carefully split and the scion, which has been cut to a wedge-shape, rather deeply inserted so that the cambiums coincide. Worsted is the best material for tying and the cuts should be covered with wax and shaded from sunshine by paper caps until union is complete and growth resumed. Walnuts may also be successfully grafted by using shoots for both stock and scion that have not become woody, or by terminal grafting in spring just before growth begins.

ROOT-GRAFTING, i.e. the grafting of shoots upon pieces of root, has a wider application than herbaceous grafting and it can be successfully applied to a wide range of woody plants. The exact method depends largely upon the relative size of stock and scion, choice falling upon the one that permits the greatest amount of cambium tissue to be brought into contact. Good roots or pieces of roots are secured while the plants are dormant. Where large fleshy roots are concerned, as with Tree Paeonies, the root has a triangular notch cut in it about 1½ in. long and the scion is similarly cut to fit and bound in place. Where the root and scion are of approximately the same diameter a cleft- or saddle-graft is made but at times a splice-graft is better. Clematis varieties are largely root-grafted, roots of *Clematis Vitalba* or *C. Viticella* being used as stock. Plants of the Bignonia group which do not readily come from cuttings, varieties of Wisteria, and Rhododendrons, are also frequently root-grafted, using roots of common species of their genus as stocks, and so are named varieties of Gypsophila such as Bristol Fairy. At one time when varieties of Hollyhocks were included among florist's flowers, they too were so increased. The method gives an opportunity of grafting apples, &c., in the depth of winter in the shelter of the potting shed which is frequently made use of. As the graft is buried in moist soil as soon as made there is no need to apply grafting wax, and the worsted used for tying has usually rotted by the time union is effected and the normal increase in diameter begins. *See also* **Propagation.**

**GRAFTING CLAY** consists of 2 parts clay and 1 of cow-dung with some finely cut hay which prevents the cracking and falling-off of the mixture. These ingredients are thoroughly kneaded together, adding water as is necessary to bring the mixture to the consistency of putty. The mixture should be made some weeks before it is needed and kept moist by making a cavity in the top of the heap and filling it with water. After the junction of graft and scion is covered with the grafting clay it may be necessary to syringe it occasionally and smooth it over to close any cracks.

**GRAFTING WAX.** Wax is better for use with small and delicate plants than clay and may be used for all purposes. The wax must not be injurious to the cut tissues either by drying or burning them up, nor must it crack or run off when subjected to natural heat and moisture.

On the whole, for general purpose a grafting wax which is applied in a lukewarm state by means of a paint-brush or broad label is the most satisfactory; grafting waxes to be applied cold are less suitable where they have to stand over winter since frost appears to penetrate through the soft waxes more readily. A good Grafting Wax for application while warm may be made from 1 part tallow, 2 parts beeswax, 4 parts resin, melted together and thoroughly mixed, then poured into cold water and kneaded with the hands until the whole becomes white and of the consistency of soft putty. Many other recipes are used, e.g. 14 parts black pitch, 14 parts Burgundy pitch, 8 parts of beeswax, 7 parts of tallow, 14 parts of yellow ochre, the various ingredients except the ochre being melted together, the ochre being stirred in while the mixture is still liquid.

**Gra'hami,** in honour of (1) Robert Graham, 1786–1845, Professor of Botany, Glasgow and Edinburgh; (2) Colonel Graham, U.S.A. Boundary Commission, 1851 (Sonora); (3) George John Graham, 1803–78, who travelled in Mexico, 1827–9.

**GRAIN.** Seeds of plants of the grasses (Gramineae), especially those used for food.

**GRAINS OF PARADISE.** *See* **Aframomum Granum-paradisi, A. Melegueta.**

**GRAM, GREEN.** *See* **Phaseolus Mungo** in Suppl.

**GRAM, HORSE.** *See* **Dolichos biflorus.**

**GRAM'INEAE.** Monocotyledons. The family of grasses, of about 5,000 species in 400 genera, of world-wide distribution. Tufted or creeping herbaceous plants, rarely shrubby or tree-like. Stem round, usually hollow and swollen at nodes. Leaves alternate, in 2 ranks, the sheath clasping the stem, its margins usually free, rarely joined to form a longer or shorter tube; blade usually narrow-linear, sometimes oblong or oval, margins often rough to the touch, veins parallel; at the junction of sheath and blade is a frequently membranous tongue, the ligule, which may be reduced to hairs, or rarely almost absent. Flowers perfect or sometimes unisexual and plants monoecious or dioecious, in small spikes (spikelets) which are arranged in spike-like or branching panicles; spikelets of one or more flowers, enclosed in chaffy or membranous glumes; usually 2 flowerless outer glumes enclose or subtend 1 or pairs of flower-bearing (but sometimes empty) inner glumes one of which, the flowering glume, is boat-shaped, the other, the pale (palea), flat with inturned edges, arranged on opposite sides of a slender rachis (rachilla). Stamens 3 (rarely 1, 2, 6, or more). Ovary 1-celled, ovule 1; stigmas usually 2, feathery. Fruit 1-seeded, usually adherent to the pale, and sometimes to the flowering glume. The nutritious foliage and starchy seeds, often also rich in protein, make many species of this family extremely valuable food plants for man and beast; the leaves of some species are used in paper-making and for their fibre, and the woody species have very numerous uses in their native countries. A few genera contain ornamental garden plants and for lawn-making other species are unsurpassed; some grasses too are among the most valuable sand-binders. References will be found under Agrostis, Aira, Alopecurus, Ammophila, Andropogon, Anthoxanthum, Arrhenatherum, Arundinacea, Arundo, Asperella, Avena, Bambusa, Briza, Bromus, Calamovilfa, Chloris, Chusquea, Coix, Cortaderia, Cymbopogon, Dactylis, Dendrocalamus, Deschampsia, Desmazeria, Eleusine, Elymus, Eragrostis, Erianthus, Festuca, Glyceria, Gynerium, Hierochloe, Holcus, Hordeum, Lagurus, Lamarckia, Lygeum, Melica, Miscanthus, Molinia, Oryza, Oryzopsis, Panicum, Pennisetum, Phalaris, Phragmites, Phyllostachys, Poa, Saccharum, Sasa, Shibataea, Sorghastrum, Sorghum, Stenotaphrum, Stipa, Trichloris, Tricholaena, Triticum, Uniola, Zea, Zizania.

**gramin'eus -a -um,** grass-like.

**graminifo'lius -a -um,** with grassy foliage.

**gram'inis -is -e,** grass-like.

**GRAMMAN'GIS** (probably from the markings on the flower). FAM. *Orchidaceae.* A genus allied to Cymbidium and to Grammatophyllum in which it is often included. As here defined the genus is monotypic and found in Madagascar. Compost and temperatures should be as for Cymbidiellas but a more decided rest should be given and the plants should be grown in pots or baskets.

**G. Ellis'ii.\*** *fl.* fragrant, 20 to 30, glossy, on a stout, arching infl. from base of pseudobulb, about 2 ft. long; sep. about 1¼ in. long, ⅝ in. broad, almost oblong, shortly acuminate, margins undulate, tips reflexed; upper sep. arched, yellow thickly marked with oblique striations and flecks of chocolate-red, dull yellow at tips; pet. about 1 in. long, whitish shading to and tipped with rose-purple; lip 3-lobed, shorter than pet., whitish, streaked and marked with purplish-red, somewhat saccate at base, side lobes rounded, erect, yellowish-white, mid-lobe bluntly roundish-triangular with several white ridges; pet. arranged as in *Lycaste Skinneri;* column terete, whitish; pollinia 2. *Pseudobulbs* stout, 4-angled, 5 to 8 in. h. clothed with membranous sheaths. *l.* 3 to 5, from top of bulbs, 15 to 24 in. long, 2 to 3 in. wide, not strictly deciduous. 1859. (L. 338; W.O.A. 147 and B.M. 5179 as *Grammatophyllum Ellisii*.)

**G. Hut'toni.** A synonym of *Cymbidium Huttoni.*

**G. stapeliiflo'ra.** A synonym of *Cymbidium Huttoni.*

E. C.

**GRAMMAN'THES.** *See* **Vauanthes.**

**GRAMMATOCAR'PUS** (*grammata,* letters, *karpos,* fruit; in allusion to the markings on the fruit). FAM. *Loasaceae.* A single species of twining, downy, annual herb constitutes the genus which is allied to and requires the same treatment as Loasa.

**G. volub'ilis.** Twining herb with opposite, 2- or 3-pinnate l. *fl.* yellow, axillary, cal. tube long, linear, lobes 5, spreading, linear-spatulate; pet. 5, saccate. Summer. Chile. (B.M. 5028; S.B.F.G. 238.)

**GRAMMATOPHYL'LUM** (*grammata,* letters, *phyllon,* leaf: in reference to the markings on the flowers of some species). FAM. *Orchidaceae.* A small genus of rather large, handsome, epiphytic orchids. Natives of Malaya, New Guinea, Philippines. Flowers showy, on long pedicels; sepals and petals sub-equal, free, spreading; lip affixed above the base of the column, erect, concave, the lateral lobes rather broad, erect, loosely embracing the column, the mid-lobe short, recurved-spreading, narrow or dilated; column erect, rather shorter than the lip; raceme loosely many-flowered; scape long, simple. Leaves distichous, often very long. Horticulturally the genus falls into 2 sections, the one of which *G. speciosum* may be taken as typical, with tall leafy stems not unlike those of *Cyrtopodium punctatum,* but larger, and the other with well-defined pseudobulbs. In both sections the leaves are long and strap-shaped, the inflorescence is produced from the base of the bulb or stem, the petals are slightly narrower than the sepals, and the lip is comparatively small with erect, prominent side lobes, the mid-lobe being somewhat tongue-like and pointed. The flowers are not brilliantly coloured, green or greenish-yellow with dull red or chocolate-red markings, but are attractive from their number. All require a warm moist atmosphere throughout the year, with a winter night temperature not less than 65° F. Those with pseudobulbs require a rest in winter, but the rest must not be too severe. The species without pseudobulbs are apparently, under cultivation, often unable to complete their growths fully in the one season, and therefore, should have a higher winter temperature. Compost should be made of 3 parts of Osmunda fibre, 1 part of Sphagnum moss, and 1 part of loam fibre (really fibrous), well mixed with broken pot-sherds. With large plants pieces of broken red brick, up to half-bricks, may be used to advantage. In the tall-stemmed section, such as G. speciosum, there are probably 6 species. Some of those with pseudobulbs described here may possibly yet prove to be local varieties rather than true species. Particularly noticeable in the speciosum group is the presence of malformed flowers at the base of the spike. They are set at wider intervals than the perfect flowers and consist of 4 segments (2 sepals and 2 petals) and an apparently abortive column. Mr. J. H. Veitch in his *Traveller's Notes* describes the extraordinary size to which the plants may attain and only large houses will accommodate well-grown plants. Confusion still exists in the classification of the species. G. Fenzlianum and G. Rumphianum have by some been regarded as synonyms or forms of G. scriptum.

**G. el'egans.*** *fl.* showy, 6 or 7 on an erect peduncle 1 ft. h.; *sep.* sepia-brown, with ochre-yellow margins, oblong; *pet.* same colour, narrower; *lip* yellow, with brown markings in front and a hairy disk, 3-fid, front lobe wedge-shaped and emarginate; column white, with a pair of brown lines below stigma. *l.* elongated, distichous. *Pseudobulbs* rather large, oblong. South Sea Is. 1883.

**G. Ellis'ii.** A synonym of *Grammangis Ellisii*.

**G. fastuo'sum.** A synonym of *G. speciosum*.

**G. Fenzlia'num.** *fl.* 2¼ in. across, somewhat distant; *sep.* and *pet.* pale yellowish-green, spotted brown; *pet.* narrower and reflexed; *lip* yellowish, obliquely striped with brown, mid-lobe reflexed; between the side lobes is a channelled, white plate; *scapes* 3 to 4 ft. long, many-fld. *l.* 1 to 1½ ft. long, oblong or lanceolate-oblong. *Pseudobulbs* 4 to 6 in. long. Amboyna.

**G. gigan'teum.** A synonym of *G. speciosum*.

**G. Guliel'mi II.** A synonym of *G. Rumphianum*.

**G. Measuresia'num.** A form of *G. Rumphianum*.

**G. multiflo'rum.*** *fl.* 2 in. across, greenish-yellow suffused or blotched brown-purple; racemes long, many-fld.; bracts oblong, scale-like; *sep.* oblong, obtuse; *pet.* similar, acute, narrower; *lip* 3-lobed, downy; mid-lobe oblong, rounded; side ones erect, subfalcate, with 4 elevated lamellae in middle. Summer. *Pseudobulbs* 8 to 12 in. h. *l.* 4 or 5, 15 to 18 in. long. Manila. 1838. (B.R. 25, 65.) var. **tigri'num**, *fl.* yellow, spotted with purple. Summer. E. Indies. 1840. (B.R. 28, 69.)

**G. pantheri'num.** *fl.* as large as those of *Cymbidium eburneum*, spotted; *sep.* and *pet.* narrow-cuneate-oblong, obtuse; *lip* cordate at base, 3-fid, with triangular segs., naked, without lines of hairs or velvet, mid-lobe acute. New Guinea. 1878.

**G. papua'num.*** *fl.* 30 or more, large; *sep.* and slightly broader *pet.* nearly 2 in. long; *pet.* 1 in. broad, broad-oblong, rounded, yellowish-green, thickly marked with bold spots of brown-red, colour dimly seen on reverse; *lip* small in comparison, 3-lobed, central lobe triangular, yellow suffused with red, the larger side lobes curve upward, their points and margins meeting, yellow with reddish lines yellowish-green outside; *lip* may be likened to a funnel with part of the edge developed into a tongue; column short, stout, curved; pedicels and ovary about 4 in. long. Bracts small, membranous, yellowish. The 3 or 4 (perhaps more) basal *fl.* are set at wider intervals and have but 2 sep. and 2 pet. larger than in perfect fl., colour dull. *Stems* 8 to 10 ft. h. *l.* 24 to 30 in. long, strap-shaped. *infl.* 6 to 8 ft. h. Spring. New Guinea. 1910.

**G. Roempleria'num.** A synonym of *Eulophiella Roempleriana*.

**G. Rumphia'num.** *fl.* erecto-patent, 25 to 30 on a scape; *sep.* and *pet.* pale yellowish-white, blotched with brown; *lip* yellowish-white, lined dark violet, pilose inside, 3-lobed. *l.* lanceolate-oblong, 1 ft. or more long. *Pseudobulbs* tufted, oblong-conical, 9 in. long when fully grown. Moluccas. (B.M. 7507.) SYN. *G. Gulielmi II.* var. **Measuresia'num,*** *fl. sep.* and *pet.* emerald-green, blotched and spotted dark brownish-purple; side lobes of *lip* light yellow with oblique brown lines, the front lobe white with 3 brown lines at apex. Philippine Is. 1889. SYN. *G. Fenzlianum Measuresianum, G. Seegerianum* (of gardens).

**G. scrip'tum.** *fl. sep.* and *pet.* yellow and red-spotted, equal, spreading, oblong, obtuse; *lip* lined with pale purple; raceme many-fld.; scape very long, rising from the base of the pseudobulb. *l.* lanceolate, 3-nerved. *Pseudobulbs* transversely articulated, deeply ribbed. Allied to *G. multiflorum*. Moluccas.

**G. Seegeria'num** (Seeger's). A garden name for *G. Rumphianum Measuresianum*.

**G. specio'sum.*** *fl.* nearly 6 in. across; *sep.* and *pet.* undulated, ovate-oblong, rich yellow, blotched and marked purple-red; *lip*

3-lobed, streaked red; scape often nearly 6 ft. h. growing from the base of the stem. Winter. *l.* distichous, lorate, acute, 1½ to 2 ft. long. Stems sometimes 9 to 10 ft. h. Java. 1837. (B.M. 5157.) SYN. *G. fastuosum, G. giganteum.*

E. C.

**GRANADILLA.** Fruit of *Passiflora edulis* or *P. quadrangularis.*

**granaten'sis -is -e,** of Granada, Cent. America.

**gran'dis -is -e** (**grandi-** in compound words), large.

**granit'icus -a -um,** of hard quartz rocks.

**Grant-Duff'ii,** in honour of Sir M. E. Grant-Duff, F.L.S., M.P., 1829–1906, Governor of Madras, collected in Algeria, &c.

**Grant'ii,** in honour of James Augustus Grant, 1827–92, Scottish explorer, who, with J. H. Spake, investigated the sources of the Nile.

**granula'tus -a -um,** composed of, or appearing as though covered with, grains.

**granulo'sus -a -um,** see **granulatus.**

**GRAPE.** Fruit of *Vitis vinifera*, the vine (q.v.).

**GRAPE HYACINTH.** See **Muscari.**

**GRAPE, SEASIDE.** See **Coccoloba uvifera.**

**GRAPE SUGAR.** See **Glucose.**

**graph-,** in compound words, signifying marked with lines (written upon).

**GRAPHIO'LA.** A rather peculiar genus of fungi which is classified among the Smuts. The only one of interest in Great Britain is *G. phoenicis* which causes a disease of Palms in conservatories. On the fronds appear black, round pustules which soon produce a tuft of long yellow hair-like threads. It would be wise to cut off the first frond which develops the disease and to spray the plant with Bordeaux mixture.

D. E. G.

**GRAPH'IUM.** The genus received its name from the imperfect stage of the fungus but it is now known to be a stage of *Ceratostomella* which has perithecia with long thin necks. The fungus causing Dutch Elm disease which was at first called *G. ulmi* is now known as *Ceratostomella ulmi. See also under* **Ulmus, Diseases.**

D. E. G.

**GRAPPLE-PLANT.** See **Harpagophytum procumbens.**

**GRAPTOPET'ALUM weinberg'ii.** A synonym of *Sedum Weinbergii.*

**GRAPTOPHYL'LUM** (*grapho*, to write, *phyllon*, leaf; in allusion to the markings on the leaves). FAM. *Acanthaceae*. A genus of about 10 species of evergreen glabrous shrubs, natives of Australia and the Pacific Is. Leaves opposite, entire or rarely dentate, generally spotted. Flowers red, stalked. Stove temperatures are needed. For treatment *see* **Eranthemum.**

**G. Earl'ii.** Shrub of 10 to 15 ft., glabrous. *l.* oblong to ovate-lanceolate, narrowed to a short stalk, entire or nearly so. *fl.* red, solitary or few in l.-axils; cor. tube about 1 in. long, lobes lanceolate. Queensland.

**G. horten'se.** Caricature Plant. *l.* elliptic, curiously marbled with white, the markings often resembling faces. *fl.* crimson, inflated at throat; racemes axillary or terminal. Habitat? Cultivated widely in India. 1780. (B.R. 1227 as *Justicia picta*.) var. **lurido-sanguin'eum**, *l.* purplish, veins blood-red (B.M. 1870 as *J. picta lurido-sanguinea*); **ig'neum**, *l.* splashed with red.

**G. Nor'tonii.** Habit of *G. hortense* of which it is sometimes regarded as a variety. *l.* dark green, markings lurid red or partly yellow.

**GRASS GUM TREE,** Grass Tree. *See* **Xanthorrhoea.**

**GRASS MOTH.** *See* **Antler Moth.**

**GRASS OF PARNASSUS.** *See* **Parnassia palustris.**

**GRASS SNAKE** (*Natrix natrix*) is sometimes found in gardens, especially those bordering on commons and marshy areas. It is not harmful, feeding principally on Frogs. It attains a length of 3 ft. or more, and its body is greyish-green with black markings on the back and with a trace of a yellow or orange collar round the neck. It is not a poisonous snake like the Viper or Adder, *Vipera berus*, but invariably meets the same fate from ignorant and unobservant people. Irregular masses of its soft-shelled eggs—each the size of a pigeon's egg—are sometimes found during the autumn and winter in leaf-mould heaps, and should be left undisturbed.

G. F. W.

**GRASSES, LAWN.** The principal grasses for lawns in gardens are Brown-top (Agrostis), Chewing's, Hard, and Fine-leaved Fescues, Smooth- and Rough-stalked Meadow-grass (*Poa pratensis* and *P. trivialis*) for ornamental lawns in open sites; for rougher lawns Rye-grass (*Lolium perenne*) may be included, and under trees Rye-grass, Crested Dogstail, and *P. nemoralis* may be added. On very acid soils *P. annua* forms much of the turf, for example, in large towns. Plants of Yorkshire fog (*Holcus* sp.) and Cocksfoot (*Dactylis glomerata*) should be regarded as weeds and eliminated, as well as Rye-grass except as mentioned above. *See* **Lawn.**

**GRASSES, ORNAMENTAL.** Various grasses find a place in gardens for purposes other than their value as lawn plants. Several besides the Bamboos are of noble proportions and graceful habit and are very ornamental in large borders or as isolated lawn plants; some are valuable on the rock-garden or for their foliage in the border, or for edgings; some have a double value : in the border for their graceful spikes or panicles which, being dried, may also be used with everlasting flowers, &c., for indoor decoration in winter. For this purpose they should be cut on a fine day before the seeds ripen and gradually dried in a cool place. Most of the annual species may be treated as biennials, sown in July or August, instead of March or April, where they are to remain, and will then form larger clumps, with larger spikes and more of them. The individual species are dealt with in their alphabetical position in this work and information concerning them should be sought there.

The Bamboos are distributed over the following genera : Arundinaria, Bambusa, Dendrocalamus (tender), Phyllostachys, Sasa, Shibataea, and though not a true Bamboo, Chusquea may also be included among them for its similar garden value.

Other tall ornamental grasses for lawn or bank plants and other more or less isolated positions will be found under Arundo, Cortaderia, Elymus, Erianthus, Gynerium, Saccharum, Zea.

Somewhat dwarfer plants more suitable for borders, or in some instances for pots, or for the water-side, are under Agrostis, Aira, Andropogon, Arrhenatherum, Asperella, Briza, Bromus, Calamovilfa, Chloris, Coix, Cymbopogon, Dactylis, Deschampsia, Desmazeria, Eleusine, Eragrostis, Festuca, Glyceria, Hierochloe, Holcus, Hordeum, Lagurus, Lamarckia, Melica, Miscanthus, Molinia, Panicum, Pennisetum, Phalaris, Phragmites, Poa, Stipa, Trichloris, Tricholaena, Uniola. Several of these produce inflorescences useful for winter

bouquets, others have variegated forms less vigorous than the normal form and more amenable to use in the garden.

Useful edging plants are provided by *Dactylis glomerata variegata*, *Festuca ovina*, *Molinia caerulea variegata*.

On the rock-garden few grasses can be admitted but some species of Festuca will be found valuable for contrast and for increasing the similitude of the garden to the alpine picture.

*gratianopolita'nus -a -um*, of the neighbourhood of Grenoble.

**GRATIO'LA** (diminutive of *gratia*, grace, in reference to medicinal qualities). FAM. *Scrophulariaceae*. A genus of about 24 species of free-flowering, mostly perennial, herbs related to Mimulus, mostly natives of Cent. Europe, temperate Australia, and N. America. Leaves opposite. Flowers white or pale, tubular, 2 lipped, upper lip notched or 2-cleft, lower 3-cleft; calyx 5-partite, the segments overlapping; stamens 2; pedicels axillary, solitary. A rich moist soil suits these hardy plants which are easily propagated by dividing the roots in spring.

**G. au'rea.** Annual about 4 in. h., branched from base. *l.* broad-linear, toothed, dotted above, sessile. *fl.* golden-yellow, peduncles scarcely as long as *l.* May. N. America. 1828. (L.B.C. 1399.) Useful for moist banks near the water.

**G. carolinen'sis.** A synonym of *G. virginiana*.

**G. officina'lis.** Perennial. About 1 ft. h. *l.* lanceolate, toothed. *fl.* white, striped purple, small. May. Europe. 1568. Once used for treatment of bruises. Useful for margins of ponds.

**G. pilo'sa.** Annual, 1 to 2 ft. h. *l.* ovate or ovate-lanceolate sparingly but sharply toothed, base broad, sessile. *fl.* white, about ⅓ in. long; cor. scarcely exceeding cal.; tube oblong. July. N. America. 1827.

**G. ramo'sa.** About 9 in. h. *l.* lanceolate or linear-lanceolate, acute, sharply coarsely toothed. *fl.* white; cor. twice as long as the linear cal. teeth; pedicels as long as or longer than *l.* May to August. N. America. 1821. SYN. *G. quadridentata*.

**G. virginia'na.** 6 to 9 in. h. *l.* oblong-lanceolate, acute, sometimes toothed, usually glabrous, narrowed to base. *fl.* tube yellowish; lobes white, about ⅓ in. long, twice as long as cal. August. N. America. 1759.

F. P.

*gra'tus -a -um*, pleasing.

**GRAVEL.** *See* **Drives.**

**GRAVEL PLANK.** A board running along the bottom of a wooden fence.

**GRAVEL WALKS.** *See* **Paths, Drives.**

*graveo'lens*, strong-smelling.

**GRAVES'IA** (in honour of C. L. Graves who wrote on the plants of Northern France and collected in Madagascar). FAM. *Melastomataceae*. A genus of dwarf plants with striking foliage, natives of Madagascar. Leaves ovate-oblong, membranous, 5-nerved. Flower-parts in fives; stamens 10, equal. Cymes many-flowered, in umbellate cymes, scape solitary, erect. For cultivation *see* **Bertolonia,** in which genus the species of Gravesia are sometimes placed.

**G. gutta'ta.** *l.* ovate, 3 to 6 in. long, 2 to 3 in. wide, profusely dotted with rose spots in lines on a rich dark-green ground. 1864. (B.M. 5524 as *Bertolonia guttata*.) var. **Alfred Bleu,** *l.* brilliantly spotted and lined, especially nerved, bright red; **Legrellea'na,** *l.* without spots but main veins and some cross-veins outlined in white (SYN. *G. Legrelliana*); **margarita'cea,** a synonym of *Salpinga margaritacea*; **super'ba,** *l.* cordate-ovate, acute, thickly spotted with large reddish-purple spots, less regularly arranged and interspersed with numerous reddish-purple dots. SYN. *Bertolonia superbissima*.

F. G. P.

**GRAVIS'IA** (*gravis*, heavy, the leaf sheaths hold water). FAM. *Bromeliaceae*. A genus of 6 species of north-east S. America and Trinidad. Herbaceous perennials with or without a short stem. Related to Aechmea but with more than 5 pores to the pollen grains (instead of 4) and sessile flowers with free sepals. Treatment as for Aechmea.

G. ex'sudans. *fl.* orange, exuding a white greasy substance; bracts golden; scape erect with scattered crimson lanceolate bract leaves. *infl.* dense, almost hemispherical. *l.* oblong, about 3 ft. long, 1½ in. wide, grey-lepidote, spiny. 2 ft. h. Brazil. 1824. (L.B.C. 801 as *Bromelia exsudans*; B.H. 1879, 352, t. 18 as *Hohenbergia exsudans*.)

## GRAY ALDER. *See* Alnus incana.

## GRAY PLUM. *See* Parinarium excelsum.

**GRAY'IA** (in honour of Dr. Asa Gray, 1810–88, great American botanist, for many years Professor of Botany at Harvard University, and friend of Sir Joseph Hooker). FAM. *Chenopodiaceae*. A genus of 2 species of rigid, erect, branched shrubs, closely related to Atriplex, natives of NW. America. Leaves alternate, sessile, linear, obovate or spatulate, obtuse, entire, rather fleshy. Male flowers minute, in close clusters, axillary, pedicellate; female flowers racemose. Fruit large for the size of the plant, pendulous. *G. polygaloides* grows in any rich soil, is hardy, and may be increased by seed or cuttings.

G. polygaloi'des. Small, erect bush; branches ascending or forked, spiny at apex. *l.* ½ to ¾ in. long, ascending, oblong-lanceolate or obovate, wedge-shaped at base. *fr.* rose, compressed; cal. in fruit nearly ½ in. long. California. 1894. (H.I.P. 271.) SYN. *G. spinosa*.

G. spino'sa. A synonym of *G. polygaloides*.

**GREASE BANDING** is not only valuable in the orchard where trees are banded to capture the wingless females of the Winter, Mottled Umber, and March Moths, but it provides a measure for preventing certain other pests from ascending the stems of trees and shrubs. Grease-bands may be attached to the stems of standard Roses to deter Ants from reaching the Aphis-infested shoots, to standard Rhododendrons to prevent the wingless Vine and Clay-coloured Weevils from feeding on the foliage, and to standard and half-standard fruit-trees to prevent the wingless and immature Capsid Bugs, which tend to fall to the ground during spraying, from regaining the shoots and leaves.

The number of Winter and related Moths may be reduced in a garden and orchard by the routine banding of standard and half-standard trees. The modern greases, which are of vegetable origin, may be applied directly to the bark of all but very young fruit-trees. The band of grease should be at least 4 in. wide, and applied at a height above ground of at least 18 in. so that soil is not splashed up during heavy rainstorms nor dead leaves blown on to the grease, thereby avoiding the formation of 'natural bridges' over which the wingless female Moths can cross. In orchards used for grazing the bands should be placed as high as possible to prevent cattle from rubbing against the grease.

The grease should be applied by the end of September every year and the bands kept clear of dead leaves by periodic scraping or handpicking. It is advisable to renew the grease in early February so that the bands are tacky to capture the spring-emerging March moth females. Fresh grease may be added to the original band every year. A reliable grease should be harmless to the bark, reasonable in price, and not unduly affected by weather so that it remains tacky throughout the winter and spring months, and does not run on warm sunny days.

G. F. W.

## GREAT BURNET. *See* Sanguisorba officinalis.

## GREAT SPEARWORT. *See* Ranunculus Lingua.

## GREATER CELANDINE. *See* Chelidonium majus.

## GREEK VALERIAN. *See* Polemonium caeruleum.

## GREEN ALDER. *See* Alnus viridis.

**GREEN CAPSID BUG** (*Lygus pabulinus*). This Capsid, which closely resembles the Apple Capsid (q.v.), has a very wide range of host plants including many fruit and ornamental trees and shrubs, herbaceous perennials, annuals, and numerous weeds. The bugs are partial to Currants and Gooseberry and as a result of their feeding on the terminal bud a number of side shoots are encouraged and a badly shaped bush results. The adult bug is bright green and clothed with dusky hairs. The female inserts her eggs in the tissues of young shoots of fruit-trees and bushes during September and October. The eggs hatch in April and early May, and the young active, slender, yellowish-green bugs feed on the young terminal leaves causing well-defined spots to develop. When about half-grown, they crawl away from their woody winter hosts to herbaceous plants, Strawberry, Potatoes, and weeds. On these secondary hosts the bugs become fully winged adults, and eggs are laid in the stem of their summer hosts. The eggs hatch in July and August and the second-brood bugs feed on the plants until fully grown, when they migrate to the winter hosts upon which the winter eggs are laid.

CONTROL. *Winter Treatment.* Infested fruit-trees and bushes should be sprayed between the middle and end of March with a mineral oil or petroleum wash at a strength of 7½ per cent. to destroy the eggs. The wash should be applied thoroughly and with considerable pressure to ensure the wetting of the branches and shoots.

*Spring and Summer Treatment.* Spray or dust the infested plants with a nicotine-soap wash or nicotine dust as soon as the young bugs are observed, or when signs of their feeding are apparent on the young foliage. The ground beneath should receive a spraying or dusting immediately after the branches are sprayed as many of the bugs fall to the ground on the approach of the sprayer and will otherwise continue to develop and feed upon weeds. The presence of a grease-band on the trunks of standard and half-standard trees will trap these immature bugs as they endeavour to reascend the sprayed trees. All weeds in fruit plantations and shrub borders should be dug in or kept in check by regular hoeing during July to destroy all possible summer host plants of this species.

A. G. F. W.

## GREEN DRAGON. *See* Arisaema Dracontium.

## GREEN LEAF-WEEVIL. *See* Phyllobius Weevil.

**GREEN MANURING.** The digging into the soil of growing plants is one of the best and cheapest way of increasing its organic matter and humus, especially useful on poor sandy soils. Whatever is chosen for the purpose must be a crop that grows quickly and yields a large quantity of green soft growth at such a time that it can be dug in when the soil is moderately moist and warm enough to favour decomposition. Such a crop, of course, adds nothing to the mineral constituents of the soil (and equally takes nothing away), but it takes up available nitrogen and returns it in a form not quickly washed out of the soil, as nitrates are with drainage water, and a very considerable quantity of carbon compounds which on decomposition yield the very important humus. If the crop was a leguminous one it will actually add to the nitrogenous reserves in the soil as well as help to conserve them. Suitable crops are mustard, rape, rye, *Trifolium incarnatum*, and vetch. The choice must depend largely upon the length of time available for occupation of the ground by the green crop which must be dug in while in full growth before seed is produced. Annual weeds dug in before they seed are, of course, a form of green-manure. The immediate result of digging in a heavy green-manuring crop may be a depression of fertility for the bacteria which immediately begin to act upon it make a great demand upon the available nitrogen in the soil. This is a passing phase which can be corrected by a light dressing of a quick-acting nitrogenous manure such as sulphate of ammonia; it soon passes and the soil is eventually much richer than it was before the green-manuring. *See* **Compost-heap** which enables the first stages of decay to be carried on without competing with crops for nitrogen.

### GREEN PUG MOTH (*Chloroclystis rectangulata*).

The looper caterpillars of this small moth feed during May and June on the blossoms of Apple, Apricot, Cherry, and Pear. It is a common pest in the southern counties though frequently overlooked. The caterpillar is pale yellowish-green with red or green markings along the back making it a conspicuous insect when seen in the blossoms. The moths are on the wing in June and July, and the female lays her eggs singly on the trunk upon which they remain until the following spring. The young larvae bore into the fruit-buds and feed within, later eating the petals and stamens of the developing flowers. When fully fed they descend to the ground and pupate in the soil. This pest is controlled by a pre-blossom application of arsenate of lead. A post-blossom spray is less effective since most of the injury will have been done before it is applied.

G. F. W.

**GREENBOTTLES,** of which the common species, *Lucilia caesar*, is the most familiar, breed in carrion and excrement. The shiny, greenish or bluish-green flies visit the blossoms of certain hardy fruits, e.g. Apple and Pear, and act as pollinating agents of minor importance. Another species, *L. bufonivora*, breeds in Toads. The eggs are laid on the head or body of the Common Toad, and the white, legless, peg-shaped maggots eat their way from the nostrils into the brain and eventually devour the entire body. Half-blinded Toads are generally found to have been attacked by this fly, and have recovered.

G. F. W.

*Green'ei,* in honour of Dr. Greene, 1793–1862, of Boston, U.S.A.

**GREENFLIES.** *See* **Aphis.**

**GREENGAGE.** A variety of Plum (q.v.).

**GREENHEART.** *See* **Ocotea Rodioei.**

**GREENHOUSE.** A greenhouse may be defined as a glass structure especially devoted to the cultivation or exhibition of plants that never require a high temperature. It is distinguished from a conservatory by the occupants being almost exclusively grown in pots and tubs, whereas many plants are permanently planted out in the conservatory. The term has a wide application for it may include houses in which the plants are grown from youth to maturity or may mean a structure set apart for the exhibition of plants previously grown to the flowering stage in other houses or frames; it may apply to the cold house from which frost is excluded or to the cool greenhouse where a minimum night temperature of 45 to 50° F. is maintained; it may be of any shape, span-roofed, lean-to, or hip-roofed. Plants available for greenhouse decoration throughout the year are almost innumerable and include a large proportion of the most beautiful plants in cultivation. If sufficient plants, carefully selected to give variety and advanced or retarded to keep a succession, are available, a fine display may be ensured throughout the year. Nearly all the 'florists' flowers' and annuals can be grown in pots if desired and there are very numerous and attractive plants from Australia, S. Africa, the Himalaya, China, Tibet, and Japan suitable for the purpose. Many hardy flowering plants and shrubs may

be lifted from the open ground and forwarded to flower in early spring in such houses. Where other houses and frames are devoted to the preparation of flowering plants, the exhibition house may be kept at a temperature scarcely warm enough for those making their annual growth, but one at which the flowers will last longer.

Whatever house is used and for whatever purpose, save for very special plants with peculiar requirements, one essential is plenty of light, and this must be borne in mind in its construction; another is that provision must be made for admitting air in any quantity that circumstances demand. That the house should be soundly constructed, free from draughts, arranged so that no noxious fumes from the stoke-hole enter it, and free from drip and defects in the glass, goes without saying. (*See also* **Glazing.**) If the soil is very heavy or wet the house should be raised above the general level so as to ensure perfect drainage.

SHAPE AND ASPECT. Plenty of light and air being essential, it follows that the site of the house should be an open one. The house may be of any size, but for the majority of plants the best shape is the span-roof, for that admits light on all sides, and plants are less likely to

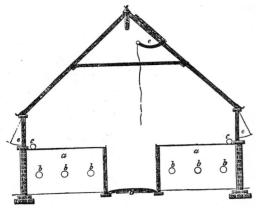

Section of Span-roofed house. The pipes *b* and *c* may be arranged to suit conditions.

draw or grow to one side than in houses of other types. Opinions differ as to the best direction for the run of the house, but most prefer that it should run north and south, on the ground that the long sides are then more open to morning and evening light and less to direct sun-rays at midday in summer. The construction should be such that there are no large, heavy, wooden rafters or sashbars to obstruct the light, and for this reason iron-work is often employed. Where wood is used, teak or western red cedar are the best, but good deal may be used if it is kept like iron thoroughly and regularly painted. The simplest form of house is a plain span 10 to 12 ft. wide with side stages and a middle path (*d*), with a height to the eaves of 5 ft., 3 ft. of which is brick or concrete, and 8 to 10 ft. at the ridge. The glazed portion of the sides should be arranged so as to open at will, either by pivots or by hinges beneath the eaves, and ventilators should be provided on both sides at the ridge (*e*). With this arrangement ventilation is possible without draughts irrespective of the direction of the wind. There should also be bottom ventilators in the walls, level with, or slightly below, the hot-water pipes so that the in-coming air is warmed before reaching the plants.

The stages or benches (*a*) should be fixed about 3 ft. from the ground and may be constructed of slate slabs supported on iron standards and angle-irons, or of rectangular flat tiles or of reinforced concrete. Where such stages are used there should be a space of about 3 in. between the back of the stage and the wall to allow free passage of warm air from the lower ventilators between the plants and the glass, and a raised surround so that pea gravel or other material capable of retaining moisture may be placed on the bench on which the pots will stand, but provision should be made for surplus water to drain away. Wooden-slatted stages have certain disadvantages for they perish rapidly unless kept regularly painted or are made of teak or other durable wood, but with some plants which are the better for a dry atmosphere, if kept in good repair they are an advantage. Currugated iron covered with moisture-retaining material may also be used and for some plants, such as Calceolarias, Cinerarias, and Cyclamens, that enjoy cool, moist conditions, solid-bricked beds filled with soil and surfaced with ashes give the best conditions.

For a show house about 18½ ft. wide allowing for a 6-ft. bed in the middle, 3-ft. wide benches at the sides and two 3-ft. paths would be suitable. The height at the eaves should be 6 ft., 3 ft. being glazed, and at the ridge

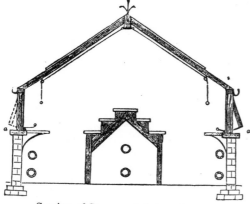

Section of Span-roofed show house.

12 ft., or there might be a lantern about 2 ft. wide rising 2½ ft. higher at the top, making the extreme height 14½ ft. Ventilation, &c., should be as already indicated. In the show house the paths should be paved or tiled or made of channelled bricks, which will retain a certain amount of water at will, enabling the atmosphere to be kept sufficiently humid. The middle bed may be covered with gravel and used for standing the taller plants, it may be partly planted out, or it may be the site of tiered benches. Supporting pillars should be used for climbers, for roof-climbers should form an important feature. When planning the house, planting quarters should be provided either by building a narrow bed between the hot-water pipes and the wall bringing it up to within a few inches of the under-side of the stage or by arranging a separate compartment opposite each rafter. The staging should be removable opposite each such station to allow for planting and subsequent attention.

In constructing a lean-to house advantage can be taken of an existing wall. Lean-to houses have the disadvantage that the plants get full light only on one side. If, however, they face south they are more economically heated and the back wall gives an ideal position for many beautiful shrubby plants which could not be accommodated in an ordinary span-roofed house, e.g. *Cassia corymbosa*, *Streptosolen Jamesonii*, and *Tibouchina semidecandra*. The size of the house must determine the internal arrangements. There will usually be a front bench, a path, and a narrow bed for the plants on the back wall, but in larger houses there may be room for a stage between the path and the back wall or even a border wide enough for shrubs to be planted without depriving the plants on the wall of light.

Hip-roofed or three-quarter-span houses have one advantage over lean-to houses in that it is possible to admit

light on both sides and usually to obtain more height and width.

GROWING-HOUSES. Where an exhibition house has to be continuously supplied it will be necessary to provide at least 2 growing-houses, or 1 house may be divided into

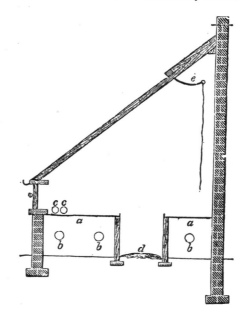

Section of Lean-to house.

2 or 3 parts by a glass partition. The growing-house should have a wall 1 ft. high with the roof coming down to rest upon it. An exterior flight of steps should lead to the middle path which should be 3½ ft. below the level of the ground. Side benches similar to those already described should be fitted but they may be somewhat wider. One division should be warm with a winter temperature of 55 to 60° F., the other cool with a winter temperature of 45 to 55° F. and no artificial heat in summer except

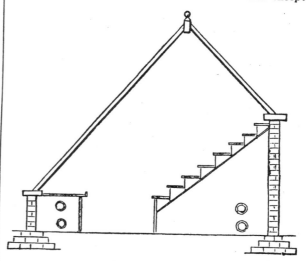

Section of Hip-roofed house.

in very damp weather or when gentle bottom heat is needed for propagation. The warmer end may be used for gentle forcing in spring, the cooler for hardening off before bringing plants into the exhibition house and for resting plants, as well as for their ordinary purposes of growing and propagation. In these houses, sections of the roof should be made to lift like hinged frame-lights to facilitate the movement of plants in and out without recourse to the steps.

FRAMES. A few frames also are of great value for many plants may be grown in them. They should be of different depths (*see* **Frames**).

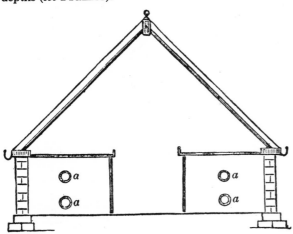

Section of Growing house.

SHADING is an important item and is best effected by roller blinds either of fine tiffany or by wooden blinds made of strips 1½ in. wide with ½ in. space between them bound together by cords or made to roll up and down, but they need to run on supports 1 ft. above the surface of the glass. It is also desirable to have a space between the tiffany and the glass. Permanent shading is never satisfactory. Continual shade, especially in spring and autumn, when dull days are frequent, may be very injurious. On the other hand the blinds need constant attention, for unless drawn before the sun becomes fierce, as it may unexpectedly do at short notice in summer and even spring, much harm may be done to flowers and tender foliage. The ends of the houses may be permanently shaded but are better shaded by tiffany hooked on when needed. The blinds may be of woolly material for use in winter to conserve heat in severe weather.

In order that light should not be impeded the glass should be kept clean. Fogs especially are apt to result in a sooty deposit being left on the glass, so robbing the plants of essential light, and if dust is allowed to accumulate the same condition occurs and great harm may be done in a short time.

HEATING. *See* **Heating.** Self-registering thermometers should be placed in every house.

VENTILATION. The art of giving the right amount of air at the right time can only be acquired by long experience. The position of the ventilators has already been indicated. They should all open from inside or by means of gearing operated from within or from outside, giving a wide range of opening.

Plenty of air should be given whenever it can be done without lowering the temperature unduly or when to give it entails the admission of damp or fog. When cold or strong winds are blowing, only the ventilators on the opposite side from that which is exposed thereto should be opened. Bottom air can always be given by the ventilators in the brickwork except when the thermometer registers frost or the wind is very cold.

Not quite so much air will be needed in the growing-houses as in those where the plants are in flower or where flowering is past. Even here, however, ventilators in the roof and in the sides between the roof and ground should be freely used. When nights are cool and the sun bright and strong during the day, early closing of the ventilators

will economize heat and keep the temperature from falling too quickly or too low.

When it is not advisable to remove frame-lights altogether they may be raised to various heights by blocks of wood, or in span-roofed frames by graduated stays.

WATER TANKS should be arranged at convenient places either inside or outside the house where the water may stand before use. If thought desirable the temperature of the water may be maintained by means of hot-water pipes run through the tank, but the hardier types of plants are not adversely affected by water somewhat lower in temperature than the air, though very tender plants may be.

GENERAL NOTES. Greenhouse plants vary so much in habit, growth, and needs that they require different methods of treatment and different composts. Notes on such points will be found under the names of the plants concerned and the following are only generalities which must usually be attended to.

Watering requires extreme care and the question 'How often should this plant be watered?' cannot be answered, except by saying, 'Whenever it needs it'. It is almost impossible to tell anyone how to water properly, but the cultivator who takes a real interest in his plants will soon know their requirements and act accordingly, treating each plant individually. On no account should a plant, except when it is resting, and not always then, be allowed to become dry. Often a plant will suffer so much damage from being dry for only one day that it will not recover for a year. Generally, if the pot in which a plant is growing gives a hollow ring when tapped it may be said to be dry, but this is not always a true test, and one can only tell correctly after long experience. Care, too, must be exercised not to over-water, as quite as much damage may be done that way. The great art is to give a plant just sufficient at the time it is beginning to require it.

Pots used for potting should be perfectly clean and dry and the drainage material should be clean, sufficient, and properly arranged. If the drainage becomes blocked it must be renewed, otherwise the soil will become sour and the plant will suffer. To prevent this, the drainage should be covered with some loose material such as dry leaves or moss. Worms are sometimes troublesome in pots. They can usually be got at by carefully knocking the plant out of the pot, taking care not to injure the roots or break the ball. If this cannot be done, watering with soot-water or clear lime-water will kill them.

When potting, the compost should be neither too wet nor too dry. It is in good condition if when a handful is well squeezed it remains in a lump which falls to pieces when it is dropped. Sufficient room must be left between the surface of the soil in the pot and the rim to enable it to hold a good quantity of water. The plants should be well centred in the pot, not buried too deeply nor potted too high, and the surface of the soil should be left level. Care must be taken that the compost is worked well among the roots, filled in evenly in the pot, and made sufficiently firm to suit the plant.

Plants when potted on should always be kept a little closer and warmer than they have previously been accustomed to, until they have recovered from the check. One good soaking should be given and the plants then be allowed to go without water for a time, but not allowed to become dry. If in summer and the foliage seems inclined to flag, the plants should be gently syringed overhead 3 or 4 times a day.

Freshly potted plants are often killed by over-watering. The soil round a freshly potted plant contains no roots or very few and there is nothing to absorb the moisture; if it be kept wet it will become sour, and when the plant begins to send fresh roots into it they will be poisoned and rot. It will be best to keep the plant rather on the dry side till its roots obtain good hold and are capable of absorbing the moisture.

All plants should be watered before potting for if the ball be dry at that time it can never be got moist again by ordinary means after potting.

The gravel on which the plants stand should be sprinkled with water daily, except in damp weather, in the cool greenhouse and more often in the warm, and may need it 3 or 4 times a day in hot summer weather, and at the same time the floor should be damped down and the foliage syringed overhead, those that are in flower very lightly, others more vigorously. Many fear to syringe plants in flower, believing that the flowers will damp off or become discoloured. This is a mistake, for if the syringing be done when the air is dry and with full ventilation on and the blinds down, syringing is of the greatest benefit. It must of course be done carefully to avoid bruising and only perfectly clean water must be used. Watering should be done with a rose-can to avoid washing the soil out of the pots. In summer, watering is best done after 4 p.m. Greenwich time, in winter in the morning.

Cleanliness is most important. The need for cleansing the glass and using clean pots and crocks has already been referred to. Dead foliage and flowers should be regularly removed as they harbour fungus pests. Cleanliness in the house removes the harbourage of many noxious insects.

Never allow a plant to spoil for want of a stake. Weak-stemmed or top-heavy plants need stakes and if a plant throws up several stems each should have a stake. Thin stakes should be used provided they are sufficiently strong. Bamboos are light, strong, and durable, and can be had in various sizes.

Arrangement must depend largely upon the taste of the person in charge. To put two similar colours together often spoils both. Fine foliage plants dotted among flowering plants often enhances their effect. Above all, overcrowding must be avoided: the individual plants should stand so as to show their form and character.

Finally, continual vigilance must be exercised to watch for and deal with pests (see **Greenhouse Pests**). Success with plants under glass depends more, even than with plants in the open, upon constant attention to details, monotonous, trivial, and fiddling perhaps, but making all the difference between good and bad cultivation.

In houses for special crops see under the plants concerned.

## Greenhouse plants

**Greenhouse plants** can be divided into two general groups, hard-wooded and soft-wooded.

HARD-WOODED PLANTS include all plants of a shrubby habit and most climbers. Many of them are difficult to cultivate, particularly if their special requirements are not attended to or are not sufficiently understood, and suitable positions are not provided. Watering, particularly, is an operation too often carried out indifferently and answerable for more casualties than any other single detail in treatment. The majority of the hard-wooded plants flower in spring and summer, and treatment varies according to the condition of the plants in their growing, resting, and flowering times. Healthy, floriferous species from Australia and S. Africa are only secured if constant attention is given throughout the preceding summer and winter. Nearly all repotting should be attended to just after the annual growth begins, a season varying with different species. A somewhat closer, warmer atmosphere and more humidity may be allowed for a month afterwards to encourage the growth of roots into the new soil. Afterwards more air must be admitted gradually and in bright summer weather a thin, temporary shading should be given. The aim, with hard-wooded plants, should be to encourage summer growth to the fullest extent, and to ensure its thorough ripening in autumn. Without this the production of flowers subsequently will be poor compared with what is possible with good cultivation. In addition to this rather difficult group, there are numerous evergreen shrubs and small trees of an ornamental character, well fitted for mixing with other plants as permanent occupants of greenhouses, and a large proportion may be cultivated in comparatively small pots. When any need pots of larger sizes, they should be shifted in spring or early autumn, and, if possible, kept a little closer for a few days afterwards.

SOFT-WOODED PLANTS include all with herbaceous stems, whether annual or perennial plants with bulbs and corms or other underground storage organs and indeed any that cannot be included among hard-wooded plants.

[In the Lists (not exhaustive) of plants which may be grown in the cold and cool greenhouses, Alpine-house Plants, Annuals, Ferns, Orchids, Hardy Herbaceous Perennials, Succulents, and Water Plants, lists of which will be found under these headings, have been omitted. Unless otherwise indicated the cold house is suitable.

Abbreviations: *b*, blue; *bk*, black; *br*, brown; *c*, cream; c-h, cool house; *g*, green; *gr*, grass; *l*, lavender or lilac; *m*, magenta; *mv*, mauve or heliotrope; *o*, orange; *p*, purple; *pi*, pink; *r*, red; *v*, violet; *w*, white; *y*, yellow. The numerals show the height in feet.]

JANUARY. See also DECEMBER. Azalea (*r* and *w*; 1–3); Camellia japonica vars. (c-h; *r*, *w*, *pi*; up to 20); Abutilon insigne (c-h; *p-r*; 6); A. megapotamicum (c-h; *r*, *y*, and *br*; 3); Barosma lanceolata (c-h; *w* and *r*; 3); Bouvardia jasminiflora (c-h; *w*; 2); Daphne odora (c-h; *w* and *pi*; 1); Epacris purpurascens (c-h; *w* and *r*; 2–3); Erica canaliculata (c-h; *w*; 2–3); E. hyemalis (c-h; *pi* and *w*; 2); E. melanthera (c-h; *pi*; 2); Gardenia Thunbergii (c-h; *w*; 4–5); Leucopogon australis (c-h; *w*; 2–4); L. Richei (c-h; *w*; 3–4); Monochaetum Hartwegianum (c-h; *pi*); Muraltia Heisteria (c-h; *p*; 2–3); Mussaenda luteola (c-h; *y* and *o*; 5–6); Rhododendron javanicum (c-h; *o* and *r*; 4).

FEBRUARY. As for January and Acacia dealbata (*y*; 8); A. retinodes (c-h; *y*; 20); A. pulchella (c-h; *y*; 6); Barosma pulchella (c-h; *r* or *p*; 1–3); Boronia pinnata (c-h; *pi*; 1–3); Diosma ericoides (c-h; *w* and *r*; 3–10); Enkianthus quinqueflorus (c-h; *r* and *pi-w*; 3–10); Pittosporum undulatum (*w*; 10).

MARCH. *Acacia, many sp. (c-h; *y*; various); Acrotriche ovatifolia (c-h; *w*; ½–1); Anthyllis Barba-Jovis (c-h; *y*; 4–8); *Barosma serratifolia (c-h; *w*; 1–3); *Boronia pinnata (c-h; *pi*; 1–3); *Bossiaea disticha (c-h; *y-r*; 1½); Bouvardia flava (c-h; *y*; 1½); *Cantua pyrifolia (c-h; *y-w*; 3); *Correa cardinalis (c-h; *r* and *g*; 3); Daphne japonica (c-h; *w* and *pi-p*; 1); *D. odora (c-h; *p-w* and *p*; 1); *Diosma ericoides (c-h; *w* and *r*; 1–3); Enkianthus sp. (*r* and *pi*; 3–10); *Epacris impressa (c-h; *w-r*; 2–3); *E. purpurascens and other sp. (c-h; *w* and *r*; 2–3); *Erica, several S. African sp. q.v. (c-h; various); Eriostemon myoporoides (c-h; *pi*; 1–2); E. scaber (c-h; *w* and *pi*; 1½); Gardenia Thunbergii (c-h; *w*; 4–5); *Gastrolobium bilobum (c-h; *y* and *r-p*; 3–4); *Gnidia pinifolia (c-h; *c-w*; 1); *Grevillea lavandulacea (c-h; *pi*; 2); *G. Thelemanniana (c-h; *r* and *y*; 3–5); *Indigofera australis (c-h; *pi*; 3–4); *Leucopogon australis (c-h; *w*; 2–4); *L. lanceolatus (c-h; *w*; 6–10); *Macleania speciosissima (c-h; *r* and *y*); Oxylobium cuneatum (c-h; *y* or *o*; 2); Prostanthera Sieberi (c-h; *m*; 5–6); *Rhododendron javanicum (c-h; *o* and *r*; 4); Tetratheca hirsuta (c-h; *pi*; ½–1½).

APRIL. Plants marked * in March and Abutilon Darwinii (c-h; *o*; 4); Acrotriche cordata (c-h; *w*; 1); Agathosma ciliata (c-h; *w*; 1–2); A. erecta (c-h; *v*; 1–2); A. punctata (c-h; *v*; 2–3); Anopterus glandulosus (c-h; *w*; 6); Anthyllis Hermanniae (c-h; *y*; 2–4); Athrixia capensis (c-h; *r-p*; 1); Barosma scoparia (c-h; *w* and *r*; 3); Bossiaea rhombifolia (c-h; *y* and *r*; 1–3); Burtonia scabra (c-h; *p*; 2); Calceolaria fuchsiifolia (*y*; 1–2); Camellia japonica and vars. (c-h; *w*, *r*, *pi*; up to 20); Celastrus lucidus (c-h; *w*; 1–3); Chorizema sp. (c-h; *o*, *r*, or *y*; 1–2); Cneorum pulverulentum (*y*; 1–3); Correa pulchella (c-h; *pi*; 6); Gaultheria fragrantissima (*w* or *p*; 4); Goodia lotifolia (c-h; *y* and *r*; 2–4); Hovea Celsii and other sp. (c-h; *b* or *v-p*; 3–10); Michelia Figo (c-h; *p*; 2–4); Mimulus glutinosus (c-h; *br* or *pi*; 5); Oxylobium cuneatum (c-h; *p*, *y*, and *r*; 6); O. obtusifolium (c-h; *o*, *y*, and *r*; 1–3); O. trilobatum (c-h; *y*; 2); Pimelea ferruginea (c-h; *r* to *pi*; 1–2); P. hypericina (*w*; 8–10); Polygala myrtifolia (c-h; *p*; 4–6); Protea cordata (c-h; *p*; 1); P. speciosa (c-h; *y-w*; 3–6); Pultenaea rosea and other sp, (c-h; various; 2–3); Rhododendron q.v. (various).

MAY. Many flowering in March and April. Acacia sp. q.v. (*y*; various); *Acrophyllum venosum (c-h; *pi-w*; 6); Acrotriche divaricata (c-h; *w*; ½–1); Adesmia boronioides (c-h; *y* and *p*; 4); Albizzia lophantha (*y*; 6–10); Anopterus glandulosa (c-h; *pi-w*; 3); Aotus gracillima (c-h; *y* and *r*; 3); Backhousia myrtifolia (c-h; *w*; 10–16); Barnardesia rosea (c-h; *pi*; 1½); *Barosma serratifolia (c-h; *w*; 1–3); *Baueria rubioides (c-h; *r*, *pi*, or *w*; 1–2); Beaufortia decussata (c-h; *r*; 3–10); B. purpurea (c-h; *p-r*; 4); Boronia sp. (c-h; various); Boissaea disticha (c-h; *y-r*; 1½); B. linophylla (c-h; *o* and *r*; 2–4); B. rhombifolia (c-h; *y* and *r*; 1–3); *Bunchosia odorata (c-h; *y*; 7); Burtonia villosa (c-h; *p*; 2); Camellia japonica and vars. (various); *Celastrus lucidus (c-h; *w*; 1–3); *Chorizema sp. (c-h; various); Darwinia macrostegia (c-h; *w* and *pi*; 2–3); Dillwynia sp. (c-h; *r*, *o*, or *y*; 2–6); *Diosma ericoides (c-h; *w* and *r*; 1–3); Enkianthus quinqueflorus (c-h; *r* and *pi-w*; 3–10); *Epacris longiflora (c-h; *r* and *w*; 2–4); E. pulchella (c-h; *r* or *pi*; 1–3); *Erica, many sp., q.v. (c-h; various); Gastrolobium bilobum (c-h; *y*; 3–8); G. villosum (c-h; *o* and *p*; 2–4); *Goodia lotifolia (c-h; *y* and *r*; 2–4); Grevillea alpina (*r* and *y*; 2); G. fasciculata (c-h; *r* and *y*; 4); G. macrostylis (c-h; *r* and *y*; 4–6); G. Thelemanniana (c-h; *r* and *y*; 3–5); Hovea Celsii (c-h; *b*; 2–4); *Indigofera australis (c-h; *pi*; 3–4); Lachnaea eriocephala (c-h; *pi-w*; 1–2); Leucopogon Richei (c-h; *w*; 3–4); *Luculia Pinceana (c-h; *w*; 6); *Mimulus glutinosus (c-h; *br* or *r*; 3); Myrtus Ugni (c-h; *w*; 4); *Oxylobium ellipticum (c-h; *y*; 2–3); Pelargonium abrotanifolium (*w* or *r*; 3); P. cordatum (*p* and *w*; 3); P. ionidiflorum (*v*; 6); P. quercifolium (*r* and *p*; 3); Petrophila acicularis (c-h; *w*, *r*; 2); P. rigida (c-h; *w*; 2–3); P. Serruriae (c-h; *w*; 3–4); Pimelea arenaria (*w*; 1–2); P. ferruginea (*pi*; 1½–2); P. imbricata (*w*; 1½); P. linifolia (*w-pi*; 1–3); P. rosea (*pi* to *w*; 1–2); P. spectabilis (*pi*; 3–4); Pittosporum viridiflorum (c-h; *y-g*; 6); Platylobium angulare (c-h; *y*; 1–1½); P. obtusangulum (c-h; *o-y*; 3–4); Podalyria calyptrata (c-h; *pi*; 3–6); Polygala myrtifolia (c-h; *p*; 4–6); Pomaderris elliptica (c-h; *y*; 4–8); Protea compacta (c-h; *pi*; 6); Psoralea pinnata and other sp. (c-h; *b* and *w*; 3–6); Pultenaea flexilis (c-h; *y*; 2–3); *Rhododendron sp., q.v. (various); Sparmannia africana (c-h; *w*; 8–12); *Sphaeralcea miniata (*r*; 1); Stenanthera pinifolia (c-h; *r-y* and *g*; 2–3).

June. In addition to those marked * in the May list: Acacia pulchella (c-h; *y*; 3–8); Acmadenia tetragona (c-h; *w*; 1–2); Adenandra sp., q.v. (c-h; *w* and *pi*; 1–3); Adesmia microphylla (c-h; *y*; 1); *Anthospermum aethiopicum (c-h; *w*; 1–3); Asystasia bella (c-h; *l*; 6); *Baeckia Camphorosmae (c-h; *w* or *pi*; 2); *Berzelia lanuginosa (c-h; *w*; 1–2); *Calceolaria sp., q.v. (*y*, &c.; various); *Ceratostema longiflorum (c-h; *r*; 3–4); *C. speciosum (c-h; *o-r*; 3–4); Chrysocoma Coma-aurea (c-h; *y*; 2); Coronilla glauca (*y*; 5–6); *Cowania plicata (c-h; *pi*; 6–7); *Crowea saligna (c-h; *r*; 2–3); *Cytisus canariensis (*y*; 2–6); Daphne odora (*r-p*; 2–6); Darwinia fimbriata (c-h; *pi*; 1–2); Dichroa febrifuga (c-h; *b* to *v*; 3–6); Discaria serratifolia and other sp. (*g-w* or *y-g*; various); Embothrium coccineum (*r*; 3 to many); *Fuchsia sp., q.v. (various); Gompholobium grandiflorum (*y*; 3); *G. polymorphum (c-h; *o-y* to *r*; 2); *G. venustum (*p*; 1–2); *Goodia pubescens (c-h; *y* and *r*; 1–2); Grevillea acanthifolia (c-h; *r*; 4); G. robusta (c-h; *o*; 5); G. rosmarinifolia (*r*; 6–7); Hakea acicularis (c-h; *w* or *pi*; 5–10); H. cucullata (c-h; *r*; 12–14); H. saligna (c-h; *w*; 12); H. suaveolens (c-h; *w*; 8–15); Hovea Celsii (c-h; *b*; 2–4); *Hypocalyptus obcordatus (c-h; *p*; 1–2); Iochroma fuchsioides (c-h; *o-r*; 5); *I. lanceolata (c-h; *b* to *p*; 4–8); Lachnaea buxifolia (c-h; *w*; 2); *L. purpurea (c-h; *p*; 2); *Leschenaultia biloba (c-h; *b*; 1); *L. formosa (c-h; *r*; 1); *Leucopogon verticillatus (c-h; *pi* or *w*; 3–6); *Lippia citriodora (*w*; 3); *Melianthus major (c-h; *br*; 4–6); * Luculia Pinceana (c-h; *w*; 4–6); Myrtus Luma (c-h; *w*; 3); *Nerium Oleander (*r*; 6–14); *Oxylobium Callistachys (c-h; *y*; 3–4); *O. ellipticum (c-h; *y*; 2–3); Pelargonium sp., q.v. (various); Persoonia ferruginea (c-h; *y*; 3–4); P. rigida (c-h; *y*; 3–4); *Phaenocoma prolifera (*r-p*; 4); Philesia buxifolia (*r*; ½–¾); Pimelea glauca (c-h; *p-w*; 1½); P. hispida (c-h; *pi*; 2–4); *P. rosea (c-h; *pi* to *w*, 1–2); *Prostanthera Lasianthos (c-h; *p*; 12); Protea cynaroides (c-h; *w* to *pi*; 2–6); *P. latifolia (c-h; *r*; 5–6); *Psoralea aculeata (c-h; *b* and *w*; 2–3); P. pinnata (c-h; *b* and *w*; 3–6); *Rafnia triflora (c-h; *y*; 3–4); Rhododendron sp. (various); Rhodomyrtus tomentosa (c-h; *pi*; 5–6); Rhus succedanea (*y*; 6); *Salvia albocaerulea (c-h; *w* and *b*; 3); *S. Goudotii (c-h; *r*; 2); *S. Grahamii (c-h; *r*; 2); *S. Heeri (c-h; *r*; 2–3); *S. rutilans (c-h; *r*; 2–3); *Sarmienta repens (c-h; *r*; creeping); *Selago Gillii (c-h; *pi*; ½); *Senecio argenteus (c-h; *y*; 1–2); *Solanum atropurpureum (c-h; *p* and *y*); *S. Capsicastrum (*w*; 1–2); S. giganteum (c-h; *b*; 10–25); *S. marginatum (c-h; *w* and *p*; 3–4); *S. Pseudocapsicum (c-h; *w*; 4); *S. pyracanthum (c-h; *b* to *v*; 3–6); Sophora secundiflora (c-h; *v*; 6); *Talinum Arnotii (c-h; *y*); *Vaccinium leucobotrys (c-h; *w*; 4–7); Witsenia corymbosa (c-h; *p-b*); Xanthosia rotundifolia (c-h; *w*; 1–2).

July. To those marked * in the June list add: Abutilon pulchellum (c-h; *w*; 8); A. venosum (c-h; *o*, veined *r*; 10); Acacia dealbata (*y*; 10–20); A. Farnesiana (c-h; *y*; 6–10); A. glauca (c-h; *w*; 5–10); A. mollissima (c-h; *y*; 10–20); Acridocarpus natalitius (c-h; *y*); Acronychia Cunninghamii (c-h; *w*; 7); Adenanthos obovata (c-h; *r*; 5); Astelma eximium (c-h; *r*; 3); Astephanus triflorus (c-h; *w*); Berkheya grandiflora (c-h; *y*; 2); Berzelia lanuginosa (c-h; *w*; 1–2); Borbonia barbata (c-h; *y*; 3–4); B. crenata (c-h; *y*; 3–6); Boronia crenulata (c-h; *r*; 1); B. serrulata (c-h; *pi*; 1–6); Bossiaea linophylla (c-h; *o* and *p*; 1–4); Bouvardia leiantha (c-h; *r*; 2); B. triphylla (c-h; *r*; 2–3); Brunia nodiflora (c-h; *w*; 1–3); Bunchosia argentea (c-h; *y*; 10); Burseria spinosa (c-h; *w*; 10); Burtonia conferta (c-h; *v*; 2); Calceolaria sp. (various); Candollea cuneiformis (c-h; *y*; 7); Celastrus lucidus (c-h; *w*; 1–3); Chorizema diversifolia (c-h; *o-r*; 2); Coronilla coronata (c-h; *y*; 1–2); Crotalaria cajanifolia (c-h; *y*; 4–6); Cytisus racemosus (c-h; *y*; 3); Diosma ericoides (c-h; *w* and *r*; 1–3); Erica sp. (various); Eugenia buxifolia (c-h; *w*; 5–10); Gazania uniflora (c-h; *y*; 1); Gomphocarpus fruticosus (c-h; *w*; 5–7); Gompholobium venustum (c-h; *p*. 1–3); Goodia lotifolia (c-h; *y* and *r*; 2–4); Grewia occidentalis (c-h; *p*; 10); Hakea dactyloides (c-h; *w*; 7); H. suaveolens (c-h; *w*; 4); Lightfootia ciliata (c-h; *b*; ¾); Luculia Pinceana (c-h; *w*); Mahernia incisa (c-h; *r* to *y*; 2–4); Oxylobium ellipticum (c-h; *y*; 2–3); Platylobium formosum (c-h; *y*; 4); Podalyria calyptrata (c-h; *p*; 6); Pultaenea stricta (c-h; *y*; 1–3); Rhododendron javanicum (c-h; *o* and *r*; 4); Salvia chamaedryoides (c-h; *b*; 1); S. fulgens (*r*; 2–3); Sphaeralcea elegans (c-h; *v* and *p*); Styphelia tubiflora (c-h; *r*; 5); Tephrosia capensis (c-h; *p*); Tetratheca pilosa (c-h; *p*; 1–1½); Tweedia caerulea (c-h; *b*; 2–3); Westringia rosmariniformis (c-h; *b*).

August. * Acmena floribunda (c-h; *w*; 4); Acradenia Frankliniae (c-h; *w*; 8); Babingtonia Camphorosme (c-h; *pi*; 7); Befaria aestuans (c-h; *p*; 10–15); B. ledifolia (c-h; *p*; 3–4); Berzelia lanuginosa (c-h; *w*; 1–2); *Bossiaea linophylla (c-h; *o* and *p*; 1–4); *Bouvardia leiantha (c-h; *r*; 2); *Brachylaena nerifolia (c-h; *y*; 2); *Burseria spinosa (c-h; *w*; 10); *Calceolaria sp. (various); Cassia corymbosa (*y*; 6); *Celastrus lucidus (c-h; *w*; 1–3); *Ceratostigma Griffithii (c-h; *b*; 3); Chaetogastra strigosa (c-h; *pi-p*; 1); Cloanthes stoechadis (c-h; *g-y*; 2); *Cneorum pulverulentum (*y*; 1–3); *Coronilla glauca (*y*; 4); Crotalaria Cunninghamii (c-h; *y-g* and *p*; 3); Crowea seligna (c-h; *pi*; 1–2); Cytisus canariensis (c-h; *y*; 2–4); Datura arborea (c-h; *w*; 7–10); Dombeya Burgesiae (c-h; *w* and *pi*; 10); Dracophyllum capitatum (c-h; *w*; 1–1½); Duvalia polita (c-h; *br-p*, *br*, or *r* and *o*); *Erica sp. (various); Embothrium coccineum (*r*; 3); Eutaxia myrtifolia (c-h; *y*; 2–6); *Fuchsia sp. (various); Gazania uniflora (c-h; *y*; 1); *Gomphocarpus fruticosus (c-h; *w*; 5–7); Gompholobium Knightianum (c-h; *pi* or *p*; 1); G. polymorphum (c-h; *r*, *y*, and *p*); Goodia pubescens (c-h; *y* and *r*; 1–2); Grevillea Banksii (c-h; *r*; 15); Grewia occidentalis (c-h; *p*; 10); Grindelia glutinosa (*y*; 2); Hakea suaveolens (c-h; *w*; 4); Iochroma fuchsioides (c-h; *o-r*; 5); I. lanceolata (c-h; *p-b*; 4–5); Leschenaultia biloba (c-h; *b*; 1); L. formosa (c-h; *r*; 1); Leucopogon verticillatus (c-h; *w* or *pi*; 3–6); Limonium profusum (c-h; *p* and *w*; 2); Luculia Pinceana (c-h; *w*); Mahernia incisa (c-h; *r* to *y*; 2–4); Melianthus major (c-h; *br*; 4–6); Myrtus Luma (c-h; *w*; 3); *Nerium Oleander (c-h; *r*; 6–12); Oxylobium Callistachys (c-h; *y*; 3–4); *O. ellipticum (c-h; *y*; 2–3); *Pelargonium sp. and vars. (various); Phaenocoma prolifera (c-h; *r*; 4); Phylica plumosa (c-h; *w*; 2); Protea cynaroides (c-h; *g-w*); Rhododendron javanicum (c-h; *o* and *r*; 4); Salvia sp. as in July list; Selago Gillii (c-h; *pi*; 4); Solanum sp. as in July list; Sparmannia africana (c-h; *w*; 6); Talinum Arnotii (c-h; *y*); Vaccinium leucobotrys (c-h; *w*; 4–7).

September. To those marked * in August add: Abutilon megapotamicum (*r*, *y*, and *br*; 3); Bouvardia angustifolia (c-h; *r*; 2); B. longiflora (c-h; *w*; 2–3); Bredia hirsuta (c-h; *pi*); Colquhounia coccinea (c-h; *r*); Mussaenda luteola (c-h; *y* and *o*; 5–6); Protea mellifera (c-h; *pi* or *w*; 6).

October. *Abutilon megapotamicum (*r*, *y*, and *br*; 3); Bocconia frutescens (c-h; *g*; 3–6); *Bouvardia leiantha (c-h; *r*; 2); *Brachylaena nerifolia (c-h; *y*; 2); *Breda hirsuta (c-h; *pi* or *w*); Bursaria spinosa (c-h; *w*; 10); *Calceolaria bicolor (*y* and *w*; 2–3); C. scabiosaefolia (*y*; 3); *Erica sp. (various); Fuchsia macrostemma (*r*; 6–12); *F. microphylla (c-h; *r*; 2); F. simplicicaulis (c-h; *pi-r*; 3); Grindelia glutinosa (*y*; 2); *Luculia gratissima (c-h; *pi*; 9–12); *Mimulus glutinosa (c-h; *br* or *pi*; 5); Monochaetum Humboldtianum (c-h; *r-p*); Mussaenda luteola (c-h; *y* and *o*; 5–6); Nerium Oleander (c-h; *r*; 6–14); *Pelargonium comptum (c-h; *pi* and *p*; 2); *Phylica plumosa (c-h; *w*; 2); *Rhododendron javanicum (c-h; *o* and *r*; 4); *Salvia boliviana (c-h; *r*; 4); *S. Greggii (c-h; *pi*; 3); Vaccinium erythrinum (c-h; *r*; 1½).

November. In addition to those marked * in the October list Boebera incana (c-h; *y*; 1½); Brachyotum confertum (c-h; *p* and *c*); Chaenostoma linifolia (c-h; *w* or *y*; 1); Daphne odora (c-h; *w* and *pi*; 3).

December. Abutilon insigne (c-h; *p-r*; 6); A. megapotamicum (c-h; *r*, *y*, and *br*; 3); A. striatum (c-h; *o-y*; 10); Bouvardia jasminiflora (c-h; *w*; 2); Bursaria spinosa (c-h; *w*; 10); Camellia japonica (c-h; various; up to 20); Daphne japonica (c-h; *w* and *pi*; 3); Erica canaliculata (c-h; *pi*; 2–4); E. gracilis (c-h; *p-r*; 1); E. hyemalis (c-h; *pi* and *w*; 2); E. ramentacea (c-h; *p-r*; 1½); Leonotis Leonurus (c-h; *r*; 3–6); Leucopogon australis (c-h; *w*; 2–4); L. Richii (c-h; *w*; 3–4); Mimulus glutinosus (c-h; *br* and *pi*; 5); Monochaetum Hartwegianum (c-h; *pi*); M. Humboldtianum (c-h; *r-p*); Mussaenda luteola (c-h; *y* and *o*; 5–6); Rhododendron javanicum (c-h; *o* and *r*; 4).

Soft-wooded Plants include all those with stems and leaves of more or less sappy growth and are mostly propagated by cuttings in that state, or by seeds. A large number of florists' flowers are included in this group and, as many of them are growing throughout the winter, a position where all possible light can reach them should be allotted to them. Many soft-wooded plants are easily grown but they are sensitive to improper treatment such as allowing them too little space, giving too little air, or too much heat, or too much shade. Many are annually raised from seed and good strains of Calceolarias, Celosias, Cinerarias, Mignonette, Primulas, Rhodanthes, &c. (*see* **Annuals**), should be among them. These should be sown at different periods so as to prolong the flowering season. Continuous growth without check is an important condition in their successful cultivation. Other soft-wooded plants which, however, become somewhat hard with age, are either propagated each year, or sometimes treated as perennials, e.g. Chrysanthemums, Eupatoriums, Fuchsias, Pelargoniums, and Salvias. An open rich soil is a general requirement for these and plenty of air and water in summer after the plants become established. Some may be forced into flower (*see* **Forcing, Shrubs for forcing**) including Lily of the Valley, *Dicentra spectabilis*, all attractive and easily grown in a cold house.

JANUARY. Begonia natalensis (c-h; *pi*; $1\frac{1}{2}$); Calceolaria Burbidgei (*y*; 2–4); Canarina Campanula (c-h; *y-p* or *o*; 3–4); Clivia × cyrtanthiflora (c-h; *pi* or *y*; 2); C. Gardenii (c-h; *r-o*, *y*; 2); Eupatorium atrorubens (c-h; *r* and *l*; 3); E. ianthinum (c-h; *p*. 3); E. Weinmannianum (*w*; 4).

FEBRUARY. As for January.

MARCH. Clianthus Dampieri (c-h; *r* with *bk* or *p* blotch; 2); Clivia miniata (c-h; *o*; 1–2); Ranunculus Lyallii (c-h; *w*; 2–4); Utricularia Endressii (c-h; *l* and *y*; $\frac{1}{4}$–1).

APRIL. *Arisaema nepenthioides (c-h; *y*; *br*, and *g*; 2); A. tortuosum (c-h; *g* striped *w*; 4); Cyclamen persicum (c-h; *w* and *p*; 1); Darlingtonia californica (c-h; *g*; 1–$1\frac{1}{2}$); *Clivia × cyrtanthiflora (c-h; *pi* or *y*; 2); *C. miniata (c-h; *o*; 1–2); *Manulea rubra (c-h; *y*; 1–2); Pelargonium pulchellum (c-h; *w* and *r*; 2–3); *Ranunculus Lyallii (c-h; *w*; 2–4); *Sarracenia Drummondii (*p*; 1); S. flava (*y*; 1); S. purpurea (*p*; 1); *Viola pedunculata (*y*).

MAY. In addition to those marked * in April: Abronia fragrans (*w*; 1–2); Aneilema sinicum (c-h; *b*; 1); Anigozanthus flavidus (*y-g*; 3–5); A. pulcherrimus (*y* and *r*; 3); A. rufus (*p* and *w*; 3); Arum palaestinum (c-h; *bk* and *y-w*, spotted *p*; 1–$1\frac{1}{2}$); Astilbe japonica (*w*; 1–2); Blumenbachia lateritia (*r*; $\frac{1}{2}$); Chironia jasminoides (c-h; *r* or *p*; 1–2); Clivia nobilis (c-h; *r* and *y*; $1\frac{1}{2}$); Eupatorium riparium (c-h; *w*; 2–3); Nolana georgiana (*w*; 1); Stylidum bulbiferum (c-h; *g-p*; 1); Utricularia Endressii (c-h; *l* and *y*; $\frac{1}{4}$–1).

JUNE. Actinotus helianthi (c-h; *w*; 2); *Agapanthus orientalis and other sp. (*b*; 2–3); *Arisaema candidissimum (*w-pi*; $2\frac{1}{2}$); A. concinnum (*w* and *g* or *p*; 1–2); Commelina coelestis (*b*; $1\frac{1}{2}$); Chironia floribunda (c-h; *p*; 2); *Drosera binata (c-h; *w*; $\frac{1}{2}$); *D. capensis (c-h; *p*; $\frac{1}{2}$); *Hedychium Gardnerianum (*g-y*; 3–5); *Hibiscus militaris (c-h; *pi*; 2–4); *Linum flavum (*y*; 1–$1\frac{1}{2}$); *L. Macraei (*o*; 1); *Lotus Jacobaeus (c-h; *p* and *y*; 1–3); *Manulea rubra (c-h; *y*; 1–2); *Mirabilis Jalapa (various; 2); Musschia aurea (c-h; *y*; 1–2); *Pelargonium Bowkeri (c-h; *p* and *y*; 1); *P. fissum (c-h; *pi*; 1); *P. glaucifolium (c-h; *bk-p* edged *g-y*; $1\frac{1}{2}$); *P. elongatum (c-h; *p-c*; $\frac{1}{2}$); *P. zonatus (c-h; various); *Senecio pyramidalis (c-h; *y*; 2); *Solanum sisymbrifolium (c-h; *b* or *w*; 4); *Sonchus gummifer (c-h; *y*; 2–3); *Stachys coccinea (c-h; *r*; 1–2); *Stylidium spathulatum (c-h; *y*; $\frac{1}{2}$); Thysanotus tuberosus (c-h; *p*); Trichinium Manglesii (c-h; *w* or *p*; $\frac{1}{2}$ –1).

JULY. Plants marked * in June list and Aneilma biflora (c-h; *b*; 1); Arisaema galeatum (c-h; *g* and *p*; 1); Astilbe rubra (c-h; *pi*; 4–6); Begonia Sutherlandii (c-h; *o-r*; 1–2); Blumenbachia contorta (c-h; *o-r*; 2); Calotis cuneifolia (c-h; *b*; 1); Chironia linoides (c-h; *r*; 1–2); Commelina elliptica (c-h; *w*; $1\frac{1}{2}$ –2); Drosera spathulata (c-h; *p*; $\frac{1}{4}$); Francoa appendiculata (*r*; 2); F. ramosa (*w*; 2–3); F. sonchifolia (*pi*; 2); Hedychium flavosum (c-h; *o*; 3); Hibiscus coccineus (c-h; *r*; 4–8); Lotus australis (c-h; *pi*, *w*, or *p-r*; 2); Oxalis elegans (c-h; *p*; $\frac{1}{2}$); O. lasiandra (c-h; *r*; $\frac{3}{4}$–$1\frac{1}{2}$); Salvia cacaliifolia (c-h; *b*; 3); S. coccinea (c-h; *r*; 2); Senecio speciosus (c-h; *p*; $\frac{3}{4}$–1); Stylidium graminifolium (c-h; *p*; $\frac{1}{2}$–$1\frac{1}{2}$); Swainsonia galegifolia (c-h; *r*; 2); S. Grayana (c-h; *pi*; 2–3); Verbena venosa (c-h; *l* or *p*; 2); Wahlenbergia tuberosa (c-h; *w* and *p*; $\frac{1}{2}$–2).

AUGUST. Agapanthus orientalis, &c. (*b*; 2–3); Amphicome arguta (*r*; 3); *A. emodi (*pi* and *o*; 1–$1\frac{1}{2}$); *Astilbe rubra (*pi*; 4–6); Begonia Sutherlandii (c-h; *o-r*; 1–2); Calotis cuneifolia (c-h; *b*; 1); Clivia miniata (c-h; *o*; 1-2); *Coelestina ageratoides (*b*; 1); Cyanella odoratissima (c-h; *pi*; 1); *Drosera binata (c-h; *w*; $\frac{1}{2}$); Francoa ramosa (*w*; 2–3); Hedychium Gardnerianum (*g-y*; 3–5); Hibiscus coccineus (c-h; *r*; 4–8); H. militaris (c-h; *pi*; 2–4); *Linum flavum (*y*; $\frac{1}{2}$–$1\frac{1}{2}$); L. Macraei (*o*; 1); *Lotus Jacobaeus (c-h; *p* and *y*; 1–3); *Manulea rubra (c-h; *y*; 1–2); M. tomentosa (c-h; *o*; 1); Mirabilis Jalapa (c-h; various; 2); Oxalis lasiandra (c-h; *r*; $\frac{3}{4}$ to $1\frac{1}{2}$); *Pelargonium as in June; Senecio pyramidalis (c-h; *y*; 2); Solanum sisymbriifolium (c-h; *b* or *w*; 4); Sonchus gummifer (c-h; *y*; 2–3); Stachys coccinea (c-h; *r* 1–2); *Stokesia cyanea (*b*; 1–$1\frac{1}{2}$); *Verbena venosa (c-h; *l* or *p*; 2); Wahlenbergia tuberosa (c-h; *w* and *pi*; $\frac{1}{2}$–2).

SEPTEMBER. Plants marked * in August list and Amicia Zygomeris (*y* splashed *p*; 8); Calceolaria arachnoidea (*p*; 1); C. Burbidgei (*y*; 2–4); Disporum pullum (c-h; *br*; $1\frac{1}{2}$); Pinguicula caudata (c-h; *p*; $\frac{1}{2}$).

OCTOBER. *Amicia Zygomeris (*y*, splashed *p*; 8); Amphicome emodi (*pi* and *o*; 1–$1\frac{1}{2}$); *Astilbe rubra (*pi*; 4–6); *Calceolaria Burbidgei (*y*; 2–4); Coelestina ageratoides (*b*; 1); *Oxalis variabilis (c-h; *w* or *r*; $\frac{1}{4}$); *Pinguicula caudata (c-h; *pi*; $\frac{3}{4}$).

NOVEMBER. Plants marked * in October and Centropogon fastuosus (c-h; *pi*; 2).

DECEMBER. Clivia × cyrtanthiflora (c-h; *p* or *y*; 2); Oxalis variabilis (c-h; *w* or *r*; $\frac{1}{4}$).

BULBOUS PLANTS. Many plants raised from bulbs, corms, or tubers are well fitted for cultivation in the greenhouse. Some of them need a decided rest period, others may remain green throughout the year. The notes on cultivation given under each genus will be a guide to their particular needs. Hardy bulbs, particularly Hyacinths, Narcissi, and Tulips, are best started into growth outdoors and brought into the house when the foliage appears above ground to continue their growth and flower. After flowering they should be cared for so that the foliage remains green and the new bulb is properly developed for the future.

JANUARY. Eucharis subedentata (*w*; $1\frac{1}{2}$); Freesia (c-h; various); hardy bulbs forwarded under glass.

FEBRUARY. As for January and Cyclamen Coum (*r*; $\frac{1}{4}$); C. vernum (*r*; $\frac{1}{4}$); Haemanthus natalensis (c-h; *g*; bracts *p*).

MARCH. As for February and Arisaema nepenthoides (c-h; *y*, *br*, and *g*; 2); Crinum Moorei (*g* and *r*); Elisena longipetala (c-h; *w*; 3); Hymenocallis calathina (c-h; *w*); Lachenalia bulbifera and other sp. (c-h; *g*, *y*, *o*, *r*; 1); Tigridia sp. (c-h; *y*, *p*, *l*, *r*; $1\frac{1}{2}$).

APRIL. Crinum Moorei (c-h; *g* and *r*; $2\frac{1}{2}$); * Ferraria Ferrariola (*g-br*; $1\frac{1}{2}$); F. undulata (*g-br*; $1\frac{1}{2}$); Hesperantha radiata (c-h; *w*; $\frac{1}{2}$); *Hymenocallis calathina (c-h; *w*; $1\frac{1}{2}$); *Hypoxis stellata (c-h; *w* and *b*; $\frac{3}{4}$); *Ixia sp. (various; 1–$1\frac{1}{2}$); *Lachenalia sp. (various; 1–$1\frac{1}{2}$); *Oxalis rosea (c-h; *pi*; $\frac{1}{2}$–1); O. versicolor (c-h; *w* and *r*; $\frac{1}{2}$); Streptanthera elegans (c-h; *pi-w*, *p*, and *c*; $\frac{3}{4}$); Sparaxis grandiflora (c-h; *p*, *w*, or variegated; 1–2); *Tigridia atrata (c-h; *p*, *g*, or *br*; 2); *T. Meleagris (c-h; *p* and *r*; $1\frac{1}{2}$); *T. van Houttei (c-h; *y*, *p*, and *l*; 1); *Zantedeschia africana (c-h; *w*; 2).

MAY. Plants marked * in April list and Babiana sp. (various; $\frac{1}{2}$–1); Caliphruria Hartwegiana (*g-w*; 1); Geissorhiza grandis (c-h; *y* and *r*; 1); G. inflexa (*y* and *p*; $1\frac{1}{2}$); G. Rochensis (c-h; *b* and *r*; $\frac{3}{4}$); Gladiolus cuspidatus (c-h; variable; 2–3); G. floribundus (c-h; *w* and *p* varying to *pi-w* and *r*; 1); Moraea edulis (v; 4); M. tricuspis (*g-w*; 1); Romulea speciosa (c-h; *pi*, *y*, and *v*); Sparaxis tricolor (c-h; *y* spotted *br*., &c.; 1–$1\frac{1}{2}$); Vallota purpurea (c-h; *r*; 2–3); Watsonia Meriana (c-h; *p* or *r*; $\frac{3}{4}$–2); Zephyranthes Andersonii (c-h; *o-r*; $\frac{1}{4}$).

JUNE. Albuca aurea (c-h; *y*; 2); *A. Nelsoni (c-h; *w* striped *r*; 4–5); Anomalesia Cunonia (c-h; *r* and *bk*; 2); *Arthropodium sp. (c-h; *w*; 1–3); Babiana sp. (various; $\frac{1}{2}$–$\frac{3}{4}$); *Brunsvigia Cooperi (c-h; *y* edged *r*; $1\frac{1}{2}$); *B. Josephineae (c-h; *r*; $1\frac{1}{2}$); B. multiflora (c-h; *r*; 1); *Crocosmia aurea (*o-r*; 2); *Ferraria Ferrariola (*g-br*; 2); *Gladiolus sp. (c-h; various; 1–3); Hesperantha radiata (c-h; *w* $\frac{1}{2}$); Hypoxis stellata (c-h; *w* and *b*; $\frac{3}{4}$); Ixia sp. (various; $\frac{1}{2}$–1); *Lilium sp. (c-h; various; 1–4); *Littonia modesta (c-h; *o*; 2–6); *Lycoris Sewerzowi (c-h; *br-r*; 1); Moraea unguiculata (*w* and *p-y*; 1); Nerine sarniensis (c-h; *r*; 1); Ornithogalum thyrsoides (c-h; *y*; $\frac{1}{2}$–$1\frac{1}{2}$); Scilla chinensis (*pi-p*; 1); Sisyrinchium iridifolium (*y-w*; $\frac{1}{4}$–1); Sprekelia formosissima (c-h; *r* or *w*; 2); *Tigridia pavonia (*o*; 1–2); *Watsonia densiflora (c-h; *pi*; $1\frac{1}{2}$–2) and other sp.; *Zantedeschia sp. (c-h; various).

JULY. Plants marked * in June list and Brodiaea sp. (*b*, *w*, *v*; 1–$1\frac{1}{2}$); Cypella Herbertii (*y*; 1); Drimiopsis Kirkii (c-h; *w*; $\frac{3}{4}$); Nerine flexuosa (c-h; *pi* and *r*; 2).

AUGUST. Albuca Nelsoni (c-h; *w* striped *r*; 4–5); Arthropodium pendulum (c-h; *w*; $1\frac{1}{2}$); Brunsvigia Cooperi (c-h; *y* edged *r*; $1\frac{1}{2}$); B. Josephineae (c-h; *r*; $1\frac{1}{2}$); Crocosmia aurea (*o-r*; 2); Cyrtanthus sanguineus (c-h; *o-r* and *y*); Eucomis bicolor (*g* and *p*; $1\frac{1}{2}$); Gladiolus sp. (various); Lilium sp. (various); Lycoris aurea (c-h; *y*; 1); L. Sewerzowi (c-h; *br-r*; 1); Thysanotus junceus (c-h; *p*; 1–2); Zephryanthes citrina (c-h; *y*; $\frac{1}{2}$).

SEPTEMBER. Amaryllis Belladonna (variable; 2); Boophone toxicaria (c-h; *pi*; 1); Crinum Moorei (c-h; *g* and *r*; 2); Crocosmia aurea (*o-r*; 2); Gladiolus sp. (c-h; various); Lycoris aurea (c-h; *y*; 1); Nerine sarniensis (c-h; *pi*; 2–$2\frac{1}{2}$); Polianthes tuberosa (*w*; 3–4); Urginea maritima (*w* and *g-p*; 4); Zephyranthes candida (*w*; $\frac{1}{2}$–$\frac{3}{4}$).

OCTOBER. As September.

NOVEMBER. Amaryllis Belladonna (variable; 2); Crinum Macowani (c-h; *w* tinged *p*; 2); C. Moorei (c-h; *g* and *r*; 2); Gladiolus psittacinus (c-h; *r*, *y*, *g*, and *p*; 3); G. Saundersii (c-h; *r* and *w*; 2–3).

DECEMBER. Hardy bulbs forwarded under glass; Eucharis subedentata.

CLIMBERS AND PILLAR PLANTS are indispensable for the decoration of the greenhouse of any size. Some of them, however, are more than usually susceptible to the attacks of insects, and if these pests are allowed to obtain a footing, considerable injury may be done to the plants beneath. The best preventive measure is to take the plants down from the wires each winter, and thoroughly wash them, and in summer to keep careful watch upon them and occasionally sponge them. Climbers should be planted out as soon as large enough to establish themselves, but they should first be prepared in pots. As already pointed out proper provision should have been made for them in the construction of the house. An open compost of sandy peat and loam is generally the best compost for them and any special need may be met by top-dressing. They usually need a plentiful supply of water during summer but little in winter during the resting period. One or two wires fixed near each other on each rafter, the plants being restricted to covering them, is best for they must not be allowed to obstruct the light from the plants beneath. Fuchsias are amongst the best plants for pillars and rafters. Tea and Noisette Roses are also good if they obtain plenty of light, and where there is room for them Bougainvilleas, Cestrums, Kennedyas, Passifloras, *Streptosolen Jamesonii*, and Swainsonias may well be included.

Other climbing or pillar plants suitable for such houses are:

JANUARY. Abutiloni nsigne (c-h; *p-r*; 6); Jasminum primulinum (*y*).

FEBRUARY. As January.

MARCH. Fuchsia penduliflora (c-h; *r*); Hibbertia dentata (c-h; *y*).

APRIL. Abutilon Darwini (c-h; *o*; 4); Cestrum fasciculatum (c-h; *p-r*); Hibbertia dentata (c-h; *y*); Hydrangea petiolaris (c-h; *w*); Kennedya prostrata (c-h; *r*); Lonicera sempervirens (c-h; *r* and *y*).

MAY. Billardiera longiflora (c-h; *g-y*, becoming *pi*); B. scandens (c-h; *c*, turning *p*); Bougainvillea speciosa (c-h; *l*); Clianthus puniceus (*r*); Cestrum sp. (various); Cobaea scandens (c-h; *p*); Hibbertia dentata (c-h; *y*); Hydrangea petiolaris (c-h; *w*); Lonicera sempervirens (c-h; *r* and *y*); Mitraria coccinea (*r*).

JUNE. Adlumia cirrhosa (*pi*); Billardiera sp. (c-h; various); Bougainvillea glabra (c-h; *pi*); B. speciosa (c-h; *l*); Cestrum sp. (c-h; various); Cobaea scandens (c-h; *p*); Fuchsia sp. (various); Grammatocarpus volubilis (*y*); Hibbertia perfoliata (c-h; *y*); Ipomoea Learii (c-h; *b*); Maurandya Barclayana (*v-p* and *g*); Mitraria coccinea (*r*); Phygelius capensis (*r*); Solanum jasminoides (*b-w*); Streptosolen Jamesonii (c-h; *o*); Teucrium fruticans (*b-l*).

JULY. As June and Candollea cuneifolius (c-h; *y*; 7); Ipomoea hederacea (*b*) and other sp.; Maurandya scandens (*p-v*); Plumbago capensis (*l* to *b*); Tropaeolum sp. (various).

AUGUST. As July.

SEPTEMBER. Blumenbachia chuquitensis (*r* and *y*); Cestrum purpureum (*r-p*); Cobaea scandens (c-h; *p*); Fuchsia sp. (various); Ipomoea sp. (various); Lapageria rosea (c-h; *pi-r*); Plumbago capensis (c-h; *b*); Streptosolen Jamesonii (c-h; *o*); Tropaeolum sp. (various).

OCTOBER. As September and Boussingaultia baselloides (*w* becoming *bk*).

NOVEMBER. Abutilon (c-h; various); Boussingaultia baselloides (*w* becoming *bk*); Fuchsia (c-h; various); Lapageria rosea (c-h; *pi-r*); Plumbago capensis (c-h; *b*).

DECEMBER. Abutilon insigne (c-h; *p-r*); A. striatum (c-h; *o-y*); Cobaea penduliflora (c-h; *g*); Jasminum primulinum (*y*).

## GREENHOUSE THRIPS (*Heliothrips haemorrhoidalis*).

This Thrips is confined in the British Isles to glasshouses where it is injurious to many ornamental plants, and especially to Azaleas. Its presence on the plants is quickly detected from the characteristic mottling of the upper surface of the leaf and by minute globules of red, later black, liquid that cover the underside of the leaves. Breeding is continuous throughout the year in heated glasshouses, and severe injury is done to Azaleas grown for Easter flowering. The minute eggs are inserted in the leaf tissue, and the young nymphs feed in small colonies between the veins on the lower leaf surface. All stages are spent on the foliage, which soon becomes scarred as a result of the puncturing of the tissues and the abstraction of the cell contents.

Plants in good health are less affected than those grown under unfavourable environmental conditions, so that it is desirable to avoid draughts, dryness at the roots, and intense sunlight. Regular spraying of the foliage with clear water tends to wash the delicate nymphs off the plants when they are unable to regain the shoots. Heavily infested plants should be sprayed with nicotine and soap wash applied to the underside of the leaves where the insects congregate and feed. Dusting

with nicotine dust is equally effective on Azaleas, and the deposit of dust may be readily removed by syringing the foliage with clear water a few days after the application. Routine fumigation of the house with nicotine vapour tends to reduce attacks of this and other species of Thrips.

G. F. W.

## GREENHOUSE WHITE FLY (*Trialeurodes vaporariorum*).

The Snowy or Ghost Fly is the most familiar pest to owners of glasshouses, in which nearly all kinds of plants are liable to attack, especially Tomatoes. The presence of the mealy winged, moth-like, White Flies is quickly detected, while the signs of attack are pale and mottled leaves which become sticky with honeydew excreted by the young 'scale' stages and interferes with the normal functions of the foliage. The growth of non-parasitic fungi—Sooty Moulds—is encouraged by the honeydew-drenched upper leaf surface, which appear as if dusted with soot. The eggs are laid in circular groups on the underside of the leaves, and hatch in 10 to 14 days into pale green, flattish larvae which, after crawling over the leaves for a short time, settle down to a sedentary existence and assume a scale-like appearance. The adult White Fly emerges through a T-shaped slit in the pupal-case. There are several generations a year, the duration of the immature stages being variable and depending upon temperature. Overlapping of the stages

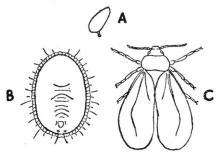

Greenhouse White fly (*Trialeurodes vaporariorum*)
A egg. B larva. C perfect insect. All much enlarged.

occurs, and eggs, larvae, pupae, and adults are present over the greater part of the year. This White Fly, which must not be confused with the Cabbage and the Rhododendron White Flies (q.v.), will attack plants in the open during the summer months.

The most effective method of control is the biological one by the introduction of a Chalcid parasite, *Encarsia formosa*, the female of which lays an egg in the larval or scale-stage of the White Fly causing it to turn black and die (*see* **White Fly Parasite**).

Spraying is not successful owing to the difficulty of wetting the 'scales' on the underside of the leaves, but the adults are readily destroyed by dusting the terminal leaves upon which they congregate with nicotine dust.

Fumigation with either hydrocyanic acid gas or tetrachlorethane is effective. The former is a deadly poison and carelessness in its use may lead to a fatal accident. The latter is far less dangerous and is suitable for use in the houses of amateurs. Certain plants, including Azalea, Chrysanthemum, and Cineraria, are, however, intolerant of the fumes of tetrachlorethane and must be removed from the house prior to fumigation (*see* **Fumigation**).

G. F. W.

## GREENO'VIA

(in honour of George Bellas Greenough, geologist, 1778–1855). FAM. *Crassulaceae*. Closely related to Sempervivum but calyx 20- to 32-parted, petals and carpels 20 to 32; stamens twice as many; petals yellow; scales absent. A genus of four species natives of the Canary Is., and therefore tender, with the habit of Sempervivum. Cultivation as for Aichryson.

**G. au'rea.*** Rosette 2 to 5 in. across, widely expanded during growth, half-closed and urn-shaped during the resting season. *l.* broad at base and apex, glaucous, fleshy with thin transparent edges, about 2 to 4 in. long, $1\frac{1}{4}$ to $2\frac{1}{4}$ in. wide. *fl.* golden, about 30-parted, and 1 in. across. Stem erect, 1 to $1\frac{1}{2}$ ft. long, covered with obovate clasping leaves, branching at top, downy; branches often horizontal, 4 to 10 in. long. March, April. Offsets on short horizontal stems, rare. Canary Is. 1815. (P.S. 96; B.M. 4087 as *G. rupifraga*; B.R. 892 and L.B.C. 1368 as *Sempervivum calyciforme.*) SYN. *Sempervivum aureum.*

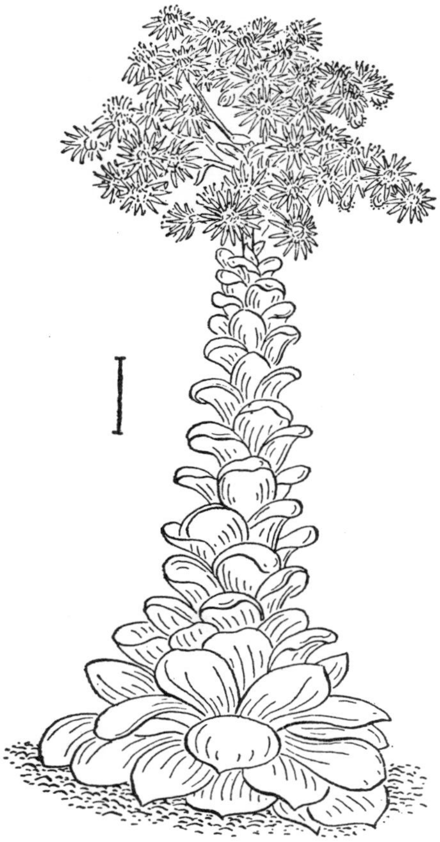

*Greenovia aurea*

**G. dodrenta'lis.** Differs from *G. aurea* by its generally much smaller and less dense rosettes, the many offsets produced, its 20-parted fl., and its lower stature. February, March. Canary Is. 1927. (P.S. 97.)

**G. rupif'raga.** A synonym of *G. aurea.*

**GREENWEED.** *See* **Genista tinctoria.**

***Gregg'ii,*** in honour of Dr. J. Gregg who collected in Mexico, *c.* 1889.

**GREGOR'IA Vitalia'na.** A synonym of *Douglasia Vitaliana.*

**GREIG'IA** (in honour of Samuel Alexjewitsch Greig, 1827–87, President, Russian Horticultural Society). FAM. *Bromeliaceae.* A genus of about 9 species of large herbs producing a crown of spiny Pine-apple-like leaves, natives of the Andes from Chile to Costa Rica with one in Juan Fernandez, closely related to Cryptanthus but with a simple inflorescence. Fruit a large whitish berry. *G. sphacelata* is usually grown as a stove-plant but may be planted out in a warm well-drained place in summer.

**G. sphacela'ta.** 3 ft. or more h. *l.* numerous, 6 ft. long, $1\frac{1}{4}$ in. wide, in a large rosette about 12 ft. across, sword-shaped, slender-pointed, fringed with stiff spines. *fl.* rose, about 3 in. long, sessile, overlapping one another in dense heads; bracts large, tinged green. Chile. 1865. (G.F. 1865, 474.) SYN. *Billbergia sphacelata.*

**GREVILL'EA** (after Chas. F. Greville, 1749–1809, a founder of the Royal Horticultural Society, once Vice-President of the Royal Society). FAM. *Proteaceae.* A genus of about 230 species of evergreen trees and shrubs, confined to Australia, Tasmania, and New Caledonia. Leaves alternate, very diverse in size and shape, varying from simple to compound. Flowers in axillary or terminal racemes or panicles, hermaphrodite. There are no petals and the perianth (often termed calyx) is usually tubular at the base but with an opening on one side through which the usually long style is protruded. In the majority the style is the most conspicuous feature of the flower.

Grevilleas for most of the British Isles are greenhouse plants, but a few are hardy in S. Surrey and several are grown out of doors in Cornwall, a number which could no doubt be considerably increased. When grown in pots they like a peaty soil or one at least free from chalk or lime, and for three or four of the summer months they may be placed in the open air, the pots being plunged in ashes. Some of the species are not of the easiest cultivation and many have been introduced to our gardens only to disappear. Cuttings frequently do not readily take root and many species can only be successfully propagated by grafting on young seedlings of *G. robusta,* seeds of which are easily obtained.

As might be expected the Grevilleas are very successfully grown in California, S. Africa, and the Riviera.

**G. acanthifo'lia.*** Shrub of several ft.; shoots soon quite glabrous. *l.* 2 to 3 in. long, 1 to $1\frac{1}{4}$ in. wide, 2-pinnately lobed, the primary lobes $\frac{1}{2}$ to $\frac{3}{4}$ in. long, each again cut into 3 triangular lobes, all spine-tipped, dark dull-green, soon glabrous. *fl.* pink, $\frac{1}{2}$ in. long with the style standing out $\frac{5}{8}$ in. beyond the perianth, crowded on terminal or axillary racemes $1\frac{1}{2}$ to 3 in. long. May. New S. Wales. 1820. (B.M. 2807.)

**G. alpes'tris.** A synonym of *G. alpina.*

**G. alpi'na.*** Bushy shrub, 2 to 4 ft.; shoots hairy. *l.* crowded, dark green, downy above, silky hairy beneath, narrowly oblong or oval to linear, $\frac{1}{3}$ to 1 in. long, $\frac{1}{12}$ to $\frac{1}{4}$ in. wide, margins recurved, apex blunt. *fl.* few, in short terminal clusters; perianth $\frac{1}{2}$ in. long, red at the swollen base, yellow upwards; style protruding $\frac{1}{4}$ in. April, May. Australia. 1854. (B.M. 5007 as *G. alpestris.*) One of the hardier species.

**G. annulif'era.*** Shrub up to 8 ft., quite glabrous. *l.* 3 to 5 in. long, pinnate; segs. 7 to 11, $\frac{1}{2}$ to $1\frac{1}{4}$ in. long, $\frac{1}{12}$ in. wide, awl-shaped, sharply pointed, glaucous beneath. *fl.* sulphur-yellow, in racemes 3 or 4 in. long, 2 in. wide, a few forming a terminal panicle; perianth $\frac{1}{3}$ in. long, lobes strongly recurved; style 1 in. long, semicircular. July. W. Australia. 1880. (B.M. 6687.)

**G. arenar'ia.** Shrub up to 6 ft.; shoots densely downy. *l.* $\frac{3}{4}$ to $1\frac{1}{2}$ in. long, $\frac{1}{6}$ to $\frac{3}{8}$ in. wide, narrowly obovate-oblong, tapered at base to a short stalk, apex rounded, mucronate, densely downy beneath. *fl.* few in a terminal cluster; perianth $\frac{1}{2}$ in. long, abruptly bent over, purple; style protruded 1 in. Spring. New S. Wales. (B.M. 3285.)

**G. asplenifo'lia.*** Tall shrub or small tree, 12 to 15 ft. *l.* 4 to 10 in. long, $\frac{1}{3}$ to 1 in. wide, linear, coarsely triangular-toothed, slender-pointed, silvery or yellowish hairy beneath. *fl.* crowded densely on underside of stalkless axillary spikes, 1 to 2 in. long; perianth reddish-pink, $\frac{1}{4}$ in. long, silky downy outside; style protruding $\frac{3}{4}$ in. Spring. New S. Wales. (B.M. 7070.) SYN. *G. longifolia.* Foliage is imported from S. France for florists' use.

**G. Banks'ii.** Tree or slender shrub, 15 to 20 ft. *l.* 4 to 10 in. long, pinnately lobed; lobes 5 to 11, linear to narrowly lanceolate, $1\frac{1}{2}$ to $3\frac{1}{2}$ in. long, $\frac{1}{5}$ to $\frac{3}{8}$ in. wide, white-silky beneath. *fl.* crowded on a terminal raceme or panicle up to 4 in. long; perianth downy outside, bright red; tube $\frac{5}{8}$ in. long, much recurved; style $1\frac{1}{2}$ in. long. Queensland. 1868. (B.M. 5870.)

**G. bipinnatif'ida.** Shrub 3 to 5 ft.; shoots usually appressed hairy. *l.* broadly ovate in general outline, 3 to 5 in. long, nearly as wide, 2-pinnately lobed, main divisions in $5\frac{1}{2}$ to $10\frac{1}{2}$ pairs, ultimate lobes triangular, slenderly spine-tipped; stalk 1 to $2\frac{1}{2}$ in. long. *fl.* erect in terminal racemes or panicles, up to 6 in. long; perianth deep pink, softly downy outside; tube $\frac{5}{8}$ in. long; style protruding $1\frac{1}{2}$ in. Winter or early Spring. W. Australia. (B.M. 8510.)

**G. Ca'leyi.** Shrub to 6 ft. and more; shoots, l.-stalks, and infl. densely furnished with soft reddish hairs. *l.* pinnate, 3 to 6 in. long; divisions up to more than 20, oblong-linear, blunt, $\frac{3}{4}$ to $1\frac{1}{2}$ in. long, tinged red when young, downy beneath. *Racemes* axillary, 1-sided, 2 to 4 in. long; perianth $\frac{1}{3}$ in. long, brownish-red, tinged purple; style protruded 1 in. June. New S. Wales. 1825. (B.M. 3313.)

**G. ericifo'lia.** Small shrub of spreading habit; shoots downy or woolly. *l.* linear, stalkless, $\frac{3}{4}$ to $1\frac{1}{4}$ in. long, $\frac{1}{12}$ in. wide, more or less crooked, pointed, downy when young, margins recurved. *fl.* few in terminal racemes, often on short side shoots; perianth $\frac{3}{8}$ in. long, bellied and bright red towards base; lobes yellow, strongly incurved; style stout, $\frac{3}{4}$ in. long. Mid-winter. New S. Wales. (B.M. 6361.)

**G. fascicula'ta.** Shrub up to 4 ft. or more; shoots slightly downy at first. *l.* linear to linear-lanceolate, ¾ to 1½ in. long, ⅛ to ¼ in. wide, stalkless, margins recurved, silky pale brown beneath. *fl.* few in clusters terminating erect, short, lateral twigs; perianth bright-red, yellow-tipped, ⅓ in. long; style scarcely protruded. May. W. Australia. (B.M. 6105.)

**G. glabra'ta.** Quite glabrous, erect, slender shrub up to 6 ft. *l.* 1 to 1½ in. long, broadly cuneate, shortly 3-lobed, lobes coarsely, sharply toothed. *fl.* in axillary racemes 1 to 2 in. long, several forming a large terminal pyramidal panicle 4 to 6 in. h.; perianth small; style white, ½ in. long; stigma pink. W. Australia.

**G. Hillia'na.** Tree up to 70 ft. *l.* very variable, lower ones obovate-oblong to oval, 6 to 8 in. long or 3-lobed or pinnatifid; uppermost l. entire, broadly linear, 4 to 6 in. long, all glabrous. *fl.* densely packed in cylindrical axillary spikes, 5 to 7 in. long, 1 to 1¼ in. wide; perianth pale green, ¼ in. long, silky; style ⅝ in. long. July. Queensland. 1862. (B.M. 7524.) Valuable timber tree.

**G. Hookeria'na.** Tall rigid shrub; shoots grey-woolly. *l.* 4 to 6 in. long, pinnatifid; segs. in 3 to 9 pairs, 1½ to 3 in. long, linear, grey-downy beneath and like the mainstalk only 1/12 to ⅛ in. wide. *fl.* very densely set on 1-sided racemes 2 to 3 in. long; perianth ⅓ to ½ in. long, yellowish; style 1 in. long, crimson. January. W. Australia. 1886. (B.M. 6879.)

**G. ilicifo'lia.** Shrub 6 ft. or more h. and wide; shoots grey-downy. *l.* variable, cuneate, lobed and sharply toothed at the end, 1 to 2½ in. long, holly-like, sometimes longer and deeply, narrowly, pinnately lobed, silky beneath. *Racemes* dense, ovate, 1-sided, many-fld.; perianth greenish-grey with appressed down; style long-exserted. Australia.

**G. intrica'ta.** Glabrous shrub 6 to 10 ft.; shoots slender, pendulous. *l.* 4 to 6 in. long, stalk and rachis very slender, 1/20 in. thick with 2 to 4 pairs of twice- or thrice-forked segs. scarcely wider than stalk, hooked at tip when young, 2 to 3 in. long. *fl.* small, ⅛ in. long, packed in terminal conical racemes 1 to 2 in. long; perianth white, yellow in bud. May. W. Australia. 1871. (B.M. 5919.)

**G. juniperi'na sulphu'rea.** A synonym of *G. sulphurea.*

**G. lavandula'cea.*** Low compact shrub; shoots silky downy. *l.* ½ to 1 in. long, ⅛ to ⅜ in. wide, stalkless, pointed, cuneate, margins recurved, silky-downy beneath. *fl.* in terminal clusters of 3 to 8; perianth rich rose, ½ in. long, bellied, downy outside, lobes much recurved; style protruding 1 in. Spring. S. Australia. 1848. (L.P.F.G. ii. 56 as *G. rosea.*)

**G. linea'ris.** Shrub 5 or 6 ft.; shoots minutely silky-downy. *l.* linear, 1 to 1½ in. long (sometimes twice as much), ⅛ to ¼ in. wide, margins recurved, tapered at both ends, silky downy beneath. *fl.* borne in small clusters at the end of short lateral twigs; perianth pink or white, ⅓ in. long; style much recurved, ⅜ to ½ in. long. Spring. New S. Wales. 1795. (B.M. 2661.)

**G. longifo'lia.** A synonym of *G. asplenifolia.*

**G. macrosty'lis.*** Shrub 4 to 6 ft.; shoots closely downy. *l.* scarcely stalked, 1 to 1½ in. long, nearly as wide, ovate but deeply 3- or 5-lobed, lobes triangular, sharply pointed, silky beneath. *fl.* few in terminal clusters; perianth ½ to ⅝ in. long, crimson at base, apex much recurved, yellow; style 1½ in. long. May, June. W. Australia. 1868. (B.M. 5915.)

**G. mucronula'ta.** Large shrub; shoots slender, downy. *l.* ovate or obovate, ½ to ¾ in. long, abruptly to taper-pointed, upper surface rough, lower silky-downy. *fl.* few in terminal and axillary clusters; perianth greenish-white; tube about ½ in. long, hairy inside, points rolled back; style ¾ in. long, purple, hairy. April, August. New S. Wales. 1820.

**G. oleoi'des.** Shrub of erect habit; shoots covered with close, silky hairs. *l.* linear, 2½ to 3½ in. long, ⅛ to ⅓ in. wide, sharply pointed, silky-downy beneath. *fl.* 8 to 14 in short-stalked, terminal clusters 2 in. wide; perianth bright carmine, tubular base ½ in. long, hairy; style 1¼ in. long. New S. Wales. (B.M. 8741.) Hardy in Cornwall.

**G. ornithop'oda.** Quite glabrous shrub a few ft. h., with slender drooping branches. *l.* 3 to 4 in. long, 3-lobed at apex, lobes 1 to 1½ in. long, ⅛ to ¼ in. wide, linear, pointed, curving outwards. *fl.* in drooping axillary racemes, 1½ to 2 in. long, ¾ in. wide; perianth white, ⅓ in. long; style short, constricted, yellowish. April. W. Australia. 1850. (B.M. 7739.)

**G. Preiss'ii.** A synonym of *G. Thelemanniana.*

**G. pulchel'la.*** Spreading shrub 2 to 3 ft.; shoots zig-zag, slender, more or less hairy. *l.* 2 to 3 in. long, 1 to 1½ in. wide, stalkless, linear-oblong in main outline, but lobed to midrib; lobes in 7 to 11 pairs, coarsely and sharply toothed at apex. *fl.* white, crowded in cylindral racemes up to 2 in. long, ½ in. wide; perianth slender; style very crooked, downy, scarcely longer than the perianth. April. W. Australia. (B.M. 5979.)

**G. punic'ea.*** Shrub of erect habit; shoots hairy. *l.* 1 to 2½ in. long, ⅓ to ⅝ in. wide, oblong-lanceolate, tapered to both ends, glossy green above, silvery or rusty-red downy beneath. *fl.* in terminal short-stalked clusters; perianth bright red, tubular, ½ to ⅝ in. long, lobes much recurved; style 1½ in. long. March to June. New S. Wales. (B.M. 6698.)

**G. robus'ta.*** Tree sometimes over 100 ft.; shoots silvery downy. *l.* in adult trees 6 to 9 in. long, pinnate; in young vigorous plants 1 to 1½ ft. long and often 2-pinnate; segs. 1 to 2 in. long, triangular to lanceolate, silky beneath. *fl.* golden-yellow in 1-sided racemes 3 to 4 in. long (rarely or never seen in Britain.) Popular shrub in pots for indoor decoration, sub-tropical bedding &c. New S. Wales. (B.M. 3184.) Much grown in S. Africa and California.

**G. ro'sea.** A synonym of *G. lavandulacea.*

**G. rosmarinifo'lia.** Shrub 6 to 7 ft., shoots slender, downy. *l.* deep green, rosemary-like, ⅛ in wide, linear, pointed, 1 to 2 in. long, stalkless, dark green, silvery hairy beneath. *fl.* red, of various shades, crowded in terminal clusters 1 to 1½ in. across; perianth ½ in. wide, style ¾ in. long. Summer. (B.M. 5971.) Hardy in S. Surrey.

**G. × semperflo'rens** (*G. sulphurea* × *G. Thelemanniana*). Shrub of 6 ft. h., young shoots densely hairy. *l.* linear, simple or forked near apex, 1¼ to 1¾ in. long, silky-hairy beneath. *fl.* orange-yellow at base, limb rose-tinted, apex green, about ⅞ in. long, in many-fld. racemes about 1½ in. long, axillary, or terminal. Of garden origin. 1927. Hardy in SW. England.

**G. seric'ea.** Shrub 5 ft., shoots slender, silky when young. *l.* oblong-lanceolate to linear-lanceolate, ¾ to 1¼ in. long, ⅛ to ⅜ in. wide, pointed, cuneate, silky hairy beneath. *fl.* crowded in stalked, terminal clusters, 1 to 1½ in. wide; perianth pink, tube ¼ in. long, lobes much recurved; style sharply bent over, ⅝ in. long. New S. Wales. 1791. (B.M. 3798 as *G. dubia.*)

**G. sulphu'rea.** Shrub up to 6 ft., shoots softly downy. *l.* densely set, ½ to 1 in. long, linear, almost needle-like, prickly pointed, margins revolute, silky-downy beneath. *fl.* pale yellow in terminal clusters of a dozen or more; perianth tubular, silky, ½ in. long; style 1 in. long. May, June. New S. Wales. (L.B.C. 1723.) Scarcely hardy near London, but begins to be so in S. Surrey. SYN. *G. juniperina sulphurea.*

**G. Thelemannia'na.*** Shrub 3 to 5 ft., shoots softly downy. *l.* 1 to 2 in. long, pinnate or 2-pinnate; lflets. linear or filiform, grooved beneath, 1/16 in. wide. *fl.* in terminal racemes 2 in. long and wide; perianth-tube pink, lobes recurved, yellowish-green; style 1 to 1¼ in. long, red. W. Australia. 1838. (B.M. 5837 as *G. Preissii.*)

**G. thyrsoi'des.** Shrub 4 to 5 ft., shoots slightly silky-downy. *l.* pinnate, 2 to 4 in. long, with 6 to 14 pairs of linear divisions, 1 to 1½ in. long, stiff, scabrous. *infl.* up to 1 ft. long, with a few short-stalked racemes near the end; perianth ½ in. long, rose; style 1 in. long. W. Australia. Grown in the open air in Cornwall.

**G. Wilson'ii.** Erect shrub, 3 to 5 ft. *l.* 2- or 3-pinnate, mainstalk short, ultimate segs. narrow-linear, ½ to 1 in. long, rigid, sharply pointed. *fl.* in erect racemes or panicles on a stalk ½ to 1 in. long; perianth ½ to ¾ in. long, bright red, swollen at base, curled at end; style very long. W. Australia.

W. J. B.

**GREW'IA** (in honour of Nehemiah Grew, 1641–1712, investigator of the anatomy of plants). FAM. *Tiliaceae.* A genus of about 90 species of trees and shrubs found in Asia, Africa, and Australia, usually stellately downy. Leaves alternate, 3- to 9-nerved. Flowers in small, stalked clusters; sep. and pet. 5; stamens numerous. Fruit a drupe. Most of the species are tropical or sub-tropical and have never been in cultivation.

**G. occidenta'lis.** Small tree or shrub, young shoots stellately hairy. *l.* oval, ovate, 1 to 4 in. long, bluntly toothed, 3-nerved, glabrous above, axil-tufted beneath. *fl.* in stalked clusters of 2 to 6, each 1 to 1¼ in. across, pink or purplish; sep. linear, longer than the pet. S. Africa. 1690. (B.M. 422.) Greenhouse.

**G. oppositifo'lia.** Small deciduous tree, shoots stellately hairy. *l.* alternate, bluntly toothed, pointed, 2 to 4 in. long, downy beneath, 3-nerved. *fl.* 1 to 1½ in. across, yellowish, produced opposite the l. in stalked clusters of 8 to 20; sep. linear, ¾ in. long. *fr.* blackish, the size of a small pea. Himalaya. Rather tender.

**G. parviflo'ra.** Deciduous shrub, 6 to 10 ft., shoots stellately downy. *l.* ovate, sometimes 3-lobed, 2 to 5 in. long, pointed, toothed, rough above, downy beneath. *fl.* creamy-yellow, ½ in. wide, in axillary umbels of about 6, on leafy shoots. July, August. *fr.* roundish, orange or red, ¼ in. wide. China, Korea. 1888. Hardy.

W. J. B.

**GREY DAGGER MOTH** (*Acronycta psi*) is widely distributed over the British Is., and its caterpillars commonly attack the foliage of Apple, Plum, Raspberry, and Rose. The moths are on the wing during June and July, when the eggs are laid on the leaves. The caterpillar is easily recognized by a large hump just before the middle of the back and a smaller one near the tail. Its colour is greyish-black, with a conspicuous yellow line down the back and reddish spots on either side. It feeds during early autumn, and pupates in cocoons attached to twigs, in cracks in the bark, and elsewhere above ground.

It is seldom necessary to apply a special spray against this pest, whose caterpillars are readily destroyed by a Derris wash.

G. F. W.

**GREY GUM.** *See* **Eucalyptus resinifera.**

**GREY MOULD FUNGUS.** This is the name given to the fungus *Botrytis cinerea* which appears as a greyish furry mould on a great many different kinds of plants. It thrives in moist soil conditions and is generally only serious in wet weather or very humid glasshouses or frames. It can flourish as a saprophyte on all kinds of dead tissues and may later begin to attack the living leaves, stems, and fruits, &c. Strawberries when ripe may suffer serious loss in damp weather. Grapes, Figs, Peaches, and similar fruits under glass are quickly destroyed by it in moist atmospheres and especially if the fruits are wounded. Cuttings of Pelargonium and other plants in frames are likely to be affected. The fungus first produces the grey mould consisting of masses of conidia which are formed on the conidiophore, and viewed through the microscope rather resemble a bunch of Grapes in shape. Later the mycelium forms the dense black or grey compact masses known as sclerotia (q.v.); these constitute the resting stage of the fungus. One of the serious diseases due to this fungus is Gooseberry Dieback (q.v.) but there are others on Tomato, &c. It is said that the fungus does not readily attack healthy green tissues but only those grown soft or weak from some other cause. The control of the fungus consists in removing all infected and dead tissues and avoiding excessively moist air conditions. Outdoors the plants should not be grown too soft and should have plenty of room to encourage air circulation. Indoors the ventilation should be enough to avoid excessive humidity.

D. E. G.

**GREY SQUIRREL** (*Sciurus carolinensis*) is an extremely destructive rodent which has been introduced from time to time into this country from N. America. It has now become established in many parts of the British Is., and favours mixed deciduous woods rather than coniferous. It occurs also in parks, and invades gardens, nurseries, and orchards to a distance of at least half a mile from any wood. It is larger than our native Red Squirrel, silvery-grey with russety-brown areas, the eyes being prominent and the ears small. Its food consists of shoots and buds; nuts, fruits, and seeds; bulbs and roots; and young birds and eggs.

Every effort should be made to keep down these rodents by shooting and trapping, and persistence in these methods will check any marked increase. A careful watch should be kept in all districts hitherto free of these rodents for their first appearance, and measures should be taken immediately to kill them before a new colony is formed.

G. F. W.

**GREY'IA** (in honour of Sir George Grey, 1812–98, Governor-General of Cape Colony, &c.). FAM. *Sapindaceae*. A genus of 3 species of shrubs or small trees, natives of S. Africa. Leaves alternate. Fruit a 5-valved, many-seeded capsule. *G. Sutherlandii* requires cool greenhouse conditions with full sunshine, and the roots to be kept on the dry side during the resting period. Propagated by cuttings of half-ripe shoots.

**G. Sutherland'ii.*** Shrub or small tree. *l.* crowded at end of the twigs, 2 to 3 in. long, broadly ovate to rounded, cordate, deeply jaggedly toothed, glabrous. *fl.* scarlet, crowded in erect terminal racemes 4 to 6 in. long, half as wide; pet. 5; stamens 10, very conspicuous, red, with dark purple anthers. Natal. 1859. (B.M. 6040; n.s. 374.)

W. J. B.

**GRI'AS** (*grao*, to eat; the fruit being edible). FAM. *Lecythidaceae*. A genus of about 4 species of tall, scarcely branched evergreen trees of Trop. America. Leaves very long, oblong, entire. Flowers white, large; petals 4 or 5, leathery; stamens numerous, in several rows on the disk. The trees which need stove conditions grow quickly in a compost of sandy loam. They can be propagated by cuttings of the ripe wood in spring.

**G. cauliflo'ra.** Anchovy Pear. Tree of 30 to 50 ft. *l.* alternate, lanceolate to spatulate, sometimes up to 3 ft. long, drooping, glossy green. *fl.* yellow, 2 in. across, very fragrant, on short peduncles from the old stem. *Berry* ovate, 2 to 3 in. long, russet-brown, edible. W. Indies. 1768. (B.M. 5622.)

**G. zamoren'sis.** *l.* ovate-lanceolate, 1 to 2 ft. long. Peru. 1879. A noble foliage plant.

F. G. P.

***Griersonia'nus -a -um,*** in honour of R. C. Grierson, of the Chinese Maritime Customs at Tengyueh.

**GRIFFI'NIA** (in honour of William Griffin, d. 1827). FAM. *Amaryllidaceae*. A genus of 7 species of bulbous plants, natives of Brazil. Leaves broad, usually stalked, netted. Flowers in umbels, white or lilac, upper segments of perianth broader than others, directed upwards, two of the lower spreading at right angles, the third directed downwards; 5 stamens declinate, with erect under upper segments. Spring and summer flowering. Well-drained fibrous loam suits these plants which need warm-house conditions and a period of rest when water should be withheld for the bulbs to ripen thoroughly.

**G. Blumena'via.** A synonym of *Hippeastrum Blumenavia.*

**G. drya'des.** *Bulb* large. *l.* oblong-lanceolate, 12 in. long. *fl.* purplish-lilac, whitish towards centre, about 4 in. across; umbel large, loose, 10- to 13-fld.; scape stout, 18 in. long. 1868. (B.M. 5786.)

**G. hyacinth'ina.** *Bulbs* ovate, of moderate size. *l.* ovate-oblong, 6 to 8 in. long, with lattice-like veining; stalked. *fl.* about 3 in. across, upper seg. blue at top, white towards base; umbel 9- or 10-fld.; scape rather longer than *l.* 1815. (G.C. 1874, 17.) var. **max'ima,** *l.* broadly ovate-oblong, *fl.* in a close, 10- to 12-fld. umbel, white tipped rich blue, 5 in. across; **micran'tha,** *fl.* scarcely 1 in. long. 1880.

**G. interme'dia.** *Bulb* ovoid, longer than in *G. hyacinthina. l.* oblong, acute, wedge-shaped at base, narrowed to stalk. *fl.* pale lilac, 1½ to 2 in. long; tube short; segs. oblanceolate; umbel 6- to 10-fld.; scape slender, 1 ft. long. (B.R. 990.)

**G. Libonia'na.** *Bulb* 1 in. thick. *l.* 5 or 6, with *fl.*, oblong acute, 3 to 4 in. long, sessile. *fl.* pale lilac, 1 to 1¼ in. long; tube scarcely developed; stamens 5 only; umbel 6- to 8-fld.; scape 2-edged, 12 in. long. 1843.

**G. orna'ta.** *l.* elliptic-oblong, margins much recurved. *fl.* delicate bluish-lilac, passing to nearly white; pedicels long; umbel 20- to 24-fld. forming a spreading head 8 to 9 in. across; scape 12 to 18 in. long, 2-edged. 1876. (B.M. 6367.)

**G. parviflo'ra.** *Bulb* ovoid, 2 to 3 in. thick. *l.* 3 or 4, with *fl.*, oblong, acute, 6 in. long, narrowed to a 6 in. stalk. *fl.* pale lilac, ¾ to 1 in. long, segs. lanceolate-clawed; umbel 10- to 15-fld.; scape nearly 1 ft. long. 1815. (B.R. 511.)

***Griffithia'nus -a -um, Griffithii,*** in honour of William Griffiths, 1810–45, Superintendent, Calcutta Botanic Garden.

**GRINDE'LIA** (in honour of David H. Grindel, 1766–1836, German botanist). FAM. *Compositae*. A genus of about 20 species of hardy or nearly hardy biennial or perennial shrubby or herbaceous plants, natives of N. America and extra-tropical S. America. Leaves alternate. often rigid, toothed or ciliately toothed, sessile or stem-clasping. Flower-heads radiate, yellow, 1 to 2 in. across, solitary at ends of branches. Plants easily grown in peat and loam. Propagated by seed sown in spring or autumn in a cool greenhouse or frame, by cuttings and by division.

**G. argu'ta.** Herbaceous perennial with unbranched stems about 12 in. h. *Lower l.* spatulate; *upper* linear-oblong, toothed, 1-nerved. *fl.-heads* yellow. July to September. Mexico. 1822. (B.R. 781 as *G. angustifolia.*) Hardy.

**G. chiloen'sis.** Glabrous, clammy, shrubby perennial up to 2 ft. h. *l.* variable, narrow-lanceolate to obovate, more or less stem-clasping, up to 5 in. long, upper smaller. *fl.-heads* yellow, up to about 3 in. across, rays up to 50, covered before opening with a thick glutinous varnish; disk orange-yellow; involucral scales in about 4 series, outer narrowed to a fine point. July, August. Argentine. 1852. (B.M. 9471.) SYN. *G. speciosa.* Nearly hardy.

**G. glutino'sa.** Shrubby, about 2 ft. h. *l.* evergreen, ovate-oblong, toothed. *fl.-heads* yellow; involucre clammy. January to December. Peru. 1803. (B.R. 187.) Nearly hardy.

**G. grandiflo'ra.** A form of *G. squarrosa*.

**G. inuloi'des.** Shrubby, about 18 in. h. *l.* oblong-lanceolate, acute, toothed near end, not clammy. *fl.-heads* yellow. June to September. Mexico. 1815. (B.M. 3737; B.R. 248.) Nearly hardy.

**G. specio'sa.** A synonym of *G. chiloensis*.

**G. squarro'sa.** Herbaceous biennial or perennial, 2 to 3 ft. h. *l.* oblong or lower spatulate, toothed, stem-clasping. *fl.-heads* yellow to orange, 1½ in. across, covered with glutinous matter before opening; involucral scales filiform, spreading, revolute. N. America. 1811. (B.M. 4628 as *G. grandiflora*; 1706 as *Donia squarrosa*.) Hardy.

*Grisebachia'nus -a -um, Grisebach'ii,* in honour of Heinrich Rudolf August Grisebach, 1814–79, Professor of Botany at Göttingen.

**GRISELIN'IA** (in honour of Franc. Griselini, 1717–83, Italian botanist). FAM. *Cornaceae*. A small genus of trees and shrubs, natives of New Zealand and Chile. Leaves alternate, often oblique, oblong, subquadrate or lanceolate, thick, leathery, shining, entire, spiny-toothed or angled, veins inconspicuous, netted. Flowers minute, dioecious, in axillary panicles. Griselinias need a light, rich loam. They are somewhat tender, especially *G. lucida*, are valuable for their shining evergreen foliage, and are especially good near the sea. *G. littoralis* is propagated by cuttings of half-ripe shoots in gentle heat or of rather harder wood under hand-lights.

**G. littora'lis.** Shrub of 20 ft. *l.* ovate or oblong, 1 to 3 in. long, less oblique at base than *G. lucida*, wedge-shaped or narrowed into the slender leaf-stalk; veins very obscure beneath. New Zealand. 1872. var. **variega'ta,** *l.* variegated.

**G. lu'cida.** Shrub of 8 to 10 ft. *l.* very obliquely ovate, obovate, or oblong, entire, blunt at tip, very unequal towards base, one side much narrower than other; veins distinct beneath. New Zealand. Tender except in very favoured districts. var. **macrophyl'la,** a large-leaved form of robust habit.

*gris'eus -a -um,* grey.

**GRO'BYA** (in honour of Lord Grey of Groby, d. 1836, patron of horticulture). FAM. *Orchidaceae*. A genus containing 3 species of epiphytic orchids, natives of Brazil. Flowers yellow or greenish, tinged and spotted purple, in short racemes from base of bulb; petals broader than sepals, forming with the upper sepal a sort of helmet overhanging the lip, the lower sepals connate at base; lip small, 3-lobed. Leaves grass-like, plicate, ribbed. Pseudobulbs clustered. Cultivation as for the Mexican Laelias.

**G. Amherst'iae.** *fl.* 6 to 15; sep. ¾ in. long; pet. slightly less but broader; sep. greenish-brown; pet. flushed and spotted purple-brown; lip purplish, apex of mid-lobe shortly recurved and crenate, lateral lobes rounded. *Pseudobulbs* ovoid, 1 to 1½ in. h., clustered. *l.* 4 to 6, almost linear, 8 in. long. (B.R. 1740.)

**G. fascif'era.** *fl.* numerous, scapes arching or drooping; sep. yellow; pet. yellow spotted purple-brown, narrow; mid-lobe of lip more sparsely spotted than side lobes, side lobes banded with purple spots, ligulate-oblong, obtuse. Spring. *Pseudobulbs* pyriform. *l.* linear-ligulate. 1911. Allied to *G. galeata*.

**G. galea'ta.** *fl.* more numerous than in *G. Amherstiae*, green, purple-flushed; pet. obliquely rhomboid, rounded at top, forming a helmet with the dorsal sep., lateral sep. deflexed, connate at base; lip 3-lobed, side lobes linear, mid-lobe cuneate-truncate, more or less lined purple with a toothed disk and shining warts. *Pseudobulbs* clustered, 1 to 2 in. h., round-oval. *l.* 3 or 4, 8 to 12 in. long, narrow. 1836.

E. C.

*Groeneveld'tii,* in honour of William Groeneveldt, 1881–? Dutch official in East Indies.

*groenland'icus -a -um,* of Greenland.

**GROMWELL.** See **Lithospermum**.

*Grono'vii,* in honour of J. Fr. Gronovius, 1690–1760, of Leiden.

**GROSSULA'RIA.** Included in Ribes.

*grossularioi'des,* Gooseberry-like.

*gros'sus -a -um, grossi-,* in compound words, very large.

**GROTTO.** A favourite feature of late Georgian and Victorian gardens.

**GROUND BEETLES.** An important group of Beetles (FAM. *Carabidae*), which occur almost entirely in the soil and are found beneath stones, under bark, in decayed wood, in rough herbage, and elsewhere. Both the adult beetles and their grubs are predaceous and feed upon a variety of soil-inhabiting creatures (insects, young Slugs, Snails, and Mites). The grubs of many Ground Beetles are mistaken for the harmful Wireworms, which they somewhat resemble, but the former are more active and possess sharp calliper-like jaws, longer legs, and a pair of bristle-like appendages on the penultimate abdominal segment. Some species of Ground Beetles in the adult stage are, however, harmful

*Carabid or Ground Beetle*

in Strawberry plantations and beds, and the ripening fruits are attacked by the following species: *Ophonus pubescens*, *Pterostichus madidus*, *P. vulgaris*, and *Abax ater*. These beetles are mainly nocturnal in their habits, and rest during the day beneath stones, litter, and herbage. The best method of control is that of reducing the harbourage for the beetles in the vicinity of the plantation by keeping the ground well cultivated between the plants until the litter is spread, by clearing out ditches and the bases of hedgerows, and by avoiding the placing of a Strawberry bed adjacent to a wood from which the beetles migrate. A few beetles are trapped when jam-jars baited with fresh meat are sunk to their rims in the ground among the plants.

G. F. W.

**GROUND CHERRY.** *See* **Prunus fruticosa.**

**GROUND CISTUS.** *See* **Rhodothamnus Chamaecistus.**

**GROUND ELDER.** *See* **Aegopodium, Weed-killers**.

**GROUND FLEAS.** *See* **Springtails.**

**GROUND HEMLOCK.** *See* **Taxus canadensis.**

**GROUND IVY.** *See* **Nepeta hederacea.**

**GROUND LAUREL.** *See* **Epigaea repens.**

**GROUND NUT.** *See* **Apios tuberosa, Arachis hypogaea.**

**GROUND RATTAN CANE.** *See* **Rhapis excelsa.**

**GROUND TISSUE,** the cells which build up the structure of the body of a plant except the skin (epidermis) and the vascular bundles. *See* **Growing Point.**

**GROUNDSEL.** *See* **Senecio.**

**GROUNDSEL TREE.** *See* **Baccharis halimifolia.**

**GROWING POINT.** A mass of cells at the extreme tips of roots and shoots, in a state of, or capable of, active division. These cells are commonly of uniform size but in most plants other than flowering plants at the apex of the mass is a single large cell or a group of large cells from which the others are derived. Usually the cells from which the epidermis and the vascular bundles are derived, known respectively as the dermatogen and plerome, are early distinguishable from the periblem which lies between them and from which much of the ground tissue arises.

**GROWTH** is increase of size rendered permanent by the addition of new material, as by the stretching of already existing cell-walls subsequently thickened by the addition within of layers of cellulose by the protoplasm, and particularly by the production of fresh protoplasm and cell-division at the growing-points, leading to increase in length and the formation of leaves, &c., and in the cambium layers, leading to increase in diameter of stems and roots and the production of protective layers of cork. As a rule in larger plants the early activity of the plant is mainly directed to increase in the organs of vegetation, later it is directed to the development of flowers and the complicated apparatus by which new individuals are produced and distributed by fruits and seeds.

**GRUB.** Common name for larva of an insect, especially of the beetle and weevil families.

**GRUBBER OR GRUBBING AXE.** An implement somewhat similar to the ordinary pick but having both ends flattened and made wedge-shaped, useful for up-rooting trees. One point, for cutting roots or splitting wood is in line with the handle, the other is placed in a transverse direction for clearing roots of soil. *See also* **Daisy Grubber.**

*grui'nus -a -um,* crane-like.

**GRUSO'NIA** (in honour of Hermann Gruson of Magdeburg, whose large collection of cacti is still maintained in that town). FAM. *Cactaceae.* Plants with cylindrical, jointed, ribbed stems, resembling a Cereus; areoles very spiny, borne along the ribs; glochids only present in the areoles on the ovary. Flowers yellow. Grows easily in a warm, dry position. For cultivation *see* **Cactus** (terrestrial).

**G. Bradtiá'na.** The only species. Mexico. (B.R.C. 1, t. 33.) SYN. *Cereus Bradtianus, Opuntia Bradtiana, O. cereiformis.*

V. H.

**GRYLLOTAL'PA.** See **Mole Cricket.**

**GRYL'LUS.** See **Crickets.**

**GUAIA'CUM** (Guaiac, the S. American name). FAM. *Zygophyllaceae.* A genus of about 8 species of tall evergreen trees or shrubs in the W. Indies and the warmer parts of N. America. Leaves opposite, equally pinnate; leaflets entire. Flowers blue or purple, solitary in the leaf-axils. Guaiacums need stove treatment and rich, sandy, fibrous loam. They can be increased by April cuttings in sand under a hand-glass in heat.

**G. arbor'eum.** About 40 ft. h. *lflets.* in 7 to 14 pairs, oval-oblong, blunt, unequal at base, usually alternate. *fl.* blue, in loose racemes. July. Cartagena. 1816.

**G. officina'le.** Lignum Vitae. Tree of 30 ft. with smooth bark, variegated green and white. *lflets.* in 2 pairs, obovate or oval, blunt. *fl.* blue, in pairs; sep. hairy; pet. 3 times as long. July. (B.R. 25, 9.) This is the source of the greenish-brown, hard, heavy wood, which has a peculiar acid aromatic scent, and is used by turners. It produces gum guaiacum, a fragrant resin used, like the bark and wood, medicinally.

**G. sanc'tum.** *l.* obliquely elliptic-lanceolate. *fl.* blue; sep. smooth, half as long as pet. West Indies. Of similar use to *G. officinale.*

F. G. P.

*guamen'sis -is -e,* of Guam.

**GUANO.** See **Manures.**

**GUARD CELLS.** The two cells (one in the fruits of Mosses) which guard the apertures (stomata) in the epidermis of stems, leaves, &c. (not developed in underground or submerged structures or in aerial roots). They differ from the usual epidermal cells by containing chlorophyll and by their crescent form. They alter the size of the stoma by changes in their bulk and so increase or diminish the rate of interchange of gases between the external air and that in the internal intercellular spaces, so that the intake of carbonic acid gas and oxygen and the exhalation of water vapour is varied according to the condition of the guard cells. *See* **Stoma.**

**GUAR'EA** (*Guara,* native Cuban name). FAM. *Meliaceae.* A genus of about 80 species of tall evergreen trees, natives of tropical America. Leaves pinnate, with opposite or alternate leaflets. Flowers white or reddish, in axillary panicles, racemes, or spikes. For treatment *see* **Guaiacum.**

**G. grandifo'lia.** Tree of 30 ft. *lflets.* in many pairs, oval-oblong, 8 to 9 in. long. *fl.* scarcely ½ in. long, silky without, in long racemes. February. French Guiana. All parts with musky odour, especially the bark. SYN. *G. grandiflora.*

**G. ramiflo'ra.** Tree of 20 ft. *lflets.* ovate-lanceolate. *fl.* whitish in lateral racemes, very short, from sides of branches. Porto Rico 1822.

**G. trichilioi'des.** Tree of 20 ft. *lflets.* lanceolate-ovate, slender-pointed, with 6 or 7 prominent lateral veins beneath. *fl.* white in long racemes. June, July. West Indies. 1822. SYN. *G. Swartzii.*

F. G. P.

*guatemalen'sis -is -e,* of Guatemala, Central America.

**GUATTE'RIA** (in honour of John B. Guatteri, 1739-93, Italian botanist, Professor at Parma). FAM. *Annonaceae.* A genus of about 50 species of evergreen trees or shrubs, natives of the warmer parts of America. Leaves alternate, entire, without stipules. Flowers yellowish-white, greenish, or dusky, solitary, or clustered in leaf axils. They need stove conditions and a compost of loam, peat, and sand, and are readily struck from cuttings in sand, under glass, in heat.

**G. Our'egou.** Tall tree. *l.* obovate-oblong, cuspidate, shining above, almost smooth beneath, with prominent veins. *fl.* with triangular, acute, cal. segs.; pet. rusty-velvety, obovate, inner longer, solitary or 2 to 4 in clusters on short peduncles. Caribbean Is.

F. G. P.

**GUAVA.** Fruit of *Psidium Guajava* and *P. Cattleianum,* edible and astringent.

*guayaquilen'sis -is -e,* of Guayaquil, Ecuador.

**GUAYOTA.** See **Gonolobus edulis.**

**GUAZU'MA** (name of Mexican origin). FAM. *Sterculiaceae.* A genus of about 5 species of evergreen hairy trees allied to Theobroma, natives of the tropics. Leaves often oblique, unequally dentate. Flowers small, white, pink, or yellow, in axillary cymes on short peduncles. A compost of peat and loam suits them and cuttings of ripe shoots root freely in heat. They need stove conditions.

**G. tomento'sa.** Tree, stellately hairy. *l.* oblong-lanceolate, 3 to 4½ in. long, obliquely cordate, slender-pointed, serrate, downy beneath. *fl.* yellow, numerous, in terminal and axillary panicles 2½ in. across and longer than l. India.

**G. ulmifo'lia.** Bastard Cedar. Wide spreading tree with habit of Elm, 40 to 60 ft. *l.* ovate to oblong-lanceolate, somewhat pointed, puberulous beneath, like branchlets, when young, finally glabrous. *fl.* yellow with 2 purple awns at tip of pet. August. W. Indies. 1739. In sleep the blades of the l. hang straight down, the stalks remaining stiff and straight.

F. G. P.

*Gueldenstaedtia'nus -a -um,* in honour of A. J. von Güldenstädt, 1741–85, who botanized in Caucasus.

**GUELDER ROSE.** See **Viburnum Opulus.**

**GUERNSEY LILY.** See **Nerine sarniensis.**

**GUETTARD'A** (in honour of John Étienne Guettard, 1715–86, who published, in 1747, a catalogue of plants in the neighbourhood of Étampes). FAM. *Rubiaceae.* A genus of about 40 species of evergreen shrubs or small trees, mostly natives of Trop. America. Leaves opposite or whorled, ovate or lanceolate. Flowers sessile, on side of the branches of the inflorescence and in the forks; calyx deciduous; corolla salver-shaped, tube cylindrical, lobes 4 to 9, oval-oblong. Fruit drupe-like. Stove conditions and a compost of peat and loam are needed for them and they can be increased by cuttings in heat.

**G. odora'ta.** Shrub of 6 to 10 ft. *l.* oval, narrowed to both ends. *fl.* reddish, about 1 in. long, very fragrant at night, hairy without; in 2-branched cymes. Summer. Trop. America. 1818.

**G. scab'ra.** Tree. *l.* obovate, mucronate, leathery, roughly hairy above, netted and downy beneath; stipules lanceolate, slender pointed, quickly falling. *fl.* white, peduncles compressed, hairy, much exceeding l.-stalks. W. Indies. 1818.

**G. specio'sa.** Tree to 30 ft. with horizontal spreading branches. *l.* broadly ovate, rounded or cordate at base, downy beneath. *fl.* white, very fragrant of cloves, large; cymes often from bare shoots, velvety, much shorter than l. June, July. Trop. Asia. (B.R. 1393.)

F. G. P.

**GUEVI'NA.** *See* **Gevuina.**

*guianen'sis -is -e,* of Guyana, S. America.

*Guicciard'ii,* in honour of Jacops Guicciardi, who collected plants in Greece.

**GUICHENOT'IA** (in honour of Antoine Guichenot, French gardener and traveller). FAM. *Sterculiaceae.* A genus of about 6 species of evergreen shrubs, natives of W. Australia. Leaves opposite, entire. Calyx of 5 sepals, membranous, each sepal 3- or 5-ribbed, constituting the chief beauty of the flower; petals 5, very small; fruit a 5-valved capsule. Greenhouse shrubs of simple cultivation; easily propagated by cuttings of half-ripened shoots.

**G. ledifo'lia.** Evergreen shrub 3 to 5 ft., shoots l. and infl. covered with soft, velvety, whitish down. *l.* linear, 1 to 1½ in. long, ⅓₂ to ¼ in. wide, blunt-ended, margins revolute. *fl.* 3 to 6 short axillary racemes; cal. white, ¼ in. long, ribbed; pet. very small. W. Australia. 1868.

**G. macran'tha.** Shrub a few ft. h., shoots, l., and infl. downy. *l.* 1 to 2½ in. long, ⅓₂ to ¼ in. wide, blunt, margins very revolute. *fl.* in axillary racemes of 2 or 3; cal. ⅓ to ⅔ in. long, purple, strongly ribbed; anthers almost black-purple. March. W. Australia. 1847. (B.M. 4651.)

W. J. B.

*Guilfoyl'ei,* in honour of W. R. Guilfoyle, 1840–1912, of Chelsea, Director, Botanic Gardens, Melbourne, Australia.

**GUILIEL'MA** (in honour of Queen Frederica Guilielma Carolina of Bavaria). FAM. *Palmaceae.* A genus of 1 or 2 species of Trop. American Palms, with slender, ringed stems and armed with very sharp spines. Leaves pinnate, hairy, spiny. Flower-spike branched. Fruit ovate, about as large as a peach, produced in large pendulous bunches. For cultivation of these stove palms *see* **Bactris.**

**G. Gasipa'es.** Stems tall, slender, densely spiny. *l.* of young plants 2-fid, very spiny; of mature plants in a crown, pinnate, 2 to 4 ft. long; pinnae about 1 ft. long, 1 in. wide, broader at the 2-fid tip, deep green, veins with slender black bristles above; stalks broadly sheathing at base, thickly armed with long, sharp spines. Amazon, Costa Rica. SYN. *G. speciosa, G. utilis, Bactris Gasipaes.*

**GUINEA CORN.** *See* **Sorghum vulgare.**

**GUINEA GRASS.** *See* **Panicum maximum.**    A

**GUINEA PEACH.** *See* **Sarcocephalus esculentus.**

**GUINEA WHEAT.** *See* **Zea Mays.**

*guineen'sis -is -e,* of Guinea, Africa.

**GUIZO'TIA** (in honour of Fr. P. G. Guizot, 1787–1874, of Nimes). FAM. *Compositae.* A genus of 5 species of Trop. African annuals. Leaves opposite or upper ones alternate. Flower-heads yellow, terminal in upper axils, heterogamous: involucral bracts sometimes in 2 series: receptacle convex or conical: ray florets ligulate, 3-toothed at tip. Achenes glabrous. *G. abyssinica* will grow well in any rich soil treated as other annuals. Ranil oil is expressed from the seed of *G. abyssinica.*

**G. abyssin'ica.** About 6 ft. h. *l.* stem-clasping, lanceolate, distantly toothed. *fl.-heads* golden yellow, 2 in. across, rather handsome; involucre simple, of 5 bracts. August, September. 1806. (B.M. 1017 as *Verbesina sativa.*) SYN. *G. oleifera, Veslingia sativa.*

*Guliel'mi,* in honour of the Emperor William of Germany.

**GULU'BIA** (native name in Ternate). FAM. *Palmaceae.* A genus of 2 species of tall Palms. For characters see *G. costata.*

**G. costa'ta.** Tree of 80 to 90 ft. *l.* regularly pinnatisect, in old plants up to 10 ft. long, 3 ft. wide, segs. very numerous, linear-lanceolate, slender-pointed. *Spadix* branched, branches fastigiate. Aru, &c.

**GUM.** Gums (including mucilages) are secreted by many plants. They belong to the same group of carbohydrates as the starch and inulin and are apparently usually waste products secreted in intercellular spaces, rounded and closed, or forming long canals, escaping only when cut into. At times they appear to be formed as the result of some derangement of the usual functions of the plant through the attack of fungi, bacteria, &c. The following are among the gums of value for various purposes. Gum Ammoniacum obtained from *Dorema ammoniacum*; Angico gum from *Piptadenia rigida*; a gum like Gum Arabic from *Acacia Senegal* and other species; Gum Benzoin from *Styrax Benzoin*; Gum Galbanum from *Ferula galbaniflua* and *F. rubricaulis*; Gum Opopanax from the roots of species of Opopanax; Gum Olibanum (really a resin also called Frankincense) from *Boswellia Carteri*; and Gum Tragacanth from *Astragalus gummifer* and other species. The stems of the Cherry and the Plum and other species of Prunus frequently produce gum. (*See* **Gummosis.**)

**GUM, BLUE.** *See* **Eucalyptus Globulus.**

**GUM CISTUS.** *See* **Cistus villosus.**

**GUM ELEMI TREE.** *See* **Amyris elemifera.**

**GUM TREE.** *See* **Eucalyptus, Nyssa.**

**GUM TREE, CAPE.** *See* **Acacia horrida.**

*Gum'bletonii,* in honour of William Gumbleton of Belgrove, Queenstown, Ireland, amateur gardener.

*gum'mifer -fera -ferum,* producing gum.

**GUMMING.** *See* **Gummosis.**

**GUMMOSIS.** A condition that arises on certain trees following wounding, severe pruning (especially on Stone Fruits), infections of bacterial and fungi, mechanical injury, heavy moist soils, and insect attacks, especially Bark Beetles, Shot Hole Borers, and the caterpillars of Goat and Wood Leopard Moths. It is frequently seen on such trees as Plums, Cherries, and Peaches. The gum may form in clear tear-like drops or may ooze out until it forms an irregular mass almost as large as a walnut. It may remain soft in damp weather but in dry will shrink and harden. Sooty black mould fungi may grow on the surface, and some have been thought to be the cause of the trouble, but this is unlikely. Disease-causing fungi in a branch may produce cankers and be attended by a certain amount of gumming but when the trouble shows on most of the branches of a tree such as a cherry, the cause is most likely to be found in malnutrition. In stone fruit trees frost injury or other wounding is followed by the exudation of gum and in conifers by resin, but in these instances the exudate covers the wound and protects it while healing. This, however, is not the condition gummosis is meant to indicate; in gummosis the tree is in ill health and even small shoots show the exudation of gum. Where stone fruit trees are affected by gumming the cause of the trouble is obscure but it appears to be some functional disorder rather than attack by a parasite. The probable cause is malnutrition either through unsuitable soil or from poor root action such as would occur if the root system suffers water-logging for long periods in spring. The same reasons are advanced for the condition seen in Plums where the fruit develops a gum-like substance in the flesh and usually near the stone, sometimes oozing out and appearing on the surface as shining globules of gum. Some varieties, e.g. Victoria Plum, are very susceptible. Where such maladies occur careful cultivation should be done to encourage the trees to keep their vigour or to regain it, so that the fruit and foliage can keep steady and uniform growth. On heavy soils attention to drainage is necessary so as to avoid water-logging in wet weather or drying out in periods of drought. Much can be done by this thorough cultivation, by supplying humus and fertilizers to the soil, and by ensuring that the soil contains sufficient lime.

D. E. G.

**GUNDEL'IA** (in honour of Andrew Gundelsheimer, German botanist, who accompanied Tournefort in his journey into the Levant, 1709). Fam. *Compositae*. A genus of 1 species, a thistle-like plant with milky juice. It grows in sandy-peat soil, is propagated by division, and is hardy.

**G. Tournefort'ii.** About 15 in. h. *l.* alternate, sessile, pinnatifid with spiny lobes and teeth. *fl.-heads* purplish, large, in terminal clusters. E. Asia. 1739.

**GUN'NERA** (in honour of J. E. Gunnerus, 1718–73, Norwegian bishop and botanist). Fam. *Haloragidaceae*. A genus of about 30 species of herbaceous perennials widely distributed mostly in the S. Hemisphere. Leaves all radical, ovate or cordate-roundish, simple or lobed, crenate, somewhat fleshy-leathery, stalked. Flowers greenish, minute in dense spikes or panicles. The species differ from one another remarkably in the size which they attain, some being quite small, needing to be searched for when growing among grass, others being the most majestic in size of all herbs hardy in the British Is. All need a damp sunny position and the large species are the better for some shelter from winds. The large species make magnificent plants for deep rich soil on the margins of lakes and slow streams and, provided the supply of water to the roots is ample, need no special feeding, though annual dressings of decayed cow manure are a help. The crowns should be covered in winter with the dead leaves and possibly, in places with a very severe winter climate, with bracken which, when the young leaves begin to force their way through in spring, should be trodden in over the roots to help the plants with their decay. The great spikes of tiny fruits tinged red have some attraction, but the removal of the inflorescences before they have developed fully aids the production of large leaves. The small species, only about 3 in. high, form good carpeters during summer in damp places but they have no other value unless it be the contrast between them as pygmies with their giant congeners. The small Gunneras from New Zealand are not dependably hardy but *G. magellanica* seems to be able to survive our winters unprotected. Propagated by seed or division in spring. **A**

**G. arena'ria.** Mat-forming, much branched with a stout rhizome covered with old l.-bases. *l.* broadly ovate to oblong, with coarse rounded teeth or almost lobed, thick, leathery, about ¾ in. long; stalk longer, stout, usually glabrous. *fl.* monoecious, on separate spikes; female hidden among l. at fl.-time. *fr.* about ⅛ in. long about twice as large as in *G. dentata.* New Zealand.

**G. chilen'sis.*** Crowns large. *l.* large, 4 to 5 ft. across, lobed and deeply toothed, stalks stout, prickly, 3 to 6 ft. or more long. *fl.* reddish, in a large panicle, very numerous. Chile. 1849. (F.d.S. 1897.)

**G. denta'ta.** Mat-forming in moist soils, with a much branched stout rhizome covered with old l.-bases. *l.* densely tufted, 1 to 3 in. long including the broad, flat, hairy stalk, blade ovate to elliptic-oblong, ⅛ to 1 in. long, coarsely toothed, rounded at base. *fl.* monoecious in separate spikes; female spikes very short, hidden among l. at fl.-time. New Zealand.

**G. magellan'ica.** Carpet-forming, about 3 in. h. *l.* radical, reniform, crenate; stalked. *Spikes* almost globose, the male about as high as l., female short, sessile. Magellan district, S. America. (Gn. 16 (1879), 413.)

**G. manica'ta.*** The largest species. Crown as large as a man's body. *l.* 4 to 6 ft. or more across, more kidney-shaped than in *G. chilensis,* lobed and coarsely toothed; stalks stout, 4 to 8 ft. long, prickly. *fl.* in long stout panicles, longer than in *G. chilensis.* S. Brazil. 1867. (I.H. 1884, 128.) **A**

**G. monoi'ca.** Mat-forming with creeping hairy stolons. *l.* in a rosette, rounded heart-shaped, ½ to 1 in. wide, slightly 3- or 5-lobed, irregularly toothed, thinly hairy; stalk ½ to 1½ in. long. *fl.* monoecious, male in upper part of panicle; peduncle 1½ to 2 in. long. New Zealand.

**G. perpen'sa.** About 18 in. h. *l.* reniform, toothed, shorter than the fruiting scape. *fl.* green. August. S. Africa. (B.M. 2376.)

**G. scab'ra.** A synonym of *G. chilensis.* **A**

F. P.

**Gunn'ii,** in honour of R. C. Gunn, 1808–81, of Tasmania.

**GUNNY.** Jute, furnished by *Corchorus capsularis* and *C. olitorius.*

**GURA'NIA** (anagram of Anguria). Fam. *Cucurbitaceae*. A genus of about 70 species of tall climbing perennial herbs or shrubs, natives of warm regions. Tendrils simple. Leaves entire, lobed, or 3- or 5-foliolate. Flowers dioecious (or rarely monoecious), yellow or red, the staminate in clusters, stamens 2, the pistillate solitary or in heads. *G. malacophylla* can be grown in large pots of rich soil in the stove or warm greenhouse and trained up the rafters.

**G. malacophyl'la.** Monoecious. Stem terete, hairy when young. *l.* broadly ovate, more or less deeply 3- or sometimes 5-lobed, minutely toothed, hairy. *Male fl.* reddish, in a globose head on a long-haired peduncle; cal. tube densely hairy without. *Female fl.* produced later, stalked, solitary or in groups of 2 or 3 in axils of very hairy young shoots. Upper Amazon. 1893. (B.M. 8085; 9415.)

F. G. P.

**GURJUN BALSAM.** Furnished by species of Dipterocarpus.

**gurwa'licus -a -um,** of Garwhal. NW. Himalaya.

**Gusdorf'ii,** in honour of H. A. Gusdorf, 1868–1933, of the Netherlands Army.

**Gusson'ei,** in honour of G. Gussone, 1787–1866, Director, Botanic Gardens, Palermo.

**GUSTAV'IA** (in honour of Gustavus III, King of Sweden and patron of Linnaeus). Fam. *Lecythidaceae*. A genus of about 11 species of evergreen trees and shrubs, natives of Trop. America. Leaves large, alternate, ovate or spatulate, glossy. Flowers showy; petals 6 to 8; peduncles 1-flowered. Fruit a few-seeded berry. Rich loamy soil and stove conditions suit them. Cuttings of ripened shoots root freely in sand under glass in heat.

**G. gracil'lima.** Tree with slender glabrous trunk. *l.* closely set, 1 to 2 in. long, slender-pointed, spreading and recurved, toothed, narrowed to a slender stalked, margin waved, midrib prominent beneath. *fl.* rose-red, 4 in. across, solitary or in pairs on stout peduncles 1 to 2 in. long, thickened upwards. September. (B.M. 6151.)

**G. insig'nis.** A synonym of *G. superba.*

**G. pterocarp'a.** Closely allied to *G. superba,* but with smaller white *fl.,* with large cal. lobes, more leathery less toothed *l.,* and a winged ovary. Guiana. (B.M. 5239.)

**G. specio'sa.** *l.* oblong-lanceolate, slender pointed, about 3¼ in. long, entire, plotted above, netted beneath, narrowed to base. *fl.* white, fragrant; pet. 6; pedicels hairy, clustered. Colombia.

**G. super'ba.** Shrub of 3 to 4 ft. *l.* obovate-lanceolate, slender-pointed, narrowed to base, glossy, dark green, sessile or nearly so. *fl.* cream-white, 5 to 6 in. across, spreading, tinged rose without; filaments rose; anthers orange. June. Trop. America. 1858. (B.M. 5069 as *G. insignis.*)

F. G. P.

**GUTIERREZ'IA gymnospermoi'des.** A synonym of *Xanthocephalum gymnospermoides.*

**GUT'TA,** from the Malayan name of *Palaquium Gutta.*

**GUTTA-PERCHA.** Obtained from *Bassia pallida, Maytenus phyllanthoides, Mimusops Balata, Palaquium Gutta.*

**GUTTA-SUNDEK.** A good gutta-percha obtained from *Payena Leerii.*

**A→**

**gutta'tus -a -um,** covered with small dots, as if sprinkled: the dots are frequently oil glands.

**Guttenberg'ii,** in honour of Hermann von Guttenberg, 1881– , of Trieste.

**GUTTIFERA'CEAE.** Dicotyledons. A family of about 650 species of trees or shrubs and a few herbs grouped in about 40 genera growing mainly in the tropics with some in temperate regions. The name of the family has reference to the oil glands and ducts which frequently cause the appearance of pellucid spots in the foliage. Leaves are usually opposite or whorled but may be alternate. Flowers with 4 or 5 imbricate sepals and 4 or 5 imbricate or convolute free petals; stamens usually many in bundles; ovary superior of 3 to 5 carpels with many ovules on a parietal placenta. Fruit variable. Many species of this family are useful timber trees. Calophyllum, Caraipa, Clusia, Garcinia yield resin. The fruits of Mammea (Mammee or St. Domingo Apricot) and Garcinia (e.g. Mangosteen) are esteemed in the tropics. The genera dealt with here are Ascyrum, Calophyllum, Clusia, Garcinia, Haronga, Hypericum, Kielmeyera, Mammea, Mesua, Ochrocarpos, Pentadesmia, Rheedia, Vismia.

***guttula'tus -a -um,*** covered with small dots.

**GUZMA'NIA** (in honour of A. Guzman, Spanish naturalist). FAM. *Bromeliaceae.* A genus of between 80 and 90 species of herbaceous perennials, natives of north-western S. America and the W. Indies, mostly, at one time, placed under Caraguata. Usually stemless herbs branching from the axils of the lower leaves, with the habit of Tillandsia to which they are nearly related, but with connate petals. For treatment *see* **Tillandsia**.

**G. Andrea'na.** About 2 ft. h. *l.* arching, green, 16 in. long, 1¼ in. wide, rather papery, in a loose rosette. *fl.* yellow, about 2 in. long, numerous in a spike-like, rather lax panicle, slightly longer than l.; stem and bracts carmine-rose. March. Andes of Pasto. 1884. (B.M. 7014 and R.H. 1886, p. 176 as *Caraguata Andreana.*)

**G. angustifo'lia.** *l.* erect or nearly so, 6 in. long, ¼ in. wide in a dense rosette, lanceolate, channelled from the ovate base to the narrowed tip. *fl.* yellow, large, few, in a dense spike about 2½ in. long; bracts red, large, oblong-lanceolate; peduncle short with a few reduced l. Costaria, Ecuador. 1884. SYN. *G. Bulliana.*

**G. Belea'na.** *l.* circinate, 2 to 2½ ft. long, 1¼ in. wide, bright green, slender-pointed, dilated at base, tinged violet above, scaly beneath. *fl.* white, few, about 2 in. long, in a compound spreading panicle; peduncle about 2 ft. long. Origin? 1891. (R.H. 1891, 114 as *Caraguata Beleana.*)

**G. cardina'lis.** Related to *G. lingulata* with brilliant red fl., the bracts around the infl. all decurved. Colombia. (R.H. 1883, 12 as *Caraguata cardinalis.*)

**G. conif'era.** *l.* lanceolate, acute, 2 to 2½ ft. long, 2½ to 3 in. wide, in a dense rosette. *fl.* pale yellow, over 2 in. long, just exceeding the bright scarlet bracts, in a dense, conical head, 8 to 10 in. long; peduncle erect. Ecuador. 1894. (B.M. 7359 as *Caraguata conifera.*)

**G. Devansaya'na.** *l.* about 2 ft. long, ¾ in. wide, dilated at base, striped purple. *fl.* pale yellow, tightly packed within broad, slender-pointed, scarlet bracts. Ecuador. (B.H. 1883, 113, t. 8, 9.)

**G. erythrole'pis.*** *l.* deep green, like those of *G. monostachya. fl.* white, bracts uniformly purplish-red (cf. *G. monostachya*). Cuba, Jamaica. 1855. (F.d.S. 1089.)

**G. Fuerstenbergia'na.** *l.* about 15 in a rosette, lanceolate, 12 in. long, ½ in. wide. *fl.* whitish, 1 in. long in a simple, cylindrical, dense spike 3 in. long, sterile at apex, bracts bright red. July. Andes of Ecuador. 1883.

**G. Lin'deni.** *l.* up to 24 in. long, 3 to 3½ in. wide, marked above with transverse, wavy lines, green above, red beneath. *fl.* whitish, in a many-fld., tall, narrow panicle, branches densely fld., ovoid or elliptical, erect, up to 2½ in. long. N. Peru. 1878. (I.H. 1878, 55, t. 309 as *Massangea Lindeni*; B.H. 1883, p. 121 as *Schlumbergia Lindeni.*)

**G. lingula'ta.** About 1 ft. h. *l.* broad at base, lingulate, about 18 in. long, recurved. *fl.* white, in a simple, few-fld. corymb surrounded by numerous large, broadly lanceolate, brilliant scarlet bracts. Colombia, &c. 1880. var. **splen'dens,** *l.* more or less lined with vinous red.

**G. Melino'nis.** About 8 in. h. *l.* lorate, 1 ft. long, 1½ to 2 in. wide, tinged violet brown beneath, in a dense rosette. *fl.* yellow, 1¼ in. long, in a dense, simple, oblong spike, 3 in. long; peduncle much shorter than l.; bracts red. French Guiana. 1879. SYN. *G. Melinoki.*

**G. monostach'ya.*** *l.* broad-linear, sword-shaped, 18 in. long, ¾ in. wide, involute, concave, base sheathing, in a rosette. *fl.* pure white on an erect scape, 12 to 24 in. long, with numerous bright, pale yellow-green bracts streaked with blackish-purple towards top, tipped red, rich scarlet at extreme apex. Summer. S. and Cent. America. 1820. (B.M. 5220 and L.B.C. 462 as *G. tricolor.*) A widely spread species which has given rise to several good garden varieties.

**G. Morrenia'na.** About 3 ft. h. *l.* 3½ ft. long, 3 in. wide with recurved, slender-pointed tips in a rosette, outer dark green passing by violet shading into the violet l. ground infl. *fl.* yellow, in a large, compact head, bracts bright red; peduncle 4 to 6 in. long. Peru. 1882. (R.H. 1887, p. 12 as *Caraguata Morreniana*; B.H. 1883, 46, as *Schlumbergia Morreniana.*)

**G. musa'ica.** *l.* ligulate, 1 ft. long, 2 in. wide, apex recurved, yellowish-green with irregular patches of dark green. *fl.* with pet. snow-white, sep. brownish ivory tipped white, in a sub-globose, about 25-fld. head; peduncle erect, bracts scarlet. (B.M. 6675; I.H. 1877, t. 268 as *Caraguata musaica.*)

**G. Osya'na.** Stem short, robust. *l.* lanceolate, 18 in. long, somewhat channelled, leathery. *fl.* yellow; pet. twice as long as sep.; lobes erect, 1½ in. long; bracts orange-salmon, overlapping, reflexed, 2½ in. long; spike many-fld., globose, 3½ in. wide. Ecuador. 1885. (B.H. 1885, p. 254 as *Caraguata Osyana.*) SYN. *Caraguata magnifica* of gardens.

**G. sanguin'ea.** About 12 in. h., stemless. *l.* lanceolate, outer 12 in. long, acute, falcate, thin, lower part green, upper half or more much tinged bright red on both sides, rosette dense. *fl.* 2½ to 3 in. long, clustered at base of centre of l.-rosette, yellowish white in the long tube, lobes white, ovate. Colombia. (B.M. 6765 and R.H. 1883, p. 468 as *Caraguata sanguinea.*)

**G. tric'olor.** A synonym of *G. monostachya.*

**G. Van Volxem'ii.** 2 to 3 ft. h. *l.* 18 in. long, 3½ in. wide, in a rosette, acute, sharply pointed. *fl.* yellowish-white, in close spikes about 1 ft. long, 3½ in. wide; bracts crimson. Colombia. 1879. (I.H. 1878, 326 as *Caraguata Van Volxemii.*)

**G. vires'cens.** About 18 in. h. *l.* lanceolate, about 18 in. long, 1¼ in. wide, scaly beneath, unarmed. *fl.* pale yellowish-green, about 2¼ in. long, many, in a close panicle; peduncle about 16 in. long. March. Venezuela. 1857. (B.M. 4991 as *Puya virescens.*) SYN. *Pitcairnia virescens, Caraguata virescens.*

**G. Zahn'ii.** About 18 in. h. *l.* linear-ligulate, 20 in. long, yellow with crimson stripes, semi-transparent, upper part bright crimson. *fl.* pale yellow in dense, oblong, compressed panicles 9 in. long, 4 in. wide. Costa Rica. 1870. (B.M. 6059 as *Caraguata Zahnii.*)

***gymn-*** in compound words signifying naked, as *gymnocarpus*, naked fruiting, *gymnospermus*, naked seeded.

**GYMNABIC'CHIA.** FAM. *Orchidaceae.* Hybrids between species of Gymnadenia and Bicchia (Platanthera), e.g. *G.* × *Schweinfurthii*, a natural hybrid between *Gymnadenia conopsea* and *Bicchia* (*Platanthera*) *albida.*

**GYMNACAMP'TIS.** FAM. *Orchidaceae.* Hybrids between species of Anacamptis and Gymnadenia, e.g. *G.* × *Aschersonii*, a natural hybrid between *Anacamptis pyramidalis* and *Gymnadenia conopsea.*

**GYMNADE'NIA** (*gymnos*, naked, *aden*, gland; the glands of the caudicle are uncovered). FAM. *Orchidaceae.* A small terrestrial genus, closely allied to Platanthera and Habenaria. As defined by R. Brown, the flowers have a spurred lip, the anther cells are contiguous, the glands of the stalks of the pollen masses are naked, and approximate. The genus contains about 20 species. The British species, *G. albida* and *G. conopsea,* which call for mention here, are widely distributed in Europe and N. Asia.

**G. al'bida.** Differs from *G. conopsea* by its white fl. which have an equally tricuspidate lip, and a swollen obtuse spur not equalling the lip. 6 in. h. *Spike* dense, cylindrical. *l.* lanceolate. Roots comparatively free or uniting into a deeply divided tuber. Europe, England. (E.B. 1461.) SYN. *Satyrium albidum, Orchis albida, O. alpina, O. parviflora, Habenaria albida, Coeloglossum albidum.*

**G. conop'sea.** *fl.* numerous, purple, small, fragrant, closely set in an oblong or cylindrical spike; upper sep. and pet. hooded; lateral sep. spreading; lip with three almost equal entire rounded lobes; spur slender cylindrical, twice as long as the ovary. Stem 12 to 18 in. or more h. *l.* linear-lanceolate, keeled. Tuber palmate. (E.B. 1460.) SYN. *Plantanthera conopsea, Habenaria conopsea.* Under cultivation, though said to prefer a chalky soil, it does not seem particular. var. **al'ba,** *fl.* white, spurred; **ecalcara'ta,** *fl.* white, spurless. See also *Orchigymnadenia.*

**G. odoratis'sima.** *fl.* fragrant, violet-red; lip half as long as ovary. Resembles *G. conopsea,* but smaller. Europe. (R.I.F.G. 421.)

**G. rupes'tris.** *fl.* 8 to 12, lilac with darker veinings on lip; spur ½ in. long. *l.* three, narrow. 6 to 9 in. h. Japan. 1873. Requires temperature, &c., of the Odontoglossum house. Japan. 1873.

E. C.

**GYMNAGLOS'SUM.** Fam. *Orchidaceae.* Hybrids between species of Coeloglossum and Gymnadenia, e.g. *G.* × *Jacksonii*, a natural hybrid between *G. conopsea* and *Habenaria* (*Coeloglossum*) *viride*.

**GYMNAPLATAN'THERA.** Fam. *Orchidaceae.* Hybrids between species of Gymnadenia and Platanthera, e.g. *G.* × *Jacksonii*. See above.

**GYMNE'MA** (*gymnos*, naked, *nema*, filament; there being no corona the filaments are exposed). Fam. *Asclepiadaceae.* A genus of about 25 species of climbing evergreen shrubs or sub-shrubs with milky sap, natives of the warmer parts of the world, with opposite leaves and small yellow flowers. The plants need stove conditions and a well-drained compost of fibrous loam and sandy peat. Cuttings of firm side shoots made in spring will root in sand in heat.

**G. lactif'erum.** *l.* ovate, bluntly slender-pointed, usually oblique; stalks short. *fl.* small, the throat of cor. crowned with 5 small fleshy tubercles; umbels shorter than l.-stalks. July. Trop. Asia. The Singalese use the sap as a substitute for cow's milk.

**G. tin'gens.** *l.* cordate to oval, slender-pointed. *fl.* pale yellow, numerous; umbels or corymbs often twin. July. Trop. Himalaya. 1823.

**GYMNIGRITEL'LA.** Fam. *Orchidaceae.* Hybrids between species of Gymnadenia and Nigritella.

**GYMNOCALY'CIUM** (*gymnos*, naked, *kalyx*, a bud; referring to the naked flower-buds). Fam. *Cactaceae.* Low, strongly ribbed plants, characterized by the 'chin', a projection of the tubercle below the areole; flowers from young areoles, bell-shaped, usually large for the size of the plants, pink, occasionally yellow; fruits oval, scaly but with no hairs or spines. All are natives of S. America. For cultivation *see* **Cactus** (terrestrial).

**G. Bodenbenderia'num.** Plant very low and wide, brownish-green, tubercles prominent; radial spines 3 to 5, black, turning grey, curved; one central pressed down on the 'chin'. *fl.* pinkish. Argentina.

**G. denuda'tum.** Plant hemispherical; ribs 5 to 8 very broad and low, hardly tuberculate; spines 5, all radial, slender, curved. *fl.* white or pale pink. Brazil, Argentina, Uruguay. (B.R.C. 3, f. 163.) Syn. *Echinocactus denudatus.*

**G. gibbo'sum.** Plants usually taller than wide, glaucous; ribs 12 to 14, strongly tuberculate; spines 7 to 12, all radial, curved. *fl.* pink. Argentina. (B.M. 3561, 4443; B.R. 137; L.B.C. 1524.) var. **caespito'sum** is a form which makes offsets at base.

**G. hybopleu'rum.** A variety of *G. multiflorum*.

**G. Kurtzia'num.** Plants round, depressed, bare at crown; ribs 10 to 18, tuberculate; radial spines 8, recurved, up to 1½ in.; one longer central. *fl.* white, reddish at base. Argentina. (B.R.C. 3, f. 174.)

**G. Leea'num.** Plants depressed, glaucous green, tuberculate; radial spines about 11, short, curved, one straight central. *fl.* large, greenish-yellow. Argentina, Uruguay. (B.M. 4184.) Syn. *Echinocactus Leeanus.*

**G. lorica'tum.** Large, low, hemispherical plants, greyish-green; ribs 13, low, rounded; spines about 7, pressed against the stem, up to 1 in. long. *fl.* pink. Argentina. Syn. *G. Spegazzinii.*

**G. Mihanovich'ii.** Plants hemispherical, greyish-green banded in red; ribs 8, prominent, tubercles low; spines 5 or 6, spreading, all radial. *fl.* yellowish-green, tinged red. Paraguay. (B.R.C. 3, f. 159.)

**G. Mos'tii.** Plants hemispherical, dark green; ribs 11 to 14, broad, strongly tuberculate; radial spines 7 to 9, one central spine, similar. *fl.* pink. Argentina. (B.R.C. 3, t. 17; Add. 83.)

**G. multiflo'rum.** Plants globular or shortly columnar; ribs 10 to 15, tuberculate; spines 7 to 10, spreading, all radial, stout, somewhat flattened. *fl.* pale pink. Brazil, Uruguay, Paraguay, Argentina. (B.R.C. 3, t. 18; B.M. 4181; Add. 83.) This plant is rather variable and a number of varieties are listed.

**G. Netrelia'num.** Plants globular, sometimes branching from the base; ribs 14, tuberculate; spines 5 to 8, all radial, very small. *fl.* lemon-yellow. Uruguay, Argentina. (B.R.C. 3, f. 160.)

**G. platen'se.** Plants small, low, depressed, dull bluish-green; ribs 8 to 12, tuberculate; spines 3 to 6, short, pressed against the stem. *fl.* whitish. Argentina. (B.R.C. 3, t. 18, 19; f. 176, 177.) Syn. *Echinocactus platensis.*

**G. Quehlia'num.** Very similar to *G. platense* and sometimes considered a variety of it.

**G. saglio'ne.** Plants often large; ribs 13 to 22, low, broad, divided into large low tubercles; spines 8 to 10, brown, 1½ in. long, curved; one or more centrals. *fl.* white or pinkish. Argentina, Bolivia. (B.R.C. 3, t. 17; f. 165.)

**G. Schickendant'zii.** Small plants; ribs 7, tuberculate; spines all radial, 6 or 7, spreading, the larger ones flattened. *fl.* white or pinkish. Argentina. (B.R.C. 3, t. 19; G.C. 33 (1903), 170.)

*Gymnocalycium multiflorum*

**G. Spegazzin'ii.** A synonym of *G. loricatum.*

**G. Stuckert'ii.** Plants globose depressed, small; ribs 9 to 11; spines all radial, flattened, spreading, up to 1 in. long. *fl.* whitish. Argentina. (B.R.C. 3, f. 180.)

V. H.

**GYMNOCLA'DUS** (*gymnos*, naked, *klados*, a branch; in reference to the branches bare of twigs during winter). Fam. *Leguminosae.* A genus of 2 deciduous trees, one N. American, the other Chinese, related to Gleditschia, with flowers in terminal panicles or racemes, the calyx tubular, 5-lobed, petals 5, equal, leaves 2-pinnate, entire, fruits large thick pods. *G. dioica* is quite hardy but grows slowly in the British Is., and flowers but seldom. It needs a deep rich loam. *G. chinensis* is tender and likely to grow outdoors only in the mildest parts. The name Coffee-tree applied to *G. dioica* comes from the seeds having been used as a substitute for coffee by the early settlers in N. America.

**G. canaden'sis.** A synonym of *G. dioica.*

**G. chinen'sis.** Soap-tree. Tree up to 40 ft. h. *lflets.* smaller than in *G. dioica*, hairy on both surfaces. *fl.* lilac-purple, before l., perfect and unisexual fl. on same tree. *fr.* 3 to 4 in. long, very thick, containing a soft substance, used by the Chinese women for washing the face. China. 1888. (H.I.P. 1412.)

**G. dioi'ca.*** Kentucky Coffee Tree. A tree up to 60 ft. h. with a narrow rounded head, shoots downy when young. *l.* up to 3 ft. long, 2 ft. wide, with 3 to 7 pairs of pinnae; lflets. ovate, 1½ to 2½ in. long, lowest pairs larger. *fl.* dioecious, greenish-white; female panicles 8 to 12 in. long, male 2½ to 4 in. June. E. and Cent. U.S.A. 1748. (R.H. 1897, 491.) Young leaves pink, autumn colour clear yellow. A very fine foliage tree. var. **variega'ta**, *l.* marked with white spots.

**GYMNOGRAM'MA** (*gymnos*, naked, *gramma*, writing; referring to the sporangia). Fam. *Polypodiaceae.* A genus of about 60 species of ferns resembling Cheilanthes in habit and growth, sori linear, without indusia, veins free, fronds not powdery below. Most of the species seen under this name belong to Pityrogramma. For treatment *see* **Pityrogramma.**

**G. flexuo'sa.** *sti.* 6 to 18 in. long, flexuose, slender. *Fronds* 3 to 4 ft. long, scandent, 3- to 4-pinnate; pinnae reflexed, outline subdeltoid; segs. flabellately branched; rachis zigzag, branched. Cent. America to Peru. 1865.

**G. Matthew'sii.** *sti.* 4 to 6 in. long, dark chestnut-brown, densely brown-hairy. *Fronds* 3-pinnatifid, leathery, 1 to 1½ ft. long, 4 to 5 in. broad, oblong-lanceolate; pinnae 2 in. long, 1 in. broad, cut to midrib below into oblong, blunt pinnules, with broad, rounded lobes, hairy both sides. *Sori* brown. Peru. (H.S. 5, 290.)

**GYMNOLO'MIA** (*gymnos*, naked, *loma*, fringe; the pappus is much reduced or absent). FAM. *Compositae*. A genus of about 16 species of erect herbs, mostly natives of Mexico and Cent. America. Lower leaves rarely almost all opposite, upper rarely almost all alternate, entire, toothed or lobed. Flower-heads stalked, solitary or in a loose corymb. Half-hardy or greenhouse plants. For cultivation *see* **Helianthus.**

G. macula'ta. A synonym of *Wulffia maculata.*

G. multiflo'ra. Annual 1 to 3 ft. h. *l.* narrow linear to lanceolate. *fl.-heads* yellow. Autumn. New Mexico. SYN. *Heliomeris multiflora.*

G. triplinerv'ia. About 3 ft. h. *l.* ovate, with a narrow point, crenate, 3-nerved, hispidly hairy on both sides; stalked. *fl.-heads* yellow, axillary, long-pedunculate; pappus crown-like. July to September. Bogota. 1825. SYN. *Gymnopsis triplinervia.*

**GYMNOPET'ALUM** (*gymnos*, naked, *petalon*). FAM. *Cucurbitaceae*. A genus of about 6 species of tendril climbers, natives of Trop. Asia and Java. *G. cochinchinensis* is grown for its ornamental fruits (gourds) and needs the same treatment as Momordica.

G. cochinchinen'sis. Slender climber, stems grooved, much branched, tendrils filiform. *l.* 1 to 3 in. long, 1 to 2 in. wide. *fl.* white, small, monoecious; cal. teeth long, linear-awl-shaped; cal. hairy. *fr.* bright red, ovoid, 10-ribbed, narrow at base, and produced into a long point at apex. Java. SYN. *Scotanthus tubiformis.*

F. G. P.

**GYMNOP'TERIS** (*gymnos*, naked, *pteris*, fern; referring to the absence of indusia). FAM. *Polypodiaceae*. A genus of 9 species of ferns closely related to Gymnogramma with hairy pinnate fronds. Sori long linear, along the veins, without indusia. The fronds are devoid of powder which is so attractive a feature in some of the species of closely related genera but the reddish or silvery hairs which cover them make them equally attractive.

G. his'pida. *rhiz.* creeping. *sti.* 3 to 6 in. long, pilose. *Fronds* deltoid, 3-pinnatifid, 2 to 3 in. each way; lower pinnae much the largest, cut to rachis; upper pinnules close, ligulate, blunt, with pale brown tomentum beneath; rachis scaly. New Mexico. SYN. *Gymnogramma hispida.*

G. Muel'leri. *sti.* wiry, 3 to 4 in. long, densely clothed with rusty-brown scales. *Fronds* pinnate, 4 to 10 in. long, 1 to 3½ in. broad; pinnae sessile, roundish or oblong, 1½ in. long, ½ in. broad, entire, thick, leathery, lower often auricled; densely matted beneath with brownish scales. *Sori* abundant, narrow, in several rows nearer margin than midrib, eventually connivent. Australia. (H.S. 5, 295; B.C.F. 2, 264.) SYN. *Gymnogramma Muelleri.* Greenhouse or Stove. When young resembles *Ceterach officinarum.*

G. ru'fa. *sti.* tufted, 4 to 12 in. long, hairy. *Fronds* 12 to 18 in. long, 3 to 5 in. broad, pinnate; pinnae distant, stalked, rounded, 1 to 2½ in. long; rachis pilose. Trop. America. 1793. (L.F. 1, 6.) SYN. *Gymnogramma rufa.*

G. tomento'sa. *sti.* tufted, 6 to 12 in. long, villose. *Fronds* 6 to 12 in. long, deltoid, 2-pinnate; upper pinnae simple, stalked, 1 to 2 in. long, ½ to 1 in. broad; lower 1 to 4 in. long. Brazil to Peru. 1831. (L.F. 1, 6.) SYN. *Gymnogramma tomentosa.*

G. vesti'ta.* *sti.* wiry, 3 to 6 in. long, densely clothed with matted, rusty-brown, silky scales. *Fronds* 6 to 12 in. long, 1 to 1½ in. broad, pinnate; pinnae opposite or alternate, close to midrib with a little space between each, entire, bluntish, oblong or cordate at base, thick but flaccid, covered on both sides with velvety hairs, at first silvery, afterwards rusty-brown. *Sori* usually forked, over whole under-surface. China, N. India. Stove or greenhouse. (B.C.F. 2, 277.) SYN. *Gymnogramma vestita.*

**GYMNOSPERM'AE.** One of the 2 great divisions of the flowering or seed-bearing plants, the other being the Angiospermae. It is characterized by the ovules not being enclosed in an ovary (naked) and by the absence of a perianth, except in the Gnetaceae. Cotyledons 2 or more, flowers strictly 1-sexual. The Gymnosperms include, in addition to families known only as fossils, the Cycadaceae, Ginkgoaceae, Gnetaceae, and Pinaceae and Taxaceae which together form the class Coniferae.

**GYMNOSPORANG'IUM.** A genus of Rust fungi (Uredinales). Nearly all the species are heteroecious, forming their teleutospores on Cupressus and Junipers and the aecidial stage on members of the Rosaceae. A common one in Great Britain is *G. clavariaeforme* which alternates between *Juniperus communis* and Hawthorns.

The aecidial stage is often seen on ornamental Hawthorns on which the twigs are swollen and distorted and cluster cups are easily seen on the swollen parts. On the Juniper the other stage causes swelling of the affected parts and bladder-like structures then grow out and release the teleutospores. At all times either stage when seen should be cut out and burnt.

D. E. G.

**GYMNOSTACH'YS** (*gymnos*, naked, *stachys*, spike; from the leafless scape). FAM. *Araceae*. A genus of a single Australian tuberous-rooted perennial herb with grass-like leaves and a flattened naked scape as long as the leaves with clusters of spikes near its apex, each with a leafy bract at its base. Greenhouse temperature suits it, and a compost of peat and loam.

G. an'ceps. Root a fusiform tuber. *l.* erect, grass-like, rather rigid, 1 to 3 ft. long, veins prominent. *fl.* white, small, rather scattered on the spike; perianth segs. ovate, short; spikes 1 to 3 in. long, curved or drooping. Australia. 1820.

**GYMNOSTACH'YUM** (*gymnos*, naked, *stachys*, spike). FAM. *Acanthaceae*. A genus of about 25 species of erect evergreen shrubs, natives of Malaya and the E. Indies. Leaves sometimes near base of stem, entire or nearly so, sometimes prettily marked. Flowers tubular in erect spike-like racemes. The following are mainly of value in the stove for their foliage. For cultivation *see* **Eranthemum.**

G. ceylan'icum. Stem very short, downy. *l.* oval or obovate, spreading horizontally, long-stalked, dark green with midrib and main veins banded white. *fl.* white, tipped green and yellow, in scattered clusters on the 1 ft.-long raceme. Winter. Ceylon. (B.M. 4706.)

G. decur'rens. Stems short, branching. *l.* ovate, 4 in. long, 2 in. wide, abruptly contracted into the stalk, often with whitish band along the purplish midrib. *fl.* white, lined violet in a terminal panicle of many-fld. spikes. Malaya. 1894.

G. venus'tum. About 5 in. h. *l.* ovate, long-pointed, 4 to 6 in. long; l.-stalk winged. *fl.* deep purple about 1 in. long in a large downy panicle about 8 in. long, 12 in. wide, rarely in a simple spike. September. Khasia Hills. (B.R. 1380 as *Justicia venusta.*)

**GYM'NOTHRIX, GYMNOTRIX.** See **Pennisetum.**

**GYNAECEUM.** Pistil or female organ of flower.

**GYNANDROP'SIS** (*gyne*, female, *andros*, male, *opsis*, appearance; the stamens appear to be inserted on top of the ovary). FAM. *Capparidaceae*. A genus of about 12 species of annual herbs, natives of the tropics, closely related to Cleome, but with a long (not short) gynophore, 6 (not 4 to 10) stamens, 3 to 7 leaflets, and white or purplish flowers. Cool greenhouse or half-hardy plants with similar requirements to Cleome.

G. coccin'ea. 6 to 9 ft. h. *l.* palmatipartite, long-stalked. *fl.* scarlet in a many-fld. terminal raceme. Summer. Colombia. 1878. (I.H. 1878, 310.) Cool house.

G. pentaphyl'la. 2 ft. h., not spiny. *l.* quinate; segs. obovate-lanceolate or elliptic-lanceolate. *fl.* white; pet. obovate, 4 times as long as cal.; stamens attached about middle of gynophore. June, July. E. and W. Indies. 1640. Greenhouse. (B.M. 1681 as *Cleome pentaphylla.*)

G. specio'sa. About 2 ft. h., rather velvety near top. *l.*flets. 5 to 7, oblong, slender-pointed, somewhat toothed. *fl.* violet, showy. Mexico. SYN. *Cleome speciosa* of H.B.K.

**gynandrous,** having stamens and pistil united in a column, as in, e.g. orchids.

**GYNE'RIUM** (*gyne*, female, *erion*, wool; referring to the hairy spikelets of the female plants). FAM. *Gramineae*. A small genus of aquatic reed-grasses closely allied to Cortaderia but with leaves distributed along the stems instead of being crowded at the base. Being a native of Trop. America, it needs a warm greenhouse where it may be grown in a large pot standing in water. The large plumes are attractive.

G. argen'teum. See **Cortaderia argentea.**

G. juba'tum. See **Cortaderia Quila.**

**G. saccharoi'des.** *See* **G. sagittatum.**

**G. sagitta'tum.** Moa Grass. Coarse reed-grass 12 to 30 ft. h., with creeping rootstock, stem tufted, about 1 in. thick at base. *l.* about 5 ft. long, 1 in. wide, distributed up the stem, the lower soon dying. *Panicle* 5 to 6 ft. long, arched. September. Trop. America. 1894. (B.M. 7352 as *G. saccharoides.*)

**GYNOPHORE.** The stalk of an ovary within the calyx.

**GYNOPLEU'RA** (*gyne*, female, *pleura*, side; the style arises from the side of the ovary). FAM. *Passifloraceae.* A genus of about 7 species of hairy herbs, shrubby at base, natives of Chile. Leaves alternate, sessile, linear, oblong or spatulate, entire, with wavy teeth, or subpinnatifid. Flowers yellow or blue, often showy, in clusters or panicles; calyx tube straight or slightly curved, bell- or top-shaped, lobes 5, oblong; petals obovate or spatulate, broader than calyx lobes; corona slightly toothed; stamens 5. The species described below are best treated as annual herbs for the greenhouse or garden and grown in a compost of sandy peat and fibrous loam with a little leaf-mould, the seed being sown in March.

**G. hu'milis.** Low-growing, slender, much-branched annual. *l.* obovate-oblong, about 1 in. long, blunt, coarsely toothed, narrowed to base, pale green, silky-hairy. *fl.* white, striped purplish-red, about $\frac{3}{8}$ in. across, crowded in corymbs at tips of branches. September. Chile. 1898. (B.M. 7645.) Hardy.

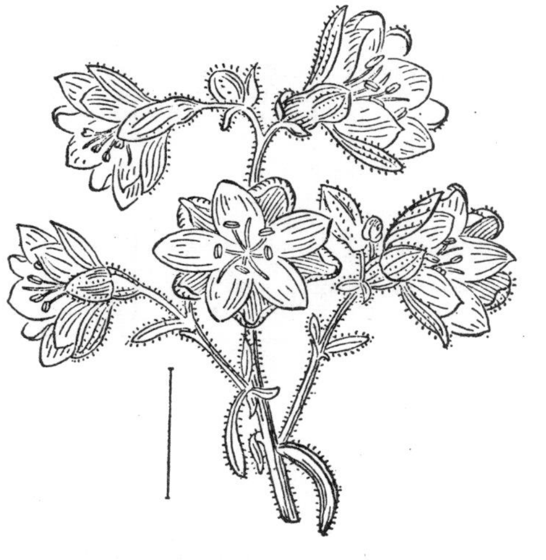

*Gynopleura linearifolia*

**G. linearifo'lia.** 12 to 18 in. h. *l.* linear, 2 to 3 in. long, blunt, toothed, recurved. *fl.* greenish-purple with 5 inner segs. pale purplish-blue; panicle several-fld. September. Chile. 1831. (B.M. 3362 as *Malesherbia linearifolia.*)

**GYNOPO'GON.** A synonym of Alyxia.

**GYNU'RA** (*gyne*, female, *oura*, tail; the stigma is long and rough). FAM. *Compositae.* A genus of about 20 species of perennial herbs, natives of the tropics of the Old World. Leaves alternate, sometimes toothed or pinnately lobed or dissected. Flower-heads solitary or in corymbs at ends of branches, receptacle flat, pitted or shortly fibrillose, involucral bracts 10 to 12, narrow, in 1 series. A compost of sandy loam and peat suits them and they may be propagated by cuttings.

**G. auranti'aca.*** 2 to 3 ft. h. Stem and *l.* covered with small violet hairs, shown especially on young l. around fl.-head. *fl.-heads* brilliant orange, about $\frac{1}{2}$ in. wide; florets tubular. February. Java. 1880. (I.H. 436.) Half-hardy. var. **ova'lis,** *fl.-heads* yellow. E. Indies. (B.R. 101 as *Cacalia ovalis.*)

**G. bi'color.** 2 to 3 ft. h., erect. *l.* broad- or ovate-lanceolate, slightly downy, rather thin, purple beneath; stalk short. *fl.-heads* short, terminal, involucre cylindrical, florets orange, tubular, slightly swelling. Moluccas. 1799. (B.M. 5123.)

**G. sarmento'sa.** Loosely twining. Stem reddish. *l.* ovate, elliptic, or lanceolate, more or less acute, almost entire or with wavy teeth; stalked or upper sessile. *fl.-heads* dull orange, numerous, narrow, $\frac{1}{2}$ in. long, in panicles. India. 1892. (B.M. 7244.)

***gypsic'ola,*** living on limestone.

**GYPSOPH'ILA** (*gypsos*, gypsum, *philos*, friendship; *G. repens* occurs on gypsum rocks). FAM. *Caryophyllaceae.* A genus of about 50 species mainly in the eastern Mediterranean region, one widely distributed in Australia and New Zealand. Annual or perennial herbs or subshrubs allied to Dianthus but with membranous stripes between the sepals, and to Tunica (q.v.). Leaves linear to lanceolate, opposite, often blue-green. Inflorescence many-flowered, corymbose or panicled. Flower small, 5-partite, sometimes dioecious; calyx bell-shaped or widened at the mouth; petals more or less spreading without scales at the base of blades, white or bright rose; stamens 10, free; styles 2 or 3; ovary 1-celled. Growing well in dryish soil, and tolerant of lime, and doing well when old brick rubbish is mixed with the soil. The root run should be deep for the roots are large, and the site a sunny one. All except the double-flowered forms are readily raised from seed, and all may be increased by cuttings of either shoots or roots. The varieties of *G. paniculata* may be grafted on roots of that species or cuttings of side branches made as soon as they begin to harden may be rooted in sand. All are hardy though some larger species may suffer in very severe winters. **A**

**G. acutifo'lia.** Habit of *G. paniculata* but fl. larger. Perennial. Stem erect or ascending, 1 to 3 ft. h., smooth, branched from base. *l.* broadly lanceolate to linear-lanceolate, very sharply pointed, mostly 3-nerved, blue-green, entire. *fl.* white to rose, 2 or 3 times as large as in *G. paniculata* in light, graceful panicles; cal. white with 5 reddish or greenish stripes. July, August. E. and S. Russia, Caucasus. Grown also for the Saponine in the thick root. Border.

**G. alpige'na.** Densely tufted perennial closely allied to *G. repens,* but only about 1 in. h.; fl. usually solitary. Pyrenees, Java. Rock-garden.

**G. arietioi'des.** Dense mat-forming with habit of *Silene exscapa. l.* grey-green, very small. *fl.* freely produced, pearl-white. Mts. of Persia. 1920. var. **caucas'ica,** smaller and even more compact than type. Caucasus. 1935. Rock-garden.

**G. cerastioi'des.** Tufted green perennial, about 2 or 3 in. h. *Lower l.* spatulate, on long petioles; *upper* obovate. *fl.* white, red-veined, about $\frac{3}{8}$ in. across, in loose corymbs; pet. notched. May to October. Himalaya. (B.M. 6699.)

**G. curvifo'lia.** Stems about 18 in. long. Related to *G. libanotica* which it much resembles but l. awl-shaped, $\frac{1}{3}$ to 1 in. long, and cal. teeth more acute, cal. about $\frac{1}{7}$ in. long. *fl.* summer. Asia Minor.

**G. el'egans.*** Glabrous annual, 12 to 20 in. h. with much-branched, spreading panicles. *l.* near base oblong-spatulate, the upper linear-lanceolate, acute, connate at base. *fl.* rose or pink; cal. hemispherical, teeth ovate; pet. wedge-shaped, about $\frac{1}{5}$ in. long; pedicels long, slender. May to September. Asia Minor. 1828. Variable in colour. var. **al'ba,** *fl.* white; **al'ba grandiflo'ra,** *fl.* white, larger than type; **carmin'ea,** *fl.* deep pink; **kermesi'na,** *fl.* bright pink; **ro'sea,** *fl.* rose. *See* **G. silenoides.**

**G. fastigia'ta.** Perennial, sometimes sub-shrubby, branched from base with many non-flowering shoots and erect, almost simple fl.-stems 12 to 18 in. h., whitish-hairy above. *l.* linear, rather thick, lower $1\frac{1}{2}$ to 3 in. long. *fl.* white or reddish, in a flat corymb; cal. bell-shaped, smooth; pet. obcuneate, about $\frac{1}{8}$ in. long, rounded. June to August. Cent. Europe. 1801. (F.d.S. 131.)

**G. frankenioi'des.** Glandular-downy, prostrate, tufted perennial, about 5 in. h., with slender branches. *l.* clustered, awl-shaped, about $\frac{1}{2}$ in. long. *fl.* pink, solitary in upper axils of shoots and terminal; cal. tubular-bell-shaped, teeth oblong; pet. wedge-shaped. June to September. Lebanon.

**G. fraten'sis.** *See* **G. repens.**

**G. glauc'a.** Habit of *G. repens*, 3 to 4 in. h. *l.* linear, about $\frac{1}{2}$ in. long, fleshy, obtuse, almost without nerves. *infl.* glandular; cal. about $\frac{1}{8}$ in. long, whitish-downy. *fl.* similar to *G. repens.* Caucasus.

**G. libanot'ica.** Perennial with woody base, about 10 in. h., blue-green with numerous slender oblong panicles, often clammy. *l.* fleshy, rigid, oblong, about $\frac{3}{8}$ in. long. *fl.* pink on filiform pedicels; cal. bell-shaped, teeth acute. July to September. Lebanon.

**G. Mangin'i.** Perennial with thick, fleshy roots with habit of *G. acutifolia. l.* smooth, blue-green. *fl.* pale-rose, rather large, in small panicles. Siberia. 1898.

**G. microphyl'la.** Prostrate perennial. *l.* clustered, linear, about $\frac{1}{8}$ in. long or less, obtuse, ciliate at base. *fl.* in few-fld. terminal cymes; pet. white, scarcely $\frac{1}{4}$ in. long. Siberia.

**G.×monstro'sa** (*G. repens*×*G. Steveni*). Taller than *G. repens* with more branches. *infl.* making growth up to 3 ft. Rock-garden.

**G. mura'lis.** Annual with very slender much-branched stems about 6 in. h., smooth or somewhat downy. *l.* linear, about ½ in. long, narrowed to both ends. *fl.* pink, veined; cal. bell-shaped, teeth rounded; pet. obovate. July to October. Cent. Europe, Asia Minor, Siberia. (F.G. 381.) Border and walls.

**G. na'na.** Tufted perennial, clammy-hairy. *l.* elliptic-linear, narrowed to base. *fl.* 1 to 5 from axils of upper l. or terminal; cal. teeth to beyond middle, oblong, obtuse; pet. rose, obovate, notched, 2½ times as long as cal. Summer. Greece.

**G. Oldhamia'na.** Glabrous perennial from a woody rootstock, up to 30 in. h., stems panicled above. *l.* narrow-oblong to oblong-lanceolate from a wedge-shaped base, 1½ to 3 in. long, rather leathery, dull grey-green. *fl.* pink or deep pink, fragrant, in a large panicle up to 12 in. long; cor. about ⅓ in. across; pet. oblanceolate, rounded at apex. August. NE. Asia, Manchuria, Korea. 1911. (B.M. 9484.) Hardy.

**G. ortegioi'des.** Perennial, with numerous much-branched stems, 8 to 20 in. h., pruinose. *l.* awl-shaped, up to ⅜ in. long. *fl.* sessile in terminal racemes; cal. obconic-tubular, about ⅛ in. long, teeth lanceolate; pet. obovate, white with purple veins, small. September. Syria.

**G. pacif'ica.** Perennial, with habit of *G. paniculata*, up to 4 ft. h. *fl.* pink, large. September. Siberia.

**G. panicula'ta.*** Perennial with deep thick roots, more or less blue-green. Stem 15 in. to 4 ft. h., generally 4-angled, mostly smooth. *l.* lanceolate to linear-lanceolate, about 2½ in. long, sessile, usually 3-nerved, margin rough, tip acute. *fl.* very small, white or sometimes pinkish, in very large, loose panicles; cal. shortly bell-shaped, deeply lobed with roundish ovate teeth; pet. oblong, obtuse; pedicels smooth, filiform. June to August. E. Europe, Siberia. 1759. var. **Bristol Fairy,*** more robust than var. **flore ple'no,** *fl.* double, white, panicles larger, produced earlier than in older double form. 1925; **compac'ta,** less tall and spreading than type; **flore ple'no,** *fl.* double; **Rosenchleirer,*** 1½ ft. h., compact, bushy, *fl.* double, ⅓ in. across, at first white, later rosy-pink. 1935. SYN. var. Rosy Veil.

**G. perfolia'ta.** Habit of *G. paniculata* but usually taller, much branched from base, smooth. *Lower l.* oblong-lanceolate to ovate-lanceolate, 3 to 4 in. long, about 1 in. wide, clasping stem at base. *fl.* twice as large as those of *G. paniculata* in much-branched, loose, many-fld. panicles. July, August. Spain. 1817.

**G. petrae'a.** Tufted grey-green perennial, creeping and woody at base. *Basal l.* in rosettes at lower part of fl.-stem linear, thickish, 1 to 2 in. long. Stem erect or ascending, 4 to 6 in. h., with 2 or 3 pairs of l., the lower as long as the basal l., the upper much shorter; nodes tinged violet. *fl.* white, in half-round to oblong heads; cal. bell-shaped, violet-tinged nerves; pet. ovate. June to August. Carpathian Mts. SYN. *Banffya petraea, G. transsylvanica.*

**G. prostra'ta.** A synonym of *G. repens.*

**G. re'pens.*** Perennial to half-shrubby forming a large tufted plant with long rootstock, much branched, with many non-flowering shoots. Stems 3 to 6 in. h., smooth, often tinged reddish, with loose corymbs. *l.* lanceolate-linear, 1-nerved, sea-green, somewhat fleshy. *fl.* about ⅓ in. across, white or rose; cal. teeth ovate-oblong, with purplish-red middle nerve; pet. obovate-cuneate. June to August. European Alps. 1774. (B.M. 1448.) SYN. *G. prostrata.* var. **fraten'sis,** near var. *rosea*, but of denser habit with reddish-brown stems; **monstro'sa,** *see* **G.×monstrosa**; **ro'sea,** *fl.* rose-pink.

**G. Rokejek'a.** Glabrous, blue-green, perennial 15 to 24 in. h., woody at the base. Stem slender, branched from base. *l.* fleshy, 1-nerved, lower oblanceolate-oblong, obtuse, upper linear-lanceolate, acute, often channelled. *fl.* pink to violet, in loose panicles; cal. bell-shaped; pet. elliptical-oblong about ⅛ in. long. March to May. Arabia, Egypt, Syria.

**G. scorzonerifo'lia.** Habit of *G. paniculata.* Grey-green perennial, sometimes hairy below. Stem robust, cylindrical. *l.* broad-oblong, 5-nerved, connate at base, obtuse. *fl.* purple, small, in much-branched loose panicles; cal. teeth ovate, obtuse, pet. shorter than cal. July to September. SE. Europe to Cent. Asia.

**G. silenoi'des.** Similar to *G. elegans* but perennial. Asia Minor.

**G. Ste'veni.** Perennial. Allied to *G. repens* but taller, up to 2 ft. h., with fl. only about half size of *G. repens*; pet. broad-linear, entire. July. Caucasus. 1818.

**G. Struth'ium.** Prostrate, much-branched perennial, branches longer than in *G. repens* and twisted, the leafy shoots many, short. *l.* narrow-linear, 3-angled, fleshy, acute. *fl.* rose, clustered; pet. small, spatulate twice as long as obtuse sep. S. Europe. Liable to cross with *G. repens.*

**G.×Sundermannii*** (*G. petraea*×*G. repens*). Distinct from *G. petraea* by its looser infl. and from *G. repens* by the longer linear l., the denser infl., and smaller fl. *fl.* white. Of garden origin. 1898.

**G. transsylvan'ica.** A synonym of *G. petraea.*

**G. trichot'oma.** A synonym of *G. scorzonerifolia.*

***gy'rans,*** revolving.

***gyrobul'bon,*** having spirally twisted bulbs.

***gyro'sus -a -um,*** gyrose, bent backwards and forwards like the anthers of Cucurbitaceae.

# H

***Haagea'nus -a -um,*** in honour of J. N. Haage, 1826–78, of Erfurt, seed-growers.

***Haast'ii,*** in honour of Sir Johann Franz Julius von Haast, 1824–87, Government geologist, who collected plants in New Zealand.

**HABENA'RIA** (*habena*, a thong or strap; the spur is long and strap-shaped in some, not all, species). FAM. *Orchidaceae.* Habenaria and Platanthera though kept separate by some are so closely allied that horticulturally no good purpose would be served by separating them. So close is the resemblance that species have been transferred from one genus to the other and then replaced; in fact Dr. Lindley, though dividing Platanthera into sections, said that the only ground for separation was the absence of fleshy processes on the lower part of the stigma in Platanthera and their presence in Habenaria. Bonatea is often included under Habenaria and is only treated separately in this work because long usage has familiarized the generic name; as with Platanthera, it is difficult to distinguish it readily from Habenaria. The group is widely distributed in both hemispheres, Platanthera more widely perhaps in the cool and subtropical zones, Habenaria in the warmer regions. It is difficult to estimate the number of species: 600 have been computed, but that number is probably exceeded. The common characters are: Tubers or, in some species, fleshy roots, from which spring erect flowering stems usually leafy or bracteose; flowers spicate or racemose, few or many, usually white, or white and green, sepals sub-equal, free, or cohering towards the base, the petals often smaller, sometimes narrow, sometimes deeply 2-lobed, the upper halves often helping with the dorsal sepal to form a hood over the column, lip continuous, and often very shortly connate with the column, the blade spreading or tapered, pendulous in many, entire or in 3 to 5 divisions. In several species the side divisions have their outer margins pectinate, fringed, or ciliate. The lip is produced into a spur usually long and slender, occasionally short and saccate. Column short without a foot. Rostellum often strangely modified, sometimes rivalling the petals in development, particularly in Bonatea. The leaves may be 2, broad and comparatively large at the base of the stem, or narrower, tapered, forming a rosette, or they may ascend the stem. A few species are decidedly of horticultural value from the beauty and almost fantastic shape of the flowers, though bright colouring is absent from the group, if a few species—*H. carnea* and its allies—from the East are excepted. Our British species are well worth growing if only for the delicious scent of their flowers. They are not particular as to soil, but should have a moderately shady and well-drained though damp position. It is probable that other species could be acclimatized if obtained from countries with temperatures and a winter season coinciding with our own. Compost for exotic species of warm climates may be made of 1 part of cut Osmunda fibre, 2 of fibrous loam, and 1 of Sphagnum moss cut fine and well mixed with a little coarse sand or finely crushed crocks. The size of the pots must be varied according to the dimensions the species attain. A 3½- or 4-in. pot is large enough for the smaller species, a 5- to 7-in. size will be required for the larger forms. Drainage must be good. The tuber should be placed from ½ to 1 in. below the surface of the compost. Once growth begins, disturbance should be avoided and water must not be given too frequently; allow the compost to become moderately dry between applications until vigour of growth denotes full root-action, then water liberally. Shading will be required, but after flowering, as the growth begins to die, decrease the frequency of the waterings, and when growth is decayed, or just before, place on a shelf in a light position. Water may be occasionally required in the winter to prevent the tubers from shrivelling, particularly with those tropical African and eastern species which require a warm temperature. Their winter temperature should not fall below 60° F. If well ripened and away from the hot-water pipes water may not be required. Thrips and red spider must be combatted by light fumigations, the use of the syringe, or dipping; with due care the last method is preferable. Propagation is slow as the tubers seldom develop more than 1 new one each season. A number of species should succeed well in a greenhouse with a winter temperature of 45 to 50° F., but like many other tuberous-rooted orchids Habenarias are not as a whole very amenable under cultivation.

For natural hybrids between Habenaria and allied genera see Gymnaglossum, Gymnaplatanthera, Orchicoeloglossum, Orchiplatanthera, and Orchiseraphias.

**H. bifo'lia.** *fl.* white, fragrant; *pet.* connivent, blunt; lip, linear, entire; anther cells parallel; spur twice length of ovary; spike slender. June to August. *l.* at base 2, elliptic; stem-*l.* smaller. 12 in. h. Europe, including Britain, N. Africa, N. Asia. SYN. *Platanthera bifolia.*

**H. blephariglot'tis.** *fl.* white, beautifully fringed, spur long, slender, borne in spikes. Very similar to *H. ciliaris* but stronger. May, June. N. America. 1820. (L.B.C. 925.)

**H. Bona'tea.** A synonym of *Bonatea speciosa.*

**H. can'dida.** A synonym of *H. subpubens.*

**H. car'nea.*** *fl.* larger than in *H. pusilla*; helmet beautiful pink; lip deeply cleft and darker than sep. and pet.; spur 1½ in. long; scape erect, 12 in. h., 3- to 5-fld. *l.* small, dark green, thickly spotted white. Penang. 1891. Stove. (J.R.H.S. 16, ccix.) var. **nivo'sa,** *fl.* white, *l.* not spotted. SYN. *H. carnea alba.*

**H. chloran'tha.** *fl.* white, larger than in *H. bifolia,* anther cells spreading at base. May, June. Taller and stouter than *H. bifolia.* Europe, including Britain, N. Asia. (E.B. 1463.) SYN. *Platanthera chlorantha.*

**H. cilia'ris.*** *fl.* orange-yellow or whitish, fragrant, in dense clusters; lip beautifully fringed; pet. denticulate. 18 to 24 in. h. N. America. 1796. (B.M. 1668.)

**H. cinnabari'na.** *fl.* orange-red, backs of sep. spotted red; densely clustered; scape erect, 6 in. h. *l.* erect, linear, 6 in. long. Madagascar. 1893. Stove.

**H. conop'sea.** *See* **Gymnadenia conopsea.**

**H. crista'ta.** *fl.* 10 to 20, much smaller than in *H. ciliaris,* golden yellow; lip deeply fringed; spur thin, shorter than ovary. Late spring. 12 in. h. N. America. 1806. (L.B.C. 1661.)

**H. decip'iens.** *fl.* 1½ in. long, with a pendent spur 4 to 5 in. long; lip white, much longer than the green sep., cuneate, 3-lobed; pedicels long; scapes erect, few-fld. September to November. *l.* radical, Plantain-like. India. Before 1891. (B.M. 7228 as *H. longecalcarata.*) Cool house.

**H. denta'ta.*** *fl.* pure white, 10 or more, about 1 in. across the sep.; dorsal sep. hooding the smaller pet.; lateral sep. divergent, their lower margins rounded; the upper straight, tapered; lip narrow at base then broadly reniform, nearly 1 in. wide, side lobes with denticulate margins; mid-lobe linear; spur 1½ in. long, white passing into green. Stem about 24 in. h., glaucous green, clothed above with sheathing bracts. *l.* 4 or 5, at intervals, the largest placed centrally, 4 in. long by 1 in. wide, tapered, glaucous green. India, Burma. (A.B.G.C. 8, 405; B.M. 9663.) SYN. *H. geniculata.*

**H. dilata'ta.** *fl.* 10 to 20, white, in dense slender spikes. Summer. *l.* narrow. 12 to 24 in. h. N. America. 1823. (H.E.F. 2, 95.)

**H. Elliot'tii.** *fl.* green; spur long, thin. *l.* bright green, lanceolate, on strong stem. Madagascar. 1897. Stove.

**H. Elwes'ii.** *fl.* greenish-yellow, 2 in. long; pet. bifurcate from base; lip glabrous, with 3-filiform segs.; raceme lax-fld. *l.* erect. Nilghiri Hills. 1896. (B.M. 7478.) Hardy?

**H. fimbria'ta.*** *fl.* many, lilac-purple, prettily fringed, on a long spike. Summer. Stem 12 to 24 in. h. *l.* 2 to 6 in. long. N. America. 1789. (B.R. 405.)

**H. folio'sa.** *See* **Orchis foliosa.**

**H. genicula'ta.** A synonym of *H. dentata.*

**H. gigan'tea.** A synonym of *H. Susannae.*

**H. Haviland'ii.** *fl.* 14 to 20, green with a white lip. Stems 2 ft. h. *l.* 12 in. long by 2½ in. wide. Borneo. Before 1915.

**H. Hellebori'na.*** *fl.* green, flesh-colour, sessile, distant, horizontal; lip much larger than sep. or pet., semi-circular; column short, broad, concealed under the dorsal sep. and pet. September. *l.* oblong-lanceolate, sub-acute, not plaited, 5-nerved, deep green. Sierra Leone. 1870. (B.M. 5875 as *Eulophia Helleborina.*) Stove.

**H. Hookeria'na.** *fl.* greenish-white. Spikes slender, 20- to 30-fld., 6 to 12 in. h. or more. *l.* 2, rounded, large, often 6 in. across. June. America. 1822. (L.B.C. 1623 as *H. orbiculata.*)

**H. inci'sa.** *fl.* rich purple, small, fragrant, thickly set in oblong, terminal racemes. June. Stem-*l.* obtusely lanceolate, deep green. 1 to 1½ ft. h. N. America. 1826. SYN. *Platanthera incisa.*

**H. leonen'sis.** A synonym of *H. subpubens.*

**H. longecalcara'ta.** A synonym of *H. decipiens.*

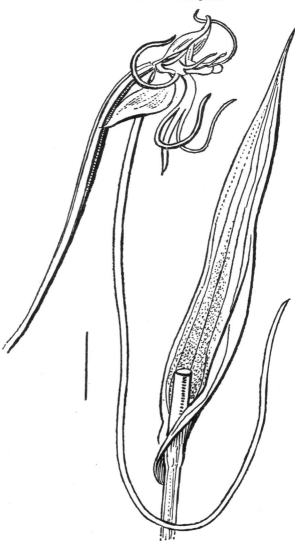

*Habenaria longicauda*

**H. longicau'da.*** *fl.* greenish-white; lateral sep. ¾ to 1 in. long; dorsal hooded; pet. divided, the upper division connivent with the dorsal sep. the lower 1 in. long, very narrow, slightly longer than the upper; side lobes of lip over 1 in. long, linear, mid-lobe slightly shorter and wider, linear; spur slightly compressed, 6 to 10 in. long. Stem, robust, leafy, 18 to 36 in. long including the raceme. *l.* narrow, 6 to 10 in. long. Guiana. 1830. (B.M. 2957.)

**H. Lugard'ii.*** *fl.* 12 to 20 or more, white and greenish; sep. reflexed; pet. hooded; lip narrowly 3-lobed; spur drooping, 8 in. long, white tinted in places with green, almost transparent. Stem about 2 ft. h., the *fl.* rather closely set and mixed with lanceolate bracts. *l.* 2, 4 in. long, 6 in. wide, sub-orbicular, flat on the compost. S. Cent. Africa. (B.M. 7798.) Watering, as with others of similar habit, should be effected by immersing the pot to the rim as required. A handsome species.

**H. macran'tha.** Very similar to *H. splendens* but distinct by its smaller *fl.* and the relatively longer free portion of the stigmatic arms. Abyssinia, Arabia.

**H. macrocerati'lis.*** *fl.* greenish-white; sep. and pet. nearly ½ in. long, upper sep. concave, lower ovate-oblong; pet. divided, upper portion connivent with the dorsal sep., lower longer, ascending or arched, 1 in. long, narrow, lobes of lip narrow, 2 outer 1 in. long, strongly curved, mid-lobe shorter and broader; spur slender, 4 to 6 in. long. Stem leafy, 15 to 30 in. h. *l.* 3 to 6 in. long, 1 to 3 in. wide. Surinam, W. Indies, Costa Rica, Mexico, &c. 1805. (B.M. 2947 as *H. macroceras.*) SYN. *Orchis Habenaria, O. longicornu.*

**H. milita'ris.** A synonym of *H. pusilla.*

**H. orbicula'ta.** A synonym of *H. Hookeriana.*

**H. proce'ra.** *fl.* 12 to 30, white, 1 to 1½ in. long, tips of sep. and spur green; lip 3-lobed, side lobes filiform; spur 4 in. long, pendulous, thickened at apex. Stem 18 to 24 in. h. *l.* 6 or 7, lanceolate-oblong, undulate. Sierra Leone. 1835. (B.R. 1858.)

**H. psyco'des.** *fl.* varying from rose to crimson, very fragrant, fringed; spikes 4 to 10 in. long. June. N. America. 1826. A very showy species, allied to *H. fimbriata,* but with smaller *fl.*

**H. pusil'la.*** *fl.* lateral sep. green, oblong, acute, reflexed, and revolute; pet. green with dorsal sep. forming a helmet; lip scarlet, side lobes oblong-dolabriform, spreading, front lobe 2-fid; raceme lax. *l.* linear, acute, 8 to 9 in. long, ½ in. broad. 1 ft. h. or more. Cochin China. 1886. (Gn. 43 (1893), t. 908; J.H. 16 (1888), p. 25; W.O.A. 281, all as *H. militaris.*) Stove.

**H. radia'ta.** *fl.* 2 or more; sep. green; pet. triangular, white; lip about 1 in. across, 3-fid, mid-lobe narrow; side lobes each expanded fan-wise, with its outer margin strongly fringed, 12 to 15 in. h. *l.* linear-lanceolate. Japan. Perhaps a form of *H. dentata.*

**H. radi'cans.** A synonym of *H. repens.*

**H. renifor'mis.** *fl.* green, about ⅓ in. across; spike 3 to 6 in. long, 4- to 6-fld. *l.* 1 or 2, radical, ½ to ⅔ in. long, fleshy, orbicular or oblong. India, &c. SYN. *Aopla reniformis, Herminium reniforme.* Stove.

**H. re'pens.** Aquatic or sub-aquatic. *fl.* small, green, in oblong spikes. Lower parts of stem submerged, upper parts erect and leafy. *Larger l.* 3 to 6 in. long, narrow. Tubers absent but roots attain considerable length. W. Indies, Carribean Gulf, &c., in marshy ditches. (H.I.P. 2686.)

**H. rhodocheil'a.*** *fl.* scape 6 to 15 in. long; raceme about 12-fld.; sep. green, united into a hood-like process; lip large, bright cinnabar-red. August. S. China. 1884. (B.M. 7571.) Sometimes considered a form of *H. pusilla.*

**H. Robinson'ii.*** Differs from *H. pusilla* by its white *fl.* and long aristate bracts of infl. Philippines. 1915.

**H. robus'ta.** A synonym of *H. Susannae.*

**H. Roebelen'ii.*** Habit of *H. pusilla,* but sep., pet., spur, and column red, lip bright scarlet. *l.* 3½ to 6 in. long, ½ in. broad, olive green, margins undulate. Annam. 1912.

**H. rotundifo'lia.** *fl.* rosy-purple; lip white, spotted purple, 3-lobed, mid-lobe obcordate, apiculate, side lobes sub-falcate; spur acute; spikes large, compact. Summer. 1½ to 3 ft. h. N. America.

**H. salaccen'sis.** *fl.* sep. greenish, spreading; pet. reddish, very narrow; lip long, 3-lobed; spur, reflexed, narrow, tipped orange; column short; spike ovate, 5 to 6 in. long. April. *l.* 4 to 5 in. long, lanceolate, acuminate, striate, upper shorter. 12 to 14 in. h. Root a tuber and 3 or 4 fleshy fibres. Mt. Salak, Java. (B.M. 5196.) Stove.

**H. splen'dens.*** *fl.* 3 to 12; dorsal sep. ovate-elliptic, shortly acuminate, narrow, about 1 in. long, lateral as long, obliquely lanceolate, dilated at base, recurved, all green; pet. pure white alined in front of the dorsal sep., sickle-shaped with front of dorsal sep. exposed between their lower portions; lip white, narrowly clawed then separating into 3 divisions, mid-lobe narrow, entire, nearly 1 in. long, side lobes divergent, narrow rib-like, their outer edges developed into 8 to 12 simple or forked filiform growths; spur cylindrical, twisted, curved, 1½ to 2½ in. long. Stem 12 to 20 in. h. *Lower l.* much reduced; *stem-l.* broadly lanceolate, sheathing at base, 6 in. long, 2 in. wide, upper gradually smaller. Uganda, Rhodesia, Zambesia. 1895. (B.M. 9350.)

**H. subpu'bens.** *fl.* 4 or 5, white; sep. ovate-acute, nearly equal, dorsal horizontal; pet. hooded, obtuse; lip entire; spur twice as long as ovary, 2-lobed at apex. August. 1 ft. h. Sierra Leone. 1844. SYN. *H. candida.* Stove.

**H. Susan'nae.*** *fl.* 4 to 8, 3 to 4 in. across, white; pet. narrow; lip 3-lobed, outer strongly fringed, inner narrowly tongue-shaped; spur 4 in. or more long. Widely distributed. India, Malaya, S. China. 1834. (B.M. 3374 as *H. gigantea.*) SYN. *H. robusta.* var. **sumatra'na,** *fl.* white. Sumatra. 1893.

**HABER'LEA** (in honour of Karl Konstantin Haberle, 1764–1832, Professor of Botany at Pesth). FAM. *Gesneriaceae.* A genus of 1 or 2 tufted herbs related to Ramonda, natives of the Balkans. Leaves in a rosette. Flowers umbellate, nodding, 5-lobed, tubular; lobes unequal, 3 large, 2 small; stamens 4, didynamous, included. Cultivation as for Ramonda; a plant for a shady nook in well-drained rich leaf-mould on the rock-garden, or in alpine house.

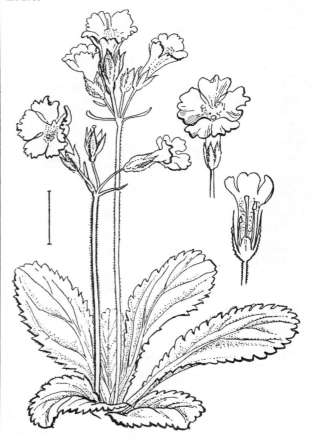

*Haberlea Ferdinandi-Coburgi*

**H. Ferdinandi-Coburg'i.*** Habit of *H. rhodopensis* but larger. *fl.* 3 or 4 on a scape, pale lilac, tube darker above than beneath, throat hairy-white, spotted yellow; cal. and pedicels hairy. Balkans. 1911.

**H. rhodopen'sis.*** Softly hairy, tufted perennial. *l.* in a basal rosette, obovate or ovate-oblong, 2 to 3 in. long, spreading, hairy, toothed, obtuse. *fl.* 2 to 5 in a drooping umbel; peduncle 4 to 6 in. h., usually several from a rosette; pale lilac, about 1 in. long, 1 in. across. April. Thrace. 1880. (B.M. 6651.) var. **virgina'lis,*** *fl.* a beautiful white. Hardy.

**HABIT.** General appearance of a plant, e.g. compact, straggling, tufted, shrubby; manner of growth.

**HABITAT.** Kind of locality in which a plant grows, e.g. woodland, river-side; native country.

**HABLITZ'IA** (in honour of C. von Hablitz, Prussian author and traveller). FAM. *Chenopodiaceae.* A single species of climbing herb, native of the Caucasus. It grows in ordinary soil, is hardy, and can be increased by seeds or division.

**H. tamnoi'des.** Climbing herbaceous perennial. *l.* alternate, triangularly cordate, slender-pointed, entire, membranous. *fl.* small, green, in branching cymes. July to October. Caucasus. 1828.

**HABRAN'THUS** (*habros,* delicate, *anthos,* flower). FAM. *Amaryllidaceae.* A genus of about 12 species of S. American bulbous plants closely related to Hippeastrum and sometimes combined with it or with Zephyranthes. In Hippeastrum the spathe is divided into 2 equal parts free to the base and on opposite sides of the peduncle, in Habranthus it sheaths the base of the pedicel and is usually extended into a free part on 1 side of the pedicel only, and this free part may be split into 2. Flowers usually solitary, sometimes 2, very rarely 4; perianth oblique and declinate (cf. Pyrolirion and Zephyranthes where they are erect), its tube short, segments nearly alike or of 4 sizes, stamens 6 of 4 different lengths. For cultivation *see* **Zephyranthes.**

**H. And'ersoni.** *l.* narrow-linear, acute, green or somewhat glaucous, 5 to 6 in. long. *fl.* golden or copper, brownish-red at base, striped without, about 1½ in. long, pedicels 1¼ in. long or more; scape reddish, 3 to 4 in. long. May. Uruguay, Argentine, Brazil? 1829. (B.R. 1345; L.B.C. 1677; S.B.F.G. s. 2, 70.) Greenhouse or half-hardy. var. **au'reus** has golden, **cu'preus,** copper-coloured, fl.; **texa'nus,** *fl.* yellow, segs. round. Texas, probably introduced. (B.M. 3596.)

**H. brachyan'drus.** *l.* about 1 ft. long. *fl.* pale pink, deep blackish-red at base, about 3½ in. long, nearly erect; tube short; segs. ½ in. wide; stamens under 1 in. long; scape about 1 ft. long, slender. S. Brazil. 1890. (B.M. 7344 as *Hippeastrum brachyandrum.*)

*Habranthus cardinalis*

**H. cardina'lis.** *l.* ligulate, 5½ in. long, up to ⅓ in. wide, long-pointed, shining green, keeled beneath. *fl.* solitary, bright red; tube funnel-shaped, about 1 in. long, greenish near base; segs. broadly oblong-lanceolate, about 1¼ in. long, slightly spreading; anthers lilac; pedicels about ¾ in. long; spathe rose-pink, about ⅞ in. long; scape cylindrical, 4½ in. long, rose near base. June. America? 1913. (B.M. 8553 as *Zephyranthes cardinalis.*)

**H. gracilifo'lius.** *l.* sub-cylindric, deeply channelled above, about 18 in. long, very slender, shining green. *fl.* rose, about 1½ in. long, tube green, not scented, closing at night; pedicels 2 to 2½ in. long; spathe about half as long; scape 7 to 8 in. long, purplish at base. January. Uruguay. 1821. Hardy. (B.M. 2464.) var. **Boothia'nus,** *fl.* pink, nodding, *l.* glaucous. Brazil. 1822. (B.R. 1967.)

**H. hesper'ius.** A synonym of *Hippeastrum advenum.*

**H. long'ipes.** *l.* linear. *fl.* pale-red, about 3 in. long; segs. lanceolate, spreading; stamens short; spathe 1 in. long; pedicels 4 in. long; scape 3 in. long. Uruguay. 1898. Greenhouse.

**H. praten'sis.** A synonym of *Hippeastrum pratense.*

**H. robus'tus.** *l.* rather glaucous, channelled. *fl.* purplish-rose, becoming white, 3½ in. long; tube almost absent; outer segs. broader than inner; spathe ⅞ in. long, rather shorter than pedicel; scape stout. Argentine. 1828. (B.M. 9126; L.B.C. 1761; S.B.F.G. s. 2, 14.) Greenhouse.

*Habranthus robustus*

**H. texa'nus.** A variety of *H. Andersoni.*

**H. versico'lor.** *l.* 3 or more, nearly 1 ft. long, ½ in. wide, acute. *fl.* rose at first then white suffused rose, red at tip and streaked red below, middle nerve green, 2 in. long; pedicel 1¼ in. long, pale green; spathe and scape at first rose, then red; spathe 1½ in. long; scape 5 in. long. Winter. Uruguay?, Brazil. 1821. (B.M. 2485.) Hardy.

**HABROTHAM'NUS.** Included in **Cestrum.**

*habrot'richus -a -um,* having soft hairs.

**HACKBERRY.** *See* **Celtis.**

**HACKEL'IA** (in honour of P. Hackel, Professor of Agriculture, Leitmeritz, writer on Flora of Bohemia). FAM. *Boraginaceae.* A genus of about 40 species of usually perennial herbs in the N. temperate zone, with alternate leaves and paniculate inflorescences. Calyx usually cut to about ¾; corolla cylindrical or funnel-shaped, cell-shaped or rotate; stamens included. *H. nipponica* might find a place on the rock-garden for its late-flowering habit. Seed or division.

**H. nippon'ica.** Densely tufted perennial, 3 to 4 in. h., shaggy hairy. *Lower l.* linear, about 2 in. long, obtuse; *stem-l.* ¼ to 1 in. long. *fl.* blue in a corymbose infl.; cor. salver-shaped, about ¼ in. acros: Japan.

*Hackenberg'ii,* in honour of Karl Gunther Hackenberg, 1892– , of the Netherlands army.

**HACQUET'IA** (in honour of Balthasar Hacquet, 1740–1815, author of *Plantae Alpinae Carniolicae*). FAM. *Umbelliferae*. A genus of a single species of tufted alpine herbaceous perennial. Leaves radical, 3-foliolate. Flowers in a simple umbel with a foliose involucre. *H. Epipactis* grows best in a stiffish loam and resents disturbance. Division should therefore be made only from strong plants just before growth begins in spring. It is a pleasant compact plant for the rock-garden.

**H. Epipact'is.**\* Tufted perennial 3 to 6 in. h. *l.* all radical, palmately 3-foliolate; lflets. wedge-shaped, 2- or 3-cleft, clear green. *fl.* yellow in a simple umbel, shortly pedicellate, at the apex of the 1 to 3 scapes; involucre of 5 to 6 obovate l. longer than the umbels. April. Europe. 1823. (B.M. 7585; L.B.C. 1832.) SYN. *Dondia Epipactis*.

**HADE'NA olera'cea.** *See* **Tomato Moth.**

*hadriat'icus -a -um,* of countries bordering the Adriatic Sea.

*haema-,* in compound words, signifying blood-red.

*haema'leus -a -um,* blood-red.

**HAEMAN'THUS** (*haema*, blood, *anthos*, flower; referring to the colouring of some species). FAM. *Amaryllidaceae*. A genus of over 50 species of bulbous plants, natives of S. and Trop. Africa. Bulb usually large with thick skin. Stem short, thick. Leaves broad, obtuse, often more or less leathery or fleshy. Inflorescence a dense, many-flowered umbel, perianth tube cylindrical, lobes narrow, often spreading; stamens 6, often long exserted. Fruit a berry. Some species are nearly hardy, and several will grow in a cool greenhouse, but a temperature of 50 to 60° F. suits them better in the growing season. A mixture of sandy loam and fibrous peat suits them and they flower better if under-potted. It is therefore unnecessary to shift them every year. As the bulbs grow and the strong roots increase weak manure water should be given. Species with well-developed bulbs should have the bulbs quite buried in the soil. The species flower at different seasons and it is important that, after flowering, they should have a period of growth, followed by a period of rest. When in flower, the blossoms will last longer in cool quarters. Propagation is effected by offsets which are usually produced freely. They should be removed and potted when new growth begins and kept in a close pit or house until established. The offsets will reach flowering size sooner if given the temperature recommended above. Many hybrids and variations are known to occur among these curious plants.

**H. abyssin'icus.** A synonym of *H. multiflorus*.

**H. al'biflos.** About 1 ft. h. *l.* oblong, strap-shaped, margins ciliate. *fl.* white. June. S. Africa. 1791. (B.M. 1239.) SYN. *H. virescens.* var. **pubes'cens,** *l.* hairy all over. 1774. (L.B.C. 702 as *H. pubescens*.)

**H. albo-macula'tus.** Bulb compressed, 2 in. across. *l.* 2, with fl., ligulate, over 12 in. long, about 3 in. wide, fleshy, deep green, much spotted white. *fl.* white, about 1¼ in. long; segs. linear, ascending, twice as long as tube; in dense heads 2 to 3 in. across, the bracts 6 or 7, white, veined green; scape 3 to 4 in. long, glabrous. S. Africa. 1878.

**H. Allison'ii.** Habit of *H. coccineus.* *fl.* pure white in very large umbels. Transvaal. 1894. SYN. *H. candidus.*

**H.×Androm'eda** (*H. Katherinae*×*H. magnificus*). *fl.* crimson.

**H. Baur'ii.** Dwarf. *Bulbs* 3 to 4 in. across. *l.* 2, nearly orbicular, 5 to 6 in. long, spreading on ground, dark green. *fl.* white, in a dense umbel 2 in. across, nearly sessile between l.; bracts broad, white, rather longer than fl., broadly obovate, ciliate. November. S. Africa. 1886. (B.M. 6875.)

**H. can'didus.** A synonym of *H. Allisonii.*

**H. car'neus.** *Bulb.* 2 to 3 in. across. *l.* 2, developed after fl., obtuse, 4 to 6 in. long, softly hairy. *fl.* pink, rarely white ½ in. long, in a dense globose umbel, 2 to 3 in. across; scape 6 to 12 in. long, mottled purple. Summer. S. Africa. 1819. (B.M. 3373; B.R. 509.)

**H. cinnabari'nus.** *l.* 4 in a radical rosette, oblong, 6 to 8 in. long; stalked. *fl.* red in a 20- to 40-fld. umbel; scape slender, about 1 ft. long. April. W. Africa. 1855. (B.M. 5314.)

**H.×Clark'ei** (*H. albiflos*×*H. coccineus*). Of garden origin with intermediate characters between the parents.

**H. coccin'eus.** Bulb compressed, about 3 in. wide. *l.* 2, fully developed after flowering, tongue-shaped, nearly erect, 18 in. to 2 ft. long, 6 to 8 in. wide. *fl.* in a dense globose umbel 2 to 3 in. wide, bright red, 1 in. long; bracts 6 to 8, about 2½ in. long, red; scape 6 to 9 in. long minutely spotted reddish-brown. September. S. Africa. 1731. (B.M. 1075; L.B.C. 240.) var. **carina'tus,** *l.* about 12 in. long, narrow; **coarcta'tus,** bracts shorter. (B.R. 181 as *H. coarctatus*.)

**H. deform'is.** *Bulb* 4 to 5 in. wide, slightly compressed. *l.* about 2 pairs, 3½ to 4 in. long and broad, dark green, smooth, hairy above, downy beneath. *fl.* white, numerous, in a compressed head parallel to bulb, about 3 in. h.; bracts about 6, equal, longer than fl., obovate-oblong, obtuse, ciliate, white; stamens exserted, anther pale yellow. March. Natal. 1869. (B.M. 5903.)

**H. incarna'tus.** Close to *H. tigrinus,* but with broader l., more slender scape, bracts smaller, narrower, and less coloured; *fl.* smaller, flesh-coloured. S. Africa. 1865. (B.M. 5532.)

**H. insig'nis.** A variety of *H. magnificus*.

**H. Kalbrey'eri.** A synonym of *H. multiflorus*.

**H. Katheri'nae.** *Bulb* globose, 2 to 3 in. wide. *l.* on separate stem, 3 to 5, oblong, 9 to 14 in. long, or more in cultivation, 4 to 6 in. wide, veins distinct. *fl.* deep red, 2½ in. long, in a dense umbel 6 to 7 in. wide; stamens exserted; scape about 12 in. long, spotted near base. Natal. (B.M. 6778.)

**H. Linden'ii.** Closely related to *H. cinnabarinus.* *l.* 6 to 8, nearly evergreen; stalks long, winged; blade 10 to 12 in. long, 3 to 5 in. wide, lanceolate or ovate-oblong, acute, base rounded, folded each side of midrib. *fl.* scarlet, 100 or more in a globose umbel 6 to 8 in. across; perianth 2 in. across, tube ⅞ in. long, lobes 1¼ in. long, linear-lanceolate; scape 18 in. long. Congo. 1890. (G.C. 8 (1890), 437, f. 85.) var. **imperia'lis,** perianth segs. longer; **Laurent'ii,** like *imperialis* but *fl.* salmon. A variable plant in colour, &c., of which many forms have been named.

**H. Lynes'ii.** *Bulb* about 2 in. h., dotted red. *l.* 5, developing fully after fl., ovate-elliptic, shortly pointed, about 5 in. long. *fl.* in a globose umbel about 6 in. wide, with over 50 fl. on a scape about 5½ in. h. spotted red at base; filaments which form the conspicuous part of the infl. bright red, about 1 in. long; perianth tube vermilion, segs. very narrow-linear, about ⅓ in. long, yellow except at the red base. June. Sudan. 1921. (B.M. 8975.) Stove.

**H. magnif'icus.** *Bulb* up to 4 in. thick. Stem robust up to 1 ft. long. *l.* 6 to 8, oblong, about 1 ft. long, bright green, undulate, 12- to 16-nerved, narrowed to a short stalk, developed mostly after fl. *fl.* bright scarlet, about 1 in. long, segs. linear, double as long as tube, in a dense globose head; stamens scarlet, 1 in. long; bracts 6 to 8 ovate or oblong, bright green, about 2 in. long. July. Natal. 1838. SYN. *H. Rouperi.* var. **insig'nis,** bracts shorter than fl., about ⅞ in. long. (B.M. 4745 as *H. insignis.*); **superb'us,** *l.* 5 or 6, narrow, with fl.

**H. Mann'ii.** Near *H. cinnabarinus* but l. on a separate stem after fl. *fl.* crimson-scarlet; scape about 1 ft. h. Spring. Guinea. 1877. (B.M. 6364.)

**H. multiflo'rus.** *Bulb* globose, about 3 in. thick. *l.* 3 or 4 on a short spotted stem, oblong, about 12 in. long, acute; stalked. *fl.* deep red, in dense umbels about 6 in. across, with up to 100 fl.; stamens long exserted; scape 1 to 3 ft. h., separate from l. April. Trop. Africa. 1783. (B.M. 961, 1995, and 5881 as *H. abyssinicus.*) SYN. *H. Kalbreyeri.* var. **superb'us,** more brilliantly coloured.

**H. natalen'sis.** *Bulb* about 3 in. thick. *l.* 7 to 9, oblong, about 12 in. long, with sheathing scales at base of plant coloured and dotted. *fl.* pale green, about 1 in. long; stamens and styles orange; in a dense, globose head; bracts oblong, obtuse, about 2 in. long, reddish-brown. February. Natal. 1862. (B.M. 5378.)

**H. Nelson'ii.** *Bulb* red, oblong, compressed. *l.* sessile, oblong, 12 in. long, 4 in. wide, downy above, glabrous beneath. *fl.* red, in a globose head about 3 in. across; scape 1 ft. long, hairy. Transvaal. 1898. (B.M. 9293.)

**H. pubes'cens.** A variety of *H. albiflos.*

**H. punic'eus.** *Bulb* almost globose, about 2 in. thick. *l.* 2 to 4, oblong, about 9 in. long, acute, about 12-nerved, narrowed to a short stalk; with fl. *fl.* bright scarlet, rarely white, with yellow or orange anthers; segs. twice as long as tube; in a dense head; bracts ovate or oblong; scape about 12 in. long. June. S. Africa. 1722. (B.M. 1315.)

**H. rotundifo'lius.** *Bulb* 3 or 4 in. thick. *l.* 2, spreading, nearly round, 5 to 6 in. long and as broad. *fl.* pale red, 1 in. long, in a dense compressed umbel 1½ to 2 in. across; scape bright red, 6 in. long. May. S. Africa. 1790. (B.M. 1618.)

**H. tigri'nus.** *l.* after the fl., tongue-shaped, about 12 in. long, ciliate, spotted reddish-brown near base beneath. *fl.* deep crimson; tube very short; in dense, rather small heads about 2 in. across; bracts about 2 in. long, obtuse, bright red; scape up to 3 ft. h. spotted red-brown. April. S. Africa. 1790. (B.M. 1705.)

**HAEMA'RIA.** Included in **Anoectochilus.**

*haematochi'lus -a -um,* with a blood-red lip.

*haemato'des,* blood-red.

**HAEMATOX'YLON** (*haema*, blood, *xylon*, wood). FAM. *Leguminosae.* A genus of 2 or 3 species related to Caesalpinia and Gleditschia. Leaves evergreen, with spines in axils. The species require stove conditions and a compost of sand and peat. *H. campechianum* can be propagated by rather firm young cuttings in sand with bottom heat under glass. It is the source of the dye-stuff haematoxylin which is made from the deep dull brownish-red heart-wood of the tree broken up into chips before use, the sap-wood being discarded.

**H. campechia'num.** Campeachy Wood. Tree of 20 to 40 ft. *l.* abruptly pinnate, clustered, red when young; lflets. small, obcordate. *fl.* small, yellow, in axillary racemes. Cent. America, Colombia, W. Indies. 1724.

F. G. P.

**HAEMODORA'CEAE.** Monocotyledons. A family of 9 genera with about 30 species, natives of Australia, S. Africa, and Trop. America. Related to Liliaceae. Perennial herbs with alternate, usually distichous leaves, sheathing at base. Flowers in a panicle of several cymes, regular or zygomorphic, trimerous. Stamens 3, attached to inner perianth leaves. Carpels 3, united, sometimes inferior; ovules few in each cell. Fruit a capsule. The roots of some yield a red colouring-matter. The genera dealt with here are: Haemodorum, Lachnanthes, Lanaria, Lophiola, Rhodohypoxis, Wachendorfia, Xiphidium.

**HAEMODO'RUM** (*haema*, blood, *doron*, gift). FAM. *Haemodoraceae.* A genus of 17 Australian perennial herbs with base of stem usually somewhat swollen. Flowers in a glabrous inflorescence, black, red, livid green, or orange; ovary inferior with only 2 or 3 ovules in each cell. Greenhouse plants increased by division of the roots in spring. The rhizomes of some species were eaten by the Australian aborigines.

**H. planifo'lium.** 2 to 3 ft. h. *Lower l.* grass-like, flat; *upper* short, few. *fl.* livid-purple or greenish at base on forked racemes forming a compact panicle. August. 1810. (B.M. 1610.)

**H. teretifo'lium.** Differs from *H. planifolium* by the very long, almost terete, slender l. from a sheathing base. August. 1822.

*Haenkea'nus -a -um,* in honour of Thaddeus Hänke, 1761–1817, of Bolivia, who collected in S. America and the Philippines.

**HAG TAPER.** *See* **Verbascum Thapsus.**

**HAGBERRY.** *See* **Prunus Padus.**

*Hagen'ii,* in honour of B. Hagen, 1853–1919, physician, who collected in the Pacific Is.

*Ha'geri,* in honour of Friedrich Hager, d. 1874, German paper merchant, who collected plants with Th. von Heldreich.

**HA-HA.** A form of boundary fence or wall sunk in a ditch below the general ground-level in order to permit an unobstructed view of the park or country beyond the garden. It was much used by the celebrated landscape gardener 'Capability' Brown, and the name is said to have originated owing to the surprise occasioned on coming across the concealed fence.

J. E. G. W.

*Hahn'ii,* in honour of M. Hahn, collector for the Jardin des Plantes, Paris, in Mexico.

**HAIR.** Elongated outgrowth from the epidermis, consisting of one cell, or a row of cells, sometimes branched, forked or spreading in a starlike manner at apex (stellate-hairs).

**HAIR GRASS.** *See* **Aira, Deschampsia.**

**HAIR ORCHID.** *See* **Eria coronaria.**

**HAIRBELL.** *See* **Harebell.**

**HAIRY-ROOT DISEASE.** Sometimes seen in apple stocks where tufts of fine fibrous roots are produced. The condition is reported to be due to the attack of a bacterium similar to that causing Crown-gall. The disease has only once been suspected in Great Britain.

D. E. G.

**HA'KEA** (after Baron von Hake, 1745–1818, German patron of botany). FAM. *Proteaceae.* A genus of over 100 species of evergreen trees and shrubs confined to Australia and Tasmania. Leaves alternate, varying in shape from acicular and terete to flat and oblong, and from entire to deeply lobed, usually with several parallel veins running lengthwise and of hard texture. Flowers 2-sexual, arranged in pairs clustered in the leaf-axils. Perianth tubular at the base with four concave lobes, to the base of which the stalkless anthers are attached. In many species the elongated style, after protruding from a slit of the perianth, is the most conspicuous feature of the inflorescence.

Although some 20 species are grown in the garden of Tresco Abbey, Scilly, and some in the Cornish gardens, the genus requires cool greenhouse treatment in most parts of the country. They like a compost of loam, peat, and silver sand and require very firm potting. In summer water is needed frequently while the plants are growing but must be given with great care at other times. Cuttings of well-ripened shoots will root in sandy peat under a bell-glass if placed in a cool house until they have callused, then given bottom heat.

**H. acicular'is.** Shrub or small bushy tree, shoots sometimes silky. *l.* terete, needle-like, 1 to 3 in. long, ⅛ in. thick, stiff, sharply pointed. *fl.* white or pinkish, few in stalkless axillary clusters; stalks silky-downy, ⅛ to ¼ in. long. May to July. Australia, Tasmania. SYN. *H. sericea.*

**H. ceratophyl'la.** Shrub up to 6 ft. or more; shoots slightly downy. *l.* 2 to 4 in. long, very variable in shape, usually cuneate at base, becoming irregularly lobed and toothed in upper half, but some quite entire. *fl.* yellowish-white, few in axillary clusters; style short. W. Australia.

**H. cuculla'ta.*** Shrub erect, 12 to 14 ft., shoots softly downy. *l.* stalkless, roundish to kidney-shaped, 2 to 4 in. wide, leathery, concave, minutely toothed, glaucous. *fl.* crowded in l.-axils; perianth red; style 1½ in. long. W. Australia. 1824. (B.M. 4528.) SYN. *H. Victoriae.*

**H. dactyloi'des.*** Tall shrub of erect growth, shoots silky-downy. *l.* oblanceolate to oblong-lanceolate, 2 to 4 in. long, ⅛ to ⅝ in. wide, 3-veined, tapering to a short stalk. *fl.* white, with yellow stigmas, crowded in axillary clusters which (the l. being closely set) make leafy cylindrical spikes up to 7 in. long. April to July. W. Australia. 1790. (B.M. 3760.)

**H. ellip'tica.** Rounded, bushy shrub, 8 to 15 ft. or a small tree; shoots covered with rust-coloured down. *l.* nearly or quite stalkless, oval, 1½ to 3½ in. long, shortly hard-pointed, veins 5 or 7. *fl.* white, crowded in axillary, globose clusters. *fr.* ovoid, 1 in. long, with a small beak. W. Australia. Notable for the bronzy young shoots.

**H. ferrugin'ea.** Shrub 6 ft. or more; shoots densely downy. *l.* stalkless, narrowly elliptic to ovate-lanceolate, 2 to 3 in. long, ⅜ to 1 in. wide, with a short horny point, entire or slightly crenate, mostly downy when young. *fl.* white, about ½ in. long, rather fragrant, crowded in axillary clusters ¾ to 1 in. wide; style reflexed at point. Summer. W. Australia. (B.M. 3424.) SYN. *H. repanda.*

**H. flex'ilis.** A synonym of *H. nodosa.*

**H. flo'rida.** Erect shrub of stiff habit, 5 to 6 ft., shoots and l. downy at first. *l.* linear-lanceolate, 1 to 2 in. long, ⅛ to ¼ in. wide, edged by a few prickly teeth, slender-pointed. *fl.* white, in axillary short-stalked clusters. July. W. Australia. 1803. (B.R. 2579.) Resembles *H. linearis* in foliage, but that species is glabrous and differs in its more slender, more prominently beaked *fr.*

**H. gibbo'sa.** Rather tall shrub, shoots and young l. densely hairy. *l.* 1 to 3 in. long, terete, stiff, sharply pointed. *fl.* cream, in stalkless axillary clusters; individual stalks short, densely downy. Takes its name from the ovoid-globose fr. which has a short, thick, oblique or incurved beak. New S. Wales. 1790. SYN. *H. lanigera.*

**H. incrassa'ta.** Shrub 2 to 3 ft., shoots downy. *l.* linear-oblong to narrowly lanceolate, 1½ to 3 in. long, about ¼ in. wide, tapered to both ends, entire. *fl.* very small, downy, in axillary clusters. Its name alludes to the much-thickened stalk of the fr., a thickening which extends also to that part of the shoot from which it springs. W. Australia. (H.I.P. 442.)

**H. lanig'era.** A synonym of *H. gibbosa.*

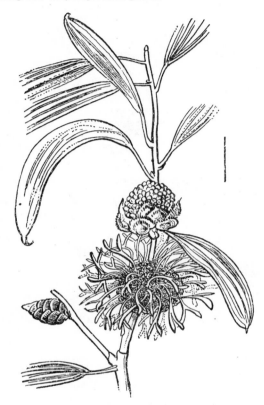

*Hakea laurina*

**H. lauri'na.*** Sea Urchin. Shrub 10 ft. and upwards, occasionally a small tree up to 30 ft. *l.* narrowly lanceolate to narrowly oblong, 4 to 6 in. long, ⅜ to 1 in. wide, 3-veined, cuneate. *fl.* red, packed in axillary, stalkless, globose heads 1 to 2½ in. across, the styles golden-yellow, ½ to ¾ in. long. W. Australia. 1830. (B.M. 7127.) Magnificent on the Riviera and probably the handsomest in the genus.

**H. linea'ris.** Bushy, glabrous shrub. 5 to 6 ft., shoots minutely downy when young. *l.* linear to lanceolate, 1 to 3 in. long, ⅛ to ½ in. wide, entire or with margins sparsely set with short sharp teeth; apex spine-tipped; stalk very short. *fl.* white, in axillary rounded clusters ¾ to 1 in. wide; styles not very markedly exposed. May to August. New S. Wales. 1824. (B.R. 1489.)

**H. microcar'pa.** Shrub up to 6 ft., of dense, rounded habit; shoots and l. glabrous or minutely downy. *l.* mostly terete, but also flat and linear-lanceolate, 1 to 4 in. long. *fl.* yellowish-white, fragrant, numerous in axillary clusters 1 in. across; style not much exserted. May. Australia, Tasmania. (B.R. 475.)

**H. multilinea'ta.** Tall shrub. *l.* linear to narrowly lanceolate, the longest 6 to 8 in. long and ⅓ in. wide; others only 3 to 5 in. long, but broader; all are stiff, grey-downy, numerously veined. *fl.* pink, in dense, cylindrical, spike-like racemes 1½ to 3 in. long, glabrous. Australia. (G.C. 19 (1896), 85.) var. **grammatophyl'la,** raceme densely downy.

**H. myrtoi'des.** Bushy shrub 6 to 8 ft., shoots at first minutely downy. *l.* ovate-lanceolate, stalkless, ½ to ¾ in. long, sharply pointed, very closely set. *fl.* red, in close axillary stalkless clusters shorter than l. and forming a cylindrical leafy spike 4 in. long; stalks purple; anthers orange-yellow; style very long, bright red. February. W. Australia. 1849. (B.M. 4643.)

**H. nit'ida.** Dense shrub, 6 to 8 ft., shoots and l. glabrous. *l.* obovate, oblong, or nearly lanceolate, 1½ to 4 in. long, ⅓ to 1 in. wide, apex spine-tipped, margins rather sparsely set with sharp teeth, but

sometimes entire, bright green. *fl.* white, in axillary globose clusters, each with a mainstalk ¼ to ¾ in. long. April. W. Australia. 1803. (B.M. 2246.)

**H. nodo'sa.** Shrub 4 to 10 ft., rarely twice as high, glabrous except for the sometimes minutely silky young shoots. *l.* 1 to 2 in. long, terete or slightly flattened, shortly and sharply pointed. *fl.* yellow, small, in axillary clusters. Victoria. SYN. *H. flexilis.*

**H. oleifo'lia.** Shrub or round-headed tree, 15 to 20 ft., shoots downy. *l.* 1 to 2½ in. long, oblong-lanceolate, cuneate, apex rounded except for a minute point, shortly stalked. *fl.* white, in dense axillary clusters; style not very long, mainstalk woolly. W. Australia. 1794.

**H. pugioniform'is.** Shrub 6 ft. or more, shoots and l. glabrous or minutely silky. *l.* cylindrical, linear, 1 to 2 in. long, ᵗ₂ in. wide, stiff, sharply pointed. *fl.* white, in small axillary clusters; stalks and perianth hairy. May, June. Australia, Tasmania. 1796. (L.B.C. 353.)

**H. repand'a.** A synonym of *H. ferruginea.*

**H. ruscifo'lia.** Shrub up to 6 or 8 ft., shoots shaggy, the long spreading hairs mixed with short fulvous down. *l.* ½ to 1 in. long, about one-third as wide, rather closely set, oval-lanceolate, sharply pointed, cuneate, veinless, downy, becoming nearly glabrous. *fl.* white, small, in dense clusters at end of short leafy shoots. W. Australia.

**H. salig'na.** Erect shrub up to 12 ft., shoots and l. almost or quite glabrous. *l.* 2 to 4 in. long, ¼ to ½ in. wide, entire, oblong-lanceolate, cuneate, tapered to a long fine point. *fl.* white, very fragrant, crowded in axillary very short-stalked clusters; each fl. has a slender stalk ¼ in. long; style exserted about ⅓ in., incurved. March to July. Queensland, New S. Wales. 1791.

**H. scopa'ria.** A variety of *H. sulcata.*

**H. seric'ea.** A synonym of *H. acicularis.*

**H. suaveo'lens.** Shrub 8 to 15 ft., shoots silky-downy. *l.* erect, pinnate, with few or many segments 1 to 2 in. long, or sometimes undivided and 3 to 4 in. long, terete, grooved above. *fl.* small, white, sweet-scented, in axillary dense racemes towards end of shoots; mainstalk ½ to ¾ in. long. Summer. W. Australia. 1803.

**H. sulca'ta.** Shrub 6 to 7 ft., shoots silky-downy when young. *l.* linear, terete, 2 to 4 in. long, stiff, sharply pointed. *fl.* pale yellow, small, in dense axillary globose clusters ¾ to 1½ in. wide; stigmas yellow. W. Australia. 1820. var. **scopa'ria,** *l.* mostly longer, sometimes 8 in.; shoots more downy. 1849. (B.M. 4644 as *H. scoparia.*)

**H. Victor'iae.** A synonym of *H. cucullata.*

W. J. B.

*hakeoi'des,* Hakea-like.

*Hale'i,* in honour of J. P. Hale, *c.* 1889, land-owner in Lower California, who collected Cacti with Mrs. Brandegee.

**HALE'NIA** (derivation doubtful). FAM. *Gentianaceae.* A genus of about 100 species of annual and biennial herbs, distributed chiefly in the tropical and sub-tropical regions with a few in the temperate zones. Flowers 4-partite, bell-shaped, with the pits at the base of the petals prolonged, in some species, into a spur. Inflorescence a terminal panicle of axillary cymes. The species mentioned are tender annuals.

**H. ellip'tica.** Erect, 9 to 24 in. h. *Basal l.* spatulate-obovate, 1 to 2 in. long; *stem-l.* ovate, almost sessile. *fl.* pale violet-blue, about ½ in. long, including the spur; cal. lobes lanceolate. Himalaya.

**H. Perrotte'tii.** Similar to *H. elliptica* but with a longer style and shorter spurs. India.

*halepen'sis -is -e, halep'icus -a -um,* from Aleppo (Haleb), N. Syria.

**HALES'IA** (in honour of Stephen Hales, 1677–1761, author of *Vegetable Staticks*). FAM. *Styracaceae.* A genus of 5 species of ornamental deciduous small trees, 3 or 4 N. American, 1 Chinese. Related to Pterostyrax from which it is distinguished by the 2- to 4-winged fruits and the parts of its flowers in fours, not fives. Leaves rather large, ovate-oblong, slender-pointed, more or less toothed, on slender petioles. Flowers white, showy, drooping, on slender pedicels in clusters from the axils of the fallen leaves of the preceding year. Fruits with 2 or 4 wings, stone 1- to 3-seeded. Well suited for almost any position, hardy, but best in one somewhat sheltered, and liking best a deep, sandy, moist soil. Increased by layers or by seeds.

## KEY

1. *Fr. 4-winged; cor. lobes shallow*       2
1. *Fr. 2-winged; cor. lobes long*       H. diptera
2. *Tree of erect habit; cor. ¾ to 1 in. long*       H. monticola
2. *Tree of spreading habit; cor. ½ to ¾ in. long*       H. carolina

*Halesia carolina*

**H. caroli'na.\*** Snowdrop Tree, Silver-bell Tree. Large shrub or tree to 30 ft. with spreading habit; young shoots with starry hairs. *l.* ovate-lanceolate, 2 to 5 in. long, starry grey-downy beneath, minutely toothed, abruptly slender-pointed. *fl.* pure white, 5 or 6 in a cluster, about ½ in. long, on stalks ½ to 1 in. long, drooping, on previous years' wood. May. *fr.* almost pear-shaped, 4-winged, 1¼ in. long. SE. United States. 1756. (B.M 910 and L.B.C. 1173 as *H. tetraptera*.) var. **glabres'cens,** *l.* oblong-oval, 3 to 4 times as long as wide, finally glabrous, *fl.* smaller, shoots less downy. Syn. *H. parviflora* of gardens; **Meehan'i,** *fl.* smaller with more cup-shaped cor. and shorter pedicels, *l.* thicker, pale, distinctly wrinkled. 1892; **stenocarp'a,** cor. deeply lobed.

**H. corymbo'sa.** A synonym of *Pterostyrax corymbosa.*

**H. dip'tera.** Tree of 10 ft. *l.* large, ovate, acute, minutely distantly toothed. *fl.* white, about 1 in. long, deeply lobed, cal. very downy. Spring. *fr.* with 2 large opposite wings and 2 obsolete ones. N. America. 1758. (L.B.C. 1172.) Less floriferous than *H. carolina.*

**H. montic'ola.** Tree up to 100 ft. in wild state, upright, bark flaking, shoots soon glabrous. *l.* elliptic or oblong-ovate, slender-pointed, soon smooth except on veins. *fl.* in clusters of 2 to 5, bell-shaped, longer than in *H. carolina* as are the fr. May. Cent. United States. 1930. var. **ro'sea,** *fl.* pale rose.

**H. tetrap'tera.** A synonym of *H. carolina.*

## HALF-HARDY PLANTS. Plants requiring protection during winter. Such plants are found in all sections—annual, biennial, and perennial, among herbs, shrubs, and trees.

*Halica'cabum,* ancient Greek name.

*halimifo'lius -a -um,* Halimium-like.

## HALIMIOCIS'TUS. Fam. *Cistaceae.* Hybrids between Halimium and Cistus. Characters intermediate.

**H.×Ingwersen'ii** (*Halimium umbellatum×Cistus hirsutus*). Shrub to 1½ or 2 ft., shoots slender, woolly. *l.* ¾ to 1¼ in. long, ⅛ to ⁷⁄₁₆ in. wide, linear, bluntish, downy. *fl.* white, ¾ to 1 in. wide, terminating

numerous slender stalks 3 to 5 in. long, the whole forming a large panicle 6 to 12 in. wide; sep. covered with white wool. 1929.

**H.×Sahuc'ii\*** (*Cistus salvifolius×Halimium umbellatum*). Shrub 1 to 1½ ft. *l.* linear to linear-lanceolate, ½ to 1 in. long, ¹⁄₁₂ to ⁷⁄₁₆ in. wide, downy. *fl.* white, 1¼ in. across, in clusters of 2 to 5; sep. 4 or 5 (rarely 3) rounded at base. June. S. France. 1929.

**H.×wintonen'sis\*** (*Cistus salvifolius × Halimium formosum*). Shrub of bushy, rather spreading habit, 1½ to 2 ft., shoots woolly. *l.* oval-lanceolate, 3-nerved, ¾ to 2 in. long, woolly. *fl.* 2 in. across, white, with a zone of crimson-maroon and a yellow patch in the centre, remaining open after midday. May, June.

W. J. B.

**HALIM'IUM** (Greek *halimos* (*Atriplex Halimus*) in allusion to the shape and colour of leaves). Fam. *Cistaceae.* A genus of about 10 species of evergreen shrubs, sub-shrubs, or herbaceous plants, closely akin to Helianthemum and often included in it. The leading characters are similar and both differ from Cistus in the 3-valved capsules, but Halimium has a very short straight style and sometimes 3 sepals, whereas in Helianthemum the style is elongated and curved and the sepals always number 5. Natives of the Mediterranean region and W. Asia. Cultivation as for Cistus. The following Key is adapted from Grosser's Monograph of Cistaceae in *Das Pflanzenreich,* where fuller descriptions will be found.

### KEY

1. *Plant herbaceous; fl. solitary, yellow*       H. canadense
1. *Plant shrubby*       2
2. *Fl. white*       H. umbellatum
2. *Fl. yellow*       3
3. *Lvs. linear; fl. pale yellow*       H. Libanotis
3. *Lvs. lanceolate, ovate, or oblong*       4
4. *Lvs. all alike*       5
4. *Lvs. on fl.-shoots green, others grey and smaller*       H. ocymoides
5. *Sep. scaly*       H. halimifolium
5. *Sep. not scaly*       6
6. *Lvs. silvery-scaly; peduncle, &c., with purplish bristles*       H. atriplicifolium
6. *Lvs. not scaly*       7
7. *Peduncles, &c., short-haired*       H. alyssoides
7. *Peduncles, &c., silky-haired; sep. purplish-bristly*       H. formosum

*Halimium alyssoides*

**H. alyssoi'des.\*** Shrub about 2 ft., of spreading habit, shoots slender, grey-downy. *l.* narrowly obovate to ovate-lanceolate, ⅛ to

$\frac{1}{2}$ in. wide, grey-downy. *fl.* $1\frac{1}{2}$ in. wide, bright unspotted yellow, terminal, and axillary; sep. 3, ovate, $\frac{1}{3}$ in. long, hairy. May, June. SW. Europe. (S.C. 81 as *Helianthemum scabrosum.*)

**H. atriplicifo'lium.** Shrub about 4 ft., of spreading habit, shoots downy. *l.* broadly ovate, blunt, 3- or 5-nerved, 1 to 2 in. long, $\frac{3}{4}$ to $1\frac{1}{4}$ in. wide, silvery-scaly above. *fl.* 2 to 8, golden-yellow with a brown spot at base, $1\frac{1}{2}$ in. across; sep. 3, ovate-lanceolate, about $\frac{1}{3}$ in. long, hairs reddish or white; peduncles, &c., sticky. June. S. Spain. 1659. Syn. *Helianthemum atriplicifolium.*

**H. canaden'se.** Herbaceous perennial, 1 to 2 ft. *l.* oblong to oblong-lanceolate, pointed, scarcely stalked, $\frac{1}{2}$ to $1\frac{1}{4}$ in. long, rough and dark green above, grey-downy beneath. *fl.* solitary or rarely in pairs, bright yellow, $\frac{3}{4}$ to $1\frac{1}{2}$ in. across; sep. hairy. May to July. Eastern N. America. 1799. (S.C. 21.) Syn. *Helianthemum canadense.*

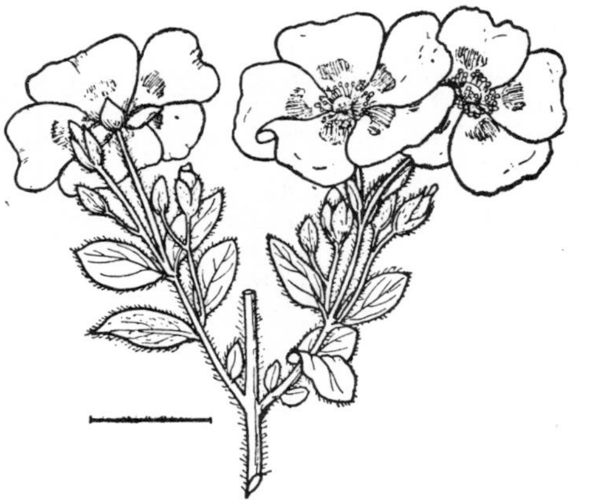

*Halimium lasianthum formosum*

**H. formo'sum.** *See* **H. lasianthum formosum.**

**H. halimifo'lium.** Shrub 3 to 4 ft., shoots scaly and downy. *l.* narrowly obovate to oblong, $\frac{3}{4}$ to 2 in. long, cuneate, grey-downy and scaly. *fl.* bright yellow, $1\frac{1}{2}$ in. wide, with only a tiny spot at the base, borne in slender, long-stalked, erect, few-fld. clusters; sep. 3 to 5, more or less scaly and downy, never silky. June. Mediterranean region. 1650. (S.C. 4.) var. **lasiocalyci'num,** shoots slender, hairs long interspersed with starry down. Morocco.

**H. lasian'thum formo'sum.*** Low, spreading shrub, $1\frac{1}{2}$ to 3 ft., much wider; wholly grey-downy with white hairs intermixed. *l.* oblong to obovate, $\frac{1}{2}$ to $1\frac{1}{2}$ in. long, $\frac{1}{4}$ to $\frac{1}{2}$ in. wide, 3-nerved, blunt. *fl.* $1\frac{1}{2}$ in. across, rich yellow, each pet. with a crimson blotch near the base; sep. 3, ovate, slender-pointed. May onwards. Portugal. 1780. (S.C. 50.) var. **con'color,** *fl.* unspotted.

**H. lasiocalyci'num.** A variety of *H. halimifolium.*

**H. Libano'tis.** Erect shrub, 2 to 3 ft., shoots slender. *l.* linear, stalkless, $\frac{1}{2}$ to $1\frac{5}{8}$ in. long, $\frac{1}{16}$ to $\frac{3}{16}$ in. wide, margin revolute, glabrous above, white or grey-downy beneath. *fl.* in terminal twos or threes on axillary shoots, yellow, 1 in. wide; sep. ovate, pointed, glabrous, $\frac{1}{4}$ in. long. June. Mediterranean region.

**H. ocymoi'des.** Shrub 2 to 3 ft., shoots slender, white with down and silky hairs. *l.* narrowly obovate or oblong, 3-nerved, $\frac{1}{2}$ to 1 in. long, $\frac{1}{8}$ to $\frac{1}{4}$ in. wide, white at first with dense down. *fl.* rich yellow, 1 to $1\frac{1}{4}$ in. wide, in erect, few-fld. panicles 3 to 9 in. h.; pet. triangular, purple at the base; sep. 3, oval, lanceolate. June. Portugal, Spain. 1880. (S.C. 13.) Syn. *Helianthemum algarvense.*

**H. umbella'tum.*** Erect shrub up to $1\frac{1}{2}$ ft., shoots viscid and downy. *l.* linear, stalkless, $\frac{1}{2}$ to $1\frac{1}{4}$ in. long, $\frac{1}{12}$ to $\frac{1}{8}$ in. wide, bright green above, white-downy beneath. *fl.* white, $\frac{3}{4}$ in. across, in erect terminal clusters; pet. obcordate, yellow-stained at base; sep. 3, ovate. June. Mediterranean region. 1731. (B.M. 9141.)

W. J. B.

**HALIMODEN'DRON** (*halimos*, maritime, *dendron*, tree; grows in dry naked salt-fields in Siberia). Fam. *Leguminosae.* The single species is a very spiny deciduous shrub, silky when young, related to Caragana but with lilac flowers in short racemes and stalked, inflated pods. It thrives in sandy soil. Seedlings are difficult to raise as the roots quickly suffer from damp. It should therefore be grafted on standards 3 or 4 ft. high of *Caragana arborescens*, when the rounded head of silvery foliage and pendent branches covered with purplish flowers in June and July make it a charming hardy shrub.

**H. argen'teum.** Shrub of 4 to 6 ft. *l.* hoary, abruptly pinnate with 2 pairs of lflets., rachis spine-tipped, persistent. *fl.* purplish, rather large, in 2- to 4-fld. racemes at the old nodes. May to July. Siberia. 1779. (B.M. 1016 as *Robinia Halimodendron.*)

**HALLER'IA** (in honour of Albrecht von Haller, 1708–77, author of *Stirpes Helveticae*, &c.). Fam. *Scrophulariaceae.* A genus of about 5 species of glabrous evergreen shrubs distributed through Africa. Leaves ovate or oblong. Flowers scarlet in few-flowered terminal cymes; calyx bell-shaped with 3 to 5 short, broad lobes; corolla tubular, widened towards the oblique, short-lobed limb. Hallerias need greenhouse protection, a light rich soil, plenty of water in summer, and good ventilation at all times. Propagation by cuttings under a hand-glass.

**H. lu'cida.** African Honeysuckle. Evergreen shrub of 4 to 6 ft. *l.* ovate, long-pointed, toothed. *fl.* reddish, large, drooping; cor. 2-lipped. June. S. Africa. (B.M. 1744.)

***Hallia'nus -a -um,*** in honour of Dr. G. R. Hall, American physician who lived in Japan and introduced *Malus Halliana*, &c., into America.

***Hallie'ri,*** in honour of Johann Gottfried Hallier, 1868–1932, Dutch botanist at Buitenzorg and Leiden.

***Hall'ii,*** in honour of Elihu Hall, 1822–82, of U.S. America, who botanized with Parry in Rocky Mts.

***haloph'ilus -a -um,*** salt loving.

**HALOPHYTES.** Plants which grow naturally in soils containing a high percentage of salt in the soil-water, i.e. plants of the sea-coast, of sand dunes near the sea, and of salt steppes. The salt in the water makes the solution available to the plants too strong to permit rapid intake of water by the roots and this with the danger of the too great accumulation of salt in the cell-sap, slowing up the plant processes and perhaps killing the cells, renders means of checking transpiration an absolute necessity. We thus find that such plants usually have long tap-roots, are more or less fleshy, have sunk stomata, thick cuticle, wax, reduced foliage, and other characters typical of xerophytes. Some families of plants consist largely of halophytes, e.g. Aizoaceae, Chenopodiaceae, Frankeniaceae, Plumbaginaceae, Rhizophoraceae, and most large families provide a few examples of halophytes as well. Thus *Crithmum maritimum* and *Eryngium maritimum* of the Umbelliferae, *Arenaria peploides*, *Silene maritima* of Caryophyllaceae, *Calystegia Soldanella* of Convolvulaceae, *Glaucium luteum* of Papaveraceae, Crambe, and *Cakile maritima* of Cruciferae, *Aster Tripolium* of Compositae, and so on, serve to illustrate the halophytes of our own British flora.

**HALORAGIDA'CEAE.** Dicotyledons. A family of about 90 species distributed over 8 genera occurring over the world, especially in Australia, often marsh or water plants, always with small and sometimes solitary flowers, but varying much in habit from gigantic herbs to small water plants. Flowers sometimes 1-sexual, regular, usually 4-merous; perianth in 1 or 2 whorls or absent; stamens 8 or fewer; carpels 1 to 4 with ovary inferior. Fruit a nut or drupe. The genera dealt with here are Gunnera, Myriophyllum, Proserpinaca.

***Hamadry'as,*** a tree nymph.

**HAMAMELIDA'CEAE.** Dicotyledons. A family of about 20 genera, chiefly in warm temperate and subtropical regions. Shrubs or trees with alternate, simple, generally stipulate leaves, with generally small flowers in clusters or racemes. Sepals usually 4 or 5, rarely 6 or 7; petals when present as many; stamens 4 or 5 or more, perigynous or epigynous, ovary 2-celled. Fruit a woody 2-valved capsule with 1 to several often winged seeds. The genera mentioned here are Bucklandia, Corylopsis, Disanthus, Distylium, Fortunearia, Fothergilla, Hamamelis, Liquidambar, Loropetalum, Parrotia, Rhodoleia, Sinowilsonia, Trichocladus.

**HAMAME'LIS** (ancient Greek name for a pear-shaped fruit). Witch-hazel. FAM. *Hamamelidaceae.* A genus of about 6 species in N. America or E. Asia. Shrubs or small trees with stellate pubescence, deciduous, short-stalked, toothed, somewhat oblique leaves with rather large stipules which quickly fall, and flowers in short-stalked few-flowered clusters in the leaf-axils. Sepals and petals 4; petals long and narrow, yellow. Seeds 2, black, shining, shot out to a considerable distance when ripe. With the exception of *H. virginiana* the species flower in spring before the leaves and are valuable for their bright yellow, abundantly produced conspicuous flowers which can withstand zero frosts without injury. All are perfectly hardy and do best in a rich, light, well-drained but moist loam. It is an advantage to mix peat or leaf-mould with it when planting. A sunny site is best with a backing of evergreen shrubs, but *H. mollis* will succeed in light shade. They can be propagated by grafting on seedlings of *H. virginiana* in early April under glass (temperature of 55 to 60° F.) using scions about 3 or 4 in. long taken from firm, well-ripened shoots. Seeds may also be used and usually take 2 years to germinate. Seedlings of both *H. japonica* and *H. mollis* often differ from their parent in shade of flower and to some extent in habit. Layering is also sometimes resorted to and if special forms are desired either layering or grafting must be practised. Pruning is rarely necessary except when a tree form is desired, and care should be taken to preserve the characteristic habit of growth. The foliage of *H. virginiana* and *H. mollis* goes a good yellow in autumn.

KEY
1. Lvs. densely softly hairy; cordate          H. mollis
1. Lvs. becoming smooth or nearly so; less distinctly cordate  2
2. Flowering in autumn; lvs. bright green beneath  H. virginiana
2. Flowering in early spring          3
3. Lvs. obovate with about 5 pairs of veins; pet. about ½ in. long          H. vernalis
3. Lvs. broad-ovate with about 7 pairs of veins; pet. about ¾ in. long          H. japonica

**H. arbo'rea.** A variety of *H. japonica.*

**H. incarna'ta.** A synonym of *H. japonica rubra.*

**H. japon'ica.*** Shrub of about 8 ft. with spreading little-branched stems, stellate-hairy when young. *l.* broad-ovate, 2 to 3½ in. long, 1½ to 2½ in. wide, finally glabrous or slightly hairy beneath, un-equal at base. *fl.* yellow in roundish heads on the leafless branches, slightly scented; pet. linear, about ⅔ in. long, ⅟₁₆ in. wide, wavy; cal. often purple within; bracts reddish. China, Japan. var. **arbo'rea,*** taller, less-branched, up to 20 ft., *fl.* golden yellow, cal. deep claret. Japan. 1862. (B.M. 6659 as *H. japonica*); **flavo-purpuras'cens**, pet. red or reddish towards base, cal. deep purple within. Japan. 1919; **ru'bra**, pet. suffused dull red, cal. deep purple within. 1919; **Zuccarinia'na,*** tall as *arborea* but more erect; pet. lemon-yellow, cal. green within. Japan. (B.M. n.s. 420.)

**H. mol'lis.*** Shrub of 10 ft. or more, with stout spreading branches densely downy when young. *l.* roundish or broad-obovate, obliquely cordate at base, 3 to 5 in. long, with wide teeth, densely stellate-hairy. *fl.* deep golden yellow, very fragrant; pet. linear, about ⅔ in. long, not wavy; cal. red-brown, smooth within, hairy without. January, February. China. 1879. (B.M. 7884.) var. **pal'ida**, pet. pale yellow. 1932. *H. mollis* is the best of the witch-hazels. Foliage yellow in autumn.

**H. verna'lis.** Suckering shrub of about 6 ft. with upright branches. *l.* obovate, wedge-shaped or truncate at base, coarsely toothed above middle, glabrous, green or grey beneath, 2 to 4 in. long. *fl.* light yellow, sometimes reddish towards base; cal. dark red within. January, February. Missouri, Louisiana. 1910. (B.M. 8573; Add. 261.)

**H. virginia'na.** Witch-hazel. Shrub or small tree up to 15 ft. with shoots downy at first. *l.* obovate, 3 to 6 in. long, coarsely dentate, almost smooth. *fl.* in short-stalked clusters, bright yellow, about ⅔ in. long; cal. dull brownish yellow within, scented. September, October. *fl.* often hidden by foliage. Eastern N. America. 1736. Foliage bright yellow in autumn. Decoctions of the bark and leaves have reputed medicinal properties.

**HAMATOCAC'TUS** (*hamatus*, hooked, *Cactus*; referring to the hooked central spine). FAM. *Cactaceae.* Plants round or elongated with a flabby texture, ribbed, ribs often spiralled; spines radial and central, 1 usually hooked. Flowers funnel-shaped with a short slender tube. Fruit small, round, red, dehiscing by a basal pore. For cultivation see **Cactus** (terrestrial).

**H. setispi'nus.** Plants with about 13 thin, high ribs, with wavy edges; radial spines 12 to 16, up to 1½ in. long, some white, some brown; centrals longer, 1 to 3. *fl.* yellow with a red centre. Texas, Mexico. (B.R.C. 3, f. 110–14.) var. **cachetia'nus** has whiter, thinner radial spines and a longer central.

V. H.

**hama'tus -a -um,** hooked at tip.

**HAMBURGH PARSLEY. See Parsley.**

**HAME'LIA** (in honour of Henry Louis du Hamel du Monceau, 1700–82, a celebrated French botanical writer). FAM. *Rubiaceae.* A genus of about 8 species of handsome

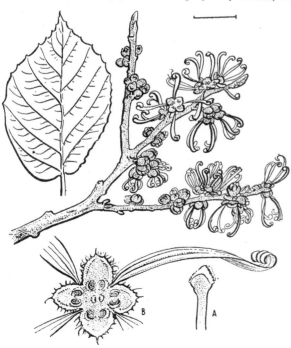

*Hamamelis mollis.* A, stamen. B, flower enlarged

*Hamelia ventricosa* (p. 952)

free-flowering shrubs, natives of trop. and sub-trop. America. Leaves opposite or whorled, stalked, ovate-oblong, acute at both ends, thin. Flowers yellow, reddish, or scarlet in terminal forking cymes, sessile or on short pedicels; corolla tubular or bell-shaped, 5-ribbed, contracted at base; stamens at base of corolla; ovary 4- or 5-celled. Fruit a berry. Hamelias need stove conditions and a compost of sandy peat and loam. Nearly ripe shoots will root in early summer in sand under glass with bottom heat. SYN. Duhamelia.

**H. pa′tens.** Shrub of 5 to 10 ft. *l.* in whorls of 3, oval-oblong, downy. *fl.* almost scarlet, in a terminal pedunculate cymose umbel. August. S. America. 1752. (B.M. 2533.) SYN. *H. coccinea.*

**H. ventrico′sa.** Shrub of about 8 ft. *l.* 3 or 4 in a whorl, oval-oblong, slender-pointed, glabrous. *fl.* yellow, tubular, about 1 in. long, bell-shaped, ventricose, pedicels long; racemes terminal. September. S. America. 1778. (B.M. 1894; B.R. 1195.) SYN. *H. grandiflora, Duhamelia ventricosa.*

F. G. P.

*Hamelin′ii,* in honour of Mr. Hamelin who collected *Bulbophyllum Hamelinii* and sent it to Messrs. Sander from Madagascar, 1893.

**HAMILTON′IA** (in honour of William Hamilton, eminent American botanist). FAM. *Rubiaceae.* A genus of 3 or 4 species of ornamental evergreen shrubs, natives of the warmer parts of China and India and of the E. Indies. Leaves opposite, ovate-lanceolate, short-stalked. Flowers white or blue, clustered or in umbels; corolla funnel-shaped; stamens at equal height; ovary 4- or 5-celled. Differing from Leptodermis by the form of the inflorescence and by the fruit-wall being 5-lobed at apex not base. Hamiltonias need stove conditions and a compost of loam and peat. Half-ripe cuttings root freely in sand under a glass with moist bottom heat. The following are all probably forms of *H. suaveolens,* the chief differences being in the colour of the flowers.

**H. scab′ra.** Shrub of 4 to 6 ft. *l.* ovate-lanceolate, shortly slender-pointed, rough on both sides. *fl.* azure-blue, very fragrant; infl. densely hairy. Winter. Nepal. 1823. (B.R. 1235 as *Spermadictyon azureum.*) SYN. *S. scabrum.*

**H. specta′bilis.** Differs from *H. scabra* by the l. smooth above, fl. lilac-blue. India to China. (R.H. 1872, 191.)

**H. suaveo′lens.** Shrub of 4 to 6 ft. *l.* broad-lanceolate, 3 to 6 in. long. *fl.* pure white, sessile in corymbose heads, very fragrant. October. India to China. 1818. (B.R. 348 as *Spermadictyon suaveolens.*)

F. G. P.

*Hamiltonia′nus -a -um,* in honour of F. Buchanan-Hamilton, British botanist.

**HAMMER.** An indispensable tool in the garden. A good form has a rather short stout head quite flat on the driving face with the other end like a claw turned back sufficiently to enable nails to be withdrawn by its aid.

*hamulo′sus -a -um,* hamulose, covered with little hooks.

**HANABUSAY′A.** *See under* **Symphyandra asiatica.**

*Han′buryi,* in honour of Daniel Hanbury, student of drug plants.

*Hanceia′nus -a -um,* in honour of H. Fletcher Hance, 1827–86, British Consul in China.

*Hancock′ii,* in honour of W. Hancock, 1847–1914, of the Chinese Customs.

**HANCORN′IA** (commemorative). FAM. *Apocynaceae.* A genus of 1 species of small, laxly branched tree, native of Brazil, the milky sap of which when exposed to air hardens into a kind of caoutchouc. Cultivation as for Tabernaemontana.

**H. specio′sa.** Tree of 20 ft. *l.* opposite, small, oblong, abruptly pointed at apex, acute at base. *fl.* resembling a Jasminum, in terminal few-fld. cymes on short peduncles, fragrant.

**HAND-BARROW.** *See* **Barrow.**

**HAND-GLASSES.** Small glazed coverings for protecting tender plants or for propagating, the top part being readily removed so as to give ready access to whatever is inside. Various shapes have been made with square, hexagonal or octagonal, bases, the square being the most useful. The frames may be of wood, copper, or cast iron and if kept painted they last a long time. Air may be admitted by tilting the movable top or removing it. Hand-glasses for propagating should be glazed airtight.

**HAND PLANT.** *See* **Cheirostemon platanoides.**

**HAND-WEEDING.** Weeding by hand is less necessary since sowing in drills is now the general practice and most weeds can be kept in check by hoeing, and since paths and drives can be kept clean by weed-killers, but it cannot be altogether dispensed with, and in spite of the use of selective weed-killers it is often necessary on lawns. Weeds are best pulled up when the ground is moist; they can be most readily removed then and with less damage to the growing crop.

**HANGING.** Plants and cuttings put into the soil by means of the dibber and left so that their bases are not in contact with the earth are said to be hanging. Hanging should be avoided; cuttings so treated nearly always fail to emit roots and consequently perish.

A→

**HAN′RYI,** in honour of Hippolyte Hanry, b. 1807, student of the flora of S. France.

**HAPLOCARPH′A** (*haploos,* single, *karphe,* scale; alluding to the pappus). FAM. *Compositae.* A genus of 4 or 5 stemless perennials with a woody rhizome, natives of S. Africa. Radical leaves numerous, entire or lyrate, white-hairy beneath. Scapes longer than the leaves, 1-headed. Flower-heads yellow, rather large, radiate; ray-florets female, ligulate; disk-florets perfect; receptacle flat, naked. Achenes differing from those of Arctotis by the absence of dorsal cavities. Pappus of several very delicate narrow scales. The 2 species mentioned require winter protection. They will grow in any good soil. They bear much resemblance to a stemless Arctotis and flower freely. They can be increased by cuttings of the young shoots produced from the crown.

**H. Leichtlin′ii.** *l.* lyrate-pinnatisect, 6 to 12 in. long, 2 to 2½ in. wide. *fl.-heads* 2 to 2½ in. across; involucral scales free, outer cobwebby-hairy, inner tipped purple; ray-florets stained purple beneath; disk deeper yellow than ray; scape about 1 ft. long. 1883.

**H. scapo′sa.** *l.* oblong, obtuse, 3 to 10 in. long, 1½ to 4 in. wide, tapering to base, nearly entire, white-woolly beneath. *fl.-heads* 2 in. across; involucral scales linear, woolly, blunt; ray- and disk-fl. clear yellow; scape 12 to 18 in. long, thickly woolly. Natal, &c.

**HAPLOPAP′PUS** (*haploos,* simple, *pappos,* down; referring to the absence of the outer pappus). FAM. *Compositae.* Sometimes erroneously spelt 'Aplopappus'. A genus of over 100 species of shrubs and herbs with alternate leaves and yellow flower-heads, widely distributed in N. and S. America. *H. ericoides* is rather tender and shrubby and is increased by cuttings. *H. spinulosus* is hardy and propagated by division. They are sun-lovers and succeed in ordinary soil.

A

**H. cilia′tus.** Perennial, 2 to 5 ft. h., erect, stout, branched, very leafy. *l.* oval or lowest obovate, 1 to 3 in. long, ½ to 1½ in. wide, sharply toothed, teeth bristle-pointed. *fl.-heads* few, clustered, sometimes nearly sessile, 1 to 1½ in. across, yellow. August, September. Missouri to Texas.

**H. cro′ceus.** Perennial, with stout, erect stem of about 18 in. Basal *l.* up to 12 in. long; *stem-l.* ovate-oblong to lanceolate, sometimes stem-clasping. *fl.-heads* showy, saffron-yellow; rays about 1 in. long; inner involucral bracts ragged. June to October. Rocky Mts. Hardy.

**H. ericoi′des.** * Evergreen shrub, 3 to 5 ft., shoots erect, downy and glutinous when young. *l.* very small, heath-like, ⅛ to ⅓ in. long, filiform, stalkless, in clusters at each joint. *fl.-heads* borne in a terminal cluster of racemes several in. across; each fl.-head is ⅓ in. wide and has 5 bright yellow ray-florets; disk also yellow. August, September. California. (G.C. 201 (1896), 301.) Wall, except in milder counties.

**H. spinulos'us.** Grey, woolly, perennial sub-shrub, 1 to 2 ft., with erect, crowded shoots springing from a woody rootstock. *l.* 1 in. long, pinnate-lobed, lobes ₁₆ in. wide, linear, pointed. *fl.-heads* bright yellow, 1 to 1¼ in. across; ray-florets very numerous and overlapping, the whole forming a showy, corymbose, leafy panicle 3 to 5 in. across. August. NW. and Cent. United States. 1871. (B.M. 6302.)

W. J. B.

**HAPLOPHRAG'MA** (*haploos*, simple, *phragma*, partition; in allusion to the flat dissepiment of the capsule). FAM. *Bignoniaceae*. A genus of 1 or 2 species of E. Indian trees or large shrubs with rusty hairy twigs. Leaves opposite, large, odd pinnate. Flowers in many-flowered panicles which are also very hairy; calyx constricted at apex; corolla bell-shaped, lobes equal, slightly wavy at margin; stamens 4, didynamous, slightly exserted, anther lobes spreading, 5th stamen very small, sterile; disk annular; ovary densely hairy. Too large for any but large greenhouse. For treatment *see* **Spathodea.**

**H. adenophyl'lum.** Tree. Young growths woolly. *lflets.* 5 to 7, broadly elliptic, acute or obtuse, entire, hairy. *fl.* brownish-yellow, 2 in. across, hairy without; panicles terminal. E. Indies. SYN. *Bignonia adenophylla, Heterophragma adenophyllum.*

F. G. P.

**HAPLOPHYL'LUM.** *See* **Ruta suaveolens.**

**HARD FERN.** *See* **Blechnum Spicant.**

**HARDENBERG'IA** (in honour of the Countess of Hardenberg, sister of Baron Hugel, the celebrated traveller). FAM. *Leguminosae.* Three species of evergreen twiners confined to Australia and Tasmania. Leaves alternate, of 1, 3, or 5 leaflets very variable in shape and size. Flowers papilionaceous, small, violet or purple, sometimes white or pink, generally crowded on slender

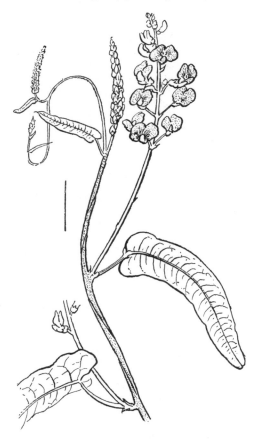

*Hardenbergia violacea*

racemes. Easily grown in a compost of peat, loam, and sand, they can be trained up the rafters of a cool greenhouse or to pyramidal or balloon shapes in pots. Both species are hardy in Scilly and *H. violacea* is grown on walls in Cornwall. Propagation is by late summer cuttings.

**H. Comptonia'na.*** Evergreen twiner up to 7 or 8 ft. *l.* of 3 or 5 lflets. varying from broadly ovate to narrowly lanceolate and from 2 to 5 in. long by ⅛ to 2 in. wide. *Racemes* axillary and terminal, 3 to 5 in. (in rare instances 8 to 10 in.) long. *fl.* violet-blue, standard ⅜ in. wide with a white, green-spotted blotch at the base; wings obovate. January to April. W. Australia. 1803. (B.M. 8992; B.R. 26, 60 as *H. digitata.*)

**H. monophyl'la.** A synonym of *H. violacea.*

**H. viola'cea.** Evergreen shrub found wild growing over low bushes. *l.* simple, cordate-ovate to narrowly lanceolate or linear. 1½ to 5 in. long, ½ to 1½ in. wide; stalk ½ to 1¼ in. long. *Racemes* axillary, 2 to 5 in. long. *fl.* often in pairs, standard ⅓ in. across, cordate, notched at the top, purple to violet with a yellow basal spot; wings and keel small. March, April. Australia, Tasmania. 1790. (B.M. 2169 as *Kennedya ovata*; B.R. 1336 as *K. monophylla.*) SYN. *H. monophylla.*

W. J. B.

**HARDENING-OFF.** The process of gradually accustoming plants to a drier atmosphere and greater fluctuations of temperature, especially to lower temperatures. Plants which have been forced, or freshly propagated, or raised in a higher temperature than that to which they will be exposed when put into their permanent quarters should be hardened off by gradual steps, as, e.g. by giving more and more air on successive days.

**hardy,** capable of passing the whole of life without protection. When the term is used in this Dictionary without qualification it implies that the plant is hardy in the neighbourhood of London. *See* **Half-hardy, Tender.**

**HARDY PERENNIALS.** Though all plants with a longer life than 2 years and hardy within the meaning of this Dictionary are strictly speaking hardy perennials, the term is usually reserved horticulturally for herbaceous plants with a perennial rootstock excluding bulbs and the like. Hardy herbaceous perennials is a better term and where it is used in schedules for shows it is advisable to state what hardy herbaceous perennials, such as bulbous plants, are excluded, if this is the intention.

**HARDY PLANTS.** Hardy plants may be of annual, biennial, or perennial duration and of any habit from minute herbs scarcely rising above the soil surface to tall trees. The ordinary garden term is, however, usually attached to herbs of various heights, bulbous plants, and shrubs or sub-shrubs of small dimensions. The treatment of many of the most popular of these is easy, provided due preparation of the soil is made at the outset, the borders kept clean, and the plants supported to prevent damage by wind. Some of the plants are well fitted for massing in large beds; the majority, however, are best grown in mixed borders in the private garden, the dwarfer and more delicate ones being reserved for special positions, especially on the rock-garden. Most hardy plants of this description provide the best display of flowers in spring or autumn, the somewhat cooler temperature and greater humidity experienced then suiting them better than the generally hotter, drier summer. These plants are not only valuable for their flowers in the mixed border but many of them give a good supply of flowers for cutting, especially in early autumn when glass-house flowers are scarce, and even for this alone their cultivation is important. A large number of hardy plants, particularly the bulbous ones, flower early in spring and may be used for furnishing flower-beds for that season before they are planted with their summer occupants. This entails space for preparation of the plants ready for the purpose, but if a special part of the garden can be set aside for hardy spring flowers where they can be kept all the summer, they succeed much better than if annually disturbed. Hardy bulbs may be planted permanently and left alone in such positions, while annuals and perennials can be renewed as becomes necessary. An open woodland site with deciduous trees often affords a suitable place for this type of garden, provided care is taken in the choice of plants for it. Many hardy spring flowers may be propagated annually from seed, or by division of old plants in autumn. Plants such as Myosotis, Primrose, Polyanthus, Silene, and Wallflower should be sown in June or a little later and be prepared in the open for planting in autumn. Dwarf perennials which may be associated with them also need propagating, among them *Alyssum saxatile*, *Arabis albida*, Aubrietias, Daisies, and dwarf Phloxes. All these may be divided to multiply them, either just after flowering or in August, providing against hot, dry weather. Perennials of this type are not usually of value for filling geometrical beds for summer display, but whole beds may sometimes be filled with advantage with such plants as the varieties of *Anemone × elegans* (*japonica*), Asters, especially the dwarfer species, Border Carnations, Delphiniums, Bearded Irises, tall Lobelias, Penstemons, tall Phloxes, Pyrethrums. Named varieties of these must, of course, be raised vegetatively, but most hardy plants are readily raised from seed. The seeds may be sown in pots and placed in a frame with very slight heat from February through the summer, or they may be sown outdoors after mid-March when germination is tolerably certain. Forwarding in frames is sometimes an advantage, but it is important that young plants thus treated should be fully exposed to light and not allowed to become drawn. Many are, however, more readily propagated by division, and this is usually best done in early autumn or as new growth begins in spring.

Where a 'Mixed Border' is to be planted with hardy plants it is important that the ground should be deeply trenched, and this is best done in the autumn previous to planting. Manure should be added during the digging and the surface should be left rough. The ground will then be in good order for planting in early spring. A moderately rich and fairly heavy soil suits most of the plants likely to be a success in such a border. The border should not be less than 10 to 12 ft. wide and a greater width will give better provision for the taller plants. If evergreen shrubs are planted irregularly according to their height they will give a furnished appearance to the border during the winter after the herbaceous plants have died down and protection from wind and strong sun in summer. The border should be planted so as to give interest at all seasons without repeating the same effect in different parts, and for this previous knowledge of heights, colours, times of flowering, and general form of the available plants will be required. There should be a general rise from the front to the back of the border, but too formal an attempt to secure this should be avoided. Generally the tall Asters, Delphiniums, Helianthus, and such plants as *Chrysanthemum maximum* would go to the back of the border, plants reaching 2 to 3 ft. high about the middle, and dwarf plants like Aubrietias, Pinks, Thrifts, and Saxifrages in front. The number of different plants suitable for the mixed border is legion. Spring-flowering bulbs should be there with their positions marked so that they are not disturbed after the foliage dies down. Vacant spaces may be filled by sowing seeds of annuals of suitable size and colouring. Supporting by stakes and twiggy sticks should be attended to betimes, care being taken that the supports are not conspicuous nor disposed so as to alter the natural habit of the plant. Annual digging is not to be recommended, but occasional stirring of the surface soil with the hoe and pricking over with a fork is to be recommended about March, when also a dressing of decayed leaves or compost will be beneficial. Plants should have room to grow and those that are apt to

spread unduly should be curbed, or better, taken up and pieces from the outside of the clump planted in their place. If alpine plants are used they should be near the front of the border with small compartments made for them and special soil, and they should be planted so that water drains away from their crowns. Occasionally in heavy soils, and more frequently in light, thorough watering may be needed, but in an average year this should not often be necessary if the soil has been properly prepared and the plants mulched.

There are many hardy plants that require constantly wet conditions but they cannot usually be included in a mixed border. For these *see* **Water Plants.**

**HARE** (*Lepus europaeus*). A destructive animal to fruit and forest trees, the bark of which it is apt to eat, especially during periods of intense cold and snow, and to garden crops and grass. *See* **Rabbit.**

G. F. W.

**HAREBELL.** *See* **Campanula rotundifolia.**

**HAREBELL, AUSTRALIAN.** *See* **Wahlenbergia gracilis.**

**HARE'S EAR.** *See* **Bupleurum.**

**HARE'S FOOT.** *See* **Ochroma Lagopus.**

**HARE'S FOOT FERN.** *See* **Davallia canariensis.**

**HARE'S TAIL.** *See* **Lagurus ovatus.**

**HARICOT.** The ripe seeds of *Phaseolus vulgaris*. *See* **Bean, French.**

**HARIO'TA.** *See* Supplement.

*Harland'ii,* in honour of Dr. W. A. Harland, ?–1857, who botanized in China.

*Harm'sii,* in honour of Dr. H. Harm, 1870– , of the Botanical Museum, Berlin.

*Haroldia'nus -a -um,* in honour of Prof. Harold W. Pearson, Professor of Botany, S. Africa.

**HARONG'A** (native name in Madagascar). FAM. *Guttiferae.* A genus of a single evergreen shrub needing stove conditions and a compost of sandy loam and peat. It may be propagated by cuttings of young shoots inserted in sand under a glass in heat.

**H. madagascarien'sis.** Shrub of 10 ft. with round branches. *l.* elliptic-lanceolate, entire. *fl.* yellow, in very large branching terminal corymbs. Trop. Africa, Madagascar. 1822.

F. G. P.

**HARPAGOPHY'TUM** (Greek, grapple plant). FAM. *Pedaliaceae.* A genus of about 4 species of procumbent, hairy, perennial herbs, natives of S. Africa and Madagascar. Leaves opposite or alternate, deeply cut. Flowers axillary, solitary, short-stalked, the stalks glandular at base. Fruit beset with large woody grapples about 1 in. long, pointed and barbed which make it well fitted for distribution by animals and exceedingly troublesome to wool growers. Greenhouse in ordinary soil.

**H. procumb'ens.** Grapple Plant. Stems many, prostrate. *l.* palmatifid, lobes deeply cut, sinuate, 5-nerved; stalked. Cor. tube blue, limb purple. S. Africa.

**HARPA'LIUM.** Included in **Helianthus scaberrimus.**

**HARRIMANEL'LA.** Included in **Cassiope.**

**HARRIS'IA** (in honour of William Harris, Superintendent of Public Gardens, Jamaica). FAM. *Cactaceae.* Plants with weak, slender stems; ribs rounded; spines usually long. Flowers large, with a long tube, nocturnal; fruit round, scaly or smooth. These cacti should be grown rather warm. Sometimes called Eriocereus. For cultivation *see under* **Cactus** (terrestrial).

**H. adscen'dens.** Stems erect, much-branched, branches very long, slender, clambering; ribs low, broken up into tubercles; areoles large, with about 10 long, stout, brown spines. *fl.* white, up to 6 or 7 in. long. Brazil. (B.R.C. 2, f. 226.) SYN. *Cereus adscendens.*

**H. Bonpland'ii.** Stems weak, strongly 4-angled; areoles with 6 to 8 sharp, long spines, red, turning grey. *fl.* white, large. Brazil. (B.R.C. 2, t. 24.) SYN. *Cereus Bonplandii.*

**H. erioph'ora.** Stem slender, branched; areoles distant, spines long, brown with dark tips. *fl.* purplish. *fr.* yellow, edible. Cuba. (B.R.C. 2, t. 18.) SYN. *Cereus eriophorus.*

**H. Jusbert'ii.** Probably a hybrid of *H. Bonplandii*; frequently used as a stock for grafting.

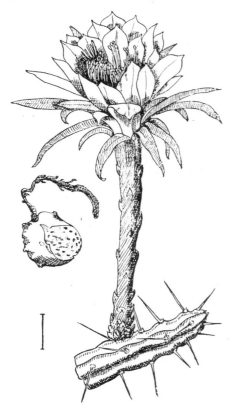

*Harrisia Martinii*

**H. Martin'ii.** Stem slender, clambering, old stems spineless; areoles on young stems with short radial spines and a long, stout central. *fl.* white. Argentina. (B.R.C. 2, t. 19, 20.) SYN. *Cereus Martinii.*

**H. platygo'na.** Stem slender, much-branched, with 6 to 8 low ribs, spines brown changing to grey; only one central spine. *fl.* white. Argentina? SYN. *Cereus platygonus.*

**H. portoricen'sis.** Stem slender, little-branched, with 11 low ribs; areoles with grey to brown spines with darker tips. *fl.* white. Porto Rico. (B.R.C. 2, t. 17.) SYN. *Cereus portoricensis.*

**H. tortuo'sa.** Stem erect at first, with about 7 ribs arranged spirally; spines 6 to 10, stout, spreading. *fl.* white, freely borne. *fr.* large, round, red. Argentina. (B.R.C. 2, t. 21.) SYN. *Cereus tortuosus.*

V. H.

**Harrisia'nus -a -um,** in honour of T. Harris, Esq., of Kingsbury, who, about 1840, imported and grew plants from Mexico.

**Harrison'iae,** in honour of Mrs. Arnold Harrison, amateur gardener of Aigburth, Liverpool, in mid-nineteenth century.

**Harrisonia'nus -a -um, Harrisonii,** in honour of Arnold Harrison of Aigburth, Liverpool.

**Harrovia'nus -a -um,** in honour of George Harrow, 1858–1940, foreman in Messrs. Veitch's Coombe Wood Nursery.

**Harrya'nus -a -um,** in honour of Sir Harry James Veitch, 1840–1924, head of Messrs. J. H. Veitch and Son, Chelsea.

**HART'IA** (in honour of Sir Robert Hart, 1835–1911, Inspector-General of Chinese Maritime Customs). FAM. *Theaceae.* Closely related to Stewartia from which it is distinguished by the greater degree of union in the stamens and the more numerous seeds. For cultivation *see* **Stewartia.** Greenhouse conditions are required except in mild districts.

**H. sinen'sis.** Evergreen shrub or tree eventually up to 50 ft.; young shoots silky hairy at first, finally smooth. *l.* alternate, elliptic to ovate, 3 to 5 in. long, 1 to 2 in. wide, glandular-toothed, dark green above, prominently veined, paler and at first silky-hairy beneath; l.-stalk, hairy, ¾ in. long, winged. *fl.* on short axillary shoots, white, 1 to 1½ in. across; pet. 5, margins jagged; stamens many, united at base into a short tube, anthers golden. June. *fr.* conical, woody, ¾ in. long. W. China. 1912. (H.I.P. 2727.)

**Hart'ii,** in honour of John Hinchley Hart, 1847–1911.

**HARTMAN'NIA.** Included in **Oenothera** (q.v.).

**HARTOG'IA** (in honour of J. Hartog, an early Dutch gardener in S. Africa and Ceylon). FAM. *Celastraceae.* A genus of 2 or 3 species, 1 or 2 of which are natives of S. Africa, the other of Madagascar. Shrubs with opposite, leathery, glaucous leaves with revolute toothed margins. They are related to Cassina and Elaeodendron but the seeds have no endosperm. They need greenhouse treatment and a sandy loam.

**H. capens'is.** Small evergreen tree or shrub up to 12 or 15 ft.; shoots greyish, glabrous. *l.* opposite, 2 to 3½ in. long, ¼ to ⅞ in. wide, lanceolate often bluntish, cuneate, toothed. *fl.* white, in small axillary clusters ¾ in. long and wide, the parts mostly in fours but occasionally in fives; pet. ⅛ in. long. S. Africa. 1800. var. **latifo'lia,** *l.* 3½ in. long by 1½ in. wide. Cool greenhouse. The wood is highly valued for fancy furniture and for veneering.

W. J. B.

**HART'S-TONGUE.** *See* **Phyllitis Scolopendrium.**

**HARTWEG'IA** (in honour of Theodor Hartweg, 1812–71, collector in Cent. America, &c., for the Horticultural Society of London). FAM. *Orchidaceae.* A genus of about 5 species of tufted epiphytes in Mexico, Guatemala, and Cent. America. The pseudo-bulbs are fleshy, stem-like, with a single leaf. The flower-spikes are produced from the junction of the bulb and leaf as in Arpophyllum. Though small the flowers are attractive, particularly in 2 of the species, by their bright colouring. The genus is allied to Arpophyllum and Epidendrum, the base of the lip being connate with the column. Temperatures, compost, and general treatment should be as for Cattleyas. As they are small, the plants may be placed in pans and suspended near the glass.

**H. gem'ma.** *fl.* several, small, bright amethyst-purple. *Pseudobulb* stem-like, 2 in. h. *l.* thick, semi-terete, channelled, acute, greenish, blotched with dull blackish-purple or violet. Cent. America. 1878.

**H. Kienas'tii.** *fl.* whitish, veined with red-purple; lip saccate at base, the sides united to the column, above which it is sharply reflexed and has the sides infolded. Habit much as in *H. gemma*. *l.* mottled dark and light green. Mexico. 1877. SYN. *Ponera Kienastii, Scaphyglottis Kienastii.*

**H. purpu'rea.** *fl.* 8 to 12, small, bright purple-rose, lip ovate, connate with the column base. Stem 2 to 4 in. long. *l.* as long or longer, narrowly triangular, olive green-grey, marked and flecked with red. Mexico, Guatemala. 1837. (Ref. B. 94.)

E. C.

**Hartwig'ii,** in honour of August Karl Julius Hartwig, 1823–1913, German writer on horticultural subjects.

**HARVEST BUGS.** *See* **Mites.**

**HARVEST-MEN.** *See* **Spiders.**

**Harveya'nus -a -um,** in honour of (1) Mr. J. C. Harvey of Mexico who collected there *c.* 1904; (2) W. H. Harvey, 1811–65, physician, author of *Flora Capensis.*

**Haselburgh'ii,** in honour of Dr. von Hasselburgh of Stralsund, grower of Cacti, *c.* 1885.

**HASHISH.** The dried leaves of Hemp, *Cannabis sativa.*

**Haspan,** name in Ceylon.

**Hasseltia'nus -a -um, Hasselt'ii,** in honour of J. C. van Hasselt, 1797–1823, physician, collected in E. Indies, and of A. C. van Hasselt, 1848–1909, of the Dutch army.

**hasta'tus -a -um, hasti-,** in compound words; hastate, formed like the head of a halberd or spear.

**HASTINGS'IA** (in honour of S. Clinton Hastings of San Francisco, California, friend of Californian botany). Fam. *Liliaceae.* A genus of 2 species of bulbous plants, related to Schoenolirion, natives of Western N. America. Bulb tunicated. Leaves rather fleshy. Scape nearly naked. Flowers white or greenish in many-flowered dense panicles or racemes; perianth segments distinct, 3-nerved; stamens 6; carpels 3; style short; ovary oblong-ovate, not deeply 3-lobed. Treatment as for Camassia.

**H. al'ba.** Stout, 2 to 3 ft. h. *l.* lorate, 1½ in. or less wide. *fl.* white or greenish-white, ¼ in. or less long, in a dense-fld. raceme about 12 in. long; stamens as long as segs. California and northward. (Armstrong, W. W. F. 11.) Dry soils.

**H. bracteo'sa.** *l.* narrower than in *H. alba. fl.* larger, white, bracts narrow, nearly as long as fl.; stamens half as long as perianth segs. Oregon. Marshes.

**HATCHET CACTUS.** *See* **Pelecyphora.**

**HATIO'RA** (named after Thomas Hariot, a botanist of the 16th cent.; the genus, having been redefined, is renamed). Fam. *Cactaceae.* Epiphytic plants with cylindrical stems divided into short joints; areoles scattered, the terminal one large and woolly; flowers terminal, small, opening only in bright sunlight.    **A**

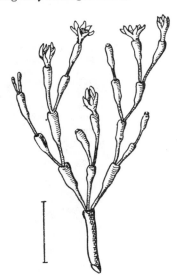

*Hatiora salicornoides*

**H. salicornoi'des.** Stems long, branchlets cylindrical or club-shaped, thinner below; a few bristles in the areoles. *fl.* small, salmon. Brazil. (B.M. 2461; L.B.C. 369; B.R.C. 4, t. 23.) Syn. *Rhipsalis salicornoides.* For cultivation *see* **Cactus.**    **A**

V. H.

**HAULM,** a stem of such plants as Beans, Peas, Potatoes.

**HAUMAKAROA.** *See* **Nothopanax simplex.**

**HAUSTARIUM.** A sucker-like structure used by many parasitic plants as a means of attachment to their host and a food-absorbing organ. Many parasitic Fungi with intercellular mycelium send out short knob-like or branched structures into the cells of their host and the Powdery Mildews (e.g. Erysiphe), the mycelium of which grows on the surface of the host, send similar haustoria into the epidermal cells. Haustoria are also formed by flowering parasites where the stem comes in contact with the host as in Dodder (Cuscuta), Mistletoe (into the cortex of the tree on which it grows), and so on.

D. E. G.

**HAUTBOIS, HAUTBOY.** *See* **Fragaria elatior.**

**havanen'sis -is -e,** of Havana.

**HAW.** Fruit of the hawthorn, *Crataegus* sp.

**HAWKBIT.** *See* **Leontodon.**    **A**

**Hawk'eri,** in honour of Lieut. Hawker, R.N., who sent home plants from the South Sea Is. (*c.* 1886).

**HAWK-FLIES.** *See* **Hover Flies.**

**HAWK-MOTHS** (family *Sphingidae*) are moderate-sized to very large strikingly coloured moths. There are in the British Is. 17 species, some of which are rare immigrants, others less rare but non-resident, and their visits are very irregular. Their flight is powerful, and they hover over flowers as they feed on the wing, pushing their long tubular proboscis down into the blossoms for nectar. Most species fly at dusk, but some in bright sunshine (Humming-bird Hawk, *Macroglossa stellatarum*, and the Narrow- and Broad-bordered Bee Hawks, *Hemaris bombyliformis* and *H. fuciformis*).

The caterpillars vary considerably in colour, their bodies being often ornamented with oblique coloured lines, while the skin may be smooth or granulated, and there is always an obliquely projecting horn or tail borne on the 8th abdominal segment. The chrysalis occurs as a rule in an earthen cell, though some may pupate in a loose cocoon among leaves on the ground.

The food plants of these caterpillars cover a wide variety, and include fruit (Eyed Hawk—q.v.), deciduous (Lime Hawk and Poplar Hawk) and coniferous trees (Pine Hawk); hedge plants (Privet Hawk); Fuchsia and Impatiens (Elephant Hawk); Potatoes and other solanaceous plants (Death's Head Hawk); and weeds, especially Bedstraws (Bedstraw Hawk and Humming-bird Hawk) and Willowherb, *Epilobium* (Small Elephant Hawk).

Of the several species represented in this country, only a few are of economic importance, namely, the Eyed Hawk, *Smerinthus ocellatus* (q.v.), whose caterpillars often strip the foliage of Apple-trees during August and September; the Privet Hawk, *Sphinx ligustri*, which may be found feeding on Privet hedges in July and August, and will also attack Lilac and Laurustinus bushes; the Poplar Hawk, *Smerinthus populi*, which attacks Aspen, Poplar, and Willow from July to September; the Lime Hawk, *Dilina tiliae*, which devours the foliage of Lime and Elm in July and August; the Death's Head Hawk, *Acherontia atropos*, which occurs sporadically on Potato foliage in gardens and fields during August and September, while the moths were known at one time to filch the honey from the old straw-skep Beehives; and the Elephant Hawk, *Deilephila elpenor*, which attacks outdoor Fuchsias in July and August, and is often found feeding on *Impatiens fulva*.

The day-flying Humming-bird and Bee Hawks are frequently seen hovering in bright sunshine over garden plants and visiting the flowers of Lithospermum and Rhododendron and of wild plants, e.g. Bugle, *Ajuga*;

Ground Ivy, *Nepeta*; and Ragged Robin, *Lychnis*. The apex of the abdomen in these 3 species is provided with an expanded, sharply cut tuft of hairs, while the wings of the 2 species of Bee Hawks resemble those of Clearwing Moths, being devoid of scales except round the margins.

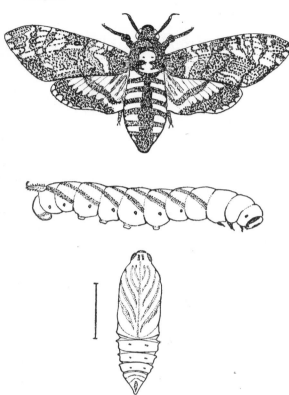

*Death's Head Hawk-Moth*

Attacks of Hawk-Moth caterpillars on cultivated plants rarely become severe in this country, and may be controlled either by hand-picking the young larvae or lightly spraying the foliage of infested fruit-trees and hedges with arsenate of lead.

G. F. W.

## HAWK'S-BEARD. *See* Crepis.

## HAWKWEED. *See* Hieracium.

**HAWORTH'IA** (in honour of Adrian Hardy Haworth, 1768–1833, an English authority and writer on succulent plants). FAM. *Liliaceae*. Small succulent plants, natives of S. Africa, at one time included in Aloe but later separated from that genus on account of the 2-lipped flower. The plants may be stemless or with a short stem; the leaves are numerous, arranged in a rosette or a close spiral; they show all stages from thin leathery slender forms to very succulent, almost cylindrical types; in some (*H. arachnoides*) the leaves curl over and protect the centre of the plant during dry periods; others (*H. truncata*) are 'window' plants, that is, the leaves have translucent tips and in their native habitat are usually buried in the soil with only the tips exposed. The flowers of Haworthia are of little interest horticulturally being inconspicuous and sparsely distributed along a slender peduncle; botanically they are not of great importance as they resemble each other closely even in species distinguished by markedly differing leaves. They are tubular with free lobes, 3 of which curve upwards and 3 downwards so that the flower is definitely zygomorphic; the colour varies from white to greenish, striped with green or dull pink.

Haworthias must be protected from frost but a high temperature is not necessary, a minimum of 40 to 45° F. being sufficient; the kinds with harder leaves will stand full sun, but the more tender-leaved species need light shade; all types benefit by a few weeks out of doors during the summer and are best in an open frame where they can be protected from heavy rain if necessary. The compost used should consist of good loam, sharp sand, leaf-mould, or peat, and the plants should be repotted at least every 2 years as the thick fleshy roots die off annually and if left will tend to make the soil sour; new roots are formed in autumn which is the best time to repot most species.

Propagation is easy from offsets which are freely produced by most species; leaf-cuttings can sometimes be struck but are difficult; seed is not recommended unless it is known to be of pure strain as Haworthias hybridize very readily. For pests *see under* **Aloe,** mealy bug being especially destructive.

Berger described 60 species but the number has been greatly increased in recent years by new discoveries and by reclassification; many varietal forms have been given names but the constancy of these forms is open to doubt and there may be unsuspected hybrids in cultivation. Any of the newer Haworthias that can be obtained are worth growing.

**A**

**H. al'bicans.** Rosette stemless. *l.* spreading, wide at the base, 3 in. long, tapering, keeled, whitish-green with a few tubercles on the keel; margin smooth, whitish, horny. (B.M. 1452 and S.-D. 5. 1 as *Aloe albicans*.)

**H. angustifo'lia.** Rosette stemless. *l.* ascending, very narrow, tapering, keeled, uniform green.

**H. arachnoi'des.** Rosette stemless. *l.* succulent, narrow, keeled, pale green with darker translucent parallel lines ending in a very long, toothed, soft bristle and with long hair-like teeth along the edges and top of the keel. (B.M. 756 and S.-D. 12. 2 as *Aloe arachnoides*.)

**H. atrovi'rens.** Rosette stemless, making offsets. *l.* spreading, short, wide and thick, tapering to a point, dark glossy green; edge with small teeth. (S.-D. 10. 2 as *Aloe atrovirens*.)

**H. attenua'ta.** Rosette stemless, making offsets. *l.* slender, tapering, very thick; a few scattered white tubercles on the face, back with white tubercles in horizontal lines. (S.-D. 6. 12 as *Aloe attenuata*.)

**H. Bolus'ii.** Similar to *H. arachnoides* but the l. more translucent towards the tip and bristles more numerous.

**H. Chalwin'ii.** Stem 6 to 8 in. h. *l.* erect, in a close spiral, very thick, slender, keeled; face smooth, back with white tubercles in longitudinal rows. (B.M. 8828.)

**H. coarcta'ta.** Stem 6 to 8 in. h., making basal offsets. *l.* in a close spiral, erect, short and wide, keeled, smooth on face with a few white tubercles in longitudinal rows on back. (S.-D. 6. 17 as *Aloe coarctata*.)

**H. columna'ris.** Rosette stemless, making offsets freely. *l.* erect, 1¼ in. long, very succulent, almost cylindrical, bluntly rounded, faintly keeled, translucent green with small, pale scattered dots.

**H. cymbiform'is.** Rosette stemless, making offsets freely. *l.* spreading, nearly as broad as long, narrowing suddenly to a sharp tip, keeled towards top; pale green with darker veins towards tip. (B.M. 802 as *Aloe cymbiformis*.)

**H. fascia'ta.** Rosette stemless, making offsets. *l.* spreading, 2 in. long, slender, tapering, thick, keeled, dark green with a smooth face and white raised horizontal lines across back. (S.-D. 6. 15 as *Aloe fasciata*.)

**H. glabra'ta.** Rosette stemless, making offsets. *l.* spreading, recurved, 3 in. long, slender, tapering, obscurely keeled; dark green with scattered white tubercles on back but none on face. (S.-D. 6. 13 as *Aloe glabrata*.)

**H. glau'ca.** Stem short. *l.* erect, narrow, flat on face, keeled on upper half of back, pale glaucous green, without markings. (S.-D. 17. 2 as *Aloe glauca*.)

**H. Herr'ei.** Stem 4 to 6 in. h. *l.* erect in a close spiral, long and very narrow, dark grey-green without markings.

**H. laetevi'rens.** Rosette stemless, making offsets freely. *l.* 1 in. long, tapering gradually to a long bristle at tip, sharply keeled, pale green with darker veins running vertically and horizontally. (S.-D. 10. 3 as *Aloe laetevirens*.)

**H. margaritif'era.** Rosette stemless, making offsets. *l.* broad at base, tapering gradually, keeled; face flat or concave, dull green with white tubercles more or less in transverse lines on face and back. (S.-D. 6. 5 as *Aloe margaritifera*.) Very variable in size and position of tubercles especially; a number of forms have been given varietal names.

**H. Maughan'ii.** Similar to *H. truncata*, but the truncated leaves are arranged in a rosette, not 2-ranked.

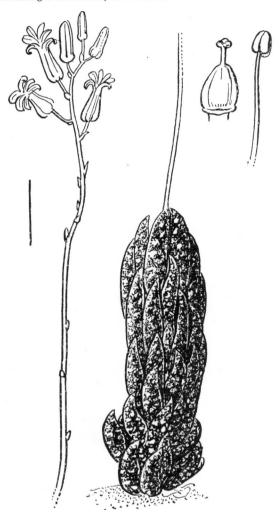

*Haworthia Chalwinii* (p. 957)

**H. pilif'era.** Rosette stemless. *l.* very succulent, thicker above, almost club-shaped, upper surface slightly flattened, coming to an abrupt point ending in a long soft bristle; edge with small transparent teeth; pale green, translucent, with darker vertical lines coming up from base.

**H. Rad'ula.** Rosette stemless. *l.* 2 in. long, ½ in. wide, tapering gradually to a slender tip, dark green with minute white scattered tubercles, edge rough. (B.M. 1345 and S.-D. 6. 8 as *Aloe Radula*.)

**H. Reinward'tii.** Stem 4 to 6 in. h., making basal offsets. *l.* erect, in a close spiral, short, broad and thick, keeled on back; face smooth, back with prominent white tubercles, edge rough. (S.-D. 6. 16 as *Aloe Reinwardtii*.)

**H. retu'sa.** Rosette stemless. *l.* few, very succulent, short, triangular in cross-section; face vertical then recurved so that upper half is horizontal, ending in a bristle; translucent dark green with paler longitudinal lines. (B.M. 455 and S.-D. 9. 3 as *Aloe retusa*.)

**H. rig'ida.** Stem 3 to 4 in. h. *l.* erect, in a close spiral, wide at base, tapering, recurved; face flat, back keeled; dull green becoming reddish when old, with minute scattered tubercles of same colour. (B.M. 1337 and S.-D. 4. 3 as *Aloe rigida*.)

**H. seta'ta.** Similar to *H. arachnoides*.

**H. tessella'ta.** Rosette stemless, making offsets freely. *l.* few, very thick, broad at base, tapering to a sharp tip, recurved; dark translucent green with paler longitudinal and horizontal lines, back with small tubercles, edge slightly toothed. (S.-D. 8. 1 as *Aloe tessellata*.)

**H. tortuo'sa.** Stem 4 to 5 in. h., making offsets. *l.* in 3 ranks, spirally arranged and twisted, erect or recurved, dull green with small green tubercles. (S.-D. 4. 2 as *Aloe tortuosa*.)

**H. trunca'ta.** Rosette stemless. *l.* few, round or oval in cross-section, top flat as if abruptly cut off, dull green, upper surface translucent (a 'window' plant). There are 2 forms varying only in size.

**H. tur'gida.** Stem short. *l.* recurved, short, almost cylindrical, tapering to a blunt point, translucent green with paler coalescing lines at tip. (S.-D. 9. 5 as *Aloe turgida*.)

**H. visco'sa.** Stem 4 to 6 in. h., branching from base. *l.* in 3 ranks, closely overlapping, broad at base, folded along midrib, compressed, uniform dull dark green, sticky. (B.M. 814 and S.-D. 3. 3 as *Aloe viscosa*.)

V. H.

**HAWTHORN.** *See* **Crataegus Oxyacantha.**

**HAWTHORN, CHINESE.** *See* **Photinia serrulata.**

**HAWTHORN, WATER.** *See* **Aponogeton distachyus.**

**HAYLOCK'IA** (in honour of Dean Herbert's gardener, at Spofforth, Matthew Haylock). FAM. *Amaryllidaceae.* A genus of a single species of bulbous plant, closely related to Zephyranthes, native of the neighbourhood of Montevideo, distinct from Zephyranthes by the absence of a scape, the ovary and spathe being within the neck of the bulb. Half-hardy. A mixture of sandy loam with a little peat or leaf-mould suits it and it can be propagated by offsets.

**H. pusil'la.** *Bulb* 1 in. across, globose, dark brown. *l.* linear, spreading, channelled above, developed after flowering. *fl.* solitary, greenish-yellow or white, sometimes tinged red without, erect, regular; tube 1 to 2 in. long, very slender, limb funnel-shaped, 1 to 1¼ in. long. July. 1830. (B.M. 7693; B.R. 1371.)

**HAYNALD'IA** (in honour of Stephen Franz Ludwig Haynald, 1816–91, Cardinal Bishop of Koloesa, an ardent botanist). FAM. *Campanulaceae.* A genus of 5 species of Brazilian perennial herbs sometimes included in Lobelia. Petals sp. free above, 2 lowest wholly separate. Seeds winged. For treatment *see* **Lobelia.**

**H. thapsoi'dea.** Herbaceous perennial. Stem erect, 6 to 8 ft. h. leafy, simple. *l.* broadly lanceolate, narrowed to stalk; lower 12 to 18 in. long, all downy, ciliate, toothed. *fl.* large overlapping; cor. rose-purple, hairy or silky; raceme large, pyramidal; pedicels reflexed in flower. June. Organ Mts. 1843. (B.M. 4150.) Greenhouse.

*Hayn'ei,* in honour of F. G. Hayne, b. 1832, Professor of Botany, Berlin.

*haza'ricus -a -um,* of Hazara, Afghanistan.

**HAZEL.** *See* **Corylus Avellana.**

**HAZEL BUD-MITE.** *See* **Nut Gall-mite.**

**HAZEL, WITCH.** *See* **Hamamelis.**

**HEAD.** A group of flowers very closely placed together, especially, as in the families Compositae and Dipsaceae, when enclosed in a ring of bracts forming an involucre.

**HEADACHE TREE.** *See* **Premna integrifolia.**

**HEADING or HEARTING.** Many varieties of *Brassica oleracea*, i.e. Cabbages, Savoys, &c., form heads or hearts by ceasing to unfold their central leaves. This occurs most readily in full light and therefore in summer, and in compact rather than very loose soil.

**HEADING-BACK.** The removal of the top branches of a tree or shrub as a means of renewing its vigour, or so as to allow of re-grafting. With old trees heading back should not be too severe in 1 year but should be spread over 2 or 3 years.

**HEART AND DART MOTH.** *See* **Surface caterpillars.**

**HEART-ROT.** A term used to describe the symptoms seen in several different diseases. For example, heart-rot of Sugar-beet has been shown to be due to deficiency of Boron in the soil; the rotting of the heart-wood of Coniferous trees is due to the attack of the fungus *Fomes annosus* (see **Bracket Fungi**).

D. E. G.

**HEARTSEASE.** See **Viola tricolor.**

**HEARTWOOD.** The central part of the wood of Dicotyledons and Conifers, hardened or altered by age, frequently of a different colour from the outer sap-wood.

**HEAT.** Heat is an essential condition for all the vital processes of a plant. Movement, including the movements associated with growth, absorption of water, and nutrient substances by roots, respiration, transpiration, photosynthesis, the action of diastase and other enzymes in the plant, and all other functions depend upon it among other things. For each function there is a degree of temperature at which it is carried on with the greatest efficiency: this is called the optimum temperature for that function in the particular plant. The optimum temperature is not the same for the performance of every function, nor is it the same for any particular function in every kind of plant. Any departure from the optimum temperature for a function, up or down, results in a slowing of the performance of that function. For plants natives of temperate regions the optimum temperature for most functions lies between 75 and 85° F. The minimum lies a few degrees above freezing-point, round about 42° F., and the maximum, at which the performance of the function ceases, lies between 110 and 120° F. The minimum temperature for plants which inhabit the tropics is higher, nearer 55° F., while inhabitants of arctic regions may become active at very little above freezing-point.

Exposure to too high a temperature results in injury or death, and the same is true for exposure to too low a temperature. In both instances the temperature which the plant will withstand depends largely upon the amount of water it, or any particular part of it, contains, as well as upon the general constitution of the plant. Thus dry seeds will withstand a temperature of 160° F., but if soaked in water they are killed at about 128° F. Bulbs of Narcissus are killed by prolonged exposure to 114° F. and most plants are severely damaged or killed at an air temperature of about 125° F. continued for a time, or if in water at about 112° F. Dry seeds exposed to the temperature at which air becomes solid, or even lower, come through the ordeal uninjured and winter buds of many trees escape injury at temperatures much below freezing-point.

When a plant is exposed to very low temperature some of the water escapes from the cells into the intercellular spaces and there freezes. In some instances if thawing takes place gradually at a short interval, the water is reabsorbed by the cells and no injury results, although a sudden thaw would result in damage or death. This is not always the case, however, for even a short exposure at freezing-point results in death in such plants as Cucurbits and Dahlias, no doubt because the withdrawal of water from the cells results in their disorganization or even possibly too great a concentration in the cells of substances which do not pass out with the water, for water alone appears to escape into the intercellular spaces. One type of injury is frequently seen after severe frosts, even in trees and shrubs of the northern forests. The water in the trunk, especially in the sap wood, becomes frozen and expanding as it turns into ice, causes the splitting of the bark and sometimes the wood itself, often on the side exposed to icy winds. Some shrubs are particularly prone to this type of damage, e.g. Rhododendrons and *Erica vagans.*

Since the optimum temperature for each function is not the same, it follows that the best temperature for a plant, that is, the best compromise for the performance of its various functions, varies at different stages of its life. Speaking generally a higher temperature is required to start the germination of a seed than is necessary for the plant that is derived from it, and perhaps no process better illustrates the differences in temperature requirements among different plants than germination, itself the result of the performance of several different functions. The following figures show the minimum temperatures for germination of some common seeds:

White Mustard, Norway Maple, Sweet Violet, between 32 and 34° F.; Beet, Cress, Onion, Rye-grass, between 34 and 42° F.; French beans, Maize, Sunflower, between 42 and 54° F.; Tomato, Tobacco, Vegetable Marrow, between 54 and 62° F.; Cucumber, Melon, and most tropical plants, above 62° F. These figures do not, of course, give the precise amount of heat required to bring about germination at these temperatures, for they do not show the length of time taken to complete the process. For instance, Maize takes much longer than the French bean at a given temperature, and Sunflower longer still, Melons take longer than Cucumbers, and so on. They do serve to illustrate the different minimum requirements of various plants and to show one reason why times and places for sowing seeds of different plants must differ.

**HEAT INJURY.** Direct heat injury to plants is not very common in this country. Under glass, however, grapes may suffer from Scald (see **Grape Scald**). Lettuces and Potatoes may in hot seasons show Tipburn where the leaf tips become browned. Apples sometimes show Scald on one side of the fruit due to hot sunshine but the reason certain fruits are so affected is somewhat obscure. In general, heat injury to outdoor plants in this country is connected with some fault in the root action predisposing the plant to such injury. Bulbs laid out to dry in hot sun are frequently damaged and may be killed. Extreme wilting due to a greater loss of water than can be made good at the time by absorption of water from the soil occasionally occurs especially with shallow-rooting plants.

A

**HEATH.** See **Erica.**

**HEATH GARDEN.** A very pleasant feature can be made in suitable soils and situations by planting hardy heaths (see **Calluna, Daboecia,** *and* **Erica**) either alone or in combination with a few plants which thrive in similar conditions. While hardy heaths may be grown on the rock garden or in formal beds or even, as far as the dwarf forms are concerned, as edgings to beds, they are much more effective when planted in large stretches in an open situation, especially if the ground is slightly undulating. This kind of planting should be attempted only in suitable soils, light, lime-free, and with a certain amount of moisture (but only temporary) in the lower parts. The undulations may be emphasized by planting the low-growing heaths in the depressions and the tall ones towards the ridges. No heaths grow well in soils permanently wet, and if any part of the area to be planted is under water for a long period, that should be avoided so far as the heaths themselves are concerned and given over to bog-plants. On the other hand, some heaths flourish on the margins of wet spots which may well be used for them. Such a garden, using the many hardy heaths available may, except in very cold districts, be a source of pleasure the year round. Some of the heaths will normally be in flower in all months of the year except perhaps May, and even this usually flowerless period, so far as heaths are concerned, can be tided over by planting a dwarf thyme which is of similar habit and will not appear incongruous in such surroundings. Even after flowering the dead inflorescences of some of the heaths add to the colour of the garden, as do the contrasting greens (and in some instances, purples), peculiar to the different species and varieties of this group of plants.

None of the species or varieties should be planted in a dot-like or haphazard fashion, but in irregular groups of the same kind and variety as large as the available space will permit, and so that the different groups run into one another. The plants should be put in so that within a short time the whole surface of the ground is hidden by their growth. Some, e.g. *Erica × darleyensis*, will in time cover an area many feet in diameter, but though this is so, rather close planting should be the rule in making a heath garden. The choice of species must be determined by the climate, for there is considerable difference in the degree of cold the different species will stand. *Calluna vulgaris, Erica carnea, E. × darleyensis, E. cinerea*, and *E. Tetralix* are generally uninjured by our most severe winters, while the taller heaths and *E. vagans* and *E. ciliaris*, as well as *Daboecia cantabrica* may be more or less damaged. Such plants as dwarf conifers, Bruckenthalia, *Polygala Chamaebuxus*, dwarf Cytisus, and Genista species, Thymus, Arctostaphylos, and dwarf Gaultherias make suitable companions for the heaths if some are desired in such a garden. Reference to the descriptions in the Dictionary will give information regarding the season, colour, height, best position, and so on, so that the greatest value can be obtained by the planting, and interest spread over the whole area instead of being confined to distinct parts of it at different seasons. Almost as important as soil and suitable plants and planting is the position of such a garden in relation to its surroundings. Severe formality seems so apart from the nature of the heaths that though the plants are beautiful individually the expression of their beauty is best appreciated away from bricks and mortar and the hard edges of formal beds and gravel paths. The labour involved in the upkeep of such a garden is not great, provided reasonable care has been taken to have the site free from perennial weeds at the outset. The plants themselves do much to smother other weeds; rarely indeed are they attacked by any pest; they are permanent occupiers of the ground requiring no replanting; the dwarfer species need occasional clipping over to prevent them becoming leggy; and they need little else.

**HEATH, ST. DABEOC'S.** *See* **Daboecia cantabrica.**

**HEATH, SEA.** *See* **Frankenia.**

**HEATHER.** *See* **Calluna vulgaris.**

*Heath'ii,* in honour of Dr. Rodier Heath, d. 1940, an ardent collector of succulent plants who worked with Dr. N. E. Brown.

**HEATING.** Very little scientific work has been undertaken in heating as applied to glasshouse structures. It is, therefore, in the main only possible to collect information on different systems of heating under varying conditions from growers and others.

The temperatures required in glass structures will vary with the crop grown, the period of growth, time of year, and weather conditions. With the majority of crops a buoyant atmosphere is favourable to satisfactory growth; a stagnant atmosphere to disease. Therefore, it is generally better to provide artificial heat and keep the ventilators slightly open, instead of closing the ventilators and reducing artificial heat. In dull weather with a low light intensity it is usually desirable to keep the temperature at the minimum, because a high temperature under conditions of poor light would induce poor weak growth. In bright sunny weather the temperature may be allowed to rise above the normal maximum (with the majority of plants) as the bright sunlight balances the high temperature and induces normal growth. Although thermostats may be used for the control of heating and ventilation, intelligent modification of temperatures will give the best results.

For the propagation of plants the ideal method of producing heat is probably by means of a 'hotbed' of fermenting material. If properly made this gives a gentle moist heat, whilst most other systems give a dry heat which has to be counteracted by various means. The temperature of the soil for the growth of plants is probably as important as the temperature of the air. With plants in pots, boxes, and small raised borders the temperature of the soil very quickly becomes the same as the temperature of the air in the glasshouse. But with houses where the plants are grown in the soil *in situ* on the floor of the house, it may take several weeks for the soil to equal the temperature of the air if the house has been unheated during the winter. Work at the Cheshunt Research Station suggests a minimum soil temperature of 57° F. for tomatoes. A number of experiments have been carried out on soil heating with electric cables or hot-water pipes; and there are now a number of both private and commercial installations with various systems of soil heating. This has been used mainly for pre-warming soil for tomatoes, for salad crops in frames, and for propagating cases. With a hotbed, the soil is warm and this may be one of the reasons for the success of this method of heating.

The majority of glasshouses and frames are heated by means of hot water, circulated in 4-in. cast-iron pipes. These, owing to their rough surface, radiate slightly more heat than wrought-iron or steel pipes.

The heat radiated by these pipes must be sufficient to equal the total loss of heat by the house through the glass and brickwork (when the required temperature has been obtained the heat lost through the floor is negligible).

When estimating the number of pipes required in a house it should be remembered that large houses are easier to heat than small ones, that badly fitting houses require more heat than sound ones, and that heat will be lost more quickly on a windy day than on a calm one.

It is possible to find the approximate amount of heat lost by a house by using the following approximations:

When the velocity of the wind is 15 m.p.h. then in 1 hour, when the difference in temperature between the air inside and outside the house is 1° F.

1 sq. ft. of glass loses 1 B.T.U.
1 „ „ brick „ $\frac{1}{2}$ „

Where 1 B.T.U. (British Thermal Unit) is the heat required to raise 1 lb. water through 1° F.

*The heat lost by a glasshouse* is estimated as follows:

Calculate the area of glass in sq. ft. (*g*) and also calculate the area of brickwork in sq. ft. (*b*).

Add together the number of sq. ft. of glass and half the number of sq. ft. of brickwork (i.e. $g + \frac{1}{2}b$).

Multiply this result by the difference required in temperature between inside of the house (*T*° F.) and the outside air (*t*°) (i.e. multiply by *T–t*).

*The amount of piping required* can be roughly calculated by using the approximation that 1 sq. ft. of surface area of pipe radiates 2 B.T.U. an hour for each 1° F. difference in temperature between the temperature of the pipe and the temperature of the house.

The amount required is estimated as follows:

Estimate the average temperature of the pipe (*P*° F.)— subtract from this the temperature required in the house (*T*° F.). Then multiply the result by 2. Now divide the total heat lost by the house by this result (i.e. divide total heat lost by $2 \times (P - T)$).

This result gives the amount of surface area required. From this, the total length of piping can be calculated.

EXAMPLE:

*Dimensions of house*

Length . . . 100 ft.
Width . . . 28 „

Height of brickwork . . . 2 ft.
„ „ glass to eaves . . 3 „
„ „ ridge . . . 8 „

i.e. area of brickwork = 512 sq. ft. approx.
area of glass = 4,192 sq. ft. approx.

*Temperatures*

Average temperature of air outside taken as 30° F.
Required temperature of air inside house . 60° F.
Average temperature of pipes . . . 180° F.

*Piping*

Diameter 4 in.

*Heat lost by the glasshouse*

= (No. of sq. ft. of glass + ½ no. of sq. ft. of brick) × (60−30)
= (4192 + ½ of 512) × 30
= (4192 + 256) × 30
= 4448 × 30 B.T.U. per hour
= *133,440* B.T.U. per hour.

The difference between the temperature of the pipes and the temperature of the house is (180−60)° F. i.e. 120° F.

∴ Amount of piping required is 133,440 ÷ 240 = 556 sq. ft.

Now the surface area of 1 ft. length of 4-in. pipe = $\pi\frac{1}{3} \times 1$ sq. ft. (as 4 in. = $\frac{1}{3}$ ft.).

∴ Length of piping required = $556 \div \frac{\pi}{3}$ ($\pi = \frac{22}{7}$)

$$= \frac{556 \times 3 \times 7}{22}$$

= approx. 530 ft.

∴ for a 100-ft. house the minimum no. of rows of pipes required is 5.

OR the approximate length, $l$, of piping required can be calculated directly as follows:

The heat radiated by pipes = heat lost by glass + heat lost by bricks.

∴ $\pi\frac{1}{3} \times l \times 2 \times (180-60) = (4192 \times 1 + \frac{1}{2}$ of $512) \times (60-30)$

∴ $\frac{2\pi l}{3} \times 120 = 4448 \times 30$

$$l = \frac{4448 \times 30 \times 3}{2\pi \times 120},$$

$l$ = approximately 530.

Alternatively tables can be consulted, e.g. for a 1,000 cu. ft. house:

| Temp. required in house °F. | B.T.U. | Feet of 4-in. pipe |
|---|---|---|
| 45 | 5,550 | 30 |
| 50 | 7,200 | 39 |
| 55 | 8,900 | 48 |
| 60 | 10,700 | 58 |
| 65 | 12,800 | 69 |
| 70 | 14,800 | 81 |

The above figures are based on a heat emission of 185 B.T.U. per ft. run of 4-in. pipe.

*Electric Heating of Glasshouses* (*The Electrification of Agriculture and Rural Districts*, Golding, p. 197).

Watts loading is given by the sum of:

Cub. capacity of house in cub. ft. multiplied by *X*.
Area of brick in sq. ft. multiplied by *Y*.
Area of glass in sq. ft. multiplied by *Z*.

*Required temperature when 32° F. outside*

| Constant | 45° | 50° | 55° | 60° | 65° F. |
|---|---|---|---|---|---|
| Cub. cap. *X* | 0·2 | 0·3 | 0·4 | 0·5 | 0·6 |
| Brick *Y* | 1·5 | 2·0 | 2·5 | 3·0 | 3·5 |
| Glass *Z* | 4·0 | 5·5 | 7·0 | 8·5 | 10·0 |

EXAMPLE:

Greenhouse cap. 3,000 cub. ft.
Glass 800 sq. ft.; brick 250 sq. ft.
Maintained at 45° F. with outside temperature 32° F.
*X* = 0·2, *Y* = 1·5, *Z* = 4·0.

Watts loading = $(3,000 \times 0·2) + (250 \times 1·5) + (800 \times 4·0)$
= 600 + 375 + 3,200
= 4,175 watts or approx. 4¼ kilowatts.

METHODS. The most suitable method of heating depends on the locality, the size and arrangement of the houses, and the crops to be grown. The control of soil and air temperature affects the incidence of disease, and the resistance of plants to disease, as well as the quantity and quality of the crop and the period of cropping. It must be remembered that different crops require different temperatures and conditions, varying according to the weather conditions and the stage of growth of the plants. The system of heating should be not only suitable for, but also readily adjustable to, changing conditions. Since fuel constitutes the second heaviest cost in growing crops under glass, it is essential that the system adopted should be efficient and well managed.

The main methods of heating the air in glasshouses are: (*a*) hot water circulated by the thermo-syphon system, (*b*) hot water with pulsometers, (*c*) steam, (*d*) steam injected into water (steam-cum-water), (*e*) hot air, (*f*) flues for heating, (*g*) electricity.

*Hot water* circulated by the thermo-syphon system is the method in most common use, and has hitherto been considered the most satisfactory for glasshouses with an area of one acre or less. On a large nursery, the disadvantages of this system are the necessity for a number of scattered stokeholes, involving extra labour for management and the distribution of fuel. On the other hand, a breakdown only affects a small area.

*Hot water with pulsometers or centrifugal electric pumps.* This system has in the past only been applicable to nurseries of two acres or more, as it has been considered necessary to have steam and electricity for the pulsometers in case of the failure of either source of power. With the easier and more certain supply of electric power now available in many places this system is worthy of consideration even in small nurseries. The circulation of water by means of pulsometers gives a rapid control of heat and enables the heating to be done from one or two central stokeholes, thus saving labour and other costs. The pumps should be fitted on the main return pipes and not on the main flows. The stokeholes may have a large number of small boilers collected together, or they may be fitted with a few large boilers. This system enables hot-water pipes to be used in the ground for soil heating without any additional pumps or separate system of heating.

*Steam.* This system is only worth consideration in a nursery of two acres or more, as a steam-boiler involves more or less continual attention. The chief advantages of steam heating are: (*a*) any number of houses can be heated from one boiler-house; (*b*) the control of temperature is quickly effected; (*c*) heat may be conserved in the boiler; (*d*) the heating pipes are of small diameter and therefore less costly; (*e*) the levels of the pipes are not important; (*f*) the steam can be used for other purposes such as soil sterilizing, pumping, &c. The main disadvantages are that steam-pipes can only be kept at the high temperature of approximately 212° F., whilst hot-water pipes are usually from 80 to 180° F., a breakdown involves rapid loss of heat. A stoker is required night and day.

*Steam-cum-water.* This arrangement is only suitable for a large nursery and has the advantage over steam alone that the pipes are maintained at a lower temperature. It is a system which may be economically sound for a nursery with scattered blocks of houses but its success depends on the availability of cheap fuel. Incidentally, it cannot be sound practice to turn water into steam, and then convert it back into hot water, unless temperature control or other considerations offset the extra fuel consumption.

Where the heating arrangements in an old and scattered nursery have to be reorganized and a central stoke-hole used, this method may be more economical than repiping all the houses.

Where widely different temperatures are required in adjoining houses as sometimes occurs in bulb forcing, the steam-cum-water system may be convenient and even economical.

*Hot Air.* Trial installations have been made adopting the method of conducting warmed air into the houses. At present this system seems to be less satisfactory and more expensive than the use of hot-water pipes.

*Flues for Heating.* Most of the early glasshouses and frames when not heated with fermenting material were heated with long flues extending part of the way or all the way down the houses. This system has now been almost completely superseded, although it is still used to some extent in rhubarb-forcing sheds in the West Riding of Yorkshire.

*Electricity.* This method has been used in a few instances and is very efficient, but at present too costly, especially as some alternative system is really necessary in case of breakdown. For the amateur's small greenhouse electricity may be the most satisfactory method of heating.

Air or space heating may be done by using tubular heaters, immersion heaters in a water system, with possibly pumps for more effective circulation, or electrode boilers. For the amateur the immersion heater in a water system is well worth consideration. All these systems can easily be thermostatically controlled.

As previously indicated electricity can be conveniently used for raising early salad crops by means of soil-heating cables, or (with A.C. electricity supply) by a low-voltage transformer and galvanized steel wire, run at 20 to 30 volts. There is a possibility of developing a system of soil sterilization by using the buried wires and laying a corresponding set of wires on the surface, the electricity being used to produce the necessary heat (approx. 212° F. for 20 min.).

BOILERS. The main types of low-pressure boilers in use on commercial nurseries are: (*a*) tubular, (*b*) sectional, and (*c*) Lancashire. On the smaller nurseries tubular boilers are probably the most satisfactory, because although some of them are perhaps not quite so efficient as sectional boilers, they are more easily repaired in case of breakdown. This may not be so important with modern methods of repair by electric welding. Boilers should be purchased with a 30 to 50 per cent. margin on the maker's specification to allow for adverse weather conditions and loss of efficiency with age. On a small nursery several small boilers interconnected may be better than one large boiler, since they give a better control of heat, save fuel, and are safer in case of breakdown.

The magazine type of boiler is worth consideration as this can be thermostatically controlled. This boiler has one or two magazines or hoppers containing a reserve of graded fuel arranged in such a way that by means of gravity the fuel is fed at the appropriate rate to the fire. There are no 'moving parts' and little to go wrong. The alternative is the automatic stoker which can be fitted to almost any type of large boiler but is not suitable for a small glasshouse. The automatic stokers are made for particular types of fuel and only fuel of the right grade can be used. Anthracite, coke, or small bituminous fuel can be used on the appropriate machines. The fuel is loaded into a hopper and conducted to the underside of the fire-box by a large screw. The speed of the screw can be varied, and the fuel is burnt in conjunction with forced draught. The forced draught can be regulated by means of a thermostat in the glasshouses, and the fire kept alight on a warm day by a time switch which turns on the forced draught for a short period—say, every half-hour. This is undoubtedly a most satisfactory and economical way of heating large boilers, and gives a very high efficiency in the combustion of fuel compared with hand firing.

The types of boilers most commonly used in gardens are small sectional boilers and for the single small house, the horse-shoe type boiler.

One or two growers have used Lancashire type steam-boilers modified to heat water for normal circulation in the pipes. By an adjustment, these boilers can be used for producing steam for steam-sterilizing in the winter. For the hot-water heating, boilers of this type are not quite as efficient as ordinary hot-water boilers, but this may be compensated for by the advantage that they can be used for steam-sterilizing.

*Position of boilers.* Boilers on nurseries are best placed about 12 ft. from the lower end of the houses; this leaves a clear road along the end of the houses, and minimizes the risk of fumes injuring the plants. This position also lessens the shadow cast by the chimneys and other structures. Where a central heating system is adopted the boilers are, of course, placed wherever is most convenient.

*Setting of boilers.* With a view to controlling the combustion of the fuel, conserving heat, and eliminating waste, the setting and protection of the boilers and the arrangement of the dampers and flues is very important. Boilers should be set so that there is no escape of heat except through the boiler. To ensure this, the following precautions are worthy of consideration when installing tubular boilers: the surrounding brickwork and covering should be made with a 9-in. wall or two 4½-in. walls, hollow or packed. The top of the boiler should have the usual fire tiles, then a 3-in. space, and then slabs. It may also be worth painting the brickwork with black varnish or tar to make it less porous. The whole should be covered from the weather.

*Flues.* The flues should be smooth on the inside and have a good rise to the shaft. They must be as large as the maximum damper opening, and if possible they should come from the bottom of the boiler, so as to retain a pocket of hot air in the boiler.

*The Dampers* must fit well, as cold air entering here checks the draught of hot air and gases entering the shaft. The dampers should be easily accessible, otherwise they may be neglected.

*The Chimney* should be higher than the surrounding structures. It should be smooth inside and of an internal square measure not less than the combined square measure of the damper openings at their maximum aperture. When not in use during the summer, the dampers, chimneys, and boilers should be kept open and as dry as possible to prevent rusting. All ashes should be cleared out of the fire-box or the production of sulphur fumes will cause corrosion.

GENERAL MANAGEMENT. In order to maintain efficiency in any heating system, regular inspection and overhaul of all taps and valves are necessary. All boilers should be emptied and washed out at least once a year. If the tubes have 'scale' inside, it should be removed in an acid bath. Even a very thin scale will mean a loss of efficiency and the burning of several extra tons of coal a year. It pays to have all dampers, &c., correctly adjusted, as 1 lb. of carbon monoxide going to waste takes 4,500 potential heat units with it.

Finally it is essential to have the most suitable kind and grade of fuel for the type of boiler in use.

SELECTION OF FUEL. The main fuels available for glasshouse heating are coal, coke, and oil. The value of fuel and its suitability for any particular purpose are determined by its carbon-hydrogen content. A horizontal type of steam-boiler with a long traverse for gases needs a long flame fuel, i.e. one having a large percentage of hydrogen in relation to percentage of carbon, e.g. steam-coal. Anthracite, with high carbon and low hydrogen and therefore a short flame, is the type of fuel required for boilers having short flues and little traverse between the tubes and the chimney.

The price of fuel by the ton is not a satisfactory gauge of its value. Bearing in mind its analysis, i.e. carbon and hydrogen content, moisture, ash content, and the fusion point of the ash (clinker) the cost per British Thermal Unit is the best guide. Typical analyses of some of the commoner fuels are as follows :

| Description | % Volatile gases | B.T.U. per lb. |
| --- | --- | --- |
| Dry steam-coal | 8–20 | 12,500 |
| Best anthracite | 8 | 15,000 |
| Furnace coke | Volatile gases driven off | 12,600 |
| Gas coke | | 12,700 |
| Fuel oil | | 18,500 |

The moisture content of cokes has been liable to great variation in the past, and figures over 10 per cent. have been by no means uncommon. This has frequently been due to the prevalence of careless hand-quenching by means of a hosepipe after manufacture. Coke made in continuous vertical gas retorts is dry-cooled and practically moisture free. In modern coke-oven practice, a predetermined quantity of water is employed in the 'quenching towers' and the resultant coke therefore contains very little moisture. Coke is liable to pick up moisture in transit, but as a rule the amount is not serious.

The damping of coke is to be deprecated, since a certain number of B.T. units will be lost in the evaporation of the moisture when the coke is burnt. With coal slack, damping may be advantageous under certain conditions, due to the binding effect of the moisture on the coal dust.

A mixed fuel, such as gas coke with 25 per cent. small coal, may be worth consideration. Forced draught, which can be economically employed in large nurseries, makes it possible to use low-priced fuel, such as coke breeze, dust of bituminous coal, &c.

Automatic stokers or magazine-fed boilers may also use low-price fuel.

For the ordinary low-pressure boilers used for most glasshouses where there is no night stoker, good anthracite is probably the best fuel in winter, and coke and 25 per cent. small coal in the summer. In larger nurseries where a night stoker is employed, a low-priced fuel with forced draught may be the most economical. In the purchase of this type of fuel, colliery certificates should be asked for as a guarantee of the source of origin.

By the substitution of special fire-bars some boilers can burn low-priced fuel with forced draught, the whole being thermostatically controlled.

*Gas* has been used to heat hot-water boilers for small houses but great care must be taken as coal-gas is deadly to plants.

*Fuel oil.* By employing thermostats, the use of fuel oil provides a very efficient control of temperature but involves a larger capital outlay than with an efficient solid fuel installation. Where there are heavy 'standby' charges, such as is the case in growing chrysanthemums, oil fuel is worth investigation. For an even and heavy load oil is more expensive than coal. Coal would therefore probably be best for propagating houses but these might be linked to an oil-heating system in the summer.

Centralized stokeholes, with water circulated by means of pulsometers or centrifugal electric pumps, are practically essential for economic heating with oil. Where oil is installed it is important that the flame should not impinge on the metal of the boiler as this causes a loss of efficiency and injures the boiler.

Small glasshouse heaters are available that burn paraffin, some are part of a small hot-water system. These are suitable for very small houses, but are not as easily controlled as other methods mentioned.

STOKING. When solid fuel is used, the efficiency of the stoking is one of the most difficult things to ensure. High efficiency in the combustion of the fuel depends on the observance of a number of practical points. The draught should pass up through the body of the fire, otherwise some of the gases will probably be cooled below the point of combustion (flash-point). Air-leaks in front through badly fitting doors are a regular source of loss. When opening the furnace door the damper should be closed somewhat to lessen the draught of cold air. The damper should fit well and should be opened only to the minimum necessary to retain a bright fire, so conserving a pocket of hot air in the fire-box. Burning fuel should completely cover the furnace bars, since gaps allow cold draughts to enter the fire-box and cool the gases below combustion-point; these go up the chimney unburnt, usually as smoke. The depth of the fire should, if possible, never be greater than 6 to 8 in. and perfectly even. Overloading with fuel means cooling the combustion chamber with a loss of gases which may amount to 16 per cent. One bright spot should be left to ignite the gases after the addition of fuel. The furnace doors should, obviously, be opened as little as possible.

There are several mechanical stokers now on the market which are worthy of consideration, since they enable these conditions to be maintained relatively easily, and also provide a means of using low-priced fuel.

Where the fires have to be 'banked' for the night, in addition to leaving one bright spot to ignite the gases, it is a help if some fine fuel is placed on the part of the fire near the furnace door. This checks the tendency of the draught to be stronger in front than in other parts of the fire.

METHODS OF REGULATING TEMPERATURE. The temperature of heated glass structures is regulated by the adjustment of ventilation and sources of artificial heat to maintain a suitable temperature. As already indicated, this varies with the crop, period of growth, weather conditions, sunlight, &c.

There are thermostatically controlled ventilators, but at present, on a large scale, ventilation will have to be carried out by hand. Ventilators should be sufficient in number, suitably placed, and easily accessible. In large houses it is an advantage if these can be opened with a lever on the outside.

For most crops it is essential that ventilators are so arranged that no stagnant patches of air remain in the houses; and that ventilation can be given without undue draught. The use of fans has been tried for blowing air into, and for extracting air from houses, but these are not a commercial proposition at present.

Most small glasshouses in gardens have inadequate means of ventilation.

When tomatoes are grown in large blocks of houses, it is often necessary to turn on the heat in the summer to obtain a circulation of air; and not because the heat itself is required.

*Arrangement of hot-water pipes.* The majority of houses are heated by means of hot-water pipes which convey the heat from the fire. The arrangement of these pipes is of great importance.

The actual arrangement of the pipes will depend on the locality and the crops, but from the points of view of healthy plant growth and effective distribution of the heat, a number of warm pipes is better than a few hot pipes. There has been a tendency in the past to use too few pipes to maintain adequate temperatures in commercial houses. The pipes should be arranged so that an even distribution of heat is obtained. In most districts at least five 4-in. pipes are needed to heat a tomato house 28 ft. wide. When buying hot-water pipes the weight per 9-ft. length should be specified. This should be a minimum of 84 lb.

With a thermo-syphon system of heating, the 'flow' pipes should rise evenly at least 1 in. in 10 ft. and the returns fall correspondingly. Overhead flows are used

More satisfactory radiation would be obtained if it were possible to arrange them separately. Pipes are generally arranged with the flow pipes on the sides of the house, which is probably the coldest place, but when several houses are built in one block some rearrangement of pipes is necessary, otherwise the warmest pipes will be under the gutters where there is least cubic capacity to heat. 'Screw-down' and diaphragm valves should be provided to enable satisfactory control of the water circulating in the pipes, and also to make it possible to isolate a boiler for repair without necessarily emptying the whole hot-water system.

In modern houses the hot-water pipes are generally

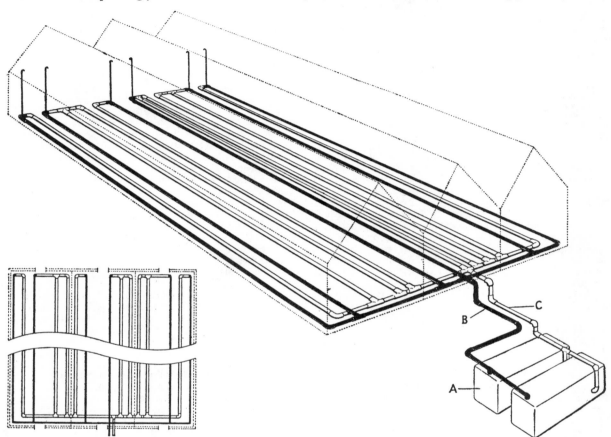

*Diagram showing arrangement of pipes for heating three houses.* A, *boilers.* B, *flow pipes in black.* C, *return pipes in outline*

for some crops, such as carnations, and have the additional advantage of enabling the boilers to be at ground-level. The main flows and returns should be separated in the houses to facilitate ease of repair and a better distribution of heat, and not one above the other as is usually the case. It is usual to place the heating pipes a few inches above ground-level, because in a glasshouse where tomatoes are grown in the ground the soil gradually rises due to the addition of manures, &c., and in a few years pipes originally placed at ground-level would tend to become buried. All pipes outside the houses should be 'lagged' with non-conducting material to check loss of heat. Asbestos lagging is undoubtedly best, but otherwise cow manure, clay, and sacking are satisfactory. One hundred ft. of 4-in. pipe which remains unlagged for 3,000 hours of heating may mean a loss equivalent to 5 tons of fuel.

The heat radiated from a pipe depends (among other things) on the difference in temperature between the surrounding air and the pipe. If pipes are arranged in 'banks' of 3 or 4, these pipes will keep each other warm.

connected with joints made of cement and tow. This is very satisfactory and permanent. 'Expansion joints' are also used which join the pipes together by an arrangement of rubber rings and collars. This is a more expensive method, but an advantage where alterations in the arrangement of the pipes are likely. This type of joint is worth having in reserve in case of breakdown as these can be used whilst there is still water in the pipes. Where these joints are used it is essential to support the pipes carefully.

Recently, growers have been using old ships' tubes and welding these together. This is a common practice in Holland, and is a cheap and satisfactory system for commercial growers.

Arrangements can be made for heating the water for watering by taking the cold-water pipe through a main flow pipe for 10 to 20 ft. The water standing in the pipe when the tap is first turned on would normally be too hot to use and should be run off.

The thermostatic control of heating has been mentioned in various connexions and this is a great advantage, particularly in maintaining night temperatures. The thermometer should be where the plants are growing and not high up on a purlin post or on the end of the house.

For certain purposes it may be desirable to keep houses cold in summer. For shading, movable blinds of wooden slats or hessian are the most satisfactory, as permanent shading such as whiting is usually too dense in dull weather. Where colder conditions are necessary, the blinds should be raised about 1 ft. above the glass, and an arrangement made for water to flow gently down the glass roof under the blind.

FRAMES. Frames may be heated by hot-water pipes as for glasshouses. Pits made up of 6×4-ft. lights generally need one 4-in. flow at the back and one 4-in. return in front. Pits made up of Dutch lights measuring 59× 31¾ in. can generally be heated by a similar coil of 2- or 3-in. pipe. By this method the crop is usually ready at the back of the frame 2 or 3 days before the front.

Mr. F. A. Secrett has devised a special system of heating Dutch lights for forcing seakale and for the production of lettuces with a view to obtaining even distribution of heat all over the frame and so enabling the crop to be cut all at once. This involves the use of T-irons on which are placed tiles to support the soil. In a chamber below 2 pipes run in a 6-in. iron gutter containing water. This provides a warm, moist atmosphere somewhat similar to that obtained from a hotbed. The initial cost is high, but may be worthwhile for high-value crops. As previously mentioned frames may also be heated by means of buried electric cables or with the aid of a transformer and galvanized steel wire. Experiments seem to indicate that heating at night only, gives as good results, at less cost, than the use of continuous heating and a thermostat. Fermenting material is now seldom used for glasshouses, but is used for frames. For this purpose fresh strawy stable or farm-yard manure is mixed with about an equal quantity of manure that has been stacked for about 6 months, or with leaves. This is watered when first mixed, and as necessary, at 2 or 3 subsequent turnings. A hotbed is usually made 9 in. to 1 ft. larger than the frame to be heated, and about 1 ft. deep, when first made and thoroughly trodden. Soil or old hotbed material (terreau) is usually used inside the frame to a depth of about 4 in.

The Dutch growers take a trench out under the centre of a row of lights measuring about 18 in. wide by 1 ft. deep and fill this with fermenting manure and then cover with soil. This is an economical and satisfactory method for cucumbers, and although uneven in heating can be used for seed raising. Fermenting manure can also be used for packing round frames placed over early strawberries.

*Ventilation.* Frames should generally be ventilated after a frost, when the best method is to prop up the lights alternately at the top and at the bottom. For normal ventilation the lights would be opened or raised according to the direction of the wind. For growing lettuces in cold Dutch lights, early in the year, ventilation is seldom given except after frost.

*Covering.* Archangel mats, straw mats, hessian, and straw have all been used in severe weather to protect frames from the cold. It is possible that the sewing-machine for making straw thatch will provide suitable straw mats for this purpose. Mats of this type last longer if dipped in preservative such as a solution of copper sulphate every year.

C. E. H.

A→

**HE'BE.** Included in **Veronica.**

**HEBECLIN'IUM.** *See* **Eupatorium.**

**HEBENSTREIT'IA** (in honour of John Ernest Hebenstreit, 1703–57, Professor of Botany in the University of Leipsig). FAM. *Scrophulariaceae.* A genus of about 30 species of shrubs, undershrubs, and annuals, all but one natives of S. Africa. Leaves alternate, or the lower ones opposite; flowers closely packed in spikes opening from the base upwards; corolla tubular at the base, with a 1-lipped, 4-lobed limb, stamens 4. Greenhouse plants, thriving in the ordinary compost of loam, peat, and sand. Propagation by soft wood cuttings; annuals by seed.

**H. au'rea.** A synonym of *H. integrifolia.*

**H. como'sa.** Perennial herb, 2 to 4 ft., stems stout, angular, minutely downy. *l.* sessile, numerous, 1 to 2½ in. long, ¼ to ⅓ in. wide, linear-lanceolate, coarsely toothed, midrib prominent beneath, glabrous. *fl.* ½ in. long, in slender, erect terminal spikes 2 to 6 in. long; cor. slenderly tubular, white or yellow, limb with an orange-red blotch on throat. September. S. Africa. 1889. (B.M. 7895.) var. **serratifo'lia,** *l.* more strongly toothed than usual, but in this respect the species is very variable. (R.G. 1901, p. 191.) There is also (not in cultivation) an entire-leafed var. called **integrifo'lia.**

**H. crassifo'lia.** Annual, much-branched, 6 to 9 in. h., branches stout, spreading, downy. *l.* linear or oblong, ¼ to ⅜ in. long, obtuse, rather fleshy, entire, glabrous, sometimes clustered. *fl.* ½ in. long; cor. tube narrow, lobes narrow, oblong, short; spikes 1 to 4 in. long, many-fld., oblong or elongated. S. Africa.

**H. denta'ta.** Sub-shrub, 1 to 2 ft., shoots finely downy. *l.* linear to lanceolate-linear, ½ to 1½ in. long, $\frac{1}{12}$ to ⅛ in. wide, toothed. *fl.* in terminal spikes up to 6 in. long; cor. ½ in. long, yellow or white, blotched with orange on the 4-lobed limb; tube slender; lobes linear-oblong. March to October. S. Africa. 1770. (B.M. 483.)

**H. frutico'sa.** Sub-shrubby plant up to 1½ ft., base woody. *l.* linear-lanceolate, up to 1 in. long, ⅛ in. wide, toothed, glabrous. *fl.* in terminal spikes 2 to 5 in. long; cor. white with an orange blotch on the limb, tube slender, limb ¼ in. wide, 4-lobed. August. S. Africa. 1816. (B.M. 1970.)

**H. integrifo'lia.** Perennial or sometimes annual plant ½ to 2 ft., shoots downy. *l.* filiform or linear-filiform, entire, ½ to 1¼ in. long, glabrous or scabrid. *fl.* in cylindrical, terminal spikes 3 to 6 in. long; cor. ⅝ in. long, yellow, limb stained red. May to September. S. Africa. 1796. (A.B.R. 252 as *H. aurea.*) SYN. *H. scabra, H. tenuifolia.*

**H. scab'ra.** A synonym of *H. integrifolia.*

**H. tenuifo'lia.** A synonym of *H. integrifolia.*

***hebephyl'lus -a -um,*** with leaves like a species of Hebe.

**HEBERDE'NIA.** Included in **Myrsine.** *H. excelsa* is *M. Heberdenia.*

***hebra'icus -a -um,*** Hebrew.

**HECH'TIA** (in honour of J. H. G. Hecht, Prussian Counsellor, d. 1837). FAM. *Bromeliaceae.* A genus of nearly 30 species of often caulescent herbaceous perennials with crowded, long, narrow, recurved, very spiny leaves, and compound spikes of insignificant flowers. The genus differs from Dyckia botanically by having dioecious flowers. The plants produce offsets from the base and call for the same treatment as Tillandsia. The species are distributed over Mexico and neighbouring countries and though several have been introduced, none is widely grown.

**H. argen'tea.** *l.* in a dense rosette, sharply recurved, rigid, about 12 in. long, densely silvery on both surfaces. *fl.* white, small, in globose clusters on a tall spike. Mexico. (B.M. 7460.)

**H. cordylinoi'des.** A synonym of *H. stenopetala.*

**H. Desmetia'na.** About 4 ft. h. *l.* ensiform, thick, recurved, about 18. in. long, spiny, sparingly scaly above, densely beneath. *fl.* red, ½ in long, in a branched panicle about 2 ft. long, leafy below. Mexico. 1894. (B.M. 7340 as *Dyckia Desmetiana.*)

**H. Elemee'tii.** A synonym of *Ochagavia Lindleyana.*

**H. pitcairniifo'lia.** A synonym of *Fascicularia pitcairniifolia.*

**H. stenopeta'la.** About 6 ft. h. *l.* in a rosette, lanceolate, recurved, 2 ft. long, pale, scaly beneath, spines large. *fl.* white, small, in a branched panicle. Mexico. 1881. (B.M. 6554.)

***hecisto-,*** in compound words, signifying viper-like.

***Hec'tori,*** in honour of Sir James Hector, F.R.S., 1834–1907, Director, Geological Survey of New Zealand.

**HED'ERA** (ancient Latin name for Ivy). FAM. *Araliaceae*. A genus of some 7 species of evergreen climbers, attaching themselves to their support by means of aerial roots. Leaves alternate, long-stalked, more or less leathery. Flowers small, bisexual, in umbels, the parts in fives. Fruit a berry, mostly black, with 2 to 5 seeds. Young shoots, calyx and flower-stalks furnished with scale-like stellate hairs, with the number of 'rays' varying in different species. In its creeping state and as long as it produces aerial roots, the ivy is quite sterile. It bears flowers and fruits only when it has reached the top of its support and ceased to climb. The leaves then become entire and the growth become bushy. Plants raised from these fertile growths make bushy shrubs several feet high and flower and fruit freely in that state. Such plants are generally distinguished from the creeping form as 'var. *arborescens*'. A vigorous hybrid between *H. Helix* and *Fatsia japonica* has been raised, *see* **Fatshedera**.

*Hechtia Desmetiana* (p. 965)

The ivies are all natives of the northern part of the Old World. The *H. australiana* of von Mueller, a Queensland tree with enormous *pinnate* leaves, which is included in the original issue of this Dictionary, is now placed in a separate genus—Kissodendron.

The growth of ivy on trees of any value or beauty is to be deprecated, but an old decayed or worthless one may well be given up to it, for, when such a tree becomes ivy-laden, it makes a most pleasant winter picture. For covering unsightly walls or buildings or for bleak walls facing north in cold districts, no evergreen is so good.

The ivies are of the easiest cultivation, thriving in full sunshine or shade, in all but the worst soils, and are readily propagated by cuttings. Grafting should be avoided. They need clipping back hard when on walls. This is best done in April just before growth begins and the opportunity of brushing out dead leaves, &c., should

then be taken. The hairs sometimes cause irritation to tender skins and those likely to be affected may well wear gloves when doing the clipping. **A**

**H. amuren'sis.** A synonym of *H. colchica*.

**H. australia'na.** A synonym of *Kissodendron australianum*.

**H. canarien'sis.** Canary Island Ivy. Strong high climber. *l.* 5 to 8 in. wide, 3- to 5-lobed, cordate at the base, of leathery texture. Hairs with about 15 rays; *l.* of fertile state ovate, not or only slightly lobed, smaller. Canary Is. N. Africa. var. **azo'rica,** *l.* 5- to 7-lobed, lobes ovate, blunt. Azores. Tender.

**H. chrysocarp'a.** *l.* broadly ovate, shallowly lobed or entire, cordate at base, 2 to 4 in. long and wide. In the fertile state the *l.* is smaller, not lobed, and comparatively much narrower. *fr.* yellow. SE. Europe, Asia Minor. Distinct by its yellow *fr.* SYN. *H. Helix poetica, H. poetarum.*

**H. cine'rea.** A synonym of *H. nepalensis*.

**H. col'chica.*** *l.* ovate, cordate or rounded at base, entire or slightly lobed, 3 to 8 in. long, leathery. Hairs with up to 25 rays. In the fertile state the *l.* are smaller, often broadly cuneate at base. In *l.* the finest of all ivies; a strong grower. The arborescent form makes fine wide bushes. Caucasus, Asia Minor. SYN. *H. amurensis, H. Roegneriana.* var. **denta'ta,** *l.* slightly toothed, thinner. There is a handsome variegated form of this (**variega'ta**).

**H. He'lix.** Common Ivy. Evergreen climber up to 100 ft. *l.* of sterile shoots 2 to 4 in. long, broadly ovate to triangular, 3- to 5-lobed, dark green with pale veins. On fertile shoots the *l.* are not lobed and more strictly ovate, and the stems cease emitting aerial roots. Hairs with 5 or 6 rays. *fl.* in globose umbels, 1½ to 2½ in. wide, yellowish-green. October. *fr.* ¼ in. wide, globose, dull inky-black. Europe (Britain). (E.B. 633.) For the hybrid with *Fatsia japonica, see* **Fatshedera**.

The ivy has sported into numerous forms, many of them extraordinarily distinct from the typical one, but their nomenclature is very much involved in gardens and nurseries and only the most marked varieties are mentioned here. For a more detailed study see Shirley Hibberd's Monograph *The Ivy.* var. **angula'ris,** *l.* bright green, medium size, lobes triangular, pointed; its sub-var. **au'rea** is one of the best yellow-leaved ivies; **arbores'cens,** Tree Ivy, the fertile shoots can be rooted from cuttings like the climbing ones and in this way take on a wide bushy shape 6 or 8 ft. across, making a useful evergreen shrub for shady places. There are white- and yellow-variegated forms; **Cavendish'ii,** dwarfish, *l.* small, angularly lobed, margins creamy-white; **chrysophyl'la,** *l.* variegated with yellow, wholly yellow, or wholly green on the same plant; **conglomera'ta,** dwarf, slow-growing, *l.* crowded, small. (R.H. 1890, 163.); **deltoi'dea,** *l.* medium size, triangular, with 3 obtuse lobes, basal ones overlapping; **digita'ta,** *l.* deeply 5- or 7-lobed; lobes slender, pointing forward and spreading out like fingers; **elegantis'sima,** a synonym of var. *marginata rubra;* **Emerald green,** *l.* particularly vivid, glossy green, useful for walls; **hibern'ica,** a synonym of *H. hibernica;* **loba'ta major,** *l.* 5-lobed, middle lobe very large, pointed; **margina'ta,** name given to a group of ivies with small *l.* margined white, creamy-white, or yellow; in the form **ru'bra** the margin becomes deep rosy-red in autumn; **mi'nor** has the smallest *l.* in the group; **min'ima,** smallest of the ivies, *l.* crowded, ½ to 1 in. across with 3 or 5 angular lobes; **ova'ta,** *l.* ovate, rounded at base, scarcely, if at all, lobed, rich green; **palma'ta,** *l.* 5-lobed, lobes triangular, spreading; **peda'ta,** *l.* 5-lobed, middle lobe long, narrow, finger-shaped; side lobes narrow but spreading; **pennsylvan'ica,** a synonym of var. *digitata* or *minima;* **poet'ica,** a synonym of *H. chrysocarpa;* **purpu'rea,** *l.* bronzy-purple in autumn mottled with dull green; chief veins white; **sagittaefo'lia,** *l.* arrow-head-shaped, 5-lobed, central lobe, large, triangular; **scot'ica,** a synonym of *H. hibernica;* **taurica,** a synonym of var. *minima* or *digitata;* a form of *H. chrysocarpa* also goes by this name; **tric'olor,** a synonym of var. *marginata rubra.*

**H. hibern'ica.** Irish Ivy. Strong growing, high climber. *l.* very dark green, 3 to 6 in. wide, with usually 5 triangular lobes; often rather cordate at the base. Hairs with 8 to 12 rays. Very common; useful ground cover for under trees and shady places. Ireland, Scotland. var. **macula'ta,** *l.* variegated yellowish-white. SYN. *H. Helix hibernica, H. scotica.*

**H. himala'ica.** A synonym of *H. nepalensis*.

**H. japon'ica.** Japanese Ivy. *l.* triangular to ovate, up to 2 in. long, slightly 3-lobed, often more or less cordate at the base. Hairs with 15 to 20 rays. *l.* of fertile state, oblong-ovate, 2 to 4 in. long. *fr.* small, black. Japan. var. **variega'ta,** *l.* thinly edged with white. Not a robust grower. SYN. *H. rhombea.*

**H. nepalen'sis.** *l.* triangular, ovate to ovate-lanceolate, slender-pointed, 2 to 4½ in. long, 1 to 2½ in. wide, often with a side lobe at each side near base and several large teeth; greyish-green. In the fertile state the *l.* is entire and proportionally narrower. Hairs with 15 to 20 rays. *fr.* yellow or red. Himalaya. (R.H. 1884, 84.) SYN. *H. cinerea, H. himalaica.*

**H. poeta'rum.** A synonym of *H. chrysocarpa*.

**H. rhom'bea.** A synonym of *H. japonica*.

**H. Roegneria'na.** A synonym of *H. colchica*.

W. J. B.

**hedera'ceus -a -um,** ivy-like.

**HEDGE HYSSOP.** *See* **Gratiola.**

**HEDGE MUSTARD.** Common name for *Sisymbrium officinale.*

**HEDGE NETTLE.** *See* **Stachys.**

**HEDGEHOG CACTUS.** *See* **Echinocactus.**

**HEDGEHOG HOLLY.** *See* **Ilex Aquifolium ferox.**

**HEDGEHOG THISTLE.** *See* **Echinocactus.**

**HEDGES.** Continuous screens of trees or shrubs planted close together at regular intervals, used for giving shelter or seclusion, hiding boundary fences, keeping out cattle, or dividing up the garden into separate sections.

Previous to the planting of a hedge, the ground must be well prepared by trenching and the addition of well-rotted manure if the soil is poor or shallow. A hedge planted to keep out cattle will need to be supplemented by a fence for some time until the hedge is well established, while in exposed situations, as for example, sites near the sea, it will be advisable to give the hedge some protection from the wind in the form of wattle hurdles during its early stages of growth. If the hedge plants used are of any considerable size, they should be staked.

Young hedges are much improved and their growth encouraged if the soil is kept open and free from weeds by frequent hoeing.

For real permanence English yew and holly are among the finest of all hedge plants but are somewhat slow growing in their early stages and consequently expensive in initial outlay. The most satisfactory planting size for these and most hedge plants is 3 to 4 ft. high. The distance apart will depend upon the height and bushiness of the specimens used and will vary from 15 to 30 in. from centre to centre.

A somewhat cheaper evergreen hedge may be formed by conifers such as *Thuya Lobbii* and *Chamaecyparis Lawsoniana.* Both of these grow more quickly than yew or holly but are less amenable to close clipping and are shorter-lived. *Thuya occidentalis* is sometimes used but is less satisfactory. *Cupressus macrocarpa* has become more popular than it deserves, owing to its rapid growth, but except in mild maritime districts it is liable to be badly browned and even killed during a severe winter, while in localities which suit it, it grows over-vigorously, entailing constant clipping if it is to be kept within bounds.

Perhaps the most frequently planted of all hedge plants is the oval-leaved privet, which certainly makes a satisfactory hedge but its roots are apt to be very troublesome by their habit of invading adjacent borders; and it has now become so common that most gardeners will prefer to plant a more interesting subject.

Among deciduous plants suitable for hedges, beech and hornbeam are perhaps the best of all since they retain their leaves through most of the winter. Beech does well in chalky districts and hornbeam where there is stiff clay, but both are good on medium or light loams.

Where space is limited evergreen bush-honeysuckles such as *Lonicera nitida* and *L. yunnanensis* make neat and close-growing hedges, although the effect is thin for a year or two after planting. Box is also a good hedge plant in chalky districts.

Where cost is important, quickthorn makes a cheap but effective hedge as also does the Myrobalan or Cherry Plum (*Prunus cerasifera*), planted in a single or a double row one foot apart. Ornamental hedges may also be formed by using some of the flowering shrubs as hedge-plants especially in less formal parts of the garden. In order to get the full benefit of the blossom of these plants, more space and freedom of growth must be allowed than for a close-clipped hedge. Suitable subjects are to be found in *Berberis Darwinii, B. Gagnepainii, B. stenophylla, Prunus Pissardii,* Lilac, Rose species and hybrid briers, *Escallonia Ingramii, E. macrantha.* Varieties of Escallonia are particularly suitable for maritime localities where other plants which may be used for hedges will include *Fuchsia Riccartonii,* Veronica in variety, Pittosporum, *Griselinia littoralis.*

J. E. G. W.

**HEDRAEAN'THUS** = **Edraian'thus.** *See* **Wahlenbergia.**

**hedraian'thus -a -um,** having sessile flowers.

*Hedwig'ii,* in honour of John Hedwig, 1730–99, muscologist, Professor of Botany, Leipsig.

**HEDYCH'IUM** (*hedys,* sweet, *chion,* snow; the flowers of *H. coronarium,* the first species described, are fragrant and white). FAM. *Zingiberaceae.* A genus of nearly 40 species of erect perennial herbs, natives of S. and E. Asia, one in Madagascar. Plants often large, with numerous reed-like stems. Leaves 2-ranked, mostly large, sessile or upper stalked, lanceolate or linear-lanceolate. Flowers in many-flowered spikes, white, yellow, or red, with a long corolla tube, narrow segments, a long filament, anthers without a spur at the base, lip long, 2-lobed, its lobes entire. Hedychiums are valuable both for their foliage and often very sweetly scented flowers and several are nearly hardy, and will, in favoured climates, stand the winter on a south border with a little protection. They are good also for sub-tropical bedding treated in the same way as Cannas, and for planting out in a wide conservatory border using a compost of good loam with a little well-decayed manure and enough sharp sand to ensure good drainage. *H. Gardnerianum* is perhaps the most satisfactory for these purposes as it is one of the hardiest, but *H. Greenei, H. flavum,* and *H. Forrestii* would all serve. For large pots or tubs the plants need planting in spring in a rich soil, plenty of water and liquid manure when growing, and repotting in the second year into pots or tubs slightly larger. When flowering is over the spikes should be cut down, and if it is desired to increase them the rhizomes should be divided when repotting is done. Where a heated tank is used for growing tropical water-plants the pots or tubs may be placed in the water to a depth of 2 or 3 in.; where no such convenience exists the plants should be watered 2 or 3 times a day while growing.

KEY

| | |
|---|---|
| 1. *Infl. dense, usually little longer than wide, fl. hiding the base* | 2 |
| 1. *Infl. longer than wide, fl. not hiding the base* | 8 |
| 2. *Fl. 3 to 5 within the bracts* | 3 |
| 2. *Fl. one only within the bracts* | H. ellipticum |
| 3. *Staminodes oblong; bracts densely overlapping* | 4 |
| 3. *Staminodes linear; bracts not overlapping* | H. Elwesii |
| 4. *Lip wide* | 5 |
| 4. *Lip longer than wide* | 7 |
| 5. *Lip white or nearly so* | 6 |
| 5. *Lip and filament yellow* | H. flavum |
| 6. *Lip widely obcordate* | H. coronarium |
| 6. *Lip elliptic, narrower* | H. Forrestii |
| 7. *Lip yellowish, base red* | H. flavescens |
| 7. *Lip white, base yellow* | H. chrysoleucum |
| 8. *Filament not, or little, longer than lip* | H. spicatum |
| 8. *Filament longer than lip* | 9 |
| 9. *Lip small, nearly round* | H. coccineum |
| 9. *Lip oblong, wedge-shaped or obovate* | 10 |
| 10. *Lvs. glabrous* | 11 |
| 10. *Lvs. hairy beneath* | 12 |
| 11. *Lvs. glaucous beneath* | H. gracile |
| 11. *Lvs. not glaucous beneath; lip rounded at apex, 2-lobed* | H. Gardnerianum |
| 12. *Filaments white* | H. thyrsiforme |
| 12. *Filaments orange* | H. peregrinum |

**H. acumina'tum.** A variety of *H. spicatum.*

**H. angustifo'lium.** A variety of *H. coccineum.*

**H. car'neum.** A variety of *H. coccineum.*

**H. chrysoleu'cum.** About 5 ft. h. *l.* lanceolate to oblong-lanceolate, long-slender-pointed, 10 to 15 in. long, sessile. *fl.* fragrant, in a dense spike, greenish-yellow; cor. tube over 3 in. long, lobes 1½ in. long, twisted, reflexed; staminodes spreading, white with yellow base, lip widely ovate, 2-lobed, white with orange median stripe; filaments deep orange. August. E. Indies. 1850. (B.M. 4516.)

**H. coccin'eum.** 4 to 6 ft. h. *l.* narrow-linear, with long point, 10 to 20 in. long, 1½ to 2 in. wide, sessile. *fl.* in a usually close spike with a stout rachis; cor. red; tube as long as cal. tube, about 1 in., lobes reflexed, flesh-coloured; lip round, ⅘ in. across, 2-fid, colours various. India, Burma. 1815. A variable plant. var. **angustifo'lium,** *l.* 1 to 1¼ in. wide, glaucous beneath, *fl.* dull red or salmon, lip large (B.M. 2078 as *H. angustifolium*); **car'neum,** *l.* larger than in type, up to over 3 in. wide, *fl.* rose or pink, lip large with dark spots. (B.M. 2637 and L.B.C. 693 as *H. carneum.*)

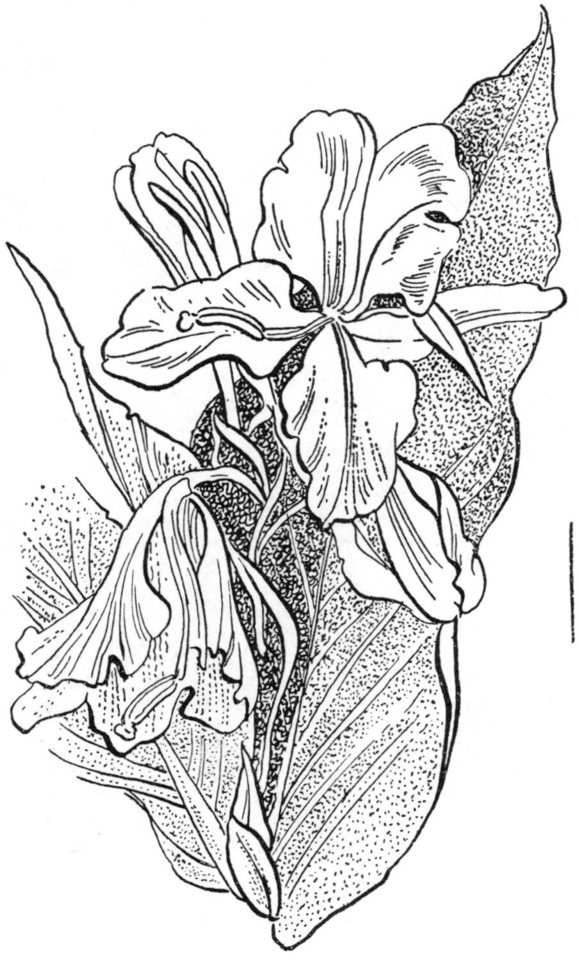

*Hedychium coronarium*

**H. coronar'ium.** 3 ft. or more h. *l.* oblong-lanceolate or lanceolate, slender-pointed, downy beneath, up to 2 ft. long. *fl.* sweet-scented, in an ellipsoid spike up to 8 in. long; cor. pure white, tube over 3 in. long, lobes lanceolate, about 1¼ in. long, variously bent, staminodes white, nearly 2 in. long; lip wide, obcordate, white, sometimes with a little yellow. May. India. 1791. (B.M. 708.)

**H. ellip'ticum.** About 5 ft. h. *l.* elliptic or oblong with a short slender point, about 12 in. long, petiole nearly 1 in. long. *Spike* many-fld., dense; cor. yellowish-white, tube about 3 in. long, lobes 1 in. long, narrow-linear; lip white, 2-fid; filament purple. August. N. India. 1804. (L.B.C. 1881.)

**H. Elwes'ii.** Up to 6 ft. h. *l.* oblong, with long, slender point, 15 in. long, over 3 in. wide, downy on midrib beneath. *fl.* in a loose spike about 6 in. long, cor. shining yellow, tube over 2 in. long, lobes narrow-lanceolate, about 1 in. long; lip obovate about 1½ in. long; filament bright red. Khasia Hills. 1894.

**H. flaves'cens.** 6 to 8 ft. h., stem reddish at base. *l.* lanceolate, slender-pointed, 10 to 15 in. long, downy beneath. *fl.* in a dense spike, 6 to 8 in. long; cor. pale-yellow, tube about 3 in. long, lobes linear, 1½ in. long, greenish; lip reddish-yellow at base; filament yellow. July. Bengal.

**H. flav'um.** About 5 ft. h. *l.* oblong or oblong-lanceolate or lanceolate, 12 to 14 in. long, glabrous above, paler beneath *fl.* in a dense spike about 6 in. long; cor. yellow or orange, tube about 3 in. long, lobes linear, about 1½ in. long; lip widely obovate, sometimes 2-lobed, yellow with orange patch in centre and at base; filament yellow. N. India. 1822. A closely related form with filament longer than lip and cor. tube twice as long as cal. has been described as **H. subditum,** and the form with an entire, not 2-fid, lip **as H. urophyllum.** (B.M. 3039 as *H. flavum.*)

**H. Forrest'ii.** 2 to 4 ft. h. *l.* narrow-lanceolate, about 20 in. long, 2½ in. wide, slender-pointed. *fl.* in a cylindrical spike 8 to 10 in. long, white; cor. tube 1½ to 2 in. long, lobes narrow, about 1½ in. long; lip and staminodes broad-elliptic about 1¼ in. long. China. Near *H. coronarium* but fl. narrower.

**H. Gardneria'num.** 6 ft. or more h., white pruinose all over (like mature rachis, &c.) when young. *l.* lanceolate or oblong-lanceolate, narrowed to a slender point, 8 to 15 in. long, 4 to 5 in. wide. *fl.* in a spike about 14 in. long; cor. lemon, tube about 2 in. long, lobes narrow-linear; lip wedge-shaped, sometimes 2-lobed, 1 to 1¼ in. long, yellow; filament bright red. Summer. N. India. 1819. (B.R. 774; B.M. 6913.)

**H. gra'cile.** Dwarf, barely 18 in. h. *l.* lanceolate, slender-pointed, about 5 in. long, 1¼ in. wide, glaucous beneath. *fl.* in a spike 3 to 4 in. long; cor. greenish-white, tube slender, 1 in. long, lobes very narrow; lip small; filament red. September. India. 1820. (B.M. 6338.)

**H. Green'ei.** 2 to 6 ft. h. *l.* 8 to 10 in. long, 2 in. wide, oblong-acuminate, somewhat hairy beneath. Spike about 5 in. long, densely fld. Bracts 2 to 3 in. long, ovate, 2- or 3-fld. Cor. tube 1½ to 2 in. long, lobes linear, up to 1½ in. long; staminodes linear, red; lip 1½ in. long, shortly 2-fid, red. W. Bhutan. 1911.

**H. peregri'num.** About 3 ft. h. *l.* elliptic or oblong-lanceolate, slender-pointed, softly downy beneath, about 14 in. long, 3 in. wide, sessile. *fl.* in a spike about 8 in. long; bracts pale brown, 2-fld.; cor. tube white, 2 in. long, lobes greenish-yellow, narrow-spatulate, 1½ in. long; lip white, 2-lobed, 1½ in. long; filament long, orange. Madagascar. 1883.

**H. spica'tum.** About 3 ft. h. *l.* lanceolate or oblong-lanceolate, slender-pointed, 4 to 15 in. long, more or less hairy beneath. *fl.* in a loose spike about 8 in. long, yellow; cor. tube over 3 in. long, lobes linear, 1 in. long, reflexed; lip white, reddish at base, obovate, 2-lobed; filament red. October. India. 1810. (B.M. 2300.) var. **acumina'tum,** *l.* distinctly stalked, softly hairy beneath; spike few-fld., slender, cor. tube at top, lobes, staminodes, and filament purple. (B.M. 2969; L.B.C. 1795 as *H. acuminatum.*)

**H. subdi'tum.** *See* **H. flavum.**

**H. thyrsiform'e.** Nearly 6 ft. h. *l.* oblong-lanceolate to narrow-lanceolate, slender-pointed, 8 to 14 in. long, paler and hairy beneath; upper short-stalked. *fl.* in dense spike, about 4 in. long, white; cor. tube about 1 in. long, lobes 1 in. long, narrow-linear; staminodes white, linear-lanceolate; lip 2-lobed; filament, nearly 3 in. long, whitish. India. (B.R. 767 as *H. heteromallum.*)

**H. urophyl'lum.** *See* **H. flavum.**

**H. yunnanen'se.** *l.* ovate-oblong, 8 to 16 in. long, 4 in. wide, entire, glabrous above. Bracts 1-fld., orange. Cor. tube 2 in. long, slender, lobes linear, 1½ in. long, twisted; lip obovate, 2-fid to middle, lobes triangular, obtuse; cal. 1 in. long; filament 1¾ in. long; ovary hairy. August. Yunnan, Indo-China. 1907.

**HEDYSA'RUM** (Greek name used by Dioscorides). FAM. *Leguminosae.* A genus of about 70 species of biennial or perennial herbs or sub-shrubs, distributed over the N. Hemisphere. Leaves unequally pinnate; leaflets entire, often with pellucid dots, without stipels. Flowers large, papilionaceous, purple, white, yellowish-white, or rarely yellow; stamens joined; peduncles with spike-like racemes. Fruit a lomentum. The Hedysarums are hardy and easily grown in ordinary soil in a sunny situation. They are deep rooting and a deep stony soil suits them best, and once planted they should be left alone. Increased by seeds or by layers. The following species are herbaceous unless otherwise stated.

**H. borea'le.** Erect or somewhat spreading herb, 1 to 3 ft. h. *lflets.* in 5 to 10 pairs, oblong or oblanceolate, glabrous. *fl.* violet-purple to white; cal. teeth ovate, acute, shorter than tube. Canada, N. United States. Rock-garden or border.

**H. capita'tum.*** Decumbent, 1 to 2 ft. long. *lflets.* in 7 pairs, lower obovate, emarginate, up to ¼ in. long, upper oblong-elliptic, obtuse. *fl.* reddish to purple in a capitate raceme; standard as long as keel; peduncles axillary, longer than l. Sicily. Rock-garden.

**H. coronar'ium.*** French Honeysuckle. Biennial (occasionally perennial). Spreading, up to 3 or 4 ft. h. *lflets.* in 3 to 5 pairs, elliptic or roundish, hairy beneath and on margins. *fl.* deep red, fragrant, in crowded ovate spikes or racemes. Summer. Europe. 1596. var. **al'bum,** *fl.* white.

**H. elonga'tum.** A synonym of *H. sibiricum.*

**H. exalta'tum.** A synonym of *H. obscurum.*

**H. flaves'cens.** 1½ to 2 in. h., erect, arching. *fl.* yellowish in drooping racemes. June, July. Turkestan. 1900.

**H. flexuo'sum.** Much like *H. coronarium* but fl. tinged blue. S. Spain.

*Hedysarum coronarium* (p. 968)

**H. hu'mile.** Closely related to *H. coronarium* but lflets. more numerous and narrower. *fl.* with wings half length of keel, red. Europe.

**H. Macken'zii.** More or less decumbent, perennial. *lflets.* oblong, hoary hairy on both sides. *fl.* violet-purple, large, in long racemes; cal. teeth awl-like, as long as or longer than tube. Colorado. 1878. (B.M. 6386.) Rock-garden or border.

**H. microca'lyx.** Tall sub-shrub. *l.* up to 1 ft. long; lflets. in 8 to 10 pairs, oblong or ovate-oblong, ¾ to 1½ in. long, stalked. *fl.* bright violet-red, 1 in. long; cal. teeth small; standard narrow-oblong, as long as narrow-linear wings; raceme up to 1 ft. long, many-fld., peduncle long. June. Himalaya. (B.M. 6931.)

**H. multiju'gum.** Deciduous shrub up to 5 ft. of loose, open habit; shoots zigzag, downy. *l.* 4 to 6 in. long; lflets. 17 to 41, ovate, oblong, or obovate, ½ to ¾ in. long. *Racemes* axillary, erect, 6 to 12 in. long, borne successively from June to September. *fl.* 8 to 10, papilionaceous, ¾ in. long, rosy magenta; cal. ¼ in. long, split on one side. *Pod* circular, 1-seeded. Mongolia, 1883. var. **apicula'tum,** *lflets.* pointed. (B.M. 8091.) Easily propagated by layers.

**H. obscu'rum.*** Perennial herb about 12 in. h. *lflets.* in 5 to 9 pairs, ovate, rather thin, glabrous. *fl.* large, rich red-violet, in a long, loose raceme. Summer. European Alps. 1640. (B.M. 282.) Rock-garden.

**H. seri'ceum.** Almost stemless. *lflets.* in 3 or 4 pairs, elliptic, silky beneath. *fl.* purple in 6 to 8 pairs on raceme; keel longer than wings, shorter than standard; cal. teeth awl-shaped. Cent. Russia, Caucasus. SYN. *H. grandiflorum.*

**H. sibi'ricum.** Perennial herb, erect, up to 4 ft. h. *lflets.* in 4 to 9 pairs, ovate-lanceolate, glabrous, apiculate. *fl.* purple, drooping, in long racemes. June, July. Siberia. 1798. (B.M. 2213; B.R. 808 as *H. alpinum.*) Border. var. **albiflo'rum,** *fl.* white.

**H. sikkimen'se.** Up to 6 in. h. *lflets.* 21 to 27, ¼ to ½ in. long, linear-oblong, glabrous above, hairy with raised veins beneath. *fl.-heads* dense, 1 to 2 in. long. *fl.* bright red, ½ to ⅝ in. long. *Pods* 1- to 3-jointed. Sikkim.

**HEDYSCE'PE** (*hedys*, sweet, *skepe*, covering). FAM. *Palmaceae.* A genus of a single species of tall Palm, native of Lord Howe Is. For cultivation *see* **Howea.**

**H. Canterburya'na.*** Trunk 30 to 35 ft. h. *l.* long, pinnate, in a dense head; segs. numerous, nearly equal, slender-pointed. *Spadix* paniculately branched, branches about 6 in. long; male fl. with outer segs. narrow-lanceolate, about ⅛ in. long, inner broader, striate; female fl. with outer segs. about ¼ in. long and broad, inner ovate and shorter. *fr.* ellipsoid, pericarp hard when dry. Lord Howe Is. SYN. *Kentia Canterburyana.*

**HEEL.** A young shoot removed from its parent so as to have a small portion of older tissue at the base is said to have a 'heel'. In many plants a cutting with a heel roots more readily than one without and if the shoot is taken with a heel from the side of a stem the heel gives a greater surface in contact with the soil than if the shoot is cut straight across.

**HEELING IN.** The temporary insertion of shoots or the roots of plants in the soil to keep them moist until the time for putting them into their permanent positions arrives, or until the mature crop such as Broccoli, or Leeks, lifted and so treated can be used, its season being thus prolonged. Shoots for grafting are often heeled in to retard their growth and thus have the stock, already planted, in advance of the scion when grafting is done.

**HEER'IA el'egans.** A synonym of *Schizocentron elegans*; **H. ro'sea,** of *Heterocentron roseum.*

***Heer'ii,*** in honour of Oswald Heer, 1809–83, director, Botanic Garden, Zurich.

**HEIM'IA** (in honour of Geheimerath Dr. Heim of Berlin, d. 1834). FAM. *Lythraceae.* A genus of about 12 species of erect, leafy herbs or sub-shrubs, with 4-angled branches, natives of the warmer parts of Africa and America. Leaves opposite or rarely in whorls of 3, or alternate, entire. Flowers yellow, purple, or blue, in axillary or 3-forked panicles, sometimes capitate. *H. salicifolia* needs no special soil. It is apt to be cut to the ground in severe winters but usually springs again from the base. A warm, sunny corner is the best place for it. Propagated by cuttings in late summer.

**H. salicifo'lia.** Shrub of 2 ft. (up to 6 ft. in wild) erect, much-branched, smooth. *l.* linear, opposite (alternate in upper part of stem), 1 to 2 in. long. *fl.* yellow, ⅓ to ½ in. across, solitary in l.-axils. July to September. N. and S. America. 1821. SYN. *Nesaea salicifolia.* var. **grandiflo'ra,** *l.* wider. *fl.* 1 to 1½ in. across. Buenos Aires. 1839. (B.R. 27, 60.) May be grown as a half-woody perennial but shrubby in milder districts.

**HEIN'SIA** (in honour of Heinsius, philologist and translator of Theophrastus). FAM. *Rubiaceae.* A genus of 3 or 4 species of evergreen shrubs, natives of Trop. Africa. Leaves opposite, short-stalked, oblong or elliptic-lanceolate, slender-pointed, stipules free. Flowers white, rather large, solitary or in 3- to 6-flowered terminal cymes; sepals leafy. *H. jasminiflora* is a beautiful much-branched, unarmed, glabrous shrub for the stove, needing the same treatment as Gardenia.

**H. jasminiflo'ra.*** Shrub of 5 to 8 ft. *l.* oval-oblong or ovate, slender-pointed, on short stalks. *fl.* white, salver-shaped, numerous; infl. somewhat racemose. February. Sierra Leone. 1824. (B.M. 4207.)

F. G. P.

**HEISTE'RIA** (in honour of Laurence Heister, 1683–1758, Professor of Botany at Helmstadt). FAM. *Olacaceae.* A genus of about 23 species of glabrous trees and shrubs, natives of W. Trop. Africa and Trop. America. Leaves entire, leathery. Flowers small, in leaf-axils. *H. coccinea* requires stove conditions and a compost of loam, sand, and peat. Firm cuttings will root in sand with brisk bottom heat.

**H. coccin'ea.** Partridge Berry. Tree of 15 ft. *l.* alternate, lanceolate with rounded base. *fl.* white, 2 to many in l.-axils; cal. dark purple or scarlet. Winter. W. Indies. 1822.

F. G. P.

**HEKETARA.** *See* **Olearia Cunninghamii.** A

***Heldreich'ii,*** in honour of Theodor von Heldreich, 1822–1902, Director, Botanic Garden, Athens, investigator of the Flora of Greece, Crete, and Asia Minor.

***hel'ena,*** of Helenendorf, Transcaucasia.

***Hel'enae,*** in honour of Helen, daughter of Sir W. Macgregor of Australia; or of Helen, wife of Dr. E. H. Wilson.

**HELE'NIUM** (*Helenion*, ancient Greek name used for a plant by Hippocrates). FAM. *Compositae.* A genus of about 30 species of erect annual or perennial herbs, closely resembling Helianthus and, like it, natives of N. and Cent. America. Differing from Helianthus by the long, not 4-angled, fruits which are usually silky-hairy and by the naked receptacle, that of Helianthus having pale-like bracts. Stems usually branched in upper part. Leaves alternate, often decurrent, entire or with a few teeth, gland-dotted. Flower-heads rayed, solitary or in corymbs; ray-florets pistillate or neutral; disk-florets perfect, 4- or 5-toothed; involucral bracts joined at base. Pappus of 5 bristles. Hardy plants for borders in any ordinary good garden soil, flowering freely. Propagated by division or by seed. All the following are perennial.

**H. autumna'le.*** Sneezeweed. 4 to 6 ft. h. Stem winged. *l.* lanceolate, 3 to 4 in. long, acute at both ends, smooth, mostly toothed. *fl.-heads* yellow, 1 to $1\frac{1}{2}$ in. across; rays 3-cleft, somewhat drooping; disk usually yellow. August to October. Canada, E. United States. 1729. (B.M. 2994.) A variable plant. var. **compac'tum,** about 3 ft. h., *fl.-heads* clear yellow, disk brownish-black; July onwards; **grandice'phalum,** 5 ft. h., *fl.-heads* large, rays clear yellow, September, October; **grandiceph'alum atropurpu'reum,** *fl.-heads* almost entirely crimson; **grandiflo'rum,** 6 ft. h., *fl.-heads* large, bright yellow, late; **pu'milum,** 1 to 2 ft. h., *fl.-heads* yellow, June onwards; **pumilum magnif'icum,** up to 3 ft., *fl.-heads* larger than in *pumilum*, pale yellow; **stria'tum,*** 5 to 6 ft. h., *fl.-heads* in large panicles, rays gold and crimson, September; **super'bum,** 5 ft. h., *fl.-heads* bright yellow, rays with wavy margins.

**H. Bigelo'vii.** About 2 ft. h. Stem winged, nearly smooth. *Lower l.* spatulate; *upper* narrow- or oblong-lanceolate. *fl.-heads* $1\frac{1}{2}$ to $2\frac{1}{2}$ in. across; rays rich yellow, $\frac{3}{4}$ in. long; disk brown; peduncles slender. July to September. California. var. **auranti'acum,** rays golden-yellow.

**H. Bolan'deri.*** 1 to 2 ft. h. Stem winged, somewhat hairy, leafless in upper part, rarely branched with 2 or 3 heads. *l.* ovate to spatulate-lanceolate, lower obovate. *fl.-heads* about 3 in. across; rays bright yellow, about 1 in. long; disk dark brown; peduncles thick, hollow. June to August. California. 1891. (R.H. 1891, p. 377.)

**H. Hoopes'ii.** 1 to 3 ft. h. Stem stout, not winged, branched in upper part. *l.* lanceolate, long-pointed, smooth, rather thick, entire. *fl.-heads* about 3 in. across; rays bright orange, scarcely drooping; disk yellow; involucral bracts long, narrow. June to September. Rocky Mts. (R.H. 1902, p. 108.) Useful for cutting.

**H. nudiflo'rum.** $1\frac{1}{2}$ to 3 ft. h. Stem rather rough, leafy, winged. *Lower l.* spatulate, winged. *fl.-heads* 1 to $1\frac{1}{2}$ in. across, numerous in corymbs; stalks short; rays wedge-shaped, drooping, yellow, brown-purple or striped. July to October. SE. United States. var. **atropurpu'reum,** *fl.-heads* with purple rays; **grandiceph'alum stria'tum,** *fl.-heads* 2 in. across, with rays striped yellow and brown (not to be confused with *H. autumnale striatum*).

***Heleoch'aris,*** beauty of the marsh.

***Hel'feri,*** in honour of Dr. J. F. Helfer of Prague, who collected in the Andaman Is. *c.* 1840.

**HELIAM'PHORA** (*helios*, sun, *amphora*, pitcher). FAM. *Sarraceniaceae.* A genus of a single species of 'pitcher plant', native of British Guiana, with the characters given below. Best grown in small pots in a mixture of peat, Sphagnum, and sand, surfaced with Sphagnum, the pot plunged to the rim in moss and covered with a bell-glass with an ample water-supply. Propagated by single crowns taken from the rhizome.

**H. nu'tans.** Perennial of 1 to 2 ft. *l.* in a radical rosette, forming a tubular pitcher enlarging upwards with a wide oblique mouth and a very small lid, hairy within, winged down front, conspicuously veined red. *fl.* white or pale rose, nodding, on a few-fld. scape, sep. 5 (rarely 4). spreading; style straight. Roraima, British Guiana. 1881. (B.M. 7093.)

**HELIANTHEL'LA** (diminutive of Helianthus). FAM. *Compositae.* A genus of about 13 species of perennial herbs, natives of N. America, distinguished from Helianthus by the laterally compressed fruits. Stems usually unbranched. Leaves alternate or sometimes opposite, linear or lanceolate, entire, usually sessile. Flower-heads solitary or few at top of stem, rayed; ray-florets yellow, sterile; disk-florets yellow or brown. *H. quinquenervis* is hardy, not particular as to soil, propagated by seed or by division.

**H. quinquener'vis.** 2 to 4 ft. h., nearly smooth. *l.* mostly opposite, 4 to 9 in. long; upper sessile. *fl.-heads* solitary or few, 3 to 5 in. across, solitary or few on long peduncles; rays 15 to 20, pale yellow, $1\frac{1}{2}$ in. long; involucral bracts large, leafy. June to September. Rocky Mts.

**HELIAN'THEMUM** (from the Greek *helios*, sun, and *anthemon*, flower). FAM. *Cistaceae.* A genus of about 100 species of evergreen shrubs and sub-shrubs, also herbaceous plants and annuals, inhabiting Europe, N. Africa, W. Asia, and N. America. Including Crocanthemum and Tuberaria. Leaves mostly opposite, but sometimes partly (rarely wholly) alternate, entire. Flowers with 5 sepals, 5 petals, numerous stamens, and 3-valved capsules. All are sun-loving plants disliking shade and damp places; they prefer a free, open, light soil and are often found wild on limestone formations. Most of the species are hardy, or fairly hardy, and the shrubby ones are easily increased by softish cuttings placed in gentle heat. The genus is closely related to Cistus which is distinguished by its 5- or 10-valved capsule (*see also* **Fumana, Halimium,** and **Halimiocistus**).

**H. algarven'se.** A synonym of *Halimium ocymoides.*

**H. alpes'tre.** Shrub of tufted habit, 3 to 5 in., shoots hairy. *l.* oval-lanceolate to obovate, cuneate, $\frac{1}{4}$ to $\frac{3}{5}$ in. long, $\frac{1}{12}$ to $\frac{1}{6}$ in. wide, green and slightly hairy on both sides. *fl.* in terminal racemes of 2 to 7, wholly bright yellow, $\frac{1}{2}$ to $\frac{3}{4}$ in. wide; fl.-stalk and sep. hairy. June, July. Mts. of Cent. and S. Europe. 1818. (S.C. 2.) Charming for the rock-garden.

*Helianthemum apenninum versicolor*

**H. apenni'num.** Spreading shrub up to 18 in., shoots and l. grey or white with thick down. *l.* linear to linear-oblong, $\frac{1}{2}$ to $1\frac{1}{4}$ in. long, $\frac{1}{8}$ to $\frac{1}{6}$ in. wide. *fl.* in terminal racemes of 3 to 10, white, 1 to $1\frac{1}{4}$ in. across. June. Europe (SW. England), Asia Minor. (S.C. 62.) SYN. *H. polifolium*, *H. pulverulentum.* var. **ro'seum,** *fl.* rosy-red (SYN. *H. rhodanthum*, S.C. 7); **versico'lor,** *l.* shorter, lanceolate, fl. in variable shades of rose to reddish. (S.C. 26.)

**H. Brew'eri.** Annual herb up to 4 in., stems 2- or 3-branched. *l.* from obovate and 1 in. long at the base to narrowly lanceolate above. *fl.* yellow, $\frac{1}{2}$ in. wide, few in an erect raceme. Europe (Anglesey). (E.B. 166.) Often regarded as a var. of *H. guttatum* from which it differs in not having a bract at the base of each fl.-stalk; also dwarfer.

**H. Broussonet'ii.** Loosely tufted sub-shrub with erect branches hoary when young, densely leafy above. *l.* oblong to oblong-lanceolate, $\frac{1}{2}$ to $1\frac{1}{4}$ in. long, ashy-green above, hoary beneath. *fl.* orange, in terminal and lateral racemes, 3- to 15-fld.; sep. downy. June. Canary Is.

**H. ca'num.** Compact tufted shrub up to 6 in., but twice as wide, shoots and l. downy and slightly hairy. *l.* ovate-oblong to lanceolate, $\frac{1}{4}$ to $\frac{3}{4}$ in. long, grey beneath. *fl.* yellow, not blotched, $\frac{1}{2}$ in. wide, in terminal racemes of 3 to 6 or more; sep. and fl.-stalk hairy. June. Europe (British Is.). (E.B. 167; S.C. 77 as *H. vineale.*)

**H. Chamaecis'tus.** A synonym of *H. nummularium.*

**H. cro'ceum.** A synonym of *H. glaucum croceum.*

**H. Fuma'na.** A synonym of *Fumana nudifolia.*

**H. glau'cum.** Spreading shrub up to 1 ft., more in width. *l.* stalked, roundish to ovate-oblong and oblanceolate, $\frac{1}{2}$ to 1 in. long, white or glaucous with starry down on both sides. *fl.* yellow, 1 in. wide, in many-fld. racemes. June. Europe, N. Africa. 1815. Distinguished from *H. vulgare* by its starry down on both sides of the l. var. **cro'ceum,** *fl.* bright yellow, sep. more starry downy. Syn. *H. croceum* (S.C. 53).

**H. globulariaefo'lium.** Herbaceous perennial of tufted growth. *l.* 1 to 2 in. long, spoon-shaped, pointed, tapered to a stalk about as long as the blade, hairy. *fl.* yellow, $1\frac{3}{4}$ in. across, in clusters of 3 to 7 terminating a stalk 6 to 9 in. long; pet. spotted with dark red at the base. Summer. SW. Europe. 1752. (B.M. 4873 as *H. Tuberaria.*)

**H. grandiflo'rum.** A synonym of *H. vulgare grandiflorum.*

**H. gutta'tum.** Annual herb with erect branching stems 4 to 12 in. h., slender, hairy. *l.* stalkless or nearly so, narrowly lanceolate, 1 to 2 in. long, hairy. *fl.* yellow, with or without a red spot at the base of the pet., $\frac{1}{3}$ to $\frac{5}{8}$ in. wide, in terminal and axillary racemes with a bract at the base of each fl.-stalk. Summer. Europe (Channel Is.). (E.B. 165.)

**H. lunula'tum.** Sub-shrubby plant, 4 to 8 in., woody at the base, of tufted habit, shoots downy and hairy. *l.* oval-oblong or obovate, $\frac{1}{3}$ to $\frac{5}{8}$ in. long, $\frac{1}{8}$ to $\frac{3}{16}$ in. wide, glabrous above margins and under-surface hairy. *fl.* yellow, $\frac{1}{2}$ in. wide, solitary on slender, terminal, hairy stalks $\frac{1}{2}$ to 1 in. long; pet. roundish with a crescent-shaped (lunulate) stain at the base. June, July. Italy.

**H. nummula'rium.** Spreading semi-shrubby plant usually 1 ft. or less h. but up to 2 ft. or more wide. *l.* $\frac{3}{4}$ to 2 in. long, $\frac{1}{8}$ to $\frac{1}{2}$ in. wide, oblong, green above, grey with down beneath. *fl.* yellow, 1 in. wide, on many-fld. terminal racemes. June, July. Europe (England). Very many vars. have been raised in gardens with fl. ranging in colour from white and pale yellow to rose, coppery-red, and crimson; also from single to very double. Many of the vars. figured by Sweet in his *Cistineae* (1825–30) are no longer in cultivation but they have been succeeded by others quite as good, sometimes more beautiful. Some are hybrids with *H. glaucum.* Syn. *H. Chamaecistus.* var. **grandiflo'rum** (Syn. *H. grandiflorum*) is botanically distinct in the l. being green and thinly hairy beneath, not grey-downy; **Surreja'num** is a curious deformed var. originally found near Croydon, the pet. linear, $\frac{1}{8}$ in. wide, notched at the apex.

*Helianthemum Tuberaria*

The following 6 garden forms are a useful selection; **The Bride,** white; **stramin'eum,** sulphur-yellow; **Fireball,** bright red; **cu'preum,** coppery-red; **muta'bile,** pale rose; **venus'tum,** crimson.

**H. oelan'dicum.** Dwarf, tufted plant a few in. h., shoots thinly hairy. *l.* oblong to lanceolate, $\frac{1}{4}$ to $\frac{1}{2}$ in. long, ciliate. *fl.* yellow, $\frac{1}{4}$ to $\frac{1}{3}$ in. across in terminal clusters of up to 4; sep. nearly as long as the pet. July. N. Europe. Near *H. alpestre* which has its pet. more apart.

**H. polifo'lium.** A synonym of *H. apenninum.*

**H. pulverulen'tum.** A synonym of *H. apenninum.*

**H. scabro'sum.** A synonym of *Halimium alyssoides.*

**H. Tubera'ria.** Herbaceous perennial, branching and spreading near the ground. *l.* oblong-ovate, blunt, cuneate, 3-nerved, $1\frac{1}{2}$ to 3 in. long, white-tomentose beneath; stalk grooved, up to 1 in. long. *fl.* yellow, $1\frac{1}{2}$ in. across, in clusters of about 5 towards the top of an erect, slender stalk 4 to 12 in. h. June, July. S. Europe. (S.C. 18.)

**H. vinea'le.** A synonym of *H. canum.*

**H. vulga're.** A synonym of *H. nummularium.*

W. J. B.

**HELIAN'THUS** (*helios*, sun, *anthos*, flower). Fam. *Compositae.* A genus of about 55 species of annual or perennial herbs, natives of N. America, Chile, and Peru. Leaves large, simple, rough-haired, usually opposite below, alternate above. Flower-heads large, solitary or in corymbs; ray-florets yellow or reddish, sterile; disk-florets perfect, yellow, brown, or purplish. Receptacle low, flat to convex. Achenes without wings, glabrous. The Sunflowers are hardy and easily grown in most soils in sunny places; they do not thrive in shade. The perennial species are gross feeders and it is advisable to lift them every second or third year and give them fresh quarters, otherwise they deteriorate and the double forms become less double. The division may take place either in spring or summer. Several species produce edible tubers but those of *H. tuberosus* (the Jerusalem Artichoke) are most in favour as a vegetable (*see* **Artichoke, Jerusalem**). The annual species may be sown where they are to grow or singly in small pots about March and planted out when ready. Varieties of the common Sunflower (*H. annuus*) are sometimes grown for their oily seeds and do best in rich, deeply cultivated soil, sown in rows about $2\frac{1}{2}$ ft. apart and 9 in. apart in the rows, earthing up if in places exposed to wind. Four to 6 lb. of seed is needed to sow an acre. Although not much used for the purpose the stems possess considerable value for paper-making, and produce a fine fibre of some textile value. The oil expressed from the seed is used as a substitute for olive-oil and the cake made from the residue is used for feeding stock and poultry. Where seed is to be saved the heads should be cut off as they mature and laid in an airy shed to dry. Mice and rats are very fond of the seeds.

The perennial species are in many instances liable to spread widely and measures should be taken to restrict them when they are grown in borders. They may be effectively employed as a rule at the back of the herbaceous border and several are useful to grow in grass in wild-gardening.

In comparatively recent years, reddish or partly reddish varieties of *H. annuus* have become available. These red sunflowers originated in a red wild plant of *H. annuus lenticularis* found in 1910 by Mrs. T. D. A. Cockerell at Boulder, Colorado. *H. annuus* is self-sterile and the red wild form was therefore crossed with the common yellow sunflower and with the wild yellow *H. annuus lenticularis* and eventually plants true to the red colouring were produced, some entirely chestnut-red, some with the ends of the rays yellow, some with a ring of red. Various other shades have been produced by introducing Sutton's primrose variety and variations in stature by crossing with *H. debilis.* Details will be found in *Science* for 1913–15. An account of the perennial species and varieties by Daniel Dewar is given in J.R.H.S. 15 (1892), pp. 26–38. Natural hybridization appears to occur frequently between the species, and consequently the exact status of seedlings cannot always be determined.

Slugs and rabbits are fond of young sunflower plants and need to be guarded against. There is sometimes a rot of the base of the stem due to the fungus *Sclerotinia sclerotiorum* probably owing to wet conditions and carelessness in leaving carrots and similar vegetables affected by this fungus lying on and near the surface of the soil. The Grey Mould fungus *Botrytis cinerea* may in wet seasons damage the foliage and flower-heads.

**H. altis′simus.** A synonym of *H. giganteus*.

**H. angustifo′lius.** Slender perennial, 2 to 5 ft. h., sparsely leafy. *Lower l.* lanceolate; *upper* linear-lanceolate, 1 to 7 in. long, ⅛ to ⅓ in. wide, sessile, shining dark green above, smooth beneath. *fl.-heads* 1½ to 2 in. across, numerous; rays about 18, golden-yellow, 1 in. long, disk dark purple; involucral scales linear-lanceolate, ciliate. September, October. E. United States. (B.M. 2051.)

**H. an′nuus.*** Common Sunflower. Annual, 3 to 12 ft. h., rough-haired. *l.* broadly ovate, acute, 4 to 12 in. long, lower heart-shaped, coarsely toothed, 3-nerved. *fl.-heads* large, up to 14 in. across (disk up to 10½ in.); rays of various colours, numerous. July to September. W. United States. 1596. (B.R. 1265 as *H. lenticularis*.) A variable species. var. **califor′nicus,** 6 ft., *fl.-heads* large, double; **citri′nus,** about 5 ft., *fl.-heads* single, rays primrose; **globo′sus fistulo′sus,** *fl.-heads* very large, globose; **Golden Nigger,** about 4 ft., *fl.-heads* with deep-golden rays, black disk; **na′nus fl. pl.,** about 3 ft. h., *fl.-heads* double; **Russian Giant,** 8 to 12 ft. h., single *fl.-heads* very large; **variega′tus,** *l.* variegated; **Red,** rays usually with a band of chestnut-red round disk, sometimes with more colour (*see* introduction).

**H. argophyl′lus.** Annual of 4 to 5 ft., very near *H. annuus* of which it is probably a form differing by its dense silky hairiness and needing constant selection. Texas. (R.H. 1857, 431.)

**H. atroru′bens.** Perennial of 2 to 5 ft. Stem purple, rough, with whitish hairs. *Radical l.* flat, hairy; *stem-l.* twisted and wavy, hairy and warted. *fl.-heads* scattered, about 2 in. across; rays yellow, 10 to 16, about 1 in. long, slender-pointed; disk dark red. SE. United States. 1732. SYN. *H. sparsifolius*. Tolerant of some shade.

**H. califor′nicus.** Perennial of 3 to 8 ft. *l.* lanceolate, rough on both sides, toothed. *fl.-heads* about 2½ in. across, in a loose panicle; rays yellow. California. Moist places. Not to be confused with *H. annuus californicus*.

**H. cilia′ris.** Perennial of about 5 ft. *fl.-heads* large; rays bright golden-yellow; disk dark brown; free-flowering. Texas to Mexico.

**H. coloraden′sis.** Perennial of tufted growth, 6 ft. h. Stems reddish, glaucous. *l.* long-lanceolate, rough, with a few distant teeth. *fl.-heads* with bright orange rays and yellow disk; involucral bracts long, slender, ciliate at base. Colorado.

**H. cucumerifo′lius.** A synonym of *H. debilis*.

**H. de′bilis.*** Annual 1 to 3 ft. h., branched. Stem hairy. *l.* ovate to deltoid or obscurely hastate, sometimes more or less heart-shaped, 1 to 3 in. long, glossy, usually toothed, stalks slender. *fl.-heads* 2 to 3 in. across, terminal on branches; rays usually yellow, ½ in. or more long, disk ½ in. or more across. Summer. S. United States. 1883. (B.M. 7432.) var. **Dazzler,** *fl.-heads* rich chestnut, tipped orange, disk darker; **Excelsior,** *fl.-heads* yellow with zones of red, brown, and purple; **Orion,** *fl.-heads* deep yellow, rays twisted; **plumo′sus,** *disk-fl.* ligulate, pale to deep yellow; **purpu′reus,** *ray-fl.* pink to purple. These are excellent for cut-flowers.

**H. decapet′alus.** Bushy perennial, 4 to 6 ft. h. Stems smooth below, rough above. *Lower l.* opposite, broadly ovate, thinnish, glabrous above, rough beneath, up to 6 in. long; *upper* smaller, narrower, 2 to 3 in. long. *fl.-heads* about 2 in. across; rays 12 to 14 or more, sulphur-yellow, acute, 1 to 1½ in. long; peduncles slender; involucral bracts linear, slender-pointed, ciliate. Autumn. Mid. United States and Canada. (B.M. 3510.) In cultivation this has given rise to var. **multiflo′rus,** somewhat taller, with broader, firmer *l.*, more ovate than in type and fl.-heads 2 to 5 in. across, rays rich yellow, and involucral bracts lanceolate and leafy. (B.M. 227 as *H. multiflorus*.) Of this there are several forms; **Bouquet d′Or,** about 4 ft. h., fully double, rays quilled, rich golden-yellow; **fl. pl.,** almost completely double; **ma′jor,** *fl.-heads* larger than in type; **maximus,*** 6 ft. h., *fl.-heads* very large, single, rays pointed, disk brown, with a double form; **maximus fl. pl.,** 3 to 5 ft. h., outer rays longer than inner; **Soleil d′Or,*** all rays quilled like a Cactus Dahlia. A dwarf form with pale-yellow fl. has also been offered.

**H. divarica′tus.** Perennial 4 to 6 ft. h., branched near top. Stem smooth or round, green or purplish. *l.* ovate, slender-pointed, usually appressed, opposite-decussate. *fl.-heads* with 8 to 15 orange rays 1 to 1½ in. long, acute; disk yellow; involucral bracts half as long as rays, linear, acute, ciliate. July to September. E. United States, Canada. 1759. (SYN. *H. decapetalus niger*.)

**H. doronicoi′des.** Perennial, 5 to 8 ft. h., rough and densely hairy. *l.* ovate, oblong, 4 to 8 in. long, narrowed to both ends, rough on both sides, toothed, sessile. *fl.-heads* crowded on short peduncles; rays yellow, 12 to 20, broad; involucral bracts lanceolate, acute, ciliate on back and margins. September, October. Mid. United States. 1759. (B.M. 2778 as *H. pubescens*.)

**H. ex′ilis.** Perennial of 1 to 2 ft. Stem slender, often unbranched. *l.* ovate-lanceolate to linear-lanceolate. *fl.-heads* yellow, rays ½ in. long; peduncles shaggy beneath heads; involucral bracts lanceolate, hairy in lower half. California.

**H. gigan′teus.** Perennial up to 12 ft. h. Stem stout, rough or bristly, purplish, branched from middle. *Lower l.* lanceolate, tapered to both ends, 3 to 7 in. long, toothed, rough on both sides, stalked; *upper* almost sessile or stalks winged. *fl.-heads* several, 1½ to 3 in. across, cupped; rays 10 to 20, deep yellow, 1 to 1½ in. long; disk purplish; involucral bracts lanceolate, narrowed to acute tip, ciliate on back and margins. September, October. Canada, Mid. United States. 1714. (B.M. 7555.) SYN. *H. altissimus, H. decapetalus sulphureus elatior.* A var. with fleshy tubers (var. *subtuberosus*) occurs in Canada, once used as food by Indians.

**H. gros′se-serra′tus.** Perennial, 7 to 9 ft. h. or more. Stem smooth, glaucous. *l.* lanceolate, slender-pointed, coarsely toothed, green above, woolly beneath, thin-stalked. *fl.-heads* many, 1 to 3 in. across in a cyme; rays 10 to 20, deep yellow, about 1 in. long; involucral bracts narrow. September, October. Mid. United States. Sometimes confused with *H. giganteus*.

**H. × H. G. Moon*** (*H. decapetalus multiflorus* × *H. laetiflorus*). About 4 ft. h., less liable to run than many perennial species; rays soft yellow, very broad, disk small; *fl.-heads* numerous. August, September. Of garden origin.

**H. hirsu′tus.** Densely hairy perennial, 2 to 4 ft. h. *l.* ovate-lanceolate, thick, very rough, pale beneath. *fl.-heads* several, 2 to 3 in. across; rays yellow, 12 to 15. August, September. E. United States.

**H. laetiflo′rus.** Perennial of 5 to 7 ft. or more, very leafy. Stem stiff, rough or bristly. *l.* broadly ovate, 9 to 12 in. long, narrowed to both ends, distinctly 3-veined, dark green, sometimes coarsely toothed, thinnish, stalked. *fl.-heads* usually several on rather short peduncles; rays 15 to 25, bright yellow, 2 to 2½ in. long, nearly ovate-lanceolate; disk yellow; involucral bracts in 3 or 4 series, 3 to 4 in. long, ciliate. August to October. Mid. United States. 1810. More apt to run even from forms of *H. scaberrimus*, and needing restraint. var. **Daniel Dewar,** rays bright orange, drooping; **Miss Mellish,** very vigorous, rays bright orange-yellow in 2 rows; **Rev. Wolley Dod,** up to 7 ft., rays deep yellow, late; **semi-ple′nus,** 3 to 4 ft., rays orange-yellow, in 2 or more rows.

**H. laeviga′tus.** Perennial of 3 to 5 ft., branching. Stem deep purple, smooth, often glaucous. *l.* lanceolate, 3 to 6 in. long, acute, usually entire, sessile or nearly so. *fl.-heads* few or solitary, 1 to 1½ in. across; rays 6 to 10, about 1 in. long; involucral bracts narrow-lanceolate. September, October. E. United States. Not inclined to run.

**H. lenticula′ris.** The wild form of *H. annuus*.

**H. macrophyl′lus.** A variety of *H. strumosus*.

**H. Maximilia′nii.** Perennial of 7 to 8 ft. Stems rough. *l.* usually alternate, lanceolate, rigid, entire or nearly so, nearly sessile. *fl.-heads* large on short, densely hairy peduncles in axils of upper *l.*; rays golden-yellow, 15 to 30, 1 to 1½ in. long; involucral bracts lanceolate, acute. September, October. Mid. United States. (R.H. 1895, 397.) Related to *H. giganteus*.

**H. mol′lis.** Hoary perennial, 3 to 4 ft. h., branched from near base, very leafy. *l.* nearly all opposite, ovate, cordate or clasping at base, 3 to 5 in. long. *fl.-heads* solitary or few, 2 to 3 in. across; rays 15 to 25, yellow; disk yellow. August, September. Mid. United States. 1805. (B.B. ed. 2, 3, 484.) var. **corda′tus,** *l.* broader and thicker, cordate. 1899.

**H. multiflo′rus.** *See* **H. decapetalus.**

**H. Nuttall′ii.** Perennial of 2 to 4 ft. Stems usually unbranched. *Lower l.* lanceolate, 3 to 6 in. long; *upper* linear, toothed or entire. *fl.-heads* much as in *H. giganteus*; involucral bracts glabrous or hairy at base only. Rocky Mts. 1899. Wet soil plant.

**H. occidenta′lis.** Perennial of 3 to 4 ft. Stem slender, branched, roughly hairy, leafy near base. *Lower l.* ovate or lanceolate-oblong, blunt, rather leathery, entire or nearly so, 3-nerved, stalked. *fl.-heads* usually solitary on long peduncles; rays orange-yellow, 1 in. long, ovate; disk yellow; involucral bracts lanceolate, acute, hispid. Mid. United States. Near *H. atrorubens*.

**H. orgya′lis.** A synonym of *H. salicifolius*.

**H. Pa′rishii.** Closely related to *H. californicus*. *l.* lanceolate, slender-pointed, strigose to densely white-hairy beneath; upper *l.* longer than the short peduncles. *fl.-heads* yellow, 2 to 3 in. across, in a terminal corymbose panicle; rays 15 to 20, 1 to 1½ in. long; involucral bracts more or less grey-hairy, shorter than in *H. californicus*. California.

**H. parviflo′rus.** Slender, glabrous perennial, leafy. *l.* thin, mostly lanceolate, 3 to 7 in. long, ½ to 1½ in. tissues as long as wide, scabrous above. *fl.-heads* ½ to 1¼ in. across, many; rays 5 to 10. July to September. California.

**H. pu′milus.** Perennial of 2 to 3 ft. Stem rough and hairy. *l.* in 5 to 7 pairs only, ovate-lanceolate, 1 to 4 in. long. *fl.-heads* few to a stem, peduncles short; rays pale yellow; disk yellow. E. Rocky Mts.

**H. rig′idus.** A synonym of *H. scaberrimus*.

**H. salicifo'lius.*** Perennial of 6 to 10 ft. Stem smooth, purplish, glaucous, very leafy. *l.* alternate, narrow-linear, 6 to 12 in. long, recurved, thin, glabrous, entire or nearly so; lower stalked. *fl.-heads* many in a large panicle, rather small; rays deep golden-yellow, about 1 in. long; disk purple; involucral bracts narrow-linear, spreading, minutely ciliate. September, October. Mid. United States. 1879. (Gn. 25 (1884), 511 as *H. orgyalis.*) A fine foliage plant for the large border, flowering best in hot summers.

**H. scaber'rimus.** Perennial of running habit, about 3 to 4 ft. h. Stem rough. *Lower l.* broadly lanceolate, 6 to 12 in. long, slender-pointed, slightly toothed, rough-haired, narrowed to a winged stalk; *upper* rather thicker. *fl.-heads* 2½ to 4 in. across; peduncles long; rays bright yellow, numerous, about 1½ in. long; disk sometimes yellowish at first, becoming brown, involucral bracts short, ovate, acute, somewhat spreading. August to October. Mid. United States. (B.M. 2020 as *H. diffusus*; B.M. 2668 and B.R. 508 as *H. atrorubens.*) SYN. *H. rigidus, Harpalium rigidum.* var. **aesti'vus,** early fl., rays golden-yellow, ½ to 1 in. long, disk purplish. SYN. var. *praecox*; **el'egans,** 6 ft. h., rays orange-yellow, ½ to 1 in. long, narrow, end September; **Latest of All,** up to 6 ft. h., rays clear yellow in a double row, acute; **prae'cox,** *see* var. **aestivus.**

**H. sparsifo'lius.** A synonym of *H. atrorubens.*

**H. strumo'sus.** Perennial of 3 to 7 ft. Stem often glaucous, usually branching. *l.* ovate-lanceolate, 3 to 8 in. long, rough above, entire or toothed. *fl.-heads* freely produced, 2½ to 4 in. across; rays deep yellow, 10 to 20. September, October. Canada, United States. var. **macrophyl'lus,** *l.* downy beneath. (B.M. 3689 as *H. mollis.*)

**H. tomento'sus.** Perennial of about 4 ft. Stem branching, sturdy. *l.* hairy, lanceolate, rarely ovate, decurrent to base of stalk, dark green, resin-dotted. *fl.-heads* in small panicles on slender pedicels; rays bright yellow, ¾ in. long, hairy and resin-dotted at back; disk yellow. September. SE. United States. (B.B. ed. 2, 3, 486.)

**H. tubero'sus.** Jerusalem Artichoke, Topinamber. Perennial with irregular, round, purplish or whitish tubers. Stem 6 to 8 ft. or more, stout, hispid. *l.* alternate, ovate, sometimes somewhat heart-shaped at base, 4 to 8 in. long, toothed, rough above, finely downy beneath. *fl.-heads* few to several, 2 to 3 in. across; peduncles rather short; rays deep yellow; bracts lanceolate, hairy. Achenes downy. October. Upper Canada, Arkansas, Georgia. 1617. (B.M. 7545.) var. **fusiform'is,** tubers long. *See* **Jerusalem Artichoke.**

**HELICHRY'SUM** (*helios*, sun, *chrysos* golden). FAM. *Compositae.* SYN. Elichrysum; including Aphelexis. A genus of about 300 species distributed over the warm and temperate regions of the Old World, the greatest concentrations being in S. Africa and Australia. They vary from annuals to herbaceous perennials, sub-shrubs, and shrubs, nearly always more or less downy to woolly. Leaves alternate, varying from tiny and scale-like to several inches long. Flower-heads solitary to clustered, ranging from a fraction of an inch to 1 or 2 in. in diameter, surrounded by an involucre of often very ornamental bracts. These bracts are dry and hard and retain these characteristics for long, indefinite periods. Some of the most beautiful of them are collected and dried for preservation and marketed as 'everlastings' or 'immortelles'. Shoots intended for this purpose should be gathered and suspended heads downwards in a dry, cool place.

A small proportion of species are hardy and should be grown in a well-drained, sunny spot, but the majority of those that have been introduced range from half-hardy to greenhouse plants. The most woolly species are not always easy to grow and are intolerant of excessive moisture. The purely shrubby types can be raised from cuttings.

**H. anatol'icum.** A synonym of *H. plicatum.*

**H. angustifo'lium.** Perennial sub-shrub with a woody base and erect, slender leafy shoots 8 to 15 in. h., white with close, soft down. *l.* ½ to 1½ in. long, from thread-like to $\frac{1}{20}$ in. wide, white-downy. *fl.-heads* yellow, ⅛ to ¼ in. wide, numerous in terminal clusters 1 to 2 in. across. June to August. S. Europe.

**H. Antenna'ria.** Erect shrub 5 to 9 ft. and as much wide under cultivation, shoots soon glabrous. *l.* obovate, ¾ to 1½ in. long, soon glabrous and dark green above, grey-white beneath. *fl.-heads* cylindrical, ¼ in. long, ¼ in. across, pale greenish-white, in terminal corymbs 1 to 2 in. wide; involucre of about 20 bracts, woolly. Tasmania. (B.M. 9152 as *Ozothamnus Antennaria.*) Has lived in a sheltered corner at Kew for 20 years.

**H. apicula'tum.*** Shrub 1½ to 2 ft., shoots springing from a woody base, covered with soft silvery wool. *Lower l.* oblong-cuneate; *upper* ones linear to oblanceolate, ½ to 2 in. long. *fl.-heads* about ⅝ in. across, bright yellow, hemi-spherical, 1 to several terminating erect, leafy stems 6 to 10 in. long. Australia, where it is widely spread, Tasmania. 1804. (B.R. 240 as *Gnaphalium apiculatum.*)

**H. arena'rium.** Yellow Everlasting. Herbaceous perennial with a slightly woody base and erect stems 6 to 12 in. h. *l.* linear to narrowly spatulate, 1 to 2 in. long, $\frac{1}{12}$ to ¼ in. wide, white-woolly; base stem-clasping. *fl.-heads* ¼ in. wide, bracts yellow, centre orange, crowded in terminal corymbs 1 to 3 in. wide. August. Europe. 1719. Hardy. The fl., popularly known as 'immortelles', are extensively used for decorative purposes, funeral wreaths, &c.

**H. bellidioi'des.** Prostrate shrub, stems very slender, much-branched. *l.* ⅛ to ½ in. long, spatulate to obovate, white with cottony down beneath. *fl.-heads* mostly solitary, terminal, ½ to ¾ in. wide on erect, slender stalks 1 to 5 in. long; bracts white, florets very numerous. (J.R.H.S. 39, lxviii.) var. **prostra'tum.** Chiefly distinguished by the fl.-heads being sessile or having very short stalks instead of the slender, comparatively tall ones of the type. New Zealand. Half-hardy. Alpine house.

*Helichrysum bracteatum*

**H. bractea'tum.** Annual, half-hardy herb, 2 to 4 ft., sometimes perennial, stems glabrous or slightly hairy, branching towards the top. *l.* linear- to oblong-lanceolate, stalkless, 1½ to 5 in. long. *fl.-heads* solitary, terminal, 1½ in. across, the pink or yellow bracts being the most conspicuous feature; the florets form a central, circular, yellow disk ½ in. across. June to August. Australia. 1799. Half-hardy. var. **al'bum,** *fl.-heads* pure white (B.M. 3857 as *H. niveum*); **atrococcin'eum,** *fl.-heads* dark scarlet; **atrosanguin'eum,** *fl.-heads* dark blood-red; **au'reum,** *fl.-heads* golden-yellow; **bi'color,** *fl.-heads* yellow, scales tipped red, l. roughly ciliate (B.R. 1814); **compos'itum,** *fl.-heads* double, variously coloured; **macran'thum,** *fl.-heads* white, rose-coloured outside; **niv'eum,** a synonym of var. *album*; **monstro'sum,** *fl.-heads* double.

**H. corda'tum.** Shrub with long, flexuose, loosely and irregularly branched stems covered with white wool. *l.* thinly disposed, cordate-ovate, 1 to 2½ in. long, dark green above, white-woolly beneath; stalk up to 1 in. long. *fl.-heads* ¼ in. wide, white, very small and numerous in clusters forming large, crooked, open, zigzagged panicles often over 1 ft. long. W. Australia.

**H. dealba'tum.** Tufted, sub-shrubby perennial sending up flowering stems 6 to 12 in. h. *Basal l.* oblong-lanceolate, ½ to 1¼ in. long, glabrous and green above, cottony-white beneath. *fl.-heads* solitary at the top of a slender stalk; involucre 1 to 1½ in. across, pure white; disk of florets yellow. August. Tasmania. 1888. Half-hardy.

**H. diosmifo'lium.** Shrub 4 to 6 ft. or small tree 10 to 20 ft., shoots viscous, downy. *l.* densely set, narrowly linear, ⅓ to ¾ in. long, $\frac{1}{20}$ to $\frac{1}{12}$ in. wide, glossy green above, grey-downy beneath, margins recurved. *fl.-heads* very numerous, ¼ in. wide, in dense, terminal corymbs 1 to 2 in. across; bracts pure white. New S. Wales, Queensland. SYN. *Ozothamnus thyrsoideus.* Similar in habit to *H. rosmarinifolium.*

**H. ela'tum.*** Erect shrub up to 7 or 8 ft., stems stout, white-felted. *l.* narrow-elliptic to lanceolate or ovate, 2 to 4 in. long, ¾ to 1¼ in. wide, white-woolly beneath, dark green and ultimately glabrous above. *fl.-heads* in a terminal cluster or panicle of sometimes 12 or more with the silvery-white or pink linear-lanceolate bracts of the involucre, which is 1½ in. across, the chief feature. Australia.

**H. ericifo'lium.** Shrub or undershrub, 1 to 1½ ft., much divided into very slender, erect branches, shoots downy to glabrous. *l.* heath-like, ⅛ to ¼ in. long, filiform. *fl.-heads* sessile, in terminal clusters, ¼ to ⅓ in. wide, bracts silvery-white. March, April. S. Africa. 1774. (B.M. 435 as *Gnaphalium ericoides.*)

**H. ericoi'des.** Tufted shrub of close habit, 4 to 12 in. h., densely branched. *l.* about $\frac{1}{12}$ in. long, ovate, blunt, appressed to, and completely covering, the stem, glabrous above, concave and downy beneath. *fl.-heads* terminal, solitary in pairs or threes, $\frac{1}{4}$ in. long, bracts silvery-white. S. Africa. 1796. SYN. *Aphelexis ericoides.* This dainty little Cupressus-like shrub must not be confounded with *H. ericifolium.* Greenhouse.

**H. feli'num.** Shrub 2 to 5 ft. Stems erect, sparsely branched, grey-woolly. *l.* densely set, variable in size and shape, from $\frac{3}{8}$ to 2 in. long and from $\frac{1}{8}$ to $\frac{1}{2}$ in. wide; in shape from linear- to ovate-lanceolate; very woolly beneath, rough above. *fl.-heads* $\frac{3}{8}$ in. wide, in terminal, globose, close clusters $\frac{3}{4}$ to $1\frac{1}{4}$ in. across or in more open, wider corymbs; bracts white or pink; central disk yellow. S. Africa. 1791. (B.R. 243 as *Gnaphalium congestum*.) Greenhouse.

**H. foe'tidum.** Herb with branching stem up to 2 ft. h. *l.* stem-clasping, entire, acute, downy beneath. *fl.-heads* pale yellow. June to September. S. Africa. 1692. (B.M. 1987 as *Gnaphalium foetidum*.)

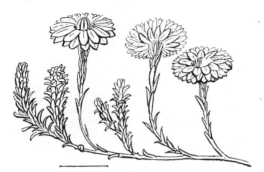

*Helichrysum frigidum*

**H. frig'idum.*** Densely tufted sub-shrub a few in. h., base woody. Stems very slender, densely clothed like the l. with silky white down. *l.* $\frac{1}{8}$ to $\frac{1}{4}$ in. long. *fl.-heads* sessile, solitary, terminal, $\frac{1}{2}$ to $\frac{3}{8}$ in. across, involucral bracts pure white. May, June. Corsica. 1875. (B.M. 6515.) Alpine house or a sunny spot in rock-garden, covered in winter with a sheet of glass to prevent excessive dampness.

**H. glomera'tum.** Shrub 3 to 8 ft., shoots slender, spreading, grooved, white with down. *l.* variable in size and shape, $\frac{1}{4}$ to $1\frac{1}{4}$ in. long (mostly $\frac{1}{4}$ to $\frac{3}{4}$), roundish to broadly ovate, entire, white-downy beneath. *fl.-heads* $\frac{1}{10}$ in. wide, in axillary and terminal globose clusters $\frac{3}{4}$ in. across; florets 8 to 12. New Zealand. Hardy only in the south and west.

**H. gran'diceps.** *See* **Leucogenes grandiceps.**

**H. grandiflo'rum.** Sub-shrub with a woody base, 1 to $2\frac{1}{2}$ ft., stem and l. grey-woolly. *l.* crowded towards the base, densely set, obovate- to roundish-oval, 1 to 3 in. long, $\frac{1}{2}$ to $1\frac{1}{4}$ in. wide, 3- or 5-nerved. *fl.-heads* $\frac{3}{8}$ in. wide, creamy-white, packed in terminal, globose, branched clusters 1 to 2 in. across. S. Africa. 1731. Greenhouse.

**H. graveo'lens.** Herbaceous perennial up to $1\frac{1}{2}$ ft., base rather woody. *l.* oblanceolate, linear-oblong, $1\frac{1}{2}$ to 3 in. long, $\frac{1}{4}$ to $\frac{1}{2}$ in. wide, sessile, 3-veined, densely greyish-white-woolly. *fl.-heads* $\frac{1}{4}$ in. wide, yellow, terminating a leafy stem, 6 to 12 in. long in a cluster of axillary corymbs that form a flattish corymb 2 or 3 in. across. Greece, Tauria. 1877. (G.F. 26, 889.) Half-hardy.

**H. Guliel'mii.*** Perennial herb up to 2 ft., all parts except the inflor. covered with white wool. *l.* 3 to 5 in. long, $\frac{1}{2}$ to $\frac{3}{4}$ in. wide, lanceolate- to linear-oblong. *fl.-heads* $1\frac{1}{2}$ in. across, on stalks 3 to 5 in. long, terminal and axillary, forming altogether impressive corymbs 5 or 6 in. across; bracts white to deep rosy-red; central disk yellow. E. Trop. Africa. 1892. (B.M. 7789.) Warm greenhouse.

**H. hu'mile.*** Shrub 6 in. to 2 ft., shoots slender, often unbranched. *l.* $\frac{1}{4}$ to $\frac{3}{4}$ in. long, subulate, appressed to the stem, cottony beneath. *fl.-heads* 1 to 2 in. across, terminal, the bracts pale pink to deep rose, linear-lanceolate; disk yellow. May, June. S. Africa. 1795. (A.B.R. 652 as *Xeranthemum humile*.) SYN. *Aphelexis humilis, A. macrantha.* var. **grandiflo'rum,** *fl.-heads* larger, habit dwarf, freely branched; **purpu'rea,** *fl.-heads* dark purple.

**H. lana'tum.** Sub-shrub with a woody base, with erect stems 12 to 18 in. h. *l.* sessile, obovate to oblanceolate, covered thickly with soft flannel, 1 to 3 in. long, $\frac{1}{4}$ to 1 in. wide. *fl.-heads* bright lemon-yellow, crowded in short-stalked clusters $\frac{1}{2}$ to $\frac{5}{8}$ in. across, forming terminal corymbs 2 to 3 in. wide. S. Africa. Remarkable for its flannel-like l. Half-hardy. SYN. *H. thianschanicum* of gardens.

**H. ledifo'lium.** Shrub of stiff, erect growth, 3 to 5 ft., shoots yellow, downy, viscous. *l.* $\frac{1}{2}$ to $\frac{1}{2}$ in. long, $\frac{1}{20}$ to $\frac{1}{16}$ in. wide, densely set, sessile, linear-oblong, much-recurved, yellow underneath. *fl.-heads* white, densely packed in terminal clusters $\frac{1}{2}$ to 1 in. wide, often so abundant as to cover the shrub. Tasmania. 1930. SYN. *Ozothamnus ledifolius.* Hardy on the south coast.

**H. Leontopo'dium.** *See* **Leucogenes Leontopodium.**

**H. Mann'ii.** Biennial, 2 ft. or more, with a clean stem half its height. *l.* densely set, ovate-lanceolate, pointed, 3 to 6 in. long, $\frac{3}{4}$ to $1\frac{1}{2}$ in. wide. *fl.-heads* 1 in. wide, crowded in a terminal cluster 6 to 8 in. across; involucral bracts white, closely appressed to the disk of bright yellow florets. W. Trop. Africa. 1861. (B.M. 5431.) This magnificent species is probably not now in cultivation. It is closely akin to the S. African *H. foetidum.* Warm greenhouse.

**H. Milligan'ii.*** Small perennial plant with a woody base and a tuft of l. about 2 in. across, sending up an erect, leafy, woolly shoot 3 to 6 in. h., bearing a terminal fl.-head. *l.* obovate to oblanceolate, $\frac{1}{4}$ to 1 in. long, those on the stem narrowest. *fl.-head* $1\frac{1}{2}$ in. across; bracts shining white, narrowly elliptical, pointed, sometimes tinged red. Tasmania.

**H. monstro'sum.** A variety of *H. bracteatum.*

**H. na'num.*** Perennial sub-shrub, 3 to 6 in., with a tufted woody base. Stems whitish, glabrous. *l.* linear to filiform, $\frac{1}{2}$ to $1\frac{1}{4}$ in. long, grey, glabrous, sessile. *fl.-heads* golden-yellow, tightly packed in terminal globose or hemispherical clusters $\frac{1}{2}$ to 1 in. across. S. Africa. A dainty little plant. Greenhouse.

**H. obcorda'tum.** Shrub 3 to 5 ft., shoots downy or nearly glabrous. *l.* broadly obovate or almost circular, $\frac{1}{8}$ to $\frac{1}{4}$ in. long, sometimes narrower and longer, very shortly stalked, dark glossy green above, pale beneath. *fl.-heads* very small, golden-yellow, in hemispherical, compound, terminal racemes 1 to 2 in. across. July, August. Australia, Tasmania. 1929.

**H. odoratis'simum.** Shrub 6 to 18 in., much-branched at the often tufted base; fl.-stems erect. *Basal l.* $1\frac{1}{2}$ to 4 in. long, $\frac{1}{4}$ to $\frac{3}{4}$ in. wide, oblanceolate to linear, 3-nerved; *upper* ones smaller and narrower, all white-woolly. *fl.-head* yellow, $\frac{1}{8}$ in. wide, crowded in terminal clusters or corymbs $\frac{3}{4}$ to 2 in. wide. S. Africa. Greenhouse.

**H. orienta'le.*** Perennial sub-shrub with a woody, tufted base and erect leafy flowering shoots, 6 to 18 in. h. *l.* oblanceolate-obovate to linear, 1 to 3 in. long, $\frac{1}{8}$ to $\frac{1}{2}$ in. wide, covered with loose white down. *fl.-heads* $\frac{1}{2}$ in. wide, in terminal clusters 1 to 3 in. across, straw-coloured-yellow. August. SE. Europe. 1835. Hardy. Very near *H. plicatum* but with paler fl.

**H. plica'tum.*** Perennial with a woody root-stock sending up erect, downy, grooved, slender-flowering stems 1 to $1\frac{1}{2}$ ft. *l.* narrowly spatulate or linear, $1\frac{1}{2}$ to 5 in. long, loosely downy. *fl.-heads* about $\frac{1}{4}$ in. wide, golden-yellow, closely packed in terminal corymbose clusters $1\frac{1}{2}$ to 2 in. across. SE. Europe. 1877. (G.F. 1877, 26, t. 889.) Hardy. SYN. *H. anatolicum.*

**H. rosmarinifo'lium.*** Snow in Summer. Shrub 6 to 9 ft., shoots glutinous, ribbed, more or less downy. *l.* closely set, linear, $\frac{1}{4}$ to $1\frac{1}{2}$ in. long, $\frac{1}{12}$ in. wide, dark green and glutinous above, whitish-downy beneath. *fl.-heads* snow-white, about $\frac{1}{8}$ in. wide, in rounded corymbs $\frac{1}{2}$ to 2 in. across, terminating short lateral twigs. June. Victoria, Tasmania. SYN. *Ozothamnus rosmarinifolius.* Hardy in Cornwall.

**H. rupes'tre.** Sub-shrub 1 to 2 ft. Stems vividly white-downy. *l.* linear to oblanceolate, $\frac{3}{4}$ to 2 in. long, $\frac{1}{16}$ to $\frac{3}{16}$ in. wide, partly stem-clasping, white-downy, margins revolute. *fl.-heads* bright yellow, $\frac{1}{4}$ in. wide, closely set in terminal clusters or corymbs 1 to 3 in. across. Mediterranean region. (R.H. 1894, 460.) Hardy.

**H. scorpioi'des.** Perennial with a semi-woody base, and erect, herbaceous, slender, softly woolly shoots 6 to 16 in. h. *l.* oblanceolate to linear, $\frac{3}{4}$ to $3\frac{1}{2}$ in. long, woolly white. *fl.-heads* yellow, solitary, terminal, 1 in. across, hemispherical. Australia, Tasmania. 1838. Greenhouse.

**H. scutellifo'lium.** Shrub 4 or 5 ft., shoots slender, fulvous-downy. *l.* grey-green, very minute, $\frac{1}{16}$ in. wide, scale-like, closely recurved, orbicular-like tiny knobs densely stuck on the shoots. *fl.-heads* yellow, $\frac{1}{8}$ in. wide, in clusters of 3 to 5. A very curious species. Tasmania. 1929. SYN. *Ozothamnus scutellifolius.* Greenhouse.

**H. Sela'go.** Freely branching, Cupressus-like shrub, 6 to 15 in. h., shoots densely packed. *l.* closely appressed to, and completely hiding, the stem, overlapping, ovate to triangular, $\frac{1}{10}$ to $\frac{1}{8}$ in. long, dark polished green and convex above, woolly inside, showing at the margins. *fl.-heads* terminal, solitary, sessile; bracts $\frac{1}{16}$ in. long, dull white. New Zealand. Hardy in mid-Sussex.

**H. serot'inum.** Tufted, sub-shrubby, much-branched; branches erect, appressed hairy; flowering shoots 1 to $1\frac{1}{4}$ in. long. *l.* up to $\frac{3}{4}$ in. long; linear, obtuse, margins revolute, at first woolly, green, finally glabrous. *fl.-heads* golden-yellow, in a dense corymb with fastigiate branches, involucral bracts about $\frac{1}{4}$ in. long, yellowish, woolly. SW. Europe. Rock-garden.

**H. sesamoi'des.*** Slender shrub 1 to 2 ft. Stems erect, often fasciculate. *Lower l.* 1 to $2\frac{1}{4}$ in. long, filiform, loosely set, downy beneath; *upper l.* appressed to the stem, $\frac{1}{8}$ to $\frac{1}{2}$ in. long. *fl.-heads* solitary, terminal, on slender stems 8 to 15 in. h.; involucre 1 to $1\frac{1}{2}$ in. across; bracts lanceolate, satiny, white, rosy, pale lemon, or mottled. April. S. Africa. 1739. (A.B.R. 242, 279 as *Xeranthemum sesamoides*.) SYN. *Aphelexis sesamoides.* Greenhouse.

**H. splen'didum.*** Shrub 2 to 5 ft., shoots velvety-white. *l.* linear, $\frac{3}{4}$ to $1\frac{1}{2}$ in. long, $\frac{1}{12}$ to $\frac{1}{4}$ in. wide, softly downy on both sides, densely set. *fl.-heads* $\frac{1}{8}$ in. wide, very bright yellow, closely packed in terminal, globose or hemispherical clusters, 1 to $1\frac{1}{2}$ in. wide. S. Africa. var. **monta'num,** shrub 6 to 12 in. h. *l.* shorter and thicker.

**H. Stoech'as.*** Goldy-locks. Perennial sub-shrub with a woody root-stock, sending up erect, slender stems 1 to 2 ft., silvery-white with down. *l.* sessile, linear, $\frac{3}{4}$ to 2 in. long, dark green above, silvery underneath. *fl.-heads* yellow, $\frac{1}{6}$ in. wide, crowded in terminal, rounded corymbs 1 to 2 in. across. Summer. S. Europe. 1629. Hardy.

**H. triner've.** A synonym of *Gnaphalium trinerve.*

W. J. B.

**HELICO'DEA.** Included in **Billbergia.**

**HELICODIC'EROS** (*helix*, spiral, *dis*, twice, *keras*, horn; the basal divisions of the leaf twist and stand erect like horns). FAM. *Araceae.* A genus of a single tuberous herb related to Dracunculus but with the male and female flowers separated by rudimentary ones on the spadix. Leaves pedately cut. For cultivation *see* **Arum.** *H. muscivorus* is nearly hardy but is apt to be damaged in severe winters.

**H. musciv'orus.** *l.* pedately cut, lobes entire. *Peduncle* 12 to 18 in. long; spathe dark purple-brown, hairy within; blade ovate, flat, longer than the spadix. April. Corsica, Balearic Is. 1777. (B.R. 831 as *Arum crinitum.*)

***helicoid,*** twisted like a snail's shell.

**HELICO'NIA** (Mt. Helicon in Greece, consecrated to the Muses). FAM. *Musaceae.* A genus of about 30 American perennial herbs allied to Musa but with 2-ranked leaves, flowers in terminal many-flowered spikes, cells of ovary with only 1 ovule, fruit a capsule dividing into 3 nuts. The flowers are inconspicuous but the foliage is handsome. They require stove treatment and a rich, loamy, open soil. Plenty of water is needed during the growing season but none when the plants die down in winter. Shade is necessary in summer otherwise the foliage is liable to damage by the sun. Propagation may be by seed but more readily by division of the root-stocks when growth begins in spring. Separate pieces should be put into 5-in. pots and grown on rapidly in a moist stove temperature, repotting into pots of larger size as becomes needful or they may be planted out in the stove. **A**

KEY

| | |
|---|---|
| 1. *Bracts wide-ovate-lanceolate, boat-shaped, distant* | 2 |
| 1. *Bracts narrow-lanceolate, boat-shaped* | 3 |
| 2. *Rachis and pedicels smooth* | H. Bihai |
| 2. *Rachis and pedicels downy* | H. humilis |
| 3. *Tall, 6 ft. or more h., l. large* | 4 |
| 3. *Scarcely 3 ft. h., l. usually under 20 in. long* | 5 |
| 4. *Lvs. green* | H. brasiliensis |
| 4. *Lvs. purple beneath* | H. metallica |
| 5. *Lvs. long-stalked* | 6 |
| 5. *Lvs. sessile or short-stalked* | 7 |
| 6. *Lvs. linear-oblong, about 2 in. wide* | H. angustifolia |
| 6. *Lvs. linear-lanceolate, 1 to 1½ in. wide* | H. psittacorum |
| 7. *Infl. sessile* | H. choconiana |
| 7. *Infl. stalk, peduncle glabrous* | H. aurantiaca |

**H. angustifo'lia.** About 3 ft. h. *l.* linear-oblong, slender-pointed, up to 2 ft. long. *infl.* about 6 in. long; bracts red. *fl.* white, pedicels orange. Brazil. 1846. (B.M. 4475.) SYN. *H. bicolor.*

**H. auranti'aca.** About 2½ ft. h. *l.* oblong, about 10 in. long, glabrous. *infl.* erect, about 3 in. long; lower bracts orange, green-tipped; upper yellowish-red. *fl.* greenish-red with red pedicels. S. Mexico. 1861. (B.M. 5416 as *H. brevispatha.*)

**H. aureo-stria'ta.** A synonym of *H. Bihai.*

**H. bi'color.** A synonym of *H. angustifolia.*

**H. Biha'i.** Up to 18 ft. h. *l.* oblong, about 4 ft. long, long-stalked, glabrous, sometimes with curved yellow veins (var. **aureo-stria'ta**). *infl.* about 2 ft. long, 1 ft. wide; bracts scarlet, tipped yellow. *fl.* green or yellow. July, August. S. America and Pacific Is. 1786. (B.R. 374; L.B.C. 252.) SYN. *H. aureo-striata.* var. **trium'phans,** *l.* dark green with distant black stripes. *See* **H. illustris.**

**H. brasilien'sis.** Up to 8 ft. h. *l.* oblong, long-stalked, glabrous. *infl.* long; peduncle straight; rachis flexuose; bracts tipped red. *fl.* greenish-yellow or red. September. Brazil, Guiana. 1820. (H.E.F. 190.)

**H. brevispath'a.** A synonym of *H. aurantiaca.*

**H. choconia'na.** About 3 ft. h. *l.* linear-oblong, about 8 in. long. *infl.* sessile, about 3 in. long; bracts scarlet. *fl.* pale yellow, 2 in. long. Guatemala.

**H. hu'milis.** Related to *H. Bihai*, about 4 ft. h. *l.* oblong-acute, about 2 ft. long, glabrous. *Rachis* flexuose; bracts red, tipped green. *fl.* yellowish-white. Trinidad, Brazil. (B.M. 5613.)

**H. illus'tris.** *l.* 1½ to 2 ft. long, ovate-lanceolate, veins bright pink. var. **Edwardus Rex** and **rubricau'lis** belong here, the latter with stem, l.-stalk, and veins, bright red. **H. San'deri** seems related but is less robust and the l. are marbled with red. The exact position of these plants, in the absence of fl., remains doubtful, but they are probably forms of *H. Bihai.* They are handsome foliage plants.

**H. metal'lica.** 9 or 10 ft. h. *l.* oblong, up to 2 ft. long, long-stalked, veins bronzy-red above, purple beneath. *Peduncle* erect; rachis somewhat flexuose; bracts green. *fl.* shining red with green tips. Colombia. 1856. (B.M. 5315.) SYN. *H. vinosa.*

**H. psittaco'rum.** About 2½ ft. h. *l.* linear-lanceolate, about 18 in. long, long-stalked. *Infl.* 2½ to 3 in. long; rachis somewhat flexuose; bracts shining red. *fl.* greenish-yellow with black spots near tips. August. W. Indies, S. America. 1797. (B.M. 502.) A variable plant in size.

**H. San'deri.** *See* **H. illustris.**

**H. trium'phans.** A form of *H. Bihai.*

**H. vino'sa.** A synonym of *H. metallica.*

**HELICOPHYL'LUM.** *See* **Eminium.** Helicophyllum the older name had already been used for a genus of mosses.

**HELICTER'ES** (*helikter*, a twisted bracelet; from the screw-shaped carpels). FAM. *Sterculiaceae.* A genus of about 40 species of hairy trees or shrubs found in the warmer regions, especially in America. Leaves entire or toothed. Flowers axillary, solitary or clustered. Capsules often with starry hairs. *H. Isora* needs stove conditions, and a compost of loam and peat. Propagated by cuttings in sand in heat.

**H. Isor'a.** Shrub of about 6 ft. *l.* like those of hazel, hairy at first, later glabrous above. *fl.* orange-red. September. E. Indies. (B.M. 2061.)

F. G. P.

**HELI'NUS** (*helinos*, a tendril; in reference to the spiral tendrils by which it climbs). FAM. *Rhamnaceae.* An African genus of 2 or 3 species of shrubby climbers. Leaves alternate, petals and stamens 5. The following species requires cool greenhouse conditions but is of no great garden value.

**H. ova'tus.** Climbing shrub up to 15 ft., shoots supported by spiral tendrils. *l.* round-ovate, 1 to 1½ in. long, apex rounded, base cordate; stalk very slender, $\frac{1}{4}$ to $\frac{3}{8}$ in. long. *fl.* borne on axillary, stalked, clusters of 4 to 6 on side twigs 2 to 4 in. long, branching out at right angles; cor. $\frac{1}{4}$ in. wide, yellowish-green to white. *fr.* an obovate-globose nut $\frac{1}{4}$ in. wide. S. and E. Africa. 1862. (R.B. 146.)

W. J. B.

***helio-,*** in compound words, signifying of the sun, as Helianthus, Heliotropium.

**HELIOCAR'PUS** (*helios*, sun, *karpos*, fruit; the valves of the capsule ciliate all round). FAM. *Tiliaceae.* A genus of 4 species of trees, natives of Trop. America. Leaves evergreen, 3-lobed, toothed. Flowers small in terminal panicles. *H. americanus* needs the stove house and a compost of sandy loam and fibrous peat. Half-ripe shoots will root in sand under a bell-glass in summer.

**H. america'nus.** Sunfruit. Tree of 14 to 20 ft. *l.* cordate, 3-lobed, serrate. *fl.* purple, small. July. 1733.

**HELIOCE'REUS** (*helios*, sun, *Cereus*, the sun Cereus). FAM. *Cactaceae.* Stems weak, procumbent; 3- or 4-

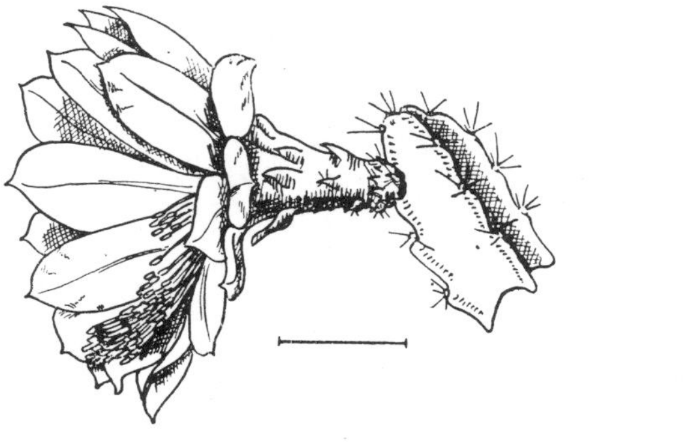

*Heliocereus speciosus* (p. 976)

angled, areoles in the crenations of the ribs; spines short. Flowers large, red, diurnal, scented. Showy plants easily grown in a warm place. **A**

**H. amecaen'sis.** A white counterpart of *H. speciosus*, possibly a local variety perpetuated in cultivation. Mexico. (B.M. 8277.) SYN. *Cereus amecaensis.*

**H. elegantis'simus.** Stems erect, then decumbent, 3 or 4-angled, areoles large with yellow felt and short, sharp spines. *fl.* red. Mexico. (B.R.C. 2, t. 17.) SYN. *Cereus coccineus.*

**H. specio'sus.** Stems clambering, ribs undulate, areoles distant, with felt and short, slender spines. *fl.* scarlet, lasting several days. Mexico. (B.M. 2306; B.R. 28, 49; L.B.C. 924; B.R.C. 2, t. 17.) SYN. *Cereus speciosissimus.* Crossed with Epiphyllum, the species has given some beautiful hybrids.

V. H.

**HELIOPHIL'A** (*helios*, sun, *philein*, to love; from the habitat). FAM. *Cruciferae.* Cape Stock. A genus of about 60 species of annual and perennial sub-shrubs, natives of S. Africa. Leaves various. Flowers of various colours in long leafless racemes; pods stalked or sessile, 2-celled, 2-valved; seeds in a single row, often winged, their cotyledons twice folded transversely. The annuals may be sown in March or April in the open border or raised under glass and planted out. *H. scandens* needs the greenhouse.

**H. amplexicau'lis.** Annual, about 9 in. h. *Lower l.* opposite; *upper* alternate, cordate, oblong, entire, stem-clasping. *fl.* small, white to purplish. June to September. 1774.

**H. coronopifo'lia.** Annual, 1 to 2 ft. h. *l.* pinnately lobed; lobes linear, entire. *fl.* blue-violet, spreading. June to September. 1778.

**H. crithmifo'lia.** Perennial herb, 6 to 12 in. h., velvety. *l.* pinnatipartite, with a channelled, linear rachis, 2 to 3 in. long, lobes in 2 to 4 pairs, rather remote, acute, somewhat fleshy. *fl.* purple, small, or in var. **parviflo'ra**, white; pedicels glabrous, ½ in. long; stamens not toothed. S. Africa.

**H. leptophyl'la.** Blue-green, glabrous. Stems ascending, branched from base, 12 to 20 in. h., branches terete, sparsely leafy. *l.* filiform, 1 to 2 in. long, erect. *fl.* bright blue with yellow throat, about ½ in. across, pet. obovate, obtuse; racemes loosely many-fld., pedicels filiform. Namaqualand.

**H. linearifo'lia.** Erect or decumbent sub-shrub, 1 to 3 ft. *h.*, glabrous or slightly hairy, branches slender. *l.* linear, about 1 in. long, ¹⁄₁₂ in. wide, entire. *fl.* blue, claws of pet. yellow; racemes 10- to 16-fld. *Pod* 3-nerved. S. Africa. Half-hardy.

*Heliophila longifolia*

**H. longifo'lia.** Glabrous annual. Stem sometimes branched, up to 18 in. h. *l.* narrow-linear, sometimes 3- or 4-fid in upper half, up to 10 in. long, ⅛ in. wide; segs. long. *fl.* blue with whitish or yellowish base, about ¾ in. across; pet. roundish-obovate. *Pod* moniliform, often curved. S. Africa. (B.M. 8886.) Half-hardy.

*Heliophila pilosa*

**H. pilo'sa.** Variable usually roughly hairy annual, 6 to 24 in. h., erect or spreading. *l.* opposite below as a rule, upper alternate, lanceolate to linear, lower pinnatifid. *fl.* sky-blue with yellow centre, varying to lilac. June, July. 1820. (B.M. 2526 as *H. striata*.) var. **incis'a**, *l.* 3-cut at apex (rarely 5-cut), lobes linear or slenderpointed. (B.M. 496 as *H. arabioides*.)

**H. scand'ens.** Stems slender, twining. *l.* lanceolate. *fl.* white, sometimes rose-tinted, large, racemose. Natal. 1887. (B.M. 7668.)

**HELIOP'SIS** (*helios*, sun, *opsis*, like). FAM. *Compositae.* A genus of about 7 species of American annual or perennial herbs. Leaves stalked, all opposite or upper sometimes alternate. Flower-heads radiate, rather large, rays yellow, pistillate, disk florets 2-sexual, receptacle conical. Achenes without a pappus (a pappus is present in the nearly related genus Zinnia). The following species are perennial and hardy, needing treatment as for Helianthus. Good on dry soils. Excellent for cutting.

**H. helianthoi'des.** 3 to 6 ft. h. *l.* ovate-lanceolate, coarsely toothed, smooth on both sides or roughish above. *fl.-heads* terminal, about 3 in. across; peduncles long. Autumn. N. America. 1714. (B.M. 3372 as *H. laevis*.) var. **Pitcheria'na**, dwarfer and more bushy, up to 3 ft. h., flowering more freely.

**H. lae'vis.** A synonym of *H. helianthoides.*

**H. scab'ra.** 2 to 4 ft. h. Much like *H. helianthoides* but l. rough all over, the upper sometimes entire. *fl.-heads* less numerous than in *H. helianthoides.* August. N. America. 1824. (B.R. 592 as *H. canescens*.) A rather variable plant. var. **gratis'sima**, 4 ft., *fl.-heads* large, double, bright pale yellow; **imbrica'ta**, 2½ ft., *fl.-heads* golden-yellow, 3 in. across; **incompara'bilis**, about 3 ft., *fl.-heads* semi-double, orange-yellow; **ma'jor**, larger in all parts than type (several very similar forms have been offered with names indicating large size); **vitelli'na**,* 3 ft., *fl.-heads* double, golden-yellow; **zinniiflo'ra**, 2½ ft., *fl.-heads* large, deep yellow, free and continuous in fl.

**HELIOSPERM'A** (*helios*, sun, *sperma*, seed; from form of seed). FAM. *Caryophyllaceae.* A genus of about 8 species of perennial, loosely tufted herbs with the habit of small-flowered Silenes, all European. Related to Melandrium but flowers with 3 (never 5) styles, and crested seeds. They like rich light soil and can be propagated by seed or division.

KEY
1. *Claw of pet. ciliate* H. alpestre
1. *Claw of pet. not ciliate* 2
2. *White woolly* H. glutinosum
2. *Bright green* H. quadrifidum

**H. alpes'tre.** Perennial tufted with woody root-stock, with many sterile leafy shoots, fl.-stem 4 to 8 in. h., smooth, or with more or less clammy rings. *Lower l.* oblanceolate narrowed to a stalk; *upper* lanceolate to linear-lanceolate, ciliate at base. *fl.* about ½ in. across, white; cal. short, bell-shaped to club-shaped; pet. 4- to 6-cleft, obovate, with 2 teeth at base of blade. June to August. E. Europe. var. **grandiflo'ra,** *fl.* larger; **ro'sea,** *fl.* pale rose. A double-fld. form is also known.

**H. erioph'orum.** A synonym of *H. glutinosum.*

**H. glutino'sum.** White woolly glandular perennial forming a loose mat. Stem about 4 in. h. *Lower l.* spatulate, mostly rounded at tip; *upper* lanceolate to linear, about 1 in. long. *infl.* many-fld. *fl.* white, about ⅓ in. across; pet. 4-lobed, the side lobes short; cal. teeth rounded, glandular-hairy. May, June. Tyrol, &c. SYN. *Silene Heufleri, S. Veselskyi.*

**H. quadrifi'dum.** Smaller than *H. alpestre*; bright green, about 3 to 6 in. h., clammy above. *Lower l.* small, lanceolate to spatulate, petiole long; *upper* larger, narrow-linear, usually smooth. *fl.* about ¼ in. across, white; pedicels long; cal. about ⅛ in. long, oblong-turbinate, teeth blunt; pet. obovate, 4-toothed. July, August. S. Europe. var. **monachor'um,** 2 in. h., densely glandular. Balkans; **pudibund'um,** *fl.* at first white, becoming rose; **pusil'lum,** about 2 in. h., smaller in all parts than type, fl. white, pedicels slender.

**HE'LIOTHRIPS haemorrhoida'lis.** *See* **Greenhouse Thrips.**

**HELIOTROPE.** *See* **Heliotropium.**

**heliotropic,** bending towards the light. Heliotropism is the phenomenon shown by the change of position of growing, and other parts of plants able to move, owing to the direction in which the rays of light fall upon them. Young stems, e.g. may grow towards the light (the heliotropism is then said to be positive), so growing up into the air and taking such a position that the leaves are adequately exposed to light; others grow horizontally under the influence of light and so spread their leaves to catch the rays of light; a few, like the young climbing branches of Ivy and the hypocotyledonary stem of Mistletoe appear to grow away from the light (i.e. are negatively heliotropic), as do most roots. The leaves of some plants, e.g. Scarlet Runner, Robinia, Sensitive Plant, change their position according to the intensity of the rays of light falling upon them, in very bright sunlight presenting only the edges of their leaves to the source of light, in light of more moderate intensity their upper surface. The position of most leaves is, however, fixed while they are young and capable of movement, and is such as to catch the rays of best intensity for their work. The directive action of light thus, through their power of response, results in the organs of a plant being placed in the position where their functions can be best carried out.

**HELIOTROP'IUM** (*helios*, sun, *trope*, turning; from the old idea that the inflorescence turned with the sun). FAM. *Boraginaceae.* Turnsole. A genus of about 220 species of annual herbs, sub-shrubs, or rarely shrubs distributed over the warmer parts of the world. Leaves alternate, rarely nearly opposite. Flowers blue or white in circinate, secund spikes; corolla salver-shaped; stamens 5, in throat of corolla, not exserted; ovary 4-celled ripening to a fruit of 4 nutlets. The only Heliotropes commonly grown in this country are the derivatives of *H. corymbosum* and *H. peruvianum*, cultivated for their delightfully fragrant flowers. *H. peruvianum* is the predominant form but the larger-flowered *H. corymbosum* is the parent of many forms and there are probably hybrids between the two. Heliotropes do not require a great amount of heat at any time but are very quickly damaged by cold and severely when the temperature reaches freezing-point. Both types can be grown as dwarf decorative plants in small pots, or as large pyramidal or standard specimens. Some varieties are dwarf and excellent for summer-flowering in beds and old plants of the taller varieties may be trained up the back wall of a warm greenhouse. Seeds or cuttings may be used as means of propagation, but cuttings must be used for named varieties. Young growing shoots taken in August or in early spring make the best cuttings. Old plants growing in heat will provide cuttings which root quickly in a close frame and their points may be used for further cuttings in preference to those from less vigorously growing plants. The young plants should be potted singly and grown in a temperature of about 60° F. repotting as becomes necessary according to the shape and size of the plants desired. Cuttings intended for standards should be taken in autumn and kept growing all winter, with a single stem until the desired height is reached, when the points may be stopped and the side branches which are soon produced used to form a head. Old plants may be grown as standards for several years in comparatively small pots if reduced and potted up each year in new soil. The heads may be made by tieing the branches to each other or by training on trellises. Large pyramids may be grown from autumn-struck cuttings in a single year if due attention is paid to their training. They should be got into their full-sized pots as soon as possible and trained to a pyramidal trellis. Small decorative plants for the greenhouse stages may be grown to flower in 5-in. pots by keeping them pinched when young. Cuttings of varieties for bedding should be taken about mid-August and put in rather thickly in pots or pans and placed in a close frame. The resulting plants should be kept as stock from which to propagate in spring and then thrown away since young plants are best. They should not be planted out until well into June since they are extremely tender. Standards, &c., intended for winter-flowering are best placed outside in a warm position in summer to ripen the wood thoroughly. They should be housed in September and kept in a temperature of 55° F. in winter.

**H. anchusifo'lium.** Summer Heliotrope. Sub-shrub about 2 ft. h. with terete, hairy branches. *l.* elliptic, obtuse, hairy, margins undulate. *fl.* like those of *H. peruvianum* but scentless. May. Argentine. 1829. (B.M. 8480.)

**H. convolvula'ceum.** Showy annual of about 2 ft. *l.* lanceolate to nearly ovate, sometimes linear; stalk short. *fl.* white, fragrant, opening at night; cor. limb large, angularly lobed; peduncles short, l. opposed and terminal. Summer. New Mexico. 1867. (B.M. 5615.) Hardy.

**H. corymbo'sum.** Shrub to 4 ft. *l.* oblong-lanceolate, proportionately narrower than in *H. peruvianum.* *fl.* lilac; fragrant, twice as large as in *H. peruvianum*; sep. long, subulate; cor. tube twice as long as cal.; infl. much larger than in *H. peruvianum* and more open. May to September. Peru. 1808. (B.M. 1609.) Greenhouse. A parent of the garden Heliotropes.

**H. curassav'icum.** Sub-shrub of about 9 in. *l.* linear-lanceolate, smooth, glaucous. *fl.* white or bluish with yellow open throat, rather large; spikes usually in pairs, densely fld. June, July. United States and W. Indies. 1731. (B.M. 2669.) Greenhouse or stove.

**H. inca'num.** Shrub of 2 to 3 ft. *l.* ovate, acute, thick, wrinkled and roughly hairy above, softer and hoary beneath. *fl.* white; cor. tube twice as long as cal., bristly hairy; peduncles hairy; spikes forked. June. Peru. Greenhouse. var. **glab'rum** has broadly elliptical rough but glabrous l. and purple fl. 1884. (G.C. 22 (1884) 809, f. 140.)

**H. in'dicum.** Annual of about 1 ft. *l.* ovate or oval, rather heart-shaped, sometimes toothed or undulate; stalks winged. *fl.* bluish in usually single densely fld. spikes, 9 to 13 in. long. June to August. W. Indies. 1713. (B.M. 1837.) Stove.

**H. lu'teum.** Shrub to 6 ft. *l.* stalked. *fl.* green and yellow, salver-shaped. June to October. N. Africa, &c. 1779. (B.R. 464 as *Tournefortia fruticosa.*) Greenhouse.

**H. peruvia'num.** Common Heliotrope. Cherry Pie. Shrub to 6 ft. *l.* oblong-lanceolate, wrinkled, margins somewhat waved, hairy; stalked. *fl.* violet or lilac, very fragrant; cor. tube about as long as cal.; spikes terminal, branched into 3 or 4, densely fld. May to September. Peru. 1757. (B.M. 141.) Greenhouse. A parent of the garden Heliotropes.

**H. rega'le.** A large-fld. race of *H. peruvianum.*

**H.×Voltairea'num.** Dwarf compact form nearly related to *H. peruvianum*, said to be a hybrid.

**HELIP'TERUM** (*helios*, sun, *pteron*, wing; referring to the plumed pappus). FAM. *Compositae.* A genus of over 40 species, comprising shrubs, sub-shrubs, perennials, and annuals, 12 natives of S. Africa, the others of Australia and Tasmania. Leaves nearly always alternate, usually woolly or downy entire. Flowers in heads surrounded by a large, often richly coloured involucre of numerous scarious, overlapping bracts surrounding a circular, central cluster of florets. These bracts persist for a long time after the flowers are dead and justify the inclusion of this genus with the 'everlastings'. With the exception of the annuals they are not easily cultivated. For one thing the English climate is against them. They like a dry, sunny atmosphere and a light, well-drained loamy soil. Greenhouse.

**H. anthemoi'des.** Glabrous perennial with numerous stems, erect, simple, rather slender, rarely over 1 ft. h. *l.* linear to linear-lanceolate, about ½ in. long, crowded, often dotted. *fl.-heads* solitary, involucre hemispherical, spreading, ¾ to 1 in. across; outer bracts short, broad, scarious, tinged brown, inner with broad claws and petal-like blades about ¼ in. long or more, white; receptacle flat; fl. all perfect. *Achenes* densely silky-hairy; pappus bristles 15 to 20, plumose. Queensland to Tasmania. Greenhouse.

**H. canes'cens.** Straggling sub-shrub, 1 to 2 ft. Stems slender, virgate. *l.* erect, oblong or lanceolate, ¼ to ⅓ in. long, grey-woolly, but variable in size and shape. *fl.-heads* 1¼ in. across, usually solitary, erect on a slender stalk; involucral bracts rosy, deep red-brown and white. Autumn to Spring. S. Africa. 1794. (B.M. 420 as *Xeranthemum canescens.*)

**H. corymbiflo'rum.** Annual, freely branching, about 15 in. h. *l.* lanceolate. *fl.-heads* nearly 1 in. wide, top-shaped, in small corymbs, rays mostly white. Australia. (G.F. 13, 430.)

**H. Cot'ula.** Slender, erect, branching annual, 6 to 20 in., loosely hairy at first. *l.* narrowly linear, 1 in. long, 1/16 to 1/12 in. wide. *fl.-heads* solitary, terminal, 1 in. across; involucral bracts ovate, white or yellow, disk yellow, ⅓ in. across. May. W. Australia. (B.M. 5604.)

**H. exim'ium.*** White-woolly shrub, 1½ to 3 ft. *l.* 2 to 3 in. long, 1½ to 2 in. wide, broadly ovate, pointed, softly woolly, closely set, partly stem-clasping. *fl.-heads* 1 to 1¼ in. across, globose, in crowded terminal clusters of 10 to 24, involucral bracts ½ in. long, bright crimson, very numerous; florets yellow, crowded, forming a disk ¾ in. across. July. S. Africa. 1794. (B.M. 300 and A.B.R. 654 as *Gnaphalium eximium*; B.R. 532 as *Astelma eximium.*)

**H. gnaphalioi'des.** Sub-shrub, decumbent, but sending up erect shoots, 1 to 1½ ft., densely downy. *l.* linear, semi-cylindrical, 2 to 2½ in. long, 1/12 in. wide, thickly white-downy. *fl.-heads* ½ in. long, ⅓ in. wide, long-stalked, erect; involucral bracts ¼ in. long, ovate-lanceolate, red-brown, finally much reflexed; florets yellow. June. S. Africa. 1824. (B.M. 2710 as *Gnaphalium modestum.*)

**H. Humboldtia'num.*** Annual, 1 to 2 ft. high, at first woolly. *l.* linear to linear-lanceolate, pointed, partly stem-clasping, 1½ to 3 in. long, ⅛ to ¼ in. wide. *fl.-heads* bright yellow, ⅛ in. wide, crowded densely in terminal flattish or rounded clusters, making a compound infl. 3 or 4 in. across. Summer. W. Australia. 1863. (B.M. 5350 as *H. Sandfordii.*)

**H. incan'um.** Perennial, 6 to 12 in. high, often found in large tufts, shoots and l. white with wool. *l.* crowded at the base of the stem, 2 to 5 in. long, about ⅛ in. wide, narrow-linear. *fl.-heads* solitary, terminal on tall slender stalks, 1½ in. wide; involucral scales much imbricated, ovate, outer ones silvery-white or tinged with brown; disk pale or bright yellow. Australia, Tasmania. (B.M. 2881 as *Elichrysum incanum.*)

**H. Mangles'ii.*** Erect, glabrous, much-branched annual, 1 to 2 ft. *l.* glaucous, ovate to oblong, base cordate, stem-clasping, 1 to 4 in. long. *fl.-heads* 1 to 1½ in. across, on slender branching stalks; involucral bracts closely imbricated, oblong, varying in colour; purple, rich rosy-red, pinkish; disk-florets yellow. Summer. W. Australia. (B.R. 1703; B.M. 3483, 5283, 5290, as *Rhodanthe Manglesii. Rhodanthe maculata* probably belongs here.) Greenhouse, but, raised from seed in March and grown on in pots, it can be planted in the open for its summer fl. 'Double'-fld. forms both deep rose and white are known.

**H. ro'seum.** Glabrous annual, 1 to 2 ft. h., branched, branches erect, each terminated by a single large head. *l.* linear, small, numerous. *fl.-heads* with many pointed rays, pink. Australia. (B.M. 4081.) var. **al'bum,** *fl.* white; **grandiflo'rum** with larger fl.-heads than is commonly seen in the type; and **ple'num** with 'double' fl.-heads are known.

**H. Sandford'ii.** A synonym of *H. Humboldtianum.*

**H. speciosis'simum.*** Sub-shrub, 1 to 2 ft. Stem stout, often unbranched, softly woolly like the l. *l.* elliptic-oblong or oblong, base partly stem-clasping, 1½ to 2½ in. long, ½ to ¾ in. wide. *fl.-heads* 1½ to 2 in. across, solitary on stout, erect stalks up to 1 ft. long; involucre of numerous, glistening white or straw-coloured, pointed bracts; disk ⅝ in. across. September. S. Africa. 1787. (A.B.R. 51 as *Xeranthemum speciosissimum.*)

**HELIX.** *See* **Snails.**

***He'lix,*** old Greek and Latin name for a twining plant.

**HELLEBORE.** *See* **Helleborus, Veratrum.**

**HELLEBORINE.** *See* **Epipactis, Serapias.**

**HELLEB'ORUS** (name used by Hippocrates and other Greek writers). Hellebore. FAM. *Ranunculaceae.* A genus of 18 or 20 herbaceous perennials, erect, with long-stalked generally pedate leaves, often winter-green, natives of S. Europe and W. Asia. Flowers large with 5 (or 6) sepals, green or coloured, and tubular nectaries. Nearly related to Eranthis but differing greatly in habit. They will grow in any ordinary garden soil but are best in a moist, well-drained, rich loam in partial shade, and do not object to lime. A top-dressing of well-rotted compost after flowering benefits them and when once planted they should remain undisturbed. They should not be allowed to become very dry in summer and then either watering or, better still, mulching should be resorted to. Most species flower in winter or in very early spring. Propagation by seed is slow but seedlings are more readily established than older plants and in the wild garden self-sown seedlings often succeed well. Strong, healthy stock can be increased by division of the roots which should be done as soon after flowering as possible. Seeds should be sown as soon as ripe.

*H. niger*, the Christmas rose, is frequently lifted and put under glass for flowering, but it will not stand much forcing. The plants may also be flowered in the open with less fear of weather damage if covered by a frame or cloche, or the forward buds may be picked and opened in water in a warm house. The flowers of the later Lenten roses do not behave so well when cut but will last long if floated on the surface of water in a bowl.

A large number of varieties of Lenten rose have been raised by crossing in the first place and by seeds from these crosses. Hybrids have been recorded among plants growing wild, as, for instance, between *H. atrorubens* and *H. odorus* with flowers with purple-brownish-green colouring outside and greener within, *H. purpurascens*

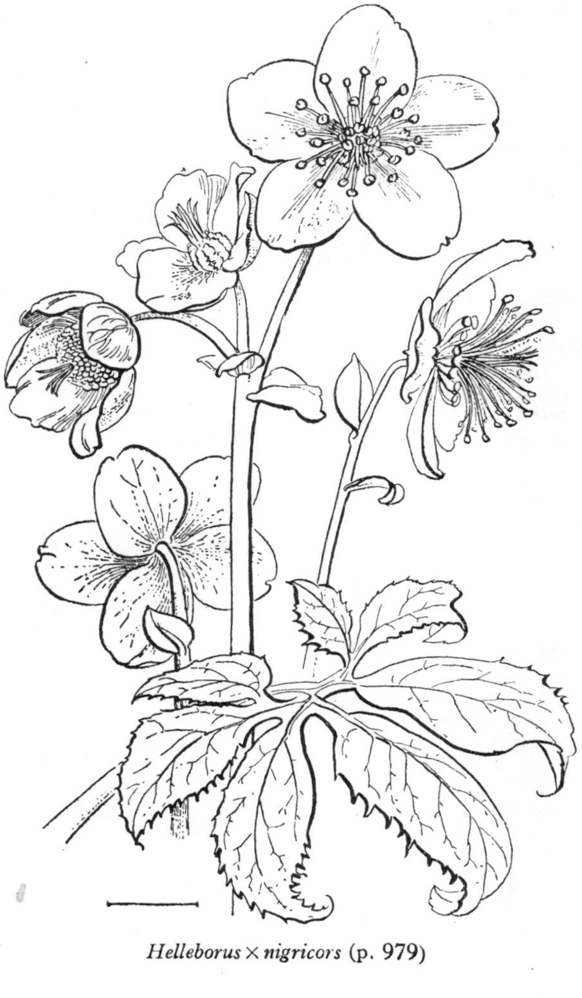

*Helleborus × nigricors* (p. 979)

and *H. viridis* with flowers of the colour of *H. viridis* but double as large, and so on. Among the garden-raised varieties *H. abchasicus*, *H. guttatus*, *H. orientalis*, *H. purpurascens*, *H. viridis*, and others have played a part, and some good varieties of these hybrids are offered under the name of *H. hybridus*, *H. orientalis*, &c. *H.* × *Heyderi* is *H. abchasicus* × *H. guttatus* with large flowers pale greenish-rose to deep purple with more or less distinct reddish spots. *H.* × *intermedius* (*H. atrorubens* × *H. dumetorum*) has purplish-green flowers, green inside with purple-tinged margins to the sepals. *H.* × *graveolens* (*H. atrorubens* × *H. odorus*) has blackish-green flowers shading to purple at the margins and with a glaucous tinge overlying the black-green within. *H.* × *nigricors* (*H. corsicus* × *H. niger*) has many-fld. inflorescences of pale green flowers in February. (Raised 1931.)

The fullest account of the genus is in Schiffner's *Monographia Hellebororum* published at Halle in 1890 where several of the species are finely figured.

Hellebores may suffer from attacks by leaf-spotting fungi, chief of which are *Coniothyrium hellebori* and *Phyllosticta helleborella*. The first makes small brown spots and the second rather large black blotches on the leaves and sometimes stems. If either is noticed in the early stages and the infected leaflets or leaves removed the trouble may be checked, but it is sometimes necessary to spray with a Bordeaux mixture.

KEYS

```
 1. Stem leafy; radical lvs. none                              2
 1. Radical lvs. long-stalked; fl.-stem direct from rhizome with
      l.-sheaths only or foliose bracts                        4
 2. Lvs. 3-partite, segs. not again divided, broad-ovate       3
 2. Lvs. many-partite, pedate with lanceolate segs.  H. foetidus
 3. Lvs. with large spiny teeth                       H. corsicus
 3. Lvs. with distant small teeth or almost entire     H. lividus
 4. Bracts undivided, oval, pale, margin entire; fl. white or
      rose                                                     5
 4. Bracts foliose, much-divided                              6
 5. Lvs. dark green, segs. cuneate, broadest above middle,
      teeth not sharp-pointed                           H. niger
 5. Lvs. pale green, segs. broad-lanceolate, broadest
      about middle, teeth sharp-pointed            H. macranthus
 6. Carpels free to base, narrowed almost to a stalk          7
 6. Carpels more or less joined at base                      11
 7. Lvs. very large, not winter-green; fl. green, very
      large, sep. broad                            H. cyclophyllus
 7. Lvs. winter-green; fl. coloured                           8
 8. Anthers more or less mucronate                            9
 8. Anthers truncate or rounded at top                      10
 9. Fl. rose-red, anthers long-pointed            H. antiquorum
 9. Fl. white, anthers frequently indistinctly pointed  H. olympicus
10. Fl. more or less deep carmine-red; lvs. glabrous   H. abchasicus
10. Fl. pale greenish-yellow-brown; lvs. hairy
      or glabrous                                    H. orientalis
10. Fl. white, densely spotted red; lvs. glabrous    H. guttatus
11. Fl. clear green or yellowish-green with mixture of
      purple                                                 12
11. Fl. muddy dark green, purple-green, or cloudy purple     14
12. Lvs. generally winter-green, segs. broad          H. odorus
12. Lvs. not winter-green, smooth or nearly so; fl. medium-
      sized or small                                         13
13. Lvs. smooth, pedate, bright green, finely
      toothed; fl. small, yellow-green, sep. nar-
      row, stigma bent                             H. dumetorum
13. Lvs. smooth or hairy, coarsely toothed; fl. yellow-
      green or green, stigma erect                     H. viridis
14. Lvs. distinctly pedate, segs. undivided; fl.
      generally small, sep. narrow, stigma bent
      outwards                                       H. atrorubens
14. Lvs. almost digitate, segs. almost always 2- or
      3-partite; fl. large, sep. broad              H. purpurascens
```

**H. abchas'icus.** Glabrous evergreen. *l.* about 1 ft. across, pedate, leathery; lflets. 5 to 7, ovate-lanceolate, deep green or tinged violet, doubly toothed; petiole about 8 in. long. *Peduncle* taller than l., tinged red, 4- or 5-fld. *fl.* nodding, purple (or green within), 2½ to 3 in. across; sep. touching or overlapping, oval, margin wavy; nectary rather compressed, green striped purple; anthers yellowish. January to March. Caucasus. (G.F. 593 as *H. colchicus*.) Variable in colour. var. **coccin'eus**, maroon-crimson; **veno'sus**, deep rose-purple with distinct veining.

**H. altifo'lius.** A variety of *H. niger*.

**H. angustifo'lius.** A synonym of *H. macranthus*.

**H. antiquo'rum.** Glabrous evergreen. *l.* 1 or 2, radical, sub-pedate, leathery; lflets. 5 to 7, ovate-lanceolate, sharply toothed. *Peduncle* usually shorter than l., striped red below, 3- or 4-fld.

*fl.* 2½ in. across, cup-shaped, nodding, rose-purple, greenish at base; sep. wide-ovate, acuminate; nectaries 10 to 15, yellowish-green; anthers yellowish-white. Early spring. Bithynian Olympus, Asia Minor. Related to *H. orientalis* and sometimes regarded as a variety of that species. (Gn. 16 (1879), 60; B.R. 28, 34 as *H. orientalis*.)

**H. atroru'bens.** Glabrous or somewhat hairy, deciduous. *l.* (radical), pedate, about 1 ft. across; lflets. usually 9, broadly lanceolate, broadest at or below the middle, acuminate, sharply toothed, somewhat shiny green above, paler below; petiole about 12 in. long, reddish-striped. *Peduncle* taller than l., 2- to 9-fld., often tinged red. *fl.* usually under 2 in. across, flattish, scentless, dull purple without, greenish-purple within; sep. oblong-ovate; nectaries 15 to 20, green. March to May. SE. Europe. (P.F.G. 82.) Often confused with *H. purpurascens* which is offered in catalogues and is figured in B.M. 4581, under this name. SYN. *H. atropurpureus*.

**H. caucas'icus.** A name variously applied to *H. guttatus*, hybrids of *H. olympicus*, &c.; should be dropped.

**H. col'chicus.** Name applied to cultivated forms of *H. abchasicus*.

**H. cor'sicus.** Glabrous evergreen, sub-shrubby. *l.* from stems, glaucous, about 18 in. h., thick, leathery, with 3 spinose-toothed lflets., bluish-green; petioles 4 to 8 in. long. *infl.* branched, about 20-fld. *fl.* nodding, about 2 in. across, cup-shaped, yellowish-green; sep. broad-ovate, obtuse; nectaries funnel-shaped, greenish-yellow. March, April. Corsica, Sardinia, Balearic Is. (S.B.F.G. s. 2. 190; B.R. 24, 54 as *H. lividus*.) See **H.** × **nigricors** above.

**H. cyclophyl'lus.** Deciduous. *l.* about 16 in. across, usually solitary, varying from almost palmate to pedate with 7 to 9 broad-lanceolate, deeply divided segs., bright green above, paler, hairy, and with prominent veins beneath; petioles 8 to 12 in. long. *Peduncles* as tall as l., 3- or 4-fld. *fl.* 2½ in. across, saucer-shaped, sub-erect, sweet-scented, yellow-green, glaucous; sep. broad; anthers yellowish-white. April, May. Greece.

**H. dumeto'rum.** Glabrous, deciduous. *l.* (radical) 2 or 3, about 8 in. across, pedate; lflets. 11 to 13, broad-lanceolate, somewhat arched, broadest about the middle, teeth small; petiole about 8 in. long. *Peduncle* about as high as l., many-fld. *fl.* about 1½ in. across, nodding, flattish, yellowish-green; sep. narrow, obtuse, not over-lappig; nectaries 8 to 12, slender. March to May. SE. Europe. (S B.F.G. 109.)

**H. foe'tidus.** Glabrous evergreen, sub-shrubby, about 2 ft. h. Stem leafy. *l.* rather leathery, dark shining green, pedatisect with 7 to 10 narrow-lanceolate segs., sharply toothed; petiole about 4 in. long. *infl.* branching, large, many-fld. *fl.* nodding, cup-shaped, small, glandular without, green, inner sep. obtuse, purplish; nectaries funnel-shaped, short-stalked. March to May. W. and S. Europe, including Britain. (E.B. 613.)

**H. gutta'tus.** Glabrous. *l.* (radical) usually 2, very similar to those of *H. abchasicus* but paler green, sub-pedate, of 5 to 7 ovate-lanceolate, sharply toothed segs. *Peduncle* about 16 in. h., flecked purplish-brown with 3 to 5 fl. *fl.* nodding, over 3 in. across, white within, pale rose near margin, greenish near base, with numerous dull purple spots, unspotted purple without; nectaries 15 to 20, compressed, greenish-yellow. January to March. Georgia, Caucasus. SYN. *H. orientalis guttatus*. A parent of several good hybrids.

**H. istri'acus.** A variety of *H. odorus*.

**H. Koch'ii.** A synonym of *H. orientalis*.

**H. liv'idus.** Very near *H. corsicus* but margin of l. almost entire, not spiny-toothed. Balearic Is. (B.M. 72, 7903.) var. **pic'tus** has white-spotted l.

**H. macran'thus.** Differs from *H. niger* which it otherwise resembles by its frequently more robust growth, broad-lanceolate (not oblong-cuneate) ashy-grey-green l.-segs. with rigid sub-spiny teeth and larger white (rarely rose-tinged) fl. with narrower sep. (overlapping only to the middle), and longer style. January, February. Italy to Greece. (S.B.F.G. s. 2. 186 as *H. niger vernalis*.) SYN. *H. niger angustifolius*, *H. niger maximus*.

**H. ni'ger.** Christmas Rose. Glabrous evergreen. *l.* (radical) peda-tisect, with 7 to 9 lobes; leathery, dark green, segs. ovate-cuneate, distantly toothed near apex; petiole about 5 in. long, frequently spotted or tinged red. *Peduncle* about as tall as l., 2- or 3-fld. *fl.* large, somewhat nodding, white or tinged rose, saucer-shaped; sep. broad-ovate; nectaries yellow, 2-lipped; anthers short. January, February. Cent. and S. Europe, W. Asia. 16th cent. (B.M. 8; S.B.F.G. s. 2. 186.) var. **altifo'lius** has very long-stalked l. taller than the fl., larger l. with more numerous cuneate segs. more distinctly toothed, petioles and peduncles red-spotted, fl. larger (up to 4 in. across) and frequently tinged rose; **angustifo'lius** and **max'imus**, synonyms of *H. macranthus*. See **H.** × **nigricors** above.

**H. occidenta'lis.** See **H. viridis**.

**H. odo'rus.** Pubescent, usually evergreen. *l.* (radical) usually solitary, leathery, rather large, pedate (or in young plants sub-palmate), segs. 7 to 11, broad-lanceolate, dull green above, shining, paler with prominent veins below, regularly double-toothed. *Peduncle* taller than l., often brownish, few-fld., 18 in. h. *fl.* about 2 in. across, nodding, cup-shaped, fragrant, yellowish-green; sep. broad-ovate, overlapping; stamens yellowish-white; nectaries green. February, March. Balkans. 1817. (B.R. 1643.) var. **istri'acus** has 12 to 16 less hairy, narrower lflets., fewer and smaller fl. with narrower segs.

**H. olym'picus.** More or less hairy evergreen. *l.* (radical) 2, large, leathery, dull shining green, more or less pedate; lflets. 7 to 9, broad-lanceolate with small double teeth; petiole 16 to 20 in. long. *Peduncle* as tall as l., 2- or 3-fld. *fl.* nodding on long pedicels, smaller than in *H. antiquorum*, white with green tinge, green at base; sep. ovate, overlapping. March, April. Bithynian Olympus, Asia Minor. (B.R. 28, 58.) This has been confused with *H. antiquorum* to which, and to *H. guttatus*, it is related.

*Helleborus orientalis*

**H. orienta'lis.** Hairy or glabrous evergreen. *rhiz.* much branched. *l.* (radical) 1 or 2, large to very large (up to 16 in. or more across), leathery, more or less pedate, with 5 to 11 elliptic-lanceolate or widely elliptic lflets. cuneate at base, doubly serrate; petiole long. *Peduncle* usually shorter than l., 3- or 4-fld. *fl.* up to 2½ in. wide, basin-shaped, cream at first then pale brownish-yellow-green, more or less nodding; sep. broadly ovate, overlapping. February to April. Greece, Asia Minor. 1839. (J.R.H.S. 63, 152 as *H. Kochii*.) A plant much confused but distinct among the eastern species by the colour of its fl.

**H. purpuras'cens.** Hairy, deciduous. *l.* (radical) usually 2, about 12 in. across, palmate; lflets. 5, broadly wedge-shaped, each deeply 3- to 6-lobed, bluish-green, coarsely double-toothed; petiole as high as l. *Peduncle* scarcely as high as fl., up to 3-fld. *fl.* about 2 in. across, more or less nodding, basin-shaped, dull purplish, veined outside, greenish-purple within; sep. broad, ovate; nectaries 15 to 20, yellow-green; stamens whitish-green. March. Hungary. 1817. (B.M. 3170; S.B.F.G. s. 2.142; B.M. 4581 as *H. atrorubens*.) *See also* **H. atrorubens.**

**H. vi'ridis.** Somewhat hairy or glabrous, deciduous. *l.* about 10 in. across, pedate; lflets. 7 to 11, undivided, lanceolate, irregularly toothed, dull green above, paler with prominent veins beneath. *Peduncle* at 10 in. h., equalling l., round, 5- or 6-fld. *fl.* of medium size, cup-shaped, nodding, scentless, bright green; sep. wide, overlapping; nectaries yellowish-green, shorter than the yellowish-white stamens. February. Ireland eastwards to Serbia. A variable plant. The British form (occurring also in France and Spain) has been distinguished under the name *H. occidentalis.* It is distinct by its broader l.-segs. with large teeth and glabrous lower surface, smaller fls. with narrow sep. without the 'bloom' present on the more widely spread type. (E.B. 44.)

*hellen'icus -a -um,* of Greece.

*hellwigien'sis -is -e,* of the Hellwig Mts., New Guinea.

*Hellwig'ii,* in honour of Franz Carl Hellwig, 1861–89, student of the flora of Germany.

**HELMET FLOWER.** *See* **Aconitum, Coryanthes, Scutellaria.**

**HELMHOLTZ'IA** (in honour of Hermann Helmholtz, 1821–94, German Professor of Botany). FAM. *Philydraceae.* A genus of 2 species of tufted herbaceous perennials, one native of Australia, the other of the Pacific Is. Greenhouse protection is needed and a compost of well-drained sandy loam and peat with plenty of water. Increased by division or by seeds.

**H. glaber'rima.** About 3 ft. h. *l.* ensiform, slender-pointed, equitant, 1 in. wide. *fl.* white, in panicles. Pacific Is. (B.M. 6056 as *Philydrum glaberrimum.*)

F. P.

**HELMINTHOSTACH'YS** (*helminthos,* worm, *stachys,* spike; from the arrangement of the sporangia). FAM. *Ophioglossaceae.* A monotypic genus containing a curious and handsome fern closely related to Botrychium, with sporangia in small crested clusters in a long, loose spike. *H. zeylanica* is somewhat difficult to grow, requiring a constantly moist place with a stove temperature all the year round. The best compost for it consists of 2 parts rich loam, 1 of leaf-mould, 1 of sand. Propagation is very slow as it rarely forms double crowns and has very rarely been raised from spores. It is deciduous and care must be taken that neither root nor rhizome becomes dry during the resting season; both are succulent and are seriously damaged by loss of water. It is of little value as a pot plant and should be grown in a moist place in a warm fernery where it will not be disturbed during the resting season.

**H. zeyla'nica.** *rhiz.* thick, creeping. *sti.* often 1 ft. long. *Fronds* with palmate-pinnate barren segs., often in 3 main divisions, stalked and again forked or pinnate, the ultimate divisions linear-oblong, 3 to 4 in. long, nearly 1 in. wide. *Fertile spike* solitary, arising from base of barren seg., 3 to 4 in. long, ½ in. wide. Himalaya to Queensland. 1861. (H.G.F. 28.) SYN. *H. dulcis.*

*helo'des,* of bogs.

*helodox'a,* glory of the marsh.

**HELO'NIAS** (*helos,* swamp; from the natural habitat). FAM. *Liliaceae.* A genus of a single species with a short thick tuberous root-stock, stalked basal leaves, and a hollow, bracteate scape with a somewhat dense spike of small pink rather starry flowers with 6 persistent segments, and 6 stamens; capsule 3-lobed, dehiscent. Hardy. A plant for the bog-garden, easily propagated by division.

**H. bulla'ta.** *l.* many at base, thin, dark green, 6 to 15 in. long, ½ to 2 in. wide, with fine, parallel veins, short-stalked. *fl.* about 30, pink or purplish, ½ in. across, 6-lobed, anthers blue, in a close raceme about 3 in. long. April, May. *Scape* 12 to 24 in. long, stout. Eastern N. America. (B.M. 747; L.B.C. 961.) SYN. *H. latifolia.*

**HELONIOP'SIS** (*Helonias, opsis,* like). FAM. *Liliaceae.* A genus of 4 species of perennial herbs, natives of Japan and Formosa. Leaves all basal, stalked, oblong or lanceolate with a scarious sheath, arising from a short, thick, horizontal rhizome. Flowers solitary or few at top of scape, rather large, slightly nodding; perianth segments distinct or scarcely joined at base, oblong or narrow, nearly equal, spreading; stamens 6, purple-blue; style long, tipped red; stigma entire, purple (in Helonias style short, stigma 3-cleft); scape erect, simple. Any fairly moist good garden soil suits these hardy plants which may be increased by division in autumn.

**H. brevisca'pa.** *l.* spatulate, slender-pointed. *fl.* blush-white; segs. obovate, scape 6 to 8 in. long, bearing fl. in a tight head on very short pedicels; bracts short. May. Japan. (G.C. 37 (1905) 178; Gn. 68 (1905) 52.)

**H. japon'ica.** *l.* oblanceolate, 3 to 4 in. long, 1 in. broad, brownish towards tips. *fl.* rose, ½ in. long; segs. free, narrow; stamens very shortly exserted; raceme 2- to 10-fld., short, pedicels longer than fl. April. Japan. 1881. (B.M. 6986.)

**H. umbella'ta.** *l.* oblanceolate, mucronate. *fl.* 3 to 10 in umbel; segs. obtuse, scarcely 1/12 in. wide; scape 3 to 5 in. long. Formosa.

*helvet'icus -a -um,* of Switzerland.

*helvo'lus -a -um,* reddish-yellow.

**hel'vus -a -um,** honey coloured.

*Heloniopsis breviscapa* (p. 980)

*Heloniopsis japonica* (p. 980)

**HELWING'IA** (in honour of Georg A. Helwing, 1666–1748, German writer on the Botany of Prussia). FAM. *Cornaceae.* A genus of 3 species in E. Asia. They are glabrous shrubs of no particular beauty, but interesting from the position of the flowers, which, the pedicels being adnate to the midrib, appear to arise from the upper surfaces of the leaves. Hardy or nearly so. Needing only ordinary soil.

**H. chinen'sis.** Somewhat taller than *H. japonica,* with ovate-lanceolate l. about 4½ in. long, and fl. on longer pedicels. West China. 1910.

**H. japon'ica.** About 4 ft. h. *l.* alternate, ovate, slender-pointed, sometimes stipulate; stalked. *fl.* small, greenish, 3- to 5-parted, clustered on midrib of l., *fr.* a drupe. Japan. SYN. *H. rusciflora.* The young l. are used as a vegetable in Japan.

**H. rusciflo'ra.** A synonym of *H. japonica.*

**HELXI'NE** (possibly from *helko,* to tear, from the catching of the fruits in cloth). FAM. *Urticaceae.* A single species of herbaceous rapidly creeping habit, native of Corsica. Stems very slender; leaves small, bright glossy green, entire, roundish. Flowers very small and inconspicuous, the pistillate in axils of lower, the staminate of upper leaves. Grows very readily in cool, moist places as over shady rocks in the rock garden, and also as a pot plant in a moist atmosphere. Soon blackened by frost but usually some part of the plant survives even severe winters. Readily propagated by cuttings and apt to cover and swamp other plants, but useful as a carpet of green in suitable places.

**H. Soleirol'ii.** Stems creeping, slender, reddish. *l.* bright green, flat, nearly round. Sardinia, Corsica. (R.H. 1917, 235.)

*helxinoi'des,* Helxine-like.

**HEMEROCAL'LIS** (*hemera,* a day, *kallos,* beauty; the flowers last a day only.) Day Lily. FAM. *Liliaceae.* A genus of about a dozen species of herbaceous perennial plants mostly natives of temperate E. Asia. Related to Hosta and Phormium. Plants with sessile, linear, 2-ranked, almost grass-like leaves and large, more or less funnel-shaped yellow to reddish-orange flowers in, often close, corymbs at the top of usually tall smooth scapes. Perianth segments united at base into a narrow tube, free parts spreading, inner often wider than outer. The flowers are usually numerous and open successively so that though the individual flowers last 1 day, rarely 2, the plants have a long period of beauty. *H. citrina* opens in mid-afternoon and remains open at night. All are hardy and in some the foliage, being yellowish-green as it comes up in early spring, is very ornamental. They succeed in any ordinary soil and even in grass in moist soils and are thus useful both in the border and in the wild garden; as they take a year or two to become thoroughly established they should not be disturbed frequently. Many of the species are self-sterile and seedlings often vary from their parents. Some, like the common form of *H. fulva,* which has been propagated vegetatively for hundreds of years, all plants of which are therefore virtually parts of 1 self-sterile individual, do not set seed. Crossing readily occurs between several of the species and this, together with the variation already referred to within the species, has resulted in the production of many new forms extending the colour range of large-flowered robust plants considerably. A list of the best of these will be found in the Supplement. Propagation by division of the clumps is easy either in spring or autumn.

An excellent account of these fine plants will be found in *Daylilies,* by Dr. A. B. Stout (1934) with descriptions of all known forms.

KEY

| | |
|---|---|
| 1. *Scape branched near top except when fl. is solitary* | 2 |
| 1. *Scape not branched; fl. sessile or nearly so* | 12 |
| 2. *Scapes shorter than lvs. or scarcely longer; fl. few; roots fleshy* | 3 |
| 2. *Scapes longer than lvs., much branched* | 5 |
| 3. *Bracts inconspicuous* | 4 |
| 3. *Bracts more or less herbaceous* | H. Forrestii |
| 4. *Lvs. flat; fl. 1 to 3* | H. nana |
| 4. *Lvs. folded; fl. 1 to 5* | H. plicata |
| 5. *Flowering from mid-May* | 6 |
| 5. *Flowering from mid-June* | 7 |
| 6. *Roots fleshy and thickened; rhizomes spreading* | H. flava |
| 6. *Roots slender and fibrous; plants compact* | H. minor |
| 7. *Fl. pale yellow* | 8 |
| 7. *Fl. orange, brownish, or reddish* | 9 |
| 8. *Roots scarcely thickened* | H. Thunbergii |
| 8. *Roots thickened and tapering* | H. citrina |
| 9. *Fl. orange* | 10 |
| 9. *Fl. brownish or reddish* | 11 |
| 10. *Scapes with thick short branches near top; roots scarcely thickened* | H. exaltata |

10. *Scapes with many slender branches; fl. small; roots fleshy* H. multiflora
11. *Fl. brownish or rosy-red* H. fulva
11. *Fl. orange or orange-yellow* H. aurantiaca
12. *Fl. light orange; main roots thickened; scape shorter than lvs.* H. Dumortieri
12. *Fl. orange; main roots slender; scape slightly longer than lvs.* H. Middendorffii

**H. auranti'aca.** *l.* green, about 28 in. long, 1 in. wide. Plant moderately vigorous. *fl.* 8 to 15, orange, often with a purplish flush about the middle of the segs., wide funnel-shaped, somewhat starry, about 4 in. across, closely clustered at top of the 3-ft. scape. June, July. Japan? var. **ma'jor** is a more vigorous plant with up to 24 fl. about 4½ in. across, bright orange without the purplish flush. (Gn. 48 (1895), 400.)

**H. Baron'i.** A garden name for *H. citrina* or a hybrid near thereto.

**H. citri'na.** *l.* dark green, about 30 in. long. Plant vigorous and compact. *fl.* 30 to 60, pale lemon or sulphur, tinged brown at back, with a long tube, about 5 in. wide at mouth; segs. narrow, on short branches at top of 3½-ft. stem; scented. July, August. (Add. 482.) The name Baroni often attached to this plant is that of the author of the name *H. citrina*, but it is also used for one of the many hybrids between *H. citrina* and *H. Thunbergii*, much like *H. citrina* but with wider segs.

**H. dis'ticha fl. pl.** A double form of *H. fulva*.

**H. Dumortier'i.** *l.* about 18 in. long, 1 in. wide. Plant vigorous, forming a dense clump. *fl.* soft apricot-orange, tinged brown outside, flattish funnel-shaped, about 3½ in. wide, scarcely stalked, in clusters of 2 to 8 at top of the stem which is rather shorter than l. May, June. Japan. 1832. (Add. 462; Gn. 31 (1887) 280.) SYN. *H. rutilans, H. Sieboldii.*

**H. exalta'ta.** *l.* 3 ft. long, up to 2 in. wide or more, recurving. Plant compact, vigorous. *fl.* about 12, light orange, wide funnel-shaped, about 4 in. across at mouth; segs. spatulate, clustered on short branches near top of 4 or 5 ft. scape; not scented. June, July. Japan. 1934. (Add. 595.)

**H. fla'va.** *l.* dark green, about 24 in. long, arching. Plant very vigorous, spreading underground. *fl.* 8 to 12, clear lemon-yellow, short funnel-shaped, 3½ in. wide at mouth, fragrant, on rather closely branched scapes about 3½ ft. h. May to July. China? 1570. (B.M. 19; Add. 457.) Somewhat variable. var. **ma'jor** has darker foliage and pet. more reflexed at tips, wavy. **A**

**H. Forrest'ii.** *l.* narrow, about ½ in. wide, 18 in. long, arching at ends. *fl.* about 8, cadmium-yellow, glistening within; tube short; segs. narrow, spreading, on slender scapes, usually branched and shorter than l. June, July. China. 1910. (Add. 481.)

**H. ful'va.** *l.* green, erect, 3 ft. long. Plant vigorous forming a clump, with spreading rhizomes. *fl.* 10 to 14, orange-brick-red with a median apricot line on each petal, wide funnel-shaped, about 4½ in. across, pet. broad, wavy, tips reflexed, on branched scapes about 4 ft. h. June to August. Origin? 1576. (B.M. 64; S.B.F.G. 28 as *H. disticha*.) The typical form does not seed and has long been propagated solely by division; the varietal name **'Europa'** has been proposed for it. Several variants are now known including the double-fld. **flore ple'no** with fl. 5 or 6 in. across. Japan. 1860. SYN. *H. disticha fl. pl.*; and the less double **Kwanso fl. pl.** which is both variegated and double-fld. Japan. 1864. A form is also grown under this name with similar fl. but with green l. var. **Cypria'na** has bright glossy green foliage, a greater number of fl. than in type, each about 4½ in. across, brownish outside. July to September. China. 1906; **macula'ta** has slightly paler fl. with a darker median band. China. 1897. (Add. 460.)

**H. gramin'ea.** A synonym of *H. minor*.

**H. Kwan'so.** *See* **H. fulva.**

**H. × luteo'la.** A hybrid between *H. aurantiaca major* and *H. Thunbergii* of which there are several forms with apricot-yellow or cadmium-yellow fl. and dense clumps of dark green drooping foliage.

**H. Middendorf'fii.** Of the habit of *H. Dumortieri* but distinct by the taller scapes just overtopping the foliage, the conspicuous bracts in the almost capitate infl. with almost cup-shaped bright orange fl. with spatulate pet., and the absence of fleshy roots. E. Siberia, Japan. 1866. var. **ma'jor** is rather more vigorous and has more numerous fl.

**H. mi'nor.** *l.* grass-like, medium green, deciduous. Plant forming a dense clump, flowering sparsely. *fl.* 2 to 5, lemon-yellow, flushed brown outside, starry, short funnel-shaped, about 2¾ in. across at mouth, on shortly branched scapes about 10 in. h. or more. May, June. E. Asia. 1759. (Add. 458; B.M. 873 as *H. graminea*.) SYN. *H. gracilis, H. graminifolia.*

**H.×Muel'leri** (*H. citrina* × *H. Thunbergii*). *fl.* starry, fragrant, primrose, about 4 in. across, on branched 4-ft. scapes. July, August.

**H. multiflo'ra.** *l.* dark green, about 30 in. long, ¾ in. wide, recurved. Plant compact. *fl.* very numerous (75 to 100), glistening chrome yellow within, tinged brownish-red without, about 3 in. wide, with narrow segs. on a slender branched scape, 4 ft. h. August, September. Honan, China. 1934. (Add. 464.)

**H. na'na.** *l.* linear, flattish, up to about 15 in. long. Plant dwarf, forming a close clump. *fl.* 1 to 3, clear orange within, reddish-brown without, funnel-shaped, with narrow segs., about 3 in. across, fragrant, on slender scape 10 to 20 in. long. June. Yunnan, China. 1914. (J.R.H.S. 45 (1916), 40; B.M. 8968.)

**H.×ochroleu'ca** (*H. citrina* × *H. Thunbergii*). *fl.* lemon-yellow, fragrant, starry, about 3½ in. across on branched scapes, 3½ ft. h. July, August. See also **H. × Muelleri.**

**H. plica'ta.** Resembling *H. Forrestii* in habit but with narrower l., about ¼ in. wide, folded (not flat), bracts very small, perianth segs. rather wider. W. China.

**H. ru'tilans.** A synonym of *H. Dumortieri*.

**H. Siebold'ii.** A synonym of *H. Dumortieri*.

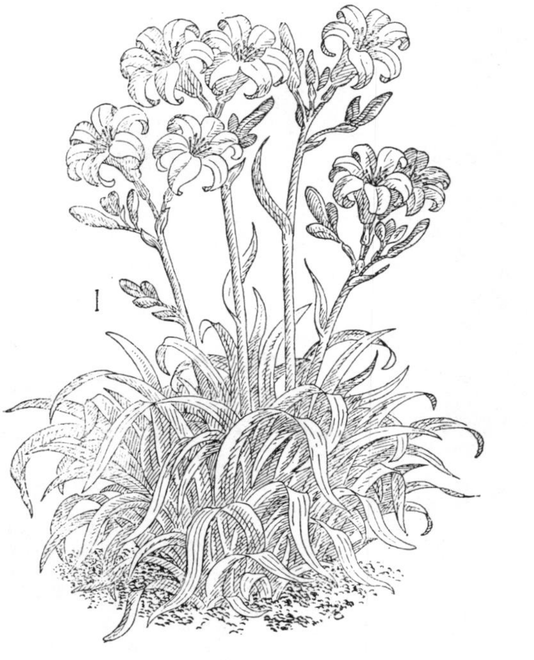

*Hemerocallis Thunbergii*

**H. Thunberg'ii.** *l.* dark green, narrow, about 30 in. long. Plant vigorous, compact. *fl.* 12 to 24, sulphur-apricot, deeper in throat, short funnel-shaped, fragrant, on scapes about 3½ ft. h., branched near top. July, August. Japan. 1890.

***hemi-*,** in compound words, signifying half, or partly.

**HEMIAN'DRA** (*hemi*, half, *andros*, a male; in allusion to the dimidiate anthers). FAM. *Labiatae*. Three species of shrubs or undershrubs, natives of W. Australia. Cool greenhouse plants thriving in a compost of loam, peat, leaf-soil, and sand, with plenty of light and air. Easily propagated by cuttings of half-ripened shoots.

**H. pung'ens.** Spreading, sometimes creeping, evergreen shrub, 1 to 2 ft., varying from glabrous to hairy and downy. *l.* opposite, stalkless, linear or linear-lanceolate, ½ to 1 in. long, ⅛ to ¼ in. wide, apex pungent. *fl.* solitary, axillary; upper lip of cal. prickly; cor. pink, pinkish-lilac, sometimes white, variable in size but ordinarily about ⅝ in. long, funnel-shaped at the base; limb ¾ in. wide, 2-lipped, lower lip 2- or 3-lobed, dotted with crimson; upper lip 4-lobed. Summer. W. Australia. (F.d.S. 985.)

W. J. B.

**HEMICHAE'NA** (*hemi*, half, *chaino*, to gape; in allusion to the 2-lipped corolla.) FAM. *Scrophulariaceae*. Monotypic genus, represented by a shrub in Cent. America. Leaves opposite; stamens 4, in pairs of unequal length; fruit an ovoid capsule. A compost of open loam suits it, and a cool greenhouse. It might prove hardy in the south-west.

**H. frutico'sa.** Evergreen shrub, 3 to 5 ft., shoots glandular-downy. *l.* 4 to 8 in. long, 2 to 2½ in. wide, oblong-lanceolate, pointed, toothed, base partly stem-clasping. *fl.* usually in clusters of 3, axillary; stalk ¾ to 1 in. long; cal. obliquely tubular, ½ in. long; cor. golden-yellow, base tubular, 1¼ in. long, limb 5-lobed, 1¼ in. wide, speckled with red in the throat. July. Guatemala (at 10,000 ft.), Costa Rica. 1871. (B.M. 6164.)

W. J. B.

**HEMIGE′NIA** (*hemi*, half, *genea*, to beget; in allusion to the single lobe of the anthers). Fam. *Labiatae.* A genus of 23 species of shrubs and undershrubs, all natives of Australia. Leaves opposite; calyx with 2 bracts beneath; stamens in 2 pairs. Light loamy soil suits *H. purpurea* which needs the protection of a cool greenhouse. It can be increased by cuttings.

**H. purpu′rea.** Heath-like, evergreen shrub or undershrub, shoots slender. *l.* in whorls of 3 or 4, narrowly linear, up to ½ in. long, grooved on upper side, glabrous. *fl.* solitary in upper l.-axils, purple; cal. 5-toothed; cor. ⅓ in. long, 2-lipped, downy outside; lower lip 3-lobed, twice as long as the 2-lobed upper lip. *fr.* 4 nuts protected by the persistent cal. New S. Wales. Flowers more or less all the year.

W. J. B.

**HEMIGRAM′MA** (*hemi*, half, *gramma*, writing; from the arrangement of the sori). Fam. *Polypodiaceae.* Six species of ferns sometimes included under Acrostichum. For cultivation *see* **Acrostichum.**

**H. decur′rens.** *sti.* firm, glossy, 1 to 1½ in. long, chestnut-brown, scaly at base. *Barren fronds* usually entire, but sometimes with a spatulate terminal pinna 1 ft. long and 3 in. broad and one or two similar but smaller ones on each side, usually connected at the base, coriaceous. *Fertile fronds* similar, but with much smaller pinnae. Hong Kong, Formosa. Syn. *Acrostichum Harlandii.* A handsome species.

**H. taccifo′lia.*** *cau.* woody, densely scaly. *sti.* of barren fronds 1 to 4 in. long, scaly. *Barren fronds* from 1 to 2 ft. long, 3 to 12 in. broad, simple, oblong-lanceolate, entire, copiously pinnate, with oblong-lanceolate pinnae, 1 to 6 in. long, ½ to 1½ in. broad, upper narrowly decurrent, lower forked at base on under side. *Fertile fronds* simple, 6 to 12 in. long, ⅛ in. broad, or pinnate, with forked linear pinnae. The 3-lobed form of this species is sometimes known as *Acrostichum trilobum.* Philippines. Stove. (H.I.P. 907.) Syn. *Gymnopteris taccaefolia.*

**HEMIGRAPH′IS** (*hemi*, half, *graphos*, written). Fam. *Acanthaceae.* A genus of about 20 dwarf, annual or perennial herbs, natives of SE. and E. Asia. Leaves opposite, sometimes toothed. Flowers rather small, solitary or rarely twin in spikes; calyx with 5 segments often more or less connate below middle; corolla tube slender, somewhat shortly widened above, limb of 5 spreading lobes; stamens 4, didynamous included. Foliage plants. For cultivation *see* **Ruellia**, to which this is related.

**H. angustifo′lia.** Erect herb. *l.* lanceolate, 5 in. long, 1 in. wide, irregularly and deeply toothed or lobed, slender-pointed. *fl.-spikes* terminal, cone-like, with obtuse bracts. Malaya. Stove.

**H. colora′ta.** Small, spreading, hairy perennial. *l.* cordate-ovate, bullate, crenate, silvery-grey above, purplish beneath, stalk 1½ in. long. *fl.* small, white, ½ in. long, in terminal spikes. India. 1885. Stove.

**H. latebro′sa.** Spreading, hairy annual, up to 2 ft. h. *l.* ovate, coarsely serrate, stalk long. *fl.* bright blue; cor. tube ¾ in. long. India. 1834. (B.M. 3389 as *Ruellia elegans.*) Syn. *Ruellia latebrosa.* Stove.

**H. repan′da.** Prostrate herb. *l.* narrow-linear, lobed. *fl.* in cone-like spikes; cor. hairy within. Malaya. For hanging baskets. Stove.

**H. stenophyl′la.** *l.* linear, 8 to 10 in. long, ½ in. wide, scalloped. *Spikes* long; cor. narrow-funnel-shaped. E. Indies. For hanging baskets. Stove.

**HEMIME′RIS interme′dia.** A synonym of *Alonsoa incisifolia.*

*hemionitid′eus -a -um,* supposed to be like a mule, barren.

**HEMIONI′TIS** (old Greek name used by Dioscorides, from *hemionos*, a mule; supposed to be barren). Fam. *Polypodiaceae.* A genus comprising 8 species of tropical ferns, found in both hemispheres. Sori along the veins. Much reticulated. The species are admirably suited for growing in Wardian cases. They are easily grown plants of dwarf habit. When grown in pots, all these singular Ferns require is a mixture of 2 parts of fibrous, soft peat, and 1 part of sand, or where the peat obtainable is of a somewhat close nature the mixture is benefited by the addition of 1 part of chopped Sphagnum. It is

essential, on account of the few roots which they produce, that these plants should be kept in small pots, and that the drainage should be perfect. All are liable to Aphis attacks, which are easily checked by slight fumigations; occasionally, also, Thrips may make their appearance on the foliage, and may be checked by a dip in a weak solution of lemon oil. *H. arifolia* is one of the most distinct species.

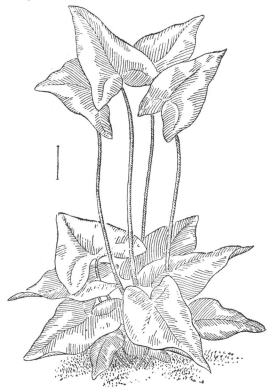

*Hemionitis arifolia* (p. 984)

*Hemionitis palmata* (p. 984)

Propagation is readily effected by spores, which germinate freely, and by means of the young plants that most kinds produce at the base and at the notches of the segments of the fronds, which, for propagation, should be firmly laid on the surface of the soil recommended above.

**H. arifo'lia.** *cau.* erect. *sti.*, of barren fronds, 2 to 4 in. long; of fertile, about 1 ft. long, densely fibrillose at base. *Fronds* 6 to 9 in. long, 1 to 2½ in. broad, ovate or oblong-lanceolate, acuminate, subentire, base narrowed, cordate. *Sori* confined to veins. Trop. Asia. (L.F. 7, 38; B.C.F. 2, 283.)

**H. corda'ta.** A synonym of *H. arifolia.*

**H. palma'ta.** *cau.* erect. *sti.*, of barren fronds, 4 in.; of fertile, 6 to 12 in. long, hairy. *Fronds* 2 to 6 in. each way, palmate, with 5 nearly equal lanceolate divisions; both surfaces villous. W. Indies. 1793. (H.E.F. 53; L.F. 7, 37.)

**H. pinna'ta.** A synonym of *H. Smithii.*

**H. Smith'ii.** *sti.* 6 to 9 in. long, glossy, dark chestnut-brown, clothed with soft yellowish hairs. *Fronds* 5 to 6 in. long, 3 to 4 in. broad, apex deeply pinnatifid, below this 2 to 3 pairs of distinct pinnae, upper oblong-lanceolate, lowest larger and forked at base, all repand. Jamaica, Costa Rica. (H.I.P. 1687.)

**HEMIORCH'IS** (*hemi*, half, *Orchis*; the plant calls to mind an Orchis). FAM. *Zingiberaceae.* A genus of 3 perennial herbs with the habit of Kaempferia, natives of N. India and Burma. Leaves oblong, sheathing. Flowering stem dwarf, slender, sheathed at base. The short filament with a declined anther distinguishes it from Globba and Mantisia, to which it is nearly related. Stove treatment is necessary. For cultivation *see* **Alpinia.**

**H. burman'ica** of Bot. Mag., *see* **H. rhodorrhachis.**

**H. rhodorrhach'is.** Rather weakly. Leafy stems with 5 or 6 sheaths at base. *l.* oblong to oblong-lanceolate, slender-pointed, about 8 in. long, green above, pale beneath. Flowering stems about 6 in. long, purplish-red above, with 5 sheaths; cor. red, lip ovate-orbicular, whitish-yellow with reddish dots; the spike produced before the l. Khasia Hills. 1889. (B.M. 7120, as *H. burmanica.*)

**HEMIPHRAG'MA** (*hemi*, half, *phragma*, partition; referring to the division of the capsule). FAM. *Scrophulariaceae.* A genus of a single species of herb native of the Himalaya. Rather tender but given winter protection it grows well on the rock-garden in well-drained loam, forming a spreading mat.

**H. heterophyl'lum.** Prostrate perennial, spreading widely when suited. *l.* of branches rounded-cordate, small, with dense clusters of awl-shaped l. in their axils. *fl.* small, pink, usually sessile and solitary; cor. 5-lobed, bell-shaped. Himalaya. Tender.

**HEMIPI'LIA** (*hemi*, half, *pilion*, cap; the pollinia being partly covered). FAM. *Orchidaceae.* A genus of about 10 species allied to Cynorchis and Habenaria, natives of Burma, N. India, Yunnan, &c. Flowers few in a raceme, sepals of nearly equal length, dorsal concave, lateral spreading, oblique; petals smaller, entire; lip continuous with column, spreading, rather broad, base lengthened into a spur; column very short. Stems with one basal leaf. Treatment as for the more tender Habenarias.

**H. amethysti'na.** *fl.* numerous, ½ in. wide, white and purple; sep. and pet. small, lower sep. with a middle greenish stripe; lip marked rose-purple; scape erect, 8 in. long. *l.* ovate, cordate, 4 in. long, yellowish-green marbled brown. Tuber small, fleshy. Burma. 1897. (B.M. 7521.)

**H. calophyl'la.** *fl.* 6 to 8; sep. and pet. white and green, rarely purple; dorsal sep. hooded; pet. smaller than sep.; lip dark wine-purple, ½ in. wide; scape 5 to 7 in. h., green, spotted reddish-brown. July. *l.* 2 to 3 in. long, 1¼ to 1½ in. wide, sessile on tuber, the narrowed base buried in ground, dark green mottled brown. Moulmein. 1886. (B.M. 6920.)

E. C.

**HEMIP'TELEA** (*hemi*, half; *ptelea* wing; in allusion to the winged fruit). FAM. *Ulmaceae.* Monotypic genus closely akin to Zelkova, q.v. for cultivation, but armed with stout spines sometimes branched and up to 4 or 5 in. long.

**H. Da'vidi.** Small shrubby deciduous tree, shoots hairy. *l.* alternate, oval, 1 to 2½ in. long, with 7 to 15 teeth on each side and with pale hairs on upper surface springing from a circular depression, slightly hairy beneath. *fl.* unisexual and bisexual, small, green, of no beauty. *fr.* an obliquely conical nut ¼ in. long, slightly winged. China, Korea. 1908.

W. J. B.

**HEMIP'TERA.** *See* **Insects.**

*hemisphae'ricus -a -um,* half ball-shaped.

**HEMITE'LIA** (*hemi*, half, *teleos*, perfect; referring to the indusium). FAM. *Cyatheaceae.* A genus of tree ferns related to Alsophila and Cyathea with the globose sori on the backs of the fronds on a vein, the indusium being scale-like on the lower side of the sorus, often indistinct and soon falling. The fronds are large, shining, pinnate or much cut. The genus contains about 100 very beautiful species in tropical and sub-tropical regions of the world. With few exceptions these ferns require stove temperatures. Most of them are strong growers with trunks up to 15 ft. long, and they need large structures in which to develop their imposing broad and shining foliage. They are not difficult to grow in pots or planted out in a mixture of about equal parts of peat, loam, and sand. During the growing season besides heat they need much moisture both at the root and on their trunks. They

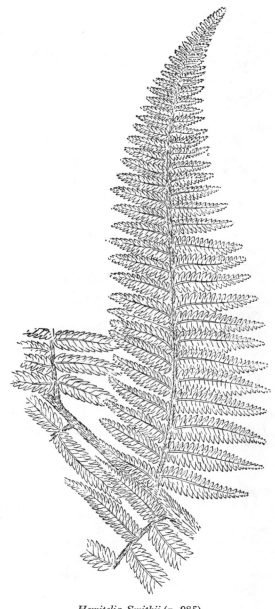

*Hemitelia Smithii* (p. 985)

are propagated by spores and sometimes by offsets which are at times produced on the trunks of some species.

**H. capen'sis.** *cau.* 12 to 14 ft. h., scaly at base, often bearing multifid pinnae. *Fronds* ample, sub-membranaceous, 2- or 3-pinnate; primary pinnae petiolate, ovate-oblong; pinnules sub-sessile, 2 to 3 in. long, ½ in. wide, oblong-acuminate, deeply pinnatifid or again pinnate; lobes linear-oblong, acute, strongly serrated. *Sori* frequently solitary at base of lobe or pinnule, rarely 3 or 4; large, prominent. S. Africa, Brazil, Java. Greenhouse. (B.C.F. 2, 289.)

**H. grandifo'lia.*** *sti.* aculeate. *Fronds* ample, pinnate; pinnae sessile, 1 to 1½ ft. long, elongate-oblong, acuminate, 1 to 2 in. broad; lobes broad-oblong, obtuse, serrate at apex. *Sori* on free veins, in a continuous line, intermediate between costule and margin. W. Indies, &c. 1852. Stove. (L.F. 8, 59; H.S. 1, 14.)

**H. guianen'sis.** A synonym of *H. multiflora.*

**H. hor'rida.** *sti.* strongly aculeate. *Fronds* 7 to 10 ft. long, pinnate; pinnae sessile, 1 to 2 ft. long, broad, oblong-lanceolate, deeply pinnatifid; lobes 3 in. long, oblong-lanceolate, acuminate. *sori* on free veinlets, forming a continuous line just within margin. W. Indies, &c. 1843. Stove. (L.F. 8, 60; H.S. 1, 15.)

**H. Karstenia'na.** *sti.* muricate and scaly at base. *Fronds* ample, pinnate; pinnae sessile, 6 to 12 in. long, 2 in. broad. *Sori* in 2 oblique lines, meeting towards rachis. Caracas. Stove.

**H. Lin'deni.** *Fronds* pinnate; pinnae short-stalked, thin, 6 to 12 in. long, 1 to 1¼ in. broad, acute, margins cleft into regular, short lobes having their apex directed upwards. *Sori* in 2 or 3 irregular series on margins of pinnae. Caracas. 1894. (I.H. 1895, 46.)

**H. multiflo'ra.** *sti.* muricate, scaly. *Fronds* ample, 3-pinnatifid; pinnae oblong-lanceolate, 1 to 1½ ft. long; pinnules 3 to 4 in. long, ligulate, ¾ in. broad, cut down to a narrow wing. *Sori* small, medial. S. America. 1824. Stove. var. **Para'dae** is larger and more robust than the type, with glabrous 2-pinnate fronds without a wing, rachis marked with white spots, sori marginal, abundant. Colombia. 1877. (I.H. 1877, 280 as *H. guianensis Paradae.*)

**H. seto'sa.** *sti.* short, grey, muricate; basal scales dark brown; rachises grey-straw, naked, smooth. *Fronds* ample, 3-pinnate; pinnae oblong-lanceolate, 1 to 1½ ft. long, lower smaller, lowest dimorphous, with pinnate subulate segs.; pinnules ligulate, 3 to 4 in. long, ¾ in. broad, cut down to rachis below; segs. ⅛ in. broad, bluntish, falcate, barren broad, fertile narrower; green, glabrous. *Sori* costular; indusium small, depressed, glabrous. Brazil. Stove.

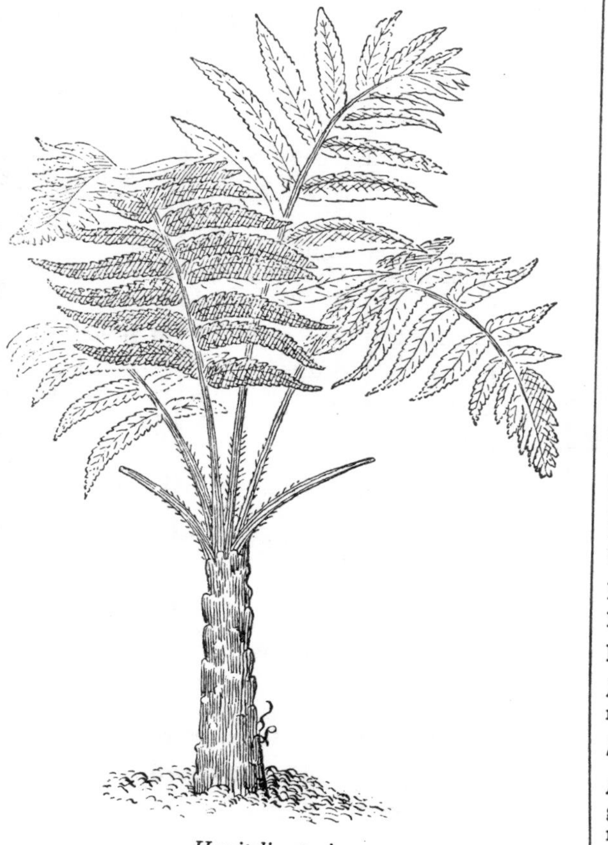

*Hemitelia speciosa*

**H. Smith'ii.*** *sti.* below densely crinite, with rigid, elongate, serrulate scales; rachis and costa below sparsely pilose, with lax, rufous, deciduous scales above, strigose-villose *Fronds* 2-pinnate; primary pinnae linear-elongate, acute, sub-falcate, serrate or crenate, glabrous, the costules beneath paleaceous or pilose or glabrous. *Sori* on fork of veins; indusium hemispherical. New Zealand. Tree-like, unarmed. Greenhouse. (B.C.F. 2, 295.) SYN. *Cyathea Smithii.*

**H. specio'sa.*** *cau.* 20 to 24 ft. h. *sti.* tuberculate-submuricate. *Fronds* ample, pinnate, very long, pinnatifid at end; pinnae firm, satiny, 8 to 12 in. long, 1 to 1½ in. broad, elongate-ensiform, acuminate. *Sori* in a sinuous continued chain or line just within margin. Trop. America. Stove. (H.S. 1, 13; B.C.F. 2, 297.)

**H. Walk'erae.*** *Fronds* ample, 2- or 3-pinnate; pinnae 1½ ft. long; pinnules 3 to 4 in. long, cleft nearly or quite to midrib; lobes oblong, very blunt, entire or slightly notched. *Sori* in lowest fork of veins close to midrib; indusium large, roundish. Ceylon (at 6,000 ft. elevation). (H.I.P. 647.)

***hemitricho'tus -a -um,*** half-hairy.

**HEMIZO'NIA** (*hemi*, half, *zonia*, ring; the bracts half-enclose the fruits). FAM. *Compositae.* A genus of Californian annual or perennial herbs, glandular and heavily scented. Leaves alternate, narrow, lowest sometimes opposite. Flowers yellow or white in many heads; disk florets surrounded by a circle of chaffy often somewhat united bracts or chaffy throughout. Ray achenes fertile without pappus, disk achenes sterile or fertile with or without pappus. Hardy border plants.

**H. corymbo'sa.** Tarweed. 12 to 18 in. h., glandular-hairy, sweet-scented. *l.* oblong or linear, ¾ to 3½ in. long, pinnate; lobes linear, sometimes toothed; upper l. linear, entire, up to ½ in. long. *fl.-heads* ½ to ⅝ in. across; rays bright yellow, ⅛ to ⅓ in. long, oblong-wedge-shaped. California.

**HEMLOCK.** *See* **Conium maculatum.**

**HEMLOCK SPRUCE.** *See* **Tsuga canadensis.**

**HEMP.** *See* **Cannabis sativa.**

**HEMP AGRIMONY.** *See* **Eupatorium cannabinum.**

**HEMP, BOMBAY.** *See* **Crotalaria.**

**HEMP, BOW-STRING.** *See* **Sansevieria zeylanica.**

**HEMP, MADRAS.** *See* **Crotalaria juncea.**

**HEMP, MANILA.** *See* **Musa.**

**HEMP, MAURITIUS.** *See* **Furcraea foetida.**

**HEMP-NETTLE.** *See* **Galeopsis.** **A**

**HEMP, SISAL.** *See* **Agave.**

**HEMP, SUNN.** *See* **Crotalaria juncea.**

***Hempel'ii,*** in honour of G. Hempel, 1847–1904, who collected Cacti in Mexico and S. America.

***Hemsleya'nus -a -um,*** in honour of W. Botting Hemsley, 1843–1924, botanist at Kew.

**HEN-AND-CHICKENS.** A form of the common Daisy with branches from the head, bearing secondary heads. A similar form of the Pot Marigold is not uncommon.

**HEN-AND-CHICKENS HOUSELEEK.** *See* **Sempervivum sobiliferum.**

**HENBANE.** *See* **Hyocyamus niger.**

***Henchmann'ii,*** in honour of Mr. Henchman, nurseryman of Clapton, Middlesex.

***hendecaphyl'lus -a -um,*** eleven-leaved.

***Henderson'ii,*** in honour of (1) A. Henderson, d. 1879, gardener at R.H.S. Gardens, Chiswick, later nurseryman; (2) Louis Fourniquet Henderson, 1853–?, who collected with Mr. Howell in Oregon.

**HENNA PLANT.** *See* **Lawsonia inermis.**

*Henningsia'nus -a -um,* in honour of P. Hennings, 1841–1908, Professor, Botanic Gardens, Berlin.

**HENRIETTEL'LA** (diminutive of Henriettea). FAM. *Melastomataceae.* A genus of about 15 species of shrubs related to Ossaea. Flowers solitary or clustered, 4- or 5-meris; petals coherent in a cone; limb of calyx hairy, lobes small; anthers short, obtuse. Treatment as for Melastoma.

**H. fascicula'ris.** Shrub of 6 to 10 ft. *l.* elliptical, 4 to 6 in. long, narrowed to base, pointed, 3-nerved, ciliate, minutely hairy on both sides. *fl.* white, in many-fld. clusters; pet. tapered. Jamaica. SYN. *Ossaea fascicularis.*

*Hen'ryi, Henrya'nus -a -um,* in honour of Dr. Augustine Henry, 1857–1930, who collected many plants in inland China; author with Elwes of *Forest Trees of Great Britain.*

*Henschel'ii,* in honour of A. W. E. T. Henschel, 1790–1856, botanist of Breslau.

**HEP** or **HIP.** The fruit of the Dog Rose.

**HEPAT'ICA** (*hepar,* the liver, from the supposed curative effect of the plant on that organ). FAM. *Ranunculaceae.* A genus of 3 species closely related to Anemone, with which it is often combined, and distinguished by the 3 simple sessile leaves of the involucre growing close beneath the calyx; distributed through the N. Temperate Zone and growing in half-shady woods. The plants are of tufted growth, flowering before the leaves appear in spring but remaining green through winter. The leaves are 3- to 5-lobed, sometimes toothed; the scapes 1-flowered; and the fruits hairy.

All the species are suited for half-shady places and do well on limey woodland soils. They are suitable for the rock-garden and can be grown in pots, a rich sandy loam with leaf soil suiting them. They are readily increased by division of the clumps and can be raised from seed sown in very shallow drills in moist soil in a shady situation in the open, transplanting in autumn or spring when large enough.

**H. acutilo'ba.*** Similar to *H. triloba* in fl. and habit, 4 to 9 in. h., but with lobes of l. and involucre more or less acute. March, April. Quebec to Missouri. SYN. *Anemone acutiloba.*

**H. angulo'sa.** A synonym of *H. transsilvanica.*

**H. trilo'ba.*** *l.* cordate, 3-lobed, rarely toothed, obtuse, 4 to 6 in. h. *fl.* blue, white, or pink, ⅓ to ¾ in. broad, sep. usually 8 to 10, oval or oblong, obtuse, longer than stamens. February, March. Scandinavia, France, Pyrenees, Russia, Siberia, China, Japan, N. America. The common Hepatica has long been grown in England and there are many varieties, including **al'ba,** white, **caeru'lea,** blue; **marmora'ta,** with white spots on l.-lobes, blue, **ru'bra,** reddish-pink, with double forms of each, the white being especially uncommon, and **Barlow'i** with rounded sky-blue fl. (B.M. 10 as *Anemone Hepatica.*)

**H. transsilvan'ica.*** *l.* 3-lobed, lobes toothed and sometimes themselves lobed, glabrous beneath when old, and somewhat shining. 8 to 12 in. h. *fl.* light blue or whitish, 2 in. broad, sep. often 3-toothed; February, March. Roumania. Larger in all parts than *H. triloba.* A pinkish variety is known. (B.M. 5518 as *Anemone angulosa.*)

**HEPIA'LIS.** *See* **Swift Moth.**

*hepta-,* in compound words, signifying seven.

**HEPTAPLEU'RUM.** *See* **Schefflera.**

**HERAC'LEUM** (*Heracleon,* ancient Greek name of the plant, from Hercules). FAM. *Umbelliferae.* A genus of about 70 species of large, sometimes gigantic, biennial or perennial herbs, natives of the N. Temperate regions and tropical mountains. Leaves cut into large segments. Flowers white in compound umbels, the outer flowers of the umbels larger than others, petals often notched. Fruits much dorsally compressed; carpels flat, with flat membranous wings. The Heracleums are sometimes grown in shrubberies or the rougher parts of the pleasure grounds or on the borders of ponds, &c., for their impressive appearance, but they are too coarse for the herbaceous border. Any ordinary soil suits them but they attain their largest size in deep woodland or somewhat moist soil. They are hardy and easily reproduced by seed or by division. *H. Sphondylium,* the Cow-Parsnip or Hogweed, is a common weed of hedgerows and open woodlands. Several species have been introduced; the following are perhaps the most striking.

**H. em'inens.** A synonym of *H. platytaenium.*

**H. flaves'cens.** Perennial, 5 to 6 ft. h. *l.* more numerous and more divided than in *H. persicum. fl.* yellowish. Austria. 1889.

**H. gigan'teum.** A synonym of *H. villosum.*

**H. lana'tum.** Perennial, 4 to 8 ft. h. Stem grooved, hairy. *l.* 3-sect, very large, smooth above, coarsely hairy beneath; largest segs. 4 to 10 in. across, unequally lobed, lobes slender-pointed. *fl.* white, umbels 6 to 10 in. across. *fr.* nearly ½ in. long. N. America, W. Asia. var. **vesti'tum,** densely woolly in upper part. SYN *H. maximum.*

**H. Lehmannia'num.** Stout biennial; 3 to 7 ft. h. *l.* glabrous above, hairy beneath; lower l. pinnatisect; segs., in 2 or 3 pairs, lobes shortly ovate, acute, coarsely toothed. *fl.* many, dull pink; umbels large. Turkestan.

**H. Mantegazzia'num.*** Cartwheel Flower. Gigantic perennial up to 12 ft. h. Stem coppery-red. *l.* 3 ft. long, forming a tuft 12 ft. across, deeply cut, lobes oblong, notched. *fl.* white, very numerous (up to about 10,000), in umbels 4 to 4½ ft. across. Caucasus. 1893.

**H. per'sicum.** Biennial up to 12 ft. h. *l.* pinnate or 2-pinnate, large, glabrous above, shortly hairy beneath; lobes in 3 or 4 pairs, lower stalked, all cut into lanceolate, long-pointed segs. *fl.* white in large, hairy umbels. Persia, &c. 1888.

**H. platytae'nium.** Biennial of 4 to 5 ft. *l.* often 2 ft. long, glabrous or nearly so above, cobwebby beneath; lower 3-sect, segs. stalked, heart-shaped, broadly palmately lobed, lobes blunt; upper 3-partite. *fl.* white, in umbels up to 1 ft. across, many-fld., softly hairy. W. Asia. 1871. (G.C. 1871, 875 as *H. eminens.*)

**H. pubes'cens.** Related to *H. persicum.* Biennial. *l.* pinnatisect, glabrous above, hairy beneath; segs. in 2 or 3 pairs, lobed; lobes elliptic, shortly pointed, lower stalked. *fl.* in many-rayed umbels, white, pedicels, &c. bristly hairy. Asia Minor. var. **Wilhelms'ii** has spine-tipped fr.

**H. pyrena'icum.** 2 to 3 ft. Stem angled and grooved, hollow, branched above. *l.* roundish heart-shaped in outline, palmatifid; lobes toothed, more or less downy and green above, hairy beneath. *fl.* white, outer radiate; umbels 20- to 30-rayed, rays long. Pyrenees. Wild garden.

**H. sibi'ricum.** 5 to 6 ft. h. *l.* pinnate, roughly hairy; lflets. ovate or oblong. *fl.* yellowish; umbels large. Summer. Europe, Asia. 1789.

**H. villo'sum.** Perennial up to 12 ft. h. *l.* sinuately pinnatifid, long-pointed, sharply toothed, woolly beneath. *fl.* white or whitish in many-rayed umbels. *fr.* ciliate, woolly on back. Caucasus. SYN. *H. giganteum.*

**HERB,** a plant of which the stem dies to the ground at the end of the season. Herbs may be annual, biennial, or perennial. **A**

**HERB CHRISTOPHER.** *See* **Actaea spicata.**

**HERB GARDEN.** A garden devoted to medicinal, pot- or sweet-herbs. It may be of a purely practical nature forming an adjunct to the kitchen garden, or it may take the form of a separate ornamental garden often of formal design and based on that of early Knot Gardens or Parterres in which herbs were grown in Tudor and Elizabethan times. These were usually edged with shrubby or half-shrubby plants of a dwarf nature such as Box, Lavender, Lavender-Cotton, Winter Savory, Hyssop, and so on which were kept closely trimmed.

The majority of herbs require a warm, light, and well-drained soil and a position receiving plenty of sun. *See* **Herbs, Pot-herbs, Sweet-herbs,** and the notes under each plant in its alphabetical position.

J. E. G. W.

**HERB OF GRACE.** *See* **Ruta graveolens.**

**HERB PARIS.** *See* **Paris quadrifolia.**

**HERB PATIENCE.** *See* **Patience.**

**HERB ROBERT.** *See* **Geranium Robertianum.**

**HERBACEOUS BORDER.** A characteristic feature of the English garden, which in its true sense is a border consisting solely of hardy herbaceous perennials which can be cut down to the ground in winter and will come up again the following year. If the border is restricted to such plants, the general maintenance is much simpler and more economical than if it is supplemented by bedding plants, Dahlias, &c., although the latter undoubtedly promote a more continuous display. Herbaceous borders require a reasonable depth of good soil, a sunny aspect, and shelter from wind. They may be arranged to run alongside a wall or hedge; or form double borders divided by a grass walk and perhaps backed by yew hedges; or, under less formal circumstances, with curving margins (provided that the curves are justified by common sense and not meaningless worm-like lines).

An edging of paving-stone about 15 to 18 in. wide between the border and grass walk will be an advantage to allow of plants such as Nepeta which overhang the edge and make mowing difficult.

The narrower the border, the shorter will be the season over which it will be possible to arrange for a satisfying display. For example, to provide for a succession of blossom from early summer to late autumn a width of 14 ft. will be advisable. Where this cannot be obtained, it will be far better to have a really good show of colour at certain definite periods, rather than attempt a prolonged succession which at no time is really satisfactory.

Much has been written on colour schemes for the herbaceous border but the most important factor in its success, apart from proper cultural attention, is to arrange the planting in such a way as to ensure that a unified picture is at all times presented, by the use of some dominating characteristic or colour note. For example, we may bring about a sense of cohesion by arranging for some particular subject to predominate at each season. In early summer, for instance, Lupins might be freely planted to form the principal feature, for mid-summer Delphiniums, to be followed by Phloxes in August, and Michaelmas Daisies in the autumn. A sense of unity may also be promoted by the free use of grey-foliaged plants.

Borders in which the colouring is intended to pass gradually from one shade to another are apt to be disappointing and difficult to work in practice. On the other hand, those confined to some particular shade or combination of nearly related colours as, for example, all white, or bronze borders will usually give a very pleasing effect.

Combinations of colours such as rose-pink and 'Paul Crampel' red, which are not near enough to harmonize nor yet far enough apart to form a pleasing contrast, should be avoided.

The following are among the best herbaceous perennials for use in the herbaceous border.

Dwarf: *Nepeta × Faassenii, Dianthus* Mrs. Sinkins, *D.× Allwooddii* in var., *Campanula carpatica, Sedum spectabile,* New Dwarf Hybrid Asters, *Armeria* Bees Ruby, *Heuchera* in var., *Erigeron, Geum, Papaver* Peter Pan, *Prunella grandiflora, Statice latifolia, Stokesia cyanea, Catananche coerulea, Trollius,* dwarf vars. of *Veronica, Viola cornuta, Potentilla, Linum narbonnense.*

Medium: *Phlox decussata, Scabiosa caucasica, Helenium pumilum, Gaillardia, Coreopsis, Papaver orientale, Eryngium Oliverianum, Aster amellus, Tradescantia, Campanula persicifolia, Salvia × superba, Rudbeckia Newmanni, Sidalcea, Delphinium* Belladonna in var., *Pyrethrum, Anemone hupehensis* and *A. elegans,* Lupins, *Achillea Eupatorium, Gypsophila, Galega, Chrysanthemum maximum, Oenothera, Lythrum.*

Tall: *Delphinium, Verbascum, Anchusa azurea, Helianthus, Rudbeckia, Chrysanthemum uliginosum,* Hollyhocks, *Helenium, Crambe cordifolia, Bocconia.*

In preparing a planting scheme, it is best to draw out the borders on paper to a scale of ¼ or ½ in. to 1 ft. each, marking them out in 1-ft. squares. Each group of plants may then be plotted in detail, and the number required quickly reckoned.

J. E. G. W.

**HERBACEOUS PERENNIALS.** Perennial plants which die down to the ground annually.

**HERBACEOUS PLANTS.** Plants which do not form a persistent woody stem. They may be annual, biennial, or perennial.

*herba'ceus -a -um,* herbaceous, thin, green, as the tissue of leaves; having the characters of a herb.

**HERBAL.** Book devoted to the description of plants, their uses, perfumes, medicinal properties, &c., especially old books of this nature.

**HERBARIUM.** A collection of dried plants systematically arranged.

**HERBARY.** Old name for part of a garden devoted to growing Herbs.

**HERBERT'IA** (in honour of Dr. Wm. Herbert, 1778–1847, Dean of Manchester, a distinguished botanist, famous for his knowledge of bulbous plants). Fam. *Iridaceae.* A genus of about 14 species of plants with corms, allied to Tigridia, natives of Texas, Chile, and

*Herbertia amatorum* (p. 988).

S. Brazil. Flowers blue or violet, short-lived, at the top of a short scape; perianth short-tubed, 6-parted, outer segments triangular, acute and reflexed, the shorter inner ones rounded and erect; style 3-lobed only at apex. Half-hardy, needing a sunny position with a compost of sandy loam and peat. Propagation by seeds and by offsets.

**H. amator'um.*** Corm globose, brown. *l.* linear, narrowed to base, 7 to 8 in. long, $\frac{1}{8}$ to $\frac{3}{8}$ in. wide. *fl.* about 2 in. across, inner segs. violet with a brown spot at base, outer dark violet, claw marked with a white spot, tube green; scape 12 to 20 in. long, branches slender, about 5 in. long. Montevideo. 1903. (B.M. 8175.)

**H. caeru'lea.*** A synonym of *H. Drummondiana*.

**H. Drummondia'na.** Corm small, ovoid. Stem simple or forked, about 9 in. h. *l.* broad, plicate, about 6 in. long. *fl.* violet, about 2 in. across; sep. white on claws; pet. small. June to August. Texas. 1839. (B.M. 3862 as *H. caerulea*; 3779 as *Alophia Drummondiana.*) SYN. *Trifurcia caerulea*.

**H. platen'sis.** Corm large. Stem 4 ft. long, erect. *l.* ensiform, glaucous, 2 ft. long, ribbed. *fl.* light china-blue, large. May to September. La Plata.

**H. pulchel'la.** Corm globose, about $\frac{1}{2}$ in. wide. About 9 in. h. *l.* linear-ensiform, acute at both ends, ribbed. *fl.* blue-purple, outer white at base, flecked lilac; segs. bearded at base. Chile, S. Brazil. 1827. (S.B.F.G. 222.)

**HERBS.** In some gardens the cultivation of Herbs does not receive the attention their usefulness merits. Some herbs are rarely required except for a small amount of their leaves for flavouring but in many instances the flavour cannot be obtained from any other material. The herbaceous perennials, such as Horehound and Mint, should be cut on a dry day in summer, when the flowers are just fully opened, and dried slowly in a cool shed for winter use. The annuals and evergreen perennials are best in a green state but several of these answer their purpose when dried and some should, consequently, be kept in reserve. Herbs should always be dried slowly, and not placed in the sun or in fire heat. To preserve the flavour the leaves should be rubbed off when quite dry, put in wide-mouthed bottles, and closely corked. A piece of ground specially devoted to Herbs is the best arrangement in the garden (*see also* **Herb Garden**), at least for the cultivation of those of which only small quantities are needed. Plenty of room should be allowed for getting amongst them to gather any particular sort, and to keep the soil hoed. Part of the space might be devoted to the annual sorts instead of sowing them amongst other plants in different parts of the garden. The following list includes most of the useful Herbs grown for flavouring purposes: Angelica, Anise, Balm, Basil (Bush and Sweet), Borage, Burnet, Caraway, Chervil, Chives, Clary, Coriander, Dill, Fennel, Horehound, Hyssop, Lavender, Lovage, Marigold, Marjoram (Sweet), Mint, Parsley, Purslane, Rosemary, Rue, Sage, Savory (Summer and Winter), Southernwood, Tansy, Tarragon, Thyme. *See also* **Pot-herbs, Sweet-herbs.**

***Herbst'ii,*** in honour of Messrs. Herbst and Rossiter of Rio de Janeiro, Brazil, *c.* 1859.

***hercoglos'sus -a- um,*** coiled tongue.

**HERCULES CLUB.** *See* **Aralia spinosa.**

**HERITIE'RA** (in honour of Charles Louis l'Héritier, 1746–1800, a celebrated French botanist). FAM. *Sterculiaceae*. A genus of 4 species of evergreen trees, natives of the shores of Trop. Asia and Australia. Leaves undivided, leathery, pinnately veined, silvery-white beneath. Flowers 1-sexual, small, in axillary panicles; calyx 4- to 6-toothed; petals absent; stamens united in a column bearing 5 anthers at top; ovaries mostly 5; style short, carpels woody when ripe. Heritieras grow best in sandy loam under stove conditions and can be propagated by large ripened cuttings which root freely in sand in moist heat in a propagating frame.

**H. littora'lis.** *l.* large, oval-oblong, rounded at base, leathery, silvery beneath. *fl.* reddish; staminate cal. urn-shaped, downy; pistillate large, cal. bell-shaped. *fr.* oblong, polished, winged, compressed and rounded at apex. Trop. coasts of Old World. 1780. The wood is very hard, tough, and durable and sinks in water. It is used in Bengal for furniture and for boat-building.

**H. macrophyl'la.** Looking Glass Tree. Evergreen tree. *l.* oblong to oblong-lanceolate, up to 10 in. long or more, base wedge-shaped or roundish, acuminate, bright-green above, opaque silvery beneath; stalk long. *fl.* small, greenish, in open panicles shorter than l. *fr.* nearly globose, rough, with abrupt flattened beak. India. (B.M. 7192.)

F. G. P.

**HERMANN'IA** (in honour of Paul Hermann, 1646–95, once Professor of Botany at Leyden; travelled in Ceylon and Batavia). FAM. *Sterculiaceae*. A genus of about 80 species of shrubs or sub-shrubs, mostly natives of S. Africa; a few, not in cultivation, are natives of N. Africa, Texas, and Mexico. Closely related to Mahernia which is sometimes combined with it. Leaves alternate, from entire to pinnatifid. Flowers rather small, yellow to orange and red, often in leafy racemes and panicles; petals and stamens 5, the former usually erect; calyx bell-shaped, 5-lobed. Fruit a leathery, 5-celled, many-seeded capsule. All the cultivated species are cool greenhouse plants, propagated by soft cuttings in gentle heat, but they are not much grown at the present time.

**H. althaeifo'lia.** Diffuse shrub, 2 to 4 ft., downy throughout, shoots angled. *l.* oval to obovate or rhomboid, blunt, shallowly toothed, 1 to 3 in. long, $\frac{1}{2}$ to $1\frac{1}{2}$ in. wide; stalk up to $1\frac{1}{2}$ in. long. *fl.* yellow or orange, $\frac{1}{2}$ in. long, 2 to 3 on a stalk, forming collectively stalked leafy panicles 3 to 12 in. long. Summer. S. Africa. 1728. (B.M. 307.)

**H. can'dicans.** Sub-shrub up to 3 ft., shoots very downy. *l.* ovate, oval or oblong, $\frac{1}{2}$ to $1\frac{1}{2}$ in. long, $\frac{1}{4}$ to 1 in. wide, margins more or less wrinkled, veins sunken above, under surface clothed with soft down. *fl.* bright yellow, nodding, $\frac{3}{8}$ in. long, borne in terminal racemes and panicles up to 6 or 8 in. long. March to June. S. Africa. (Gn. 71 (1907), 15.)

**H. conglomera'ta.** Much-branched shrub up to 2 ft., shoots and l. shaggy with grey hairs. *l.* $\frac{1}{2}$ to 1 in. long, roundish to widely obovate, plaited obtuse, bluntly toothed; stalk $\frac{1}{8}$ to $\frac{1}{3}$ in. long. *fl.* yellow, crowded in a cluster at end of the branches; cal. and ovary hairy. S. Africa. 1868. (Ref. B. 217.)

**H. crista'ta.*** Sub-shrub, sending up semi-woody, angled shoots 1 to 2 ft. h. from a woody rootstock; all the parts furnished with starry down. *l.* 1 to 2 in. long, $\frac{1}{4}$ to 1 in. wide, pointed, irregularly toothed, scarcely stalked. *fl.* nodding, solitary in the upper l.-axils, bright brick-red to crimson, $\frac{3}{4}$ in. long; capsule $\frac{3}{4}$ in. long, 5-angled, ridges spiny. Autumn. S. Africa. 1890. (B.M. 7173.)

**H. denuda'ta.** Glabrous, straggling shrub, 2 to 3 ft. *l.* lanceolate to oblanceolate, 1 to $1\frac{1}{2}$ in. long, $\frac{1}{4}$ to $\frac{1}{2}$ in. wide, pointed, upper part coarsely toothed. *fl.* nodding, thinly disposed in terminal racemes and panicles up to 8 in. long; cor. yellow, $\frac{1}{4}$ in. long. June to August. S. Africa. 1820.

**H. fascicula'ta.** A synonym of *H. linearifolia*.

**H. flam'mea.*** Shrub 2 to 3 ft., shoots slender, stellately hairy. *l.* cuneate, apex truncate and usually toothed, $\frac{1}{2}$ to 1 in. long, $\frac{1}{4}$ to $\frac{1}{2}$ in. wide, downy especially at first. *fl.* scented at night-time, nodding, in terminal racemes several in. long; cor. rich red, $\frac{1}{2}$ in. long. Summer. S. Africa. 1794. (B.M. 1349.)

**H. linearifo'lia.** Much-branched, rigid shrub, 1 to 2 ft., shoots slender, glabrous, viscous. *l.* clustered to solitary at the nodes, linear, $\frac{1}{4}$ to $\frac{7}{8}$ in. long, $\frac{1}{12}$ in. or less wide, glabrous, slightly viscous. *fl.* wine-red, $\frac{1}{2}$ in. long, nodding, scattered and few on racemes several in. long. S. Africa. 1868. (Ref. B. 289 as *H. fasciculata.*)

**H. scopa'ria.** Sub-shrubby, prostrate plant, sending up thinly bristly shoots 1 to 2 ft. h. *l.* $\frac{1}{2}$ to $1\frac{1}{2}$ in. long, $\frac{1}{16}$ to $\frac{1}{8}$ in. wide, linear or narrowly cuneate, pointed, often toothed near apex, thinly bristly beneath and on margins. *fl.* nodding, $\frac{1}{3}$ in. long, orange, 1 to 6 in terminal, often clustered, racemes. April. S. Africa. 1870. (Ref. B. 195.)

W. J. B.

**hermaphrodite,** having both stamens and pistil in one flower.

**HERMINIER'A** (in honour of F. L. l'Herminier, 1779–1883, apothecary in Guadeloupe). FAM. *Leguminosae*. A genus of 1 species, a tall shrub which grows in thick masses in beds of shallow stagnant waters in the Upper Nile country. Closely related to Aeschynomene and sometimes included with it. Best grown in a pot partially submerged in a warm-water tank. Propagated by seeds.

**H. Elaphrox'ylon.** Ambash. Pith-tree. *l.* unequally pinnate, without stipels. *fl.* large; cor. bright orange, papilionaceous; cal. 2-lipped; stamens in 2 bundles of 5 each with uniform anthers. *Pod* linear, nearly flat, curved spirally, separating at the square articulations. Trop. Africa. SYN. *Aeschynomene Elaphroxylon.*

F. G. P.

**HERMIN'IUM** (*hermin*, bedpost; alluding to the knob-like root). FAM. *Orchidaceae.* Musk Orchis. A genus of about 20 small-flowered orchids in the temperate or alpine regions of Europe and Asia. Closely allied to Orchis but the perianth is without a spur and the anther cells are distant at their base, the glands of the stalks of the pollinia protruding below the cells. *H. Monorchis* is best grown on dry chalky banks and propagated by division.

**H. alpi'num.** *fl.* 8 to 15, white or greenish-brown; lip ovate, repand, twice as large as the acute pet.; spike shorter than l. May. *l.* linear, grass-like. Mts. of Europe. 1824. (B.R. 1499 as *H. cordatum.*)

**H. Monor'chis.** *fl.* greenish-yellow, small, numerous, with musky odour; spike dense; lip deeply 3-lobed, base saccate. July. *l.* 2, radical, oblong or lanceolate. 3 to 6 in. h. Europe (Britain), Siberia, Himalaya. (E.B. 1466.)

E. C.

**HERMODAC'TYLUS** (from *Hermes*, Mercury, *dactylos*, finger; in reference to the form of the root). A monotypic genus related to Iris, in the Mediterranean region, naturalized in England and Ireland. Habit and flower-form that of a bulbous Iris; distinguished from Iris by its 1- (instead of 3-) celled ovary, and the almost hand-like form of the underground portion with swollen fibres. This plant is quite hardy and not particular as to soil or aspect so long as the site is well drained.

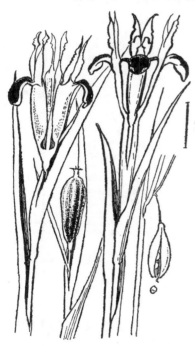

*Hermodactylus tuberosus*

**H. tubero'sus.*** Snake's Head. Stem weak, slender, hollow, about 1 ft. long. *l.* outer ring scale-like, lanceolate, inner, 2 or 3, weak, glaucous, tetragonal, erect. *fl.* solitary; limb 2 to 2½ in. deep; falls with orbicular, obtuse, lurid purple, veinless lamina, ½ to ¾ in. broad, not exceeding half the oblong, spatulate, greenish-yellow claw, ¾ to 1 in. broad at middle; standards erect, under 1 in. long, rhomboid, unguiculate; blade entire or tricuspidate; spathe with usually only 1 large green valve, often overtopping the flower. April, May. Levant. Before 1600. (B.M. 531.) SYN. *Iris tuberosa.*

**HERNAN'DIA** (in honour of Francisco Hernandez, physician to Philip II of Spain, writer on the Flora of Mexico). FAM. *Hernandiaceae.* A genus of 8 species of tropical evergreen trees grown chiefly for their handsome foliage. Leaves cordate, peltate, smooth. Flowers yellowish, monoecious, in panicles; sepals petaloid. Hernandias need stove conditions and a compost of sandy loam and peat. Ripe cuttings with leaves intact root freely in sand under a propagating frame with brisk bottom heat.

**H. cordig'era.** Large tree, with spreading branches. *l.* few near ends of branches, large, oval, entire, obtuse, long-stalked. *fl.* yellowish in groups of 3; lateral male, middle female; stamens 4. *fr.* a 1-seeded drupe. New Caledonia.

**H. Moerenhoutia'na.** Small tree. *l.* alternate, elliptic to broadly ovate-cordate, 3 to 5 in. long, leathery, obtuse, entire, smooth above, hairy on veins beneath. *fl.* dirty yellow, 3 in each involucre, 2 male, 1 female; peduncles axillary. October. Pacific Is. (B.M. 5839.)

**H. sono'ra.** Tree to 50 ft. *l.* simple, roundish, centre red. *fl.* whitish-green, in corymbs. India. 1693. Used for sub-tropical bedding. The sap of the l. is a powerful depilatory, destroying hairs without pain.

**HERNANDIA'CEAE.** Dicotyledons. A family of 24 tropical trees in 4 genera, closely related to Lauraceae but with the ovary inferior. Fruit winged with 1 seed. Leaves alternate, without stipules. The only genus dealt with here is Hernandia.

**HERNIAR'IA** (*hernia*, rupture; in allusion to use in treating rupture). FAM. *Caryophyllaceae.* A genus of 8 or 10 species of herbs, either small or with a short-lived perennial rootstock, except *H. rotundifolia*, natives of Cent. and S. Europe, N. Africa, and W. Asia with 1 species in S. Africa. Leaves opposite. Flowers green, small, crowded in little axillary cymes. Of little beauty but of use in carpet-bedding and for covering rocks, retaining its deep green colour throughout the year, even in dry seasons and on the poorest soils. For cultivation, *see* **Paronychia.**

**H. glab'ra.** Rupturewort. Stems much-branched, spreading on ground, several in. long. *l.* small, opposite, oblong-ovate or rarely orbicular. *fl.* summer. Europe (Britain), N. and W. Asia. (E.B. 1171.)

**H. hirsu'ta.** *l.* elliptic, otherwise similar to *H. glabra* but for being hairy all over. Britain to W. Asia.

**H. inca'na.** Habit of *H. hirsuta* but villosely hairy; *l.* ovate-oblong. S. France, Italy.

**H. rotundifo'lia.** Rootstock woody in old plants, stem persistent, forming a thick mat. *l.* oblong-spatulate to obovate about ¼ in. long, almost glabrous, upper smaller. *fl.* many, very small, in dense paniculate spikes. July to September. Italy.

**HERON'S BILL.** *See* **Erodium.**

**HERPES'TIS.** *See* **Bacopa.**

*herpet'icus -a -um,* ring-worm like.

**HERPOT'RICHIA.** *See* **Pine diseases.**

**HERRAN'IA** (in honour of General Herran, a President of the Republic of New Granada). FAM. *Sterculiaceae.* A genus of 4 or 5 species of evergreen trees or shrubs natives of Trop. S. America and closely related to Theobroma, the Cocoa plant.

**H. albiflo'ra.** Evergreen tree 20 to 25 ft. or a tall shrub, often unbranched; young shoots downy. *l.* clustered at top of the stem, 5- or 6-foliolate; lflets. radiating, 8 to 16 in. long, 2½ to 6 in. wide, oblanceolate, acuminate, cuneate; stalk 8 to 15 in. long, downy, angled. *fl.* borne close to stems several years old, followed by ovoid-pointed fr. 5 in. by 2 in., containing many seeds embedded in well-flavoured pulp which are themselves mixed with those of *Theobroma Cacao* and the product said thereby to be improved. A noble plant, but probably not now in cultivation. Stove or warm greenhouse.

W. J. B.

*Herrar'ai,* in honour of Professor F. L. Herrara of the University of Cuzco, Peru.

**HERRER'IA** (in honour of Gabriel A. de Herrera, 1470–1539, Spanish agriculturist). FAM. *Liliaceae*. A genus of 3 species of Brazilian climbing plants with a tuberous rootstock. Leaves crowded on very short lateral branches lanceolate or linear. Flowers in many-flowered axillary racemes, small, scented. Peat, sand, and loam mixed suits these greenhouse plants which can be increased by cuttings or by seeds.

**H. Salsaparil'ha.** Stem climbing, roughly hairy, up to 8 ft. *l.* lanceolate. *fl.* green, yellow, about ½ in. across, in panicles; perianth segs. ovate-obtuse. Brazil. 1824. (B.M. 1042 as *H. parviflora.*)

**HERSCHEL'IA.** Included in **Disa.**

***Hers'ii,*** in honour of Joseph Hers, who sent plants from China, *c.* 1920, to the Arnold Arboretum.

***Hertrich'ii,*** in honour of William Hertrich, Director, Huntington Gardens, San Marino, U.S. America, 1902–47.

**HESPERALO'E** (*hesperos*, western, *Aloe*; alluding to the aspect of the plants and their native habitats). FAM. *Liliaceae*. Two species of Yucca-like shrubs natives of Texas and Mexico, differing from Yucca by their short-lived greenish or red flowers. They require greenhouse conditions, a light loamy soil, and all the sunshine possible.

**H. funif'era.** Shrub often forming clusters of stems. *l.* 3 to 4 ft. long, less concave than in *H. parviflora*, marginal fibres much coarser. *Panicle* up to 10 ft. branched near the top; fl.-stalks and perianth purplish-green, the latter 1 in. long; style scarcely exserted. Mexico. 1900. (I.H. 11 as *Yucca funifera.*) SYN. *H. Davyi.*

**H. parviflo'ra.** The typical form of this species has probably not reached cultivation in Britain, but is represented by the variety described below. The type differs from it in the perianth being more slender and especially in the style being well exserted. (*H. yuccaefolia*, not of B.M. 7723.) var. **Engelmann'i.** Evergreen Yucca-like shrub, developing clusters of sucker growths. *l.* spreading, 3 to 4 ft. long, about 1 in. wide, linear, pointed, thick and leathery, concave above, bright green with white threads hanging from the margin. *fl.* in a slender panicle up to 6 ft. long; perianth oblong-campanulate, about 1 in. long, ⅜ in. wide, bright rosy-red, golden-yellow within; style not or only slightly exserted. July. Texas. 1882. (B.M. 7723 as *H. yuccaefolia.*) SYN. *H. Engelmanni.*

W. J. B.

**HESPERAN'THA** (*hesperos*, evening, *anthos*, flower). FAM. *Iridaceae*. A genus of about 30 species of usually rather dwarf herbs, natives of Trop. and S. Africa, related to Geissorrhiza but with a short style. Leaves sword-shaped, curled. Flowers very fragrant, opening in evening, in loose spikes; perianth salver-shaped, tube slender, covered by bracts, segments as long as tube, nearly equal, spreading; filaments short. For cultivation *see* **Ixia.**

**H. angus'ta.** *l.* narrower than in *H. falcata*. *fl.* uniformly white. Spring.

**H. Buhr'ii.** About 10 in. h. *fl.* several, white within, pink without; anthers golden-yellow. May, June. S. Africa. 1936. Fl. open from noon onwards.

**H. cinnamo'mea.** About 6 in. h. *l.* falcate, curled. *fl.* white within, reddish-brown without. Spring. 1787. (B.M. 1054.)

**H. falca'ta.** 6 to 12 in. h. *l.* somewhat sickle-shaped, 3 to 12 in. long, up to ⅜ in. wide, striated. *fl.* 3 to 10, tube and segs. each about ⅜ in. long, inner segs. and outer segs. within white, outer segs. shining brown without. April. (B.M. 566 as *Ixia falcata.*)

**H. graminifo'lia.** Smooth, about 6 in. h. *l.* linear. *fl.* greenish-white. Autumn. 1808. (B.M. 1254 as *H. pilosa nuda.*)

**H. longitu'ba.** About 1 ft. h. *l.* 2 or 3, grass-like, glabrous, 6 to 9 in. long. *fl.* 3 to 8; inner segs. white, outer tinged reddish-brown, ½ to ⅝ in. long; spathe valves tinged red. 1877.

**H. pilo'sa.** Stem smooth, about 6 in. h. *l.* linear, hairy. *fl.* white within; outer segs. speckled red without. Spring. 1811. (B.M. 1475.)

**H. radia'ta.** About 6 in. h. *l.* fistulous. *fl.* nodding, white within; outer segs. striped reddish-brown. April to June. 1794. (B.M. 573 as *Ixia radiata.*)

**H. Stanford'iae.** About 12 in. h. *l.* 3, falcate. *fl.* erect, bright yellow; scape smooth. April, May. S. Africa. 1936. Fl. open from noon to sunset.

**HES'PERIS** (old Greek name used by Theophrastus, from *hesperos*, evening, when the flowers of some species are fragrant). FAM. *Cruciferae*. A genus of about 24 species of erect biennial or perennial herbs, natives of Europe and W. and N. Asia. Leaves ovate or oblong, entire, toothed or lyrate. Flowers of various colours in loose racemes without bracts, fragrant. Pods long, round or 4-angled; valves flattish, keeled, 3-nerved. Seeds many, sometimes margined. Differs from Matthiola and Cheiranthus mainly in the embryo. *H. matronalis* is freely increased by seed, but its beautiful double forms must be propagated by division or by cuttings. The single forms grow readily in any moist, well-drained soil but the double ones are less easily satisfied; a moist sandy loam with leaf-soil suits them best.

**H. matrona'lis.*** Damask Violet; Dame's Violet; Sweet Rocket. Perennial 2 to 3 ft. h. *l.* ovate-lanceolate or lanceolate, mainly radical, 3 to 4 in. long, tapering to base or shortly stalked. *fl.* of various colours, fragrant in evening. S. Europe eastwards to Siberia. (E.B. 103.) A variable plant, the double varieties of which are especially good. The single varieties are excellent for the wild garden. var. **alba ple'na,*** *fl.* double white; **fl. pleno,** *fl.* double purple; **candis'sima,** *fl.* pure white, single; **niv'ea,** *fl.* white; **purpu'rea,** *fl.* purple.

**H. niv'ea.** A variety of *H. matronalis.*

**H. trist'is.** Biennial about 18 in. h., branched in upper part of stem. *Radical l.* stalked; *upper* sessile, ovate, entire, or toothed, 2 to 4 in. long. *fl.* whitish or cream, brownish-red or purple, fragrant at night, pedicels very long. Spring, summer. E. Europe. 1629. (B.M. 730.) A plant for the wild garden, old walls, and so on.

**H. viola'cea.** Annual or biennial of 6 to 12 in. *Radical l.* oblong, entire or repand, rarely to runcinate; *upper* lanceolate, acute, almost entire. *fl.* violet, obovate, clawed; pedicels as long as cal.; raceme almost paniculate. June. Asia Minor.

**HESPEROCAL'LIS** (*hesperos*, evening, *callis*, beauty). FAM. *Liliaceae*. A genus of a single species of Californian bulbous plant with a short, woody stem, covered with the remains of old leaves, and thick, linear, margined, radical leaves. Related to Hemerocallis and Leucocrinum. Greenhouse protection or treatment as a half-hardy plant is necessary with general conditions as for Yucca.

**H. undula'ta.** *l.* radical, long linear, wavy, thick, with a broad white margin. *fl.* whitish, fragrant, large in a simple raceme, pedicels short; perianth funnel-shaped, tube cylindrical, lobes oblong-spatulate, longer than tube, somewhat spreading; stamens 6; scape erect, unbranched. February, March. Colorado, California. 1882. (A.W.W.F. 30.)

**HESPEROCHI'RON** (*hesperos*, evening or western, *Chiron*, Chironia). FAM. *Hydrophyllaceae*. A genus of 2 or 3 perennial, dwarf, stemless herbs with succulent basal leaves and short thick roots, natives of Western N. America. Flowers solitary, on axillary peduncles, large, saucer- or bell-shaped, white, pink, or blue. Rock-garden plants, with a long resting period, needing good ordinary well-drained soil.

**H. californ'icus.** *l.* many in a radical rosette, 1 to 2 in. long, more or less oblong, entire. *fl.* white with dark stripes; cor. oblong-bell-shaped, ½ to ⅝ in. long. July. California, in wet places. 1823. (B.R. 833 as *Nicotiana nana.*)

**H. pu'milus.*** *l.* radical, spatulate, 2 to 2½ in. long, ½ to ⅝ in. wide, entire, hairy beneath. *fl.* white, pink, or bluish with violet veins and a yellow base, nearly rotate; lobes longer than tube; tube hairy within. Idaho to Oregon. 1888. (Gn. 18 (1880), 3.) SYN. *Villarsia pumila.*

**HESPEROME'CON.** A synonym of Platystigma.

**HESPEROSCOR'DON, HESPEROSCOR'DUM.** Included in **Brodiaea.**

**HESPEROYUC'CA.** Included in **Yucca.**

**HESSE'A** (in honour of Paul Hesse, botanical traveller). FAM. *Amaryllidaceae*. A genus of about 8 species of bulbous S. African plants with linear or subulate leaves and many-flowered umbels on a solid scape. Flowers small, pink, segments of perianth free or nearly so, spreading; stamens inserted at the base of the segments. For cultivation of these greenhouse bulbs *see* **Strumaria.**

**H. crisp'a.** About 3 in. h. *l.* filiform, straight. *fl.* pink; perianth segs. wavy. April to August. 1790. (B.M. 1363 as *Strumaria crispa.*)

**H. Duparquetia'na.** *l.* lorate, about 1 ft. long. *fl.* white with segs. crimson keeled, flat, narrow, about 2 in. long; perianth tube short; umbels about 20-fld. Kalahari region.

**H. filifo'lia.** About 6 in. h. *l.* filiform. *fl.* white; perianth segs. acute. November. 1774. (B.R. 440 as *Strumaria filifolia.*)

**H. gemma'ta.** About 1 ft. h. *l.* lanceolate, ciliate. *fl.* pale yellow; segs. wavy, channelled; peduncles long; scape flexuous. August. 1812. (B.M. 1620 as *Strumaria gemmata.*)

**H. stellar'is.** About 6 in. h. *l.* linear-acute, entire. *fl.* pink; segs. spreading alternately, bearded at ends. October, November. 1794. SYN. *Amaryllis stellaris, Strumaria stellaris.*

**HETAE'RIA.** Included in **Anoectochilus.**

**HETERAN'THERA** (*heteros*, variable, *anther*). FAM. *Pontederiaceae.* A genus of about 11 species of ornamental aquatic perennial herbs in Trop. Africa, Australia, and America. Leaves roundish, long-stalked, or linear. Flowers blue or white, small, produced from a spathe in the axil of a sheathing leaf-stalk; perianth salver-shaped with a long, slender tube and a 6-lobed limb. *H. limosa* may be grown by the side of a pond or brook in a sheltered place; the other species require the same treatment as other tender aquatics. Propagated by division or seed.

**H. callaefo'lia.** Stem creeping, 1 ft. h. *l.* broadly cordate, smooth. *Spadix* 4 in. long, thickly covered with small white fl.; spathe summer. Summer. Trop. Africa.

**H. du'bia.** A synonym of *H. graminea.*

**H. gramin'ea.** Water Star Grass. Stem slender, floating or creeping, branched, 2 to 3 ft. long. *l.* linear, flat, elongated, acute, sheathing at base. *Spadix* 1- or 2-fld.; perianth light yellow; segs. narrow, small. July, August. Useful for tropical aquaria when l. remain submerged and fl. float on the surface of the water. N. America. 1823. SYN. *H. dubia, Commelina dubia, Leptanthus gramineus, Schollera graminea.*

**H. Kotschya'na.** Glabrous, 5 to 12 in. h. *l.* cordate, 1 to 3 in. long, ½ to 2 in. broad, stalks 2 to 8 in. long. Spadix 2 to 4 in. with several whitish fl. July. Australia, E. Africa. 1913.

**H. limo'sa.** Stem often branched at base, 6 to 15 in. long, fleshy. *l.* ovate, or ovate-oblong, blunt, rounded at base, entire, smooth, stalks 2 to 5 in. long. *Spathe* 1-fld.; perianth white or blue; peduncle 1 ft. or more long. July. Trop. America. (B.M. 6192.) SYN. *Leptanthus ovalis.* Half-hardy.

**H. reniform'is.** Mud Plantain. Stem creeping, rooting at nodes, 6 to 18 in. long. *l.* deeply cordate or reniform, 1 to 2 in. broad, entire, smooth, stalks 2 to 9 in. long. *Spathe* 2- to 5-fld., white or pale blue, about ¼ in. across. Summer. S. and Cent. America. SYN. *Leptanthus reniformis.* Greenhouse. Shallow water.

**H. spica'ta.** Stem creeping. *l.* erect, cordate, stalks long. *fl.* violet-blue, spike 2 or 3 in. long. Summer. Cuba.

**H. zosterifo'lia.** Stem trailing. *l.* very close, small, oblong, smooth, entire, sessile. *fl.* pale blue, axillary. S. America. 1925. Something like *Elodea densa.* A good tropical aquarium plant.

F. P.

***hetero-***, in compound words, implying diverse, as *heterophyllus*, having leaves of diverse forms.

**HETEROCEN'TRON** (*heteros*, variable, *kentron*, spur). FAM. *Melastomataceae.* A genus of about 4 species of erect or prostrate, sometimes hairy, herbs or sub-shrubs, natives of the mountains of Mexico and Guatemala. Leaves cordate, lanceolate or obovate-lanceolate, membranous. Flowers pink or white; petals 4, ovate or obovate, obtuse or slender-pointed. *H. roseum* is an ornamental plant requiring a warm greenhouse but useful in the alpine house in autumn or out-doors in summer, flowering also in the stove in winter. A compost of sandy loam and peat suits it and it may be propagated by cuttings in February or March.

**H. el'egans.** A synonym of *Schizocentron elegans.*

**H. ro'seum.** Sub-shrub of 1 ft. or more. *l.* opposite, elliptic, obtuse, entire, penni-nerved, slightly scabrid above, tapering to a rather long stalk. *fl.* bright rose, nearly 1 in. across; in a terminal compound panicle of numerous corymbs; pet. 4, spreading, rhomboid-orbicular, rather concave, shortly clawed. Autumn, early winter. Mexico. (B.M. 5166 as *H. mexicanum.*) SYN. *Heeria rosea.*

**heterochlamydeous,** having both calyx and corolla in the flower.

***heterochro'mus -a -um,*** of diverse colours.

**HETEROD'ERA mario'ni.** *See* **Root-knot eelworm,** *also* **Potato Pests, Potato Root eelworm.**

***hetero'don,*** having varying teeth.

**heteroecious,** having two homes, as, e.g. many Rust Fungi which are parasitic in one stage on one host, and in another upon a host of an entirely different character. Thus *Puccinia graminis* has one stage on *Berberis vulgaris*, another on wheat; species of Gymnosporangium have one stage on species of Juniperus and pass the rest of their life on some tree belonging to the family Rosaceae.

**heterogamous,** having, in a capitulum, the ray-florets either neuter or female, those of the disk male.

***heterolep'idus -a -um,*** having varying scales.

**HETEROM'ELES** (*heteros*, different, *mele*, apple tree). FAM. *Rosaceae.* Monotypic and nearly akin to Photinia but differs in having flowers with only 10 stamens.

**H. arbutifo'lia.** Californian Maybush. Evergreen tree up to 30 ft. or a shrub, young shoots downy. *l.* oblanceolate to oblong or elliptical, 2 to 4 in. long, stiff and leathery, spine-toothed. *fl.* white, ⅜ in. wide, borne in a cluster of corymbs making a terminal panicle up to 6 in. wide. August. California. 1796. (B.R. 491 as *Photinia arbutifolia.*) Very handsome in fruit. Not very hardy but succeeds from S. Surrey southwards and westwards.

W. J. B.

**HETEROPAP'PUS** (*heteros*, various, *pappus*, down; the pappus of the ray-florets differs from that of the disk). FAM. *Compositae.* A genus of about 4 species of erect herbs, natives of Manchuria, Formosa, and Japan, closely related to Aster but with the pappus of the ray-florets chaffy, of the disk of 1 or 2 rows of slender bristles. Leaves alternate, entire or with large teeth. Flower-heads rather large, loosely panicled or solitary, at apex of branches; ray-florets white or bluish. Cultivation as for Aster.

**H. decip'iens.** A form of *H. hispidus.*

**H. his'pidus.** Stem hispid, about 1 ft. h. *l.* oblong-lanceolate, roughly hairy, ciliate, lower ovate. *fl.-heads* white or purple, disk yellow, solitary at ends of branches; involucral scales oblong, overlapping. Distribution as genus. 1804. Purple form, 1863. (G.F. 425.) Hardy.

***heterophyl'lus -a -um,*** having leaves of different shapes.

**HETEROP'TERIS** (*heteros*, various, *pteron*, wing; the wings of the fruit vary in form). FAM. *Malpighiaceae.* A genus of about 90 species of tropical shrubs, mainly S. American, one in W. Africa. Leaves opposite, usually entire and glandular-dotted beneath, with short stalks and small stipules. Flowers yellow or purple, small, often in racemes or panicles; calyx 5-parted; petals clawed; stamens 10, perfect but unequal. Fruit of 1 to 3 samaras, wings somewhat semi-circular. Allied to Banisteria but usually erect. For cultivation *see* **Banisteria.**

**H. chrysophyl'la.** Twining climber, branches clothed with dense appressed rusty hairs. *l.* opposite, oval or oval-oblong, entire, leathery, glabrous above, with several glands near margin and golden-brown down beneath. *fl.* orange, becoming reddish, in axillary umbel-like panicles, shorter than l., cal. covered with rusty down and with 8 oblong, bright green, shining, prominent glands. March. Brazil. 1833. (B.M. 3237.) SYN. *Banisteria chrysophylla.*

**H. purpu'rea.** Low climbing shrub. *l.* oval, smooth, glaucous beneath, stalks with 2 glands at middle. *fl.* purple, few, in corymbs or racemes on slender pedicels jointed below the middle. *fr.* 1 in. long with half-obovate-oblique wings. W. Indies, Venezuela. 1759.

**H. seric'ea.** Climber. *l.* ovate, obtuse, bright golden-downy on both surfaces at first, later glabrous above. *fl.* yellow, in racemes. July. Brazil. 1810. SYN. *Banisteria sericea.*

F. G. P.

**HETEROSPATH'E** (*heteros*, variable, *spathe*; the spathes are unequal). FAM. *Palmaceae.* A genus of several species of smooth-stemmed Palm remarkable for the length of the tapered segments of its pinnate leaves. *H. elata* needs stove conditions, with rich sandy loam and leaf-mould. It is propagated by seeds.

**H. ela′ta.** *l.* tufted, pinnatisect, gracefully spreading; segs. ½ in. wide, somewhat distant, bright green on both surfaces, narrowed to a long, slender, tapering point. Amboyna. 1880.

**HETEROSPERM′UM** (*heteros*, variable, *sperma*, seed). **FAM.** *Compositae*. A genus of about 5 species of small annuals, mostly natives of the warmer parts of America, related to Coreopsis. Leaves opposite, pinnately or ternately cut, rarely entire. Flower-heads yellow, small; rays 3 to 5, little exserted. Treatment as for Coreopsis.

**H. Xant′i.** Hardy annual. Habit and aspect of Bidens sp. with finely cut l. Intermediate between Bidens and Coreopsis. Lower California. 1897. (G.F. 48, 135.)

**HETEROSPO′RIUM echinula′tum.** A fungus causing Ring-spot disease of Carnations (q.v.).

**heterosporous,** bearing different kinds of spores, as Selaginella.

**HETEROSTYLISM.** Having more than 1 length of style (and stamens) in different plants of the same species; e.g. in Primula the stamens are half-way up the tube of the corolla and the stigma at the mouth in one form (pin-eyed) of the flower; the stamens at the mouth of the corolla, the stigma reaching only half-way up the tube in the other (thrum-eyed). In Lythrum there are 3 forms of flower and several other genera of plants provide further examples. The phenomenon is connected with the avoidance of self-fertilization. See Darwin on *Forms of Flowers*.

**HETEROTHE′CA** (*heteros* variable, *theca*, sheath; from the shape of the achenes). **FAM.** *Compositae*. A genus of about 5 species of erect herbs, natives of N. America and Mexico. *H. inuloides* grows in ordinary garden soil but needs protection in winter. Propagated by seeds or division.

**H. inuloi′des.** Perennial of 1 to 1½ ft. h. *l.* ovate-oblong, entire, hairy and ciliate; basal l. ovate, obtuse, bluntly toothed, stem-l. variable, somewhat stem-clasping. *fl.*-heads yellow, large in loosely spreading corymbs; peduncles very hairy, involucral bracts many, roughly hairy; receptacle honey-combed. Summer. Mexico. (S.B.F.G. 246 as *Diplocoma villosa*.)

**HETEROT′OMA** (*heteros*, variable, *tome*, cut; the corolla being unequally cut). **FAM.** *Campanulaceae*. A genus of about 10 species of annual or perennial herbs, natives of Mexico. Leaves alternate, stalked. Flowers blue, yellow, or orange, in terminal racemes; base forming a spur involving corolla and 2 sepals; corolla tube split to base at back; stamens free of corolla or two adnate at base; ovary 2-celled, ovules many. Fruit a capsule dehiscing by 2 lobes in upper part. Treatment as for half-hardy species of Lobelia.

**H. lobelioi′des.** * Bird Plant. Stem woody at base, branching, hairy. *l.* ovate-lanceolate, toothed. *fl.* about 2 in. long, single on axillary peduncles; cor. tube red, limb golden-yellow, 3-lobed; lower lip of cal. adnate to cor. tube, with 2 narrow green lobes projecting beyond it; staminal column erect, as long as cor. Summer. Mts. of Mexico and Cent. America. 1861. (F.d.S. 1454; B.M. 7849.)

**HETEROT′RICHUM** (*heteros*, variable, *trichos*, hair). **FAM.** *Melastomataceae*. A genus of about 12 species of often hispid-hairy or glandular shrubs, natives of Guiana, Colombia, and the W. Indies. Leaves large, ovate-cordate or oblong, entire or toothed, stalked. Flowers white or pink, in terminal, or sometimes lateral, panicles; petals 6 or 8; stamens 12 or many; calyx bell-shaped or globose with 4 to 8 teeth. *H. macrodon* needs stove conditions and a compost of sandy loam and peat. Increased by cuttings.

**H. macro′don.** * Shrub of 7 to 8 ft., branches and l.-stalks covered with rufous hairs. *l.* in very unequal pairs, cordate-ovate, slenderpointed, toothed, 7-nerved, paler beneath. *fl.* in terminal cymes of 10 to 12; pet. 8, pure white, red at base, obovate, overlapping;

stamens 16. Autumn. Caracas, Colombia. (B.M. 4421.) SYN. *Octomeris macrodon*. Handsome shrubs flowering when quite small.

F. G. P.

**HETEROTROP′A.** Included in **Asarum.**

**A→**

**HEUCH′ERA** (in honour of Johann Heinrich Heucher, 1677–1747, Professor of Medicine, Wittenberg). **FAM.** *Saxifragaceae*. Alum Root. A genus of about 70 species of perennial herbs, natives of N. America from Mexico almost to the Arctic. Leaves in a radical tuft, heart-shaped, 5- to 9-lobed, crenate, long-stalked. Flowers rather small in loose panicles; calyx tube often bell-shaped, urn-shaped, cylindrical, turbinate, or saucer-shaped, often oblique; petals 5 or none, small, often shorter than calyx; stamens 5. Fruit an inferior capsule, 2-beaked. The genus is related to Mitella and Tiarella, and like those is attractive by its foliage and by the light, diffuse arrangement of its flowers, the conspicuous part of which is the coloured calyx. Any good sweet garden soil which does not dry out in spring suits the Heucheras and they will put up with some shade though best in the sun. They are readily divided in spring, but where more than 1 species is grown crossing is apt to occur so that seed cannot generally be relied upon. *H. sanguinea* has given, perhaps by crossing with other species, a number of very effective varieties and the hybrid race *H × brizoides* is a favourite for its light effect. Heuchera has also crossed with Tiarella—*see* **Heucherella.** Species like *H. hispida*, grown especially for their foliage, should have the inflorescences pinched out as they appear.

**H. america′na.** Clammy-hairy, about 18 in. h. Basal *l.* roundish heart-shaped, 5- to 7-lobed, mottled at first, becoming green and glabrous above; long-stalked. *infl.* an open panicle; sep. reddish; pet. greenish-white; stamens much longer than sep. Summer. N. America. 1656. (B.B. ed. 2,2, 226.)

**H. bractea′ta.** Densely tufted, 4 to 6 in. h. Basal *l.* roundish kidney-shaped, lobes roundish with cuspidate teeth. *infl.* dense, an almost spike-like panicle; sep. oblong, obtuse; pet. slightly longer, oblanceolate. Summer. Colorado. Rock-garden.

**H.× brizoi′des.** A group of mostly pink or red flowered hybrids between *H. americana × H. sanguinea* and probably *H. micrantha*. See **Heucherella.**

**H. caules′cens.** A synonym of *H. villosa*.

**H. cylin′drica.** Tufted. *l.* roundish heart-shaped, lobes shallow, teeth ovate, cuspidate-ciliate. *infl.* in a spike-like panicle; about 12 to 20 in. h.; sep. oblong; pet. yellowish-green, minute. Summer. NW. America. 1830. (B.R. 1924.)

**H. erubes′cens.** A synonym of *H. micrantha*.

**H. glab′ra.** Tufted. *l.* heart-shaped, glabrous, lobes acute, teeth unequal, acute. *infl.* in a loose panicle, 12 to 18 in. h. *fl.* white, small. Summer. NW. America.

**H. his′pida.** Satin-leaf. *l.* roundish heart- or kidney-shaped, 5- to 9-lobed, lobes shallow, rounded, teeth broad, ciliate, tinged crimson in winter. *fl.* veined purple on pale brown, oblique; sep. spatulate, blunt, pet. spatulate, often shorter than sep., stamens about equal to sep. *infl.* 2 to 3 ft. h. Summer. Virginia, Carolina. 1826. (B.B. ed. 2, 2, 227.) SYN. *H. Richardsonii*.

**H. macrophyl′la.** A synonym of *Tiarella macrophylla* as a rule. The true plant is probably not in cultivation.

**H. micran′tha.** Basal *l.* roundish heart-shaped, bluntly lobed, crenate, almost glabrous, teeth horny. *infl.* a loose panicle about 2 ft. h., clammy-hairy. *fl.* very small, yellowish-white. Summer. Brit. Columbia to California. 1827. (B.R. 1302.) A parent of some good garden hybrids. var. **ro′sea**, scape slender, coral-red, hairy, *fl.* blush-white.

**H. pilosis′sima.** Stem short, plant covered with long, spreading, glandular hairs. *l.* ovate-heart-shaped, lobes blunt, toothed. *fl.* with linear pet., twice as long as cal. teeth. California.

**H. pubes′cens.** Tufted, downy as though covered with powder. *l.-lobes* rather acute, teeth mucronate. *fl.* rather large, crowded on the short branches of the panicle, pale red variegated with yellow; scape 9 to 12 in. h. E. United States. 1812. SYN. *H. ribifolia*. Evergreen, *l.* marbled bronzy-red in winter.

**H. ribifo′lia.** A synonym of *H. pubescens*.

**H. Richardson′ii.** A synonym of *H. hispida*.

**H. rubes′cens.** Tufted. *l.* kidney-shaped or roundish heart-shaped, glabrous or rarely slightly glandular, thick, often shining. *fl.* purplish-red; sep. oblong, blunt, rather shorter than spatulate pet., in an open panicle. W. United States, Oregon, southwards.

**H. sanguin'ea.*** Coral Bells. *l.* heart-shaped or roundish, 5- to 7-lobed; lobes toothed, ciliate; stalks with spreading hairs. *fl.* deep or bright red, somewhat bell-shaped, stamens shorter than sep.; panicle open, scape 9 to 18 in. h., hairy below, glandular above. June to September. N. Mexico, Arizona. 1882. (B.M. 6929; Gn. 26 (1884), 360.) Flower colour very variable, var. **al'ba,** *fl.* white; **atrosanguin'ea,** *fl.* dark red; **grandiflo'ra,** *fl.* larger, glowing coral-scarlet. SYN. *H. robusta*; **ro'sea,** *fl.* rose-red; **splen'dens,** *fl.* dark crimson. These are garden varieties and several others have been raised, giving a great range of colour. Hybrids have been raised with *Tiarella cordifolia*. Plants offered as **H. hy'brida** may be hybrids or sometimes seedlings of this species, sometimes, as **H. Zabelia'na,** much taller with pale pink long-stalked fl.

**H. villo'sa.** *l.* roundish heart-shaped, deeply 5- to 7-lobed, lobes broadly triangular, acute. *fl.* pinkish, small, in a loose panicle on scapes 1 to 3 ft. h., stem, and l.-stalks rusty-hairy; pet. spatulate-linear, about as long as stamens. August, September. N. America. 812. (B.B. ed. 2, 2, 226.)

**HEUCHEREL'LA.** FAM. *Saxifragaceae.* Hybrids between species of Heuchera and Tiarella, more or less intermediate between the 2 genera.

**H. × tiarelloi'des*** (*Heuchera × brizoides × Tiarella cordifolia*). Tufted perennial about 4 in. h., stoloniferous. *l.* more or less orbicular, with 7 shallow lobes, 3 to 4 in. long, crenate, ciliate, often mottled brown when young. *fl.* in a narrow panicle about 5 in. long, carmine, small, bell-shaped; peduncle up to 16 in. long, reddish, hairy. Summer. Of garden origin at Nancy. 1917. A white-fld. hybrid of similar parentage (but the Heuchera parent had white fl.) has also been introduced as var. **al'ba.** This is not stoloniferous, and the infl. is somewhat taller. 1925. Neither plant sets seed, and both are hardy and easily propagated by division.

***Heuffel'ii,*** in honour of the Hungarian botanist, Johann Heuffel, 1800–57, physician.

**HE'VEA** (*Heve*, native name in Brazil). FAM. *Euphorbiaceae.* A genus of about 18 species of S. American trees with milky juice. Leaves long-stalked, alternate, leaflets 3, entire, stalked. Flowers monoecious, in loose panicles, small; calyx 5-toothed; corolla absent; stamens 5 to 10 united into a column by their filaments; ovary 3-celled, ovules 1 in each cell. Seeds about 1 in. long. *H. brasiliensis* is very widely cultivated in damp tropical forests as a source of rubber, being one of the chief rubber-producing trees, and some other species, e.g. *H. guianensis* and *H. pauciflora*, are also sometimes cultivated for rubber. *H. brasiliensis* is usually raised from seed which must be sown as soon as ripe, but it may be raised from cuttings of half-ripe wood in heat. It grows in suitable conditions to its full height of 60 ft. in about 8 years and yields rubber from 6 years old for several years. In our stoves it needs sandy loam.

**H. brasilien'sis.** Para Rubber. Tree to 60 ft. *l.* light green. *fl.* greenish-white, finely downy. May. Brazil. 1823. (H.I.P. 2573, 2575.)

**HEWARD'IA.** Included in *Adiantum.*

**HEWIT'TIA** (in honour of Mr. Hewitt, who wrote in the *Madras Journal of Science*, 1837). FAM. *Convolvulaceae.* A genus of a single species widely spread in the tropics, with the characters set out below. Fruit a globose, dehiscent, 4-valved capsule, 1-celled, 4-seeded. Distinct from Calystegia by the bracts being shorter than the calyx. *H. bicolor* should be raised from seed sown in spring on a hotbed, potted singly in pots, and trained to sticks. It needs a warm greenhouse except in very warm and sheltered places.

**H. bi'color.** Twining herb. *l.* broadly cordate, angled or 3-lobed, entire. *fl.* white or pale yellowish with dark purple centre, 1 to 3 on an axillary peduncle; sep. acute, outer broad; cor. bell-shaped, limb 5-angled; pedicels short. 1812. (B.M. 2205 and B.R. 318 as *Convolvulus bicolor.*) SYN. *Palmia bicolor.*

***hexa-,*** in compound words, signifying 6, as *hexapetalus*, with 6 petals.

**HEXACEN'TRIS.** Included in **Thunbergia.** *See* **T. mysorensis.**

**HEXADES'MIA** (*hex*, six, *a*, without, *desmos*, a bond or thong; in allusion to the 6 separate pollen masses). FAM. *Orchidaceae.* A small genus of about 12 epiphytic, branched Orchids, natives of Mexico, Cent. America, the W. Indies, and Brazil, allied to Scaphyglottis. Flowers small, fascicled or racemose from apex of pseudobulbs. Leaves fleshy. Compost as for Odontoglossums. May be grown with Cattleyas throughout the year or in the cool house in summer.

**H. crurig'era.** *fl.* small, white, with a purple-tipped column; freely produced in racemes ¼ to ½ in. long. Tufted. *Pseudobulbs* fusiform, 1 to 3 in. long, diphyllous. *l.* fleshy, slender, pointed, 2 to 4 in. long. Costa Rica, Guatemala. 1843. (Ref. B. 92.)

**H. fascicula'ta.** *fl.* 1 to 5, about ½ in. across in a loose fascicle; sep. and pet. greenish, brown-flushed; lip broadly tongue-shaped, yellowish-white. *Pseudobulbs* clavate, compressed, slender below, 2 to 4 in. long or more, diphyllous. *l.* tongue-shaped, 2 to 4 in. long. Mexico.

**H. micran'tha.** Near *H. crurigera* in habit but racemes longer and fl. smaller with a green disk to lip. Costa Rica, Guatemala. 1884.

E. C.

**HEXAGLOT'TIS** (*hex*, six, *glotta*, tongue; from the 6 spreading lobes of style). FAM. *Iridaceae.* A genus of 2 or 3 species of herbs with a tunicated corm, natives of S. Africa. Leaves 1 or 2, linear, or nearly terete. Flowers yellow, 3 or 4 in cluster on a panicle with a few spicate branches; perianth segments free, nearly equal, twisting as they fade; filaments very short, flattened, connivent. Cultivation of these greenhouse plants as for Ixia.

**H. longifo'lia.** About 18 in. h. *fl.* yellow; segs. oblong, spreading; filaments united into a tube. May. 1766. (B.M. 695 as *Moraea flexuosa.*) SYN. *Homeria flexuosa.*

***hexag'onus -a -um,*** 6-angled.

**A→**

**HEXIS'IA** (*exisoein*, equal or alike; lip and sep. similar). FAM. *Orchidaceae.* A genus of 3 or 4 epiphytic orchids found from Brazil to Mexico. Flowers of medium size; sepals nearly equal, narrow, dorsal free, lateral produced in a very short chin, petals like dorsal sepal; lip erect, connate with column at base; lateral lobes obscure, mid-lobe lanceolate, spreading, equalling sepals; column short. Pollinia 4. Racemes terminal, few-flowered; peduncles short. Leaves narrow, rather stiff. The compost should be as for Odontoglossums and the plants in pans which can be suspended. Atmospheric moisture is required throughout the year. Winter night temperature 60° F.

**H. bidenta'ta.** *fl.* bright scarlet, about ½ in. across; sep. and pet. linear, acute; lip narrow-obovate-oblong; racemes short, arising from nodes. *l.* linear-oblong, not exceeding joints. Stem ascending or drooping, jointed, joints 1 to 2 in. long. Panama, Colombia. 1887. (B.M. 7031.)

**H. imbrica'ta.** Much like *H. bidentata* but with shorter joints and l. *fl.* scarlet. Brazil, Guiana. 1836. (Sert. Orch. 40 as *Diathonaea imbricata.*)

E. C.

***Hey'deri,*** in honour of Herr Heyder, 1808–84, a noted cultivator of Cacti in Berlin.

**HEYN'EA** (in honour of Dr. Heyn, German botanist). FAM. *Meliaceae.* A genus of 3 or 4 species of Indian or E. Indian trees and shrubs. Leaves odd-pinnate, leaflets opposite, entire. Flowers rather small in terminal or axillary panicles; calyx 4- or 5-toothed; petals 4 or 5, oblong, nearly erect; staminal tube 8- to 10-fid, lobes linear, 2-fid, with anthers between the linear teeth; ovary 2- or 3-celled, immersed in disk. Fruit a capsule, 1-seeded. Requires stove conditions.

**H. triju'ga.** Tree, sometimes large. *l.* 4 to 15 in. long; lflets. 5 to 11, 2 to 6½ in. long. *fl.* white in panicles nearly as long as l. Nepal. 1807. (B.M. 1738.)

***Heynea'nus -a -um,*** in honour of the botanist-missionary, Benjamin Heyne, who collected near Travancore in the early 19th century.

***hi'ans,*** gaping.

**HIBBERT'IA** (in honour of George Hibbert, a distinguished patron of botany, d. 1838). FAM. *Dilleniaceae*. A genus of about 70 species of evergreen shrubs, natives chiefly of Australia but represented also in Tasmania, New Caledonia, and Madagascar. Leaves alternate, sometimes heath-like. Flowers yellow or white, solitary, mostly terminal; sepals and petals 5, stamens indefinite, rarely under 12. The flowering season often extends over 2 or 3 months. All the species described below except *H. Baudouinii* require cool greenhouse conditions; several are grown out of doors in Cornwall and Scilly. *H. Baudouinii* is a stove plant. **A**

KEY
1. *Lvs. flat or nearly so* — 2
1. *Lvs. small, narrow with revolute margins* — H. pedunculata
2. *Lvs. not perfoliate* — 3
2. *Lvs. perfoliate* — H .perfoliata
3. *Plant more or less erect* — 4
3. *Plant trailing or climbing* — 7
4. *Shoots downy* — 5
4. *Shoots glabrous* — 6
5. *Stamens all on one side of carpels; lvs. minutely hairy beneath* — H. bracteata
5. *Stamens all round carpels; lvs. silky-hairy beneath* — H. montana
6. *Lvs. 6 to 12 in. long* — H. Baudouinii
6. *Lvs. 1 to 2 in. long* — H. Cunninghamii
7. *Lvs. 1½ to 2 in. across* — H. volubilis
7. *Lvs. 1 to 1½ in. across* — 8
8. *Lvs. 1½ to 3 in. long* — H. dentata
8. *Lvs. 1 to 1½ in. long* — H. grossulariifolia

**H. Baudouin'ii.** Small shrub, almost or quite glabrous. Stems erect, stout. *l.* clustered towards end of shoots, linear-lanceolate, 6 to 12 in. long, 1 to 1½ in. wide. *fl.* 1 to 1½ in. across in axillary erect spikes 6 to 9 in. h., scarcely stalked; sep. ciliate; pet. bright yellow. New Caledonia. 1873. (B.M. 6053.) Remarkable and beautiful species, probably not now in cultivation.

**H. bractea'ta.** Erect, much-branched undershrub; young shoots downy. *l.* narrow-oblong to oblanceolate, ½ to ⅞ in. long, 1/12 to 1/8 in. wide, shortly pointed, cuneate, minutely downy beneath. *fl.* yellow, ¾ in. wide, terminal on lateral twigs; sep. densely silky; pet. notched. May, June. New S. Wales. Hardy in Scilly.

**H. corifo'lia.** *See* **H. pedunculata.**

**H. crena'ta.** A synonym of *H. grossulariifolia*.

*Hibbertia Cunninghamii*

**H. Cunningham'ii.** Slender-stemmed, flexuose, glabrous shrub. *l.* linear, 1 to 2 in. long, 1/16 to ⅛ in. wide, pointed, base dilated and clasping the stem. *fl.* yellow, 1 to 1½ in. wide, borne on bracted, axillary stalks up to 1 in. long; sep. ¼ in. long; pet. obovate, slightly notched. Summer. W. Australia. (B.M. 3183.) SYN. *Candollea Cunninghamii*.

**H. denta'ta.** Shrub with trailing or twining stems, downy when young. *l.* 1½ to 3 in. long, ¾ to 1½ in. wide, ovate-oblong, sparsely toothed, base rounded. *fl.* 1 to 1½ in. across, bright yellow; pet. obovate, mucronate; sep. ½ in. long, ovate. Spring, summer. New S. Wales, Victoria. 1814. (B.M. 2338.)

**H. grossulariifo'lia.** Slender-stemmed, diffuse, trailing shrub. *l.* 1 to 1½ in. long, ½ to 1 in. wide, broadly ovate to oval, coarsely toothed, base truncate or rounded, apex blunt or rounded, downy beneath. *fl.* yellow, 1 in. across, solitary on slender downy sfalks up to 2 in. long; cal. silky-hairy; pet. obovate. Summer. W. Australia. 1816. (B.M. 1218.) SYN. *H. crenata*.

*Hibbertia dentata*

**H. monta'na.** Shrub of tufted habit, 1 to 1½ ft., shoots erect, slender, downy. *l.* ½ to 1 in. long, linear-oblong, cuneate, minutely pointed, silky-hairy beneath. *fl.* yellow, ¾ in. wide, stalkless, surrounded by 2 or 3 roundish bracts at base; pet. obovate, notched. W. Australia. Hardy in Scilly.

*Hibbertia grossulariifolia*

**H. peduncula'ta.** Diffusely branched, heath-like shrub, 2 ft. *l.* narrowly linear, blunt, ¼ to ½ in. long, densely arranged, margins revolute. *fl.* yellow, ¾ to 1 in. wide, on slender stalks up to 1 in. long; sep. ¼ to ½ in. long; pet. obovate, slightly notched. June. New S. Wales. (The form figured in B.M. 2672 as *H. corifolia* and in B.R. 1001 as *H. pedunculata*, Bentham distinguishes as var. **corifo'lia**, 'stems short, diffuse or prostrate'.)

**H. perfolia'ta.*** Quite glabrous, erect or sometimes rather trailing shrub. *l.* 1 to 2½ in. long, ½ to 1½ in. wide, ovate, base completely surrounding stem, often more or less toothed. *fl.* bright yellow, 1½ in. wide, on a stalk 1 to 2 in. long; sep. ⅓ to ½ in. long, lanceolate, pointed; pet. obovate. May. W. Australia. (B.R. 29, 64.)

**H. volu'bilis.*** Prostrate or twining shrub up to 4 ft., young shoots silky. *l.* 1½ to 4 in. long, ½ to 1½ in. wide, obovate to lanceolate, cuneate, glabrous above, silky-hairy beneath. *fl.* rich yellow, unpleasantly scented, 1½ to 2 in. across; sep. up to 1 in. long, pointed, silky-hairy; pet. obovate. Summer. New S. Wales, Queensland. 1790. (A.B.R. 126; B.M. 499 as *Dillenia speciosa*.)

W. J. B.

*Hibbertia volubilis*

**hibern'icus -a -um,** Irish.

**hibern'us -a -um,** winter-flowering or winter-green.

**HIBIS'CUS** (ancient Greek name used by Dioscorides for the Marsh Mallow). FAM. *Malvaceae*. A genus of about 150 species of herbs, shrubs, or trees, often roughly hairy with star-shaped hairs, rarely glabrous, natives of the tropics with a few in temperate regions. Leaves of various forms, often deeply divided, stipulate. Flowers usually large and showy mostly marked by a deeper colour at base. Filaments usually short and crowded along the greater part of the long staminal column. Bracteoles usually persistent, occasionally dropping very quickly. A few species of this large genus are hardy but most need a warm greenhouse or stove. The latter group succeed best either in large pots or planted out. A compost of peat and fibrous loam, not broken too small, in about equal parts with a little charcoal or sand suits them. The plants should be kept rather dry in winter and in spring should be lightly cut in and started in moist, brisk heat. Throughout the summer they need plenty of heat and water. Some species succeed in the greenhouse all the summer, but need a higher temperature than that provides in winter. They are propagated by seed and by cuttings in a close frame in spring. *H. Rosa-sinensis Cooperi*, grown for its foliage, needs the same treatment as other stove plants in winter. The hardy species grow best in sandy, deep rich soil, and need a warm position in a sunny place. *H. Trionum* is readily raised from seed. The shrubby species, *H. syriacus* may also be readily raised from seed sown in March in light soil with gentle heat. They are, however, usually raised from cuttings or layers since the named varieties do not come true. Mature wood of the current season is taken in early autumn, dibbled in sandy soil in pots plunged in warm bottom-heat and kept close when they root in about 14 days. These cuttings need shade from sun on bright days. Layers should be made at midsummer or at latest by early autumn. Grafting on seedling stocks in spring is also sometimes done.

**H. Abelmos'chus.** Annual or biennial, rough-hairy. *l.* of various form, palmately 5- to 7-lobed, lobes spreading, oblong-lanceolate, coarsely toothed; bracteoles 6 to 12, linear, ¾ in. long or less. *fl.* 4 in. across, yellow, centre crimson; cal. 15-toothed. Summer. *fr.* bristly. India. Grown for fl. and in tropics for the musk-scented seeds. Variable. Tender.

**H. africa'nus.** A synonym of *H. Trionum*.

**H. × Arch'eri** (*H. Rosa-sinensis × H. schizopetalus*). *fl.* red, much like those of *H. Rosa-sinensis*. (Gn. 55 (1899), 310.) Of garden origin.

**H. calyci'nus.** Shrub, stems slender, hairy. *l.* roundish, slightly 3-lobed, toothed. *fl.* large, bell-shaped, yellow with a purple base, broadly obovate. Natal. SYN. *H. chrysanthus*. Greenhouse.

**H. Camero'ni.** Shrub about 1 ft. h. *l.* heart-shaped, 5-lobed, coarsely toothed, lobes acute, narrowed at base. *fl.* rose; cal. large, inflated, 5-lobed; pet. obliquely wedge-shaped, truncate, crimson blotched at base. Madagascar. (B.M. 3936.) Stove.

**H. cannabi'nus.** Annual or perennial, glabrous, prickly. *Lower l.* heart-shaped, not lobed; *upper* deeply palmately lobed, lobes narrow, toothed. *fl.* large, yellow with crimson centre, on short, axillary peduncles; sep. lanceolate, bristly, glandular; cor. spreading. *fr.* bristly. Old World. Grown for its fibre, a form of jute.

**H. coccin'eus.** Perennial herb, 4 to 8 ft. h. *l.* 5-lobed, lobes lanceolate, remotely toothed, tips entire; stalks long. *fl.* 5 to 6 in. across, rose-red; column of stamens very long. July, August. Marshes of Florida and Georgia. (B.M. 360 as *H. speciosus*.) Greenhouse.

**H. diversifo'lius.** Tall, rigid, herbaceous perennial, stiffly hairy with prickly branches and l.-stalks. *l.* broad-heart-shaped or nearly orbicular, angular or 5-lobed, lobes shallow, toothed. *fl.* in axillary or terminal racemes, primrose-yellow with dark red centre; sep. linear-lanceolate, bristly; cor. larger than cal. Tropics. (B.R. 381.) Tender. May be grown as an annual.

**H. esculen'tus.** Gombo, Okra. Annual, 2 to 3 ft. h. *l.* heart-shaped, 3- to 5-lobed; lobes oblong, toothed; stalks 6 in. long, bristly. *fl.* yellow with crimson centre, axillary, solitary, peduncle 1 in. long. Summer. *fr.* 6 to 10 in. long, smooth, edible, used in cookery. Tropics. Half-hardy. var. **specio'sus,** sulphur-yellow with large blood-red blotch at base. (G.F. 1894, 623.)

**H. Hama'bo.** Shrub 6 to 10 ft. h., hairy. *l.* roundish, abruptly pointed, with irregular shallow teeth, white tomentose beneath, green- or grey-hairy above. *fl.* 3 in. across, yellow with darker base, solitary in axils of upper l. Japan.

**H. heterophyl'lus.** Shrub of 6 ft. h. with prickly branches. *l.* entire or deeply 3-lobed, lanceolate or elliptic-oblong, 5 to 6 in. long, usually toothed, sometimes white beneath. *fl.* white with a purple centre, 3 to 4 in. long, on short peduncles in the upper axils. Australia. 1803. (B.R. 29; Gn. 2 (1885), 478 as *H. grandiflorus*.)

**H. Huegel'ii.** Erect, stellately hairy shrub. *l.* heart-shaped, 3- to 5-lobed, lobes obovate, obtuse, deeply sinuate; stalked. *fl.* rose, solitary; involucel 10- to 12-lobed, lobes subulate; cal.-teeth lanceolate, style exserted; stigma 5-fid. Australia. var. **quinquevul'nera.** *fl.* rose with 5 dark red spots at base. (B.M. 5406.)

**H. lavateroi'des.** Stellately hairy annual, 1 to 2 ft. h., little branched. *l.* ovate-deltoid, acute, base cordate, toothed, about 2½ in. long; stalked. *fl.* purple with rose suffusion, hairy without, about 1½ in. across; involucel 10-leaved; peduncle 1-fld., solitary. Mexico.

**H. Man'ihot.** Perennial. Stout up to 9 ft. h. *l.* palmately deeply 5- to 7-lobed, often 1 ft. long, lobes linear, slender-pointed, coarsely toothed. *fl.* 6 to 7 in. across, sulphur-yellow with purple centre; pet. roundish, abruptly narrowed at base. Summer, autumn. China, Japan. 1715. (B.M. 1702, 3152, 7752; Gn. 53 (1898), 127.) Best grown as an annual, seed being sown in heat early. Greenhouse. var. **dissec'tus,** *l.* cut nearly to stalk. A

**H. milita'ris.*** Perennial herb, 2 to 4 ft. h. *l.* heart-shaped, toothed, somewhat 3-lobed, downy beneath. *fl.* 3 to 5 in. across, rose, or whitish, on axillary, jointed, 1-fld. pedicels. Summer. SE. United States. (B.M. 2385.) Hardy.

**H. Moscheu'tos.** Swamp Rose-Mallow. Vigorous perennial, 3 ft. or more h. Stem hairy. *l.* ovate, slender-pointed, toothed, softly hairy beneath, glabrous above in age. *fl.* 4 to 8 in. across, light rose, l.-stalk and peduncle often joined; bracteoles and cal. downy. Summer. *fr.* globose-ovoid, glabrous. E. United States. (B.M. 882 as *H. palustris*; B.R. 1463.) Hardy. var. **ro'seus,** *fl.* rose. Naturalized in France. *See* **H. oculiroseus.**

**H. muta'bilis.** Small tree without prickles. *l.* 5-angled, 4 in. across, heart-shaped, toothed, downy. *fl.* white or pink on opening in morning, becoming deep red by night, 3 to 4 in. across, on axillary peduncles 4 to 5 in. long. China. 1690. (B.R. 589.) A double-fld. form is known.

**H. oculiro'seus.** Resembles *H. Moscheutos* but *fl.* white with dark red centre, fr. ovoid-comic, pointed. E. United States. Hardy. (Add. 88.)

**H. palus'tris.** A synonym of *H. Moscheutos*.

**H. radia'tus.** Shrub with prickly branches. *l.* palmate, or rarely not lobed, lobes 3 to 5, broadly lanceolate; stalk prickly, as long as blade. *fl.* solitary in l.-axile, on short peduncles, very large, yellow with large deep crimson centre. Summer. India, Java. Stove. var. **Lind'leyi,** *fl.* deep purple. (B.R. 1395 as *H. Lindleyi*); **fl.-ru'bro,** *fl.* rose-purple. (B.M. 5098.)

**H. Rosa-sinen'sis.*** Shrub up to 8 ft. h., glabrous. (A tree in sub-tropics.) *l.* ovate, narrowed to tip, coarsely toothed in upper part; bracteoles linear, free, as long as cal., usually 7. *fl.* 4 to 5 in. across, typically bright rose-red with a projecting red staminal column, but very variable in colouring and with single, semi-double, or wholly double fls. in cultivation. Summer. China, &c. (B.M. 158.) Stove or greenhouse. A large number of varieties have been offered, among them var. **Coo'peri** with vivid green l. splashed and blotched with dark olive-green, creamy-white, and crimson with a feathery reddish-carmine margin.

*Hibiscus Rosa-sinensis*

**H. ro'seus.** A variety of *H. Moscheutos.*

**H. Sabdarif'fa.** Jamaica Sorrel; Roselle. Nearly glabrous annual with reddish stems 5 to 7 ft. h. *Basal l.* ovate, not lobed; *upper* digitately 3-lobed; stalks long; lobes lanceolate-oblong, toothed and sometimes lobed. *fl.* solitary, almost sessile in l.-axils; cal. and bracts, fleshy, red; pet. yellow. Tropics of Old World. The fleshy cal. is cooked, making a jelly with cranberry flavour. Tender.

**H. schizopet'alus.*** Glabrous shrub with slender drooping branches. *l.* ovate-elliptic, toothed; bracteoles minute. *fl.* brilliant orange-red, pendulous on slender, long-jointed peduncles; pet. deeply cut; staminal column slender projecting about 2 in. beyond cor. E. Trop. Africa. (B.M. 6524.) Stove.

**H. Scot'tii.** Shrub or small tree. *l.* ovate, entire, 3-lobed, or toothed. *fl.* 3½ in. across, bright golden-yellow with carmine eye. Socotra. (B.M. 7816.)

**H. syri'acus.*** Deciduous shrub about 6 ft. h. or more, much-branched, glabrous or nearly so. *l.* triangular- or rhomboid-ovate, rather small; lower ones mostly 3-lobed, with rounded teeth; bracteoles 6 or 7, linear. *fl.* about 3 in. across, bell-shaped, solitary in axils of l. of young shoots, on short peduncles, very variable in colour. Late summer. Syria, &c. 1596. (B.M. 83 as *Althaea fruticosa.*) Hardy. Many varieties have been offered with flowers white to very deep purple and single, semi-double, or double. Lateral shoots closely spurred in on Continent but rarely pruned in England. A selection of varieties will be found in the Supplement.

**H. tilia'ceus.** Shrub or small tree. *l.* roundish heart-shaped with a short point, scarcely toothed, white-hairy beneath; bracteoles 10, persisting. *fl.* yellow, 2 to 3 in. long. Tropics. (B.R. 232.) Stove.

**H. Trio'num.*** Bladder Ketmia. Bushy annual, 12 to 24 in. h., usually hispid. *l.* 3- to 5-parted, mid-lobe much largest, lobes linear, coarsely notched; radical l. not lobed. *fl.* yellow or white with brown-purple centre; cal. becoming inflated in fr. Summer. Tropics of Old World. (B.M. 209.) Syn. *H. africanus.* Half-hardy.

**H. venus'tus.** Tall shrub. *l.* orbicular, about 17 in. across, lobed. *fl.* cream, about 3 in. across. Tahiti. 1891. (B.M. 7183.) Stove.

**H. Waim'eae.** Tree to 25 ft. with slender grey twigs with pro-minent l.-scars, at first dull purple and hairy. *l.* wide elliptic-ovate or roundish, 3½ to 8 in. long, blunt, toothed, glabrous above, downy with purplish veins beneath; stalk 1½ to 4 in. long. *fl.* solitary in

upper axils, white, limb spreading; segs. about 4½ in. long; cal. tubular, 1¼ to 1½ in. long, split on one side, lobes triangular; staminal tube over 6 in. long, red, like the free spreading filaments, in upper part; involucral bracts 6 to 8, reflexed, linear-awl-shaped. Autumn. Hawaiian Is. 1911. (B.M. 8547.)

**HICKORY.** *See* **Carya.**

**HICKORY PINE.** *See* **Pinus aristata.**

**HIDAL'GOA** (in honour of Senor Hidalgo, a Mexican naturalist). FAM. *Compositae.* A genus of 3 species of herbs or sub-shrubs, natives of Brazil and Costa Rica, related to Dahlia but differing in habit, in the large achenes of the ray-florets, and in the sterile disk-florets which have entire or very shortly 2-lobed styles. *H. Wercklei* needs greenhouse treatment and should be grown as a perennial. It needs ordinary soil and climbs by means of long leaf-stalks which twist round objects of support.

*Hidalgoa Wercklei*

**H. Werck'lei.** Climbing. *l.* opposite, broadly ovate, pinnately ternatisect, 1½ to 2½ in. long, teeth tipped reddish-brown. *fl.-heads* solitary, 2½ in. across; ray-florets about 10, bright scarlet above, dirty yellow beneath, 3-toothed, spreading, oblong; disk yellow; peduncles solitary in l.-axils. Costa Rica. 1898. (B.M. 7684.) SYN. *Childsia Wercklei.*

*hiema'lis, -is -e,* of the winter, usually indicating plants flowering in winter.

*hieraciifo'lius -a -um,* with Hieracium-like leaves.

**HIERAC'IUM** (name used by the Greek Dioscorides for another plant). FAM. *Compositae.* Hawkweed. A genus of perennial herbs, natives of Europe and N. Africa with a few in America. The number of species is vari-ously computed by different botanists, the genus occupy-ing several volumes in some floras but few of the species are of horticultural value, and some, if introduced into the garden, multiply fast and spread far by their para-chuted fruits and become an ineradicable nuisance. Leaves entire or toothed. Flower-heads yellow or rarely orange-red; all florets ligulate; involucral bracts more or less overlapping. Some British species are ornamental on old walls. Propagated by division in spring or by seeds. Hardy.

**H. alpi′num.** *l.* oblong to lanceolate, slightly toothed. *fl.-heads* solitary, bright yellow, on stems about 6 in. h. with 1 or 3 small narrow l. Mts. of Europe, N. Asia.

**H. auranti′acum.** *l.* elliptical, entire, acute, hairy. *fl.-heads* orange to orange-red, ½ to 1 in. across, short-stalked, in a terminal corymb of 8 to 10, on a stem 12 to 18 in. h. June to September. Europe, naturalized in Britain. (E.B. 823.) Of striking colour but apt to become a weed.

**H. bombyci′num.** Perennial. Stem ascending, up to 15 in. h. *l.* elliptical, narrowed to a winged stalk. *fl.-heads* large, 1 or 3; involucral bracts hairy. Spring. Cent. Spain. Rock-garden.

**H. macula′tum.** *l.* ovate-lanceolate, strongly toothed, hairy, spotted with black. *fl.-heads* yellow, in cymes on a branched, many-lvd. stem 18 in. h.; florets toothed. Summer, autumn. (E.B. 849.)

**H. marmor′eum.** Perennial, about 12 in. h., more or less grey-hairy, leafy, branched above. *l.* 10 to 14, green, toothed, rough above; lower oblong-oval, large, more or less stalked, upper much shorter, broadly cordate at base. *fl.-heads* 1 or 2 on each branch. July, August. Serbia, Bulgaria. Probably a hybrid, *H. umbellatum* × *H. pannosum* × *H. racemosum*. Rock-garden.

**H. Pilosel′la.** Mouse-ear Hawkweed. Wide mat-forming. *l.* oblong to lanceolate, entire, narrowed to base, often stalked, grey-hairy. *fl.-heads* solitary on short peduncles, lemon, often tinged red without; involucral bracts and peduncles near top closely white downy with short, spreading black hairs. Europe including Britain, Asia, N. Africa. (E.B. 822.) A pest on lawns.

**H. villo′sum.*** Spreading. *l.* oblong, silvery glaucous, shaggy, scarcely toothed; upper ovate or oblong-ovate, semi-stem-clasping. *fl.-heads* 1½ to 2 in. across, bright yellow, on leafy stems about 1 ft. h. June to August. Cent. Europe. (E.B. 839.)

*Hiern′ii,* in honour of W. P. Hiern, 1839–1925, British botanist.

**HIEROCH′LOE** (*hieros,* sacred, *chloa,* grass; in N. Europe these grasses are strewn before church doors on saints′ days). Fam. *Gramineae.* A genus of about 13 species of grasses, natives of the temperate and arctic regions. Related to Anthoxanthum but with staminate (not sterile) lateral florets and rather spreading (not contracted) panicles, and, like that, containing cumarin and smelling like new-mown hay, more powerfully, however, in *H. odorata* and *H. redolens* than in *Anthoxanthum odoratum.* Leaf blades flat; panicles terminal; spikelets with one perfect terminal and 2 lateral staminate florets, usually shining brown. Hardy grasses growing freely in damp spots and propagated by seed or division.

**H. alpi′na.** About 1 ft. h. *Lower l.* very narrow. *Panicle* 1 to 2 in. long, one lateral floret scarcely, or only short-awned, the other long-awned from middle. July. Alpine mountain tops in N. Hemisphere. 1827.

**H. borea′lis.** A synonym of *H. odorata.*

**H. odora′ta.** Holy Grass. Vanilla Grass. Strongly fragrant. Root-stock creeping. Slender, 1 to 2 ft. h., smooth. *l.* short lanceolate. *Panicle* 2 to 5 in. long, somewhat 1-sided; spikelets chestnut; staminate florets ciliate, lower palea bristle-pointed at or near tip. June, July. Europe, including Britain, N. America. (E.B. 1695 as *H. borealis.*)

**H. redo′lens.** Strongly scented. Densely tufted, 2 to 3 ft. h. *l.* sometimes slightly scabrid. *Panicle* 6 to 10 in. long, nodding; branches capillary, slightly hairy, lower 2 to 3 in. long. Tasmania, &c. 1882.

*Hieronymia′nus -a -um,* in honour of Georg Hieronymus, 1846–1921, student of the Argentine flora.

*hierren′sis -is -e,* from Hierro, in Canary Is.

*Higgins′iae,* in honour of Mrs. Vera Higgins, editor of Cactus Journal of England, &c.

*Hildebrand′ii,* in honour of Mr. H. H. Hildebrand, who collected plants in India and Shan States.

*Hildebrandt′ii,* in honour of Mr. J. M. Hildebrandt, who collected on the east coast of Trop. Africa, *c.* 1872–7.

**HILL GOOSEBERRY.** *See* **Rhodomyrtus tomentosa.**

**HILLEBRAND′IA** (in honour of Dr. William Hillebrand, author of a Flora of Hawaii and discoverer of the plant). Fam. *Begoniaceae.* A genus of a single species of tall, branched, succulent herb, clothed everywhere with long reddish hairs, native of the Sandwich Is., differing from Begonia in the ovary being free in the upper part and bearing petaloid organs in the female flowers. Flower showy, in a stalked corymb, monoecious; petals 5; stamens many; styles 5, fleshy. Capsule not winged, opening at top. Treatment as for stove species of Begonia.

**H. sandwicen′sis.** Rootstock tuberous. Stem 3 to 4 ft. h. *l.* 4 to 8 in. long and wide, obliquely rounded, deeply heart-shaped at base, sinus very narrow, basal lobes overlapping. *fl.* white, tinged rose or rose, about ½ in. across; peduncles 6 to 12 in. long. May. 1886. (B.M. 6953.)

**HIL′LIA** (in honour of Sir John Hill, 1716–75, botanical writer). Fam. *Rubiaceae.* A genus of 10 ornamental evergreen shrubs, some of which are epiphytic, natives of Trop. America and the W. Indies. Branches smooth, often rooting. Leaves opposite, fleshy, short-stalked, stipules intrapetiolar, thin, caducous. Flowers white, fragrant, large, solitary at ends of branches; calyx usually falling; stamens of equal length. The 2 species mentioned grow up the mossy trunks of trees and require stove conditions.

**H. longiflo′ra.** Shrub of 2 ft. *l.* ovate. *fl.* white, very fragrant; cor. tube long, segs. 6, twisted. February. W. Indies, &c. 1789. (B.M. 721.) Syn. *H. parasitica.*

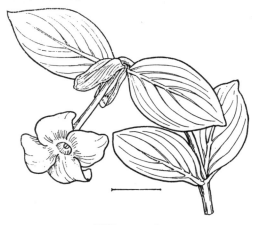

*Hillia tetrandra*

**H. tetran′dra.** Shrub of 3 to 4 ft., roots bearing small tubers. *l.* obovate to spatulate-lanceolate, 1½ to 2 in. long, wedge-shaped at base, rounded at apex, midrib thickened in lower half, abruptly slender above; sessile. *fl.* white, fragrant; cor. tube 1 to 1½ in. long, lobes roundish-obovate, ¼ to ⅓ as long as tube. June. Jamaica. 1793. (B.M. 7355.)

**HILUM.** Scar left on the seed where it was joined to the fruit.

*himala′icus -a -um, himalayen′sis -is -e,* of the district of the Himalaya, N. India.

**HIMANTOGLOS′SUM** (*himas,* strap, *glossa,* tongue; from the length of the petals). Fam. *Orchidaceae.* A small genus closely allied to Orchis and sometimes included therein but distinct by the lip twisted spirally in the bud, spur very short and pollen glands connate. For treatment *see* **Orchis.**

**H. hirci′num.** Lizard Orchis. Tubers ovoid. *l.* mostly radical, oblong, obtuse. Stem 1 to 5 ft. h., erect. *fl.* large, strongly scented of goats; sep. and pet. forming a green hood about ⅓ in. long; lip white, spotted purple at base, 1½ in. long, side lobes slender, mid-lobe about 1 in. long, ⅛ in. wide, green; spike 6 to 17 in. long; bracts 1 to 2 in. long. July, August. Middle Europe (rare in Britain), N. Africa. Syn. *Orchis hircina, Aceras hircina, Loroglossum hircinum.*

**H. longibractea′tum.** Sep. and pet. green, obtuse, lateral sep. spotted brown; lip fleshy, 4-lobed, lilac to purple-blue, crisped at base, 4 times as long as the thick conical spur, lobes obtuse, crenate; bracts longer than fl.; spike long, many-fld. May. *l.* oblong, narrowed at base. N. Mediterranean. 1818. (B.R. 357.) Syn. *Aceras longibracteata, Orchis longibracteata.*

E. C.

**HINAU.** *See* **Elaeocarpus dentatus.**

**HINDS'IA** (in honour of R. Brinsley Hinds, botanist on the Sulphur Expedition, 1836–42). FAM. *Rubiaceae.* A genus of 3 erect evergreen sub-shrubs, natives of Brazil, which have sometimes been included in Rondeletia. Leaves ovate or ovate-lanceolate, stalked. Flowers rather large, violaceous, in terminal cymes, with short bracteolate pedicels; corolla more funnel-shaped than in Rondeletia, with a beard in the mouth of the tube. For cultivation *see* **Rondeletia.**

*Hindsia longiflora*

**H. longiflor'a.** Shrub of 2 ft. *l.* ovate-lanceolate, coarsely hairy beneath. *fl.* blue, sometimes white; panicle leafy, its branches 3-fld. May. 1841. (B.M. 3977 as *Rondeletia longiflora*.)

*Hindsia violacea*

**H. viola'cea.** Downy shrub of 3 ft. *l.* broad-ovate. *fl.* ultramarine in clusters. May. 1844. (B.R. 30, 40.)

**HIP.** Fruit of the Rose.

**HIPPEAS'TRUM** (*hippeus*, a knight, *astron*, a star; application not evident). FAM. *Amaryllidaceae.* A genus of about 75 species of S. American bulbous plants, closely related to Amaryllis, Habranthus, Pyrolirion, and Zephyranthes. Bulb tunicated. Leaves linear or strap-shaped. Flowers declinate, funnel-shaped, segments of 4 different sizes, stamens clustered, of 4 different lengths; spathes of 2 equal and opposite simple valves free of one another to the base; peduncle 2- to several-fld., rarely only 1, each with a bract below it. Fruit a 3-celled capsule. Often placed under Amaryllis.

Few plants are more gorgeous in winter and spring than some of the species of Hippeastrum and the numerous hybrids that have been obtained by crossing them, some having flowers of the richest deep crimson, blood red, or orange scarlet, while in the latest developments there are whites and pinks. Species and hybrids have been crossed and intercrossed until variety of colouring, striping, mottling, and blending, breadth of petal, size, substance, and perfect form have been attained far beyond the expectations of the most sanguine of the original hybridizers. When once established and of sufficient size, the flowering of the bulbs annually is almost certain; and they do not require much space, nor does their general cultivation call for extraordinary skill. Propagation is readily effected by seeds for the raising of new varieties, and this method is also largely used for raising plants for ordinary decoration. Particular varieties are increased by means of the offsets that spring from the base of established bulbs.

In cross-pollinating for seed, care should be taken to keep the different colours pure, for this seems to give the best results. Thus crimson should be crossed with crimson, and the same rule followed with other colours. Plants intended to produce seed should be stood apart from the others and their anthers should be removed before they open to shed the pollen.

Seeds should be sown in well-drained pans as soon as ripe, using a light compost and covering the seeds lightly. In a temperature of 60 to 65° F. the seed soon germinates, and when large enough to handle the seedlings should be pricked off into 6-in. pots, about 10 in a pot. Plunged in a bed with bottom heat of about 70° F. and with a moist air and temperature of 60 to 65° F., they will make rapid progress. When large numbers are being raised pans or boxes should be used instead of pots for the young seedlings. When the leaves are about 6 in. long the seedlings should be potted into 4-in. pots in which they can be flowered for the first time. They should be plunged up to the rim in a hotbed well up to the roof-glass. If large numbers are being grown, they may be planted out in a bed with bottom heat instead of being potted singly; this will minimize the attention they will require. In 12 months they should be lifted and placed in 4- or 5-in. pots, using a compost of 3 parts of good medium loam that has been stacked for a year to 1 of well-decayed leaf-soil or peat with enough clean sand to keep the whole open, and a 5-in. potful of bone-meal to each bushel of the compost. After potting they should be plunged to the rim in a bed or stood on the bench with a moist bottom, well up to the roof-glass. It is very important to give water sparingly at the root until the plants have made a quantity of fresh roots, and this applies to their treatment whenever they are repotted. When the pots are well filled with roots, the plants enjoy ample supplies of water and should be fed twice a week with dilute liquid manure or clear soot-water, alternating with some good mixed fertilizer.

Hippeastrums are more or less evergreen, though for convenience flowering bulbs are dried off and rested every year; but young seedlings should never be dried off until they have reached flowering size, though in the winter they will need less water at the root. When the weather is suitable they should be syringed twice a day with soft water, getting well beneath the leaves. With good cultivation a few of the strongest should flower in the second year, and the bulk of them in the third year from the sowing of the seed.

Any specially good seedling can be increased by means of offsets. This is best done when the old bulbs are being repotted, but they should on no account be taken off unless they part readily from the parent bulb. Care should be taken to injure the roots as little as possible. The offsets should be put into suitable pots, working the compost very carefully between the roots, and very little water should be given until they have well rooted. This method is not greatly used now since in good strains the seedlings come very true to colour.

With a large collection Hippeastrums may be had in flower for several months. If wanted to flower early in the year the first batch should be started about the middle of December in a temperature of 55 to 60° F., plunging the pots to the rim in a plunge bed with a bottom heat of about 70 to 75° F. For early flowering, plants should be chosen that do not need repotting, and it is important to select from those that were started early in the previous season: as they finished their growth early they are naturally in better condition to respond to early forcing. The plants should be examined for faulty drainage, replacing some of the top soil with fresh compost. The bulk of the collection should be overhauled in January and February, repotting such as require it and top-dressing the remainder. When repotting all dead roots and decayed parts at the base of the bulb should be removed, and the bulbs should be examined for mealy bugs which harbour under the loose outer scales, washing them if necessary in a solution of soft soap and water. Pots from 4 to 7 or even 8 in. should be used, according to the size of the bulbs. The soil should be worked carefully among the roots and pressed firmly about the bulb, using the fingers, not a rammer, for the purpose. When finished about half the bulb should be covered. The pots should then be plunged up to the rims in a bed of peat fibre, with a bottom heat of 70 to 75° F. at command. The temperature of the house to begin with should be not more than 55 to 60° F. No water should be given for at least a fortnight after repotting, and then very sparingly until a quantity of new roots has been formed. Plants that have not been repotted should show the flower-spike (along with foliage) in about 3 weeks from being started, and then the temperature may be raised 5°. Generally a minimum of 60° F., rising with sunheat to 65 or 70° F., will suit them throughout the growing season. When in flower they may be removed to a warm greenhouse or conservatory, where, in cooler and more airy conditions, the flowers will last much longer.

After flowering the plants should be returned to the growing house and from then onwards should have every attention as regards watering and feeding to ensure good bulbs for the next season. A moist growing atmosphere must be maintained, and the foliage should be syringed twice a day, once before air is put on in the morning, and again when the house is shut up in the afternoon. Light shading should be given during the hottest part of the day.

When no more leaves are developed growth may be regarded as having finished and water should be gradually withheld and ventilation increased both day and night, having regard to the weather, of course. With the bulk of the plants this stage will be reached in September, though with those started early in the year it may be reached before that. During the rest-period the bulbs are best stored in their pots in any dry warm building where the temperature does not fall below 40° F. If a house is devoted to them alone they may be left in it during the rest period.

Though special conditions are necessary to obtain the best results, it is still possible to grow Hippeastrums in an ordinary greenhouse, where, of course, growth is much slower, and flowers cannot be had so early in the season.

All inferior seedlings should be marked during the flowering season and thrown away.

The only important disease of Hippeastrums, as well as of Amaryllis, is the virus known as *Spotted Wilt*. The symptoms appear on the leaves as pale yellow or whitish spots which may coalesce and form large patches so that the leaves yellow and die. There may also be reddish streaks which run along the leaf edges and kill them. Control largely depends on keeping down insects and destroying affected plants as soon as they are seen to be infected. *See* **Tomato Spotted Wilt.**

Hippeastrums are very subject to attacks of thrips, red spider mites, and mealy bugs. The former two are usually due to wrong cultural conditions, dry atmospheric conditions favouring both these pests. They can, to a great extent, be prevented by maintaining a moist atmosphere, and by regular syringing. Thrips can also be controlled by frequent light fumigations with nicotine. In bad attacks it may be necessary to sponge the leaves and check red spider mites by using a sulphur vaporizer. Mealy bug is a much more serious pest and if not promptly and constantly dealt with will soon ruin a collection. They can be controlled by sponging and carefully cleaning the bulbs during the rest-period. Where a collection is free from this pest great care should be taken not to introduce it with plants from an outside source. Bulb mite is sometimes troublesome due to wrong cultural conditions. If it occurs the bulbs should be carefully washed and repotted in fresh compost. Basal rot may also occur; the cause of this is somewhat obscure, but is probably caused by over-watering and faulty drainage.

**J. C.**

KEY

| | |
|---|---|
| 1. *Lvs. linear* | 2 |
| 1. *Lvs. lorate* | 9 |
| 2. *Fls. openly funnel-shaped* | 3 |
| 2. *Fls. narrowly funnel-shaped* | 8 |
| 3. *Stigma trifid* | 4 |
| 3. *Stigma capitate; umbel 3- or 4-fld.* | H. pratense |
| 4. *Umbels 2-fld.* | 5 |
| 4. *Umbels 3- to 6-fld.* | 6 |
| 5. *Fls. yellow* | H. Elwesii |
| 5. *Fls. rose* | H. roseum |
| 6. *Fls. yellow or red* | 7 |
| 6. *Fls. bright red; erect; segs.* $\frac{1}{4}$ *in. wide* | H. bifidum |
| 7. *Fls. yellow, tinged red, erect; segs.* $\frac{1}{2}$ *in. wide* | H. Bagnoldi |
| 7. *Fls. red, ascending or horizontal; segs.* $\frac{1}{4}$ *in. wide* | H. advenum |
| 8. *Fls. ascending, 2 in. or more long; scape 12 to 18 in. long* | H. bicolor |
| 8. *Fls. erect,* $1\frac{1}{2}$ *to 2 in. long; scape 6 to 12 in. long* | H. phycelloides |
| 9. *Perianth tube long* | 10 |
| 9. *Perianth tube short* | 11 |
| 10. *Fls. sulphur or cream* | H. solandriflorum |
| 10. *Fls. white, tinged yellow in throat* | H. candidum |
| 11. *Perianth closed with a distinct neck at throat* | 12 |
| 11. *Perianth not closed in at throat* | 18 |
| 12. *Stigma trifid* | 13 |
| 12. *Stigma capitate* | 17 |
| 13. *Fls. pale yellow, netted green; tube about* $\frac{3}{4}$ *in. long* | H. calyptratum |
| 13. *Fls. crimson, striped or not with green or yellow* | 14 |
| 14. *Fls. striped or rayed* | 15 |
| 14. *Fls. not striped* | 16 |
| 15. *Fls. red with yellow rays* | H. organense |
| 15. *Fls. striped green and yellow* | H. psittacinum |
| 16. *Fls. crimson with a green base and blotch of deep purple above the green* | H. aulicum |
| 16. *Fls. dull crimson, base green, unspotted* | H. Forgetii |
| 17. *Fls. cream, dotted all over with crimson; scape 2-fld.* | H. pardinum |
| 17. *Fls. red below, greenish above; scape 4-fld.* | H. Cybister |
| 18. *Stigma capitate* | 19 |
| 18. *Stigma trifid* | 26 |
| 19. *Perianth tube very short* | 20 |
| 19. *Perianth tube* $\frac{1}{2}$ *to 1 in. long* | 24 |
| 20. *Fls. mainly red* | 21 |
| 20. *Fls. lilac; segs. narrow; scape 4- to 12-fld.* | H. procerum |
| 21. *Fls. not striped* | 22 |
| 21. *Fls. pale red with dark red stripes* | H. Andreanum |

22. *Fls. red, white or whitish at base, large* — 23
22. *Fls. red, bell-shaped, rather small* — H. miniatum
23. *Fls. bright red with large white star at base* — H. Reginae
23. *Fls. bright red, greenish-white at base; segs. tipped white* — H. Leopoldii
24. *Lvs. bright green, reddish or purplish at base* — 25
24. *Lvs. dark green with ivory-white midrib. Fls. about 3 in. across* — H. reticulatum
25. *Fls. 4 in. across; tube $\frac{1}{2}$ in. long, pale brownish-pink; style exserted* — H. stylosum
25. *Fls. 4 to 5 in. across; tube 1 in. long, colour variable* — H. equestre
26. *Lvs. 6 to 8* — 27
26. *Lvs. 2; fls. white, with double broad red streak in middle of segs.* — H. breviflorum
27. *Fls. whitish with double red streaks; tube about 1 in. long* — H. vittatum
27. *Fl.-segs. keeled green; base green; colour variable* — H. rutilum

**H.×Ackermann'ii.** A hybrid near *H. aulicum.*

**H. adve'num.** Bulb $1\frac{1}{2}$ in. thick. *l.* linear, 1 ft. long, glaucous green. *fl.* yellow or red, horizontal or ascending, $1\frac{1}{2}$ to 2 in. long; segs. $\frac{1}{4}$ in. broad; umbel 2- to 6-fld. Winter. Chile. (B.M. 1125 and B.R. 849 as *Amaryllis advena.*) SYN. *Habranthus hesperius.*

**H. Albert'i.** A variety of *H. Reginae* with double fl.

**H. ambig'uum.** A variety of *H. solandriflorum.*

**H. Andrea'num.** *l.* lorate, after fl. *fl.* pale red with dark red stripes; 4 in. long with short tube; spathe pink; umbel 4- to 6-fld.; scape 1 to $1\frac{1}{2}$ ft. long. Colombia. 1876. SYN. *Amaryllis Andreana.*

**H. au'licum.*** *l.* broad strap-shaped, not glaucous, closely striate, rather obtuse; with fl. *fl.* large, 5 to 6 in. long, rich crimson, green at base with a dark blotch of deep purple above the green; segs. slender-pointed, striate; scape 1 to $1\frac{1}{2}$ ft. long, rounded, glabrous, usually 2-fld. Brazil, Paraguay. (B.M. 2983, 3311 as *Amaryllis aulica.*) var. **platypet'alum,** more robust with broader perianth segs. (B.R. 1038.)

**H. Bagnol'di.** Bulb 2 in. thick, tunic nearly black. *l.* linear, glaucous, 12 in. long. *fl.* yellow, tinged red, erect or nearly so, $1\frac{1}{2}$ to 2 in. long; tube very short; segs. $\frac{1}{2}$ in. wide; umbel 4- to 6-fld.; scape 1 ft. long. Argentina, Chile. (B.R. 1396 as *Habranthus Bagnoldi.*) var. **puncta'tum** has drooping fl., tube green, segs. milky-white with numerous small red dots, revolute at tips. Chile. 1885. (G.F. 1163, f. 3 as *Habranthus punctatus.*)

**H. bi'color.** Bulb globose, 2 in. across. *l.* about 4, with fl., linear-obtuse, $1\frac{1}{2}$ to 2 ft. long. *fl.* bright red, yellowish green towards base, ascending, narrow-funnel-shaped; umbel 4- to 9-fld.; scape slender, 1 to $1\frac{1}{2}$ ft. long. October. Chile. (B.M. 2399 as *Amaryllis cyrtanthoides*; B.R. 809 as *A. ignea*; B.R. 1943 as *Phycella biflora.*) var. **magnif'ica** has fl. over 3 in. long.

**H. bif'idum.** Bulb about $1\frac{1}{2}$ in. thick. *l.* 2 or 3, linear, slightly glaucous, 12 in. long, after fl. *fl.* bright red, erect or nearly so, about 2 in. long; tube very short; segs. $\frac{1}{2}$ in. wide, blunt; umbel 3- to 6-fld.; scape 12 in. long. March. Argentina, Uruguay. 1825. (B.M. 2639 as *Habranthus angustus*; B.M. 2599 as *H. bifidus*; B.R. 1148 as *H. intermedius*; B.R. 1638 as *H. kermesinus.*)

**H. Blumena'via.** Bulb about $1\frac{1}{2}$ in. thick, globose. *l.* 3 to 5 in. long, narrow-oblong to oblong-oval, 1 to 2 in. wide; stalk about 2 in. long. Scape up to 8 in. long, somewhat compressed, pale mauve below, green above. *fl.* 4 or 5, spreading then drooping; on pedicels about 1 in. long; perianth funnel-shaped, white with mauve-crimson lines and bands running downwards; tube short; segs. about 3 in. long, upper elliptic, others narrower; all obtuse, margins crisped; stamens declinate. SE. Brazil. 1866. (B.M. 9504; 5666 as *Griffinia Blumenavia.*)

**H. brachyan'drum.** A synonym of *Habranthus brachyandrum.*

**H. breviflo'rum.** *l.* 2, lanceolate, membranous, about 3 ft. long. *fl.* white, striate, tinged yellowish-green without with a central broad red streak, the streak with a white line down middle within; scape rounded, glaucous. April. Argentina. 1836. (B.M. 3549.) Stove.

**H. calyptra'tum.** Bulb 3 in. thick. *l.* 5 or 6, lorate, acute, bright green, $1\frac{1}{2}$ to 2 ft. long, 2 in. broad. *fl.* pale yellow netted green; tube $\frac{3}{4}$ in. long; segs. 4 in. long, oblong, clawed, acute, about $1\frac{1}{2}$ in. wide; umbel 2- or 3-fld.; scape 2 ft. long. Brazil. 1816. (L.B.C. 864 as *Amaryllis calyptrata.*)

**H. can'didum.** Allied to *H. solandriflorum* but fl. white, tinged yellow in throat, segs. narrower, crisped near tips. Argentina. 1929. (B.M. 9184.)

**H. Cy'bister.** *l.* strap-shaped, $1\frac{1}{4}$ in. wide, after fl., reddish at base. *fl.* red below, greenish above; segs. broad below, pale-striped within, long, narrowed above; filaments very long, reddish towards base; pedicels over 1 in. long; scape 4-fld., robust, rounded, over 2 ft. long, reddish below. Bolivia. 1840. (B.M. 3872 as *Sprekelia Cybister.*)

**H. Elwes'ii.** *l.* linear, with the fl. about 10 in. long, $\frac{1}{6}$ in. wide. *fl.* pale yellow, claret coloured at base within; spreading lobes 3 in. across; stamens half as long as perianth-lobes; scape 2-fld., cylindrical. Argentina. 1903. (B.M. 8614.)

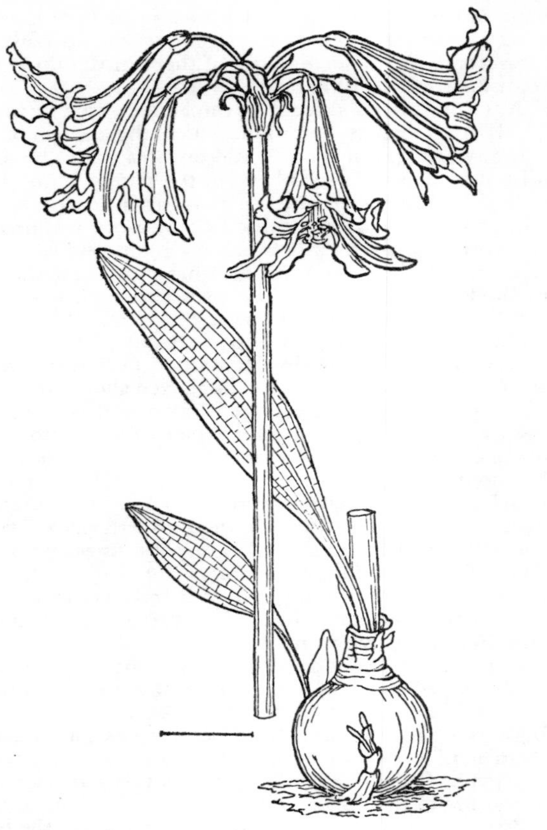

*Hippeastrum Blumenavia*

**H. eques'tre.*** Bulb globose, about 2 in. thick, tunic brown, neck short. *l.* lorate, about 2 in. wide, developing fully after fl., then about 18 in. long. *fl.* bright green, red at base, 4 to 5 in. across, tube 1 in. long, green; segs. broadened from base, then pointed; scape 2- to 4-fld., 1 to 2 ft. long, rounded, glaucous. Widely distributed in S. America, Guiana to Peru, W. Indies, naturalized in other tropical regions. Winter and spring. (B.M. 305; B.M. 2315 as *H. spathaceum.*) A variable species which crosses freely. var. **ful'gidum,** *fl.* bright orange, margined white (*see also* **H. rutilum**); **ignes'cens,** deep scarlet, barred white, throat white; **ma'jor,** very large bright orange, green at base. (B.R. 234.); **pyrrochro'um,** *fl.* deep red, greenish-yellow in throat. Para. 1863. (I.H. 1864, 420 as *H. pyrrochroum.*); **splen'dens,** larger in all parts, red. SYN. *H. Wolteri.* Double forms, e.g. **flore ple'no** with rich orange fls., have also been raised.

**H. Forget'ii.** Related to *H. pardinum.* Bulb rather small, neck 3 in. long. *l.* 6, with fl., 2 ft. long, $1\frac{1}{2}$ in. wide, light green. *fl.* dull crimson, base green, unspotted; about 6 in. across, segs. keeled with green in lower half; tube under $\frac{1}{4}$ in. long; stigma 3-lobed; scape 2-fld., slender, about 2 ft. long. Winter. Peru. 1909.

**H. ful'gidum.** A variety of *H. rutilum.*

**H. ignes'cens.** A variety of *H. equestre.*

**H. × John'soni** (*H. Reginae × H. vittatum*). *fl.* deep dull red; segs. with white stripe down keel. Robust and free-flowering. 1799. Raised by Mr. Johnson, an English watch-maker. (B.M. n.s. 122.)

**H. Leopold'ii.** Bulb 2 or 3 in. thick. *l.* lorate, $1\frac{1}{2}$ to 2 ft. long. *fl.* 6 to 7 in. across, bright red, greenish-white in throat; segs. white towards tip, 2 in. wide, keel 2-fid, white, in lower half; tube short; filaments white; scape stout, usually 2-fld. Peru. 1869. (G.C. 1870, 733 as *Amaryllis Leopoldii.*)

**H. minia'tum.** *fl.* red, bell-shaped; tube $\frac{1}{4}$ of fl; scape 2- to 5-fld., smooth, about 1 ft. long, *l.* rather shorter. July. Peru. 1832. (S.B.F.G. s. 2, 213 as *Habranthus miniatus.*) Stove.

**H. organen'se.** Bulb somewhat stoloniferous. *l.* lorate, usually somewhat glaucous. *fl.* large, red, with yellow rays; sep. wider than pet.; tube short, closed at mouth. Brazil. 1830. (B.M. 2983 as *Amaryllis aulica glaucophylla.*) Very variable in colour, size, length of style, and in the cutting of the scales at the throat.

**H. pardi'num.*** Bulb and l. much as in *H. Forgetii.* *fl.* over 6 in. across, spreading, rich cream dotted all over with crimson; tube very short; scape $1\frac{1}{2}$ ft. long, 2-fld., glaucous. Peru. 1866. (B.M. 5645.) Greenhouse. var. **tric'olor,** whitish and greenish chequered red without, dull crimson chequered white within, lower part of fl. white with a few red spots.

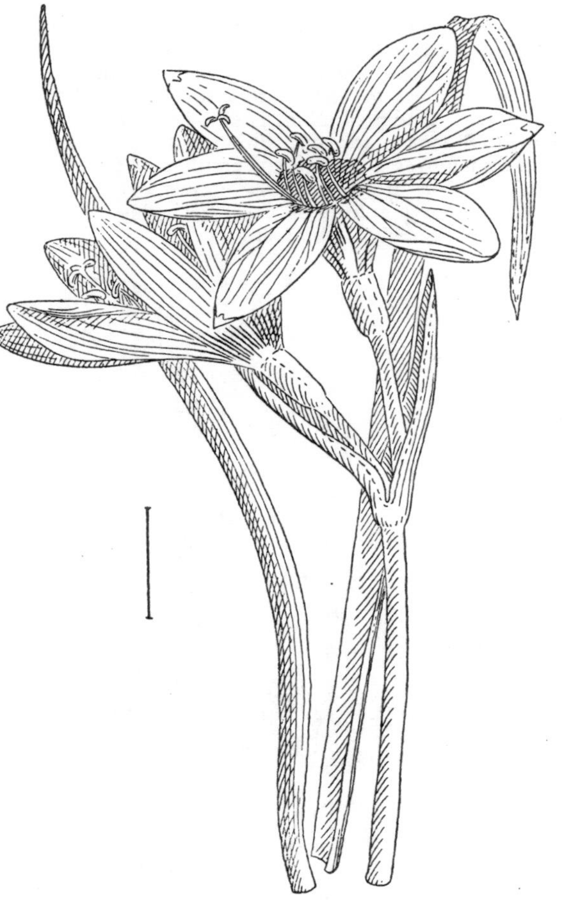

*Hippeastrum Elwesii* (p. 1000)

**H. phycelloi'des.** *l.* 3 or 4, linear, glaucous, with fl. *fl.* bright red, base yellowish, erect; segs. oblanceolate; tube ¾ in. long; scape 3- to 6-fld., 6 to 12 in. long. Chile. 1830. (B.R. 1417 as *Habranthus phycelloides.*)

**H. praten'se.*** *l.* dark green, linear, about 10 in. long. *fl.* bright scarlet sometimes feathered yellow at base, about 2½ to 3 in. across; scape 3- or 4-fld., about 1 ft. long. Chile. 1840. (B.R. 28, 35 as *Habranthus pratensis.*) Hardy in favoured districts.

**H. proc'erum.** Bulb large, neck 10 to 12 in. long. *l.* about 12, falcate, ensiform, 2 to 3 ft. long, 1½ to 2 in. wide. *fl.* lilac, tube very short; segs. 5 to 6 in. long, less than 1 in. wide; scape 4- to 12-fld., 1 to 1½ ft. long, 2-edged, stout. Winter. Brazil. 1863. (F.d.S. 2077–8 as *Amaryllis procerum*; B.M. 5883 as *A. procera.*)

**H. psittaci'num.** Bulb 3 to 4 in. thick, neck long. *l.* 6 to 8, with fl., eventually about 2 ft. long. *fl.* green and scarlet striped; segs. 4 to 5 in. long; scape 2- to 4-fld., 2 to 3 ft. long. Brazil. (B.M. 3528; B.R. 199; L.B.C. 1204.)

**H. pulverulen'tum.** A variety of *H. rutilum.*

**H. pyrrochro'um.** A variety of *H. equestre.*

**H. Regin'ae.** Mexican Lily. Bulb 2 to 3 in. thick. *l.* eventually 2 to 3 ft. long, 1½ in. wide. *fl.* bright red, with large greenish-white star in throat; segs. 4 to 5 in. long, tube about ½ in. long, green; scape 2- to 4-fld., 1 ft. long. May. Brazil. 1725. (B.M. 453 as *Amaryllis Reginae.*)

**H. reticula'tum.** Bulb globose, neck short. *l.* dark green with ivory-white midrib, 1 ft. long, 2 in. wide, with fl. *fl.* soft pink and white, veins darker, about 3 in. across; scape 5- or 6-fld. Brazil. 1677. (B.M. 2113.) Stove.

**H. ro'seum.** *l.* narrow. *fl.* rose, drooping; segs. spreading. September. Chile. 1831. (L.B.C. 1771 as *Habranthus pumilus.*) SYN. *Zephyranthes pumila.* Stove.

**H. ru'tilum.** Bulb 2 to 3 in. thick. *l.* 6 to 8, lorate, 1 ft. long. *fl.* bright crimson, keeled green half-way, tube green; filaments red; segs. 3 to 4 in. long; tube ¾ in. long; scape 2- to 4-fld., 1 ft. long. Brazil, Venezuela. 1810. (B.R. 23 and L.B.C. 1449 as *Amaryllis rutila.*) var. **acumina'tum,** *fl.* red, *l.* with ashy bloom. SYN. *H. pulverulentum*; **citri'num,** *fl.* bright yellow; **croca'tum,** *fl.* saffron, segs. undulate; **ful'gidum,** larger than type, deep crimson. (B.M. 1943 as *Amaryllis miniata*; B.M. 2475 as *H. sub-barbatum.*)

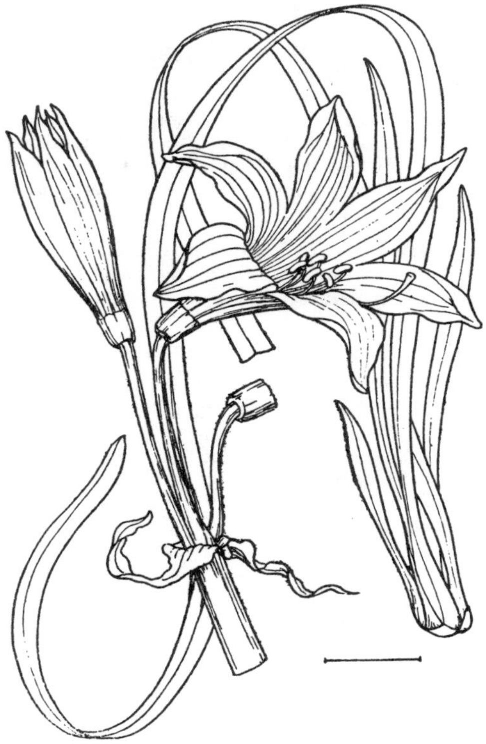

*Hippeastrum pratense*

**H. solandriflo'rum.** Bulb ovoid, 3 to 4 in. thick, neck short. *l.* rather narrow, 1 to 2 in. wide, 1 to 2 ft. long, with fl. *fl.* large, drooping; tube nearly as long as segs., cylindrical, slender, pale green; segs. oblong, sulphur or cream, greenish, or sometimes purple in middle without; scape somewhat flattened, 2- to 4-fld., 2 to 3 ft. long. S. America. 1839. (B.M. 2573, 3771.) Stove.

**H. stylo'sum.** Bulb globose, 3 in. thick, tunic pale, neck short. *l.* 4 to 6, as in *H. equestre*, but more glossy, purplish at base. *fl.* 4 in. across, pale brownish-pink, with specks and veins deeper; anthers straw-coloured, striped red; tube ½ in. long; segs. under 1 in. wide; style long exserted; scape 3- to 8-fld., 1½ to 2 ft. long. Guiana, Brazil. 1821. (B.M. 2278; B.R. 719.) Stove. var. **nu'dum,** stamens much exserted, spreading.

**H. sub-barba'tum.** A synonym of *H. rutilum fulgidum.*

**H. vitta'tum.** Bulb globose, 3 in. thick. *l.* 6 to 8, after fl. 2 ft. long, bright green. *fl.* whitish with double red stripes, keel white, 4 to 5 in. across; segs. obovate-oblong, about 1½ in. across; tube about 1 in. long; scape 3- to 6- fld., up to 3 ft. h. Peru. (B.M. 129.)

**HIP'PIA** (*hippos*, a horse; application doubtful). FAM. *Compositae.* A genus of about 4 species of herbs or branching sub-shrubs, natives of S. Africa, with alternate usually deeply pinnately cut leaves. They are tender perennials needing a compost of loam and peat, and may be propagated by seeds or cuttings.

**H. frutes'cens.** Sub-shrub, about 6 in. h. Hairy. *l.* pinnatifid. *fl.-heads* very small, yellow, rayless. February to August. 1710. (B.M. 1855.)

***hippo-,*** in compound words, signifying horse.

**HIPPOBRO'MUS** (*hippos*, a horse, *bromus*, a bad smell; in allusion to the unpleasant odour of all its parts when bruised). FAM. *Sapindaceae.* A monotypic genus. Leaves alternate. Flowers polygamous or dioecious; stamens 8, abortive in the females. *H. alatus* likes a loamy soil and is best raised from seed, though cuttings of moderately ripe shoots may root. Greenhouse.

**H. ala'tus.** Evergreen shrub or tree, 10 to 30 ft. *l.* 3 to 6 in. long, equally pinnate; lflets. 8 or 10, obovate or bluntly ovate, ¾ to 2 in. long, ½ to ⅞ in. wide, oblique, coarsely toothed, especially towards apex or entire, glabrous or nearly so. *fl.* ¼ in. wide, crowded in axillary panicles 1 to 2½ in. long, colourless. *fr.* globose, ⅓ in. wide, black. S. Africa.

W. J. B.

**HIPPOCASTANA'CEAE.** Dicotyledons. A family of 3 genera with about 25 species of deciduous trees or shrubs with opposite digitate or pinnate leaves without stipules, found in temperate regions of the N. Hemisphere. Flowers in terminal panicles, irregular, with 4 or 5 free or connate sepals, 4 or 5 unequal clawed petals, 5 to 9 distinct stamens, 3-celled superior ovary with 2 ovules in each cell. Fruit 3-valved, dehiscent, usually with 1 very large seed. Aesculus is the only genus in cultivation.

**HIPPOCRA'TEA** (in honour of the Greek writer on medicine, Hippocrates, *c.* 460 B.C.). FAM. *Hippocrateaceae*. For characters see family. Stove conditions are necessary.

**H. obtusifolia.** Climbing shrub. *l.* elliptic or oblong, obtuse, 2 to 5 in. long, 1 to 2½ in. wide, crenate or entire, leathery, glabrous. *fl.* greenish, small, in dichotomous cymes shorter than l. Summer. India, Malaya, Australia, Trop. Africa. SYN. *H. volubilis, Celastrus volubilis.*

**HIPPOCRATEA'CEAE.** Dicotyledons. A family of 3 genera with about 150 species of mostly climbing shrubs, natives of tropical and sub-tropical regions, allied to Celastraceae. Leaves simple, opposite or alternate, with or without stipules. Flowers in cymes, small, greenish, regular. Sepals and petals 5, stamens usually 3, sometimes 5 with 2 sterile; ovary superior, 3-celled with 2 to 10 ovules in each cell. Fruit a berry or 3-winged. The genera in cultivation are Hippocratea and Salicia.

**hippocrepiform,** horseshoe-shaped.

**HIPPOCRE'PIS** (*hippos,* horse, *krepis,* shoe; from the shape of the pod). FAM. *Leguminosae.* A genus of about 12 species of herbs or low shrubs, natives of Europe, N. Africa, and W. Asia. Leaves unequally pinnate; leaflets entire, without stipels. Flowers papilionaceous, yellow, honeyed, on axillary peduncles. Pods flat, curved, breaking into horseshoe-shaped joints. Easily grown in ordinary well-drained soil and increased by division or seeds. *H. balearica* needs greenhouse or frame protection in winter and is the better for some peat in the compost.

**H. balea'rica.** Shrubby, erect, 1 to 2 ft. h. *fl.* yellow in an umbel on a peduncle longer than l. Minorca. 1776. (B.M. 427.) Half-hardy.

**H. como'sa.** Stem spreading, herbaceous. *l.*flets. 7 to 11, obovate, obtuse. *fl.* as in *H. balearica.* Spring, summer. S. and W. Europe, including Britain. N. Africa. (E.B. 380.) Hardy. Rock-garden.

**HIPPOMA'NE** (*Hippomanes,* old Greek name for a kind of spurge used by Theophrastus; meaning mad after horses). FAM. *Euphorbeaceae.* A genus of a single species of very poisonous tree with milky juice. Sandy loam and peat compost suits it. It needs stove conditions and may be propagated by cuttings in sand under a glass in heat.

**H. Mancinel'la.** Manchineel; Manzanillo. Tree of 40 to 50 ft. *l.* ovate or elliptical, shining green, toothed, with a single gland at junction of stalk and blade. *fl.* small and inconspicuous, 1-sexual. W. Indies. 1690. (G.F. 510.)

**HIPPOPH'AE** (*Hippophaës,* an old Greek name for a prickly spurge). Sea Buckthorn. FAM. *Elaeagnaceae.* A genus of 2 species of hardy deciduous shrubs or trees natives of temperate parts of Europe (including Britain) and Asia, distinguished from Shepherdia by alternate (not opposite) leaves and 4 (not 8) stamens, and from Elaeagnus by dioecious flowers with 2 (not 4) sepals and short (not long) perianth tube. The whole of the young growth is covered with silvery scales or stellate hairs. Leaves simple, exstipulate, narrow. Flowers small, staminate, sessile, pistillate, shortly stalked, in short racemes on last season's growth, produced before the leaves. Fruits yellow, drupe-like, with a bony stone. Both species succeed in ordinary soil, or by the water's edge, or even on the seashore. *H. rhamnoides* is not in-frequently used as a hedge-plant in maritime districts. To secure the ornamental fruits which, since they are so sour that birds will not eat them, last longer than almost any other berries, male and female plants must be sufficiently close to one another for the wind to carry the pollen. One male plant is sufficient among about 8 female. Since the sex of seedlings cannot be ascertained until they flower, where plants are desired for the beauty of their fruits it is desirable to propagate by layers, though where quantities of plants for hedges are required they can be readily raised from seed.

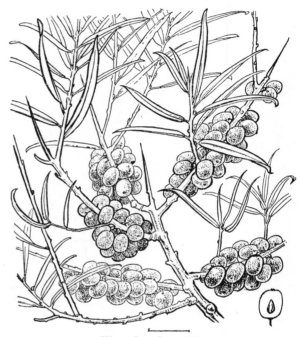

*Hippophae rhamnoides*

**H. rhamnoi'des.\*** Shrub or tree up to 40 ft., usually much smaller. Young growth silvery, often spiny. *l.* almost sessile, linear, 1 to 2½ in. long. *fl.* April. *fr.* nearly round or ovoid, ⅓ in. across, orange-yellow. September to February. Europe (Britain) to E. Asia. (E.B. 1245; B.M. 8016.)

**H. salicifo'lia.** Tree up to 45 ft., with drooping twigs. Young growth scaly and brown-hairy. *l.* linear-oblong, dull green above, mid-rib brown beneath. *fr.* pale yellow. Himalaya. 1822. Less ornamental in fruit than *H. rhamnoides.*

**hippophaeoi'des,** resembling Hippophae.

**HIPPURIDA'CEAE.** Dicotyledons. A family of a single species, *Hippuris vulgaris* (see below), allied to Halorragidaceae. Aquatic with whorled leaves and flowers with perianth of 1 stamen and 1 inferior carpel with 1 seed.

**HIPPUR'IS** (old Greek name used by Dioscorides, from *hippos,* horse, *oura,* tail). FAM. *Hippuridaceae.* A genus of a single almost cosmopolitan (including Britain) aquatic herb with creeping rhizomes and erect shoots rising above the water. The axillary flowers consist of 1 stamen and 1 carpel. Fruits 1-seeded. A useful plant for the cold aquarium but too liable to spread in wet places outdoors unless the roots are confined. Easily increased by division of the rhizomes.

**H. vulgar'is.** Common Marestail. Stem slender, glabrous, 8 to 20 in. h. *l.* crowded in whorls, linear, strap-shaped, entire, ½ to 1 in. long, 1/12 to ⅛ in. wide, sessile. *fl.* minute. Summer. (E.B. 516.)

F. P.

**HIPTA'GE** (*hiptamai,* to fly, the samaras being 3-winged). FAM. *Malpighiaceae.* A genus of about 4 species of climbing shrubs, natives of Trop. Asia. Leaves opposite, leathery, entire, without glands; stalked; without stipules. Flowers white in terminal and axillary racemes on erect peduncles; calyx 5-partite; petals clawed; stamens 10, declinate. Stove conditions and a compost of peat and loam suit them and they may be increased by cuttings.

**H. Madablo'ta.*** *l.* ovate-oblong, acute. *fl.* somewhat resembling those of *H. obtusifolia* but larger and very fragrant; outer pet. oblong. April. Trop. Asia. 1793. (Wight, Ill. 50.)

**H. obtusifo'lia.** Large shrub to 20 ft. *l.* oblong, obtuse. *fl.* with 5 pet., lower more expanded, upper reflexed, uppermost tinged rose with yellowish base, other 4 white, fragrant. China. 1810.

F. G. P.

**HIRAE'A.** (in honour of J. N. de la Hire, 1685–1717, physician of Paris). FAM. *Malpighiaceae.* A genus of over 50 species of mostly climbing shrubs, natives of the warmer parts of America. Leaves entire, stipulate. Flowers in axillary umbels, or terminal racemes, small or of medium size, rosy lilac or yellow, sepals 4 or 5; petals longer than calyx, reflexed, often toothed; stamens 10, alternate longer, filaments joined at base. Fruit a samara. Cultivation as for Banisteria.

**H. Wiedsea'na.** Branches flattish, reddish-hairy. *l.* obovate or obovate-lanceolate, 4 to 5 in. long, glabrous and shining above, velvety beneath; stalk 2-glandular. *fl.* in 4-fld. axillary umbels; pet. about ⅓ in. long, glabrous. Brazil.

*hirci'nus -a -um,* of a goat, with the odour of a goat.

**HIR'CULUS.** Included in **Saxifraga.**

*hirsutis'simus -a -um,* very hairy.

*hirsu'tulus -a -um,* somewhat hairy.

*hirsu'tus -a -um,* hairy.

*hirtel'lus -a -um,* somewhat hairy.

*hirti-,* in compound words, referring to hairiness.

*hir'tipes,* having a hairy stalk.

*hir'tulus -a -um,* somewhat hairy.

*hir'tus -a -um,* hairy.

*hirundina'ceus -a -um,* pertaining to the swallow.

*His'lopii,* in honour of an amateur botanist in Rhodesia.

*hispan'icus -a -um,* Spanish.

*hispidis'simus -a -um,* very bristly.

*hispid'ulus -a -um,* somewhat bristly.

*his'pidus -a -um* (*hispidi-,* in compound words), with rather stiff hairs, bristly.

**HISTIOP'TERIS** (*histion,* sail, *pteris* fern; from the form of the fronds). FAM. *Polypodiaceae.* A genus of 8 species of ferns. Sorus linear, marginal, with a marginal indusium. Differing little from Pteris in habit but with the veins anastomizing and forming unequal areoles, those near the margins of the fronds sometimes free. For treatment *see* **Pteris.**

**H. inci'sa.** Bat's-wing Fern. *sti.* stout, erect, straw-coloured or light brown. *Fronds* several ft. long, 2- or 3-pinnate, uppermost pinnae simply pinnate with entire, linear-oblong pinnules; next with numerous pinnatifid pinnules 2 to 3 in. long, about ¾ in. broad in opposite pairs, lowest often close to stem, smaller and with segs. dilated; lowest pinnae often very large and compound. *Sori* interrupted or continuous, often reaching points of segs. Tropics. 1823. Greenhouse. (F.S.A. (2) 133.) SYN. *Pteris incisa, P. Vespertilionis, Ritobrochia Vespertilionis.* var. *auri'ta* has lowest pinnules simple, close to stem at base of pinnae. (B.C.F. 3, 278.) SYN. *Pteris aurita.*

*his'trio,* an actor, from the varied colouring.

*histrion'icus -a -um,* pertaining to the stage or to actors.

**HLADNIK'IA.** Included in **Pleurospermum.**

**HOAR'EA.** Included in **Pelargonium.** *H. atra* is a synonym of *P. hirsutum melananthum.*

**hoary,** covered with grey or whitish hairs.

*Hochreutine'ri,* in honour of Benedict Pierre Georges Hochreutiner, 1873–    , botanist at Geneva.

*Hochstett'eri,* in honour of Christian F. Hochstetter, 1787–1860, botanist of Stuttgart.

*Hodgkinson'ii,* in honour of Dr. Hodgkinson of Wilmslow, *c.* 1900.

*Hodg'sonii,* in honour of Brian H. Hodgson, F.R.S., 1800–94, East India Co.'s resident in Nepal.

**HOES** and **HOEING.** There are numerous forms and varieties of Hoes adapted for the special purposes for which they may be required, and the condition or nature of the soil, whether light or heavy. They are indispensable garden implements for drawing drills for seeds, thinning and cleaning crops, breaking the surface of the soil, earthing up, &c. The principal forms are the Draw Hoe and the Dutch or Thrust Hoe, both of which are manufactured in many widths. Draw Hoes were originally all made with a short neck and a circular eye for fixing the handle in. In using these the soil gets much clogged on and around the eye. A great improvement, which prevents this clogging considerably, has been effected by the almost general use of the shape known as the Swan-necked. In this, the handle is inserted in a socket, which is connected with the blade by a curved solid neck. The blades should be made of steel plates, welded on iron necks. The width of the blade varies from 2 in. to 9 in. in the different sizes. Hoes with a flat, triangular head, and 3 points, are sometimes used for making drills; and the Spanish or Vernon Hoe, now rarely seen, is a form with only 1 point. The Onion Hoe is a small hoe of the Draw Hoe type with a swan-neck and a short handle, very useful for weeding and singling small plants. Dutch Hoes are very useful for destroying weeds, or for loosening the surface, where the soil is not too stiff or wet. A workman, in using the Dutch Hoe, walks backwards, and, consequently, does not tread on the ground after it is finished, as he does with the Draw Hoe. It is well adapted for light work on a fairly even surface and for hoeing flower-beds to loosen the surface while standing on the adjoining walk instead of the soil. A combination Draw Hoe, or Mattock and Fork, sometimes termed a Pickfork, is useful for loosening and breaking hard lumps of soil, and the forked part is frequently utilized with advantage in unloading manure. Another and stronger form of a similar description is also made, and in light soils is sometimes used for lifting potatoes. The Sproughton Hoe is an improved Dutch Hoe, as it is worked in the same way, with the advantage that, having a double edge, it may be effectively moved either backwards or forwards. When the person using the Hoe is standing up, the flat of the blade lies on the surface of the ground, and is easily moved backwards or forwards without bending the back. Another advantage is that the Hoe is self-cleaning, i.e. does not clog with soil if it is damp, and works itself bright quickly, doing its work expeditiously and well. If it is desired to remove any large or noxious weed by the roots, the pointed end is handy for that purpose. Hoeing forms a considerable portion of routine work in gardens. Nearly all crops are much benefited by the surface soil being kept loose; and large numbers of seedling weeds are destroyed, at the same time, by running the Hoe through in dry weather. The thinning of crops is much practised with Draw Hoes. It should only be entrusted to workmen who understand the use of the implement, as otherwise many plants will be cut up that should have remained.

**HOFFMAN'NIA** (in honour of G. F. Hoffmann, 1761–1826, Professor of Botany, Göttingen). FAM. *Rubiaceae*. A genus of about 45 species of herbs or shrubs, natives of Trop. America. Leaves opposite, or in whorls of 3 or 4; stipules interpetiolar, small, broadly triangular or transversely oblong-linear, deciduous. Flowers white, yellow or red, small, in axillary, few-flowered cymes. The species dealt with are handsome foliage plants, often known under the sectional name Campylobotrys; they will grow well in sandy soil and most will thrive outdoors in summer but need greenhouse protection in winter, or stove conditions. They may be propagated by cuttings put into sandy soil under a bell-glass with bottom heat.

**H. dis'color.** About 6 in. h. *l.* lurid green with a satiny or velvety sheen above, rich red-purple beneath. The branches, peduncles, petals, and teeth of the cal. also red. Mexico. 1850. (B.M. 4530 as *Campylobotrys discolor*.) Stove.

**H. Ghiesbreght'ii.** Herb with long, green branches, 2 to 4 ft. h. *l.* broadly oblong-lanceolate, 12 in. or more long, decurrent and narrowed to base so as to be perfoliate, somewhat plicate; rich dark velvety-green above, very slightly downy, dull red-purple with prominent veins beneath. *fl.* yellow, spotted red, inconspicuous, in cymes on short, axillary peduncles. S. America. 1861. (B.M. 5383 as *Higginsia Ghiesbreghtii*.) var. **variega'ta**, *l.* blotched with yellow, creamy-white, and red.

**H. peduncula'ta.** 2 to 3 ft. h. *l.* elliptical, acute, wedge-shaped at base, almost smooth above, rusty-hairy beneath; stalk long. *fl.* yellow, variegated with red, rotate, in few- to 8-fld. racemes, peduncles as long as, or longer than, l.-stalks. Jamaica.

**H. reful'gens.** 1 to 2 ft. h. with erect, purple branches. *l.* narrow-obovate, narrowed to base, 3 to 5 in. long, sessile, dull green tinged red above, especially toward margins, pale red beneath, over 1 in. across, in solitary cymes; cor. lobes longer than tube; peduncles purple-red, shorter than l. S. America. (B.M. 5346 as *Higginsia refulgens*.)

**H. rega'lis.** Shrub of 1 ft. with 4-angled, somewhat fleshy stems. *l.* roundish-ovate, slender-pointed, entire, somewhat leathery, glabrous, shining dark green above, reddish-purple beneath. *fl.* clustered, unattractive. Mexico. 1859. (B.M. 5280 as *Higginsia regalis*.)

**H.×Roez'lii.** Stem 2 to 3 in. h., glabrous, stout, 4-angled. *l.* roundish-ovate, 4 to 8 in. long, 2½ to 6 in. wide, margins downy, puckered all over, dark green and purplish with satiny lustre above, pale purple beneath. *fl.* dark red, about ½ in. across in racemes. 1878. Mexico. (B.M. 9025.) Stove.

*Hofmann'ii,* in honour of Herr Hofmann, Austrian botanist, who discovered *Symphyandra Hofmannii, c.* 1880, in Bosnia.

**HOG NUT.** *See* **Carya glabra.**

**HOG PLUM.** *See* **Spondias lutea** *and* **Ximenia americana.**

**HOHENBERG'IA** (in honour of Herr Hohenberg, *c.* 1830). FAM. *Bromeliaceae*. A genus of about 30 species of usually epiphytic herbs distinguished from Androlepis by the naked filaments of the stamens and from Wittmackia by the compound inflorescence: natives of S. America and the W. Indies. Leaves usually broad, spiny, in a rosette, more or less recurved, from among which the inflorescence rises. For treatment *see* **Aechmea.**

**H. augus'ta.** *l.* broad-linear, up to 4 ft. long, 5½ in. wide, blunt, toothed, bright green, irregularly spotted dull green. *fl.* blue, fragrant, small; sep. with a spiny tip; infl. a globose, woolly cone, panicled. S. Brazil. 1883. (R.H. 1881, 437 as *H. ferruginea*.) SYN. *Aechmea augusta*.

**H. capita'ta.** A synonym of *Aechmea exsudans*.

**H. erythrostach'ys.** A synonym of *H. stellata*.

**H. Legrellia'na.** A synonym of *Aechmea recurvata*.

**H. stella'ta.** *l.* broad-linear, up to 3 ft. long, 3 in. wide, recurved, dull green, margin spiny. *fl.* violet; scape erect, stout, 8 to 10 in. h. with a panicle of many fl. with blood-red bracts. Brazil, Trinidad. 1868. (B.M. 5668 as *Aechmea glomerata*.) SYN. *H. erythrostachys*.

**HOHE'RIA** (*hoihere*, a Maori name). FAM. *Malvaceae*. A genus (as now generally accepted) of 4 small trees or shrubs, 3 of which are evergreen and 1 deciduous, natives of New Zealand. Leaves alternate, toothed, of firm texture. Flowers white, in axillary clusters, stalks

jointed about the middle. Calyx 5-toothed; petals 5; stamens numerous, in 5 clusters. Fruit carpels 5, falling away from a central axis when ripe.

Easily cultivated in any good, well-drained soil, but tender. None is genuinely hardy although they may successfully pass through a series of mild winters in our average climate. But they are all admirable for such areas as S. Sussex and S. Hants, and thence westward. Propagation is by layers and cuttings.

KEY
1. Deciduous shrub      H. Lyallii
1. Evergreen shrub or small tree      2
2. Lvs. 1 to 2 in. long, linear-oblong to oblong, often blunt      H. angustifolia
2. Lvs. ovate or ovate-lanceolate      3
3. Lvs. ovate, 3 to 5 in. long      H. populnea
3. Lvs. ovate-lanceolate to lanceolate, 2 to 4 in. long      H. sexstylosa

**H. angustifo'lia.** Slender, evergreen tree up to 30 ft. *l.* 1 to 2 (rarely 3) in. long, oblong to linear-oblong, blunt or pointed, sharply toothed. *fl.* white, ½ in. across, in axillary clusters of 2 to 4. Often regarded as a var. or sub-var. of *H. populnea*; it blossoms earlier. New Zealand.

**H. Lyal'lii.**\* Deciduous shrub or small tree, all the vegetative parts more or less starry-downy. *l.* 2 to 4½ in. long, cordate-ovate, jaggedly toothed, pointed. *fl.* pure white, 1½ in. across, in axillary clusters of 2 to 5; pet. overlapping; stamens numerous; anthers yellow. June, July. New Zealand. 1871. Hardy near London, except that it may be cut back in unusually severe winters. (B.M. 5935 as *Plagianthus Lyallii*.) SYN. *Gaya Lyallii*. var. **glabra'ta**, shoots, l., &c., slightly downy, soon glabrous; less sturdy in habit; *fl.* more cup-shaped; **ribifo'lia**, *l.* deeply lobed or cut, not so slender-pointed, more downy.

**H. popul'nea.**\* Evergreen small tree or shrub, 10 to 30 ft., shoots, fl.-stalks, and cal. downy. *l.* 3 to 5 in. long, half as wide, ovate, unevenly, sharply, and strongly toothed, bright green. *fl.* pure white, ¾ to 1 in. across, borne very profusely in axillary clusters. September. *fr.* a cluster of 5 winged carpels. New Zealand. (J.R.H.S. 38, ccxlvii.) Not hardy except in favoured localities. var. **lanceola'ta**, a synonym of *H. sexstylosa*.

*Hoheria sexstylosa*

**H. sexstylo'sa.** Evergreen shrub or small tree. *l.* leathery, shining green, ovate-lanceolate to lanceolate, sharply pointed and toothed, 2 to 4 in. long. *fl.* pure white, ¾ to 1 in. wide, very profuse. Often regarded as a variety of *H. populnea*. Earlier flowering. July, August. New Zealand. (B.M. 8843 as *H. populnea lanceolata*.)

W. J. B.

**HOLBOEL'LIA** (in honour of Frederick Louis Holboell, 1765–1829, Superintendent, Botanic Garden, Copenhagen). FAM. *Lardizabalaceae*. A genus of about 5 species of evergreen twining plants with ornamental foliage, natives of N. India and China, related to Stauntonia but with corymbose clusters of flowers with petals and free stamens. Glabrous, woody twiners with long-stalked, digitate leaves, few-fld. axillary racemes, fls. with 6 petaloid sepals and 6 small nectaries, 1-sexual. Male flowers with 6 free stamens, female with small staminodes and 3 carpels. Fruits fleshy, indehiscent pods with black seeds in several rows. *H. coriacea* is hardy, *H. latifolia* less so, requiring a cool house except in very mild localities; the other species have not been sufficiently tried. Propagation is by seed, layers, or soft-wood cuttings. No special soil is required.

KEY
1. Lflets. 3
1. Lflets. generally more than 3     H. coriacea
2. Lflets. 3 to 7; fls. 1 to 1½ in. long     2
2. Fls. about ¾ in. long     H. grandiflora
3. Lflets. 5 to 9, glaucous, veins beneath inconspicuous H. Fargesii
3. Lflets. 3 to 7, green and net-veined beneath     H. latifolia

**H. coria'cea.** Vigorous twiner of 20 ft. or more, with purplish stem. *l.* of 3-stalked lflets. 2½ to 6 in. long, 1 to 3 in. wide, the middle one largest, oval or obovate, side leaflets ovate, dark, glossy green, conspicuously veined beneath. *fl.*, male purplish, ½ in. long, in terminal groups of corymbs, female greenish-white tinged purple, in clusters of 3 or 4 in lower leaf-axils. April, May. *fr.* purple, about 2 in. long. W. China. 1907. (B.M. n.s. 447.)

**H. cunea'ta.** A synonym of *Sargentodoxa cuneata*.

**H. Farges'ii.** *lflets.* 5 to 9, oblong-lanceolate or oblanceolate, 2 to 5 in. long, glaucous with inconspicuous veins beneath. *fl.* about ¾ in. long, coloured as in *H. coriacea*. Cent. China. 1907. (H.I.P. 2848.)

**H. grandiflo'ra.** *lflets.* 3 to 7, oblong to oblanceolate, 2½ to 5½ in. long, acuminate, glaucous and reticulate beneath. *fl.* white, 1 to 1½ in. long, fragrant. May. *fr.* 3 to 5 in. long, purple, edible. W. China. 1908.

**H. latifo'lia.** *lflets.* 3 to 7, ovate-oblong to oblong, 2 to 5 in. long, green and reticulate beneath. *fl.* about ¾ in. long, in short racemes, fragrant, male greenish-white, female purplish. March. *fr.* 2 to 3 in. long, purple, edible. Himalaya. 1840. (B.R. 32, 49.) Syn. *Stauntonia latifolia*.

**HOL'CUS** (*Holkos*, old Greek name of a grass). Fam. Gramineae. A genus of about 8 species of annual or perennial grasses, natives of Europe, temperate Asia, and N. and S. Africa. Flowers in a loose panicle; spikelets compressed, 2-flowered. Some species are weeds of grass-land, the soft hairy foliage being disliked by cattle, and they often escape into cultivated land. *H. lanatus* and *H. mollis*, the 2 British species, are sometimes lawn weeds.

**H. lana'tus albo-variega'tus.** Neat tufted perennial. *l.* soft, hairy, with broad central and narrow green stripes, the intermediate spaces and margin clear silvery-white.

*Holdt'ii,* in honour of Fredrich von Holdt, who raised the hybrid *Robinia* × *Holdtii* in Colorado.

*Holfordia'nus -a -um,* in honour of R. S. Holford of Westonbirt.

*hollan'dicus -a -um,* of NE. New Guinea.

**HOLLOW-HEART DISEASE.** See **Potato, Hollow-heart disease.**

**HOLLY.** See **Ilex Aquifolium.**

**HOLLY, AMERICAN.** See **Ilex opaca.**

**HOLLY FERN.** See **Polystichum Lonchitis.**

**HOLLY LEAF MINER,** *Phytomyza ilicis,* disfigures leaves of Hollies. The small, black flies appear towards the end of May, when the females lay their eggs singly on the underside of the leaves near the midrib. The young maggots tunnel into the tissues, forming the familiar brownish or yellowish blisters. They are fully fed by the following March or April, and the white, flattened, oval puparia may be seen partially exposed in the mine.

It is not possible to take any remedial measures against this pest on tall trees owing to the difficulty of reaching the topmost branches. Attacked Holly hedges should be clipped in autumn, and the prunings burned. Specimen

trees, which are rendered unsightly by this miner, should have the blistered leaves removed and burned, the heavily infested shoots pruned off, and the underside of the leaves sprayed with a nicotine and soap wash to destroy the mining maggots. Spraying the foliage with a paraffin emulsion during egg-laying period—mid-May to mid-June—tends to repel the female flies, but will prove effective only when several applications are made.

G. F. W.

**HOLLY OAK.** See **Quercus Ilex.**

**HOLLY, SEA.** See **Eryngium maritimum.**

**HOLLYHOCK** (*Althaea rosea*). The Hollyhock has long been grown in England and at one time took its place among the florists' flowers and was given special classes at exhibitions, named varieties being propagated by cuttings, by division, and by eyes taken from side shoots when they were getting firm in July and August and rooted under a shaded hand-glass in light soil. Many fine varieties were raised by crossing and selection, attention being specially devoted to double forms. The onset of Hollyhock rust, which is more liable to damage old plants than young seedlings and which proved impossible to control effectively, led to its almost complete disappearance as a florists' flower, though not of good forms for garden decoration, for which it is still a favourite.

Seed saved from the finest plants should be sown as soon as ripe in pots or pans in gentle heat, or in the open air in June or July, and transplanted into 3-in. pots and wintered in a cold frame, or in well-drained soil in the open. Propagation by cuttings, which gives better plants than division, is done by taking side shoots about 3 in. long from sides of the old root at almost any time, placing them singly in small pots of light sandy soil, and keeping them close and shaded until roots are formed. If done in winter gentle bottom heat should be given. Division is effected after flower is over, by separating the crown so as to have one or more buds and as many roots as possible to each piece. Choice varieties may be propagated by grafting small pieces on roots from vigorous seedlings in spring, using the whip method of grafting.

Any good garden soil will suit hollyhocks but it should be well prepared and, if poor, enriched. The young plants if wintered under glass must be given plenty of light and air, but little water, and must not be starved for root room. They should be gradually hardened off in March and planted out about mid-April where they are to flower. Three feet apart each way will not be too much. For late flowering planting may be delayed a month. The plants may need protection at first on cold nights and they need plenty of water during the summer. A top-dressing of compost manure is beneficial when the flower-spikes appear. Strong plants may be allowed 2 or 3 spikes but weak ones should have but 1. The spikes should be staked before there is danger of damage from strong winds (6 ft. stakes are suitable) and the growths should be tied in at frequent intervals. When flowering is over the spikes should be cut down to about 6 in. from the ground. Unless the soil is dry and winter conditions are not usually severe the old roots should be lifted and stored in frames but where conditions are favourable they may be left outdoors, but owing to the liability to attacks of the rust fungus (see below) old plants are rarely a success.

*DISEASES.* The chief Hollyhock disease is Rust, caused by the fungus *Puccinia malvacearum* which also attacks many other malvaceous plants such as the wild mallows and Lavatera. On the Hollyhock the signs are brownish-black pustules on the under-surfaces of the leaves and on the stems, this being the teleutospore stage of the fungus which is the only one formed. This rust is difficult to control and spraying or soil treatments seem to be of little use. The teleutospores overwinter in the crown of the plant and reinfect in the spring. Search for resistant or immune plants has so far met with no success. Plants which are weak or suffering from drought are severely affected so that every effort should be made to keep them vigorous, and it is best to raise fresh seedlings each year so as to have a succession of strong young plants. Destroy infected leaves as far as possible. Hollyhock disease is not seen in the neighbourhood of industrial towns, a freedom thought to be due to fumes of sulphur dioxide, &c., in the atmosphere having a fungicidal effect on the rust.

(D. E. G.)

**HOLM OAK.** *See* **Quercus Ilex.**

**HOLMSKIOLD'IA** (in honour of Theodor Holmskiold, 1732–94, Danish botanist). FAM. *Verbenaceae.* A genus of 3 glabrous or hoary shrubs with opposite leaves. Flowers in short-stalked axillary cymes or clustered at ends of shoots; calyx thin, coloured; corolla cylindrical, curved, its limb oblique, shortly 5-lobed; stamens 4, anthers exserted. Fruit an obovoid drupe. *H. sanguinea* is a stove evergreen for a light, rich soil. Cuttings root readily in sandy soil under glass, in heat.

**H. sanguin'ea.** Evergreen shrub of about 4 ft. *l.* ovate, slender-pointed, nearly entire; stalked. *fl.* scarlet in a raceme of a few 2- to 4-fld. whorls; cal. large, rotate-bell-shaped; cor. tube incurved, long. India. 1792. (B.R. 692.)

F. G. P.

*holo-,* in compound words, signifying completely.

**HOLODIS'CUS** (*holos,* entire, *diskos,* disk; in allusion to the entire disk of the flower). FAM. *Rosaceae.* Allied to Spiraea in which it is often included, but with a fruit of 5 achenes, not follicles. A genus of deciduous, simple-leaved, more or less pubescent shrubs with about 14 species in Western N. and Cent. America. Flowers very small, in terminal panicles; leaves deeply serrate or lobed, exstipulate. The species mentioned are hardy and succeed in good loamy soil not apt to become too dry in summer, where they form handsome bushes and flower freely.

**H. dis'color.*** Shrub of 4 to 10 ft. h. with spreading, arching branches. *l.* broad-ovate, about 2 to 4 in. long, somewhat lobed, white tomentose beneath. *fl.* about ⅛ in. across, creamy-white, in large drooping panicles up to 8 in. long and 6 in. wide. July. Western N. America. 1827. (B.R. 1365 as *Spiraea ariaefolia.*) var. **ariaefo'lia*** has l. greyish-green and pubescent beneath. This is the commonly cultivated form and is very handsome.

**H. dumo'sus.** Shrub of about 3 ft. h. with erect branches. *l.* obovate, pubescent above, whitish tomentose below, about 1½ in. long. *fl.* as in *H. discolor* but panicle ovoid, narrow, 2 to 8 in. long. July. Utah, N. Mexico. 1879. SYN. *Spiraea dumosa.*

**HOLOGY'NE.** Included in **Coelogyne.**

*hololeu'cus -a -um,* wholly white.

**HOLOSCHOEN'US.** Included in **Scirpus.**

*holoseric'eus -a -um,* covered all over with silky hairs.

*Holos'tea,* ancient Greek plant name.

*Holst'ii,* in honour of C. H. E. W. Holst, 1865–94, German gardener who travelled in E. Africa.

**HOLY HERB.** *See* **Verbena officinalis.**

**HOLY THISTLE.** *See* **Silybum Marianum.**

*Holzmannia'nus -a -um,* in honour of Timoleon Holzmann, b. 1843, student of Greek botany.

**HOMALAN'THUS** (*homalos,* smooth, *anthos,* flower). FAM. *Euphorbiaceae.* A genus of about 18 species of evergreen shrubs, natives of Malaya, Pacific Is., and Australia. Leaves entire, long-stalked. Flowers 1-sexual, inconspicuous, in terminal racemes with the female flowers at base. Treatment as for stove species of Euphorbia.

**H. fastuo'sus.** *l.* peltate. *fl.* greenish. Philippines. 1866.

**H. gigan'teus.** *l.* densely downy beneath. *fl.* with pedicels of female 3 times as long as of male. Java. 1866.

**H. Leschenaultia'nus.** A synonym of *H. populneus.*

**H. polyan'drus.** Erect shrub; branches terete. *l.* alternate, broadly ovate, clear glaucescent green above, rich wine-purple beneath. Lord Howe Is. 1876.

**H. populifo'lius.** Queensland Poplar. Shrub of 6 ft. *l.* 2 to 4 in. long and wide, glaucous, at first enclosed between 2 lanceolate, greenish stipules which soon fall, gland-tipped above; stalks slender, red; l. copper-coloured when young; orange-red in autumn. *fl.* pale green and yellow; racemes 2 to 4 in. wide; female fls. 4 or 5, staminate numerous, generally in threes. Australia. 1825. (B.M. 2780 as *Omalanthus populifolius.*)

**H. popul'neus.** Similar to *H. populifolius,* but with glandular stigmas. Trop. Asia. SYN. *H. Leschenaultianus.*

F. G. P.

**HOMALOCEPH'ALA** (*homalos,* level, *kephale* head; referring to the flat top to the plant). FAM. *Cactaceae.* Large plants, broad but low, strongly ribbed; ribs thin but widening under each areole; areoles with dense white felt when young; radial spines 6, spreading and recurved, flattened, annulate, reddish; central spine longer and flatter. Flowers bell-shaped, pink, scented, lasting several days. For cultivation *see* **Cactus** (terrestrial).

**H. texen'sis.** The only species. Texas, New Mexico, Mexico. (B.R.C. 3, t. 19.) SYN. *Echinocactus texensis.*

V. H.

**HOMALOME'NA** (*homalos,* flat, *nema,* thread (?); from the shape of the stamens). FAM. *Araceae.* A genus of about 80 species of herbaceous or shrubby plants, natives of Asia and Trop. Africa, differing from Chamaecladon, where the ovary is 2-celled, by the 3- or 4-celled ovary. Leaves ovate- or triangular-heart-shaped or lanceolate; stalks often long with a long sheath. Flowers on a spadix without an appendix, included in the straight spathe, often shortly stalked; male inflorescence cylindrical or fusiform, female shorter and narrower; spathe cylindrical or convolute below, its blade convolute or gaping, slender-pointed. Handsome foliage plants needing treatment like Caladium.

**H. insig'nis.** *l.* 1 ft. long, 6 in. wide, elliptic-oblong, obtuse or with a short mucro, rounded at base, green above, tinged purple beneath; stalks brownish-purple, channelled, 3 to 5 in. long, sheathed to middle. *Spathe* green, 3½ to 4 in. long, obtusely keeled at back. compressed-rostrate at tip; spadix white, 3 in. long. Borneo. 1885. (I.H. 1885, 560.)

**H. pelta'ta.** 3 ft. h. *l.* deeply cordate, about 24 in. long, 16 to 17 in. wide, basal lobes rounded, rather hairy. *Spathe* persistent, 6 to 7 in. long, constricted in middle, slender-pointed, pinkish, spotted greenish within; spadix about as long as spathe, cream. Colombia. 1877. (G.C. 1877, 273.)

**H. pictura'ta.** 4 to 5 in. h. *l.* heart-shaped, the 2 basal lobes rounded, ovate or oblong, pointed, midrib marked by a narrow silvery-white band. *Spathe* green; spadix white. Colombia. 1873. (G.F. 1877, 891.)

**H. Roez'lii.** 6 in. h. *l.* ovate-oblong, rounded or tapering at base, sparsely spotted yellow; stalks long. *Spathe* olive-brown without, creamy within. Colombia. 1873. (G.C. 1874, 804 as *Curmeria Roezlii.*)

**H. rubes'cens.** 1 to 2 ft. h. *l.* heart-arrow-shaped, dark green, purplish beneath; stalk deep red. *Spathe* subcylindrical, convolute, reddish-purple without, whitish within. Java. 1870. (G.F. 1869, 634.) SYN. *H. rubrum.*

**H. Siesmeyeria'num.** *l.* slightly arrow-shaped, veins, midrib, and margins tinged red beneath; stalks purplish-red, long, glabrous. *Spathe* purplish-red without, white within, tube and limb indistinguishable; peduncle purplish-red. Malaya. 1885.

**H. Wallis'ii.** *l.* ovate-oblong, slightly oblique, rounded and tapering slightly at base, abruptly slender-pointed, margin white, sprinkled with golden blotches above. *Spathe* about 3 in. long, narrowed in middle, reddish; spadix red, nearly as long as spathe. Colombia. 1877. (B.M. 6571.) SYN. *Curmeria Wallisii.*

**H. Wendland'ii.** *l.* heart-arrow-shaped, about 18 in. long, 12 in. wide, dark green above, paler and polished beneath; stalk 2½ ft. long, dark red at base. Costa Rica.

**HOMALONE'MA.** A synonym of Homalomena.

*Hombron'ii,* in honour of Jacques Bernard Hombron, 1798–1852, surgeon on the Astrolabe expedition.

**HOME′RIA** (in honour of the Greek Homer, *c.* 850 B.C.). FAM. *Iridaceae.* A genus of 6 species of S. African plants with tunicated corms. Basal leaf usually solitary, linear-ensiform, overtopping flowers. Flowers on a leafy branching scape, showy and enduring, usually orange-red, copper-coloured, or yellow; segments free to base, connivent in a cup, then spreading; filaments united into a cylindrical tube; spathes cylindrical, few-flowered. Cultivation as for **Ixia.**

**H. auranti′aca.** A variety of *H. collina.*

**H. colli′na.** About 1½ ft. h. *l.* narrow, convolute, concave, in the flowering plant usually cauline. *fl.* reddish-yellow at base. Summer. 1793. (B.M. 9487; B.M. 1033 as *Moraea collina.*) Variable. var. **auranti′aca**, 1 ft. h., *fl.* orange-red, yellow. 1810. (B.M. 1612 as *Moraea collina miniata minor.*); **minia′ta**, scape up to 20 in. h., with several clusters of fl. *l.* linear, without a central band. *fl.* tawny-red with yellow centre. (S.B.F.G. 152; A.B.R. 404 as *Moraea miniata.*); **ochroleu′ca,** *fl.* pale yellow.

**H. el′egans.** 1½ ft. h. *l.* broader than in *H. collina.* *fl.* yellow and dull blue or orange-brown. Summer. 1797. (B.M. 1283 as *Moraea spicata.*)

**H. linea′ta.** 2 ft. h. *l.* broadly linear, somewhat leathery, acute, midrib white. *fl.* red, yellow. 1825. (S.B.F.G. 178.)

**H. ochroleu′ca.** A variety of *H. collina.*

**homo-,** in compound words, signifying similar, as *homolepis,* having similar scales.

**HOMOCLA′DIUM platycla′dum.** A synonym of *Muehlenbeckia platyclados.*

**homogamous,** having all the flowers in a capitulum hermaphrodite.

**homogeneous,** having a uniform nature or consistence.

**HOMOGLOS′SUM** (*homos,* equal, *glossa,* tongue; from the nearly equal perianth segments). FAM. *Iridaceae.* A genus of about 10 species of herbs, natives of S. and Trop. Africa, sometimes included in Antholyza but distinct by the lobes of the perianth similar in form, and either nearly equal or the 5 lower gradually smaller, the upper lobe not hooded. Corm nearly globose.

*Homoglossum Merianella*

Leaves few, linear or awl-shaped. Stem unbranched with a loose terminal spike of 1 to 7 flowers. Bracts ¾ to 2½ in. long, outer longer than inner, herbaceous. Perianth-tube curved, basal part very slender. Seeds many, flat, winged all round. Cultivation as for Antholyza.

**H. Gaw′leri.** Much like *H. Watsonium* but with perianth segs. yellow from the base half-way up. S. Africa. (B.M. 569 as *Gladiolus Watsonius* var.) Cf. *H. Huttonii* which is sometimes confused with *H. Gawleri.*

**H. Hut′tonii.** 1 to 2 ft. h. *l.* 1 or 2, awl-shaped (not linear), 8 to 18 in. long, grooved. *fl.* in a loose 2- or 3-fld. spike; bracts 1½ to 2 in. long; perianth about 3 in. long, crimson, streaked yellowish in throat; tube curved; segs. more or less overlapping, directed forward, upper lobe about 1½ in. long, elliptic-ovate, lower lobes ¾ to 1 in. long, lanceolate, acute. S. Africa. *See* **H. Gawleri** with which this has been confused.

**H. Merianel′la.** Flames. Corm of medium size. Hairy. Stem 1 to 2 ft. h. *l.* 4 to 6, narrow-linear, rigid, strongly ribbed, short. *fl.* in a very loose, 1-sided, 3- to 6-fld. spike; bright red; tube about 1½ in. long; segs. broadly oblong, 1½ in. long, blunt. April to June. S. Africa. 1795. (B.M. 9510; B.M. 574 as *Gladiolus hirsutus roseus.*) SYN. *Antholyza Merianella.*

**H. revolu′tum.** A synonym of *H. Watsonium.*

**H. watsonioi′des.** Erect, 2 to 3 ft. h., with usually 2 small l. *l.* 4, linear, 1 to 1½ ft. long, erect, firm. *fl.* 4 to 10 in a very loose, 1-sided spike; bright scarlet; tube about 1½ in. long; segs. oblong or ovate, acute, 1 in. long; bracts lanceolate. June. Kilimanjaro. 1886. (B.M. 6919 as *Antholyza watsonioides.*) SYN. *Gladiolus watsonioides.*

**H. Watson′ium.** Corm globose, up to nearly 1 in. thick. Stem about 18 in. h. *l.* narrow-linear, stiff; stem-l. with a long smooth sheath. *fl.* in a very loose, 2- to 4-fld., 1-sided spathe; bracts lanceolate, very long; perianth bright red; tube up to 2 in. long; segs. oblong, acute, spreading. February, March. S. Africa. (B.M. 450 as *Gladiolus Watsonius.*) SYN. *Antholyza revoluta* of Baker, *Gladiolus praecox, H. revolutum* of Baker.

**HOMOGY′NE** (*homos,* similar, *gyne,* female; the female flowers resemble the others). FAM. *Compositae.* A genus of 3 species of stemless perennial herbs, natives of the mountains of Europe. Leaves radical, broad, heart-shaped, angular or with wavy margins. Flower-heads white or purple, tassel-like on scapes with 1 or 2 heads and 1 or 2 distant leaves. Hardy, needing a damp (not wet) soil on border, rock-garden, or in woodland.

**H. alpi′na.** Alpine Coltsfoot. 3 to 6 in. h. *l.* kidney-shaped, toothed, glossy, evergreen. *fl.-heads* clear rose-purple, disk-like; solitary on an almost naked scape. Austria. 1710. (T.A.P.E. 33; B.M. 84 as *Tussilago alpina.*)

**H. dis′color.** About 6 in. h. *l.* roundish, base heart-shaped, margin with acute rounded teeth; thick, firm, smooth and shining above, veins evident, densely shortly hairy beneath. *fl.-heads* purple on a terete purple scape clothed with whitish wool. Austria to Italy. 1633. (T.A.P.E. 32.) SYN. *Tussilago discolor.*

**H. sylves′tris.** Habit of *H. alpina.* *l.* kidney-shaped, 7- to 9-lobed, sharply toothed, nearly glabrous; lobes 3-toothed. *fl.-heads* as in *H. alpina.* Carinthia, Carniola.

**A→**

**HOMOP′TERA.** *See* **Insects.**

**HONCKEN′YA** (in honour of G. A. Honckeny, 1724–1805, author of a flora of Germany). FAM. *Tiliaceae.* A genus of 2 or 3 species of shrubs, covered with starry down, natives of Trop. Africa. Leaves entire or lobed. Flowers large, bluish-violet, in terminal racemes. Stove conditions and a mixture of loam and peat suit them. Cuttings of young shoots in sand, under a hand-glass, in heat can be used for propagation.

**H. ficifo′lia.** *l.* variable, 3- to 7-lobed, cordate, roundish or oblong, with coarse rounded teeth. *fl.* bluish-violet, subsolitary or in short racemes. Trop. Africa. 1898. (B.M. 7836 as *Clappertonia ficifolia.*)

F. G. P.

*hondoen′sis -is -e,* of Hondo, Japan.

**HONESTY.** *See* **Lunaria annua.**

**HONEY.** *See* **Bee, Hive Nectary,.**

**HONEY-BEE.** *See* **Bee, Hive.**

**HONEY-BERRY.** *See* **Melicocca bijuga.**

**HONEY-FLOWER, CAPE.** *See* **Protea mellifera.**

**HONEY FUNGUS** or **HONEY AGARIC** (*Armillaria mellea*) belongs to the family Agaricaceae in the class Basidiomycetes. This fungus has been called many other names such as Bootlace Fungus, Shoestring Fungus, Collar-rot Fungus, &c. It is mainly confined to the underground parts of plants and lives commonly on dead tree-stumps and other debris from which it may attack the living roots of many kinds of plants. All kinds of trees may be attacked and even herbaceous plants, such as Rhubarb, Daffodil, &c., may be affected where the soil is heavy and keeps wet.

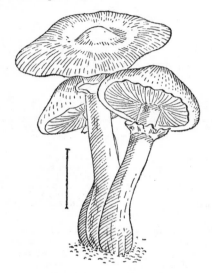

*Honey Fungus*

As the trouble is in the roots, when such plants as Rhododendron, Privet, &c., begin to die, it is useless to examine the leaves and upper parts without examining the underground portions. Signs of the fungus will usually be found at the collar just below ground-level or in the roots. When the bark of such places is lifted the fungus can be seen as thin, white, fan-like sheets of growth and from such a badly infected centre the fungus will put out long, shiny, black, cord-like strands so as to reach and infect other trees. These black cords are properly called rhizomorphs and give rise to the name Bootlace Fungus. When seen they provide unmistakable evidence of the presence of *Armillaria mellea*.

From dead infected stumps the fungus in the later months of the year sends up fruits which have honey-coloured caps with brown scales and long yellowish stems possessing a ring towards the upper part. The gills of these fruits will liberate spores to infect other dead stumps and debris. It is thought these spores are not dangerous from an infection point of view, but they infect old stumps which again send out rhizomorphs which infect living plants. It is essential to remove all stumps and roots of trees or hedgerows when clearing land for fruit-plantations, to drain the land, and to see that wooden posts and stakes are well creosoted at their lower ends. Where trees die from this disease be sure to lift *all* the roots for burning.

It may be that the fungus can attack only injured roots or those of trees weakened through poor health. Certainly the fungus is more serious on badly drained land or in trees not thriving through some unsuitable soil condition. Important points in checking it are: (1) Thorough destruction of old stumps. (2) Destruction of all parts of any infected root system. (3) Careful attention to efficient drainage so as to avoid prolonged water-logging even in winter. With a small area vacant of other plants a thorough watering of the freshly forked soil with 2 per cent. formalin solution (1 pint commercial formalde-hyde to 6 gals. water) may be worth trying. A method sometimes used with an infected tree is to dig a trench 2 ft. deep outside the root system throwing the earth inwards and possibly watering with formalin inside the circle.

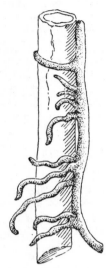

*Honey Fungus Mycelium*

When a Privet or other hedge dies from this disease all infected plants need burning. The old soil should then be dug out in a trench, say, 3 ft. wide and 18 in. deep, and replaced with fresh soil which should be well limed. This can be replanted with young healthy trees, taking care to injure the roots as little as possible.

D. E. G.

**HONEY GARLIC.** *See* **Allium siculum.**

**HONEY GUIDES.** Lines or spots on the petals which act as finger-posts pointing to the location of nectar, usually in flowers in which the nectary is not exposed.

**HONEY LOCUST.** *See* **Gleditschia triacanthos.**

**HONEY PALM.** *See* **Jubaea.**

**HONEY, SHAM.** Spiny spots in a flower looking like drops of nectars, as in Cleome, Lopezia, Parnassia.

**HONEYDEW.** The excretion of a sticky nature by green-flies and some of their relatives. It is apt to clog the stomata of leaves upon which it falls and serves as a pabulum upon which sooty moulds flourish and further interfere with the functions of the leaf.

**HONEYSUCKLE.** *See* **Lonicera.**

**HONEYSUCKLE, AFRICAN.** *See* **Halleria lucida.**

**HONEYSUCKLE, BUSH.** *See* **Diervilla.**

**HONEYSUCKLE, JAMAICA.** *See* **Passiflora laurifolia.**

**HONEYWORT.** *See* **Cerinthe.**

*hongkongen'sis -is -e,* of Hongkong.

**hooded,** arching so as to form a cover like a hood, cucullate.

**HOOD'IA** (in honour of Mr. Hood, a cultivator of succulent plants, *c.* 1830). FAM. *Asclepiadaceae.* Much-branched plants with very stout, leafless stems divided into many low tubercles, each tipped with a spine or bristle. Flowers large and showy, the corolla cup- or saucer-shaped, circular, not divided into lobes (as in Stapelia, q.v.) but with 5 points. **A**

**H. Bain'ii.** Up to 1 ft. h., bushily branched, glaucous with pale-brown spines. *fl.* 2½ to 3 in. across, cup-shaped, pale yellow. Cape Province and SW. Africa. (W. & S. 1124, 1157, 1158; B.M. 6348.)

**H. Dreg'ei.** Stems with 20 to 24 tuberculate ribs, with stiff bristles. *fl.* 1½ in. across, 5 lobes more distinct, pale brown, completely covered on the inside with white hairs. Cape Province. (W. & S. 1123, 1139–42.)

**H. Gor'doni.** Up to 1½ ft. h., stout, erect, glaucous green with slender brown spines. *fl.* nearly circular, with 5 slender points, pale purple with faint yellowish stripes. SW. Africa. (W. & S. 1119, 1120, 1122, 1153, 1154; B.M. 6228 except dissections.)

**H. macran'tha.** Stems up to 3 ft. h., the thickest stems 4 in. across. *fl.* 8 in. across, bright purple. SW. Africa. (W. & S. 1121, 1125–9.)

**H. Trieb'neri.** Stems dwarf, not more than 8 in. h. *fl.* very shallow, green and pink. SW. Africa. (W. & S. 1160–3.)

V. H.

**HOODIOP'SIS** (the genus closely resembles Hoodia). FAM. *Asclepiadaceae*. Stems similar to those of Hoodia but with fewer angles; the flower differs in the much greater length of the corolla lobes.

**H. Trieb'neri.** Stems erect, branching, with about 7 angles divided into tubercles and tipped with hard spines. *fl.* with 5 lobes, 4 in. across; densely papillate inside, deep wine-red. (W. & S. 1168–70.)

V. H.

*Hoogia'nus -a -um,* in honour of John Hoog, head of the famous firm of Dutch bulb-growers, Messrs. van Tubergen, and nephew of the founder.

**HOOK CLIMBERS.** Plants which climb by hooking on to supports, e.g. Rose, Bramble, Cleavers.

**HOOK'ERA.** *See* **Brodiaea.**

*Hook'erae,* in honour of Lady Hooker, wife of Sir W. J. Hooker, d. 1872.

*Hook'eri, Hookeria'nus -a -um,* in honour of Sir W. J. Hooker, 1785–1865, Director of Kew, or of his son Sir Joseph D. Hooker, 1817–1911, traveller in the Himalaya, who succeeded his father as Director of Kew.

**HOOP ASH.** *See* **Celtis occidentalis crassifolia.**

**HOOP PINE.** *See* **Araucaria Cunninghamii.**

**HOOP WITHY.** *See* **Rivina.**

*Hoop'esii,* in honour of Thomas Hoopes, who, *c.* 1859, botanized on Pike's Peak, N. America.

**HOP.** *See* **Humulus Lupulus.**

**HOP-DAMSON APHIS** (*Phorodon humuli*) or 'Hop Fly' was until recent years one of the most destructive pests in hop-gardens and in damson and plum orchards, but modern methods of pest control have considerably reduced its importance. The winter is passed in the egg stage on Bullace, Damson, Plum, and Sloe. The eggs hatch in spring, and the young Aphides immediately cause the leaves to curl. Winged forms appear later and fly off to Hops, where they suck the sap of the young tender leaves. Hop-gardens may be invaded by this pest from late May to August, and the later infestations are more serious for the Aphides crawl into the cones and feed within them. Winged forms appear on Hops in autumn, and return to the woody hosts for egg-laying.

This pest is completely controlled on fruit-trees by thorough and forceful application of 5 per cent. tar-distillate wash applied in December. A spring application of a nicotine and soap wash before leaf-curling begins will reduce an attack, while nicotine dusting will destroy many of the Aphides within the curled leaves of their woody hosts. The measures adopted in hop-gardens are spraying and dusting of the leaves as soon as the pest is detected—early application being specially desirable owing to the great speed of increase of this Aphis.

G. F. W.

**HOP DOG** (*Dasychira pudibunda*) or Pale Tussock Moth may occur in hop-gardens during August, September, and October. The conspicuous and brilliantly coloured caterpillars have hairy greenish bodies furnished with 4 thick brushes of yellow hairs, interspersed with black velvety patches on the back and another reddish tuft at the tail. They feed also on the leaves of Apple, Birch, Hazel, Oak, and other trees. When fully fed they spin cocoons between the leaves, and the greyish moths are on the wing in May and June.

It is seldom that serious damage is done to the plants by these caterpillars owing to their late appearance in the season, and it is not often found necessary to take remedial measures against them.

G. F. W.

**HOP HORNBEAM.** *See* **Ostrya.**

**HOP-TREE.** *See* **Ptelea trifoliata.**

**HO'PEA** (in honour of Dr. John Hope, 1725–86, Scottish botanist). FAM. *Dipterocarpaceae*. A genus of nearly 50 species of tropical trees. Leaves simple; stipules small or minute, soon falling. Flowers in one-sided spikes or racemes; calyx often glabrous; petals hairy without. Stove conditions and ordinary potting compost are needed.

**H. odora'ta.** Evergreen tree with yellowish-brown very durable wood. Glabrous except in infl. *l.* ovate-lanceolate. *fl.* fragrant, in axillary grey-hairy panicles; *pet.* ciliate; anthers oblong; ovary narrowed to conical style. March, April. India eastwards.

*Hopea'nus -a -um,* in honour of Thomas Hope, 1770–1831, or Louise Hope, his wife, of Deepdene, Dorking.

**HOPLOCAMP'A testudin'ea.** *See* **Apple Saw-fly.**

**HOPLOPHY'TUM.** Included under **Aechmea.**

*Hop'pei,* in honour of David Heinrich Hoppe, 1760–1846, apothecary and professor at Regensburg, student of the flora of Mid-Europe.

*Hoppenstedt'ii,* in honour of Signor Hoppenstedt, landowner in Mexico.

*hordea'ceus -a -um,* Barley-like.

**HORD'EUM** (ancient Latin name for barley). FAM. *Gramineae*. A genus of about 16 annual or perennial grasses, natives of Europe, Asia, N. Africa, and temperate America with terminal bristly spikes, consisting of many 1-flowered spikelets growing 3 together on each joint of the rachis, the middle one sessile and fertile, the others usually stalked, often consisting of awns alone. The rachis breaks up at the joints at maturity. Here belongs barley (*H. sativum*) and a number of weeds, usually of neglected places gone out of cultivation. *H. jubatum*, grown for its ornamental feathery spikes, is an annual, and may be sown outdoors in rather dry soil.

**H. juba'tum.** Squirrel tail grass. Tufted annual. Stem slender about 9 to 12 in. h. *l.* narrow, acute, rough, sheath smooth, ligule almost absent. *Spike* about 2 in. long, narrow except for the spreading awns about 2½ in. long. June. N. and S. America, Siberia. 1782.

**HOREHOUND** (*Marrubium vulgare*). Hardy and easily grown, being best in a poor soil. It may be raised from seed sown in the open in March, by division of roots in spring, or by cuttings put in a shady place outside. The plants should be planted 10 to 15 in. apart, and the ground be kept clean between them. They will last for several years, the annual growths being cut when the flowers open (which will be in the second year from seed) and dried in a cool shed. Horehound tea made by pouring boiling water on the leaves is used for alleviating coughs. The fresh Horehound is also candied and is used in making Horehound ale. Its use in cookery has passed out of fashion for the flavour is too strong for modern taste. It has a good reputation as a bee plant.

*horizonta'lis -is -e,* growing parallel with the earth's surface.

**HORMID'IUM** (*hormos,* a necklace; in allusion to the small pseudobulbs clustered at the sides of the rhizome). FAM. *Orchidaceae.* A genus embracing about 7 species of dwarf, stove, Trop. American, epiphytic Orchids, often included under Epidendrum (q.v. for cultivation). Flowers variously disposed; lateral sepals broader; petals like the dorsal sepal or very narrow; lip broadly connate with the base of the short column. Leaves small, leathery or slightly fleshy. The pollen masses (4) are more distinct than in Epidendrum with a slightly different arrangement.

**H. pseudopyg'maeum.** *fl.* borne in short spikes, white, marked with red on the lip, slightly stronger in growth and l. than *H. tripterum.* Costa Rica. 1899.

**H. pyg'maeum.** A synonym of *H. tripterum.*

**H. trip'terum** is often met with in cultivation. *fl.* small, solitary or few; greenish or greenish-white, hardly ½ in. across; lip white, somewhat reniform. *rhiz.* creeping, branching, clothed with scale l. *Pseudobulbs* fusiform, 1 to 1¾ in. h., set at intervals of 1 to 2 in. on the rhiz., 2-phyllous, 1 to 2 in. long. Brazil. 1829. (B.M. 3233 as *Epidendrum pygmaeum.*) SYN. *Coelogyne triptera, Epidendrum caespitosum, E. uniflorum, Hormidium pygmaeum.*

E. C.

**HORM'INUM** (old Greek name for a kind of sage). FAM. *Labiatae.* A monotypic genus related to Salvia but with the upper stamens present as well as the lower, the anthers joined in pairs as in Monarda and with a ring of hairs in the corolla-tube. A hardy herbaceous plant growing well in any well-drained open border or on the rock-garden, and readily increased by seed or by division.

**H. pyrena'icum.** Stems erect, 6 to 12 in. h. *l.* nearly all radical, ovate, obtuse, deeply roundish-toothed. *fl.* bluish-purple, nearly 1 in. long, nodding on short pedicels, in distant 6-fld. second whorls. Summer. Pyrenees to Tirol. 1820. (S.B.F.G. 252.) var. **ro'seum** has rosy-purple fl.

**HORMONES.** It has long been suggested that there exist in plants various compounds that regulate their growth, substances that move about the plant and determine the response made to a particular environmental condition. Darwin postulated the existence of such a substance to account for the results of one-sided illumination which he observed and described, and others considered there must be flower-producing, root-forming, stem-forming, and growth-inhibiting substances produced in plants. What these substances actually were was not known, nor indeed was it known whether there were such substances, and if there were, where they were produced. Later it was discovered that seedlings of oats grown in the light produced a substance in the growing tips of the plant capable of bringing about the curvature of the plant towards the light. This substance is not produced when the seedlings are grown in the dark. The substance is produced in exceedingly small amounts, perhaps as little as 1 part in 100,000,000 of the watery sap of the plant. Search for other materials which would affect growth led to the discovery by Kögh in Holland of two such active substances in urine which were named Auxin A and Auxin B, and the general name of Auxines has been at times applied to these and other hormones or growth-regulating substances. It was further found that both these Auxines could be extracted from germinating barley, yeast, and certain vegetable oils, and these were doubtless the source of their presence in urine. The discovery of a third such substance—3-indole acetic acid—in urine was followed by active search for other organic compounds which might have similar powers of regulating plant growth in some direction, and a considerable number have been discovered and made synthetically in the chemical laboratory. It seems improbable that many of these are identical with the substances that are formed in the plant, although their action may be similar. It appears that in many instances their action depends upon the presence of some other specific substance, it may be acting at the same time, or it may be taking up action when the first substance has prepared the way, just as some enzymes do, in, e.g. changing starch to sugar and vice versa. It is certain too that while minute amounts of some of these growth-regulating substances bring about certain reactions, stronger solutions do not act with proportionately greater vigour and may indeed bring about entirely different results. From which it is clear that these growth-substances must be applied with the very greatest care, and that their use for any specific purpose must be preceded by searching and carefully controlled experiments. For various reasons only some of the substances of this nature hitherto discovered can be used in horticultural practice, and even these are in many instances highly specific in their action. Thus alpha-naphthalene acetic acid is very effective in inducing the production of seedless berries on holly if sprayed on the open flowers in a solution of 10 to 15 parts in a million of water, but it has not this effect on tomatoes. On the other hand indole acetic acid used at the rate of 1,000 parts to a million of water is effective in setting fruit on a large number of plants. Beta-naphthoxyacetic acid will bring about a good development of tomato fruits even after the flowers have fallen some days. Experiments are being made with growth-regulating substances with the object of reducing the proneness to drop prematurely, and some success has been attained with certain varieties of apples and plums, but general directions cannot yet be given and the same applies to their use as selective weed-killers. With the last there is the further complication that the reaction of plants depends largely upon the stage of growth reached, and also upon environmental conditions such as temperature and humidity. It is, however, certain that some plants are extremely sensitive to such substances as Methoxone, but the concentration and rate of application must be worked out to suit each crop and each local climate. In other ways growth-regulating substances have found some application, e.g. in inhibiting sprouting of potatoes in store by dusting with a 3 per cent. alpha-naphthyl-dimethyl-ether on powdered diatomaceous earth, using 200 grammes of the powder to 50 kilos of potatoes. Attempts to delay the opening of flowers of fruit-trees with the object of avoiding frost damage have been successful at times but the results have not been uniform. Many successful attempts to hasten root-production by treating cuttings with growth-regulating substances have been made, and some small success in inducing root-development in cuttings which have ordinarily proved very difficult to root, but here again much remains to be done in finding the best substance to use for particular plants, and the best manner of using it both as regards strength, and the state of the plant to which it is applied.

Cut and dried formulae for the use of growth-regulating substances are at the present stage of little use, for new substances are continually being discovered and their range of effective action is still a matter for extended experiment. Furthermore, actual knowledge of the constitution of the substances that act in the plants in nature is very incomplete, and until much more is known it can scarcely be safe to give directions for the general use of growth-regulating substances.

A→

**HORN MANURE.** *See* **Manures.**

**HORN OF PLENTY.** *See* **Fedia Cornucopiae.**

**HORNBEAM.** *See* **Carpinus Betulus.**

**HORNED POPPY.** *See* **Glaucium flavum.**

**HORNED RAMPION.** *See* **Phyteuma.**

**HORNET** (*Vespa crabro*) is the largest of the 7 British species of Wasps, and is distinguished by its larger size and colour—brown and orange-yellow instead of black and bright yellow. Hornets are less widely distributed than Wasps, but they often abound in wooded areas and in country districts where they build their nests in tree-holes, beneath thatch, and under the eaves of houses. They feed on fruit to a much less extent than Wasps, but they destroy quantities of many kinds of insects while beekeepers often suffer through the raiding of their hives. Owing both to the swift flight of these insects and to the fact that they remain fully active on moonlight nights, it is more difficult to trace them to their nests than Wasps. An effort should be made to discover the site and to destroy the colony if hives are raided or if the nest is situated near human habitations. (*See* **Wasps**.)

G. F. W.

**HORN-NUT.** *See* **Trapa nutans.**

*hornot'inus -a -um*, of the current year.

*Hornschuch'ii*, in honour of Christian F. Hornschuch, 1793–1850, writer on mosses.

**horny**, hard, of the consistence of horn.

*hor'ridus -a -um*, very thorny.

**HORSE BEAN.** *See* **Vicia Faba.** A

**HORSE GENTIAN.** *See* **Triosteum.**

**HORSE MANURE.** The excrement of horses is richer in nitrogen than that of cows but less rich than that of sheep. Both cows and sheep digest the fibrous matter of their food more completely than do horses, and consequently horse-dung, being also more porous and open, ferments more quickly and is therefore better fitted for the making of hotbeds and shows its value as a source of nitrogen (of which the mixed solid and liquid excrement mixed with the litter used in the stable contains about 0·7 per cent., phosphatic acid about 0·3 per cent. and potash about 0·4 per cent.) more quickly but with less lasting results than either cow, sheep, or poultry manure. Pig manure is wet and decomposes less readily than that of horses and sheep though its composition is much the same, save for the water content. Poultry manure is much richer in nitrogen, &c., but nitrifies slowly owing to the small amount of fibrous organic material contained.

Horse manure is especially valuable in mushroom growing (*see* **Mushroom**) and for this purpose it is important to obtain it from stable-fed animals not dosed with medicine. Stable litter is to be preferred for hotbeds when the whole of the droppings are left in it. Horse-dung is of less value for making manure-water than that of sheep, deer, or cows, but the drainage from a large heap in wet weather is usually of good quality and should not be wasted. Horse-dung may be used nearly fresh especially on cold, heavy soils, but on soils well drained it is better to have been previously well turned and moistened if any part is dry. If a heap is allowed to become very hot and white in the middle, great loss of nitrogen is certain and most of the value of the dung is dissipated. Horse-dung is a good top dressing for growing crops, its effects being quickly apparent.

**HORSE-CHESTNUT.** *See* **Aesculus.**

**HORSEHAIR, VEGETABLE.** *See* **Tillandsia usneoides,** the soft tissues of the dead parts of which decay and leave the hard, hanging from trees on which the plant grew, like tufts of hair. Used for packing.

**HORSE-HAIR WORMS.** A name applied to species of the genera Gordius and Mermis, belonging to a group of Round Worms or Nemathelminthes. They resemble animated horsehairs and live as larvae a parasitic life in various kinds of insects such as Water Beetles and Grass-hoppers. They are often seen after rain twining in Gordian knots on plants.

**HORSE-RADISH** (*Cochlearia Armoracia*). A hardy perennial, naturalized in Britain and widely grown in the temperate parts of the Old World from early times for the use of its roots, scraped into fine shreds for culinary purposes. Most of the horse-radish used in this country is imported but excellent produce can be grown here especially if grown in good deep, rich, moist soil. Propagation is easily effected by pieces of the root 2 or 3 in. long, with or without a good crown. The soil for the growing of horse-radish must be deeply worked for at least 2 ft. Planting must be done in early spring. Trenches should be dug 2 or 3 ft. deep, the top 15 in. of the soil being thrown into the bottom, a layer of good manure on top of this and dug in, and the trench is then filled with the soil which was before in the bottom. If several trenches are being made, the first trench may be dug to the full depth and filled from the second and so on. The pieces for planting are put on top of the good soil at the bottom of the trench 12 in. apart. Another method is to plant on the flat, making holes 15 in. deep with a crowbar, dropping the propagating piece to the bottom and filling in with good soil. Subsequent treatment is the removal of side shoots and hoeing to keep the bed free from weeds. Some of the roots may be ready after a year's growth but usually 2 or 3 years are needed. The quicker the necessary growth is made, i.e. straight roots 10 to 12 in. long, 1½ to 2 in. thick, the better they will be for use. The roots must be completely removed when lifting takes place since any piece left will grow. Fresh plantings should be made each year on a new site.

Another method is sometimes used but the complete removal of all pieces of root is very difficult. Raised narrow beds are made like those for Asparagus and enriched by large dressings of manure. Straight roots 6 to 9 in. long are laid horizontally 1 ft. apart with the crown end towards the outside of the bed and covered with 6 in. of soil. The branches from these roots grow down and when the large roots are ready the spade is laid horizontally beneath them and the whole is lifted out. The secondary roots should be lifted for use in making a fresh bed. A

**HORSE-RADISH TREE.** *See* **Moringa oleifera.**

**HORSESHOE VETCH.** *See* **Hippocrepis comosa.**

**HORSETAIL.** *See* **Equisetum.**

*Horsfal'liae*, in honour of Mrs. Horsfall of Liverpool, *c.* 1834.

**HORSFIELD'IA** (in honour of Dr. Thomas Horsfield, 1773–1859, American botanist, who collected in Java). FAM. *Araliaceae.* A genus of 2 species of tall evergreen prickly shrubs, natives of Java. Leaves alternate, stalked, cordate or peltate, 3- to 5-lobed, or palmately 5- to 9-fid, hairy or woolly beneath. Flowers in head-like umbels, small. For treatment *see* **Trevesia.**

H. aculea'ta. *l.* cordate, 5-lobed, upper 3-lobed, covered with starry hairs beneath. *fl.* greenish-yellow, in a terminal panicle densely covered with starry hairs.

*Horst'ii*, in honour of Dirk Willem Horst, 1846–?, who travelled in Molucca, &c.

**HORTENS'IA.** A synonym of Hydrangea; name in honour of Hortense van Nassau.

*horten'sis -is -e*, of or belonging to a garden.

**HORTEN'SIS opuloi'des.** A synonym of *Hydrangea macrophylla.*

## HORTICULTURE. The science and practice of Gardening.

**HOSACK'IA** (in honour of David Hosack, 1769–1835, Professor of Botany, New York). FAM. *Leguminosae*. A genus of about 45 species of herbaceous annuals or perennials, rarely sub-shrubs, mostly natives of Western N. America. Related to Lotus and sometimes included in that genus but with small, scarious stipules never leaflet-like as in Lotus, lobes of calyx shorter than tube, and keel obtuse. Leaves unequally pinnate, rarely trifoliolate. Flowers usually in umbels, yellow or reddish. The 2 species mentioned are hardy, suitable for the rockgarden, and needing only ordinary garden soil. Propagation by seeds or division.

**H. bi′color.** Glabrous perennial about 18 in. h. *lflets.* 7 to 9. *fl.* 6 to 10 in umbel, standard and keel yellow, wings often white. Summer. *Pod* slender. Washington, California. 1823. (B.R. 1257; B.M. 2913 as *Lotus pinnatus*.)

**H. crassifo′lia.** Perennial of 2 to 3 ft., nearly glabrous. *lflets.* 9 to 15, thickish, oval to ovate. *fl.* greenish-yellow or purplish, in many-fld. umbels. June. *Pod* thickish. California. (B.R. 1977 as *H. stolonifera*.)

*Ho′sei,* in honour of Bishop G. F. Hose, 1838–1922, of Singapore; or Charles Hose, 1863–1929, who travelled in Sarawak.

**Hose-in-hose,** of a gamosepalous calyx of colour and form like the corolla or with a second corolla within the first as in a form of the Primrose and Azalea.

*Hoss′ei,* in honour of Carl Curt Hosseus, 1878–?, who collected in Siam, &c.

**HOST PLANT.** A plant upon which another grows, sending suckers into it and deriving its food, either wholly or partially, from it. *See* **Parasitic Plant.**

**HOS′TA** (in honour of Nicolaus Thomas Host, 1761–1834, physician to the Emperor, Vienna). Plantain Lily. SYN. *Funkia*. FAM. *Liliaceae*. Handsome herbaceous perennials with fascicled tuberous roots, natives of E. Asia, especially Japan, and hardy in this country. Leaves mostly radical, large, stalked. Flowers large, tubular with 6 usually spreading lobes, white to dark lilac. Stamens declinate, on the tube, or hypogynous. Racemes simple, generally taller than leaves, usually 15- to 20-flowered. The flowers are usually short-lived, but are produced in succession, and apart from the flowers the foliage is often very handsome. The dwarfer species and varieties may be used for edging but the greatest value of Plantain Lilies is as woodland or shrubbery plants where the clumps in semi-shade are excellent throughout the summer until frosts cut them down, or on lawns or in borders. They can be grown in pots for greenhouse or conservatory decoration. The soil should be well manured and not liable to dry out readily. Propagation is by the division of healthy clumps by cutting through with a sharp spade in winter, or, better, when the growth begins in spring. There is still much confusion in gardens, and in botanical literature, among Plantain Lilies. Prof. L. H. Bailey has, in *Gentes Herbarum*, vol. ii, done much to clarify their classification and a good account of his work with some additions has been given by W. T. Stearn in *Gard. Chron.*, 1931, pp. 27 ff. The following key has been modified from this work for inclusion here. Further study will no doubt result in name changes. A

KEY

1. *Fl. white, 4 in. long, trumpet-shaped, ascending;*
 *lvs. cordate, glossy green*     H. plantaginea
1. *Fl. more or less drooping, shorter*     2
2. *Perianth tube suddenly expanded from a narrow*
 *base; lvs. dark green*     H. ventricosa
2. *Perianth tube gradually expanded, lilac to white*     3
3. *Lvs. glaucous or blue-green, broad-ovate-cordate, veins*
 *usually more than 8 each side of midrib*     4
3. *Lvs. green, tapered at base, with usually not more than*
 *8 veins each side of midrib*     5

4. *Infl. longer than l., fl. open widely*     H. Fortunei
4. *Infl. usually shorter than l.; fl. narrow*     H. glauca
5. *L.-blade often over twice as long as wide, stalk not*
 *winged*     H. lancifolia
5. *L.-blade not more than twice as long as wide*     6
6. *Lvs. lanceolate, stalk winged; infl. much above l.*     H. rectifolia
6. *Lvs. oval or ovate, plant dwarf*     7
7. *Lvs. ovate, pointed, wavy, marked with white*     H. undulata
7. *Lvs. oval*     8
8. *Lvs. acute, flat; fl. pale lilac*     H. Sieboldiana
8. *Lvs. blunt, flat; dark lilac*     H. decorata

**H. coeru′lea.** A synonym of *H. ventricosa*.

**H. decora′ta.** Differs from *H. rectifolia* by its broader-oval, blunt l. abruptly narrowed to the stalk, and from *H. undulata* by its usually leafless scape and its flat l. not splashed with white. *l.* about 8 in. h. *Scape* up to 24 in. h., 12- to 24-fld. Japan. (B.M. 9395.) var. **margina′ta** has white-margined l.

**H. Fortu′nei.** *l.* rather less glaucous than *H. glauca*, cordate-ovate, blade 5 to 8 in. long, up to 6½ in. wide; stalk about as long. *fl.* pale lilac, funnel-shaped, open at mouth, about 1½ in. long; racemes overtopping l.; bracts up to 1½ in. long. July. Japan. 1876. SYN. *Funkia Sieboldii* of gardens. var. **gigan′tea** is larger in all parts, up to 42 in. h.; **marginato-al′ba** has white-margined l.; **robus′ta** is another strong form.

**H. glau′ca.** *l.* glaucous or blue-green, blade up to about 12 in. long, 9 in. wide, petiole as long. *fl.* pale lilac, narrow-funnel-shaped, about 2 in. long, in racemes of about 15 fls. scarcely taller than foliage. June. Japan. 1830. (B.R. 25, 50 as *Funkia Sieboldiana*; L.B.C. 1869 as *Hemerocallis Sieboldtiana*.) Commonly called *Funkia Sieboldiana* in gardens.

**H. grandiflo′ra.** A synonym of *H. plantaginea grandiflora*.

**H. lanceola′ta.** A synonym of *H. lancifolia*.

*Hosta lancifolia*

**H. lancifo′lia.** *l.* ovate-lanceolate, acute, green, blade about 5 in. long, 2 in. wide; stalk narrow, longer than blade. *fl.* pale lilac, 1½ in. long, funnel-shaped with segs. spreading; raceme 6- to 10-fld.; scape slender. July to September. Japan. 1829. (L.B.C. 1658 as *Hemerocallis lancifolia*.) SYN. *H. japonica, Funkia lanceolata*. A variable plant in height and in other characters. var. **albo-margina′ta** has white-margined l. (B.M. 3657.); **for′tis** is of strong growth with infl. up to 3 ft. h. and fl. earlier; **tardiflo′ra** is dwarf in growth (10 to 15 in.), sometimes dense-fld., fl. in September, October. (B.M. 8645 as *Funkia lancifolia tardiflora*.) SYN. *F. tardiflora*.

**H. plantagin′ea.** *l.* ovate-cordate, green, 12 to 20 in. long including stalk; stalk winged, wings incurved. *fl.* white, 4 in. or more long, ascending, trumpet-shaped, fragrant, in short racemes, well above l.; bracts sheathing base of fl. August, September. China, Japan. 1830. (B.M. 1433 as *Hemerocallis japonica.*) SYN. *Funkia subcordata, F. spathulata*. var. **grandiflo′ra** has longer fl. than in type. SYN. *Funkia grandiflora*; **japon′ica,** a form with proportionately narrower and more acuminate l.

**H. rectifo′lia.** *l.* green, more or less erect, about 12 in. long, blade about 6 in. long, 3 in. wide, the broad-winged stalk as long. *fl.* dark lilac, about 2 in. long, funnel-shaped, widely opened; racemes many-fld. about 12 in. long, well overtopping foliage. July. Japan. 1897. (G.C. 91 (1932), 23.) SYN. *Funkia longipes* of gardens.

**H. Sieboldia′na.** *l.* ovate, slender-pointed, tapering below, to a sheathing petiole, striated, green. *fl.* whitish, tinged with purple and green, 1 to 1½ in. long, funnel-shaped, nodding; racemes taller than foliage, 8 to 9 in. long, 6-to 10-fld. August. Japan. (B.M. 3663.)

**H. spathula'ta.** A synonym of *H. plantaginea.*

**H. subcorda'ta.** A synonym of *H. plantaginea.*

**H. tardiflo'ra.** A variety of *H. lancifolia.*

*Hosta Sieboldiana* (p. 1012)

**H. undula'ta.** *l.* green, splashed white; blade ovate, about 6 in. long, 3¼ in. wide, waved, stalk rather longer. *fl.* pale lilac, about 2 in. long on a somewhat leafy scape about 30 in. *h.* August. Japan. 1834. (Lowe, Beaut. lvd. Pl. 34 as *Funkia Sieboldiana variegata.*)

**H. ventrico'sa.** *l.* ovate-cordate, green, blade about 9 in. long, sometimes up to 8 in. wide, stalk often longer, edges not incurved. *fl.* dark lavender specked white within, 1½ to 2 in. long, tube suddenly expanded from a narrow base; raceme 10- to 15-fld. on a stiff stem up to 3 ft. long. May. E. Asia. 1790. (B.M. 894 as *Hemerocallis coerulea.*) SYN. *H. ovata, Funkia ovata, F. coerulea.* var. **margina'ta** has white-margined *l.* A yellow-margined form is also known.

**HOTBEDS** are special beds in which the temperature is raised above the normal by heat obtained from fermenting material, by hot-water pipes, or by electrical methods. The last two methods are comparatively recent and on the whole less satisfactory so far as the regulation of soil moisture is concerned, though more amenable to regulation of temperature, than the old method. Hotbeds are occasionally made for encouraging growth of tender plants in the open but find their chief application for plants under cloches, in frames, or in glass-houses. They are extremely useful, especially in spring, for forwarding early vegetables, for propagating and growing-on all sorts of soft-wooded plants, and for the cultivation of such plants as cucumbers and melons, for they provide both moist and a genial temperature without, if properly made, the great fluctuations to which normal soil is subject. Cuttings of bedding plants produce roots more readily and grow faster on a hotbed than if merely placed in a structure with fire-heat.

To prepare a bed of the best quality fresh stable litter should be secured and mixed thoroughly with at least an equal quantity of newly collected leaves. Stable litter by itself heats much too violently and does not last long; the mixture with leaves makes the heating process slower but more lasting. If any part of the heap is dry it should be well watered during the mixing and the heap turned every other day for a week, breaking up any clods as the work proceeds. It should be then ready for the making of the hotbed by building a heap the shape of the frames to be used with a width of 2 ft. all round (putting the largest litter on the outside), or for placing in a pit of sufficient depth. The whole should be firmly and evenly trodden so as to ensure that no one part settles more closely than another and to secure uniform temperature all through. The temperature of the heap is largely dependent upon the activity of the bacteria and fungi which bring about fermentation and this depends to a great extent upon the amount of oxygen and water available. Constancy and equal distribution of air and water are thus necessary for the maintenance of regular temperature.

All rank steam must be allowed to pass off before plants are placed in the frames and shading should be applied during sunshine if steam is likely to arise. Some top ventilation night and day should be allowed for a short time after the beds are made. No seed sowing should be done until the temperature falls to 85° F. or for the hardier plants to 75°. Hotbeds on the soil surface made for propagating should be not less than 2 or 3 ft. thick beneath the frames and apart from the material placed in the frames themselves. A layer of ashes over the surface is useful for the plunging of small pots.

The beds should be made on a well-drained site sheltered from cold winds by a fence or wall or tall hedge and near a water-supply. For planting direct sifted old hotbed manure to the depth of 4 to 6 in. may be used above the hotbed proper or equal parts of this material and good garden loam.

When the temperature tends to fall below the minimum required, as a result of the bed itself becoming cool or because of severe weather, hot manure should be heaped outside the frames from the level of the bed to the level of the lights, repeating this measure when necessary.

It is, of course, useless to have warm soil if the air around the plants is cold and it is therefore necessary to cover the frames closely at night with mats, straw-mats being most useful, to prevent loss of heat by radiation and to keep out frosts.

For other methods of soil heating, *see* **Heating.**

**HOTEI'A.** Included in **Astilbe.** *See* **A. japonica.**

**HOTTENTOT BREAD.** *See* **Dioscorea elephantipes.**

**HOTTENTOT CHERRY.** *See* **Maurocenia capensis.**

**HOTTENTOT FIG.** *See* **Mesembryanthemum edule.**

**HOTTENTOT'S HEAD.** *See* **Stangeria eriopus.**

**HOTTO'NIA** (in honour of P. Hotton, 1648–1709, a Dutch botanist, Professor at Leiden). FAM. *Primulaceae.* A genus of 2 species of hardy perennial aquatic herbs, natives of Europe, N.W. Asia, and N. America. Stem spongy with many air spaces, leaves much divided into capillary segments, submerged. Flowers white or lilac, honeyed, in whorls, forming a terminal raceme. Fruit globular, 5-valved, many-seeded. They grow well in shallow ponds and are useful aquarium plants, being good oxygenators. Propagated by division in spring or by seeds sown at the same season.

**H. infla'ta.** Stem entirely submerged, branched. *l.* almost or quite sessile, ovate or oblong, divided almost to midrib into narrowly linear, entire segs., ½ to 2 in. long. *Peduncles* several in a cluster at ends of stems and branches, partly aerial, hollow, jointed, 3 to 8 in. h., 1 in. thick. *fl.* white in whorls of 2 to 10, small; first fl. cleistogamous. June to August. N. America.

**H. palus'tris.*** Featherfoil; Water Violet. 1 to 2 ft. *h.* *l.* submerged. deeply pinnatifid, with linear segs. *fl.* lilac with a yellow eye, primrose-shaped, dimorphic; whorls numerous. June. Europe, including Britain, W. Siberia. (E.B. 1128.)

F. P.

**HOT-WATER TREATMENT.** A method of controlling various plant diseases and animal pests. So far as plant diseases are concerned the treatment is used for certain seedborne diseases to kill fungus and bacterial parasites living in the seed tissues or on the seed coat and also on certain herbaceous plants to kill the disease-causing organisms living in them. E.g. the Mint Rust fungus, *Puccinia menthae*, is controlled by hot-water treatment of selected runners and shoots which are thus rendered free of the fungus (see **Mint diseases**). Where animal pests are concerned the treatment consists in immersing the plants in water at a constant temperature of 110° F. for a certain time from 20 min. to 3 hrs. It is used for controlling (1) Eel-worms in bulbs (Narcissus), and dormant stools, and rooted cuttings (Chrysanthemum); (2) Tarsonemid Mites in bulbs (Narcissus, Amaryllis) and in runners (Strawberry); and (3) the Large and Lesser Bulb Fly maggots in Narcissus. The capacities of the baths used range from 7 lb. to 10 cwt. of Narcissus bulbs, and are well suited to all needs. Electric-, gas-, and oil-heated baths are obtainable fitted with a thermostat for temperature control. The treatment is successful provided that (i) the operation is done at the right time, (ii) an accurate thermometer is used, (iii) the proper type of bath is used for the particular purpose, (iv) the temperature is maintained at a constant level throughout the period of immersion, (v) the correct type of container for bulbs is used. The types of baths available and the technique employed to obtain effective results are described in Bulletin 105 of the Ministry of Agriculture on 'The Efficiency of Baths used for the Hot-water Treatment of Narcissus Bulbs'.

D. E. G. and G. F. W.

**HOULLET'IA** (in honour of M. Houllet, 1811–90, assistant curator under Decaisne, Jardin des Plantes, Paris). FAM. *Orchidaceae*. A genus of about 10 species of ornamental epiphytic orchids, natives of Colombia and Brazil. Scapes from the base of the pseudobulbs. Perianth spreading; sepals nearly free; petals a little smaller, clawed; lip 3-lobed, fleshy, with the hypochil and epichil well defined by a constriction continuous with the base of the column, which is erect, arched, and clavate. Though allied to Stanhopea considerable differences are apparent. In Houlletia the scapes are usually erect (arched or drooped in some species) and the sepals and petals are of greater substance. The hypochil bears 2 horn-like processes which are bent backward and are not nearly as large and prominent as are the horns in many Stanhopeas. The pseudobulbs are similar but smaller in Houlletia and the single leaf is narrower and contracted into a longer petiole. Compost and temperatures are similar to those given for Stanhopea, but pots should take the place of baskets as the taller leaves render suspension difficult. Careful watering is necessary particularly when growth first begins; when growth is finished a rest is required with infrequent waterings. The winter night temperature should be from 55 to 60° F. When young the plicate leaves may be attacked by thrips which should be got rid of by dipping or light fumigation.

**H. Brocklehurstia'na.*** *fl.* nodding, fragrant, 3 to 3½ in. wide; pet. orange-brown with darker spots; lip yellow, spotted dark brown, hypochil whitish with purple spots, epichil tongue-shaped, recurved, flushed and spotted purple-brown, its basal angles pointed; spikes about 6-fld. Summer. *Pseudobulbs* short, rounded. *l.* broad, pale green, 18 to 30 in. long including long petiole. Brazil. 1841. (B.M. 4072.) SYN. *H. stapeliaeflora*.

**H. chrysan'tha.** A synonym of *H. Wallisii*.

**H. Landsberg'ii.*** *fl.* fleshy, 3 in. wide; sep. orange with small red spots; pet. smaller, notched; lip white, tinged purple, narrow, with 4 horn-like lobes; peduncle purplish, stout, 4 in. long, drooping. *l.* 12 in. long, 4 in. wide, strongly ribbed. *Pseudobulbs* 1 in. long. Costa Rica. 1891. (B.M. 7362.)

**H. Lowia'na.** *fl.* 1 to 3, about 3 in. h., less in width, soft creamy-yellow, the inner surfaces of sep. and pet. covered with minute purple dots; sep. concave, larger than the flat tapered pet. which have a semicircular sinus on their upper margins; lip ivory-white,

spotted with magenta on the hypochil and sparsely so on the hastate epichil, the barbs of which are narrow and linear, two similar but larger processes extend backwards from the hypochil. Peduncles short, bent forwards or sideways. *Pseudobulbs* shortly pyriform, furrowed; said to be diphyllous. *l.* cuneate-oblong-lanceolate, acute, plaited, unequal. Colombia. 1874. (G.C. 20 (1896), 716.)

**H. odoratis'sima.*** *fl.* 2½ in. wide; sep. and pet. orange-brown, striped paler; lip white, tipped yellow, epichil hastate. *l.* light green. Habit much as in *H. Brocklehurstiana* but smaller. New Granada. var. **antiquen'sis,*** sep. much wider, lip very long, almost sagittate, white, tinged pale yellow, spike erect, many-fld., l. and pseudobulb dark green. Antioquia. 1870. (W.O.A. 316.); **xanthi'na,** sep. and pet. orange-yellow, lip sulphur and white. 1884.

**H. pic'ta.*** *fl.* 7 to 10, cinnamon brown, 3½ in. wide; sep. narrow-oblong, tips rounded; pet. rather smaller, narrowed to base; lip shorter than pet., jointed in middle, epichil hastate with blunt apex recurved, hypochil with ascending spurs, little shorter than column; column yellow; blotched brown at back. Habit much as in *H. Brocklehurstiana*. *Pseudobulbs* clustered, about 3 in. long, narrow, ovoid, compressed. New Granada. (B.M. 6305.)

**H. San'deri.** *fl.* 2 to 4, malodorous, inverted, almost globular, sep. partially concealing the pet., creamy-white passing to yellow at base of lip; scape 9 to 12 in. h. Resembling *H. Brocklehurstiana* in growth but smaller. Peru. Before 1910. (B.M. 8346.)

**H. tigri'na.** *fl.* sep. greenish-yellow barred with brown; pet. smaller, rich yellow, barred crimson; lip white, dotted brown and barred light purple; raceme decumbent, few-fld. *Pseudobulbs* 2 in. long, somewhat ovate, with long dark-green obtuse l. Colombia. 1852. (I.H. 612.)

**H. Wallis'ii.** *fl.* large, 2½ in. wide; sep. and pet. golden-yellow, much spotted chocolate; lip rich yellow, freckled crimson, epichil with horn-like basal angles; spike from base of the flask-shaped pseudobulbs, 6- to 8-fld. *l.* solitary, narrow elliptic, plaited. Colombia. 1869. (I.H. 18, 71 as *H. chrysantha*.)

E. C.

**HOUND'S TONGUE.** *See* **Cynoglossum.**

**HOUSELEEK.** *See* **Sempervivum.**

A→

**HOUS'TONIA** (in honour of Dr. William Houston, 1695–1733, writer on American plants). FAM. *Rubiaceae*. A genus of about 50 species of hardy herbaceous tufted perennials, natives of N. America and Mexico. Leaves small, opposite. Flowers white, purple, or blue, dimorphic; parts in fours; corolla gamopetalous; stamens 2. Fruit a capsule opening at top. They are excellent plants for growing between large stones where they will flower nearly all the year round, and for moist shady places. A compost of leaf-soil and sand suits them. *H. caerulea* forms a good pot plant under cold frame treatment or for the alpine house, and may be used for surfacing soil in pots in which bare-stemmed hardy plants are grown. Propagation is by division in early autumn or by seeds.

**H. caeru'lea.** Bluets. Small tufted perennial, 3 to 6 in. h. *l.* ovate-lanceolate, narrowed at base; radical l. spatulate, slightly hairy. *fl.* light blue, sometimes white; cor. salver-shaped, ½ in. across; peduncles 1-fld., long. June onwards. Virginia. 1785. (B.M. 370.) May be treated as an annual or biennial. var. **al'ba,** *fl.* white. (B.M. 2822 illustrates probably a form of this species as *H. serpyllifolia*.)

**H. longifo'lia.** About 6 in. h. or more. *l.* linear-oblong, lowest tapered to base and ciliate; stipules entire or 2- or 3-toothed. *fl.* pale lilac or white in leafy panicles; stamens included. August. N. America. 1828. (B.M. 3099.)

**H. purpu'rea.** Tufted perennial, 3 to 18 in. h. *l.* roundish-ovate to lanceolate, short-stalked. *fl.* purple, funnel-shaped, on many-fld. peduncles. July, August. Mid. United States. Related to *H. longifolia*. (L.B.C. 1621.)

**H. serpyllifo'lia.** Prostrate, widely creeping, about 3 in. h. *l.* spatulate, rather hairy. *fl.* deep violet-blue or white, larger than in *H. caerulea*, on long, terminal 1-fld. peduncles. Early summer. 1826.

**HOUT'TEA** (in honour of Louis van Houtte, 1810–76, well-known Belgian nurseryman). FAM. *Gesneriaceae*. A genus of 3 species of shrubs, natives of Brazil, closely related to Isoloma. Leaves opposite, crenulate, pale or ashy-hairy beneath. Flowers scarlet or spotted; corolla tube cylindrical. For treatment *see* **Gesneria.**

**H. Gard'neri.** Glabrous perennial about 2 ft. h. *l.* thick, fleshy, elm-like. *fl.* red, downy on long axillary 1-fld. peduncles; 3 cal. segs. slender-pointed. July, August. 1841. (B.M. 4121 as *Gesneria Gardneri*.)

**H. pardi'na.** Downy perennial about 18 in. h. *l.* elliptic, thickish, serrate, hairy beneath. *fl.* orange-red, tube curved, limb spreading, spotted; peduncles axillary, 1-fld. August to October. 1847. (B.M. 4348 as *Gesneria pardina.*)

**HOUTTUYN'IA** (in honour of Martin Houttuyn, 1720–94?, a Dutch naturalist). FAM. *Saururaceae.* A genus of a single perennial, herbaceous water-plant in the Himalayan region, China, and Japan. Rootstock creeping, leaves broad, simple. Flowers small, naked in spikes subtended by a corolla-like spathe with 4 ovate, spreading, white flaps. A hardy plant in sheltered positions growing best in shallow water or moist loamy soil. Propagated by division in spring, or from seeds. The plant is of interest in that it seeds parthenogenetically.

**H. califor'nica.** *See* **Anemopsis californica.**

**H. corda'ta.** Stem leafy, angular, erect, 6 to 24 in. h. *l.* broad, simple, alternate, ovate-cordate, bluish-green, 5-nerved. Involucre resembling a cor. of 4 white, ovate, spreading, elliptical lflets., inserted immediately below the oblong spadix, which bears several naked, closely packed fl., stamens 3; peduncle terminal, solitary. June. 1820. (B.M. 2731.) SYN. *Gymnotheca chinensis, Polypara cochinchinensis.*

F. P.

**HO'VEA** (in honour of A. P. Hove, a Polish botanist and collector for Kew). FAM. *Leguminosae.* A genus of about a dozen species of evergreen shrubs confined to Australia and Tasmania. Leaves alternate, entire or prickly toothed. Flowers blue or purple, in axillary clusters or shortly racemose. They require cool greenhouse conditions similar to Acacias or Callistemons and although not much grown at the present time are very charming.

**H. Cel'sii.*** Shrub 3 to 6, sometimes up to 10 ft., shoots reddish with minute down. *l.* mostly oblanceolate to obovate, 1 to 3 in. long, ⅛ to ¼ in. wide, blunt ended, cuneate. *fl.* blue, in axillary clusters of 2 to 4 very freely borne on lateral leafy shoots; standard pet. ½ in. across with a white basal patch; cal. and stalks rusty-downy. March. W. Australia. 1818. (B.M. 2005.) SYN. *H. elliptica.*

**H. chorizemifo'lia.*** Shrub of several ft., shoots rusty-downy. *l.* oblong-ovate to oval, ¾ to 3 in. long, ½ to 1 in. wide, margins sparsely stiffly spine-toothed, glabrous, and net-veined beneath. *fl.* 2 to 6 in the l.-axils; standard pet. ½ in. wide, intense blue with a basal white patch; wings ¼ in. long. April. W. Australia. (B.R. 1524.) Very distinct by its holly-like l.

**H. ellip'tica.** A synonym of *H. Celsii.*

**H. lanceola'ta.** A variety of *H. longifolia.*

**H. longifo'lia.** Erect shrub, 8 to 10 ft., shoots softly downy. *l.* linear-oblong, pointed, cuneate, ¾ to 3 in. long, ⅛ to ⅜ in. wide, margins recurved, reddish-downy beneath. *fl.* in short axillary downy clusters, sometimes solitary, sometimes racemose; standard pet. ⅜ in. across, pale blue with a basal yellow patch; wings wholly blue. Australia. 1805. (B.R. 614 (and as *H. racemulosa,* 29. 4).) var. **lanceola'ta,** *l.* thicker, broader, densely downy beneath. (B.M. 1624 as *H. lanceolata.*); **panno'sa,** parts almost woolly, l. large, leathery, fl. large, shortly stalked. (B.M. 3053 as *H. pannosa.*)

**H. pun'gens.*** Shrub 1 to 3 ft., shoots hairy. *l.* linear, ½ to 1¼ in. long with a prickly mucronate tip, margins rolled under. *fl.* 1 to 3, axillary, short-stalked, deep violet-purple; standard pet. ⅜ in. wide, notched at top, and with a whitish patch at base. Spring. W. Australia. 1837. (P.M.B. 6, 101.)

W. J. B.

**HOVEN'IA** (in honour of David Hoven, a senator of Amsterdam). FAM. *Rhamnaceae.* A single species native of Japan. Flowers 5-parted; petals enclosing stamens; disk hairy, style 3-parted. The branches of the inflorescence become fleshy and contorted at maturity, turn red, and are edible. It grows well in sandy loam and is fairly hardy but apt to be cut at the tips in winter. Cuttings of ripe wood will root in sand under a bell-glass.

**H. dul'cis.** Japanese Raisin Tree. Deciduous tree of about 30 ft., branches erect, young shoots downy. *l.* alternate, oval or cordate, 4 to 7 in. long, 3 to 6 in. wide, tapering to tip, unequally toothed, downy beneath. *fl.* greenish-white, small, in axillary and terminal cymes, 2 to 3 in. wide; peduncles sub-cylindric, reflexed, smooth, about 1 in. long, thickening after flowering, containing a sweet red pulp in which the 3-celled leathery indehiscent fr. is often partially embedded. Himalaya, China. 1812. Cultivated in Japan. (B.M. 2360.) SYN. *H. inaequalis.*

**HOVER FLIES** or Hawk Flies (FAM. *Syrphidae*) are well known for their habit of hovering over flowers in bright sunshine during summer and autumn. The females lay their white or yellowish eggs on leaves and shoots of plants infested with Aphides. The legless, peg-shaped, slug-like, greenish or brownish maggots wriggle and loop along the leaves feeding voraciously upon Aphides, the bodies of which are sucked dry and cast aside. When fully fed, they pupate in a pear-shaped puparium, which is firmly attached to the leaves or to some neighbouring support. The winter is spent either in the maggot stage amongst dead leaves and rubbish or in the pupal stage. The adults of many species resemble Wasps in their general coloration having black-and-yellow-banded bodies. They feed on pollen and nectar and are useful pollinating agents of fruit blossom.

G. F. W.

**HOW'EA** (from Lord Howe Is. where alone the genus is found). FAM. *Palmaceae.* A genus of 2 species of very attractive Palms related to Linospadix, differing by the flowers having very numerous stamens with erect, basifixed anthers, the female flowers having no staminodes and the ovule erect. Spineless Palms with stout, erect, ringed stems. Leaves equally pinnatisect in a dense terminal crown, the segments narrow, slender-pointed. Spadix 2 to 3 ft. long, 1 to 5 from the single spathe. Fruit 1½ in. long, olive-shaped. The Howeas (usually called Kentias in the market) are the most popular of Palms for general decorative work and among the most satisfactory for growing in rooms as well as in the warm greenhouse. They are raised from seeds imported from Lord Howe Is. The seeds should be sown as soon as received in a warm house in a compost of light soil, watered liberally, and given a temperature of about 80° F. The seedlings should be potted into small thumb-pots when the first leaf is developed and given a night temperature of 65° F. and moderate shade. They may be shifted on into slightly larger pots in 3 or 4 months and thenceforward have a temperature of about 60° F. They require ample water when growing. A good rich loam lightened by peat serves them well and they are the better for manure water periodically. *H. Forsteriana* is the better of the two species for room decoration.

**H. Belmorea'na.*** Curly Palm. Stem up to 35 ft. in the wild. *l.* 6 to 8 ft. long, with numerous long slender segments, more or less erect. *fl.* on thick, simple, drooping spikes. *fr.* oblong or elliptical, 1 to 1½ in. long, with a hard pericarp when dry. (B.M. 7018, 8760.) SYN. *Kentia Belmoreana.*

**H. Forsteria'na.*** Flat or Thatch Leaf Palm. Closely resembling the former species in male fl. and fr., but l. segs. rather fewer, crown of l. less crowded, segs. drooping. SYN. *Kentia Forsteriana.*

***Howell'ii,*** in honour of Thomas Howell who in 1884 rediscovered *Picea Breweriana,* &c., in California.

**HOY'A** (in honour of Thomas Hoy, one-time gardener to the Duke of Northumberland at Sion House). FAM. *Asclepiadaceae.* A genus of about 70 species of climbing or decumbent evergreen shrubs, most abundant in Malaya but found also in India, China, and the hotter parts of Australia. Leaves opposite, fleshy or leathery. Flowers usually of medium size or large, corolla rotate. Hoyas are interesting and ornamental plants with handsome wax-like flowers in umbel-like clusters. Most of them grow better in an intermediate temperature than where it is very hot. They are better trained on a wall or where more moisture is present than on the rafters of the house or in any dry position. *H. carnosa,* a fine species, is the one most frequently grown. It sometimes attaches itself to a wall, like Ivy, and grows freely when planted out at the base. It is quite easy to manage and usually improves with age. *H. bella* is a slender plant needing a little more heat. It is well adapted for growing in hanging baskets or over pieces of dead tree fern placed in the middle of pans. Propagation of most species is usually by cuttings or layers. *H. bella,* however, is best grafted on a stronger-growing species, doing better thus than on its own roots. Cuttings should be taken in spring, or later in the year, from shoots of the preceding summer's growth, placed in a compost of peat and sand, and plunged in bottom heat in a close frame. Slight shade and careful watering are necessary. The rooted cuttings should be shifted into larger pots with a similar compost, and the points of the shoots should be stopped when new growth begins. For layers good-sized shoots should have a few leaves removed and be layered in pots of soil until rooted. When rooted they should be potted on into pots of a suitable size according to their strength, or the stronger-growing species may be planted out in rather rough peaty soil, taking care that drainage is efficient. They do not need much shade nor a too close atmosphere, and they should be allowed to rest in winter by having less water and a temperature not exceeding 50° F., starting them again in spring. The flower-stalks should not be removed as the flowers of the next year are formed upon them as well as upon the young wood when it is growing well. Plants that attach themselves to walls will sometimes maintain themselves there even when the main root in the soil dies away. Mealy bug is sometimes troublesome but this can usually be controlled by a fine jet from the hose-pipe or by hand-picking. All the species mentioned below are climbers, unless it is otherwise stated.

**H. angustifo'lia.** Slender climber, young shoots sparsely hairy. *l.* linear-lanceolate, 4 to 6 in. long, ⅓ in. wide, fleshy, acute, deep green. *fl.* white with a small purple eye, about ¾ in. across; umbels 8- to 12-fld.; pedicels about 1 in. long. China.

**H. austra'lis.** *l.* obovate or sub-orbicular, obtuse or shortly pointed, leathery, deep green. *fl.* white, tinged pink, fragrant of Honeysuckle; in deflexed umbels. October. Queensland, New S. Wales. 1863. (B.M. 5820.)

**H. bel'la.*** Dwarf, shrubby, slender, about 1½ ft. h., forming a drooping mass. *l.* small, dark green above, short-stalked. *fl.* waxy-white with a rose-crimson or violet centre, in many-fld. short-stalked umbels. India. 1847. (B.M. 4402.) Syn. *H. Paxtonii.*

**H. burman'ica.** Dwarf shrub to 15 in., branches pale, terete. *l.* ovate-lanceolate, 2 to 3 in. long, slender-pointed, slightly concave, glabrous, glaucous green. *fl.* small, yellow with reddish-purple flush at base; pedicels short; umbels few-fld., axillary and terminal. India, Burma.

**H. carno'sa.*** Wax Flower. *l.* oval-oblong, slender-pointed. *fl.* pinkish-white; cor. fleshy, bearded within; umbels pendulous; peduncles short; pedicels downy. Summer. Queensland. 1802. (B.M. 788 as *Asclepias carnosa.*) var. **variega'ta,** *l.* variegated.

**H. cinnamomifo'lia.** Stem long, branching, twining to 10 ft. h. *l.* ovate, large, slightly peltate, slender-pointed, thick; stalks very thick, short, 3 middle veins very conspicuous. *fl.* pale yellow-green, large; segs. broadly ovate, acute; segs. of corona deep purple-red, ovate, acute, thick, fleshy. July. Java. 1847. (B.M. 4347.)

**H. coria'cea.** Glabrous twiner. *l.* elliptical or elliptic-ovate, acute, leathery, dark green. *fl.* brownish-yellow in large umbels; pedicels slightly hairy. Java. 1838. (B.M. 4518.)

**H. corona'ria.** *l.* oval, acute, leathery, hairy beneath, margins recurved; stalks terete, hairy. *fl.* yellow with 5 red spots at base of corona, large, in axillary umbels. Java. 1856. (B.M. 4969.) Syn. *H. grandiflora.*

**H. Cumingia'na.** *l.* close, flat, cordate, slightly downy beneath, sessile. *fl.* greenish-yellow or white; corona rich purplish-brown; umbels short, axillary. Spring, summer. Malaya. (B.M. 5148.)

**H. Engleria'na.** Branches angled, partly pendent. *l.* lanceolate or narrowly ovate-lanceolate, stalk short. *fl.* whitish, ⅓ in. across, fragrant; cor. fleshy, deeply 5-lobed, usually in 4-fld. terminal umbels. Siam. Somewhat resembles *H. linearis* but with smaller *l.* and different habit.

**H. frater'na.*** Stem terete. *l.* elliptical, 6 to 12 in. long, thick, leathery, fleshy, glabrous, shining dark green above, margins recurved, apex acute, base sub-cordate, midrib broad, prominent. *fl.* brownish-red, in dense umbels; peduncles thickened at base, shorter than *l.* Java. (B.M. 4684.)

**H. fusco-margina'ta.** *l.* ovate-lanceolate, about 8 in. long, fleshy, margins tawny. *fl.* pale yellow to yellowish-green; umbels many-fld.; peduncles about 2 in. long. Habitat?

**H. globulo'sa.*** *l.* oblong, rounded at base, slender-pointed, leathery, more or less hairy. *fl.* pale straw, or cream, in globose umbels; corona pink at base. April. Sikkim. 1880. (G.C. 17 (1882), 741.) Succeeds with same treatment as *H. carnosa.*

**H. gonoloboi'des.** Climber with reddish-brown bristly hairs. *l.* cordate-ovate, slender-pointed, rather thin, hairy on both sides. *fl.* brownish, rotate; lobes ovate, obtuse; umbels on bristly hairy peduncles. India? 1884.

**H. Griffith'ii.*** Stem climbing, flexuous. *l.* distant, elliptic to oblanceolate, 4 to 10 in. long; stalk very short. *fl.* dull rose-red with yellowish edges without, paler and yellowish within with 3 faint pink stripes on each seg., 1 to 1½ in. across; umbel many-fld., peduncle stout, 1 to 1½ in. long. July. E. Bengal. 1875. (B.M. 6877.)

**H. imperia'lis.*** Tall climber with downy stems and *l.* *l.* elliptical or linear-oblong, obtuse with a short point, 6 to 9 in. long, slightly hairy. *fl.* reddish-brown or dull purple, about 3 in. across, waxy, rather hairy near the white corona; umbels 8 to 9 in. across, 8- to 10-fld., drooping, on long peduncles. Borneo. 1847. (B.M. 4397.) Needs rich soil and a rather high temperature.

**H. Kerr'ii.** Stems smooth, pale. *l.* orbicular-obcordate, rounded or broadly wedge-shaped at base, leathery, dull dark green above, paler beneath with soft hairs, margin ciliate; stalk very stout. *fl.* creamy-white and rose-purple, becoming brownish, glabrous without, densely hairy within; lobes of corona rose-purple. Summer. Siam. 1926. (B.M. 9322.)

**H. lacuno'sa.** Branches terete, rooting. *l.* elliptic-lanceolate, slender-pointed, midrib and few veins depressed above; stalk thick, short. *fl.* greenish-yellow, rotate, velvety-hairy within; lobes finally reflexed; umbel flattish, many-fld.; peduncle usually shorter than *l.* March to June. East Indies. 1854. (B.M. 4826.) var. **pallidiflo'ra,** *fl.* almost colourless. *l.* broader than in type, veins obsolete. Java. (B.M. 5272.)

**H. lasian'tha.*** *l.* ovate with short point; veins obsolete. *fl.* yellow; cor. reflexed, densely shaggy within; umbels terminal, peduncles long. July. Borneo. 1858. (B.M. 5081 as *Plocostemma lasianthum.*)

**H. Lauterbach'ii.** Stems and *l.* hairy. *fl.* dark brownish-red without, emerald green within, large, hairy. New Guinea. 1896.

**H. linea'ris.*** Branches pendulous, slender. *l.* cylindrical, rather pointed, deeply grooved beneath, dark green; stalk short. *fl.* white; umbel terminal, loose, sessile. Autumn. Himalaya. A good basket plant. var. **sikkimen'sis,** stems weak and flaccid. *l.* hairy, soft. *fl.* nearly ½ in. across, cal. lobes small, cor. lobes recurved, umbel 10- to 13-fld., loose. Sikkim. 1883. (B.M. 6682.)

**H. longifo'lia Shepherd'ii.** *l.* 2 to 6 in. long, ⅓ in. wide, with a short point, dark green and channelled above, paler and roundish beneath, suddenly bent downwards at apex of the short stalk. *fl.* small, delicate white and rose, in umbels about 2 in. across. June. Sikkim, Khasia Hills. 1860. (B.M. 5269.)

**H. multiflo'ra.** Stout, glabrous climber. *l.* linear-oblong, acute at both ends, stalk short. *fl.* straw-yellow and white, tipped buff, silky within; corona lobes entire on inner angles; umbels many-fld., terminal and axillary; peduncles 1 to 2 in. long. August. Malacca. 1838. (B.M. 5173 as *Centrostemma multiflorum.*) Syn. *Cyrtoceras multiflorum, C. floribundum.*

**H. ovalifo'lia.** *l.* narrow oval, about 6 in. long, fleshy, dark green, margins revolute. *fl.* bright yellow; corona red; umbels large. Summer. India. 1840. (P.F.G. 1, 23.)

**H. pal'lida.** A synonym of *H. parasitica.*

**H. parasit'ica.** *l.* variable, elliptic to lanceolate or ovate, fleshy, dark green. *fl.* pale yellow or straw; corona pink, very fragrant; umbels of moderate size. Summer. India. 1815. (B.R. 951 as *H. pallida.*)

**H. Pax'tonii.** A synonym of *H. bella.*

**H. Pott'sii.** *l.* cordate, slender-pointed, rusty above, paler beneath. *fl.* pale yellow, slightly downy, fragrant; corona white with yellow centre; umbels globose. India. 1824. (B.M. 3425; L.B.C. 1609.) var. **trinerv'is.** *l.* oblong, light yellowish-green, variable in size. *fl.* pale greenish-yellow. China.

**H. purpu'reo-fus'ca.** *l.* ovate, with a short point, fleshy, dark green. *fl.* ashy-brown; corona rich purplish-brown; umbels large, dense. September. Java. 1849. (B.M. 4520.)

**H. Rid'leyi.** *l.* ovate to lanceolate or oblong, acute, wedge-shaped at base, 3 to 5 in. long, fleshy, leathery; stalk thick. *fl.* pearly pinkish white; downy within; corona lobes sharply acute; umbels 3 in. across. Java on trees. (F.d.S. 579.)

**H. Shepherd'ii.** A variety of *H. longifolia.*

**H. trinerv'is.** A variety of *H. Pottsii.*

**H. viridiflo'ra.** A synonym of *Dregea volubilis.*

F. G. P.

*Hrubya'nus -a -um,* in honour of Baron Hruby.

*Hualta'ta,* Chilean name of *Senecio Hualtata.*

*Hubert'ii,* in honour of Hubert Winkler, 1875– ?, who travelled in the Cameroons, &c.

*Hubsch'ii,* in honour of Anton Hubsch, German traveller in Brazil, *c.* 1881–7.

**HUCKLEBERRY.** *See* **Gaylussacia.**

**HUCKLEBERRY, BLUE.** *See* **Gaylussacia frondosa.**

**HUDSON'IA** (in honour of Wm. Hudson, author of *Flora Anglica*, 1730–93). FAM. *Cistaceae.* A genus of 3 species of low evergreen shrubs, natives of Eastern N. America. Leaves alternate, small or scale-like. Flowers yellow, solitary, terminal; sepals 3; petals 5, soon falling. Of little garden value and difficult to cultivate, although hardy enough. They grow wild in poor sandy soil.

**H. ericoi'des.** Bushy evergreen shrub, 6 to 9 in., heath-like. *l.* ¼ to ⅓ in. long, awl-shaped, erect, hairy, grey-green. *fl.* bright yellow, ½ in. wide, solitary on a very slender, silky stalk, ½ in. long; sep. silky. May. Nova Scotia to N. Carolina. 1805. (L.B.C. 192.)

**H. tomento'sa.** Shrub of tufted growth, wholly hoary with down, 8 to 12 in. *l.* narrow-oblong, $\frac{1}{12}$ in. long. *fl.* bright yellow, ⅓ in. wide, stalkless or nearly so; sep. blunt. May, June. Shores of the Great Lakes and sea-shores of N. America. 1826. (S.C. 36.)

***hudson'icus -a -um,*** of Hudson's Bay.

***Hueb'neri,*** in honour of F. Hübner of Leipzig, d. 1888.

**HUEGEL'IA.** A synonym of Trachymene; name in honour of Karl, Baron von Hügel, 1794–1870, who travelled in Philippines, &c. Now included in **Didiscus** (q.v.) **A**

**HUERN'IA** (in honour of Justus Heurnius, 1587–1652, a Dutch missionary who was the first collector of Cape plants. Named by Robert Brown who spelt the name incorrectly). FAM. *Asclepiadaceae.* Stems short, succulent, leafless, 4- or 5-angled. The genus is characterized by the flower which has a 10-pointed corolla, there being shorter points between each of the main lobes; the flowers are solitary or several together from the base of the stem; in general structure they resemble Stapelia (q.v.). For cultivation *see* **Stapelia.**

**H. as'pera.** Stems procumbent, obtusely angled, with small teeth. *fl.* bell-shaped, dense purple inside, the surface being covered with papillae. Probably Tanganyika. (W. & S. 837–9; B.M. 7000.)

**H. barba'ta.** Stems erect, 4 or 5-angled, glaucous green with long green teeth. *fl.* pale yellow spotted with red; the cor. lobes sharply pointed, the tube deep with hairs in the throat. S. Africa. (W. & S. 1014–20 and Pl. 30; B.M. 2401 as *Stapelia barbata.*)

**H. Hislop'ii.** Stems thin, fluted, with short teeth. *fl.* pale buff with red dots, papillose; cor. lobes with slender points, tube deep. Rhodesia. (W. & S. 1006–8.)

**H. Hys'trix.** Stems short, 5-angled, pale green or purplish; teeth conical, spreading. *fl.* yellow, banded and dotted with red; the inner surface densely covered with spine-like fleshy processes, banded like the spines of a porcupine. Natal. (W. & S. 936–47; B.M. 5751 as *Stapelia Hystrix.*)

**H. kenien'sis.** Stems prostrate or ascending, green or reddish, 5-angled, angles rounded, spines very short. *fl.* bell-shaped, the lobes not spreading, pale outside and deep dark purple inside, papillose. Kenya. (W. & S. 840–50.)

**H. Loesneria'na.** Stems short, stout, acutely 4-angled, green or purplish. *fl.* bell-shaped but spreading at the mouth, dull yellow with very narrow brownish-red lines, with short stiff fleshy processes on the inner surface. Transvaal. (W. & S. 954–7.)

**H. ocula'ta.** Stems acutely 5-angled with stout fleshy spines. *fl.* bell-shaped, not spreading much at the mouth; very dark purple inside except at the base of the tube which is white. SW. Africa. (W. & S. 861–4 & Pl. 24; B.M. 6658.)

**H. Pillan'sii.** Stems ovoid or cylindrical, densely covered with tubercles in 20 to 24 vertical rows, spines long and bristle-like. *fl.* with widespread, slender lobes, covered on the inner surface with small fleshy processes, pale yellow dotted with crimson. Cape Province. (W. & S. 1021–4.)

**H. primuli'na.** Stems short and stout, glaucous, 4- or 5-angled, angles sharp, toothed. *fl.* with broad, widespread lobes, smooth, yellow with no markings. Cape Province. (W. & S. 851–8.)

**H. Schneideria'na.** Stems with 5 or 6 obtuse angles and acute teeth. *fl.* cup-shaped with widespreading lobes; inner surface pale brownish with black hairs, papillose, tube black within. Nyasaland and Portuguese E. Africa. (W. & S. 859, 860.)

**H. somal'ica.** Related to *H. oculata* but cor. lobes rugulose. Stems about 2½ in. h., 5-angled, angles with long teeth. Pedicels ½ in. long; cor. 1⅓ in. across, tube bell-shaped, glabrous, brownish-purple within; lobes recurved, brownish-purple, deltoid, acute, glabrous without. Somaliland. (B.M. 7730.)

**H. Thuret'ii.** Stems glaucous, 4- or 5-angled, angles more or less tuberculate with short teeth. *fl.* cup-shaped with widespread lobes, quite smooth inside, pale buff with numerous small red dots. S. Africa. (W. & S. 915–23.)

**H. Verek'eri.** Stems 5- to 7-angled, teeth very long, flattened laterally. *fl.* with very slender, widespread lobes; tube shallow, white at the base, red at the throat, and the lobes pale yellow with minute purple bristles. S. Rhodesia. (W. & S. 865–6, and Pl. 25.)

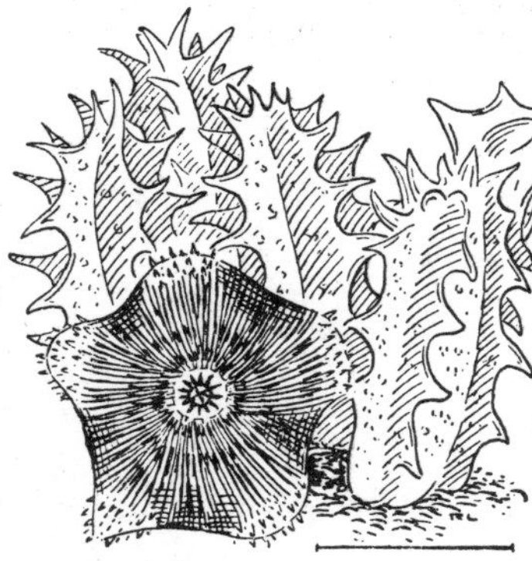

*Huernia somalica*

**H. zebri'na.** Stems 5-angled, angles compressed, with stout conical teeth. *fl.* with a short tube and thickened fleshy ring at the mouth, the lobes short and spreading; yellow with broad broken bands of purple-brown. Zululand, Transvaal. (W. & S. 978–88.) var. **magniflo'ra,** *fl.* larger, with paler bands. (W. & S., Pl. 27.)

V. H.

**HUERNIOP'SIS** (resembling Huernia). FAM. *Asclepiadaceae.* The 3 species now included in this genus partly resemble Huernia in that the corolla has a definite tube and are distinguished from the other Stapelieae by the curious form of the corolla lobes, which are indented at the base so that the mouth of the tube appears to be 10-pointed. The stems are prostrate, more or less clavate, obtusely 4-angled, with spreading teeth.

**H. atrosanguin'ea.** *fl.* dark blackish-crimson, without markings, but minutely papillate. Bechuanaland. (W. & S. 1037, 1045, 1046.) SYN. *Caralluma atrosanguinea.*

**H. decip'iens.** *fl.* smaller, brownish-crimson mottled with yellow. SW. Africa. (W. & S. 1033–6, 1038, 1039, 1042–4.)

V. H.

***Huet'ii,*** in honour of A. Huet du Pavillon, 1829–1907.

***Hugh'ii,*** in honour of Mr. Hugh Low, orchid dealer and raiser.

***Hugo'nis,*** in honour of Father Hugh Scallon, R.C. Missionary in W. China, *c.* 1899.

***huillen'sis -is -e,*** of Huilla, Portuguese W. Africa.

***Hullett'ii,*** in honour of R W. Hullett, 1843?–1914, who collected in Malaya.

**HUL'SEA** (in honour of G. W. Hulse, United States Army Surgeon, who collected in California). FAM. *Compositae.* A genus of a few species of balsam-scented biennial and perennial herbs. Leaves mainly basal usually with broad stalks. Flower-heads rather large, radiate, yellow or purple; involucral bracts in many series, narrow, acute; receptacle flat. Achenes linear, cuneate, flattened or 3-angled, soft downy; pappus of 4 truncate scales. Well-drained ordinary soil on rock-garden in sunny position. Propagation by seed.

**H. na'na.** Perennial, 2 to 7 in. h. Root-stock stout. *l.* narrow to broadly linear, irregularly crinkled or toothed, 1 to 3 in. long; stem-l. few and small. *fl.-heads* single on end of stems, about 1 in. across, clammy-downy or cottony; rays yellow, many, linear, about ⅓ in. long; involucre slightly hairy, ½ in. h., bracts narrow-oblong. *Scales* of pappus fringed. Mts. of California.

**HULTHE'MIA.** Included in **Rosa.** *See* **R. persica.**

**HUMA'TA** (*humus*, soil; from the creeping habit of these ferns). FAM. *Polypodiaceae*. A genus of over 40 species related to Davallia with small leathery fronds, the barren ones usually once pinnatifid; indusia large, attached by the base only. Mostly Malayan, but a few extending beyond. Cultural treatment is similar to that of Davallia, but a few special notes may be helpful. *H. alpina* requires warm temperature and moist atmosphere, but no overhead syringing, and to be grown on a pyramid of fibrous peat. *H. angustata* also needs stove treatment; it grows on tree trunks in its native country. *H. parvula*, a species only a few inches high, is of very neat habit; it requires only a very shallow pan and care to keep the rhizomes on the soil surface. These ferns have often been grouped under Davallia.

**H. alpi'na.** *rhiz.* creeping, scaly. *sti.* 2 to 4 in. long. *Fronds* 2 to 3 in. long, 1 to 1½ in. broad, deltoid; upper segs. of barren frond slightly dentate, blunt at apex of fertile fronds, distant, deeply, and sharply toothed; lower cut nearly to rachis with sharply toothed lobes. *Sori* in teeth on both sides. Malaya. (B.C.F. 2, 119.)

**H. angusta'ta.** *rhiz.* creeping, scaly. *Fronds* sub-sessile, 3 to 8 in. long, ¼ to ⅜ in. broad, linear, slightly crenate; barren ones entire. *Sori* in a row along margin. Malaya. (B.C.F. 2, 120.)

**H. assam'ica.** *rhiz.* stout, wide-creeping, densely clothed with light brown scales. *sti.* naked, 1 to 3 in. long. *Fronds* 6 to 12 in. long, spear-shaped, 3-pinnatifid; pinnae shortly stalked; pinnules crowded, glabrous. *Sori* close to margins of ultimate lobes; as broad as deep. N. India, Yunnan. SYN. *Acrophorus assamicus*, *Leucostegia assamica*. Stove.

**H. Griffithia'na.** *rhiz.* wide-creeping, densely scaly. *sti.* erect, wiry, elongated. *Fronds* deltoid, with an attenuated apex, 9 to 12 in. long, 4 to 8 in. broad; pinnae acuminate; pinnules oblong-lanceolate, obtuse; lobes short and blunt. *Sori* large, cup-shaped, sub-marginal. N. India to China, Formosa. (H.S.F. 1, 49 B.)

**H. heterophyl'la.** *rhiz.* creeping, scaly. *Fronds* shortly stalked, 3 to 6 in. long, 1 in. broad, glabrous; barren ovate-lanceolate, entire, or slightly lobed at base; fertile narrower, and deeply sinuate-pinnatifid. Malaya. (L.F. 8, 19.)

**H. par'vula.** *rhiz.* wide-creeping, scaly. *sti.* 1 to 2 in. long, or fronds sub-sessile, ½ to ¾ in. long by ½ in. broad, deltoid, 2- or 3-pinnate, with all divisions almost filiform. *Sori* at sinuses of ultimate forks. Malaya. 1868. (B.C.F. 2, 147.)

**H. pectina'ta.** *rhiz.* creeping, scaly. *sti.* 2 to 4 in. long, erect, scaly. *Fronds* 4 to 8 in. long, 2 to 3 in. broad, ovate-lanceolate, deeply cut into long, parallel, linear-oblong, entire, or incise-pinnatifid pinnae. *Sori* oblique in 2 sub-marginal rows. Malaya, Polynesia.

**H. re'pens.*** *rhiz.* wide-creeping, climbing. *Fronds* simply pinnate, 8 to 18 in. long, ½ to 1½ in. broad; pinnae ¼ to ½ in. long, half as broad. *Sori* marginal, large. Trop. E. Asia, Australia. 1869. (H.G.F. 7.) SYN. *Davallia hemiptera*, *D. pedata*.

**H. Tyerman'ni.*** Allied to *H. Griffithiana*. *rhiz.* wide-creeping, densely scaly; scales linear, white. *sti.* 2 to 3 in. long, naked, reddish. *Fronds* 4 to 6 in. long, deltoid, 3- to 4-pinnatifid; lower pinnae largest, stalked, deltoid, unequal-sided; lowest pinnules stalked, cuneate-oblong or deltoid, upper segs. falcate-deltoid, entire, lower cuneate-oblong, pinnatifid. *Sori* at base of ultimate lobes, 1/16 broad. China. 1871. (G.C. 1871, 870.) var. **farca'ta** has fronds forked at tips.

**H. vesti'ta.** *Fronds* like *H. repens*, but the barren have segs., except those of lower pinnules, blunt and scarcely toothed; lobes of fertile segs. (in teeth of which sori are placed) narrower and more sharply toothed. Malaya. Stove. (H.S. 1, 41.)

**HUMBLE BEES** (*Bombus* species) resemble Wasps so far as their social life is concerned, for the colonies die out every autumn and only the fertilized queens survive the winter. The queens reappear in spring and form new colonies, usually underground, in ditch sides, grassy banks, heaps of dry moss, and elsewhere. The queen constructs a number of cells, some being partially filled with a paste of pollen as food for the larvae, others stocked with honey for her own consumption. These bees are of the greatest benefit to the fruit-grower owing to their pollinating habits, for they work industriously upon fruit blossom even during inclement weather, when Hive Bees will not venture far from their hives. They are known, however, on occasion to rob flowers (e.g. Beans and Antirrhinums) of the nectar by boring a hole at the base of the calyx, thereby defeating the provisions for pollination.

Humble Bees were introduced into New Zealand many years ago for the purpose of pollinating the Clover to ensure seed production. The biology of these bees is described in a well-illustrated manual entitled *The Humble Bee* by F. W. L. Sladen (London, 1912).

G. F. W.

**HUMBLE PLANT.** *See* **Mimosa pudica.**

***Humblot'ii,*** in honour of M. Leon Humblot, French naturalist, who collected in Madagascar, Great Comoro Is., &c., *c.* 1884.

***Humboldtia'nus -a -um, Humboldt'ii,*** in honour of Fr. W. H. Alexander von Humboldt, 1769–1859, explorer of Cent. America; ***humboldtia'nus*** is also used to refer to Humboldt Bay in New Guinea.

**HU'MEA** (in honour of Lady Hume, of Wormleybury, Herts.). FAM. *Compositae*. A genus of 4 Australian herbs or shrubs with alternate, entire leaves and numerous small flower-heads in a loose, terminal panicle or compact corymb. *H. elegans* is very ornamental, when well grown, both for greenhouse decoration and for sub-tropical gardening. It is a biennial. The seed should be sown in July in light, finely sifted soil and placed in a cold frame. When the seedlings appear they should be potted, taking care not to injure the roots. The young plants should be grown on in a frame or cool house with plenty of light and air, and the roots should be kept nearly dry through the winter. In spring gradually encourage growth and pot on, the final pots being about 9 in. in diameter. They rarely succeed unless carefully treated in potting and watering. Except in very warm weather syringing is apt to be harmful. They are too tender to trust outdoors until June and when put out they should be staked and protected from rough winds. When the young plants are once established a rich compost of loam and decayed manure, with a little charcoal added, should be used.

**H. el'egans.*** Biennial, 5 to 6 ft. h. *l.* large, oblong or lanceolate, stem-clasping, often decurrent. *fl.-heads* brownish-red, pink, or crimson, minute, very numerous in a large, loosely branched, terminal, drooping panicle. July to October. Australia. (Gn. 31 (1873), 280.) Coolhouse or summer-bedding.

***Humea'nus -a -um,*** in honour of David Hume, gardener Edinburgh Botanical Gardens, killed on service, 1914 (*Roscoea Humeana*); or of W. Burnley Hume, amateur gardener.

***humifu'sus -a -um,*** spreading over ground.

***hu'milis -is -e,*** dwarfer than most of its kindred.

**HUMMING-BIRD HAWK MOTH.** *See* **Hawk Moths.**

***humulifo'lius -a -um,*** with hop-like foliage.

**HU'MULUS** (*humus*, ground; the plants being prostrate if not supported). FAM. *Urticaceae*. Hop. A genus of 2 species of hardy perennial herbaceous twiners easily grown in ordinary garden soil but most vigorous in good deep loam. Leaves opposite, broad, 5- to 7-nerved. Flowers dioecious, males in panicles, females in spikes. The heads of fruit of *H. Lupulus* are used in brewing and the young blanched shoots as a pot-herb. Propagation is by seed or by division in spring. The climbing stems make a pleasant screen in summer. SYN. Lupulus.

**H. japon'icus.** *l.* palmately 5- to 7-lobed, margins toothed. *fl.* male in long, loose panicles, female in short, ovoid spikes, on long peduncles, with cordate, cuspidate bracts which do not enlarge in fruit. Japan. 1886. (H.G.F. 1886, f. 43.) var. **lutes'cens,** *l.* bronzy or golden. 1898; **variega'tus,** *l.* spotted. A

**H. Lu'pulus.** Stem angled, rough. *l.* cordate, toothed, rough. *fl.* greenish-yellow; males in loose axillary panicles; females in short-stalked, axillary, roundish spikes. Temperate Europe, including Britain, Asia, N. America. (E.B. 1284.) var. **au'reus,** *l.* golden. SYN. var. *luteus*.

**HUMUS.** The amorphous black substance which results from the decay of vegetable matter in the soil. Earth containing a high percentage of humus is often called Vegetable Mould or Black Earth from its colour.

**HUNGARIAN LOTUS.** *See* **Nymphaea thermalis.**

*hunga'ricus -a -um,* Hungarian.

**HUNNEMAN'NIA** (in honour of John Hunneman, English botanist and introducer of plants to Britain, d. 1839). FAM. *Papaveraceae.* A single species of perennial, woody at base, native of Mexican highlands, with erect, glaucous stem, slenderly branched, and large solitary long-stalked yellow flowers. Sepals 2, caducous; petals 4, spreading; stamens many. Fruit 1-celled, siliqua-like, with numerous seeds. Seed should be sown in spring in the open border or in autumn, the seedlings being protected through winter. A rich, deep soil is required, and it must be well drained.

**H. fumariifo'lia.** Half-hardy erect perennial, 2 to 3 ft. h., woody at base only. *l.* 2 to 4 in. long, 3-ternate, segs. linear, obtuse, glaucous; stalk keeled beneath. *fl.* 2 to 3 in. across, yellow; pet. concave, widely obovate or almost round. July to October. Mexico. 1827. (B.M. 3061; S.B.F.G. 276.) Some large-fld. forms have been selected. Flowers useful for cutting. May be treated as an annual.

*Hunnewellia'nus -a -um,* in honour of a New England family interested in horticulture.

**HUNTER'S NUT.** *See* **Omphalea megacarpa.**

**HUNTLEY'A** (in honour of the Rev. J. T. Huntley). FAM. *Orchidaceae.* A small genus of epiphytic orchids in Cent. America, Brazil; closely allied to Bollea and with that genus often included under Zygopetalum. The scapes are 1-flowered; sepals and petals similar; the fleshy arched column is produced into a short foot to which the bases of the lateral sepals are affixed, as is the shortly clawed spreading lip which is more or less 3-lobed with a transverse fleshy crest distinctly fimbriated. Pollinia 4. Pseudobulbs are absent, leaves large, distichously arranged, with prominent veins. The foliage characters are very similar to those of Bollea, Pescatorea, and Warscewiczella, and similar treatment and compost should be given. The whole group has been considered difficult to cultivate successfully, usually because the rather soft fleshy texture of the foliage is not considered. If possible a lean-to house with a south-west by west aspect should be given them. A moist atmosphere must be maintained throughout the year. Winter temperature should be 65 to 70° F. at night, 70° F. by day, unless advantage can be taken of the winter sunshine. In summer the day temperature will range higher but shading and ventilation must be manipulated to prevent excessive or dry heat; a dry hot atmosphere is most harmful. The absence of pseudobulbs precludes any attempt at resting, and liberal watering is required through the summer with avoidance of waterlogged compost. For this reason, and the fact that root disturbance should be avoided as much as possible, baskets are preferable to pans or pots. With large plants masses of roots are formed and when re-basketing becomes absolutely necessary the dead roots should be cut away close to the rhizome beneath the centres of the plants. With the use of baskets old compost can often be removed and replaced with new for a long period. Compost should consist of 3 parts of clean Osmunda and 2 parts of Sphagnum moss well mixed with the addition of charcoal nodules and finely pounded pot sherds. The syringe may be freely but lightly used. The flowers of the whole group, though produced singly on rather short scapes, are among the most beautiful and interesting of orchids. Propagation is by the division of plants, sufficiently large, in the late spring. Attacks by red spider and thrips are usually indicative of too dry an atmosphere or the admission of direct sunlight. Shading, however, must not be so heavy as to induce gloom.

**H. albidoful'va.*** Near to *H. meleagris,* of which it has been regarded as a variety. The lower parts of the sep. and pet. are whitish, the upper fulvous-brown, lip white tipped with rosy-carmine or purple. Brazil. 1868. (I.H. 1868, 556.) SYN. *Zygopetalum meleagris albidofulvum.*

**H. Burt'ii.*** *fl.* 3 to 4 in. across; sep. and pet. elliptical, pointed, whitish, passing at base to yellow, upper part marked with red-brown; pet. with a somewhat radiating, reddish blotch at base; lip white at base, then red-brown with brighter veins, the crest white with purplish incurved tooth-like hairs. *l.* 10 to 15 in. long. Costa Rica. 1867. (B.M. 6003 as *Batemannia Burtii.*) var. **Wallis'ii** is a synonym of *H. Wallisii.*

**H. can'didum.** A synonym of *Warscewiczella candida.*

**H. ceri'na.** A synonym of *Pescatorea cerina.*

**H. Gusta'vi.*** Near to *H. meleagris* in habit. *fl.* yellow; sep. suffused with red except near base; pet. with a transverse red blotch; the front lobe of the lip covered with minute red spots. New Granada. 1877. (X.O. 3, 216, 34 as *Batemannia Gustavi.*)

**H. lu'cida.** *fl.* 2 in. across; sep. whitish at base then purplish-brown; pet. light purplish-brown, each with a transverse crescent-shaped greenish band; lip yellow, purplish centrally, crest orange-yellow. *l.* 6 to 8 in. long. British Guiana. 1886.

**H. meleag'ris.*** *fl.* 3 in. across; sep. and pet. similar, broadly ovate-lanceolate, whitish at base, passing into yellow in centre, heavily flushed and marked with red-brown; lip cordate, apiculate, white with the front part yellowish-brown, crest yellowish or white, fringed. *l.* 10 to 15 in. long, 1½ to 2 in. wide, bluish-green. Brazil. 1838. (B.R. 25, 14 as *Batemannia meleagris.*)

**H. viola'cea.** A synonym of *Bollea violacea.*

**H. Wallis'ii.*** *fl.* 4 in. across; sep. green shaded with brown, yellowish near base; pet. similarly coloured but streaked with red at their bases; lip greenish, brownish-red on the anterior area, crest whitish with a red-brown fimbriation. *rhiz.* ascending. *l.* 10 to 15 in. long. Sometimes considered a variety of *H. Burtii.* New Granada. 1873. SYN. *Batemannia Burtii Wallisii.* var. **ma'jor,*** *fl.* larger, 5 in. or more across, more highly coloured, lip reticulated chiefly at margins with blackish-purple. New Granada, Ecuador? 1880. (W.O.A. 185 as *Batemannia Wallisii major.*)

E. C.

**HUNTSMAN'S CUP.** *See* **Sarracenia purpurea.**

*hupehen'sis -is -e,* from Hupeh, China.

**HUPIRO.** *See* **Coprosma foetidissima.**

**A**

**HU'RA** (its S. American name). FAM. *Euphorbiaceae.* A genus of 2 Trop. American trees with glossy evergreen alternate simple leaves. Flowers monoecious, without petals. *H. crepitans* has a round hard-shelled fruit about as large as an orange which when ripe and in a dry atmosphere bursts with a loud noise, throwing the seeds many feet. It can be grown in stove conditions in light loamy soil and propagated by cuttings in sand in heat under a close-frame. The abundant milky juice is poisonous.

**H. crep'itans.** Sand-box Tree. Tree of 30 to 100 ft. *l.* poplar-like, hairy, long-stalked. *fl.* small, reddish; stamens numerous in 2 or 3 whorls; style long. 1733.

**HURTLE-BERRY** or **HURTS.** *See* **Vaccinium Vitis-Idaea.**

**HUTCHINS'IA** (in honour of Miss Hutchins of Bantry, 1785–1815, a student of Cryptogamic Botany). FAM. *Cruciferae.* A genus of 8 species of small annual or perennial herbs, natives of the N. Temperate regions. Leaves pinnate. Flowers very small, white; sepals equal at base; petals equal, entire; stamens not toothed. Fruit oblong or ovate, laterally compressed, cells 2-seeded. Plants for the rock-garden in open, well-drained sandy situations. Propagation by seed or division. All of the following are sometimes offered under the generic name Noccaea.

**H. alpi'na.** Tufted perennial, 1 to 3 in. h. *l.* pinnatifid, glabrous. *fl.* in clusters about 1 in. h.; style very shortly exserted. May to July. Pyrenees, &c. 1775. (T.A.P.E. 8.)

**H. Auerswal'dii.** Stem flexuous, 2 to 6 in. h., leafy to apex. *l.* purplish beneath; segs. narrow, of upper l. linear, slender-pointed. *fl.* larger than in *H. alpina* with spreading pedicels, whitish; anthers yellow. May, June. Spain.

**H. brevicau'lis.** Similar to *H. alpina* but smaller in all parts. High Alps.

**H. stylo'sa.** Annual of about 3 in. h., tufted. Dry walls or dry slopes of rock-garden. Sows itself freely. (B.M. 2772.)

*Hu'teri,* in honour of Rupert Huter, b. 1834, priest of Ried, Tirol, student of the flora of Dalmatia, &c.

*Hut'tonii,* in honour of Mr. J. Hutton, who collected *Cyrtanthus Huttonii,* &c., in S. Africa, *c.* 1860, or of Henry Hutton, d. 1868 in Java, who collected for Messrs. James Veitch.

## HYACINTH. *See* Hyacinthus.

## HYACINTH, GRAPE. *See* Muscari.

## HYACINTHEL'LA. *See* Supplement.

**A→**

*hyacinth'us -a -um, hyacinthi'nus -a -um,* dark purplish-blue.

**HYACIN'THUS** (ancient Greek name used by Homer and others, the flower being said to spring from the blood of the dead Hyakinthos). FAM. *Liliaceae.* A genus of about 30 species, mostly natives of the Mediterranean region especially in its eastern part, with a few in Trop. and S. Africa. It is related to Scilla and Chionodoxa but with Muscari it is distinguished by the segments of the perianth (which are free in Scilla) being shorter than the perianth tube and from Muscari by the funnel- or bell-shaped or almost cylindrical tube without any constriction in its upper part, whereas in Muscari the globose or more or less ovate perianth is distinctly constricted above. Bulbs tunicated flattish or ovate. Leaves linear or broadly linear, glabrous. Inflorescence a raceme, usually many-flowered, bracts small. Flowers of medium size or small; perianth deciduous, tubular-bell-shaped to almost globose with 6 spreading teeth, either short or reaching nearly to the middle of the tube; stamens included, attached to the perianth tube except near the tip; style and stigma short; seeds usually 2 in each of the 3 cells of the capsule. The species mentioned below are grown in the same way as other hardy bulbs. The florist's forms which are commonly understood as Hyacinths are derived from *H. orientalis* and its variety *provincialis*; the Roman hyacinth which lends itself so well to early forcing is *H. orientalis albulus.* These hyacinths are largely imported, the former mainly from Holland, though recent experimental work has shown that first-class bulbs for their special purpose can be and are now grown in certain districts of England, particularly Lincolnshire; the Roman hyacinths from S. France. By forcing and careful management hyacinths may be had in flower from Christmas until May, and their lasting qualities, fragrance, and variety of colour have made them very popular, though their stiff appearance recommends them less nowadays than it did when spring bedding was practised in almost every garden. Propagation by seed is rarely attempted except for the production of new varieties. Seed is sown in light sandy soil in September covered with about ½ in. of similar soil and protected during winter. The seedlings need 4 to 6 years to reach the flowering stage. The usual and sole method when stock true to its parent is required is by offsets which should be taken off soon after the old bulb is lifted and planted 2 in. deep in sandy soil. They usually flower in the third year. Special measures are adopted by nurserymen to increase the number of offsets produced. A basal cross-cut passing through the basal plate and the bases of the scales, made before planting the bulb, is one method. Another is to scoop out the base of the bulb with a special knife. Small bulbs are produced in considerable numbers on the edges of the cuts made which can be taken off and grown on after the bulbs are lifted. The flowering of the bulbs treated is naturally considerably interfered with, but the small bulbs so formed reproduce the parent bulb exactly in much greater abundance than naturally formed offsets would do. It has also been found that mature leaves taken off and inserted in sandy soil under glass with some heat form bulbs at their bases.

Hyacinths should be grown in pots for forcing for exhibition and for greenhouse or indoor decoration. For the last purpose single varieties are sometimes grown in hyacinth glasses. For spring flowering in the open they are best grown in masses.

ROMAN HYACINTHS usually reach this country much earlier than the large-flowered varieties. The bulbs should be planted soon after they arrive, 3 or 4 in a 5-in. pot of good light soil with enough sand to ensure good drainage, and just covered with soil. The pots should be watered and stood outside on an ash standing ground and covered to a depth of 6 in. with well-washed ashes. When the pots are filled with roots they are brought into heat and the growth of the tops is encouraged by frequent syringing. Flowering will begin in November, and by potting at intervals and bringing into heat at different times they may be had in flower into February or later, if potted up at the same time as the large-flowered varieties. The Roman hyacinths are much better for cutting than the large-flowered varieties. Some growers force the bulbs in boxes and move the plants into pots just before the flowers open. This does not affect the flowers much but bulbs severely forced are of little value afterwards.

LARGE-FLOWERED HYACINTHS. *Cultivation in pots.* Bulbs are usually available in September, and they should then be potted singly into 5-in. or 6-in. pots, according to the size of the bulbs, and treated thereafter like the Roman hyacinths, being brought into heat when well rooted with the crown just beginning to expand. The potting compost should be fibrous loam and well-decayed manure in equal parts with sand to lighten it. The compost should be filled lightly into the pot and the bulb pressed into it so that the base is firmly held. Flowering will begin in December if carefully forced, and a succession can be had by potting at intervals until the end of November. Forcing should be done in full light. If retardation is necessary in March and April it can be effected by housing in a pit or house with a north aspect. When growing, plenty of water is needed, and when the flower-spikes appear manure water may be used.

*Cultivation in glasses* has to a large extent given place to cultivation in bowls of fibre (*see* **Tulip**). Special glasses with a rather narrow neck and a cup-like rim hold the bulbs with no more than their base in the water, into which the roots become submerged. Rain-water with a little charcoal in it is used for filling the glasses and the bulbs rest on moss. When the bulbs are in position the glasses are kept in a cool, dark place until roots are formed. A little additional water and a light place thereafter will be all that is needed until the bulbs flower. Single varieties are best for this method of growing.

*Cultivation outdoors.* Smaller bulbs may serve outdoors than those used for forcing. They should be planted in well-dug, moderately rich soil in October, but only well-decayed manure should be added to enrich it. Planting should be 9 in. apart and 3 in. deep. Protection should be given in severe weather after the flower-shoots appear. Bulbs so grown may be used another year though they are rarely so satisfactory as those specially grown. After forcing they are fit only for planting in shrub or mixed borders. Staking may be necessary in exposed places. Hard, heavy bulbs should be chosen rather than those of large size, but of proportionately light weight. **A**

A list of varieties will be found in the Supplement.

*DISEASES.* Hyacinths may suffer from Storage Rot caused by a Green Mould (*Penicillium* sp.) similar to the rotting seen in Gladiolus and Daffodil (q.v.), but it should not be serious if the bulbs are stored in good conditions and dampness is avoided. A well-known disease is Yellows (*Bacterium hyacinthi*) in which the bulbs rot before or soon after planting so that no growth occurs or the growth is stunted and the plant does not flower properly. Identification of the disease is obtained by cutting an affected bulb crosswise, when yellow spots are seen in the tissues of the closely packed scales and are thus roughly arranged in circles. If the bulb is cut lengthwise it will show yellow stripes traversing the scales down to the basal plate. These yellow spots and stripes contain a yellow slimy liquid which oozes out. It is difficult to tell the disease in the dry bulb but where it is suspected among growing plants care should be taken to destroy the plant and the soil around it. In propagating hyacinths by scoring and scooping, the knife ought to be disinfected by dipping in a solution of disinfectant such as Lysol or wiping the knife on a rag soaked in such fluid. Varieties most susceptible to the disease are L'Innocence, Grandesse, Queen of the Blues, Grand Lilas. Another bacterial disease is Soft Rot (*Bacterium carotovorum*) which is much quicker in its effect than Yellows. The growth is stopped and the foliage and flower-buds soon yellow and shrivel up and the whole top may fall over. In a few days the entire bulb may become a rotten, dirty-white, foul-smelling mass. Exactly how infection occurs is not known but over-feeding with nitrogenous manures causing soft growth and forcing in hot, very moist conditions will render the plants more likely to infection. Overwatering in such conditions helps the bacterium to spread and it may then enter the bulb at the nose and work downwards. Even outdoor hyacinths should not be heavily manured. Whenever soft rot appears, affected plants with some surrounding soil should be lifted and burnt. Bulbs intended for forcing should not be brought into a high temperature too early. Sound, clean bulbs should be chosen and rotten and dead tissues should be carefully burnt. L'Innocence, Perle Brilliant, and Grand Maître are prone to soft rot, but Queen of the Pinks is said to be fairly resistant to it. Black Slime disease (*Sclerotinia bulborum*) can be recognized by decay of the bases of the leaves so that they turn yellow and fall over when the plant is flowering. The bulb rots and shows a white fluffy fungus mycelium which later forms smooth black sclerotia between the bulb scales. Finally the bulb disintegrates into a dry black mass of rotted tissues. Such plants should be immediately lifted and burnt but it should be mentioned that this disease is so far very rare in Great Britain. Hyacinths sometimes show a non-parasitic trouble called Loose Bud in which at an early stage of growth the flower-stalk is broken at its base leaving the inflorescence quite loose. The flower-truss and its short stem remains the same size and may be carried up some inches by the leaves and still looks fresh. It can, however, be lifted out of the leaves and looks like a short peg a couple of inches long. No parasite is present but the young stalk has parted from the bulb. The condition may not be noticed for some weeks until it is obvious that growth is not proceeding and that the inflorescences can be easily lifted out. The real reason for the trouble is unknown. Vigorous varieties seem to be prone to it but it may occur in most kinds. Outdoor bulbs can be affected but it is more common in forced ones. Some writers suppose that the leaves growing quickly from some cause exercise a tight grip on the plump bud and drag it upwards, thereby wrenching it away from its base. Rapid temperature change from low to high may aggravate such a condition but at present no definite proof of any theory has been brought forward.

(D. E. G.)

**H. amethysti'nus.*** Bulb ovate, about $\frac{3}{4}$ in. thick. Stem 4 to 10 in. h. *l.* 6 to 8, narrow-linear. *infl.* rather loose, 4- to 10- or 15-fld. *fl.* bright blue, about $\frac{2}{5}$ in. long, on pedicels about as long as the bracts, narrow cylindrical, somewhat wider upwards, teeth ovate. Spring. Pyrenees. 1759. (B.M. 2425.) A white-fld. form is known in gardens.

**H. azu'reus.*** Bulb ovate to broadly ovate, tunic brown. Stem 4 to 8 in. h. *l.* 2 to 5, somewhat fleshy, linear, broadest near the blunt tip. *infl.* dense. *fl.* bright blue, about $\frac{1}{5}$ in. long, nodding, later erect, tube-, bell-, or tubular-bell-shaped, twice as long on the broadly ovate segs. March, April. Asia Minor. A white-fld. form has arisen in an English garden.

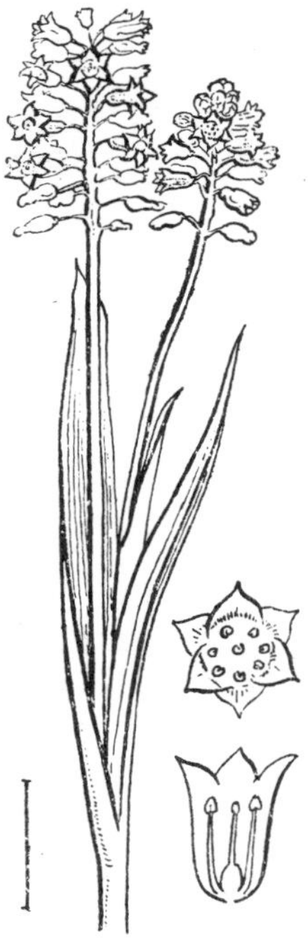

*Hyacinthus azureus*

**H. can'dicans.** A synonym of *Galtonia candicans.*

**H. corymbo'sus.** *l.* 5 or 6, 2 to 4 in. long, nearly cylindrical, about $\frac{1}{12}$ in. thick, fleshy, pale green. *fl.* lilac-rose, $\frac{1}{2}$ in. long, in a rather close, 4- to 9-fld. raceme, on a scape 2 to 3 in. long. Autumn. S. Africa. 1793. (B.M. 991 as *Massonia corymbosa.*)

**H. fastigia'tus.** A synonym of *H. Pouzolzii.*

**H. hyacinthoi'des.** *See* **H. spicatus.**

**H. linea'tus.** *l.* 2 or (rarely) 3, oblong-lanceolate, acute, 3 to 4 in. long, falcate. *fl.* blue, $\frac{1}{8}$ to $\frac{1}{6}$ in. long, bell-shaped in a 6- to 12-fld. raceme about 1 in. long on a scape 2 to 4 in. long. Spring. Asia Minor. 1887. (G.F. 1887, 446, f. 114.)

**H. orienta'lis.*** Common Hyacinth. Bulb often large, ovate to flattish globose, with purple or whitish tunic. Stem 6 to 12 in. long, stout or rather weak. *l.* 4 to 6, linear-lanceolate, $\frac{2}{5}$ to $\frac{4}{5}$ in. wide, bright green, hooded at tip, infl. in cultivation very many-fld., in nature 5- to 15-fld. *fl.* of various colours, about 1 in. long, nodding, fragrant, funnel-shaped with a cylindrical tube, segs. oblong-spatulate, spreading or recurved. Spring. *Seeds* 8 to 12 in each cell. Italy eastwards to Mesopotamia. The wild form is a very graceful plant perhaps not now in cultivation. The sturdy, symmetrical form of the florists' Hyacinth is largely a matter of cultivation. They have been derived from the type and its variety *provincialis* (q.v.). var. **al'bulus,*** Roman Hyacinth, bulb of medium size with whitish tunic, l. erect, usually rather narrow, stem rather weak, perianth white, with long, cylindrical tube and rather narrow segs. S. France. Very useful for early forcing; **provincia'lis,*** *l.* narrower, stem weak. *infl.* looser. *fl.* smaller than in type. S. France.

**H. Pouzolz'ii.** *l.* 3 to 6 or more, subulate, weak, 6 in. long, with fl. bright lilac, $\frac{1}{4}$ to $\frac{1}{3}$ in. long in a few-fld. raceme, in nature often in a corymb, on an erect scape shorter than l.; segs. oblong-lanceolate. March, April. Corsica, Sardinia. 1882. (B.M. 6663 as *H. fastigiatus.*)

**H. roma'nus.*** Roman Squill. Bulb ovate, large. Stem 6 to 12 in. long. *l.* 4 to 5, more or less erect, somewhat fleshy, grass green, much longer than stem. *infl.* rather loose, 20- to 30-fld., pedicels erecto-patent. *fl.* bell-shaped, $\frac{1}{4}$ to $\frac{3}{8}$ in. long, blue or white; segs. lanceolate, acute. April. S. France, eastwards to Balkans, N. Africa. 1596. (B.M. 939 as *Scilla romana.*) SYN. *Bellevallia romana.*

**H. spica'tus.** *l.* 6 to 8, linear, 3 to 4 in. long, $\frac{1}{4}$ in. wide, narrow at base, somewhat fleshy. *fl.* 6 to 12, in a dense, spike-like raceme, dull blue; segs. erecto-patent, lanceolate; scape 1 to 3 in. long. February. Greece, Crete. (B.R. 1869.) This name appears to be untenable as an earlier *H. spicatus* (now *Scilla hispanica patula*) was described. *H. hyacinthoides* appears to be the earliest valid name.

*Hyacinthus orientalis.* Wild form (p. 1021)

**HYAENA'NCHE.** *See* **Toxicodendrum globosa.**

*hyali'nus -a -um,* hyaline, transparent or nearly so.

**HYALOSE'MA.** Included in **Bulbophyllum.**

*hyberna'lis -is -e,* of or belonging to winter.

**HYBER'NIA defolia'ria.** *See* **Mottled Umber Moth.**

**HYBRID.** A plant raised by crossing 2 species. A plant of hybrid origin is indicated by the sign ×. If a graft hybrid (q.v.) the sign + is used.

**HYBRIDIZING.** A term used rather loosely for crossing of any 2 plants, though strictly a hybrid is as defined above. There is, however, no real distinction between hybridizing and crossing of varieties save that the latter is usually more easily effected than the former, but crossing may occur not only between varieties of a species and between different species of the same genus, but also in many instances between 2 species belonging to different but related genera. *See* **Crossing, Plant-breeding, Pollination.**

**HYDNA'CEAE.** A family of large fleshy fungi of which the genera are distinguished by the fact that the hymenium is spread over spines or protuberances on the under-surface of the cap. They usually grow in woods and sandy places but some species, e.g. *Hydnum erinaceus,* grow on trunks and branches and are said to cause a rot of Oak-trees. *H. repandum* is common in Great Britain and when fresh is considered excellent for eating.

D. E. G.

**HYDNOCARP'US** (*Hydnon,* truffle, *karpos,* fruit; the fruit somewhat resembles a truffle). FAM. *Flacourtiaceae.* A genus of about 12 species of trees, natives of Trop. Asia. Leaves serrate or entire; stipules deciduous. Flowers solitary or in few-flowered clusters; sepals and petals 5. Fruit a globose berry; seeds many. Stove conditions are required. The oil from the seeds is used medicinally and the fruits as fish poison in SE. Asia.

**H. Wightia'nus.** Tall tree; shoots and racemes slightly downy. *l.* elliptic, often deeply toothed, leathery. *fl.* white, 4 to 9 in. long, up to 1 in. across; pet. ciliate. *fr.* up to 4 in. across. S. India. The fruit is used to intoxicate fish, and the oil from the seeds is used in treating cutaneous diseases.

**HYDNOPHY'TUM** (*Hydnon,* the Greek name used by Theophrastus for the truffle, *phyton,* a plant; the tuber-like stock resembles a truffle). FAM. *Rubiaceae.* A genus of about 30 species of very curious, epiphytic, glabrous shrubs, with deformed, fleshy, tuberous, simple or lobed bases, which are excavated and inhabited by ants; natives of the Indian Archipelago, Trop. Australia, and Fiji Is. Leaves opposite, leathery, obtuse. Flowers white, sessile, small, axillary, solitary or fascicled; corolla funnel- or salver-shaped, with a short or long tube. Drupe small, with 2 stones. For treatment of these stove plants, *see* the closely allied genus **Myrmecodia.** **A**

**H. Forb'esii.** Stems short, terete. Tuber prickly. *l.* sub-sessile, obovate, obtuse or slightly acute. *fl.* tubular, axillary, very shortly pedicellate. July. *fr.* coral red, ellipsoid, crowned with the cal. limb, produced in October. New Guinea. 1886. (B.M. 7218.)

**H. longiflo'rum.** Stems proper terete; the base swollen and tuber-like. *l.* opposite, 2 to 2½ in. long, ovate, fleshy, green. *fl.* tubular, ¼ in. long, in axillary clusters. August. Fiji. 1891. (B.M. 7343.)

F. G. P.

**HYDRAN'GEA** (*hydor,* water, *aggeion,* vessel; in allusion to the cup-shaped fruit). FAM. *Saxifragaceae.* A genus of about 35 species of shrubs, sometimes tree-like, sometimes climbing, natives of N. and S. America and E. Asia. Leaves opposite or in threes, toothed in all but one of the cultivated species; the same species (*H. integerrima*) is evergreen, the rest deciduous. Flowers in terminal corymbs or panicles, bisexual, small, with 4 or 5 sepals and petals, and usually 10 (but up to 20) stamens. In many species, but not all, a proportion of the flowers (mostly marginal) are quite sterile. These have no stamens or pistil, but consist of 3 to 6 flat, spreading sepals, giving them a diameter of 1 to 2 in. Under cultivation, and sometimes in a wild state, the corymbs may consist entirely of sterile flowers and are then very showy. Whilst the majority have white sterile flowers, some are pink and several have a tendency to blue (see note on *H. macrophylla*). Fruit a small 2- to 5-celled capsule, many-seeded, opening at top.

Except that a few species are rather tender, the Hydrangeas are easily cultivated, thriving in well-drained loamy soil. Sheltered positions are desirable and some, like *H. macrophylla* and *H. Sargentiana,* prefer shady situations. Most are easily propagated by cuttings of half-ripened, leafy twigs in gentle heat, but large-leaved species like *H. quercifolia* and *H. Sargentiana* are more conveniently layered.

CULTIVATION IN POTS. Hydrangeas may be propagated annually to produce one head of flowers each—a method largely practised with the varieties of *H. macrophylla*—or they may be grown as shrubby plants several years in succession. Cuttings should be inserted in small single pots, and plunged in a close, warm frame. They may be taken in spring, from young growths that are not bearing flowers, and be grown on throughout the summer and well ripened in autumn by exposure outside. Another plan is to let the old plants grow all the season, and put in strong points as cuttings when partially ripened. If this plan is followed, the formation of roots only should be encouraged, by plunging in a little bottom heat, but not in an enclosed frame. Select the tops of the strongest and most prominent shoots for cuttings, and insert them in August. When they are rooted, gradually harden off, and expose them to full sunshine and plenty of air in autumn to ensure thorough ripening. When the leaves fade water should be withheld, and the plants kept dry in a cool greenhouse all the winter. In February, or earlier if desired, they may be potted into 5- or 6-in. pots and started by placing in a higher temperature and applying more water. The embryo buds, formed the previous autumn, will soon begin to expand; but it is not usual for all to flower, as they may not have been sufficiently strong. As a rule the corymb of flowers appears after the fourth pair of leaves; and should the plant develop so far without the embryo being seen, it may be thrown away, unless required for another year. Late autumn-struck cuttings produce useful dwarf-flowering plants in spring, not exceeding 1 ft. in height. Those propagated in spring and grown on in pots for the next year are much stronger and taller in proportion. A new stock should be propagated annually and the old ones thrown away, unless required for bush specimens or for supplying cuttings, when they may be cut down, repotted, and grown on in pots, or be planted out in the open air. Hydrangeas like a rich soil, such as loam and decayed cow or other manure in equal parts. Any quantity of water may be applied in the growing season; and artificial manure, given just as the flowers are developing, invariably proves beneficial. The flowers sometimes turn blue, certain soils having the property of changing the normal colour, in consequence of the presence of some chemical constituent. Water, in which alum has been dissolved, is used artificially to cause the same change in colour. The most satisfactory results are given by the use of aluminium sulphate. A 5-in. pot may have $\frac{3}{4}$ oz. of ground crystals applied to its surface, a 6-in. pot $1\frac{1}{2}$ oz. The application is better done when the compost is prepared, using $2\frac{1}{2}$ lb. of crystals to 1 cwt. of soil. For plants in the open ground the application should be made in November at the rate of 1 to 2 lb. to a plant, more, up to 10 lb. for very large, less for small plants. In some gardens, plants that produce red flowers one year may develop blue ones the next, and this without any influence or skill on the part of the cultivator.

*DISEASES.* Occasionally Hydrangea leaves may show brown spots due to Leaf Spot caused by the fungus *Septoria hydrangeae*, but this is not likely to be serious. A more likely trouble, especially under glass, is the Powdery Mildew (*Oidium hortensiae*) which should be easily got rid of with increased ventilation and careful watering to avoid excessive humidity. It should not be necessary to spray, but if this is done Bordeaux mixture is suitable.

(D. E. G.)

KEY

1. *Climbing by aerial roots*   2
1. *Erect. Lvs. toothed*   4
2. *Deciduous. Lvs. toothed*   3
2. *Evergreen. Lvs. entire*   H. integerrima
3. *Lvs. cordate or rounded at base. Stamens 15 to 20*   H. petiolaris
3. *Lvs. broadly wedge-shaped at base. Stamens about 10*   H. anomala
4. *Fl. in panicles*   5
4. *Fl. in flat or hemispherical corymbs*   6
5. *Lvs. lobed*   H. quercifolia
5. *Lvs. not lobed*   H. paniculata
6. *Ovary inferior. Capsule with cal. at apex*   7
6. *Ovary partly superior. Capsule with cal. about or above the middle*   17
7. *Corymb not enclosed in an involucre before expanding*   8
7. *Corymb enclosed in an involucre before expanding*   H. involucrata
8. *Branches glabrous or nearly so when young*   9
8. *Branches densely hairy*   12
9. *Lvs. glabrous or nearly so*   10
9. *Lvs. hairy beneath*   11
10. *Lvs. up to 8 in. long*   H. arborescens
10. *Lvs. up to about 5 in. long; somewhat downy beneath*   H. × canescens
11. *Lvs. densely greyish-hairy beneath. Ray-fls. usually few*   H. cinerea
11. *Lvs. densely white-hairy beneath. Ray-fls. usually many*   H. radiata
12. *Hairs on branches harsh, spreading*   H. Sargentiana
12. *Hairs on branches stiff, appressed*   13
13. *Lvs. heart-shaped or rounded at base*   14
13. *Lvs. wedge-shaped at base*   15
14. *Lvs. abruptly pointed; stalks up to 6 in. long. Corymbs 4 to 6 in. across*   H. longipes
14. *Lvs. shortly pointed, coarsely toothed; hairs beneath brown. Corymbs up to 12 in. across*   H. robusta
15. *Lvs. toothed, greyish and densely strigose beneath*   H. strigosa

15. *Lvs. finely toothed*   16
16. *Stems and l.-stalks covered with spreading hairs. Lvs. densely hairy beneath*   H. villosa
16. *Lvs. greyish-white and densely roughly strigose beneath*   H. aspera
17. *Fertile fl. blue or pink*   18
17. *Fertile fl. white*   20
18. *Corymb sessile with lvs. at base*   H. Davidi
18. *Corymb stalked, usually without bracts*   19
19. *Lvs. obovate to broadly elliptic, glabrous or almost so*   H. macrophylla
19. *Lvs. ovate or elliptic to lanceolate, slightly hairy on both surfaces*   H. serrata
20. *Lvs. softly white hairy beneath*   H. heteromalla
20. *Lvs. nearly glabrous or roughly hairy beneath*   21
21. *Bark of 2-year old shoots brown or greyish-brown, not peeling*   H. xanthoneura
21. *Bark of 2-year old shoots peeling*   22
22. *Lvs. hairy beneath*   H. Bretschneideri
22. *Lvs. glaucous beneath, silky-strigose on veins*   H. hypoglauca

**H. altis′sima.** A synonym of *H. anomala*.

**H. anom′ala.** Strong deciduous climber, 40 ft. or more, clinging to its support by aerial roots; bark peeling. *l.* 3 to 5 in. long, ovate or oval, toothed, downy in vein-axils beneath; stalk 1 to 3 in. long. *Corymbs* 6 to 10 in. across with a few sterile fl. $\frac{3}{4}$ to $1\frac{1}{2}$ in. across; fertile fl. yellowish-white, stamens about 10. June. Himalaya, 1839, China. 1908. SYN. *H. altissima.* Closely akin and similar to *H. petiolaris,* but with fewer stamens.

**H. arbores′cens.** Shrub usually 3 to 4 ft., shoots slightly downy at first. *l.* ovate or oval to roundish, pointed, 3 to 7 in. long, 2 to 6 in. wide, bright green above, glabrous except for a little down beneath; stalks 1 to 3 in. long. *Corymbs* flattish, 4 to 6 in. across; sterile fl. few or absent; fertile ones very small, crowded, dull white. July, August. N. United States. 1736. (B.M. 437.) var. **grandiflo′ra,\*** *fl.* all sterile, pure white, in heavy, rounded clusters.

**H. as′pera.** Shrub up to 6 ft. or more, sometimes small-tree-like, of stiff habit; shoots downy. *l.* 4 to 9 in. long, one-third as wide, oblong, slender-pointed, finely toothed, densely grey-downy beneath, upper surface harsh. *Corymbs* 6 to 8 in. across; sterile fl. 1 to $1\frac{1}{2}$ in. wide, the 4 to 6 sep. blue or white, often toothed. Himalaya, China.

**H. Bretschneid′eri.\*** Shrub to 10 ft. of spreading habit, shoots loosely downy at first, older bark peeling. *l.* 3 to 5 in. long, oblong to ovate, base rounded or cuneate, slender-pointed, hairy on veins beneath. *Corymbs* 4 to 8 in. across; sterile fl. numerous, $\frac{3}{4}$ to $1\frac{1}{2}$ in. wide, sep. 3 or 4, rounded to obovate, white, turning rosy; fertile fl. dull white. July. China. 1882. (B.T.S.I. 624.) SYN. *H. pekinensis, H. vestita pekinensis.*

**H. × canesc′ens** (*H. arborescens × H. radiata.*) Intermediate between parents in several respects but very near *H. cinerea* from which it differs by its smaller *l.* having a thinner down beneath. Sterile fl. few.

**H. ciner′ea.** Shrub up to 6 ft., shoots downy. *l.* broadly ovate, oval or ovate-oblong, 3 to 6 in. long, shortly pointed, bright green above, covered with grey down beneath; stalk up to 3 in. long. *fl.* in corymbs up to 6 or 7 in. wide, very small; sterile fl. few or absent. July. SE. United States. 1906. var. **ste′rile,\*** *fl.* all sterile in fine trusses 3 to 6 in. across. 1910. This var. and its parent species differ from *H. arborescens* chiefly by the grey, downy under-surfaces of the *l.*

**H. cyane′ma.** A synonym of *H. robusta*.

**H. Da′vidi.\*** Shrub 6 to 7 ft., shoots downy, slender. *l.* 3 to 7 in. long, one-third as wide, oblong-lanceolate, long and slenderly pointed, cuneate, conspicuously toothed, downy on midrib and veins beneath. *fl.* in loose corymbs 5 to 10 in. across, sterile ones white, 1 to 2 in. wide, fertile fl. blue. June, July. China. 1908.

**H. heteromal′la.** Shrub up to 10 ft., shoots very downy. *l.* oval to ovate-lanceolate, 4 to 8 in. long, $1\frac{1}{2}$ to 3 in. wide, finely toothed, covered with close white down beneath; stalks up to 2 in. long, reddish. *Corymbs* 4 to 8 in. across; sterile fl. $\frac{3}{4}$ to $1\frac{1}{2}$ in. wide, white, with sep. oval or obovate; fl.-stalks bristly downy. June, July. Himalaya. 1821. SYN. *H. vestita.*

**H. Horten′sia.** See **H. macrophylla**.

**H. hypoglau′ca.** Shrub up to 9 ft., shoots glabrous, purplish-brown. *l.* $2\frac{1}{2}$ to $4\frac{1}{2}$ in. long, half as wide, ovate to ovate-oblong, shortly pointed, dull green above, glaucous and bristly on veins beneath. *Corymbs* 5 or 6 in. across; sterile fl. marginal, 1 to $1\frac{1}{4}$ in. wide; sep. 4, oval, white; fertile fl. $\frac{1}{4}$ in. wide, white; fl.-stalk bristly. China. 1901.

**H. integer′rima.** Evergreen climber up to 50 ft., adhering to its support by aerial roots. *l.* leathery, entire, oval or slightly obovate, pointed, 2 to 6 in. long, half as wide, dark green, glabrous; stalk 1 to $1\frac{1}{4}$ in. long. *Panicles* terminal and axillary, rather columnar, up to 6 in. long with occasional sterile white fl. 1 in. across; fertile fl. very small, greenish. Chile. 1927. Interesting for its climbing, self-supporting habit, and toothless *l.,* but lacking floral attractiveness. (B.M. n.s. 153.)

**H. involucra′ta.** Shrub 3 to 6 ft., shoots, young *l.,* fl.-stalks, and ovary, all bristly. *l.* 4 to 9 in. long, roundish-ovate to oblong, slender-pointed, finely toothed. *Corymbs* 3 to 5 in. across, enclosed in bud state by about 6 broadly ovate bracts about 1 in. long; sterile fl. marginal, white or bluish; fertile fl. small, blue or pink. August, September. Japan. About 1840. Rather tender. var. **horten'sis,** *fl.* double.

**H. long'ipes.** Shrub 6 to 8 ft. of lax habit; shoots slender, loosely downy. *l.* roundish-ovate, rounded or cordate at the base, abruptly slender-pointed, 3 to 7 in. long, bristly on both surfaces, especially on veins beneath; stalks up to 6 in. long. *Corymbs* flattish, 4 to 6 in. across; sterile fl. ¾ to 1½ in. wide, white; fertile small, white; stalks bristly. July, China. 1901. Remarkable for its long l.-stalks.

**H. macrophyl'la.** Common Hydrangea. Shrub rounded, up to 8 ft. by 12 ft. in mild districts, usually much smaller, shoots glabrous, stout. *l.* 4 to 8 in. long, broadly ovate or oval, short-pointed, coarsely toothed, shining green, strongly ribbed. *fl.* in flat corymbs normally about 6 in. across, but often much larger; fertile fl. small; sterile 1 to 1½ in. wide, pink or blue. July to September. Japan. 1790. (B.M. 438.) Syn. *H. hortensis, H. opuloides.* var. **Horten'sia,** all fl. of sterile showy type, corymb much more rounded; **Maries'ii,** sterile fl. marginal, rosy-pink, 2 to 3 in. wide, corymb flat; **ni'gra,** stems dark purple, almost black, *fl.* nearly all sterile, bright rose. There are many other garden-raised vars. with personal or colloquial names. *See* Supplement.

The fl. are blue in some soils, pink in others. Chemical preparations can be obtained to mix with the soil which will ensure the production of blue fl. *See* introductory note.

**H. niv'ea.** A synonym of *H. radiata.*

**H. opuloi'des.** A synonym of *H. macrophylla.*

*Hydrangea paniculata*

**H. panicula'ta.** Shrub or small tree, 12 to 30 ft., usually much smaller in Britain and often kept low by pruning. *l.* often in threes on vigorous plants, oval or ovate, pointed, toothed, 3 to 6 in. long, half as wide, bristly on the veins beneath. *Panicles* pyramidal, erect, 6 to 18 in. h., outer fl. sterile, ¾ to 1¼ in. wide, white turning

purplish; small fertile ones yellowish-white. Japan, China. 1861. var. **grandiflo'ra,** *fl.* all or nearly all sterile, crowded in panicles up to 12 in. tall. By hard pruning in late winter, reducing the young shoots of each branch to 1 or 2 and giving generous treatment at the root, huge panicles 18 in. by 12 in. may be had.

**H. pekinen'sis.** A synonym of *H. Bretschneideri.*

*Hydrangea petiolaris*

**H. petiola'ris.** Strong deciduous climber 60 to 80 ft., clinging by aerial roots like ivy; bark peeling. *l.* 2 to 4½ in. long, pointed, roundish-ovate, rounded to cordate at base, sharply and finely toothed; stalk nearly as long as blade. *Corymbs* 6 to 10 in. wide; sterile fl. marginal 1 to 1¾ in. wide, white; fertile fl. small, dull white; stamens 15 to 20. June. Japan. (B.M. 6788; B.T.S. 1, 628.) Syn. *H. scandens, H. tileaefolia.* Does well on a lofty north wall, or may be planted to cover a tree stump when it will remain shrubby.

**H. plantanifo'lia.** A synonym of *H. quercifolia.*

*Hydrangea quercifolia* (p. 1025)

**H. quercifo'lia.*** Shrub up to 6 ft., shoots stout, woolly. *l.* broadly oval or broadly ovate to roundish, 3- to 7-lobed, sometimes boldly, sometimes slightly, finely toothed, 4 to 8 in. long, two-thirds to about as wide, dull green above, whitish-downy beneath. *Panicle* pyramidal, erect, 4 to 12 in. h.; fertile fl. $\frac{1}{8}$ in. wide; sterile ones 1 to $1\frac{1}{2}$ in. wide, white turning purplish. July. SE. United States. 1803. (B.M. 975.) Distinguished by its large, handsomely scalloped l. An extra large-leaved form is called **platanifo'lia** in gardens.

**H. radia'ta.** Shrub up to 6 ft., shoots soon glabrous. *l.* ovate to oval, slenderly pointed, 2 to 5 in. long, half as wide, covered beneath with close, pure white felt. *fl.* in rounded corymbs, 4 to 6 in. wide; sterile fl. few, 1 to $1\frac{1}{4}$ in. across; fertile ones small, numerous, white. July. N. and S. Carolina. 1786. Remarkable for the snow-white undersurface of the l. Syn. *H. nivea.*

**H. robus'ta.** Shrub 8 to 15 ft., shoots downy. *l.* 5 to 11 in. long, 3 to $7\frac{1}{2}$ in. wide, ovate or oval, short-pointed, coarsely toothed, bristly downy beneath; stalk $1\frac{1}{2}$ to 4 in. long. *Corymbs* nearly 12 in. across; sterile fl. 1 to $2\frac{1}{2}$ in. wide, white; sep. ovate, orbicular, or obovate, toothed; fertile fl. small, blue. Himalaya. 1850. (B.M. 5038.) A fine species both in fl. and l. but tender. Should be tried in the south-west. Syn. *H. cyanema.*

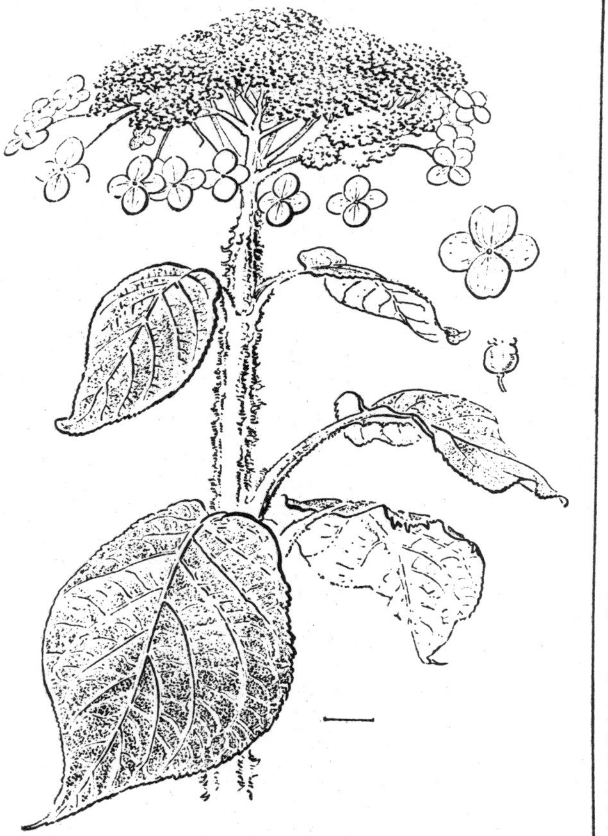

*Hydrangea Sargentiana*

**H. Sargentia'na.** Tall, ungainly shrub, 6 to 10 ft., shoots very stout, ribbed, densely clothed with stiff, bristly hairs. *l.* ovate, base rounded or cordate, shortly pointed, 6 to 10 in. long, 3 to 7 in. wide, dull green above, pale, bristly beneath; stalk bristly, up to $4\frac{1}{2}$ in. long. *Corymbs* flattish, 6 to 10 in. across, with white sterile fl. $1\frac{1}{4}$ in. wide at margins; fertile fl. rosy-lilac. July, August. China. 1908. (B.M. 8447.) Remarkable for its large l. and curious bristliness. Grows best in shade.

**H. scan'dens.** A synonym of *H. petiolaris.*

**H. serra'ta.*** Shrub to 4 or 5 ft., shoots slender. *l.* oval, ovate, or lanceolate, 2 to 4 in. long, cuneate, slender-pointed, with appressed hairs on both surfaces. *Corymbs* 2 to $2\frac{1}{2}$ in. across; sterile fl. $\frac{1}{2}$ to $\frac{3}{4}$ in. wide; sep. over-lapping, variously coloured, blue, pink, or white. July, August. Japan, Korea. Syn. *H. Thunbergii.* Has been much confused with *H. macrophylla,* but l. much smaller, thinner, and dull green, *inflor.* smaller. var. **acumina'ta,** *l.* more slenderly pointed, *ray-fl.* usually blue; **pubes'cens,** *l.* more downy, *ray-fl.* pink or white; **rosal'ba,** *l.* ovate to obovate, *ray-fl.* white or pink, often toothed. Syn. var. *Lindleyana*; **stella'ta,** downy on both surfaces, *ray-fl.* with numerous sep. (*flore pleno*).

**H. strigo'sa.** Shrub up to 9 ft., shoots covered with grey, appressed bristles. *l.* 3 to 8 in. long, one-fourth as wide, lanceolate to oblong-lanceolate, slender-pointed, toothed, thinly bristly above, more densely so beneath. *Corymbs* 7 or 8 in. across; sterile fl. 1 to $1\frac{1}{2}$ in. wide, the 4 sep. obovate, often toothed, pale purplish-blue or white; fertile fl. small, white. June. China. 1907. (B.M. 9324.) Rather tender but grows freely in Sussex.

**H. Thunberg'ii.** A synonym of *H. serrata.*

**H. tileaefo'lia.** A synonym of *H. petiolaris.*

**H. vesti'ta.** A synonym of *H. Bretschneideri* or *H. heteromalla.*

**H. villo'sa.** Shrub up to 9 ft., shoots, l.-stalks, and fl.-stalks densely hairy. *l.* 4 to 9 in. long, oval to oblong-lanceolate, long and slenderly pointed, finely and regularly toothed. *Corymbs* terminal and axillary, 6 in. across; sterile fl. few, $1\frac{1}{2}$ in. wide; sep. 4, obovate, toothed; fertile fl. $\frac{1}{8}$ to $\frac{1}{4}$ in. wide. August. China. 1908.

**H. xanthoneu'ra.** Shrub 8 to 15 ft., of loose thin habit, shoots slightly downy and warty. *l.* in pairs or threes, 3 to 6 in. long, ovate or oval, shortly slender-pointed, pale beneath with whitish, appressed hairs on the veins. *Corymbs* 5 or 6 in. wide, with marginal sterile fl. $1\frac{1}{4}$ in. wide, creamy white; fertile fl. $\frac{1}{4}$ in. wide, dull white. June. China. 1904. var. **Wilson'ii,** *l.* oblong, glossy, sterile fl. white, becoming deep pink.

**HYDRAS'TIS** (derivation doubtful). Fam. *Podophyllaceae.* A genus of 2 species of herbaceous perennials with erect, hairy stems and palmately lobed leaves. Flowers greenish-white, small, solitary; sepals petaloid, soon falling; petals none; stamens many; carpels becoming joined in fruit which is bright red. Hardy in good, rich loam and leaf-soil, growing best in a moist shady place but not readily established. Propagated by seed sown in moist sandy loam in shade in autumn or early spring, or by division of established plants.

**H. canaden'sis.** Golden Seal; Orange Root. About 1 ft. h. Stem simple, hairy. *l.* 5- to 7-lobed, cordate at base, 4 to 8 in. across, doubly toothed veins. *fl.* as described above. May, June. N. America. 1759. (B.M. 3019, 3232.) The roots are used medicinally after grinding.

**HYDRIL'LA** (*hydor,* water). Fam. *Hydrocharitaceae.* A genus of 1 species of aquatic plant, native of Cent. Europe, Asia, and Australia. A plant for indoor aquaria or outdoor pools, growing submerged and forming large masses; said to be a good oxygenator.

**H. verticilla'ta.** *l.* linear or oblong, toothed or entire, 4 to 8 in a whorl, $\frac{1}{4}$ to $\frac{1}{2}$ in. long on the slender, much-branched stems. *fl.* dioecious, very small; male solitary, short-stalked in a sessile spathe; sep., pet., and stamens 3; female 1 or 2, sep. and pet. 3; stigmas 3; ovary extending beyond spathe into a beak.

F. P.

***hydro-,*** in compound words, signifying water.

**HYDROCARBONS.** Like the carbohydrates (q.v.) many hydrocarbons form part of the store of food laid up for future use in the plant, especially in seeds and fruits. The particular form of these compounds of carbon, hydrogen, and oxygen (in which as contrasted with the carbohydrates the proportion of carbon is greater than of hydrogen and oxygen and their energy value, weight for weight, also greater) varies from plant to plant, but they are usually free fatty acids mixed with glycerin compounds (known as glycerides) of fatty acids. It is to these stores of fats and oils as reserve foods that many tropical, sub-tropical, and warm temperate plants owe their commercial value, i.e. coconut, oil-palms, olives, ground-nuts, cotton-seed, castor-oil, and soy-bean. A few plants of cooler regions also store oil in seeds, e.g. sunflower and flax, but speaking generally, oils and fats are more commonly stored by plants of warm countries than of cool. Instances occur, however, in cold regions, as in some conifers, where the starch present in the plant in summer is converted into oil in winter. These fats and oils are made available for the use of the plant as a source of energy or as material for growth by a fat-enzyme which converts them into a fatty acid and glycerin which is further converted into sugar or starch.

In addition to the fats and fixed oils, other types of

hydrocarbons are formed in various parts of plants which have no direct food value, but to which the odours of plants are chiefly due: here belong the essential and volatile oils, turpentine, camphor-oil, oil of cloves, almond oil, mustard oil.

**HYDROC'ERA** (*hydor*, water, *ceras*, horn). FAM. *Balsaminaceae.* A genus of a single species of aquatic needing a rich, loamy soil in large pans or pots of water in a warm part of the stove. Increased by seeds sown in spring.

**H. angustifo'lia.*** Water Balsam. *l.* alternate, narrow. *fl.* variegated red, white, and yellow, large, irregular; sep. 5, coloured; pet. 5, outer front ones largest, concave; stamens 5; peduncles axillary, short, 1- to 3-fld. July to September. Trop. Asia. 1810. SYN. *Tytonia natans.*

F. P.

**HYDROCHA'RIS** (*hydor*, water, *charis*, grace; a pretty water plant). FAM. *Hydrocharitaceae.* A genus of a single species of floating water plant distributed over Europe and N. Asia. *H. Morsus-ranae* grows well in any still water. It may be readily increased by runners which root at the nodes or by seeds.

**H. Mor'sus-ranae.** Stems floating with floating tufts of l. rooting below, roots fibrous. *l.* tufted, orbicular, entire, cordate at base, rather thick, about 2 in. across, stalked. *fl.* rather large, outer segs. pale green, shorter and narrower than the inner white ones; peduncles of male plant rather short, 2- or 3-fld.; pedicel of female longer, perianth with short tube. Summer. (E.B. 1444.)

F. P.

**HYDROCHARITA'CEAE.** Monocotyledons. A family of about 55 species of water plants (some marine) in 13 genera, world-wide in distribution. Leaves mostly ribbon-like, sometimes floating, usually alternate, sometimes whorled. Flowers almost always 1-sexual, usually dioecious, regular, sepals 3, petals 3, stamens 3 (or 6, 9, 12, or 15), the inner and outer whorls sometimes forming staminodes; carpels 2 to 15, ovary inferior. Fruit with many seeds. The genera dealt with are Hydrilla, Hydrocharis, Limnobium, Ottelia, Stratiotes, Vallisneria.

**HYDROC'LEYS** (*hydor*, water, *kleis*, key). FAM. *Alismataceae.* A genus of 3 or 4 species of glabrous, aquatic herbs, natives of Trop. S. America. Leaves clustered, floating, ovate- or cordate-orbicular, veins converging at apex; stalks thick, sheathing at base. Flowers solitary, large, on a long, thick peduncle, hermaphrodite; perianth segments 6, 3 outer persistent, 3 inner larger, yellow, deciduous; stamens numerous, hypogynous, in many series. *H. Commersonii* is easily grown in the stove in a tub or cistern of water and is readily increased by seeds or runners.

**H. Commerson'ii.** *l.* broadly ovate or nearly round, 2 to 3 in. long, up to 2¾ in. wide, obtuse, leathery, cordate at base; stalks round, 4 to 6 in. long. *fl.* solitary, axillary; sep. narrow-ovate, obtuse; pet. broadly obovate-wedge-shaped, large; stamens many, fertile or sterile. May. Venezuela, Brazil. (B.M. 3248 and B.R. 1640 as *Limnocharis Humboldtii.*) SYN. *Vespuccia Humboldtii.*

F. P.

**HYDROCOT'YLE** (*hydor*, water, *kotylis*, a small cup; from the form of the leaves). FAM. *Umbelliferae.* A genus of about 40 species of dwarf water-side plants with minute flowers, sometimes offered, but of no horticultural importance. *H. vulgaris* is a common British plant called the Marsh Pennywort, with round leaves.

**HYDROCYANIC ACID** (HCN) or Prussic Acid, is found in some plants either free or in combination (as in the kernels of bitter almonds and cherries) in the glucoside amygdalin. In contact with water amygdalin is decomposed by the action of the enzyme emulsin into hydrocyanic acid, benzaldehyde (oil of bitter almonds), and glucose. It is a very powerful poison and because of this hydrocyanic acid gas has been used for the destruction of various insects, especially under glass, including aphides, scale insects, and white-fly. It has been used also abroad for trees, &c., growing in the open, by erecting tents over them. Owing to its terribly poisonous properties—for a very small quantity is deadly to human life—it must be used with the very greatest care. Except in great dilution it is also deadly to plants. For the main precautions to be taken in its use in glasshouses *see* **Fumigation.** Several methods of generating the gas have been proposed, the one in general use is by the action of sulphuric acid (the crude acid diluted with twice its bulk of water, pouring the acid into the water, not vice versa), on sodium cyanide. The diluted sulphuric acid is placed in saucers or jars at various points in the house so that the gas is evenly distributed when generated, and the sodium cyanide accurately weighed for each jar is dropped into the acid, beginning with the container farthest from the exit and proceeding quickly to the others in turn until the exit door is reached. The fumigation should not begin until after sunset. The air of the house should be as dry as possible consistent with the plants it contains; the ventilators should be tightly closed and all possible vents stopped up before fumigation begins. The doors should all be locked so that it is impossible for anyone to enter the house before it has been ventilated in the morning. The morning ventilation is greatly facilitated if the ventilators can be opened from outside. The temperature should be kept uniform through the night, rising if anything rather than falling.

To ascertain the amount of sodium cyanide required the size of the house must be accurately known. This is calculated by multiplying the length by the breadth of the house and the product by the average height, all measurements being in feet. The average height is found by adding the height at the eaves to the height at the ridge and dividing the sum by 2. Thus the cubic contents of a house 100 ft. long, 20 ft. wide, 4½ ft. high at the eaves and 10 ft. at the ridge will be $100 \times 20 \times \frac{14\frac{1}{2}}{2} = 14{,}500$ c.ft. Where very tender plants are concerned ¼ oz. of sodium cyanide to each 1,000 ft. is all that will be safe to use; for less succulent plants the usual dose will be ½ oz. A house of the size postulated would therefore need 3½ to 7 oz. of sodium cyanide, divided equally among the containers, and this must be accurately weighed out.

An easier and on the whole safer method is by the use of calcium cyanide which, in contact with moisture, gives off hydrocyanic acid gas. This is sometimes called cyanogas and is in the form of a powder which can be distributed with less trouble than is involved by the sodium cyanide method. The special grade of fineness made for the purpose should be used according to the directions given with it. The precautions necessary are the same as those given above and it is equally important to measure the house and the material accurately. Another grade of cyanogas has been prepared for pumping into rat holes and burrows of other vermin, and still another for treating heaps of soil against wireworms, &c., which has been used with some success.

**HYDROE'CIA mica'cea.** *See* **Rosy Rustic Moth.**

**HYDRO'LEA** (*hydor*, water, *elaia*, oil; from the habitat and character of the plants). FAM. *Hydrophyllaceae.* A genus of 20 annual or perennial herbs or sub-shrubs sometimes included under Nama. Natives of warm regions except Africa. Leaves alternate, ovate or lanceolate, entire, often with spines in axils. They thrive in damp boggy soil in the greenhouse. Propagated from seed, or by cuttings in sand under glass.

**H. corymbo'sa.** Stem 1 to 2 ft. h. *l.* oblong-lanceolate, glabrous, nearly sessile. *fl.* in a terminal corymbose cyme, blue; sep. linear-lanceolate, rough-hairy. Summer. S. Carolina to Florida.

**H. ova'ta.** Perennial. Stem erect, 1 to 3 ft. h. *l.* ovate, short-stalked, 1 to 2½ in. long, ½ to 1¼ in. wide. *fl.* in terminal clusters 1 in. or more across, purplish or white; sep. lanceolate, very hairy. Summer. SE. United States.

**H. quadrival'vis.** Stem ascending, 1 to 2 ft. h., downy above, with slender spines in the l.-axils. *l.* linear-elliptic, acute, 1 to 3 in. long. *fl.* in axillary clusters, blue, ⅛ to ¼ in. across, almost sessile. Summer. N. Carolina. 1824. SYN. *Nama quadrivalvis.*

**H. spino'sa.** Stem 1 to 2 ft. h. with sharp spines in l.-axils. *l.* lanceolate, greasy-looking. *fl.* in terminal corymbose clusters, pale blue. June, July. S. America. 1791. (B.R. 566.)

**H. zeylan'ica.** *l.* lanceolate, bright green, short-stalked. *fl.* axillary, pale blue with white spot in centre. Summer. India and other tropical parts of Old World.

F. P.

**HYDROPEL'TIS.** *See* **Brasenia.**

*hydroph'ilus -a -um,* water-loving.

**HYDROPHYLLA'CEAE.** Dicotyledons. A family of about 170 species of annuals or under shrubs in 17 genera, chiefly American. Leaves usually alternate, rarely opposite, without stipules. Flowers often showy, perfect, regular, sepals and petals usually 5, joined; corolla rotate, bell- or funnel-shaped; stamens 5 attached to corolla; ovary superior, carpels 2. Fruit a capsule, usually many-seeded. The genera dealt with are Decemium, Emmenanthe, Hesperochiron, Hydrolea, Hydrophyllum, Nama, Nemophila, Phacelia, Romanzoffia, Wigandia.

**HYDROPHYL'LUM** (*hydor,* water, *phyllon,* leaf; the leaves very watery in spring). FAM. *Hydrophyllaceae.* A genus of 7 species of perennial herbs, natives of N. America. Leaves alternate, large, stalked, lobed or divided. Flowers in cymose clusters; calyx without appendages (cf. Decemium); corolla bell-shaped, 5-cleft; style 2-fid at apex. Fruit a globose capsule with 1 to 4 brownish seeds. Hardy plants for damp places. Propagated by division or seeds.

**H. appendicula'tum.** A synonym of *Decemium appendiculatum.*

**H. canaden'se.** Perennial herb about 1 ft. h. *l.* palmately 5- to 7-lobed, Maple-like, with the long stalk about 10 in. long, sharply remotely toothed. *fl.* greenish-white, about ¼ in. long, in terminal or axillary crowded cymes; pedicels short. Eastern N. America. 1759. (B.R. 242.)

**H. virginia'num.** Almost glabrous perennial herb, up to 2 ft. h. *l.* oval, with stalk up to 12 in. long, with 3 to 5 segs.; upper 3-lobed, lobes acute, toothed. *fl.* whitish or blue, in crowded terminal or axillary circinate clusters; cal. lobes narrow-linear, bristly ciliate; cor. about ⅜ in. long. Eastern N. America. 1739. (B.R. 331.)

**HYDROPHYTE.** An aquatic plant.

*Hydropi'per,* ancient name for the Water pepper.

**HYDROS'ME.** Included in **Amorphophallus.**

**HYDROTAE'NIA** (*hydor,* water, *tainia,* band; the segments have a triangular nectar-secreting bar at base). FAM. *Iridaceae.* A genus of 3 or 4 species of plants closely related to Tigridia, natives of Mexico and Peru. The chief distinguishing mark between them and Tigridias is the absence of the spreading portion of the perianth segments so that the perianth here is bell-shaped. For treatment *see* **Tigridia.**

**H. Meleag'ris.** About 18 in. h. *l.* solitary, straight-veined, plicate. *fl.* much like *Fritillaria pyrenaica,* 4 or 5 in a leafy convolute spathe 2½ in. long; segs. marked with a few interrupted crimson bands, slightly clawed. Mexico. (B.R. 28, 39.) Greenhouse. SYN. *Tigridia Meleagris.*

**H. Van Hout'tei.** About 12 in. h. *l.* few, ensiform, plicate, upper shorter. *fl.* about 1½ in. across, outer segs. larger, yellow with broad basal blotch and marginal veins purple, inner segs. lilac, veined purple; spathes terminal on branches of stem. S. Mexico. 1875. (F.d.S. 2174 as *Tigridia Van Houttei.*)

*Hyea'nus -a -um,* in honour of Jules Hye-Lessen, a noted orchid-grower.

*hyema'lis.* *See hiemalis.*

**HYGROMETER.** An instrument for ascertaining the humidity of the air. For horticultural purposes a simple form consisting of 2 carefully calibrated mercury thermometers mounted side by side, the bulb of one being covered with thin muslin and having round the neck over the muslin, twisted or tied loosely, a piece of lamp wick or similar material led into a vessel of water about 3 in. from the bulb and somewhat to the side so that its vapour shall not affect the other thermometer, answers well. Readings of the 2 thermometers are taken and compared with tables giving the amount of moisture in the atmosphere as shown by the difference in the readings of the 2 thermometers. As the humidity of the air is a factor in predicting frost, the hygrometer may be used as a frost predictor, and horticultural hygrometers are commonly fitted with a revolving scale between the 2 thermometers indicating the probability of frost within the following few hours.

**HYGROPH'ILA** (*hygros,* moist, *phileo,* to love; from the habitat of some species). FAM. *Acanthaceae.* A genus of about 14 tropical and sub-tropical herbs, allied to Barleria with opposite, lanceolate or ovate, entire leaves, and purple flowers in terminal heads or axillary whorls. Sandy loam is the best compost for *H. spinosa* which needs a sunny position in the greenhouse and to be kept moderately dry, otherwise leaf rather than flowers will result. Propagation is by seed sown in August for flowering in the next year, or by division in spring.

**H. spino'sa.** Herbaceous, roughly hairy perennial of about 2 ft., somewhat spiny. *l.* lanceolate, about 7 in. long, ciliate, with long, white hairs. *fl.* blue-purple in spiny axillary whorls, spines about 6, straight and stout; bracts up to 1 in. long, lanceolate; cor. 1 in. long, tube swollen at apex, deeply 2-lipped. India. 1781. SYN. *Asteracantha longifolia, Barleria longifolia.*

**HYLEMY'IA brunnes'cens.** *See* **Carnation, Fly.**

**HYLESI'NUS fraxi'ni.** *See* **Fraxinus, Ash-bark beetle.**

**HYLI'NE** (*hyle,* a wood; from the habitat). FAM. *Amaryllidaceae.* A genus of 2 species of bulbous plants with the habit of Hymenocallis, natives of Brazil. Differing from Hymenocallis by the free perianth segments and numerous ovules. For treatment *see* **Hymenocallis.**

**H. Wors'leyi.** *l.* 1½ ft. long, 2 in. wide. *fl.* 8 in. long, white, segs. narrow, on a 2-fld. scape, 15 in. h. Brazil. 1899.

**HYLO'BIUS abie'tis.** *See* **Pinus Pests, Pine Weevil.**

**HYLOCE'REUS** (*hyle,* wood, meaning forest Cereus). FAM. *Cactaceae.* Epiphytic climbing plants with aerial roots; stems 3-angled or winged; areoles in the notches, very distant; spines inconspicuous. Flowers very large, white, nocturnal; stamens very numerous. Fruit large, spineless with leafy scales. These plants prefer semi-shade and very warm conditions. **A**

**H. Lemair'ei.** Stems climbing, margins slightly undulate, areoles far apart. *fl.* pinkish. W. Indies. (B.M. 4814; B.R.C. 2, t. 31.) SYN. *Cereus Lemairei.*

**H. Napoleo'nis.** Stems much-branched, 3-angled, angles acute, not horny. *fl.* very large, white, scented, diurnal. W. Indies, S. Mexico. (B.M. 3458.) May be related to *H. triangularis.*

**H. Purpu'sii.** Stems erect, covered with glaucous bloom; margins horny. *fl.* pink. Mexico. SYN. *Cereus Purpusii.*

**H. triangula'ris.** Stems climbing, jointed, triangular, margin nearly straight, not horny. *fl.* white, 8 in. long. Jamaica. SYN. *Cereus triangularis.*

**H. trigo'nus.** Stems climbing, jointed, triangular, margin strongly undulate, not horny. *fl.* large, white. W. Indies. SYN. *Cereus trigonus.*

**H. unda'tus.** Stems climbing, triangular, more or less undulate, margin horny with age. *fl.* very large, white. W. Indies. (B.M. 1884; B.R. 1807.) SYN. *Cereus undatus, C. triangularis* (of gardens). Commonly cultivated throughout the Tropics.

V. H.

**HYLOME'CON** (*hyle,* wood, *mekon,* poppy). FAM. *Papaveraceae.* A genus of a single species of herbaceous perennial with a short rhizome, native of temperate E. Asia. Leaves with usually 2 or 3 pairs of leaflets, the upper smaller. Flowers rather large, golden-yellow, bracteate. Related to Chelidonium but with bracts and a simple stem and to Stylophorum from which it differs by the absence of bracteoles and the usually solitary peduncles. Sepals 2, petals 4, stamens many. *H. japonicum* is hardy and can be propagated by seed sown outdoors in April or by division. A deep soil, with plenty of decaying leaf-mould, suits it.

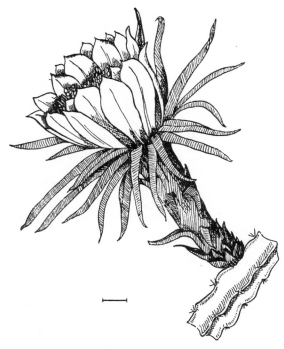

*Hylocereus undatus* (p. 1027)

**H. japon'icum.** Herbaceous perennial up to 12 in. h., at first somewhat hairy, later glabrous. *l.* lanceolate-oblong, up to 10 in. long, irregularly toothed; lflets. 1 to 3 in. long, half as wide, sessile or nearly so; l.-stalks slender. *fl.* golden, 1½ to 2 in. across; peduncles erect, 1½ to 3 in. long, slender; stamens yellow, about half as long as pet. June. Japan, &c. 1870. (B.M. 5830 as *Stylophorum aponicum*.) SYN. *H. vernalis*.

**hyloph'ilus -a -um,** wood-loving.

**HYMENAE'A** (Hymen, god of marriage; alluding to the twin leaflets). FAM. *Leguminosae*. A genus of about 8 species of evergreen trees, natives of Trop. America. Leaflets 2, leathery. Flowers white, large or medium. Hymenaeas are handsome trees, needing stove treatment and a compost of rich loam and peat. Firm cuttings will root, during spring, in sand in bottom heat.

**H. Courba'ril.** Anime Resin. Locust Tree. Tree of 40 to 60 ft. *lflets.* oblong-ovate, oblique, with a long slender point. *fl.* yellow, striped purple. S. America. 1688. Furnishes a valuable resin and a hard, close-grained, brown wood used for building in its native country.

**HYMENAN'DRA** (*hymen*, membrane, *andros*, man; the anthers are joined by a membrane). FAM. *Myrsinaceae*. A genus of one stout evergreen shrub, native of NE. India with handsome foliage. It needs stove conditions and treatment like Ardisia.

**H. Wallich'ii.** Shrub of 2 to 4 ft. *l.* large, leathery, glossy, toothed, with pellucid dots. *fl.* pink in compound lateral umbels; cor. wheel-shaped, 5-parted.

**HYMENAN'THERA** (*hymen*, membrane, *anther*; the anthers are terminated by a membrane). FAM. *Violaceae*. A genus of 4 or 5 species of evergreen or partially evergreen rigid shrubs or small trees, natives of Australia and New Zealand. Leaves alternate, often clustered, small, entire or toothed; stipules deciduous. Flowers small, axillary, frequently polygamous, of no beauty; sepals and petals 5, anthers nearly stalkless, connate into a tube with a membranous appendage at apex. Fruit a berry

with 1 or 2 nearly globular seeds. A compost of 2 parts sandy peat and 1 of fibrous loam suits them, and young cuttings root readily in sand under a bell-glass.

**H. angustifo'lia.** Erect, slender shrub, 5 ft. or more h., shoots at first downy then warted. *l.* linear-oblanceolate, ½ to 1¼ in. long, 1/16 to 1/12 in. wide, dark green, becoming purplish, more or less evergreen. *fl.* yellowish, ½ in. wide, solitary or in pairs in l.-axils, often 1-sexual. May. *fr.* white with purple markings, globose. Tasmania. SYN. *H. dentata angustifolia*. As hardy as *H. crassifolia*.

**H. chatham'ica.** Of similar habit to *H. crassifolia* but with lanceolate l. 3 to 4 in. long, quite evergreen, conspicuously veined, toothed. New Zealand. Hardy only in mild parts of British Is.

**H. crassifo'lia.** Dense much-branched rounded shrub 3 to 6 ft. h. and twice as wide; shoots downy at first. *l.* alternate or tufted, linear-spatulate, ½ to 1 in. long, entire. *fl.* brownish, small; pedicels solitary, axillary. May. Berries white, oblong-obtuse, ¼ in. long, very ornamental. New Zealand. 1875. (B.M. 9426; G.C. 3 (1875), 237.) Hardy in S. England.

**H. denta'ta.** Shrub of 6 ft. *l.* oblong-elliptical to linear, obtuse or acute, leathery, sessile or narrowed to a short stalk. *fl.* yellow, small, axillary, solitary. April. New S. Wales. 1824. (B.M. 3163.) Tender. var. **angustifo'lia,** a synonym of *H. angustifolia*.

**H. obova'ta.** A shrub of up to 12 ft. *l.* obovate, 1 to 2 in. long, short-stalked, usually entire. *fr.* purplish. New Zealand. Rather tender.

**HYMENIUM.** Spore-bearing surface of certain fungi. The typical spores of a fungus-fructification are formed in or on special structures according to the kind of fungus. For example, they are borne in asci in Ascomycetes, on basidia in Basidiomycetes. A layer of asci or a layer of basidia, sometimes interspersed with sterile cells or paraphyses, is called a hymenium.

D. E. G.

**HYMENOCAL'LIS** (*hymen*, membrane, *kallos*, beauty; in reference to the membrane uniting the stamens). FAM. *Amaryllidaceae*. A genus of about 40 species of bulbous plants, natives of America, mainly S. America, with 1 in W. Africa. Leaves sessile and lorate, or stalked and oblong. Flowers in umbels, usually pure white, fragrant; perianth tube straight, long, scarcely widened at throat; segments 6; stamens 6, united into a distinct cup or corona, the free parts of the filaments slender; ovary 3-celled with 2 ovules in each cell. Nearly related to Pancratium in which there are many ovules in each cell, and often confused with this Old World genus in gardens. The species with short, incurved filaments, usually under 1 in. long, beyond the edge of the large cup are sometimes referred to as Ismenes: they are *H. Amancaes, H. Andreana, H. calathina, H. Macleana*. These may be grown in the open border if sheltered from cold winds in well-drained soil, but are scarcely safe to leave out through the winter except in favoured districts; elsewhere they should be taken up, placed in sand, and kept in a shed or frame for the winter. The stove species like *H. macrostephana* need a strong, loamy soil, well drained, with plenty of pot-room, the bulbs being buried just below the surface and they must always be kept moist, especially in summer. The greenhouse species, however, should be kept dry during the winter resting-period, being given the same treatment as the stove species otherwise, except as regards temperature. The plants may be flowered annually if well treated. **A**

**H. adna'ta.** A synonym of *H. littoralis*.

**H. Aman'caes.** About 2 ft. h. *l.* sheathing about half the length of the scape, net-veined. *fl.* bright yellow, large, nodding, salver-shaped; tube green in lower, yellow in upper part; segs. linear-lanceolate, narrow, starry; scape compressed, 2-edged, even. Chile, Peru. (B.M. 1224 as *Pancratium Amancaes*.) Greenhouse.

**H. amoe'na.** A synonym of *H. ovata*.

**H. Andrea'na.** About 18 in. h. *l.* linear, pale green, glabrous. *fl.* white, solitary; tube green, cylindrical, erect, curved at top, 4½ to 5 in. long; segs. linear, 3½ to 4 in. long; corona broadly funnel-shaped, nearly 3 in. long, 3 to 4 in. across, with green stripes; scape slender. Ecuador. 1876. (R.H. 1884, 468; Gn. 25 (1884), 454 as *Ismene Andreana*.) Greenhouse.

**H. Borskia'na.** A synonym of *H. undulata*.

**H. calathi'na.*** *l.* few, in 2 ranks, sheathing scape, obtuse, veins parallel. *fl.* white, very fragrant, tube and upper part of style green, about 3 in. long, opening successively with intervals of 10 to 14 days. March, April. Brazil. 1796. (B.M. 1561 as *Pancratium calathinum.*) Greenhouse.

*Hymenocallis calathina*

**H. caribae'a.** Bulb globose, 3 to 4 in. across. *l.* 12 or more, in several ranks, lorate, acute, 2 to 3 ft. long, 2 to 3 in. wide, narrowing to 1 in. at base. *fl.* 6 to 12, white; tube 2 to 3 in. long; segs. linear, 3 to 3½ in. long; corona obconic, 1 in. long, with 2 small teeth between free parts of filaments which are 1½ to 2 in. long; scape rather shorter than l., 2-edged. June. W. Indies. 1872. (B.M. 826 as *Pancratium caribaeum*; L.B.C. 558 as *P. declinatum.*) Stove.

**H. Chore'tis.** A synonym of *H. glauca*.

**H. concin'na.** Much like *H. caribaea* but evergreen and smaller in all parts. *l.* 1 in. wide. Mexico. 1893. Stove.

**H. cordifo'lia.** *l.* broad, Eucharis-like, 2½ ft. long. *fl.* white, about 20 in umbel; tube 4 in. or more long; segs. 2 in. long; corona inconspicuous. Venezuela. 1899. (R.H. 1899, 445.) Stove.

**H. crassifo'lia.** *l* 6 to 8, lorate, obtuse, 2 ft. long, 2 in. wide, bright green. *fl.* white, 4 in a sessile umbel; segs. linear, 3½ in. long; scape 2 ft. h. SE. United States. 1871. (Ref. B. 331 as *Pancratium crassifolium.*) Greenhouse.

**H. × Daphne** (*H. calathina* ♂ × *H. speciosa*). *fl.* white, large. Raised by Mr. van Tubergen of Haarlem before 1900.

**H. deflex'a.** *l.* ensiform, 12 in. long, 2 in. wide, acute. *fl.* 3 or 4 in a sessile umbel; tube curved, 1½ to 2 in. long, segs. linear, 3 to 4 in. long; corona funnel-shaped, 2 to 3 in. long, with recurved processes 1 in. or more long; scape 2-edged. Peru. 1839. SYN. *Ismene deflexa.* Stove.

**H. eucharidifo'lia.** *l.* 4, oblong, about 1 ft. long, thin, bright green, nearly sessile. *fl.* white; tube slender, green, 4 in. long; segs. linear, deeply channelled, 3 to 3½ in. long; corona funnel-shaped, 1¼ in. long; umbel 4- or 5-fld.; scape 1 ft. long, 2-edged. May. Trop. America. 1884. Stove.

**H. expan'sa.** About 2 ft. h. *l.* linear-lanceolate, striped. *fl.* sessile, more or less 3-cornered, pale green, 4½ in. long; segs. linear. November. Habitat? (B.M. 1941 as *Pancratium expansum.*) Stove.

**H. × festa'lis** (*Elisena longipetala* ♀ × *H. calathina*). Vigorous. *fl.* white; scape about 18 in. h. Raised by Mr. Worsley of Isleworth, about 1910. Nearly hardy.

**H. glau'ca.** About 1 ft. h. *l.* strap-shaped, erect, 6 in. long, about 2½ in. wide, glaucous. *fl.* white with a long green tube; corona white, rotate, margin jagged; scape 3-fld. August. Mexico. 1837. SYN. *H. Choretis, Choretis glauca.* Stove.

**H. Harrisia'na.** About 12 in. h. *l.* sessile. *fl.* white, tube very long and slender; segs. very narrow-linear, corona well formed; stamens green; umbels few-fld. June. Mexico. 1838. (B.M. 6562.) Greenhouse.

**H. Horsman'nii.** *l.* few, thin, oblanceolate from a narrow base, 1 ft. long. *fl.* white, tube 4 to 5½ in. long; segs. very narrow, 2½ in. long; corona rotate, less than 1 in. long; peduncle 3 to 4 in. long with 1 to 3 fls. July. Mexico. 1883. Stove.

**H. hu'milis.** *l.* linear, 4 to 6 in. long, ⅛ in. wide. *fl.* solitary, tube 1¼ in. long, widened at top; segs. linear, 2 in. long; corona funnel-shaped, ⅝ in. long; peduncle rather shorter than l. Florida. 1888. Greenhouse.

**H. la'cera.** About 18 in. h. *l.* linear-oblong, streaked. *fl.* white, segs. linear-lanceolate; corona spreading, closely toothed; scape 2-edged, 10- to 12-fld., longer than l. May. Florida. 1803. (B.M. 827 as *Pancratium rotatum.*) SYN. *H. rotata.*

**H. littora'lis.** About 12 in. h. *l.* rather broad. *fl.* white; tube 3 to 4 in. long; segs. narrow; corona deep, wavy. May. S. America. 1758. (B.M. 2621.) SYN. *H. adnata.*

**H. Maclea'na.** About 2 ft. h. *l.* broad, arching, deep green. *fl.* yellowish marked with green; tube slender; segs. and style longer than corona. Lima. 1837. (B.M. 3675 as *Ismene Macleana*; B.R. 27, 12 as *I. virescens.*) Greenhouse. Nearly hardy.

**H. macrostepha'na.** About 2 ft. h. *l.* broad-lanceolate, 2½ to 3 ft. long. *fl.* white, tube green, about 3 in. long, fragrant; umbel 6- to 8-fld. February. S. America. 1879. (B.M. 6436.) Stove.

**H. Moritzia'na.** Compact, evergreen. *l.* erect, distichous or nearly so, Eucharis-like, 2½ ft. long. *fl.* 20 or more in umbel, fragrant; tube very long, greenish. La Guayra. Much like *H. eucharidifolia* but larger in all parts. Stove.

**H. ova'ta.** 1 to 2 ft. h. *l.* 6 to 8, 10 in. long, midrib thick, fleshy, blade pale green beneath. *fl.* white, tube greenish-white; fragrant. October. Guiana. 1790. (B.M. 1467 as *Pancratium amoenum*; B.R. 43 as *P. ovatum.*) SYN. *P. fragrans.* Stove.

**H. Palm'eri.** *l.* linear, 1 ft. long, ¼ in. wide. *fl.* solitary, tube 3½ to 4 in. long; segs. as long as tube, only 1/12 in. wide; corona funnel-shaped with long-pointed lobes, 1 to 1¼ in. long; peduncle slender, under 1 ft. long. Florida. 1888. Greenhouse.

**H. quitoen'sis.** A synonym of *Leptochiton quitoensis.*

**H. schizostepha'na.** *fl.* resembling that of *H. caribaea* but having very stout filaments winged at base, forming an irregular corona appearing as though torn. Brazil. 1899. (B.M. 7762.) Stove.

**H. senegam'bica.** *l.* sessile, ensiform, 2 ft. long, 1½ to 2 in. wide at middle, narrowed to 1 in. at base, arched, acute. *fl.* 6 to 8 in umbel, sessile, tube slender, 5 to 6 in. long; segs. narrow-linear, about 4 in. long; corona funnel-shaped, 1 in. long; free filaments 2 to 2½ in. long, anthers 1 in. long. Guinea. The only species native in the Old World. Nearly hardy.

**H. specio'sa.** *l.* 1½ to 2 ft. long, 3 to 4 in. wide in widest part, very dark green. *fl.* white, very fragrant especially in evening; scape shorter than l., 2-edged. W. Indies. 1759. (B.M. 1453 as *Pancratium speciosum.*) Stove.

**H. Sulphur Queen.** *See* **H. Amancaes.**

**H. tenuifo'lia.** A synonym of *Leptochiton quitoensis.*

**H. tubiflo'ra.** *l.* narrow-oblong, acute, about 8 to 12 in. long, narrowed to a stalk 6 to 12 in. long. *fl.* many in umbel, sessile; tube erect, slender, 6 to 8 in. long; segs. linear, about 4 in. long; corona narrow-funnel-shaped, 1 in. long; scape compressed 1 ft. long. Guiana, Trinidad. 1803. SYN. *Pancratium guianense.* Greenhouse.

**H. undula'ta.** About 1 ft. h. *l.* 2½ ft. long, dull green. *fl.* white, 7 in an umbel; corona very thin, transparent. April. La Guayra. 1845. SYN. *H. Borskiana.* Stove.

**H. vires'cens.** A synonym of *H. Macleana.*

**HYMENOCYS'TIS.** *See* **Woodsia fragilis.**

***hymeno'des,*** of membranous texture.

**HYMENODIC'TYON** (*hymenum*, a membrane, *dictyon*, net; seeds covered with a netted membrane). FAM. *Rubiaceae.* A genus of 4 or 5 species of trees, natives of Trop. Asia and Africa. Leaves opposite, deciduous. Flowers small, in racemose panicles, the bracts enlarged and coloured white. For treatment *see* **Cinchona.**

**H. excel'sum.** Tree of 30 ft. *l.* oblong, downy; floral-l. white, blistered. *fl.* in large axillary and terminal panicles. Summer. India. 1820. The bark is very astringent and is used for tanning. SYN. *H. utile.*

F. G. P.

**HYMENO'DIUM.** Included in **Elaphoglossum.**

**HYMENOLAE'NA.** A synonym of Woodsia.

**HYMENOLE'PIS** (*hymen*, membrane, *lepis*, scale; from the nature of the indusia). FAM. *Polypodiaceae*. A genus of about a dozen species of ferns with simple uniform fronds having the sori in a patch at the narrowed apex; tropical in distribution. For treatment *see* **Acrostichum.**

**H. platyrhyn'chos.** *sti.* tufted, very short. *Fronds* 12 to 16 in. long, 1 in. broad, simple. *Sori* in a patch at the apex, 1 to 2 in. long, ⅜ in. broad, which does not reach to the entire edge; lower part narrowed gradually, with naked surfaces, leathery. Luzon. (H.C.F. 99.) Stove.

**H. spica'ta.** *rhiz.* woody, short creeping. *sti.* 1 to 2 in. long, firm. *Fronds* 6 to 18 in. long, ½ to 1 in. broad, upper part contracted, fertile, entire; lower part narrowed very gradually. Malaya. (L.F. 2, 64.) Greenhouse.

**HYMENOMYCE'TES.** One of the large section of Basidiomycetous Fungi having the hymenium (spore-bearing surface) exposed from the first or from very early during development, as, for example, in the Agaricaceae, Hydnaceae, Polyporaceae, &c.

D. E. G.

**HYMENOPHYLLA'CEAE.** A family of slender ferns, with about 650 species in 4 genera, in tropical and temperate regions. Mostly creeping. Leaves pinnate, but 1 cell thick except in the veins, and without stomata. The sporangia are sessile and are surrounded by a cup-shaped indusium on the edge of the leaf at the termination of a vein. The sporangia have a complete oblique or transverse annulus and dehisc longitudinally. The species are found chiefly in damp woods. The genera in cultivation are Hymenophyllum and Trichomanes.

**HYMENOPHYL'LUM** (*hymen*, a membrane, *phyllon*, a leaf). Filmy Fern. FAM. *Polypodiaceae*. A genus of about 320 species of ferns, widely distributed. Fronds delicately membranous, simple or compound, never with anastomosing veins. Sori marginal, more or less sunk in the frond, or exserted; indusia inferior, more or less deeply 2-lipped or 2-valved, toothed, fringed, or entire; receptacle elongated, columnar, exserted or included. Except where otherwise stated, the species described below require stove treatment.

With the exception of the beautiful *H. fuciforme* and *H. pulcherrimum* nearly all are of creeping habit. Having shallow-rooting rhizomes, they succeed best when growing on the surface of a rock and allowed to run under the moss which covers it. The great majority of these plants are natives of New Zealand, Tasmania, and Chile, where they exist in a climate naturally cool and humid, and of the E. and W. Indies, where they occur under trees at high elevations; in such situations they are permanently subject to the influences of shade and moisture, and to a comparatively cool temperature. The fronds show considerable variation.

Hymenophyllums are particularly well adapted for growing in fern-cases in towns; they are all the more valuable by reason of their fronds, though apparently delicate, not being, like that of most other Ferns, affected by fogs which prove so destructive to plants in general. They require constant moisture, produced more by condensation than by mechanical waterings to which they are decidedly averse, especially the species with hairy or woolly fronds, which suffer greatly from being syringed overhead. It is especially to be deprecated in the case of *H. hirtellum*, *H. scabrum*, *H. sericeum*, and *H. tunbridgense*. For *H. sericeum* the material most suited is a piece of sandstone, or any other porous stone, over which its tiny rhizomes can run freely without, however, clinging to it. A successful method is to make a large pit under a spreading tree, with bed of cement to cover the bottom, and hold, say, 1 in. of water over the whole surface; all the ferns should be placed on bricks or on inverted pots, and the whole is covered with a 3-light frame. Condensation is free and much time is saved as no overhead syringing is required.

Hymenophyllums require but little light, and only a small depth of soil, as their slender rhizomes, mostly wiry, have the greatest objection to being buried under the loose material in which they grow. When the plants are cultivated in pots or in pans the compost should be of sandy peat, chopped Sphagnum, and small pieces of sandstone, in about equal parts, with an additional sprinkling of coarse crock dust, the whole being made so light and permeable as to be prevented under any circumstances from becoming sour through the accumulated moisture resulting from the repeated sprinklings and waterings necessary to produce condensation. Some species, especially among the dwarfest, succeed best when established on a piece of sandstone without any other material.

Hymenophyllums are propagated but slowly, commonly by the division of their rhizomes, an operation which is safe enough, although it is one requiring a little patience. Draughts must be carefully avoided at all times of the year, and air should only be very sparingly admitted into the case.

No Hymenophyllum is more effective than *H. demissum*; it is a suitable companion for the Killarney Fern. The lively green colour of its young fronds, which, with age, turn to the deepest dark green, and the vigorous habit and constitution of the plant are special recommendations.

*H. dichotomum* delights to send its tiny rhizomes through a coating of moss covering either a piece of rock or a block of wood or Tree-Fern.

*H. dilatatum Forsterianum* is very free-growing; its wiry rhizomes are particularly fond of moss and decaying vegetable matter. It produces fronds in great abundance.

*H. hirsutum* succeeds best on a block of wood and in an upright position; it requires a very humid but airy situation, and great care must be taken at all times that no water touches its fronds.

*H. polyanthos* does not require such a close temperature as do most Hymenophyllums; the airiest place in the house suits it best. It is provided with exceedingly slender, wiry rhizomes, which make their way through partly decayed vegetable matter; on that account it makes a beautiful object on a block of wood, its slender, elegantly arching fronds then showing themselves to great advantage.

*H. tunbridgense* is one of the most difficult of Hymenophyllums to manage. It dislikes water over the fronds, and does best either in a mixture of equal parts of peat and silver-sand or on a block of sandstone, the principal object being to have it pressed hard on to the material upon which it is intended to grow. The treatment giving the most satisfactory results consists in laying the sheet of *Hymenophyllum* upon a porous piece of stone without any soil, and laying a slab over it, leaving it in that state for 3 to 4 weeks, after which the plant has usually taken hold of the new stone, when the slab is removed.

**H. abrup'tum.** *sti.* about ¼ in. long, very slender. *Fronds* ½ to 1 in. long, ¼ to ½ in. broad, oblong, pinnatifid nearly to rachis; pinnae linear, about ¼ in. long. *Sori* 1 or 2 to a frond, terminal on apex. Trop. America, Patagonia. 1859. (H.S. 1, 31.)

**H. aerugino'sum.*** *sti.* 1 to 2 in. long, hairy. *Fronds* 2 to 3 in. long, about, or scarcely, 1 in. broad, lanceolate or ovate-acuminate, 3-pinnatifid; pinnae often much imbricate, lower flabellate, cut nearly to rachis; surface and margin pubescent. *Sori* terminal on segs. Tristan da Cunha. (H.S. 1, 34; B.C.F. 2, 303.)

**H. asplenioi'des.** *sti.* 1 to 2 in. long, slender. *Fronds* 2 to 4 in. long, ½ to 1 in. broad, pendulous, oblong in general outline, pinnatifid nearly to rachis. *Sori* 1 to 4, terminal on segs. Trop. America. 1859. (H.C.F. 56.)

**H. attenua'tum.** A synonym of *H. magellanicum*.

**H. austra'le.** *sti.* 2 to 4 in. long, erect, margined with a broad, crisped wing. *Fronds* 4 to 8 in. long, 3 to 4 in. broad, triangular, 3-pinnatifid; lower pinnae 1½ to 2 in. long, triangular-rhomboid, cut to a narrow, crisped centre. *Sori* 6 to 20 to a pinna, terminal and axillary on segs. on both sides. N. India to Malaya, Australia, New Zealand, and Antarctic Is. SYN. *H. crispatum*, *H. fimbriatum* (H.S. 1, 36), *H. flexuosum*, *H. javanicum*. var. **flexuo'sum** has fronds 10 to 12 in. long, broadly lanceolate, 4-pinnatifid; ultimate segs. narrow, undulate. New Zealand.

seaweed-like, 3 to 5 in. long, 1 to 1½ in. broad, with simple, prominent veins, brownish-rosy in age. *Sori* 6 to 12 each side of frond, at tips of sinuses. Chile. (L.F. 8, 5; H.S. 1, 31.)

*Hymenophyllum australe*

*Hymenophyllum demissum*

**H. axilla're.** *rhiz.* very slender. *Fronds* 3 to 8 in. long, 1 in. broad, narrow-oblong, flaccid, pendent, 3-pinnatifid; main rachis winged throughout or above only; lower pinnae varying from ½ in. long with simple segs. to 1½ in. long with pinnatifid pinnules and several segs. *Sori* 2 to 12 to a pinna, terminal on lateral segs. W. Indies, Venezuela.

**H. bad'ium.** *sti.* 2 to 3 in. long, winged above. *Fronds* erect, 4 to 12 in. long, 2 to 3 in. broad, oblong or broadly lanceolate, 3-pinnatifid; main rachis broadly winged; lower pinnae cut to rachis into several pinnules each side, lowest deeply incised. *Sori* 2 to 12 to a pinna, terminal on segs. on both sides. India, &c. (F.B.I. 282.)

**H. bival've.** *sti.* 2 to 4 in. long, wiry. *Fronds* ovate-triangular, 3-pinnatifid, 3 to 8 in. long, 2 to 3 in. broad; lower pinnae triangular-acuminate; ultimate segs. linear, ⅛ to ¼ in. long, spinulose-dentate. *Sori* very numerous, often 6 to 8 on a single pinnule. Australia, New Zealand. (H.S. 35 D.)

**H. Borya'num.** A synonym of *H. ciliatum.*

**H. Catheri'nae.** A synonym of *H. lineare.*

**H. caudicula'tum.** *sti.* 4 to 6 in. long, wiry, broadly winged above. *Fronds* 6 to 12 in. long, 2 to 3 in. broad, ovate-acuminate, 3-pinnatifid; lower pinnae rhomboidal-lanceolate, erecto-patent, divided to rachis. *Sori* 2 to 12 to a pinna, at apex of segs. on both sides. Brazil, Peru, and Chile. (Gn. 48 (1895), 228.)

**H. chiloen'se.** A synonym of *H. dicranotrichum.*

**H. cilia'tum.\*** *sti.* 1 to 2 in. long, ciliately and decurrently winged above. *Fronds* oblong, acuminate, 3-pinnatifid, 2 to 6 in. long, 1 to 2 in. broad at centre; lower pinnae oblong or rhomboidal, with a broad central individual portion. *Sori* 2 to 12 on a pinna, at end of lateral segs. on both sides. Trop. America, Trop. Africa, Sikkim, New Zealand. 1859. (F.B.I. 305.) SYN. *H. Boryanum, H. Plumieri.*

**H. crispa'tum.** A synonym of *H. australe.*

**H. cris'pum.** Closely allied to *H. axillare*, distinguished by crisped fronds, on slender, wingless stipes. Trop. America.

**H. cruen'tum.** *rhiz.* slender, creeping, simple, slightly sinuate. *sti.* slender, naked, 3 to 6 in. long. *Fronds* delicately transparent,

**H. demis'sum.\*** *sti.* 4 to 6 in. long, erect, firm. *Fronds* 4 to 12 in. long, 3 to 4 in. broad, ovate-triangular, 3- or 4-pinnatifid; lower pinnae 2 to 3 in. long, triangular-rhomboid, divided nearly to rachis. *Sori* 20 to 30 to a pinna, terminal and axillary in segs. on both sides. New Zealand, Philippines, Malaya. 1858. Greenhouse. (L.F. 8, 7.)

**H. dichot'omum.\*** *sti.* 2 to 3 in. long, winged on both sides. *Fronds* broadly triangular, 2- or 3-pinnatifid, 4 to 6 in. long, 2 to 3 in. broad; lower pinnae thrice as long as broad, segs. crisped and sharply toothed or torn. *Sori* numerous in axils of segs. Antarctic America. (H.S. 1, 36.)

**H. dicranot'richum.\*** *Fronds* triangular or broadly lanceolate, about 2 in. long and 1 in. broad, dull green, with conspicuous dark veins, 2-pinnatifid; pinnae ciliate on margins and slightly hairy beneath. *Sori* solitary at base of pinnae on upper side. Chiloé. (H.S. 1, 32.)

**H. dilata'tum.** *sti.* 2 to 4 in. long, erect, wiry. *Fronds* 6 to 12 in. long, 4 to 6 in. broad, ovate-lanceolate, 3-pinnatifid; lower pinnae rhomboid-lanceolate, divided nearly to rachis. *Sori* 2 to 12 to a pinna, terminal or axillary on segs. on both sides. Malaya, Trop. Australia, Polynesia, New Zealand. var. **Forsteria'num** has larger fronds with undulate pinnae. Brazil?

**H. elegan'tulum.** *sti.* 1 to 4 in. long, ciliate. *Fronds* flaccid, pendulous, 6 to 18 in. long, 2 to 6 in. broad, linear-oblong and pinnate or broadly oblong and 2-pinnate; rachis free; lower pinnae in the 2-pinnate form often with several pairs of pinnules; pinnules 1 to 3 in. long, deeply pinnatifid principally on upper side; ultimate segs. densely hairy. *Sori* 6 to 12, terminal on lateral segs. Ecuador, Colombia.

**H. falkland'icum.** *sti.* ½ to ¾ in. long, filiform. *Fronds* oblong, pinnatifid, 1 to 2 in. long, ⅜ to ½ in. broad; pinnae erecto-patent, sessile, upper simple, lower deeply 2- or 3-fid; lobes ciliate-dentate. *Sori* solitary. Falkland Is. (B.C.F. 2, 312.) Greenhouse.

**H. ferrugin'eum.** *sti.* 1 to 3 in. long, wiry, erect, tomentose. *Fronds* 3 to 8 in. long, 1½ to 2 in. broad, ovate-lanceolate, 3-pinnatifid; main rachis slightly winged above; lower pinnae spreading, divided nearly to rachis into numerous alternate pinnules, again deeply divided into broad, linear segs., surface and margins tawny-pubescent. *Sori* 2 to 12 to a pinna, terminal on lateral segs. New Zealand, Chile.

**H. fimbria'tum.** A synonym of *H. australe.*

**H. flabella'tum.** *sti.* 2 to 4 in. long, firm, erect. *Fronds* 4 to 12 in. long, 2 to 4 in. broad, ovate-acuminate, 3-pinnatifid, flaccid; lower pinnae 1 to 2 in. long, broadly rhomboid-acuminate, divided to rachis. *Sori* 6 to 20 to a pinna, terminal on lateral segs. Australia, New Zealand, Samoa. 1859: SYN. *H. nitens.* Greenhouse.

*Hymenophyllum falklandicum* (p. 1031)

**H. flexuo'sum.** A variety of *H. australe.*

**H. fucifor'me.*** *rhiz.* thick, decumbent, resembling crowns. *sti.* strong, erect, narrowly winged above. *Fronds* erect, glaucous, 1 to 2 ft. long, 4 to 6 in. broad, triangular-lanceolate, 3-pinnatifid; main rachis winged; lower segs. sometimes forked. *Sori* numerous, small, disposed in axils of segs. Chile, Juan Fernandez. (H.S. 1, 36.)

**H. fucoi'des.** *sti.* 2 to 4 in. long, wiry, ciliate. *Fronds* oblong, 3-pinnatifid, 4 to 6 in. long, 1½ to 2 in. broad; main rachis winged above and ciliate; secondary rachis winged throughout; pinnae rhomboid, acuminate, with long, narrow, spinulose-toothed, entire or forked segs. *Sori* not more than 4 to a pinna, usually confined to segs. on upper side. Trop. America, Samoa. (H.C.F. 63.)

**H. hirsu'tum.*** *sti.* 1 to 2 in. long, slender. *Fronds* linear-oblong, once pinnatifid, 2 to 6 in. long, about ½ in. broad, slender, flaccid, often pendulous, hairy over surface; pinnae short, close. *Sori* 1 to 4 on a pinna. Trop. America, S. Africa, Madagascar.

**H. hirtel'lum.** *sti.* 1 to 4 in. long, tomentose. *Fronds* ovate-acuminate, 3-pinnatifid, 3 to 6 in. long, 2 to 3 in. broad; lower pinnae rhomboid-lanceolate, with a narrow central undivided portion; lower pinnules pinnatifid, with long, narrow-linear ciliate segs. *Sori* 2 to 12 to a pinna, at end of lateral segs. on both sides. W. Indies, Mexico, &c. 1859. (L.F. 8, 7; H.S. 1, 31.)

**H. javan'icum.** A synonym of *H. australe.*

**H. linea're.*** *rhiz.* slender, hairy, thread-like. *sti.* 1 to 2 in. long, erect, wiry. *Fronds* pendulous, flaccid, 2 to 8 in. long, 1 to 2 in. broad, pinnate or 3-pinnate; pinnae deeply cut into simple or forked linear lobes, with margins and surface densely hairy. *Sori* 2 to 6 to a pinna, terminal on lateral segs. W. Indies. (F.S.A. (2) 5.) SYN. *H. Catherinae, H. elegans.*

**H. magellan'icum.** *sti.* erect, wiry, 2 to 4 in. long, naked or winged. *Fronds* oblong-triangular, 3 to 6 in. long, 2 to 4 in. broad, 3-pinnatifid; lower pinnae broadly triangular, with deeply cleft pinnules, with several toothed segs. each side. *Sori* very small, 6 to 10 to a pinna, terminal on segs. of upper ones. Chile, Chiloé, S. Brazil. (H.S. 1, 36 B as *H. attenuatum.*)

**H. multif'idum.*** *sti.* wiry, naked, 2 to 4 in. long. *Fronds* broadly lanceolate, 2 to 6 in. long, 1 to 5 in. broad, 3-pinnatifid; main rachis winged above, wingless below; ultimate segs. narrow. *Sori* 2 to 12 to a pinna, terminal on lateral segs. of upper ones on both sides. New Zealand, Australia, Polynesia, Celebes.

**H. ni'tens.** A synonym of *H. flabellatum.*

**H. pectina'tum.*** *sti.* naked, 2 to 4 in. long, very wiry. *Fronds* oblong, pinnate, glaucous green, 3 to 6 in. long, ½ to 1½ in. broad, with conspicuous venation; main rachis only winged towards apex; pinnae deeply cleft on upper side into long, narrow, parallel, simple or slightly forked segs. *Sori* 6 to 8 to a pinna, terminal on lower segs. of upper side. Chile, Chiloé. (H.S. 1, 34; B.C.F. 2, 323.) var. **superb'um** is particularly fine.

**H. pelta'tum.** Differs from *H. tunbridgense* in the more ovoid and turgid indusium, in the darker green and more rigid fronds, with the pinnae pinnatifid on the upper side chiefly. Britain. Hardy. (H.B.F. 44; E.B. 1841.) SYN. *H. Wilsoni, H. unilaterale.*

**H. Plumie'ri.** A synonym of *H. ciliatum.*

**H. polyan'thos.*** *sti.* 2 to 3 in. long, slender. *Fronds* 2 to 8 in. long, 1 to 3 in. broad, ovate-oblong, 3-pinnatifid; lower pinnae triangular-rhomboid, cut to narrow centre. *Sori* 2 to 12 to a pinna, terminal or axillary on segs. of both sides. Tropics. 1824. (H.S. 1, 37 B; L.F. 8, 8.) SYN. *H. protrusum.*

**H. protru'sum.** A synonym of *H. polyanthos.*

**H. pulcher'rimum.*** *sti.* 3 to 4 in. long, wiry, erect, winged down to base. *Fronds* 6 to 12 in. long, 4 to 6 in. broad, ovate-triangular, 3- or 4-pinnatifid; lower pinnae 2 to 3 in. long, lanceolate-rhomboid. *Sori* numerous, axillary and terminal on segs. of both sides. New Zealand. Greenhouse. (H.S. 1, 37; B.C.F. 2, 112.)

**H. ra'rum.** *sti.* very slender, 1 to 3 in. long. *Fronds* flaccid, pendent, 2 to 6 in. long, 1 to 2 in. broad, oblong, 2-pinnatifid; pinnae simple, linear or forked or pinnatifid. *Sori* large, terminal on segs. of upper pinnae. New Zealand, Tasmania. Greenhouse. (F.S.A. (2) 3 as *H. fumarioides.*)

**H. scab'rum.** *sti.* 2 to 4 in. long, wiry, ciliate. *Fronds* 6 to 15 in. long, 2 to 5 in. broad, ovate-acuminate, 3-pinnatifid; lower pinnae 2 to 3 in. long, oblong-rhombid, acuminate, divided nearly to rachis. *Sori* 6 to 20 to a pinna, terminal on lateral segs. on both sides. New Zealand. 1859. Greenhouse.

**H. seric'eum.** *sti.* 2 to 4 in. long, wiry. *Fronds* pendent, 6 to 24 in. long, 2 to 3 in. broad, elongate-oblong, obtuse or acuminate, simply pinnatifid; pinnae 1 to 2 in. long, numerous, opposite, very variable in division. *Sori* numerous to a pinna, small, terminal on apex of pinnae and lateral segs. Trop. America. 1859. (L.F. 8, 8.)

**H. subtilis'simum.** A synonym of *H. ferrugineum.*

**H. tunbridgen'se.*** *sti.* ½ to 1½ in. long. *Fronds* oblong-lanceolate, 1 to 3 in. long, ½ to 1 in. broad, pinnate throughout; pinnae distichous, flabellate-pinnatifid; lobes linear, 1/12 to ¼ in. long, spinulose, serrate, as is the compound indusium. Temperate regions (Britain). Hardy. (H.B.F. 43; E.B. 1840.)

**H. unilatera'le.** A synonym of *H. peltatum.*

**H. Wilsoni.** A synonym of *H. peltatum.*

**HYMENOP'TERA.** An order of Insects (q.v.) including, Ants, Bees, Gall-wasps, Ichneumon Flies, Sawflies, Wood-wasps, Wasps, &c.

**HYMENOSPO'RUM** (*hymen*, membrane, *sporos*, seed, the seeds have a membranous wing). FAM. *Pittospora-ceae.* A single evergreen Australian shrub or tree constitutes this genus, which differs from Pittosporum by its large yellow flowers and the flat winged seeds, the seeds of Pittosporum being thick and without a wing. It needs greenhouse protection in most parts but is hardy in Scilly. For cultivation see **Pittosporum.**

**H. fla'vum.*** Evergreen shrub or tree, 10 to 25 ft., shoots glabrous. *l.* mostly alternate, obovate to ovate-oblong, 3 to 6 in. long, cuneate, slender-pointed, sometimes downy beneath. *fl.* fragrant, bright yellow, about 1 in. wide, in terminal corymbs 4 to 8 in. across; main-stalk 1½ to 2 in. long; sep. 5, ovate-lanceolate, ½ in. long; cor. 1½ in. long, tubular with a limb of 5 obovate, spreading lobes, silky behind; stamens 5, downy. April. Seeds winged. Queensland, New S. Wales. (B.M. 4799 as *Pittosporum flavum.*)

W. J. B.

**HYMENOSTACH'YS.** Included in **Trichomanes.**

**HYMENOX'YS.** See **Baeria coronaria.**

**HYOPHOR'BE** (*hys*, pig, *phorbe*, food; the fruits are eaten by swine). FAM. *Palmaceae.* A genus of 3 or 4 species of Palms, natives of Mauritius, with stout, un-armed stems, sometimes swollen beneath the terminal crown of leaves. Leaves pinnatisect, pinnae opposite, mostly linear-lanceolate, margins recurved near base and thickened throughout; stalk channelled. Flowers dioecious, white or yellow, on a short, much-branched spadix. Fruit pear- or olive-shaped, 1-seeded. For treatment of these ornamental palms, see **Areca.** A

**H. amaricau'lis.*** Very stout, up to 60 ft. in nature, bottle-shaped near base. *l.* pinnate, at first erect, then spreading, 4 to 6 ft. long; pinnae stout, in 40 to 60 pairs, about 2 in. wide, closely set, acute; stalk deep maroon, glaucous, with an orange line along outer edges of midrib. *fl.* white. *Seed* elliptic, about ½ in. long. Mauritius. (I.H. 462–3.) SYN. *Areca speciosa.*

**H. in'dica.** A synonym of *Chrysalidocarpus lutescens.* A

**H. Verschaffelt'ii.*** 25 to 30 ft. h. in nature, swollen about half-way up. *l.* 4 to 6 ft. long, nearly erect, gracefully arching at top; pinnae in 30 to 50 pairs, about 2 ft. long, 1 in. wide; stalk 3 in. long, slightly grooved above, with a yellow band from the upper part of the l.-sheath to the end of the blade. *fl.* orange-yellow. *Seed* cylindrical, about ⅜ in. long. Mauritius. (G.C. 1870, 418.)

**HYOSCY′AMUS** (*Hyos Kyamos*, Hog's Bean, ancient Greek name used by Dioscorides). FAM. *Solanaceae.* A genus of about 11 species of biennial or perennial erect herbs natives of N. Africa, Europe, and Asia. Flowers with an obliquely bell-shaped or shortly funnel-shaped corolla, 5-lobed. Capsule enclosed in a large calyx, erect, opening by a circular raised ring immediately below the hardened top. *H. niger* is of no particular value except for its medicinal properties and is poisonous to fowls. It grows in any ordinary soil and is apt to appear in un-expected places.

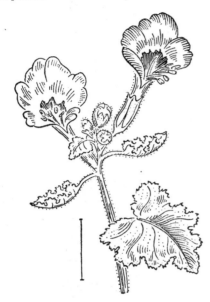

*Hyoscyamus albus*

**H. al′bus.** Annual or biennial. 2 to 3 ft. h. Habit of *H. niger. l.* lobed and toothed, hairy. *fl.* yellow without coloured veins, purple in throat. Summer. Europe. (F.G. 230.)

**H. ni′ger.** 1 to 2 ft. h., annual or biennial. *l.* rather large, sessile, upper stem-clasping, ovate, regularly pinnatifid; stalks short. *fl.* pale dingy yellow with purplish veins. Summer. *Capsule* 2-celled, many-seeded. Europe (including Britain) to India. (E.B. 936.) The l. and young tops are used in medicine and it has been long grown for its narcotic properties.

**HYOSE′RIS** (*hys*, pig, *seris*, salad). FAM. *Compositae.* A genus of 3 or 4 species of nearly stemless herbs, natives of S. Europe and the Mediterranean region. Leaves radical, pinnatifid. Scape 1-headed, leafless. Flower-heads homogamous, yellow; involucre cylindrical-bell-shaped, inner bracts in 1 row, equal, outer few and short; receptacle plain, naked; florets all rayed. Achene glabrous. *H. foetida* is a rock-plant, not unlike Taraxacum, but smaller; it is best in a sunny, well-drained spot with a fairly moist soil.

**H. foet′ida.** Perennial. *l.* pinnatifid with 10 to 12 pairs of lobes, glabrous or somewhat hairy on veins beneath; lobes more or less triangular and toothed. *fl.-heads* yellow. Mts. of S. Europe. SYN. *Aposeris foetida.*

**HYOSPA′THE** (*hys*, pig, *spathe*; Hog palm is the common name in Brazil). FAM. *Palmaceae.* A genus of reed-like, unarmed Palms, natives of Brazil. Leaves few in a terminal crown, irregularly pinnatisect; segments broad. Flowers green, minute; spadices 2 or 3, short-stalked; spathes 2, lower keeled. For treatment of *H. elegans*, which need a stove, *see* **Bactris.**

**H. el′egans.** *l.* 3 to 4 ft. long, nearly entire when young, but with age becoming irregularly pinnatisect. *fl.-spikes* produced below l., monoecious. *fr.* violet, olive-shaped. Para. The l. are used in thatching.

**HYPECO′UM** (*hypecoon*, Greek name used by Dioscorides). FAM. *Papaveraceae.* A genus of 15 species

distributed through the N. Temperate regions of the Old World. Annual rather dwarf herbs with more or less glaucous, usually glabrous, foliage. Leaves forming a basal rosette, pinnatipartite, segments more or less pinnately cut, stem-leaves of similar form. Flowers usually small, in a dichasial cyme; sepals lanceolate or ovate, toothed at apex, deciduous; petals 4 usually yellow, outer pair usually 3-lobed, inner 3-fid; stamens 4, their filaments winged; fruit siliqua-like, 2-valved. Hypecoums need only ordinary soil, are hardy and may be raised by sowing where they are to flower in spring for summer-flowering, autumn for spring-flowering.

**H. grandiflo′rum.** Hardy annual about 10 in. h. *l.* 4 to 6 in. long; segs. narrow-linear. *fl.* orange, about ½ in. across; outer pet. 3-lobed, mid-lobe somewhat hooded, side lobes oblong-linear. Summer. Mediterranean region. (G.F. 1060.)

**H. procum′bens.** Hardy annual about 1 ft. h. *l.* with many pinnate lobes themselves 2-pinnatifid, stalked; stem-l. less divided, stalks shorter. *fl.* bright yellow about ⅓ in. across in groups 2 to 5 on the many scapes which are at first erect but procumbent in fruit; outer pet. somewhat 3-lobed, the mid-lobe largest. Spring, summer. *Pods* flat, curved. S. Europe. 1596. (S.B.F.G. 217.)

*hypenan′thus -a -um*, with bearded flowers.

*hyperbor′eus -a -um*, northern.

**HYPERICA′CEAE.** *See* **Guttiferae.**

**HYPE′RICUM** (old Greek name, used by Dioscorides). St. John's Wort. FAM. *Guttiferae.* A large genus of shrubs, sub-shrubs, and herbs (of which only those of perennial habit are noticed here) with rounded, winged, or angular stems; sessile or sub-petiolate, deciduous or evergreen, opposite or whorled leaves nearly always punctate with pellucid glands; yellow or yellowish perfect flowers consisting of 5 equal or unequal sepals, 5 imbricate, contiguous or separated petals, 3 or 5 discrete or connate styles and (usually) numerous stamens, which in some species are free but in others in 3 or 5 bundles. Fruit capsular and, except in *H. Androsaemum*, membranous. Many members of the genus are excellent garden plants. Generous displays of flowers may be had from them from spring till autumn and they are of the easiest culture in any reasonably good, well-drained but moisture-retentive soil, always providing that the temperature of a neighbourhood is in accord with the hardiness of species planted there. A sunny position is preferred by most. Hypericums are readily propagated from seed, cuttings, rooted runners for species which provide them, and, in vigorous and quickly spreading kinds, like *H. calycinum*, by simple division.

KEY

| | | |
|---|---|---|
| 1. | *Shrubs* | 2 |
| 1. | *Sub-shrubs (in the suffruticose sense) and perennial herbs* | 22 |
| 2. | *Up to 6 ft. or more h.* | 3 |
| 2. | *Less than 6 ft.* | 6 |
| 3. | *Fl. with 3 styles* | H. densiflorum |
| 3. | *Fl with 5 styles* | 4 |
| 4. | *Fl. 2½ in. or more across* | 5 |
| 4. | *Fl. ½ in. across* | H. lobocarpum |
| 5. | *Sep. obtuse* | H. Hookerianum |
| 5. | *Sep. sharply pointed* | H. Leschenaultii |
| 6. | *Shrubs between 3 and 6 ft. h.* | 7 |
| 6. | *Shrubs under 3 ft. h.* | 18 |
| 7. | *Stems rounded* | 8 |
| 7. | *Stems winged, edged, or angular* | 10 |
| 8. | *Lvs. up to 3 in. long, ovate* | H. elatum |
| 8. | *Lvs. up to 2 in. long, elliptic-lanceolate* | 9 |
| 9. | *Lvs. pointed at both ends, arranged in 2 rows* | H. glandulosum |
| 9. | *Lvs. sometimes pointed at both ends, arranged in 4 rows* | H. floribundum |
| 10. | *Stems winged or edged* | 11 |
| 10. | *Stems 4-angled* | 15 |
| 11. | *Stems 2-winged* | 12 |
| 11. | *Stems 2-edged* | 13 |
| 12. | *Stems 2-winged only at apices* | H. inodorum |
| 12. | *Stems 2-winged for whole length* | H. aureum |
| 13. | *Shrub up to 5 ft. h.* | H. prolificum |
| 13. | *Shrubs up to 3 or 4 ft. h.* | 14 |
| 14. | *Fls. 1 in. across* | H. uralum |
| 14. | *Fls. 2 in. across* | H. patulum |
| 15. | *Stamens in 5 bundles* | H. lysimachioides |

| | |
|---|---|
| 15. *Stamens free* | 16 |
| 16. *Styles 5* | H. Kalmianum |
| 16. *Styles 3* | 17 |
| 17. *Lvs. nearly linear, sharply pointed* | H. glomeratum |
| 17. *Lvs. lanceolate, obtuse* | H. nudiflorum |
| 18. *With rounded stems* | 19 |
| 18. *With stems other than rounded* | 20 |
| 19. *Styles 5; fls. $\frac{1}{2}$ in. across or less* | H. aegypticum |
| 19. *Styles 5; fls. about 2 in. across* | H. kouytchense |
| 19. *Styles 3* | H. chinense |
| 20. *Stems winged and warted* | H. balearicum |
| 20. *Stems angled or 2-edged* | 21 |
| 21. *Slightly angled, fls. about $\frac{3}{4}$ in. across* | H. empetrifolium |
| 21. *2-angled, fls. about $1\frac{3}{4}$ in. across* | H. reptans |
| 22. *Sub-shrubs* | 23 |
| 22. *Perennial herbs* | 42 |
| 23. *Hairy or downy or at least with hairy or downy lvs.* | 24 |
| 23. *Smooth or at least with smooth lvs.* | 29 |
| 24. *Hairiness general or nearly so* | 25 |
| 24. *Lvs. puberulent-glandular at edge* | H. orientale |
| 25. *Plant hairy except for inflorescence* | H. lanuginosum |
| 25. *Hairiness general* | 26 |
| 26. *Plant glaucous or partly so* | 27 |
| 26. *No part of plant glaucous* | 28 |
| 27. *Wholly glaucous* | H. rhodopeum |
| 27. *Lower l.-surface glaucous* | H. hirsutum |
| 28. *Plant whitish-tomentose; lvs. undulate* | H. tomentosum |
| 28. *Plant papillose-puberulent; lvs. truncate at base* | H. confertum |
| 29. *Lvs. grey-powdered* | H. ericoides |
| 29. *Plants free from powder* | 30 |
| 30. *Plants with membranous capsules* | 31 |
| 30. *Plant with berry-like capsule* | H. Androsaemum |
| 31. *Fls. not in specific arrangements* | 32 |
| 31. *Fls. in racemes or cymes* | 33 |
| 32. *Fls. terminal and solitary, rarely in twos or threes, 3 in. or more across* | H. calycinum |
| 32. *Fls. terminal, 1 to 3; 1 in. across* | H. Buckleyi |
| 33. *Fls. in short, leafy racemes* | H. cuneatum |
| 33. *Fls. in cymes* | 34 |
| 34. *Plants with round stems* | 35 |
| 34. *Plants with 2-winged, 2-angled, or 2-edged stems* | 40 |
| 35. *Plants glaucous or partly so* | 36 |
| 35. *Plants not glaucous in any part* | 39 |
| 36. *Wholly glaucous* | H. olympicum |
| 36. *Lvs. more or less glaucous* | 37 |
| 37. *Both surfaces glaucescent* | H. fragile |
| 37. *Lower surface glaucous* | 38 |
| 38. *Lvs. linear* | H. hyssopifolium |
| 38. *Lvs. rounded or broadly ovate* | H. nummularium |
| 39. *Lvs. in whorls* | H. Coris |
| 39. *Lvs. opposite* | H. galioides |
| 40. *Plant glaucous; stems 2-edged* | H. rumelicum |
| 40. *Plants not at all glaucous* | 41 |
| 41. *Lvs. (bruised) smell unpleasantly; stems 2-angled* | H. hircinum |
| 41. *Lvs. odourless; stems slightly winged at apices* | H. Richeri |
| 42. *Fls. yellow or yellowish* | 43 |
| 42. *Fls. pinkish or orange-coloured* | H. anagalloides |
| 43. *Plants with angled, winged, or 2-edged stems* | 44 |
| 43. *Plants with rounded stems* | 51 |
| 44. *With 4-angled stems* | 45 |
| 44. *With winged or 2-edged stems* | 47 |
| 45. *Fls. with 5 styles* | H. Ascyron |
| 45. *Fls. with 3 styles* | 46 |
| 46. *Sep. oval, obtuse* | H. quadrangulum |
| 46. *Sep. linear-lanceolate, acute* | H. japonicum |
| 47. *Stems 4-winged* | H. tetrapterum |
| 47. *Stems 2-winged or 2-edged* | 48 |
| 48. *Stems 2-winged, erect* | H. elegans |
| 48. *Stems 2-edged* | 49 |
| 49. *Stems erect* | H. perforatum |
| 49. *Stems prostrate, procumbent, or ascending* | 50 |
| 50. *Styles about half length of ovary; lvs. bordered with black dots* | H. humifusum |
| 50. *Styles about equal in length to ovary; lvs. not bordered with black dots* | H. napaulense |
| 51. *Plants glaucous in whole or in part* | 52 |
| 51. *No part of plant glaucous* | 54 |
| 52. *Plant wholly glaucous* | H. polyphyllum |
| 52. *Lower l.-surface glaucous* | 53 |
| 53. *Lvs. roundish or oval* | H. Elodes |
| 53. *Lvs. linear or oblong* | H. linarifolium |
| 54. *Plant prostrate, smooth* | H. repens |
| 54. *Plants erect or ascending* | 55 |
| 55. *Plant velvety-downy* | H. Kotschyanum |
| 55. *Plant smooth* | H. montanum |

**H. acu'tum.** A synonym of *H. tetrapterum.*

**H. adenophyl'lum.** A synonym of *H. olympicum.*

**H. aegypt'icum.** Attractive evergreen shrub, hardy only in mild areas. *l.* crowded, ovate or obovate, acute, $\frac{1}{8}$ to $\frac{1}{4}$ in. long. *fl.* $\frac{1}{4}$ to $\frac{1}{2}$ in. across, solitary, terminating short shoots or forming leafy racemes; pet. more erect than spreading; sep. oblong, erect, about $\frac{1}{8}$ in. long; styles 3. August. Mediterranean region; not Egypt. (B.M. 6481.)

**H. anagallidioi'des.** A synonym of *H. tetrapterum.*

**H. anagalloi'des.** Creeping, prostrate or procumbent annual or perennial herb. *l.* elliptic to broadly oval, obtuse, $\frac{3}{16}$ to $\frac{9}{16}$ in. long. *fl.* in few-fld. terminal cymes; cor. uniform pinkish or orange, $\frac{3}{8}$ in. across; pet. narrow, about $\frac{3}{16}$ in. long; sep. unequal, elliptic, shorter than pet. Summer. *Capsule* ovate, 1-celled. Western N. America. (F.B., W.W.F., 293.) SYN. *H. tapetoides.*

**H. Androsae'mum.** Tutsan. Sub-shrub, up to 3 ft. with angled or slightly winged shoots. *l.* up to 4 in. long and $2\frac{1}{2}$ in. wide, ovate or oval-lanceolate, cordate, blunt, pale beneath, obscurely punctate-pellucid. *fl.* about $\frac{3}{4}$ in. across, in terminal cymes of 3 to 9; styles 3; cal. nearly as wide as cor. June to August or later. *fr.* a black, berry-like capsule. Europe including Britain. (E.B. 264.) SYN. *H. officinale.* Known for centuries as a medicinal plant.

**H. angustifo'lium.** A synonym of *H. linarifolium.*

**H. Ascy'ron.** Herbaceous perennial, from 2 to 6 ft. h. with 4-angled stems. *l.* stem-clasping, ovate-oblong or ovate-lanceolate, sub-acute, 2 to 5 in. long. *fl.* 1 to $2\frac{1}{2}$ in. across, in 3- to 12-fld. cymes; sep. unequal, ovate to ovate-oblong; stamens in 5 bundles. July. *Capsules* ovoid. North-eastern N. America, Cent. and E. Asia. (B.B. ii. 2, 529.) SYN. *H. pyramidatum.* var. **Vilmorin'ii,** *fl.* up to 4 in. across. Korea. (B.M. 8557.)

**H. au'reum.** A synonym of *H. frondosum.*

**H. axilla're.** A synonym of *H. galioides.*

**H. balear'icum.** Compact evergreen shrub, not more than 2 ft. h. with slightly winged, warted stems. *l.* oblong to obovate, rounded at apex, tapered to base, warty beneath, margin wavy, up to 1 in. long. *fl.* terminal, solitary, 1 to $1\frac{1}{2}$ in. across, fragrant. June to September. Attractive but only reliably hardy in milder districts. Balearic Is. 1714. (B.M. 137.)

**H. Buck'leyi.** Smooth sub-shrub, erect or ascending, up to about 1 ft. h. with obscurely 4-angled shoots. *l.* obovate or elliptic, rounded at apex, $\frac{1}{4}$ to $\frac{3}{4}$ in. long, becoming a pretty red in autumn. *fl.* 1 to 3 terminal; cor. $\frac{3}{4}$ to 1 in. across, pet. narrowly obovate; sep. half length of pet.; styles 3, connate. June, July. *Capsule* conic, nearly $\frac{1}{2}$ in. long. Cent. United States. 1889. Rare in nature and, though apparently quite hardy, uncommon in gardens.

**H. calyca'tum.** A synonym of *H. japonicum.*

**H. calyci'num.*** Rose of Sharon, Aaron's Beard. More or less evergreen, very vigorous, stoloniferous sub-shrub about 1 ft. h., procumbent or ascending, with obscurely 4-angled shoots. *l.* ovate-oblong, almost leathery, glaucous beneath, 2 to 4 in. long. *fl.* terminal, solitary or, rarely, in pairs or threes; cor. up to $3\frac{1}{4}$ in. across, pet. obovate; sep. roundish and about $\frac{3}{4}$ in. long; stamens in 5 bundles; styles 5. June to September. SE. Europe, W. Asia Minor. 1676. (B.M. 146.) One of the most beautiful and hardiest species which will grow almost anywhere, even under large trees.

**H. chinen'se.** Evergreen or half-evergreen shrub about 2 ft. h. with round stems. *l.* sessile, oblong, 1 to 3 in. long. *fl.* terminal, solitary or in cymes of 3 to 7; cor. bright yellow, $1\frac{1}{2}$ to 2 in. across; sep. oblong, blunt, black-spotted; stamens in 5 bundles; styles connate, 5-branched, at apex. August, September. China, Japan. 1753. (B.M. 334.) SYN. *H. monogynum, H. sinense.* Not reliably hardy.

**H. confer'tum.** Sub-shrub, almost herbaceous, papillose-puberulent, up to 1 ft. h., ascending then procumbent. *l.* of stems up to $\frac{3}{8}$ in. long, lanceolate or ovate-lanceolate, acute or blunt, truncate at base; of axillary twigs half as long, revolute. *fl.* in terminal, almost sessile cymes. Fls. $\frac{3}{4}$ in. across, pet. spreading, meeting at their bases, oblong or oval, blunt or rounded at apex; cal. fringed with stalked glands. June, July. Syria, Cyprus. Too tender for outdoor cultivation except in the mildest districts.

**H. coria'ceum.** A synonym of *H. Leschenaultii* and *H. lysimachioides.*

**H. Cor'is.*** Evergreen, smooth, nearly upright sub-shrub, 1 ft. or more h. with round shoots. *l.* in whorls of 3 to 5, linear, obtuse, often mucronulate, recurved, about 1 in. long. *fl.* in cymes forming a loose terminal panicle; cor. golden-yellow finely streaked red, about $\frac{3}{4}$ in. across; sep. linear-oblong, about $\frac{1}{4}$ in. long, erect in fruit. July, August. S. Europe, Spain to Corsica and Italy. (B.M. 6563.) 1640. SYN. *H. verticillatum.* A pretty little plant but will not withstand severe frost.

**H. cunea'tum.** Diffuse sub-shrub herbaceous rather than the shrubby, 8 to 16 in. h. with red stems. *l.* cuneate, slightly wavy at margin, darker above than beneath, sparsely dotted with black. *fl.* in short, leafy racemes; cor. $\frac{3}{4}$ in. across; sep. linear-lanceolate. April to July. W. Asia Minor, Syria. var. **frag'ile** has dense racemes, minute but otherwise similar l., brittle stems about 4 in. h. Not to be confused with *H. fragile.* Only half-hardy. Very rare in cultivation.

**H. delphinen'se.** A synonym of *H. quadrangulum.*

**H. densiflo'rum.** Evergreen, upright shrub up to 4 ft. h. in Britain, 6 ft. in nature. Shoots 2-angled. *l.* linear to linear-oblong, acute, recurved, $\frac{1}{2}$ to 2 in. long. *fl.* very numerous in dense cymose panicles; cor. $\frac{3}{8}$ to $\frac{5}{8}$ in. across; sep. unequal oblong, to elliptic-oblong. July to September. *Capsule* ovoid, up to $\frac{1}{4}$ in. long. SE. United States, Texas. 1889. (G. and F. 3, 527.) SYN. *H. prolificum densiflorum.* Not very attractive.

**H. diversifo'lium.** A synonym of *H. hyssopifolium.*

**H. ela'tum.** Half-evergreen shrub up to 5 ft. h. with reddish, rounded, horizontally spreading or declining branches and 2-winged stems. *l.* ovate, occasionally notched, stem-clasping, sub-petiolate or sessile, slightly glaucous beneath, aromatic when bruised, 1 to 3 in. long, $\frac{1}{2}$ to 2 in. wide. *Cymes* few-fld., terminal or axillary near ends of shoots; cor. 1 in. across; sep. very unequal, ovate, slightly punctate, reflexed in fr.; 3, sometimes 4 long styles. July to October. Madeira and Canary Is. 1762. SYN. *H. grandifolium, H. erectum, H. multiflorum* (of gardens), *Androsaemum Webbianum.* Vigorous but not quite hardy. (B.M. n.s. 376.)

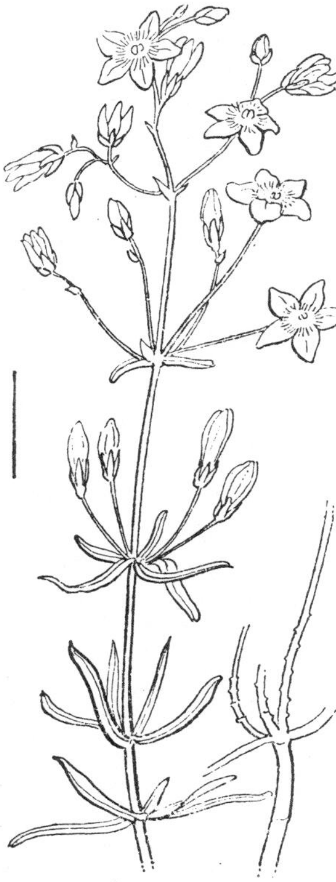

*Hypericum Coris* (p. 1034)

**H. el'egans.** Upright perennial herb, 6 to 12 in. h. with dark-spotted and slightly 2-winged stems. *l.* ovate-lanceolate, cordate, somewhat stem-clasping, $\frac{3}{4}$ to 1 in. long. *fl.* in terminal cymose panicles; cor. up to 1 in. across; sep. ovate-lanceolate, acute, punctate-pellucid, glandular-ciliate; anthers black-spotted. June, July. Cent. Europe, W. Siberia. SYN. *H. Kohlianum.*

**H. Elo'des.** Marsh St. John's Wort. Herbaceous perennial with creeping, rooting stems and ascending branches from 4 to 12 in. h. for boggy ground. *l.* rounded or oval, half stem-clasping, villose, revolute, $\frac{1}{3}$ to $\frac{3}{4}$ in. long. *fl.* in cymes forming a loose terminal cluster; cor. pale yellow, about $\frac{1}{3}$ in. across; sep. oval, sharp-pointed, glandular-ciliate, one-third length of pet.; stamens in 3 bundles. June to August. Europe, Britain, Portugal to Switzerland, and Italy. (E.B. 276 as *H. Helodes.*) SYN. *Helodes palustris.*

**H. elonga'tum.** A synonym of *H. hyssopifolium elongatum.*

**H. empetrifo'lium.** Evergreen, beautiful shrub with slightly angled stems sometimes erect and 12 to 15 in. h., often prostrate. *l.* nearly always in whorls of 3, linear, $\frac{1}{4}$ to $\frac{1}{2}$ in. long. *fl.* in terminal, few-fld. cymes forming loose panicles; cor. bright golden-yellow, $\frac{1}{2}$ to $\frac{3}{4}$ in. across; sep. short, oblong, obtuse, edged with black glands. July to September. SE. Europe, Asia Minor. 1788. (B.M. 6764 (erect form), S.B.F.G. 774 (prostrate form).) Half-hardy in most localities.

**H. erect'um.** A synonym of *H. elatum.*

**H. ericoi'des.** Evergreen sub-shrub, 3 to 6 in. h., much resembling a low Heath. *l.* whorled, imbricate, much recurved, linear-oval, mucronate, grey-powdered, about $\frac{1}{8}$ in. long. *fl.* in terminal, few-fld. cymes; cor. $\frac{1}{2}$ in. across; pet. obtuse or truncate, nearly twice as long as cal., apices dotted with black; sep. oval-lanceolate, acute, sparsely fringed and bearing stalked glands; styles 3, divergent. June to August. *Capsule* ovate, 3-angled. Spain, possibly Portugal. Not quite hardy. (B.M. n.s. 36.)

**H. fimbria'tum.** A synonym of *H. Richeri.*

**H. floribun'dum.** Bushy shrub, up to 3 ft. h., with round, smooth, erect branches. *l.* crowded, elliptic-lanceolate or pointed at both ends, 1 to 2 in. long. *fl.* in many-fld. cymes; cor. $1\frac{1}{2}$ to 2 in. across; pet. concave or hooded; sep. unequal, ovate-lanceolate, much shorter than pet.; stamens in 3 bundles; styles 3. July to October. Madeira, Canary Is. SYN. *Webbia floribunda. H. floribundum* of gardens is *H. Hookerianum Rogersii.*

**H. folio'sum.** A synonym of *H. prolificum.*

**H. frag'ile.** Pretty, very floriferous sub-shrub with round stems from 6 to 9 in. long. *l.* ovate or oval, smooth, glaucescent, $\frac{1}{8}$ to $\frac{1}{4}$ in. long. *fl.* in 3- to many-fld. terminal cymes; cor. about 1 in. across; sep. linear-lanceolate, ciliate. July, August. SE. Europe. Rare in gardens.

**H. frondo'sum.** Beautiful, dense, deciduous, branching shrub with 2-winged stems, 3 to 4 ft. h. *l.* oblong to ovate-oblong, mucronate, more or less glaucous, 1 to 3 in. long. *fl.* sessile in many-fld. cymes, orange-yellow, 1 to 2 in. across; sep. leaf-like, unequal, shorter than pet.; styles 3, connate. July, August. *Capsule* ovate, pointed, red, about $\frac{1}{2}$ in. long. SE. and S. United States. (B.M. 8498 as *H. aureum.*) SYN. *H. prolificum aureum. H. prolificum* has pedicellate fl.

**H. galioi'des.** Evergreen, rounded, bushy sub-shrub from 2 to 3 ft. h. with round stems. *l.* crowded, linear, acute, recurved, $\frac{3}{4}$ to 2 in. long, $\frac{1}{8}$ to $\frac{1}{6}$ in. wide. *fl.* solitary, or usually in terminal and axillary cymes forming a leafy panicle on each branch; cor. $\frac{1}{4}$ to $\frac{3}{4}$ in. across; pet. narrow, cuneate at base; sep. linear or linear-spatulate; styles 3. July to October. *Capsule* conic, ridged. SE. United States. 1790. SYN. *H. axillare.* (G.C. 24 (1898) 301.)

**H. glandulo'sum.** Upright shrub, 3 to 4 ft. h., smooth except for the downy young shoots. *l.* crowded towards upper part of stems, mostly sessile, elliptic-lanceolate, pointed at both ends, serrulate with black glands, shining, up to $1\frac{1}{2}$ in. long and $\frac{1}{2}$ in. wide. *fl.* crowded in short, compact, terminal cymes; cor. $\frac{3}{8}$ to $\frac{3}{4}$ in. across, dull, pale yellow within, reddish and shining without, flat, sprinkled with black glands especially at edges; sep. unequal, lanceolate, acute, serrulate with large, black glands; styles 3. April to July. Madeira and neighbouring islands.

**H. glomera'tum.** Shrub with 4-angled stems up to 3 ft. h. *l.* sessile, linear to narrow-oblong, sharp-pointed, pale beneath, $\frac{3}{4}$ to $1\frac{1}{2}$ in. long. *fl.* in compact, terminal cymes; cor. up to 1 in. across; pet. spatulate; sep. leafy, narrow-oblong, acute. August. E. United States: N. Carolina. Before 1905.

**H. grac'ile** (of Boissier). A variety of *H. lanuginosum.*

**H. grandifo'lium.** A synonym of *H. elatum.*

**H. Helo'des.** A synonym of *H. Elodes.*

**H. Hen'ryi.** A variety of *H. patulum.*

**H. hirci'num.** Stinking St. John's Wort. Half-evergreen, bushy and rounded sub-shrub from 2 to 4 ft. h. with erect, 2-angled stems. Whole plant, particularly the foliage, when bruised, redolent of goats. *l.* sessile, ovate to ovate-lanceolate, acute or obtuse, 1 to $2\frac{1}{2}$ in. long. *fl.* solitary or in threes, terminal and axillary; cor. 1 to $1\frac{1}{2}$ in. across; pet. 3 times as long as sep.; sep. lanceolate, falling before fruit is ripe; stamens in 5 bundles, longer than pet. May to July. *Capsule* ovoid, pointed. Cent. Europe, Mediterranean region. 1640. (E.B. 266.) SYN. *Androsaemum hircinum.* var. **pu'milum** about 1 ft. h., l. smaller, habit compact. SYN. *H. hircinum minor.*

**H. hirsu'tum.** Hairy St. John's Wort. Erect sub-shrub, $1\frac{1}{4}$ to $3\frac{1}{2}$ ft. h., with rounded stems, short branches, covered with short, yellowish hairs. *l.* oval-oblong, with pellucid dots, hairy; stalk short. *fl.* in terminal cymes forming a pyramidal panicle; cor. pale yellow, $\frac{1}{2}$ to $\frac{3}{4}$ in. across; pet. about 3 times as long as cal., slightly longer than stamens; sep. lanceolate, ciliolate-glandular. Europe (including Britain), Caucasus, Armenia, Siberia. (E.B. 274.) SYN. *H. villosum.*

**H. Hookeria'num.** More or less evergreen shrub of about 6 ft. h. in cultivation, more in nature. Handsome when well grown. *l.* sessile, ovate, oblong or rounded, blunt or pointed, dark and glaucescent above, paler beneath, 1 to 4 in. long, $\frac{1}{2}$ to 2 in. wide. *fl.* in terminal cymose clusters of 6 or more; cor. brilliant yellow, saucer-shaped, up to $2\frac{1}{2}$ in. across; pet. firm, broadly obovate; sep. obovate, obtuse; stamens in 5 bundles. August to October. *Capsule* broadly ovate, ridged longitudinally. S. India, Sikkim Himalaya, Assam. Before 1853. (B.M. 4949 as *H. oblongifolium.*) Hardy, but appreciates shelter. var. **Leschenaul'tii,** a synonym of *H. Leschenaultii*; **Rogers'ii,*** *fl.* 2 to 3 in. across, of good substance, cup-shaped. A handsome plant reaching 10 ft. h. in favoured localities. Victoria Mts., Burma. SYN. *H. floribundum, H. Rogersii,* of gardens; **Rowallane Hybrid** (*H. Hookerianum Rogersii* × *H. Leschenaultii*), 5 to 6 ft. h., *l.* ovate-lanceolate, dark-green, $2\frac{1}{2}$ in. long, glaucous beneath, *fl.* in threes at ends of branches, buttercup-yellow, 3 in. across, bowl-shaped. Of garden origin. 1940.

**H. humifu'sum.** Trailing St. John's Wort. Smooth perennial herb, usually prostrate and sometimes ascending or erect up to 8 in. h. *l.* sessile, oval-oblong or elliptic-lanceolate, blunt, often slightly mucronate, pale below, edged with black dots, only upper ones pellucid-punctate, $\frac{1}{8}$ to $\frac{1}{4}$ in. long. *fl.* solitary or in few-fld., loose, terminal cymes; cor. tinted red, about $\frac{1}{4}$ in. across, pet. a little longer than cal., slightly black-dotted; sep. unequal, more or less black-dotted often glandular-dentate. June to September. W. and Cent. Europe, S. India, S. Africa. (E.B. 271; B.M. 8773 as *H. laeve* forma *rubra.*) SYN. *H. rubrum* Common, but attractive, garden weed in Britain.

**H. hyssopifo'lium.** Smooth sub-shrub 1 to 2 ft. h. with rounded, reddish, erect or ascending stems and short branches. *Lower l.* linear-oblong, narrowing to base; *upper* clustered, linear, obtuse, recurved; all leathery, pale green above, glaucous beneath, up to $\frac{3}{4}$ in. long, $\frac{1}{4}$ in. wide. *fl.* in terminal cymes forming elongated pannicles; cor. 1 in. across; pet. glandular-ciliate at apex, 3 or 4 times as long as sep.; sep. elliptic-lanceolate, obtuse or subacute, thickly glandular-ciliate; styles 3. June to August. *Capsule* elliptical, sharp-pointed, $\frac{1}{8}$ to $\frac{1}{4}$ in. long. S. Europe, Caucasus, Armenia, Asia Minor, Syria, Siberia. (B.M. 3277.) Syn. *H. diversifolium.* var. **elonga'tum** has a sub-corymbose infl. and narrower l.

**H. inodo'rum.** Leafy evergreen shrub, 3 to $4\frac{1}{2}$ ft. h., with arching unbranched stems which are rather flattened or slightly 2-winged towards apex. *l.* ovate to ovate-oblong, rounded at apex, 1 to 2 in. long. *fl.* solitary or in small terminal cymes; cor. about 1 in. across; pet. narrow, thin; sep. linear; stamens longer than pet.; styles 3. July to September. E. Europe, Caucasus. 1870. Syn. *H. ramosissimum.* Allied to *H. hircinum* but without its unpleasant smell.

**H. japon'icum.** Smooth, tufted or prostrate perennial herb with 4-angled stems up to 15 in. long. *l.* stem-clasping, oval or ovate. *fl.* in terminal cymes; cor. $\frac{1}{2}$ in. across; pet. equal to cal.; sep. linear-lanceolate, acute, glandular and pellucid-punctate at apex. Summer. S. and E. Asia, Australia, New Zealand. Syn. *H. pusillum, H. calycatum.*

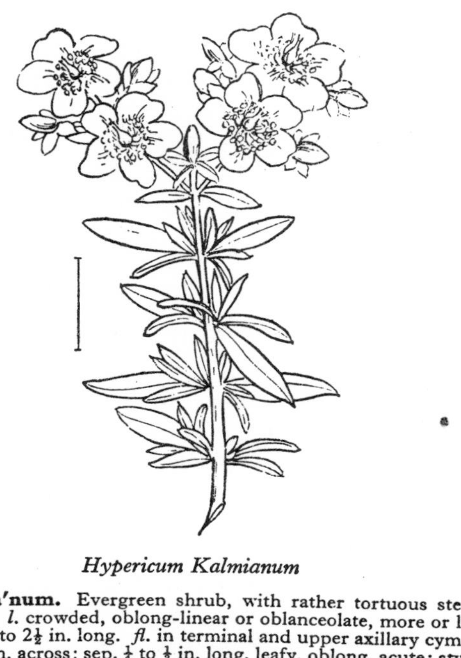

*Hypericum Kalmianum*

**H. Kalmia'num.** Evergreen shrub, with rather tortuous stems 2 to 3 ft. h. *l.* crowded, oblong-linear or oblanceolate, more or less glaucous, 1 to $2\frac{1}{2}$ in. long. *fl.* in terminal and upper axillary cymes; cor. $\frac{1}{2}$ to 1 in. across; sep. $\frac{1}{4}$ to $\frac{1}{3}$ in. long, leafy, oblong, acute; styles 3, connate below. August. *Capsule* ovoid, furrowed lengthwise. E. United States, Canada. 1759. (B.M. 8491.)

**H. Kohlia'num.** A synonym of *H. elegans.*

**H. Kotschya'num.** Grey, velvety-downy, round-stemmed, perennial herb from 6 to 12 in. h. *l.* of stem $\frac{1}{2}$ to 1 in. long, oblong, obtuse, with several nerves; of axillary shoots crowded, linear, recurved. *fl.* in few-fld. cymes which form a rather loose, short panicle; cor. about 1 in. across; sep. obtuse, papillose beneath. June. Asia Minor, Syria.

**H. kouytchen'se.** Much-branched, more or less prostrate, glabrous shrub about 2 ft. h. Shoots tinged red or brown, terete or only slightly compressed. *l.* elliptic, ovate, 1 to 3 in. long, acute, glaucous beneath, with scattered translucent dots. *fl.* yellow, up to $2\frac{1}{4}$ in. across; sep. ovate-lanceolate, acute; pet. obovate-oblong, not overlapping, slightly toothed on one side near apex. Autumn. W. China. 1907. (B.M. 9345.) Less hardy than *H. patulum.*

**H. lanugino'sum.** Downy St. John's Wort. Round-stemmed sub-shrub $1\frac{1}{2}$ to 3 ft. h. and covered, except for the smooth infl., with fine grey tomentum. *l.* stem-clasping, subcordate, oblong or oblong-lanceolate, only sparsely pellucid-punctate, black-dotted marginally, $\frac{3}{4}$ to 2 in. long. *fl.* in cymes forming a broad, fairly compact, terminal panicle; cor. $\frac{1}{2}$ to $\frac{3}{4}$ in. across; pet. $\frac{5}{16}$ in. long, 3 times as long as sep.; sep. obtuse. glandular-denticulate. May to July. Greece, Asia Minor, Syria. var. **grac'ile,** panicle looser, sep. somewhat acute.

**H. Leschenault'ii.*** Evergreen in nature but in colder climates a half-evergreen or deciduous shrub. *l.* sessile, firm, rounded-obovate, rather obtuse, smooth, glaucous, punctate beneath, $1\frac{1}{2}$ to $2\frac{1}{2}$ in. long and about half as wide. *fl.* terminal, solitary or, more usually, in cymes of 3 or more; cor. very rich yellow, up to 3 in. across; pet. concave, rounded-obovate, slightly overlapping, 1 in. or so wide; sep. spreading, ovate-lanceolate or oblanceolate, acute or acuminate, about $\frac{1}{2}$ in. long; stamens numerous, in 5 bundles; styles 5, divergent. July to September or later. *Capsule* almost 1 in. long. Malay Archipelago; in cultivation 1882. (B.M. 9160.) Syn. *H. Hookerianum Leschenaultii, H. triflorum.* One of the finest species which, under cultivation in the open, rarely reaches more than 6 ft. and seldom as much. Hardier than its reputation allows but should be sheltered by the company of other shrubs. *See* **H. Hookerianum.**

**H. linarifo'lium.** Flax-leaved St. John's Wort. Perennial herb with erect or ascending stems from 4 to 18 in. long, often reddish, 2-angled at first. *l.* sessile or nearly so, semi-stem-clasping, oblong or linear, obtuse, glaucous beneath, usually thick, often recurved, edged with black dots, not pellucid-punctate, $\frac{1}{2}$ to 1 in. long, $\frac{1}{12}$ to $\frac{1}{8}$ in. wide. *fl.* in cymes forming a loose (usually) terminal cluster; cor. tinted with red, $\frac{1}{2}$ to $\frac{3}{4}$ in. across; pet. 3 times longer than sep.; sep. lanceolate and sharp-pointed or elliptical and blunt, nearly equal, glandular-ciliate and black-dotted; styles 3, divergent. June, July. Madeira and Canary Is., SW. Europe including SW. England. (E.B. 272.) Syn. *H. nubigenum, H. angustifolium.*

**H. lobocarp'um.** Erect shrub up to 6 ft. with angled shoots. *l.* sessile or nearly so, narrow-oblong or oblanceolate, obtuse or mucronulate, recurved, 1 to $2\frac{3}{4}$ in. long. *fl.* in many-fld. cymes forming a terminal elongated panicle or flattish cluster; cor. about $\frac{1}{3}$ in. across; pet. wedge-shaped; sep. oblong, more or less obtuse; styles 5, convergent. August, September. *Capsule* oblong, 5-angled, $\frac{1}{4}$ in. long. E. United States. 1898. (G. and F. 10, 453.)

**H. lysimachioi'des.** Smooth evergreen or sub-evergreen shrub 3 ft. or more h. with spreading branches and angled shoots. Apt to be cut to the ground in hard winters. *l.* subsessile, ovate to ovate-oblong, acute or subacute, glaucous beneath, $\frac{3}{4}$ to $1\frac{1}{2}$ in. long. *fl.* in loose, terminal, leafy cymes; cor. about $1\frac{1}{4}$ in. across; pet. lanceolate; sep. linear-lanceolate, about $\frac{1}{3}$ in. long; stamens in 5 bundles. August, September. West temperate Himalaya. 1904.

**H. macula'tum.** A synonym of *H. quadrangulum.*

**H. monogyn'um.** A synonym of *H. chinense.*

**H. monta'num.** Erect perennial herb from $1\frac{1}{4}$ to $3\frac{1}{4}$ ft. h. *l.* oval or oblong, blunt or acute, pale (but not glaucous) beneath, semi-stem-clasping, edges black-dotted, only upper pellucid-punctate, 1 to $1\frac{3}{4}$ in. long. *fl.* in cymes forming a dense terminal cluster; cor. pale, $\frac{5}{8}$ to $\frac{7}{8}$ in. across; pet. about twice as long as cal.; sep. lanceolate, pointed, shortly dentate-glandular. June to August. Europe (including Britain), Caucasus, Armenia, China. Algeria. (E.B. 275.) Syn. *H. glandulosum.*

**H.×Moseria'num** (*H. calycinum×H. patulum*). *l.* ovate, obtuse, mucronulate, glaucous beneath, about 2 in. long. *fl.* in terminal clusters; cor. rich golden-yellow, up to $2\frac{1}{2}$ in. across; pet. broad and overlapping; sep. unequal, leafy, oval to oblong; stamens in 5 bundles, anthers reddish. July to October. *Capsule* obconic. Raised by Moser about 1887. (Gn. 54 (1898), 490.) Desirable shrub, liable to be badly cut in winter. var. **tric'olor,** *fl.* smaller, *l.* edged red, variegated white.

**H. multiflo'rum.** A synonym of *H. elatum.*

**H. napaulen'se.** Prostrate diffuse perennial herb with slender, rounded stems from 1 to 2 ft. long and obscurely 2-edged shoots. *l.* sessile or sub-petiolate, stem-clasping, oval or ovate, obtuse, thin, glaucous beneath, $\frac{1}{2}$ to $\frac{3}{4}$ in. long. *fl.* in loose, few-fld. cymes; cor. $\frac{1}{3}$ in. across; pet. without glands or almost so; sep. lanceolate, shortly dentate; sep. 5, connate at base; stamens in 3 bundles. Summer. India, Burma. Syn. *H. pallens, H. setosum, H. nepalense.*

**H. nepalen'se.** A garden synonym for *H. napaulense* and *H. uralum.*

**H. nubige'num.** A synonym of *H. linarifolium.*

**H. nudiflo'rum.** Erect shrub of 1 to 3 ft. with 4-angled shoots. *l.* elliptic-oblong to oblong-lanceolate, obtuse, thin, $\frac{3}{4}$ to $2\frac{1}{2}$ in. long. *fl.* in loose, naked, terminal, cymose clusters; cor. $\frac{1}{2}$ to $\frac{3}{4}$ in. across; sep. elliptic-oblong or elliptic-lanceolate; styles 3, connate. July, August. *Capsule* conic-ovate, $\frac{1}{4}$ in. long. SE. United States. 1897.

**H. nummular'ium.** Smooth, rampant sub-shrub with numerous slender stems from 4 to 12 in. long. *l.* rounded or sometimes broadly oval, shortly petiolate, glaucous beneath, rarely pellucid-punctate, $\frac{1}{3}$ to $\frac{1}{2}$ in. long. *fl.* rarely solitary, usually in few-fld. terminal cymes; cor. $\frac{3}{4}$ in. across; pet. 3 or 4 times as long as cal.; sep. elliptic, somewhat obtuse, glandular-ciliate. July to September. E. France, Italy, Pyrenees, N. Spain. (W.A.P. 4.)

**H. oblongifo'lium.** A synonym of *H. Hookerianum* and of *H. patulum oblongifolium.*

**H. officina'le.** A synonym of *H. Androsaemum.*

**H. olym'picum.** Upright, ascending or sometimes decumbent, glaucous sub-shrub up to $1\frac{1}{2}$ ft. *l.* sessile, oblong-lanceolate, glaucous, markedly pellucid-punctate, $\frac{3}{8}$ to 1 in. or more long. *fl.* in 1- to 5-fld. terminal cymes; cor. $1\frac{1}{2}$ to 2 in. across; pet. oblong-obovate, more than twice as long as cal. outer sep. ovate, rigidly pointed, inner ovate and acute; stamens in 3 bundles. July, August. SE. Europe, Syria, Asia Minor. (B.M. 1867.) Syn. *H. adenophyllum.* var. **citri'num,** *fl.* extremely pale yellow; even more beautiful than type. Very attractive.

**H. orienta'le.** Erect sub-shrub, 6 to 12 in. h., with slender, straight or more or less crooked stems. *l.* stem-clasping, linear- or obovate-oblong, obtuse, ciliate-glandular, $\frac{1}{2}$ to 1 in. long. *fl.* in small terminal cymes; cor. 1 in. across; sep. ovate-oblong, dentate. Summer. Asia Minor.

**H. origanifo'lium.** A synonym of *H. rhodopeum.*

**H. pal'lens.** A synonym of *H. napaulense.*

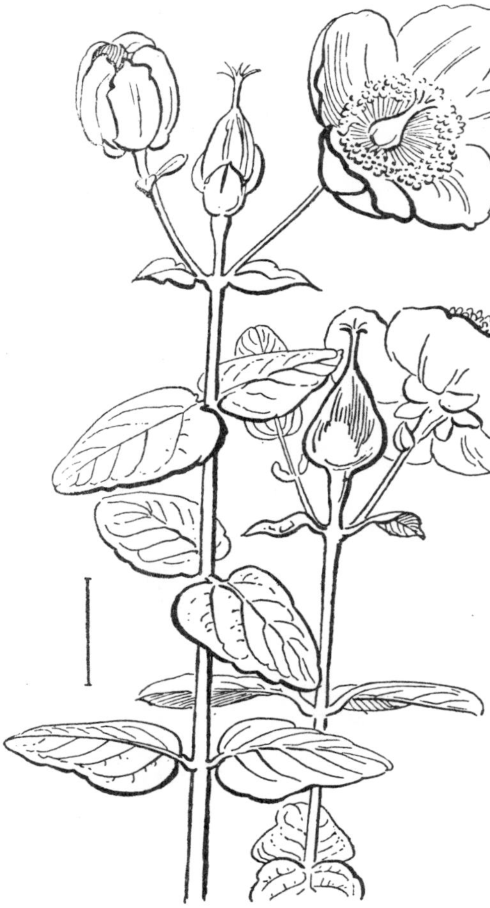

*Hypericum patulum Forrestii*

**H. pat'ulum.** Evergreen, spreading shrub, from $1\frac{1}{2}$ to 3 ft. h. in Britain, up to 6 ft. in nature; shoots smooth, purplish, spreading or somewhat drooping, 2-edged. *l.* ovate, ovate-lanceolate or ovate-oblong, sub-acute, glaucous beneath, $1\frac{1}{2}$ to $2\frac{1}{2}$ in. long. *fl.* rarely solitary, usually in terminal cymes; cor. bright golden-yellow, $1\frac{1}{2}$ to 2 in. across; pet. roundish, overlapping, of good substance; sep. sub-orbicular, about $\frac{1}{3}$ in. long; stamens in 5 bundles, shorter than the upright styles. July to October. *Capsule* ovate, more or less longitudinally grooved about $\frac{1}{2}$ in. long. Himalaya, China, Japan. 1862. (B.M. 5693.) var. **Forrest'ii,*** closely resembles var. *Henryi* but has somewhat larger, more substantial fl. of somewhat better form. China; **Hen'ryi,*** *fl.* up to $2\frac{1}{2}$ in. across. *l.* ovate or ovate-oblong, obtuse, 2 to 3 in. long, hardy and vigorous. China. 1898; **oblongifo'lium,** *fl.* $1\frac{3}{4}$ in. across, pet. a little more than twice length of sep., *l.* up to 4 in. long. SYN. *H. oblongifolium*; **ura'lum,** a synonym of *H. uralum.*

**H. perfora'tum.** Upright perennial herb, 1 to 2 ft. h. with 2-edged stems. *l.* sessile, elliptic, oblong or linear, recurved, very punctate-pellucid, pale beneath, black-dotted, $\frac{1}{2}$ to 1 in. long. *fl.* in cymes forming a loose, many-fld., terminal cluster; cor. $\frac{1}{2}$ to 1 in. across; petals black-dotted, twice as long as sep.; sep. lanceolate, pointed, more or less dotted black. May to August. *Capsule* oval, as long as pet. Europe, N. Africa, W. Asia, Himalaya, Siberia. (E.B. 268.) SYN. *H. vulgare.* Garden weed in Britain, though quite a pretty one.

**H. polyphyl'lum.** Beautiful, low, perennial herb with almost prostrate, procumbent or ascending stems from 6 to 12 in. long. *l.* narrowly ovate or elliptic, pointed or sub-acute, smooth, glaucous, $\frac{1}{8}$ to $\frac{1}{3}$ in. long. *fl.* in dense terminal cymes; cor. $1\frac{1}{2}$ to 2 in. across, golden-yellow often marked scarlet; pet. oval, obovate or oblong, obtuse or truncate; sep. much shorter than pet., ovate or lanceolate. July to September. SW. Asia Minor. (N.F.S. 8, 276.)

**H. prolif'icum.** Hardy, floriferous, compact shrub, up to 5 ft. h., with 2-angled twigs. *l.* narrow-oblong or oblanceolate, acute, glossy, 1 to 3 in. long. *fl.* in many-fld. cymes from terminal axils; cor. up to 1 in. across; sep. obovate; stamens separate; styles 3, connate at base. July to September. *Capsule* 3-celled, oblong, $\frac{1}{2}$ in. long. SE. and E. Cent. United States. About 1850. (G. and F. 3, 526.) SYN. *H. foliosum.* Closely allied to *H. densiflorum*, distinct by having broader l. and larger fl.

**H. pusil'lum.** A synonym of *H. japonicum.*

**H. pyramida'tum.** A synonym of *H. Ascyron.*

**H. quadran'gulum.** Stoloniferous perennial herb, 8 to 16 in. h., with 4-angled stems. *l.* sessile, lower oval or oval-oblong, obtuse or subacute, pale beneath, bordered with black dots, upper semi-stem-clasping, not punctate-pellucid, $\frac{3}{4}$ to 1 in. long. *fl.* in cymes forming dense terminal clusters; cor. $\frac{3}{4}$ to 1 in. across, black-dotted, 3 or 4 times as long as sep.; sep. oval-elliptic, obtuse, with some black dots. June to September. *Capsule* oval. Europe, Britain, W. Siberia. (E.B. 370.) SYN. *H. quadrangulare, H. maculatum, H. delphinense, H. tetragonum,* &c.

**H. re'pens.** Closely tufted herbaceous perennial, 6 to 8 in. h., densely leafy. *l.* narrow. *fl.* yellow, in long racemes. Asia Minor.

**H. rep'tans.*** Mat-forming, vigorous, shrubby. *l.* oval, thin, smooth, light green, yellow or red in late autumn. *fl.* golden yellow, $1\frac{3}{4}$ in. across, tinged crimson without. Autumn. Sikkim. Best planted on a mound so that stems hang down.

**H. rhodo'peum.*** Prostrate sub-shrub with rounded, puberulent, glaucous, ascending or procumbent shoots up to 6 in. long. *l.* sessile ovate or oval, soft, glaucous, puberulent, pale beneath, $\frac{1}{2}$ to $\frac{7}{8}$ in. long, about half as wide. *fl.* in few-fld. cymose clusters; cor. shining yellow, $1\frac{1}{4}$ to $1\frac{3}{4}$ in. across; pet. sparsely black-dotted at margin, oblong, obovate-oblong, subacute, obtuse or truncate; sep. ovate, obtuse, much shorter than pet.; stamens numerous. May, June. SE. Europe, Asia Minor. SYN. *H. origanifolium.* Very floriferous but so vigorous that it needs occasional checking.

**H. Rich'eri.** Smooth sub-shrub from 8 to 18 in. h. with erect or ascending stems slightly winged at upper ends. *l.* oval, oval-lanceolate or ovate, sessile, semi-stem-clasping, edged with black dots, obscurely and irregularly punctate-pellucid, $\frac{3}{4}$ to $1\frac{1}{2}$ in. long. *fl.* in cymes forming a fairly dense, few-fld., terminal cluster; cor. $1\frac{3}{4}$ to $2\frac{1}{4}$ in. across; pet. oval, acute, dotted with black, 3 times as long as sep.; sep. lanceolate, sharply pointed, fringed and dotted black. June to August. *Capsule* broadly oval. Cent., S., and E. Europe. (T.S.A.P. 13.) SYN. *H. fimbriatum, H. transsilvanicum.*

**H. Rogers'ii** of gardens. See *H. Hookerianum Rogersii.*

**H. ru'brum.** A synonym of *H. humifusum.*

**H. rumel'icum.** Smooth, glaucous sub-shrub with rigid, sparingly black-dotted and 2-angled stems from 4 to 18 in. h. *l.* sessile, linear-oblong or oblong-lanceolate, obtuse, firm, often recurved, sparsely dotted with black, not punctate-pellucid, $\frac{7}{16}$ to $2\frac{1}{4}$ in. long, and from $\frac{1}{16}$ to $\frac{5}{16}$ in. wide. *fl.* in few-fld. terminal cymes, usually forming elongated panicles; cor. about $1\frac{1}{4}$ in. across; pet. twice as long, dotted with black and black-glandular-denticulate; sep. lanceolate, acuminate, dotted black and fringed with short glandular hairs. June, July. Balkans, Serbia, Macedonia, Thessaly.

**H. seto'sum.** A synonym of *H. napaulense.*

**H. sinen'se.** A synonym of *H. chinense.*

**H. tapetoi'des.** A synonym of *H. anagalloides.*

**H. tetrap'terum.** Stoloniferous perennial herb from 8 to 12 in. h., stems 4-winged, dotted with black. *l.* semi-stem-clasping, elliptic, sometimes rounded, very obtuse, slightly dotted with black at borders, abundantly punctate-pellucid, 1 in. or more long. *fl.* in cymes forming a dense terminal cluster; cor. $\frac{3}{8}$ to $\frac{3}{4}$ in. across; pet. slightly dotted with black at margins, longer than sep.; sep. lanceolate-acuminate, black-dotted. June to August. Europe, Asia Minor, N. Africa. SYN. *H. acutum.* (E.B. 270 as *H. quadrangulum.*) Closely akin to *H. quadrangulum*, distinct by its lanceolate-acuminate sep. and 4-winged stems.

**H. tomento'sum.** More or less white-tomentose sub-shrub with rounded, slender, ascending or decumbent stems from 4 to 12 in. long which branch freely towards apex. *l.* oval, obtuse, undulate, white-tomentose, semi-stem-clasping, $\frac{1}{4}$ to $\frac{1}{3}$ in. long. *fl.* in cymes forming loose terminal clusters; cor. $\frac{1}{2}$ to $\frac{3}{4}$ in. across; pet. up to twice the length of sep.; sep. lanceolate, acuminate, shortly ciliate-glandular. June, July. *Capsule* oval, slightly longer than cal. S. Europe from Spain to Italy, N. Africa from Morocco to Tunisia.

**H. transsilvan'icum.** A synonym of *H. Richeri.*

**H. tric'olor.** A synonym of *H. Leschenaultii.*

**H. triflo'rum.** A synonym of *H. Leschenaultii.*

**H. ura'lum.** Half-evergreen shrub, 2 to 3 ft. h., with slightly winged shoots. *l.* ovate to oval, glaucous beneath, aromatic when bruised, 1 to $1\frac{1}{2}$ in. long. *fl.* in terminal cymes of from 3 to 15 fl.; cor. cup-shaped, golden-yellow, 1 in. or so across; pet. rounded, overlapping; sep. broadly oval, $\frac{3}{16}$ in. long; stamens in 5 bundles; styles 5. August, September. *Capsule* conical, $\frac{1}{2}$ in. long. Nepal, W. China. 1820. (B.M. 2375.) SYN. *H. patulum uralum, H. nepalense* (Hort.). Once considered a variety of *H. patulum.* No hardier than *H. patulum*, fl. smaller, habit arching.

**H. villo'sum.** A synonym of *H. hirsutum*.

**H. vulga're.** A synonym of *H. perforatum*.

F. S.

**HYPERTROPHY.** The condition where a plant organ becomes abnormally enlarged. This often occurs when some part of a plant is invaded by a fungus parasite with the result that the affected tissues are irritated and grow to a great size. Examples are seen in Cabbage, Finger and Toe disease (swollen roots), Witches' brooms on Cherries (swollen branches), Crown Gall in Apples (swollen roots), Pocket Plums (enlarged fruits), Peach-leaf blister (enlarged parts of leaves), and so on.

D. E. G.

**HYPHA** (pl. *Hyphae*). A fungus thread. The vegetative part of many fungi is composed of filaments, threads, or hyphae which are usually much branched and ramify through soil, debris, or as parasites through the cells of other plants in search of food which they absorb directly through their walls. Most of this absorption occurs near the growing tip of the hypha. When a fungus spore germinates it produces a germ tube, which grows and branches, and in time forms the mass of hyphae known as a mycelium. This vegetative growth later becomes aggregated in parts to form fructifications which, despite their complex appearance, are simply masses of inter-woven hyphae. Other hyphae produce spores by simple abstriction from their tips and are then known as conidio-phores. Some fungal hyphae possess no cross-walls (septa), a characteristic used in separating certain groups for classification, e.g. Phycomycetes which have no septa except in the conidiophores (*see* **Fungi**).

D. E. G.

*hyphaema'ticus -a -um,* blood-red.

**HYPHAE'NE** (*hyphaino*, to entwine; in allusion to the fibres of the fruit). Fam. *Palmaceae*. A genus of 9 species of Trop. African palms with fan-shaped leaves and tall or medium stems which are frequently branched, un-armed. Leaves in a terminal crown, orbicular or nearly so, with sword-shaped acute or 2-fid segments. Flowers dioecious, males in twos, females solitary. *H. thebaica* is difficult to grow. It is best in rich sandy loam. It is increased by seed. **A**

**H. crini'ta.** Stem simple 8 to 20 ft. long. *l.* fan-shaped, fibrous between segs. covered at first with white down; margins and upper surface of nerves scabrid; stalks sheathing at base, deeply channelled above. *fr.* obovate, flattish, shortly stalked. Natal. Syn. *H. natalensis, H. Petersiana.* Greenhouse.

**H. theba'ica.** Doum Palm. About 40 ft. h. *l.* large, fan-shaped, in crowns at ends of the branches of the stem. *fr.* orange-yellow. Egypt. 1828. (F.d.S. 2152–3.) The very hard wood is used in making various domestic utensils.

*hypnoi'des,* moss-like.

*hypo-* in compound words, signifying under, as *hypophyllus*, growing under the leaf.

**HYPOCALYM'MA** (*hypo*, under, *kalymma*, a veil; in allusion to the calyx falling off like a veil or cape). Fam. *Myrtaceae*. A genus of about 12 evergreen shrubs. Leaves opposite, entire, or with crisped margins; flowers not, or very shortly, stalked; calyx lobes and petals 5; stamens numerous. Cool greenhouse shrubs requiring conditions and soil the same as for Australian Acacias. *H. robustum* is hardy in Scilly.

**H. angustifo'lium.** Bushy glabrous shrub up to 3 ft., shoots grey, angled, very slender. *l.* ½ to 1¼ in. long, 1/16 in. or less wide narrowly linear. *fl.* stalkless, white or pale pink with a deep pink centre, stalkless, in pairs at one or both l.-axils; pet. about ⅛ in. wide. May. W. Australia. 1840. Syn. *H. suave.*

**H. robus'tum.** Shrub 3 to 4 ft., entirely glabrous. *l.* stalkless, narrowly linear, ½ to 1 in. long, 1/12 to ¼ in. wide, midrib thick and broad above. *fl.* rich pink, ½ in. across, stalkless, axillary, usually in pairs, forming leafy spikes 4 to 10 in. long; pet. roundish-ovate; stamens 30 to 40. May. W. Australia. 1843. (B.M. 8435; B.R. 29, 8.)

**H. sua've.** A synonym of *H. angustifolium*.

W. J. B.

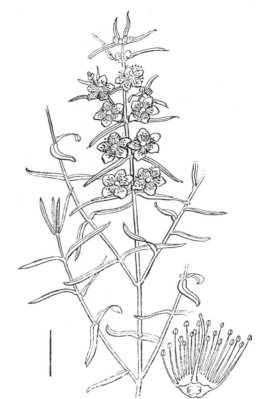

*Hypocalymma robustum*

**HYPOCALYPT'US** (*hypo*, under, *kalypto*, to hide; named from a covering to the unopened flower observable in most of the species so called by Thunberg, but which are now referred to Podalyria). Fam. *Leguminosae*. A genus of 2 species of evergreen shrubs natives of S. Africa. Flowers with a widely bell-shaped calyx with 5 short teeth, hollowed at base; standard roundish, re-flexed, longer than wings and keel; stamens 10, monadel-phous; pod linear, flat, thickened at back; many-seeded. It needs greenhouse treatment and a compost of loam and peat. Cuttings of side shoots taken in April will root in sand under a close frame. The second species, *H. sophoroides*, is a beautiful shrub up to 15 ft., very similar in general appearance to *H. obcordatus*; flowers crimson with a large yellow spot on the standard. It does not appear to be in cultivation.

**H. obcorda'tus.*** Evergreen shrub up to 15 ft., shoots ribbed, very leafy. *l.* 3-foliate; lflets. obovate or obcordate, ¾ to 1½ in. long, ⅜ to 1 in. wide, base cuneate, apex notched and mucronate. *fl.* densely packed in erect, terminal, hairy racemes 2 to 3 in. long; standard ¾ in. wide, crimson, rosy-purple or lilac with a yellow spot at the base; wings obovate; keel nearly hidden, darker. May, June. S. Africa. 1790. (B.M. 3894; and B.M. 1913 and B.R. 128 as *Crotalaria purpurea*.)

W. J. B.

**HYPOCHIL.** The lower part of the divided lip of some Orchids. *See* **epichil, mesochil**.

**HYPOCHOE'RIS** (derivation doubtful). Fam. *Compositae*. A genus of about 50 species of annual or perennial herbs, distributed over temperate regions. Leaves mainly in a basal rosette. Flower-heads yellow, homogamous; peduncles long; florets all ligulate; involucral bracts in many series; receptacle flat. *H. uniflora* is one of the few species worth growing, and that, on the rock-garden.

**H. uniflo'ra.** Perennial. *Rosette l.* oblong-lanceolate, toothed, hairy; *stem-l.* 1 or 2. *fl.-heads* yellow; involucre very hairy; peduncles usually 1-fld., occasionally 2 or 3. *Achenes* beaked. Alps of Europe. (T.A.P.E. 38.)

*hypochondri'acus -a -um,* of melancholy appearance, with sombre-coloured flowers.

*hypochry'sus -a -um,* golden beneath.

**HYPOCOTYLE.** The part of the stem between the cotyledons and the root; it becomes swollen into a storage organ in some plants, e.g. Radish.

**hypocrateriform,** salver-shaped; having a long, slender corolla tube with a flat limb, like the Primrose.

**HYPOCYR'TA** (*hypo*, under, *kyrtos*, curved, gibbous; referring to the swollen lower part of the corolla tube). FAM. *Gesneriaceae.* A genus of about 12 species of often much-branched shrubs, mostly natives of Brazil, with opposite, entire or slightly toothed leaves and flowers with a deeply 5-parted calyx and corolla with a swollen tube. For cultivation of these stove plants *see* **Gesneria.**

**H. glab'ra.** Stem unbranched, erect, fleshy, purple. *l.* elliptic, obtuse, glossy, minutely downy. *fl.* rich scarlet with orange-yellow limb; tube much swollen, axillary. June, July. S. America. 1846. (B.M. 4346.)

**H. pul'chra.** Stem erect, about 5 in. h. *l.* ovate, 4 to 5 in. long, base cordate, dull green clouded with brown and with sunken nerves above, wine-red beneath with prominent veins. *fl.* with cal. scarlet; cor. yellow, much swollen. June. Colombia. 1894. (B.M. 7468.) A beautiful foliage plant.

**H. strigillo'sa.** Stem erect, hairy above, about 2 ft. h. *l.* oblong, slender-pointed, strigillose. *fl.* scarlet and yellow, solitary in l.-axils; cor. much swollen. May. Brazil. (B.M. 4047.)

**HYPODER'RIS** (*hypo*, under, *derris*, skin; from the indusium of the circular sori). FAM. *Polypodiaceae.* A genus of 4 species of fern closely related to Woodsia. Sori sub-globose in lines parallel with the secondary veins; indusium calyciform, margin fimbriate. Easily grown in a warm, moist atmosphere in a compost of 1 part fibrous loam, 2 of peat, and 1 of silver sand. They grow larger in shady places but also thrive in strong light. They need much water at the root from May to October. They are of robust habit.

*Hypoderris Brownii*

**H. Brown'ii.** *Fronds* simple, somewhat heart-shaped, pinnately veined, 10 to 12 in. long. Trinidad. SYN. *Woodsia Brownii.*

**HYPOEST'ES** (*hypo*, under, *estia*, house; the bracts cover the calyx). FAM. *Acanthaceae.* A genus of over 40 species of evergreen shrubs or perennial herbs, natives of S. Africa and the tropics. Leaves entire or toothed. Flower-heads often sessile or shortly stalked. For treatment *see* **Adhatoda.**

**H. arista'ta.** Erect herb, 2 to 3 ft. h. *l.* stalked, ovate, about 3 in. long, acute, entire, downy. *fl.* rose-purple, about 1 in. long; cor. tube slender, downy, with a somewhat bell-shaped throat, lobes short, lateral lobes striped, mid-lobe spotted with purple, lower lobe smaller striped white. February. S. Africa. 1874. (B.M. 6224.) Greenhouse.

**H. involucra'ta.** A synonym of *Peristrophe speciosa.*

**H. sanguinolen'ta.** Herb of 6 to 12 in. Stems downy. *l.* oblong to obovate, obtuse, margin wavy, entire, downy, dark green with fiery-red veins. *fl.* pale purple, with white throat and dark purple markings; cor. resupinate, tube slender, curved. Madagascar. (B.M. 5511.) Warm greenhouse. SYN. *Eranthemum sanguinolentum.* Beautiful foliage plant. It should be frequently propagated by cuttings which root readily, and make good plants in small pots. Should be carefully looked over for scale insects which are very fond of it.

A→

**hypogenous,** growing upon the under-surface of anything.

**hypogynous,** growing from below the ovary, as the petals and stamens of the buttercup. Cf. epigynous, perigynous.

*hypolepido'tus -a -um,* scaly beneath.

**HYPOLE'PIS** (*hypo*, under, *lepis*, a scale; from the position of the sori). FAM. *Polypodiaceae.* A genus of about 50 species of ferns. Sori marginal, small, sub-globose, uniform, distinct, in the sinuses of the frond; indusium membranous, of same shape as sorus, formed out of the reflexed margin of the frond. All the species require stove or greenhouse temperature. They thrive best when associated with stones, over and amongst which their creeping rhizomes run, although they do not cling to the stones. All are easy to grow and when in pots should have rough peat with a good sprinkling of small stones and silver sand for they require an abundant supply of water at the roots all the year round. The drainage must be perfect otherwise the plants suffer rapidly. They should be grown in a fairly shaded place: direct rays of the sun damage the soft, papery fronds. Propagation by spores is easy, as it is also by the division of the rhizomes. *H. repens* produces spores so freely that it may become a troublesome weed in a fernery.

**H. amaurorach'is.** A synonym of *H. punctata.*

**H. anthriscifo'lia.** A synonym of *H. sparsisora.*

**H. dis'tans.*** *sti.* 6 in. h., slender, flexuose. *Fronds* about 1 ft. long, 4 to 5 in. broad, ovate-lanceolate, 2-pinnate; pinnae spreading, at right angles to rachis; pinnules oblong, cut half-way down. *Sori* small, 2 to 4 to a pinnule. New Zealand. 1861. (H.S. 2, 95.) Greenhouse.

**H. Millefo'lium.** *rhiz.* stout, wide-creeping. *sti.* erect, about 6 in. long, pale brown. *Fronds* broadly triangular, 1 ft. or more in length, 4 to 6 in. broad, stalked, slightly hairy below; pinnae stalks slightly winged; ultimate segs. sharply toothed. *Sori* in lower sinuses only. New Zealand. (H.S. 2, 95.) Greenhouse.

**H. puncta'ta.*** *rhiz.* thick, hairy. *sti.* 1 to 1½ ft. long, like rachis, dark purplish. *Fronds* handsome, very hairy, elongate-triangular, 3 ft. long; 2 ft. broad at base; pinnae distinctly stalked, lowest opposite, others alternate; pinnules undulate, notched. *Sori* abundant, conspicuous, solitary in notches of lobes. Australia. Greenhouse. SYN. *H. amaurorachis.*

**H. radia'ta.** A synonym of *Adiantopsis radiata.*

**H. re'pens.** *sti.* 1 to 2 ft. long, strong, erect, more or less prickly. *Fronds* 3 to 4 ft. long, 4-pinnatifid; lower pinnae 1 to 2 ft. long, 6 to 12 in. broad, ovate-acuminate; pinnules lanceolate; segs. cut nearly to rachis. *Sori* 2 to 6 to a seg. Trop. America. 1824. (H.S. 2, 90; L.F. 4, 11.) Stove.

**H. rugulo'sa.** *rhiz.* wide-creeping, firm, villose. *sti.* scattered, 1 to 2 ft. long, firm, erect, polished, viscid. *Fronds* 1 to 4 ft. long, 6 to 2 ft. broad; lower pinnae sometimes 1 to 2 ft. long, deltoid; pinnules close, lanceolate; rachis deep purplish-brown, densely viscid; under side slightly hairy. *Sori* copious, marginal. New Zealand, Australia, &c. SYN. *Polypodium rugulosum, Phegopteris rugulosa.* Greenhouse.

**H. sparsiso'ra.** *rhiz.* stout, wide-creeping. *sti.* strong, erect, straw-colour, 1 to 2 ft. long, rough. *Fronds* thin, 6 to 10 ft. long; lower pinnae 1 ft. or more in length, 4 to 6 in. broad; pinnules spear-shaped, distant; segs. cut to midrib into small, oblong, deeply pinnatifid divisions. *Sori* 2 to 4 together in lower sinuses. Bourbon, Mauritius, &c. (H.S. 2, 95 as *H. anthriscifolia, Microlepia anthriscifolia*; F.S.A. (2) 117.) Greenhouse.

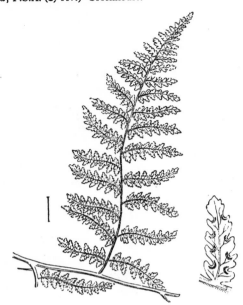

*Hypolepis sparsisora*

**H. tenuifo′lia.** *sti.* 1 ft. long, erect. *Fronds* 4 to 5 ft. long, 4-pinnatifid; lower pinnae ovate-acuminate, 1 to 1½ ft. long, 6 to 9 in. broad; pinnules lanceolate. *Sori* 2 to 6 to an ultimate division. Java to Australia. 1824. (H.S. 2, 89c, 90A.) Stove.

*hypoleu′cus -a -um,* whitish beneath.

**HYPOLYT′RUM** (*hypo*, beneath, *elytron*, sheath; having 2 or 3 small scales included within a larger one). FAM. *Cyperaceae*. A genus of about 40 species widely distributed in the tropics. Leaves flat, rather thin, 3-nerved, gradually narrowed to each end. Spikes in panicles with rigid branches; bracts long, leaf-like. The 2 species mentioned are herbaceous stove plants suitable for table decoration. A compost of sandy loam and peat suits and they must have shade and moisture to grow them well. Propagation by seed or cuttings.

**H. latifo′lium.** 2 to 4 ft. h. *l.* broad-lanceolate. *fl.* rich brown in a rather dense terminal cluster. Ceylon. 1877. (B.M. 6282.)

**H. Schraderia′num.** Grass-like, stout. *l.* tufted, 2½ in. long, 2 in. wide, entire, green with purple margins. Brazil. 1893. (I.H. 1895, 25, f. 5.)

F. G. P.

**HYPONOMEU′TA.** *See* **Ermine Moths.**

*hypophyl′lus -a -um,* hypophyllous, growing on the under side of a leaf.

*Hypop′itys,* growing beneath pines.

**HYPOX′IS** (*hypo*, beneath, *oxys*, sharp; in reference to the base of the capsule). FAM. *Amaryllidaceae*. A genus of about 60 species of dwarf rhizomatous or cormous herbaceous perennials with grass-like leaves, natives of Trop. Asia, Australia, Madagascar, Trop. and S. Africa, and Trop. and N. America. Flowers yellow, star-shaped; perianth tube none; segments 6, almost equal, spreading; stamens 6; ovary 3-celled. Sandy loam and peat or leaf-soil forms the best compost for them, and they may be increased by offsets. Few are much worth growing.

**H. colchicifo′lia.** Corm globose, 2 in. across. About 1 ft. h. *l.* 6 to 8, tufted, oblong or oblong-lanceolate, up to about 8 in. long, 1½ to 2 in. wide, glabrous. *fl.* bright yellow within, greenish-yellow and slightly hairy without, about 1¼ in. across; segs. oblong-lanceolate; peduncle slender, 3- or 4-fld. Autumn. S. Africa. 1884.

**H. ela′ta.** A synonym of *H. hemerocallidea.*

**H. erec′ta.** A synonym of *H. hirsuta.*

**H. hemerocallid′ea.** *l.* many, 1 to 1½ ft. long, spreading, revolute, thinly hairy above, thickly beneath. *fl.* golden-yellow, 2 in. across; scapes numerous, shorter than l., many-fld., pedicels slender, 1½ in. long. June. Natal. 1862. (B.M. 5690 as *H. elata.*)

**H. hirsu′ta.** About 6 in. h., hairy. *l.* linear-lanceolate. *fl.* yellow, small, starry; scape 1- to 6-fld. June, July. N. America. 1752. (B.M. 710 as *H. erecta.*) var. **al′ba,** *fl.* white.

**H. latifo′lia.** *l.* scale-like in lower part, then broad-lanceolate, about 6 in. long, slender-pointed; upper narrowest becoming 2 ft. long. *fl.* bright yellow within, green without, large; racemes many-fld. Natal. 1854. (B.M. 4817.)

**H. longifo′lia.** About 1½ ft. h. Tufted. *l.* many, outer 2 ft. long, spreading on ground, inner sheath sub-erect, broad, membranous, 2 to 4 in. long, blade very slender, flaccid, bright green, slightly hairy on margin and keel. *fl.* golden-yellow within, green and hairy without; outer segs. lanceolate, inner rather wider; scapes several, much shorter than l., umbel 4- or 5-fld. August. Algoa Bay. 1871. (B.M. 6035.)

**H. stella′ta.** About 9 in. h. *l.* linear-lanceolate, keeled. *fl.* white within; outer segs. green keeled without; scapes 1- to 4-fld. S. Africa. 1752. (B.M. 662, 1223.)

**HYPSE′LA.** *See* Supplement.

**HYP′TIS** (*hyptios*, resupinate; the limb of the corolla is turned on its back). FAM. *Labiatae*. A genus of about 300 species of Trop. American herbs, or shrubs of various habit. Calyx teeth 5, usually more or less acute; corolla somewhat 2-lipped, lower lobe deflexed abruptly; stamens 4, didynamous. *H. suaveolens* is a greenhouse or half-hardy annual, calling for no special treatment and of no great merit.

**H. suaveo′lens.** *l.* ovate, or lower cordate, doubly toothed or almost sinuate. *fl.* pale blue; cor. shortly exserted; heads few-fld. in a panicle, terminal or axillary. W. Indies, &c. 1889. SYN. *Ballota suaveolens.*

**HYSSOP** (*Hyssopus officinalis*). A partially evergreen bushy herb, native of S. Europe, its leaves and young growth having a pleasantly mint-like odour. It is grown for the use of its flowers and tops which are steeped in water to make an infusion sometimes employed in removing phlegm. At one time a kitchen herb used for flavouring broths but now usually thought too strongly flavoured, but young parts still sometimes sparingly used in salads. An oil distilled from the leaves is used in perfumery and in flavouring liqueurs. There are three varieties with, respectively, blue, red, and white flowers. They may be increased by seed sown in April, by division in spring or autumn, or by cuttings in spring, inserted in shade. Plants raised from seed or cuttings should, when large enough, be planted out, 1 ft. apart each way, and kept watered until established. They grow best in a sunny place in a light, rather dry soil. They need cutting back occasionally but no further attention. They are sometimes used as edging plants. The Hyssop of the Bible is the Caper Plant, *Capparis spinosa.*

**HYS′SOPUS** (*Hyssopos*, the old Greek name used by Hippocrates). FAM. *Labiateae*. A genus of a single species of shrub related to Satureia, but with conspicuously exserted stamens, and to Thymus but with a 15-ribbed, tubular calyx with 5 equal teeth. For treatment, &c., see Hyssop.

**H. officina′lis.** 1 to 2 ft. h. *l.* opposite, narrow-elliptic or linear, entire. *fl.* bluish-purple, rarely white; whorls 6- to 15-fld. in terminal, secund spikes. Mediterranean region and Cent. Asia. Long cultivated. (B.M. 2299.) var. **al′bus,** *fl.* white; **ru′ber,** *fl.* red.

**HYSTERION′ICA** (late flowering?). FAM. *Compositae*. A genus of about 12 species of herbaceous perennials or under-shrubs, usually rough with long, spreading hairs. Leaves narrow-linear, acute, scattered. *H. linearifolia* is a neat compact plant, freely producing its flower-heads in any ordinary garden soil.

**H. linearifo′lia.** About 1 ft. h. *fl.-heads* yellow, solitary, on long stalks. May to October. Uruguay. 1828. SYN. *Neja gracilis.*

**HYS′TRIX.** A synonym of Asperella.

*Hys′trix,* porcupine-like.

# I

*ianthi'nus -a -um,* bluish-purple, or violet.

*-ianthus -a -um,* in compound words signifying bluish-purple or violet; ianthine.

**IBBETSO'NIA.** *See* **Cyclopia.**

*iber'icus -a -um,* Spanish or Georgian (Caucasus).

**IBERIDEL'LA.** *See* **Thlaspi rotundifolia.**

*iberid'eus -a -um,* Iberis-like.

**IBER'IS** (*Iberia*, ancient name of Spain where many species occur wild). **FAM.** *Cruciferae.* A genus of about 40 species of annual or biennial herbs and sub-shrubs, natives of S. Europe and W. Asia. Stems round, usually smooth. Leaves alternate, linear or obovate, entire or pinnately cut. Flowers white or purple, in racemes or corymbs; petals 4, the two outer largest. Fruit a flat siliqua, rounded at base, entire or emarginate at apex. All the species are easily grown in good well-drained ordinary soil so long as they have plenty of sun and are not overcrowded. Some of the sub-shrubs are somewhat impatient of our winter damp but they can be accommodated on raised situations in the rock-garden and on dry walls for which they are admirably adapted. The annuals and biennials should be sown in light sandy soil in March and April for summer flowering, and in August or September for flowering in spring. The sub-shrubby species are, for the most part, compact free-flowering plants which, besides the uses suggested above, are well adapted for the front of borders. They can be raised from seed or from cuttings which root readily or by division.

KEY

| | | |
|---|---|---|
| 1. | *Annual or biennial; stems not woody at base* | 2 |
| 1. | *Perennial; stems woody at base* | 8 |
| 2. | *Infl. racemose in fruit* | 3 |
| 2. | *Infl. corymbose in fruit* | 6 |
| 3. | *Lobes of pod erect* | 4 |
| 3. | *Lobes of pod divergent* | 5 |
| 4. | *Lvs. toothed near tip* | I. amara |
| 4. | *Lvs. more deeply cut into narrow lobes* | I. pectinata |
| 5. | *Lvs. toothed near tip* | I. odorata |
| 5. | *Lvs. pinnately cut* | I. pinnata |
| 6. | *Lvs. in dense rosettes; fls. pink* | I. Bernardiana |
| 6. | *Lvs. not in dense rosettes* | 7 |
| 7. | *Lvs. linear, entire* | I. linifolia |
| 7. | *Lvs. lanceolate, lower toothed* | I. umbellata |
| 8. | *Fruits in racemes* | 9 |
| 8. | *Fruits in corymbs* | 12 |
| 9. | *Fl. in racemes* | 10 |
| 9. | *Fl. in corymbs* | 11 |
| 10. | *Plant very vigorous and spreading* | I. correaefolia |
| 10. | *Plant less vigorous with smaller lvs.* | I. sempervirens |
| 11. | *Lvs. entire* | I. saxatilis |
| 11. | *Lvs. toothed* | I. gibraltarica |
| 12. | *Fl. pink or purple* | 13 |
| 12. | *Fl. white; lvs. not ciliate* | 14 |
| 13. | *Stems more or less prostrate* | I. contracta |
| 13. | *Plant rather bushy; lvs. ciliate* | I. Tenoreana |
| 14. | *Stem tall, bushy* | I. semperflorens |
| 14. | *Stem about 6 in. h., bushy* | I. Pruiti |
| 14. | *Stems decumbent, ascending at tips* | I. Jordanii |

**I. ama'ra.*** Candytuft. Annual, erect, branching, 6 to 12 in. h. *l.* lanceolate, toothed towards apex, acute. *fl.* white, at first in corymbs but the infl. finally lengthening to a raceme. *fr.* nearly round. Summer. W. Europe, including Britain. (E.B.149.) var. **corona'ria** has larger fl. and infl. than type and there are several fine forms, e.g. **Empress,** excellent for cutting; **Giant Snowflake,** with trusses about 6 in. long; **hyacinthiflo'ra,** with fine trusses and large fl.; **Spiral White,** with solid columnar trusses, and the dwarf forms **Little Prince** and **Tom Thumb** about 6 in. h. and compact in habit.

**I. Bernardia'na.** Annual, about 6 in. h. *l.* spatulate, lobed, deep glossy green, in dense compact rosettes. *fl.* pink, in corymbs. Pyrenees. SYN. *I. Bubanii.*

**I. Buba'nii.** A synonym of *I. Bernardiana.*

**I. cappadoc'ica.** A synonym of *Ptilotrichum cappadocicum.*

**I. contrac'ta.** Glabrous, rather prostrate sub-shrub, about 6 in. h. *l.* linear, toothed, slightly narrowed to base. *fl.* white. May. *fr.* in a much-contracted corymb. Spain. 1824. var. **ro'sea,** *fl.* pink or purplish.

**I. corifo'lia.** A variety of *I. saxatilis.*

**I. corona'ria.** A variety of *I. amara.*

**I. correaefo'lia.*** Evergreen sub-shrub with numerous, procumbent branches making a close mat often over a yard across, about 8 in. h. *l.* spatulate, about 1 to 1½ in. long, obtuse, entire, smooth. *fl.* white in large compact flat heads later lengthening to about 3 in., very free. May, June. This is related to *I. sempervirens* and is often known as such. It is quite hardy, long-lived, neat, and the best form for making large masses on banks or dry walls. By some it is regarded as a hybrid.

**I. Garrexia'na.** A variety of *I. sempervirens.*

*Iberis gibraltarica*

**I. gibraltar'ica.*** Evergreen sub-shrub with spreading, somewhat straggling branches up to about 1 ft. h. *l.* wedge-shaped, ¾ to 2 in. long, up to ½ in. wide, blunt, toothed near apex, smooth, those on flower-stems much smaller and narrower. *fl.* white, often tinged pink or red, in corymbs, the fl.-stems often branched. May to July. Gibraltar. 1732. (B.M. 124.) Not very hardy. Should be planted in full sun. Plants under this name are frequently untrue.

**I. Jordan'ii.** Tufted with several almost prostrate branches 3 to 6 in. long. *fl.* in terminal corymbs of white fl. larger than in *I. correaefolia.* Anatolia.

**I. linifo'lia.** Annual or perennial, 8 to 12 in. h., glabrous. *l.* linear, entire, lower somewhat toothed. *fl.* pink in rounded terminal corymbs. June to September. S. Europe.

**I. odora'ta.** Annual of 6 to 12 in. *l.* linear, ciliate below, widening somewhat upwards and there with several short lobes. *fl.* white, fragrant. *fr.* smooth. Greece, Syria.

**I. panduraefor'mis.** A synonym of *I. pectinata.*

**I. pectina'ta.** Annual or biennial, 6 to 12 in. h., branched. *l.* pinnatifid with linear blunt lobes, dark green, sometimes downy and ciliate. *fl.* white, in dense umbel-like racemes; pet. 4 times as long as sep. *fr.* downy. France. SYN. *I. affinis, I. panduraeformis.*

**I. petrae'a.** See **I. saxatilis, I. Tenoreana.**

**I. pinna'ta.** Annual or biennial, 6 to 12 in. h. *l.* oblong-linear, pinnately cut into linear, blunt lobes. *fl.* white, fragrant, in corymbs. Cent. and S. Europe. The name has been wrongly applied to forms of the perennial *I. sempervirens.*

**I. Pru'iti.** Perennial sub-shrub, glabrous, about 6 in. h. *l.* obovate-spatulate, entire, or slightly toothed, forming a central rosette, not ciliate. *fl.* pure white, in compact corymbs. May, June. Sicily. Not very hardy. Its pure-white fl. and glabrous l. distinguish it from *I. Tenoreana.*

**I. saxat'ilis.*** Evergreen sub-shrub, 3 to 6 in. h. Stems ascending. *l.* linear, almost cylindric, entire, somewhat fleshy, acute, ciliate. *fl.* white, in corymbs, often tinged purple especially as they fade. May to July. Pyrenees to Sicily. 1739. var. **corifo'lia** has glabrous l. and white fl. (B.M. 1642 as *I. corifolia*.)

**I. semperflo'rens.** Evergreen sub-shrub to 2 ft. h., bushy, glabrous. *l.* narrow-obovate, rather fleshy, blunt, ¾ to 2½ in. long, entire. *fl.* white, fragrant, in crowded corymbs 1 to 2 in. across. November to April. *Pod* scarcely notched. Sicily, Italy. 1679. The most tender of the sub-shrubby species, but handsome.

**I. sempervi'rens.*** Evergreen sub-shrub, spreading, forming a glabrous leafy mat, 9 to 12 in. h. like *I. correaefolia* but smaller. *l.* numerous, oblong, blunt, narrowed to base, smooth. *fl.* white in corymbs 1½ to 2 in. across, lengthening later. Spring, summer. *Pod* notched. S. Europe. 1731. var. **Garrexia'na**, has narrow l., often acute, and more slender; usually dwarfer. S. Europe. 1820. The type is quite hardy, *Garrexiana* hardy in most places. A variable plant, some forms of which are much more compact in habit though not less floriferous. Some have been named, like **Little Gem, Snowflake,** and all are worthy for the rock-garden or the border. var. **ple'na,** double-fld. A poor thing. Variegated forms are known.

**I. Tenorea'na.*** Evergreen perennial, with hairy ascending shoots 4 to 8 in. h., rather tortuous. *l.* in lower part obovate, narrowed at base, upper oblong-linear, all somewhat fleshy, ½ to 1½ in. long, ciliate. *fl.* purplish or whitish in flat clusters, 1 to 2 in. across. May. Pyrenees to Sicily. 1822. (B.M. 2783.) Forms of *I. sempervirens* are often offered for this.

**I. umbella'ta.*** Candytuft. Annual 6 to 12 in. h. *l.* lanceolate, slender-pointed, lower toothed, upper entire. *fl.* variable, typically purple, in terminal umbels. Spring, summer. S. Europe. 1596 or earlier. (B.M. 106.) A variety of colours can be had and they breed true and are mostly named from the colour. var. **Dunnet'tii** is very dark purple. var. **na'na** is dwarf and compact and this form can also be had in various colours.

A→

*Ibo'ta,* Japanese name.

**ICACI'NA** (in allusion to resemblance to the Icaco (Chrysobalanus)). FAM. *Icacinaceae.* A genus of 3 or 4 species of Trop. African climbing or twining shrubs with ovate, entire, alternate leaves without stipules and hairy flowers in terminal panicles. *I. Mannii* needs the stove, and grows well in rich sandy loam and leaf-soil. It can be increased by cuttings.

**I. Mann'ii.** Stem slender, climbing, from a large tuberous root 6 to 12 in. across, terete and glabrous. *l.* elliptic, 5 to 7 in. long, suddenly narrowed to a long point, rounded at base, entire, thin, glabrous or downy only on midrib beneath; stalk short. *fl.* yellow, ¼ in. long, in short silky axillary cymes together forming a terminal panicle; pet. linear-oblong; stamens exserted. October. Guinea. 1865. (B.M. 6260.)

**ICACINA'CEAE.** Dicotyledons. A family of about 200 species in 38 genera, natives of the tropics, formerly placed in Olacaceae from which it is markedly different. Trees and shrubs (often tall climbing), rarely herbs. Leaves alternate, usually entire, often leathery. Flowers in compound panicles, regular, usually perfect; calyx of 4 or 5 united sepals, petals 5 or 4, usually free; stamens 5 or 4, alternating with petals; ovary superior, of 3 (5 or 2, rarely many) united carpels, usually 1-celled with 2 ovules. Fruit usually a 1-seeded drupe or sometimes a samara. The genera treated here are Cassinopsis, Icacina, and Villaresia, the last, in *V. Congonha,* one of the sources of Maté-Tea.

**ICE PLANT.** *See* **Mesembryanthemum crystallinum.** Applied also at times to *Sedum spectabile.*

*ichangen'sis -is -e,* of the district of Ichang, China.

**ICHNEUMON FLIES** (Order *Hymenoptera*), being almost entirely parasites of insects, are beneficial to man. The name Ichneumon is often loosely applied to include members of other families, e.g. *Braconidae,* and *Chalcidae,* which have certain resemblances in structure and similar habits of parasitism. The most familiar Ichneumons are the reddish-brown species of *Ophion,* which are attracted to artificial light and enter rooms, and which parasitize certain Noctuid Moth caterpillars. The head of Ichneumon Flies is separated from the thorax by a short neck giving great mobility to this organ, the antennae are long, the female has a prominent ovipositor,

while the thorax is separated from the abdomen by a petiole or stalk giving the insect the appearance of having a waist. There are two pairs of membranous wings, the fore-wings being larger than the hind. The eggs are laid in, on, or near the body of the host insect, and the resulting grubs feed within the victim's body. Pupation takes place within a cocoon in or outside the host. Among the many hundreds of species, mention is made here of 2 only, namely, *Pimpla pomorum,* which parasitizes the Apple-blossom Weevil, *Anthonomus pomorum*; and *Rhyssa persuasoria,* the *Sirex* Woodwasp parasite, which is the largest species found in Britain. The female *Rhyssa* thrusts her rapier-like ovipositor through the bark and solid wood of living Coniferous trees to deposit her eggs on or near the burrowing *Sirex* larva. Caterpillars and other insects found to be parasitized should be left untouched to allow the parasites to emerge and to continue their work of destruction of insect pests (*see* **Braconid Wasps, Chalcid Wasps**).

G. F. W.

**ICHNOCAR'PUS** (*ichnos,* a vestige, *karpos,* fruit; the follicles being very slender). FAM. *Apocynaceae.* A genus of 9 species of tall climbing shrubs, natives of Malaya, E. Asia, and N. Australia. For cultivation *see* **Dipladenia.**

**I. frutes'cens.** *l.* opposite, oblong-lanceolate, glabrous. *fl.* purple, small; cor. salver-shaped; peduncles axillary, very long, racemose. July, August. Trop. Asia, Australia. 1759.

*icos-,* in compound words signifying twenty.

*icter'icus -a -um,* jaundiced, sickly yellow.

*ictu'rus -a -um,* like a marten's tail.

*idae'us -a -um,* of Mt. Ida, Crete.

*Ida-may'a,* in honour of Ida May Burke, *c.* 1867, daughter of the discoverer of the plant in California.

*-ides, -oi'des,* similar to.

A→

**IDE'SIA** (in honour of Eberhard Ysbrant Ides, *c.* 1720, a Dutch traveller in China). FAM. *Flacourtiaceae.* The only species is a deciduous tree with long-stalked alternate, toothed leaves. Flowers usually dioecious, without petals, in large terminal panicles; sepals 3 to 6, yellowish, hairy; stamens numerous; pistillate flowers with roundish ovary, styles 5, spreading. Fruit a many-seeded berry. The tree is best propagated by seed, is hardy, and handsome when bearing ripe fruit.

**I. polycar'pa.*** Tree up to 40 feet, usually smaller, with spreading branches. *l.* cordate, shortly pointed, toothed, about 6 in. long, 5 in. wide, but on vigorous shoots much more, long-stalked, dark green and smooth above, glaucous, and hairy near base beneath. *fl.* yellow-green; male panicles 5 or 6 in. long, female, longer and looser. June, July. *fr.* about ⅓ in. across, nearly round, dark brown, finally deep red. Japan, China. 1864. (B.M. 6794.) var. **vesti'ta,** *l.* very downy when young. Szechwan. 1908. A variety with cut and crisped leaves (**cris'pa**) has been recorded.

A→

*igna'vus -a -um,* slothful.

*ig'neus -a -um,* fiery-red.

*ignora'tus -a -um,* unknown.

*ika'riae,* of the Island Ikaria, Aegean Sea.

**I'LEX** (Latin name of *Quercus Ilex*). FAM. *Aquifoliaceae.* Holly. Including Prinos. A genus of about 300 species of evergreen and deciduous trees and shrubs inhabiting temperate and tropical regions of the world. Leaves alternate, simple, entire, or toothed. Flowers small, usually dull white and with little attraction, sometimes yellowish or greenish, produced during spring or early summer in the leaf-axils of the preceding year's growth, ranging from solitary to numerous in stalked clusters. The plants are usually 1-sexual and some of the best garden varieties of the common holly, being male, never produce fruits. Fruit an ovoid, oval, or globose drupe (commonly called a berry) containing 2 to 8 nutlets. The common holly, *I. Aquifolium*, has innumerable varieties and is certainly the best of our native evergreens for garden use. It submits to training into almost any shape and soon recovers if severely pruned to preserve the desired form. Pruning or clipping, whether of trained trees or hedges should be done in September or April. Holly is best transplanted at the beginning of May, or better in early autumn when there will be sufficient time for new roots to be formed before

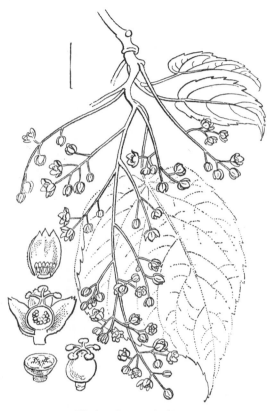

*Idesia polycarpa* (p. 1042)

winter, and the atmosphere is likely to be moist; in spring they will then start into growth without a check. Holly does not transplant well when old but it is a long-lived tree when established in good soil and left undisturbed at the root. In transplanting it is always advisable to lift the plants with good balls of earth and preserve the roots intact. If large plants have to be moved and the roots are injured, or are almost shaken free of soil it is a good plan to reduce the leafy growth, if need be to the extent of one-half. Avoid planting in very dry, windy weather, but if it is done in such conditions give a good watering at the roots and overhead as soon as planting is finished, and if the weather continues dry repeat the waterings at intervals. The common holly makes one of the handsomest and most enduring hedges though it is slow-growing at first, taking 8 or 10 years from seed to make a hedge 4 ft. high, and is consequently less frequently planted than its many merits warrant. It is not unusual to allow a long stem to run up and form a tree at intervals along a holly hedge. For hedge-making the plants should have been properly prepared in the nursery and well-furnished to the base. If such plants are chosen, though the first cost may be somewhat greater than if indifferent ones are purchased, a satisfactory hedge will soon be formed and become not only a useful fence but an en-

during thing of beauty. The plants may be from 2 to 5 ft. high when planted and whether for hedge-making or for specimen plants the ground should be thoroughly prepared by trenching before planting is embarked upon. Holly may be propagated by seed, by grafting, and by cuttings. For propagation by seed it is necessary to collect the fruits when ripe and mix them with sand until the following spring or autumn, and occasional turning of the heap is an advantage. After this prolonged exposure to all weathers the outer covering of the fruit rots and the seed is then ready for sowing in drills of moist sandy compost, sowing the sand and seeds of the heap together and covering the mixture with fine soil to the depth of about 1 in. A few boughs or a lath blind placed over the beds will serve as a protection to the seedlings from frost or bright sun which is apt to injure them. The seedlings are allowed to remain in the beds for 2 years and are then lined out into nursery rows about 1 ft. apart, where again they will stand for about 2 years. By then, 15 to 18 in. high, the plants will require more room and they should be transplanted to provide it. Frequent transplanting encourages the formation of fibrous roots and more certainty of moving with safety at later stages, for left undisturbed but few fibrous and many long roots liable to damage when moving is attempted, will be made. The numerous varieties can only be increased by grafting or budding or by cuttings. Grafting and budding are done upon stocks of the common type raised from seed, grafting in March, budding with a pushing bud in May or with a dormant one in August. Cuttings are taken from mature wood of the current season, made 2 or 3 in. long, cut clean below a joint and having the lower leaves removed, and dibbled in on a warm sheltered border in August and covered with a hand-light or frame. It is important that they should be made quite firm at the base. They will need watering with a fine-rose water-pot 2 or 3 times a week and shade from sun with mats, but only enough ventilation to allow surplus moisture to escape, until they have rooted. Plants raised from cuttings take a little longer to grow in the first season or two, but when established are to be preferred, for shoots from the base belong to the same variety, not to a different stock as they do with grafted or budded trees. The pendulous varieties must be worked at the desired height on stocks of the common type.    **A**

KEY

1. *Lvs. evergreen*    2
1. *Lvs. deciduous*    21
2. *Fr. black*    3
2. *Fr. red or yellow*    4
3. *Young shoots round; lvs. acute, sparsely toothed*    I. crenata
3. *Young shoots angled; lvs. usually bluntish, often entire*    I. glabra
4. *Fr. very numerous, ⅛ in. wide*    I. micrococca
4. *Fr. usually ¼ in. or more wide*    5
5. *Lvs. often over 2 in. wide*    6
5. *Lvs. usually not over 1½ in. wide*    11
6. *Lvs. 4 to 9 in. long*    7
6. *Lvs. 2 to 6 in. long*    8
7. *Lvs. shining; teeth shallow*    I. latifolia
7. *Lvs. dull green; teeth small, spine-tipped*    I. insignis
8. *Lvs. with winged l.-stalk, spines short*    I. Perado
8. *L.-stalk not winged*    9
9. *Lvs. obovate or oval, coarsely toothed*    I. paraguariensis
9. *Lvs. acute*    10
10. *Lvs. rectangular with large strong spines*    I. cornuta
10. *Lvs. broadly oval, dull dark green*    I. platyphylla
11. *Fl. clustered in axils of last year's branches*    12
11. *Fl. solitary or with solitary stalked infl. on young branches*    19
12. *Lvs. spiny, at least at tip*    13
12. *Lvs. toothed, or entire, but obtuse*    16
13. *Fl. and fr. stalked; lvs. 1 to 3 in. long*    I. Aquifolium
13. *Fl. and fr. almost stalkless*    14
14. *Lvs. crowded, more or less rhomboidal; teeth few, strong*    I. Pernyi
14. *Lvs. elliptic to ovate; teeth spiny, rather small*    15
15. *Shoots densely hairy; lvs. 1 to 2 in. long*    I. ciliospinosa
15. *Shoots minutely downy; lvs. 2 to 5 in. long*    I. dipyrena
16. *Lvs. wrinkled above, ¾ to 2 in. long*    I. rugosa
16. *Lvs. smooth above*    17

17. *Lvs. quite entire, 2 to 4 in. long*     I. integra
17. *Lvs. toothed*     18
18. *Shoots smooth; lvs. 2 to 5 in. long*     I. corallina, I. Fargesii
18. *Shoots downy; lvs. ½ to 1½ in. long*     I. vomitoria
19. *Lvs. toothed*     20
19. *Lvs. entire, 1½ to 3 in. long*     I. pedunculosa
20. *Lvs. dull green, spiny toothed, 1½ to 3½ in. long*     I. opaca
20. *Lvs. bright green, blunt-toothed, ½ to 1¼ in. long*     I. yunnanensis
21. *Fr.-stalks ¾ to 1½ in. long, drooping; lvs. slender-pointed*     I. geniculata
21. *Fr.-stalks short*     22
22. *Shoots downy*     I. serrata
22. *Shoots smooth*     23
23. *Fr. black, ⅜ in. wide; lvs. 2½ to 4 in. long*     I. macrocarpa
23. *Fr. orange or red*     24
24. *Lvs. more or less downy beneath, at least on midrib*     25
24. *Lvs. smooth beneath, little toothed*     I. laevigata
25. *Lvs. 2 to 6 in. long, sharply toothed, pale green*     I. montana
25. *Lvs. 1 to 3 in. long, bluntly or doubly toothed*     26
26. *Nutlets smooth on back; lvs. not on short spurs*     I. verticillata
26. *Nutlets ribbed on back; lvs. often on short spurs*     I. decidua

**I. Aquifo'lium.\*** Common Holly. Evergreen, a shrub in its young state, eventually becoming a tree 30 to 80 ft., mostly 1-sexual. *l.* 1 to 3 in. long, ovate to oval, dark glossy green, very spiny-toothed and wavy-margined when young, becoming entire and flatter in upper part of old trees. *fl.* small, dull white, densely clustered in l.-axils. May, June. *fr.* bright red, ¼ in. wide. Europe (Britain), N. Africa, W. Asia. (E.B. 316.) This, the most beautiful and, in gardens, the most useful of native evergreens, has broken up into very numerous vars. differing greatly in shape, size, and colouring of l., also in habit. Bird-lime is obtained from the bark of holly. Some of the larger-leaved varieties mentioned below are no doubt derived from crosses with other species, see *I. Perado* and *I. platyphylla* (q.v.). The varieties fall into two groups, those with green leaves and those with variegated leaves. A number of these have received names of Latin form and are sometimes listed as though they were distinct species. Catalogue names not found under species should be sought in the following list of varieties which contains all the most marked forms. The varieties marked † bear male, those marked ‖ female flowers. A mixture of both male and female plants is usually necessary for effective fruit production.

I. Green-leaved Varieties. **altaclaren'sis,**† bark purplish, *l.* up to 4½ in. long, 3 in. wide, slightly glossy; **angustifol'ia,** see **myrtifolia; balea'rica,**‖ 10 ft. h., *l.* ovate, acute, flat, shiny, entire or spiny toothed, *fl.* in few-fld. umbels. 1815; **Besson'ii,** *l.* spineless, obovate-lanceolate, rather less rigid and paler green than most varieties; **camelliaefo'lia,**‖ *l.* dark glittering green, up to 5 in. long, 2 in. wide, almost entire; **chinen'sis,**†‖ distinct by its long narrow *l.*, 3 to 4½ in. long, 1½ in. wide, ovate-lanceolate, very spiny, a wild Chinese var. 1901; **costa'ta,** Grecian Holly, *l.* oblong-acute, 2½ in. long, 1½ in. wide, spines rather distant and spreading; **crassifo'lia,**‖ dwarf, bushy, slow-growing, bark purple, *l.* dull green, very thick, tips and margins recurved, teeth prominent, serrate; **crisp'a,**† *l.* spirally twisted, bark purple, a variegated form; **crispa pict'a**† has

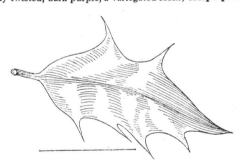

*Ilex Aquifolium donningtonensis*

yellow-centred *l.*; **donningtonen'sis,**† free in growth, pyramidal. *l.* lanceolate, sometimes sickle-shaped, 2 in. long, ¾ in. wide, spines few or none; **fe'rox,**† Hedgehog Holly, bark purple, *l.* ovate-oblong, to narrow-ovate, 2 in. or more long, slender-pointed, very spiny on surface and margin of the dark green l.; **Fish'eri,**† *l.* 4 in. long, 3 in. wide, strongly spiny; **Fox'ii,** small-growing, *l.* ovate, stoutish, 2 to 2½ in. long, spines rather distant, flat, numerous; **fructu-luteo,**‖ *fr.* yellow; **hasta'ta,** *l.* ¾ to 1½ in. long, ½ in. wide, spines large in 1, 2, or occasionally more pairs near l.-base, upper half of l. forming a large, entire, oblong-bluntish lobe. Syn. *latispina minor, latispina sana, latispina pygmaea;* **Henderson'ii,**‖ bark purplish, *l.* about 2¼ in. long, 1⅛ in. wide, oblong-elliptic, dull green with sunken veins, usually entire; **heterophyl'la,** strong-growing, *l.* ovate or elliptic-ovate, 2½ in. long, 1 to 1½ in. wide, twisted nr. point, entire or spiny; **Hodgins'ii,**‖ *l.* very broadly ovate, 3 to 4 in. long, 2½ in. wide, spines strong but distant and irregularly placed; **latispi'na,**† *l.* ovate, 2 to 3 in. long, point long, slender, deflexed, spines 1 to 3, ¼ to ¾ in. long (see also **hastata**); **laurifo'lia,**‖

tall, rather irregular, bark purple, *l.* ovate to elliptic, 2 to 3 in. long, usually entire, deep green, glossy; **maderen'sis,**† rather tender, *l.* tender or ovate-oblong, 3 in. long, 1¼ in. wide, point short, slender, margin regularly spiny, flat; **Marnock'ii,**‖ *l.* dark, shining, similar to *camelliaefolia* but wider; **monstro'sa,**† *l.* oblong, long,

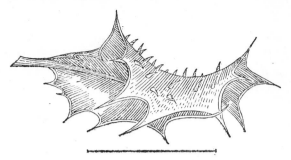

*Ilex Aquifolium ferox*

slender-pointed, spines strong, mostly directed upwards; **myrtifo'lia,**‖ *l.* ovate-lanceolate, 1 to 1½ in. long, half as wide, usually moderately spiny, sometimes entire. Syn. *angustifolia;* **nob'ilis,** vigorous. *l.* roundish-ovate, 2¾ to 3¾ in. long, spines bold, distant; **ova'ta,**† slow-growing, *l.* ovate, 2½ in. long, teeth regular, angular, scarcely spiny; **pend'ula,**‖ Weeping Holly, branches stiff, arching to pendulous; **platyphyl'la,** *l.* broadly ovate, 3½ in. long, 2¼ in. wide, spines often irregularly placed round margin; **recurv'a,**† rather dwarf, *l.* ovate, about 1¼ in. long, ½ in. wide, spiny with usually a long apical spine. Syn. *tortuosa;* **scot'ica,**‖ *l.* oval, up to 3 in. long, deep lustrous green, twisted, entire (there is a golden variety of this); **serratifo'lia,**‖ near *myrtifolia,* *l.* lanceolate, 1½ in. long, ½ in. wide, stiff, midrib curved, spikes numerous, regular, stoutish; **Shephard'ii,**‖ near *Hodginsii,* *l.* up to 4 in. long, 2½ in. wide, bright green;

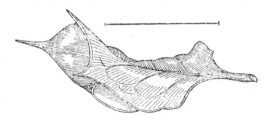

*Ilex Aquifolium tortuosa*

**tortuo'sa,**† Screw Holly, vigorous, of dense habit, *l.* 2 in. long, 1 in. wide, once spirally twisted, margin revolute, rarely spiny (*see also* **recurva**); **Whittingtonen'sis,**† graceful, *l.* lanceolate or elliptic-ovate, 2¼ in. long, ⅝ in. wide, sometimes slightly recurved, spines numerous, stiff; **Wilson'ii,**‖ vigorous and sturdy, *l.* up to 5 in. long, nearly 3 in. wide, leathery, rather dull green.

II. Gold or Silver Variegated Leaves. **albo-pict'a,** see **argentea medio-picta; argent'ea elegantis'sima,**† *l.* elliptic or elliptic-ovate, about 2¼ in. long, spines few, distant, unequal, margin creamy-white, centre dark green with grey blotches. Syn. *elegantissima;* **argentea marginat'a,**‖ *l.* broadly ovate, 2 to 2½ in. long, usually spiny, margin irregular, narrowish silvery-grey, centre dark green, slightly mottled. Syn. *albo-marginata, argentea lato-marginata, variegata argentea;* **argentea marginata pendula,**‖ Perry's Weeping Holly, branches pendulous; **argentea medio-pict'a,**‖ bark green, *l.* ovate or wedge-shaped, 1½ to 2 in. long, about 1 in. wide, spines strong, spreading, margin dark green, centre creamy-white Syn. *albo-picta,* Silver Milkmaid; **argentea regin'a,\***† Silver Queen, bark purplish, best white-variegated variety; **argentea strict'a,** *l.* oblong-elliptic, 2 to 2½ in. long, 1½ in. wide, spiny, rather wavy, margin broadly unequally creamy-white, centre mottled with flakes of green and greyish-green; **au'rea angustifo'lia,**† *l.* elliptic-oblong, slender-pointed, 1½ to 2½ in. long, about 1 in. wide, spiny, margin wavy, deep gold, centre pale green; **au'rea latifo'lia,** *l.* ovate, 2 to 2½ in. long, spines strong, spreading, margin deep gold, narrow, irregular, centre splashed pale green; **aurea macula'ta,** *l.* oblong-ovate, about 2½ in. long, spines triangular, distant margin green, centre creamy-yellow. Syn. *maculata aurea;* **aurea marginata bromeliaefo'lia,**‖ *l.* ovate, spines flattish, distant, terminal long; margin yellow, unequal, centre mottled pale green on dark. Syn. *bromelicefolia aureo-marginata;* **aurea marginata fruct'u-lut'eo,**‖ *l.* ovate, 2½ in. long, spines coarse, distant, margin greenish-yellow, centre green, blotched grey, berries yellow; **aurea pen'dula,** Golden Weeping, *l.* margin golden, centre green; **aurea picta latifo'lia,** Golden Milkmaid, *l.* ovate or broadly ovate, 2 in. long or more, up to 1½ in. wide, spines variable, margin deep glossy green, irregular, often narrow, centre a large branching deep yellow blotch; **aurea regi'na,**† Golden

Queen, *l.* broadly ovate, 2½ to 3 in. long, 1⅛ to 2 in. wide, spines very broad, variously directed, margin broad, deep golden-yellow, continuous, centre usually much-mottled grey and green. SYN. *aurea marginata, latifolia marginata, reginae*; **Cook'ii,**|| *l.* ovate, flat, spines rather weak, margin greenish-yellow, narrow, centre very dark green blotched greenish-yellow; **crispa picta,**† *see* **crispa; ferox argent'ea,**† Silver-striped Hedgehog, *l.* ovate, more or less convex; very spiny towards front and edges, margin and spines creamy-white, centre deep green. SYN. *ferox argentea variegata*; **flavesc'ens,**|| Moonlight Holly, *l.* suffused with yellow, especially when young; **Golden King,** like Golden Queen but with larger more deeply coloured l.; **handsworthen'sis,**|| *l.* elliptic-oblong, 2½ to 3 in. long, free-growing, l.-margins and strong spines creamy-white, even, centre mottled green and grey-green; **heterophylla aureo-picta,** *l.* ovate, flat, entire, 2½ in. long, margin dark green, centre with a broad, unequally developed feathery blotch of bright yellow; **Hodgins'ii aurea,**|| *l.* broadly oblong-ovate, margin broad, golden, centre mottled dark and grey-green; **Lawsonia'na,**|| *l.* ovate or bluntly elliptical, 2½ to 3¼ in. long, spines distant, centre marked with broad bands and blotches of yellow on dull green. SYN. *Lawsoniana variegata*; **Madame Briot,*** *l.* broad-oblong-ovate, 2½ to 3 in. long, 1¼ to 1½ in. wide, spines strong, wavy or spreading, margin narrow, golden, centre mottled yellow and green, sometimes wholly golden; **maderen'sis variega'ta,** *l.* ovate or obovate, 2 to 2½ in. long, spines distant, flat or wavy, margin dark green, centre a feathered golden blotch mixed with pale green; **scot'ica au'rea,** *l.* obovate, about 1½ in. long, nearly entire, somewhat wavy, margin broad, golden, centre mottled dark green; **Watereria'na,**† dense, dwarf, *l.* oblong, ovate or obovate, often oblique, 1¾ to 2½ in. long, spiny or entire, margin a broad sometimes broken golden band, centre dark green, mottled or streaked yellowish- and greyish-green.

**I. Cassi'ne.** A synonym of *I. vomitoria.*

**I. ciliospino'sa.** Evergreen shrub, 12 to 15 ft., shoots downy. *l.* 1 to 2 in. long, half as wide, ovate to oval, slender-pointed, numerously and slenderly toothed, the teeth pointing forward, dark dull green. *fr.* red, ¼ in. long, ovoid. China. 1908.

**I. coralli'na.** Evergreen tree to 20 ft. *l.* lanceolate to oblong-lanceolate, 2½ to 6 in. long, sharply toothed, slender-pointed. *fr.* small, red, clustered, almost sessile, ⅛ to ⅙ in. across. China. 1900.

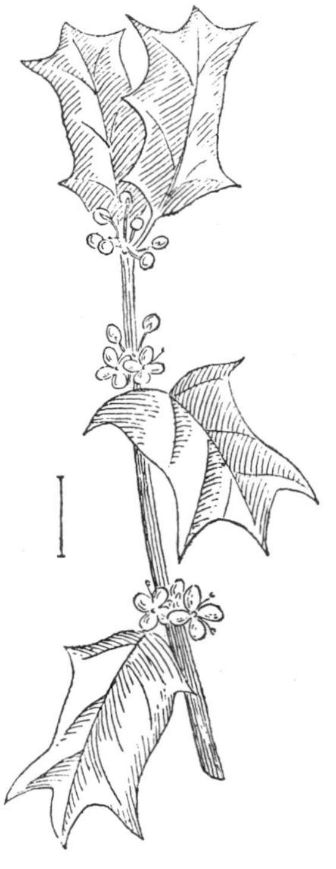

*Ilex cornuta*

**I. cornu'ta.*** Horned Holly. Evergreen shrub of dense bushy growth, 8 to 10 ft., usually more in width. *l.* dark shining green, 2 to 4 in. long, 1 to 3 in. wide, somewhat rectangular, with a large strong spine at each corner, one at the end and 2 smaller ones, much recurved, in the middle. *fl.* small, dull white. April. *fr.* globose, red, ⅜ in. wide. China. 1846. (B.M. 5059.)

**I. crena'ta.** Evergreen, stiff, very variable shrub, sometimes a small tree up to 20 ft., shoots minutely downy. *l.* oblong-lanceolate, glabrous, ½ to 1¼ in. long, cuneate, sharply pointed, sparsely toothed. *fr.* globose, ⅙ in. wide, black. Japan. 1864. The tree form known as **ma'jor** has larger l. and fr. ¼ in. wide. var. **Maries'ii,** very compact shrublet, annual growth under 1 in. *l.* orbicular or broadly ovate, ¼ in. wide. 1879; **variega'ta,** *l.* spotted with, or wholly, yellow.

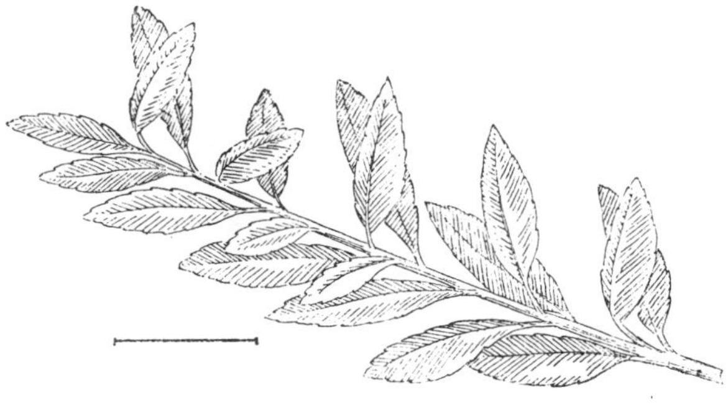

*Ilex crenata*

**I. decid'ua.** Deciduous shrub, usually 5 to 10 ft., or a small tree up to 30 ft., shoots grey, glabrous. *l.* 1 to 2½ in. long, one-third as wide, oval to obovate, tapered to both ends, bluntly toothed, midrib downy. *Male fl.* on slender stalks ½ in. long. *fr.* globose, orange to scarlet, ¼ in. wide. SE. United States. 1760. (S.S. i. t. 49.) SYN. *Prinos deciduus.*

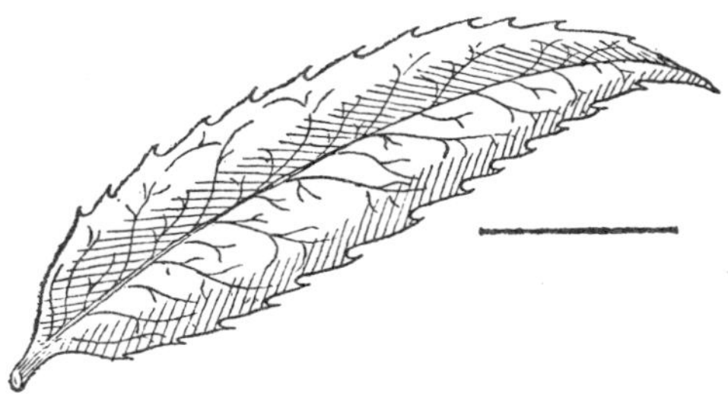

*Ilex dipyrena*

**I. dipyre'na.** Evergreen tree up to 40 ft., shoots angular, minutely downy. *l.* oblong to narrowly oval, 2 to 5 in. long, ¾ to 1½ in. wide, cuneate, spine-tipped, very spiny-toothed when young, becoming entire in the upper part of tree when old; dull green. *fl.* numerous, in clusters. *fr.* oval, red, ⅓ in. long. Himalaya. 1840.

**I. Farges'ii.** Evergreen tree, 15 to 20 ft., glabrous. *l.* 2 to 5 in. long, ⅜ to 1⅛ in. wide, narrowly cuneate, sparsely toothed towards the slender apex, dull green. *fr.* red, globose, ¼ in. wide, often in threes or fours in a l.-axil. China. 1900. Very distinct by its long narrow l. (B.M. 9670.)

**I. genicula'ta.*** Deciduous shrub, 5 to 8 ft., shoots glabrous. *l.* ovate to oval-lanceolate, 1½ to 2½ in. long, half as wide, slender-pointed, sharply toothed, downy on chief veins and midrib beneath. *fr.* globose, cinnabar-red, ⅙ in. wide; stalk slender, ¾ to 1½ in. long. Autumn colour yellow. Japan. 1926. Distinct by the long fr.-stalks.

**I. glab'ra.** Inkberry. Evergreen shrub, 2 to 6 ft., shoots erect, angular, minutely downy. *l.* narrowly obovate to oblanceolate, nearly or quite toothless, ¾ to 1½ in. long, ⅓ to ⅝ in. wide, dark glossy green, glabrous. *fr.* globose, ¼ in. wide, black. N. America. 1759. (L.B.C. 450.) SYN. *Prinos glaber.*

**I. insig'nis.*** Evergreen glabrous small tree, shoots stout, reddish at first, becoming silvery-grey and lustrous. *l.* 5 to 9 in. long, 2 to 3 in. wide, ovate to oblong, slender-pointed, cuneate, dark dull green, edged with small spine-tipped teeth. *fr.* bright red, roundish-oval, ⅜ in. long, scarcely stalked. Himalaya. 1880. Cool greenhouse.

**I. integ'ra.** Evergreen tree 30 to 40 ft., shoots glabrous, angled. *l.* oval to obovate, 2 to 4 in. long, ¾ to 1¼ in. wide, cuneate, tapering to a blunt apex, quite devoid of teeth, dark lustrous green. *fr.* deep red, globose, ⅜ in. wide. Japan. 1864. Distinct in the evergreen class by its entire l. SYN. *Othera japonica.*

**I. laeviga'ta.** Winterberry. Deciduous shrub, up to 6 or (rarely) 8 ft., shoots glabrous. *l.* 1½ to 2½ in. long, ½ to ¾ in. wide, narrowly oval, obovate or lanceolate, slender-pointed, cuneate, obscurely toothed. *fr.* rather flattened, globose, ⅓ in. wide, orange-red, solitary. E. United States. 1812. SYN. *Prinos laevigatus.*

**I. latifo'lia.** Evergreen tree, 50 to 60 ft., shoots very thick, glabrous. *l.* 4 to 8 in. long, 1½ to 3 in. wide, oblong, very stout, dark shining green, shallow-toothed. *fl.* green, densely clustered in l.-axils. June, July. *fr.* red, globose, ½ in. wide, in clusters. Not very hardy, best in a cool greenhouse or in SW. counties. (B.M. 5597.)

**I. macrocar'pa.** Deciduous glabrous tree, 30 to 50 ft., *l.* broadly ovate to oval, 2½ to 4 in. long, 1¼ to 1¾ in. wide, cuneate, short-pointed, finely shallowly toothed, dark green. *fr.* black, ⅝ in. wide.

globose. China. 1907. One of the largest of Prinos group; quite hardy. (B.M. n.s. 72.)

**I. manot'risha.** Evergreen shrub. *l.* elliptic, 3 to 4 in. long, crenulate. *fl.* yellow-green; male on very short branches forming a panicle; pedicels downy. *fr.* scarlet, abundant. Formosa. (B.M. n. 5. 84.)

**I. micrococ'ca.** Evergreen tree up to 50 ft. or a large shrub. *l.* ovate-lanceolate to ovate-oblong, 3 to 6 in. long, 1 to $2\frac{1}{2}$ in. wide, glabrous, toothed (often indistinctly); base rounded to subcordate, apex slender-pointed. *fl.* white, very copiously borne in stalked umbels. *fr.* globose, $\frac{1}{8}$ in. wide, dark crimson. China. Cult. 1930. Distinct by its very numerous stalked umbels of very small fr.

**I. monta'na.** Deciduous shrub or a tree up to 40 ft., shoots glabrous. *l.* ovate to oval or lanceolate, 2 to 6 in. long, $\frac{3}{4}$ to $2\frac{1}{2}$ in. wide, sharply toothed, pale green, only midrib and veins downy. *fr.* $\frac{3}{8}$ in. wide, globose, bright orange-red. E. United States. 1899. (S.S. i. t. 59.) SYN. *I. dubia-monticola, I. monticola.* Prinos group. var. **mol'lis,** *l.* softly downy beneath.

**I. op'aca.** American Holly. Evergreen tree 40 to 50 ft., trunk girthing 6 to 9 ft., shoots finely downy. *l.* dull green above, yellowish beneath, oval, $1\frac{1}{2}$ to $3\frac{1}{2}$ in. long, half as wide, armed with broad spine-tipped teeth. *Male fl.* 3 to 9 in slender-stalked axillary cymes. *fr.* globose, red, $\frac{1}{4}$ in. across, usually solitary. United States. 1774. (S.S. i. t. 45.) var. **xanthocarp'a,** *fr.* yellow. 1901.

**I. paraguarien'sis.** Evergreen tree, 15 ft. or more. *l.* obovate or oval, coarsely and shallowly toothed especially towards the apex, leathery, 2 to 5 in. long, 1 to $2\frac{1}{2}$ in. wide. *fl.* in axillary stalked clusters, green, $\frac{1}{4}$ in. wide. *fr.* $\frac{1}{5}$ in. wide. (B.M. 3992.) This is the famous Brazilian tree from whose l. an infusion is made by pouring boiling water over them, making the extraordinarily popular beverage known as Paraguay, Maté or Yerba Tea. The tree has no horticultural interest.

**I. pedunculo'sa.** Evergreen glabrous shrub or small tree, 20 to 30 ft. *l.* $1\frac{1}{2}$ to 3 in. long, about half as wide, ovate or oval, slender-pointed, not toothed, dark glossy green. *fl.* in slender-stalked cymes. *fr.* bright red, $\frac{1}{4}$ in. wide; stalk 1 to $1\frac{1}{2}$ in. long. Japan. 1893. var. **continenta'lis,** *l.* 4 or 5 in. long, stouter, inconspicuously toothed when young, cal. ciliate. Both are distinct by the long fr.-stalks.

**I. Pera'do.** Evergreen tree of medium size. *l.* 3 to 5 in. long, half as wide, oval, ovate, or obovate, sometimes entire, sometimes sparsely toothed, dark glossy green, and leathery. *fr.* deep red, roundish-oval, $\frac{1}{3}$ in. wide, clustered in the l.-axils, each on a stalk about $\frac{1}{3}$ in. long. No doubt one parent of some of the large-leaved garden vars. Canary Isles, Azores. 1760. Distinguished from common holly by its distinctly winged l.-stalk and shorter teeth.

**I. Per'nyi.*** Evergreen small tree up to 30 ft., or a shrub, young shoots minutely downy. *l.* densely set, $\frac{5}{8}$ to 2 in. long, $\frac{3}{8}$ to 1 in. wide, quadrangular-ovate with a long triangular apex and 1 to 3 spines on each side, brilliant black-green. *fl.* pale yellow. *fr.* stalkless or nearly so, red, roundish-oblong, $\frac{1}{4}$ in. wide. China. 1900. (G.C. 45 (1909), 75.) var. **Veitch'ii,** *l.* larger, $1\frac{1}{2}$ to 2 in. long, with 4 or 5 rigid spines each side.

**I. platyphyl'la.** Evergreen tree, 30 ft. and upwards. *l.* 3 to 6 in. long, 2 to $3\frac{1}{2}$ in. wide, very stout and stiff, broadly oval, pointed, spiny on the margins or entire, dullish dark green. *fr.* deep red, $\frac{3}{8}$ in. wide. Canary Is. 1760. The type may not be in cultivation now

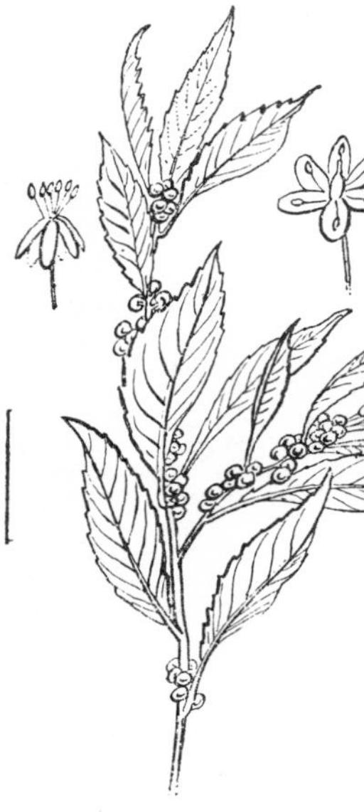

*Ilex verticillata*

and is probably rather tender, but it and *I. Perado* have hybridized with *I. Aquifolium* and given birth to the large, dullish-leaved garden varieties like *atrovirens, balearica, maderensis, nigrescens,* &c.

**I. rugo'sa.** Low, spreading, sometimes prostrate evergreen shrub. *l.* narrowly ovate-oblong to lanceolate, $\frac{3}{4}$ to 2 in. long, $\frac{3}{8}$ to $\frac{3}{4}$ in. wide, tapering to both ends, glabrous, wrinkled above. *fr.* roundish-oval, $\frac{1}{4}$ in. wide, red, short-stalked. Japan. 1895. Very distinct in habit but suffers too much from late spring frosts to be of value.

**I. serra'ta.** Deciduous shrub, 12 to 15 ft., young shoots downy, *l.* oval, ovate, sometimes obovate, 1 to 3 in. long, $\frac{1}{3}$ to 1 in. wide, finely toothed; soft with minute down at first beneath. *fr.* red, globose, $\frac{1}{6}$ in. wide. Japan. 1893. SYN. *I. Sieboldii.* var. **leucocarp'a,** *fr.* white, *l.* shorter and broader; **xanthocarp'a,** *fr.* yellow.

**I. verticilla'ta.*** Deciduous shrub 5 to 10 ft., of spreading growth; shoots glabrous. *l.* oval, obovate, or lanceolate, tapered at both ends, $1\frac{1}{2}$ to 3 in. long, $\frac{1}{2}$ to 1 in. wide, shallowly, often doubly, toothed, downy on veins beneath. *fl.* several in l.-axils. *fr.* red, globose, $\frac{1}{4}$ in. wide. Eastern N. America. 1793. (B.M. 8832.) SYN. *Prinos verticillatus.* var. **chrysocarp'a,** *fr.* yellow.

**I. vomito'ria.** Cassina. Evergreen shrub or small tree up to 25 ft., shoots downy. *l.* $\frac{1}{2}$ to $1\frac{1}{2}$ in. long, half as wide, oval to ovate-oblong, slightly toothed, glabrous; stalk $\frac{1}{12}$ to $\frac{1}{8}$ in. long. *fr.* $\frac{1}{5}$ in. wide, scarlet, globose. SE. United States. 1700. (S.S. i. t. 48.) SYN. *I. Cassine* (of Walter, not Linn.)

**I. yunnanen'sis.** Evergreen shrub, 10 to 12 ft., shoots densely downy. *l.* $\frac{3}{4}$ to $1\frac{1}{4}$ in. long, about half as wide, ovate, rounded at base, pointed, bluntly toothed, brownish-red when young, afterwards bright green. *fr.* $\frac{1}{4}$ in. wide, red. China. 1901. Akin to *I. crenata.*

W. J. B.

***ilicifo'lius -a -um,*** with holly-like leaves.

***ilici'nus -a -um,*** holly-like.

**ILLAWARRA PALM.** *See* **Archontophoenix Cunninghamiana.**

**ILLAWARRA PINE.** *See* **Callitris cupressiformis.**

**A**

***illecebro'sus -a -um,*** alluring, charming.

**ILLECEB'RUM** (*illecebra*, attraction, charm). FAM. *Caryophyllaceae.* A genus of a single species. *I. verticillatum* is a hardy, glabrous, much-branched annual needing a moist peat soil, native of the warmer parts of Britain, &c.

**I. verticilla'tum.** Annual, 1 to 3 in. h. *l.* opposite, obovate, green. *fl.* shining white, in axillary whorls. Summer. W. Europe, including Britain, N. Africa.

**ILLIC'IUM** (*illicium*, allurement; in allusion to the enticing aromatic odour of the plants). FAM. *Magnoliaceae.* Anise Trees. A genus of about 20 species of evergreen shrubs, natives of E. and S. Asia, Malay States, and S. United States. Leaves alternate, leathery, entire. Flowers axillary, usually solitary; petals numerous (up to 30). Fruit a star-shaped ring of 1-seeded carpels. *I. floridanum* and *I. anisatum* are hardy only in the milder counties. They like a light moist loam to which peat may be added. Propagated by layers or cuttings.

**I. anisa'tum.** Star Anise. Shrub or small tree; wood and l. very aromatically fragrant. *l.* 2 to 4 in. long, $\frac{3}{4}$ to $1\frac{1}{2}$ in. wide, narrowly oval to lanceolate, cuneate, shortly stalked, apex blunt. *fl.* 1 to $1\frac{1}{2}$ in. wide, crowded, axillary; pet. up to 30, linear, $\frac{1}{8}$ in. wide, pointed, pale greenish-yellow, not fragrant. Japan, Formosa. 1790. (B.M. 3961.) SYN. *I. religiosum.* A form with variegated l. has been offered (var. **fol. var.**).

**I. florida'num.** Aniseed Tree. Evergreen shrub 6 to 10 ft. *l.* 3 to 5 in. long, 1 to 2 in. wide, narrowly oval to lanceolate, tapered to both ends, glabrous. *fl.* 2 in. across, solitary in several of the terminal l.-axils, each on a slender stalk 1 to 2 in. long, nodding; pet. 20 to 30, maroon-purple, linear to narrow-lanceolate. May. *fr.* about 1 in. across. SE. United States. 1771. (B.M. 439.)

**I. religio'sum.** A synonym of *I. anisatum.*

**I. ve'rum.** Star Anise. Small evergreen tree. *l.* oblanceolate to narrowly elliptic, cuneate, abruptly tapered to a blunt or pointed apex, glabrous, 4 to 6 in. long, 1 to 2 in. wide; stalk about $\frac{1}{2}$ in. long. *fl.* $\frac{5}{8}$ in. wide, very shortly stalked, globose and only about $\frac{3}{8}$ in. wide on account of the 10 ciliolate sep. and pet. being very concave, pink outside, red inside, but the colour is scarcely seen. S. China. 1883. (B.M. 7005.) Warm greenhouse.

W. J. B.

***illini'tus -a -um,*** smeared or smirched.

***illus'tris -is -e,*** bright, brilliant.

*ilven'sis -is -e,* of Elba (Ilva being the ancient name).

**IMAGO** (pl. *imagines*). The mature, usually winged stage of an insect, e.g. butterfly, beetle, wasp.

**IMANTOPHYL′LUM.** A synonym of Clivia.

*imber′bis -is -e,* without hairs, beardless.

*imbrica′tus -a -um,* imbricate, overlapping each other, like tiles.

*imereti′nus -a -um,* of Imeretie, W. Caucasus.

*immacula′tus -a -um,* without spots.

*immargina′tus -a -um,* immarginate, having no rim or edge.

**IMMORTELLES.** *See* **Everlastings.**

**IMMUNITY.** Plants of the same species may differ very much in their susceptibility or resistance to disease. This susceptibility or resistance depends on a definite genetic character transmitted by heredity according to Mendel's law. Plants completely resistant to certain diseases are spoken of as 'immune' and the immunity prevails despite heavy infection or poor growing conditions, but although a plant may be immune to one disease it may not necessarily be immune to another. The selection of immune plants is a valuable method of combating diseases but they frequently lack the most desirable qualities of fruit, flower, &c., and it is the work of plant breeders to endeavour to improve these qualities in resistant plants. A good example of immunity to disease is that of Potato varieties immune to Wart disease, the destructive effect of which was avoided by the discovery and development of such varieties.

D. E. G.

*impar,* unequal.

**imparipinnate,** pinnate but having an odd or terminal leaflet, unequally pinnate.

**IMPA′TIENS** (*impatiens,* impatient; in allusion to the elastic valves of the seed-pod which bring about the violent discharge of the seed when ripe). FAM. *Balsaminaceae.* A genus of about 500 species of annual or biennial herbs or sub-shrubs, natives mostly of the mountains of Asia and Africa, and rarely of Europe, N. America, N. Asia, and S. Africa. Stem often with swollen nodes, brittle, succulent, and hollow. Leaves usually alternate. Branches many-flowered, peduncles axillary; flowers purple, yellow, pink, or white, often showy; petals 4, outer 2 alternate with sepals, upper one arched and with a terminal notch, lower one spurred at base. Fruit a many-seeded capsule with elastic valves which when ripe at the slightest touch roll up inwards with great suddenness, scattering the seeds in every direction. Comparatively few of the species are now in cultivation though many are worthy of a place in our gardens. The hardy annuals are easily raised from seed and grow well in any ordinary good soil, some needing a moist place. The stove and greenhouse species are also easily raised from seed but can also be propagated by cuttings which usually root easily in a close frame. *I. Balsamina* needs the usual treatment of a tender annual (*see also* **Balsam**). *I. Sultani* succeeds in the cool greenhouse or in a window in summer, but needs a higher temperature such as an intermediate or warm house can afford in winter. Cuttings of strong, healthy shoots root quickly in the propagating frame at almost any season. They are best put singly into small pots and afterwards somewhat restricted at the roots by being given only small shifts, pots of 5 or 6 in. being large enough for the final potting and capable of carrying very decorative plants, using a rich open soil. *I. flaccida* and *I. Holstii* succeed under the same treat-

ment. The dwarf *I. Jerdoniae* needs special treatment. It should be planted in a basket in April in a compost of peat and loam and be suspended in a moist stove temperature until it begins to flower, when it should be removed to a drier position. In November, when the leaves drop and the stems swell, the plants should be hung near the glass in a house with a rather dry atmosphere of about 55° F., and should there remain quite dormant until the following April.

A

*Impatiens amphorata*

**I. amphora′ta.** Annual of 3 to 6 ft. Stem succulent, branched above. *l.* elliptic-ovate or lanceolate, 3 to 6 in. long, finely roundish-toothed, bright green, edges and midrib often pink. *fl.* pale purple-tinged and speckled rose-red, 1¼ in. long; sep. greenish, broadly roundish-heart-shaped, acute; standard orbicular, spurred behind; lip cylindrical-saccate, tip rounded with a red incurved spur ¾ in. long; lateral lobes rounded, pendulous, obtuse; racemes terminal, 2 to 5 in. long, many-fld. August, September. W. Himalaya. (B.M. 6550.) Hardy.

**I. Balfour′ii.** Glabrous perennial, slender, branched, 2 to 3 ft. h. *l.* ovate-lanceolate, 3 to 5 in. long, with a long point, teeth many, minute, recurved but not glandular. *fl.* rose and yellow in a loose terminal raceme; sep. nearly orbicular, small, white tinged rose; wings pale yellow on basal lobe, bright rose on end lobe; lip 1¼ in. long, spur somewhat incurved, blunt, horn-like. Summer. W. Himalaya. (B.M. 7878.) Tender.

**I. Balsami′na.\*** Balsam. Annual, about 18 in. h. *l.* oblong-oval, deeply toothed; stalks glandular. *fl.* red, large; standard rounded; wings very broad, terminal lobe sessile, large, side lobe rounded; lip small, cone-shaped, spur incurved of variable length. India, Malaya, China. 1596. (B.M. 1256 as *I. coccinea.*) SYN. *Balsamina hortensis.* Variable in stature, form of leaf, size and colour of fls., both in the wild and in its cultivated forms, of which at present the best known is **camelliaeflo′ra,** with large double fls. of various colours both self and spotted. Tender. *See* **Balsam.**

**I. biflo′ra.** Annual of 2 to 3 ft. *l.* ovate or oval, coarsely toothed; stalked. *fl.* orange, thickly spotted reddish-brown in loose panicles at ends of branches, drooping on slender pedicels; spur strongly inflexed, longer than broad, acutely cone-shaped. July to October. N. America, naturalized along rivers in Britain. (E.B. 314 as *I. fulva.*) Hardy annual for moist shady places. Frequently produces cleistogamous fl., sometimes only those.

**I. can′dida.** A variety of *I. Roylei.*

**I. chinen′sis.** Annual of about 2 ft. *l.* opposite, lanceolate, bristly toothed, sessile. *fl.* red, solitary or twin in l.-axils; spur long, very slender. July, August. India. 1840. (B.M. 4631 as *I. fasciculata.*) SYN. *I. setacea.* Greenhouse.

**I. cornig′era.** A synonym of *I. Roylei.*

**I. fascicula′ta.** A synonym of *I. chinensis.*

**I. flac′cida.** Glabrous annual of 6 to 18 in. *l.* dark shining green, ovate or lanceolate, 2 to 5 in. long; stalked. *fl.* rose-purple, flat, about 2 in. long, usually solitary; sep. ovate; standard broad, spurred, 2-lobed; wings broad, 2-lobed; lip boat-shaped, spur 1¼ in. long, slender, curved. India, Ceylon. 1861. (B.M. 5276 and a purple-fld. form B.M. 5625 as *I. latifolia.*) var. **al′ba,** *fl.* white. Greenhouse.

**I. ful′va.** A synonym of *I. biflora.*

**I. glandulif′era, I. glandulig′era.** Synonyms of *I. Roylei.*

**I. grandiflo'ra.** Stout, glabrous, branching perennial. *l.* ovate-lanceolate, 3 to 6 in. long, with wavy margin and wrinkles between veins; lower part of blade and stalk glandular. *fl.* bright rose-red with crimson stripes on wings, about 3 in. across, solitary; sep. green, roundish-ovate; standard roundish, erect, shortly spurred below tip; lip 1¾ in. long, swollen, white, netted purple with an abrupt incurved spur 1 in. or more long; wings very large. Madagascar. (B.M. 7826.) Stove.

**I. Hawk'eri.** Herbaceous, branched, up to 2 ft. h. Stems dull red. *l.* opposite or ternate, ovate, 4½ in. long, sharply toothed; shortly stalked. *fl.* brownish-red, large, very showy, solitary or in corymbs in l.-axils, about 3 in. across; sep. and pet. broad, side lobes oblong, claws white with blue markings; spur red, recurved, 3 in. long. Summer, autumn. Sunda Is. 1886. (B.M. 8247.) Intermediate house.

**I. Herzog'ii.** Stout branching, glabrous herb with 4-angled green stems. *l.* opposite near base, in whorls of 5 to 7 above, ovate to ovate-lanceolate, 2½ to 5½ in. long, long-pointed, toothed, sometimes ciliate near base; stalk with awl-shaped glands at base. *fl.* numerous, axillary, scarlet, 1½ to 2¼ in. across, spur very slender, 2 to 2¾ in. long, red, incurved. New Guinea. 1909. (B.M. 8396.) Warm house or stove. Near *I. Hawkeri. See* **I. × kewensis.**

**I. Hols'tii.*** Much like *I. Sultani.* Nearly glabrous, sub-shrubby, branched, 2 to 3 ft. h., branches striped red. *l.* ovate to lanceolate, acute, the rounded teeth with a bristle between. *fl.* scarlet, 1¾ in. across, flat, solitary or twin on the peduncles; sep. 3, lateral small, scale-like; standard broadly obcordate; lateral pet. deeply 2-lobed, lobes obovate-spatulate; spur slender, 1½ in. long. Summer. E. Trop. Africa. (B.M. 8029.) Cultivation as for *I. Sultani*, than which it is more vigorous with larger, brighter fls. var. **Liegnitzia'na,** more compact, free flowering with a clearer colour than in type. Excellent pot plant; may be grown outdoors in summer. A hybrid with *I. Sultani* (**I. × Holstanii**) is known. *See also* **I. × kewensis.**

**I. Hookeria'na.** Perennial up to 3 ft. h., much-branched. Stem fleshy. *l.* ovate-lanceolate, large, toothed, pale-green; stalk long. *fl.* large, white streaked purple on the large lower pet., 3- to 6-fld. peduncles from axils of upper l.; spur longer than fl., bent, horn-shaped. Autumn, winter. Ceylon. 1852. (B.M. 4704.) Stove.

**I. javen'sis.** Hairy annual (?) related to *I. chinensis* but stems creeping, branched. *l.* ovate, acuminate, toothed, glaucous beneath, acute at base. *fl.* solitary in l.-axils; peduncles as long as l.; spur long. All year. High mts. of Java.

**I. Jerdon'iae.** Annual about 9 in. h. *l.* oval, near upper part of gouty stems. *fl.* large, in clusters of 6 to 8 in. l.-axils; sep. green, lateral pet. bright yellow; lip bright red. Summer. E. Indies. 1852. (B.M. 4739.) See introduction. Stove.

**I.×kewen'sis** (*I. Herzogii*×*I. Holstii*). Intermediate between parents.

**I. Maria'nae.** Annual. Stem thickish, hairy. *l.* oblong-wedge-shaped, acute, deep green, paler between veins. *fl.* light purple, rather large, in cymes; standard with a hairy ridge up to a projection about one-third below top; lip with a longish, slender, hooked spur. June. Assam. 1881. Greenhouse.

**I. mira'bilis.** Curious in habit with a thick trunk up to 4 ft. h. and 7 or 8 in. through in its native country. *l.* tufted at apex of stem, ovate, about 12 in. long, fleshy, crenate. *fl.* golden-yellow, very large, curiously inflated, axillary; lateral pet. coalescing in 1. August. Langkawi Is. 1891. (B.M. 7195.) Warm house.

**I. Noli-tange're.** Touch-me-not. Annual of about 18 in. *l.* ovate, coarsely toothed. *fl.* yellow spotted red within, large; peduncles 3- or 4-fld. July. Europe, including Britain, Siberia, W. Asia. (E.B. 313.) Syn. *I. Noli-me-tangere.* Hardy. Plant for moist places.

**I. Oliver'i.** Glabrous perennial of 4 to 8 ft., bushy, up to 10 ft. through. Stems pale green. *l.* in whorls of 4 to 8, oblanceolate, up to 8 in. long, more or less acute, toothed-ciliate. *fl.* pale lilac or rose, up to 2½ in. across, almost white without on 1-fld. peduncles about 2½ in. long; lateral sep. ovate, much shorter than pet.; lip ovate, funnel-shaped, abruptly short-pointed; spur slender, 1¾ in. long, curved. Trop. E. Africa. (B.M. 7960.) Cool greenhouse or outdoors in summer.

**I. Petersia'na.** Much like *I. Holstii*, but reddish-brown or bronzy in all parts, l.-blade, and stalk, peduncles and pedicels longer. Stem hairy. *l.* elliptic. *fl.* carmine-red; pet. entire. W. Trop. Africa. (R.H. 1910, 452.)

**I. platypet'ala.** Annual of about 18 in. h. or more. Stem stout, succulent, branched, usually reddish-purple. *l.* in whorls, oblong-lanceolate, sharply toothed, hairy beneath. *fl.* rose, large, on 1-fld. axillary peduncles shorter than l.; spur very slender, sickle-shaped. Summer. Java. 1844. (B.R. 32, 68.)

**I. Roy'lei.** Annual of 6 to 8 ft. Stem stout, succulent, branched. *Lower l.* opposite; *upper* whorled, all ovate or ovate-lanceolate, about 4 in. long, sharply toothed. *fl.* dark purple on 3- to 6-fld. peduncles in axils of upper l., very numerous; standard 2-lobed; wings broad; lip saccate, very obtuse; spur short. August. India. 1839. Naturalized here and there in Britain. (B.M. 4020 and B.R. 26, 22 as *I. glandulifera.*) Hardy. var. **can'dida,** *fl.* white, more or less spotted crimson. (B.R. 27, 20 as *I. candida.*); **macrochi'la,** *upper l.* alternate, stalks glandular, *fl.* rose. 1838. (B.R. 26, 8 as *I. macrochila.*); **moscha'ta,** *l.* coarse-toothed, only slightly glandular. Syn. *I. moschata*; **pallidiflo'ra,** *l.* 6 to 8 in. long, *fl.* pale pink spotted red, larger than in type. (B.M. 7647.); **White Queen,** *fl.* white or almost so.

**I. scab'rida.** Annual of 2 to 3 ft. Stem purplish, slightly angled. *l.* lanceolate, toothed, slender-pointed, hairy. *fl.* yellow with minute purple dots; peduncles 2- to 6-fld. July. India. 1827. (B.M. 4051; B.R. 26, 9 as *I. tricornis.*) Hardy.

**I. seta'cea.** A synonym of *I. chinensis.*

**I. Sulta'ni.*** Glabrous, erect, branched perennial, 12 to 24 in. h., branches rather succulent, green. *l.* elliptic or lanceolate, narrowed to a stalk about 1 in. long, lower l. alternate, upper usually whorled; all stalked. *fl.* scarlet, large, flat; standard obovate to roundish, rather smaller than other pet.; lateral pet. cleft to base into 2 equal lobes; lip with a long, slender, curved spur. Flowering almost continuously. Zanzibar. (B.M. 6643.) var. **Epis'copi,** *fl.* rich purple carmine shot brilliant rose. 1896. A good pot plant. *See* introduction, and *see also* **I. Holstii.**

**impatient,** sometimes used of plants which cannot withstand an excess of any condition, as impatient of drought or of over-watering.

***impedi'tus -a -um,*** tangled.

**IMPERA'TA.** A synonym of Miscanthus.

***Impera'ti,*** in honour of Ferrante Imperato, apothecary in Naples, 1550–1625.

***impera'tor,*** Emperor.

**IMPERATO'RIA.** A synonym of Peucedanum.

***Imperatric'is,*** in honour of the Empress Josephine.

**imperfect,** of flowers lacking either stamens or pistils.

***imperia'lis -is -e*** very noble.

***implex'us -a -um,*** tangled or interlaced.

***impo'nens,*** deceptive.

***impres'sus -a -um,*** sunken, as veins may be.

***impudi'cus -a -um,*** immodest.

***Imray'i,*** in honour of Dr. Imray who collected in the island of Dominica.

***Imschootia'nus -a -um,*** in honour of Herr A. van Imschoot of Ghent, Belgium, *c.* 1895.

***in-,*** in compound words signifying not, as *inermis,* not armed.

***inaequa'lis -is -e*** (*inaequi-,* in compound words), unequal.

**INARCHING.** *See* **Grafting.**

***Inaya'tii,*** in honour of Khan Inayat, Mr. Duthie's chief plant-collector who discovered many new plants in N. India, *c.* 1897.

***inca'nus -a -um,*** quite grey.

***incarna'tus -a -um,*** flesh-coloured.

**INCARVIL'LEA** (in honour of Pierre d'Incarville, 1706–57, French Missionary in China and botanical correspondent of the great French botanist Bernard de Jussieu). Fam. *Bignoniaceae.* A genus of about 6 species of erect glabrous perennials with usually pinnate leaves and terminal clusters of large 2-lipped, tubular flowers, differing from Amphicome by the awl-shaped calyx segments and the winged seeds (calyx in Amphicome truncate or shortly toothed, seeds surrounded by a ring of hairs or a narrow fringe). Corolla lobes 5, broad, spreading, stamens 4, included. Fruit a capsule opening on one side only. Hardy or nearly so in light warm soils which are deep, rich, and well drained, for stagnant moisture in winter is fatal to their well-being. Protection by a covering of bracken is worth while in winter. Propagated by seed or division. Seedlings take about 3 years to reach flowering size.

**I. brev'ipes.** A variety of *I. grandiflora*.

**I. compac'ta.** Habit usually compact. *l.* unequally pinnate, fleshy, segs. short, ovate-acute. *fl.* bright rose-pink, about 2½ in. long, funnel-shaped. Summer. NW. China. 1881. (G.F. 1068.) Very shy to flower.

*Incarvillea Delavay*

**I. Delava'yi.\*** Stem very short, scarcely branched or not. *l.* few, radical, 12 to 18 in. long, pinnate; lflets. 6 to 8, rather distant, 4 to 5 in. long, toothed, dark green. *Scape* sometimes 3 ft. h. on old plants. *fl.* 3 to 13, bright rose-red, tube 3 in. long, decurved, limb 3 to 3½ in. across. May, June. W. China, Tibet. 1893. (B.M. 7462.) var. **Bees' Pink,** *fl.* pale pink.

**I. grandiflo'ra.** Dwarfer than *I. Delavayi* with shorter, rounder lflets., entire or nearly so. *Scapes* shorter, with 1 or 2 fl. *fl.* rich rose-red, nearly 4 in. across, yellow in tube, blotched white in throat. May, June. W. China. 1898. var. **brev'ipes,** pedicels much shorter than peduncles, *fl.* brilliant crimson.

**I. lu'tea.** *l.* mostly radical, pinnate, 8 to 15 in. long, stalks long; lflets. broadly lanceolate, toothed. *Scapes* stout, 2 to 4 ft. long, 6- to 20-fld. *fl.* yellow, limb paler than tube, 2 in. across. June. SW. China. 1910. (G.C. 50 (1911) suppl. Aug. 19.)

**I. Ol'gae.** Somewhat shrubby, 2 to 4½ ft. h. *l.* opposite, pinnate, 2 to 4 in. long; lflets. narrow-oblong, pinnatifid. *fl.* in loose clusters on short stalks, pale pink, about 1 in. long, 1 in. across, bell-funnel-shaped. Summer. Turkestan. 1880. (B.M. 6593.)

**I. sinen'sis.** 1 to 2 ft. h. *l.* alternate, 2- or 3-pinnate with narrow segs. *fl.* in loose terminal racemes, nearly sessile, large, scarlet or reddish-purple. China. Greenhouse, tender. Best grown as an annual or biennial, flowering quicker than most from seed.

**I. varia'bilis.** Shrubby perennial of about 2 ft. *l.* alternate, 2 to 4 in. long, ovate, pinnate, short-stalked; lflets. in 6 to 8 pairs, lobes entire or slightly divided. *fl.* in loose, erect racemes, bright rose, tube about 1 in. long, slightly curved, limb over 1 in. across. August. W. China. 1898. (B.M. 7651.) Hardy only in warm districts.

**INCENSE.** See **Styrax officinalis.**

*inci'sus -a -um,* incised, having the margins sharply and deeply cut.

**included,** enclosed in anything.

*incompara'bilis, -is -e,* unequalled.

**incomplete,** lacking some part.

*inconspic'uus -a -um,* small.

**incumbent,** lying upon anything, as distinct from accumbent, lying against.

*incurv'us -a -um,* incurved, curved inwards as the rays of some Chrysanthemums.

**indefinite.** (1) In great number; stamens are said to be indefinite when too numerous to count; (2) growth of stem continued by a persistent terminal as in Pines (compare definite growth); (3) an inflorescence with lowest or outermost flowers opening first.

*indehis'cens,* indehiscent; as of a fruit not opening in a definite manner when ripe.

**INDIAN ALMOND.** See **Terminalia Catappa.**

**INDIAN BLUE Waterlily.** See **Nymphaea stellata cyanea.**

**INDIAN BUTTER TREE.** See **Madhuca butyracea.**

**INDIAN CORN.** See **Zea Mays.** For cultivation *see* Supplement under **Sweet Corn.**

**INDIAN CRESS.** See **Tropaeolum majus.**

**INDIAN CUP.** See **Sarracenia.**

**INDIAN CURRANT.** See **Symphoricarpos orbiculatus.**

**INDIAN FIG.** See **Opuntia.**

**INDIAN FLOWERING FERN.** See **Helminthostachys.**

**INDIAN GARLAND FLOWER.** See **Hedychium.**

**INDIAN HAWTHORN.** See **Raphiolepis.**

**INDIAN HILL GUAVA.** See **Rhodomyrtus tomentosa.**

**INDIAN HORSE CHESTNUT.** See **Aesculus indica.**

**INDIAN (or EGYPTIAN) LOTUS.** See **Nymphaea Lotus.**

**INDIAN MALLOW.** See **Sida, Urena.**

**INDIAN MILLET.** See **Panicum miliaceum.**

**INDIAN MULBERRY.** See **Morinda citrifolia.**

**INDIAN PHYSIC.** See **Magnolia Fraseri, Gillenia trifoliata.**

**INDIAN PINK.** See **Dianthus chinensis, Silene californica, Spigelia marilandica.**

**INDIAN RUBBER.** See **Landolphia, Manihot.**

**INDIAN SHOT.** See **Canna indica.**

**INDIARUBBER PLANT.** See **Ficus elastica.**

*in'dicus -a -um,* of India.

**indigenous,** native.

**INDIGOF'ERA** (from *indigo,* a blue dye, *fero,* to bear). FAM. *Leguminosae.* A genus of some 300 species of deciduous shrubs and herbs found in America, Africa, Asia, and Australia, a few hardy or half-hardy, but mostly requiring stove or greenhouse treatment. Comparatively few are in cultivation. Leaves alternate, pinnate, rarely 3-foliolate or simple. Flowers papilionaceous, usually pink or purple, ¼ to ¾ in. long, borne often numerously in slender racemes that spring from the leaf-axils successively, usually between midsummer and October. Several species, especially *I. tinctoria,* yield the dark-blue dye, indigo.

Provided the temperature is suitable they are easily

cultivated in an open well-drained loamy soil and given a sunny position. The genus has in recent years been augmented in gardens by several handsome shrubby species from China, and they, with a few Himalayan species longer known, practically represent the genus under cultivation.

**I. amblyan'tha.** Shrub up to 6 ft., shoots angled, appressed-hairy. *l.* 4 to 5 in. long; lflets. 7 to 11, narrowly oval, ½ to 1½ in. long, downy. *Racemes* 3 to 4½ in. long, erect, slender, borne successively in the l.-axils from June to Oct. *fl.* ¼ in. long, closely packed, pale rose to deep pink. *Pod* 1 to 1¾ in. long, downy. China. 1907.

**I. A'nil.** Erect shrub of 2 to 4 ft. *lflets.* in 3 to 7 pairs, oval or oblong, nearly smooth beneath. *fl.* pinkish in axillary racemes shorter than l. Summer. W. Indies, Trop. America. Before 1731. (B.M. 6506.) Stove.

**I. atropurpu'rea.** Shrub of about 5 ft. *lflets.* in 5 to 10 pairs, oval, retuse, mucronulate, margins wavy. *fl.* dark purple to crimson, in slender, axillary racemes. August. Nepal. 1816. (B.M. 3065; B.R. 1774.) Tender.

**I. austra'lis.*** Shrub of 3 to 4 ft. *lflets.* in 5 to 7 pairs, elliptic-obtuse, glabrous. *fl.* rose, in racemes scarcely as long as l. March to June. Australia. 1790. (B.R. 386; L.B.C. 149; B.R. 991 as *I. angulosa*; B.M. 3000 as *I. sylvatica.*) Greenhouse. A good pot plant of neat habit.

**I. deco'ra.*** Shrub 1 to 1½ ft., shoots slender, reddish-brown. *l.* 4 to 6 in. long, with 7 to 13 lflets. which are ovate-lanceolate to oval, bristle-tipped, 1 to 2½ in. long, slightly downy beneath. *Racemes* erect, axillary, 6 in. long, carrying 20 to 40 fl., each ⅝ to ¾ in. long; standard pet. white, with pale crimson near the base; wing pet. pink. July, August. China, Japan. 1845. Very charming but tender, cut back to ground level in winter. (B.M. 5063.) var. **al'ba,** *fl.* white (G. and F. 7, 375).

**I. Dielsia'na.** Shrub 3 to 5 ft., shoots angled. *l.* 2½ to 5 in. long; lflets. 7 to 11, oval-oblong to obovate, bristle-tipped, ½ to ⅞ in. long, appressed-downy above and beneath. *Racemes* 5 to 6 in. h., slender, closely set with fl., each nearly ½ in. long, pale rose; cal. and pet. downy. China. 1906.

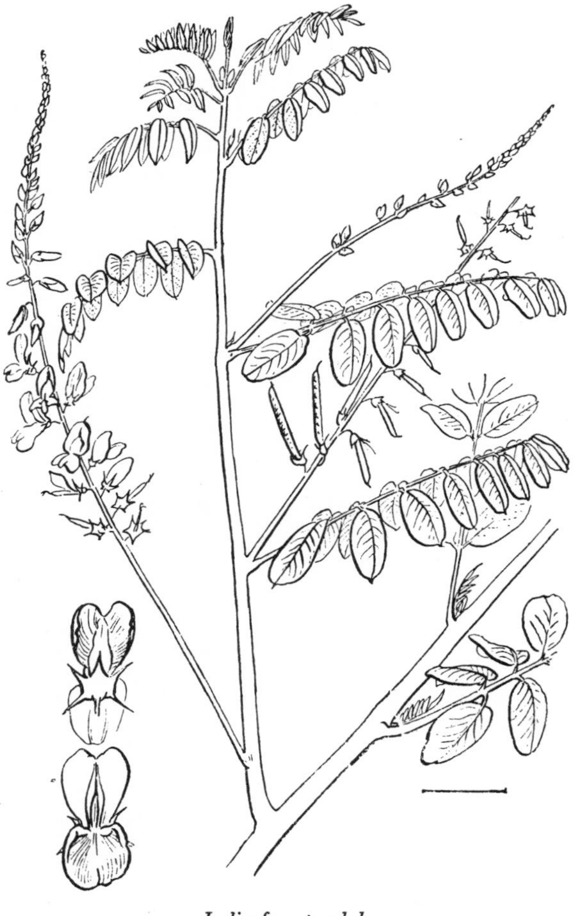

*Indigofera pendula.*

**I. Dos'ua.** About 18 in. h. *lflets.* in 10 to 15 pairs, oval, retuse, mucronulate, covered, like branches, with reddish-brown hairs. *fl.* bright red, in axillary racemes shorter than l. Summer. India. Greenhouse. This name is sometimes applied to *I. Gerardiana*, a hardier plant. Variable in habit. var. **stric'ta,** more erect. *fl.* violet-red.

**I. Gerardia'na.*** Shrub up to 8 ft. in mild localities but cut back to ground level in colder ones and then 2 to 4 ft. h. *l.* 2 to 4 in. long with 13 to 21 lflets. each about ½ in. long, obovate or oval, with appressed grey hairs beneath. *Racemes* axillary, borne successively from June to September, 3 to 5 in. long, with 20 to 30 fl., each ½ in. long, rosy-purple. Himalaya. 1840. (B.R. 28, 57 as *I. Dosua.*) Graceful and attractive at its best.

**I. hebepet'ala.** Shrub about 4 ft. in open ground, but considerably taller in mild climates where it is not cut back to ground level in winter. *l.* 7 to 9 in. long; lflets. 5 to 11, broadly oval, 1 to 2½ in. long, apex rounded, appressed-hairy beneath. *Racemes* 3 to 9 in. long, bearing 20 to 60 fl., each ½ to ⅝ in. long; standard dark crimson, wing pet. and keel. August, September. Himalaya. Before 1881. (B.M. 8208.)

**I. Kirilow'i.** Shrub 3 ft. or more. *l.* 4 to 6 in. long with 7 to 11 lflets. which are broadly oval, roundish, or obovate, bristle-tipped, ½ to 1¼ in. long. *Racemes* axillary, erect, 4 to 6 in. long. *fl.* 20 to 30 crowded on the terminal half, rose with dark spots at base of standard pet., ¾ in. long. June, July. China, Korea. 1899. (B.M. 8580.)

**I. pen'dula.*** Shrub of spreading habit, 8 to 10 ft. *l.* 8 to 10 in. long; lflets. 19 to 27, oblong to oval, ¾ to 1¼ in. long, appressed-hairy beneath. *Racemes* pendulous, slender, 10 to 18 in. long, springing from l.-axils successively during August, September. *fl.* ⅓ to ½ in. long, rosy-purple, closely set at 6 or 8 to the inch. *Pod* 2 in. long. China. 1914. (B.M. 8745.)

**I. Potanin'ii.** Shrub 4 to 6 ft. *l.* 3 to 6 in. long with 5 to 9 lflets. which are oval, ovate, or oblong, ½ to 1¼ in. long, appressed-hairy beneath. *fl.* rosy-pink, ⅜ in. long, in axillary racemes, 2 to 5 in. long; cal. hairy, with 5 awl-shaped lobes. June, July. China. 1911.

**I. pulchel'la.** Shrub of 5 ft. *lflets.* in 5 pairs, obovate-elliptic, flat, slightly hairy. *fl.* purple-red, in axillary racemes longer than l. E. Indies. 1819. (B.M. 3348 as *I. violacea.*) Greenhouse.

**I. tincto'ria.** Sub-shrub of 4 to 6 ft. *lflets.* in 4 to 7 pairs, obovate, hairy beneath. *fl.* with pale standard and red wings and keel, in axillary racemes, shorter than l. July. E. Indies. 1731. Stove. Much grown in warm countries at one time as a source of indigo.

**I. viola'cea.** A synonym of *I. pulchella.*

W. J. B.

***indivi'sus -a -um,*** undivided.

**INDUMENTUM.** The hairy covering of a plant of whatever kind.

**induplicate,** having the margin bent abruptly inwards and the external faces of the edges applied to each other without twisting.

***indura'tus -a -um,*** hard.

**INDUSIUM.** The membranous covering arising above or below the sporangia in ferns.

***ine'brians,*** to make drunk.

***iner'mis -is -e,*** unarmed; destitute of spines or prickles.

***infecto'rius -a -um,*** dyed.

**inferior,** growing below some organ, as the ovary when the calyx, petals, and stamens take their rise above it. (Cf. superior.)

***infes'tus -a -um,*** troublesome.

***infla'tus -a -um,*** puffed up.

**INFLORESCENCE.** The arrangement of the flowers on the flower-stem.

***infortuna'tus -a -um,*** poisonous.

***infra-,*** in compound words, signifying below.

***infrac'tus,*** curved inwards.

**infundibuliform,** funnel-shaped.

**ING'A** (native name of one species in W. Indies). FAM. *Leguminosae*. A genus of about 160 species of unarmed trees and shrubs, related to Calliandra, natives of the warmer parts of S. America, especially Brazil and Guiana. Distinct from Acacia by the united stamens. Leaves abruptly pinnate, with 2 to 5 pairs of rather large leaflets, usually with glands between them. Flowers not papilionaceous, in heads, spikes, racemes, or umbels, from the leaf-axils, usually white or yellowish; stamens many, in one bundle, exserted. Pod narrow, more or less completely indehiscent. Stove conditions and a compost of peat and loam suit them and abundance of water is needed during the summer months but scarcely any in winter.

**I. dul'cis.** A synonym of *Pithecolobium dulce*.

**I. Harris'ii.** A synonym of *Calliandra Harrisii*.

**I. pulcher'rima.** A synonym of *Calliandra Tweediei*.

**I. puncta'ta.** Small tree. *lflets.* in 2 or 3 pairs, oblong, slender-pointed, shining. *l.* and shoots glabrous, shoots warted. *fl.* in axillary spikes on twin peduncles; *cor.* silky hairy. Venezuela, Brazil.

**INJECTION.** A modern method used for treating trees which develop non-parasitic nutritional disorders, such as Chlorosis (in which the leaves become sickly and generally appear yellow or yellowish-white), due to a deficiency of some essential chemical element. The injection is done by boring holes in different places in the trunk or branches after which a glass tube is placed in the hole and sealed round. A rubber tube connects this glass tube to a container placed higher up from which flows a supply of the missing substance into the trunk; for instance, iron can be supplied by a weak solution of ferric chloride. Another way is to insert the iron as a powder, this being done by placing powdered ferric citrate into the holes and plugging them with grafting wax. Almost all necessary elements can be introduced into trees by these methods.

D. E. G.

**INKBERRY.** *See* **Ilex glabra**.

*innomina'tus -a -um,* unnamed.

**INOCAR'PUS** (*inos*, fibre, *karpos*, fruit; in allusion to the fibrous pericarp). FAM. *Leguminosae*. A genus of 3 species of evergreen trees, natives of the E. Indies and the islands of the Pacific. Leaves simple, leathery, pinnately nerved with very short stalks. Flowers yellow or white, in axillary spikes; calyx tubular; petals 5. Stove treatment is necessary with a compost of loam and peat. Cuttings of half-ripe wood will root in sand.

**I. ed'ulis.** Otaheite Chestnut. Tree of about 20 ft. *l.* alternate. *fl.* white; pet. 5 united into a short tube. Summer. *fr.* a fibrous pod, 1-seeded. Pacific Is. 1793.

**INOCULATION.** Term sometimes used for budding.

**INO'DES.** Included in **Sabal**.

*ino'dorus -a -um,* scentless.

*inophyl'lus -a -um,* fibrous-leaved.

*inopina'tus -a -um,* unexpected.

*in'ops,* poor, deficient.

*in'quinans,* defiled, filthy.

*inscalp'tus -a -um,* cut into, carved.

**INSECTICIDES.** This term is frequently used in its widest sense to include not only substances designed for the destruction of insects but chemicals that are used to destroy related pests, e.g. Red Spider and Gall-mites (Acaricides), Woodlice and Millepedes, and even Earthworms (Vermicides) and Slugs and Snails (Molluscicides).

For general purposes, insecticides may be grouped as: (I) Direct or Contact Washes which are used for destroying Sucking Insects (Aphides, Capsid Bugs, Leafhoppers, Scale Insects, Mealy Bugs, and Thrips), and Egg-killing Washes or Ovicides; and (II) Protective Washes or Stomach Poisons for controlling leaf-eating Caterpillars, Beetles (e.g. Chafers), Weevils, and Sawfly larvae, while Poison Baits are employed against Slugs, Woodlice, and the soil-inhabiting Cutworms or Surface Caterpillars and Leatherjackets.

There may appear some overlapping in this classification of insecticides for some may occur in both classes, e.g. nicotine is usually classed as a Contact Poison, but it will act both as a Stomach Poison and as a Repellent: and such chlorinated hydrocarbons as D.D.T. act both as a contact and an internal poison. **A**

An insecticide must destroy the pest without harming the living plant which is its host; the toxic material should be amenable to application in the form of either a solution (e.g. nicotine), suspension (e.g. lead arsenate), or emulsion (e.g. refined petroleum oils), or a powder of sufficiently fine division to allow freedom of 'flow' in the dusting machine; and it should be stable in a concentrated form to avoid loss of toxicity during storage and economical in price.

Developments in the manufacture of insecticides are constantly taking place, and new materials are being investigated with a view to improving field performance of both washes and dusts. In recent years Rotenone as the active principle in such plants as *Derris*, *Lonchocarpus*, and *Tephrosia* (see Fish-poison Plants) has been discovered, with the result that an entirely new group of insecticides has developed, and various organic products have also been produced, including the chlorinated hydrocarbons (D.D.T. or Dichloro-diphenyl-trichlorethane, Gammexane or Benzene hexachloride, and others under chemical formulae, e.g. $C_{10}H_6Cl_8$), Acaricides (e.g. A.B. 30 or Azo-benzene), and Soil Insecticides (e.g. D-D or Dichloropropane-Dichloropropylene), and many others.

The term 'Fumigant' indicates an insecticide applied as a gas, but the use of toxic gases and vapours differs so much in practice from the application of washes and dusts that this group has been dealt with separately (*see* **Fumigation** and under **Insecticides** in Suppl.

Certain insecticides, e.g. arsenate of lead, Paris green, and nicotine, are extremely poisonous to man and animals and should be handled with great caution. Under the Pharmacy and Poisons Act of 1933, and the Poison Rules 1935, amateur gardeners and horticulturists may purchase these poisons only from a chemist's shop, or from a shop of a listed seller of Part II Poisons, and the amateur cannot purchase through the post any of the poisons of which the sale involves the signing of the Poisons Book.

Lists of officially approved insecticides and fungicides are published from time to time in the Ministry of Agriculture's official Journal *Agriculture*, and should be consulted before purchases are made.

(I) CONTACT WASHES are applied chiefly against insects which pierce the tissues of plants and suck the sap or tap the food-conducting channels by means of their needle-like stylets. Owing to this method of feeding it is not possible to poison their food, and it is therefore essential to wet their bodies with the spray fluid to kill them. The so-called Winter and Delayed Dormant egg-killing washes are included in this category, for their aim is to destroy the eggs of insects on deciduous hard-wooded trees and shrubs by applying a cover-wash, so that death follows either as a result of suffocation of the developing embryo or from its caustic action on the shell. Success depends upon thoroughness in application, high pressure, and on the wetting and spreading powers of the wash. Contact washes, other than those with ovicidal properties, should be applied as soon as the pest is observed, especially against those Aphides which are readily controlled before the leaves upon which they feed begin to curl, but are later protected from the action of the insecticide within tightly curled foliage. The wash must be directed to that part of the plant upon which the insects are feeding, and such pests as Leaf-hoppers, Aphides, and Scales tend to congregate upon the lower surface of the leaves so both sides of the leaves must be wetted.

A considerable number of insecticides are more conveniently purchased under proprietary names, and should be obtained only from reliable firms and used strictly according to the manufacturer's instructions. An increasing number of washes are being standardized under the Ministry of Agriculture's scheme for the approval of proprietary products, and must conform to certain standards set up by this official body.

Among the principal Contact Poisons are:

(1) *Nicotine*, a plant alkaloid, which is obtained from the Tobacco plant (*Nicotiana Tabacum*) and is used both in the form of sprays and dusts. The active agent is the vapour, which affects the insect through its breathing-pores and causes paralysis of the nervous system. It is poisonous to men and animals, so that reasonable care must be taken to avoid applying nicotine-containing sprays and dusts either directly or indirectly, as by drip from overhanging branches or drift from powder-dusters, to herbs, salad crops, maturing leaf vegetables, ripening fruit, or to plants in full bloom because of the danger of poisoning pollinating insects. Washes must contain a spreading agent (e.g. soft soap) to ensure the complete wetting of the insect's body. In insecticidal dusts the nicotine is absorbed on a finely divided carrier (e.g. Kaolin) from which, when the dust is applied to the plant in temperatures above 60° F., nicotine is freely volatilized. There are various grades of dust containing 2–4 per cent. nicotine, especially suitable under the right conditions of high temperature, low humidity, and a calm atmosphere for destroying Caterpillars and Sawfly larvae within rolled leaves, Aphides within tightly curled foliage, and Leaf-hoppers occurring on the lower surface of basal leaves where thorough wetting is difficult or impossible to accomplish.

Nicotine-soap washes are used chiefly against Thrips, Capsid Bugs, Leaf-hoppers, Aphides, Scale insects, Mealy Bugs, and Leaf-miners, while nicotine dusts are specially effective in destroying insects sheltered within curled, twisted, and rolled leaves.

(2) *Derris* is one of the Rotenone-containing fish and arrow poison plants and is obtained from the roots of *Derris elliptica* and *D. malaccensis*, the chief sources of which are in the Malay Peninsula. The Derris root is finely ground, and used either as a suspension in water or mixed with a suitable carrier as a dust. Derris extracts or liquid Derris are available, but the instability of these preparations is a disadvantage. Derris preparations are non-poisonous to human beings, and are used to replace nicotine in circumstances where it is inadvisable to use a poisonous wash or dust. Stress is laid upon the toxicity of these preparations to fish, so that the greatest care should be taken that these insecticides do not reach, even in small quantities, rivers, streams, or fish-ponds.

Derris washes and dusts are used against sucking insects, and are effective also in controlling *young* caterpillars on Roses and tender-leaved plants, and especially against Raspberry Beetle outbreaks in cultivated Blackberry, Loganberry, and Raspberry plantations.

(3) *Pyrethrum* insecticides are prepared from the flower-heads of *Chrysanthemum cinerariifolium*, and have the advantage of being non-poisonous to man and warm-blooded animals. The name 'Dalmatian Insect Powder' suggests that formerly supplies were obtained from the Balkans, and this still forms the chief ingredient in household insecticides. The earlier Pyrethrum extracts quickly lost toxicity on exposure, but this has been overcome to a considerable extent though it is inadvisable to buy larger stocks of these preparations than are necessary for a season's requirements. The active principle is Pyrethrin which causes rapid paralysis of the insect. The great advantage of Pyrethrum washes is that they may be applied to ripe fruits and mature vegetables of all kinds, especially against Aphides on ripening Currants and Gooseberry and salad crops, and against Sawfly larvae attacking the foliage of ripening Strawberries, while good control of Red Spider Mite on glasshouse plants is possible with regular applications.

(4) *Quassia* is purchased in the form of wood-chippings from either the Jamaican *Picraena excelsa* or Surinam *Quassia amara*. While extracts used as insecticides are non-poisonous to man, their application to food crops is inadvisable owing to the extremely bitter taste imparted to the sprayed foliage. Against insects Quassia extracts are highly specific, and, while many species do not appear to be affected, others (notably certain species of Aphides and of Sawflies, especially *Hoplocampa* sp.) are readily destroyed. The principle Quassin is extremely slow in its action on insects, which die slowly in a state of coma. Quassia extracts form the basis of bird-repelling washes, and are used to deter birds from injuring the buds of fruit and ornamental trees and shrubs and from devouring coloured fruits and berries.

(5) *Mineral oil emulsions* are more generally known under the name of 'White-oils'. They are highly refined petroleum oils of high boiling-point which, during the refining process, become colourless. These washes are supplied by insecticide manufacturers ready for use and should be diluted strictly according to the maker's instructions. Both Summer and Winter White-oil emulsions are available, the former for use during the growing season, the latter as an egg-killing wash on deciduous fruit-trees. 'White-oils' may be used on a wide range of plants, but should never be applied to glaucous-foliaged plants (e.g. Carnation) since they destroy the 'bloom', nor frequently to such plants as Tomato owing to the danger of Oedema or 'Dropsy' developing on the foliage, while their incompatability with sulphur washes, e.g. lime sulphur, should be borne in mind to avoid leaf and bud injury. They are effective against many pests, chiefly Scales and Mealy Bugs, and Red Spider on glasshouse crops.

(6) *Lime sulphur* and especially liver of sulphur (potassium sulphide) have been used for many years against Red Spider and Gall-mites, and against various scale insects on fruit-trees. Commercial lime sulphurs are readily available, and have replaced the less satisfactory home-made products. The standard required of the commercial product is that it does not contain less than 24 per cent. of dissolved sulphur in the form of polysulphides. Some varieties of fruit, particularly Apples and Gooseberries, are sulphur-shy, and require lower concentrations to avoid injury to fruits and foliage, while certain varieties are too intolerant to allow even one application of lime sulphur.

With contact washes it is necessary to distinguish between those preparations which are applied during the period of active growth and those applied during the dormant season. The former group has already been discussed, and the latter, more generally known as *Winter washes*, will now receive consideration.

*Winter washes* may be conveniently divided into those possessing cleansing powers only (e.g. caustic soda), which can destroy mosses, lichens, and algae on trees; those with cleansing and feebly ovicidal powers (e.g. lime sulphur and lime washes); and those with cleansing and strongly ovicidal properties (e.g. tar oils and petroleum oils with or without the addition of dinitro-ortho-cresol and organic thiocyanates). Some egg-killing washes are specific in their action upon the eggs of insects and mites. For instance, tar oils, though effective against the eggs of Aphides, Psyllids, and some other fruit pests, are ineffective against the eggs of Red Spider Mites, and only feebly effective against those of Capsid Bugs and Moths, and winter petroleum washes do not kill the eggs of some fruit-infesting species of Aphides or of Psylla, but are invaluable against those of the fruit-tree Red Spider Mite.

The successful control of fruit pests during the dormant season by means of ovicidal washes will depend upon the thoroughness in application and high pressure to ensure the wetting of all parts of the trees. Ovicides are applied chiefly to fruit-trees and bushes, and have a limited use in the flower garden, though they may be applied to deciduous trees and shrubs, and to Roses at concentrations not exceeding 5 per cent.

(7) *Tar oils* should bear a specification approved by the Ministry of Agriculture and the Association of British Insecticide Manufacturers, and should be applied only during the season of dormancy otherwise severe bud injury may result. Concentrated washes should be diluted to 5 per cent. for Soft and Stone fruits for application in December and to 7–8 per cent. on Apples and Pears, while 10 per cent. concentrations are occasionally recommended for cleaning neglected Apple-trees of mosses and lichens and in severe attacks of Woolly Aphis and Bark Beetles. Miscible tar oils are unsuitable for use with very hard and saline waters, and stock emulsions should be substituted.

(8) *D.N.O.C.* or *D.N.C.* (Dinitro-ortho-cresol) petroleum emulsions are known as 'dual-purpose' or 'omnibus' washes, for they are less selective in their action upon the eggs of fruit pests and provide, in a single application, an effective control of Aphides, Psylla, Capsid Bugs, Winter Moths, and the fruit-tree Red Spider Mite. Concentrations ranging from $4\frac{1}{2}$ to 8 per cent. are employed, and there is a wider limit of application than with tar oils. Spraying may be carried out from December to the end of February or early March on Apple. The tendency of these washes to stain makes it advisable to wear old clothes and gloves and to smear the face with petroleum jelly prior to spraying.

(9) *Thiocyanate petroleum emulsions* resemble D.N.O.C. washes in that they are 'dual-purpose' in their action upon fruit pests and control the widest range of pests in their egg stage. These washes show up well on sprayed trees, there is no staining of clothing or skin, they are the least damaging of all ovicides to turf and under-crops, and they may be used over a longer period, namely, December to April.

(10) *Petroleum oils*, though effective against the eggs of Capsid Bugs and Red Spider Mites, are not suitable for controlling Aphis and Psylla outbreaks. Concentrations of $7\frac{1}{2}$ per cent. applied in March to Apples will result in good control being effected not only against the eggs of Capsids and Red Spider Mites but against those of the Winter Moth group of Caterpillars. Lime sulphur applications should not follow too closely upon petroleum oil sprays otherwise there is risk of severe injury to the buds and foliage. It may be advisable to omit the pre-blossom lime sulphur application on Apples sprayed as late as the end of March with a winter petroleum.

(II) STOMACH POISONS and PROTECTIVE WASHES are applied either in the form of a fine mist to the foliage of plants attacked by leaf-eating Caterpillars, Sawfly larvae, Chafers, and Weevils so that an even and fine film of arsenical particles is deposited on the leaf surface, or mixed (e.g. Paris green) with an attractive bait, mainly Bran, for the control of Woodlice, Cutworms or Surface Caterpillars, and Leatherjackets.

(1) *Lead arsenate* is obtainable in the form of a paste or powder, the former being used at the rate of 1 lb. to 20 gallons of water, and the latter at half that strength. This substance is insoluble in water, and requires to be kept agitated during its application to ensure constant suspension of the arsenical particles in the spraying machine or spray-tank. Arsenical washes and dusts are poisonous to man and stock, and should never be applied either directly or indirectly on herbs, salad crops, maturing leaf vegetables, ripening fruit, to trees in grazed grass orchards, or, owing to the danger of poisoning Hive Bees and other pollinating insects, to plants in bloom. A thick paste of lead arsenate may be used for painting the scions on newly grafted fruit-trees to avoid injury by the bud-destroying Clay-coloured Weevil, and to the stems of Climbing Roses to prevent damage to the rind by the same pest. Lead arsenate may safely be combined with lime sulphur and nicotine, provided that soft soap is not added to the combined wash, but that some other spreader is used.

(2) *Paris green* has been superseded as a fruit-tree spray by lead arsenate, but is a most effective stomach poison for use in poison baits. The main constituent is copper aceto-arsenite, which readily breaks down on treatment with water to form water-soluble arsenic which has disastrous results on foliage. Paris green must be thoroughly mixed with the attractant, namely, bran or dried blood, at the rate of 1 lb. to 28 lb. of the former or 56 lb. of the latter. A dry bait with dried blood as the attractant is more effective against Woodlice, while a moistened, but not wet, mixture proves more attractive to Cutworms and Leatherjackets. The bait is distributed evenly and thinly over the soil towards evening at the rate of 1 oz. to the square yard. All reasonable precautions should be taken to prevent injury to dogs, cats, poultry, and wild birds.

(3) *Sodium fluoride* forms the basis of many Cockroach baits, and has been recommended as a substitute for arsenicals in poison baits, but has the disadvantage of possessing certain deleterious properties upon man which limits its wide use as an insecticide.

(4) *Sodium arsenite* forms the active principle in certain sweetened poison baits used chiefly against Ants.

III. SPRAY WETTERS, SPREADERS, ADHESIVES, and EMULSIFIERS. The success of many insecticides, more particularly contact washes, depends upon their powers of wetting and spreading, thus enabling the spray to cover the entire surface sprayed, i.e. the pest and the plant. These terms have been used to embrace many types of auxiliary spray materials owing to the action of wetting and spreading being so closely related that it is difficult to distinguish the mode of action of the one from the other. The action of such agents is to lower the surface tension of the liquid in which they are dissolved, thus enabling the entire surface sprayed to be covered. A considerable number of *Wetters* and *Spreaders* are available, some of which possess the properties of both. For instance, soap (known commercially as Horticultural Potash Soft Soap), Saponin, Casein, sulphonated lorol, sulphite lye, flour paste, and numerous synthetic proprietary preparations possess both wetting and spreading powers, though some (e.g. soft soap) are incompatible with certain washes because they are precipitated as curd when added to lead arsenate and lime sulphur and by hard waters.

*Adhesives* increase the retention or tenacity of spray deposits, and prevent them being washed off readily from foliage during rainy periods. The American term 'Sticker' is applied to substances that improve spray retention. Coarse particles of sulphur and arsenic are readily removed from glossy leaves by heavy rain, and even by high winds, and the addition of milk products (e.g. Casein), flour, gelatine, glue, and fish oils prevent this loss of spray material.

*Emulsifiers* are necessary to produce miscibility of oils with water and, while most wetters and spreaders (especially soft soap) act as emulsifiers, some stabilizer is required to prevent the breaking down of the oil-in-water or the water-in-oil combination.

IV. SOIL INSECTICIDES aim at destroying pests in the soil without unduly affecting other organisms, e.g. beneficial nitrifying bacteria, or plant roots. The term 'Soil Sickness' is applied to a condition in which the crop fails to grow satisfactorily though supplied with a full range of nutrients, and generally occurs in soils in which one crop has been grown continuously without any system of rotation being practised. Soil treatment consists both of physical and chemical methods, the former by the use of Heat—Steam Sterilization—which is confined to the treatment of glasshouse borders, and relatively small quantities of potting composts, the latter by means of chemicals.

The following chemicals are used for the partial sterilization of soil against animal organisms:

(1) *Naphthalene* in the form of crude or 'Drained Salts' and the finer grades of 'Whizzed' naphthalene. Some grades are dark brown, others are pink, reddish, or bluish, and may contain tar acids which are toxic to plants if used too frequently or in excessive quantities inducing the condition known as 'Naphthalene-sick' soil. At normal concentrations naphthalene acts as a repellent thus allowing seeds to germinate and young plants to become established before the soil pest begins its depredations. The substance decomposes rapidly in certain moist, rich soils and disappointing results may then follow its application. Some pests, e.g. Swift Moth caterpillars, are more intolerant of naphthalene than others, and effective control of these creatures is possible. The rate of application is 2 to 4 oz. to the square yard, and the substance should be thoroughly incorporated with the top spit during digging and trenching operations, or lightly forked, hoed, or watered in immediately after its distribution over the soil surface.

(2) *Formaldehyde* has been used for the partial sterilization of glasshouse soils for many years, especially against fungi and Eelworms, and as a seed disinfectant. It is volatile and soluble, and is used at a dilution of 2 per cent. Its value against Eelworms and other soil pests is extremely limited for it gives only partial control, but a stimulating effect upon plants shown by soils treated with it may tend to mask the injuries caused by nematodes.

(3) *Carbon disulphide* was originally employed in 1872 in France against the Vine Phylloxera, and was popular on the Continent for many years as a soil fumigant. It has the advantages of being reasonable in price, volatile, and possessing good insecticidal properties, but its disadvantage as a fumigant in warehouses against pests of stored products is its inflammability. To overcome the fire hazard, the preparation of an emulsion with sulphonated castor oil is recommended and employed against Root-knot Eelworm and Millepedes in glasshouse borders, and Chafer larvae in the restricted area of a lawn. The concentrated liquid is effective in controlling Chafer grubs and Weevil larvae in forest nursery beds, Ant's nests, and the root form of Woolly Aphis.

(4) *Paradichlorbenzene* is recommended as a soil fumigant provided that high soil temperatures prevail to aid its volatilization, and that sufficient time is allowed to elapse between treatment and sowing and planting on account of its retarding effect upon plant growth. A few crystals placed upon the crocks of potted Auriculas infested with Root Aphis is effective against this pest, and against Root Mealy Bugs on pot plants. It forms the chief ingredient in liquid dressings for Furniture and Death-watch Beetles in furniture and timber roofs of ancient buildings.

(5) *Calcium cyanide* in its commercial form of 'Granular' cyanide has proved successful against Wireworms and other soil pests, but its poisonous nature is a distinct disadvantage in restricting its use except by the most careful operators.

(6) *Calomel* or *Mercurous chloride* is widely employed against certain Dipterous pests of vegetables. The pure form is used as a seed dressing for Onions using powdered calomel equal in weight to the seed, and making a paste with starch as an adhesive. Four per cent. calomel dust is applied both as a dust round Brassicas immediately after planting out, and again 14 days later, allowing 1½ oz. to 10 plants against Cabbage Root Fly (q.v.); and along the rows of Onions when the seedlings are 1½ in. high, the doses being repeated in 10 days, using ½ lb. to every 25 yards run of row, against Onion Fly (q.v.).

Further details may be found in *The Scientific Principles of Plant Protection*, by Dr. H. Martin, 1940, and *Chemistry of Insecticides and Fungicides*, by D. E. H. Frear, 1943.

G. F. W.

**INSECTS.** No other group of animals is of such importance in the garden as are Insects. By their numbers and widespread distribution they force themselves upon the notice of the least observant. The degree and amount of damage they cause to plants is very great and, at times, catastrophic, and such infestations can be checked only when preventive and curative measures are based on a knowledge of the habits and life-cycle of the species concerned. The wide range of plants grown in gardens encourages a greater number of pests to persist than in open fields where farm crops are chiefly annuals, rotation is practised, and conditions are less sheltered. Insects are perhaps most noticed on account of the injuries they inflict on plants, but there are many species which are directly or indirectly beneficial either owing to their predatory or parasitic habits, destroying injurious species and thereby balancing nature (Ladybirds and their grubs, Braconid, Chalcid, and Ichneumon 'wasps' and Tachinid flies), to the services they render by flower-visiting and pollen-carrying, thereby securing pollination of blossoms (Hive, Humble, and Solitary Bees), or to their saprophagous habits (Dung Beetles and many Fly maggots) whereby plant tissues are broken down in the soil making them available to lower organisms for the production of humus and plant foods.

No more than a general outline of the Class *Insecta* is attempted here, but fuller information on the more common insect and allied pests will be found throughout the Dictionary under their special titles, e.g. Winter Moths, Wasps, &c. See also *A General Textbook of Entomology*, by A. D. Imms.

The term Insect is often used to include other pests, for instance, Millepedes, Red Spider Mites, and Woodlice (*all of which see*), but it should be confined to the group of animals characterized by the possession of a hard, jointed, horny external skeleton within which are situated the various body organs (food canal, heart, respiratory and nervous systems, muscles, and sexual organs). The body is divided into three main segments, namely, the Head, which bears the antennae (feelers), eyes, and mouth parts; the 3 segments constituting the Thorax, which bears three pairs of jointed legs, and may be provided also with 1 or 2 pairs of wings; and the segmented Abdomen, which contains part of the food canal and reproductive organs and, in certain instances, bears external appendages (e.g. callipers of Earwigs, cornicles of Aphides, and cerci of Cockroaches). Extending down within the upper or dorsal length of the insect is a long tube that pumps the blood and is comparable to the heart of the higher animals, while down the lower or ventral portion of the body is the main nerve chain, which is a series of nerve fibres, the largest of which—the ganglion—is situated in the head and corresponds to the brain.

The method of breathing in Insects is different from that in the higher animals, and is performed by a tracheal system. Air is taken in through minute holes (spiracles) arranged along the sides of the body which lead into tubes (tracheae and tracheoles) that pass to every part, thus enabling air to flow freely in and out in a manner comparable with the blood system through arteries and veins in the higher animals.

The mouthparts of insects are of two main types, namely, Biting and Sucking, and in devising methods for the control of pests it is essential to know the method of their feeding.

Insects with Biting Mouth parts include Earwigs, Cockroaches, Crickets, the larval (immature) stages of Butterflies and Moths ('caterpillars') and Sawflies ('false caterpillars'), and the adult and larval stages ('grubs') of Beetles and Weevils. All leaf-eating types may be destroyed by the use of Stomach Poisons (see **Insecticides**) which, in the form of arsenical particles (lead arsenate), are either dusted or sprayed on the foliage to form an even distribution of poison that is devoured with the food. There are numerous other insects which possess biting jaws, including many soil pests (Wireworms, Cockchafer, and some Weevil grubs), leaf-mining caterpillars and maggots, tunnelling caterpillars (Goat and Wood Leopard Moths), and boring beetles (Bark Beetles) which are of necessity controlled by other means.

Insects with Sucking Mouth parts include Capsid Bugs, Aphides (Green Flies and Plant Lice), White Flies, Psyllids (Suckers), Scale Insects, and Mealy Bugs, all of which pierce the tissues of plants with the aid of needle-like stylets and abstract the cell contents or tap the food-conducting channels. It is not possible to poison their food, so they are destroyed by means of fumigants (under glass) and by the aid of Contact Washes (see **Insecticides**), which kill on contact with the insect's body by blocking the breathing-pores, causing suffocation, or by acting on the nervous system, producing paralysis.

Insects undergo a series of changes or metamorphoses, which may be complete or incomplete. Complete metamorphosis comprises four stages—the egg (ovum), the larva (generally known as the caterpillar, grub, or maggot), the pupa (chrysalis), and the adult. In those insects which undergo these changes, there is little or no resemblance between the immature (larval) and the adult stages. Examples are Butterflies and Moths, Beetles and Weevils, two-winged Flies, Sawflies, Wasps, Bees, and Ants.

Insects which undergo little or no true pupal stage include Earwigs, Cockroaches, Crickets, Thrips, Capsid Bugs, Aphides, Scales, and Mealy Bugs, in which the immature (nymphal) stages resemble in miniature their parents, though the wings (if present in the adult) are at first absent and later vestigial, and are sexually immature. Many such insects continue to be active from the time they are hatched until they die.

The injurious stages of insects are the larva, or the adult, or both. For instance, the caterpillars of Butterflies and Moths are destructive to plants in general owing to their habit of defoliation, mining leaves, buds, and shoots, feeding on roots and underground portions, and of boring into branches and stems, whereas the adults are harmless to plant life owing to their exclusively nectar-sucking type of mouth parts. On the other hand, the adults of many Beetles and Weevils are as destructive as their grubs, as witness the Cockchafer and Vine Weevil whose larvae are serious soil pests and the adults defoliators.

The Classification of Insects is based upon the type of metamorphosis (complete or incomplete), the mouth parts (biting, sucking, or piercing), the absence or presence of one or two pairs of wings, and the characters afforded by the antennal (feelers) and tarsal (leg) joints. Systematists recognize 24 Orders, of which those of importance to horticulturists are indicated by an asterisk.

## CLASS INSECTA

### Sub-class Apterygota

Wingless, primitive insects undergoing little or no metamorphosis.

Order:

| 1. Diplura (double-tailed) | . . Bristle-tails. |
| 2. Thysanura (fringed-tailed) | . Fish-insects and Fire-brats. |
| 3. Protura (first, tailed). | |
| 4. *Collembola (glue, peg) . | . Springtails. |

### Sub-class Pterygota

Winged insects, with occasional wingless forms, metamorphosis varied but rarely wanting.

*Div. 1. Exopterygota*

Incomplete metamorphosis rarely accompanied by a pupal stage, with wings developing externally, the young known as nymphs.

Order:

| 5. *Orthoptera (straight-winged) | Cockroaches, Crickets, Locusts, Grasshoppers. |
| 6. Isoptera (equal-winged) | . Termites or White Ants. |
| 7. Plecoptera (folded wings) | . Stone-flies. |
| 8. Embioptera (Embia, winged) | . Web-spinners. |
| 9. *Dermaptera (skin-winged) | . Earwigs. |
| 10. Ephemeroptera (living a day, winged) . . . | . May-flies. |
| 11. Odonata (toothed) . | . Damsel- and Dragon-flies. |
| 12. Psocoptera (Psocus, winged) | . Psocids or Book-lice. |
| 13. Anoplura (unarmed tail) | . Bird- and Sucking-lice. |
| 14. *Thysanoptera (fringe-winged) | Thrips or Thunder-flies. |
| 15. *Hemiptera (half-winged) | |
| (a) Heteroptera (dissimilar wings) . . . | . Plant Bugs. |
| (b) Homoptera (similar wings) | Leaf-hoppers, Aphides (Plant Lice), Psyllids (Suckers), White Flies, Scales, and Mealy Bugs. |

*Div. 2. Endopterygota*

Complete metamorphosis always accompanied by a pupal stage, wings developing internally, and with specialized larvae.

Order:

| 16. Neuroptera (nerve-winged) . | Alder-flies, Lace-wings, Ant-lions. |
| 17. Mecoptera (long-winged) | . Scorpion-flies. |
| 18. Trichoptera (hair-winged) | . Caddis-flies. |
| 19. *Lepidoptera (scale-winged) . | Butterflies and Moths. |
| 20. *Coleoptera (sheath-winged) . | Beetles and Weevils. |
| 21. Streptsiptera (twisted wings) | Stylops. |
| 22. *Hymenoptera (membrane-winged) | Sawflies, Gall-wasps, Ichneumon-flies, Ants, Bees, and Wasps. |
| 23. *Diptera (two-winged) . | . Flies. |
| 24. Aphaniptera (not apparently winged) . . . | . Fleas. |

G. F. W.

**INSECT POWDER, DALMATIAN.** See **Chrysanthemum cinerariifolium.**

**INSECTIVOROUS PLANTS.** *See* **Carnivorous Plants.**

**INSECTS AND FLOWERS.** *See* **Pollination.**

**INSERTION OF LEAF.** The manner in which the leaf is united to the stem. It may be without a stalk (sessile) or by means of a stalk (petiolate or stalked); the base may clasp the stem (amplexicaul) or partly so (semi-amplexicaul); it may form a sheath round it (sheathing), or it may be joined round the stem so that the stem appears to grow through it (perfoliate); the tissues of the leaf may be continued down the stem so as to form wings (decurrent).

*insig'nis -is -e,* striking, remarkable.

*insitit'ius -a -um,* grafted, foreign.

*insu'bricus -a -um,* of N. Italy.

*in'sulans,* of an island.

*integer'imus -a -um,* undivided or without teeth.

*integri-,* in compound words, signifying without division of any kind.

**INTEGUMENT.** A covering layer or skin.

*inter-,* in compound words, signifying between, as *intercostal,* between the veins.

**INTERCELLULAR SPACE.** A space between the cells of a plant, normally occupied by air; these spaces afford a means by which gases pass from one part of the plant to another.

**INTERFASCICULAR CAMBIUM.** The cambium extending between the vascular bundles of stems and roots of Dicotyledons, giving rise to new vascular bundles. *See* **Cambium.**

**INTERMEDIATE HOUSE.** A glasshouse where a temperature between that of the stove and the greenhouse is normally maintained. *See* **Greenhouse.**

*interme'dius -a -um,* between extremes.

**INTERNAL BREAKDOWN.** Generally applied to the brown discoloration of the flesh followed by darkening of the skin, seen in Apples and Pears. This often occurs in cold storage and is also seen in Plums, Peaches, &c., and in Pears at times follows premature picking. A pressure gauge has been devised in America for ascertaining the best state at which to harvest apples and pears for particular purposes such as cold store, export, &c. It should not be confused with a very similar condition seen when Apples are over-ripe and past their season.

D. E. G.

**INTERNODE.** The space on the stem intervening between two nodes.

**interpetiolar,** between the leaf-stalks.

*interrup'tus -a -um,* interrupted; not continuous.

*intra-,* in compound words, signifying within, as *intramarginalis,* within the margin.

*intrica'tus -a -um,* tangled.

*intror'sus -a -um,* introrse; turned towards the axis to which it belongs, as of an anther with its valves turned towards the middle of the flower (cf. *extrorsus*).

**INTUMESCENCES.** Distensions of tissue usually seen on leaves but occasionally on stems and fruits due to the abnormal elongation of cells. There is no parasite concerned in these growths which are usually the result of some faulty condition of the environment leading to certain cells becoming distended with cell sap. The areas containing these cells are swollen and raised in whitish pimples or blisters which may rupture the epidermis of leaf or stem but later collapse and become brown and powdery owing to drying and death of the swollen cells. On pea pods they may appear as warty outgrowths, on apple branches as Burr Knots (under Apple Diseases) or even in apple fruit cores as woolly streaks of tissue. In frame-grown cuttings and plants such as Pelargoniums these blister-like intumescences have been given the name Dropsy or Oedema (q.v.). With plants grown under glass the cause is generally excessively moist atmospheric conditions, while in plants out of doors it is usually due to too vigorous root action possibly combined with too hard cutting-back.

D. E. G.

*In'tybus,* chicory or endive.

**IN'ULA** (ancient Latin name used by Horace, &c.). FAM. *Compositae.* A genus of about 60 species of herbaceous plants, natives of Europe, Asia, and Africa, mostly in temperate regions. Leaves radical or alternate, entire or toothed, sometimes large. Flower-heads yellow, rays rarely white; involucre hemispherical, scales overlapping except at their spreading points; ray-florets numerous, ligulate, linear; disk-florets very numerous, perfect, tubular; receptacle flat or nearly so, areolate or honeycombed. Most species grow freely in ordinary garden soil in sunny positions and are readily increased by seed or by division at planting-time in spring or autumn. Some, like *I. Helenium* and *I. macrocephala,* are rather coarse and are best grown in the wild garden. The following are all perennial. *I. crithmoides* is often called Golden Samphire and is a native English plant of salt marshes, but is not of horticultural importance.

**I. acau'lis.** Tufted, stemless. *l.* oblong-spatulate, obtuse, entire, 1 to 1½ in. long, ⅜ in. wide, rigidly ciliate-pectinate. *fl.-heads* yellow, solitary, smaller than in the related *I. salicina;* involucral bracts ciliate, reflexed, purple within. July, August. Asia Minor.

**I. ensifo'lia.** Erect, about 9 in. h. *l.* linear, slender-pointed, many-nerved, glabrous, sessile. *fl.-heads* yellow, of medium size, solitary or several on a stem; involucral scales lanceolate, leaf-like, erect, cobwebby beneath. August. Caucasus, &c. 1791.

**I. glandulo'sa.** A synonym of *I. orientalis.*

**I. grandiflo'ra.** About 2 ft. h., unbranched. *l.* oblong, hairy, glandular-toothed, sessile. *fl.-heads* large, orange-yellow, solitary; involucral scales linear, rusty-hairy. Summer. Caucasus, Persia. 1810.

**I. Hele'nium.** Elecampane. Vigorous, 3 to 4 ft. or more h. Stem branched and downy above, furrowed. *l.* large, ovate, toothed, downy beneath, rugose, stem-clasping, lowest stalked. *fl.-heads* bright yellow, solitary, large. Summer. Europe, including Britain, N. Asia. (E.B. 766.) Formerly much used in medicine. Rootstock candied.

**I. hir'ta.*** Erect, somewhat branched, about 12 in. h., hairy. *l.* lanceolate-oblong, rigid, entire, hairy on veins and margin. *fl.-heads* bright orange-yellow, usually in ternate corymbs; involucral scales ciliate, linear-lanceolate, outer longest. June to August. S. Europe. 1759. Borders.

**I. Hook'eri.** 1 to 2 ft. h., sparingly branched. *l.* oblong-lanceolate, 3 to 4 in. long, minutely toothed, hairs short above, longer beneath; sessile or shortly stalked. *fl.-heads* pale yellow, slightly scented, 2½ to 3½ in. across; rays numerous, 1 in. or more long, bluntly 3-toothed at tip; involucral bracts broad, shaggy. August to October. Sikkim Himalaya. 1849. (B.M. 6411.)

**I. limonifo'lia.** *rhiz.* long, covered with remains of l. Stem with a terminal sub-corymbose panicle up to 1 ft. h., sub-shrubby, with appressed grey hairs. Basal *l.* entire, ovate or oblong-spatulate, obtuse, stalk short; *stem-l.* larger. *fl.-heads* discoid, hemispherical, yellow; involucral l. leaf-like, linear, obtuse. June. Crete.

**I. macroceph'ala.** 4 to 6 ft. h. Stem 1-, rarely 2-headed. *l.* oblong, minutely toothed. *fl.-heads* similar to those of *I. Helenium* but twice as large. SE. Europe. Near *I. Royleana.*

**I. magnif'ica.** Robust perennial up to 6 ft. h. Stem loosely hairy, striate, black purple. *l.* elliptic-ovate to ovate, toothed, lowest up to 12 in. long, 7 in. across, long-stalked, upper small and sessile, dark green and glabrous above, softly hairy beneath. *fl.-heads* in a corymb, 6 in. across; rays female, golden-yellow, narrow-linear; disk-florets deep yellow tipped orange; involucral bracts lanceolate, up to 2 in. long. E. Caucasus. 1925. var. **cyclophyl'la,** involucral bracts short, broadly rounded, about ⅜ in. long, spreading or reflexed. (B.M. 9227.)

**I. monta'na.** About 9 in. h., erect, hairy. *l.* lanceolate, entire, basal l. narrowed to stalk. *fl.-heads* yellow, solitary; involucral bracts oblong-lanceolate, obtuse, hairy without, inner bracts linear. Summer. S. Europe.

**I. Oculis-Chris'ti.*** About 12 in. h. or more. *l.* broadly lanceolate, obtuse, at most slightly toothed, rather downy. *fl.-heads* bright golden-yellow, about 3½ in. across, involucre very downy. Summer. E. Europe. 1759. Borders.

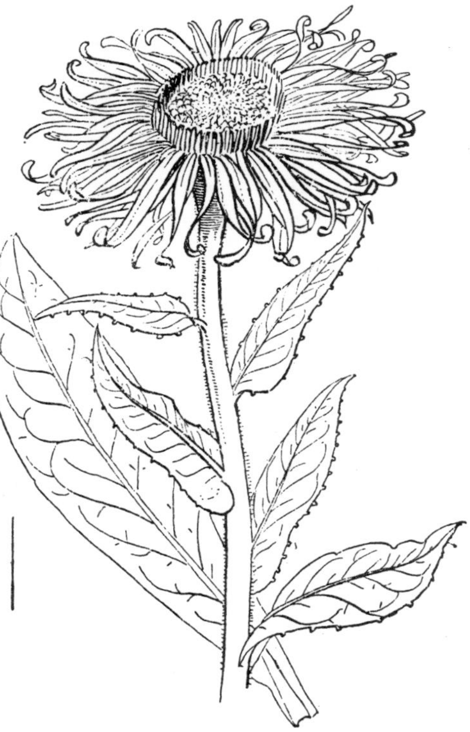

*Inula orientalis*

**I. orienta'lis*.** Hairy, 18 to 24 in. h. *l.* oblong, almost entire, sessile, teeth glandular. *fl.-heads* orange-yellow, rays wavy; involucral scales hairy, lanceolate. June to August. Caucasus. 1804. (B.M. 1907; B.R. 334.) SYN. *I. glandulosa.* Useful for cutting. Borders. var. **lacinia'ta,** rays cut; **super'ba,** *fl.-heads* larger than in type.

**I. Roylea'na.** About 2 ft. h., unbranched, leafy. *l.* ovate, narrowed to winged stalk, hairy, slightly toothed. *fl.-heads* deep golden-yellow, large; buds black. August to October. Himalaya. (G.C. 38 (1905), 265.)

**I. salici'na.** About 18 in. h. Stems erect, corymbosely branched. *l.* lanceolate, roughly ciliate on margins, tip somewhat recurved; half stem-clasping. *fl.-heads* solitary or in corymbs, yellow; involucral scales ovate-lanceolate. July to September. S. Europe. 1648.

**I. squarro'sa.** Erect, slightly branched, about 1 ft. h. *l.* oblong, slender-pointed, more or less rough-toothed. *fl.-heads* solitary or in corymbs; involucral scales ovate. France, &c. 1768.

**I. thapsoi'des.** Robust, about 3 ft. h., silky-hairy. *l.* large, oblong, entire or minutely toothed, stalk short. *fl.-heads* orange-yellow, discoid, small, in a densely congested corymb. August. Caucasus, N. Persia.

**I. visco'sa.** Erect, clammy-hairy, about 18 in. h. *l.* lanceolate, toothed, sessile with cordate auricles. *fl.-heads* yellow in few-fld. panicles; involucral bracts linear. July. S. Europe. 1596.

***-inus,*** suffix implying resemblance.

***inu'tilis -is -e,*** useless.

***invenus'tus -a -um,*** without charm.

***invi'sus -a -um,*** not visible.

**INVOLUCEL.** A small or secondary involucre.

***involucra'tus -a -um,*** having an involucre.

**INVOLUCRE** (1). A ring or rings of bracts surrounding several flowers. (2) At one time used as a synonym of indusium in ferns.

***involu'tus -a -um,*** involute, rolled inwards, as leaves in a bud.

***invol'vens,*** rolled up.

**IOCHRO'MA** (*ion*, violet, *chroma*, colour; from the colour of flowers). FAM. *Solanaceae.* A genus of about 20 species of attractive shrubs or small trees, natives of Cent. and S. America. Flowers clustered; corolla tubular, the limb 5-lobed; fruit a globose or ovoid-conical, pulpy berry. Young or specially vigorous plants may have leaves considerably larger than the dimensions here given. Easily cultivated shrubs requiring the shelter of a greenhouse. They may be taken out of doors in late summer. Several species are grown in the open in California. Increased by cuttings.

**I. coccin'ea.** Shrub with downy young shoots. *l.* oblong to ovate, 3 to 5 in. long, slender-pointed, veins downy beneath. *fl.* pendulous in a nearly or quite terminal cluster of 8 or more; cor. scarlet, 1½ to 2 in. long, the limb ¾ in. across, narrow, shallowly lobed; pale yellow in the throat. Cent. America. (F.d.S. 1261.)

**I. fla'va.** Bushy shrub up to 7 ft., shoots glabrous. *l.* ovate-lanceolate, glabrous above, finely downy beneath, tapering to both ends. *fl.* in drooping axillary clusters; cor. pale yellow, tubular, 1½ in. long; limb narrow, 5-toothed. Colombia. About 1894. (R.H. 1898, 360.)

**I. fuchsioi'des.*** Shrub 5 ft. or more, glabrous. *l.* obovate, inclining to ovate or oblong, 2 to 4 in. long, blunt, tapered to a short stalk. *fl.* drooping, in axillary clusters; cor. tubular, 1½ to 2 in. long, ⅜ in. wide, orange-scarlet, yellow in throat; limb ⅝ in. across, shallowly 5-toothed. Andes. 1843. (B.M. 4149 as *Lycium fuchsioides.*)

**I. grandiflo'ra.** Shrub several ft. h., shoots downy. *l.* 3 to 5 in. long, 2 to 3½ in. wide, ovate-cordate, pointed, downy. *fl.* in terminal pendulous clusters of 6 to 8; cor. tube cylindrical, 1½ in. long, the limb 1¼ in. across with 5 spreading pointed lobes, rich glowing purple. Autumn. Ecuador, Peru. About 1846. (B.M. 5301.)

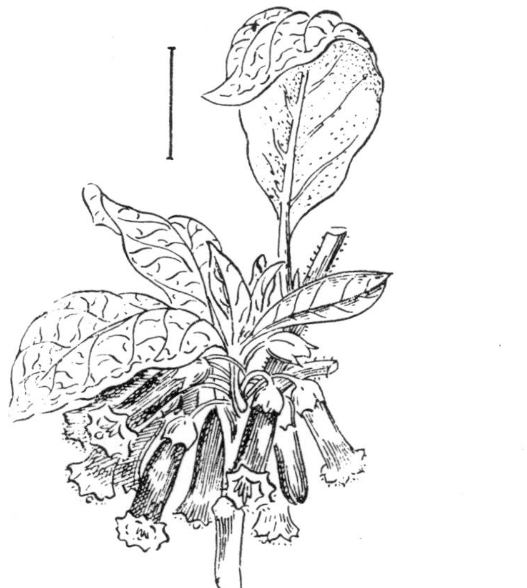

*Iochroma lanceolata*

**I. lanceola'ta.*** Shrub 4 to 8 ft., shoots stellately downy. *l.* up to 6 in. long, one-third to half as wide, oblong-lanceolate, pointed, base tapering to a grooved stalk ¾ in. long, stellately downy beneath. *fl.* crowded in a nearly terminal, scarcely stalked cluster; cor. deep blue varying to purplish, 1½ in. long, slenderly tubular; limb 5-toothed, ⅜ in. across. Colombia. 1847. (B.M. 4338 as *Chaenestes lanceolata.*)

**I. tubulo'sa.*** Shrub 4 to 6 ft., shoots, l. and infl. downy. *l.* ovate to oblong, 2 to 5 in. long, half as wide, pointed, greyish-green. *fl.* in axillary pendulous clusters of up to 20; cor. deep blue-purple, cylindrical, 1½ in. long by ¼ in. wide; limb ½ in. across, paler, with 5 very shallow teeth. August. Trop. America. (B.R. 1845, 20.)

W. J. B.

**IODINE** is one of the chemical elements found in plants in small amounts, especially in marine plants, but whether it plays any direct role in their economy is doubtful.

**ioen'sis -is -e,** of Iowa.

**ionan'drus -a -um,** with violet anthers.

**IO'NE** (*Ione*, one of the Nereids). Fam. *Orchidaceae.*
A genus of about 10 epiphytic orchids, in the Himalaya
chiefly but also found in Burma and Siam, allied to Bulbophyllum and sometimes included in that genus, separated
as the lip is fixed and the 4 pollinia are attached in
pairs to the 2 glands. The lateral sepals, usually connate, are placed under the comparatively large lip, petals
smaller than sepals. The genus has not the attraction of
Bulbophyllum: the flowers, though often many on a spike,
are small and lack bright colouring. The habit is that
of Bulbophyllum, the pseudobulbs bearing a single
leathery leaf. The compost and cultural treatment
should be that given Bulbophyllums.

**I. flaves'cens.** Dwarf. *fl.* yellow; lip deep yellow. Burma. 1914.

**I. grandiflo'ra.** Dwarf. *fl.* dull purple. Burma. 1902.

**I. palea'cea.** *fl.* greenish and reddish. Assam. 1877. (B.M. 6344.)

**I. scario'sa.** *fl.* whitish, stained with pink, bracts glumaceous,
keeled; spike 5 to 12 in. h. *Pseudobulbs* small, ovate. *l.* 2 to 4 in.
long, narrow. N. India. (A.B.G.C. 8, 219.) Syn. *Sunipia scariosa.*

**I. siamen'sis.** *fl.* greenish, sparsely marked purple. Siam. 1902.

E. C.

**IONID'IUM** (*ion*, violet, *eidos*, resemblance; the flowers
are violet-like). Fam. *Violaceae.* A genus of about 40
species of herbs or sub-shrubs, mostly natives of sub-
tropical America. Leaves alternate or rarely opposite.
Flowers solitary with the small sepals somewhat decurrent, petals unequal, lower twice or 3 times as long
as others, concave and keeled. Some species are of
economic importance the roots being used as substitutes
for Ipecacuanha, but few are of horticultural importance.
They need greenhouse treatment and a compost of peat
and loam. The shrubby species will root in sand under a
bell-glass. The herbs are increased by seeds or division.

**I. capen'se.** Cape Violet. Stems erect, shrubby, 6 to 12 in. h. *l.*
alternate, obovate, scarcely toothed, hairy. *fl.* white; sep. acute,
ciliate. Summer. S. Africa. 1824.

**I. Ipecacuan'ha.** About 18 in. h. *l.* ovate-oblong. *fl.* white;
peduncles axillary, drooping; lower lip very large, emarginate. July.
S. America. 1822. The roots furnish white Ipecacuanha.

**I. polygalifo'lium.** Shrubby, diffusely branched, procumbent,
about 1 ft. h. *l.* opposite, lanceolate, almost entire. *fl.* greenish-
yellow or white; sep. ovate-oblong, acute, hairy. Summer. S.
America. 1797.

**ionocent'rum,** violet-spurred.

**IONOPSID'IUM** (*ion*, violet, *opsis*, like; from faint
resemblance to some tufted species of Violet). Fam.
*Cruciferae.* A genus of 2 species of small annual herbs
related to Cochlearia, one a native of Portugal, the other
of Sicily and Algeria. Leaves spatulate or orbicular,
entire or 3-lobed. Flowers violet, white, or flesh-coloured,
small, on long peduncles; sepals spreading, equal at base,
pouch broadly oblong, laterally compressed. *I. acaule*

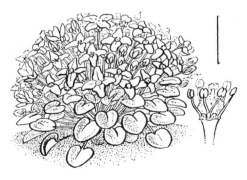

*Ionopsidium acaule*

is a neat and pretty annual for the rock-garden and fitted
also as a pot plant for window gardening. Seed should be
sown in the open in pots in spring or summer and the
plants grown in a shady place. It freely sows itself.

**I. acau'le.** 2 or 3 in. h., tufted, annual. *fl.* lilac or white with
violet tinge. Summer and winter. Portugal. 1845. (B.R. 32, 51.)

**IONOP'SIS** (*ion*, violet, *opsis*, like; flowers resemble a
violet in form). Fam. *Orchidaceae.* A small genus of epiphytic, stemless, tufted orchids, natives of W. Indies and
Trop. America from Mexico to Brazil, requiring stove temperature. Flowers small in racemes or panicles; sep. and
pet. connivent, the bases of lateral sep. forming a sac; lip
large, fleshy, fan-shaped. Leaves few, fleshy, narrow, pointed.
Pseudobulbs small or absent. The compost should be
of two parts Osmunda fibre, two parts of Sphagnum cut
fine, and finely crushed crocks. Wood blocks may be
used but small pans that can be suspended answer better.
Water liberally when growing, but though water is
required in winter stagnant compost must be avoided.
Winter temperature should not fall below 60° F.

*Ionopsis paniculata*

**I. panicula'ta.\*** *fl.* snow-white or delicate rose; scape panicled,
18 in. h.; pet. obtuse; lip hairy, rounded, 2-lobed, much longer than
sep. *l.* linear-lanceolate, keeled. Brazil, 1865. (B.M. 5541.) var.
**max'ima,** has larger fl., pet. striped purple. Brazil. 1887. (L. 114.)

**I. tene'ra.** A synonym of *I. utricularioides.*

**I. utricularioi'des.** *fl.* white or flushed rose, with pink stain at
base of lip, racemose; sep. and pet. acute, sub-equal; lip hairy,
2-lobed, much longer than sep. *l.* rigid, acute, furrowed, keeled at
base. Trop. America. 1825. (B.R. 1904 as *I. tenera.*) var. **zona'lis,**
lip rosy with broad transverse purplish-violet zone at base. Brazil.
1857.

**I. zona'lis.** A synonym of *I. utricularioides zonalis.*

E. C.

**ionos'ma,** violet-scented.

**IOSTEPHA'NE** (*ion*, violet, *stephane*, wreath; the ray-florets are violet). FAM. *Compositae*. A genus of 2 species of roughly hairy herbaceous perennials, natives of Mexico, related to Rudbeckia. *I. heterophylla* is a handsome plant, needing some protection for its tuberous roots in severe weather, such as a cover of a large pot. Propagated by division or by seeds sown in spring.

**I. heterophyl'la.*** Clammy hairy perennial about 18 in. h. *Basal l.* many, spreading, oblong, acute, tapered to stalk, toothed; *stem-l.* few, lanceolate or linear-lanceolate, entire, sessile. *fl.-heads* nodding, rays 15 to 20, lilac, neuter, hairy beneath; disk-florets hermaphrodite, funnel-shaped, paleaceous, oblong, acute; peduncles 1-fld., densely hairy. Autumn. 1829. (S.B.F.G. s. 2, 32 as *Echinacea heterophylla*.)

**IPECACUANHA.** The roots of *Cephaelis Ipecacuanha* (q.v.) provide an emetic used as a specific for dysentery. White Ipecacuanha is a product of *Ionidium Ipecacuanha* (q.v.).

**A→**

**IPHIGE'NIA** (after the daughter of Agamemnon). FAM. *Liliaceae*. A genus of 5 species of bulbous plants related to Ornithoglossum but with flat filaments. Leaves few, linear, scattered, upper bracts like. Flowers small, erect, solitary or in corymbs; segments 6, starry, deciduous; stamens 6; fruit a capsule. *I. indica* is widely distributed in the SE. Asiatic Monsoon area, 1 other occurs in New Zealand, the other 3 in widely separated parts of Africa. Stove conditions are needed and treatment as for Ornithoglossum. Of little horticultural interest.

**I. in'dica.** Stem flexuous, 3 to 10 in. long. *l.* few, lower 6 to 8 in. long. *fl.* reddish or purplish, few or many on pedicels 1 to 2 in. long; perianth ¼ to ⅓ in. long. June. India, &c. 1818.

**IPOMOE'A** (*ips*, bindweed, *homoios*, similar). FAM. *Convolvulaceae*. A genus of about 300 species of evergreen and deciduous twining or creeping herbs, rarely trees or shrubs, distributed over the warmer parts of the world. Closely related to Convolvulus but with 1 capitate or 2 or 3 globose, not 2 linear or ovate stigmas, and to Calonyction and Quamoclit but with funnel-shaped corolla tube with usually included stamens. Leaves alternate, entire, lobed or divided. Flowers often showy; corolla salver-shaped, bell-shaped, or tubular, limb spreading, entire or angular; calyx with obtuse lobes; ovary 2- to 4-celled, 4-ovuled. Pharbitis sometimes included here has narrow-pointed, calyx lobes, and a 3-celled, 6-ovuled ovary. Some of the stove species are among the prettiest plants for covering trellises or pillars, particularly over paths where the beautifully coloured flowers can be seen to advantage. They are free-growing plants liking plenty of root-room, best secured by planting them out in the border inside the house; where this cannot be done large pots or boxes must be substituted. The hardier species succeed in the open-air during summer if forwarded a little in a warm frame and afterwards planted out in a sheltered place. The annual species, whether needing the stove, or half-hardy, can be raised readily from seed sown early in spring in a warm house. It is a good plan to sow 2 or 3 seeds in a small pot and when the seedlings are up to transfer them bodily to a larger pot without disturbing the roots. They should be trained up temporary stakes until established and finally planted out. A compost of fibrous loam, rotten manure, and leaf-soil somewhat lumpy should be used for them. Evergreen Ipomoeas may be propagated by cuttings of side-shoots in peaty soil, in brisk bottom heat, or by layers. *I. Horsfalliae* does not strike readily but can be increased by layers or better by grafting pieces on its own roots or on the roots of some other vigorous species such as *I. pandurata*.

**I. Aiton'ii.** Evergreen twiner to 10 ft. *l.* cordate, roundish, 3-lobed, lobes acute. *fl.* pale purple; cor. bell-shaped with a thickened tube; peduncles many-fld., longer than l.-stalks. April to October. S. Africa. (B.R. 1794.) Stove.

**I. ala'tipes.** Glabrous perennial climber. *l.* cordate, 2 to 3 in. long, slender-pointed, lobes obtusely rounded at base with a deep obtuse sinus. *fl.* salmon, 3 in. across; cal. large, ovate, 1 in. or more long; pedicels wingless, very twisted, frequently glandular; peduncles axillary broadly winged each side, 2- to 4-fld. June. Panama. 1862. (B.M. 5330.) Stove.

**I. albive'nia.** Evergreen twiner. *l.* roundish-cordate with somewhat raised veins, woolly beneath. *fl.* pure white, large, solitary at ends of branches, tube deep purple within. August, September. Algoa Bay. 1824. (B.R. 1116 as *Convolvulus albivenius*.) Stove.

**I. angustifo'lia.** Annual, much-branched, rambling. *l.* linear-oblong, 2 to 3 in. long, less than ½ in. wide, slender-pointed, glabrous. *fl.* white or cream, bright purple in throat, scarcely ¾ in. across; peduncle filiform, solitary, usually 2-fld., pedicels slender, upper fl. opening first. Trop. regions. 1778. (B.M. 5426; B.R. 317 as *I. denticulata*.) Greenhouse. SYN. *I. filicaulis*.

**I. arbores'cens.** Erect, tree-like, 15 to 18 ft. h., velvety, pubescent. *l.* ovate-cordate. *fl.* white, 2 in. long; sep. oval, obtuse, downy. *Seeds* black with tufts of long white hairs on dorsal angles. Mexico. 1880. Requires cool dry atmosphere as of Cactus house.

**I. au'rea.** Slender twiner, woody at base, roots white, tuberous. *l.* digitately 5-lobed. *fl.* golden yellow, 2 to 4 in. across, funnel-shaped with a wide expanded limb. Lower California. 1900.

*Ipomoea Batatas*

**I. Batat'as.** Sweet Potato. Creeping, rarely climbing. Roots tuberous. *l.* variable, usually angular and lobed. *fl.* white without, purple within, about 1 in. long; peduncles equalling or longer than l.-stalks, 3- or 4-fld. E. Indies. 1797. SYN. *Batatas edulis*. Stove or greenhouse. Widely grown in warm countries in many varieties for the edible tubers.

**I. bignonioi'des.** Deciduous twiner. Roots tuberous. *l.* 3-lobed, lower rounded, overlapping. *fl.* dark purple, funnel-shaped, limb curled; peduncles many-fld., nodding, shorter than l.-stalks. July Cayenne. 1824. (B.M. 2645 as *Batatas bignonioides*.) Stove.

**I. bilo'ba.** Prostrate or climbing up to 40 ft. Perfectly glabrous. *l.* often broader than long, 1 to 4 in. across, orbicular or broadly obovate or oblong, emarginate or shortly obtusely 2-lobed, thick and fleshy, prominently veined; stalks 1 to 4 in. long. *Peduncles* 1- to 3-fld., about as long as l.; sep. ovate; cor. 1 to 2 in. across, broadly bell-shaped, purplish or pinkish, base tubular. Trop. shores. SYN. *I. Pes-Caprae*.

**I. Bon'a-nox.** A synonym of *Calonyction aculeatum*.

**I. bonarien'sis.*** Branching twiner, stems purplish. Roots tuberous. *l.* cordate, palmately 3- to 5-lobed. *fl.* purplish-lilac; peduncles axillary, solitary, 3- to 7-fld. corymbose. Summer. Buenos Aires. About 1826. (B.M. 3665; B.R. 27, 13 as *I. ficifolia*.) SYN. *I. Perringiana*. Stove.

**I. cathar'tica.** A synonym of *Pharbitis cathartica*.

**I. Cavanilles'ii.** Deciduous twiner. Roots tuberous. *l.* quinate; lflets. ovate, entire, unequal. *fl.* pale whitish-red; cor. lobes obtuse, crenate; peduncles 1- to 3-fld. August. Hab.? 1815. SYN. *Batatas Cavanillesii*. Stove.

**I. chryorrhiz'a.** Probably a form of *I. Batatas*. The cultivated Kumarah of New Zealand.

**I. chrysei'des.** Evergreen twiner, slightly woody; branches smooth or nearly so. *l.* ovate-cordate, sub-hastate, entire or often angled, 3-lobed. *fl.* yellow, small; peduncles stiff, 2- to 7-fld. July to October. Trop. Asia, Africa, Australia. 1817. (B.R. 270.) Stove.

**I. coccin'ea.** A synonym of *Quamoclit coccinea*.

**I. cras'sipes.** 4 ft., clothed with soft short hairs. *l.* oblong-lanceolate, entire, acute. *fl.* purple; sep. very unequal; peduncles 1-fld., 2-bracteate, thickened above. August. S. Africa. 1842. (B.M. 4068.) Greenhouse.

**I. dasysper'ma.** Annual, glabrous, sometimes tuberculate twiner of 6 to 8 ft. *l.* cordate-ovate, 3-sect, central lobe 3-partite, lateral 2- or 3-partite or sometimes pedate. *fl.* salver-shaped, 3 to 4 in. across, pale or sulphur yellow, with 5 narrow greenish plaits, tube and throat purple; peduncles axillary, 1- to 3-fld. with a few minute bracts. Trop. Asia and Africa. 1815. (B.M. 8788; B.R. 86 as *I. tuberculata*.) Stove.

**I. deco'ra.** Herbaceous perennial, 3 ft. h., woody at base. *l.* oval, velvety. *fl.* white, rosy-purple in centre, large. E. Africa. 1879. Stove.

*Ipomoea dasysperma* (p. 1059)

**I. digita'ta.** Perennial climber or trailer to 20 or 30 ft. Roots tuberous. *l.* 5- to 7-partite; segs. elliptic, sometimes spatulate, entire. *fl.* pink or pinkish-purple, 5-lobed, 1½ to 3 in. wide, broadly bell-shaped, numerous in 2-branched cymes. July to September. Tropics. 1799. (B.M. 3685 and B.R. 62, 333 as *I. platensis*.) SYN. *Batatas paniculata.* var. **insig'nis,** *l.* not palmately divided, slightly cut or entire, sometimes purplish beneath. (B.M. 1790; B.R. 75 as *I. insignis.*)

**I. ficifo'lia.** A synonym of *I. bonariensis.*

**I. filicau'lis.** A synonym of *I. angustifolia.*

**I. fistulo'sa.** Sub-shrub, 4 to 8 ft. h., branching. *l.* entire or nearly so, 4 to 6 in. long, rather thick. *fl.* pinkish-purple, about 3 in. long, bell-shaped. July to September. Brazil. SYN. *I. texana.* var. **Goodetl'ii** has lavender-pink *fl.* with darker throat. Stove.

**I. Gerrard'ii.** Evergreen twiner, 10 to 15 ft. long. *l.* roundish, cordate. *fl.* pure white with yellow throat, very fragrant, large, freely produced. Natal. 1857. (B.M. 5651.) Stove.

**I. glaucifo'lia.** Deciduous twiner. Tuberous rooted. *l.* sagittate, truncate, stalks long. *fl.* small, purplish, tube inflated; segs. ovate, acute; peduncles 2-fld., as long as *l.* May. Mexico. 1732. SYN. *Batatas glaucifolia.* Stove.

**I. gossypioi'des.** Annual, more or less erect. *l.* on long stalks. *fl.* rose with reddish-purple throat, showy. S. Argentine. 1897. Greenhouse.

**I. grandiflo'ra.** A synonym of *Calonyction aculeatum.*

**I. ×Harding'ii.** Herbaceous perennial twiner with scabrous tuberous root. *l.* 3-lobed (sometimes obscurely 5-lobed), cordate at base, middle lobe ovate, acute, covered with short hairs. *fl.* rose-purple with deep purple throat and markings, racemose. July, August. 1839. (P.M. 11, 217.) Of garden origin.

**I. hedera'cea.** A synonym of *Pharbitis hederacea.*

**I. hederifo'lia.** A synonym of *Quamoclit coccinea hederifolia.*

**I. heterophyl'la.** Deciduous tuberous-rooted twiner, very hairy. *l.* 5-palmate, lobes or lflets. ovate-spatulate, acute. *fl.* blue; peduncles solitary, axillary, with 3 sessile *fl.* July. Cuba. 1817. SYN. *Batatas heterophylla.* Stove.

**I. Horsfal'liae.*** Showy, handsome evergreen twiner. *l.* 5-digitate, lflets. lanceolate, entire, with undulate margins. *fl.* deep rich rose, glossy; peduncles as long as *l.*-stalks, with dichotomous cymes. Winter. W. Indies. 1833. (B.M. 3315.) var. **Briggs'ii,** *fl.* rich magenta-crimson, flowering more freely, and rooting more freely from cuttings than type. SYN. *I. Briggsii, I. Lady Briggs.* Stove.

**I. imperia'lis.** A synonym of *Pharbitis × imperialis.*

**I. Jal'apa.** Evergreen twiner, tuberous-rooted. *l.* membranous, cordate, entire, slender-pointed. *fl.* red, white, or light pinkish-purple; cor. long, tubular; tube ventricose above; peduncles 2-fld., longer than stalks. August. S. United States. 1733. SYN. *Batatas Jalapa.* Greenhouse or half-hardy. The root sometimes weighs 40 or 50 lb. and is said to be as purgative as that of *I. Purga,* the Jalap of commerce.

**I. Kerb'eri.** A synonym of *Quamoclit Kerberi.*

**I. Lear'ii.** A synonym of *Pharbitis Learii.*

*Ipomoea Horsfalliae*

**I. leptophyl'la.** Bush Moon-flower. Perennial, erect or ascending, 2 to 4 ft. h., tuberous-rooted. *l.* simple, entire, linear, 2 to 4 in. long, ¼ in. wide, acute, shortly stalked. *fl.* rose-pink, purple in throat; cor. funnel-shaped, about 3 in. long; peduncles short, 1- or 2-fld. Texas, New Mexico. Greenhouse. Roots very large, 10 to 100 lb.

**I. linifo'lia.** Annual, slender twiner or creeper. *l.* narrow-oblong, lower often sub-cordate, ovate-oblong, 1½ to 2½ in. long. *fl.* yellow, small; peduncles 1 to 3 in. long, few- or many-fld. May. Malaya, Queensland. 1827. SYN. *Skinneria caespitosa.* Stove.

**I. macrorrhi'za.** Trailer or climber with large woody rootstock. *l.* entire, repand or lobed, ovate-cordate, whitish with soft down. *fl.* cream with a magenta throat, 3 in. long; inner sep. twice as long as outer; peduncles 1- to 5-fld. August, September. Mexico. 1814. (B.R. 342.) Greenhouse.

**I. microdac'tyla.** Glabrous woody twiner, 12 to 15 ft. h. Stems often with corky bark. *l.* 3- to 5-lobed, or nearly entire. *fl.* scarlet, salver-form, 1½ in. long, limb as broad, slightly 5-lobed; stamens slightly exserted. Florida, Cuba. Greenhouse.

**I. murica'ta.** Stems filiform, 1 ft. h., branched, from an oblong, fusiform tuberous root. *l.* multifid almost to base; segs. often again divided, glabrous, sessile. *fl.* lilac to rose; sep. muricate at back of base; peduncles axillary, 1-fld. June, July. S. America. 1840. (B.M. 4301.) Stove.

**I. mutab'ilis.** A synonym of *Pharbitis mutabilis.*

**I. Nation'is.** A synonym of *Quamoclit Nationis.*

**I. Nil.** A synonym of *Pharbitis hederacea.*

**I. obscu'ra.** Annual twiner with round reddish stems. *l.* broadly cordate, 1 to 3 in. long, acute, entire, slightly downy beneath and at edge. *fl.* white with 5 cream plaits and a purple eye, slightly pentagonal, tube as long as cal.; peduncles axillary 1- or sometimes 3-fld. India, Ceylon, Malaya, &c. 1732. (B.R. 239.) Stove.

**I. palma'ta.** Deciduous twiner with white tubercular stem and tuberous root. *l.* 5-palmate, lobes ovate, obtuse, middle one largest. *fl.* white or purplish, white; peduncles 3-fld. June. Guinea. 1823. SYN. *Batatas senegalensis.* Stove.

**I. pandura'ta.*** Man of the Earth. Wild Potato Vine. Perennial twiner with long tuberous roots. *l.* cordate, entire, occasionally angular or hastately 3-lobed, slender-pointed, rather downy beneath. *fl.* white with purple-throat, large; peduncles many-fld. June to August. United States, &c. 1776. (B.M. 1939 as *Convolvulus panduratus*; B.M. 1603 as *C. candicans*.) Hardy.

**I. panicula'ta.** A synonym of *I. digitata.*

**I. Perringia'na.** A synonym of *I. bonariensis.*

**I. Pes-Cap'rae.** A synonym of *I. biloba.*

**I. Pes-tig'ridis.** Twining annual. *l.* deeply 5- to 9-lobed, lobes elliptic, slender-pointed, narrowed to base, hairy. *fl.* pink in dense bracteate heads; cor. funnel-shaped, somewhat hairy without; sep. lanceolate, acute, hairy. April, May. Trop. Asia, Africa. 1732. Tender. var. **longibracea'ta,** twining up to 6 ft., covered with long yellow hairs, *fl.* white within, violet in throat, tube purple, over 2 in. wide, the 5-lobed bracts 1 to 1¼ in. long. Trop. Africa. 1917. (B.M. 8806.) SYN. *I. lophantha.*

**I. platen'sis.** A synonym of *I. digitata.*

**I. pulchel'la.** Evergreen twiner, about 10 ft. h. *l.* quinate; lflets. elliptic, slender-pointed, glaucous beneath, stalked. *fl.* purple; cor. lobes emarginate, plicate; peduncles twisted, 1- to 3-fld. Winter. Ceylon. (B.M. 4305.) Stove.

**I. Pur'ga.** True Jalap. Twiner. Root tuberous. *l.* sagitto-cordate, slender-pointed, glabrous. *fl.* purplish-rose; cor. limb broad, flat; peduncles generally 1-fld., longer than l.-stalks. Autumn. Xalapa, Mexico. (B.R. 33, 49 as *Exogonium Purga*.) Greenhouse. Jalap is obtained by grinding dried slices of the roots to powder.

*Ipomoea Pes-tigridis longibracteata* (p. 1060)

**I. purpu'rea.** A synonym of *Pharbitis purpurea*.

**I. Quam'oclit.** A synonym of *Quamoclit pinnata*.

**I. Robert'sii.** Twining perennial. *l.* broad ovate-cordate, 3 to 4 in. long, membranous, slender-pointed, dull green, downy; stalked. *fl.* nearly white without with pale pink stripes, 3 to 4 in. long, limb white within with faint stripes of pale pink and 5 lanceolate, rosy-pink rays; peduncles 1-fld. July. Queensland. 1883. (B.M. 6952.) Stove.

**I. rubro-caeru'lea.** A synonym of *Pharbitis tricolor*.

**I. setif'era.** Glabrous perennial. *l.* cordate-sagittate, emarginate, mucronulate. *fl.* white or purple, fragrant, showy and borne profusely; outer sep. with a bristle; peduncles 2- to 4-fld. Guiana, &c. 1894. Greenhouse.

**I. seto'sa.** Brazilian Morning Glory. Deciduous twiner, bristly. *l.* cordate, 3-lobed, middle lobe contracted below to a narrow neck. *fl.* purplish-red, salver-shaped; peduncles robust, many-fld., 3-forked. Brazil. (B.R. 335.) Greenhouse.

**I. sim'plex.** Perennial herb, stems 6 to 10 in. long from a sub-globose tuber as large as an apple. *l.* alternate, nearly sessile, 3 in. or more long, narrow-lanceolate, tapered at both ends, margins waved. *fl.* rose, cor. tube slightly enlarged upwards to the broad limb; clustered on short peduncles. S. Africa. 1844. (B.M. 4206.) Greenhouse or succulent house.

**I. sinua'ta.** Evergreen twiner, woody at base. Stem, l.-stalks, and peduncles very hairy. *l.* deeply 7-partite; segs. sinuate or pinnatifid. *fl.* white, throat reddish, bell-shaped; cal. as long as cor. tube; peduncles 1-fld., longer than l. June to September. Trop. America. 1813. Greenhouse.

**I. stans.** Erect, branching shrub with woody rootstock. *l.* oblong, hastate, deeply toothed at base, almost sessile, finely downy. *fl.* pink or purple, solitary on axillary peduncles. Mexico. Greenhouse, or half-hardy.

**I. terna'ta.** Habit of *I. Horsfalliae*. *l.* 3-foliolate; lflets. elliptic or elliptic-oblong, stalked. *fl.* white, 3 in. across, in axillary few-fld. cymes. W. Indies. 1884. Syn. *I. Horsfalliae alba, I. Thomsoniana*. Stove.

**I. Thomsonia'na.** A synonym of *I. ternata*.

**I. tric'olor.** A synonym of *Pharbitis tricolor*.

**I. Tweed'iei.** Evergreen twiner to 6 ft. *l.* cordate, acute, entire. *fl.* purple; cor. tube long; sep. ovate, acute, unequal; peduncles 1- or 2-fld. June, July. Panama. 1838. (B.M. 3978.) Stove.

**I. tyrianthi'na.** A synonym of *Pharbitis tyrianthina*.

**I. veno'sa.** Deciduous twiner. Roots tuberous. *l.* digitate; lflets. entire, slender-pointed, stalked. *fl.* purple; peduncles with an ovate-cordate, solitary l. at base of each pedicel. July. Mascarene Is. 1820. Syn. *Batatas venosa*. Stove.

**I. versicol'or.** A synonym of *Quamoclit lobata*.

**I. Wood'ii.** Woody climber. Root tuberous. *l.* cordate, tinged purple. *fl.* rose-purple, large, in short-stalked clusters. Zululand. 1894. Greenhouse.

F. G. P.

**IPOMOP'SIS.** Included in **Gilia.**

**IP'SEA** (*ips*, a gall-fly, from a fancied resemblance). Fam. *Orchidaceae*. A monotypic terrestrial genus confined to Ceylon. Compost should consist of 3 parts fibrous loam to 1 of leaf-mould and finely cut Sphagnum moss with (according to the nature of the loam) an addition of coarse sand. When growth is finished a decided rest is necessary in a temperature of 50 to 55° F. In summer a cool position in the intermediate house is suitable.

*Ipsea speciosa*

**I. specio'sa.*** Daffodil Orchid. *Pseudobulbs* cormlike, sub-globose. *l.* deciduous; 6 to 12 in. long, less than ⅛ in. broad, tapering below into a slender petiole. *Scapes* erect, 7 to 15 in. h., 1-, 2-, or more-fld. *fl.* golden-yellow with a few red lines on the disk of the lip; sep. and smaller pet. 1½ to 1¾ in. long; lateral sep. connate at their bases forming a short spur; lip 3-lobed, lateral lobes triangular ascending, mid-lobe broadly obcordate with 5 waved keels on disk; column clavate. Pollinia 8. Spring. Ceylon. 1866. (B.M. 5701.) Syn. *Pachystoma speciosum*.

**I. Thompsonia'na.** A synonym of *Ancistrochilus Thompsonianus*.

E. C.

**irenae'us -a -um,** peaceful.

**IRESI'NE** (*eiros*, wool; the branches being woolly). FAM. *Amaranthaceae.* A genus of about 20 species of erect herbs or sub-shrubs, natives of the hotter parts of America, nearly allied to Achyranthes and sometimes included with it, but differing by the 1-, not 2-, celled anthers. Leaves opposite, stalked, and in the cultivated species very handsome. Flowers white or greenish, inconspicuous, with 3 bracts. Iresines are important in bedding-out schemes for their striking foliage. They are easily propagated for the purpose in spring in a close frame or propagating-pit. The stock plants should be secured by putting in a quantity of cuttings in 5-in. pots in a close frame in August: they soon root and the resulting plants should be kept rather dry through the winter in a temperature of 55°. An increase of heat and moisture in March will cause the production of strong cuttings which will make good plants by June. Iresines are rather tender and should, therefore, not be planted out before the beginning of June, except in localities where there is no fear of late frosts. A warm season suits the plants best, bringing the foliage to perfection, particularly that of *I. Herbstii.* Aphis and Red Spider Mite are apt to be troublesome, especially while the plants are indoors.

**I. Biemuel'leri.** Twigs and *l.* rose-carmine. Probably of garden origin.

**I. Herbst'ii.** Stem and branches bright carmine, almost transparent, 12 to 18 in. h. *l.* somewhat cordate, deeply 2-lobed at apex, concave, deep maroon above, midrib and main veins broadly margined carmine, deep crimson beneath. S. America. 1864. (B.M. 5499 as *Achyranthes Verschaffeltii.*) var. **aureo-reticula'ta,** stems, l.-stalks, and main veins vinous red, *l.* green, blotched gold; **brilliantis'sima,** *l.* rich crimson; **Wallis'ii,** *l.* small, ovate-reniform, cleft at apex, recurved, blackish-purple, plant very dwarf.

**I. Lin'denii.** *l.* narrow, ovate-acuminate or oblong-lanceolate, rich deep blood-red with a central amaranth band, veins less curved than in *I. Herbstii.* Ecuador. 1868. (F.d.S. 1737.) SYN. *I. acuminata.* var. **formo'sa,** *l.* golden, veined crimson, pencilled green. Both type and variety compact and handsome.

F. G. P.

**IRIAR'TEA** (in honour of Bernardo de Iriarte, 1734–1814, Spanish botanist). FAM. *Palmaceae.* A genus of 7 to 8 species of tall spineless Palms having their stems raised on stilt roots, natives of Trop. S. America. Leaves odd-pinnate, leaflets wedge-shaped which is the mark of distinction from Ceroxylon to which they are closely related. They are raised from imported seed and potted in a compost of sand and loam, the pots being plunged in a tank of water. Rarely seen and difficult to cultivate.

**I. deltoi'dea.** *l.* with pinnae about 2 in. wide, sessile, erose at tip, apical seg. much the largest, 6 to 12 in. long and nearly as much wide. Peru. SYN. *I. robusta.*

**I. exorrhiz'a.** About 35 ft. h. with a crown. *l.* of 15 to 20 pairs of lflets. about 20 in. long 1½ in. wide. *Spadices* from between the l., 1 to 4. *fl.* yellow. S. America. SYN. *I. Bungerothii.*

**I. gigan'tea.** *l.* with large fan-shaped pinnae, oblique, praemorse, light green, lowermost *l.* recurved. Hab.? (G.C. 1872, 1105.) A noble species.

**I. ventrico'sa.** About 80 ft. h. *l.* 8 to 12 ft. long, pinnae repand-sinuate. *Spathes* 10 to 12, deciduous; spadices 3 to 4 ft. long. *fr.* globose, as large as a cherry. Brazil. (I.H. 400.)

**IRIDA'CEAE.** Monocotyledons. A family of about 800 species in 57 genera, natives of temperate and tropical regions of the world, especially in S. Africa and Trop. America. Most are rhizomatous or tuberous herbs with equitant leaves in 2 ranks, the flowers being terminal and perfect. The perianth is of 6 segments, petaloid and united below into a long or short tube, stamens 3 opposite the outer perianth segments, ovary inferior, 3-celled as a rule with usually many ovules on an axile placenta. Fruit a capsule. A family of great horticultural importance containing many showy plants. The genera referred to are Acidanthera, Anomalesia, Antholyza, Aristea, Babiana, Belamcanda, Bobartia, Calydorea, Chamelum, Chasmanthe, Cipura, Crocosmia, Crocus, Curtonus, Cypella, Dierama, Diplarrhena, Eleutherine, Ferraria, Freesia, Galaxia, Giessorhiza, Gelasine, Gladiolus, Herbertia, Hermodactylus, Hesperantha, Hexaglottis, Homeria, Homoglossum, Hydrotaenia, Iris, Ixia, Klattia, Lapeyrousia, Libertia, Marica, Melasphaerulea, Micranthus, Moraea, Nemastylis, Neomarica, Nivenia, Orthosanthus, Patersonia, Petamenes, Rigidella, Romulea, Schizostylis, Sisyrinchium, Solenomeles, Sparaxis, Strephanthera, Symphyostemon, Synnotia, Syringodea, Tigridia, Trimeza, Tritonia, Watsonia, Witsenia.

**irides'cens,** iridescent.

**iridioi'des,** Iris-like.

**IRIDORCH'IS gigant'ea.** A synonym of *Cymbidium giganteum.*

**Irio,** ancient Latin name for a cruciferous plant.

**IRIS** (the Greek name used by Theophrastus). FAM. *Iridaceae.* A genus of about 200 species of perennial herbaceous plants with creeping, tuberous or bulbous root-stocks, natives of the North temperate regions. Related to Moraea from which it is distinguished by the perianth pieces united into a tube (often short or very short) at the base, and to Hermodactylus which has a 1- instead of 3-celled ovary. Leaves chiefly radical, equitant, sword-shaped, or linear. Flowers in sheaths; perianth 6-cleft; segments in 2 whorls; 3 outer (the falls) reflexed, often bearded at base; 3 inner (standards) erect, usually smaller than outer; tube usually short; stamens 3, inserted at base of outer perianth segments. Fruit a 3-celled leathery capsule. The species of Iris are mostly hardy and their showy flowers, remarkable alike for their

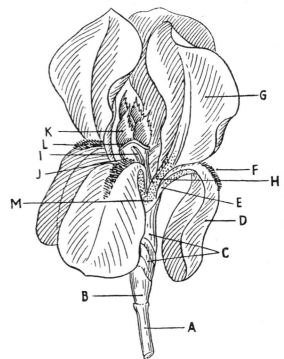

*Diagram of Iris Flower*

A, pedicel; B, ovary; C, spathes; D, falls; E, haft of falls; F, beard; G, standards; H, haft of standards; I, anther; J, style; K, crests of style; L, stigma; M, perianth tube.

structure and the blending of colours which many show, have recommended them strongly to horticulturists from early times. Two distinct types of growth are seen in the genus—in the one the underground structure is a more or less stout rhizome producing annual shoots from the terminal buds of its branches and roots from their lower side, and in the other bulbs or bulb-like corms. The flowering season of the various species is spread over a great part of the year. *I. unguicularis* in one or other of its different varieties is in flower from October to March. This species needs planting in poor well-drained warm situations and succeeds well at the foot of a south wall. Several of the bulbous Irises also flower in winter or early spring if planted in sheltered places or in a cool greenhouse, including *I. alata*, *I. Histrio*, *I. histrioides*, *I. persica*, *I. Danfordiae*, *I. Vartani*, *I. sindjarensis*, followed by *I. reticulata*, *I. Bakeriana*, and *I. Rosenbachiana*. *I. bucharica* and *I. orchioides* are among the bulbous Irises flowering in April when the dwarf bearded Irises begin, followed by the taller ones carrying on in their various species and varieties until mid-June. In the period from late April to mid-June the great majority of Irises of the Apogon, Pogoniris, and Oncocyclus groups open their flowers while the varieties of *I. Kaempferi* and the lovely *I. laevigata* flower well into July. A few flowers may be expected in autumn from some of the bearded Irises but without these and the curious and sometimes monocarpic *I. dichotoma*, which normally flowers in August, the flowering period of Irises which can be grown in any garden begins in October and lasts without intermission, save in extreme winters, until near the end of July, a range covered by the species of few other genera.

The genus can be conveniently divided into 11 groups the characters of which are embodied in the Key given below. They are (1) Apogon; (2) Evansia; (3) Pogoniris; (4) Oncocyclus; (5) Regelia; (6) Pseudevansia; (7) Pardanthopsis, all with a rhizomatous root-stock; (8) Nepalensis with a root-stock consisting of a bud covered with bristly fibres and with thick persistent roots; (9) Juno; (10) Xiphion, both with a bulbous root-stock, the Junos having thick persistent roots while in the Xiphions the roots die off annually; and (11) Gynandriris with the root-stock a corm, represented by a single species, *I. Sisyrinchium*.

The species comprising each of these groups (indicated in the Key and by the number following each species in the descriptions corresponding with the number given above) not only have many distinct structural characters in common but in a considerable degree have common cultural requirements.

The latter statement is not well borne out in group 1, the Apogon group, for considerable range of habitat, especially in regard to moisture conditions, is found within the group. The treatment needed by *I. unguicularis* has already been alluded to but generally moist soil or marshy and even permanently wet soil is needed by the greater part of them. The interesting series of species of American origin, *I. Douglasiana*, *I. missouriensis*, *I. tenax*, &c., need moist soil but are intolerant of stagnant water; the water-side or a moist border suits several, e.g. *I. sibirica* and its relatives, *I. graminea*, *I. aurea*, *I. ochroleuca*, *I. chrysographes*, *I. Delavayi*; marshy situations suit *I. spuria*, *I. versicolor*, *I. Pseudacorus*, *I. fulva*; while *I. laevigata* does best in shallow water, and *I. Kaempferi* in shallow water in summer and with water below the level of their rhizomes in winter.

Group 2, the Nepalensis group, likes plenty of moisture in summer, but are best lifted in October with their fleshy roots intact, stored in sand until spring, and then planted in March.

Group 3, the bearded Irises, are plants for full sun, well-drained soil containing lime, and planted so that their rhizomes are partly exposed on the soil surface. Most of this group are quite hardy but a few, especially those which produce their leaves before winter sets in, are apt to suffer in severe winters. Some of these make

magnificent plants if grown in borders in a large, airy house without artificial heat.

The cushion Irises, Group 4, the most striking of all for their curious colouring, are perhaps the most difficult to cultivate and are best grown planted out in well-drained calcareous soil, fertile but not freshly manured, and in good heart, in frames facing south and fully exposed, so that they can be covered by lights from the time the leaves begin to die in July until October, during which time no rain should fall upon the soil in which they are planted. Planting should be done by mid-October and most species of the group flower in April or May. Some have had moderate success by lifting the plants in mid-July and storing the rhizomes in thoroughly dry sand in a dry, sunny house until planting time comes again in October. Care must be taken that the roots which have begun to form in July, and are still unbranched, are not damaged if the lifting method is attempted. The plants must be preserved from excessive wet in autumn and winter.

Like the species of group 4, those of group 5, the Regelia Irises and the hybrids between the species of these groups (known as Regelio-cyclus Irises), must be kept dry during the summer months but the Regelia Irises, starting into growth later than the Oncocyclus, are less liable to suffer damage by winter frosts; still, it is well to protect them in severe weather. Group 6, the Pseudevansia group, needs much the same treatment with thorough summer roasting.

The solitary species in group 7, *I. dichotoma*, on the other hand, given a sunny position and a moderate amount of moisture while it is growing and flowering in August, is not so pernicketty. Its main drawback is the extreme freedom with which its evanescent flowers are produced, not infrequently leading to its death after flowering. Group 8 contains two species, *I. nepalensis* and *I. Collettii*, which are best lifted in October, keeping their roots intact, stored in dry sand, and replanted in well-drained rich soil in a sunny place.

The species of groups 9 and 10 have bulbous root-stocks and their cultivation does not differ from that of other small bulbs, but the bulbs of the Juno group (9) having persistent fleshy roots need handling with care lest the roots are damaged in lifting, storing, or planting. It will be seen in the descriptions of the species that several flower in winter, or have well-developed foliage, like *I. Histrio*, combined with early flowering habit and these are best grown in frames or in the cold greenhouse to prevent damage to the foliage. The solitary species in group 11, *I. Sisyrinchium*, which has a corm, though abundant in its natural habitat, has never taken kindly to cultivation in Britain.

Propagation of nearly all the species is readily effected by seeds which many produce freely. In the bulbous species flowering may be expected in 3 or 4 years from seed sown in the autumn of the year it ripens; in the rhizomatous species it may need only 18 months if the plants are kept growing.

The time of planting is important and is mentioned above for most groups. It is usually just before the time when the development of new roots begins. In the Pogoniris group the best time for replanting and division of rhizomes is immediately after flowering, unless the plants have to be kept out of the ground and the roots to become dry when September or October will be found to be best. All the named varieties of species of this and other groups must be propagated vegetatively for they are of mixed parentage and do not breed true from seed. The bulbous species form offsets which afford good means of increase, though the offsets in some species are very small and need 2 or 3 years to reach flowering size.

Few Irises respond readily to attempts to force them into flower but when the flower can be felt within the basal sheath in the bearded Irises gentle forcing will bring it on more quickly. The bulbous Irises of the Xiphion group, *I. Xiphium* (Spanish Iris), *I. Xiphioides* (English Iris), *I. tingitana*, may also be gently forced and these were at one time grown largely for cutting for market but have been almost superseded by the Dutch Irises raised by crossing *I. tingitana* and the early flowering vigorous variety *praecox* of *I. Xiphium*, and as the raisers, Messrs. var. Tubergen, state other forms of *I. Xiphium*. **A**

Irises for table decoration, &c., should be cut while still in the bud. They open freely in water and last longer so cut than if allowed to open on the plant. The buds of *I. unguicularis* are best cut when first visible.

A vast number of varieties of some species, e.g. *I. Kaempferi*, and of hybrids between species of the Pogoniris group especially, and to a less extent between species of the Apogon group, have been raised and these form the bulk of the Irises seen in gardens. Raisers in France, Germany, England, and of late years N. America have all played a part in the development of garden Irises and the number extending the colour range, and size of flower and improving the habit of these varieties is constantly being added to. The history of these developments will be found at length in the publications of the Iris Society of Great Britain and the Iris Society of America and lists of varieties of merit will be found in the Supplement to this Dictionary. Crossing is by no means difficult provided the structure of the flower (see figure) is understood. Seed should be sown as soon as ripe, and while haphazard crossing may chance to give good results, more is to be expected as the result of careful selection of parents with a clear idea of the object desired. Constitution, amenability to the climate, floriferousness, number and arrangement of flowers, durability of flowers and length of flowering period, and stiffness of stem are among the characters in addition to flower colour, form, and size that need to be taken into consideration in attempts at raising new varieties. The general characters and cultivation of Irises are well dealt with by W. R. Dykes in *The Genus Iris* and in *The Handbook of Garden Irises*.

The vast number of varieties of bearded Irises which have been raised in gardens from the latter half of the 19th century onwards rendered necessary a garden classification for the better understanding of the group. At first an endeavour was made to group them about the wild species to which they bore most resemblance but it was soon found that the crossing between the species which was taking place closed up the gaps between the wild species and caused this method of classifying the varieties to be inadequate. About 1920 the British Iris Society and the Royal Horticultural Society devised an artificial mode of classifying these Irises which has been found of much value in basing the main groups solely upon the colour of the flowers as seen in the mass growing in the garden. This classification has been followed in the main wherever Irises have been grown. Minor deviations from it have been introduced in various places from time to time, and a certain amount of personal opinion has to determine the particular group into which some 'border-line varieties' should be placed, but it still affords a workable basis of arrangement and is given in its original form. In each colour group or 'Class' three sub-classes provide for differe.ices in height—tall varieties, 18 in. high and upwards; semi-dwarf varieties, from 10 to 16 in. high; dwarf varieties, up to 9 in. high. Some of the Classes are, as will be seen, divided in sections to admit a nearer approximation of variations within the main colour characteristic of the Class. A well known though possibly old variety is named as an example.

CLASS I. *White or nearly white varieties*: Albicans, White Knight.

CLASS II. *White feathered with purple*. Here are 8 subdivisions, viz. A. White ground and B. Yellow ground each with (a) Colour confined to margins of segments, or (b) Colour suffused over the segments, and in each of these the feathering or suffusion may be either (1) blue-purple (lavender or lilac) or (2) red-purple (rose or pink). Mme. Chereau illustrates the white ground feathered with blue-purple group and Zouave the yellow ground suffused with blue-purple. The yellow-ground varieties are not numerous even now.

CLASS III. *White Standards, Coloured Falls*. In this class colour may be confined to the veins as in Duchesse de Nemours, or it may be confluent over the falls as in Rhein Nixe.

CLASS IV. *Purple Bicolor Varieties with Standards paler than Falls*. Here are 4 subdivisions marked by (a) Standards pale blue-purple (lavender), e.g. Lord of June; (b) Standards dark blue-purple, e.g. Souvenir de Mme. Gaudichau; (c) Standards pale red-purple, e.g. Standards pale red-purple, e.g. Mrs. F. C. Stern; (d) Standards dark red-purple, e.g. Kharput.

CLASS V. *Standards and Falls Coloured of the same (or almost the same) shade of blue- or red-purple*. Here are again 4 subdivisions: (a) Pale blue-purple, e.g. Corrida; (b) Dark blue-purple, e.g. Goldcrest; (c) Pale red-purple, e.g. Queen of May; Dark red-purple, e.g. Kochii.

CLASS VI. *Standards of shot shades*. Here the colouring of the standards is a mixture of two shades, one of which is always yellow and the chief subdivisions are according to the predominance of yellow in the colouring: (a) Yellow scarcely perceptible (1) pale blue or lavender, e.g. Quaker Lady, and (2) pale pink or rose, e.g. Ramona; (b) Bronze, with colour about equally balanced, e.g. Alcazar; (c) Yellow obvious, with (1) Purple predominating, e.g. Prosper Laugier, and (2) Yellow predominating, e.g. Iris King.

CLASS VII. *Standards Yellow, Falls Blue-, Red-, or Brown-Purple*. In this class are 4 divisions. (a) Standards pale yellow, falls with vein colour distinct, e.g. Gracchus; (b) Standards pale yellow, falls with vein colour suffused over surface, e.g. Loreley; (c) Standards dark yellow, falls with vein colour distinct, e.g. Rialgar; (d) Standards dark yellow, falls with vein colour suffused over surface, e.g. Fro.

CLASS VIII. *Standards and Falls Yellow*. Here are 2 divisions: (a) Standards dark yellow, e.g. Yellow-hammer; (b) Standards pale yellow, e.g. Amber.

*DISEASES*. On bulbous Irises Green Mould or Bulb Rot (*Penicillium* sp.) is mainly a storage trouble and may destroy the bulbs rapidly where the stores are poorly ventilated and damp. The fungus is often hidden beneath the scales but affected bulbs are usually softer and the basal plate rots away so that they can be picked out and discarded before planting. The disease known as Ink or Bulb Scab caused by the fungus *Mystrosporium adustum* appears as inky-black spots or blotches on the outer scales of bulbs of *I. reticulata* and attacks the inner fleshy part making black sunken areas which increase and cause the bulb to rot away. The only reliable control is to strip the outer scales from the bulbs before planting and to discard any that show the black lesions; no dipping treatment has yet been found of any use. The foliage of *I. reticulata* is not attacked but the same fungus may cause black spots on and severely damage the leaves of Dutch Irises without attacking the bulbs. The Virus disease known as Mosaic or Stripe is rare on non-bulbous Irises in this country, but is well known on some of the bulbous species especially *I. tingitana* and the variety known as 'Wedgewood'. It causes yellow streaking in the foliage and flower stems, dwarfing the plant and 'breaking' the flowers so that darker patches than normal appear on the petals. In glasshouses insects must be kept down and all affected plants should be rogued out. Mosaic on forced Irises must not be confused with yellowish streaking caused by low temperatures early in the season but mosaic, if present, will show much later.

On rhizomatous Irises the most serious trouble is Soft Rot or Rhizome Rot due to *Bacterium carotovorum* in which the leaves begin to yellow at the tip following a wet bacterial rot present in the bases of the leaves and the rhizome below them. The rhizome affected is soon reduced to wet, evil-smelling pulp, but long before this the disease can be detected by a softness of the rhizome felt when pressing the skin. Wet badly drained soils predispose the plants to attack and help to spread the disease. In hot weather the affected rhizomes may dry out but the trouble recurs with warm wet weather. The remedy is to cut off the affected part of the rhizome with its leaves and burn it, then sprinkle the cut surface and the remaining leaf bases with copper-lime dust (*see* **Fungicides**). Deep planting must of course be avoided. A dressing of superphosphates is beneficial. Leaf Spot is a well-known disease on bearded Irises, due to the fungus *Didymellina* (*Heterosporium*) *gracile*, and also occurs on bulbous species and more rarely on Gladioli and Narcissi. It attacks the leaves forming brown spots surrounded by a yellowish marginal band and these rapidly enlarge and turn grey with age. In damp conditions and on shady sites the trouble may be severe but in many places, especially in the southern counties, the disease does not appear until after flowering time and is not considered serious. Where, however, it becomes very bad before flowering, it is necessary to dust the plants with copper-lime dust or spray with Bordeaux mixture and a spreader (*see* **Fungicides**). Usually, however, it is sufficient to take away and burn all diseased leaves in the autumn and again in the spring as growth starts. Rust due to *Puccinia iridis* is not common in this country but may occasionally be seen as yellowish-brown pustules on the leaves. If affected leaves are carefully removed and burnt this rust should never be a cause for alarm.

(D. E. G.)

*IRIS SAWFLY* (*Rhadinoceraea micans*) is a pest of *I. laevigata* during late May, June, and July, and occurs frequently on the wild yellow Iris *I. Pseudacorus*. The leaden-grey larvae feed along the leaf-margins from which large portions are eaten out. Pupation takes place in the soil beneath or near the host plants, and the adult Sawflies are on the wing during early and mid-summer.

Attacked leaves should be lightly sprayed with arsenate of lead to which is added a 'sticker' in the form of 2 oz. gelatine to every 10 gallons of wash to prevent the loss of the arsenical particles through rain. Dusting with nicotine dust is also effective, but neither of these insecticides, nor Derris preparations, should be used on plants growing in or near waters stocked with fish owing to the danger of poisoning them, and Pyrethrum extracts should be substituted.

(G. F. W.)

KEY

| | | |
|---|---|---|
| 1. | *Root-stock a bulb or corm* | 2 |
| 1. | *Root-stock a rhizome or bud covered with bristly fibres* | 30 |
| 2. | *Root-stock a corm; stamens adherent to style branches* (Gynandriris *group*) | I. Sisyrinchium |
| 2. | *Root-stock a bulb* | 3 |
| 3. | *Bulb with fleshy roots persisting in resting season* (Juno *group*) | 4 |
| 3. | *Bulb without persistent roots* (Xiphion *group*) | 18 |
| 4. | *Plant stemless* | 5 |
| 4. | *Plant with evident stem* | 8 |
| 5. | *Lvs. very short at flowering time* | 6 |
| 5. | *Lvs. broad, falcate at flowering time* | 7 |
| 6. | *Haft of falls without wings* | I. Rosenbachiana |
| 6. | *Haft of falls with upturned wings* | I. persica |
| 7. | *Fl. blue or white* | I. alata |
| 7. | *Fl. smaller, usually greenish-yellow* | I. palestina |
| 8. | *Falls winged* | 9 |
| 8. | *Falls not winged* | 13 |
| 9. | *Falls with hairy middle ridge* | I. Tubergeniana |
| 9. | *Middle ridge of falls not hairy* | 10 |
| 10. | *L.-margin conspicuously white-horny* | 11 |
| 10. | *L.-margin not white-horny* | I. sindjarensis |
| 11. | *Stem tall with narrow distant lvs.* | I. Aitchisonii |
| 11. | *Stem dwarf with broader close-set lvs.* | 12 |
| 12. | *Fl. blotched white, crests small, triangular* | I. Willmottiana |
| 12. | *Fl. yellow, crests large, squarish* | I. caucasica |
| 13. | *Fl. 1 or 2, falls yellow, standards purple* | I. Fosteriana |
| 13. | *Fl. usually more than 2, colouring different* | 14 |
| 14. | *Lvs. with inconspicuous edge* | I. orchioides |
| 14. | *Lvs. with conspicuous horny edge* | 15 |
| 15. | *Falls yellow, standards white* | I. bucharica |
| 15. | *Fl. blue or purple* | 16 |
| 16. | *Stem short; lvs. narrow* | I. linifolia |
| 16. | *Stem 12 to 15 in. long; lvs. broader* | 17 |
| 17. | *Haft of falls widened abruptly into blade, deep violet* | I. warleyensis |
| 17. | *Haft of falls widened gradually into blade, pale violet* | I. coerulea |
| 18. | *Bulb with smooth outer coat; stem well developed* | 19 |
| 18. | *Bulb with netted outer coat; stem very short or absent* | 24 |
| 19. | *Perianth tube very short* | 20 |
| 19. | *Perianth tube ½ in. or more long* | 21 |
| 20. | *Blade of falls much shorter than fiddle-shaped haft; pedicel long* | I. Xiphium |
| 20. | *Blade of falls narrowed to triangular haft; pedicel short* | I. xiphioides |
| 21. | *Fl. yellow* | I. juncea |
| 21. | *Fl. not yellow* | 22 |
| 22. | *Falls bearded* | I. Boissieri |
| 22. | *Falls not bearded* | 23 |
| 23. | *Standards rounded, blunt* | I. filifolia |
| 23. | *Standards lanceolate, pointed* | I. tingitana |
| 24. | *Lvs. with 8 ribs at equal intervals* | I. Bakeriana |
| 24. | *Lvs. with 4 ribs irregularly spaced* | 25 |
| 25. | *Standards reduced to mere bristles* | I. Danfordiae |
| 25. | *Standards and falls of about equal length* | 26 |
| 26. | *Fl. yellow* | I. Winogradowii |
| 26. | *Fl. not yellow* | 27 |
| 27. | *Fl. in late autumn; haft of falls narrow* | I. Vartani |
| 27. | *Fl. in spring* | 28 |
| 28. | *Bulb with few offsets, each of considerable size* | I. reticulata |
| 28. | *Bulb with many small offsets* | 29 |
| 29. | *Fl. before lvs.* | I. histrioides |
| 29. | *Fl. overtopped by lvs.* | I. Histrio |
| 30. | *Root-stock a bud covered with bristly fibres, and with thick persistent roots* (Nepalensis *group*) | 31 |
| 30. | *Root-stock a rhizome* | 32 |
| 31. | *Perianth tube 1½ in. long; stem long* | I. nepalensis |
| 31. | *Perianth tube very short; stem almost absent* | I. Collettii |
| 32. | *Falls bare without crest or beard* (Apogon *group*) | 33 |
| 32. | *Falls hairy or with a crest or beard or both* | 71 |
| 33. | *Lvs. linear* | 34 |
| 33. | *Lvs. sword-shaped* | 57 |
| 34. | *Stem not exceeding 3 in. long or absent* | 35 |
| 34. | *Stem over 3 in. long* | 36 |
| 35. | *Perianth tube 3 to 5 in. or more long; lvs. $\frac{1}{12}$ to $\frac{1}{3}$ in. wide* | I. unguicularis |
| 35. | *Perianth tube ½ to 1 in. long; falls oblong* | I. ruthenica |
| 36. | *Stem hollow* | 37 |
| 36. | *Stem solid* | 43 |
| 37. | *Standards erect* | 38 |
| 37. | *Standards spreading* | 40 |
| 38. | *Lvs. glaucous on both sides* | 39 |
| 38. | *Lvs. glossy above, glaucous beneath* | I. Forrestii |
| 39. | *Spathes narrow, dry, brown at flowering time* | I. sibirica |
| 39. | *Spathes broad not dry, brown at flowering time* | I. orientalis |
| 40. | *Lvs. glaucous on both sides* | 41 |
| 40. | *Lvs. glossy above, glaucous beneath* | I. Bulleyana |
| 41. | *Stems much longer than lvs.* | I. Delavayi |
| 41. | *Stems about as long as lvs.* | 42 |
| 42. | *Pedicels long; perianth tube much shorter than ovary* | I. Wilsonii |
| 42. | *Pedicels short; perianth tube about ½ length of ovary* | I. chrysographes |
| 43. | *Stem 18 to 24 in. long* | 44 |
| 43. | *Stem up to about 12 in. long, usually less* | 49 |
| 44. | *Standards developed* | 45 |
| 44. | *Standards reduced to bristles* | I. setosa |
| 45. | *Perianth tube much ribbed* | 46 |
| 45. | *Perianth tube not distinctly ribbed* | 47 |
| 46. | *Lvs. glossy above, glaucous beneath* | I. Clarkei |
| 46. | *Lvs. glaucous on both sides* | I. prismatica |
| 47. | *Pedicels long: standards blunt, notched at apex* | 48 |
| 47. | *Pedicels short; standards pointed* | I. montana |
| 48. | *Plant sturdy; lvs. at least as long as stem, persistent* | I. longipetala |
| 48. | *Plant slender; lvs. shorter than stem, dying in autumn* | I. missouriensis |
| 49. | *Spathes very long; rhizome bristly* | I. Grant-Duffii |
| 49. | *Rhizome not bristly* | 50 |
| 50. | *Stigma triangular or tongue-shaped* | 51 |
| 50. | *Stigma 2-toothed; falls fiddle-shaped* | I. Sintenisii |
| 51. | *Stems simple* | 52 |
| 51. | *Stems branched; perianth tube linear, about ½ in. long* | I. Douglasiana |
| 52. | *Perianth tube short funnel-shaped* | 53 |

**I. acutilo'ba** (4). 8 in. h. *l.* ¼ to ½ in. wide, curved, 3 to 4 in. long. *fl.* 1; falls creamy-white with thick brownish veins and brown signal patch, lanceolate, 1 to 1½ in. long, ½ in. wide, reflexed, beard purple; standards similar in colour, erect, much broader and longer than falls; tube 1 in. long, green, mottled purple; pedicel very short. June. Transcaucasia. (G.F. 1874, 812.) Variable in colouring. Allied to *I. Ewbankiana* but with reflexed falls. See **I. Polakii.** *I. Helenae* with rose-tinged fl. is sometimes regarded as a distinct species. (B.M. 9333.)

**I. Aitchison'ii** (9). Stem 12 to 24 in. h., 1- to 4-fld. *l.* linear, subterete, 1 to 1½ ft. long at flowering time, ½ to 1 in. wide. *fl.* bright lilac or yellow, 1½ to 2 in. long; falls ½ in. wide, blade obovate; standards spreading, 3-cuspidate, less than 1 in. long; tube 1 to 1½ in. long; spathes 1-fld., 2 to 2½ in. long. March, April. Punjab, Afghanistan. 1898. (Gn. 54 (1898), 102.)

**I. ala'ta** (9).* *l.* sub-erect, lanceolate, acuminate, finally 1 ft. long. *fl.* bright lilac-purple; falls oblong, about 2 in. long, 1 in. wide, bright yellow at throat; standards oblanceolate-spatulate, 2 in. long, spreading horizontally; tube cylindrical, 3 to 6 in. long; spathe sessile, valves lanceolate, 3 to 4 in. long. November to January. Spain, Algiers, &c. 1801. (B.R. 1876; D.I. 40; B.M. 6352 as *Xiphium planifolium.*) var. **al'ba,** fl. pure white; **margina'ta,** fl. dark blue, falls edged white. Other colour forms are sometimes grown.

**I. Albert'i** (3). *rhiz.* stout. Stem branched, bracts leafy. *l.* ensiform, 1½ to 2 ft. long, slightly glaucous. *fl.* pale lavender-purple or yellowish; falls obovate-wedge-shaped, 2 in. long, densely bearded, haft veined dull brown and lilac; standards roundish, over 1 in. wide, abruptly narrowed to a canaliculate claw; tube under 1 in. long. *infl.* loose, overtopping *l.* May. Turkestan. (B.M. 7020; D.I. 38.)

**I. al'bicans** (3). *rhiz.* stout. Stem 15 to 18 in. h. *l.* stiffer than in *I. germanica,* broader and often twisted. *fl.* white; standards without hairs; spathe valves at most dry near tip at flowering time; *infl.* with shorter branches than in *I. germanica.* May. Dykes considers it a native of Yemen, but widely distributed in Mahomedan countries, commonly planted on graves. 1858. (D.I. 35a.) Often confused with *I. germanica alba* and *I. florentina.* var. **Madon'na** has blue fl. and purple-tinted spathes. (D.I. 35b.)

**I. albopurpu'rea.** See **I. laevigata.**

**I. amoe'na** (3). A hybrid group with white standards, falls veined dull violet-blue on a white ground. (S.B.F.G. s. 2, 165.)

**I. an'glica.** A synonym of *I. xiphioides.*

**I. antilibanot'ica** (4). 2 ft. h. *l.* sickle-shaped, $\frac{1}{4}$ to $\frac{3}{8}$ in. wide, grey-green, 1 ft. long. *fl.* solitary, large; falls deep plum with blackish signal patch, $2\frac{1}{2}$ in. long, reflexed, beard pale yellow; standards pale reddish-violet, erect, $3\frac{1}{2}$ in. long, broad with recurved margins. May. Anti-Lebanon. 1936.

**I. aphyl'la** (3). About 1 ft. h. Stems forked below middle, sometimes at base. *l.* ensiform, falcate, glaucous green, as long as stem. *fl.* dark lilac, $2\frac{1}{2}$ in. deep; falls obovate, $\frac{3}{4}$ to $1\frac{1}{4}$ in. wide, reflexed half-way, narrowed to a claw, beard white, tipped blue, base yellow; standards erect, slightly wider than falls, abruptly narrowed to a long claw; spathes green or flushed purple. Spring, sometimes also autumn. E. Europe, Caucasus. (B.M. 2361 and B.R. 801 as *I. furcata*; 5806 as *I. biflora.*) Quite leafless during winter. Variable. **I. benacen'sis** is a form with long, narrow spathes streaked red-purple, and narrow red-purple falls.

**I. arena'ria.** A variety of *I. flavissima.*

**I. assyria'ca.** An albino form of *I. sindjarensis.*

**I. atho'a.** A synonym of *I. Reichenbachii.*

**I. atrofus'ca** (4). Differs from *I. Bismarckiana* by the absence of purple flush on spathes, the red-black dots and veins which nearly obscure the falls, the round black signal patch, the scattered dingy yellow beard tipped brown, and the grey standards less thickly veined and dotted red-black. May. Palestine. 1893. (G.C. 35 (1904), 266 as *I. Haynei*; B.M. 7379 as *I. atropurpurea atrofusca.*)

**I. atropurpu'rea** (4). About 8 in. h. *l.* linear, glaucous, 6 in. long. *fl.* purplish-black; falls oblong-wedge-shaped, 2 in. long, $1\frac{1}{2}$ in. wide, signal patch greenish-yellow, beard yellowish tipped black; standards erect, rounded with a claw, 3 in. long; tube green; spathes 1-fld. May. Syria. 1889. (I.H. 1889, 51; G.F. 1891, 1361.)

**I. at'tica.** A variety of *I. pumila.*

**I. auranit'ica** (4). About 2 ft. h. *l.* narrow. *fl.* large; falls bright or bronzy, orange-yellow veined brown, 3 in. long, $2\frac{1}{4}$ in. wide, reflexed, signal patch purplish-brown; standards erect, domed, 4 in. wide, coloured as falls. May. Syria.

**I. au'rea** (1). Stem stout, 3 to 4 ft. h., bearing 2 sessile clusters of fl. *l.* ensiform, about 2 ft. long. *fl.* golden-yellow, deeper than in *I. Monnieri*; falls oblong, crisped at edge; standards oblanceolate, 3 in. long, edges waved. Late June. Kashmir. 1847. (B.R. 33, 59; D.I. 16.)

**I. Bakeria'na** (10). *l.* 2, awl-shaped, hollow, 4 to 6 in. long at flowering, tip horny. *fl.* solitary, violet-scented; falls white with violet spots and bright violet margins and with inconspicuous yellow streak down claw; standards deep violet, erect, oblanceolate; tube 3 to 6 in. long. January, February. Asia Minor, Mesopotamia. 1887. (B.M. 7084; Gn. 37 (1890), 462.) Easily distinguished from *I. reticulata* by the 8-angled l.

**I. baldschuan'ica.** *See* **I. Rosenbachiana.**

**I. balka'na.** A purple-fld. form of *I. Reichenbachii.*

**I. barba'ta.** A name covering all the tall bearded Irises.

**I. Bar'numae** (4). Stem 1-headed, 1 to 6 in. long with a single l. *l.* weak, 6 in. long at flowering, $\frac{1}{4}$ to $\frac{1}{3}$ in. wide, glaucous. *fl.* falls dark claret-purple with darker veins, 2 in. long, $1\frac{1}{4}$ in. wide, oblong-wedge-shaped, beard yellow tipped purple; standards erect, $3\frac{1}{4}$ in. long, $2\frac{3}{4}$ in. wide, deep red-purple; tube greenish, $\frac{1}{2}$ in. long; spathe 2 in. long, tinged purple. May. Egypt to Palestine. 1888. (B.M. 7050.) var. **urmien'sis** is a fine form with yellow fl. (B.M. 7784 as *I. chrysantha.*) SYN. *I. urmiensis. See* **I. Polakii.**

**I. Bar'toni.** A synonym of *I. kashmiriana.*

**I. basal'tica.** A synonym of *I. susiana.*

**I. benacen'sis.** *See* **I. aphylla.**

**I. biflo'ra.** A form of *I. aphylla* or a synonym of *I. subbiflora.*

**I. Biliot'tii** (3). $2\frac{1}{2}$ to 3 ft. h. *l.* darker green, more rigid and more distinctly striated than in *I. germanica*, which it resembles in habit. *fl.* fragrant; falls reddish-purple with fine blackish veins, $3\frac{1}{2}$ in. long, $1\frac{1}{2}$ in. wide, wedge-shaped-spatulate; standards bluish-purple with fine blue veins, $3\frac{1}{2}$ in. long, 2 in. wide, connivent; styles white, ovate with triangular, reddish-purple crests; spathes long, narrow, green, dry only at tip. June. NE. Asia Minor. 1887.

**I. Bismarckia'na** (4). Stem stout, leafy, 12 to 15 in. h. *l.* ensiform, 8 in. long, glaucous green. *fl.* large; falls ash-grey with darker veins and a dark signal patch at base, orbicular; standards sky-blue with blackish veins. May. N. Palestine. 1890. (B.M. 7986; 6960 as *I. sari lurida.*) SYN. *I. sari nazarensis.*

**I. Bloudow'ii** (3). Closely related to *I. flavissima* with light-yellow fl. very rarely produced in this country. 4 to 6 in. h. April. Altai Mts.

**I. Boissier'i** (10). About 12 in. h. *l.* linear, 12 in. long, channelled, yellowish-green. *fl.* 1 or 2; falls rich red-purple with red-purple veins 2 in. long, $\frac{3}{4}$ in. wide, signal patch yellow, with yellow hairs on patch and haft; standards obovate, erect, purple in upper, reddish in lower part, $1\frac{1}{2}$ in. long, $\frac{5}{8}$ in. wide. June. N. Portugal. 1876. (B.M. 7097.)

**I. Bornmuel'leri.** A synonym of *I. Danfordiae.*

**I. bosni'aca.** A synonym of *I. Reichenbachii.*

**I. bractea'ta** (1). 8 to 10 in. h. *l.* few to a tuft, 1 to 2 ft. long, $\frac{1}{4}$ to $\frac{1}{3}$ in. wide, rigid. *fl.* bright yellow; falls 2 in. long, $\frac{1}{2}$ in. wide, with 4 distinct brown-purple veins; standards shorter, oblanceolate; tube very short; spathes 2-fld. May. Oregon. 1888. (B.M. 8640; J.R.H.S. 42, clxviii.)

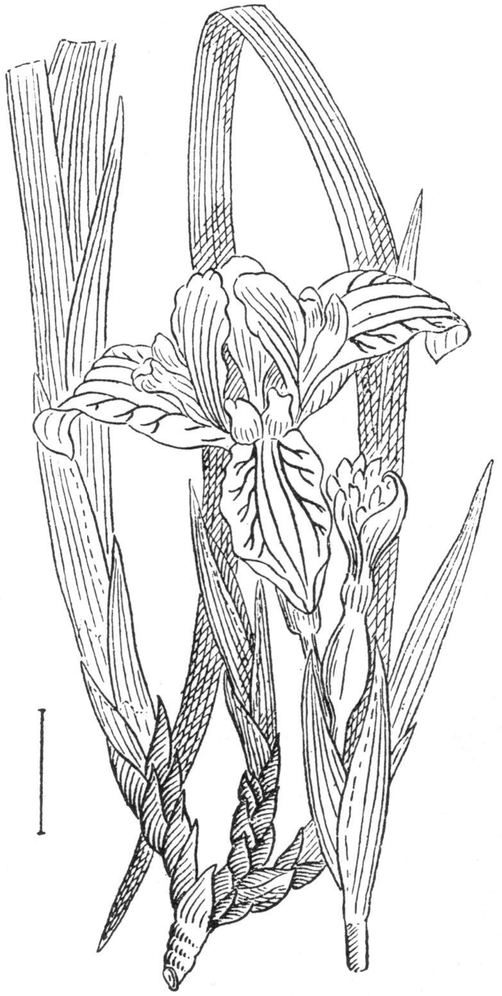

*Iris bracteata*

**I. bucha'rica** (9).* 12 to 18 in. h. *l.* lanceolate, 8 to 12 in. long, 2 to $2\frac{1}{2}$ in. wide, deeply channelled, glossy above, glaucous beneath, edge horny. *fl.* 5 to 7 in l.-axils; falls golden-yellow, nearly round, over 1 in. wide; standards small, white, broadly lanceolate, mucronate, spreading; tube $1\frac{1}{2}$ to 2 in. long. April. Bokhara. 1902. (B.M. 7914; D.I. 41.)

**I. Bulleya'na** (1). Stem 15 to 18 in. long, hollow, leafy in lower part. *l.* linear-ensiform, 18 in. long, $\frac{1}{2}$ in. wide, glossy above, glaucous beneath. *fl.* 1 or 2; falls bright blue-purple in veins and blotches on cream ground, uniform towards margins; obovate, spreading; standards lilac, shorter than falls, oblanceolate, canaliculate, somewhat divergent. June. W. China. (D.I. 6.) Moist soil.

**I. carolinia'na.** A synonym of *I. versicolor.*

**I. caucas'ica** (9). Stem 1- to 3-fld. or very short. *l.* 4 to 6, sharply falcate, 4 to 6 in. long, glossy above, glaucous beneath. *fl.* scentless; falls pale yellow, obovate, $1\frac{1}{2}$ in. long, $\frac{1}{2}$ in. wide, reflexing only in upper third; standards deflexed, deeply toothed; styles broad, pale yellow, with deltoid crests; spathes 1-fld. February, March. Caucasus to Persia. (S.B.F.G. 255; B.M. n.s. 405.) Loamy soil. var. **coeru'lea,** *see* **I. coerulea.**

**I. cengial'ti** (3). Closely related to *I. pallida* but more slender and with pale-brown spathes. *l.* 6 to 9 in. long, yellowish-green. *fl.* sky-blue flushed violet. May, June. NE. Italy. var. **illy'rica** has glaucous l. SYN. *I. illyrica.* **I. Sweer'tii** is a pale almost albino form of *I. cengialti.* (S.B.F.G. s. 2, 254.)

**I. Chamaei'ris** (3). Stem 1 to 10 in. long, 1-headed. *l.* 4 to 6 in a tuft, about $\frac{1}{2}$ in. wide, pale green. *fl.* 1 or 2; falls oblong-spatulate, $\frac{3}{4}$ in. wide, blue, purple, yellow, or white tinged and veined brown, beard usually bright orange-yellow; standards erect or converging, oblong, clawed, 1 in. wide, margins crisped; tube about 1 in. long. April, May. S. Europe. (B.M. 6110 as *I. olbiensis.*) SYN. *I. lutescens*. Very variable in colour and stature. Differs from *I. pumila* by the distinct stem, shorter perianth tube, and greener, more inflated spathes. Often confused in gardens.

**I. chinen'sis.** A synonym of *I. japonica*.

**I. chrysan'tha.** A synonym of *I. Barnumae urmiensis*.

**I. chrysograph'es** (1). Stem 15 to 18 in. long, hollow, 2-fld. *l.* linear-ensiform, acuminate, 18 to 20 in. long, ½ in. wide. *fl.* with short thick tube; falls deep violet more or less marked by golden veins, limb about 2¼ in. long, 1 in. wide; standards oblanceolate, narrow, deep violet, somewhat spreading. June. Szechwan, Yunnan. 1911. (B.M. 8433; D.I. 4.) Moist soil. See also **I. Dykesii.**

**I. chrysophoeni'cia** (1). One of the many forms related to *I. versicolor* found in the Mississippi delta, this having purple falls with a distinct yellow area near the base of the limb passing into the haft and narrower somewhat spreading standards similarly coloured. June. 1936. (Add. 452.)

**I. Clark'ei** (1). Distinguished from *I. sibirica* by the solid, branching stem, l. shining above, glaucous beneath, and the green, wholly herbaceous spathe valves. Himalaya. 1908. (B.M. 8323; D.I. 5.)

**I. coeru'lea** (9). Distinguished from *I. orchioides* by the distinct horny margin of the l. *fl.* grey-blue passing to green then yellow on the patch near the crinkled white crest. Stem 15 in. h. with 3 to 5 fl. in l.-axils. April. Turkestan. 1889. SYN. *I. caucasica coerulea, I. orchioides coerulea*.

**I. Collet'tii** (8). Nearly related to *I. nepalensis* but with broader, deep green, not glaucous, l., and a very short (up to 2 in.) stem. *fl.* lavender, tube short. May. N. Burma, Siam, Yunnan. (B.M. 7889.)

**I. confu'sa** (2). Of similar habit to *I. Wattii* with leafy stems having a tuft of l. at apex from which in the succeeding year the 6- to 8-branched infl. arises, but with smaller fl. about 2 in. across faintly tinged mauve, having yellow stains and orange spots on the fimbriate crest and wavy crenate segs.; falls about 1 in. long, ⅜ in. wide; spathe valves about ½ in. long. Up to 3 ft. h. *l.* 1½ to 2 in. wide, smooth. April. W. China. Greenhouse.

**I. creten'sis.** *See* **I. unguicularis.**

**I. cre'tica.** *See* **I. unguicularis.**

**I. crista'ta** (2). About 6 in. h. Stem very short, 2-fld. *l.* about 4, distichous, broad in middle, linear. *fl.* tube 1½ to 4 in. long; falls obovate, blunt, reflexing, ½ in. long, ½ in. wide, pale lilac, throat and crest deep yellow; standards erect, oblanceolate, rather shorter and narrower than falls. May. E. United States. 1756. (B.M. 412; L.B.C. 1366; D.I. 25.) **I. lacus'tris** is a smaller more compact plant with more slender rhiz.

**I. cu'prea.** A synonym of *I. fulva*.

**I. cypria'na** (3). About 3 ft. h., often with a bent stem. *l.* ensiform, glaucous. *fl.* bright lilac, fragrant, 6 to 7 in. across; falls broadest at apex, beard white tipped yellow and with yellow base; tube rather longer and segs. more obovate than in *I. pallida*. May. Cyprus. 1885. *See* **I. trojana.**

**I. Danford'iae** (10).* Stem very short, 1-headed, spotted brown. *l.* 4-angled, 1 ft. long, hollow, after fl. *fl.* bright yellow, 1 to 2 in. across; standards minute, erect, less than ¾ in. long; tube 1½ to 3 in. long. January, February. Cicilian Taurus. 1889. (B.M. 7140; Gn. 37 (1890), 462 as *I. Bornmuelleri.*)

**I. darwas'ica** (5). About 1 ft. h. Stem 1-headed. *l.* linear, thin, glaucous, about 1 ft. long, ¼ in. wide. *fl.* hyaline-greenish with claret-purple veins; falls elliptic-lanceolate, cuspidate, 2¼ in. long, ½ in. wide, bearded to middle with blue; standards oblong, claw sometimes faintly bearded. April, May. Turkestan. 1885. (B.M. 7029 as *I. Suwarowi.*)

**I. Delavay'i** (1). Stem 3 to 4 ft. h., hollow. *l.* 2½ ft. long, glaucous. *fl.* purple-violet, blotched white, 2½ in. across; falls rounded oval, emarginate; standards small, lanceolate, reflexed. June. Yunnan. 1895. (B.M. 7661.) Semi-aquatic.

**I. deserto'rum.** A synonym of *I. spuria halophila*.

**I. dichot'oma** (7). Stem 2 to 3 ft. h., slender, much-branched, branches often in pairs. *l.* ensiform, distichous, erect. *fl.* dull greenish-white, opening once in afternoon, spirally twisting after flowering; falls oblong, ½ in. wide, haft white, spotted purple; standards oblanceolate, deeply emarginate; clusters 5- or 6-fld. August. Siberia, N. China. 1784. (B.M. 6428; B.R. 246; S.B.F.G. 96.) Often flowers so freely that it fails to make lateral growth and dies.

**I. Douglasia'na** (1).* Stem 6 to 12 in. h., slender, pink near base, bearing a terminal and 1 or 2 lateral fl.-clusters. *l.* evergreen, about 4 in a tuft, linear, thick, rigid, strongly ribbed, pink near base. *fl.* 1½ to 2 in. deep, extremely variable in colour; falls with a slight median ridge and 4 parallel dark lines, ½ to ¾ in. wide, as long as haft, reflexing; standards rather shorter, erect, lanceolate, clawed. May. California. 1873. (B.M. 6083; D.I. 8; Gn. 50 (1896), 272.)

**I. Du'thiei.** A synonym of *I. kumaonensis*.

**I. Dykes'ii** (1). Closely related to *I. chrysographes* but larger in all parts. Up to 20 in. h. *l.* over 32 in. long, ⅗ in. wide, dark green. *fl.* later than in *I. chrysographes*, dark blue-purple with golden median line in lower half; tube 1¼ in. long; filaments shorter than in *I. chrysographes*, anthers larger. China? 1922. (B.M. 9282.)

**I. ensa'ta** (1). Stem flattened, about 1 ft. long, firm. *l.* tufted, linear, firm, glaucous, ¼ to ½ in. wide, eventually 18 to 24 in. long. *fl.* in a single 1- to 3-fld. cluster, varying from white with greenish veins to dark purple, about 2 in. deep; all segs. oblanceolate; falls reflexed, marked with yellow and veined at throat; standards erect, ¼ in. wide, rather darker than falls. April, May. Temperate Asia. (B.M. 2331 as *I. Pallasii*; B.R. 26, 1 as *I. fragrans*; B.M. 2528 as *I. longispatha*; S.B.F.G. s. 2, 187 as *I. biglumis.*)

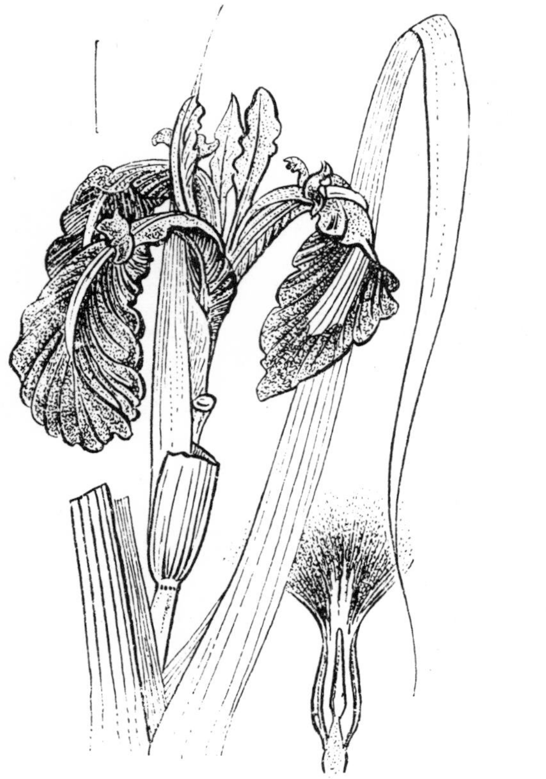

*Iris Dykesii*

**I. errat'ica.** A synonym of *I. Pseudopumila*.

**I. Eulefeld'ii.** A synonym of *I. scariosa*.

**I. Ewbankia'na** (4). Stem 2 to 4 in. h. *l.* very narrow, falcate, 6 to 8 in. long, glaucous. *fl.* about 3¼ in. across, creamy-white with conspicuous brown-purple veins; falls lanceolate, pointed, spreading, beard yellow, signal patch small, nearly black; standards obovate-lanceolate, pointed, erect. May. Asia Minor, N. Persia. 1901. (G.C. 29 (1901), 407.)

**I. filifo'lia** (10). Stem slender, terete, 12 to 18 in. h., 2-fld. *l.* 6 or more, lower filiform, over 1 ft. long, outer scale l. at base mottled deep purple. *fl.* bright deep purple, 2½ in. deep; blade of falls orbicular, shorter than the fiddle-shaped haft, signal patch orange; standards obovate, emarginate, erect; tube 1 in. long; spathe 3 in. long with pale-green lanceolate valves. June. S. Spain, NW. Africa. 1869. (B.M. 5928 as *Xiphion filifolium*, 5981 as *X. tingitanum.*) *See also* **I. Xiphium.**

**I. fimbria'ta.** A synonym of *I. japonica*.

**I. flaves'cens** (3). *fl.* lemon-yellow, almost white. A bearded Iris probably of garden origin.

**I. flavis'sima** (3). *rhiz.* much-branched. Stem 3 to 4 in. h., slender, erect, 1- to 3-fld. *l.* tufted, few, linear, 3 to 4 in. long. *fl.* bright yellow striped with purplish-brown on hafts; falls oblong, beard orange; standards rather shorter, narrow. May. Hungary to NE. Asia. 1802. (B.R. 549 as *I. arenaria.*) *See* **I. Bloudowii.**

**I. florenti'na.** An albino form of *I. germanica* (q.v.) with white fl. showing traces of blue on the falls and with spathe valves almost entirely dry. One of the plants grown near Florence for Orris root, its rhizomes having emetic qualities and being used as the basis for many perfumery powders. The Fleur-de-Lis of French Heraldry. (B.M. 671.)

**I. foetidis'sima** (3). Stinking Gladwyn. Stem compressed, 2 ft. h. *l.* ensiform, as long as stem, firm. *fl.* bluish-lilac, 2 in. deep in sessile lateral clusters; falls obovate, ¾ in. wide; standards erect, oblanceolate, shorter than falls, ⅓ in. wide. June. W. Europe, including Britain. (E.B. 1494.) The dehiscing capsule showing the large, persistent orange seeds is very ornamental. Moist shady places.

**I. folio'sa** (1). Stem flexuous, up to 6 in. long only. *l.* ensiform, 18 in. long, 1 in. wide, glaucous. *fl.* lavender with white near base of falls, about 5 in. across; falls ovate, haft greenish, hairy near base of blade, $3\frac{1}{2}$ in. long, $1\frac{1}{4}$ in. wide; standards oblanceolate, spreading, $2\frac{1}{2}$ in. long, $\frac{5}{8}$ in. wide. June, July. SE. United States. (D.I. 20.) Syn. *I. hexagona Lamancei.*

**I. Fontane'sii.** *See* **I. tingitana.**

**I. Forres'tii** (1). Stem 12 to 18 in. long, hollow, usually 1-headed. *l.* narrow-linear, about 16 in. long, glossy above, glaucous beneath. *fl.* lemon to yellow with brown-purple veins on haft of falls; falls oblong-ovate, blade 2 in. long, 1 in. wide; standards nearly erect, oblanceolate, shorter than falls. Yunnan. 1909. (D.I. 3; G.C. 47 (1910), 418.)

**I. Fosteria'na** (9). Stem 1- or 2-headed, 6 to 8 in. long at flowering time. *l.* few, lanceolate, acuminate, falcate, striate on outside. *fl.* falls pale yellow, $1\frac{1}{2}$ to 2 in. long, blade orbicular, about $\frac{3}{4}$ in. wide; standards bright purple, 1 in. long, oblanceolate, more or less horizontal; spathes 1-fld. April. Afghan-Russian border. (B.M. 7215.)

**I. frag'rans.** *See* **I. subbiflora.**

**I. ful'va** (1). Stem 2 to 3 ft. h., forked low down, angular in lower part with l. at forks. *l.* narrow-ensiform, bright green. *fl.* bright reddish-brown, 2 to $2\frac{1}{2}$ in. deep; all segs. equally reflexed when fully out; falls oblanceolate, $\frac{3}{4}$ to 1 in. wide, blunt, narrowed to a short claw, velvety above with reddish-brown hair on keel; standards broad, truncate, emarginate, 2 in. long, $\frac{3}{4}$ in. wide. June, July. S. United States. (B.M. 1496; D.I. 21.) Syn. *I. cuprea.*

**I. Gates'ii** (4).* Habit and l. of *I. susiana. fl.* falls delicate pale grey derived from fine purple veins on creamy-white, sometimes sky-blue with darker veins, 4 to 5 in. wide, throat densely hairy; standards round, erect, coloured as falls, 4 to 5 in. across. May. Asia Minor. 1889. (B.M. 7867; G.C. 8 (1890), 17; Gn. 43 (1893), 130.) The largest fld. of all Irises but of somewhat sombre colouring.

**I. german'ica** (3). Common Iris. Stem 2 to 3 ft. h., glaucous, forked half-way down. *l.* few, tufted ensiform, glaucous, partly developed in winter. *fl.* fragrant, $2\frac{1}{2}$ to 3 in. deep; falls bright purple, reflexed half-way down, claw white with brownish veins, beard yellow; standards obovate, deep lilac, erect. May. Origin uncertain, long cultivated. (B.M. 670.) This description applies to the commonest form but others differing mainly in colour are also common: **Amas** has deep-purple falls with a beard of bluish-white orange-tipped hairs and nearly orbicular light-blue standards, l. scarcely developed in winter. Syn. *I. macrantha*; **florenti'na,** *see* **I. florentina; Fontarabie,** dwarfer than type with large fl. having distinctly blue standards and a brighter yellow beard; **Kharput** has young l. with a red edge and long narrow reddish-purple segs.; **Koch'ii** and **nepalen'sis** are deep reddish-purple with falls almost black, *nepalensis* being taller in stem and foliage than *Kochii* (D.I. 36) and having a more marked light area on the haft of the falls. (B.R. 818 as *I. nepalensis.*) Syn. *Purple King, I. atropurpurea*; **Siwas** has weak yellow-green l. and blue fl., beard less yellow. The name *germanica* is sometimes applied (like *I. barbata*) to the whole group of tall, bearded Irises, but should be restricted as here defined.

**I. gigan'tea.** A synonym of *I. ochroleuca.*

**I. gracil'ipes** (2). Stem branched, 8 to 10 in. long, slender. *l.* ensiform, about 12 in. long, $\frac{1}{3}$ in. wide. *fl.* pinkish-lilac, rather fleeting; falls obovate, about 1 in. long, $\frac{1}{2}$ in. wide, emarginate, with a wavy orange crest; standards, oblanceolate, spreading, $\frac{1}{4}$ in. wide; tube $\frac{1}{2}$ in. long, funnel-shaped. May. Japan. 1902. (B.M. 7926.)

**I. gramin'ea** (1). Stem 2-edged, about 9 in. h., solid. *l.* about 4, tufted, linear, much longer than fl. *fl.* scented of ripe plums, bright lilac-purple, $1\frac{1}{2}$ to 2 in. deep; falls roundish, $\frac{1}{2}$ in. wide, throat veined blue-purple on white, haft dull yellow; standards erect, purple, $\frac{1}{4}$ in. wide; clusters terminal, 1- or 2-fld. Cent. and S. Europe. 1597. (B.M. 681.)

**I. Grant-Duf'fii** (1). *rhiz.* spiny. Stem 6 in. long, 1-headed, about 2-leaved. *l.* linear, under 1 ft. long, $\frac{1}{8}$ in. wide. *fl.* about $2\frac{1}{2}$ in. long; falls yellow, $\frac{1}{2}$ in. long, haft yellowish-white veined lilac; standards similar, oblanceolate, clawed; tube $\frac{1}{4}$ in. long; spathes 1-fld. April, May. Palestine. 1888. (B.M. 7604.) var. **Ascherson'ii** has greenish-yellow fl., falls edged by a line of nearly black dots.

**I. Griffith'ii** (3). Close to *I. Chamaeiris* but with fl. tube about 2 in. long, segs. purple, spathes long, green. April, May. Afghanistan. 1892.

**I. Gueldenstadtia'na.** A synonym of *I. spuria halophila.*

**I. halophil'a.** A synonym of *I. spuria halophila.*

**I. Hartweg'ii** (1). Related to *I. tenax* with many yellow fl. (D.I. 10.)

**I. Hayn'ei.** A synonym of *I. atrofusca.*

**I. Hel'enae.** *See* **I. acutiloba.**

**I. hexag'ona** (1). Stem 3 to 4 ft. h., forked, leafy, with 3 or 4 heads of fl. *l.* ensiform, 2 to 3 ft. long, 1 to $1\frac{1}{2}$ in. wide. *fl.* lilac, 3 to $3\frac{1}{2}$ in. deep; falls obovate, clawed, blade 4 to $4\frac{1}{2}$ in. long, about 2 in. wide; standards oblanceolate, $\frac{1}{2}$ in. wide, rather shorter than falls, tube $\frac{3}{4}$ to 1 in. long, funnel-shaped; spathes often 5 to 6 in. long. June, July. S. United States. (B.M. 6787.) Rather tender. White-fld. forms occur.

**I. His'trio** (10).* Stem very short. *l.* usually 2, 6 to 8 in. long at flowering time, eventually 12 in. long. *fl.* falls much streaked and spotted lilac on paler ground, with yellow median line, about $1\frac{1}{2}$ in. long, haft gradually narrowed downwards; standards lilac, oblanceolate, divergent; spathe 1-fld., valves 3 to 4 in. long. Winter. Palestine. 1873. (D.I. 46; Gn. 33 (1888), 558; B.M. 6033 as *Xiphion Histrio.*) Bulb produces many small offsets.

**I. histrioi'des** (10).* Distinguished from *I. Histrio* by *l.* very short at flowering time, spreading often wider falls, and erect standards. The general colour is bluer than in *I. Histrio* as a rule and the l. stouter. January. (Gn. 42 (1892), 42; J.R.H.S. 58 (1933) 16; B.M. 9341.) Variable. var. **sophenen'sis** has narrow segs. Amassia, Asia Minor. 1885.

**I. Hoogia'na** (5).* Stem 18 to 30 in. h., 1.-headed. *l.* as in *I. stolonifera. fl.* 2 or 3, about 5 in. deep, uniformly pale grey-blue or somewhat darker, rarely white; falls somewhat recurved, haft veined, beard golden-yellow. May. Turkestan. 1913. (B.M. 8844.) One of the most beautiful of Irises.

**I. Hook'eri.** *See* **I. setosa.**

**I. Hookeria'na** (6). Stem about 5 in. long. *l.* appearing with fl., eventually 1 ft. long, $\frac{3}{4}$ to 1 in. wide. *fl.* 2, falls bluish-purple, narrow-obovate, 2 in. long, $\frac{7}{8}$ in. wide, reflexed, densely bearded; standards bluish-purple, narrower than falls, 2 in. long, $\frac{3}{4}$ in. wide; styles blue, very concave, crests toothed, revolute. May. N. India. 1887. (B.M. 7276.)

**I. ibe'rica** (4). Stem 3 to 6 in. h. *l.* few, in a basal tuft, falcate, 3 in. long, glaucous, linear. *fl.* solitary; segs. nearly equal, ovate, obtuse, $1\frac{1}{2}$ to 2 in. wide, narrowed to a short claw; falls reflexing from near base, concave, closely veined as in *I. susiana* with dark purplish-brown, signal patch velvety, uniformly dark purple; standards erect, white or pale lilac without veining. May. Russian Turkestan, N. Persia. (B.M. 5847.) Somewhat variable in colouring but with falls distinct in form.

**I. illy'rica.** *See* **I. cengialti.**

**I. imbrica'ta** (3). 12 to 20 in. h. *l.* pale yellow-green. *fl.* rather crowded, yellowish-green veined with brown on haft; falls obovate, $2\frac{1}{2}$ in. long, $1\frac{1}{4}$ in. wide; standards roundish-oblong. April, May. Turkestan, N. Persia. (B.R. 31, 35; B.M. 7701 as *I. obtusifolia.*) Confused with *I. flavescens* but distinct by its membranous, inflated green spathes dry only at tip.

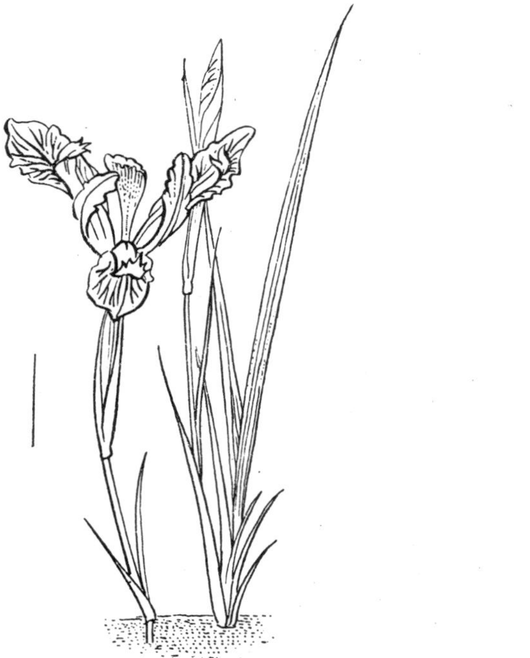

*Iris innominata*

**I. innomina'ta** (1). Stem $4\frac{1}{2}$ in. long, wiry. *l.* grassy, tufted, $\frac{1}{8}$ in. wide, dark green, nearly as long as scape. *fl.* golden-buff veined light brown, solitary; falls about $\frac{5}{8}$ in. wide; standards 1 in. long, slightly paler than falls. June. Oregon. 1935. (J.R.H.S. 61, 389; B.M. 9628.)

**I. japon'ica** (2). Stem 1 to $1\frac{1}{2}$ ft. h., upper half a loose panicle with erecto-patent branches. *l.* in a fan-like tuft, ensiform, dark-green. *fl.* lilac, 1 to $1\frac{1}{2}$ in. deep; falls oblong-spatulate, $\frac{3}{4}$ in. wide, crisped, and irregularly cut on margins of segs., spotted with yellow and white in middle and with a petaloid crest reaching half-way up also fringed; standards plain lilac. April. Japan, China. (B.M. 373 as *I. chinensis.*) SYN. *I. fimbriata.*

**I. jun'cea** (10). Stem flexuous, terete, 1 ft. h., with 1 or 2 fl. *l.* many, terete, slender, 18 to 24 in. long. *fl.* deep yellow, 1½ to 2 in. deep; blade of falls orbicular, 1 in. wide, as long as the broad haft; standards oblanceolate, spreading, shorter than falls, ½ in. wide; tube 1½ to 2 in. long; spathe 2 to 3 in. long, valves lanceolate, acuminate. June. N. Africa. (Gn. 54 (1898), 470; B.M. 5890 as *Xiphion junceum.*) var. **numid'ica** has paler fl.

**I. Juno'nia** (3). Distinguished from *I. pallida* by the shorter narrower l. 12 to 14 in. long, 1¾ in. wide in middle and by the spathe valves dry only in upper half. *fl.* lavender, beard white tipped orange, 3½ in. long, 1¾ in. wide; standards paler with reflexed sides. About 2 ft. h. June. Asia Minor.

**I. Kaemp'feri** (1).* Stem 2 ft. or more, 2-fld., often branched with a second head of fl. *l.* 2 to 2½ in. long, ensiform, with a distinct midrib. *fl.* of various colours, large; falls in the wild type deep red-purple, about 3 in. long, standards of same colour but shorter and narrow-oblanceolate. July. Japan. 1857. (B.M. 6132; Gn. 9 (1876), 476; 16 (1879), 198; 21 (1882), 424; D.I. 19.) Fl. often very large in the cultivated varieties, up to 10 in. across in the double varieties with the standards and sometimes the style arms spreading and of similar form to the falls. *See* **I. laevigata.**

**I. kamaonen'sis** (6). *rhiz.* red-skinned. Plant compact. *l.* linear, erect, about 6 in. long at flowering time, eventually 18 in. *fl.* falls purple mottled lilac, oblong-ovate, beard white, sometimes tipped yellow; standards paler, erect, clawed; tube striped purple, cylindrical, 2 to 2½ in. long; spathes 1- or 2-fld.; peduncle very short. May. Cent. Himalaya. 1887. (D.I. 30; B.M. 6957 as *I. Kingiana.*) SYN. *I. Duthiei.*

**I. kashmiria'na** (3). Stem 2 ft. long with several clusters of fl. *l.* ensiform, glaucous, 1½ ft. long, over 1 in. wide. *fl.* fragrant, white, 3 in. long; standards and falls about 1½ in. wide, beard white tipped yellow; falls reflexing half-way down; spathes 3 in. long, 2- or 3-fld. June. Kashmir, Afghanistan, &c. 1875. (B.M. 9378; 6869 as *I. Bartoni.*)

**I. Kingia'na.** A synonym of *I. kumaonensis.*

**I. Koch'ii.** *See* **I. germanica.**

**I. Korolkow'i** (5). Stem 1 to 1½ ft. h., leafy in lower part, fl.-head single, 2- to 3-fld. *l.* linear, glaucous, as long as stem. *fl.* 2½ in. deep, creamy-white tinged brown with numerous dark-brown veins; blade of falls oblong, 1½ in. long, 1 in. wide, claw bearded; standards rather wider, oblong, clawed, erect. May. Turkestan. 1874. (B.M. 7025; D.I. 28.)

**I. Krela'gei.** *See* **I. reticulata.**

**I. lacus'tris.** *See* **I. cristata.**

**I. laeviga'ta** (1).* Related to *I. Kaempferi* but l. without distinct midrib. *fl.* clear uniform blue; blade of falls 2½ in. long, 2 in. wide; standards erect, oblanceolate, 2½ in. long. June. *Capsules* 2 in. long with blunt ends (tapered in *I. Kaempferi*) and semicircular, not nearly circular seeds. Japan. A very lovely Iris. var. **albopurpu'rea,** standards white, falls mottled. (B.M. 7511 as *I. albopurpurea.*)

**I. Leichtlin'ii.** A synonym of *I. stolonifera.*

**I. linifo'lia** (9). Related to *I. caucasica* but with linear l.; falls grey-white tinged green; standards minute. Turkestan. 1905.

**I. longipet'ala** (1). Stem 2 to 3 ft. h., solid, compressed, usually with 1 fl.-cluster, occasionally 2 or 3. *l.* narrow, ensiform, firm, 1 to 1½ ft. long. *fl.* white veined violet, 2½ to 3 in. deep; falls obovate, clawed, spreading and drooping, 1 to 1¼ in. wide, narrowed to a short claw with bright-yellow keel and violet veins on a white ground; standards erect, oblanceolate, spatulate, 2 to 3 in. long, ¾ in. wide. May, June. California. 1862. (B.M. 5298.)

**I. Lortet'ii** (4). *l.* ensiform, thin, glaucous, under 1 ft. long at flowering time. *fl.* falls pale greyish-lilac spotted and striped reddish-brown, signal patch dark crimson with short yellow hairs down haft, 3 in. wide; standards pale grey, veined and dotted reddish-brown, wavy, 3 to 4 in. across, erect-inflexed; spathes 1 to 6 in. long, 1-fld.; pedicel short. May. Lebanon. 1890. (B.M. 7251; D.I. 27; Gn. 43 (1893), 130.)

**I. lupi'na.** *See* **I. sari.**

**I. lu'rida** (3). Stem about 18 in. h., deeply forked. *l.* 6 to 8 in. long. *fl.* about 3 in. deep; falls oblong, reddish-purple in upper, veined purple in lower half on a yellow ground, about 1 in. wide, beard bright yellow; standards oval, dull purple with a veined yellow claw, crisped, 2¾ in. long, 1¼ in. wide; spathe green flushed purple, usually 2-fld. April. E. Europe. 1758. Probably of garden origin. (B.M. 986.)

**I. lutes'cens.** A form of *I. Chamaeiris.*

**I. macrosi'phon** (1). Stem 3 to 6 in. long, 1-headed. *l.* linear, 1 ft. long, finely ribbed. *fl.* often lilac but sometimes white or cream, about 2 in. deep; falls obovate-wedge-shaped, ¾ in. wide; standards rather shorter; spathes 1- to 3-fld. May. California, Oregon. 1890. (D.I. 12.)

**I. Madon'na.** *See* **I. albicans Madonna.**

**I. Mar'iae** (4). A close ally of *I. atropurpurea* with a continuous rhizome, dark purple fl. with a dark beard and a more prominent signal patch than in *I. Barnumae.* Palestine. 1894. (G.F. 1893, f. 1394 a; J.H. 28 (1894), 302 as *I. Helenae.*)

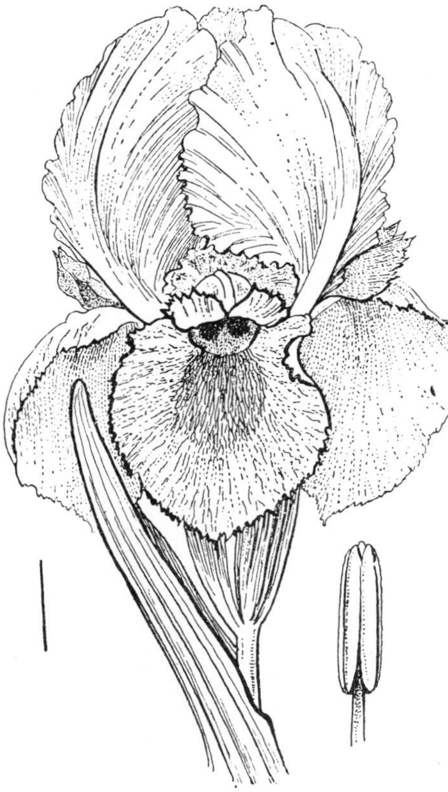

*Iris Lortetii*

**I. me'da** (4). *l.* glaucous, not rigid, 4 to 5 in. long at flowering time, ⅛ in. wide. *fl.* falls lilac-purple or greenish-yellow with a brown signal patch and many brown veins, beard dense, yellow; standards longer than falls, erect; spathe 2 to 2½ in. long, 1-fld. May. Persia. 1888. (B.M. 7040.)

**I. melli'ta** (3). *l.* 3 to 5 in. long, narrow. Related to *I. pumila* but of variable height up to 5 in., and with sharply keeled narrow spathes 2 to 3 in. long. *fl.* pale smoky-brown with fine red-brown veins passing to red-purple shot with blue towards margins; falls much reflexed, beard white tipped blue; standards longer and wider than falls; tube 2 in. or more long. April, May. SE. Europe. (B.M. 8515.) var. **rubromargina'ta** has red-edged l.

**I. mesopotam'ica** (3). 3 to 4 ft. h. Stem branched, erect. *l.* 18 to 24 in. long, 2 in. wide, deep green. *fl.* large, light blue, redder towards middle, standards paler; falls obovate, beard white passing to orange on haft; standards obovate; spathes thin but dry only in upper half. June. Syria? SYN. *I. Ricardi.* Less hardy than *I. pallida.* Stem often too weak to hold the large fl. erect, a character which is sometimes handed on to its hybrids.

**I. Miles'ii** (2). Stem 3 ft. long, branched, arising with a distichous cluster of reduced l., and bearing 2 to 4 clusters of fl. *l.* 7 or 8, ensiform, pale green, 2 to 3 in. wide, gradually tapering. *fl.* 2 to 4 in a cluster, pale reddish-lilac with dark veins and blotches and an orange or yellow much-cut crest, 3½ to 4 in. across. June, July. Temp. Himalaya. 1881. (B.M. 6889.) Vigorous and hardy with leafless rhizomes in winter.

**I. minu'ta** (1). A very small species. *l.* linear, about ½ in. wide, 4 in. long at flowering time, eventually 12 to 15 in. *fl.* solitary, yellow; falls brownish at edges. April, May. Japan. (B.M. 8293.)

**I. missourien'sis** (1). Similar to *I. longipetala,* but holding fl. well above l. and entirely leafless in winter. May, June. Rocky Mts. 1880. (B.M. 6579; Gn. 50 (1896), 186.)

**I. Monnier'i** (1). Stems stout, terete, 3 to 4 ft. h. *l.* firm, suberect, lanceolate, about 2 ft. long. *fl.* yellow, fragrant, clustered, 3 to 3½ in. deep; falls roundish, 1½ to 1¾ in. wide, as long as claw; standards spreading, oblanceolate-spatulate, 3 in. long, 1 in. wide; spathes 2-fld. June, July. Crete. (R.L. 236.) Closely allied to *I. ochroleuca* and perhaps a form of that species.

**I. monta'na** (1). Related to *I. missouriensis* but with stems shorter than l. which are 12 to 18 in. long, ⅓ in. wide, *fl.* deep or pale lavender, standards oblanceolate, not emarginate. May, June. United States. (D.I. 22.)

**I. nazaren'sis.** A synonym of *I. Bismarckiana.*

**I. neglec'ta** (3). A hybrid group of tall bearded Irises with blue or lilac standards and falls closely veined. *l.* ribbed. (B.M. 2435.)

**I. nepalen'sis** (8). Stem 6 to 12 in. h. with 1 to 3 clusters of fl. *l.* linear, ensiform, moderately firm with a median rib on one side and 2 ribs on the other, gradually narrowed to an acuminate tip. *fl.* pale lilac, 1½ to 2 in. deep; falls with reflexing oblong blade as long as haft with a waved median ridge, yellow on haft; standards oblanceolate, clawed, rather shorter than falls. July. Himalaya. 1828. (D.I. 39; S.B.F.G. s. 2, 11.)

**I. obtusifo'lia.** A synonym of *I. imbricata.*

**I. ochroleu'ca** (1). Stem 3 ft. h., stout, slightly flattened. *l.* ensiform, 1 in. wide, firm, dark green. *fl.* clustered, 3 to 3½ in. deep; falls roundish-obovate, abruptly reflexed, 1½ to 1¾ in. wide, white, flushed yellow in middle, emarginate, haft yellow on face without veins, green on back; standards white with orange centre, erect, about 3 in. long, oblanceolate, emarginate. June, July. Asia Minor ? (B.M. 61.)

**I. olbien'sis.** See **I. Chamaeiris.**

*Iris orchioides*

**I. orchioides** (9). Stem 1 to 1¼ ft. long with 3 to 6 solitary, axillary fls. *l.* about 6, lanceolate, 6 to 9 in. long at flowering time and by glossy above, glaucous beneath. *fl.* 2 to 3 in. across; falls bright yellow with a deep green blotch on each side of crest running down the narrow oblong haft; standards yellow, under 1 in. long with a long filiform haft, horizontal or drooping; tube 1½ to 2 in. long; spathes 1-fld., 2 in. long. March, April. Turkestan. 1880. (B.M. 7111.) var. **coeru'lea,** see **I. coerulea;** **ocula'ta** has blade of falls more spotted; white (**al'ba**) and pale yellow (**sulphu'rea**) forms occur.

**I. orienta'lis** (1). Closely related to *I. sibirica,* distinguished by the stem and foliage of about equal height, the 2-, not many-fld., purple spathes which are only slightly dry at flowering time and by the short pedicels. May, June. E. Asia, Japan. (D.I. 1b: B.M. 1604 as *I. sibirica sanguinea.*) Sometimes distinguished as *I. extrem-orientalis.*

**I. palesti'na** (9). Similar to *I. alata* but smaller. Variable in colour being yellow, greenish, or blue (**caeru'lea**) with a few veins of a deeper shade. Winter. Syria.

**I. pal'lida** (3). Distinct from *I. germanica* by its pale glaucous foliage, dry silvery spathes at flowering time and the short perianth tube. May, June. Stem 2 to 3 ft. h. *fl.* fragrant. (B.M. 685.) var. **dalmat'ica** has broader l. about 2 in. wide, very glaucous, and large lavender fl.

**I. paradox'a** (4). Stem 2 to 6 in. long, 1-headed. *l.* linear, falcate, 3 to 6 in. long at flowering time, ¼ in. wide. *fl.* falls pale purple covered along middle with black-purple velvety hair and veined black-purple near edge, 1 to 2 in. long, ½ in. wide; standards white veined and dotted deep blue-violet, erect, 2 to 3 in. long, 1½ to 2 in. wide with a short claw; tube ½ to ¾ in. long; spathe 1-fld., 2 to 3 in. long. May. Georgia, N. Persia. 1888. (B.M. 7081; Gn. 32 (1887), 584.)

**I. pers'ica** (9). Stem very short with 1, occasionally 2, fl. *l.* 4 or 5 in a basal tuft, linear, recurved, 2 to 3 in. long at flowering time. *fl.* violet-scented; falls oblong-spatulate, ½ in. wide, pale greenish-blue with a bright yellow, smooth keel, margins waved. February. Asia Minor to S. Persia. (B.M. 1; Gn. 33 (1888), 558.) A variable plant. var. **ala'tica,** resembling var. *Sieheana* but with wings of haft of fall horizontal instead of encircling style branches; **Isaacson'i,** *fl.* creamy-white with greenish tinge without purple blotch on falls; **is'sica,** *fl.* bright yellow; **purpu'rea,** *fl.* reddish-purple with darker blotch on falls; **Siehea'na,** *fl.* blotched brown-purple on greyish ground; **stenophyl'la,** *fl.* pale grey-blue with blotches of blue-black, sometimes 2-fld., *l.* narrow, ciliate. (B.M. 7734.); **tau'ri,** *fl.* dark violet-purple, with white veins on haft and middle of falls, *l.* scarcely ciliate and not white-edged. (B.M. 7793; G.C. 29 (1901), 191.)

**I.×plica'ta** (3). A hybrid group with standards and falls white except for veins of colour on edges of segs., otherwise like *I. pallida.* (B.M. 870 as *I. aphylla pallida.*)

**I. Polak'ii** (4). Dr. Stapf reduces *I. Barnumae* to a variety of a species, *I. Polakii,* of which he recognizes 3 forms: var. **Barn'umae,** tall, with more or less uniformly violet fl.; **protony'ma,** shorter with dark purple to maroon fl. and very narrow l. (B.M. 9279.) SYN. *I. acutiloba;* and **urmien'sis,** *fl.* yellow.

**I. prismat'ica** (1). Stem 1½ to 2 ft. h., slender, solid, terete. *l.* linear, 2 ft. long, tufted, moderately firm. *fl.* 2 or 3 in terminal cluster, solitary on branches; deep bright lilac-blue; falls roundish, under 1 in. wide, much shorter than the strap-shaped haft; standards oblanceolate, clawed, erect, shorter than the falls. May. Much like *I. sibirica* but with solid stem, longer pedicels projecting beyond the dry, narrow, 1 in. long spathe valves and widely spreading rhiz. United States. (B.M. 1504; D.I. 7.)

**I. Pseudac'orus** (1). Yellow Flag, Water Flag. Stem 2 to 3 ft. h., stout, terete, forked low down. *l.* ensiform, glaucous, 1 in. wide. *fl.* large, almost scentless, clustered, bright yellow, 2 to 2½ in. deep; falls roundish, 1¼ to 1½ in. wide, bright orange-yellow with a deeper spot at throat and radiating brown veins, haft green down back; standards oblanceolate, spatulate, erect, about ½ in. long. May, June. Europe, including Britain, W. Asia. (E.B. 1495.) var. **acori-form'is** has falls veined brown; **al'ba,** *fl.* cream with brownish veins near tip; **Bastar'di,** *fl.* without deeper blotch.

**I. Pseudopu'mila** (3). Related to *I. Chamaeiris* with a stem longer than the tube but with narrow spathe valves, 1-fld., perianth tube 2 to 3 in. long. *l.* greyish-green, 6 to 8 in. long, stem 4 to 7 in. long. *fl.* purple, yellow, or white. April. S. Italy, Sicily. **I. Statel'lae** is closely related with very pale yellow fl. as is also **I. errat'ica** with pale yellow fl. (B.M. 6894 as *I. Statellae.*)

**I. pu'mila** (3). 4 to 5 in. h., almost stemless. *l.* ensiform, about 4 in a tuft, slightly glaucous. *fl.* small, solitary, variable in colour, about 2 in. deep; falls oblong, clawed, reflexing about half-way down, beard dense on haft and lower part of keel; standards erect, as large as falls, rather paler. April. Europe, Asia Minor. 1596. (B.M. 1209; D.I. 32; L.B.C. 1506 as *I. taurica.*) Much variation in colour occurs. var. **at'tica** has pale straw yellow fl. tinged green with a brownish spot on falls. SYN. *I. attica;* **azu'rea** and **caeru'lea,*** blue (B.M. 1261), and various other colour forms are available.

**I. Pur'dyi** (1). Near *I. bracteata* but the pale straw-brown, lined fl. have a longer narrow tube (1¼ to 1½ in. long) double the length of the ovary, longer, broader l., and a straight-edged instead of pointed style. May, June. (D.I. 11.) Sometimes confused with *I. Douglasiana.*

**I. Reichenbach'ii** (3). Stem 6 to 10 in. long. *l.* 3 to 6 in. long at flowering time, eventually longer. *fl.* with falls and standard almost chocolate, beard bluish-white (**I. balkana**) or falls yellow, beard orange; tube 1 to 1½ in. long, funnel-shaped. April. Balkans. (D.I. 34; B.M. 8812.) SYN. *I. bosniaca, I. serbica.*

**I. reticula'ta** (10). *l.* 2 to 4 in a tuft, as high as fl. at flowering, eventually 1 ft. long or more, ¹⁄₁₂ in. wide, 4-angled. *fl.* deep violet-purple, falls with raised orange ridge bordered white, reflexed, ½ in. long, ⅜ in. wide, haft 1½ in. long, channelled; standards erect, oblanceolate, 2½ in. long; tube 3 to 6 in. long; spathes 1-fld., sessile. February, March. Caucasus. (B.M. 5577; D.I. 45.) A variable species. var. **al'ba,** *fl.* white; **Cantab,** *fl.* Cambridge Blue with orange markings; **cyan'ea,** *fl.* blue of various shades, more or less like type; **Krela'gei,** *fl.* red-purple, often earlier; the commonest form. (L.B.C. 1829; S.B.F.G. s. 2, 189.) Many good seedlings have recently been raised, the result of crossing different forms together, such as **Royal Blue, Hercules, Aurora.** Some variants approach *I. Histrio,* &c.

**I. Ricar'di.** A synonym of *I. mesopotamica.*

**I. Rosenbachia'na** (9). Stem very short with 1 to 3 fl. in l.-axils. *l.* 3 to 6, linear-lanceolate, acute, deep green, 1 to 2 in. long at flowering, eventually 9 in. long, 2 in. wide. *fl.* falls long, oblong, usually deep velvety purple with an orange crest, 2 to 2½ in. long, ½ in. wide; standards 1 in. long, coloured as falls, horizontal or drooping; style broad, 1 in. long. January to March. Turkestan. 1886. (B.M. 7135.) A variable plant with fl. in various striking combinations of purple, yellow, and white. var. **baldschuan'ica** is smaller and later with pale primrose fl. veined and blotched brown-purple. SYN. *I. baldschuanica.*

**I. rubromargina'ta.** *See* **I. mellita.**

**I. ruthen'ica** (1). Stem slender, 1 to 8 in. h., 1- or 2-fld. *l.* linear, acuminate, about 6 in. long at flowering, eventually 12 in., grassy. *fl.* fragrant, 1½ in. deep, 3 in. across; falls broad-oval, spreading, creamy-white with bright-bluish veins, ½ in. wide; standards lanceolate, deep violet, erect, ¼ in. wide. May. Transylvania and Siberia to China. 1804. (B.M. 1123 and 1393; D.I. 13; L.B.C. 1650.)

**I. sambuci'na** (3). Probably of hybrid origin, with deciduous l., branched many-fld. stems about 2 ft. long, fl. violet or bluish with bluish style-branches, beard orange, spathes not wholly dry. June. Habitat? 1758. (B.M. 787 as *I. squalens.*)

**I. sar'i** (4). Stem 3 to 6 in. long, 1-headed, with 2 reduced l. *l.* about 6 in a tuft, linear, about 9 in. long at flowering time, ¼ to ⅓ in. wide, pale. *fl.* falls 3 in. long, 1½ in. wide, blade lanceolate, wavy or toothed at margin, yellow or greenish with brown-red veins, signal patch dark red, reflexed half-way, with a diffuse beard down haft; standards wider and a little longer, round, with a short haft, almost entirely suffused with red-brown; tube 1½ in. long; spathe 1-fld., 3 in. long. May. Asia Minor. 1876. (D.I. 26; B.M. 7904 as *I. lupina.*) Variable in colour, sometimes with a bluish instead of a yellow ground. var. **lu'rida** and **nazaren'sis.** *See* **I. Bismarckiana.**

**I. scario'sa** (3). Stem about 6 in. h. with 1 or 2 fl. *l.* very glaucous. *fl.* red-purple with darker veins on falls; beard yellow on haft, white on blade; tube brown-purple; spathe 2 in. long, scarious. May. Caspian east to Altai. (B.M. 6902 as *I. Eulefeldii.*) SYN. *I. Eulefeldii.*

**I. seto'sa** (1). Stem 6 to 24 in. h., rather stout, solid, branching low down. *l.* thin, lower 1 to 2 ft. long, about ½ in. wide. *fl.* purple, 2 to 2½ in. deep; falls orbicular, 1 in. wide, reflexing half-way down; standards erect, ½ in. long, narrowed to a fine point. May, June. E. Siberia to Japan, N. America. 1844. (D.I. 23; B.M. 2326 as *I. brachycuspis*; 2356 as *I. tripetala.*) A very variable species in height, in presence or absence of colouring, in l.-bases and spathes, and to some extent in the form of the fl.

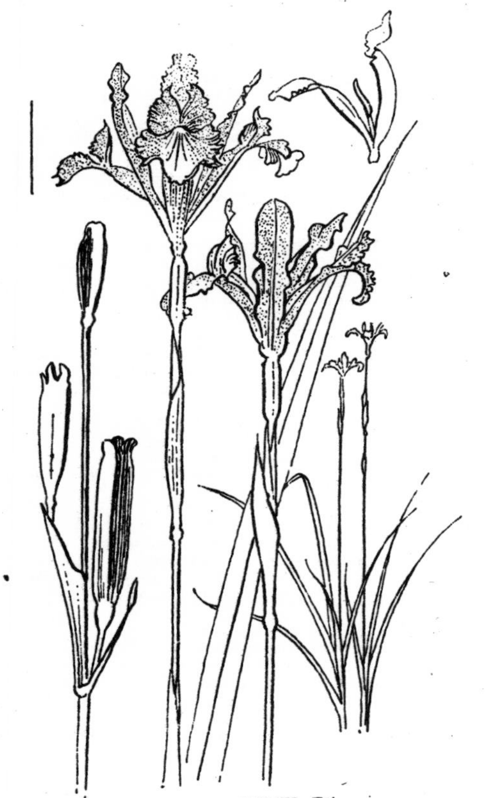

*Iris sibirica*

**I. sibi'rica** (1).* Tufted. Stem much taller than l., hollow, often with one side branch. *l.* linear, 1 to 2 ft. long, ¼ in. wide. *fl.* 2 to 5 in a terminal head, blue-purple, lavender, or grey, occasionally white, about 3 in. deep, 2½ in. across; falls roundish-oblong, about ¾ in. wide, reflexed; standards broad-lanceolate, shorter than falls, erect; tube ½ in. long; spathes small, brown, dry at flowering. June. Cent. Europe, Russia. 1596. (D.I. 1; B.M. 50.) A variable species. Several white forms are known as **al'ba** (B.M. 438) and **Snow Queen.** For var. **orienta'lis,** *see* **I. orientalis.**

**I. sikkimen'sis** (6). Related to *I. kumaonensis*. Stem 4 to 6 in. long with 2 or 3 fl. *l.* 4 to 8 in. long at flowering time, eventually 12 to 18 in., ½ to ¾ in. wide, ensiform. *fl.* falls dark violet, mottled, 2½ in. long, 1 in. wide; blade obovate; beard white tipped orange; standards pale mauve, oblong, emarginate, 2 in. long, ¾ in. wide; tube 1½ to 2 in. long, deep purple. May. Sikkim. (D.I. 31.)

**I. sindjaren'sis** (9). *l.* about 12, crowded, lanceolate, distichous, 8 to 10 in. long, striated below, glossy above. *fl.* bluish-white; falls oblong-wedge-shaped, 2 in. long, with radiating darker lilac lines and a small yellow crest; standards deflexed, 1 in. long; tube 2 to 2½ in. long. February, March. Mesopotamia. 1890. (B.M. 7145; Gn. 69 (1906), 134.)

**I. Sintenis'ii** (1). Stem round, 4 to 12 in. long, 2-fld. *l.* linear, acuminate, 8 to 18 in. long, ¼ to ½ in. wide. *fl.* bluish-purple; blade of falls elliptical, veined and dotted on a white ground; standards erect, oblanceolate, emarginate; tube short. May, June. SE. Europe, Asia Minor. (D.I. 71a.) SYN. *I. Uromovii.*

**I. Sisyrin'chium** (11). Corm small. Stem terete, 6 to 12 in. long, 1- to 3-headed. *l.* 2, linear, arching, 6 to 12 in. long. *fl.* lilac, fugitive; falls with central yellow spot bordered white; standards shorter, ⅛ to ¼ in. long; tube 1 in. long. May, June. Mediterranean region to India. (B.M. 1407 as *Moraea Sisyrinchium*; S.B.F.G. 110 as *M. Tenoreana*; B.M. 6096 as *Xiphion Sisyrinchium.*) Rarely permanent in England.

**I. Sofara'na** (4). *fl.* similar to *I. susiana* but falls creamy-white with many dark purple veins, elliptic, standards nearly white with thin dark purple veins and dots, orbicular. May. Lebanon. 1899. (G.C. 54 (1913), 377.)

**I. spu'ria.** Stem 1 to 2 ft. h., little branched, stout, round. *l.* erecto-patent, linear-ensiform, unpleasantly scented when bruised, 1 ft. long, ½ in. wide. *fl.* clusters sessile or nearly so, bright lilac, 1½ to 2 in. long; blade of falls rounded, under 1 in. wide, scarcely deflexed, keel from base of blade down haft bright yellow, haft faintly streaked purple on white ground; standards oblanceolate, shorter than falls, bright lilac. June, July. Europe, Asia, Algeria. (D.I. 15, 17b; B.M. 58, 1131 as *I. halophila*; 1514 as *I. desertorum.*) A widely spread species, variable in colour, form, and habit but with the general characters described. The form often known as *I. halophila* or *I. Gueldenstadtiana* (*fl.* white, dull yellow, or pale purplish) has narrower fl.-segs. and is dwarfer than many. *I. aurea, I. Monnieri,* and *I. ochroleuca* are sometimes regarded as forms of this species.

**I. squa'lens** (3). Similar to *I. sambucina* but with cloudy yellow fl., the falls veined with yellowish white on a bluish- or reddish-lilac ground. Of hybrid origin. (B.M. 187 as *I. sambucina.*)

**I. Statel'lae.** *See* **I. Pseudopumila.**

**I. stolonif'era** (5). *rhiz.* spreading, slender, red-skinned. Stem 12 to 24 in. h., 1- to 3-fld. *l.* ensiform, dark blue-green, ribbed. *fl.* pale or dark blue edged or shot with brown-veining, heavy or faint; falls obovate, reflexed, wavy at margin, 2½ to 3 in. long. 1½ in. wide; beard bright yellow or blue; standards obovate, erect, about as large as falls; tube 1 in. long, tinged purple. May. Bokhara, Turkestan. 1884. (D.I. 29; Gn. 52 (1897), 222; B.M. 7861 as *I. Leichtlinii.*)

**I. stylo'sa.** A synonym of *I. unguicularis.*

**I. subbiflo'ra** (3). Stem 8 to 12 in. long. *l.* ensiform 4 to 8 in. long. *fl.* bright violet-purple; blade of falls obovate, 1½ in. long, 1 in. wide, reflexing; beard bluish and white; standards erect 2 in. long, over 1 in. wide; spathe 1- or 2-fld., more or less dry in upper part. April. SW. Europe. 1596. (B.M. 1130; D.I. 33.) SYN. *I. biflora, I. fragrans.*

**I. susia'na** (4).* Mourning Iris. Stem 1 to 1½ ft. h. *l.* ensiform, pale green, rather firm, about 12 in. long, 1 in. wide. *fl.* solitary; falls like standards in size and shape, blade round, 1½ to 3 in. wide, narrowed to a wedge-shaped short haft, with dense fine spots and lines of brown-black on a whitish ground tinged with lilac; falls reflexing, beard broad, brown-black, signal patch purple-black, velvety; standards erect, much spotted on brighter lilac. May. Levant. 1573. (B.M. 91; Gn. 39 (1891), 340.)

**I. Suwar'owi.** A synonym of *I. darwasica.*

**I. Sweer'tii.** *See* **I. cengialti.**

**I. tau'ri.** A synonym of *I. persica tauri.*

**I. tecto'rum** (2). 12 in. or more h. *l.* ensiform, about 12 in. long, thin, pale green. *fl.* bright lilac, 1½ to 2 in. deep; falls over 1 in. wide, obtuse, crisped at edge, with deep lilac veins on a paler lilac groundwork, narrowed into a haft as long as blade, crest white and lilac, ½ in. deep, deeply cut; standards spreading, rather shorter than falls, blade orbicular, plain lilac; spathe single, terminal, 2- or 3-fld. May, June. Japan. 1872. (B.M. 6118; D.I. 24; Gn. 50 (1896), 272.) A white form (**al'ba**) occurs.

**I. te'nax** (1).* Stem 12 in. h., slender. *l.* linear, moderately firm, fibres very tough. *fl.* often 2, from grey to reddish-claret with middle ridge of falls yellow, 2 to 3 in. deep; falls lanceolate, clawed, blade ¾ to 1 in. wide, reflexed; standards nearly as long, ¼ in. wide, lanceolate. May. Washington, Oregon. (B.M. 3343; B.R. 1218; D.I. 9.) N. American Indians used the fibres in weaving.

**I. tingita'na** (10).* Stem stout, terete, 18 to 24 in. long. *l.* linear with a clasping purple-spotted sheath, over 1 ft. long, upper gradually smaller. *fl.* lilac-purple, 3 in. deep; blade of falls orbicular, shorter than the fiddle-shaped haft; standards erect, linear-lanceolate; tube about 1½ in. long, spathes 2-fld., 5 to 6 in. long, valves lanceolate, acuminate. April, May. Morocco. (B.M. 6775; Gn. 36 (1889), 294.) The largest of its group. var. **Fontane'sii,** deep violet-blue with an orange blotch.

**I. troja'na** (3). Stem 2 ft. or more long, erect, branched. *l.* longer than in *I. germanica*, wider than in *I. cypriana* with which it is sometimes confused. *fl.* about 5 in. deep, 4 in. wide, fragrant; falls obovate, red-purple, reflexed, beard white tipped yellow, yellow near base; standards obovate, pale blue, flushed purple; buds long, pointed; spathes dry only near tip; tube as long as ovary. May, June. Troad? 1888. (D.I. 37.)

**I. Tubergenia'na** (9). *l.* ribbed, glaucous. *fl.* falls bright yellow, 2 in. long with a fimbriate crest; standards minute, 3-toothed. March. Turkistan. 1899. (Gn. 66 (1904), 1.) Allied to *I. caucasica* and *I. orchioides*.

**I. tubero'sa.** A synonym of *Hermodactylus tuberosus*.

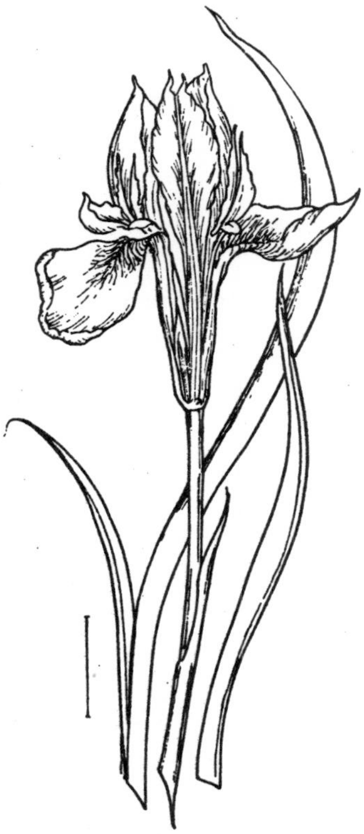

*Iris unguicularis*

**I. unguicula'ris** (1).* Stem very short or absent. *l.* in a basal tuft, linear, erect, firm, 18 to 24 in. long, ¼ to ½ in. wide. *fl.* fragrant, 3 in. deep, bright lilac; falls obovate, reflexed, 1 in. wide, gradually narrowed into a linear haft, keeled yellow, streaked lilac on white ground at throat; standards nearly of same shape and size, lilac, erect; tube very long, slender. November to March. Algeria, E. Mediterranean. (D.I. 14; Gn. 24 (1883), 68; 46 (1894), 248; B.M. 5773 as *I. stylosa*.) Several variations in colour and habit occur. Colour forms are **al'ba,** *fl.* white; **grandiflo'ra,** *fl.* deep purple, large; **lilaci'na,** *fl.* pale lilac, rather small; **margina'ta,** *fl.* violet, edged white; **specio'sa,** *fl.* deep violet with bright yellow keel and base of falls veined violet-purple on a white ground; **creten'sis** has very narrow foliage and usually smaller *fl.* (B.M. 6343; 9369 as *I. cretensis*.) SYN. *I. angustifolia*; **la'zica** has wider, ensiform *l.*, green spathes, perianth tube 3 to 4 in. long, stem 3 to 4 in. long, *fl.* dark purple. Lazistan.

**I. urmien'sis.** A synonym of *I. Barnumae urmiensis*.

**I. Uromo'vii.** A synonym of *I. Sintenisii*.

**I. variega'ta** (3). Stem 15 in. h., branched; terminal head 3-, lateral 2-fld. *l.* ensiform, 8 to 18 in. long, 1 in. wide, ribbed. *fl.* of medium size; falls obovate, about ¾ in. wide, reflexed, yellow with much brown veining and colouring, beard bright yellow; standards erect, rounded, oblong, bright yellow; tube ¾ in. long. May, June. SE. Europe. 1597. (B.M. 16; Gn. 14 (1878), 12.)

**I. Varta'ni** (10). *l.* 2, 8 to 18 in. long, dark green, 4-sided. *fl.* fragrant, pale slaty-lilac; falls lanceolate, ½ in wide, veined lilac on a paler ground, crest wavy, yellow; standards erect, ⅛ in. wide; tube nearly white, 2½ in. long; peduncle very short. December, January. Palestine. 1885. (B.M. 6942.)

**I. ver'na** (1). Similar to *I. pumila* but without a beard. Stem very short. *l.* ensiform, glaucous, purple at base, 4 to 6 in. long at flowering time. *fl.* blue, falls obovate, 1½ in. long, ⅓ in. wide, haft hairy, orange, dotted brown; standards obovate, erect. April, May. S. United States. 1748. (B.M. 8159, L.B.C. 1855; S.B.F.G. 68; Add. 456.)

**I. versicol'or** (1). Stem 18 to 24 in. h. terete, forked low down; fl.-clusters terminal and 2 or 3 lateral. *l.* ensiform, rather glaucous. *fl.* claret-purple; falls 2 to 3 in. long, ¾ to 1 in. wide, blade oval, reflexing, wedge-shaped at base; standards oblanceolate-spatulate, 1½ in. long, light claret-purple. May, June. N. America. 1732. (B.M. 21; 703 as *I. virginica*; B.M. 8465 as *I. caroliniana*.) SYN. *I. caroliniana*. var. **kermesi'na,** *fl.* rich red-purple, almost crimson. *See also* **I. chrysophoenicea.**

**I. vica'ria** (9). About 2 ft. h. *fl.* white tinged pale blue, many in l.-axils. April. Cent. Asia. 1936.

**I. virgin'ica.** A synonym of *I. versicolor*.

**I. Vivia'ni.** A variety of *I. Xiphium*.

**I. warleyen'sis** (9). Related to *I. orchioides*. Stem about 12 in. long with 3 to 5 fl. in l.-axils. *l.* 6 or 7, about 6 in. long, 1 to 1½ in. wide, margin distinctly horny. *fl.* deep violet edged white; falls nearly round with wavy whitish crest and orange signal patch; standards narrow with sharp projecting point, horizontal. April. Bokhara. 1901. (B.M. 7956; F. & S. 3, 344; D.I. 42.)

**I. Watsonia'na** (1). Stem 15 to 20 in. h., 8- or 9-fld. *l.* as in *I. Douglasiana*, 28 in. long, ¾ in. wide, arching, not persistent. *fl.* violet or lavender-purple with blue suffusion down middle of both falls and standards and yellow or cream patch on blades; tube shorter than in *I. Douglasiana*; ovary more sharply angled than in *I. tenax* which otherwise the flower much resembles. May. Western N. America. (G.C. 55 (1914), 391.)

**I. Watt'ii** (2). Habit of *I. confusa* but with leafy bracts. Stem 3 ft. h., bearing 40 to 50 fl. *l.* thin, ribbed, 1 to 2¼ in. wide. *fl.* soft lavender-lilac; falls 2 in. long, 1⅜ in. wide, reflexed, haft spotted violet-blue, crests yellow or orange; standards horizontal, 1½ in. long, ¾ in. wide, margins wavy; style branches nearly erect, crests large, fringed; spathe valves 1 in. long. April. Assam, W. China. (B.M. 9590.)

**I. West'ii.** A synonym of *I. susiana*.

**I. Willmottia'na** (9). Allied to *I. caucasica* but with wider, less channelled *l.* and narrower, not inflated spathe valves. *fl.* varying from deep lavender to bright blue or white, the white central patch blotched and veined blue. March, April. E. Turkistan. 1899. (Gn. 66 (1904), 1.) var. **al'ba,** *fl.* white.

**I. Wils'onii** (1). Stem about 2 ft. h., hollow, 2-fld. *l.* linear-ensiform, 2 ft. long, ½ in. wide, upper part drooping. *fl.* resembling those of *I. sibirica* but yellow and with divergent, not erect standards; blade of falls ovate, haft broad, veined brown; standards lanceolate, frilled. June. W. China. 1909. (B.M. 8340; D.I. 2.)

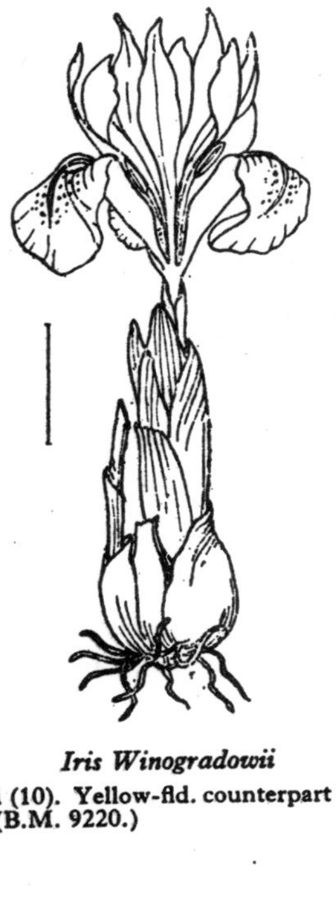

*Iris Winogradowii*

**I. Winogradow'ii** (10). Yellow-fld. counterpart of *I. reticulata*. W. Caucasus. 1927. (B.M. 9220.)

**I. xiphioi′des** (10).* English Iris. Stem 1 to 2 ft. h. 2- or 3-fld. *l.* about 6 from base, 3 or 4 from stem below spathe, lower 1 ft. long, ⅛ to ¼ in. wide, deeply channelled. *fl.* deep blue with golden patch on fall, but varying from white, mauve, and lavender through blue; blade of falls roundish oblong, rather longer than the broad-winged haft; standards erect, shorter than falls, blade nearly round, tapering to haft; tube ¼ to ½ in. long; spathe about 3 in. long; pedicels 1 to 3 in. long. June, July. Pyrenees. 1570. (B.M. 687; Gn. 31 (1887), 212.) SYN. *I. anglica, Xiphion latifolium.*) Many colour varieties flowering about a fortnight later than *I. Xiphium* have been raised.

**I. Xiph′ium** (10).* Spanish Iris. Stem 1 to 2 ft. h., 1 -or 2-fld. *l.* 4 to 6 below spathe valves, lowest 12 in. or more long, glaucous, deeply channelled. *fl.* about 4 in. wide; blade of falls orbicular, reflexing, 1 in. wide and deep, variable in colour, white, yellow, or blue, with yellow or orange patch on blade; standards oblanceolate, ⅛ to ¼ in. wide, erect; tube almost absent; spathe valves 4 to 5 in. long; pedicels about as long as spathe. May, June. S. France to Portugal. 1596. (B.M. 686; Gn. 20 (1881), 442.) SYN. *I. hispanica.* An early flowering form (var. **prae′cox**, April, May) has been misnamed *I. filifolia* in gardens. var. **lusitan′ica**, Thunderbolt Iris, *fl.* yellow; **Vivia′ni**, *fl.* large, white, falls sulphur yellow. Many colour forms are offered, and this species and probably especially its var. *praecox*, has, by crossing with other species of the same group, e.g. *I. tingitana*, given rise to the Dutch Irises which flower at the end of May and in early June. (D.I. 43.)

**IRIS GARDEN.** A garden devoted mainly or entirely to irises can form an interesting and ornamental feature, but in planning such a garden the wide differences of soil conditions demanded by the various types of irises must be taken into account (*See* **Iris**).

The bearded section is usually employed to provide the main display, and varieties of this group delight in a well-drained soil and sunny situation. If, however, the ground is moist, or includes a pond or stream, this should offer good opportunities for the cultivation of the handsome Japanese irises.

The period of interest will be extended by planting early flowering bulbous irises such as *I. histrioides* and *I. reticulata.* These will do best in light soil in a raised border facing south or south-west. The winter-flowering *I. unguicularis* might also be included where it can be accommodated at the foot of a south wall in poor gravelly soil.

Although bearded Irises may sometimes look well in formal beds, where a formal-shaped enclosure demands such an arrangement, Irises as a whole are seen to best advantage arranged informally in broad groupings, backed by planting and set off by a grass margin.

J. E. G. W.

**IRIS ROOT** or **ORRIS ROOT.** *See* **Iris florentina.**

**IRISH HEATH.** *See* **Daboecia cantabrica.**

**IRON** is one of the chemical elements essential for plant-life. It is present in the plant only in small quantities but without it no chlorophyll is produced, and in circumstances leading to deficient supplies of iron plants become chlorotic and food manufacture is interfered with or altogether ceases. The green colour of plants suffering from chlorosis, as is not infrequent in very calcareous soil, is produced if iron is supplied to the soil (as, e.g., by a dressing of 4 oz. to the square yard of ferrous sulphate) or by spraying the affected foliage with a weak solution of ferric chloride or by injecting the stem. Iron sulphate is sometimes used as a fungicide.

**IRON SHRUB.** *See* **Sauvagesia erecta.**

**IRON TREE.** *See* **Parrotia persica.**

**IRON WEED.** *See* **Vernonia.**

**IRONBARK.** *See* **Eucalyptus leucoxylon.**

**IRONWOOD.** *See* **Mesua ferrea, Ostrya virginiana.**

**IRONWORT.** *See* **Sideritis.**

*irregular′is -is -e*, irregular, of flowers with parts of dissimilar size.

**A→**

*irrig′uus -a -um*, watered.

**IRRITABILITY** or sensitiveness to the impact of various external forces is one of the properties of all living matter and it is often manifested by movements sufficiently marked as to be evident without special apparatus. By virtue of the irritability of its protoplasm the parts of the plant are put in such relation with their environment that they are best able to do their normal work. Any change in direction or intensity of the forces acting upon the plant acts as a stimulus bringing about a more or less direct response. Among the stimuli causing movement are (1) pressure or contact, as seen, e.g. in the leaves of Mimosa, Drosera, and Dionaea, the stamens of Berberis, Kalmia, Cistus, the stigmatic lobes of Mimulus and Bignonia, tendrils of various plants; (2) variations of temperature bringing about the opening and closing of such flowers as Crocus and Tulip, and in the leaves of Oxalis and Mimosa; (3) variations in intensity of light, as in the movements of leaves of *Desmodium gyrans* and of the Scarlet Runner; (4) variations in the direction of light seen in the curvature of stems towards the light and of roots away from it (*see* **Heliotropic**); (5) directive influence of the pull of gravity, seen in the direction of growth of primary stems away from the pull of gravity and of primary roots towards it, while most leaves take up a horizontal position (*see* **Geotropism**); (6) differences in degree of moisture in surroundings, causing growth of roots towards the moister part of the surroundings (*see* **Hydrotropism**).

*irrit′ans*, causing discomfort.

*irrora′tus -a -um*, dewy.

*Irving′ii*, in honour of Dr. Irving, 1816–55, who collected in W. Africa.

**ISABE′LIA** (in honour of H. I. H. Isabel, Countess d' Eu). FAM. *Orchidaceae.* A genus of a single species of epiphyte allied to Neolauchia. Treatment as for Cattleya. The small size and creeping habit of the plant renders a small raft or piece of tree-fern stem fixed obliquely in a pot the best support.

**I. virgina′lis.** *fl.* 1 or 2, very small, lateral sep. forming a short chin; lip free, concave. Pollinia 8. Winter, spring. Brazil. (B.M. 8787.)

**ISABELLA GRAPE.** *See* **Vitis Labrusca.**

*Isabel′lae*, in honour of Miss Isabel Forrest, sister of George Forrest, the botanical collector.

*isabelli′nus -a -um*, greyish drab.

**I′SATIS** (old Greek name used by Dioscorides). FAM. *Cruciferae.* A genus of about 30 species of erect, branched, annual, biennial, or perennial herbs, natives of S. Europe and W. Asia. Leaves entire; stem leaves sagittate. Flowers often yellow, in loose racemes, without bracts. They succeed in ordinary good garden soil.

**I. alpi′na.** Perennial, 4 to 12 in. h., freely branched, glabrous and glaucous, very leafy. *Lower l.* in rosette, obovate; *stem-l.* oblong, auricled, stem-clasping. *fl.* yellow, large, in corymbs. *fr.* elliptic, about ½ in. long, with reflexed pedicels. Europe.

**I. Boissieria′na.** Hardy annual about 1 ft. h. *Upper l.* oblong, acute, heart-shaped-sagittate, acute; *lower* wedge-shaped-oblong, acute, sinuate-toothed. *fl.* yellow, in a corymbose raceme. Turkestan. 1876.

**I. glau′ca.** Hardy perennial of 2 to 4 ft., glaucous. *Radical l.* oblong, about 1 ft. long, stalked; *stem-l.* small. *fl.* yellow, in a large panicle. June. *fr.* about ½ in. long, ¼ in. wide, downy. Asia Minor to Persia.

**I. tincto′ria.** Common Dyer's Weed. Woad. Biennial, 2 to 4 ft. h. *Upper l.* sagittate, sessile; *lower* ovate, stalked; all glaucous. *fl.* yellow in long, erect racemes. June. Europe, including Britain, N. Asia. (E.B. 161.) Yields a blue dye; used by Ancient Britons to stain their bodies.

*Ischae′mum*, styptic.

**ISCHA'RUM** (*ischein*, to check; the upper part of the spadix appears to be checked in growth and ill-nourished). FAM. *Araceae.* A genus sometimes united to Biarum consisting of a few tuberous herbs. Needing greenhouse treatment. For cultivation, *see* **Typhonium.**

**I. angusta'tum.** Tuber as large as a small potato. *l.* long, thick, oblong-lanceolate, subacute, stalked. *Spathe* 6 in. long, sheathing part nearly white, blade black-purple, erect; spadix slender, female part short, neutral part ½ in. long, white, male part black-purple. December. Syria. 1860. (B.M. 6355.)

**I. exim'ium.** *l.* broad, simple. *Spathe* dark purple within, green spotted red without. W. Cilicia. 1898. (G.C. 23 (1898), f. 49.)

**I. Pyra'mi.** *l.* elliptic-obovate, obtuse, obliquely nerved, narrowed to stalk. *Spathe* dark velvety-purple, short, broad-lanceolate, twisted, slender-pointed; tube swollen; spadix as long as spathe. January. Syria. 1861. (B.M. 5324.)

**ISCHNOSI'PHON.** *See* **Monotagma.**

**ISER'TIA** (in honour of P. E. Isert, a German surgeon). FAM. *Rubiaceae.* A genus of 15 species of shrubs and trees, natives of Brazil, Guiana, Colombia. Leaves large, opposite, rarely ternate or whorled, thick, leathery, slender-pointed. Flowers scarlet or red, rarely yellow or white, rather large, in many-flowered, thyrsoid, terminal, corymbose cymes, shortly stalked. *I. coccinea* is a handsome stove evergreen shrub needing a compost of peat and loam with a little charcoal and silver sand. Increased by cuttings inserted in sandy soil, in heat, in spring and summer.

**I. coccin'ea.** Shrub of 8 to 12 ft. *l.* oval, narrowed to both ends, downy beneath. *fl.* scarlet, velvety outside, 1 in. long in a terminal, many-fld. panicle. July. Guiana. 1820.

***island'icus -a -um,*** Icelandic.

**ISLE OF WIGHT BEE DISEASE.** *See* Supplement.

**ISME'NE.** Included in **Hymenocallis.** *I. Andreana* and *I. quitoensis*, synonyms of *Leptochiton quitoensis.*

***iso-,*** in compound words, signifying equal, as *isophyllus*, having equal leaves.

**isobilateral,** applied to leaves having both surfaces alike.

**ISOCHI'LUS** (*isos*, equal, *cheilos*, lip; referring to the form of the lip). FAM. *Orchidaceae.* A genus of 4 or 5 epiphytic tufted species occurring in the W. Indies and Trop. America from Mexico to Brazil. Flowers small or medium-sized, rose or red in 1 row in spike-like racemes; lip free from column, narrowed at base, with slight S-like curvature. Stems with leaves in 2 rows. Temperature, compost, &c., should be as for Cattleyas, but the slender stems forbid any attempt to give a decided rest.

**I. linea'ris.** *fl.* 5 to 15, purplish, rose, small, in short spikes. Spring. *l.* 2 to 2½ in. long, narrow, on slender stems 1 to 1½ ft. h. Mexico to Brazil. 1791. (B.R. 745; L.B.C. 1341.) var. **al'ba,** *fl.* white; **ma'jor,** more robust, *fl.* darker.

E. C.

**ISOETA'CEAE.** Lycopodiales. A family of 1 genus, Isoetes, which see for characters.

**ISOE'TES** (*isos*, equal, *etos*, the year; the plants are evergreen). FAM. *Isoetaceae.* A genus of about 50 species of stemless perennials, mostly aquatics, with short, stout rhizomes and awl-shaped leaves, distributed over the temperate and tropical fresh waters of the world. Roots numerous, branching dichotomously. Leaves sheathing at base with a large sporangium sunken in the tissue near the base, the outer leaves producing microspores, the inner macrospores. The germination of the spores, &c., is similar to that seen in Selaginella. The British *I. lacustris* is sometimes offered for aquaria, in which it must be grown submerged. An interesting but not particularly beautiful plant.

**I. lacus'tris.** Quillwort. *l.* 10 to 20, 2 to 6 in. long, 4-angled, awl-shaped, deep green, of 4 chambered tubes; capsules partly covered by the edges of the l.-sheath. N. Europe, including Britain, W. Siberia, N. America.

**ISOLE'PIS.** *See* **Scirpus.** *I. gracilis*, a synonym of *Scirpus cernuus.*

**ISOLO'MA** (*isos*, equal, *loma*, border; the corolla lobes are equal). FAM. *Gesneriaceae.* A genus of about 50 species of tropical herbaceous plants, natives of America, distinct from Gesneria by the absence of well-formed tubers, the form of the fruits and the anthers, and the 5 equal lobes of the floral disk, and from Achimenes by the more tubular form of the flowers and the lobed disk. Several species form underground runners thickly covered with scale leaves. Leaves opposite, usually with longish hairs. Flowers often scarlet, orange, or spotted, usually axillary; corolla tube somewhat enlarged above, segments 5, almost equal. Cultivation as for Gesneria. Some may be offered under the name Kohleria or Tydaea and some of the latter group have been separated into a genus Sciadocalyx, having an umbrella-like expansion of the cup-shaped calyx, but this distinction is difficult to uphold and all are here included in Isoloma. Several of the Isolomas and their hybrids can be raised from seed to flower the same year, or may be propagated in the same way as Achimenes and Gesnerias.

The species appear to hybridize readily with one another and probably with Gesneria and Achimenes, and many of the plants in cultivation are probably of hybrid origin. See, for instance, figures in *The Garden*, vol. xv, p. 376; xxxiv, p. 440, showing early hybrids still worth growing. Some of those raised on the Continent have received Latin names, as *Eeckhautii*, *gigantea*, *Ortgiesii.* Among the hybrids is a section with the corolla lobes much cut and jagged round the edges.

**I. amab'ile.** Erect, hairy, 1 to 2 ft. h. *l.* ovate, tapering to stalk, bluntly serrate, purplish on veins. *fl.* large, hairy, dark rose, much-dotted and blotched; peduncles axillary, solitary, at least as long as l. Colombia. 1855. (B.M. 4999.) A parent of many hybrids.

**I. bogoten'se.*** Erect, slightly hairy, little-branched, 1 to 2 ft. h. *l.* sometimes whorled, ovate-cordate, toothed, rich velvety-green with white or pale green mottling, whitest in middle. *fl.* orange and yellow, much spotted with red; peduncles much longer than l., axillary, 1-fld. Autumn, early winter. Bogota. 1844. (B.M. 4126 and B.R. 31, 42 as *Achimenes picta.*)

**I. Cecil'iae.** Much like *I. amabile* but l. roundish, cordate at base, coarsely toothed. *fl.* large, bright rose with darker spots, tube white with rose spots within; peduncles 1-fld., 1 to 3 in l.-axils. Colombia. 1877. (I.H. 1876, 178.)

**I. Deppea'num.** 2 to 3 ft. h. *l.* lanceolate, slender-pointed, 3 to 6 in. long, 1¼ to 2¼ in. wide, toothed, harshly hairy and bright green above, softly white, hairy beneath. *fl.* small, orange-red, about 1 in. long, ½ in. across, in 3- to 4-fld. hairy umbels. Summer. Mexico. (B.M. 3725 as *Gesneria elongata* var.)

**I. digitaliflo'rum.** Erect, hairy. *l.* large, ovate-acuminate. *fl.* very large, deflexed, tube rose-purple above, white beneath, lobes green dotted purple, in short, terminal panicles. Colombia. (I.H. 1870, 17.) A parent of many hybrids.

**I. el'egans.** Softly hairy, often reddish. *l.* ovate-oblong, slender-pointed, unequal at base, crenate. *fl.* purple, throat and lobes yellowish within, spotted purple; cor. tube 1½ in. long, slightly incurved; umbels 3- or 4-fld. in l.-axils. Guatemala. (F.d.S. 489 as *Moussonia elegans*; G.F. 1854, 101 as *M. formosa.*)

**I. erian'thum.** Erect, softly hairy, 2 to 4 ft. h. *l.* ovate-lanceolate, toothed; stalk long. *fl.* 1½ to 2 in. long, orange-red or cinnabar-red, lobes rounded, lower 3 spotted; peduncles several-fld. Colombia. (B.M. 7907.) SYN. *I. hirsutum.* May be had in flower in the warm greenhouse during most of the year by continuously rooting strong tops in the close frame.

**I. hirsu'tum** of gardens. A synonym of *I. erianthum.*

**I. honden'se.** Erect, about 1 ft. h. *l.* ovate, acute, toothed, hairy; stalks about ½ in. long. *fl.* small, hairy; cor. yellow, about 1 in. long, tube red-hairy; peduncles 1 to 3 in l.-axils, longer than l. December or at any time by forcing or retarding. Honda, Colombia. 1845. (B.M. 4217 as *Gesneria hondensis.*)

**I. hypocyrtiflo'rum.** *l.* ovate-cordate, bluntish, velvety, emerald-green, traversed by silvery ribs. *fl.* orange-red, downy, nearly globose, about 1 in. long, nearly closed at mouth; peduncles 1 or 2 in l.-axils, long. Ecuador. 1866. (B.M. 5655 as *Gloxinia hypocyrtiflora.*) SYN. *Pearcea hypocyrtiflora.*

**I. ignora'tum.** Erect, hairy. Stem fleshy. *l.* in whorls of 3, oblong, narrowed to stalk, deeply crenate. *fl.* small, tubular, reddish, hairy; peduncles 1 or 2 in axils of small upper l. Mexico. (G.F. 1852, 1.)

*Isoloma bogotense* (p. 1075)

**I. jalisca'num.** Downy, decumbent, about 1 ft. h. *l.* oblonglanceolate, 1 to 3 in. long. *fl.* scarlet, about 1 in. long, tube downy, contracted at mouth; in 2- to 4-fld. axillary umbels, peduncles about 1 in. long. Mexico. 1896.

**I. Lindenia'num.** Erect, hairy. *l.* ovate, olive-green, veins bright green with silvery borders. *fl.* rather large, white with deep violet band on lower side of throat, yellow and purple marking on upper lip; cor. tube short; peduncles axillary, 1-fld. Trop. America. 1868. (G.F. 589.)

**I. longifo'lium.** *l.* sometimes alternate, narrowed to both ends, crenate. *fl.* orange-red; in a terminal raceme; peduncles whorled. Syn. *Gesneria longifolia.*

**I. longipeduncula'tum.** Silky-hairy. *l.* in whorls of 3, elliptic, nearly sessile. *fl.* orange-scarlet spotted in mouth; cor. tube 1 to 1½ in. long; cal. segs. spreading; peduncles 1-fld., erect, 1 or 2 in l.-axils. Mexico. (I.H. 287 as *Kohleria lanata.*)

**I. × Luciani**\* (*I. digitaliflorum × I. pardinum*). Hairy, robust, hairs crimson. *fl.* large, crimson, much spotted; cal. lobes spreading; peduncles 2- or 3-fld. erect, solitary, axillary. 1874. (I.H. 1874, 182 as *Sciadocalyx Luciani.*)

**I. magnif'icum.** *fl.* crimson-black streaked; peduncles long, 1-fld., axillary. Colombia. (F.d.S. 1013 as *Locheria magnifica.*)

**I. mol'le.** Hairy shrub, 1½ ft. h. *l.* ovate, slender-pointed, toothed. *fl.* red, densely hairy, funnel-shaped; in 3- to 5-fld. umbel, pedicels long, peduncle short, axillary. Winter. Caracas. 1819. (B.M. 3815 as *Gesneria mollis.*)

**I. ocella'tum.** Stem shortly hairy. *l.* large, ovate, slender-pointed, wrinkled, veiny. *fl.* small, bright red, downy, drooping, lobes with white spots with black centre; peduncles red, erect, 1-fld., axillary, shorter than l. Panama. 1847. (B.M. 4359 as *Achimenes ocellata.*)

**I. pardi'num.** *fl.* scarlet with dark spots on lobes; in 3- or 4-fld. axillary umbels; peduncles short. Mexico. (I.H. 1873, 152 as *Tydaea pardina.*)

**I. pic'tum.**\* Velvety-hairy, about 3 ft. h. *l.* sometimes in whorls of 3, ovate, slender-pointed, toothed, red-purple beneath. *fl.* scarlet, yellow beneath and at contracted mouth, very hairy and velvety, in a long, terminal raceme; peduncles short. Colombia. 1848. (B.M. 4431 as *Gesneria picta.*)

**I. × pyramida'le.**\* Near *I. Luciani* but with more fl. in umbel. Tall, robust, and stem densely red-hairy. 1861.

**I. rubricau'le.** *l.* elliptic. *fl.* rather small, scarlet, tubular; cal. lobes long, acute; peduncles 1-fld., solitary, little longer than l. Venezuela.

**I. rupes'tre.** Allied to *I. longifolium.* Stem woolly, whitish. *fl.* hairy, tube cylindric, in clusters in upper l.-axils; peduncles 1-fld. Nicaragua. 1871.

**I. Schiedla'num.** Stem reddish, 1½ ft. h. *l.* in whorls of 3, softly downy, paler beneath. *fl.* scarlet, somewhat bell-shaped, hairy, lobes yellow with lines of red dots; peduncles clustered, shorter than l., 1- to 3-fld. November. Mexico. (B.M. 4152 as *Gesneria Schiedlana.*)

**I. Seeman'nii.** Little branched, about 2 ft. h. *l.* sometimes in whorls of 3, lower large, broadly ovate, coarsely toothed, acute; stalks rather long. *fl.* small, reddish-orange, tube cylindrical, hairy, lobes spotted deep red; peduncles clustered. October. Panama. 1848. (B.M. 4504 as *Gesneria Seemannii.*) Allied to *I. longifolium.*

**I. Trian'aei.** *fl.* large, crimson with contracted yellow mouth, lobes spreading; in 1- to 4-fld. umbels; peduncles thick, long, axillary. Colombia. (G.F. 1854, 52.)

**I. triflo'rum.** 1½ to 2 ft.. h. *l.* ovate, 1½ to 6 in. long, slenderpointed, toothed, dark green above, wrinkled, veiny and downy beneath; stalks woolly. *fl.* yellow, clothed with shaggy red hair, tube swollen; in 3-fld. umbels; peduncles solitary, axillary, very short; pedicels long. Summer. Colombia. 1846. (B.M. 4342 as *Gesneria triflora.*)

**I. tubiflo'rum.** Hairy. *l.* large, ovate, short-stalked, slightly toothed, veiny and pale beneath. *fl.* yellow tinged red, small, tube much contracted at mouth; peduncles 2 in l.-axils, longer than l.-stalks. Colombia. 1846. Allied to *I. hondense.*

**I. Warscewicz'ii.** Hairy. *l.* ovate or cordate, oblique. *fl.* scarlet, tube swollen, mouth yellow spotted crimson; peduncles 3- to 8-fld., axillary, shorter than pedicels. Colombia. (B.M. 4843 as *Sciadocalyx Warscewiczii.*)

**ISOM'ERIS** (*isos*, equal, *meris* part; the parts of the flowers, however, are very unequal). FAM. *Capparidaceae*. Monotypic genus; perhaps not now in cultivation in Britain. Greenhouse, needing sandy loam and leaf-mould, and propagated by cuttings of ripe shoots in autumn.

**I. arbor'ea.** Deciduous bush with disagreeable odour, 3 to 10 ft., young shoots grey-downy. *l.* alternate, 3-foliolate; lflets. ½ to 1½ in. long, ⅛ to ⅜ in. wide, oblong, pointed, glaucous. *fl.* in bracted racemes up to 6 in. long; cal. 4-lobed, persistent; cor. yellow, pet. 4, erect, ¼ to ½ in. long; stamens 6, much exserted; style still more exserted. May. *fr.* an obovoid or pear-shaped, inflated, longstalked capsule 1½ in. long, many-seeded. California. 1839. (B.M. 3842.) var. **globo'sa**, capsule globose, shoots not glaucous.

**ISOMET'RUM** (*isos*, equal, *metron*, measure; from the equal corolla segments). FAM. *Gesneriaceae*. A genus of 2 species of dwarf perennial herbs with thickened rhizomes, natives of W. China, related to Didissandra but with the segments of the corolla nearly equal and spreading. Leaves in a basal rosette, coarsely toothed or somewhat lobed, peduncles longer than leaves, whitish hairy and glandular with a few longer brown hairs.

*Isometrum Farreri*

Inflorescence umbellate and bracteate, corolla lobes 5, rounded, almost equal; stamens 4, anthers joined in pairs. For treatment see Ramondia.

**I. Far'reri.** *l.* in a basal rosette, obovate-lanceolate or narrowly ovate, to 1½ in. long, ⅝ in. wide, white-hairy with some brown hairs beneath; stalked. *fl.* shrimp-pink toned brown, in a 5- to 7-fld. umbel; cor. segs. about ⅛ in. long. July, August. Kansu. 1915. (B.M. 8917.) SYN. *Oreocharis Henryana* of Farrer not Oliver.

**ISONAN'DRA Gut'ta.** *See* **Palaquium Gutta.**

**ISOPLEX'IS** (*isos*, equal, *pleko*, to plait; the upper segment of the corolla is equal in length to the lip). FAM. *Scrophulariaceae.* Two species of evergreen semi-woody shrubs closely akin to Digitalis (fox-glove). Leaves long, narrow, alternate, toothed. Flowers in erect, dense, terminal racemes; corolla tubular at base, limb 5-lobed, 2-lipped; stamens 4. These shrubs require cool greenhouse conditions and should be given a compost of good loam, silver sand, and leaf-mould.

**I. canarien'sis.*** Evergreen bushy shrub, 4 to 6 ft., shoots erect, stout, downy. *l.* oval-lanceolate, 5 in. long, 1 to 2 in. wide, downy especially beneath. *fl.* numerous in terminal erect spikes up to 1 ft. long; cor. orange-yellow, 1½ in. wide. May, June. Canary Is. 1698. (B.R. 48 as *Digitalis canariensis.*) Grown in the open air in Scilly. Differs from *I. sceptrum* by its clearer-coloured, larger, and more open cor.

**I. scep'trum.** Evergreen shrub 4 to 6 ft. *l.* 6 to 10 in. long, obovate to oval-oblong, pointed, toothed, downy beneath, tapering to a broad stalk. *fl.* closely packed in a broad raceme 4 or 5 in. h. terminating an erect, stout peduncle, each springing from the axil of a linear-lanceolate bract; cor. yellow, netted with tawny veins, 1 in. wide. July, August. Madeira. 1777. (S.E.B. 73 as *Digitalis sceptrum.*)

**ISOPO'GON** (*isos*, equal, *pogon*, beard; the inflorescence has a beard-like fringe). FAM. *Proteaceae.* A genus of about 30 species of evergreen shrubs, all natives of Australia. Leaves either entire or pinnately divided, stiff in texture. Flowers 2-sexual, crowded densely in terminal or axillary heads or 'cones'. Perianth sessile, slenderly tubular, the limb with 4 linear or oblong segments. Fruit a small, dry, hairy nut. These shrubs require cool greenhouse conditions similar to Acacias. About half a dozen species are cultivated in the open air in Scilly.

**I. anemonifo'lius.** Shrub 4 to 6 ft., young shoots downy. *l.* 1½ to 4 in. long, pinnately or 3-fidly divided or lobed, segs. linear, ⅛ in. wide, pointed, the whole tapering to a long stalk. *fl.* yellow, densely packed in a globose solitary terminal head 1½ in. wide, or sometimes in 2 or 3 smaller ones. July. New S. Wales. 1791. (B.M. 697 as *Protea anemonifolia.*)

**I. attenua'tus.** Shrub 2 to 3 ft. *l.* 4 to 6 in. long, ⅓ to ⅔ in. wide, entire, oblanceolate, broadest towards the pointed apex, tapering thence to base, glabrous. *fl.* rather pale yellow, crowded in hemispherical heads 1 to 1½ in. across and terminal or in the upper l.-axils. W. Australia. (B.M. 4372.)

**I. Bax'teri.*** Erect shrub of several ft., shoots densely, softly downy. *l.* up to 2½ in. long and wide, deeply 2- or 3-lobed and much undulated, segs. sharply pointed and pointing in all directions; hard and stiff in texture. *fl.* soft rose, crowded in flattened-globose terminal heads 1½ to 2 in. across; perianth very hairy. March, April. W. Australia. 1830. (B.M. 3539.)

**I. cunea'tus.** Shrub 4 to 8 ft., young shoots at first silky. *l.* entire, 3 to 4 in. long, ½ to 1½ in. wide, oblanceolate to ovate-oblong, minutely pointed, scarcely stalked. *fl.* pale purple, crowded in a flattish terminal head 1 to 1½ in. across; perianth 1 in. long. Spring. W. Australia. 1829. (B.M. 3421 as *I. Loudoni.*)

**I. latifo'lius.** Stout bushy shrub up to 10 ft. and about as much wide. *l.* entire, 3 to 4 in. long, obovate to oval-oblong, tapered at base to a short stalk, shortly pointed, glabrous. *fl.* pink, in large flattened-globose terminal heads; perianth 1½ in. long. W. Australia. (J.R.H.S. 36, 296.)

**I. longifo'lius.** Shrub 2 to 8 ft., mostly glabrous. *l.* linear to oblanceolate, 4 to 6 in. long (sometimes twice as much), 1 in. wide, entire or 2- or 3-lobed towards the end. *fl.* yellow, crowded in a stalkless, globose, terminal head 1½ in. across, perianth silky. W. Australia. 1823. (B.R. 900.)

**I. Lou'doni.** A synonym of *I. cuneatus.*

**I. ro'seus.** Bushy shrub, 2 to 4 ft., shoots downy and hairy. *l.* once or twice ternately divided, or merely pinnate, 1 to 3 in. long including the stalk; segs. linear, pointed, $\frac{1}{16}$ to ⅛ in. wide. *fl.* pink, glabrous, compacted into a solitary terminal head 1½ in. across or sometimes into 5 or 6 axillary heads and then only ½ in. across. April. W. Australia. 1840. (B.M. 4037 as *I. scaber.*)

**I. sphaeroceph'alus.*** Shrub of several ft., habit erect, shoots and young leaves downy. *l.* entire, 2 to 4 in. long, up to ⅓ in. wide, linear to linear-lanceolate, abruptly narrowed to a sharp point, base tapered, dull green. *fl.* yellow, densely packed in heads 1¾ in. across, sometimes terminal and solitary, more often in 2 or 3 of the uppermost l.-axils also. Spring. W. Australia. (B.M. 4332.)

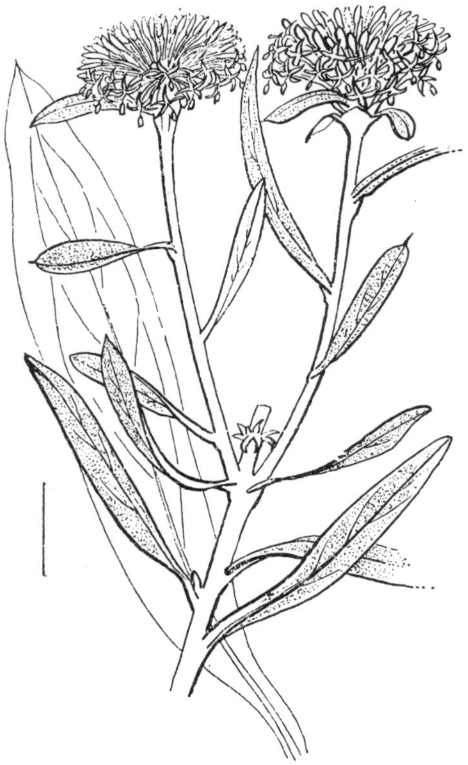

*Isopogon cuneatus*

**ISOPY'RUM** (*isos*, equal, *pyros*, wheat; the fruits somewhat resemble wheat grains). FAM. *Ranunculaceae.* A genus of about a dozen tufted perennial herbs, natives of the mountains of Europe, India, China, and Japan. Leaves much divided ternately, leaflets 3-lobed, thin. Flowers white, usually solitary or in loose panicles; carpels 2, rarely 3, spreading in fruit, thus differing from Paraquilegia, where there are usually 5. *I. thalictroides* needs woodland soil with light shade and can with care be grown on the rock-garden. It can be divided in autumn or raised from seed.

**I. adiantifo'lium.** Rootstock slender, horizontal, scaly. *Radical l.* long-stalked, stipellate at top of stalk; terminal seg. simple, lateral segs. compound, their lflets. 5 to 7, obtuse, crenate, shortly stalked; *stem-l.* opposite or whorled. *fl.* white, ½ in. across; pet. long-clawed; carpels 3. N. India.

**I. grandiflo'rum.** A synonym of *Paraquilegia grandiflora.*

**I. microphyl'lum.** A synonym of *Paraquilegia microphylla.*

**I. thalictroi'des.** Tufted. Rootstock creeping, roots clustered. *l.* much divided; lflets. 3-lobed, coarsely toothed, stalks dilated at base. Stem slender, 9 to 15 in. h. *fl.* white, small, nodding, in spreading panicles. March. Europe. 1759.

**ISOTHE'CA** (*isos*, equal, *theka*, cell; from the equal anther lobes). FAM. *Acanthaceae.* A genus of a single W. Indian species. Flowers in a terminal thyrse. Stamens with parallel lobes. Treatment as for Justicia.

**I. al'ba.** Erect, glabrous. *l.* elliptic, slender-pointed, base wedge-shaped, about 9 in. long, veins conspicuous beneath; stalk 2 in. long. *fl.* white, cor. tube 1¾ in. long, glabrous; stamens slightly exserted. Trinidad. 1921.

**ISOTO'MA** (*isos*, equal, *toma*, section; the corolla segments are equal). FAM. *Campanulaceae.* A genus of 8 species of herbs of various habit, 6 natives of Australia, 1 of W. Indies, 1 of Pacific Is. Leaves simple or pinnate, sometimes entire. Flowers in axillary or terminal racemes; pedicels 1-flowered; 2 anthers with an awn or hairy, 3 larger, naked. Fruit a capsule, dehiscing by 2 lobes at apex. Cultivation as for Lobelia.

**I. axilla'ris.** Perennial, 1 ft. h. *l.* pinnatifid, toothed, sessile. *fl.* blue, tube long, green, limb flat; peduncles axillary, long, 1-fld. Autumn. Australia. 1824. (B.M. 2702 as *Lobelia senecioides.*) Greenhouse. var. **subpinnatif'ida,** *l.* lobes longer than in type, often again pinnatifid. (B.M. 5073 as *I. senecioides subpinnatifida.*)

**I. Brown'ii.** Annual, 1 ft. h.; stem almost simple. *l.* linear, entire. *fl.* purple, in racemes. Autumn. W. Australia. 1829. (B.M. 3075 as *Lobelia hypocrateriformis.*) Greenhouse.

*Isotoma longiflora*

**I. longiflo'ra.** Perennial. *l.* obovate-lanceolate, coarsely toothed, hairy. *fl.* white; cor. tube very long, slender. Summer. W. Indies. (B.R. 1200 as *Lobelia longiflora.*) Very poisonous.

**I. petrae'a.** Glabrous perennial, branched, about 1 ft. h. *l.* lanceolate or ovate-lanceolate, accuminate, usually laciniate. *fl.* white, tinged pink, 1½ in. long, segs. horizontal or reflexed, lower 3 yellowish at junction. Australia. Greenhouse.

**I. senecioi'des subpinnatif'ida.** A synonym of *I. axillaris.*

**ISOTRE'MA.** Included in **Aristolochia.**

**ISOTRO'PIS** (*isos*, equal, *tropis*, keel; referring to the keel of the flower). Fam. *Leguminosae.* A genus of 8 species of herbs or undershrubs with diffuse or ascending stems, natives of Australia. Leaves alternate, simple or 1-foliolate, stipules minute or linear-falcate. Flowers papilionaceous, solitary on axillary peduncles or in a terminal raceme. Needing greenhouse conditions and treatment as for Chorizema.

**I. stria'ta.** Hairy perennial or undershrub, 6 to 18 in. h., with some branches leafless and dichotomous. *l.* sparse, lower obovate or wedge-shaped, obtuse, truncate, or broadly 2-lobed; upper narrower and sometimes acute. *fl.* with large yellow standard streaked purple, keel and wings purple. Spring. (L.B.C. 1953 as *Chorizema spartioides.*)

*is'sicus -a -um,* of Issus, Cilicia.

*-issimus -a -um,* as suffix, implying in a superlative degree.

*istri'acus -a -um,* from Istria, Austria.

**ITALIAN ALDER.** *See* **Alnus cordata.**

**ITALIAN MILLET.** *See* **Setaria italica.**

**ITALIAN POPLAR.** *See* **Populus nigra.**

*ital'icus -a -um,* Italian.

**I'TEA** (from Itea, the Greek name of the Willow). Fam. *Saxifragaceae.* A genus of trees and shrubs with 10 species in NE. Asia and 1 in N. America. Flowers white, small, in terminal or axillary racemes or panicles; sepals 5, persistent; petals 5, narrow; stamens 5; ovary superior, 2-celled, styles joined, ovules numerous. Fruit a capsule with flattened seeds. Leaves alternate, toothed, without stipules. Branches with interrupted pith. Propagated by cuttings of fairly ripe wood with a keel in July or August in gentle heat. Old plants of *I. virginiana* may be divided. A good deep loam or sandy peat, with plenty of moisture, is necessary for the best results.

**I. ilicifo'lia.*** Evergreen shrub, with smooth shoots, about 12 to 15 ft. h. *l.* resembling holly but thinner, 2 to 5 in. long, dark glossy green above, paler and hairy in vein axils beneath. *fl.* greenish-white, crowded on pendulous, arching racemes, 6 to 14 in. long. August. W. China. 1895. Tender except in favoured districts where it makes a very fine shrub. (B.M. 9090.)

**I. virginia'na.** Deciduous shrub 3 to 6 ft. h. with many erect stems, downy when young, branched at top. *l.* narrow oval or oblong, 1½ to 4 in. long, toothed, bright green above, paler and slightly hairy beneath, remaining long on plant in autumn. *fl.* creamy-white, ⅓ to ½ in. across, crowded on erect, cylindrical, downy racemes 2 to 6 in. long at ends of leafy twigs. July. E. United States. 1744. (B.M. 2409.) Foliage sometimes colours bright red in autumn. Hardy.

**I. virgin'ica.** A synonym of *I. virginiana.*

**I. yunnanen'sis.** Evergreen shrub very similar to *I. ilicifolia* but with few spines on the proportionately narrow *l.* which are 2 to 4 in. long. *fl.* dull white racemes arching, cylindrical, about 7 in. long, July. Yunnan. 1918.

**ITHURIEL'S SPEAR.** *See* **Brodiaea laxa.**

**ITHYCAU'LON** (*ithys*, straight, *caulon*, stem; from the habit of the plants). Fam. *Polypodiaceae.* A genus of about 10 species of ferns related to Davallia, natives of Trop. America. For treatment *see* **Davallia.**

**I. inaequa'le.** *rhiz.* creeping. *sti.* stout, 2 to 3 ft. long. *Frond* 2 to 3 ft. long, 12 to 18 in. wide, ovate lanceolate, 4-pinnatifid, glabrous; lower pinnae 9 to 12 in. long, 4 to 8 in. wide; pinnules 3 to 5 in. long, 1 to 2 in. wide, cut nearly to rachis into oblong, toothed lobes. *Sori* 2 to 12 to a seg., in the teeth near margin. Trop. America. Greenhouse. (H.S. 1, 57.) Syn. *Davallia brasiliensis, Saccoloma inaequale.*

**I'VA** (after *Ajuga Iva*, because of its similar smell). Fam. *Compositae.* A genus of about 15 species of herbs, shrubs, or annuals, natives of N. and Cent. America and the W. Indies. Lower leaves opposite, upper alternate. Marginal flowers of each head few, female; disk flowers 2-sexual. Often found wild on sea shores and in saline soil. Of little garden value. Both the following species are hardy.

**I. frutes'cens.** Marsh Elder. Shrub or sub-shrub, 3 to 10 ft. *l.* oval to oblong-lanceolate 4 to 6 in. long, 1 to 2 in. wide, pointed, toothed, 3-nerved, scarcely stalked; upper smaller and alternate. *fl.-heads* greenish, ⅛ in. wide, axillary, forming small-leaved axillary racemes. July to September. E. United States. 1880.

**I. xanthiifo'lia.** Annual herb, 3 to 6 ft., much branched, downy. *l.* mostly opposite, broadly ovate, slender-pointed, broadly tapered at base, largest 6 in. long, grey-downy beneath. *fl.-heads* greenish, 1/12 in. wide, stalkless or nearly so, borne in terminal and axillary spikes or panicles 2 to 4 in. long. July to September. N. America.

**IVES'IA.** Included in **Potentilla.**

**IVORY, VEGETABLE.** *See* **Phytelephas macrocarpa.**

**IVORY NUT PALM.** *See* **Phytelephas macrocarpa.**

**IVY.** *See* **Hedera.**

**IVY, GROUND.** *See* **Nepeta Glechoma.**

**IVY, POISON.** *See* **Rhus radicans.**

**IVY-LEAVED BELL-FLOWER.** *See* **Wahlenbergia hederacea.**

**IVY-LEAVED FERNS.** *See* **Hemionitis.**

**IVY-LEAVED PELARGONIUM.** *See* **Pelargonium peltatum.**

**IVY-LEAVED TOADFLAX.** *See* **Linaria Cymbalaria.**

A

**IXAN'THUS** (*Ixos*, Mistletoe, *anthos*, flower; the flower is glutinous). FAM. *Gentianaceae*. A genus of a single species of erect biennial herb, a native of the Canary Is. Well-drained fibrous peat is the best soil for it and it needs a light, airy place in the cool greenhouse. Seed should be sown in spring.

**I. visco'sus.** Erect, about 18 in. h. with opposite, decussate branches. *l*. ovate-lanceolate, entire, 3- or 5-nerved, upper often connate. *fl*. 5-cleft, yellow, salver-shaped, tube white, twice as long as cal. June, July. (B.M. 2135 as *Gentiana viscosa*.)

**IX'IA** (Greek name used by Theophrastus for bird-lime; here referring to the clammy sap). FAM. *Iridaceae*. A genus of about 30 species of S. African plants closely related to one another with slender stems, usually unbranched, arising from a corm with a single tunic, narrow, ensiform leaves, and flowers in simple or branched spikes. Perianth tube long, slender, segments 6, equal, forming a regular, salver-shaped corolla, stamens 3, usually free, shorter than the perianth segments. Fruit a small capsule. At one time many plants now distributed over several genera were included in this. Ixias are usually not quite hardy but their bright colours and fragrance qualify them for wide planting outdoors wherever the climate permits. The green-flowered *I. viridiflora* with its black centre is particularly striking and many seedlings of merit have been raised in gardens, improvements upon the wild forms. The best time for planting outdoors is November or later, in a sunny, well-drained south border or under a south wall, putting in the corms about 6 in. deep and covering them with light litter until early spring. They should be lifted and dried off as soon as the leaves die down.

For cultivation in pots, for which they are particularly suited, 6 to 8 corms should be planted in a 5-in. pot in October. A mixture of sandy loam and leaf-soil should be used and the corms should be planted firmly and covered with about 1 in. of soil. The pots may be plunged or stood on ashes in a cool frame and will require but little water during winter, until the flower spikes appear when the plants should be fully exposed to light and given plenty of air but draughts must be avoided. At no time will they need a high temperature. After flowering they should be dried off gradually, and stored dry until the next planting season. Propagation is by seed or by offsets. Offsets usually flower in their second year, and should be planted at the same time as the parents. Seed should be sown also in autumn and the seedlings (which should remain in the pans for the first year) should flower in the third or fourth year.

**I. arista'ta.** Corm globose. Stem 12 to 18 in. long. *l*. 3 or 4, linear, firm, 4 to 6 in. long, strongly ribbed. *fl*. many, in a loose spike; tube about ¾ in. long, segs. whitish or tinged rose, about ¾ in. long. April, May. 1800. (B.M. 589.) var. **el'egans**, *l*. narrower, *fl*. smaller. (G.F. 46 as *Wurmea elegans*.)

**I. au'lica.** About 2 ft. h. *fl*. rose, many. April. 1774. (B.M. 1013 as *I. capillaris aulica*.)

**I. capilla'ris.** About 18 in. h. *fl*. lilac; spathe scarious, papery, with 5 rib-like streaks each ending in a tooth. April. 1774. var. **incarna'ta**, *fl*. flesh-colour. (B.M. 617 as *Morphixia capillaris*.) SYN. *I. scariosa*.

**I. columella'ris.** See *I. maculata*.

**I. flexuo'sa.** A variety of *I. polystachya*.

**I. leucan'tha.** Very near *I. patens*. About 18 in. h. *l*. narrow. *fl*. white, 1-sided; spathe toothed, shorter than tube. May. 1779.

**I. macula'ta.*** Corm about ¾ in. thick, globose. Stem about 12 or up to 20 in. h. *l*. about 4, linear, strongly nerved. *fl*. in a dense, many-fld. spike, orange, segs. spotted blackish or purplish. April, May. (B.M. 539 as *I. conica*.) SYN. *I. capitata*. var. **ochroleu'ca**, *fl*. large, cream with large reddish-brown spots in middle. 1780. (B.M. 1281.) **I. columella'ris** has purple fl. with bluish spots. SYN. *Morphixia columellaris*.

**I. monadel'pha.*** Corm rather small. Stem about 12 in. h., sometimes branched. *l*. linear, rather wide. *fl*. few in a spike, variable in colour but usually blue or violet with violet or green spots, filaments joined. April, May. 1792. Variable. var. **cur'ta**, *fl*. large, orange with greenish-red spots; **grandiflo'ra**, *fl*. very large, lilac with blue spots; **latifo'lia**, *fl*. blue with brown spots; **purpu'rea**, segs. small, bright red; **versic'olor**, bright yellow with large, black spots and rays. All these have been described as species.

**I. odora'ta.*** About 1 ft. h. *fl*. in a many-fld. spike, yellow, fragrant; perianth salver-shaped, longer than spathe. May, June. 1757. (B.M. 1173 as *I. erecta lutea*.) SYN. *Morphixia odorata*.

**I. panicula'ta.*** Corm large, ¾ in. thick. Stem about 12 in. h., branched. *Basal l*. 2. *fl*. creamy-white in a loose, many-fld. spike, tube 3 in. long, straight, widened above, often reddish at base. April to June. 1774. (B.M. 256 as *I. longiflora*; 1502 as *Tritonia longiflora*.) Variable. var. **rochen'sis**, *fl*. with much shorter and more dilated tube. (B.M. 1503 as *Tritonia rochensis*.); **tenuiflo'ra**, *fl*. smaller, self-coloured. (B.M. 1275 as *Tritonia tenuiflora*.)

**I. pa'tens.*** Stem up to 18 in. h., often branched. *l*. broad. *fl*. in a many-fld. dense spike, bell-shaped to spreading, pink; style longer than stamens. April. 1779. (B.M. 522.)

**I. polystach'ya.*** About 18 in. h. *fl*. white, somewhat greenish at base, not spotted; segs. spreading, about ⅔ in. long. May, June. 1757. var. **flexuo'sa**, *fl*. reddish to lilac. (B.M. 624 as *I. flexuosa*.)

**I. scario'sa.** A synonym of *I. capillaris*.

**I. specio'sa.*** About 6 in. h. *fl*. dark red, bell-shaped; stigma longer than stamens. May, June. 1778. (B.M. 594 as *I. crateroides*.)

*Ixia viridiflora*

**I. viridiflo'ra.*** About 12 in. h. *l*. linear-ensiform. *fl*. green, spotted at base, in a many-fld. spike. May, June. 1780. (B.M. 549 as *I. maculata viridis*.) var. **amethysti'na**, segs. whitish to bluish upwards. (B.M. 789 as *I. maculata amethystina*.)

**IXIAN'THES** (*ixos*, bird-lime, *anthos*, flower; in allusion to the viscous corolla). FAM. *Scrophulariaceae*. A monotypic genus; for characteristics see below. Cool greenhouse shrub.

**I. retzioi'des.*** Evergreen shrub 4 to 7 ft., shoots downy, erect, terete, densely leafy. *l*. alternate or whorled, 3 to 4 in. long, about ¼ in. wide, oblanceolate to linear, toothed, leathery. *fl*. on axillary stalks up to 1 in. long forming a mass of blossom 3 or 4 in. long and wide; cor. sulphur-yellow, 1¼ in. wide, bellied at base, limb 5-lobed, lobes roundish-obovate; stamens 2, short, with 2 or 3 staminodes. June. S. Africa. 1891. (B.M. 7409.)

W. J. B.

**IXIOLIR'ION** (*Ixia*, *lirion*, lily; in allusion to a likeness to Ixia). FAM. *Amaryllidaceae*. A genus of perhaps 3 species of bulbous plants from W. and Cent. Asia, allied to Alstroemeria and Bomarea, which, however, have no distinct rootstock. Leaves very narrow, mostly at base of stem. Flowers regular in loose racemes; segments 6, free to the base; usually deep blue or violet; stamens shorter than perianth, attached to the claws; fruit a 3-celled capsule. They grow best in a well-drained, dry, sunny border with a light, fairly rich soil but may be grown in pans with some success. If grown in the open they need protection in spring so that the foliage is not damaged by late frosts. The bulbs may be carefully lifted in autumn and stored in a dry place.

**I. Kolpakowskia'num.** *l.* linear, about 1 ft. h. *fl.* blue or white, trumpet-shaped with a long, narrow tube made by the narrower parts of the narrow acute segs. Summer. Lake Sairan. 1878. (G.F. 953 as *Kolpakowskia ixiolirioides*.)

**I. Ledebour'ii.** A synonym of *I. montanum.*

**I. monta'num.** 12 to 18 in. h. *l.* broadly linear. *fl.* blue, about 2 in. across, sometimes in a panicle; segs. more or less spreading or recurved. June. Cent. Asia. 1844. (B.R. 1844, 66.) SYN. *I. tataricum.* A plant variable in colour of fls. and in width of l. var. **macranth'um,** *fl.* deep blue shaded purple; **Sintenis'ii,** *fl.* lighter blue.

**I. Pal'lasii.** A synonym of *I. montanum.*

**I. tata'ricum.** A synonym of *I. montanum.*

**IXO'DIA** (*ixodes*, viscid, in reference to the glutinous secretion on the plant). FAM. *Compositae.* A genus monotypic or, according to some authors, of 2 Australian species. Flower-heads much resembling those of an Achillea. Cool greenhouse. Propagated by cuttings.

**I. achilleoi'des.** Evergreen shrub, 1 to 3 ft., shoots angular, glabrous and, like other parts, glutinous. *l.* linear, ½ to 1 in. long, sessile. *fl.-heads* numerous, ⅓ in. wide, in terminal corymbs 1 to 2 in. across; there are no ray-florets, their place and functions being taken by the white petal-like inner bracts of the involucre; disk ⅛ in. wide, yellow. June. Victoria, S. Australia. 1803. (B.M. 1534.) var. **ala'ta,** very distinct by its strong growth, its l. up to 2 in. long and ⅜ in. wide, corymbs 3 to 5 in. across and fl.-heads ⅜ in. wide, superior to the type but joined to it, according to Bentham, by many intermediate forms. SYN. *I. alata.*

W. J. B.

**IXOR'A** (name of a Malabar idol to which the flowers of some species are offered). FAM. *Rubiaceae.* A genus of about 150 species of evergreen shrubs or small trees, mostly natives of Trop. Asia and Africa, extending to America, Australia, and the Pacific Is. Leaves evergreen, opposite or rarely ternate, or whorled, leathery, sometimes sessile. Flowers in terminal corymbs on bracteate pedicels; corolla yellow, orange, scarlet, pink, or white, salver-shaped with a long, slender tube, somewhat barbed in the throat. Fruit a hard, fleshy berry. Related to Pavetta but with the style 2-fid at the tip, not entire or nearly so. The Ixoras are amongst the most handsome and striking of stove flowering plants. They are usually of compact, bushy habit, needing little training, and have by no means unattractive foliage. Propagation is by cuttings which are best taken in spring, though they will root at almost any time. The cuttings should be short-jointed and moderately firm; they should be inserted singly in small pots which should then be plunged in a close frame with a bottom heat of about 80° F. and kept shaded. Roots soon form, as a rule, and the little plants should then be hardened to the open house and potted into 5-in. pots where, if given a high temperature and abundant moisture, they soon grow. Some of the species and hybrids can be flowered in pots of this size. A compost of fibrous peat with a little leaf-soil and plenty of silver sand suits Ixoras at all stages, being used rather fine for cuttings and in a rough state for older plants. They are the better for almost any amount of heat and moisture in summer but a cooler and rather drier atmosphere should be given in autumn and winter for ripening the growths. The branches should then be cut back to about one joint, but some may need to be left longer to secure symmetry. Plants in large pots will do well for several years without repotting if fed liberally with manure water when growing. Young plants grow freely if plunged in a bed of fermenting material, but this should not be allowed to become very hot. A little shade from bright sunshine is advisable in summer, but in dull weather all possible light should be given. Many of the following are of garden origin though they have received

Latin names, and can be raised true to type only by vegetative means. **A**

**I. acumina'ta.** Shrub of 3 to 6 ft. *l.* broad-lanceolate, slender-pointed, glabrous. *fl.* white, fragrant, large; tube 1½ in. long; corymbs large, crowded, almost sessile. N. India.

**I.×amab'ilis.** *fl.* pinkish, suffused with orange. An attractive plant of garden origin.

**I. amboini'ca.** *l.* ovate-oblong, large, undulate, slender-pointed, glabrous; stalk short. *fl.* orange-yellow in trichotomously branches corymbs. Amboina.

**I. armeni'aca.** Dwarf and compact. *fl.* pale yellow flushed salmon. 1890. Of garden origin.

**I. × auranti'aca.** *fl.* orange-red. Growth compact. Of garden origin.

**I. barba'ta.** Shrub of 6 ft. *l.* elliptic-oblong, acute, rather leathery, glossy, stalk short; stipules ovate, slender-pointed; one pair of l. only slightly smaller at base of main peduncle. *fl.* in sub-corymbose panicles; cal. tube globose, reddish-green; cor. tube greenish-white, 1½ in. long, slender, slightly curved; segs. white within; mouth with a delicate fringe of hairs. July. Andaman Is. 1823. (B.M. 2505, 4513.)

**I. Burbidg'ei.** Habit of *I. fulgens.* *fl.* orange-scarlet, in dense terminal and axillary cymes. 1883. Habitat?

**I.×Chelson'ii.** Dwarf branching shrub. *fl.* bright orange-salmon shaded pink in very large round corymbs. Summer. Of garden origin.

**I. chinen'sis.** Shrub of 2 to 3 ft. *l.* oval-lanceolate, with a long, slender point, firm. *fl.* light orange in many-fl., much branched, crowded cymes; cor. tube ¾ to 1 in. long. Summer. Moluccas, China. 1822. A very variable plant with white, pink, yellow, and orange forms. (B.R. 100 as *I. blanda*; B.R. 782 as *I. crocata*; B.M. 169 as *I. coccinea*.) SYN. *I. stricta.* var. **al'ba,** *fl.* pure white; **ro'sea,** up to 4 ft. h., *l.* dark shining green, oblong, narrowed to base, hairy beneath, *fl.* pale pink, becoming reddish in age, in large, loose, very much-branched cymes. Summer. Bengal. 1819. (B.M. 2428.) SYN. *I. rosea*; **ru'tilans,** vigorous, *fl.* tube reddish-crimson, lobes rich orange or salmon-red, corymbs larger than in type, compact. The form of this, **Prince of Orange,** has cinnabar-red fl. Of garden origin. (G.F. 1015.)

**I. coccin'ea.*** Shrub of 3 to 4 ft. *l.* heart-shaped, oblong, acute, shining, sessile. *fl.* bright red, in very large umbellate corymbs; cor. tube nearly 2 in. long. Summer. E. Indies. 1814. (B.R. 154 as *I. grandiflora*; B.R. 782 as *I crocata*.) The fl. and bark are made into an eye-lotion and the l. used in treating sores, ulcers, &c., in its native country. A variable species. Here belong var. **Bandhu'ca,** *fl.* deep scarlet, cor. tube over 1 in. long, corymbs rather contracted. India. 1815. (B.R. 513 as *I. Bandhuca*.); **Dixia'na,** *fl.* dark orange in very large corymbs, freely produced. Of garden origin. 1868; **Fras'eri,*** *l.* dark green, *fl.* brilliant reddish-salmon, cor. tube carmine, in numerous large, globular corymbs. Of garden origin; **Mors'ei,** *fl.* bright orange, sometimes shaded scarlet, in large corymbs. 1884; **Pil'grimii,*** *fl.* bright orange-scarlet, shaded crimson, corymbs round, 7 in. across. 1880. Of garden origin, derived from *I.×Williamsii* and needing less heat than *I. coccinea.*

**I.×Co'lei*** (*I. chinensis×I. coccinea*). Robust. *l.* roundish, dark green. *fl.* white, numerous, in round corymbs, remaining long in fl. Of garden origin.

**I. concin'na.*** *fl.* bright salmon-pink at first, becoming deep salmon-pink, in large compact corymbs. 1882. Malaya.

**I. conges'ta.** Shrub of 4 ft. *l.* broad-oblong or elliptic, 6 to 12 in. long, acute, slender-pointed. *fl.* bright orange, becoming reddish; segs. rounded; sessile or nearly so, in corymbs. Burma, Singapore. 1845. (B.M. 4325 as *I. Griffithii*.)

**I. conspic'ua.** *fl.* buff-yellow, becoming bright orange; corymbs large. 1886. Of garden origin.

**I. deco'ra.** *fl.* yellow, flaked rosy-crimson, large, in large corymbs. 1882. Of garden origin.

**I. em'inens.** *fl.* clear buff changing in age to light salmon-pink, large. 1885. Of garden origin.

**I. exim'ia.** *fl.* buff, becoming salmon-pink; cor. tube long; corymbs large. 1881. Of garden origin.

**I. fer'rea.** Tree to 20 ft. *l.* oblong, acute, 4 to 6 in. long; stalks short. *fl.* few, pink in axillary, sessile, contracted corymbs; cor. tube ⅓ in. long. W. Indies. 1793.

**I. Findlaya'na.** Compact, free-growing shrub. *fl.* white, very fragrant. E. Indies. 1883.

**I. formo'sa.** *fl.* orange-red, freely produced; corymbs large, globose. Of garden origin.

**I. ful'gens.*** Shrub of 3 to 4 ft., branches slender, polished. *l.* linear-lanceolate, slender-pointed; stalks short. *fl.* clear orange-scarlet, or orange becoming scarlet; on short pedicels in dense terminal corymbs. Java, &c. (B.M. 4523 as *I. salicifolia*.) var. **variega'ta,** *l.* marked with a feathered greying stripe along mid-rib. 1882.

**I. Gem'ma.** *fl.* rich orange-yellow, in large compact corymbs. 1885. Of garden origin.

**I. illus'tris.** *fl.* bright orange-salmon, in large corymbs. 1881. Of garden origin.

**I. insig'nis.** Dwarf. *fl.* deep rosy-crimson, shaded orange; corymb compact. Of garden origin.

**I. javan'ica.*** Shrub of 3 to 4 ft. with forking coral-red branches. *l.* ovate-oblong, slender-pointed. *fl.* orange-red; cor. tube long, slender; corymbs dense, in long trichotomous peduncles. Summer. Java. 1846. (B.M. 4586.)

**I.×kewen'sis.** Shrub of 4 ft. *l.* elliptic, pale yellowish-green, 6 to 9 in. long. *fl.* orange-scarlet; in large corymbs. Of garden origin.

**I. lanceola'ria.** Shrub of 2 ft. *l.* lanceolate, up to 9 in. long, slender-pointed, rather leathery; patent; veins nearly at right angles to midrib, parallel. *fl.* greenish-white, in rather loose, pedunculate, trichotomously branched corymbs. April. India. 1847. (B.M. 4399.)

**I. laxiflo'ra.** Shrub of 3 to 4 ft. *l.* oblong-lanceolate, up to 9 in. long, slender-pointed; stalk short. *fl.* very fragrant, small, in large, terminal, trichotomously branched panicles; cal. deep red; cor. white, fringed pink; cor. tube 1½ in. long, slender, segs. spreading. Summer. Upper Guinea. (B.M. 4482.)

*Ixora lutea*

**I. lu'tea.*** Habit of *I. coccinea.* *l.* oblong-elliptic, mucronate, unequally heart-shaped at base, pale green, margins slightly recurved. *fl.* pale yellow, sessile, in lax-fld. corymbs. Differs from *I. coccinea* by its looser corymbs and the larger ovate-rhomboid cor. lobes. Of garden origin. (B.M. 8439 as *I. coccinea lutea*.)

**I. macrothyr'sa.*** Glabrous rigid shrub. *l.* linear-oblong to oblong-lanceolate, about 12 in. long, 1½ to 2 in. wide, deep green, slender-pointed. *fl.* deep red, becoming tinged crimson with age; corymbs very large. Sumatra. 1878. (B.M. 6853; Gn. 13 (1878), 312 as *I. Duffii*.)

**I. ocula'ta.** Shrub of 2 to 3 ft. *l.* obovate, dark green. *fl.* orange-salmon with deeper-coloured eye. Origin unknown.

**I. odora'ta.** Shrub of 3 ft. *l.* broadly ovate or obovate-lanceolate, spreading, 6 to 12 in. long; lower l. stalked, upper more ovate, smaller, sessile. *fl.* white, soon becoming yellow-brown, very fragrant, 4 to 5 in. long, in large panicles 1 ft. or more across. May. Madagascar. 1844. (B.M. 4191.)

**I. orna'ta.** *fl.* bright orange-salmon, freely produced. 1881. Of garden origin.

**I. parviflo'ra.** *l.* oblong or elliptic, 3 to 6 in. long, obtuse; stalk very short. *fl.* white, tube short, lobes oblong; clusters sub-globose. August. 1800. India.

**I.×pictura'ta** (*I. chinensis×I.×Williamsii*). Habit and foliage of *I.×Williamsii*, corymb, &c., of *I. chinensis.* 1880. Of garden origin.

**I. Pil'grimii.** *See* **I. coccinea.**

**I. plu'mea.** *l.* oblanceolate, 4 to 5 in. long, slender-pointed, wedge-shaped at base, rather leathery; stipules broad-ovate, long-cuspidate. *fl.* white; cal. tube short, rounded, lobes linear; cor. tube slender; corymb 3 to 5 in. across, peduncles short. Java, Malaya.

**I. prin'ceps.** *l.* 6 to 7 in. long, 2 in. wide. *fl.* buff-white, becoming deep reddish-orange, very freely produced. Java.

**I. profu'sa.** *fl.* rosy-salmon, in dense, very large corymbs. 1883. Of garden origin.

**I. regi'na.** Dwarfer and more compact than *I. Williamsii.* *l.* ovate, slender-pointed. *fl.* rich violet-salmon, in large dense corymbs. Of garden origin.

**I. salicifo'lia.** A synonym of *I. fulgens.*

**I. salmon'ea.** *fl.* buff and salmon. 1892. Of garden origin.

**I. sanguin'ea.** *l.* dark green. *fl.* crimson, shaded deep violet, in many-fld. large corymbs. Of garden origin.

**I. specio'sa.** *fl.* yellow-buff becoming orange-salmon. 1886. Of garden origin.

**I. specta'bilis.** *l.* broad elliptic-lanceolate, 2 to 5 in. long, glabrous, stalked, the upper oblong, stem clasping. *fl.* white, in trichotomous corymbs; cal. teeth; cor. lobes narrow. Burma.

**I. splen'dens.*** *l.* elliptic-obtuse, 3½ in. long, 1½ in. wide. *fl.* bright copper-scarlet, very brilliant; cor. tube 1½ in. long; corymbs very large. Of garden origin.

**I. splen'dida.** *fl.* brilliant orange-crimson in large corymbs. 1883. Of garden origin. (I.H. 463.)

**I. stric'ta.** A synonym of *I. chinensis.*

**I. Thwaites'ii.** Shrub or small tree in the wild. *l.* broad-lanceolate, but variable, 3 to 8 in. long, rather leathery, abruptly slender-pointed; stalk scarcely ⅓ in. long; stipules reddish. *fl.* white or cream; tube slender, 1¼ in. long; lobes spreading, ¾ in. across; corymb compact, peduncle short. Ceylon. 1859. (B.M. 5197 as *I. jucunda*.)

**I. umbella'ta.** Much-branched glabrous shrub of 3 to 4 ft., twigs terete. *l.* elliptic or oblong-elliptic, 6 to 10 in. long, with a short blunt point, base round, mid-rib prominent beneath. *fl.* white; cal. deeply lobed, ciliate (like bracteoles); cor. tube slender, throat slightly hairy within. Java. 1889. (B.M. 8577.)

**I. undula'ta.** Shrub of 3 to 4 ft. *l.* elliptic or lanceolate, slender-pointed, undulate. *fl.* white; cor. tube ½ in. long; in a terminal panicle, its branches corymbose at tips. Summer. Bengal, &c. 1820.

**I. venus'ta.** *fl.* bright orange, becoming salmon-buff, large. Of garden origin.

**I.×West'ii.** *fl.* pale rose, becoming bright rose, in sub-globose trusses 4 to 6 in. across. 1882. Of garden origin.

**I.×Wil'liamsii.*** Free-growing and flowering. *fl.* reddish-salmon in large corymbs. Requires less heat than many. A parent of many beautiful garden forms, itself of garden origin.

# J

**JABORANDI.** The drug obtained from *Pilocarpus Jaborandi*.

**JABORO'SA** (*Jabarose*, the Arabic name of the allied Mandrake). FAM. *Solanaceae*. A genus of 6 or 7 species of perennials, one from Mexico, the others from the Andes and temperate S. America. Leaves runcinate-pinnatifid or more deeply cut, or toothed. Flowers white or yellowish; corolla bell-shaped or tubular. *J. integrifolia* needs a warm place in a light sandy soil and is not to be entirely depended upon for hardiness. It may be increased by division, by cuttings of young shoots under a hand-light, or by seeds sown in spring.

**J. integrifo'lia.** Creeping plant about 6 in. h. *l.* large, oval, nearly entire, dark green, stalked. *fl.* greenish-white, about 2 in. long, segs. acute; peduncles as long as l.-stalks. Buenos Aires. (B.M. 3489.)

**JACA.** *See* **Artocarpus integrifolia.**

**JACARAN'DA** (name of 1 species in Brazil). FAM. *Bignoniaceae*. A genus of about 50 species of ornamental shrubs and trees, somewhat resembling the fine-leaved species of Acacia in habit. Leaves opposite, 2-pinnate. Flowers blue or violet, showy, in panicles which are usually terminal; corolla tubular at base, much dilated above, bell-shaped, tube swollen in lower part. A compost of sandy peat and fibrous loam suits them provided it is thoroughly drained. Cuttings of half-ripe shoots will root in early summer in sand or sand and peat in heat, kept shaded until well rooted. Stove or warm greenhouse conditions are necessary for these plants.

**J. chelon'ia.** *l.* 2-pinnate, fern-like, ornamental. *fl.* large, blue, in narrow terminal panicles, 12 in. long. Paraguay, Argentina. Wood veined rose, valuable for cabinet work.

**J. cuspidifo'lia.** Larger in all parts than *J. ovalifolia* which it otherwise much resembles. *fl.* brighter blue. Brazil, Argentina.

*Jacaranda jasminoides*

**J. jasminoi'des.** Shrub to 20 ft. *l.* 2-pinnate, downy. lflets. ovate-rhomboid, acute, very unequal. *fl.* downy without, dark purple, with short tube; limb tubular-bell-shaped, 1½ in. long, with pale spot under upper lip. June. Mexico. 1824. (B.R. 1103 as *J. tomentosa*.)

**J. ovalifo'lia.*** Shrub of about 10 ft. *l.* 2-pinnate, about 18 in. long; pinnae opposite, in many pairs, each with 10 to 28 pairs of trapezoid-oval-oblong mucronate, downy lflets. *fl.* blue, drooping; cor. silky; panicles erectly pyramidal, large, naked, terminal. Brazil. 1818. (B.M. 2327; B.R. 631.) SYN. *J. mimosifolia, Bignonia caerulea*. Valuable for conservatory decoration or sub-tropical bedding. It will tolerate pruning to keep it in shape. var. **al'ba**, *fl.* white.   **A**

*Ja'cea.* Spanish name of *Centaurea Jacea.*

**JACINTH.** *See* **Hyacinth.**

**JACK TREE.** *See* **Artocarpus integrifolia.**

*Jack'ii*, in honour of John George Jack, b. 1861, of Canada, dendrologist at the Arnold Arboretum.

**JACK-IN-A-BOX.** *See* **Hernandia sonora.**   **A**

*Jack'mani*, in honour of G. Jackman of Woking, *c.* 1865.

**JACKSO'NIA** (after George Jackson, Scottish botanist). FAM. *Leguminosae*. A genus of about 30 species of Australian shrubs, mostly leafless; leaves when present simple (i.e. 1-foliolate); shoots often flattened and leaf-like. Flowers papilionaceous. Cool greenhouse, in as sunny a place as possible. Grow in light loam. The two following species are cultivated in Scilly.

**J. hor'rida.** Shrub, tall and much branched, shoots angular and flattened; branchlets leaf-like, often twice or thrice forked; ultimate segs. ⅓ to 1 in. long, linear, sharply pointed, rigid, flat with a raised midrib. *fl.* yellow. ⅓ in. long, 1 to 3 at the base of the branchlets or in short racemes. *Pod* covered with soft brown down, ⅓ in. long, turgid. Queensland. Formidably armed.

**J. scopa'ria.*** Broom-like shrub, 10 to 12 ft., shoots glabrous, erect, much clustered, angled like those of common broom but much more slender. *l.* usually absent except in the seedling state; when present ¾ to 2 in. long, entire. *fl.* yellow, ⅓ in. long, copiously borne in clusters of 3 to 6 nearly or quite terminal. Summer. *Pod* flat, oblong, ⅓ to ½ in. long. Queensland, New S. Wales. 1803. (L.B.C. 427.)

W. J. B.

**JACOBAE'A.** Included in **Senecio.**

**JACOBEA LILY.** *See* **Sprekelia formosissima.**

**JACOBIN'IA** (Jacobina, in S. America, near Bahia). FAM. *Acanthaceae*. A genus of perhaps 40 species of glabrous herbs or, rarely, shrubs, natives of the hotter parts of America. Leaves opposite, entire. Flowers sometimes solitary, sometimes in clusters or spikes; calyx with 5 linear, or awl-shaped segments; corolla 2-lipped; stamens 2 with 2 hairy structures on the corolla tube representing the 2 often found in allied genera, without appendages to the anther-lobes which are seen in the related Justicia; style filiform. *J. Ghiesbreghtiana, J. pauciflora,* and *J. × penrhosiensis,* often known as Libonias in gardens, are good winter-flowering plants for greenhouse decoration. Old plants from which it is intended to propagate should be started into growth by placing in a little heat early in spring and from these the cuttings should be taken, put into sandy soil and kept close until rooted. They should then be potted off singly, and grown throughout the summer in a frame, giving plenty of air to induce sturdy, short-jointed growth, stopping several times to induce a bushy habit. The compost should be 3 parts good loam, 1 of leaf-soil or peat with enough sand to keep the whole open; 5- or 6-in. pots are large enough to flower the plants in. Light shading may be given in hot weather, but by early autumn full sun will be needed so that the wood may be thoroughly ripened. Old plants may be grown for several years but should be cut back after flowering, and follow the same routine as the young plants put into the frame, but young plants usually make more shapely growth. They require an intermediate temperature when flowering, and they must be well watered, otherwise loss of leaves will occur. Red Spider Mites are apt to attack them and are difficult to dislodge but frequent spraying with clean water throughout the summer is usually an effective check. For cultivation of other species *see* **Justicia.**

J. C.

**J. au′rea.** Stem obtusely 4-angled, about 6 ft. h. *l.* ovate-cordate, decurrent into a long stalk. *fl.* yellow, tubular, cut half-way into 2 lips; thyrse large, terminal, compact; bracts and sep. linear-awl-shaped. July. Honduras. 1848. (B.M. 4444 as *Cyrtanthera catalpaeflora.*)

**J. carn′ea.** About 6 ft. h. *l.* ovate-acuminate. *fl.* flesh-coloured; thyrse compact; bracts and sep. ovate-lanceolate. August, September. Brazil. 1827. (B.M. 3383; B.R. 1397 as *Justicia carnea.*) Syn. *J. magnifica carnea.* Greenhouse.

**J. chrysostepha′na.** Stem obtusely 4-angled. *l.* ovate, slender-pointed, not decurrent into the stalk, midrib and nerves beneath bright red. *fl.* yellow in a terminal corymb smaller than in *J. aurea,* cor. 2-lipped. Winter. Mexico. 1870. (B.M. 5887 **as** *Cyrtanthera chrysostephana.*) *See note on* **J. coccinea.**

**J. coccin′ea.** About 5 ft. h. *l.* elliptic. *fl.* scarlet, crowded in a terminal spike; upper lip lanceolate, reflexed at end. February. Brazil. (B.M. 432 as *Justicia coccinea.*) This, *J. carnea,* and *J. chrysostephana* are best from cuttings put in in spring. They grow and flower freely without special treatment but need plenty of air and a moderate temperature after they have made good growth, otherwise they are apt to become lanky.

**J. Ghiesbreghtia′na.** 1 to 1½ ft. h. *l.* ovate-lanceolate, bright green, glabrous. *fl.* scarlet, in very loose terminal panicles. Winter. Mexico. 1843. (G.F. 98 as *Sericographis Ghiesbreghtiana.*) Needs a good rest in August and September and open-air treatment then, otherwise it flowers indifferently.

**J. Linden′ii.** Glabrous sub-shrub. *l.* oval, slender-pointed. *fl.* orange-yellow, in terminal heads. Mexico. 1890. (R.H. 1870, 250 as *Justicia Lindenii.*)

**J. magnif′ica.** *See* **J. carnea** *and* **J. Pohliana.**

**J. Mohint′li.** A synonym of *J. spicigera.*

*Jacobinia pauciflora*

**J. pauciflo′ra.** Downy sub-shrub, 1 to 2 ft. h. Stems round. *l.* elliptic or elliptic-oblong. *fl.* scarlet, tipped yellow, about 1 in. long, numerous, drooping, or nearly horizontal, tubular, lips short. Brazil. 1862. (B.H. 1863, 2.) Syn. *Libonia floribunda.* Treat like *J. Ghiesbreghtiana.*

**J.×penrhosien′sis** (*J. Ghiesbreghtiana×J. pauciflora*). *l.* more acute and *fl.* brighter crimson and larger than in *J. pauciflora.* Winter. (R.H. 1876, 50.) A fine pot plant.

**J. Pohlia′na.** Much like *J. carnea* but stronger in growth and more leafy. *l.* ovate-oblong or ovate, about 6 in. long, almost cordate at base. *fl.* bright crimson. Brazil. var. **na′na** is dwarfer; **veluti′na,** *l.* and bracts softly hairy. *fl.* pink, 2 in. long. Treatment as *J. carnea.*

**J. seric′ea.** Whitish-silky. *l.* oblong, slender-pointed. *fl.* red, 2 in. long, downy, in terminal spikes. Peru.

**J. spicig′era.** Bushy sub-shrub. *l.* long-ovate, sometimes faintly toothed, thick and minutely downy. *fl.* bright orange, tubular, 1½ in. long, slightly swollen at base of tube, lower lip deflexed, spirally curved. Mexico. 1886. Syn. *J. Mohintli.* Treatment as *J. Ghiesbreghtiana.*

**J. suberec′ta.** Of low spreading habit, herbaceous, velvety. *l.* nearly sessile, ovate, about 2½ in. long. *fl.* bright scarlet, about 1¼ in. long, downy without, 2-lobed at apex; in 1- to 10-fld. cymes. Uruguay. 1909. (B.M. 8350.) Good basket plant for warm house.

***Jacobinia′nus -a -um,*** in honour of G. A. von Jacobi (1805–74) of Berlin.

### JACOB'S LADDER. *See* **Polemonium caeruleum.**

### JACOB'S STAFF. *See* **Verbascum Thapsus.**

### JACQUEMON′TIA (in honour of Victor Jacquemont, 1801–32, French naturalist and traveller in the E. Indies). Fam. *Convolvulaceae.* A genus of about 60 species of twining or prostrate herbs or sub-shrubs, natives of Trop. America and Africa. Leaves entire, often cordate, rarely dentate or lobed. Flowers Convolvulus-like, blue, white, or rarely violet, sometimes loosely or densely cymose, sometimes capitate, rarely solitary or loosely racemose. Treatment as for Ipomoea.

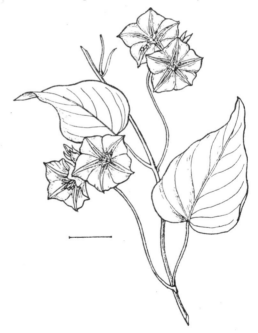

*Jacquemontia pentantha*

**J. pentan′tha.** Twining perennial of 6 to 8 ft., somewhat shrubby at base. *l.* oblong-cordate, slender-pointed, somewhat repand, smooth. *fl.* rich violet-blue, sessile; peduncles 5- to 12-fld. July to September. Mexico to Brazil. 1808. (B.M. 2151 as *Convolvulus pentanthus.*) Syn. *J. violacea.* var. **canes′cens,** downy, *fl.* blue; sep. oblong, obtuse. Summer. Bogota. 1846. (B.R. 1847, 27 as *Convolvulus canescens.*) Syn. *J. canescens.*

**J. viola′cea.** A synonym of *J. pentantha.*

***Jacquesia′nus -a -um,*** in honour of M. Jacques, head gardener at Neuilly, France.

### JACQUIN′IA (in honour of Nicholas Joseph de Jacquin, 1727–1817, Professor of Botany, Leyden). Fam.

*Myrsinaceae.* A genus of about 30 species of evergreen shrubs, natives of Trop. America, allied to Theophrasta. Leaves alternate or whorled, entire, crowded near ends of branches, margins revolute. Flowers white, yellow, orange, or purple, solitary or racemose at ends of branches; corolla salver-shaped with 5 appendages alternate with lobes at throat. Fruit a leathery berry. Stove conditions and a compost of sandy peat with a small quantity of fibrous loam suits them. Cuttings of ripe shoots, made in summer, in sand under a close frame with moist bottom heat afford means of propagation.

**J. armillar'is.** Bracelet Wood. Shrub or tree. *l.* wedge-shaped, spatulate or obovate-oblong, obtuse or retuse, sometimes mucronate, nearly veinless. *fl.* white in racemes or corymbs. June. W. Indies. 1768. The shining yellow and brown seeds are made into bracelets in the W. Indies.

**J. auranti'aca.** Shrub of 3 to 6 ft., branches somewhat whorled. *l.* obovate-lanceolate, slender-pointed, point sharp. *fl.* orange in racemes. April to September. Sandwich Is. 1796. (B.M. 1639.)

**J. keyen'sis.** Small evergreen tree, 12 to 15 ft. h. *l.* wedge-shaped, spatulate or obovate, 4 in. long, 1½ in. wide, usually whorled. *fl.* small, white, honey-scented, in racemes. Winter. Trop. America.

**J. ruscifo'lia.** Shrub of 8 to 10 ft. *l.* whorled, lanceolate, about 3 in. long, glabrous, rigidly spiny, margin somewhat revolute. *fl.* red, small, solitary or in small umbels, terminal, nodding. Havana.

**jagged,** coarsely cut.

**JAGGERY.** *See* **Arenga.**

**JALAP.** *See* **Ipomoea Purga.**

**JALAPA.** A synonym of Mirabilis. From Xalapa, Mexico.

*jalisca'nus -a -um,* of Jalisco, a province of Mexico.

**JAMAICA DOGWOOD.** *See* **Piscidia.**

**JAMAICA EBONY. Brya Ebenus.** **A**

**JAMAICA HONEYSUCKLE.** *See* **Passiflora laurifolia.**

**JAMAICA HORSE-BEAN.** *See* **Canavalia ensiformis.**

**JAMAICA PAROQUET BUR. Triumfetta.** **A**

**JAMAICA PEPPER.** *See* **Allspice, Pimenta officinalis.**

**JAMAICA PLUM.** *See* **Spondias lutea.**

**JAMAICA ROSE.** *See* **Meriania.**

*jamaicen'sis -is -e,* of Jamaica, W. Indies.

**JAMBOS'A.** Included in **Eugenia.** From the native Hindu name.

**JAMES'IA** (in honour of Dr. Edwin James, 1797–1861, American botanist, who discovered *J. americana*). FAM. *Saxifragaceae.* A genus of 3 deciduous shrubs related to Deutzia but with a superior ovary. Flowers in terminal cymes, sepals 5, petals 5, convolute, hairy inside, stamens 10, carpels 3 to 5, fruit a 3- to 5-valved capsule with many seeds. *J. americana* is hardy and grows well in a sunny position in an open not very rich soil. Increased by seeds, or by cuttings of ripened shoots placed in sandy loam.

**J. america'na.** Roundish shrub of 4 to 6 ft. *l.* opposite, 1 to 3 in. long, coarsely toothed. *fl.* about ½ in. across, white, fragrant, in many-fld. cymes about 2 in. wide. May. Western N. America. 1865. (B.M. 6142.) Foliage turns orange and scarlet in autumn.

*Jamesia'nus -a -um,* in honour of James, brother of George Forrest (q.v.).

**JAMESON'IA** (in honour of Dr. William Jameson, 1796–1873, Professor of Botany, Quito). FAM. *Poly-* *podiaceae.* A genus of about 18 species of S. American ferns allied to Gymnogramme. Sori oblong on the flabellate veins on back of the pinnae, remote from the edge. The species described succeed under greenhouse treatment in an open compost of 2 parts fibrous peat, 1 part chopped Sphagnum, 1 part silver sand. They need abundant water at the roots but should not be syringed overhead. Propagation by division or by the abundant spores which germinate freely in warmth. Not very decorative. The species described have been called varieties of *J. imbricata.*

*Jamesia americana*

**J. canes'cens.** A stouter plant than *J. imbricata,* the upper part of the fronds densely clothed with long, yellowish-brown hair, hiding the hoary pinnae. S. America.

**J. imbrica'ta.** *rhiz.* woody, creeping, black. *sti.* wiry, slender, 3 to 6 in. long. *Fronds* 6 to 18 in. long, ⅛ to ¼ in. broad, pinnate; pinnae close, roundish, often spreading horizontally; margins incurved. Andes, New Grenada to Peru.

**J. Pearc'ei.** Habit of *J. imbricata. Fronds* rather more than 1 in. wide; pinnae ⅛ in. long, oblong, densely hairy beneath, margins revolute. Ecuador.

**J. vertica'lis.** Habit of *J. imbricata. sti.* 12 in. long. *Fronds* 6 to 9 in. long, ½ in. wide; pinnae oblong-triangular, naked; rachis shortly downy. S. America.

*James'onii,* in honour of Mr. Jameson who collected *Gerbera Jamesonii,* near Barberton, S. Africa.

**JANATSI.** *See* **Debregeasia.**

*janeiren'sis -is -e,* of Rio de Janeiro, S. America.

**JANKAE'A** (in honour of Victor de Janka, student of the flora of the Danube region). FAM. *Gesneriaceae.* A genus of a single Greek species with the habit of Haberlea and Ramondia, differing from Haberlea by its shortly bell-funnel-shaped not 2-lipped corolla, and 4 straight, equal, not didynamous stamens with reflexed filaments, and from Ramondia which has a rotate corolla and 5 very short stamens. It is not easy to please but should succeed in rough, coarse, sandy peat with plenty of grit, in a spot overhung by a rock so that rain does not fall on the foliage nor moisture hang round the collar; or better still in the alpine-house. Propagated by seed or by leaf-cuttings taken in July and given heat.

**J. Heldreich'ii.** Perennial. Rosette solitary. Stem covered with reddish hair. *l.* rather thick, ovate, entire, about 1 in. long, obtuse, covered above with silky white appressed hair, beneath with reddish-brown hair. *fl.* violet, about ¾ in. long, bell-shaped, 4-lobed to middle, lobes almost equal; cal. lobes 4, ovate, obtuse; stamens 4, filaments straight. *fr.* a capsule twice as long as cal. Olympus, Greece.

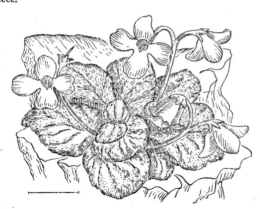

*Jankaea Heldreichii*

*Janows'kii,* in honour of R. F. Janowski, 1880– ?, who collected in New Guinea.

*Jansenia'nus -a -um,* in honour of P. J. Jansen, 1872– ? or P. Jansen, 1882– ?, Dutch botanists.

**JAN'THE.** *See* **Celsia bugulifolia.**

*januen'sis -is -e,* of Genoa, N. Italy.

**JAPAN LACQUER.** Varnish Tree. *See* **Rhus vernicifera.**

**JAPAN LAUREL.** *See* **Aucuba.**

**JAPAN PEPPER.** *See* **Zanthoxylum piperitum.**

**JAPAN WAX.** *See* **Rhus succedanea.**

**JAPANESE ALDER.** *See* **Alnus japonica.**

**JAPANESE CEDAR.** *See* **Cryptomeria japonica.**

**JAPANESE CHERRIES.** Under this name many varieties of cherries originating in the far east, especially in Japan, are in cultivation in Britain. A great deal of confusion exists as to the botanical status and nomenclature of many of them, for though it is certain that they have all been derived from wild species of Japan and China, it is by no means clear in many instances from which wild species they have taken origin or, indeed, what the limits of the supposed parent species really are. The opinions of various botanists who have assayed the task of assigning the cultivated forms to wild parents have differed markedly and with them the botanical names bestowed upon them. The species which seem most clearly differentiated are here described under **Prunus** and include *P. campanulata* with the reddest flowers of any cherry, too tender, however, for wide cultivation in Britain; *P. subhirtella* (Higan), very variable in habit and colour of flower, with, in addition to the normal erect form, *pendula,* one of the most striking and beautiful of weeping trees, and *autumnalis,* flowering in October and in favourable periods until spring; *P. yedoensis* (Yoshino), the first to flower with masses of single, nearly white flowers, with pinkish calyces; *P. Sargentii* (also called *P. sachalinensis*) with rose or shell-pink flowers and copper-red young leaves in spring and brilliant scarlet and crimson leaves in autumn; *P. Sieboldii* (Takasago) with

very hairy leaves and semi-double pinkish-white flowers nearly as early as Yoshino, often placed under *P. serrulata*; *P. incisa* (Fuji), also early flowering with rather small single flowers produced in great profusion; *P. speciosa* (Oshima-Zakura) with large single white flowers in long-stalked corymbs; *P. serrulata* with usually reddish or brownish-green leaves when unfolding, glabrous or nearly so, is the group to which the majority of the varieties cultivated in Britain belong, and *P. Sieboldii* and *P. speciosa* already mentioned are often included with it. Some botanists have separated the varieties with leaves green when unfolding and with long bristle-tipped teeth to the leaves under the name *P. Lannesiana,* but it is impossible to make this division when a large number of varieties are considered, for there is no such hard and fast line between them, and they may all be better considered varieties (i.e. clones) under the species *P. serrulata,* the name Lindley gave to the first white double-flowered cherry introduced into England from China in 1822—probably the first 'Japanese cherry' to reach Europe. It is only comparatively recently that the Japanese Cherries have been widely planted. Perhaps the variety Fugenzo, first known here as James H. Veitch, introduced in 1892, gave an impetus to the planting of ornamental cherries here and the early years of the 20th century have seen the introduction of very many others. Several have taken a part in introducing and popularizing them but none more actively than Mr. Collingwood Ingram of Benenden, Kent, who has collected and studied them for many years and whose articles in the *Journal of the Royal Horticultural Society,* vol. 50 and 54 and in other horticultural Journals have added much to our knowledge of them. His book *Ornamental Cherries* (1948), with numerous plates, brings his observations and conclusions up to date and should be consulted for full descriptions of the varieties in cultivation in Britain at the present time. Other important books are the excellent pamphlet, *The Oriental Flowering Cherries,* 1934, by Paul Russell; *Die Japanischen Bergkirschen,* by M. Miyoshi, 1916; and *The Cherries of Japan,* by E. H. Wilson, 1916.

Miyoshi recognized about 120 varieties and many more names have appeared in various lists, but some of these are quite redundant and others belong to varieties too much alike. The variations are seen not only in flower colour, form, and fragrance, but in habit of growth and in spring and autumn colouring of the foliage. The differences in habit and size make these cherries fit into many situations, some being well-fitted for planting as roadside trees as well as for decorating the garden, and the variety Cheal's Weeping or Kiku-Shidare is useful on banks if worked low down, while the upright Amanogawa is a striking form for formal planting. None of these will come true from seed, but all seem at home grafted or budded on seedlings of the British *Prunus Avium,* and that species is generally better for the purpose than seedlings of *P. serrulata.* In America grafting is often done on pieces of the roots of year-old seedlings of *P. Avium,* but in Britain stem grafting or budding is the common practice. The working is best done low down so that the scion itself forms the stem and many root if the union is covered. Cuttings are difficult or impossible to root, but layering may be done with success with some and perhaps all varieties. These cherries are not very particular as to soil though it should be well-drained and is best of a loamy nature. When once established they may be grown with mown grass up to their stems and so may be planted as lawn trees, and they may be successfully transplanted at almost any size and age. Miss Mountain has drawn up the following key giving the important characters and differences between some of the most distinct and well-known varieties, including some outside the *P. serrulata* group. *See also* Supplement.

KEY

| | |
|---|---|
| 1. *Plant with small hairs in some parts* | 2 |
| 1. *Plant (adult) smooth, except the bud scales* | 4 |
| 2. *Fl. single; pet. 5* | 3 |
| 2. *Fl. semi-double; pet. 7 to 15* | Takasago |
| 3. *Style and calyx hairy* | Yoshino |
| 3. *Cal. hairy, style smooth. Old bark satiny red-brown* | Juddii |
| 3. *Style and cal. smooth* | Fudan-Zakura |
| 4. *Pet. 5 to 11* | 5 |
| 4. *Pet. 12 to 15* | 16 |
| 4. *Pet. more than 16* | 22 |
| 5. *Fl. white* | 6 |
| 5. *Fl. pink, at least when young* | 10 |
| 5. *Fl. and buds yellowish* | Ukon |
| 5. *Fl. yellowish with green and pink streaks* | Gioiko |
| 6. *Fl. fragrant* | 7 |
| 6. *Fl. without scent; pet. 5* | 9 |
| 7. *Young lvs. coppery* | Takinioi |
| 7. *Young lvs. green* | 8 |
| 8. *Pet. 5; fl. small* | Jo-nioi |
| 8. *Perfect pet. 5; several stamens petaloid; fl. large* | Shirotae |
| 9. *Fl. very large* | Tai-haku |
| 9. *Fl. small* | Washi-no-o |
| 10. *Pet. 5* | 11 |
| 10. *Pet. 5 to 12* | 13 |
| 11. *Young lvs. coppery, teeth usually simple, even, long-pointed* | Ruirin |
| 11. *L.-teeth coarse, often double, short-pointed* | 12 |
| 12. *Bark at all ages reddish-brown* | Sargentii |
| 12. *Bark greyish (a smooth form of Yoshino)* | Hillieri |
| 13. *Branches fastigiate* | Amanogawa |
| 13. *Branches more or less spreading* | 14 |
| 14. *L.-teeth coarse, frequently double, points very long. Fl. pendent* | Shirotae |
| 14. *L.-teeth with medium points. Fl. not pendent* | 15 |
| 15. *Winter-buds slim. L.-teeth even, usually simple* | Mikuruma-gaeshi |
| 15. *Winter-buds round, plump. L.-teeth often double* | Ojochin |
| 16. *Most fl. yellow, green and pink* | Gioko |
| 16. *Fl. pink* | 17 |
| 17. *Styles usually several* | Horinji |
| 17. *Style usually single* | 18 |
| 18. *Cal. tube short, wide* | 19 |
| 18. *Cal. tube long narrow* | 20 |
| 19. *Young lvs. coppery, colour persisting as they unfold* | Troyame |
| 19. *Young lvs. bronze, becoming olive-green as they unfold* | Hokusai |
| 20. *Winter-buds plump, frequently blunt-ended* | Kokonoye |
| 20. *Winter-buds usually slim* | 21 |
| 21. *L.-teeth large, coarse, irregular* | Yedo |
| 21. *L.-teeth otherwise* | Shujaku |
| 22. *Fl. very pale pink or white, from first* | 23 |
| 22. *Fl. deep pink at least when young* | 26 |
| 23. *Style usually single, not leafy, much longer than stamens* | Prunus serrulata |
| 23. *Styles leafy, usually 2 or more* | 24 |
| 24. *Young lvs. coppery, colour persisting as they unfold* | Shirofugen |
| 24. *Young lvs. green or slightly golden bronze* | 25 |
| 25. *L.-teeth very long-pointed. Fl. almost white* | Shimidsu |
| 25. *L.-teeth not long-pointed. Fl. pink when young* | Ichiyo |
| 26. *Pet. 50 to 100. Fl. 1¼ to 1½ in. across* | 27 |
| 26. *Pet. 15 to 45* | 28 |
| 27. *Tree weeping* | Kiku-shidare |
| 27. *Tree not weeping* | Asano |
| 28. *Young lvs. deep copper while folded* | 29 |
| 28. *Young lvs. green, yellow, or light bronze* | 30 |
| 29. *Lvs. fading to light copper before fl. fall. Tree with many thin crossing branches* | Fugenzo |
| 29. *Lvs. retaining deep colour as they expand. Stamens with pink connectives prolonged* | Kanzan |
| 30. *Cal. lobes long narrow* | 31 |
| 30. *Cal. lobes short broad* | Ichiyo |
| 31. *Styles longer than stamens, hidden among pet. Young lvs. light bronze, becoming golden as they expand* | Pink Perfection |
| 31. *Style usually 3. Young lvs. olive-green while folded* | Daikoku |

**JAPANESE DWARF TREES.** Trees grown in miniature form reproducing, except in size, the form of the species they represent. The art of producing such plants was developed by the Japanese and most of the best examples have been imported from Japan. Many kinds of trees have been grown in this way including Conifers, Maples, Beeches, Oaks, Pears, Plums, Cherries, Wisterias, Cycads. These dwarf trees are grown in china pots so that the root run is greatly restricted. They are rarely produced by manipulations from the seedling stage but appear to be mainly plants obtained from the wild which have been subject to many adverse conditions or gnarled pieces of trees which have been rooted and subsequently trained by continual pinching,

pruning, and twisting of shoots until they have attained the desired form. These trees are hardy for the most part and should spend much of their time in the open, but it is better to protect them from spring frosts since frost does not discriminate between the shoots that should and those that should not die. These dwarf trees need pruning in February, especially those with deciduous foliage, and during summer to have the shoots pinched back several times so as to retain the shape of the plant. Pines are not pinched back but need pruning in spring, but other conifers need pinching. Other evergreen are pinched back and pruned after spring-flowering, or in February if flowering is late. Repotting needs doing every fifth year, into a pot the same size as the old one, loosening the earth round the bole, treating them in the same way as heaths or other hard-wooded plants, and cutting away any very vigorous roots. The pots must be thoroughly drained. The compost should be a mixture of leaf-mould, peat, and garden-soil, the work being done in February or March. Watering must be done whenever necessary but not frequently in winter. After repotting (or the annual resurfacing needed if the trees are in shallow pans) a copious watering should be given. Such trees may be used on a terrace or for indoor decoration but should not be allowed to remain indoors too long as the conditions there frequently lead to loss of foliage.

**JAPANESE HORSE-CHESTNUT.** *See* **Aesculus turbinata.**

**JAPANESE MAPLE.** *See* **Acer palmatum.**

**JAPANESE MEDLAR.** *See* **Eriobotrya japonica.**

**JAPANESE OAK.** *See* **Lithocarpus glabra.**

**JAPANESE PAGODA TREE.** *See* **Sophora japonica.**

**JAPANESE TOAD LILY.** *See* **Tricyrtis hirta.**

**JAPÁNESE YEW.** *See* **Taxus cuspidata.**

*japon'icus -a -um,* Japanese.

*Jarckia'nus -a -um,* in honour of Herr Jarck who sent *Aerides Jarckianum* to Dresden from the Philippines, *c.* 1914.

**JAROSSE.** *See* **Lathyrus sativus.**

**JARRAH.** *See* **Eucalyptus marginata.** **A**

**JASIO'NE** (a name given by Theophrastus to the Convolvulus). FAM. *Campanulaceae.* A genus of about 12 species of herbs, natives of temperate Europe and the Mediterranean region, with considerable likeness to Globularia. Leaves often in a rosette, alternate, narrow. Flowers in a terminal head with an involucre of bracts, blue, rarely white, deeply 5-parted; anthers connate at base into a tube. A somewhat sandy soil suits these hardy rock-garden plants which should, so far as the perennial species are concerned, be sown in autumn, the annuals in March. The perennials may also be increased by division.

**J. amethysti'na.** Tufted perennial, 1 to 4 in. *l.* in a basal rosette, oblong or linear-spatulate, toothed. *fl.* in a congested head; cor. grey; segs. linear-lanceolate; stigmas blue; involucral bracts usually entire. May to August. Sierre Nevada, Spain.

**J. hu'milis.** About 4 in. h. with unbranched stems. *Basal l.* in a rosette, linear-obovate, flat, entire. *fl.* blue on short peduncles. Summer. Pyrenees. 1824.

**J. Jank'ae.** Tufted perennial. Stem sometimes branched, naked above, sometimes hispid near base. *l.* lanceolate or linear-oblong, not wavy; stalks long. *fl.* blue, in heads; involucral bracts, with thickened margin, remotely toothed. Summer. Hungary.

**J. monta'na.** Sheep's-bit Scabious. Annual (or biennial), 6 to 12 in. h. Stem erect, unbranched. *l.* lanceolate, wavy, hairy. *fl.* pale blue or white in globose heads; peduncles naked. Summer. Europe, including Britain. (E.B. 683.)

**J. peren'nis.** Perennial, about 12 in. h. Stems erect, unbranched. *Basal l.* obovate; *stem-l.* oblong-linear, flat; all rather hairy. *fl.* blue, stalked, in large, sub-globose heads; peduncles naked. Summer. W. Europe. 1787. (B.M. 2198; B.R. 505.)

**JASMINE.** *See* **Jasminum.**

**JASMINE, BOX.** *See* **Phillyrea.**

**JASMINE, CAPE.** *See* **Gardenia.**

**JASMINE, CAROLINA.** *See* **Gelsemium.** A

**JASMINE, ROCK.** *See* **Androsace Chamaejasme.**

**JASMINE, WINTER.** *See* **Jasminum nudiflorum.**

***jasminoi'des,*** Jasmine-like.

**JASMI'NUM** (Latinized Persian name). FAM. *Oleaceae.* A genus of some 200 species of climbing, trailing, or erect shrubs inhabiting temperate, tropical, and subtropical regions. Leaves opposite or alternate, simple, 3-foliolate, or pinnate; leaflets toothless. Flowers yellow, white, or rarely reddish, sometimes solitary, more often in cymose clusters of 3 to many, usually fragrant; corolla tubular with 4 to 9 lobes; stamens 2; fruit a berry, usually black, normally twin (i.e. the 2 carpels remain united) but often only 1 develops.

Provided their requirements as to climate and temperature are met—and in that respect they vary from hardy to greenhouse and stove plants—the jasmines are easily cultivated. They succeed in good well-drained loam and are easily propagated by cuttings. Some, like *J. officinale*, are genuine, self-supporting twiners, but others are rambling or trailing shrubs which in gardens need the support of a wall, pergola, arbour, or merely stakes to show them at their best. Species grown under glass can be trained to wires near the roof.

**J. amplexicau'le.** Climber about 5 ft. h. *l.* simple, cordate-oblong, shining. *fl.* white in dense cymes; cal. teeth awl-shaped, downy. January. India, China. 1819. (B.R. 436 as *J. undulatum*.) Stove.

**J. azor'icum.** Shrubby twiner with terete branches. *lflets.* ovate, sub-cordate, undulate. *fl.* white; pet. 5, as long as cor. tube. Summer, autumn. Azores. 1724. (B.M. 1889.) Greenhouse.

**J. Beesia'num.** Deciduous or semi-evergreen climber, producing a tangle of slender, grooved, slightly downy stems. *l.* simple, opposite, ovate-lanceolate to lanceolate, 1½ to 2 in. long, dark dull green, slightly downy. *fl.* fragrant, 1 to 3 together, ⅝ to ¾ in. long, rose. May. *fr.* ⅓ in. wide, black, shining. China. 1910. (B.M. 9097.)

**J. disperm'um.** Deciduous climber, glabrous save at nodes. *l.* opposite, pinnate; lflets. lanceolate, usually in 2 pairs with a much larger terminal one; lateral 1 to 1¾ in. long, terminal up to 3½ in. long, ciliate. *fl.* white or slightly tinged pink, fragrant, in axillary and terminal cymes; cal. ⅛ in. long, shortly 5-toothed (teeth not long as in *J. officinale*); cor. tube ⅝ in. long, lobes 5, obovate, spreading, about ⅓ in. long. N. India to Yunnan. 1848. (B.M. 9567.) Cool greenhouse.

**J. Far'reri.** Widespreading, evergreen shrub, 6 to 8 ft., shoots angled, downy, purplish. *l.* alternate, 3-foliolate; lflets. ovate-lanceolate, terminal one up to 4 in. long and ¾ to 1⅝ in. wide, side ones much smaller, stalkless. *fl.* in terminal clusters of up to 12; cor. bright yellow, ¾ in. long, ⅝ in. wide; cal. downy, funnel-shaped, with 5 triangular-teeth. May, June. Burma. 1919. (B.M. 9351.) Cultivated wrongly as *J. Giraldii* at first. Hardy.

**J. flor'idum.** Evergreen shrub of rambling growth, shoots angled, glabrous. *l.* alternate, usually 3-foliolate; lflets. oval, obovate, or ovate, ½ to 1½ in. long, glabrous. *fl.* in terminal many-fld. clusters; cor. yellow, ½ to ¾ in. long, lobes 5, pointed; cal. lobes 5, ⅛ in. long, awl-shaped. July, September. *fr.* black, ⅛ in. wide. China. 1850. (B.M. 6719.) Warm wall.

**J. fru'ticans.** Evergreen or semi-evergreen shrub, mostly 3 to 6 ft. (higher against a wall); shoots angled, glabrous. *l.* alternate, 3-foliolate; lflets. narrow-oblong or linear-obovate, ⅓ to ¾ in. long, deep green, glabrous except on the margins. *fl.* 3 to 5 in a cluster terminating short twigs; cor. yellow, ⅝ in. long and wide; cal. with slender lobes. June, July. *fr.* black, globose, ¼ in. wide. Mediterranean region. 1570. (B.M. 461.) Hardy.

**J. Giral'dii.** *See* **J. Farreri.**

**J. gracil'limum.*** Branches long, slender. *l.* ovate-cordate, acute, hairy; stalked. *fl.* white, large, fragrant; pet. 9, elliptic-oblong in globose, drooping, many-fld. panicles. Winter. N. Borneo. 1881. (B.M. 6559.) Stove.

**J. grandiflo'rum.** Straggling bush. *l.* pinnate; lflets. of equal size, outer 3 to 5 confluent, bluntish. *fl.* white, reddish beneath, similar to *J. officinale* but larger. June to October. Sub-trop. Himalaya. 1629. (B.R. 91.) Warm greenhouse. Related to *J. officinale* but differing by the large fl. and confluent lflets. as well as by its tenderness.

**J. hirsu'tum.** A synonym of *J. multiflorum.*

**J. hu'mile.** Italian Jasmine. Evergreen shrub, 3 to 4 ft., shoots erect. *l.* usually 3-foliolate. *fl.* yellow, in clusters of 2 to 4. SE. Europe. 1656. (B.R. 350.) Hardy. *J. revolutum* and *J. Wallichianum* are sometimes regarded as vars. of this species. They are distinguished by their taller growth, and more numerous fl. and lflets.

**J. multiflo'rum.** Straggly, downy shrub. *l.* cordate, mucronate, hairy beneath and on stalk, the upper forming an involucre beneath the umbel. *fl.* white, large, fragrant; pet. 6 to 9, lanceolate; umbels terminal, sessile. Summer. China, India. 1759. (B.M. 1991 as *J. hirsutum.*) SYN. *J. pubescens.* Greenhouse.

**J. nit'idum.** Climber with slender stems. *l.* simple, lanceolate, 3 in. long. *fl.* white, fragrant, ¾ in. long, in short, few-fld. racemes. Admiralty Is. 1898. Stove.

**J. nudiflo'rum.*** Deciduous shrub of loose, rambling shape, 12 ft. against a wall; shoots 4-angled, slender, glabrous. *l.* opposite, 3-foliolate; lflets. oval-oblong, ½ to 1¼ in. long, deep glossy green, margins minutely hairy. *fl.* yellow, solitary, axillary; cor. ¾ to 1 in. wide, 6-lobed; cal. 6-lobed, lobes linear. November to February. China. 1844. (B.M. 4649.) One of the best mid-winter-flowering, hardy shrubs. var. **au'reum,** *l.* blotched yellow.

**J. officina'le.*** Common Jasmine. Semi-evergreen or deciduous climber, up to 30 or 40 ft. if trained, shoots very slender, angled. *l.* opposite, pinnate; lflets. usually 5 or 7, occasionally 9, oblong-ovate, ½ to 2½ in. long, stalkless except the large terminal one. *fl.* white, very fragrant, in terminal clusters of 3- to 8-fld. cymes; cor. ¾ in. long and wide, 4- or 5-lobed. June to September. Persia, N. India, China. 1548. (B.M. 31.) Hardy. A perfume is extracted from the fl. var. **affin'e,** *fl.* larger, more numerous in the cyme. (B.R. 31, 25 as *J. affine.*); **au'reum,** *l.* blotched with yellow; **grandiflo'rum,** *see* **J. grandiflorum.**

**J. Park'eri.*** Evergreen shrub of tufted habit, 8 to 12 in., shoots grooved, minutely downy. *l.* alternate, pinnate, ½ to 1 in. long; lflets. 3 or 5, oval or ovate, ⅛ to ⅜ in. long, stalkless. *fl.* solitary, terminal or axillary; cor. yellow, ½ to ⅝ in. long, ½ in. wide; cal. 1/10 in. long, minutely downy, lobes awl-shaped. June. NW. India. 1923. Very distinct by its dwarfness and solitary fl. Rock-garden. Hardy.

**J. polyan'thum.*** Deciduous or evergreen climber up to 20 ft., shoots glabrous. *l.* opposite, 3 to 5 in. long, pinnate; lflets. 5 or 7, terminal one 1½ to 3 in. long, lanceolate; side ones scarcely half as large, tufted in the vein-axils beneath. *Panicles* axillary, many-fld., 2 to 4 in. long, very fragrant; cor. white inside, rosy outside, ¾ in. long and wide, lobes obovate. China. 1891. (B.M. 9545; R.H. 1891, 270.) Cool greenhouse or walls in the mildest counties.

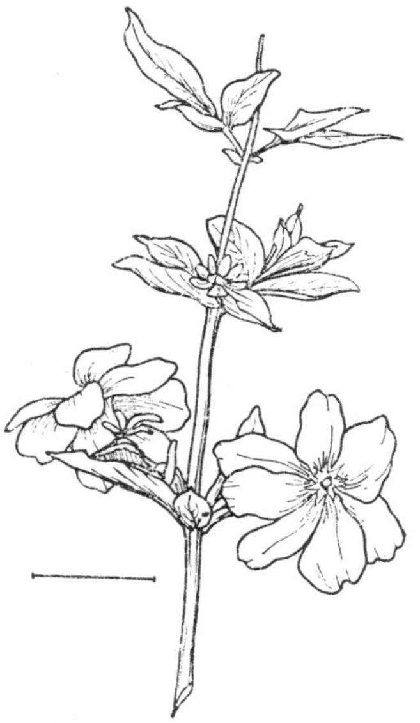

*Jasminum primulinum*

**J. primuli'num.*** Evergreen rambling shrub, up to 15 ft. if trained, shoots 4-angled, glabrous. *l.* opposite, 3-foliolate; lflets. lanceolate to narrowly oval, 1 to 3 in. long. *fl.* solitary on short, bracteate shoots; cor. 1½ to 1¾ in. long, bright yellow, 6- to 10-lobed, lobes rounded. March, April. *fr.* unknown. China. 1900. (B.M. 7981.) Not known in a wild state. Cool greenhouse or against a warm wall in the mildest localities.

**J. pubes'cens.** A synonym of *J. multiflorum*.

**J. pubig'erum.** Evergreen climbing shrub. *l.* alternate, pinnate; lflets. 7, ovate-lanceolate or oblong with a slender point, sessile, downy at first. *fl.* yellow; pet. 5 or 6, obtuse; peduncles long, 1-fld., in terminal corymbs, downy. Summer, autumn. NW. India. 1827. Nearly hardy. Closely related to *J. revolutum* but with smaller fl.

**J. Reeves'ii.** A synonym of *J. revolutum*.

**J. revolu'tum.**\* Nearly or quite evergreen shrub of spreading habit; shoots glabrous, stout. *l.* alternate; lflets. 3, 5, or 7, ovate or oval, ¾ to 1½ in. long, terminal one longer, dark dull green. *fl.* fragrant, in terminal clusters of 6 to 12 or more, often augmented by axillary clusters, making a many-fld. infl. 5 in. wide; cor. yellow, ½ to 1 in. wide; cal. triangular-lobed. June to September. Himalaya, Afghanistan. 1812. (B.M. 1731.) Hardy. SYN. *J. Reevesii, J. triumphans. See* **J. humile.**

**J. rex.** Glabrous climber, young branches round, green. *l.* simple, broad-oblong, 4 to 8 in. long, slender-pointed, dark green above, paler beneath. *fl.* white, 2 in. or more across, salver-shaped, in drooping 2- or 3-fld. cymes forming a terminal panicle, scentless; cal. lobes 6, linear; cor. tube about 1 in. long, slender, lobes 8 (or 9), obovate-oblong, spreading. Winter. SW. Siam. 1921. (B.M. 8934.) Stove.

**J. Sam'bac.**\* Evergreen twiner. *l.* cordate to oblong, acute or obtuse, waved, almost sessile, rather thin. *fl.* white, fragrant, usually in small, 3-forked cymes. Almost continuous. India. 1665. (B.R. 1.) B.M. 1785 shows a double-fld. form (var. **flore ple'no**). Stove.

**J. simplicifo'lium.** Climber or tree. *l.* oblong, shining. *fl.* white, terminal; cor. segs. 6 to 8, linear, acute, as long as tube. June, July. Australia. 1800. (B.M. 980; B.R. 606 as *J. gracile*.) Stove. var. **linearifo'lium**, *l.* narrower than in type.

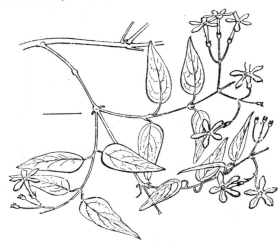

*Jasminum smilacifolium*

**J. smilacifo'lium.** Large climbing shrub, with glabrous shoots. *l.* ovate, 7 in. long, base obtuse, very thick; stalk ¾ in. long. *fl.* white with pink tinge, tube about 1 in. long, lobes ¾ in. long, acute; cymes up to 20-fld. Malacca.

**J. ×stephanen'se** (*J. Beesianum*×*J. officinale*). Vigorous climber, 15 to 20 ft., shoots angled, slender. *l.* simple to pinnate; lflets. (rarely more than 5) dull green, downy beneath. *fl.* fragrant, in terminal clusters; cor. soft pale pink, ½ in. long and wide. June, July. Of garden origin. (R.H. 1927, 644.) Hardy.

**J. triner've.** Climbing shrub with terete glabrous branches. *l.* ovate, 3-nerved at base, long acuminate; stalk jointed in middle. *fl.* white, 1 in. long, axillary or terminal, stalked, solitary or in groups of 3 to 9; cal. lobes awl-shaped; cor. lobes 6 to 8, linear-lanceolate, shorter than tube. Java.

**J. triumph'ans.** A synonym of *J. revolutum*.

**J. undula'tum.** A synonym of *J. amplexicaule*.

**J. Wallichia'num.** Nearly evergreen shrub; shoots slender, angled, glabrous. *l.* alternate; lflets. 7 to 13, lanceolate to ovate, ½ to 1½ in. long, terminal one much the largest. *fl.* numerous in terminal and axillary clusters; cor. yellow, ⅝ in. long, ½ in. wide; cal. triangular-lobed. June to September. Nepal. 1812. (B.M. 1409.) Hardy.

W. C. B.

**Jataman'si,** Sanskrit name for a kind of Spikenard.

**JATEORHI'ZA** (*iatos*, healing, *rhiza*, root; from the medicinal properties). FAM. *Menispermaceae*. A genus of 2 species, perennial herbs, natives of Trop. Africa or Madagascar. Leaves large, membranous, palmately lobed. Flowers dioecious, the male in long, slender, racemose panicles usually sessile on the short lateral branches, female in simple or nearly simple racemes. For treatment *see* **Cocculus.** *J. palmata* is the source of Columba-root, a drug acting as a bitter tonic without stimulative effects; used in cases of indigestion.

**J. Colum'ba.** A synonym of *J. palmata*.

**J. palma'ta.** Columba Root. Herbaceous perennial. Root a cluster of fusiform, somewhat branched, fleshy, curved, descending tubers. *l.* alternate, younger thin, pellucid, usually 3-lobed. *fl.* pale green. Mozambique. (B.M. 2970–1 as *Cocculus palmatus*.) SYN. *J. Columba, Menispermum palmatum, M. Columba.*

F. G. P.

**JAT'ROPHA** (*iatros*, physician, *trophe*, food; the species have medicinal properties). FAM. *Euphorbiaceae*. A genus of about 160 species of tall herbs and shrubs, rarely trees, many of them of economic importance, widely distributed throughout warm regions but most abundant in S. America. Several species have been used in medicine, mainly locally. Leaves alternate, stipulate. Flowers in cymes. Sandy peat and fibrous loam constitute the best compost for Jatrophas. Cuttings of firm young shoots dried before insertion will root in sandy soil with brisk bottom heat, and seeds also germinate readily.

**J. Cur'cas.** French Physic Nut, Barbados Nut, Purging Nut. Shrub up to 10 ft., deciduous. *l.* 3- to 5-lobed, almost glabrous, stalks long, stipules minute. *fl.* small, yellowish-green, in corymbiform, many-fld. cymes. Trop. America. Cultivated in Trop. America for the seeds which contain a purgative oil, used also in cooking and soap-making. The seeds are eaten in Mexico.

**J. diversifo'lia.** A synonym of *J. integerrima*.

**J. gossipifo'lia.** *l.* lobed above middle, 5 to 6 in. wide; segs. usually obovate, slender-pointed, doubly serrate or crenate, densely glandular. *fl.* beautiful reddish-purple, in many-fld. panicles. Summer. Trop. America, Africa. 1690. (B.R. 746; L.B. 6, 117.) SYN. *J. staphisagrifolia*. Reputed remedy for leprosy.

**J. integer'rima.** 3 ft. h. *l.* ovate, slightly lobed at base, slender-pointed. *fl.* red in sub-cymose racemes. Summer. Cuba. 1809. (B.M. 1464.) SYN. *J. diversifolia*.

**J. multif'ida.** Coral Plant, Physic Nut. 3 ft. h. *l.* palmate, 11-lobed, lobes pinnatifid, wedge-shaped, smooth; stipules setaceous, multifid. *fl.* scarlet. July. S. America. 1696.

**J. pandurifo'lia.** 4 ft. h. *l.* oblong, somewhat fiddle-shaped, entire, angular at base, with 2 teeth each side, slender-pointed. *fl.* scarlet in many-fld. cymes. Summer. W. Indies. 1800. SYN. *J. acuminata, J. hastata.*

**J. podag'rica.** Guatemala Rhubarb. Erect, branched, 18 in. h., gouty at base. *l.* peltate-cordate, 5-lobed, glabrous; lobes sub-ovate, blunt; stipules fringed with glands. *fl.* orange-red, in terminal, long-stalked cymes; cal. teeth and pet. blunt. Colombia. 1847. (B.M. 4376.)

**J. spathula'ta.** Shrub of 5 to 6 ft., stoloniferous, with fleshy branches. *l.* spatulate, entire or 3-lobed, nearly glabrous. *fl.* dioecious, pale rose, clustered. S. America. Succulent house-plant.

**J. u'rens.** 2 to 4 ft. h. *l.* roundish-cordate, 3- to 5-lobed, lobes toothed, cut or pinnatifid, often discoloured. *fl.* red. June to September. Trop. America. (G.C. 14 (1880), 753.)

F. G. P.

*javalen'sis -is -e*, of the Javali Mine, Nicaragua.

*javan'icus -a -um*, of Java, E. Indies. Many variations of this name occur.